HOLT

American Anthem

Edward L. Ayers
Robert D. Schulzinger
Jesús F. de la Teja
Deborah Gray White

Senior Consulting Author
Walter Robertson III
Dunkirk High School

HOLT, RINEHART AND WINSTON
A Harcourt Education Company
Orlando • **Austin** • New York • San Diego • London

Authors

Edward L. Ayers

Edward L. Ayers is president of the University of Richmond. He was named National Professor of the Year in 2003 and his book *In the Presence of Mine Enemies: The Civil War in the Heart of America, 1859–1863* won the Bancroft Prize and the Beveridge Prize in 2004. *The Promise of the New South: Life After Reconstruction* was a finalist for the Pulitzer Prize and the National Book Award. Ayers is also the creator of the acclaimed Web project, "Valley of the Shadow: Two Communities in the American Civil War," a comprehensive examination of everyday life before and during the Civil War in two small communities on either side of the Mason-Dixon Line.

Jesús F. de la Teja

Jesús F. de la Teja is chair of the history department at Texas State University at San Marcos, Texas, as well as the State Historian of Texas. Prof. de la Teja has a number of books either in progress or recently published on colonial history of Mexico and Spanish borderlands including *Texas: Crossroads of North America* and *San Antonio de Béxar: A Community on New Spain's Northern Frontier,* which was the 1996 winner of the Presidio La Bahia Award. A Fellow of the Texas State Historical Association, Prof. de la Teja has received Texas State's Excellence Award for teaching. He earned undergraduate and Master's degrees from Seton Hall and a Ph.D. from the University of Texas, Austin. Prof. de la Teja participated in a MacArthur Foundation grant for scholarly work on Texas colonization and independence.

ISBN-13 978-0-55-400235-4
ISBN-10 0-55-400235-3

1 2 3 4 5 6 7 8 9 048 10 09 08 07

Deborah Gray White

Deborah Gray White is Distinguished Professor of History at Rutgers University. She received her undergraduate degree from SUNY Binghamton, her Master's from Columbia University, and a Ph.D. from the University of Illinois at Chicago. A specialist in American history and the history of African Americans, she is the author of several books including: *Ar'n't I a Woman?: Female Slaves in the Antebellum South; Too Heavy A Load: Black Women in Defense of Themselves, 1894–1994;* and *Let My People Go: African Americans 1804–1860.*

Robert D. Schulzinger

Robert D. Schulzinger is Director of the International Affairs Program and Professor of History at the University of Colorado, Boulder. Dr. Schulzinger, a member of the U.S. State Department's Historical Advisory Committee, received his undergraduate degree from Columbia University, and a Master's and Ph.D. from Yale. He has written extensively on post-World War II history; his books include *A Time for War: The United States & Vietnam, 1941–1975.*

Senior Program Consultant

Sam Wineburg

Sam Wineburg is Professor of Education at Stanford University, where he directs the only Ph.D. program in History Education in the nation. Educated at Brown and Berkeley, he spent several years teaching history at the middle and high school level before completing a doctorate in Psychological Studies in Education at Stanford. His book *Historical Thinking and Other Unnatural Acts: Charting the Future of Teaching the Past* won the Frederic W. Ness Award from the Association of American Colleges and Universities.

Senior Consulting Author

Walter Robertson III

Walter Robertson III has taught history courses for over ten years. Currently, he teaches Advanced Placement history courses at Dunkirk High School in Dunkirk, New York. After serving in the U.S. Army, Robertson received a Fulbright Scholarship to Tanzania. His B.A. is from Syracuse University, and his Master's in history is from the University of Wisconsin. One of the authors of *Down the Street, Around the World: A Starter Kit for Global Awareness,* published by the American Federation of Teachers, Robertson has been the Chairman of the Social Studies Committee for the New York State United Teachers since 2003.

Consultants

Program Consultant

Kylene Beers, Ed.D
Senior Reading Researcher
School Development Program
Yale University
New Haven, Connecticut

Academic Consultants

John Ferguson
Senior Religion Consultant
Assistant Professor
Political Science/Criminal Justice
Howard Payne University
Brownwood, Texas

Gregory Massing
*Constitutional Law
    Consultant; author,
    Holt's* Civics in Practice
Adjunct Professor
Boston College Law School
Chestnut Hill, Massachusetts

Walter Schroeder
Geography Consultant
Assistant Professor Emeritus
Department of Geography
University of Missouri
Columbia, Missouri

Program Advisers

Academic Reviewers

Raymond Hyser, Ph. D.
James Madison University
Harrisonburg, Virginia

Michael S. Mayer, Ph.D.
Department of History
University of Montana
Missoula, Montana

Silvana Siddali, Ph.D
Department of History
St. Louis University
St. Louis, Missouri

Rebecca Tannenbaum, Ph.D
Department of History
Yale University
New Haven, Connecticut

Senior Consulting Writer

Peter Lacey
Sunderland, Massachusetts

Educational Reviewers

Gina Capelli
Liberty High School
Brentwood, California

Brent Duggins
Glenwood High School
Chatham, Illinois

Conrad Graf
Wayne High School
Fort Wayne, Indiana

Traci S. Lipscomb
Rustburg High School
Rustburg, Virginia

Nancy A. Llombart
Lakeview High School
St. Clair Shores, Michigan

Kris Oliveira
Clovis West High School
Fresno, California

Robert M. Rodrigues
Chartiers Valley High School
Bridgeville, Pennsylvania

Avon Ruffin
Winston-Salem Forsyth County
    Schools
Winston-Salem,
    North Carolina

Glenda Watanabe
Banning High School
Wilmington, California

New York Teacher Reviewers

Nelson Acevedo
New York Department
    of Education
Curriculum Instructional
    Specialist
New York, New York

Bob Van Amburgh
Instructional Supervisor
City School District of Albany
Albany, New York

Tim Backus
K-12 Supervisor of Social Studies
South Colonie Central High
    School
Albany, New York

Arthur Brown Jr.
Social Studies Specialist
New York City Department
    Education, Region 1
New York, New York

Ann-Jean Paci
Retired Assistant Principal
Sheepshead Bay High School
Brooklyn, New York

Anthony Powell
Social Studies Department Chair
Edmund Miles Middle School
Amityville, New York

Walter Robertson III
Dunkirk High School
Dunkirk, New York

Field Test Teachers

Melanie Adamek
Niagara Wheatfield High School
Sandborn, New York

David Breen
Fels High School
Philadelphia, Pennsylvania

Jackie Burris
Asheville High School
Asheville, North Carolina

Patrick Eviston
Colonel White High School
Dayton, Ohio

Dena Grevis
Libbey High School
Toledo, Ohio

Ernesto Quiroz
Fillmore High School
Fillmore, California

Judith L. Spurlock
Meadowdale High School
Dayton, Ohio

James Toby
Everett High School
Lansing, Michigan

Robyn Webb
Elsik High School
Houston, Texas

iv

Contents

Key Idea 4 The skills of historical analysis include the ability to: explain the significance of historical evidence; weigh the importance, reliability, and validity of evidence; understand the importance of multiple causation; understand the importance of changing and competing interpretations of different historical developments.

UNIT 1

Beginnings–1763
Beginnings of America

CHAPTER 1 — The World Before 1600

New York State Learning Standards

Key Idea 3 Study about the major social, political, economic, cultural, and religious developments in New York State and United States history involves learning about the important roles and contributions of individuals and groups

History's Impact Video Series
The World Before 1600

CHAPTER 2 — European Colonies in America

New York State Learning Standards

Key Idea 1 The study of New York State and United States history requires an analysis of the development of American culture, its diversity and multicultural context, and the ways people are unified by many values, practices, and traditions.

Key Idea 3 Study about the major social, political, economic, cultural, and religious developments in New York State and United States history involves learning about the important roles and contributions of individuals and groups.

History's Impact Video Series
European Colonies in America

UNIT 6
1898–1920
Becoming a World Power

New York State Learning Standards

Key Idea 2 Important ideas, social and cultural values, beliefs, and traditions from New York State and United States history illustrate the connections and interactions of people and events across time and from a variety of perspectives.

Key Idea 3 Study about the major social, political, economic, cultural, and religious developments in New York State and United States history involves learning about the important roles and contributions of individuals and groups.

History's Impact Video Series
Entering the World Stage

New York State Learning Standards

Key Idea 2 Important ideas, social and cultural values, beliefs, and traditions from New York State and United States history illustrate the connections and interactions of people and events across time and from a variety of perspectives.

Key Idea 3 Study about the major social, political, economic, cultural, and religious developments in New York State and United States history involves learning about the important roles and contributions of individuals and groups.

History's Impact Video Series
The First World War

UNIT 7

1919–1940

A Modern Nation

CHAPTER 19 **From War to Peace** **620**

New York State Learning Standards

Key Idea 1 The study of New York State and United States history requires an analysis of the development of American culture, its diversity and multicultural context, and the ways people are unified by many values, practices, and traditions.

Key Idea 2 Important ideas, social and cultural values, beliefs, and traditions from New York State and United States history illustrate the connections and interactions of people and events across time and from a variety of perspectives.

History's Impact Video Series
From War to Peace

CHAPTER 20 **The Roaring Twenties** **644**

New York State Learning Standards

Key Idea 1 The study of New York State and United States history requires an analysis of the development of American culture, its diversity and multicultural context, and the ways people are unified by many values, practices, and traditions.

Key Idea 2 Important ideas, social and cultural values, beliefs, and traditions from New York State and United States history illustrate the connections and interactions of people and events across time and from a variety of perspectives.

History's Impact Video Series
The Roaring Twenties

CHAPTER 21 **The Great Depression Begins** **670**

New York State Learning Standards

Key Idea 3 Study about the major social, political, economic, cultural, and religious developments in New York State and United States history involves learning about the important roles and contributions of individuals and groups.

History's Impact Video Series
The Great Depression Begins

UNIT 9

1954–1975

A Nation Facing Challenges

Features

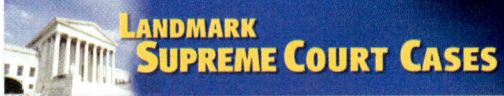

LANDMARK SUPREME COURT CASES

TRACING HISTORY

HISTORY & Geography

American Liberty

Maps

Interpret maps to see where important events happened and analyze how geography has influenced history.

✴Interactive Maps

Go online to extend your learning with interactive maps.

Charts and Graphs

Charts, Graphs, and Time Lines

Analyze information presented visually to learn more about history. To examine key facts and concepts, look for this special logo:

BATTLE OF THE SOMME

Duration of battle: July 1-Nov. 18, 1916

Total Allied casualties: about 630,000

British casualties on day 1: about 57,000

Total German casualties: about 650,000

GRAPHS

TIME LINES

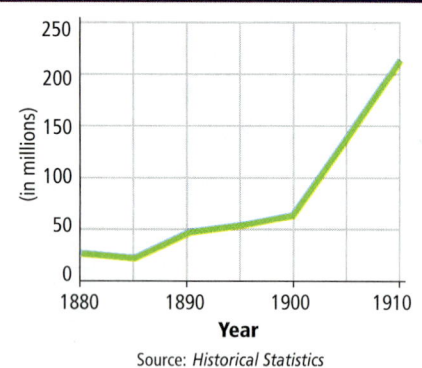

U.S. OIL PRODUCTION, 1880–1910

(in millions)

Year

Source: *Historical Statistics of the United States*

Primary Sources

Relive history through eyewitness accounts, literature, and documents.

Reading like a Historian

When I asked Kevin, a 16-year-old high school junior, what he needed most to do well in history class, he had little doubt: "A good memory."

"Anything else?"

"Nope. Just memorize facts and stuff, know 'em cold, and when you get the test, give it all back to the teacher."

"What about thinking—does thinking have anything to do with history?"

"Not really. It's all pretty simple. Random stuff happened a long time ago. People wrote it down. Others copied it and put it in a book. Poof—history."

I was saddened but not surprised by Kevin's answers. I've spent nearly twenty years studying how high school kids learn history. Over the years I've met many Kevins, students who knew history as nothing but a grim list of names and dates—one random fact after another.

In *American Anthem, New York Edition* we have created a textbook that I hope will change the way students such as Kevin learn history. To explore the past and feel its excitement, you must learn to read like a historian.

Senior Program Consultant

Gilbert Stuart painted this portrait of George Washington in 1796, while Washington was president. Historians consider this painting a primary source because it was created during Washington's lifetime.

Be a History Detective

Names, facts, and dates: this is what history has become for a lot of you. But the funny thing is that when you ask historians what they do, an entirely different picture emerges. They see themselves as detectives searching for clues to a puzzle that can never be entirely solved.

Asking questions Traced back to its earliest meaning, the word *history* (in Greek, *istor*) is about *inquiry*. To engage in inquiry means trying to figure things out, asking questions open to debate. Inquiry is about as far from mindless memorization as you can get.

Even when historians are able to piece together the basic story of what happened in the past, rarely do they all line up in agreement about what an event means or what caused it. Historians argue amongst themselves about the past's meaning and what it has to tell us in the present. The past may be over, but history is a moving target.

Facts and Their Meaning

Where do facts fit into this picture? Facts are important but hardly the whole story. To historians, history is an argument about what facts *mean*.

If history already happened, you might ask, what's there to argue about? It turns out, a lot. Was the American Revolution a fight against tyranny or an attempt by the well bred to preserve their social position? Was the Civil War fought over the issue of slavery or was it a conflict over states' rights? Was the "Progressive Era" really so progressive? Could the Vietnam War have been prevented?

Reviewing sources Take, for example, a story you probably know—or think you do. Pocahontas, a beautiful Native American woman, falls in love with the handsome English captain John Smith, and later saves his life just as her dad, Powhatan, is ready to club him to death.

Do you believe it?

The facts are these: John Smith wrote two different accounts of his time in Jamestown, one in 1608, the other in 1624. In his first book, he talks about meeting Chief Powhatan, but there is no mention of any threat. In fact he says the opposite: Powhatan "kindly welcomed me with such good wordes, and great Platters . . . assuring me his friendship." Nor is there any mention of being saved by a young Indian girl—anyway, Pocahontas was only 11 or 12, hardly the gorgeous teenager of cartoon fame—and no hint of any love affair anywhere. Only when Smith published a second book in 1624, well after Pocahontas had already married another colonist, John Rolfe, had a son, became ill, and died in 1617, do we hear of Smith's dramatic rescue by the Indian princess. So which account should we believe, the one Smith wrote in 1608 or 1624?

Weighing opinions Different opinions swirl around this question, and there are actually good reasons for believing a number of them. But while everyone is entitled to an opinion, not every opinion is entitled to being believed. In history, a persuasive opinion is backed up by evidence. It is evidence that distinguishes a solid interpretation from a wild guess. *American Anthem* offers you numerous opportunities to develop the critical reading skills you'll need to analyze evidence like a historian.

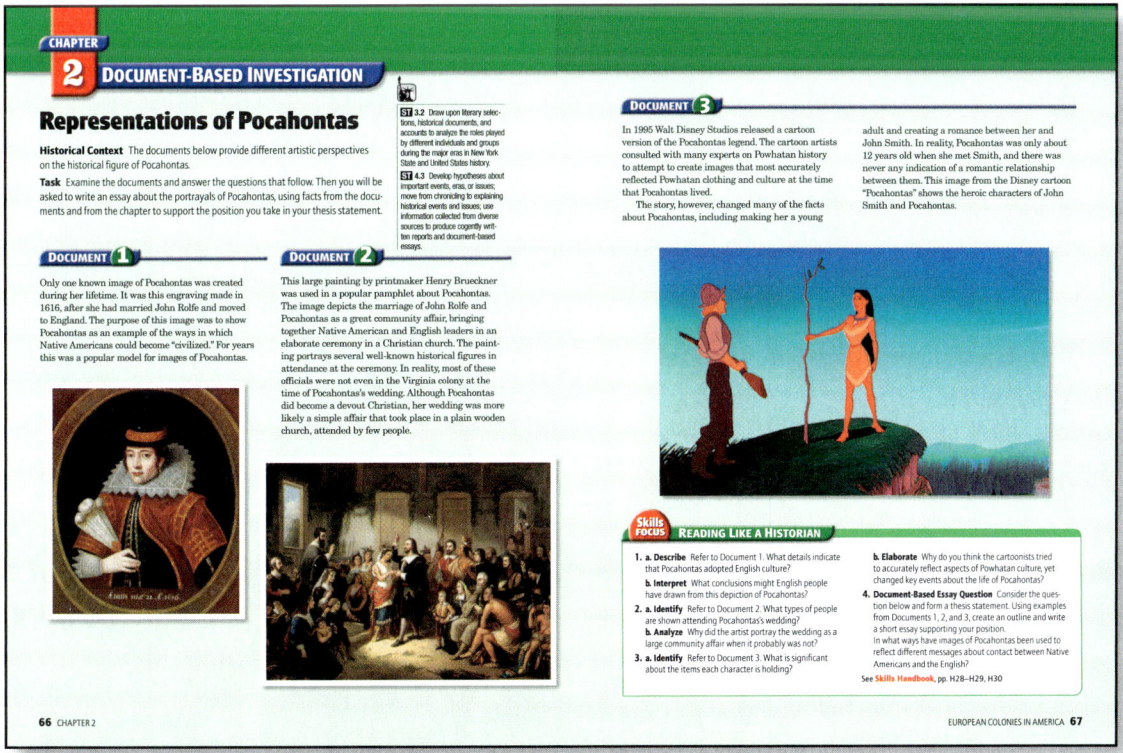

Document-Based Investigations give you opportunities to inquire like a historian. You will study a series of documents and then draw your own conclusions about what they mean.

Evidence in History

To find evidence in history we can't talk to the dead. What we can do is examine what they left behind—their diaries, letters, telegrams, secret memos, and in the modern era, their tape recordings and computer records. This is what historians mean when they talk about reading *primary* sources. These sources are considered to be primary—*most important, appearing in the first position, essential*—because they are written by the people we are trying to understand. Their words come to us directly, without being filtered by someone else.

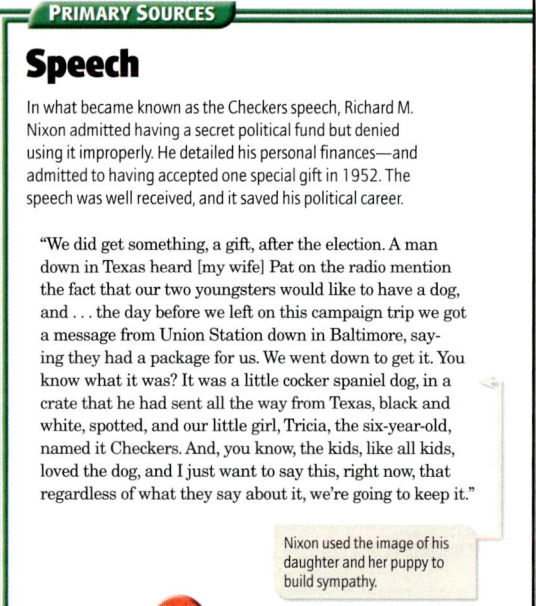

Speech

In what became known as the Checkers speech, Richard M. Nixon admitted having a secret political fund but denied using it improperly. He detailed his personal finances—and admitted to having accepted one special gift in 1952. The speech was well received, and it saved his political career.

"We did get something, a gift, after the election. A man down in Texas heard [my wife] Pat on the radio mention the fact that our two youngsters would like to have a dog, and . . . the day before we left on this campaign trip we got a message from Union Station down in Baltimore, saying they had a package for us. We went down to get it. You know what it was? It was a little cocker spaniel dog, in a crate that he had sent all the way from Texas, black and white, spotted, and our little girl, Tricia, the six-year-old, named it Checkers. And, you know, the kids, like all kids, loved the dog, and I just want to say this, right now, that regardless of what they say about it, we're going to keep it."

Nixon used the image of his daughter and her puppy to build sympathy.

Skills FOCUS   READING LIKE A HISTORIAN

1. **Analyzing Primary Sources** What was the gift that Nixon admitted to having received?

2. **Drawing Conclusions** [...] speech was effective at e[...]

See **Skills Handbook**, pp. H12[...]

Primary sources are important pieces of historical evidence—and must be read with a historian's critical eye.

Counterpoints features ask you to analyze different points of view about key historical issues.

How Historians Read

Learning to read like a historian is different from the other kind of reading you do, like reading your driver's ed manual or your math book. In practically every country, a red road sign means stop. In math 2 + 2 = 4 no matter where you live—in Dallas, San Francisco, or Paris. But because history is always written from a particular perspective, its meanings change from place to place and from one era to the next. Even the book you're holding, while trying to balance different perspectives, makes choices that reflect its perspective: where to begin its story, where to end it, which events to narrate and which to leave out.

Points of view In our chapter covering the Revolutionary War, the rebellious American colonists are referred to as "patriots." Would you expect them to be so described in a British textbook? When you come to the chapters on World War II, D-Day is a large part of the story on the war in Europe. In Russian textbooks, D-Day—referred to as the "opening of the second front"—barely gets mentioned. There, the big story is the siege of Stalingrad, in which the Red Army held off the Nazis for six months, and in the process lost a million of its own citizens—but not before causing the collapse of Hitler's Sixth Army.

It is only natural that historians today have different points of view. The people at the time

Tactics of Change

Martin Luther King's commitment to nonviolence never wavered.

"[V]iolence . . . seeks to annihilate rather than convert . . . Nonviolence is a powerful and just weapon . . . which cuts without wounding and ennobles the man who wields it."

Martin Luther King Jr., 1964

Malcolm X was blunt and uncompromising. He inspired hatred from some and respect from others.

"[N]ow you're facing a situation where the young Negro's coming up. They don't want to hear that 'turn-the-other-cheek' stuff, no. . . . There's new thinking coming in. There's new strategy coming in . . . It'll be ballots, or it'll be bullets. It'll be liberty, or it will be death."

Malcolm X, 1964

Skills FOCUS   READING LIKE A HISTORIAN

Identifying Points of View What does King mean when he says that nonviolence "cuts without wounding"? To what is Malcolm X referring when he speaks of "ballots" or "bullets"?

See **Skills Handbook**, pp. H28–H29

did too. The Counterpoints features found in this book show that as history was being made, people disagreed about what was happening and what to do.

Reading for perspective Perspective means a place to stand, and each one of us has to stand somewhere. Where the authors of this book stand is revealed in the words they choose—just think about the difference between calling this book "American Anthem," versus, say, "American Dilemma" or "American Crisis." But determining perspective means paying more attention to words than you're probably used to.

Attention to detail Consider two facts: first, Harry Truman became the 32nd president; and second, he never went to college. The moment we try to combine them, we no longer have two neutral bits of information. We have a historical interpretation. Think about the sentence, "Harry Truman became the 32nd president *but* he never went to college." Change one little word—substitute *because* for *but*—and see what happens. The first sentence suggests that the lack of a college education was something Truman had to overcome. The second seems to say that Truman's humble education *caused*, or at least partially caused, his success. Two completely different ideas rest on one word. Without paying attention, you'd miss it.

The Role of Thinking

The book you are holding offers an interpretation of history, but not the final word. It does its best to combine perspectives, but like any book, it can never escape the fact that it was written by human beings living in a particular time and place. As such, it records the unrecognized assumptions, biases, and blind spots of our time. In reading like a historian, one of your goals is to treat this book like any other account of the past. You should analyze it, evaluate the evidence it offers for its assertions, and read it carefully—more carefully than you've ever read a history textbook before. The thread connecting all of these goals is the very thing that escaped Kevin: the role of thinking.

Kevin's right. Without thinking, history *is* meaningless. But when you add thinking—an ingredient only you can provide—the past springs to life. That is what reading like a historian is all about.

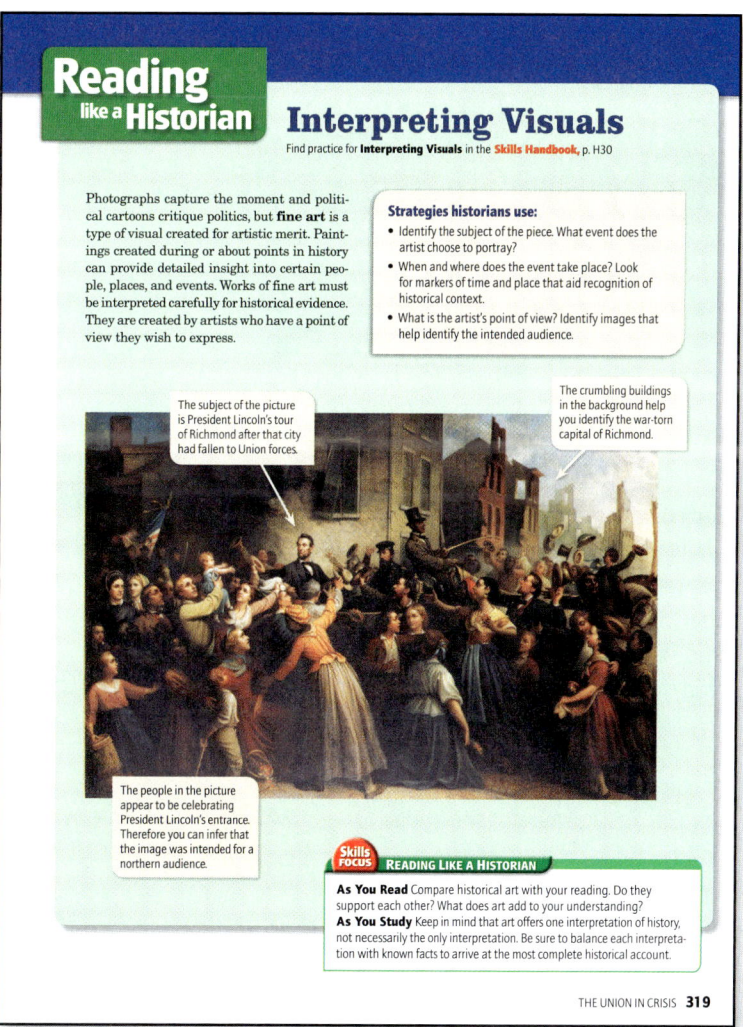

Reading like a Historian — Interpreting Visuals

Find practice for **Interpreting Visuals** in the **Skills Handbook**, p. H30

Photographs capture the moment and political cartoons critique politics, but **fine art** is a type of visual created for artistic merit. Paintings created during or about points in history can provide detailed insight into certain people, places, and events. Works of fine art must be interpreted carefully for historical evidence. They are created by artists who have a point of view they wish to express.

Strategies historians use:
- Identify the subject of the piece. What event does the artist choose to portray?
- When and where does the event take place? Look for markers of time and place that aid recognition of historical context.
- What is the artist's point of view? Identify images that help identify the intended audience.

The subject of the picture is President Lincoln's tour of Richmond after that city had fallen to Union forces.

The crumbling buildings in the background help you identify the war-torn capital of Richmond.

The people in the picture appear to be celebrating President Lincoln's entrance. Therefore you can infer that the image was intended for a northern audience.

Skills Focus — READING LIKE A HISTORIAN

As You Read Compare historical art with your reading. Do they support each other? What does art add to your understanding?
As You Study Keep in mind that art offers one interpretation of history, not necessarily the only interpretation. Be sure to balance each interpretation with known facts to arrive at the most complete historical account.

THE UNION IN CRISIS **319**

A historian looks at all evidence critically. Valuable information comes not only from text-based documents, but also from paintings, photographs, political cartoons, and other visual media.

How to Use Your Textbook

American Anthem, New York Edition was created to make your study of United States history an enjoyable, meaningful experience. Take a few minutes to become familiar with the book's easy-to-use structure and special features.

Unit

Each unit of study focuses on a particular time period. Unit openers list the chapter titles and the years the chapters cover. They also provide an overview of the main themes covered in the unit. A historic photograph or illustration previews the material you are about to explore.

Prepare to Read

Each unit begins with an opportunity to reinforce important skills first taught in the Skills Handbook. Taking the time to review these skills will help you as you read the unit.

Reading Skills Call-outs give practical how-to instruction about the skill. Test-taking tips show you how reading skills can help you when taking exams.

Reading Like a Historian This book provides strategies to help you think like a historian. Each call-out applies one of the strategies to the passage or visual being analyzed.

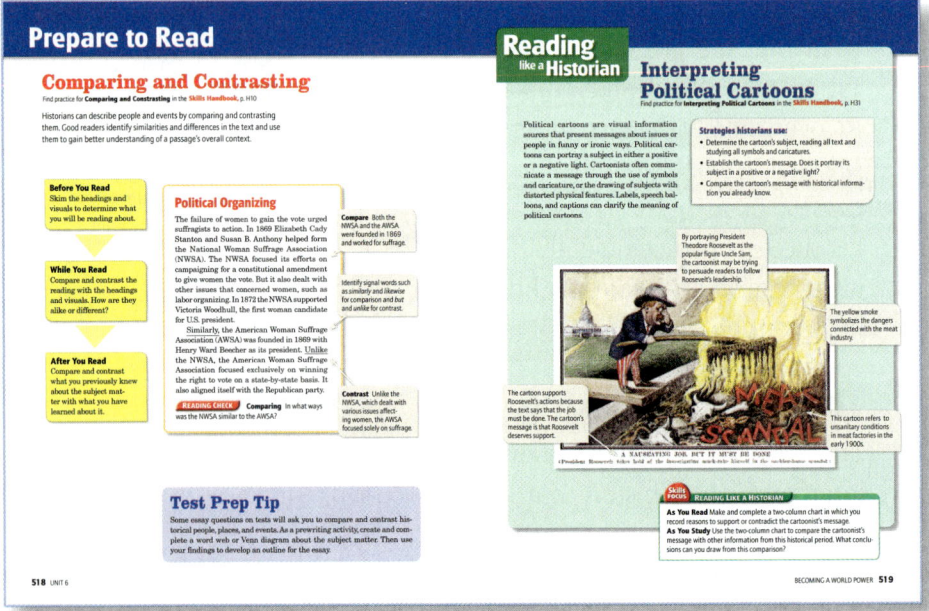

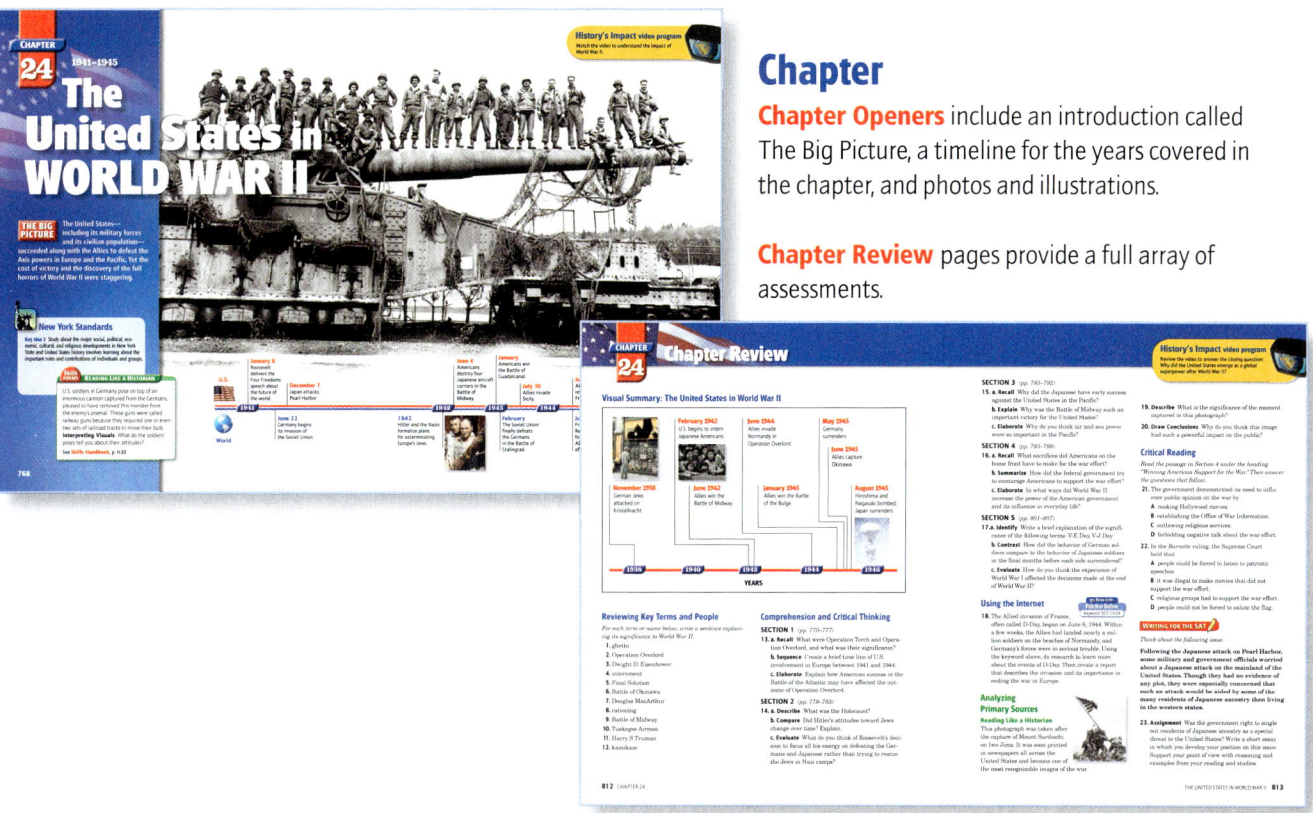

Chapter

Chapter Openers include an introduction called The Big Picture, a timeline for the years covered in the chapter, and photos and illustrations.

Chapter Review pages provide a full array of assessments.

Section

Section opener pages include a Main Idea statement, Focus Questions, and Key Terms and People. In addition, each section includes the following special features:

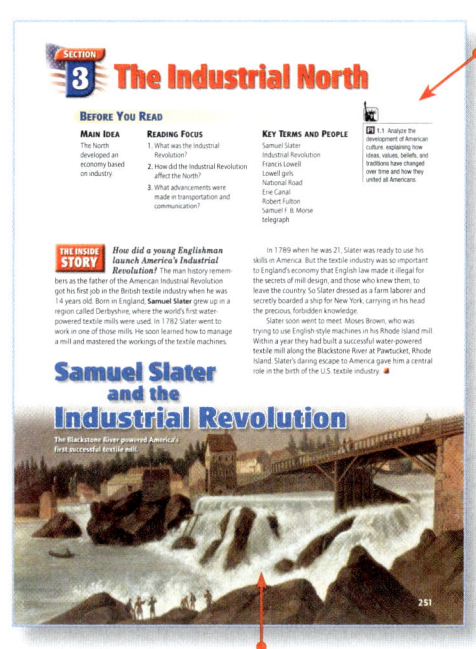

The Inside Story introduces each section with a compelling story from history.

New York Learning Standards for Social Studies Performance Indicators appear on the section opener.

Focus on New York features highlight connections between events in New York and United States history.

Reading Check questions provide opportunities to review and assess your understanding.

Section Assessments help you to check your understanding of a section's main ideas. There is also assessment practice online.

Scavenger Hunt

American Anthem, New York Edition contains a great deal of information about U.S. history. Before you begin your journey into the past, take a minute to familiarize yourself with this book and its contents. This will help make your journey easier.

1 How many units and chapters are in the book? How do you know?

2 Where in *American Anthem, New York Edition* do you find the atlas?

3 The Reading Like a Historian Skills section of the Skills Handbook offers students exposure to and practice in various skills, such as analyzing primary sources. Where in the book do you find additional Reading Like a Historian skill practice?

4 Where and how do you find key terms and people for Chapter 11, Section 2?

5 Where in *American Anthem, New York Edition* do you find strategies for various kinds of test questions?

6 *American Anthem, New York Edition* was created to help you meet all of the social studies standards. Where do you find a description of these standards?

7 Where do you find review questions to help you study?

8 Where do you look to find information about interactive maps and other map essentials?

9 Where do you look to find a list of all of the primary sources used?

10 Where can you find reading support for each unit?

New York State Standards

Welcome to Holt, Rinehart and Winston's *American Anthem, New York Edition.* Throughout this course, you will study the people and events that helped shape our country from prehistory to the present, with an emphasis on the development of the modern United States. To ensure successful study, you will follow the New York State Learning Standards for Social Studies and the more detailed standards outlined in the New York Social Studies Core Curriculum. The Board of Regents approved the New York State Learning Standards for Social Studies as a guide for what students should achieve throughout the year.

Your United States history course will focus on Social Studies Standard 1—History of the United States and New York. Standard 1 requires that you learn about the people, events, and ideas that have helped shape the United States and the state of New York. Standard 1, which is listed on pages ST2–ST3 of this book, is further divided into four Key Ideas. These Key Ideas describe the kinds of information that you will be learning and the kinds of skills that you will be practicing.

Each Key Idea is organized into two parts—Performance Indicators and Sample Tasks. Performance Indicators identify what you must do to demonstrate proficiency within each Key Idea. Sample Tasks provide suggested strategies of fulfilling the Performance Indicators so that you will master each Key Idea.

State Capitol in Albany, New York

New York State Standards

Standard 1—History of the United States and New York

Students will learn a variety of intellectual skills to demonstrate their understanding of major ideas, eras, themes, developments, and turning points in the history of the United States and New York.

KEY IDEA 1: The study of New York State and United States history requires an analysis of the development of American culture, its diversity and multicultural context, and the ways people are unified by many values, practices, and traditions.

PI 1.1 Analyze the development of American culture, explaining how ideas, values, beliefs, and traditions have changed over time and how they united all Americans.

PI 1.2 Describe the evolution of American democratic values and beliefs as expressed in the Declaration of Independence, the New York State Constitution, the United States Constitution, the Bill of Rights, and other important historical documents.

KEY IDEA 2: Important ideas, social and cultural values, beliefs, and traditions from New York State and United States history illustrate the connections and interactions of people and events across time and from a variety of perspectives.

PI 2.1 Discuss several schemes for periodizing the history of New York State and the United States.

PI 2.2 Develop and test hypotheses about important events, eras, or issues in New York State and United States history, setting clear and valid criteria for judging the importance and significance of these events, eras, or issues.

PI 2.3 Compare and contrast the experiences of different groups in the United States.

PI 2.4 Examine how the Constitution, United States law, and the rights of citizenship provide a major unifying factor in bringing together Americans from diverse roots and traditions.

PI 2.5 Analyze the United States involvement in foreign affairs and a willingness to engage in international politics, examining the ideas and traditions leading to these foreign policies.

PI 2.6 Compare and contrast the values exhibited and foreign policies implemented by the United States and other nations over time with those expressed in the United Nations Charter and international law.

Lower Manhattan, New York City

KEY IDEA 3: Study about the major social, political, economic, cultural, and religious developments in New York State and United States history involves learning about the important roles and contributions of individuals and groups.

PI 3.1 Compare and contrast the experiences of different ethnic, national, and religious groups, including Native American Indians, in the United States, explaining their contributions to American society and culture.

PI 3.2 Research and analyze the major themes and developments in New York State and United States history (e.g., colonization and settlement; Revolution and New National Period; immigration; expansion and reform era; Civil War and Reconstruction; the American labor movement; Great Depression; World Wars; contemporary United States).

PI 3.3 Prepare essays and oral reports about the important social, political, economic, scientific, technological, and cultural developments, issues, and events from New York State and United States history.

PI 3.4 Understand the interrelationships between world events and developments in New York State and the United States (e.g., causes for immigration, economic opportunities, human rights abuses, and tyranny versus freedom).

KEY IDEA 4: The skills of historical analysis include the ability to: explain the significance of historical evidence; weigh the importance, reliability, and validity of evidence; understand the concept of multiple causation; understand the importance of changing and competing interpretations of different historical developments.

PI 4.1 Analyze historical narratives about key events in New York State and United States history to identify the facts and evaluate the authors' perspectives.

PI 4.2 Consider different historians' analyses of the same event or development in United States history to understand how different viewpoints and/or frames of reference influence historical interpretations.

PI 4.3 Evaluate the validity and credibility of historical interpretations of important events or issues in New York State or United States history, revising these interpretations as new information is learned and other interpretations are developed. (Adapted from *National Standards for United States History*)

Adirondack State Park

New York Social Studies Core Curriculum

In addition to the Learning Standards, Key Ideas, and Performance Indicators, the New York State Education Department has developed a more detailed set of standards known as the New York Social Studies Core Curriculum. The Core Curriculum lists expectations for student mastery of content and skills during the course of United States History and Government.

The Core Curriculum, which is listed on pages ST4–ST6, is organized chronologically across seven historical units, each of which covers a specific period of history. Each unit lists specific content, concepts and themes, and connections to key historical people, places, and events in United States history and government. The content of the Core Curriculum provides the basis for the New York State Regents examination in United States History and Government.

Unit One: Introduction

I. Geography

  A. The physical/cultural setting in the Americas

  B. Role/influence of geography on historical/cultural development

  C. Geographic issues today

  D. Demographics

Unit Two: Constitutional Foundations for the United States Democratic Republic

II. The Constitution: The Foundation of American Society

  A. Historical foundations

  B. Constitutional Convention

  C. The Bill of Rights

  D. Basic structure and function: three branches and their operation

  E. Basic constitutional principles

  F. Implementing the new constitutional principles

III. The Constitution Tested: Nationalism and Sectionalism

  A. Factors unifying the United States, 1789–1861

  B. Constitutional stress and crisis

  C. Territorial expansion through diplomacy, migration, annexation, and war; Manifest destiny

  D. The Constitution in jeopardy: The American Civil War

Ossining, New York

Niagara Falls

Fort Ticonderoga

NEW YORK STATE STANDARDS

Farm near Delhi, New York

Standards Practice and Plan

What events in United States history have led to the events of today? What effect have resources, environment, and technology had on the course of United States history? What can we learn from historical documents about the actions and intentions of the American people? What role does bias play in historical interpretation?

The New York State Education Department Board of Regents adopted the Learning Standards for Social Studies to help answer these questions. Social Studies Standard 1 covers the history of the United States and New York. The key ideas (KI), performance indicators (PI), and sample tasks (ST) for Standard 1 highlight the outstanding people and events and the fundamental concepts of United States and New York history. You are required to master these concepts for the United States History and Government Regents Exam. All high school students in New York must pass this exam to graduate.

Standards Practice and Plan is your guide. This assessment workbook introduces you to the components of Standard 1 that you are required to master. Use this resource to help you learn and analyze the information presented in your United States history course.

Standards Practice and Plan helps you by

- **Breaking down the learning.** This workbook examines a different key idea every week. A practice question is presented for each day of the week. Each question allows you to explore one or more performance indicators.
- **Connecting the performance indicators and sample tasks to your United States history textbook.** References at the end of each question direct you to relevant material in your textbook. You can use these references to find answers and review important information. Questions move consecutively through your textbook, so you learn key ideas and performance indicators as you learn the text.
- **Using different information sources.** Each section includes questions derived from maps, charts, graphic organizers, images, and primary sources. These questions expose you to different forms of historical documentation and require you to think about historical information in a variety of ways.
- **Giving you answers.** *Standards Practice and Plan* includes an Answer Key against which you can check your mastery of United States and New York history.

KEY IDEA 3 Study about the major social, political, economic, cultural, and religious developments in New York State and United States history involves learning about the important roles and contributions of individuals and groups.

MONDAY  PI 3.1

1 The first Americans were most likely

(Chapter 1.1)

(1) Aztecs

(2) Maya

(3) Anasazi

(4) hunter-gatherers from Asia

TUESDAY PI 3.1

2 Before European colonization, North American indigenous peoples *(Chapter 1.2)*

(1) established one vast culture in the American Northeast that slowly spread west

(2) formed large, clustered civilizations in the American Southwest and Northeast

(3) developed many distinct cultures with different languages, religious beliefs, and economic systems across the continent

(4) split into many small tribal units across the continent that traded peaceably and shared a common language and religious system

WEDNESDAY PI 3.2

3 Which of the following European countries did not establish major settlements in North America?

(Chapters 2.1, 2.2)

(1) Spain

(2) Holland

(3) England

(4) Portugal

THURSDAY  PI 3.2

4 Social contract theory *(Chapter 3.3)*

(1) sought to guarantee liberty by dividing the powers of government

(2) led to the growth of new Protestant denominations in the mid-1700s

(3) questioned the authority of any church to persecute those who did not accept its teachings

(4) held that if a government did not protect citizens and their rights, then citizens were justified in overthrowing it

FRIDAY PI 3.2, PI 3.3

It is not the cause of a poor printer, nor of New York alone, which you are now trying. No! It may in its consequences affect every freeman that lives under a British government on the mainland of America. It is the best Cause. It is the cause of liberty."
—Trial of John Peter Zenger, 1735

5 What significant contribution did the trial of John Peter Zenger make to the development of American democratic values?
(Chapter 3.3)

(1) It set a precedent for trial by jury.

(2) It set a precedent for freedom of the press.

(3) It set a precedent for freedom of religious worship.

(4) It set a precedent for criticism of colonial governments.

KEY IDEA 1 The study of New York State and United States history requires an analysis of the development of American culture, its diversity and multicultural context, and the ways people are unified by many values, practices, and traditions.

MONDAY

 PI 1.1, PI 1.2

1 Colonists objected to the Stamp Act, the Townshend Acts, the Tea Act, and the Intolerable Acts because all of these

(Chapter 4.1)

(1) led to a boycott of American goods

(2) resulted in less government involvement from Britain

(3) threatened the colonies' power of self-government

(4) jeopardized the colonists' security and ability to settle western lands

TUESDAY

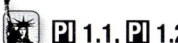 PI 1.1, PI 1.2

2 From which of the following Enlightenment thinkers did the authors of the Declaration of Independence adopt many of their principles? *(Chapter 4.2)*

(1) John Locke

(2) Sir Isaac Newton

(3) Jonathan Edwards

(4) Jean-Jacques Rousseau

WEDNESDAY

 PI 1.2

3 What does this cartoon illustrate?

(Chapter 5.3)

(1) the American Revolution

(2) colonial resistance to British policies

(3) conflicts between colonists and Native Americans

(4) the struggle over ratification of the U.S. Constitution

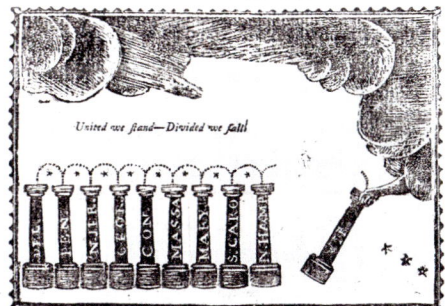

THURSDAY

 PI 1.1, PI 1.1

4 How does the First Amendment affect religious liberty in the United States?

(Chapter 5.3)

(1) It gave states the power to regulate religion.

(2) It gives Congress the power to make laws regarding any religion or religious practice.

(3) It guarantees citizens the right to hold any religious belief and forbids the establishment of state churches.

(4) It guarantees citizens the right to hold any religious belief but gives states the right to establish official state churches.

FRIDAY

 PI 1.2

5 What was the significance of *Marbury* v. *Madison*? *(Chapter 6.3)*

(1) It upheld the president's power to appoint judges.

(2) It led to the formation of new positions in the judiciary branch.

(3) It established the Supreme Court's right to declare a law unconstitutional.

(4) It established the Supreme Court's right to refuse presidential appointments.

KEY IDEA 3 Study about the major social, political, economic, cultural, and religious developments in New York State and United States history involves learning about the important roles and contributions of individuals and groups.

MONDAY
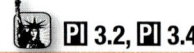 **PI 3.2, PI 3.4**

> *The American continents ... are henceforth not to be considered as subjects for future colonization by any European powers.*
> Monroe Doctrine, 1823

1 **The Monroe Doctrine was** *(Chapter 7.1)*

(1) an invitation for foreign colonization

(2) a policy of active U.S. involvement in Europe

(3) a plan for reorganizing the U.S. government

(4) an effort to keep the United States out of European affairs and European countries from colonizing the Americas

TUESDAY
 PI 3.2

2 **A Boston newspaper called James Monroe's presidency "the era of good feelings" because** *(Chapter 7.1)*

(1) the United States embraced a new spirit of isolationism

(2) it was characterized by economic growth and feelings of nationalism

(3) the administration focused on existing states, not expansion into new territories

(4) European nations and the United States entered into economic and diplomatic partnerships

WEDNESDAY
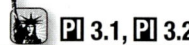 **PI 3.1, PI 3.2**

3 **What was the significance of Andrew Jackson's policy toward Native Americans in the 1830s?** *(Chapter 7.2)*

(1) It contributed to the development of an independent Cherokee state.

(2) It led to the forced removal of thousands of Native Americans from the southeastern United States.

(3) It ended in a war that eliminated most of the Native American population east of the Mississippi River.

(4) It prompted a new series of treaties guaranteeing mutual respect and cooperation between Native Americans and the United States.

THURSDAY
 PI 3.2, PI 3.3

4 **The Industrial Revolution refers to a period from the mid-1700s to the mid-1800s when** *(Chapters 7.3, 7.4)*

(1) cities in both the North and South grew at a faster rate

(2) American business owners rebelled against British business owners

(3) technological developments changed the way of life in both the North and the South

(4) agriculture and handcrafts gave way to machine production and manufacturing

FRIDAY
 **PI 3.1**

5 **The Second Great Awakening revived religious fervor by encouraging** *(Chapter 8.1)*

(1) people that their destiny lay in their own hands

(2) a return to traditional values and strict adherence to church rules

(3) the codification of Christian doctrine as law at all levels of government

(4) the establishment of new churches based on public displays of faith and denial of material wants

KEY IDEA 2 Important ideas, social and cultural values, beliefs, and traditions from New York State and United States history illustrate the connections and interactions of people and events across time and from a variety of perspectives.

MONDAY
 P 2.2, P 2.3

1 **What effect did the Great Irish Famine have on the United States?** *(Chapter 8.2)*

(1) United States citizens undertook a massive relief effort.

(2) More than 1 million Irish immigrated to the United States.

(3) Trade between Europe and the United States decreased by more than half.

(4) The United States government began using federal monies to provide foreign aid.

TUESDAY
 P 2.1, P 2.2

2 **During the 1800s the United States underwent which two significant economic and social processes?** *(Chapter 8.2)*

(1) revolution and expansion

(2) reformation and unionization

(3) militarization and privatization

(4) industrialization and urbanization

WEDNESDAY
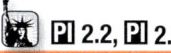 P 2.2, P 2.3

3 **According to the map, routes along the Underground Railroad** *(Chapter 8.4)*

(1) began in free states

(2) ran only from east to west

(3) originated in slave states

(4) led only to territories where slavery was permitted

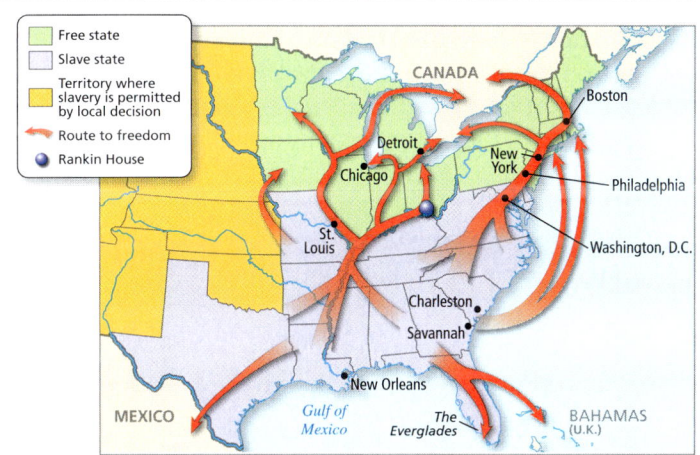

Legend:
- Free state
- Slave state
- Territory where slavery is permitted by local decision
- Route to freedom
- Rankin House

CANADA, Boston, Detroit, New York, Chicago, Philadelphia, St. Louis, Washington, D.C., Charleston, Savannah, New Orleans, MEXICO, Gulf of Mexico, The Everglades, BAHAMAS (U.K.)

THURSDAY
 P 2.2

4 **Manifest destiny can best be described as the belief that the United States** *(Chapter 9.1)*

(1) had the right and obligation to spread across the entire continent

(2) was destined to advance freedom and democracy around the world

(3) had a mission to industrialize and advance capitalism around the world

(4) was entitled to oversee political and economic developments throughout the Western Hemisphere

FRIDAY
 P 2.3

5 **What group, founded by Joseph Smith, migrated west when its practices came under attack in the mid-1800s?** *(Chapter 9.1)*

(1) Quakers

(2) Mormons

(3) Christians

(4) Seventh-Day Adventists

KEY IDEA 3 Study about the major social, political, economic, cultural, and religious developments in New York State and United States history involves learning about the important roles and contributions of individuals and groups.

 **MONDAY** PI 3.1, PI 3.3

1 What significant social effect did the Kansas-Nebraska Act have on settlement in those territories? *(Chapters 10.1, 10.2)*

(1) It caused a rapid decline in settlement.

(2) It contributed to a rapid growth in urbanization.

(3) It established a precedent for deciding the slavery issue peaceably by ballot.

(4) It led to violence between competing waves of proslavery and Free-Soil settlers.

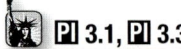 **TUESDAY** PI 3.1, PI 3.3

2 Which of the following people led a raid on the U.S. arsenal at Harpers Ferry with the intention of starting a slave revolt? *(Chapter 10.2)*

(1) Dred Scott

(2) John Brown

(3) Preston Brooks

(4) Steven Douglas

WEDNESDAY PI 3.1, PI 3.3

3 This map illustrates the national split caused by Abraham Lincoln's election, which led to the *(Chapters 10.3, 10.4)*

(1) Freeport Doctrine

(2) call for a new election

(3) secession of southern states

(4) formation of the Republican party

Candidate	Political Affiliation	Electoral Votes	Popular Votes
Abraham Lincoln	Republican	180	1,868,452
John C. Breckinridge	Southern Democratic	72	847,953
John Bell	Constitutional Union	39	590,631
Stephen A. Douglas	Northern Democratic	12	1,375,157

Striped pattern shows state where electoral votes went to two candidates as indicated by the colors.

 **THURSDAY** PI 3.1, PI 3.3

4 Which of the following groups of people did the Emancipation Proclamation free? *(Chapter 11.3)*

(1) enslaved persons in U.S. territories

(2) enslaved persons in other countries

(3) enslaved persons throughout the United States

(4) enslaved persons in areas in rebellion against the United States

 **FRIDAY** PI 3.2, PI 3.3

5 What unconstitutional action did Abraham Lincoln take when he jailed critics of the war and the draft? *(Chapter 11.3)*

(1) Lincoln declared martial law.

(2) Lincoln suspended habeas corpus.

(3) Lincoln issued a declaration of war.

(4) Lincoln issued an executive order opposing the First Amendment.

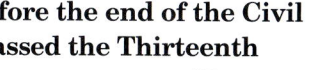

WEEK 6

 KEY IDEA 3 Study about the major social, political, economic, cultural, and religious developments in New York State and United States history involves learning about the important roles and contributions of individuals and groups.

MONDAY PI 3.1, PI 3.2

1 **During the Civil War people from states and territories west of the Mississippi River** *(Chapter 11.4)*

(1) remained neutral

(2) sided only with the Union

(3) sided only with the Confederacy

(4) fought for both the Union and the Confederacy

TUESDAY PI 3.2

2 **Early in 1865, before the end of the Civil War, Congress passed the Thirteenth Amendment to** *(Chapter 11.5)*

(1) abolish slavery

(2) establish the electoral college system

(3) grant citizenship to former enslaved persons

(4) guarantee former enslaved persons the right to vote

WEDNESDAY PI 3.1, PI 3.2

3 **In March 1865 the Freedmen's Bureau was established to** *(Chapter 12.1)*

(1) lead enslaved persons to freedom in the North

(2) advocate for civil rights on behalf of former enslaved persons

(3) help black and white southerners uprooted by the Civil War

(4) combat the influx of carpetbaggers and scalawags in the South

THURSDAY  PI 3.2, PI 3.3

4 **What was the key difference between Reconstruction under Andrew Johnson and Reconstruction under Congress?** *(Chapter 12.2)*

(1) Johnson's Reconstruction ensured a role for freedmen in southern government.

(2) Congressional Reconstruction helped preserve the old Confederate power structure.

(3) Johnson's Reconstruction involved harsher penalties against the former Confederate states.

(4) Congressional Reconstruction made it more difficult for southern states to rejoin the Union.

FRIDAY PI 3.2, PI 3.3

5 **This image illustrates the shift in the Reconstruction South from** *(Chapter 12.3)*

(1) Democratic control to Republican control

(2) plantations to sharecropping and tenant farming

(3) industrialization to an emphasis on agricultural businesses

(4) an agrarian plantation system to an industrialized economy

KEY IDEA 3 Study about the major social, political, economic, cultural, and religious developments in New York State and United States history involves learning about the important roles and contributions of individuals and groups.

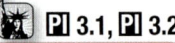 **MONDAY**  PI 3.1, PI 3.2

1 **Americanization refers to** *(Chapter 13.1)*

(1) policies restricting interaction among Native American groups

(2) efforts by the U.S. government to remove Native Americans from U.S. territories

(3) practices meant to isolate Native Americans in cultural pockets on their reservations

(4) programs designed to dissolve Native American tribal identities and acculturate Native Americans

TUESDAY PI 3.1, PI 3.2

2 **Which of the following industries drew many people west in the mid-1800s?**

(Chapter 13.2)

(1) mining

(2) trading

(3) shipping

(4) manufacturing

WEDNESDAY  PI 3.1, PI 3.2

3 **In the late 1800s most of the railroad lines shown**

(Chapter 14.1)

(1) linked the United States and Canada

(2) were clustered in the Pacific Time Zone

(3) were clustered in the Central and Eastern Time Zones

(4) extended only as far west as places in the Mountain Time Zone

THURSDAY PI 3.2, PI 3.3

4 **Corporate trusts and monopolies, such as John D. Rockefeller's Standard Oil, were extensions of business practices grounded in** *(Chapter 14.2)*

(1) philanthropy

(2) mass marketing

(3) laissez-faire capitalism

(4) governmental regulation

FRIDAY 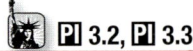 PI 3.2, PI 3.3

5 **What effect did industrialization have on working conditions in the United States?**

(Chapters 14.2, 14.3)

(1) Workers enjoyed income equality across classes.

(2) Laborers worked eight-hour days in well-paying jobs.

(3) Employers provided workers with benefits, such as sick leave.

(4) Workers labored long hours in poor conditions at low-paying jobs.

KEY IDEA 3 Study about the major social, political, economic, cultural, and religious developments in New York State and United States history involves learning about the important roles and contributions of individuals and groups.

 **MONDAY** PI 3.1, PI 3.2

1 In the late 1800s workers responded to poor conditions and wages by *(Chapter 14.3)*

(1) creating blacklists

(2) organizing labor unions

(3) taking over control of factories

(4) pushing for anti-immigrant legislation

 **TUESDAY** PI 3.2, PI 3.3

2 All of the following inventions reshaped life in the late 1800s except *(Chapter 14.4)*

(1) airplanes

(2) telephones

(3) typewriters

(4) electrical lighting

WEDNESDAY PI 3.1, PI 3.2

3 This map shows how immigrants in the late 1800s changed the face of Chicago—and other cities—by *(Chapter 15.1)*

(1) pushing out earlier immigrants

(2) building cultural enclaves around the cities

(3) settling in ethnic neighborhoods within cities

(4) integrating into existing neighborhoods and adopting local customs

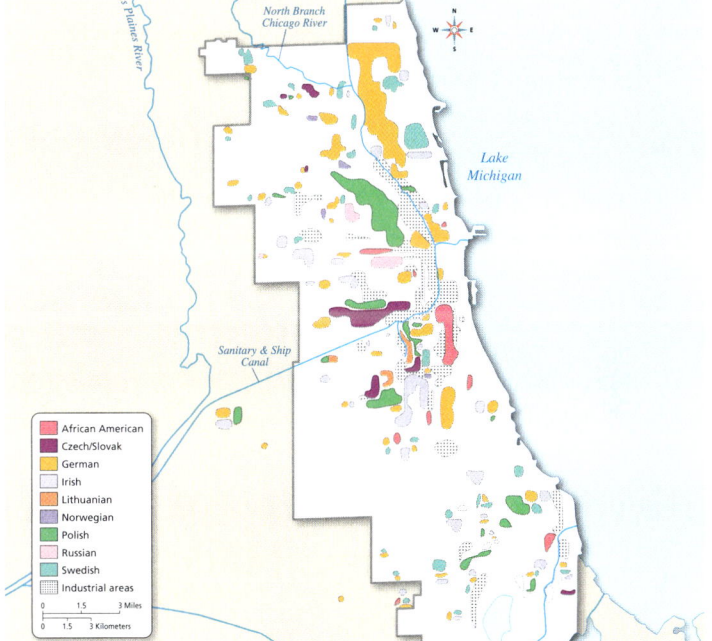

 THURSDAY PI 3.1, PI 3.3

4 In the late 1800s urban political machines often gained power by *(Chapter 15.3)*

(1) changing to the gold standard

(2) offering jobs, housing, and other help to immigrants

(3) organizing labor leaders and reformers to combat corruption

(4) promising to reduce immigration and competition for jobs

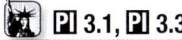 **FRIDAY** PI 3.1, PI 3.3

5 In the case *Plessy* v. *Ferguson*, the Supreme Court *(Chapter 15.4)*

(1) legalized slavery in all U.S. territories

(2) overturned the "separate but equal" standard

(3) legalized segregation and established the "separate but equal" standard

(4) declared Jim Crow laws unconstitutional, which led to voting rights reform

 **KEY IDEA 1** The study of New York State and United States history requires an analysis of the development of American culture, its diversity and multicultural context, and the ways people are unified by many values, practices, and traditions.

MONDAY PI 1.1

1 Jacob Riis' photographs in *How the Other Half Lives* shocked many people in the early 1900s by revealing the *(Chapter 16.1)*

(1) conditions of urban poverty

(2) need for workplace reforms

(3) cultural practices of immigrants

(4) standard of living in western European nations

TUESDAY PI 1.2

2 The Seventeenth Amendment had an important effect on the American democratic process by *(Chapter 16.1)*

(1) reducing the voting age to 18

(2) introducing the electoral college

(3) guaranteeing all citizens the right to vote

(4) giving voters the power to elect their senators directly

WEDNESDAY  PI 1.1, PI 1.2

3 This cartoon illustrates Theodore Roosevelt's determination to *(Chapter 16.3)*

(1) become president of the United States

(2) break up trusts that were not in the public interest

(3) persuade voters to embrace his Square Deal platform

(4) discourage competition by promoting de-regulation of business

NO MOLLY-CODDLING HERE

THE GRANGER COLLECTION, NEW YORK

THURSDAY  PI 1.1

4 Upton Sinclair's *The Jungle* exposed *(Chapter 16.3)*

(1) child labor in the textile industry

(2) child labor in the mining industry

(3) poor sanitation and unsafe working conditions in the meatpacking industry

(4) poor sanitation and unsafe working conditions in the iron and steel industry

FRIDAY PI 1.1, PI 1.2

5 In what year did women gain full voting rights? *(Chapter 16.4)*

(1) 1868

(2) 1896

(3) 1920

(4) 1965

WEEK 10

KEY IDEA 2 Important ideas, social and cultural values, beliefs, and traditions from New York State and United States history illustrate the connections and interactions of people and events across time and from a variety of perspectives.

MONDAY PI 2.2, PI 2.5

1 **Secretary of State John Hay's Open Door Policy was meant to** *(Chapter 17.1)*

(1) isolate China and its products from the rest of the world

(2) allow unrestricted Chinese immigration to the United States

(3) give the United States exclusive trading privileges with China

(4) give all nations, including the United States, equal trading rights in China

TUESDAY PI 2.5, PI 2.6

2 **The interests of the United States in Asia, Latin America, and the Pacific islands in the 1800s can best be described as** *(Chapters 17.1, 17.2, 17.3)*

(1) diplomatic

(2) imperialist

(3) democratic

(4) commercial

WEDNESDAY PI 2.5, PI 2.6

3 **Both Theodore Roosevelt's "Big Stick" diplomacy and William Taft's dollar diplomacy were designed to** *(Chapter 17.3)*

(1) help Cuba remain independent

(2) protect U.S. interests and influence in Latin America

(3) increase European intervention in Latin America

(4) establish permanent military bases in countries around the world

THURSDAY PI 2.2, PI 2.5

4 **In 1917 the United States entered World War I as a result of the** *(Chapter 18.2)*

(1) British defeat at Gallipoli

(2) sinking of the *Lusitania*

(3) German invasion of Belgium

(4) sinking of three American merchant ships by German U-boats

FRIDAY PI 2.4, PI 2.5

5 **This poster, used by the Committee on Public Information to build and maintain support for the war effort, is an example of which of the following?** *(Chapter 18.3)*

(1) war bonds

(2) legislation

(3) propaganda

(4) executive order

NEW YORK STATE STANDARDS PRACTICE

KEY IDEA 2 Important ideas, social and cultural values, beliefs, and traditions from New York State and United States history illustrate the connections and interactions of people and events across time and from a variety of perspectives.

MONDAY  PI 2.2

1 After World War I communism and other radical ideas that threatened American norms led to the Red Scare and

(Chapter 19.1)

(1) renewed confidence in labor unions

(2) the start of the Bolshevik Revolution

(3) an attack known as the Palmer Raids

(4) greater understanding between earlier and more recent immigrants

TUESDAY PI 2.2

2 Warren Harding and Calvin Coolidge would have likely agreed on the ideas of

(Chapter 19.3)

(1) limiting big business and funding more public works projects

(2) promoting business and limiting government regulatory power

(3) increasing government oversight and strictly enforcing business regulations

(4) regulating business only when it conflicts with the public interest and supporting the nation's farmers

WEDNESDAY PI 2.2

3 This cartoon about the Scopes trial illustrates one of the most dramatic conflicts between supporters of the separation of church and state and

(Chapter 20.1)

(1) fundamentalism

(2) social Darwinism

(3) transcendentalism

(4) Protestant revivalism

GATHERING DATA FOR THE TENNESSEE TRIAL

THURSDAY 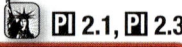 PI 2.1, PI 2.3

4 All of the following were renowned figures during the Harlem Renaissance except

(Chapter 20.2)

(1) Billy Sunday

(2) Langston Hughes

(3) Zora Neale Hurston

(4) James Weldon Johnson

FRIDAY PI 2.2

5 In the 1920s the growth of radio, film, and the automobile contributed to the

(Chapter 20.3)

(1) Great Depression

(2) end of World War I

(3) suffrage movement

(4) development of a common American culture

KEY IDEA 3 Study about the major social, political, economic, cultural, and religious developments in New York State and United States history involves learning about the important roles and contributions of individuals and groups.

MONDAY 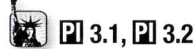 **PI** 3.1, **PI** 3.2

1 What potential issue does this chart illustrate?

(Chapter 21.1)

(1) The distribution of wealth and income were well balanced.

(2) The boom of the Roaring Twenties hid great economic disparity.

(3) Only a small percentage of workers invested in the stock market.

(4) Few workers earned enough income to participate in the new consumer culture.

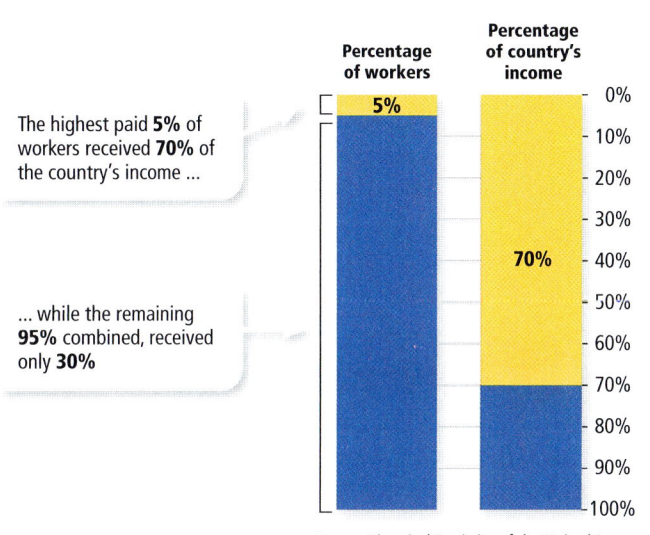

DISTRIBUTION OF WEALTH, 1929

Percentage of workers

Percentage of country's income

The highest paid **5%** of workers received **70%** of the country's income ...

5%

70%

... while the remaining **95%** combined, received only **30%**

Source: *Historical Statistics of the United States*

TUESDAY  **PI** 3.2, **PI** 3.3

2 Which of the following contributed to the Great Depression? *(Chapters 21.1, 21.2)*

(1) labor shortages

(2) the stock market boom

(3) business and farm foreclosures

(4) increases in consumer spending

WEDNESDAY **PI** 3.2

3 Which of the following compounded the devastation of the Great Depression?

(Chapter 21.2)

(1) World War II

(2) the Red Scare

(3) an influenza epidemic

(4) drought and dust storms in the Great Plains

THURSDAY  **PI** 3.1, **PI** 3.2

4 During the 1930s many people who lived in the Dust Bowl states *(Chapter 21.2)*

(1) migrated east

(2) migrated west

(3) joined labor unions

(4) went to work on the railroads

FRIDAY  **PI** 3.2, **PI** 3.3

5 Henry Ford revolutionized the manufacturing industry by introducing which of the following? *(Chapter 21.2)*

(1) the automobile

(2) the assembly line

(3) welfare capitalism

(4) the concept of buying on credit

KEY IDEA 1 The study of New York State and United States history requires an analysis of the development of American culture, its diversity and multicultural context, and the ways people are unified by many values, practices, and traditions.

MONDAY PI 1.2

1 All of the following were part of Franklin Roosevelt's New Deal except the
(Chapters 21.3, 22.1)

(1) Securities Act

(2) Smoot-Hawley Tariff Act

(3) Civilian Conservation Corps

(4) Public Works Administration

TUESDAY PI 1.2

2 One major criticism of the New Deal was that the programs *(Chapter 22.1)*

(1) failed to alleviate unemployment

(2) gave too much power to the executive branch

(3) did not include provisions for banking reforms

(4) ceded too much federal decision-making to state governments

WEDNESDAY PI 1.1, PI 1.2

3 Social Security represented a major change in the relationship between the federal government and the citizenry because it *(Chapter 22.2)*

(1) restructured the federal tax system

(2) set up a national pension and healthcare system for all American workers

(3) provided immediate economic relief in the form of paid jobs on public works projects

(4) promised a government-funded pension and unemployment insurance for many American workers

THURSDAY PI 1.1

4 One key difference between the American Federation of Labor and the Committee for Industrial Organization was that the *(Chapter 22.2)*

(1) CIO represented the interests of unskilled workers

(2) AFL represented the interests of unskilled workers

(3) CIO won every confrontation with American business

(4) AFL represented unions organized across broad industries

FRIDAY PI 1.1, PI 1.2

5 This graph supports the statement that the 1935 National Labor Relations Act *(Chapter 22.2)*

(1) helped increase union membership

(2) restricted workers' rights to organize

(3) encouraged company-sponsored unions

(4) discouraged the organizing of unions across industries

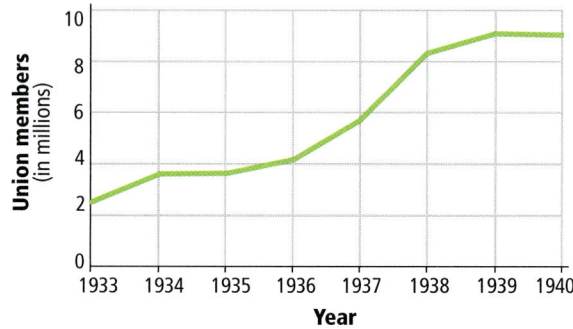

GROWTH OF UNION MEMBERSHIP, 1933 - 1940

Source: *Historical Statistics of the United States*

KEY IDEA 2 Important ideas, social and cultural values, beliefs, and traditions from New York State and United States history illustrate the connections and interactions of people and events across time and from a variety of perspectives.

MONDAY
PI 2.2, PI 2.5

1 Which of the following events changed American public opinion in support of U.S. involvement in World War II?
(Chapter 23.3)

(1) Japan's invasion of China

(2) Italy's invasion of Ethiopia

(3) Japan's attack on Pearl Harbor

(4) the sinking of the USS *Reuben James*

TUESDAY
PI 2.3, PI 2.6

2 During World War II, African Americans
(Chapter 23.4)

(1) did not serve in the military

(2) served in the military in segregated units

(3) served in the military without discrimination

(4) served in the military in noncombat capacities only

WEDNESDAY
PI 2.5, PI 2.6

3 After World War II the United States, Great Britain, France, and the Soviet Union organized which of the following bodies to deal with the Nazis responsible for the Holocaust?
(Chapter 24.2)

(1) United Nations

(2) Yalta Conference

(3) International Military Tribunal

(4) North Atlantic Treaty Organization

THURSDAY
PI 2.3, PI 2.4

4 Which of the following actions on the part of the United States conflicted with constitutional liberties?
(Chapter 24.4)

(1) the policy of food rationing

(2) the declaration of war on Japan

(3) the internment of Japanese Americans

(4) the bombing of Hiroshima and Nagasaki

FRIDAY
PI 2.2, PI 2.5

5 This image shows a mushroom cloud from what new weapon used by the United States during World War II?
(Chapters 23.4, 24.5)

(1) atomic bomb

(2) neutron bomb

(3) hydrogen bomb

(4) thermonuclear bomb

KEY IDEA 2 Important ideas, social and cultural values, beliefs, and traditions from New York State and United States history illustrate the connections and interactions of people and events across time and from a variety of perspectives.

MONDAY

 PI 2.5

1 Aid given by the United States under the Marshall Plan was part of a broader Cold War policy of *(Chapter 25.1)*

(1) détente

(2) containment

(3) brinkmanship

(4) dollar diplomacy

THE MARSHALL PLAN

Purpose: A U.S. financial aid program to rebuild the economies of European countries in order to create stable conditions for democratic governments.

Total amount of aid: $13.4 billion

Number of countries that received aid: 17

Countries that received the most aid: Great Britain, France, and Italy

TUESDAY

 PI 2.2, PI 2.5

2 In 1949 twelve nations, including the United States, formed the North Atlantic Treaty Organization in reaction to the *(Chapter 25.1)*

(1) Korean War

(2) Cuban missile crisis

(3) Soviet blockade of Berlin

(4) formation of the Warsaw Pact

WEDNESDAY

 PI 2.5, PI 2.6

3 The Universal Declaration of Human Rights, adopted by the United Nations in 1948, did all of the following except *(Chapter 25.2)*

(1) ban the use of weapons of mass destruction

(2) declare that all human beings are born free and equal

(3) mandate an end to torture, slavery, and inhumane punishment

(4) demand civil rights, such as the right to assembly and the right to a fair trial

THURSDAY

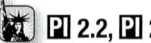 PI 2.2, PI 2.6

4 McCarthyism was empowered primarily by *(Chapter 25.3)*

(1) Ethel and Julius Rosenberg

(2) the public's fear of communism

(3) propaganda films made in Hollywood

(4) the conflict surrounding the Vietnam War

FRIDAY

 PI 2.5, PI 2.6

5 In the 1950s President Eisenhower warned that the arms industry in the United States had *(Chapter 26.2)*

(1) adjusted slowly to the demands of modern war

(2) become a permanent, vast, military-industrial complex

(3) fallen behind the technological advancements of the Soviet arms industry

(4) focused too much on technological development and not enough on maintaining conventional arms

KEY IDEA 2 Important ideas, social and cultural values, beliefs, and traditions from New York State and United States history illustrate the connections and interactions of people and events across time and from a variety of perspectives.

 **MONDAY** 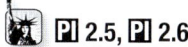 PI 2.1, PI 2.2

1 John F. Kennedy's presidency was largely dominated by a period of volatile international relations know as the *(Chapter 27.1)*

(1) Cold War

(2) Red Scare

(3) Iron Curtain

(4) Great Society

TUESDAY  PI 2.5, PI 2.6

2 The Bay of Pigs invasion was orchestrated by the CIA to *(Chapter 27.1)*

(1) support the French in Vietnam

(2) overthrow Fidel Castro in Cuba

(3) regain control of the Suez Canal

(4) restore independence to South Korea

 **WEDNESDAY** PI 2.3, PI 2.4

3 During the 1950s and 1960s, the Supreme Court under Chief Justice Earl Warren did all of the following except *(Chapter 27.2)*

(1) ban racial segregation in the nation's schools

(2) rule that legislative districts must have equal populations

(3) extend the Bill of Rights to cover the actions of state governments

(4) deny people the right to lawyers during routine police questioning

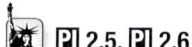 **THURSDAY** PI 2.5, PI 2.6

4 Lyndon Johnson's guideline for intervention in Latin America was known as the *(Chapter 27.3)*

(1) Great Society

(2) New Frontier

(3) Pueblo incident

(4) Johnson Doctrine

FRIDAY  PI 2.2, PI 2.3

5 Which Great Society program provided housing for low-income Americans? *(Chapter 27.3)*

(1) Civil Rights Acts

(2) Voting Rights Act

(3) Omnibus Housing Act

(4) Economic Opportunity Act

MAJOR GREAT SOCIETY PROGRAMS

Year Enacted	Legislation	Purpose and Provisions
1964	Economic Opportunity Act	created the Job Corps, VISTA, and eight other programs to fight the "war on poverty"
1964	Tax Reduction Act	cut income tax rates up to 30%, with the greatest cuts going to lower-income
1964	Civil Rights Act	outlawed discrimination in housing, employment, and public accomodations; authorized federal government to enforce desegregation
1965	Elementary and Secondary School Act	provided aid to school systems based on number of students from low-income homes
1965	Social Security Amendments	established Medicare and Medicaid
1965	Voting Rights Act	ended the requirement that voters pass literacy tests and allowed federal supervision of voter registration
1965	Omnibus Housing Act	provided housing for low-income Americans
1965	Water Quality Act	required states to clean up rivers and lakes
1965	Higher Education Act	provided scholarships and low-interest loans for college students

KEY IDEA 3 Study about the major social, political, economic, cultural, and religious developments in New York State and United States history involves learning about the important roles and contributions of individuals and groups.

MONDAY  PI 3.2

1 The arrest of Rosa Parks in 1955 led to integrated *(Chapter 28.1)*

(1) buses

(2) public schools

(3) universities and colleges

(4) lunch counters and restaurants

TUESDAY PI 3.1, PI 3.2

2 James Farmer of CORE and Martin Luther King Jr. of SCLC drew on what principle of Mohandas Gandhi when organizing the civil rights movement? *(Chapter 28.2)*

(1) political action

(2) massive resistance

(3) nonviolent resistance

(4) public accommodations

WEDNESDAY PI 3.2

"I have a dream that one day this nation will rise up and live out the true meaning of its creed: 'We hold these truths to be self-evident; that all men are created equal.' …
I have a dream that my four little children will one day live in a nation where they will not be judged by the color of their skin, but by the content of their character.
I have a dream today!"
—Martin Luther King Jr., August 28, 1963

3 During what event in 1963 did Martin Luther King Jr. give this speech? *(Chapter 28.2)*

(1) Selma march

(2) Freedom Rides

(3) March on Washington

(4) Birmingham campaign

THURSDAY PI 3.2

4 Lyndon Johnson strongly supported the Civil Rights Act of 1964, which *(Chapter 28.2)*

(1) made harming civil rights workers a federal crime

(2) eliminated the use of literacy tests for voting registration

(3) made segregation in institutions of higher education illegal

(4) banned discrimination in employment and in public accommodations

FRIDAY PI 3.2

5 The voter registration efforts of Freedom Summer followed the passage of the *(Chapter 28.3)*

(1) Civil Rights Act

(2) Voting Rights Act

(3) Equal Rights Amendment

(4) Twenty-fourth Amendment

KEY IDEA 3 Study about the major social, political, economic, cultural, and religious developments in New York State and United States history involves learning about the important roles and contributions of individuals and groups.

MONDAY
 PI 3.3, PI 3.4

1 In 1964 the Tonkin Gulf Resolution expanded presidential powers by
(Chapter 29.1)

(1) stripping Congress of its power to declare war

(2) giving the president the power to declare war even in peacetime

(3) making the president the commander-in-chief of the armed forces

(4) giving the president the power to make war in Southeast Asia without a declaration of war

TUESDAY
 PI 3.1, PI 3.2

2 The Equal Rights Amendment (ERA), which passed Congress but failed to win ratification in enough states, promised
(Chapter 30.1)

(1) equal treatment of men and women only in the public sector

(2) equal opportunities for men and women only in the workplace

(3) equal treatment for men and women in all spheres of society

(4) equal opportunities for men and women only in institutions of higher education

WEDNESDAY
 PI 3.2, PI 3.3

3 The American Indian Movement (AIM) and the larger Red Power movement were responses to the federal government's
(Chapter 30.1)

(1) termination policy

(2) urbanization policy

(3) Americanization policy

(4) Native American self-determination policy

THURSDAY
 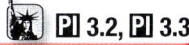 **PI 3.2, PI 3.3**

4 Which Latino leader became a national figure after heading the Great Grape Boycott? *(Chapter 30.2)*

(1) César Chávez

(2) Rodolfo Gonzales

(3) Henry B. Gonzalez

(4) José Angel Gutiérrez

FRIDAY
 PI 3.1, PI 3.2

*"I have endured in the rugged mountains /
Of our country / I have survived the toils
and slavery of the fields. / I have existed /
In the barrios of the city / In the suburbs
of bigotry / In the mines of social snobbery
/ In the prisons of dejection / In the muck
of exploitation / And / In the fierce heat
of racial hatred. / And now the trumpet
sounds, / The music of the people stirs the
/ Revolution. . . . "*

—Rodolfo "Corky" Gonzales,
"I Am Joaquín"

5 This song became an anthem for which of the following movements? *(Chapter 30.2)*

(1) labor movement

(2) Chicano movement

(3) Red Power movement

(4) Black Power movement

KEY IDEA 2 Important ideas, social and cultural values, beliefs, and traditions from New York State and United States history illustrate the connections and interactions of people and events across time and from a variety of perspectives.

MONDAY  **P1** 2.3, **P1** 2.4

1 As president Richard Nixon supported and worked for all of the following except
(Chapter 31.1)

(1) affirmative action

(2) forced desegregation

(3) social welfare programs

(4) environmental protections

TUESDAY  **P1** 2.1, **P1** 2.6

2 Richard Nixon's presidency was characterized by a foreign policy primarily based on
(Chapter 31.1)

(1) détente

(2) glasnost

(3) containment

(4) shuttle diplomacy

WEDNESDAY  **P1** 2.2

3 The political cartoon shows Richard Nixon hiding behind the seal of the President of the United States. This cartoon was symbolic of Nixon's attempt to protect himself during the Watergate scandal by invoking
(Chapter 31.2)

(1) executive privilege

(2) checks and balances

(3) presidential pardons

(4) the Fifth Amendment

Speaking of sanctuaries ...

THURSDAY  **P1** 2.2

4 An accident at Three Mile Island in Pennsylvania brought attention to the
(Chapter 31.3)

(1) hazards of toxic waste

(2) need for energy conservation

(3) safety risks of nuclear power

(4) nation's dependence on fossil fuels

FRIDAY **P1** 2.1, **P1** 2.5

5 All of the following occurred during Jimmy Carter's presidency except the
(Chapter 31.3)

(1) SALT II talks

(2) Iran-Contra affair

(3) Camp David Accords

(4) Iranian hostage crisis

KEY IDEA 2 Important ideas, social and cultural values, beliefs, and traditions from New York State and United States history illustrate the connections and interactions of people and events across time and from a variety of perspectives.

MONDAY PI 2.2, PI 2.3

1 In the 1980s who became a hero of a growing movement known as the New Right? *(Chapter 32.1)*

(1) Ronald Reagan

(2) Gerald Ford

(3) Richard Nixon

(4) John Anderson

TUESDAY  PI 2.1, PI 2.2

2 The Reaganomics of the 1980s emphasized *(Chapter 32.1)*

(1) supply-side economics

(2) corporate tax increases

(3) reduced military spending

(4) more federal spending on social programs

WEDNESDAY PI 2.2, PI 2.6

And then I hear the noise. Pick, pick, pick. Chuck, chuck, chuck. Growing louder and louder as hundreds of hammers and chisels attack the wall, taking it down chip by chip. I laugh and laugh—and cry at the same time.

—BBC reporter Tim Weber, November 9, 1989

3 This quotation about the end of the Cold War refers to the *(Chapter 32.3)*

(1) velvet revolution

(2) fall of the Berlin Wall

(3) Soviet withdrawal from Afghanistan

(4) meltdown at the Chernobyl nuclear plant

THURSDAY PI 2.2, PI 2.5, PI 2.6

4 Which of the following statements best describes the United States' interest in Iraq's invasion of Kuwait? *(Chapter 32.3)*

(1) Iraq formed a nonmilitary buffer between Kuwait and Iran.

(2) Iraq had rich supplies of petroleum on which the United States depended.

(3) Kuwait had rich supplies of petroleum on which the United States depended.

(4) Iran, Iraq, and Kuwait were allies, making it difficult for the United States to choose sides.

FRIDAY 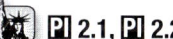 PI 2.1, PI 2.2

5 In 1977 Steve Jobs and Steve Wozniak of Apple Computer launched the computer revolution by *(Chapter 32.4)*

(1) creating the first computer chips

(2) introducing the computer to military engineers

(3) developing computer software that was more user-friendly

(4) making the computer small enough to be usable at home

KEY IDEA 3 Study about the major social, political, economic, cultural, and religious developments in New York State and United States history involves learning about the important roles and contributions of individuals and groups.

MONDAY

 PI 3.2, PI 3.3

1 Which of the following did not contribute to a major Republican victory in the 1994 mid-term elections? *(Chapter 33.1)*

(1) welfare reform

(2) tax increases

(3) Clinton's failed health-care plan

(4) Clinton's failure to deliver on several campaign promises

TUESDAY

 PI 3.1, PI 3.3

2 Critics of the North American Free Trade Agreement contended primarily that *(Chapter 33.1)*

(1) trade between Mexico and the United States would decline

(2) Mexican immigration into the United States would increase

(3) American businesses would not be able to sell more goods in Mexico and Canada

(4) lower wages and fewer regulations in Mexican factories would drive American factories out of business

WEDNESDAY

 PI 3.2, PI 3.3

3 The 2000 presidential election illustrated in this map ended with *(Chapter 33.2)*

(1) a narrow electoral victory for Al Gore

(2) an overwhelming electoral victory for Al Gore

(3) a narrow popular-vote victory for George W. Bush

(4) a narrow electoral victory for George W. Bush

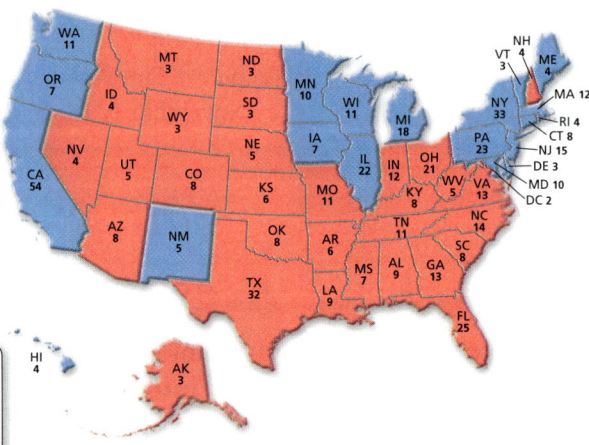

Candidate	Political Affiliation	Electoral Votes	Popular Votes
George W. Bush	Republican	271	50,455,156
Albert A. Gore	Democratic	266	50,992,335
TOTAL		537	105,396,641

THURSDAY

 PI 3.3, PI 3.4

4 The attacks on the World Trade Center on September 11, 2001, led to all of the following except *(Chapter 33.3)*

(1) war in Afghanistan

(2) passage of the USA Patriot Act

(3) a military alliance with the Taliban

(4) formation of the Department of Homeland Security

FRIDAY

 PI 3.2, PI 3.3

5 Which of the following did George W. Bush cite as an impending crisis resulting from the graying of the American population? *(Chapter 33.4)*

(1) declining work force

(2) failure of the Social Security system

(3) inadequate prescription drug coverage

(4) collapse of the private healthcare industry

KEY IDEA 2 Important ideas, social and cultural values, beliefs, and traditions from New York State and United States history illustrate the connections and interactions of people and events across time and from a variety of perspectives.

MONDAY 2.3

1 **The Bracero Program** *(Issue 1)*

(1) assimilated immigrants into American culture

(2) created a seasonal, circular migration pattern

(3) offered humanitarian protection to immigrants

(4) placed various limitations on U.S. immigration

TUESDAY 2.3

2 **What is a central debate about the role of women in the military?** *(Issue 2)*

(1) whether they should serve in combat roles

(2) whether they should serve in leadership roles

(3) whether they should be allowed in the military at all

(4) whether they should receive the same pay as men for the same work

WEDNESDAY 2.2

3 **What does this cartoon imply about the future of social security in America?**

(Issue 4)

(1) Age restrictions on social security will be lifted.

(2) An ongoing surplus will fund social security indefinitely.

(3) Social security will become less of an issue as Americans age.

(4) Most of the money behind social security eventually will dry up.

THURSDAY 2.2

4 **The 1998 shootings at Columbine High School in Colorado focused attention on which of the following potential causes of violent crime?** *(Issue 5)*

(1) human nature

(2) drugs and alcohol

(3) violence in the media

(4) race and class conflict

FRIDAY  2.3

5 **Which of the following groups of people is least likely to interpret U.S. outsourcing as a positive economic trend?** *(Issue 7)*

(1) investors

(2) foreign workers

(3) domestic workers

(4) market economists

ANSWER KEY

WEEK 1
1. (4)
2. (3)
3. (4)
4. (4)
5. (2)

WEEK 2
1. (3)
2. (1)
3. (4)
4. (3)
5. (3)

WEEK 3
1. (4)
2. (2)
3. (2)
4. (4)
5. (1)

WEEK 4
1. (2)
2. (4)
3. (3)
4. (1)
5. (2)

WEEK 5
1. (4)
2. (2)
3. (3)
4. (4)
5. (2)

WEEK 6
1. (4)
2. (1)
3. (3)
4. (4)
5. (4)

WEEK 7
1. (4)
2. (1)
3. (3)
4. (3)
5. (4)

WEEK 8
1. (2)
2. (1)
3. (3)
4. (2)
5. (3)

WEEK 9
1. (1)
2. (4)
3. (2)
4. (3)
5. (3)

WEEK 10
1. (4)
2. (2)
3. (2)
4. (4)
5. (3)

WEEK 11
1. (3)
2. (2)
3. (1)
4. (1)
5. (4)

WEEK 12
1. (2)
2. (3)
3. (4)
4. (2)
5. (2)

WEEK 13
1. (2)
2. (2)
3. (4)
4. (1)
5. (1)

WEEK 14
1. (3)
2. (2)
3. (3)
4. (3)
5. (1)

WEEK 15
1. (2)
2. (3)
3. (1)
4. (2)
5. (2)

WEEK 16
1. (1)
2. (2)
3. (4)
4. (4)
5. (3)

WEEK 17
1. (1)
2. (3)
3. (3)
4. (4)
5. (4)

WEEK 18
1. (4)
2. (3)
3. (1)
4. (1)
5. (2)

WEEK 19
1. (2)
2. (1)
3. (1)
4. (3)
5. (2)

WEEK 20
1. (1)
2. (1)
3. (2)
4. (3)
5. (4)

WEEK 21
1. (1)
2. (4)
3. (4)
4. (3)
5. (2)

WEEK 22
1. (2)
2. (1)
3. (4)
4. (3)
5. (3)

Skills Handbook

To maximize your study and enjoyment of U.S. history, use the Skills Handbook to review and practice a variety of Reading, Social Studies, and Reading Like a Historian skills.

New York Learning Standards

Key Idea 4 The skills of historical analysis include the ability to: explain the significance of historical evidence; weigh the importance, reliability, and validity of evidence; understand the importance of multiple causation; understand the importance of changing and competing interpretations of different historical developments.

A mural showing the construction of a dam

Becoming an Active Reader

by Dr. Kylene Beers

Words surround us. In fact, it's unlikely that you can escape written words during a typical day. Each day, you see printed words in books, magazines, and newspapers; on television and the Internet; at home and in shops and restaurants; and along roads and interstates. Just as you are doing now, every day and in almost every place, you are reading. But just as words can be found in different places, so too can words be used for different purposes. Some words are used to educate, others to inform, and still others to entertain. You will read a textbook such as this one differently from how you would read an advertisement for a new video game or a letter from a friend.

Because you read material differently depending on your purpose for reading, it is important to learn and use various skills and strategies to improve your recognition and comprehension of material. In this Handbook, there are opportunities to learn reading skills that you can master and use throughout *American Anthem* to gain greater understanding of your reading.

① Key Terms and People   At the beginning of each section you will find a list of terms, people, and events that you will need to know. Watch for these words as you read.

② Reading Focus and **Reading Check**   The Reading Focus questions act as a type of outline for each section, and the Reading Check questions offer opportunities to assess what you have learned as you go.

③ Academic Vocabulary   When we use a word that is important in all classes, not just in social studies, we define it in the margin under the heading Academic Vocabulary. Because you will see these academic words in other texts, you will benefit by learning what the words mean while reading this book.

Read Like a Skilled Reader

How can you become a more skilled reader? For starters, you first need to *think* about how to become a better reader. You also can use the following ideas and strategies.

Skilled readers . . .
- Preview what they are supposed to read before they begin reading. They look for titles of chapters and sections, listings of main ideas and focus questions, key terms and information in the margin such as Academic Vocabulary, and visuals such as charts, graphs, maps, and photographs.
- Construct tables or K-W-L charts into which they organize ideas from the reading. They write notes in the tables or charts as they read.

- Use clues from the text, such as the signal words shown below, to help determine or cement understanding.
  Sequencing words: *first, second, third, before, after, sooner, later, next, then, following that, earlier, finally*

  Cause and effect words: *because, so, since, due to, as a result of, the reason for, therefore, brought about, led to, thus, consequently*

  Comparison and contrast words: *likewise, similarly, also, as well as, unlike, however, on the other hand*

Read Like an Active Reader

Active readers know that it is up to them to figure out what the text means. Here are some steps you can take to become an active and successful reader.

Predict what will happen next on the basis of what already has happened in the text. When your predictions do not match what happens in the text, reread to clarify meaning.

Question what is happening as you read. Constantly ask yourself why events happen, what certain ideas mean, and what causes events to occur.

Summarize smaller parts of a chapter. Do not try to summarize an entire chapter! Instead, read some of the text and summarize. Then move on.

Connect events in the text to what you already know or have read.

Clarify your understanding by pausing occasionally to ask questions and check for meaning. You may need to reread to clarify or read further to collect more information to gain understanding.

Visualize people, places, and events in the text. Envision events or places by drawing maps, making charts, or taking notes about what you are reading.

Building Your Vocabulary

As you know, skilled readers implement various strategies and use the text itself to answer questions and clarify meaning. Becoming a skilled reader means that you understand not only how ideas relate but also the words that shape the ideas.

Within this textbook, there are two main types of words. The first, academic words, are words that are important in all classes, not just in social studies. Academic words are found in the margin of most sections under the heading Academic Vocabulary. A second type includes words used primarily in social studies. A sampling of both types appears in the chart below.

By understanding the prefixes, suffixes, roots, and **etymologies,** or origins, of words, you can gain greater understanding of words and how they are related to one another. You can see such relationships by grouping previously unfamiliar words in a notebook, on note cards, or on a word wall.

A **word wall** is just what it sounds like it is—a wall of words. Each day, students add words to a wall, grouping them alphabetically or in categories. Over the course of a school year, a word wall becomes like a large dictionary, with words attached to a wall, to a whiteboard, or to a bulletin board.

Academic Word/Definition	Etymology
authority—firm self-assurance	from the Latin *auctoritas,* meaning "opinion, decision, power"
federal—national	from the Latin *foedus,* meaning "compact" or "league"
hypothesis—an idea that is based on facts and is used as a basis for reasoning	from the Greek *hypotithenai,* meaning "to put under, suppose"
interpret—to understand in light of circumstances	from Latin *interpretari* and *interpres,* meaning "agent, negotiator, interpreter"
revolution—a drastic and far-reaching change	from the Latin *revolvere,* meaning "to revolve or roll back"
technique—method	from the Greek *technikos,* meaning "technical"

Social Studies Word/Definition	Prefix/Suffix
civilization—the culture of a particular time or place	Suffix *–ation,* meaning "action" or "resulting state"
century—a period of 100 years	Prefix *cent,* meaning "hundred"
democracy—governmental rule by the people, usually through majority rule	Prefix *demo,* meaning "people"
geography—the study of Earth's physical and cultural features	Prefix *geo,* meaning "Earth"; suffix *graph,* meaning "to write, draw"
independence—the state of being free from rule	Prefix *in,* meaning "not"; root *depend,* meaning "to need"; suffix *–ence,* meaning "action," "state," or "process"
society—a group of people who share common traditions	Prefix *soci,* meaning "to join," "companions"

Identifying Main Idea and Details

Define the Skill

The **main idea** is the central thought in a passage. It is general and conveys the key concept that the author wants you to know. The main idea can come at the beginning, middle, or end of a passage, though you usually find it near the beginning. The main idea can be one or two sentences and can be implied or directly stated.

Details are facts that support or explain the main idea. Details are specific and provide additional information, such as the *who, what, when, where, why,* and *how.* These include facts, statistics, examples, explanations, and descriptions.

Learn the Skill

Use the following strategies to identify main ideas and details in the reading.

Life in Colonial America

Early British settlers and newcomers from many countries were creating a new American culture. As Crèvecoeur had noticed, it was not British or European, but something new.

Colonial cities Colonial cities were lively, exciting places. Some had paved streets and sidewalks lit by oil lamps. Ships from foreign ports were anchored in the harbors. People waited eagerly for letters from relatives and the latest British newspapers and magazines, with gossip and drawings of new fashions.

Many colonial cities had libraries, bookshops, and impressive public buildings. City dwellers could go to plays or concerts. They shopped in markets for country produce and luxury goods from Europe. Schools taught music, dancing, drawing, and painting.

1 **Identify the topic by examining the title or other headings.** A section heading usually describes the topic.

2 **Find the topic sentence that summarizes the passage's main idea.** Then restate the main idea in your own words.

3 **Look for details that support the main idea.** Supporting details usually follow the main idea and provide more information about it.

Apply the Skill

1. Identify the main idea of the passage and restate it in your own words.
2. What details support the main idea?
3. How do the details add to the main idea?

Summarizing

Define the Skill

Summarizing is the process of condensing what you read into a briefer, easier-to-understand format. A good summary should include only a passage's main ideas and its most important supporting details. When summarizing, remember to use your own words. Knowing how to summarize can help you understand and recall the main ideas of what you read.

Learn the Skill

Use the following strategies to summarize the reading.

1 Identify main ideas in the passage.
Often, a main idea is located at the beginning of a passage or a paragraph.

2 Look for key supporting details.
Include only the most important details in the summary.

Different worlds The economic differences between the primarily industrial North and the primarily agricultural South led to even greater differences between the two regions. Trade and industry encouraged urbanization, and so cities grew in the North much more than in the South. Moreover, the Industrial Revolution and the revolutions in transportation and communication had the greatest impact on the North, where new technology was seized by businesses in pursuit of efficiency and growth.

By contrast, in the South, after the widespread use of the cotton gin, there was relatively little in the way of technological development. Many Southerners saw little use in labor-saving devices, for example, when they had an ample supply of enslaved people to do their bidding.

3 Ask questions and look up unfamiliar words.
Then restate the passage's main idea and most important details in your own words.

Apply the Skill

1. What is the main idea of the second paragraph? How do you know?
2. What details support the main idea in the second paragraph?
3. Write a brief summary of the above passage, including only the main ideas and most important details.

READING SKILL

Making Inferences

Define the Skill

Inferences are implied, or unstated, ideas drawn from details in the reading. Making inferences means using clues in the text to connect implied ideas with stated facts and your own prior knowledge and common sense. Learning how to make inferences will help you gain greater understanding about particular historical people, places, and events from the reading.

Learn the Skill

Use the following strategies to make inferences about the reading.

1 Identify main ideas and details.
Note stated facts and information in the reading.

2 Identify implied ideas in the text.
What ideas are suggested but not directly stated in the reading? Statistics and opinionated language can lead to implied understanding.

> The vote in November 1860 was almost completely along sectional lines. Lincoln won every northern state—although he and Douglas split the electoral vote in New Jersey. In the South, Breckinridge and Bell split the vote, with the Lower South going entirely to Breckinridge. What was troubling, however, was that the split in the Democratic Party allowed Lincoln to be elected president with less than 40 percent of the popular vote. Even more worrisome was the fact that of the nearly 2 million votes Lincoln received, only 26,000 came from slave states.
>
> Many Northerners celebrated Lincoln's victory. "The great revolution has finally taken place," one free-soiler wrote. "The country has once and for all thrown off the domination of the slaveholders." Many Southerners looked at the results with concern. "A party founded on the ... hatred of African slavery is now the controlling power," the *New Orleans Delta* warned the slaveholding South.

3 Compare stated and unstated ideas with your prior knowledge.
Use facts from the reading, your common sense, and what you already know about a topic or an event to make a valid inference about it.

Apply the Skill

1. From a national perspective, what was troubling about Lincoln's election in 1860?
2. What can you infer about the effect of Lincoln's election on the future of the South?
3. Using the reading and your prior knowledge, explain the effect that multiple candidates can have on a general election.

Sequencing

Define the Skill

By **sequencing** events in chronological, or time order, you can gain greater and more accurate understanding of them. Learning to sequence also can help you understand relationships among events, including how a past event may influence a pending one and eventually lead to a future outcome.

Learn the Skill

Use the following strategies to sequence the reading.

1 Examine all text and visuals for specific dates.
Times of the day, seasons of the year, and people's ages are helpful in determining the specific sequence of events, which is known as absolute chronology.

2 Look for words signal.
Clue words such as *by, in, after, first, last, before, next, then, soon,* and *finally* help indicate the general sequence of events, which is known as relative chronology.

3 Identify events that occurred at the same time.
Words such as *while, meanwhile,* and *during* signal the occurrence of simultaneous events.

Carnegie and Steel **Andrew Carnegie** lived a true rags-to-riches story. Born in 1835 in Scotland to poor parents, Carnegie immigrated to the United States when he was 12. At age 17, he took a job with the Pennsylvania Railroad. He advanced quickly and began investing in the iron, oil, railroad, and telegraph industries. He soon founded his own company and rose to the top of the steel business.

Carnegie held down costs by using vertical integration, buying supplies in bulk, and producing items in large quantities. By 1899 the Carnegie Steel Company dominated the American steel industry. In 1901 Carnegie sold the company to banker J.P. Morgan for $480 million. After retiring, Carnegie began to devote his time to philanthropy, or charity.

Apply the Skill

1. In what year did Carnegie take a job with the Pennsylvania Railroad? How long after that did he build Carnegie Steel Company into the nation's dominant steel business?
2. To what cause did Carnegie devote himself after his retirement?
3. Use information from the reading to produce a time line of significant events from Carnegie's life.

Identifying Cause and Effect

Define the Skill

By using **cause and effect,** you can determine why certain events occurred and whether events are related and, if so, how they are related.

A cause is an action that makes another event happen. Often, a cause will be directly stated in the text, but sometimes it will be implied. An effect is something that happens as a result of a cause. One cause may have more than one effect. Similarly, one effect may have more than one cause. Identifying causes and effects can help you better understand what you read.

Learn the Skill

Use the following strategies to identify cause and effect in the reading.

1 Identify the causes of events.
Look for a reason or reasons that prompted a given event to occur. Words such as *since, because, so, therefore,* and *due to* can signal a causal relationship among events.

2 Identify the effects of events.
Look for phrases and clue words that indicate consequences, such as *thus, brought about, led to, consequently,* and *as a result.*

3 Connect causes and effects.
Consider why certain causes led to an event, and why the event turned out as it did. Remember that an event can be both a cause and an effect.

War Breaks Out

Since Russia had promised to protect Serbian Slavs, the Russian army quickly began to mobilize, or prepare for war. Germany viewed Russia's mobilization as an act of aggression against its ally Austria-Hungary and thus declared war on Russia. Then Germany declared war on France, Russia's ally. All-out war was about to begin.

The Germans take Belgium Germany made the first move in the war, following the Schlieffen Plan. On August 14, 1914, German troops crossed the German border into the neutral country of Belgium. Kaiser Wilhelm II believed that he had to catch Belgium and France by surprise. Germany's invasion of Belgium drew a new, powerful nation into the conflict. Because the British had planned to defend Belgium, Great Britain declared war on Germany.

Apply the Skill

1. Why did the Russian army begin to mobilize for war?
2. What was the effect of Russia's mobilization? Explain.
3. List an effect of Germany's decision to invade the neutral nation of Belgium.

Comparing and Contrasting

Define the Skill

You usually can find the greater meaning of certain time periods, people, places, and events by **comparing and contrasting** information and details from them. Comparing involves looking at both the similarities and differences between two or more people, places, or events. Contrasting means examining only the differences between them. Learning to compare and contrast effectively can give you a deeper contextual understanding of the reading.

Learn the Skill

Use the following strategies in comparing and contrasting parts of the reading.

1 Identify similarities in the reading.
Words such as *also, both, all, like, likewise, similar,* and *as* can signal comparison between people, places, and events.

2 Identify differences in the reading.
Words such as *unlike, different, but, however, not, though, only,* and *while* can indicate differences between people, places, and events.

The Effects of the Crash

In the aftermath of the crash, American business and political leaders rushed to calm the panic and reassure the nation. One business leader wrote optimistically in the days following Black Tuesday, "The recent collapse of stock market prices has no significance as regards the real wealth of the American people as a whole." President Hoover also downplayed the effects of the crash. He and many others firmly believed that the economy would soon recover from the shock and return to prosperity.

The impact on individuals No one denied, however, that the stock market collapse had ruined countless individual investors. Some had lost years of gains. Many saw huge fortunes disappear before their eyes.

Margin buyers were particularly hard hit. When stock prices began to fall, brokers demanded that they pay back the borrowed money. To "make" these margin calls, investors were forced to sell their shares for far less than they had paid for them. Some lost their savings trying to make up the difference.

3 Analyze the information.
Identify relationships between similarities and differences in the text. What do they tell you about a topic in a big-picture sense?

Apply the Skill

1. How did President Hoover's initial reaction to the stock market crash compare to the reactions of other business and political leaders?
2. What did all parties agree was an effect of the stock market collapse?
3. Which group of investors was hit hardest by the stock market collapse? Explain.

Identifying Problem and Solution

Define the Skill

By **identifying problem and solution,** you can better understand the challenges that people have faced over time and the means by which they have resolved such difficulties. Learning to effectively identify problems and solutions is a valuable skill that you can apply to your understanding of history.

Learn the Skill

Use the following strategies to identify problems and solutions in the reading.

1 Identify the problem. Note the problem to be solved. Some problems are directly stated, while others are not.

2 List all possible solutions to it. Because there is usually more than one way to solve a problem, identify and weigh all of the alternatives. Then consider the advantages and disadvantages of each.

Trade and economic development

World War II had raised a number of concerns about the financial relationships between countries. These problems had helped bring about the Great Depression. Now they threatened to limit trade and create conflict between nations. Many leaders hoped that solving these problems would lead to greater prosperity around the world. This, in turn, would promote peace.

Even before the war was over, representatives of many of the world's great powers met at a conference in Bretton Woods, New Hampshire. Out of this conference came an agreement to create two organizations—the **World Bank** and the **International Monetary Fund** (IMF). Both began operating in 1947.

The World Bank aimed to help poor countries build their economies. It provided grants of money and loans to help with projects that could provide jobs and wealth.

Economic policy was the focus of the IMF. The IMF was designed to encourage economic policies that promoted international trade.

3 Evaluate the chosen solution. Later, use what you know about the topic and your own common sense to evaluate a solution's effectiveness.

Apply the Skill

1. What problems did world leaders identify after World War II?
2. What solution did world leaders offer to these problems?
3. What did world leaders hope to accomplish by solving the problem?

Drawing Conclusions

Define the Skill

Historical writing often features cause-and-effect relationships between and among events. In some cases, however, outcomes in the text are implied. In such instances, you can use facts and your own knowledge and experience to **draw conclusions** about the reading. In drawing conclusions, you analyze the reading and form opinions or make judgments about its meaning.

Learn the Skill

Use the following strategies to draw conclusions from the reading.

1 Identify the main idea and supporting details. Read the passage carefully to find clue words and establish meaning.

2 Connect the reading and your prior knowledge. Look for connections between stated facts, implied ideas, and what you already know about the topic.

Creating the Great Society Now that he was an elected president, Johnson pushed even harder for his plans. On inauguration day, he told aides at an inaugural ball, "Don't stay up late. There's work to be done. We're on our way to the Great Society."

Johnson had a personal interest in providing education for the children of the poor. In 1965 Congress passed the Elementary and Secondary School Act, the first large-scale program of government aid to public schools. The Higher Education Act created the first federal scholarships for college students. In February 1965 the Office of Economic Opportunity launched Head Start, an education program for the pre-school children of low-income parents.

The president also persuaded Congress to pass the Omnibus Housing Act in 1965. To oversee this and other federal housing programs, Congress created the Department of Housing and Urban Development (HUD). Johnson appointed Robert Weaver to head this new department, making him the first African American to be part of a president's cabinet.

3 Summarize the reading. Summarize the reading in your own words. Then draw a conclusion that states an opinion or makes a judgment about what the reading means to you.

Apply the Skill

1. What can you conclude about Johnson's interest in education?
2. What led Johnson to push even harder for his plans after he became an elected president?
3. What did Johnson mean when he said, "Don't stay up late. There's work to be done. We're on our way to the Great Society"?

Making Generalizations

Define the Skill

A generalization is made by combining details from a passage with a reader's prior knowledge. People **make generalizations** by looking for people, events, or ideas that share something in common and identifying their connection. As a reader, look for a generalization if an author suggests that a series of facts are connected. Look for clue words, including *all, none, every,* and *never*. Other clue words that sometimes show a generalization are *most, many, few, some, usually,* and *sometimes*.

Learn the Skill

Use the following strategies to make generalizations from the reading.

1 Look for the main idea of the passage.
Find similarities between paragraphs that link main ideas together.

> **John Lewis** took part in some of the first sit-ins in 1960. He was also a Freedom Rider in 1961 and participated in the ill-fated Selma march in 1965. The leader of the Student Non-violent Coordinating Committee in the early 1960s, Lewis was later elected to many terms representing the people of Atlanta, Georgia, in Congress.
>
> As a staff member of Southern Christian Leadership Conference, **Andrew Young** played major roles in the 1963 Birmingham campaign and the Selma march. In 1972, he became Georgia's first black member of Congress since Reconstruction. Young later served as U.S. ambassador to the United Nations and as mayor of Atlanta.
>
> **Jesse Jackson** was a close adviser to Martin Luther King, Jr. and was with him at the motel in Memphis on the day King was assassinated. Jackson later founded his own civil rights organization, Operation PUSH, and became an international figure for his work on behalf of poor and oppressed peoples around the world. His strong campaigns for the Democratic presidential nomination in the 1980s raised the real possibility that the nation might one day have a black president.

2 Locate supporting details.
Listing facts will help you determine what people, places, or events are being grouped together.

3 Identify a common thread and relate it to your prior knowledge.
Determine which words (*most, few,* etc.) will be most useful for a generalization. Then compare the generalization against what you already know about the subject.

Apply the Skill

1. What is the main idea of the passage?
2. Make a generalization based on the passage above.
3. What facts support that generalization?

Interpreting Time Lines

Define the Skill

A **time line** chronologically organizes events that occurred during a specific period of time. It has a beginning date and an ending date. The **time span** is the years between the beginning date and the ending date. **Time intervals** mark shorter increments of time within the time span. They appear at regular intervals, such as every 10 or 20 years. Two time lines can be used to list events that happened within a certain time span but at different places. These are called **parallel time lines**.

By organizing events chronologically, time lines can help you see how events are related. Seeing how events are related can help you find cause and effect relationships among the events and remember them. Time lines also allow you to compare, contrast, and draw conclusions about historical events.

Learn the Skill

Use the following strategies to read the time line.

1 Identify the time span of the time line. Look at the beginning date and the ending date to determine the time period.

TIME LINE

The English in North America

1607 Captain John Smith and more than 100 colonists settle Jamestown.

1639 Connecticut settlers adopt the Fundamental Orders of Connecticut, which allowed men who were not church members to vote.

1619 Virginia's House of Burgesses becomes the first legislature in America.

1620 The Pilgrims sign the Mayflower Compact.

2 Determine the time intervals of the time line. Check to see whether the years are evenly spaced. Determine whether the time is divided by decades, by centuries, or by another division.

3 Analyze the events on the time line. Recognize the types of events that the time line describes and determine how they are related.

Apply the Skill

1. What is the time span of the time line?
2. What are the time intervals of the time line?
3. How are the events on the time line related?

Interpreting Charts

Define the Skill

Charts, including simple charts, tables, and diagrams, are visual representations of information, such as facts and statistics. Historians use charts to organize, condense, simplify, and summarize information. **Simple charts** combine or compare information.

Tables classify information by groups. Numbers, percentages, dates, and other data can be classified in the columns and rows of a table for easy reference and comparison. **Diagrams** illustrate processes or steps so that they are easier to understand. Knowing how to read and use charts allows you to interpret, compare, analyze, and evaluate historical information.

Learn the Skill

Use the following strategies to interpret the chart.

1 **Identify the type of information presented in the chart.**
Read the title and any column headings to understand what the chart is about. The title of this chart is "The English Colonies in America."

2 **Look at the way information is organized.**
Charts can be organized alphabetically, chronologically, or in other ways.

3 **Analyze the information found in the chart.**
Interpret, compare, and contrast the information in the chart to draw conclusions and make inferences or predictions.

THE ENGLISH COLONIES IN AMERICA

Joint-stock colonies were established by groups of investors who pooled their money hoping to make a profit.	Virginia* (1607) Massachusetts* (1620)
Royal colonies were under the direct control of the king of England, who appointed a governor.	Delaware (1664)
Proprietary colonies were established by private individuals, or Lord Proprietors, who had power to make and execute laws.	New Hampshire* (1623) New Jersey* (1630) Pennsylvania* (1634) Maryland* (1632) North Carolina* (1655) South Carolina* (1670) Georgia* (1732)
Self-governing colonies were independent of the king or a joint-stock company.	Connecticut (1634) Rhode Island (1636)

* Later became a royal colony

Apply the Skill

1. How is the information in the chart organized?
2. According to the chart, what is one difference and one similarity between the colonies of Virginia and Pennsylvania?

Interpreting Pie and Bar Graphs

Define the Skill

Graphs are diagrams that present statistical or numeric data. They can display amounts, trends, ratios, and changes over time. A **pie graph** is a circular chart that shows how individual parts relate to the whole. The circle of the pie symbolizes the whole amount. The slices of the pie represent the individual parts of the whole. A **bar graph** compares quantities. A single bar graph compares one set of data. A double bar graph compares two sets of data. Knowing how to interpret graphs will allow you to better understand and evaluate historical data as well as recognize historical trends.

Learn the Skill

Use the following strategies to interpret the pie graph.

Use the following strategies to interpret the bar graph.

1 Identify the subject of the pie graphs.
Read the title and the legend to determine the subject of the pie graphs.

1 Read the title and the legend.
This will allow you to determine the subject of the graph.

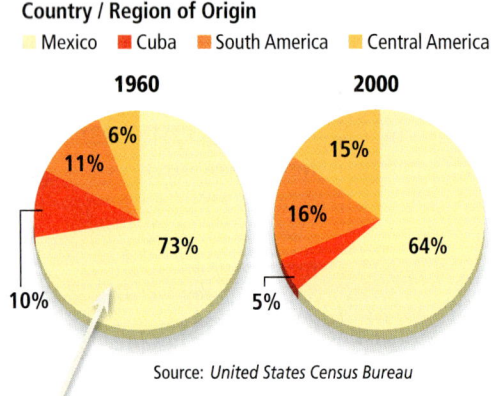

HISPANIC IMMIGRANTS TO THE UNITED STATES

Country / Region of Origin
■ Mexico ■ Cuba ■ South America ■ Central America

1960

2000

Source: *United States Census Bureau*

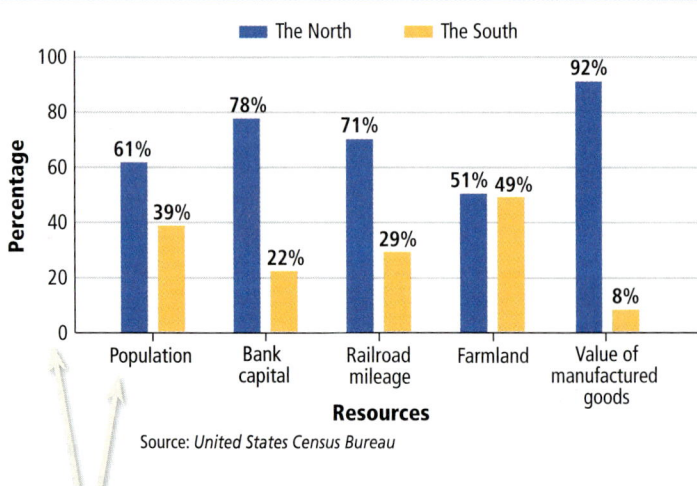

NORTHERN AND SOUTHERN RESOURCES

■ The North ■ The South

Source: *United States Census Bureau*

2 Read the statistics.
Compare the sizes of each piece within each graph. Then compare the pieces across the graphs.

3 Draw conclusions
Determine what the statistics tell about the subject of the pie graphs.

2 Examine the labels.
Read the horizontal and vertical axis labels. These tell what the bar graph measures and the unit of measurement.

3 Analyze the bar graph.
Compare the amounts shown on the bar graph. Draw conclusions about what this information tells about the subject.

Apply the Skill

1. What information do the pie graphs compare?
2. What information does the bar graph compare?
3. What conclusions can you draw from the data in the bar graph?

Interpreting Line Graphs

Define the Skill

A **line graph** is a visual representation of data organized so that you can see the pattern of change over time. On a line graph, usually the **vertical axis** shows quantities and the **horizontal axis** shows time. People may use line graphs to track changes in events such as population growth or the stock market. Line graphs show time in intervals so they are not always exact and may require that you estimate quantities. Knowing how to interpret line graphs can help you recognize historical trends.

Learn the Skill

Use the following strategies to interpret a line graph.

1 **Read the title of the graph.** The title tells you the subject or purpose of the graph.

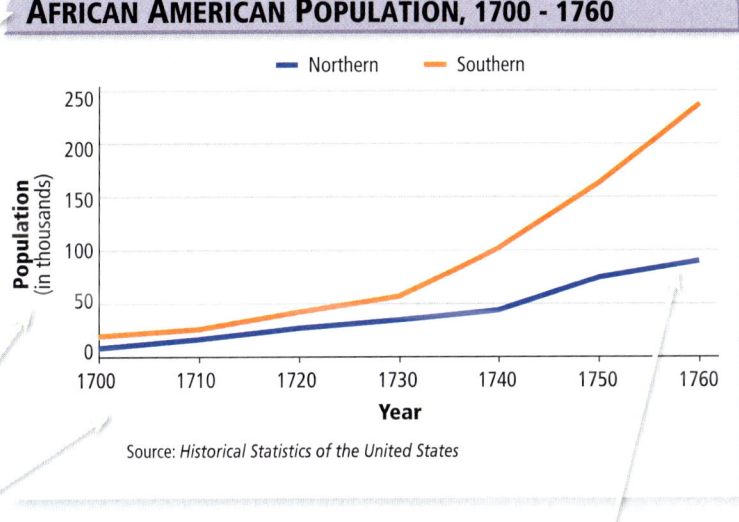

AFRICAN AMERICAN POPULATION, 1700 - 1760

— Northern   — Southern

Source: *Historical Statistics of the United States*

2 **Read the horizontal and vertical axis labels.** The labels explain what the line graph measures and what is the unit of measurement.

3 **Analyze the statistics on the graph.** Look at the slant of the line. The closer the line is to being parallel to the horizontal axis, the slower the change. The closer the line is to being perpendicular to the horizontal axis, the quicker the change.

Apply the Skill

1. About how big was the African American population in the South in 1740?
2. About how many more African American people lived in the South than in the North in 1760?
3. What conclusion can you draw about the African American population in the North?

Interpreting Infographics

Define the Skill

An **infographic** is a way of presenting a large amount of information in a graphic, or visual, form. Infographics often combine different types of information, such as text, illustrations, maps, charts, tables, graphs, and diagrams. You need to be able to understand what each piece of information is conveying on its own and how each piece works together to convey a larger point. Infographics help readers understand the importance of an event, an object, or a place. An infographic can be a two-dimensional or a three-dimensional model. Some infographics are interactive. Different types of infographics have different uses. For example, tables and charts organize information, whereas pictorial infographics are memorable and bring history to life.

Learn the Skill

Use the following strategies to interpret infographics.

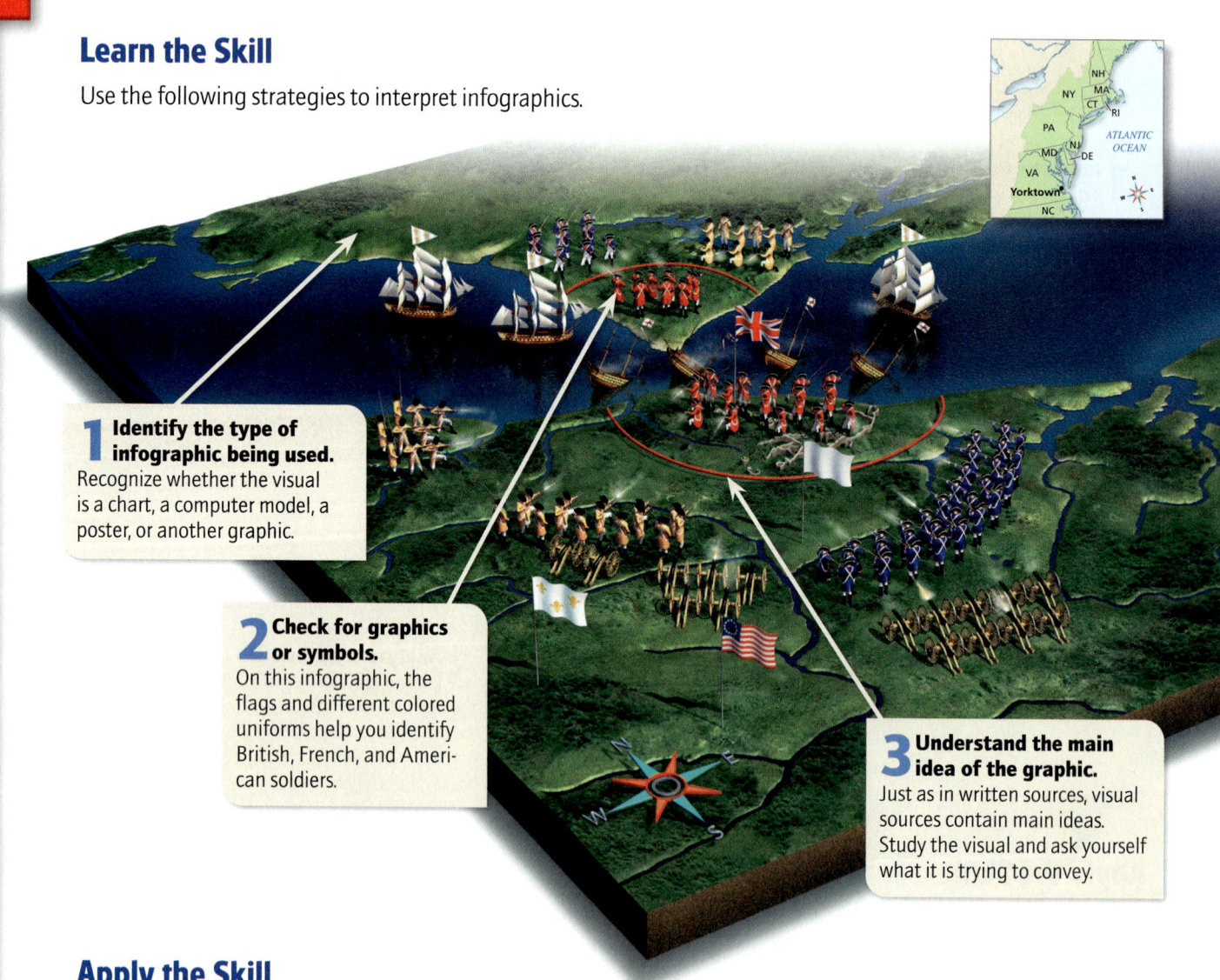

1 **Identify the type of infographic being used.**
Recognize whether the visual is a chart, a computer model, a poster, or another graphic.

2 **Check for graphics or symbols.**
On this infographic, the flags and different colored uniforms help you identify British, French, and American soldiers.

3 **Understand the main idea of the graphic.**
Just as in written sources, visual sources contain main ideas. Study the visual and ask yourself what it is trying to convey.

Apply the Skill

1. What type of infographic is this?
2. What do the ships represent?
3. Why did the British surrender at Yorktown?

Interpreting Movement Maps

Define the Skill

Different types of maps are used for different purposes. **Movement maps** show motion or travel from one point to another. They can track sea voyages, explorations, or migrations. They can span a week, a few months, or thousands of years. Understanding how to read and interpret a movement map can help you learn more about historical events, their chronology, and the geographical locations they affected.

Learn the Skill

Use the following strategies to interpret movement maps.

1 **Read the title and legend to learn the subject and purpose of the map.** Use that prior knowledge and the map to draw conclusions. What area does the map cover? What time period does the map cover? The legend explains what the symbols and the colors on the map mean

2 **Identify and understand the patterns of movement shown on the map.** Trace the path of movement from start to end. What does the map tell you about the explorers' movements?

3 **Analyze the information.** What do you already know about the subject?

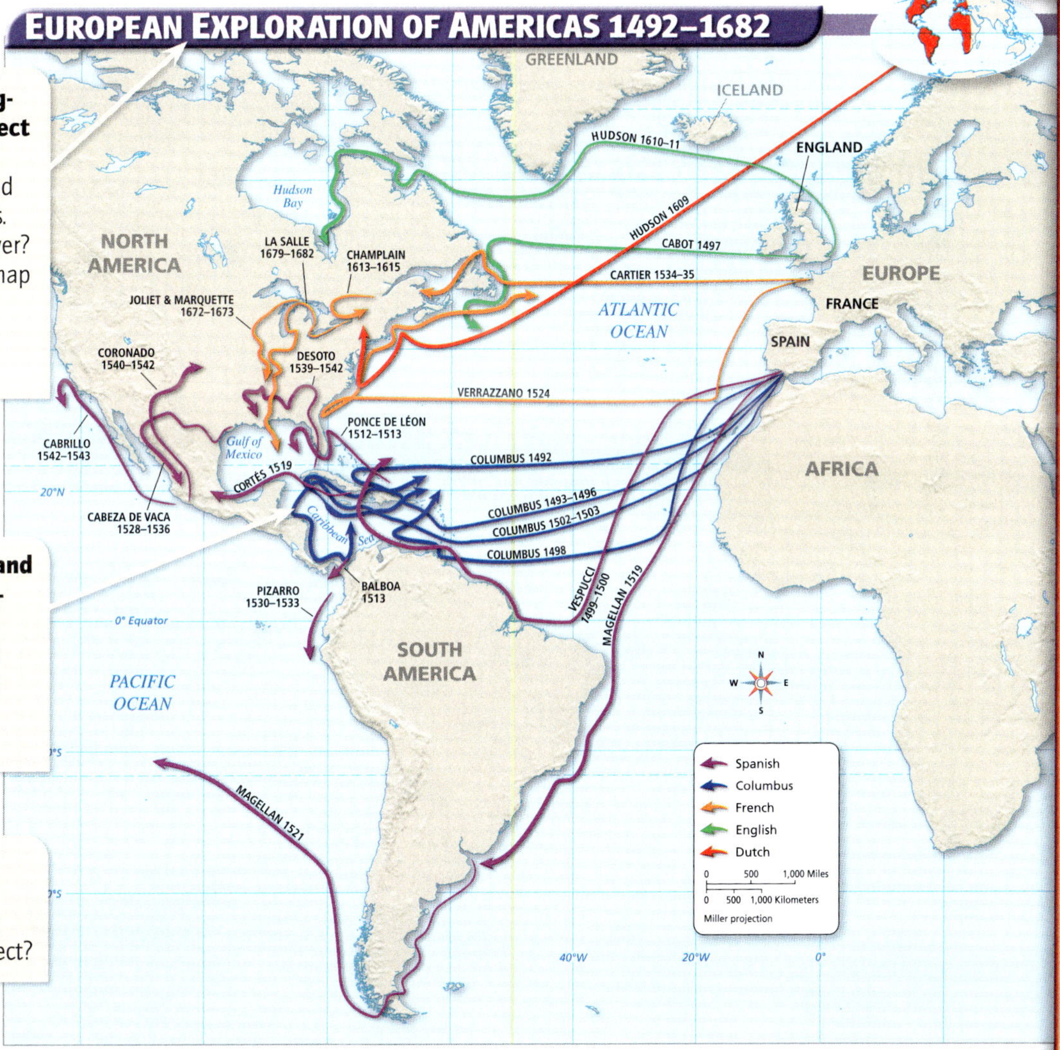

EUROPEAN EXPLORATION OF AMERICAS 1492–1682

GREENLAND
ICELAND
Hudson Bay
HUDSON 1610–11
ENGLAND
NORTH AMERICA
LA SALLE 1679–1682
CHAMPLAIN 1613–1615
HUDSON 1609
CABOT 1497
CARTIER 1534–35
EUROPE
JOLIET & MARQUETTE 1672–1673
ATLANTIC OCEAN
FRANCE
CORONADO 1540–1542
DESOTO 1539–1542
SPAIN
CABRILLO 1542–1543
VERRAZZANO 1524
PONCE DE LÉON 1512–1513
Gulf of Mexico
COLUMBUS 1492
AFRICA
20°N
CORTÉS 1519
CABEZA DE VACA 1528–1536
Caribbean Sea
COLUMBUS 1493–1496
COLUMBUS 1502–1503
COLUMBUS 1498
PIZARRO 1530–1533
BALBOA 1513
VESPUCCI 1499–1500
MAGELLAN 1519
0° Equator
SOUTH AMERICA
PACIFIC OCEAN
MAGELLAN 1521

N
W E
S

Legend:
- Spanish
- Columbus
- French
- English
- Dutch

0   500   1,000 Miles
0   500   1,000 Kilometers
Miller projection

40°W   20°W   0°

Apply the Skill

1. Describe the path that Magellan took.
2. What patterns can you find?
3. How do the patterns you found relate to the present-day Americas?

SOCIAL STUDIES SKILL

Interpreting Historical Maps

Define the Skill

A map is a representation of features on Earth's surface. Historians use different types of maps to locate historical events, to demonstrate how geography has influenced history, and to illustrate human interaction with the environment.

A **historical map** provides information about a place at a certain time in history. It can illustrate information such as population density, economic activity, political alliances, battles, and movement of people and goods. Knowing how to use historical maps can help you learn how places have changed over time. For example, these historical maps show how the Treaty of Paris changed North America after the French and Indian War.

Learn the Skill

Use the following strategies to interpret historical maps.

1 Read the title and legend. The title will help you identify the subject and the purpose of the map. The legend explains the meaning of the symbols and the colors on the map.

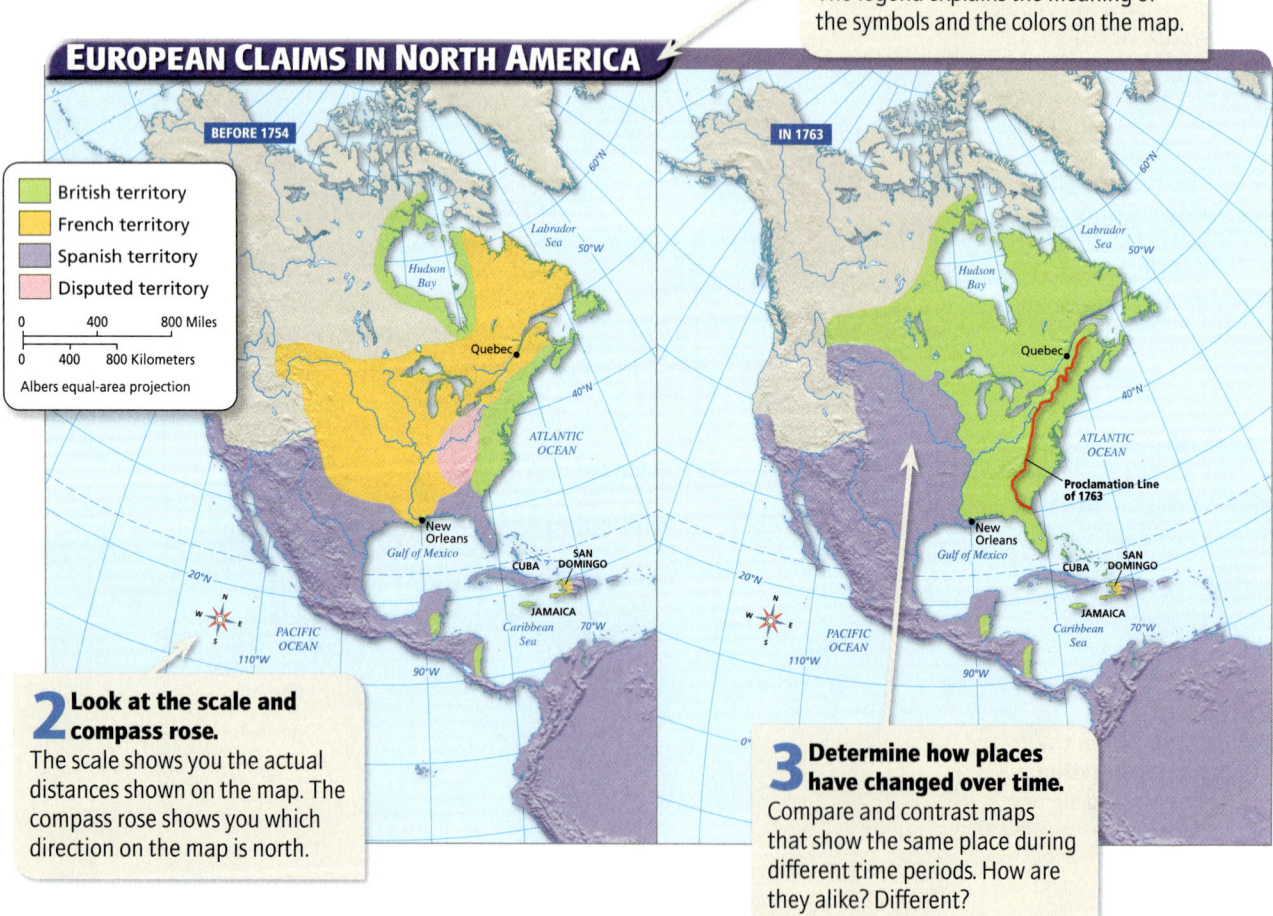

EUROPEAN CLAIMS IN NORTH AMERICA

2 Look at the scale and compass rose. The scale shows you the actual distances shown on the map. The compass rose shows you which direction on the map is north.

3 Determine how places have changed over time. Compare and contrast maps that show the same place during different time periods. How are they alike? Different?

Apply the Skill

1. What is the purpose of these historical maps?
2. Which country claimed Quebec before 1754? Which country claimed Quebec in 1763?

Interpreting Cartograms

Define the Skill

A distribution map show how data, such as population, is spread over a certain area. A **cartogram** is a type of distribution map that distorts the sizes and shapes of state, regions, or countries to reflect some value *other* than physical size. For example, a cartogram may display information about the population of a region or the gross national products of several countries. The cartogram is a tool for making visual comparisons. At a glance, you can see how each country, region, or state compares with another in a particular value.

Learn the Skill

Use the following strategies to interpret cartograms.

1 Read the title and legend.
Identify the value illustrated by the cartogram.

2 Determine what countries, regions, or states the cartogram shows.
Find the largest and smallest land areas on the cartogram. Compare the sizes of the land areas on the cartogram with the way they appear on a political map.

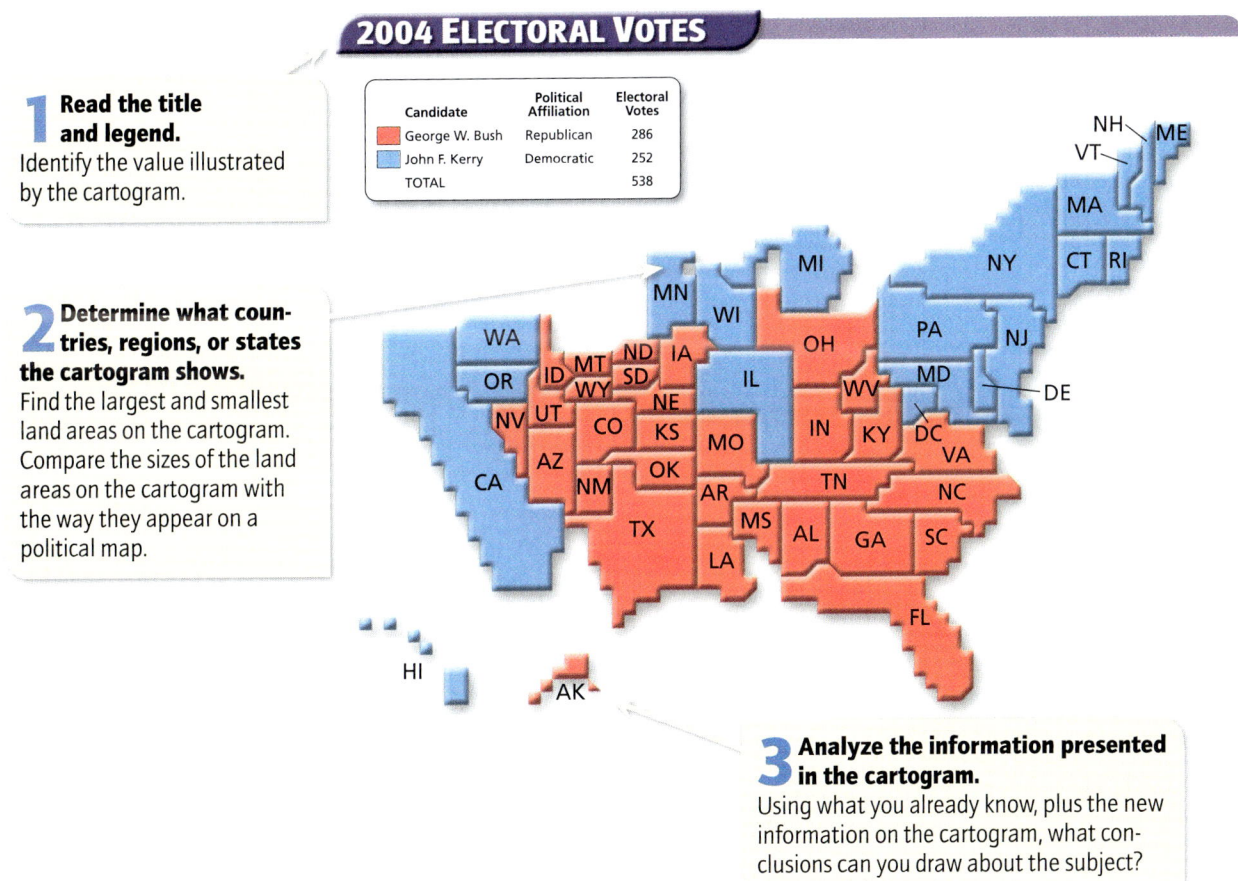

2004 ELECTORAL VOTES

Candidate	Political Affiliation	Electoral Votes
George W. Bush	Republican	286
John F. Kerry	Democratic	252
TOTAL		538

3 Analyze the information presented in the cartogram.
Using what you already know, plus the new information on the cartogram, what conclusions can you draw about the subject?

Apply the Skill

1. On the cartogram, is Pennsylvania or Missouri more distorted in size when compared with a political map?
2. What does this cartogram tell about the populations of Massachusetts and South Dakota?

Analyzing Costs and Benefits

Define the Skill

Government officials use cost-benefit analyses to help them decide which programs to fund. A **cost-benefit analysis** is a process that measures whether a project or a policy is worthwhile by calculating and comparing its benefits with its costs to society. Basic economic indicators including employment, gross domestic product, and inflation can be used in the analysis. All costs and benefits are expressed in terms of money. Some costs and benefits, however, such as time or safety, cannot be directly measured by how much money is earned or lost. Mathematical formulas are used for these types of costs and benefits to determine how to express their monetary value. One obstacle to cost-benefit analysis is that people may sometimes disagree about the value of the costs and the benefits.

Learn the Skill

Use the following strategies to analyze costs and benefits.

1 Identify and calculate the costs.
What are the different costs of the project? Add those together to calculate the total cost.

2 Identify and calculate the benefits.
Determine the benefits of the proposed project. Calculate the total amount of money the project will save or earn for society.

3 Analyze the costs and the benefits and draw conclusions.
Compare the costs with the benefits. Divide the total benefits by the total costs to determine the benefits-to-cost ratio. If the ratio is more than 1, the project will earn money. If the ratio is less than 1, the project will lose money.

JOB CORPS: COSTS AND BENEFITS TO SOCIETY PER PARTICIPANT

Costs (1995 Dollars)	
Cost of Government-Funded Pay, Food, and Clothing for Participant	$2,361
Program Operating Costs	$14,128
Benefits (1995 Dollars)	
Participant Earns Government-Funded Pay, Food, and Clothing	$2,361
Additional Earnings and Benefits	$27,531
Reduced Crime in Community	$1,240
Reduced Use of Other Job Training Programs	$2,186

Apply the Skill

1. What is the total cost of Job Corps per participant?
2. What is one benefit of Job Corps?
3. How much money will society earn or lose for each dollar the government spends on Job Corps?
4. Will the program earn or lose money?

Evaluating Information on the Internet

Define the Skill

The **Internet** is an international computer network that connects schools, businesses, government agencies, and individuals. Every Web site on the Internet has its own address, called a **URL**. Each URL has a domain. The **domain** tells you the type of Web site you are reading. Common domains in the United States are .com, .net, .org, .edu, and .gov. A Web site with the domain .edu means that it is sponsored by an educational institution. The collection of web sites throughout the world is called the **World Wide Web**.

The Internet can be a valuable research tool. Unlike the information in books and newspapers, much of the content on the Internet is not checked for accuracy. Anyone can post information on the Web, so it is important to know how to evaluate the content of Internet resources. Evaluating the content found on the Internet will help you determine the accuracy and reliability of the information.

Learn the Skill

Use the following strategies to evaluate information on the Internet.

3 Identify the author and check for bias.
Determine the author's credentials. Is he or she an expert in the field? Decide whether the Web site presents balanced information or is overly biased towards a certain point of view.

1 Identify the Web site's domain.
Determine who sponsors the Web site. Web sites sponsored by reputable organizations, educational institutions, and government agencies usually provide accurate and reliable information.

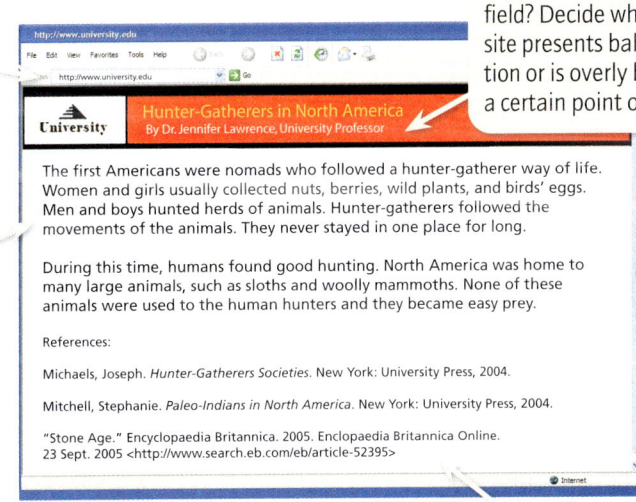

2 Understand the purpose of the site.
Find out whether the purpose of the site is to inform, to persuade, or to entertain.

4 Check the author's sources.
For any research-based information, the author should provide a list of sources he or she used. You can also consult the author's sources for your own research.

Apply the Skill

1. What is the domain of the Web site? Do you think the information on the Web site will be reliable? Why or why not?
2. Who is the author of the Web site? What are the author's credentials?
3. Do you think this Web site presents a balanced point of view or a biased point of view? Explain your response.

Major Historical Concepts

To think like a historian, you need to be aware of some basic concepts of history—about how history happens and how historians think about the past. Keep these five major historical concepts in mind as you read this textbook.

Continuity and Change in History

Change happens at different rates at different times Historical change doesn't happen at a uniform rate. Some periods see great, sweeping changes that affect the course of history for hundreds of years to come. At other times, the changes are gradual and harder to see.

Some aspects can change while others remain the same Change happens at different rates in different places, too. Just because one part of society changes that doesn't mean all of society will change. For example, after the United States gained its independence, states in the North gradually became more industrialized and outlawed slavery, while states in the South remained largely agricultural and kept slavery.

Change is complicated Historical change affects all areas of life, not just politics or technology. Beliefs and values are also subject to change. Once, women were not permitted to join the armed forces. Today the debate is not over whether women should be allowed to join but what role the hundreds of thousands of military women should have.

Understanding Cause and Effect in History

The limitations of cause and effect One event may have several causes. A proximate, or immediate, cause may seem obvious, such as Germany's invasion of Poland as the proximate cause of World War II. But there also may be deeper causes, such as the war reparations that Germany was forced to pay after the Treaty of Versailles officially ended World War I. It may not always be immediately possible to identify a direct cause for an event or to identify all of the deeper causes.

What causes events? Inflation in Germany after World War I made paper money almost worthless (above left), hastening Adolf Hitler's rise to power.

The Civil Rights Movement involved millions of people and changed American politics, voting patterns, schooling, and entertainment.

The destruction of the USS *Maine* may have been an act of war or it may have been a chance occurrence.

The Role of Chance in History

The impact of historical events   An explosion sunk the USS *Maine* in Havana harbor in 1898. The Spanish and the U.S. governments disagreed about the cause of the explosion, which killed all the men aboard. The Spanish-American War ensued, and "Remember the Maine!" became an American battle cry. Chance events can have unexpected and sometimes enormous consequences. Many factors may influence the direction of history, but change just one of those factors and the outcome itself may change. If the USS *Maine* had not exploded there may not have been a Spanish-American War.

Understanding Historical Events in Context

Events as they happened   Historians strive to place events in the context of their time, understanding them the way the participants would have. This means understanding the ideas and beliefs of the time and not imposing modern day values on the past. We may still disagree with the actions people took in the past, such as enslaving human beings or denying women the right to vote, but historians need to understand why people acted as they did.

Drawing Lessons from History

Comparing the present with the past   Past decisions and the consequences of historical events reverberate through our own time. Decisions made almost 150 years ago—leading up to and during the Civil War—still affect how different regions of the country view one another. Some things have changed; some have stayed the same.

Abraham Lincoln was a divisive President in his time; now he is a beloved figure.

Lessons we have learned   We can get a better sense of how to meet the challenges we face today by knowing how people in the past met or failed to meet similar challenges. For example, after the stock market crash of 1929 and the Great Depression that followed, the practice of buying stocks on borrowed money was severely restricted. Today many of the laws that make up the fabric of our nation came from lessons learned in difficult times. Historians are careful not to think the past holds all the answers. No situation is exactly like any other, and we need to be careful not to draw lessons too hastily, or too confidently.

Traders on the New York Stock Exchange are still bound by laws developed in response to the stock market crash of 1929.

Themes of History

Understanding history means understanding the connections between time, places, events, and people. Throughout *American Anthem,* you will find opportunities to make those connections and identify themes that will help you grasp the larger patterns of events across time.

Government and Democracy

The United States was founded on such ideals as human equality, limited government, and democratic representation. Today, as when our nation was founded, the American government is separated into three branches—the executive branch, the legislative branch, and the judicial branch. For over two hundred years, these three branches have worked under a system of checks and balances so that no one branch ever becomes too powerful.

Our Constitution defines the structure of our government.

Individual Rights and Responsibilities

When America was founded, only white men with property could vote in elections or hold office. Over the past two centuries, women and African Americans have fought for and won the right to vote and participate in our democracy. Today, American citizens can register to vote when they are eighteen years old. Voting is one of our most precious individual rights and responsibilities as citizens of the American democracy.

Voting is the most fundamental way citizens exercise both their rights and their responsibilities.

Economic Development

In the United States, the abundance of natural resources, a free-enterprise economic system, and government regulation protecting both private property and the public good all work together to ensure our country's economic success. The offer of social mobility and economic success through hard work has attracted immigrants to the United States from around the world.

Many innovators, such as Thomas Edison, have contributed to America's cultural and economic development.

Immigrants from many nations choose to become citizens of the United States.

Immigration and Migration

People from many nations, representing an extraordinary range of ethnic, racial, national, and religious groups, have come to the United States and become American citizens, making our country the most diverse in the world. At many times in our nation's history, people have also migrated within the country's borders, seeking new opportunities and a better way of life.

Cultural Expressions

A diverse nation has given rise to a diverse culture, drawing on the traditions of many different groups. This blending and remixing of cultural expression among ethnic, racial, and religious groups is the source of tremendous strength and creativity, but it also sometimes causes conflict.

Global Relations

Early American foreign policy reflected the country's origins as a British colony, prompting America to try to remain separate from the affairs of European nations. By the 1900s, however, the United States emerged as a world superpower, with allies and responsibilities around the world.

U.S. leaders can make an important difference in the world.

Science and Technology

A spirit of innovation in science and technology has had an enormous effect on our country's economy and culture. Throughout our history, American inventions have vastly improved quality of life and standards of living not only here but across the globe.

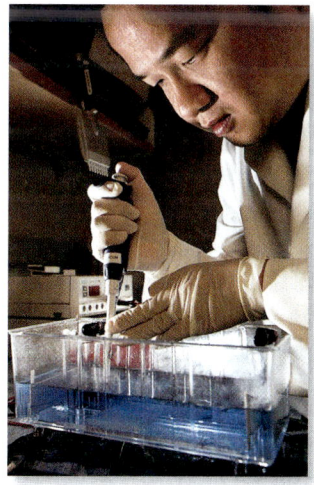

Medical and computer science are important parts of our nation's past and future.

Uniquely American art forms, such as jazz and blues music, have come from cultural diversity.

Analyzing Primary Sources

Define the Skill

Primary sources are documents or other artifacts created by people present at historical events either as witnesses or participants. You can identify a primary source by reading for first person clues, such as *I, we,* and *our.* Quotation marks signify a speech or writing. These types of sources are valuable to historians because they give information about an event or a time period. All primary sources include a point of view because they were written or created by one person or group. Points of view may differ. For example, a Union soldier writing about a Civil War battle may have a different point of view than a Confederate soldier writing about the same battle. Historians compare primary sources to understand an event from all sides in order to write an accurate historical interpretation.

Primary sources can include:
- Letters
- Photographs
- Diaries
- Newspaper stories
- Pamphlets, books, or other writings
- Court opinions
- Autobiographies
- Pottery, weapons, and other artifacts
- Government data, laws, and statutes
- Speeches

Learn the Skill

Use the following strategies to analyze primary sources.

1 Identify the author or creator of the primary source.
There is little information given about Beverly. His role is unclear. A historian should ask more questions about this primary source.

2 Determine the historical event the primary source is describing.
Ask yourself whether Beverly's details match what you already know about Bacon's Rebellion.

Virginian Robert Beverly on Bacon's Rebellion—

"Four things may be reckoned to have been the main ingredients towards this intestine commotion [violent outbreak]. First, The extreme low price of tobacco, and the ill usage of the planter in the exchange of goods for it, which the country, with all their earnest endeavors, could not remedy. Secondly, The splitting the colony into proprieties, contrary to the original charters; and the extravagant taxes they were [charged]. Thirdly, The heavy restraints and burdens laid upon their trade by act of Parliament in England. Fourthly, The disturbance given by the Indians."

3 Compare what you already know to details in the primary source.
Often a primary source will enhance your knowledge of an event. Which detail in this source tells you something new?

Apply the Skill

1. What is Robert Beverly's point of view?
2. List two details about Bacon's Rebellion provided by this source.
3. How would this source help a historian write a historical interpretation of Bacon's Rebellion?

Artifacts are also primary sources. This is a twelve shilling note from Pennsylvania, 1777.

Use the following strategies to analyze primary sources.

1 **Identify the author or creator of the primary source.**
In 1777, the colonies each printed their own money. The monetary system was based on a system of pounds, shillings, and pence.

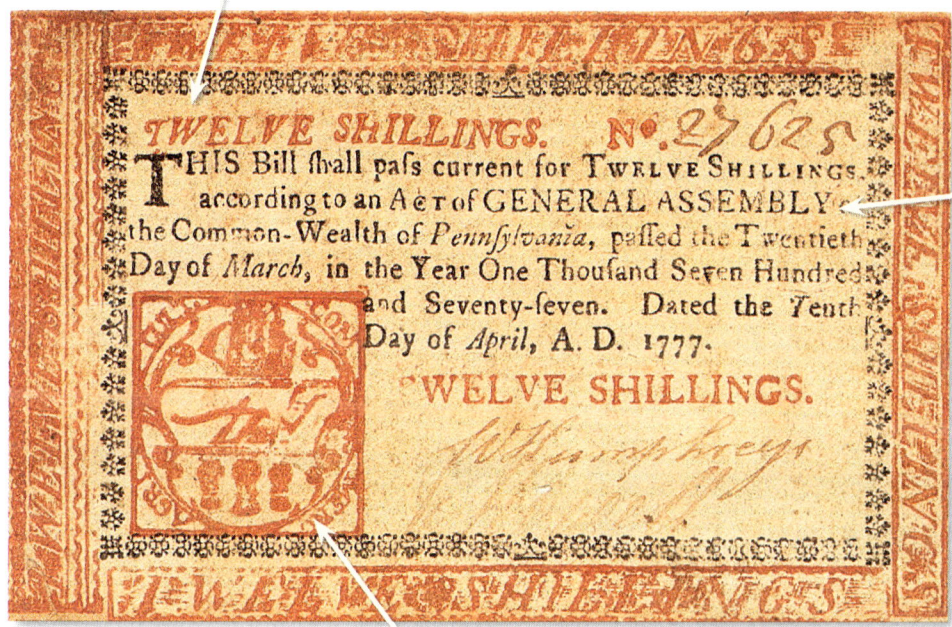

2 **Determine the time period that the primary source is describing.**
The paragraph printed on the money tells under whose authority it was printed. It also states when the act was passed, dating the note in 1777.

3 **Compare what you already know to details in the primary source.**
The seal on the note shows a ship, a plow, and bundles of wheat. What can these icons tell you about the colony of Pennsylvania?

Apply the Skill

1. Who is the creator of this primary source?
2. What can you infer about colonial money by viewing this primary source?
3. How would this source be useful to a historian?

Interpreting Visuals

Define the Skill

Visuals can be important historical sources, so interpreting visuals in vital to reading like a historian. Visuals may offer an accurate portrayal of the details of a historical figure or event. Or they may represent an exaggerated or biased point of view. Knowing and understanding an artist or photographer's point of view can sometimes reveal more to a historian than the actual image itself.

To analyze an image, first determine the medium. Is the image a photograph, a piece of fine art, a poster, an advertisement, or a cartoon? What might this tell you about the image's audience? Next, look at the credit line and title, which will tell you who created the image and possibly what the artist intended it to mean. Look or details that could convey meaning. Then study the subject of the visual. Who or what is being portrayed? Are there symbols or familiar landmarks in the image? Why might those elements have been chosen? Finally, compare the image with what you know about the historical time it depicts.

Learn the Skill

Use the following strategies to analyze visuals.

1 Who or what is the subject?
Queen Elizabeth I

2 Examine the details. What is the historical context of this picture? Behind Queen Elizabeth are images of the English fleet defeating the Spanish Armada in 1588.

3 How is the subject depicted? The queen is portrayed in a positive light, as a beautiful, poised woman in rich clothes and luxurious surroundings.

4 Does the image agree or disagree with known historical facts? The right panel behind Elizabeth shows ships sinking in bad weather, which was a historical factor in the Armada's defeat.

Apply the Skill

1. What symbols of power and rule are included in the picture?
2. Elizabeth was 55 years old when the English fleet defeated the Spanish Armada, yet she is portrayed as young and beautiful in this painting. Why might that be so?

Interpreting Political Cartoons

Define the Skill

Political cartoons are another kind of visual found in the historical record. These differ from visuals such as photographs and fine art because political cartoons often exaggerate characteristics of subjects or events in order to convey a specific message, either about politics in particular or society in general. Historians use political cartoons to understand how a particular person or event was perceived at the time. To interpret political cartoons, examine all the elements while considering the social, political, and historical context of the time.

Learn the Skill

Use the following strategies to interpret political cartoons.

1 Identify the cartoon's subject. This cartoon shows Congressman Preston Brooks (D, SC) attacking Senator Charles Sumner (R, MA). The two disagreed about the Kansas-Nebraska compromise over slavery.

4 Compare the message with historical knowledge. Does the cartoon agree or disagree with facts you already know? Preston attacked Sumner in a nearly empty Senate chamber, not in front of a crowd of witnesses as shown in the cartoon.

2 Read any text and study all symbols. Do they provide any clues about point of view? The caption uses the phrase "Southern Chivalry" to describe the beating; this is a use of irony, or meaning the opposite of what is actually stated.

SOUTHERN CHIVALRY — ARGUMENT versus CLUB'S.

3 Establish the cartoon's message. How is the subject portrayed? Preston Brooks is portrayed in a negative light, attacking a helpless Sumner on the floor of the Senate.

Apply the Skill

1. Does this cartoon look as though it was created by a supporter of slavery or a supporter of abolition?
2. Are there any features in this carton that are exaggerated?
3. Which of the two men is portrayed as the aggressor? Which is portrayed as the victim?

Interpreting Literature as Historical Evidence

Define the Skill

Historians can sometimes use literature written during a particular time period to gain detailed insights into certain people, places, and events. For example, a novel about an upper-class New York City family in the late 1800s can provide historical details about the lifestyle of that social class. Some literature is activist, meaning that its purpose is to inspire an emotional or social response.

Learn the Skill

Use the following strategies to interpret literature.

1 Identify the author's point of view or bias. Does the author have experiences that make the description more reliable? Reflect on what you already know about the book or author before you begin to read.

2 Look for descriptive passages. This sentence gives descriptive details about workers in meat-packing factories. Do these details make the account historically believable?

Excerpt from *The Jungle,* by Upton Sinclair—

The men would tie up their feet in newspapers and old sacks, and these would be soaked in blood and frozen, and then soaked again, and so on until by night time a man would be walking on great lumps the size of feet of an elephant. Now and then, when the bosses were not looking, you would see them plunging their feet and ankles into the steaming hot carcass of the steer, or darting across the room to the hot-water jets.

4 Compare details in the literature with known facts about the event. Sinclair was one of many writers in the early 1900s who investigated businesses and industry. Sinclair's work led to the passage of The Pure Food and Drug Act in 1906, to protect consumers from contaminated beef.

3 Determine whether the literature is meant to describe a certain historical event or to elicit an emotional response. Here, the author wants to elicit an emotional response from the audience. What effect does this strategy have on the usefulness of the literature as an historical interpretation?

Apply the Skill

1. What is the author's point of view or bias?
2. What is the goal of the literature selection?
3. What can historians learn about factory work by reading this selection?

Recognizing Bias

Define the Skill

To ensure an effective analysis of primary sources, historians must learn to recognize bias and the source of bias. Bias is a point of view that is slanted by personal or political beliefs. Every primary source reflects bias, from either the person who created the source or the person viewing the source. Bias appears in primary sources for a variety of reasons and gives clues about an author's intent or background.

For example, the author may be trying to justify an action or sway an opinion. Sometimes an author expresses a personal view without knowing that it is biased. Bias can help historians understand the different attitudes during a certain time in history. To avoid bias, a historian must examine different points of view and primary sources. It is important to look at many sources on the same incident or issue in order to achieve a balanced analysis.

Learn the Skill

Use the following strategies to recognize bias.

1 Identify the document. This section gives you the context of the statement. Think about how speeches at public celebrations are different from other primary sources, such as private letters.

2 Examine the author's point of view. What bias does the author express? Identify the author and his occupation. What can this tell you about the author's possible goals?

Dr. H. W. Harkness, Sacramento Newspaper Publisher, at the ceremony to celebrate the first transcontinental railroad—

❝The east and west have come together. Never, since history commenced her record of human events, has she been called upon to note the completion of a work so magnificent.❞

4 Compare the primary source with historical evidence. In what ways is the primary source different from other historical accounts? In what ways is it similar?

3 Consider the author's goal. This claim is not a true claim. The speaker is using rhetoric, or the skill of using language effectively and persuasively. Consider whether rhetoric is appropriate for this event.

Apply the Skill

1. What is the author's goal in this statement?
2. Explain how a historian could use this document in preparing a historical account of the celebration marking the completion of the transcontinental railroad.

Evaluating Sources

Define the Skill

Historians must constantly evaluate sources to determine their credibility. Credible sources help historians produce an accurate and reliable historical account. Historians use several criteria for evaluating sources:

- They consider the author or producer of a source.
- They think about where, when, and why a source was created.
- They assess the level of bias in a source.
- They acknowledge that sources are more reliable if the author was close in time and place to a given event.

Learn the Skill

Use the following strategies to evaluate sources.

1 Identify and learn the background of the author of the source. Quotes almost always include the name of the speaker or writer. This title also gives context information.

President Woodrow Wilson, in a speech to Congress, April 2, 1917—

“We shall fight for the things which we have always carried nearest our hearts, for democracy. . . [and to] bring peace and safety to all nations and make the world itself at last free.”

3 Determine whether the source was meant to be public or private. The use of quotation marks and the word "we" help show that this is a primary source. This speech was given to Congress, but who was Wilson really addressing?

2 Examine the context of the source. Consider when, in relation to the event, the source was created. In January, 1917, Germany resumed its submarine warfare. By April, they had sunk five U.S. submarines. Wilson justifies the U.S. entry into World War I by saying that the "peace and safety" of the world is at stake.

Apply the Skill

1. Who is the producer of the source?
2. What is the context of the source? Is the source meant to be public or private?
3. In what way is the source biased? What is the goal of the speaker?
4. How would you evaluate the source, on the basis of its credibility?

Analyzing Secondary Sources

Define the Skill

Secondary sources are accounts produced after a historical event by people who rely on primary sources. Secondary sources often contain summaries and analyses of events and time periods. Your textbook can be considered a secondary source, as can many other history books.

When a historian produces a secondary source, it often contains an interpretation of a historical event, or what the historian thinks actually happened and why. Historians build their interpretations on the basis of available facts and their own analysis. These secondary sources can be analyzed to determine whether they present a complete and accurate accounting of events.

Other kinds of secondary sources include:
- Encyclopedia entries
- Web sites
- Articles and essays by historians
- Biographies

Learn the Skill

Use the following strategies to analyze secondary sources.

1 Identify the source.
This is an encyclopedia article.

2 Summary
Secondary sources offer summaries of historical facts.

"World War I." Encyclopedia Britannica. 2005. Encyclopedia Britannica Online School Edition. 22 Sept. 2005

World War I, *also called* **First World War,** *or* **Great War**—an international conflict that in 1914–18 embroiled most of the nations of Europe along with Russia, the United States, the Middle East, and other regions. The **war** pitted the Central Powers—mainly Germany, Austria-Hungary, and Turkey—against the Allies—mainly France, Great Britain, Russia, Italy, Japan, and, from 1917, the United States. It ended with the defeat of the Central Powers. The **war** was virtually unprecedented in the slaughter, carnage, and destruction it caused.

World War I was one of the great watersheds of 20th-century geopolitical history. It led to the fall of four great imperial dynasties (in Germany, Russia, Austria-Hungary, and Turkey), resulted in the Bolshevik Revolution in Russia, and, in its destabilization of European society, laid the groundwork for **World War II.**

3 Analysis
Secondary sources analyze historical facts and draw conclusions.

4 Consequences
Since they are produced after an event is over, secondary sources can take a longer view of an event's consequences.

Apply the Skill

The first paragraph of the article offers a summary of the subject, World War I. The second paragraph contains an analysis of the importance and effects of the war. Answer these questions based on the excerpt:

1. What important information about World War I can be found in the first paragraph?
2. What are some of the consequences of World War I listed in the article?

Many Web sites are secondary sources, and their use is becoming more common and accepted among historians. Web sites, however, require special care in analysis. Because the World Wide Web uses open architecture, meaning that anyone can post information without any kind of review process, it is harder to determine whether information on these sites is accurate. Pay close attention to the stated source of any historical Web site, as well as the date it was last updated.

Among Web domain extensions, .gov and .edu are considered the most reliable for academic work. Some .org and .com sites are also good resources, but they require careful study to determine their credibility.

The domain extensions that appear in a Web address can help. These include the following:
- **.gov**—a government site
- **.org**—usually a nonprofit organization
- **.edu**—educational entities such as colleges and universities
- **.com**—for-profit and commercial entities, including book publishers

Learn the Skill

Use the following strategies to analyze secondary sources.

1 What kind of secondary source is it?
This is a biography on a Web site.

2 Determine the author or the publisher of the secondary source.
What do you know about the person's or organization's credibility? The content of this biography is provided by the Smithsonian Institution, a credible source.

3 How does the author or publisher handle primary source material?
Is primary source material drawn from a range of sources for balance? The fine art portrait is identified and sourced. The biography also notes that conflicting opinions exist about General MacArthur and presents generalizations of those opinions.

4 When numbers and statistics are used, examine them carefully.
Are they offering a complete picture or just one part of the story? This biography does not use numbers or statistics, but in other historical writings, visual representations of data would need to be analyzed.

http://www.hrw.com/si/social/si_1914/index.html

SMITHSONIAN INSTITUTION

Spotlight: Biography

The Korean War

The Korean War (1950–1953) is often referred to as America's "forgotten war," because it did not capture the nation's attention as had World War II, nor did it arouse controversy as did the war in Vietnam. In fact, although the Korean War was much shorter than the Vietnam War, the casualties were almost as high, with 54,000 Americans killed and 103,000 wounded. Total casualties for the war reached 1.9 million. In 1995, more than forty years after the conflict ended, a memorial honoring the sacrifices and services of Korean War soldiers was dedicated on the Mall in Washington, D.C., directly across from the Vietnam Veterans' Memorial.

Douglas MacArthur (1880–1964)

Howard Chandler Christy (1873–1952)
Oil on canvas, 1952, NPG.78.271
National Portrait Gallery,
Smithsonian Institution, Washington, D.C.
Gift of Henry Ostrow

Though General Douglas MacArthur is perhaps best known for his participation in the Korean War, his military service actually began a half-century earlier. In fact, his was one of the longest and most controversial careers of any American military officer. Douglas MacArthur was the son of another famous soldier, Arthur MacArthur II, who led troops in the Civil War, the Spanish American War, and in the Philippines. Encouraged by his father's military successes as well as an ambitious mother, MacArthur entered the United States Military Academy at West Point and graduated at the head of

American Beginnings to 1789   American Nation from 1790 to 1865   The Expanding Nation from 1865 to 1914

Apply the Skill

1. What information do you learn about General Douglas MacArthur?
2. This source does not list an author. What information would you look at to help you determine whether this is a credible secondary source?

Analyzing Bias in Historical Interpretation

Define the Skill

When reading works of historical interpretation to determine their credibility and usefulness, it is important to read critically, looking for **bias in historical interpretation.** Most historians try to filter out their own biases when writing history. But they may not succeed, since they may not be aware of their biases. Bias can affect the way a historian tells a story, what facts are included or excluded, which events are highlighted or ignored, and how he or she treats primary sources.

Learn the Skill

Read the excerpt from Theodore Roosevelt's history of the War of 1812 between Great Britain and the United States. Then use the following strategies to analyze bias in historical interpretation.

1 Does the author have a background in the subject matter? Theodore Roosevelt was a graduate of Harvard and a New York state Assemblyman in 1882. He would later serve as secretary of the Navy, and become President of the United States in 1901.

2 Is emotional language used to support a particular point of view? This emotional language demonstrates Roosevelt's pro-American bias.

Theodore Roosevelt, *The Naval War of 1812,* published in 1882—

"But the wrongs done by the Americans were insignificant compared with those they received. Any innocent merchant vessel was liable to seizure at any moment; and when overhauled by a British cruiser short of men was sure to be stripped of most of her crew. . . . If a captain lacked his full complement there was little doubt as to the view he would take of any man's nationality. The wrongs inflicted on our seafaring countrymen by their impressment into foreign ships formed the main cause of the war."

3 Are credible primary sources used to support the text? Are footnotes or cited quotations used? This assertion is not backed up by a primary source or factual citation. The event happened more than 40 years before Roosevelt was born and he cannot have first-hand knowledge of it.

Apply the Skill

1. Who is the author? What important information is found in his background?
2. Are there examples of emotional language in the excerpt? If so, what are they?
3. Is there bias in this passage? Explain your answer.

Evaluating Historical Interpretation

SKILLS HANDBOOK

Define the Skill

Historians and others evaluate historical interpretations to determine credibility, the level of bias, and the relevance of the material. A historical interpretation is a way to explain the past. These interpretations can change over time as historians learn more about the people and events of the past. Historians use several criteria for evaluating historical interpretations.

- Consider the age of the interpretation and its current relevance to the material. Some sources, such as encyclopedias, are updated periodically to include new material.
- Assess the level of bias in the interpretation.
- Determine the credibility of the interpretation.

Learn the Skill

Use the following strategies to evaluate historical interpretation.

1 Identify the author or publisher of the source to determine credibility.
The introduction tells you the author's name and his profession. A book by a history professor is almost always a credible source.

2 Consider when the source was created.
This book was published in 2003, so it probably uses current scholarship.

excerpt from *In the Presence of Mine Enemies: War in the Heart of America, 1859–1863,* by Edward L. Ayers, Professor of History, published in 2003—

Together, the stories of Augusta [County, Virginia] and Franklin [County, Pennsylvania] tell of a war both simpler and less straightforward than general accounts reveal. The Civil War was like all wars in that it elevated the worst human emotions and called them virtues. People let themselves be driven by arrogance and revenge as well as by ideology and principle. People watched themselves descend into rage and numbness, knowing themselves unworthy of their feelings. People invoked the Constitution and the Declaration of Independence against enemies invoking the same icons.

3 Examine the level of bias in the interpretation.
Does it detract from the overall credibility? The author's research was based on the people and public records of two counties, one in the North and the other in the South. He is using primary sources and presenting potentially opposing viewpoints. This creates a less-biased source.

Apply the Skill

1. Who is the author of the interpretation?
2. How does bias affect the interpretation?
3. Explain why the source would be valuable to current students.

Analyzing Alternative Interpretations of the Past

Define the Skill

Interpretations of past events can differ in many ways. An interpretation may reflect an extreme bias for one view or another, or it may reflect two different schools of thought. Historians are often faced with alternative interpretations of a time or event in the past. When faced with opposing viewpoints, good historians do additional research to find the accuracies in each account.

Learn the Skill

Use the following strategies to analyze interpretations.

1 Look for information about the author or the source that may give clues to possible bias.
Andrews is a historian while Hacker is an economics professor. How could the different careers affect the authors' point of view?

Charles M. Andrews, historian—

"Primarily, the American Revolution was a political and constitutional movement and only secondarily one that was either financial, commercial or social. At bottom, the fundamental issue was the political independence of the colonies, and in the last analysis the conflict lay between the British Parliament and the colonial assemblies…"

2 Define the main points in each argument.
This will help you compare the interpretations.

3 Discount rhetoric or emotional language that is not factual.
Here, Hacker uses rhetoric to demean the "political and constitutional concepts" that Andrews supports.

Louis M. Hacker, economics professor—

"The struggle was not over high-sounding political and constitutional concepts; over the power of taxation or even, in the final analysis, over natural rights. It was over colonial manufacturing, wild lands and furs, sugar, wine, tea, and currency, all of which meant, simply, the survival or collapse of English mercantile capitalism within the imperial-colonial framework of the mercantilist system."

4 In what ways do the interpretations differ?
Summarize each interpretation to compare them. However, you should read additional information, opinions, or studies before you decide with which interpretation to agree.

Apply the Skill

1. Summarize the two interpretations presented above.
2. What can comparing these interpretations tell you about historical interpretation in general?

Making Oral Presentations

Define the Skill

Historians sometimes make oral presentations. These include speeches, lectures, or interviews. Oral presentations often support a version of or a conclusion about an issue and are given from outlines or note cards. They should be more dynamic than simply reading a written essay aloud. Historians must perform thorough research, make notes, and carefully organize their presentations. As a student of history, an oral presentation allows you to present information on a topic you have researched to an audience.

Learn the Skill

Use the following strategies to make oral presentations.

1 Identify a historical topic you would like to present.
Choose a central idea or theme on which to focus your research. Research the topic to gather relevant facts and vivid details. Include visual aids, such as maps, charts, or pictures, to add to your presentation.

5 Practice reading your presentation aloud.
Make sure that you are comfortable speaking and that your statements are clear. Although you do not want to read directly from your notes while giving an oral presentation, it may be helpful to write sentences in your introduction to get you started.

Topic: Watergate

Introduction: On a summer night in 1972, a bungled break-in would cause the downfall of an American president. My hypothesis is that President Nixon, although a flawed person, was the victim of incompetent subordinates.

Body: Talk about Nixon's top aides
  a. H. R. Haldeman
  b. John Ehrlichman

2 Organize your information into an introduction, a body, and a conclusion.
The introduction should clearly state your topic and hypothesis while also generating interest with the listener. The body features the main points of your argument. The conclusion summarizes your main points and draws on those points to formulate a personal opinion about your topic.

3 Proofread your notes to ensure that they are well organized and grammatically correct.
Clearly label your notes. Using the terms introduction, body, and conclusion on your note cards helps you make an organized presentation.

4 Express arguments clearly and persuasively.
Write key words and clues in your notes to use as talking points. It may be helpful to structure this section in outline form. Also, look at how the opening sentence could catch the listeners' attention.

Apply the Skill

1. Name the three parts of a well-organized oral presentation.
2. What is the topic and hypothesis of this oral presentation?
3. List two visual aids that could be used to add interest and clarity to this presentation.

Making Written Presentations

Define the Skill

Written presentations are one of the ways that historians present their scholarship. Historians must perform careful research and cite all sources in written presentations. They also try to write about a small part of an event. This is called narrowing the focus, and it helps historians make important points and explore new facets of history. For example, a historian might not make a written presentation about World War II, which would take thousands of pages to fully cover. He or she would probably write about one aspect of the war, such as a certain battle. As a student, a written presentation is a way for you to present information on a topic you have researched.

Learn the Skill

Use the following strategies to make written presentations.

1 Identify a historical topic.
Be sure to narrow the focus of your idea or theme. Also, clearly state your topic. Make sure that any facts you include relate specifically to this topic.

5 Proofread your written presentation to ensure that it is well organized and grammatically correct.
Proofreading your notes and your presentation is always important to prevent errors. Read your presentation aloud to make sure that your statements are clear.

2 Formulate a hypothesis.
This will be the main idea of your presentation. Once you have determined your hypothesis, research will be easier. Find and organize facts, data, and details to support your hypothesis.

Topic: The Camp David Accords, 1978

Hypothesis: The Camp David ~~Accounts~~ Accords were an important first step in establishing peace in the Middle East.

Fact: By signing the agreement, Egypt recognized Israel as a country.

Bibliography: World Book Encyclopedia, 2003 edition; Volume 1, p. 582a

4 Clearly state your hypothesis and the facts that support it in your writing.
This will help you organize your presentation. Good historians show both sides of any argument, so be sure to include all relevant facts.

3 Keep a bibliography of sources as you research.
A bibliography is a list of all sources used or cited in a written presentation. You must cite your sources to retain credibility and avoid plagiarism.

Apply the Skill

1. What is the hypothesis in the written presentation notes above?
2. List an area of history you would like to research.
3. Narrow the focus to a small part of this area, and write a sample hypothesis for your written presentation.

Strategies for Multiple Choice

You can improve your test-taking skills by practicing these strategies for multiple-choice questions. Read the skill-specific tips and samples on the left page. Then practice the skill on the right page. A multiple-choice question usually consists of a single *stem* and four *answer options*. Only one option is the correct answer. The other, incorrect options are *distracters*.

LEARN

1 **Read the stem carefully to determine what it is asking.**

2 **Read carefully when a question is phrased in the negative.**
Some standardized tests phrase questions in the negative. Take care with questions that contain words such as *not* and *except*.

3 **Look for key words and facts within a stem.**

4 **Consider options such as *all of the above* and *none of the above* as you would any other possible response.**
If you choose *all of the above*, ensure that all of the choices are correct.

5 **If two options contradict each other, one of them is likely to be the correct answer.**

6 **Eliminate the answer options that you know are incorrect.**

7 **Watch for modifiers.**
Options that include superlative words such as *always* or *never* are usually incorrect. Superlatives indicate that the correct answer must be an undisputed fact. In social studies, that is rarely the case.

1 **2**

Stem

Answer Options

1. Which of the following was *not* a cause of colonial unrest with Britain?

   (1) the Boston Massacre

   (2) the Olive Branch petition

   (3) passage of various taxes, such as the Sugar Act, on the colonies

   (4) the presence of British soldiers in the colonies

2. On April 18, 1775, the <u>first</u> shots of the Revolutionary War were fired at

   (1) Concord

   (2) Lexington

   (3) Philadelphia

   (4) all of the above **4**

3 Many shots were fired during the Revolution, but you are looking for those that were fired *first*.

3. During the Revolutionary War, a Loyalist was someone who

   (1) remained loyal to Britain

   (2) wanted freedom from Britain

   (3) fought alongside the Continental Army

   (4) lived mainly in New England and Virginia

5

4. Many changes occurred as a result of the Revolutionary War, including

   (1) more rights for women

   (2) voting rights for <u>all</u> men

   (3) Spanish control of the colonies

   (4) the formation of the United States

6 Absolute words such as *all*, *none*, and *every* often signal an incorrect option.

7 You can eliminate **(3)** if you recall that Spain controlled Florida after the Revolutionary War.

Answers: 1 (2), 2 (2), 3 (1), 4 (4)

Directions: *Read the following questions and choose the best answer.*

1. Which of the following were considered border states in the Civil War?
   (1) Kentucky
   (2) Maryland
   (3) all of the above
   (4) none of the above

2. What existing invention was put to use in the Civil War to aid communication?
   (1) e-mail
   (2) telephone
   (3) the telegraph
   (4) the Pony Express

3. The Emancipation Proclamation freed all
   (1) enslaved people
   (2) debtors from their debts
   (3) enslaved people in rebelling states
   (4) enslaved people who had escaped to the North

4. Prison camps during the Civil War did not
   (1) lack food
   (2) have disease
   (3) have overcrowding
   (4) have sanitary conditions

Strategies for Secondary Sources

You can improve your test-taking skills by practicing these strategies for secondary sources. Read the skill-specific tips and samples on the left page. Then practice the skill on the right page. A secondary source is a written source or a visual created after an event by a person who was not present at the event. The creators of secondary sources research primary sources and other secondary sources to learn about historical events. A biography is an example of a secondary source, as is a history textbook.

LEARN

① Identify the type of secondary source.
Is it an encyclopedia entry, a Web site, a scholarly article, or another type of source?

② Identify the author of the secondary source.
Note how much time has passed between the event and the time when the author writes about it. Is the author qualified to write about the topic?

③ Look at the title and topic sentence to preview the content of the passage.

④ Recognize the historical event or people involved.

⑤ Ask yourself whether the author uses any primary sources or other secondary sources for support.

⑥ Read the questions before rereading the passage so that you know what information you need to find.

—Paul Johnson, *A History of the American People*, p. 445

Lincoln's object was not merely to put his name and his case before the American people, as well as Illinois voters. It was also to expose the essential pantomime-horse approach of a man who tried to straddle North and South. He succeeded in both. He put to Douglas the key question: 'Can the people of a United States territory, in any lawful way, against the wish of a citizen of the United States, exclude slavery from its limits prior to the formation of a state constitution?' If Douglas said yes, to win Illinois voters, he lost the South. If he said no, to win the South, he lost Illinois. Douglas' answer was: 'It matters not what way the Supreme Court may hereafter decide as to the abstract question whether slavery may or may not go into a territory under the Constitution; the people have the lawful means to introduce it or exclude it as they please, for the reason that slavery cannot exist a day or an hour unless it is supported by the local police regulations.' This answer won Douglas Illinois but lost him the South and hence, two years later, the presidency.

1. Johnson uses primary source quotes to
- **(1)** identify the two senatorial candidates
- **(2)** show the similarities between the viewpoints of Lincoln and Douglas
- **(3)** describe the many issues that Lincoln and Douglas debated
- **(4)** show how Lincoln forces Douglas to state his position on slavery

Answer: 1 (4)

Directions: *Read the following passage and use your knowledge of U.S. history to answer the questions below.*

—from *In the Presence of Mine Enemies: War in the Heart of America, 1859–1863*
By Edward L. Ayers

Michael Hanger, the young carpenter from Augusta in the 5th Virginia Infantry, described the situation he and his comrades faced [in his diary]. "5 O'Clock A.M. we can hear the cannon firing from the hills in front, and a little below us. The Yankees are endeavoring to draw us in that direction. The Junction is strongly fortified . . . in every possible direction." Put into position, Hanger and his comrades lay there for three and a half hours . . .

Things got worse the next day. "It is now raining very hard and has been all night. The wounded on the battlefield must have suffered greatly last night. It is a very muddy and disagreeable day . . ." Hanger gave no fuller evaluation of the battle. He did not say who had won and lost. He only listed the names of the men in his company who had been wounded. He did not give the name the battle was to bear. The Confederates called it Manassas, after the nearby town; the Union called it Bull Run, naming it after the nearby river, as became its custom.

1. What primary source does Ayers use?
(1) accounts by Union generals
(2) the diary of Michael Hanger
(3) Michael Hanger's military record
(4) accounts by Confederate generals

2. What historical event is Michael Hanger describing?
(1) the Battle of Bull Run
(2) the burning of Atlanta
(3) the Battle of Yorktown
(4) Michael Hanger's death

3. Ayers uses primary sources to
(1) analyze the impact of the battle
(2) provide descriptive details of the battle
(3) support political viewpoints of the time
(4) give personal details about fellow soldiers

4. How did the outcome of this battle affect the Union army?
(1) The victory boosted the soldiers' morale.
(2) The soldiers realized that it would be a short war.
(3) The Union army decreased training for its soldiers.
(4) The Union army increased training for its soldiers.

Strategies for Political Cartoons

You can improve your test-taking skills by practicing these strategies for political cartoons. Read the skill-specific tips and samples on the left page. Then practice the skill on the right page. Political cartoons are primary sources. They use comedic images to poke fun at political figures and issues. Cartoons can provide helpful context to the opinions and values of the time.

LEARN

1 Identify the characters and issues being portrayed.
This figure represents an anarchist.

2 Read the caption and any other labels to better understand the subject.

3 Identify any exaggerated images or ideas.
The wild character of the anarchist is a common exaggeration from the time period.

4 Identify common symbols used to help you recognize the subject of the cartoon.

5 Identify the cartoonist's point of view.
Recognize whether the subject is portrayed positively or negatively.

6 Identify the message the cartoonist wanted to send with this cartoon.
Does the cartoonist agree or disagree with the situation?

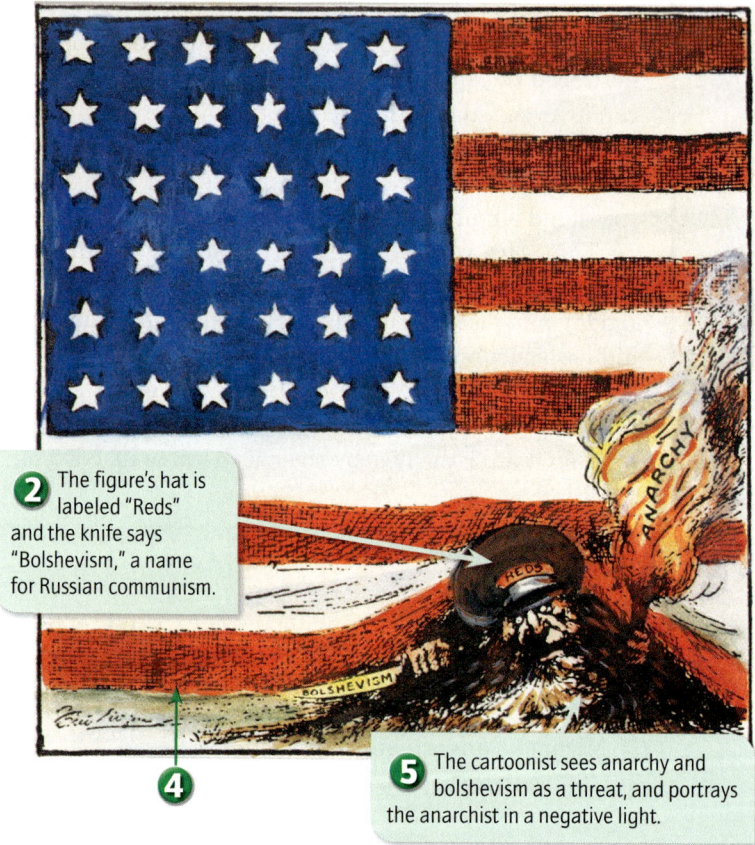

2 The figure's hat is labeled "Reds" and the knife says "Bolshevism," a name for Russian communism.

5 The cartoonist sees anarchy and bolshevism as a threat, and portrays the anarchist in a negative light.

1. Which sentence best summarizes the message of this cartoon?
   (1) Immigration is anarchy.
   (2) Anarchy is not welcome in the United States.
   (3) Immigrants and anarchists are hiding under the U.S. flag.
   (4) Immigration should be restricted and anarchists should be deported.

2. Which word summarizes the cartoonist opinion regarding immigration practices?
   (1) positive
   (2) criminal
   (3) beneficial
   (4) dangerous

Answers: 1 (4), 2 (4)

Directions: *Interpret the following cartoon and answer the questions below.*

1. The symbol the artist uses for the Teapot Dome oil scandal is

(1) a steamship

(2) a steamroller

(3) a runaway train

(4) a horse and buggy

2. Who might the figures running from the scandal represent?

(1) ordinary citizens

(2) politicians implicated or involved in the scandal

(3) people harmed by the illegal oil deals

(4) those who brought the scandal to the public's attention

3. What effect does the artist think the scandal will have on President Warren G. Harding?

(1) It will help him.

(2) It will crush him.

(3) It will bypass him.

(4) It will not affect him.

4. Which sentence best summarizes the message of this cartoon?

(1) President Harding was a criminal.

(2) Being involved with an oil company will crush politicians.

(3) The Teapot Dome scandal was a minor incident.

(4) The Teapot Dome scandal will negatively impact those involved.

Strategies for Charts

You can improve your test-taking skills by practicing these strategies for charts. Read the skill-specific tips and samples on the left page. Then practice the skill on the right page. Charts are used to organize and summarize large amounts of information. The table, one of the most common types of charts, organizes data into columns and rows.

LEARN

1 Read the title or heading of the chart.
Find out the topic and information covered in the chart.

2 Find row and column headings.
Identify the information represented, how it is organized, and how the information is related.

3 Look for similar trends or data patterns between rows and columns.
Also look for data that does not conform to the patterns.

4 Make generalizations and draw conclusions from information in the chart.
One generalization you could make from this chart is that many countries wanted to prevent future conflict.

1 ⟶

PROGRAMS FOR A SAFER WORLD

As World War II came to an end, the countries of the world began seeking ways to prevent the problems and conflicts that helped lead to war. Leaders in the United States and other countries paved the way in establishing the following:

2 The first column lists the names of the programs. The second column gives details about each program's purpose.

3 The program in this row is the only one that does not relate directly to economic reconstruction.

World Bank (1944)	• Organization for providing loans and advice to countries for the purpose of reducing poverty
International Monetary Fund (1944)	• System for promoting orderly financial relationships between countries • Designed to prevent economic crises and to encourage trade and economic growth
United Nations (1945)	• Organization in which member nations agree to settle disputes by peaceful means • Replaced the League of Nations
General Agreement on Tariffs and Trade (1946)	• Agreement among member nations on rules and regulations for international trade • Focused on reducing tariffs and other trade barriers

1. Which generalization could you make from the information on this chart?

(1) After World War II, many countries believed that financial agreements between countries would help to limit disputes.

(2) After World War II, the World Bank primarily dealt with military issues.

(3) After World War II, these programs were developed to promote problems and conflicts between countries.

(4) After World War II, the wealthy countries around the world would receive loans from poorer countries.

Answer: 1 (1)

Directions: *Interpret the following chart and answer the questions below.*

EUROPE'S JEWISH POPULATION

	c. 1933	c. 1950	Percent Decrease
Europe	9,500,000	3,500,000	63
Selected Countries			
Poland	3,000,000	45,000	98.5
Romania	980,000	28,000	97
Germany	565,000	37,000	93.5
Hungary	445,000	155,000	65
Czechoslovakia	357,000	17,000	95
Austria	250,000	18,000	93
Greece	100,000	7,000	93
Yugoslavia	70,000	3,500	95
Bulgaria	50,000	6,500	87

Source: *United States Holocaust Memorial Museum*

1. Which of the following statements about this chart is true?
- **(1)** The data includes every country in Europe.
- **(2)** The data shows Jewish population loss in Poland during the Holocaust.
- **(3)** The data covers the years 1933 to 1980.
- **(4)** The data shows Jewish population losses around the world.

2. Which statement is NOT true about this chart?
- **(1)** Poland lost more Jews than any other country on the chart.
- **(2)** Bulgaria lost the least number of Jews of any other country on the chart.
- **(3)** From 1933 to 1950, Hungary lost more Jews than any other country shown on the chart.
- **(4)** Hungary had the smallest percentage drop in Jewish population from 1933 to 1950.

3. What trend is shown in this chart?
- **(1)** The Holocaust reduced overall Jewish population in Europe by 75 percent.
- **(2)** Jewish population losses during the Holocaust were concentrated in Central and Eastern Europe.
- **(3)** Jewish population in Europe increased during the Holocaust.
- **(4)** all of the above

4. Which generalization could you make from the data on this chart?
- **(1)** The Holocaust dramatically reduced Europe's Jewish population.
- **(2)** The Holocaust dramatically increased Europe's Jewish population.
- **(3)** The total population of Europe decreased by 65 percent.
- **(4)** The total population of Poland decreased by 98.5 percent.

Strategies for Line and Bar Graphs

You can improve your test-taking skills by practicing these strategies for line and bar graphs. Read the skill-specific tips and samples on the left page. Then practice the skill on the right page. Graphs are used to show the relationship among numerical data. Line graphs illustrate how quantities and trends change over time. Bar graphs compare groups of numbers within categories.

LEARN

❶ **Read the title of the graph to determine its main idea.**

❷ **Study the label on the vertical axis.**
The vertical axis usually indicates the type of information in the graph.

❸ **Examine the label on the horizontal axis.**
The horizontal axis usually tells you the time period the graph covers.

❹ **If a legend accompanies the graph, study it.**
The legend provides additional information. Legends specify what the colors, patterns, or symbols on the graph mean.

❺ **Identify any trends or patterns that the graph reveals.**

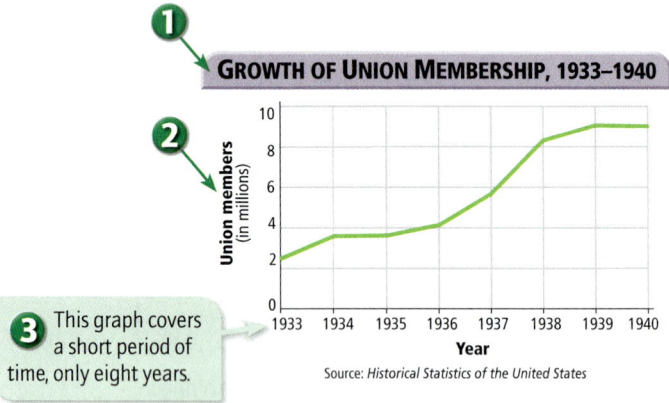

GROWTH OF UNION MEMBERSHIP, 1933–1940

❸ This graph covers a short period of time, only eight years.

Source: *Historical Statistics of the United States*

1. Which statement correctly describes the trend in union membership?

   (1) Union membership grew the most between 1933 and 1935.

   (2) Union membership grew the most between 1934 and 1936.

   (3) Union membership grew the most between 1936 and 1938.

   (4) Union membership grew the most between 1938 and 1940.

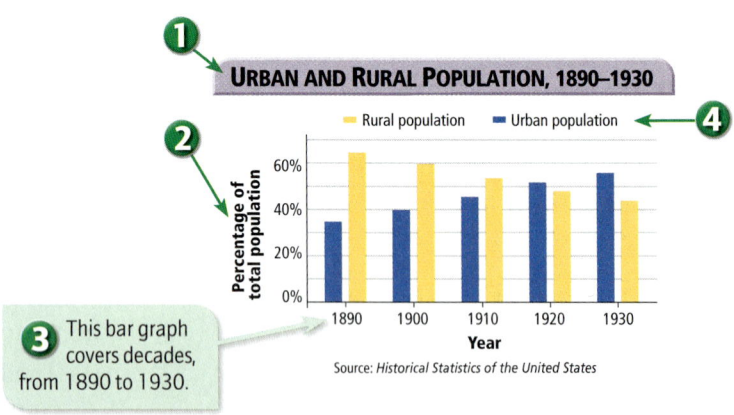

URBAN AND RURAL POPULATION, 1890–1930

❸ This bar graph covers decades, from 1890 to 1930.

Source: *Historical Statistics of the United States*

2. Which of these statements describes the rural population between 1890 and 1930?

   (1) The rural population was lower in 1890 than in 1930.

   (2) The rural population was higher in 1890 than in 1930.

   (3) The rural population and the urban population increased at the same rate.

   (4) The rural population and the urban population declined at the same rate.

Answers: 1 (3), 2 (2)

Directions: *Use the line graph and the bar graph to answer the questions below.*

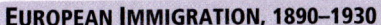

EUROPEAN IMMIGRATION, 1890–1930

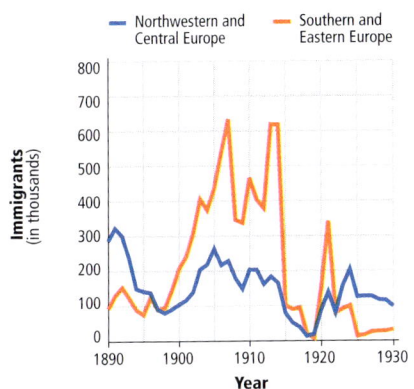

Source: *Historical Statistics of the United States*

AMERICAN INVOLVEMENT IN VIETNAM, 1965–1972

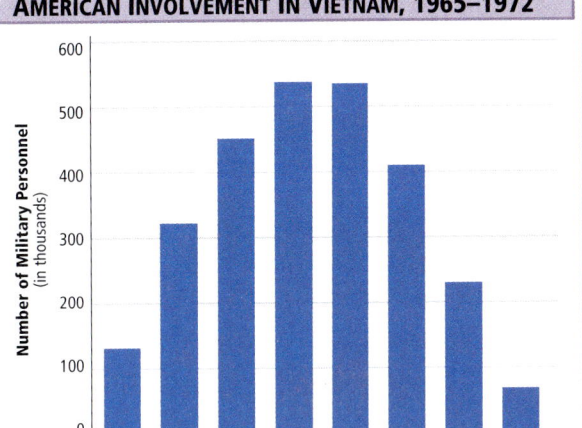

Source: *United States Department of Defense*

1. Between 1900 and 1910, most European immigrants came from
   (1) Southern and Eastern Europe.
   (2) Northern and Central Europe.
   (3) Southern and Central Europe.
   (4) Northern and Eastern Europe.

2. Which of the following describes a trend in European immigration to the United States between 1920 and 1930?
   (1) More European immigrants came from Northern and Eastern Europe.
   (2) More European immigrants came from Southern and Central Europe.
   (3) The number of immigrants coming from Southern and Eastern Europe decreased.
   (4) The number of immigrants coming from Northern and Central Europe remained about the same.

3. How did the number of U.S. military personnel in Vietnam change between 1966 and 1967?
   (1) It decreased by more than 100,000.
   (2) It increased by more than 100,000.
   (3) It increased by more than 200,000.
   (4) It decreased by more than 200,000.

4. Which of the following statements describes the number of U.S. military personnel in Vietnam from 1969 to 1972?
   (1) The number of U.S. military personnel in Vietnam did not change.
   (2) The number of U.S. military personnel in Vietnam increased slightly.
   (3) The number of U.S. military personnel in Vietnam decreased dramatically.
   (4) The number of U.S. military personnel in Vietnam increased dramatically.

Strategies for Pie Graphs

You can improve your test-taking skills by practicing these strategies for pie graphs. Read the skill-specific tips and samples on the left page. Then practice the skill on the right page. A pie, or circle, graph shows how parts are related to a whole. Slices of a pie graph should add up to 100% and are proportional to their percentage.

LEARN

1 **Read the title of the graph to learn the topic and time period it covers.**

The title explains that the topic is the presidential election of 1800.

2 **Be sure the slices add up to 99–100%.**

Compare the slices. Are they similar or do they vary widely? Pie graphs don't always indicate numbers, so you may have to estimate.

3 **Look for the legend or labels to explain what the different slices represent.**

The labels indicate the number of electoral votes won by each candidate.

4 **If there are two graphs, compare and contrast them to identify and understand trends.**

5 **Draw conclusions about what might cause similarities or differences between slices or graphs.**

The narrow margin of victory suggests that the country was evenly divided.

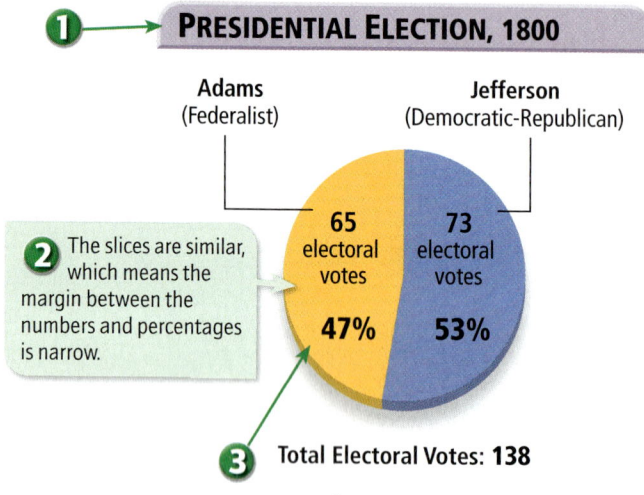

1 **PRESIDENTIAL ELECTION, 1800**

Adams (Federalist)   Jefferson (Democratic-Republican)

2 The slices are similar, which means the margin between the numbers and percentages is narrow.

65 electoral votes — 47%
73 electoral votes — 53%

3 Total Electoral Votes: **138**

Source: *The National Atlas of the United States of America*

1. Which sentence best describes the political atmosphere surrounding the election of 1800?

(1) The election race was calm, as a clear Republican victory was expected.

(2) The election race was vicious, but a clear Federalist victory was expected.

(3) U.S. citizens were almost evenly divided between the two candidates

(4) The Federalist party had an overwhelming lead in the election race

Answer: 1 (3)

PRACTICE

Directions: *Interpret the following circle graph and answer the questions below.*

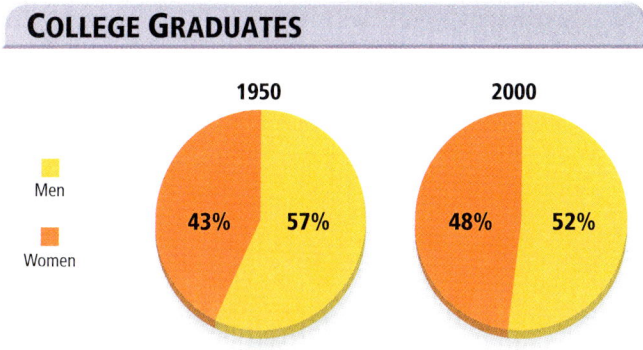

Source: *United States Census Bureau*

1. What do the different colors of the slices represent?

   (1) 1950 and 2000

   (2) men and women

   (3) the percentages of each slice

   (4) women who graduated and women who did not graduate

2. What comparison do these two graphs make?

   (1) the number of male versus female students who graduate from college

   (2) the number of women who graduate from college versus the number of women who vote

   (3) the gender of college graduates in 1950 versus 2000

   (4) the percentage of women who graduate from high school versus the percentage of women who graduate from college

3. From these graphs you can conclude that

   (1) More women than men graduated from college in 2000.

   (2) Fewer men than women graduated from college in 1950.

   (3) Women made up a smaller percentage of all college graduates in 2000 than in 1950.

   (4) Women made up a larger percentage of all college graduates in 2000 than in 1950.

4. What might explain the trend of women to close the gap on men in college graduations?

   (1) More men earned college degrees in 2000 than in 1950.

   (2) More men than women earned college degrees in 1950.

   (3) Women no longer thought they needed college degrees in 2000.

   (4) Women found a college degree more important to earn in 2000 than in 1950.

Strategies for Political and Thematic Maps

You can improve your test-taking skills by practicing these strategies for political and thematic maps. Read the skill-specific tips and samples on the left page. Then practice the skill on the right page. Political maps show countries and the political divisions within them. For example, a political map might show provinces, states, counties, or major cities. They may also highlight physical features, such as mountains or bodies of water.

A thematic map shows patterns of movement, battles, or other special features. Special symbols, such as icons or arrows, are often used on these types of maps.

LEARN

1 **Read the title or heading of the map to find the topic and other information that is shown.**

2 **Find the map legend to find out what different colors or symbols on the map mean.**
Also, read any labels on the map. These can give you details about the purpose of the map.

3 **Look for any special features on the map.**
These may include a locator or an inset map. The arrows on this map show migratory patterns.

4 **Use the compass rose to find directions on the map.**
If there is no compass rose on the map, you must use your prior knowledge of geography to determine direction and location. The map scale can also help in estimating the distance between two places.

5 **Note the lines of longitude and latitude.**
These help determine location on a map.

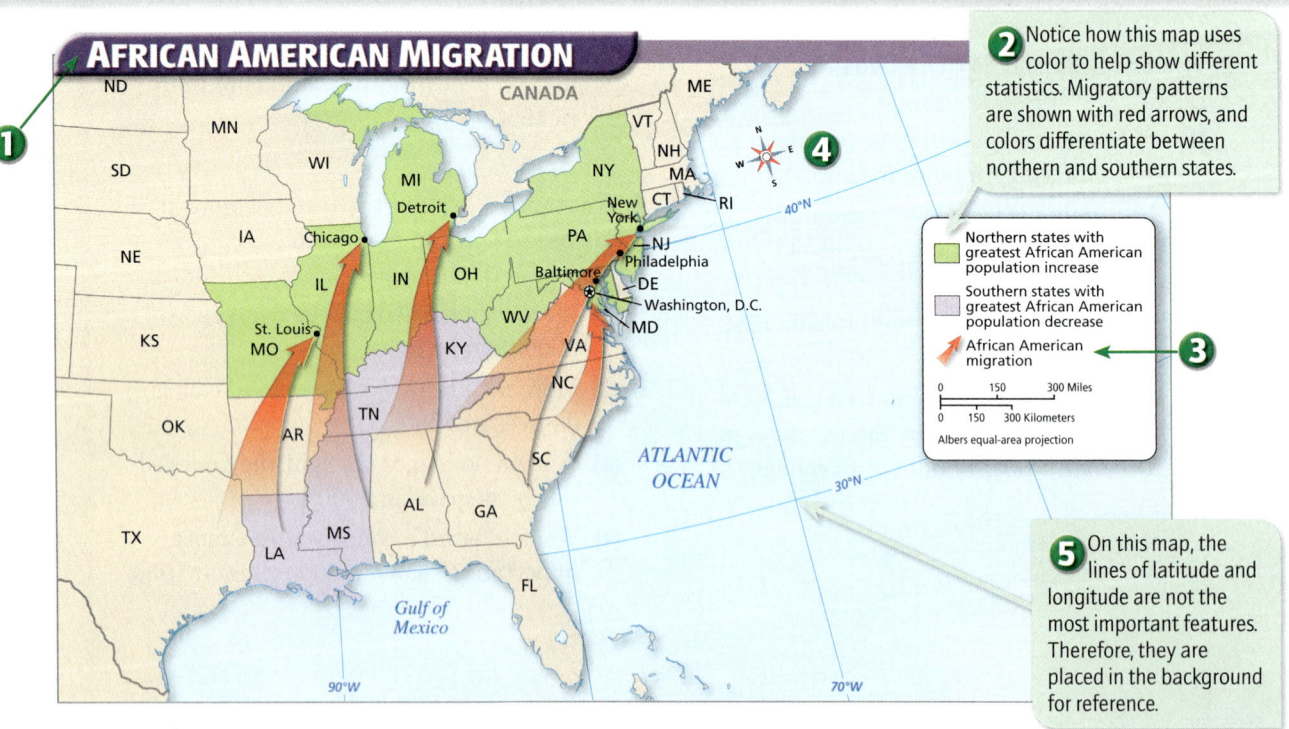

2 Notice how this map uses color to help show different statistics. Migratory patterns are shown with red arrows, and colors differentiate between northern and southern states.

Legend:
- Northern states with greatest African American population increase
- Southern states with greatest African American population decrease
- African American migration

0   150   300 Miles
0   150   300 Kilometers
Albers equal-area projection

3

5 On this map, the lines of latitude and longitude are not the most important features. Therefore, they are placed in the background for reference.

1. Which statement about the information on the map is correct?

(1) Many African Americans left the East in the early 1900s.

(2) Many African Americans left the West in the early 1900s.

(3) Many African Americans left the North in the early 1900s.

(4) Many African Americans left the South in the early 1900s.

Answer: 1 (4)

Directions: *Interpret the following thematic map and answer the questions below.*

1. Which statement about the United Kingdom is correct?

(1) The United Kingdom was neutral.

(2) The United Kingdom was controlled jointly by the Allied and Axis powers.

(3) The United Kingdom was controlled by the Axis powers.

(4) The United Kingdom was controlled by the Allied powers.

2. In what year did Axis troops advance into the Union of Soviet Socialist Republics?

(1) 1938

(2) 1939

(3) 1940

(4) 1941

3. Which of the following accurately shows the order of German occupation?

(1) Yugoslavia, France, Poland

(2) Poland, France, Yugoslavia

(3) France, Poland, Yugoslavia

(4) Yugoslavia, Lithuania, France

4. All of the following statements about the map are true except:

(1) Neither Bulgaria nor Finland were neutral countries.

(2) Both Spain and Turkey were neutral countries.

(3) Axis powers controlled most of Europe.

(4) Allied powers controlled most of Europe.

Strategies for Time Lines

You can improve your test-taking skills by practicing these strategies for time lines. Read the skill-specific tips and samples on the left page. Then practice the skill on the right page. A time line is a type of chart which shows events as they occurred in their chronological order. Time lines are a useful visual tool for learning sequence and cause-and-effect.

LEARN

1 **Read the title to learn the subject and time period of the time line.**

2 **Look for the beginning and end dates on the time line.**
Think about what you already know about this time period before you begin reading.

3 **Read the events on the time line in chronological order.**
Try to understand the connections between the events.

4 **Note the intervals between events.**
Are there long or short breaks between events?

5 **Make inferences about the time period from the information on the time line.**

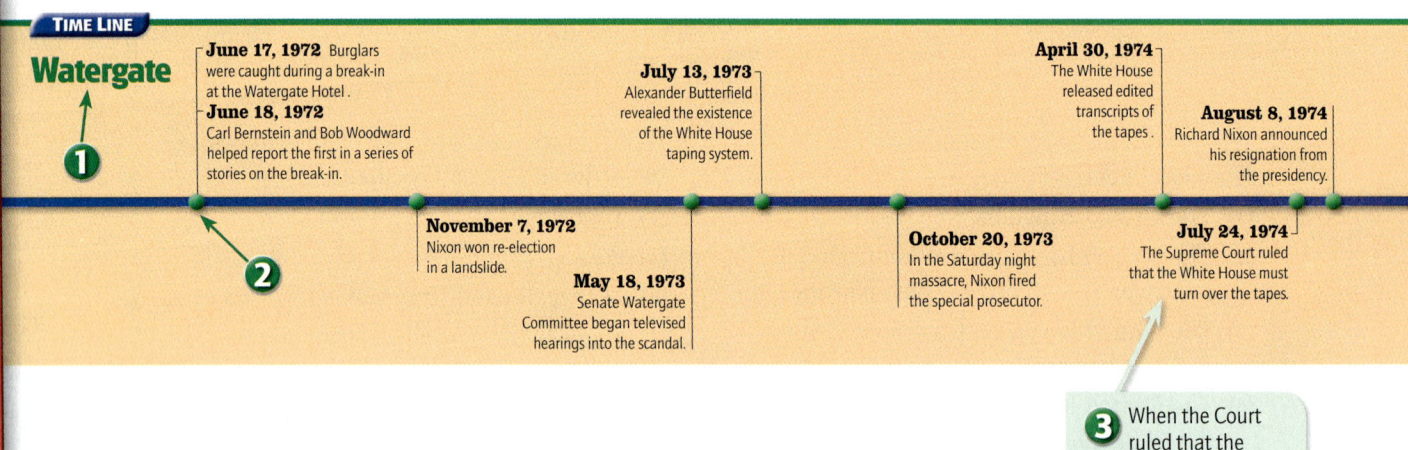

TIME LINE

Watergate

1

2

June 17, 1972 Burglars were caught during a break-in at the Watergate Hotel.
June 18, 1972 Carl Bernstein and Bob Woodward helped report the first in a series of stories on the break-in.

November 7, 1972 Nixon won re-election in a landslide.

May 18, 1973 Senate Watergate Committee began televised hearings into the scandal.

July 13, 1973 Alexander Butterfield revealed the existence of the White House taping system.

October 20, 1973 In the Saturday night massacre, Nixon fired the special prosecutor.

April 30, 1974 The White House released edited transcripts of the tapes.

July 24, 1974 The Supreme Court ruled that the White House must turn over the tapes.

August 8, 1974 Richard Nixon announced his resignation from the presidency.

3 When the Court ruled that the tapes had to be turned over, Nixon realized that he had to resign.

1. What can you infer about the reaction of the American public to Watergate?

(1) The public was not affected by the scandal.

(2) The public supported President Nixon's policies.

(3) The public did not think that the break-in was wrong.

(4) The public was disappointed and probably angered by the scandal.

Answer: 1 (4)

Directions: *Interpret the following time line and answer the questions below.*

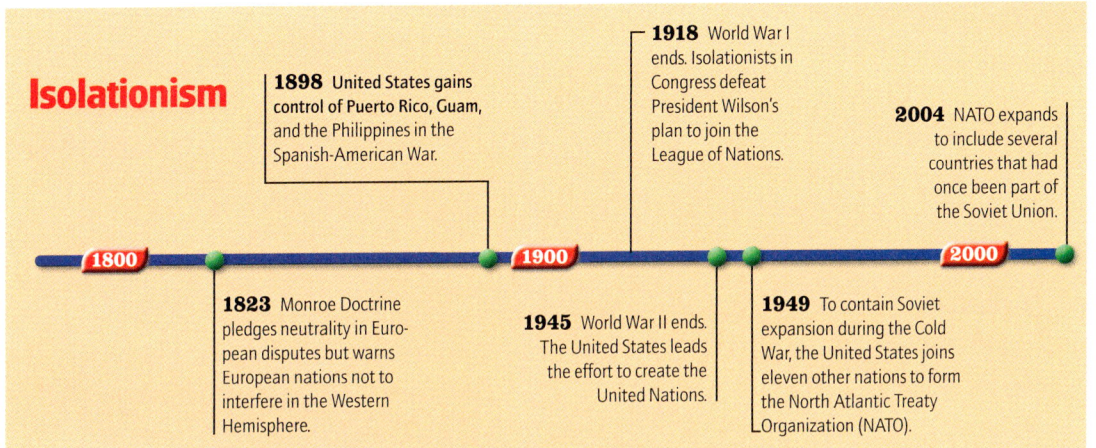

Isolationism

1898 United States gains control of Puerto Rico, Guam, and the Philippines in the Spanish-American War.

1918 World War I ends. Isolationists in Congress defeat President Wilson's plan to join the League of Nations.

2004 NATO expands to include several countries that had once been part of the Soviet Union.

1800   1900   2000

1823 Monroe Doctrine pledges neutrality in European disputes but warns European nations not to interfere in the Western Hemisphere.

1945 World War II ends. The United States leads the effort to create the United Nations.

1949 To contain Soviet expansion during the Cold War, the United States joins eleven other nations to form the North Atlantic Treaty Organization (NATO).

1. What time period does this time line cover?
   (1) the 1800s
   (2) the 1900s
   (3) the 2000s
   (4) all of the above

2. American foreign policy in the 1800s
   (1) did not exist
   (2) was isolationist
   (3) was involved with the politics of other countries
   (4) took on a leadership role to the rest of the world

3. In what way did American foreign policy change as time passed?
   (1) It became more isolationist.
   (2) America opened relations with every country immediately.
   (3) America slowly became more involved with other countries.
   (4) The United States government thought creating a group of "united nations" would not be helpful and wanted to deal with countries on a one-on-one basis.

4. What can you infer is one reason why the United States wanted to create a group of united nations?
   (1) They wanted to return to their isolationist stance.
   (2) They had just finished a second world war and were looking for a way to keep and encourage peace.
   (3) They wanted to foster trade relations.
   (4) They did not want to participate in any international debates.

Strategies for Constructed Response

You can improve your test-taking skills by practicing these strategies for constructed-response questions. Read the skill-specific tips and samples on the left page. Then practice the skill on the right page. Constructed-response questions are based on different types of documents. These can include excerpts, political cartoons, charts, graphs, maps, time lines, posters, and other visuals.

Each document is investigated through one or more open-ended, short-answer questions, which build from simple to complex and evaluate critical-thinking skills. The first question usually requires an answer that can be found in the document. The second question often asks you to connect the information presented in different parts of the document. The third question often requires an answer that is built on information that is not in the document, but is related to the subject of the document.

LEARN

1 **Read the title of the document to identify the subject presented.**

2 **Study the document.**
The callouts give you more information about the subject of the map. Each callout on this map identifies the conflict in the area.

3 **Read the questions and then study the document again to locate the answers.**

4 **Answer the questions carefully.**
Complete sentences are not necessary unless the directions say to use them.

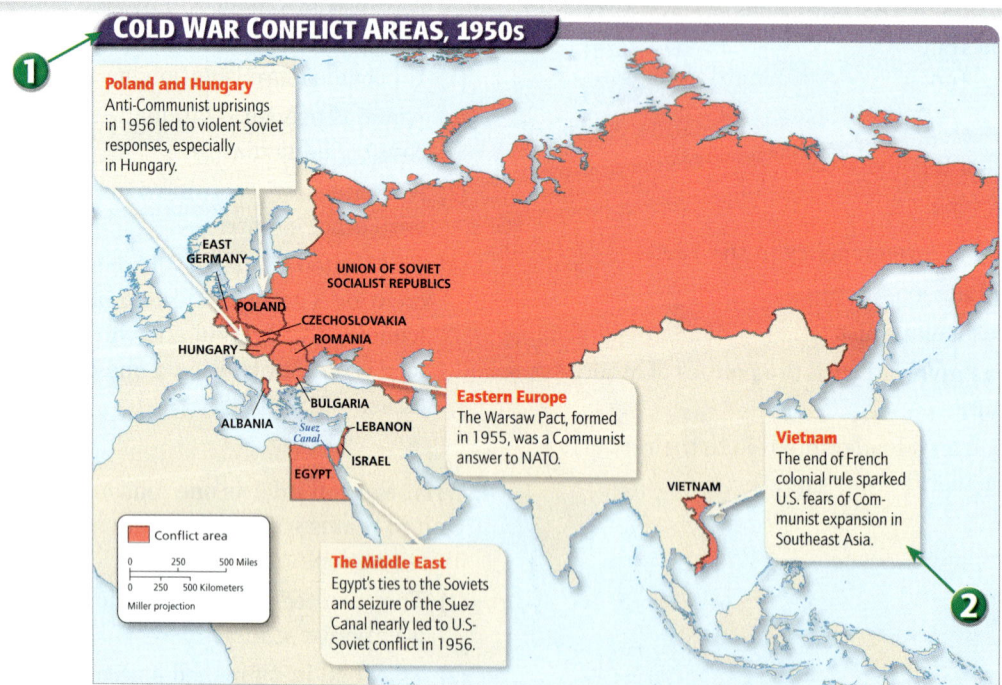

COLD WAR CONFLICT AREAS, 1950s

1

Poland and Hungary
Anti-Communist uprisings in 1956 led to violent Soviet responses, especially in Hungary.

Eastern Europe
The Warsaw Pact, formed in 1955, was a Communist answer to NATO.

Vietnam
The end of French colonial rule sparked U.S. fears of Communist expansion in Southeast Asia.

2

The Middle East
Egypt's ties to the Soviets and seizure of the Suez Canal nearly led to U.S.-Soviet conflict in 1956.

EAST GERMANY, POLAND, CZECHOSLOVAKIA, ROMANIA, HUNGARY, BULGARIA, ALBANIA, Suez Canal, LEBANON, ISRAEL, EGYPT, UNION OF SOVIET SOCIALIST REPUBLICS, VIETNAM

Conflict area
0 250 500 Miles
0 250 500 Kilometers
Miller projection

1. What was considered the Communist answer to NATO? _____ the Warsaw Pact

2. How was the conflict in the Middle East different than the conflicts in Poland and Hungary?
In the Middle East, Egypt was friendly to the Soviet Union.
In Poland and Hungary, there were anti-communist uprisings.

3. Which conflict area will the U.S. military be most involved with in the 1960s? _____ Vietnam

Directions: *Look at the following chart and answer the questions below.*

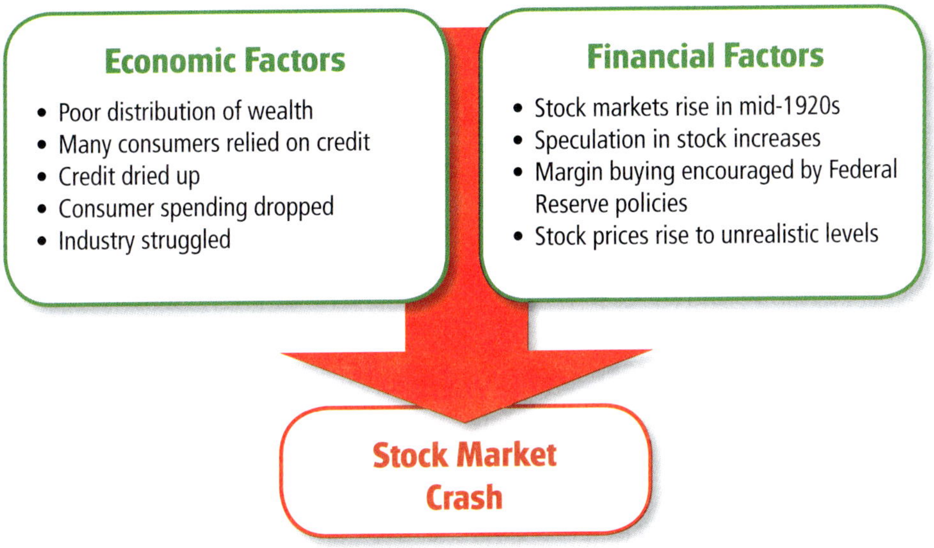

Economic Factors

- Poor distribution of wealth
- Many consumers relied on credit
- Credit dried up
- Consumer spending dropped
- Industry struggled

Financial Factors

- Stock markets rise in mid-1920s
- Speculation in stock increases
- Margin buying encouraged by Federal Reserve policies
- Stock prices rise to unrealistic levels

Stock Market Crash

1. What was one economic factor that led to the crash of the stock market?

_____

_____

2. How was credit spending both an economic and financial factor in the stock market crash?

_____

_____

3. How did the crash of the stock market affect the American economy?

_____

_____

Strategies for Extended Response

You can improve your test-taking skills by practicing these strategies for extended-response questions. Read the skill-specific tips and samples on the left page. Then practice the skill on the right page. Extended-response questions usually focus on a document. Documents can be articles, historical documents, charts, graphs, photographs, political cartoons, and other information sources. Documents can be primary or secondary sources. Some extended-response questions ask you to analyze or summarize the information presented in the document. Others require you to complete a chart, graph, or diagram. In most standardized tests, a document has only one extended-response question.

LEARN

1 **Read the title of the document to learn what the document is about.**

2 **Read the extended-response questions carefully.**

3 **Study and analyze the document.**
This chart lists important New Deal programs undertaken in response to the stock market crash and the Great Depression.

4 **Analyze any partial or a sample answers provided.**
Your answers should take the same form as this sample answer.

5 **Take notes and jot down ideas in outline form.**
Use your notes and outline to prepare for writing an essay or other extended piece of writing.

MAJOR NEW DEAL PROGRAMS

Relief	
Civilian Conservation Corps (CCC), 1933	provided jobs on conservation projects to young men whose families needed relief
Works Progress Administration (WPA), 1935	provided many different types of jobs on public works projects for those needing relief
Social Security Act, 1935	established pensions for retirees, unemployment benefits, and aid for certain groups of low-income or disabled people

Reform	
Securities and Exchange Commission (SEC), 1934	provided increased government regulation of the trading on stock exchanges
National Labor Relations Act, 1935	established the National Labor Relations Board (NLRB) to enforce labor laws

Recovery	
Tennessee Valley Authority (TVA), 1933	promoted development projects in the Tennessee River Valley
Federal Housing Administration (FHA), 1934	provided loans for renovating or building homes

1. In the right-hand column, briefly explain the function of each New Deal program listed in the left-hand column. One entry has been completed for you.

2. This chart explains several important New Deal programs introduced to respond to the stock market crash and the Great Depression. Write a short speech for Franklin D. Roosevelt discussing why these programs are necessary and what he hopes they will accomplish.

Directions: *Use the time line and your knowledge of American history to answer questions 1 and 2.*

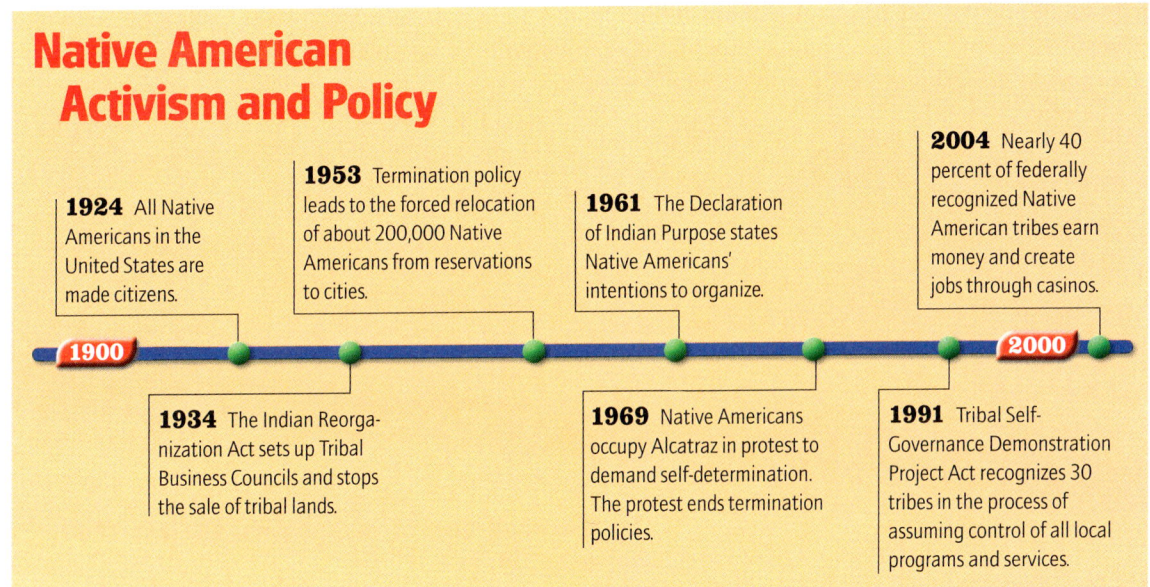

Native American Activism and Policy

1924 All Native Americans in the United States are made citizens.

1953 Termination policy leads to the forced relocation of about 200,000 Native Americans from reservations to cities.

1961 The Declaration of Indian Purpose states Native Americans' intentions to organize.

2004 Nearly 40 percent of federally recognized Native American tribes earn money and create jobs through casinos.

1900

2000

1934 The Indian Reorganization Act sets up Tribal Business Councils and stops the sale of tribal lands.

1969 Native Americans occupy Alcatraz in protest to demand self-determination. The protest ends termination policies.

1991 Tribal Self-Governance Demonstration Project Act recognizes 30 tribes in the process of assuming control of all local programs and services.

1. Make a chart as shown below on a separate sheet of paper. Complete the chart by listing major events in Native American history since 1800 and explaining each event's significance to the relationship between Native Americans and the United States government.

Year	Event	Significance

2. Identify major changes in United States government policy toward Native Americans as shown on the time line. Write a short essay discussing the difference between Americanization and termination policies, analyzing each policy's effects on the formation of Native American social and political movements.

Strategies for Document-Based Questions

You can improve your test-taking skills by practicing these strategies for document-based questions. Read the skill-specific tips and samples on the left page. Then practice the skill on the right page. A document-based question consists of the analysis of several written and visual documents. Such documents may include excerpts, quotations, maps, charts, graphs, time lines, political cartoons, and so on. These documents are followed by short-answer questions. Students use their answers to these questions and information from the documents to produce an essay on a certain topic.

LEARN

1. **Read carefully the "Background" to understand the documents that you will be analyzing.**

2. **Read the "Task" portion, which describes in detail the steps you will follow in answering document-based questions and formulating an essay about a given topic.**

3. **"Part A: Short-Answer Questions" signifies the first part of the document-based question.**

4. **Examine and study each document.**

5. **Read and answer each of the document-specific questions.**

Background   In the late 1800s and early 1900s women in the United States made many important social and political gains.

Task   Using information from the documents and your knowledge of United States history, answer the questions that follow each document in Part A. Your answers to the questions will help you write the Part B essay, in which you will be asked to:

> **Describe challenges facing women in the late 1800s and early 1900s.**

Part A: Short-Answer Questions

Study each document carefully. Then answer the question or questions that follow each document in the space provided.

DOCUMENT 1

> *"... The women, dissatisfied as they are with this form of government, that enforces taxation without representation—that compels them to obey laws to which they have never given their consent—that imprisons and hangs them without a trial by a jury of their peers, that robs them, in marriage, of the custody of their own persons, wages and children—are this half of the people left wholly at the mercy of the other half, in direct violation of the spirit and letter of the declarations of the framers of this government, every one of which was based on the immutable [undeniable] principle of equal rights to all."*

1. What were Susan B. Anthony's beliefs about women's voting rights?

   She believed that women should have

   the same voting rights as men.

DOCUMENT 2

5

2. What does this political cartoon represent?

It represents tough choices facing women

in their home and work lives.

Part B: Essay **6**

Using the documents, your answers to the questions in Part A, and your knowledge of U.S. history, write a well-organized essay about challenges facing women in the late 1800s and early 1900s.

6 Write your essay.
Include an introductory paragraph that frames your argument, a main body with details that explain it, and a closing paragraph that summarizes your position. Include specific details or documents to support your ideas.

Rubric
The best essays will note challenges such as voting rights (Document 1), and the tough choices relating to women's careers and home life. (Document 2).

Background In the 1920s, new forms of media emerged that enabled people to share the same information and enjoy the same pastimes.

Task Using information from the documents and your knowledge of U.S. history, answer the questions that follow each document in Part A. Your answers to the questions will help you write the Part B essay, in which you will be asked to:

> **Describe the growth of popular American culture in the 1920s.**

DOCUMENT 1

1. What does this magazine cover convey about American culture during the 1920s?

DOCUMENT 2

2. What can you tell about the popularity of films from this picture?

Part B: Essay

Using the documents, your answers to the questions in Part A, and your knowledge of U.S. history, write a well-organized essay about the growth of popular American culture in the 1920s.

Beginnings of AMERICA

Beginnings–1763

Themes

Cultural Expressions
The Native Americans' ancient ways of life changed with the arrival of European settlers. As settlements developed into colonies, colonists began to form a distinct, American culture.

Immigration and Migration
People first migrated to America many thousands of years ago and lived throughout the continent before Europeans arrived and began to form colonies.

The voyage of the Mayflower marked a new beginning for not just the settlers on board but for America as well.

THE GRANGER COLLECTION, NEW YORK

Identifying Main Idea and Details

Find practice for **Identifying Main Idea and Details** in the **Skills Handbook,** p. H5

The main idea is the most important idea of a passage. Details support, illustrate, or develop the main idea.

Before You Read
Look at headings and the Reading Check questions.

While You Read
Look for topic sentences in each paragraph. These are often the main ideas.

After You Read
Ask yourself questions. What was the main idea? What was the author trying to get across?

Quakers Settle Pennsylvania

This section head tells you the topic—how the Quakers came to settle Pennsylvania.

Another one of Charles II's land grants became William Penn's colony, Pennsylvania. Penn planned to build a colony that would give him and other Quakers a haven. From the king's perspective, it was an opportunity to get rid of an unpopular group.

The Quakers Of all the various groups of Nonconformists—Protestants who did not follow the Church of England—the Quakers upset people the most. Officially called the Society of Friends, their name came from their founder, George Fox. He urged them to "tremble [quake] at the name of the Lord."

Main idea The Quakers' religious beliefs upset the members of other groups.

Quakers believed in direct, personal communication with God. That meant no ministers and no hierarchy of priests and bishops, as in the Anglican and Roman Catholic Churches. They had no set worship service. Instead, members of the congregation spoke up in Quaker meetings. They preached their beliefs in the streets and sometimes interrupted other groups' church services

Detail The Quakers believed in direct communication with God, without a hierarchy priests and bishops.

READING CHECK **Identifying Main Ideas and Details** Why did the Quakers upset members of other religious groups?

Test Prep Tip

Short answer questions on tests often ask you to find details that support a passage's main idea. To find supporting details, use clue words such as *who, what, when, where, why,* and *how.* Turn section headings into questions. An example for this passage might be "Why did the Quakers settle Pennsylvania?

Reading like a Historian

Analyzing Primary Sources

Find practice for **Analyzing Primary Sources** in the **Skills Handbook,** p. H28

Primary sources are documents created by people who were present at historical events either as witnesses or as participants. These sources can range from letters and diary entries to newspaper stories and photographs.

Strategies historians use:

- Find clues in the text. Look for words that identify a primary source, such as *I*, or note quotation marks that indicate a passage is someone's speech or writing.
- What does the source say about the event or time period described?
- Identify the author and analyze the type of source. Is this the kind of document in which primary sources are often found?

Quotation marks, as well as the word *I*, help you determine that what you are reading is a primary source.

"From a child I was fond of reading, and all the little money that came into my hands was ever laid out in books…This bookish inclination at length determined my father to make me a printer, though he had already one son (James) of that profession. In 1717 my brother James returned from England with a press and letters to set up his business in Boston…[My] father was impatient to have me bound to my brother. I stood out [tried to avoid being bound] some time, but at last was persuaded, and signed the indentures when I was but twelve years old. I was to serve as an apprentice until I was twenty-one years of age…**"**

— *Autobiography of Benjamin Franklin*, 1771-1790

Benjamin Franklin is the writer. The passage describes his early life. It also tells us that people in Franklin's time learned a trade such as printing by being indentured, or legally contracted to work for someone.

The word *Autobiography* means "to write the story of one's own life." An autobiography is always considered a primary source.

Skills FOCUS   READING LIKE A HISTORIAN

As You Read Paraphrase the primary source in your own words to make sure you understand any difficult language.

As You Study Use your prior knowledge and information in the chapter to assess the source.

The WORLD Before 1600

THE BIG PICTURE During the Ice Age, nomads crossed a land bridge connecting Asia and North America. Since then, people of various cultures have made the Americas their home. Meanwhile in Europe and Africa, cultures that would one day explore the world and build colonies in the Americas were coming into contact.

New York Standards

Key Idea 3 Study about the major social, political, economic, cultural, and religious developments in New York State and United States history involves learning about the important roles and contributions of individuals and groups.

Skills FOCUS READING LIKE A HISTORIAN

This detail from Portugal's Monument of Discovery shows Prince Henry the Navigator at the forefront of many famous Portuguese explorers. The monument is shaped like the prow of a ship and was built for the 500th anniversary of Henry's death.
Drawing Conclusions Why do you think Portugal built this monument?

See **Skills Handbook**, p. H12

U.S.

38,000– 10,000 BC
The first people migrate to North America.

500 BC
Adena culture begins in the Ohio River Valley.

800 BC

World

History's Impact video program
Watch the video to understand the impact of different cultures.

100 BC
Hopewell
Mound Builders
inherit Adena
traditions.

1000
Mississippian
society spreads
across the
southeast
and southern
Midwest.

200 BC   AD 400   1000   1600

400 BC
The Maya build
great stone
cities in Central
America.

500
Roman
Empire
collapses.

1440
Atlantic slave
trade begins.

1492
Columbus lands
on an island in the
Caribbean.

The Early Americas

BEFORE YOU READ

MAIN IDEA

People arrived on the American continents thousands of years ago and developed flourishing societies.

READING FOCUS

1. According to scientists and historians, how and when did the first migration to the Americas occur?
2. What kind of cultures developed in Central and South America?
3. What characterized the earliest cultures of North America?

KEY TERMS AND PEOPLE

nomad
hunter-gatherer
agricultural revolution
Olmec
Maya
Toltec
Aztec
Inca
pueblo
clan

1.1 Compare and contrast the experiences of different ethnic, national, and religious groups, including Native American Indians, in the United States, explaining their contributions to American society and culture.

The First AMERICANS

THE INSIDE STORY *How do we learn about prehistoric people in the Americas?*

Prehistory means the time before written records were kept. So with no ancient scrolls or stone tablets to refer to and certainly no books or newspapers or Web sites, how do we know about the first people in our part of the world?

Information about early American cultures comes mainly from archaeology. Archaeology is the scientific study of the remains of past human life. Archaeologists carry out digs to unearth ancient towns and campsites. They examine pottery, tools, bones, and other physical evidence.

One important piece of archaeological evidence is a distinctive stone spear point called the Clovis point. Because these spear points have been found throughout the Americas, scientists have developed theories of early human migration based upon them.

Some archaeological evidence is controversial. For example, ancient burial grounds might hold valuable clues about the peoples who settled the Americas. Yet some groups do not want scientists disturbing these sites. Many Native Americans consider them sacred places and believe the bones of their ancestors should remain untouched.

▲ **The discovery of artifacts like this spear straightener help researchers reconstruct the past.**

Evidence may also be interpreted in different ways. As you will read, most scholars agree that the first people in North America crossed a land bridge from Siberia to Alaska. But other scholars argue that ancient humans arrived in South America by boat. A 9,000-year-old skeleton known as Kennewick Man aroused even more controversy. The skeleton did not appear to be Asian, and so certain scholars suggested that some early Americans may actually have come from Europe. Some Native American groups, however, claimed Kennewick Man as an ancestor.

All these ideas and interpretations suggest that future archaeologists will have plenty to study! ◢

Migration to the Americas

As recently as 10,000 years ago, during the last Ice Age, thick sheets of ice covered many parts of the world. So much of the earth's water was frozen that sea levels dropped, exposing land along the coasts.

Today the waters of the Bering Strait divide modern Alaska from Siberia in northeast Asia. During the Ice Age, though, a land bridge connected Asia and North America. Historians call this ancient land area Beringia.

Scholars agree that hunters from Siberia crossed the land bridge and arrived in North America. This probably took place between 12,000 and 40,000 years ago, and small groups of people crossed at different times.

Hunters and gatherers These first Americans were **nomads,** people who move from place to place. They followed a **hunter-gatherer** way of life. This meant that women and girls collected nuts, berries, wild plants, and birds' eggs. Men and boys went on extended hunts, following herds of animals. When the animals moved, the hunter-gatherers did too, never staying in one place for long.

The newcomers found good hunting in the cool grasslands along the edges of the ice sheets. North America was home to many huge animals, including giant sloths, fierce saber-toothed cats, and elephantlike woolly mammoths. Wolves and camels roamed the land, too. None of these animals were accustomed to human hunters. That made them easy prey for the hunters, who drove them off cliffs or killed them with sharp, stone-tipped spears.

The Ice Age ended as the climate grew warmer. The glaciers gradually melted away, leaving large lakes and layers of rich soil. Thick forests grew up in eastern North America.

The combination of climate change and skillful hunters wiped out most of the huge Ice Age animals. Humans had to find new food supplies, so bands of hunter-gatherers moved southward. By at least 11,000 years ago, archaeologists say, people were living in both North and South America.

The agricultural revolution Over time, Native Americans began to plant and harvest crops. Farming led them to settle into villages rather than move from place to place. This

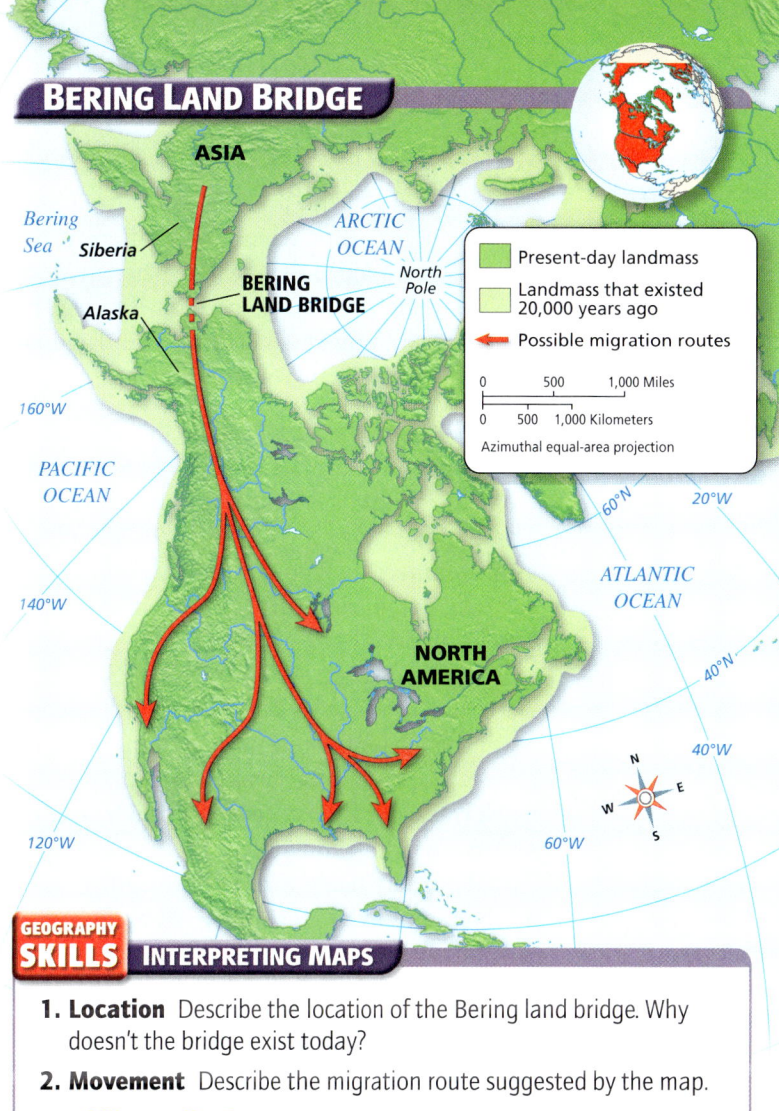

BERING LAND BRIDGE

ASIA

Bering Sea · Siberia

ARCTIC OCEAN

North Pole

Alaska

BERING LAND BRIDGE

160°W

PACIFIC OCEAN

140°W

NORTH AMERICA

120°W

ATLANTIC OCEAN

60°N   20°W

40°N

40°W

60°W

- ▢ Present-day landmass
- ▢ Landmass that existed 20,000 years ago
- → Possible migration routes

0   500   1,000 Miles
0   500   1,000 Kilometers
Azimuthal equal-area projection

GEOGRAPHY SKILLS   INTERPRETING MAPS

1. **Location** Describe the location of the Bering land bridge. Why doesn't the bridge exist today?
2. **Movement** Describe the migration route suggested by the map.

See **Skills Handbook**, p. H19

dramatic change in the way people lived is called the **agricultural revolution**. Scientists believe it began in parts of the Americas at least 7,000 years ago.

By about 2,000 years ago, ancient American farming was based on three basic crops: corn (maize), beans, and squashes such as pumpkins. To supply meat, men still hunted seasonally, but they also began raising animals.

A settled way of life led to other changes in culture. With a more dependable food supply, populations grew. People developed crafts such as pottery making and weaving. Native Americans also developed ways to govern their villages and distribute wealth.

READING CHECK   **Identifying Cause and Effect** How were Siberian hunters able to reach North America thousands of years ago?

ACADEMIC VOCABULARY
distribute divide among several

Cultures of Central America and South America

Central and South America are dotted with archaeological sites from many different cultures. Three major cultures flourished in Mesoamerica, the area from present-day central Mexico into Central America. A fourth important culture arose in South America.

The Olmec The first major Mesoamerican society grew up around 1200 BC in the steamy tropical lowlands along the Gulf of Mexico. The **Olmec** culture is called the mother culture of Mesoamerica. This is because the Olmec's religion, art, agriculture, and social organization influenced later peoples.

The Olmec were engineers and artists. They were also the first in Mesoamerica to develop a writing system. Their most striking works of art are huge sculpted heads made of basalt, a black volcanic rock. Some heads weigh as much as 40 tons and stand 10 feet high.

ACADEMIC VOCABULARY

technique
method

Like many early farmers, the Olmec used a "slash-and-burn" technique. They cut down and burned the trees on a plot of land. The ashes made the soil fertile for a few years. Then the farmer moved on to a new patch of land, allowing the old plot to regain its fertility. Over time, villagers cleared large areas of land.

The Maya and the Toltec Olmec culture gradually declined for reasons that remain unclear. Among the societies that succeeded it were the **Maya**, who began their rise around 400 BC. Their cities were religious centers with stone pyramids, palaces, temples, and sacred ball courts. Painted carvings of warriors, gods, and jaguars decorated the buildings.

Mayan civilization reached its height between about AD 250 and 900. Religious centers grew into city-states with thousands of people. Priests studied the stars and devised several calendars. The Maya also developed a writing system and a number system that used the concept of zero.

By about 1500, Mayan civilization had declined, but the culture never disappeared. Some 4 million Mayan-speaking people still live in southern Mexico and Guatemala today.

About AD 900, while the Maya were beginning to decline, the **Toltec** came to dominate central Mexico. These people were known for their skills as warriors, artisans, and builders. Toltec influence can be seen in the architecture of late Mayan cities such as Chichén Itzá, whose ruins still stand in southern Mexico.

The Aztec In the 1400s power in the central valley of Mexico shifted to a group of invaders from the north. These were the warlike Mexica,

---

TIME LINE

Early Cultures of the Americas

Long before Europeans arrived in the Americas, a wide variety of cultures existed in Mesoamerica and South America.

c. 500 BC–AD 500
The Adena and Hopewell built huge earth mounds, such as this serpent mound (right) in present-day Ohio.

Olmec

Adena and Hopewell

Anasazi and Hohokam

c.1200 BC–400 BC
The Olmec were the first major Mesoamerican society, influencing later cultures.

c. 200 BC–AD 1300
The Anasazi and Hohokam people lived in the Southwest. The Anasazi built multi-story adobe buildings called pueblos. This pueblo (left) built into a cliff is a distinctive example.

better known as the **Aztec.** The Aztec built their capital, Tenochtitlán (tay-nawch-teet-LAHN), on an island in a shallow lake. With canals, broad central plazas, and busy marketplaces, it was a dazzling sight. To supply food to the growing city, farmers tended floating gardens, called *chinampas,* in the lake.

The Aztec conquered many neighboring peoples. They demanded regular payments of tribute such as food, fine woods, furs, feathers, and slaves. Slaves and captives taken in war usually became victims in religious sacrifices. The Aztec, like other early peoples, believed in many gods. To honor these deities, Aztec priests ritually left offerings of food, flowers, and even human hearts. The scale of human sacrifice made many people in the empire hate their Aztec rulers.

The Inca While the Aztec were conquering Mesoamerica, a group called the **Inca** rose to power in the Andes Mountains of South America. The Inca conquered their neighbors along the coast and built a vast empire connected by roads and bridges. At its height, the Inca empire was the largest in the Americas, including perhaps 12 million people.

READING CHECK **Sequencing** In what ways did Olmec culture influence later cultures in Mesoamerica?

The Earliest Cultures of North America

Early Native Americans encountered many different environments in North America—forests, deserts, and fertile land. In each region, different kinds of societies developed. Some Native Americans remained hunter-gatherers. Others settled in farming villages.

Peoples of the Southwest The early cultures of the dry Southwest probably developed more than 2,000 years ago. Trade and common ways of living linked these cultures with nearby Mexico. Groups in this region all grew corn, beans, and squash, and women typically made pottery.

The Hohokam people in south-central Arizona were one such group. To farm in the desert, they dug irrigation ditches that brought water from rivers to the fields. Some Hohokam sites had temple mounds and ball courts, like those in Mexico but simpler.

Another group, the Anasazi, settled in the area where present-day Arizona, New Mexico, Colorado, and Utah meet. Anasazi culture soon spread eastward. One of its distinctive features was multistory adobe buildings. When Spaniards arrived in the 1500s, they called the buildings **pueblos,** meaning "towns."

THE IMPACT TODAY

Government
Present-day Mexico City stands on the original site of Tenochtitlán.

c. 600–1500
The Mississippian people were an advanced farming society in the Southeast and southern Midwest.

c. 900–1500
The Toltec came to dominate what is now central Mexico as the Maya began to decline.

c.1400–1521
The Aztec empire dominated the central valley of present-day Mexico.

Aztec

Toltec

Mississippian

Maya

Inca

c. 400 BC–AD 1500
The Maya made many advances such as a writing system and a number system that used the concept of zero. This pyramid (below) was part of the Mayan city of Chichén Itzá.

c. 1100–1532
The Inca empire stretched across South America. At its height the empire included perhaps 12 million people.

Skills FOCUS **INTERPRETING TIME LINES**

Sequencing Which culture existed for the longest period of time?

See **Skills Handbook,** p. H14

The Anasazi built some of their pueblos on flat mesas and on steep cliffs. Major pueblos, some with hundreds of rooms, were located in Chaco Canyon. Miles of roads linked them with distant Anasazi settlements. Traders carried food and luxuries such as turquoise.

By about 1300, the Anasazi culture was beginning to decline. So were other ancient societies of the Southwest. One reason may have been a great drought in the late 1200s. Wars or invasions may also have contributed. Dispersing eastward, some Anasazi groups settled in present-day New Mexico, becoming the ancestors of today's Pueblo Indians.

The Mound Builders Complex early societies also developed in eastern North America, from the Atlantic Ocean to the Mississippi. River. These people lived in small farming villages, probably run by the leaders of clans, or groups of people related by blood. As these groups grew and flourished, their villages became more complex.

The Ohio River valley was the center of two highly organized farming societies, Adena and Hopewell. Both groups are known as Mound Builders because they buried clan members in large earth mounds.

Adena culture got its start sometime before 500 BC. The Adena people had a wide-ranging trade network that brought them goods from distant places. They obtained copper and pearls, for example, to adorn the rings and ornaments that were buried with important people.

By about 100 BC, Adena culture had been absorbed by the Hopewell culture. Hopewell people were skillful artists who carved realistic human statues and ceremonial pipes depicting animals. They also worked with copper, shells, mica, and other materials from as far away as the Great Lakes and the Gulf of Mexico.

By about AD 400 or 500, the trade network that linked Hopewell settlements was falling apart. Mound-building traditions, however, continued for hundreds of years.

Mississippian culture The last major mound-building culture in North America was the Mississippian. Theirs was the most advanced farming society north of Mexico. The Mississippians grew maize and beans, and they introduced a new farming tool—the hoe.

All across the Southeast and southern Midwest, the Mississippians built towns. These had impressive ceremonial temple-mounds and broad central plazas. The homes of rulers and nobles stood on pyramids around the central square. The greatest Mississippian cities were Cahokia, near present-day St. Louis, and Moundville, in Alabama.

By about 1100, Cahokia was a great population center, perhaps as large as London. Until the late 1800s, its central pyramid was the largest structure in the United States.

READING CHECK **Drawing Conclusions** How did the landscape and climate of the Southwest affect early peoples there?

SECTION 1 ASSESSMENT

go.hrw.com
Online Quiz
Keyword: SD7 HP1

Reviewing Ideas, Terms, and People

1. **a. Recall** Where did the original settlers in the Americas come from?
   b. Analyze What changes in the environment led to the **agricultural revolution**?

2. **a. Identify** What is Mesoamerica?
   b. Sequence Trace, in order, the development of different cultures in Central and South America.

3. **a. Recall** What two cultures are known as Mound Builders, and why?
   b. Make Generalizations What were the typical characteristics of the early cultures of the Southwest?
   c. Evaluate What achievements marked the Mississippians as having an advanced culture?

Critical Thinking

4. **Sequencing** Copy the chart below and fill it in to show the differences before and after the agricultural revolution.

Before	After

FOCUS ON SPEAKING

5. **Persuasive** As a member of a hunter-gatherer band long ago, write a speech explaining why a particular location will be a good place for your group to settle.

North American Cultures in the 1400s

BEFORE YOU READ

MAIN IDEA

A variety of complex societies existed in different regions of North America before European explorers arrived in the early 1500s.

READING FOCUS

1. How did regional differences among Native Americans shape their diverse cultures?
2. What Native American customs were shared among several groups?
3. How did trading networks link Native American societies?

KEY TERMS AND PEOPLE

Pueblo
Kwakiutl
Iroquois
longhouse
kinship
matrilineal
division of labor
shaman
barter

PI 1.1 Compare and contrast the experiences of different ethnic, national, and religious groups, including Native American Indians, in the United States, explaining their contributions to American society and culture.

Taking Out History's TRASH

THE INSIDE STORY

How do ancient trash heaps help us learn about early North Americans?
Archaeologists study ancient towns, campsites, and burial sites. They examine pottery, weapons, tools, bones, and other physical evidence. One of the best places to find useful information is an ancient trash heap, called a midden.

For years, archaeologists have studied the shell middens of the Calusa Indians at a site in Pineland, Florida. The Pineland site was a Calusa village for more than 1,500 years. Calusa Indian influence stretched across most of Florida during the sixteenth century, when Europeans arrived in North America. The Pineland site is particularly significant because it offers a distinct look at Indian life in North America before Europeans arrived.

At the Pineland site, huge shell mounds still overlook the ocean. From these mounds, archaeologists have learned many things about the Calusa. For example, they know from the large quantities of discarded shells that the Calusa people were hunter-gatherers who looked to local streams and bays for their food, rather than farming. ◢

◀ **Archaeologists unearth the secrets of the Calusa Mound Builders at Florida's Pineland site.**

Regional Differences Among Native Americans

ACADEMIC VOCABULARY

influence to have an effect on

The Calusa people in Florida were just one of many Native American groups scattered across the continent. North America has great differences in climate, geography, and resources. These diverse environments influenced the Native American cultures that formed across the continent.

When Europeans reached North America in the 1500s, fewer people lived there than in either Mesoamerica or South America. Historians' estimates of the population north of Mexico range from fewer than 1 million to as many as 10 million.

The Southwest The Pueblo peoples of the Southwest inherited many Anasazi traditions. Groups like the Zuni, Hopi, and Acoma lived in many-roomed pueblos. Each pueblo was governed by a council of religious elders. Pueblo groups grew corn, beans, squash, and cotton in the river and creek bottoms in the desert. They also made distinctive pottery and baskets.

Two groups of newcomers later arrived in the Southwest. The Apache and the Navajo were nomadic hunters from the plains farther north. Learning from their Pueblo neighbors, the Navajo gradually took up farming. They also became skillful weavers.

The Northwest Coast and California In contrast to the dry Southwest, the Northwest Coast was cool and rainy. Tall trees and wild plants grew in the moist climate. The forests supplied wild game, such as moose, deer, and bear. Abundant salmon swam in the swift rivers. Hunters went to sea in dugout canoes, using harpoons to hunt whales.

Native Americans in the Northwest Coast, including the Kwakiutl (kwah-kee-YOO-tuhl) and Haida (HY-duh), became skilled woodworkers. They built large, sturdy houses from cedar planks. Later, after acquiring iron tools, they began to carve totem poles, masks, and other wooden crafts.

Their rich resources made these peoples aware of wealth and luxuries. They owned luxury goods, such as fine blankets. Families also held feasts called potlatches, where they showed off their wealth by giving valuable gifts to their guests.

South of the Northwest Coast lay the California region. California was home to the Pomo, Hupa, and Yurok, among others. These people lived in small communities of 50 to 300, speaking more than 100 languages.

California had many food sources available year-round, so farming was not necessary. Instead, the people fished and hunted.

The Far North The Native Americans of the far North—also known as the Arctic and Subarctic—were probably the most recent migrants from Asia. The ancestors of modern Inuit (I-NOO-wuht) probably came by boat about 1,500 years ago. The Aleuts (a-lee-OOTs) settled much earlier on what are now the Aleutian Islands.

Much of the land in the Far North is tundra, treeless plains that are partially frozen for much of the year. Despite the lack of vegetation, animals were plentiful, so the Inuit and Aleuts lived mainly by hunting. On the coast, people hunted seals, seabirds, and whales. Inland, they hunted caribou, beaver, and bear.

Archaeological evidence from early sites in the Far North is rare. Perhaps this is because rising sea levels after the end of the Ice Age covered settlements on the coast.

The Great Basin and the Plateau Two dryland regions lay to the east of the mountain ranges of the Pacific coast. In the Great Basin, Native Americans such as the Ute (YOOT) and the Shoshones (shuh-SHOHNS) faced severe challenges—little rain, few trees, no large rivers, and little wild game.

Native Americans in the Great Basin remained hunter-gatherers. Some lived in caves. They found food by digging roots and gathering acorns, piñon nuts, and other seeds. They also hunted small animals such as rabbits. Not surprisingly, populations were small.

Although the Plateau, the high plains region to the north, is fairly arid, it gets more rain and has more forests than the Great Basin. The Plateau is crossed by rivers brimming with Pacific salmon and other fish. Groups such as the Nez Percé (NEZ PUHRS) lived in villages along these abundant rivers.

The Great Plains Some of the best-known Native American groups—the Sioux (SOO), Pawnee, and Cheyenne (shy-AN)—lived on

NATIVE AMERICAN CULTURE AREAS

Legend:
- Far North
- Northwest Coast
- Plateau
- Great Plains
- Eastern Woodlands
- Great Basin
- California
- Southwest
- Southeast

0   300   600 Miles
0   300   600 Kilometers
Albers equal-area projection

INUIT
INGALIK
INUIT
EYAK
TAGISH
TLINGIT
140°W
HAIDA   TONGASS
HAISLA   CARRIER
50°N
HEILTSUK
KWAKIUTL
NOOTKA   SHUSWAP
SQUAMISH   NOOKSACK
MAKAH   CHIMAKUM
130°W   COAST   COLUMBIA
SALISH   SPOKANE
CHINOOK   YAKIMA
KLICKITAT
WALLA WALLA
YAQUINA   NEZ
MOLALA   PERCÉ
UMPQUA
TOLOWA   MODOC   NORTHERN
40°N   HUPA   PAIUTE
ACHOMAWI
YUKI   NORTHERN
WAPPO   MAIDU   SHOSHONE
MIWOK   WASHO   WESTERN
COSTANOAN   SHOSHONE
ESSELEN   MONO
YOKUTS   KAWAIISU   UTE
CHUMASH
MOHAVE   HOPI (PUEBLO)
NAVAJO   APACHE
ZUNI (PUEBLO)
NAKIPA   YUMA   APACHE
30°N   PIMA   SUMA
COCHIMI   JUMANO
SERI
IGNACIENO   YAQUI
120°W
TARAHUMARA
WAICURA
LAGUNERO
GUACHICHIL
MESOAMERICA

ROCKY MOUNTAINS

HAN
DOGRIB
SASCHUTKENNE

INUIT

CHIPEWYAN

SWAMPY
CREE

**NORTH
AMERICA**

BLACKFOOT   PLAINS
CREE   PLAINS
OJIBWAY
CROW   MANDAN
TETON SIOUX
CHEYENNE   SANTEE
SIOUX   SAUK
OMAHA   FOX
PAWNEE
ARAPAHO   IOWA
MISSOURI   ILLINOIS
KANSA
Cahokia
OSAGE
KIOWA
COMANCHE
WICHITA
CADDO
TONKAWA
KARANKAWA

*Hudson
Bay*
Arctic Circle
50°W

MONTAGNAIS

MICMAC

ALGONQUIAN
OTTAWA
HURON
IROQUOIS
POTAWATOMI
KICKAPOO   MIAMI
SUSQUEHANNA
SHAWNEE   POWHATAN
CHEROKEE
CHICKASAW
TUSKEGEE   CHERAW
CREEK   CUSABO
ALABAMA
CHOCTAW   APALACHEE
MOBILE

PEQUOT
MOHEGAN
MASSACHUSET
WAMPANOAG
60°W
NARRAGANSET
MOHAWK
ONEIDA
ONONDAGA
CAYUGA
SENECA
DELAWARE

BEOTHUK

*ATLANTIC
OCEAN*

N
W   E
S

SEMINOLE
CALUSA

Tropic of Cancer   TAINO
90°W   80°W

Gulf of Mexico

70°W

110°W   100°W

*PACIFIC
OCEAN*

**GEOGRAPHY
SKILLS** INTERPRETING MAPS

Although we refer to them collectively as Native Americans, the
people who lived in North America in the 1500s were not a single
people, but many different groups with different ways of life.
Region Name each culture area and identify one group that is a part
of that area.

See **Skills Handbook**, p. H20

the Great Plains west of the Mississippi River. Prairie grasses and wildflowers grew on this flat terrain, and trees lined the wide rivers. The Plains were also home to the last of the great herds of North American animals—deer, antelope, elk, and most importantly, bison, also known as buffalo.

Because the tough roots of prairie grasses made farming difficult, the culture of early Plains Indians depended on hunting buffalo. Hunting improved after the introduction of the bow and arrow by about AD 950.

Descendants of the Mississippian culture, such as the Caddo and the Wichitas, moved into the southern Plains region. These groups brought new crops and built new villages, especially in the fertile valleys of the Mississippi River and its tributaries.

The Eastern Woodlands

In the 1400s, thick forests covered what is now the eastern United States, from the Atlantic Ocean west to the Mississippi. Because of these forests this region is known as the Eastern Woodlands. The Native Americans in this huge area lived in distinct cultural groups, and their homelands often centered in river basins. Hills and mountain ranges made travel hard. Thus, each group developed its own traditions and tools and often a separate language.

In the Northeast, the **Iroquois** (EER-uh-kwoy) included several Native American nations, including the Mohawks and Oneidas. All these people spoke Iroquois languages, and they shared a common culture. They were often at war, however, mainly over territory.

The Iroquois lived in large villages, which were sometimes surrounded by palisades—walls of upright wood poles. **Longhouses** provided shelter. These were large wooden buildings with a central aisle and living spaces on either side. The longhouse was so key to their culture that the Iroquois called themselves "people of the longhouse."

Other groups in the Eastern Woodlands spoke Algonquian languages. These groups included the Chippewa (or Ojibwa), Fox, and Sauk (SAWK).

All woodland groups learned to make the best use of local resources. In the oak forests, for example, they made flour from bitter acorns. They hunted forest animals for meat and furs and built traps to catch fish in the rivers.

The Southeast

In the Southeast, most Native Americans had lived in settled farming villages for hundreds of years. A warm climate, fertile land, and plenty of rain allowed them to grow several crops a year. The Choctaw were one of many groups in this region. They lived in thatched-roof log cabins plastered with mud.

Some peoples carried on the Mississippian culture into the 1500s and even later. One group carved shells with mysterious designs that may have had religious meaning, which archaeologists have found near temple mounds.

Differences in Geography, Differences in Dwellings

People used the materials at hand to build their homes. In the arid Southwest, people used sun-dried clay bricks, called adobe, to build entire villages. Taos Pueblo of New Mexico (top) was built between 1000 and 1450. In contrast, longhouses of the Northeast were built of wooden frames covered with bark. The material was not as lasting as adobe, but it was plentiful. The longhouse above is a replica.

READING CHECK **Drawing Conclusions** How did the environment make life easier in some regions than in others?

Preserving Native American Cultures

America's newest national museum is devoted to America's earliest inhabitants. The National Museum of the American Indian, a part of the Smithsonian Institution, opened in Washington, D.C., in 2004. The museum focuses on the study of Native American cultures from all over North and South America, from the oldest artifacts to current art forms.

The origins of the museum go back many years. In 1897 an electrical engineer named George Gustav Heye (HY) was working in Arizona. He became fascinated with Native American cultures. For the rest of his life, he used his wealth to build the world's largest private collection of Indian objects.

Heye spent time with various nations, including the Seneca in New York State. They named him *O'owah*, meaning "Screech Owl." In North Dakota, the Hidatsa also gave him an Indian name after he returned a sacred object lost to the nation years earlier.

In 1922 Heye opened a museum in New York City. The collections of that museum are the basis for the new Smithsonian museum.

Making Inferences Why might Heye have been able to aquire such a large number of Indian artifacts?

Northwest Indians attend a ceremony in traditional dress.

Native American Customs

Based on the records of early explorers and settlers, scholars are able to say quite a bit about how Indian societies worked before European contact. Generalizations are risky because Native Americans organized their villages and societies in different ways. Some cultures were complex, while others remained simpler. Their homes ranged from skin tents to adobe pueblos to the Iroquois longhouse. Still, Native Americans in North America shared a number of ideas and customs.

Family relations At the heart of Native American society were families. Most villages and nations were organized into clans on the basis of **kinship**, or blood relations. Sometimes kinship ties were based on the mother's family, sometimes on the father's. Kinship often determined how property would be inherited. It also determined status and who one could or could not marry.

Housing patterns and social arrangements in many societies depended on the position of women. Among the Iroquois, for example, several different clans might live in a village. But all the women in one longhouse came from a single clan. Iroquois society was **matrilineal**—property was inherited through the mother. In the longhouse, each woman and her family had their own living quarters. A man married into a particular longhouse.

Similarly, among the Hopi in the Southwest, a man went to live with his wife's family when he married. He took seeds from his mother's crops with him and raised a crop for his new household. That also helped spread different crop varieties.

Social and political structures Social organization varied greatly from group to group. Some cultures, such as the Pacific Coast and Mississippian, had strict social classes. In other groups, there was more equality.

Most clans or nations were headed by chiefs. Villages were usually run by a council of elders with wisdom and experience.

Land use Native Americans' concept of land ownership was very different from that of Europeans. Mainly, they did not believe that land should be bought and sold. Some societies viewed land as a gift of the Great Spirit to humans. It was to be used and shared by the village or group for farming or hunting.

FOCUS ON NEW YORK

GOVERNMENT
Native American nations sometimes joined together to form protective trading groups. In 1570 five Iroquois nations—the Mohawks, Oneidas, Onondagas, Cayugas, and Senecas, all of whom were based in New York—formed the League of Five Nations. The League of Five Nations later served as a model for the American system of representative democracy.

This does not mean that there was no sense of territoriality. For example, the Iroquois nations often went to war over hunting grounds. Other groups, however, often shared the use of an area of land.

Division of labor Even in the earliest hunter-gatherer groups, certain people did certain kinds of work. This is called **division of labor.** In ancient times, as you have read, men and boys hunted animals. Women and girls gathered plants, nuts, and berries.

With the agricultural revolution, mainly women took over planting and cultivating food crops. During years of gathering wild plants, they had learned which plants were edible and how they grew. This knowledge helped groups invent tools for farming.

In the Southwest, the division of labor was different. Both women and men were in charge of farming. Women looked after children and cooked. As artisans, women wove cloth and made pottery and baskets. Men were woodcarvers and probably metalworkers.

Religious beliefs Despite many differences in culture, Native Americans shared some spiritual and religious ideas. One was a spiritual connection to the natural world. An Indian of the Wabanaki nation in New England said, "The Great Spirit is our father, but the Earth is our mother." In many belief systems, a tree stood at the center of the earth. For the Iroquois it was a white pine; for the Sioux, a flowering tree was at the center of the sacred hoop.

Animals, particularly bears, were thought to be powerful spirits. Hunters carried out rituals to honor the spirit of an animal they were about to kill. Clans chose an animal as their symbol and spirit guide.

Native Americans told many stories. Some explained the creation of the world or the origin of their own people. Some related the deeds of heroes, often twins. Other stories were about deities or spirits, often those associated with crops, rivers, and other aspects of nature.

In many cultures, **shamans** were people believed to have spiritual and healing powers. When Europeans arrived, they called shamans medicine men.

READING CHECK **Making Generalizations**
How did gender differences influence the division of labor in Native American societies?

Trading Networks Link Native American Societies

You might think that with different languages and different ways of living, Native American groups kept apart. What brought them together, though, was trade. From their earliest days in North America, hunting bands sometimes met during their seasonal migrations. Probably to show good will, different bands exchanged gifts and spear points. Exchanging gifts as a sign of friendship or peace became a tradition.

Later, people began to travel deliberately to exchange goods. The main trade items were food, raw materials, and luxury goods. Native Americans usually traded by a **barter** system, an exchange of goods without using money. In a few places, shells were used as money.

Reasons for trade Native Americans learned to take advantage of the unique natural resources of their own lands. That led to specialization among different peoples. For example, groups with fertile land could produce extra food to trade with areas where food was scarce. Other groups had access to desirable minerals such as flint, copper, or turquoise. People who lived near lakes or oceans collected shells and pearls. Cotton was a useful trade item in the Southwest because cloth and seeds were light and easy to carry.

Some groups mastered skills that others did not have. Basket weavers, for example, might trade with pottery makers. Exchanging handicrafts as well as raw materials helped people in different areas to meet their needs.

Trading networks In the previous section, you read that the Adena and Hopewell people, the early inhabitants of Ohio, traded widely. The Hopewell trade network was particularly vast, covering about two-thirds of what is now the United States. Exotic minerals and other goods passed from trader to trader until they reached the Hopewell heartland.

Because of the distances involved and the hardships of travel, it could take years to bring some items to Ohio. Still, the Hopewell people prized bear's teeth and obsidian, a shiny black volcanic glass, from the Rocky Mountains. They obtained copper from the Great Lakes, thin sheets of mica from the Appalachian Mountains, and shells from the Atlantic seacoast.

Trade Covered Thousands of Miles

Native American trading networks covered great distances. Today archaeologists find trade objects many miles from their original homes.

This Mississippian ornamental collar is made of shell. Shell objects were sometimes found many miles from the ocean.

The obsidian of this knife blade came from present-day Wyoming, but the knife blade was found in Ohio.

Native American traders used canoes to transport their wares along rivers. They also traveled on foot, carrying goods in backpacks. By the 1400s there were well-worn paths through the forests. Thousands of miles of trade networks crisscrossed North America.

One of the most famous of these trading paths began in Iroquois country and ran southward through mountain valleys as far south as present-day North Carolina. It crossed the territory of the Shawnee, Choctaw, Cherokee, and other nations.

Trading networks varied in size. In California, for example, many different bands lived in a fairly small area with very diverse environments. That encouraged an active trading network. People on the coast made trade items out of shells. They traded with people in the interior for stone objects.

Exchange of ideas Along with foodstuffs, raw materials, and more exotic goods, trade networks carried ideas from place to place. The presence of temple mounds and pyramids in Mississippian society, for example, suggests that Mississippians may have borrowed Mesoamerican building practices. In the Southwest, meanwhile, the Pueblo peoples adopted certain religious ideas that came from Mexico. They wove these ideas into their own belief systems just as they wove brilliantly colored Mexican macaw feathers into their ritual headdresses.

READING CHECK **Summarizing** What role did trade play in Native American societies?

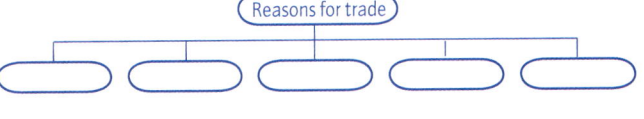

SECTION 2 ASSESSMENT

go.hrw.com
Online Quiz
Keyword: SD7 HP1

Reviewing Ideas, Terms, and People

1. **a. Recall** What were the two main language groups in the Eastern Woodlands?
   b. Compare and Contrast What were the differences and similarities between Pacific Coast and Great Basin cultures?
2. **a. Define** Write a brief definition for each of the following terms: **kinship, division of labor**.
   b. Explain What role did **shamans** play in Native American society?
   c. Elaborate How was the natural world important in Native Americans' religious views?
3. **a. Recall** What goods did Native Americans trade?
   b. Summarize Why did Native American groups in North America trade with one another?

Critical Thinking

4. **Sequencing** Copy the flowchart below and identify the reasons why Native Americans established trading networks.

Reasons for trade

FOCUS ON SPEAKING

5. **Persuasive** As a member of a Native American group in inland California, write a speech persuading a coastal group to trade shells for your spear points.

African Cultures before 1500

BEFORE YOU READ

MAIN IDEA

Trade was a major factor in the development of African societies south of the Sahara.

READING FOCUS

1. What powerful West African trading kingdoms arose between 300 and 1500?
2. How did trade shape kingdoms in East Africa?
3. How did African society change as a result of the slave trade?

KEY TERMS AND PEOPLE

Islam
oral tradition
Mansa Musa
Muslims
Askia Muhammad
lineage
plantation

 1.4 Understand the interrelationships between world events and developments in New York State and the United States (e.g., causes for immigration, economic opportunities, human rights abuses, and tyranny versus freedom).

Would you cross the Sahara on a camel? Crossing the sands of the Sahara has always been dangerous. Nevertheless, even in ancient times, traders made the trip in search of gold and other riches. One of the greatest ancient travelers, Ibn Battutah, crossed the desert mainly because he was curious. He visited Mali, the great West African trade empire, and the rich cities of East Africa. Ibn Battutah's accounts are the only record of those cultures in the fourteenth century.

Ibn Battutah was an Arab scholar from Tangier, in North Africa. His first trip, in 1325, was a pilgrimage to Mecca, the spiritual center of Islam. For almost 30 years, he traveled in the Muslim world, from Spain to India. He met rulers, merchants, scholars, and ordinary people.

Ibn Battutah made new friends wherever his travels took him. Along the way he found many different places to stay, including inns, mosques, and people's homes. Mali was his last trip across the Sahara desert. Even with a camel caravan, it was a dangerous journey. "That desert has many devils . . . ," Ibn Battutah wrote. "There is only sand blown by the wind. You see mountains of sand in a place, then you see they have moved to another."

West African Trading Kingdoms

Even today, the Sahara is a fearsome barrier to travelers. It divides northern Africa from the southern part of the continent. As a result, Mali and other societies south of the desert developed independently.

Crossing the Sahara

A modern-day salt caravan makes tracks across the Sahara.

WEST AND CENTRAL AFRICA, 1100–1500

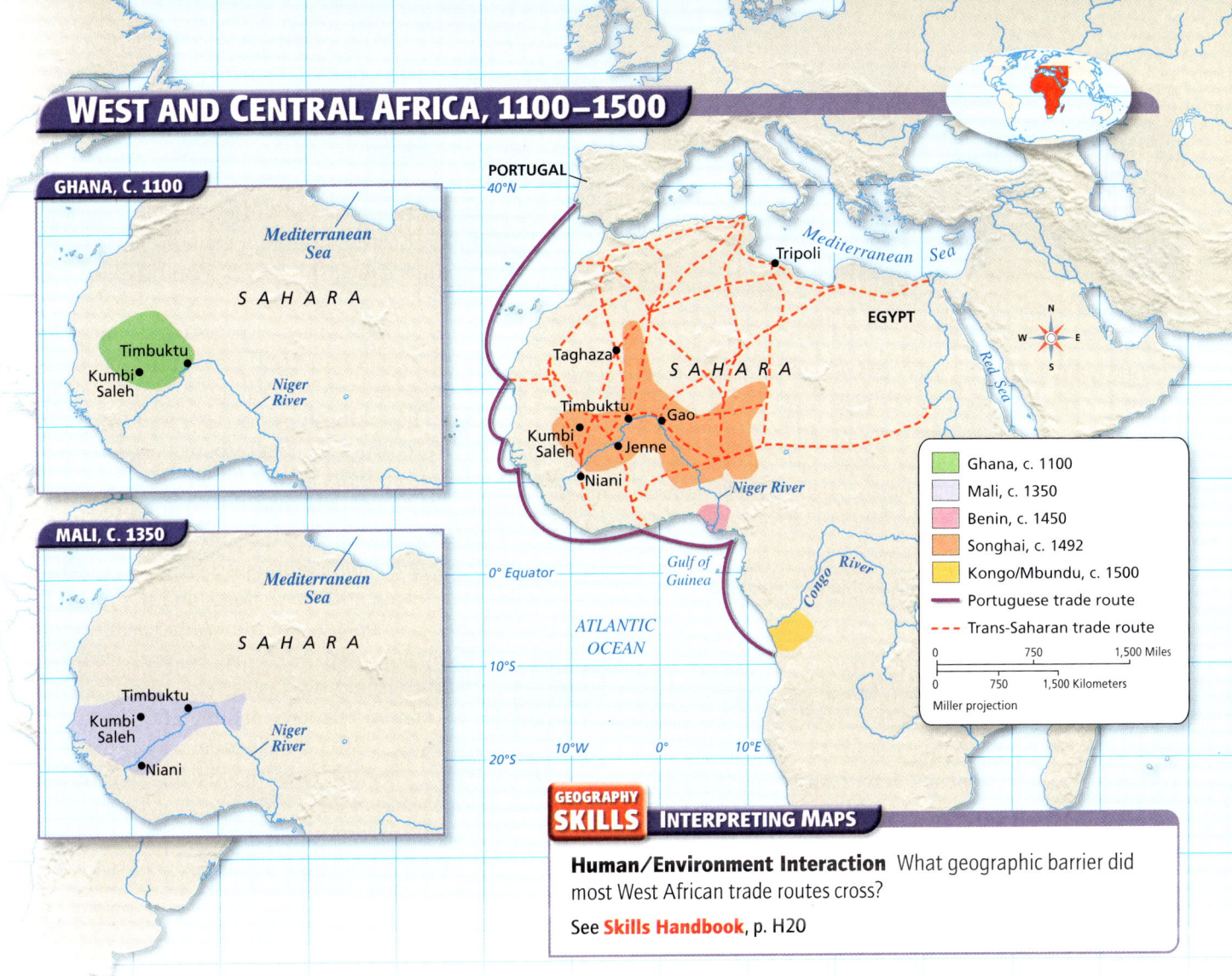

GHANA, C. 1100

MALI, C. 1350

PORTUGAL
40°N

Mediterranean Sea

SAHARA

Timbuktu
Kumbi Saleh

Niger River

Tripoli

Mediterranean Sea

EGYPT

Taghaza

SAHARA

Timbuktu
Kumbi Saleh
Jenne
Gao
Niani

Niger River

Gulf of Guinea

ATLANTIC OCEAN

Congo River

0° Equator

10°S

20°S

10°W   0°   10°E

🟩	Ghana, c. 1100
⬜	Mali, c. 1350
🟥	Benin, c. 1450
🟧	Songhai, c. 1492
🟨	Kongo/Mbundu, c. 1500

Portuguese trade route
--- Trans-Saharan trade route

0   750   1,500 Miles
0   750   1,500 Kilometers
Miller projection

GEOGRAPHY SKILLS INTERPRETING MAPS

Human/Environment Interaction What geographic barrier did most West African trade routes cross?

See **Skills Handbook**, p. H20

Trans-Sahara trade Despite the dangers, trading caravans have crossed the Sahara since ancient times. The African interior had valuable resources that made the trip worthwhile. The most precious were gold and ivory. In return, Arabs from North Africa traded salt from mines in the desert. For people in the interior, salt was probably as precious as gold.

Several great trading empires in West Africa thrived thanks to gold and salt. These empires grew up in the savanna, or grasslands, near a great bend of the Niger River.

Desert traders brought something else important to West Africa—the religion of Islam. Founded by the prophet Muhammad, Islam began in Arabia in the 600s. Later, Arab traders brought the teachings of Islam into West Africa. Some peoples in West Africa accepted Islam. Others, however, continued to practice traditional African religions.

Ghana The earliest West African trading state was Ghana, which probably arose about AD 300. Located along the trade route for gold and salt, Ghana grew very wealthy. It also grew powerful, conquering many nearby areas.

Because African languages were not written, what we know about Ghana's early history is largely from **oral tradition** —history passed down by storytellers. These sources tell us that Ghana kept its traditional religions rather than converting to Islam.

Mali In about 1240, a great warrior named Sundiata conquered Ghana and established the new state of Mali. Mali's most famous ruler was **Mansa Musa** (MAHN-sah moo-SAH), who held power from about 1307 to 1332. Unlike the people of Ghana, the people of Mali were **Muslims**, or followers of Islam. The university in the city of Timbuktu was a center of Islamic learning.

THE IMPACT TODAY

Government
When the modern African nations of Ghana and Mali became independent, they took the names of ancient West African trading kingdoms. The modern nations do not include the same territories as the earlier states.

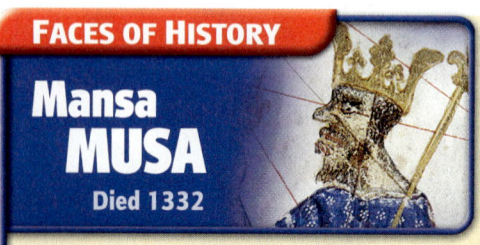

Born into a ruling family, Mansa Musa inherited the kingdom of Mali from his father in about 1307. Musa greatly influenced the lives of his people. He encouraged education, agricultural development, industry, and trade. Rich in gold, Mali grew wealthy through trade. Mansa Musa protected traders, creating a large army to guard trade routes. Mali soon expanded into a vast empire.

As a Muslim, Mansa Musa encouraged the spread of Islam in Mali, but he did not force his people to practice Islam. In 1324 he took a pilgrimage to Mecca. He brought thousands of fellow travelers and vast riches to distribute during his trip. Mansa Musa's travels made the world aware of Mali's great riches.

Explain How did Mansa Musa influence life in Mali?

Mansa Musa was deeply religious. In 1324 he decided to make the hajj, a pilgrimage to the holy city of Mecca in Arabia. Mansa Musa's journey across Africa made the outside world aware of Mali's fabulous wealth.

Songhai By the mid-1400s, Mali was weakening. Another kingdom, Songhai, gained control of much of the Niger River valley. Songhai became larger than either Ghana or Mali. Its most famous ruler was **Askia Muhammad**, who reigned from 1493 until 1528. A devout man, he encouraged a revival of Muslim learning.

The power of Songhai began to fail in the late 1500s. By then, patterns of trade were shifting to routes in the coastal regions.

Coastal kingdoms By about 1300, the settlement of Benin (buh-NEEN) was becoming a powerful state. Benin grew rich from foreign trade. It eventually ruled a large area of the West African forest region. Benin was famous for its brilliant artists. They created beautiful statues of heads and other bronze artwork.

At about the same time, the kingdom of Kongo was growing up farther south, along the Congo River in Central Africa. Kongo territory spread along the Atlantic coast and far inland. The kingdom thrived in part by trading in salt and palm oil.

READING CHECK **Sequencing** What was the first great trading state in West Africa?

Kingdoms in East Africa

Across the African continent, trade was important in the growth of kingdoms. The people of East Africa looked to Egypt, India, and the Middle East for trading partners. Their trading ships sailed the Red Sea and crossed the Indian Ocean.

Like West Africa, East Africa had gold mines. Traders also sold exotic products such as cinnamon, rhinoceros horn, and tortoise shell. They shipped enslaved Africans abroad, too. In return they bought porcelain, silk, and jewels from India and China.

Nearby Arabia strongly influenced cultures in East Africa, especially along the coast. Many Arab merchants settled in the coastal cities, bringing their customs and the religion of Islam. People in the interior generally kept their traditional religions. Several wealthy Muslim city-states also grew up along the coast and on offshore islands. They included Mombasa, Kilwa, and Zanzibar.

Soon, a new culture developed in East Africa. African and Arab traders even spoke a new language. Called Swahili, it mixed Arabic words with the language patterns of the local Bantu people.

READING CHECK **Identifying Cause and Effect** How did geography affect trade in East Africa?

African Society and the Slave Trade

Visitors to Africa were amazed by the wealth and lavish lifestyles of African rulers. Most had large courts and many officials, servants, and entertainers.

Strong families were another central feature of African society. People were loyal to their clan and to those with the same **lineage**, or ancestry. They felt loyalty to their village as well. People working in certain crafts also formed tightly knit groups.

Among ordinary people, class distinctions existed, but they were not rigid. The biggest division was between people who were free and those who were not. Men and women could be enslaved if they were captured in war, found guilty of a crime, or in debt. In most African societies, however, slaves could work their way into freedom. They had social mobility, meaning that they could move from a low status to a higher one.

The Portuguese in West Africa The nature of slavery changed drastically after Europeans arrived on the African continent in the late 1400s. In the next section, you will read about the adventurous Portuguese sailors who explored the west coast of Africa. Mainly, they were looking for a sea route to India. But they had also heard stories of fabulous gold in wealthy African kingdoms. They hoped to return to Portugal with gold.

The Portuguese established trading posts and later built forts on the Atlantic coast. They found riches in an area called the Gold Coast, but many of their other ventures were not as profitable as they had hoped.

Then the Portuguese, and later the Spanish, set up **plantations**, or large-scale farms, on several islands off the African coast. During the 1500s, they also started sugar plantations on Caribbean islands and elsewhere in the Americas. It was not only the Spanish and Portuguese who launched these ventures but also the British, French, and Dutch.

Plantation agriculture requires large numbers of workers because it is so labor-intensive. Planters first tried to use Native Americans, but diseases and harsh working conditions took a heavy toll. Then Europeans turned to importing Africans.

The Atlantic slave trade begins Slavery had existed in Africa and other parts of the world for hundreds of years. Historians point out that Europeans did not deliberately come to Africa to enslave Africans. The Atlantic slave trade arose primarily in response to the demand for cheap labor. It also grew out of European views that black Africans were inferior.

Slavery was already widespread in Mediterranean countries when the Portuguese arrived in Africa in the 1400s. They began taking Africans back to Europe to show that they had actually found a new land. At first, they treated Africans well and trained them as guides and interpreters. Soon, however, the Portuguese began using Africans as servants and eventually as slaves. By one estimate, about 50,000 African captives had been sent to southern Europe by the 1550s.

The slave trade across the Atlantic began in the sixteenth century when planters in the Americas began to demand more workers for their plantations. The Portuguese and other traders in Africa persuaded a few African rulers and merchants to supply them with slaves. Merchants cooperated in order to keep the

Linking TO Today

The Door of No Return

The Atlantic slave trade affected people and societies all over the world. Today many visitors to West Africa visit the fortresses and dungeons formerly used to imprison captives before sea voyages. One of the best known is on the coastal island of Gorée (gaw-RAY) in the modern-day nation of Senegal.

Gorée is home to the House of Slaves and its Door of No Return. Some experts doubt that the House of Slaves, built in 1776, was used to hold people before they were shipped across the ocean. Historian Philip Curtin describes it as "architecturally one of the finest houses on Gorée, certainly not a place where slaves would be kept."

Still, the Door of No Return has become a powerful symbol for tens of thousands of visitors every year. UNESCO, the UN agency that promotes cultural preservation, named Gorée a World Heritage Site in 1978. World leaders have traveled to the island, including former South African president Nelson Mandela, U.S. presidents Bill Clinton and George W. Bush, and Pope John Paul II.

Drawing Conclusions What does the Door of No Return symbolize?

The Door of No Return can be seen at the end of the dark passage flanked by the double staircase.

CAUSES AND EFFECTS OF THE ATLANTIC SLAVE TRADE

CAUSES
- Settlers in the Americas needed many workers for labor-intensive plantation agriculture.
- Planters wanted cheap labor.
- Europeans thought Africans were inferior.

EFFECTS
- Historians estimate that 20 million Africans landed in the Americas.
- Historians estimate that millions of Africans died on slave ships crossing the Atlantic.
- Millions were deprived of their freedom, causing tremendous human suffering.
- The American economy became dependent on slavery.
- In the nineteenth century, conflicting views over slavery led to the Civil War in the United States.

traders' business. Some rulers cooperated in exchange for European firearms. Others were motivated by a desire to weaken rival African leaders.

African suppliers did not round up all those who were enslaved, however. Europeans took some people captive during conflicts with North African Muslims. European traders also conducted slave raids and kidnappings. Some European colonists in Africa took part in these activities as well. Although the Portuguese had begun the trade, by the 1600s the English, French, and Dutch were also heavily involved in the slave trade.

The impact on African society The Atlantic slave trade went on for 400 years and devastated societies in West Africa. Although there are no firm figures, historians estimate that some 20 million enslaved Africans were shipped to the Americas. Probably several million more were sent to Europe, Asia, and the Middle East. Countless others died while marching from the interior to the coast, or while crammed aboard slave ships crossing the Atlantic Ocean.

The human cost of the slave trade was tremendous. Slavery deprived millions of people of their basic freedom. It also affected African society in many ways. Slave hunters took some of the strongest young people—the future leaders. Slave raids made people fearful and discouraged them from planning for the future. The slave trade also interrupted normal political and economic development because parts of Africa suffered enormous losses in population.

In addition, the slave trade weakened traditional bonds and divided Africans from one another. Traders hired young men as kidnappers. Rulers conducted wars against their own people and their neighbors in order to gain captives. The forced labor of millions of Africans enriched other parts of the world—but it did not enrich Africa itself.

READING CHECK **Identifying the Main Idea** How did the demand for slave labor begin?

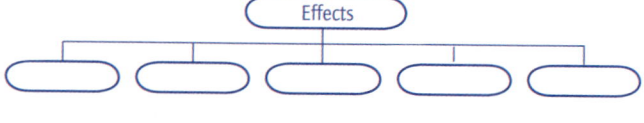

go.hrw.com
Online Quiz
Keyword: SD7 HP1

SECTION 3 ASSESSMENT

Reviewing Ideas, Terms, and People

1. **a. Identify** What were the great West African trading empires?
   b. Analyze What kinds of products were exchanged in the trans-Sahara trade?

2. **a. Describe** What were the trading patterns in East Africa?
   b. Make Inferences How did nearby Arabia influence cultures in East Africa?

3. **a. Recall** Who were the first European explorers on the Atlantic coast of Africa?
   b. Explain What factors led to the Atlantic slave trade?

Critical Thinking

4. **Identifying Cause and Effect** Copy the chart below and list the effects of the slave trade on African societies.

```
        Effects
  ┌────┬────┬────┬────┬────┐
  ◯    ◯    ◯    ◯    ◯
```

FOCUS ON WRITING

5. **Expository** As an African ruler in the 1500s, write a letter to your royal counselors explaining why you are sending all European traders out of your country.

Europe and Exploration

BEFORE YOU READ

MAIN IDEA

Renaissance ideas changed Europeans' medieval outlook and inspired them to explore the world.

READING FOCUS

1. What changes took place in Europe during the Middle Ages?
2. What happened during the Renaissance and the Protestant Reformation?
3. What did Europeans hope to find during the Age of Exploration?

KEY TERMS AND PEOPLE

Middle Ages
Crusades
Magna Carta
Renaissance
Martin Luther
Reformation
Protestants
Queen Isabella
caravel

PI 1.4 Understand the interrelationships between world events and developments in New York State and the United States (e.g., causes for immigration, economic opportunities, human rights abuses, and tyranny versus freedom).

THE INSIDE STORY

Would you dare to sail an unknown ocean? People in medieval Europe were very superstitious. Most were uneducated and knew little about the world outside their villages. They believed in magic and witchcraft. They told stories about dragons and other fantastic monsters. They thought that evil spirits lurked in the deep dark forests around their own villages. Who could even imagine what horrible beasts might exist in places they had never seen?

Even well-educated mapmakers drew pictures of sea serpents and other fabulous creatures in unexplored parts of the world. At the edges of the Atlantic Ocean, maps said simply, "Here there be monsters."

Not surprisingly, sailors were some of the most superstitious people in the late medieval world. Uncertain of what lay beyond the horizon, most sea captains tried to stay in sight of land. But in the Age of Exploration, sea captains sailed into parts of the world that no one—as far as they knew—had ever explored.

Many sailors were afraid of these unknown waters. Some believed that the ocean water at the Equator was boiling hot and filled with sea monsters that would swallow their ships. In spite of their fears, hundreds of sailors did sign on to sail into unknown seas on the early voyages of discovery.

Sailing the BOILING SEAS

▶ Medieval maps often showed sea monsters, like this detail at right, illustrating sailors' fears of the unknown.

23

The Middle Ages

Monsters and boiling seas were not the only fearsome things during the **Middle Ages**, the period of European history from about AD 500 to 1500. This time, also known as the medieval period, began when the old Roman Empire collapsed, creating widespread lawlessness.

Feudalism and the manorial system

During the early Middle Ages, life was frightening for Europeans. Invaders occupied Spain and attacked other nations in central Europe. In the north, Vikings from Scandinavia raided the coasts.

Because no governments were strong enough to protect people, local nobles took over. A system of feudalism developed, mainly in France, England, and Germany. The feudal system involved interdependency between lords and vassals, or nobles of lower rank. Feudal lords ruled large estates, or manors, and gave parcels of land to vassals in exchange for their loyalty and military service.

The Crusades The Roman Catholic Church was the leading institution in medieval Europe. Religion dominated the lives of the people, most of whom had few material comforts.

Many devout believers made pilgrimages to Christian shrines and holy places. A number of these holy places were in Palestine, the area known as the Holy Land. Muslim Turks, however, ruled that region. In 1095 Pope Urban II called on Christian kings and knights to go to war to recapture those lands. Thousands answered his call. The holy wars that followed were known as the **Crusades**, and they continued until 1291.

At first the Crusaders did gain territory, but the Muslims eventually won back the region. However, the Crusades did open Europeans' eyes to the rest of the world. Soldiers who had never traveled farther than the next village suddenly experienced new lands and peoples.

The Crusades also gave a boost to trade between Europe and the Middle East. People now wanted exotic luxury goods such as fruits, spices, sugar, silks, perfumes, and carpets. Merchants in European cities, especially in Italy, made fortunes. These rich merchants, along with successful artisans, made up a growing middle class in the towns. Towns grew into bustling market centers.

New nation-states Early in the Middle Ages, Europe was divided among hundreds of nobles. Barons, earls, dukes, counts—each ruled a piece of land and hoped to rule more. By the late Middle Ages, though, things were changing. Many nobles had lost their fortunes (and even their lives) in the Crusades. At the same time, the new middle-class townspeople did not owe loyalty to a feudal lord. It was the king who gave their town a charter (a document defining its territory), and it was the king who collected taxes from them.

In England, France, and Spain, those developments allowed strong rulers to unify their lands. They began creating nation-states—countries with strong central governments and homogeneous, rather than diverse, populations. With taxes from the towns, rulers could hire their own armies. They chose royal officials from the educated middle class and made policies for all their subjects.

In England, however, some barons acted to curb the king's powers. In 1215 they forced the unpopular King John to sign the **Magna Carta**. This document established several important principles of government, such as no taxation without representation and the right to trial

Magna Carta

- Signed by King John in 1215
- Guaranteed certain rights to the barons
- Restricted the power of the king
- Established no taxation without representation
- Established the right to trial by jury of one's peers
- Set forth the basic principles of English and, later, American law

by a jury "of one's peers [equals]." At first only the barons enjoyed these rights, but gradually they were extended to ordinary people.

Later in the 1200s, the English also began to develop a parliament, a representative assembly that could make laws. This evolved gradually into two "houses" that met separately. The House of Lords was a council of nobles and bishops. The House of Commons included knights and townspeople.

READING CHECK **Identifying Cause and Effect** What events helped strong nations arise toward the end of the Middle Ages?

The Renaissance and the Protestant Reformation

As the Middle Ages came to an end, the stage was set for great changes in Europe. Increased trade with the East opened people's minds to new ideas. Prosperity brought population growth and better education. In the 1300s a new era of learning and creativity began. This period is called the **Renaissance** (REN-uh-sahns), a term that comes from the French word for "rebirth."

The Renaissance The Renaissance began in the wealthy city-states of Italy. In the 1400s and 1500s, though, it spread northward to the rest of Europe.

Renaissance scholars took a fresh interest in ancient knowledge that had been lost during the Middle Ages. They studied anew the classics of ancient Greece and Rome. Inspired by those civilizations, artists and writers created works of lasting beauty. Merchants who had become rich from international trade supported their work.

The Renaissance was not just a time of intense creativity in the arts. It was truly a new beginning in ways of thinking as well. In the medieval period, many people accepted misery as their lot in life and hoped for rewards in heaven. Now people showed more interest in a meaningful life on earth. They valued individuals and their personal achievements.

Scientists also began to question long-accepted teachings of the Catholic Church—for example, the idea that the earth was at the center of the universe. It was a big change from the way people thought during the Middle Ages.

PRIMARY SOURCES

Sketch by Leonardo da Vinci

Leonardo da Vinci thought that flight would require flapping wings. This sketch shows one of his ideas for a device that would test the strength of beating wings.

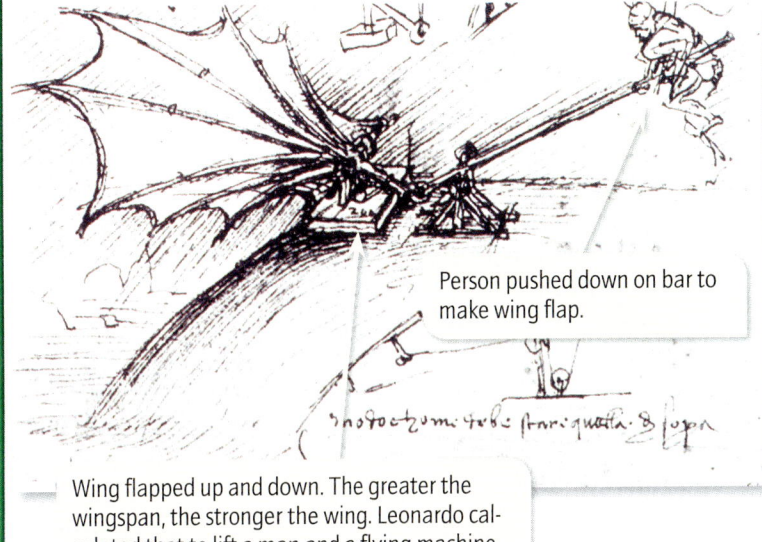

Person pushed down on bar to make wing flap.

Wing flapped up and down. The greater the wingspan, the stronger the wing. Leonardo calculated that to lift a man and a flying machine weighing 400 pounds, it would take a wingspan of about 12 feet.

Skills FOCUS **READING LIKE A HISTORIAN**

1. **Interpreting Visuals** How do the wings in the sketch differ from wings on today's airplanes?

2. **Evaluating Sources** Do you think Leonardo's wings would have worked?

See **Skills Handbook**, pp. H30, H34

The Protestant Reformation It was not only scientists who challenged the authority of the church. Many people felt that some members of the clergy had become lazy and corrupt. Devout Catholics complained that the church was failing to provide proper spiritual guidance.

Discontent with the church reached its peak in northern and central Europe. In 1517 a German monk named **Martin Luther** strode to a church in the town of Wittenberg and nailed a list of arguments to the door. Luther criticized some church practices and called for a public debate. He hoped to bring about reforms, but his actions set off a religious revolution.

Luther's calls for reform launched a movement that became known as the **Reformation**. Those who joined in protesting against the Roman Catholic Church became known as **Protestants**. They soon broke with Catholicism and formed their own churches.

Reform ideas spread beyond the German states to other parts of Europe, including Switzerland, England, Scotland, Scandinavia, and the Netherlands. By the mid-1500s Protestants began to dominate northern Europe, while the Catholic Church still controlled most of southern Europe. Central Europe was divided.

Christianity in Spain

Spain was also divided along religious lines for many years. In the 700s a few small Christian kingdoms controlled northern Spain. Islam, meanwhile, had taken root in most of the Iberian Peninsula—present-day Spain and Portugal. There the Muslims, known as Moors, introduced cultural advances rare in medieval Europe.

By the 1100s, however, Muslim rule was declining. At the same time, the Crusades were inspiring Christian rulers to try to win back the Iberian Peninsula. This movement was known as the Reconquista, or Reconquest. One by one, Muslim kingdoms fell.

In 1469 a royal marriage united the two largest Christian kingdoms. **Queen Isabella** of Castile-León married King Ferdinand of Aragón. Their goal was to unite all of Spain as a Catholic kingdom. They believed that Spain could be a strong nation-state only if it had a single religion.

Granada, the last Muslim stronghold, fell in 1492. That same year, Spain's rulers ordered all Jews to convert or leave the country. In 1497 Muslims in Portugal were also ordered to convert or leave. Meanwhile, Christians suspected of defying the church risked punishment by the Spanish Inquisition, a famously harsh court.

READING CHECK **Summarizing** What happened to the Catholic Church during the Renaissance?

The Age of Exploration

The Renaissance changed the way that Europeans looked at themselves and the world around them. They had seen new places and were curious about them. Advances in science and technology encouraged people to ask questions and think boldly. A desire to explore seized the rulers of unified nation-states—France, England, Spain, and Portugal. They dreamed of increasing their wealth and power by finding new sources of trade.

Some historians suggest that the religious spirit of the Crusades and the Reconquista also spurred the Age of Exploration that began in the 1400s. Catholic explorers hoped not only to make voyages of discovery but also to spread Christianity.

The travels of Marco Polo

During the Middle Ages, some of the boldest travelers had been traders from the Italian city-states of Venice and Genoa. Many Italian merchants crossed the Mediterranean Sea to trade with Muslims, who brought spices and other goods from Asia. Only a few Europeans traveled to China and India themselves, crossing the mountains and deserts of central Asia until they finally reached the Far East. Trading trips such as these took many years.

The most famous of these travelers was a young Venetian named Marco Polo. He set out for China in 1271 with his father and uncle, who had made the trip once before. The Polos stayed in China for almost 17 years, while Marco worked for the emperor Kublai Khan.

Their return trip, partly by sea, took them to many parts of Southeast Asia and India. All along the way, Marco took note of people, places, and customs. After finally getting home to Venice, Marco dictated the story of his travels. The book became instantly popular, and it influenced later explorers.

Prince Henry the Navigator

One of the leading figures in the Age of Exploration was Prince Henry of Portugal, known as the Navigator. He had heard tales of African gold, and in 1419, he set up a school and naval observatory to encourage exploration.

Henry brought in mapmakers, experienced sailors, shipbuilders, and instrument makers. He also began to sponsor many expeditions in the Atlantic Ocean and down the west coast of Africa. He hoped to find gold, compete with the Muslims for trade in Africa, and spread Christianity. He also hoped to find a sea route to India. That would let Portugal and other countries trade directly with the East instead of going through Italian merchants.

Caravel

A special type of ship called the caravel enabled European explorers to sail across huge oceans and up small rivers. Though small, caravels were sturdy. They featured important advances in sailing technology.

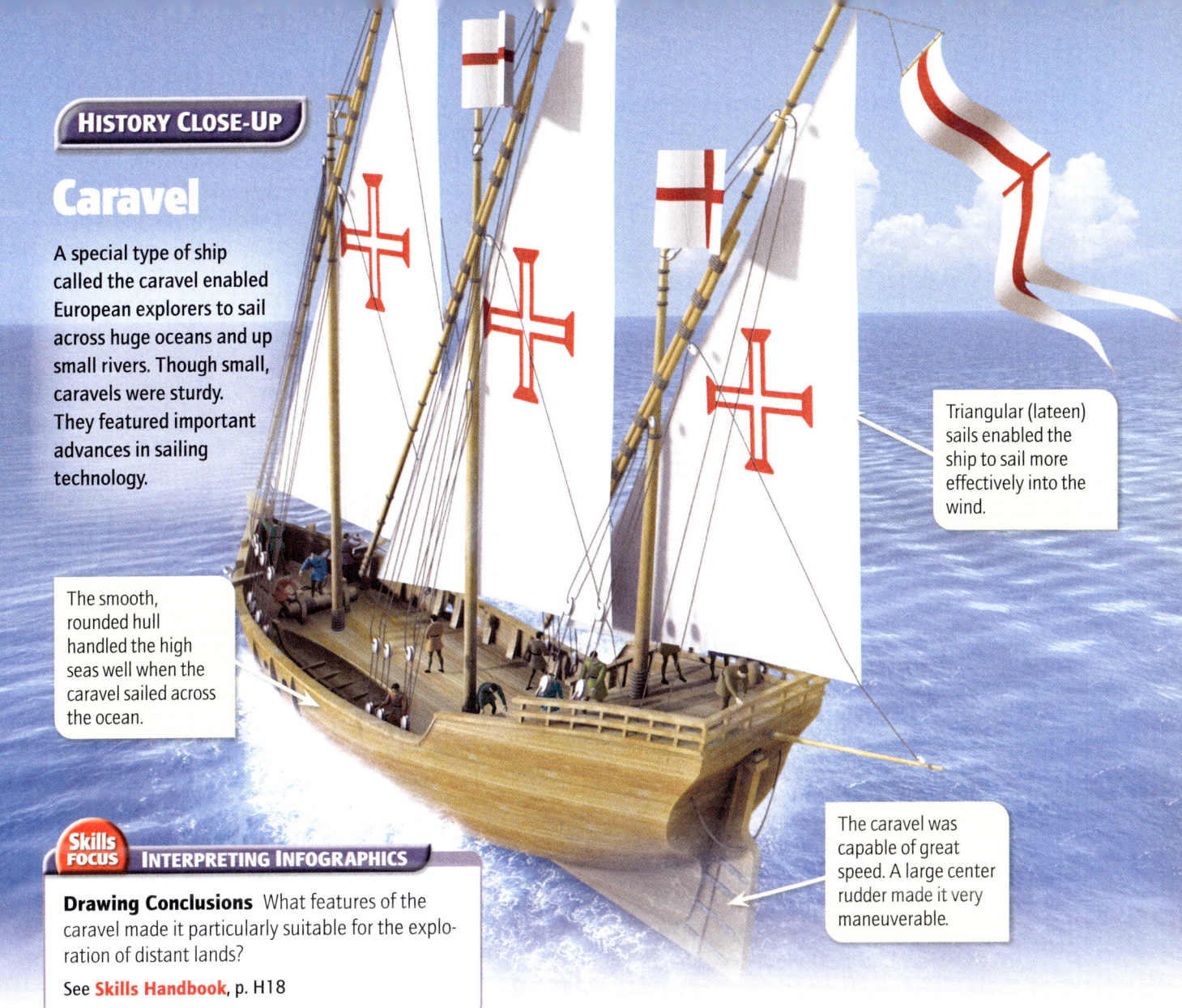

Triangular (lateen) sails enabled the ship to sail more effectively into the wind.

The smooth, rounded hull handled the high seas well when the caravel sailed across the ocean.

The caravel was capable of great speed. A large center rudder made it very maneuverable.

Skills FOCUS **INTERPRETING INFOGRAPHICS**

Drawing Conclusions What features of the caravel made it particularly suitable for the exploration of distant lands?

See **Skills Handbook**, p. H18

Henry's ships traveled farther and farther south along Africa's west coast. In the 1440s, Portuguese sea captains discovered several rivers, set up colonies, made accurate maps, and brought back gold dust from West Africa. As you read in Section 3, they also began to bring Africans to Portugal as servants.

In 1448 the Portuguese set up the first European trading post in Africa. They traded for gold, ivory, pepper, and palm oil. They also started sugar plantations on the islands of Cape Verde and São Tomé.

Better sailing technology One reason that Portugal's expeditions were so successful was because sailors had a new kind of ship. Prince Henry's school in southern Portugal had developed the **caravel**, a vessel both sturdy and

swift. Along with square sails, caravels used triangular (lateen) sails, which helped them maneuver and sail against the wind. Caravels also had large cargo holds, so they could carry more goods than older ships.

There were other advances in technology, too. Previously sailors had relied on coastal landmarks to pinpoint their location. They worried about losing their way if they sailed out of sight of land. Now mariners began to use improved navigational instruments, which made longer sea voyages possible. With an astrolabe, for example, sailors could determine their latitude using the sun and stars.

Ship captains also began to use improved versions of the magnetic compass. Because the compass always showed north, they could accurately plot their course even at night or on cloudy days.

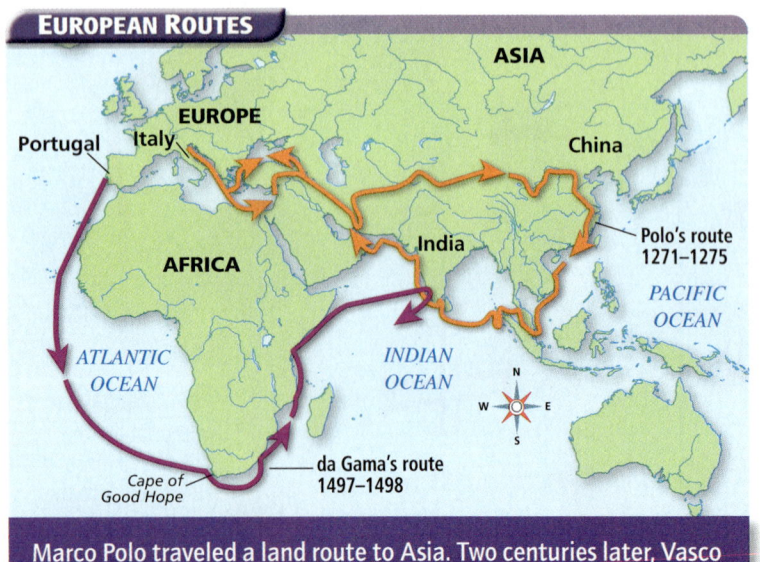

EUROPEAN ROUTES

Marco Polo traveled a land route to Asia. Two centuries later, Vasco da Gama discovered a sea route.

Looking for a sea route to Asia The overland trip to Asia remained long, difficult, and dangerous. Many Europeans still hoped to find a southern sea route to India. Again, Portugal led the way.

In early 1488, a Portuguese explorer named Bartolomeu Dias was sailing down Africa's west coast near the southern tip of the continent. A sudden storm blew his ships off course, and he lost sight of land for almost a month. Eventually, Dias realized that he was no longer traveling south but north. He had rounded the southern tip of Africa!

Dias returned home without going farther. He reportedly chose the name Cape of Storms for the point of land he had reached. The Portuguese king, however, signaling his pleasure in the discovery, called it the Cape of Good Hope.

About 10 years later, another Portuguese explorer, Vasco da Gama, led another historic expedition. Da Gama showed great skill at navigating. In 1498 he landed on the coast of India, finding the sea route so many had sought.

Da Gama's success was a challenge to other European rulers. The opening of a new trade route helped make Portugal a world power. It also led to the decline of trans-Sahara trade and the African trading empires.

As soon as da Gama returned to Portugal, another expedition was organized to return to India. This fleet was led by Pedro Álvars Cabral. On its way to the Cape of Good Hope, the fleet sailed southwest in the Atlantic. There the crew became the first Europeans to spot the coast of what is now Brazil. The fleet then turned eastward and continued on to India. En route, however, several ships and sailors were lost, including Bartolomeu Dias.

Though this voyage met bad luck, Cabral set up trading posts in India and brought back spices. More importantly, his sighting of Brazil gave Portugal a land claim in the Americas.

READING CHECK **Identifying the Main Idea** Why did the Portuguese and other Europeans want to find a sea route to India?

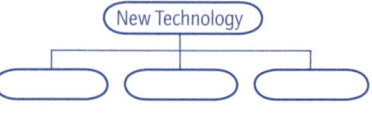

SECTION 4 ASSESSMENT

go.hrw.com
Online Quiz
Keyword: SD7 HP1

Reviewing Ideas, Terms, and People

1. a. Describe What were the **Crusades**?
   b. Explain What did lords and vassals offer each other under the feudal system?
   c. Elaborate What was the relationship between the growth of towns and the rise of nation-states?

2. a. Define Write a brief definition for each of the following terms: **Renaissance, Reformation**.
   b. Contrast How did the worldview of people in the Renaissance differ from the outlook during the **Middle Ages**?

3. a. Recall What were Prince Henry's contributions to the Age of Exploration?
   b. Explain What motivated the Portuguese to find a sea route to India?

Critical Thinking

4. Sequencing Copy the chart below and use it to show the advances in seafaring technology that aided Portuguese exploration.

New Technology

FOCUS ON WRITING

5. Persuasive As Prince Henry, write a letter to persuade one of your ship captains to attempt the dangerous trip around the Cape of Good Hope.

Cultures Make Contact

BEFORE YOU READ

MAIN IDEA

Columbus's voyages to the Americas established contact with Native Americans and led to European colonies and an exchange of goods and ideas.

READING FOCUS

1. When did Vikings visit North America, and why was their stay brief?
2. Why were Columbus's voyages to the Caribbean significant?
3. What impact did European exploration have on Native Americans?
4. What was the Columbian Exchange, and how did it affect both Europe and America?

KEY TERMS AND PEOPLE

Vikings
Leif Eriksson
Christopher Columbus
Tainos
colonization
Columbian Exchange

PI 1.2 Research and analyze the major themes and developments in New York State and United States history (e.g., colonization and settlement; Revolution and New National Period; immigration; expansion and reform era; Civil War and Reconstruction; the American labor movement; Great Depression; World Wars; contemporary United States).

THE INSIDE STORY

Why did the queen of Spain sponsor Christopher Columbus's voyage? The explorer Christopher Columbus was incredibly stubborn in believing that he could reach Asia by sailing west. Still, it took many years to find someone who had enough faith to finance his expedition. That someone was Queen Isabella of Spain, one of the strongest monarchs of the time.

Columbus and Isabella came from different worlds but were somewhat alike in both looks—auburn hair and blue eyes—and personality. From their first meeting in 1486, Isabella was sympathetic to his plans. Nonetheless, the final decision took six years. Isabella named a royal committee to investigate his idea, but they advised against it. She continued to encourage Columbus, sending occasional gifts of money. She told him to try again after the Reconquista was over.

In early 1492, an impatient Columbus offered the Spanish rulers one last chance. He added other demands—property, a title, and a share of trade. They said no, so Columbus packed his maps and left. Then, at the last minute, Luis de Santangel, a royal finance official, changed Isabella's mind. The whole voyage, he said, would not cost as much as entertaining a visiting king or queen for a week! Nevertheless, Santangel said he could raise the money. Isabella quickly sent a royal guard to bring Columbus back. History had been made.

▲ **Christopher Columbus's persistence with Queen Isabella (seated) finally paid off in 1492.**

Vikings Visit North America

Hundreds of years before Columbus planned his first voyage, the Norse from Scandinavia dominated the northern seas. The Norse, better known as **Vikings**, were sea raiders who terrorized the coasts of western Europe. The Vikings were also bold explorers in the North Atlantic Ocean.

In the late 900s, Vikings from Norway reached the island of Greenland in North America. Although Greenland today is largely ice covered, the climate was warmer then. Vikings led by Erik the Red established settlements there in 986.

In about 1000, Erik's son, **Leif Eriksson,** also headed to Greenland. He and his group missed their destination, however, and sailed further west than they had intended. Leif landed on a coast, probably in eastern Canada, where many grapevines and wild grasses grew. He named the place Vinland because of its abundant grapevines.

A few years later, other Viking explorers tried to establish a colony in Vinland. That led to the first known European contact with Native Americans. According to Scandinavian sagas—tales of legendary figures—the Viking settlers didn't find a warm welcome. Indeed, they left just three years later, after warfare with the natives. The Vikings continued to make trips to Vinland for timber, but they never settled there again.

READING CHECK **Summarizing** What was the Viking experience in America?

Columbus Voyages to the Caribbean

In the 1400s other Europeans knew nothing of the Vikings' journeys to North America. People in Europe had no inkling that the Americas even existed. That changed—and the whole world changed—as a result of one man's determination to find a sea route to India.

Christopher Columbus The explorer **Christopher Columbus** was born and raised in the Italian trading city of Genoa. As a young man, he went to sea and served on both merchant ships and warships. In 1476, when his ship sank in battle, he ended up in Portugal. This was a stroke of luck because the Portuguese, as you read in Section 4, were the leaders in exploration.

At the time, Vasco da Gama had not yet made his historic voyage to India. But many Portuguese mariners were sailing south along the African coast in hope of reaching the Indies. Some thought about trying a different course—sailing west. Because no one knew that the American continents were in the way, the idea of sailing west to reach Asia seemed promising. Yet no one dared venture far into the unknown Atlantic Ocean.

Columbus was the exception. He made it his life goal to lead a westward voyage. He needed ships and crews, though. As you read in the "Inside Story," it took many years before he convinced Queen Isabella of Spain to back his "Enterprise of the Indies."

In the meantime, Columbus studied sailing and navigation techniques. He also read many books dealing with travel and geography, including Marco Polo's *Travels.* After careful study, he concluded that the distance to Japan was only about 2,400 nautical miles. Unfortunately, Columbus made major errors in calculating the size of the world and the width of the Atlantic Ocean.

The first voyage On August 3, 1492, Columbus set sail. He had about 90 men, two caravels (the *Niña* and the *Pinta*), and his flagship, the *Santa Maria*. After three weeks on the open sea, the crew was frightened and restless. Some were near mutiny. Then they began to see birds and floating tree branches, which made them believe they were nearing land.

Columbus Describes Contact

When Christopher Columbus landed in what he thought was part of Asia, he met people who had never before been seen by Europeans. Columbus's views and descriptions of these people, whom he came to call "Indians," would shape European views of Native Americans for centuries to come.

A main goal of early explorers was to convert Native Americans to Christianity.

"I gave them [Indians] a thousand good, pleasing things which I had brought, in order that they might be fond of us, and furthermore might be made Christians and be inclined to the love and service of their Highnesses and of the whole Castilian [Spanish] nation and try to help us and to give us of the things which they have in abundance and which are necessary to us."

—Columbus's Letter on His First Voyage

Columbus thought the Indians he met had gold and other riches.

Skills FOCUS   READING LIKE A HISTORIAN

1. **Analyzing Primary Sources** How did Columbus's goal of gaining riches for Spain affect his treatment of the Indians?

2. **Evaluating Sources** Do you think Columbus's plan worked?

See **Skills Handbook**, pp. H28–29

Then, before dawn on October 12, 1492, a sailor shouted, "Tierra! Tierra!," or "Land! Land!" The three ships anchored off a small island in the Caribbean. Columbus named the island San Salvador.

Because the distance he had sailed was about what he had calculated in error, Columbus believed he was in the Indies. When the local people, the Tainos, greeted him, Columbus called them *los Indios,* or "Indians." He gave them gifts of red caps, glass beads, and bells.

The Tainos lived simply in thatched huts in the jungle. They grew vegetables, wove cotton, and made pottery. Columbus was disappointed not to find the rich cities he expected. But he still hoped to pick up Asian spices, silks, and other treasures on the larger islands nearby.

The crews soon set off, taking six Tainos with them as guides. The local Indians promised that plenty of gold lay ahead. The fleet stopped at Cuba, then sailed to another large island, which Columbus named *La Isla Española* ("The Spanish Isle"). Today it is Hispaniola (Haiti and the Dominican Republic).

There at last they found gold, which encouraged Columbus. But the *Santa Maria* went aground on a coral reef and sank. With his two remaining ships, Columbus returned to Spain.

Columbus would later make three more trips to the Americas. Although his voyages changed history, Columbus never understood why. When he died in 1506, he still believed he had explored part of Asia.

READING CHECK   **Making Inferences** Why did Columbus continue to think he was in Asia?

Impact on Native Americans

Columbus's voyages set off a wave of European colonization in the Americas. As you might imagine, colonization had a profound impact on the native peoples of the Americas.

Colonies in Hispaniola When the *Santa Maria* ran aground off Hispaniola in December 1492, Columbus took it as a sign from God that he was meant to establish a colony there. Because it was Christmas Day, he called it *Villa de la Navidad* ("Christmas Town") and had his men build a fort. As he departed for Spain, he told them to trade for gold, treat the natives well, and find a place to build a town.

Columbus came back to La Navidad the following year, intending to organize new colonies. But upon his return, he was shocked and dismayed. Many of his men had behaved wildly in his absence and made the Tainos so angry that the Indians had killed them all. This incident soured relations between the Spaniards and the Tainos, who had seemed so peace-loving.

Deciding to find another site for a colony, Columbus sailed east along the coast. There he established Isabela, named after the queen. Still believing he was in Asia, Columbus hoped to set up a trading post to exchange European goods for gems, precious metals, and spices. The site was a poor choice, however. It had malaria-carrying mosquitoes and no fresh water.

Things went badly in Isabela. Columbus's brothers ran the settlement while he explored other islands. Some of the Spanish officers rebelled against them. Then, under pressure to supply more gold, Columbus and his brothers captured Indians to sell as slaves. Colonization turned into the conquest of Hispaniola. In March 1495 the Spaniards marched inland with dogs, horses, and muskets. The Indians were unable to unite against them.

BARTOLOMÉ DE LAS CASAS

READING LIKE A HISTORIAN

Bartolomé de Las Casas is shown at his desk. His many writings included a plea for "enlightenment to those who are in a position to do something about what has been happening."
Interpreting Visuals How is his relationship to Native Americans shown in this painting?

Eventually, Ferdinand and Isabella decided that Columbus was a better admiral than he was an administrator. He lost his post as governor of Hispaniola in 1500. Unfortunately, the people of the islands were in for more suffering under other governors.

Native American labor Columbus's first reaction to meeting the native Tainos was to note "how easy it would be to convert these people [to Christianity] and to make them work for us." That view set a pattern for later Spanish and other European explorers.

As you know, the Spaniards who came to the Caribbean were mainly interested in finding gold. Because mining required much physical labor, they recruited Indians to help. It was an easy step from forced labor to enslavement.

Slavery was also a response to pressure from Spain to make a profit from Columbus's voyages. Early in 1494, along with gold, fine woods, and parrots, Columbus sent 26 Indians back to Spain. He said that they should be taught Spanish so they could be interpreters. Columbus also suggested starting a trade in Indian slaves. Slavery was common in many societies at the time. Europeans were also receptive to the idea of enslaving non-Christians because they could then be converted.

Trade in Indian slaves Not everyone approved of enslaving Indians. One opponent was Queen Isabella, who stated that Caribbean Indians belonged to the monarchs and could not be owned by anyone else in Spain. As a result, many Indians were sent instead to plantations off the coast of Portugal. Later, after the Portuguese, French, and Dutch set up plantations on Caribbean islands, Indians who were enslaved were often kept as local labor.

The best-known defender of the Indians was a priest and friar named Bartolomé de Las Casas. He settled in Hispaniola in 1502 and later became a missionary to the Indians. He dedicated his life to protecting them from mistreatment by the settlers. Las Casas won the admiration of King Ferdinand of Spain. In the decades that followed, the Spanish government passed laws protecting the Indians, but enforcement of these laws proved difficult.

READING CHECK **Summarizing** What impact did Spanish colonization have on Native Americans?

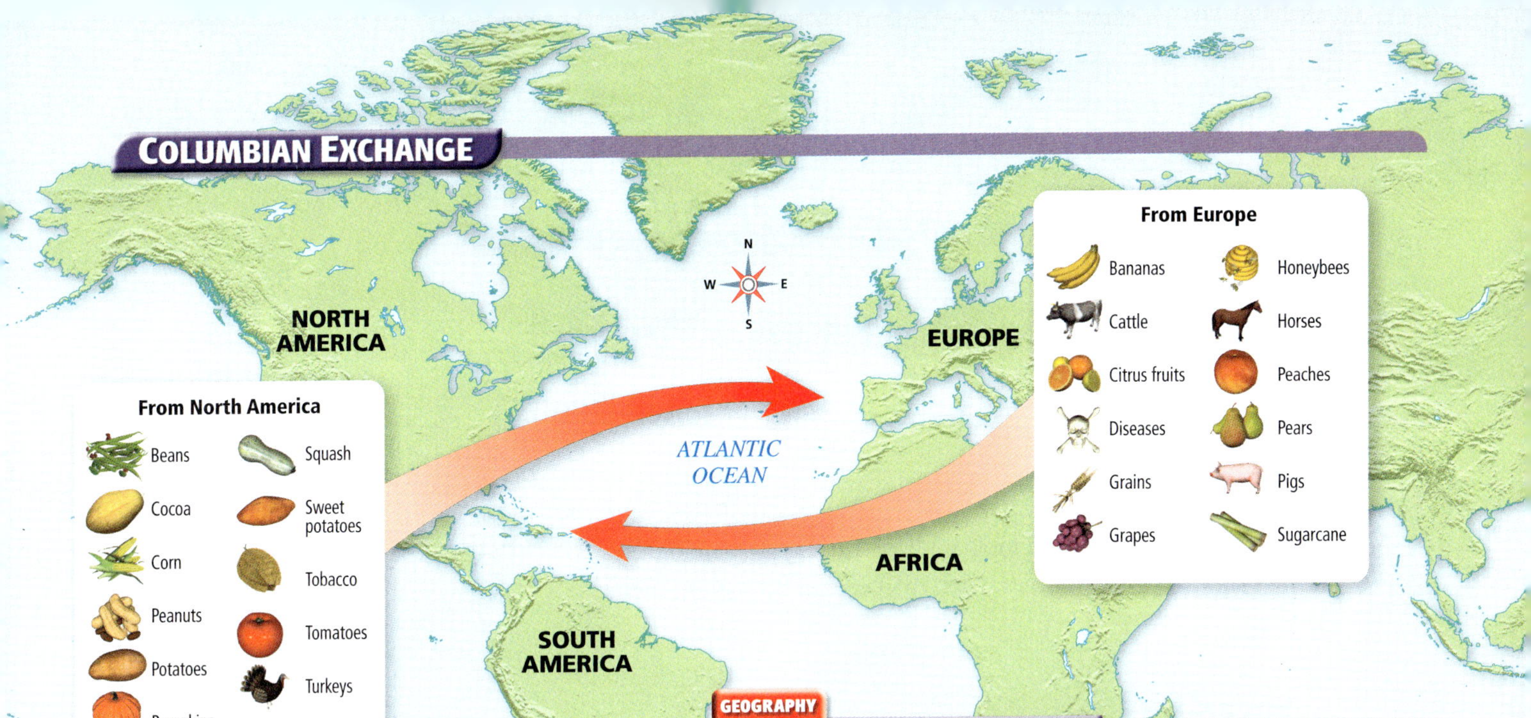

COLUMBIAN EXCHANGE

NORTH AMERICA

From North America

- Beans
- Cocoa
- Corn
- Peanuts
- Potatoes
- Pumpkins
- Squash
- Sweet potatoes
- Tobacco
- Tomatoes
- Turkeys

EUROPE

ATLANTIC OCEAN

AFRICA

SOUTH AMERICA

From Europe

- Bananas
- Cattle
- Citrus fruits
- Diseases
- Grains
- Grapes
- Honeybees
- Horses
- Peaches
- Pears
- Pigs
- Sugarcane

GEOGRAPHY SKILLS **INTERPRETING MAPS**

The Columbian Exchange affected cultures on both sides of the Atlantic.

1. **Regions** What kinds of items were exchanged?
2. **Movement** How do you think these items came to be exchanged?

See **Skills Handbook**, p. H19

The Columbian Exchange

Interaction between Europeans and Native Americans—and eventually Africans—led to the exchange of plants, animals, languages, and technology. Deadly germs were exchanged, too, bringing new epidemics to the Americas. Because all these transfers came about after Columbus's voyages, they are known as the Columbian Exchange (see map above).

Many crops that Native Americans grew were unfamiliar in Europe. Europeans took home corn, beans, squash, tomatoes, cacao (chocolate), peanuts, and other foods when they returned from their voyages.

European explorers and settlers brought certain foods of their own to the Americas, too. Domestic animals and new technology also crossed from Europe to the Americas. Europeans brought horses, which later became central to Plains Indian culture. Indians also learned about guns from Europeans.

The Columbian Exchange had some tragic consequences as well. Native Americans had no resistance to European diseases. Thousands died of smallpox and measles.

READING CHECK **Identifying Cause and Effect** Identify one effect of the Columbian Exchange.

SECTION 5 ASSESSMENT

go.hrw.com
Online Quiz
Keyword: SD7 HP1

Reviewing Ideas, Terms, and People

1. **a. Identify** Who was **Leif Eriksson**?
   b. Explain Why didn't the **Vikings** stay in North America?
2. **a. Recall** How did **Columbus** plan to reach the Indies?
   b. Make Inferences What qualities do you suppose Columbus had?
3. **a. Recall** Where did Columbus first establish colonies?
   b. Predict How do you think the Caribbean Indians viewed Europeans?
4. **a. Define** What is meant by the term **Columbian Exchange**?
   b. Evaluate How was the Columbian Exchange both beneficial and harmful?

Critical Thinking

5. **Identifying Cause and Effect** Copy the chart below and show the factors that contributed to the enslavement of the Indians in the Caribbean.

Enslavement of Indians

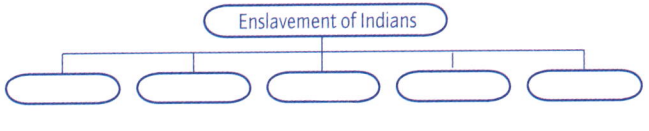

FOCUS ON WRITING

6. **Descriptive** Write a letter to a friend in Europe in the 1500s describing the fruits and vegetables you are sending from the Americas and how they can be used.

Migration throughout the World

Historical Context The documents below provide information on early migration throughout the world.

Task Examine the documents and answer the questions that follow. Then you will be asked to write an essay about why people migrated, using facts from the documents and from the chapter to support the position you take in your thesis statement.

ST 4.3 Develop hypotheses about important events, eras, or issues; move from chronicling to explaining historical events and issues; use information collected from diverse sources to produce cogently written reports and document-based essays.

DOCUMENT 1

Many different groups have been inspired to migrate in order to spread their religious beliefs. After the founding of Islam, Arab Muslims traveled far beyond their original homeland in Southwest Asia to spread their faith. They were particularly successful in Africa, where the faith spread to key kingdoms of northern and eastern Africa, helping to solidify the Islamic Empire. This image shows one of the earliest mosques built in Africa.

DOCUMENT 2

Most scientists believe that the earliest Americans came to this continent from Asia. In all likelihood, the early migrants were looking for food. Clovis spear points like the one shown here are among the oldest artifacts found on the North American continent. They are often found in places where the earliest Americans killed woolly mammoth. This Clovis point was discovered in New Mexico and has been dated at 11,500 BC.

The Age of Exploration was pushed in part by the desire of European nations to build their own empires. In the following letter from 1497, an Italian priest writes to the duke of Milan to report on John Cabot's trip to America and the effects it might have on England's economic power. At the time, many European leaders still thought the Americas were part of Asia. Although Cabot's exploration did not yield great riches, it did lay the foundation for later English migration to the Americas.

"[H]is Majesty [England's King Henry VII] has gained a great part of Asia without a stroke of the sword . . . And they say that the land is fertile and temperate, and think that the red wood grows there, and the silks, and they affirm that there the sea is full of fish that can be taken not only with nets, but with fishing-baskets, a stone being placed in the basket to sink it in the water . . .

[Cabot and] his partners say that they can bring so many fish that this kingdom will have no more business with Iceland, and that from that country there will be a very great trade in the fish which they call stock-fish . . . [H]e thinks of going, after this place is occupied, along the coast farther toward the east . . . where he believes all the spices of the world grow, and where there are also gems . . .

And in the spring he says that his Majesty will arm some ships, and will give him all the criminals, so that he may go to this country and plant a colony there. And in this way he hopes to make London a greater place for spices than Alexandria."

For the next 100 years many more explorers and migrants came to the Americas, often at great risk to themselves. The majority of these early migrants died prematurely, but they helped lay the foundation for more stable settlements. In 1604 French explorer Samuel de Champlain, who established a successful North American fur trade for his home country, commented on the many personal motivations he observed behind exploration and migration.

"The inclinations [motives] of men differ according to their varied dispositions [personalities]; and each one in his calling has his particular end in view. Some aim at gain, some at glory, some at the public weal [good]. The greater number are engaged in trade, and especially that which is transacted on the sea."

Skills FOCUS   READING LIKE A HISTORIAN

1. **a. Identify** Refer to Document 1. Why did Arabs build mosques in Africa?
   b. Interpret Why might someone leave their home to spread a religious faith?

2. **a. Identify** Refer to Document 2. How old is the artifact shown in this photograph?
   b. Analyze How did need for food influence migration?

3. **a. Identify** Refer to Document 3. Where did the writer think Cabot had explored?
   b. Infer Why would a country seeking to build wealth send criminals to their colonies?

4. **a. Identify** According to Champlain, what was the main personal motive of most migrants?
   b. Elaborate What do you think Champlain's personal motives probably were? Explain.

5. **Document-Based Essay Question** Consider the question below and form a thesis statement. Using examples from Documents 1, 2, 3, and 4, create an outline and write a short essay supporting your position.
   What motivated early world explorers to migrate to other continents?

See **Skills Handbook**, pp. H28–H29, H30

Visual Summary: The World Before 1600

Early Native American Cultures

- Scientists disagree on when and how the first Americans arrived.
- One theory is that the first Americans crossed a land bridge from Asia to America.
- Early Mesoamerican cultures include Olmec, Maya, and Aztec.
- Early North American cultures include Hohokam, Anasazi, Adena, Hopewell, and Mississippian.

North American Cultures in the 1400s

- Native Americans in North America establish diverse cultures based on geography.
- Some North American cultures share characteristics, including social structure, religious beliefs, and technology.
- Trading networks allow North American groups to share goods and ideas.

Africa

- Major kingdoms include Ghana, Mali, Songhai, Benin, and Kongo.
- Portuguese traders arrive in Africa in 1400s.
- European slave trade begins in late 1400s.

Europe

- Magna Carta establishes basic principles of government in 1215.
- The Renaissance begins around 1300.
- The Age of Exploration begins in the late 1400s.
- Christopher Columbus voyages to the Caribbean in 1492.
- The Reformation begins in 1517.

Reviewing Key Terms and People

Match each lettered definition with the correct numbered item below.

a. Exchange of goods without using money

b. People who move from place to place with the seasons

c. Group of people related by kinship

d. Change from hunting and gathering to farming

e. German monk who challenged the Catholic church and started the Protestant Reformation

f. Scandinavian sea raiders and explorers

g. Leader of the expedition to the Americas that included the flagship *Santa Maria*

h. The process of going to and settling in a place

i. A movement to change the Catholic church

j. Document that established several important principles of government

1. Martin Luther
2. colonization
3. Vikings
4. Reformation
5. Christopher Columbus
6. nomads
7. Magna Carta
8. agricultural revolution
9. barter
10. clan

Comprehension and Critical Thinking

SECTION 1 *(pp. 6–10)*

11. a. **Recall** How did the first people arrive in North America?

    b. **Analyze** What were the main effects of the agricultural revolution?

History's Impact video program
Review the video to answer the closing question: How has American history been shaped by people of different cultures and traditions?

SECTION 2 *(pp. 11–17)*

12. a. Define Write a brief definition of *shaman*.

b. Contrast What were the main differences between Native American religious beliefs and European religious beliefs?

c. Predict How could Native Americans' view of land ownership work in favor of Europeans when Europeans established colonies in the Americas?

SECTION 3 *(pp. 18–22)*

13. a. Identify What two valuable resources were instrumental in the development of West African trading empires?

b. Make Inferences Why were people along the African coast more heavily influenced by foreign religions, while people in the interior generally kept their traditional religions?

c. Evaluate Do you think trade with Europe ultimately helped or hurt Africa? Why?

SECTION 4 *(pp. 23–28)*

14. a. Recall What were the Crusades?

b. Explain In what ways was the Renaissance a rebirth for Europe?

c. Rank Of feudalism, the Crusades, the Reformation, and the Renaissance, which do you think had the biggest impact on European exploration?

SECTION 5 *(pp. 29–33)*

15. a. Describe Describe Columbus's career as an explorer and governor.

b. Explain How did the actions of the Spaniards cause the La Navidad colony to fail?

c. Evaluate Who do you think benefited most from the Columbian Exchange, Native Americans or Europeans? Why?

Using the Internet

go.hrw.com
Practice Online
Keyword: SD7 CH1

16. The lives and living conditions of Native Americans changed greatly after the arrival of Europeans. Using the keyword above, do research to learn about Native Americans in the United States today. Choose a group that you read about in this chapter. Then create an outline of a report that presents this information.

Analyzing Primary Sources

Reading Like a Historian This is part of Columbus's description of encountering the Tainos.

> ❝I gave them a thousand good, pleasing things which I had brought, in order that they might be fond of us, and furthermore might be made Christians and be inclined to the love and service of their Highnesses and of the whole Castilian [Spanish] nation and try to help us and to give us of the things which they have in abundance and which are necessary to us.❞
>
> —Columbus's Letter on his First Voyage

17. Identify Who was Columbus referring to when he wrote "their Highnesses"?

18. Draw Conclusions What were Columbus's goals in giving the Tainos "pleasing things"?

Critical Reading

Read the passage in Section 4 that begins with the heading "The Middle Ages." Then answer the following question.

19. According to the passage, the leading institution in medieval Europe was

A. the military.

B. the nation-state.

C. the Catholic Church.

D. the nobility.

FOCUS ON WRITING

Narrative Writing *Narrative writing tells a story. It uses precise detail and often describes events in sequential order. To practice narrative writing, complete the assignment below.*

Writing Topic: How Europeans viewed Native Americans

20. Assignment Imagine that you are a European explorer who has landed in North or South America. Based on what you have read in this chapter, write a paragraph describing your first encounter with Native Americans, your reactions to these people, and your thoughts about further contact.

European Colonies in America

THE BIG PICTURE Following Columbus's voyages, European nations competed to establish colonies in the Americas. By 1733 England, France, and Spain had founded extensive and diverse colonies. These settlements had disastrous consequences, however, for Native Americans.

New York Standards

Key Idea 1 The study of New York State and United States history requires an analysis of the development of American culture, its diversity and multicultural context, and the ways people are unified by many values, practices, and traditions.

Key Idea 3 Study about the major social, political, economic, cultural, and religious developments in New York State and United States history involves learning about the important roles and contributions of individuals and groups.

Skills FOCUS **READING LIKE A HISTORIAN**

Together, European colonists and Native Americans take part in a traditional harvest meal. Artist Jennie Brownscombe painted this symbolic interpretation of *The First Thanksgiving* in 1914.
Interpreting Visuals Describe the positive and negative relationship between Europeans and Native Americans shown in this painting.

See **Skills Handbook**, p. H30

1500

1513
Ponce de León begins exploring Florida.

1521
Cortés conquers the Aztecs in Mexico.

1530–1536
Pizarro defeats the Incas in Peru.

History's Impact video program

Watch the video to understand the impact of religious freedom.

1607
Jamestown colonists arrive in Virginia.

1620
Pilgrims settle in Plymouth.

1680
Pueblo Revolt begins in New Mexico.

1733
Georgia, the last of the original 13 British colonies, is founded.

1550 **1600** **1650** **1700** **1750**

1588
England's navy defeats the Spanish Armada.

1685
Huguenots are denied freedom of worship in France.

1713
Queen Anne's War ends. England takes parts of present-day eastern Canada from France.

European Settlements in North America

BEFORE YOU READ

MAIN IDEA

In the 1500s and 1600s, European nations, led by Spain, continued to explore, claim territory, and build settlements in America.

READING FOCUS

1. Which Spanish conquistadors explored North America, and what were they seeking?
2. How did Spain build an empire?
3. What other nations explored North America?

KEY TERMS AND PEOPLE

Treaty of Tordesillas
conquistador
Juan Ponce de León
Hernán Cortés
Francisco Vásquez de Coronado
missionary
Sir Francis Drake
Peter Minuit

PI 3.2 Research and analyze the major themes and developments in New York State and United States history (e.g., colonization and settlement; Revolution and New National Period; immigration; expansion and reform era; Civil War and Reconstruction; the American labor movement; Great Depression; World Wars; contemporary United States).

SPAIN or PORTUGAL?

◄ At Tordesillas in 1494, Spain and Portugal divided the world for exploration.

THE INSIDE STORY

How did two European sea powers carve up the Americas?

In 1493 Queen Isabella of Spain came to the pope with a problem. Columbus had just returned from his successful first voyage, and the queen wanted to move quickly to secure Spain's claim to the Americas. Spain's chief rivals, the skilled navigators of Portugal, were eager to seize land in the New World, as were other European powers. The queen wanted the Roman Catholic Church's stamp of approval on her claims before others rushed in.

Pope Alexander VI, a Spaniard himself, was happy to help. He drew an imaginary north-south line of demarcation from pole to pole in the Atlantic Ocean. Spain would control all the lands west of the line that did not have a Christian ruler. Portugal got the lands to the east.

At the time, of course, the ocean was a great mystery. Europeans did not know what lands might lie within it and across it. They did not know that Columbus had stumbled upon two giant continents. So the pope drew his line in the water, dividing the ocean's unknown lands between the two Catholic countries in the hope of keeping the peace.

King John II of Portugal protested. The line was so far east that it gave Portuguese navigators little room even to explore Africa. So in 1494, Spanish and Portuguese diplomats met at Tordesillas, Spain, and signed a treaty moving the line more than 800 miles west.

The **Treaty of Tordesillas** (tawr-day-SEE-yahs) gave Spain the best deal by far. The treaty did give Portugal a claim to Brazil, but Spain got the rest of the Americas. Not surprisingly, England, France, and Holland did not accept this division of the world. European explorers also found that other people—Native Americans—already held a claim to the Americas.

Spanish Conquistadors

A wave of Spanish exploration in the Americas followed the Treaty of Tordesillas. Because Columbus had landed in the Caribbean, the Caribbean islands became Spain's base for exploration in the early 1500s.

The Spanish explorers of the 1500s were called **conquistadors** (kahn-KEES-tuh-dawrz), from the Spanish for "conquerors." They traveled to lands an ocean away for "God, gold, and glory"—in other words, to spread Christianity, find wealth, and win fame. Just as the Portuguese had led the way in finding the sea route to India, Spanish conquistadors pioneered the exploration of the "New World."

Ponce de León and Florida
Juan Ponce de León (wahn pahn-suh-day-lee-OHN) was a Caribbean settler who had sailed with Columbus in 1493. He explored the island of Puerto Rico and became its governor. In 1513 Ponce de León left Puerto Rico, searching not only for gold but also for a "fountain of youth." According to legend, this miraculous fountain was on an island called Bimini.

On Easter Sunday 1513, Ponce de León landed on a lush, green coast. He claimed the area for Spain, naming it "La Florida"—from *Pascua Florida,* the Spanish term for the Easter celebration. It was the first time Spanish explorers had touched mainland North America.

Cortés and the Aztec
The search for gold led the conquistadors to the great Native American empires you read about earlier. In 1519 **Hernán Cortés** (ayr-NAHN cawr-TEZ) and his soldiers landed on the Gulf Coast of Mexico. Their goal was to conquer the Aztec Empire.

Remembering ancient legends, the Aztecs thought that the invaders might be messengers from the gods. Cortés took advantage of this belief as well as the resentment of peoples the Aztecs had conquered. The Spaniards marched across Mexico, gathering allies. One of Cortés's most valuable helpers was Malinche, an Aztec woman who served as his interpreter.

Moctezuma, the Aztec ruler, sent gifts of gold to welcome the Spanish. Other Aztec nobles saw the danger and tried to resist. But in 1521, after a long, violent siege, the Aztec capital, Tenochtitlán, fell to the Spanish.

The Spanish in America

Conquistadors appeared large and frightening mounted on horseback. Horses, native to Europe, had never been seen before in the Americas.

War dogs were another terrifying Spanish weapon.

Conquistadors traveled to America in the 1500s. Bringing horses and guns from Spain, they conquered huge Native American empires.

The fall of the Aztec Empire devastated Mexican peoples and their culture. Many Aztecs died, and their cities were destroyed. The conquest also brought other changes, including a new language, Spanish, and a new religion, Christianity. Some aspects of the native Mexican cultures remained, but many ancient ways disappeared forever.

Tales of golden cities

Cortés's success in conquering the Aztecs inspired other quests for gold in North America. In 1527 a Spanish expedition of about 400 men landed near present-day Tampa, on the west coast of Florida. A series of misfortunes eventually reduced the expedition to just four known survivors. They included the treasurer of the expedition, Álvar Núñez Cabeza de Vaca. From the present-day Texas coast near Galveston, they traversed the continent, probably reaching present-day New Mexico and Arizona. They arrived at the Pacific coast of Mexico in 1536.

Cabeza de Vaca and his men told their stories to Spaniards when they reached Mexico. Some historians infer that their tales gave rise to the legend of the Seven Golden Cities of Cíbola, cities rich in gold. Later explorers in the Southwest looked for these cities in vain.

Other Spanish explorers

Several later expeditions went in search of the Seven Golden Cities. Hernando de Soto landed in Florida in 1539 and traveled through the Southeast as far north as the present-day Carolinas and Tennessee. De Soto then headed west and became the first European to see the Mississippi River. Crossing the river, he reached present-day Arkansas. In 1542 he died of a fever, and his men buried him in the Mississippi River.

Other expeditions probed the American Southwest. In search of the Seven Cities, **Francisco Vásquez de Coronado** set out in 1540. He conquered some Pueblo peoples but found no gold. His group then split up. One of Coronado's men became the first European to see the Grand Canyon. Others explored present-day Arizona, New Mexico, Texas, Oklahoma, and Kansas.

Expeditions also set out by sea from Mexico. From 1542 to 1543, Juan Rodríguez Cabrillo (cuh-BREE-oh) sailed north, exploring the coast of California. He sailed into what are now San Diego and Monterey bays, visited the Channel Islands, and spent the winter there.

The Spanish quests for gold came up empty. After finding no gold in the American Southwest, Spain then turned to mining in Mexico.

The nation's oldest city

Although Ponce de León had landed in Florida in 1513, he had not established permanent settlements there. Years later, in 1565, the conquistador Pedro Menendez de Avilés founded St. Augustine in Florida. St. Augustine was strategically placed to defend the treasure that Spanish fleets were bringing to Spain. Today it is the oldest city in the United States.

READING CHECK Identifying the Main Idea
What were the main goals of Spanish explorers?

Spain Builds an Empire

While the conquistadors were exploring North America, the government of Spain was beginning to establish colonial governments. To govern the vast areas of land they claimed, Spain set up viceroyalties. A viceroyalty was a province ruled by a representative of the monarch. The viceroyalty of New Spain included much of the American Southwest and present-day Mexico, along with Florida, Central America, part of Venezuela, and some Caribbean islands.

Social structure

The Spanish conquest of the Americas caused a new social structure to emerge. Those who came from Spain, known as *peninsulares*, considered themselves superior to the *creoles*. Creoles were people born in the Americas of pure Spanish descent. Many Spanish settlers married local Native American women, and their mixed families were known as mestizos. Lower on the social scale were people of mixed Spanish and African descent, pure-blooded Indians, and Africans.

A key element of the Spanish American social structure were the <mark>missionaries</mark>, church members who teach and convert others to a religion. Spain sent Roman Catholic missionaries to establish missions—large plantations centered around a church—along the California coast and throughout the Southwest. There priests taught Christianity to Native Americans along with European farming, herding, and crafts. Many Native Americans came to the missions—or were forced to come—to live and work for the priests.

EUROPEAN EXPLORATION OF AMERICAS, 1492–1682

GREENLAND

ICELAND

HUDSON 1610–11

ENGLAND

Hudson Bay

LA SALLE 1679–1682

CHAMPLAIN 1613–1615

HUDSON 1609

NORTH AMERICA

CABOT 1497

JOLIET & MARQUETTE 1672–1673

CARTIER 1534–35

EUROPE

FRANCE

CORONADO 1540–1542

DESOTO 1539–1542

ATLANTIC OCEAN

SPAIN

VERRAZZANO 1524

CABRILLO 1542–1543

PONCE DE LÉON 1512–1513

AFRICA

COLUMBUS 1492

20°N

CORTÉS 1519

Gulf of Mexico

COLUMBUS 1493–1496

CABEZA DE VACA 1528–1536

COLUMBUS 1502–1503

Caribbean Sea

COLUMBUS 1498

PIZARRO 1530–1533

BALBOA 1513

VESPUCCI 1499–1500

MAGELLAN 1519

0° Equator

SOUTH AMERICA

PACIFIC OCEAN

N
W · E
S

20°S

MAGELLAN 1521

The Treaty of Tordesillas divided the New World, giving any lands west of the line to Spain and east of the line to Portugal.

40°S

➤	Spanish
➤	Columbus
➤	French
➤	English
➤	Dutch

0   500   1,000 Miles
0   500   1,000 Kilometers
Miller projection

40°W   20°W   0°

60°S

go.hrw.com
Interactive Map
Keyword: SD7 CH2

GEOGRAPHY SKILLS INTERPRETING MAPS

1. **Region** Which French explorers investigated the interior?

2. **Movement** Why was Hudson searching for a Northwest Passage? Do you think he could have found one?

3. **Movement** Which country launched the most expeditions?

See **Skills Handbook**, p. H19

120°W   100°W   80°W   60°W

Land and labor At first, Spanish colonists tried to use Native Americans as laborers. Under Spain's *encomienda* system, landowners received grants from the king, which gave them the right to control the people of a certain area. The word *encomienda* comes from the Spanish word for "entrust." Under the encomienda system, the king expected the landowners to convert the Native Americans to Christianity and teach them European ways. The Native Americans, for their part, were to work as laborers.

Officially, Native Americans were to be treated humanely. In reality, many were enslaved and worked to death on huge estates called *haciendas*. As Native American populations declined from disease and ill treatment, landowners came to depend upon the labor of enslaved Africans. Indians and Africans also were forced to work in the silver mines that came to dominate New Spain's economy.

The Pueblo Revolt In 1598 the king of Spain sent Juan de Oñate (wahn day oh-NYAH-tay) to settle New Mexico, which Coronado had abandoned a half-century before. Oñate founded the first Spanish settlements in New Mexico. Missionary work was a major part of these settlements. The Spanish missionaries wanted to replace the native religions with Christianity.

In 1680 the Pueblo Indians revolted against the Spanish missionary system. A shaman named **Popé** (poh-PAY) led the revolt, encouraging other Pueblos to rebel and take back their traditional ways of life. Many villagers joined the Pueblos.

The Pueblo Revolt began in August 1680 with an attack on Santa Fe, the Spanish capital, in what is now New Mexico. After a 10-day siege, the Spanish settlers fled the city. Popé then tried to restore traditional ways and wipe out every trace of Spanish culture.

Pueblo control of Santa Fe did not last. In 1692 Spanish soldiers retook the area. Pueblo culture, however, remained strong.

READING CHECK **Identifying Cause and Effect** What effects did Spanish conquest and colonization have on Native Americans?

Other Nations Explore

Spain soon faced competition from other European explorers in North America. England's King Henry VII sent out his country's first voyage of exploration in 1497. The captain was John Cabot, an Italian navigator. Cabot crossed the Atlantic and landed in Newfoundland. Like Columbus, Cabot thought he had reached Asia. He claimed the land for England.

By the early 1500s England had come to realize that North America was a separate continent. In 1508 Cabot's son Sebastian launched a

A Powerful Queen

Under the rule of "Good Queen Bess"—Elizabeth I—England developed a strong navy. Elizabeth I gave her sea captains unofficial permission to raid rival ships and ports. *What does this painting of the queen attempt to convey about her reign and her character? Refer to details in the painting.*

voyage looking for a Northwest Passage, a short-cut water route to the Pacific Ocean. A route through North America remained the goal of many later explorers because it would create a shorter sea route to Asia.

England's navy England did not act on Cabot's North American claim until the reign of Queen Elizabeth I (1558–1603). Elizabeth built England into a sea power. Her daring ship captains attacked Spanish ships to steal their gold and silver.

The most famous of these naval captains was **Sir Francis Drake.** In 1577 he circumnavigated the globe, plundering Spanish ships and towns on the Pacific coast of South America along the way.

During this time, religious conflicts between Catholic Spain and Protestant England erupted in war. In 1588 the Spanish king sent a fleet of ships, the Spanish Armada, to invade England. Bad weather and England's superior navy defeated the supposedly invincible Armada. The defeat of the Spanish Armada opened the Atlantic Ocean and North America to English colonizing expeditions.

New France France also joined the colonial rivalry in North America. In 1524 the French king sent Giovanni da Verrazano to explore the Atlantic coast. He explored from the present-day Carolinas as far north as Maine.

Ten years later, an explorer named Jacques Cartier (CAHR-tyay) discovered the St. Lawrence River and claimed the land that is now Quebec. On his second voyage, Cartier sailed up the river to an island he named Montréal.

Like so many explorers before them, the French hoped to find gold. Instead, they found that New France was rich in other resources: fish and furs. In 1608 Samuel de Champlain (sham-PLAYN) founded a fur trading post at Quebec, France's first permanent settlement in the New World.

In 1666 a French noble, the Sieur de la Salle, emigrated to become a fur trader. He explored the Great Lakes region and followed the Mississippi Valley to its mouth. He claimed the territory for France, naming it Louisiana after France's king, Louis XIV.

New Netherland The Netherlands, though a small country, had a large fleet of merchant ships that traded in Africa and Asia. After it declared independence from Spain, the Netherlands sought to explore North America.

In 1609 the Dutch sent English explorer Henry Hudson to look for a Northwest Passage. What he actually found is now called the Hudson River. The Dutch claimed territory along the Atlantic coast and founded the colony of New Netherland. In 1626 **Peter Minuit** was named the colony's director general and purchased Manhattan Island from a group of Native Americans.

**FOCUS ON
NEW YORK**

ECONOMICS
In 1626 Peter Minuit purchased Manhattan Island from Native Americans in exchange for goods valued at 60 guilders, or about $200 in today's money. Settlement began later that year in the area Minuit named New Amsterdam. Manhattan held strategic value for the Dutch, who fortified the southern tip of the island to defend their fur trade operations in the Hudson River.

READING CHECK **Identifying the Main Idea** How did other nations challenge Spain's claim to North America?

SECTION 1 ASSESSMENT

go.hrw.com
Online Quiz
Keyword: SD7 HP2

Reviewing Ideas, Terms, and People

1. a. Identify What was the **Treaty of Tordesillas**?
   b. Contrast In what ways did the expeditions of **Ponce de León** and **Cortés** differ?
   c. Predict How might the **conquistadors'** exploration and conquest of the Americas affect the future of the region?

2. a. Recall What was the Pueblo Revolt?
   b. Making Inferences What differing reactions do you think Native Americans had to the encomienda system and to the Spanish **missionaries**?

3. a. Recall What other European nations explored North America after Spain began its explorations?
   b. Analyze What issue made England and Spain become enemies, and what happened as a result?

Critical Thinking

4. Sequencing Copy the chart below and make a time line of major explorations after Columbus.

Hudson claims Dutch lands on Atlantic coast.

FOCUS ON SPEAKING

5. Expository Assume the role of a sea captain who must appear before a European monarch to ask the king or queen to sponsor an expedition to the Americas. Write out the petition you would make at court. Include an explanation of how the monarch will benefit from your voyage.

The English in Virginia

BEFORE YOU READ

MAIN IDEA

After several failures, the English established a permanent settlement at Jamestown, Virginia.

READING FOCUS

1. Why were the first English colonies established?
2. What helped the Jamestown colony survive?
3. How did Virginia grow and change during the 1600s?

KEY TERMS AND PEOPLE

joint-stock company
John Smith
Powhatan
Pocahontas
John Rolfe
headright
House of Burgesses
indentured servant
Bacon's Rebellion

PI 3.3 Prepare essays and oral reports about the important social, political, economic, scientific, technological, and cultural developments, issues, and events from New York State and United States history.

The Lost Colony of Roanoke

THE INSIDE STORY

What happened to the colonists of Roanoke Island? Sir Walter Raleigh was an adventurer, a poet, and a favorite of Queen Elizabeth at court. With her permission, he sent several expeditions to the Atlantic coast of North America. He named the entire region Virginia—after Elizabeth, known as the "virgin queen."

Early attempts at settlement failed, but in 1587 Raleigh sent out a new expedition of soldiers and more than 100 settlers, mostly families. The group's governor, John White, wanted to create a self-sufficient colony. They settled on Roanoke Island, a three-mile-wide strip of land off present-day North Carolina, and became friendly with Manteo, leader of the local Croatoan Indians. Soon after the colonists landed on Roanoke, White's granddaughter Virginia Dare was born. She was the first English child born in North America.

The English settlers had landed too late in the season to plant crops, so White headed back to England for supplies. What happened next is one of the great mysteries in American history.

England was at war with Spain, so White had to wait three long years before obtaining a ship to return to Roanoke. In August 1590 he and his men approached Roanoke Island. They saw a light in the darkness and rowed toward it, blowing a trumpet and singing English songs to let the settlers know they were friends. There was no answer.

In the morning they landed and found the village in ruins, overgrown with trees and shrubs. The only clue White found was the word *Croatoan* carved on a post. The settlers

▲ John White puzzles over the only clue to the fate of his lost colony.

had buried chests full of pictures, books, maps, and other goods. These chests now lay strewn about, destroyed.

White hoped to find the settlers, including his family, on nearby Croatoan Island, but bad weather forced him away. No trace of the lost colony was ever found.

People have tried to solve the mystery of Roanoke Island ever since. Perhaps the settlers sought refuge with local Indians, or were killed by Indians. Maybe they were wiped out by a violent storm or severe drought. But so far, no one knows the true fate of the lost colony of Roanoke. ◼

The First English Colonies

Despite the tragedy on Roanoke, England continued to seek a permanent foothold in America. English settlers wanted to come to the New World for many reasons. With economic problems at home, they yearned for new opportunities. Many English farm workers were unemployed, and small farmers were struggling. In the wealthy class, large plots of land had been divided among heirs for generation after generation, until land became scarce. Some young men who did not inherit land sought new adventures in America.

King James's charter Sir Walter Raleigh never returned to North America after Roanoke was destroyed, although he still had faith that England could colonize North America. His charter rights were transferred to the London Company, a group of English merchants. Another group, the Plymouth Company, was interested in charter rights farther north.

In 1606 King James I issued a charter that divided America between the two groups. The Plymouth Company and the London Company were joint-stock companies, business entities in which investors pooled their money hoping to make a profit. The companies were responsible for governing and maintaining their colonies. In return, the investors got most of the colony's profit.

READING CHECK **Making Inferences** What did English settlers hope to gain by going to America?

The Jamestown Colony

Establishing a colony and outfitting an expedition was an expensive and risky venture. Several people, including Raleigh, tried and failed. Most could not afford to try again. The colonists at Jamestown, the first English colony to survive, went through many difficult years.

The first settlers Late in 1606 the London Company sent three ships and 144 male colonists to Virginia. About 100 survived the crossing. In 1607 they sailed some 60 miles up the broad James River and built the Jamestown colony. The settlers named both the colony and the river after King James. One of the leaders was Captain **John Smith**, a young explorer.

Soon it became clear that Jamestown's location was a problem. It was a low, swampy area filled with malaria-carrying mosquitoes. Moreover, Jamestown was inside the territory of the powerful Powhatan Confederacy, a group of Algonquian (al-GAWN-kwee-en) peoples named for their leader, **Powhatan**.

Jamestown faced other difficulties, too. Some settlers died of malaria or dysentery from drinking unsafe water. Others became too weak to work. In addition, some of the settlers spent more time looking for treasure than growing food. Many of the adventurers were English gentlemen who were not used to physical labor. By January 1608, when more English colonists arrived, only 38 of the original settlers were alive.

Captain John Smith John Smith had become an important member of the colony. He helped trade for food with Indians, built houses, and explored the area. During one of his explorations, he later wrote, he had been captured by some Powhatans. As they were about to kill him, Smith said, Powhatan's young daughter **Pocahontas** begged her father to save him. Later, Pocahontas helped keep peace between the settlers and the Powhatans.

Smith became leader of Jamestown in 1608 and tried to impose military discipline on the colony. He laid down the law:

HISTORY'S VOICES

❝You must obey this now for a Law, that he that will not worke shall not eate (except by sickness he be disabled) for the labours of thirtie or fortie honest and industrious men shall not be consumed to maintaine an hundred and fiftie idle loyterers.❞

—John Smith, *Generall Historie of Virginia, New England, & the Summer Isles*

Smith also organized raids to steal food from the local Native Americans. The colonists got through the winter with only a few deaths, but Smith was burned in an accident with gunpowder and had to return to England.

The starving time The London Company, now called the Virginia Company, was determined to make Jamestown profitable. It sold stock to new settlers, offering free ship passage to those who would work for the company for seven years. More settlers set out in 1609—in time for one of Jamestown's worst periods.

A Foothold in the New World

English settlers founded Jamestown about 60 miles up the James River, out of view of Spanish ships. The fort shown in this 1607 drawing helped protect colonists from the Powhatan Indians.

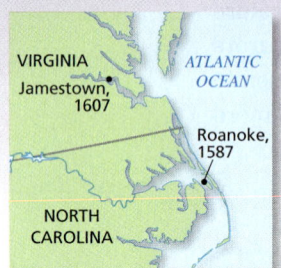

The settlers called the winter of 1609–1610 the "starving time." The Powhatan Indians, resentful of earlier raids, killed the colonists' livestock and prevented them from hunting. Many English colonists in Jamestown died that winter.

THE IMPACT TODAY

Economics

Facing declining tobacco use and increased foreign competition, modern farmers in tobacco-growing states such as Virginia, North Carolina, and Kentucky are reducing their dependence on tobacco by switching to alternative crops, from hot peppers to blueberries, with the help of federal grants.

Growing tobacco One crop finally made Jamestown and the Virginia colony profitable: tobacco. Tobacco was a native plant grown in North America and the islands of the West Indies. It was important in Native American ceremonies throughout the continent.

The first English settler to grow tobacco in Virginia was **John Rolfe**. Rolfe conducted experiments with tobacco to find out the best way to grow and cure the leafy plants, helping to make it profitable to ship the crop to England.

In 1613 while Pocahontas was being held captive by colonial officials, Rolfe proposed marriage. Pocahontas converted to Christianity, changed her name to Rebecca, and the two married. Their marriage finally secured peace between the settlers and the Powhatans.

The Virginia Company thought that the charming Pocahontas would be a good advertisement for Virginia. In 1616 she and Rolfe sailed to England, where she met the king and was welcomed in English society.

Conflicts with Native Americans By 1622, relations between the settlers and the Powhatan Confederacy had worsened. Both Pocahontas and Powhatan were dead. English farmers were taking over more and more land to grow tobacco, their profitable new crop.

In an effort to protect Indian lands, the Powhatans launched a surprise attack on Jamestown in the spring of 1622. Many settlers were killed, including John Rolfe. Continued conflict kept the colony from turning a profit, which led the king to end the Virginia Company's charter.

Still, the settlement struggled on. Attacks persisted for the next 20 years. The last Powhatan attack came in 1644. By then the Virginia settlers were strong enough to resist them.

READING CHECK **Drawing Conclusions**
What was wrong with the location of Jamestown?

Virginia Grows and Changes

During its 15-year existence, the Virginia Company struggled to attract settlers and turn a profit. But persistent problems, including near-bankruptcy and perceived mismanagement, persuaded England finally to revoke the charter and make Virginia a royal colony.

The headright system Starting in 1618, the Virginia Company offered **headrights**, 50-acre grants of land that colonists could obtain in various ways. The head of a family received one headright for each family member and servant he had. People who paid the passage to America for another person—a new servant, for example—got an additional headright.

The Virginia Company brought in skilled artisans to help the colonial economy grow. Since most early settlers were men, the company also sent about 100 women who agreed to marry the colonists. That would make society more stable.

Soon Virginia began to thrive again. By the 1640s Virginia had a non-native population of about 8,000. Between 1640 and 1650 that number doubled.

The House of Burgesses

Since the Middle Ages, English people had been proud of the political rights they had gained from Magna Carta. The first charter of Virginia promised settlers the same basic English rights. Now the Virginia Company acted on that promise.

In July 1619, representatives from the various communities in Virginia met in an assembly called the **House of Burgesses** (BUHR-juhs-ez). Membership in the House of Burgesses was granted only to white male landowners. The group had the power to raise taxes and make laws, but the governor still had the right to veto those laws.

This system was much more restrictive than the representative government we know today. Yet the House of Burgesses was significant because it was America's first legislature, or lawmaking body.

Colonial workers

The majority of workers in Virginia were **indentured servants**. Employers hired indentured servants to work under contract for a certain number of years, usually four to seven. The employer, in return, would pay for food, shelter, and, most importantly, the worker's journey to America. When a servant's term of indenture expired, he or she was supposed to be given a suit of clothes as well as tools or land.

Soon indentured servants and former servants were a large part of the Virginia population. Many former indentured servants became successful farmers or artisans. But

many others found themselves without a job or a good future. They were a restless group of unemployed men, moving from place to place in search of work.

About one-fourth of the indentured servants in the Chesapeake Bay region were young women. Most worked as household servants. Because men greatly outnumbered women in the colony, most women married soon after their indentures were over.

In August 1619, a Dutch ship landed at Jamestown. John Rolfe noted that it carried about 20 Africans. At first, Africans generally were regarded as indentured servants. In time, their situation changed to permanent servitude as Africans and their descendants became trapped in the institution of slavery.

By the late 1600s, the number of indentured servants was decreasing. Employers saw many advantages to using slave labor instead of indentured servants. Slaves who had been kidnapped from Africa, for example, could never go back home. Nor did the employers have to pay enslaved Africans as they had paid indentured servants. If slaves escaped, they could not blend into the white population.

Conflicts among settlers

As Virginians moved westward, clashes with Native Americans continued. Conflicts among the colonists themselves also occurred.

Increasingly, settlers on the frontier had different interests from the large landholders

FACES OF HISTORY

POWHATAN

1550?–1618

When the first English colonists arrived in Virginia, Chief Powhatan ruled the Powhatan federation of Indians. Chief Powhatan controlled the territory from Jamestown to the Potomac River.

Powhatan did not welcome the English settlers. His followers led several small-scale raids on the fort and in 1608 captured Captain John Smith. Smith described Powhatan as "a tall well proportioned man." Chief Powhatan eventually let Smith return to Jamestown, and over time, relations with the colonists improved. Chief Powhatan even let his sons and his daughter, Pocahontas, visit the English settlement to trade goods.

Summarizing How did Powhatan deal with the English settlers?

Bacon's Rebellion

The rebellion led by farmer Nathaniel Bacon threatened the power of Virginia's colonial government. Virginian Robert Beverley later wrote about the incident and its causes.

"Four things may be reckoned to have been the main ingredients towards this intestine commotion [violent outbreak]. First, The extreme low price of tobacco, and the ill usage of the planters in the exchange of goods for it, which the country, with all their earnest endeavors, could not remedy. Secondly, The splitting the colony into proprieties, contrary to the original charters; and the extravagant taxes they were [charged]. Thirdly, The heavy restraints and burdens laid upon their trade by act of Parliament in England. Fourthly, The disturbance given by the Indians."

Skills FOCUS   READING LIKE A HISTORIAN

1. **Drawing Conclusions** According to Beverley, what role did economics play in the rebellion?
2. **Identifying Points of View** Based on this excerpt, do you think Beverley was sympathetic to the farmers' cause? Explain your answer.

See **Skills Handbook**, pp. H28–H29

in the eastern tidewater region of Virginia—and from their royal government. Virginia's governor, Sir William Berkeley, wanted good relations with Native Americans on the frontier in order to protect his fur trade with them. Settlers, however, wanted to expand westward into land reserved for the Indians.

In the end, Berkeley's actions led to an uprising. Nathaniel Bacon was a well-to-do tobacco planter on the frontier. After his slave overseer was killed in an Indian attack in 1676, Bacon formed a small army and launched what became known as **Bacon's Rebellion**. Although Bacon was an aristocrat himself, his "army" was mostly former indentured servants.

Governor Berkeley declared Bacon a rebel. Bacon's army then attacked Jamestown and took control, apparently with popular support. In back-and-forth fighting, the town was burned. Berkeley fled. Then Bacon suddenly became ill and died. His rebellion collapsed.

Nevertheless, Bacon's Rebellion had lasting effects. The House of Burgesses opened more frontier land to settlers. In addition, landowners began to rely on slave labor, fearing uprisings from freed indentured servants.

READING CHECK **Summarizing** What were some key developments in the Virginia colony during the 1600s?

SECTION 2 ASSESSMENT

go.hrw.com
Online Quiz
Keyword: SD7 HP2

Reviewing Ideas, Terms, and People

1. **a. Identify** What was Sir Walter Raleigh's role in the colonization of Virginia?
   b. Explain What happened to the lost colony at Roanoke?

2. **a. Identify** What roles did **John Smith**, **Powhatan**, and **Pocahontas** have in the development of the Virginia colony?
   b. Summarize What factors led to hardships for the English settlers at Jamestown?
   c. Evaluate Why was it so difficult for settlers to establish a successful colony?

3. **a. Recall** What did the Virginia Company do to attract settlers to America?
   b. Explain How did the system of indentured servitude affect the population of Virginia?
   c. Predict Why was the establishment of the **House of Burgesses** important?

Critical Thinking

4. **Identifying Cause and Effect** Copy the chart below and show the aftereffects of Bacon's Rebellion.

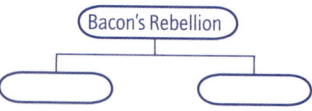

FOCUS ON WRITING

5. **Persuasive** Write a newspaper editorial for a Virginia newspaper in which you argue for or against the opening of more lands in western Virginia for the growth of new English settlements.

The Northern Colonies

BEFORE YOU READ

MAIN IDEA

The Pilgrims founded colonies in Massachusetts based on Puritan religious ideals, while dissent led to the founding of other New England colonies.

READING FOCUS

1. Why did the Puritans flee England?
2. How did dissent among the Puritans threaten the New England colonies?
3. What was life like in New England?

KEY TERMS AND PEOPLE

Mayflower Compact
Puritans
William Bradford
John Winthrop
Great Migration
Roger Williams
Anne Hutchinson
royal colony
Pequot War
King Philip's War

PI **1.2** Describe the evolution of American democratic values and beliefs as expressed in the Declaration of Independence, the New York State Constitution, the United States Constitution, the Bill of Rights, and other important historical documents.

THE INSIDE STORY

How will the new colony be ruled? The passengers could scarcely wait to get off their ship and begin building their new homes on solid land in America. First, though, they had important business to conduct.

For two long months in 1620 the *Mayflower* had pitched its way across the stormy Atlantic Ocean. The ship carried English Christians who were looking for a place where they could worship as they pleased. Others on the ship simply wanted a new way of life. They would need to cooperate in order to survive in the wilderness.

The adventurers had landed too far north—at the tip of present-day Cape Cod, Massachusetts. The *Mayflower* settlers realized they were out of the jurisdiction of their Virginia charter or of any authority they knew. But they believed in the rule of law. They believed that the colony needed a government structure.

So, even before they landed, they established rules to keep order in the new settlement. On November 11, 1620, the 41 men signed the **Mayflower Compact**. Promising allegiance to England's King James, they agreed to make "just and equal laws . . . for the general Good of the Colony."

The compact was remarkable in a couple of ways. The settlers agreed to be ruled by a government chosen by the consent of the people. They agreed to obey all laws made for the good of the whole group.

Today we take these ideas for granted. Yet at a time when authority rested with kings and queens, the Mayflower Compact was a historic step toward self-government. ◼

The Mayflower Compact

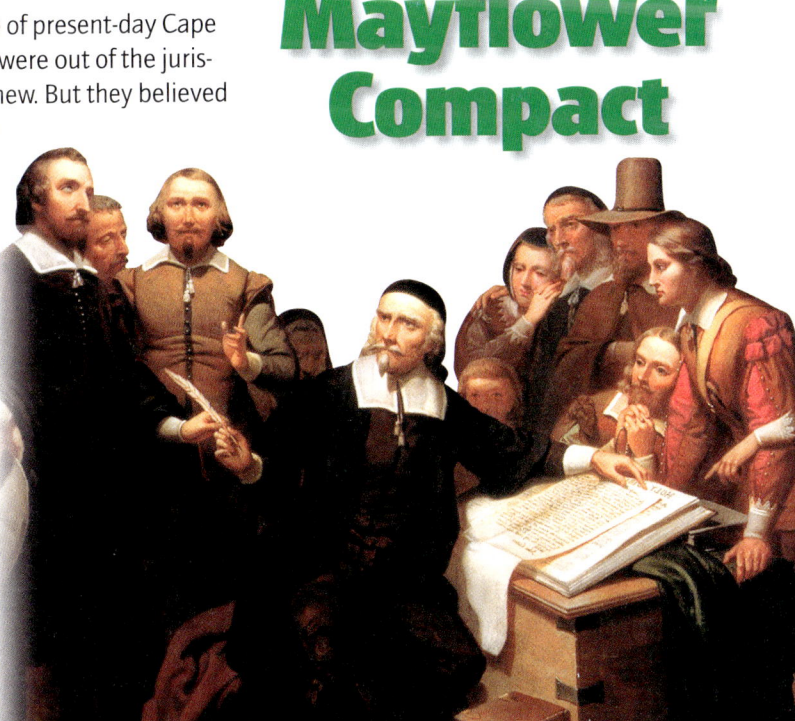

▶ **The Mayflower Compact united the Pilgrims in "a civil Body Politick."**

Puritans Flee to Freedom

The Protestant Reformation eventually led to the establishment of the Church of England, also known as the Anglican Church. The English monarch served as head of this new government-sponsored church.

The new form of worship had some elements of Roman Catholicism. Queen Elizabeth I introduced more Protestant ideas from groups such as the Calvinists. That did not satisfy some Protestants, however.

Puritans and Separatists

Some English Protestants wanted to "purify" the church by making further reforms. These people were known as **Puritans**. For example, they wanted a simpler church service. They also objected to the wealth and power of bishops.

Other, more strict Puritans wished to remove all traces of Catholicism from their religious practice. The Separatists, as these people were called, wanted a total separation from the Church of England.

The Church of England, however, was the official church of the land. English subjects were required to attend services and pay taxes to support the church. Those who wanted to worship in another way were often persecuted for their beliefs. These dissenters were fined or put in prison.

Founding Plymouth Colony

One group of Separatists moved to the Netherlands in 1608. Dutch society was well known for its religious tolerance. After a few years, though, the English were ready to leave. Earning a living was hard. Their children were becoming more Dutch than English. Moreover, war with Spain seemed near. The Separatists decided to move to America.

A group of merchants formed a joint-stock company to support Puritans moving to the New World. Each colonist had a share in the company. A Virginia Company charter granted them land in North America to settle. After seven years, land and profits would be divided among the colonists and the other investors.

In the end, however, only half of the Pilgrims from the Netherlands were on the small ship *Mayflower* when it set sail in September 1620. These 35 people referred to themselves as "saints." **William Bradford** headed the group. The voyagers included 66 others, many of

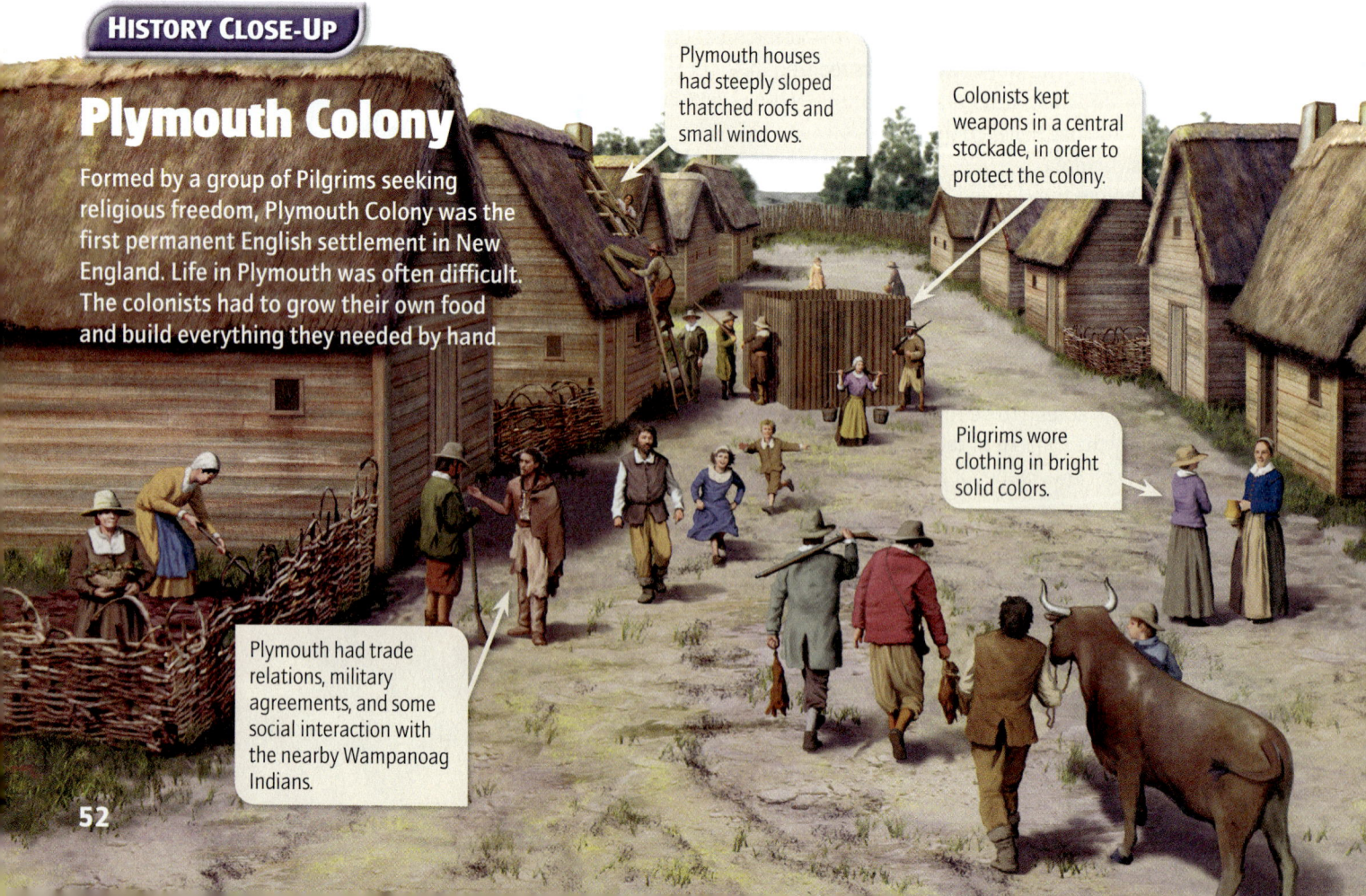

HISTORY CLOSE-UP

Plymouth Colony

Formed by a group of Pilgrims seeking religious freedom, Plymouth Colony was the first permanent English settlement in New England. Life in Plymouth was often difficult. The colonists had to grow their own food and build everything they needed by hand.

Plymouth houses had steeply sloped thatched roofs and small windows.

Colonists kept weapons in a central stockade, in order to protect the colony.

Pilgrims wore clothing in bright solid colors.

Plymouth had trade relations, military agreements, and some social interaction with the nearby Wampanoag Indians.

whom were not Separatists. The "saints" called them strangers. Bradford later wrote about the departure from the Netherlands:

HISTORY'S VOICES

❝So they left that goodly and pleasant city which had been their resting place nearly twelve years; but they knew they were pilgrims, and looked not much on those things, but lift up their eyes to the heavens . . . and quieted their spirits.❞

—William Bradford, *Of Plymouth Plantation*

Their sponsor, the Virginia Company, had intended the expedition to land near the Hudson River. Instead, because of a storm or poor navigation, the ship had landed at Cape Cod, where they signed the Mayflower Compact. After exploring the area for several weeks, the expedition founded Plymouth Colony on a sheltered harbor just south of present-day Boston.

Winter took a toll. By the spring of 1621, about half the group had died of hunger, cold, or illness. The rest survived with the aid of the local Wampanoag (wahm-puh-NO-ahg) Indians.

The next year life improved. The first corn harvest was so successful that the Pilgrims held a harvest feast with their Wampanoag neighbors, which we now commemorate as

Skills FOCUS INTERPRETING INFOGRAPHICS

Making Inferences What does this picture tell you about life in Plymouth Colony?

See **Skills Handbook**, p. H18

Women baked bread in outdoor ovens.

Thanksgiving Day. Bradford was chosen governor of Plymouth in 1621. He led the colony until just before his death in 1657.

Plymouth Colony never grew very large, but it remained self-governing until 1691. Then it became part of the Massachusetts Bay Colony.

"A City upon a hill" The success of the Plymouth settlement, combined with continued religious persecution and economic hard times, encouraged thousands of other Puritans to move to "New England." Some Puritan merchants managed to get a charter from the king and organize the Massachusetts Bay Company. Its chief goals were to make a profit and to create a refuge for Puritans.

The company bought out the other investors and chose **John Winthrop** to lead the new colony. Winthrop took charge of a fleet of 11 ships and some 700 people that set out for New England in 1630. Most were families planning to make a new home. Aboard the *Arbella,* Winthrop put forth his vision of the colony as a model for the world:

HISTORY'S VOICES

❝For we must consider that we shall be as a City upon a hill. The eyes of all people are upon us.❞

—John Winthrop, *A Model of Christian Charity*

The Massachusetts Bay Colony grew faster than Plymouth. Puritan colonists soon established other towns nearby. The colony's capital was the port city of Boston. Other early towns included Salem, Watertown, and Concord.

The Massachusetts Bay Colony charter included some provisions for colonial government. It created a Massachusetts General Court, which had the ability to elect officers and make laws. Eventually, this court turned into a kind of self-government, although only male members of the court could vote or hold office. Each town elected representatives to the court. The members of the court in turn elected a council, headed by Winthrop, which held all legislative, judicial, and executive power.

The success of the Plymouth and Massachusetts Bay colonies inspired what is called the **Great Migration**. Between 1620 and 1643 some 20,000 English men and women crossed the Atlantic Ocean to settle in New England.

READING CHECK **Comparing** How were the Plymouth and Massachusetts Bay colonies founded?

ACADEMIC
VOCABULARY

fundamental
original, essential
radical relating to
extreme change

Dissent Among the Puritans

The Puritans came to America to find religious freedom for their form of worship, which they believed to be the true and pure religion. Their community, ways of life, and laws were deeply rooted in their religious beliefs. As in England, citizens were expected to attend church and pay taxes to support it. They obeyed strict codes of behavior, dress, and speech. Hard work and little or no play was generally the rule—and in America, they had the freedom to make their own rules and live by them.

In the Massachusetts Bay Colony, church and government were closely linked and dissent was not permitted. In time, dissenters left the colony and settled new towns in other parts of New England.

Connecticut and Rhode Island Thomas Hooker, a powerful Puritan minister, believed that "in matters which concern the common good," a government "chosen by all" was best. His differences with Winthrop's government finally led Hooker and his congregation to leave the colony. They headed west and settled in the fertile Connecticut River Valley. In 1639 the group adopted America's first written constitution: the <u>Fundamental</u> Orders of Connecticut. The document extended voting rights to all free men, not just church members.

Roger Williams was a man of strong convictions who clashed with authorities in Boston. A <u>radical</u> Separatist minister, he believed in religious tolerance. He believed that church and government matters should be separate. Williams also was a friend to the Narragansett Indians and thought that settlers should buy land, not take it. He purchased land from the Narragansetts and established a settlement he called Providence, in what is now Rhode Island. Government and church were separate, and people of all faiths, including Jews, were welcome.

Anne Hutchinson caused an even bigger uproar. She believed that people did not need a minister's teaching in order to be spiritual. Challenged by the Massachusetts governor, Hutchinson declared:

HISTORY'S VOICES

❝Now if you do condemn me for speaking what in my conscience I know to be truth, I must commit myself into the Lord.❞

—Trial of Anne Hutchinson, 1637

COUNTERPOINTS

Separation of Church and State

Roger Williams's belief that the government had no right to interfere in religious matters was considered radical and even dangerous in his day.

❝ [M]agistrates, as magistrates, have no power of setting up the form of church government, electing church officers, [or] punishing with church censures . . . And on the other side, the churches as churches, have no power . . . of erecting or altering forms of civil government, electing of civil officers, [or] inflicting civil punishments. ❞

Roger Williams, 1644

To John Winthrop, the colony of Massachusetts and its government were inseparable from the religious beliefs of its people.

❝ We must be knit together in this work, as one man. . . For we must consider that we shall be as a City upon a hill. The eyes of all people are upon us. . . [I]f we shall deal falsely with our God in this work we have undertaken, . . . we shall be made a story and a byword throughout the world. ❞

John Winthrop, 1630

Skills
FOCUS **READING LIKE A HISTORIAN**

Analyzing Primary Sources Why does Winthrop believe the colonists' religion should guide their decisions as they build the colony?

See **Skills Handbook**, pp. H28–29

Hutchinson was imprisoned, tried, and banished from Massachusetts Bay Colony. She and her husband, Will, and other Massachusetts leaders migrated to Rhode Island.

Anne Hutchinson's brother-in-law, a minister, left Massachusetts in 1638 to start a settlement in what is now New Hampshire. In 1679 New Hampshire became a **royal colony,** under direct control of the king. It was the last of the New England colonies to be created. Maine remained part of Massachusetts until 1820.

Witchcraft trials in Salem
In 1692 a series of bizarre events brought a crisis to the Massachusetts colony. It started in Salem Village, where several girls exhibited strange behaviors and claimed to have been bewitched. Belief in witches was common in the 1600s.

The girls accused several women of witchcraft, including respected church members and a West Indian servant. After some forced confessions, hysteria gripped the town. Wild rumors and hearsay led to the arrest of hundreds of people in the colony. Nineteen people were executed, and others died in jail. Then as quickly as it came, the witch scare passed. The witch trials were condemned, and the remaining prisoners were freed.

READING CHECK **Summarizing** What colonies were founded by Puritan dissenters?

Life in New England

The Puritan colonies set high ideals for themselves. Those ideals shaped their daily lives, their governments, and their school systems.

Education and public schools
The American public school system began in the New England colonies. Puritans wanted their children to read well enough to understand the Bible and to have skill in a trade or craft.

In the 1640s the Massachusetts General Court passed several education laws. One gave town officials, called selectmen, the right to ensure that children and apprentices got a proper education. Other laws required towns to set up elementary and grammar schools.

Most children learned reading, writing, and some arithmetic in a "dame school," taught by a woman in her home. Often that was the only education a girl received. Boys had opportunities for

Anne Hutchinson set sail for America in 1634 with her family, settling in the Massachusetts Bay Colony. A smart and kind leader in her community, Hutchinson decided to hold informal meetings in her home, where she and her visitors discussed their faith.

In these meetings Hutchinson contradicted church leaders by stating her belief that grace was all that was needed for salvation. Church leaders branded her a heretic and banned her from the colony. Hutchinson, her family, and a number of her followers established a new colony in what would become Rhode Island. Eventually, Hutchinson and most of her family died in a conflict with Native Americans.

Drawing Conclusions Why was Anne Hutchinson banned from the Massachusetts Bay Colony?

further schooling. By the early 1700s, boys could attend two New England colleges: Harvard in Massachusetts and Yale in Connecticut.

Colonial government
England's colonies began with differing political arrangements. Some colonies were owned by individuals, others by joint-stock companies. During the late 1600s and early 1700s most became royal colonies under the direct rule of the English king.

The town was the center of life in the New England colonies. Typically, a town was built around a central grassy area called the common. The meeting house and schoolhouse faced the common, and cattle grazed there.

Town government was the most relevant to people's daily lives. They met in a town meeting to elect selectmen, choose delegates to the colonial assembly, set taxes, and deal with local problems such as roads. The town meeting was the closest thing to democracy in the colonies. Voting was limited to church members and property owners.

Relations with Native Americans
The more the English settlements expanded, the more they came into conflict with Native Americans. Relations at first had been friendly. A Patuxet Indian named Squanto had helped the Plymouth colonists survive, for example.

By the mid-1600s, the colonists were less dependent on the Indians. Fishing, trade, and

Government
Many towns in New England have kept their town-meeting government to this day. In old town halls, set on colonial town commons, selectmen (and women) meet to make local laws and hear issues brought by citizens.

NORTHERN COLONIES

Northern colonies

0   25   50 Miles
0   25   50 Kilometers
Albers equal-area projection

Penobscot River

MAINE
(part of Massachusetts Colony)

Lake Champlain

NEW HAMPSHIRE

Portsmouth, 1623

Salem, 1626

Boston, 1630

MASSACHUSETTS

Plymouth, 1620

Providence, 1636

Hartford, 1636

CONNECTICUT

RHODE ISLAND

New Haven, 1638

Hudson River

Connecticut River

ATLANTIC OCEAN

70°W

GEOGRAPHY SKILLS   INTERPRETING MAPS

About 93,000 colonists lived in the northern colonies by 1700.

1. **Human-Environment Interaction** Why do you think Hartford was built near a river?

2. **Location** Which colony was established first?

See **Skills Handbook**, p. H20

shipbuilding were becoming more important than the fur trade. At the same time, the Native Americans now had guns. As settlers took more land for farms and scattered the wild game, the Native Americans began to resist.

Puritan attitudes changed, too. Some still wanted to convert the Native Americans to Christianity and teach them English ways. The missionary John Eliot translated the Bible into Algonquian. But others decided that Indians were heathens and that it was their religious duty to drive them out or kill them.

In 1637 conflicts erupted in the Connecticut River Valley over land and over the Pequot Indians' trade with the Dutch. The **Pequot War** ended with a brutal massacre. Some 90 colonists, with their Narragansett and Mohegan allies, attacked a Pequot fort. They set it on fire, then killed all those who fled. The war nearly wiped out the Pequot people.

In 1675 Indians again resisted English settlers in **King Philip's War**. The Wampanoag leader Metacomet, known to the English as King Philip, led his people and others in attacks that destroyed colonial towns. In return, the colonists burned villages and crops.

The war was costly for both sides. Many settlers—perhaps 600—died in the fighting. Nearly all the Wampanoag and Narragansett Indians were killed, and their villages were destroyed. Survivors fled or were sold as slaves. The war left southern New England open to white settlers.

READING CHECK **Summarizing** How did New England colonists' relations with Native Americans change over time?

SECTION 3 ASSESSMENT

go.hrw.com
Online Quiz
Keyword: SD7 HP2

Reviewing Ideas, Terms, and People

1. **a. Describe** What was the **Mayflower Compact**?
   b. Summarize Why did the **Puritans** want to leave England?

2. **a. Identify** What did **Anne Hutchinson** and **Roger Williams** have in common?
   b. Analyze How did the treatment of dissenters both help and harm colonization in New England?

3. **a. Recall** What led to war between the New England colonists and the local Native Americans?
   b. Evaluate How did the Puritans' treatment of Native Americans conflict with their values?

Critical Thinking

4. **Identifying Cause and Effect** Copy the chart below and identify the reasons for the Great Migration.

Great Migration

FOCUS ON SPEAKING

5. **Persuasive** As a supporter of Roger Williams, write a speech urging Massachusetts Bay officials to buy rather than take land from Native Americans.

American Literature

ST 3.2 Draw upon literary selections, historical documents, and accounts to analyze the roles played by different individuals and groups during the major eras in New York State and United States history.

About the Reading Tituba, a slave from Barbados, was among the first people accused of witchcraft in Salem. In Ann Petry's 1964 novel, *Tituba of Salem Village*, the Reverend Parris threatens and beats Tituba until she confesses to being a witch.

AS YOU READ **Consider what could have prompted the witch scare.**

Excerpt from

Tituba of Salem Village

by Ann Petry

The Trial of George Jacobs *painted by Tompkins Matteson in 1855 shows the hysteria over witchcraft extending into the courtroom.*

I am doomed, Tituba thought. Even if the master were the kind who would risk his own life and his family's safety to protect his slave, even so he couldn't possibly save me from hanging. Anyone who saw me touch one of these girls in the middle of one of their fits, and saw them suddenly become well because I touched them, would believe me to be a witch.

"Now will you confess?" Parris asked between clenched teeth.

"What do you want me to say, master?"

"What is it you do to these children?"

"She bewitches us," Abigail said. "She and Goody Good and old Gammer Osburne. They were the first ones to come in the house after Goody Sibley baked the witch cake."

"Witch cake!" the master said, horror in his voice. "What devil's work is this?" He took hold of Abigail's arm. "What are you talking about?"

Abigail told him about the baking of the witch cake, how Goody Sibley and John had fed it to the dog, how the dog had yelped and run out of the house. Right after that, Tituba and Good and Gammer Osburne had entered the keeping room. All of them at the same time. "They were the witches, drawn to the house by the witch cake," she said primly.

"You did this in my house?" he asked scowling. "The black art was used—in my house? Why this is

going to the Devil for help against the Devil—"

Abigail, frightened, said, "We didn't know what else to do. There have been so many things, so many strange things—We didn't mean any harm." She wept piteously and ran out of the room.

"I'll have you hanged," the master shouted, glaring at Tituba, "and Good and Osburne along with you. When this story gets out, it will ruin me in the parish."

Skills FOCUS — READING LIKE A HISTORIAN

1. **Drawing Conclusions** Why was Reverend Parris angry at Tituba?

2. **Literature as Historical Evidence** How does this story illustrate the hysteria that took place in Salem?

See **Skills Handbook**, p. H32

Jamestown and Plymouth

The historical development of any community, sometimes its very survival, depends on its geography. Does it have access to important natural resources? Is there safe and convenient access to other communities? What is the climate like? Early English colonists to North America had these and other considerations in mind when they founded their colonies. But in a new land, there was much they didn't know. They would have to adapt to their new surroundings or die.

Near the Sea Plymouth and Jamestown were sited near the ocean for easy access to the ships that would carry trade goods to and from England.

Plymouth

ATLANTIC OCEAN

Jamestown

Jamestown

Jamestown was built 36 miles upriver from the ocean. This location protected it from storm waves and enemy warships.

Williamsburg (1698)

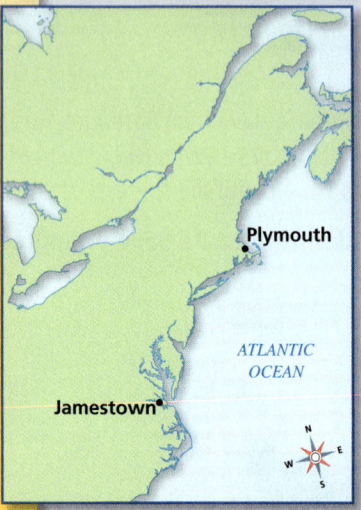

Tobacco Virginia's warm climate and moist, well-drained soil was well-suited for tobacco growing.

Mosquitos Nearby swamps were infested with mosquitoes, which carry malaria. An epidemic broke out just two months after the colonists arrived. Frequent outbreaks of malaria eventually led colonists to move their capital to Williamsburg.

Fields The colonists grew food for themselves and tobacco for export. From 1618 to 1623, the colony's population grew from 400 to 4500 because of the tobacco boom.

Jamestown (1607)

James River

Plymouth

Plymouth's site, on high ground in a protected harbor, was chosen after the Pilgrims spent months searching the shores of Cape Cod Bay.

New York Standards

ST 2.3 Examine the effects of immigration of various Native American groups.

ST 4.3 Develop hypotheses about important events, eras, or issues.

Coastal Farms In 1627, settlers were given farmland along the coast. As the population grew, settlers formed separate communities such as this one at Duxbury.

Indian Trail Plymouth's location near an Indian village proved vital. The Wampanoag Indians showed colonists how to grow crops adapted to the local environment, as well as where to trap beaver and catch fish. This helped the newcomers survive the first harsh winters.

INDIAN TRAIL

Plymouth Bay

Abandoned Indian Village

Plymouth Colony (1620)

Furs Plymouth's rocky, sandy soil meant that colonists could not grow enough crops for export. Instead, they supplied England with beaver fur for hatmaking.

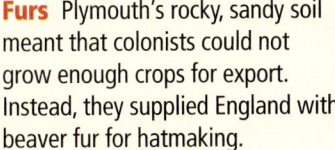

GEOGRAPHY SKILLS **INTERPRETING MAPS**

go.hrw.com
Practice Online
Keyword: SD7 CH2

1. **Location** What was important in deciding the location of a new colony?

2. **Human-Environment Interaction** How did each colony take advantage of its environment for trade?

See **Skills Handbook,** p.H20

The Middle and Southern Colonies

BEFORE YOU READ

MAIN IDEA

Events in England during and after the English Civil War led to a new wave of colonization along the Atlantic coast south of New England.

READING FOCUS

1. What brought about a new era of colonization in America?
2. Why were new southern colonies founded?
3. Why did the Quakers settle Pennsylvania?
4. Why was Maryland founded?

KEY TERMS AND PEOPLE

Quaker
William Penn
Restoration
proprietary colonies
Peter Stuyvesant
James Oglethorpe
Lord Baltimore
Toleration Act

P1 3.4 Understand the interrelationships between world events and developments in New York State and the United States (e.g., causes for immigration, economic opportunities, human rights abuses, and tyranny versus freedom).

William Penn's Quaker Colony

THE INSIDE STORY

Why did William Penn settle the colony of Pennsylvania? Imagine if the president and Congress each raised an army and began fighting each other. That's roughly what happened in England in the 1640s, when the armies of King Charles I clashed with the armies of Parliament in several years of civil war. Parliament's forces finally triumphed, and their strict Puritan leader, Oliver Cromwell, set up a new government. Cromwell's efforts to broadly reform government and society met with resistance, however, and after his death the monarchy was restored under King Charles II.

During the civil wars, Admiral William Penn the Elder at first supported Parliament but secretly switched sides, possibly giving ships and loans to help restore the monarchy. After the Restoration, the king knighted Admiral Penn. When Penn died in 1670, he was owed a substantial sum of money by King Charles.

Penn's son William had been a problem for his patriotic father. Inspired by a traveling preacher, the younger Penn had joined a new Christian sect known as the **Quakers**. A fervent Quaker, **William Penn** wrote dozens of books and pamphlets promoting his simple faith, social reform, and freedom of ideas. He boldly criticized power and wealth in society and in the English church. Like other Quakers, he was jailed for his beliefs.

Despite his clashes with English authorities, Penn was granted a large and valuable tract of land in North America, in payment for the debt owed to his father. Penn's land stretched across thickly forested hills west of the Delaware River. He named his new colony Pennsylvania, or "Penn's woods." It would be a refuge for Quakers and others suffering religious persecution.■

◄ **William Penn used pamphlets to attract settlers to his colony.**

A New Era of Colonization

During the English Civil War and the years of Oliver Cromwell's rule, little colonization occurred in America. With peace and stability came a new era of English colonization in the middle and southern part of the Atlantic coast of North America.

Charles II and the Restoration In 1660, two years after Cromwell died, a new Parliament invited the son of Charles I to become king. Charles II, "the merry monarch," rode into London, greeted by fireworks and dancing in the streets. His reign, from 1660 to 1685, is called the **Restoration** because it restored the English monarchy.

A new period of colonization began under Charles II. The king owed money and favors to those who had supported him during the civil war, including William Penn's father. What better way to repay those favors than to give gifts of land in America? Thus, the king established **proprietary colonies**, grants of land to loyal friends. The friends became Lords Proprietors of their colonies—that is, owners with executive powers. Four new proprietary colonies were established: New York, New Jersey, Carolina, and Pennsylvania. Unlike joint-stock companies, these new American colonies were governed not by investors or colonial legislatures but by their Lords Proprietors.

New Netherland becomes New York

One of Charles's first grants was to his brother James, the duke of York. It included the large swath of land between the Connecticut and Delaware rivers. The grant ignored the fact that the Dutch already claimed the area as New Netherland.

The town of New Amsterdam was a thriving settlement. Because of the Dutch colony's religious tolerance, some English settlers from New England, including Anne Hutchinson, had moved there.

Political tensions existed between England and the Netherlands, however. In addition, New Netherland had the <u>distinct</u> disadvantage of being located between English colonies in New England and those farther south. In 1664 an English fleet sailed into the harbor and demanded that New Netherland surrender.

Peter Stuyvesant, the unpopular governor of New Netherland, surrendered almost without a fight. The Dutch took the colony back briefly in 1673, but by 1674 New Netherland was firmly in English hands. James renamed it New York.

FOCUS ON NEW YORK
GOVERNMENT
Stuyvesant wanted to fight the British. He surrendered, however, when Dutch citizens, resentful of his sometimes heavy-handed rule, refused to join him. Stuyvesant spent the rest of his life in New York on his farm "the Bouwerie," from which New York City's neighborhood "the Bowery" takes its name.

TIME LINE

Upheaval Causes English to Journey West

1642
Monarchists battled the armies of Parliament in the English Civil War, which raged until 1651.

1653
After the English Civil War, Oliver Cromwell brought unpopular reforms but encouraged tolerance of Puritans.

1640 1650 1660

1660
After the Restoration of Charles II to the monarchy, English colonization expanded in America.

Skills FOCUS **INTERPRETING TIME LINES**

Upheaval delayed English colonization of America. *What events affected colonization by England?*
See **Skills Handbook**, p. H14

MIDDLE AND SOUTHERN COLONIES

Middle colonies
Southern colonies

0 50 100 Miles
0 50 100 Kilometers
Albers equal-area projection

Albany, 1624
NEW YORK
Hudson River
PENNSYLVANIA
New York, 1626
Philadelphia, 1682
NEW JERSEY
MARYLAND
Delaware River
DELAWARE
VIRGINIA
Chesapeake Bay
Richmond, 1645
Williamsburg, 1633
James River
Norfolk, 1682
ATLANTIC OCEAN
APPALACHIAN MOUNTAINS
NORTH CAROLINA
SOUTH CAROLINA
(separated from North Carolina in 1729)
Georgetown, 1665
GEORGIA
(founded in 1733)
Charles Town, 1670

N E S W

GEOGRAPHY SKILLS | **INTERPRETING MAPS**

By 1733 nine middle and southern colonies had been founded.

Location What geographic element formed the western border of the southern colonies?

See **Skills Handbook**, p. H20

New York was unusual in the diversity of its settlers. They included not only the English and Dutch but also Scandinavians, Germans, French, Native Americans, and enslaved Africans brought by the Dutch West India Company. James, a Roman Catholic, allowed religious tolerance.

At first New York did not have a representative assembly. That angered New Englanders who had settled on Long Island. Power was mainly in the hands of large land-owning families, both friends of James and the original Dutch "patroons," who had been given tracts of land in return for bringing settlers. Still, the colony grew and prospered under English rule. A treaty in 1684 made an alliance with the Iroquois, which protected the fur trade.

Soon after receiving his land, James gave a large tract of land south of the Hudson River to two proprietors. Sir George Carteret (cahr-tuh-RET) and Sir John Berkeley were his political allies. Carteret was from the Channel Island of Jersey and so named the new territory New Jersey. Over the next few years, arguments among settlers over rights and property occurred. Berkeley sold his portion of New Jersey to English Quakers, who settled the Delaware Valley. After continued disputes over land titles, the crown revoked the proprietors' charters. New York and New Jersey became royal colonies by the early 1700s.

READING CHECK **Summarizing** How did New York eventually become an English colony?

New Southern Colonies

Charles II gave large land grants to other friends and supporters. In charters issued in 1663 and 1665, eight men became the co-owners of Carolina. This land was part of the territory once claimed for Virginia, which stretched south to Spanish Florida. The name *Carolina* came from *Carolus*, the Latin form of *Charles*.

The Carolinas The new proprietors first gave themselves large estates. To attract settlers, they offered a representative assembly as well as religious toleration for all Christians. In that way, they hoped to draw settlers from other, less tolerant, colonies.

Settlement was slow, however, and some proprietors dropped out. One proprietor,

Anthony Ashley Cooper, persuaded others to pay to bring in boatloads of settlers. In 1670 they founded Charles Town (modern-day Charleston, South Carolina), the future capital of the colony.

The southern and northern parts of Carolina developed very differently. Southern Carolina had the port of Charles Town and the prosperous estates of aristocratic landowners. Large plantations grew up along the rivers. Rice and indigo were the major crops in Southern Carolina. They were shipped out of Charles Town along with other products.

Some plantation owners from the West Indies moved to the colony. They brought enslaved Africans with them. The colony's economy became dependent on slave labor.

By contrast, settlers in northern Carolina were mainly small farmers who did not import Africans as slaves. The region did not have a good harbor like the one at Charles Town.

In 1729 seven of the proprietors sold their interests in the land in the northern part of the colony to the Crown. The king then made North Carolina and South Carolina two separate royal colonies.

Georgia By the 1680s, English colonies lined most of the Atlantic coast south of New France. Colonists were moving steadily westward. The Spanish Empire held most of the Southeast and Southwest. Some English military experts wanted a military "buffer zone" between the Carolinas and Spanish Florida. That led to the establishment of Georgia, the last of the original 13 colonies.

The need for a buffer colony fit nicely with a plan being developed by an English general, **James Oglethorpe**. Oglethorpe was a humanitarian, a person who is interested in improving people's lives. As a member of the English Parliament, he had investigated the horrendous conditions in English prisons. He was especially concerned about honest people who were thrown in prison for being unable to pay their debts. Oglethorpe proposed starting a new colony for debtors to give them a new start in life.

In 1732 he and 20 other trustees received a charter for the Georgia colony from King George II. The next year, Oglethorpe arrived with a boatload of colonists and founded the city of Savannah, Georgia.

Unlike the founders of other colonies, the trustees of Georgia governed but did not own land or expect a profit. At first the trustees set out rigid rules for colonists regarding land ownership, slavery, and personal behavior. Eventually, those rules were relaxed. Slavery was legalized in 1751, the year before Georgia became a royal colony.

Georgia's early settlers included former debtors as well as impoverished craftspeople from Britain and religious refugees from Germany and Switzerland. The population grew, and by 1770 the colony had more than 20,000 people, nearly half of them enslaved Africans.

READING CHECK **Comparing and Contrasting** How were the colonies of Carolina and Georgia similar, and how were they different?

Quakers Settle Pennsylvania

As you have read, one of Charles II's land grants became the colony of Pennsylvania. Penn wanted the colony to be a haven for Quakers. From the king's <u>perspective</u>, it was a way to get rid of an unpopular group.

The Quakers Of all the various groups of Nonconformists—Protestants who did not follow the Church of England—the Quakers upset people the most. Officially called the Society of Friends, their name came from their founder, George Fox. He urged them to "tremble," or quake, "at the name of the Lord."

Quakers believed in direct, personal communication with God. They had no ministers and no hierarchy of priests and bishops, as in the Anglican and Roman Catholic churches. Instead of formal services with many rituals, Quakers held simple meetings in which members of the congregation rose to speak.

Quakers also believed in the equality of all men and women. That was a threat in a society with strict social classes based on wealth and power. Finally, they were pacifists who refused to fight in wars. For these beliefs, Quakers were jailed and persecuted in England. They were not entirely welcome in the existing American colonies, either, except in Rhode Island.

A tolerant colony Penn left for America in 1682 with a plan in mind for a "Holy Experiment" that would reflect his beliefs. He would

Technology

Since its construction in the early 1900s, the statue of William Penn atop Philadelphia's graceful City Hall remained the city's tallest structure. According to tradition, nothing could be taller. In 1987 the 548-foot limit was broken, as the first modern skyscraper rose above Penn.

Promoting Religious Tolerance

The Reformation in Europe triggered tense, sometimes violent conflicts among members of various Christian sects. The upheaval forced thousands of Europeans to flee their home countries. Many came to America and chose to settle in the Middle Colonies.

The Dutch were known for their religious tolerance, and Dutch settlers in New York and New Jersey continued this practice under English rule. Other settlers in these colonies included Lutherans from Sweden, Huguenots from France, and Jews from Portugal.

Pennsylvania, founded by Quakers on the principle of religious tolerance, attracted many groups, including Presbyterians, Amish, and Mennonites. In Delaware, the succession of Swedish, Dutch, and English rule, with their varying religions, promoted tolerance.

Today, the First Amendment guarantees freedom of religion. This tradition, begun in Rhode Island, was strengthened in the diverse Middle Colonies.

Making Comparisons How did changes in governing powers affect religious tolerance in the Middle Colonies?

A woman offers a religious testimony at this Quaker meeting from the mid-1600s.

build a new city, with spacious streets laid out in an orderly grid pattern. He called it Philadelphia, Greek for "City of Brotherly Love."

One enthusiastic Quaker settler, Gabriel Thomas, described how the city grew:

HISTORY'S VOICES

❝Since that time, the Industrious (nay Indefatigable) Inhabitants have built a Noble and Beautiful City, and called it Philadelphia, which contains about two thousand Houses, all Inhabited, and most of them Stately, and of Brick, generally three Stories high, after the Mode in London, and as many as several Families in each . . .❞

—*An Historical and Geographical Account of the Province and Country of Pennsylvania, in America* (1698)

Throughout the 1600s, while wars in Europe ruined farms and trade and religious clashes caused social upheaval, Penn advertised the colony widely. He offered opportunities and land at reasonable prices.

Members of small German Protestant sects such as the Amish and Mennonites were happy to find religious tolerance in Pennsylvania. The colony's rich farmlands attracted thousands of other Germans. Their numbers soon reached about 100,000, roughly one third of Pennsylvania's population.

After a 1685 law ended religious tolerance in France, some 15,000 French Protestants, called Huguenots, fled to America. Many of

these skilled and well-educated people settled in Philadelphia and other colonial cities.

Like Roger Williams in Rhode Island, Penn recognized the Native Americans' right to the land. In 1682 he made an agreement with the Delawares, who sold him land as a way of protecting themselves against the Iroquois.

While Pennsylvania grew and prospered, some people were unhappy with Penn's one-man rule. In 1701, before returning to England, Penn granted a Charter of Liberties, which set up a representative assembly.

Delaware In 1638 a small colony of Swedes settled near what is now the city of Wilmington, Delaware. Swedish rule was brief. In 1655 the Dutch took New Sweden. The colony was later seized by England.

When William Penn received his original land grant in America, he was informed that it lacked access to the Atlantic Ocean. So in 1682 he persuaded the duke of York to make him proprietor of an area along the Delaware River and bay, which would later become the colony of Delaware. Control of these waterways would provide a major trade route for ships going in and out of the port of Pennsylvania.

READING CHECK **Identifying Cause and Effect** What events in Europe encouraged immigration to Pennsylvania?

The Founding of Maryland

The founding of the Church of England as the nation's official church made life difficult for many Roman Catholics in England. Although they were a small minority, English Catholics included some influential families. When George Calvert, the first **Lord Baltimore**, converted to Catholicism, thereby ending his political career, he sought land in America, as a haven for Catholics and for personal wealth.

In the 1620s Calvert founded a settlement in modern-day Newfoundland, Canada, but found it too cold. He traveled to Jamestown but was banned because of his religion. He then asked King Charles I for land near the broad Chesapeake Bay. He died before it was granted, but in 1632, his son Cecilius Calvert, also Lord Baltimore, received the rights. His new colony was named Maryland, perhaps for Queen Henrietta Maria or for the biblical Virgin Mary.

In fact, Maryland attracted many more Protestant settlers than Catholic ones, and clashes between the groups were common. As a result, in 1649 the colonial assembly passed the **Toleration Act**. It protected the right of all Christians to practice their religion.

READING CHECK **Making Inferences** What made English Catholics want to immigrate to America?

THE ENGLISH COLONIES IN AMERICA

QUICK FACTS

Joint-stock colonies were established by groups of investors hoping to make a profit.	Virginia (settled 1607) Plymouth Colony (settled 1620)
Self-governing colonies were run independently of the king or of any joint-stock company.	Massachusetts Bay Colony (settled 1630) Rhode Island (settled 1636) Connecticut (settled 1635; Hooker 1636)
Proprietary colonies were founded by private individuals, or Lord Proprietors, who were granted the power to make and execute laws.	Maine* (settled 1623) New Hampshire (settled 1623) New York (settled 1624; English 1664) New Jersey (settled 1624; charter 1664) Maryland (charter 1632) Pennsylvania (settled 1682) Delaware (English 1664; to Penn 1682) Carolinas (charters 1663–65; divided 1712) Georgia (charter 1732) *Part of Massachusetts 1691–1820
Royal colonies were under the direct control of the king of England, who appointed a governor over the colony.	The following later became royal colonies: Virginia (1624) New Hampshire (1679) New York (1685) Massachusetts (1691) New Jersey (1702) South Carolina (1721) North Carolina (1729) Georgia (1752)

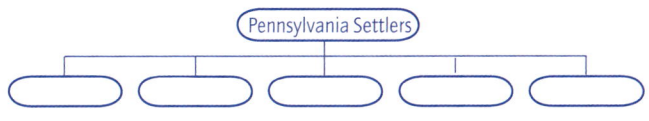

SECTION 4 ASSESSMENT

go.hrw.com
Online Quiz
Keyword: SD7 HP2

Reviewing Ideas, Terms, and People

1. a. Identify What events helped revive English colonization of America?
b. Analyze What effect did Charles II have on settlement patterns in the region south of New England?
c. Evaluate In giving proprietary colonies to his supporters, what assumptions did Charles II make about the land?

2. a. Describe What two reasons did **James Oglethorpe** have for founding the Georgia colony?
b. Compare How did the economies in the northern and southern parts of Carolina differ?

3. a. Recall Who were the **Quaker** people, and why were they persecuted in England?
b. Make Generalizations In what ways was Pennsylvania unique among the colonies?
c. Rate How important were location and natural resources in Pennsylvania's development? Explain.

4. a. Identify Who was **Lord Baltimore**?
b. Make Inferences Why do you suppose Catholics wanted to leave England after the founding of the Church of England?
c. Rate How did Maryland's **Toleration Act** compare with the practice of religious tolerance in Pennsylvania?

Critical Thinking

5. Identifying Supporting Details Copy the chart below and identify the groups of colonists in Pennsylvania.

Pennsylvania Settlers

FOCUS ON WRITING

6. Persuasive Write an advertisement that will persuade new settlers to move to your colony.

Representations of Pocahontas

Historical Context The documents below provide different artistic perspectives on the historical figure of Pocahontas.

Task Examine the documents and answer the questions that follow. Then you will be asked to write an essay about the portrayals of Pocahontas, using facts from the documents and from the chapter to support the position you take in your thesis statement.

ST 3.2 Draw upon literary selections, historical documents, and accounts to analyze the roles played by different individuals and groups during the major eras in New York State and United States history.

ST 4.3 Develop hypotheses about important events, eras, or issues; move from chronicling to explaining historical events and issues; use information collected from diverse sources to produce cogently written reports and document-based essays.

DOCUMENT 1

Only one known image of Pocahontas was created during her lifetime. It was this engraving made in 1616, after she had married John Rolfe and moved to England. The purpose of this image was to show Pocahontas as an example of the ways in which Native Americans could become "civilized." For years this was a popular model for images of Pocahontas.

DOCUMENT 2

This large painting by printmaker Henry Brueckner was used in a popular pamphlet about Pocahontas. The image depicts the marriage of John Rolfe and Pocahontas as a great community affair, bringing together Native American and English leaders in an elaborate ceremony in a Christian church. The painting portrays several well-known historical figures in attendance at the ceremony. In reality, most of these officials were not even in the Virginia colony at the time of Pocahontas's wedding. Although Pocahontas did become a devout Christian, her wedding was more likely a simple affair that took place in a plain wooden church, attended by few people.

In 1995 Walt Disney Studios released a cartoon version of the Pocahontas legend. The cartoon artists consulted with many experts on Powhatan history to attempt to create images that most accurately reflected Powhatan clothing and culture at the time that Pocahontas lived.

The story, however, changed many of the facts about Pocahontas, including making her a young adult and creating a romance between her and John Smith. In reality, Pocahontas was only about 12 years old when she met Smith, and there was never any indication of a romantic relationship between them. This image from the Disney cartoon "Pocahontas" shows the heroic characters of John Smith and Pocahontas.

Skills FOCUS — READING LIKE A HISTORIAN

1. a. Describe Refer to Document 1. What details indicate that Pocahontas adopted English culture?

b. Interpret What conclusions might English people have drawn from this depiction of Pocahontas?

2. a. Identify Refer to Document 2. What types of people are shown attending Pocahontas's wedding?

b. Analyze Why did the artist portray the wedding as a large community affair when it probably was not?

3. a. Identify Refer to Document 3. What is significant about the items each character is holding?

b. Elaborate Why do you think the cartoonists tried to accurately reflect aspects of Powhatan culture, yet changed key events about the life of Pocahontas?

4. Document-Based Essay Question Consider the question below and form a thesis statement. Using examples from Documents 1, 2, and 3, create an outline and write a short essay supporting your position.
In what ways have images of Pocahontas been used to reflect different messages about contact between Native Americans and the English?

See **Skills Handbook**, pp. H28–H29, H30

Visual Summary: European Colonies in America

England
• Major explorers in North America: Cabot, Drake, Raleigh
• Colonies founded along Atlantic coast

France
• Major explorers in North America: Cartier, Champlain, La Salle
• Colonies founded in Quebec and Louisiana

Spain
• Major explorers in North America: Ponce de Léon, Cabeza de Vaca, de Soto, Coronado
• Colonies founded in American Southeast and Southwest

The Netherlands
• Major explorer in North America: Hudson
• Colonies founded in New Netherland and Delaware (both later become English colonies)

THE GRANGER COLLECTION, NEW YORK

Reviewing Key Terms and People

Identify the correct term or person from the chapter that best fits each of the following descriptions.

1. Person sent by a church to teach and convert others to a religion
2. Conquistador who conquered the Aztec peoples
3. English explorer who plundered Spanish ships and towns
4. Leader of a major Indian confederacy near the Jamestown colony
5. People who worked for a certain number of years in return for being brought to America
6. An uprising of unemployed and unhappy colonists in Virginia
7. English explorer who helped the Jamestown colony survive
8. English colonist who helped found Rhode Island
9. Protestants who wanted to purify the established Church of England
10. The flood of English immigrants who came to New England from the 1620s to the 1640s
11. English colonist who started a colony to give Quakers a refuge from religious persecution

Comprehension and Critical Thinking

SECTION 1 *(pp. 40–45)*

12. **a. Recall** What were the three main goals of the Spanish conquistadors?

   b. Analyze How did Spanish conquistadors and missionaries treat Native Americans?

   c. Predict How will French settlers probably get along with Native Americans? Why?

SECTION 2 *(pp. 46–50)*

13. **a. Describe** What was life like in Jamestown during the starving time?

   b. Make Generalizations What is the historical significance of Virginia's House of Burgesses?

History's Impact video program

Review the video to answer the closing question: How has a desire to worship freely influenced American history?

c. Rank Think about Spain's and England's reasons and methods for establishing colonies in the Americas. Was one better than the other? Why or why not?

SECTION 3 *(pp. 51–56)*

14. a. Define What was the central agreement of the Mayflower Compact, and where were the settlers when they signed it?

b. Contrast How did the Puritans' laws and government in the Massachusetts Bay Colony conflict with their reasons for moving to America?

c. Elaborate How was Rhode Island different from most of the other colonies?

SECTION 4 *(pp. 60–65)*

15. a. Identify Which two colonies were the most tolerant of other religions?

b. Contrast How were the colonies established under England's King Charles II different from earlier American colonies?

c. Evaluate The names of many towns and colonies started with "New" (New Amsterdam, New York, New Jersey). What does this say about Europeans' intentions in the Americas?

Using the Internet

go.hrw.com
Practice Online
Keyword: SD7 CH2

16. The development of each of the English colonies was shaped by its geography and by the people who lived there. Using the keyword above, do research to learn more about one of the colonies. Then, from the viewpoint of a colonist, write an diary entry about how your colony is changing over time. Note how the land is being put to use. Describe how factors such as religion, culture, values, family life, and work are affecting the colony's development.

Analyzing Primary Sources

Reading Like a Historian When John Smith became the leader of Jamestown, he told the colonists:

> ❝You must obey this now for a Law, that he that will not worke shall not eate (except by sickness he be disabled) for the labours of thirtie or fortie honest and industrious men shall not be consumed to maintain an hundred and fiftie idle loyterers.❞
>
> —John Smith, *Generall Historie of Virginia, New England, & the Summer Isles*

17. Describe What problem was Smith trying to address in this passage?

18. Evaluate Was Smith's new law too harsh? Why or why not?

Critical Reading

Read the passage in Section 3 that begins with the heading "Relations with Native Americans." Then answer the question that follows.

19. The last paragraph of the passage says that King Philip's War was "costly for both sides." This means

A. the war was fast and easy for both sides.

B. the colonists suffered very little.

C. both sides lost a lot in the war.

D. Native Americans had few losses.

WRITING FOR THE SAT

Think about the following issue.

During most of the 1600s and early 1700s, English subjects were required to support the Church of England by paying taxes and by attending services regularly—regardless of their personal beliefs. Many nonconformists, such as Puritans and Quakers, left England for the colonies in pursuit of religious freedom.

20. Assignment Given the uncertainty of life in the English colonies, what does it say about many colonists' religious faith that they were willing to move to the colonies? Write a short essay in which you develop your position on this issue. Support your point of view with reasoning and examples from your studies.

CHAPTER

3

1650–1763

Colonial Life

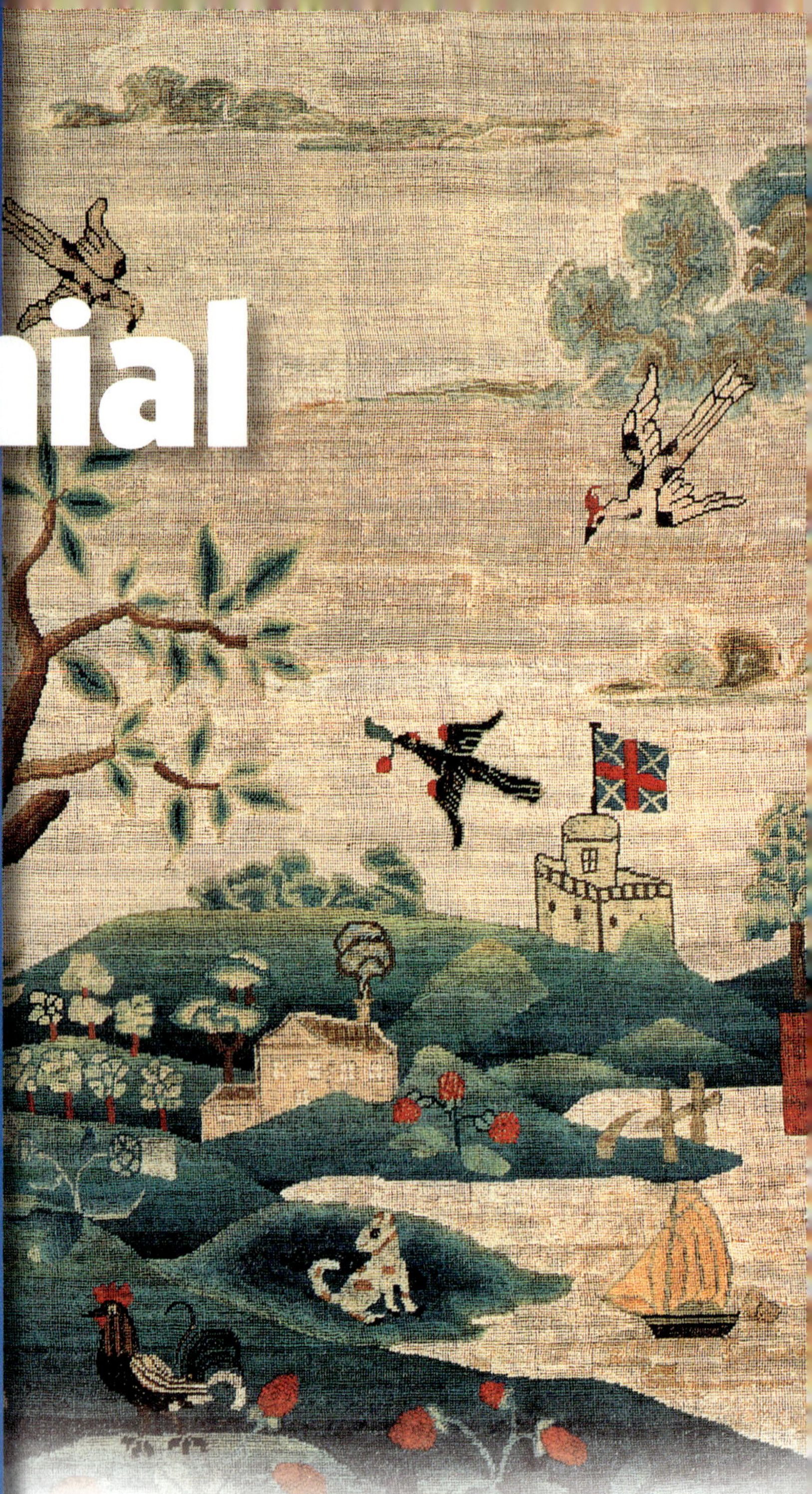

THE BIG PICTURE For more than 100 years, England's colonies in America grew steadily. Over time, the colonies developed their own economies, political systems, traditions of local government, and sense of self-reliance. Colonists maintained economic, political, and personal ties with Great Britain. But as time wore on, serious strains between the colonists and Britain began to appear.

New York Standards

Key Idea 1 The study of New York State and United States history requires an analysis of the development of American culture, its diversity and multicultural context, and the ways people are unified by many values, practices, and traditions.

Key Idea 3 Study about the major social, political, economic, cultural, and religious developments in New York State and United States history involves learning about the important roles and contributions of individuals and groups.

Skills FOCUS **READING LIKE A HISTORIAN**

Bostonians graze their cattle and enjoy some recreation on Boston Common in this 1750 embroidery. Beacon Hill, home to many prominent residents, can be seen in the background.
Interpreting Visuals In what ways do you think the city's common served the community?

See **Skills Handbook**, p. H30

U.S.

1643 Massachusetts, Plymouth, Connecticut, and New Haven colonies form the New England Confederation.

1650

World

1651 England passes the first of the Navigation Acts.

History's Impact video program

Watch the video to understand the impact of the French and Indian War.

PHOTOGRAPH © 2005 MUSEUM OF FINE ARTS, BOSTON

1691
New charter makes Massachusetts, including Maine and Plymouth, a royal colony.

1739
British minister George Whitefield helps launch the Great Awakening with his preaching.

1754
The French and Indian War begins. Benjamin Franklin proposes the Albany Plan of Union to unite the colonies.

1670 **1690** **1710** **1730** **1750** **1770**

1685
Charles II dies; his brother James becomes king of England.

1701
England goes to war against Spain.

1715
After a reign of 72 years, King Louis XIV of France dies.

1759
Invading British forces capture the French Canadian stronghold of Quebec.

1763
The Treaty of Paris ends the Seven Years' War in Europe.

Political Life in the Colonies

BEFORE YOU READ

MAIN IDEA

British mercantilist policies and political issues helped shape the development of the American colonies.

READING FOCUS

1. What is mercantilism?
2. How did the Glorious Revolution and the English Bill of Rights affect political developments in the colonies?
3. How did government in the colonies change under the policy of salutary neglect?

KEY TERMS AND PEOPLE

mercantilism
balance of trade
Navigation Acts
Dominion of New England
William and Mary
Glorious Revolution
English Bill of Rights
confederation
salutary neglect

 PI 3.4 Understand the interrelationships between world events and developments in New York State and the United States (e.g., causes for immigration, economic opportunities, human rights abuses, and tyranny versus freedom).

 **THE INSIDE STORY**

Why did molasses matter?

Colonial merchants and ship captains knew that the rugged coast of New England had thousands of bays and coves where small boats could come ashore. That made it easy for smugglers to bring in goods and avoid certain British taxes. Smuggling made life much harder for British customs officials trying to enforce trade laws.

One of those trade laws was the Molasses Act of 1733. Molasses is a dark, sweet syrup made when raw sugar is processed. Colonists used it in cakes and pies and poured it over pancakes. Most important of all, molasses was distilled to make rum. Rum was the most popular drink in the colonies. The yearly consumption averaged more than

four gallons per person! Rum was also one of the northern colonies' most valuable products, and many gallons were exported every year.

The Molasses Act made the colonists furious. They bought about half their molasses and sugar from planters in the Caribbean. The new law put a high tax on imports of such foreign sugar. Its goal was to make the colonists buy sugar from the British West Indies. Instead, smuggling became so widespread that tax revenues dropped. British officials decided not to try to enforce the act. ◢

SMUGGLING MOLASSES

▼ **A merchant ship loaded with goods is launched at Salem Harbor, Massachusetts.**

PEABODY ESSEX MUSEUM, SALEM, MASSACHUSETTS

Mercantilism

Colonists began smuggling because they felt England was taxing them unfairly. From the English perspective, however, taxing the colonies was a good way to make money. After all, profit was one of England's major <u>incentives</u> for establishing colonies in America.

The economic policy of **mercantilism** held that a nation's power was directly related to its wealth. The American colonies were valuable to England because the colonists could supply raw materials and could buy English goods. That would achieve another goal of mercantilism, a favorable **balance of trade**. Balance of trade is the relationship between a country's imports and exports. A country with a favorable balance of trade makes money by exporting more products than it imports.

To preserve its balance of trade, England had to prevent its colonies from trading with other nations. As a result, the interests of England and its colonies soon clashed. In theory, the mercantilist system could bring the colonies <u>prosperity</u>, too. The colonists, however, did not see it that way.

The English only wanted certain American products, such as fur and timber. But the colonies produced other goods, such as wheat and fish, that England did not want. In addition, colonists often could get better prices for their goods from the French, Spanish, or Dutch. They resented England's attempts to control what they could buy and sell.

The Navigation Acts

Beginning in 1651, the English government passed several laws to control colonial trade and ensure the colonies remained profitable—for England. Together, these laws are called the **Navigation Acts**.

The first act targeted trade with the Dutch. It said that all goods coming to England from Asia, Africa, or America must be carried in English ships. England did not strongly enforce this act, but it set a pattern for later laws.

In 1660 Parliament added a new provision: Not only must the ship be English, so must its captain and most of its crew. This act also listed a number of colonial products that could be sent only to England or another English colony.

Then in 1663, Parliament passed a new law. It required that almost everything being shipped to the colonies pass through England so England could tax these goods.

In 1673 Parliament tightened its control even more. Merchants now had to pay a tax, or duty, on certain goods—called "enumerated articles." Parliament sent officials to the colonies to collect these taxes.

Effects of the Navigation Acts The Navigation Acts had mixed results for both England and its colonies. For England, the laws increased revenues, but at the same time it increased the costs of law enforcement in America. For the colonists, the demand for ships stimulated certain industries, such as lumber and shipbuilding. On the other hand, the Navigation Acts also meant more English involvement in colonial affairs.

Most colonists resented the Navigation Acts. Many ignored them, and many prominent merchants took part in smuggling.

ACADEMIC VOCABULARY
incentive motivational factor
prosperity economic well-being

READING CHECK Identifying the Main Idea
What was the principal goal of mercantilism?

Rising Tensions Between England and America, 1651–1689

QUICK FACTS

THE NAVIGATION ACTS, 1651, 1660, 1663, 1673

England passed laws restricting colonial trade:
- All goods coming to England had to be carried on English ships.
- Captain and most of the crew on the ship had to be English.
- Certain products could be shipped only to England.
- American merchants had to pay a tax on certain goods.

Colonists' Reaction Some colonists began smuggling goods and refusing to pay their taxes.

PEABODY ESSEX MUSEUM, SALEM, MASSACHUSETTS

The Glorious Revolution and the English Bill of Rights

The New England colonies, especially Massachusetts, did not behave as the English thought they should. When the English restored the monarchy under King Charles II, Puritans in Massachusetts at first refused to accept him as their king. Some even suggested that not all English laws applied to the colonies.

New Englanders also broke mercantilist laws that harmed their own economies. New England fishers competed with those from England. Some New Englanders began to compete with English manufacturers. The first successful ironworks in the colonies began at Saugus, Massachusetts, in 1646.

Royal officials looked for ways to control the colonies. First, King Charles took away Massachusetts' control over New Hampshire. In 1684, as the colony still refused to enforce the Navigation Acts, the king took back its charter and made it a royal colony.

The Dominion of New England

King Charles II died in 1685. His brother James became king and tightened royal control even more. First, he created the **Dominion of New England**. It was a kind of supercolony that included all of New England, New York, and New Jersey. James's long-range plan was to divide and rule the rest of the American colonies in the same way.

The king appointed Sir Edmund Andros as governor of the Dominion. Andros was an experienced colonial governor but treated the colonists as if they were disobedient children. His arbitrary decisions soon made people angry. He demanded the return of the colonial charters. Colonists saw the charters as basic to their political rights. The new Dominion had no elected assembly, only an appointed council.

Andros infuriated the colonists in other ways, too. In Puritan Boston, he ordered Anglican services to be held in the Old South Meetinghouse. Andros also strictly enforced the Navigation Acts. He imposed new taxes on land and on imported wine, rum, and brandy.

The Glorious Revolution

Meanwhile, James II was making himself equally unpopular in England. James was a Roman Catholic who hoped to make England Catholic again. He also wanted an absolute monarchy.

James's daughters Mary and Anne were Protestant. But his second wife, a Catholic, gave birth to a son in early 1688. This made leaders in Parliament fear the beginning of a Catholic dynasty. So, they invited Mary and her Dutch husband, William of Orange, to become co-rulers of England. This change of leadership became known as the **Glorious Revolution**.

The Glorious Revolution was essentially peaceful. Although William came from Holland with an army, James's supporters quickly deserted him. The ex-king fled to France.

Before being crowned, **William and Mary** jointly accepted a document that became known as the **English Bill of Rights**. This historic document allowed Parliament to set limits on

Rising Tensions, continued

THE DOMINION OF NEW ENGLAND, 1865

To gain more control over the colonies, King James II created the Dominion of New England. The Dominion combined several northern colonies under the rule of a royal governor, Edmund Andros.

Colonists' Reaction Colonists were angry because they lost their colonial charters. Used to governing themselves, they resented the king's governor, Edmund Andros.

Colonial leaders arrest Governor Andros.

the monarchs' powers. It protected freedom of speech for members of Parliament and gave them control of taxes. Later, these ideas would influence American politics.

Colonists' reactions News of the Glorious Revolution reached America in the spring of 1689. It led to several small uprisings in the colonies. Colonial leaders in Massachusetts acted quickly. They arrested Andros and his government and sent them back to England. Almost a century later, John Adams wrote, "It ought to be remembered that there was a revolution here, as well as in England, and that we, as well as the people of England, made an original, express contract with King William."

That ended the Dominion of New England. Connecticut and Rhode Island got their charters back. A new charter in 1691 made Massachusetts a royal colony that included Maine and Plymouth. Although Massachusetts was a royal colony, its colonial assembly still had a voice in choosing the governor's council.

The Glorious Revolution also sparked a rebellion in New York. Many merchants, especially the Dutch, disliked the Navigation Acts. Others were unhappy that the colony had no elected assembly.

Royal officials in New York delayed the announcement of England's new rulers. But when word of Andros' arrest came from Boston, small farmers, city workers, and others joined a rebel government. In the end, royal rule returned to New York, but the colony was at last granted an elected assembly.

READING CHECK **Identifying Supporting Details** How did Governor Andros provoke colonists' disapproval?

Government in the Colonies

Local rebellions after the Glorious Revolution showed English officials that colonists would resist arbitrary rule like that of Andros. Some colonies regained their elected assemblies. On the other hand, many more were now under tighter control as royal colonies.

Some of the colonists insisted that, as English citizens, they had all the rights that citizens enjoyed in England itself. This was not true. In fact, the English Bill of Rights did not apply in the colonies. Still, the Glorious Revolution gave colonists ideas about their rights and self-rule.

Steps toward self-rule Since the first settlements, the colonists had claimed their rights as English citizens. Colonists had taken small steps toward self-government during the English Civil War. For example, Massachusetts coined its own money, the pine-tree shilling.

The colonies even made an early move toward unity. Several joined forces to form the United Colonies of New England, also called the New England Confederation, in 1643. A **confederation** is a group in which each member keeps control of its own internal affairs. They cooperate on other actions, such as defense.

Neglect by England The Glorious Revolution had shifted considerable power to Parliament. But Parliament dealt mainly with issues in England. The monarch and his or her officials made

King William and Queen Mary accepted the English Bill of Rights and jointly ruled England.

THE GLORIOUS REVOLUTION, 1688

In England, William and Mary took the throne from King James II in a peaceful revolution.

Colonists' Reaction Colonists overthrew Governor Edmund Andros in 1689 and got their charters back.

most colonial policy. In 1696 an agency known as the Board of Trade was set up to handle colonial affairs. The board consisted of royal councilors and other high officials.

The Board of Trade had many roles. It had a hand in the appointment of colonial governors. It wrote laws for the colonies and sent them to Parliament for passage. It could review laws passed by colonial legislatures. It worked with other agencies to enforce the Navigation Acts.

The colonies had some say in their own government. They had agents to present their point of view to the Board of Trade. Like modern lobbyists trying to influence Congress, they tried to protect their colony's interests.

Many English officials were involved in colonial policy, but they did not rule the colonies very strictly. The politician Edmund Burke later termed this situation salutary neglect. In other words, the colonies benefited by being left alone.

At the same time, England's attention began to turn away from the colonies. War with Spain broke out in 1701. Later, supporters of the ex-king James II tried to put one of his relatives back on the throne. Because England's attention was focused elsewhere, colonial governments gained some independence.

Colonial governments in the 1700s In the colonists' daily lives, local governments were more influential than faraway English officials. New Englanders held town meetings.

In other colonies, the county or parish was the unit of local government. Many colonists saw their elected assembly as a basic right.

Most colonial assemblies were modeled on the Parliament in London. They were bicameral, that is, with two houses. The governor's council was the upper house. The council had executive and legislative powers. It was also the supreme court of the colony.

The elected assembly was the lower house, much like Parliament's House of Commons. As the Commons gained power after the Glorious Revolution, colonial assemblies also won important rights. Members had freedom of speech in debates. Most importantly, they won the right to pass money bills. That meant the governor depended on the assembly for his salary.

Each colony had a governor. In royal colonies the governor was appointed by the monarch. In proprietary colonies, the proprietor chose a governor. Members of the governor's council were chosen in the same way. They were usually rich and influential men.

On paper, colonial governors had great power. They could veto acts of the assembly. They commanded military forces, made treaties, and chose many minor officials. On the other hand, they lacked ways of backing up their decisions. No doubt many kept in mind the fate of Governor Edmund Andros.

READING CHECK **Comparing** How were colonial assemblies similar to Parliament?

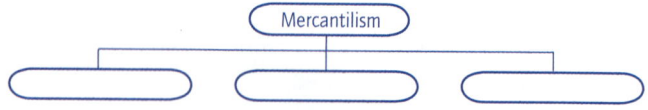

Reviewing Ideas, Terms, and People

1. a. Identify What were the principles behind the policy of mercantilism?
b. Summarize What were the main provisions of the Navigation Acts?
c. Evaluate Which benefited more from the Navigation Acts—England or the American colonies?

2. a. Describe What circumstances led to the Glorious Revolution in England?
b. Make Inferences Why did colonists revolt in reaction to the Glorious Revolution?

3. a. Recall What early move toward unity did the New England colonies make in 1643?
b. Analyze What was the effect of salutary neglect?

Critical Thinking

4. Analyzing Copy the chart below and show the basic principles of mercantilism.

Mercantilism

FOCUS ON SPEAKING

5. Expository Suppose you are a merchant in New England. Explain why you are resisting English law and disobeying the Navigation Acts. Read your explanation aloud to the class.

BEFORE YOU READ

MAIN IDEA

A commerce-based economy developed in the northern colonies, while the southern colonies developed an agricultural economy.

READING FOCUS

1. What were the characteristics of northern colonial economies?
2. What were the characteristics of southern colonial economies?
3. What was the impact of slavery in the colonies?

KEY TERMS AND PEOPLE

triangular trade
Middle Passage
cash crop
Eliza Lucas
yeoman
Olaudah Equiano
Stono Rebellion

PI 1.1 Analyze the development of American culture, explaining how ideas, values, beliefs, and traditions have changed over time and how they united all Americans.

Slavery in the Northern Colonies

▼ Phillis Wheatley was still enslaved when she published *Poems on Various Subjects, Religious and Moral.*

THE INSIDE STORY

How did slavery affect the North?

The economies of the southern colonies came to depend on the work done by enslaved Africans. They worked on the plantations of the South, growing tobacco, rice, and indigo. But slave labor was more widespread in the northern and middle colonies than most people realize. Enslaved Africans worked in homes, workshops, and farms in New England and throughout the middle colonies.

In addition, New England ship captains were major players in the slave trade with West Africa. Even Quaker merchants in Philadelphia owned slaves, and some took part in the slave trade. The first poet of African American ancestry was Phillis Wheatley, who was kidnapped in Africa at age 7 and bought as a slave by a Boston family. Her exceptional talents made her famous, and she later gained her freedom.

Enslaved workers in the North were a smaller percentage of the population than they were in the southern colonies. In New England the percentage was less than 5 percent, but it was higher in the middle colonies, where farms were larger. In the North, enslaved Africans more often lived in urban areas and worked as household servants or artisans. Some northern farms, however, were very large, with many African American workers. Most of the northern states began to abolish slavery gradually after the American Revolution, but in some places that process took many years.

THE GRANGER COLLECTION, NEW YORK

Northern Colonial Economies

Agriculture was the main economic activity in colonial America. However, colonists often found that English crops and methods did not succeed in their new home. Climate, land, and other factors influenced farming in different regions. Those factors also steered some colonists into other ways of making a living.

Farming Much of the soil in New England was thin and rocky. The winters were long, and the growing season short. Many colonists practiced subsistence farming—growing just enough food for their own family. Some raised extra corn or apples or cattle to trade with their neighbors. There was rarely enough to produce an export crop.

Farther south, the middle colonies had better land and a milder climate. Farmers here grew enough wheat to sell grain and flour to other colonies and to send abroad. They also raised cattle and hogs for export.

The colonies' most productive farmers were the German colonists known as the Pennsylvania Dutch (from the word *Deutsch*, which means "German"). These settlers used fertilizer and crop rotation. As in Europe, women worked in the fields alongside men.

Natural resources For early colonists, North America's most valuable resources were its thick forests and the fur-bearing animals in them. Colonial traders got beaver furs and deerskins from Native American trappers.

The number of fur-bearing animals soon declined. Colonists turned to other resources, such as timber and fish. Lumber mills cut logs into planks, shingles, and siding for ships and houses. Timber was one of the raw materials that the colonies sent to England.

As a result of the Navigation Acts, many coastal towns became centers for shipbuilding. It was less expensive to build ships in the colonies than it was to build them in England. Shipyards built both merchant ships and small fishing boats. An estimated 33,000 colonists worked as shipbuilders, the largest single group in the work force.

Some of the fish catch was exported to Europe and the West Indies. The rest was eaten at home. New England sailors began the whaling industry in the early 1700s, sailing from ports such as Nantucket. Whales provided oil for lamps as well as materials used in perfumes, candles, and women's corsets.

Colonial industries Under mercantilism, colonial industries were not supposed to compete with those in England. That discouraged the growth of industries. So did a shortage of capital for investment.

Because English goods were expensive, colonists made many things at home. Small industries developed. Mills, run by waterpower, ground grain into flour. Distilling rum and brewing other alcoholic beverages were major commercial activities. Ironworks developed where there were local supplies of iron ore. Other small companies made bricks, leather goods, and glass. Importing cloth from England was too expensive for many people, so cloth making became another small-scale industry. Families wove wool and linen cloth for personal use as well as for sale to merchants.

THE IMPACT TODAY

Daily Life

Today the Pennsylvania Dutch are mostly Amish and Old Order Mennonites. These groups still travel by horse and buggy and farm using teams of horses. Their use of a variation of the German language is seen as a sign of humility and a way to keep the outside world at bay.

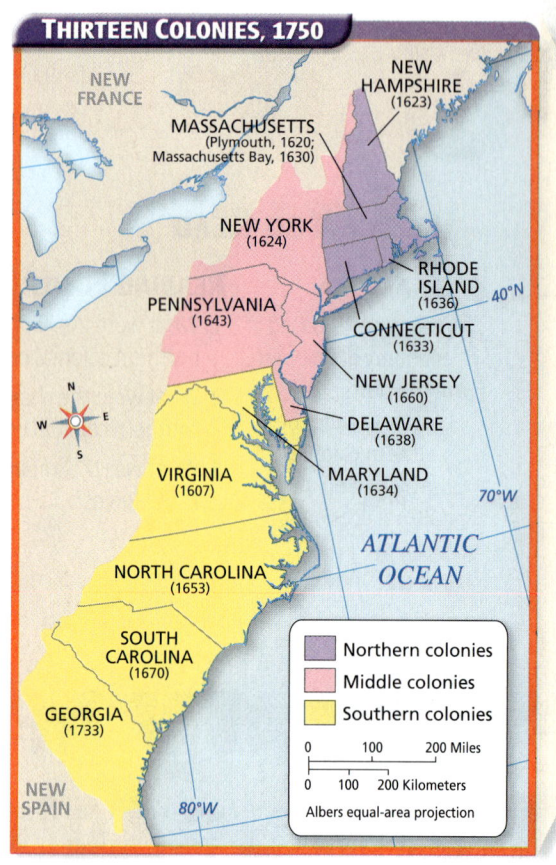

THIRTEEN COLONIES, 1750

NEW FRANCE

NEW HAMPSHIRE (1623)

MASSACHUSETTS (Plymouth, 1620; Massachusetts Bay, 1630)

NEW YORK (1624)

RHODE ISLAND (1636)

CONNECTICUT (1633)

NEW JERSEY (1660)

PENNSYLVANIA (1643)

DELAWARE (1638)

MARYLAND (1634)

VIRGINIA (1607)

NORTH CAROLINA (1653)

SOUTH CAROLINA (1670)

GEORGIA (1733)

NEW SPAIN

ATLANTIC OCEAN

40°N

70°W

80°W

Northern colonies
Middle colonies
Southern colonies

0   100   200 Miles
0   100   200 Kilometers
Albers equal-area projection

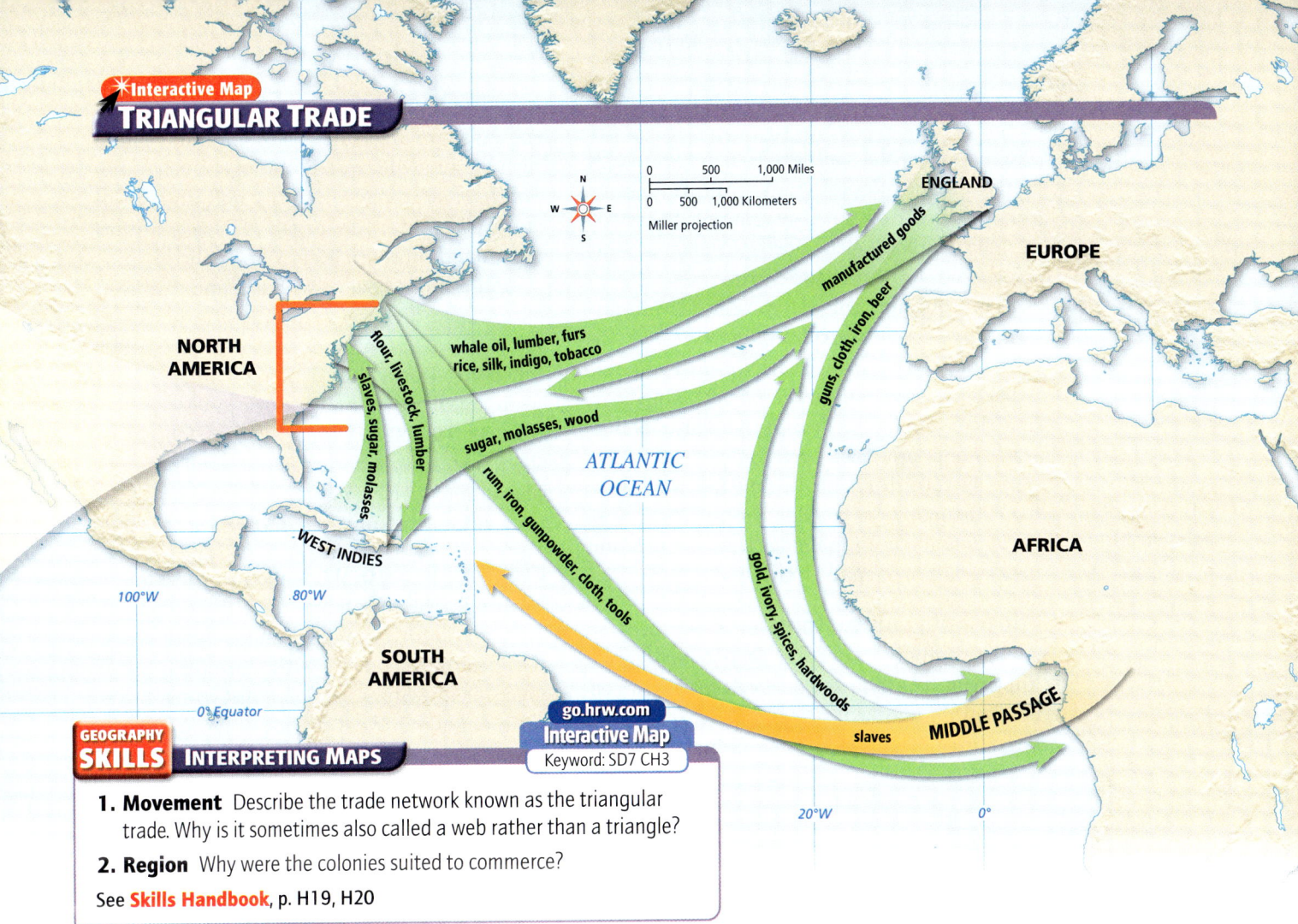

0   500   1,000 Miles
0   500   1,000 Kilometers
Miller projection

ENGLAND

EUROPE

NORTH AMERICA

manufactured goods

whale oil, lumber, furs
rice, silk, indigo, tobacco

flour, livestock, lumber

guns, cloth, iron, beer

slaves, sugar, molasses

sugar, molasses, wood

ATLANTIC OCEAN

AFRICA

rum, iron, gunpowder, cloth, tools

WEST INDIES

100°W   80°W

gold, ivory, spices, hardwoods

SOUTH AMERICA

slaves   MIDDLE PASSAGE

0° Equator

20°W   0°

GEOGRAPHY SKILLS INTERPRETING MAPS

go.hrw.com
Interactive Map
Keyword: SD7 CH3

1. **Movement** Describe the trade network known as the triangular trade. Why is it sometimes also called a web rather than a triangle?

2. **Region** Why were the colonies suited to commerce?

See **Skills Handbook**, p. H19, H20

Trade and commerce Good harbors, inexpensive ships, and a tradition of seafaring encouraged the development of commerce. The port cities of Boston, New York, and Philadelphia were thriving centers of trade. Merchant ships from the colonies traded along the coasts and across the Atlantic. Traders also traveled the inland rivers.

The trade routes that linked the Americas, Europe, Africa, and the West Indies are often described as the **triangular trade**. In that triangle, ships carried rum from New England to Africa to trade for enslaved Africans. Traders shipped the Africans to plantations in the West Indies and traded them for sugar and molasses. Finally, traders shipped the sugar and molasses back to New England to be made into rum.

The term **Middle Passage** is the name used by historians to describe the horrific journey that enslaved Africans made across the Atlantic. The trip from West Africa to the Indies was the middle leg of the triangle.

Historians today, however, think that real trade patterns were not that simple. They believe the patterns were more like a spider web than a neat triangle. Coastal trade linked the colonies and the West Indies. The fertile mid-Atlantic colonies sent grain, fruits, and vegetables to other colonies. Northern merchants exported flour, fish, lumber, and manufactured goods to the West Indies.

The northern colonies sent furs and timber to England. Defying the Navigation Acts, they also sold fish, fruit, and meat in southern Europe and to other colonies in the West Indies that did not belong to England. The southern colonies sent other goods to England. Overseas trade grew quickly in the 1700s. By 1770, the value of exports had increased to nearly four times the value of exports in 1700.

READING CHECK **Identifying the Main Idea**
What factors helped trade become the basis for northern colonial economies?

Southern Colonial Economies

Products from the southern colonies were very important in colonial trade. Still, the region remained rural, with economies based on agriculture. Unlike the northern colonies, only a few cities formed in the South.

The southern colonies produced valuable cash crops—agricultural products grown to be sold. One was tobacco, America's most valuable export. Indigo, a plant used to make a blue dye, and rice were also grown in the South. Southerners also produced naval stores—products such as rope, tar, and turpentine that were used to <u>maintain</u> wooden ships. There was great demand in England for these crops—and great profit to be made from them.

The plantation system
As tobacco became an increasingly important crop, a way of life known as the plantation system developed in Virginia and Maryland. A plantation is a large farm, usually in a warm climate, with an unskilled labor force that grows one cash crop, such as sugar or tobacco. The plantation system soon became widespread through much of the South. Eventually, a wealthy and influential class of planters emerged. These planters dominated southern society and politics.

Plantations needed workers, and this need encouraged the growth of slavery. A few huge plantations had hundreds of workers, either indentured servants or slaves. Most farms were smaller and had a work force of fewer than 30. The bulk of these workers labored in the fields, although men and women on large plantations performed other necessary tasks such as shoemaking, weaving, and carpentry.

Rice and indigo
While tobacco was king in Virginia, rice and indigo were the dominant crops in South Carolina. The low-lying coastline and marshes of South Carolina proved ideal for growing rice. Some historians think that enslaved West Africans brought the knowledge of rice growing to America.

ACADEMIC VOCABULARY

maintain keep in an existing state

HISTORY CLOSE-UP

South Carolina Rice Plantation, 1730–1750

On early rice plantations like this one, nearly all tasks were done by hand. Enslaved Africans performed the arduous work of planting, harvesting, and cultivating the rice.

Slaves lived in small, one-room buildings. The slave cabins were often built in rows.

The kitchen building was separate from the main house.

The main plantation house was usually built on high ground, facing the river.

The winnowing house was used to separate the rice from the chaff, or outer covering.

Growing rice in swampy fields was difficult and dangerous. Mosquitoes bred in the wet coastal conditions, and they could carry malaria, a deadly disease. Free workers would not tolerate these conditions. Rice planters turned instead to enslaved Africans to do the work. Many enslaved Africans already knew successful methods of rice growing. In addition, many of them had more resistance to malaria.

The other major crop in South Carolina was indigo, a plant from the West Indies whose seeds were used to produce a deep blue dye. Indigo was widely used for military uniforms and men's coats.

The first successful indigo crop was grown in South Carolina by **Eliza Lucas**. In 1739 at about age 17, she was left to manage her father's plantations while he returned to military duty in the West Indies. Lucas experimented with crops such as ginger, figs, and indigo. She wrote about her experiences in 1740.

HISTORY'S VOICES

❝Wrote my Father a very long letter on his plantation affairs and . . . on the pains I had taken to bring the Indigo, Ginger, Cotton . . . and had greater hopes from the Indigo (if I could have the seed earlier next year from the West Indies) than any of the rest of the things I had tryd.❞

—Letterbook of Eliza Lucas Pinckney, 1740

The new crop soon became profitable. Demand in England was so great that Parliament offered a bonus to indigo growers. By 1754 South Carolina exported a million pounds annually.

In 1744 Eliza Lucas married a widowed planter, Charles Pinckney. Their two sons became well-known politicians and soldiers. One was a signer of the Constitution.

Small farms Southern economies rested on the plantation system and its valuable crops. Most farmers did not live on plantations, however, but on small farms. Even small farmers sometimes had a few enslaved Africans who worked in the fields alongside them.

These independent **yeoman** (YOH-muhn) farmers raised livestock and exported beef and pork. They grew corn, wheat, fruit, and vegetables for the home market. Small-scale farmers also grew tobacco but had to sell it through the large planters.

READING CHECK **Contrasting** How did the plantation system differ from the work patterns of yeoman farmers?

The Impact of Slavery

English and Spanish settlers needed workers for their plantations and haciendas. Some colonists tried to enslave Native Americans. Due to disease and other problems, such efforts often failed. In the 1600s, indentured servants from England and Europe supplied most labor in the colonies. But former indentured servants began to pose problems in the colonies. Eventually, colonists came to depend on the work of enslaved Africans instead.

The African slave trade By the 1600s Portugal, Spain, France, Holland, and England were involved in the trans-Atlantic slave trade. Most captured Africans were taken to colonies in the Caribbean and South America, then to

Tasks on a Rice Plantation

❶ **Planting** Slaves planted rice by hand in the spring.

❷ **Watering** Rice is grown in flooded fields, so rice plantations were built near natural water sources.

❸ **Canal Building** Plantation owners had slaves construct canals to direct the water to the fields. Canals and floodgates controlled the flow of water to the rice fields.

❹ **Harvesting** Slaves harvested rice in the fall.

❺ **Pounding** Getting the rice ready to sell was hard work. First, slaves pounded the rice.

❻ **Winnowing** Then they brought it to the winnowing house, where they dropped it through a grating in the floor. The rice grains fell to the ground below and were collected. Later, rice mills did this task.

❼ **Shipping** The river also provided a way to transport rice to buyers.

Skills FOCUS **INTERPRETING INFOGRAPHICS**

Early South Carolina rice plantations like this one were often built near natural water sources.

Making Inferences How did the location near the river help with growing rice?

See **Skills Handbook**, p. H18

Olaudah Equiano
1750–1797

Born in western Africa in present-day Nigeria, Olaudah Equiano was taken from his family at the age of 11 and sold into slavery. African slave traders forced Equiano onto a slave ship sailing to the Caribbean and then to Virginia. A lieutenant in the British navy purchased Equiano from a Virginia planter. Working on ships under the command of his slaveholder, Equiano eventually earned enough money to buy his freedom in 1766. As a free man, Equiano traveled as a missionary and spoke out against slavery. He visited many countries in Europe, Latin America, and Africa, and also traveled to India. In 1789 Equiano published his autobiography, *The Interesting Narrative of the Life of Olaudah Equiano, or Gustavus Vassa, the African.* By describing the horrors of the Middle Passage, Equiano's book encouraged readers to call for an end to slavery.

Explain How did Equiano fight slavery?

North America. Only a small percentage—perhaps 5 percent—came directly to the North American colonies.

Some Africans who later gained freedom described the horrifying conditions of the passage across the Atlantic—the dreaded Middle Passage. Kidnapped Africans were chained together in dark, foul-smelling quarters below the decks of the ship. Some ship captains tried to keep their prisoners healthy to make them more valuable. Others packed men, women, and children into such a small space that they could not sit or stand.

One African, **Olaudah Equiano**, later wrote about the horrific conditions on a crowded slave ship.

HISTORY'S VOICES

❝The closeness of the place, and the heat of the climate. . . almost suffocated us. . . . The shrieks of the women, and the groans of the dying, rendered the whole a scene of horror almost inconceivable.❞

—Olaudah Equiano, *The Interesting Narrative of the Life of Olaudah Equiano*, 1789

Three of his companions threw themselves overboard, choosing death by drowning over slavery. When Africans arrived in the Americas, they faced still more terrors—the auction block and an uncertain future.

Slavery in North and South The number of Africans in the English colonies grew quickly during the 1700s because of births as well as the slave trade. By 1760 the African population was about 250,000—10 times greater than it had been in 1700.

The agricultural economy determined where most Africans lived. Percentages were smallest in New England, Pennsylvania, and Delaware, where most people were independent yeoman farmers. There, Africans lived mainly in cities and worked as servants or artisans.

Because the Dutch had been active in the slave trade, New York and New Jersey had larger African populations. Many were skilled craftsworkers such as carpenters, shoemakers, and barrel makers.

Populations of enslaved Africans were largest in colonies with plantation agriculture. In parts of Virginia and Maryland, they made up as much as 30 percent of the population. North Carolina, with its many small farms, still had a sizable population of enslaved Africans.

In South Carolina, the large demand for workers on rice plantations caused the population of enslaved Africans to grow dramatically. By the mid 1700s, there were approximately twice as many enslaved Africans as whites in South Carolina.

Why slavery continued As you read earlier, the first Africans arrived in colonial Virginia in 1619. Many African workers were treated as indentured servants at first. Gradually, their terms of indenture grew longer until they lasted a lifetime. While white servants were freed, black servants often were not. Under the laws of several colonies, they lost other rights as well.

The line dividing blacks and whites became sharper, partly because the English settlers considered themselves naturally superior to the enslaved Africans. By the mid-1600s in Virginia and Maryland, most African servants were servants for life. Their children also became servants for life.

Historians disagree about why slavery continued for so long in the Americas. For planters, slave labor had obvious economic advantages. It cost less to hold slaves than to pay the expenses of indentured servants. The children of enslaved Africans supplied the next generation of workers. Also, the number of people who chose to take up indentures dropped steadily in the late 1600s.

Nevertheless, the institution of slavery troubled some colonists. But others justified the practice by pointing out that Africans themselves captured and sold their own people. Still others, such as Virginia colonist Peter Fontaine, justified slavery for economic reasons.

HISTORY'S VOICES

❝. . . to live in Virginia without slaves is morally impossible. Before our troubles, you could not hire a servant or slave for love or money, so that, unless you are robust enough to cut wood, to go to mill, to work at the hoe, etc., you must starve. . .This of course draws us all into the original sin and curse of the country of purchasing slaves.❞

– Letters of Peter Fontaine, 1757

Resisting slavery Writers at the time often portrayed enslaved Africans as contented and obedient. In fact, however, many enslaved Africans physically resisted brutal treatment and abuse. Others protested by committing small acts of sabotage, such as burning a barn or breaking tools. Some ran away but were often recaptured and killed or severely punished.

Southern planters lived in fear of slave revolts. Small-scale rebellions were frequent. The major revolt in the colonial period is known as the **Stono Rebellion**. In 1739 about 100 enslaved Africans in South Carolina took weapons from a firearms shop and killed several people before they were apprehended.

AFRICAN POPULATION IN THE COLONIES, 1700–1760

Source: *Historical Statistics of the United States*

Skills FOCUS **INTERPRETING GRAPHS**

Summarize the growth in African population in the northern and southern colonies as described by this chart. What was the difference in African population by 1760?

See **Skills Handbook**, p. H17

Some skilled artisans escaped slavery by buying their freedom. They hired out their labor, gradually earning and saving enough money to buy freedom for themselves. Sometimes they earned enough to buy freedom for their families as well.

READING CHECK **Identifying Cause and Effect** Why did the use of indentured servants decline, while slavery continued?

SECTION 2 ASSESSMENT

go.hrw.com
Online Quiz
Keyword: SD7 HP3

Reviewing Ideas, Terms, and People

1. **a. Describe** What is meant by the **triangular trade**?
   b. Contrast Why did agriculture in the middle colonies differ from that in New England?
   c. Evaluate In what ways was the ocean valuable to economies in the northern colonies?

2. **a. Identify** What were the four major exports of the southern colonies?
   b. Explain Why did southern economies remain rural and agricultural?
   c. Predict How would the value of tobacco and rice exports influence slavery in the southern colonies?

3. **a. Describe** What was the **Middle Passage**?
   b. Sequence Trace the changes that took place in the labor force in the American colonies in the 1600s and 1700s.

Critical Thinking

4. **Comparing** Copy the chart below and list the major products and activities in the economies of the northern and southern colonies.

Northern Colonies	Southern Colonies

FOCUS ON WRITING

5. **Descriptive** As a new immigrant from England to the American colonies, write a letter home explaining which colony you would like to live in and why.

America's Emerging Culture

BEFORE YOU READ

MAIN IDEA

Enlightenment ideas and the Great Awakening brought new ways of thinking to the colonists, and a unique American culture developed.

READING FOCUS

1. What impact did the Enlightenment have in the colonies?
2. How was the Great Awakening significant?
3. How did the colonies become more diverse in the 1700s?
4. What was life like in colonial America?

KEY TERMS AND PEOPLE

Benjamin Franklin
Enlightenment
John Locke
social contract
Great Awakening
Jonathan Edwards
George Whitefield

PI 1.1 Analyze the development of American culture, explaining how ideas, values, beliefs, and traditions have changed over time and how they united all Americans.

Benjamin Franklin's Humble Beginnings

THE INSIDE STORY

What was Benjamin Franklin like as a young man? People today remember **Benjamin Franklin** as one of the most famous Americans in history. But in 1723 he was just a 17-year-old printer's apprentice, trying to get away from a harsh older brother. As a boy, Franklin wanted to go to sea, but his father did not approve. Franklin did not want to join his father's candlemaking business, either. Since he loved to read, he was finally apprenticed to his older brother as a printer. The job suited him, but he and his brother did not get along. When Franklin decided to leave, his brother made sure that no other printer in Boston would hire him. So the young Benjamin Franklin set off alone for the big city—colonial Philadelphia.

Franklin made his way to Philadelphia by boat. Years later, in his *Autobiography*, he made fun of his first appearance in the city: "I was in my Working Dress . . . I was dirty from my Journey; my Pockets were stuff'd out with Shirts & Stockings." He had no idea of prices in the city. For three pennies at a bakery, he was surprised to get "three great Puffy Rolls." With two bread rolls under his arm, Franklin strolled down the street eating the third. He finally gave the others to a woman and child he had met on the boat. Soon, Franklin found work with a printer. It was the beginning of an amazing career. ◼

▶ **Young Benjamin Franklin, newly arrived in Philadelphia**

The Enlightenment and the American Colonies

In the 1400s the Renaissance had changed Europeans' outlook on the world. Similarly, in the late 1600s, new ways of thinking changed ideas about government and human rights. These new ways of thinking gave rise to a European movement called the **Enlightenment**. Because the Enlightenment emphasized a search for knowledge, the period is also known as the Age of Reason.

The Scientific Revolution

A revolution in science in the 1500s and 1600s helped lay the foundation for the Enlightenment. Using what is now called the scientific method, scientists used observation and experiments to look for natural laws that governed the universe.

For example, Sir Isaac Newton showed that certain physical laws—such as the force of gravity—seemed to operate everywhere in the universe. Other scientists looked for order and method in nature. The Swedish scientist Linnaeus devised a method for classifying plants and animals that is still the basis for scientific names today.

The Enlightenment in Europe

Thinkers in Europe, especially in France and England, admired this new approach to science. They thought that logic and reason could also be used to improve society, law, and government.

In England, the philosopher **John Locke** wrote in defense of the Glorious Revolution. In his *Two Treatises of Government* (1690), he said that it was the duty of government to protect the citizens' natural rights. These natural rights were life, liberty, and property.

Locke also said that in a civil society, people had a **social contract** with their government. The social contract theory held that if a government (or ruler) did not protect citizens and their rights, then the people were justified in overthrowing the government.

In France, social critics admired English rights and freedoms. English laws limited the power of the ruler, while France still had an absolute monarchy. To limit the French monarchy, the Baron de Montesquieu (MOHN-tehs-kyoo) suggested that the powers of government be divided. This would prevent any person or group from gaining too much power.

KEY POLITICAL THINKERS OF THE EUROPEAN ENLIGHTENMENT

John Locke *Two Treatises of Government* (1690)	Developed a theory that government should protect citizens' natural rights, which included life, liberty, and property. Wrote that government and the people were bound by a social contract
Baron de Montesquieu *The Spirit of the Laws* (1748)	Outlined theories of government, including a republican democracy in which power would be divided to avoid tyranny
Jean-Jacques Rousseau *The Social Contract* (1762)	Argued that true democracy would require many people to share political power

Many Enlightenment thinkers were deists, who believed in God but not in traditional Christian teachings. They questioned the authority of any church to persecute those who did not accept its teachings. The French writer Voltaire used satire and wit to make fun of intolerance and prejudice.

Enlightenment philosophers such as Jean-Jacques Rousseau wanted to apply their ideas to education, which they believed would improve society. Others sought reforms in criminal justice and in conditions for the poor.

The Enlightenment in America

The ideas of the Enlightenment began in the educated upper classes of Europe but soon spread beyond the European continent. Locke in particular was widely read in the American colonies. His ideas influenced Thomas Jefferson and Benjamin Franklin, among others. Jefferson used Locke's theories in 1776 when he wrote the Declaration of Independence:

HISTORY'S VOICES

❝We hold these truths to be self-evident, that all men are created equal, that they are endowed by their Creator with certain unalienable Rights, that among these are Life, Liberty and the pursuit of Happiness.❞

—The Declaration of Independence, 1776

Other early American leaders used Enlightenment ideas when they drafted the United States Constitution.

FACES OF HISTORY

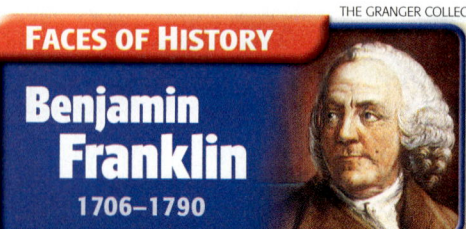

Benjamin Franklin
1706–1790

One of the most famous Americans in history, Benjamin Franklin was a man of many talents. He worked as a printer, publisher, author, inventor, scientist, politician, and diplomat. In all of these roles he helped shape American history.

As an inventor and scientist, Franklin exemplified the Enlightenment ideals of science and reason. His curious mind led him to invent bifocal glasses and the lightning rod, among other things. As a politician, Franklin helped draft the Albany Plan of Union and revised the first draft of the Declaration of Independence. During the American Revolution, Franklin served as a diplomat. Then at age 81, he was the oldest delegate at the Constitutional Convention.

Evaluate Why do you think Benjamin Franklin is one of the most famous Americans in history?

ACADEMIC VOCABULARY

displaced took the place of

Both Benjamin Franklin and Thomas Jefferson were interested in science and invention, applying reason to ask questions and find answers. Franklin was typical of the Enlightenment ideal of self-improvement and optimism. While still a printer's apprentice, he spent half his money on books, including one by Locke.

Enlightenment thinkers questioned common beliefs and deep-rooted superstitions. Benjamin Franklin, for example, did many experiments with electricity. In the most famous experiment, he flew a kite in a thunderstorm to prove that lightning was a form of electricity. Franklin was then able to collect the electricity from the lightning and conduct experiments with it. These experiments made him famous as a scientist, but they were controversial, too. Some people still did not believe that lightning was a form of electricity.

READING CHECK **Comparing** What was the connection between science and the Enlightenment?

The Great Awakening

Enlightenment ideas also led some people in the colonies to question long-accepted religious beliefs. They looked for rational, scientific explanations for how the universe worked.

At the time, many Christian denominations taught that human beings were essentially wicked. Only God's grace or their own faith and good works could save them. Most Enlightenment thinkers, however, believed humankind was essentially good, or at least capable of learning to be good.

Changes in religious attitudes Such Enlightenment ideas disturbed the traditional religious establishment. Strict groups, such as the Puritans, were dismayed by the growing tolerance for other beliefs. Even in the 1700s, Puritan New England still appeared very strict to people in other colonies. But the Puritans themselves were already worried about the decline of religious fervor in their communities. Church membership was declining.

In addition, many colonies were becoming prosperous from business and trade. Some religious leaders worried that material values and concern for making money had displaced spiritual values. Clergy looked for new ways to bring people back to the church. That set the stage for one of the great social movements in American history.

A revival of religion That movement was a religious revival in the colonies known as the **Great Awakening**. Beginning in New England and New Jersey in the 1720s and 1730s, the Great Awakening eventually swept through all the colonies. One of its leaders was the Puritan minister **Jonathan Edwards**. Emphasizing the individual's personal relationship with God, Edwards appealed to his listeners' fears and emotions. His most famous sermon painted a terrifying picture of the agonies that sinners would suffer if they did not repent.

Like so many other American thinkers of the time, Edwards was influenced by the philosophies of men such as John Locke and Sir Isaac Newton. Like them, Jonathan Edwards valued rational thought. His fiery sermons displayed his belief in the rational, or logical, aspects of religion.

In 1739 a British Methodist minister, **George Whitefield**, traveled to America. As he had done in England, Whitefield held open-air meetings that were intended to move audiences to feel the religious spirit. Thousands came to hear him. Whitefield preached his way through the colonies. Unlike Edwards, he did not frighten his audiences, but his strong voice moved people to cry and confess their sins.

Sermon

In this 1741 sermon, clergyman Jonathan Edwards asked people to think about how God views their sinful acts.

> Edwards used vivid images to stir his listeners' emotions and imaginations.

Skills FOCUS **READING LIKE A HISTORIAN**

1. **Analyzing Primary Sources** What imagery does Edwards use to describe his view of God's relationship with sinners?

2. **Contrasting** How does this sermon bring forth the idea of both God's anger and his forgiveness?

See **Skills Handbook**, pp. H10, H28–H29

"The God that holds you over the pit of hell much as one holds a . . . loathsome insect over the fire abhors [hates] you, and is dreadfully provoked; his wrath toward you burns like fire; he looks upon you as worthy of nothing else but to be cast into the fire; he is of purer eyes than to bear you in his sight; you are ten thousand times more abominable [horrible] in his eyes than the most hateful venomous serpent is in ours. You have offended him infinitely more than ever a stubborn rebel did his prince, and yet it is nothing but his hand that holds you from falling into the fire every moment."

> Great Awakening preachers believed that people would turn toward evil without the help of God.

Although Benjamin Franklin and George Whitefield did not agree about religion, they became good friends. In his *Autobiography* Franklin describes one of Whitefield's crowded meetings in Philadelphia:

HISTORY'S VOICES

"He had a loud and clear Voice, and articulated his Words & Sentences so perfectly that he might be heard and understood at a great Distance . . . He preached one evening from the top of the Court House Steps . . . I computed that he might well be heard by more than Thirty-Thousand."

—*The Autobiography of Benjamin Franklin, 1793*

The Great Awakening led to an increase in church membership in the 1700s. It also resulted in the growth of new Protestant denominations in America. Puritan beliefs formed the basis of the Congregational Church. By the mid-1700s, the evangelistic movements of the Great Awakening helped the Methodist, Baptist, and Presbyterian churches to become well established.

The Great Awakening had other key effects on the colonies. Although its leaders sometimes disagreed on religious matters, overall the Great Awakening still forged one of the first links uniting the colonies. It also led to the creation of several respected centers of learning, including Princeton, Brown, and Rutgers colleges, as well as Dartmouth College.

READING CHECK **Summarizing** How did the Great Awakening influence religious attitudes in the colonies?

The Colonies Become More Diverse

The first colonists in New England, Virginia, and the Carolinas came primarily from England. Other colonies, especially New York and Pennsylvania, attracted people from more diverse backgrounds. Dutch influence remained strong in New York.

Non-English colonists In the early 1700s, large numbers of Scots and Scots-Irish (Scots from Northern Ireland) emigrated to the colonies. They settled mainly in the middle colonies and the Carolinas and were pioneers in settling the mountainous back country. Mostly strict Presbyterians, they had little love for the

FOCUS ON NEW YORK

DAILY LIFE

New York City continues to be a place of great diversity. Today, its population is 11 percent African American, 10 percent Puerto Rican, 9 percent Italian, 5 percent Irish, 5 percent Dominican, and 4.5 percent Chinese. The city also includes the nation's largest Jewish community.

English government. They were always ready to fight for their political rights.

Religious unrest in Europe and religious tolerance in the colonies attracted Germans, French Huguenots, and Jews to America. Many German colonists were skilled farmers and artisans. They established weaving mills, ironworks, and glassworks. French colonists also brought their craft and scientific skills to the colonies. Jewish communities grew up in the cities of Newport, Philadelphia, New York, and Charleston.

The new American As often happens, it took a newcomer to recognize what America was becoming. Hector St. John de Crèvecoeur (krehv-CUHR) was a French immigrant who looked carefully at his adopted country.

HISTORY'S VOICES

❝What then is the American, this new man? He is neither an European, nor the descendant of an European . . . He is an American . . . Here individuals of all nations are melted into a new race of men, whose labours and posterity will one day cause great changes in the world.❞

—*Letters from an American Farmer*, 1782

READING CHECK **Identifying the Main Idea** Describe the growing ethnic, religious, and occupational diversity in colonial America.

Life in Colonial America

Early English settlers, along with newcomers from many countries, were creating a new American culture. As Hector St. John de Crèvecoeur had noticed, it was not English or European, but something new.

Colonial cities Colonial cities were lively, exciting places. Some had streets paved with cobblestones and sidewalks lit by oil lamps. Ships from foreign ports anchored in the harbors. People waited eagerly for letters from relatives. They also enjoyed the latest English newspapers and magazines with gossip and drawings of new fashions.

Many colonial cities had libraries, bookshops, and impressive public buildings. City dwellers could go to plays or concerts. They shopped in markets for country produce and luxury goods from Europe. Schools taught music, dancing, drawing, and painting as well as more traditional academic subjects.

In some ways, city life was easier for women than rural life was. They were freed from the hard work of farming, such as milking cows or working in their gardens, even though they still had many daily household tasks to perform. Women in more prosperous households had more time for reading and writing. Both men

American Civil Liberty

Freedom of the Press

Freedom of the press was not an English tradition. Instead, it developed in the American colonies. In 1734 a New York printer named John Peter Zenger printed several newspaper articles in the *New York Weekly Journal* criticizing the royal governor. Officials burned the paper and arrested Zenger.

Under English law, Zenger could have been found guilty simply for publishing the articles. But Zenger's lawyer, Andrew Hamilton, argued that the articles could not be considered libel—an unlawful attack of character—if they were true. He insisted that the jury's decision could potentially "affect every freeman that lives under a British government on the mainland of America."

The judge tried to uphold the law as written, but the jury agreed with Hamilton and freed Zenger. The case of *Crown* v. *Zenger* was an important step towards freedom of the press. The precedent it set eventually led to the acceptance of truth as a defense in cases of libel.

Identifying Cause and Effect How did the *Zenger* case influence the British colonies?

This tapestry commemorates both the *Zenger* case and victory for a free press.

THE METROPOLITAN MUSEUM OF ART

and women spent many hours writing letters to keep in touch with friends and family.

Popular culture People in colonial America worked hard but had time for play, too. Many got their work done in sociable ways, such as in quilting bees or barn raisings. Northern colonists went ice-skating and sledding in winter. Others enjoyed horse racing and hunting.

People made their own entertainments. Visiting neighbors was a favorite pastime. Social events in the colonies often included getting together with neighbors to dance or listen to music.

Colonial communications Printers in the colonies were also publishers. They printed and distributed newspapers, books, advertisements, and political announcements. The first American printer set up a printing press in Cambridge, Massachusetts. In 1640 he published the *Bay Psalm Book* for use in Puritan church services.

Communications were slow between the colonies and with England. Letters to England went by ship, taking many weeks. The ever-inventive Benjamin Franklin helped improve the postal service between colonies. The postal service also carried newspapers.

Influential newspapers were published in Boston, New York, and Philadelphia. Printing was so expensive, however, that only the most pertinent information was included in their pages. This usually meant that classified advertisements and reports of crop prices filled most columns of colonial newspapers.

Some newspaper publishers were careful not to disagree with royal officials, but others were bolder. In 1734 British royal officials arrested publisher John Peter Zenger for printing material critical of the New York governor. In the court case that followed, Zenger won the first important victory for freedom of the press in the American colonies. (See American Civil Liberty on the opposite page.)

African American culture In spite of the difficulties of their lives, enslaved Africans created their own culture and society. This was especially true on larger plantations. Their community grew to include others nearby.

African Americans tried to build a strong family structure. But the realities of slavery split husbands and wives, parents and children, who were often sold separately and sent away. Kinship networks had always been important in many African cultures. Now they became essential as a way of looking after those who had lost their real families.

Religion was another strength of the community. Many African Americans were Christians but also kept older African beliefs. The slave community preserved music and dance traditions as well. African music, foods, and other traditions gradually became a part of American culture.

READING CHECK **Summarizing** In what ways were African families in the colonies affected by slavery?

SECTION 3 ASSESSMENT

go.hrw.com
Online Quiz
Keyword: SD7 HP3

Reviewing Ideas, Terms, and People

1. a. Define What was the **Enlightenment**?
   b. Explain What was John Locke's view of the relationship between people and government?
   c. Elaborate How did Locke's ideas influence British colonists in North America?

2. a. Identify Who was **George Whitefield**, and why was he important?
   b. Compare How did **Jonathan Edwards** and Whitefield differ in their appeals to colonial audiences?
   c. Evaluate What influence did the **Great Awakening** have on colonial religion?

3. a. Recall Where did the Scots-Irish settle in the colonies?
   b. Make Generalizations What skills did later immigrants bring to the colonies?

4. a. Recall What kinds of entertainment were popular in the American colonies?
   b. Compare How did the issues in Zenger's trial compare with the issues in the arrest of Edmund Andros?

Critical Thinking

5. Analyzing Copy the chart below and then list the different influences on colonial culture.

Influences on Colonial Culture

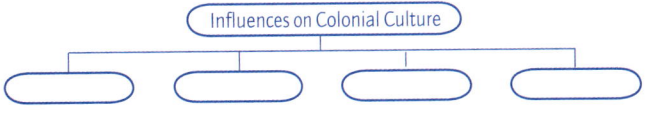

FOCUS ON WRITING

6. Expository Write a letter to the editor of a colonial newspaper. Explain why you think that it was right or wrong for John Peter Zenger to criticize a royal official.

The French and Indian War

BEFORE YOU READ

MAIN IDEA

The French and Indian War established British dominance in North America but put a strain on the relationship with the colonists.

READING FOCUS

1. How did France develop an empire in North America?
2. Why did Spain and England clash in North America?
3. What were major events in the French and Indian War?
4. What were the effects of the French and Indian War on all those involved?

KEY TERMS AND PEOPLE

George Washington
Iroquois League
Albany Plan of Union
Marquis de Montcalm
William Pitt
Treaty of Paris
George Grenville
Pontiac
Proclamation of 1763

PI 3.3 Prepare essays and oral reports about the important social, political, economic, scientific, technological, and cultural developments, issues, and events from New York State and United States history.

First Steps to FAME?

THE INSIDE STORY

What will the French say? A small expedition set out on horseback from Virginia in October 1753. It included four frontiersmen, two translators, and one 21-year-old major in the Virginia militia. The officer's name was **George Washington**. On orders from King George II, the governor of Virginia had sent Washington to the Ohio Valley to warn the French that they were on British lands and must leave.

The group traveled north through snow and rain to a French fort near Lake Erie. The French officers greeted Washington formally, but they said no to the king's message. Now Washington had to get home to Virginia in mid-winter.

A few months later, in the spring of 1754, Washington was sent back with a company of soldiers. The Virginians built a small log fort, Fort Necessity, near the French stronghold of Fort Duquesne, but they were badly outnumbered. When a much larger French force attacked, Washington had to surrender. ■

France in North America

The first permanent French settlement in North America was a fur-trading post started in 1608 at Quebec by Samuel de Champlain. Later that century, La Salle claimed the Mississippi basin for France. He named the region Louisiana, after the French king Louis XIV.

To protect the fur trade, Champlain made alliances with the Algonquians and Hurons. In 1609 the French helped those allies in raids against the Iroquois Mohawks.

Instead of building towns along the coast, French fur traders and missionaries traveled deep into the interior. They formed close ties with Native American fur trappers. Traders lived in Native American villages, learned their languages, and married local women.

As early as the 1600s, English and French traders in the Great Lakes region fought over the fur trade. They also clashed over the rich fishing grounds off Nova Scotia and over islands in the Caribbean.

France had built outposts from the Great Lakes to the Mississippi Valley by the early 1700s. French forts at Detroit, Niagara, Kaskaskia, and New Orleans bordered the English colonies to the west.

While the French were forming alliances with Native Americans, the English were doing the same thing. The power struggle between the two nations and their allies meant constant battles along the frontier.

READING CHECK **Identifying the Main Idea**
What was the basis of the economy in France's colonies in America?

Spain and England Clash

Spain and England clashed in North America, especially in the area known as La Florida. It included much of Georgia and South Carolina, the Florida peninsula, and land along the Gulf Coast.

Spain wanted its territory in La Florida as a defense against France and England. La Florida did not have gold, silver, or particularly fertile soil. But holding this territory allowed Spain to guard the sea routes for Spanish treasure ships returning from Mexico.

In the late 1500s, Franciscan friars began to establish missions along the Atlantic coast. By the mid-1600s, the Spanish were operating nearly 40 missions in Florida and Georgia.

As English colonies expanded southward, they threatened the Spanish missions and settlements. Carolina slave raiders began to attack the Spanish missions. By 1700 the Spanish presence in Florida had been reduced to the areas of St. Augustine and Pensacola.

READING CHECK **Contrasting** How did Florida differ from Spain's colonies in Mexico?

The French and Indian War

The French and Indian War lasted from 1754 to 1763 and became part of a larger war between France and Great Britain called the Seven Years' War. War between France and Great Britain broke out in the colonies first, then spread to the European continent. The French joined with Native Americans to attack the British in North America. Spain and its colonies were also involved.

THE IMPACT TODAY

Government
Before 1707 England and Scotland were officially separate nations. In 1707 they joined together as the Kingdom of Great Britain. Today the nation is known officially as the United Kingdom of Great Britain and Northern Ireland. The United Kingdom includes England, Scotland, Wales, and Northern Ireland.

Young Washington delivered a message to the French to withdraw from the Ohio Valley. Washington, who volunteered for this duty, earned both a bonus and wide recognition.

The Iroquois League An alliance of Native Americans called the **Iroquois League** allied itself with Britain. The League had formed nearly 200 years earlier in what is now upstate New York. The Mohawk, Oneida, Onondaga, Cayuga, and Seneca peoples—often at war with each other—formed an alliance in 1570. According to tradition, a prophet named Dekanawidah led the Five Nations to "plant the Tree of Great Peace" and unite as the Iroquois League. The Tuscarora joined in 1722 as the sixth nation.

The Iroquois League had a constitution and a council of leaders. Its unity allowed the Iroquois League to resist European takeover. Although most northeastern Native Americans had allied with the French, the Iroquois League saw the Europeans as enemies.

The Albany Plan In the early 1750s conflict with France erupted in the Ohio River Valley. The French built Fort Duquesne (doo-KAYN) at the point where the Allegheny and Monongahela rivers join to form the Ohio—the site of Pittsburgh today. But a Virginia-based land company planned to bring settlers there. In 1754 George Washington and his militia made an unsuccessful attempt to take this land back from France. This was the first skirmish of the French and Indian War.

Later in 1754, at the urging of British officials, delegates from New England, New York, Pennsylvania, and Maryland met in Albany. Their main goal was to win the support of the Iroquois League against the French. At the same time, they wanted to achieve some sort of unity among the colonies. Benjamin Franklin proposed the **Albany Plan of Union** as a way to colonial unity. Each colony would keep its own constitution, while a grand council would deal with military issues, Native American relations, and western settlement. Although the Albany Plan of Union was never approved, it was the first atttempt to unite the colonies.

The war continues The early war went badly for the British. Their commander, General Edward Braddock, tried again to capture

PRIMARY SOURCES

Political Cartoon

In 1754 Benjamin Franklin published this political cartoon to encourage support for the Albany Plan of Union.

JOIN, or DIE.

The colonies are represented as divided parts of a snake. Some people thought Franklin chose a snake to reflect the winding eastern coastline.

The slogan meant that the colonies should join together because they were on the verge of war with France.

Skills FOCUS   READING LIKE A HISTORIAN

1. **Analyzing Primary Sources** What image did Franklin use to represent the colonies?
2. **Drawing Conclusions** Why do you think Franklin chose to present his message through a cartoon?

See **Skills Handbook**, pp. H12, H28–H29

Fort Duquesne in 1755. George Washington was his chief aide, leading about 250 Virginia militia.

In unfamiliar territory, the British soldiers were easy targets for an ambush by the French and their Native American allies. Almost 1,000 were wounded or killed, including Braddock. George Washington then assumed command of the army and proved a heroic leader, even though two horses were shot out from under him.

In New York, the **Marquis de Montcalm**, the French commander, won victory after victory. He captured Fort Oswego on Lake Ontario and Fort William Henry on Lake George in 1756. Montcalm's greatest battle was at Fort Ticonderoga in 1758, when his 3,800 men turned back a British force of 15,000.

William Pitt became the British secretary of state in 1757 and took control of directing the war. British officers in America began to force colonists into the army, seize supplies, and send soldiers to stay in colonists' houses. The colonists resented this and resisted. Pitt then relaxed some policies, sending more British soldiers to America.

In 1758 British and colonial troops recaptured Fort Duquesne. Their Native American allies began to desert the French. The next year the British took back Fort Ticonderoga and captured Fort Niagara and Crown Point on Lake Champlain.

Next, General James Wolfe besieged Quebec. Montcalm thought that the city's location on a steep bluff would protect it. But the British found a path up the cliff from the river. In the battle that followed, both commanders were killed. Quebec surrendered in September 1759. That was the turning point in the war, and France surrendered the following year.

THE FRENCH AND INDIAN WAR IN NEW YORK

French possession
British possession
French fort
British fort
French movement
British movement
Battle

0   40   40 Miles
0   40   80 Kilometers
Albers equal-area projection

Quebec

NEW FRANCE

Montreal

St. Lawrence River

Fort Frontenac

Fort Crown Point (St. Frédéric)

Lake Champlain

Fort Ticonderoga (Carillon)

Lake Ontario

Fort Niagara

Fort Oswego

Fort William Henry

NH

Fort Stanwix

Fort Edward

Fort Herkimer

Fort Hunter

NY

Albany

MA

GEOGRAPHY SKILLS **INTERPRETING MAPS**

Construction of French forts in the Ohio Valley antagonized the British into declaring war on the French.

1. **Movement** What is the pattern of fighting shown on this map?
2. **Human-Environment Interaction** Why did the British army have difficulty fighting in the American colonies? Why didn't the French army have the same difficulty?

See **Skills Handbook**, p. H20

The peace treaty The **Treaty of Paris**, signed in 1763, ended the Seven Years' War in Europe and the French and Indian War in North America. Britain gained all French land east of the Mississippi River—including much of what is now Canada. This victory gave Britain the basis of what would become a mighty empire.

Spain gave up control of Florida to Britain but got a major prize from its ally France—the huge Louisiana Territory, including the city of New Orleans. An earlier secret treaty between the two monarchs had made the transfer, but the Treaty of Paris confirmed it. France kept two islands near Canada and regained some Caribbean islands.

READING CHECK **Drawing Conclusions**
What was the goal of the Albany Plan of Union?

FOCUS ON NEW YORK

CULTURE

To commemorate the 250th anniversary of the French and Indian War, New York is hosting a series of events through the year 2010. These events—including reenactments—will highlight key turning points of the war.

Effects of the War

The war brought some important benefits to the colonists. Ironworkers, shipbuilding, and farmers profited by supplying the army. Carolinians and Georgians benefited from the acquisition of Florida, which could no longer serve as a haven for runaway slaves.

Though they had been unwilling to unite at first, the war forced the colonists to work together. Their common effort increased the colonists' self-confidence.

The war brought Britain an empire, but at a great cost. British officials decided that the colonists should pay some of those expenses.

After King George III took the throne in 1760, his new prime minister, **George Grenville**, wanted to be strict with the colonies. His policies would alienate the colonists even further.

Pontiac's Rebellion The Treaty of Paris gave Britain control over the Great Lakes region, but its native peoples resisted the takeover. Their leader was **Pontiac**, an Ottawa chief in what is now Michigan. At first Pontiac welcomed colonial and British troops who were taking over French forts. But he later realized that the British were not as friendly toward Native Americans as the French. He made a daring plan to drive them out.

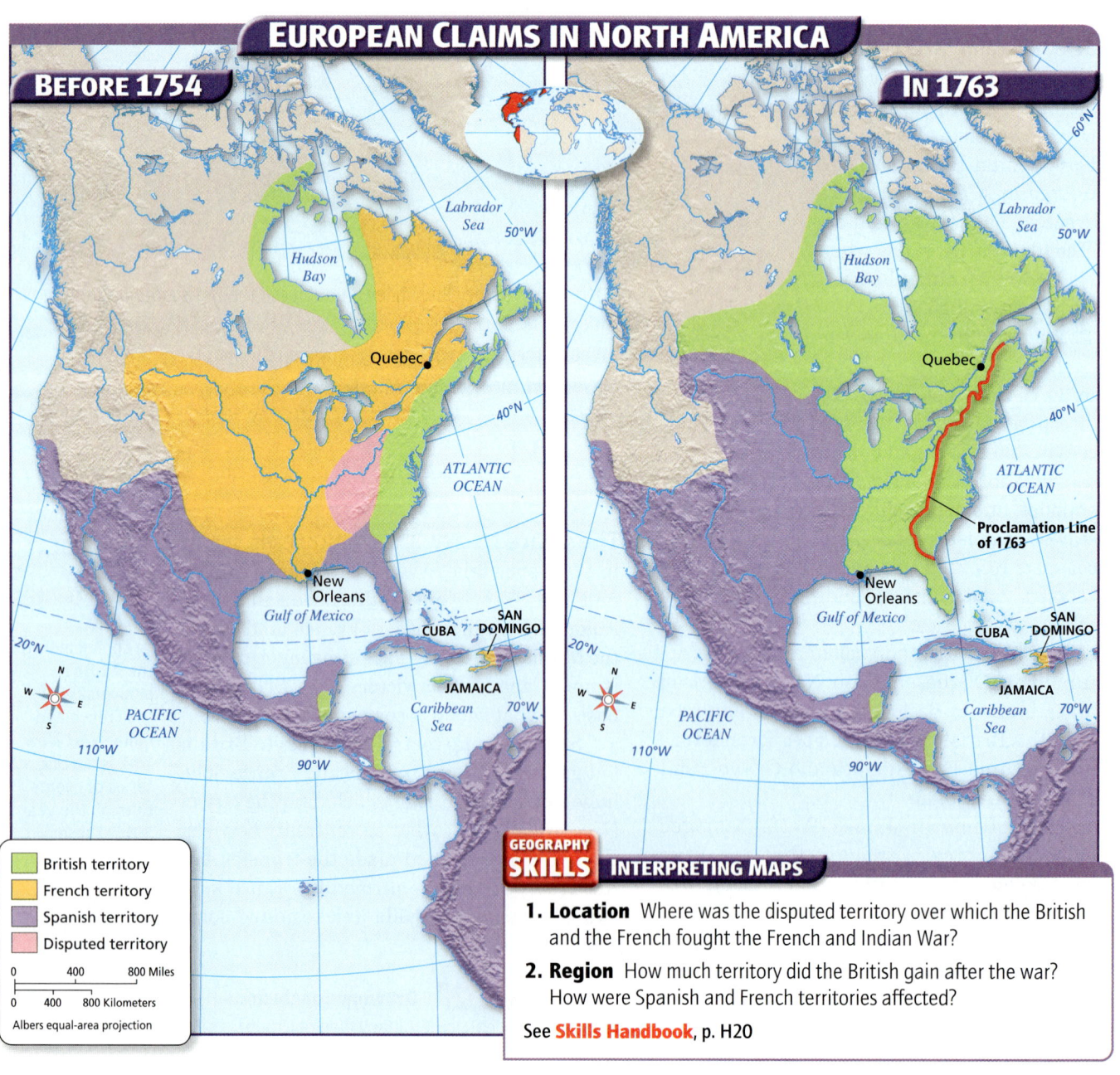

EUROPEAN CLAIMS IN NORTH AMERICA

BEFORE 1754

IN 1763

Proclamation Line of 1763

- British territory
- French territory
- Spanish territory
- Disputed territory

0   400   800 Miles
0   400   800 Kilometers
Albers equal-area projection

GEOGRAPHY SKILLS INTERPRETING MAPS

1. **Location** Where was the disputed territory over which the British and the French fought the French and Indian War?

2. **Region** How much territory did the British gain after the war? How were Spanish and French territories affected?

See **Skills Handbook**, p. H20

In 1762 Pontiac put together an alliance of almost all the Native Americans in the Upper Midwest. His strategy was for each group to overcome the nearest British fort and then attack the surrounding settlements. Pontiac expected help from the French, but that help never arrived and the siege failed.

The war went on for several years. Pontiac's forces wiped out forts and settlements, but the British held on. In 1766 Pontiac agreed to a peace treaty.

The Proclamation of 1763

As soon as the French left, American traders and settlers crossed the mountains into the Ohio Valley. To avoid conflicts with the Native Americans there, officials decided to stop colonists from moving west. With the **Proclamation of 1763**, they drew a line along the Appalachian Mountains, reserving land on the western side for Native Americans.

This appealed to British officials because it gave them control of migration westward. It also slowed the movement out of cities, which were centers of trade and prosperity.

Effects on Native Americans

Overall, the war was a disaster for the Native Americans of the Ohio Valley, no matter which side they had chosen. Most had supported the losing French. Even the Iroquois League, who had been allies of the British, had been weakened by the war.

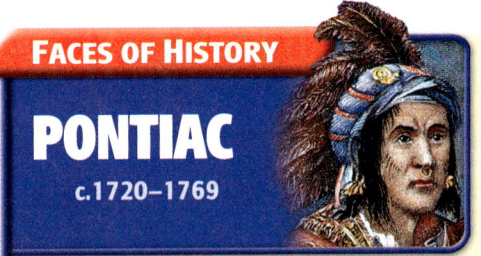

FACES OF HISTORY

PONTIAC
c.1720–1769

Pontiac was born in present-day Michigan to parents from two different Native American groups in the area, the Ottawa and the Ojibwa.

Pontiac traveled widely, meeting with various Native American groups. By 1755 he ruled as chief of a strong organization that united the Ottawas, Ojibwas and Potawatomies.

When the British began to settle in the region, Pontiac rallied the various Native American groups to oppose the newcomers. Pontiac and other Native American leaders laid siege to the British Fort Detroit for six months. While the siege was not successful, Pontiac won fame for his leadership.

Draw Conclusions Why was Pontiac considered a great leader?

The British believed the Iroquois had given only half-hearted support and no longer felt as friendly toward their former allies.

Although the Proclamation of 1763 was meant to slow western settlement, it did take away some native lands. Plus, settlers often ignored the Proclamation altogether. Later treaties continued to push the line of white settlement farther and farther west.

READING CHECK **Summarizing** What were the major effects of the French and Indian War?

SECTION 4 ASSESSMENT

go.hrw.com
Online Quiz
Keyword: SD7 HP3

Reviewing Ideas, Terms, and People

1. a. Identify What was the role of Samuel de Champlain in French settlement in North America?
   b. Compare How did the French colonies in North America differ from the British colonies?

2. a. Recall Why was Florida an important part of Spain's North American empire?
   b. Summarize What led to clashes between the British and Spanish in Florida?

3. a. Identify What were the roles of **George Washington**, Edward Braddock, Marquis de Montcalm, and **William Pitt** in the French and Indian War?
   b. Interpret Which country lost the most territory as a result of the French and Indian War?

4. a. Recall What was Pontiac's strategy to defeat the British? Did he succeed?

b. Make Inferences Why did British officials want to slow migration out of cities?
c. Predict How might the colonists' new self-confidence affect their relationship with British officials?

Critical Thinking

5. Sequencing Copy the chart below and make a time line of major events and battles in the French and Indian War.

The French and Indian War | 1754 | 1756 | 1758 | 1760 | 1762

FOCUS ON WRITING

6. Persuasive As a colonial newspaper editor, write an editorial either defending or attacking the British policy of drafting colonists and quartering soldiers in people's homes.

African Traditions in the Colonies

Historical Context The documents below provide different perspectives on how Africans carried their traditions to the colonies.

Task Examine the documents and answer the questions that follow. Then you will be asked to write an essay about African culture in the colonies, using facts from the documents and from the chapter to support the position you take in your thesis statement.

ST **4.3** Develop hypotheses about important events, eras, or issues; move from chronicling to explaining historical events and issues; use information collected from diverse sources to produce cogently written reports and document-based essays.

DOCUMENT 1

Most African cultures have strong musical traditions. Enslaved Africans used drums for dancing and sometimes for sending coded messages. For this reason, drums were outlawed in some parts of the colonies. The drum on the left was made by an enslaved African who lived in Virginia. Created from local materials, the style of its carvings is very similar to drums found in Africa, such as the drum on the right.

DOCUMENT 2

The rhythm of the drum was often used in traditional African religious ceremonies. One of the most common types of spiritual worship that was carried to the colonies was the ring shout, in which worshippers dance and chant, often shouting as they sing. This style of worship was very different from the quieter styles typical of most European churches. Colonist John Watson commented upon observing this style of worship among a group of free blacks near Philadelphia.

"In the blacks' quarters, the coloured people get together, and sing for hours together, short scraps of disjointed affirmations, pledges, or prayers, lengthened out with long repetitious choruses. These are all sung in the merry chorus-manner of the southern harvest field, or [corn]husking-frolic method, of the slave blacks; and also very greatly like the Indian dances. With every word so sung, they have a sinking of one or the other leg of the body alternately; producing an audible sound of feet at every step . . . If some, in the meantime sit, they strike the sounds alternately on each thigh . . . [T]he example has already visibly affected the religious manner of some whites. From this cause, I have known in some camps meetings from 50 to 60 people crowd into one tent, after the public devotions have closed, and there continues the whole night, singing tune after tune, . . . scarce one of which were in our hymn books. Some of these from their nature, (having very long repetition choruses and some short scraps of matter) are actually composed as sung and are almost endless."

This watercolor painting titled *The Old Plantation* was created by an unknown artist. It shows enslaved Africans from South Carolina around 1790. The image contains numerous examples of African cultural traditions that carried over to the colonies.

This instrument may be a Yoruba *gudugudu*, a drum made by stretching animal skin over a hollowed-out piece of wood.

In African societies it was common to dance barefoot while wearing colorful head scarves. These head scarves are patterned after the style used by West African groups such as the Yoruba.

COLONIAL WILLIAMSBURG FOUNDATION

This image may be showing a marriage ceremony. In some African societies, couples jumped over a stick or broom when they wed. Slaves in American societies came to refer to getting married as "jumping the broom."

This instrument is similar to the *molo*, an ancestor of the banjo, used by the Yoruba.

Skills FOCUS   READING LIKE A HISTORIAN

1. a. Identify Refer to Document 1. How are the two drums similar?
b. Interpret Why might some people in the colonies view drums as dangerous?

2. a. Describe Refer to Document 2. According to the writer, what other group has a dance style similar to that of the African Americans?
b. Analyze In what ways did the ring shout affect white society?

3. a. Describe Refer to Document 3. What is happening in the image?

b. Interpret How does the image reflect the strength of cultural traditions?

4. Document-Based Essay Question Consider the question below and form a thesis statement. Using examples from Documents 1, 2, and 3, create an outline and write a short essay supporting your position.
How did African culture survive in the colonies, even under slavery?

See **Skills Handbook**, pp. H28–H29, H30

Visual Summary: Colonial Life

Political
- The Navigation Acts and the Dominion of New England: two attempts by England to exert more control over the colonies
- Salutary neglect of the colonies brought about colonial self-government

Economic
- Northern economy: farming, shipbuilding, trade, commerce
- Southern economy: plantation farming (tobacco, rice, indigo)
- Slavery in the northern and southern colonies provided agricultural workers, servants, and artisans.

Military
- The French and Indian War (1754–1763): France and England clash over territory in North America
- Treaty of Paris (1763) redraws lines in North America; England and Spain claiming the most territory

Life in the Colonies

Social
- The Great Awakening increased church membership
- The European Enlightenment spread to the colonies, bringing ideas of law and individual rights
- Immigration from other countries increased diversity in the colonies

Reviewing Key Terms and People

For each term or name below, write a sentence explaining its significance to colonial life.

1. mercantilism
2. balance of trade
3. Navigation Acts
4. salutary neglect
5. triangular trade
6. Middle Passage
7. Enlightenment
8. Benjamin Franklin
9. Great Awakening
10. George Washington
11. Albany Plan of Union

Comprehension and Critical Thinking

SECTION 1 *(pp. 72–76)*

12. a. Recall What was the Glorious Revolution?

b. Explain How were the policies of William and Mary different from those of James II?

c. Evaluate How did salutary neglect change the relationship between Britain and the colonies?

SECTION 2 *(pp. 77–83)*

13. a. Identify Name two major industries in the northern colonies.

b. Compare How were northern colonial economies different from southern colonial economies?

c. Evaluate Why was slavery more prevalent in the southern colonies than in the northern colonies?

History's Impact video program

Review the video to answer the closing question: Why was victory in the French and Indian War so important for the British?

SECTION 3 *(pp. 84–89)*

14. a. Recall What was the Enlightenment?

b. Explain How did the Great Awakening change religious life in the colonies?

c. Elaborate What were some other important aspects of colonial society?

SECTION 4 *(pp. 90–95)*

15. a. Identify What was the central conflict of the French and Indian War?

b. Summarize What were the terms of the Treaty of Paris?

c. Predict How might the terms of the Treaty of Paris continue to affect the relationship between Great Britain and the American colonies?

Using the Internet

go.hrw.com
Practice Online
Keyword: SD7 CH3

16. Colonial life was different from life today in many ways, but it was remarkably similar in others. The lack of electricity made simple tasks much more challenging. But children played games similar to those played by children today, and adults looked for ways to lighten the burdens of daily life. Using the keyword above, do research to learn more about daily life in colonial times. Then create a report that describes what you learned and how the lives of the colonists were similar to and different from our lives today.

Analyzing Primary Sources

Reading Like a Historian John Adams wrote the following passage in 1775, recalling the colonial rebellion against Governor Edmund Andros.

> ❝It ought to be remembered that there was a revolution here, as well as in England, and that we, as well as the people of England, made an original, express contract with King William.❞

—John Adams, *Novanglus Letters*, 1775

17. Identify What was the contract between the American colonies and King William?

18. Make Inferences In 1775 America was on the brink of revolution against Great Britain. Why was Adams referring back to the Governor Andros incident, which had happened a century earlier?

Critical Reading

Read the passage in Section 4 that begins with the heading "The Albany Plan" and study the political cartoon. Then answer the questions that follow.

19. According to the passage, the Albany Plan of Union was the idea of

A Benjamin Franklin.

B George Washington.

C the Iroquois League.

D Great Britain.

20. The passage and the political cartoon suggest that uniting the colonies was important because

A they shared one constitution.

B they were stronger together than they were apart.

C there was too much distance between the colonies.

D one colony had all the power.

21. According to the passage, the Albany Plan of Union was significant because

A it formed the framework for the Constitution.

B it was approved by the British and all the colonial assemblies.

C it was the first attempt to unite the colonies.

D it helped the colonists defeat the British.

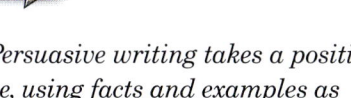
FOCUS ON WRITING

Persuasive Writing *Persuasive writing takes a position for or against an issue, using facts and examples as supporting evidence. To practice persuasive writing, complete the assignment below.*

Writing Topic The rising tensions between Great Britain and its colonies during the years 1650–1763

22. Assignment Given what you have read in the chapter, were the colonists justified in protesting British policies? Write a short essay in which you develop your position on this issue. Support your point of view with reasoning and examples from your reading and studies.

CHAPTER 1 — The World before 1600
Beginnings to 1600

MAIN IDEA Native Americans inhabited the Americas for thousands of years before the arrival of Europeans. Then in the 1400s, an age of exploration began in Europe. European sailors traveled to Asia, Africa, and the Americas.

SECTION 1 The first Americans developed societies in North, Central, and South America, adapting to the land and creating a way of life that remained undisturbed for thousands of years.

SECTION 2 Differences in geography shaped North American cultures prior to European settlement. Groups across North America were linked by trade.

SECTION 3 Wealthy African empires established trade routes across the Sahara. When European explorers first arrived in Africa in the 1400s, they wanted to trade for gold and other riches. Eventually, they began a slave trade from Africa that lasted for hundreds of years and caused extreme human suffering.

SECTION 4 The Renaissance in Europe was characterized by new ways of thinking and the desire to explore other worlds. Explorers set sail from Europe, hoping to find gold and spread Christianity.

SECTION 5 Searching for a westward route to Asia, Christopher Columbus landed on a new continent. The colonies he built in the Caribbean marked the beginning of European colonization in the Americas.

CHAPTER 2 — European Colonies in America
1500–1733

MAIN IDEA Spain was the first European nation to claim land in the Americas. In the 1700s, however, England had joined with Scotland to form a powerful nation known as Great Britain. By 1733 Great Britain claimed 13 colonies along the Atlantic seaboard of North America.

SECTION 1 Spanish conquistadors established an empire in the Americas. France, England, Portugal, and the Netherlands also sent explorers to America.

SECTION 2 In 1607 the English established a colony at Jamestown, Virginia. It was the first permanent English settlement in North America. By the mid-1600s, the Virginia colony was thriving.

SECTION 3 To escape religious persecution in England, the Pilgrims settled Plymouth Colony in Massachusetts. Other colonies in the North soon followed.

SECTION 4 A new phase of British colonization in America began, leading to the establishment of the Middle Colonies and the Southern Colonies. These colonies were founded for a variety of reasons, from religious freedom to personal profit.

CHAPTER 3 — Colonial Life

1650–1763

MAIN IDEA Life in the colonies was shaped by the policies enforced by Great Britain, the economies that emerged in the various regions, and the distinctive American culture that was beginning to form. Struggles over territory eventually led to the French and Indian War.

SECTION 1 Great Britain's mercantilist policies gave it a strong hold over the colonies. Although the colonies formed governments, final political authority rested with Parliament and the British monarch.

SECTION 2 Colonial economies were shaped by local natural resources. Commerce and shipping dominated in the North, while the South relied on agriculture and building plantations to grow cash crops.

SECTION 3 The Enlightenment and the Great Awakening led to new ways of thinking in the colonies. During this time a unique colonial culture began to take shape in the thirteen colonies.

SECTION 4 Great Britain, France, and Spain fought for dominance in North America during the French and Indian War. Several Native American groups formed alliances with France during the war. However, Great Britain's eventual victory established a large British territory east of the Mississippi River.

Forming a NEW Nation

1763–1815

Themes

Government and Democracy
American colonists fought Great Britain in the Revolutionary War and won the opportunity to forge a new nation and form a democratic government.

Rights and Responsibilities
Americans adopted the Constitution of the United States and the Bill of Rights to ensure responsible government and to protect the rights of the individual.

George Washington (right) and his officers pledge their allegiance to an independent United States of America.

Prepare to Read

Summarizing

Find practice for **Summarizing** in the **Skills Handbook,** p. H6

Summarizing is a way of condensing information by conveying only the most important points. Summarizing can help you recall what you read.

Before You Read
Read headings and the review questions to determine what the passage will be about.

While You Read
Identify the main idea of the passage. Then look for the key details that support it.

After You Read
To summarize the passage, restate the main idea and key supporting details in your own words.

The Role of Women

Even before independence was declared, American women had been active in boycotts and other protests. Once the fighting began, Patriot women found many other ways to take part.

A few, like Deborah Sampson, disguised themselves as men to become soldiers in the Continental Army. Mary Hays was nicknamed "Molly Pitcher" for bringing water to the troops at the battle of Monmouth in New Jersey on a blistering hot day. Stories say that she took over her husband's gun when he was overcome by the heat. Many other women also carried food and water to the soldiers on the battlefields.

Women also served as couriers, scouts, and spies. One teenager, 16-year-old Sybil Ludington, learned of a planned British attack on Danbury, Connecticut. On her horse Star, she made a 40-mile night ride to spread the alarm.

READING CHECK **Summarizing** In what ways did women participate in the Revolutionary War?

The heading tells you the topic—women's roles in the Revolutionary War.

Main Idea Patriot women contributed in many ways to the battle for independence.

Details Patriot women served as soldiers, couriers, scouts, and spies.

Test Prep Tip

Multiple choice and short answer questions on tests ask you to summarize what you have read. Try breaking lengthier text into shorter summaries by noting the main idea of each paragraph or passage as you read.

Recognizing Bias in Primary Sources

Find practice for **Recognizing Bias in Primary Sources** in the **Skills Handbook,** p. H33

Bias is a point of view that is slanted by personal or political beliefs. Every primary source reflects a bias—of the person who created it. Bias may appear in primary sources for a variety of reasons. An author may be trying to argue for or justify some course of action. An author may also be expressing a personal view without knowing that it is biased.

Strategies historians use:

- Examine clues such as dates as well as words such as *our* and *we* to recognize bias in primary sources.
- Compare the primary source with other sources and with historical evidence. Is the passage consistent with other historical accounts?
- Learn about the author's background and beliefs to determine what particular bias he or she may have.

The author of this passage is justifying the action of colonists to take up arms against Great Britain.

How does this account of history compare with what you already knew about it?

❝We have not raised armies with ambitious designs of separating from Great Britain and establishing independent states . . . In our own native land, in defence of the freedom that is our birthright . . . for the protection of our property, acquired solely by the honest industry of our forefathers and ourselves, against violence actually offered, we have taken up arms.❞

—from *Declaration of the Causes and Necessity of Taking Up Arms,* July 6, 1775

Dates can help you determine context. In 1775 the colonies were struggling against Great Britain. This passage was written from the colonists' point of view.

Skills FOCUS **READING LIKE A HISTORIAN**

As You Read Examine a passage once without regard to bias. Then reread the passage, looking for examples of bias. What differences did you note between your first and second readings?

As You Study Use what you know about bias to add context to important historical events. Construct a chart showing the author of a primary source, his or her point of view, and examples of bias.

The Revolutionary ERA

THE BIG PICTURE Great Britain began to increase taxes on the American colonists, who protested because they were not represented in Parliament. Small rebellions, mostly in the form of boycotts, led to tighter controls, which triggered all-out war.

New York Standards

Key Idea 1 The study of New York State and United States history requires an analysis of the development of American culture, its diversity and multicultural context, and the ways people are unified by many values, practices, and traditions.

Key Idea 3 Study about the major social, political, economic, cultural, and religious developments in New York State and United States history involves learning about the important roles and contributions of individuals and groups.

Skills FOCUS **READING LIKE A HISTORIAN**

Cannon fire lights up the early morning sky in *The Battle of Princeton*, a 1777 painting by early American artist James Peale. The victories at Trenton and Princeton helped Americans believe that their independence was more than just words on paper.

Identifying Points of View Why do you think Peale chose to commemorate this battle?

See **Skills Handbook**, pp. H28–H29

U.S.

World

October 1763
The Proclamation of 1763 bars colonists from settling in Indian lands west of the Appalachians.

1765

1765
Parliament passes the Stamp Act, angering colonists.

History's Impact video program

Watch the video to understand the impact of the Declaration of Independence today.

March 1770
Five protesters are killed by British soldiers in the Boston Massacre.

April 1775
Revolutionary War begins with battles of Lexington and Concord.

July 4, 1776
Congress approves the Declaration of Independence.

October 19, 1781
British surrender at Yorktown, ending the war.

1770 — 1775 — 1780 — 1785

1775
King George III issues a proclamation banning overseas trade for American colonies.

1778
Following the Battle of Saratoga, France formally recognizes the U.S. and promises military help.

1783
Treaty of Paris ends the Revolutionary War. Britain signs subsidiary treaties with America and allies France and Spain.

The Road to Revolution

BEFORE YOU READ

MAIN IDEA

A series of increasingly restrictive laws angered many American colonists, leading to rebellion against Britain.

READING FOCUS

1. Why did Great Britain pass new laws in America?

2. How did the colonists respond to the new laws? How did their response lead to even stricter measures?

3. Why did the First Continental Congress meet?

4. What was the significance of the battles at Lexington and Concord?

KEY TERMS AND PEOPLE

Samuel Adams
Stamp Act
Quartering Act
writs of assistance
Boston Massacre
Committees of Correspondence
Intolerable Acts
First Continental Congress
minutemen

P1 1.2 Describe the evolution of American democratic values and beliefs as expressed in the Declaration of Independence, the New York State Constitution, the United States Constitution, the Bill of Rights, and other important historical documents.

The Boston TEA PARTY

◄ Colonists in crude disguises destroy tea at Boston Harbor.

THE INSIDE STORY

How did tea start a rebellion in Boston?

In 1773 Parliament passed the Tea Act, which was designed to help a struggling British company and reduce smuggling. Because of colonial boycotts, the British East India Company had millions of pounds of unsold tea. Colonists instead were drinking smuggled Dutch tea or making "liberty tea" from dried raspberry or currant leaves.

Under the new law the East India Company was allowed to sell tea directly to the colonists. This meant East India Company tea was actually cheaper than smuggled tea. Still, the colonists resisted. In November 1773 three ships arrived in Boston Harbor. Bostonians allowed the ships to dock but not unload.

On the night of December 16, 1773, a large and angry crowd gathered in downtown Boston. They demanded that the tea ships be sent back to London. Then another group of people arrived, disguised as Indians. In fact, they were Samuel Adams and about 70 others. Protected by the crowd, they boarded the ships. They broke open the chests of tea and dumped them into the harbor. Hundreds of Bostonians watched from the shore, enjoying the Boston Tea Party. The loss of the valuable cargo infuriated British officials and brought more repressive laws. ■

Britain Passes New Laws

By the time the Boston Tea Party took place, tensions had been rising between Great Britain and its colonies for some time. As you read in the previous chapter, colonists had rebelled against arrogant royal officials such as Edmund Andros. They had also disobeyed laws they did not like, such as the Navigation Acts.

Then the French and Indian War created even more tension between Britain and the colonies. Colonists had fought beside British soldiers, who treated them poorly and refused to learn how to fight in the American wilderness. Families also resented being forced to house British soldiers.

After the war, Parliament tried to deny the colonists access to western lands with the Proclamation of 1763. But colonists thought they had a right to those lands because they had helped defeat the French. Resentment of this and other British laws would increase over the next decade, eventually leading the American colonies to revolution.

Grenville and the Sugar Act
The French and Indian War left Britain with a huge debt and with an army of 10,000 in the colonies. The British government said the troops were there to protect the colonies from lingering threats after the war. But many colonists felt the British troops were in fact there to intimidate them. Colonists also felt that they did not need British protection because they had been defending themselves for over 150 years.

The issue of British soldiers became even more of a problem for the colonists when Prime Minister George Grenville decided that the colonists should pay for the troops themselves. Grenville's plan was to tax the colonies to raise money. The first law Parliament passed to accomplish this was the Sugar Act, which put a tax on sugar and molasses imported from the French and Spanish West Indies. Northern merchants especially disliked the Sugar Act. They feared that the new tax would hurt the rum industry because the molasses used to make rum would be more expensive.

Other colonists raised a different issue. In the Boston town meeting, **Samuel Adams** said that making colonists pay taxes without a representative in Parliament changed them from being "free Subjects to the miserable state of

BOYCOTTING BRITISH GOODS

Skills FOCUS READING LIKE A HISTORIAN

To protest unpopular British laws, some colonial women boycotted, or refused to buy, British goods. The British illustration shown here criticized women's boycotts.

Identifying Point of View How are the women depicted here?

tributary Slaves." The cry of "no taxation without representation" became a major issue in the years before the Revolutionary War.

The Stamp Act brings protests
Looking for another way to raise money, Grenville next proposed a stamp tax. Passed early in 1765, the Stamp Act required a government tax stamp on all legal documents, such as contracts and licenses. Newspapers, almanacs, and even printed sermons and playing cards had to have the official stamps.

The Stamp Act proved to be a very bad idea. It was the first time Parliament had taxed Americans directly, and colonists protested the law openly. In part this was because the people the Stamp Act affected most—lawyers, merchants, printers, ministers, innkeepers—were the same people who led public opinion. In many places mobs forced stamp agents to resign. In Philadelphia colonists even conducted a mock hanging of a dummy representing a stamp agent.

In Virginia, a young lawyer named Patrick Henry made a fiery speech to the House of Burgesses. Henry proposed that Virginians should pay only the taxes voted by their own assembly. Then the Massachusetts assembly organized the Stamp Act Congress to protest the Stamp Act. In October 1765, delegates from nine colonies met in New York to send a petition to the king and Parliament. The petition stated that Parliament did not have the right to tax the colonies without representation.

In response to the new laws, a group called the Sons of Liberty organized protests. At first this group had been made up of unskilled workers, artisans, and small farmers. Now the group included prominent citizens such as merchants and lawyers. One protest tactic was to boycott, or refuse to buy, British goods. This had started with the Sugar Act. Women joined the protests as Daughters of Liberty. They stopped buying British goods and wore clothes of homespun cloth. They also put pressure on merchants who did not join the boycott.

As merchants in Great Britain saw sales drop because of boycotts, they asked Parliament to repeal the Stamp Act. Parliament did eventually repeal the act, but still insisted it had the right to tax the colonies.

Another unpopular law passed in 1765 was the **Quartering Act**, which said that colonists must find quarters, or living space, for the British soldiers stationed in America. The colonists saw the Quartering Act as another attack on their rights.

ACADEMIC VOCABULARY

imported bought from another country

Townshend Acts Many powerful people in Britain thought that Parliament was giving in to the colonists too often. So in 1767 a new government minister, Charles Townshend, came up with a new way to tax the colonies. He proposed a tax on lead, paint, paper, glass, and tea that were imported from Britain. The money raised would pay the costs of the army in America and the salaries of colonial officials. But the Townshend Acts angered the colonists. To them, it was another case of taxation without representation.

The Townshend Acts also brought back **writs of assistance**, which Parliament had used unsuccessfully in the colonies in the 1600s. A writ gave customs officers the right to search colonial homes for smuggled goods—without a search warrant. This violated the right to privacy in one's house, a cherished right in Britain. In a protest against writs, James Otis wrote:

HISTORY'S VOICES

"A man's house is his castle; and while he is quiet, he is as well guarded as a prince in his castle. This writ, if it should be declared legal, would totally annihilate [destroy] this privilege. Customhouse officers may enter our houses when they please; we are commanded to permit their entry. Their menial servants may enter—may break locks, bars, everything in their way . . ."

–James Otis, speech before Superior Court of Massachusetts, 1761

READING CHECK **Making Inferences** Why did colonists object to writs of assistance?

Tensions between Britain and America, 1765–1775

STAMP ACT, 1765

British Action Great Britain passed a law requiring colonists to pay tax—in the form of stamps—on certain documents.

Colonists' Reaction Refusing to use the stamps, colonists burned them and started riots. In 1765 the colonists formed a Stamp Act Congress asking Parliament to repeal the law.

TOWNSHEND ACTS, 1767

British Action Britain passed a series of four laws declaring its authority over the colonies. The Townshend Acts suspended one colonial representative assembly and also set up strict measures for collecting taxes in the colonies.

Colonists' Reaction The colonists resented the threat to their self-government and protested what they considered "taxation without representation."

BOSTON MASSACRE, 1770

British Action British troops quartered in Boston opened fire after being harassed by an angry mob of colonists. Five colonists died.

Colonists' Reaction Boston colonists, including Samuel Adams, demanded the removal of British troops from Boston.

The Colonists Respond

Customs officials strictly enforced the new laws. But Boston merchants were used to avoiding customs duties. Now they joined with merchants in Philadelphia and New York in nonimportation agreements. Some southern merchants and planters joined them.

The plan worked. Most of the Townshend Acts were repealed in March 1770. Parliament kept the tax on tea, however, to show that it still had the right to tax the colonies. But by then the colonists' anger was growing. The first serious confrontation happened in Boston on the same day that the Townshend Acts were repealed, though that news had not yet reached America.

The Boston Massacre Seeing the British soldiers on their streets angered the people of Boston. The troops were a reminder of British control and arrogance. Laborers especially disliked them, since the poorly paid soldiers took part-time jobs when they were off duty. Street fights were common.

On March 5, 1770, a crowd of colonists began to throw snowballs at the sentry guarding the customs house. A British officer brought soldiers to help, but the scuffle went on. Workers taunted the British soldiers—known as Redcoats for their red uniforms—calling them "lobster scoundrels."

Accounts disagree about what happened next. Someone shouted "Fire!" and the British soldiers fired into the crowd. Five people died, including an African American sailor named Crispus Attucks, who may have led the crowd.

Colonial leaders called the event the **Boston Massacre**. They played it up as a deliberate attack on innocent civilians. The soldiers were put on trial for murder. To make sure that the law was followed, attorney John Adams (a cousin of Samuel) agreed to represent the soldiers in this unpopular case. All the soldiers were freed except for two who were given a light punishment. To avoid more violence, the troops moved out of Boston.

Samuel Adams and his fellow radicals made sure that no one would forget the Boston Massacre. A few years later, Adams introduced the idea of **Committees of Correspondence** to spread the news of British injustices from colony to colony. By communicating with each other, the committees became the basis of a political network to unify the colonies.

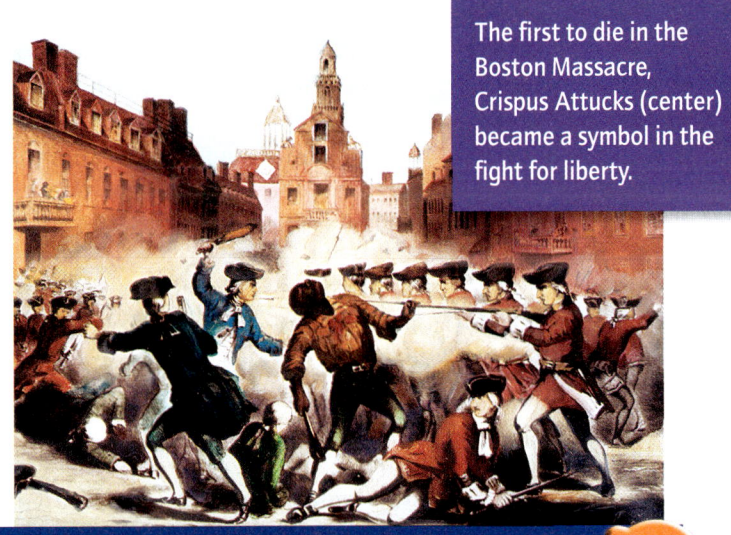

The first to die in the Boston Massacre, Crispus Attucks (center) became a symbol in the fight for liberty.

QUICK FACTS

TEA ACT, 1773	INTOLERABLE ACTS, 1774	BATTLES OF LEXINGTON AND CONCORD, 1775
British Action Great Britain restructured the tax on tea to give a special advantage to the British East India Company. Under the Tea Act, colonial tea merchants would lose business.	**British Action** In response to colonial protests, Britain passed a series of laws designed to punish the colonies, especially Massachusetts. The laws essentially took away the power of self-government in Massachusetts.	**British Action** 700 British troops advance toward Concord to seize the colonists' military supplies.
Colonists' Reaction In what became known as the Boston Tea Party, colonists dumped shiploads of British tea into Boston Harbor.	**Colonists' Reaction** The First Continental Congress convened in Philadelphia and sent a list of grievances to Great Britain.	**Colonists' Reaction** In Lexington, about 70 minutemen fight the British, and in Concord hundreds of colonists force the British troops to withdraw. It is the beginning of the Revolutionary War.

The Tea Act and the Intolerable Acts

Another new prime minister, Lord North, took office in 1770. At first he tried policies to keep the colonies quiet. Then at his request, Parliament passed the Tea Act. As you have read, the Tea Act led to the Boston Tea Party.

The Tea Act also led to one of the earliest organized political efforts by American women. In 1774 a group of women gathered in Edenton, North Carolina, and agreed to boycott tea. A British political cartoon satirized the women because, at the time, politics was not considered a proper activity for women.

Angry officials in London wanted the colonists to pay for the Boston Tea Party. Some British politicians, such as William Pitt and Edmund Burke, warned that stricter laws would unite the colonists. But Lord North insisted. In 1774 Parliament passed a series of laws, the Coercive Acts, to punish the rebellious colonists. In the colonies, these laws were called the Intolerable Acts.

The first of the Intolerable Acts closed the port of Boston. Another gave the royal governor much more control over Massachusetts. He could hire and fire local officials, and limit town meetings. Still another act imposed more rules for quartering soldiers.

The Quebec Act An additional annoyance for the colonists was a law known as the Quebec Act. Britain had won French territory in Canada after the French and Indian War. Incorporating that territory into British North America proved difficult, however. Settlers in Canada were used to French law. In addition, the scattered French settlements were difficult to protect from Native Americans.

Parliament attempted to solve these problems with the Quebec Act. This act expanded the province of Quebec southward to the Ohio River and west to the Mississippi, including the scattered French settlements there. The Roman Catholic Church would be legal, and French Catholics were guaranteed their rights.

American colonists were alarmed. They assumed that the Quebec Act would limit their chances to settle on the western frontier. They also felt the act threatened their security against the French.

READING CHECK **Summarizing** How did colonists respond to increasingly strict laws from Britain?

The First Continental Congress

As some British political leaders had predicted, the Intolerable Acts brought more unity among the colonies. Other colonies sent food and money to support the people of Massachusetts. Colonists also organized boycotts.

In September 1774 delegates met in Philadelphia at the First Continental Congress. In attendance were Patrick Henry, George Washington, John and Samuel Adams, and John Jay. They agreed that each colony would have one vote, despite differences in size.

John Adams, who kept careful notes at the Congress, reported a speech by Patrick Henry:

HISTORY'S VOICES

"The distinctions between Virginians, Pennsylvanians, New Yorkers, and New Englanders are no more. I am not a Virginian but an American."

—Patrick Henry, quoted in *The Works of John Adams*

In many ways, the First Continental Congress did bring the colonists together as Americans. All the delegates agreed that Parliament was exerting too much control. Still, their views varied from moderate to radical. One delegate suggested a plan for union under British authority, much like the Albany Plan of Union. The delegates, however, rejected that proposal by a very close vote.

The Congress then issued a Declaration of Rights protesting Great Britain's actions. This document reflected the delegates' mixed views toward Britain. In the document, the Congress accepted Parliament's right to regulate trade. But the Declaration of Rights also called for the removal of British troops and the repeal of taxes and the Intolerable Acts.

Boycotts had worked before, so the Congress used those tactics again. They agreed not to import or use British goods and to stop most exports to Britain. The Continental Congress also formed a force of minutemen, colonial soldiers who would be ready to resist a British attack with short notice.

After taking these actions, the Continental Congress agreed to meet again in the spring. At that time they would decide if further action was necessary.

READING CHECK **Making Inferences** Why did colonists accept British regulations on trade but not taxes?

The Battles of Lexington and Concord

Before the Continental Congress could meet again, however, war began. Minutemen in Massachusetts had been drilling on their village commons and stockpiling gunpowder and weapons. The British commander in Boston, General Thomas Gage, was waiting for reinforcements. He knew that colonial militias all across the Massachusetts countryside were preparing for a conflict.

Gage was also becoming more hostile to the unruly American colonists. He wrote to a British official that "conciliating, moderation, reasoning is over. Nothing can be done but by forceable means." In preparation Gage sent several of his officers to survey the local countryside. He also organized small groups of British soldiers to take short marches in the hopes that the colonists would see his well-trained troops and be intimidated by them.

Then in April 1775, new orders came from Great Britain. King George III wanted to take action against the colonists. The king ordered General Gage to arrest colonial leaders, particularly Samuel Adams and John Hancock. Gage also began to prepare the British troops to capture the colonists' gunpowder. The gunpowder was stockpiled in Concord, a town several miles west of Boston.

To accomplish this Gage planned a surprise attack for the night of April 18, 1775. At 10 o'clock that night, about 700 British troops crossed the Charles River in small boats and set out by road for Concord.

Battle of Lexington

British troops fired at minutemen on Lexington Green.

The minutemen are shown leaving. Eight were killed and ten were wounded.

Skills FOCUS — INTERPRETING VISUALS

In this 1775 engraving American troops on Lexington Green scatter under British fire in the first battle of the Revolutionary War.

Interpreting Visuals How does this engraving show the relative experience of American and British troops?

See **Skills Handbook**, p. H30

Spreading the alarm Colonial leaders had watched Gage's preparations, so they knew something was about to happen. A secret system of alarm riders was already in place to warn the minutemen of any unusual activity among the troops in Boston. The alarm riders were a group of about 30 men who were ready to ride their horses across the countryside to warn their fellow colonists about any action taken by the British troops.

The most famous of these riders was Paul Revere, a Boston silversmith and engraver who belonged to the Sons of Liberty. On the night of April 18, he and William Dawes learned about the British movements. They set off toward Lexington to warn Adams and Hancock.

Revere crossed the river to Charlestown, got a horse from friends, and started for Lexington. On the way, he escaped from two British guards who chased him. Revere later told how in Medford he "awaked the captain of the minute men and after that, I alarmed almost every house, till I got to Lexington."

Dawes set off from Boston. At about midnight, he met Revere in Lexington at the house where Adams and Hancock were staying. They warned the two leaders, then set off for Concord. A young doctor, Samuel Prescott, another of the Sons of Liberty, caught up with them on the road. As Dawes and Prescott went to warn people in a nearby house, Revere rode on. British officers surrounded him and tried to arrest them all. Prescott and his horse jumped a low stone wall and escaped to warn the minutemen at Concord. Dawes also escaped.

The British captured Revere and continued along the route toward Lexington. But soon they heard the guns of the colonial militia. They took Revere's horse and let him go. He escaped back to the house where Adams and Hancock were staying.

Lexington and Concord

The alarm riders had awakened the countryside. Alarm bells everywhere began to ring. Besides, 700 armed British soldiers could not move along a quiet country road without being heard. By the time the British reached Lexington, the militia had been waiting a long time. In fact, some colonists had already left. Still, about 70 minutemen remained waiting for the British soldiers on the Lexington town green.

When the British troops arrived, the minutemen realized they were badly outnumbered. Their captain ordered them to leave. But then, according to colonial accounts, British soldiers charged toward them. According to one account, Major Pitcairn, leading the British troops, shouted at the minutemen, "Ye villains, ye rebels, disperse!" Then from somewhere on the Lexington town green, a shot rang out.

More shots followed, and the militia fled. Eight Americans were killed, and others were wounded. The first shots of the Revolutionary War had been fired—although to this day no one is sure whether it was the colonists or the British who fired first.

The British next moved on to Concord. There the scene was very different. Hundreds of minutemen had assembled at Concord. Most of their store of gunpowder had already been used or hidden in the woods. The militia backed away from the narrow bridge as the British advanced toward them. The two sides exchanged gunfire.

Finally, the British turned and retreated toward Boston. All along the way, angry militia

THE IMPACT TODAY

Daily Life

Each year, the Boston Marathon takes place on Patriot's Day, a day in April that commemorates Paul Revere's 1775 ride.

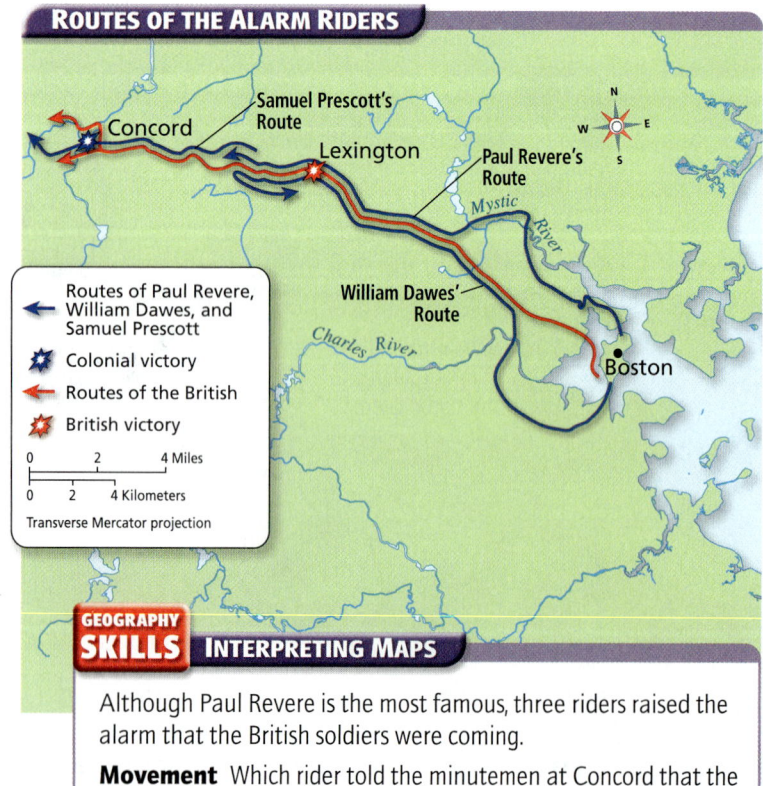

ROUTES OF THE ALARM RIDERS

Samuel Prescott's Route

Concord

Lexington

Paul Revere's Route

Mystic River

William Dawes' Route

Charles River

Boston

Routes of Paul Revere, William Dawes, and Samuel Prescott

★ Colonial victory

Routes of the British

✹ British victory

0   2   4 Miles
0   2   4 Kilometers

Transverse Mercator projection

GEOGRAPHY SKILLS   INTERPRETING MAPS

Although Paul Revere is the most famous, three riders raised the alarm that the British soldiers were coming.

Movement Which rider told the minutemen at Concord that the British soldiers were approaching?

See **Skills Handbook**, p. H19

The Battle of Lexington

The colonists and the British troops saw the Battle of Lexington very differently. British officer John Pitcairn gave General Gage this account of the battle.

"I gave directions to the troops to move forward, but on no account to fire, or even attempt it without orders; when I arrived at the end of the Village, I observed drawn up upon a Green near 200 rebels; when I came within about 100 yards of them, they began to file off towards some stone walls on our right flank. The Light Infantry, observing this, ran after them. I instantly called to the soldiers not to fire, but surround and disarm them, and . . . some of the rebels who had jumped over the wall fired four or five shots at the soldiers . . . and at the same time several shots were fired from a meeting house on our left. Upon this . . . the Light Infantry began a scattered fire, and continued in that situation for some little time, contrary to the repeated orders both of me and the officers that were present."

 Skills FOCUS **READING LIKE A HISTORIAN**

1. **Analyzing Primary Sources** Why do you think Pitcairn is emphasizing that the British soldiers did not fire first?
2. **Identifying Points of View** How does this source compare to other points of view you read about in this section?

See **Skills Handbook**, pp. H28–H29

---

hid behind barns, stone walls, and fences, firing at the British soldiers as they passed. At the end of the day, the number of British casualties was far greater than the number of colonial casualties.

The shot heard 'round the world Many years later, on July 4, 1837, Ralph Waldo Emerson wrote a poem for the dedication of the Battle Monument at Concord. Emerson's grandfather had fought at the Battle of Concord. In the poem, Emerson wrote an unforgettable phrase to describe the importance of the battle: "Here once the embattled farmers stood/ And fired the shot heard 'round the world."

 READING CHECK **Sequencing** Trace, in order, what happened on April 18 and April 19, 1775.

---

 go.hrw.com
Online Quiz
Keyword: SD7 HP4

SECTION 1 ASSESSMENT

Reviewing Ideas, Terms, and People

1. **a. Identify** How did the Sons and Daughters of Liberty respond to new British laws?
   b. Analyze In what ways did the French and Indian War increase tensions between the British and the colonists?
   c. Evaluate Why did the **Stamp Act** anger colonists more than other taxes?

2. **a. Describe** What happened at the Boston Tea Party? Why did it happen?
   b. Make Inferences Why did colonists pay more for smuggled Dutch tea?
   c. Evaluate Were the colonists justified in dumping the British tea into Boston Harbor?

3. **a. Identify** Who were the major colonial leaders at the **First Continental Congress**?
   b. Summarize What actions did the First Continental Congress take?
   c. Predict Was the meeting of the Congress a final step toward independence? Why or why not?

4. **a. Recall** What did alarm riders do?
   b. Summarize Describe what happened at the Battles of Lexington and Concord.
   c. Evaluate Why did Emerson refer to the Battle of Concord as "the shot heard 'round the world"?

Critical Thinking

5. **Sequencing** Copy the chart below and make a time line of the events and laws leading up to the battles at Lexington and Concord.

Lexington and Concord

FOCUS ON SPEAKING

6. **Persuasive** As a delegate to the First Continental Congress meeting *before* the Battles of Lexington and Concord, make a speech explaining what course you think the colonies should take next.

Declaring Independence

BEFORE YOU READ

MAIN IDEA

As a revolutionary ideology grew and conflicts with Britain continued, the Second Continental Congress declared American independence.

READING FOCUS

1. What actions did the Second Continental Congress take?

2. How did violence in Boston push the colonies closer to revolution?

3. What revolutionary ideology lay behind the writing of the Declaration of Independence?

4. How did colonists' reactions to the Declaration of Independence differ?

KEY TERMS AND PEOPLE

Second Continental Congress
Thomas Jefferson
Continental Army
John Adams
Battle of Bunker Hill
Loyalist
Thomas Paine
Common Sense
Virginia Declaration of Rights
Abigail Adams

PI 1.2 Describe the evolution of American democratic values and beliefs as expressed in the Declaration of Independence, the New York State Constitution, the United States Constitution, the Bill of Rights, and other important historical documents.

"Give Me LIBERTY"

COLONIAL WILLIAMSBURG FOUNDATION

THE INSIDE STORY

Were Americans ready for the Revolution? Patrick Henry was known as a fiery speaker and a radical leader. His brilliant arguments in the courtroom made him a successful lawyer. As early as 1765, speaking against the Stamp Act, Henry criticized the king and Parliament and defended the colonies' right to self-government.

Ten years later in early 1775, Massachusetts minutemen were organizing a self-defense force. Grandfathers and teenagers were drilling with muskets on the village commons. On March 23, 1775, Patrick Henry once again stirred up his audience in the Virginia Convention of Delegates:

"Gentlemen may cry, Peace, Peace—but there is no peace. The war is actually begun! The next gale that sweeps from the north will bring to our ears the clash of resounding arms! Our brethren are already in the field! Why stand we here idle? What is it that gentlemen wish? What would they have? Is life so dear, or peace so sweet, as to be purchased at the price of chains and slavery? Forbid it, Almighty God! I know not what course others may take; but as for me, give me liberty or give me death!"

Henry's rousing speech inspired Virginians to raise a militia. Only a few weeks after his speech, as you have read, fighting began at Lexington and Concord. ◼

◀ **Patrick Henry's words fanned the flames of revolution.**

The Second Continental Congress Takes Action

In May 1775, a few weeks after Lexington and Concord, the **Second Continental Congress** met in Philadelphia as planned. New members included Benjamin Franklin, John Hancock, and **Thomas Jefferson**. When the group convened, delegates' attitudes toward Britain was mixed. Many still felt loyalty toward King George III, blaming his ministers and Parliament for bad policies. All delegates rejected Parliament's authority to tax the colonies, but only a few actually wanted independence. During the next months they made several crucial decisions.

Creating a Continental Army
War had already begun, and New Englanders and British troops were fighting around Boston. The Congress agreed to support the war, even though its members did not agree on the final goal. The Congress made the New England forces the core of a **Continental Army**.

Then in June 1775 the Congress chose George Washington to lead the new army. **John Adams** of Massachusetts suggested Washington for the position, pointing out his "skill and experience as an officer" in the French and Indian War. Adams also noted Washington's "independent fortune, great talents, and excellent universal character."

War or peace?
In July the Congress issued two very different documents. The differing positions in these documents reflected the colonists' divided feelings. The first, called *A Declaration of the Causes and Necessity of Taking Up Arms*, explained why Americans were at war. It accused Parliament of having "an inordinate passion for power." It also charged General Gage with "cruel aggression." Finally, the document concluded:

HISTORY'S VOICES

❝We have not raised armies with ambitious designs of separating from Great Britain and establishing independent states. . . . In our own native land, in defence of the freedom that is our birth-right . . . for the protection of our property, acquired solely by the honest industry of our forefathers and ourselves, against violence actually offered, we have taken up arms.❞

–*A Declaration of the Causes and Necessity of Taking Up Arms*, July 6, 1775

THE SECOND CONTINENTAL CONGRESS, 1775

- Formed the Continental Army; appointed George Washington commander in chief

- Issued a Continental (national) currency

- Wrote *A Declaration of the Causes and Necessity of Taking Up Arms*

- Proposed reconciliation with King George III in the Olive Branch Petition

---

A few days later, the Congress sent King George III what became known as the Olive Branch Petition. Its authors called themselves the king's "faithful subjects in the Colonies." They begged him to use his "royal authority and influence" to reach a "happy and permanent reconciliation."

Despite the petition, the king declared the colonies to be in rebellion. In response, Parliament passed a harsh law banning colonial trade outside the British Empire.

READING CHECK **Contrasting** How did the actions of the Second Continental Congress reflect the delegates' differences of opinion?

More Violence in Boston

Even while the Continental Congress was meeting, fighting continued in several parts of the colonies. The British at first treated these encounters as local rebellions. Then colonial forces expanded the war.

On May 10, 1775, as the Continental Congress was just beginning, the Green Mountain Boys captured the British fort at Ticonderoga in New York. The Green Mountain Boys were a local Vermont militia organized by Ethan Allen. Other members of this militia captured the fort at Crown Point a few days later. Both forts were on the strategic Lake Champlain–Lake George route to Canada.

The siege of Boston
After the battles at Lexington and Concord, British troops withdrew back into Boston. Several thousand British troops occupied the town. The Americans quickly put together a larger army, bringing

CHARLES TOWN

BOSTON

together some 15,000 militia from all over New England. The standoff at Boston led to the first major battle of the Revolutionary War, the **Battle of Bunker Hill**.

Boston could be attacked from several hills overlooking the city. Dorchester Heights was to the south. Bunker Hill and Breed's Hill were across the river in Charlestown. General Gage was planning to occupy the hills as soon as reinforcements arrived.

But a colonial force led by Colonel William Prescott moved quickly to fortify the hills. While under attack from British cannons across the river and warships in the harbor, they hastily built a fort on Breed's Hill.

On June 17, 1775, British troops led by General William Howe tried to dislodge the colonists from the hilltop. Some 2,500 troops stormed the hill twice as the colonists fired from behind barricades. The colonists were short of ammunition and so waited until the enemy was a few yards away, then fired with deadly aim. One commander shouted the now-famous phrase, "Don't fire until you see the whites of their eyes!"

On the third British attempt, the colonists ran out of gunpowder. They retreated to nearby Bunker Hill (which gave the battle its name).

About 1,000 British soldiers and about 400 American colonists were killed or wounded.

Although the British won, the brave defense at the Battle of Bunker Hill gave the colonists confidence in their ability to fight the better-trained and better-equipped British army.

Washington takes command

Two weeks after the Battle of Bunker Hill, George Washington took command of the Continental Army in Boston. The army was seriously short of heavy weapons and gunpowder, so Washington sent Henry Knox to Fort Ticonderoga to bring back captured British weapons. Knox was a former Boston bookseller who was now in charge of artillery for the Continental Army. Using troops, horses, and oxen, Knox moved more than 50 cannons and mortars across 300 snowy miles to Boston.

As a result, by March 1776, Washington had enough guns and ammunition to take Dorchester Heights. From there he forced the British to evacuate Boston and the harbor. From Boston, the British sailed for Halifax, Nova Scotia, along with about 1,100 **Loyalists**, colonists whose sympathies were with the king and Britain. This first test proved Washington's ability as a general.

Other battles There were clashes in other colonies, too. In the winter of 1775–1776 Benedict Arnold led a small Continental force through the snowy wilderness in an unsuccessful attack on the city of Quebec.

In the southern colonies, colonial victories discouraged a British invasion there. In December 1775, a colonial victory over a British force in the Battle of Great Bridge in Virginia ended British rule in that colony. In February 1776, Scottish Loyalists waving broadswords attacked a colonial force at Moores Creek, North Carolina. But well-armed colonists were waiting. Their victory ended British control in North Carolina. In June, British ships launched an attack on a fort at Sullivan's Island near Charleston, South Carolina, but the fort's commander held them off.

READING CHECK **Making Inferences** Why was the Continental Army short of gunpowder and weapons?

The Declaration of Independence

The events of 1775 pushed more American colonists toward supporting independence. They were angry at the king's reaction to the Olive Branch Petition. They also learned that the British were recruiting Native Americans and African Americans to fight against them. In addition, they heard that the king was hiring mercenary soldiers from the German state of Hesse.

By the spring of 1776, some colonists were still doubtful, but their leaders were becoming certain of their cause. When the Continental Congress met again, it opened seaports to foreign trade except with Britain.

Revolutionary ideology The colonists still thought of themselves as British. Even though they lived an ocean away, they believed they were entitled to all the rights that British citizens had claimed over the years. Those rights, such as trial by jury, went as far back as the Magna Carta. But many of Parliament's recent laws seemed to differentiate between the rights of citizens in Britain and those in America. That was why colonists refused to pay taxes imposed by a Parliament where they had no representative.

Colonial leaders knew the philosophy of Enlightenment thinkers such as John Locke. The idea of natural rights was part of their revolutionary ideology. Under Locke's theory of the social contract, the present British government was failing to protect the rights and liberties of its citizens in America. That would justify a rebellion against it.

A matter of *Common Sense* One powerful voice speaking out for independence was a British journalist who had been in America for only two years. **Thomas Paine** came to America on the advice of Ben Franklin, whom he met in London. Early in 1776 Paine published a pamphlet called ***Common Sense***. In it he condemned

PRIMARY SOURCES

Common Sense

In January 1776 many colonists were divided about their relationship with Great Britain. Then Thomas Paine published *Common Sense*, a pamphlet that stated in easy-to-understand terms why the colonies should break free from Britain. This widely read document strengthened support for the American Revolution.

"Any submission to, or dependence on, Great Britain, tends directly to involve this continent in European wars and quarrels, and set us at variance [odds] with nations who would otherwise seek our friendship, and against whom we have neither anger nor complaint. As Europe is our market for trade, we ought to form no partial connection with any part of it. 'Tis the true interest of America to steer clear of European contentions, which she can never do while by her dependence on Britain she is made the weight in the scale of British politics."

Paine used direct language to make his arguments for independence from Great Britain.

Skills FOCUS **READING LIKE A HISTORIAN**

1. **Analyzing Primary Sources** According to Paine, what is a major problem with remaining under British rule?
2. **Drawing Conclusions** Why do you think Paine named his pamphlet *Common Sense*?

See **Skills Handbook**, pp. H12, H28–H29

KEY DOCUMENTS THAT INFLUENCED THE DECLARATION OF INDEPENDENCE

QUICK FACTS

Magna Carta (1215)	Guaranteed civil and political freedoms to feudal lords. These freedoms later became fundamental for all English citizens.
Mayflower Compact (1620)	Established the first colonial government in the colonies.
English Bill of Rights (1689)	Placed limits on the English king's power and more power in the hands of a representative government.
John Locke's *Two Treatises of Government* (1690)	Declared rights of life and property to be part of "natural law." Justified the overthrow of government if these rights were denied.
Thomas Paine's *Common Sense* (1776)	Argued that American colonists should not only rebel against unfair taxation but also declare independence from Britain.

monarchy and particularly the rule of George III. Paine called for an American declaration of independence, not just a protest against taxes.

Thomas Paine was a brilliant political writer, and his words stirred many colonists. Within a few months, the 50-page pamphlet sold more than 100,000 copies. It was one of the first American bestsellers.

Virginia calls for independence
In May 1776 the Virginia Convention of Delegates issued a declaration of citizens' rights called the **Virginia Declaration of Rights**. This was the first official call for American independence. It would influence not only the Declaration of Independence but also the Bill of Rights in the U.S. Constitution and many state constitutions.

Drawing on Locke's idea of natural rights, the Virginia declaration stated:

HISTORY'S VOICES

❝ That all men are by nature equally free and independent and have certain inherent rights,. . . namely, the enjoyment of life and liberty, with the means of acquiring and possessing property, and pursuing and obtaining happiness and safety. ❞

–Virginia Declaration of Rights

On June 7, 1776, Richard Henry Lee of Virginia then presented three resolutions to the Continental Congress. The first stated that the colonies should be independent. The second resolution stated that Americans needed to form foreign alliances for support. Finally, the third resolution recommended that the colonies form a plan for unification.

Writing the Declaration
Congress discussed the Virginia proposals, and no one seriously objected. That showed how far their thinking had moved toward independence. Moderates such as John Dickinson did urge people to wait to be certain of foreign help.

Finally, the delegates named a committee to write a draft of a declaration of independence. Its members were John Adams, Robert Livingston, Roger Sherman, Thomas Jefferson, and Benjamin Franklin. Jefferson was chosen to write the draft.

Jefferson was young, but Adams wrote that he came to Congress with "a reputation for literature, science, and a happy talent of composition." In fact, Adams told him, "You can write ten times better than I can." In addition, Jefferson was a Virginian, which was an advantage to him politically.

Adams and Franklin did make some changes in Jefferson's draft, however. Then the Congress as a whole made some more. They toned down some of his language about the king. Because of pressure from some southern colonies, they also cut out an entire section attacking the slave trade. The colonial economy depended on the slave trade, so including it in the Declaration of Independence would have opened up the signers to charges of hypocrisy. Jefferson later noted that the Declaration did not present new ideas but simply stated "an expression of the American mind."

On July 2, 1776, the final document was presented to the Congress, which voted to declare independence. Two days later, on July 4, they approved the entire document. Copies were sent out and read in public. Crowds in Philadelphia, New York, Boston, and other cities cheered and rang church bells. Now, in British eyes, the colonists were all rebels.

READING CHECK **Identifying Cause and Effect** How did Enlightenment thinking influence the Declaration of Independence?

Reactions to Independence

Not everyone was convinced of the need for American independence, however. Until the last minute, many colonists hoped for a compromise that would let the colonies remain part of Great Britain.

In addition, colonists living on the western frontier had not previously been part of political quarrels. They feared that a fight for independence would expose them to Indian attack, since any fighting against the British would draw men away from the defense of the frontier. Therefore, many frontier settlers did not support American independence.

Even after the Declaration, some colonists remained loyal to Britain. During the war, Britain would enlist the help of Loyalists to fight against the Patriots, those who supported independence. The Declaration of Independence forced the colonists to take sides. Would they be Patriots fighting for independence? Or would they be Loyalists?

The Loyalists Probably about a quarter of the colonists remained loyal to Great Britain and the king for the course of the Revolutionary War. Patriots called these Loyalists Tories, which was the name of the more conservative political party in Great Britain.

Loyalist feelings varied from region to region and from family to family. Most New Englanders and Virginians were strongly on the Patriot side. Feelings were mixed in the middle colonies and especially in New York. Loyalists were strong in southern colonies such as Georgia and South Carolina.

Close ties to Great Britain mattered, too. Loyalist sympathies were strong among people who had been government officials or belonged to the Anglican Church. Landowners, merchants, doctors and lawyers could be found on both sides. Most debtors, small farmers, and shopkeepers were Patriots.

In many places it was dangerous to be a Loyalist—at least publicly. Local Patriots sometimes harassed Loyalists, attacking their farms and

COUNTERPOINTS

Loyalist and Patriot

Benjamin Franklin was a Patriot who believed that the British Parliament should not make laws in the colonies. He expressed his views in a letter to his son.

Benjamin Franklin's son, William Franklin, was a Loyalist who took his responsibilities as royal governor of New Jersey seriously.

" I think that all laws until they are repealed ought to be obeyed and that it is the duty of those who are entrusted with the executive part of government to see that they are so. "

William Franklin,
1771

" I am indeed of opinion, that the parliament has no right to make any law whatever, binding on the colonies . . . I know your sentiments differ from mine on these subjects. You are a thorough government man, which I do not wonder at, nor do I aim at converting you. I only wish you to act uprightly and steadily. "

Benjamin Franklin,
1773

Skills FOCUS | **READING LIKE A HISTORIAN**

Identifying Points of View How did Benjamin Franklin and William Franklin differ in their views of the British government?

See **Skills Handbook**, pp. H28–H29

Abigail ADAMS
1744–1818

Intelligent and outspoken, Abigail Adams is best known for the eloquent letters she wrote to John Adams while he was away attending to his duties.

Abigail's letters show an active interest in politics. In 1775 she encouraged her husband to support the growing independence movement. Abigail also urged him to support the education of women and the abolition of slavery. In one of her most famous letters, she reminded John to "remember the ladies" when planning the new nation's government.

Interpret What do Abigail Adams's letters tell us about her political beliefs?

A cheer for the Patriots When the news of the Declaration of Independence reached Boston in July 1776, **Abigail Adams**, the wife of John Adams, had no doubts about how she felt. In one of her famous letters to John, who was then a delegate serving in the Continental Congress, Abigail described hearing the Declaration of Independence read from the State House in Boston.

HISTORY'S VOICES

❝Great attention was given to every word. As soon as he ended, the cry from the balcony was 'God save our American States,' and then three cheers which rent the air. The bells rang . . . the cannons were discharged, the platoons followed, and every face appeared joyful . . . After dinner the King's Arms were taken down from the State House, and every vestige of him from every place in which it appeared, and burnt in King Street. Thus ends royal authority in this State. And all the people shall say Amen.❞

—Abigail Adams, letter, 1776

Abigail Adams continued to write letters to her husband throughout the Revolutionary War and later during the early years of the new American republic.

READING CHECK **Making Inferences** Why did Loyalists leave the colonies?

property, or even driving them out of town. Families were sometimes bitterly divided. Some states passed laws taking away Loyalists' property.

During the war, several regiments of Loyalists fought with the British. Others left the country for Canada, Great Britain, or British-held islands in the Caribbean. Some simply lived quietly and avoided politics. After the American Revolution ended, perhaps 100,000 more Loyalists left the United States, mainly to settle in Canada.

SECTION 2 ASSESSMENT

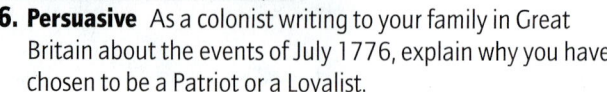

go.hrw.com
Online Quiz
Keyword: SD7 HP4

Reviewing Ideas, Terms, and People

1. a. Describe What were the delegates' points of view when the **Second Continental Congress** began?
b. Evaluate Should King George III have rejected the Olive Branch Petition?

2. a. Identify Who were the Green Mountain Boys?
b. Explain Explain the events at the **Battle of Bunker Hill**, focusing on why the battle was a British victory.
c. Predict How did the Battle of Bunker Hill encourage the American cause?

3. a. Recall What British actions in 1775 pushed the colonists toward independence?
b. Analyze What was the effect of Paine's *Common Sense* on colonial thinking?
c. Elaborate How did ideas from the Enlightenment become part of revolutionary ideology?

4. a. Describe What was the position of **Loyalists** after the Declaration of Independence?

b. Make Inferences Why would a farmer or shopkeeper tend to be a Patriot?
c. Evaluate What were the strengths of the Declaration of Independence? What were some weaknesses?

Critical Thinking

5. Contrasting Copy the chart below and fill in reasons why someone would choose the Loyalist or Patriot side.

Loyalist	Patriot

FOCUS ON WRITING

6. Persuasive As a colonist writing to your family in Great Britain about the events of July 1776, explain why you have chosen to be a Patriot or a Loyalist.

The Declaration of Independence

In Congress, July 4, 1776
The unanimous Declaration of the thirteen united States of America,

When in the Course of human events, it becomes necessary for one people to dissolve the political bands which have connected them with another, and to assume among the Powers of the earth, the separate and equal station to which the Laws of Nature and of Nature's God entitle them, a decent respect to the opinions of mankind requires that they should declare the causes which **impel** them to the separation.

We hold these truths to be self-evident, that all men are created equal, that they are **endowed** by their Creator with certain unalienable Rights, that among these are Life, Liberty, and the pursuit of Happiness. That to secure these rights, Governments are instituted among Men, deriving their just powers from the consent of the governed, That whenever any Form of Government becomes destructive of these ends, it is the Right of the People to alter or to abolish it, and to institute new Government, laying its foundation on such principles and organizing its powers in such form, as to them shall seem most likely to effect their Safety and Happiness. Prudence, indeed, will dictate that Governments long established should not be changed for light and transient causes; and accordingly all experience hath shown, that mankind are more disposed to suffer, while evils are sufferable, than to right themselves by abolishing the forms to which they are accustomed. But when a long train of abuses and **usurpations**, pursuing invariably the same Object **evinces** a design to reduce them under absolute **Despotism**, it is their right, it is their duty, to throw off such Government, and to provide new Guards for their future security.—Such has been the patient sufferance of these Colonies; and such is now the necessity which constrains them to alter their former Systems of Government. The history of the present King of Great Britain is a history of repeated injuries and usurpations, all having in direct object the establishment of an absolute **Tyranny** over these States. To prove this, let Facts be submitted to a **candid** world.

He has refused his Assent to Laws, the most wholesome and necessary for the public good.

He has forbidden his Governors to pass Laws of immediate and pressing importance, unless suspended in their operation till his Assent should be obtained; and when so suspended, he has utterly neglected to attend to them.

Vocabulary

impel force
endowed provided
usurpations wrongful seizures of power
evinces clearly displays
despotism unlimited power
tyranny oppressive power exerted by a government or ruler
candid fair

He has refused to pass other Laws for the accommodation of large districts of people, unless those people would **relinquish** the right of Representation in the Legislature, a right **inestimable** to them and **formidable** to tyrants only.

He has called together legislative bodies at places unusual, uncomfortable, and distant from the depository of their Public Records, for the sole purpose of fatiguing them into compliance with his measures.

He has dissolved Representative Houses repeatedly, for opposing with manly firmness his invasions on the rights of the people.

He has refused for a long time, after such dissolutions, to cause others to be elected; whereby the Legislative Powers, incapable of **Annihilation**, have returned to the People at large for their exercise; the State remaining in the mean time exposed to all the dangers of invasion from without, and **convulsions** within.

He has endeavored to prevent the population of these States; for that purpose obstructing the Laws of **Naturalization of Foreigners**; refusing to pass others to encourage their migration hither, and raising the conditions of new **Appropriations of Lands**.

He has obstructed the Administration of Justice, by refusing his Assent to Laws for establishing Judiciary Powers.

He has made Judges dependent on his Will alone, for the **tenure** of their offices, and the amount and payment of their salaries.

He has erected **a multitude of** New Offices, and sent hither swarms of Officers to harass our people, and eat out their substance.

He has kept among us, in times of peace, Standing Armies without the Consent of our legislature.

He has affected to render the Military independent of and superior to the Civil Power.

He has combined with others to subject us to a jurisdiction foreign to our constitution, and unacknowledged by our laws; giving his Assent to their Acts of pretended legislation:

For **quartering** large bodies of armed troops among us:

For protecting them, by a mock Trial, from Punishment for any Murders which they should commit on the Inhabitants of these States:

For cutting off our Trade with all parts of the world:

For imposing taxes on us without our Consent:

For depriving us in many cases, of the benefits of Trial by Jury:

For transporting us beyond Seas to be tried for pretended offences:

EXPLORING THE DOCUMENT Colonists had been angry over British tax policies since just after the French and Indian War. **Why were the colonists protesting British tax policies?**

For abolishing the free System of English Laws in a neighboring Province, establishing therein an **Arbitrary** government, and enlarging its Boundaries so as to **render** it at once an example and fit instrument for introducing the same absolute rule into these Colonies:

For taking away our Charters, abolishing our most valuable Laws, and altering fundamentally the Forms of our Governments:

For suspending our own Legislature, and declaring themselves invested with Power to legislate for us in all cases whatsoever.

He has **abdicated** Government here, by declaring us out of his Protection and waging War against us.

He has plundered our seas, ravaged our Coasts, burnt our towns, and destroyed the lives of our people.

He is at this time transporting large armies of **foreign mercenaries** to complete the works of death, desolation and tyranny, already begun with circumstances of Cruelty & **perfidy** scarcely paralleled in the most barbarous ages, and totally unworthy the Head of a civilized nation.

He has constrained our fellow Citizens taken Captive on the high Seas to bear Arms against their Country, to become the executioners of their friends and Brethren, or to fall themselves by their Hands.

He has excited domestic **insurrections** amongst us, and has endeavored to bring on the inhabitants of our frontiers, the merciless Indian Savages, whose known rule of warfare, is an undistinguished destruction of all ages, sexes and conditions.

In every stage of these Oppressions We have **Petitioned for Redress** in the most humble terms: Our repeated Petitions have been answered only by repeated injury. A Prince, whose character is thus marked by every act which may define a Tyrant, is unfit to be the ruler of a free People.

Nor have We been wanting in attention to our British brethren. We have warned them from time to time of attempts by their legislature to extend an **unwarrantable jurisdiction** over us. We have reminded them of the circumstances of our emigration and settlement here. We have appealed to their native justice and **magnanimity**, and we have **conjured** them by the ties of our common kindred to disavow these usurpations, which, would inevitably interrupt our connections and correspondence. They too have been deaf to the voice of justice and of **consanguinity**. We must, therefore, **acquiesce** in the necessity, which denounces our Separation, and hold them, as we hold the rest of mankind, Enemies in War, in Peace Friends.

We, therefore, the Representatives of the united States of America, in General Congress, Assembled, appealing to the Supreme Judge of the world for the **rectitude** of our intentions, do, in the Name, and by Authority of the good People of these Colonies, solemnly publish and declare, That these United

Vocabulary

arbitrary not based on law

render make

abdicated given up

foreign mercenaries soldiers hired to fight for a country not their own

perfidy violation of trust

insurrections rebellions

petitioned for redress asked formally for a correction of wrongs

unwarrantable jurisdiction unjustified authority

magnanimity generous spirit

conjured urgently called upon

consanguinity common ancestry

acquiesce consent to

rectitude rightness

EXPLORING THE DOCUMENT Here the Declaration calls the king a tyrant. **What do you think *tyrant* means from this passage?**

Colonies are, and of Right ought to be Free and Independent States; that they are Absolved from all Allegiance to the British Crown, and that all political connection between them and the State of Great Britain, is and ought to be totally dissolved; and that as Free and Independent States, they have full Power to levy War, conclude Peace, contract Alliances, establish Commerce, and to do all other Acts and Things which Independent States may of right do. And for the support of this Declaration, with a firm reliance on the Protection of Divine Providence, we mutually pledge to each other our Lives, our Fortunes and our sacred Honor.

EXPLORING THE DOCUMENT Here is where the document declares the independence of the colonies. **Whose authority does the Congress use to declare independence?**

EXPLORING THE DOCUMENT The Congress adopted the final draft of the Declaration of Independence on July 4, 1776. A formal copy, written on parchment paper, was signed on August 2, 1776.

EXPLORING THE DOCUMENT The following is part of a passage that the Congress removed from Jefferson's original draft: "He has waged cruel war against human nature itself, violating its most sacred rights of life and liberty in the persons of a distant people who never offended him, captivating and carrying them into slavery in another hemisphere, or to incur miserable death in their transportation thither." **Why do you think the Congress deleted this passage?**

John Hancock	Benjamin Harrison	Lewis Morris
Button Gwinnett	Thomas Nelson, Jr.	Richard Stockton
Lyman Hall	Francis Lightfoot Lee	John Witherspoon
George Walton	Carter Braxton	Francis Hopkinson
William Hooper	Robert Morris	John Hart
Joseph Hewes	Benjamin Rush	Abraham Clark
John Penn	Benjamin Franklin	Josiah Bartlett
Edward Rutledge	John Morton	William Whipple
Thomas Heyward, Jr.	George Clymer	Samuel Adams
Thomas Lynch, Jr.	James Smith	John Adams
Arthur Middleton	George Taylor	Robert Treat Paine
Samuel Chase	James Wilson	Elbridge Gerry
William Paca	George Ross	Stephen Hopkins
Thomas Stone	Caesar Rodney	William Ellery
Charles Carroll of Carrollton	George Read	Roger Sherman
George Wythe	Thomas McKean	Samuel Huntington
Richard Henry Lee	William Floyd	William Williams
Thomas Jefferson	Philip Livingston	Oliver Wolcott
	Francis Lewis	Matthew Thornton

The Revolutionary War Begins

BEFORE YOU READ

MAIN IDEA

While the colonies and the British began with different strengths and weaknesses, the Revolutionary War demonstrated Washington's great leadership.

READING FOCUS

1. What groups of people played a part in the Revolutionary War?
2. What major revolutionary battles took place in the North?
3. In what ways was the Battle of Saratoga a British setback?
4. How did Washington's leadership at Valley Forge influence the course of the Revolutionary War?

KEY TERMS AND PEOPLE

Redcoats
Battle of Saratoga
Valley Forge
inflation
Marquis de Lafayette

PI 3.3 Prepare essays and oral reports about the important social, political, economic, scientific, technological, and cultural developments, issues, and events from New York State and United States history.

Deborah Sampson, SOLDIER

THE INSIDE STORY

Who is that young soldier? Older soldiers in the Fourth Massachusetts Regiment felt protective toward Robert Shurtleff. The new recruit was strong, but he seemed very young to his fellow soldiers. Shurtleff was so young that he did not even have to shave! He also kept to himself, seldom joining in the teasing and rough talk that went on in camp. All the same, the young soldier proved to be brave in battle. In the fighting in New York, he was slightly wounded several times but never complained. He insisted on taking care of his wounds himself.

What the soldiers didn't realize about Robert Shurtleff was that "he" was actually a woman, Deborah Sampson. Dressed in men's breeches and shirt and with her hair cut short, the 21-year-old Sampson had joined the army posing as a man. Her disguise worked partly because she stood about 5 foot 7 inches, tall for a woman in the 1700s. She was also physically strong from doing farmwork as an indentured servant. As long as she looked and acted like a male soldier, it never occurred to anyone that Private Shurtleff was a woman. She guarded her secret until she came down with a fever. In the hospital, the truth was discovered. Sampson received an honorary discharge in October 1783, went home, and married a farmer, Benjamin Gannett. She later received a soldier's pension. ◢

▲ **Sampson, shown here in the only known portrait of her, disguised herself to become a soldier.**

The People behind the American Revolution

After declaring independence, the colonies and the Congress next took steps toward forming a nation. The colonies adopted constitutions and established new state governments. But first, the American colonists had to win the Revolutionary War. Many people would play a role.

Continentals and Redcoats When the war began, the British seemed to have an overwhelming military advantage. Britain was a world power with an army of well-trained soldiers, known as **Redcoats** for their red uniforms.

Compared with that, American prospects looked bad. Washington's Continental Army and state militias together had only about 19,000 soldiers. He had no navy except for some merchant ships armed with guns. Raising and keeping an army was a constant problem.

Finding and paying for supplies and military equipment was even harder. Congress was always short of money. The army depended heavily on captured British guns and ammunition. Soldiers and their commanders constantly complained about shortages of food, clothes, and gunpowder.

On the other hand, the British army included many hired German soldiers. They had no loyalty to their cause, while colonists were fighting for their homes and liberty. Moreover, the Royal Navy had been allowed to decline after the French and Indian War. Many of its ships were old and in poor condition.

The role of women Even before independence was declared, American women had been active in boycotts and other protests. Once the fighting began, Patriot women found many other ways to take part.

A few, such as Deborah Sampson, disguised themselves as men to become soldiers in the Continental Army. Mary Hays was nicknamed Molly Pitcher for bringing water to the troops at the battle of Monmouth in New Jersey on a blistering hot day.

Women also served as couriers, scouts, and spies. Sybil Ludington, a 16-year-old girl, learned of a planned British attack on Danbury, Connecticut. On her horse Star, she made a 40-mile night ride to spread the alarm.

ACADEMIC VOCABULARY

prospects
expectations for the future

STRENGTHS AND WEAKNESSES OF THE CONTINENTAL AND BRITISH ARMIES

QUICK FACTS

Continental Army	British Army
Strengths • Strong military leadership • Fighting on home territory • Alliance with France	**Strengths** • Well-trained military • Ample resources • Alliances with Loyalists
Weaknesses • Small, untrained military • Shortages of resources • Weak central government	**Weaknesses** • Fighting in unfamiliar territory • Fighting far from home

Many women participated in the revolution in less dramatic but still vital ways. Catherine Greene, the wife of General Nathanael Greene, turned their home into a hospital. Some women in Philadelphia raised money to supply the army with food and clothing.

Many women did what was considered "women's work" such as laundry or nursing. At home, women knit wool stockings and made bandages for the troops. Some melted down their pewter pots and pitchers to make bullets. As in all wars, women kept their homes, farms, and shops running while the men were at war.

The role of African Americans African Americans, both free and enslaved, fought on both sides of the Revolutionary War. Before the war began, some British officials had tried to win over African Americans. Governor Dunmore of Virginia, for example, offered enslaved Africans their freedom if they joined the British army. As the war went on, many did. Some also enlisted in the Royal Navy. Northern Patriot militias also promised freedom in exchange for military service.

Black Americans fought at Lexington, Concord, and Bunker Hill. At first the Continental Army did not officially accept them. Soon, the need for soldiers overcame that prejudice. Volunteers were supposed to prove that they were freemen, but many recruiters did not ask.

New England regiments had the most African Americans because more free blacks lived there. Connecticut and Rhode Island had all-black regiments. James Middleton, the only black commissioned officer in the Continental Army, led a Massachusetts regiment.

African American soldiers generally received the same pay, clothing, and rations as whites. They served in both the army and the navy. Most African American soldiers, however, were given menial duties, kept at low ranks, and were not encouraged to re-enlist.

The role of Native Americans The Iroquois League had long been allies of the British. Now Britain expected their help. The Iroquois hoped that a British victory would slow American settlements on their lands.

But the French and Indian War had weakened the league. Only four of the Six Nations helped the British. Joseph Brant, a Mohawk leader, did become a British officer. He and his

Many years before he became the first president of the United States, George Washington earned a reputation as an exceptional military leader. In 1752 he joined the Virginia militia and led troops in the French and Indian War. Years later, as an early supporter of American independence, Washington began to recruit and train a militia when tensions rose with the British.

Leading the Continental Army, Washington made some early tactical mistakes, such as allowing the British to occupy New York City. Nevertheless, his ability to inspire and manage his army helped the Americans achieve victory in the end.

Predict How do you think Washington's military experience prepared him for the presidency?

sister Mary brought the Mohawks, Senecas, Onandagas, and Cayugas to help in campaigns in upstate New York. Oneidas and Tuscaroras, however, sided with the Americans.

On the frontiers, Loyalists and Native Americans sometimes fought together. In the mountains of Virginia and the Carolinas, the Cherokees attacked some settlements. Patriot militias fought back fiercely and tried to force the Cherokees to move west.

READING CHECK **Summarizing** What advantages did Britain have at the beginning of the war?

Revolutionary Battles in the North

The British reacted to the Declaration of Independence with a great show of military strength. Their losses and forced retreat from Boston in March 1776 had made them realize that they were engaged in a real war.

The British fight back After his unexpected defeat by Washington in Boston, General Howe returned to New York with a huge force. Howe was now the commander of British forces in America. More than 300 ships and approximately 30,000 British soldiers arrived in New York in August 1776. For the next few years, Revolutionary battles were centered in New York, New Jersey, and Pennsylvania.

Before the campaign began, General Howe and his brother Admiral Richard Howe tried to make peace. They wrote to Washington and offered a pardon to the rebels if they would give in and promise loyalty. Washington refused.

Howe's forces soon defeated the Americans and captured Long Island, taking many Americans prisoner. But Howe did not follow up on the victory. Washington took advantage of a heavy fog to take his remaining men across the river to Manhattan Island. As fall went on, the British moved steadily northward on the island as Washington's men retreated to the rocky heights at the northern end.

In the Battle of Harlem Heights, American forces won a few small encounters that helped their morale. Then Howe's army forced them to retreat across New Jersey. There they crossed the Delaware River into Pennsylvania.

In traditional European warfare, armies did not fight in the winter. Howe's men settled down in winter quarters at various towns in New Jersey, including Trenton and Princeton. The Hessians, the German mercenaries, were guarding Trenton, on the Delaware River.

But Washington did not follow European fighting methods. Instead, on Christmas night of 1776, he and his men crossed the icy Delaware River to Trenton. After celebrating Christmas, the Hessians were asleep. The Americans took them by surprise, occupied the town, and captured weapons and ammunition. Moving on, Washington then drove the British out of Princeton. In January 1777 the Continental Army went into winter quarters.

Campaigns in New York When fighting began again in the spring of 1777, Britain's plan was to cut New England off from the rest of the colonies. To do this, troops commanded by General John Burgoyne planned to meet General Howe's troops at Albany. But Howe changed his plans and decided to attack Philadelphia first. The city was the American capital, so Howe hoped its capture would hurt Patriot morale. He also hoped its sizeable Loyalist population would help him.

Howe took an army of 15,000 by sea from New York to Chesapeake Bay. In September he met Washington and his army of 11,000 in southeastern Pennsylvania. The British won the Battle of Brandywine Creek, but the Americans escaped without serious casualties.

From there Howe easily captured Philadelphia, where he and his troops settled comfortably for the winter. The Continental Congress fled the city. Washington and his exhausted troops settled into quarters at Valley Forge, Pennsylvania, for the winter of 1777–1778.

READING CHECK **Making Inferences** Why did Howe return to New York with so many ships and troops?

A British Setback at Saratoga

In the meantime, General Burgoyne was conducting a campaign in upstate New York. His strategy was to lead part of his force down the Hudson River valley to Albany. The rest would travel up the Saint Lawrence River into Lake Ontario and take the Mohawk valley. Burgoyne expected to meet Howe's army at Albany.

Things went well for the British at first. Burgoyne's army easily recaptured Fort Ticonderoga on July 5, 1777, a serious loss for the Americans. In response, Congress sent a new general, Horatio Gates, to lead the Continental Army in New York.

The other British force, however, met strong local resistance along the Mohawk River. When they attacked Fort Stanwix in early August, a band of Patriot farmers and their Oneida allies rallied to help the fort's defenders. But they were ambushed by British troops and their Iroquois allies in one of the bloodiest battles of the war. Then an American force led by Benedict Arnold arrived to hold the fort.

Burgoyne was now very short of supplies. Because of Howe's delays, no reinforcements arrived from the south. In early October, with only 5,000 men left, Burgoyne found himself at Saratoga, New York, surrounded by an American force of 17,000 under General Gates. He twice tried to break through Continental lines to reach Albany but could not. On October 17, 1777, Burgoyne surrendered to Gates.

The **Battle of Saratoga** is considered the turning point of the Revolutionary War. News of the American victory encouraged the colonists and surprised the British and Europeans. Most importantly, the victory at Saratoga convinced France to support the American cause.

READING CHECK **Summarizing** How did General Gates achieve victory at Saratoga?

FOCUS ON NEW YORK
CULTURE
At Saratoga National Historic Park in New York, people can visit the Saratoga battlefield. The Saratoga Monument stands in the nearby village of Victory.

Battle of Quebec

Montreal

Battle of Ticonderoga, 1775

Capture of Ticonderoga, 1777

Burgoyne

NH

Battle of Concord

Battle of Lexington

Battle of Saratoga

Battle of Bunker Hill

Capture of Fort Stanwix

Albany

MA

Boston

Lake Ontario

NY

CT

RI

Washington

Battle of Harlem Heights

New York

40°N

PA

Philadelphia

Valley Forge

Battles of Trenton and Princeton

NJ

MD

Howe

DE

70°W

VA

Legend
- Colonial troop movement
- Colonial victory
- British troop movement
- British victory

0   40   80 Miles
0   40   80 Kilometers
Albers equal-area projection

GEOGRAPHY SKILLS — INTERPRETING MAPS

go.hrw.com
Interactive Map
Keyword: SD7 CH4

1. **Location** How does the the pattern of battles and troop movements reflect Britain's war strategy?

2. **Movement** Why was the Battle of Saratoga a turning point?

See **Skills Handbook**, p. H19

Washington's Leadership at Valley Forge

For Washington and his tired army, the winter of 1777–1778 at **Valley Forge** was a low point of the Revolution. The winter weather was bitterly cold, and some 12,000 men were housed in makeshift huts and tents. Food was scarce. Washington's soldiers shivered in worn, ragged uniforms. Many of the men became ill, and hundreds died.

The winter at Valley Forge was a tough test of Washington's leadership, but he met the challenge. His firm character and common sense helped hold his troops together. In spite of many defeats, Washington always managed to keep a national army in the field. This was in part because his men greatly admired him.

Washington enforced discipline strictly. At the same time, he was always insisting that the Congress treat the army better.

Money problems Paying for the war was an ongoing problem. Congress did not have the power to make people pay taxes. Most currencies were based on supplies of "hard money"—gold and silver—which was scarce. Congress and the states printed paper money with little to back it up. As a result, paper money became almost worthless, and prices soared. This situation is known as **inflation**.

Because Continental money was worth very little, some farmers and merchants instead chose to trade with the British, who had gold and silver coin. This caused problems. For example, the food shortages at Valley Forge

Winter at Valley Forge

George Washington (right), saw that his troops remained ready for battle, despite the harsh winter at Valley Forge. In this painting, he watches as his troops perform a series of drilling exercises. Even more important, Washington was able to inspire his men with his leadership.

in 1776, Paine wrote another series of papers called *The American Crisis*. To rally his troops at Valley Forge, Washington read Thomas Paine's ringing words aloud:

HISTORY'S VOICES

❝The summer soldier and the sunshine patriot will, in this crisis, shrink from the service of their country; but he that stands it now, deserves the love and thanks of man and woman.❞

—Thomas Paine, *The American Crisis*
(December 19, 1776)

Help arrives from Europe The American struggle for liberty found support in Europe. Several European officers joined the American cause. One was Baron Friedrich von Steuben of the Prussian army. In the cold, snowy winter at Valley Forge, he drilled Washington's troops. By spring, Washington's men were a well-trained fighting force.

Washington also acquired an invaluable aide, a 20-year-old French noble, the **Marquis de Lafayette**. Lafayette was like a son to Washington. In the next section you will learn how Lafayette's help became crucial in the outcome of the Revolutionary War.

occurred partly because some Philadelphia merchants would not sell their goods to the Continental Army.

Encouraging words Earlier in 1776 Thomas Paine's *Common Sense* had inspired many American colonists to support a declaration of independence from Great Britain. After the retreat across New Jersey

READING CHECK **Summarizing** How did the winter at Valley Forge affect the army?

---

go.hrw.com
Online Quiz
Keyword: SD7 HP4

SECTION 3 ASSESSMENT

Reviewing Ideas, Terms, and People

1. **a. Describe** What kind of work did Patriot women undertake in the Revolution?
   b. Summarize What was the role of African Americans in the Revolution?
   c. Evaluate How did the fact that Americans were fighting for independence affect their fighting capability?

2. **a. Describe** What was Burgoyne's strategy for cutting New England off from the other colonies?
   b. Make Generalizations In general, what was the year 1776 like for the Continental Army?

3. **a. Identify** What roles did William Howe, John Burgoyne, and Horatio Gates play in the **Battle of Saratoga**?
   b. Analyze What factors contributed to the British defeat at Saratoga?
   c. Predict How do you think the victory at Saratoga will affect the course of the war?

4. **a. Identify** What factors made the winter at **Valley Forge** so difficult for the Americans?

b. Draw Conclusions What impact did Washington's character have on events at Valley Forge?

Critical Thinking

5. **Summarizing** Copy the chart below, fill it with details from the section, and then analyze the role of women, African Americans, and Native Americans in the Revolutionary War.

African Americans	Women	Native Americans

 FOCUS ON WRITING

6. **Descriptive** As either a British soldier at Saratoga or an American soldier at Valley Forge, write a letter home describing one day on the battlefield to your family. Use details from the section in your description.

American *Literature*

ST 3.2 Draw upon literary selections, historical documents, and accounts to analyze the roles played by different individuals and groups during the major eras in New York State and United States history.

THOMAS PAINE (1737–1809)

About the Reading During the Revolutionary War Thomas Paine wrote a series of articles called *The American Crisis.* The following is from an article written on September 12, 1777, shortly after the Battle of Brandywine Creek.

AS YOU READ Consider how the various modes of public communication during wartime have the ability to influence public support.

Excerpt from

The American Crisis

by Thomas Paine

General Howe planned to stamp out both the Continental Army and the Revolution at the Battle of Brandywine Creek.

Gentlemen of the city and country, it is in your power, by a spirited improvement of the present circumstance, to turn it to a real advantage. Howe is now weaker than before, and every shot will contribute to reduce him. You are more immediately interested than any other part of the continent: your all is at stake; it is not so with the general cause; you are devoted by the enemy to plunder and destruction: it is the encouragement which Howe, the chief of plunderers, has promised his army . . .

Our army must undoubtedly feel fatigue, and want a reinforcement of rest though not of valor. Our own interest and happiness call upon us to give them every support in our power, and make the burden of the day, on which the safety of this city depends, as light as possible. Remember, gentlemen, that we have forces both to the northward and southward of Philadelphia, and if the enemy be but stopped till those can arrive, this city will be saved, and the enemy finally routed. You have too much at stake to hesitate. You have been invaded, have likewise driven off the invaders. Now our time and turn is come, and perhaps the finishing stroke is reserved for us. When we look back on the dangers we have been saved from, and reflect on the success we have been blessed with, it would be sinful either to be idle or to despair.

I close this paper with a short address to General Howe. You, sir, are only lingering out the period that shall bring with it your defeat. You have yet scarce began the war, and the further you enter, the faster will your troubles thicken. What you now enjoy is only a respite from ruin; an invitation to destruction; something that will lead on to our deliverance at your expense. We know the cause which we are engaged in, and though a passionate fondness may make us grieve at every injury which threatens it, yet, when the moment of concern is over, the determination to duty returns. We are not moved by the gloomy smile of a worthless king, but by the ardent glow of generous patriotism.

Skills FOCUS **READING LIKE A HISTORIAN**

1. **Identifying the Main Idea** Who was Paine's audience? What were his purposes in writing?
2. **Literature as Historical Evidence** What does Paine claim motivates the British army? How might you assess the validity of these claims?

See **Skills Handbook**, pp. H5, H32

An American Victory

BEFORE YOU READ

MAIN IDEA

A strengthened Continental Army, along with European allies, helped the colonists achieve a victory at Yorktown.

READING FOCUS

1. What Revolutionary War battles took place in the West and South?
2. Why did France and other European nations assist the Americans?
3. What led to the British surrender at Yorktown?
4. How did the Revolution affect American culture?

KEY TERMS AND PEOPLE

George Rogers Clark
Nathanael Greene
Charles Cornwallis
Count de Rochambeau
Bernardo de Gálvez
Battle of Yorktown
Treaty of Paris

PI 1.1 Analyze the development of American culture, explaining how ideas, values, beliefs, and traditions have changed over time and how they united all Americans.

THE INSIDE STORY

How did a spy trick the British? Like many enslaved people, James Armistead had the last name of a slaveholder. Later, he added another name—Lafayette. In 1781 Armistead volunteered to serve with the Marquis de Lafayette, expecting to be a servant. But Lafayette realized that the young African American could do much more, and Armistead became a spy. Pretending to be a runaway, he found work in the camp of Benedict Arnold, who had become a traitor. He also won the trust of British general Cornwallis, who asked him to spy on the Americans! Armistead became a double agent. He gave accurate information to the Americans and inaccurate information to the British. His efforts helped defeat the British at the crucial battle of Yorktown.

In one instance, the Americans forged a fake order for reinforcements. Armistead took the crumpled paper to Cornwallis, saying he had found it on the road. It made Cornwallis think that American forces were stronger than they actually were. After the surrender, Cornwallis visited Lafayette and was very surprised to see his spy as an aide to the French general.

Lafayette admired Armistead's courage and resourcefulness. He wrote, "His Intelligences from the Enemy's Camp were Industriously Collected and More faithfully deliver'd." He then asked the Virginia Assembly to give Armistead his freedom. When they agreed, Armistead added Lafayette's name to his own. He became a farmer in Virginia. The two met once again 40 years later when the Frenchman returned to the United States. ◼

Spying for the Revolution

▶ James Armistead (right) spied for Continental Army commander Lafayette (left) during the last phase of the Revolutionary War.

Revolutionary Battles in the West and South

The Revolutionary War changed in several ways after the Battle of Saratoga. The Northeast was fairly quiet, with British troops occupying New York. Washington's army—now a better, more disciplined fighting force—waited nearby. Meanwhile, the action shifted to the South and the western frontier.

War in the West In 1779 the Americans won some important victories in the area north and west of the Ohio River, largely due to the efforts of **George Rogers Clark**, a pioneer on the western frontier in Kentucky. In 1778 Clark persuaded Governor Patrick Henry of Virginia to send an expedition to deal with the British in the West. Clark led a small force down the Ohio River. His men captured the British settlements at Fort Kaskaskia and Cahokia on the Mississippi River in present-day Illinois. Although the British held the settlement of Vincennes, the people there were French and Clark won their loyalty. In 1779 he and his men captured the fort and its commander in the Battle of Vincennes.

War in the South In 1778 the British shifted their strategy. They had expected to win the war quickly and crush the rebels. Now, instead of sending more troops and supplies, British

Interactive Map
BATTLES OF THE AMERICAN REVOLUTION, 1778–1781

Legend:
- Colonial troop movement
- Colonial victory
- British troop movement
- British victory

0   50   100 Miles
0   50   100 Kilometers
Albers equal-area projection

Lake Ontario
Lake Michigan
Lake Erie
Detroit
Hamilton
Pittsburgh
NY
PA
Valley Forge
NJ
MD
DE
Washington & Rochambeau
Battle of Vincennes
Clark
Ohio River
St. Louis
Clark
Battle of Cahokia
Kaskaskia
Mississippi River
APPALACHIAN MOUNTAINS
VA
Lafayette
Williamsburg
Battle of Yorktown
Cornwallis
Battle at Guilford Court House
NC
Cornwallis
Battle of Cowpens
Battle of King's Mountain
SC
Clinton & Cornwallis
Battle at Charleston
Campbell
GA
Battle at Savannah
ATLANTIC OCEAN
40°N
35°N
30°N
80°W
75°W

go.hrw.com
Interactive Map
Keyword: SD7 CH4

GEOGRAPHY SKILLS **INTERPRETING MAPS**

1. **Human-Environment Interaction** How did Clark, a frontiersman, move his troops west?
2. **Place** What important battles did the colonists win in the west?
3. **Region** Where did the British concentrate their attacks?

See **Skills Handbook**, p. H19

officials had a different strategy. They hoped that the many Loyalists in America would rise up to support them.

Because the British believed that Loyalist sympathies were strongest in the South, they planned a campaign there. However, they discovered that Patriots were as strong and determined in Virginia as in New England. Many Loyalists lived in the Carolinas and Georgia, but they were often reluctant to help.

The British also faced frequent surprise raids by small bands of Patriots. These fighters struck quickly, then disappeared into the woods. The most famous was Francis Marion, who was nicknamed the Swamp Fox for his daring raids from the Carolina marshes.

Then at King's Mountain on the border between the Carolinas, local Patriots defeated a Loyalist force. A new American commander, **Nathanael Greene**, took charge. In March 1781 Greene and Lafayette's troops met British commander **Charles Cornwallis**'s army in a brutal battle at Guilford Court House, North Carolina. Cornwallis won, but British losses were so great that he stopped the campaign.

READING CHECK **Identifying the Main Idea** Why did the British decide to move the war into the South?

America's European Allies

Americans wanted recognition as a sovereign nation from Europe. European nations could also provide the Americans with money and supplies to fight the war. Gates's victory at Saratoga made a European alliance possible. France became America's strongest ally, but help also came from Spain and the Netherlands.

Alliance with France France was happy to see its old enemy, Great Britain, losing part of its empire. France also hoped that a British defeat in America would help restore French power in Europe.

At first the French government helped the Americans by sending gunpowder, artillery, and muskets. Then in 1776 the Americans sent Benjamin Franklin to France. In his fur cap and homespun coat, he became a favorite with both aristocrats and the ordinary people. Franklin was in Paris when the news of Saratoga reached there in December 1777. As a

★ **Interactive**
HISTORY CLOSE-UP

The Battle of Yorktown

General Cornwallis brought his troops to Yorktown thinking the British navy could protect him there, but he was wrong. Instead, the combined American and French forces surrounded the British, attacking them and cutting off their support. Cornwallis surrendered on October 19, 1781.

YORKTOWN

result of Saratoga and Franklin's diplomatic skill, France soon signed two treaties. One formally recognized the United States as a nation. The other promised military help.

In 1780 Lafayette helped persuade the French government to send a 6,000-soldier army to help the Americans against the British. The troops were led by a French general, the **Count de Rochambeau** (roh-shahm-BOH).

Help from Spain Spain did not become a direct ally of the Americans, but they did join the war in 1779 as an ally of France. At that time **Bernardo de Gálvez**, an experienced officer, was the Spanish governor of Louisiana. After Spain declared war, Gálvez began to attack British forts on the Mississippi and along the Gulf Coast in West Florida, which had once belonged to Spain. He went on to defeat the British in the southern cities of Baton Rouge, Natchez, Mobile, and Pensacola.

READING CHECK **Making Inferences** Why did the Spanish want to help the Americans?

French ships blocked the British navy from bringing reinforcements to Cornwallis.

The British purposely sank dozens of their own ships. This formed a barrier.

American and French troops surrounded the British.

Skills FOCUS **INTERPRETING INFOGRAPHICS**

go.hrw.com
Interactive
Keyword: SD7 CH4

Weary from hard-fought victories in the West, Cornwallis hoped to await aid in Virginia.

1. **Movement** Why couldn't Cornwallis escape Yorktown by land?
2. **Movement** How did Washington use French allies to put Cornwallis under siege?

See **Skills Handbook**, p. H18

Victory at Yorktown

Washington and Rochambeau received word in January 1781 that there was trouble in Virginia. Benedict Arnold, who had been a hero for the Continental Army at Saratoga, had become a traitor. Arnold had been helping the British cause by leading British troops in raids on Patriot warehouses.

Washington was shocked and disappointed by Arnold's treachery. He sent Lafayette to Virginia to stop him. Then he and Rochambeau planned a massive march into Virginia.

After giving up his Carolina campaign, General Cornwallis moved into Virginia. But Lafayette's forces gradually forced the British to the coast. In July 1781 Cornwallis took his army to the Yorktown Peninsula in Chesapeake Bay. There they built a fort and waited for British ships to take them to Charleston or New York.

A siege at Yorktown Washington saw an opportunity to trap Cornwallis. He sent a message to Admiral de Grasse, who commanded France's Caribbean fleet. Washington asked him to establish a blockade in Chesapeake Bay (see the illustration above). The blockade would prevent British ships from rescuing Cornwallis's men.

Washington instructed Lafayette to keep Cornwallis's army trapped on the peninsula so they could not escape by land. Meanwhile, Washington and Rochambeau traveled south with a huge French and American army.

Cornwallis, with 7,000 troops, now faced a combined French and American army of more than 17,000. The **Battle of Yorktown** lasted about three weeks. With his army bombarded by land and sea, Cornwallis had little choice but to surrender. He did so on October 19, 1781, ending the fighting.

In effect, the war for independence was over, although the British still occupied several American cities. It took several years to agree on the terms of a peace treaty.

The Treaty of Paris Some royal officials still hoped that America would remain part of the British Empire. But the American diplomats, who included Benjamin Franklin and John Adams, insisted on independence.

The Americans negotiated a peace treaty with Britain. The <mark>Treaty of Paris</mark> was signed on September 3, 1783. In it, Britain formally recognized the United States as an independent nation. The treaty also declared the Mississippi River the western boundary of the United States. Britain agreed to leave its forts in the West. Spain and France also made peace with Britain in the Treaty of Paris. In return for its help during the war, Spain regained control of Florida.

After all the trouble caused by taxes, in the Treaty of Paris the United States now promised to pay what Americans owed British merchants. The treaty also allowed Loyalists to claim property losses.

READING CHECK **Making Generalizations** What territory did Great Britain lose in the Treaty of Paris?

Revolution Changes America

The American Revolution brought many changes to American society. Politics became more democratic as more men gained the right to vote. In some states, all adult male taxpayers could vote. In others, owning any kind of property—not just land—gave a man the right to vote.

The Revolution also introduced new ideas of equality. The Declaration of Independence stated that "all men are created equal." Americans never again wanted to be ruled by a monarch or an aristocratic upper class.

Women's rights Equality, however, still did not include American women. The words in the Declaration of Independence applied only to white males. Even though women had done important work during the Revolution, the war did not bring them new rights. Abigail Adams had touched on the issue of women's rights in one of her letters to John Adams. While the Continental Congress was still debating the Declaration of Independence, she had written to her husband:

HISTORY'S VOICES

❝Remember the Ladies, and be more generous and favourable to them than your ancestors. Do not put such unlimited power into the hands of the Husbands . . . If [particular] care and attention is not paid to the Ladies we are determined to foment a Rebellion, and will not hold ourselves bound by any Laws in which we have no voice, or Representation.❞

–Abigail Adams, letter of March 31, 1776

Women did not gain rights after the war, as Adams had hoped. Married women still could not sign contracts or own property. The law stated that a married woman's property belonged to her husband.

The slavery question The American struggle for freedom also raised questions about slavery. Many African Americans who had fought for the Patriot cause believed they had earned their freedom.

Worries over the morality of slavery were not new. Benjamin Franklin and Dr. Benjamin Rush had formed an antislavery organization in Philadelphia in 1775. Others in Pennsylvania, especially Quakers and Mennonites, had long opposed slavery. In 1780 Pennsylvania passed a law for the gradual abolition of slavery. During the 1780s the New England states also abolished slavery.

Such changes came more slowly in the South, however. Jefferson had written an antislavery section in the Declaration of Independence in 1776, but southern delegates removed it. After the war, both Virginia and Maryland made it easier to grant freedom to enslaved people. Several southern states also passed laws limiting the slave trade.

Impact on religion Before the war, many colonies had official churches that everyone paid taxes to support. Now changes came for many religious groups.

New laws endorsed a separation of church and state. In Virginia, Thomas Jefferson wrote a Statute for Religious Freedom (1786). It said that "no man shall be compelled to frequent [attend] or support any religious worship, place, or ministry."

The state church in Virginia and Maryland had been the Anglican Church. After the war American Anglicans reorganized as the Protestant Episcopal Church. New England states kept their relationship with the Congregational Church, but outsiders no longer had to pay to support the church.

For the Roman Catholic Church, the Revolutionary War led to a certain amount of acceptance. Catholics had often faced prejudice, but the arrival of French Catholic soldiers helped change many people's attitudes.

A new nation Economically, the war left the new nation with some problems. The Revolution had cost a lot of money, and Congress had borrowed from foreign sources and American citizens. Now the money needed to be repaid.

At the same time, the 13 colonies—now states—wanted to retain their sovereign power. They had just escaped one tyrannical government, and they did not want to create another. So, setting up a central government to deal with debt and other national issues was going to be complicated. Soon, the Continental Congress would meet again. This time the delegates would discuss economic issues and a new system of government.

READING CHECK **Making Generalizations**
How did the war affect American politics?

THE GREAT SEAL OF THE UNITED STATES

The Latin phrase "E Pluribus Unum" means "out of many, one." It refers to the joining of the colonies into one nation.

The bald eagle holds the olive branch of peace in one talon and the arrows of war in the other.

Skills FOCUS **READING LIKE A HISTORIAN**

On June 20, 1782, the Continental Congress approved an official seal of the United States. The original sketch (top) and today's seal (bottom) are shown here.

Interpreting Visuals What do the symbols in the Great Seal of the United States signify?

SECTION 4 ASSESSMENT

go.hrw.com
Online Quiz
Keyword: SD7 HP4

Reviewing Ideas, Terms, and People

1. a. Recall In what ways did the Revolutionary War change after the Battle of Saratoga?
b. Explain What gains did Americans make in the West?
c. Evaluate Was Britain's move into the South a good idea?

2. a. Recall What kind of aid did France give to the American Patriots?
b. Make Inferences Why did other European nations choose to help the Americans against Great Britain?

3. a. Identify Who were Lafayette and **Rochambeau**, and what role did they play in the **Battle of Yorktown**?
b. Explain How did American forces trap Cornwallis at Yorktown?
c. Evaluate Do you think the Americans could have won the war without the help of the French?

4. a. Recall What actions regarding slavery did states take after the war?

b. Elaborate How did the war change colonial churches?
c. Predict What issues faced the new nation?

Critical Thinking

5. Sequencing Copy the chart below and make a time line of major events and battles leading up to the victory at Yorktown.

Victory at Yorktown

FOCUS ON WRITING

6. Expository Write an answer to Abigail Adams's letter in which you give some ideas about the status of women after the Revolutionary War.

Patriots and Loyalists

Historical Context The documents below provide different views of events during the American Revolution.

Task Examine the documents and answer the questions that follow. Then you will be asked to write an essay about Patriot and Loyalist views, using facts from the documents and from the chapter to support the position you take in your thesis statement.

ST 3.2 Draw upon literary selections, historical documents, and accounts to analyze the roles played by different individuals and groups during the major eras in New York State and United States history.

ST 4.3 Develop hypotheses about important events, eras, or issues; move from chronicling to explaining historical events and issues; use information collected from diverse sources to produce cogently written reports and document-based essays.

DOCUMENT 1

In the years leading up to the Revolution, Patriots used tactics such as tarring and feathering to humiliate British officials without causing permanent harm to them. This image, published in 1774, expressed Loyalist horror at the tarring and feathering of British tax agent John Malcolm by suspected members of the Sons of Liberty. The Tree of Liberty, a popular image among Patriot artists, is portrayed with a hangman's noose on it to represent the hypocrisy of the Patriots.

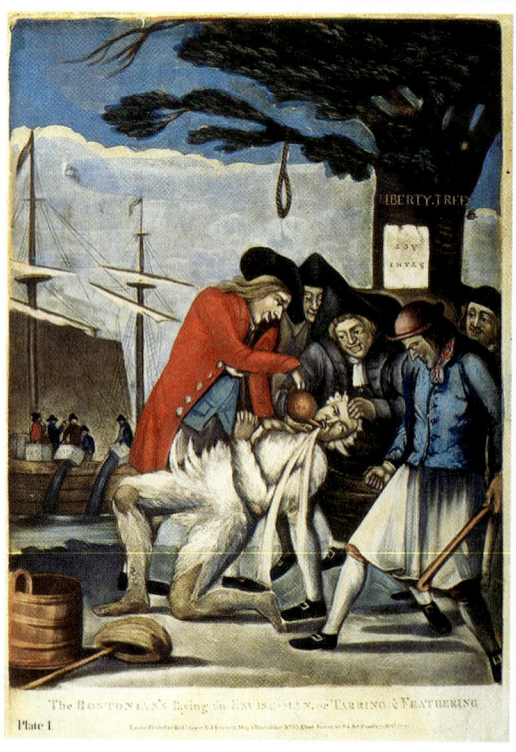

DOCUMENT 2

The Patriots took a very different view of efforts to humiliate the British. Published in 1775, this image by a Patriot artist celebrates a New York barber who half-shaved a British officer, then forced him into the street to be laughed at by observers. The officer is shown running out of the barber shop not only half-shaven but also without his wig, which all important men wore.

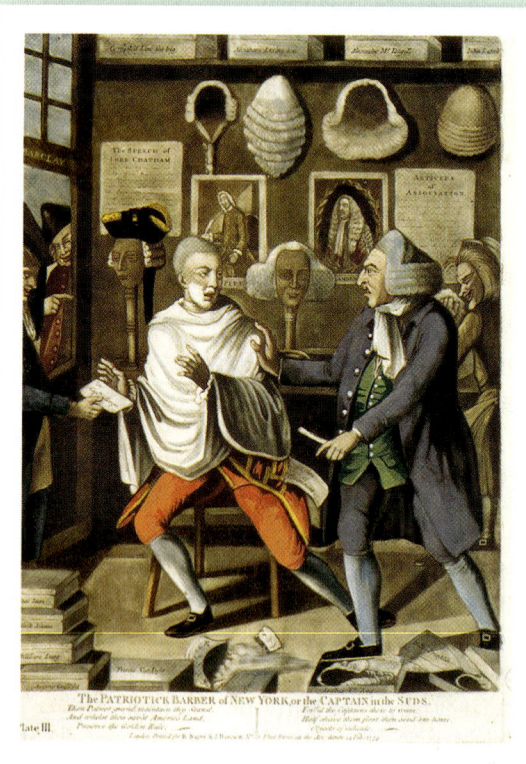

This image was published in 1779, three years into the war, and was titled "The Horse America Throwing his Master." It shows King George III being thrown by his horse, which represents the United States. The crop used to whip the horse is shown here as having swords, bayonets, and tomahawks on the end. These were weapons used by British soldiers and their Indian allies against the Patriots. At right, a Patriot soldier marches into the scene carrying a flag with 13 stars on it.

THE HORSE AMERICA, *throwing his Master.*

Pub.ᵈ as the Act directs, Aug.ᵗ 1.ˢᵗ 1779. by W.ᵐ White, Angel Court, Westminster.

Skills FOCUS | **READING LIKE A HISTORIAN**

1. **a. Describe** Refer to Document 1. What was the purpose of the actions taken against John Malcolm?
   b. Analyze Why do you think the artist saw the Patriots' actions as hypocritical?

2. **a. Identify** Refer to Document 2. Why was the British officer shown as bald in addition to being half-shaven?
   b. Elaborate Why do you think the Patriots supported humiliation as a tactic against British officials?

3. **a. Identify** Refer to Document 3. What does the flag in the image represent?

   b. Interpret Do you think this image was created by a Patriot or a Loyalist? Explain.

4. **Document-Based Essay Question** Consider the question below and form a thesis statement. Using examples from Documents 1, 2, and 3, create an outline and write a short essay supporting your position. How did Patriots and Loyalists view the American Revolution differently?

   See **Skills Handbook**, pp. H10, H28–29, H30, H31

Chapter Review

Visual Summary: The Revolutionary Era

The Road to Revolution
- Great Britain and the American colonies clash over "taxation without representation."
- The First Continental Congress meets.
- Battle of Lexington: "The Shot Heard 'round the World"

Declaring Independence
- The Second Continental Congress meets.
- Violence continues in Boston.
- Colonists draft and sign the Declaration of Independence.

The Revolutionary War Begins
- Major battles take place in the North.
- The war turns in the colonies' favor at the Battle of Saratoga.
- Washington's troops regroup during the winter at Valley Forge.

An American Victory
- Colonists win major victories in the West and South.
- France and Spain become allies of the American colonists.
- The Battle of Yorktown ensures American victory.

Reviewing Key Terms and People

For each term or name below, write a sentence explaining its significance to the Revolutionary era.

1. Stamp Act
2. Intolerable Acts
3. First Continental Congress
4. battles of Lexington and Concord
5. Second Continental Congress
6. Loyalist
7. *Common Sense*
8. Thomas Jefferson
9. Battle of Saratoga
10. Valley Forge
11. Marquis de Lafayette
12. Treaty of Paris

Comprehension and Critical Thinking

SECTION 1 *(pp. 106–113)*

13. **a. Identify** What objects required stamps under the Stamp Act?

    b. Sequence Create a brief time line of the events leading up to the battles of Lexington and Concord.

    c. Analyze How did the American colonists win the Battle of Concord?

SECTION 2 *(pp. 114–120)*

14. **a. Recall** When did the Second Continental Congress meet?

    b. Compare What were the arguments for war during the Second Continental Congress? What were the arguments for peace?

    c. Evaluate Did the American colonies make the right decision in declaring their independence from Great Britain?

History's Impact video program
Review the video to answer the closing question:
How does the Declaration of Independence affect
American life today?

SECTION 3 *(pp. 125–130)*

15. a. Describe How did American women help with revolutionary efforts?

b. Compare What were the strengths of the Continental Army? What were the strengths of the British Redcoats?

c. Analyze Why was the Battle of Saratoga considered a turning point in the war?

SECTION 4 *(pp. 132–137)*

16. a. Recall What happened at the Battle of Yorktown?

b. Analyze How did America's European allies help shift the balance in the Revolutionary War?

c. Predict The Revolutionary War brought many changes to America. How do you think those changes affected the new nation in the years after the war?

Using the Internet

go.hrw.com
Practice Online
Keyword: SD7 CH4

17. Revolutionary battle sites still exist across the eastern seaboard of the United States. Using the keyword above, do research on a significant Revolutionary War site that tourists can visit today. Then create a brochure that teaches tourists the significance of your site and encourages them to visit.

Analyzing Primary Sources

Reading Like a Historian On July 6, 1775, the Second Continental Congress issued a document called *A Declaration of the Causes and Necessity of Taking Up Arms*, which explained why the colonists were at war. Read the excerpt below and answer the questions that follow.

> ❝We have not raised armies with ambitious designs of separating from Great Britain and establishing independent states . . . In our own native land, in defence of the freedom that is our birthright . . . for the protection of our property, acquired solely by the honest industry [work] of our fore-fathers and ourselves, against violence actually offered, we have taken up arms.❞

18. Identify Name three reasons why the colonists were at war.

19. Analyze How is the position of this document different from the position the colonists later took in the Declaration of Independence?

Critical Reading

Read the passage in Section 4 under the heading "Revolution Changes America." Then answer the questions that follow.

20. Which of the following statements about women's rights after the Revolution are true?

A Married women could not sign contracts or own property.

B Women could vote in Massachusetts.

C Women were not offered higher education.

D Women could not vote in any state.

21. In the years following the Revolution,

A American Anglicans reorganized as the Protestant Episcopal Church.

B women were given the right to vote.

C all men and women had the right to vote.

D Thomas Jefferson wrote the Declaration of Independence.

WRITING FOR THE SAT

Think about the following issue.

The British army in America was well trained and had access to many resources from Great Britain. In contrast, the Continental Army often lacked resources and was not as well trained. Nevertheless, the Americans were able to win independence from Great Britain in 1783.

22. Assignment Given that the British were a well-trained, well-equipped fighting force, how were the Americans able to win independence from Britain? Write a short essay in which you develop your position on this issue. Support your point of view with reasoning and examples from your reading and studies.

Creating a New GOVERNMENT

THE BIG PICTURE The Articles of Confederation, under which the thirteen colonies had united to win independence, proved insufficient to govern the new nation. Delegates from 12 states met at the Constitutional Convention in Philadelphia and fashioned a newer, stronger form of government, which has endured for more than 200 years.

New York Standards

Key Idea 1 The study of New York State and United States history requires an analysis of the development of American culture, its diversity and multicultural context, and the ways people are unified by many values, practices, and traditions.

 Skills FOCUS READING LIKE A HISTORIAN

The artist Junius Brutus Stearns captured the gravity of the task set before the nation's founders in his 1856 painting *Washington Addressing the Constitutional Convention.* **Interpreting Visuals** What does this painting tell you about the crafters of the Constitution?

See **Skills Handbook**, p. H30

 U.S.

November 1777
Congress adopts Articles of Confederation.

1775

 **World**

1778
British explorer Captain James Cook lands in Hawaii, meeting people like this Sandwich Islander.

History's Impact video program

Watch the video to understand the impact of the Bill of Rights.

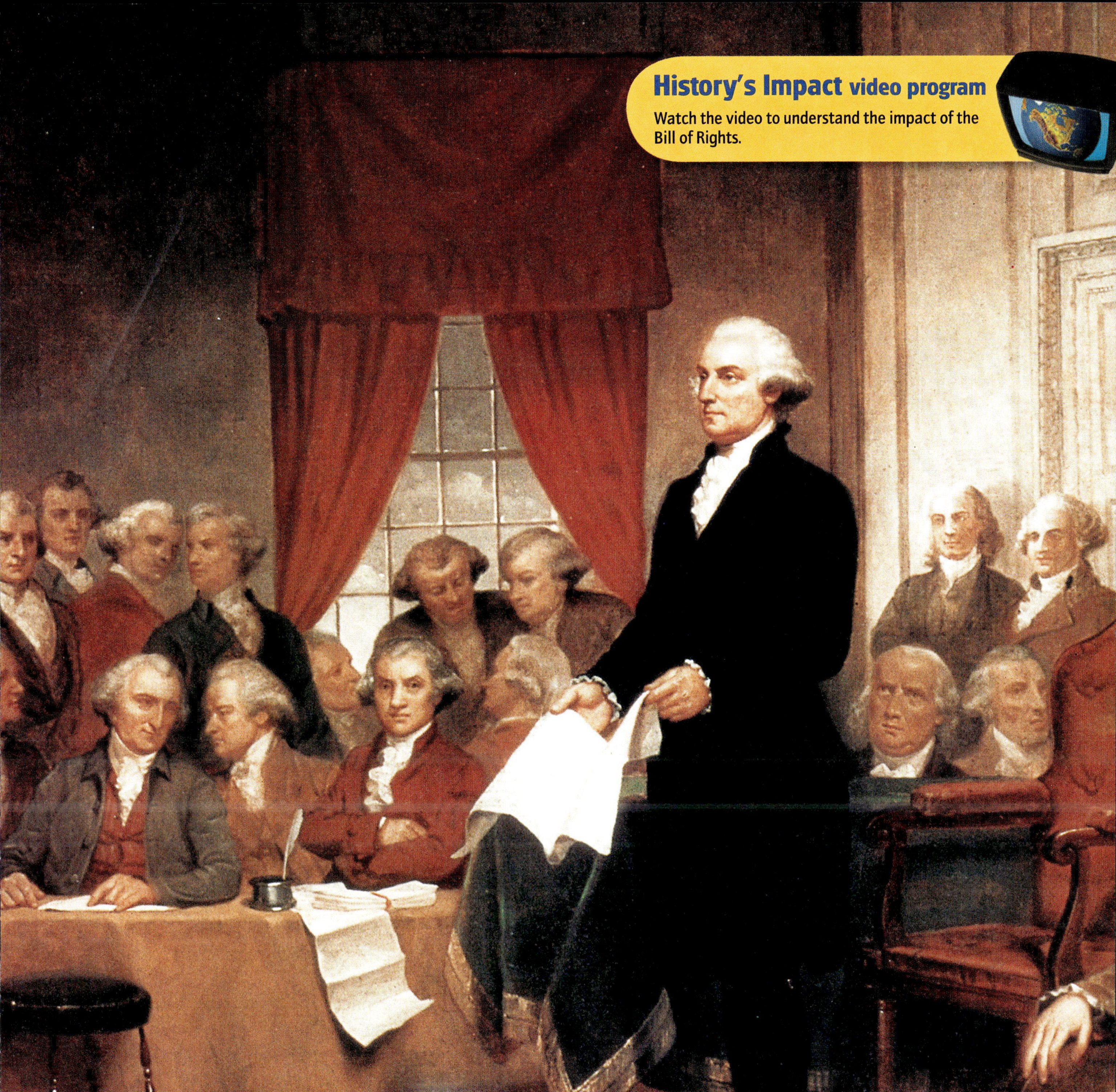

1780

September 1781
Spanish settlers found the city of Los Angeles.

March 1781
Articles of Confederation go into effect.

1784
Russians settle in the Aleutian Islands of present-day Alaska.

1785
Land Ordinance of 1785 creates plan for surveying and selling land in the Northwest Territory.

1785

May 1787
Constitutional Convention meets in Philadelphia.

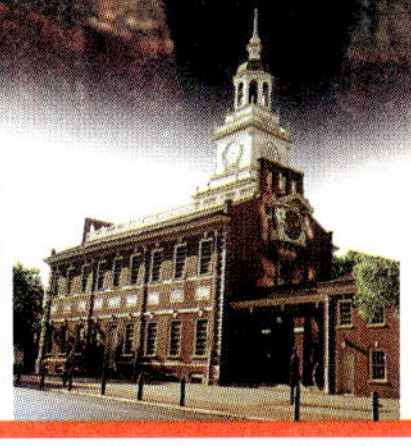

1789
First U.S. Congress meets in New York.

July 1789
The French Revolution begins with the capture of Bastille prison.

1790

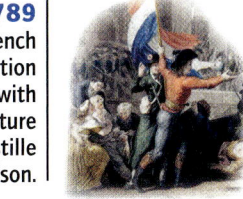

The Articles of Confederation

BEFORE YOU READ

MAIN IDEA

In order to carry on the war and build a new nation, Americans had to create a framework of government, but their first attempt had many weaknesses.

READING FOCUS

1. What were some key aspects of the new American republic?
2. What was the structure of the new national government?
3. What problems did the Confederation face?
4. What did the government accomplish in the Northwest Territory?

KEY TERMS AND PEOPLE

legislative branch
judicial branch
executive branch
republic
Articles of Confederation
Land Ordinance of 1785
Northwest Ordinance

PI **1.1** Analyze the development of American culture, explaining how ideas, values, beliefs, and traditions have changed over time and how they united all Americans.

The States, UNITED

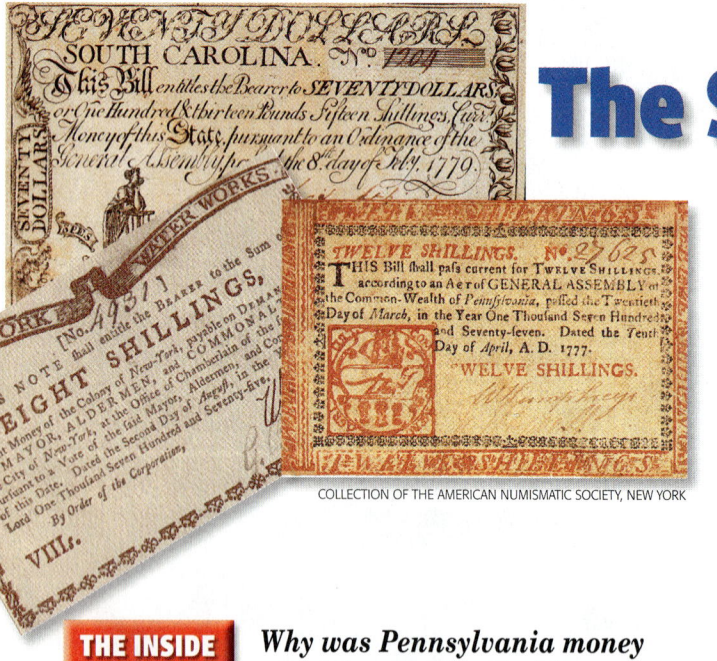

COLLECTION OF THE AMERICAN NUMISMATIC SOCIETY, NEW YORK

◄ **Almost as though they were separate nations instead of separate states, some states had their own currencies.**

THE INSIDE STORY *Why was Pennsylvania money worthless in New York?* In 1774, at the First Continental Congress, Patrick Henry declared bravely: "The distinctions between Virginians, Pennsylvanians, New Yorkers, and New Englanders are no more. I am not a Virginian but an American."

Patrick Henry's words were inspiring. Yet even after the Americans won the Revolutionary War and the 13 colonies became states, they were still struggling to unite as Americans. Loyalty to one's state remained stronger than any feeling of national unity.

In many ways, each state behaved like a small country. Some had their own navies and made treaties with foreign nations. Small states and large states were at odds. Some

states, including New York and New Hampshire, argued over land claims. Trade and the economy caused most clashes among states.

Financial chaos reigned in the early years. For starters, many states printed their own paper money. If you had a pocket full of paper money printed in Pennsylvania, you could not spend it in New York or Virginia. States also imposed tariffs, or import taxes, on goods shipped from other states. An out-of-state ship that docked at a Virginia port without paying the tariff could be seized and sold.

The lack of unity made commerce especially difficult in certain states. James Madison wrote: "New Jersey, placed between Philadelphia and New York, was likened to a cask tapped at both ends; and North Carolina, between Virginia and South Carolina, to a patient bleeding at both arms."

Soon the states would attempt to come together under a new national government. If Americans were truly to unite, they would need to invent a government that would address the needs of all the states. Americans would also need to find a balance between state and national government. ◢

The American Republic

While Americans were fighting for independence from Britain, they were also setting up new governments. Most of the 13 states wrote new constitutions. These state constitutions echoed many prized British rights, including representative government, the rule of law, limits on government power, and individual liberties.

New state governments Despite differences among the states, their governments had many similarities. Each state government had three branches. The **legislative branch** made the laws. The **judicial branch** interpreted the laws. The **executive branch**—the governor—carried out the laws. Remembering their experience with authoritarian royal governors, the states chose to limit the governor's power. Instead, elected legislatures held more power.

Republicanism Above all, Americans did not want a king or any other supreme authority over them. Going back to the ideas of John Locke, they wanted a **republic**, a political system without a monarch. It would rule "with the consent of the governed." No government in the world at that time was based on this idea. The ideal of republicanism was that hard-working, property-owning citizens would be active in government. Reality, of course, was different. Women, African Americans, Native Americans, and poor white laborers seldom owned property or took part in government.

Republican motherhood The Revolutionary War did bring a shift in women's roles. During the war, women ably managed farms and businesses. Some women fought in battle or defended their homes with axes and muskets. American women had become politically active for the first time before the war, organizing boycotts and later supporting the war effort.

The idea of republican motherhood developed from these roots. People recognized that women had the first opportunity to educate children in civic virtues and responsibilities. Republican motherhood encouraged mothers to raise their sons to be patriotic future leaders and their daughters to be intelligent, patriotic, and competent so they could run households and educate their own children.

Judith Sargent Murray, a contemporary author, maintained that young women should

REPUBLICAN MOTHERHOOD

The Sedgwick home is pictured in the background.

The book suggests the importance of education to the Sedgwick family.

Skills FOCUS READING LIKE A HISTORIAN

The Sedgwicks, a prominent Federalist family in Massachusetts, valued education. In this painting, Pamela Dwight Sedgwick is pictured with her daughter, Catharine, who became a writer.

Interpreting Visuals Why did the family choose to include a book in this portrait?

See **Skills Handbook**, p. H30

be educated in reasoning, not just household skills. After infancy, she noted, boys and girls were given very different educations:

HISTORY'S VOICES

❝ How is the one exalted, and the other depressed, by the contrary modes of education which are adopted! the one is taught to aspire, and the other is early confined and limited. As their years increase, the sister must be wholly domesticated, while the brother is led by the hand through all the flowery paths of science. ❞

—Judith Sargent Murray, quoted in *Founding Mothers*

READING CHECK **Making Inferences** Why did the states create weak executive branches?

ACADEMIC VOCABULARY

constitutions documents containing the basic laws and principles of a state or nation

A New National Government

The states formed their new governments quickly during the Revolutionary War, but the Continental Congress found it more difficult to agree upon a structure for a national government. Yet some kind of central government was needed to carry on the war and make agreements with foreign governments. As they worked out a plan, the Congress set up a completely new kind of government structure.

The Articles of Confederation
In 1776, while one congressional committee was writing the Declaration of Independence, another committee was trying to work out a plan of union. John Dickinson of Pennsylvania led the effort. Dickinson was a moderate who had once hoped for peace with Great Britain. Now he drafted a plan for a new American government.

For more than a year Congress debated whether to adopt the **Articles of Confederation**, America's first national constitution. As its name indicates, the document established a confederation—an association of independent, sovereign states with certain common goals.

Congress formally adopted the Articles of Confederation in November 1777. It took a while longer for each of the 13 states to ratify the document because of disputes over western lands.

Powers of the new government
In March 1781 the Articles of Confederation finally went into effect. The states retained most of their power under the Articles. The document provided for only a weak national government. Unlike the state governments, the central government had only one branch: the Continental Congress, which was a legislative body. There was no executive or judicial branch. Each state also had only one vote in Congress, regardless of population.

Under the Articles, Congress did have certain powers. It could establish national policies and conduct foreign relations, including relations with Native American nations. Congress could borrow and coin money and set up post offices. It also had the power to establish an army and declare war.

READING CHECK **Summarizing** Under the Articles of Confederation, what powers did the central government have?

ACADEMIC VOCABULARY

ratify officially approve
amend make changes

The Confederation Faces Problems

The powers of Congress, however, were just words on paper. It was difficult, and often impossible, for the government to make these words a reality. Nine of the 13 states had to agree on any major law. All 13 states had to agree to amend the Articles of Confederation.

Financial problems
The new government's major problems involved money. Although there were large war debts to pay, the government did not have the power to impose or collect taxes. Congress did ask the states for money but only received about one-sixth of what it requested. This meant the government could not pay to support an army or navy. Nor could it repay money borrowed from foreign governments and from individual Americans during the Revolutionary War. Some soldiers who had fought in the war actually went unpaid.

In 1781 Congress set up a department of finance run by Philadelphia merchant Robert Morris and his business associate, Haym Salomon. Both men had worked hard during the war to raise money for the army. Salomon loaned thousands of dollars to the government and to several government leaders, most of which was never repaid.

Morris and others who wanted a stronger national government suggested amending the Articles of Confederation to allow Congress to place a 5 percent tax on imports. The plan

QUICK FACTS
WEAKNESSES OF THE ARTICLES OF CONFEDERATION

- Congress could not impose taxes

- Congress could not regulate trade

- Nine of 13 states needed to agree to pass laws

- All states had to agree to amend the Articles

- No executive branch to enforce laws passed by Congress

- No judicial branch to interpret laws passed by Congress

The Articles of Confederation

John Jay, president of the Continental Congress and part of the committee sent to negotiate peace with Great Britain, had grave misgivings about the Articles of Confederation.

Concerned that trouble would result from attempts to change the government, Richard Henry Lee of Virginia defended the Articles of Confederation.

" I think Sir that the first maxim of a man who loves liberty should be, never to grant to Rulers an atom of power that is not most clearly & indispensably necessary for the safety and well being of Society . . . [T]he Confederation should not be presumptuously called an infallible system for all times and all situations . . . no change should be admitted until proved to be necessary by the fairest, fullest & most mature experience. **"**

Richard Henry Lee, 1785

" To oppose popular prejudices, to censure the proceedings, and expose the improprieties [wrongdoing] of states is an unpleasant task, but it must be done. Our affairs seem to lead to some crisis, some revolution. . . . [W]e are going and doing wrong, and therefore I look forward to evils and calamities. . . . **"**

John Jay, 1786

Skills FOCUS READING LIKE A HISTORIAN

Identifying Points of View Both men fear "calamities" and troubles ahead, but for each, those troubles are different. What does each man fear?

See **Skills Handbook**, pp. H28–H29

---

failed. To amend the Articles required unanimous consent, and one state would not support the import tax.

Problems with the states Congress had very little power over the individual states. States could make their own agreements with foreign nations or Native Americans. They might set taxes on trade with neighboring states and refuse to honor contracts made in other states. As you read earlier, some states even issued their own money.

Because there was no national court system, Congress could not settle disputes between states. States sometimes refused to recognize laws or court decisions made in other states. A criminal could escape the law simply by fleeing across a state line.

Problems with foreign nations Because it was so weak, Congress also had trouble taking advantage of the territory that the United States had won in the 1783 Treaty of Paris. The British continued to occupy their forts in the Great Lakes region. With the help of Native American allies, they kept American settlers out of parts of the Northwest Territory.

In addition, Congress had difficulty negotiating with Spain about the right to travel on the Mississippi River and use the port of New Orleans. People in the South and West, especially Kentucky and Tennessee, depended on the Mississippi River to take their produce to market. Disagreements also continued about the border with Spanish Florida.

Economic problems Money problems plagued not only the government but also private citizens and businesses in every state. The end of the war was a disaster for New England's valuable trade with Britain and the British West Indies. Traders lost the advantage of being part of the British Empire and now had to pay high customs duties.

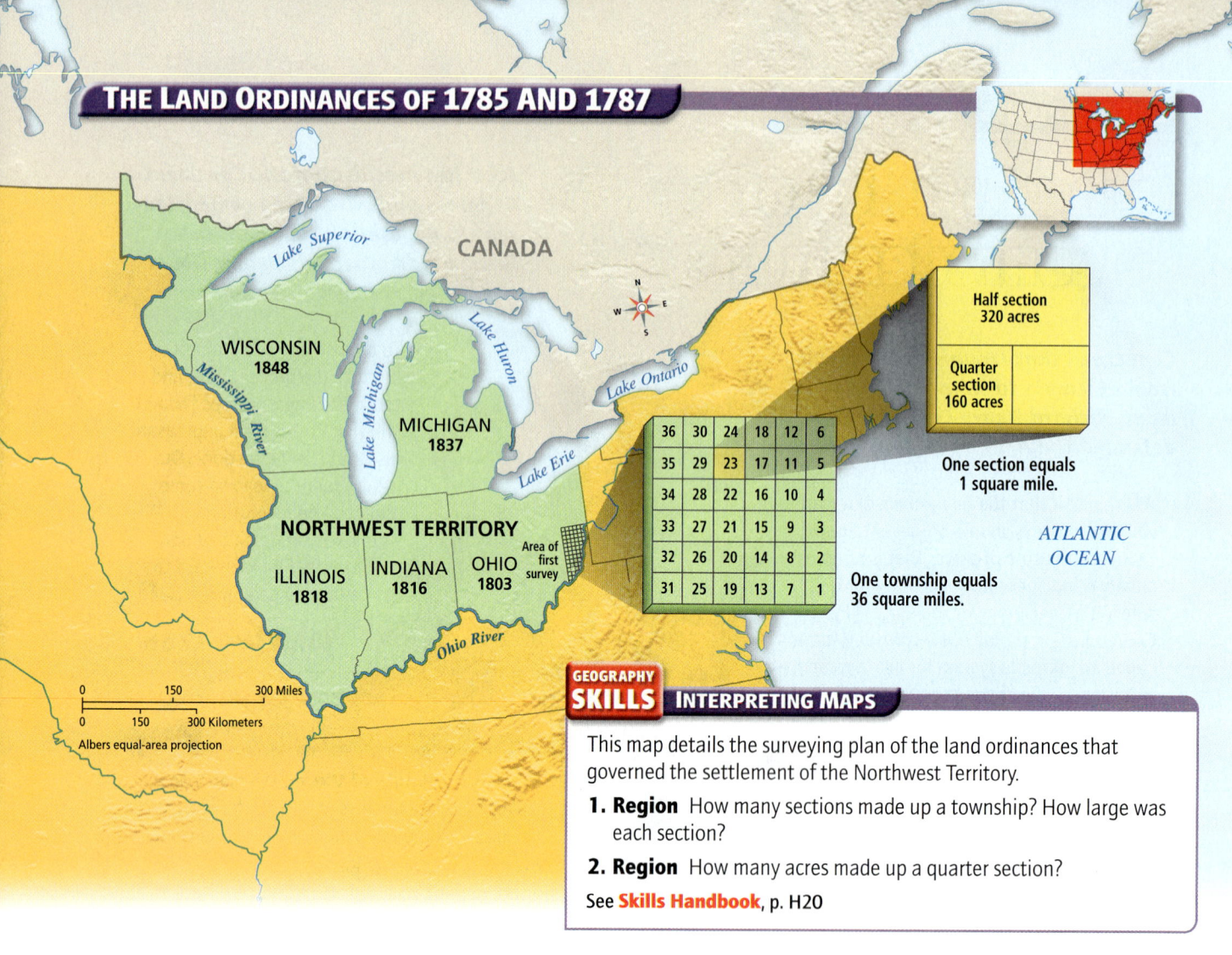

THE LAND ORDINANCES OF 1785 AND 1787

WISCONSIN 1848

MICHIGAN 1837

NORTHWEST TERRITORY

Area of first survey

ILLINOIS 1818   INDIANA 1816   OHIO 1803

Lake Superior
Lake Michigan
Lake Huron
Lake Erie
Lake Ontario
Mississippi River
Ohio River

CANADA

ATLANTIC OCEAN

36	30	24	18	12	6
35	29	23	17	11	5
34	28	22	16	10	4
33	27	21	15	9	3
32	26	20	14	8	2
31	25	19	13	7	1

One township equals 36 square miles.

Half section 320 acres

Quarter section 160 acres

One section equals 1 square mile.

0   150   300 Miles
0   150   300 Kilometers
Albers equal-area projection

GEOGRAPHY SKILLS INTERPRETING MAPS

This map details the surveying plan of the land ordinances that governed the settlement of the Northwest Territory.

1. **Region** How many sections made up a township? How large was each section?

2. **Region** How many acres made up a quarter section?

See **Skills Handbook**, p. H20

Before the war, Great Britain had paid bonuses to support key colonial industries, such as indigo and naval stores. The end of that aid from Britain hurt southern economies. Also, because many African Americans had left during the war, there were fewer workers.

In addition, the paper money issued during the war was not backed by gold or silver. That led to inflation—a huge rise in prices as the value of paper money fell. Congress could not collect taxes, but the states could—and did. Some states required that people pay their taxes in gold or silver, not the nearly worthless paper money. People who could not pay their debts were jailed. The laws especially hurt poor farmers who were already in debt. Frustrated farmers began rebellions in several places.

READING CHECK **Summarizing** What money problems did the national government face under the Articles of Confederation?

The Northwest Territory

Even though the Confederation was a weak government, some of its actions did have long-lasting effects. One notable accomplishment was establishing a pattern for settlement in western lands.

Western land claims In colonial times, several colonies, particularly New York and Virginia, claimed huge, unmapped areas of land west of the Appalachian Mountains. But others had fixed western boundaries. They worried that western land claims would create huge neighboring states.

After the Revolutionary War, settlers streamed into the lands west of the Appalachians. People on the frontier already were at odds with people from the East over taxes and policies toward Native Americans. Now the question was how to organize settlement of the vast western lands.

The Articles of Confederation did not address the question of new states. Congress had to find a way to bring western land and settlers into the political structure. Before that could happen, states had to give up their western land claims to the central government. During the 1780s and early 1790s, most states did so. Selling those lands could bring the Confederation badly needed money.

Dividing western lands In 1784 Thomas Jefferson came up with a proposal to divide the Northwest Territory—the land north and west of the Ohio River—into 10 districts. When the population in any district reached 20,000, its people would be able to send a representative to Congress. Later, the district could be admitted as a state. This original plan never fully went into effect, however.

The next year Congress drew up a plan for surveying, selling, and settling the territory. Under the **Land Ordinance of 1785**, the land would be surveyed and divided into a neat grid of townships, each 6 miles square (see map on opposite page). Within a township were 36 sections, each 1 mile square. The government would own four of the sections, while a fifth would be sold to support public schools. Surveyors planted "witness trees" to mark the corners of a section.

The Land Ordinance of 1785 changed the landscape of the Northwest Territory. As the United States expanded farther west, the same regular grid was used in other territories. This model ended many boundary disputes.

Land was to be sold at auction for at least $1 an acre. Buying a whole section was too expensive for most ordinary settlers and small farmers, who had to buy smaller parcels. Congress also sold some good land directly to land speculators.

In 1787 Congress passed another law for western settlement, the **Northwest Ordinance**. It was meant to encourage orderly settlement and the formation of new states, all controlled by law. The Northwest Ordinance also promised settlers religious freedom and other civil rights. Significantly, slavery was not allowed in the Northwest Territory.

A single governor was put in charge of the Northwest Territory, but the law said that it could later become three to five states. With a population of 5,000 adult males, a district could become a territory and send a nonvoting representative to Congress. With a population of 60,000, the territory could write a constitution and apply to become a state.

READING CHECK **Summarizing** How could a territory become a state?

Daily Life
When the Northwest Territory was divided into states, the square townships remained. Many of these townships still exist in midwestern states.

SECTION **1** **ASSESSMENT**

go.hrw.com
Online Quiz
Keyword: SD7 HP5

Reviewing Ideas, Terms, and People

1. a. Define What are the characteristics of a **republic**?
b. Make Inferences Why was having a written constitution so important to Americans?
c. Predict What possible changes might result from the idea of republican motherhood?

2. a. Describe What kind of government did the **Articles of Confederation** create?
b. Evaluate Was one vote per state a weakness of the new government? Why or why not?

3. a. Identify What kinds of problems did Congress face?
b. Explain Why was it so difficult to amend the Articles of Confederation?

4. a. Describe What did the survey plan for the Northwest Territory look like?
b. Interpret What were the goals of the land laws for the Northwest Territory?

c. Elaborate How might the new land laws influence settlement in the Northwest Territory?

Critical Thinking

5. Contrasting Copy the chart below and list the powers and the weaknesses of the Confederation government.

Powers	Weaknesses

FOCUS ON WRITING

6. Persuasive As a newspaper editor in a state with large western land claims, such as New York or Virginia, write an editorial in which you support or oppose giving up your state's land claims to the central government. Use details from the section to support your argument.

Drafting the Constitution

BEFORE YOU READ

MAIN IDEA

The Constitutional Convention tried to write a document that would address the weaknesses of the Articles of Confederation and make compromises between large and small states and between the North and South.

READING FOCUS

1. What different points of view emerged at the Constitutional Convention?

2. What compromises did the delegates make at the Constitutional Convention?

3. How does a system of checks and balances prevent any one branch of the federal government from becoming too powerful?

KEY TERMS AND PEOPLE

James Madison
Constitutional Convention
Virginia Plan
New Jersey Plan
Great Compromise
Three-Fifths Compromise
checks and balances

P1 1.2 Describe the evolution of American democratic values and beliefs as expressed in the Declaration of Independence, the New York State Constitution, the United States Constitution, the Bill of Rights, and other important historical documents.

THE INSIDE STORY

Why did farmers rebel at a courthouse in Massachusetts? Times were hard after the war. To pay off the state's war debts, the Massachusetts legislature raised taxes and demanded that the taxes be paid in hard currency, not paper money. That hurt farmers in western Massachusetts, who used paper money and a barter system. Some lost their farms because they owed taxes. Some were thrown in debtors' prison.

Fed up, the farmers protested. If the courts were shut down, judges could not order the farms to be sold to pay debts. So in September 1786, Daniel Shays, a veteran who had fought at Bunker Hill, led a crowd to close the courthouse at Springfield. In January 1787, Shays led a larger group of angry farmers to break into the military arsenal at Springfield, where hundreds of guns were stored. After a short battle with Massachusetts militia, Shays and his men retreated. Four were killed.

Shays's Rebellion was only one of several taxpayers' revolts to happen during this period. The unrest alarmed some national leaders. ◼

▶ **Shays's forces were easily defeated, but the rebellion rang alarm bells among the nation's leaders.**

Shays's Rebellion

THE GRANGER COLLECTION, NEW YORK

The Constitutional Convention

Frustration with the Articles of Confederation had been building for years, not only among farmers but also among veterans, merchants doing business between states, and creditors of the Continental Congress who had gone unpaid. A group of army officers stationed at Newburgh, New York, even launched a conspiracy in 1783 to overthrow the government, but George Washington declined the offer to lead the revolt. By fall 1786 conditions were so bad that as Shays's Rebellion began, Washington and **James Madison** were convening a meeting of five states in Annapolis, Maryland, to discuss the situation.

Washington himself had concerns about the Articles. In August 1786, he expressed these worries in a letter to John Jay, a prominent lawyer and diplomat.

HISTORY'S VOICES

❝I do not conceive we can exist long as a nation without having lodged somewhere a power, which will pervade the whole Union in as energetic a manner as the authority of the State governments extends over the several States.❞

—George Washington, Aug. 1, 1786

After the Annapolis meeting Congress called all the states to meet in Philadelphia in May 1787. According to Congress, the purpose of the Philadelphia convention was to revise the Articles of Confederation. Many states, however, sent delegates who supported a stronger central government.

A historic meeting The hot summer of 1787 was a turning point in American history. Only a few delegates arrived in Philadelphia on May 14, the day the **Constitutional Convention** was scheduled to begin. Traveling to Philadelphia over bad roads from distant states took some delegates several weeks. The meeting did not officially begin until the end of May.

Delegates from 12 states attended some or all of the meetings. (Politicians in Rhode Island opposed a stronger government and so never took part.) Each state had one vote. Decisions were made by a simple majority.

The delegates agreed to keep their discussions secret so that they could speak freely. The official secretary took only incomplete notes,

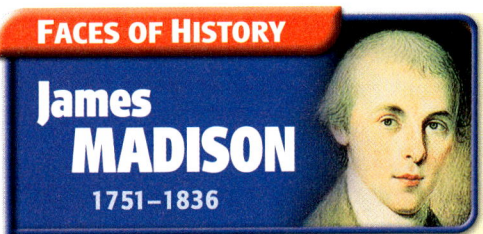

FACES OF HISTORY

James MADISON

1751–1836

History remembers James Madison as the Father of the Constitution because of his central role at the Constitutional Convention. The detailed diary he kept during the hot summer of 1787 remains the best primary account of the Constitutional Convention. Each night Madison stayed up late to transcribe his notes, recording important speeches and votes. "Nor was I unaware of the value of such a contribution," Madison wrote, "[to] the cause of liberty throughout the world." Not only a notetaker, Madison also was one of the convention's most active participants, drafting the highly influential Virginia Plan. Later, his eloquent support of the Constitution in *The Federalist* helped bring ratification.

Interpret Why is Madison called the Father of the Constitution?

but several other delegates kept personal diaries. The best account of the convention is the detailed diary kept by James Madison. Madison took notes about the delegates, their speeches, and their votes. Because of the enormous role he played in planning and writing the final document, Madison earned the title Father of the Constitution.

The convention delegates, known today as the Framers, also included John Dickinson, Alexander Hamilton, Robert Morris, Charles Cotesworth Pinckney, and Edmund Randolph. Leading the group were George Washington and Benjamin Franklin, the most admired men in America. The convention unanimously chose Washington as its president. His strength and character made him a symbol for people in every state. His leadership would bring the convention respect and legitimacy.

The delegates were all men, and they were mostly in their thirties and forties. The youngest delegate was 26-year-old Jonathan Dayton of New Jersey. Benjamin Franklin, at 81, was the oldest.

As a group, the delegates were well-educated. Many were trained as lawyers, and about half had attended college. Others were merchants, physicians, and planters. Most had been in their state's legislature or held state office. Some had signed the Declaration of Independence. Many had served in the Revolution. Most of the delegates were wealthy.

There were a few surprising absences from the Constitutional Convention. Several of the most fervent Patriots, such as Samuel Adams, opposed creating a stronger national government. Patrick Henry, whose fiery speeches had helped start the Revolution, also refused to attend the convention. John Adams and Thomas Jefferson did favor the convention's work but did not attend because they were on diplomatic missions abroad.

Controversial plans Almost as soon as the Constitutional Convention began, it became clear that most delegates were ready to do much more than revise the Articles of Confederation. They were ready to frame an entirely new government.

The most historic and difficult issues would involve finding a balance between the large and small states. The convention delegates would also have to find a balance between various northern and southern interests. Of tremendous importance was the emerging battle between those who wanted a strong national government and those who wanted to protect states' rights. But many smaller disagreements would make the convention long and often frustrating.

Edmund Randolph of Virginia boldly took the lead. He presented a plan that Madison had devised called the **Virginia Plan**. This plan proposed an entirely new form of national government. Many parts of Randolph's Virginia Plan were controversial, however. Government would have three separate branches: executive, legislative, and judicial. The legislature would choose an executive to carry out the laws. It would also set up a court system to interpret the laws.

Under the Virginia Plan, the national legislature would be bicameral, meaning it would have two houses, or groups of representatives. Voters would choose members of the lower house, who would then select the upper house. Members of the lower house would be chosen in proportion to each state's population. The national government would have the authority to make the states follow its laws.

THE IMPACT TODAY

Government

Today the United States has a bicameral legislature. The upper house is the Senate and the lower house is the House of Representatives. All states except Nebraska have bicameral legislatures.

ACADEMIC VOCABULARY

proportion
proper or equal share

The Constitutional Convention

Key Delegates at the Constitutional Convention

1. Roger Sherman
2. Alexander Hamilton
3. Benjamin Franklin
4. James Madison
5. George Washington
6. James Wilson

152

Smaller states quickly objected to parts of the Virginia Plan. They were afraid of the "tyranny" of their large neighbors. For example, Virginia, the largest state in terms of population, could have 10 times as many representatives as Delaware, the smallest.

Delegates argued about Randolph's plan for several weeks. To counter it, William Paterson of New Jersey proposed a "small state" plan. The **New Jersey Plan** kept many features of the Articles of Confederation but gave Congress additional powers. The plan proposed a unicameral, or one-house, legislature. Each state would have equal representation in the legislature. The New Jersey Plan also suggested a "plural executive"—that is, two or three top executives chosen by Congress. The executive would appoint members of a supreme court. These suggestions triggered weeks of debates throughout the hot Philadelphia summer.

READING CHECK **Identifying Points of View** Why did some Patriots refuse to attend the Constitutional Convention?

Compromises at the Convention

The Virginia Plan and New Jersey Plan set the stage for major disagreements. While most delegates favored parts of the Virginia Plan, it was clear that many compromises would have to be made to satisfy smaller states.

The Great Compromise After days of argument, it looked as if the convention was at a stalemate. Some large states were hinting that they might withdraw and form their own nation. A separate committee was set up to find a way to balance the interests of large and small states.

Finally, the Connecticut delegates—Oliver Ellsworth, Roger Sherman, and Dr. William Samuel Johnson—came up with a compromise. It stated: "The two ideas . . . ought to be combined; that in one branch the people ought to be represented; in the other the States." That is, the upper house, the Senate, would

This painting shows the Framers signing the Constitution on September 17, 1787. A key accomplishment of the convention was the agreement to create a bicameral, or two-house, legislature. This agreement is called the Great Compromise.

THE GREAT COMPROMISE

Virginia Plan
(Large-state plan)

- Gave more power to state government
- Bicameral legislature
- The number of representatives for each state would be based on population.

New Jersey Plan
(Small-state plan)

- Gave more power to national government
- Unicameral legislature
- Each state would have an equal number of representatives.

THE GREAT COMPROMISE

- Bicameral legislature
- In the lower house, the number of representatives for each state is determined by population.
- In the upper house, each state has an equal number of representatives.

have two representatives from each state. In the other house, representation would be based on states' population.

Today this answer may seem obvious. But it was such a major step for the convention that it is known as the **Great Compromise**. It is also called the Connecticut Compromise.

Compromises on slavery As part of the Great Compromise, delegates also had to decide on how to count population. Enslaved African Americans made up a large proportion of the population in several southern states—as much as 30 to 40 percent. Counting them in full would have given those states much greater representation in Congress. But because some taxes were based on population, it would also increase taxes.

Southern states at first wanted to count all slaves for representation purposes but none for taxation. Northern states objected. In the **Three-Fifths Compromise**, delegates agreed that all whites plus three-fifths of the slave population (referred to as "all other persons") would be counted for both representation and taxation. Native Americans were not counted.

The slavery question brought up other issues. Many people opposed slavery as immoral. Thomas Jefferson, himself a slaveholder, had tried to include a protest against it in the Declaration of Independence. Some delegates spoke eloquently about including a ban on slavery in the Constitution.

In the hope of maintaining unity between North and South, however, the delegates did not consider including a ban on slavery in the Constitution. As another compromise, they agreed to a clause allowing the slave trade to continue for 20 years. Another clause, known as the fugitive slave clause, stated that a slave who fled to another state had to be returned to his or her original state.

Other compromises Because the delegates were devising a government like no one had ever seen before, they had to consider many details. Here are some of the questions they had to answer:

- Who should choose the executive? Should the office be held by one man, or several?
- Who should be eligible to be president? How old should he be? Must the president be American-born?
- Who can declare war, the president or the U.S. Congress?
- What should be the term of office for the president and for members of Congress?
- Can a president be removed from office?
- Who can be a member of Congress? How old should they be? Must they be wealthy?
- Should government officials be required to belong to a certain religious faith?
- Should voters be required to own property?

Over the summer, all of these questions were raised, along with many others. Some were debated for a few hours. Other questions took weeks to resolve.

READING CHECK **Making Inferences** What benefits did the southern states gain from the Three-Fifths Compromise?

Checks and Balances

In late July 1787, a five-man committee consisting of Oliver Ellsworth, Nathaniel Gorham, Edmund Randolph, John Rutledge, and James Wilson sat down to write a final document. Their draft would include the decisions and compromises that had already been made.

By then many delegates were tired of arguing, tired of being away from home, and tired of the stiflingly hot weather. They took a 10-day holiday. George Washington and Robert Morris (in whose Philadelphia home Washington was staying) went trout fishing.

Balancing powers On August 6, delegates returned to read the draft of the Constitution that the committee had written. For more than a month they picked over the details and made changes. One big point of debate was the balance between the powers of Congress and those of the president (as the executive was now called). A related question was what powers the states should have and what powers the federal government should have.

All the delegates had taken part in a rebellion against the authority of a king. As a result, they had given much greater powers to Congress than to the president. In the first draft, Congress chose the president for one seven-year term. Popular election had been suggested, but it was voted down.

ACADEMIC VOCABULARY
federal national

Then at the end of August, James Madison said he could not support the document in its present form. This was a major blow because the entire convention had been working from his basic plan. Alarmed, they named another committee, with one delegate from each of the states. Madison represented Virginia.

The outcome was another compromise. Instead of allowing people to elect the president directly, the state legislatures would choose electors, who would then choose a president. That removed the presidency one step from the popular vote. It also took away some of the overwhelming power given to Congress.

At almost the last minute, delegates created the office of vice president. That position would go to the person who came in second in the electoral vote. (The delegates did not foresee the rise of political parties.)

These last-minute changes were important in setting up **checks and balances** among the legislative, executive, and judicial branches of government. This meant that the Constitution provided each branch with power to slow or stop an action taken by one of the other branches. These checks and balances ensured that no one branch of the government would dominate the others.

For example, the committee gave the president the power to make treaties and name judges and ambassadors. But the Senate had to give its "advice and consent" to these actions. The committee also gave the president the power to veto a law passed by Congress. But Congress could still pass any law over the president's veto provided that two-thirds of each house agreed to do so. (See the diagram on this page for more examples of checks and balances among the three branches of the federal government.)

Planning the court system The issue of the court system provoked fewer arguments. Congressional representation and the role of the president were far more divisive. But the courts were still important. Delegates wanted to keep judges and courts independent, maintaining a separation of powers.

FOCUS ON NEW YORK

GOVERNMENT
The Framers used the New York State Constitution of 1777 as a model for parts of the Constitution of the United States. The New York State Constitution called for a popularly elected executive who could veto laws. New York's first state constitution helped shape the office of President as we know it today.

QUICK FACTS

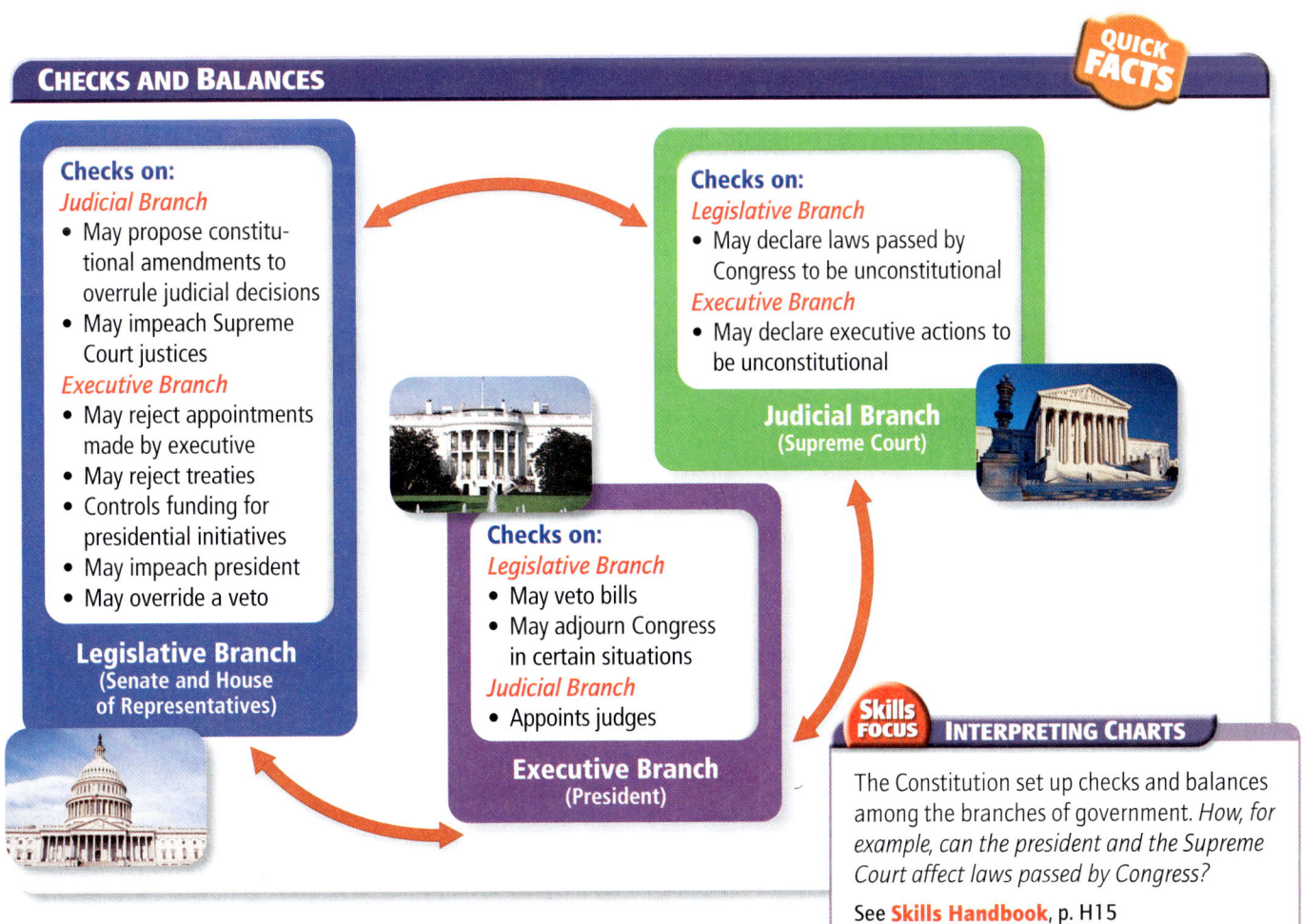

CHECKS AND BALANCES

Checks on:
Judicial Branch
- May propose constitutional amendments to overrule judicial decisions
- May impeach Supreme Court justices

Executive Branch
- May reject appointments made by executive
- May reject treaties
- Controls funding for presidential initiatives
- May impeach president
- May override a veto

Legislative Branch
(Senate and House of Representatives)

Checks on:
Legislative Branch
- May veto bills
- May adjourn Congress in certain situations

Judicial Branch
- Appoints judges

Executive Branch
(President)

Checks on:
Legislative Branch
- May declare laws passed by Congress to be unconstitutional

Executive Branch
- May declare executive actions to be unconstitutional

Judicial Branch
(Supreme Court)

Skills FOCUS **INTERPRETING CHARTS**

The Constitution set up checks and balances among the branches of government. *How, for example, can the president and the Supreme Court affect laws passed by Congress?*

See **Skills Handbook**, p. H15

At first, the delegates gave the choice of federal judges to the Senate. Then they decided to split the responsibility between the two other branches. The president would nominate judges, but the Senate would have to approve them. Judges could not be fired arbitrarily.

Final decisions As the Constitutional Convention drew to a close, a Committee on Style worked out the wording of the final draft. Madison and others gave the credit for the document's elegant language and clarity to Gouverneur Morris of Pennsylvania. Morris wrote the famous opening phrase, "We, the people of the United States."

The U.S. Constitution set out a plan of government that had never been seen before, with three separate branches. Today the basic structure of the federal government remains exactly as the Framers envisioned it over 200 years ago. The legislative branch (the House of Representatives and the Senate) makes the laws. The executive branch (the president and his advisers) carries out those laws. The judicial branch (the Supreme Court and lower courts) interprets the laws as they relate to the Constitution.

When it was time to sign the Constitution, Benjamin Franklin urged the delegates to overlook the parts of the document that they did not like because it was as close to a perfect Constitution as he thought possible:

HISTORY'S VOICES

❝I confess that there are several parts of this constitution which I do not at present approve, but I am not sure I shall never approve them. For having lived long, I have experienced many instances of being obliged to change opinions even on important subjects . . . It therefore astonishes me, Sir, to find this system approaching so near to perfection as it does . . . Thus I consent, Sir, to this Constitution because I expect no better, and because I am not sure that it is not the best.❞

—Benjamin Franklin, quoted in James Madison's journal

Franklin urged the meeting to "act heartily and unanimously" in signing the Constitution and trying to make it work. But some of those who had worked hardest to draft the document could not, at the last minute, bring themselves to sign it. They were George Mason and Edmund Randolph of Virginia and Elbridge Gerry of Massachusetts. They would not sign because the Constitution lacked a bill of rights. Other delegates who had misgivings went ahead and signed the document anyway.

In all, 39 delegates from 12 states signed the Constitution. Then the Constitutional Convention adjourned on Monday, September 17, 1787. Now it was time for the American people to approve the document.

READING CHECK **Identifying Supporting Details** Name three instances of checks and balances in the Constitution.

SECTION 2 ASSESSMENT

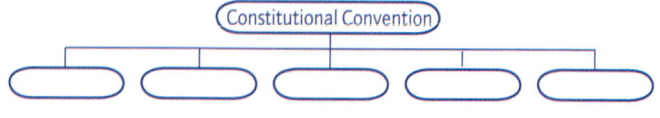
go.hrw.com
Online Quiz
Keyword: SD7 HP5

Reviewing Ideas, Terms, and People

1. **a. Recall** What were the main points of the **Virginia Plan** and the **New Jersey Plan**?
   b. Summarize How did Shays's Rebellion reveal weaknesses of the Articles of Confederation?
   c. Rate What were the most radical changes suggested in the Virginia Plan?

2. **a. Define** What was the **Great Compromise**?
   b. Explain Explain the issues the **Three-Fifths Compromise** addressed.
   c. Evaluate Did large states gain more from the Great Compromise or did small states?

3. **a. Identify** Identify the three branches of government and the role of each of them.
   b. Interpret Give one example of **checks and balances** between Congress and the president.

c. Develop How did the delegates' thinking about the office of president change during the course of the convention?

Critical Thinking

4. **Identifying Supporting Details** Copy the chart below and fill in the major issues that caused controversy at the Constitutional Convention.

Constitutional Convention

FOCUS ON SPEAKING

5. **Persuasive** As a delegate to the Constitutional Convention, write a speech in which you outline what you think ought to be the requirements for a senator.

Ratifying the Constitution

BEFORE YOU READ

MAIN IDEA

Federalists and Antifederalists struggled over the principles of the new Constitution. But the promise of adding a Bill of Rights brought about ratification.

READING FOCUS

1. What arguments for and against the Constitution were put forth by Federalists and Antifederalists?
2. What ideas were published in *The Federalist*?
3. Why was adding a Bill of Rights significant in the ratification process?

KEY TERMS AND PEOPLE

Federalist
Antifederalist
Alexander Hamilton
Brutus
Bill of Rights
Publius
The Federalist
John Jay
delegated powers
reserved powers

PI **1.2** Describe the evolution of American democratic values and beliefs as expressed in the Declaration of Independence, the New York State Constitution, the United States Constitution, the Bill of Rights, and other important historical documents.

A Rising Sun or a Setting Sun?

THE INSIDE STORY

Will the Constitution succeed?
It was the final day of the Constitutional Convention: September 17, 1787. The aging Benjamin Franklin, always a shrewd politician, knew it was important for the convention delegates to appear united. But down to the last minute, some delegates were still arguing. Local loyalties were still strong.

Franklin offered a final persuasive speech, read aloud by another delegate. He said that the new Constitution might not be perfect, but it was the best one possible.

Then the convention's oldest delegate made a motion that the meeting approve the Constitution unanimously. Although individual delegates still disagreed, every state present said yes. Delegates stepped forward, one at a time, to sign the document. Stories say there were tears in Franklin's eyes as he picked up the quill pen. He looked toward the chair where George Washington had sat to preside over the meeting. The image of a sun was painted on the back.

James Madison described the scene: Franklin remarked that painters had trouble showing the difference between a rising and a setting sun. He went on, "I have often and often in the course of Session . . . looked at that [sun] behind the president without being able to tell whether it was rising or setting. But now at length I have the happiness to know that it is a rising and not a setting Sun."

◀ **The sunburst on the back of Washington's chair symbolized faith in the new Constitution.**

Federalists and Antifederalists

The delegates who met at Philadelphia in May 1787 expected to revise the Articles of Confederation and make the government stronger. Instead, they essentially threw out the Articles and wrote a new Constitution. The new Constitution put forth a framework for a strong national government with certain powers left to the states. It declared that the Constitution would be the "supreme law of the land."

The Philadelphia Convention had been held in secret. As the meeting continued through the summer of 1787, people wondered what it would produce. When the Constitution was finally published, the drastic changes surprised and angered some people. Many remembered British tyranny and feared the idea of a too-powerful national government. That led to a 10-month struggle over ratification.

Supporters and opponents of the new Constitution immediately began to present their arguments. Supporters of the Constitution, once called nationalists, were now known as Federalists. Opponents of the Constitution were called Antifederalists.

The Federalist viewpoint

Supporters of the new Constitution had an advantage from the beginning. To begin with, they had been studying and defending their points of view all during the Constitutional Convention. They had their arguments ready.

The Federalists also had strong leaders such as Madison, John Dickinson, and the brilliant young **Alexander Hamilton**. Born in the West Indies, Hamilton had been Washington's aide during the Revolutionary War. Federalists also had the backing of George Washington and Benjamin Franklin.

Like Franklin, most Federalists admitted that the Constitution was not perfect but was the best they could do. They believed that a strong national government was necessary for the survival of the republic. They wanted government to end chaos and be a check on the kind of mob rule seen during Shays's Rebellion. At the same time, they pointed out that the separation of powers in the Constitution put limits on government power.

The Federalist cause was generally popular in the cities, but Federalists were outnumbered in the general population. Especially in the rural western parts of the states, some people saw the Federalists as an educated, wealthy, urban elite. They distrusted them.

Still, the Federalists were well organized and knew how to gather political support. As soon as the Constitution was written, they quickly began to work for its ratification.

The Antifederalist viewpoint

Although they outnumbered the Federalists, those who had doubts about the Constitution were at a disadvantage. First, the term "Antifederalists" suggested that they were simply *against* something, without a plan of their own. In a sense, that was true. Many Antifederalists admitted there were flaws in the Articles of Confederation. They wanted a new government, but not the one outlined in the Constitution. Mainly, Antifederalists tried to warn people about flaws in the proposed government.

The Antifederalists were less organized and less unified than their opponents. They were more diverse, coming from different economic backgrounds and social classes. Their core consisted of farmers and planters.

Antifederalists did agree on one central issue: They distrusted any central authority. They were afraid that a strong national government would lead to a kind of tyranny—exactly what they had fought against in the Revolution. Antifederalists worried that the central government outlined in the Constitution would abuse both states' rights and individual liberties. They did not trust any government to protect the people's rights. Many also thought the new government favored the educated and wealthy over ordinary people.

Some opponents argued that a republic could not succeed in a nation as large as the United States. They also criticized specific features such as the role of the president, the number of congressional representatives, and the length of senatorial terms.

The Antifederalists had many strong leaders. Some, like Samuel Adams, Patrick Henry, and Richard Henry Lee, had opposed the convention from the beginning. Mercy Otis Warren, the colonial writer, warned it would create tyranny. In a typically fiery speech at the

Political Cartoon

This political cartoon was published soon after the ninth state, New Hampshire, ratified the Constitution.

The pillars represent the colonies in the order in which they ratified the Constitution.

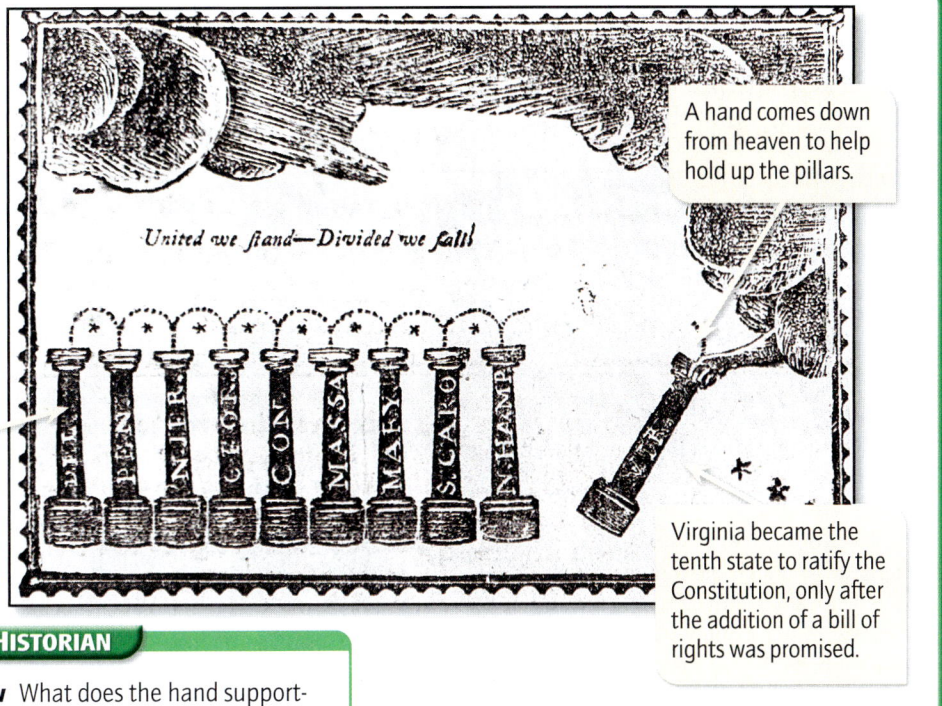

United we stand—Divided we fall

A hand comes down from heaven to help hold up the pillars.

Virginia became the tenth state to ratify the Constitution, only after the addition of a bill of rights was promised.

Skills FOCUS **READING LIKE A HISTORIAN**

Identifying Points of View What does the hand supporting the pillar reflect about the artist's view of the new country and its Constitution?

See **Skills Handbook**, pp. H28–H29

Virginia ratifying convention, Patrick Henry even claimed that the convention delegates did not have the authority to create a completely new government.

HISTORY'S VOICES

❝My political curiosity . . . leads me to ask, who authorised them to speak the language of, *We, the People*, instead of *We, the States*? . . . The Federal Convention ought to have amended the old system—for this purpose they were solely delegated . . . You must therefore forgive the solicitation of one unworthy member, to know what danger could have arisen under the present confederation, and what are the causes of this proposal to change our Government.❞

—Patrick Henry, June 1788

George Mason, who had refused to sign the Constitution, also worked actively against its ratification. So did Robert Yates, a delegate from New York. Under the name **Brutus**, Yates wrote a number of anti-Constitution essays.

The ratification process The concerns of the Antifederalists led them to demand the addition of a **Bill of Rights**. Because they did not trust government, they wanted to spell out some basic rights in the Constitution to make sure those rights would be protected. Adding a Bill of Rights became the main focus of the struggle over ratification.

The Framers knew that getting unanimous agreement would be hard. Article VII of the Constitution explained what must be done to bring the constitution into effect. Only 9 of the 13 states had to ratify, or approve, the Constitution. Some people thought that nine states were not enough to authorize a complete change of government. But the Confederation Congress, which was still technically the American government, approved.

To make ratification more likely, the Framers bypassed the state legislatures, which would lose considerable power to the new national government. Instead, they called for special ratifying conventions in each state. In the fall of 1787 the battle over ratification began.

READING CHECK **Drawing Conclusions** Why did their experience as colonists make some people suspicious of central government?

Federalist vs. Antifederalist

In Federalist No. 45, James Madison argued that the states were too powerful under the Articles of Confederation.

❝ Was, then, the American Revolution effected, was the American Confederacy formed, was the precious blood of thousands spilt, . . . not that the people of America should enjoy peace, liberty, and safety, but that the government of the individual States . . . might enjoy a certain extent of power, and be arrayed with certain dignities and attributes of sovereignty?❞

James Madison, 1787

Patrick Henry spoke against the proposed Constitution, saying it took power away from the states.

❝ Here is a resolution as radical as that which separated us from Great Britain. It is radical in this transition; our rights and privileges are endangered, and the sovereignty of the states will be relinquished. ❞

Patrick Henry, 1788

THE THOMAS GILCREASE INSTITUTE OF AMERICAN HISTORY AND ART, TULSA, OKLAHOMA

COLONIAL WILLIAMSBURG FOUNDATION

Skills FOCUS READING LIKE A HISTORIAN

Distinguishing Fact from Opinion Which parts of these quotations are fact, and which parts are opinion?

See **Skills Handbook**, pp. H28–H29

The Federalist Papers

In late 1787, people in New York opened their newspapers to find a series of essays written under the pen name **Publius**. By spring, 85 essays on government had appeared. Addressed "To the People of the State of New York," they were first published in New York newspapers. Later, the essays circulated widely in other states and were collected in a book called **The Federalist**, also known as the Federalist Papers.

The anonymous Publius discussed and defended each part of the Constitution. The main goal of the essays was to persuade New York delegates to ratify the document by explaining the advantages it would bring. But they were also brilliant explanations of republican government and politics.

Writing The Federalist Publius was in fact three leading Federalists: James Madison, Alexander Hamilton, and **John Jay**. Their

names were kept secret until 1802. Hamilton and Madison wrote most of the essays in *The Federalist*, and Jay supplied a few. Historians are still not entirely certain of the authorship of every essay in *The Federalist*.

Ideas in The Federalist Madison, on whose ideas the Constitution was based, wrote about political theory in his essays. Hamilton offered practical arguments for a strong government.

In *Federalist* No. 1, Hamilton introduced the series. He told his readers that the decision they were about to make was important for the whole world. He noted:

HISTORY'S VOICES

❝ . . . it seems to have been reserved to the people of this country . . . to decide the important question, whether societies of men are really capable or not of establishing good government from reflection and choice, or whether they are forever destined to depend for their political constitutions on accident and force. ❞

–*The Federalist* No. 1

Hamilton also listed the subjects of future essays, including how the Constitution would help preserve republican government, liberty, and property.

In *Federalist* No. 10, Madison warned against the dangers of factions—groups with specific, often opposing, interests. Factional fights had torn apart some European governments. But Madison argued that factions were a natural part of American society and that suppressing such groups would destroy liberty. Instead, a republican government would help balance their influence. In *Federalist* No. 51, Madison explained how the separation of powers described in the Constitution would limit government powers.

The Constitutional Convention had spent less time discussing the judiciary than the other branches. In *Federalist* No. 78, Hamilton said that the lack of a judiciary was one flaw in the Articles of Confederation. He explained the importance of an independent judiciary. He also discussed the Supreme Court's power to consider whether a law is constitutional.

READING CHECK **Summarizing** What were the main arguments made by the authors of *The Federalist*?

Adding a Bill of Rights

Even before the Constitution was signed, it was clear that the lack of a bill of rights was going to cause trouble. The three delegates who refused to sign the Constitution in Philadelphia had been the first indication that there might be problems.

For example, George Mason had written Virginia's Declaration of Rights. He said he could quickly write a national one. On the other hand, Roger Sherman of Connecticut pointed out that most state constitutions already had bills of rights and he believed that was enough. Others agreed, and the convention voted down all moves to add a bill of rights. As a result, Mason did not sign the Constitution. He never <u>deviated</u> from his opposition, hurting his friendship with Madison and Washington.

The fight for ratification When the ratification battle began, the Federalists were better prepared than their opponents. They quickly organized and gained control of several state conventions, especially in small states.

Pennsylvania's convention met first, but Delaware moved more quickly. On December 7, 1787, Delaware became the first state to ratify the Constitution, with a unanimous "yes" vote. Pennsylvania followed days later, approving it by two to one. Within the first two weeks of 1788, New Jersey, Georgia, and Connecticut also had ratified it.

Massachusetts was a bigger challenge. Elbridge Gerry led a strong opposition there. Yet the Massachusetts vote had the potential to influence delegates in other states with large Antifederalist forces, such as New York, Virginia, and North Carolina. Federalists went to work to persuade prominent men such as John Hancock. By a close 187–168 vote, Massachusetts ratified on February 6, 1788. Its resolution, however, included a number of suggested amendments.

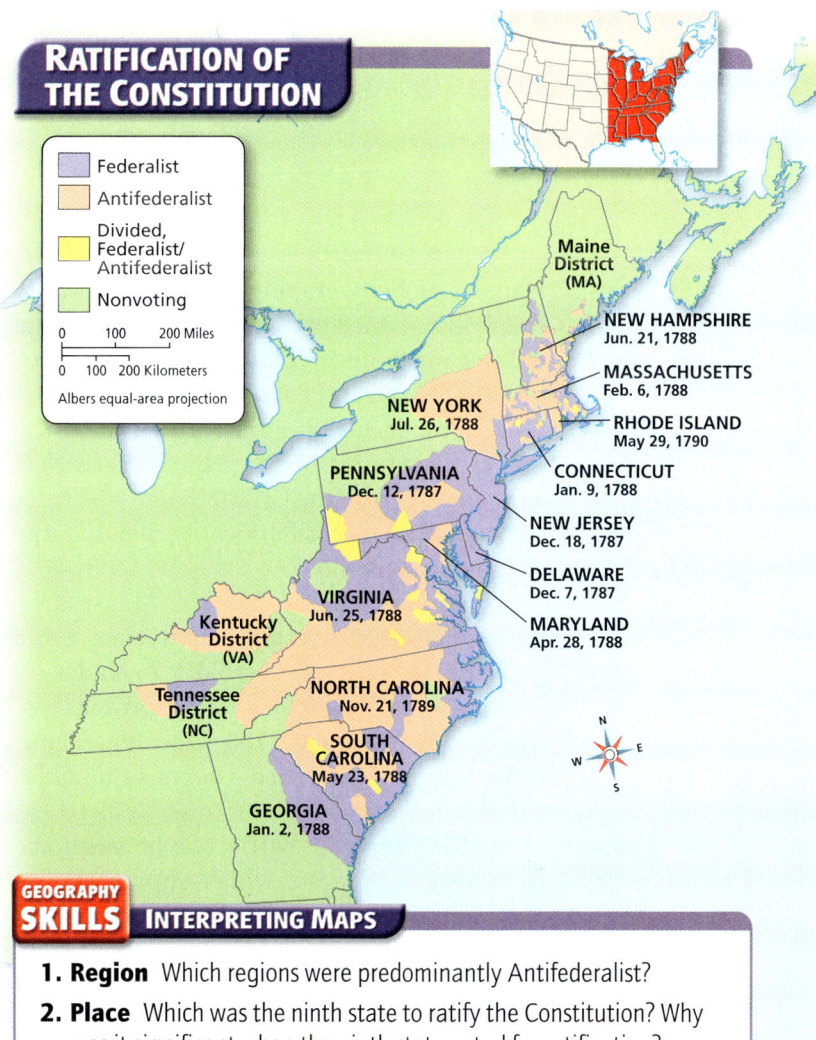

RATIFICATION OF THE CONSTITUTION

- Federalist
- Antifederalist
- Divided, Federalist/Antifederalist
- Nonvoting

0   100   200 Miles
0 100 200 Kilometers
Albers equal-area projection

Maine District (MA)
NEW HAMPSHIRE Jun. 21, 1788
MASSACHUSETTS Feb. 6, 1788
RHODE ISLAND May 29, 1790
NEW YORK Jul. 26, 1788
PENNSYLVANIA Dec. 12, 1787
CONNECTICUT Jan. 9, 1788
NEW JERSEY Dec. 18, 1787
DELAWARE Dec. 7, 1787
MARYLAND Apr. 28, 1788
VIRGINIA Jun. 25, 1788
Kentucky District (VA)
Tennessee District (NC)
NORTH CAROLINA Nov. 21, 1789
SOUTH CAROLINA May 23, 1788
GEORGIA Jan. 2, 1788

GEOGRAPHY SKILLS **INTERPRETING MAPS**

1. **Region** Which regions were predominantly Antifederalist?
2. **Place** Which was the ninth state to ratify the Constitution? Why was it significant when the ninth state voted for ratification?

See **Skills Handbook**, p. H21

American Civil Liberty

The First Amendment

The First Amendment protects freedom of religion, freedom of speech, freedom of the press, and the right to peaceably assemble. For over 200 years, these have been familiar rights to Americans.

In recent years, some people have wondered: Do First Amendment rights apply on the Internet? People can create Web sites on almost any topic. While many people feel some sites contain indecent or dangerous material, in the United States the First Amendment guarantees freedom of speech on the Internet.

Many other countries also encourage freedom of speech on the Internet. Some, however, strictly limit how their citizens use this technology. For example, China does not allow criticism of the government or support for oppressed religious minorities. The government of Saudi Arabia also limits Internet use. Leaders identify Web sites that they consider offensive and block access to them.

Contrasting Why is Internet access not limited in the United States as it is in some other countries?

Americans young and old exercise their First Amendment rights to assemble at a peace rally.

Federalists were less worried about New Hampshire but were unpleasantly surprised. Ratification failed on the first vote. The state did not ratify until June 1788. In the meantime, Maryland and South Carolina said yes.

That made up the nine states needed for the Constitution to go into effect. But without New York and Virginia, the United States would not be much of a country. Ratification of both large states was a must.

Virginia was oddly divided. Many large landowners opposed the Constitution, while some frontier people supported it. To Madison's great relief, the state narrowly approved "his" Constitution in June 1788. Like Massachusetts, Virginia demanded a promise to add a bill of rights.

In New York the battle was between the New York City area, which supported the Federalists, and the rest of the state. Governor George Clinton led a strong Antifederalist force, while Hamilton and his allies worked tirelessly for ratification. They even hinted that the city might secede and ratify separately. Some opponents began to see that being

outside the Union would be an economic disaster for the state. New York at last ratified in July by a vote of only 30–27.

With 11 states, the new government could now go ahead. In September 1788, the Congress of the Confederation took its final actions. It set dates in early 1789 for elections to choose members of Congress and presidential electors. The last two states, North Carolina and Rhode Island, did not join the Union until after the new government was already at work.

Constitutional amendments Several crucial states had ratified the Constitution only because they were promised a bill of rights. Once the new Congress was elected, it needed to add that bill of rights in the form of amendments to the Constitution. Article V of the Constitution gave either Congress or state conventions the right to propose amendments.

It was not only the Antifederalists who wanted a bill of rights. It was in the Federalists' interests to support one, too. Besides, most Federalists did not oppose a bill of rights. They simply did not think one was necessary.

Now Madison took charge of getting a bill of rights through Congress. In fact, he insisted on bringing up the issue. On June 8, 1789, Madison spoke to Congress and proposed some amendments. He pointed out that in England the constitution limited only the king's power, not Parliament's. These changes, he said, would protect against all abuses of power:

HISTORY'S VOICES

❝ . . . if all power is subject to abuse, that then it is possible the abuse of the powers of the General Government may be guarded against in a more secure manner than is now done. . . . We have in this way something to gain, and, if we proceed with caution, nothing to lose. ❞

–James Madison, June 8, 1789

In September 1789 Congress approved 12 amendments based on the ideas Madison had presented. As the Constitution required, they were sent to the states for approval. By the end of 1791, the state had approved 10 of them. These 10 amendments became the Bill of Rights.

The Bill of Rights The Bill of Rights protected both individuals and states against what people feared might be too much government power. The first eight amendments dealt with individual civil liberties. The Ninth Amendment stated that listing certain rights given to the people did not mean that other rights did not exist as well.

Most of the amendments echoed the rights spelled out in the Virginia Declaration of Rights. The First Amendment guaranteed civil liberties such as freedom of speech, the press, and religion. The amendments addressed problems from British colonial rule, such as the quartering of soldiers and illegal searches. Some amendments drew on rights provided in ancient English law, such as trial by jury. The complete text of the Constitution and the Bill of Rights follows this chapter.

States' rights Most of the amendments in the Bill of Rights listed things that no government, state or federal, could do. The final amendment addressed the actions that states could take. It answered Antifederalist fears about the loss of states' rights and sovereignty.

The Tenth Amendment defined two kinds of government powers. The Constitution gives certain powers to each branch of the national government. Those are the **delegated powers**. Some powers are expressly stated. Other powers are implied.

The Tenth Amendment also defined the **reserved powers**. Those are powers that the Constitution does not specifically give to the federal government or deny to the states. The Tenth Amendment says that the reserved powers belong to the states or to the people.

READING CHECK **Making Inferences** Why did Madison lead the fight for a bill of rights?

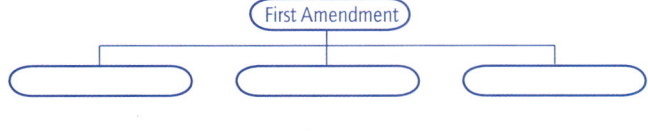

go.hrw.com
Online Quiz
Keyword: SD7 HP5

SECTION 3 ASSESSMENT

Reviewing Ideas, Terms, and People

1. a. Identify Identify three leaders on each side of the Federalist–Antifederalist debate.
b. Make Generalizations What were the Antifederalists' main objections to the Constitution?
c. Evaluate Why was the lack of the **Bill of Rights** so important in the ratification struggle?

2. a. Recall Who were the authors of *The Federalist*?
b. Explain In *Federalist* No. 10, what was Madison's attitude toward factions in a republic?
c. Predict What might Madison say about the role of factions, or political parties, in politics today?

3. a. Recall Which state was first to ratify the Constitution? Which states were crucial to the Constitution's success?
b. Summarize What kinds of rights were promised in the first eight amendments to the Constitution?

c. Evaluate How has the Bill of Rights been important in American history since 1791?

Critical Thinking

4. Identifying Supporting Details Copy the chart below and use it to show examples of First Amendment rights.

First Amendment

FOCUS ON WRITING

5. Persuasive As a member of the Congress elected in 1789, describe five or six amendments you would propose to add to the Bill of Rights. Explain your reasons.

Forming a Government

Historical Context The documents below provide different information about the debates that led to ratification of the U.S. Constitution.

Task Examine the documents and answer the questions that follow. Then write an essay about the Constitution. Use facts from the documents and from the chapter to support the position you take in your thesis statement.

ST 4.1 Analyze important debates in American history (e.g., ratification of the United States Constitution), focusing on the opposing positions and the historical evidence used to support these positions.

ST 4.3 Develop hypotheses about important events, eras, or issues; use information collected from diverse sources to produce cogently written reports and document-based essays.

DOCUMENT 1

During the Constitutional Convention, Virginia delegate James Madison took extensive notes, including these notes on whether the Constitution should ban any further importation of slaves.

"**Mr. Sherman** [Connecticut]: was for leaving the clause as it stands. He disapproved of the slave trade; yet as the States were now possessed of the right to import slaves, as the public good did not require it to be taken from them, & as it was expedient to have as few objections as possible to the proposed scheme of Government, he thought it best to leave the matter as we find it . . . He observed that the abolition of slavery seemed to be going on in the U.S. & that the good sense of the several States would probably by degrees [complete] it . . .

Mr. E[l]lsworth [Connecticut]: As he had never owned a slave could not judge of the effects of slavery on character: He said however that if it was to be considered in a moral light we ought to go farther and free those already in the Country . . . As population increases poor laborers will be so plenty as to render slaves useless. Slavery in time will not be a speck in our Country . . .

Mr. Pinckney [South Carolina]: If slavery be wrong, it is justified by the example of all the world. He cited the case of Greece Rome & other ancient States; the sanction given by France, England, Holland & other modern States . . . In all ages one half of mankind have been slaves. . . . An attempt to take away the right as proposed will produce serious objections to the Constitution which he wished to see adopted . . ."

DOCUMENT 2

The delegates also discussed the powers of the presidency (the executive), which was at one point to be elected by Congress (the legislature). They debated whether to have one president or several, how long a term should be, and whether to limit the number of terms.

"**Mr. Strong** [Massachusetts]: supposed that there would be no necessity, if the Executive should be appointed by the Legislature, to make him ineligible a [second] time; as new elections of the Legislature will have intervened; and he will not depend for his [second] appointment on the same [set] of men as his first was [received] from . . .

Mr. Williamson [North Carolina]: was for going back to the original ground; to elect the Executive for 7 years and render him ineligible a second time . . . He did not like the Unity in the Executive. He had wished the Executive power to be lodged in three men taken from three districts into which the States should be divided. . . . Another objection [against] a single Magistrate [executive] is that he will be an elective King, and will feel the spirit of one. He will spare no pains to keep himself in for life, and then will lay a train for the succession of his children. It was pretty certain he thought that we should have a King; but he wished no precaution to be omitted that might postpone the event as long as possible. Ineligibility a second time appeared to him to be the best precaution. With this precaution he had no objection to a longer term than 7 years. He would go as far as 10 or 12 years . . . "

DOCUMENT 3

The Federalist was a collection of essays by James Madison, Alexander Hamilton, and John Jay supporting ratification of the new Constitution. In *Federalist* No. 69, Hamilton addressed fears that a strong president would be like a monarch.

"[The president] is to be elected for four years, and is to be re-eligible as often as the people of the United States shall think him worthy of their confidence. In these circumstances there is a total dissimilitude [lack of similarity] between him and a king of Great Britain, who is an hereditary monarch, possessing the crown as a patrimony descendible to his heirs forever; but there is a close analogy between him and a governor of New York, who is elected for three years, and is re-eligible without limitation or intermission . . .

The President . . . would be liable to be impeached, tried, and, upon conviction of treason, bribery, or other high crimes or misdemeanors, removed from office; and would afterwards be liable to prosecution and punishment in the ordinary course of law. The person of the king of Great Britain is sacred and inviolable; there is . . . no punishment to which he can be subjected without involving the crisis of a national revolution."

DOCUMENT 4

The table below summarizes the 10 amendments that make up the Bill of Rights.

THE BILL OF RIGHTS	
1st Amendment	Protects freedom of religion, speech, press, assembly, petition
2nd Amendment	Protects the right to bear arms
3rd Amendment	Provides restrictions on quartering soldiers in citizens' homes
4th Amendment	Bans unreasonable searches or seizures
5th Amendment	Protects citizens against self-incrimination and being tried twice for the same crime; prohibits government from depriving citizens of life, liberty, or property without due process of law
6th Amendment	Protects citizens' rights to a swift and fair trial
7th Amendment	Guarantees right to trial by jury
8th Amendment	Protects citizens against cruel and unusual punishment
9th Amendment	States that citizens have rights beyond those specifically written in the Constitution
10th Amendment	States that all powers not given to the government are reserved to the states, or to the people

Skills FOCUS READING LIKE A HISTORIAN

1. **a. Identify** Refer to Document 1. Which of these delegates objected most strongly to the slave trade?
   b. Evaluate How does this debate reflect different attitudes toward slavery in the North and the South?

2. **a. Identify** Refer to Document 2. Why does Williamson think the executive should be three people?
   b. Predict What problems might have developed if Williamson's plan had been adopted?

3. **a. Recall** Refer to Document 3. According to Hamilton, how is the United States president different from the king of Great Britain?
   b. Infer Why might this essay have convinced some people to support the Constitution?

4. **a. Identify** Refer to Document 4. Which amendment guarantees freedom of expression?
   b. Analyze Why do you think some states thought that a Bill of Rights was essential?

5. **Document-Based Essay Question** Consider the question below and form a thesis statement. Using examples from Documents 1, 2, 3, and 4, create an outline and write a short essay supporting your position.
   What roles did debate and compromise play in the development and ratification of the Constitution?

See **Skills Handbook**, pp. H14, H28–29

Visual Summary: Creating a New Government

The Articles of Confederation (ratified 1781)

- America's first written constitution
- A loose union of sovereign states
- Designed to make the central government weak because early leaders feared tyranny

The U.S. Constitution (ratified 1788)

- Replaced the Articles of Confederation
- Provided representation for all states
- Established three branches of government (executive, legislative, judicial) with separation of powers to avoid tyranny
- Created checks and balances among the three branches
- Bill of Rights later added (ratified 1791)

Reviewing Key Terms and People

Identify the correct term or person from the chapter that best fits each of the following descriptions.

1. The Father of the Constitution
2. Compromise at the Constitutional Convention that counted three-fifths of enslaved Africans when determining representation in Congress
3. Compromise at the Constitutional Convention that established a bicameral legislature
4. A political system without a monarch that rules with the consent of the governed
5. System that helps prevent one branch of government from becoming too strong
6. Branch of government that makes the laws
7. Branch of government that carries out the laws
8. Branch of government that interprets the laws
9. Supporters of the Constitution, also known as nationalists
10. Opponents of the Constitution
11. Name for the first 10 amendments to the Constitution
12. Name of the 1785 plan for surveying, selling, and settling the Northwest Territory
13. Series of newspaper articles in support of the proposed Constitution
14. Powers given to the branches of the national government under the Constitution

History's Impact video program

Review the video to answer the closing question: How does the Bill of Rights protect the personal freedoms of Americans?

Comprehension and Critical Thinking

SECTION 1 *(pp. 144–149)*

15. a. Identify What was a republican mother?

b. Explain What does it mean to *ratify* something?

c. Draw Inferences What fear led the new republic to limit the powers of its central government?

SECTION 2 *(pp. 150–156)*

16. a. Recall What was Shays's Rebellion?

b. Summarize What compromises were made at the Constitutional Convention?

c. Elaborate How do checks and balances prevent any one branch of government from becoming too powerful?

SECTION 3 *(pp. 157–163)*

17. a. Identify What were the Federalist Papers?

b. Summarize What did Federalists believe? What did Antifederalists believe?

c. Evaluate Why was the Bill of Rights necessary for ratification of the Constitution?

Using the Internet

go.hrw.com
Practice Online
Keyword: SD7 CH5

18. Using the keyword above, research a leader of the Constitutional Convention or a noted Federalist or Antifederalist. Then write a short biography of the person you chose. Be sure to explain why your person supported or did not support ratification of the Constitution.

Analyzing Primary Sources

Reading Like a Historian Judith Sargent Murray wrote the following about the differences in boys' education and girls' education.

> **❝**How is the one exalted, and the other depressed, by the contrary modes of education which are adopted! The one is taught to aspire, and the other is early confined and limited. As their years increase, the sister must be wholly domesticated, while the brother is led by the hand through all the flowery paths of science.**❞**
>
> —Judith Sargent Murray, quoted in *Founding Mothers*

19. Make Inferences What does the phrase "the flowery paths of science" suggest?

20. Draw Conclusions What is Judith Sargent Murray's opinion about differences in the education of boys and girls?

Critical Reading

Read the passage in Section 1 that begins with the heading "Economic problems." Then answer the questions that follow.

21. How did the end of the war with Great Britain affect the economy of the southern states?

A Southerners could now sell more indigo and naval stores to Great Britain.

B British financial aid to certain American industries ended, hurting those industries.

C Enslaved Africans who had sided with the British returned to plantation work.

D Southern plantations stopped producing indigo.

22. What led to inflation after the Revolutionary War?

A American paper money was not backed by gold or silver.

B Farmers had a lot of extra money to spend.

C The central government imposed high taxes.

D Currency in Great Britain lost value.

FOCUS ON WRITING

Expository Writing *Expository writing gives information, explains why or how, or defines a process. To practice expository writing, complete the assignment below.*

Writing Topic The U.S. Constitution

23. How was the U.S. Constitution an improvement upon the Articles of Confederation? Write a short essay in which you develop your position on this issue. Support your explanation with reasoning and examples from your reading and studies.

The Constitution of the UNITED STATES

THE BIG PICTURE The Constitution has remained the central document of American government for more than two centuries. It established three branches of government—legislative, executive, and judicial. The first 10 amendments, known as the Bill of Rights, focus on personal liberties.

New York Standards

Key Idea 3 Study about the major social, political, economic, cultural, and religious developments in New York State and United States history involves learning about the important roles and contributions of individuals and groups.

 READING LIKE A HISTORIAN

Tourists line up to view the Declaration of Independence and the Constitution of the United States in the rotunda of the National Archives Building in Washington, D.C. Above them hangs a mural depicting the Founders. **Interpreting Visuals** How does this photograph link the past with the present?

See **Skills Handbook**, p. H30

169

The Constitution of the United States

Preamble

The short and dignified preamble explains the goals of the new government under the Constitution.

We the People of the United States, in Order to form a more perfect Union, establish Justice, insure domestic Tranquility, provide for the common defense, promote the general Welfare, and secure the Blessings of Liberty to ourselves and our Posterity, do ordain and establish this Constitution for the United States of America.

Note: The parts of the Constitution that have been lined through are no longer in force or no longer apply because of later amendments. The titles of the sections and articles are added for easier reference.

Article I The Legislature

Section 1. Congress

All legislative Powers herein granted shall be vested in a Congress of the United States, which shall consist of a Senate and House of Representatives.

Section 2. The House of Representatives

1. Elections The House of Representatives shall be composed of Members chosen every second Year by the People of the several States, and the Electors in each State shall have the Qualifications requisite for Electors of the most numerous Branch of the State Legislature.

2. Qualifications No Person shall be a Representative who shall not have attained to the Age of twenty five Years, and been seven Years a Citizen of the United States, and who shall not, when elected, be an Inhabitant of that State in which he shall be chosen.

3. Number of Representatives Representatives and direct Taxes shall be apportioned among the several States which may be included within this Union, according to their respective Numbers, which shall be determined by adding to the whole Number of free Persons, including those bound to Service[1] for a Term of Years, and excluding Indians not taxed, three fifths of all other Persons.[2] The actual Enumeration[3] shall be made within three Years after the first Meeting of the Congress of the United States, and within every subsequent Term of ten Years, in such Manner as they shall by Law direct. The Number of Representatives shall not exceed one for every thirty Thousand, but each State shall have at Least one Representative; and until such enumeration shall be made, the State of New Hampshire shall be entitled to choose three, Massachusetts eight, Rhode-Island and Providence Plantations one, Connecticut five, New-York six, New Jersey four, Pennsylvania eight, Delaware one, Maryland six, Virginia ten, North Carolina five, South Carolina five, and Georgia three.

4. Vacancies When vacancies happen in the Representation from any State, the Executive Authority thereof shall issue Writs of Election to fill such Vacancies.

5. Officers and Impeachment The House of Representatives shall choose their Speaker and other Officers; and shall have the sole Power of impeachment.

Legislative Branch

Article I explains how the legislative branch, called Congress, is organized. The chief purpose of the legislative branch is to make laws. Congress is made up of the Senate and the House of Representatives.

The House of Representatives

The number of members each state has in the House is based on the population of the individual state. In 1929 Congress permanently fixed the size of the House at 435 members.

Vocabulary

[1] **those bound to Service** indentured servants

[2] **all other Persons** slaves

[3] **Enumeration** census or official population count

Section 3. The Senate

1. Number of Senators The Senate of the United States shall be composed of two Senators from each State, ~~chosen by the Legislature thereof,~~ for six Years; and each Senator shall have one Vote.

2. Classifying Terms Immediately after they shall be assembled in Consequence of the first Election, they shall be divided as equally as may be into three Classes. The Seats of the Senators of the first Class shall be vacated at the Expiration of the second Year, of the second Class at the Expiration of the fourth Year, and of the third Class at the Expiration of the sixth Year, so that one third may be chosen every second Year; ~~and if Vacancies happen by Resignation, or otherwise, during the Recess of the Legislature of any State, the Executive thereof may make temporary Appointments until the next Meeting of the Legislature, which shall then fill such Vacancies.~~

3. Qualifications No Person shall be a Senator who shall not have attained to the Age of thirty Years, and been nine Years a Citizen of the United States, and who shall not, when elected, be an Inhabitant of that State for which he shall be chosen.

4. Role of Vice-President The Vice President of the United States shall be President of the Senate, but shall have no Vote, unless they be equally divided.

5. Officers The Senate shall choose their other Officers, and also a President pro tempore,[4] in the Absence of the Vice President, or when he shall exercise the Office of President of the United States.

6. Impeachment Trials The Senate shall have the sole Power to try all Impeachments.[5] When sitting for that Purpose, they shall be on Oath or Affirmation. When the President of the United States is tried, the Chief Justice shall preside: And no Person shall be convicted without the Concurrence of two thirds of the Members present.

7. Punishment for Impeachment Judgment in Cases of Impeachment shall not extend further than to removal from Office, and disqualification to hold and enjoy any Office of honor, Trust or Profit under the United States: but the Party convicted shall nevertheless be liable and subject to Indictment, Trial, Judgment and Punishment, according to Law.

The Vice President

The only duty that the Constitution assigns to the vice president is to preside over meetings of the Senate. Modern presidents have usually given their vice presidents more responsibilities.

EXPLORING THE DOCUMENT If the House of Representatives charges a government official with wrongdoing, the Senate acts as a court to decide if the official is guilty. *How does the power of impeachment represent part of the system of checks and balances?*

Vocabulary

[4] **pro tempore** temporarily

[5] **Impeachments** official accusations of federal wrongdoing

---

FEDERAL OFFICE TERMS AND REQUIREMENTS

QUICK FACTS

Position	Term	Minimum Age	Residency	Citizenship
President	4 years	35	14 years in the United States	natural-born
Vice President	4 years	35	14 years in the United States	natural-born
Supreme Court Justice	unlimited	none	none	none
Senator	6 years	30	state in which elected	9 years
Representative	2 years	25	state in which elected	7 years

Section 4. Congressional Elections

1. Regulations The Times, Places and Manner of holding Elections for Senators and Representatives, shall be prescribed in each State by the Legislature thereof; but the Congress may at any time by Law make or alter such Regulations, except as to the Places of choosing Senators.

2. Sessions ~~The Congress shall assemble at least once in every Year, and such Meeting shall be on the first Monday in December, unless they shall by Law appoint a different Day.~~

Section 5. Rules/Procedures

1. Quorum Each House shall be the Judge of the Elections, Returns and Qualifications of its own Members, and a Majority of each shall constitute a Quorum[6] to do Business; but a smaller Number may adjourn[7] from day to day, and may be authorized to compel the Attendance of absent Members, in such Manner, and under such Penalties as each House may provide.

2. Rules and Conduct Each House may determine the Rules of its Proceedings, punish its Members for disorderly Behaviour, and, with the Concurrence of two thirds, expel a Member.

3. Records Each House shall keep a Journal of its Proceedings, and from time to time publish the same, excepting such Parts as may in their Judgment require Secrecy; and the Yeas and Nays of the Members of either House on any question shall, at the Desire of one fifth of those Present, be entered on the Journal.

4. Adjournment Neither House, during the Session of Congress, shall, without the Consent of the other, adjourn for more than three days, nor to any other Place than that in which the two Houses shall be sitting.

Section 6. Payment

1. Salary The Senators and Representatives shall receive a Compensation for their Services, to be ascertained by Law, and paid out of the Treasury of the United States. They shall in all Cases, except Treason, Felony and Breach of the Peace, be privileged from Arrest during their Attendance at the Session of their respective Houses, and in going to and returning from the same; and for any Speech or Debate in either House, they shall not be questioned in any other Place.

2. Restrictions No Senator or Representative shall, during the Time for which he was elected, be appointed to any civil Office under the Authority of the United States, which shall have been created, or the Emoluments[8] whereof shall have been increased during such time; and no Person holding any Office under the United States, shall be a Member of either House during his Continuance[9] in Office.

Vocabulary

[6] **Quorum** the minimum number of people needed to conduct business

[7] **adjourn** to stop indefinitely

[8] **Emoluments** salary

[9] **Continuance** term

Vocabulary

[10] **Bills** proposed laws

EXPLORING THE DOCUMENT The Framers felt that because members of the House are elected every two years, representatives would listen to the public and seek its approval before passing taxes. *How does Section 7 address the colonial demand of "no taxation without representation"?*

EXPLORING THE DOCUMENT The veto power of the president is one of the important checks and balances in the Constitution. *Why do you think the Framers included the ability of Congress to override a veto?*

Section 7. [How a Bill Becomes a Law]

1. Tax Bills All **Bills**[10] for raising Revenue shall originate in the House of Representatives; but the Senate may propose or concur with Amendments as on other Bills.

2. Lawmaking Every Bill which shall have passed the House of Representatives and the Senate, shall, before it become a Law, be presented to the President of the United States: If he approve he shall sign it, but if not he shall return it, with his Objections to that House in which it shall have originated, who shall enter the Objections at large on their Journal, and proceed to reconsider it. If after such Reconsideration two thirds of that House shall agree to pass the Bill, it shall be sent, together with the Objections, to the other House, by which it shall likewise be reconsidered, and if approved by two thirds of that House, it shall become a Law. But in all such Cases the Votes of both Houses shall be determined by yeas and Nays, and the Names of the Persons voting for and against the Bill shall be entered on the Journal of each House respectively. If any Bill shall not be returned by the President within ten Days (Sundays excepted) after it shall have been presented to him, the Same shall be a Law, in like Manner as if he had signed it, unless the Congress by their Adjournment prevent its Return, in which Case it shall not be a Law.

3. Role of the President Every Order, Resolution, or Vote to which the Concurrence of the Senate and House of Representatives may be necessary (except on a question of Adjournment) shall be presented to the President of the United States; and before the Same shall take Effect, shall be approved by him, or being disapproved by him, shall be repassed by two thirds of the Senate and House of Representatives, according to the Rules and Limitations prescribed in the Case of a Bill.

HOW A BILL BECOMES A LAW

1 A member of the House or the Senate introduces a bill and refers it to a committee.

2 The House or Senate Committee may approve, rewrite, or kill the bill.

3 The House or the Senate debates and votes on its version of the bill.

4 House and Senate conference committee members work out the differences between the two versions.

5 Both houses of Congress pass the revised bill.

Section 8.
Powers Granted to Congress

1. Taxation The Congress shall have Power To lay and collect Taxes, **Duties**,[11] **Imposts**[12] and **Excises**,[13] to pay the Debts and provide for the common Defense and general Welfare of the United States; but all Duties, Imposts and Excises shall be uniform throughout the United States;

2. Credit To borrow Money on the credit of the United States;

3. Commerce To regulate Commerce with foreign Nations, and among the several States, and with the Indian Tribes;

4. Naturalization and Bankruptcy

To establish an uniform **Rule of Naturalization**,[14] and uniform Laws on the subject of Bankruptcies throughout the United States;

5. Money To coin Money, regulate the Value thereof, and of foreign Coin, and fix the Standard of Weights and Measures;

6. Counterfeiting To provide for the Punishment of counterfeiting the **Securities**[15] and current Coin of the United States;

7. Post Office To establish Post Offices and post Roads;

8. Patents and Copyrights To promote the Progress of Science and useful Arts, by securing for limited Times to Authors and Inventors the exclusive Right to their respective Writings and Discoveries;

9. Courts To constitute Tribunals inferior to the supreme Court;

10. International Law To define and punish Piracies and Felonies committed on the high Seas, and Offences against the Law of Nations;

Linking TO Today

Native Americans and the Commerce Clause

The commerce clause gives Congress the power to "regulate Commerce with . . . the Indian Tribes." The clause has been interpreted to mean that the states cannot tax or interfere with businesses on Indian reservations, but that the federal government can. It also allows Native American nations to develop their own governments and laws. These laws, however, can be challenged in federal court. Although reservation land usually belongs to the government of the Indian group, it is administered by the U.S. government.

Drawing Conclusions How would you describe the status of Native American nations under the commerce clause?

Vocabulary

[11] **Duties** tariffs

[12] **Imposts** taxes

[13] **Excises** internal taxes on the manufacture, sale, or consumption of a commodity

[14] **Rule of Naturalization** a law by which a foreign-born person becomes a citizen

[15] **Securities** bonds

6 The president signs or vetoes the bill.

7 Two-thirds majority vote of Congress is needed to approve a vetoed bill. Bill becomes a law.

ANALYSIS SKILL **ANALYZING INFORMATION**

Why do you think the Framers created this complex system for adopting laws?

Vocabulary

[16] Letters of Marque and Reprisal documents issued by governments allowing merchant ships to arm themselves and attack ships of an enemy nation

11. War To declare War, grant **Letters of Marque and Reprisal**,[16] and make Rules concerning Captures on Land and Water;

12. Army To raise and support Armies, but no Appropriation of Money to that Use shall be for a longer Term than two Years;

13. Navy To provide and maintain a Navy;

14. Regulation of the Military To make Rules for the Government and Regulation of the land and naval Forces;

15. Militia To provide for calling forth the Militia to execute the Laws of the Union, suppress Insurrections and repel Invasions;

16. Regulation of the Militia To provide for organizing, arming, and disciplining, the Militia, and for governing such Part of them as may be employed in the Service of the United States, reserving to the States respectively, the Appointment of the Officers, and the Authority of training the Militia according to the discipline prescribed by Congress;

17. District of Columbia To exercise exclusive Legislation in all Cases whatsoever, over such District (not exceeding ten Miles square) as may, by Cession of particular States, and the Acceptance of Congress, become the Seat of the Government of the United States, and to exercise like Authority over all Places purchased by the Consent of the Legislature of the State in which the Same shall be, for the Erection of Forts, Magazines, Arsenals, dock-Yards, and other needful Buildings;—And

18. Necessary and Proper Clause To make all Laws which shall be necessary and proper for carrying into Execution the foregoing Powers, and all other Powers vested by this Constitution in the Government of the United States, or in any Department or Officer thereof.

The Elastic Clause

The Framers of the Constitution wanted a national government that was strong enough to be effective. This section lists the powers given to Congress. The last portion of Section 8 contains the so-called elastic clause.

THE ELASTIC CLAUSE

The elastic clause has been stretched (like elastic) to allow Congress to meet changing circumstances.

Section 9. Powers Denied Congress

1. Slave Trade ~~The Migration or Importation of such Persons as any of the States now existing shall think proper to admit, shall not be prohibited by the Congress prior to the Year one thousand eight hundred and eight, but a Tax or duty may be imposed on such Importation, not exceeding ten dollars for each Person.~~

2. Habeas Corpus The Privilege of the **Writ of Habeas Corpus**[17] shall not be suspended, unless when in Cases of Rebellion or Invasion the public Safety may require it.

3. Illegal Punishment No **Bill of Attainder**[18] or **ex post facto Law**[19] shall be passed.

4. Direct Taxes No **Capitation**,[20] or other direct, Tax shall be laid, unless in Proportion to the Census or enumeration herein before directed to be taken.

5. Export Taxes No Tax or Duty shall be laid on Articles exported from any State.

6. No Favorites No Preference shall be given by any Regulation of Commerce or Revenue to the Ports of one State over those of another; nor shall Vessels bound to, or from, one State, be obliged to enter, clear, or pay Duties in another.

7. Public Money No Money shall be drawn from the Treasury, but in Consequence of Appropriations made by Law; and a regular Statement and Account of the Receipts and Expenditures of all public Money shall be published from time to time.

8. Titles of Nobility No Title of Nobility shall be granted by the United States: And no Person holding any Office of Profit or Trust under them, shall, without the Consent of the Congress, accept of any present, Emolument, Office, or Title, of any kind whatever, from any King, Prince, or foreign State.

Section 10. Powers Denied the States

1. Restrictions No State shall enter into any Treaty, Alliance, or Confederation; grant Letters of Marque and Reprisal; coin Money; emit Bills of Credit; make any Thing but gold and silver Coin a Tender in Payment of Debts; pass any Bill of Attainder, ex post facto Law, or Law impairing the Obligation of Contracts, or grant any Title of Nobility.

2. Import and Export Taxes No State shall, without the Consent of the Congress, lay any Imposts or Duties on Imports or Exports, except what may be absolutely necessary for executing it's inspection Laws: and the net Produce of all Duties and Imposts, laid by any State on Imports or Exports, shall be for the Use of the Treasury of the United States; and all such Laws shall be subject to the Revision and Control of the Congress.

3. Peacetime and War Restraints No State shall, without the Consent of Congress, lay any Duty of Tonnage, keep Troops, or Ships of War in time of Peace, enter into any Agreement or Compact with another State, or with a foreign Power, or engage in War, unless actually invaded, or in such imminent Danger as will not admit of delay.

EXPLORING THE DOCUMENT Although Congress has implied powers, there are also limits to its powers. Section 9 lists powers that are denied to the federal government. Several of the clauses protect the people of the United States from unjust treatment. *In what ways does the Constitution limit the powers of the federal government?*

Vocabulary

[17] **Writ of Habeas Corpus** a court order that requires the government to bring a prisoner to court and explain why he or she is being held

[18] **Bill of Attainder** a law declaring that a person is guilty of a particular crime

[19] **ex post facto Law** a law that is made effective prior to the date that it was passed and therefore punishes people for acts that were not illegal at the time

[20] **Capitation** a direct uniform tax imposed on each head, or person

Article II The Executive

Section 1. The Presidency

1. Terms of Office The executive Power shall be vested in a President of the United States of America. He shall hold his Office during the Term of four Years, and, together with the Vice President, chosen for the same Term, be elected, as follows:

2. Electoral College Each State shall appoint, in such Manner as the Legislature thereof may direct, a Number of Electors, equal to the whole Number of Senators and Representatives to which the State may be entitled in the Congress: but no Senator or Representative, or Person holding an Office of Trust or Profit under the United States, shall be appointed an Elector.

3. Former Method of Electing President ~~The Electors shall meet in their respective States, and vote by Ballot for two Persons, of whom one at least shall not be an Inhabitant of the same State with themselves. And they shall make a List of all the Persons voted for, and of the Number of Votes for each; which List they shall sign and certify, and transmit sealed to the Seat of the Government of the United States, directed to the President of the Senate. The President of the Senate shall, in the Presence of the Senate and House of Representatives, open all the Certificates, and the Votes shall then be counted.~~

THE ELECTORAL COLLEGE

11 Number of Electors

WA 11
OR 7
ID 4
MT 3
WY 3
ND 3
SD 3
MN 10
WI 10
MI 17
NH 4
VT 3
ME 4
NY 31
MA 12
RI 4
CT 7
NJ 15
DE 3
MD 10
NV 5
UT 5
CO 9
NE 5
IA 7
IL 21
IN 11
OH 20
PA 21
WV 5
VA 13
CA 55
KS 6
MO 11
KY 8
NC 15
TN 11
SC 8
Washington, D.C. 3
AZ 10
NM 5
OK 7
AR 6
MS 6
AL 9
GA 15
TX 34
LA 9
FL 27
AK 3
HI 4

GEOGRAPHY SKILLS INTERPRETING MAPS

Place Which two states have the most electors?

The Person having the greatest Number of Votes shall be the President, if such Number be a Majority of the whole Number of Electors appointed; and if there be more than one who have such Majority, and have an equal Number of Votes, then the House of Representatives shall immediately choose by Ballot one of them for President; and if no Person have a Majority, then from the five highest on the List the said House shall in like Manner choose the President. But in choosing the President, the Votes shall be taken by States, the Representation from each State having one Vote; A quorum for this purpose shall consist of a Member or Members from two thirds of the States, and a Majority of all the States shall be necessary to a Choice. In every Case, after the Choice of the President, the Person having the greatest Number of Votes of the Electors shall be the Vice President. But if there should remain two or more who have equal Votes, the Senate shall choose from them by Ballot the Vice President.

4. Election Day The Congress may determine the Time of choosing the Electors, and the Day on which they shall give their Votes; which Day shall be the same throughout the United States.

5. Qualifications No Person except a natural born Citizen, or a Citizen of the United States, at the time of the Adoption of this Constitution, shall be eligible to the Office of President; neither shall any Person be eligible to that Office who shall not have attained to the Age of thirty five Years, and been fourteen Years a Resident within the United States.

6. Succession In Case of the Removal of the President from Office, or of his Death, Resignation, or Inability to discharge the Powers and Duties of the said Office, the Same shall devolve on the Vice President, and the Congress may by Law provide for the Case of Removal, Death, Resignation or Inability, both of the President and Vice President, declaring what Officer shall then act as President, and such Officer shall act accordingly, until the Disability be removed, or a President shall be elected.

7. Salary The President shall, at stated Times, receive for his Services, a Compensation, which shall neither be increased nor diminished during the Period for which he shall have been elected, and he shall not receive within that Period any other Emolument from the United States, or any of them.

8. Oath of Office Before he enter on the Execution of his Office, he shall take the following Oath or Affirmation:—"I do solemnly swear (or affirm) that I will faithfully execute the Office of President of the United States, and will to the best of my Ability, preserve, protect and defend the Constitution of the United States."

 **EXPLORING THE DOCUMENT** The youngest elected president was John F. Kennedy; he was 43 years old when he was inaugurated. (Theodore Roosevelt was 42 when he assumed office after the assassination of McKinley.) *What is the minimum required age for the office of president?*

Presidential Salary

In 1999 Congress voted to set future presidents' salaries at $400,000 per year. The president also receives an annual expense account. The president must pay taxes only on the salary.

Section 2. Powers of Presidency

1. Military Powers The President shall be Commander in Chief of the Army and Navy of the United States, and of the Militia of the several States, when called into the actual Service of the United States; he may require the Opinion, in writing, of the principal Officer in each of the executive Departments, upon any Subject relating to the Duties of their respective Offices, and he shall have Power to grant **Reprieves**[21] and **Pardons**[22] for Offences against the United States, except in Cases of Impeachment.

2. Treaties and Appointments He shall have Power, by and with the Advice and Consent of the Senate, to make Treaties, provided two thirds of the Senators present concur; and he shall nominate, and by and with the Advice and Consent of the Senate, shall appoint Ambassadors, other public Ministers and Consuls, Judges of the supreme Court, and all other Officers of the United States, whose Appointments are not herein otherwise provided for, and which shall be established by Law: but the Congress may by Law vest the Appointment of such inferior Officers, as they think proper, in the President alone, in the Courts of Law, or in the Heads of Departments.

3. Vacancies The President shall have Power to fill up all Vacancies that may happen during the Recess of the Senate, by granting Commissions which shall expire at the End of their next Session.

Section 3. Presidential Duties

He shall from time to time give to the Congress Information of the State of the Union, and recommend to their Consideration such Measures as he shall judge necessary and expedient; he may, on extraordinary Occasions, convene both Houses, or either of them, and in Case of Disagreement between them, with Respect to the Time of Adjournment, he may adjourn them to such Time as he shall think proper; he shall receive Ambassadors and other public Ministers; he shall take Care that the Laws be faithfully executed, and shall Commission all the Officers of the United States.

Section 4. Impeachment

The President, Vice President and all civil Officers of the United States, shall be removed from Office on Impeachment for, and Conviction of, Treason, Bribery, or other high Crimes and Misdemeanors.

Article III   The Judiciary

Section 1.   Federal Courts and Judges

The judicial Power of the United States shall be vested in one supreme Court, and in such inferior Courts as the Congress may from time to time ordain and establish. The Judges, both of the supreme and inferior Courts, shall hold their Offices during good Behavior, and shall, at stated Times, receive for their Services a Compensation, which shall not be diminished during their Continuance in Office.

Section 2.   Authority of the Courts

1. General Authority   The judicial Power shall extend to all Cases, in Law and Equity, arising under this Constitution, the Laws of the United States, and Treaties made, or which shall be made, under their Authority;—to all Cases affecting Ambassadors, other public Ministers and Consuls;—to all Cases of admiralty and maritime Jurisdiction;—to Controversies to which the United States shall be a Party;—to Controversies between two or more States —between a State and Citizens of another State; —between Citizens of different States;—between Citizens of the same State claiming Lands under Grants of different States, and between a State, or the Citizens thereof, and foreign States, Citizens or Subjects.

2. Supreme Authority   In all Cases affecting Ambassadors, other public Ministers and Consuls, and those in which a State shall be Party, the supreme Court shall have original Jurisdiction. In all the other Cases before mentioned, the supreme Court shall have appellate Jurisdiction, both as to Law and Fact, with such Exceptions, and under such Regulations as the Congress shall make.

FEDERAL JUDICIAL SYSTEM QUICK FACTS

Supreme Court

Reviews cases appealed from lower federal courts and highest state courts

Courts of Appeals

Review appeals from district courts

District Courts

Hold trials

Judicial Branch

The Articles of Confederation did not set up a federal court system. One of the first points that the Framers of the Constitution agreed upon was to set up a national judiciary. In the Judiciary Act of 1789, Congress provided for the establishment of lower courts, such as district courts, circuit courts of appeals, and various other federal courts. The judicial system provides a check on the legislative branch: It can declare a law unconstitutional.

3. Trial by Jury The Trial of all Crimes, except in Cases of Impeachment, shall be by Jury; and such Trial shall be held in the State where the said Crimes shall have been committed; but when not committed within any State, the Trial shall be at such Place or Places as the Congress may by Law have directed.

Section 3. Treason

1. Definition Treason against the United States, shall consist only in levying War against them, or in adhering to their Enemies, giving them Aid and Comfort. No Person shall be convicted of Treason unless on the Testimony of two Witnesses to the same overt Act, or on Confession in open Court.

2. Punishment The Congress shall have Power to declare the Punishment of Treason, but no Attainder of Treason shall work **Corruption of Blood**,[23] or Forfeiture except during the Life of the Person attainted.

Article IV Relations among States

Section 1. State Acts and Records

Full Faith and Credit shall be given in each State to the public Acts, Records, and judicial Proceedings of every other State. And the Congress may by general Laws prescribe the Manner in which such Acts, Records and Proceedings shall be proved, and the Effect thereof.

Section 2. Rights of Citizens

1. Citizenship The Citizens of each State shall be entitled to all Privileges and Immunities of Citizens in the several States.

2. Extradition A Person charged in any State with Treason, Felony, or other Crime, who shall flee from Justice, and be found in another State, shall on Demand of the executive Authority of the State from which he fled, be delivered up, to be removed to the State having Jurisdiction of the Crime.

3. Fugitive Slaves No Person held to Service or Labour in one State, under the Laws thereof, escaping into another, shall, in Consequence of any Law or Regulation therein, be discharged from such Service or Labour, but shall be delivered up on Claim of the Party to whom such Service or Labour may be due.

The States

States must honor the laws, records, and court decisions of other states. A person cannot escape a legal obligation by moving from one state to another.

EXPLORING THE DOCUMENT The Framers wanted to ensure that citizens could determine how state governments would operate. *How does the need to respect the laws of each state support the principle of popular sovereignty?*

FEDERALISM

National
- Declare war
- Maintain armed forces
- Regulate interstate and foreign trade
- Admit new states
- Establish post offices
- Set standard weights and measures
- Coin money
- Establish foreign policy
- Make all laws necessary and proper for carrying out delegated powers

Shared
- Maintain law and order
- Levy taxes
- Borrow money
- Charter banks
- Establish courts
- Provide for public welfare

State
- Establish and maintain schools
- Establish local governments
- Regulate business within the state
- Make marriage laws
- Provide for public safety
- Assume other powers not delegated to the national government or prohibited to the states

ANALYSIS SKILL | **ANALYZING INFORMATION**

Why does the power to declare war belong only to the national government?

Section 3. New States

1. Admission New States may be admitted by the Congress into this Union; but no new State shall be formed or erected within the Jurisdiction of any other State; nor any State be formed by the Junction of two or more States, or Parts of States, without the Consent of the Legislatures of the States concerned as well as of the Congress.

2. Congressional Authority The Congress shall have Power to dispose of and make all needful Rules and Regulations respecting the Territory or other Property belonging to the United States; and nothing in this Constitution shall be so construed as to Prejudice any Claims of the United States, or of any particular State.

Section 4. Guarantees to the States

The United States shall guarantee to every State in this Union a Republican Form of Government, and shall protect each of them against Invasion; and on Application of the Legislature, or of the Executive (when the Legislature cannot be convened), against domestic Violence.

EXPLORING THE DOCUMENT In a republic, voters elect representatives to act in their best interest. *How does Article IV protect the practice of republicanism in the United States?*

National Supremacy

One of the biggest problems facing the delegates to the Constitutional Convention was the question of what would happen if a state law and a federal law conflicted. Which law would be followed? Who would decide? The second clause of Article VI answers those questions. When a federal law and a state law disagree, the federal law overrides the state law. The Constitution and other federal laws are the "supreme Law of the Land." This clause is often called the supremacy clause.

Article V — Amending the Constitution

The Congress, whenever two thirds of both Houses shall deem it necessary, shall propose Amendments to this Constitution, or, on the Application of the Legislatures of two thirds of the several States, shall call a Convention for proposing Amendments, which, in either Case, shall be valid to all Intents and Purposes, as Part of this Constitution, when ratified by the Legislatures of three fourths of the several States, or by Conventions in three fourths thereof, as the one or the other Mode of Ratification may be proposed by the Congress; Provided that no Amendment which may be made prior to the Year One thousand eight hundred and eight shall in any Manner affect the first and fourth Clauses in the Ninth Section of the first Article; and that no State, without its Consent, shall be deprived of its equal Suffrage in the Senate.

Article VI — Supremacy of National Government

All Debts contracted and Engagements entered into, before the Adoption of this Constitution, shall be as valid against the United States under this Constitution, as under the Confederation.

This Constitution, and the Laws of the United States which shall be made in Pursuance thereof; and all Treaties made, or which shall be made, under the Authority of the United States, shall be the supreme Law of the Land; and the Judges in every State shall be bound thereby, any Thing in the Constitution or Laws of any State to the Contrary notwithstanding.

The Senators and Representatives before mentioned, and the Members of the several State Legislatures, and all executive and judicial Officers, both of the United States and of the several States, shall be bound by Oath or Affirmation, to support this Constitution; but no religious Test shall ever be required as a Qualification to any Office or public Trust under the United States.

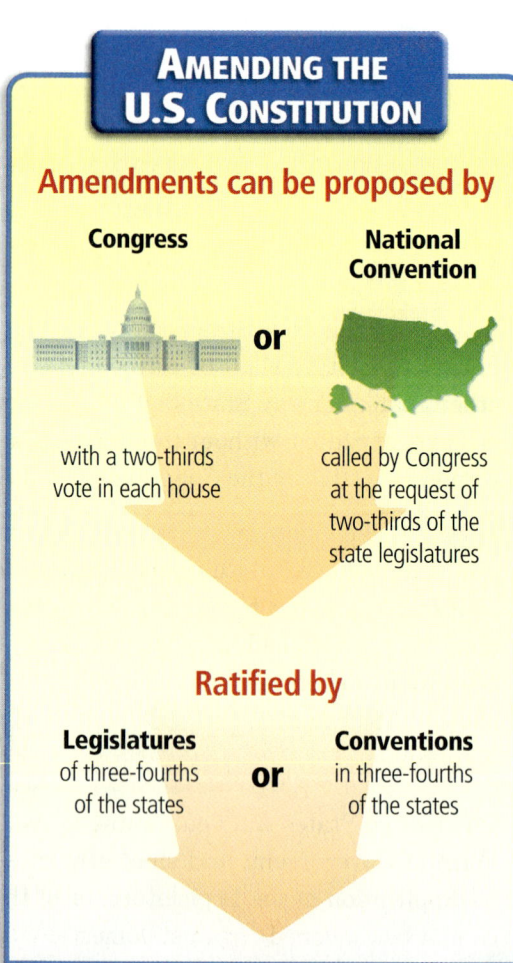

AMENDING THE U.S. CONSTITUTION

Amendments can be proposed by

Congress or **National Convention**

with a two-thirds vote in each house

called by Congress at the request of two-thirds of the state legislatures

Ratified by

Legislatures of three-fourths of the states or **Conventions** in three-fourths of the states

Amendment is added to the Constitution.

Article VII | Ratification

The Ratification of the Conventions of nine States, shall be sufficient for the Establishment of this Constitution between the States so ratifying the Same.

Done in Convention by the Unanimous Consent of the States present the Seventeenth Day of September in the Year of our Lord one thousand seven hundred and Eighty seven and of the Independence of the United States of America the Twelfth In witness whereof We have hereunto subscribed our Names,

George Washington—
President and deputy from Virginia

Delaware

George Read
Gunning Bedford Jr.
John Dickinson
Richard Bassett
Jacob Broom

Maryland

James McHenry
Daniel of St. Thomas
  Jenifer
Daniel Carroll

Virginia

John Blair
James Madison Jr.

North Carolina

William Blount
Richard Dobbs Spaight
Hugh Williamson

South Carolina

John Rutledge
Charles Cotesworth
  Pinckney
Charles Pinckney
Pierce Butler

Georgia

William Few
Abraham Baldwin

New Hampshire

John Langdon
Nicholas Gilman

Massachusetts

Nathaniel Gorham
Rufus King

Connecticut

William Samuel
  Johnson
Roger Sherman

New York

Alexander Hamilton

New Jersey

William Livingston
David Brearley
William Paterson
Jonathan Dayton

Pennsylvania

Benjamin Franklin
Thomas Mifflin
Robert Morris
George Clymer
Thomas FitzSimons
Jared Ingersoll
James Wilson
Gouverneur Morris

Attest:
William Jackson,
  Secretary

Ratification

The Articles of Confederation called for all 13 states to approve any revision to the Articles. The Constitution required that 9 out of the 13 states would be needed to ratify the Constitution. The first state to ratify was Delaware, on December 7, 1787. Almost two-and-a-half years later, on May 29, 1790, Rhode Island became the last state to ratify the Constitution.

Constitutional Amendments

Note: The first 10 amendments to the Constitution were ratified on December 15, 1791, and form what is known as the Bill of Rights.

Bill of Rights

One of the conditions set by several states for ratifying the Constitution was the inclusion of a bill of rights. Many people feared that a stronger central government might take away basic rights of the people that had been guaranteed in state constitutions.

EXPLORING THE DOCUMENT The First Amendment forbids Congress from making any "law respecting an establishment of religion" or restraining the freedom to practice religion as one chooses. *Why is freedom of religion an important right?*

Rights of the Accused

The Fifth, Sixth, and Seventh Amendments describe the procedures that courts must follow when trying people accused of crimes.

Vocabulary

[24] **quartered** housed

[25] **Warrants** written orders authorizing a person to make an arrest, a seizure, or a search

[26] **infamous** disgraceful

[27] **indictment** the act of charging with a crime

Amendments 1–10. The Bill of Rights

Amendment I

Congress shall make no law respecting an establishment of religion, or prohibiting the free exercise thereof; or abridging the freedom of speech, or of the press; or the right of the people peaceably to assemble, and to petition the Government for a redress of grievances.

Amendment II

A well regulated Militia, being necessary to the security of a free State, the right of the people to keep and bear Arms, shall not be infringed.

Amendment III

No Soldier shall, in time of peace be **quartered**[24] in any house, without the consent of the Owner, nor in time of war, but in a manner to be prescribed by law.

Amendment IV

The right of the people to be secure in their persons, houses, papers, and effects, against unreasonable searches and seizures, shall not be violated, and no **Warrants**[25] shall issue, but upon probable cause, supported by Oath or affirmation, and particularly describing the place to be searched, and the persons or things to be seized.

Amendment V

No person shall be held to answer for a capital, or otherwise **infamous**[26] crime, unless on a presentment or **indictment**[27] of a Grand Jury, except in cases

FUNDAMENTAL LIBERTIES

Freedom of Religion

Freedom of Speech

arising in the land or naval forces, or in the Militia, when in actual service in time of War or public danger; nor shall any person be subject for the same offence to be twice put in jeopardy of life or limb; nor shall be compelled in any criminal case to be a witness against himself, nor be deprived of life, liberty, or property, without due process of law; nor shall private property be taken for public use, without just compensation.

Amendment VI

In all criminal prosecutions, the accused shall enjoy the right to a speedy and public trial, by an impartial jury of the State and district wherein the crime shall have been committed, which district shall have been previously ascertained[28] by law, and to be informed of the nature and cause of the accusation; to be confronted with the witnesses against him; to have compulsory process for obtaining witnesses in his favor, and to have the Assistance of Counsel for his defence.

Amendment VII

In suits at common law, where the value in controversy shall exceed twenty dollars, the right of trial by jury shall be preserved, and no fact tried by a jury, shall be otherwise reexamined in any Court of the United States, than according to the rules of the common law.

Amendment VIII

Excessive bail shall not be required, nor excessive fines imposed, nor cruel and unusual punishments inflicted.

Amendment IX

The enumeration in the Constitution, of certain rights, shall not be construed to deny or disparage others retained by the people.

Amendment X

The powers not delegated to the United States by the Constitution, nor prohibited by it to the States, are reserved to the States respectively, or to the people.

Trials

The Sixth Amendment makes several guarantees, including a prompt trial and a trial by a jury chosen from the state and district in which the crime was committed.

Vocabulary

[28] **ascertained** found out

EXPLORING THE DOCUMENT The Ninth and Tenth Amendments were added because not every right of the people or of the states could be listed in the Constitution. *How do the Ninth and Tenth Amendments limit the power of the federal government?*

Freedom of the Press

Freedom of Assembly

Freedom to Petition the Government

ANALYSIS SKILL **ANALYZING INFORMATION**

Which amendments guarantee these fundamental freedoms?

AMENDMENTS TO THE U.S. CONSTITUTION

The Constitution has been amended only 27 times since it was ratified more than 200 years ago. Amendments help the structure of the government change along with the values of the nation's people. Read the time line below to learn how each amendment changed the government.

1870
Amendment 15
Prohibits national and state governments from denying the vote based on race

1791
Bill of Rights
Amendments 1–10

1865
Amendment 13
Bans slavery

1790 | **1820** | **1870**

1795
Amendment 11
Protects the states from lawsuits filed by citizens of other states or countries

1804
Amendment 12
Requires separate ballots for the offices of president and vice president

1868
Amendment 14
Defines citizenship and citizens' rights

Amendments 11–27

Amendment XI

Passed by Congress March 4, 1794. Ratified February 7, 1795.

The Judicial power of the United States shall not be **construed**[29] to extend to any suit in law or equity, commenced or prosecuted against one of the United States by Citizens of another State, or by Citizens or Subjects of any Foreign State.

Amendment XII

Passed by Congress December 9, 1803. Ratified June 15, 1804.

The Electors shall meet in their respective states and vote by ballot for President and Vice-President, one of whom, at least, shall not be an inhabitant of the same state with themselves; they shall name in their ballots the person voted for as President, and in distinct ballots the person voted for as Vice-President, and they shall make distinct lists of all persons voted for as President, and of all persons voted for as Vice-President, and of the number of votes for each, which lists they shall sign and certify, and transmit sealed to the seat of the government of the United States, directed to the President of the Senate;—the President of the Senate shall, in the presence of the

President and Vice President

The Twelfth Amendment changed the election procedure for president and vice president.

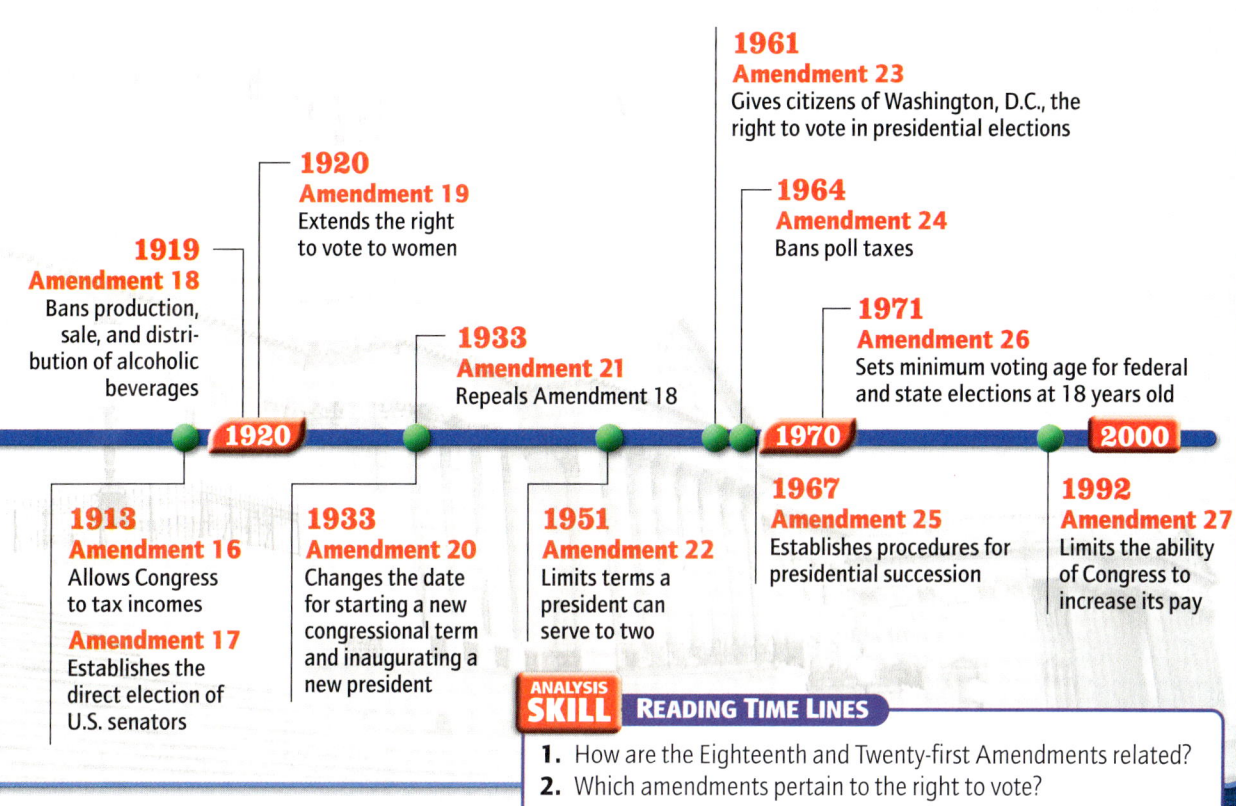

1919
Amendment 18
Bans production, sale, and distribution of alcoholic beverages

1920
Amendment 19
Extends the right to vote to women

1961
Amendment 23
Gives citizens of Washington, D.C., the right to vote in presidential elections

1964
Amendment 24
Bans poll taxes

1933
Amendment 21
Repeals Amendment 18

1971
Amendment 26
Sets minimum voting age for federal and state elections at 18 years old

1920

1970

2000

1913
Amendment 16
Allows Congress to tax incomes

Amendment 17
Establishes the direct election of U.S. senators

1933
Amendment 20
Changes the date for starting a new congressional term and inaugurating a new president

1951
Amendment 22
Limits terms a president can serve to two

1967
Amendment 25
Establishes procedures for presidential succession

1992
Amendment 27
Limits the ability of Congress to increase its pay

ANALYSIS SKILL **READING TIME LINES**

1. How are the Eighteenth and Twenty-first Amendments related?
2. Which amendments pertain to the right to vote?

Senate and House of Representatives, open all the certificates and the votes shall then be counted;—The person having the greatest number of votes for President, shall be the President, if such number be a majority of the whole number of Electors appointed; and if no person have such majority, then from the persons having the highest numbers not exceeding three on the list of those voted for as President, the House of Representatives shall choose immediately, by ballot, the President. But in choosing the President, the votes shall be taken by states, the representation from each state having one vote; a quorum for this purpose shall consist of a member or members from two-thirds of the states, and a majority of all the states shall be necessary to a choice. And if the House of Representatives shall not choose a President whenever the right of choice shall devolve upon them, before the fourth day of March next following, then the Vice-President shall act as President, as in case of the death or other constitutional disability of the President.—The person having the greatest number of votes as Vice-President, shall be the Vice-President, if such number be a majority of the whole number of Electors appointed, and if no person have a majority, then from the two highest numbers on the list, the Senate shall choose the Vice-President; a quorum for the purpose shall consist of two-thirds of the whole number of Senators, and a majority of the whole number shall be necessary to a choice. But no person constitutionally ineligible to the office of President shall be eligible to that of Vice-President of the United States.

Amendment XIII

Passed by Congress January 31, 1865. Ratified December 6, 1865.

1. Slavery Banned Neither slavery nor **involuntary servitude,**[30] except as a punishment for crime whereof the party shall have been duly convicted, shall exist within the United States, or any place subject to their jurisdiction.

2. Enforcement Congress shall have power to enforce this article by appropriate legislation.

Amendment XIV

Passed by Congress June 13, 1866. Ratified July 9, 1868.

1. Citizenship Defined All persons born or naturalized in the United States, and subject to the jurisdiction thereof, are citizens of the United States and of the State wherein they reside. No State shall make or enforce any law which shall abridge the privileges or immunities of citizens of the United States; nor shall any State deprive any person of life, liberty, or property, without due process of law; nor deny to any person within its jurisdiction the equal protection of the laws.

2. Voting Rights Representatives shall be apportioned among the several States according to their respective numbers, counting the whole number of persons in each State, ~~excluding Indians not taxed~~. But when the right to vote at any election for the choice of electors for President and Vice-President of the United States, Representatives in Congress, the Executive and Judicial officers of a State, or the members of the Legislature thereof, is denied to any of the ~~male~~ inhabitants of such State, ~~being twenty-one years of age~~, and citizens of the United States, or in any way abridged, except for participation in rebellion, or other crime, the basis of representation therein shall be reduced in the proportion which the number of such ~~male~~ citizens shall bear to the whole number of ~~male~~ citizens ~~twenty-one years of age~~ in such State.

3. Rebels Banned from Government No person shall be a Senator or Representative in Congress, or elector of President and Vice-President, or hold any office, civil or military, under the United States, or under any State, who, having previously taken an oath, as a member of Congress, or as an officer of the United States, or as a member of any State legislature, or as an executive or judicial officer of any State, to support the Constitution of the United States, shall have engaged in insurrection or rebellion against the same, or given aid or comfort to the enemies thereof. But Congress may by a vote of two-thirds of each House, remove such disability.

4. Payment of Debts The validity of the public debt of the United States, authorized by law, including debts incurred for payment of pensions and bounties for services in suppressing insurrection or rebellion, shall not be questioned. But neither the United States nor any State shall assume or pay

The Thirteenth, Fourteenth, and Fifteenth Amendments are often called the Reconstruction Amendments. This is because they arose during Reconstruction, the period of American history following the Civil War. A key aspect of rebuilding the Union was extending the rights of citizenship to former slaves.

The Thirteenth Amendment banned slavery. The Fourteenth Amendment required states to respect the freedoms listed in the Bill of Rights, thus preventing states from denying rights to African Americans. The Fifteenth Amendment gave African American men the right to vote.

African Americans vote in an election during Reconstruction.

 ANALYSIS SKILL **ANALYZING INFORMATION**

Why were the Reconstruction Amendments needed?

any debt or obligation incurred in aid of insurrection or rebellion against the United States, ~~or any claim for the loss or emancipation of any slave~~; but all such debts, obligations and claims shall be held illegal and void.

5. Enforcement The Congress shall have the power to enforce, by appropriate legislation, the provisions of this article.

Amendment XV

Passed by Congress February 26, 1869. Ratified February 3, 1870.

1. Voting Rights The right of citizens of the United States to vote shall not be denied or abridged by the United States or by any State on account of race, color, or previous condition of servitude.

2. Enforcement The Congress shall have the power to enforce this article by appropriate legislation.

Amendment XVI

Passed by Congress July 2, 1909. Ratified February 3, 1913.

The Congress shall have power to lay and collect taxes on incomes, from whatever source derived, without apportionment among the several States, and without regard to any census or enumeration.

Amendment XVII

Passed by Congress May 13, 1912. Ratified April 8, 1913.

1. Senators Elected by Citizens The Senate of the United States shall be composed of two Senators from each State, elected by the people thereof, for six years; and each Senator shall have one vote. The electors in each State shall have the qualifications requisite for electors of the most numerous branch of the State legislatures.

2. Vacancies When vacancies happen in the representation of any State in the Senate, the executive authority of such State shall issue writs of election to fill such vacancies: *Provided*, That the legislature of any State may empower the executive thereof to make temporary appointments until the people fill the vacancies by election as the legislature may direct.

3. Future Elections This amendment shall not be so construed as to affect the election or term of any Senator chosen before it becomes valid as part of the Constitution.

Amendment XVIII

Passed by Congress December 18, 1917. Ratified January 16, 1919. Repealed by Amendment XXI.

1. Liquor Banned After one year from the ratification of this article the manufacture, sale, or transportation of intoxicating liquors within, the importation thereof into, or the exportation thereof from the United States and all territory subject to the jurisdiction thereof for beverage purposes is hereby prohibited.

2. Enforcement The Congress and the several States shall have concurrent power to enforce this article by appropriate legislation.

3. Ratification This article shall be inoperative unless it shall have been ratified as an amendment to the Constitution by the legislatures of the several States, as provided in the Constitution, within seven years from the date of the submission hereof to the States by the Congress.

EXPLORING THE DOCUMENT The Seventeenth Amendment requires that senators be elected directly by the people instead of by the state legislatures. *What principle of our government does the Seventeenth Amendment protect?*

Prohibition

Although many people believed that the Eighteenth Amendment was good for the health and welfare of the American people, it was repealed 14 years later.

WOMEN FIGHT FOR THE VOTE

To become part of the Constitution, a proposed amendment must be ratified by three-fourths of the states. Here, suffragists witness Kentucky governor Edwin P. Morrow signing the Nineteenth Amendment in January 1920. By June of that year, enough states had ratified the amendment to make it part of the Constitution. American women, after generations of struggle, had finally won the right to vote.

ANALYSIS SKILL **ANALYZING INFORMATION**

What right did the Nineteenth Amendment grant?

Amendment XIX

Passed by Congress June 4, 1919. Ratified August 18, 1920.

1. Voting Rights The right of citizens of the United States to vote shall not be denied or abridged by the United States or by any State on account of sex.

2. Enforcement Congress shall have power to enforce this article by appropriate legislation.

Amendment XX

Passed by Congress March 2, 1932. Ratified January 23, 1933.

1. Presidential Terms The terms of the President and the Vice President shall end at noon on the 20th day of January, and the terms of Senators and Representatives at noon on the 3d day of January, of the years in which such terms would have ended if this article had not been ratified; and the terms of their successors shall then begin.

Women's Suffrage

Abigail Adams and others were disappointed that the Declaration of Independence and the Constitution did not specifically include women. It took many years and much campaigning before national suffrage for women finally was achieved.

2. Meeting of Congress The Congress shall assemble at least once in every year, and such meeting shall begin at noon on the 3d day of January, unless they shall by law appoint a different day.

3. Succession of Vice President If, at the time fixed for the beginning of the term of the President, the President elect shall have died, the Vice President elect shall become President. If a President shall not have been chosen before the time fixed for the beginning of his term, or if the President elect shall have failed to qualify, then the Vice President elect shall act as President until a President shall have qualified; and the Congress may by law provide for the case wherein neither a President elect nor a Vice President shall have qualified, declaring who shall then act as President, or the manner in which one who is to act shall be selected, and such person shall act accordingly until a President or Vice President shall have qualified.

4. Succession by Vote of Congress The Congress may by law provide for the case of the death of any of the persons from whom the House of Representatives may choose a President whenever the right of choice shall have devolved upon them, and for the case of the death of any of the persons from whom the Senate may choose a Vice President whenever the right of choice shall have devolved upon them.

5. Ratification ~~Sections 1 and 2 shall take effect on the 15th day of October following the ratification of this article.~~

6. Ratification ~~This article shall be inoperative unless it shall have been ratified as an amendment to the Constitution by the legislatures of three-fourths of the several States within seven years from the date of its submission.~~

Amendment XXI

Passed by Congress February 20, 1933. Ratified December 5, 1933.

1. 18th Amendment Repealed The eighteenth article of amendment to the Constitution of the United States is hereby repealed.

2. Liquor Allowed by Law The transportation or importation into any State, Territory, or Possession of the United States for delivery or use therein of intoxicating liquors, in violation of the laws thereof, is hereby prohibited.

3. Ratification ~~This article shall be inoperative unless it shall have been ratified as an amendment to the Constitution by conventions in the several States, as provided in the Constitution, within seven years from the date of the submission hereof to the States by the Congress.~~

Amendment XXII

Passed by Congress March 21, 1947. Ratified February 27, 1951.

1. Term Limits No person shall be elected to the office of the President more than twice, and no person who has held the office of President, or acted as President, for more than two years of a term to which some other person was elected President shall be elected to the office of President more than once. ~~But this Article shall not apply to any person holding the office of President when this Article was proposed by Congress, and shall not prevent any person who may be holding the office of President, or acting as President, during the term within which this Article becomes operative from holding the office of President or acting as President during the remainder of such term.~~

2. Ratification ~~This article shall be inoperative unless it shall have been ratified as an amendment to the Constitution by the legislatures of three-fourths of the several States within seven years from the date of its submission to the States by the Congress.~~

After Franklin D. Roosevelt was elected to four consecutive terms, limits were placed on the number of terms a president could serve.

EXPLORING THE DOCUMENT From the time of President George Washington's administration, it was a custom for presidents to serve no more than two terms in office. Franklin D. Roosevelt, however, was elected to four terms. The Twenty-second Amendment restricted presidents to no more than two terms in office. *Why do you think citizens chose to limit the power of the president in this way?*

Amendment XXIII

Passed by Congress June 16, 1960. Ratified March 29, 1961.

1. District of Columbia Represented The District constituting the seat of Government of the United States shall appoint in such manner as Congress may direct:

A number of electors of President and Vice President equal to the whole number of Senators and Representatives in Congress to which the District would be entitled if it were a State, but in no event more than the least populous State; they shall be in addition to those appointed by the States, but they shall be considered, for the purposes of the election of President and Vice President, to be electors appointed by a State; and they shall meet in the District and perform such duties as provided by the twelfth article of amendment.

2. Enforcement The Congress shall have power to enforce this article by appropriate legislation.

Voting Rights

Until the ratification of the Twenty-third Amendment, the people of Washington, D.C., could not vote in presidential elections.

Poll taxes were used to deny impoverished Americans, including many African Americans and Hispanic Americans, the right to vote. Poll taxes were outlawed by the Twenty-fourth Amendment.

The American GI Forum Says: BUY YOUR POLL TAX

1939 Poll Tax Receipt

ANALYSIS SKILL   ANALYZING INFORMATION
How did poll taxes deny poor Americans the opportunity to vote?

Amendment XXIV

Passed by Congress August 27, 1962. Ratified January 23, 1964.

1. Voting Rights The right of citizens of the United States to vote in any primary or other election for President or Vice President, for electors for President or Vice President, or for Senator or Representative in Congress, shall not be denied or abridged by the United States or any State by reason of failure to pay poll tax or other tax.

2. Enforcement The Congress shall have power to enforce this article by appropriate legislation.

Amendment XXV

Passed by Congress July 6, 1965. Ratified February 10, 1967.

1. Succession of Vice President In case of the removal of the President from office or of his death or resignation, the Vice President shall become President.

2. Vacancy of Vice President Whenever there is a vacancy in the office of the Vice President, the President shall nominate a Vice President who shall take office upon confirmation by a majority vote of both Houses of Congress.

Presidential Disability

The illness of President Eisenhower in the 1950s and the assassination of President Kennedy in 1963 were the events behind the Twenty-fifth Amendment. The Constitution did not provide a clear-cut method for a vice president to take over for a disabled president or upon the death of a president. This amendment provides for filling the office of the vice president if a vacancy occurs, and it provides a way for the vice president—or someone else in the line of succession—to take over if the president is unable to perform the duties of that office.

3. Written Declaration   Whenever the President transmits to the President pro tempore of the Senate and the Speaker of the House of Representatives his written declaration that he is unable to discharge the powers and duties of his office, and until he transmits to them a written declaration to the contrary, such powers and duties shall be discharged by the Vice President as Acting President.

4. Removing the President   Whenever the Vice President and a majority of either the principal officers of the executive departments or of such other body as Congress may by law provide, transmit to the President pro tempore of the Senate and the Speaker of the House of Representatives their written declaration that the President is unable to discharge the powers and duties of his office, the Vice President shall immediately assume the powers and duties of the office as Acting President.

Thereafter, when the President transmits to the President pro tempore of the Senate and the Speaker of the House of Representatives his written declaration that no inability exists, he shall resume the powers and duties of his office unless the Vice President and a majority of either the principal officers of the executive department or of such other body as Congress may by law provide, transmit within four days to the President pro tempore of the Senate and the Speaker of the House of Representatives their written declaration that the President is unable to discharge the powers and duties of his office. Thereupon Congress shall decide the issue, assembling within forty-eight hours for that purpose if not in session. If the Congress, within twenty-one days after receipt of the latter written declaration, or, if Congress is not in session, within twenty-one days after Congress is required to assemble, determines by two-thirds vote of both Houses that the President is unable to discharge the powers and duties of his office, the Vice President shall continue to discharge the same as Acting President; otherwise, the President shall resume the powers and duties of his office.

Amendment XXVI

Passed by Congress March 23, 1971. Ratified July 1, 1971.

1. Voting Rights   The right of citizens of the United States, who are eighteen years of age or older, to vote shall not be denied or abridged by the United States or by any State on account of age.

2. Enforcement   The Congress shall have power to enforce this article by appropriate legislation.

Amendment XXVII

Originally proposed September 25, 1789. Ratified May 7, 1992.

No law, varying the compensation for the services of the Senators and Representatives, shall take effect, until an election of representatives shall have intervened.

Expanded Suffrage

The Voting Rights Act of 1970 tried to lower the voting age from 21 to 18. However, the Supreme Court ruled that the act applied to national elections only, not to state or local elections. The Twenty-sixth Amendment set the minimum voting age for all elections at 18.

Constitution Review

Visual Summary: The Constitution of the United States

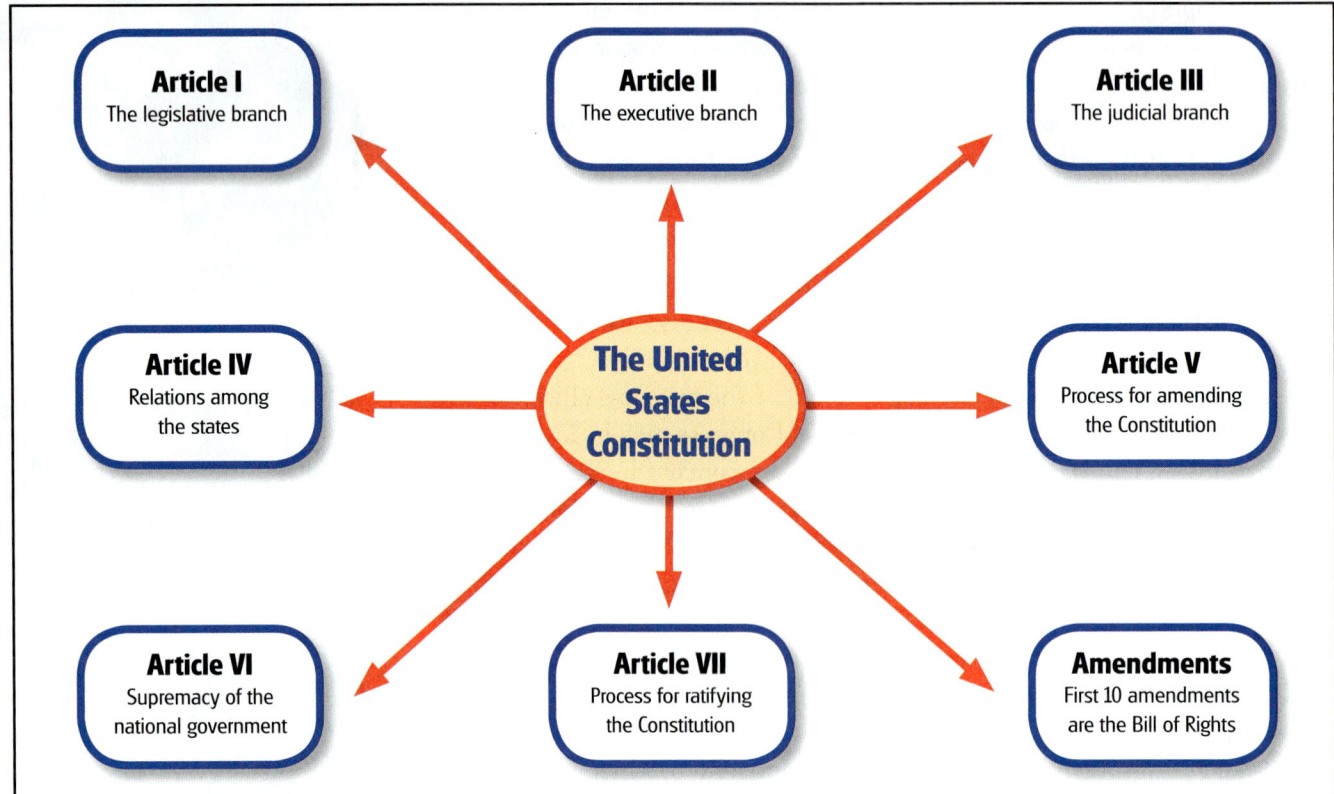

Article I The legislative branch

Article II The executive branch

Article III The judicial branch

Article IV Relations among the states

The United States Constitution

Article V Process for amending the Constitution

Article VI Supremacy of the national government

Article VII Process for ratifying the Constitution

Amendments First 10 amendments are the Bill of Rights

Reviewing Key Terms and People

For each term or name below, write a sentence explaining its significance to the U.S. Constitution.

1. pro tempore
2. quorum
3. bills
4. elastic clause
5. writ of habeas corpus
6. ex post facto law
7. executive branch
8. State of the Union
9. federalism
10. national supremacy
11. Bill of Rights

Comprehension and Critical Thinking

ARTICLE I *(pp. 171–177)*

12. **a. Recall** What is the focus of Article I?

    b. Make Inferences Why do you think Congress fixed the size of the House of Representatives at 435 members in 1929?

    c. Elaborate Describe how a bill becomes a law, explaining how the process is an example of checks and balances in the Constitution.

ARTICLE II *(pp. 178–180)*

13. **a. Identify** Which branch of government is the focus of Article II of the U.S. Constitution?

    b. Compare What are the main powers of the president, and how do they compare to the main powers of the legislature?

    c. Evaluate Do you think the electoral college is the best way to elect the president? Explain.

ARTICLE III *(pp. 181–182)*

14. a. Describe Which branch of government is the focus of Article III of the U.S. Constitution?

b. Analyze How are cases appealed to the Supreme Court in the federal judicial system?

c. Elaborate How does the judicial system provide a check on the legislature?

ARTICLE IV *(pp. 182–183)*

15. a. Describe What is the focus of Article IV of the U.S. Constitution?

b. Analyze Why must states honor the laws of other states?

c. Evaluate How well does the system of federalism balance the powers of states and the national government?

ARTICLE V *(p. 184)*

16. a. Identify What does Article V of the U.S. Constitution discuss?

b. Explain What is the process for amending the U.S. Constitution?

ARTICLE VI *(p. 184)*

17. a. Describe What happens if a state law and a federal law conflict with each other?

b. Analyze Why do you think the idea of national supremacy was included in the Constitution?

ARTICLE VII *(p. 185)*

18. a. Recall How many states are needed to ratify the Constitution?

b. Compare Why was the number of states needed to ratify the Constitution different from the number of states needed to revise the Articles of Confederation?

Using the Internet

go.hrw.com
Practice Online
Keyword: SD7 CH5

19. Each of the 50 states sends representatives to the Senate and the House of Representatives. Using the keyword above, locate congressmembers representing your state or your congressional district. Then conduct research to find out if they have sponsored a bill, how they voted on recent legislation, issues that interest them, or their viewpoints on pending legislation. Create a chart to display your research.

Analyzing Primary Sources

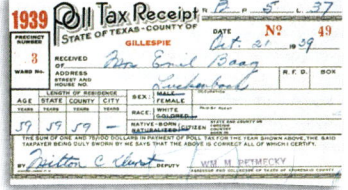

Reading Like a Historian This poll tax receipt was issued in 1939 to a voter in Texas. Poll taxes were later outlawed by the Twenty-fourth Amendment.

20. Recall What was a poll tax?

Explain Why were poll taxes outlawed by the Twenty-fourth Amendment?

Critical Reading

Review the timeline in this section titled "Amendments to the U.S. Constitution." Consider the 27 amendments on the time line and then answer the questions that follow.

21. The purpose of Amendment 15 was

A to prohibit national and state governments from denying the vote based on race.

B to extend voting rights to women.

C to repeal Amendment 14.

D to ban production, sale, and distribution of alcoholic beverages.

22. What do the amendments have in common?

A Each amendment gave a different group of people the right to vote.

B Each amendment helped the structure of government change along with the values of the nation's people.

C Each amendment helped the Constitution remain unchanged for 200 years.

D Each amendment was eventually repealed.

FOCUS ON WRITING

Expository Writing *Expository writing gives information, explains why or how, or defines a process. To practice expository writing, complete the assignment below.*

Writing Topic **The preamble to the Constitution**

23. What does the preamble state? What does it tell you about the Framers' intentions? Write a brief paragraph that answers these questions. Include quotations from the text of the preamble.

Forging the New REPUBLIC

THE BIG PICTURE In the last decade of the 1700s, debates over the size and role of the federal government led to the emergence of rival political parties. Thomas Jefferson's election as president in 1800 marked the rise of the Democratic-Republican Party.

New York Standards

Key Idea 1 The study of New York State and United States history requires an analysis of the development of American culture, its diversity and multicultural context, and the ways people are unified by many values, practices, and traditions.

Key Idea 3 Study about the major social, political, economic, cultural, and religious developments in New York State and United States history involves learning about the important roles and contributions of individuals and groups.

Skills FOCUS READING LIKE A HISTORIAN

President George Washington celebrates his second inauguration at Independence Hall, Philadelphia, in 1793. As the country's first president, Washington not only led the nation but also set the style and tone for the office. **Interpreting Visuals** What image, style, or tone does this painting suggest?

See **Skills Handbook**, p. H30

1791
Pierre Charles L'Enfant is hired to plan the new national capital.

The Bill of Rights is added to the Constitution.

U.S.

1790 **1795**

World

1793
Thousands are killed during the Reign of Terror in France.

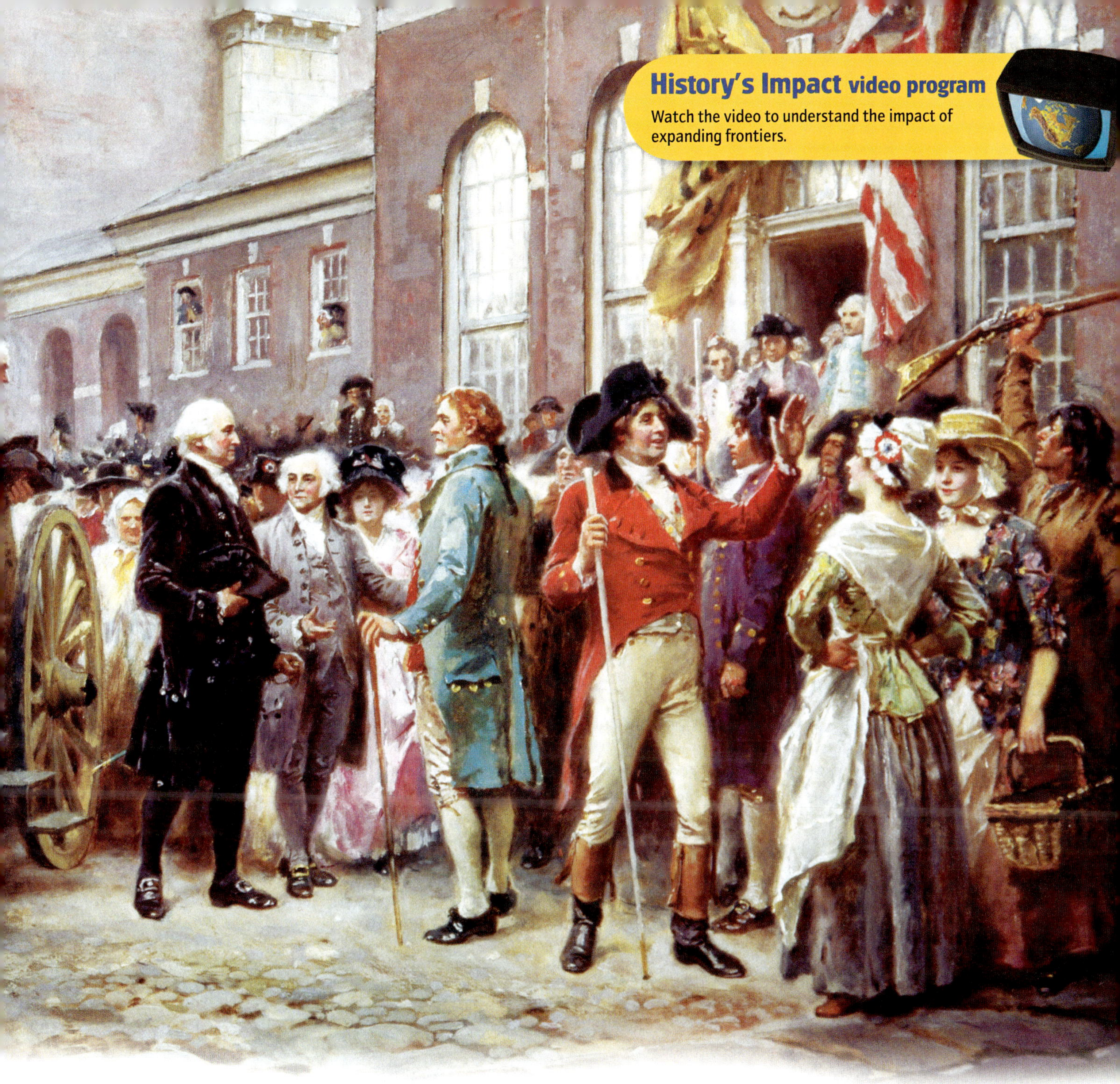

History's Impact video program

Watch the video to understand the impact of expanding frontiers.

July 1798
Congress passes the Alien and Sedition Acts.

1800

1801
The United Kingdom of Great Britain and Ireland is formed.

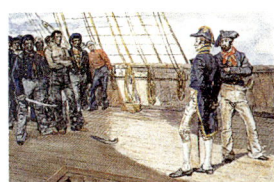

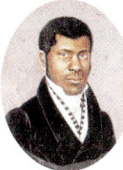

1803
Haitian liberator Pierre Toussant-Louverture dies in a French prison.

May 1804
Lewis and Clark set off to explore the continent west of the Mississippi.

1805

June 1807
British ship fires on American frigate *Chesapeake*.

1807
Great Britain outlaws the slave trade in its empire.

1810

June 1812
United States declares war on Great Britain.

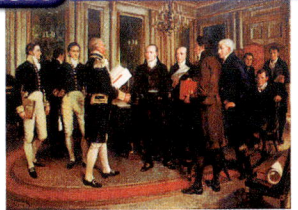

1814
Treaty of Ghent ends war between Great Britain and the United States.

1815

SECTION 1
Washington Becomes President

BEFORE YOU READ

MAIN IDEA

President Washington and other leaders tried to solve the new nation's economic problems. This led to the rise of political parties.

READING FOCUS

1. What steps did Congress and the president take to organize the new government?
2. What was Alexander Hamilton's plan to settle the nation's debts?
3. What was the debate over the national bank?
4. How did the first political parties form?

KEY TERMS AND PEOPLE

cabinet
Alexander Hamilton
Judiciary Act of 1789
strict construction
loose construction
Bank of the United States
Whiskey Rebellion
two-party system
Democratic-Republicans

 PI 1.2 Describe the evolution of American democratic values and beliefs as expressed in the Declaration of Independence, the New York State Constitution, the United States Constitution, the Bill of Rights, and other important historical documents.

 **THE INSIDE STORY**

How did Americans welcome the new president? The new government was slow getting started. Even after electors voted unanimously for Washington, it took months for Congress to make the results official. Washington had already packed his bags for the trip from Virginia to New York, the temporary capital. As he waited, both he and his wife, Martha, had serious doubts about the coming months.

After the war, Washington had looked forward to a quiet life as a farmer at Mount Vernon. Now it seemed that responsibility for the success of the new nation rested on his shoulders. To make things worse, he was short of money and had to borrow to pay for his trip. He wrote gloomily that he approached the presidency "with feelings not unlike those of a culprit who is going to his place of execution."

Finally, on April 14, the election results were official, and Washington set out for New York. As his coach passed through towns and villages on the trip north, enthusiastic crowds cheered him. Men on horseback rode alongside the coach, stirring up dust from the dirt roads. He stopped in small towns to make speeches. He led parades and went to lavish dinners.

The emotions of the people were almost overwhelming. At last Washington reached New York, and the joyful celebrations reached a peak on the historic day of the nation's first presidential inauguration. ◼

A Born Leader

▶ **Washington's stately image has come to symbolize the presidency.**

The President's Cabinet

Washington appointed four cabinet members, pictured with him here:

1. Henry Knox
2. Thomas Jefferson
3. Edmund Randolph
4. Alexander Hamilton
5. George Washington

THE GRANGER COLLECTION, NEW YORK

Organizing the Government

No one doubted that George Washington would become the first president of the United States. The whole time that the Constitutional Convention had debated the role of the president, most people had Washington in mind for the job. Indeed, when the presidential electors met in February 1789, Washington won unanimously. John Adams, who received the second highest number of votes, became vice president.

Inauguration day, April 30, 1789, began with the sound of cannons and church bells. The streets of New York were hung with banners. Washington stepped onto the balcony of Federal Hall on Wall Street and took his oath of office. He was formally dressed in a brown suit of American-made broadcloth, to encourage American business. He also wore white silk stockings and silver-buckled shoes, and his graying hair was powdered white.

Washington spoke briefly, and then the celebrations began. Fireworks lit up the sky over New York City. The new president joined members of Congress at a church service in Saint Paul's Church.

Washington chooses a cabinet In his inaugural address, Washington spoke modestly about his lack of administrative experience. But the former commander in chief was certainly an experienced leader. His dignity and quiet power, along with his impressive height, gave him an air of authority.

Washington knew that what he did as president would set a pattern for later administrations. For example, the Constitution mentions the "heads of the executive departments" but did not specify what those departments should be. So, in 1789 Congress created the first three executive departments—state, treasury, and war. The leaders of these departments would become known as the president's **cabinet**.

For the cabinet positions, Washington chose men he knew and trusted. Henry Knox, who had been in charge of weaponry in the Revolutionary War, became secretary of war. Thomas Jefferson became secretary of state, and Alexander Hamilton became secretary of the treasury. Edmund Randolph of Virginia was attorney general, the president's legal adviser.

There were personal and political clashes in the brand-new government. Washington and

John Adams, the vice president, were old opponents. They avoided working closely with each other. Similarly, Hamilton and Jefferson—both brilliant men—disagreed about policies. They were also very different in personality and grew to dislike each other intensely.

Many compromises had been made in writing the Constitution. Many questions about the direction the country should take had not been answered. Deep differences remained. The Federalists, led by Hamilton, envisioned a strong centralized nation, with prospering cities and businesses and a role in world affairs. But others preferred a smaller central government, more rural than urban, with a good deal of power left to the states. Led by Jefferson and Madison, these people were known as Jeffersonian Republicans.

The first Congress Only 10 states had joined the government by this time, so the first Congress was small. The Constitution stated that Vice President Adams would preside over the Senate. That was the vice president's only job at the time.

As you read earlier, Congress quickly debated a Bill of Rights and sent proposed amendments to the states. By 1791 the 10 amendments known as the Bill of Rights became an important part of the Constitution.

The Constitution left the structure of the federal court system up to Congress. In the **Judiciary Act of 1789**, Congress organized the judicial branch. It had a six-person Supreme Court with one chief justice and five associates. Washington named John Jay as the first chief justice of the United States. Congress also created district courts and courts of appeal.

READING CHECK **Making Generalizations**
What kind of government did Democratic-Republicans want and what kind did Federalists want?

Settling the Nation's Debts

The Treasury secretary, **Alexander Hamilton**, faced enormous problems. The new government owed money to foreign nations, to private lenders, and even to former soldiers.

Hamilton thought the secret of stable government was a wealthy aristocratic class. To win their support, he had to make the government's financial position more secure, both at home and abroad. Financial stability, he said, would help

HISTORY'S VOICES

❝to promote the increasing respectability of the American name; to answer the calls of justice; . . . to furnish new resources, both to agriculture and commerce; to cement more closely the union of the States; to add to their security against foreign attack; to establish public order.❞

—Alexander Hamilton,
Report on the Public Credit, 1790

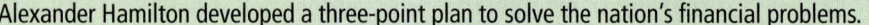

HAMILTON'S ECONOMIC PLAN

QUICK FACTS

Alexander Hamilton developed a three-point plan to solve the nation's financial problems.

Point	Arguments For	Arguments Against
1. Pay the national debt Take on foreign and domestic debt by replacing creditors' old low-value bonds with new, interest-bearing bonds. Take over most of the states' $25 million Revolutionary War debts	• Would build confidence in the new nation • Would free up state money for business and trade	• Would reward rich speculators and punish ordinary citizens who had sold their bonds at low prices • Southern states had already paid their war debts, and resented being taxed to pay the Northern debt.
2. Raise money to pay the debt Pass the Tariff of 1789 and a new excise tax	• Would raise money for the new nation and help manufacturers	• Some people resented these new taxes and tariffs
3. Standardize the banking system Create a national bank and a national mint	• Would raise money for the new nation and help manufacturers	• The Constitution did not specifically say the federal government could create a national bank.

Hamilton's economic plan Hamilton's plan had several features. He wanted the federal government to take on all debt from the Revolutionary War—including the debts of both the states and national government. To do that, he had to find ways to bring the government more income, or revenue. Finally, he wanted to establish a national bank, which would control credit and make loans to the government.

Hamilton's ideas were controversial. The government had sold bonds to merchants and farmers and army officers and soldiers, promising to pay back the money in a certain number of years. But during the hard times after the war, many people holding the bonds needed cash. They sold their bonds to speculators, who paid far less than the actual face value of the bonds. Speculators were betting that the bonds would regain their value.

Under Hamilton's plan, the government would pay the face value to the speculators who now held the bonds. The speculators would make a profit, while those people who originally held the bonds had lost money. Some people thought this was unfair.

Imposing new taxes Unlike the Articles of Confederation, the Constitution gave Congress the power to impose taxes. So far, however, most government income had come from sales of lands in the West.

To increase revenue, Hamilton proposed two different kinds of taxes. One was a tariff, a tax on imported goods. Congress quickly passed the Tariff of 1789.

In 1791 Congress also passed the first excise tax, which is a tax on the production or sale of a certain product. The 1791 tax was on liquor, sugar, snuff, and carriages. It would prove to be very unpopular.

Hamilton's plan to pay off the states' debts was also controversial. Northern states had greater debts than most of the southern states. If the national government assumed all state debts, people in the South would have to pay taxes to pay off other states' debts. Jefferson and others objected to the plan, and Congress voted it down several times.

Compromise leads to a new capital Hamilton tried to change Jefferson's mind about his economic plan. He also needed to win over southerner James Madison, who led

FACES OF HISTORY

Benjamin BANNEKER
1731–1806

The son of a former slave, Benjamin Banneker taught himself advanced mathematics. At the age of 30, he built a precise wooden clock and, at the age of 58, he accurately predicted a solar eclipse. His scientific and mathematical skills helped him earn an appointment by George Washington to survey land for the new capital in Washington, D.C.

Banneker worked closely with Pierre L'Enfant, the architect in charge of planning the new nation's capital. When L'Enfant was dismissed from the project because of his temper, he took the plans with him. Banneker recreated the drawings from memory. These recreated plans were used to complete the work on the city.

Explain How did Banneker help build the city of Washington, D.C.?

the opposition in Congress. Over dinner, they crafted a compromise.

In 1790 the nation's capital had moved from New York to Philadelphia. But many Virginians wanted it in the South. Now the three men agreed that the capital would be moved to the new Federal City in the South by 1800. In return, southerners in Congress would allow Hamilton's debt bill to pass.

Washington was pleased because the historic bargain allowed him to choose an area on the Potomac River between Virginia and Maryland, near his Mount Vernon home. In March 1791 Washington chose a French engineer, Pierre Charles L'Enfant, to plan the new capital's layout. At Jefferson's suggestion, he named Benjamin Banneker, an African American mathematician, as a member of the planning commission.

L'Enfant conceived a grand and elegant plan for the city. The overall plan included wide boulevards radiating out from the Capitol, like spokes of a wheel. Washington, who had been a professional surveyor, admired L'Enfant's plan. Jefferson, however, had already designed and built several beautiful buildings. He disliked L'Enfant's grand, imperial style and drew his own plan for a simpler town. Although L'Enfant was eventually dismissed from the project, much of his plan was followed.

READING CHECK **Summarizing** How did Hamilton increase revenue?

Debating a National Bank

The most controversial part of Hamilton's plan was the national bank. The debate made clear that Jeffersonian Republicans and Federalists had opposing viewpoints about government. Like many debates during the Constitutional Convention, the disagreement centered on how much power the central government should have.

A broader debate arose over two ways of viewing the Constitution: **strict construction** and **loose construction**. People who favor strict construction believe that the government should only do what the Constitution specifically states it can do. On the other hand, those who favor loose construction think that the government can take reasonable actions that are not outlined in the Constitution—as long as those actions are not specifically prohibited.

Hamilton's bank plan The Constitution (Article I, Section 8) listed a number of specific, or expressed, powers that are granted to Congress. When Hamilton proposed a national bank, he pointed to the clause in the Constitution that allows Congress to pass all laws that are "necessary and proper" to carry out its assigned powers.

This broad interpretation of the Constitution was a prime example of loose construction. From Hamilton's point of view, the "necessary and proper" clause allowed actions that follow the intent of the Constitution even though those actions are not specifically named in the Constitution. This clause has allowed the government to expand its powers and to adjust to changing times. To this day, it is still a question for debate.

Jefferson opposes the bank Jeffersonian Republicans continued the Antifederalists' arguments against a strong central government. Jefferson himself, although he admired Washington and Madison, was lukewarm about the Constitution in its final form.

Jefferson wanted a small central government with more power left to the states. He favored limiting government powers to only

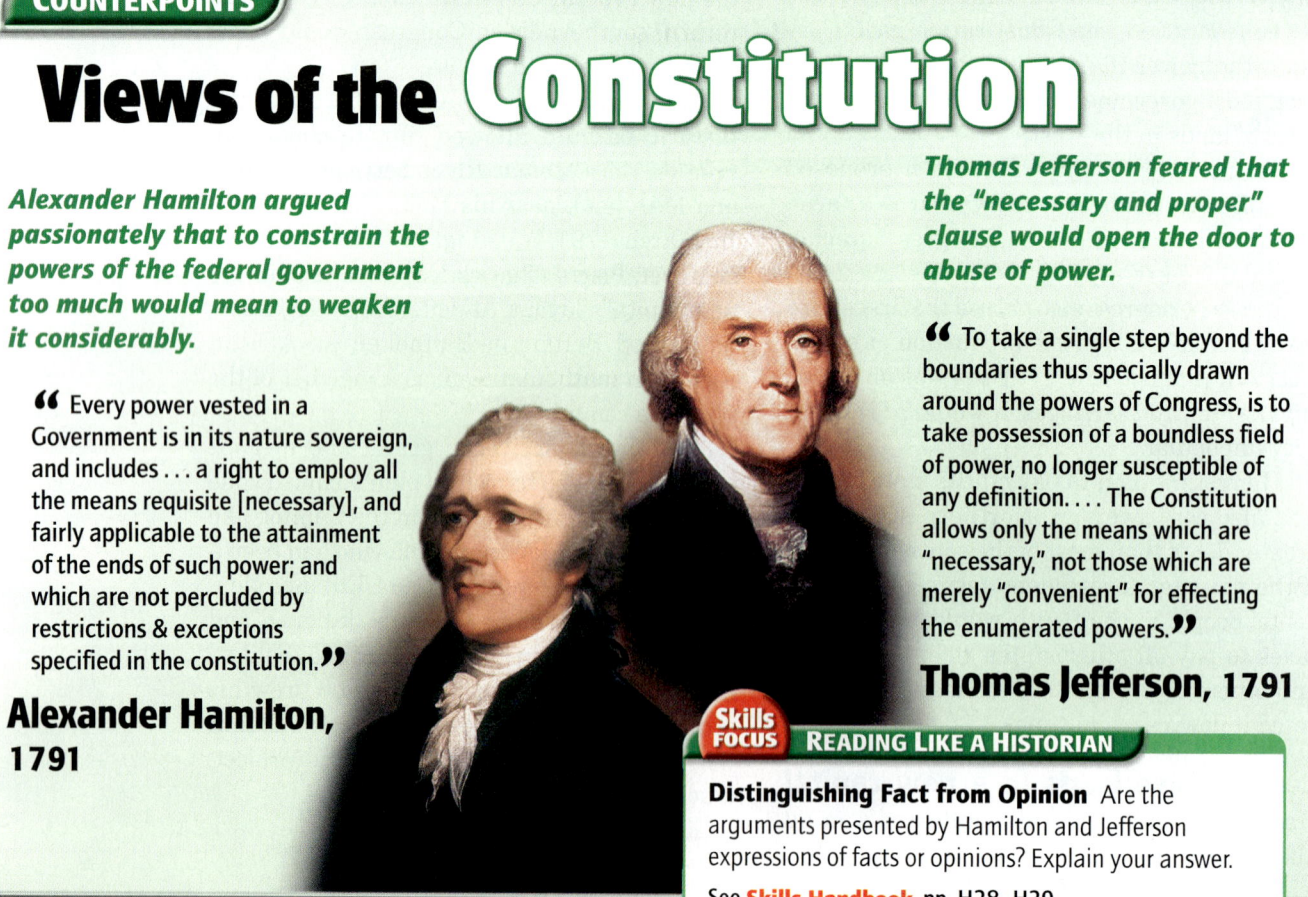

COUNTERPOINTS

Views of the Constitution

Alexander Hamilton argued passionately that to constrain the powers of the federal government too much would mean to weaken it considerably.

66 Every power vested in a Government is in its nature sovereign, and includes . . . a right to employ all the means requisite [necessary], and fairly applicable to the attainment of the ends of such power; and which are not percluded by restrictions & exceptions specified in the constitution. 99

Alexander Hamilton, 1791

Thomas Jefferson feared that the "necessary and proper" clause would open the door to abuse of power.

66 To take a single step beyond the boundaries thus specially drawn around the powers of Congress, is to take possession of a boundless field of power, no longer susceptible of any definition. . . . The Constitution allows only the means which are "necessary," not those which are merely "convenient" for effecting the enumerated powers. 99

Thomas Jefferson, 1791

Skills FOCUS **READING LIKE A HISTORIAN**

Distinguishing Fact from Opinion Are the arguments presented by Hamilton and Jefferson expressions of facts or opinions? Explain your answer.

See **Skills Handbook**, pp. H28–H29

THE GRANGER COLLECTION, NEW YORK

those specifically spelled out in the Constitution—and that would not include the power to form a national bank.

Washington signs the bank bill The bank proposal made others uneasy as well. Its directors were to be private bankers, who would clearly gain more influence and wealth from it. Madison, Randolph, and others joined Jefferson in opposing it. Speaking to Congress, Madison said that the right to regulate trade had little to do with a national bank.

Despite the opposition, Congress passed the bill and sent it to the president to sign. Jefferson urged Washington to veto the bank bill. While Washington admitted that he was "greatly perplexed," he did not want to use the presidential veto.

Hamilton eventually persuaded President Washington to be flexible. Washington signed the bill to charter the first **Bank of the United States** in February 1791.

READING CHECK **Summarizing** Why did Jefferson oppose the national bank?

FACES OF HISTORY

Alexander HAMILTON
1757?–1804

Although Alexander Hamilton scorned party politics, his policies and his quarrels with Thomas Jefferson contributed to the formation of the first political parties in the United States. Hamilton worked zealously to form a strong central government in the United States. To build the government's strength, Hamilton proposed economic policies that profited the business class rather than the common people. According to Hamilton, the government would benefit most with support from the business class. When Britain and France went to war, Hamilton clashed with Jefferson about foreign policy. Hamilton wanted the United States to abandon its alliance with France, whereas Jefferson contended that the United States should honor the alliance. Despite Jefferson's insistence, Hamilton persuaded President Washington that the United States should remain neutral during the conflict. As the disagreements between Hamilton and Jefferson intensified, government leaders chose sides. Those who supported Hamilton formed the Federalist Party.

Interpret What did Hamilton believe would make the United States a strong nation?

First Political Parties Form

Hamilton and Jefferson had personal differences. But their rift between the two leaders also reflected a deep split among national leaders. The people themselves were divided along the same lines as they were during the battle over ratifying the Constitution. Soon, another of Hamilton's controversial financial plans—the excise tax—led to a violent clash between supporters and opponents of strong government.

The Whiskey Rebellion Farmers and settlers in the woods and mountains of the western frontier had always resented the wealth and power of people in the East. They felt their interests were ignored. They disliked being told how to act by easterners—including the national government in Philadelphia.

In 1794 farmers on the frontier in western Pennsylvania objected violently to Hamilton's excise tax on whiskey. Their livelihoods depended on turning their surplus grain into rye whiskey. Whiskey was easier to transport

◄ In this painting Washington (seated atop the white horse) directs the Western Army at Fort Cumberland, Maryland.

207

than grain and could be sold for more money. The rebel farmers led an uprising known as the **Whiskey Rebellion**.

The farmers attacked tax collectors. They burned the barns of people who gave away the location of stills where whiskey was made. A crowd of more than 2,000 angry farmers threatened Pittsburgh, then a small town. There was talk of setting up an independent nation.

Washington took command. He wanted to make it clear that armed rebellion against the national government would not be tolerated. To help the Pennsylvanians, he called out the militia from Virginia, Maryland, and New Jersey. That raised a force of some 13,000 or more men. Washington sent one last order to the rebels to stop. He and Hamilton rode west to lead the troops into Pennsylvania.

Instead of resisting the huge militia force, the surprised farmers scattered in all directions. The militia caught and arrested them. Two were later convicted of treason, but Washington eventually pardoned them. A pleased Washington said that the rebel farmers had been taught a lesson "without spilling a drop of blood." He had also shown that the federal government would take action within a state.

Political parties develop The Constitution did not anticipate political parties. Most of the Framers thought parties were dangerous to national unity. Washington opposed political parties as well. In *The Federalist*, James Madison had warned about factions.

In the 1790s, however, Americans became politically divided. The Whiskey Rebellion showed that some people did not agree with Washington's policies.

Both sides—Jeffersonian Republicans and Federalists—were starting to act like political parties. The Federalists under Hamilton took the lead. They established local associations. They gave political offices and other favors to their supporters. Jeffersonian Republicans went even further than the Federalists in setting up their party organizations. In various states, Jeffersonian Republicans worked together to influence elections.

Each side justified its actions as necessary to resist what they considered the dangerous ideas of the other. By forming these two groups, early American leaders were well on their way to establishing a **two-party system**.

Jeffersonian Republicans were later called **Democratic-Republicans** to emphasize that they favored popular government. However, none of the Framers or other early leaders were in favor of a government as democratic as it eventually became. They did not completely trust the mass of ordinary and largely uneducated people.

THE IMPACT TODAY

Government

Jefferson's Democratic-Republican Party eventually developed into the modern Democratic Party. The modern Republican Party was founded in the 1850s.

READING CHECK **Identifying Cause and Effect** What was the main cause of the Whiskey Rebellion?

SECTION 1 ASSESSMENT

go.hrw.com
Online Quiz
Keyword: SD7 HP6

Reviewing Ideas, Terms, and People

1. **a. Identify** Who were the members of Washington's first cabinet?
   b. Explain How did Washington influence the role of future presidents?
   c. Predict What were likely to be the results of the compromises made while writing the Constitution?

2. **a. Describe** What were the main features of Hamilton's economic plan?
   b. Analyze Which leaders objected to paying the states' debts, and what were their objections?

3. **a. Recall** Why did Hamilton and Jefferson disagree on the bank bill?
   b. Compare Describe the two opposing points of view on how to interpret the Constitution.
   c. Evaluate How would the country's growth have been limited if leaders had always followed **strict construction**?

4. **a. Identify** Who were some of the leading Republicans in the 1790s?
   b. Explain What events and points of view during the 1790s showed that a **two-party system** was developing?

Critical Thinking

5. **Comparing** Copy the chart below and compare the points of view of Federalists and Republicans.

Federalists	Republicans

FOCUS ON WRITING

6. **Persuasive** As a newspaper editor in either Philadelphia or Virginia, write an editorial explaining why the national capital should be located in your region.

Challenges of the 1790s

BEFORE YOU READ

MAIN IDEA

The United States faced many challenges during the 1790s. It tried to remain neutral in European wars while dealing with conflicts with Native Americans in the Northwest Territory.

READING FOCUS

1. Why did Washington want to remain neutral in response to events in Europe?

2. What conflicts took place in the Northwest Territory?

3. What challenges did John Adams face as president, and what was the XYZ affair?

KEY TERMS AND PEOPLE

Neutrality Proclamation
Jay's Treaty
Pinckney's Treaty
Little Turtle
Battle of Fallen Timbers
Treaty of Greenville
sectionalism
XYZ affair
Alien and Sedition Acts
Virginia and Kentucky
   Resolutions
nullification

PI 3.4 Understand the interrelationships between world events and developments in New York State and the United States (e.g., causes for immigration, economic opportunities, human rights abuses, and tyranny versus freedom).

THE INSIDE STORY

How would the Americans respond to a French Revolution?

Just as the new U.S. government was getting organized, the people of France launched a revolution of their own. In France, the king had absolute power. The monarch and a few noble families owned most of the country's land and wealth. Only nobles had a voice in government.

There was an immense gap between this privileged upper class and the rest of the people. Most were poor peasants or urban laborers who paid high taxes to support the nobles' grand estates.

In early 1789 France exploded into horrific bloodshed. People protested against food shortages, high prices, and taxes. On July 14, 1789, a crowd of angry Parisians stormed the Bastille prison, a hated symbol of royal power. Soon, a revolutionary government took over. It limited the king's power and made France a constitutional monarchy.

The Americans faced a difficult question. Should they support another country's revolution against an oppressive monarchy? Or, should the United States remain neutral?

Remaining Neutral

The overthrow of the French monarchy alarmed other European rulers. Austria and Prussia declared war on France. Other nations, including Great Britain and Spain, soon joined them.

But in the United States, many people celebrated the news from France. After all, help from the French military had been vital in winning the Revolutionary War. Democratic-Republicans thought that the revolution in France meant the end of monarchy and a turn toward liberty. They also feared that if the French

Revolution Abroad

▼ French revolutionaries seize the Bastille, where arms and munitions were stored.

Keeping the Peace

The United States attempted to remain neutral in foreign conflicts following the French Revolution. Three agreements supported this goal:

1793 Neutrality Proclamation
The United States would be "friendly and impartial" toward France and Great Britain.

1794 Jay's Treaty
Britain relinquished control of the Northwest to the United States and agreed to pay for its attacks on American merchant ships.

1795 Pinckney's Treaty
Spain gave the United States the right to use the Mississippi River and port of New Orleans. Spain and the United States settled the northern boundary of Florida.

Skills FOCUS   **INTERPRETING TIME LINES**

How might Jay's Treaty and Pinckney's Treaty have helped the United States remain neutral?

See **Skills Handbook**, p. H14

Revolution failed, it meant a failure of republican government everywhere.

The more conservative Federalists were horrified. Hamilton had always had a great deal of respect for monarchy and not much for democracy. But the Federalists seemed to be in the minority.

A declaration of neutrality
Once war in Europe began, both France and Britain tried to draw the United States into the conflict. One crucial issue was trade by sea. Britain was a major sea power, while France was not. The French needed American ships on their side.

The new French government called on old alliances as well as public sympathy for the republican cause. Nevertheless, Washington wanted to remain strictly neutral. He did agree to recognize the new government in France, however. Jefferson explained:

ACADEMIC VOCABULARY

deny to refuse

HISTORY'S VOICES

❝We surely cannot deny to any nation the right whereon our own government is founded, that every nation may govern itself according to whatever form it pleases.❞

— Thomas Jefferson, letter to Gouverneur Morris, 1792

Washington was convinced that the future growth and prosperity of the United States depended on staying neutral. In April 1793, he issued the **Neutrality Proclamation.** It committed the United States to "pursue a conduct friendly and impartial towards the belligerent powers." He held to the Neutrality Proclamation for the rest of his presidency.

Genet defies neutrality
Republican newspapers harshly attacked the president and the proclamation. They spread rumors that the Federalists wanted a return to monarchy. Then France's new ambassador to the United States, Edmund Genet, tried to convince ordinary American citizens to support the French. Pro-French mobs held street rallies. Eventually, Genet openly defied the Neutrality Proclamation. He enlisted an American crew to fight on a French ship against the British.

Washington, who had a quick temper, was furious. Even Jefferson thought that Genet had gone too far. Washington demanded that France replace Genet with a new ambassador.

More diplomatic challenges
For years, Jefferson had wanted to resign as secretary of state. Now Washington could no longer convince him to stay. Jefferson's departure meant that there was no one in the cabinet to balance Hamilton's point of view.

Then close on the heels of the French crisis came trouble with Britain. In early 1794 the British began to seize American merchant ships in the West Indies, claiming they carried French goods or were sailing to a French port. They threw the American sailors into prison.

In addition, in the Northwest Territory the British were stirring up trouble among the Native Americans.

Washington sent Chief Justice John Jay to negotiate with the British. In **Jay's Treaty** (1794), the British agreed to pay for damages to American ships. They also agreed to leave their forts, giving the United States control of the Northwest. In return, the United States agreed to pay debts owed the British.

Jay's Treaty was wildly unpopular. It did pave the way to settle another problem, however. Spain was now worried that the United States and Britain would unite against Spain in North America. This concern aided diplomat Thomas Pinckney in his negotiations with Spain. **Pinckney's Treaty** (1795) with Spain settled many border and trade disputes between the United States and Spain.

READING CHECK **Summarizing** Why did many Democratic-Republicans sympathize with the French revolutionaries?

Conflicts in the Northwest Territory

After the Revolution, settlers poured across the Appalachians into the western lands. The Land Ordinance of 1785 and the Northwest Ordinance established patterns for dividing and settling the Northwest Territory. This land, however, was already home to many Native American nations.

The government put pressure on Iroquois, Choctaw, Chickasaw, and Cherokee leaders, sometimes forcing them to sign treaties giving up land. Other Native American nations formed confederations to resist white settlement. In the early 1790s violence broke out in Ohio and Indiana. A large force of American soldiers moved in but were turned back by a confederation of Miamis and Shawnees. Their war chief was Michikinqua, or **Little Turtle**.

In 1791 Arthur St. Clair, the governor of the Northwest Territory, brought an army to

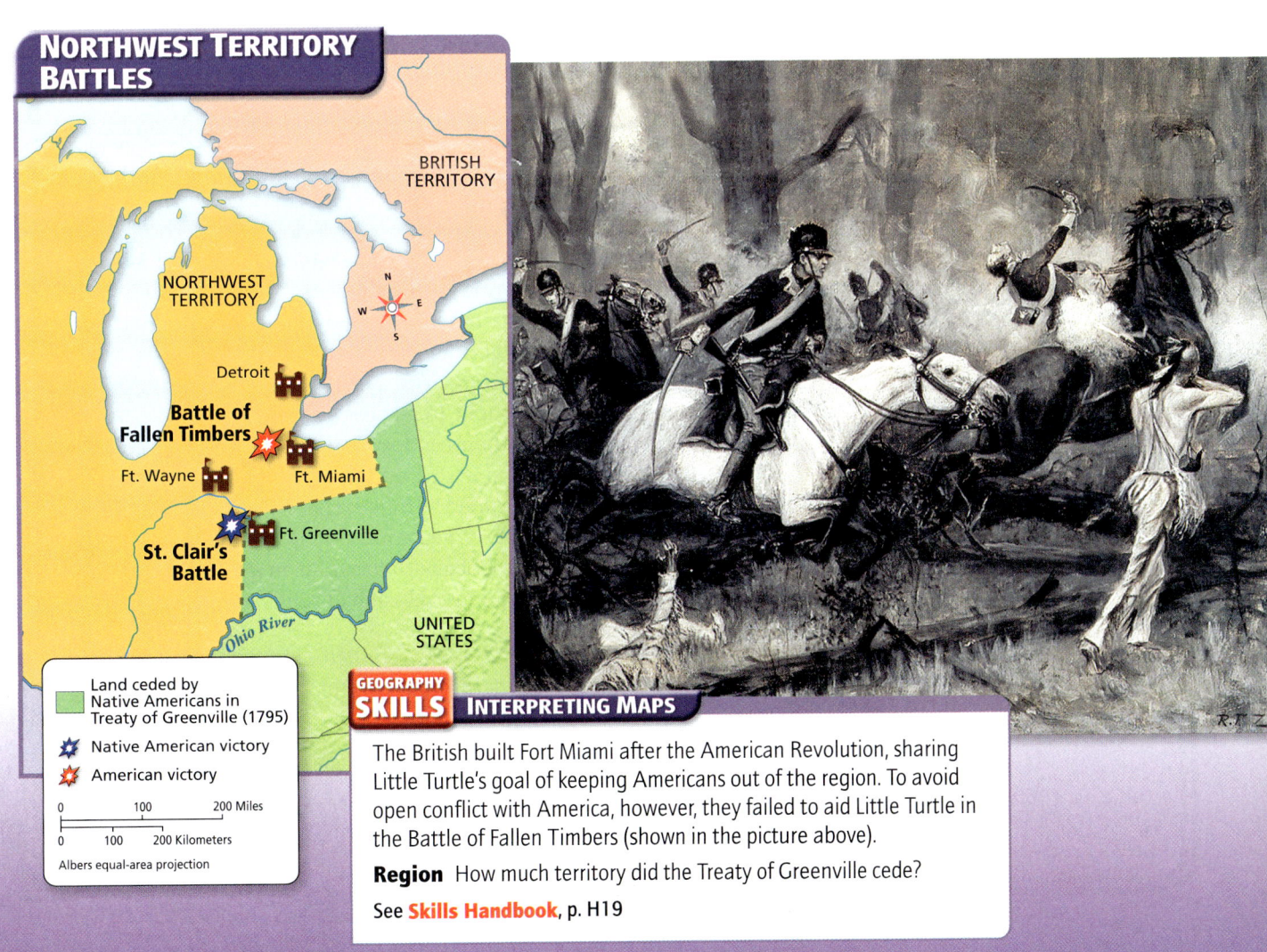

NORTHWEST TERRITORY BATTLES

BRITISH TERRITORY

NORTHWEST TERRITORY

Detroit

Battle of Fallen Timbers

Ft. Wayne

Ft. Miami

St. Clair's Battle

Ft. Greenville

Ohio River

UNITED STATES

Land ceded by Native Americans in Treaty of Greenville (1795)

★ Native American victory

★ American victory

0   100   200 Miles
0   100   200 Kilometers
Albers equal-area projection

GEOGRAPHY SKILLS **INTERPRETING MAPS**

The British built Fort Miami after the American Revolution, sharing Little Turtle's goal of keeping Americans out of the region. To avoid open conflict with America, however, they failed to aid Little Turtle in the Battle of Fallen Timbers (shown in the picture above).

Region How much territory did the Treaty of Greenville cede?

See **Skills Handbook**, p. H19

force the Miamis, Shawnees, and Delawares to give up their lands for settlement. In November 1791 Little Turtle and his forces met St. Clair's army and won the greatest victory Native Americans had ever achieved over white armies.

U.S. General Anthony Wayne, a hero of the Revolution, then brought some 4,000 troops into the Ohio Valley. There they built forts and brought in supplies. Little Turtle realized that he could no longer expect help from the British. He urged his people to negotiate with the Americans, but he lost their support.

At the **Battle of Fallen Timbers** in 1794, the American forces won a decisive victory over the Miamis. In the **Treaty of Greenville** (1795) the Miamis gave up large territories in Ohio and parts of Indiana, Illinois, and Michigan. The treaty also recognized the Miamis' claim to the land they still had. Little Turtle himself turned to trying to maintain peace.

READING CHECK **Making Inferences** What did the loss of British support mean for Indians in the Ohio Valley?

President Adams and the XYZ Affair

In 1792 Washington reluctantly agreed to a second term in office. He was getting older and his health was not good. He wanted only to go home to Mount Vernon. In addition, Washington was no longer the universally admired hero that he had been just a few years before. His insistence on neutrality was unpopular, and many of his policies were harshly criticized by ardent Democratic-Republicans.

By 1796 nothing could persuade Washington to consider a third term as president. His Farewell Address was a long letter published in a Philadelphia newspaper. In it he continued to warn against getting involved in party politics and foreign affairs.

The election of 1796 Even though some people criticized him harshly, Washington was still a unifying symbol for the country. With his retirement, the rivalry between the two parties became more intensely political.

PRIMARY SOURCES

Washington's Farewell Address

In 1796 George Washington announced that he would not seek a third term in office. In his Farewell Address, he gave his advice on several subjects of importance to the future of the country. Following are some of his comments regarding the role of religion and politics.

"Of all the dispositions [moods] and habits which lead to political prosperity, religion and morality are indispensable supports. In vain would that man claim the tribute of patriotism who should labor to subvert these great pillars of human happiness—these firmest props of the duties of men and citizens. The mere politician, equally with the pious [religious] man, ought to respect and to cherish them. A volume could not trace all their connections with private and public felicity [truth]. . . . And let us with caution indulge the supposition that morality can be maintained without religion. Whatever may be conceded to the influence of refined education on minds of peculiar structure, reason and experience both forbid us to expect that national morality can prevail in exclusion of religious principle."

Washington emphasized the influence of religion on moral and ethical behavior.

Skills FOCUS **READING LIKE A HISTORIAN**

1. **Comparing** According to Washington, what is the relationship between religion and morality?
2. **Analyzing Primary Sources** According to Washington, what is religion's role in building the country?

See **Skills Handbook**, pp. H10, H28–H29

Jefferson was the clear choice as the Democratic-Republican candidate. Although Hamilton was the most prominent Federalist leader, many of his plans, including the excise tax, were unpopular. Hamilton also had no interest in the presidency. So the Federalists chose John Adams as their candidate.

Since before the Revolutionary War, Adams had been an outstanding leader. He had played a major role in creating the United States and in handling diplomacy in Europe. But to some people, Adams seemed cold, distant, and not well suited for the presidency.

As a result, while the Federalists easily won a majority of presidential electors, Adams did not have their full support. **Sectionalism**, or loyalty to one's region, played a role. Adams was best known in New England. In the South, many Federalists preferred his running mate, Thomas Pinckney of South Carolina.

The vote of the electors revealed a serious flaw in the new Constitution. Adams won with only a few votes more than Jefferson: 71 to 68. According to the Constitution, that meant that Adams's vice president would be the candidate who came in second: Jefferson, his greatest political rival.

More problems with France

Relations with European nations were still a problem. Jay's and Pinckney's treaties had settled some conflicts with Britain and Spain. But Jay's Treaty made relations with revolutionary France more tense. French ships began to seize U.S. merchant vessels at sea. President Adams sent Charles Cotesworth Pinckney (older brother of Thomas) as the diplomatic representative of the United States, but the French turned him away. This was a serious insult.

Some angry Federalists wanted war. In 1797 Adams sent three distinguished American diplomats to France: Pinckney, Elbridge Gerry, and John Marshall. Again, the U.S. representatives were insulted. Rather than meeting with them, the French foreign minister, Prince Talleyrand, sent three minor diplomats who demanded bribes and a loan.

An angry President Adams sent a report to Congress, naming the three French agents as "X, Y, and Z." When the **XYZ affair** became public, many Americans wanted war. A popular slogan was: "Millions for defense but not one cent for tribute!"

FACES OF HISTORY

John ADAMS
1735–1826

John Adams entered Harvard College at the age of 15 and later became a respected lawyer. He rose to prominence as a Patriot during the Revolutionary War. Despite his good reputation, Adams was often critical of himself. When Thomas Jefferson pressed him to write the Declaration of Independence, Adams refused, insisting that he was "obnoxious, suspected, and unpopular." In reality, however, others respected him for his wisdom and honesty.

After serving as Washington's vice president, Adams was elected to the presidency. Although he strengthened the military and avoided war with Great Britain and France during his term, Adams's presidency is mainly remembered for its partisan conflict. Remarkably, Adams and Thomas Jefferson both died on July 4, 1826, the fiftieth anniversary of the adoption of the Declaration of Independence.

Summarize What characterized Adams's presidency?

Pulling back from outright war, Congress cut off trade with France. It canceled wartime treaties it had made with pre-revolutionary France, authorized building warships, and allowed the U.S. navy to capture French vessels at sea. Congress's actions persuaded the new French government, headed by a young general named Napoleon Bonaparte, to sign treaties on trade. The president and Congress had skillfully avoided a costly war with France.

Censoring free speech

Indignation over the XYZ affair brought new support for the Federalists. It also brought new suspicions about the Democratic-Republicans' pro-French sympathies and a general resentment of foreigners. That mood allowed Congress to pass measures aimed at protecting the country from foreign enemies and domestic dissent during what was expected to be a war with France.

The series of four laws are known as the **Alien and Sedition Acts**. The three alien laws were aimed mainly at French and Irish refugees, most of whom supported France. Those measures increased the period of residency required for citizenship from 5 years to 14; required foreigners to register with the government; and allowed the president to jail or expel any foreigner thought to be "dangerous to the peace and safety" of the country.

XYZ Affair

- France had attacked American merchant ships. French agents (referred to as X, Y, and Z) demanded bribes. The XYZ affair nearly brought France and the United States to war.

Alien and Sedition Acts (1798)

- The Alien Acts allowed the president to order foreigners considered to be a threat to national security to be jailed or deported.

- The Sedition Act made it a crime to speak against the government. Its target was the Democratic-Republicans, who historically had supported the French.

Virginia and Kentucky Resolutions (1798 and 1799)

- Some people saw the Alien and Sedition Acts as unconstitutional. The Virginia and Kentucky Resolutions nullified, or declared void, the Alien and Sedition Acts.

The Sedition Act outlawed any opposition to government policies by actions or by "false, scandalous, or malicious writing." In effect, it prohibited any criticism of public officials, a clear contradiction to the First Amendment rights of free speech and a free press.

Adams used the Alien and Sedition Acts cautiously. No aliens were deported, but nine Democratic-Republican newspaper editors and a member of Congress were convicted under the Sedition Act.

In an attempt to be rid of the hated laws, Jefferson and Madison drafted the Virginia and Kentucky Resolutions. In these resolutions, Jefferson and Madison argued that the Alien and Sedition Acts were unconstitutional.

They hoped that state legislatures would nullify the laws, or declare them void. Many supporters of states' rights believed that nullification of federal laws by states was legal. In the end, however, only Virginia and Kentucky passed the resolutions.

The end result of these actions was a deeper and more bitter political divide in Congress and the country. As you will read in the next section, Jefferson would eventually be elected president, and the new Congress would allow the Alien and Sedition Acts to expire.

READING CHECK **Identifying Cause and Effect** How did the XYZ affair lead to the Alien and Sedition Acts?

SECTION 2 ASSESSMENT

go.hrw.com
Online Quiz
Keyword: SD7 HP6

Reviewing Ideas, Terms, and People

1. **a. Recall** What major event occurred in France from 1789 to 1793?
   b. Compare How did Federalists and Democratic-Republicans react to the situation in France?
   c. Evaluate Was Edmund Genet's influence a threat to the United States? Why or why not?

2. **a. Identify** Who was Little Turtle?
   b. Summarize What happened in Ohio and Indiana as settlers moved into the Northwest Territory?

3. **a. Describe** How did Washington's retirement influence party politics?
   b. Explain What was the XYZ affair? How did it affect American public opinion?

c. Rate Were the Alien and Sedition Acts effective weapons against foreign interference and internal turmoil? Explain.

Critical Thinking

4. **Analyzing** Copy the chart below and list the important points of each of these three treaties.

Jay's Teaty	Pinckney's Treaty	Treaty of Greenville

FOCUS ON WRITING

5. **Supporting a Position** You are a journalist who has been arrested under the Sedition Act for criticizing President Adams. Write a speech defending your right to criticize the president.

Jefferson's Presidency

BEFORE YOU READ

MAIN IDEA

The rise of political parties influenced the election of 1800, bringing Thomas Jefferson and a new outlook to the presidency.

READING FOCUS

1. Why was the transfer of power in the election of 1800 significant?
2. What changes did Jefferson make when he took office?
3. What was the impact of the Louisiana Purchase?
4. How did the role of the Supreme Court change?

KEY TERMS AND PEOPLE

Aaron Burr
Twelfth Amendment
Louisiana Purchase
Lewis and Clark expedition
Meriwether Lewis
William Clark
Sacagawea
Zebulon M. Pike
Judiciary Act of 1801
judicial review

P1 1.1 Analyze the development of American culture, explaining how ideas, values, beliefs, and traditions have changed over time and how they united all Americans.

A TIED ELECTION

THE INSIDE STORY

Will Aaron Burr be president? Under the Constitution's plan for selecting a president, electors from each state voted for two candidates. The one with the most votes became president and the runner-up became vice president. This worked fine in the first election, because Washington was the unanimous choice. In 1796 the rise of political parties led to an uncomfortable situation. President John Adams, a Federalist, served with his political rival, Thomas Jefferson, as vice president. Politics became even more confusing in the bitterly contested election of 1800.

The Democratic-Republicans intended Jefferson to be president with Aaron Burr as vice president. In a close election, however, Jefferson and Burr each received 73 votes. A tied vote meant the House of Representatives would decide the outcome. Because Federalists were in control of the House until after the inauguration, they had to decide which Democratic-Republican they disliked less. Many despised and feared Jefferson. A few others, especially Alexander Hamilton, distrusted Burr even more.

The honorable thing for Burr to do was to concede to Jefferson, his party leader. But he did not. Over six days and nights, House members took vote after vote. Finally, on the 36th ballot, Jefferson won the presidency. Burr blamed Hamilton for his loss and never forgave him. ◢

▲ **Thomas Jefferson (left) won the election of 1800 against rival party candidate President John Adams (right) but first had to triumph over a member of his own party, Aaron Burr.**

The Election of 1800

The dawn of a new century brought many changes to the young American nation. One important political event was the presidential election of 1800. This contest marked the first time that power passed from one American political party to another.

The 1800 election matched Democratic-Republican Thomas Jefferson against Federalist John Adams, just as in the election of 1796. This time, however, **Aaron Burr** was the Democratic-Republican candidate for vice president and Charles Cotesworth Pinckney was the Federalist candidate. Each party believed that the republic's survival depended on the success of their

THE ELECTION OF 1800: POWER CHANGES HANDS

QUICK FACTS

Federalists

John Adams and Charles C. Pinckney

- Wanted a strong federal government
- Thought the country should be ruled by the elite
- Emphasized manufacturing
- Believed in loose interpretation of the Constitution
- Supported Great Britain

Democratic–Republicans

Thomas Jefferson and Aaron Burr

- Wanted a limited national government that shared power with state and local governments
- Believed the country should be ruled by ordinary citizens
- Emphasized agriculture
- Believed in strict interpretation of the Constitution
- Supported France

THE IMPACT TODAY

Daily Life

One famous example of negative campaigning is Lyndon Johnson's "daisy" TV ad of 1964. It featured a small girl with a daisy, fading to the image of a nuclear explosion. It was meant to raise fears that his opponent, Barry Goldwater, would risk nuclear war.

candidates. As a result, the campaign was vicious. Supporters of each side made their arguments in letters and newspaper editorials, which often made wild accusations and spread scandalous stories.

Federalists claimed that Jefferson was dangerously pro-French. They warned that if the Democratic-Republican candidate were in office, the violence and chaos of the French Revolution would follow. Federalists also accused Jefferson of wanting to destroy organized religion because of his interest in science and philosophy.

The Democratic-Republicans attacked the Federalists as well. Unpopular Federalist policies such as the Alien and Sedition Acts were easy targets for criticism. Democratic-Republicans also claimed that Adams wanted to crown himself king and that the Federalists would try to limit Americans' rights.

When the votes were counted, the election ended in a tie. At the time, political parties did not specify who was the party's preferred candidate for president. When Jefferson and Burr each received the same number of votes, an unprecedented electoral crisis began.

The Constitution made it clear that ties would be decided by the House of Representatives. But the House was deadlocked as well. Vote after vote took place, but each ended in a tie. Alexander Hamilton urged Federalists to

support Jefferson and finally, on the 36th vote, Jefferson was chosen as the third president of the United States.

The problems with the voting system led Congress to propose the **Twelfth Amendment**, which was ratified in 1804. This amendment said that electors must cast separate ballots for president and vice president.

Hard feelings over the election continued for years. Burr blamed Hamilton for his loss, and when Hamilton helped prevent Burr from being elected governor of New York, Burr challenged him to a duel. In July 1804 the duel was fought, and Hamilton died. The news shocked the country and ended Burr's political career.

READING CHECK **Drawing Conclusions**
How did the Alien and Sedition Acts hurt Federalists?

Jefferson Makes Changes

The election was finally decided just two weeks before inauguration day. Although both sides had bitterly fought, Jefferson's inaugural address urged unity and tolerance. He spoke of the special blessings that Americans enjoyed, and then said:

HISTORY'S VOICES

❝With all these blessings, what more is necessary to make us a happy and a prosperous people? Still one thing more, fellow-citizens—a wise and frugal government, which shall restrain men from injuring one another, shall leave them otherwise free to regulate their own pursuits of industry and improvement, and shall not take from the mouth of labor the bread it has earned.❞

—Thomas Jefferson, Inaugural Address, March 4, 1801

Jefferson considered his election victory the "revolution of 1800." His actions as president were not revolutionary, but he did succeed in reducing the size and influence of the federal government.

The members of Jefferson's cabinet shared his belief in a smaller government. His closest ally was James Madison of Virginia, who became secretary of state. Treasury Secretary Albert Gallatin had economic ideas that differed vastly from policies of the past.

Under the Federalists, Hamilton's economic plans had increased the level of public debt and established a federal tax system. In order to reduce the size of the government, the

Jefferson administration changed the tax system in 1802. With the new system, only customs duties and the sale of lands in the western United States produced revenue for the government. Gallatin also reduced the size of the executive department staff.

Jefferson did not think there should be a large standing army in peacetime, as the army could be a threat to civil liberties. Accordingly, he shrank the size of the army and navy, although he did help found the U.S. Military Academy at West Point in 1802.

The president later reversed course and began a naval buildup in response to the plight of merchants. Their ships started coming under attack from the so-called Barbary pirates from North Africa, who demanded tribute from U.S. merchant ships in the Mediterranean Sea.

READING CHECK **Making Inferences** How did cutting taxes fit with Jefferson's ideals?

The Louisiana Purchase

Many issues linked the United States with France. The new ruler of France was General Napoleon Bonaparte, who wanted to build a French empire. He hoped to regain France's former lands in North America to the west of the Mississippi River, a region called the Louisiana Territory. Those lands had gone to Spain in the Treaty of Paris in 1763. In 1800 in a secret treaty, Spain returned Louisiana to France along with the port city of New Orleans.

Jefferson had hoped that the United States could take control of Louisiana and New Orleans and was very concerned by this treaty. Access to New Orleans and the Mississippi River was vital to American commerce. In order to sell their products, farmers in the West needed to ship their goods down the Mississippi to New Orleans. In Pinckney's

ACADEMIC VOCABULARY

commerce purcase and sale of commodities

GEOGRAPHY SKILLS **INTERPRETING MAPS**

go.hrw.com
Practice Online
Keyword: SD7 CH6

1. **Movement** About how long was Lewis and Clark's route?
2. **Region** What new problems do you think the Louisiana Purchase might present for the United States and for Native Americans?

See **Skills Handbook**, p. H19

Westward Expansion

Of the 10 most populous cities in the United States today, six are in the West. Conquest of the West began with Spanish colonizers in the 1700s. Study the time line to learn about how the American West grew.

ST 2.3 Examine the effects of immigration on various Native American groups.

THE GRANGER COLLECTION, NEW YORK

1804–1806 With Sacagawea as a guide, Lewis and Clark traveled some 8,000 miles exploring the Louisiana Purchase. Fur trappers and settlers would soon follow.

1700

1700s Spanish colonizers built mission settlements in what are now Texas, New Mexico, and California.

Treaty, Spain had promised to protect American access to the river. In 1802, however, Spanish officials suddenly closed the lower Mississippi and New Orleans to American shipping. The officials soon turned over control of the area to France.

President Jefferson had to act quickly to protect American trade. He sent James Monroe to Paris to try to purchase New Orleans and West Florida. At the meeting, Monroe was stunned when French foreign minister Talleyrand offered to sell the United States all of the vast Louisiana Territory.

Napoleon had come to realize that controlling a North American empire might be difficult. The French colony of Haiti, in the Caribbean, had been taken over by enslaved Africans who revolted against French rule. Napoleon was afraid of future trouble in North America. He decided to abandon his claims in North America and to focus instead on waging war in Europe.

Jefferson had authorized James Monroe and Robert Livingston, the American ambassador, to buy only New Orleans, not all of Louisiana. But Monroe and Livingston did not have time to write to Jefferson for his approval, however, or Napoleon might change his mind. On April 30, 1803, they signed an agreement with France to buy the land. The final price of the territory included in the **Louisiana Purchase** was about 80 million francs, or $15 million. The purchase almost doubled the territory of the United States.

A constitutional puzzle The Louisiana Purchase was a remarkable bargain, but it raised many questions. Jefferson himself had to reconsider his long-held position in favor of strict construction of the Constitution. Jefferson believed that the Constitution should be interpreted based only on its precise meaning. Nowhere did the Constitution directly give Jefferson the authority to buy new territory for the nation, yet common sense told him that it was clearly a good idea.

Jefferson and his advisers finally decided that the right to acquire territory was implicit in the president's constitutional power to make treaties. Some Federalists in Congress, however, called the Louisiana Purchase unconstitutional. They also feared it would result in more states dominated by Democratic-Republicans. Yet even Hamilton agreed that the purchase was good for the country. Congress quickly approved it.

Lewis and Clark explore the West
Americans knew very little about the people and the land of this enormous new territory to the West. In fact, they did not even know the exact size and boundaries of the land they had purchased. Jefferson wanted to learn more

ACADEMIC VOCABULARY
implicit suggested or implied

1838–1839 To make room for white settlers, the United States forcibly relocated thousands of Native Americans from the East to Oklahoma.

1800

1900

1836 Narcissa Whitman and her husband, Marcus, were among the first settlers of Oregon Territory, where they founded a mission.

1930s Route 66 became a major migration path to California for Americans fleeing an economic disaster and catastrophic Midwest dust storms.

about the area. He also wanted to see if there was a river route that could be taken across the country to the Pacific Ocean.

Jefferson sent out a number of expeditions to explore the West and make contact with the Native Americans there. The most famous was the Corps of Discovery, usually called the **Lewis and Clark expedition**. Its leaders were **Meriwether Lewis**, Jefferson's secretary, and **William Clark**, an experienced frontiersman. Their ultimate goal was to reach the Pacific Ocean. Jefferson wanted Lewis and Clark to map the country and survey its natural history, including plants, animals, and landforms.

The expedition, made up of about 50 skilled frontiersmen, left St. Louis in May 1804 and traveled up the Missouri River. The men made their way west across the continent, over lands that they had never before seen. They paddled along raging rivers, trudged across plains and rugged mountains, and hiked through thick forests. Along the way, they acquired a valuable guide: a young Shoshone woman, **Sacagawea**, the wife of a French Canadian fur trapper.

In November 1805 the expedition finally reached the west coast of North America. Clark called the sight of the Pacific Ocean one of "the grandest and most pleasing prospects which my eyes ever surveyed."

The group spent the winter on the coast and started home in the spring, finally reaching St. Louis in September 1806. Jefferson was delighted to hear of the expedition's success. Many Americans had feared that the entire expedition had died along the way. In fact, only one man had died—of appendicitis.

Lewis and Clark had kept detailed journals of everything they encountered, including 120 species of plants and animals that they had never seen. They sent many boxes of specimens back to Jefferson. Other members of the expedition made notes and sketches.

After the exploration and further mapping of the territory, the United States claimed ownership of land extending as far to the southwest as the Rio Grande, in what is now Texas. These land claims would later lead to disagreement between the United States and Spain.

Another explorer in the West was a young army lieutenant, **Zebulon M. Pike**. His 1805 expedition traveled 2,000 miles to explore the upper Mississippi Valley, looking for the source of the river. In 1806 Pike's group traveled to the Southwest. They explored the Arkansas and Red Rivers and gathered information about the economy and defenses of Spanish New Mexico and Texas. Pike reported back that the central plains were too dry for settlement.

READING CHECK **Identifying Problems and Solutions** What constitutional question did the Louisiana Purchase raise?

Thomas JEFFERSON
1743–1826

Although Thomas Jefferson is well known today as the writer of the Declaration of Independence, few people knew it at the time. As president, Jefferson sought to smooth the discord that brought him to office, declaring, "We are all Republicans—we are all Federalists."

Jefferson was a man of many talents and contradictions. He was not only a politician but also a gifted architect, scholar, scientist, and writer. He was a poor public speaker, however, and preferred to communicate in writing. Even though he was a wealthy and educated Virginia planter, he truly believed in republican simplicity. He dressed casually, walked to his inauguration, and kept state dinners informal.

Explain How did Jefferson's actions reflect his beliefs?

The Role of the Supreme Court Changes

In the election of 1800 the Federalists had lost control of both the presidency and Congress. As a result, they tried to increase their hold on the third branch of government: the judiciary.

Federalist legislators in Congress passed the **Judiciary Act of 1801** shortly before their terms ended. This act created new positions in the judicial branch. Departing President John Adams hurried to fill them with Federalists.

Adams worked late into the night of March 3, 1801, to sign the commissions for these new judges. These documents had to be delivered to the new judges in order to make the appointments official. But not all were delivered before Jefferson took office the next day. James Madison, the new secretary of state, refused to deliver the remaining commissions to the so-called midnight judges.

One of the undelivered commissions was for William Marbury, who turned to the Supreme Court for help. He asked the Court to order Madison to deliver his commission.

The Court ruled that the Constitution only gave the Supreme Court the power to hear certain kinds of cases. The Constitution did not give the Court the power to force Madison to deliver Marbury's commission. Therefore, the Court said, the law that gave it that power—the Judiciary Act of 1789—was unconstitutional. *Marbury* v. *Madison* was important because it established the Supreme Court's right to declare that a law violates the Constitution. This power is known as **judicial review**.

READING CHECK **Making Inferences** Why did Adams appoint the midnight judges?

SECTION 3 ASSESSMENT

go.hrw.com
Online Quiz
Keyword: SD7 HP6

Reviewing Ideas, Terms, and People

1. **a. Recall** Why was the Twelfth Amendment passed?
   b. Summarize What were the issues in the election of 1800?
   c. Evaluate Why was the election important in American politics?

2. **a. Describe** What were Jefferson's goals in office?
   b. Contrast How were Adams and Jefferson different in manner and outlook?
   c. Evaluate Why do you think Jefferson urged unity and tolerance in his inaugural address?

3. **a. Identify** What roles did Lewis, Clark, Sacagawea, and Pike play in exploring the Louisiana Territory?
   b. Summarize How did the Louisiana Purchase come about?
   c. Elaborate Given Jefferson's strong feelings about strict construction, how could he justify the Louisiana Purchase?

4. **a. Recall** Who were the midnight judges?
   b. Analyze What were the main points of the Supreme Court's decision in *Marbury* v. *Madison*?

   c. Rate How did this decision relate to the system of checks and balances?

Critical Thinking

5. **Predicting** Copy the chart below and use it to show different ways in which the Louisiana Purchase would affect American government and society.

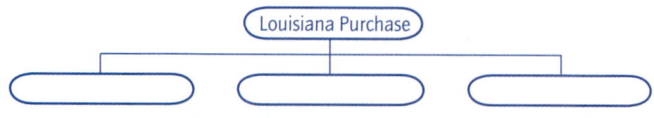

Louisiana Purchase

FOCUS ON WRITING

6. **Persuasive** As a political campaign worker in 1800, write a speech promoting the campaign of either Adams or Jefferson.

LANDMARK SUPREME COURT CASES

Constitutional Issue: Judicial Review

ST 1.2 Analyze the decisions leading to major turning points in United States history, comparing alternative courses of action, and hypothesizing, within the context of the historic period, about what might have happened if the decision had been different.

Marbury v. *Madison* (1803)

Why It Matters *Marbury* v. *Madison* established the Supreme Court's power to decide whether laws passed by Congress are constitutional. This power, known as judicial review, remains the central job of the Supreme Court today.

Background of the Case

In the fall of 1800, President John Adams rushed to sign commissions filling 58 new government positions with members of his own party before he left office. Adams's secretary of state, John Marshall, sealed the commissions but failed to deliver 17 of them. The new secretary of state, James Madison, refused to deliver some of these commissions. One of the men who did not receive his commission, William Marbury, brought suit in the Supreme Court. He claimed that the Judiciary Act of 1789 gave the Supreme Court the power to order Madison to deliver his commission.

THE IMPACT TODAY How the Supreme Court (shown in the artist's sketch above) interprets the Constitution through judicial review remains an issue in government today. As in Madison's day, the debate involves strict constructionists and loose constructionists.

The Decision

In *Marbury* v. *Madison*, the Supreme Court ruled that it did not, in fact, have the power to order Madison to deliver Marbury's commission. This is because the Constitution had designated the Supreme Court an appellate court. With very few exceptions, it hears only appeals from decisions issued by other courts. Although the Judiciary Act of 1789 had tried to expand the Supreme Court's powers, that expansion violated the Constitution and could not be allowed. John Marshall, then chief justice of the Supreme Court, explained this landmark decision:

> **"** It is emphatically the province and duty of the judicial department to say what the law is. **"**

In other words, *Marbury* v. *Madison* established that the Supreme Court has the authority to declare an act of Congress unconstitutional.

go.hrw.com
Research Online
Keyword: SS Court

CRITICAL THINKING

1. **Analyze the Impact** Using the keyword above, find *Federalist* No. 78. Read paragraphs 9 through 14. Did Hamilton anticipate the constitutional question decided in *Marbury* v. *Madison*? Would he have agreed with Marshall's opinion?

2. **You Be the Judge** Given what you have read about checks and balances in the Constitution, do you think it is important for the Supreme Court to have the power of judicial review? How might our government be different today if the Supreme Court did not have this power?

7. Reaching the Pacific Finding no ocean-going ships to take them home, the Corps spends the winter at Fort Clatsop before the long trip back.

4. Great Falls, June 1805 The Corps' boats are stopped by a series of great waterfalls. Two wagons made on the spot are loaded with canoes and baggage and pulled over 18 miles.

Columbia River

PACIFIC OCEAN

6. Canoe Camp, September–October 1805 A Nez Percé chief shows Clark how to use fire to hollow out canoes. The Columbia River and its tributaries now carry the Corps to the Pacific.

5. Over the Rockies With horses carrying their baggage, the Corps struggles through snowstorms over the steep trails. On September 17, they reach their highest point, 7,032 feet above sea level.

Lewis and Clark's Journey to the Pacific

"Your mission is to explore the Missouri river [to locate] the most direct and practicable water communication across this continent," President Thomas Jefferson wrote to Meriwether Lewis in 1803. Under orders to map a route across the Louisiana Purchase, Lewis and Clark and the Corps of Discovery traveled up the Missouri River, across the Rocky Mountains, and down rivers to reach the Pacific Ocean. Along the way, they met Native Americans and cataloged geography, plants, and animals. Their mission stands as one of history's greatest explorations.

GEOGRAPHY FACTS

- The expedition traveled about 8,000 miles. Today the trip by car would be about 4,300 miles.
- It took 53 days for the expedition to travel 250 miles across the Rocky Mountains.
- The expedition discovered and described new species including: 10 plants, 11 birds, and 11 mammals.
- Lewis and Clark determined there was no all-water route across North America.

New York Standards

ST 4.3 Develop hypotheses about important events, eras, or issues.

3. Fort Mandan, Winter 1804–1805
The Corps spends a very cold winter with the Mandan people, surviving on their beans, corn, and squash. Sacagawea joins them as a Shoshone translator. Six canoes replace the large keelboat.

1. Camp Dubois, May 14, 1804
A 55-foot keelboat and two smaller pirogues carry the 44 members of the expedition, a Newfoundland dog, and supplies.

2. Council Bluffs, August 1804
Now entering the Great Plains, the Corps continues to pole, pull, row, and sail their boats upriver.

Missouri River

Journals Clark illustrated his descriptions with drawings like this one of the pheasant-tailed grouse.

GEOGRAPHY SKILLS **INTERPRETING MAPS**

go.hrw.com
Interactive Map
Keyword: SD7 CH6

1. **Human-Environment Interaction** Over the course of the trip, how did the environment affect the Corps' mode of travel?

2. **Region** Describe some of the different regions the Corps traveled through.

See **Skills Handbook**, p. H20

SECTION 4 — The War of 1812

BEFORE YOU READ

MAIN IDEA

In the early 1800s, Americans unified to face Great Britain in war once again and to battle resistance from Native Americans over attempts to seize their lands.

READING FOCUS

1. What violations of American neutrality led to the War of 1812?
2. How did Tecumseh resist American settlers?
3. How did the War of 1812 begin? How did the war affect the new nation?

KEY TERMS AND PEOPLE

impressment
Embargo Act
William Henry Harrison
Tecumseh
War Hawks
Andrew Jackson
Battle of New Orleans
Treaty of Ghent

PI 3.2 Research and analyze the major themes and developments in New York State and United States history (e.g., colonization and settlement; Revolution and New National Period; immigration; expansion and reform era; Civil War and Reconstruction; the American labor movement; Great Depression; World Wars; contemporary United States).

The Burning of the White House

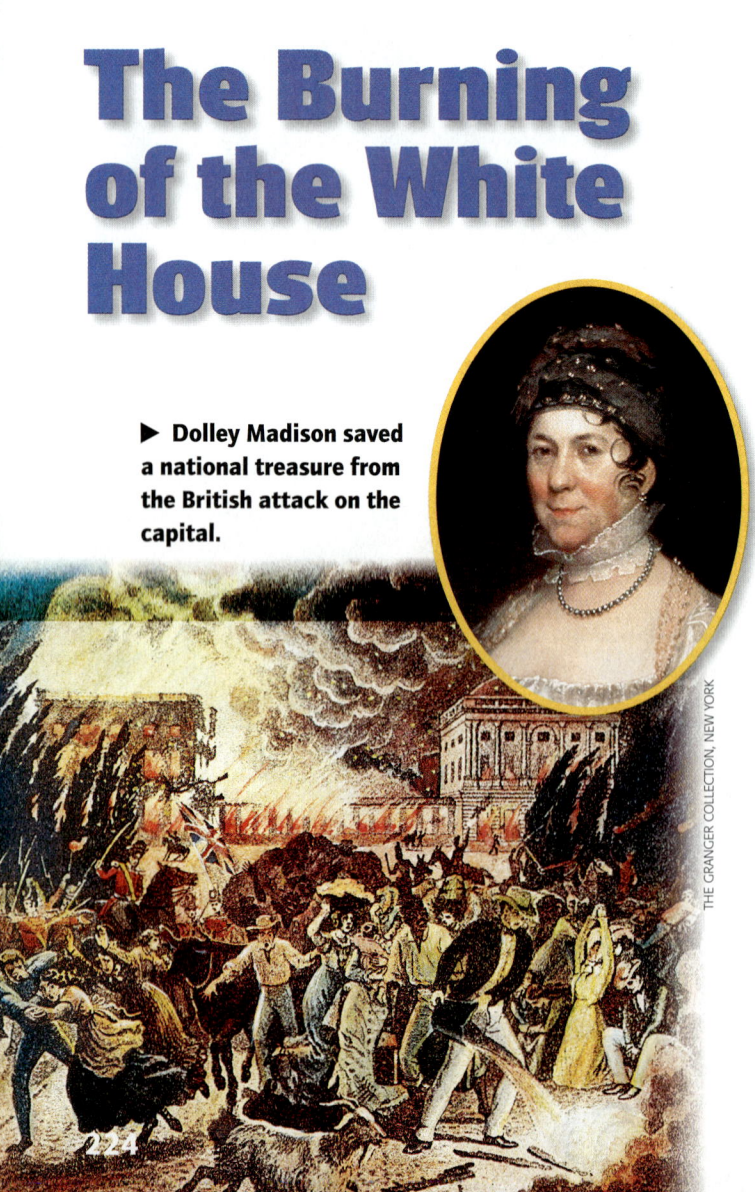

► Dolley Madison saved a national treasure from the British attack on the capital.

THE GRANGER COLLECTION, NEW YORK

THE INSIDE STORY

How did Dolley Madison save an American treasure? In August 1814 the British fleet sailed into Chesapeake Bay and headed toward Washington City. Few soldiers were left to defend the capital, and government officials fled as the British approached.

On August 23 James Madison left the President's House to be with the army in the field. He left his wife, Dolley, to look after herself and the government papers in his office. The next day the First Lady was alarmed to receive two hastily written notes telling her to prepare to flee the advancing attack.

By August 25 there was still no sign of the president. Finally, Dolley found a wagon, filled it with silver and other valuables, and sent them to safety at a bank. An impatient friend had to wait while she made one last brave gesture.

"I insist on waiting until the large picture of General Washington is secured, and it requires to be unscrewed from the wall." Finally, she had to break the picture frame and roll up the canvas.

The precious portrait saved, Dolley Madison fled the President's House. The British easily took the city and set fire to major buildings, including the White House. ◼

Violating Neutrality

How did the United States and Great Britain find themselves at war again so soon after the Revolution? Unresolved tensions between the two nations, both on the Northwest frontier and on the seas, caused the Americans and the British to lock in battle once again.

As early as 1803, the United States became caught in the middle of British trade disagreements. When the

Napoleonic Wars broke out between France and Great Britain, American merchant shipping was affected.

Then in 1806 and 1807, France and Britain tried to cut off each other's access to European ports. Both nations ignored American neutrality. If American ships sailed directly to Europe, the British navy might stop them. If ships stopped in Britain, the French would seize them. American captains saw the British as the more serious threat. One reason was the practice of **impressment**. Ordinary sailors in the Royal Navy were badly paid and brutally treated. To find crews, men were often impressed—kidnapped and forced to work on ships. Many deserted whenever they could.

British captains claimed they had the right to stop and search American ships for deserters. But while looking for British sailors, they often took Americans as well. In 1807 the British ship *Leopard* stopped the American frigate *Chesapeake*. When the Americans refused to let the ship be searched, the *Leopard* opened fire. The British then seized four Americans.

Americans were furious about the *Chesapeake* incident. To avoid war, President Jefferson proposed and Congress passed a drastic law. The **Embargo Act** prohibited exports to foreign countries. Many captains evaded the act, but the ban on trade was a disaster for the economy. Goods piled up in warehouses, ships sat in the harbors, people lost their jobs, and businesses failed.

The 1808 presidential election took place in the hard times after the hated Embargo Act. James Madison, Jefferson's ally, won easily. A new law reopened all trade except that with Britain and France. Still, conflicts over commerce were pushing the country toward war.

READING CHECK **Summarizing** What were the consequences of the Embargo Act?

Tecumseh Resists Settlers

Another factor leading to war was the ongoing conflict between settlers and Native Americans in the Northwest Territory. Things had been fairly quiet since the the Battle of Fallen Timbers. But as anti-British feelings grew in the United States, the British tried to rebuild their old alliances with Native Americans.

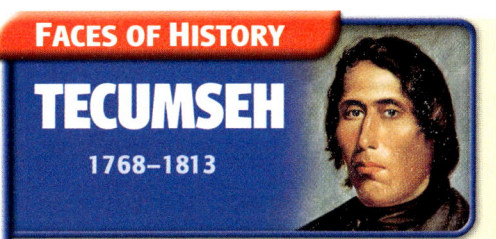

Born in present-day Ohio, Tecumseh tried to organize all Native Americans in opposition to the advancement of settlers. He believed that the land belonged to all Native Americans and that the United States had no right to take or purchase land from an individual tribe. Sadly, Tecumseh's efforts to unite Native Americans failed.

When the War of 1812 erupted, Tecumseh joined the British and was given the rank of brigadier general. He led a large group of Native Americans in the siege of Fort Meigs, defeating the American forces. However, Tecumseh died fighting in the Battle of the Thames when his forces were defeated by General William Harrison.

Summarize Describe Tecumseh's efforts against American settlers.

New policies **William Henry Harrison** was a Virginian who joined the army and fought in the Indian wars. He later became the Northwest Territory's delegate to Congress.

In 1800 Harrison was named governor of the new Indiana Territory. He was supposed to carry out President Jefferson's new Native American policy. Under this policy, Native Americans could choose either to become farmers and join white society or to move west of the Mississippi. As Harrison implemented the policy, Native Americans made treaties in which they lost millions of acres of tribal lands in Michigan, Indiana, and Illinois.

New Indian leaders Two Shawnee brothers emerged as leaders who could bring Native Americans together. One was a religious leader called the Prophet, or Tenskwatawa. Thousands came to hear him speak against white culture at Prophetstown, where the Wabash River met Tippecanoe Creek in present-day Indiana. He taught his followers to reject white culture.

Tecumseh, or Shooting Star, was the Prophet's brother and an inspiring leader. In 1809 he began to unite his brother's followers. But in 1811, while Tecumseh was away, Harrison's army attacked. Both sides suffered heavy losses, and Prophetstown was burned. The Battle of Tippecanoe made Harrison a national hero. He and Tecumseh would meet again.

READING CHECK **Making Inferences** Why did the British and Native Americans become allies?

ACADEMIC VOCABULARY
prohibited did not allow

The War of 1812 Begins

Ever since the incident with the *Chesapeake* and the *Leopard*, some American politicians had been calling for war. Known as **War Hawks**, most came from the western states. They were less concerned with world affairs than they were with frontier events. They hated the British and even hoped for a conquest of Canada.

War is declared Henry Clay, a leading War Hawk, became Speaker of the House in 1811. Under pressure from Congress, President Madison finally gave in. The United States declared war on Great Britain in June 1812.

The War of 1812 was fought on land and on sea, from Canada to Louisiana. Much of the war took place along the U.S.–Canadian border. The British also staged a massive blockade of the American coast and New Orleans.

Gains and losses The American navy won several surprising victories against the Royal Navy. In August 1812 the USS *Constitution* sank the British *Guerrière*. British gunfire bounced off the ship's oak hull, giving it the nickname Old Ironsides.

The naval war moved into the Great Lakes. Captain Oliver Hazard Perry hastily built new ships and gathered a small fleet. In September 1813 he anchored at the end of Lake Erie and waited for British ships to arrive. When the Battle of Lake Erie was over, Perry reported, "We have met the enemy and they are ours."

Soon after war was declared, American forces made several unsuccessful invasions of Canada. Tecumseh then joined the British in a campaign to capture Detroit and invade Ohio.

General Harrison, the hero of Tippecanoe, took command of U.S. forces in the Northwest Territory. After the American victory at Lake Erie, the British began a retreat from Detroit. Harrison's army followed them.

In October 1813, Harrison met British and Indian forces at the Battle of the Thames in

One surprising victory occurred when the British invaded Albany and the Hudson Valley. The U.S. Navy defeated a larger British squadron on Lake Champlain. This decisive victory halted the invasion and secured Lake Champlain for the United States.

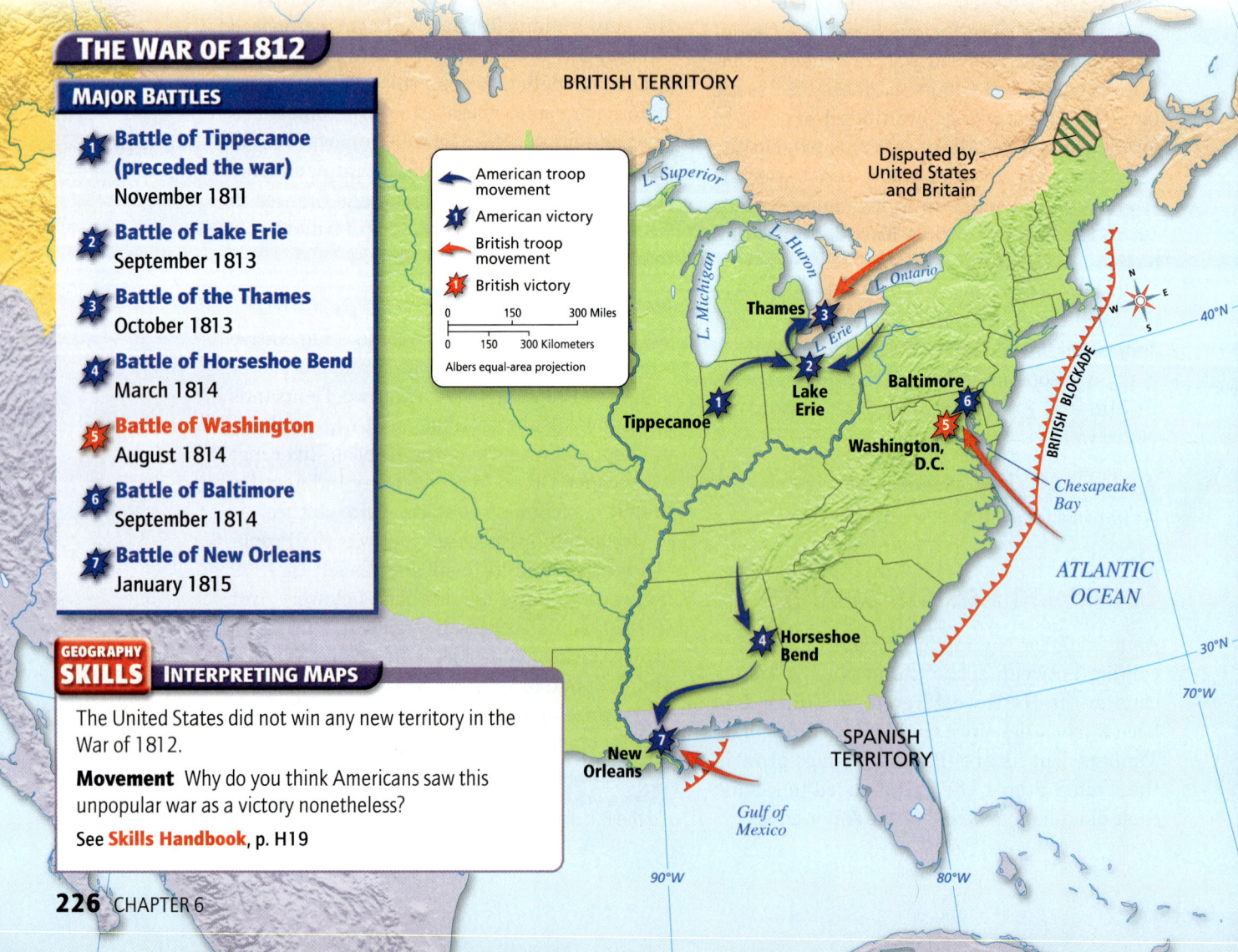

THE WAR OF 1812

MAJOR BATTLES

1. **Battle of Tippecanoe (preceded the war)**
   November 1811
2. **Battle of Lake Erie**
   September 1813
3. **Battle of the Thames**
   October 1813
4. **Battle of Horseshoe Bend**
   March 1814
5. **Battle of Washington**
   August 1814
6. **Battle of Baltimore**
   September 1814
7. **Battle of New Orleans**
   January 1815

American troop movement
American victory
British troop movement
British victory

0   150   300 Miles
0   150   300 Kilometers
Albers equal-area projection

BRITISH TERRITORY

Disputed by United States and Britain

L. Superior
L. Michigan
L. Huron
L. Ontario
L. Erie

Thames
Lake Erie
Tippecanoe
Baltimore
Washington, D.C.
Chesapeake Bay
Horseshoe Bend
New Orleans
SPANISH TERRITORY
Gulf of Mexico
ATLANTIC OCEAN
BRITISH BLOCKADE

40°N
30°N
70°W
90°W
80°W

GEOGRAPHY SKILLS INTERPRETING MAPS

The United States did not win any new territory in the War of 1812.

Movement Why do you think Americans saw this unpopular war as a victory nonetheless?

See **Skills Handbook**, p. H19

Ontario. The Americans outnumbered the enemy. Tecumseh was killed in the battle, ending the British–Native American alliance. Native Americans at once lost their greatest leader and their power in Ohio and Indiana.

Native Americans suffered another tragic loss in the South. There Tecumseh had organized the Creeks to resist settlers. Tennessee militia leader **Andrew Jackson** led a force against them. In March 1814, at the Battle of Horseshoe Bend, Jackson massacred Creek women, children, and warriors. He then seized the fort at Pensacola in Spanish Florida.

One British tactic was to make quick strikes against coastal cities. In August 1814 the British fleet sailed into Chesapeake Bay. Soldiers quickly marched to Washington, where they burned several major buildings.

The British then bombarded Fort McHenry, which guarded Baltimore harbor. After an overnight battle, a young lawyer, Francis Scott Key, was so overjoyed to see the American flag still flying that he started scribbling a poem that became America's national anthem: "The Star-Spangled Banner."

In the South, a British force landed near New Orleans in December. But Jackson got there first with an army of militia, pirates, and regular soldiers. In January 1815 the **Battle of New Orleans** made him a hero.

Treaty of Ghent By then, however, the peace treaty had been signed. In 1814 diplomats met in Ghent, Belgium, to finalize the **Treaty of Ghent**, which was signed in December. American and British diplomats were eager for peace. The Napoleonic Wars had been costly for England. In America, New Englanders were near rebellion over the war. No territory changed hands, but Americans had proved themselves as a nation.

 **READING CHECK** **Making Inferences** Why did the War Hawks want war?

CAUSES AND EFFECTS OF THE WAR OF 1812

CAUSES

- British impressment of American sailors
- International conflicts over commerce
- British military aid to Native Americans on the Northwest frontier

EFFECTS

- Britain and France gain respect for United States
- National pride grows
- U.S. manufacturing increases
- Native American resistance declines

SECTION 4 ASSESSMENT

go.hrw.com
Online Quiz
Keyword: SD7 HP6

Reviewing Ideas, Terms, and People

1. **a. Define** Explain the policy of **impressment** and its importance.
   b. Make Inferences What was the purpose of the **Embargo Act**?
   c. Evaluate Why were threats to merchant shipping a cause for war?

2. **a. Identify** What roles did **Tecumseh**, the Prophet, and **William Henry Harrison** play in the struggle for the western frontier?
   b. Summarize What was Jefferson's policy toward Native Americans in the Northwest Territory?
   c. Predict How did British and Native American alliances contribute to the move toward war?

3. **a. Define** What was the **Treaty of Ghent**?
   b. Analyze What losses did Native Americans suffer in the War of 1812?
   c. Evaluate Why did Americans see the end of the war as a victory?

Critical Thinking

4. **Identifying Cause and Effect** Copy the chart below and use it to make a time line of major battles in the War of 1812.

The War of 1812

1811   1812   1813   1814

FOCUS ON WRITING

5. **Persuasive** Prepare a speech for a debate in which you argue for or against going to war in 1812.

The First American Political Parties

Historical Context The documents below provide different perspectives on political parties in the federal period.

Task Examine the documents and answer the questions that follow. Then you will be asked to write an essay about the development of the first American political parties, using facts from the documents and from the chapter to support the position you take in your thesis statement.

ST 3.3 Compare and analyze the major arguments for and against major political developments in New York State and United States history.

ST 4.3 Develop hypotheses about important events, eras, or issues; move from chronicling to explaining historical events and issues; use information collected from diverse sources to produce cogently written reports and document-based essays.

DOCUMENT 1

In 1796 George Washington decided not to seek re-election for a third term as president of the United States. In his famous Farewell Address, Washington warned Americans to avoid divisions based on political parties and geography. Below is a short excerpt from his address.

"I have already intimated to you the danger of Parties in the State, with particular reference to the founding of them on Geographical discriminations. Let me now . . . warn you in the most solemn manner against the baneful effects of the spirit of Party, generally . . .

The alternate domination of one faction over another, sharpened by the spirit of revenge natural to party dissention . . . is itself a frightful despotism. . .

It serves always to distract the Public Council and enfeeble the Public Administration. It agitates the Community with ill founded jealousies and false alarms, kindles the animosity of one party against another, foments occasionally riot and insurrection."

DOCUMENT 2

In the election of 1800 between Thomas Jefferson and John Adams, presidential power was transferred between political parties for the first time in the young nation's history. The electoral vote was sharply divided along geographic lines, as the map below shows.

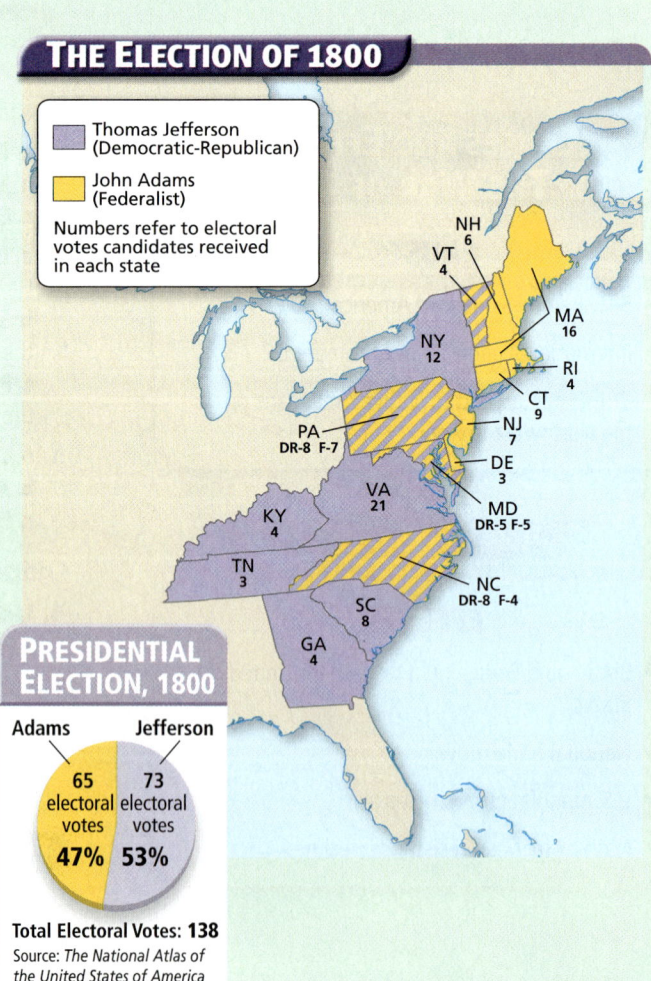

THE ELECTION OF 1800

- Thomas Jefferson (Democratic-Republican)
- John Adams (Federalist)

Numbers refer to electoral votes candidates received in each state

NH 6
VT 4
MA 16
NY 12
RI 4
CT 9
PA DR-8 F-7
NJ 7
DE 3
VA 21
MD DR-5 F-5
KY 4
TN 3
NC DR-8 F-4
SC 8
GA 4

PRESIDENTIAL ELECTION, 1800

Adams: 65 electoral votes 47%
Jefferson: 73 electoral votes 53%

Total Electoral Votes: 138

Source: *The National Atlas of the United States of America*

DOCUMENT 3

In 1798 one of the most controversial issues in the U.S. Congress was the passage of the Alien and Sedition Acts. The Federalist government believed that Democratic-Republican criticism of Federalist policies was disloyal and that foreigners, or aliens, would sympathize with France during war. The political cartoon below depicts Congress in 1798. Roger Griswold, a Federalist, is using his cane to attack Matthew Lyon, a Democratic-Republican, who is retaliating with tongs.

THE GRANGER COLLECTION, NEW YORK

DOCUMENT 4

The presidential campaign of 1800 was a bitter political struggle. Each party made accusations against the other. Democratic-Republicans believed the Federalist president John Adams wanted to turn the country into a monarchy. Federalists worried that Thomas Jefferson might have ties to revolutionary France. In Jefferson's Inaugural Address (1801), he called for the country to unite around common goals.

"Every difference of opinion is not a difference of principle. We have called by different names brethren of the same principle. We are all Republicans, we are all Federalists. If there be any among us who would wish to dissolve this Union or to change its republican form, let them stand undisturbed as monuments of the safety with which error of opinion may be tolerated where reason is left free to combat it . . .

Let us, then, with courage and confidence pursue our own Federal and Republican principles, our attachment to union and representative government."

Skills FOCUS READING LIKE A HISTORIAN

1. **a. Identify** Refer to Document 1. Name three ways Washington believed political parties could negatively affect the nation.
   b. Interpret Why might Washington have considered political parties based on geography to be dangerous?

2. **a. Identify** Refer to Document 2. According to the pie graph, what percentage of electoral votes did Jefferson receive? What percentage did Adams receive?
   b. Analyze What regional voting pattern can you identify using the map?

3. **a. Describe** Refer to Document 3. How does this cartoon characterize the political divisions in the United States in 1798?
   b. Analyze Why did the Democratic-Republicans

respond so strongly against the Sedition Act? Why did the Federalists believe it was necessary?

4. **a. Recall** Refer to Document 4. What does Jefferson believe about political parties?
   b. Analyze Why might Jefferson have made this plea for unity in his inaugural address?

5. **Document-Based Essay Question** Consider the question below and form a thesis statement. Using examples from Documents 1, 2, 3, and 4, create an outline and write a short essay supporting your position.
   Explain and analyze the development of the first American political parties during the period 1794–1801. Did the presence of political parties help or harm the nation?

See **Skills Handbook**, pp. H21, H28–H29, H31

Visual Summary: Forging the New Republic

Government
- President Washington forms his cabinet.
- Judiciary Act of 1789 establishes the Supreme Court. *Marbury* v. *Madison* defines the Court's role.
- Congress creates the Bank of the United States.

Conflicts
- Native Americans fight against white settlement in Northwest Territory.
- United States and Great Britain fight the War of 1812.

Forging the New Republic

Expansion
- Louisiana Purchase roughly doubles the size of the United States.
- Lewis and Clark explore the west.

THE GRANGER COLLECTION, NEW YORK

Reviewing Key Terms and People

Complete each sentence by filling the blank with the correct term or person.

1. The idea that the powers of the central government should be limited to those specifically spelled out in the Constitution is called _____.

2. The Secretary of State, the Secretary of War, and the Secretary of the Treasury made up President Washington's _____.

3. The _____ set up the Supreme Court with one chief justice and five associates.

4. Loyalty to one's geographic region, sometimes more than to one's country, is called _____.

5. The idea that state legislatures can decide not to follow laws passed by the central government is called _____.

6. _____ led Native American forces in the Battle of Tippecanoe.

7. _____ is the right of the Supreme Court to declare that a law violates the Constitution.

8. _____ states that the central government can do certain things as long as the Constitution does not specifically prohibit them.

9. Jefferson's vice president, _____, killed Alexander Hamilton in a duel.

10. _____ tried unsuccessfully to resist the expansion of American settlement in the Northwest Territory.

11. The War of 1812 was ended by the _____.

12. _____ commanded American troops at the Battle of New Orleans.

13. _____ was the act of kidnapping men and forcing them to work on ships.

Comprehension and Critical Thinking

SECTION 1 *(pp. 202–208)*

14. a. **Identify** What roles did Pierre Charles L'Enfant and Benjamin Banneker have in the creation of Washington, D.C.?

History's Impact video program

Review the video to answer the closing question: How has the American spirit of exploration affected the history of the nation?

b. Contrast What were the main differences between the Federalists and the Democratic-Republicans?

c. Predict How would President Washington's actions during the Whiskey Rebellion help determine the actions of presidents facing similar situations in the future?

SECTION 2 *(pp. 209–214)*

15. a. Recall Why were Americans generally sympathetic to France after the French Revolution? Why did those sympathies change to hostility?

b. Summarize How did the U.S. government respond to the XYZ affair?

c. Evaluate Should a democratic government be allowed to pass a law like the Sedition Act? Why or why not?

SECTION 3 *(pp. 215–220)*

16. a. Identify What changes did Jefferson make during his presidency?

b. Analyze In what ways was Federalist opposition to the Louisiana Purchase an example of party politics?

c. Evaluate Defend this statement: "The Supreme Court should have the right to declare that a law violates the Constitution."

SECTION 4 *(pp. 224–227)*

17. a. Describe What British actions helped trigger the War of 1812?

b. Make Inferences Why did Native Americans resist Jefferson's policy for Indian affairs?

c. Evaluate What was ultimately accomplished by the War of 1812?

Using the Internet

go.hrw.com
Practice Online
Keyword: SD7 CH6

18. The War of 1812 was the new country's first war against a European nation. Using the keyword above, do research to learn more about this war. Pick one topic related to the war and create a detailed report on this element or event in the conflict.

Analyzing Primary Sources

Reading Like a Historian When Native Americans in the Northwest Territory were being forced to give up their land in the early 1800s, Tecumseh mourned for his people:

❝ The Great Spirit gave this great island to his red children. He placed the whites on the other side of the big water. They were not contented with their own, but came to take ours from us. They have driven us from the sea to the lakes—we can go no farther. ❞

—Tecumseh, Shawnee leader

19. Identify What is "the big water"?

20. Interpret What does Tecumseh mean by "they have driven us from the sea to the lakes"?

Critical Reading

Read the passage in Section 1 that begins with the heading "Political parties develop." Then answer the following question.

21. In the third paragraph the passage reads: "Each sides justified its actions as necessary to resist the dangerous ideas of the other." Here the word *justified* means

A. claimed to be proper.

B. denied.

C. invented.

D. told many people about.

WRITING FOR THE SAT

Think about the following issue.

In his Farewell Address, George Washington warned the new nation to beware of party politics and involvement in the affairs of foreign countries.

22. Assignment Was Washington right or wrong about the danger of party politics and involvement in the affairs of other countries? Write a short essay in which you develop your position on these questions. Support your view with logical reasoning, examples from your reading, and current events.

The Revolutionary Era
1763–1783

MAIN IDEA Angered by a series of new British laws, the colonists fought the Revolutionary War and eventually gained independence from Great Britain.

SECTION 1 The British Parliament passed the Stamp Act, Sugar Act, Quartering Act, and other laws to raise money in the colonies. The colonists rebelled, claiming Great Britain had no right to tax them without colonial representation in Parliament.

SECTION 2 With the Declaration of Independence, drafted by Thomas Jefferson, the colonists declared their independence from Great Britain in 1776.

SECTION 3 The Revolutionary War proved costly for both sides. Facing a better trained and equipped British army, the colonists relied on strong leadership and a fierce belief in their cause to sustain them until key victories began to turn the tide.

SECTION 4 Fighting ceased in October 1771, and the Treaty of Paris was signed in 1783, granting American independence and setting the Mississippi River as the western boundary of the United States.

Creating a New Government
1776–1789

MAIN IDEA Creating a new American government proved to be a difficult task. The first national constitution, the Articles of Confederation, had many weaknesses. At the Constitutional Convention, American leaders worked to build compromises between the states.

SECTION 1 The Articles of Confederation established a weak central government and left a good deal of power in the hands of individual states. Unable to impose taxes or settle disputes between the states, the Confederation government was largely ineffective.

SECTION 2 After the Articles of Confederation failed to establish an effective national government, delegates to the Constitutional Convention met to draft a new constitution. Key compromises between small and large states helped delegates agree upon the U.S. Constitution, which created a federal system of government and balanced the power of the national government among three branches.

SECTION 3 Federalists and Antifederalists began heated debates over the Constitution. Eventually, the addition of the Bill of Rights led to ratification. The Bill of Rights is the term for the first 10 amendments to the Constitution.

Forging the New Republic
1789–1815

MAIN IDEA In its early years, the United States faced many challenges, including the emergence of political parties and conflicts with Native Americans and Great Britain.

SECTION 1 George Washington became the first president of the United States in 1789. Disputes over the National Bank and differing views on the proper interpretation of the Constitution led to the emergence of political parties.

SECTION 2 As president, Washington maintained American neutrality in European conflicts. However, violence broke out in the western frontier in response to American settlement in Native American territory.

SECTION 3 Thomas Jefferson became president in 1800. Among his accomplishments was the Louisiana Purchase, which doubled the size of the United States in 1803.

SECTION 4 British impressment of American sailors, disputes over trade, and conflicts in the Northwest Territory led to the War of 1812. The Treaty of Ghent ended the war in 1814. The United States had proven itself as a nation once again.

Developing a National Identity

Themes

Cultural Expressions
Americans took pride in their new nation and eagerly sought to change their lives and society through religious movements and reforms in education and other institutions.

Immigration and Migration
European immigrants flooded eastern cities, and Americans increasingly migrated to the western regions of the country.

Economic Development
The growth of factories and manufacturing established the North as an industrial power, while southern economies continued to rely mainly on agriculture.

An early steam locomotive powers a railroad in New Jersey, one of the first railroads in the country.

233

Making Inferences

Find practice for **Making Inferences** in the **Skills Handbook,** p. H7

Often meaning is implied, or hinted at in a text. When meaning is implied, good readers connect facts with their own experiences to make inferences.

Before You Read
Skim the text to determine what it will be about. Then think about what you already know about the subject.

While You Read
Note ideas directly stated in the reading, as well as those that may be implied.

After You Read
Review ideas expressed in the text and make connections to your prior knowledge. What can you infer from or about the text?

The revolution spreads

Throughout the early and middle 1800s, industrialization spread slowly from the textile to other industries in the North. In the 1830s, steam engines became better and more widely available, and their power helped make the textile industry the fastest growing part of the American economy.

Industrialization in the North led to the urbanization of the North. People left the farm and moved to cities where they could work in the mills and factories. In 1820, only 7 percent of Americans lived in cities. Within 30 years, the percentage more than doubled.

The North underwent a dramatic and rapid change. In a few decades, it evolved from a region of just small towns and farms into one including large cities and factories—all as a result of the Industrial Revolution.

READING CHECK **Making Inferences** How did industrionalization change peoples' ways of life?

Implied Industrial jobs in the North offered greater opportunities than rural jobs.

Directly stated Between 1820 and 1850 the number of Americans living and working in northern cities more than doubled.

Test Prep Tip

Tests often contain passages from which you may be asked to infer meaning, such as future events or an author's purpose. Because making inferences means choosing the most likely explanation from the facts available, try to balance information in the text with prior knowledge so that you arrive at the most informed inference.

Reading like a Historian

Interpreting Visuals

Find practice for **Interpreting Visuals** in the **Skills Handbook,** p. H30

Visuals such as photographs, illustrations, advertisements, or political cartoons are an important part of the historical record. These sources provide rich detail about historical events and the people who participated in them. The first **historical photographs** date from the invention of photography around 1830.

Strategies historians use:

- Identify the subject. Look for captions. Who or what is being portrayed?
- Some historical photographs are staged or posed. Others show people as they are. Both types contain important information.
- Study the visual details. What do they tell you about the image historical context?

The row of tiny houses indicates the living conditions of the people pictured.

The people in this photograph are not posing. The photo is probably an accurate record of life.

Enslaved African Americans at rest on a Sunday in 1860.

The caption tells you what the subject of this picture is.

Skills FOCUS READING LIKE A HISTORIAN

As You Read Examine the historical photographs. Describe what they depict. How do photographs support the text? How do the photographs help you understand the material?

As You Study Compare historical photographs of different scenes and events. Look for details that will indicate historical context.

CHAPTER 7

1815–1840

From Nationalism to Sectionalism

THE BIG PICTURE The War of 1812 filled Americans with national pride and confidence in the future. Yet against the backdrop of an emerging national identity, two distinct economic systems were developing in the North and South. Nationalism gave way to sectionalism as the two sections disagreed over various issues such as slavery.

New York Standards

Key Idea 1 The study of New York State and United States history requires an analysis of the development of American culture, its diversity and multicultural context, and the ways people are unified by many values, practices, and traditions.

Key Idea 3 Study about the major social, political, economic, cultural, and religious developments in New York State and United States history involves learning about the important roles and contributions of individuals and groups.

 Skills FOCUS READING LIKE A HISTORIAN

Americans have been celebrating Independence Day ever since they first declared their freedom in 1776. Here they are shown celebrating in *Fourth of July at Centre Square, Philadelphia, 1819*, by John Lewis Krimmel. **Interpreting Visuals** How do you think the painting illustrates a spirit of nationalism?

See Skills Handbook, p. H30

COURTESY THE PENNSYLVANIA ACADEMY OF THE FINE ARTS, PHILADELPHIA

U.S.

March 1816 James Monroe is elected president.

1815

World

1815 Napoleon is defeated at the Battle of Waterloo.

History's Impact video program

Watch the video to understand the impact of economic change.

1820
The Missouri Compromise admits one free state and one slave state into the Union.

1823
The Monroe Doctrine warns European powers away from the Americas.

1828
Andrew Jackson is elected president.

May 1830
The Baltimore & Ohio Railroad opens.

1838
U.S. troops begin the forced removal of the Cherokee people from Georgia along the Trail of Tears.

1840
Samuel F. B. Morse patents the telegraph.

1820

1825

1830

1835

1840

1821
Mexico wins independence from Spain.

1825
Bolivia, named for South American liberator Simón Bolívar, gains its independence.

1832
British Reform Act gives urban centers more power.

1833
Slavery is outlawed in the British Empire.

1837
Queen Victoria begins her reign in the United Kingdom.

The Rise of Nationalism

BEFORE YOU READ

MAIN IDEA

Nationalism contributed to the growth of American culture and influenced domestic and foreign policies.

READING FOCUS

1. What were the characteristics of the new American culture?
2. How did nationalism influence domestic policy?
3. How did nationalism guide foreign policy?
4. What was the Missouri Compromise?

KEY TERMS AND PEOPLE

Alexis de Tocqueville
Noah Webster
nationalism
sectionalism
McCulloch v. *Maryland*
James Monroe
John Quincy Adams
Adams-Onís Treaty
Monroe Doctrine
Missouri Compromise

PI 1.1 Analyze the development of American culture, explaining how ideas, values, beliefs, and traditions have changed over time and how they united all Americans.

A Bold Move

▲ **Lady Liberty and the liberty cap and pole she carries were powerful revolutionary symbols that citizens of the young nation could rally behind.**

THE INSIDE STORY

How did the United States defy the monarchs of Europe?
Between 1803 and 1815, a series of wars fought by or against France under the French emperor, Napoleon, had seriously threatened the monarchies of Europe. Soon after Napoleon's defeat in 1815, the major European powers, including Great Britain and Russia, formed a loose alliance known as the Concert of Europe. Their goals were to keep a balance of power in Europe and to suppress revolutionary ideas.

At the same time, revolutions were breaking out in South America, as colonies declared their independence from Spain. Although the United States declared neutrality, it supplied the rebels with ships and supplies. In 1822 President James Monroe was the first to give diplomatic recognition to the new nations. But both Great Britain and the United States were worried that France would send troops to reconquer Spain's colonies.

John Quincy Adams, Monroe's secretary of state, was an experienced diplomat who had been living abroad since he was a teenager. He was worried about territorial threats from other European nations. Russia, for example, claimed much of the Pacific Coast of North America. Adams wanted to stand up to the monarchs of Europe. He declared "that the American continents are no longer subjects for any new European colonial establishments." He also said that the United States should act on its own, instead of following like "a [rowboat] in the wake of a British man-of-war." Those brave words led to the statements made in the Monroe Doctrine, which declared the Americas off limits to European colonization. ■

A New American Culture

The Monroe Doctrine was a bold statement. After all, the United States was still a very young nation in 1823. Moreover, the population of the country was a tiny fraction of what it would become. There were fewer than 10 million Americans at the time. The overwhelming majority of them still lived in rural areas along or near the East Coast. The largest city, New York, was home to only about 120,000 people. The next largest cities, Philadelphia and Baltimore, were about half that size. But the young country was growing rapidly.

A country "in constant motion" Americans were hard at work building their new nation. As they went about their lives, they slowly developed their own unique culture. Culture is the ways of life of a particular group of people. It includes the group's language, art, music, clothing, food, and other aspects of daily life. The rise of a distinctly American culture during the early 1800s is important because the culture that developed then still influences the way Americans live today.

One of the most insightful observers of the emerging American culture was the French philosopher **Alexis de Tocqueville**. In his book *Democracy in America*, Tocqueville wrote of the seemingly limitless energy of Americans. He keenly observed that

HISTORY'S VOICES

❝[Americans] all consider society as a body in a state of improvement . . . in which nothing is, or ought to be, permanent . . . America is a land of wonders, in which everything is in constant motion and every change seems an improvement.❞

—Alexis de Tocqueville, *Democracy in America*

Instead of imitating European cultures, as they had done for generations, Americans began doing things in a distinctly American way. A new American culture was emerging.

American art and literature The rise of American culture was especially significant in the worlds of art and literature. Before the 1800s, American artists and writers were paid little respect, even by their fellow Americans. That changed with the emergence of talented Americans whose work honored American life.

In 1825 the painter Thomas Cole helped establish the Hudson River school, a group of artists whose landscapes both depicted and celebrated the American countryside. The works of Cole and other American artists came to be admired in both America and Europe.

ACADEMIC VOCABULARY

generation the average length of time between the birth of parents and that of their offspring

A New American Style of Art

The first uniquely American style of art began with the Hudson River school, a group of landscape artists inspired by the wilderness of the Hudson River Valley. Their paintings reflected pride in the grandeur of the American landscape. *A View of the Mountain Pass Called the Notch of the White Mountains (Crawford Notch)* was painted by Thomas Cole around 1839.

The notch that is the subject of this painting allowed travelers to pass through a New Hampshire mountain range.

A tree stump was a common symbol of the Hudson River school—a reminder of the fragility of life.

People, although depicted tiny in scale, were always linked to the land.

▲ **James Monroe,** president from 1817 to 1825, secured the nation's borders with the Monroe Doctrine.

▲ **John Quincy Adams,** as secretary of state under Monroe, extended the territory of the United States. He became the nation's sixth president.

▲ **John Marshall,** chief justice of the United States from 1801 to 1835, established the supremacy of federal law over state law.

▲ **John C. Calhoun** served as Monroe's secretary of war, as vice president twice, and as a member of Congress. He was a dominant political figure and a strong advocate of states' rights.

▶ **Henry Clay** was a passionate nationalist during the several decades he spent in Congress. He proposed the American System to help unify the young nation.

American authors also gained respect in the early 1800s. Three writers in particular—Washington Irving, James Fenimore Cooper, and William Cullen Bryant—proved that Americans could create literature and that people on both sides of the Atlantic would respect American works.

Even Americans' unique version of the English language earned respect. In 1828 this new American English was published by lexicographer **Noah Webster** in *An American Dictionary of the English Language.* Webster's dictionary defined thousands of words that had never been included in a dictionary before. Clearly, Americans were forming a new culture—with a language all its own.

READING CHECK **Making Inferences** Why do you think Europeans initially held little respect for American writers and painters?

Nationalism Influences Domestic Policy

As a uniquely American culture developed, so too did a sense of nationalism. **Nationalism** is the belief that the interests of the nation as a whole are more important than regional interests or the interests of other countries. A spirit of nationalism replaced the tendency toward **sectionalism,** or the belief that one's own section, or region, of the country is more important than the whole.

In the early 1800s, feelings of nationalism swept the country. These feelings were soon reflected in government policies.

John Marshall John Marshall served as chief justice of the United States from 1801 until 1835—longer than any other chief justice. Marshall was a firm believer in the importance of a strong national government. His Court made two key rulings that both reflected growing feelings of nationalism and promoted nationalism by strengthening the national government.

Two key rulings In 1819 the case of *McCulloch* v. *Maryland* came before the Supreme Court. The case pitted the State of Maryland against the national government. In his ruling, Chief Justice Marshall sided with the national government. He made it clear that national interests were to be put above state interests. You can read more about *McCulloch* v. *Maryland* at the end of this section.

In 1824 the Marshall Court issued another ruling that enhanced the national government's power over the states. This case involved the cutting-edge transportation technology of the day: steamboats.

Rival steamboat companies were operating in New York. Aaron Ogden had received permission from the State of New York to run his business. Thomas Gibbons had a license from the national government to run his. Gibbons sued Ogden, and the case of *Gibbons* v. *Ogden* went to the Supreme Court.

Marshall's court ruled in favor of Gibbons, who was licensed by the national government. Thus, Marshall again declared that national law was superior to state law. Marshall further declared that the Constitution gives the national government the sole right to regulate interstate commerce, or trade between states.

In these two rulings, John Marshall's Supreme Court established the power of the national government over state governments. In matters of the Constitution, therefore, nationalism had triumphed over sectionalism.

The American System
Perhaps the most nationalistic domestic policy of the early 1800s was a plan championed by Henry Clay, the speaker of the U.S. House of Representatives. His plan was called the American System. The American System sought to implement several policies to unify the young country. These policies included a tariff to protect American industries, the sale of government lands to raise money for the national government, the maintenance of a national bank, and government funding of internal improvements or public projects such as roads and canals.

The American System was never implemented as a unified policy, although the national government did establish tariffs and a bank. But the fact that it was proposed and partially put in practice demonstrates how nationalist feelings and a desire to tie the country together were very much on the minds of Americans of the early 1800s.

READING CHECK **Identifying the Main Idea**
What domestic policies in the early 1800s promoted nationalism?

Nationalism Guides Foreign Policy

American foreign policy in the early 1800s reflected the feelings of nationalism that spread through the nation. Americans were proud of their victory in the War of 1812 and confident in the strength of their young but growing country. They were determined to take their place on the world stage.

The Era of Good Feelings
In 1816 voters elected **James Monroe** to the presidency. As president, Monroe would serve from 1817 to 1825. During his presidency, the economy grew rapidly, and a spirit of nationalism and optimism prevailed. One Boston newspaper called the time the "Era of Good Feelings."

Diplomatic successes
The good feelings at home were matched by successful diplomacy abroad. Monroe's administration achieved a series of brilliant diplomatic successes that helped secure the territory and borders of the United States.

In 1818 the United States concluded the Rush-Bagot Treaty with Britain. The treaty provided for the nearly complete disarmament of the eastern part of the border between the United States and British Canada. Monroe also convinced Britain to draw the western part of the border between the United States and Canada along the 49th parallel.

In 1819 Secretary of State **John Quincy Adams** reached an important agreement with Spain. Under the **Adams-Onís Treaty**, the United States acquired Florida and established a firm boundary between the Louisiana territory and Spanish territory farther to the west.

Thus Adams expanded the country to the south and east and defined its borders to the north and west. Further, Adams convinced Spain and Russia to give up their claims to the disputed Oregon Country and negotiated a treaty with Britain that would allow American settlers to travel to Oregon for 10 years.

The Monroe Doctrine
Although the Monroe administration had achieved stunning diplomatic successes, the United States still faced a foreign policy problem. The problem arose in Europe but concerned hemispheric neighbors in Central America and South America.

ACADEMIC VOCABULARY
implement to execute or carry out

Spain had colonized Central and South America in the 1600s and 1700s. In the early 1800s had Spain neglected its colonies because it was fighting France, which, under Napoleon, was expanding in Europe. Many colonies took the opportunity to declare independence. But after Napoleon was defeated, Spain and other European powers considered retaking control of the former colonies in the Americas.

This concerned Great Britain, which had developed a thriving trade with the former Spanish colonies. It also concerned the United States. American lawmakers wanted to deter any foreign country from taking lands in the Americas that the United States might someday claim, such as the Pacific Northwest.

President Monroe and Secretary of State John Quincy Adams responded by declaring a new foreign policy for the United States. In time, it would be called the Monroe Doctrine. A doctrine is a policy. The **Monroe Doctrine** stated that the United States would view any European attempts to further colonize the Americas "as dangerous to our peace and safety." In Monroe's message to Congress, delivered on December 2, 1823, he stated:

HISTORY'S VOICES

❝The American continents . . . are henceforth not to be considered as subjects for future colonization by any European powers.❞

—Monroe Doctrine, 1823

Monroe also stated that the United States would not "interfere in the internal concerns" of Europe. In essence, the Monroe Doctrine stated that the United States would stay out of European affairs and that it expected Europe to stay out of American affairs.

The Monroe Doctrine was a bold statement to the old, great powers of Europe. It confirmed that American nationalism was to be felt well beyond the shores of the young nation.

READING CHECK **Summarizing** What were the major diplomatic achievements of the Monroe administration?

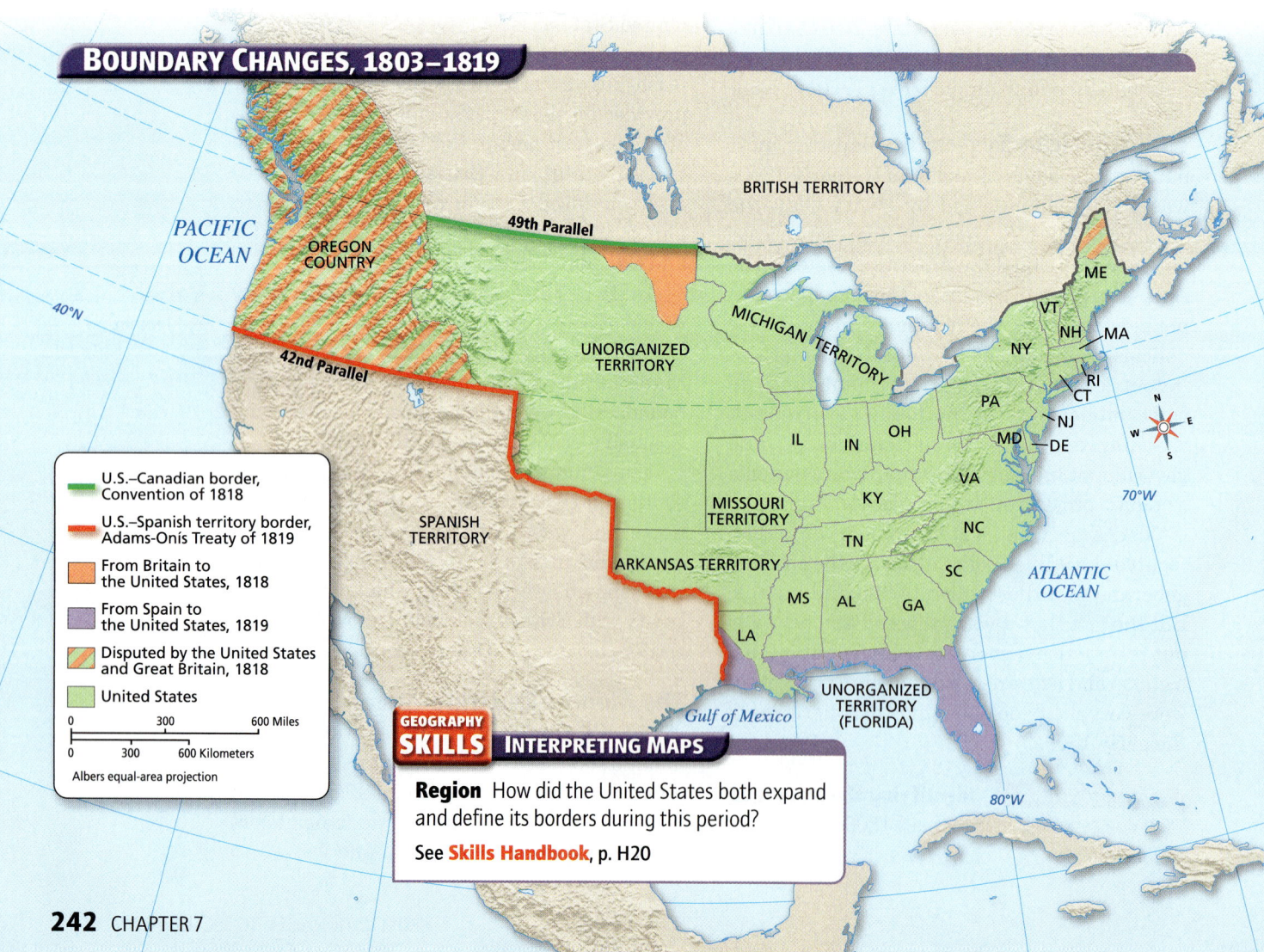

BOUNDARY CHANGES, 1803–1819

PACIFIC OCEAN

BRITISH TERRITORY

OREGON COUNTRY

49th Parallel

42nd Parallel

40°N

UNORGANIZED TERRITORY

MICHIGAN TERRITORY

ME
VT
NH — MA
NY
RI
CT
PA
NJ
MD — DE
OH
IL   IN
VA
KY
MISSOURI TERRITORY
NC
TN
SC
ATLANTIC OCEAN
70°W

SPANISH TERRITORY

ARKANSAS TERRITORY

MS   AL   GA

LA

Gulf of Mexico

UNORGANIZED TERRITORY (FLORIDA)

80°W

Legend:
- U.S.–Canadian border, Convention of 1818
- U.S.–Spanish territory border, Adams-Onís Treaty of 1819
- From Britain to the United States, 1818
- From Spain to the United States, 1819
- Disputed by the United States and Great Britain, 1818
- United States

0   300   600 Miles
0   300   600 Kilometers
Albers equal-area projection

GEOGRAPHY SKILLS **INTERPRETING MAPS**

Region How did the United States both expand and define its borders during this period?
See **Skills Handbook**, p. H20

The Missouri Compromise

Americans' feelings of nationalism were fueled by the pride they took in the rapid growth of American settlement. By 1818 settlers had even spread beyond the Mississippi River into Missouri. Most newcomers to Missouri had migrated from the South. About 1 in 6 settlers were enslaved African Americans.

When the Missouri Territory applied to join the union, it caused an uproar. In 1819 there were 22 states in the Union. In half of the states—the "slave states" of the South—slavery was legal. In the other half of the states—the "free states" of the North—slavery was illegal. This exact balance between slave states and free states gave them equal representation in the U.S. Senate. If Missouri were admitted as a slave state, the balance would be upset.

The situation was resolved by what became known as the **Missouri Compromise** of 1820. Under this agreement, Missouri was admitted to the Union as a slave state and Maine was to be admitted as a free state. Thus, the balance between the number of free states and slave states was preserved. The agreement also banned slavery in the northern part of the Louisiana Territory. The Missouri Compromise

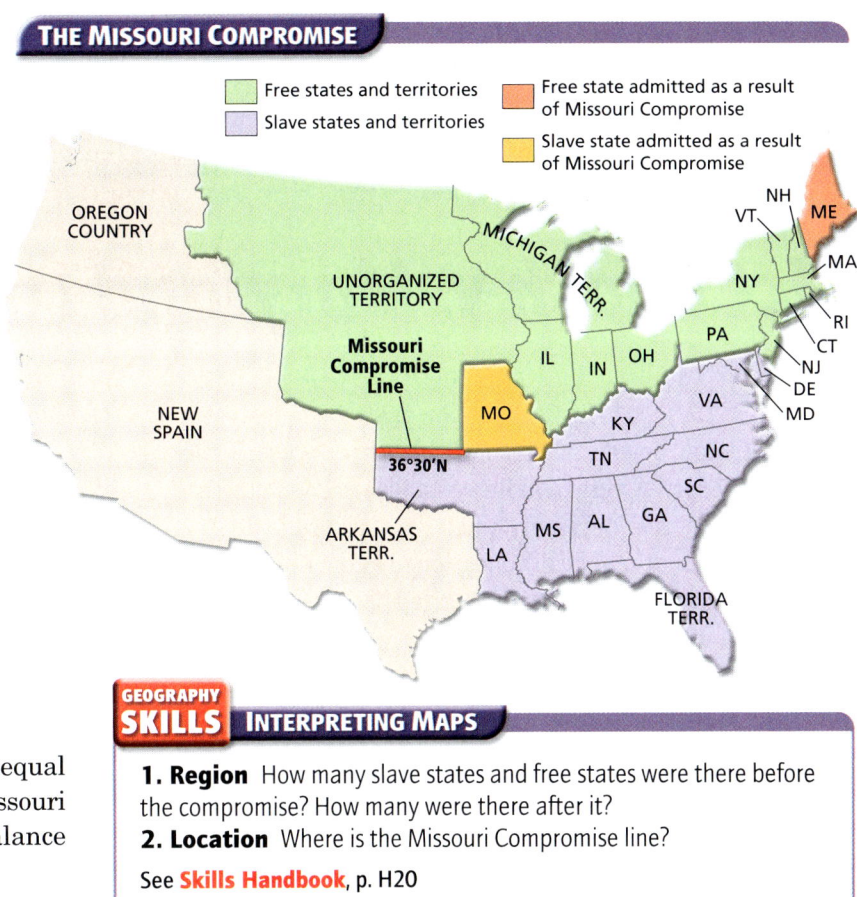

THE MISSOURI COMPROMISE

- Free states and territories
- Slave states and territories
- Free state admitted as a result of Missouri Compromise
- Slave state admitted as a result of Missouri Compromise

GEOGRAPHY SKILLS **INTERPRETING MAPS**

1. Region How many slave states and free states were there before the compromise? How many were there after it?
2. Location Where is the Missouri Compromise line?

See **Skills Handbook**, p. H20

kept the balance between slave and free states. It was disturbingly clear, however, that feelings of sectionalism in the North and the South were beginning to emerge.

READING CHECK **Identifying the Main Idea** Why was the Missouri Compromise adopted?

go.hrw.com
Online Quiz
Keyword: SD7 HP7

Reviewing Ideas, Terms, and People

1. a. Describe How did Alexis de Tocqueville describe the American people?

b. Compare What did Thomas Cole and **Noah Webster** have in common?

2. a. Identify Who was John Marshall?

b. Compare What did *McCulloch* v. *Maryland* and *Gibbons* v. *Ogden* have in common?

3. a. Recall What was the **Adams-Onís Treaty**?

b. Analyze What was the purpose of the **Monroe Doctrine**?

4. a. Describe Why would adding only Missouri to the Union have created an imbalance in the Senate?

b. Make Inferences What does the Missouri Compromise imply about Americans' views toward slavery?

Critical Thinking

5. Identifying Cause and Effect Copy the diagram below and identify the effects of nationalism.

Nationalism

FOCUS ON WRITING

6. Expository Write a paragraph explaining why Alexis de Tocqueville's description of Americans does or does not describe Americans today. Give details that support your position.

ST **1.2** Analyze the decisions leading to major turning points in United States history, comparing alternative courses of action, and hypothesizing, within the context of the historic period, about what might have happened if the decision had been different.

McCulloch v. Maryland (1819)

Why It Matters The Constitution gives the federal government certain powers and reserves all other powers to the states. *McCulloch* v. *Maryland* first established congressional authority under the "necessary and proper" clause to do things that are not specifically mentioned in the Constitution but that fall within Congress's authorized powers.

Background of the Case

After the War of 1812, President Madison asked Congress to create the Bank of the United States, a national bank for the entire country. Other banks established by the states resented the competition. In 1818 the Maryland legislature put a tax on the Baltimore branch of the national bank. James McCulloch, a bank officer in the Baltimore branch, refused to pay the tax. The case raised two issues: Did Congress have the authority to create a national bank? Was Maryland's tax on the bank protected by the Constitution?

The Decision

In his ruling, Chief Justice John Marshall carefully analyzed the balance of power between the federal government and the states. The Constitution does not specifically give Congress the power to create a bank, but it does give Congress the power to collect taxes, borrow money, regulate commerce, raise an army and navy, and to make "all laws which shall be necessary and proper for carrying into execution the foregoing powers." Marshall noted that a national bank was a reasonable way for Congress to carry out its specified powers. If a state could tax the bank, Marshall argued, then it would have the power to destroy the bank, which would defeat "all the ends of government" under the Constitution. The Court ruled that Maryland's tax on the bank was therefore unconstitutional.

THE IMPACT TODAY Many federal activities are not specifically mentioned in the Constitution but are "necessary and proper" for carrying out Congress's authority. One example is Congress's power to draft Americans into military service. This power supports the constitutional authority of Congress to raise and support an army.

CRITICAL THINKING

go.hrw.com
Research Online
Keyword: SS Court

1. **Analyze the Impact** Using the keyword above, research one of the laws listed below. What is the purpose of the law? What provisions in the Constitution gave Congress the power to enact the law?
   - Americans with Disabilities Act
   - Clean Air Act of 1970

2. **You Be the Judge** Congress passed a law making it a federal crime to bribe an official of a state or local entity that receives at least $10,000 in federal funds. Does Congress have the power under the "necessary and proper" clause to create a federal crime even when there is no connection between the bribe and the federal money? Explain your answer in a short paragraph.

The Age of Jackson

BEFORE YOU READ

MAIN IDEA

President Andrew Jackson's bold actions defined a period of American history.

READING FOCUS

1. What path led to Andrew Jackson's presidency?
2. How did the Indian Removal Act lead to the Trail of Tears?
3. Why was the national bank a source of controversy?
4. How did a conflict over the issue of states' rights lead to a crisis?

KEY TERMS AND PEOPLE

Democratic Party
Jacksonian Democracy
spoils system
Indian Removal Act
Worcester v. *Georgia*
Trail of Tears
Second Bank of the
   United States
states' rights
John C. Calhoun
secede
nullification crisis

PI 3.2 Research and analyze the major themes and developments in New York State and United States history (e.g., colonization and settlement; Revolution and New National Period; immigration; expansion and reform era; Civil War and Reconstruction; the American labor move- ment; Great Depression; World Wars; contemporary United States).

THE INSIDE STORY

How should guests behave at the White House? Andrew Jackson won the presidency in 1828 as the candidate of the common man. Rough-hewn voters in the West and South, especially, thought of him as one of their own. So when the new president threw open the doors of the White House to anyone who wanted to attend his inaugural reception in 1829, thousands showed up to get a glimpse of their hero—and of the White House.

An estimated 20,000 well-wishers pushed and shoved their way into the White House staterooms. They trampled the carpets with muddy boots and climbed on the uphol- stered sofas and chairs. They broke china, smashed glass- ware, and bloodied more than a few noses. Finally, harried servants brought tubs of punch, ice cream, and lemonade outside, as people climbed through open windows to escape the riotous scene. The new president himself fled to the safety of a hotel.

Jackson's opponents denounced the day as "the reign of King Mob." One of Jackson's colleagues, however, was more forgiving. He called it "a proud day for the people." ◢

Party at the
WHITE
HOUSE

◀ **A crowd converges upon the White House to celebrate Jackson's inauguration.**

Path to the Presidency

Andrew Jackson's early life was as rambunctious as his inauguration. As a teenager, he served in the army during the Revolutionary War. As a young man, he was known to be "roaring, rollicking" and "mischievous."

Jackson moved to Tennessee in 1788. There he practiced law, became a successful land speculator, and served in a variety of government offices, including the House of Representatives and in the Senate.

The War of 1812 brought Jackson the opportunity to vent his boundless energy as a soldier. He was commissioned into the U.S. Army and ordered to march his troops toward New Orleans. Jackson drove himself and his soldiers hard. They thought their commander was tough as hickory wood, and Jackson became known as Old Hickory.

Later in the war, Jackson was given command of military operations in the South. In December 1814 and January 1815, Jackson led the American forces that drove off the British invasion at the Battle of New Orleans. The battle made Jackson nationally famous and popular as the "Hero of New Orleans." General Jackson planned to use his popularity to win the presidency.

In 1824 Jackson ran for president as a member of the Democratic-Republican Party. Other candidates of the party included John Quincy Adams and Henry Clay.

Jackson won the popular vote. But he did not win a majority of the electoral votes. As a result, the winner of the election was to be determined by a vote in the House of Representatives.

In the House vote, Clay gave his support to Adams. This gave Adams enough votes to win the election and become president in 1825. Adams immediately named Clay as his secretary of state. Jackson and his supporters suspected Adams and Clay had made a secret deal. They called it a "corrupt bargain." Jackson vowed to defeat Adams in the next election.

Jackson and his supporters created a new political party that came to be known, in time, as the **Democratic Party**. Adams and his supporters became the National Republicans.

Adams did not enjoy great popularity as president. His administration was weakened by scandal and by relentless criticism from Jackson's supporters. Also, Adams himself seemed to many Americans to be out of touch with the people.

In contrast, Jackson was a popular war hero who seemed very much to be "a man of the people." In the 1820s voting restrictions in many states—such as the requirement for property ownership—were being lifted, allowing poor people to become voters. These new voters were strong Jackson supporters.

In the election of 1828, Jackson easily defeated the unpopular Adams. The Age of Jackson had begun.

Andrew Jackson was supported by ordinary, working Americans. In time, such political power exercised by ordinary Americans became known as **Jacksonian Democracy**.

One of Jackson's first acts in office was to replace many officials with his supporters. Rewarding supporters in this way is called the **spoils system**. Jackson faced criticism, but in fact he only replaced about 1 in 10 officials.

READING CHECK **Identifying Cause and Effect** How did his military career help Jackson become president?

The Indian Removal Act

By the time Andrew Jackson became president, the land east of the Mississippi River was largely settled by white Americans. In the Southeast, however, huge expanses of land were still controlled by Native American groups.

Five major Native American groups lived in the southeastern United States: the Cherokee, Choctaw, Chickasaw, Seminole, and Creek. White Americans sometimes called these groups the "five civilized tribes" because many of their members had adopted aspects of European and American culture. The Cherokee,

Andrew Jackson, "man of the people," said that "the people are the government, administering it by their agents."

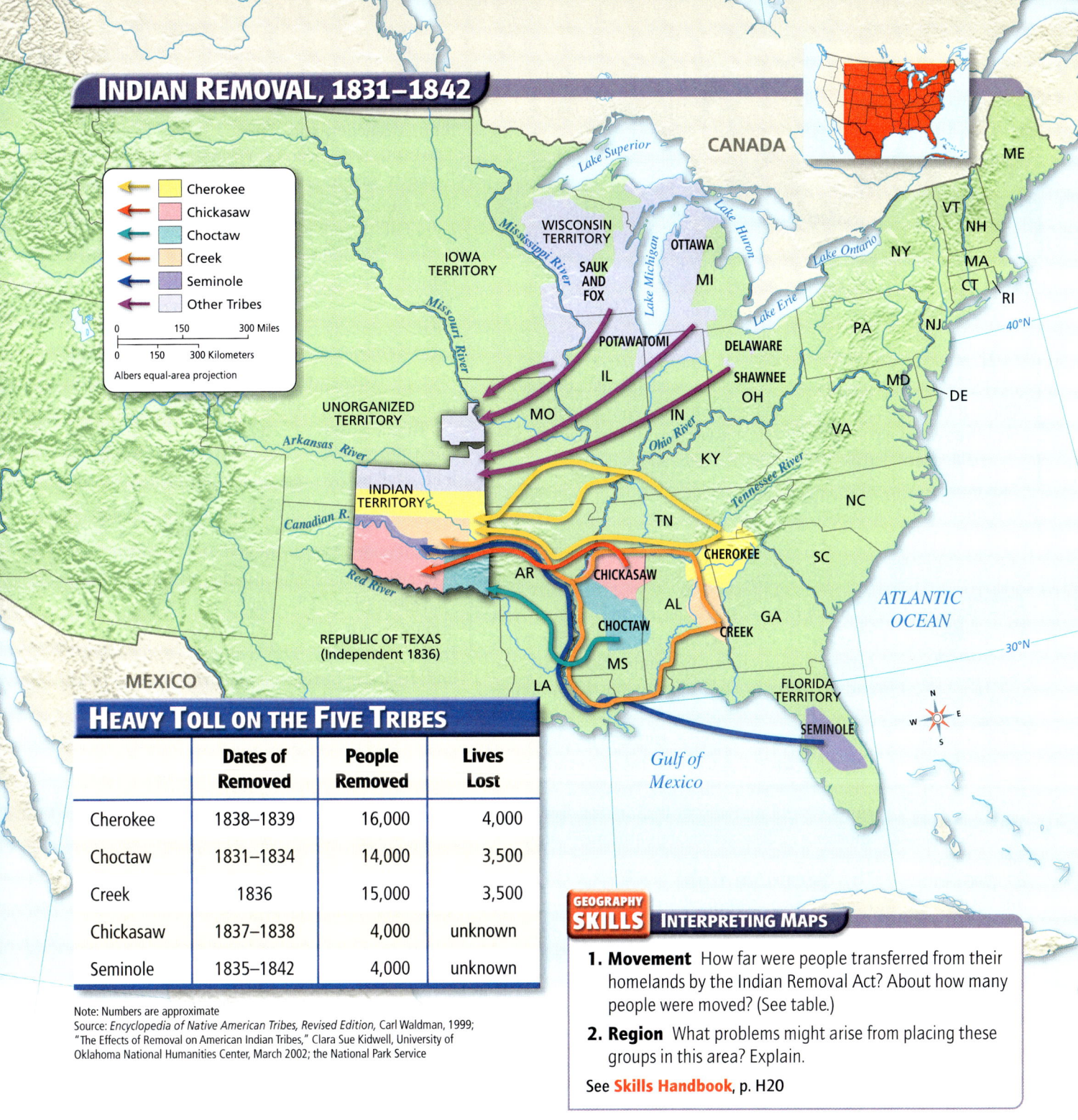

INDIAN REMOVAL, 1831–1842

CANADA

	Cherokee
	Chickasaw
	Choctaw
	Creek
	Seminole
	Other Tribes

0   150   300 Miles
0   150   300 Kilometers
Albers equal-area projection

CANADA

Lake Superior
WISCONSIN TERRITORY
IOWA TERRITORY
OTTAWA
MI
Lake Michigan
Lake Huron
Lake Ontario
Lake Erie
ME
VT
NH
NY
MA
CT
RI
40°N

Mississippi River
SAUK AND FOX
POTAWATOMI
IL
DELAWARE
SHAWNEE
OH
PA
NJ
MD
DE

Missouri River
UNORGANIZED TERRITORY
MO
IN
Ohio River
KY
VA

Arkansas River
INDIAN TERRITORY
Canadian R.
Red River
AR
TN
Tennessee River
NC
CHEROKEE
SC

CHICKASAW
AL
CHOCTAW
GA
CREEK
ATLANTIC OCEAN
30°N

REPUBLIC OF TEXAS (Independent 1836)

MEXICO
LA
MS
FLORIDA TERRITORY

Gulf of Mexico
SEMINOLE

N E S W

HEAVY TOLL ON THE FIVE TRIBES

	Dates of Removed	People Removed	Lives Lost
Cherokee	1838–1839	16,000	4,000
Choctaw	1831–1834	14,000	3,500
Creek	1836	15,000	3,500
Chickasaw	1837–1838	4,000	unknown
Seminole	1835–1842	4,000	unknown

Note: Numbers are approximate
Source: *Encyclopedia of Native American Tribes, Revised Edition,* Carl Waldman, 1999; "The Effects of Removal on American Indian Tribes," Clara Sue Kidwell, University of Oklahoma National Humanities Center, March 2002; the National Park Service

GEOGRAPHY SKILLS **INTERPRETING MAPS**

1. **Movement** How far were people transferred from their homelands by the Indian Removal Act? About how many people were moved? (See table.)

2. **Region** What problems might arise from placing these groups in this area? Explain.

See **Skills Handbook**, p. H20

for example, learned English, built towns, and established a written constitution. A Cherokee named Sequoya created a writing system for the Cherokee language.

Although some white Americans respected these peoples, many viewed them as inferior. Above all else, though, farmland was becoming scarce in the East, and white settlers coveted the Indians' lands.

The Indian Removal Act President Jackson concluded that the best action was to relocate the nations so that the southeast would be open to white settlement. In 1830 Congress passed, and Jackson signed into law, the **Indian Removal Act**, which called for the relocation of the five nations to an area west of the Mississippi River called Indian Territory—land in what is now present-day Oklahoma.

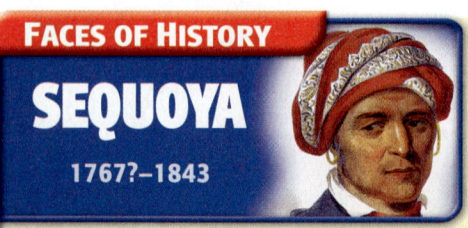
Little is known with certainty about Sequoya's early years, including when or where he was born. Settling in Georgia, he worked at various trades—farmer, trader, silversmith. Sequoya believed that knowledge was key to Cherokee independence and that written language was a way for his people to acquire that knowledge. In 1809 he set out to create a system of writing for the Cherokee language. By 1821 he had created 86 characters that represented all the syllables of the Cherokee language. Soon the Cherokee were teaching the system in their schools and publishing their own books and newspapers. Sequoya's work helped unite eastern and western Cherokee around a shared language and preserved Cherokee cultural traditions.

Summarize Why do you think Sequoya believed written language was important?

THE IMPACT TODAY

Government

Today there are three federally recognized Cherokee communities, two in Oklahoma and one in North Carolina. The largest is the Cherokee Nation of Oklahoma, which has about 125,000 members. The Cherokee are by far the largest Native American group in the United States today.

Under the supervision of the U.S. Army, the Choctaw, the Creek, and the Chickasaw were forced to march west, hundreds of miles, to Indian Territory. Conditions on the marches were miserable. Exposure, malnutrition, and disease took their toll. About one-fourth of the Choctaw and the Creek—men, women, and children—died on the long trek. The Chickasaw's forced journey to Indian Territory was shorter and less deadly, but still miserable.

The Seminole fight back The Seminole reacted to attempts at their removal with armed force. Seminole women and children hid from the soldiers in the dense Florida swamps, while Seminole men conducted hit-and-run attacks on the American soldiers. About 3,000 Seminole were forced to move to Indian Territory, but many more continued to resist. They were never officially defeated, and their descendants still live in Florida today.

The Trail of Tears While the Seminole resisted removal with armed force, the Cherokee fought in the American court system. They sued the federal government, claiming that they had the right to be respected as a foreign country. The case reached the Supreme Court in 1831. Chief Justice John Marshall, however, refused to hear the case. He ruled that the Cherokee had no right to bring suit since they were neither citizens nor a foreign country.

The Cherokee, however, had another plan of attack. Samuel Austin Worcester was a white man, a teacher, and a friend to the Cherokee. The state of Georgia, carrying out the Indian Removal Act, ordered Worcester to leave Cherokee land. He refused and brought suit on behalf of himself and the Cherokee.

In 1832 John Marshall's Supreme Court issued its decision in **Worcester v. Georgia**. Many whites were stunned when Marshall ruled against Georgia, denying them the right to take Cherokee lands. Jackson was outraged. He reportedly stated, "John Marshall has made his decision—now let him enforce it."

To get around the Court's ruling, government officials signed a treaty with Cherokee leaders who favored relocation, even though they did not represent most of the Cherokee people. Under this treaty, the Cherokee were herded by the U.S. Army, like the other nations before them, on a long and deadly march west.

Of the 16,000 Cherokee forced to leave their homes, about 4,000 died on the march to the Indian Territory. The Cherokee suffered so badly—from hunger, exposure, disease, and bandits—that their exodus became known as the **Trail of Tears,** a term that has become synonymous with all of the nations' suffering.

READING CHECK **Summarizing** How did the Indian Removal Act affect the people of the "five civilized tribes"?

The National Bank

A hotly contested issue of Jackson's presidency concerned the **Second Bank of the United States**, a national bank overseen by the federal government. Congress established the Bank in 1816 and gave it a 20-year charter. The purpose of the Bank was to regulate state banks, which had grown rapidly since the First Bank of the United States went out of existence in 1811.

Jackson and other Americans strongly opposed the Second Bank of the United States. They thought that the Constitution did not give Congress the authority to create it in the first place.

Opponents recognized that state banks were more inclined to make loans to poorer farmers in the South and West—the very people who supported Jackson. By contrast, they viewed the national bank as an institution devoted to the interests of wealthy northern corporations. Jackson so despised the bank that he called it a "monster," adding, "I will kill it."

In the summer of 1832 Henry Clay and Daniel Webster, National Republicans who opposed Jackson, introduced a bill to renew the Bank's charter. The timing of the bill, during an election year, was deliberate. They hoped that Jackson's opposition to the bill would hurt his chances of reelection. Jackson promptly vetoed the bill. In the election of 1832, Clay challenged Jackson for the presidency, and the controversy over the Bank became a major campaign issue.

Nevertheless, Jackson won re-election, defeating Clay in a landslide. At the beginning of his second term, Jackson ordered his secretary of the Treasury to take the money out of the Bank and deposit it in select state banks. Critics called these banks "pet banks" because they were loyal to Jackson.

Nicholas Biddle, the president of the Second Bank of the United States, opposed the pet-bank initiative, but there was little he could do. In 1836 the Second Bank of the United States was reduced to just another state bank.

READING CHECK **Identifying Points of View** Why did Jackson oppose the Second Bank of the United States?

Conflict over States' Rights

The controversy over the Second Bank of the United States was largely a dispute over how power should be divided between the federal government and state governments. Those who favored giving more power to the states invoked the concept of **states' rights**, based on the Tenth Amendment's provision that powers "not delegated to the United States by the Constitution, nor prohibited by it to the States" are reserved to the states.

The tariff controversy

In 1816 Congress passed a tariff on British manufactured goods. It raised the tariff in 1824 and 1828. The tariff was welcomed by industry leaders of the northern states. Because the tariff increased the price of British goods, it encouraged Americans to buy American goods.

The agricultural southern states despised the tariff. It forced southerners to buy northern goods instead of the less expensive British goods they were accustomed to. Moreover, southern cotton growers, who exported most of their crop to Britain, opposed interference with international trade.

The controversy over the tariff helped drive a wedge between Jackson and his vice president, **John C. Calhoun**. Calhoun, a southerner,

© COLLECTION OF THE NEW-YORK HISTORICAL SOCIETY [neg. 42459]

Battle over the National Bank

Jackson compared the Second Bank of the United States to an "undemocratic, hydra monster" and a "hydra of corruption." A hydra is a serpentlike monster in Greek mythology that grew back two heads for every one cut off. *Why did Jackson oppose the Bank?*

charged that the tariff benefited northern states at the expense of southern states. Outraged southerners referred to the 1828 tariff as the Tariff of Abominations.

Calhoun advanced the idea that a state could nullify, or reject, any law passed by Congress—such as the tariff law—that the state thought violated the Constitution or was not in the best interests of the state. The concept that states have the right to reject federal laws is called the nullification theory.

The Hayne-Webster debate

The issue of nullification and states' rights was the focus of one of the most famous debates in Senate history. It took place in 1830 between Senator Robert Hayne of South Carolina and Senator Daniel Webster of Massachusetts.

Hayne maintained that the federal government was a compact, or agreement, among the states. Nullification, he said, gave states a lawful way to protest federal legislation.

Webster responded that the United States was one nation, not merely an agreement of states. His impassioned reply ended with the words, "Liberty *and* Union, now and forever, one and inseparable!" The thundering defense of the Union made Webster a nationally famous figure overnight.

The nullification crisis

In 1832 Congress passed another tariff, and the nullification theory was put to the test. South Carolina declared the tariff law "null and void" and threatened to **secede**, or withdraw, from the Union if the federal government tried to enforce the tariff. This event is known as the **nullification crisis**.

Calhoun felt so strongly about the issue that he resigned the vice presidency and became a senator from his home state of South Carolina. Jackson felt just as strongly. He stated:

HISTORY'S VOICES

"I consider the power to annul a law of the United States, assumed by one State, incompatible with the existence of the Union . . ."

—Andrew Jackson, 1832

Jackson demanded and received the Force Bill from Congress that empowered him to use military force to collect the tariff in South Carolina. But South Carolina declared that bill null and void as well. The situation was resolved by Henry Clay, who worked out a compromise in which tariffs would be reduced over a period of 10 years. But the issues of nullification and of states' rights would be raised again and again in the years to come.

READING CHECK **Identifying the Main Idea** What was the nullification crisis?

SECTION 2 ASSESSMENT

go.hrw.com
Online Quiz
Keyword: SD7 HP7

Reviewing Ideas, Terms, and People

1. a. Recall How did the Battle of New Orleans help Andrew Jackson's political career?
b. Analyze How did the "corrupt bargain" lead to the creation of a new political party?

2. a. Identify What were the "five civilized tribes"?
b. Draw Conclusions What does the passage of the **Indian Removal Act** indicate about American attitudes toward Native Americans?
c. Elaborate What do you think modern Americans should learn from the **Trail of Tears**?

3. a. Recall Why did Jackson want to destroy the **Second Bank of the United States**?
b. Draw Conclusions What are two reasons that Nicholas Biddle might have had for trying to save the national bank?

4. a. Define What is a tariff?
b. Contrast How did the northern and southern views of the American tariff on British manufactured goods differ?

c. Evaluate What are arguments for and against the nullification theory?

Critical Thinking

5. Comparing and Contrasting Copy the diagram and compare and contrast the controversies over the Second National Bank and the Tariff of Abominations.

Similarities	Differences

FOCUS ON WRITING

6. Persuasive Write an editorial in which you make the case for or against the concept of nullification. Support your argument with examples from the section.

The Industrial North

BEFORE YOU READ

MAIN IDEA

The North developed an economy based on industry.

READING FOCUS

1. What was the Industrial Revolution?
2. How did the Industrial Revolution affect the North?
3. What advancements were made in transportation and communication?

KEY TERMS AND PEOPLE

Samuel Slater
Industrial Revolution
Francis Lowell
Lowell girls
National Road
Erie Canal
Robert Fulton
Samuel F. B. Morse
telegraph

PI **1.1** Analyze the development of American culture, explaining how ideas, values, beliefs, and traditions have changed over time and how they united all Americans.

How did a young Englishman launch America's Industrial Revolution? The man history remembers as the father of the American Industrial Revolution got his first job in the British textile industry when he was 14 years old. Born in England, **Samuel Slater** grew up in a region called Derbyshire, where the world's first water-powered textile mills were used. In 1782 Slater went to work in one of those mills. He soon learned how to manage a mill and mastered the workings of the textile machines.

In 1789 when he was 21, Slater was ready to use his skills in America. But the textile industry was so important to England's economy that English law made it illegal for the secrets of mill design, and those who knew them, to leave the country. So Slater dressed as a farm laborer and secretly boarded a ship for New York, carrying in his head the precious, forbidden knowledge.

Slater soon went to meet Moses Brown, who was trying to use English-style machines in his Rhode Island mill. Within a year they had built a successful water-powered textile mill along the Blackstone River at Pawtucket, Rhode Island. Slater's daring escape to America gave him a central role in the birth of the U.S. textile industry. ◼

Samuel Slater
and the
Industrial Revolution

The Blackstone River powered America's first successful textile mill.

The Industrial Revolution

Samuel Slater's trip to America was an important event in one of the most dramatic changes in all of history. This change was so far-reaching that historians considered it a revolution. The **Industrial Revolution** was the birth of modern industry and the social changes that accompanied it. The Industrial Revolution occurred over a period of several decades from the middle of the 1700s to the middle of the 1800s.

The Industrial Revolution began in Great Britain's textile industry. There, for centuries, cloth had been made in workers' homes, using simple, human-powered machines. Plant fibers were spun into thread on spinning wheels. The thread was woven into cloth on looms.

Then in the late 1700s, a series of inventions radically transformed the industry. These inventions mechanized both spinning and weaving. British inventors created machines that used power from running water and steam engines to spin and weave cloth.

These powered spinning and weaving machines revolutionized the British textile industry. By 1800 textile companies had built hundreds of mills to house the new, large machines and produced volumes of cloth that could only have been dreamed of a few decades earlier. What was once a human-powered industry based in workers' homes was now a machine-powered industry based in huge mills. The Industrial Revolution had begun.

A key development of the Industrial Revolution was the replacement of human power with machine power. At the beginning of the Industrial Revolution, water power was far more important than steam power. But the steam engine became more and more important during the 1800s.

The steam engine was invented in England in 1698. But it didn't come into its own until the late 1700s. That's when Scottish inventor James Watt radically improved the existing engine, making it much more efficient and reliable. It was Watt's steam-engine design that powered the Industrial Revolution in Britain, and, not long after, in the United States.

> **READING CHECK** **Sequencing** What events led to the birth of the Industrial Revolution in the British textile industry?

The North Industrializes

To keep their economic advantage, the British made it illegal for anyone with knowledge of industrial machines to leave the country or for anyone to export any industrial machines. Samuel Slater <u>violated</u> these laws when he brought knowledge of the new industrial machines to America. Slater and Moses Brown, a Pawtucket, Rhode Island, merchant, built a water-powered spinning mill on the Blackstone River. Their mill was the first successful textile mill in the country, and its construction marks the beginning of the Industrial Revolution in the United States.

Lowell The Industrial Revolution spread rapidly from Pawtucket throughout New England. By 1810 there were more than 60 mills spinning thread in New England. In 1813 in Waltham, Massachusetts, the first factory to

ACADEMIC VOCABULARY
violate to break or disregard, as in a law

TIME LINE

Industrial Revolution

1793 Eli Whitney invents the cotton gin, a machine for cleaning cotton. This revolutionized cotton production.

1793 Samuel Slater builds the nation's first successful textile mill, harnessing river water to power the machinery.

1797 Eli Whitney begins manufacturing muskets with interchangeable parts, devising the basis for mass production.

252 CHAPTER 7

bring all processes of cloth production under one roof was built. But it was Lowell that became the center of textile production.

The city was named for **Francis Lowell**, a wealthy Boston textile merchant. Workers began building mills and other buildings in Lowell, Massachusetts, in 1822. Within two years, the mills at Lowell were turning out great amounts of cotton cloth—and earning great profits. The city continued to grow as more and more textile firms opened mills there. Lowell soon had 40 mill buildings and 10,000 looms. People came from other countries to visit this wonder of American industry.

The majority of the workers in the Lowell mills were young women. Most of them had been recruited from local farms. They made relatively good wages for the time period, but they worked hard for it—often as long as 14 hours a day, 6 days a week.

The women's lives were strictly regulated by the ringing of bells. One worker described it this way:

HISTORY'S VOICES

❝Up before day, at the clang of the bell—and out of the mill by the clang of the bell—into the mill, and at work, to the obedience of the ding-dong bell—just as though we were so many living machines.❞

—Anonymous story in the *Lowell Offering*, a literary magazine by and for the mill girls

These hard-working young women came to be known as the **Lowell girls**. Despite their long hours, they developed a lively society in the boardinghouses in which they lived, forming friendships and clubs.

The revolution spreads Throughout the early and middle 1800s, industrialization spread slowly from the textile industry to other industries in the North. In the 1830s steam engines became better and more widely available, and their power helped make industry the fastest-growing part of the U.S. economy.

Industrialization in the North led to urbanization. People left the farm and moved to cities where they could work in the mills and factories. In 1820 only 7 percent of Americans lived in cities. Within 30 years, that percentage more than doubled.

The North underwent dramatic and rapid changes. Within a few decades, it evolved from a region of small towns and farms into one including large cities and factories—all as a result of the Industrial Revolution.

READING CHECK **Making Generalizations**
What part of the United States was most affected by the Industrial Revolution?

Transportation and Communication

The development of American industry in the early 1800s went hand in hand with the development of transportation networks. Businesses needed ways to transport raw materials to their growing number of factories and mills and to ship their finished goods to market.

Roads and canals In 1811 construction began on the **National Road**. When the road was completed in 1841, it stretched 800 miles west

1807 Robert Fulton launches the *Clermont*—and the first successful steamboat passenger service in America.

THE GRANGER COLLECTION, NEW YORK

1844 Samuel Morse uses this telegraph key to send the world's first telegraph message.

c. 1830 The Lowell, Massachusetts, textile mills keep working thanks to the innovation of employing farm girls.

Skills FOCUS **ANALYZING THE TIME LINE**

What was a common feature of the advances made during the Industrial Revolution?
See **Skills Handbook**, p. H14

The Erie Canal

With its endpoints in Albany and Buffalo, New York's Erie Canal linked the young nation's East and West. Canal travel encouraged trade, tourism, and western farming and settlement. After the canal opened in 1825, nearby cities and towns grew. Freight and passenger traffic, as shown in the painting below, boosted local economies.

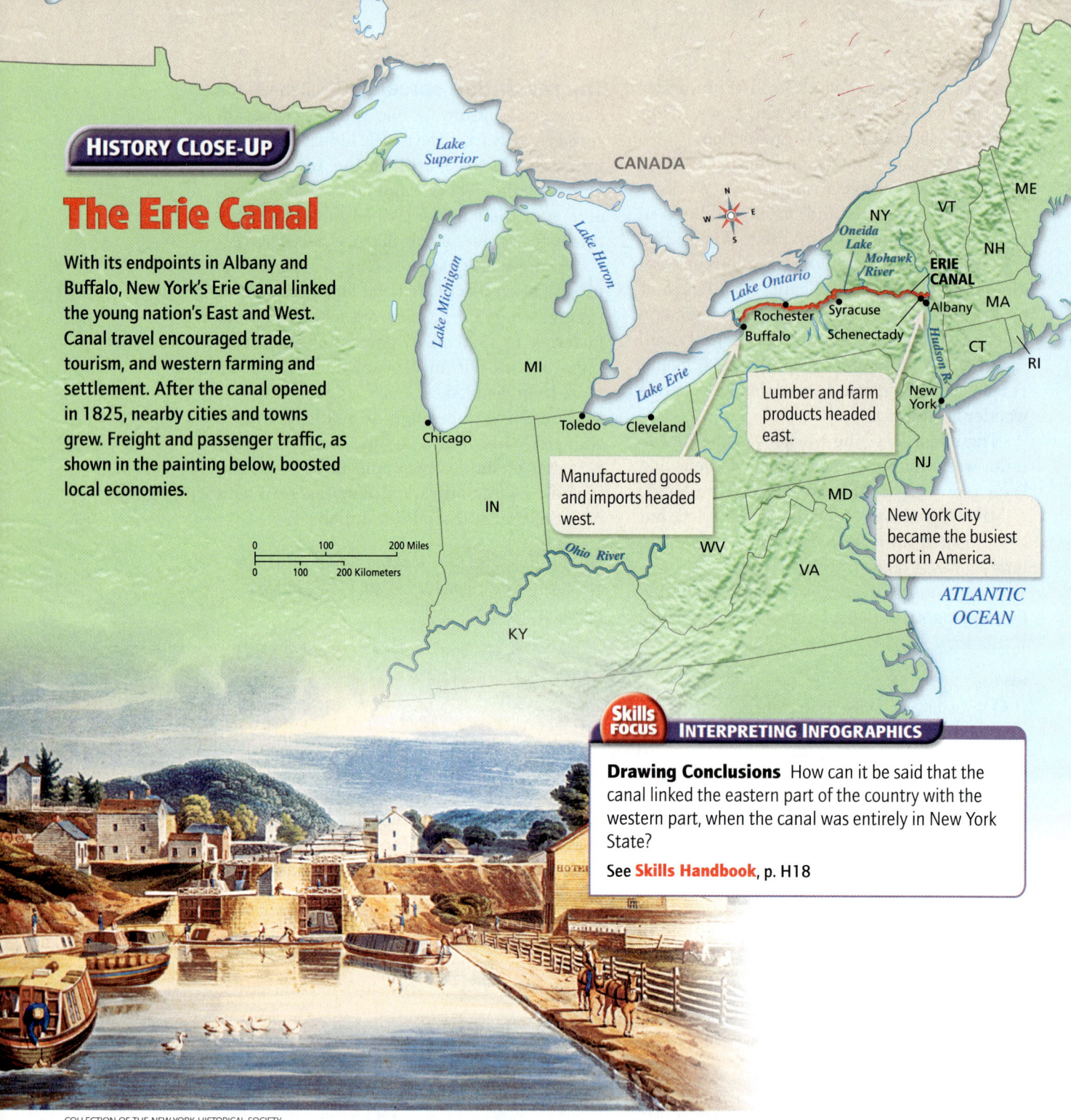

Lumber and farm products headed east.

Manufactured goods and imports headed west.

New York City became the busiest port in America.

INTERPRETING INFOGRAPHICS

Drawing Conclusions How can it be said that the canal linked the eastern part of the country with the western part, when the canal was entirely in New York State?

See **Skills Handbook**, p. H18

COLLECTION OF THE NEW-YORK HISTORICAL SOCIETY

from Cumberland, Maryland, to Vandalia, Illinois. Most roads were not so ambitious. They were much shorter and crudely made. Still, by 1840 a network of roads connected most of the cities and towns throughout the United States, promoting travel and trade.

In 1825 the 363-mile-long **Erie Canal** opened, connecting the Great Lakes with the Hudson River—and with the Atlantic Ocean. The canal provided a quick and economical way to ship manufactured goods to the West and farm products to the East. The cost of shipping by canal barge was one-fifth of the cost of shipping by wagon, and shipping time was cut in half.

The Erie Canal also led to the establishment of New York City as a great trading city. Located where the Hudson River meets the Atlantic Ocean, New York was at the perfect geographic location to serve as a gateway between domestic and foreign trade.

The success of the Erie Canal set off a canal craze in the United States. Within 15 years, more than 3,000 miles of canals formed a dense network in the northeast.

The steamboat The first successful steamboat service was run by **Robert Fulton**. In 1807 Fulton began operating a regular passenger service on the Hudson River with his boat, *The North River Steamboat of Clermont*, usually called the *Clermont*. The success of the *Clermont* inspired others to build and operate steamboats. Within a decade, dozens of steamboats were puffing up and down the Ohio, the Mississippi, and other rivers.

The railroad The first steam-powered train ran in the United States made its first trip in 1830. It was not a long trip, since there were only 23 miles of track in the entire country at the time. In 1831 the first scheduled passenger train service began in Charleston, South Carolina. By 1835 states had issued more than 200 contracts to build railroad lines. By 1840 there were about 3,000 miles of track in the country.

The speed, power, reliability, and carrying capacity of the railroad quickly made it a preferred means of travel and transport. The Iron Horse soon became the most important component of the American transportation network. Its success led to a general decline in roads and brought about the end of the canal craze.

Advances in communication Advances in communication rivaled advances in transportation during the early 1800s. In 1811 a German printer used steam to power a printing press. Steam-powered presses were soon built in the United States, enabling publishers to print material much faster and in much greater volumes than ever before. Another important advance in communications involved the postal service. With the growing use of steamboats and the railroad, mail delivery was faster and more widely available. In 1800 there were fewer than 1,000 post offices. By 1840 there were more than 12,000.

The greatest advancement in communication was the brainchild of **Samuel F. B. Morse**. In 1840 he patented the first practical telegraph. A **telegraph** is a device that sends messages using electricity through wires. Communication by telegraph was instantaneous, and newspapers, railroads, and other businesses were quick to grasp its advantages.

Telegraph wires would soon crisscross the nation, adding a network of rapid communication on top of an already advanced network of transportation. Thus, the Industrial Revolution was accompanied by a transportation revolution and a communications revolution.

READING CHECK **Summarizing** What key advancements in transportation and communication were made in the early 1800s?

FOCUS ON NEW YORK

SCIENCE AND TECHNOLOGY

Fulton first experimented with steam-powered ships while in France. There he met U.S. Ambassador Robert Livingston, a fellow New Yorker, and the two men became partners. The *Clermont* traveled between New York City and Albany powered by an engine specially built by British inventor James Watt.

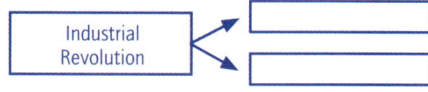

SECTION 3 ASSESSMENT

go.hrw.com
Online Quiz
Keyword: SD7 HP7

Reviewing Ideas, Terms, and People

1. **a. Describe** Describe the birth of the **Industrial Revolution** in Great Britain.
   b. Analyze Why was the use of steam and water power an important part of the Industrial Revolution?
   c. Elaborate What effects of the Industrial Revolution can you identify in your own life today?
2. **a. Identify** Who were **Samuel Slater** and Moses Brown?
   b. Make Inferences Why do you think industrialization spread from the textile industry to other industries?
   c. Evaluate Do you think the **Lowell girls** were treated fairly? Explain your answer.
3. **a. Describe** What were the major economic and social effects of the **Erie Canal**?
   b. Draw Conclusions Why do you think that railroads became more important than roads and canals?

c. Evaluate What do you think was more important in the development of the nation, the transportation revolution or the communications revolution? Give reasons for your answer.

Critical Thinking

4. **Identifying Cause and Effect** Copy the diagram and identify the effects of the Industrial Revolution in the United States.

Industrial Revolution → [ ] [ ]

FOCUS ON WRITING

5. **Persuasive** What do you think was the most important invention of this time period? Identify and defend your choice in a persuasive paragraph.

The Land of Cotton

BEFORE YOU READ

MAIN IDEA

During the early 1800s, the South developed an economy based on agriculture.

READING FOCUS

1. Why was cotton king in the South?
2. How did the cultivation of cotton lead to the spread of slavery?
3. What key differences developed between the North and the South?

KEY TERMS AND PEOPLE

Eli Whitney
cotton gin
Cotton Belt
King Cotton

PI 3.3 Prepare essays and oral reports about the important social, political, economic, scientific, technological, and cultural developments, issues, and events from New York State and United States history.

Revolution in a COTTON BOX

▲ **With a cotton gin, a worker could clean 50 times more cotton than by hand.**

THE INSIDE STORY

How did Eli Whitney help transform the South? When Catherine Greene was 44, her husband, the Revolutionary War general Nathanael Greene, died suddenly in 1786, leaving her to raise their five children alone. Caty had a lively personality, and she was strong-willed. Determined to save her family from ruin, she faced the challenge of running the family plantation in Georgia.

In 1792, with her finances stabilized, Greene hired a young graduate of Yale University to tutor her children. In his spare time, the tutor, **Eli Whitney**, also tinkered with machines. Greene encouraged his experiments.

Not many Georgia planters at the time grew cotton because separating the seeds from the fluffy cotton fibers was so slow and expensive. In 1793, Whitney designed a wooden cylinder with teeth like a wire comb. When turned by a hand crank, it combed the seeds out of the cotton. But the sticky cotton soon jammed the machines. Greene suggested adding a stiff brush that cleaned the teeth as the cylinder turned. The cotton gin was born.

Whitney got a patent for his invention in 1794 and tried to set up a factory. Greene borrowed money to help him. But many farmers just copied the machine. In the end, neither the inventor nor his patron made any money from the cotton gin. But the South was transformed. The gin led to the spread of cotton farming throughout the region and triggered an increased demand for slave labor in the cotton-growing states. ◾

"King Cotton"

The **cotton gin** (*gin* is short for *engine*) was actually quite a simple machine. It was so simple, in fact, that cotton farmers routinely built their own, copying Eli Whitney's design and infringing on his patent. Even so, the cotton gin had a major impact on life in the South.

A type of plant called long-staple cotton grew well in the West Indies, where many of the earlier cotton plantations were established. American growers were disappointed, however, when they tried the plant in the southern United States. The plants could not survive southern winters. As a result, growers turned to a hardier variety of cotton called short-staple cotton. It could stand the cold, but it was harder to clean than long-staple cotton. Whitney's cotton gin solved the problem and made the large-scale production of cotton possible.

The demand for cotton was increasing both at home and abroad. In the United States, the booming textile industry of the North bought cotton to weave into cloth to sell to the growing American population. Overseas, the greatest demand came from Great Britain. There, the mechanized textile industry, exploding in the midst of the Industrial Revolution, demanded ever-increasing amounts of cotton to feed its hundreds of mills.

The combination of the new cotton gin and the huge demand for cotton encouraged many Americans farmers to begin growing cotton. Southerners moved south and west to acquire land for cotton farms in the Carolinas, Tennessee, Georgia, Alabama, Mississippi, and Louisiana. Beginning in the 1820s, the number of acres devoted to cotton cultivation soared. A nearly uninterrupted band of cotton farms called the **Cotton Belt** stretched across the South, all the way from Virginia in the East to Texas in the West.

Growing cotton was a way to get rich relatively quickly. One man at the time described the mania for growing cotton:

ACADEMIC VOCABULARY

acquire come into possession or control of

HISTORY'S VOICES

❝Young men who come to this country, 'to make money,' soon catch the mania, and nothing less than a broad plantation, waving with the snow white cotton bolls, can fill their mental vision, as they anticipate by a few years in their dreams of the future, the result of their plans and labours.❞

—J. H. Ingram, *The South-West*

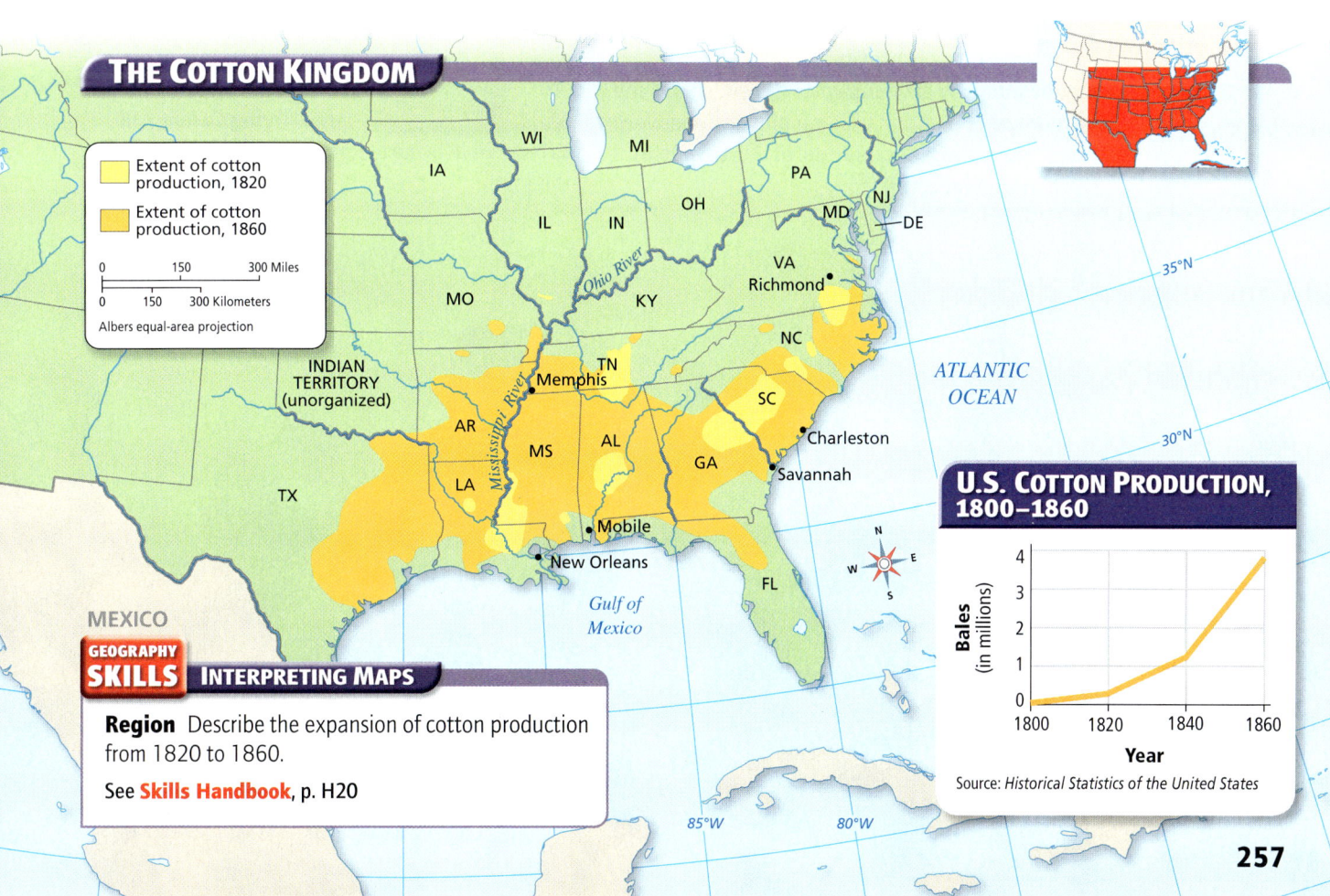

THE COTTON KINGDOM

Extent of cotton production, 1820
Extent of cotton production, 1860

0   150   300 Miles
0   150   300 Kilometers
Albers equal-area projection

WI, IA, MI, PA, OH, NJ, MD, DE, IL, IN, MO, VA, Richmond, KY, NC, INDIAN TERRITORY (unorganized), TN, Memphis, SC, ATLANTIC OCEAN, AR, Charleston, MS, AL, Savannah, GA, LA, TX, Mobile, New Orleans, FL, MEXICO, Gulf of Mexico

35°N, 30°N, 85°W, 80°W

U.S. COTTON PRODUCTION, 1800–1860

Bales (in millions) — 4, 3, 2, 1, 0
Year — 1800, 1820, 1840, 1860

Source: *Historical Statistics of the United States*

GEOGRAPHY SKILLS INTERPRETING MAPS

Region Describe the expansion of cotton production from 1820 to 1860.

See **Skills Handbook**, p. H20

Numbers tell the story of the cotton boom. With few exceptions, cotton was America's largest and most valuable export from 1807 until the end of the 1800s. Cotton became so important to the economy of the South that by 1855 cotton became more than a crop—it gained royal status. Senator James H. Hammond of South Carolina stood on the Senate floor and pronounced that "Cotton is king." Soon, people called the crop **King Cotton**.

READING CHECK Identifying the Main Idea
Why was cotton called King Cotton?

The Spread of Slavery

Even with the use of the cotton gin, farming cotton was a labor-intensive enterprise. The land had to be prepared, and the cotton seeds had to be planted. The growing plants had to be tended. Finally, of course, the crop had to be picked, cleaned, and formed into bales.

The first cotton farms were small and run by families who didn't own slaves. They were soon followed by wealthier planters who bought huge tracts of land and used enslaved African Americans to raise and pick the cotton that made the planters rich.

These wealthier planters grew cotton and other crops on plantations. As the amount of money made by growing cotton grew, so did the number of plantations. Some plantations were huge, including thousands of acres. Others were more modest.

The growth of cotton farming led directly to an increase in demand for enslaved African Americans. Although the importation of enslaved people had been banned in 1808, they were routinely smuggled into southern ports like Charleston, South Carolina, and New Orleans, Louisiana. These people, and the children of enslaved parents, were cruelly bought and sold by slave traders to provide ever more workers for the cotton fields.

In 1810 there were about 1 million enslaved African Americans in the United States. Most lived in Virginia, the Carolinas, and Tennessee. By 1840 that number had more than doubled to nearly 2.5 million.

As cotton farms spread, so too did slavery. The enslaved population grew in Georgia, Alabama, and Mississippi. Overall, enslaved African Americans accounted for about one-third of the population of the South.

Most southerners were not slaveholders. About one-fourth of the white families in the South owned slaves. Most had fewer than 20. Only a handful of large plantation owners kept hundreds of African Americans in bondage.

Planters knew that the more slaves they used as laborers, the more cotton they could grow, and the more money they could make. Thus, there was a powerful economic incentive to maintain slavery in the South.

READING CHECK Identifying Cause and **Effect** What led to the spread of slavery throughout the South?

Slavery and King Cotton

Artist William Henry Brown painted this scene of enslaved workers on a Mississippi cotton plantation in 1842. *Examine the painting carefully. What does it tell you about the lives and working conditions of enslaved African Americans?*

Differences between the North and the South

Cotton was king in the South, but it wasn't the only crop grown there. Sugarcane, sugar beets, tobacco, and rice were also important crops. Together, these crops led the economy of the South. By 1840 the South was a thoroughly agricultural region.

In contrast, the North's economy was not nearly as reliant on agriculture. Farming was an important activity and had been since colonial times, but the Industrial Revolution made manufacturing and trade the base of the North's economy.

Different worlds The economic differences between the primarily industrial North and the primarily agricultural South led to even greater differences between the two regions. Trade and industry encourage urbanization, and so cities grew in the North much more than in the South. Moreover, the Industrial Revolution and the revolutions in transportation and communication had the greatest impact on the North. Northern businesses seized new technology in pursuit of efficiency and growth.

By contrast, in the South after the widespread use of the cotton gin, there was relatively little in the way of technological progress. Many southerners saw little need for labor-saving devices, for example, when they had an ample supply of enslaved people to do their work.

These different ways of life led to the development of different points of view. In the North, urban dwellers were exposed to many different types of people and a constantly changing landscape. They tended to view change as progress. In the South, where the landscape was less prone to change and where the population was less diverse, people tended to place a higher value on tradition.

Aggravating the differences between the North and the South was physical distance. Relatively few southerners had the means or motivation to travel extensively in the North, and relatively few northerners had ever visited the South. Thus, to most northerners, the South was a distant and different, almost foreign, place. Southerners had the same feelings about the North.

Differences over slavery The greatest difference between North and South, however, concerned slavery. In the South, where slavery was legal, it was viewed by most white people as an absolutely vital part of the economy, a natural situation, and, to many, a practice sanctioned by their Christian religion. In the North, where slavery was illegal, ever increasing numbers of people viewed it as evil.

Americans of the time were well aware of the differences between the two regions of their country. Yet few could know that the differences would eventually lead the two regions to fight each other in a bloody conflict called the Civil War.

READING CHECK **Contrasting** What were the major differences between the North and the South?

SECTION 4 ASSESSMENT

go.hrw.com
Online Quiz
Keyword: SD7 HP7

Reviewing Ideas, Terms, and People

1. **a. Identify** Where did the demand for cotton grown in the South come from?
   b. Analyze What factors led to the establishment of the **Cotton Belt**?

2. **a. Describe** How did the spread of cotton farming lead to the spread of slavery?
   b. Evaluate Do you think there was much opposition to slavery in the South? Why or why not?

3. **a. Recall** Besides cotton, what other major crops were grown in the South?
   b. Compare and Contrast How were the North and the South similar and different?
   c. Elaborate How did people in the South justify the continuation of the inhumane institution of slavery?

Critical Thinking

4. **Comparing and Contrasting** Copy the diagram and identify similarities and differences between the North and the South.

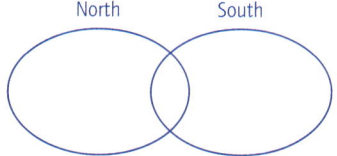

North   South

FOCUS ON WRITING

5. **Expository** Write a paragraph that explains why cotton became fundamental to the economy of the South.

Jackson and Presidential Power

Historical Context The documents below provide different information on Andrew Jackson and presidential power.

Task Examine the documents and answer the questions that follow. Then you will be asked to write an essay about how Andrew Jackson changed presidential power. Use facts from the documents and from the chapter to support the position you take in your thesis statement.

ST 3.2 Draw upon literary selections, historical documents, and accounts to analyze the roles played by different individuals and groups during the major eras in New York State and United States history.

ST 4.3 Develop hypotheses about important events, eras, or issues; move from chronicling to explaining historical events and issues; use information collected from diverse sources to produce cogently written reports and document-based essays.

DOCUMENT 1

In his time, Andrew Jackson was an extremely popular president. The public generally supported his policies and his expansion of power. During the nullification crisis, Jackson threatened to send troops to South Carolina if necessary to force it to obey federal law. The song "Jackson and the Nullifiers" became a popular tune that reflected how much the country supported him.

When we our glorious Constitution form'd,
These Southern men declined it,
But soon they found they were unarmed,
And petitioned to sign it.
Sing Yankee doodle doodle doo,
Yankee doodle dandy,
Now like the snake torpid in a brake [lazy in a marsh],
They think Nullification it is handy.
Without their trade we are not afraid,
But we can live in peace and plenty,
But if to arms they sound alarms,
They may find it not so handy.
Sing Yankee doodle doodle doo,
Sing Yankee doodle dandy,
For Jackson he is wide awake,
He says the Union is so handy.
Our country's cause, our country's laws,
We ever will defend, Sir,
And if they do not gain applause,
My song was never penned, Sir.
So sound the trumpet, beat the drum,
Play Yankee doodle dandy,
We Jackson boys will quickly come,
And be with our rifles handy.

DOCUMENT 2

Some critics believed that Jackson had expanded the power of the presidency to a level not intended by the U.S. Constitution. This cartoon reflected those views.

One of Jackson's major goals was to destroy the Bank of the United States, which he saw as harming poor Americans. As you read in Section 2, he used his presidential power of veto and public support to end the national bank and replace it with smaller banks that he approved. This cartoon shows Jackson fighting a hydra that represents the national bank. The hydra is a mythological beast whose heads grow back when cut off. In this cartoon, the heads of the hydra are politicians who oppose Jackson's fight with the bank.

Andrew Jackson strikes the hydra with a cane labeled "veto."

Nicholas Biddle, the president of the Second Bank of the United States, is shown as the biggest head on the hydra.

THE GRANGER COLLECTION, NEW YORK

Skills FOCUS READING LIKE A HISTORIAN

1. **a. Identify** Refer to Document 1. According to the song, what were the people willing to do to show their support for Jackson?
   b. Analyze In the song, southern men are depicted as favoring nullification. What lines in the song express the opposite view?

2. **a. Identify** Refer to Document 2. To whom is Jackson being compared in this image?
   b. Elaborate Do you think the cartoonist thought that Jackson's expansion of power was a positive or negative development? Explain your answer.

3. **a. Identify** Refer to Document 3. Who does the cartoonist seem to support in this image?
   b. Interpret Why do you think Nicholas Biddle is shown as the biggest head of the hydra?

4. **Document-Based Essay Question** Consider the question below and form a thesis statement. Using examples from Documents 1, 2, and 3, create an outline and write a short essay supporting your position. How did Andrew Jackson change the power of the presidency?

See **Skills Handbook**, pp. H28–29, H31

Visual Summary: From Nationalism to Sectionalism

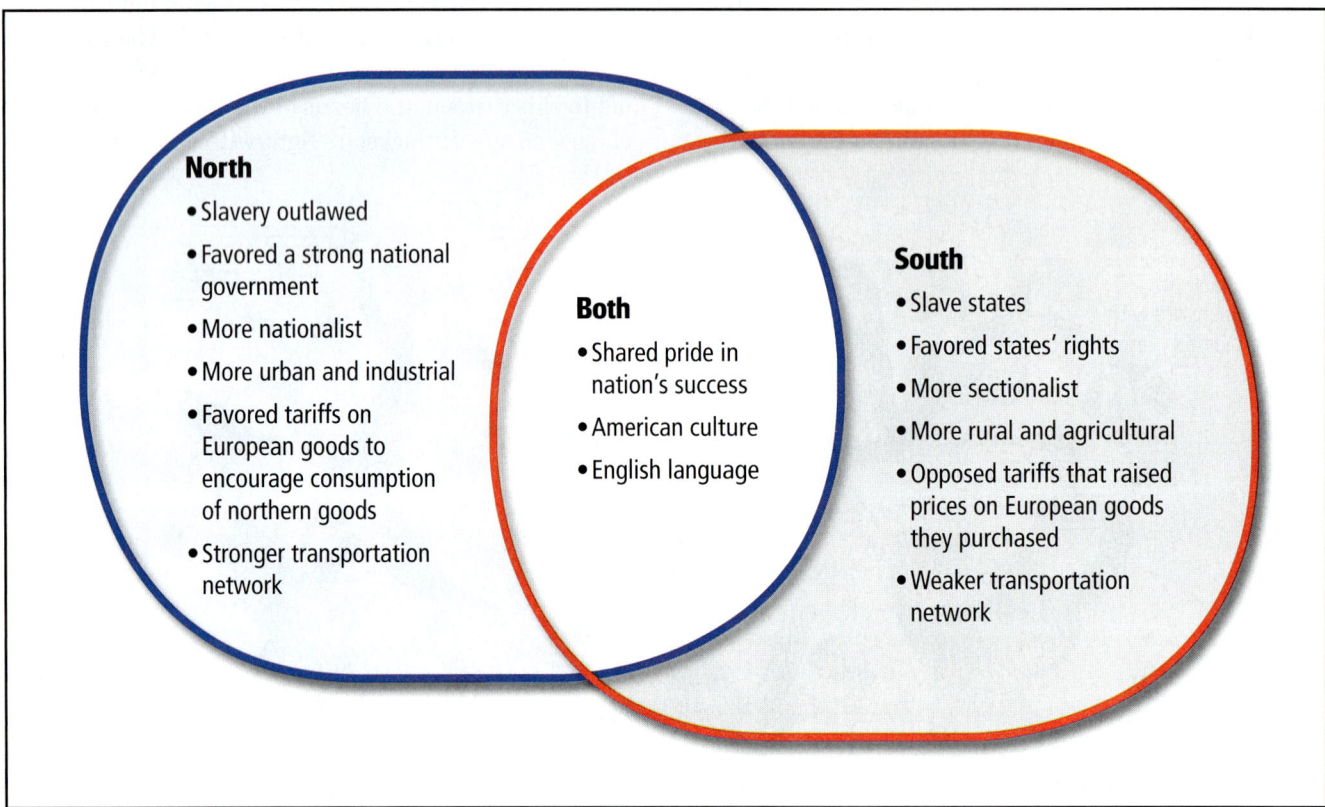

North
- Slavery outlawed
- Favored a strong national government
- More nationalist
- More urban and industrial
- Favored tariffs on European goods to encourage consumption of northern goods
- Stronger transportation network

Both
- Shared pride in nation's success
- American culture
- English language

South
- Slave states
- Favored states' rights
- More sectionalist
- More rural and agricultural
- Opposed tariffs that raised prices on European goods they purchased
- Weaker transportation network

Reviewing Key Terms and People

Identify the correct term or person from the chapter that best fits each of the following descriptions.

1. Waterway linking Great Lakes and Hudson River
2. To leave the Union
3. The birth of modern industry
4. Patented the first successful telegraph
5. Englishman who brought water-powered mill technology to the United States
6. Inventor and operator of the *Clermont*
7. United States' warning to European countries not to interfere in the Americas
8. Eli Whitney's invention
9. South Carolina's rejection of federal laws
10. Band of cotton farms in the South
11. 1830 law that resulted in the Trail of Tears

Comprehension and Critical Thinking

SECTION 1 *(pp. 238–243)*

12. **a. Recall** What replaced feelings of sectionalism in the early 1800s?

    b. Analyze How did growing nationalism affect foreign and domestic policies?

    c. Elaborate How did the Missouri Compromise reflect growing sectionalism in the United States?

SECTION 2 *(pp. 245–250)*

13. **a. Identify** What was Jacksonian Democracy?

    b. Contrast How did the Seminole and the Cherokee resist the Indian Removal Act?

    c. Elaborate How did the issues of states' rights and nullification affect Jackson's presidency?

History's Impact video program
Review the video to answer the closing question:
How did the economic differences between the
North and the South help lead to the Civil War?

SECTION 3 *(pp. 251–255)*

14. a. Describe How did the Industrial Revolution reach the United States?

b. Make Inferences Why did the Industrial Revolution affect the North much more than it did the South?

c. Evaluate What effects did the Industrial Revolution have on the United States?

SECTION 4 *(pp. 256–259)*

15. a. Recall What did the cotton gin do?

b. Draw Conclusions Why did slavery spread throughout the South?

c. Predict What do you think are some likely effects of the fundamental differences between the North and the South?

Using the Internet

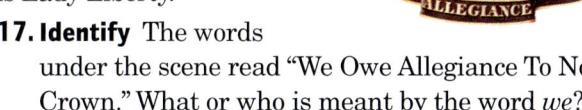

go.hrw.com
Practice Online
Keyword: SD7 CH7

16. During the early 1800s, Americans built thousands of miles of canals. Using the keyword above, do research to learn about the Erie Canal and its impact on New York and the rest of the country. As you do your research, find out what role New York governor DeWitt Clinton played in the development of the Erie Canal. Then create a report that describes how the Erie Canal helped New York and the rest of the country grow.

Analyzing Primary Sources

Reading Like a Historian

This work was painted in the early 1800s by John A. Woodside of Philadelphia. The woman in the painting is Lady Liberty.

17. Identify The words under the scene read "We Owe Allegiance To No Crown." What or who is meant by the word *we*?

18. Analyze Study the painting. How does the artist convey a feeling of patriotism and nationalism?

Critical Reading

Read the passage at the end of Section 1 that begins with the heading "The Missouri Compromise." Then answer the questions that follow.

19. What led to the Missouri Compromise?

A the fact that slavery was illegal in Missouri

B the effort to abolish slavery in the South

C the desire to maintain a balance in the Senate between free and slave states

D the need to admit Maine as a slave state

20. How did the Missouri Compromise affect the Louisiana Territory?

A It banned slavery in all of the territory.

B It allowed slavery in all of the territory.

C It banned slavery in part of the territory and allowed it in another.

D It left the question of slavery in the territory undecided.

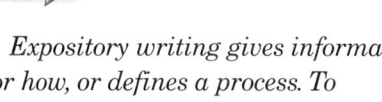

FOCUS ON WRITING

Expository Writing *Expository writing gives information, explains why or how, or defines a process. To practice expository writing, complete the assignment below.*

Writing Topic Differences between the North and the South

21. Assignment Based on what you have read in this chapter, write a paragraph that explains how differences between the North and the South developed in the early 1800s.

A Push for REFORM

THE BIG PICTURE The religious revival called the Second Great Awakening set off one of the great periods of social reform in American history. Some reformers sought to improve conditions in prisons, factories, and the increasingly crowded cities. Other reformers worked to extend women's rights and to end slavery in the United States. Inspired to do good works, the reformers changed the face of America.

New York Standards

Key Idea 3 Study about the major social, political, economic, cultural, and religious developments in New York State and United States history involves learning about the important roles and contributions of individuals and groups.

 Skills FOCUS READING LIKE A HISTORIAN

The religious fervor that swept the nation can be seen in the 1836 engraving *Methodist Camp Meeting*, by E. W. Clay. Religious meetings attracted huge crowds. The humble settings helped drive home the preacher's message.
Interpreting Visuals Examine the response of the people in the crowd. How are they affected by the speaker?

See **Skills Handbook**, p. H30

1833
Oberlin becomes the first American college to admit women.

William Lloyd Garrison founds American Anti-Slavery Society.

 U.S.

1830   1835

 World

1833
Parliament outlaws slavery throughout the British Empire.

History's Impact video program

Watch the video to understand the impact of reformers.

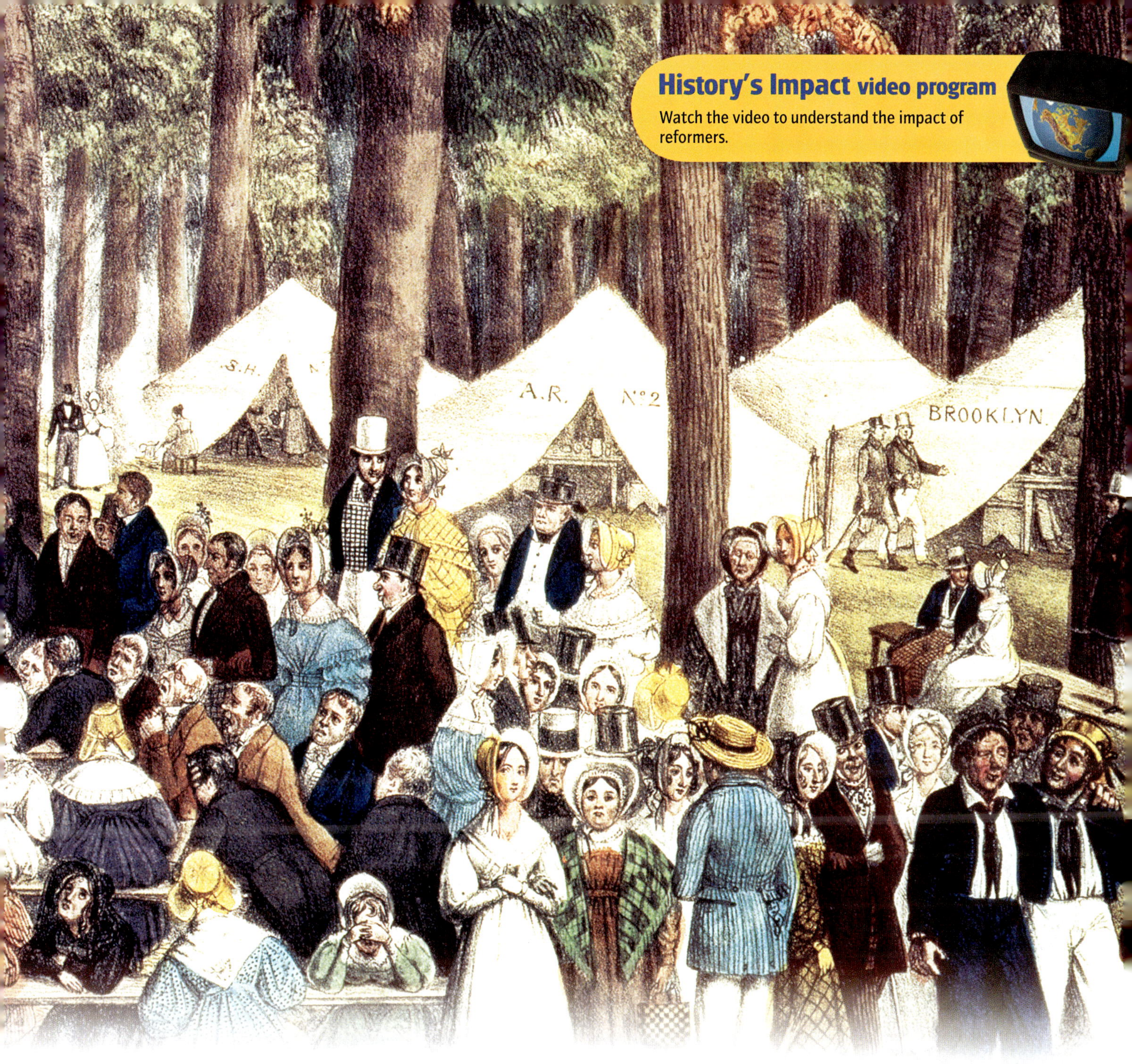

[NEG. #44227] COLLECTION OF THE NEW-YORK HISTORICAL SOCIETY

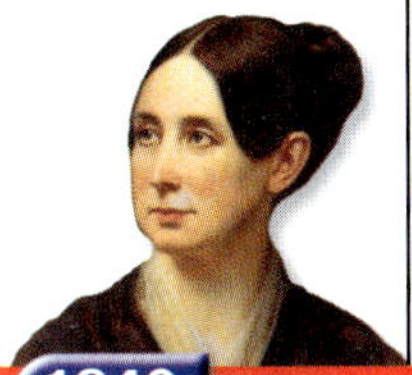

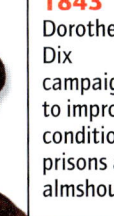

1843 Dorothea Dix campaigns to improve conditions in prisons and almshouses.

1845 Abolitionist Frederick Douglass publishes his *Autobiography*.

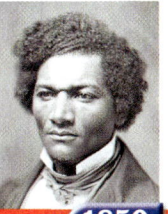

1852 Massachusetts passes mandatory school attendance law.

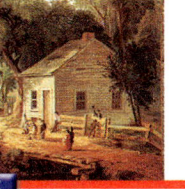

1860 One in six Americans lives in a city.

Some 30 percent of Americans work in manufacturing.

1840 — 1845 — 1850 — 1855 — 1860

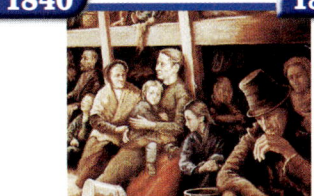

1845 Blight devastates Ireland's potato crop, leading to famine.

1848 Social revolutions demanding constitutional government break out across much of Europe.

1859 Charles Darwin's *On the Origin of Species* is published.

New Movements in America

BEFORE YOU READ

MAIN IDEA

A revival in religion in the early 1800s helped lead to an era of reform.

READING FOCUS

1. How did religion help lead to reform?
2. What role did Horace Mann play in reforming education?
3. What role did Dorothea Dix play in reforming prisons?
4. What are transcendentalism and utopianism?

KEY TERMS AND PEOPLE

Charles Grandison Finney
Second Great Awakening
Reform Era
temperance movement
Horace Mann
Dorothea Dix
transcendentalist movement
Ralph Waldo Emerson
Henry David Thoreau
utopian movement

PI 3.2 Research and analyze the major themes and developments in New York State and United States history (e.g., colonization and settlement; Revolution and New National Period; immigration; expansion and reform era; Civil War and Reconstruction; the American labor movement; Great Depression; World Wars; contemporary United States).

THE INSIDE STORY

What was happening in western New York? In the 1820s and 1830s it seemed that people in every small town were finding a new interest in religion. Crowds flocked to prayer meetings to hear fiery preachers. So many religious revivals took place that the area was called the Burned-Over District—scorched by the flames of religion. Revival meetings were personal, public, and emotional. Unlike in many traditional churches, women were welcome to pray and even preach in public.

Several religious movements began in the Burned-Over District. Joseph Smith published the Book of Mormon based on information he says he translated from golden plates delivered by an angel. Smith's teachings led to the founding of the Church of Jesus Christ of Latter-day Saints, or the Mormons. Another revivalist was William Miller, who prophesied the Second Coming of Christ. His followers developed into the Seventh-day Adventist Church. Western New York was also home to Shaker farms, utopian communities like Oneida, and advocates of Spiritualism.

Other reform movements found support too. Western New York was a stronghold for the antislavery movement. Homes and churches were "stations" on the Underground Railroad, which helped slaves escape to Canada. The movement for women's rights also took root here.

FUELED BY THE Fires of Religion

▼ **American Methodists flock to a camp meeting.**

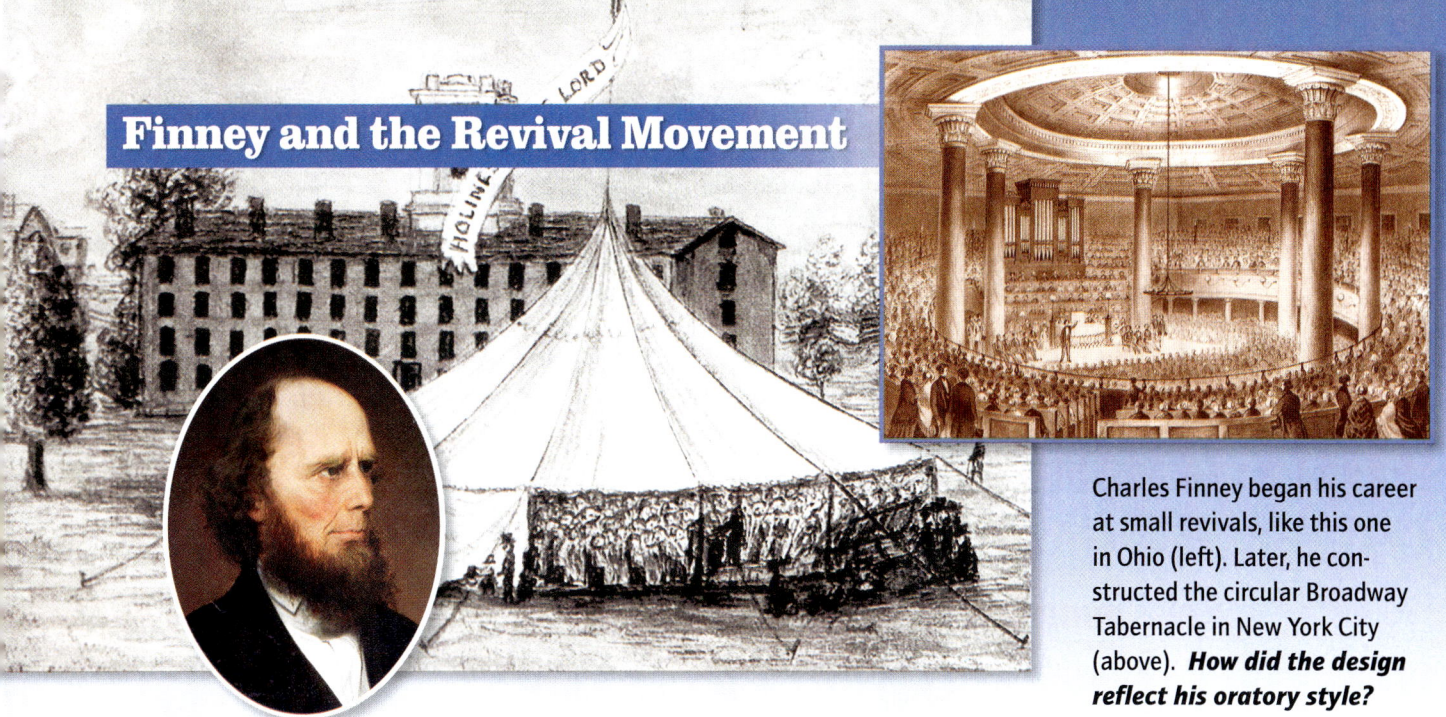

Finney and the Revival Movement

Charles Finney began his career at small revivals, like this one in Ohio (left). Later, he constructed the circular Broadway Tabernacle in New York City (above). *How did the design reflect his oratory style?*

Religion Sparks Reform

The most famous—and the most colorful—character of the Burned-Over District was a preacher named **Charles Grandison Finney**. Finney led revivals, or meetings designed to revive, or reawaken, religious feelings. Finney held revivals throughout the Burned-Over District in the 1820s and 1830s. In his memoirs, the charismatic preacher attributed his success to his way of speaking:

HISTORY'S VOICES

❝The more experience I had, the more I saw the results of my method of preaching, the more I conversed with all classes, high and low, educated and uneducated, the more was I confirmed in the fact that God had led me, had taught me, had given me right conceptions in regard to the best manner of winning souls . . . Indeed, people have often said to me: 'Why, you do not preach. You talk to the people.'❞

—Charles Grandison Finney

Finney talked to many people. At his revivals, hundreds, and sometimes thousands, of people would embrace his teachings.

The Second Great Awakening Finney was just one of many preachers who found willing audiences during the 1820s and 1830s. Across the country, but especially in the North, Americans attended revivals and joined churches in record numbers. By 1850, twice as many Americans attended church than they had at the birth of the country.

This religious movement was called the **Second Great Awakening**. A similar movement, the First Great Awakening, had taken place in the American colonies in the 1700s.

Many preachers of the Second Great Awakening were Protestant. They did not teach strict adherence to church rules, or obedience to a minister. Rather, preachers told people that "their destiny lay in their own hands." People were urged to live well and to work hard.

Further, followers were told that they had the opportunity and the responsibility to do God's work on earth. Through dedication and hard work, they were told, they could create a kind of heaven on earth. Participants in the Second Great Awakening took these beliefs to heart. Across the country, tens of thousands of Americans became determined to reform, or reshape, American life.

Thus, the Second Great Awakening helped launch a remarkable period in American history. The **Reform Era**, which lasted from about 1830 until 1860, was a time in which many Americans attempted to reshape American society. Inspired by the Second Great Awakening, the men and women who participated in the many different movements of the Reform Era are called reformers.

The temperance movement One of the main goals of the reformers was to reduce the use of alcoholic beverages. This movement is called the **temperance movement**. *Temperance* means "moderation."

Reformers wrote books, plays, and songs about the evils of alcohol, which they linked to sickness, poverty, and the breakup of families. Reformers also founded temperance societies, or clubs, and persuaded many Americans to sign temperance pledges. In 1851 reformers persuaded legislators in the state of Maine to outlaw alcohol. Over the next several years, some 12 states followed suit.

READING CHECK **Identifying Cause and Effect** How did the Second Great Awakening help launch the Reform Era?

Reforming Education

Prior to the 1840s, American schools were either private schools or common schools—free public schools were students learned basic reading, writing, and mathematics skills. Most families could not afford private schools, and the quality of teaching in common schools was generally poor.

The common-school movement Most reform-minded Americans wanted more children to be educated. They held that educated people made better decisions and that widespread education was fundamental to a democratic society. Education reformers organized themselves into "friends of education" groups and began the common-school movement to extend and improve public schools.

Horace Mann The greatest school reformer of the Reform Era was **Horace Mann**. In 1837 he became the first secretary of education in the state of Massachusetts.

Mann advocated a new, highly organized approach to education. He envisioned systems in which states would fund and supervise locally controlled schools. Because education was so important to the individual and to society as a whole, Mann advocated compulsory attendance. He also championed the creation of so-called normal schools, where teachers would receive training.

McGuffey Reader

The *McGuffey Readers* included a variety of short stories and excerpts from well-known books to help students learn reading skills.

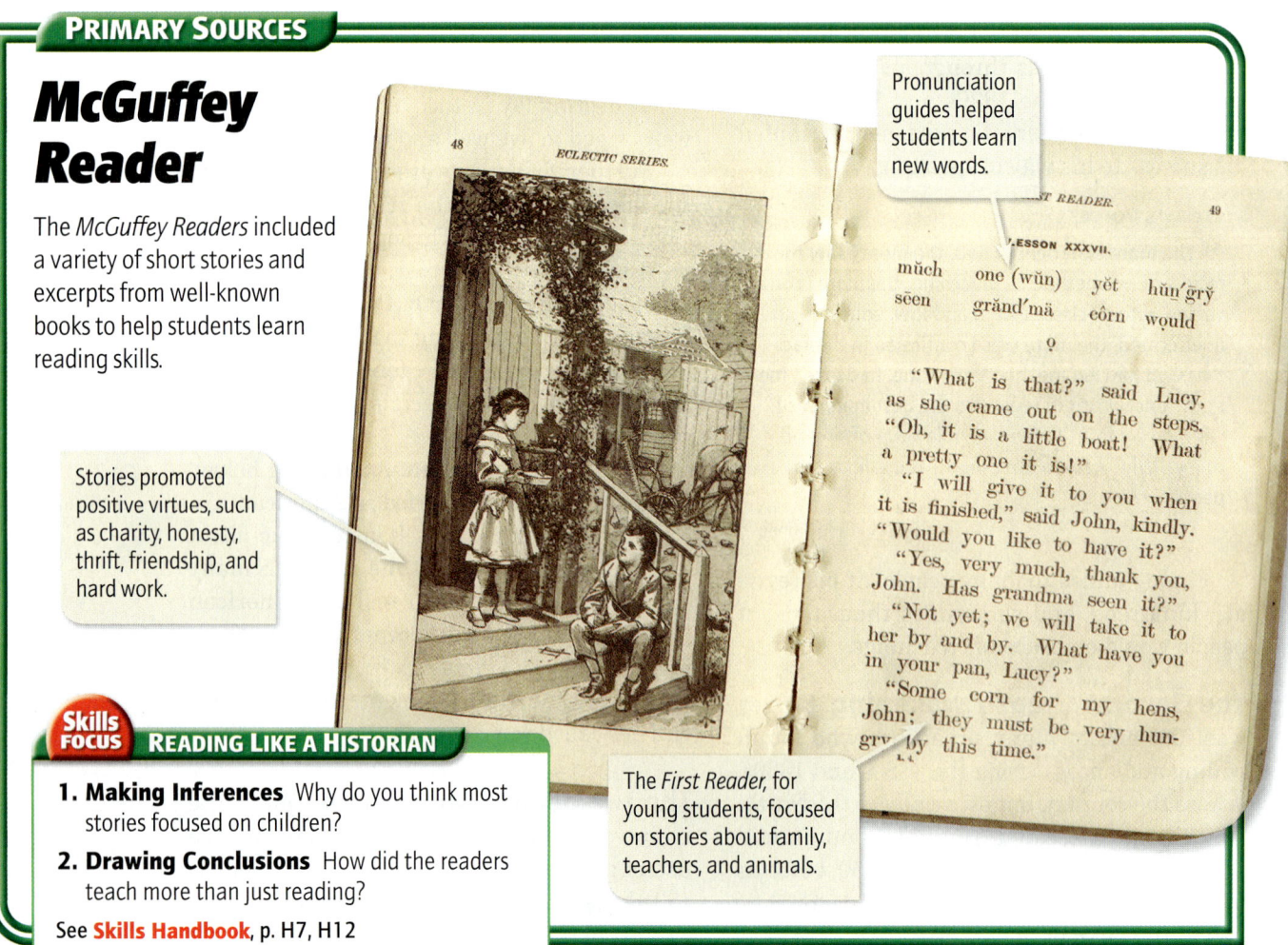

Pronunciation guides helped students learn new words.

Stories promoted positive virtues, such as charity, honesty, thrift, friendship, and hard work.

The *First Reader*, for young students, focused on stories about family, teachers, and animals.

Skills FOCUS **READING LIKE A HISTORIAN**

1. **Making Inferences** Why do you think most stories focused on children?

2. **Drawing Conclusions** How did the readers teach more than just reading?

See **Skills Handbook**, p. H7, H12

Mann's work transformed education in Massachusetts. In 1839 Massachusetts created the country's first normal school. In 1852 it passed the first compulsory attendance law in the United States.

Other states copied Mann's education work in Massachusetts. By 1860, six in ten white children attended school—almost twice the rate of 30 years earlier. Education reform, however, did nothing to help Native American children, who lived within their tribes. Nor could it help African American children, nearly all of whom were slaves. Still, the school reformers' efforts laid the groundwork for education in the United States to the present day.

William McGuffey One of the most well known of the education reformers was William McGuffey. McGuffey wrote and published a series of textbooks called *Eclectic Readers*, which became popularly known as *McGuffey Readers*. These books, written for different grade levels, taught reading and moral and intellectual values. *McGuffey Readers* were so popular—well over 100 million were sold—that nearly every American student in the middle and late 1800s used them in school.

READING CHECK **Identifying the Main Idea** What was the goal of the common-school movement?

Reforming Prisons

Dorothea Dix was a reformer who campaigned for humane treatment of prisoners and the mentally ill. Dix visited a jail in Cambridge, Massachusetts, to teach Sunday school to prisoners in 1841. What Dix saw there appalled her. Mentally ill people and nonviolent criminals were confined with violent criminals. All were held in horribly crowded, unsanitary conditions and were often abused by their jailers.

Dix visited prisons and almshouses, or charity homes for the very poor, throughout Massachusetts. Everywhere she went, she found inhumane conditions.

In 1843 Dix petitioned the state legislature to do something about "the condition of the miserable, the desolate, the outcast" in prisons and almshouses across the state. Moved by Dix's plea, the Massachusetts legislature created state-supported institutions to house and treat mentally ill people, separate from

criminals. Dix and her supporters convinced other state governments to create similar institutions. Before Dix began her work, there were no professional treatment centers in the United States for the mentally ill. By the time of her death, more than 100 such institutions were built across the country.

READING CHECK **Summarizing** What were Dorothea Dix's main achievements?

Transcendentalism and Utopianism

One of the most remarkable movements of the Reform Era took place in New England. It was called the **transcendentalist movement**. Members of this movement believed in a philosophy called transcendentalism.

Transcendentalism is the belief that knowledge is found not only by observation of the world but also through reason, intuition, and personal spiritual experiences. Thus, by transcending, or going beyond, observation, people can have a deeper and truer understanding of the world.

Ralph Waldo Emerson The leading transcendentalist was **Ralph Waldo Emerson**. Emerson gave sermons and lectures and wrote essays and poems. In his work, Emerson expressed the transcendental belief that people should

FACES OF HISTORY

Dorothea DIX
1802–1887

A fast learner who loved to read, Dorothea Dix began teaching young students by the time she was 14. At 19 Dix opened her own school in Boston. In addition, she dedicated her spare time to helping prison inmates and the mentally ill.

While traveling in Europe, Dix met a number of reformers. Returning home, she toured a local jail where the mentally ill were chained in a dungeon. Dix demanded reforms in the treatment of prisoners and the mentally ill. She traveled the nation visiting jails and lobbying for reforms. With her support, the first state hospital was opened in New Jersey. When the Civil War erupted, Dix volunteered to lead the Army Nursing Corps for the Union.

Explain How did Dorothea Dix care for the less fortunate?

be self-reliant and trust their intuition. Such thinking, he said, would lead to a sense that all people and all of nature were connected. Thus, the transcendentalist would support social reform. Emerson's rich writing style and the power of his ideas made him one of America's most renowned and important authors.

Henry David Thoreau

Another major transcendentalist was **Henry David Thoreau**. Thoreau, like Emerson, firmly believed in the power of self-reliance and individual thought.

In 1845 Thoreau began living alone in a cabin on the shore of Walden Pond, near Concord, Massachusetts. By living simply, Thoreau hoped to live a meaningful life.

ACADEMIC VOCABULARY
ideal honorable or worthy goal

Thoreau held that people should act according to their own beliefs, even if they had to break the law. In 1846 Thoreau refused to pay a tax he thought would promote slavery, and he spent a night in jail. Later, in an essay titled "Civil Disobedience," Thoreau stated "that government is best which governs least."

"Civil Disobedience" became an enormously influential essay. In the twentieth century, it inspired Mohandas Gandhi of India to develop a doctrine of nonviolent resistance that helped free his country from British rule. In the United States, civil rights leader Martin Luther King Jr. put Thoreau's and Gandhi's ideas and methods to work on behalf of African Americans in the 1960s.

Utopianism

Some reformers believed in creating new communities that would be free of social ills. These communities became known as utopian communities, after the word *utopia*, which means "a perfect society." Reformers built more than 90 utopian communities in the United States during the **utopian movement** of the first half of the 1800s.

One such community was led by Robert Owen, a British social reformer. In 1825 he purchased the town of Harmonie, Indiana, and renamed it New Harmony. There he attempted to build a utopian community. Unfortunately, the residents of the community failed to implement Owen's <u>ideals</u>, and the community failed three years later.

Another famous utopian community was founded by transcendentalists in Massachusetts in 1841. Brook Farm emphasized equality among all its members. However, the community failed in 1847 due to mounting debts.

Most utopian communities were small and short-lived. A notable exception were those built by the Shakers, a Christian sect that established communities beginning in the late 1700s. In the 1830s, nearly 6,000 Shakers lived in more than a dozen communities throughout the United States.

 **READING CHECK** **Comparing** How were the transcendentalist and the utopian movements similar and different?

SECTION 1 ASSESSMENT

go.hrw.com
Online Quiz
Keyword: SD7 HP8

Reviewing Ideas, Terms, and People

1. **a. Identify** Who was **Charles Grandison Finney**?
   b. Analyze How did the **Second Great Awakening** inspire the **Reform Era**?

2. **a. Identify** Who was **Horace Mann**?
   b. Evaluate How successful was the common-school movement?

3. **a. Recall** Why did **Dorothea Dix** begin her campaign?
   b. Contrast How were mentally ill people and prisoners treated differently after Dix's work?

4. **a. Identify** Who were two important members of the **transcendentalist movement**?
   b. Make Inferences How did transcendentalism support reform?
   c. Evaluate How successful was the **utopian movement**?

Critical Thinking

5. **Summarizing** Copy the chart below and identify the major movements and leaders of the Reform Era.

Movement				
Leader				

 **FOCUS ON WRITING**

6. **Persuasive** Identify one aspect of American life today that you think should be reformed. Write an editorial explaining what should change, why it should be changed, and how reformers could best accomplish that change.

American *Literature*

ST 3.2 Draw upon literary selections, historical documents, and accounts to analyze the roles played by different individuals and groups during the major eras in New York State and United States history.

About the Reading From 1845 to 1847, Henry David Thoreau, a New England transcendentalist, retreated from society to live in seclusion on Walden Pond near Concord, Massachusetts. The following excerpt is taken from a collection of Thoreau's writings from his time at Walden.

AS YOU READ Put yourself in Thoreau's place and think about the reasons why he may have wanted to live in seclusion.

Excerpt from

Walden

by Henry David Thoreau

The surface of the earth is soft and impressible by the feet of men; and so with the paths which the mind travels. How worn and dusty, then, must be the highways of the world, how deep the ruts of conformity! I did not wish to take a cabin passage, but rather to go before the mast and on the deck of the world, for there I could best see the moonlight and the mountains. I do not wish to go below now.

I learned this, at least, by my experiment; that if one advances confidently in the direction of his dreams, and endeavors to live the life which he has imagined, he will meet with a success unexpected in common hours. He will put some things behind, will pass an invisible boundary; new, universal, and more liberal laws will begin to establish themselves around and within him; or the old laws be expanded, and interpreted in his favor in a more liberal sense, and he will live with the license of a higher order of beings. In proportion as he simplifies his life, the laws of the universe will appear less complex, and solitude will not be solitude, nor poverty poverty, nor weakness weakness.

It is a ridiculous demand which England and America make, that you shall speak so that they can understand you. Neither men nor toad-stools grow so. As if that were important, and there were not enough to understand you without them. As if Nature could support but one order of understandings . . . I desire to speak somewhere *without* bounds; like a man in a waking moment, to men in their waking moments; for I am convinced that I cannot exaggerate enough even to lay the foundation of a true expression.

Skills FOCUS **READING LIKE A HISTORIAN**

1. **Summarizing** What does Thoreau mean when he writes that he desires "to speak somewhere without bounds"?

2. **Literature as Historical Evidence** How does Thoreau's call for personal renewal and self-reliance reflect a larger call for reform in the 1830s and 1840s?

See **Skills Handbook**, p. H6

Walden Pond, Massachusetts, where Thoreau lived for two years

Early Immigration and Urban Reform

BEFORE YOU READ

MAIN IDEA

A wave of Irish and German immigrants entered the United States during a period of urbanization and reform.

READING FOCUS

1. Why did many Irish and Germans immigrate to the United States in the 1840s and 1850s?
2. What was life in the United States like for the new immigrants?
3. How did urbanization and industrialization lead to reform?

KEY TERMS AND PEOPLE

Great Irish Famine
push-pull model of immigration
nativism
Know-Nothings
tenements
wage earners
urban working class
labor movement
Martin Van Buren

 PI 3.4 Understand the interrelationships between world events and developments in New York State and the United States (e.g., causes for immigration, economic opportunities, human rights abuses, and tyranny versus freedom).

DISCRIMINATION Set to Music

▲ This song described the descrimination that Irish immigrants sometimes faced.

THE INSIDE STORY

How could immigrants find a job? Music hall singers in the 1860s could always please an audience with the song "No Irish Need Apply." The song tells how a boy from Ireland tries to get a job, even though the ad says, "No Irish need apply." The employer insults him, but the angry young Irishman fights him and makes him apologize. In the song's chorus, he remains proud of his heritage: "But to me it is an honor / To be born an Irishman."

Irish immigrants in the mid-1800s faced widespread discrimination. Newspaper ads and signs in shop and factory windows read "No Irish need apply" or "Protestants only." Some historians question how widespread these signs actually were. But American workers resented the Irish for taking scarce jobs, especially low-paying jobs on the docks or as day laborers. Others mistrusted the Irish for being Roman Catholic.

The signs were aimed mainly at Irish Catholic men. In general, Irish women found jobs as cooks or maids more easily. Eventually, Irish immigrants overcame prejudice to find their place in American society. ■

Irish and German Immigrants

The sadness of the song "No Irish Need Apply" is apparent. What makes the song even sadder, though, is that many of the Irish immigrants who faced this prejudice were desperate refugees fleeing one of the great disasters of the modern age.

Irish immigration Since the 1700s, the poor people of Ireland had relied on the potato as their staple, or major, food crop. In fact, most people of Ireland ate little else. From 1845 to 1849, a disease, or blight, struck the crop, severely restricting the potato harvest.

The results were devastating. Deprived of their primary food source and receiving little relief from the ruling British government, Ireland's poor faced starvation. By 1850 about 1 million had died during the **Great Irish Famine**.

Desperate to save themselves and their families, more than 2 million people left Ireland. By 1854, about 1.5 million of them had settled in the United States.

German immigration The other major group of immigrants to the United States in the mid-1800s were the Germans. Like the Irish, many Germans were fleeing conditions in their homeland. Unlike the Irish, they had not faced famine. Instead, they left Germany for many different reasons. Some fled economic depression and overpopulation, which made jobs scarce. Others left to escape religious persecution, harsh tax laws, or military service. Still others fled their country after a revolution in 1848 failed. Many Germans came to the United States in search of free land and business opportunities.

Pushed and pulled All immigration can be described using the **push-pull model of immigration**. In this model, factors that cause people to leave their homeland are "pushes." Factors that cause people to move to a particular country are called "pulls." Various pushes and pulls led to a record number of immigrants to the United States, including about 3 million Irish and German immigrants by 1860.

READING CHECK **Summarizing** What caused German and Irish immigrants to be pushed from their homelands?

The Lives of Immigrants

The lives that immigrants built in the United States varied widely. Wealthy people with family or other connections in the United States did well. The majority of immigrants, however,

FOCUS ON NEW YORK

DAILY LIFE

In the late 1800s Ellis Island in New York Harbor was the main port of entry for thousands of immigrants into the United States. Over time, New York's immigrant heritage has grown. In the 2000 census, about 2.1 million New Yorkers indicated they had German ancestry and another 2.4 million claimed Irish ancestry. Nationally, about 30 million Americans claimed Irish ancestry and another 43 million Americans claimed German ancestry.

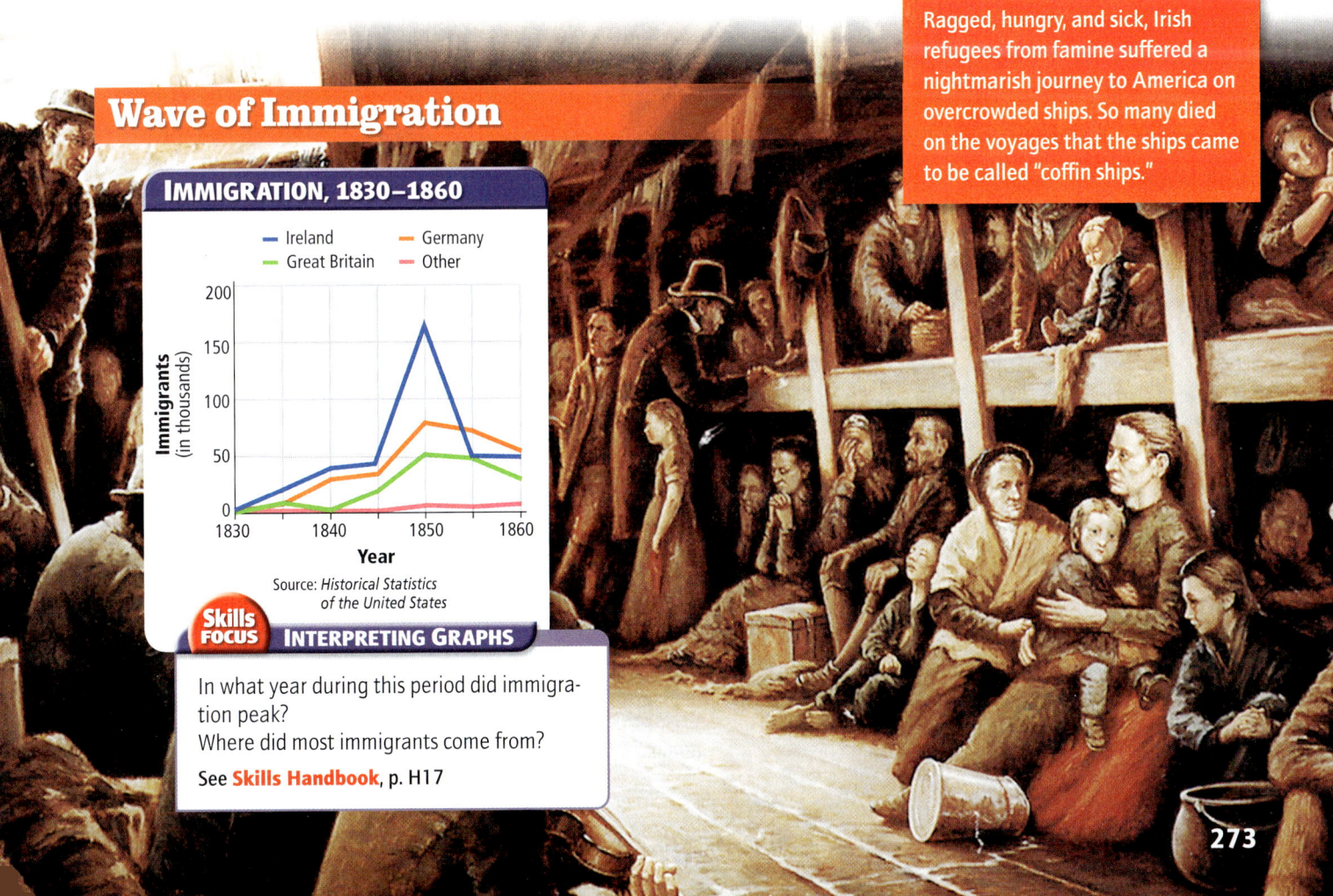

Ragged, hungry, and sick, Irish refugees from famine suffered a nightmarish journey to America on overcrowded ships. So many died on the voyages that the ships came to be called "coffin ships."

Wave of Immigration

IMMIGRATION, 1830–1860

- Ireland
- Germany
- Great Britain
- Other

Immigrants (in thousands) / Year

Source: *Historical Statistics of the United States*

Skills FOCUS **INTERPRETING GRAPHS**

In what year during this period did immigration peak?
Where did most immigrants come from?

See **Skills Handbook**, p. H17

273

had little or no money and often no one to turn to for help. They faced a difficult struggle to survive in, what was to them, an alien and often hostile land.

Hostility toward the Irish

Many immigrant groups to the United States have faced <u>discrimination</u>. Few immigrant groups, however, met the hostility that the Irish did.

Why were the Irish treated so harshly? One reason was their sheer numbers. More than 1.3 million Irish immigrants arrived between 1846 and 1855. The country's population in that period averaged 24 million. The largest city at the time, New York, was home to only half a million people. Many Americans viewed the influx of so many people from a single foreign country as a threat to their way of life.

The Irish were also resented because of their poverty. Because desperate Irish immigrants would work for very low wages, they posed a threat to American workers.

Above all else, though, Irish immigrants were resented because they were Roman Catholic. The United States at the time was predominantly Protestant. Many Americans believed that the Roman Catholic religion was at odds with democratic principles. Samuel F. B. Morse, who invented the first practical telegraph, was one such American. Describing Roman Catholicism as "Popery," he reflected the biased view of many Americans of the time.

HISTORY'S VOICES

❝Popery cannot tolerate our form of government . . . Popery does not acknowledge the right of the people to govern; but claims for itself the supreme right to govern all people and all rulers by divine right . . . It does not tolerate liberty of conscience nor liberty of opinion.❞

—Samuel F. B. Morse

As the number of Irish immigrants grew, so too did these feelings of <mark>nativism</mark>, or opposition to immigration. The growth of nativism was a marked change in Americans' attitudes. For generations, immigrants had been generally welcomed as adding to the population and prosperity of a growing country. Besides, most Americans were descended from immigrants— many just a generation or two in the past. But the influx of a huge number of poor, Catholic, Irish immigrants in such a short time changed many Americans' views. They began to regard immigrants as a threat to their way of life.

TWO PORTRAYALS OF IMMIGRATION

© COLLECTION OF THE NEW-YORK HISTORICAL SOCIETY

Skills FOCUS **READING LIKE A HISTORIAN**

These images show two portrayals of Irish immigrants.
Interpreting Visuals Which image is more likely to create bias against Irish immigrants? Explain your answer.

MUSEUM OF THE CITY OF NEW YORK

The Know-Nothings Anti-immigrant sentiment was promoted by well-funded and well-organized social and political groups. One such group was a secret fraternal organization called the Know-Nothings. The group earned its name because its members, when asked about their group's activities, answered by saying, "I know nothing."

The Know-Nothings reorganized themselves into a political party. The American Party would boast of more than 1 million members by the 1850s. They achieved remarkable political success in a short time, claiming more than 40 congressional seats. When they won elections in Massachusetts, one newspaper trumpeted the news.

❝ . . . [In Massachusetts] are heard the voices of her native born children, declaring for the perpetuity AMERICAN INSTITUTIONS, and AMERICAN LIBERTIES. The [people] have spoken in a voice of thunder, in favor of Americans ruling America . . . the warm pulsation of the people's heart beats only for FREEDOM . . . and PROTESTANTISM. ❞

—*Daily Evening Journal,* November 14, 1854

The American Party even ran a presidential candidate in 1856. Eventually disagreements over slavery and related political issues fractured the party, and it ceased to exist by the time of the Civil War.

A different German experience Nearly as many Germans as Irish immigrated to the United States in the mid-1800s. Fortunately for the Germans, they did not encounter the same hostility that greeted Irish immigrants. Why not? Whereas most Irish immigrants were poor and Catholic, most German immigrants were middle class and Protestant.

German immigrants spread across the country. They could afford to travel far inland, seeking free or cheap land, reunions with relatives, or other opportunities in the heartland. Many settled in the Midwest, but large German immigrant communities could be found from New York to Texas. German immigrants worked as farmers, artisans, factory workers, and in other occupations.

READING CHECK **Contrasting** How were Irish immigrants treated differently than German immigrants?

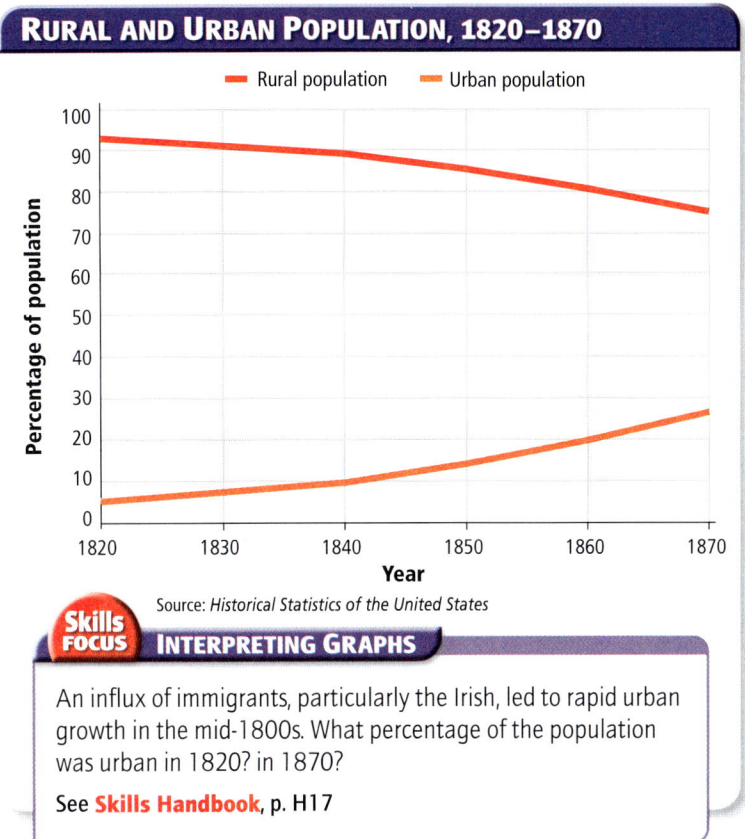

RURAL AND URBAN POPULATION, 1820–1870

— Rural population   — Urban population

Source: Historical Statistics of the United States

Skills FOCUS **INTERPRETING GRAPHS**

An influx of immigrants, particularly the Irish, led to rapid urban growth in the mid-1800s. What percentage of the population was urban in 1820? in 1870?

See **Skills Handbook**, p. H17

Reform, Urbanization, and Industrialization

Immigrants to the United States in the middle 1800s arrived in a country undergoing two dramatic changes. One was urbanization. In 1800 about 1 in 20 Americans lived in urban areas; by 1860 about 1 in 6 did. The other change was industrialization. In 1800 nearly everything in the country was made by hand. By 1860 about one-third of all goods were made by machine. The parallel forces of urbanization and industrialization caused tremendous social change and resulted in important reform movements.

Growing city populations The arrival of so many Irish immigrants in the 1840s and 1850s was a major factor in the growth of some American cities. Most Irish immigrants, unable to afford to travel far from where they landed in America, settled in northeastern cities such as New York and Boston. By 1850 Irish immigrants accounted for one-fourth of the population of these cities. Even today, both have large Irish American populations.

Immigration

In the past, most immigrants to the United States came from European nations. Today growing numbers of immigrants come from Mexico, Central America, South America, and Asia.

In 2003 more than 244,000 people born in Asia moved to the United States. Nearly 116,000 people came from Mexico, and almost 110,000 others were born in Central or South America.

No matter where immigrants are born, they leave their homes in search of a better life. They may hope to find better economic opportunities or political or religious freedom.

In earlier eras, immigrants entered the country through specific immigration centers. Europeans entered the United States at Ellis Island in New York Harbor. Asian immigrants came to Angel Island, near San Francisco. Today, immigrants arrive to the United States like any other travelers, often by plane.

Comparing What do today's immigrants share with those of the past?

Immigrants becoming U.S. citizens at a naturalization ceremony

Urbanization and reform By the mid-1800s, large American cities were home to some tremendously wealthy people. They had made fortunes in trade or in new industries. It was not uncommon for this richest 1 percent of the population to control more than half of the wealth of a city. The vast majority of urban Americans, however, were very poor.

Many city-dwellers lived in **tenements**, or poorly made, crowded apartment buildings. Lacking adequate light, ventilation, and sanitation, tenements were very unhealthy places to live. Disease spread rapidly in the crowded conditions.

The plight of tenement dwellers sparked preliminary efforts at reform. In some cities, local boards of health were established to set sanitation rules. Enforcement was often uneven, however, and the poorer neighborhoods—which were in the greatest need—received less attention than richer ones.

Local reform societies did what they could to alleviate the suffering but only reached a fraction of those who needed help. For the most part, the poor of America's large cities fended for themselves, helping their families, neighbors, and friends as best they could.

Conditions in the poorer districts of American cities would remain unsatisfactory throughout the mid-1800s. Serious efforts at reforming cities would not begin until late in the century.

ACADEMIC VOCABULARY

preliminary prior to the main action; introductory

Industrialization and reform Between 1820 and 1860, the percentage of Americans who worked in manufacturing and related fields soared from 5 percent to about 30 percent. This fundamental shift in the economy had far-reaching social effects. Previously, most Americans had worked on farms. People worked for themselves, kept the profits they earned, and made much of what they needed.

Americans who worked in factories faced a far different economic situation. They were **wage earners**. That is, instead of earning income from their own enterprise, they were paid a set amount by business owners. Instead of making the things they needed, they had to buy them—using their limited wages—from merchants in the city where they lived.

In addition to immigrants flooding the cities, many Americans were leaving farms to work in factories. A new social class arose: the **urban working class**. Most of them were poor and uneducated. Many were immigrants.

As a rule, the relatively wealthy business owners wanted to maximize their profits. The results were low wages, long hours, and unsafe working conditions for workers. In response, workers began to organize into groups to demand higher wages, shorter hours, and safer working conditions. These efforts by workers to improve their situation was one of the great reform movements of the Reform Era. It is called the **labor movement**.

The American labor movement began in the 1820s. During that decade skilled workers, such as carpenters and masons, formed organizations to regulate their pay. The advent of widespread factory work in the 1830s contributed to the early development of the labor movement.

Most workers' organizations were local and short-lived. Not until 1834 was an attempt made to create a national labor organization. In New York City, several smaller groups united to form the National Trades Union. It lasted only until the Panic of 1837, an economic crisis that left as many as one-third of American workers out of a job.

The labor movement faced fierce opposition from business owners. Moreover, many government officials were business owners themselves, or at least sympathized with the owners whose prosperity they thought essential to the well-being of the nation.

Labor reformers did enjoy some victories. One of their major campaigns was the Ten-Hour Movement, a campaign to limit the working day to 10 hours from the more common 12 hours—or more. In 1837 President Andrew Jackson declared a 10-hour workday for some federal employees. President **Martin Van Buren** extended the rule to others in 1840. In the mid-1840s, New Hampshire became the first state to limit the workday to 10 hours. Other states followed New Hampshire's example.

Working Conditions

A cotton mill boss whips a young worker in this 1853 woodcut. Workers in this period also faced long hours, low wages, and unsafe conditions. *How did workers try to improve their conditions?*

Despite this success, laborers remained very much at the whim of business owners. It would be decades before they made substantial progress in improving their work conditions.

READING CHECK **Identifying the Main Idea**
What reforms arose in response to urbanization and industrialization?

---

go.hrw.com
Online Quiz
Keyword: SD7 HP8

SECTION 2 ASSESSMENT

Reviewing Ideas, Terms, and People

1. a. Recall How did the **Great Irish Famine** affect the United States?
 b. Draw Conclusion What factors do you think pulled Irish and German immigrants to the United States?

2. a. Recall Why were Irish immigrants discriminated against?
 b. Compare Why were German immigrants treated differently than Irish immigrants?

3. a. Explain What was life like for the **urban working class**?
 b. Evaluate What factors limited the success of the early labor movement?

Critical Thinking

4. Comparing and Contrasting Copy the diagram below and compare and contrast Irish and German immigration.

	Irish Immigrants	German Immigrants
Reasons for Immigrating		
Places Settled		
Economic Standing		
Religious Beliefs		

FOCUS ON WRITING

5. Expository Write a dialogue that might have taken place between a leader of the labor movement and a business owner in the 1830s. The dialogue should reflect each person's position on the 10-hour workday.

The Great Irish Famine

Because of the potato crop failure and mass starvation between 1845 and 1851, over a million Irish emigrated to America. They traveled weeks in crowded ships to reach the chaos of American port cities, where they had imagined great opportunities awaited them. Most of these immigrants were too poor to buy farmland and were not eager to return to an agricultural life. They settled in Irish neighborhoods in New York, Boston, Philadelphia, and Baltimore—the port cities where they disembarked. Many others found their way to the interior cities of Chicago, St. Louis, and Cincinnati.

IRISH IMMIGRATION TO THE UNITED STATES	
1845	44,821
1846	51,752
1847	105,536
1848	112,934
1849	159,389
1850	164,004
1851	221,253
1852	159,548
1853	162,649
1854	101,606
1855	49,627
Total	1,333,128

Source: *Historical Statistics of the United States: Colonial Times to 1970*

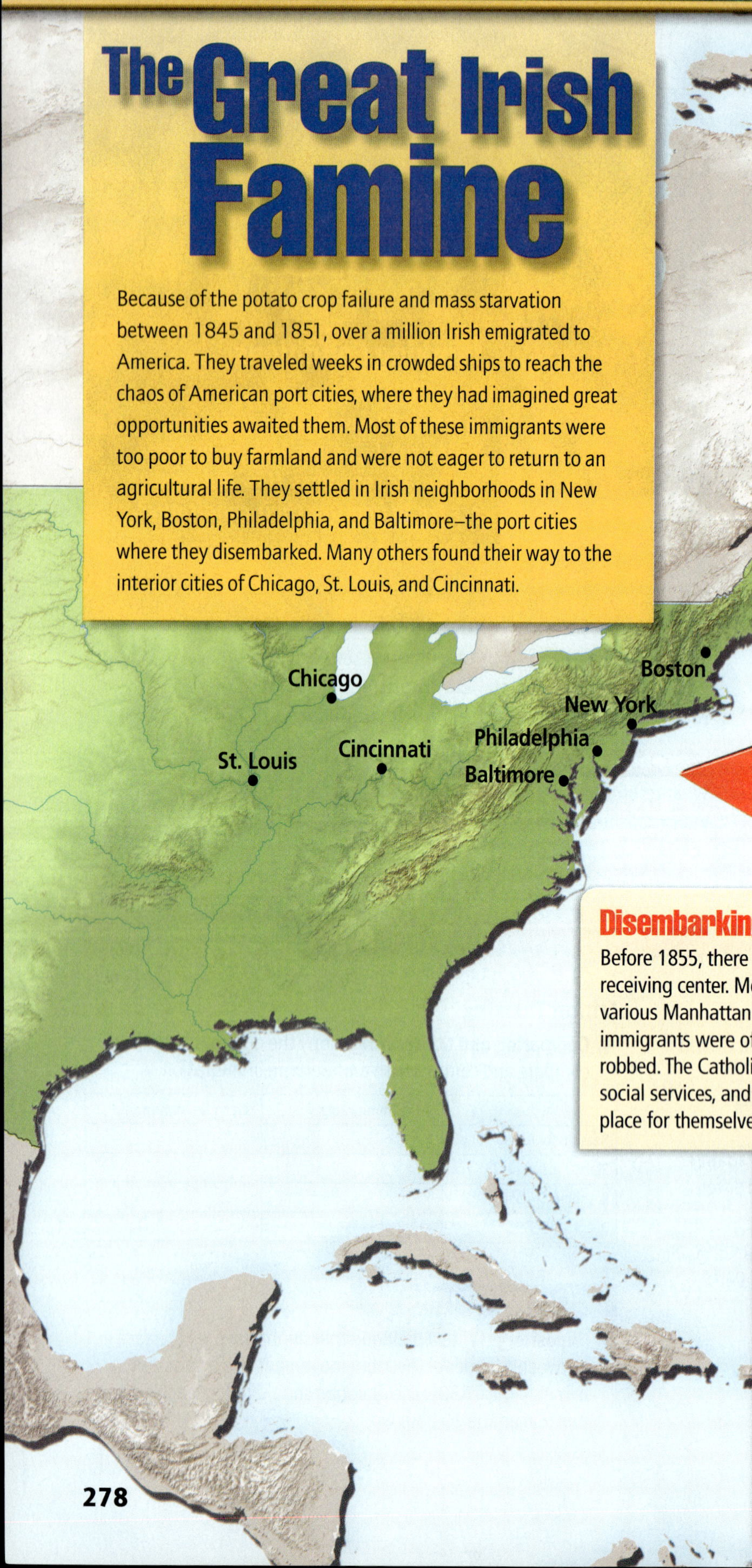

Chicago

Boston

New York

St. Louis • Cincinnati

Philadelphia

Baltimore

Disembarking

Before 1855, there was no central immigrant-receiving center. Most ships let passengers off at various Manhattan docks. There, the unprotected immigrants were often taken advantage of or robbed. The Catholic Church helped them with social services, and eventually the Irish forged a place for themselves.

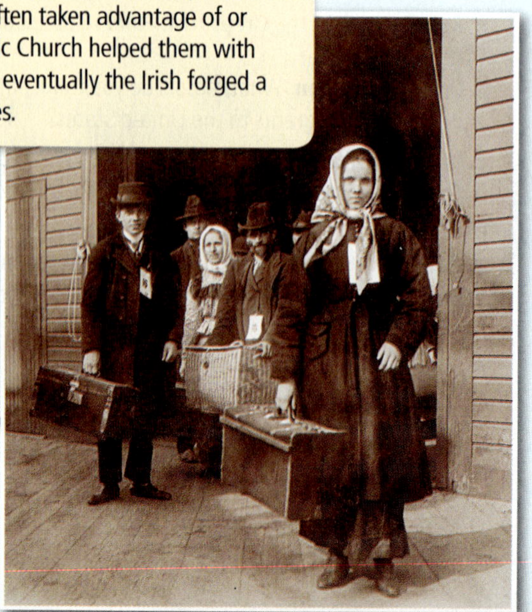

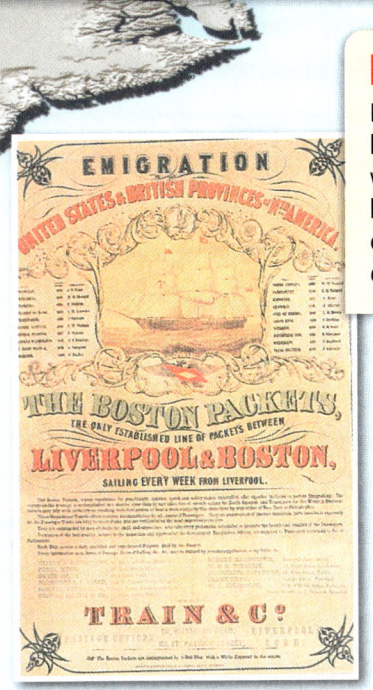

Eviction and Emigration

In the 1800s, Irish farmers rented their land from English landowners. They had little time to tend their own crops, so they came to depend on potatoes, which were easy to grow. Potatoes made up 60 percent of the Irish diet. When blight destroyed this crop several years in a row, farmers spent their money on food instead of rent. Many were then evicted and had little choice but to emigrate. Most left for North America by way of Liverpool, England.

Dublin

IRELAND

Liverpool

ENGLAND

London

Coffin Ships

Although laws limited the number of passengers on a ship, captains avoided the law by loading passengers at more than one port. Packed into windowless compartments, with disease spreading and food and water scarce, many passengers died during the crossing.

GEOGRAPHY SKILLS   INTERPRETING MAPS

1. **Human-Environment Interaction** How did the potato blight lead to mass Irish emigration?
2. **Movement** Describe the passage and the reception for Irish immigrants to America.

See **Skills Handbook**, p. H20

SECTION 3

Women and Reform

BEFORE YOU READ

MAIN IDEA

After leading reform movements to help others, some American women began to work on behalf of themselves.

READING FOCUS

1. What limits were placed on women's lives in the early 1800s?
2. What role did women play in the movements of the Reform Era?
3. Why was the Seneca Falls Convention important?

KEY TERMS AND PEOPLE

cult of domesticity
reform societies
Catharine Beecher
Seneca Falls Convention
Elizabeth Cady Stanton
Lucretia Mott

P1 **3.2** Research and analyze the major themes and developments in New York State and United States history (e.g., colonization and settlement; Revolution and New National Period; immigration; expansion and reform era; Civil War and Reconstruction; the American labor movement; Great Depression; World Wars; contemporary United States).

THE INSIDE STORY

Why was Elizabeth Cady Stanton angry? When Elizabeth Cady's only brother died, her father sighed, "Oh my daughter, I wish you were a boy." She tried to please him. She got the best education available to women at the time and studied law in his office. In 1840 at age 25, she married an abolitionist, Henry Stanton. Their marriage vows omitted the word *obey*.

On their honeymoon the Stantons traveled to London for a world antislavery convention, but its organizers refused to allow women to participate in convention debates. Elizabeth Cady Stanton and Lucretia Mott, another rejected delegate, decided that in order for their voices to be heard, they must work for their own rights. In 1848 they organized and directed the first women's rights convention, in Seneca Falls, New York. About 300 people attended, including abolitionist Frederick Douglass.

At the meeting, Stanton presented a Declaration of Sentiments. It echoed the Declaration of Independence—but with some important differences: "We hold these truths to be self-evident, that all men and women are created equal, that they are endowed by their Creator with certain inalienable rights . . ."

Although Lucretia Mott and Henry Stanton both objected, the Seneca Falls declaration also called for the right to vote. It said that women should have "immediate admission to all the rights and privileges which belong to them as citizens of the United States." The statement concluded that these demands were likely to meet with ridicule. Not surprisingly, that was exactly what happened. ◢

CRUSADER
for Women's Rights

▶ Reformist Elizabeth Cady Stanton and her children, about 1848

Limits on Women's Lives

The Seneca Falls declaration was widely ridiculed. So, too, were the women who supported it. The handful of men who dared to speak out for the equal treatment of women were treated with even worse disdain. This surprised no one. A combination of legal, economic, and cultural factors limited what American women in the early 1800s could achieve.

Legal limits Legally, women in the United States were denied many of the basic rights and responsibilities of U.S. citizenship. With few exceptions, women could not vote or hold public office. Other than marraige, they could not enter into legal contracts. When married couples with children divorced, the law awarded custody of the children to the father.

Economic limits With few exceptions, married women were not allowed to own property. Real property, such as land and buildings, businesses, and even household goods, was legally owned by husbands.

In the early 1800s, many American women took jobs outside of their homes for the first time. The Industrial Revolution led to a record number of working women. In 1816 the federal government determined that more than 60,000 of the 100,000 industrial workers in the country were women. Even this did not help most women economically. Wages were low. Moreover, the wages of married women were legally the property of their husbands. Single women were expected to turn over most of their earnings to their families.

Cultural limits The legal and economic limits placed on women both reflected and promoted a widely held view that women were inferior to men. Women, most men believed, should attend only to household and family duties—and to their husbands. Matters outside the home—business, government, politics—should be the province of men, who could handle such weighty matters.

The cultural limits placed on women intensified during the Industrial Revolution. The view that "a woman's place is in the home" became more widespread. This was largely a response to the belief that industrialization was threatening family life by taking women out of the household to work. A movement arose to urge women to remain in the home environment. Books and magazines praised the virtues of women staying at home, caring for their families, and obeying their husbands. Some historians gave this movement a name: the **cult of domesticity**.

READING CHECK **Identifying the Main Idea**
What limits were placed on American women in the early 1800s?

Women in the Reform Era

Despite the many limits placed on their lives, American women often took the lead in reshaping life in the nation. They played important roles in all of the great reform movements of the Reform Era.

All of the reform movements were rooted to some degree in the Second Great Awakening. This religious revival opened many doors for women. The movement de-emphasized obedience to a minister and celebrated good works. Women were therefore able to participate more fully in religious affairs. Many formed groups, such as Bible-reading and missionary societies, that served as extensions of their involvement in churches.

Reform societies Some of these women's church societies evolved into reform societies. **Reform societies** were groups that were organized to promote social reforms. The number of reform societies grew rapidly in the 1830s and 1840s.

The New York Female Reform Society was formed in 1834.

HISTORY'S VOICES

❝It is the imperious [dominant] duty of ladies everywhere and of every religious denomination to cooperate in the great work of moral reform.❞
—Statement of the New York Female Reform Society

Similar societies sprang up throughout the Northeast. Tens of thousands of women joined these groups.

By moral reform, the groups meant promoting good behavior. Society members would visit poor neighborhoods, almshouses, jails, and other places to provide religious instruction and encouragement. Some reform society members established homes for

THE IMPACT TODAY

Economics
In 2004 about 46 percent of the American labor force consisted of women.

orphaned girls, homeless young women, and other women in need.

Education reform As in other reform movements, women led the movement to reform education. **Catharine Beecher** ran a school for women, the Hartford Female Seminary, in Massachusetts. Later, she opened the Western Female Institute in Cincinnati, Ohio. Beecher worked to create normal schools and to send teachers west to educate frontier children.

Oberlin College in Ohio became the first American college to welcome women as well as men in 1833. In 1837 Mary Lyon established the first women's college in the United States, Mount Holyoke College in Massachusetts. Many women became teachers during the Reform Era. This gave them a fundamental role in shaping American life.

Other reforms Urban reforms during the Reform Era were implemented largely by female reform societies. Through visits and the establishing of homes for girls and women in need, women worked to improve the lives of the urban poor.

Women's contributions to the labor movement arose from their firsthand experiences as workers. By 1850 about 225,000 American women were at work in the country's mills and factories, toiling long hours for low wages, often in unsafe conditions. Some of the earliest labor strikes were held by women, such as the Lowell Girls, who were attempting to better their working conditions.

Many participants in the temperance movement were women. Because women were economically dependent on men, they and their children were often the victims of men's excessive alcohol consumption. Thus, they knew firsthand of the dangers of alcohol abuse.

READING CHECK **Summarizing** How did women contribute to reform?

The Seneca Falls Convention

The **Seneca Falls Convention** was held in July 1848 in Seneca Falls, New York. It was the first women's rights convention held in America. Many historians mark it as the beginning of the modern American women's movement.

PRIMARY SOURCES

Declaration of Sentiments

The writer used the same words that are in the Declaration of Independence, but included women.

In 1848 women's rights supporters met in Seneca Falls, New York, and produced a document calling for greater expansion of women's rights, especially the right to vote. Modeled after the Declaration of Independence, the Declaration of Sentiments was a landmark in the women's movement.

Like the Declaration of Independence, the Declaration of Sentiments included a list of grievances.

"We hold these truths to be self-evident: that all men and women are created equal; that they are endowed by their Creator with certain inalienable rights; that among these are life, liberty, and the pursuit of happiness; that to secure these rights governments are instituted, deriving their just powers from the consent of the governed . . .

The history of mankind is a history of repeated injuries . . . on the part of man toward woman, having in direct object the establishment of an absolute tyranny over her . . .

Having deprived her of this first right as a citizen, the elective franchise, thereby leaving her without representation in the halls of legislation, he has oppressed her on all sides."

Skills FOCUS **READING LIKE A HISTORIAN**

1. **Analyzing Primary Sources** Why do you think the writer modeled this document after the Declaration of Independence?

2. **Identifying Points of View** Why did the writer believe that voting rights were so important?

See **Skills Handbook**, pp. H28–29

A desire for political power Over the years, countless American women had fought for many different kinds of reforms. But the limits placed on them—especially their prohibition from participating in government by voting or holding public office—restricted their influence and accomplishments. As a result, many women wanted to obtain political power in order to advance the reforms.

Other women, however, thought that political power should be available to women, not just so that they could achieve reform but because it was fair and reasonable.

Moreover, women reformers had long worked for the rights of others. They were especially active in the abolitionist movement to end slavery. It was a short leap from thinking about racial equality to equality between the sexes. Thus, the time was right for women—who had long worked to improve the lives of others—to fight to improve their own lives.

The convention Elizabeth Cady Stanton and Lucretia Mott organized the Seneca Falls Convention. Mott was a prominent abolitionist. A Quaker, she helped found several antislavery groups and organized antislavery conventions. Stanton, like Mott, was also a dedicated and experienced abolitionist.

Mott and Stanton had attended the World's Anti-Slavery Convention in London in 1840. Mott and Stanton's husband, Henry, were official delegates. They were shocked to learn that Mott, because she was a woman, would not be allowed to participate in convention debates. Worse, women even had to be segregated from men. This experience drove Mott and Stanton to take action. They determined to call a convention on behalf of women's rights.

The women's rights convention was held near Stanton's home in Seneca Falls, New York. It was attended by about 300 people. The convention produced the Declaration of Sentiments, written by Stanton. Exactly 100 participants—68 women and 32 men—signed the Declaration of Sentiments, which publicly stated their belief that "all men and women are created equal." The struggle for the equality of American women had begun.

READING CHECK **Making Inferences** How do you think the Seneca Falls Convention affected the women's movement for equal rights?

THE GRANGER COLLECTION, NEW YORK

FACES OF HISTORY

Lucretia MOTT
1793–1880

Raised as a Quaker, Lucretia Mott was strongly committed to her faith. At Quaker meetings, Mott was encouraged to speak out against social problems. In the 1830s Mott traveled the country making speeches against slavery. In 1840 Mott attended the World's Anti-Slavery Convention in England but was not allowed to speak, simply because she was a woman.

Back in the United States, Mott began to demand equal treatment for women. In 1848 Mott and Elizabeth Cady Stanton organized a convention in Seneca Falls, New York. The convention issued a Declaration of Sentiments, demanding women's equality. Throughout the rest of her life, Mott continued to fight for social justice and women's equality.

Summarize What causes did Lucretia Mott support?

SECTION 3 ASSESSMENT

go.hrw.com
Online Quiz
Keyword: SD7 HP8

Reviewing Ideas, Terms, and People

1. **a. Recall** What was the **cult of domesticity**?
   b. Draw Conclusions How did industrialization help lead to the cult of domesticity?
   c. Predict What do you think would happen to the cult of domesticity after this time period? Why?

2. **a. Describe** Describe the purpose and activities of **reform societies**.
   b. Compare What did all of the reform movements in which women participated have in common?
   c. Evaluate How important was the growth in the number of women teachers in the early 1800s? Why?

3. **a. Identify** Who organized the **Seneca Falls Convention**?
   b. Analyze What was the purpose of the Seneca Falls Convention?
   c. Evaluate Do you think the Declaration of Sentiments changed anyone's attitude toward women? Why or why not?

Critical Thinking

4. **Identifying Cause and Effect** Copy the diagram below and identify the causes of the women's rights movement.

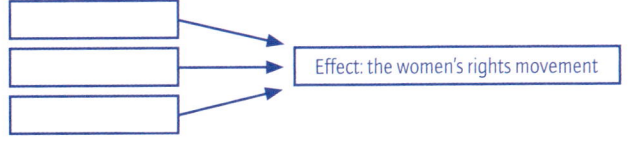

Effect: the women's rights movement

FOCUS ON WRITING

5. **Persuasive** Reread the excerpt from the Declaration of Sentiments on the opposite page. Then write a paragraph explaining why you think any of the grievances are or are not valid today.

Fighting against Slavery

BEFORE YOU READ

MAIN IDEA

The movement to end slavery dominated the Reform Era.

READING FOCUS

1. What was life like for enslaved African Americans in the South?
2. How did people in the South fight against slavery?
3. What were the major developments in the abolition movement?

KEY TERMS AND PEOPLE

free blacks
Nat Turner
Underground Railroad
Harriet Tubman
abolition movement
William Lloyd Garrison
David Walker
Sojourner Truth
Frederick Douglass

PI 3.2 Research and analyze the major themes and developments in New York State and United States history (e.g., colonization and settlement; Revolution and New National Period; immigration; expansion and reform era; Civil War and Reconstruction; the American labor movement; Great Depression; World Wars; contemporary United States).

THE INSIDE STORY

What stories come from slavery? Most of the thousands of enslaved Africans in the Americas never had a chance to tell their stories. No one but their families and fellow slaves knew what they endured. Nevertheless, some outstanding African Americans made themselves heard. For example, abolitionist leader Frederick Douglass wrote a powerful autobiography in 1845. Opponents of slavery helped others tell their stories, either as written narratives or as oral history.

By the 1930s, during the Great Depression, African Americans who had experienced slavery were growing old. A federal government project recorded their stories. In 1937 in Lafayette, Indiana, an interviewer talked with John W. Fields, an 89-year-old former slave who was still working. Fields explained how important education was:

"In most of us colored folks was the great desire to [be] able to read and write. We took advantage of every opportunity to educate ourselves. The greater part of the plantation owners were very harsh if we were caught trying to learn or write. It was the law that if a white man was caught trying to educate a negro slave, he was liable to prosecution entailing a fine of fifty dollars and a jail sentence. We were never allowed to go to town and it was not until after I ran away that I knew that they sold anything but slaves, tobacco, and whiskey. Our ignorance was the greatest hold the South had on us."

Born into Slavery

▶ Enslaved African Americans taking a Sunday rest by their cabins in South Carolina, 1860

The Lives of Enslaved African Americans

Including the colonial period, slavery had been an American institution for two centuries. Enslaved African Americans were held in every colony, northern and southern. In the North, slavery continued to exist in some form until the 1840s. By 1860 nearly 4 million African Americans lived in slavery in the South. While the majority of white southerners were not slaveholders, the southern economy depended on the labor of slaves.

Some differences existed in the lives of enslaved people—where they lived, how they were treated, and what work they were made to do. Nevertheless, it is clear that work, want, fear, and hope dominated all of their lives.

A life of work Generally, slaveholders viewed slaves as property, not as people. For slaveholders, buying slaves and providing, even minimally, for them was a major expense. Slaves who could not or would not perform the tasks demanded of them were of little use to slaveholders. Therefore, work was the dominant fact in the lives of enslaved people.

Men, women, and children were expected—or forced—to work whenever the slaveholder demanded it. For most enslaved people, this meant virtually every day of their lives, from the time they were old enough to perform chores until they were too old to be of any more use to the slaveholder.

Most enslaved people lived on farms or plantations in the South, where cotton was a leading crop. Cotton farming was labor-intensive. Many slaves worked as field hands, planting, tending, picking, processing, and loading cotton. Other jobs included constructing and repairing buildings and fences, hauling water, clearing land, and doing the many other tasks needed to keep a farm or plantation running.

Other plantation slaves worked in the slaveholder's house, performing a wide variety of servant duties like cooking and cleaning. Some enslaved people were skilled artisans, and many worked as blacksmiths, bricklayers, or carpenters.

Some slaves lived in cities. There they worked in factories and mills, in offices, and in homes. Still others worked in mines or in the forest as lumberjacks.

A life of want Enslaved people lived, for the most part, in barely tolerable conditions. One man who escaped from slavery later described what life as a slave was like.

HISTORY'S VOICES

" We lodged in huts and on the bare ground . . . In a single room were huddled, like cattle, ten or a dozen persons, men, women, and children. All ideas of refinement and decency were, of course, out of the question. There were neither bedsteads, nor furniture of any description. Our beds were collections of straw and old rags, thrown down in the corners and boxed with boards, a single blanket the only covering . . . The wind whistled and the rain and snow blew in through the cracks, and the damp earth soaked in the moisture till the floor was [muddy] as a pigsty. "

—Josiah Henson, *Uncle Tom's Story of His Life: An Autobiography of the Rev. Josiah Henson,* 1877

The food and clothing provided to slaves were typically as inadequate as the shelter. Medical care was virtually nonexistent. Sickness rarely stopped their work. Enslaved African Americans had no rights under the law, which viewed them as property.

A life of fear The way slaveholders treated enslaved people varied. Many slaveholders treated their slaves relatively well. But they generally did so in order to secure loyal service, not out of any great sense of humanity. Offering humane treatment did not make up for the inherently cruel condition of holding another human being as a piece of property.

Other slaveholders treated their slaves in a much harsher fashion. In addition to the cruel nature of slavery itself, some slaveholders would resort to a wide variety of punishments, such as beating, whipping, starving, and threatening a person's family members to ensure obedience.

A nightmarish reality for slaves was the threat of being separated from their families. Slaveholders and dealers routinely separated children from their parents, brothers from their sisters, and husbands from their wives, selling them to different slaveholders.

A life of hope One of the most remarkable facts about the life of African Americans under slavery was how they endured. Despite lives of backbreaking work and harsh punishments, African Americans developed ways to survive and bring some light into their lives.

Religion was a major source of comfort for enslaved people. A combination of African and Christian beliefs provided hope for a better life after death.

Drawing on their rich African oral tradition, enslaved people found pleasure in storytelling. Songs, too, provided inspiration and a brief respite from their hard lives. Many took pleasure in the dream that one day they might be free.

READING CHECK **Making Generalizations**
What words would you use to describe the lives of enslaved people?

The Antislavery Movement in the South

Not all African Americans in the South were held as slaves. In 1860, about 215,000 were **free blacks**. Some were former slaves who had been emancipated, or freed, by slaveholders. More typically, some were free because their ancestors had been emancipated. These men and women, however, faced harsh legal and social discrimination. Still, free blacks played a leading role in antislavery activities. Many aided people escaping slavery and spoke out for freedom. Some even spoke of their enslaved brethren revolting against their oppressors.

Slave revolts Between 1776 and 1860, about 200 slave uprisings and plots occurred in the United States. Most were short lived. An uprising led by **Nat Turner** in 1830 became the deadliest slave revolt in American history.

Turner and five accomplices killed Turner's slaveholder and his family. They then marched through Southampton County, Virginia, gaining as many as 75 followers and killing dozens more white people. A local militia captured the rebels and executed 20 of them, including Turner. Other white people in the area killed about 100 other slaves suspected of sympathizing with the revolt.

To try to prevent similar revolts, many southern communities stepped up their policing. New laws were enacted to strictly limit the movements and meetings of slaves.

Escape Some enslaved people chose a nonviolent way to end their enslavement: They escaped. They tried to reach the free states of the North or Canada or Mexico where slavery was illegal.

No one knows exactly how many slaves escaped. Perhaps 40,000 or more had fled the United States by 1860. Some estimates put the number at 100,000. Certainly, thousands attempted escape, and although most were soon captured, many did make it to freedom.

The Underground Railroad Over the years an informal, constantly changing network of escape routes developed. This so-called **Underground Railroad** had no formal organization. Sympathetic white people and free blacks provided escapees with food, hiding places, and directions to their next destination, closer to free territory. The most famous worker on the Underground Railroad was **Harriet Tubman**. Tubman had escaped slavery herself, and she helped many others on their journey to freedom.

READING CHECK **Identifying the Main Idea**
How did enslaved people resist their captivity?

The Underground Railroad

Free blacks and abolitionists helped enslaved African Americans find safety in northern states, Canada, and Mexico. This scene is an artist's re-creation showing escaped slaves reaching the house of the Reverend John Rankin. Located on the Ohio River, between free states and slaves states, the Rankin house was a key stop on the Underground Railroad.

As a "conductor," John Rankin lit a lamp in his window to tell escaping slaves that he would help them.

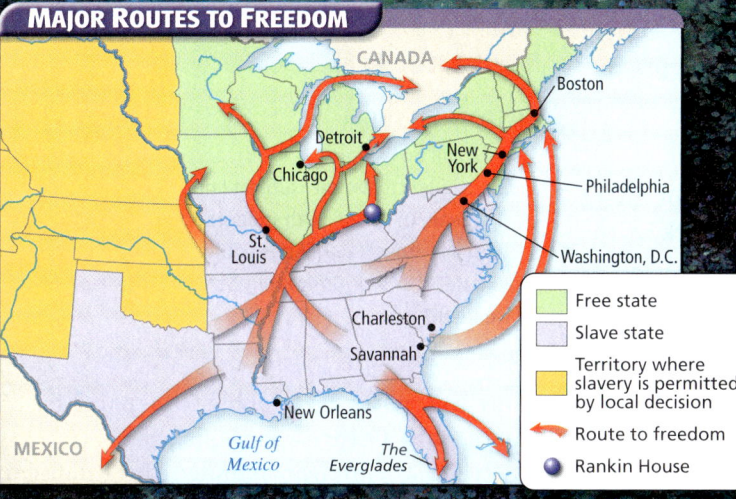

MAJOR ROUTES TO FREEDOM

CANADA

Boston
Detroit
Chicago
New York
Philadelphia
St. Louis
Washington, D.C.
Charleston
Savannah
New Orleans
MEXICO
Gulf of Mexico
The Everglades

- Free state
- Slave state
- Territory where slavery is permitted by local decision
- Route to freedom
- Rankin House

Many groups and individuals helped slaves escape bondage. Religion inspired many abolitionists.

Harriet Tubman helped hundreds of slaves escape to freedom.

Skills FOCUS **INTERPRETING INFOGRAPHICS**

1. **Making Inferences** What dangers might the enslaved people have faced along their journey?
2. **Drawing Conclusions** What might have been the shortest route to freedom from the Rankin house?

See **Skills Handbook**, p. H7, H12, H18

Escaping slaves used whatever means of transportation they could find, although much of their journey was on foot.

The Abolition Movement

The number of slaves attempting to escape their plight increased sharply during the 1830s. They may have been encouraged by a small movement that was gaining supporters in the North. The **abolition movement** was a campaign to abolish, or end, slavery. Supporters of the movement were called abolitionists.

The abolition movement was one of the the largest movement of the Reform Era of the 1830s, 1840s, and 1850s. No other movement attracted as many followers, garnered as much attention, arose such strong feelings, or had such an impact on the history of the United States. In retrospect, this is not surprising, since the lives of several million people held in slavery were at stake.

Religious roots The abolition movement had deep roots in religion. As far back as the colonial period, the Quakers condemned slavery as immoral. Elihu Embree, the son of a Quaker minister, published the first newspapers in the country devoted to the abolitionist cause. One was called *The Emancipator*. Embree proclaimed that "freedom is the inalienable right of *all men*." Many Quakers joined the abolitionist cause.

The rebirth of religious fervor in the Second Great Awakening also aided in the rise of the abolition movement. Many religious people in the North saw slavery as a moral wrong that went directly against their beliefs. Many joined reform societies to campaign against slavery. By 1836 more than 500 such groups existed.

William Lloyd Garrison Although all abolitionists wanted an end to slavery, many favored its gradual abolition. One such person, **William Lloyd Garrison**, became the leading spokesperson for the immediate abolition of slavery. Garrison had been influenced in his beliefs by a number of fellow abolitionists, including **David Walker**. In 1831 in Boston, he began publishing an abolitionist newspaper called *The Liberator*. In the first issue, he made his devotion to abolition clear.

HISTORY'S VOICES

❝I will be as harsh as truth, and as uncompromising as justice. On this subject I do not wish to think, or speak, or write, with moderation. No! No! . . . I am in earnest—I will not equivocate—I will not excuse—I will not retreat in a single inch—and I will be heard.❞

—William Lloyd Garrison

Garrison continued to publish the paper for 35 years, until slavery was abolished.

In 1833 Garrison founded the American Anti-Slavery Society, the most influential abolitionist group to call for the immediate end to slavery in the United States. By 1840, the American Anti-Slavery Society had a membership of 150,000 to 200,000.

Leading abolitionists As in other reform movements of the time, women such as **Sojourner Truth** played a significant role in the abolition campaign. Truth, along with Sarah and Angelina Grimké, were outspoken campaigners for abolition. The daughters of a South Carolina plantation owner, the Grimké sisters witnessed the suffering of slaves firsthand. Their public outspokenness against slavery earned them the disapproval of their community. They then moved to the North, where they not only fought against slavery but also for the rights of women.

Like the Grimkés, **Frederick Douglass** supported women's rights. Douglass was a featured speaker at the Seneca Falls Convention. But he is best remembered as an abolitionist

FACES OF HISTORY

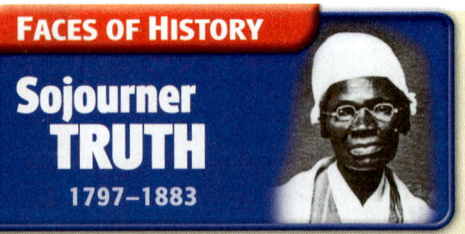

Sojourner TRUTH
1797–1883

In 1826, one year before New York outlawed slavery, a woman who would come to be known as Sojourner Truth escaped from enslavement. In later years Truth would become one of the most important figures in both the women's rights and abolitionist movements. She believed she had a mission to travel the nation ("sojourn") and speak the truth about racial and social injustices. A tall, charismatic woman, Sojourner Truth captivated audiences with fiery speeches and moving songs in support of causes in which she believed. Her memorable speech "Ar'n't I a Woman?" called for black women to be treated with the same respect as white women.

Make Inferences In what ways did Sojourner Truth's life experiences affect her views?

leader. Born into slavery in Maryland, Douglass escaped as a young man of 20. His intelligence and speech-making skills eventually earned him a place as a popular speaker to antislavery audiences. In 1845 Douglass published his autobiography, *Narrative of the Life of Frederick Douglass*. In writing about his quest to escape slavery, Douglass stated, "You have seen how a man was made a slave; you shall now see how a slave was made a man."

Douglass went on to publish an abolitionist newspaper, the *North Star*. His writing, his firsthand experience with slavery, and, above all, his powerful speeches made Douglass one of the most influential abolitionists.

Opposition to abolition The majority of white southerners did not own slaves. To the minority who were slaveholders, the abolition movement was an outrage. They viewed the movement as an attack on their livelihood, their way of life, and even on their religion.

Southern ministers constructed elaborate arguments attempting to justify slavery in biblical terms. Slaveholders and politicians argued that slavery was essential to the production of cotton and the health of the economy. To many, even in the North, this was a powerful argument. By 1860 cotton accounted for about 55 percent of the country's exports.

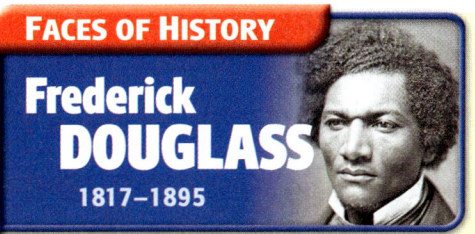

FACES OF HISTORY
Frederick DOUGLASS
1817–1895

After escaping slavery on his second attempt, Frederick Douglass made his way to Massachusetts, where he gave a speech on the horrors of slavery, which instantly made him a leading spokesman for the abolitionist cause. For the next 50 years, he used his sharp intellect, gift for writing, and strong public speaking skills to campaign against slavery and racial prejudice in America.

During the Civil War, Douglass recruited African Americans to fight for the Union. He also met with President Abraham Lincoln to protest discrimination against black soldiers. In later years, Douglass focused on land rights for former slaves, women's rights, and the movement to end lynching.

Explain What skills made Douglass a persuasive abolitionist?

Indeed, there was support for, and toleration of, slavery in the North. To northern workers, freedom for slaves might mean more competition for jobs. Still, the pressure to abolish slavery was undeniable. Frederick Douglass said the issue of slavery was "the great, paramount, imperative, and all-commanding question for this age and nation to solve."

READING CHECK **Making Inferences** What might happen as a result of the differing views of slavery in the United States?

go.hrw.com
Online Quiz
Keyword: SD7 HP8

Reviewing Ideas, Terms, and People

1. a. Recall Where did most enslaved people live?
   b. Elaborate How did enslaved people maintain their hope?
   c. Predict What do you think would bring an end to slavery in the United States?

2. a. Describe Describe the revolt of **Nat Turner**.
   b. Make Inferences What can you infer from the number of people who escaped from slavery?
   c. Elaborate What words do you think would best describe passage on the **Underground Railroad**?

3. a. Identify Who was **William Lloyd Garrison**?
   b. Contrast How was Garrison's approach to abolition different from that of earlier abolitionists?
   c. Evaluate What do you think made **Frederick Douglass** such an effective abolitionist?

Critical Thinking

4. Identifying Cause and Effect Copy the diagram below and identify the way groups of Americans reacted to slavery.

Group	Reactions to Slavery
Enslaved Africans and African Americans	
Abolitionists	
Slaveholders	

FOCUS ON WRITING

5. Expository Write a paragraph that explains what the Underground Railroad was and what its name suggests.

Reform Movements

Historical Context The documents below provide perspectives on different reform movements during the 1800s.

Task Examine the documents and answer the questions that follow. Then you will be asked to write an essay about reform movements in the 1800s, using facts from the documents and from the chapter to support the position you take in your thesis statement.

ST 3.2 Draw upon literary selections, historical documents, and accounts to analyze the roles played by different individuals and groups during the major eras in New York State and United States history.

ST 4.3 Develop hypotheses about important events, eras, or issues; move from chronicling to explaining historical events and issues; use information collected from diverse sources to produce cogently written reports and document-based essays.

DOCUMENT 1

Henry Highland Garnet was born into slavery in 1815. At age nine, he escaped and made his way to the North, where he became a leader of the abolitionist movement. He gave the following speech in 1843.

"Two hundred and twenty-seven years ago, the first of our injured race were brought to the shores of America. They came not with glad spirits to select their homes in the New World . . . Neither did they come flying upon the wings of Liberty, to a land of freedom. But they came with broken hearts, from their beloved native land, and were doomed to unrequited [unpaid] toil . . .

The propagators of the system, or their immediate ancestors, very soon discovered its growing evil, and its tremendous wickedness, and secret promises were made to destroy it. The gross inconsistency of a people holding slaves, who had themselves 'ferried o'er the wave' for freedom's sake, was too apparent to be entirely overlooked . . .

The colonists threw the blame upon England. They said that the mother country entailed the evil upon them, and that they would rid themselves of it if they could. The world thought they were sincere . . . But time soon tested their sincerity.

In a few years the colonists grew strong, and severed themselves from the British Government. Their independence was declared, and they took their station among the sovereign powers of the earth . . . When the power of Government returned to their hands, did they emancipate the slaves? No; they rather added new links to our chains . . ."

DOCUMENT 2

Besides gaining voting rights, one of the main goals of the women's rights movement was to change laws regarding rights to property. This issue drew support from women like Keziah Kendall, who owned a farm with her two sisters. Kendall wrote the following letter to an opponent of women's rights, explaining her views on the subject.

"My name is Keziah Kendall. I live many miles from Cambridge, on a farm with my two sisters, one older, one younger than myself . . . [W]e have a good estate—comfortable house—nice barn, garden, orchard & such, and money in the bank besides . . . Now we are taxed every year to the full amount of every dollar we possess—town, county, state taxes—taxes for land, for moveables, for money and all. Now I don't want to go [become a] representative or anything else, anymore than I do to be a constable or a sheriff, but I have no voice about public improvements, and I don't see the justice of being taxed anymore than the revolutionary heroes did . . . I am told . . . that if a woman dies a week after she's married that her husband takes all her personal property and the use of her real estate as long as he lives—if a man dies his wife can have her thirds [one-third of the estate] . . . I think the law is in fault here . . .

Women have joined the Antislavery societies, and why? Women are kept for slaves as well as men—it is a common cause, deny the justice of it, who can!"

The temperance movement of the 1800s focused on trying to get people to stop, or cut back on, drinking liquor. The movement used many popular images of the time to show the advantages of sobriety and the destructiveness of drunkenness. These two images show the "Tree of Temperance" and the "Tree of Intemperance," recalling the biblical story of Adam and Eve, who brought sin into the world by eating fruit from a forbidden tree. The fruits are labeled with the positive qualities of temperence and the negative qualities of drunkenness.

Positive qualities, such as Industry, Philanthropy, Goodwill, and Charity

Signs of a productive community

Well-dressed, happy children and adults

Negative qualities, such as Diseases, Ignorance, Vice, Crime, and Immorality

Drunken, unhappy people

Prohibitionists are celebrating the first major anti-liquor law, passed in Maine in 1851.

This twisted tree's roots represent different kinds of liquor. A serpent with an apple in its mouth and a mug of beer on its head suggests the serpent who tempted Adam and Eve.

Skills FOCUS — READING LIKE A HISTORIAN

1. a. Identify Refer to Document 1. According to Garnet, whom did the early colonists blame for supporting slavery?

b. Analyze In what way does Garnet see the founders of the United States as insincere?

2. a. Identify Refer to Document 2. To whom does Kendall compare herself when she complains about paying taxes without having a voice in government?

b. Explain According to Kendall, why do so many women support the antislavery movement?

3. a. Identify Refer to Document 3. How do the two images reflect the religious background of the temperance movement?

b. Contrast Based on these images, how was a temperate society different from an intemperate one?

4. Document-Based Essay Question Consider the question below and form a thesis statement. Using examples from Documents 1, 2, and 3, create an outline and write a short essay supporting your position.

How were the reform movements of the early 1800s similar to and different from one another?

See **Skills Handbook**, pp. H28–H29

Visual Summary: A Push for Reform

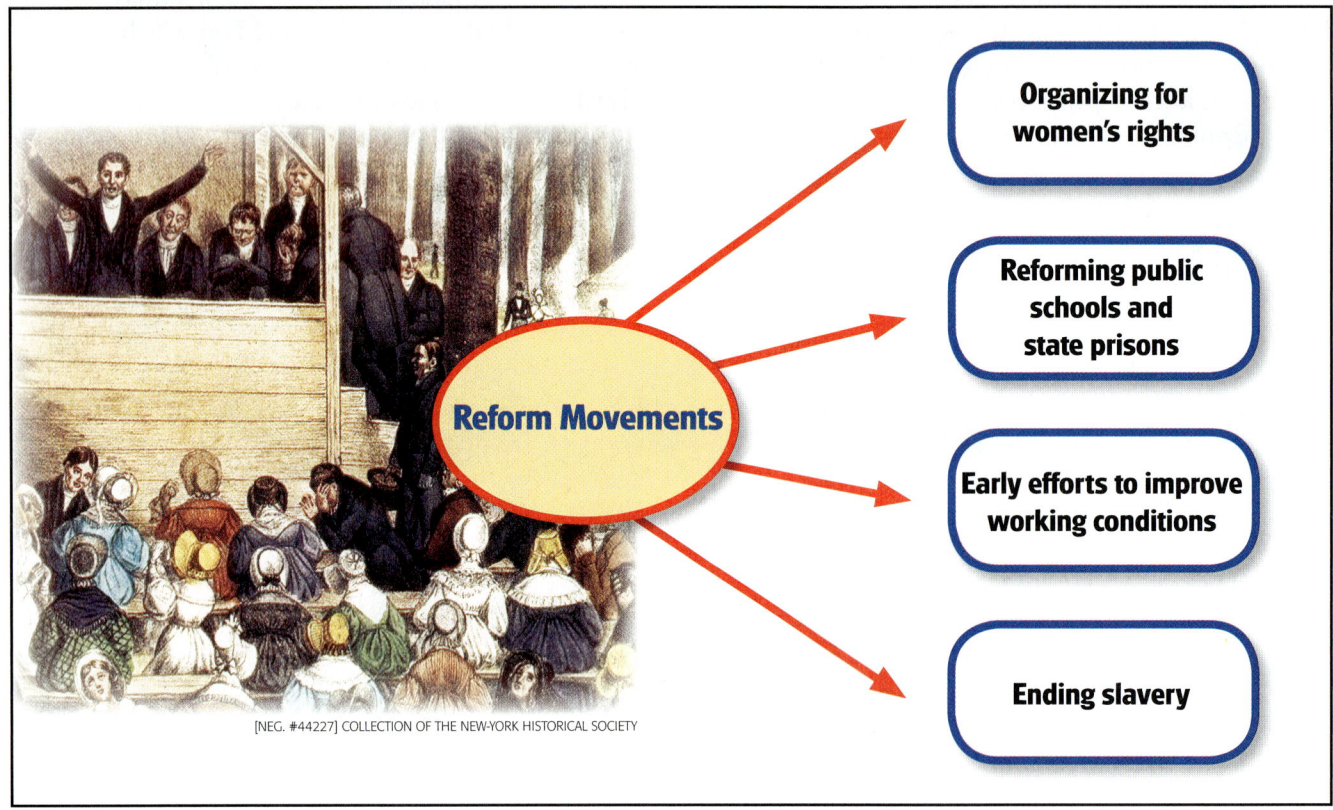

[NEG. #44227] COLLECTION OF THE NEW-YORK HISTORICAL SOCIETY

Reform Movements

- Organizing for women's rights
- Reforming public schools and state prisons
- Early efforts to improve working conditions
- Ending slavery

Reviewing Key Terms and People

For each term below, write a sentence explaining its significance to the Reform Era.

1. Frederick Douglass
2. temperance movement
3. Horace Mann
4. push-pull model of immigration
5. William Lloyd Garrison
6. utopian movement
7. Dorothea Dix
8. Seneca Falls Convention
9. Henry David Thoreau
10. free blacks
11. Lucretia Mott
12. Nat Turner

Comprehension and Critical Thinking

SECTION 1 *(pp. 266–270)*

13. **a. Recall** What was the Second Great Awakening?

b. Contrast How was it different from the First Great Awakening?

c. Evaluate Which movement of the Reform Era do you think was the most important? Why?

SECTION 2 *(pp. 272–277)*

14. **a. Define** Write a brief definition of nativism.

b. Analyze Why were Irish immigrants treated so harshly?

c. Infer What factors led many Americans to oppose immigration?

SECTION 3 *(pp. 280–283)*

15. **a. Describe** What restrictions on women existed during the 1800s?

b. Draw Conclusions Why do you think limits were placed on women?

History's Impact video program

Review the video to answer the closing question: How has American life been improved by the work of reformers?

SECTION 4 *(pp. 284–289)*

16. a. Identify What was the Underground Railroad?

b. Sequence How did the abolition movement change over the years?

c. Elaborate What did abolitionist Frederick Douglass mean when he said that the issue of slavery was "the great, paramount, imperative, and all-commanding question for this age and nation to solve"?

Using the Internet

go.hrw.com
Practice Online
Keyword: SD7 CH8

17. With the exception of Native Americans, all people who live in the United States today can trace their history back to another country. Using the keyword above, do research to learn about your family's ancestry regarding immigration. Then write a report that presents this information. Include visuals if possible.

Analyzing Primary Sources

Reading Like a Historian The American Party, also known as the Know-Nothings, opposed immigration. In 1854 they won state elections in Massachusetts. The newspaper passage below celebrates the party's victory. Read the passage and answer the questions that follow.

> ❝The people of the Old Bay State have spoken, and from Berkshire to Cape Cod, are heard the voices of her native born children, declaring for the perpetuity AMERICAN INSTITUTIONS, and AMERICAN LIBERTIES. The descendants of the heroes of BUNKER HILL, LEXINGTON, and CONCORD, have spoken in a voice of thunder, in favor of Americans ruling America . . . the warm pulsation of the people's heart beats only for FREEDOM . . . and PROTESTANTISM.❞
>
> —*Daily Evening Journal*, November 14, 1854

18. Identify What does "Bunker Hill, Lexington, and Concord" refer to?

19. Interpret In addition to being against the Irish, what else is this newspaper against?

Critical Reading

Read the passage in Section 3 that begins with the heading "Limits on Women's Lives." Then answer the questions that follow.

20. According to the passage,

A. laws and culture both placed limits on women.

B. there were legal limits, but no economic limits.

C. there were some jobs in which women were paid as much as men.

D. no one challenged the limits placed on women.

21. The first paragraph says that "The handful of men who dared to speak out for the equal treatment of women were treated with even worse disdain." The word *disdain* means

A. respect.

B. contempt.

C. generosity.

D. caution.

WRITING FOR THE SAT ✎

Think about the following issue:

In the 1800s there were many restrictions on women. In most places, they could not vote, hold public office, serve on juries, or enter into legal contracts. Most jobs were closed to them; when they worked, they did not earn as much as men. Married women could not own property; if they worked, they had to give their wages to their husbands.

22. Assignment Have conditions for women improved since the 1800s? Have women achieved complete equality with men in our society? Write a short essay in which you develop your position on this issue. Support your view with reasoning and examples from your reading and studies.

CHAPTER 9

1830–1860

Expansion Leads to Conflict

THE BIG PICTURE They were drawn by varied dreams: of gold, of religious freedom, of good farmland. They possessed a belief that settling the lands from the Atlantic to the Pacific was America's destiny. Between 1830 and 1860 Americans by the thousands migrated westward into the frontier wilderness. In 1846, souring relations led to war between Mexico and the United States, and the outcome defined America's borders.

New York Standards

Key Idea 2 Important ideas, social and cultural values, beliefs, and traditions from New York State and United States history illustrate the connections and interactions of people and events across time and from a variety of perspectives.

Skills FOCUS **READING LIKE A HISTORIAN**

Painter Albert Bierstadt spent years documenting the westward journey across the American landscape, as he did here in *Emigrants Crossing the Plains.* He compared the beauty of the Rockies with the Alps, and his popular paintings helped publicize westward expansion.

Interpreting Visuals What is the overall tone or mood of this painting?

See **Skills Handbook**, p. H30

U.S.

World

November 1830
Joseph Smith founds the Mormon Church.

1830

1834
Mexican President Antonio López de Santa Anna makes himself dictator.

History's Impact video program

Watch the video to understand the impact of Texas and the Southwest.

October 1835
The Texas Revolution breaks out at Gonzales.

1843
The missionary Marcus Whitman leads a large wagon train along the Oregon Trail.

May 1846
The United States declares war on Mexico.

January 1848
Gold is discovered at Sutter's Mill in northern California.

April 1860
Pony Express mail service begins.

1836   1842   1848   1854   1860

1842
Great Britain annexes Hong Kong.

February 1848
Mexico signs the Treaty of Guadalupe Hidalgo, ceding California and much of the Southwest to the United States.

1854
Commodore Perry and Japanese officials sign an agreement opening Japan to U.S. trade.

1857
The first transatlantic communications cable, linking Great Britain and the United States, begins operation.

Manifest Destiny

BEFORE YOU READ

MAIN IDEA

Americans in large numbers followed trails to the West in the 1840s and 1850s.

READING FOCUS

1. Why did Americans head west?
2. What were the major western trails?
3. How did the gold rush affect California?
4. What were some major effects of westward migration?

KEY TERMS AND PEOPLE

manifest destiny
John L. O'Sullivan
entrepreneur
Santa Fe Trail
Oregon Trail
Mormon Trail
James K. Polk
gold rush
California Trail
Pony Express

 2.5 Analyze the United States involvement in foreign affairs and a willingness to engage in international politics, examining the ideas and traditions leading to these foreign policies.

A Day on the Trail

▲ A westward-bound family poses with their prairie schooners.

THE INSIDE STORY

How can we cross the river with everything we own? Oregon Territory was the goal of many pioneer families. Some single women made the trip, usually traveling with a family.

Harriet Buckingham, who was just 19, kept a diary of her trip to Oregon in 1851. Buckingham was a good observer, describing the landscape and the Native American peoples she met. The wagon train included seven wagons and a carriage, along with oxen, cows, horses, and mules. They carried tents, cookstoves, and a coop full of chickens. On May 13, 1851, they reached the Platte River. One challenge was to get across the river. Another was the weather.

"We were quickly wakened this morning by the singing of the Indians. Our men all went to work with the three other companies [of wagons] building a bridge. It was completed by afternoon when we crossed. It is a matter of surprise that over 500 head of cattle & fifty wagons should cross without accident. The Waggons were all drawn over by hand & the cattle & horses swam . . . We encamped a mile from the creek. The Evening was delightful, the moon shone so clearly but before morning, it clouded up and one of the most terrifine [terrifying] storms I ever witnessed . . . The rain fell in torrents. The lightning was most vivid. We were obliged to move as soon as possible for fear of being overflown . . . we traveled on some 3 miles in water up to the axletrees."

Americans Head West

Just like Harriet Buckingham, hundreds of thousands of Americans migrated west in the 1840s and 1850s. They went for many different reasons, and they settled in many different places. Yet they all shared the dream of new opportunities and a better life.

"Multiplying millions" By 1840 the American population had grown to about six times what it had been during the American Revolution. The country's area had expanded to about twice its original size. It seemed inconceivable to most Americans that the growth and expansion they had always known would stop.

In fact, many Americans of the time believed in **manifest destiny**, the idea that the nation had a God-given right to all of North America. The term was first used by newspaper editor **John L. O'Sullivan**. In 1845 he wrote that "our manifest destiny [is to] overspread the continent allotted by Providence [God's power] for the free development of our yearly multiplying millions." Most Americans gave little thought to how manifest destiny would affect peoples already living in regions to be added to the United States.

Reasons for westward migration Many Americans who headed west in the early and mid-1800s believed in manifest destiny. But they also had more personal reasons. Mountain men, who went west to trap and trade, were among the earliest migrants. They were followed by missionaries, who hoped to convert Native Americans to Christianity. Lumberjacks and miners headed west to capitalize on the region's natural resources.

Most pioneers in the 1840s and 1850s were farmers. They moved west to farm the vast, rich land of which earlier migrants spoke. Many of them were relatively poor. They had little to lose by leaving their homes and had a chance to gain a great deal by moving west. The farmers were followed by **entrepreneurs**, people willing to invest their money in the hope of making a profit. Shopkeepers, carpenters, and other businesspeople knew that if they were among the first to practice their trade in a new settlement, they had a greater chance for success.

READING CHECK **Summarizing** What types of people headed west, and for what reasons?

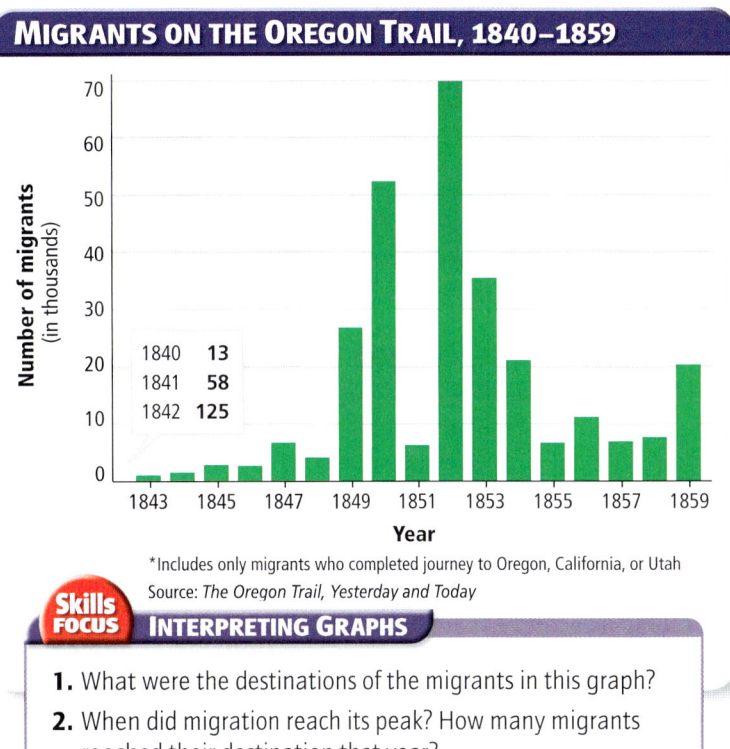

MIGRANTS ON THE OREGON TRAIL, 1840–1859

Year	Number
1840	13
1841	58
1842	125

*Includes only migrants who completed journey to Oregon, California, or Utah
Source: *The Oregon Trail, Yesterday and Today*

Skills FOCUS **INTERPRETING GRAPHS**

1. What were the destinations of the migrants in this graph?
2. When did migration reach its peak? How many migrants reached their destination that year?

See **Skills Handbook**, p. H16

Major Western Trails

Americans who migrated west had the adventure of their lives. But for some, the trip cost them their lives.

No train tracks or smooth highways led from the East to the far West in the 1840s and 1850s. Migrants reached the West by riding in wagons pulled by oxen or horses, or by walking. Some migrants actually walked hundreds of miles to reach their new homes. They took one of several routes that were well established by 1850.

The Santa Fe Trail The first major western trail was the **Santa Fe Trail**, which led from Independence, Missouri, to the town of Santa Fe, the capital of Spanish New Mexico. The Santa Fe Trail began as a commercial route, or trade route. News of the wealth of Santa Fe motivated Americans to open trade with the people there.

In 1821 a veteran of the War of 1812 named William Becknell led a small band of traders out of Arrow Rock, Missouri, bound for Santa Fe. It took them two months to complete the difficult, 800-mile journey, but they made it and sold their goods for a huge profit.

FOCUS ON NEW YORK

GOVERNMENT

New York newspaper editor John L. O'Sullivan first wrote about manifest destiny in *The United States Magazine and Democratic Review*, a journal that promoted the expansionist policies of the Democratic Party. O'Sullivan's newspaper, the *New York Morning News,* helped win New York state, and the presidency, for James K. Polk in 1844.

Other traders followed Becknell's route. They carried cloth, books, hardware and other goods to Santa Fe and returned with Mexican silver coins, wool, animals, and other items that fetched high prices in the eastern United States. In the 1820s and 1830s, about 150 traders traveled the trail each year. By the 1840s, the trading route also began to serve as a route for migrants heading west.

ACADEMIC VOCABULARY

cycle a series of events that repeats regularly

The Oregon Trail The longest and most famous trail used by the migrants was the **Oregon Trail**. The 2,000-mile trail stretched from Independence, Missouri, to the rich farming lands of the Willamette Valley in what is now the state of Oregon.

Native Americans had for centuries used parts of what would become the Oregon Trail. Lewis and Clark also followed part of the route on their historic journey to the West from 1804 to 1806. Many fur traders and mountain men also knew of the route and used it when traveling to and from the West.

Migrants first used the trail in the 1840s. It was in 1843 that the Oregon Trail became established as a major trail west. In that year Dr. Marcus Whitman, who had established a mission in what was called Oregon Country, led a huge party of migrants west. The party consisted of hundreds of people. Thereafter for decades, each spring large groups of migrants started across the trail in an annual cycle.

Danger stalked migrants on their six-month journey to Oregon. Treacherous geography and harsh weather, conflict with Native Americans, and disease took the lives of some 20,000 travelers by 1859. But tens of thousands more pioneers survived. Congress organized Oregon Territory in 1848. In 1859 Oregon became the 33rd state.

The Mormon Trail In 1830 Joseph Smith founded the Church of Jesus Christ of Latter-day Saints in New York. Its members were called Mormons. In five years, Mormon missionaries had attracted some 8,000 followers.

AMERICAN TRAILS WEST

CANADA

Fort Vancouver
Columbia River
Portland
WILLAMETTE VALLEY
Snake River
Missouri River
GREAT PLAINS
Mississippi River

The Oregon Trail ran some 2,000 miles from Independence, Missouri to Oregon Country.

CASCADE RANGE
Fort Hall
ROCKY
SOUTH PASS
Fort Laramie
North Platte River
Council Bluffs

Sacramento
Great Salt Lake
Salt Lake City
MOUNTAINS
Nauvoo

San Francisco
SIERRA NEVADA
Fort Kearney
Fort Leavenworth
Arrow Rock

Stockton
St. Louis

PACIFIC OCEAN
Colorado River
Arkansas River
Independence

Los Angeles
The Santa Fe Trail was an important commercial route, transporting silver, fur, and manufactured goods.

Fort Yuma
Santa Fe
Red River
Fort Smith

30°N
El Paso
Rio Grande

The Old Spanish Trail was a series of footpaths and horse and mule routes that together formed a trade network between the United States and Mexico.

Butterfield Overland Trail
California Trail
Mormon Trail
Old Spanish Trail
Oregon Trail
Santa Fe Trail

0   200   400 Miles
0   200   400 Kilometers
Albers equal-area projection

120°W

GEOGRAPHY SKILLS **INTERPRETING MAPS**

1. **Movement** What trails did the Old Spanish Trail link together?

2. **Human-Environment Interaction** Why was overland travel to and from the West so difficult?

See **Skills Handbook**, p. H19

The practice of men having more than one wife was among other Mormon beliefs that differed from Protestant Christianity. It also fueled hostility. Violent mobs forced the Mormons out of New York to Ohio, out of Ohio to Missouri, and out of Missouri to Illinois. There they built the community of Nauvoo, but they again faced angry neighbors. A mob killed Joseph Smith and his brother and forced the Mormons once more to seek a new home.

Brigham Young became the new leader of the Mormons. He declared that they should migrate west to find a place where they could practice their religion freely. The Mormons abandoned Nauvoo.

Between 1847 and 1853, some 16,000 Mormons migrated to the area around the Great Salt Lake in present-day Utah. The 1,300-mile route they followed became known as the **Mormon Trail**. By 1860 the Mormons had established dozens of settlements in the region. Eventually, thousands more Mormon migrants traveled the route to new settlements in the West.

READING CHECK **Comparing and Contrasting** How were the Santa Fe, Oregon, and Mormon trails similar and different?

The Gold Rush

The largest single migration west—and one of the greatest migrations in U.S. history—did not occur because of manifest destiny or a desire for new farmland or a search for religious tolerance. It resulted from a hunger for gold.

Gold fever In 1848 a carpenter discovered gold in the American River at John Sutter's sawmill in northern California. Sutter tried to keep the discovery of gold on his land a secret, but word soon spread. People as far away as Asia, South America, and Europe heard the news from American sailors. Many headed to California, dreaming of striking it rich.

News reached the United States, too, but most people dismissed it as a rumor. Then on December 5, 1848, in his State of the Union address, President **James K. Polk** made an announcement that reverberated around the country. The gold mines in California "are more extensive and valuable than was anticipated," he told the Congress. "The explorations already made warrant the belief that the supply is very

The Long Tom, shown here, became a common method of placer mining by 1850. Placer mining involved separating gold deposits from other river sediment. A Long Tom took six to eight people to work and was more efficient than panning for gold.

large and that gold is found at various places in an extensive district of country."

Polk's speech was reported in newspapers across the country. Thousands of Americans caught "gold fever." When one San Francisco newspaper wrote about what happened in California, it described what soon would happen across the nation.

HISTORY'S VOICES

❝ The whole country, from San Francisco to Los Angeles, and from the sea shore to the base of the Sierra Nevada resounds with the sordid cry of 'gold, GOLD, GOLD!' while the field is left half-planted, the house half-built, and everything neglected but the manufacture of shovels and pickaxes. ❞
—*San Francisco Californian,* May 29, 1848

Rush to California The mass migration to California of miners—and businesspeople who made money off the miners—is known as the **gold rush**. The migrants who left for California in 1849 were called forty-niners. Their numbers approached a stunning 80,000.

Many more soon followed. Although the dream of finding gold brought people from around the world, 80 percent of those arriving in California came from the United States. To reach California, most people traveled over land, following the **California Trail**. Others

Science and Technology
Millions of pounds of toxic mercury used in some gold-mining processes in the mid-1800s still pollute river beds and stream beds in California today.

booked passage on ships that sailed all the way around the southern tip of South America. Still others sailed south to Panama, crossed Central America by mule train, and then sailed north to California. By 1854 as many as 300,000 people had migrated to California.

Booming cities Upon reaching California, most miners moved into mining camps in the gold fields. Many others—especially businesspeople—settled in cities. San Francisco, the port nearest the gold fields, had a population of about 800 in 1848. One year later some 25,000 people lived there. By 1860 it was home to some 60,000 people.

The town of Stockton, located on the San Joaquin River on the way to the southern gold fields, boomed. Sacramento, located on the Sacramento River between San Francisco and the northern gold fields, also grew rapidly. When California became the 31st state in 1850, Sacramento became its capital.

ACADEMIC VOCABULARY
implications possible significance

READING CHECK **Sequencing** What were the major events that led to the widespread settlement of parts of California?

Major Effects of Westward Migration

Use of the western trails declined sharply after 1869, when railroad tracks finally ran unbroken from the east to the West Coast. By that time, however, more than 350,000 migrants had followed the overland trails to the West. Such a tremendous migration—equal to about 1.5 percent of the total American population in 1850—had significant effects.

The Oregon Treaty The presence of so many Americans in Oregon Country prompted presidential candidate James K. Polk to campaign in 1844 on the promise of securing the region for the United States. Since 1818 the United States and Britain had jointly controlled Oregon. Polk campaigned with the slogan "Fifty-four Forty or Fight!" He was referring to the line of north latitude, 54°40', that marked the northern boundary of Oregon Country. Polk's statement had dramatic implications. He was pledging war with Great Britain if it refused to give all of Oregon to the United States.

Skills FOCUS **READING LIKE A HISTORIAN**

Romanticizing Native American Life

George Catlin made this painting of a Mandan village from sketches, rather than memory, to capture "the thrilling panorama" he saw. Even so, like most of his paintings, it is a romanticized portrait of his subject.

Recognizing Bias Why might Catlin have painted the scene this way?

Polk won the presidency but retreated from his pledge. Instead, he concluded a treaty with Britain that set the boundary between the United States and British Canada at the 49th parallel. This boundary, now between the United States and an independent Canada, still exists today.

Communication links

Westward migration also led to the need for communication over long distances. Business and government officials in the West needed a way to stay in contact with their eastern counterparts. Individuals, likewise, wanted to stay in touch with the relatives they left behind.

The first answer to this need for communication was mail. A major southern route was the Butterfield Trail, over which a private stagecoach line ran. Starting in 1858 and lasting for two-and-a-half years, the Butterfield stages carried passengers and mail between St. Louis and San Francisco. The trip took more than two weeks. For about 18 months, the **Pony Express** offered somewhat quicker mail service between Missouri and California using relays of young riders on fast horses.

In 1861 the telegraph linked the East and the West. It made the Pony Express obsolete by delivering important messages much more

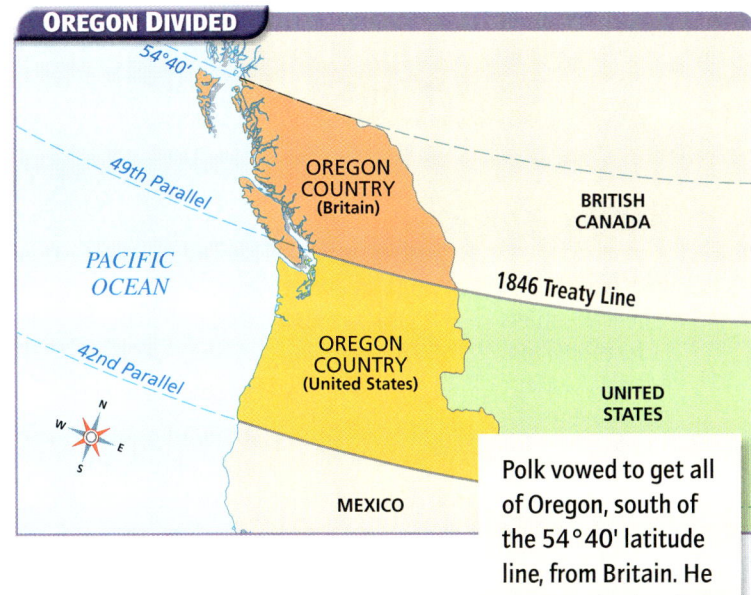

OREGON DIVIDED

Polk vowed to get all of Oregon, south of the 54°40' latitude line, from Britain. He compromised and drew the line at the 49° instead.

quickly and efficiently. Stage lines using the Pony Express's central route continued to deliver packages and routine mail, however.

In time, the greatest effect of westward migration would be on the original inhabitants of the West: Native Americans. Their lives would be forever changed.

READING CHECK **Identifying the Main Idea** What were two major effects of Americans' westward migration?

Reviewing Ideas, Terms, and People

1. a. Recall What is **manifest destiny**?
 b. Analyze Why did many farmers and **entrepreneurs** head west in the 1840s and the 1850s?
 c. Evaluate How large a role do you think a belief in manifest destiny played in people's decisions to head west?

2. a. Describe How did the **Santa Fe Trail** come into existence?
 b. Make Inferences Why did the **Oregon Trail** become so heavily traveled?
 c. Evaluate How might attitudes of migrants on the Mormon Trail have been like and unlike those of other travelers west?

3. a. Identify What was the **gold rush**?
 b. Make Inferences Why do you think Americans who went to California took different routes there?
 c. Evaluate How did the gold rush affect the United States, California, and the people in both places?

4. a. Recall About how many migrants followed overland trails to the West?

b. Make Inferences Why, do you think, did President **James Polk** retreat from his "Fifty-four Forty or Fight!" pledge?
c. Predict What effects do you think the migration that began in the 1840s would have on Native Americans?

Critical Thinking

5. Summarizing Copy the chart below and complete it to summarize the causes and effects of westward migration.

Group	Cause	Effect
mountain men		
farmers		
forty-niners		
Mormons		

FOCUS ON WRITING

6. Expository Many Americans came to California to "mine the miners." Explain what this phrase means in a paragraph.

Texas Independence

BEFORE YOU READ

MAIN IDEA

American settlers in Texas revolted against the Mexican government and created the independent Republic of Texas.

READING FOCUS

1. What system did the Spanish use to settle Texas?
2. How did Americans begin to move into Texas?
3. What were the causes and effects of the Texas Revolution?

KEY TERMS AND PEOPLE

mission system
Moses Austin
Stephen F. Austin
empresarios
Tejanos
Antonio López de Santa Anna
Texas Revolution
Sam Houston
Alamo
William Travis
Republic of Texas

PI 2.5 Analyze the United States involvement in foreign affairs and a willingness to engage in international politics, examining the ideas and traditions leading to these foreign policies.

Deep in the Heart of TEXAS

Why move to the territory of Texas? Stephen F. Austin is called the father of Texas, but other members of his family also helped Texas grow. Mary Austin Holley met her younger cousin Stephen in about 1808 when he was at school in Connecticut. She was a talented and charming woman, and the two became friends. A few years after Austin established his American colony in Texas, Holley's husband died, and she moved to Louisiana to be a governess.

Soon Mary's brother Henry Austin also settled in Texas. She thought about uniting the family there, so Stephen set aside land for her on Galveston Bay. Holley visited his colony in 1831 and loved what she saw. Soon after, she published an account of her visit—the first book about Texas by an Anglo-American. It was titled *Texas: Observations Historical, Geographical, and Descriptive, in a Series of Letters Written during a Visit to Austin's Colony.* Holley's book called Texas "a splendid country." She predicted: "There cannot be a doubt, that, in a few years, Texas will become one of the most thriving, if not the most populous, of the Mexican States."

Her book probably persuaded many Americans to come to Texas. Holley also supported her cousin's belief in Texas independence. She made several long visits to Texas and wrote more enthusiastic reports. ◼

The Spanish Settle Texas

Mary Austin Holley and the other Americans who came to Texas were far from the first people to call the region home. The original inhabitants were, of course, Native Americans. Hundreds of Native American groups had lived in Texas for thousands of years. The Indians of Texas belonged to the Plains, the Southwest, and the Southeast culture groups.

The first Europeans to visit Texas were the Spanish. Spanish explorers crossed Texas several times during the 1500s. Spain claimed Texas based on these explorations. But the Spanish, finding little wealth in the region, made little attempt to settle the land.

◄ Texas booster Mary Austin Holley attracted settlers to the state.

In 1689, however, the Spanish discovered the fort that the French explorer René-Robert Cavelier, Sieur de La Salle, had built on the Texas coast. Local Indians had destroyed the fort, but the Spanish were alarmed. They feared the French would claim Texas. So the Spanish came up with a plan to settle Texas.

The mission system The Spanish attempted to settle Texas by building missions. Missions were small settlements designed to convert Native Americans to Catholicism and make them into loyal Spanish subjects. Missions were usually accompanied by presidios, or forts, run by soldiers who were charged with protecting the missions. The Spanish had effectively used this **mission system** in Mexico, and they expected it would work well in Texas.

Between the late 1600s and late 1700s, the Spanish built about two dozen missions and presidios in Texas. They also built the towns of San Antonio and Nacogdoches (na-kuh-DOH-chuhz). Despite Spanish hopes, the missions failed, and the towns never flourished.

Most Native Americans rejected mission life, where they were expected to give up their culture, including their religion. Moreover, they soon realized that the missions could bring death. The Spanish carried diseases that the Indians had never been exposed to. Countless thousands of Native Americans—even entire nations—were wiped out by these diseases. Some Indian groups came to view the Spanish as dangerous trespassers, and they attacked Spanish missions and towns.

The mission system ends Spain built the mission system to convert Native Americans and to counter the threat of French settlement in Texas. But France, after losing the French and Indian War, ceded much of its land claim in North America to Spain in 1762. Thus, Spain no longer faced a threat to its claim to Texas. This fact, coupled with the widespread failure of the mission system to convert Native Americans into Spanish subjects, caused Spain to all but abandon the missions. By 1800 Spain still claimed Texas, but only three Spanish settlements existed in the entire region.

READING CHECK **Identifying Cause and Effect** What caused the Spanish to implement and then abandon the mission system in Texas?

Americans Move into Texas

In 1820 **Moses Austin**, a former banker from Missouri, approached Spanish colonial officials with a plan he called the Texas Venture. Austin proposed that, in exchange for land, he would build a colony in Texas. The Spanish, eager to have the land settled, agreed. Austin died before he could start his colony. One of his last wishes was that his son, **Stephen F. Austin**, carry out his plans for a colony in Texas.

The younger Austin pursued his father's plan with a great deal of enthusiasm. He found a suitable location for the colony between the Colorado and Brazos rivers. There, well-watered land would be perfect for farming and ranching. Austin had no trouble finding American settlers for his colony, even though they had to meet strict criteria. Settlers were attracted by the extremely low land prices.

Austin's Colony In 1823 Austin's Colony was officially established. Austin directed the building of a small town called San Felipe de Austin. San Felipe, as it came to be called, was the administrative, commercial, and social center of the colony. By 1824 about 300 families

FACES OF HISTORY

Stephen F. AUSTIN
1793–1836

Long considered the "father of Texas," Stephen F. Austin established the first Anglo-American colony in the Tejas (TAY-hahs) province of Mexico. Born in Virginia and raised in present-day Missouri, Austin traveled east at age 11 to attend college at Yale. Later, Austin returned to Missouri to help run his family's lead mine.

Stephen's father, Moses, had grander plans. He wanted to form an American settlement in Texas. He received permission from the Spanish colonial government for the project but died soon afterward, leaving his son to carry out his plan.

Stephen F. Austin worked energetically to recruit settlers and smooth over difficulties with the Mexican government. On one trip to Mexico, he was arrested on suspicion of disloyalty to Mexico. Yet even up to the outbreak of Texas Revolution, Austin worked for reconciliation between Mexico and the American settlers. The capital city of Texas is named for him.

Summarizing In what ways did Austin shape the course of American colonization of Texas?

lived on farms and ranches throughout the colony. The population of the colony was about 1,800 people. About 400 of these settlers were enslaved Africans.

Mexican independence Moses Austin had approached Spanish officials with his original plan for settlement. By the time his son Stephen had established the colony, however, Mexico was no longer part of New Spain. After a decade-long struggle, Mexico had become an independent country in 1821.

The *empresarios* Like the Spanish government, the new Mexican government wanted Texas settled. Mexico passed a number of colonization laws offering land grants to settlers in return for becoming loyal Mexican citizens and meeting other conditions. The government assigned large amounts of land to *empresarios*, or contractors, who recruited settlers and established colonies. Stephen Austin was the most successful *empresario*. Other *empresarios*, some from Europe, also founded colonies in Texas.

By 1830 there were more than a dozen colonies in Texas. About 30,000 settlers were living there, including several thousand enslaved Africans and 4,000 **Tejanos**, or Texans of Mexican heritage. The American settlement marked a dramatic change in the region. Just a decade earlier, there were only about 2,000 non-Indian people in Texas. Most of the settlers by 1830 were from the United States.

READING CHECK **Making Inferences** How might Mexican officials have viewed the presence of so many people from the United States in Texas?

The Texas Revolution

American settlers in Texas had to agree to certain conditions in exchange for receiving land. Most important, they had to surrender their American citizenship, swear allegiance to Mexico, adopt the Roman Catholic religion, and hold the land for seven years.

In practice, the settlers did not comply and adapt. Instead, they lived much as they had in the United States. They continued to bring in large numbers of slaves, even after Mexico outlawed slavery. The settlers thought of themselves not as Mexicans, but as Americans who happened to live in Mexico. Their loyalties and economic activities remained connected to the United States. They had few dealings with the Mexican government.

Tensions in Texas The government of Mexico grew concerned about the loyalties of the American settlers in Texas. In 1827 Mexico sent General Manuel de Mier y Terán to assess the situation. As he traveled the region, he wrote to Mexico's president about the tensions there.

HISTORY'S VOICES

❝Mexican influence is proportionately diminished until . . . it is almost nothing . . . The ratio of Mexicans to foreigners is one to ten . . . It would cause you the same chagrin [humiliation] that it has caused me to see the [extremely low] opinion that is held of our nation by these foreign colonists . . . I am warning you to take timely measures. Texas could throw the whole nation into revolution.❞
—Manuel de Mier y Terán, letter of June 20, 1828

The report prompted Mexico to bolster its authority in Texas. Mexican officials took steps to decrease American influence in the region. One such measure was an April 1830 law designed to halt American immigration into Texas. The law cancelled most *empresario*

THE GRANGER COLLECTION, NEW YORK

FACES OF HISTORY

Santa ANNA
1794–1876

Antonio López de Santa Anna was the ultimate political survivor. Born at a time when Mexico was still ruled by Spain, he joined the Spanish army in Mexico at age 16. When Mexico's war for independence erupted, Santa Anna at first fought for Spain against the Mexican rebels. In 1821 he switched sides and became a powerful figure by helping Mexico to secure its independence.

In 1832 Santa Anna organized a revolt against the Mexican government. The next year he was elected president, an office he held many times between 1833 and 1855.

When American settlers in Texas rebelled, Santa Anna marched an army under his command into the province. His disastrous leadership cost Mexico dearly. Santa Anna remained a dominant force in Mexican political life, however, by performing bravely in battle against an invading French force. He was finally driven from power by generals angry at his sale of land to the United States.

Making Inferences Why might Santa Anna's actions in Mexico's war for independence have benefited him personally?

contracts and discouraged trade between settlers and the United States by placing a high tariff on American imports. The law also banned the importation of slaves into Texas.

The Mexican government sent troops into Texas to enforce the ban on emigration from the United States and to collect taxes. The action placed <u>emphasis</u> on the fact that settlers needed to obey Mexican law. These actions infuriated the American settlers.

International tensions The tensions within Texas heightened tensions between the United States and Mexico. Throughout the early 1800s, the United States had grown in size and wealth. Mexican government officials suspected that the United States wanted to grow even more by acquiring Texas.

The United States had originally claimed Texas as part of the Louisiana Purchase. American filibusters—people who engage in a private military action in a foreign country—had invaded Texas. Now there were tens of thousands of American settlers there. Even though the United States dropped its claim to Texas, Mexicans feared that their northern neighbor would still attempt to seize Texas from Mexico.

In 1827 Joel Poinsett, the U.S. minister to Mexico, offered on behalf of the United States to buy a large part of Texas for $1 million. Mexican officials refused, but their fears of U.S. intentions in Texas were confirmed. Poinsett reported that the Mexican people "regard the United States with distrust."

The Texas Revolution begins Tensions between settlers, now calling themselves Texans, and the Mexican government grew continually worse. In 1832, at the settlement of Anahuac, armed Texans confronted a Mexican official they felt had wrongly imprisoned two settlers. This began a protest by Texans against the government of Mexico.

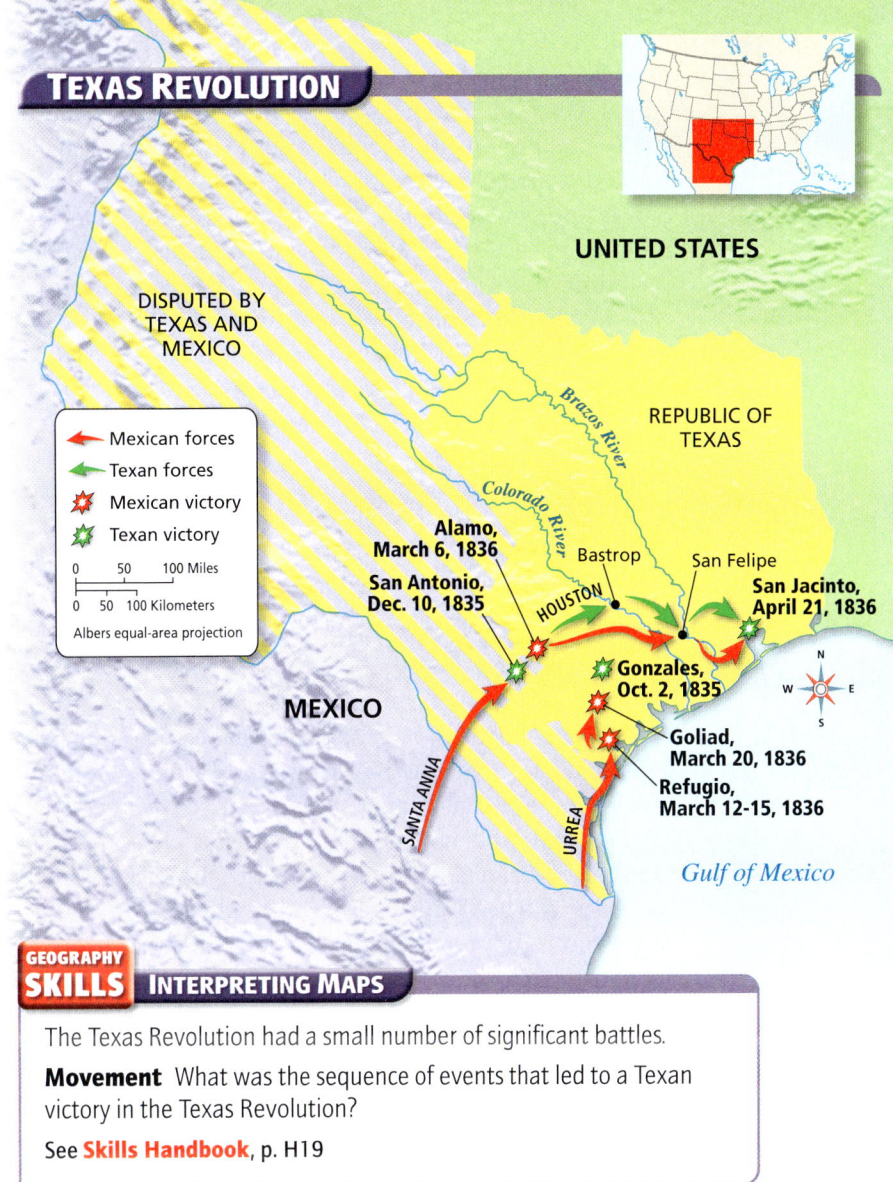

TEXAS REVOLUTION

UNITED STATES

DISPUTED BY TEXAS AND MEXICO

→ Mexican forces
→ Texan forces
✶ Mexican victory
✶ Texan victory

0   50   100 Miles
0   50   100 Kilometers
Albers equal-area projection

REPUBLIC OF TEXAS

Brazos River
Colorado River

Alamo,
March 6, 1836
Bastrop
San Felipe
San Antonio,
Dec. 10, 1835
HOUSTON
San Jacinto,
April 21, 1836
Gonzales,
Oct. 2, 1835

MEXICO

SANTA ANNA
URREA
Goliad,
March 20, 1836
Refugio,
March 12-15, 1836

Gulf of Mexico

GEOGRAPHY SKILLS INTERPRETING MAPS

The Texas Revolution had a small number of significant battles.

Movement What was the sequence of events that led to a Texan victory in the Texas Revolution?

See **Skills Handbook**, p. H19

Protest turned bloody at the town of Velasco. Some Texans on their way to join the protest at Anahuac were transporting a cannon. When Mexican soldiers ordered them to stop, the Texans attacked. After a brief conflict, the Mexicans surrendered.

In 1832 and 1833, Texans held conventions to discuss the best course of action. Many American settlers and some Tejanos believed the situation would improve if Texas became a separate Mexican state. Austin went to Mexico City to present this plan to Mexican leaders. Instead, they felt he was threatening an armed revolt. Austin was jailed and held in Mexico City for more than a year.

To make matters worse, political strife within Mexico had produced a new president. **Antonio López de Santa Anna** assumed the office as a supporter of the rights of Mexican states. Once in power, however, he changed sides and became the leader of those who wanted a strong central government. When Santa Anna enforced new laws banning state militias, some Mexican states revolted. Texans, including many Tejanos, were among those who felt that their liberties were threatened.

By the time Austin was released from jail, he had changed his mind about a peaceful resolution to the conflicts with Mexico.

HISTORY'S VOICES

> ❝War is our only recourse. There is no other remedy. We must defend our rights, ourselves, and our country by force of arms.❞
>
> —Stephen F. Austin, 1835

War came soon enough. Violence erupted at Gonzales, when Mexican forces attempted to retrieve a cannon they had loaned Texans for defense against Native Americans. The Texans refused to return the cannon. They taunted the Mexican soldiers with a battle flag that pictured the cannon along with the phrase "Come and take it." The Texans attacked the Mexican force, and it retreated. The Battle of Gonzales, fought on October 2, 1835, was small, but it was the start of something big—it was the first battle of the **Texas Revolution**.

After Gonzales, hope for a peaceful resolution between the Texans and Mexico diminished. In November, Texans met at the settlement of Washington-on-the-Brazos. At this meeting, called the Consultation, the settlers founded a government and gave **Sam Houston** the task of raising an army.

From the Alamo to independence

In December, rebel Texan forces captured the town of San Antonio, which contained a fort called the **Alamo**. In the 1700s the fort was a mission that had been converted to military use. News of its capture infuriated Santa Anna. He led an army into Texas to punish the rebels and put down the unrest there once and for all.

On February 23, 1836, Santa Anna's force of about 6,000 soldiers reached San Antonio. When some Tejanos and other Texans took refuge in the Alamo, Santa Anna demanded their surrender. The rebels' leader, **William Travis**, responded with a cannon shot.

The Mexican army laid siege to the fort. For 12 days and nights, it pounded the Alamo with cannon fire.

In the early morning hours of March 6, about 1,800 Mexican soldiers stormed the Alamo. Within four hours, they had killed nearly all of the fort's 200 defenders.

★ Interactive
HISTORY CLOSE-UP

The Battle of San Jacinto

On the afternoon of April 21, 1836, Texas forces led by Sam Houston attacked Santa Anna's army at San Jacinto, near the present-day city of Houston. The Texans' victory over the larger Mexican force ended the Texas Revolution and secured Texas' independence from Mexico.

Some panicked Mexican soldiers fled, but their escape was prevented by bodies of water on three sides of the battlefield.

About 900 Texans charged more than 1,200 Mexican soldiers in a battle that lasted less than 20 minutes.

Skills FOCUS | **INTERPRETING INFOGRAPHICS**

go.hrw.com
Interactive
Keyword: SD7 CH9

Making Inferences How might Santa Anna have anticipated the geographic trap that he and his army quickly fell into?

See **Skills Handbook**, p. H18

While the Alamo was under siege, a group of 57 Anglo Texans and two Tejanos met at Washington-on-the-Brazos. Unwilling to accept continued Mexican rule, they issued the Texas Declaration of Independence on March 2, 1836. Then they wrote a constitution for the new, independent nation.

Goliad and the Runaway Scrape

Soon after the Alamo's fall, elements of Santa Anna's army defeated other groups of Texas rebels at the Battle of Refugio and the Battle of Coleto, near Goliad. The Mexicans held the Tejanos and Anglos captured in these and other battles in the presidio at Goliad. On March 26, following Santa Anna's orders, Mexican soldiers executed more than 340 of these prisoners.

Sam Houston, the leader of the Texas forces, was not present at the Alamo or Goliad, but he quickly learned of the disasters. Knowing his army was not well trained and organized enough to defeat Santa Anna, Houston ordered a retreat to the east.

Word of Houston's retreat, coupled with news of what was called the Goliad Massacre, set the people of Texas into a panic. In what would be called the Runaway Scrape, thousands of Texans, including many Tejanos, fled Santa Anna's advancing army.

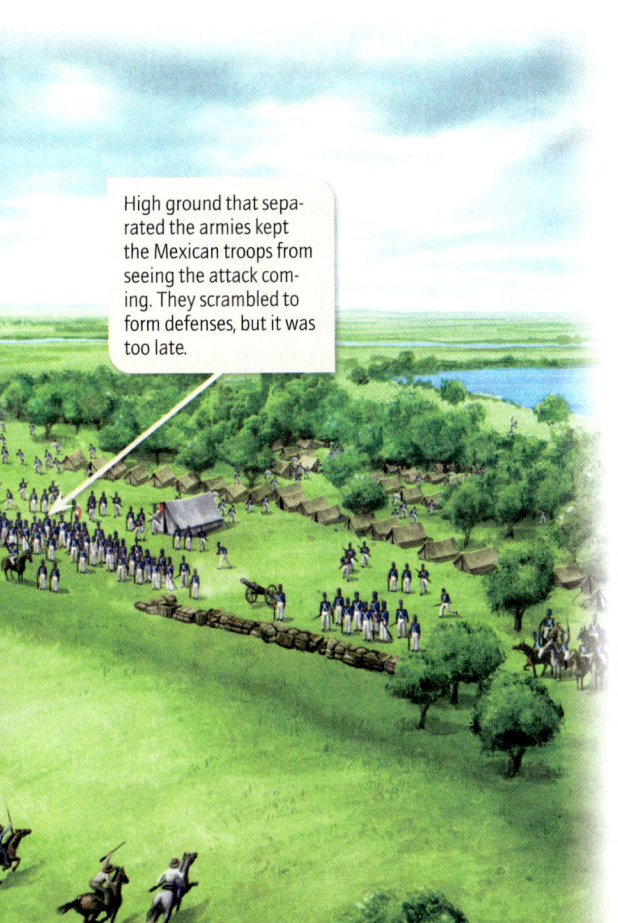

High ground that separated the armies kept the Mexican troops from seeing the attack coming. They scrambled to form defenses, but it was too late.

Texans victorious

Santa Anna's army followed Houston's forces to San Jacinto, near the coast. There, Houston managed to take the Mexican army by surprise. Shouting "Remember the Alamo!" and "Remember Goliad!" the Texans won a quick victory and captured Santa Anna. He was forced to sign the Treaties of Velasco, ending the war. The terms required Mexico to withdraw its troops and to recognize Texas' independence. Texas became a separate nation named the **Republic of Texas.**

The troubles between Texas and Mexico were far from over, however. Because Santa Anna was a prisoner when he signed the treaties, the Mexican government refused to honor all of their provisions. The Texas Revolution was over, but the fighting over Texas was not.

READING CHECK **Summarizing** What were the major events of the Texas Revolution?

Government

In most states, the common practice is to fly the state flag below the U.S. flag. Texans, proud of their state's history as an independent nation, routinely fly the state flag—the flag of the old Republic of Texas—alone.

SECTION 2 ASSESSMENT

go.hrw.com
Online Quiz
Keyword: SD7 HP9

Reviewing Ideas, Terms, and People

1. **a. Describe** How was the **mission system** organized?
   b. Analyze Why did the mission system fail?
   c. Predict How might development of the American Southwest have been different if the mission system had succeeded?

2. **a. Identify** Who was **Stephen F. Austin**?
   b. Explain Why did Americans move to Texas?
   c. Evaluate Do you think it was wise for the Spanish and then the Mexican government to allow Americans to settle in Texas? Explain.

3. **a. Recall** What factors caused tensions between American settlers in Texas and the Mexican government?
   b. Compare and Contrast How were the battles at the **Alamo** and San Jacinto similar and different?
   c. Rate How important was **Antonio López de Santa Anna** as a factor in the **Texas Revolution**? Explain your assessment.

Critical Thinking

4. **Summarizing** Copy the diagram below and complete it to elaborate on the reasons that Texans did not want to become Mexican citizens.

Why Texans did not want to become Mexican citizens
1.
2.
3.
4.

FOCUS ON WRITING

5. **Persuasive** Were the Texas rebels justified in their fight for independence, or should they have honored Mexican law and government? Write a paragraph defending your position.

War with Mexico

BEFORE YOU READ

MAIN IDEA

Soon after annexing Texas, the United States declared war on Mexico.

READING FOCUS

1. What were the arguments for and against the annexation of Texas?
2. What created tensions between the United States and Mexico in the 1840s?
3. What were the causes and effects of the Mexican-American War?

KEY TERMS AND PEOPLE

John Tyler
Zachary Taylor
Mexican-American War
Stephen Kearny
Republic of California
Bear Flag Revolt
Winfield Scott
Treaty of Guadalupe Hidalgo
Mexican Cession

P1 2.2 Develop and test hypotheses about important events, eras, or issues in New York State and United States history, setting clear and valid criteria for judging the importance and significance of these events, eras, or issues.

From REPUBLIC to STATE

THE INSIDE STORY

Will Texas join the Union? At last, Texas was an independent nation, the Republic of Texas. Texans were proud. Yet, for many, independence was just a stepping stone to what they really wanted: statehood.

In Texas' first election, war hero Sam Houston won the presidency. His election also was the first chance for Texans to decide whether they wanted to become part of the United States. Overwhelmingly, they voted yes.

Texans voted for annexation for many reasons. Many had never considered themselves to be Mexican citizens, and they longed to be part of their homeland. Joining the United States would also bring them under the protection of the U.S. Army and Navy, which could defend them against a Mexican invasion. Texas also faced economic troubles. It was in debt, and its currency had little value. Joining the Union would help the Texas economy.

The new nation of Texas faced a new battle: the fight for statehood. It would take far longer to become a state than it had taken to become an independent country.

The Annexation of Texas

Americans who believed in manifest destiny were delighted at the prospect of admitting Texas to the Union. Annexing Texas would add a large area to the country. Supporters viewed the Texas Revolution in the spirit of the American Revolution. They admired Texans for fighting for their freedom from Mexico.

▼ Lowering the Texas flag to make way for the U.S. flag

Many southerners supported annexation because Texas allowed slavery. Admitting Texas to the Union as a slave state would boost the South's political power.

Other Americans had doubts about letting Texas become a state. They were concerned that the United States would have to bear the substantial Texas debt. Many northerners opposed annexation because it would spread slavery westward and increase slave states' voting power in Congress. A major argument in Congress was that the Constitution said nothing about admitting an independent nation to the United States.

Texas remained a republic for nine years. The annexation question became a significant issue in the 1844 presidential election. When James K. Polk, the pro-annexation candidate, won the presidency, Mexico warned the United States that it would consider the annexation of Texas "equivalent to a declaration of war against the Mexican Republic." However, the outgoing president, **John Tyler**, who also favored annexation, signed the joint resolution of Congress into law three days before the end of his term, in March 1845.

Meanwhile, diplomats from France, Great Britain, Mexico, and the United States maneuvered around the Texas issue. In March 1845 Congress passed the joint resolution annexing Texas to the United States. Passing such a resolution took only a simple majority in Congress. Annexing Texas by treaty with the Republic of Texas would have required two-thirds approval in the Senate, which supporters feared would be difficult to obtain.

In the fall of 1845, Texas put the question to voters once again. The results were virtually the same: more than 7,600 in favor of annexation and 430 opposed. Texas became part of the United States on December 29, 1845.

On February 19, 1846, a simple ceremony was held at the republic's capitol building in Austin. Anson Jones, the last president of Texas, lowered its tricolored flag.

"The final act of this great drama is now performed," he said. "The Republic of Texas is no more."

READING CHECK **Summarizing** Why was the annexation of Texas controversial?

Tensions between the United States and Mexico

The annexation of Texas enraged the Mexican government. Mexico still held the position that Texas had been unfairly taken from it by foreigners during the Texas Revolution.

Mexican government officials had refused to recognize the independence of the Republic of Texas. They viewed its annexation as a theft of Mexican territory. When Congress voted for the annexation of Texas, Mexico responded by breaking off diplomatic relations with the United States.

Polk and manifest destiny In March 1845 James K. Polk became president. Polk was an enthusiastic supporter of national expansion. In fact, he had set his sights on even more territory. He wanted the nation to acquire the land between Texas and the Pacific Ocean. These territories, New Mexico and California, belonged to Mexico. But Polk thought they should become part of the United States.

HISTORY'S VOICES

❝To enlarge [the United States] is to extend the dominions of peace over additional territories and increasing millions . . . my duty [is] to assert and maintain . . . the right of the United States to that portion of our territory which lies beyond the Rocky Mountains.❞

—James K. Polk, Inaugural Address, March 4, 1845

Only a handful of Americans lived in New Mexico and California. They were sparsely populated by Mexican citizens as well. In addition, the Mexican government and army had little presence in either area. Polk sought an opportunity to acquire these remote regions.

The boundary dispute Polk also sought to secure the boundary between Texas and Mexico. At first the United States recognized the Nueces River as the boundary between Mexico and the Republic of Texas. Texans, however, claimed the boundary was farther south, at the Rio Grande. When the United States annexed Texas, it also claimed the Rio Grande as the boundary. Mexico maintained that the boundary should remain at the Nueces River.

Another dispute between the United States and Mexico involved money. The United States claimed that Mexico owed American citizens $3 million for the loss of property and life during Mexico's fight for independence from Spain. Polk wanted these problems resolved. He devised a plan to settle all of these issues in one bold move.

Slidell's trip In the fall of 1845, Polk sent a special envoy, or messenger, to Mexico. The envoy, John Slidell, arrived with a U.S. offer to cancel the $3 million in claims against Mexico in exchange for Mexico's recognition of the Rio Grande as its boundary with the United States. Further, he was authorized to pay Mexico up to $30 million to purchase New Mexico and California for the United States.

	Area disputed by the U.S. and Mexico
	Mexican territory
	Territory ceded by Mexico, Treaty of Guadalupe Hidalgo, 1848 (Mexican cession)
→	Mexican forces
→	U.S. forces
✦	Mexican victory
✦	U.S. victory

CALIFORNIA REPUBLIC

UNITED STATES

Bear Flag Revolt, June 14, 1846
Sonoma
Monterey, July 7, 1846
Los Angeles
San Pasqual, Dec. 6, 1846
KEARNY
Sacramento, Feb. 28, 1847

Bent's Fort
Fort Leavenworth
KEARNY
Santa Fe
El Brazito, Dec. 25, 1846
El Paso

Colorado River
Gila River
Rio Grande
Arkansas River
Mississippi River

New Orleans
Gulf of Mexico

PACIFIC OCEAN
Tropic of Cancer

MEXICO
Monterrey, Sept. 20–24, 1846
Buena Vista, Feb. 22–23, 1847
Mazatlán
Saltillo
Matamoros
TAYLOR
SCOTT
TAYLOR
San Luis Potosí
SANTA ANNA
Tampico
SCOTT
Mexico City, Sept. 13–14, 1847
SANTA ANNA
SCOTT
Veracruz, Mar. 9–29, 1847

0   200   400 Miles
0   200   400 Kilometers
Albers equal-area projection

GEOGRAPHY SKILLS INTERPRETING MAPS

One of the bloodiest battles fought in California was the Battle of San Pasqual, a rare loss for General Kearny. Above is California's bear flag.
Movement Describe Kearny's march from Kansas to California.

See **Skills Handbook**, p. H19

Slidell found the Mexican government in turmoil. Neither of the rivals for Mexico's presidency would consent to meet with him. An angry Slidell recommended to Polk that Mexico be punished.

READING CHECK **Contrasting** How did the U.S. position regarding Texas differ from the Mexican position?

The Mexican-American War

While Slidell was in Mexico, Polk ordered General **Zachary Taylor** to advance with his troops into the disputed territory between the Nueces River and the Rio Grande, On April 25 some of Taylor's soldiers fought a skirmish in this region with a small party of Mexican soldiers.

Polk used this event as an excuse to request that Congress declare war on Mexico. Ignoring the fact that the boundary was in dispute, the president charged that Mexicans had "invaded our territory and shed the blood of our fellow-citizens on our own soil." The United States declared war on Mexico on May 13, 1846. The **Mexican-American War** had begun.

Fighting the war The United States used an aggressive strategy to win the war. Within weeks, General **Stephen Kearny** marched west from Kansas, bound for the New Mexico territory. He easily captured the town of Santa Fe and took control of New Mexico. Kearny then headed west, hoping to gain control of California.

In California, a small group of Americans revolted against Mexican rule. The rebels defeated a small Mexican force in the village of Sonoma and forced the Mexican leader to sign a treaty turning California over to them. On June 14, 1846, the Americans declared the independent **Republic of California**. They made a crude flag for their new country that had a picture of a bear on it. Because of this flag, the uprising in California became known as the **Bear Flag Revolt**.

A month later, U.S. naval forces arrived and soon gained control of California. Meanwhile, American forces under General Taylor advanced into northern Mexico and captured important towns in the region.

Another force, under General **Winfield Scott**, landed on the Gulf coast of Mexico near Veracruz. Scott led his forces inland and marched into Mexico City in September 1847.

In a matter of months, U.S. forces had captured New Mexico and California. When Mexico's capital fell, the Mexican government was forced to give in to American demands.

Results of the war Signed in 1848, the **Treaty of Guadalupe Hidalgo** ended the Mexican-American War. Under the treaty, Mexico was forced to turn over to the United States a huge tract of land known as the **Mexican Cession**. In return, the United States agreed to pay Mexico $15 million and drop the $3 million in damages. In 1853 the Gadsden Purchase clarified the treaty boundary and transferred even more land to the United States.

President Polk was pleased with America's victory. Many other Americans, however, did not feel they could be proud of this war.

CAUSES AND EFFECTS OF THE MEXICAN-AMERICAN WAR — QUICK FACTS

CAUSES
- Annexation of Texas
- Boundary dispute
- Manifest destiny and expansionism

EFFECTS
- Treaty of Guadalupe Hidalgo
- Mexican Cession
- Gadsden Purchase

HISTORY'S VOICES

❝This is no war of defense, but one of unnecessary and offensive aggression. It is Mexico that is defending her firesides . . . not we.❞

—Henry Clay, speech of November 13, 1847

Debate continues over whether the Mexican-American War was justified, and hard feelings persist. Historians agree, however, that the war was a clear expression of America's belief in manifest destiny.

READING CHECK **Summarizing** What were the results of the Mexican-American War?

THE IMPACT TODAY

Government
A 2004 government study found that the United States failed to recognize Mexican titles to millions of acres of land in the Mexican Cession, despite agreeing to do so in the Treaty of Guadalupe Hidalgo. The resulting land disputes remain a major political issue in New Mexico.

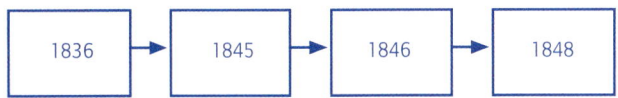

SECTION 3 ASSESSMENT

go.hrw.com
Online Quiz
Keyword: SD7 HP9

Reviewing Ideas, Terms, and People

1. a. Recall What were the major arguments for and against the annexation of Texas?
b. Explain How did the question of slavery play a role in the annexation debate?
c. Evaluate Which arguments for and against annexation were most powerful? Why do you think so?

2. a. Describe How did tensions between the United States and Mexico heighten during the mid-1840s?
b. Make Inferences Why might President Polk have expected the trip to Mexico by his envoy Slidell to be a success?
c. Evaluate Do you think Mexico was wise to break off diplomatic relations with the United States? Explain.

3. a. Identify What were the major outcomes of the **Mexican-American War**?
b. Draw Conclusions Do you think the Mexican-American War was justified in terms of protecting Texas citizens? Explain.

c. Predict What effect do you think the Mexican Cession would have on tensions between the North and the South over slavery? Explain.

Critical Thinking

4. Sequencing Complete the diagram below to trace the process by which the United States expanded its borders in the 1840s.

| 1836 | → | 1845 | → | 1846 | → | 1848 |

FOCUS ON SPEAKING

5. Persuasive Give a one-minute speech stating reasons to support or oppose the war between the United States and Mexico.

The "Real" Story of the Alamo

Historical Context The documents below provide information on what happened at the Alamo, from varying points of view.

Task Examine the documents and answer the questions that follow. Then you will be asked to write an essay about differing portrayals of the Battle of the Alamo, using facts from the documents and from the chapter to support the position that you take in your thesis statement.

ST 4.3 Develop hypotheses about important events, eras, or issues; move from chronicling to explaining historical events and issues; use information collected from diverse sources to produce cogently written reports and document-based essays; apply the skills of historiography by comparing, contrasting, and evaluating the interpretations of different historians of an event, era, or issue.

DOCUMENT 1

Because so few people survived at the Alamo, few records exist to tell what actually happened there. One of the few accounts by a survivor came from Susanna Dickinson, whose version of the attack was published in 1875.

"I knew Colonels [Davy] Crockett, [Jim] Bowie, and [William Barret] Travis well. Col. Crockett was a performer on the violin, and often during the siege took it up and played his favorite tunes . . .

Under the cover of darkness the [Mexicans] approached the fortifications, and planting their scaling ladders against our walls just as light was approaching, they climbed up to the tops of our walls and jumped down within, many of them to their immediate death.

As fast as the front ranks were slain, they were filled up again by fresh troops . . .

As we passed through the enclosed ground in front of the church, I saw heaps of dead and dying . . .

I recognized Col. Crockett lying dead and mutilated between the church and the two story barrack building, and even remember seeing his peculiar cap lying by his side.

Col. Bowie was sick in bed and not expected to live, but as the victorious Mexicans entered his room, he killed two of them with his pistols before they pierced him through with their sabres.

Col. Travis and Bonham were killed while working the cannon, the body of the former lay on the top of the church."

DOCUMENT 2

In 1955 a document appeared in Mexico that claimed to be Mexican officer José Enrique de la Peña's first-hand account of what happened at the Alamo. Some scholars have questioned the authenticity of the account, which is at odds with some legends of the Alamo. The following is the officer's account of Davy Crockett's death.

"Some seven men survived the general carnage and, under the protection of General [Manuel Fernández] Castrillón, they were brought before [Mexican President Antonio López de] Santa Anna. Among them was one of great stature . . . in whose face there was the imprint of adversity, but in whom one also noticed a degree of resignation and nobility that did him honor. He was the naturalist David Crockett . . . Santa Anna answered Castrillón's intervention in Crockett's behalf with a gesture of indignation [anger] and, addressing himself to the . . . the troops closest to him, ordered [Crockett's] execution. The commanders and officers were outraged at this action and did not support the order, hoping that once the fury of the moment had blown over these men would be spared; but several officers who were around the president and who . . . became noteworthy by an infamous deed, surpassing the soldiers in cruelty. They thrust themselves forward, in order to flatter their commander, and with swords in hand, fell upon these unfortunate, defenseless men just as a tiger leaps upon his prey . . . [T]hese unfortunates died without complaining and without humiliating themselves before their torturers."

DOCUMENT 3

The legend of the Alamo has inspired numerous books and several films. In 1960 Hollywood produced a big-budget version of the story. The film focused heavily on the American defenders, portraying the Texans as a virtually all-Anglo force. The following poster features four men, including the stars playing Jim Bowie, Davy Crockett, and William Barret Travis.

DOCUMENT 4

In 2004 filmmakers decided to retell the story of the Alamo with greater authenticity. This film version gave more attention to the Mexican view of the battle and also tried to present a more authentic portrait of the defenders, including the Tejano and African American defenders. The filmmakers worked closely with historians to make sure details such as the hair and clothing styles of the characters were accurate. This still from the film shows the actors playing Texas defenders Juan Seguín and Davy Crockett.

Skills FOCUS   READING LIKE A HISTORIAN

1. **a. Identify** Refer to Document 1. According to Dickinson, how did William Barret Travis, Davy Crockett, and Jim Bowie die?
   b. Analyze Overall, what is the impression that Dickinson gives of the attack on the Alamo?

2. **a. Identify** Refer to Document 2. According to José Enrique de la Peña, what happened to Crockett?
   b. Compare and Contrast Refer to Documents 1 and 2. How do Dickinson and de la Peña's accounts compare to one another?
   c. Evaluate Refer to Documents 1 and 2. Which one seems more reliable? Explain possible reasons.

3. **a. Contrast** Refer to Documents 3 and 4. What are some differences between the two film portrayals of the Texas defenders?
   b. Elaborate Why do you think the film version made in 2004 was so different from the one made in 1960?

4. **Document-Based Essay Question** Consider the question below and form a thesis statement. Using examples from Documents 1, 2, 3, and 4, create an outline and write a short essay supporting your position.
   How and why have versions of what happened at the Alamo differed?

   See **Skills Handbook**, pp. H28–29, H30

Visual Summary: Expansion Leads to Conflict

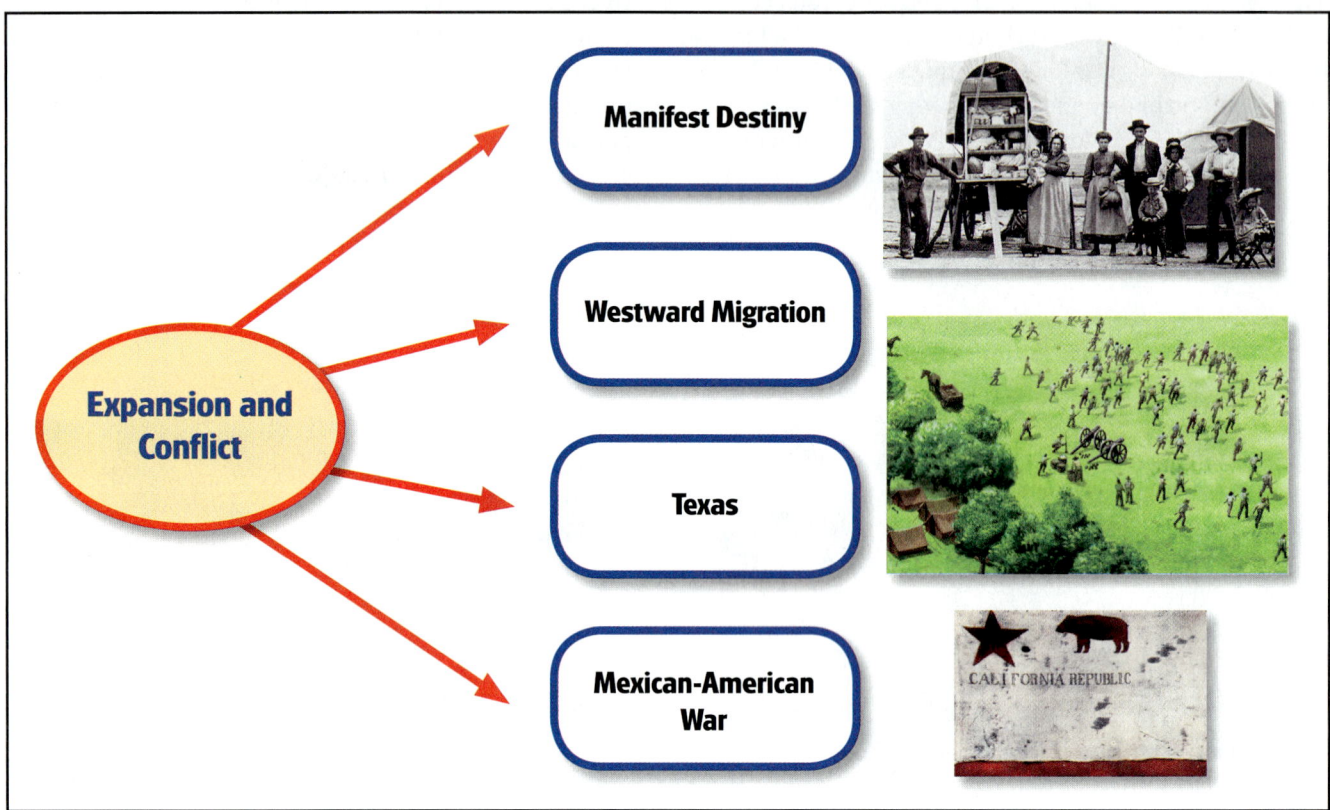

Expansion and Conflict

→ Manifest Destiny

→ Westward Migration

→ Texas

→ Mexican-American War

Reviewing Key Terms and People

Match each lettered definition with the correct numbered item below.

1. Catholic settlements with forts that were built by the Spanish to convert local Indians
2. Leader of American colonists in Texas
3. Land Mexico gave to the United States
4. Dictator of Mexico
5. 1846 uprising in California
6. Independent nation that resulted from the Treaties of Velasco
7. Belief that the United States should spread across the North American continent from coast to coast
8. Mexican fort in San Antonio that was important in the Texas Revolution
9. Longest, most famous migrant trail to the West
10. Process by which the Republic of Texas became part of the United States

a. manifest destiny
b. Oregon Trail
c. mission system
d. Antonio López de Santa Anna
e. Alamo
f. Republic of Texas
g. Stephen F. Austin
h. annexation
i. Bear Flag Revolt
j. Mexican Cession

History's Impact video program

Review the video to answer the closing question: How has the history of Texas and the Southwest been affected by different groups?

Comprehension and Critical Thinking

SECTION 1 *(pp. 296–301)*

11. a. Identify What factor triggered the largest wave of migration to the West?

   b. Analyze Why was a journey west in the 1840s and 1850s a huge adventure?

   c. Predict What effect might the railroad have on the land in the western part of the United States?

SECTION 2 *(pp. 302–307)*

12. a. Recall List at least two main goals of the Spanish mission system.

   b. Compare How were the tensions within Texas similar to those between the United States and Mexico?

   c. Evaluate How did the American losses at the Alamo affect the Texas Revolution?

SECTION 3 *(pp. 308–311)*

13. a. Recall Why was the Mexican government angry about the annexation of Texas?

   b. Make Inferences How did the recommendations of U.S. envoy John Slidell to President Polk reflect Slidell's feelings about his treatment in Mexico?

   c. Elaborate How did the United States take advantage of its military victories over Mexico?

Using the Internet

go.hrw.com
Practice Online
Keyword: SD7 CH9

14. Marcus Whitman and his wife, Narcissa, were among the first white Americans to settle in Oregon Country. They build their mission near the Columbia River and set about converting Cayuse Indians to Christianity. Using the keyword above, do research on the Whitmans' settlement and its fate. Then create a report that describes life at the mission.

Analyzing Primary Sources

Reading Like a Historian President James Polk strongly supported the territorial expansion of the United States.

> ❝To enlarge [the United States] is to extend the dominions of peace over additional territories and increasing millions . . . my duty [is] to assert and maintain . . . the right of the United States to that portion of our territory which lies beyond the Rocky Mountains . . . The world beholds the peaceful triumphs of the industry of our emigrants . . . The jurisdiction of our laws . . . should be extended over them in the distant regions which they have selected for their homes.❞
>
> —President James K. Polk, Inaugural Address

15. Identify What does Polk see as his duty?

16. Draw Conclusions What reasons does Polk give to support U.S. expansion?

Critical Reading

Read the passage in Section 1 that begins with the heading "The Gold Rush." Then answer the question that follows.

17. According to the History's Voices quotation, "the whole country" refers to

   A the Sierra Nevada.

   B the United States.

   C farmers.

   D much of California.

 FOCUS ON WRITING

Persuasive Writing *Persuasive writing takes a position for or against an issue, using facts and examples as supporting evidence. To practice persuasive writing, complete the assignment below.*

Writing Topic The annexation of Mexican land by the United States

18. Assignment Based on what you have read in this chapter, write a paragraph that either supports or opposes the way the United States acquired land from Mexico.

 **IN BRIEF** Below is a chapter-by-chapter summary of the main ideas covered in Unit 3.

 **From Nationalism to Sectionalism**
1815–1840

MAIN IDEA The outcome of the War of 1812 filled Americans with a strong sense of national pride. At the same time, the North and the South were developing very different ways of life. Sectional divisions over economic issues and slavery gradually weakened the nationalism aroused by the war.

SECTION 1 Americans' new sense of national identity was reflected in the nation's art and literature. The Monroe Doctrine and the Adams-Onís Treaty showed America's growing confidence as a nation. Despite this national pride, the Missouri Compromise in 1820 ended the Era of Good Feelings and showed that strong divisions existed over the issue of slavery.

SECTION 2 Andrew Jackson's presidency was marked by the removal of eastern Native Americans to the west of the Mississippi River. Controversies over the Second National Bank, the tariff, and states' rights showed continuing sectional divisions among Americans.

SECTION 3 Manufacturing and industry became increasingly important to the North's economy in the early 1800s. The development of roads, canals, and railroads encouraged population growth and trade.

SECTION 4 The South's economy remained heavily agricultural. The cotton gin's invention and demand for cotton in the North and Great Britain made King Cotton the South's main crop and encouraged the growth of slavery.

 **A Push for Reform**
1830–1860

MAIN IDEA The mid-1800s were a time of great reform in the United States. Inspired by a religious movement, many Americans worked to make improvements in American society.

SECTION 1 The preachers of the Second Great Awakening taught that people had a responsibility to do God's work. This message led Americans to try to make society better by working for temperance, education reform, and prison reform. Some reformers formed communities to be free of society's ills.

SECTION 2 The arrival of large numbers of Irish and German immigrants in the mid-1800s brought great change, including rapid growth in the population of northern cities. Movements arose to improve conditions in factories, clean up overcrowded cities, and aid city dwellers who needed help.

SECTION 3 Despite the severe limits society put on women in the mid-1800s, they took the lead in many reform movements. Their desire to advance reform led them to demand equality and more political power in American society.

SECTION 4 The harsh lives led by slaves in the South caused an abolition movement to develop that called for an end to slavery. Some abolitionists attacked slavery in speeches, and others helped slaves escape to freedom.

 **Expansion Leads to Conflict**
1830–1860

MAIN IDEA As increasing numbers of Americans moved west, the United States expanded its borders through annexation, war, and threats of war. By 1850 the nation stretched across North America from the Atlantic Ocean to the Pacific.

SECTION 1 Economic opportunity, coupled with a belief in the nation's manifest destiny, led many Americans westward in the mid-1800s. The largest migration took place over the Oregon Trail. In 1849 a gold rush drew thousands of people to California. American settlement in the West led to improved communications and changed the lives of Native Americans forever.

SECTION 2 Stephen Austin led the first American settlers into Mexico's Texas region in the 1820s. Tensions between American settlers and Mexico erupted into revolt, war, and freedom from Mexico in 1836. Texans formed an independent nation called the Republic of Texas.

SECTION 3 The United States annexed Texas in 1845. A dispute over Texas's southern border led to the Mexican War in 1846. After Mexico's defeat, the two nations signed the Treaty of Guadalupe Hidalgo in 1848. Mexico turned over a huge tract of land to the United States, including California and what is today the American Southwest.

1850–1877

Themes

Government and Democracy
Conflicts between the North and the South over the issue of slavery resulted in the outbreak of the Civil War.

Rights and Responsibilities
During Reconstruction, the Thirteenth, Fourteenth, and Fifteenth Amendments were added to the Constitution to extend the rights of citizenship to former slaves.

Civil War battles were more brutal than either side had anticipated and often involved tens of thousands of soldiers.

Sequencing

Find practice for **Sequencing** in the **Skills Handbook,** p. H8

Most historical writing is organized in sequence, or the order in which events occur. Sequencing allows readers to better understand both the content and the context of what they are reading, including how one event may influence another and eventually lead to a certain outcome.

Before You Read
Examine time lines in the text. What do they tell you about the subject matter?

While You Read
Note key dates and events from the text, and use them to produce your own time line.

After You Read
Compare your time line and those in the text. How are they similar? How are they different?

Lincoln's Early Politics

As a young man, Lincoln moved to New Salem, a village about 20 miles northwest of Springfield, Illinois. He took a job as a store clerk and the next year ran for a seat in the state legislature. Lincoln lost that election, but two years later he ran again and won.

In December 1834, at age 25, Lincoln began the first of four terms in the Illinois General Assembly. During his first term he studied law at home, and in 1836 he was licensed to practice law. As a member of the state legislature, Lincoln opposed resolutions that condemned the abolition movement and that called for continuing slavery in Washington, D.C.

Lincoln met Mary Todd, the cousin of his law partner and the daughter of a wealth Kentucky slaveholder, in 1840. It was a rocky courtship because Todd flirted with another local attorney, Stephen Douglas. After a broken engagement, Lincoln and Todd made up and married in 1842. By then Lincoln had retired from the legislature to devote more time to his law practice.

READING CHECK **Sequencing** Which event occurred first? Which event occurred last?

Sequence Clue words, such as *first, next, then, before, after,* and *finally,* help indicate the order of events.

Dates, times of day, and seasons of the year are helpful clues in determining sequence.

Test Prep Tip

Multiple choice, short answer, and essay questions often ask you to determine the correct sequence of events. Sometimes, though, events can occur at the same time. Signal words such as *while, meanwhile,* and *during* tell you this.

Interpreting Visuals

Find practice for **Interpreting Visuals** in the **Skills Handbook,** p. H30

Photographs capture the moment and political cartoons critique politics, but **fine art** is a type of visual created for artistic merit. Paintings created during or about points in history can provide detailed insight into certain people, places, and events. Works of fine art must be interpreted carefully for historical evidence. They are created by artists who have a point of view they wish to express.

Strategies historians use:

- Identify the subject of the piece. What event does the artist choose to portray?
- When and where does the event take place? Look for markers of time and place that aid recognition of historical context.
- What is the artist's point of view? Identify images that help identify the intended audience.

The subject of the picture is President Lincoln's tour of Richmond after that city had fallen to Union forces.

The crumbling buildings in the background help you identify the war-torn capital of Richmond.

The people in the picture appear to be celebrating President Lincoln's entrance. Therefore you can infer that the image was intended for a northern audience.

Skills Focus   READING LIKE A HISTORIAN

As You Read Compare historical art with your reading. Do they support each other? What does art add to your understanding?

As You Study Keep in mind that art offers one interpretation of history, not necessarily the only interpretation. Be sure to balance each interpretation with known facts to arrive at the most complete historical account.

The Nation Splits Apart

THE BIG PICTURE After the war with Mexico ended, one question stirred national politics: Would these new territories be slave or free? Congressional attempts to settle this question only triggered greater division. By 1860 the nation had split along sectional lines—North and South—and hostile camps took steps that would lead to war.

New York Standards

Key Idea 3 Study about the major social, political, economic, cultural, and religious developments in New York State and United States history involves learning about the important roles and contributions of individuals and groups.

 Skills FOCUS   **READING LIKE A HISTORIAN**

Nowhere was the fight over slavery more pronounced than in Kansas territory. In the Marais des Cygnes Massacre, a gang of 30 pro-slavery men rounded up a group of eleven antislavery settlers and gunned them down in a small ravine, killing five and wounding four. **Interpreting Visuals** Why weren't the victims of the massacre fighting back?

See **Skills Handbook**, p. H30

U.S.

1850
Congress reaches the Compromise of 1850, admitting California as a free state and passing the Fugitive Slave Act.

1850

World

1851
The Great Exhibition, the first World's Fair, opens in London.

History's Impact video program
Watch the video to understand the impact of Dred Scott.

1852
Harriet Beecher Stowe publishes *Uncle Tom's Cabin*, a novel about slave life.

May 1854
Kansas-Nebraska Act becomes law.

May 21, 1856
Proslavery group attacks antislavery stronghold of Lawrence, Kansas.

October 1859
John Brown seizes the federal arsenal at Harpers Ferry, Virginia.

1852 — 1854 — 1856 — 1858 — 1860

1852
Republic of South Africa is established.

1854
Japan and the United States sign an agreement opening Japan to trade.

1857
Uprising against British rule in India begins with Sepoy Rebellion.

1861
Russian serfs are emancipated.

321

The Politics of Slavery

BEFORE YOU READ

MAIN IDEA

The issue of slavery dominated national politics during the 1850s. The federal government forged policies in attempts to satisfy both North and South.

READING FOCUS

1. What factors made slavery in the United States an issue before 1850?

2. How did the Compromise of 1850 seek to settle issues between North and South ?

3. In what ways did the North and South each hope to benefit from the Kansas-Nebraska Act?

4. How did people in the North and South react to the Kansas-Nebraska Act?

KEY TERMS AND PEOPLE

radical
Millard Fillmore
Compromise of 1850
Fugitive Slave Act
Harriet Beecher Stowe
Uncle Tom's Cabin
Stephen Douglas
popular sovereignty
Kansas-Nebraska Act
free-soilers
Republican Party
nativism

PI 3.3 Prepare essays and oral reports about the important social, political, economic, scientific, technological, and cultural developments, issues, and events from New York State and United States history.

A MINISTER Defies the PRESIDENT

THE INSIDE STORY

What happened when a minister hid two enslaved people? Husband and wife William and Ellen Craft escaped from slavery in Georgia in 1848 and made their way to Massachusetts, where slavery had been outlawed. William, a skilled cabinetmaker, found work in Boston.

The Crafts joined the church of well-known abolitionist Theodore Parker and lived quietly. Parker was one of the most important ministers of his day. His powerful sermons attracted so large a crowd that he preached not from a church pulpit but from the city's enormous Music Hall. Each Sunday thousands of people gathered to hear Parker denounce slavery and call for women's rights.

After learning of the Crafts' whereabouts in 1850, their slaveholder in Georgia sent two men to Boston to capture them. William fled to the home of a local African American abolitionist. There he was guarded by barrels of gunpowder that the homeowner placed on his front porch. Ellen hid in Parker's home. When President Millard Fillmore threatened to send U.S. troops to seize the Crafts, Parker's followers put them on a ship to England. "I would rather lie all my life in jail, and starve there, than refuse to protect one of these parishioners of mine," Parker angrily informed the president. "You cannot think that I am to stand by and see my church carried off to slavery and do nothing." ◼

▶ The minister Theodore Parker (above right) issued this broadside cautioning African Americans to avoid police.

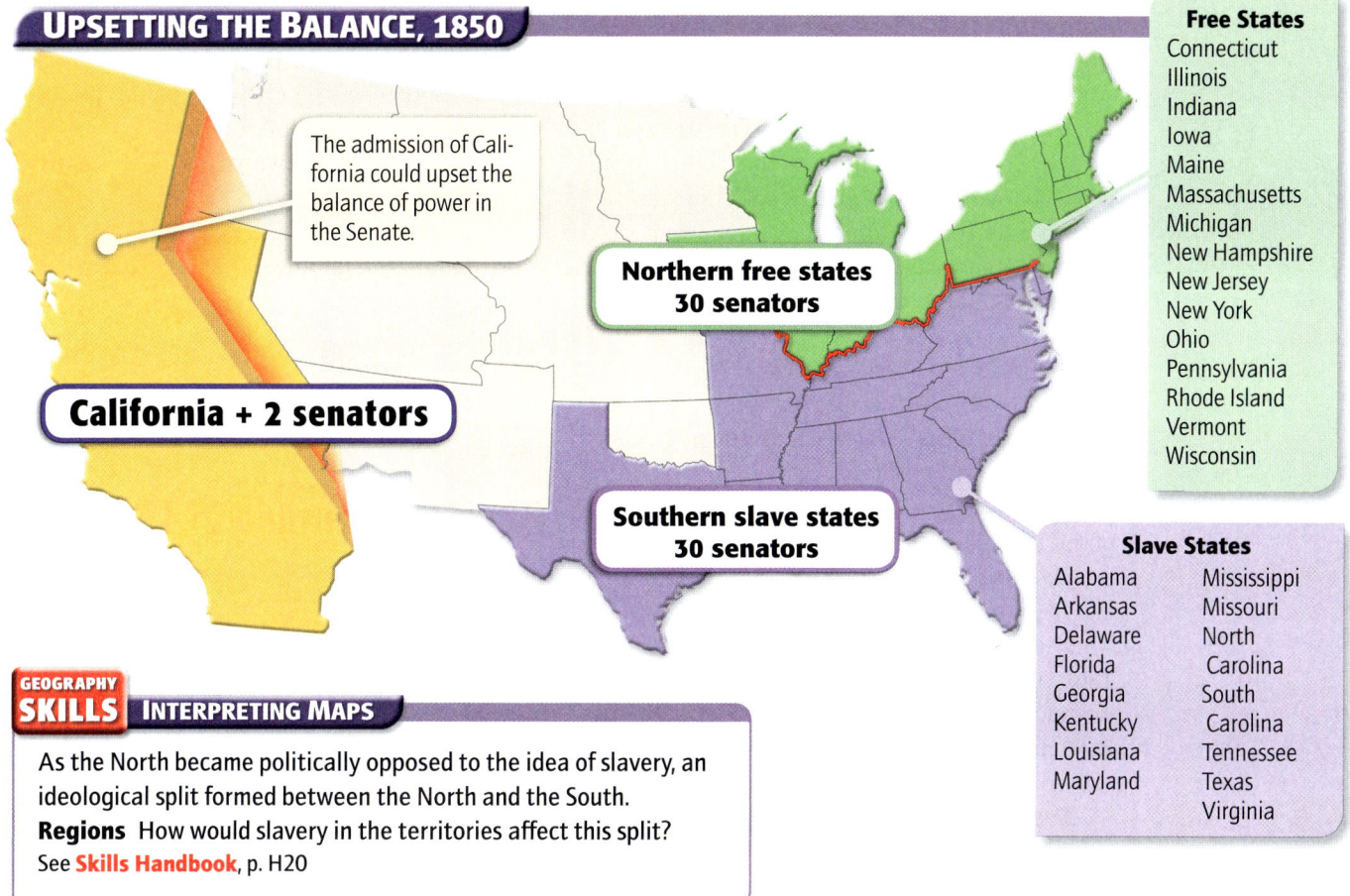

UPSETTING THE BALANCE, 1850

The admission of California could upset the balance of power in the Senate.

Northern free states 30 senators

California + 2 senators

Southern slave states 30 senators

Free States
Connecticut
Illinois
Indiana
Iowa
Maine
Massachusetts
Michigan
New Hampshire
New Jersey
New York
Ohio
Pennsylvania
Rhode Island
Vermont
Wisconsin

Slave States
Alabama	Mississippi
Arkansas	Missouri
Delaware	North
Florida	Carolina
Georgia	South
Kentucky	Carolina
Louisiana	Tennessee
Maryland	Texas
	Virginia

GEOGRAPHY SKILLS INTERPRETING MAPS

As the North became politically opposed to the idea of slavery, an ideological split formed between the North and the South.

Regions How would slavery in the territories affect this split?

See **Skills Handbook**, p. H20

Slavery in the United States

By 1850 slavery had existed for more than 200 years in America. Under British rule slavery had existed in every colony, north and south. After the Revolutionary War, the northern states began to end the practice.

Freedom in the North did not always come quickly. Some northern states freed only children born after slavery had been banned. Their mothers remained enslaved. In several northern states, slavery continued to exist in some form until the 1840s.

Even at its peak, however, northern slavery never equaled that of the South. By 1790 more than 90 percent of enslaved Americans lived to the south of the Mason-Dixon line.

By 1850 the nation was divided. Two societies existed—the North where workers labored for wages and the South where a large number of workers were enslaved. Many southerners believed the health of their economy depended on slave labor. "It is, in truth, the slave labor in Virginia which gives the value to her soil and her habitations," said Virginian Thomas Dew.

The developing debate over slavery was largely one of property rights versus human rights. Those who supported slavery believed that property rights came first. "We take it for granted, that the right of the owner to his slave is to be respected," argued Dew.

To the northerners who were truly concerned about slavery, the issue was one of basic democratic ideology. "Shall the Government be a commonwealth where all are citizens, or an aristocracy where man owns his brother man," Theodore Parker asked. "Shall a man have a right to his own limbs, his liberty, his life?"

The treatment of slaves in the South varied widely. Northern opponents of slavery emphasized its harshness. Escaped slaves told stories of mistreatment and abuse. William Wells Brown, who had once been enslaved in Missouri, wrote that the whip was used "very frequently and freely, and a small offense on the part of the slave furnished an occasion for its use."

Those opposed to slavery believed that their arguments were valid. Still, many Americans in the early 1800s thought that the property

ACADEMIC VOCABULARY

ideology set of beliefs that form the basis of a culture or political system

ACADEMIC VOCABULARY

valid meaningful or justifiable

rights of slaveholders were more important than the human rights of slaves. It was difficult for opponents of slavery to overcome the claim that slaveholders' rights were protected by the Constitution, just as the rights of all property owners were protected. This was one reason why the abolition movement was slow to gain popular support in the North.

After winning the Mexican-American War, the United States added more than 500,000 square miles of new territory. New states would eventually be formed from this vast area. Would these states ban or allow slavery?

The Missouri Compromise of 1820 had banned slavery in most of the northern part of the Louisiana Purchase. Now some antislavery activists wanted to do the same to this new territory. Other people, mainly southerners, wanted to allow slavery in the new lands. By 1850, the political argument over slavery no longer centered on its existence in the South. Instead, the debate shifted to the spread of slavery into places where it did not yet exist.

The question of the expansion of slavery was also a struggle for control of the Congress. New states would mean additional seats in the Senate and the House of Representatives, and these new legislators might work for or against slavery. If northern legislators could block the expansion of slavery and gain control of Congress, laws might be passed that would end slavery in the South.

Then in March 1850, California applied to become a state, just two years after the area had become part of the United States. At that time the number of free states and slave states were equal. The balance of political power was about to change.

READING CHECK **Summarizing** What arguments existed for and against ending or limiting the institution of slavery?

The Compromise of 1850

Only about 14,000 non-Indians lived in California in 1848. So many forty-niners moved there during the gold rush, however, that by 1850 California's population had jumped to 93,000. Residents quickly approved a constitution banning slavery and applied for statehood.

This request brought the issue of slavery to the surface. In 1820 Kentucky senator Henry Clay had crafted the Missouri Compromise. Now, nearing the end of a long political career, he hoped for one more compromise between North and South. On January 29, 1850, he introduced a plan to Congress in which he proposed compromises on several slavery issues.

The Senate debate over Clay's resolutions was one of the greatest in its history. Two political giants of the time, Daniel Webster of Massachusetts and John C. Calhoun of South Carolina, faced off. Calhoun made his opposition to compromise clear. Gravely ill and unable to speak, he sat grimly in his chair while his speech was read to the other senators.

HISTORY'S VOICES

❝The South asks for justice, simple justice, and less she ought not to take . . . Nothing else can, with any certainty, finally and forever settle the question at issue, terminate agitation, and save the Union.❞

—Senator John C. Calhoun, March 4, 1850

Three days later, Webster rose to reply. He personally opposed slavery and its spread, but he was dismayed by Calhoun's threat that the South might secede, or withdraw from the Union, over this issue. He believed that the preservation of the Union was more important than the disagreement over slavery.

TERMS OF THE COMPROMISE OF 1850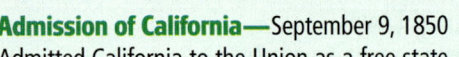

Admission of California—September 9, 1850
Admitted California to the Union as a free state.

Texas and New Mexico Act—September 9, 1850
Set the Texas-New Mexico border and organized the New Mexico Territory with slavery to be decided by its residents.

Utah Act—September 9, 1850
Organized the Utah Territory with slavery to be decided by its residents.

Fugitive Slave Act—September 18, 1850
Strengthened the Fugitive Slave Act of 1793 by imposing heavy penalties on persons who aided runaway slaves or who blocked or refused to help in their capture.

An Act Abolishing the Slave Trade in the District of Columbia—
September 20, 1850
Outlawed the buying and selling of slaves, but not slavery itself, in the nation's capital.

Source: Encyclopedia of American History

Not all northern senators agreed with Webster. New York's Senator William Seward opposed any compromise on slavery and fiercely attacked slavery itself. Seward's speech caused a stir across the nation. It established him as a **radical**, or a person with extreme views, on the slavery issue.

The debate on Clay's proposals dragged on through the summer. Calhoun's death on March 31 removed one obstacle to compromise. President Zachary Taylor, who also opposed compromise, died a few months later. His successor, **Millard Fillmore**, supported Clay's plan. Finally, in September the Senate passed five laws based on Clay's resolutions. Together, these laws formed what became known as the **Compromise of 1850**.

The Fugitive Slave Act

The issues the compromise seemed to solve were soon replaced by others. One part of the compromise itself was very controversial. The **Fugitive Slave Act** made it a federal crime to assist runaway slaves. The law also allowed the arrest of escaped slaves in states where slavery was illegal. People accused of being escaped slaves had to prove that they were not, which was often difficult or impossible. In addition, escaped slaves who had lived in the North for years were returned to slavery if caught. For example, an Indiana man was turned over to a slaveholder who claimed that he had escaped 19 years earlier.

The fugitive slave law was openly resisted by people in the North. "We must trample this law under our feet," one abolitionist urged. Many northerners who had previously been quiet on slavery issues were furious. Mobs rescued slaves from northern police stations. They threatened slave catchers. In turn, the North's reaction angered southern slaveholders. By 1851 some southern leaders were again talking of seceding from the Union.

Uncle Tom's Cabin

Among those angry northerners was **Harriet Beecher Stowe**, a magazine writer in Maine. Stowe had once lived in Cincinnati, Ohio, an important stop on the Underground Railroad. There she heard tales of slavery's cruelty and horror. In 1851 she wrote a series of short stories about slave life for an antislavery newspaper. A year later these stories were published as a novel called **Uncle Tom's Cabin**.

When Harriet Beecher Stowe met President Lincoln during the Civil War, he greeted her by saying, "So you're the little woman who wrote the book that made this great war."

Although Stowe had little firsthand knowledge of slavery or the South, her novel became an enormous success. Within a year, 300,000 copies were sold in the United States and nearly a million more in the rest of the world. The book outraged many southerners. They accused Stowe of writing lies about plantation life. "There never before was anything so detestable or so monstrous among women as this," a New Orleans newspaper declared angrily. Stowe's book raised tensions over slavery to a new height.

READING CHECK **Identifying Cause and Effect** How did the Fugitive Slave Act and *Uncle Tom's Cabin* add to tensions over slavery?

The Kansas-Nebraska Act

The Compromise of 1850 marked the end of an era of political leadership in Congress. Clay and Webster both died within the next two years. Their deaths allowed **Stephen Douglas**, a senator from Illinois, to gain power and influence. As a first-term senator, Douglas had led the fight for the passage of the Compromise

From Compromise to Conflict

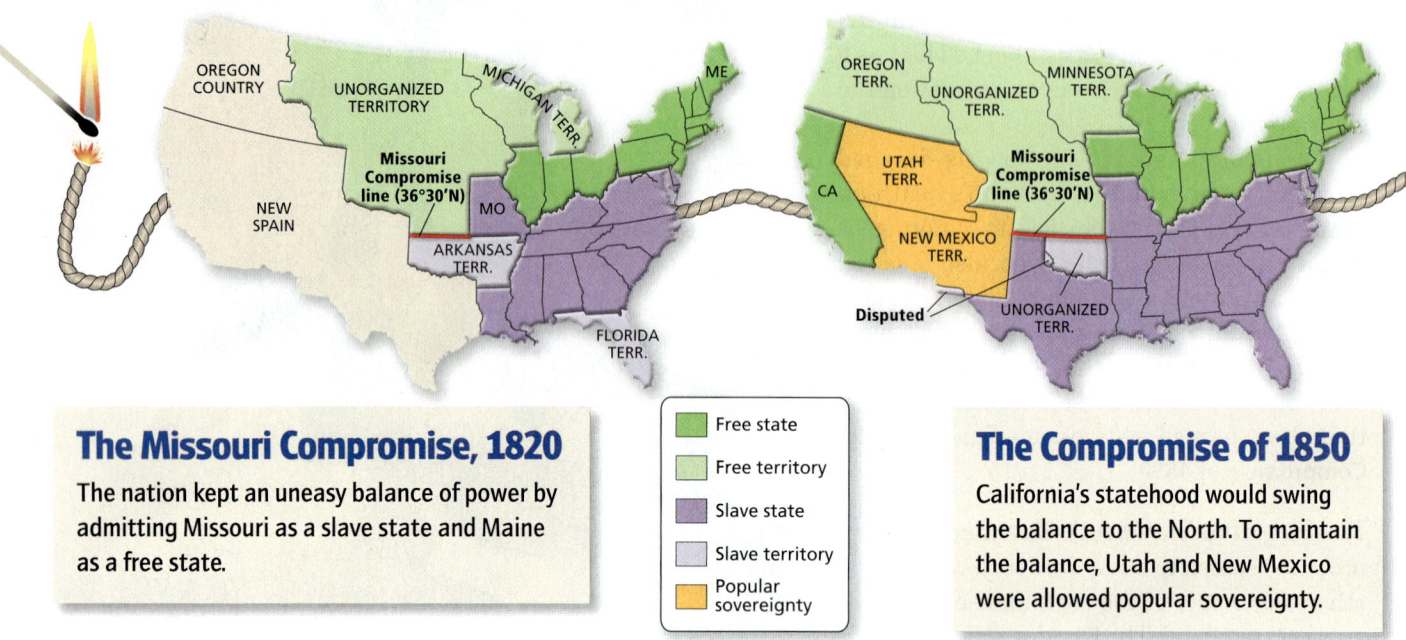

The Missouri Compromise, 1820

The nation kept an uneasy balance of power by admitting Missouri as a slave state and Maine as a free state.

Legend:
- Free state
- Free territory
- Slave state
- Slave territory
- Popular sovereignty

The Compromise of 1850

California's statehood would swing the balance to the North. To maintain the balance, Utah and New Mexico were allowed popular sovereignty.

THE IMPACT TODAY

Government

Today the principle of popular sovereignty is expressed in many states by initiatives and referendums. Initiatives allow voters to accept or reject laws proposed by citizen groups, and referendums enable voters to reject laws passed by the state legislature.

of 1850. By 1854 he was ready to assume the leadership role that would help earn the 5'4" politician the nickname "The Little Giant."

Among the issues that divided North and South was a proposed railroad to connect the new state of California to the rest of the nation. Southerners favored New Orleans, Louisiana, as the railroad's eastern end. Northerners opposed this route, afraid that a railroad which connected California to the South might help bring slavery into the territories organized by the Compromise of 1850.

Douglas believed the proposed railroad could transform Chicago, Illinois, into a major urban center. Before the northern route could be considered, however, the land it crossed had to be officially opened for settlement by the government. In 1854 Douglas introduced a bill into Congress to do that. He proposed that the region west of Iowa and Missouri be organized into the Kansas and Nebraska Territories.

Douglas needed southern support in order to get his bill passed. The Missouri Compromise had closed the Kansas and Nebraska region to slavery. Douglas knew that southerners would not agree to allow settlement in any territories that would someday become free states. For his solution, he turned to the Compromise of 1850. He proposed that as in New Mexico and Utah,

the issue of slavery in Kansas and Nebraska should be settled by **popular sovereignty**. In other words, the people there would decide whether to allow it.

This approach got Douglas the southern support he needed. Southern senators, however, had one more demand. They wanted the Missouri Compromise repealed entirely. When Douglas changed his bill to end the Missouri Compromise's limits on slavery, it took all his political skills to hold on to northern support. In May 1854 his **Kansas-Nebraska Act** became law. Lost in the controversy over the bill was Douglas's proposed railroad to the Pacific Ocean. Congress would not approve the construction of such a railroad until 1862.

READING CHECK Identifying the Main Idea
Why did Douglas introduce his Kansas-Nebraska bill?

Reactions in North and South

The North's response to the Kansas-Nebraska Act was intense. Hundreds of meetings were held to protest the law. Northerners sent numerous petitions and resolutions to Congress. "This crime shall not be consummated [completed]," read one. "Nebraska, the heart of our continent, shall forever continue free."

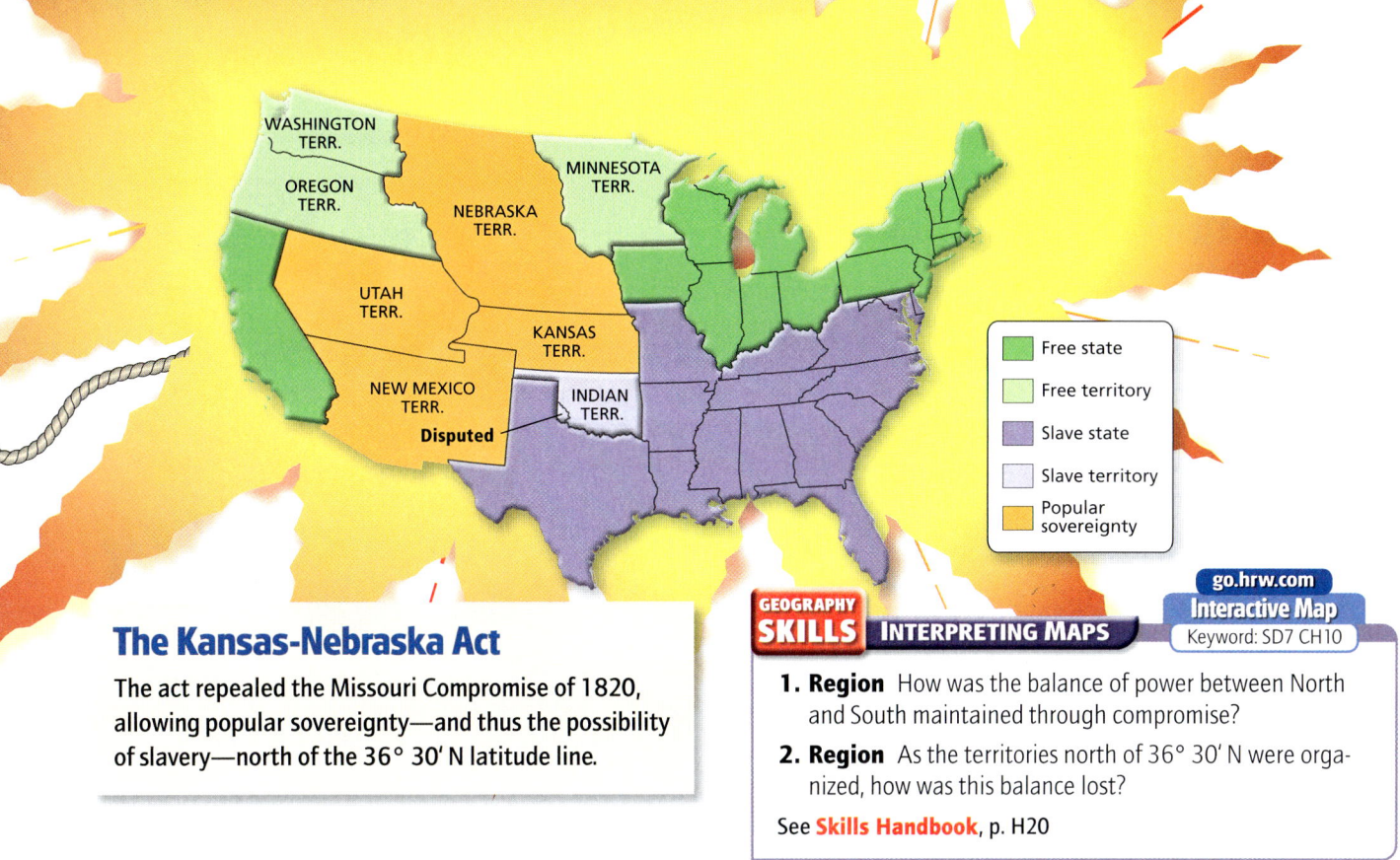

The Kansas-Nebraska Act

The act repealed the Missouri Compromise of 1820, allowing popular sovereignty—and thus the possibility of slavery—north of the 36° 30′ N latitude line.

Legend:
- Free state
- Free territory
- Slave state
- Slave territory
- Popular sovereignty

GEOGRAPHY SKILLS **INTERPRETING MAPS**

go.hrw.com
Interactive Map
Keyword: SD7 CH10

1. **Region** How was the balance of power between North and South maintained through compromise?
2. **Region** As the territories north of 36° 30′ N were organized, how was this balance lost?

See **Skills Handbook**, p. H20

Shifts in politics Some northern politicians called the Kansas-Nebraska Act a "gross violation of a sacred pledge." Such reactions caused major changes in the nation's political-party system. The controversy greatly weakened the Democratic Party. Northerners were outraged that many northern Democratic members of Congress had voted for the act. A great number of northern Democrats quit the party.

The effect on the Whig Party was even more severe. Whigs were already suffering from serious divisions. Some northern Whigs, called Conscience Whigs, opposed slavery on moral grounds. Other Whigs in both the North and the South, known as Cotton Whigs, strongly supported slavery. The deaths of Clay and Webster, the Whigs' long-time leaders, further weakened the party at a critical time in national politics.

Cotton and Conscience Whigs in Congress became bitterly divided over Douglas's proposal. After it passed, the two groups refused to work together. One Connecticut Whig resigned from the Senate in disgust. "The Whig party has been killed off . . . by that miserable Nebraska business," he complained. With their party basically dead, Cotton Whigs joined their southern Democratic allies in the Democratic Party. Many Conscience Whigs joined northern Democrats and members of the Free-Soil Party to form a new political party in order to resist the further spread of slavery.

The rise of the Republican Party The Free-Soil Party was formed in 1848 by some northern Whigs and Democrats, and members of a small antislavery party known as the Liberty Party. The Free-Soil Party took its name because opposition to the spread of slavery was its main issue. *Free soil* was a term for land on which slavery did not exist. In fact, people of all political parties who opposed slavery's spread were often called **free-soilers**.

The Kansas-Nebraska Act caused the Free-Soil Party, northern Whigs, and others to join forces. "Rally as one man for the reestablishment of liberty and the overthrow of the Slave Power," a free-soiler urged. One such rally was held in a church at Ripon, Wisconsin, in February 1854. The rally's leaders called for a new political party to be formed. From this meeting the **Republican Party** was born. In July, at a meeting in Jackson, Michigan, the new party's name was officially adopted.

By the end of 1854, Republican groups were operating in states across the North. They worked with the Know-Nothings, members of

Republican Party Today

Throughout American history, political parties have used the term *republican*. In response to the Kansas-Nebraska Act in 1854, antislavery members of several other parties joined forces. They formed the Republican Party, the same party that exists today.

The first Republican candidate for president was John C. Frémont in 1856. He lost that election, but in 1860 the Republican Party's second presidential candidate, Abraham Lincoln, was elected president of the United States.

Over time, Republican goals have shifted. During much of the nineteenth century, the party focused on rebuilding the Union, and limiting unfair business practices. During the twentieth century, the Republican Party became known for its conservative social policies and a belief in laissez-faire economic policies, which seek to minimize government interference in economic matters.

Analyzing Information How did the Republican Party gain prominence during the nineteenth century?

Delegates at the 2004 Republican National Convention

a political party officially called the American Party, to defeat Democratic candidates for Congress in the elections that year.

The Know-Nothings' **nativism**, or opposition to immigration, was troubling to some Americans. Still, the problems that the Kansas-Nebraska Act caused the Democrats and Whigs briefly gave the Know-Nothings political influence again. At first, the Republicans' association with the Know-Nothings kept

one prominent Whig, William Seward, away from the new party. Not until 1855, after he had been safely re-elected to the Senate, did Seward become a Republican. Another, much less famous northern Whig soon joined him. That politician's name was Abraham Lincoln.

READING CHECK **Summarizing** How did passage of the Kansas-Nebraska Act affect the nation's political-party system?

SECTION 1 ASSESSMENT

go.hrw.com
Online Quiz
Keyword: SD7 HP10

Reviewing Ideas, Terms, and People

1. a. Identify How was the nation divided over the institution of slavery?
  b. Analyze What effect did the Mexican-American War have on the issue of slavery in the United States? Why did it have this effect?

2. a. Describe What were the terms of the **Compromise of 1850**?
  b. Make Inferences Why would the Compromise of 1850 have been controversial in both the North and the South?
  c. Evaluate Was the Compromise of 1850 a good solution to the conflict over slavery? Explain why or why not.

3. a. Recall What is **popular sovereignty**? Why did **Stephen Douglas** include it in his Kansas-Nebraska bill?
  b. Draw Conclusions How would both the North and the South have expected to benefit from the passage of the **Kansas-Nebraska Act**?

4. a. Describe Why was the **Republican Party** founded?
  b. Make Inferences Why would some northerners have been upset over the passage of the Kansas-Nebraska Act?

Critical Thinking

5. Compare and Contrast Copy the chart below and record the reasons that northerners and southerners in Congress passed the Compromise of 1850.

Reasons for Northern Support — Compromise of 1850 — Reasons for Southern Support

FOCUS ON WRITING

6. Expository Suppose you were a northern senator during the debate on the Kansas-Nebraska bill. Write a speech stating your position and the reasons for your stand on Senator Douglas's controversial proposal.

Sectional Conflicts and National Politics

BEFORE YOU READ

MAIN IDEA

Rising tensions over slavery expanded from political rhetoric into outright violence.

READING FOCUS

1. Why did popular sovereignty lead to violent struggle in Kansas?
2. In what ways did the presidential election of 1856 illustrate the nation's growing divisions?
3. What events of Buchanan's presidency further divided the nation?
4. Why was John Brown's raid on Harpers Ferry an important event in American history?

KEY TERMS AND PEOPLE

"Bleeding Kansas"
Franklin Pierce
John Brown
Pottawatomie Massacre
guerrilla war
James Buchanan
John Frémont
Dred Scott decision
Lecompton Constitution
Robert E. Lee

PI 3.2 Research and analyze the major themes and developments in New York State and United States history (e.g., colonization and settlement; Revolution and New National Period; immigration; expansion and reform era; Civil War and Reconstruction; the American labor movement; Great Depression; World Wars; contemporary United States).

THE INSIDE STORY

What did John Doy's experience show about conditions in Kansas in the 1850s? In January 1859, John Doy and his 21-year-old son Charles, agreed to take a group of 13 escaped slaves from Lawrence, Kansas, to freedom in Iowa. Doy, an English physician, had come to Kansas in 1854 to help make the territory a free state. An active abolitionist, Dr. Doy was making the journey as a "conductor" on the Underground Railroad.

Doy and his son moved the escaped slaves in two covered wagons. They were barely 12 miles from Lawrence, however, when they were stopped by a band of slave hunters. The group seized the Doys and took them to Missouri. There Dr. Doy was tried and convicted of slave stealing and sentenced to five years in prison.

Back in Lawrence, a plan was devised to rescue Doy from jail before he could be moved to the Missouri state penitentiary. In July, a group of antislavery Kansans assembled at St. Joseph, where Dr. Doy was being held. One of them visited Doy in jail and slipped him a note about the plan to break him out. That night they

went to the jail, pretending to have captured a horse thief. Once inside, they overpowered the two jailers and freed Dr. Doy. Crossing the Missouri River in rowboats, they evaded the posse sent after them and arrived in Lawrence to a hero's welcome two days later. ◼

THE RESCUE OF DR. JOHN DOY

▶ **John Doy (seated) and the men who rescued him from "that vile iron box" he was jailed in.**

The Struggle for Kansas

The kidnapping of Dr. John Doy was one of many acts of slavery-related lawlessness that plagued Kansas Territory. By 1856 so much violence had occurred there that the territory was being called **"Bleeding Kansas."**

Northerners and southerners alike realized what the settlement of Kansas meant for the nation. "We are playing for a mighty stake," Missouri senator David Atchison noted. "If we win we carry slavery to the Pacific Ocean, if we fail we lose . . . all the territories." Northerners were just as eager to keep Kansas free. "We will engage in competition for the virgin soil of Kansas," pledged William Seward. "God give the victory to the side which is stronger in numbers as it is in right."

Pro-slavery and free-soil forces soon were fighting for control in Kansas. Each side intended to control the territory's elections and, later, a vote on a state constitution. Free-soil settlers flooded into the territory. Groups opposed to slavery raised money to help volunteers move there. People in slaveholding states also formed emigrant groups. Atchison took a leave of absence from the Senate to lead the effort to establish slavery in the new territory.

Popular sovereignty Settlement of the slavery issue by popular sovereignty did not require settlers to vote on whether to allow it. Instead, the question was settled indirectly. The voters would elect a territorial legislature, which would then pass laws on the subject. Later, a constitution had to be written and approved by voters before the territory could become a state. That constitution would either permit or ban slavery. It was through these processes that Kansas would eventually enter the Union as a slave state or as free soil.

The first election was held in November 1854 to choose the territory's delegate to Congress. About 1,700 armed Missourians crossed into Kansas and threatened violence if they were not allowed to vote. A pro-slavery delegate was elected.

Even greater voting fraud took place in elections for the territorial legislature in March 1855. In some districts the number of

Interactive

HISTORY CLOSE-UP

The Sack of Lawrence

On May 21, 1855, a pro-slavery posse arrived in Lawrence, Kansas, to arrest leaders of the "rebel" antislavery government. The posse looted and destroyed much of the town.

When posse members could not destroy the Free State Hotel with cannon shots, they set it on fire.

The posse burned the office of *The Free State*, one of Lawrence's antislavery newspapers.

ballots cast was more than twice the number of registered voters. A legislature of 36 pro-slavery candidates and 3 free-soilers was elected. "Missourians have nobly defended our rights," declared an Alabama newspaper.

The legislature met in the town of Lecompton and quickly passed a strict slave code into law. Outraged free-soilers refused to accept the new legislature. They elected an antislavery governor and legislature and set up their own government. By 1856 two governments were passing and carrying out laws, each claiming to be the legal government of Kansas.

The Sack of Lawrence

By 1855 the town of Lawrence had become a center of antislavery activity in the territory. In November, shootings of pro-slavery settlers near the town brought some 1,500 Missourians across the border. Nearby federal troops waited for the president's order to keep peace in the area. No such order was issued. The Missourians decided against attacking Lawrence only when they <u>verified</u> that it was defended by a heavily armed force of free-soilers.

Although President **Franklin Pierce** was a New Hampshire Democrat, he seemed to be under the influence of pro-slavery elements in Congress. In January 1856 Pierce condemned the free-soil government in Kansas as rebels. This prompted pro-slavery Kansas officials to charge free-soil leaders with treason.

On May 21 a pro-slavery sheriff and about 800 men rode into Lawrence to arrest them. The posse destroyed the offices of the town's two antislavery newspapers, burned the hotel and the free-soil governor's house, and looted stores and homes. Antislavery newspapers labeled the raid the Sack of Lawrence in an effort to paint the raiders as barbarians and inflame public opinion in the North.

The Pottawatomie Massacre

A related event soon inflamed public opinion in the South. Fifty-six-year-old **John Brown** was a committed abolitionist. As a young man, he had used his Pennsylvania home as a station on the Underground Railroad. After several business failures, Brown followed several of his sons to Kansas in 1855. All hoped to obtain land and

ACADEMIC VOCABULARY
verified made sure that something is accurate or true

Posse members took the printing press from the office of the antislavery newspaper *The Herald of Freedom* and dumped it in a nearby river.

Members of the posse looted homes and businesses, making off with whatever they could carry.

Skills FOCUS **INTERPRETING INFOGRAPHICS**

go.hrw.com
Interactive
Keyword: SD7 CH10

1. **Drawing Conclusions** Why did the posse want to destroy the two antislavery newspapers in Lawrence?
2. **Making Inferences** Why did some members of the posse loot private homes and businesses?

See **Skills Handbook**, p. H18

Chapter Review

Visual Summary: The Nation Splits Apart

Compromise of 1850
- California enters as a free state
- Popular sovereignty on slavery in the rest of Mexican Cession

Kansas-Nebraska Act (1854)
- Popular sovereignty on slavery
- "Bleeding Kansas"

Disputes over the spread of slavery divided the nation.

Lincoln-Douglas Debates (1858)
- National attention on slavery dispute
- National attention on Lincoln's views

Election of 1860
- Split in Democratic Party
- Antislavery Lincoln elected president
- Lower South secedes

Reviewing Key Terms and People

Complete each sentence by filling in the blank with the correct term or person.

1. An army's guns are stored in an _____ .
2. A person who holds extreme views is sometimes called a _____.
3. The _____ resulted from proposals made by Henry Clay to settle the nation's issues regarding slavery.
4. The _____ made it illegal to help runaway slaves.
5. _____ were people who wanted land to be closed to the practice of slavery.
6. A _____ involves fighting from ambush and surprise attacks.
7. The Supreme Court's ruling in the _____ widened the nation's divisions over slavery.
8. A _____ is a statement of principles.
9. In 1856, the divisions between North and South helped _____ _____ to win a three-way election for president.
10. _____ _____ was a radical settler who thought that abolitionists should use violence.
11. The convention that formed the Confederate States of America elected _____ _____ as the new nation's first president.
12. A person who supports _____ is opposed to immigrants and to immigration.
13. Fighting that involves opposing groups of citizens from the same country is called a _____ .
14. The presidential candidate who received the least votes in the South in the election of 1860 was _____ _____ .
15. The _____ proposed protecting slavery by restoring the Missouri Compromise.
16. The _____ , which would have allowed slavery in Kansas, widened sectional divisions.

History's Impact video program
Review the video to answer the closing question:
What immediate effect did the Dred Scott decision
have on the United States?

Comprehension and Critical Thinking

SECTION 1 *(pp. 322–328)*

17. a. Identify What issue was behind the question of the expansion of slavery after the Mexican War?

b. Analyze How did the Fugitive Slave Act cause more divisions between the North and South?

c. Evaluate What were Stephen Douglas's motives in pushing through the Kansas-Nebraska Act?

SECTION 2 *(pp. 329–335)*

18. a. Describe Give a description of the civil war that developed in Kansas.

b. Draw Conclusions What underlying fear caused voters to turn to James Buchanan for president in the election of 1856?

c. Predict How did John Brown's raid foreshadow future events?

SECTION 3 *(pp. 337–343)*

19. a. Recall Why did Abraham Lincoln re-enter politics after his second retirement?

b. Analyze How did Lincoln's acceptance speech for the Republican nomination for the U.S. Senate create a national issue?

c. Predict Why would the circumstances of Lincoln's election as president 1860 suggest major problems in the future?

SECTION 4 *(pp. 344–349)*

20. a. Describe What happened to the Union after the election of Abraham Lincoln as president?

b. Draw Conclusions Why didn't Lincoln support the Crittenden Compromise?

c. Evaluate How strong was the movement for secession on the South? Explain.

Using the Internet

**go.hrw.com
Practice Online**
Keyword: SD7 CH10

21. Harriet Beecher Stowe's novel *Uncle Tom's Cabin* inflamed passions on both sides before the Civil War. Using the keyword above, find excerpts from the book that you think help explain its impact on people of the 1850s. Write a review in which you analyze whether Stowe was concerned with accuracy in the characters and events she created.

Analyzing Primary Sources

Reading Like a Historian In 1859 Texas governor Sam Houston made a speech opposing secession.

> You may, after the sacrifice of countless millions of treasure and hundreds of thousands of lives, as a bare possibility, win Southern independence . . . But I doubt it . . . the North is determined to preserve this Union.

—Sam Houston, 1859

22. Identify What sacrifice is Houston referring to?

23. Make Inferences Why is Houston convinced that secession cannot succeed?

Critical Reading

Read the passage in Section 2 that begins with the heading "The Sack of Lawrence." Then answer the questions that follow.

24. According to the passage, the attack on the free-soil government of Kansas was set off by remarks made by

A. William Seward.

B. Franklin Pierce.

C. John Brown.

D. Charles Sumner.

25. In the last paragraph in this section, the term *barbarians* means

A. illegal voters.

B. fighters who conduct guerrilla war.

C. people who act in an uncivilized manner.

D. persons who support slavery.

WRITING FOR THE SAT

Think about the following issue:

Congress hoped that the Compromise of 1850 would settle disagreements between the North and South and keep the Union together.

26. Assignment: Did the Compromise of 1850 have a chance of succeeding? Write a short essay in which you develop your position on this issue. Support your point of view with reasoning and examples from your reading and studies.

1861–1865

The CIVIL WAR

THE BIG PICTURE The Civil War was fought nationwide, using new technologies and strategies, but by soldiers who were often ill equipped, underfed, and poorly trained. The conflict resulted in freedom for some 4 million enslaved people and the preservation of a nation. The costs were staggering—more than 600,000 lives lost and about $5 billion in property damaged or destroyed.

New York Standards

Key Idea 3 Study about the major social, political, economic, cultural, and religious developments in New York State and United States history involves learning about the important roles and contributions of individuals and groups.

Skills FOCUS   READING LIKE A HISTORIAN

Peter Frederick Rothermel completed this painting of Pickett's Charge, part of a bloody battle in Gettysburg, Pennsylvania, in 1871. The painting, which hangs in the state museum, is 32 feet wide and more than 16 feet high. **Interpreting Visuals** What impact do you think seeing this painting on such a large scale would have? Explain.

See **Skills Handbook**, p. H30

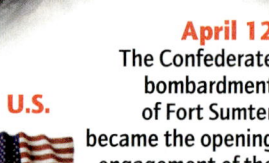

U.S.

1861

World

April 12
The Confederate bombardment of Fort Sumter became the opening engagement of the Civil War.

1861
Louis Pasteur invented pasteurization.

Benito Juárez elected president of Mexico.

History's Impact video program
Watch the video to understand the impact of the Civil War.

January 1
President Lincoln issues the Emancipation Proclamation.

July 4
Confederate stronghold of Vicksburg surrenders after a siege.

November 15
Sherman burns Atlanta and begins March to the Sea.

April 9
Lee surrenders to Grant at Appomattox.

1862 — 1863 — 1864 — 1865

1863
French troops capture Mexico City and install Austria's Archduke Maximilian as emperor.

The International Red Cross is established.

1864
Denmark surrenders disputed territory to Prussia and Austria.

1865
British surgeon Joseph Lister develops the use of antiseptics in surgery.

Preparing for War

BEFORE YOU READ

MAIN IDEA

The attack on Fort Sumter led both the North and the South to prepare for war in earnest.

READING FOCUS

1. How did the fall of Fort Sumter lead to war?
2. Why did many northerners and southerners eagerly rush to war?
3. Why was the loyalty of the border states important, and how did Lincoln obtain it?
4. What were Union and Confederate goals and strategies for the war?

KEY TERMS AND PEOPLE

Robert Anderson
artillery
border states
martial law
Anaconda Plan
cotton diplomacy
embargo

PI 3.2 Research and analyze the major themes and developments in New York State and United States history (e.g., colonization and settlement; Revolution and New National Period; immigration; expansion and reform era; Civil War and Reconstruction; the American labor movement; Great Depression; World Wars; contemporary United States).

The Reluctant Warrior

THE INSIDE STORY

Which side would a soldier choose? Robert E. Lee's family was one of the oldest and most distinguished families in Virginia. His father, "Light-Horse Harry" Lee, was an outstanding cavalry officer in the Revolutionary War, a delegate to the Continental Congress, and a friend of George Washington. Richard Henry Lee, a great uncle, had signed the Declaration of Independence. Robert E. Lee, born in 1807, lived up to the family's proud traditions. In 1829 he graduated second in his class from the U.S. Military Academy at West Point. In the Mexican-American War, General Winfield Scott called Lee "the very best soldier I ever saw in the field." He was handsome, good-humored, and a natural leader.

As war between the North and the South came nearer, Lee's loyalties were torn between his country and his state. From an army post in Texas, he wrote to his son: "I can anticipate no greater calamity for the country than a dissolution of the Union . . . I am willing to sacrifice every thing but honour for its preservation." His native state of Virginia had not yet seceded, but it did so after President Lincoln called for volunteers for the army in April 1861.

President Lincoln asked Lee to command the forces the federal government was gathering to put down the rebellion. Although Lee opposed secession, he refused Lincoln's offer. Saying that he could not take part in invading the South, Lee regretfully resigned from the U.S. Army and became commander of Virginia's state forces. In 1862 Lee assumed overall command of one of the Confederacy's main armies, the Army of Northern Virginia. ◢

◀ **Gentleman and soldier Robert E. Lee**

THE MUSEUM OF THE CONFEDERACY, RICHMOND, VIRGINIA

The Fall of Fort Sumter

On April 12, 1861, Confederate guns fired on Fort Sumter in the harbor of Charleston, South Carolina, and the Civil War began. This bloody, four-year conflict tore the nation apart and changed the course of American history.

Crisis at Fort Sumter The crisis at Fort Sumter actually began about a month earlier, on March 5. On that day, President Abraham Lincoln's first full day in office, he received a desperate message from the commander of Fort Sumter, **Robert Anderson**. Confederate leaders had demanded that he surrender the fort or face an attack. The fort's supplies were running low, and Anderson needed help.

Confederate troops had seized many forts, arsenals, and other federal government property throughout the states that had seceded. Fort Sumter was one of the few such places still in Union hands. It had become a target of the Confederate revolt. If President Lincoln turned over the fort, his surrender might reassure southerners that the North did not want war. On the other hand, it would also anger many people in the North who did not want to treat the Confederacy as if it were a separate, legitimate nation.

Lincoln made a clever decision. He would not surrender Fort Sumter. Instead, he told the Confederates that he would send only food and other nonmilitary supplies to the fort to feed the soldiers trapped there.

Now Confederate president Jefferson Davis faced a difficult decision. If he allowed the fort to be resupplied, it could hold out indefinitely and would continue to be a symbol of federal authority in the South. If he attacked the fort, however, war would begin.

The attack on Fort Sumter Davis decided to act before the supplies arrived. "You will at once demand [the fort's] evacuation," he ordered the Confederate commander in Charleston. "If this is refused, proceed, in such manner as you may determine, to reduce [destroy] it."

In the early morning of April 12, Confederate **artillery**, or large mounted guns, opened fire on the fort. The fort's defenses were no match for these massive guns, and it surrendered the next day. On April 14 the U.S. flag flying over the fort was replaced with a southern flag.

READING CHECK **Identifying the Main Idea** Why was the dispute that arose over Fort Sumter significant?

Confederates unleash cannon fire upon Fort Sumter. Captain Abner Doubleday of the U.S. Army said, "Their explosion shook the fort like an earthquake."

The Rush to War

ACADEMIC VOCABULARY

rebellion violent resistance to established government or authority

In response to the fall of Fort Sumter, President Lincoln called for 75,000 volunteers to serve for 90 days in order to put down the <u>rebellion</u>. Lincoln's old political enemy Stephen Douglas supported this action. "There are only two sides to the question," Douglas told a huge crowd in Chicago. "There can be no neutrals in this war, only *patriots—or traitors*."

Northerners rushed to enlist in the military. A woman in Boston reported people's eagerness to fight.

HISTORY'S VOICES

❝Hastily formed companies marched to camps of rendezvous, the sunlight flashing from gun-barrel and bayonet … Merchants and clerks rushed out from stores … saluting them as they passed … I had never dreamed that New England could be fired with so warlike a spirit.**❞**

—Mary Ashton Livermore in *Voices of the Civil War*

Reaction in the South was very different. Lincoln's call for volunteers forced the eight slave states that remained in the Union to choose a side. "We must either identify ourselves with the North or the South," a Virginia newspaper wrote. "The South must go with the South," a North Carolina paper argued. "Blood is thicker than water."

All the slave states that remained in the Union refused to provide troops to fight against fellow southerners. "Not one man will the State of Missouri furnish to carry on any such unholy crusade," its governor informed the president. The governors of Arkansas, Kentucky, North Carolina, Tennessee, and Virginia sent similar replies. Delaware and Maryland ignored Lincoln's request.

In the Confederate states, anger ran high. "Lincoln may bring his 75,000 troops against us," Confederate vice president Alexander Stephens said defiantly. "We can call out a million of peoples if need be, and when they are cut down we can call another."

On April 17 Virginia seceded. In May, the states of Arkansas, Tennessee, and North Carolina followed Virginia into the Confederacy. Meanwhile, leaders on both sides wondered what Delaware, Kentucky, Maryland, and Missouri would do.

READING CHECK **Making Generalizations** How did southerners react to Lincoln's call for troops to put down the rebellion?

The Border States

Delaware, Kentucky, Maryland, and Missouri were known as **border states**—slaveholding states that remained in the Union and formed its border with the Confederacy. Delaware had few slaves and slaveholders, and most people believed it would remain in the Union. In the other border states, however, secessionist sympathies were strong. Each of these states had great geographic and military importance.

Martial law in Maryland Maryland was perhaps the most critical border state. If it seceded, Washington, D.C., would be completely surrounded by Confederate territory. When some pro-secession Marylanders began burning bridges and cutting telegraph lines to harm the Union war effort, Lincoln acted quickly to ensure they did not do more damage.

For much of 1861 federal troops guarded sites in Maryland that had military value. Maryland churches were forced to fly the American flag. Newspapers that supported secession were shut down, and their editors were jailed or banished to the South.

Lincoln also placed parts of Maryland under **martial law**. This is a type of rule in which military commanders are in control and citizens' rights and freedoms are suspended. In November 1861 the military supervised new elections

FACES OF HISTORY

Abraham LINCOLN
1809–1865

Throughout his time in office, Abraham Lincoln struggled with personal tragedies while striving to hold his family and the nation together during the Civil War. In 1862 Abraham and Mary Todd Lincoln's 11-year-old son William died of typhoid fever in the White House.

Struck with grief over the loss of their son, the Lincolns sank into depression. The first lady took William's death especially hard. The president struggled in the midst of a war that was going badly to care for his wife and to grieve the loss of his son. Lincoln often resorted to humor and storytelling to overcome his grief. He explained to a friend "if it were not for these stories [and] jokes … I should die."

Summarize Why was Lincoln's presidency especially difficult?

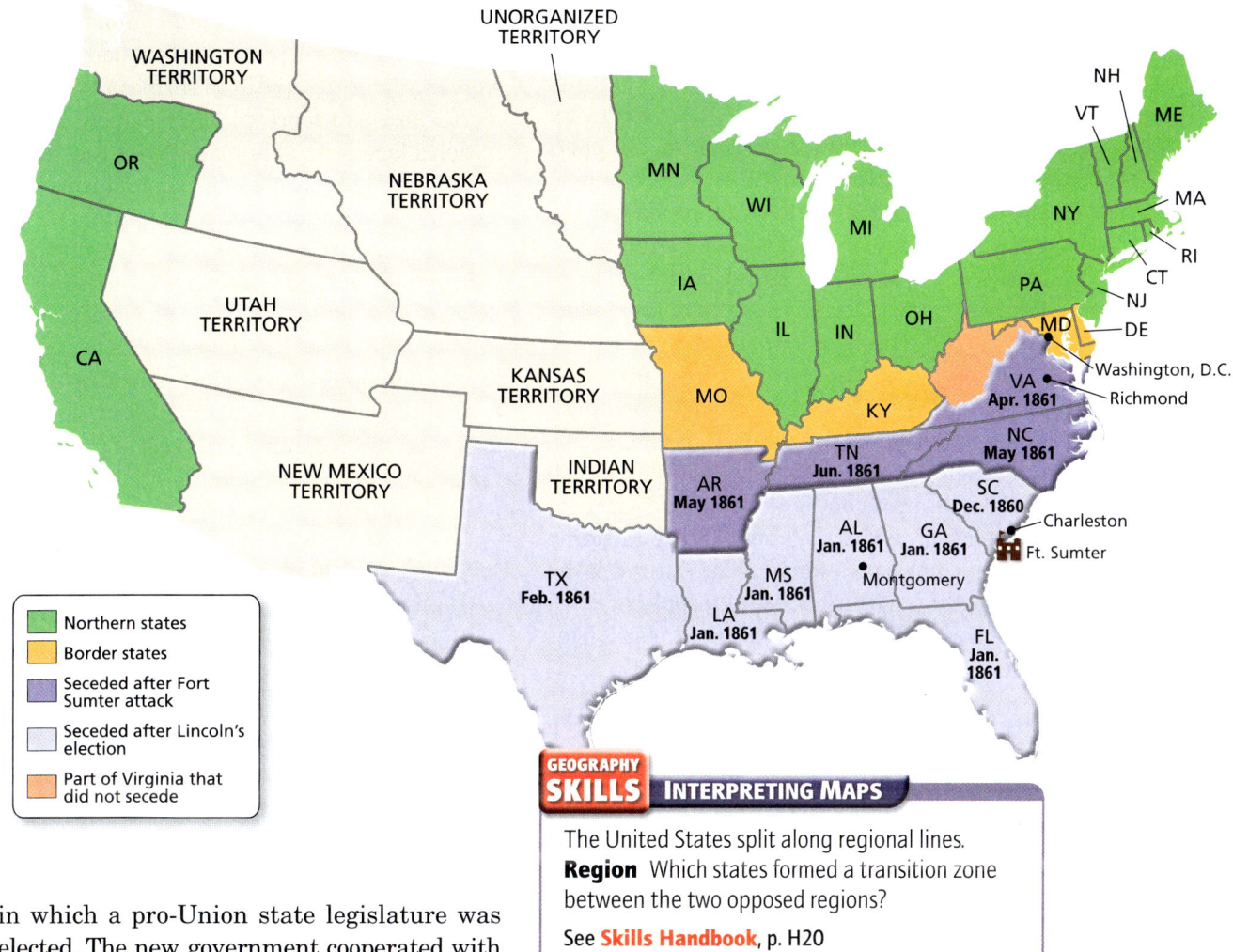

Northern states
Border states
Seceded after Fort Sumter attack
Seceded after Lincoln's election
Part of Virginia that did not secede

GEOGRAPHY SKILLS | **INTERPRETING MAPS**

The United States split along regional lines.
Region Which states formed a transition zone between the two opposed regions?

See **Skills Handbook**, p. H20

in which a pro-Union state legislature was elected. The new government cooperated with federal officials for the rest of the war.

Divisions in Missouri Missouri was important because it could control the lower Mississippi River. Missourians' loyalties were divided. Many government officials and the state's slaveholders supported secession, but most Missourians did not. Pro-Union citizens formed a militia and organized a rival government. Lincoln sent troops to aid the pro-Union forces against the secessionists. The Confederates aided the other side. The secessionists, however, never gained enough control over the state to withdraw it from the Union.

Divided loyalties in Kentucky Control of Kentucky meant control of some 700 miles of the Ohio River that formed its northern border. If Kentucky were in Confederate hands, a large part of the Union would be open to the threat of invasion. "I hope to have God on my side, but I must have Kentucky," Lincoln reportedly said.

Most of the state's government officials opposed secession, but many citizens favored joining the Confederacy. As a result, Kentucky's governor declared that the state would not choose a side in the war. Eventually, Kentucky sided with the Union after the state was invaded by Confederate troops in September 1861.

No matter which side the border states took, they all had some citizens fight for the North and others fight for the South. Nowhere was this more true than in Kentucky. One of Kentucky senator John Crittenden's sons was a Union general and the other was a general in the Confederate army. First Lady Mary Todd Lincoln, a Kentucky native, had four brothers in Confederate armies.

READING CHECK **Summarizing** Why was it important to the Union that the border states remain loyal?

Goals and Strategies

As both sides prepared to fight, their leaders announced their goals for the war. Lincoln had to define the Union's goals very carefully. He knew that most northerners were not abolitionists and that they would not support a war that centered around the dispute over slavery. He also feared that making slavery the issue in the war might push the border states to secede. Instead, he asked northerners to fight for patriotic reasons—to save the Union, not to settle the slavery issue.

The South's war goals were simple: to be left alone with slavery unchanged. This position shaped the South's military strategy. The Confederates prepared to defend the South against an invasion by the North. Southerners believed that if they held off the invading armies, northerners would soon get tired of the fighting and withdraw. Many people on both sides doubted that the war would last longer than 90 days.

The North's strategy While the South could plan a defensive war, the North faced a much more difficult task. Unless southerners returned their states to the Union voluntarily, northern armies would need to invade the South in order to crush the rebellion.

In many ways, however, the North was better equipped than the South for such a war. For example, the North had a much larger population than the South, so more northerners were available to serve in the armed forces. The North also had more than 85 percent of the nation's factories. This meant that the North would have a much easier time producing war supplies such as guns and ammunition.

The North tried to take advantage of the South's lack of industries and resources in its first plan for fighting the war. The Union strategy was developed by General Winfield Scott, the commander of the Union armies and a hero of the war against Mexico. Scott planned to seal off the South from the rest of the world. He believed this would end the rebellion with less bloodshed than any other means.

First, the Union navy would blockade the South's ports. This would prevent the Confederacy from importing the manufactured goods it so desperately needed. It would also prevent the South from exporting the cotton and other products it sold to the rest of the world. Then a fleet of Union gunboats would move down the Mississippi River and cut the Confederacy in two. With the Confederacy divided and weakened, Scott believed that southerners who did not support secession would rise up and overthrow the Confederate leaders.

Scott's plan had major flaws, however. For one thing, it was based on the false belief that most southerners did not support secession and were under the control of radical leaders. It would also take a great deal of time to form an effective blockade and capture and control the Mississippi River. Scott's plan failed to recognize that most northerners believed in and wanted a short war.

Northern journalists thought Scott's strategy absurd. They called it the **Anaconda Plan**, after the snake that slowly squeezes its victims to death. Instead, they urged Scott to send an army to capture the new capital of the Confederacy—Richmond, Virginia—which was close to Union territory. "On to Richmond!" northern newspapers cried, and a quick end to the war.

The South's strategy While the Confederates had far fewer resources than northerners, they essentially made up for this with their support for the cause. White southerners believed themselves to be fighting for their freedom and

NORTHERN AND SOUTHERN RESOURCES

Legend: The North (blue), The South (yellow)

Resources	The North	The South
Population	61%	39%
Bank capital	78%	22%
Railroad mileage	71%	29%
Farmland	51%	49%
Value of manufactured goods	92%	8%

Source: United States Bureau of the Census

Skills FOCUS **INTERPRETING GRAPHS**

1. Which side had control of the country's resources in each of the categories shown, and by how much?
2. What advantage do you think this provided?

See **Skills Handbook**, p. H16

their homeland, as the Patriots had done in the Revolutionary War. They fought to defend their new nation even though three-fourths of them did not hold slaves.

"Thank God! We have a country at last," a Mississippian declared, "to live for, pray for, fight for, and, if necessary, to die for." Many southerners viewed Union troops as vandals who were being sent to plunder the South. "Our men *must* prevail in combat, or lose their property, country, freedom, everything," one Confederate wrote.

Southerners also placed great value on their bravery and fighting ability. They were convinced of their military superiority over the armies of the North.

In fact, the South's military leaders did give the Confederacy a strong advantage over the North. Many of the nation's most talented and promising army officers were southerners. Like Robert E. Lee, most sided with their home states and fought for the Confederacy.

Cotton diplomacy Many southerners believed that their greatest strength and advantage over the North was their cotton. The South had long exported enormous amounts of cotton to the textile mills of Great Britain and France. Southerners were convinced that if war disrupted this supply, both nations would come to the Confederacy's aid to restore the cotton trade. They expected that the powerful British navy would break through any Union blockade of southern ports.

"If those miserable Yankees try to blockade us, and keep you from our cotton," one southern merchant told a British journalist, "you'll just send their ships to the bottom and acknowledge us." By "acknowledge us" he meant that Britain would recognize the Confederacy as an independent nation.

PRIMARY SOURCES

Propaganda Map

At the start of the war, General Winfield Scott developed a plan to surround the South and cut off its supplies. This 1861 map cartoon expressed confidence in Scott's plan.

Scott's strategy was called the Anaconda Plan, after the South American snake that wraps around and suffocates its prey.

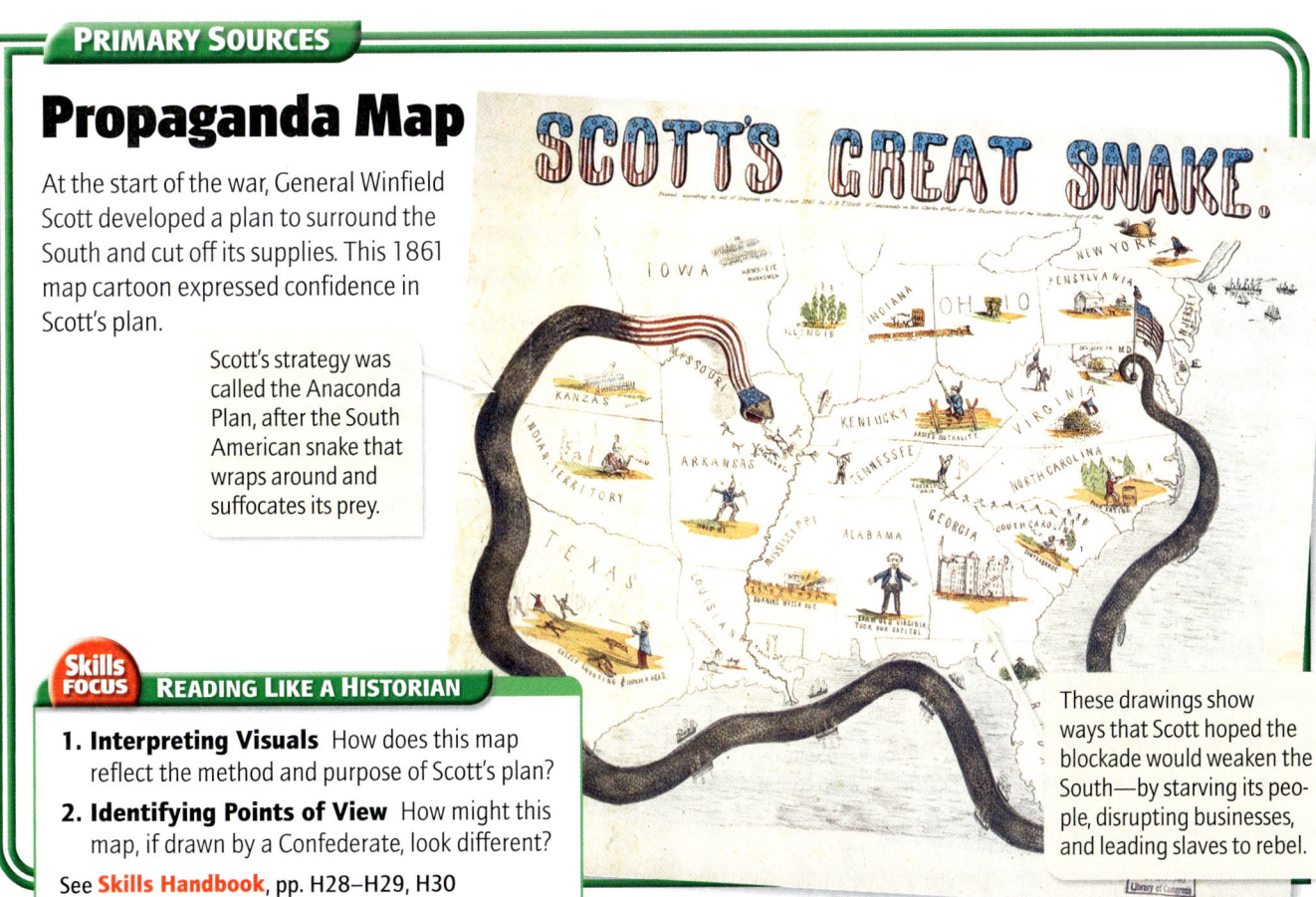

These drawings show ways that Scott hoped the blockade would weaken the South—by starving its people, disrupting businesses, and leading slaves to rebel.

Skills FOCUS   READING LIKE A HISTORIAN

1. **Interpreting Visuals** How does this map reflect the method and purpose of Scott's plan?
2. **Identifying Points of View** How might this map, if drawn by a Confederate, look different?

See **Skills Handbook**, pp. H28–H29, H30

Receiving foreign aid and the recognition of southern independence became important goals in the South's war strategy. Southerners believed that their cotton was the key to making this happen. "Our cotton is . . . the tremendous lever by which we can work our destiny," Confederate vice president Alexander Stephens declared in July 1861. This use of cotton as a tool of Confederate foreign policy was known as **cotton diplomacy**.

When Britain and France failed to recognize the Confederacy as an independent nation early in the war, Confederates deliberately stopped shipping cotton to those countries. The *Memphis Argus* instructed planters to **embargo**, or totally restrict, their export of cotton to markets overseas.

HISTORY'S VOICES

❝Keep every bale of cotton on the plantation. Don't send a thread to New Orleans or Memphis until England and France have recognized the Confederacy—not one thread.❞

—*Memphis Argus*, Memphis, Tennessee

"The cards are in our hands," the *Charleston Mercury* boasted, "and we intend to play them out to the bankruptcy of every cotton factory in Great Britain and France for the recognition of our independence."

Cotton diplomacy failed, however, in part because the British deeply resented the Confederacy's attempt to blackmail them. "[If southerners] thought they could extort our cooperation by the agency of king cotton, they had better think again," warned the London *Times*. "No English Parliament could do so base [dishonorable] a thing," Britain's foreign minister declared.

More importantly, a huge cotton crop in 1860 had allowed overseas mill owners to stockpile southern cotton. In addition, the end of southern exports raised cotton prices worldwide. These higher prices encouraged farmers in Egypt and India to grow more cotton to sell to European countries. When mill owners in Britain and France exhausted their reserves of southern cotton, they turned to Egypt and India for a new supply.

By the time southerners realized that cotton diplomacy had failed, the North's blockade had tightened, making the export of cotton nearly impossible. Further efforts to gain or block foreign involvement in the conflict, however, remained important to the actions and strategies of both sides during the Civil War.

READING CHECK **Summarizing** For what reasons did cotton diplomacy fail?

---

go.hrw.com
Online Quiz
Keyword: SD7 HP11

Reviewing Ideas, Terms, and People

1. **a. Identify** Where did the first battle of the Civil War take place?
   b. Analyze Why was this place important to both the North and the South?

2. **a. Identify** Which states joined the Confederacy after Lincoln's call for troops?
   b. Make Inferences Why did Lincoln's call for troops force the slave states that remained in the Union to choose a side?
   c. Elaborate Why were many men eager to enlist at the beginning of the war?

3. **a. Describe** What made the **border states** important?
   b. Analyze Why was Maryland the most critical border state?

4. **a. Describe** What was **cotton diplomacy**?
   b. Compare How were many southerners' views during the Civil War similar to those of Patriots during the Revolutionary War?
   c. Predict Which side do you think was better prepared for war, the North or the South? Explain why you think so.

Critical Thinking

5. **Comparing and Contrasting** Review your notes on Civil War goals and strategies. Then copy the graphic organizer below and use it to compare and contrast the North's and the South's goals and strategies.

Northern Goals and Strategies	Southern Goals and Strategies

FOCUS ON SPEAKING

6. **Persuasive** Suppose that you lived in a border state in 1861. Give a speech that makes an argument and provides reasons for or against your state seceding and joining the Confederacy.

Fighting Erupts

BEFORE YOU READ

MAIN IDEA

Widespread fighting occurred during the first two years of the Civil War.

READING FOCUS

1. What factors made the major battles in the war so bloody?
2. How did the Union carry out its strategy in the Mississippi Valley?
3. What led to the Confederate successes in the war in the East?
4. Why did Confederate forces invade the Union, and with what result?

KEY TERMS AND PEOPLE

Stonewall Jackson
infantry
First Battle of Bull Run
casualties
George McClellan
cavalry
ironclads
Ulysses S. Grant
Battle of Shiloh
Battle of Antietam

PI 3.2 Research and analyze the major themes and developments in New York State and United States history (e.g., colonization and settlement; Revolution and New National Period; immigration; expansion and reform era; Civil War and Reconstruction; the American labor movement; Great Depression; World Wars; contemporary United States).

THE INSIDE STORY *Why was an audience watching a battle?* In the summer of 1861, northerners and southerners both expected victory by the fall. In July, Lincoln sent an army southward from Washington toward Richmond, Virginia. On July 21 the Union army attacked Confederate forces about 30 miles south of Washington, near a creek called Bull Run.

Enthusiasm for the war was high in Washington. Many men and women, including members of Congress, packed picnic baskets and rode out to watch the battle. The Union army made gains at first, but fresh Confederate troops arrived, forcing the Union army to retreat.

Then a Confederate artillery shell blew up a wagon on a bridge, creating a bottleneck along the march route. The orderly retreat turned into chaos as panicked Union soldiers began to run. Terrified civilians joined the stampede away from the battlefield.

Edmund Clarence Stedman, a reporter for the *New York World,* described the scene: "Hosts of federal troops . . . were fleeing along the road . . . Army wagons, sutlers' teams [merchants' wagons], and private carriages choked the passage, tumbling against each other amid clouds of dust . . . Hacks [hired carriages], containing unlucky spectators . . . were smashed like glass . . . Those on foot who could catch [horses] rode them bareback, as much to save themselves from being run over as to make quicker time."

Picnic on the BATTLEFIELD

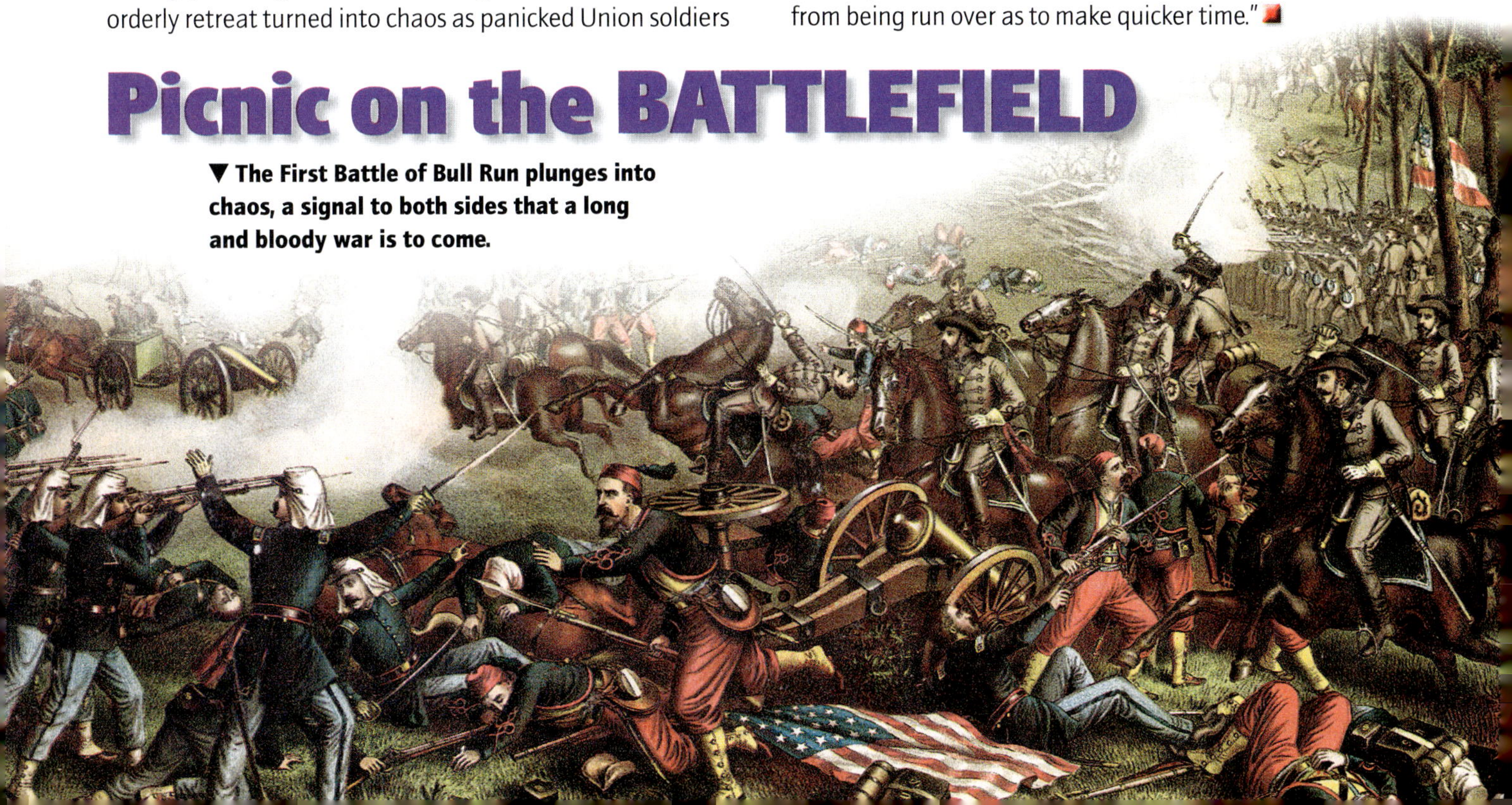

▼ The First Battle of Bull Run plunges into chaos, a signal to both sides that a long and bloody war is to come.

The New Weapons of War

Civil War soldiers used several weapons that were new to America. Although some had been developed in Europe, the American Civil War was their first major test in battlefield conditions.

Large bullets called minié balls were used by both sides and did great damage on impact.

Union balloons rose 3,500 feet and allowed observers to see up to 6 miles.

Several types of ironclads, ships covered with iron plates of armor, were used by both sides in the war.

The Major Battles Begin

General Irvin McDowell warned President Lincoln that the Union army was not ready to fight. The 90-day enlistments of the North's volunteers were nearly over, however. There would soon be no army. "You are green [inexperienced] it is true," Lincoln noted, "but they [the Confederate troops] are green, also; you are all green alike." He decided that the army must attack.

On July 16, 1861, General McDowell began to march his 35,000-man army into Virginia. Blocking his path to Richmond were 22,000 Confederate troops located near the small town of Manassas Junction. The Confederates positioned themselves on the south side of a stream called Bull Run and waited.

McDowell's troops took two and a half days to march the 25 miles between Washington and Manassas. "They were not used to journeys on foot," he later explained. Their slow pace allowed the Confederate commander, P. G. T. Beauregard, to bring in 11,000 more troops by train. By the time the Union army arrived, the two forces were about equal in size.

First Battle of Bull Run Beauregard and McDowell had each planned carefully, but their inexperienced armies could not carry out the plans. The battle became a chaotic free-for-all. At first, the Union troops pushed the Confederates back. Then some Virginia soldiers led by General Thomas Jackson rushed onto the field and stopped the Union advance. "There stands Jackson like a stone wall!" Confederate general Barnard Bee shouted to his troops. "Rally behind the Virginians!" Bee was killed soon after, but **Stonewall Jackson** had earned his famous nickname.

By late afternoon the Union troops began to fall back. When Beauregard ordered his entire line of **infantry**, or foot soldiers, to charge, the Union retreat turned into a stampede. Soldiers tossed away guns, packs, and anything else that might slow them down as they ran from the battlefield.

If the Confederates had pursued the fleeing troops, they might have been able to destroy the Union army. Instead, as one Confederate general put it, "our army was more disorganized by victory than that of the United States by defeat." The exhausted victors stayed on the battlefield after the **First Battle of Bull Run**. The Confederate army had suffered nearly 2,000 **casualties**, the military term for those killed, wounded, or missing in action. Union casualties numbered about 2,900.

The Battle of Bull Run ended most northerners' hopes for a short war. Lincoln called for a million more volunteers willing to serve for three years. The president also replaced McDowell with a brilliant 34-year-old general, **George McClellan**. McClellan immediately set about turning some 100,000 of these three-year volunteers into a real army.

THE IMPACT TODAY

Culture

The battlefield at Bull Run is today a national park. It is one of 384 Civil War battlefields that have been designated as historic sites by the U.S. or state governments.

The Union's Gatling gun, an early machine gun, could fire 200 times per minute.

The Confederate *Hunley* was the first submarine to sink an enemy vessel. The explosion sank the *Hunley*, too.

THE MUSEUM OF THE CONFEDERACY, RICHMOND, VIRGINIA

Skills FOCUS INTERPRETING VISUALS

Making Inferences How were ironclads an advantage over wooden ships?

See **Skills Handbook**, p. H30

Tactics and technology Most of the top generals on each side in the war had been trained at the U.S. Military Academy at West Point. The predominant instruction was based on the wars conducted by Napoleon in his conquest of Europe a half-century before. Such tactics often involved sending a force of infantry or **cavalry**, soldiers on horseback, to charge an enemy position. These methods had worked well in the Mexican-American War. Many Civil War generals had served in that war as young officers.

The weapons on Civil War battlefields, however, were far more deadly than those used in the 1840s. In the Mexican War, the average musket had a range of 250 yards and was accurate only to a distance of about 80 yards. In addition, it took about 25 seconds to reload the weapon. A charging enemy often could overwhelm defenders before they could fire again.

By the 1850s, however, weapon makers found that bullet-shaped ammunition traveled through the air in a much straighter line than a round ball. They also discovered that cutting a spiral groove inside a gun barrel, called rifling, made the bullet rotate after it was fired. Both changes increased range and accuracy. Rifles, as the new guns were called, were accurate to 500 yards. New systems for reloading allowed a soldier to fire about 10 times a minute.

The killing power of artillery also increased. The solid iron cannonballs of earlier years were replaced by shrapnel—shells that exploded in the air over a target, or when they struck a target. Fragments of these exploding shells ripped into any troops nearby. If enemy troops were close to defenders, cannon could fire canister—shells filled with small bits of metal. Canister turned artillery into giant shotguns that mowed down advancing troops.

Attacks against military forces with these modern weapons produced huge numbers of casualties. This clash of tactics and technology is why some historians call the Civil War the last old-time war and first modern one.

New devices of war The Civil War was the first time observation balloons were used to direct artillery fire. This gave rise to the first use of camouflage to disguise tents and guns from airborne observers. Other devices that saw limited use for the first time include machine guns, wire entanglements, flamethrowers, and gas shells called stink bombs.

Existing devices were put to new uses as well. The telegraph, invented by Samuel F. B. Morse in the 1840s, allowed generals in the field to communicate quickly with government leaders. The Civil War also marked the first time in history that railroads were used to move large numbers of troops.

ACADEMIC VOCABULARY
predominant most noticeable or important

READING CHECK **Summarizing** How did tactics, technology, and inexperience shape the fighting in the Civil War?

The Fight for the Mississippi Valley

Among the most successful new weapons of the Civil War were the Union's ironclads. These armored gunboats were critical to the North's campaign in the Mississippi River valley. Covered with heavy iron plates up to three inches thick, the boats were nearly invincible to Confederate cannon fire.

As McClellan trained the new Army of the Potomac in Washington, D.C., other Union soldiers began to carry out General Scott's plan to take control of the Mississippi River. Southern leaders expected the Union's attack to come down the Mississippi River. To resist this tactic, they invaded western Kentucky and fortified the bluffs above the river. However, the Union attacked from the Tennessee River instead.

Grant moves south In February 1862 seven Union gunboats and 15,000 troops led by General **Ulysses S. Grant** moved up the Tennessee River. The gunboats pounded Fort Henry, a Confederate fort near the Kentucky-Tennessee line, into a quick surrender.

Grant then marched his troops cross-country to capture Fort Donelson on the Cumberland River. After holding out for three days, the fort's commander tried to negotiate. Grant refused. "No terms except unconditional and immediate surrender can be accepted," he said. The fort's 12,000 defenders gave up, and the North had a much-needed victory. When newspapers reported Grant's tough remark, northerners also had a hero.

Grant's capture of Forts Henry and Donelson caused a sensation in both North and South. Two major rivers into the western Confederacy were wide open. In addition, Confederate defenses along the Mississippi River were now vulnerable to attack.

Another Union army under General Don Carlos Buell quickly advanced up the Cumberland River to capture Nashville, the capital of Tennessee. Meanwhile, Grant and about 38,000 soldiers continued south along the Tennessee River toward Corinth, Mississippi, an important railroad center.

The Battle of Shiloh By late March 1862 more than 40,000 Confederate troops from across the region had gathered at Corinth to block the Union advance. Grant, however, stopped at Pittsburg Landing, Tennessee, a small river town some 20 miles away. He was waiting for 25,000 more troops that Buell had sent from Nashville. The Confederates decided to attack before Grant's army got larger.

On April 6, 1862, the southerners surprised the Union soldiers, who were camped at Shiloh Church outside Pittsburg Landing. *Shiloh* means "place of peace" in Hebrew, but it was far from peaceful that day. After hours of fighting, the Confederates pushed the Union forces back against the Tennessee River. By nightfall the Confederates were confident they would finish off Grant's army in the morning. When Union officers suggested that their army retreat, Grant replied, "Retreat? No. I propose to attack at daylight and whip them."

Buell's troops finally arrived that night and, true to his word, Grant attacked the next morning. Now facing an army much larger than their own, the Confederates were driven back. By 2:30 p.m. the **Battle of Shiloh** was over, and the Confederate army was in retreat.

This two-day battle produced some of the bloodiest fighting yet seen in the war. About one of every four soldiers was killed or wounded. The Union army suffered some 13,000 losses, while Confederate casualties totaled more than 10,000.

The Battle of Shiloh also ended northern hopes that the rebellion would collapse on its own. Grant wrote later that after this battle, "I gave up all idea of saving the Union except by complete conquest."

The Mississippi River campaign The Battle of Shiloh opened the way for Union forces to split the Confederacy and gain complete control of the Mississippi River. Union generals began massing more than 100,000 troops at Pittsburg Landing, preparing to move south along the river. Meanwhile, a Union fleet of 24 wooden ships entered the river from the Gulf of Mexico and pushed north to capture New Orleans, Louisiana, the South's largest city. Admiral David Farragut commanded the fleet. Aboard some of his ships were 15,000 army troops led by General Ben Butler.

Two forts guarded New Orleans on opposite sides of the Mississippi River just south of the city. "Nothing afloat could pass the forts," claimed one New Orleans citizen. Indeed,

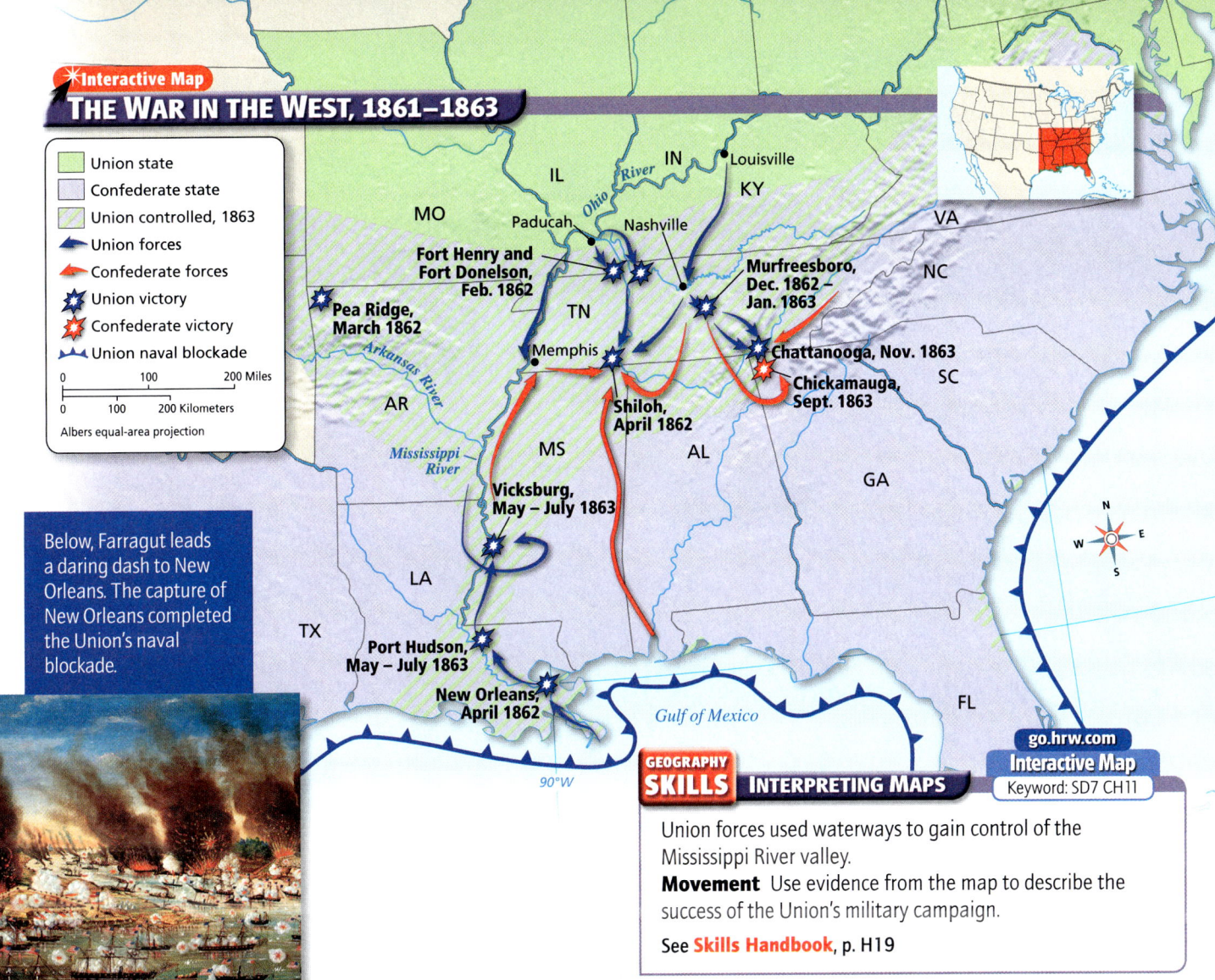

Interactive Map
THE WAR IN THE WEST, 1861–1863

Union state
Confederate state
Union controlled, 1863
Union forces
Confederate forces
Union victory
Confederate victory
Union naval blockade

0   100   200 Miles
0   100   200 Kilometers
Albers equal-area projection

IL
IN   Louisville
MO
Paducah   Nashville   KY
Ohio River
VA
Fort Henry and
Fort Donelson,
Feb. 1862
Murfreesboro,
Dec. 1862 –
Jan. 1863
NC
Pea Ridge,
March 1862
TN
Arkansas River
Memphis   Chattanooga, Nov. 1863
SC
AR
Shiloh,
April 1862
Chickamauga,
Sept. 1863
Mississippi River
MS   AL
GA
Vicksburg,
May – July 1863
LA
TX
Port Hudson,
May – July 1863
New Orleans,
April 1862
Gulf of Mexico
FL
90°W

Below, Farragut leads a daring dash to New Orleans. The capture of New Orleans completed the Union's naval blockade.

GEOGRAPHY SKILLS **INTERPRETING MAPS**

go.hrw.com
Interactive Map
Keyword: SD7 CH11

Union forces used waterways to gain control of the Mississippi River valley.
Movement Use evidence from the map to describe the success of the Union's military campaign.
See **Skills Handbook**, p. H19

after six days of heavy fire from the Union ships the forts remained standing. Finally, Farragut decided on a bold plan—to slip past the forts under the cover of darkness. At two o'clock on the morning of April 24, the Union vessels began to move. Then the moon rose and disaster struck. The Confederate soldiers in the forts saw the ships and opened fire with artillery. The lead vessel was heavily battered, but most of the ships managed to make their way past the forts.

After sinking several Confederate warships further upriver, Farragut's fleet arrived at New Orleans on April 25. The nearly undefended city quickly surrendered.

Many southerners were concerned about what the fall of New Orleans might mean for the Confederacy's future. Mary Chesnut, who was married to a Confederate general, wrote about her fears in her diary.

HISTORY'S VOICES

"New Orleans gone—and with it the Confederacy. Are we not cut in two? The Mississippi ruins us if lost…Death, not life, seems to be our fate now."

—Mary Chesnut, April 27, 1862

Farragut soon pushed north to capture the cities of Baton Rouge, Louisiana, and Natchez, Mississippi. In June, another Union fleet came downriver from Missouri and seized Memphis, Tennessee. The town of Vicksburg, Mississippi, high on a bluff, was the major river stronghold, and it remained in Confederate hands. "Ships . . . cannot crawl up hills 300 feet high," Farragut noted. An army would be needed. That assignment would fall to General Grant.

READING CHECK **Sequencing** By what process did Union forces gain control of nearly all of the Mississippi River in 1862?

Gettysburg, July 1863

PA

NJ

MD

Antietam, Sept. 1862

WV (1863)

Washington, DC

DE

1st Battle of Bull Run, July 1861

2nd Battle of Bull Run, Aug. 1862

Potomac River

Chesapeake Bay

Rappahannock River

Chancellorsville, April - May 1863

York River

Fredericksburg, Dec. 1862

Richmond

Yorktown

ATLANTIC OCEAN

Seven Pines, May - June 1862

James River

VA

Seven Days, June - July 1862

NC

This portrayal of the Battle of Antietam was painted by James Hope, a Union soldier from Vermont.

Legend:
- Union state
- Confederate state
- Gained statehood and admitted to the Union, 1863
- Union controlled, 1863
- Union forces
- Confederate forces
- Union victory
- Confederate victory
- Union naval blockade

0   25   50 Miles
0   25   50 Kilometers
Albers equal-area projection

GEOGRAPHY SKILLS INTERPRETING MAPS

go.hrw.com
Interactive Map
Keyword: SD7 CH11

1. **Movement** Which army shows the most movement?
2. **Location** Where did the Confederates invade the Union?

See **Skills Handbook**, p. H19

The War in the East

As Grant moved south through Tennessee, McClellan's army in the East was finally ready for action. General McClellan had a clever plan. Rather than march directly toward Richmond, he planned to move his army by boat down the Potomac River and across Chesapeake Bay. He would then attack the Confederate capital from the east, where its defenses were weaker. It was a good plan, but McClellan never seemed ready to fight. As the months passed and still he did not move, Lincoln lost patience. "How *long* would it require to actually get in motion?" the president asked McClellan in December 1861.

The peninsula campaign In March 1862 McClellan finally began to move his 100,000-man army. In early April the advancing Union soldiers came upon 15,000 Confederates at Yorktown, about 60 miles from Richmond. The Confederates' defenses were weak, but McClellan delayed an attack in order to ask Lincoln for more troops. The president refused. A Confederate force of 20,000 men led by Stonewall Jackson was causing trouble for Union troops elsewhere in Virginia. Lincoln was afraid that if he sent additional troops to help McClellan, those soldiers might later be needed to defend Washington. Instead, the president sent his general a clear warning.

❝It is indispensable to *you* that you strike a blow …The country will not fail to note—is now noting—that the present hesitation to move upon an entrenched enemy is but the story of Manassas [Bull Run] repeated…I have never written to you, or spoken to you, in greater kindness of feeling than now…*But you must act.***❞**

—Abraham Lincoln, April 9, 1862

McClellan ignored the president's advice. After spending another month waiting outside Yorktown, he finally attacked. The Confederates offered no resistance. Instead, they retreated toward Richmond. McClellan's delay, however, had given the Confederate commander, General Joseph Johnston, time to gather more troops.

Suddenly, on May 31, the Confederates turned and attacked the much larger Union army at a moment when the Union forces were divided by a river. Neither side won the Battle of Seven Pines, but both sides suffered heavy casualties. Johnston was among the Confederates who were wounded. General Robert E. Lee took command of Johnston's army and renamed it the Army of Northern Virginia.

As McClellan again waited for Lincoln to send more troops, the Confederates again took advantage of their opponent's caution. Although Lee's army was still greatly outnumbered by the Union forces, he sent some of his troops to help Stonewall Jackson fight in the Shenandoah Valley. Lee was gambling that McClellan would not attack while these soldiers were gone. With his now larger force, Jackson pretended that he was going to attack Washington. Lincoln ordered McClellan's reinforcements to stay and protect the capital.

This was exactly what Lee had hoped for. Jackson quickly moved his army from the Shenandoah Valley to join Lee. In late June their combined armies attacked McClellan in a series of bloody clashes called the Seven Days' Battles. Although McClellan won four of the five battles, he retreated.

The Second Battle of Bull Run

While McClellan's army sat motionless to the southeast of Richmond, Lincoln turned to General John Pope, who was forming a new Union army near Washington. In mid-July, Pope moved into northern Virginia with about 50,000 troops. Lincoln ordered McClellan to renew his attack in order to trap Lee's forces between the two Union armies. Once again McClellan did nothing. Lincoln then ordered him to withdraw his army from the Virginia peninsula and join Pope's troops.

Lee decided to act before the two Union armies could unite and create an overwhelming force. On August 29 he lured Pope into battle near Manassas, on almost the same ground where the Confederates had beaten McDowell's army a year before. At the Second Battle of Bull Run, Pope met the same fate. After Pope's defeat, Lincoln put McClellan back in command. When members of his cabinet protested, Lincoln explained, "We must use what tools we have."

READING CHECK **Identifying Cause and Effect** Why were Confederate forces able to defeat the larger Union armies that invaded Virginia?

The Union Is Invaded

The series of defeats in Virginia brought morale in the North to a new low. "The nation is rapidly sinking just now," a New Yorker wrote in his diary. "Disgust with our present government is certainly universal." In the Confederacy, General Lee sensed this situation, and an opportunity. He wrote to Confederate president Jefferson Davis, "The present seems to be the most propitious [favorable] time . . . for the Confederate army to enter Maryland."

Davis agreed. A victory on Union soil might prompt the North to ask for peace. If not, Confederate leaders hoped such a victory would at least convince Britain and France to recognize southern independence. In addition, moving the war out of Virginia would give farmers there the chance to harvest what remained of their crops, which were much needed by the troops and civilian population.

In early September 1862 Lee's army crossed the Potomac River into western Maryland, with McClellan's army in pursuit. Then a Union soldier found a copy of Lee's marching orders that had been lost by a careless Confederate officer. Now that he knew Lee's plans, McClellan exclaimed, "If I cannot whip Bobbie Lee, I will be willing to go home." When he telegraphed his good news to Lincoln, the delighted president replied, "God bless you and all with you. Destroy the rebel army, if possible."

The Battle of Antietam McClellan caught up with Lee near the town of Sharpsburg, Maryland, and prepared for battle. His 70,000 Union troops dwarfed Lee's army of 40,000. Yet again, the ever-cautious McClellan delayed for 16 hours before beginning his attack. This gave the Confederates time to organize their defenses. Finally, on September 17, 1862, the Battle of Antietam took place. Named after a creek that crossed the battlefield, Antietam was the bloodiest single-day battle of the Civil War—and of U.S. history.

Time and time again the Union troops charged the Confederate defenses. The savage fighting ended in late afternoon, when both sides became too exhausted to continue. Union and Confederate casualties combined exceeded 23,000. Lee lost almost a third of his army. McClellan had as many as 25,000 troops waiting in reserve, but he did not use them.

Had McClellan attacked Lee again the next day he would have followed Lincoln's command to "destroy the rebel army." But he did not. Instead, that night the Confederate troops began a slow retreat back to Virginia. Lincoln ordered McClellan to "cross the Potomac and give battle." Again, McClellan would not move. In early November 1862, President Lincoln relieved the general of command for the second and final time.

The Battle of Fredericksburg Lincoln replaced McClellan with General Ambrose Burnside. Soon, Burnside was marching a massive army of 110,000 men toward Richmond. He found his path blocked, however, by Lee and 75,000 Confederate soldiers on the south side of the Rappahannock River at Fredericksburg. Lee expected the Union army to cross the river above or below the town. Burnside decided instead to surprise Lee by crossing directly in front of the Confederate army.

The only thing that surprised Lee was Burnside's terrible judgment. Burnside ordered five pontoon bridges built across the river and sent his army over them to attack. He believed his superior numbers could force Lee to retreat.

On December 13, 1862, at the Battle of Fredericksburg, Burnside ordered his troops to charge Lee's army 14 times. Only the approach of darkness and the pleas of Burnside's commanders halted the horrible slaughter. The Union army lost nearly 13,000 men, more than twice the number of Confederate losses.

The disaster at Fredericksburg plunged the North into gloom. When Lincoln heard the terrible news, he said, "If there is a worse place than Hell, I am in it."

READING CHECK **Drawing Conclusions** Why was the Battle of Antietam an especially significant battle in the Civil War?

SECTION 2 ASSESSMENT

go.hrw.com
Online Quiz
Keyword: SD7 HP11

Reviewing Ideas, Terms, and People

1. a. Describe What was the outcome of the **First Battle of Bull Run**?
b. Predict Although they had many new weapons, Civil War generals relied on old battlefield strategies. How might such weapons and tactics affect the outcomes of battles?

2. a. Identify What were **ironclads**? How did the North use them?
b. Analyze Why were **Ulysses S. Grant**'s early victories in the Mississippi River valley important?

3. a. Describe What happened at the Second Battle of Bull Run?
b. Contrast How was the war in the East different from the war in the West?
c. Elaborate How would you describe **George McClellan** as a battlefield commander? Give reasons for your answer.

4. a. Recall Why did Lee cross into Maryland in 1862?
b. Evaluate Do you think Lincoln was right to relieve McClellan of his command after the **Battle of Antietam**?

Critical Thinking

5. Categorizing Review your notes on major Civil War battles. Then copy the graphic organizer below and use it to list Union and Confederate victories.

Union Victories	Confederate Victories

FOCUS ON WRITING

6. Expository Suppose you are President Lincoln. Write a letter to a friend describing your personal thoughts and feelings about the progress of the war.

The War behind the Lines

BEFORE YOU READ

MAIN IDEA

The Civil War created hardships, challenges, and opportunities for people in the North and the South.

READING FOCUS

1. How did the Emancipation Proclamation affect the Civil War?
2. How did African Americans contribute to the war effort?
3. What was life like in the military?
4. What similarities and differences existed on the home front in the North and South?

KEY TERMS AND PEOPLE

Emancipation Proclamation
emancipation
freedmen
conscription
Copperheads
habeas corpus
Clara Barton

PI 3.1 Compare and contrast the experiences of different ethnic, national, and religious groups, including Native American Indians, in the United States, explaining their contributions to American society and culture.

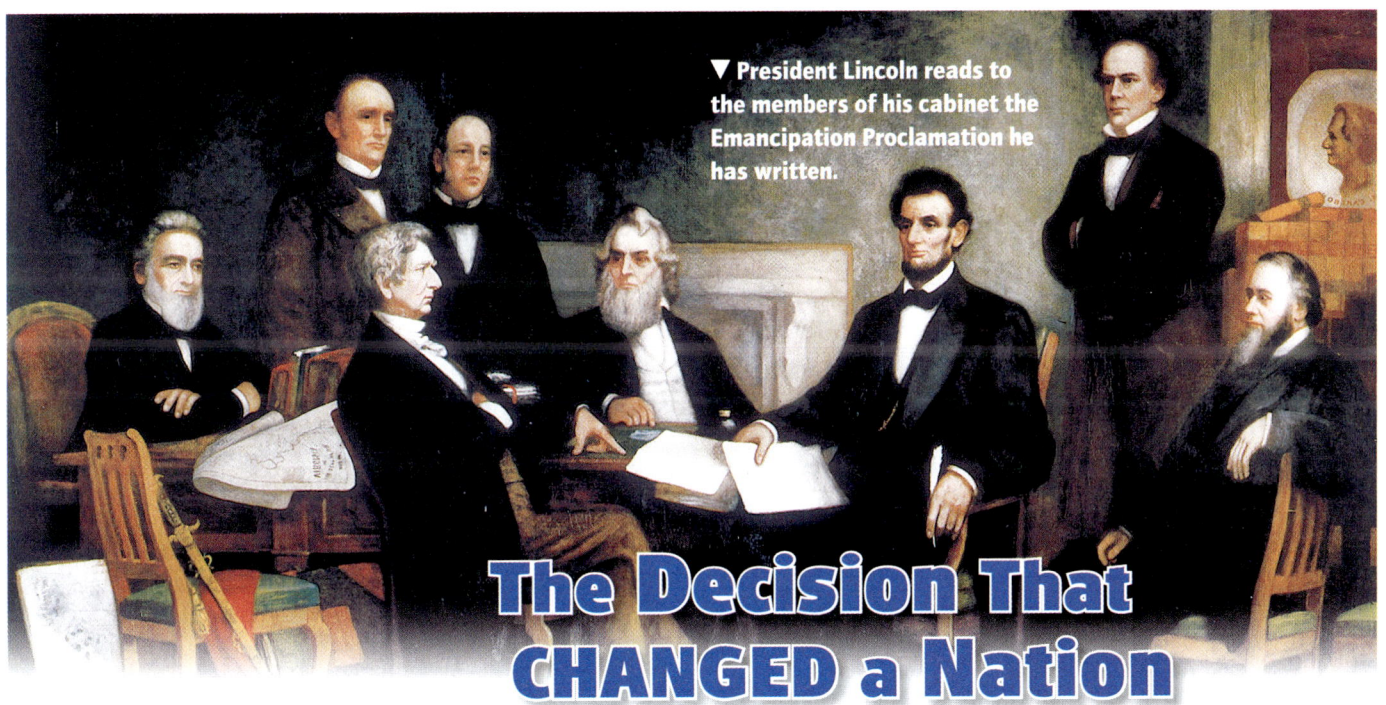

▼ President Lincoln reads to the members of his cabinet the Emancipation Proclamation he has written.

The Decision That CHANGED a Nation

THE INSIDE STORY

What great change did Lincoln make in the nation? The retreat of the Confederate army from Maryland in September 1862 allowed Abraham Lincoln to call the Battle of Antietam a victory for the North. Lincoln needed a victory because he planned a drastic action he hoped would help end the war. He had been waiting for the right time to announce this measure to the nation and the world.

The president called his cabinet together on September 22, the Monday after the battle. "I wish that we were in a better condition," he observed. "The action of the army against the rebels has not been quite what I should have best liked. But they have been driven out of Maryland."

President Lincoln then pulled from a pocket a paper he had written. He told the cabinet members in advance that he did not seek their advice about "the main matter" because he had already made up his mind, but he was willing to listen to any suggestions they might have about the wording he had used.

Then Lincoln began to read aloud from the paper he held. Finally, he reached the historic words that changed a nation—that on January 1, 1863, "all persons held as slaves within any state, or part of a state, the people whereof shall then be in rebellion against the United States shall be then, thenceforward, and forever free." ◢

The Emancipation Proclamation

As the fighting dragged on and casualties increased, northern attitudes about the war began to change. Some northerners came to believe that just saving the Union was not enough. They did not want the nation restored to what it had been before the war. These northerners argued that the South, which they blamed for causing the bloodshed and horrors of the war, should be punished by freeing its enslaved people.

Lincoln did not think that the Constitution gave him the power to take such action. Gradually, however, others convinced him that he could. They did so by noting that slavery provided the labor the South needed to continue the war. "This rebellion has its source and life in slavery," one influential Republican in Congress declared. This reasoning allowed Lincoln to use his constitutional power as commander in chief of the armed forces to end slavery in the rebelling states.

On January 1, 1863, Lincoln issued the **Emancipation Proclamation**. This document freed the slaves in all areas that were in rebellion against the United States.

Reaction to **emancipation**—the act of freeing someone from slavery—was mixed in the North. Many abolitionists were upset that the Emancipation Proclamation allowed slavery to continue in states that were not in rebellion. It did not even apply to areas of the Confederacy that had already been conquered by Union armies.

Some northerners opposed emancipation because they feared increased competition for jobs in the North. When the government had used former slaves to help harvest crops in Illinois in 1862, for example, riots broke out in protest. Calm was not restored until the government returned the former slaves to south of the Ohio River. Riots against black workers also took place in Cincinnati, Ohio; Brooklyn, New York; and several other northern cities.

Many northerners supported the Emancipation Proclamation, however, because they thought it would help shorten the war. A Cincinnati newspaper expressed pleasure that Lincoln was trying to destroy "the compulsory labor system *which feeds the enemy.*" Reactions in Union armies generally reflected those in northern society. Few soldiers were abolitionists, an Indiana colonel noted, but they were eager "to destroy everything that . . . gives the rebels strength."

Reaction overseas was also mixed. In Great Britain, where the abolition movement was strong, many felt that Lincoln had not gone far enough. "Where he has no power, Mr. Lincoln will set the negroes free," the London *Times* critically wrote. "Where he retains power he will consider them as slaves." Nevertheless, Lincoln's action ended whatever hope remained in the South for British intervention in the war. The British government was not willing to take the side of a slave power in a war that was now about ending slavery.

READING CHECK **Identifying Cause and Effect** In what ways did the Emancipation Proclamation affect the Civil War?

African American Union Soldiers

About 10 percent of the Union forces were African American. Their performance in battle proved to doubters their valor.

NOW IN CAMP AT READVILLE!
54th REGIMENT!
MASS. VOLUNTEERS, composed of men of
AFRICAN DESCENT
Col. ROBERT G. SHAW.
Colored Men, Rally 'Round the Flag of Freedom!
BOUNTY $100!
AT THE EXPIRATION OF THE TERM OF SERVICE.
Pay, $13 a Month!
Good Food & Clothing!
State Aid to Families!
RECRUITING OFFICE.
COR. CAMBRIDGE & NORTH RUSSELL STS.,
BOSTON.
Lieut. J. W. M. APPLETON, Recruiting Officer.

Juneteenth

The Emancipation Proclamation took effect on January 1, 1863—except in Texas. News of freedom did not reach African Americans there until June 19, 1865. Today that date marks a celebration that is known as Juneteenth. It is the oldest celebration of the ending of slavery in the United States.

In 1980 Juneteenth became a state holiday in Texas. It is not an official holiday anywhere else, but it is celebrated by people in Louisiana, Oklahoma, and other states.

Some of the largest Juneteenth events take place in Minneapolis, Minnesota, and Milwaukee, Wisconsin.

Juneteenth festivities take many forms. Early events included prayer services as well as family gatherings. Today Juneteenth is also celebrated with speeches, parades, picnics, and rodeos.

Drawing Conclusions Why do you think Juneteenth is celebrated so widely, even though it is an official holiday only in Texas?

Civil War re-enactors celebrate Juneteenth with a parade through Austin, Texas.

African Americans and the War

Enslaved African Americans made important contributions to the South's war effort. Their work on farms and plantations provided much of the food the South needed and released white males from labor so they could fight in Confederate armies. Many of the armies' non-combat jobs, such as cooking, nursing, driving wagons, and building defenses, were performed by slaves.

Even before the Emancipation Proclamation, thousands of slaves escaped to the safety of invading Union troops. Many were then hired by the Union army. They drove wagons, built forts, served as guides for invading forces, and performed a variety of other jobs.

The Proclamation encouraged **freedmen** (the term for emancipated slaves) to join the Union army and navy. Black sailors had been serving in the Union navy since the beginning of the war, but at first the Union army did not accept black volunteers. By the time the Emancipation Proclamation took effect, however, escaped slaves and free African Americans had been formed into Union army regiments in Louisiana, South Carolina, and Kansas. Black abolitionists called on all African American men to join in the fight.

HISTORY'S VOICES

"Let the black man get upon his person the brass letters, U.S.; let him get an eagle on his button, and a musket on his shoulder and bullets in his pocket, and there is no power on earth which can deny that he has earned the right to citizenship."

—Frederick Douglass, *Douglass' Monthly*, August 1863

African American soldiers served in segregated units that were usually commanded by white officers. At first, black regiments were used mainly for labor and guard duty, thereby freeing white soldiers to fight. In May and July of 1863, however, African American troops fought heroically in attacks at Port Hudson on the Mississippi River and at Fort Wagner in South Carolina. In both battles the African American regiments suffered terrible losses. The 54th Massachusetts Infantry, which led the charge on Fort Wagner, became one of the most famous units of the Civil War.

Nearly 180,000 African Americans served in the Union armies. More than half had been in slavery when the war began. At the end of the war, more than a tenth of Union soldiers were African American. Black troops took part in some 200 battles. More than 38,000 died serving the Union.

READING CHECK **Summarizing** What contributions did northern and southern African Americans make in the Civil War?

FOCUS ON NEW YORK

GOVERNMENT
New York's black regiments began organizing in May 1862. According to the U.S. War Department, 4,125 African American New Yorkers formed regiments of cavalry, infantry, and light and heavy artillery. New York's 20th, 26th, and 31st regiments of the U.S. Colored Troops trained on Rikers and Hart Islands.

Life in the Military

Most of the troops who died during the Civil War did not die on the battlefield or from wounds suffered there. Disease was by far the greatest killer of soldiers. For every death that resulted from battle, about two more soldiers died from disease.

Wartime medicine In a time before vaccinations and antibiotics, epidemics of mumps, measles, and smallpox swept through army camps. Soldiers who escaped infectious diseases were often sickened by conditions such as dysentery, cholera, and typhoid fever, which resulted from poor sanitation and polluted water supplies. At times, as many as one-third of an army's soldiers might be too sick to fight.

In Europe, scientists were learning that tiny organisms, today called bacteria, could spread disease, infect food and water, and enter the bloodstream through open wounds. Civil War doctors, however, knew none of these things. Doctors often went days without washing their instruments, or even their hands, passing germs from one patient to another. Soldiers sometimes tried to conceal wounds to avoid seeing the doctor.

Battlefield wounds, however, were often difficult to conceal. The minié bullet, or "minnie ball," was the most common ammunition on both sides. This heavy lead bullet inflicted great damage. Shots to an arm or leg usually shattered any bones the bullet struck. The bullets also carried dirt and germs into the wound, which often caused infection.

President Lincoln approved the creation of the United States Sanitary Commission in 1861. Within two years it had 7,000 branches across the North, staffed mainly by women volunteers. The Sanitary Commission provided nurses and ambulance drivers to the army. Its workers also collected and distributed food, clothing, and medical supplies. They inspected hospitals and army camps and offered advice on sewage disposal, hygiene, disease prevention, and nutrition.

Photograph

Civil War soldiers spent much more time in camp than on the battlefield. Camp life was boring but also dangerous due to frequent epidemics of disease.

Many soldiers had strong opinions about the war. Newspapers kept them informed about the war's progress and the political issues involved.

Writing letters home was probably the major leisure time activity in camp. Although mail delivery was often slow, letters helped morale.

Skills FOCUS READING LIKE A HISTORIAN

Analyzing Visuals What evidence in the photograph indicates that soldiers had to do their own housekeeping while in camp?

See **Skills Handbook**, p. H30

Camp life On average, soldiers spent about 75 percent of their time in camp. Conditions were often horrible. In wet weather, camps were a sea of mud. In dry weather, they were filled with clouds of dust. Soldiers crammed into tents that were designed for far fewer people. As canvas for tents became scarce in the South, Confederate soldiers were often forced to sleep on the open ground.

Days in camp were long and boring. They typically began at 5 a.m. in summer and 6 a.m. in winter. After breakfast, the men took part in up to five daily drills. During these two-hour sessions they learned and practiced battlefield maneuvers. Between drills, the troops cleaned the camp, gathered firewood, wrote letters home, and played games. Boxing matches, baseball, and card games were popular.

Troops on both sides ate well at first. In camp, soldiers' daily rations consisted of bread, fresh or salted pork or beef, coffee, and beans. When on the march, however, hard bread biscuits called hardtack and coffee or water were the main sources of nourishment. Soldiers often added to their diets whatever they could find in the area. A large army could strip the countryside of crops and livestock.

Prison camps As hard as army life was, conditions for prisoners of war were much worse. At first, neither North nor South kept large numbers of captured soldiers. Many prisoners were released if they promised to go home instead of back to their army. Others were exchanged for prisoners held by the other side.

When African Americans began joining the Union army in 1863, however, this changed. Confederate leaders declared that captured black soldiers would be enslaved or executed. This threat caused Union leaders to end prisoner exchanges. As a result, the number of prisoners held by each side increased.

Good treatment of prisoners was never a high priority for either side. The end of prisoner exchanges led to overcrowding in prison camps in both the North and the South. This caused

Andersonville

More than 56,000 Civil War soldiers died in prison camps such as this one in Georgia, mostly due to starvation, disease, and other effects of the harsh and miserable conditions.

CIVIL WAR: PRISONERS OF WAR

Union	Confederacy
POW camps: 14	POW camps: 20
Total POWs: 214,865	Total POWs: 194,793
Died in prison: 25,796	Died in prison: 30,218
Death rate: 12%	Death rate: 15.5%

Source: *The Civil War Day by Day*

conditions to worsen. A large number of major battles in 1863 and 1864 also overwhelmed camps that were already inadequate.

Andersonville and Elmira To handle the growing number of prisoners, in 1864 Confederate leaders erected a stockade in an open field near the town of Andersonville, Georgia. Built to hold 10,000 Union soldiers, by July 1864 it held more than 30,000 men within its 20-foot log walls. A single stream ran though the enclosure, serving as a sewer as well as providing water for bathing and drinking. Under these terrible conditions, about 100 prisoners died each day in the hot sun.

When word of conditions at Andersonville reached the North, Union leaders responded by limiting Confederate prisoners' food to only bread and water. As a result, the death rate at the Union's most notorious prison camp at Elmira, New York, approached that of Andersonville. Prisoners at Elmira ate rats in order to get some meat in their diets.

 **READING CHECK** **Making Generalizations** What was a soldier's life like?

THE IMPACT TODAY

Government
Humane treatment of prisoners of war is now required by the fourth Geneva Convention, an international agreement reached in 1949.

Life on the Home front

Families on both sides made sacrifices and endured hardships as a result of the war. Still, life on the home front was quite different in the North and the South.

The southern home front Shortages made life difficult for southerners. With few factories, the South had little ability to manufacture needed goods. Food production dropped as invading Union armies made farming difficult. As a result, the costs of everyday items soared. A pair of shoes that sold for $18 in 1862 cost up to $800 by 1865. Bread sold for $25 a loaf in some places.

Scarcity was only one reason for high prices, however. Another was inflation, an increase in prices resulting from an increased supply of money. To pay for the war, the Confederate government printed huge sums of paper money. Since the South had little gold to back this money, by 1863 a Confederate paper dollar was worth only about 20 cents. The Confederate government also borrowed money by selling bonds and thus fought the war on credit.

High prices and shortages brought hardship. In 1863 about 1,000 women looted shops in Richmond for food, shoes, cloth, and other items. Food riots took place in several other southern cities. Such conditions led thousands of soldiers to desert. "Men cannot be expected to fight for the government that permits their wives and children to starve," one Confederate leader noted. "Poor men have been compelled to leave the army to come home to provide for their families," a Mississippi soldier explained. "We are poor men and willing to defend our country but our families [come] first."

The Confederate draft As the one-year enlistments of the original volunteers expired, southern leaders grew concerned about maintaining the armies. Many soldiers shared the views of one Virginian, who in January 1862 wrote, "If I live this twelve months out, I intend to try mighty hard to keep out [of the army]."

Reacting to such sentiments, the Confederate Congress enacted the first military draft in American history in April 1862. The law extended the volunteers' enlistments for two more years and required three years' service from other white males aged 18 to 35. (By 1864 the ages had been changed to 17 and 50.) Men in jobs critical to the war effort at home were excused as were slave overseers on large plantations and holders of 20 or more slaves.

This **conscription**, or forced service in the military, was extremely unpopular. It seemed to violate the very principles of states' rights

ACADEMIC VOCABULARY
credit the sum of money provided by a lender

Women on the Home Front

Women took over family farms and businesses while the men were away at war. These northern women (right) are part of a local militia, prepared to defend themselves against southern invaders. *The Return to Fredericksburg after the Battle* (far right) shows southern life during the war. ***What does the painting show about the effects of the war on the home front?***

and limited national power for which southerners were fighting. A Texas senator defended the draft against such complaints.

❝The enemy are in portions of almost every state in the Confederacy...We need a large army. How are you going to get it?...No man has any individual rights, which come into conflict with the welfare of the country.❞

—Louis T. Wigfall, 1862

Many southerners found little comfort in this reasoning. A North Carolina soldier observed that "when we hear men comparing the despotism [unlimited power] of the *Confederacy* with that of the Lincoln government —*something must be wrong.*"

The governors of Georgia and North Carolina did not support the draft and attempted to block it in their states. The draft's exemption of slaveholders also provided reasons for soldiers to desert. Many agreed with a poor farmer who deserted because he would not be forced "to fight for the rich men while they were at home having a good time."

Groups of draft evaders and deserters blocked Confederate government authority in some regions of the South. Government officials placed some areas under martial law to restore order.

Copperheads and the Union draft

Although northerners did not suffer the supply shortages that southerners did, they experienced some of the other problems that plagued the South. When the Union needed more soldiers in March 1863, it also turned to the draft to find them.

Like the Confederate draft law, the Union law allowed men who could afford to do so to hire substitutes to fight in their place. In addition, those drafted could be excused by paying a $300 fee. This amount was more than seven months' wages for the average worker. As in the South, northern critics accused the draft of turning the war into a poor man's fight.

Antidraft riots erupted across the North. The worst took place in New York City in July 1863. For four days, mobs attacked draft offices and African Americans. Shouting, "There goes a $300 man," rioters even attacked well-dressed white men. The violence left more than 100 people dead.

The draft fueled an antiwar movement that had already emerged in the North. Opposition to the war was led by some members of the Democratic Party in Congress and in several state legislatures. Their supporters referred to them as Peace Democrats. Critics called them **Copperheads**, comparing them to the poisonous snake of the same name.

Copperhead newspapers called on Union troops to desert. "It is to emancipate slaves . . . that you are used as soldiers," an Iowa newspaper wrote. "Are you, as soldiers, bound by patriotism, duty, or loyalty to fight in such a cause?" These tactics seriously threatened the war effort. As a result, the federal government arrested and jailed without trials some of the most vocal critics who opposed the war, the draft, or emancipation.

These government actions were possible because in September 1862 and again a year later Lincoln suspended **habeas corpus** across the entire country. Habeas corpus is the constitutional right of an arrested person to appear in court charged with a crime. Lincoln also suspended habeas corpus in specific places at other times during the war. He justified his actions by saying that he was willing to violate the Constitution in order to save the nation. During the war, tens of thousands of people were arrested for opposing government policy.

Mary WALKER
1832–1919

Born into an abolition- ist family, Mary Edwards Walker was encouraged by her father to pursue an education. In 1855 she graduated from Syracuse Medical College, the only woman doctor in her class.

When the Civil War began, Walker tried to join the Union army but was denied a position as a medical officer. She managed to serve as an unpaid assistant surgeon, becoming the first woman surgeon in the U.S. Army. Walker worked as a field surgeon near the Union front lines for almost two years. She earned the Congressional Medal of Honor for her wartime service—the only woman to be so honored.

Make Inferences How did Walker show her support for the Union?

Women in the Civil War Women in the North and South contributed to the war in many ways. Several hundred disguised them- selves as men and enlisted in the army. A few served as spies. Most women, however, filled less dramatic but more important roles. Women on both sides took over farms, plantations, stores, and other businesses while their fathers, hus- bands, and sons served in armies. They worked as bankers and steamboat captains. Northern women produced huge amounts of food with the help of new farm equipment such as the McCormick reaper.

The need for clothes, shoes, and other supplies created about 100,000 jobs for women in northern factories. Women also worked in the South's few factories, and women on both sides performed dangerous work making ammunition for the troops.

Women formed thousands of societies to gather and send supplies to their armies. They made bandages, shirts, and bedclothes for soldiers. After the war hundreds of female teachers went south to educate former slaves.

Many women found new occupations. Hundreds were hired by the Union government as clerks. They became the first women to hold federal government jobs. Women also staffed government offices in the South. Like clerical work, nursing was a man's job before the war. During the war, however, about 3,000 women served the Union army as paid nurses.

Some women, like **Clara Barton**, who later founded the American Red Cross, cared for the wounded on the battlefield. Thousands of female volunteers worked on hospital ships or in hospitals behind the lines. In the South women nurses served as volunteers at first. In 1862 the Confederate Congress passed a law permitting women to be hired as army nurses.

READING CHECK **Comparing and Contrasting** What similarities and differences existed in conscription in the North and South?

SECTION 3 ASSESSMENT

go.hrw.com
Online Quiz
Keyword: SD7 HP11

Reviewing Ideas, Terms, and People

1. **a. Recall** What is **emancipation**?
   b. Predict How do you think the **Emancipation Proclamation** will affect people's attitudes toward the war?

2. **a. Describe** Who were **freedmen**?
   b. Make Inferences Why do you think the Union army did not accept African American volunteers at first?

3. **a. Identify** What did most Civil War soldiers die from?
   b. Draw Conclusions What do you think Union leaders hoped to accomplish by ending prisoner exchanges?
   c. Predict How could camp conditions have been improved for soldiers?

4. **a. Describe** What is **habeas corpus**, and what role did it play in the Civil War?
   b. Analyze Why was the war often called a poor man's fight?
   c. Elaborate How did the war change some women's lives?

Critical Thinking

5. **Identifying Points of View** Review your notes on the Emancipation Proclamation. Then copy the graphic organizer below and use it to identify reasons people supported or opposed the Emancipation Proclamation.

Reasons to Oppose the Emancipation Proclamation	Reasons to Support the Emancipation Proclamation

FOCUS ON WRITING

6. **Narrative** Suppose that you live in either the North or the South during the Civil War. Write a diary entry that describes your life and experiences on the home front and your feelings about the war.

American *Literature*

ST 3.2 Draw upon literary selections, historical documents, and accounts to analyze the roles played by different individuals and groups during the major eras in New York State and United States history.

Louisa May Alcott (1832–1888)

About the Reading Louisa May Alcott is most commonly known for writing *Little Women* (1868–69). When the Civil War began, Alcott volunteered as a nurse until she contracted typhoid and was sent home. *Hospital Sketches* (1863) is a published collection of letters from her time as a nurse and was one of her first significantly recognized works.

AS YOU READ **Consider how difficult it must have been for hospital staff to care for injured soldiers under such poor conditions.**

Excerpt from

Hospital Sketches

by Louisa May Alcott

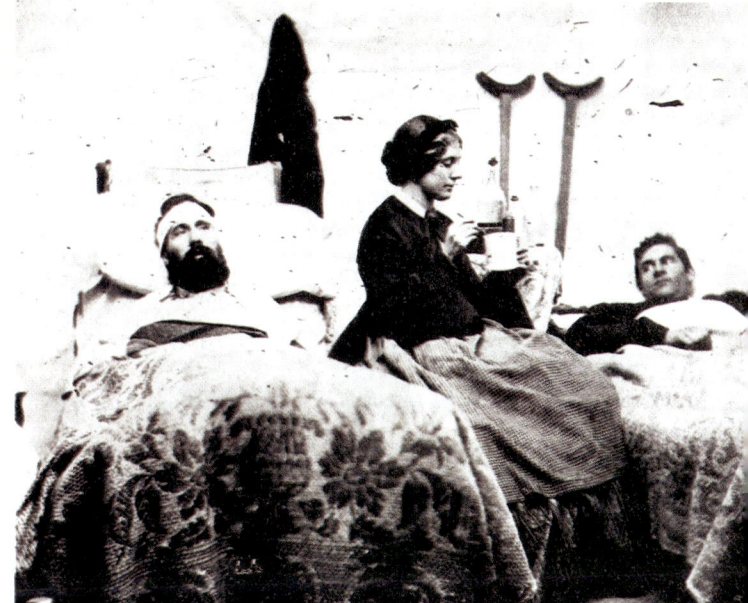

Nurse Ann Bell tends to wounded soldiers in a federal hospital in Nashville, Tennessee.

In they came, some on stretchers, some in men's arms, some feebly staggering along propped on rude crutches, and one lay stark and still with covered face, as a comrade gave his name to be recorded before they carried him away to the dead house. All was hurry and confusion; the hall was full of these wrecks of humanity, for the most exhausted could not reach a bed till duly ticketed and registered; the walls were lined with rows of such as could sit, the floor covered with the more disabled, the steps and doorways filled with helpers and lookers on; the sound of many feet and voices made that usually quiet hour as noisy as noon; and, in the midst of it all, the matron's motherly face brought more comfort to many a poor soul, than the cordial draughts she administered, or the cheery words that welcomed all, making of the hospital a home.

The sight of several stretchers, each with its legless, armless, or desperately wounded occupant, entering my ward, admonished me that I was there to work, not to wonder or weep; so I corked up my feelings, and returned to the path of duty, which was rather a "hard road to travel" just then. The house had been a hotel before hospitals were needed, and many of the doors still bore their old names; some not so inappropriate as might be imagined, for that ward was

in truth a *ballroom,* if gun-shot wounds could christen it. Forty beds were prepared, many already tenanted by tired men who fell down anywhere, and drowsed till the smell of food roused them. Round the great stove was gathered the dreariest group I ever saw—ragged, gaunt and pale, mud to the knees, with bloody bandages untouched since put on days before; many bundled up in blankets, coats being lost or useless; and all wearing the disheartened look which proclaimed defeat. . .

Skills FOCUS READING LIKE A HISTORIAN

1. **Making Inferences** What critical role did women play during the Civil War?

2. **Literature as Historical Evidence** What inferences can be made from the excerpt about the Union army and the conditions under which soldiers fought?

See **Skills Handbook**, p. H32

SECTION 4 — The War Continues

BEFORE YOU READ

MAIN IDEA

Important fighting occurred in all sections of the country as well as at sea.

READING FOCUS

1. In what ways was the war at sea an important part of the Civil War?
2. What were each side's goals in the West, and how were events there influenced by the rest of the war?
3. What three major battles took place in 1863, and why was each important?
4. Why was the fighting around Chattanooga, Tennessee, important to the outcome of the war?

KEY TERMS AND PEOPLE

Trent affair
Battle of Glorieta Pass
Battle of Pea Ridge
Stand Watie
Battle of Chancellorsville
George Meade
Battle of Gettysburg
James Longstreet
Pickett's Charge
Battle of Chickamauga

 PI 3.2 Research and analyze the major themes and developments in New York State and United States history (e.g., colonization and settlement; Revolution and New National Period; immigration; expansion and reform era; Civil War and Reconstruction; the American labor movement; Great Depression; World Wars; contemporary United States).

 **THE INSIDE STORY**

Why did a war hero become a scapegoat? It was no secret that Confederate leaders planned to send two of their number to Europe to seek British and French recognition of southern independence. So when a boat carrying James Mason and John Slidell slipped past the Union blockade of Charleston, South Carolina, in October 1861, the U.S. Navy was embarrassed. Reaching Cuba, the two men then boarded the *Trent*, a British ship bound for England. Captain Charles Wilkes, commander of the U.S. warship *San Jacinto*, decided to redeem the navy's honor. On November 8, even though he had no specific order to do so, Wilkes stopped the unarmed *Trent* at sea and seized Mason and Slidell.

Wilkes's action made him a hero in the North. Congress voted him a commendation. However, Britain demanded that Mason and Slidell be released. When Lincoln hesitated, the British government sent troops to Canada. Facing the prospect of war with Britain, Lincoln allowed the two Confederates to resume their journey. "One war at a time," the president explained. His advisers, however, did not want the United States to be humiliated by appearing to give in to a British threat. A way was found to save the nation's honor. Captain Wilkes, the recent national hero, was court-martialed for what now was labeled his great misdeed. ■

One War at a Time

◀ **A Union warship chases a Confederate blockade runner.**

The Civil War at Sea

As the *Trent* affair illustrates, the Civil War was a world event. The war's most obvious international impact was its effect on trade. In particular, the Union's naval blockade disrupted the South's trade with the rest of the world.

Blockade runners At the beginning of the war, slipping through, or "running," the Union blockade was fairly easy. Once the Union navy obtained more ships, however, the blockade became tighter and tighter. By the summer of 1862, Union warships guarded most southern ports.

To get supplies from overseas, the South depended on ships known as blockade runners. Blockade runners were built for speed. They were low, sleek vessels painted gray to make them less visible. To make the vessels even harder to see, attempts to run the blockade often took place at night, without lights. Many blockade runners burned anthracite coal for fuel, which produces no smoke.

When leaving the South, these ships were packed full of cotton. They brought this valuable material to Bermuda, the Bahamas, or Cuba, where it was unloaded and shipped to Europe. On the return trip, the blockade runners carried silk, soap, pepper, and other goods that brought high prices in the South. Later in the war, when supplies in the South were desperately low, the Confederate government required that blockade runners be at least half full of medicine, food, and military supplies.

The scarcity of many goods in the South meant that prices were high, and successful blockade runners could make enormous profits. A ship that ran the blockade could pay for itself in just one round trip. A captain could earn $5,000 in gold and a crew member $250 for the voyage. Crew members were often British citizens because, if captured, they were quickly released. Confederates who were captured trying to run the blockade faced long prison terms.

The *Monitor* and the *Merrimack* The Confederates could run the Union blockade, but they hoped to destroy it. To do so, they created a powerful ironclad ship by repairing the damaged USS *Merrimack*, which they had captured. Then they covered it with thick iron plates for armor and renamed it the *Virginia*.

When word reached the North that the Confederates were building the *Virginia*, Union officials hurried to complete their own seagoing ironclad, which they had been building in New York. On March 9, 1862, the Union's ironclad *Monitor* arrived off the Virginia coast to confront the *Virginia*.

The two ships fought for hours in the world's first battle between ironclads. Neither was able to seriously damage the other, but engine problems forced the *Virginia* to return to port. Although the battle had no winner, it changed naval warfare forever. In May the Confederates destroyed the *Virginia* to prevent its capture by McClellan's invading Union army.

Confederate raiders Unable to match the Union navy's strength, the South turned to unconventional tactics to battle the North at sea. Confederate leaders paid for the construction of 29 commerce raider ships in Europe. These vessels then roamed the world's oceans attacking Union merchant ships and disrupting the North's foreign trade.

The most famous of the Confederate commerce raiders was the CSS *Alabama*. Launched from Britain in May 1862, the *Alabama* terrorized Union shipping across the Atlantic and Pacific oceans. It was finally caught and sunk by the USS *Kearsarge* off the coast of France in June 1864. By that time, however, the *Alabama* had done enormous damage to Union trade. It captured 68 northern merchant ships during its 22 months at sea. Another of the raiders, the *Shenandoah*, captured 36 vessels.

READING CHECK **Summarizing** How did the South try to overcome the North's advantages at sea?

The War in the West

While the most important battles of the Civil War took place east of the Mississippi River, Union and Confederate forces clashed to the west of the Mississippi as well. About 90 engagements were fought in the West.

California and the territories Congress admitted Kansas to the Union as a free state in 1861 and quickly added the Dakota, Colorado, and Nevada territories as well. Between 1862 and 1864 Congress created the Idaho, Arizona, and Montana territories. Lincoln appointed pro-Union officials to head each of the new territorial governments. These actions were intended to secure the West for the Union.

To help further ensure western loyalty, Lincoln did not enforce the draft in the West or pressure the region for volunteers. Nevertheless, some 17,000 Californians joined the Union army. The state's main contribution, however, was its gold. Mines in California and in the new territories provided vast amounts of gold and silver, which helped the Union pay the costs of fighting the war.

Because the need for soldiers in the East was so great, few Union troops were available to defend the West. In early 1862 about 4,000 Confederate troops in Texas marched north.

The Confederates' goal was to conquer the lightly defended Union territories and capture their valuable mines.

Union troops and volunteers from California, Colorado, and Kansas stopped the Confederate invasion in the **Battle of Glorieta Pass** in northern New Mexico on March 28, 1862. The Confederates actually won the day-long battle. Some Colorado soldiers, however, slipped around the Confederate army during the fighting and destroyed the Confederate supply wagons. The loss of their supplies forced the invaders back to Texas. Their retreat secured the West for the Union.

Native Americans and the war More than 10,000 Native Americans took part in the Civil War. Many Cherokees fought for the Confederacy, but the war bitterly divided the Cherokees—and other nations as well—over issues of loyalty and slavery.

Some nations saw the transfer of soldiers from western forts to eastern battlefields as a chance to take back land they had lost. In 1862, for example, Sioux in Minnesota and Dakota Territory began a revolt.

When the Union moved its soldiers from Indian Territory to the East, Confederate agents soon arrived. They negotiated treaties with the Cherokees, Creeks, Choctaws, Chickasaws, and several smaller tribes. These four tribes, with aid from the Seminoles, raised about 5,000 Indian troops for the Confederate army.

Despite the treaties, most Cherokees, Creeks, and Seminoles supported the Union. Some of them tried to escape to Kansas but were attacked by Confederate Indian troops and Texas cavalry. In Kansas, Union officers organized the survivors and other Native Americans into two regiments.

About 1,000 Native Americans were among the 14,000 Confederates who took part in the war's biggest battle west of the Mississippi. This was the **Battle of Pea Ridge**, which occurred in Arkansas in March 1862. Although the Union army won the battle, Indian troops commanded by Cherokee leader **Stand Watie** fought bravely. Watie was later promoted to general, the only Native American on either side to hold this rank in the war.

Victory at the Battle of Pea Ridge helped the Union's plan to conquer the Mississippi River valley. It also exposed Indian Territory to attack. In June 1862 and again in 1863, Union Indians and other troops invaded Indian Territory and defeated the Confederate Indians. Many Indians then abandoned their treaty with the South and pledged loyalty to the Union. Watie, however, continued to resist. He waged a guerrilla campaign for the rest of the war. In fact, Watie was the last Confederate general to surrender when the war ended.

READING CHECK **Identifying Problems and Solutions** Why would some Indians have viewed the war as an opportunity and have sided with the South?

Three Major Battles

After being crushed at the Battle of Fredericksburg in December 1862, the Union Army of the Potomac was ready to fight again by spring. General Joseph Hooker was now in command.

The Battle of Chancellorsville Leaving 40,000 men at Fredericksburg to keep Confederate General Robert E. Lee's attention, Hooker moved more than 70,000 troops west and then south across the Rappahannock River, hoping to surprise the Confederates from behind.

Lee expected this and marched 40,000 soldiers west. He ordered the 10,000 troops he left in Fredericksburg to light many campfires at night so Union forces would think a much larger army was still there. Then Lee divided his army again and sent Stonewall Jackson and about 30,000 troops on a daylong march around Hooker's army to attack its right side. At 6 p.m. on May 2, 1863, Jackson's troops charged out of the woods at Hooker's troops as they cooked dinner in their camps, near a crossroads named Chancellorsville. The attack was a complete surprise. If darkness had not halted the fighting, the Union army might have been destroyed.

Battle of Chancellorsville

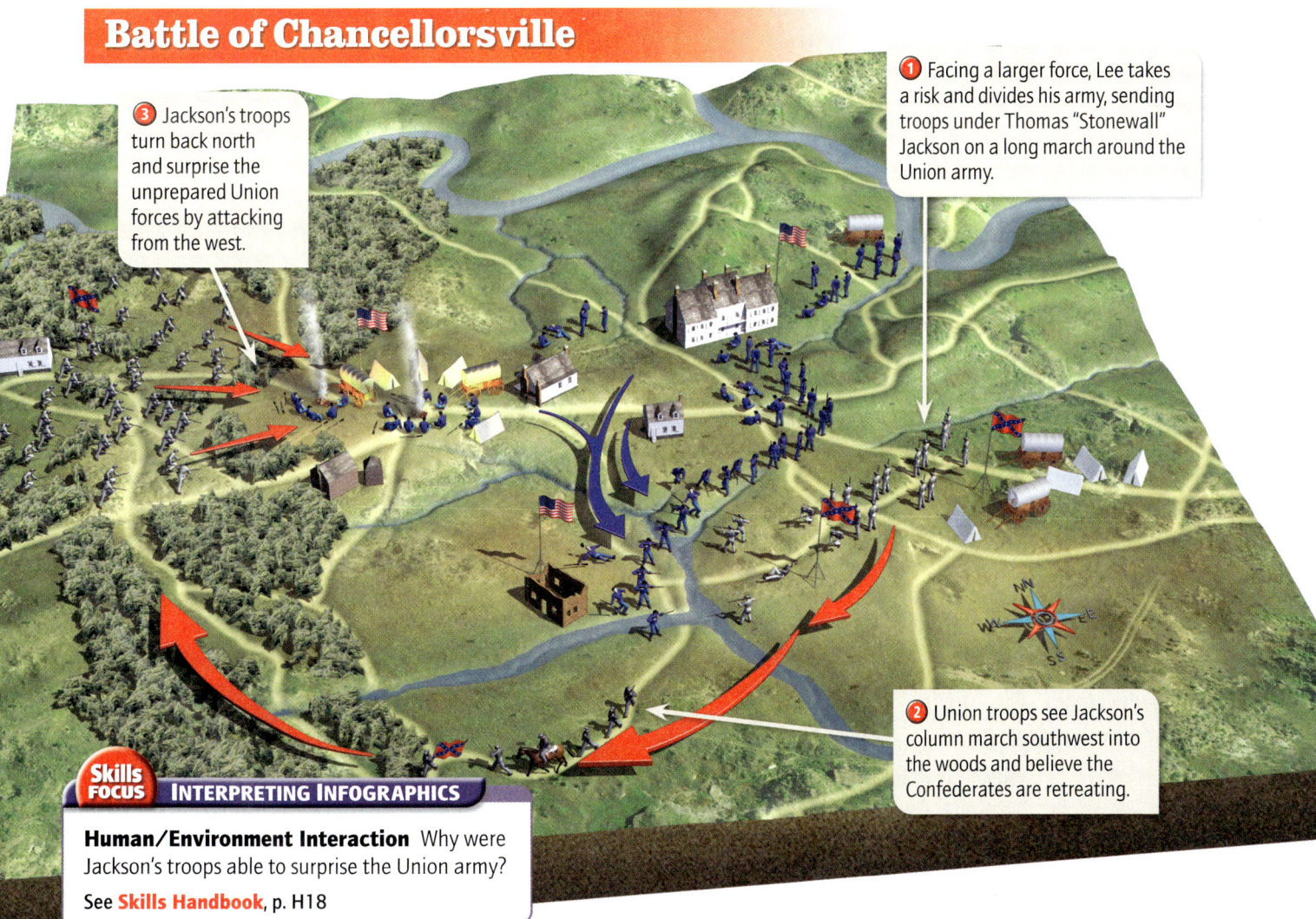

3 Jackson's troops turn back north and surprise the unprepared Union forces by attacking from the west.

1 Facing a larger force, Lee takes a risk and divides his army, sending troops under Thomas "Stonewall" Jackson on a long march around the Union army.

2 Union troops see Jackson's column march southwest into the woods and believe the Confederates are retreating.

Skills FOCUS **INTERPRETING INFOGRAPHICS**

Human/Environment Interaction Why were Jackson's troops able to surprise the Union army?

See **Skills Handbook**, p. H18

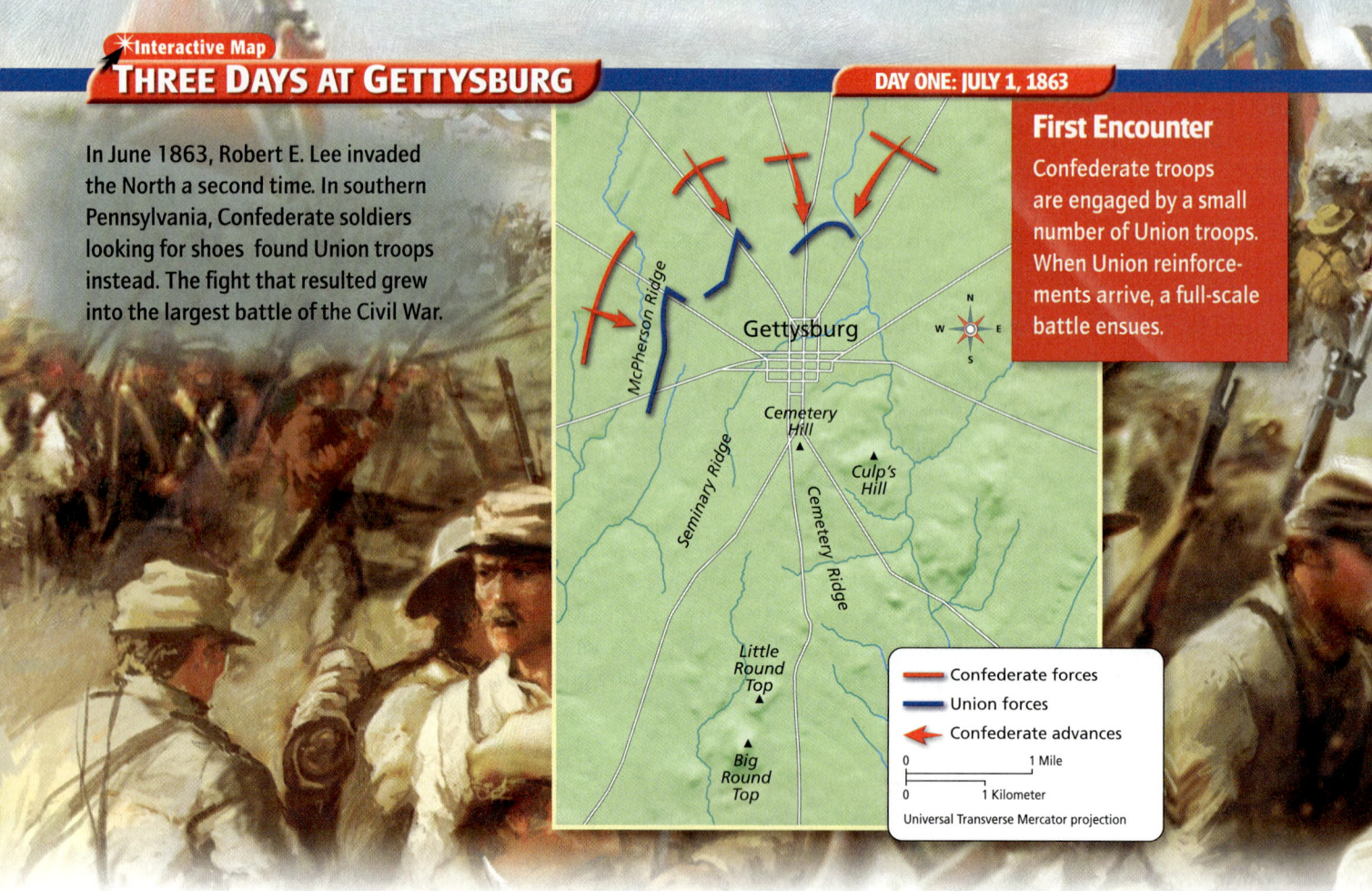

In June 1863, Robert E. Lee invaded the North a second time. In southern Pennsylvania, Confederate soldiers looking for shoes found Union troops instead. The fight that resulted grew into the largest battle of the Civil War.

DAY ONE: JULY 1, 1863

First Encounter

Confederate troops are engaged by a small number of Union troops. When Union reinforcements arrive, a full-scale battle ensues.

McPherson Ridge

Gettysburg

Seminary Ridge

Cemetery Hill

Culp's Hill

Cemetery Ridge

Little Round Top

Big Round Top

⬛ Confederate forces
⬛ Union forces
⬅ Confederate advances

0   1 Mile
0   1 Kilometer
Universal Transverse Mercator projection

The **Battle of Chancellorsville** lasted two more days. Then on May 5 Hooker retreated, having suffered more than 17,000 casualties. Lee lost nearly 13,000 men. Among them was Stonewall Jackson, the man Lee called his "strong right arm." Jackson was mistakenly shot by his own troops as he returned from scouting enemy lines on the first night of the battle. On May 10 he died from his wounds.

Chancellorsville was Lee's greatest and most brilliant victory. Defeating a force about twice its size lifted the spirits of his army. In the North, morale sank even lower. The antiwar Copperheads pointed to Chancellorsville as proof that the war could not be won.

For these reasons and others, Lee decided the time was right to invade the North again. The Union blockade and the South's shortages were beginning to seriously weaken his army. He hoped a major victory on Union soil would cause the North to finally quit the war.

The Battle of Gettysburg
In June 1863 Lee marched his army north. Hooker's army moved too, keeping itself between the enemy

force and Washington, D.C. However, Hooker did not try to block the Confederates from entering Union territory on June 24. Convinced that Hooker was as indecisive as McClellan, Lincoln replaced him with General **George Meade**.

Meanwhile, a Confederate general learned about a supply of shoes rumored to be in the nearby town of Gettysburg, Pennsylvania. His troops desperately needed shoes. On July 1 he ordered some soldiers into the town to locate and seize the shoes. There they came upon Union cavalry units who were looking for Lee's army. The skirmish that took place developed into the largest battle ever fought in North America, the three-day **Battle of Gettysburg**.

When the fighting began, both sides rushed reinforcements to Gettysburg. By early afternoon about 24,000 Confederate and 19,000 Union troops were involved. When the day ended, the southerners had pushed the Union army back onto some hills south of the town.

That night Lee and Meade arrived. General **James Longstreet** had become Lee's most trusted commander after Jackson's death. Longstreet warned Lee that the Union positions were too

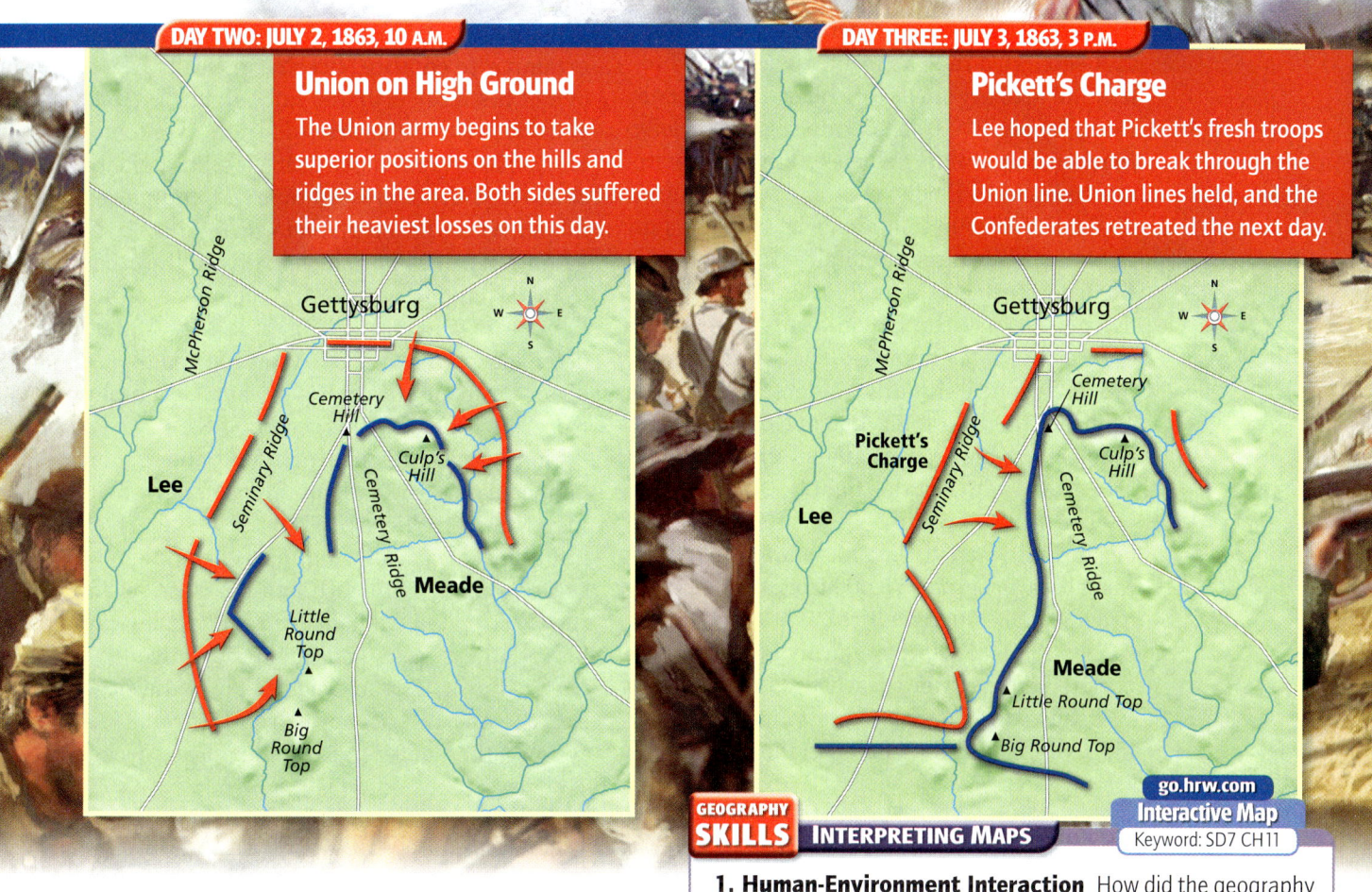

DAY TWO: JULY 2, 1863, 10 A.M.

Union on High Ground

The Union army begins to take superior positions on the hills and ridges in the area. Both sides suffered their heaviest losses on this day.

Gettysburg

McPherson Ridge

Cemetery Hill

Culp's Hill

Seminary Ridge

Lee

Cemetery Ridge

Meade

Little Round Top

Big Round Top

DAY THREE: JULY 3, 1863, 3 P.M.

Pickett's Charge

Lee hoped that Pickett's fresh troops would be able to break through the Union line. Union lines held, and the Confederates retreated the next day.

Gettysburg

McPherson Ridge

Cemetery Hill

Pickett's Charge

Culp's Hill

Seminary Ridge

Lee

Cemetery Ridge

Meade

Little Round Top

Big Round Top

GEOGRAPHY SKILLS INTERPRETING MAPS

go.hrw.com
Interactive Map
Keyword: SD7 CH11

1. **Human-Environment Interaction** How did the geography of the area play a role in the battle?
2. **Movement** Trace the mounting severity of the conflict from July 1 to July 2. What were the Confederate and Union strategies? Who had the advantage by July 3? Explain.

See **Skills Handbook**, p. H18

strong to attack. He urged Lee to retreat, make the Union army chase him, and fight the battle on ground of his own choosing.

After Chancellorsville, however, Lee had great confidence in his army. "The enemy is there and I intend to attack him there," he said, pointing to the Union lines. "If he is there, it will be because he is anxious that we should attack him," Longstreet replied, "a good reason, in my judgment, for not doing so." Ignoring this warning, Lee ordered an attack the next day.

July 2 saw some of the bloodiest fighting of the entire war. Confederate troops broke through Union defenses and tried to seize Little Round Top, an undefended hill just south of the Union's lines. The 20th Maine regiment rushed to the hill in time for a heroic defense. The day's fighting cost the Confederates some 9,000 casualties, but Lee was determined not to leave Pennsylvania without a victory. He ordered 15,000 fresh troops to attack the center of the Union lines on Cemetery Ridge the next day.

Longstreet objected. Again Lee would not be persuaded. The next day a great artillery duel took place as the Confederates tried to soften up the Union defenses for the assault. The thunder of the guns was heard in Pittsburgh, some 200 miles away.

Then in mid-afternoon, the guns fell silent. Longstreet was with one of his officers, General George Pickett, when the order came to attack. Pickett later recalled their exchange.

HISTORY'S VOICES

"He looked at me for a moment, then held out his hand. Presently clasping his other hand over mine without speaking, he bowed his head...I saw tears glistening on his cheeks and beard. The stern old war-horse, God bless him, was weeping for his men."

—General George Pickett in a letter to his fiancée

Then Pickett's troops, a line of soldiers a mile wide and three rows deep, began marching toward the Union positions a mile away. As the Confederates moved across the open field that separated the two armies, a storm of bullets and artillery shells tore huge holes in their ranks. About 300 Confederate soldiers briefly reached the Union defenses, but they were driven back or killed.

Of the 15,000 soldiers who carried out **Pickett's Charge**, less than half returned to the Confederate lines. Lee told Pickett to ready his division in case the Union army launched a counterattack. "General Lee, I have no division," Pickett replied. Finally understanding the extent of the slaughter, Lee apologized as he rode among his troops. "It's all my fault," he said. "It is I who lost this fight."

The next day, July 4, the Confederates began their retreat. Lee had suffered 28,000 casualties among his 75,000 troops. The Union had about 23,000 casualties out of some 85,000 soldiers. As Lee's battered army made its way back to Virginia, word reached Richmond that Vicksburg, the Confederate stronghold on the Mississippi River, had fallen to the Union.

The Siege of Vicksburg After several attempts to capture Vicksburg, Grant began one of his most brilliant campaigns. In April 1863 he marched his army down the west bank of the Mississippi River past Vicksburg. South of the city, Grant crossed the river and moved inland, where he fought and won five battles in 17 days. Then in May, having driven the other Confederate forces from the region, he began a siege to starve Vicksburg and its 32,000 defenders into surrender. (You can read more about Vicksburg in the History and Geography feature that follows this section.)

For weeks, Grant's artillery and Union gunboats on the river kept up a constant shelling of the city. Vicksburg's citizens dug caves into the sides of hills and moved into them to escape the rain of death and destruction. As they exhausted their food supplies, they ate horses, mules, dogs, and rats to stay alive.

On July 4, the forty-eighth day of the siege and the day Lee began his retreat from Gettysburg, the Confederate commander at Vicks-

---

The Gettysburg Address

Lincoln made this speech to dedicate a cemetery for the soldiers killed in the Battle of Gettysburg. He used the occasion to remind a war-weary nation why it was fighting.

Fourscore and seven years ago our fathers brought forth on this continent a new nation, conceived in liberty and dedicated to the proposition that all men are created equal.

Now we are engaged in a great civil war, testing whether that nation or any nation so conceived and so dedicated can long endure. We are met on a great battlefield of that war. We have come to dedicate a portion of it as a final resting place for those who died here that the nation might live. It is altogether fitting and proper that we should do this.

But, in a larger sense, we can not dedicate—we can not consecrate—we can not hallow—this ground. The brave men, living and dead, who struggled here, have consecrated it, far above our poor power to add or detract. The world will little note nor long remember what we say here, but it can never forget what they did here.

It is for us the living, rather, to be dedicated here to the unfinished work which they who fought here have thus far so nobly advanced. It is rather for us to be here dedicated to the great task remaining before us—that from these honored dead we take increased devotion to that cause for which they here gave the last full measure of devotion—that we here highly resolve that these dead shall not have died in vain, that this nation shall have a new birth of freedom, and that government of the people, by the people, for the people shall not perish from the earth.

Skills FOCUS **READING LIKE A HISTORIAN**

1. **Analyzing Primary Sources** For what reason does Lincoln say the Union is fighting the war?
2. **Identifying Points of View** How does he connect the soldiers' deaths to the need to continue the war?

See **Skills Handbook**, pp. H28–H29

burg surrendered the city and his army of 31,000 troops to Grant. Four days later, Port Hudson, Louisiana, the last Confederate fort on the Mississippi River, also surrendered to Union forces.

READING CHECK **Identifying Cause and Effect** What set of events led to the huge, three-day Battle of Gettysburg?

The Chattanooga Campaign

The losses at Gettysburg, Vicksburg, and Port Hudson plunged southerners into gloom. Their spirits improved only slightly when a Confederate army led by General Braxton Bragg won a major victory at the **Battle of Chickamauga** in northwest Georgia in September 1863. The battle resulted from a Union campaign to capture Chattanooga, an important railroad center on the Georgia-Tennessee border.

General William Rosecrans, the Union commander, had lured the Confederate army out of Chattanooga, planning to destroy it on open ground. Instead, it was the Union army that was nearly destroyed. As the Union soldiers retreated, they found the Confederates had left the road to Chattanooga unprotected. This allowed the Union army to flee to the very city it hoped to capture. By the time Bragg pursued

them, Union troops were ready to defend the city. Bragg's forces dug in on the hills around Chattanooga and tried to starve them out.

In late October, Grant arrived and opened a supply line to feed the Union troops trapped in Chattanooga. By late November 1863, he had gathered enough troops to end the Confederate siege. In the Battle of Lookout Mountain and the Battle of Missionary Ridge, his forces drove the Confederates from their positions overlooking the city. A northern journalist described the Union attack on Missionary Ridge.

HISTORY'S VOICES

❝They creep up [the mountain], hand over hand, loading and firing, and wavering and halting… Plunging shot tear away comrades on left and right…but our brave mountaineers are clambering steadily on.❞

—B.F. Taylor, November 25, 1863

These victories gave the Union forces control of Chattanooga, an important first step in Grant's plan to invade Georgia, the heart of the Lower South. Southerners were also aware of what the battles meant. "Unless something is done," one Confederate official wrote, "we are irretrievably [hopelessly] gone."

READING CHECK **Identifying Main Idea and Details** What did the Union hope to accomplish in the Battle of Chickamauga, and with what result?

THE IMPACT TODAY

Culture
Chickamauga was the first Civil War battlefield to become a national park, earning that designation in 1890. Gettysburg became a national park in 1895.

SECTION 4 ASSESSMENT

go.hrw.com
Online Quiz
Keyword: SD7 HP11

Reviewing Ideas, Terms, and People

1. a. Identify What was the *Trent* affair?
b. Draw Conclusions How did the battle between the *Monitor* and the *Virginia* change naval warfare?

2. a. Describe How did Lincoln encourage loyalty to the Union in the West?
b. Elaborate What factors might have influenced Native Americans to choose a side in the war?

3. a. Recall Why did Lee decide to invade the North in 1863?
b. Draw Conclusions Why were Vicksburg and Port Hudson important locations?
c. Evaluate Do you agree that Lee was responsible for the loss of the **Battle of Gettysburg**? Why or why not?

4. a. Identify Who was Braxton Bragg?
b. Make Inferences Why was control of Chattanooga important to the North?
c. Elaborate By the end of 1863, what was the general feeling about the war in the South? Why?

Critical Thinking

5. Comparing and Contrasting Review your notes on major Civil War battles. Then copy the graphic organizer below and use it to identify similarities and differences between them.

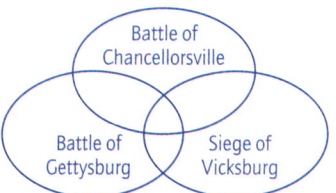

Battle of Chancellorsville

Battle of Gettysburg   Siege of Vicksburg

FOCUS ON WRITING

6. Descriptive Suppose you are a newspaper reporter who has witnessed one of the major battles discussed in this section. Write a news story that provides an account of the battle for readers in either the North or the South.

The Battle for Vicksburg

"Vicksburg is the key!" President Abraham Lincoln told his generals and military advisers. "The war can never be brought to a close until that key is in our pocket." Vicksburg, Mississippi, controlled the movement of supplies on the Mississippi River and was vital to keeping open the supply lines linking the Confederacy's eastern and western halves. The city was situated high above a hairpin bend in the river, and Union boats could not get by Confederate guns. Capturing Vicksburg would give the Union control of the Mississippi River and split the Confederacy. Beginning in the spring of 1863, General Ulysses S. Grant undertook this daunting task.

4. The Siege of Vicksburg, May 18–July 4

Grant's first two assaults on Vicksburg failed, forcing him to lay siege to the city and the 30,000 Confederate troops trapped inside. After six weeks of bombardment, the Confederates surrendered. Grant's bold campaign had given the Union control of the Mississippi River.

Vicksburg

1. Grant Crosses into Louisiana, March 29

Grant's original plan was to attack Vicksburg from the north. The swampy land, however, made the plan impossible. So Grant ordered his troops to cross the Mississippi River into Louisiana and to march south.

Mississippi River

Port Gibson

2. Grant Moves East, April 30

Union gunboats and transports moved Grant's forces back across the river into Mississippi. In a daring move Grant marched east without a supply line, allowing his troops to move quickly.

New York Standards

ST **4.3** Develop hypotheses about important events, eras, or issues; move from chronicling to explaining historical events and issues.

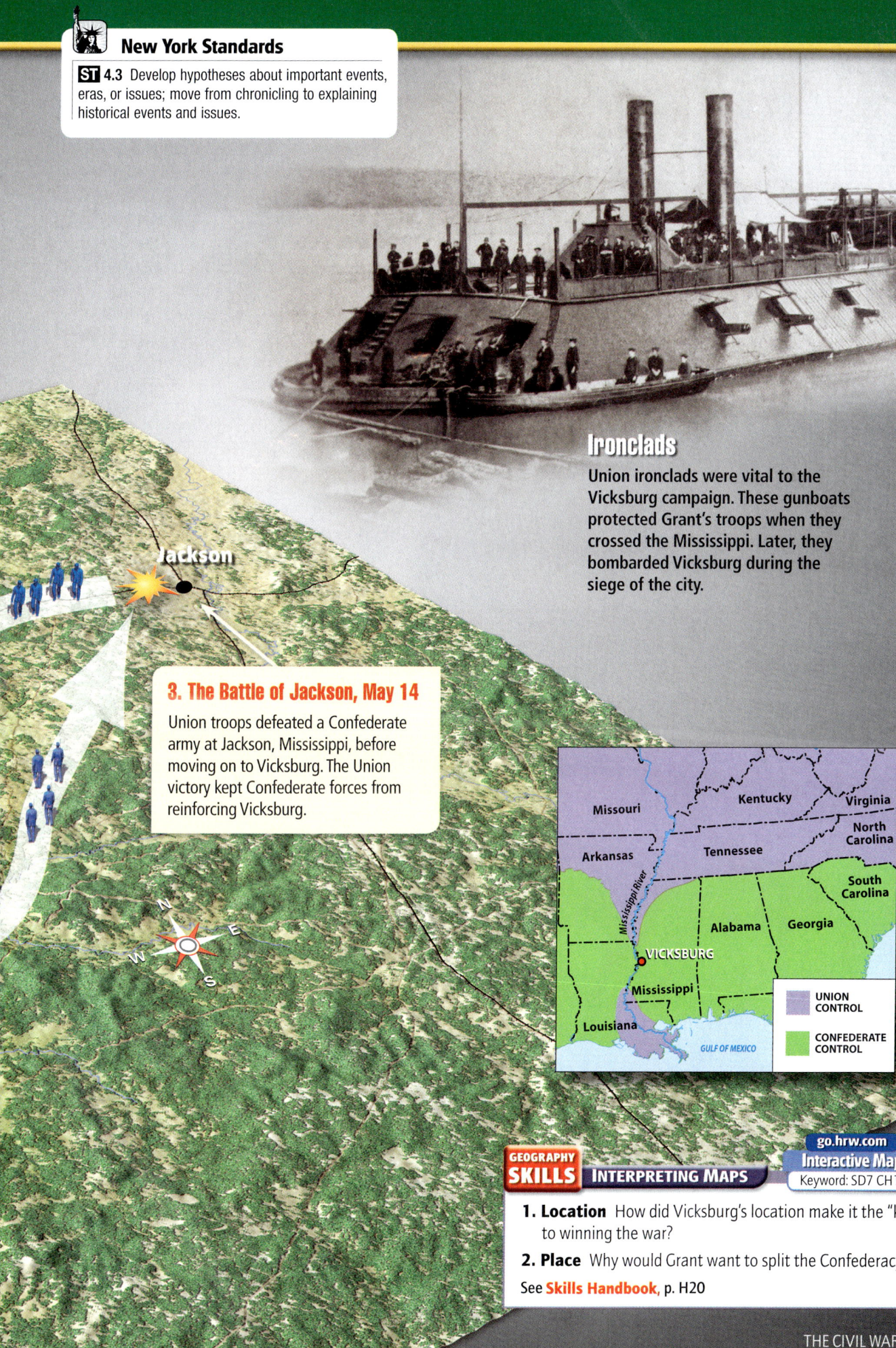

Ironclads

Union ironclads were vital to the Vicksburg campaign. These gunboats protected Grant's troops when they crossed the Mississippi. Later, they bombarded Vicksburg during the siege of the city.

Jackson

3. The Battle of Jackson, May 14

Union troops defeated a Confederate army at Jackson, Mississippi, before moving on to Vicksburg. The Union victory kept Confederate forces from reinforcing Vicksburg.

Missouri
Kentucky
Virginia
Arkansas
Tennessee
North Carolina
South Carolina
Mississippi River
VICKSBURG
Alabama
Georgia
Mississippi
Louisiana
GULF OF MEXICO

UNION CONTROL

CONFEDERATE CONTROL

GEOGRAPHY SKILLS **INTERPRETING MAPS**

go.hrw.com
Interactive Map
Keyword: SD7 CH11

1. Location How did Vicksburg's location make it the "key" to winning the war?

2. Place Why would Grant want to split the Confederacy?

See **Skills Handbook**, p. H20

BEFORE YOU READ

MAIN IDEA

Southerners continued to hope for victory in 1864, but military and political events caused those hopes to fade.

READING FOCUS

1. What tactics did Grant use against Lee to change the course of the war?
2. How did the election of 1864 affect Confederate hopes for victory in the Civil War?
3. How did the actions of Sherman and Grant help bring the war to an end?

KEY TERMS AND PEOPLE

William Tecumseh Sherman
Battle of the Wilderness
Battle of Spotsylvania
Battle of Cold Harbor
Battle of Atlanta
Thirteenth Amendment

PI 3.2 Research and analyze the major themes and developments in New York State and United States history (e.g., colonization and settlement; Revolution and New National Period; immigration; expansion and reform era; Civil War and Reconstruction; the American labor movement; Great Depression; World Wars; contemporary United States).

A CALL TO GREATNESS

THE INSIDE
STORY

Why was Grant viewed as a hero? The people in the lobby of Washington's Willard Hotel did not notice the short, rumpled man and the teenage boy as they checked in. However, the desk clerk snapped to attention as the man signed the guest register: "U.S. Grant and son, Galena, Illinois." Word spread quickly that the new head of all Union armies was in town. That evening Grant walked to the White House to call on the president, who happened to be holding a reception. Cheering erupted as the guests pushed forward to get a glimpse of the great general. Secretary of State Seward helped him stand on a sofa to be better seen.

Grant had shown absolutely no signs of greatness as a young man. His father had gotten him into West Point, hoping that a military career might provide a living for his unexceptional son. Grant left the army after the Mexican War, however, and then failed at farming, bill collecting, and even selling firewood on the streets of St. Louis. Finally, he went to work in his father's store in Galena, Illinois. Because he was Galena's only West Point graduate, the town put him in charge of raising volunteers when the Civil War began. Grant rejoined the army and never looked back. Now, less than three years later, as a reception guest noted, "The little, scared-looking man who stood on a crimson sofa was the idol of the hour."

◄ **The war revealed in Grant a talent for military leadership.**

Grant versus Lee

Ulysses S. Grant's victory over Confederate forces at Chattanooga in November 1863 convinced President Lincoln that the Union finally had a general who could crush the Confederates. In March 1864 Lincoln brought Grant to Washington and gave him command of all Union armies. Grant named one of his top officers, General **William Tecumseh Sherman**, to replace him as commander on the western front of the war.

Confederate leaders still had some hope for victory in 1864. It was a presidential election year in the North. If the South could hold out until the November election, northerners might be so tired of war that they would reject Lincoln. A new president might accept southern independence in return for peace. Robert E. Lee's plan was not necessarily to win battles but to make the cost of fighting so high for the North that Lincoln would lose the election.

Grant hoped to end the war before November. He knew that the South was running short of men and supplies. Grant told Sherman to attack the Confederate army that he was facing. "Break it up," Grant ordered, "and get into the interior of the enemy's country as far as you can, inflicting all the damage you can against their war resources."

The Wilderness and Spotsylvania

In May, Grant moved the Army of the Potomac toward Richmond. Almost at once, Lee's 61,000 troops forced about 100,000 Union soldiers into another battle near Chancellorsville. Fighting in the two-day **Battle of the Wilderness** was so fierce that the dense forest caught fire from the shooting. Many of the wounded were burned to death. Despite losses nearly twice as high as Lee's, Grant pushed south. His troops' spirits rose. For the first time, the Union army was staying on the attack after a battle.

Two days later, the armies of Grant and Lee met again in an 11-day series of clashes known as the **Battle of Spotsylvania**. The fiercest fighting took place on May 12, when Union troops attacked the strongest part of the Confederate defenses, a place that became known as the Bloody Angle. The two armies battled for some 20 hours in fighting so heavy that rifle fire cut down trees nearly two feet thick. A Union officer described the scene.

THE GENERALS

Ulysses S. Grant

- Graduated West Point in 1843
- Rank: 21 in a class of 39
- Age in May 1864: 42
- Previous major victories: Battle of Shiloh, Siege of Vicksburg, Battle of Lookout Mountain, Battle of Missionary Ridge
- Grant's wife was a cousin of Confederate general James Longstreet.

Robert E. Lee

- Graduated West Point in 1829
- Rank: 2 in a class of 46
- Age in May 1864: 57
- Previous major victories: Second Battle of Bull Run, Battle of Fredericksburg, Battle of Chancellorsville
- Lee's great uncle, Richard Henry Lee, proposed and signed the Declaration of Independence.

HISTORY'S VOICES

" Rank [a row of troops] after rank was riddled by shot and shell and bayonet thrusts, and finally sank, a mass of torn and mutilated corpses; then fresh troops rushed forward to replace the dead; and so the murderous work went on. **"**

—Colonel Horace Porter in *Voices of the Civil War*

Casualties were appalling. From May 5 to May 12, the Union army suffered 32,000 killed, wounded, or missing. Lee's losses totaled 18,000. Yet, the worst was to come.

Cold Harbor and Petersburg

Grant continued to push toward Richmond. In early June the armies fought yet again. In the first 30 minutes of fighting at the **Battle of Cold Harbor**, the charging Union soldiers suffered about 7,000 casualties. "It was not war," a Confederate general recalled later. "It was murder."

Following a month of marching and fighting, the Union army's high spirits were gone. Many soldiers at Cold Harbor pinned their names and addresses on their uniforms before the battle so their bodies could be more easily identified. "The men feel at present a great horror and dread of attacking earthworks [fortifications] again," one Union officer observed. So after failing to capture Petersburg, a rail center just south of Richmond, Grant began a siege of the

The Wilderness,
May 1864

Grant

Lee

Spotsylvania, May 1864

Cold Harbor, June 1864

VA

Richmond

Appomattox
Court House

Appomattox,
April 1865

Petersburg,
June 1864 – April 1865

Five Forks,
April 1865

NC

0   50 Miles
0   50 Kilometers

WI

MI

MD

DE

Washington, D.C.

WV

PA

NJ

40°N

OH

IN

MD

DE

Washington, D.C.

Richmond

WV

VA

APPALACHIAN MOUNTAINS

KY

TN

Nashville,
Dec. 1864

NC

Bentonville,
March 1865

Sherman

SC

Columbia,
Feb. 1865

Sherman

AR

Atlanta,
July 1864

Sherman

GA

Savannah,
Dec. 1864

MS

AL

MobileBay,
August 1864

Farragut

LA

Gulf of
Mexico

FL

ATLANTIC
OCEAN

30°N

N
W   E
S

90°W   85°W

Legend

- Union state
- Confederate state
- Union controlled
- ➤ Union forces
- ➤ Confederate forces
- ✦ Union victory
- ✦ Confederate victory
- ✦ No victor
- ➤➤ Union naval blockade

0   75   150 Miles
0   75   150 Kilometers
Albers equal-area projection

GEOGRAPHY SKILLS | **INTERPRETING MAPS**

go.hrw.com
Interactive Map
Keyword: SD7 CH11

General Sherman hoped to hasten the end of the war by destroying the Confederacy's economic base and crushing its citizens' spirits.

1. **Movement** Trace Sherman's path of destruction. How long did he wage his so-called total war?

2. **Region** About how many miles did Sherman's march cover?

See **Skills Handbook**, p. H19

city. He knew that if he prevented food from passing through Petersburg to the Confederate capital, Richmond eventually would have to surrender. Lee was content to dig in his troops and wait for the November election.

Sherman on the move As Grant pressured Lee's army in Virginia, the next phase of the war began when Sherman set out from Chattanooga on his long-expected invasion of Georgia. The Union army marched toward Atlanta, an important southern manufacturing and transportation center. About 60,000 Confederate troops, led by General Joseph Johnston, stood between Sherman's 100,000 troops and their objective. Johnston's army slowed Sherman's advance but could not stop it. By mid-July the Union army was just eight miles from the city.

At this point, President Jefferson Davis replaced Johnston with the more aggressive General John Hood. Hood attacked the Union army immediately. This was exactly what Sherman was hoping for. In the Battle of Peachtree Creek on July 20 and the **Battle of Atlanta** on July 22, Hood desperately threw his troops against the Union forces. The two battles cost him nearly a quarter of his army.

Hood pulled his weakened forces back behind Atlanta's defenses, hoping to hold out until the North's presidential election. Sherman laid siege to the city, shelling it daily with his artillery. Finally, he was able to close the last railroad line into Atlanta, forcing Hood's troops to abandon the city on September 1. The next day the Union army entered Atlanta. "Atlanta gone," Mary Chesnut wrote in her diary. "No hope. We will try to have no fear."

READING CHECK **Making Inferences** Why were Grant and Sherman eager for the armies opposing them to fight?

Confederate Hopes Fade

While Sherman was besieging Atlanta, the Democratic Party held its national convention in Chicago. The Democrats chose General George McClellan as their presidential candidate. They adopted a party platform that called for an immediate end to the war. Southerners found new hope in these events. Confederate vice president Alexander Stephens called them

"the first ray of real light I have seen since the war began." In South Carolina, the *Charleston Mercury* predicted that McClellan's election would "lead to peace and our independence."

The Republicans, hoping to broaden Lincoln's appeal, dropped Vice President Hannibal Hamlin of Maine from the ticket. In his place they chose Andrew Johnson, a pro-Union Democrat from Tennessee. Many believed it would not be enough. The Emancipation Proclamation and Grant's huge losses in Virginia had made the war highly unpopular in the North. "The people are wild for peace," a Republican Party leader reported. Lincoln himself expected to lose the election. "I am going to be beaten," he predicted gloomily, "and unless something changes, *badly* beaten."

Sherman's capture of Atlanta provided the change Lincoln hoped for. It allowed the president to defeat McClellan easily in the November election. Even soldiers in the Union army gave Lincoln a huge margin of victory. "We all want peace . . . but an *honorable* one," wrote one soldier, a Democrat, to explain why troops did not vote for the popular general.

Lincoln's victory also enabled Congress to pass the constitutional amendment that Republicans had been seeking since 1862. The **Thirteenth Amendment** to end slavery in the United States finally passed the House of Representatives on January 31, 1865. It was ratified by the states and became part of the Constitution in December 1865.

As Lincoln began his second term in March, the war seemed nearly over to all except the most die-hard secessionists. To those who called for harsh punishment of the South, Lincoln announced his intention to be forgiving.

HISTORY'S VOICES

❝With malice toward none, with charity for all, with firmness in the right as God gives us to see the right, let us strive on to finish the work we are in, to bind up the nation's wounds.❞
—Lincoln's Second Inaugural Address, March 4, 1865

Meanwhile, the task of completing what Lincoln called "the work we are in" continued on the battlefields as the long and bloody war entered its final phase.

READING CHECK **Identifying the Main Idea** Why did Confederate hopes for success in the war rise and then fall in 1864?

ACADEMIC VOCABULARY

phase a stage in a process of change or development

The War Comes to an End

One of Sherman's first acts after entering Atlanta in September 1864 was to force its citizens to leave the city. When Atlanta's mayor protested the harshness and cruelty of this order, the general replied:

HISTORY'S VOICES

❝War is cruelty, and you cannot refine it. And those who brought war into our country deserve all the curses…a people can pour out…The only way the people of Atlanta can hope once more to live in peace and quiet at home is to stop the war.❞

—William Tecumseh Sherman in *Voices of the Civil War*

THE IMPACT TODAY

Economics

In the decades following the Civil War, Atlantans rebuilt their ruined city into what today is the major commercial center of the South.

Sherman's March Sherman remained in Atlanta until after the November election. Then he set out with some 60,000 troops to march across Georgia and capture Savannah. As he abandoned Atlanta, his troops burned much of the city.

During Sherman's March to the Sea, the Union army cut a swath of destruction 300 miles long and 50 to 60 miles wide across the heart of Georgia. The soldiers slaughtered livestock, destroyed crops, tore up railroad tracks, and looted homes and businesses.

Sherman's tactics were designed to show that Union armies could now do as they wished in the South and that further resistance was hopeless. He also wanted to destroy food supplies needed by Lee's troops at Petersburg.

Arriving outside Savannah, Georgia, on December 10, Sherman began a siege of the city. Its 10,000 defenders soon slipped away, and on December 21, Union troops entered Savannah. Sherman telegraphed a holiday greeting to President Lincoln in Washington. "I beg to present you, as a Christmas gift, the city of Savannah," Sherman's telegram read.

In January 1865 Sherman brought his army north into South Carolina, which had been the first state to secede. "The whole army is burning with . . . desire to wreak vengeance on South Carolina," Sherman wrote. "I almost tremble at her fate."

In Georgia, Union troops burned relatively few private homes. In South Carolina, however, few homes in their path escaped destruction. The destruction of civilian property finally stopped when the army entered North Carolina in late February.

The fall of Richmond Sherman's army was headed north in order to join Grant at Petersburg, where the siege had been going on since June 1864. With Sherman's army added to his own, Grant hoped to surround Lee without spreading Union forces so thin that the Confederates could break through and escape. As it turned out, Grant's plan was not necessary.

By late March 1865 the number of defenders at Petersburg had shrunk to about 35,000. They were low on food, ammunition, and other supplies. Grant realized that he could break through Lee's defenses without waiting for Sherman, and on April 2 he did. With nothing now standing between Grant's army and Richmond, Confederate leaders fled the city. Union troops entered Richmond on the next day.

Meanwhile, Lee tried to escape with what was left of his army. He hoped to join another Confederate force that was retreating from Sherman in North Carolina. Grant's army pursued Lee's 13,000 remaining troops, however, and blocked their escape. When the Union forces surrounded the Confederates at the town of Appomattox Court House, Virginia, Lee decided to surrender.

Surrender at Appomattox Lee and Grant met in a home in Appomattox Court House on Sunday, April 9. The two generals chatted briefly about their service as young officers in the Mexican-American War. Then Grant presented the terms of the surrender. They were extremely generous for a conflict that had been so long, bloody, and bitter. Lee's troops merely had to turn over their weapons and leave.

Grant then offered food for Lee's starving troops. "It will be a great relief, I assure you," Lee responded. After a few more minutes of conversation, Lee, Grant, and other officers signed the surrender. Lee then returned to his troops to tell them that the war was over.

HISTORY'S VOICES

❝I have done for you all that it was in my power to do. You have done all your duty. Leave the result to God. Go to your homes and resume your occupations. Obey the laws and become as good citizens as you were soldiers.❞

—Robert E. Lee, April 9, 1865

In the Union army's camps, the troops began firing artillery to salute the victory. Grant ordered the guns silenced. "The war is over," he

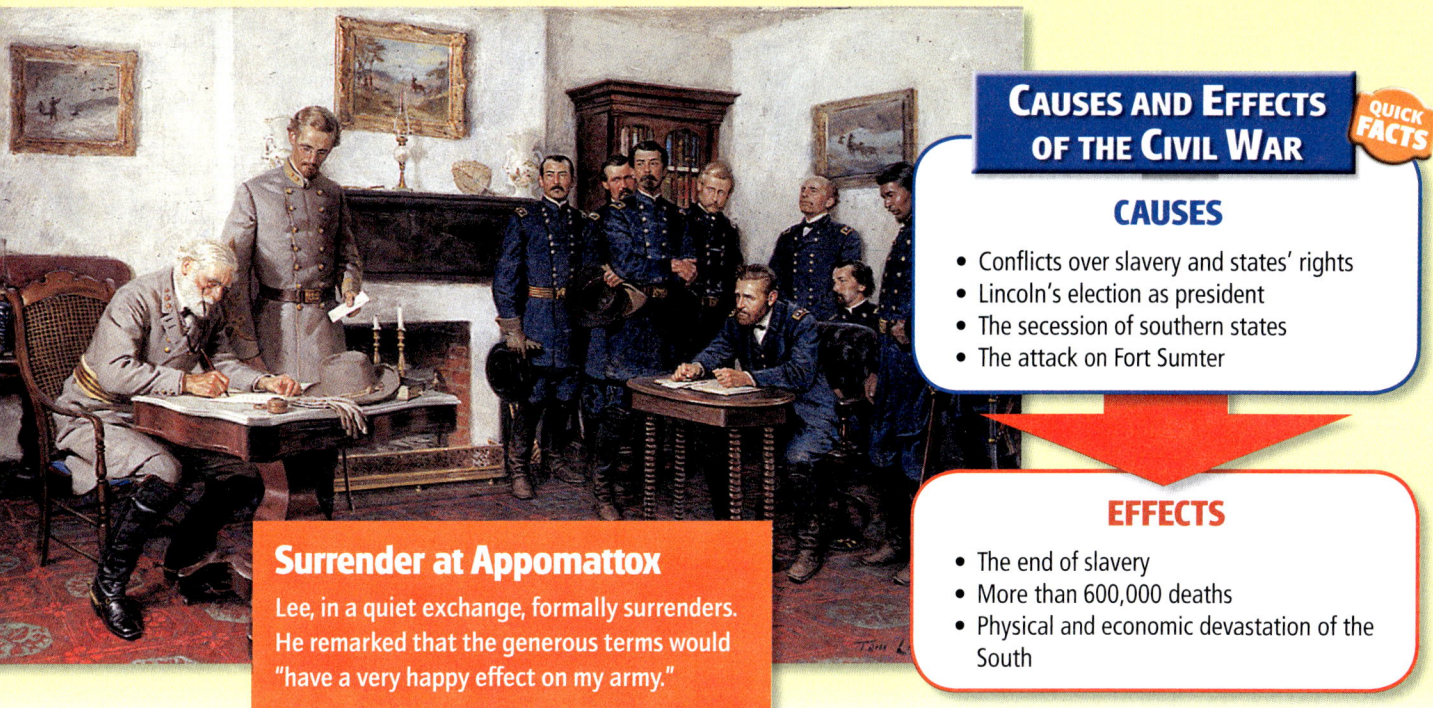

CAUSES AND EFFECTS OF THE CIVIL WAR

CAUSES
- Conflicts over slavery and states' rights
- Lincoln's election as president
- The secession of southern states
- The attack on Fort Sumter

EFFECTS
- The end of slavery
- More than 600,000 deaths
- Physical and economic devastation of the South

Surrender at Appomattox
Lee, in a quiet exchange, formally surrenders. He remarked that the generous terms would "have a very happy effect on my army."

said. "The rebels are our countrymen again." In cities across the North, however, news of Lee's surrender brought wild, joyful celebration.

In Washington, a huge crowd gathered outside the White House. Too tired for a speech, Lincoln said instead that he'd always liked "Dixie," an old tune that had become a popular song among Confederates. "We fairly captured it [yesterday]," he joked. "I now request the band to favor me with its performance."

It was not until May 26, 1865, however, that the last of the Confederate forces finally surrendered. Tragically, President Lincoln did not live to see the official end of the war. His death would change the course of American history in the months and years following the war.

READING CHECK **Sequencing** What series of events in Georgia, the Carolinas, and Virginia brought the Civil War to an end?

SECTION 5 ASSESSMENT

go.hrw.com
Online Quiz
Keyword: SD7 HP11

Reviewing Ideas, Terms, and People

1. **a. Recall** What strategy did Lee adopt in 1864, and what was his goal?
   b. Analyze Why did Lincoln put Grant in command of all the Union armies?
   c. Evaluate Was Grant's strategy as a commander effective? Why or why not?

2. **a. Identify** What did the **Thirteenth Amendment** do?
   b. Elaborate Why did Lincoln expect to be beaten for re-election in 1864? What might have changed his mind?
   c. Predict How might the nation's history be different if **William Tecumseh Sherman** had failed to capture Atlanta before the 1864 election?

3. **a. Describe** What was Sherman's march across Georgia like?
   b. Contrast How did Sherman's army behave differently in South Carolina than in Georgia?
   c. Elaborate Why do you think Grant offered Lee such generous surrender terms?

Critical Thinking

4. **Identifying Cause and Effect** Review your notes on the South's surrender. Then copy the graphic organizer below and use it to identify causes and effects of the South's surrender.

The South Surrenders

Cause	Effect

FOCUS ON WRITING

5. **Expository** Lincoln and Grant both favored generous, forgiving treatment of the South after the war. Write a paragraph explaining why you agree or disagree with their ideas about dealing with the South.

Attitudes toward the Civil War

Historical Context The documents below provide different information on communication between soldiers and civilians during the Civil War.

Task Examine the documents and answer the questions that follow. Then you will be asked to write an essay about attitudes toward the Civil War, using information from the documents and the chapter to support the position you take in your thesis statement.

ST 3.2 Draw upon literary selections, historical documents, and accounts to analyze the roles played by different individuals and groups during the major eras in New York State and United States history.

ST 4.3 Develop hypotheses about important events, eras, or issues; move from chronicling to explaining historical events and issues; use information collected from diverse sources to produce cogently written reports and document-based essays.

DOCUMENT 1

The Civil War was the first major American military conflict after the invention of photography. As a result, an extensive photographic record of the battlefield experience exists. Also, many men on each side had portraits taken of themselves before they left home for military service. Usually it was the first, and sometimes the only, photo they had ever had taken. Below are portraits of two soldiers. The photograph on the left is of a young Confederate enlisted man. The young Union soldier on the right was probably an officer.

DOCUMENT 2

As the war dragged on, life became more difficult for Confederate soldiers, and mail service was often disrupted. This letter was written by Georgia soldier Zachariah H. J. Benefield to his wife, Sarah Jane, in April 1864. At the time, he was fighting in Tennessee.

"Jane, I have no news of interest to write to you, only [that] we have had a hard march. We marched five days. It snowed and rained everyday we were camped at Zolicofer, Tennessee, eleven miles from the [state] line of Virginia . . . On Tuesday the 22 of March the snow fell two feet deep here & it has been snowing & raining ever since. We are on our road to Virginia, I think.

Jane we are faring very bad for something to eat. We get flour with the bran in it & it is half oats & [a] man can't hardly eat it. We don't get half enough of it. We steal a little . . . We can't buy nothing [because] our money [is not worth anything]. Jane, this is the fifth letter I have written to you & got no answer yet. Jane, I don't know what to think. Jane, you said you would write to me every week. If you have written to me I ain't got your letter. Jane, if you knew how bad I want to hear from you, you would write to me . . . Jane, tell brother that I am looking for a letter from him. They say that the Yankees is advancing on Richmond. Again we have to go and defend it. We are falling back out of east Tennessee. Jane, we saw a bad time, marching through the snow & rain."

DOCUMENT 3

By the final months of the war, people on both sides were growing weary of the suffering. Following are several diary entries by Union nurse Rebecca Usher, written in the spring of 1865. At the time she was stationed at a hospital in Virginia, where the fighting was still active.

"**Sat. [Jan. 21st]** – The men come in for all sorts of stores as usual and many of them complain of being hungry—they say they do not have enough to satisfy their appetites. . . . We do all we can for them—give one man a cup of tea and a slice of dry toast, another corn starch, another sage pudding, another crackers, anything we can think of to eke out their scanty meals. . . .

Thursday 16th – . . . A train filled with Rebel deserters came in last evening. It is said there were 500. One of them said they had fought us well before now but they had become convinced it was no use to hold out any longer. . . .

March 22—A man came in yesterday from Conn., who said it was the first time he had spoken to a woman in a year. The tears came into his eyes, his voice trembled, & he was entirely overcome by his feelings.

A boy from Michigan who was an orphan & had lost 3 brothers in the army came in with one of our Maine boys. He had lost his voice from the measles & was the only one of his family left. We got him a [bag of donated goods]. It seemed a great comfort to him. He smiled & appeared as pleased as a child as he examined its contents. He found a letter in it from a Yarmouth girl, which pleased him more than all."

Skills FOCUS   READING LIKE A HISTORIAN

1. **a. Describe** Refer to Document 1. How would you describe the two men?
   b. Analyze How do you think having a photograph of soldiers affected their families back home?

2. **a. Identify** Refer to Document 2. What were the main problems facing Benefield's unit?
   b. Interpret How would lack of mail have affected soldiers' morale and people's attitudes back home?

3. **a. Identify** Refer to Documents 2 and 3. What problems did Union soldiers share with the Confederates?

   b. Elaborate How do you think the Civil War had changed the soldiers that Usher described?

4. **Document-Based Essay Question** Consider the question below and form a thesis statement. Using examples from Documents 1, 2, and 3, create an outline and write a short essay supporting your position.
   How did connections between the homefront and frontlines affect civilians and soldiers during the Civil War?

See **Skills Handbook**, pp. H28-H29, H30

Visual Summary: The Civil War

Preparing for War	Early Confederate Successes	The Union Gains Advantage	The Final Phase	Results of the War
• Calls for troops • More southern states secede • Holding the border states • The Anaconda Plan • The Union blockade • Cotton diplomacy	• First Battle of Bull Run • The Peninsula Campaign • Second Battle of Bull Run	• Capture of Fort Henry and Fort Donelson • Battle of Shiloh • The Mississippi River campaign • Battle of Antietam • The Emancipation Proclamation • Siege of Vicksburg • Battle of Gettysburg • Battle of Chickamauga	• Grant's Virginia campaign • Siege of Petersburg • Battle of Atlanta • Election of 1864 • Sherman's march • Surrender at Appomattox	• The end of slavery • Restoration of the Union • Devastation of the South • More than 600,000 deaths

Reviewing Key Terms and People

Match each numbered definition with the correct lettered item at right.

1. Type of rule in which military commanders are in control and citizens' rights and freedoms are suspended
2. Southern general whose nickname reflected his bravery in battle
3. Union general who boosted the North's morale with early victories
4. Group of Democrats who opposed the war
5. Northern general who frustrated Lincoln with his hesitancy to fight
6. Announcement freeing enslaved African Americans in all areas that were in rebellion against the United States
7. Southern general who urged Lee to withdraw at Gettysburg
8. Increase in prices

9. Person who helped with the war effort by caring for soldiers wounded in battle
10. Northern general in command at Gettysburg
11. Union general who helped end the war with his invasion of Georgia

a. inflation
b. George Meade
c. Clara Barton
d. Emancipation Proclamation
e. James Longstreet
f. martial law
g. Copperheads
h. William Tecumseh Sherman
j. Stonewall Jackson
k. George McClellan
l. Ulysses S. Grant

History's Impact video program

Review the video to answer the closing question:
How did the Civil War divide and ultimately unify
the nation?

Comprehension and Critical Thinking

SECTION 1 *(pp. 356–362)*

12. a. Identify What was the Anaconda Plan?

  b. Contrast How were the initial military strategies of the North and South different?

  c. Evaluate Was the South's strategy for fighting the war a good one? Why or why not?

SECTION 2 *(pp. 363–370)*

13. a. Describe How did the new weapons used in the war affect the fighting?

  b. Analyze How did the First Battle of Bull Run change the way people viewed the war?

  c. Predict What might have happened if Lincoln had replaced McClellan with Grant earlier in the war?

SECTION 3 *(pp. 371–378)*

14. a. Define What is the draft?

  b. Analyze How did the blockade affect the South?

  c. Elaborate Why did Lincoln free slaves only in areas in rebellion against the United States?

SECTION 4 *(pp. 380–387)*

15. a. Identify What major events of the war occurred in 1863?

  b. Draw Conclusions Why were Britain and other nations concerned about the Civil War?

  c. Predict How might the war have been different if Lee had decided not to fight at Gettysburg?

SECTION 5 *(pp. 390–395)*

16. a. Recall How did Sherman help Lincoln win re-election in 1864?

  b. Contrast In what ways were Grant's and Lee's strategies different in 1864?

  c. Elaborate Why do you think Lee encouraged his soldiers to go home and become good citizens?

Using the Internet

go.hrw.com
Practice Online
Keyword: SD7 CH11

17. The Civil War was a long conflict marked by many complex battles. Using the keyword above, do research to learn more about one of the most important battles of the war. Then create a report on the fighting, people involved, or consequences of the Battle of Gettysburg.

Analyzing Primary Sources

Reading Like a Historian Read the History's Voices passage in Section 5 from Abraham Lincoln's Second Inaugural Address that begins: "With malice toward none, with charity for all."

18. Identify What is the "work we are in" that Lincoln refers to?

19. Make Inferences How do Lincoln's words show his attitude toward the South?

Critical Reading

Read the passage in Section 5 that begins with the heading "Sherman's March." Then answer the questions that follow.

20. According to the passage, one of Sherman's main reasons for being so destructive was that he

  A wanted revenge on Robert E. Lee.

  B was trying to show Grant he was a good general.

  C wanted to destroy the South's ability to fight.

  D was trying to make Britain and France stop supporting the South.

21. In the second paragraph of the passage, "Sherman's army cut a swath . . . across the heart of Georgia," the term *swath* means

  A a strike or blow.

  B an important victory.

  C an exchange of goods or services.

  D a long, broad band or strip.

FOCUS ON WRITING

Persuasive Writing *Persuasive writing takes a position for or against an issue, using facts and examples as supporting evidence. To practice persuasive writing, complete the assignment below.*

Writing Topic The Emancipation Proclamation

22. Assignment Based on what you have read in this chapter, write a paragraph that argues whether or not the Emancipation Proclamation was effective.

Reconstruction

THE BIG PICTURE Following the Civil War, Congress implemented a plan to reconstruct the South. Despite landmark constitutional amendments, gains for southern African Americans were limited. After 12 years, and in response to fierce resistance from many white southerners, the federal government declared Reconstruction over.

New York Standards

Key Idea 1 The study of New York State and United States history requires an analysis of the development of American culture, its diversity and multicultural context, and the ways people are unified by many values, practices, and traditions.

Key Idea 3 Study about the major social, political, economic, cultural, and religious developments in New York State and United States history involves learning about the important roles and contributions of individuals and groups.

Skills FOCUS   READING LIKE A HISTORIAN

Much of Atlanta had been burned during the Civil War, but following the war it became Georgia's new state capital and a center of Reconstruction activity.

Interpreting Visuals What evidence of Atlanta's revival can you see in this Reconstruction-era painting?

See **Skills Handbook**, p. H30

U.S.

1865
Upon Lincoln's death, Andrew Johnson becomes president. Johnson launches his own Reconstruction plan.

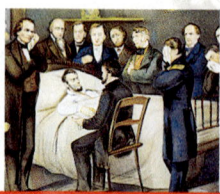

1865

World

1866
Swedish chemist Alfred Nobel invents dynamite.

History's Impact video program

Watch the video to understand the impact of the Thirteenth, Fourteenth, and Fifteenth Amendments.

February 1869
Congress passes the Fifteenth Amendment, assuring African American men the right to vote.

February 1870
Hiram R. Revels becomes the first African American U.S. Senator.

1876
Supreme Court limits Fourteenth and Fifteenth Amendments, weakening Reconstruction.

1877
Compromise of 1877 gives Rutherford B. Hayes presidency, ending Reconstruction.

1870

1875

1880

1869
The Suez Canal is completed.

1871
German states, united under Prussia, defeat France in the Franco-Prussian War.

1873
Canada's famed Mounted Police force is established.

1877
The tenth Russo-Turkish War begins.

401

Plans for Reconstruction

BEFORE YOU READ

MAIN IDEA

Northern leaders had differing ideas for dealing with the many issues and challenges of restoring the southern states to the Union.

READING FOCUS

1. What challenges faced the South after the Civil War?
2. What actions did Union leaders take during wartime to reconstruct the nation after the war's end?
3. How did Lincoln's assassination affect the nation?
4. Why did President Johnson and Congress differ over Reconstruction?

KEY TERMS AND PEOPLE

Freedmen's Bureau
Ten Percent Plan
Thaddeus Stevens
Wade-Davis Bill
pocket veto
John Wilkes Booth
Andrew Johnson

 3.2 Research and analyze the major themes and developments in New York State and United States history (e.g., colonization and settlement; Revolution and New National Period; immigration; expansion and reform era; Civil War and Reconstruction; the American labor movement; Great Depression; World Wars; contemporary United States).

An Unexpected Visitor

 **THE INSIDE STORY** *How welcome was Lincoln in the Confederate capital?* Less than 100 miles separate Richmond, Virginia, and Washington, D.C. In 1865, one city was the U.S. capital, the other the capital of the Confederacy. By early April, Richmond had been under siege for months. On April 3, Union forces finally captured the city. The next day, President Lincoln decided to pay a visit. Richmond lay in ruins. Skeletons of burned-out buildings lined the streets.

Lincoln reached the city on a navy ship with his son Tad. It was Tad's 12th birthday. They walked through the ruined streets with a small guard of soldiers. One witness said that Lincoln "was walking with his usual long, careless stride, and looking about with an interested air and taking in everything." The president visited Jefferson Davis's house and was curious about everything in it. He met with Confederate officials who remained and then toured the city.

As Lincoln, in his trademark stovepipe hat, walked the streets, most of Richmond's white citizens kept an angry silence. The newly freed African Americans reacted very differently. Hundreds emerged from the ruins. Some fell on their knees as they recognized the president, crying "Glory, hallelujah!" An African American Union soldier wrote: "It was a great deliverer among the delivered. No wonder tears came into his eyes." Lincoln told the Union commander to treat all Richmonders with compassion. ◼

In the late 1800s an artist painted a different version of Lincoln's visit to Richmond.

The South after the War

President Lincoln's visit to Richmond showed him some of the challenges facing the nation at the end of the Civil War. Richmond was in ruins, as were many other southern cities and towns. Large parts of the countryside had been devastated by the fighting and by armies passing through them. The loss of farm buildings, machinery, work animals, and other livestock was widespread.

Furthermore, formerly enslaved African Americans faced an uncertain future. Although they were now free, they had very few job opportunities, and many were unable to make a living.

Property losses In the years after the war, farms and plantations in the South were worth only about half of what they were in 1860. Farms and plantations that did survive the war suffered from neglect. This was because many small farmers died fighting the war, leaving their farms without proper care. In total, more than one-fifth of the South's white male population perished.

Plantations suffered from the loss of workers. Some slaves escaped during the war; others left after the war's end. "All was lost, except my debts," one Confederate general complained about his once prosperous plantation.

Property losses were not limited to cities and farms, however. War damage or neglect also left the South's transportation network in poor shape. Long stretches of railroad lines were useless. In Alabama, a government survey described the condition of one railroad.

HISTORY'S VOICES

"From Pocahontas to Decatur, one-hundred and fourteen miles, almost entirely destroyed, except the road-bed and iron rails, and they in very bad condition—every bridge and trestle destroyed, cross-ties rotten, buildings burned . . . and track grown up in weeds and bushes . . . About forty miles of the track was burned . . . and rails bent and twisted in such a manner as to require great labor to straighten."

—House Report 34, 39th Congress, 1865

Challenges for African Americans The nearly 4 million African Americans living in the former Confederacy had won their freedom. But they faced other problems after the war. Most had no money or education. The condition of the South's economy made job prospects bleak. Former owners needed workers but often could not afford to pay them. The South needed to find a new labor system that would replace slavery, put people to work, and make the region productive again.

Many former slaves were no longer willing to work the long hours that been required under slavery. Some women resisted work in the fields and tried to enroll their children in school instead. They wanted an education, too, and to devote more time to their families. Ways had to be found to provide educational and economic opportunities for all formerly enslaved African Americans.

How to treat the South The nation also needed to answer many legal and political questions. What place would African Americans have in political life in the South? What was the status of the Confederate states? Were they conquered territories, or were they once again states in the Union? If they were not states, how could they become states? Should Confederates be forgiven? Or, should they be punished for seceding and starting the war?

READING CHECK **Identifying the Main Idea** What were conditions like in the South in the aftermath of the Civil War?

Wartime Reconstruction

Union leaders began addressing these issues even before the South's formal surrender. For example, in March 1865 Congress created the **Freedmen's Bureau** to provide help to the thousands of black and white southerners uprooted by the fighting. The Bureau continued to function throughout the Reconstruction era, which lasted from 1865 to 1877.

Northerners disagreed over how to treat the conquered Confederacy. Many, including some members of Congress, shared the view of abolitionist Wendell Phillips. "We have a right to trample it [the South] under the heels of our boots," Phillips declared. "That is the meaning of the war." Lincoln, however, stated in his second inaugural address in 1865 that he hoped to treat the South "with malice toward none, with charity for all."

Reconstruction experiments Even before the war ended, northern leaders tested possible roles for freed African Americans in the South's economy. When planters fled regions that came under Union control, the army often seized their plantations. Sometimes, the army hired freed slaves to work on the plantations for pay. In a few cases, former slaves rented plantations. This allowed them to farm the land and to keep or sell the crops they raised. In this way, some former slaves saved enough money to buy land of their own.

The most famous wartime reconstruction experiment took place on the Sea Islands off the coast of South Carolina. When Union forces captured these islands early in the war, nearly all the white population fled to the mainland. The federal government seized their plantations, sold some of the land, and hired former slaves to farm the rest of it.

In January 1865 General Sherman divided this and other land along the South Carolina and Georgia coasts into 40-acre plots. He offered a plot to any formerly enslaved family who wanted land. By the end of the war more than 40,000 freedmen were farming in the region,

The Costs of the Civil War

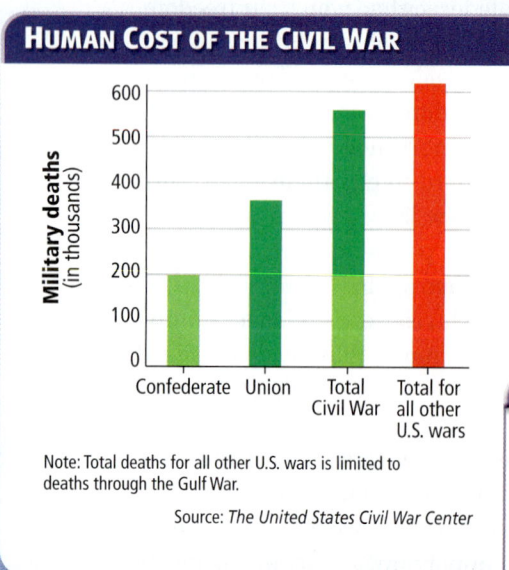

HUMAN COST OF THE CIVIL WAR

Military deaths (in thousands)

Confederate, Union, Total Civil War, Total for all other U.S. wars

Note: Total deaths for all other U.S. wars is limited to deaths through the Gulf War.

Source: *The United States Civil War Center*

FINANCIAL COST OF THE CIVIL WAR

Southern livestock killed: 40 percent	
Southern farm machinery destroyed: 50 percent	
Drop in South's total property wealth: 66 percent	
Total national wealth held by the South, 1860: 30 percent	
Total national wealth held by the South, 1870: 12 percent	

Skills FOCUS **INTERPRETING GRAPHS**

1. According to the chart, what was the South's worst financial loss of the war?
2. According to the graph, how do Civil War deaths compare with the total for all other U.S. wars?

See **Skills Handbook**, pp. H15, H16

Freedmen's Village

Union troops provided building materials to help these former slaves transform an abandoned Sea Islands plantation into a village.

on land they considered their own. Northern religious groups and other organizations sent teachers to coastal Georgia and South Carolina to start schools for the former slaves.

In Louisiana another large reconstruction experiment provided former slaves as paid workers to planters who took Lincoln's loyalty oath. The freedmen signed a <u>contract</u> to work for a year. In return, the planter agreed to provide housing, food, and medical care in addition to wages. But the planter sometimes deducted these basic items from the freedmen's wages. Little money was left over, so many freedmen could not afford to leave the plantation when their contracts ended.

Lincoln's Reconstruction plans
In 1862 Lincoln appointed military governors temporarily to rule parts of the Confederacy that were already in Union hands. To prepare these and other conquered regions for rejoining the Union, he issued a Proclamation of Amnesty and Reconstruction in December 1863.

Lincoln's proclamation offered forgiveness for the rebellion to all southerners (except high-ranking Confederate leaders) who pledged loyalty to the Union and support for emancipation. When 10 percent of a state's voters had taken this oath, they could organize a new state government. The new government was then required to ban slavery. Once these steps

were complete, Lincoln would recognize it as the state's legal government, even if the state's Confederate government was still functioning.

This procedure for readmitting seceded states became known as the **Ten Percent Plan**. Before the war ended, Lincoln had accepted three southern states back into the Union. By early 1865, Arkansas, Louisiana, and Tennessee had formed pro-Union governments and sent senators and representatives to take seats in Congress.

Opposition to Lincoln's plan
Lincoln's actions set off a great debate in Congress over who would control Reconstruction. Some members noted that admitting states to the Union was a power of Congress. They claimed it was not up to the president to make the rebel states part of the Union again. Lincoln's supporters pointed out that since secession was unlawful, the Confederate states had never legally left the Union in the first place. Therefore, Congress did not need to readmit them.

Many members of Congress did not support readmitting southern states. Massachusetts senator Charles Sumner argued that the southern states had given up their status as states when they seceded. Other members claimed that the parts of the Confederacy controlled by Union armies were conquered

ACADEMIC VOCABULARY

contract an official legal agreement between two parties

territories. According to this reasoning, Congress would decide on their admission to the Union as it did with all territories that became states.

Some members of Congress objected to the Ten Percent Plan as much too lenient. Republican **Thaddeus Stevens** of Pennsylvania noted that allowing just 10 percent of a state's voters to form a government violated the nation's principles. "The democratic doctrine that the majority shall rule is discarded and dangerously ignored," he observed. "When the doctrine that the *quality* and not the *number* of voters is to decide the right to govern, then we no longer have a republic."

For these reasons and others, Congress refused to allow senators and representatives from states organized under Lincoln's plan to take their seats. Instead, Congress responded with its own Reconstruction plan in 1864 by passing the **Wade-Davis Bill**. The bill required a majority of a state's white male citizens to pledge loyalty before elections could be held.

Lincoln, however, thought this tougher requirement would make southerners more committed to continuing the war. He killed the Wade-Davis Bill with a **pocket veto**. This is a presidential power to prevent a bill passed in the last 10 days of a legislative session from becoming law by simply ignoring it. The bill's outraged Republican sponsors, Benjamin Wade and Henry Davis, wrote a stinging criticism of Lincoln's action.

HISTORY'S VOICES

❝ [The president] must understand that our support is of a cause and not of a man; that the authority of Congress is paramount and must be respected; . . . and if he wishes our support, he must confine himself to his executive duties— to obey and execute, not make the laws— to suppress by arms armed rebellion, and leave political reorganization to Congress. ❞
—The Wade-Davis Manifesto, August 5, 1864

This attack by members of his own party hurt Lincoln deeply. It was just the first indicator, however, of the struggle that was to come.

READING CHECK **Contrasting** How did Lincoln's views on Reconstruction differ from the views of some members of Congress?

COUNTERPOINTS

Views on Reconstruction

Representative Thaddeus Stevens, a Radical Republican leader, insisted that the South be treated as a conquered territory.

❝ [W]e hold it the duty of the Government to inflict . . . punishment on the rebel belligerents, and so weaken their hands that they can never again endanger the Union . . . This can be done only by treating and holding them as a conquered people. ❞

Thaddeus Stevens, 1865

President Andrew Johnson, a southerner, argued that the southern states should not be denied their rights.

❝ [T]he policy of military rule over a conquered territory [implies] that the States [who took] part in the rebellion had by the act . . . ceased to exist. But the true theory is that all pretended acts of secession were from the beginning null and void. ❞

Andrew Johnson, 1865

Skills Focus **READING LIKE A HISTORIAN**

Recognizing Bias Why might President Johnson have been biased in favor of the South?

See **Skills Handbook**, p. H33

Lincoln's Assassination

Lincoln's popularity as a victorious wartime leader might have allowed him to win the battle with Congress for control of Reconstruction. But the president did not live long enough.

Less than a week after General Lee's surrender in Virginia, **John Wilkes Booth** shot Lincoln while the president watched a play at Ford's Theater in Washington, D.C. on April 14, 1865. Lincoln died the next morning.

Booth, a southerner, strongly supported secession and the Confederacy. His first plan had been to kidnap the president and exchange him for Confederate prisoners of war. Booth organized a group to help carry out the kidnapping. The plot failed when Lincoln's schedule changed and he did not appear at the place Booth intended to seize him. Booth decided to kill Lincoln instead.

Other plotters were assigned to assassinate Secretary of State William Seward and Vice President **Andrew Johnson** the same night. Booth hoped this would create chaos within the government and help the Confederacy win the war. Only Booth carried out his assignment successfully, however. He escaped into Virginia where he was located by Union troops and killed when he refused to surrender.

Lincoln's death produced one of the greatest outpourings of grief in the nation's history. A train carried his body back to Illinois for burial. Huge crowds gathered to pay respects at stops along the train's nearly two-week journey.

White southerners reacted to Lincoln's death with more concern than grief. They feared the effect the assassination might have on the Reconstruction program. Some southern leaders disliked Andrew Johnson even more than they disliked Lincoln. The vice president was a southerner who had sided with the Union during the war. In the eyes of many white southerners, this made him a traitor. Now this traitor to their cause would become president of the United States.

READING CHECK **Sequencing** Trace the events that led to Lincoln's assassination.

Lincoln's funeral procession traveled by train across more than 1,600 miles of countryside, making stops in major cities such as New York (above). "Now he belongs to the ages," Secretary of War Edwin Stanton said upon Lincoln's death. *Why do you think so many people were given an opportunity to participate in the funeral?*

Johnson and Congress Differ over Reconstruction

Andrew Johnson was sworn in as president a few hours after Lincoln's death. The two men shared a common background. Both had been raised in poverty without much formal schooling. Both men overcame their humble beginnings to achieve success. Johnson had been governor of Tennessee and a U.S. senator. When Lincoln sought re-election in 1864, the Republicans picked Johnson to run for vice president. Like Lincoln, Johnson never forgot his roots.

Early relations with Congress Even though Johnson was a Democrat, Republican leaders in Congress at first thought they could work with him. "Treason is a crime and crime must be punished," Johnson told Senator Wade. Senator Sumner also met with Johnson and described his attitude as excellent. "There is no difference between us," Sumner reported.

Wade, Sumner, and other Republican leaders failed to understand Johnson's views. The new president held no ill will toward the South or toward southerners. He merely despised the wealthy planter class. In addition, although Johnson opposed secession, he had always supported states' rights and limits on the power of the national government. He was not about to give Congress the control it sought over the affairs of the rebel states.

Johnson's Reconstruction plan Practical matters also convinced Johnson to keep Reconstruction under presidential control. Congress was in recess when he took office as president. Its new session did not begin until December. Johnson believed it was important to have a program to reunite the nation in place before that time.

Johnson launched his Reconstruction plan in late May. Like Lincoln's plan, it restored the rights of white southerners who took an oath of loyalty to the United States.

Johnson added to Lincoln's list of exceptions, however. Southerners who owned property worth more than $20,000 would also have to apply to the president for a pardon, just like former Confederate military and political leaders. This added measure allowed President Johnson to decide personally the punishment the planters would receive.

Unlike the Wade-Davis Bill and Lincoln's plan, the Johnson plan did not set a percentage of loyal voters that was needed to form a state government. It merely required that pledge-takers call a convention to repeal secession, amend the state constitution to abolish slavery,

and refuse to pay the debts of the Confederate government. When these steps were complete, the state could elect a governor and legislature and send representatives to Congress.

Concern over Johnson's plan Sumner, Stevens, and other leading Republicans in Congress were troubled by the president's plan. One concern was that it contained no provisions for giving freedmen a role in southern state government. Another was that once a state had qualified under Johnson's plan to hold elections, any voter could take part.

Stevens wrote Johnson in July to request that he suspend his plan. "Can you not hold your hand and wait the action of Congress?" Steven asked the president. Johnson did not even bother to answer Stevens's letter. The new president ignored one of the most powerful members of Congress and continued to push forward on his own.

When Congress met in December, Johnson told it that every former Confederate state except Texas had met his conditions for Reconstruction and had been restored to the Union. Many members of Congress were far from satisfied. A battle for control of Reconstruction was about to begin.

READING CHECK **Identifying the Main Idea** What was President Johnson's plan for Reconstruction?

SECTION 1 ASSESSMENT

Reviewing Ideas, Terms, and People

1. **a. Recall** What happened to southern farms and plantations during the Civil War?
   b. Contrast How did conditions differ for African Americans before and after the Civil War?
   c. Evaluate Do you think it was necessary to punish the former Confederate states for seceding?

2. **a. Identify** State the importance of each of the following: **Freedmen's Bureau, Thaddeus Stevens.**
   b. Interpret How well did wartime Reconstruction experiments work in employing freed African Americans?
   c. Elaborate Why did Congress feel that Reconstruction was a congressional task and not a presidential task?

3. **a. Recall** Who was **John Wilkes Booth**?
   b. Predict What effect do you think Lincoln's assassination had on Reconstruction?

4. **a. Describe** For what reasons did Congress oppose the Reconstruction plan put forward by **Andrew Johnson**?

b. Compare and Contrast In what ways were Lincoln and Johnson similar?

Critical Thinking

5. **Evaluating** Fill in the chart below, listing the major aspects of the three different Reconstruction plans. Which do you think was the best Reconstruction plan? Why?

Ten Percent Plan	Wade-Davis Bill	Johnson's Plan

FOCUS ON WRITING

6. **Expository** Write a letter to the Freedmen's Bureau in which you explain your opinion about work contracts between freed African Americans and planters. Use details from the section to support your position.

ST 3.1 Investigate how Americans have reconciled the inherent tensions and conflicts over minority versus majority rights.

Ex Parte Milligan (1866)

Why It Matters Criminal defendants have fewer constitutional protections in military courts than in civil courts. In 1866 the Supreme Court limited the power of military courts to try civilians for violating criminal law.

Background of the Case

An army court found Lambden Milligan guilty of disloyal activities during the Civil War and sentenced him to death. Milligan was not in the military and he lived in Indiana, which was not part of the Confederacy. Because his trial was run under the direction of the Indiana military commander, he did not receive some constitutional protections, such as a public trial and a trial by jury, that would have been available to him in a civilian court. On appeal, Milligan argued that the military court had no authority to try him.

The Decision

The Supreme Court held that the Constitution is not suspended during times of emergency. Even in wartime, citizens are entitled to civil trials. If a wartime commander had the right to suspend all civil rights of citizens and substitute military law for civilian law, then military law would be superior to civilian law. This was not what the Constitution intended, the justices said.

During wartime the government must have more flexibility to protect the country, the justices agreed. Martial law can be declared when the courts and civil authorities of a community no longer function. However, the Court observed that the Civil War was not being fought in Indiana, and that civil courts were available to try alleged wrongdoers. The military court, therefore, had no authority over civilians like Milligan, and the Supreme Court granted his request for discharge from confinement.

THE IMPACT TODAY After the terrorist attacks on America on September 11, 2001, the U.S. military began imprisoning suspected terrorists at a military base at Guantánamo Bay, Cuba. They were held indefinitely and interrogated without access to lawyers or courts. In 2004 the U.S. Supreme Court ruled that American-born Yaser Esam Hamdi could challenge his treatment at Guantánamo in a U.S. court.

go.hrw.com
Research Online
Keyword: SS Court

CRITICAL THINKING

1. **Analyze the Impact** Milligan wanted legal protections he could not get in a military court. Other Court cases have defined what protections are required in a civil trial. Using the keyword above, study *Gideon* v. *Wainwright*. What rule did that case create to protect the rights of criminal defendants?

2. **You Be the Judge** Should foreigners accused of terrorism be tried in civil courts or in military tribunals? What parts of *Milligan* suggest a right to trial in civil courts? In what ways is *Milligan* different, so that military tribunals might be allowed?

SECTION 2

Congressional Reconstruction

BEFORE YOU READ

MAIN IDEA

Congress took control of Reconstruction as a new, radical branch of the Republican Party was emerging.

READING FOCUS

1. How did the South respond to Reconstruction under President Johnson?
2. Why did Congress take control of Reconstruction, and what changes did it make?
3. How did Radical Reconstruction differ from earlier Reconstruction plans, and what were its effects?

KEY TERMS AND PEOPLE

Black Codes
Ku Klux Klan
Radical Republicans
Civil Rights Act
Fourteenth Amendment
Reconstruction Acts
impeachment
Horatio Seymour
Fifteenth Amendment

 1.2 Describe the evolution of American democratic values and beliefs as expressed in the Declaration of Independence, the New York State Constitution, the United States Constitution, the Bill of Rights, and other important historical documents.

Clashing over Reconstruction

THE INSIDE STORY

Why was Thaddeus Stevens so angry? Thaddeus Stevens's strong, controversial opinions made him deeply hated—and deeply admired. Stevens grew up in poverty and had a deformed foot, which he hid with a special boot. This background helped give him deep sympathy for other social "outsiders." He hated slavery and, as a lawyer, defended fugitive slaves. As a Republican member of Congress, he became one of its leaders during the Civil War.

Although a wartime ally of President Lincoln, Stevens disagreed with Lincoln's plans for the South after the war. Stevens wanted to treat the South like a defeated nation, punishing the planter class and ensuring the rights of freed slaves. His ideas were radical for the time: free schools for everyone and universal suffrage for African Americans. Until those rights were secure, he did not want to allow the southern states to rejoin the Union.

When President Andrew Johnson adopted Lincoln's forgiving approach to Reconstruction after Lincoln's death, Stevens was outraged. In September 1865 he lashed out at Johnson's gentle handling of the South: "The foundation of their institutions—political, municipal, and social—must be broken up and relaid or all our blood and treasure have been spent in vain. This can only be done by treating and holding them as conquered people." ◼

▶ Stevens viewed white southerners as "conquered rebels."

Reconstruction under President Johnson

Representative Thaddeus Stevens may have been unhappy with Johnson's handling of the Reconstruction program, but most white southerners welcomed Johnson's approach. They were relieved that he did not intend to punish them for the rebellion. In particular, they were pleased that his plan let them form new governments on their own terms.

Many white southerners wanted their society and government to remain much as they were before the war. They wanted to rebuild their society with all the advantages they had enjoyed before the war. Although the fighting had stopped, deep-rooted prejudice against African Americans did not simply vanish. Most white southerners did not intend to concede equality to the former slaves.

Johnson himself made it clear that while African Americans had rights, those rights did not include a role in government. "White men alone must manage the South," he declared.

State governments President Johnson pardoned nearly every planter and former Confederate leader who applied. So the states he restored to the Union generally restored to power their prewar leaders. They sent to Washington nine Confederate generals, two Confederate cabinet members, and Alexander Stephens, the vice president of the Confederacy. Not surprisingly, Congress refused to seat these former Confederates.

The Black Codes Southern state leaders could not restore slavery after the ratification of the Thirteenth Amendment in December 1865. But they wanted to preserve the unequal relationship between white and black southerners. Southern state legislatures passed Black Codes, which were laws designed to keep freedmen in a slavelike condition and to give planters a supply of cheap labor. However, these laws did allow freedmen certain rights, such as the right to marry or own property.

The Black Codes varied from state to state. In most states, former slaves were required to sign contracts requiring the freedman, and sometimes his family, to work for his employer for one year. If a freedman quit before the end of his contract, he forfeited his wages. Further-

more, it was illegal for any employer to hire a freedman while he was under contract with another employer.

To discourage freedmen from starting businesses, the Black Codes forbade them from renting property in cities or towns. In some states, freedmen who worked at a job other than field hand or servant had to pay a tax.

Any freedman refusing to sign a labor contract or who left his job during his contract could be arrested for being jobless. Such offenses were punished by fines. If a freedman could not pay the fine, he or she had to perform forced labor for up to a year.

In some states, freedmen could not own guns. In others, their guns and dogs were taxed. This was to prevent freedmen from hunting as a source of food. All these laws were designed keep freedmen dependent on the plantations for their existence.

PRIMARY SOURCES

Speech

In 1866 Congress refused to seat southern members until their states had been restored to the Union through the acceptance of federal Reconstruction laws. Thaddeus Stevens explained why he thought this should be so.

"[The southern states] are not out of the Union, but are only dead carcasses lying within the Union . . . Nobody, I believe, pretends that with their old constitutions and frames of government they can be permitted to claim their old rights under the Constitution. They have torn their constitutional states into atoms, and built on their foundations fabrics of a totally different character. Dead men cannot raise themselves. Dead states cannot restore their existence 'as it was' . . . Congress must create states and declare when they are entitled to be represented."

Skills FOCUS **READING LIKE A HISTORIAN**

Analyzing Primary Sources How does Stevens imply that the southern states brought their condition upon themselves?

See **Skills Handbook**, pp. H28–H29

ACADEMIC VOCABULARY

prejudice a judgment or opinion about a person or group that is formed in ignorance

Southern defiance Because the Black Codes helped retain a familiar way of life, local sheriffs and Civil War veterans supported and enforced these laws. They invaded African Americans' homes and seized guns and other property. They also abused freedmen who refused to sign labor contracts.

These activities inspired white citizens to form their own private groups, supposedly to help keep order in the South. Among these groups was the **Ku Klux Klan**. This group began as a social club in Tennessee in 1866 but soon began terrorizing African Americans and whites who were loyal to the U.S. government. Similar groups sprang up in other southern states. Local officials rarely prosecuted whites who committed violence against blacks.

READING CHECK **Summarizing** What was the purpose of the Black Codes?

Congress Takes Control of Reconstruction

At first, most northerners supported President Johnson's Reconstruction plan. They were eager to put the Civil War behind them and reunite the nation. Johnson's program seemed the easiest way to do that.

Northern opposition grows As time passed, however, northerners became disturbed by what was happening in the South. "Public sentiment [there] is still as bitter and unloyal as in 1861," the *New York Times* reported. The return of former Confederates to power seemed to confirm this view. "[The] reptile spirit of secession is still alive," a New Jersey newspaper warned, "and ready to display its fangs at any moment."

Northerners were even more troubled by the Black Codes. Most white northerners still cared little about African American rights. Many believed, however, that if southern states were allowed to abuse freedmen, the North's victory would be diminished.

Congress fights back Northern response to the Black Codes strengthened a group of senators and representatives who wanted a more thorough Reconstruction program for the South. The so-called **Radical Republicans** favored much tougher requirements for restoring the southern states' governments and wanted to reshape southern society.

Radical Republicans had pushed Lincoln to make the end of slavery a Union goal during the war. They now wanted freed slaves to have economic opportunity and political equality after the war.

The Freedmen's Bureau

The Freedmen's Bureau aided former slaves in many ways. It was most successful in founding schools, like this one in Virginia. The Freedmen's Bureau also built hospitals and provided medical assistance to freedmen.

The Right to Vote

The Thirteenth Amendment ended slavery, and the Fourteenth Amendment granted citizenship to former slaves. Voting, however, remained under the control of the states. Although southern states had to grant African Americans voting rights in order to rejoin the Union, many whites objected. Many northern states also avoided granting voting rights to blacks.

In 1870 the Fifteenth Amendment established that "the right of citizens of the United States to vote shall not be denied or abridged by the United States or by any State on account of race, color, or previous condition of servitude."

Still, states set other requirements that kept many African Americans from voting. Also, the Fifteenth Amendment did not give the vote to women. Native Americans could not vote because they were not considered citizens. Women were not granted the vote nationwide for another 50 years, and Native Americans did not have the right to vote until after World War II.

Making Generalizations Why was the Fifteenth Amendment necessary?

THE GRANGER COLLECTION, NEW YORK

Freedmen cast their votes, 1867

"The whole fabric of southern society must be changed," proclaimed Stevens, a leader of the Radical Republicans in the House.

HISTORY'S VOICES

❝We have turned loose . . . four million slaves without . . . a cent in their pockets. The infernal laws of slavery have prevented them from acquiring an education . . . This Congress is [determined] to provide for them until they can take care of themselves . . . If we leave them to the legislation of their late masters, we had better had left them in bondage.❞

—Thaddeus Stevens, September 18, 1865

When Congress reconvened in December 1865, it ignored Johnson's announcement that Reconstruction was complete. Instead, moderate Republicans, who still controlled both the House and Senate, decided to continue but improve Johnson's Reconstruction program.

Johnson versus Congress The moderates did not share the Radicals' desire to force a social revolution on the South. Yet they did see a need to help the freedmen and protect their civil rights. With this in mind, the moderates proposed two bills in January 1866.

The first bill extended the life and expanded its duties of the Freedmen's Bureau, which was about to close. The bill allowed the Bureau to continue building schools, finding land, and providing other aid to freedmen. It also gave the Bureau authority in legal disputes between whites and African Americans. The intent of this change was to remove such cases from southern state courts.

The second bill was an attack on the Black Codes. The **Civil Rights Act** gave African Americans citizenship and "equal benefit of all laws and proceedings for the security of person and property, as is enjoyed by white citizens." Anyone who denied freedmen these rights would be tried in federal courts.

Both bills easily passed Congress. President Johnson vetoed them, however, claiming they were unnecessary and unconstitutional. When Congress modified the Freedmen's Bureau Bill in response to Johnson's objections, he vetoed it again. Congressional Republicans then united to pass both bills over the president's veto.

Johnson's rigid actions in the fight over the Freedmen's Bureau and the Civil Rights Act ended all attempts by moderate Republicans to work with him. They decided instead to help the Radical Republicans to take control of Reconstruction.

READING CHECK **Identifying Cause and Effect** What developments led Congress to take control of Reconstruction?

Radical Reconstruction

Johnson claimed that the Civil Rights Act threatened the constitutional rights of the states. Congressional Republicans worried that the Supreme Court might agree and overturn the law or that a future Congress might weaken or repeal it. To prevent this, Congress passed the **Fourteenth Amendment** in June 1866 and submitted it to the states for approval.

The amendment required states to grant citizenship to "all persons born or naturalized in the United States." It promised citizens "equal protection of the laws" and barred states from depriving anyone of "life, liberty, or property without due process of law." In effect, it wrote the Civil Rights Act into the Constitution.

ACADEMIC VOCABULARY
utilize use

The election of 1866 Some northerners thought the Fourteenth Amendment went too far. Johnson saw the chance to block Congress by making control of Reconstruction an issue in the 1866 congressional elections. He toured the North, campaigning for candidates who supported his policies.

Johnson's views were discredited, however, by riots that took place in Memphis, Tennessee, and New Orleans, Louisiana, in 1866. In both cities, white mobs attacked African American soldiers and freedmen, killing dozens of people and injuring hundreds more. "You may judge [Johnson] by the terrible massacre at New Orleans," proclaimed Charles Sumner, a Radical Republican leader in the Senate. The Republicans won an overwhelming victory over the candidates favored by Johnson.

The Reconstruction Acts The election of 1866 gave the Radicals the votes in Congress to take control of Reconstruction. They quickly passed, over Johnson's veto, the first of four **Reconstruction Acts** in March 1867. This law divided the South into five military districts under the control of the U.S. Army. Only Tennessee, which Congress had readmitted to the Union in 1866, was exempt from the law.

The act required the remaining states to ratify the Fourteenth Amendment, to write new state constitutions that guaranteed freedmen the right to vote, and to form new state governments elected by all male citizens, including African Americans. A state would not be eligible for readmission to the Union until these three conditions were met.

Congress passed three more Reconstruction Acts in 1867 and 1868. These laws authorized the army to register African Americans to vote. Military commanders could also remove any elected official who did not cooperate.

Since these laws placed much of Congress's program in the hands of the army, Republican leaders worried that President Johnson might <u>utilize</u> his power as commander in chief to interfere with Reconstruction. To prevent this, Congress passed the Tenure of Office Act in March 1867. This law required Senate permission to remove any official whose appointment had required Senate approval.

President Johnson's impeachment The Tenure of Office Act set off the final battle between Johnson and the Republicans. The dispute centered around Lincoln's secretary of war, Edwin Stanton, who had stayed on in

MILITARY DISTRICTS, 1867

CANADA

Military district I
Military district II
Military district III
Military district IV
Military district V
Not part of a military district

Dates refer to year of readmission to the Union

VA (1870)
NC (1868)
TN (1866)
SC (1868)
AR (1868)
MS (1870)
AL (1868)
GA (1870)
LA (1868)
TX (1870)
FL (1868)

ATLANTIC OCEAN

MEXICO

Gulf of Mexico

30°N
80°W
90°W

0   150   300 Miles
0   150   300 Kilometers
Albers equal-area projection

GEOGRAPHY SKILLS INTERPRETING MAPS

1. **Regions** Into how many military districts was the South divided? What states made up each district?
2. **Location** In what order were the states readmitted to the Union?

See **Skills Handbook**, p. H20

the Johnson cabinet. Stanton was a strong supporter of congressional Republicans. It was difficult for Johnson to undermine Congress's program with Stanton in charge of the army.

When Johnson fired Stanton, the House of Representatives voted in February 1868 to impeach the president for violating the Tenure of Office Act. **Impeachment** is the process set forth in the Constitution for charging the president or another federal official with a crime. Once impeached by the House, the president is tried by the Senate, where a two-thirds vote is needed for conviction.

After a two-month trial, the Senate fell just one vote short of convicting President Johnson and removing him from office. The verdict allowed Johnson to remain in office.

Although his control of Reconstruction had ended, Johnson continued to issue pardons. By the end of 1868 the rights of almost all Confederate leaders had been restored.

The Fifteenth Amendment While the Senate was deciding Johnson's fate, Republicans nominated General Ulysses Grant as their presidential candidate. The election in November 1868 was close, but a half million African American votes in the South gave Grant a comfortable victory in the electoral college.

When Republicans realized that most white southern voters had supported Grant's Democratic opponent, former New York governor **Horatio Seymour**, they pushed the **Fifteenth Amendment** through Congress. The amendment, which stated that people could not be denied the right to vote because of their race, became part of the Constitution in March 1870. Many white northerners opposed the amendment because it applied to their states as well. Women also criticized the amendment because it did not give them voting rights.

Still, by extending suffrage to all African American males, the Fifteenth Amendment brought millions of potential new voters to the Republican Party. It also aimed to protect freedmen from the growing political power of pardoned former Confederates. This protection turned out to be temporary, however, because the amendment did not ban denial of suffrage for reasons other than race.

READING CHECK **Making Inferences** Why was President Johnson impeached?

DEFYING THE TENURE OF OFFICE ACT

THE LITTLE BOY WOULD PERSIST IN HANDLING BOOKS ABOVE HIS CAPACITY.

AND THIS WAS THE DISASTROUS RESULT.

THE GRANGER COLLECTION, NEW YORK

Skills FOCUS **READING LIKE A HISTORIAN**

Johnson ignored the Tenure of Office Act, arguing that the law was unconstitutional.

Identifying Points of View What outcome did the cartoonist predict for the impeachment trial? What was the actual outcome?

SECTION **2** **ASSESSMENT**
go.hrw.com
Online Quiz
Keyword: SD7 HP12

Reviewing Ideas, Terms, and People

1. **a. Recall** What events showed continuing prejudice against African Americans?
   b. Interpret Why were violent acts against African Americans often not punished?
   c. Predict What were some possible social effects of the **Black Codes**?

2. **a. Define** Write a brief definition of **Radical Republicans**.
   b. Analyze Why did President Johnson think the **Civil Rights Act** was unconstitutional?

3. **a. Recall** What did the four **Reconstruction Acts** do?
   b. Predict How do you think women might have used the **Fifteenth Amendment** to fight for their own voting rights?

Critical Thinking

4. **Recognizing Cause and Effect** Copy the chart below and record the events that led to the passage of the Fifteenth Amendment.

Passage of the Fifteenth Amendment

FOCUS ON SPEAKING

5. **Persuasive** Present a speech that Thaddeus Stevens might have given in the House of Representatives. Argue for or against President Johnson's approach to Reconstruction, using supporting details from the section.

Republicans in Charge

BEFORE YOU READ

MAIN IDEA	READING FOCUS	KEY TERMS AND PEOPLE	**P1** 3.1 Compare and contrast the experiences of different ethnic, national, and religious groups, including Native American Indians, in the United States, explaining their contributions to American society and culture.
Republican Reconstruction had a significant impact on life in the South.	1. What changes did Republican government bring to the South? 2. What was life after slavery like for African Americans? 3. How did Reconstruction affect patterns of land ownership and land use in the South?	scalawag carpetbagger Hiram Revels Southern Homestead Act sharecropping tenant farming	

Civil War Hero— and Scalawag

General James Longstreet suffered because of the choices he made after the Civil War.

THE INSIDE STORY

Why did southerners turn against General Longstreet? At first, James Longstreet was a war hero in the South. He had been an important aide to General Lee, who called him "my old war horse." Although seriously wounded and paralyzed in one arm, he served with Lee until the Confederate surrender at Appomattox.

After the war Longstreet quickly became wealthy as a cotton broker and head of an insurance company. But his hero status—and his economic fortunes—soon changed. A practical businessperson, he supported Reconstruction, believing that the best way for the South to rebuild was to cooperate with the victors. In addition, he joined the Republican Party and backed General Grant, an old friend and his wife's cousin, for president in 1868.

To many white southerners, Longstreet went from a war hero to a **scalawag**—a scoundrel and a traitor in the eyes of former Confederates. His businesses failed, and he was forced to turn to the Republican Party in order to make a living. President Grant gave Longstreet a government job in New Orleans. He later held other federal posts, including U.S. ambassador to Turkey and U.S. marshal for Georgia. ◼

Republican Government Brings Change to the South

As Congress and the army took control of Reconstruction, political power shifted in the South. General Longstreet and other white "scalawags" chose to support this change. For Longstreet, becoming a scalawag changed his life dramatically. He had to rely on the Republican Party for government jobs until he died in 1904.

Scalawags and carpetbaggers Many scalawags were farmers who had never owned slaves and had opposed secession and the war. Many also lived in areas where the population was mostly white. They joined the Republicans to prevent the old planter class from returning to power. In addition, some scalawags were planters and other formerly wealthy southerners who had been financially ruined by the war. They hoped that the new state governments would pass laws to protect them from their debts. Still others were business leaders who wanted to end the South's long dependence on plantation agriculture.

The scalawags allied with northern Republicans who came south to take part in the region's political and economic rebirth. Southern critics called these northerners **carpetbaggers**, a reference to a type of cheap suitcase made of carpet. The newcomers were scorned as low-class persons who could carry everything they owned in a carpetbag.

In fact, many carpetbaggers were educated people. Like the scalawags, they came from a variety of backgrounds, ranging from political and business leaders to teachers, Freedmen's Bureau officers, and former soldiers. Some were African American. Many carpetbaggers

Political Cartoon

A bitter war of political cartoons raged throughout the Reconstruction era. In this 1880 cartoon in the magazine *Puck,* James Albert Wales depicts the view of many traditional southern whites toward Radical Reconstruction under President Ulysses S. Grant.

Grant presides over a South that is clearly still in ruins.

President Grant rides atop a carpetbag stuffed with guns and bayonets, carried along by federal soldiers.

The woman representing "the Solid South" stumbles along a rough path, under the weight of a heavy carpetbag.

THE "STRONG" GOVERNMENT 1869—1877.

READING LIKE A HISTORIAN

Interpreting Political Cartoons What is the cartoonist's message about Reconstruction? What details does he use to convey it?

See **Skills Handbook**, p. H31

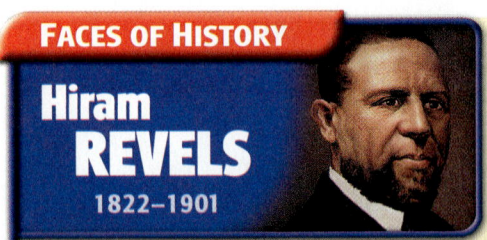
bought abandoned land cheaply or formed partnerships with planters and helped rebuild the South's economy.

African Americans in government

The carpetbaggers and scalawags allied to control southern state governments. They were joined by freedmen, who were eager to exercise the rights they had gained from the Civil Rights Act and the Fourteenth Amendment. In South Carolina and Louisiana, African American delegates outnumbered whites in the constitutional conventions that the Reconstruction Acts required. In other states, about 25 percent of the delegates were African American.

African Americans formed the largest group of Republican voters in the South. As a result, nearly 700 African Americans served in southern state legislatures during Reconstruction. Sixteen African Americans served in Congress. They included **Hiram Revels**, who took the Senate seat held by Confederate president Jefferson Davis before the war. In all, more than 1,500 African Americans held state and local offices during Radical Reconstruction.

New state governments

The state governments established under Radical Reconstruction brought many changes to the South. New state constitutions guaranteed male freedmen the right to vote. Republican governments created the region's first public school systems. They also built many hospitals as well as institutions for orphans and people with mental disabilities. These schools and other facilities were open to all southerners, although they were usually segregated by race.

The new governments eliminated property requirements for voting and officeholding. They modernized divorce laws and expanded the rights of married women. State legislatures in the Lower South enacted laws making it illegal for railroads, hotels, and other public facilities to discriminate against African Americans. The Black Codes were repealed in every state.

To help the South's economy grow, the Republicans built thousands of miles of new railroads. Railroad companies got grants of land and money from state governments. The government raised this money by increasing taxes on large landowners. At the same time, they reduced taxes on poor farmers.

Many of these changes angered the planters and Democratic Party politicians who had controlled the South for so long. Some of the freedmen were unhappy too, because the Republican governments did little to help them obtain their own land.

READING CHECK Identifying the Main Idea
Who were scalawags and carpetbaggers? What did they join together to do?

Life after Slavery for African Americans

Freedom meant a variety of things to formerly enslaved African Americans in the South. For some, it meant the chance to search for long-lost relatives who had been sold during slavery. Many freedmen traveled thousands of miles to reunite with family members.

Seeking economic opportunity

Other freedmen searched for employment, often by moving to urban areas. The African American population of the South's 10 largest cities doubled by 1870. A smaller number of freedmen moved to the North. Cities in both North and South usually offered only segregation, poor housing, and low-paying jobs.

Some former slaves went west, where they started businesses or worked as miners, soldiers, and cowboys. Most freedmen remained in the rural South, however. Whether they continued to work for their former slaveholders

THE IMPACT TODAY

Government
The 110th Congress included 42 African Americans in the House and 1 in the Senate. Only 5 African Americans, including Hiram Revels, have served in the Senate.

African Americans and Reconstruction

During the early days of Reconstruction, new doors opened for African Americans in the South. Not only did they gain political power in state legislatures and in Congress, but they were also able to enjoy the simple human privileges and joys of daily life unknown to them under slavery.

Economic Freedom A store owner (in the apron) celebrates Emancipation Day—and his economic freedom—in 1888.

Freedom of Worship African American families pose for a photograph at a church picnic.

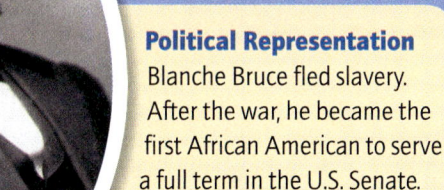

Political Representation Blanche Bruce fled slavery. After the war, he became the first African American to serve a full term in the U.S. Senate.

Educational Opportunity Students attend the Hampton Institute in Virginia, ca. 1899. The institute was founded in 1868 to provide moral training and industrial education to freedmen.

Skills FOCUS **INTERPRETING INFOGRAPHICS**

These scenes, like snapshots out of a family album, would have been virtually unimaginable to generations of families trapped in slavery. Life during Reconstruction wasn't easy, but it brought hope.

Contrasting How might the people in each of these photographs have described the changes in their circumstances after the war?

See **Skills Handbook**, p. H18

depended on how they had been treated as slaves. If the slaveholder had been violent, few of his workers were likely to remain.

One such slaveholder tried to convince a former slave family who had moved to Ohio to return to the plantation. The husband wrote back with this reply:

HISTORY'S VOICES

❝We have concluded to trust your sincerity by asking you to send us our wages for the time we served you. This will make us forget and forgive old scores, and rely on your justice and friendship in the future.❞

—Jourdan Anderson, August 7, 1865

Education and religion Denied schooling under slavery, freed African American slaves eagerly sought education. By 1877 more than 600,000 African Americans had enrolled in elementary schools in the South. The Freedmen's Bureau alone started more than 4,000 schools.

Many northern groups, both black and white, sponsored schools. A general who had commanded black troops during the war started Hampton Institute in Virginia in 1868. Hampton's system of vocational education became the model for most black colleges in the South. The American Missionary Association founded seven colleges, including Fisk University in Nashville, Tennessee. Fisk was unique at the time because it stressed higher education for freedmen instead of job training.

African Americans established other institutions themselves, especially churches. Under slavery they had been forced to worship in their slaveholders' churches. During Reconstruction freedmen founded their own churches. These churches became centers of community life for African Americans, and ministers became community leaders.

Some black churches also started schools. Morehouse College was founded in 1867 by Springfield Baptist Church in Augusta, Georgia, to prepare African Americans for careers as ministers and teachers. Morehouse moved to Atlanta in 1879. It became best known for educating Dr. Martin Luther King Jr.

The meaning of freedom Freedmen created a wide variety of other organizations to help themselves and one another. These included debating clubs, drama societies, trade associations, fire companies, and mutual aid societies. African Americans in Nashville, Atlanta, New Orleans, and other southern cities raised money to establish orphanages, soup kitchens, employment agencies, and funds to aid the poor.

Robert Fitzgerald, a black carpetbagger in Virginia, was encouraged to see freedmen taking the lead to improve themselves and gain control of their lives.

HISTORY'S VOICES

❝They tell me before Mr. Lincoln made them free they had nothing to work for, to look up to, now they have everything, and will, by God's help, make the best of it.❞

—Robert Fitzgerald, diary entry

READING CHECK **Summarizing** What were some new educational opportunities for African Americans in the 1860s and 1870s?

Reconstruction and Land Ownership

The main symbol of personal freedom and economic independence to many former enslaved African Americans was their own land. At first former slaves often claimed a right to plantation land because of the years of unpaid labor they had provided. For some freedmen, the redistribution of the planters' land seemed a logical step after emancipation.

Hopes for land fade In Section 1 you read about land redistribution in Georgia and South Carolina. Freedmen hoped this would be repeated elsewhere. But President Johnson soon returned land in the South to its original white owners.

Although some Radical Republicans wanted to give the planters' land to their former slaves, most considered this proposal too extreme. Instead, Congress passed the Southern Homestead Act in June 1866. This law set aside 45 million acres of government-owned land in southern states to provide free farms for African Americans. Few freedmen had the means to buy seed, animals, and equipment, however. As a result, only about 4,000 families took advantage of the offer, and the law was repealed in 1872.

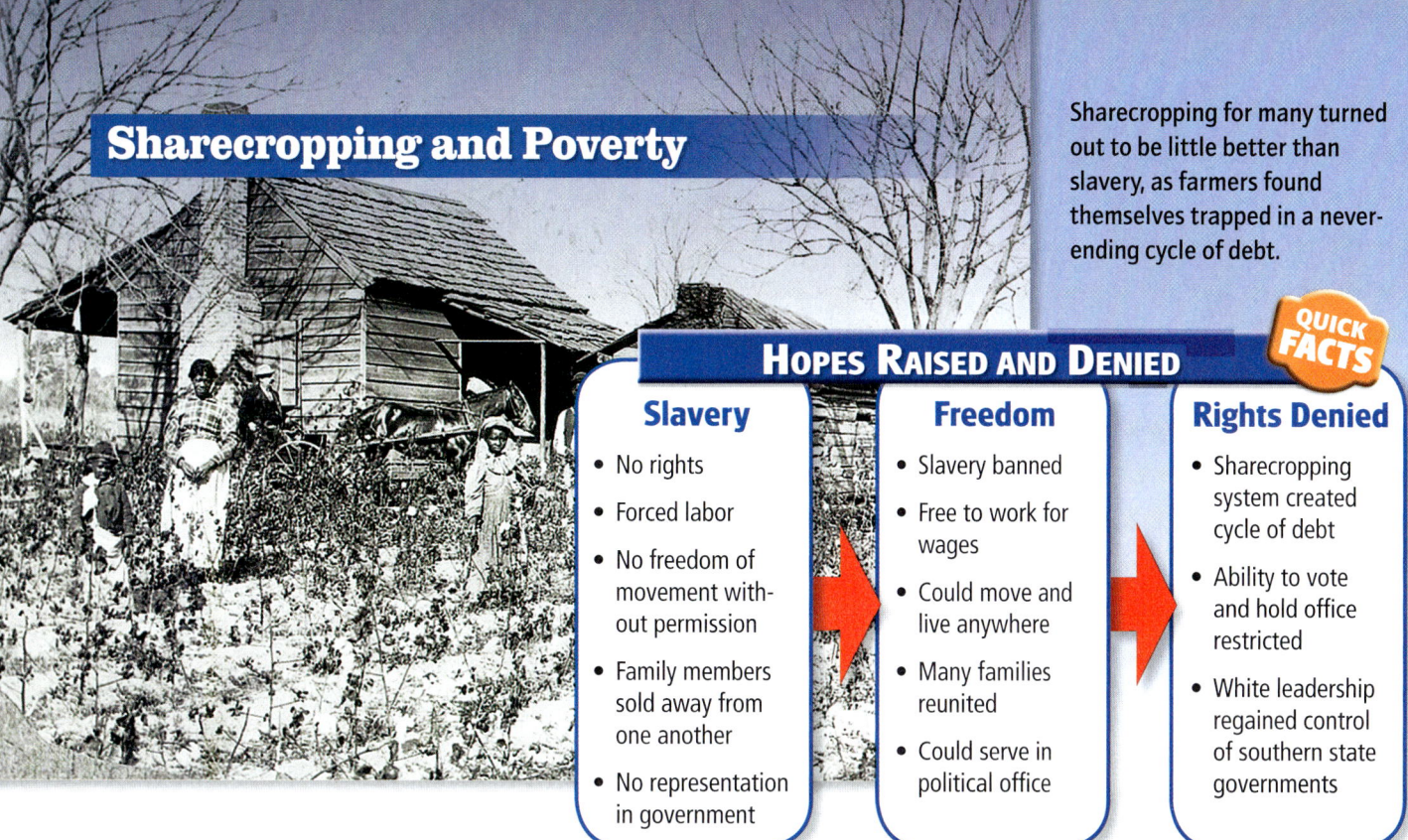

Sharecropping and Poverty

Sharecropping for many turned out to be little better than slavery, as farmers found themselves trapped in a never-ending cycle of debt.

HOPES RAISED AND DENIED

Slavery
- No rights
- Forced labor
- No freedom of movement without permission
- Family members sold away from one another
- No representation in government

Freedom
- Slavery banned
- Free to work for wages
- Could move and live anywhere
- Many families reunited
- Could serve in political office

Rights Denied
- Sharecropping system created cycle of debt
- Ability to vote and hold office restricted
- White leadership regained control of southern state governments

Freedmen who did have money to buy land often found landowners unwilling to sell to them. In part, this was because white southerners did not want to lose their supply of cheap labor. Land ownership would give former slaves economic independence. "Freedom and independence are different things," a Mississippi planter wrote in his diary. "A man may be free and yet not independent."

Still, some freedmen found ways to buy farms and other land. In Mississippi, for example, 1 in every 12 African American families owned land by 1870.

Sharecroppers and tenant farmers

Most freedmen were not content to work for the low wages planters were willing—and in many cases able—to pay. They also disliked working in supervised groups as they had under slavery. As a result, a new system gradually arose to replace the wage labor system. Instead of working for wages, freedmen began receiving a share of their employer's crop. This arrangement was known as **sharecropping**. By the end of the 1870s most freedmen and many poor white southerners were sharecroppers.

Under the sharecropping system, the employer provided land, seed, tools, a mule, and a cabin. The sharecropper provided the labor. Employers benefited because they no longer had to pay their workers. In turn, sharecroppers benefited by having a specific plot of land to farm.

A sharecropper who did well and saved some money might switch to **tenant farming**. Tenant farmers rented the land they farmed from the landowner. This arrangement allowed tenant farmers to grow whatever crops they chose. Many preferred growing food crops to cotton. Food crops increased freedmen's independence by providing not only a source of income but also food for their families as well.

Several factors combined to keep most sharecroppers and tenant farmers in poverty, however. Neither group had any income until harvest time. To meet their everyday needs, they had to promise their crop to local merchants, who then sold them other goods on credit. If the sale of the crop did not produce enough money to pay for their purchases, the merchant added the remaining debt to the next year's bill.

This system made it difficult for many sharecroppers and tenant farmers to get out of poverty and gain true independence. It also helped keep the South's economy tied to one-crop agriculture. Merchants generally gave credit only to farmers who grew certain crops. Most often they were only interested in extending credit to farmers who grew cotton.

Rise of Southern Industry

Workers process cloth in a cotton factory in North Carolina. In 1860 about 324,000 spindles turned in southern cotton mills. By 1900 that number rose to nearly 4.4 million.

A nationwide depression caused cotton prices to fall steeply in the 1870s. This prompted southern farmers to grow more cotton in an attempt to raise their incomes. Crop surpluses drove prices even lower, plunging sharecroppers and tenant farmers deeper into debt.

Industrial growth in the South Even as the rural South suffered economically, southern cities grew rapidly. As Radical Republican governments improved the South's railroad system and linked it to northern lines, Atlanta and other cities gradually became important business centers. Southern business leaders joined with northern investors to build textile mills and other manufacturing ventures.

Most of the South's industrial growth occurred after Reconstruction ended. The growth did not greatly benefit African Americans or other poor southerners. Industrial workers in the South earned far lower wages than northern workers. Most southern African Americans could not find factory work at all.

In some industries, workers lived in houses provided by their employer and bought goods on credit at the company store. Like sharecroppers and tenant farmers, they often found themselves locked in a cycle of debt.

READING CHECK **Contrasting** How did sharecropping and tenant farming differ?

---

go.hrw.com
Online Quiz
Keyword: SD7 HP12

Reviewing Ideas, Terms, and People

1. **a. Identify** Who was **Hiram Revels**?
   b. Explain What did the new state governments accomplish under Radical Reconstruction?
   c. Rate Do you think the new governments were successful in bringing change to the South?

2. **a. Describe** What organizations were created in the 1860s and 1870s to help African Americans take advantage of their freedom?
   b. Analyze Among formerly enslaved African Americans, why did freedom mean different things to different people?

3. **a. Recall** What was the **Southern Homestead Act**?
   b. Explain Why did the system of **sharecropping** make it difficult for freedmen to become economically independent?
   c. Evaluate Why was land ownership a key issue for African Americans at this time?

Critical Thinking

4. **Comparing and Contrasting** Copy the chart below and fill in some details about African American workers as sharecroppers, tenant farmers, and industrial workers. Use details from Section 3 to fill in the chart. What does your completed chart tell you about opportunities for African American workers during this time?

African Americans as sharecroppers	African Americans as tenant farmers	African Americans as industrial workers

FOCUS ON WRITING

5. **Descriptive** Write a letter from a freedman to a planter looking for workers. Describe the conditions under which you will return to work for the planter. Use details from this section in your letter.

SECTION 4

Reconstruction Collapses

BEFORE YOU READ

MAIN IDEA

A variety of events and forces led to the end of Reconstruction, which left a mixed legacy for the nation.

READING FOCUS

1. What problems caused support for Reconstruction to decline?
2. What events brought Reconstruction to an end?
3. What was Reconstruction's legacy for the South and for the rest of the nation?

KEY TERMS AND PEOPLE

Enforcement Acts
Liberal Republicans
Redeemers
Rutherford B. Hayes
Samuel J. Tilden
Compromise of 1877
New South
Solid South

P1 3.3 Prepare essays and oral reports about the important social, political, economic, scientific, technological, and cultural developments, issues, and events from New York State and United States history.

In the Shadow of Slavery

THE GRANGER COLLECTION, NEW YORK

▲ **Many African Americans after the Civil War met with violence and oppression from whites.**

THE INSIDE STORY

What was life like for African Americans in the South after the Civil War? Violence erupted in much of the Reconstruction-era South. Some angry southerners attacked newly freed African Americans and the white Americans who supported the freedmen's right to equality.

Violence was both personal and political. The Ku Klux Klan began as a social group but soon became a terrorist organization. It was the most widespread white supremacist group, but not the only one. Others included the White Liners, the White League, and the Knights of the White Camelia. These groups all used tactics such as threats, beatings, whippings, and even torture and murder. They burned down schools and churches. Race riots broke out in cities and towns.

George Houston, a tailor born in slavery, was a political activist in Alabama and a member of the state legislature. In August 1869, members of the Klan paid him a visit. A Klansman wounded his son, broke down the door, and shot him in the leg.

Houston put up a fight. He had only a gun for shooting squirrels, but "[I] cocked the barrel and shot at his head at fifteen steps . . . My wife jumped and fastened the window. Then they shot the window full of holes and the side of the house beside that. As she shut the window the balls came in the house like rain. They shot the whole side of the house."

Unlike many unfortunate victims, the Houstons were rescued eventually. After the terrifying incident, they moved away, but George Houston remained defiant: "I say the Republican party freed me, and I will die on top of it. I don't care who is pleased. I vote every time."

Problems with Reconstruction

Despite the efforts to control it, violent opposition to Reconstruction plagued the South through much of the Reconstruction era.

Terrorist groups in the South The hooded and disguised night riders of the Ku Klux Klan were the most active terrorists, but many similar organizations existed. Their members included planters, merchants, and poor white farmers and laborers. They were united by a common desire to undo the South's new hierarchy and restore the old political and social order. Although only a small minority of white southerners were members of these groups, many others supported their goals.

The groups' main target was African Americans, especially local leaders. But both blacks and whites were terrorized by threats, house burnings, and much worse. Members of these groups beat Freedmen's Bureau teachers, women as well as men. They murdered an Arkansas member of Congress and three members of the Georgia legislature, along with thousands of other people. Many state and local officials resigned in fear. A carpetbagger in North Carolina described the situation.

HISTORY'S VOICES

> ❝Of the slain, there were enough to furnish forth a battlefield, and all from those three classes, the negro, the scalawag, and the carpet-bagger—all killed with deliberation . . . shot, stabbed, hanged, drowned . . . And almost always by an unknown hand . . . execution without warning, mercy, or appeal . . . in the treachery which made a neighbor a disguised assassin.❞
>
> —Albion Tourgée, *A Fool's Errand,* 1879

The groups did not limit their attacks to white Republicans and politically active African Americans, however. They also assaulted and killed African Americans whom they regarded as too economically successful.

PRIMARY SOURCES

Political Cartoon

During the Grant administration, corruption plagued the federal government. Many politicians used their offices for financial gain. Grant was not directly involved in any scandals, but many people felt that they reflected his lack of leadership.

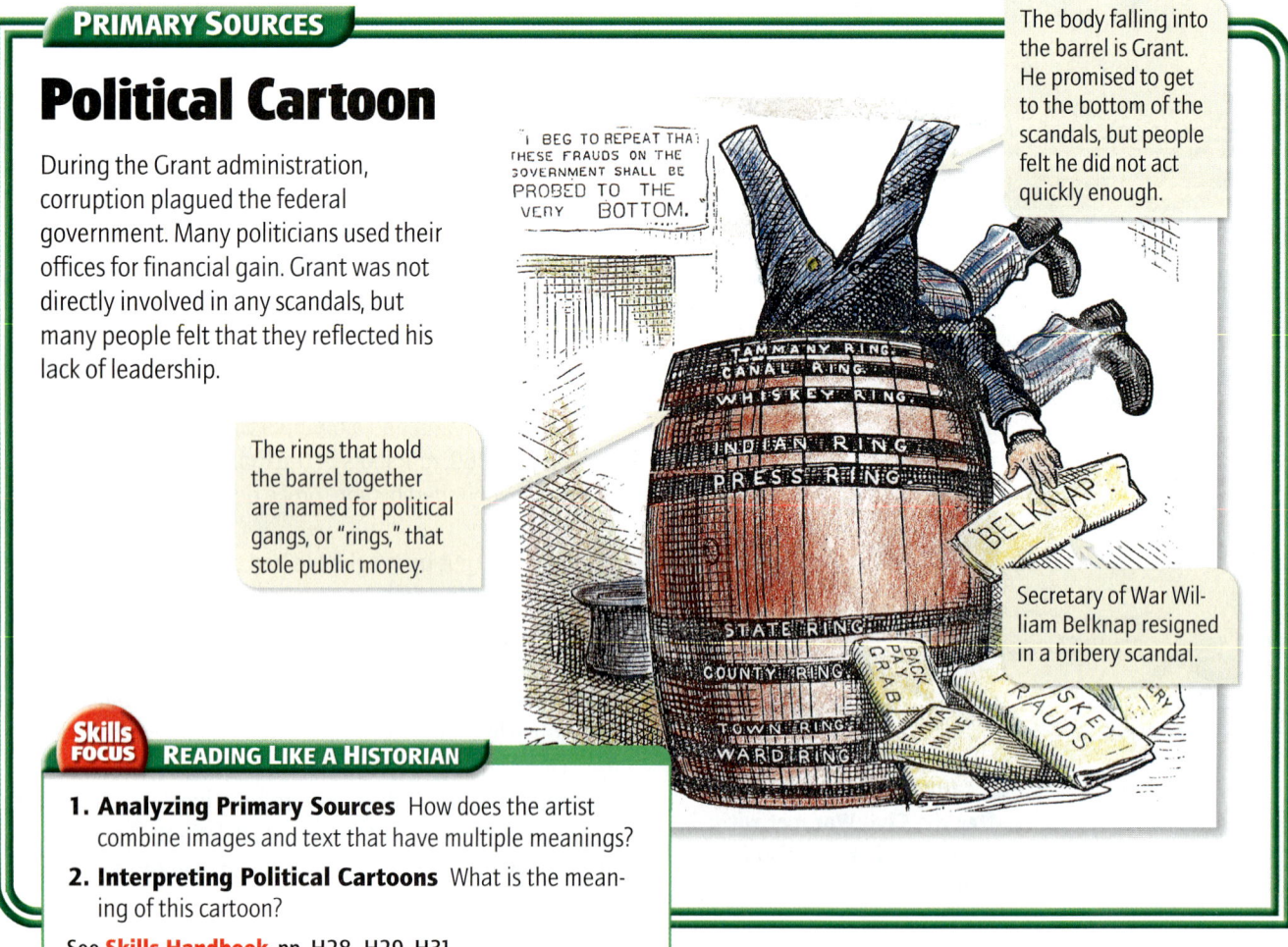

The body falling into the barrel is Grant. He promised to get to the bottom of the scandals, but people felt he did not act quickly enough.

The rings that hold the barrel together are named for political gangs, or "rings," that stole public money.

Secretary of War William Belknap resigned in a bribery scandal.

Skills FOCUS **READING LIKE A HISTORIAN**

1. **Analyzing Primary Sources** How does the artist combine images and text that have multiple meanings?
2. **Interpreting Political Cartoons** What is the meaning of this cartoon?

See **Skills Handbook**, pp. H28–H29, H31

When state governments proved unable to control this violence, Congress passed three **Enforcement Acts** in 1870 and 1871. These laws set heavy penalties, including imprisonment, for anyone attempting to prevent a qualified citizen from voting. They also banned the use of disguises to deprive any person of rights. The laws empowered the army and federal courts to capture and punish Ku Klux Klan members. Although the Klan's power was soon broken, many similar groups continued to operate.

Support for Reconstruction declines

White southerners claimed the Enforcement Acts threatened individual freedom. The laws also caused support for Reconstruction to decline in the North. Many northerners were dismayed that after so many years the army was still needed to keep peace in the South and that the Republican state governments were so ineffective. This reaction was exactly what the terrorist groups wanted.

Even southern Republicans began losing faith in Reconstruction. African Americans remained unhappy about their widespread poverty and the lack of land reform. Southerners of both races were discouraged by the region's poor overall economic condition, despite the Republicans' costly building programs and other reforms. These programs raised taxes and plunged the states into debt. Some programs, especially railroad building, also raised charges that the Reconstruction governments were inefficient and corrupt.

Conditions in the South strengthened the **Liberal Republicans**. This group broke with the party over the Enforcement Acts and the scandals that plagued the Grant administration. Although they could not block Grant's re-election in 1872, Liberal Republicans helped Democrats regain control of the House of Representatives in 1874. The Republican majority in the Senate was cut almost in half.

Economic factors also weakened support for Reconstruction. A severe five-year depression began in 1873, taking a toll on the South's economy as it was struggling to rebuild. The depression's impact in the North caused Republican leaders to pay less attention to Reconstruction and more to economic issues.

READING CHECK **Summarizing** What caused support for Reconstruction to decline?

The End of Reconstruction

By the mid-1870s it was clear to northerners and southerners alike that Reconstruction was on the decline. The most determined leaders of Reconstruction, Representative Thaddeus Stevens and Senator Charles Sumner, had died, and decisions of the Supreme Court were weakening key provisions of Reconstruction.

In 1873 the Supreme Court ruled in the *Slaughterhouse Cases* that most civil rights and freedoms remained under state control and were therefore not protected by the Fourteenth Amendment. Three years later, in *United States* v. *Cruikshank*, the Court ruled that the Fourteenth Amendment did not empower the federal government to punish whites who suppressed African Americans.

In *United States* v. *Reese* (1876), the Court determined that the Fifteenth Amendment did not protect voting rights if they were denied for some other reason than race. These three Supreme Court decisions combined to seriously weaken the goals and operations of Reconstruction.

"Redeeming" the South As support for Reconstruction declined in both the North and the South, southern Democratic leaders and their supporters grew stronger and bolder. Lawlessness and terrorism increased as they tried to regain control of their governments.

Terrorists publicly threatened, beat, and even murdered Republican candidates and their supporters in broad daylight. On election days armed Democrats stole or destroyed ballot boxes and drove African American voters from the polls. When Mississippi's governor asked for federal help to solve these problems in 1875, President Grant refused, saying that the northern public was "tired out" by the South's continuing problems.

By 1876 only South Carolina, Louisiana, and Florida remained under Republican rule. The Democrats who controlled the other southern states called themselves the **Redeemers** for having redeemed, or won back, their states from the Republicans. Many Redeemers were former Confederate leaders. Inspired by the Redeemers, Democrats in South Carolina, Louisiana, and Florida were determined to regain control of their states from the Republican leaders of Reconstruction, too.

THE ELECTION OF 1876

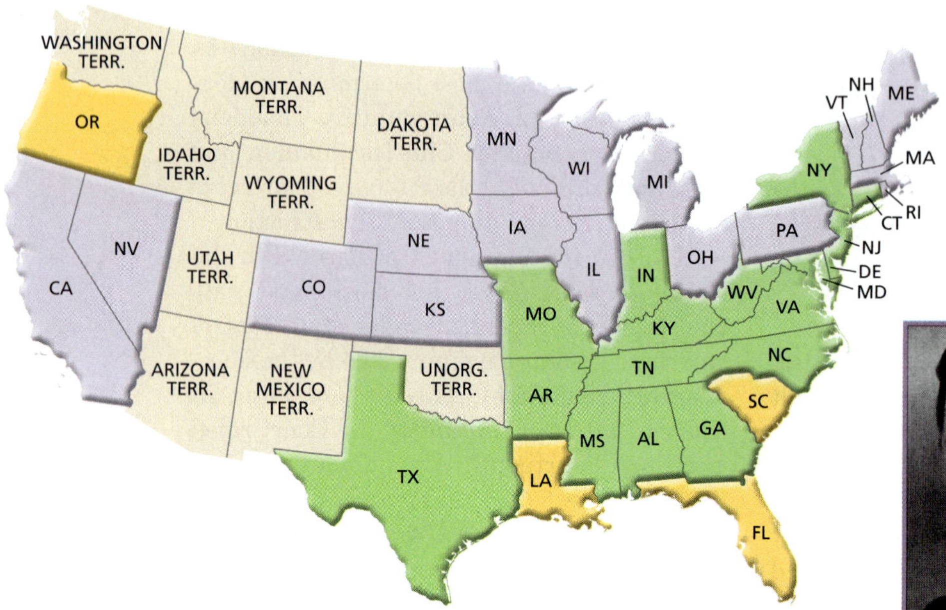

Candidate	Political Affiliation	Electoral Votes	Popular Votes
Rutherford B. Hayes	Republican	165	4,036,298
Samuel J. Tilden	Democratic	184	4,300,590
Disputed		20	

Rutherford B. Hayes

Samuel J. Tilden

GEOGRAPHY SKILLS INTERPRETING MAPS

1. **Region** What regional voting patterns can you identify on the map?

2. **Location** In which states were the electoral votes disputed?

See **Skills Handbook**, p. H20

The election of 1876 Southern Democrats' efforts in South Carolina, Louisiana, and Florida had a direct effect on the presidential election of 1876. The election pitted Ohio's Republican governor, **Rutherford B. Hayes**, against Democrat **Samuel J. Tilden**, the governor of New York.

Tilden narrowly won the popular vote. He also finished ahead in the electoral college vote, 184–165. Yet he was still one vote short of the majority he needed to win the election. This was because 20 electoral votes were disputed. All but one of the disputed votes were from the three southern states the Republicans still controlled. Tilden needed only one more electoral vote to win the majority and become president. Hayes, the Republican candidate, needed all 20 of the disputed votes.

Charges flew that massive voting fraud had taken place in Louisiana, South Carolina, and Florida. Republicans claimed that Democrats in those states had prevented African Americans from voting. Democrats complained that

election officials appointed by the Republican governments in Louisiana, South Carolina, and Florida had thrown out large numbers of votes cast by Democrats.

Nearly everyone agreed that Oregon's disputed electoral vote should go to Hayes. But each side claimed the 19 votes from Louisiana, South Carolina, and Florida. Democrats threatened to put Tilden in the White House by force if necessary. "Tilden or War," Democratic newspapers proclaimed.

Congress could not resolve the crisis on its own. In January 1877 it established an Electoral Commission to decide which candidate deserved each vote. After some political maneuvering, the Republicans gained an 8–7 majority on the 15-member commission. Not surprisingly, this commission awarded all 20 of the disputed votes to the Republican candidate, Hayes.

To get the Democratic-controlled House of Representatives to accept the Electoral Commission's decision, Democratic and Republican

THE IMPACT TODAY

Government

Close presidential election results in 2000 and 2004 resulted in claims of fraud, including alleged efforts to prevent African Americans from voting or to exclude their votes from the count. No fraud prosecutions resulted, but various federal, state, and private commissions formed to recommend election reforms.

leaders negotiated the **Compromise of 1877**. In return for Hayes becoming president, Republicans agreed to withdraw the remaining federal troops from the South. Without the protection of the federal government, the last of the Republican state governments collapsed and Reconstruction came to an end.

READING CHECK **Identifying Cause and Effect** How did the election of 1876 contribute to the end of Reconstruction?

Reconstruction's Legacy

Reconstruction and its collapse deeply affected the nation's future development. The Fourteenth and Fifteenth Amendments began permanent change in both the South and the North. These amendments, which were part of the Radicals' program to make former slaves citizens and guarantee them the right to vote, established citizenship and voting rights for northern African Americans as well. Passage of the Fifteenth Amendment also increased calls for women to have the right to vote, too.

After Reconstruction, some southerners referred to their region as the **New South**. This was because the late 1800s and early 1900s were a time of industrialization and economic change in the South. In other ways, however, the South remained as it had been before

the Civil War. The Supreme Court's decisions weakening the protections of the Fourteenth and Fifteenth Amendments encouraged those who preferred the old southern way of life.

The Redeemers, for example, found ways to return African Americans to what one white southerner called "an era of second slavery." You will learn more about the Redeemers' actions in a later chapter.

If the Civil War was fought to settle the issue of states' rights, the experience of Reconstruction showed that it failed to do so. White southerners deeply resented that the federal government controlled their states for more than a decade after the war. This resentment continued in the South for much of the next century.

Reconstruction also intensified the hostility that many white southerners had felt toward the Republican Party before and during the Civil War. For a century after Reconstruction ended, the South was so strongly Democratic that it was known as the **Solid South**. Not until the 1970s did the Republican Party begin to regain the level of support in the South that it enjoys today.

READING CHECK **Comparing and Contrasting** What changes did Reconstruction bring to the South? In what ways did the South remain unchanged?

SECTION 4 ASSESSMENT

Reviewing Ideas, Terms, and People

1. a. Recall What terrorist groups operated in the South after the Civil War? What kinds of actions did they take to oppose Reconstruction?
b. Analyze Did the **Enforcement Acts** help to carry out Reconstruction? Why or why not?
c. Evaluate Do you think northerners were right to stop supporting Reconstruction? Why or why not?

2. a. Identify Which leaders of Reconstruction had died by 1877?
b. Summarize What did the Supreme Court decide in the *Slaughterhouse Cases*, *United States* v. *Cruikshank*, and *United States* v. *Reese*?
c. Evaluate Do you think the **Compromise of 1877** was a good idea? Why or why not?

3. a. Define Write a brief definition for the following terms: **New South**, **Solid South**.

b. Analyze Why did Reconstruction bring back issues of states' rights?
c. Predict What do you think happened in the South after the end of Reconstruction?

Critical Thinking

4. Sequencing Copy the chart below and fill in the events in the North, South, and entire nation that contributed to the end of Reconstruction.

_____ _____ _____ _____ Reconstruction ends

FOCUS ON SPEAKING

6. Persuasive Suppose you are a member of the House of Representatives in 1877. Present a speech urging your fellow House members to accept or reject the Compromise of 1877.

Changed Lives during Reconstruction

Historical Context The documents below provide different information on how Reconstruction changed people's lives in the South.

Task Examine the documents and answer the questions that follow. Then you will be asked to write an essay about how Reconstruction changed people's lives, using facts from the documents and from the chapter to support the position you take in your thesis statement.

ST 4.3 Develop hypotheses about important events, eras, or issues; move from chronicling to explaining historical events and issues; use information collected from diverse sources to produce cogently written reports and document-based essays.

DOCUMENT 1

Many southerners fully expected their former slaves to continue to work for them and were shocked when they left to seek opportunities elsewhere. In this letter, freedman Jourdan Anderson, living in Dayton, Ohio, responds to a request from his former master to come back to Tennessee and work on the plantation.

"I am doing tolerably well here; I get $25 a month, with [food] and clothing; have a comfortable home for [my wife] Mandy (the folks here call her Mrs. Anderson), and the children, Milly, Jane, and Grundy, go to school and are learning well . . . We are kindly treated . . . Now, if you will write and say what wages you will give me, I will be better able to decide whether it will be to my advantage to move back again . . .

Mandy says she would be afraid to go back without some proof that you are sincerely disposed to treat us just and kindly—and we have concluded to test your sincerity by asking you to send us our wages for the time we served you . . . I served you faithfully for thirty-two years and Mandy twenty years. At $25 a month for me, and $2 a week for Mandy, our earnings would amount to $11,680. Add to this the interest for the time our wages has been kept back and deduct what you paid for our clothing and three doctor's visits to me, and pulling a tooth for Mandy, and the balance will show what we are in justice entitled to . . . If you fail to pay us for faithful labors in the past we can have little faith in your promises in the future."

DOCUMENT 2

The Reconstruction era saw many new opportunities for poor whites as well as for black southerners. The use of slaves had limited the amount of work for wages that was needed and available in the South. Now, African Americans and poor whites often competed for similar work. In the following article, a newspaper in Petersburg, Virginia, noted the changes Reconstruction brought to service employment in the city.

"Formerly a white drayman [hauler of heavy goods] or cartman or hack [buggy] driver was a sight unknown in our streets, now they share these employments with the blacks, and eventually will monopolize them . . . Formerly most, if not all, of our bars were tended by colored men, though owned by whites, now the [drinks] are mixed, as well as the rent paid, and the stock kept up by white men in many instances. Formerly, the restaurants of Petersburgh were almost exclusively in the hands of the colored people; now, we believe, there is but one establishment of the sort in the city. Formerly we had only colored barbers; now, the native whites seek, generally, barbers of their own color, and eventually they will do so exclusively."

Former slaves were often eager to seek new lives for themselves and their families. The photograph on the left shows enslaved people and their living quarters on a Georgia plantation around 1860. The photograph on the right shows a family of formerly enslaved people in Mississippi around 1870.

[NEG. #50473] COLLECTION OF THE NEW-YORK HISTORICAL SOCIETY

Skills FOCUS READING LIKE A HISTORIAN

1. a. Describe Refer to Document 1. What does Anderson ask his former master to do to prove that his offer of a job is sincere?
b. Analyze How does Anderson's letter reflect the changing expectations that former slaves had about their treatment by whites?

2. a. Identify Refer to Document 2. What had changed in Petersburg?
b. Interpret How might some whites use this information to try to convince former slaves to remain on their old plantations?

3. a. Describe Refer to Document 3. Describe the scenes in the two photographs.
b. Compare How do these two photographs reflect changes in dignity for African Americans under slavery and during Reconstruction?

4. Document-Based Essay Question Consider the question below and form a thesis statement. Using examples from Documents 1, 2, and 3, create an outline and write a short essay supporting your position.
How did Reconstruction change the lives of African American and white southerners?

See **Skills Handbook**, pp. H28–29

Visual Summary: Reconstruction

Presidential Reconstruction
- Freedmen's Bureau
- Lincoln's Ten Percent Plan
- Johnson's plans and actions

Congressional Reconstruction
- Civil Rights Act
- Fourteenth and Fifteenth Amendments
- Reconstruction Acts
- Enforcement Acts

Reconstruction Government
- Republican rule
- Scalawags and carpetbaggers
- African American elected officials
- Republican improvement programs

The Reconstruction Era

Resistance to Reconstruction
- Black Codes
- Violence against freedmen
- Violence against Republican rule
- Democratic Redeemers

Reconstruction Economics
- Labor contracts and wage-labor system
- Sharecropping and tenant farming
- Continued dependence on cotton
- African American land ownership

Reconstruction Ends
- Reconstruction's failures
- Declining support
- Liberal Republicans
- Compromise of 1877

Reviewing Key Terms and People

Match each lettered definition with the correct numbered item at right.

a. Leader of the Radical Republicans

b. White citizens that terrorized African Americans

c. Organization to assist uprooted southerners after the Civil War

d. Man who became president after Lincoln's death

e. Southerners who supported changes brought by Reconstruction

f. Northern Republicans who came to the South to take part in the region's rebirth

g. African American who became a senator

h. An attempt to provide land ownership to freed African Americans

i. A farming system that replaced the wage labor system

j. Agreement that brought Reconstruction to an end

1. sharecropping

2. Hiram Revels

3. scalawags

4. Southern Homestead Act

5. Andrew Johnson

6. carpetbaggers

7. Compromise of 1877

8. Freedmen's Bureau

9. Ku Klux Klan

10. Thaddeus Stevens

History's Impact video program

Review the video to answer the closing question: How did the three amendments passed after the Civil War help the civil rights movement a century later?

Comprehension and Critical Thinking

SECTION 1 *(pp. 402–408)*

11. a. Describe What major problems did the South face after the Civil War?

b. Analyze Why did some members of Congress oppose Lincoln's Ten Percent Plan?

c. Predict Why was Johnson's Reconstruction plan likely to provoke problems with Congress?

SECTION 2 *(pp. 410–415)*

12. a. Recall Why did the South welcome Johnson's Reconstruction plan?

b. Draw Conclusions How did Johnson's views help lead to Radical Reconstruction efforts?

c. Evaluate What were some shortcomings of the Fifteenth Amendment?

SECTION 3 *(pp. 416–422)*

13. a. Identify What changes did the new state governments make under Radical Reconstruction?

b. Analyze How did freedom change the lives of African Americans in the South?

c. Elaborate How did the sharecropping system limit the freedom of African Americans?

SECTION 4 *(pp. 423–427)*

14. a. Describe How did legal challenges contribute to the decline of Reconstruction?

b. Drawing Conclusions In what ways was the election of 1876 a victory for the Democrats?

c. Evaluate How much better off were African Americans after Reconstruction than they had been before the Civil War?

Using the Internet

go.hrw.com
Practice Online
Keyword: SD7 CH12

15. A main goal of freed African Americans after the Civil War was to get an education. Using the keyword above, do research to find out more about schools started by the Freedmen's Bureau for African Americans in the South. Then create a report analyzing the impact of these schools.

Analyzing Primary Sources

Reading Like a Historian The damage and destruction of property in the South that resulted from the Civil War was severe. In addition, many places had been neglected as people went to war or fled from areas where fighting was taking place. Re-read the History's Voices passage in Section 1 that begins, "From Pocahontas to Decatur, one hundred and fourteen miles . . ."

16. Identify What does this primary source describe?

17. Predict How would these conditions likely affect the economy of the South?

Critical Reading

Re-read the passage in Section 4 that begins with the heading "Terrorist groups in the South." Then answer the question that follows.

18. When this passage states, "The hooded and disguised night riders of the Ku Klux Klan were the most active terrorists," the term *terrorists* means

A people who favor enslaving African Americans.

B people who use violence to further their goals.

C people who are the targets of attacks.

D people who use disguises and ride at night.

WRITING FOR THE SAT

Think about the following issue:

Three constitutional amendments—the Thirteenth, Fourteenth, and Fifteenth—were passed during Reconstruction. Under Johnson's Reconstruction program, however, the southern states passed Black Codes restricting the rights of African Americans. Subsequent laws passed by the Redeemers and rulings by the Supreme Court continued to weaken the impact of the Reconstruction amendments.

19. Assignment Did Reconstruction ultimately help African Americans gain more rights? Write a short essay in which you develop your position on this issue. Support your point of view with reasoning and examples from your reading and studies.

 **The Nation Splits Apart**
1850–1861

MAIN IDEA **Slavery moved to the forefront of national politics in the 1850s. Despite efforts to find compromises between the North and the South over slavery, southern states eventually seceded from the Union and created the Confederate States of America.**

SECTION 1 In passing the Compromise of 1850 and the Kansas-Nebraska Act, Congress attempted to please both the North and the South. Despite these compromises, many northerners and southerners remained at odds over issues related to slavery.

SECTION 2 Tensions over slavery in Kansas erupted into violence in the mid-1850s. The *Dred Scott* decision in 1857 and Buchanan's actions as president widened the nation's divisions. John Brown's raid on a government arsenal in Virginia in the hope of arming a slave revolt helped to unite southerners in defense of slavery.

SECTION 3 Abraham Lincoln rose in politics in the 1840s and 1850s by opposing the spread of slavery. Lincoln won the presidency in 1860 in an election that not only widened the divisions between North and South but also split the Democratic Party as well.

SECTION 4 Following Abraham Lincoln's election as president, South Carolina seceded from the Union in December 1860. Other states of the Lower South soon followed South Carolina's lead, resulting in the creation of the Confederate States of America in 1861.

 **The Civil War**
1861–1865

MAIN IDEA **The Civil War pitted the North against the South in the bloodiest war the United States had yet seen. Fighting on many fronts, the Union eventually defeated the Confederacy in 1865.**

SECTION 1 The Confederacy attacked Fort Sumter in April 1861. President Lincoln called for troops to put down the rebellion, and both sides prepared for war.

SECTION 2 The Civil War began with decisive victories for the Confederacy in Virginia and for the Union in the Mississippi Valley. The Confederates' success in Virginia prompted Lee to invade the Union in 1862, only to be defeated at the Battle of Antietam.

SECTION 3 Hoping to weaken the Confederates' ability to fight, Lincoln granted freedom to slaves in unconquered areas of the South in 1863. Both sides resorted to unpopular drafts to raise more troops. Opposition to the war became strong in the North and in the South as well, where the hardships of war were especially harsh.

SECTION 4 The Civil War raged at sea as well as on land, where the fighting reached west of the Mississippi River and involved Native Americans. Union victories at Gettysburg and Vicksburg in July 1863 became a turning point in the war.

SECTION 5 Grant's battles with Lee in Virginia and Sherman's march through Georgia and the Carolinas weakened the South. Lincoln's re-election in 1864 ended the South's remaining hopes for victory. Lee finally surrendered to Grant in April 1865.

 **Reconstruction**
1865–1877

MAIN IDEA **Reconstruction of the South following the Civil War went through many phases and brought many changes to the region.**

SECTION 1 Even before the war ended, Union leaders developed reconstruction plans for the South. These plans fell apart after the war and Lincoln's assassination, as President Johnson and Congress differed over how the defeated South should be treated.

SECTION 2 Southern resistance to Reconstruction and the introduction of Black Codes led to Congress taking control of Reconstruction. Led by Radical Republicans, Congress passed laws to change southern society, protect the rights of the newly freed slaves, and take control from former Confederates.

SECTION 3 Former slaves enjoyed new rights and freedoms as southern state governments came under Radical Republican control. Despite much rebuilding, black and white southerners alike continued to suffer from economic problems.

SECTION 4 As northern interest in Reconstruction declined, white southerners regained control in the South. Reconstruction was ended as part of a compromise between Republicans and Democrats to settle the disputed presidential election of 1876.

Themes

Economic Development
The growth of northern steel and oil industries fueled the nation's economy, and the completion of the Transcontinental Railroad encouraged western development.

Immigration and Migration
Westward expansion led to the loss of territory for Native Americans, and in crowded northern cities, many poor immigrants faced difficult living and working conditions.

Cultural Expressions
Transportation by streetcar and subway and innovations such as the telephone and electricity changed the way many Americans lived.

This factory in Springfield, Massachusetts, supplied a bustling nation with everything from freight trains to trolley cars.

Prepare to Read

Identifying Cause and Effect

Find practice for **Identifying Cause and Effect** in the **Skills Handbook,** p. H9

As students of history, you want to know why certain events occurred. By learning to identify causes and effects, you can better understand how historical events influence one another.

Before You Read
Skim the review questions in the reading. List what you already know about the subject matter and what you would like to know about it after the reading.

While You Read
Create a table that lists the causes and effects of various events. Keep in mind that a cause may have many effects, and an effect may have more than one cause.

After You Read
Compare the two lists. How are they alike or different?

The Pullman Strike

Other unions suffered setbacks too. In 1893 the Pullman Company laid off more than half its employees. It cut the wages of the remaining employees as much as 50 percent, but it did not lower their rents.

That led to the decision by workers to go on strike with the support of **Eugene V. Debs,** the leader of the American Railway Union (ARU). He urged the members of the ARU not to work on any trains that included Pullman cars.

The government soon stepped in. It ordered the union to call off the strike because it was interfering with the delivery of U.S. mail. When ARU officials refused, many of them were jailed. Meanwhile, President Grover Cleveland called in federal troops, and the strike collapsed. As a result of their participation in the strike, most of the workers who had taken part wound up fired or blacklisted.

READING CHECK **Identifying Cause and Effect** What events led to the Pullman Strike?

Cause Employees were displeased about layoffs and wage cuts at the Pullman Company.

Effect Employees decided to go on strike against the Pullman Company.

Test Prep Tip

Multiple choice and short answer questions ask you to identify cause and effect. Signal words such as *because* and *led* to show causes. Words such as *therefore, so,* and *since* show effects. An example of an effect in this passage might be, "As a result of their participation in the strike, most of the workers who had taken part were fired or blacklisted."

Evaluating Sources

Find practice for **Evaluating Sources** in the **Skills Handbook,** p. H34

Historians understand that although certain sources are more reliable than others, bias can influence any historical source. Therefore, historians must evaluate all sources. Sources report what writers believe to have happened or what writers want readers to know. Both point of view and personal experience affect sources. Understanding how bias influences a source allows historians to know how, or whether, they will use it.

Strategies historians use:

- Who created the source? Is the author impartial in his or her writing, or influenced by his or her interests?
- What is the purpose of the source? Is it supposed to convey public or private information? Does the writer want to inform or persuade others?
- Compare the source with other sources of information, including both primary and secondary sources. Are they consistent?

Social Darwinism

A professor and minister, William Graham Sumner was the leading proponent of social Darwinism in the United States.

Note the background of each speaker. Sumner was a professor and a minister. As such, he probably lived in a middle-class setting, unlike Rauschenbusch, who lived among impoverished people.

❝If . . . men were <u>willing</u> to set to work with energy and courage . . . all might live in plenty and prosperity. But if they insist on remaining in the slums of great cities . . . there is no device . . . which can prevent them from falling victims to poverty and misery or from succumbing in the competition of life to those who have <u>great command</u> of capital.❞

Look for clue words such as *willing* that might indicate bias. Identify how bias affects each source.

Walter Rauschenbusch, lived among the poor. He found fault with the attitude of the rich toward the working class.

❝Progress slackens when a single class appropriates the social results of the common labor, fortifies its <u>evil</u> rights by unfair laws, throttles the masses by political centralization and suppression, and consumes in luxury what it has taken in <u>covetousness</u> . . . Exploitation creates poverty, and poverty is followed by physical degeneration.❞

Does the source present logical arguments? Are the cause-and-effect relationships sound? Are conclusions rational or emotional?

Skills FOCUS   **READING LIKE A HISTORIAN**

As You Read Evaluate each source and decide whether you would use it to draw conclusions or make generalizations about the historical period or subject.

As You Study After you have evaluated the source, determine the extent to which it relates to your study. Then decide how the source contributes to your historical understanding.

The American WEST

THE BIG PICTURE In opening the West for settlement, the federal government relocated Native Americans to vastly diminished homelands or eliminated them in military battles. Immigrants, African Americans, and white Americans eagerly moved into the new frontier to mine, ranch, and establish farms. New technologies and perseverance helped them survive in the new landscape.

New York Standards

Key Idea 3 Study about the major social, political, economic, cultural, and religious developments in New York State and United States history involves learning about the important roles and contributions of individuals and groups.

Skills FOCUS READING LIKE A HISTORIAN

A family of homesteaders traveling west pauses to pose for a photograph beside their covered wagon in Loup Valley, Nebraska, in 1886. **Interpreting Visuals** Using clues from the photograph, describe what the journey might have been like. What challenges might the family have faced while traveling west?

See **Skills Handbook**, p. H30

U.S.

1868
Sioux sign a treaty agreeing to live on a reservation.

1860

World

1864
The Taiping Rebellion in China leaves 20 million Chinese dead and causes mass emigration.

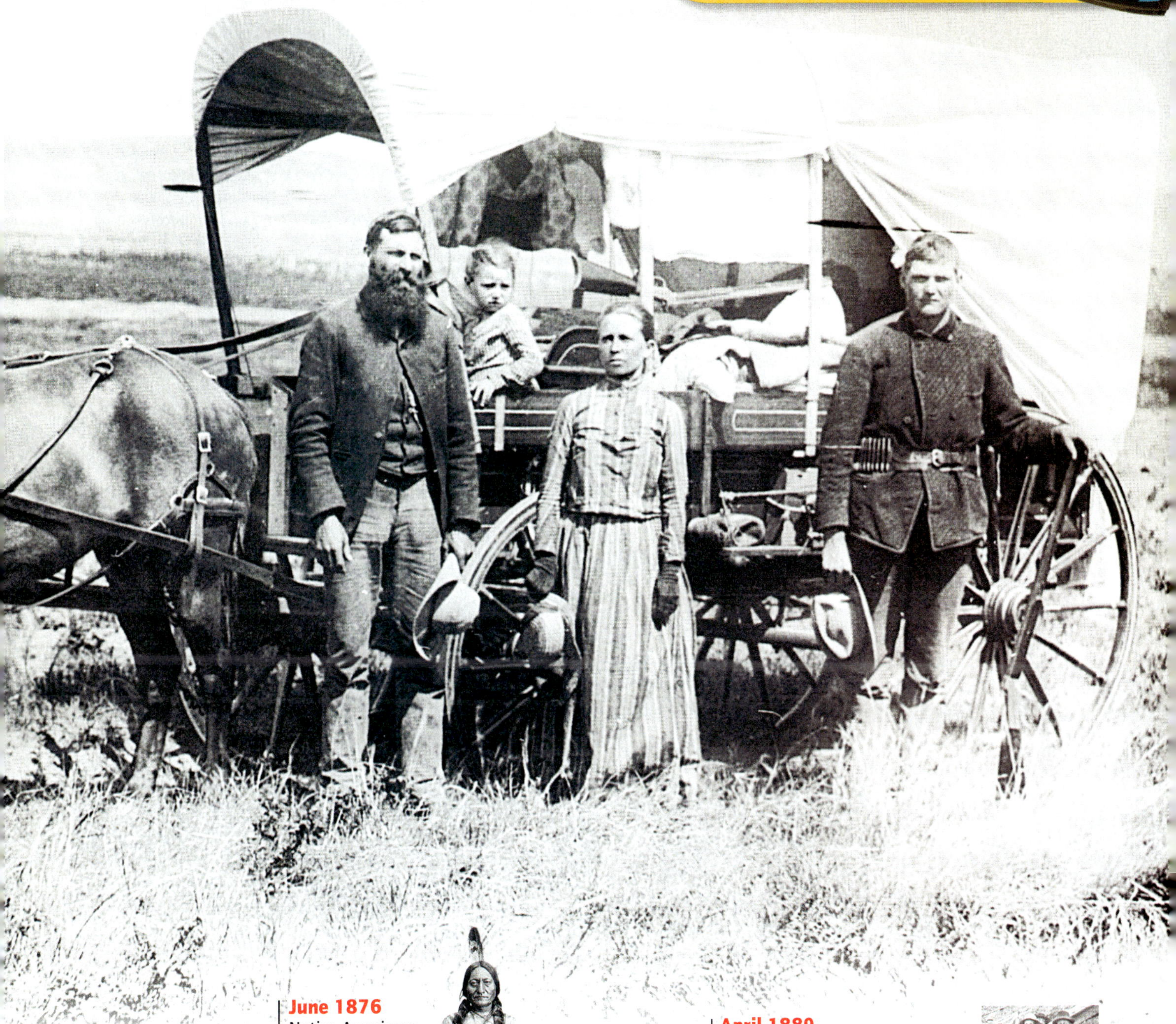

1871
Some 600,000 cattle are driven to market on the Chisholm Trail.

June 1876
Native Americans, led by Sitting Bull, defeat U.S. Cavalry force at the Battle of Little Bighorn.

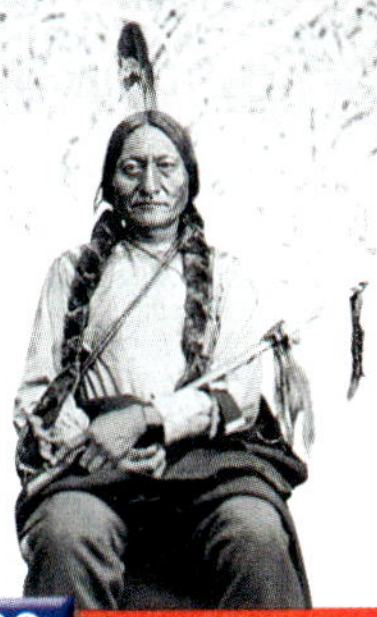

April 1889
Thousands lay claim to land during the Oklahoma Land Run.

July 1897
The Klondike gold rush begins.

1870　　　　　　**1880**　　　　　　**1890**　　　　　　**1900**

1871
Prussia consolidates German states into a unified nation.

1875
Industrial revolution causes 1 million to crowd Berlin.

1880
Crop failures and a troubled economy cause millions of Italians to emigrate to America.

1895
Guglielmo Marconi invents the radio.

437

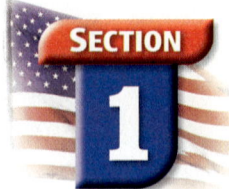

The Fight for the West

BEFORE YOU READ

MAIN IDEA

Native Americans fought the movement of settlers westward, but the U.S. military and the persistence of American settlers proved too strong to resist.

FOCUS QUESTIONS

1. How was the stage set for conflict between white settlers and Native Americans in the West?
2. What were the Indian Wars and their consequences?
3. How did Native American resistance to white settlement end?
4. What was life like on the Indian reservations?

KEY TERMS AND PEOPLE

Sand Creek Massacre
Sitting Bull
George Armstrong Custer
Battle of the Little Bighorn
Wounded Knee Massacre
Chief Joseph
Geronimo
Americanization
Bureau of Indian Affairs
Dawes Act

PI 3.1 Compare and contrast the experiences of different ethnic, national, and religious groups, including Native American Indians, in the United States, explaining their contributions to American society and culture.

The Ghost Dance

◀ Some Plains Indians hoped the Ghost Dance would help them reclaim their former ways of life.

THE INSIDE STORY

What would you do to save your culture? By the 1890s Native Americans and their cultures faced extinction. People had lost their land, homes, and food sources. In utter desperation, many Indians turned to traditional religion—and to a prophet with a new message of hope.

Wovoka, a shaman of the Northern Paiute in Nevada, became known as a healer who could bring rain. Working for white farmers, Wovoka learned about Christianity and its belief in a messiah, or savior. In 1889 he had a vision that he spoke with God in heaven, where he saw many who had died. The dream, he said, told him to bring the Indians a new message and a sacred dance. According to most surviving accounts, the message was that the people should get along and not steal or lie or go to war. They were to perform the special Ghost Dance five nights in a row. Wovoka promised that a messiah would come to save only the Indians.

Wovoka's message, and the Ghost Dance movement, spread across the central Plains. During the frenzied dances people saw visions of buffalo herds returning and white settlers leaving the West. The Ghost Dance offered hope. But as you will read, it ultimately led to tragedy. ◼

Stage Set for Conflict

The Ghost Dance was an expression of deepest grief about the loss of Native Americans' ways of life. As white settlers began streaming into the West, Native Americans and white settlers clashed over control of the land. U.S. government actions compounded the tensions.

Culture of the Plains Indians The Sioux, Blackfoot, and Cheyenne of the northern Plains and the Kiowa and Comanche of the southern Plains thrived thanks to the abundance of wild buffalo, their main source of food, clothing, shoes, shelter, and supplies. The Plains Indians lived a nomadic lifestyle, traveling the great grasslands on horseback as they followed the migrations of the buffalo herds. They did not believe that land should be bought and sold.

Most white settlers were farmers or town dwellers. They believed that land should be divided and claims given to people to farm or establish businesses. If

Native Americans would not settle down in one place, many Americans believed, then their lands were available for the taking.

Government policy In the mid-1800s the United States government's Indian policy underwent a key change. Previously the Army had forcibly removed Native Americans from the East and relocated them farther west. By the 1850s growing numbers of white settlers wanted to move into those western lands as well. So instead of pushing the Indians further westward, the government began seizing their land and sending them to reservations. The goal was to break the power of the Plains Indians and open up their lands for settlement. Americans generally agreed with this new policy.

Destruction of the buffalo For Plains Indians, being confined to reservations threatened their buffalo-centered way of life. Yet the vast herds that had supported them for countless generations now were being driven to extinction. In 1800 some 60 million buffalo had lived on the Plains. Remarkably, by 1894 perhaps as few as 25 buffalo remained. The catastrophe had several causes. White settlement reduced buffalo grazing lands and cut off migration routes. Settlers' livestock carried diseases that destroyed buffalo herds.

Yet other more deliberate actions by whites hastened the catastrophe. U.S. Army adopted a policy of encouraging the destruction of the buffalo. It sought to wipe out the Plains Indians' food supply to force them onto reservations.

One of the most dramatic causes of destruction was the hunting of buffalo for sport and profit. With the expansion of railroads across the Plains, buffalo hides could easily be shipped east, where demand for them increased in the 1870s. Hides were used to make belts for factory machines and fashionable buffalo robes.

For pleasure, railroads offered "hunting specials," allowing passengers to shoot buffalo from the train. The slaughter was so massive that in one summer, several railroads had to cancel their hunting specials. The stench of buffalo carcasses sickened passengers.

READING CHECK **Identifying Problems and Solutions** How did Americans deal with Indians that stood in the way of their westward expansion?

ACADEMIC VOCABULARY
policy plan, course of action

HUNTING ON THE PLAINS

Hunters used spears and arrows to bring down the huge beasts. Families then harvested the skin, bones, meat, and tissue, wasting little.

Strength, speed, agility, and accuracy made Plains horsemen skilled hunters, highly respected in their communities.

Skills FOCUS **READING LIKE A HISTORIAN**

Artist John Mix Stanley had a keen sense that he was chronicling a vanishing way of life as he painted *Buffalo Hunt on the Southwestern Prairies* in 1845.
Interpreting Visuals What qualities does Stanley convey about the hunters?

The Indian Wars

Tensions between the settlers and the Plains Indians escalated into decades of violence that swept the Indians from most of the West. The conflicts are known as the Indian Wars.

The Sand Creek Massacre In Colorado Territory, a band of Cheyenne raided nearby ranches in 1864. Army officials offered amnesty, or forgiveness, if they returned to their reservation at Sand Creek. Cheyenne chief Black Kettle wanted peace. He led his people back.

Before dawn on November 29, Army colonel John M. Chivington arrived at Sand Creek with about 700 troops. Black Kettle raised an American flag and a white flag as a sign of peace. But Chivington did not want peace. "It is simply not possible for Indians to obey or even understand any treaty," he said. "[T]o kill them is the only way we will ever have peace . . . in Colorado."

Chivington's troops opened fire and killed about 150 people, mostly women, children, and elderly people. After burning the camp to the ground, the troops returned to Denver with scalps, which they displayed to cheering crowds. News of the **Sand Creek Massacre** outraged many Americans. Congressional investigators condemned Chivington's actions as atrocities, but they did not punish him.

Treaties After the Sand Creek Massacre, enraged Cheyenne stepped up raids. The Sioux did as well. A swelling stream of travelers along the Bozeman Trail were passing through sacred Sioux hunting grounds. The Sioux chief Red Cloud had tried without success to negotiate an end to white encroachment in this area. In December 1866 the Sioux attacked a supply wagon train outside newly built Fort Kearny. When a patrol of some 80 soldiers tried to drive off the war party, the Sioux killed the entire group of soldiers.

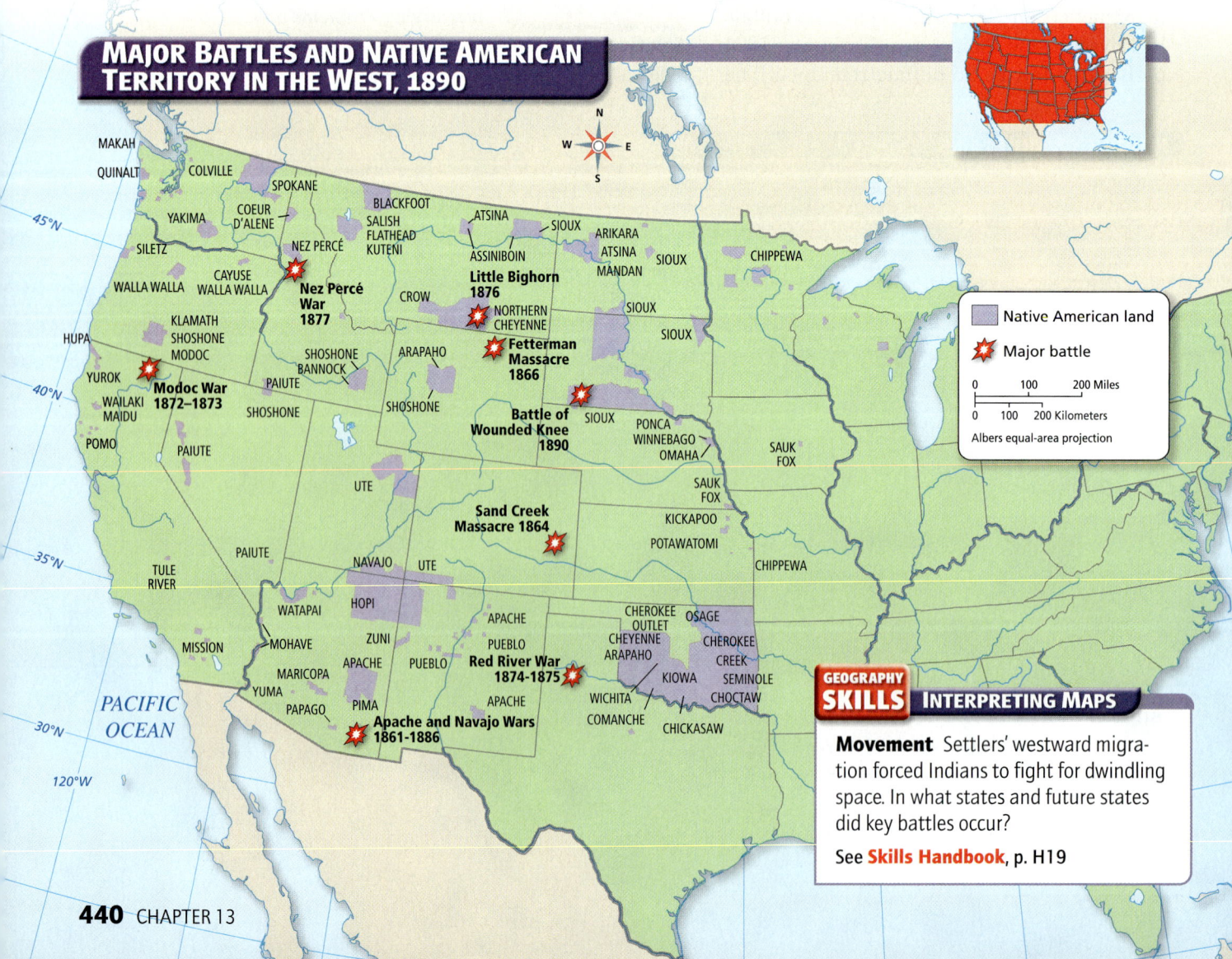

MAJOR BATTLES AND NATIVE AMERICAN TERRITORY IN THE WEST, 1890

Legend:
- Native American land
- Major battle

0 — 100 — 200 Miles
0 — 100 — 200 Kilometers
Albers equal-area projection

Nez Percé War 1877
Little Bighorn 1876
Fetterman Massacre 1866
Modoc War 1872–1873
Battle of Wounded Knee 1890
Sand Creek Massacre 1864
Red River War 1874–1875
Apache and Navajo Wars 1861–1886

GEOGRAPHY SKILLS INTERPRETING MAPS

Movement Settlers' westward migration forced Indians to fight for dwindling space. In what states and future states did key battles occur?

See **Skills Handbook**, p. H19

Finally, the government agreed to close the Bozeman Trail. In exchange, officials pressured the Sioux to sign the Second Treaty of Fort Laramie in 1868. The Sioux agreed to live on a reservation along the Missouri River.

Meanwhile, U.S. officials forced the Comanche, Kiowa, Cheyenne, and other southern nations to sign the Medicine Lodge Treaty in 1867. Those nations would be moved to reservations in what is now western Oklahoma.

Battle of the Little Bighorn For years the Lakota Sioux conducted raids against white settlers who had moved into Sioux lands. In response, the U.S. government ordered all Lakota Sioux to return to their reservation by January 31, 1876. They refused. The situation was turned over to the military.

About 2,000 Sioux, Cheyenne, and Arapaho gathered near the Little Bighorn River. The leader of the Sioux, **Sitting Bull**, conducted a ceremonial sun dance. He reportedly had a vision of a great victory over soldiers.

The brash leader of the U.S. Army troops, Lieutenant Colonel **George Armstrong Custer**, predicted victory as well. On June 25, 1876, Custer led his troops into a headlong attack against superior numbers. Custer and his troops were quickly encircled and slaughtered. The **Battle of the Little Bighorn** was a tremendous victory for the Sioux—but a temporary one. Now the U.S. government was even more determined to put down the Indian threat to settlers.

The Battle of Palo Duro Canyon In the Texas Panhandle, Colonel Ranald McKenzie caught Comanches, Kiowas, and Cheyennes preparing a winter encampment in the fall of 1874. He sent in his cavalry. Some Indians fled; others defended their scattered camps. Then McKenzie's men slaughtered more than 1,000 Indian ponies and destroyed all food stores. Starving Comanches led by Quanah Parker had no choice but to move onto the reservation in Indian Territory the following spring. The Indian Wars in the southern Plains were over.

The Ghost Dance As you read earlier, word spread that a Paiute shaman, Wovoka, had received a powerful vision in 1889. Wovoka declared that the Indian dead would live again, the buffalo would return, and the settlers would leave. Wovoka's vision developed into a religious movement. Known to outsiders as the Ghost Dance, it inspired hope among Native Americans who were suffering terribly.

In August 1890 newspapers began suggesting that the Ghost Dance was a sign of a coming uprising. A small but very vocal group of whites began asking the government for help.

In December 1890 the U.S. military ordered the arrest of Sitting Bull, who had joined the Ghost Dance movement. A skirmish broke out, and Sitting Bull was killed. Many of Sitting Bull's band of Sioux fled west. The weary Sioux surrendered to U.S. troops, who took them to Wounded Knee Creek, in modern-day South Dakota, to make camp.

The Wounded Knee Massacre The next morning, Colonel James Forsyth of the 7th Cavalry ordered the Sioux to give up their rifles. One young man named Black Coyote did not want to give up his gun, and in his struggle with the soldiers, the gun went off. Instantly, the Sioux and the soldiers began shooting.

About half of the Sioux men were killed right away. Women and children fled, but soldiers pursued them. By the end of the fight, about 300 Sioux men, women, and children lay dead. Bodies of women and children were found as far as three miles from the camp.

The **Wounded Knee Massacre** shocked many Americans. General Nelson Miles was so outraged that he removed Forsyth from command. Others in the army did not share Miles' concern, however. Three officers and 15 enlisted men received the Medal of Honor for their actions.

Wounded Knee marked the end of the bloody conflict between the army and the Plains Indians. Black Elk, a survivor of the massacre, came to realize what the loss truly meant:

HISTORY'S VOICES

❝I did not know then how much was ended. When I look back now from this high hill of my old age, I can still see the butchered women and children . . . as plain as when I saw them with eyes still young. And I can see that something else died there in the bloody mud, and was buried in the blizzard. A people's dream died there. It was a beautiful dream . . .❞

—From "Black Elk Speaks," ca. 1932

 **READING CHECK** **Identifying the Main Idea** What were the U.S. Army and the Plains Indians fighting over in the Indian Wars?

THE IMPACT TODAY

Culture
To this day Wounded Knee remains a symbol of injustice toward Native Americans. In 1973, so-called "Wounded Knee II," a standoff between the U.S. military and Indians protesting discrimination, ended in the deaths of two Indian activists.

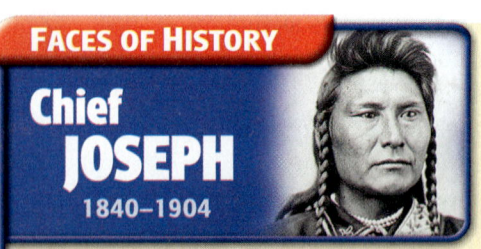

Chief JOSEPH
1840–1904

Chief Joseph became the leader of the Nez Percé in 1871. He struggled to preserve his people's way of life and their homeland in the forested Wallowa Valley. In 1877 when the U.S. government ordered the Nez Percé to relocate to a reservation, Joseph at first agreed, but then was forced to flee. He attempted to escape into Canada with about 750 of his people. On a historic journey across Idaho, Montana, Oregon, and Washington, they defeated pursuing troops who greatly outnumbered them. Traveling with families, low on supplies, the warriors managed to evade the U.S. Army for more than three months.

Ultimately, though, Chief Joseph saw that resistance was futile. To protect his hungry and exhausted people, Joseph surrendered. In the years that followed, the Nez Percé leader continued to speak out against the injustices of U.S. policy toward Native Americans.

Drawing Conclusions Why did Joseph hope to reach Canada?

Resistance Ends in the West

ACADEMIC VOCABULARY

traditional
established, customary

West of the Great Plains, Native Americans struggled to maintain their traditional ways of life. Their stories ended in tragedy as well.

Resistance in the Northwest In 1855 the Nez Percé (NEZ PUHRS) agreed to move onto a reservation in Idaho and Oregon. But in 1863, as gold miners and settlers began streaming onto the reservation, the U.S. government took back nine tenths of the Nez Percé land.

In 1877 the Indians were ordered to abandon the last portion of their Oregon homeland and move into a small section of Idaho. Their leader, **Chief Joseph,** reluctantly agreed. In the meantime, hostilities broke out among settlers and some young Nez Percé. The Indians—warriors, women, and children—were forced to flee, with the army in close pursuit.

The Nez Percé headed to Canada, fighting major battles as they fled. Less than 40 miles from the Canadian border, Joseph and his people were forced to surrender to the U.S. Army.

HISTORY'S VOICES

FOCUS ON NEW YORK

ART
At the height of the American policy attacking Native American culture, a wealthy New Yorker named George Gustav Heye was working to protect it. Heye amassed a collection of Native American art and artifacts that became the foundation of the National Museum of the American Indian, which is part of the Smithsonian Institution.

❝I am tired of fighting. Our chiefs are killed. . . It is cold, and we have no blankets. The little children are freezing to death. . . My heart is sick and sad. From where the sun now stands I will fight no more forever.❞

–Chief Joseph, statement at his surrender, 1877

Chief Joseph and his people were taken first to eastern Kansas and then to Indian Territory (present-day Oklahoma), where many died. Half of the Nez Percé were eventually returned to Idaho, but Chief Joseph and many others were sent to northern Washington State.

Resistance in the Southwest In the 1870s the government had moved the Apache peoples to the San Carlos Reservation along the Gila River in Arizona. Soldiers had forcefully stopped a religious gathering there in 1881. The Apache leader **Geronimo** fled the reservation with dozens of others.

Geronimo's band of Apache led raids on both sides of the Arizona-Mexico border for years. Geronimo briefly returned to reservation life in 1884. But soon he resumed raiding settlements. Captured one last time in September 1886, Geronimo and his followers were sent to an Apache internment camp in Florida as prisoners of war. Geronimo's surrender marked the end of armed resistance in the Southwest.

READING CHECK **Summarizing** How did Native American resistance end in the Northwest and Southwest regions?

Life on the Reservations

The U.S. government had two reasons for creating Indian reservations. First, it wanted control over all the western territories. Second, many Americans wanted Native Americans to abandon their traditional culture and religions and live like white Americans.

Americanization Starting in about 1870, the government's Indian policy changed yet again. Most government officials and reformers began to believe that Native Americans would be better off if they abandoned their culture and adopted the culture of white America. The new thinking was that instead of removal, treaties, reservations, or war, the government should pursue a policy of **Americanization**.

Americanization entailed a wholesale attack on Native American beliefs and practices, starting with tribal identity. The federal agency that managed the Native American reservations, the **Bureau of Indian Affairs** (BIA), began issuing wide-ranging orders that left few aspects of Indian culture untouched.

❝You are therefore directed to induce your male Indians to cut their hair, and both sexes to stop painting [their faces]. . . The wearing of citizens' clothing, instead of the Indian costume and blanket, should be encouraged.❞

–BIA letter to Greenville Indian School, California, 1902

The government built schools for Native American children, often hundreds of miles away from the students' homes. In these schools, students could only speak English and could not wear their traditional clothing. Every effort was made to discourage students from practicing their own culture so that they might learn to live like white Americans.

The Dawes Act Congress took a significant step in the Americanization process when it passed the **Dawes Act** in 1887. The new law broke up most reservations and turned Native Americans into individual property owners. Each head of family received 160 acres. Each single person over 18 years old received 80 acres, and each child would receive 40 acres. Any land left over would be sold.

The BIA and reformers, some well-intentioned, believed this shift would transform the Indians' relationship to the land. Ownership would provide incentives to succeed, they thought—and then the federal government could slash support for reservations.

The Carlisle Indian Industrial School was a school for assimilation in Pennsylvania. Boys and girls were taught to read, write, and learn industrial and domestic activities of white American culture. The left photo shows some Lakota boys upon their arrival at the school. *What changes do you see in them in the right photo, after they have spent some time at the school?*

The government, however, gave the less productive land to the Indians and sold off the best land. Many Native Americans received near-desert lands unsuitable for farming. But even when Indians received good land, many could not afford the tools, animals, seed, and other supplies necessary to start farms.

READING CHECK **Identifying Supporting Details** What was the Dawes Act?

SECTION 1 ASSESSMENT

go.hrw.com
Online Quiz
Keyword: SD7 HP13

Reviewing Ideas, Terms, and People

1. **a. Explain** Why was the destruction of the buffalo significant to the lives of Native Americans on the Plains?
   b. Evaluate How did U.S. government policies bring the army into conflict with Plains Indians?

2. **a. Define** What were the Indian Wars?
   b. Compare How did Americans and Indians react to the **Sand Creek Massacre** and the **Wounded Knee Massacre**?

3. **a. Identify** Which events marked the end of armed resistance by Native Americans in the Northwest and the Southwest?
   b. Draw Conclusions What factors brought about the end of the Indian resistance?

4. **a. Describe** What was the process of **Americanization**?
   b. Make Inferences What did Americanization reveal about white Americans' views of Native Americans?

Critical Thinking

5. **Identifying Cause and Effect** Copy the chart below and record causes and effects of the Battle of the Little Bighorn.

Causes   Effects

Battle of the Little Bighorn

FOCUS ON WRITING

6. **Expository** Suppose you have been living among the Lakota Sioux. Newspapers have frightened local settlers by suggesting that the Ghost Dance is a sign of a coming Indian uprising. Write a letter to the editor explaining the true meaning of the Ghost Dance.

2 Mining and Ranching

BEFORE YOU READ

MAIN IDEA

Many people sought fortunes during the mining and cattle booms of the American West.

FOCUS QUESTIONS

1. How did mining lead to new settlements in the West?
2. Why did mining become big business?
3. How and why did the cattle boom come to an end?

KEY TERMS AND PEOPLE

Comstock Lode
placer mining
hydraulic mining
hard-rock mining
Chisholm Trail
Joseph Glidden

3.2 Research and analyze the major themes and developments in New York State and United States history (e.g., colonization and settlement; Revolution and New National Period; immigration; expansion and reform era; Civil War and Reconstruction; the American labor movement; Great Depression; World Wars; contemporary United States).

Seattle Strikes it RICH

▲ Miners seeking gold in the Klondike stocked up on provisions in Seattle.

THE INSIDE STORY

Who really struck it rich in the Alaska gold rush? Gold in the Klondike! As the news spread, some 100,000 miners raced to Alaska. Several cities in the Pacific Northwest became boomtowns, but the richest by far was Seattle, Washington. Some two thirds of the prospectors passed through Seattle. Its merchants were ready, offering everything from tents to miners' shoes to "Alaska Dog Feed."

"The stores are ablaze with Klondike goods; men pass by robed in [odd] garments," a local newspaper reported

in 1897. It observed "teams of trained dogs, trotting about with sleds; men with packs upon their backs, and a thousand and one things which are of use in the Klondike trade." Women could even get advice on choosing the right outfit.

The city's success was no accident. Erastus Brainerd, a former Boston museum curator, led an energetic campaign to promote Seattle as the one-stop marketplace for miners.

Few miners hit it rich in Alaska, of course. But the Klondike Gold Rush brought a fortune to the city of Seattle. ◼

Striking Gold and Silver

The California gold rush of 1849 had captured the imaginations of many Americans. New mining strikes inspired thousands of people to rush to the West in search of fortune.

As the news of each new discovery spread, miners raced from one gold or silver strike to the next—to Idaho, Montana, the Black Hills of the Dakota Territory, Arizona, and to Cripple Creek, Colorado. Miners were excited by reports of others finding riches.

Discovering gold and silver
After the California gold rush, the first promising mining discovery occurred in Colorado. In 1858 prospectors found gold near Pikes Peak. Thousands flocked to the area. Most left disappointed.

In 1859 prospectors found silver in the Carson River valley of present-day Nevada. Thousands of miners rushed to this mine, which became known as the Comstock Lode. Over the next 20 years, miners took about $500 million worth of silver from the Comstock Lode.

The Klondike gold rush
"Gold! Gold! Gold!" shouted the headline of the *Seattle Post Intelligencer* on July 17, 1897. A huge gold strike had been made along the Klondike River in Canada's remote Yukon Territory near the Alaska border. Soon gold was discovered on the Alaska side of the border as well. Over the next year, about 100,000 Americans stampeded to the Klondike in search of riches.

Getting to the Klondike was treacherous. Canadian officials required that miners bring enough provisions for a year—nearly a ton of goods. Prospectors brought groceries, clothing, hardware, tents, packsaddles, camp stoves, bedding, and sleds. Prospectors made slow progress, having to move a year's worth of supplies—weighing as much as a ton—over rough terrain. One miner wrote about the hardship.

HISTORY'S VOICES
❝My feet are sore, my heels are blistered, my legs sore and lame, my hands, neck, shoulders, sore and chafed from rope. But boys, don't think I'm discouraged. . . there is a golden glimmer in the distance.❞

–Prospector Fred Dewey

Like the majority of gold seekers in previous gold rushes, most of the prospectors who reached the Klondike came away disappointed. The best gold-bearing creeks had already been claimed, and the reports of "gold for the taking" had been greatly exaggerated.

Mining camps
Most prospectors were men. They came from all over the United States as well as from other nations. Thousands poured into mining areas from Mexico, England, Ireland, China, and many other countries.

Almost as soon as gold was discovered, prospectors would swarm into the region. They set up camps that were little more than groups of tents or hastily built shacks. Most camps had no law enforcement. Since miners were competing against each other for gold, the intense rivalry frequently led to violence.

Some people formed their own vigilante committees to combat theft and violence, but

PRIMARY SOURCES

Letter

Many of the gold seekers were like Hunter Fitzhugh, an unemployed young man who left Kentucky for Alaska in 1897. He gave up his quest after three years. This letter describes life in his mining camp.

"I am sitting in my flannel shirt sleeves . . . at our . . . dining table, by a little bit of window made of celluloid instead of glass . . . I am the cook this week, and am at present cooking peas, evaporated potatoes, evaporated eggs, tomatoes, and cornstarch pudding . . . I washed my shirt and my other pair of socks [yesterday evening], so don't have to repeat the performance for at least two months. The sun never sets now, and all night is just the same as all day . . . To be sure I long for home and civilization, . . . but on the other hand if I was in the States I would be under the eye and hand of a boss, or out of a job . . . I may get next to a claim this year that will net me $125,000.00 . . . who knows."

Skills Focus — READING LIKE A HISTORIAN

1. **Making Inferences** What does Fitzhugh believe the future holds for him?
2. **Analyzing Primary Sources** What does Fitzhugh's description tell you about supplies and sanitary conditions in the mining camps?

See **Skills Handbook**, p. H28–29

ACADEMIC
VOCABULARY

invest put money
into in order to gain
a financial return

their methods were often excessively violent. An accused criminal could be hanged after a speedy and unofficial "trial" of sorts.

Camps become towns Some of the sprawling mining camps developed into towns. These early towns had dirt streets, wooden sidewalks, and hastily constructed buildings. Stores and saloons sprang up, seemingly overnight.

As towns developed, more women and children came to join the men. The arrival of families often turned rough-and-tumble towns into prosperous, respectable communities. Townspeople established churches, schools, newspapers—even opera houses.

> **READING CHECK** **Sequencing** How did Western mining camps evolve into towns?

Mining as Big Business

In the early days of the Gold Rush, individual prospectors worked with hand tools. Some found gold through placer mining, in which minerals are found in loose sand or gravel. The simplest form of placer mining was panning for gold. It was a cheap but tough way for an individual to try to make money.

When the surface deposits of gold ran out, miners needed more sophisticated equipment to extract gold from deeper within the earth.

Large companies were formed to <u>invest</u> in this expensive equipment. By the 1880s, mining was dominated by these big companies.

Mining companies used two methods to extract the ore. Hydraulic mining used water under high pressure to blast away dirt, exposing the minerals underneath. This method sent sediment into rivers, choking them and causing floods. Hard-rock mining required cutting deep shafts in solid rock to extract the ore.

Miners became employees of mining companies rather than lone prospectors. They dug mine shafts, built tunnels, and drilled and processed ore. For some it was better than relying on their own luck. Yet it carried plenty of risks. Countless miners died in cave-ins, underground fires, explosions, and flooded mines.

In some towns, miners began to organize unions to negotiate for safer working conditions and better pay. The mining companies bitterly resisted these efforts. In Cripple Creek, Colorado, violent conflict broke out in 1903 between members of the Western Federation of Miners and corporate mining interests determined to crush the union. When it was over, 30 men had been killed in numerous gun battles, and the union was defeated.

> **READING CHECK** **Contrasting** How did working conditions for miners change once mining companies took over?

Hydraulic mining was a large-scale form of placer mining. Miners diverted water from a high to a low elevation. The water exited a small nozzle, called a monitor, at 5,000 pounds of pressure. Hydraulic mining was banned in 1884 because of its negative effects on farmers. *How did hydraulic mining affect farmers?*

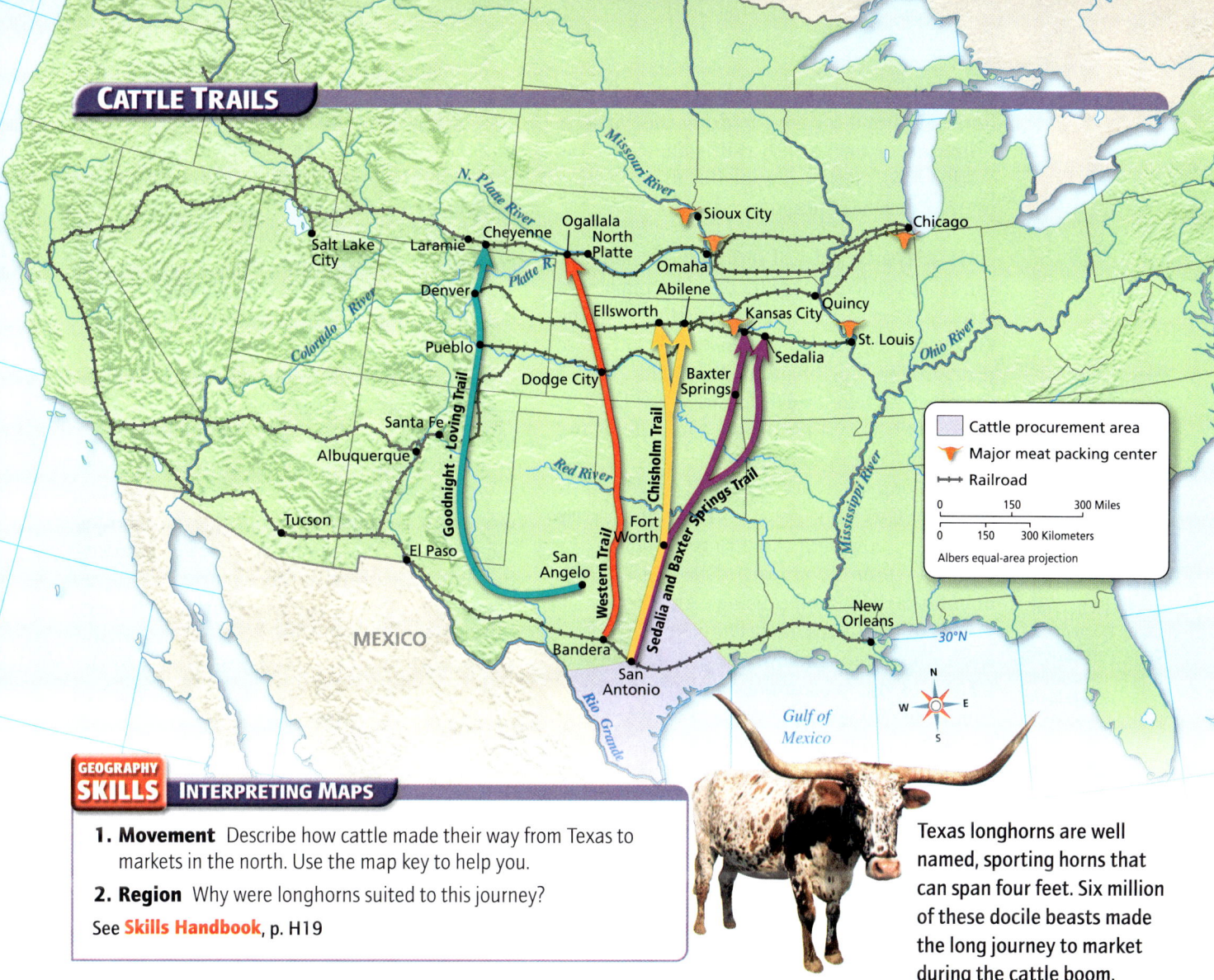

Cattle procurement area
Major meat packing center
Railroad

0   150   300 Miles
0   150   300 Kilometers
Albers equal-area projection

Texas longhorns are well named, sporting horns that can span four feet. Six million of these docile beasts made the long journey to market during the cattle boom.

GEOGRAPHY SKILLS INTERPRETING MAPS

1. **Movement** Describe how cattle made their way from Texas to markets in the north. Use the map key to help you.
2. **Region** Why were longhorns suited to this journey?

See **Skills Handbook**, p. H19

The Cattle Boom

In the decades after the Civil War, with the buffalo hunted to near extinction and most Native Americans confined to reservations, a new business came to dominate the economy of the Plains. Cattle ranching offered a way to "mine" the lush prairie grasses for profit.

Origins of Western ranching The first ranchers in the West were the Spanish, who brought cattle to the New World from Spain in the 1500s. The Spanish, and later the Mexicans, became adept at raising cattle under dry and difficult environmental conditions.

These ranchers interbred Spanish and English cattle to develop a new breed that thrived on the Plains: the Texas longhorn. Unlike other breeds, the Texas longhorn were hardy, could travel long distances without much water, and

could live on grass alone. They also had immunity to Texas fever, a disease that was deadly to other breeds of cattle.

The Spanish also introduced sheep ranching to the West. In the Southwest, Navajos and Pueblos raised sheep as well. After the Civil War, New England mills increased their demand for raw wool to produce cloth. Sheep ranchers responded to that demand by raising new breeds of sheep that produced more wool.

Cowboys complained that sheep ruined the grass for cattle by eating the roots. Conflicts between sheep owners and cattle owners sometimes became violent as they competed for grazing land on the open range.

Demand for beef After the Civil War, cities in the East clamored for beef to feed their growing populations. By 1866 a steer that might sell for as little as $4 in Texas could bring $40 up north. The age of the cattle drives had begun. Ranchers hired cowboys to drive the cattle to railheads, or towns with railroads, where the cattle could then be shipped to meatpacking centers such as Chicago.

Cattle trails Several different cattle trails ran from cattle country in Texas to major rail centers. One of the most important was the Chisholm Trail, which began in San Antonio, ran through Fort Worth, and ended in the Kansas towns of Abilene and Ellsworth. By 1871 as many as 600,000 cattle traveled along the Chisholm Trail in a single year.

The long drive north usually lasted three months. Cowboys gently urged the cattle northward, allowing them to graze along the trail for 10 or 12 miles a day. Pushing the animals faster risked causing a stampede.

About two thirds of the cowboys on the trail were white teenage boys between the ages of 12 and 18, but substantial numbers of African American and Hispanic young men worked as cowboys as well. Even a few women—usually disguised as men—rode the trails.

Ranching as big business Cattle owners often had trouble keeping track of their herds on the open range. By the 1870s, however, a new invention allowed ranchers to enclose some of their grazing lands. **Joseph Glidden** of De Kalb, Illinois, received a patent for barbed wire, a fencing material made of sharp, pointed pieces of wire, or barbs, wrapped around a strand of wire. Barbed wire made excellent fences on the Plains, where wood and stone were scarce.

Privately owned cattle ranches spread quickly across the Great Plains. Between 1882 and 1886, more than 400 cattle corporations sprang up in Wyoming, Montana, Colorado, and New Mexico. Most of these were backed by eastern and European investors. This transformed the cattle business into big business.

The enclosure of the open range led to conflicts between landless cattle owners and the ranchers and farmers who enclosed the land. Some ranchers were reckless with their enclosures, stringing barbed wire across public lands or other people's property, even blocking public roads. This set off a wave of fence cutting in 1883, which slowed the next year when the Texas legislature made fence cutting a felony.

The severe winters of 1885–1886 and 1886–1887 brought staggering losses to the cattle industry. Cattle migrating south to avoid harsh blizzards were trapped by drift fences, which stretched from eastern New Mexico and across the Texas Panhandle to Indian Territory (modern-day Oklahoma). The drift fences had been built to prevent the spread of cattle with Texas fever, but they proved deadly. Trapped by the fences, thousands of cattle perished in a disaster cattle owners called the "Big Die-up."

READING CHECK **Identifying Cause and Effect** What factors caused the Western cattle boom?

THE IMPACT TODAY

Economics

Battles over land use continue today. Often they center on whether companies should be allowed to drill for oil and natural gas or to conduct logging operations in wilderness areas previously off-limits to development.

SECTION 2 ASSESSMENT

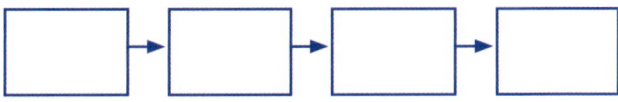
go.hrw.com
Online Quiz
Keyword: SD7 HP13

Reviewing Ideas, Terms, and People

1. **a. Recall** What difficulties did miners face in reaching the mining districts of the Klondike?
   b. Summarize How did mining lead to the establishment of new towns in the West?

2. **a. Describe** What resources did mining companies have that individual prospectors did not?
   b. Contrast How did **placer mining, hydraulic mining,** and **hard-rock mining** differ?

3. **a. Identify** What was the importance of the Texas longhorn?
   b. Make Generalizations How did ranching become established in the West?

4. **a. Describe** How did cowboys move cattle from ranch lands in southern Texas to the railroads in Kansas?

   b. Evaluate What could have been done to avoid the problems that struck the Western cattle industry?

Critical Thinking

5. **Sequencing** Copy the chart below and record the sequence of events that led to the rise and fall of the cattle drives.

   [ ] → [ ] → [ ] → [ ]

FOCUS ON WRITING

6. **Expository** Take the position of a cattle owner who owned land in Texas or one who did not. Based on your position, write a letter arguing for or against the use of barbed wire on the open range.

Farming the Plains

BEFORE YOU READ

MAIN IDEA

The government promoted the settlement of the West, offering free or cheap land to those willing to put in the hard work of turning the land into productive farms.

READING FOCUS

1. What incentives encouraged farmers to settle in the West?
2. Which groups of people moved to the West, and why did they do so?
3. What new ways of farming evolved in the West?

KEY TERMS AND PEOPLE

sod house
Homestead Act
Pacific Railway Act
Morrill Act
Frederick Jackson Turner
Benjamin "Pap" Singleton
Exoduster
dugout
James Oliver
bonanza farm

P1 3.4 Understand the interrelationships between world events and developments in New York State and the United States (e.g., causes for immigration, economic opportunities, human rights abuses, and tyranny versus freedom).

"Home, Sweet Soddie"

▶ The humble sod house had the advantage of being cool in the summer and warm in the winter. Notice the cow grazing on the roof.

THE INSIDE STORY

Could you live in a house made of dirt? Uriah Oblinger, a Civil War veteran, staked his claim in Fillmore County, Nebraska, and began to build what he called his "sod mansion." Oblinger, along with his wife, Mattie, and their baby daughter, were among the thousands of pioneer families whose first home in the West was a **sod house**, or "soddie."

Sod is a strip or block of dense grass with the roots and soil attached. The tough roots of the prairie grasses made ideal sod. With some effort it could be cut and stacked like bricks to make thick-walled homes that stayed warm in harsh prairie winters and cool in the blazing summers. In the treeless Plains, sod was a popular building material.

In a letter home, Uriah reported proudly that in nine days, he had hauled the sod, built walls, and put in window and door frames. All that was left was to put on a roof and level the floor. Most soddies had dirt floors. People sometimes smoothed and whitewashed the inside walls.

In 1873, Mattie wrote to her family in Indiana: "At Home in our own house, and a sod at that! . . . I suppose you would like to see us in our sod house. It is not quite so convenient as a nice frame, but I would as soon live in it as the cabins I have lived in. And then we are at home which makes it more comfortable." Some women hated the constant fight with insects, dirt, and leaky roofs. Others, like Mattie, were just happy to have a home that they owned. ◢

Incentives for Settlement

Major Stephen H. Long, an early visitor to the Great Plains, called the region "the Great American Desert." He believed the area was "unfit for cultivation, and of course uninhabitable by a people depending upon agriculture for their subsistence." A few decades later, with encouragement from the government, people began pouring onto the Plains to build farms.

New legislation Congress passed three acts in 1862 to turn public lands into private property. The **Homestead Act** allowed any head of household over the age of 21 to claim 160 acres of land. Each homesteader had to build a home on the land, make improvements, and farm the land for five years before being granted full ownership of the land by the government. Nearly 2 million people applied for land claims under this act. Most of the best land awarded under the Homestead Act was claimed before 1900, but the last homesteader received land in 1988.

The **Pacific Railway Act** of 1862 gave land to railroad companies to encourage the construction of railroad and telegraph lines. The **Morrill Act**, also passed by Congress in 1862, gave land to the states to provide colleges for "agriculture and the mechanic arts." Not all states actually built colleges on the land they received. Instead, many sold the land and used the proceeds to fund education. The Morrill Act was significant because it was the first time the federal government provided assistance for higher education.

Railroads encourage settlement Railroad companies lured settlers to the West. Within a few years of the passage of the Pacific Railway Act, the federal government had given the railroads some 125 million acres of public land. State and local governments had given nearly 100 million more acres.

Railroad companies reaped profits by selling some of the land to settlers. They placed ads in eastern newspapers, as well as in Europe, singing the praises of the American West. In the early 1900s railroads advertised that Montana was a farmer's paradise. In response to the ads, some 40,000 homestead claims were filed in Montana between 1906 and 1918, making it the favorite destination of homesteaders.

The Oklahoma Land Run of 1889 By the 1870s, treaties had resulted in the relocation of a number of Native American nations to Indian Territory (present-day Oklahoma). In

HISTORY CLOSE-UP

Oklahoma Land Rush

Between 1889 and 1895, five land runs drew thousands of new settlers to Oklahoma. The largest land run occurred in 1893. Settlers claimed seven million acres of land in an area known as the Cherokee Outlet on September 16, 1893.

Around 100,000 settlers rushed to claim land in the Cherokee Outlet.

Homesteaders await the trumpet calls, gunshots, and even cannon blasts that will signal the start of the land run.

1879, however, a Cherokee activist discovered that some 2 million acres in central Oklahoma had not been assigned to any nation. For 10 years settlers tried to move into these unassigned lands, despite presidential proclamations forbidding unlawful entry into Indian Territory. By the late 1880s, however, a political movement arose to open this area, and in 1889, it was opened to settlers.

On April 22, 1889, thousands of eager settlers lined up along the perimeter of these unassigned lands. At noon, federal troops gave the signal, and some 50,000 people rushed into the Oklahoma interior to stake their claim. A magazine described the founding of one town:

HISTORY'S VOICES

❝The city of Guthrie was built in . . . an afternoon. At twelve o'clock on Monday, April 22nd, the resident population of Guthrie was nothing; before sundown it was at least ten thousand. In that time streets had been laid out, town lots staked off, and steps taken toward the formation of a municipal government. At twilight the campfires of ten thousand people gleamed on the grassy slopes of the Cimarron Valley, where, the night before, the coyote, the gray wolf, and the deer had roamed undisturbed.❞

–William Willard Howard, *Harper's Weekly,* May 1889

Between 1889 and 1895, five different land runs brought countless settlers to live in Oklahoma. Not everyone who rushed there to claim land was fully prepared to settle, however. Some arrived with few provisions and no money. Many hopeful settlers became quickly discouraged and left once they realized they could not survive until the next year's crops came in.

Closing of the frontier For decades the U.S. Census Bureau had monitored the extent of American settlement. The frontier, according to the bureau, existed at a point where the population totaled fewer than 2 people per square mile.

In 1890 the Census Bureau issued a momentous report. It stated that "at present the unsettled area has been so broken into by isolated bodies of settlement that there can hardly be said to be a frontier line." In simpler terms, the federal government had declared the frontier closed.

The historian **Frederick Jackson Turner** seized on the news. Jackson believed that the existence of the frontier had made the United States distinctive. He explained his frontier thesis in an 1893 essay.

ACADEMIC VOCABULARY

thesis proposition put forth for argument

Like many frontier towns, Perry, Oklahoma, began to emerge within days of the opening of the Cherokee Outlet.

Skills FOCUS INTERPRETING VISUALS

Chaotic settlement patterns led to some conflicts between homesteaders and the people known as boomers and sooners. These were people who staked claims before the territory was legally opened to settlers. **Making Inferences** What other types of conflicts do you think might have arisen in the land rush?

See **Skills Handbook**, p. H7

"Up to our own day American history has been in a large degree the history of the colonization of the Great West. The existence of an area of free land, its continuous recession [moving back], and the advance of American settlement westward, explain American development."

–Frederick Jackson Turner

For more than a century, historians debated Turner's idea. Today most dispute it. Some point to other factors—such as slavery, immigration, and industrialization—as being more important to the country's development. Others question whether the term *frontier* should even apply to an area that was already inhabited by Native Americans.

READING CHECK **Summarizing** What did the Homestead Act do?

Migrating West

After the Civil War, most of the people moving West belonged to one of three major groups: white Americans from the East, African Americans from the South, and immigrants from foreign countries.

White settlers Most of the white settlers who moved West came from states in the Mississippi Valley, which had once been the frontier. So many people had moved to those states that cheap land was getting difficult to find. Still, those who went west were mostly middle-class farmers or businesspeople. They could afford the money for supplies and transportation.

African American settlers In the late 1870s, African Americans began a massive migration west. Some were inspired by the words of **Benjamin "Pap" Singleton**, a community builder and former slave who urged African Americans to build their own communities in the West. Others fled because of violence and oppression in the South. The withdrawal of federal troops from the South in 1877 led to segregation laws and violent attacks from groups such as the Ku Klux Klan.

Rumors soon spread throughout the South that the federal government would set aside Kansas for former slaves. The rumor turned out to be false, but some 15,000 African Americans moved to Kansas within the year in search of a peaceful life. The settlers became known as **Exodusters**. Tens of thousands of these Exodusters left the South and settled in Kansas, Missouri, Indiana, and Illinois.

European settlers The lure of economic opportunity brought thousands of Europeans to the west. Scandinavians from Sweden, Norway, and Finland poured onto the northern Plains in the 1870s, seeking farmland. Many Irish who had come to help build the railroads decided to stay and settle on the Plains. Many Russian Mennonites, members of a Protestant religious sect, brought their experience of farming on the Russian steppes, or grasslands, to the Great Plains. Huge numbers of Germans came to the United States as well. Many moved to the central part of Texas, creating a distinctive culture in that area.

Chinese settlers By the 1880s some of the Chinese immigrants who had come for the California gold rush or to build railroads had turned to farming, especially in California. Those who had experience as farmers in China introduced innovative techniques, helping to establish California's fruit industry. Although some Chinese farmed their own land, most ended up as farm laborers, usually because of laws that barred Chinese from owning land.

READING CHECK **Drawing Conclusions** Why did European immigrants move to the West?

FACES OF HISTORY

Benjamin SINGLETON
1809–1892

Born in Nashville, Tennessee, Benjamin Singleton escaped slavery and settled in the North. There, he protected runaway slaves. After the Civil War, Singleton returned to Tennessee determined to help the newly freed African Americans there purchase farmland. But white landowners refused to sell their land at fair prices.

Singleton found an answer. He established settlements in Kansas and encouraged former slaves to move west. Thousands did. These former slaves became known as Exodusters. The exodus peaked in 1879 two years after Reconstruction ended. Later in life, Singleton unsuccessfully tried to help resettle African Americans in Africa.

Sequence What steps did Singleton take to try to help African Americans gain better lives?

New Ways of Farming

The journey west was expensive and full of hardships. But once farmers staked a claim on a homestead, they faced new challenges.

First, the climate was harsh. Winters could be bitterly cold as snowstorms rushed down from Canada. Summers were fiercely hot, causing crops to shrivel and diet.

Water was scarce, forcing farmers to dig wells and install windmill-driven pumps. In the Southwest, some settlers used Hispanic and Native American irrigation techniques. Their farms stretched out in strips from water sources so that each would have water access.

Without lumber to build houses, many settlers used the earth itself. Some early settlers built **dugouts**, shelters dug into the sides of hills. They soon replaced dugouts with sturdy sod houses.

Farming in a new environment New kinds of farming equipment helped farmers meet the challenge of farming on the Plains. **James Oliver** developed a new plow with a sharper edge that helped Plains farmers plow their fields with much less effort. Machines called combine harvesters cut wheat, separated the grains from the stalks, and removed the husks from the grains all in one operation. Such equipment was expensive, and many small farmers went into debt to buy it.

Challenges for Farmers

QUICK FACTS

- **Harsh climate:** from bitter snowstorms to fierce heat and drought
- **Scarce water:** low rainfall and few rivers
- **Lumber shortage:** few wood sources for home-building or heating

Pumps powered by windmills drew water from deep underground.

Farming as big business Large companies soon saw a business opportunity on the Plains. They created giant **bonanza farms**. These farms operated like factories, with expensive machinery, professional managers, and laborers who performed specialized tasks.

Owners of bonanza farms reaped great profits during good growing seasons. During bad growing seasons, they struggled to maintain equipment and pay workers. Small family farmers with fewer expenses often handled the boom-and-bust cycles better than the big companies. By the 1890s, most bonanza farms had been broken up.

READING CHECK **Identifying Problems and Solutions** How did farmers deal with the harsh environment of the Great Plains?

SECTION 3 ASSESSMENT

go.hrw.com
Online Quiz
Keyword: SD7 HP13

Reviewing Ideas, Terms, and People

1. **a. Define** Write a brief definition of the following terms: **Homestead Act, Pacific Railway Act, Morrill Act**
   b. Evaluate Do you think the West would have been settled as quickly without U.S. government incentives? Explain.

2. **a. Identify** Which groups of people decided to move West?
   b. Explain Why did the **Exodusters** leave the South, and why did they choose to move to Kansas?
   c. Predict Which kinds of people do you think would be most successful in establishing a new farm on the Plains?

3. **a. Recall** What factors made farming different in the West than in the East?
   b. Compare and Contrast How were **dugouts** and **sod houses** similar? How were they different?
   c. Evaluate How did farmers adapt their lives because of the scarcity of resources?

Critical Thinking

4. **Comparing** How did the government and the railroads promote settlement in the West?

Government	Railroads

FOCUS ON WRITING

5. **Descriptive** Suppose you and your family are living on the prairie. Write a letter to your friend back East describing the challenges of living in a sod house.

Influences on Homesteaders

Historical Context The documents below provide different perspectives on why homesteaders moved west.

Task Examine the documents and answer the questions that follow. Then, you will be asked to write an essay about the reasons homesteaders moved west, using facts from the documents and from the chapter to support the position you take in your thesis statement.

ST 4.3 Develop hypotheses about important events, eras, or issues; move from chronicling to explaining historical events and issues; use information collected from diverse sources to produce cogently written reports and document-based essays.

DOCUMENT 1

People moved west for a great variety of reasons. Some were drawn there by so-called "pull factors"—aspects of the West that attracted people. Other people were motivated by "push factors"—conditions that made them want to leave their homes and start a new life elsewhere. Many people picked up and headed west to escape desperate poverty in eastern cities.

DOCUMENT 2

Many people who migrated west wrote letters back home to tell family members about their experiences. Uriah Oblinger was an impoverished young man from Indiana who fell in love with Mattie Thomas. To earn enough money to support a family, he kept moving farther west, looking for job opportunities and land. After they finally married in 1869, Uriah and Mattie settled a homestead in Nebraska, taking advantage of the opportunities created by the Homestead Act of 1862. During their years on the farm, Mattie wrote many letters to her family back in Indiana telling them about the opportunities in Nebraska.

"I think George & Grizzie would do well to come west if their money will not go far enough there for them . . . [W]e will be as well off as they are in a few years. We can say now that we own 160 [acres] and all it wants is improvements and I am sure it is a healthy place. Poor little Earny! It is too bad he must have the chills so much. If I was them I would be willing to sacrifice some of my enjoyments to endure a few privations for the sake of having health in my family. I am very sure they would be healthier here, but I shall not urge them to come for fear they would not be satisfied & then we would be to blame. Do you ever hear how Al Shoap likes the west? Is he in the grasshopper region? Tell Doc we will write to him soon to be patient & wait."

The U.S. government and land agents used advertisements such as posters and fliers to encourage people to move west. The following advertisement was for an offer of land being sold by a railroad company.

Skills FOCUS READING LIKE A HISTORIAN

1. a. Describe Refer to Document 1. Would the situation shown in the photograph be a push factor or a pull factor for westward migration?

b. Analyze How do you think life would be different for these families if they moved west?

2. a. Identify Refer to Document 2. How does the experience of the Oblingers illustrate both push factors and pull factors?

b. Elaborate Do you think that Mattie Oblinger's arguments for moving west are persuasive? Explain.

3. a. Identify Refer to Document 3. What is the purpose of this advertisement?

b. Interpret How might people like those in Document 1 have been influenced by the ad in Document 3?

4. Document-based Essay Question Consider the question below and form a thesis statement. Using examples from Documents 1, 2, and 3, create an outline and write a short essay supporting your position.

Why did people move west in the late 1800s?

See **Skills Handbook**, pp. H28–29, H30

Visual Summary: The American West

Cause
• Westward Expansion

Effects
• Native Americans were massacred, sent to reservations, their lands stolen, their culture destroyed
• Mining boom created new towns and businesses
• Cattle boom created new trails and ranches
• Farmers settled the Plains, building communities

Reviewing Key Terms and People

Match each lettered definition with the correct numbered item below.

a. A breed of cattle that thrived under the harsh conditions of the Great Plains

b. A law that allowed any adult head of household to claim 160 acres of land

c. Homes built on the prairie from squares of turf and soil

d. The process used to force Native Americans to abandon their traditional ways of life

e. A method used to extract minerals by cutting deep ridges in solid rock

f. African Americans who moved from southern states to Kansas after the end of Reconstruction

g. Homes built into the sides of hills on the prairie

h. One of the most important routes used to drive cattle from Texas to rail centers in Kansas

i. The federal agency that managed the Native American reservations

j. A method used to extract minerals by using water under high pressure

k. The last Sioux victory in battle against the U.S. Army

l. The violent event that marked the end of the war between the Plains Indians and the U.S. Army

m. The law that divided reservation land among individual Native Americans

1. Americanization
2. Battle of the Little Bighorn
3. Bureau of Indian Affairs
4. Chisholm Trail
5. Dawes Act
6. dugouts

7. Exodusters
8. hard-rock mining
9. Homestead Act
10. hydraulic mining
11. sod houses
12. Texas longhorn
13. Wounded Knee Massacre

History's Impact video program
Review the video to answer the closing question:
How have forms of communication changed
over time?

Comprehension and Critical Thinking

SECTION 1 *(pp. 438–443)*

14. a. Identify What was the Sand Creek Massacre, and how did people react to it?

  b. Analyze How did the Indian Wars reflect changes in U.S. government policy toward Native Americans that occurred when white Americans began moving onto the Great Plains?

  c. Elaborate Describe the differing responses of Native Americans and their leaders to the actions of the U.S. Army during the Indian Wars.

SECTION 2 *(pp. 444–448)*

15. a. Recall What was placer mining?

  b. Draw Conclusions Why did very few individuals become rich through mining?

  c. Analyze What factors caused western mining to become dominated by large corporations rather than individual prospectors?

SECTION 3 *(pp. 449–453)*

16. a. Describe What was the purpose of the Pacific Railway Act and the Morrill Act?

  b. Make Inferences Why was the federal government interested in helping the railroad companies expand throughout the West?

  c. Evaluate What effects did the expansion of the railroads have on the economy, land use, and population of the West?

Using the Internet

go.hrw.com
Practice Online
Keyword: SD7 CH13

17. During the gold and silver rushes of the late 1800s, people often abandoned mining towns as soon as the mineral deposits were exhausted. Using the keyword above, do research to learn about ghost towns of the West. Then create a report that tells the story of one town, from its founding to its decline.

Analyzing Primary Sources

Reading Like a Historian

18. Describe What do you think the stacked bags may be?

19. Draw Conclusions Why was this moment important enough to be photographed?

Critical Reading

Read the passage in Section 3 that begins with the heading "The Oklahoma Land Run of 1889." Then answer the questions that follow.

20. Why was land in Oklahoma Territory made available to settlers in 1889?

  A The federal government had purchased the land from Native Americans.

  B The Homestead Act made the land available.

  C The government gave in to pressure from settlers to open the unassigned lands.

  D Railroad companies sold the land to pay for expansion of the railroads.

21. How did the unassigned lands change at noon on April 22, 1889?

  A All lands had been claimed by that time.

  B Thousands of people rushed into the unassigned lands to stake their claims.

  C The town of Guthrie had been laid out by noon.

  D Municipal government had been formed.

 FOCUS ON WRITING

Expository Writing *Expository writing gives information, explains why or how, or defines a process. To practice expository writing, complete the assignment below.*

Writing Topic **The settlement of the West**

22. Based on what you have read in this chapter, write a paragraph that explains how Americans settled the West in the late 1800s and how the region changed as a result.

CHAPTER 14

1880–1910

The Second INDUSTRIAL Revolution

THE BIG PICTURE The growth of the railroad industry fueled the Second Industrial Revolution, making America the world's manufacturing leader. Demand for rails and railroad cars spurred expansion in coal mining and steel manufacturing. Improved communications and transportation connected distant markets—across the nation and the world.

New York Standards

Key Idea 3 Study about the major social, political, economic, cultural, and religious developments in New York State and United States history involves learning about the important roles and contributions of individuals and groups.

Skills FOCUS READING LIKE A HISTORIAN

In 1904 the St. Louis World's Fair celebrated the nation's progress since the Louisiana Purchase. Nearly 20 million visitors toured the fair's grand buildings to view such technological innovations as air conditioning and automobiles.

Making Inferences What can you infer from the fact that so many people toured the fair?

See **Skills Handbook**, p. H7

U.S.

 1880

World

1881
The Pullman Palace Car Company creates the town of Pullman, Illinois, to house its employees.

1882
Italy, Austria-Hungary, and Germany form the Triple Alliance for mutual defense.

458

History's Impact video program

Watch the video to understand the impact of the U.S. as the world's most powerful industrial nation.

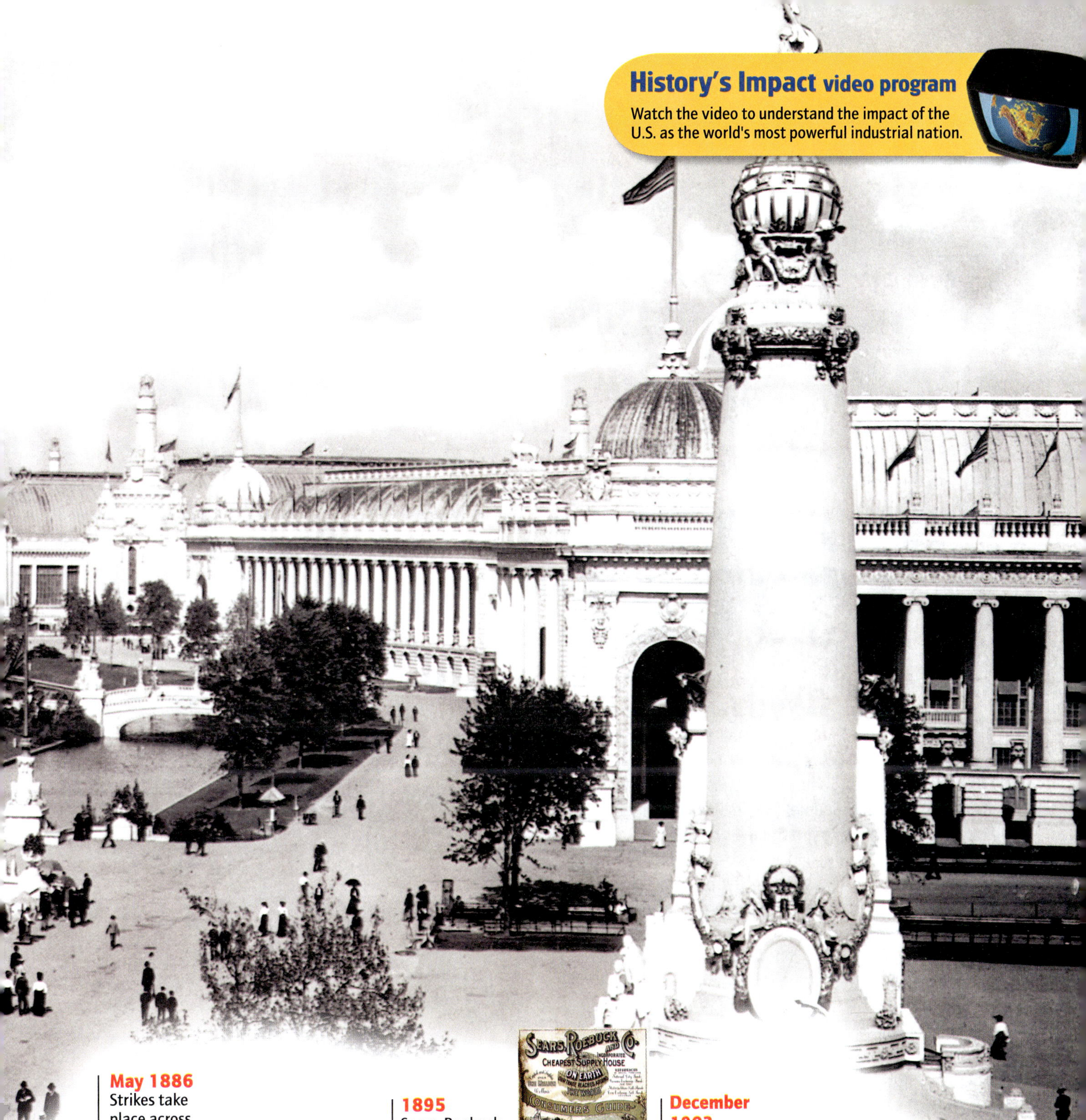

May 1886
Strikes take place across the nation.

The Haymarket Riot occurs in Chicago.

1885
German engineer Gottlieb Daimler patents a version of the modern gas engine.

1890

1890
Congress passes the Sherman Antitrust Act.

1895
Sears, Roebuck and Company produces a 532-page mail-order catalog.

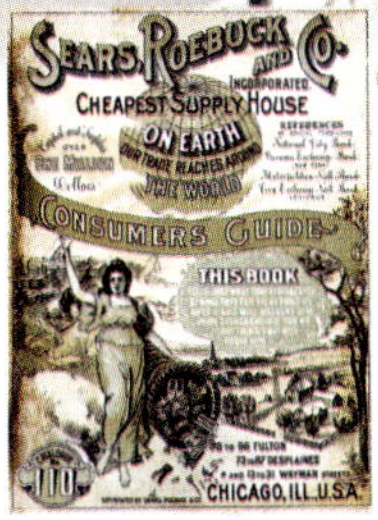

1900

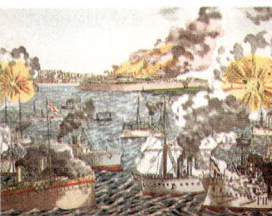

1900
The Boxer Rebellion breaks out in China.

December 1903
The Wright brothers make the first airplane flight.

1905
The Russo-Japanese War ends, and Japan emerges as a major world power.

1910

1910
Four former British colonies unite as the Union of South Africa.

Industry and Railroads

BEFORE YOU READ

MAIN IDEA

During the late 1800s, new technology led to rapid industrial growth and the expansion of railroads.

READING FOCUS

1. What new industries emerged in the late 1800s, and why were they important?

2. Why did railroads expand, and what changes resulted?

KEY TERMS AND PEOPLE

Bessemer process
Edwin L. Drake
wildcatter
transcontinental railroad

 PI 3.3 Prepare essays and oral reports about the important social, political, economic, scientific, technological, and cultural developments, issues, and events from New York State and United States history.

"TENTACLES OF STEEL"

 **THE INSIDE STORY**

Can you fight a big corporation? In May 1869 officials from the Union Pacific and Central Pacific railroads met at Promontory Summit, Utah. They pounded a symbolic golden spike into a railroad tie. The first transcontinental railroad was complete! Railroads quickly expanded.

The railroad—the Iron Horse— linked California with the rest of the country. It gave many people jobs. It let farmers ship fresh produce and meat to eastern cities. Railroad companies thus had tremendous political and financial power. All too often, though, they used their power unfairly.

One issue was rates for shipping freight. Railroads charged different rates to different shippers. They raised rates at harvest time, charging more than the crop would sell for. Nevertheless, farmers had to depend on them.

Many California farmers resented the situation. The Southern Pacific Railroad was the biggest corporation and the largest employer in the state. To farmers, the railroad was an octopus whose tentacles were reaching in all directions to strangle them.

In 1901 novelist Frank Norris published *The Octopus*. The book describes the uneven struggle between California wheat farmers and the railroads. One character in the book sees the railroad as "the terror of steel and steam . . . with tentacles of steel clutching into the soil, the soulless Force, the iron-hearted Power, the monster, the Colossus, the Octopus." Eventually, the railroads' abuses of power would lead to government regulation of their business practices.

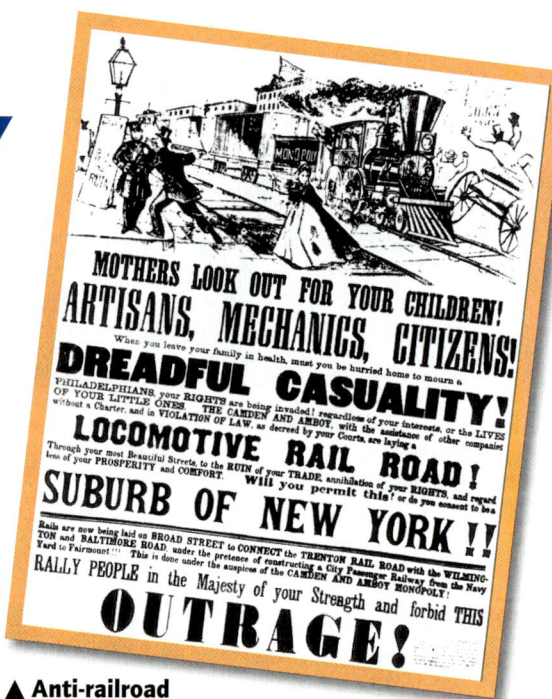

▲ Anti-railroad poster from 1843

New Industries Emerge

As you read earlier, the United States began its Industrial Revolution in the early 1800s. Water or steam power replaced animal and human sources of power. Workers made goods in factories instead of in small workshops or private homes.

In the late 1800s, new technologies helped industry grow to new heights. Electrical power replaced steam and water power. Factories became larger and produced more and more goods. Faster transportation helped move people and goods more cheaply. Industrial growth was so dramatic in the late 1800s that the period is sometimes called the Second Industrial Revolution.

Making steel In the 1850s two inventors an ocean apart were working on a new way to make steel. In the United States, William Kelly used a blast of hot air to purify molten iron and convert it to steel. Working independently in England, Henry Bessemer developed a similar method, which he quickly patented.

Using the so-called **Bessemer process,** American steel mills began working faster and more cheaply than ever before. In 1873 the United States turned out about 115,000 tons of steel. By 1910 output had soared to 24 million tons, making America the world's top producer.

Why did this matter? Steel helped transform the United States into a modern industrial economy. Steel was stronger, less brittle, and more easily shaped than iron. Thus railroads found steel to be a superior material for locomotives and rails. With steel, construction companies could build bigger bridges and taller buildings. The low cost of steel also made it desirable for ordinary items such as nails and wire.

The start of the oil industry Oil became another key commodity in the late 1800s, valued both as a fuel source and as a lubricant for factory machinery. For generations, people had been finding oil on the surface of coastal waters and lakes. It was not until the mid-1800s, though, that people put it to good use, refining it into kerosene to light lamps.

As demand for kerosene skyrocketed, companies sought to profit. One of them hired **Edwin L. Drake** to extract oil from the ground in Pennsylvania. At first people mocked Drake's drilling efforts as "Drake's Folly." Then in August 1859, his crew hit a crevice deep in the rock. As oil seeped up, the men scrambled to collect it in a bathtub. Edwin Drake had drilled the first commercial oil well. He was soon steadily pumping "black gold" to the surface.

The output from Drake's oil well was modest, but it drew plenty of **wildcatters,** or oil prospectors, to the area. Wildcatters looked for oil in other regions, too. In January 1901, a group led by Anthony F. Lucas struck a rich oil pocket

Texas Leads the Oil Boom

U.S. OIL PRODUCTION, 1880–1910

Barrels (in millions) — vertical axis: 0, 50, 100, 150, 200, 250
Year — horizontal axis: 1880, 1890, 1900, 1910

Source: *Historical Statistics of the United States*

Skills FOCUS **INTERPRETING GRAPHS**

Wooden derricks line Spindletop's Boiler Avenue in Texas in 1903. After Spindletop gushed, speculators rushed to buy area land. *About how many more barrels of oil were produced in 1910 than in 1880?*

See **Skills Handbook**, p. H17

Boiler Avenue

at Spindletop Hill near Beaumont, Texas. The oil gushed nearly 100 feet in the air for nine days before it could be capped.

The discovery at Spindletop kicked off an oil boom in Texas. Spindletop Hill bristled with oil derricks, jammed in so closely they nearly touched each other. Spindletop produced more than 17 million barrels of oil in 1902. With so many wells, though, production began to decline rapidly. By 1904 Spindletop produced only about 20 percent of what it had in 1902.

This first oil boom in Texas lasted less than 20 years, but it had long-term consequences. Many of the world's leading oil companies, such as Exxon Mobil, Gulf Oil, and Texaco, got their start at Spindletop. They would refine crude oil not only into kerosene, but also into gasoline and other fuels. These new petroleum products would become major sources of energy, fueling a revolution in transportation and industry.

READING CHECK **Drawing Conclusions** Why did steel and oil become important industries?

Railroads Expand

In the 1850s train tracks already crisscrossed the Northeast and reached into the Southeast and the Great Lakes area. In the following decades, rail service spread even farther. Between 1865 and 1890, the number of miles of railroad track jumped nearly fivefold.

The federal government aided this growth by giving thousands of acres of land to railroad companies. They used some of it for new routes and sold some to finance construction. Cheap steel also helped the railroads expand. Steel rails cost only about $12 a ton in the late 1890s, down from $50 a ton in 1877.

A transcontinental railroad In 1862 Congress authorized two companies to build rail lines to the West Coast. For the next six

Interactive Map
RAILROADS BUILT BY 1910

RAILROADS BUILT BY 1870

go.hrw.com
Interactive Map
Keyword: SD7 CH14

Pacific Time Zone
Mountain Time Zone
Central Time Zone
Eastern Time Zone
Railroad

0   200   400 Miles
0   200   400 Kilometers
Albers equal-area projection

GEOGRAPHY SKILLS **INTERPRETING MAPS**

1. **Region** How many time zones was the continental United States divided into in 1910?
2. **Movement** What region had the most railroads? Why do you think this might be so?

See **Skills Handbook**, p. H19

and a half years, workers raced to complete the first **transcontinental railroad**—one that would cross the whole country.

The Union Pacific laid tracks westward from Omaha, Nebraska. It hired thousands of Irish, German, English, African American, and Native American workers to build its part of the line. These workers could make progress fairly quickly because much of the land was prairie or gently rolling hills.

Workers for the Central Pacific laid track toward the east, starting in Sacramento, California. These workers—primarily Chinese—labored on tougher terrain. They had to cross deserts and blast through the granite mountains on the California-Nevada border. They also faced attacks by Native Americans.

On May 10, 1869, the two rail lines met at Promontory Summit in Utah Territory. At the ceremony celebrating the completion of the railroad, an official praised the achievement:

HISTORY'S VOICES

❝The east and west have come together. Never, since history commenced her record of human events, has she been called upon to note the completion of a work so magnificent.❞

—Dr. H. W. Harkness

The first transcontinental railroad was soon followed by others. Regional railroads expanded, too, uniting the country both physically and economically.

The effects of expansion The creation of a vast railroad network had several important effects. On the economic front, the railroads promoted trade and provided many jobs. In addition, the demand for rails and railcars gave a boost to steel and train manufacturers.

The railroads also sped up settlement of the West. A journey to the West Coast once took months. Now travelers could go from the Atlantic to the Pacific in just a few days. As a result, parts of the country that had been sparsely populated began to fill with residents. Wherever railroads were built, new towns sprang up and existing towns grew into bigger cities.

Railroads also led to the adoption of what we call standard time. Earlier, people kept time according to the position of the sun. When it was noon in Chicago, it was 12:07 p.m. in Indianapolis and 12:31 p.m. in Pittsburgh. The state of Michigan had at least 27 different local times. Wisconsin had even more—38!

Running a railroad, however, required accurate timekeeping. A New York school principal, C. F. Dowd, was the first to propose dividing the earth into time zones. All communities within a single time zone would set their clocks alike. Railroad officials enthusiastically embraced this idea in 1883. In 1918 Congress adopted standard time for the nation as a whole.

THE IMPACT TODAY

Economics
Rail travel has declined since the advent of cars and planes. Most U.S. trains now carry freight instead of passengers.

READING CHECK **Identifying Problems and Solutions** Why did railroads adopt standard time?

SECTION 1 ASSESSMENT

go.hrw.com
Online Quiz
Keyword: SD7 HP14

Reviewing Ideas, Terms, and People

1. a. Describe How did the **Bessemer process** change steel making in the United States?
b. Explain Why is **Edwin L. Drake** an important figure in the history of the oil industry? Why was the discovery at Spindletop important?
c. Elaborate How did the growth of the steel industry affect other industries?

2. a. Recall What role did the U.S. government play in the expansion of railroads during the late 1800s?
b. Analyze How did the **transcontinental railroad** affect the settlement of the West?
c. Evaluate How did the expansion of the railroads change life for all Americans?

Critical Thinking

3. Sequence Copy the time line below and use it to record key events in the oil and railroad industries.

1855 |————|————|————|————|————| 1905

FOCUS ON WRITING

4. Descriptive You live in a small town in the late 1800s. You know that a railroad company is planning to build tracks in your general area. Write a letter to a distant friend describing how people feel about the coming of the railroad and what benefits or drawbacks it will have for the town.

Railroads
Transform Chicago

By 1900, railroads had transformed Chicago into the hub of the nation's transportation system. The city was the primary place where eastern manufactured goods were sold and then shipped to the smaller towns of the West. It was also the place where western farm produce, lumber, and other products were processed before being shipped to distant markets around the world. Large industries and retailing businesses, eager to exploit the city's transportation advantages, took root in the city. As industries grew, so did the population, forcing the city to grow upwards and outwards.

Meatpacking Industry

The Union Stock Yards covered more than a square mile. Railroads brought in cattle and hogs from as far away as Texas. Huge packing companies processed meat and shipped it out across the country over the rails.

New York Standards

ST **4.3** Develop hypotheses about important events, eras, or issues; move from chronicling to explaining historical events and issues.

Suburbs

As Chicago grew, so did its middle classes. They migrated to the new suburbs that became stops on the steam railroads that left the city for places as far away as San Francisco.

Steel Skyscrapers

Chicago's steel industry and railroads depended on each other. Chicago's mills made steel rails, while much of the raw materials needed to make steel was brought in by train. After the Great Fire of 1871, the mills produced steel for the world's first skyscrapers.

Catalog Companies

Montgomery Ward's four-pound catalogs offered products rural customers needed. Railroad tracks ran right through the company's warehouse. Competitor Sears, Roebuck & Co. moved to Chicago because of its railroad access to all parts of the country.

Shipping Industry

From Chicago, boats carried goods east through the Great Lakes and the Erie Canal and south through a canal leading to the Mississippi River. Boats transported heavy items such as coal.

GEOGRAPHY SKILLS | **INTERPRETING MAPS**

go.hrw.com
Interactive Map
Keyword: SD7 CH14

1. **Location** How did Chicago's location make it an ideal railroad hub?

2. **Human-Environment Interaction** How did Chicago industries and people take advantage of the railroads?

See **Skills Handbook,** p. H20

The Rise of Big Business

BEFORE YOU READ

MAIN IDEA

Corporations run by powerful business leaders became a dominant force in the American economy.

READING FOCUS

1. What conditions created a favorable climate for business during the late 1800s?
2. How did business structures change?
3. Who were the leading industrial tycoons, and what did they achieve?
4. How did mass marketing change the way goods were sold?

KEY TERMS AND PEOPLE

Horatio Alger
entrepreneur
capitalism
laissez-faire
social Darwinism
monopoly
John D. Rockefeller
vertical integration
horizontal integration
Andrew Carnegie
Cornelius Vanderbilt

 PI 3.2 Research and analyze the major themes and developments in New York State and United States history (e.g., colonization and settlement; Revolution and New National Period; immigration; expansion and reform era; Civil War and Reconstruction; the American labor movement; Great Depression; World Wars; contemporary United States).

From Rags to Riches

THE INSIDE STORY

Can a book make you successful? "Strive and succeed!" That was the lesson that thousands of American boys learned from the popular novels of **Horatio Alger Jr.** It was also the title of one of his 100 or so books. Alger was one of the most popular American writer of the late 1800s. His stories inspired hundreds of young men to strive for success.

The Horatio Alger hero was poor but honest, brave, and trustworthy. He faced hardships but eventually found a good job, and sometimes fame and fortune. He was cheerful even when faced with difficulties. He worked hard, too, but it was usually sudden good luck (which he of course deserved) that brought the final happy ending.

Alger had his own success story. Born in 1832, he was the son of a Unitarian minister. His family expected him to become a clergyman, but he really wanted to be a writer. In 1867, he found his own formula for success. He released *Ragged Dick, or Street Life in New York,* first as a magazine serial and then as a book. This story of a streetwise shoe-shine boy was an immediate hit. Many other tales followed. Their plots were all very similar; only the hero's name was different. Here are a few Alger titles: *Bound to Rise, or Live and Learn; The Train Boy, or Up the Ladder; Struggling Upward, or Luke Larkin's Luck.*

◀ **This is one of 70 rooms in business tycoon Cornelius Vanderbilt II's summer cottage, built in 1895.**

A Favorable Climate for Business

Horatio Alger's novels showcased an American ideal—self-reliant individualism. His characters went from rags to riches through their own hard work. Similarly, many people in the late 1800s believed that a strong work ethic made one successful. The business world welcomed **entrepreneurs**—risk takers who use their money and talents to launch new ventures.

Belief in free markets

American entrepreneurs were working within the capitalist system. **Capitalism** is an economic system in which private businesses run most industries. Competition determines prices and wages.

By the late 1800s most business leaders believed in **laissez-faire** (le-say-FER) capitalism. The term *laissez-faire* is French for "to let do." Laissez-faire capitalism allows companies to conduct business without intervention by the government. Business leaders believed that government <u>regulation</u> would destroy individual self-reliance, reduce profits, and harm the economy.

Social Darwinism

Americans understood that there were inequalities under capitalism. But many thinkers believed that inequalities were part of a natural order. To explain why some people prospered while others did not, economists and business leaders embraced the philosophy of **social Darwinism.** This philosophy adapted the ideas of the British scientist Charles Darwin and applied them to human society.

Darwin had studied plants and animals and concluded that members of a species compete for survival. Those best adapted to their environment thrive. Less well adapted members gradually die out. Darwin called this process natural selection.

Social Darwinists believed that natural selection also applied to society. Stronger people, businesses, and nations would prosper. Weaker ones would fail. Social Darwinists believed that what they called "survival of the fittest" strengthened society as a whole. They opposed any interference with the process.

READING CHECK **Summarizing** What beliefs did social Darwinists hold?

ACADEMIC VOCABULARY
regulation rules or legal oversight

COUNTERPOINTS

Social Darwinism

A professor and minister, William Graham Sumner advocated Social Darwinism.

"If . . . men were willing to set to work with energy and courage . . . all might live in plenty and prosperity. But if they insist on remaining in the slums . . . there is no device . . . which can prevent them from falling victims to poverty and misery or from succumbing in the competition of life to those who have greater command of capital."

William Graham Sumner, c. 1885

Walter Rauschenbusch, also a minister, lived among the poor in New York City. He found fault with the attitude of the rich toward the working class.

"Competitive commerce exalts selfishness to the dignity of a moral principle. It pits men against one another in a gladiatorial game in which there is no mercy and in which ninety percent of the combatants finally strew the arena. . . . If the rich had only what they earned, and the poor had all that they earned, . . . life would be more sane."

Walter Rauschenbush, 1908

THE GRANGER COLLECTION, NEW YORK

Skills FOCUS **READING LIKE A HISTORIAN**

Identifying Points of View How does each man find fault with either the working class or the wealthy?

See **Skills Handbook**, pp. H28–H29

Business Structures Change

ACADEMIC VOCABULARY

complex complicated; made up of many parts

In the late 1800s industrialization continued on a massive scale. Businesses became larger and more <u>complex</u>. This led to changes in the way businesses were organized.

Proprietorships and partnerships At the end of the Civil War, most businesses were small. Some were run by individual owners—an arrangement called a proprietorship. Other companies were owned by two or more people in a partnership. In both proprietorships and partnerships, the owners of the company were personally responsible for all debts and obligations of the business.

Corporations The massive industries of the late 1800s needed more expert management. These industries began organizing as corporations. A corporation is a business with the legal status of an individual. It is owned by stockholders—people who buy shares of the company, or stock. The major business decisions of a corporation are made by a board of directors. The board in turn hires corporate officers to run the day-to-day operations.

A corporation has several advantages. It can raise large sums of money by selling stock. That money can be used to expand the business. Also, stockholders have limited responsibility for the corporation's debts. They can lose only the amount of money they have invested in the business. Finally, a corporation is not dependent on a single owner for its existence. It can continue to function long after its original founders leave.

Trusts and monopolies In the late 1800s competition in the marketplace was fierce. To gain dominance, some competing companies formed trusts. The companies agreed to merge and turn over their separate stocks to a board of trustees. The trustees then ran the group of companies as if it were a single corporation, and all the participants split the profits.

When a trust gained complete control over an industry, it held a monopoly. That meant it had no competition from other firms. It could raise prices on its products or lower quality much more freely than it otherwise might.

READING CHECK **Contrasting** How were proprietorships and corporations different?

Industrial Tycoons

As businesses grew ever larger in the late 1800s, many corporate leaders amassed staggering fortunes. Three of them—John D. Rockefeller, Andrew Carnegie, and Cornelius Vanderbilt—were wealthier than any Americans before them.

Rockefeller and oil John D. Rockefeller entered the oil business in 1863 and proved himself to be a superb business leader. His company, Standard Oil, started as a refinery. To increase profits, though, Rockefeller engaged in vertical integration—acquiring companies that supplied his business. Rockefeller bought barrel factories, oil fields, oil-storage facilities, pipelines, and railroad cars. This allowed him to keep his costs low and profits high.

To expand his business, Rockefeller also practiced horizontal integration. This meant taking over other companies producing the same product. Rockefeller bought as many refineries as he could. By 1879 Standard Oil refined 90 percent of all U.S. oil.

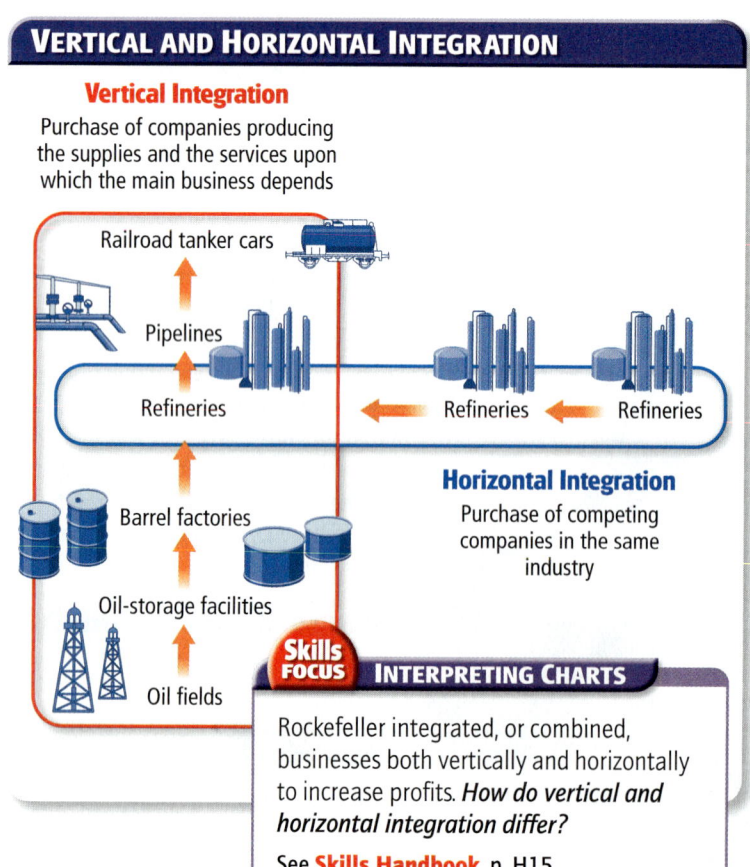

VERTICAL AND HORIZONTAL INTEGRATION

Vertical Integration
Purchase of companies producing the supplies and the services upon which the main business depends

Railroad tanker cars

Pipelines

Refineries — Refineries ← Refineries

Barrel factories

Horizontal Integration
Purchase of competing companies in the same industry

Oil-storage facilities

Oil fields

Skills FOCUS **INTERPRETING CHARTS**

Rockefeller integrated, or combined, businesses both vertically and horizontally to increase profits. *How do vertical and horizontal integration differ?*

See **Skills Handbook**, p. H15

Political Cartoon

This 1901 drawing portrays John D. Rockefeller as ruling the oil industry.

Standard Oil owned interests in all parts of the industry, including drilling, refining, and storage of oil.

Rockefeller got special rates from railroad companies, lowering his transport costs.

Rockefeller's fortune rested on Standard Oil.

© COLLECTION OF THE NEW-YORK HISTORICAL SOCIETY #77374T

Skills FOCUS   READING LIKE A HISTORIAN

1. **Interpreting Political Cartoons** What images suggest Rockefeller's wealth and power?

2. **Contrasting** How does this depiction of Rockefeller contrast with his position as a generous philanthropist?

See **Skills Handbook**, pp. H10, H31

Rockefeller tried to limit competition in other ways as well. He made special deals with railroads and shipping companies to get the lowest possible price for transporting his oil. Rockefeller could now sell his oil much more cheaply than his competitors could. In this way, he drove rival firms out of business.

At one point, Rockefeller's fortune approached $900 million. He gave away over half of it to worthy causes, though. Rockefeller donated more than $80 million to the University of Chicago. He channeled millions more into education and other good works through his Rockefeller Foundation.

Carnegie and steel Andrew Carnegie lived a true rags-to-riches story. Born in Scotland to parents that hit hard economic times when he was about 9, Carnegie immigrated to the United States when he was 12. He advanced quickly in his early jobs and began investing in the iron, oil, railroad, and telegraph industries. He soon founded his own company and rose to the top of the steel business.

Carnegie held down costs by using vertical integration, buying supplies in bulk, and producing items in large quantities. By the end of the century the Carnegie Steel Company dominated the U.S. steel industry. In 1901 Carnegie sold the company to banker J. P. Morgan for $480 million. After retiring, Carnegie began to devote his time to philanthropy, or charity.

Carnegie gave away some $350 million over his lifetime, mostly to support education. He built public libraries, financed scientific work, and established what is now Carnegie Mellon University in Pittsburgh. He also built Carnegie Hall, the famous concert site in New York City, and funded international peace efforts.

FOCUS ON NEW YORK

CULTURE

The Rockefeller Foundation, headquartered in New York City, is now active across the globe, supporting cultural activities and projects in health, agriculture, and urban development.

Carnegie believed that wealthy people had a duty toward the rest of society. He explained his philosophy, known as the Gospel of Wealth, in 1889:

HISTORY'S VOICES

❝This, then, is held to be the duty of the man of Wealth: . . . to consider all surplus revenues which come to him simply as trust funds . . . to produce the most beneficial result for the community.❞

—Andrew Carnegie

Railroad tycoons Other industrial leaders rode the railways to success. **Cornelius Vanderbilt** began investing in railroads during the Civil War. By 1872 he owned the New York Central Railroad. Soon his holdings stretched west to Michigan and north to Canada. At the height of his career, he controlled more than 4,500 miles of railroad track. He also invested heavily in steamship lines and dominated shipping along the Atlantic Coast.

Unlike Rockefeller and Carnegie, Vanderbilt supported few charities. His greatest donation was a $1 million gift to Central University in Nashville, Tennessee, which was later renamed Vanderbilt University. When Vanderbilt died in 1877, he left an estate of $100 million.

Another railroad man, George Pullman, made his fortune by designing and building railroad cars. His Pullman Palace Car Com-

pany, founded in Chicago in 1867, was known for creating sleeper cars that made long-distance travel more comfortable.

In 1881 Pullman built an entire town south of Chicago for his employees. He believed that happy workers would be productive workers. The town of Pullman had comfortable homes with indoor plumbing—a luxury for working-class families. Residents also enjoyed shops, a church, and a library.

At the same time, the Pullman Company controlled many aspects of life in the town. There were no local newspapers and no self-government. Those who spoke out against company policies might find themselves evicted from their homes.

A mixed legacy Some Americans came to view the business tycoons of the late 1800s as "robber barons." Critics have argued that these entrepreneurs profited unfairly by squeezing out competitors and using other tough tactics. Their huge mansions and luxurious lifestyles seemed like ill-gotten rewards.

Other people, though, saw men like Rockefeller, Carnegie, and Vanderbilt as "captains of industry." Admirers credited these tycoons with using their business skills to make the American economy more productive. That in turn made the American economy stronger. In addition, Rockefeller and Carnegie won praise for their generous contributions to charity.

READING CHECK **Identifying Supporting Details** How did Rockefeller and Carnegie gain a competitive edge?

Mass Marketing

The industrial tycoons of the day were not the only people bringing changes to American business. Retailers, too, looked for new ways to <u>maximize</u> their profits.

Many companies that advertised in popular magazines began targeting their messages to women. They realized that women made most purchasing decisions about household goods.

Advertisers also tried new approaches to win customers. Food companies often used wholesome farm images to convey a sense of purity. Some companies came up with clever brand names, such as Uneeda Biscuit crackers, to help customers remember their products.

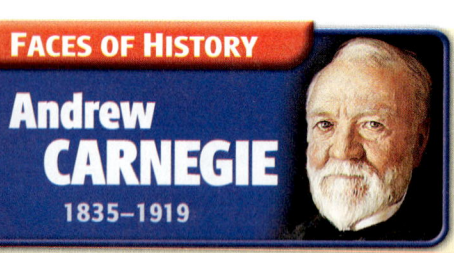

FACES OF HISTORY

Andrew CARNEGIE
1835–1919

Andrew Carnegie began his working career in the United States in a textile factory, but he soon found a job as a telegraph operator.

From there he became the assistant to a Pennsylvania Railroad official. With his savings and a small loan, Carnegie made his first investment in iron manufacturing. Carnegie also advanced his career at the railroad. He soon earned enough to invest in a variety of industries. In 1865 he resigned his job to devote himself to his business ventures. Carnegie's business boomed when he turned to steel manufacturing. His eye for efficiency and close partnerships with railroad companies made Carnegie the king of steel. In 1901 he sold his company and turned to philanthropy. His charities established over 2,500 libraries in the United States and in other English-speaking countries.

Make Inferences How do you think Carnegie's background influenced his drive for success and his charitable activities?

In the cities a new kind of store emerged that made shopping easier. This was the department store, where retailers sold many different products under one roof, grouping them into separate departments for clothing, shoes, cookware, and so on. No longer did customers have to trudge from shop to shop to purchase a variety of goods. They loved the convenience of one-stop shopping—and they loved department store prices. Because these stores bought in bulk, they could pass on the savings to their customers.

Rural dwellers, meanwhile, could purchase a huge variety of goods from mail-order companies. In 1895 Sears, Roebuck and Company produced a 507-page catalog offering everything from slippers to stoves to saddles. The 1904 Montgomery Ward catalog weighed a hefty four pounds and was mailed to roughly 3 million homes.

Mail-order customers simply made their selections, sent in their payments, and waited for the merchandise they ordered to arrive by rail or post. Now even Americans living in the countryside could buy a wide range of manufactured goods—wider than ever before—without having to travel to cities.

House in the Mail

Mass marketers sold affordable, ready-to-assemble houses through their catalogs (below). Right, a modern couple enjoys living in one of these now historic homes.

FOR BETTE

The CARLIN
No. 3031 "Already Cut" and Fitted.

Honor Bilt $1,172.00

READING CHECK **Identifying the Main Idea**
How did companies make their products available to more people in the late 1800s?

go.hrw.com
Online Quiz
Keyword: SD7 HP14

SECTION 2 ASSESSMENT

Reviewing Ideas, Terms, and People

1. **a. Define** What was **laissez-faire** capitalism?
   b. Analyze Why did business leaders oppose government regulation of business?

2. **a. Recall** Why did corporations arise?
   b. Draw Conclusions Do you think the public generally welcomed or feared **monopolies**? Explain.

3. **a. Describe** What does **vertical integration involve?** What does **horizontal integration** involve?
   b. Evaluate How would you assess the contributions—both positive and negative—made by tycoons such as **John D. Rockefeller** and **Andrew Carnegie**?

4. **a. Recall** How did companies market their products in the late 1800s?
   b. Explain What was innovative about the department store?
   c. Predict How might the rise of department stores and mail-order catalogs have affected Americans' spending habits?

Critical Thinking

5. **Comparing and Contrasting** Copy the chart below and record the main characteristics of the following types of businesses: proprietorships, partnerships, and corporations.

Proprietorship	Partnership	Corporation

FOCUS ON WRITING

6. **Expository** You are a small business owner or a consumer living in the late 1800s. You believe that trusts and big corporations have accumulated too much power. You think there should be more competition in the marketplace. Write an article for your local newspaper explaining how large corporations dominate the business world and how this affects ordinary people like you.

Workers Organize

BEFORE YOU READ

MAIN IDEA
Grim working conditions in many industries led workers to form unions and stage labor strikes.

READING FOCUS
1. What was the relationship between government and business in the late 1800s?
2. What were working conditions like for industrial workers?
3. How did workers seek changes?

KEY TERMS AND PEOPLE
Sherman Antitrust Act
sweatshop
Knights of Labor
Terence V. Powderly
xenophobia
blacklist
Samuel Gompers
American Federation of Labor
Eugene V. Debs
Grover Cleveland

PI 3.2 Research and analyze the major themes and developments in New York State and United States history (e.g., colonization and settlement; Revolution and New National Period; immigration; expansion and reform era; Civil War and Reconstruction; the American labor movement; Great Depression; World Wars; contemporary United States).

THE INSIDE STORY

Could you live on $133 a year? When the Industrial Revolution began, businesses did pretty much as they pleased. Few officials worried about the workers, and by the late 1800s there were more workers than jobs.

In October 1883 Thomas O'Donnell, a part-time textile worker, appeared before a Senate committee looking into labor conditions. He was one of many who could not find full-time work. O'Donnell's worn clothes contrasted with the formal dress of the senators. He painted a devastating picture of life for the working poor. New machines required smaller workers, encouraging the use of child labor. Factories fired adults and hired men who had sons who could work. "Whoever has a boy has work," O'Donnell said, "and whoever has no boy stands no chance."

"How much money have you got?" a senator asked. "I have not got a cent in the house," O'Donnell answered, "didn't have when I came out this morning." In fact, he, his wife, and two children had lived on only $16 for the past three months. Over the entire year, the family income had amounted to about $133 from a few weeks' work in the textile mill. O'Donnell dug clams for food and picked up wood for heating. His children were often sickly because they lacked food or clothes or shoes. For workers like O'Donnell, there seemed to be no way to escape from these conditions. ◢

"NOT A CENT IN THE HOUSE"

▼ Too small for the job, these child workers climb onto the machinery at a Georgia textile mill in 1909.

Government and Business

In the late 1800s the government maintained a hands-off attitude toward business. Most politicians, like business leaders, insisted that regulating business would harm the economy.

Nonetheless, as corporations expanded, the government grew uneasy about the power of these giants. In 1890 Congress passed the **Sherman Antitrust Act**. This act made it illegal to form trusts that interfered with free trade. It also prohibited monopolies and activities that hindered competition in the marketplace.

At first the government did not prosecute many companies under this act. Between 1890 and 1901 just 18 suits were brought, and four of those were against labor unions. The law was vague, and for a time the government stopped trying to enforce the Sherman Act.

The government paid even less attention to workers. After all, industrialization was raising the standard of living for all Americans. Yet income inequality was increasing too. By 1890 just 10 percent of the population controlled 75 percent of the nation's wealth. This meant that the rich were exceedingly rich. At the same time, many industrial workers were barely scraping by, earning less than $500 per year.

READING CHECK **Drawing Conclusions** How did government policies affect business?

Industrial Workers

The growth of industry in the late 1800s required huge numbers of workers to keep the factories running. Who were these people whose <u>labor</u> fueled American industry?

The workforce Many factory workers were immigrants. Many others were rural Americans who came to the cities to earn a living. The best factory jobs went to native-born whites or European immigrants. African Americans found more opportunities as laborers or household help, but those jobs usually paid less than factory work.

Many industrial workers were children. By 1900 about one in six children between the ages of 10 and 15 held a job outside the home. Even children as young as five sometimes worked to help make ends meet.

Working conditions Most unskilled laborers typically worked 10 hours per day, six days a week. They had no paid vacation, no sick leave, and no compensation for injuries suffered on the job. Employers pressured these tired, low-paid laborers to work as fast as possible to speed up production. This often led to terrible accidents. Most employers felt no responsibility to help those who were injured. They simply hired new workers to replace them.

Some of the worst exploitation occurred in cramped workshops set up in shabby tenement buildings. These so-called **sweatshops** were especially common in the garment industry:

HISTORY'S VOICES

❝ In [the tenements] the child works unchallenged from the day he is old enough to pull a thread. There is no such thing as a dinner hour; men and women eat while they work, and the 'day' is lengthened at both ends far into the night. Factory hands take their work with them at the close of the lawful day to eke out their scanty earnings by working overtime at home. ❞

—Jacob Riis

Some garment workers toiled in their own apartments instead of in sweatshops. But this meant that the workers—not the employers—were paying for the rent, heat, and light needed to make the clothing.

READING CHECK **Making Inferences** Why would workers agree to work in difficult conditions?

ACADEMIC VOCABULARY

labor work performed for wages

Government

The federal government and all 50 states now have child labor laws to protect minors. These laws set minimum ages for different kinds of work and limit the hours that children may work.

The Labor Movement

Union membership has declined since the late 1940s as traditionally unionized industries lost jobs and as employment in non-unionized high-tech and service industries grew. Study the time line to learn about key events in the American labor movement.

ST 2.2 Explain the contributions of specific groups of people to American society and culture.

◀ Early 1800s New England factory

1834 Young mill girls in Lowell, Massachusetts, form a union, the Factory Girl's Association, to protest wage cuts.

1794 Shoemakers in Philadelphia establish the first trade union in the United States.

▶ American Federation of Labor emblem

1886 Violence breaks out between police and union supporters in Chicago's Haymarket Square. Samuel Gompers founds the American Federation of Labor (AFL).

`1700` `1800`

Workers Seek Changes

By the late 1800s working conditions were so dismal that workers began organizing in ever-increasing numbers. By banding together, they hoped to pressure employers into making the workplace safer and paying reasonable wages.

Early organizing The labor movement had gotten its start in the late 1700s. In 1794 a group of Philadelphia shoemakers formed a trade union to protect their interests. Over the next few decades, skilled workers in other trades—carpenters, printers, blacksmiths, and so forth—also organized. These early unions remained mostly small and local, however.

National unions After the Civil War, the labor movement began to grow. The National Labor Union (NLU) organized in 1866 as a federation of small, local unions. The NLU pushed to shorten the workday to eight hours. Unsuccessful in this effort, the NLU folded in 1872.

The **Knights of Labor**, founded in Philadelphia in 1869, was a more effective group. Under the leadership of **Terence V. Powderly** in the 1880s, the Knights of Labor began to accept unskilled workers, women, African Americans, and even employers as members. It excluded only bankers, gamblers, lawyers, liquor sellers, physicians, and stockholders. By 1886 the group had more than 700,000 members.

With the motto "An injury to one is a concern of all," the Knights of Labor campaigned for many reforms. The group's constitution outlined its general goals:

HISTORY'S VOICES

❝To secure to the toilers [workers] a proper share of the wealth that they create; more of the leisure that rightfully belongs to them; more society advantages; . . . in a word, all those rights and privileges necessary to make them capable of enjoying, appreciating, defending and perpetuating the blessings of good government.❞

—Preamble to the Constitution of the Knights of Labor

The Knights of Labor also worked for the eight-hour workday, the end of child labor, and equal pay for equal work. In its early years, the organization discouraged the use of strikes, preferring boycotts and negotiation with employers. Yet soon enough, strikes would become commonplace.

The Great Railroad Strike The first major rail strike happened in 1877. Times were tough, and several northern railroads cut wages that year. Workers for the Baltimore and Ohio Railroad protested by walking off the job and blocking several freight trains. Pennsylvania Railroad employees blocked the movement of all trains on their rail lines. The strikes quickly spread to other railroads, stopping most freight traffic for more than a week.

◀ Air traffic controllers on the picket line

1981 President Ronald Reagan fires most of the nation's striking air-traffic controllers.

◀ Service Employees International president Andy Stern (right) announces the union's split from the AFL-CIO.

1900 ● ● **2000** ●

1994 Despite union protests that jobs will relocate to lower-wage Mexican factories, the North American Free Trade Agreement (NAFTA) takes effect between the United States, Canada, and Mexico.

2005 The Teamster and Service Employees International Union splits from the AFL–CIO. Shortly after, the United Food and Commercial Workers also leaves.

Several governors called out their state militias to put down the strikes. In Baltimore, the militia fired into crowds, killing 10 people. Troops in Pittsburgh killed 20 civilians, including 3 children. Protestors reacted angrily to this bloodshed. Mobs in Pittsburgh set train engines, buildings, and equipment on fire, causing more than $4 million in damage.

The arrival of U.S. Army troops put an end to the Great Railroad Strike of 1877. But the violence on the part of both strikers and the government had led to the deaths of more than 100 people.

The Haymarket Riot

The United States experienced a year of more intense strikes and turmoil in 1886. Wage cuts in many industries caused workers across the nation to go on strike. Labor demonstrations were common that year, some involving violent clashes with police. One of the worst confrontations was the Haymarket Riot.

In Haymarket Square in Chicago, crowds gathered to protest violent police action at a strike the day before. Suddenly, someone threw a bomb into the crowd. People panicked, and gunfire rang out. Before the situation calmed down, 11 people had lost their lives and more than 100 suffered injuries.

People immediately blamed foreign-born unionists for the violence. The press fanned the flames of this **xenophobia** (zeh-nuh-FO-bee-uh), or fear of foreigners. Police arrested numerous suspects and eventually charged eight men with conspiracy and murder. All had foreign-sounding names.

No evidence existed to connect these men to a crime. In fact, five of them were not even in Haymarket Square when the bomb went off. But all eight were convicted and sentenced to death. Four were hanged, and one killed himself in prison. In 1893 the new governor of Illinois pardoned the last three, believing that their guilt had not been proven.

The American Federation of Labor

Following the Haymarket Riot, employers struck back at organized labor. Increasingly, they forced employees to sign documents saying they would not join unions. Employers made and shared **blacklists**—lists of people perceived as troublemakers, whom they refused to hire. When workers protested by striking, employers replaced them with "scabs," or strikebreakers. These scabs were often African Americans or others who had been excluded by the unions.

Union members did not stop organizing, despite the risks. In 1886 a group of skilled workers led by **Samuel Gompers** formed the **American Federation of Labor** (AFL). Using strikes and other tactics, the AFL won wage increases and shorter work weeks.

THE IMPACT TODAY

Economics
In 1955 the AFL merged with another powerful union, the Congress of Industrial Organizations. Today the AFL-CIO represents more than 9 million American workers.

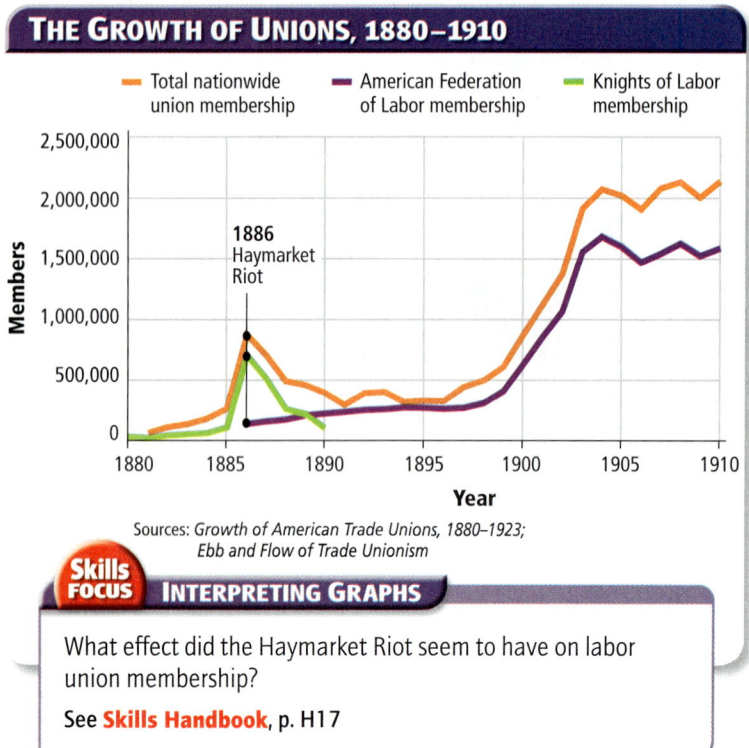

THE GROWTH OF UNIONS, 1880–1910

— Total nationwide union membership
— American Federation of Labor membership
— Knights of Labor membership

Members

2,500,000

2,000,000

1,500,000

1,000,000

500,000

0

1880   1885   1890   1895   1900   1905   1910

Year

1886 Haymarket Riot

Sources: *Growth of American Trade Unions, 1880–1923; Ebb and Flow of Trade Unionism*

Skills FOCUS   INTERPRETING GRAPHS

What effect did the Haymarket Riot seem to have on labor union membership?

See **Skills Handbook**, p. H17

The Homestead strike Although unions made some gains, conflicts with employers continued. In 1892 workers at the Carnegie Steel Company in Homestead, Pennsylvania, protested when the manager wanted to step up production. They refused to work faster, and the manager tried to lock them out. The workers then seized the plant.

Days later, gunfire erupted when private guards hired by the company tried to take control. A fierce battle raged for 14 hours, leaving 16 people dead. The governor called out the state militia to restore order, and within months, the steelworkers' union withered.

The Pullman strike Other unions suffered setbacks, too. In 1893 the Pullman Company laid off a third of its employees. It cut the wages of the remaining employees an average of 25 percent, but it did not lower their rents.

The workers went on strike with the support of **Eugene V. Debs**, the leader of the American Railway Union (ARU). He urged the members of the ARU not to work on any trains that included Pullman cars.

The government soon stepped in. It ordered the union to call off the strike because it was interfering with delivery of the U.S. mail. When ARU officials refused, many of them were jailed. Meanwhile, President **Grover Cleveland** called in federal troops, and the strike collapsed. Workers who would not quit the ARU wound up fired or blacklisted.

For the next several decades, unions struggled for progress. They would eventually gain considerable power, but the late 1800s remained the era of big business.

READING CHECK   Making Generalizations
How did employers and political leaders generally respond to the labor strikes of the late 1800s?

SECTION 3 ASSESSMENT

go.hrw.com
Online Quiz
Keyword: SD7 HP14

Reviewing Ideas, Terms, and People

1. **a. Identify** What was the **Sherman Antitrust Act**?
   b. Analyze Did the Sherman Antitrust Act curb the power of big business? Explain.

2. **a. Describe** What groups of people went to work in factories during the Second Industrial Revolution?
   b. Make Inferences Why might some employers have preferred child workers to adult workers?

3. **a. Recall** Why did more and more workers begin organizing in the late 1800s?
   b. Contrast How did the **Knights of Labor** and the **AFL** differ from earlier unions?
   c. Evaluate You read that violence often accompanied labor union strikes. Do you think this helped or hurt the cause of workers? Explain.

Critical Thinking

4. **Identifying Cause and Effect** Copy the chart below and record the causes and effects of key labor incidents.

Incident	Cause	Effect

FOCUS ON SPEAKING

5. **Persuasive** You are a factory owner and that your workers want higher wages and shorter hours. You believe that meeting these demands will drive you out of business. Give a talk to your workers to try to persuade them to accept your terms and refrain from striking.

The Age of Invention

BEFORE YOU READ

MAIN IDEA

Important innovations in transportation and communication occurred during the Second Industrial Revolution.

READING FOCUS

1. What advances in transportation were made in the late 1800s?
2. What inventions led to a communications revolution?
3. How did Thomas Edison help shape the modern world?

KEY TERMS AND PEOPLE

mass transit
Orville and Wilbur Wright
telegraph
Alexander Graham Bell
Thomas Alva Edison

PI **3.2** Research and analyze the major themes and developments in New York State and United States history (e.g., colonization and settlement; Revolution and New National Period; immigration; expansion and reform era; Civil War and Reconstruction; the American labor movement; Great Depression; World Wars; contemporary United States).

How did two bicycle mechanics change the world? On a windy December day in 1903, a one-man airplane flew over the dunes near Kitty Hawk, North Carolina. The pilot was Orville Wright. Orville and his older brother Wilbur had always been clever with machines. Bicycling was a new craze in the 1890s, and the Wrights started a successful business designing and making bicycles. Wilbur began to read about experiments with gliders—light airplanes that have no motors but are carried by the wind. In 1899 the Wright brothers began to build and test gliders. Soon they turned to powered flight.

On the morning of December 17, the brothers took turns piloting their tiny 745-pound plane. On Orville's first flight, the plane lurched up and down, stayed in the air for 12 seconds, and then nosed into the ground. It was the first true flight in an airplane. The brothers made three more flights that day. Orville's diary described the fourth trip: "The machine started off with its ups and downs as it had before, but by the time he [Wilbur] had gone over three or four hundred feet he had it under much better control and was traveling on a fairly even course." The plane traveled 852 feet in 59 seconds. The Wrights had flown into history.

A Flight Into History

▼ Orville Wright makes the first flight as his brother Wilbur watches.

Cable Cars to Light Rail

The late 1800s were the heyday of cable cars and electric streetcars in urban America. But with the rise of the automobile, many systems declined or were dismantled by the 1950s.

Today more cities are turning to light rail trains. These are electrically powered by overhead trolley wires or an electrified third rail. Los Angeles, for example, has a light-rail network linking its downtown with outlying areas.

Supporters of light rail emphasize its benefits in reducing traffic and pollution. Opponents argue that too few people use these systems.

Comparing How are some light-rail systems like old-fashioned trolleys?

Riding the light rails in Los Angeles, yesterday (right) and today.

Advances in Transportation

Railroads allowed people to travel long distances quite easily. But Americans also needed local forms of transportation. As cities grew larger in the 1800s, walking everywhere became impractical. Workers wanted faster ways of getting to and from their jobs. People wanted easier access to stores and attractions. Residents in distant neighborhoods felt isolated from the city center.

Cities responded by devising means of **mass transit**. These are public transportation systems that carry large numbers of people and make regular stops along established routes.

Streetcars The first forms of mass transit were horse-drawn passenger vehicles. By the 1830s these horsecars were rolling along rails in the street, and they became known as streetcars. Rails made the ride smoother and allowed horses to pull larger and heavier loads.

In cities with steep hills, though, streetcars needed more power than horses could provide. Andrew Smith Hallidie solved the problem in San Francisco by building the first cable car line in 1873. The cars could climb up the hills by latching onto a moving cable underground. The cable was kept in motion by a steam engine in a central station.

Soon the cable cars became a symbol of San Francisco. One visitor wrote about them admiringly in 1888:

HISTORY'S VOICES

“If any one should ask me what I consider the most distinctive, progressive feature of California, I should answer promptly, its cable-car system . . . A point of perfection [is] the amazing length of the ride that is given you for . . . a nickel. I have circled this city of San Francisco . . . for this smallest of . . . coins.”

—Harriet Harper, 1888

Other cities began to build cable car lines, but they quickly became outdated. By 1900 most had been replaced by streetcars powered by overhead electrical wires. Electric streetcars, or trolleys, were cheaper to build and faster to run than cable cars.

Subways As American cities continued to expand rapidly, traffic became a serious problem. In urban centers such as Boston and New York, traffic sometimes came to a complete standstill, with horses and electric streetcars competing for space on narrow roads. Then Boston found a solution. The city unveiled the nation's first subway line in 1897, attracting more than 100,000 riders on opening day. The local newspaper reported the event proudly:

"It was a great success. . . . The regularity with which the cars were run, the haste with which they were occupied and emptied at the . . . terminal and the machine-like precision with which they arrived and departed were undoubtedly wonderful."

—*Boston Daily Globe,* 1897

New York opened its subway in 1904 to even bigger crowds. On its first day, some 350,000 New Yorkers eagerly rode the new underground trains.

Automobiles While mass transit was taking off, inventors were also experimenting with vehicles for personal use. A breakthrough came when Nikolaus A. Otto, a German engineer, invented the internal combustion engine in 1867. Soon inventors in Europe and the United States were trying to adapt that engine to power a "horseless carriage." In 1893 Charles and J. Frank Duryea built the first practical motorcar in the United States.

The early automobiles were for the wealthy few who could afford expensive playthings. A new car cost about $2,500—at a time when the average worker made roughly $500 a year.

Airplanes Human beings had tried for hundreds of years to discover a way to fly. During the Renaissance, the Italian artist Leonardo da Vinci designed—but did not build—a flying machine. It was not until 1903 that two American brothers crafted a successful airplane.

Orville and Wilbur Wright were Ohio bicycle makers who tackled the challenge systematically. They made kites to test their wing designs. They built a wind tunnel to study the forces of wind on the wings. They figured out how to power their plane with an engine and how to control it.

On December 17, 1903, the Wright brothers tried out their airplane at Kitty Hawk, North Carolina. In freezing temperatures and a strong wind, Orville climbed into the pilot's seat. The plane took off across the beach, flying just inches above the ground and landing 120 feet from where it had started. This short trip—12 seconds in all—was the first true flight in an airplane. The Wright brothers quickly followed this success with even longer flights.

READING CHECK **Summarizing** What innovations in the late 1800s changed the way people moved from place to place?

Communications Revolution

Inventors also changed the way Americans communicated in the 1800s. In earlier times, people had face-to-face contact or relied on handwritten letters or printed materials. Communicating over long distances meant physically carrying a document from one place to another. Technology changed all this.

The telegraph In 1837 Samuel F. B. Morse patented his method of communicating by sending messages over wires with electricity. He called his invention the **telegraph.** Telegraph operators tapped out patterns of long and short signals that stood for letters of the alphabet. Using this system, known as Morse code, an operator could send a message to distant locations in mere minutes.

After the Civil War, the telegraph grew with the railroads. Telegraph wires were strung on poles along the railroad tracks. Train stations had telegraph offices inside them. Telegraphs became the fastest way to send messages.

The telephone Elisha Gray and **Alexander Graham Bell** both developed devices that could transmit voices using electricity. In 1876 the two men brought their designs to the patent office within hours of each other. Bell, however, got his design patented first. Today he is known as the inventor of the telephone.

Companies quickly found telephones to be an essential business tool. People wanted them in their homes, too. By 1900 more than a million telephones had been installed in offices and households across the nation.

The typewriter Inventors in many nations made attempts to create a writing machine. Christopher Latham Sholes, a Milwaukee printer, developed the first practical typewriter in 1867, with the help of Carlos Glidden and Samuel Soulé. Sholes later improved upon his

FOCUS ON NEW YORK

DAILY LIFE

New York's subway system is one of the world's busiest, carrying an average of 4.5 million people every weekday. The system includes more than 840 miles of track— enough to reach to Chicago if it were laid end to end.

machine by designing the QWERTY keyboard, which is still the standard in computers today. The name QWERTY comes from the first few letters found at the top left. Sholes purposely placed the most frequently used letters far apart so the keys wouldn't jam when struck.

The typewriter could produce legible documents very quickly. Businesses began to hire women as typists to manage company correspondence. This opened up new job opportunities for many American women.

READING CHECK **Identifying the Main Idea**
How did technology improve communication during the Second Industrial Revolution?

Thomas Edison

Inventors and innovators in the late 1800s were obsessed with the idea of progress. They made things work better, faster, and more cheaply. They turned seemingly impossible dreams into profit-making ventures.

One of the most amazing inventors of the era was **Thomas Alva Edison**. As a child, he had an unstoppable curiosity about how everything worked. Although he lost almost all his hearing when he was about 12, Edison did not let this discourage him. In fact, he sometimes looked upon it as a blessing because it helped him concentrate on his work.

At the age of 22, Edison declared himself an inventor. His early successes included an improved telegraph. In 1876, in a pioneering move, Edison opened his own research laboratory in Menlo Park, New Jersey. He hired several assistants to work with him, choosing men with scientific and technical expertise. He provided them with materials and equipment, and he encouraged them to think creatively.

Edison also encouraged hard work. As he said, "Genius is 1 percent inspiration, 99 percent perspiration." Laboring right alongside his assistants, Edison spent long hours testing out ideas and tinkering with designs. Even failures didn't phase him:

HISTORY'S VOICES

❝ I never quit until I get what I'm after. Negative results are just what I'm after. They are just as valuable to me as positive results. ❞

—Thomas Alva Edison

See **Skills Handbook**, pp. H7, H30

PRIMARY SOURCES

Menlo Park Lab

Thomas Alva Edison's greatest invention may have been the modern industrial research laboratory. In Menlo Park, New Jersey, Edison brought together inventors who shared ideas and helped design hundreds of inventions. Following the Menlo Park model, young companies like Bell Telephone and Eastman Kodak quickly set up their own research labs. Such facilities are now common in most industries.

Skills FOCUS **READING LIKE A HISTORIAN**

1. **Interpreting Visuals** How does this image reflect the type of work carried on at Menlo Park?

2. **Making Inferences** What would be the advantage of bringing together many inventors under one roof?

In 1879 the lab became the first building ever to be equipped for electric lighting.

Another great Menlo Park invention was the phonograph, developed in 1877. On this phonograph, sound was recorded by a stylus inscribing a piece of tinfoil wrapped around a cylinder which was turned by cranking the large wheel shown here.

Thomas Edison built Menlo Park when he was 29.

Gathering groups of inventors together to work under one roof was unheard of before Edison's time.

Within four years of setting up shop, Edison and his team had invented the first phonograph, or record player, and a telephone transmitter. Other inventions poured out of the lab so quickly that Edison became known as the Wizard of Menlo Park.

Edison's greatest bit of "wizardry" was probably his development of practical electric lighting. He first came up with an incandescent bulb that could safely illuminate homes and streetlamps. Edison realized, though, that his lightbulb wouldn't be widely used until electricity became widely available. So in 1880 he undertook a new challenge—bringing electricity to New York City.

Edison first had to design and produce by hand all the parts necessary for an electricity network—sockets, fuses, switches, power meters, and generators. In 1882 he was ready. Near Wall Street, he installed a lighting system powered by his own electric power plant. The plant could deliver electricity only to homes and offices within a square mile. Luckily, within that square mile lay some very influential customers, including the New York Stock Exchange and the major New York newspapers. Electric power plants soon arose all over the country, and new investors flocked to Edison.

In 1887 Edison built an even larger laboratory in West Orange, New Jersey. He hired hundreds of brilliant technicians for his "invention

Thomas Alva Edison prefered self instruction to formal schooling. He read widely in history, literature, and the sciences. In his spare time he built complicated models, including a working sawmill and a steam-powered railroad engine.

At the age of 14, he was earning $10 a day producing and selling his own newspaper. At the age of 20, Edison created his first invention, an electric vote-counting machine. Disappointed because few politicians were interested, Edison vowed that from then on, he would invent only things that people would buy.

Edison's next invention, a new stock ticker for reporting sales and purchases of stocks, earned him $40,000. He used the money to set up his Menlo Park laboratory. Edison also established businesses to manufacture his gadgets.

Elaborate How was the commercial failure of Edison's vote-counting machine a blessing in disguise?

factory." There, Edison and his team improved the phonograph, invented the motion picture camera and projector, and developed stronger and more powerful batteries. Over his lifetime, Edison earned more than 1,000 U.S. patents.

READING CHECK **Making Inferences** Why was Edison's lightbulb so important?

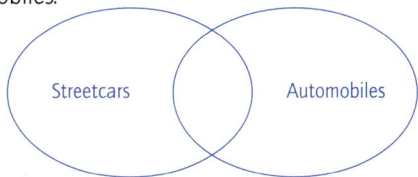

SECTION 4 ASSESSMENT

go.hrw.com
Online Quiz
Keyword: SD7 HP14

Reviewing Ideas, Terms, and People

1. **a. Recall** Name three different kinds of mass transit vehicles used in the 1800s.
   b. Explain Why were cable cars replaced in many cities by 1900?
   c. Elaborate Why would cars and airplanes be useful forms of transportation?

2. **a. Describe** How did the **telegraph** improve communication between people?
   b. Rank Which invention do you think was more significant, the telegraph or the telephone? Explain.

3. **a. Identify** What were some of the major inventions created by **Thomas Alva Edison**?
   b. Draw Conclusions How did Edison's inventions change the way Americans lived?

Critical Thinking

4. **Comparing and Contrasting** Copy the chart below and record the similarities and differences between streetcars and automobiles.

Streetcars   Automobiles

FOCUS ON WRITING

5. **Expository** You are a city official working to develop the first subway system in Boston. Write an announcement explaining how this new mode of transportation works and how it will benefit residents and visitors.

The Rights of Workers

Historical Context The documents below provide different information about the rights of workers and the needs of businesses in the 1800s.

Task Examine the documents and answer the questions that follow. Then you will be asked to write an essay about why workers and business owners were at odds in the 1800s, using facts from the documents and the chapter to support the position you take in your thesis statement.

ST **4.1** Analyze important debates in American history (e.g., regulation of big business), focusing on the opposing positions and the historical evidence used to support these positions.

ST **4.3** Develop hypotheses about important events, eras, or issues; move from chronicling to explaining historical events and issues; use information collected from diverse sources to produce cogently written reports and document-based essays.

DOCUMENT 1

Mary Harris "Mother" Jones was a passionate supporters of workers' rights. She championed labor unions from the 1870s until the 1920s, when she was more than 90 years old. The speech below, given to a group of striking coal miners in Charlestown, West Virginia, on August 15, 1912, reflects her sympathy for workers' struggles.

"Come with me and see the horrible pictures, see the horrible condition the ruling class has put these women in. Aye, they destroy women. Look at those little children, the rising generation, yes, look at the little ones, yes . . .

Go into our factories, see how the conditions are there, see how women are ground up for the merciless money pirates, see how many of the poor wretches go to work with crippled bodies . . .

I talked with a mother who had her small children working. She said to me, "Mother, they are not of age, but I had to say they were; I had to tell them [the employers] they were of age so they could get a chance to help me to get something to eat . . . "

There is a great revolution going on in the industrial world . . . The small business man is beginning to be eliminated. He has got to get down, he can't get up . . .

This fight that you are in is the great industrial revolution that is permeating the heart of men over the world."

DOCUMENT 2

One of Mother Jones's main targets was steel magnate Andrew Carnegie, whom she criticized for exploiting workers. In his autobiography, Carnegie wrote that he believed in paying workers well. He also blamed the violent Homestead strike on a handful of unreasonable union members. Below is an excerpt from *The Autobiography of Andrew Carnegie,* written in 1920.

"Taking no account of the reward that comes from feeling that you and your employees are friends and judging only from economical results, I believe that higher wages to men who respect their employers and are happy and contented are a good investment, yielding, indeed, big dividends . . .

The unjust demands of the few union men, and the opinion of the three thousand non-union men that they were unjust, very naturally led [the Homestead factory supervisor] into thinking there would be no trouble . . .

Nothing I have ever had to meet in all my life, before or since, wounded me so deeply. No pangs remain of any wound received in my business career save that of Homestead. It was so unnecessary. The men were outrageously wrong. The strikers, with the new machinery, would have made from four to nine dollars a day under the new scale—thirty per cent more than they were making with the old machinery."

One of the most controversial practices of the industrial era was using child labor. Young workers saved factory owners a lot of money because they were cheaper to hire than adults. Many adult factory workers could not earn enough to support their families unless their children also worked.

Labor leaders and social reformers called for both the end of child labor and wages that workers could live on. Many business owners resisted these changes, however, fearing they would cut into profits. This cartoon, titled "The Galley," appeared in *Puck* magazine on August 4, 1910.

THE GALLEY.

Skills FOCUS READING LIKE A HISTORIAN

1. **a. Explain** Refer to Document 1. Why did the mother lie to let her children work?
   b. Elaborate According to Mother Jones, how do modern working conditions "destroy" women?
2. **a. Identify** Refer to Document 2. What kind of worker does Carnegie think should be rewarded with good wages?
   b. Analyze According to Carnegie, in what way were the strikers being shortsighted?
3. **a. Describe** What image does the cartoonist use to depict working conditions for children?
   b. Interpret How does the cartoonist imply that factory owners are being cruel? What motive is suggested for their behavior?
   c. Evaluate Where do the cartoonist's sympathies lie?
4. **Document-Based Essay Question** Consider the question below and form a thesis statement. Using examples from Documents 1, 2, and 3, create an outline and write a short essay supporting your position.
   How were the needs of workers and business owners at odds in the Second Industrial Revolution?

See **Skills Handbook**, pp. H31, H34

Visual Summary: The Second Industrial Revolution

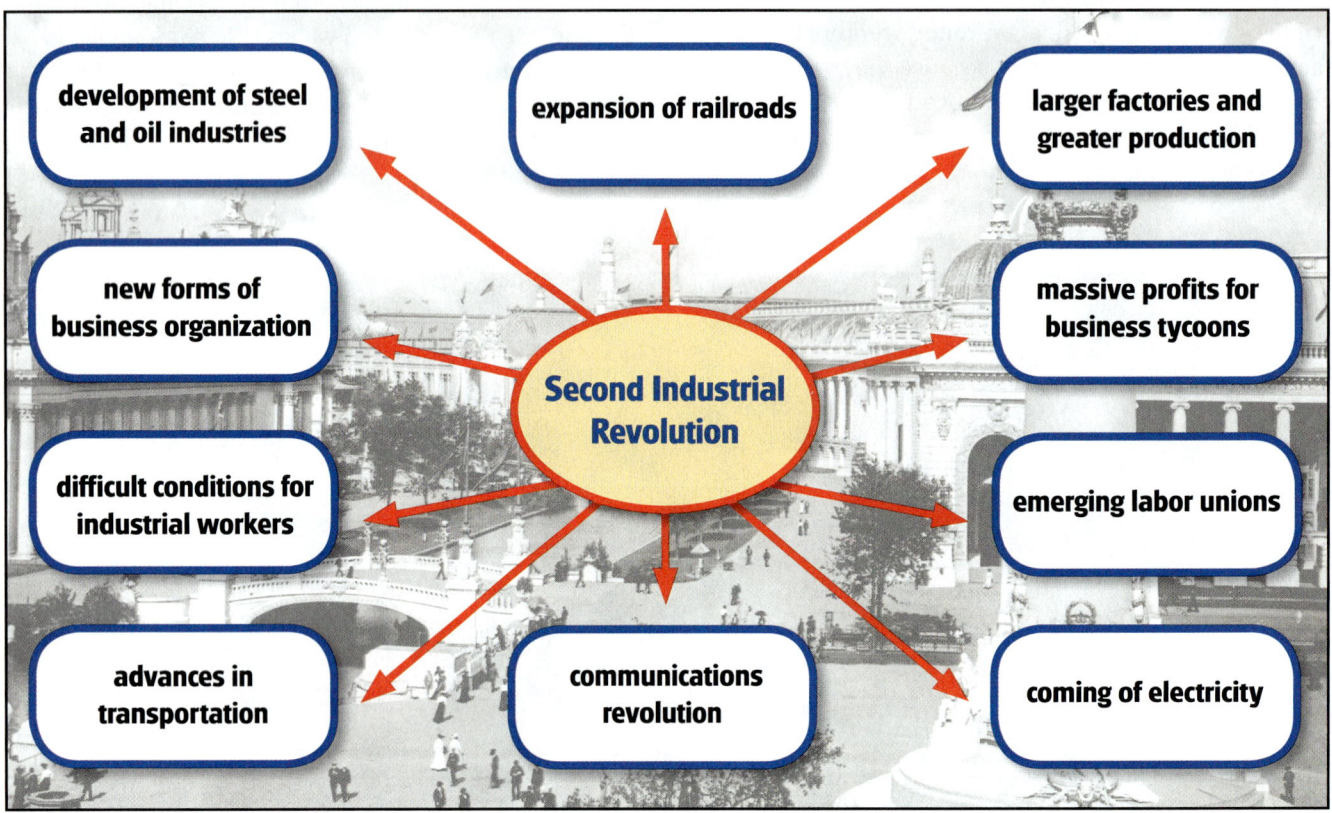

Reviewing Key Terms and People

Identify the correct term or person from the chapter that best fits each of the following descriptions.

1. Someone who invests money and takes risks to start a new business

2. A device for sending coded messages over wires with electricity

3. A form of capitalism in which the government does not intervene

4. An 1890 law that prohibited trusts from interfering with free trade

5. A philosophy holding that people compete in society and those who are stronger and more capable are the ones who prosper

6. A process of acquiring companies that provide many of the supplies and services needed for a particular industry

7. A technique developed in the 1850s for making steel faster and cheaper

8. A union of skilled workers led by Samuel Gompers in the 1880s

9. The so-called Wizard of Menlo Park, whose inventions included practical electric lighting, the phonograph, and the movie camera

10. An oil prospector

11. A tenement workshop where employees toil long hours under poor conditions for little pay

12. The owner of the Standard Oil Company and a leading philanthropist

13. A list of perceived troublemakers whom employers won't hire

14. The inventor of the telephone

History's Impact video program
Review the video to answer the closing question:
How did the Second Industrial Revolution change
life in the United States?

Comprehension and Critical Thinking

SECTION 1 *(pp. 460–463)*

15. a. Identify What new industries spurred America's industrial growth in the late 1800s?

b. Make Inferences Why do you think the federal government helped finance the first transcontinental railroad?

c. Elaborate How was steel linked to the expansion of the railroads?

SECTION 2 *(pp. 466–471)*

16. a. Recall What new kinds of business structures arose during the late 1800s?

b. Explain Name four industrial tycoons of the day and explain how they made their fortunes.

c. Develop How did American economic principles and the ideas of social Darwinists encourage the growth of big business?

SECTION 3 *(pp. 472–476)*

17. a. Describe What was the Haymarket Riot?

b. Make Generalizations What were conditions like for factory workers, and what goals did union organizers have?

c. Evaluate Why do you think employers and government officials were generally unsympathetic to the labor movement in the late 1800s?

SECTION 4 *(pp. 477–481)*

18. a. Define What is mass transit?

b. Analyze Why is Thomas Alva Edison regarded as one of the greatest inventors in history?

c. Predict How do you think American productivity was affected by advances in transportation and communication? Discuss some specific examples in your answer.

Using the Internet

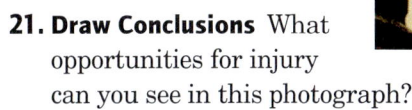

go.hrw.com
Practice Online
Keyword: SD7 CH14

19. During the late 1800s, many of the captains of industry donated millions of dollars to charitable organizations. Using the keyword above, do research to learn about Andrew Carnegie's involvement with public libraries. Then create a report that tells the story of the Carnegie libraries. Find out whether your town received funds to build a Carnegie public library.

Analyzing Primary Sources

Reading Like a Historian

From 1908 to 1912 photographer Lewis Hine documented the dangerous and difficult conditions in which child laborers worked.

20. Explain Why are these boys standing on this spinning machine?

21. Draw Conclusions What opportunities for injury can you see in this photograph?

Critical Reading

Reread the passage with the heading "Making steel." Then answer the question that follows.

22. Why was the new way to make steel known as the Bessemer process and not the Kelly process?

A Bessemer's method worked, but Kelly's did not.

B Bessemer bought the rights to the technique from Kelly.

C Bessemer did a better job of promoting the use of his method.

D Bessemer was quick to secure a patent for his technique.

WRITING FOR THE SAT

Think about the following issue:

Social Darwinists believed that the process of natural selection made society stronger as a whole. Therefore, they opposed any intervention that would interfere with that process.

23. Assignment Did the social Darwinists have the right or wrong idea about how society becomes stronger and better? Write a short essay in which you develop your position on this issue. Support your point of view with reasoning and examples from your reading and studies.

1880–1920

Life at the Turn of the 20th Century

THE BIG PICTURE In the late 1800s waves of immigrants came from Southern and Eastern Europe, settling in the cities and living and working in squalid conditions. Government was plagued by corruption. Discrimination was a daily reality.

New York Standards

Key Idea 2 Important ideas, social and cultural values, beliefs, and traditions from New York State and United States history illustrate the connections and interactions of people and events across time and from a variety of perspectives.

Key Idea 3 Study about the major social, political, economic, cultural, and religious developments in New York State and United States history involves learning about the important roles and contributions of individuals and groups.

Skills FOCUS READING LIKE A HISTORIAN

New York City's Mulberry Street in 1900 was home to a large population of Italian immigrants. They formed a tightly knit community. That helped them survive under very difficult living conditions.
Interpreting Visuals What does this photograph tell you about the way immigrants lived?

See **Skills Handbook**, p. H30

1881
Tennessee passes the first Jim Crow law.

 1880

1885
Calling for greater local participation, the Indian National Congress is founded in British-ruled India.

History's Impact video program
Watch the video to understand the impact of *Plessy* v. *Ferguson*.

May 1893
Stock market crashes, triggering depression in which 3 million lose their jobs.

February 1905
W.E.B. DuBois and others found the Niagara Movement, an early civil rights organization.

January 1910
Immigration station opens at Angel Island in San Francisco Bay.

February 1917
Congress approves a literacy test for immigrants.

1890	1900	1910	1920

1889
The Eiffel Tower opens in Paris.

1893
New Zealand becomes the first country to allow women to vote.

1907
Japan stops issuing passports to laborers headed to the U.S.

1910
Over 2 million Italians have left for the United States over 10 years.

1911
Sun Yat-sen becomes the first president of the Republic of China.

487

New Immigrants

BEFORE YOU READ

MAIN IDEA

A new wave of immigrants came to the United States in the late 1800s, settling in cities and troubling some native-born Americans.

READING FOCUS

1. How did patterns of immigration change at the turn of the century?
2. Why did immigrants come to America in the late 1800s, and where did they settle?
3. How did nativists respond to the new wave of immigration?

KEY TERMS AND PEOPLE

Ellis Island
Angel Island
benevolent society
Denis Kearney
Chinese Exclusion Act
Gentlemen's Agreement
literacy test

PI 3.4 Understand the interrelationships between world events and developments in New York State and the United States (e.g., causes for immigration, economic opportunities, human rights abuses, and tyranny versus freedom).

THE INSIDE STORY

Will they send you back to Europe? At the immigration checkpoint at Ellis Island in New York Harbor, families huddled nervously. Inspectors were waiting to check each newcomer for any disease or defect, mental or physical. They would decide whether a person would be admitted to the United States—or sent back to Europe.

Most people didn't realize that the first test came as they climbed the stairs, carrying children and bundles. Doctors were watching carefully. Did that woman seem sickly? Did that man limp? Any sign of weakness could be trouble.

The physical checkup took only a few minutes. Doctors looked at the way people spoke, walked, and behaved. They examined hands, skin, and scalp. They especially looked for diseases, such as tuberculosis, which could spread to other people. What many people feared most was the test for trachoma, an eye disease. With his fingers or with an instrument like a buttonhook, the "eye man" turned the eyelid inside-out to look for signs. Trachoma, which could lead to blindness, meant rejection.

To identify people who needed a closer look, doctors marked their shoulders with blue chalk. The letter *B* meant back, *H* meant heart, *L* meant lameness, *X* meant mental problems. Families were terribly upset when one member was sent for further tests. It could mean they would be separated, perhaps forever. ■

Buttonhook Men and Blue Chalk

▶ **An immigrant undergoes an eye exam at Ellis Island, 1905.**

Changing Patterns of Immigration

It has been said that the United States is a nation of immigrants. During the history of this country, Native Americans were the only ones who did not come from somewhere else originally. All other Americans, at some point in their family history, came to the United States as immigrants.

The old immigrants Between 1800 and 1880, more than 10 million immigrants came to the United States. These people became known as the old immigrants. Most came from Northern and Western Europe—primarily from the United Kingdom, the Netherlands, the German states, Sweden, and Norway. Most of these immigrants were Protestant Christians. Their cultures were fairly similar to those of the original American settlers.

Why did the old immigrants come to the United States? Some came to have a voice in their government. Others came to escape political turmoil. Still others sought religious freedom. Some, like the Irish, came to escape poverty and starvation.

Most immigrants, however, came in search of economic opportunity. They had limited prospects in their home countries, where jobs were scarce and nobles and the church controlled most of the land. The huge supply of open farming land in the United States—and the easy access to it—attracted millions of Northern and Western Europeans in the decades before 1880.

Europeans, however, were not the only ones to come to the United States during these early waves of immigration. About 25,000 Chinese immigrants arrived to seek their fortunes in the late 1840s and early 1850s, lured by news of the California gold rush.

After the gold rush faded, more Chinese immigrants came to help build the nation's railroads, especially the first transcontinental railroad. Many later found employment as farmers, miners, or domestic servants.

The new immigrants From 1880 to 1910, a new wave of immigration brought some 18 million people to America. Their arrival would further transform the United States.

OLD AND NEW IMMIGRANTS

QUICK FACTS

Old Immigrants	New Immigrants
• Arrived before 1880	• Arrived 1880–1910
• Came from Northern and Western Europe	• Came from Southern and Eastern Europe
• Were mainly Protestant Christians	• Were mainly Catholics, Jews, or Orthodox Christians
• Were culturally similar to the original American settlers	• Were often culturally different from the original American settlers
• Settled both in cities and in rural areas	• Generally settled in cities

Unlike the old immigrants, most of these new immigrants came from Southern and Eastern Europe. Many were Czech, Greek, Hungarian, Italian, Polish, Russian, or Slovak. Furthermore, most of these new immigrants were not Protestant Christians. Many were Roman Catholics, Orthodox Christians, or Jews. Arab, Armenian, and French Canadian immigrants also poured in by the thousands.

Smaller numbers of new immigrants came from East Asia. Chinese communities had flourished for decades in the western United States. Severe immigration laws in the 1880s reduced new Chinese arrivals to a trickle. However, an estimated 90,000 people of Chinese descent lived in the country in 1900.

Meanwhile, Japanese immigrants were beginning to appear. The earliest came around 1885, when Japan decided to let laborers leave to work on sugar plantations in the Hawaiian Islands. From Hawaii, many Japanese moved to the United States. By 1904 about 10,000 Japanese lived in the United States.

The massive flood of new immigrants dramatically changed the makeup of the American population. The United States became more diverse than ever before. In fact, by 1910 about 1 in 12 Americans had been born in a foreign country.

ACADEMIC VOCABULARY
immigration
the movement of people into foreign countries

READING CHECK **Contrasting** How did the new immigrants differ from the old immigrants?

Immigration

The number and origins of immigrants coming to the United States have been influenced by many factors, including political and economic changes abroad, as well as U.S. policies that alternately encourage or restrict immigration.

1845–1850 Some 500,000 people flee famine in Ireland to come to America.

1800

1892 Ellis Island immigration station opens in sight of the Statue of Liberty in New York Harbor.

ST 2.2 Explain the contributions of specific groups of people to American society and culture; analyze the metaphors of the "melting pot" and the "salad bowl" to explain the experiences of the first immigrant groups as compared to those of later groups.

Coming to America

The decision to move to the United States was agonizing for many immigrants. Leaving their homeland meant separation from the people they loved and the culture they knew. What brought them here?

Desire for a better life John F. Kennedy, an Irish American who became president in 1961, wrote in his book *A Nation of Immigrants*, "There were probably as many reasons for coming to America as there were people who came." Most of the new immigrants, like their predecessors, were seeking a better life. But the reasons they left their homelands varied.

Russian Jews fled to the United States in search of freedom from religious persecution. Entire villages of Jews were forced out of Russia and Eastern Europe by pogroms, organized attacks that were often encouraged by local authorities. Many of these Jews came to the United States not only to practice their religion but also to save their lives.

Many immigrants left Southern and Eastern Europe because of desperate poverty and little economic opportunity. Europe's population was rising fast. Too many people competed for too little land and too few jobs. Many Europeans heard that America was the land of opportunity. In America, it was said, all people needed to do was work hard and save their money, and they would prosper.

The journey to America The decision to come to the United States often involved the entire family. One family member—usually a father or an eldest son—might make the journey first. The family would pool their resources to buy his passage on a ship. He would then come to the United States and work, saving his earnings so he could send prepaid tickets back to the rest of his family.

For many immigrants, just getting to a departure point was a journey in itself. Travelers made their way to port cities by train, wagon, or foot. Once at the docks, they might have to wait weeks for a departing ship.

After a U.S. immigration law went into effect in 1893, immigrants had to be approved by the steamship authorities before they were allowed to come on board. They had to provide identifying information, show that they had at least $30 in cash, and indicate whether they had ever been in prison, a poorhouse, or a mental institution.

Immigrants faced one last hurdle before boarding the ship: the medical examination. Doctors employed by the steamship lines examined immigrants for any obvious diseases

1910 The Angel Island immigration center opens in San Francisco Bay, processing mainly Asian immigrants.

2000–2003 Almost 3 million legal immigrants come to the United States.

or defects. They then vaccinated all immigrants, disinfected them and their baggage, and allowed the immigrants to board the ship.

Most immigrants traveled in steerage, the cheapest way to travel. Steerage passengers were held in the bottom of the steamships in crowded and unsanitary conditions. A government report in 1911 explained how terrible these conditions were.

HISTORY'S VOICES

❝ The ventilation is almost always inadequate, and the air soon becomes foul. The unattended vomit of the seasick, the odors of not too clean bodies, the reek of food and the awful stench of the nearby toilet rooms make the atmosphere of the steerage such that it is a marvel that human flesh can endure it . . . All of these conditions are naturally aggravated by the crowding. ❞

—*Reports of the Immigration Commission,* 1911

Immigrants who survived the awful ocean crossing faced one last test before they could begin their new lives in America. They had to make it through the immigration station.

Ellis Island The U.S. government opened an immigration station in 1892 on **Ellis Island** in New York Harbor. Over the next 62 years, some 112 million immigrants would pass through Ellis Island on their way to begin a new life.

Immigrants had to pass inspection before being allowed to enter the United States. For those who traveled in first or second class, inspectors came aboard ship to check their health and review their papers.

Those who traveled in steerage had to make their way through the immigration checkpoint at Ellis Island. The inspection process usually took up to five hours. Immigrants waited nervously, fearful they would be sent back home. Doctors would scan each passenger for signs of serious disease or disability. Immigrants who did not pass the medical inspection were sent back, some penniless and without their families.

In peak years, as many as 20 percent of immigrants were held for weeks or longer at Ellis Island before being allowed to land. Sick passengers stayed at the island's hospital until they recovered. Those whose papers did not pass review were held for a hearing. About five out of every six passengers who were detained were eventually cleared to enter.

After passing inspection, immigrants were free to enter the United States and begin their new lives. Some headed off on their own, while others met family members already in the United States. One Russian Jewish immigrant remembered meeting her father for the first time, in 1910.

FOCUS ON NEW YORK

DAILY LIFE

It is estimated that nearly half of all Americans today can trace their family origins to at least one immigrant who entered the country at Ellis Island.

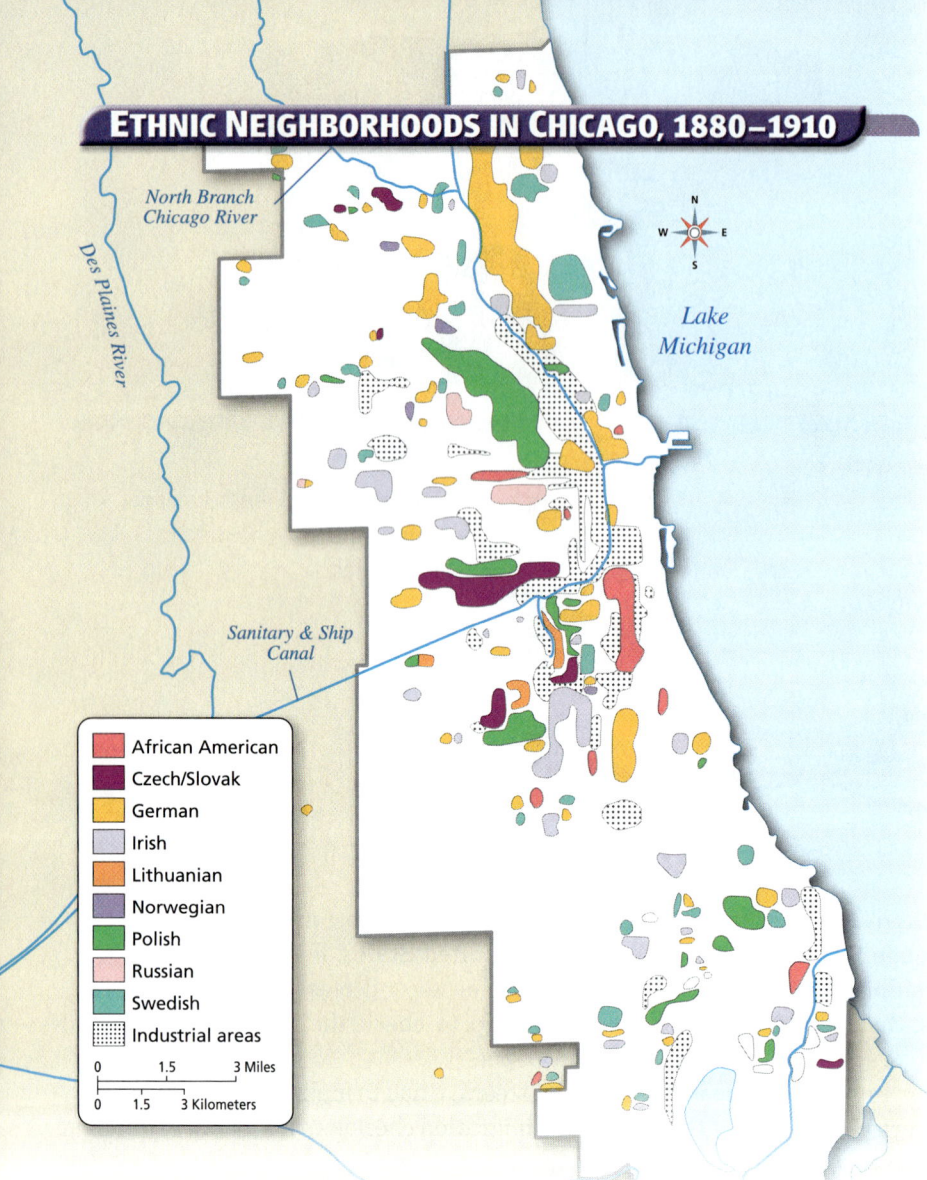

ETHNIC NEIGHBORHOODS IN CHICAGO, 1880–1910

North Branch Chicago River

Des Plaines River

Lake Michigan

Sanitary & Ship Canal

Legend:
- African American
- Czech/Slovak
- German
- Irish
- Lithuanian
- Norwegian
- Polish
- Russian
- Swedish
- Industrial areas

0   1.5   3 Miles
0   1.5   3 Kilometers

GEOGRAPHY SKILLS INTERPRETING MAPS

Around the turn of the century, three-quarters of Chicago's population consisted of immigrants and their children.
Place What were the two largest ethnic groups in Chicago at this time?
See **Skills Handbook**, p. H20

HISTORY'S VOICES

❝I saw a man coming forward and he was so beautiful I didn't know he was my father . . . Later on I realized why he looked so familiar to me. He looked exactly like I did . . . But that's when I met him for the first time. And I fell in love with him and he with me.❞

—Katherine Beychok, *Ellis Island History*

Angel Island After 1910, newcomers arriving on the West Coast were processed at **Angel Island**, an immigration station in San Francisco Bay. Some immigrants passed through Angel Island fairly quickly. But many Chinese immigrants were detained for weeks or months while awaiting a ruling on whether or not they could stay.

The people detained at Angel Island faced prisonlike conditions. Much of the time they were locked in barracks to prevent escape and were allowed outside only for supervised recreation. To relieve the boredom of life at Angel Island, some Chinese immigrants wrote poetry on the walls of their barracks. Their poems often expressed resentment and despair over their treatment.

HISTORY'S VOICES

❝Imprisoned in the wooden building day after day,

My freedom withheld; how can I bear to talk about it?

I look to see who is happy but they only sit quietly.

I am anxious and depressed and cannot fall asleep . . .

After experiencing such loneliness and sorrow,

Why not just return home and learn to plow the fields?❞

—Anonymous Chinese immigrant

For those immigrants who were finally allowed to settle in the United States, a stressful ordeal was over. Yet for many, the hard times were just beginning. Poverty and discrimination faced many new arrivals.

Building urban communities Many immigrants found themselves better off in the United States than they had been. Still, they typically experienced hardships. Most immigrants settled in crowded cities. Most could find only low-paying, unskilled jobs. As a result, new immigrants generally had no choice but to live in poor housing in teeming slums—frequently near the factories where they worked.

In the cities of the Northeast and Midwest, immigrants usually settled near others from their homeland or even their home city or province. Surrounded by people who spoke their language and shared their culture, newcomers found companionship and got help adapting to their new lives. Meanwhile, the cities became a patchwork of ethnic clusters.

In these immigrant neighborhoods, residents built institutions to keep their cultures alive. They established churches and synagogues so they could practice their religious faith. Many religious organizations provided their members with economic assistance, training courses, and child care.

In a number of cities, residents formed **benevolent societies**, aid organizations to help immigrants. Some benevolent societies helped immigrants obtain jobs, health care, or education. Some collected a few cents from members every month. In return, members received financial support if they became too ill to work, and they were buried when they died.

These benevolent societies made a huge difference in helping immigrants through difficult times. At the time, there were no state-sponsored programs to help poor and needy people. The benevolent societies filled this void. At the same time, they helped build a sense of community among immigrants.

READING CHECK **Contrasting** How did Ellis Island and Angel Island differ?

Nativists Respond

The immigrants who settled in the United States strengthened the American economy. Immigrant labor kept the factories running and helped build cities.

Many native-born Americans, however, saw the new immigrants as a threat to society. Many thought the newcomers were simply too different to fit in. Others blamed immigrants for problems such as crime, poverty, and violence. Americans who opposed immigration were known as nativists.

Nativists believed that immigrants also posed a threat to the economy. Immigrants accepted lower wages for their work. The result, claimed nativists, was a loss of jobs for native-born Americans and lower wages for everyone. Nativists opposed further immigration. They began pressing for laws that would close America's doors to newcomers.

Limiting Chinese immigration For many years people had tolerated Chinese workers, although they did not welcome them. After 1873, though, the economy worsened. Many American citizens blamed Chinese immigrants for taking away needed jobs.

PRIMARY SOURCES

Political Cartoon

This cartoon appeared in 1893. Its caption reads: "They would close to the new-comer the bridge that carried them and their fathers over."

These successful old immigrants stand opposed to new immigration.

The clothing and items carried by this immigrant are typical of a poor person from Eastern Europe.

PUCK.

LOOKING BACKWARD.
THEY WOULD CLOSE TO THE NEW-COMER THE BRIDGE THAT CARRIED THEM AND THEIR FATHERS OVER.

Skills FOCUS **READING LIKE A HISTORIAN**

1. **Interpreting Political Cartoons** Who do the shadow figures represent? (Reread the caption for clues.)
2. **Making Inferences** Was the artist a nativist?

See **Skills Handbook**, p. H31

In the late 1870s a group of unemployed workers organized the Workingmen's Party of California to oppose Chinese immigration. Their leader was **Denis Kearney**, an Irish immigrant. Kearney ended many of his speeches with the angry cry, "The Chinese must go!"

In 1879 California adopted a new state constitution that prohibited Chinese workers from holding state jobs. The new constitution also allowed local governments to ban the Chinese from their communities or to restrict them to certain districts.

Soon this anti-Chinese sentiment spread to the federal level. In 1882 Congress passed the **Chinese Exclusion Act**. This law banned Chinese immigration for 10 years. It also declared that none of the Chinese who were already in the United States could become citizens. The law was renewed in 1892. Then in 1902 Congress banned Chinese immigration indefinitely.

This ban did not completely stop Chinese immigration to the United States. Some exceptions were made. Overall, though, Chinese immigration declined sharply after 1882.

Limiting Japanese immigration

The nativists on the West Coast resented Japanese immigrants as well. As a result, in 1906 the San Francisco school board segregated its schools. Japanese students were then required to attend a separate school from white children. The Japanese government angrily protested this discrimination.

The matter went to President Theodore Roosevelt, who in 1907 negotiated the **Gentlemen's Agreement** with Japan. Japan agreed to prevent unskilled workers from immigrating to the United States. In exchange, San Francisco stopped the practice of segregating Japanese schoolchildren.

Deterring other immigrants

Some nativists opposed immigration not only from Asia but also from Southern and Eastern Europe. They claimed that those immigrants could not blend into American society because they were poor, illiterate, or non-Protestant.

Many nativists called for immigrants to pass a **literacy test**, an exam to determine whether the test takers could read English. They wanted the test to keep many of these immigrants out. In 1917 Congress passed the Literacy Test Act over President Woodrow Wilson's veto.

Americanization

Not all native-born Americans wanted to prevent immigrants from coming to the United States. Some people wanted to teach the newcomers American ways to help them assimilate into American society. Schools and voluntary organizations taught immigrants English literacy skills and subjects needed for citizenship, such as American history and government.

READING CHECK **Summarizing** Why did nativists oppose immigration?

SECTION 1 ASSESSMENT

Reviewing Ideas, Terms, and People

1. **a. Describe** Who were the new immigrants?
   b. Analyze Why did the United States seem to offer immigrants a promising future?
   c. Predict Of all the differences between new and old immigrants, which ones do you think would pose the most tensions between the two groups? Explain your reasoning.

2. **a. Recall** Where were **Ellis Island** and **Angel Island** located?
   b. Compare How were Ellis Island and Angel Island similar?
   c. Elaborate How did the practices at Angel Island reveal a bias against certain immigrants?

3. **a. Identify** Who was **Denis Kearney**?
   b. Make Generalizations How did nativists view the new wave of immigrants in the late 1800s?
   c. Evaluate How did nativism influence the law?

Critical Thinking

4. **Sequencing** Copy the chart below and record the steps taken by most immigrants in their journey to the United States. Begin with the decision to leave their homeland and end with their approval to enter the United States.

   Decide to leave homeland → → → → Enter the United States

FOCUS ON WRITING

5. **Persuasive** Suppose you are an American citizen who opposes nativist legislation such as the **Chinese Exclusion Act**. Write a letter to the editor to support your position. Consider the contributions of immigrants to U.S. history and the reasons for anti-immigrant sentiments.

SECTION 2 Urban Life

BEFORE YOU READ

MAIN IDEA

In cities in the late 1800s, people in the upper, middle, and lower classes lived different kinds of lives because of their different economic situations.

READING FOCUS

1. How did American cities change in the late 1800s?
2. How did class differences affect the way urban dwellers lived?
3. How did the settlement house movement work to improve living conditions for immigrants and poor Americans?

KEY TERMS AND PEOPLE

Elisha Otis
Frederick Law Olmsted
settlement house
Jane Addams
Lillian Wald
Social Gospel

PI 2.3 Compare and contrast the experiences of different groups in the United States.

THE INSIDE STORY

Do you enjoy a walk in the park? If so, thank Frederick Law Olmsted. He and his firm planned and built many of America's most beautiful public parks. His ideas had a strong influence on park design throughout the country.

Before becoming a landscape architect—a term he invented—Olmsted studied engineering, ran a farm, and worked as a journalist. In 1850, when he was 28, Olmsted and some friends took a walking tour of Europe. There he admired the many public and private parks as well as the elegant layouts of country estates.

By 1856 the City of New York had acquired 840 acres on what was then the edge of town. Olmsted and architect Calvert Vaux won a competition to design the city's new Central Park. Their plan kept the feel of a natural landscape but added walks and parkways so that people could stroll comfortably and enjoy the area.

Central Park was one of the first large U.S. city parks. Olmsted thought that expanses of green space and trees improved the quality of city life. "A park is a work of art," he said. Every detail—every blade of grass—mattered.

During the Civil War, Olmsted was in charge of medical supplies and sanitation for the Union army. After the war he returned to park design. For the next 30 years he created peaceful havens in Philadelphia, Detroit, Chicago, Boston, Montreal, and other cities. His firm also designed landscapes for the U.S. Capitol and White House grounds and for national parks from Maine to California. ◢

▼ **Frederick Law Olmsted designed a series of parks for the city of Boston, Massachusetts, known collectively as the Emerald Necklace.**

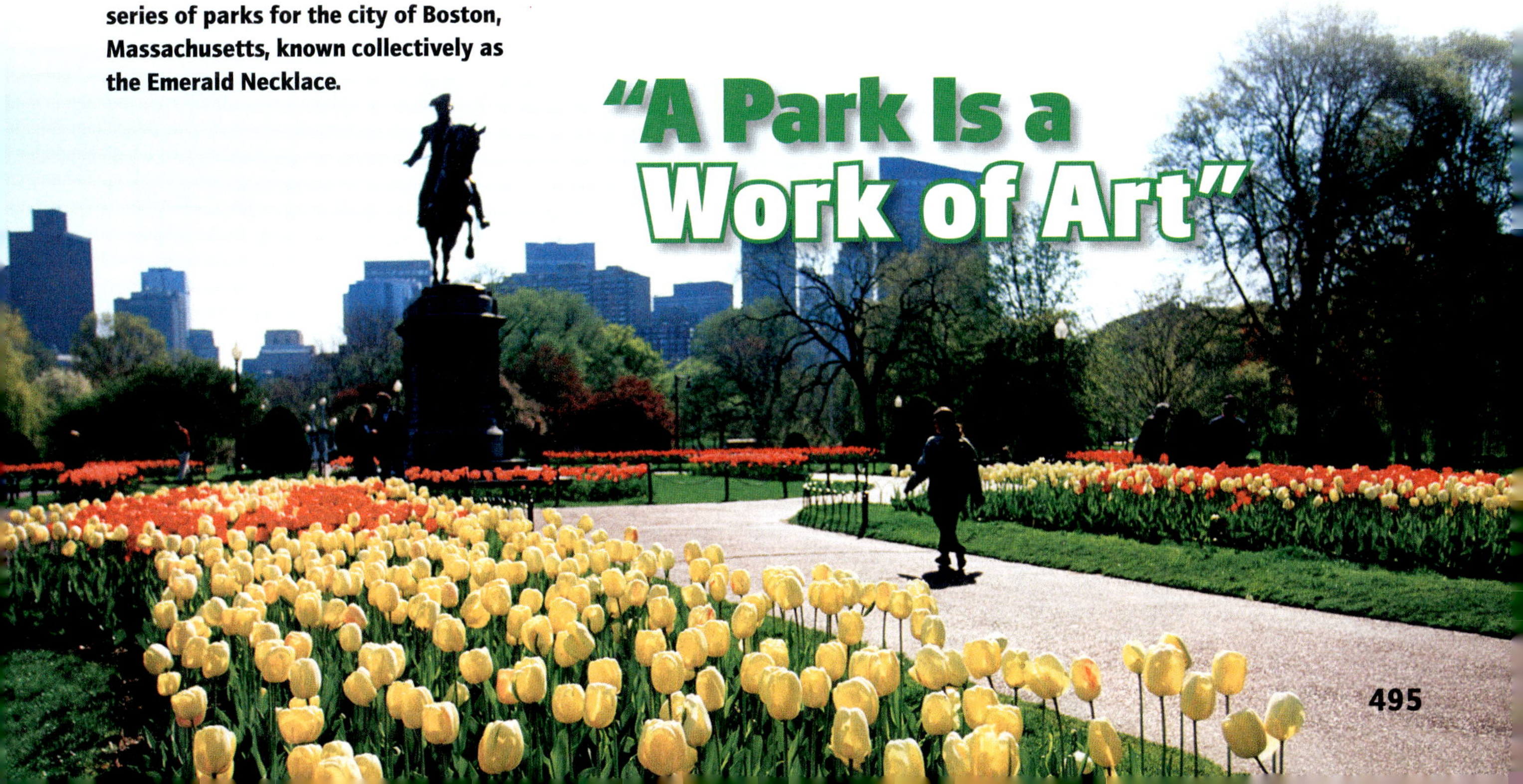

"A Park Is a Work of Art"

Early Skyscrapers

The Reliance Building Reaching 14 stories in 1894, the Reliance Building in Chicago seemed to defy gravity. Its steel skeleton supported an exterior made mostly of windows. The Reliance Building helped usher in the era of the skyscraper.

Steel beams provided strength and support for taller buildings.

Windows could be larger because steel beams, not the exterior walls, supported the structure.

Mechanical elevators allowed people to reach upper floors easily.

American Cities Change

Before industrialization, cities were compact. Few buildings stood taller than four stories. Most people lived within walking distance of their workplaces, schools, shopping districts, and places of worship. But in the late 1800s, cities began to run out of buildable space. Instead of spreading out, they began to build up. Architects started using strong steel frames, which allowed them to build taller buildings than ever before. The safety elevator, invented by **Elisha Otis,** made taller buildings practical.

With the coming of mass transit, cities expanded as people moved farther away. Middle class and wealthy people could work in the city but leave the noises and smells behind when they went home. The working poor, however, could not afford to move from the city center.

As cities grew, some people began to fear that urban areas would no longer have any green spaces. The new field of urban planning arose to deal with this challenge. Urban planners and civil engineers tried to map out the best use of space in cities. Landscape architects such as **Frederick Law Olmsted** designed city parks to provide city residents with a sense of the countryside. Olmsted designed New York City's Central Park as well as a network of Boston parks known as the Emerald Necklace and other urban parks.

READING CHECK

Identifying Cause and Effect How did the use of steel change the way architects designed buildings?

Skills FOCUS INTERPRETING INFOGRAPHICS

Because an internal steel skeleton provided structural support, the outside of the Reliance Building could be more decorative. Larger-than-usual windows let in light and air. Exterior details, such as the bands of terra cotta ornamentation, gave it an intricate look.
Making Inferences Why did the Reliance Building need stairways when it already had mechanized elevators?
See **Skills Handbook**, p. H18

Class Differences

America's booming cities provided bountiful opportunities for success in life. But the opportunities varied tremendously depending on one's status in society.

The wealthy The richest Americans in the late 1800s did not all come from old-money families with inherited wealth. Instead, they made their fortunes in industry and business. Many of these newly rich made a point of conspicuously displaying their wealth. Because of their excesses, the period from the 1870s to the 1890s is sometimes called the Gilded Age.

The well-to-do spent vast sums of money on housing. Affluent New Yorkers lined Fifth Avenue with grand houses resembling medieval castles and Italian Renaissance palaces. In the summer, they left their city homes for magnificent country estates. The oldest grandson of industrialist Cornelius Vanderbilt, for example, built a palatial summer home in Newport, Rhode Island. His "cottage" had 70 rooms.

High-society women read instructive literature that outlined proper behavior for ladies and gentlemen. The guides glorified the ideal woman as a homemaker. Her role was to organize and decorate her home, entertain, supervise a staff of servants, and offer moral and social guidance to her family. Most wealthy women stayed busy with these private activities. Some, however, lent their time and occasionally their money to social reform efforts.

The middle class The growth of new industries resulted in an increase in the urban middle class. The rise of modern corporations also caused the middle class to swell as more and more people became accountants, clerks, managers, and salespeople.

Industry and business, as well as a growing population, created a need for educated workers such as teachers, engineers, lawyers, and doctors. Before the late 1800s, however, few standards existed to ensure that these workers had appropriate qualifications. During the 1870s and 1880s, schools and organizations began to standardize the skills and knowledge needed for certain occupations. This process became known as professionalization. It brought new respect to professions such as medicine, law, and education.

Few professions accepted women as members. But women found other opportunities to work outside the home. Businesses hired women as salesclerks, secretaries, and typists.

When young, middle-class women married, they usually stopped working outside the home. Yet managing a home now involved less labor than it had previously. Women could buy many of the items their mothers had formerly made themselves, such as clothing. In addition, many middle class households employed at least one servant to manage the housework.

With less time spent on housework, many middle class women had time for other activities. Some participated in reform movements. Others joined reading clubs and other social groups. By taking part in activities outside the home, middle class women began to expand their influence into the public world.

The working class Many people in the cities lived in terrible poverty. As more people moved to the cities in search of work, the growing population kept wages low. Housing shortages meant that most workers lived in cramped conditions. In New York City, for example, about half of the population crowded into tenements, or run-down apartment buildings.

Tenements were usually within walking distance of the factories, stockyards, and ports where many of the urban poor worked. This meant that at home, as well as on the job, they had to endure pollution and filth. Sickness and untimely death were common.

Tenements lacked <u>sufficient</u> light and ventilation. Only the rooms facing the street and the back of the building had windows, and even these were a mixed blessing. They let in sunlight but also the stench from trash and sewage and the pollution from belching factories.

Housekeeping was laborious in a tenement. With no indoor plumbing, women and children had to haul water from an outdoor water pump for laundry, bathing, and cooking. Women washed clothes by boiling them on the stove and then hanging them to dry on lines strung between buildings or in the kitchen. On top of their difficult housekeeping tasks, many working-class women also labored in low-paying jobs outside the home.

 **READING CHECK** **Contrasting** How did life in the cities differ for wealthy and working-class people?

THE IMPACT TODAY
Government
Today all 50 states have laws requiring licensing for many occupations, from practicing medicine to doing electrical work to cutting hair in a barbershop or beauty salon.

The Settlement House Movement

With poverty a desperate problem, some American reformers turned to Great Britain for inspiration. In 1884 London reformers had founded the first **settlement house**, a place where volunteers provided a variety of services to people in need.

Instead of just giving handouts, settlement houses taught immigrants many skills they could use to help themselves out of poverty. They offered English classes and job-training courses. They also provided social activities, such as clubs and sports.

Soon, settlement houses began appearing in U.S. cities. One of the first was Hull House in Chicago, founded by **Jane Addams** and Ellen Gates Starr in 1889. The settlement house movement spread quickly. In New York City, **Lillian Wald** founded the Henry Street Settlement. Janie Porter Barrett established the Locust Street Social Settlement in Hampton, Virginia, the first settlement house for African Americans. By 1910 there were 400 settlement houses in U.S. cities.

Most settlement house workers were middle-class, college-educated women who lived among the people they served. In a society that barred women from working in many professions, the settlement houses gave women new opportunities to lead, organize, and improve life for others.

Many workers in the settlement houses held strong religious views. They believed in the **Social Gospel**, the idea that religious faith should be expressed through good works. They believed that churches had a moral duty to help solve society's problems.

Social Darwinists, however, criticized the Social Gospel movement. Social Darwinists such as sociologist William Graham Sumner viewed existence as a competitive struggle in which only the fittest would survive. People were poor, Sumner said, because of their own deficiencies. Therefore, social reforms could not help them.

READING CHECK **Summarizing** How did the settlement house movement work to address poverty?

SECTION 2 ASSESSMENT

go.hrw.com
Online Quiz
Keyword: SD7 HP15

Reviewing Ideas, Terms, and People

1. a. Identify Who was Elisha Otis?
b. Draw Conclusions How did elevators and steel change the way cities looked?

2. a. Describe What were conditions in tenements like?
b. Explain How did professionalization meet the needs of the developing American economy?
c. Develop How did women's roles vary from one social class to another?

3. a. Recall What was the **settlement house** movement?
b. Make Inferences Why did middle-class women get involved in the settlement house movement?
c. Elaborate How did the settlement house movement differ from earlier attempts to relieve poverty?

Critical Thinking

4. Contrasting Copy the table below and record the differences between the Social Gospel concept and social Darwinism.

Social Gospel	Social Darwinism

FOCUS ON WRITING

5. Descriptive Suppose you are a settlement house worker around 1900. Write a letter to a friend describing the people you serve, their needs, and their neighborhood.

Politics in the Gilded Age

BEFORE YOU READ

MAIN IDEA

Political corruption was common in the late 1800s, but reformers began fighting for changes to make government more honest.

READING FOCUS

1. How did political machines control politics in major cities?
2. What efforts were made to reduce federal corruption?
3. How did the Populist movement give farmers political power?

KEY TERMS AND PEOPLE

William Marcy Tweed
Thomas Nast
James A. Garfield
Chester A. Arthur
National Grange
Populist Party
William McKinley
William Jennings Bryan

PI 3.2 Research and analyze the major themes and developments in New York State and United States history (e.g., colonization and settlement; Revolution and New National Period; immigration; expansion and reform era; Civil War and Reconstruction; the American labor movement; Great Depression; World Wars; contemporary United States).

THE INSIDE STORY

Who runs the city? James Pendergast owned a hotel and saloon in an area of tenements and small factories in Kansas City, Missouri. In 1892 "Big Jim" won a seat representing this tough ward on the City Council. This became his base for building a powerful political machine—a network of friends who helped him control city government.

Pendergast spoke out for underpaid workers, such as firefighters. He made sure that poor families had food and heat. He could count on their support in return. "All there is to it," he said, "is having friends, doing things for people, and then later on they'll do things for you."

Not all of Pendergast's buddies were upstanding citizens. Some ran illegal gambling and liquor operations. But Pendergast's cronies in the police department protected them.

When "Big Jim" died in 1911, his brother Tom took over and extended machine control over the entire state Democratic Party. The Pendergast machine grew more and more corrupt. It finally collapsed in the 1930s as Tom Pendergast and others went to prison. ◢

▶ **These down-at-the-heels citizens gladly exchanged their votes for a pair of new shoes.**

Politics and Friendship

Political Machines

Before the Civil War, most cities were small and easily managed by part-time politicians. By the late 1800s, however, cities faced challenges that part-timers could not handle. Problems such as crime, inadequate water supplies, and poor sanitation needed professionals to solve them.

The solution in many cities was the political machine, an informal group of professional politicians who controlled local government. Political machines sorted out some of the biggest urban problems. However, they often resorted to corrupt methods.

Immigrants and political machines By the late 1800s, political machines controlled many major U.S. cities. They made a special point of reaching out to immigrants. They helped newcomers find jobs or housing, supplied coal in winter, and provided turkeys for holiday dinners. Machine politicians also helped immigrants become naturalized citizens. In return, these elected officials expected the people they assisted to vote for them and rally broader community support.

James Pendergast was a popular political boss in Kansas City, Missouri. He gained the loyalty of local immigrants by doing favors such as giving money to those in need. He used his connections to run for alderman. By 1900 he controlled Kansas City politics.

Political machines sometimes dominated entire counties. Stephen Powers and James B. Wells Jr. set up a political machine in Cameron County, Texas, in the 1870s. In exchange for votes, they helped Mexican Americans pay for weddings, funerals, and living expenses during hard times.

In some cities, immigrants not only backed the political machine but also became part of it. Irish Americans rose through the ranks of Boston's political machine. Two second-generation Irish immigrants even became mayor: John F. Fitzgerald (President John F. Kennedy's grandfather) and James Michael Curley.

Political Cartoon

Thomas Nast's biting political cartoons helped expose the corrupt Tammany Hall political machine. Here Boss Tweed takes money from the public, while a sign above him says tauntingly, "What are you going to do about it?"

Tweed, behind the table, collects payments from both rich and poor.

A police officer with a nightstick enforces Tweed's shady business.

SKILLS FOCUS   READING LIKE A HISTORIAN

Identifying Points of View What message was Nast trying to send about public money?
Interpreting Political Cartoons What makes Tweed look corrupt?
See **Skills Handbook**, pp. H28–H29, H31

Corruption It is appropriate for politicians to help their constituents and ask for their support. But political machines became famous for using illegal tactics to maintain control.

Machine bosses bought voter support with jobs and favors. They also engaged in election fraud. Sometimes they hired men to vote several times in an election. The hired voters would change coats or shave off their beards so they could vote more than once without detection. Hence the old Chicago joke, "Vote early and vote often."

Many machine politicians practiced graft—using their position to gain money and power dishonestly. They demanded bribes and payoffs in exchange for contracts or jobs. For example, one Chicago business leader routinely paid members of the City Council to let him maintain a monopoly over the city's streetcar system. Like other business leaders, he considered the payoffs part of the cost of doing business.

The Tweed Ring The most notorious political machine was Tammany Hall, which ran the Democratic Party in New York City. In 1863 **William Marcy Tweed** became the powerful head of Tammany Hall.

Like other political bosses, Boss Tweed used his position to rake in riches for himself and his friends, a group known as the Tweed Ring. In one case the city paid $13 million to build a new courthouse, which was several times the actual construction cost. The difference went into the pockets of Tweed and his associates.

Tweed controlled elections, corrupt judges, and big business in the city. His power seemed unbreakable—until 1871. That's when a new bookkeeper for the county gave evidence to the *New York Times* that proved how much the Tweed Ring had stolen.

Thomas Nast, a political cartoonist, attacked this corruption in *Harper's Weekly* magazine in 1871. Week after week, Nast's cartoons sharply criticized Tweed and Tammany Hall. As public opinion turned against Tweed, he is said to have demanded that the cartoons be stopped.

HISTORY'S VOICES

❝ I don't care so much what the papers write about me—my constituents can't read, but they can see the . . . pictures. ❞

—William Marcy "Boss" Tweed, 1871

Tweed was convicted for fraud and extortion in 1873. He was sentenced to 12 years' imprisonment. Tweed later escaped but was caught in Spain. Officials there recognized him from one of Nast's drawings. In 1878 Tweed died in a New York City jail.

READING CHECK **Drawing Conclusions**
Why do you think corruption flourished in New York City for so long without a public outcry?

Federal Corruption

The dominant image of government in the late 1800s was the smoke-filled back room—the clubs and parlors where corrupt politicians and business leaders made deals to enrich themselves. Much dirty business was conducted in this way, out of public view. The problem extended to the highest levels of government.

Scandals of the Grant administration

Ulysses S. Grant, the Union army's commanding general at the end of the Civil War, became president in 1869. His presidency was marred by several scandals that outraged the nation.

One of the most significant dramas was the Crédit Mobilier scandal. In the 1860s the Union Pacific Railroad set up a construction company called Crédit Mobilier to build part of the transcontinental railroad. Crédit Mobilier charged American taxpayers about $23 million more than it actually cost to build the railroad. That $23 million went into the bank accounts of the Union Pacific directors and the Crédit Mobilier stockholders.

In 1872 the *New York Sun* revealed that Crédit Mobilier had given stock to members of Congress and even to Vice President Schuyler Colfax. Corruption now tainted some of the nation's foremost leaders.

Another scandal erupted in 1875 when a new treasury secretary revealed a conspiracy to divert tax collections into private hands. The Whiskey Ring, a group that included Grant's private secretary, whiskey distillers, distributors, and government officials, stole millions of dollars of taxpayers' money. Whiskey producers paid bribes to government officials. In exchange, officials allowed them to keep millions of dollars in liquor taxes that should have gone to the federal treasury.

Many state and local governments, along with the federal government, adopted civil service reform. Here Chicago police are taking a civil service exam. **What was the purpose of the exams?**

President Hayes and reform These scandals moved reformers to action. They wanted to end the fraud under the spoils system, a long-standing practice of filling government jobs with the winning political party's supporters.

When Republican Rutherford B. Hayes became president in 1877, he wanted reform. He issued an executive order that prohibited government employees from managing political parties or campaigns. At the New York Customhouse, where corrupt Republicans controlled the jobs, two top officials ignored the order. Hayes fired them.

This outraged Roscoe Conkling, a political boss and Republican senator from New York. Conkling and his supporters, known as the Stalwarts, wanted to continue the spoils system. Reformers in the Republican Party wanted to end it.

In 1880, when Hayes decided not to run for a second term, the Republicans split over whom to nominate. They finally compromised on Ohio senator **James A. Garfield**.

Garfield's short presidency Garfield won the election, but he soon angered the Stalwarts by failing to give Conkling a cabinet appointment. The feud did not last long, however. Four months into his term, in July 1881, Garfield was shot in a Washington, D.C., railroad station. The president died in September.

The man who killed Garfield was Charles Guiteau (guh-TOH), an unstable character who had been denied a job in Garfield's administration. Guiteau believed that killing the president would help the Stalwart cause. However, the opposite happened. Garfield was succeeded by the vice president, **Chester A. Arthur**. Although Arthur had formerly supported the Stalwarts, he now turned against the spoils system.

Civil service reform President Arthur surprised many people by acting independently of the Republican Party that helped him into office. In 1883 he helped secure passage of the Pendleton Civil Service Act. The law required that promotions be based on merit, not on political connections. Although the Pendleton Act initially applied to only 10 percent of federal jobs, it was an important first step in reducing corruption in the federal government.

READING CHECK **Summarizing** How did Presidents Hayes and Arthur begin civil service reform?

The Populist Movement

Calls for reform also arose from another direction. Farmers began a movement for reform that would challenge both of the major political parties.

Farmers' hardships Farmers in the late 1800s were in a desperate situation. Crop prices were falling. Many farmers borrowed large sums to buy new equipment or more land so they could grow more crops. The resulting oversupply of farm products caused prices to fall even further. A farmer who planted 24 acres of cotton in 1894 made less money than a farmer who planted only 9 acres in 1873.

Indebted farmers found it increasingly difficult to repay their loans. Even worse, railroads began to charge enormous fees to transport crops to market. The smallest farmers often had to pay the highest shipping prices.

To many farmers, it seemed that everyone else was making money at their expense. The merchants who sold the farm equipment profited. The banks and the railroads got richer and richer. But the farmers who worked all day every day were nearly penniless. Outraged farmers decided to fight this unjust situation.

The National Grange With no one else to help them, farmers organized to help themselves. Local groups formed to provide emergency aid and other assistance to individual farmers. In time, local groups merged to form nationwide organizations.

The first major farmers' organization was the Order of Patrons of Husbandry, more commonly known as the **National Grange**. Founded in 1867 by Oliver Hudson Kelley, the Grange began as a social group. Kelley had surveyed farming conditions in the South immediately after the Civil War, and he saw how downtrodden many farmers were. He decided to create an organization in which farmers could support each other.

HISTORY'S VOICES

❝ 1. United by the strong and faithful tie of Agriculture, we mutually resolve to labor for the good of our Order, our country, and mankind.

2. We heartily endorse the motto: 'In essentials, unity; in non-essentials, liberty; in all things, charity.' ❞

—1874 Declaration of Purposes of the National Grange

The Grange campaigned to unite farmers from across the nation, transcending regional rivalries. The organization declared that "in our agricultural brotherhood and its purposes, we shall recognize no North, no South, no East, no West."

Within a few years, membership in the Grange exploded. Farmers began to realize that to save their livelihoods, they would have to fight against the railroads and operators of grain elevators who made huge profits at their expense. An 1874 Grange document urged farmers to act boldly to protect their interests.

HISTORY'S VOICES

❝ Choke monopolies, break up rings, vote for honest men, fear God and make money. So shalt thou prosper and sorrow and hard times shall flee away. ❞

—"The Ten Commandments of the Grange," *Oshkosh (WI) Weekly Times*, December 16, 1874

Around this time, the focus of the Grange shifted toward fighting for political reform. The organization's first target was railroad rates. By the late 1870s, the Grange had succeeded in persuading the state legislatures in Illinois, Iowa, Minnesota, and Wisconsin to regulate railroads and operators of grain elevators. The

business opposed regulation because it took a bite out of their profits. They challenged these Granger laws in the courts.

In 1877 the Supreme Court agreed with the Grange. In the case of *Munn* v. *Illinois*, the Court declared that state legislatures did have the right to regulate businesses that involved the public interest.

Nine years later the Court ruled again on the issue of business regulation. In the 1886 case *Wabash* v. *Illinois*, the Court ruled that the federal government had the power to regulate railroad traffic moving across state boundaries.

The *Wabash* case led Congress to approve the Interstate Commerce Act in 1887. Passage of the law had great historic significance. It marked the first time that the federal government had regulated an industry.

The <u>objective</u> of the Interstate Commerce Act was to make railroad rates fair for all customers by requiring the rates to be "reasonable and just." The act prohibited railroads from giving more favorable rates or special rebates to large shippers. It also forbade railroads from charging more for short hauls than for long hauls over the same rail line. To oversee the railroads, the act created the Interstate Commerce Commission (ICC).

ACADEMIC VOCABULARY
objective goal

The National Grange was founded in 1867. In less than a decade, more than 21,000 granges were organized on the state, county, and local levels.

Congress did not, however, give the ICC the power to enforce the provisions of the law. The ICC did not gain enforcement power until 1906, under President Theodore Roosevelt. Nonetheless, the ICC would later serve as a model for government regulation of private businesses.

The Alliance movement Other farmers' organizations formed in Texas and New York in the 1870s. As they grew and established links, they became known as the Farmers' Alliance.

Like the Grange, the Farmers' Alliance began as a way to help farmers with practical needs such as buying equipment or marketing farm products. Soon, the Alliance also began lobbying for banking reform and regulation of railroad rates.

The Alliance movement spread quickly. By 1890 more than 1 million farmers from different regions of the country had joined.

In the South, however, leaders of the Southern Alliance restricted membership to white farmers only. African American farmers therefore formed their own organization, the Colored Farmers' Alliance.

In 1890 the Colored Farmers' Alliance had more than 1 million members. It worked for the same kinds of reforms as the Southern Alliance. In addition, the Colored Farmers'

Alliance fought prejudice. It urged its members to become economically strong by avoiding debt and owning their own farms. Like other African American organizations of the time, it advocated hard work and sacrifice as the keys to gaining equality in society.

The money supply issue In order to create better economic conditions for farmers, the Farmers' Alliances wanted to expand the money supply. In other words, they wanted the government to print more money. They thought that more money in circulation would inflate prices, including the prices for crops. The resulting inflation would ease farmers' debt burden.

Paper money was originally redeemable for either gold or silver coins. But in 1873 Congress voted to adopt the gold standard, a monetary system in which the standard unit of exchange is a certain amount of gold. Under the gold standard, the government promised to redeem any bill for gold. In addition, there could only be as much money in circulation as there was gold in the treasury to back it up.

The gold standard reduced the number of dollars in circulation, and this alarmed many farmers. In the hope of expanding the supply of money, farm groups urged that money once

Growth of the Populist Movement

The Populist movement began among struggling farmers in the Midwest, South, and West. Eventually laborers joined with farmers to press for new government policies that would benefit ordinary working people. The Populist movement reached its height in the 1890s with the formation of the Populist Party.

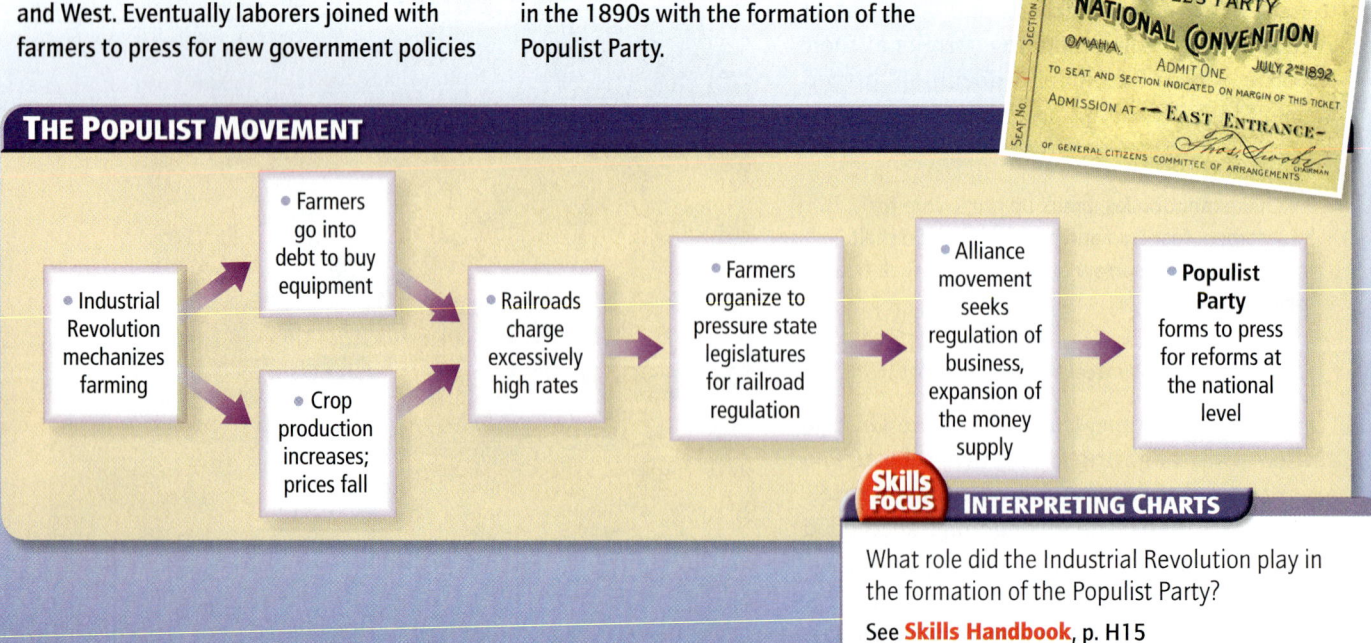

THE POPULIST MOVEMENT

- Industrial Revolution mechanizes farming → • Farmers go into debt to buy equipment / • Crop production increases; prices fall → • Railroads charge excessively high rates → • Farmers organize to pressure state legislatures for railroad regulation → • Alliance movement seeks regulation of business, expansion of the money supply → • **Populist Party** forms to press for reforms at the national level

Skills FOCUS INTERPRETING CHARTS

What role did the Industrial Revolution play in the formation of the Populist Party?

See **Skills Handbook**, p. H15

again be backed by silver as well as gold. They pressured Congress to pass laws requiring the government to buy some silver to mint coins. However, the silver did not have much impact on the money supply.

This sharply disappointed Alliance members. In the elections of 1890, they became very politically active. They stood behind any candidate who supported their position on monetary policy, and they had remarkable success. Alliance-backed candidates won more than 40 seats in Congress and four governorships.

The Populist Party Encouraged by their clout in the elections, Alliance leaders decided to form a national political party. At a convention in Omaha, Nebraska, in July 1892, the People's Party was born. This coalition of farmers, labor leaders, and reformers became more commonly known as the **Populist Party**.

The Populist Party supported National Grange and Alliance demands. The party platform called for an income tax, bank regulation, government ownership of railroad and telegraph companies, and the free (unlimited) coinage of silver. In pushing this agenda, the Populists claimed to speak for the common people rather than the ruling elite.

HISTORY'S VOICES

❝We seek to restore the government of the Republic to the hands of the 'plain people,' with which class it originated. We assert our purposes to be identical with the purposes of the National Constitution . . . We believe that the power of government—in other words, of the people—should be expanded . . . to the end that oppression, injustice, and poverty shall eventually cease in the land.❞

—Preamble to the 1892 Platform of the Populist Party

In the 1892 presidential election, the Populists backed James B. Weaver against the Republican incumbent, Benjamin Harrison, and the Democratic candidate, Grover Cleveland. Cleveland won the election, but the Populist Party won several seats in Congress as well as several state offices. This was remarkable success for a new party.

The Panic of 1893 Soon after the election, the nation plunged into an economic depression. In May 1893 one of the leading railroad companies failed. This triggered the Panic of

1893: investors pulled out of the stock market and thousands of businesses collapsed. By year's end, some 3 million people had lost their jobs. Strikes and protests swept the country.

There were many causes for this national depression, including a worldwide financial slump. President Cleveland focused on one of many causes: the Sherman Silver Purchase Act of 1890.

This law required the government to pay for silver purchases with paper money redeemable in either gold or silver. But new discoveries of silver decreased its value, and people rushed to exchange their paper money for gold. This put a huge strain on the treasury's gold reserves. To protect the gold standard and to restore confidence in the economy, Cleveland called for Congress to repeal the Sherman Silver Purchase Act. Congress did so in October 1893. Because of Cleveland's actions, the country stayed on the gold standard.

The election of 1896 Silver continued to be a controversial issue. In the presidential election of 1896, the Republicans nominated Ohio governor **William McKinley**, who believed that the gold standard was the key to the nation's prosperity. The Democrats, meanwhile, did not want President Cleveland to seek re-election because the Panic of 1893 had made him so unpopular. Instead, they nominated **William Jennings Bryan**, a former two-term U.S. congressman from Nebraska.

Economics
President Richard Nixon took the United States off the gold standard in 1971, and the dollar has been allowed to "float" according to market value ever since.

The caption of this Republican cartoon called Bryan unfit to be president because he made "sacrilegious" use of Christian symbols—the cross and crown of thorns—in his speeches. **Interpreting Political Cartoons** How does the image suggest Bryan's lack of respect?

Bryan hailed the free coinage of silver as the key to prosperity. In a famous speech, he vowed to resist the gold standard alongside business people, workers and farmers.

HISTORY'S VOICES

❝If they [Republicans] dare to come out in the open field and defend the gold standard as a good thing, we will fight them to the uttermost. Having behind us the producing masses of this nation and the world, supported by the commercial interests, the laboring interests and the toilers everywhere, we will answer their demand for a gold standard by saying to them: You shall not press down upon the brow of labor this crown of thorns, you shall not crucify mankind upon a cross of gold.❞

—William Jennings Bryan, speech to the Democratic National Convention, July 9, 1896

The Democratic Party's adoption of the free-silver platform caused the Populists to throw their support to Bryan as well. Worried that Bryan was picking up votes, many business leaders contributed millions of dollars to the Republican campaign. McKinley subsequently won the election. Free silver had not been a strong enough issue for a national victory.

The election of 1896 was the high point of influence for the Populist Party, which soon faded away. Even so, the party's platform laid the groundwork for reforms that the government would later enact. Populist language also became a mainstay in politics. Many politicians have tried to craft populist messages that suggest they are on the side of ordinary people and not special interests.

READING CHECK **Sequencing** How did the Farmers' Alliance give rise to the Populist Party?

SECTION 3 ASSESSMENT

go.hrw.com
Online Quiz
Keyword: SD7 HP15

Reviewing Ideas, Terms, and People

1. **a. Describe** What was the relationship between **William Marcy Tweed** and **Thomas Nast**?
   b. Summarize How did political machines gain power?
   c. Evaluate Do you think political machines did more harm than good? Explain.

2. **a. Recall** How did the **Crédit Mobilier scandal** tarnish the Grant administration?
   b. Elaborate In what way did the **Pendleton Civil Service Act** affect federal corruption?

3. **a. Identify** Who were **William McKinley** and William Jennings Bryan?
   b. Analyze How did farmers raise their issues from the local level to national politics?
   c. Evaluate What was the impact of the **Populist Party**?

Critical Thinking

4. **Comparing and Contrasting** What were the main similarities and differences between the **National Grange** and the Farmers' Alliances?

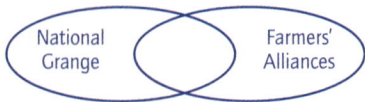

National Grange — Farmers' Alliances

FOCUS ON SPEAKING

5. **Persuasive** Imagine you are a leader of the Populist Party. Deliver a short speech in which you explain why the issue of free silver is so important to your cause.

Segregation and Discrimination

BEFORE YOU READ

MAIN IDEA

The United States in the late 1800s was a place of great change— and a place in need of even greater change.

READING FOCUS

1. What kinds of legalized discrimination did African Americans endure after Reconstruction?

2. What informal discrimination did African Americans experience?

3. Who were the most prominent black leaders of the period, and how did their views differ?

4. In what ways did others suffer discrimination in the late 1800s?

KEY TERMS AND PEOPLE

poll tax
grandfather clause
Jim Crow law
Plessy v. *Ferguson*
racial etiquette
lynching
Booker T. Washington
W. E. B. Du Bois
NAACP
debt peonage

PI 3.1 Compare and contrast the experiences of different ethnic, national, and religious groups, including Native American Indians, in the United States, explaining their contributions to American society and culture.

THE INSIDE STORY

Why did a dinner invitation cause controversy? In October 1901, soon after he became president, Theodore Roosevelt invited a national leader to dine at the White House. The invitation made headlines because that leader was an African American: Booker T. Washington. Roosevelt often consulted with him about political appointments in the South because he knew that Washington understood the complicated relationships in the region. The dinner was a small occasion with the president, his family, and a few guests. To some people, that social closeness was even more upsetting. At the time, many restaurants would not serve black people.

Washington was not the first African American to visit the White House. President Lincoln had welcomed Sojourner Truth and Frederick Douglass to discuss abolition. Black entertainers performed there in the late 1800s. But a social invitation to dinner was another matter.

When Washington died in 1915, the *New York Times* obituary noted, "Most of the criticism fell upon Colonel Roosevelt, but the incident [the White House dinner] served also to injure Dr. Washington's work in some parts of the South." ◼

ROOSEVELT AND BOOKER T. WASHINGTON

▶ **Appearing side by side, Roosevelt and Washington made a powerful statement to both the black and the white communities.**

Separate, Not Equal
These African American children in Alabama were segregated into a one-room school.

Legalized Discrimination

As you know, the Fourteenth and Fifteenth Amendments were meant to guarantee the rights of African Americans. Yet that did not happen. In the late 1800s, prejudice persisted throughout the country, and in the South, new laws made discrimination legal.

Restricting the right to vote By the time Reconstruction ended, white Democrats had regained control over the southern state legislatures. They went to great lengths to make sure that African Americans could not exercise their right to vote. One tactic was to require voters to pay a poll tax and pass a literacy test. These measures kept most African Americans from voting. Most were too poor to afford the poll tax, and many had been denied the education needed to pass the literacy test.

The laws prevented some poor or illiterate white men from voting. However, many southern state legislatures had written grandfather clauses into their constitutions. The clauses stated that a man could vote if he, his father, or his grandfather had been eligible to vote before January 1, 1867. That date is significant. Before that time, only white men had the right to vote. Freed slaves had not yet achieved that right. The grandfather clause, therefore, made sure that African Americans could not vote.

Legalized segregation Southern state legislatures also passed a series of laws designed to create and enforce segregation. These provisions were called Jim Crow laws. The name Jim Crow came from a stereotypical character in a minstrel song of the 1820s. By the 1890s the term was used for the laws discriminating against African Americans.

The first of these laws, passed in Tennessee in 1881, required separate railway cars for African Americans and whites. By the 1890s southern states had segregated many public places and services, including schools.

African Americans filed lawsuits against railroads, hotels, and theaters that refused to serve them. They wanted equal treatment under the Civil Rights Act of 1875.

HISTORY'S VOICES

❝All persons . . . shall be entitled to full and equal enjoyment of the accommodations, advantages, facilities, and privileges of inns, public conveyances on land or water, theaters, and other places of public amusement.❞

—Civil Rights Act of 1875

In 1883, however, the Supreme Court declared that the Civil Rights Act of 1875 was unconstitutional. The Court ruled that the Fourteenth Amendment—which guarantees equal protection of the law—applied only to state governments. Congress could prevent the states from denying African Americans their rights, but Congress could not outlaw discrimination by private individuals or businesses.

Thirteen years later, another key case came before the Supreme Court. This time the matter involved a Louisiana state law requiring railroads to provide "equal but separate accommodations for the white and colored races." Homer Plessy, an African American man, sat in a whites-only train compartment to test the law. He was arrested, but he appealed based on the Fourteenth Amendment.

In *Plessy v. Ferguson* (1896) the Court upheld the practice of segregation. The Court ruled that "separate but equal" facilities did not violate the Fourteenth Amendment. Only one justice, John Marshall Harlan, disagreed with the majority. The *Plessy* decision allowed legalized segregation for nearly 60 years.

READING CHECK **Summarizing** How did southern states limit the rights of African Americans?

Informal Discrimination

Laws were not the only source of racial barriers. Strict rules of behavior, called **racial etiquette**, governed social and business interactions. African Americans were supposed to "know their place" and defer to whites in every encounter. If they failed to speak respectfully or acted with too much pride or defiance, the <u>consequences</u> could be serious.

The worst consequence was **lynching**—the murder of an individual, usually by hanging, without a legal trial. Between 1882 and 1892, nearly 900 African Americans lost their lives to lynch mobs. Lynchings declined after 1892, but they continued into the early 1900s.

Lynchings could be sparked by the most minor offenses, or perceived offenses. Many, if not most, victims were innocent of any crime, and few of the killers were ever punished.

READING CHECK **Drawing Conclusions**
Why did African Americans usually go along with the system of racial etiquette?

Prominent Black Leaders

Near the turn of the century, two different approaches emerged for improving the lives of African Americans. **Booker T. Washington,** born into slavery, believed that African Americans should accept segregation for the moment. He thought they could best prosper by acquiring farming and vocational skills. He founded the Tuskegee Institute in Alabama to teach African Americans practical skills for self-sufficiency.

W. E. B. Du Bois, a Harvard-trained professor, believed in speaking out against prejudice and striving for full rights immediately. African Americans, he said, should be uplifted by the "talented tenth," their best-educated leaders. Du Bois launched the Niagara Movement in 1905 to protest discrimination. Four years later, he helped found an even more influential organization, the National Association for the Advancement of Colored People (**NAACP**).

READING CHECK **Contrasting** How did the views of Washington and Du Bois differ?

ACADEMIC VOCABULARY
consequence something that logically follows an action

Overcoming Discrimination

Booker T. Washington walked a fine line between helping African Americans to advance and trying to avoid angering white Americans.

❝ No race can prosper till it learns that there is as much dignity in tilling a field as in writing a poem . . . The opportunity to earn a dollar in a factory just now is worth infinitely more than the opportunity to spend a dollar in an opera-house. ❞

Booker T. Washington,
1895

To W. E. B. Du Bois, equality meant opportunities to achieve at the highest levels.

❝ Industrial and trade teaching is needed . . . [but] it is not needed as much as thorough common school training and the careful education of the gifted in higher institutions. ❞

W. E. B. Du Bois,
1904

SKILLS FOCUS **READING LIKE A HISTORIAN**

Identifying Points of View For those who favored gradual social change, whose approach would be more appealing? Explain your reasoning.

See **Skills Handbook**, pp. H28–H29

Mexican American workers, like these railway workers in Texas, were routinely the lowest paid of any ethnic group.

Others Suffer Discrimination

African Americans were not the only people to face racial prejudice. Mexican Americans, Asian Americans, and Native Americans all experienced legal and social discrimination in the late 1800s.

Mexican Americans Many Mexican Americans and Mexican immigrants encountered hostility from white Americans. They often did not speak English well and had to take the most menial jobs for little pay. Some worked in the mines or on railroads. Most, however, worked on farms.

Many Mexican immigrants became trapped in their jobs because of a system brought from Mexico called **debt peonage**. In this system, workers were tied to their jobs until they could pay off debts they owed their employer. Debt peonage was finally made illegal in 1911.

Asian Americans Earlier in this chapter, you read about laws that limited immigrants from Asia and denied Chinese Americans citizenship. But discrimination went further. Chinese and Japanese Americans had to live in segregated neighborhoods and attend separate schools. Esther Wong, a Chinese immigrant, noted that "only a very few Chinese could find houses in American districts, for most house owners do not want Chinese tenants." Several states also forbade marriage with whites.

Native Americans Native Americans, too, endured injustices, including continuous government efforts to stamp out their traditional ways of life. Children were sometimes sent away from their parents to be "Americanized." People living on reservations had few opportunities for economic advancement. Many Native Americans were also excluded from political activity. In a number of states, they were not considered citizens until the passage of the Indian Citizenship Act of 1924.

READING CHECK **Comparing** How were the experiences of minority groups similar?

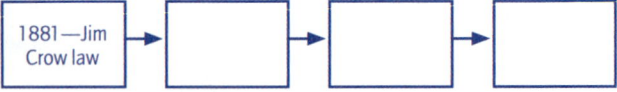

SECTION 4 ASSESSMENT

go.hrw.com
Online Quiz
Keyword: SD7 HP15

Reviewing Ideas, Terms, and People

1. **a. Define** What was a **grandfather clause**?
   b. Draw Conclusions What was the real purpose of **poll taxes**, literacy tests, and the grandfather clause?

2. **a. Describe** What was **racial etiquette**?
   b. Explain What could happen to African Americans who defied the rules of racial etiquette?

3. **a. Identify** Who was **Booker T. Washington**?
   b. Analyze What did **W. E. B. Du Bois** expect of the group he called "the talented tenth"?
   c. Predict For the time period of this chapter, do you think Washington's or Du Bois's approach would have been most beneficial for African Americans? Explain.

4. **a. Recall** What was **debt peonage**?
   b. Make Inferences How do you think segregation affected the people who were subjected to it?

Critical Thinking

5. **Sequencing** Copy the chart below and record the sequence of legal milestones from the passage of the first Jim Crow law in Tennessee to the Supreme Court's decision 15 years later in *Plessy* v. *Ferguson*. Be sure to include dates.

   1881—Jim Crow law → ☐ → ☐ → ☐

FOCUS ON WRITING

6. **Expository** Imagine that you are a newspaper editor in 1896. Write an editorial explaining what you think of the Supreme Court's decision in *Plessy* v. *Ferguson*. Address the "separate but equal" argument.

LANDMARK SUPREME COURT CASES
Constitutional Issue: Equal Protection

ST 1.2 Analyze the decisions leading to major turning points in United States history, comparing alternative courses of action, and hypothesizing, within the context of the historic period, about what might have happened if the decision had been different. Investigate decisions and actions such as: the *Plessy* v. *Ferguson* Supreme Court decision.

Plessy v. *Ferguson* (1896)

Why It Matters By the 1890s southern states had laws enforcing segregation in most aspects of daily life. *Plessy* v. *Ferguson* upheld the states' rights to regulate social and economic matters within their borders.

Background of the Case

Homer Plessy was convicted of sitting in a whites-only railway car. He had white parents and white grandparents but was considered black because he had a black great-grandparent. Plessy argued that Louisiana's Separate Car Act of 1890 violated the Thirteenth Amendment, which abolished slavery, and the Fourteenth Amendment, which requires all people to be treated equally under the law.

The Decision

The Court upheld the Separate Car Act. Justice Henry Brown maintained that the abolition of slavery did not prevent states from making legal distinctions between races. A law can recognize the obvious differences between races, he wrote, without violating their legal equality.

The Court noted that the Fourteenth Amendment requires legal equality but does not eliminate all racial distinctions and does not force people to accept a social "commingling of the races upon terms unsatisfactory to either." The lone dissenter, Justice John Marshall Harlan, wrote:

❝Our Constitution is color-blind, and neither knows nor tolerates classes among citizens. In respect of civil rights, all citizens are equal before the law. The humblest is the peer of the most powerful. The law regards man as man, and takes no account of his surroundings or of his color when his civil rights as guaranteed by the supreme law of the land are involved.❞

THE IMPACT TODAY Nearly 60 years passed before *Plessy* was formally overturned in *Brown* v. *Board of Education* (1954). Even then, segregation did not disappear overnight. Today, however, people of all races mix freely in public accommodations, as these airplane travelers are doing.

go.hrw.com
Research Online
Keyword: SS Court

CRITICAL THINKING

1. **Analyze the Impact** Using the keyword above, read about the *Brown v. Board of Education* decision, which overruled *Plessy*. What did the Court in *Brown* say about the "separate but equal" doctrine in *Plessy*? Why was the reasoning in *Brown* so significant in ending legal segregation?

2. **You Be the Judge** Until 1997 the Virginia Military Institute was an all-male, state-supported military college with a long tradition of rigorous "adversarial" training to mold character and develop leadership. Did excluding women violate the Constitution? Would it matter if Virginia also had an all-female military school? Explain.

City Life

Historical Context The documents below provide information on city life near the turn of the century.

Task Examine the documents and answer the questions that follow. Then you will be asked to write an essay about city life around 1900, using facts from the documents and from the chapter to support the position you take in your thesis statement.

ST 4.3 Develop hypotheses about important events, eras, or issues; move from chronicling to explaining historical events and issues; use information collected from diverse sources to produce cogently written reports and document-based essays.

DOCUMENT 1

Beginning in the late 1800s, more immigrants began to arrive in the United States from Eastern and Southern Europe. Few of these immigrants spoke English, and most of them settled in major cities such as New York, Boston, and Chicago. There they created ethnic neighborhoods that made the cities very diverse.

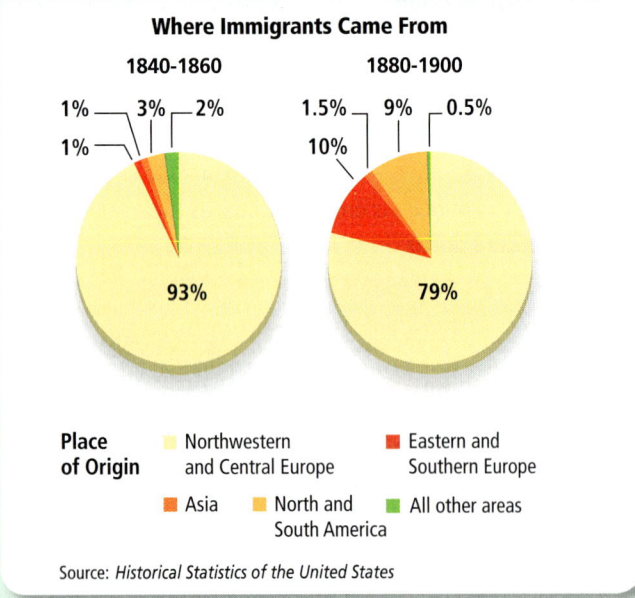

SHIFTING PATTERNS OF IMMIGRATION

Where Immigrants Came From

1840-1860

1% — 3% — 2%
1% —
93%

1880-1900

1.5% — 9% — 0.5%
10% —
79%

Place of Origin
- Northwestern and Central Europe
- Eastern and Southern Europe
- Asia
- North and South America
- All other areas

Source: *Historical Statistics of the United States*

DOCUMENT 2

In some cities, settlement houses took the lead in trying to help poor immigrants with basic needs, such as housing, education, and job training. Hull House founder Jane Addams explained how her organization viewed its role in Chicago.

"The Settlement then, is an experimental effort to aid in the solution of the social and industrial problems which are engendered [created] by the modern conditions of life in a great city. It insists that these problems are not confined to any one portion of a city. It is an attempt to relieve, at the same time, overaccumulation at one end of society and the destitution [poverty] at the other; but it assumes that overaccumulation and destitution is most sorely felt in the things that pertain to social and educational privileges. From its very nature it can stand for no political or social propaganda . . . It must be open to conviction and must have a deep and abiding sense of tolerance. It must be hospitable and ready for experiment. . . It must also be grounded in a philosophy whose foundation is the solidarity of the human race . . . Its residents must be emptied of all conceit of opinion and all self-assertion, and ready to arouse and interpret the public opinion of their neighborhood. They must be content to live quietly side by side with their neighbors, until they grow into a sense of relationship and mutual interests."

Around 1890 British writer Rudyard Kipling visited San Francisco. He was fascinated by the city's cable cars, which seemed able to effortlessly navigate steep hills and sharp turns.

"The cable cars have for all practical purposes made San Francisco a dead level. They take no count of rise or fall, but slide equably on their appointed courses from one end to the other of a six-mile street. They turn corners almost at right angles, cross other lines, and for [all] I know may run up the sides of houses. There is no visible agency of their flight, but once in awhile you shall pass a five-storied building humming with machinery that winds up an everlasting wire cable, and the initiated will tell you that here is the mechanism. I gave up asking questions. If it pleases Providence [God] to make a car run up and down a slit in the ground for many miles, and if for twopence halfpenny [two and a half cents] I can ride in that car, why shall I seek the reasons of the miracle?"

This photograph shows cable car passengers traveling along San Francisco's Sutter Street in 1905. Women were expected to take seats, but men had the option of standing and hanging onto special poles.

Skills FOCUS — READING LIKE A HISTORIAN

1. **a. Describe** Refer to Document 1. How did immigration patterns change in the late 1800s?
   b. Analyze How did this change affect major cities?

2. **a. Identify** Refer to Document 2. According to Addams, what was the purpose of the settlement house?
   b. Draw Conclusions What kind of relationship did Addams expect settlement house residents to have with their neighbors?

3. **a. Recall** Refer to Documents 3 and 4. What were some of the features of cable cars?

   b. Interpret Did Kipling really imagine that cable cars could "run up the sides of houses"? What point was he trying to make?

4. **Document-Based Essay Question** Consider the question below and form a thesis statement. Using examples from Documents 1, 2, 3, and 4, create an outline and write a short essay supporting your position. How did immigrants and new technology change American cities around 1900?

See **Skills Handbook**, pp. H15, H28–H29, H30

Visual Summary: Life at the Turn of the Twentieth Century

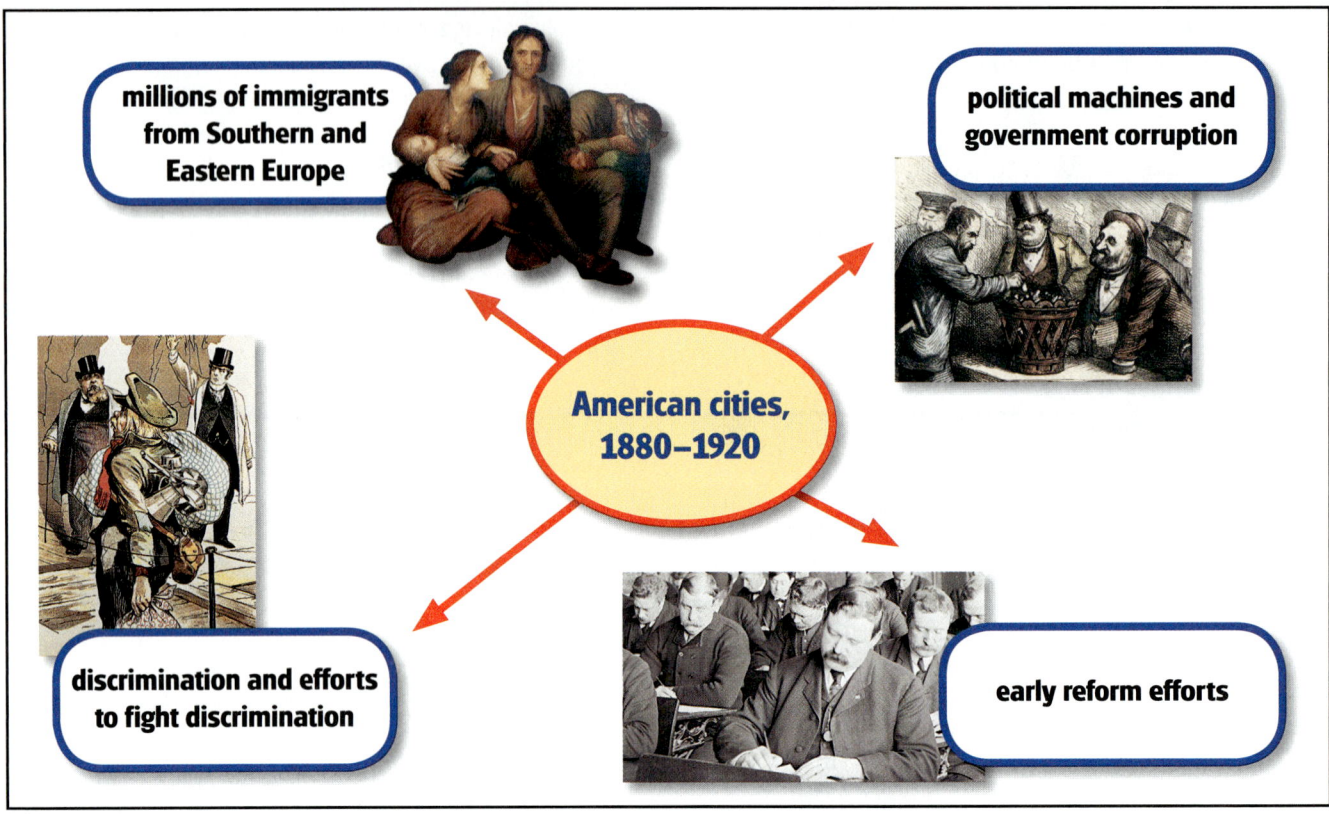

millions of immigrants from Southern and Eastern Europe

political machines and government corruption

American cities, 1880–1920

discrimination and efforts to fight discrimination

early reform efforts

Reviewing Key Terms and People

Match each lettered definition with the correct numbered item below.

a. Angel Island

b. Jane Addams

c. James A. Garfield

d. debt peonage

e. Ellis Island

f. Jim Crow laws

g. National Grange

h. poll tax

i. Thomas Nast

j. Social Gospel

1. political cartoonist who helped expose the corrupt dealings of the Tweed Ring

2. activist who founded Chicago's Hull House

3. system in which workers were tied to their jobs until they had paid off money that they owed to their employer

4. fee that citizens had to pay before voting

5. organization founded to fight for issues important to the nation's farmers

6. Ohio senator who won the presidency in 1880, but who was assassinated just four months into his term.

7. legislation that created and enforced segregation

8. idea that religious faith should be expressed through good works

9. immigration station in San Francisco Bay through which most Asian immigrants entered the United States

10. immigration station in New York Harbor through which most European immigrants entered the United States

History's Impact video program

Review the video to answer the closing question: How did *Plessy* v. *Ferguson* (1898) affect African Americans?

Comprehension and Critical Thinking

SECTION 1 *(pp. 488–494)*

11. a. Describe Where did new immigrants to America typically settle?

b. Compare What did the Gentlemen's Agreement and the Chinese Exclusion Act have in common?

c. Elaborate Why do you think that Congress passed laws banning some groups of immigrants and not others?

SECTION 2 *(pp. 495–498)*

12. a. Identify Who was Frederick Law Olmsted?

b. Explain How were the settlement house movement and the Social Gospel movement connected?

c. Develop Did all Americans live equally well during the Gilded Age? Explain.

SECTION 3 *(pp. 499–506)*

13. a. Recall What was the gold standard?

b. Analyze Information Why did farmers organize in the late 1800s?

c. Evaluate How did political machines both help and harm the public?

SECTION 4 *(pp. 507–511)*

14. a. Identify Who were Booker T. Washington and W. E. B. Du Bois?

b. Summarize In what ways did African Americans suffer both legal and informal discrimination in the late 1800s?

c. Evaluate Do you think Homer Plessy was rash or courageous for challenging the law requiring separate rail cars for African Americans and whites? Explain.

Using the Internet

go.hrw.com
Practice Online
Keyword: SD7 CH15

15. Thousands of immigrants crowded into American cities in the late 1800s and early 1900s. Using the keyword above, do research to learn about immigrants' lives in their new homes. Where did they live? How did they live? In what ways did they maintain their old traditions, and in what ways did they adapt to American society? Write a description of the ways in which immigrants tried to make their difficult living conditions more bearable.

Analyzing Primary Sources

Reading Like a Historian

Photographers captured the tension of immigrants, such as this woman at Ellis Island, trying to enter the United States.

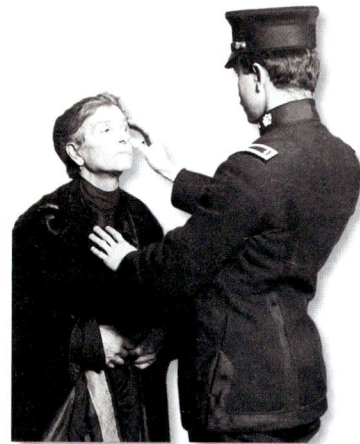

16. Identify What is happening in this picture?

17. Draw Conclusions Why did the government undertake this process?

Critical Reading

Read the passage in Section 3 under the heading "The Populist Party." Then answer the question that follows.

18. Which of the following statements is true?

A The Populist Party began as a coalition of farmers, laborers, and business leaders.

B The Populist Party campaigned for an income tax, government regulation of business, and unlimited coinage of silver.

C Populist candidates fared poorly in the elections of 1892.

D Populists believed that government regulation of banks and railroads would harm the economy.

FOCUS ON WRITING

Persuasive Writing *Persuasive writing takes a position for or against an issue, using facts and examples as supporting evidence. To practice persuasive writing, complete the assignment below.*

Writing Topic U.S. policy on inspection of immigrants

19. Assignment U.S. officials believed that wealthier immigrants were less likely to become a social burden than poor ones. First and second class passengers arriving in New York underwent a quick inspection aboard ship. Steerage passengers faced medical and legal inspections on Ellis Island. Do you think this was a reasonable policy? Write a paragraph in which you develop your position.

 **The American West**
1860–1900

MAIN IDEA In the late 1800s Americans moved West in increasing numbers. They established mining, ranching, and farming operations, but in the process they also destroyed the traditional way of life of the Native Americans they encountered.

SECTION 1 Native Americans resisted the movement of Americans westward. Nevertheless, the power of the U.S. military and the persistence of American settlers eventually proved too strong to resist.

SECTION 2 The lure of gold and silver drew thousands of miners westward, though few found the wealth they dreamed of. Meanwhile, ranchers established a thriving cattle industry on the Great Plains.

SECTION 3 The government promoted the settlement of the West by offering free or cheap land to those willing to establish productive farms. The government also gave land to railroad companies, which could either use it to extend the railroads or sell to settlers.

 **The Second Industrial Revolution**
1880–1910

MAIN IDEA In the late 1800s innovations in business and industry occurred at an ever-more rapid pace. Business leaders made vast sums of money as they consolidated their holds over industry, but ordinary workers continued to work and live in dangerous and difficult conditions.

SECTION 1 The rise of the oil and steel industries transformed industry in the late 1800s. The railroads were a direct beneficiary of these innovations.

SECTION 2 Powerful business leaders consolidated their hold over industries by developing new business structures and strategies. This often resulted in cheaper manufactured goods for consumers but also less competition in the market.

SECTION 3 While businesses made huge profits—largely free of government regulation—workers toiled in dangerous conditions for scandalously low wages. With government turning a blind eye to the condition of workers, many workers began to organize in an effort to improve their situations.

SECTION 4 Innovations in transportation and communications went hand in hand with other business transformations in the late 1800s. Automobiles, streetcars, subways, telephones, and electricity changed the way Americans lived.

 **Life at the Turn of the Twentieth Century**
1880–1920

MAIN IDEA In the late 1800s waves of immigrants were arriving from southern and eastern Europe. Government was plagued by corruption, although reformers began to make efforts to restore honesty to government. Discrimination was a daily reality for African Americans, Asian Americans, Hispanic Americans, and Native Americans.

SECTION 1 A new wave of immigrants from southern and eastern Europe came to America. They settled mainly in cities, where they lived in often squalid conditions.

SECTION 2 The middle class was growing, while a small number of wealthy people enjoyed lavish lifestyles. Most urban dwellers, however, lived in deep poverty, and reformers began working to improve their living conditions.

SECTION 3 Major cities were controlled by political machines, and corruption even crept into national government. Reforms began at the national level to restore honest government. Meanwhile, a farmer's movement to reform railroad practices soon led to a political movement at the national level.

SECTION 4 In the late 1800s African Americans experienced tremendous discrimination. Jim Crow laws enforced segregation and restricted African American voting rights, while informal racial etiquette reinforced their lower status in society. Meanwhile, Hispanic Americans, Asian Americans, and Native Americans experienced discrimination in employment, housing, and education.

Themes

Government and Democracy
Movements for social, moral, economic, and political reform responded to changes that had been brought on by industrialization, the growth of cities, and immigration.

Economic Development
Claiming Alaska, Hawaii, and new territories in the Pacific made the United States a growing economic power.

Global Relations
The United States became increasingly involved in foreign affairs, claiming new territories after the Spanish-American War and entering the fighting in World War I.

Sixteen U. S. battleships, together known as the Great White Fleet, sailed around the globe in 1907–1908 in a proud display of American naval power.

Comparing and Contrasting

Find practice for **Comparing and Constrasting** in the **Skills Handbook,** p. H10

Historians can describe people and events by comparing and contrasting them. Good readers identify similarities and differences in the text and use them to gain better understanding of a passage's overall context.

Before You Read
Skim the headings and visuals to determine what you will be reading about.

While You Read
Compare and contrast the reading with the headings and visuals. How are they alike or different?

After You Read
Compare and contrast what you previously knew about the subject matter with what you have learned about it.

Political Organizing

The failure of women to gain the vote urged suffragists to action. In 1869 Elizabeth Cady Stanton and Susan B. Anthony helped form the National Woman Suffrage Association (NWSA). The NWSA focused its efforts on campaigning for a constitutional amendment to give women the vote. But it also dealt with other issues that concerned women, such as labor organizing. In 1872 the NWSA supported Victoria Woodhull, the first woman candidate for U.S. president.

Similarly, the American Woman Suffrage Association (AWSA) was founded in 1869 with Henry Ward Beecher as its president. Unlike the NWSA, the American Woman Suffrage Association focused exclusively on winning the right to vote on a state-by-state basis. It also aligned itself with the Republican party.

READING CHECK **Comparing** In what ways was the NWSA similar to the AWSA?

Compare Both the NWSA and the AWSA were founded in 1869 and worked for suffrage.

Identify signal words such as *similarly* and *likewise* for comparison and *but* and *unlike* for contrast.

Contrast Unlike the NWSA, which dealt with various issues affecting women, the AWSA focused solely on suffrage.

Test Prep Tip

Some essay questions on tests will ask you to compare and contrast historical people, places, and events. As a prewriting activity, create and complete a word web or Venn diagram about the subject matter. Then use your findings to develop an outline for the essay.

Interpreting Political Cartoons

Find practice for **Interpreting Political Cartoons** in the **Skills Handbook,** p. H31

Political cartoons are visual information sources that present messages about issues or people in funny or ironic ways. Political cartoons can portray a subject in either a positive or a negative light. Cartoonists often communicate a message through the use of symbols and caricature, or the drawing of subjects with distorted physical features. Labels, speech balloons, and captions can clarify the meaning of political cartoons.

Strategies historians use:
- Determine the cartoon's subject, reading all text and studying all symbols and caricatures.
- Establish the cartoon's message. Does it portray its subject in a positive or a negative light?
- Compare the cartoon's message with historical information you already know.

By portraying President Theodore Roosevelt as the popular figure Uncle Sam, the cartoonist may be trying to persuade readers to follow Roosevelt's leadership.

The yellow smoke symbolizes the dangers connected with the meat industry.

The cartoon supports Roosevelt's actions because the text says that the job must be done. The cartoon's message is that Roosevelt deserves support.

This cartoon refers to unsanitary conditions in meat factories in the early 1900s.

A NAUSEATING JOB, BUT IT MUST BE DONE
(President Roosevelt takes hold of the investigating muck-rake himself in the packing-house scandal.)

Skills FOCUS — **READING LIKE A HISTORIAN**

As You Read Make and complete a two-column chart in which you record reasons to support or contradict the cartoonist's message.

As You Study Use the two-column chart to compare the cartoonist's message with other information from this historical period. What conclusions can you draw from this comparison?

The Progressives

THE BIG PICTURE As the 1900s dawned, activists called Progressives fought to make America's economic and political systems fairer. Some fought for women's suffrage. Others attacked a wide range of societal ills. The Progressive movement involved countless individuals and groups at all levels of government.

New York Standards

Key Idea 1 The study of New York State and United States history requires an analysis of the development of American culture, its diversity and multicultural context, and the ways people are unified by many values, practices, and traditions.

Key Idea 3 Study about the major social, political, economic, cultural, and religious developments in New York State and United States history involves learning about the important roles and contributions of individuals and groups.

SKILLS FOCUS   READING LIKE A HISTORIAN

Improving the living conditions of urban immigrants became a major priority for many Progressives. In this 1909 photograph, immigrant students receive instruction at the Hancock School in Boston.

Making Inferences What special challenges do you think immigrant students might have faced?

See **Skills Handbook**, p. H7

U.S.

September 1901 Theodore Roosevelt becomes president after McKinley is assassinated.

1900

World

1901 First Nobel Prize is awarded.

Lady Moon, Lady [Moon]
Sailing so high,
Drop down to Baby,
From out the blue sky.
Babykin, Babykin
Down far below,
I hear thee calling,
Yet I can not go.

Moon loves the baby
The moonlight says,
In her home, dark and [...]
Though she must stay
Kindly she'll watch thee,
Till dawns the new day

History's Impact video program
Watch the video to understand the impact of labor laws.

1904
Muckraker Lincoln Steffens exposes government corruption in *The Shame of the Cities.*

May 1909
Civil rights activists found the NAACP.

1913
Anti-Defamation League is formed to fight anti-Semitism.

January 1919
Eighteenth Amendment bans alcoholic beverages.

August 1920
Nineteenth Amendment gives women the right to vote.

1904	1908	1912	1916	1920	1924

1906
Workers form the British Labour Party.

1913
Dr. Albert Schweitzer opens hospital in the French Congo to battle diseases such as leprosy and the plague.

1915
Mohandas K. Gandhi returns to India after leading a nonviolent campaign against discrimination in South Africa.

1923
Mustafa Kemal establishes the Republic of Turkey.

Progressivism

BEFORE YOU READ

MAIN IDEA

Progressives focused on three areas of reform: easing the suffering of the urban poor, improving unfair and dangerous working conditions, and reforming government at the national, state, and local levels.

READING FOCUS

1. What issues did Progressives focus on, and what helped energize their causes?

2. How did Progressives try to reform society?

3. How did Progressives fight to reform the workplace?

4. How did Progressives reform government at the national, state, and local levels?

KEY TERMS AND PEOPLE

Jacob Riis
progressivism
muckrakers
Ida Tarbell
Lincoln Steffens
Robert M. La Follette
Seventeenth Amendment
initiative
referendum
recall

PI **3.1** Compare and contrast the experiences of different ethnic, national, and religious groups, including Native American Indians, in the United States, explaining their contributions to American society and culture.

How the OTHER HALF Lives

MUSEUM OF THE
CITY OF NEW YORK

THE INSIDE STORY

How did a photographer help the nation's urban poor? When **Jacob Riis** wrote about the lives of impoverished immigrants in New York City, he was telling a familiar story: his own. Riis emigrated from Denmark in 1870, at the age of 21. He had trouble finding jobs and lived in poverty. By 1877, however, he was a police reporter for the *New York Tribune,* a voice for social reform.

Riis went to places that were comfortably out of view of most Americans: the tenements of the Lower East Side. "Someone had to tell the facts; that is one reason I became a reporter," he said. He described a room where six adults and five children lived: "One, two, three beds are there, if the old boxes and heaps of foul straw can be called by that name; a broken stove with crazy pipe from which the smoke leaks at every joint . . . piles of rubbish in the corner. The closeness and smell are appalling."

Words could barely describe the squalor. So Riis learned to use a camera. With a new invention, flash powder, he photographed dingy rooms and hallways. He showed his photos in public lectures. His 1889 article in *Scribner's Magazine,* "How the Other Half Lives," became a best-selling book. Riis's fame helped him press the city to improve living conditions for the poor and to build parks and schools.

◄ **Jacob Riis photographed a part of America that people did not know existed—or did not want to know.**

What Was Progressivism?

Jacob Riis's book *How the Other Half Lives* stunned Americans with its photographs of desperate urban poverty. In the late 1800s, a reform movement known as **progressivism** arose to address many of the social problems that industrialization created. The reformers, called Progressives, sought to improve living conditions for the urban poor. They questioned the power and practices of big business. Progressives also called for government to be more honest and responsive to people's needs.

Reform-minded writers were the first to expose many of the social ills that Progressives targeted. Popular magazines printed journalists' firsthand accounts of injustices and horrors they had witnessed. These journalists were known as **muckrakers** because they "raked up" or exposed the filth of society.

Most of the muckrakers' articles focused on business and political corruption. **Ida Tarbell** wrote a scathing report condemning the business practices of the Standard Oil Company in *McClure's Magazine*. Tarbell revealed how John D. Rockefeller crushed his competition in his quest to gain control over the oil business. Tarbell's reports appealed to a middle-class readership increasingly frightened by the unchecked power of large businesses such as Standard Oil.

Other muckrakers wrote about insurance and stock manipulation, the exploitation of child labor, slum conditions, and racial discrimination. **Lincoln Steffens** exposed the corruption of city governments in *The Shame of the Cities* (1904). Frank Norris described the strangling power of a monopolistic railroad in his 1901 novel *The Octopus: A Story of California*. The muckrakers helped prepare the way for many reforms in the United States.

READING CHECK **Sequencing** How important were the writings of the muckrakers in the Progressive movement, and what did they write about?

Reforming Society

By 1920, more than half of all Americans lived in cities. As cities continued to grow, they were increasingly unable to provide the services people needed: garbage collection, safe housing, and police and fire protection.

PRIMARY SOURCES

Ida Tarbell

Journalist Ida Tarbell's 1903 exposé of the business practices of the Standard Oil Company was one of the triumphs of muckraking. Here Tarbell comments on the company's 1880 victory over independent oil producers who were pressured into giving up their lawsuits against Standard Oil.

> "Now, what was this loose and easily discouraged organization [of independent oil producers] opposing? A compact body of a few able, cold-blooded men—men to whom anything was right that they could get, men knowing exactly what they wanted, men who loved the game they played because of the reward. . . The withdrawal of the [law]suits was a great victory for Mr. Rockefeller. There was no longer any doubt of his power in defensive operations. Having won a victory, he quickly went to work to make it secure."

Skills FOCUS **READING LIKE A HISTORIAN**

1. **Analyzing Primary Sources** How does Tarbell describe the leaders of Standard Oil?
2. **Identifying Points of View** What do you think Tarbell hoped to achieve by publishing her articles?

See **Skills Handbook**, pp. H28–H29

Housing reforms For the reformers, these conditions provided an opportunity. In New York City, for example, activists such as Lillian Wald worked vigorously to expand public health services for the poor. Progressives scored an early victory in New York State with the passage of the Tenement Act of 1901. This law forced landlords to install lighting in public hallways and to provide at least one toilet for every two families. Outhouses were eventually banned from New York City slums.

These simple steps helped create a healthier environment for impoverished New Yorkers. Within 15 years, the death rate in New York dropped dramatically. Housing reformers in other cities and states pushed for legislation similar to New York's law.

Fighting for civil rights Some progressives also fought prejudice in society. In 1909 Ida Wells-Barnett, W. E. B. Du Bois, Jane Addams,

FOCUS ON NEW YORK

DAILY LIFE

Working in the slums of the Lower East Side helped shape the ideas of another reformer, Margaret Sanger, a New York native. Sanger founded the American Birth Control League in 1921, which was the forerunner of today's Planned Parenthood.

and other activists formed the multiracial National Association for the Advancement of Colored People (NAACP). Its purpose was to fight for the rights of African Americans.

The NAACP fought on a number of fronts. In 1913 it protested the introduction of segregation into the federal government. Two years later, the NAACP protested the film *Birth of a Nation*, by D.W. Griffith, because of its hostile stereotyping of African Americans. Attempts to ban or censor the film met with little success.

In 1913 Sigmund Livingston, a Jewish man living in Chicago, founded the Anti-Defamation League (ADL). The mission of the ADL was to fight anti-Semitism, or hostility toward Jews.

ADL began by combatting the use of negative stereotypes of Jews in print, on stage, and in films. Adolph S. Ochs, publisher of *The New York Times* and a member of the ADL, wrote a memo to newspaper editors nationwide discouraging the use of negative references to Jews. By 1920 the practice in newspapers had nearly stopped.

READING CHECK **Comparing** How were the missions of the NAACP and the ADL similar?

ACADEMIC VOCABULARY
concrete specific, particular

Reforming the Workplace

By the end of the 1800s, labor unions were actively campaigning for the rights of adult male workers. Progressive reformers took up the cause of working women and children. In 1893 Florence Kelley helped persuade Illinois to prohibit child labor and to limit the number of hours women were forced to work.

In 1904 Kelley helped found the National Child Labor Committee. The committee's mission was to persuade state legislatures to ban child labor. Yet many employers continued hiring children, and not all states enforced child labor laws.

Progressives also organized state-by-state campaigns to limit women's workdays. Kelley led a successful effort in Oregon that limited the workday in laundries to 10 hours. Utah also passed a law limiting workdays to eight hours in some women's occupations.

But unskilled workers, men and women alike, were still paid extremely low wages. In 1900 about 40 percent of working-class families lived in poverty. Labor unions and Progressives both worked to secure laws ensuring workers a minimum wage. In 1912 Massachusetts became the first state to pass such a law. Congress did not pass a national minimum-wage law until 1938.

Courts and labor laws

Business owners began to fight labor laws in the courts. In the early 1900s, the Supreme Court ruled on several cases concerning state laws that limited the length of the workday. In the 1905 case *Lochner* v. *New York*, the Supreme Court sided with business owners. The Court refused to uphold a law limiting bakers to a 10-hour workday on the grounds that it denied workers their right to make contracts with employers.

But in 1908 the Court sided with workers. In the case *Muller* v. *Oregon*, the Court upheld a state law establishing a 10-hour workday for women in laundries and factories. Louis D. Brandeis, the attorney for the state of Oregon and a future Supreme Court justice, argued the state's case. He maintained that concrete evidence showed that working long hours harmed the health of women. This research convinced the Supreme Court to uphold the Oregon law.

His defense, known as the Brandeis brief, became a model for the defense of other labor laws. It was used in the 1917 case *Bunting* v. *Oregon*, in which the Court upheld a law that extended the protection of a 10-hour workday to men working in mills and factories.

The Triangle Shirtwaist Company Fire

A gruesome disaster in New York in 1911 galvanized Progressives to fight for safety in the workplace. About 500 young women worked for the Triangle Shirtwaist Company, a high-rise factory that made women's blouses. One Saturday, just as these young workers were ending their six-day workweek, a fire erupted, probably from a discarded match.

Within moments, the eighth floor was ablaze, and the flames quickly spread to two other floors. Escape was nearly impossible. Many doors were locked to prevent theft. The flimsy fire escape broke under the weight of panic-stricken people, sending its victims tumbling to their deaths. With flames at their backs, dozens of workers leaped from the windows.

More than 140 women and men died in the Triangle Shirtwaist Company fire. Union organizer Rose Schneiderman commented on the senseless tragedy.

The Triangle Shirtwaist Fire

The fire at the Triangle Shirtwaist Company was a tragedy waiting to happen. Crowded conditions, a lack of workplace safety laws, negligent owners, and an ill-prepared fire department combined to create a scene of devastation. Most victims were immigrant girls, some as young as 15 or 16.

The fire on the eighth floor was higher than the fire department's ladders could reach.

Most exit doors had been locked by managers to prevent theft. Elevators could accommodate only 10 people at a time.

Garment workers labored long hours in tightly packed quarters.

Large amounts of fabric and paper scraps added fuel to the fire.

AFTERMATH OF THE FIRE

Why was the Triangle Shirtwaist Company fire significant?

- At least 140 people died.
- Investigators found similar hazards in workplaces across New York State.
- New state laws were passed to require dramatic new fire safety measures, factory inspections, and sanitation improvements.
- New York reforms became a model for workplace safety nationwide.

Skills FOCUS | **INTERPRETING INFOGRAPHICS**

go.hrw.com
Interactive
Keyword: SD7 CH16

The Asch Building, where the Triangle Shirtwaist Company was located, was not unusual in its lack of fire safety precautions. Typical of many urban high-rise buildings at the time, it had inadequate fire escapes, no fire alarms, and no sprinkler system.

Drawing Conclusions What was the biggest obstacle preventing the workers' escape from the Triangle Shirtwaist fire?

See **Skills Handbook**, p. H18

"This is not the first time girls have been burned alive in the city. Every week I must learn of the untimely death of one of my sister workers. Every year thousands of us are maimed. The life of men and women is so cheap and property is so sacred."

—Rose Schneiderman, April 2, 1911

FOCUS ON NEW YORK

GOVERNMENT
New York social reformer and workers' safety expert Frances Perkins helped investigate the Triangle Shirtwaist Fire. Perkins later was appointed secretary of labor by President Franklin D. Roosevelt, making her the first woman Cabinet member.

The Triangle Shirtwaist fire was a turning point for reform. With the efforts of Schneiderman and others, New York State passed the toughest fire-safety laws in the nation.

The unions During the Progressive Era, energetic new labor unions joined the fight for better working conditions. The International Ladies' Garment Workers Union (ILGWU) was founded in 1900. Unlike the American Federation of Labor (AFL), which allowed only skilled workers as members, the ILGWU organized unskilled workers. In 1909 the garment workers called a general strike known as the "Uprising of the 20,000." The strikers won a shorter workweek and higher wages. They also attracted thousands of workers to the union.

Meanwhile, the Industrial Workers of the World (IWW), founded in 1905, opposed capitalism altogether. Under the leadership of William "Big Bill" Haywood, the IWW organized the unskilled workers that the AFL ignored. Known as "Wobblies," IWW members not only used traditional strategies such as strikes and boycotts but also engaged in more radical tactics, including industrial sabotage.

At the height of its strength in 1912, the IWW led some 20,000 textile workers on strike in Lawrence, Massachusetts, to protest pay cuts. After a bitter, well-publicized 10-week strike, the mill owners gave in and raised wages.

But the IWW's success was brief. Several later strikes were terrible failures. Fearing the union's revolutionary goals, the government cracked down on the IWW's activities. Disputes among its leaders also weakened the union. Within a few years, it declined in power.

READING CHECK **Identifying Cause and Effect** What factors produced reforms in wages and workplace safety?

Reforming Government

Progressives targeted government for reform as well. They wanted to eliminate political corruption and make government more efficient.

City government reforms Cleaning up government often meant winning control of it. One of the most successful reform mayors was Tom Johnson of Cleveland, Ohio. He set new rules for the police, released debtors from prison, and supported a fairer tax system. In Toledo, Ohio, Mayor Samuel M. Jones overhauled the police force, improved municipal services, set a minimum wage for workers, and opened kindergartens for children.

Progressives also promoted new government structures as a means to improve efficiency. In 1900 a massive hurricane struck Galveston, Texas. The traditional city government proved unable to cope with the disaster, so the Texas legislature set up a five-member commission to govern the city. The commissioners were experts in their fields rather than party loyalists. Galveston's city commission was more honest and efficient than its previous government. By 1918 some 500 American cities adopted the commission plan of city government.

Another new form of government, the council-manager model, began in Staunton, Virginia, in 1908. The city council appoints a professional politician to run the city. The reform inspired cities nationwide to follow suit.

Women march in a Labor Day parade in 1912. Although not considered "ladylike behavior," some women protested their unhealthy and dangerous working conditions.

State government reforms The fight for Progressive reforms extended to the state level. In Wisconsin, a progressive governor named **Robert M. La Follette** pushed through an ambitious agenda of reforms that became known as the Wisconsin Idea.

Elected in 1900, La Follette called for electoral reforms, such as limits on campaign spending. He created state commissions to regulate railroads and utilities. He also formed commissions to oversee transportation, civil service, and taxation.

Other governors pushed for reforms in their states. In New York Charles Evans Hughes regulated public utilities and pushed through a worker safety law. In Mississippi James Vardaman limited the use of convict labor. Vardaman's reforming spirit, however, was marred by extreme racism. He exploited prejudices of poor white farmers toward African Americans to gain support for his policies.

Election reforms Progressives wanted to reform elections to make them fairer and to make politicians more accountable to voters. They pushed for the direct primary, an election in which voters choose candidates to run in a general election. Mississippi adopted the direct primary in 1903. Most other states followed.

Progressives also backed the **Seventeenth Amendment**, ratified in 1913. The amendment gave voters, rather than state legislatures, the power to directly elect their U.S. senators. Progressives believed that direct elections would undermine the influence of party bosses.

Progressives also fought for the use of the secret ballot, which printed all candidates' names on a single piece of paper. Previously, each political party printed its own ballot on colored paper, making it easy to see how people voted and to pressure them to support certain candidates. By 1900 almost all states had adopted the secret ballot.

Finally, Progressives urged states to adopt three additional election reform measures: the initiative, the referendum, and the recall. These measures have become powerful tools with which voters can influence public policy.

An **initiative** allows voters to put a proposed law on the ballot for public approval. The **referendum** allows citizens to place a recently passed law on the ballot, allowing voters to approve or reject the measure. The **recall** enables citizens to remove an elected official from office by calling for a special election. Each measure was designed to make politicians more accountable to voters.

READING CHECK **Contrasting** How does the city commission form of government differ from the city manager form?

PROGRESSIVE ELECTION REFORMS
QUICK FACTS

- **direct primary** voters select a party's candidates for public office

- **17th Amendment** voters elect their senators directly

- **secret ballot** people vote privately without fear of coercion

- **initiative** allows citizens to propose new laws

- **referendum** allows citizens to vote on a proposed or existing law

- **recall** allows voters to remove an elected official from office

go.hrw.com
Online Quiz
Keyword: SD7 HP16

SECTION 1 ASSESSMENT

Reviewing Ideas, Terms, and People

1. **a. Identify** What was **progressivism**?
   b. Summarize What were some areas of reform that the Progressives targeted?
   c. Evaluate If the **muckrakers** had not done their work, do you think reforms would have occurred? Explain.

2. **a. Explain** Why was the Triangle Shirtwaist fire important?
   b. Contrast How did the tactics of the **ILGWU** differ from those of the IWW?

3. **a. Recall** What are the differences between an **initiative**, a **referendum**, and a **recall**?
   b. Rank Which of the election reforms do you think had the greatest impact on American voters? Explain.

Critical Thinking

4. **Identifying Cause and Effect** Copy the chart below and record the effects of the work of the Progressives in three broad categories: society, workplace, and government.

   Society — Progressives — Government
   Workplace

FOCUS ON WRITING

5. **Descriptive** Suppose you are a New York newspaper reporter in 1911. Describe the events of the Triangle Shirtwaist fire.

ST 3.2 Draw upon literary selections, historical documents, and accounts to analyze the roles played by different individuals and groups during the major eras in New York State and United States history.

About the Reading The muckraking novel *The Jungle* exposed the horrific working conditions and unsanitary manufacturing practices in the meatpacking industry. The book prompted a huge federal probe and the passage of the Meat Inspection Act of 1906.

AS YOU READ **Think about the risks these factory workers dealt with on the job every day.**

Excerpt from

The Jungle

by Upton Sinclair

Sinclair exposed the nation's meatpacking plants, where workers operated in dangerous, grueling, disease-ridden conditions.

There was no heat upon the killing-floor. The men might exactly as well have worked out of doors all winter. For that matter, there was very little heat anywhere in the building, except in the cooking-rooms and such places—and it was the men who worked in these who ran the most risk of all, because whenever they had to pass to another room they had to go through ice-cold corridors, and sometimes with nothing on above the waist except a sleeveless undershirt. In summer time the chilling-rooms were counted deadly places, for rheumatism and such things; but when it came to winter the men envied those who worked there—at least the chilling rooms were kept at a precise temperature, and one could not freeze to death. On the killing-floor you might easily freeze, if the gang for any reason had to stop for a time. You were apt to be covered with blood, and it would freeze solid; if you leaned against a pillar you would freeze to that, and if you put your hand upon the blade of your knife, you would run a chance of leaving your skin on it. The men would tie up their feet in newspapers and old sacks, and these would be soaked in blood and frozen, and then soaked again, and so on until by night time a man would be walking on great lumps the size of feet of an elephant. Now and then, when the bosses were not looking, you would see them plunging their feet and ankles into the steaming hot carcass of the steer, or darting across the room to the hot-water jets. The cruelest thing of all was that nearly all of them—all of those who used knives—were unable to wear gloves, and their arms would be white with frost and their hands would grow numb, and then of course there would be accidents. Also the air would be full of steam, from the hot water and the hot blood, so that you could not see five feet before you; then, with men rushing about at the speed they kept up on the killing-floor, and all with butcherknives, like razors, in their hands —well, it was to be counted as a wonder that there were not more men slaughtered than cattle.

Skills FOCUS   READING LIKE A HISTORIAN

1. **Identifying Supporting Details** What dangers to workers and to food does Sinclair describe?
2. **Literature as Historical Evidence** What does *The Jungle* suggest about reasons workers formed unions?

See **Skills Handbook**, pp. H5, H32

SECTION 2

Women and Public Life

BEFORE YOU READ

MAIN IDEA

Women during the Progressive Era actively campaigned for reforms in education, children's welfare, temperance, and suffrage.

READING FOCUS

1. What opportunities did women have for education and work outside the home during the late 1800s?

2. How did women gain political experience through participation in reform movements?

3. How did the women's suffrage movement campaign for the vote?

KEY TERMS AND PEOPLE

Prohibition
Woman's Christian Temperance Union
Frances Willard
Carry Nation
Eighteenth Amendment
National Association of Colored Women
Elizabeth Cady Stanton
Susan B. Anthony
National American Woman Suffrage Association

PI 1.1 Analyze the development of American culture, explaining how ideas, values, beliefs, and traditions have changed over time and how they united all Americans.

THE INSIDE STORY

How did some African American women break barriers in the late 1800s? Most African American women of the 1800s could only dream of going to college. Two women dreamed it, and then did it. Alberta Virginia Scott (1875–1902) and Otelia Cromwell (1874–1972) both graduated from prestigious women's colleges.

Scott was the first known African American to graduate from Radcliffe College in Cambridge, Massachusetts. She entered Radcliffe in 1894, studying science and classics. After graduating, Scott felt she should teach in the South. In 1900 Booker T. Washington invited her to teach at Tuskegee Institute, but sadly, after a year she became ill and died.

Otelia Cromwell had a long and distinguished career as an educator. She transferred from Howard University to Smith College in Northampton, Massachusetts. After graduating in 1900, she taught public school in Washington, D.C. She then went back to school, earning a master's degree from Columbia University and a Ph.D. from Yale.

Professor Cromwell became head of the literature department at Miner Teachers College in Washington. She wrote and edited several books and articles, including a respected biography of suffragist Lucretia Mott. She retired in 1944, and in 1950 she received an honorary degree from Smith. Today Smith College hosts an annual Otelia Cromwell Day, featuring lectures, films, and workshops.

Educational PIONEERS

▶ **Otelia Cromwell was honored for her career in education.**

Opportunities for Women

By the late 1800s, women were finding more opportunities for education and employment. With greater opportunities came a desire for greater involvement in the life of the community. Many women turned outward, beyond the home, to work for change and reform in society. They sought to use their talents and skills to make life better for others as well as for themselves. In the process, women became a greater political force.

Higher education

Throughout the early 1800s, women had limited opportunities for higher education. It wasn't until 1833, for example, that a college, Oberlin College in Ohio, began admitting women as well as men. Later in the century, more colleges opened their doors to women. By 1870 about 20 percent of all college students were women. By 1900 that number had increased to more than one-third.

Most of the women who attended college at this time were members of the middle or upper classes. They wanted to be able to use their knowledge and skills after graduating. However, many professional opportunities were still denied them. The American Medical Association, for example, did not admit women members until 1915. Denied access to their professions, many of these women put their talents and skills to work in various reform movements. These movements would be the training grounds for later political activism.

Employment opportunities

Job opportunities for educated middle class women expanded in the late 1800s. Women worked as teachers and nurses—the traditional "caring professions"—but they also entered the business world as bookkeepers, typists, secretaries, and shop clerks.

In addition, businesses such as newspapers and magazines began to hire more women as artists and journalists. The businesses wanted to cater to the interests of the growing consumer group formed by educated and employed women. By 1900 the census counted 11,207 female artists, up from 412 in 1870, and 2,193 female journalists, up from a mere 35 some three decades years before.

Working class women and those without high school educations found jobs available to them in industry. Women poured into the garment industry, where they took positions that paid less than men's jobs did. Employers usually assumed that women were single and were being supported by their fathers. They also

---

TRACING HISTORY

Women's Rights

Efforts to expand women's rights began long before the Progressive Era and continued beyond it. Study the time line to learn about key events in the history of women's rights.

ST 4.1 Analyze important debates in American history (e.g. women's suffrage), focusing on the opposing positions and the historical evidence used to support these positions.

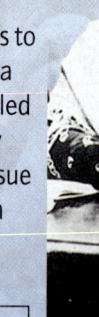

1848 Delegates to the historic Seneca Falls Convention, led by Elizabeth Cady Stanton (right), issue a bold declaration calling for equal rights for women.

1700

1800

1776 Shortly before the Declaration of Independence was drafted, Abigail Adams wrote her husband, John, urging that the new nation protect women's liberties.

1869 Women living in Wyoming Territory become the first American women to win the right to vote.

assumed that male employees were supporting families. Employers used these assumptions as reasons to pay women lower wages.

By the late 1800s these opportunities in public life began to change the way many middle-class women viewed their world. They began to see that they had a role to play in their communities and in society beyond the home.

READING CHECK **Summarizing** What new opportunities did women find outside the home in the late 1800s?

Gaining Political Experience

As in earlier times, women became the backbone of many reform movements during the Progressive Era. Women learned how to organize, how to persuade other people, and how to publicize their cause. Furthermore, participation in these movements taught women that they had the power to improve life for themselves, their families, and their communities.

Children's health and welfare Some women gained experience while campaigning for the rights of children. Many Progressive reformers worked to end child labor, improve children's health, and promote education.

Lillian Wald, founder of the Henry Street Settlement in New York City, believed the federal government had a responsibility to tend to the well being of children. She campaigned tirelessly for the creation of a federal agency to meet that goal. She was successful when the Federal Children's Bureau opened in 1912.

Prohibition Progressive women also gained political experience by participating in the **Prohibition** movement, which called for a ban on making, selling, and distributing alcoholic beverages. Reformers believed alcohol was often responsible for crime, poverty, and violence against women and children.

Two major national organizations, the **Woman's Christian Temperance Union** (WCTU) and the Anti-Saloon League, led an organized crusade against alcohol. **Frances Willard** headed the WCTU from 1879 to 1898. Willard made the WCTU a powerful force for temperance and for the rights of women.

Many reformers spread the anti-alcohol message in Protestant churches. Billy Sunday, a former baseball player turned Presbyterian evangelist, preached that the saloons were "the parent of crimes and the mother of sins." Starting in 1900, evangelist **Carry Nation** took her campaign right to the source. With a hatchet in

FOCUS ON NEW YORK

DAILY LIFE
Today, the Henry Street Settlement continues to provide social services, such as after-school programs and crisis counseling, for Manhattan's Lower East Side. The settlement also provides arts education for the community. It established the Abrons Arts Center, which offers classes in music, dance, theater, and visual arts.

1920 The Nineteenth Amendment is ratified, guaranteeing women the right to vote.

1900

1972 Congress approves the women's Equal Rights Amendment to the Constitution, but it fails to win ratification by the required 38 states.

2000

2004 Some 73 percent of women were registered to vote in the 2004 election, and a high proportion of them, about 65 percent, did vote.

Elizabeth Cady STANTON
1815–1902

Born in Johnstown, New York, Elizabeth Cady Stanton spent her life campaigning for human rights. After the Civil War, however, Stanton took a surprising stand. A devoted abolitionist, Stanton decided, along with Susan B. Anthony and Sojourner Truth, not to support the Fourteenth and Fifteenth Amendments, which granted citizenship rights and the vote to male African Americans over the age of twenty-one. Stanton rejected the amendments because they specifically excluded rights for women. Stanton's position led to a fracture in what had been a strong alliance between abolitionists and women's suffragists.

Predict How might Stanton's campaign against those amendments have affected the women's suffrage movement?

one hand and a Bible in the other, she smashed up saloons in Kansas and urged other women to do the same. Nation's fiery speeches, dramatic raids, and canny sense of publicity made her a national figure in the temperance cause.

Prohibitionists eventually won Congress to their cause. In 1917 Congress proposed the **Eighteenth Amendment**, which prohibited the manufacture, sale, and distribution of alcoholic beverages.

The states ratified the amendment in 1919. The Eighteenth Amendment proved so unpopular, however, that it was repealed in 1933.

Civil rights African American women fought for many of the same causes as white women, such as ending poverty, promoting child welfare, fighting for better wages and safer workplace conditions, and fighting alcohol abuse. Yet these women had the added burden of waging their battles in an atmosphere of discrimination. Many African American women discovered that they were not welcome in most reform organizations. So they formed their own.

One of the largest organizations of African American women was founded in 1896. The **National Association of Colored Women** (NACW) included some of the most prominent women within the African American community, such as antilynching activist Ida B. Wells-Barnett and Margaret Murray Washington of the Tuskegee Institute. Harriet Tubman, the famous conductor on the Underground Railroad during the 1850s, also became a member. By 1916 the organization had more than 100,000 members.

The NACW campaigned against poverty, segregation, and lynchings. It fought against the persistence of Jim Crow laws that denied African Americans the right to vote. Eventually, the NACW also began to campaign for temperance and women's suffrage. The organization formed settlement houses, hospitals, and schools.

READING CHECK Identifying the Main Idea
What did women learn through their reform work that would be useful to them politically?

Rise of the Women's Suffrage Movement

When the delegates to the Seneca Falls Convention met in 1848 to campaign for women's rights, little did they know how long it would take for women to win the right to vote. It took 72 more years of organizing, campaigning, and persuading before they won the right to vote.

The Fifteenth Amendment After the Civil War, suffragists, who had supported abolition, called for granting women the vote as well as newly freed African American men. They were told that women would have to wait. Abolitionist Horace Greeley urged them to "remember that this is the Negro hour and your first duty is to go through the state and plead his claims." Suffragists waited.

Many of these suffragists were not satisfied by the ratification of the Fifteenth Amendment in 1868. The amendment gave the vote to African American men but not to women. It prohibited denying the right to vote "on account of race, color, or previous condition of servitude."

Women organize Now suffragists were spurred to action. In 1869 **Elizabeth Cady Stanton** and **Susan B. Anthony** formed the National Woman Suffrage Association. The NWSA campaigned for a constitutional amendment to give women the vote. It dealt with other issues that concerned women as well, such as labor organizing. In 1872 some NWSA members supported Victoria Woodhull, the first woman presidential candidate.

Meanwhile, the American Woman Suffrage Association (AWSA) was founded in 1869, with Henry Ward Beecher as its president. Unlike the NWSA, the American Woman Suffrage

Association focused exclusively on winning the right to vote on a state-by-state basis. It also aligned itself with the Republican Party.

Very soon, suffragists began to rejoice at some victories in the West. In 1869 Wyoming Territory became the first to grant women the vote. Utah Territory followed a year later. Before women nationwide won the vote, legislators in 12 states granted women the right to vote.

Susan B. Anthony tests the law

A tireless campaigner for the women's suffrage cause, Susan B. Anthony wrote pamphlets and made speeches. She also testified before every Congress between 1869 and 1906 on behalf of women's suffrage. In 1872 she and three of her sisters staged a dramatic protest. They registered to vote, and on Election Day they voted in Rochester, New York. Two weeks later they were arrested for "knowingly, wrongfully and unlawfully" voting for a representative to the Congress of the United States.

Before her trial began, Anthony delivered an address in which she spelled out many reasons that justice required that women be given the right to vote.

HISTORY'S VOICES

> **"**One-half of the people of this nation today are utterly powerless to blot from the statute books an unjust law, or to write there a new and a just one. The women, . . . are [the] half of the people left wholly at the mercy of the other half, in direct violation of the spirit and letter of the declarations of the framers of this government, every one of which was based on the immutable [undeniable] principle of equal rights to all.**"**
>
> —Susan B. Anthony, 1872

At her trial, the judge refused to allow Anthony to testify on her own behalf, ruled her guilty, and fined her $100. Anthony refused to pay the fine, hoping to force the judge to

THE IMPACT TODAY

Government

Some 65 women served as representatives and 14 as senators in the 2005–2006 U.S. Congress. Representative Nancy Pelosi of California was minority leader in the House, the highest-ranking position ever held by a woman in Congress.

PRIMARY SOURCES

Political Cartoon

In 1912 cartoonist Laura E. Foster addressed an issue faced by even more women today: the tough choices relating to careers and home life.

The woman climbing the stairs represents women seeking career success.

The prize of Fame at the top of the stairs represents the goal that some people believed suffragists sought.

LONELINESS
ANXIETY
STRIFE
SUFFRAGE
DISAPPOINTMENT
FLATTERY
PROFESSIONAL TRIUMPH
ARTISTIC SUCCESS
CAREER
ADMIRATION
SOCIAL ACHIEVEMENT
AMBITION
HOME
CHILDREN
MARRIAGE

The words at the bottom imply the traditional women's values—home, children, marriage—the woman is leaving behind. The children represent those left behind by the woman's search for personal success.

Skills FOCUS **READING LIKE A HISTORIAN**

1. **Interpreting Political Cartoons** How do the words change as the stairs lead up to the top?
2. **Identifying Points of View** What point is the cartoonist trying to make with this cartoon?

See **Skills Handbook**, pp. H28–H29, H31

arrest her and create a case that could be tried through the courts. The judge, however, did not imprison Anthony for refusing to pay the fine, thus denying her the right to appeal her case to a higher court.

In 1875 the Supreme Court ruled that even though women were citizens, citizenship did not give them the right to vote. The Court decided it was up to the states to grant or withhold that right. Suffrage associations therefore continued their strategy of trying to persuade each state legislature to grant women the vote.

Anti-suffrage arguments Opponents of the suffrage movement put forth a variety of arguments. Some believed that voting would interfere with women's duties at home or would destroy families altogether. Others claimed that women did not have the education or experience to be competent voters. Still others believed the notion that most American women did not want to vote. They said that it was unfair for suffragists to try to force the vote on those unwilling women.

Significant business interests also opposed women's suffrage. The liquor industry feared that women would vote for Prohibition. As women became more active in other reform movements—such as food and drug safety,

ACADEMIC VOCABULARY

notion idea

worker safety, and child labor—business owners feared that women would vote for regulations that would drive up business costs.

Even some churches and clergy members spoke out against women's suffrage. They argued that marriage was a sacred bond in which the entire family was represented by the man. In that case, they believed that women did not need the vote.

Two organizations merge In 1890 the National Woman Suffrage Association and the American Woman Suffrage Association merged. They formed the **National American Woman Suffrage Association** (NAWSA) under the leadership of Elizabeth Cady Stanton. Susan B. Anthony served as NAWSA's president from 1892 to 1900. Anthony died in 1906. Her final public statement was "Failure is impossible."

Like Susan B. Anthony, most of the early suffragists did not live long enough to cast their ballots. In fact, when women nationwide finally won the vote in 1920, only one signer of the Seneca Falls Declaration—Charlotte Woodward, age 92—was still alive.

READING CHECK **Identifying Cause and Effect** What effect did the passage of the Fifteenth Amendment have on suffragists?

SECTION 2 ASSESSMENT

go.hrw.com
Online Quiz
Keyword: SD7 HP16

Reviewing Ideas, Terms, and People

1. a. Describe In the 1800s, what new opportunities did women in various social classes have outside the home?
b. Explain How did new opportunities change the way many women viewed their place in the public world?

2. a. Identify Write a sentence describing each of the following: **Prohibition, Carry Nation, Frances Willard, National Association of Colored Women**.
b. Analyze Why did many women choose to join the temperance movement?
c. Elaborate How were women's reform causes related to traditional roles in the home?

3. a. Recall What happened to **Susan B. Anthony** when she attempted to vote?
b. Analyze What effect did the Fifteenth Amendment have on the women's rights movement?
c. Elaborate Why do you think many suffragists decided to adopt a state-by-state strategy, rather than campaign for a constitutional amendment?

Critical Thinking

4. Comparing and Contrasting Copy the Venn diagram below and fill it out to show the ways in which the National Woman Suffrage Association and the American Woman Suffrage Association were similar and different.

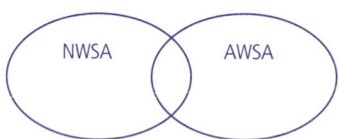

NWSA   AWSA

FOCUS ON WRITING

5. Persuasive Suppose you are a woman who has gained political experience in the abolitionist movement. Write a letter to the editor explaining your opposition to the exclusion of women from the proposed Fifteenth Amendment. Be sure to provide details to support your argument.

SECTION 3

Theodore Roosevelt's Square Deal

PI **3.2** Research and analyze the major themes and developments in New York State and United States history (e.g., colonization and settlement; Revolution and New National Period; immigration; expansion and reform era; Civil War and Reconstruction; the American labor movement; Great Depression; World Wars; contemporary United States).

BEFORE YOU READ

MAIN IDEA

Theodore Roosevelt used the power of the presidency to push for progressive reforms in business and in environmental policy.

READING FOCUS

1. What was Theodore Roosevelt's view of the role of the president?
2. How did Roosevelt attempt to regulate big business?
3. What was Roosevelt's philosophy about conserving the environment, and how did he carry out his philosophy?

KEY TERMS AND PEOPLE

Theodore Roosevelt
bully pulpit
Square Deal
Elkins Act
Hepburn Act
Upton Sinclair
Meat Inspection Act
Pure Food and Drug Act
John Muir
Newlands Reclamation Act
Gifford Pinchot

THE INSIDE STORY

Cowboy or politician? No one who knew "Teedie" Roosevelt at age 9 would have recognized the sturdy athlete who later cleaned up a corrupt New York City police department and led the Rough Riders in Cuba during the Spanish-American War. The young Roosevelt was sickly and shy. Family doctors forbade any sports or strenuous activity, so Teedie spent his time reading and studying natural history. Then as a teenager, **Theodore Roosevelt** energetically set about making himself into a new person. He took up boxing, tennis, horseback riding, and rowing. He fashioned an optimistic, vigorous personality that was to make him a successful politician.

Roosevelt came from a prominent New York family and attended Harvard University, but he grew to love the outdoors. He spent time in northern Maine and in the rugged Badlands of the Dakota territory, where he rode horses and hunted buffalo. When Roosevelt was 26, tragedy struck. Both his wife and his mother died unexpectedly. Trying to forget his grief, Roosevelt returned to his ranch in Dakota Territory.

For two years, Roosevelt lived and worked with cowboys, who came to admire his toughness as he rode in roundups and hunted bear, elk, and mountain lions. The westerners also liked the way he stood up to bullying rustlers who called him "four eyes" because of his thick glasses. After two years, Roosevelt's western adventure was over. He returned to New York and to politics. ◢

▶ **A young Theodore Roosevelt in 1880**

Prelude to the Presidency

Roosevelt's View of the Presidency

Theodore Roosevelt's rise to the governorship of New York in 1898 spelled big trouble for the Republican political machine in New York. To rid themselves of the Progressive reformer, party bosses came up with a clever plan: They got Roosevelt nominated as vice president, a job with little power at the time.

ACADEMIC VOCABULARY

framework the basic concepts that constitute a way of viewing reality

Taking office However, the party bosses—and the nation—were shocked when anarchist Leon Czolgosz (CHAWL-gawsh) fatally shot President William McKinley in 1901. Theodore Roosevelt, the energetic reformer, now held the highest office in the land.

Roosevelt was just 42 years old when he took office—the youngest person ever to become president. During the late 1800s, most presidents had taken a hands-off approach to governing. Not Teddy Roosevelt. He saw the White House as a bully pulpit—a powerful platform to publicize important issues and seek support for his policies. With great enthusiasm and energy, Roosevelt brought new momentum to the Progressive movement.

The coal strike of 1902 Soon after the new president took office, some 150,000 Pennsylvania coal miners struck for higher wages, shorter hours, and recognition of their union. The strike gave Roosevelt an opportunity to define his view of the presidency.

As winter neared, Roosevelt feared what might happen if the strike were not resolved. Northern cities depended on Pennsylvania coal for heating. The president felt compelled to use his influence "to bring to an end a situation which has become literally intolerable."

Roosevelt urged the mine owners and the striking workers to accept arbitration. In the arbitration process, two opposing sides agree to allow a third party to settle a dispute. The workers agreed to accept arbitration, but the mine owners refused. As winter drew nearer, Roosevelt threatened to take over the mines. The threat finally convinced the mine owners to agree to his arbitration plan.

After a three-month investigation, the arbitrators announced their decision. They gave the workers a shorter workday and higher pay but did not require the mining companies to recognize the union. For the first time, the federal government had intervened in a strike to protect the interests of the workers and the public. Satisfied, Roosevelt pronounced the compromise a "square deal."

The Square Deal The Square Deal became Roosevelt's 1904 campaign slogan and the framework for his entire presidency. He promised to "see that each [person] is given a square deal, because he is entitled to no more and should receive no less." Roosevelt's promise revealed his belief that the needs of workers, business, and consumers should be balanced. Roosevelt's Square Deal called for limiting the power of trusts, promoting public health and safety, and improving working conditions.

The popular president faced no opposition for the nomination with his party. In the general election Roosevelt cruised to victory, easily defeating his Democratic opponent, Judge Alton Parker of New York.

READING CHECK Identifying the Main Idea
What was Roosevelt's Square Deal?

Regulating Big Business

Roosevelt believed that big business was essential to the nation's growth, but he also believed companies should behave responsibly.

HISTORY'S VOICES

❝We demand that big business give the people a square deal; in return we must insist that when anyone engaged in big business honestly endeavors to do right he shall himself be given a square deal.❞

—Theodore Roosevelt

Roosevelt focused a great deal of attention on regulating large corporations. Addressing Congress in 1902, Roosevelt stated, "We are . . . determined that they [corporations] shall be so handled as to subserve [serve] the public good. We draw the line against misconduct, not against wealth."

Trust-busting In 1901 tycoons J. P. Morgan, James J. Hill, and E. H. Harriman joined their railroads together to eliminate competition. Their company, the Northern Securities Company, dominated railroad shipping from Chicago to the Northwest.

The following year, President Roosevelt directed the U.S. attorney general to sue the Northern Securities Company for violating the Sherman Antitrust Act. In 1904 the Supreme Court ruled that the monopoly did violate the Sherman Antitrust Act, and it ordered the corporation dissolved.

The ruling proved to be a watershed. An encouraged Roosevelt administration launched a vigorous trust-busting campaign. It filed dozens of lawsuits against monopolies and trusts that it believed were not in the public interest.

The size of the trust was not the issue. What mattered was whether a particular trust was good or bad for the American public. The Roosevelt administration went after the bad trusts: the ones that sold inferior products, competed unfairly, or corrupted public officials.

Regulating the railroads Another way to ensure that businesses competed more fairly was through regulation. Railroads commonly granted rebates to their best customers. This meant that huge corporations

Bully Pulpit

NO MOLLY-CODDLING HERE

THE GRANGER COLLECTION, NEW YORK

Skills FOCUS **READING LIKE A HISTORIAN**

Far left, Roosevelt is making good use of the bully pulpit. The cartoon shows Roosevelt as a man who will not "mollycoddle," or indulge, big business.

1. **Interpreting Political Cartoons** What does the reference to big business mean?

2. **Identifying Points of View** What does the cartoon say about Roosevelt's efforts? Explain.

See **Skills Handbook**, p. H28–H29, H31

Theodore ROOSEVELT
1858–1919

Author, athlete, and Nobel Prize–winning statesman, Theodore Roosevelt forged a presidential style that was an extension of the fascinating life he had led. Doing battle with corporate trusts and crusading for the environment were just other adventures for the battle-ready hero and nature lover.

Roosevelt embraced the "strenuous life" in what he called "the arena" of public service. Whether reforming the New York City police department, defying corrupt party bosses, or leading soldiers in the Spanish-American War, Roosevelt was always, in his words, "daring greatly." As president, Roosevelt focused on "trust-busting" and environmental conservation at home and pursued a "muscular" foreign policy, using an enlarged U.S. Navy to project American power. His intervention in Central America led to the founding of Panama and, later, the building of the Panama Canal.

"TR" even survived a brush with death in 1912. Shot in the chest by a would-be assassin, he proceeded to give a 90-minute campaign speech. He told the stunned crowd, "It takes more than that to kill a bull moose."

Interpret How did Roosevelt's life affect his style of leadership?

---

paid significantly less to ship their products than small farmers or small businesses. In 1903 Congress passed the **Elkins Act,** which prohibited railroads from accepting rebates. The Elkins Act ensured that all customers paid the same rates for shipping their products.

The **Hepburn Act** of 1906 strengthened the Interstate Commerce Commission (ICC), giving it the power to set maximum railroad rates. It also gave the ICC the power to regulate other companies that were engaged in interstate commerce.

Protecting consumers Roosevelt also responded to growing public dismay about practices of the food and drug industries. Some food producers, drug companies, and meat packers were selling dangerous products to an unknowing public.

Food producers, for example, resorted to clever tricks to pass off tainted foods. Some poultry sellers added formaldehyde, a chemical used in embalming dead bodies, to old eggs to hide their foul odor. Unwary consumers bought the tainted food and were tricked into thinking it was healthy.

Many drug companies were equally unconcerned for their customer's welfare. Some sold medicines that simply did not work. Others marketed patent, or nonprescription, medicines containing dangerous narcotic drugs. Products such as Dr. James' Soothing Syrup, intended to soothe babies' teething pain, contained the drug heroin. Gowan's Pneumonia Cure contained the addictive painkiller opium.

Few industries fell into greater public disrepute than the meatpacking business. The novelist **Upton Sinclair** exposed the wretched and unsanitary conditions at meatpacking plants in his 1906 novel *The Jungle*.

HISTORY'S VOICES

“There would be meat stored in great piles in rooms; and the water from leaky roofs would drip over it, and thousands of rats would race about on it. . . . A man could run his hand over these piles of meat and sweep off handfuls of the dried dung of rats. . . . The packers would put poisoned bread out for them; they would die, and then rats, bread, and meat would go into the hoppers together.”

—Upton Sinclair, *The Jungle*, 1906

Sinclair's novel ignited a firestorm of criticism aimed at meatpackers. Reformers and an outraged public called for change. Roosevelt ordered Secretary of Agriculture James Wilson to investigate the conditions in the packing houses. Wilson's final report made for gruesome reading.

"We saw meat shoveled from filthy wooden floors, piled on tables rarely washed, pushed from room to room in rotten box carts. In all of which processes it [the meat] was in the way of gathering dirt, splinters, floor filth, and the expectoration [saliva] of tuberculous and other diseased workers."

The Wilson report shocked the U.S. Congress into action. In 1906 it enacted two groundbreaking consumer protection laws. The first, the **Meat Inspection Act**, required federal inspection of meat shipped across state lines. The **Pure Food and Drug Act** forbade the manufacture, sale, or transportation of food and patent medicine containing harmful ingredients. The law also required food and medicine containers to carry accurate ingredient labels.

READING CHECK **Summarizing** What measures did the Roosevelt administration take to regulate business and protect consumers?

Environmental Conservation

In the late 1800s people acted as if the United States had an unending supply of natural resources. Lumber companies cleared large tracts of forest lands. Farmers plowed up the Great Plains. Ranchers' cattle and sheep overgrazed the prairies. Mining companies clogged rivers and cluttered the land with their refuse. Cities dumped sewage into rivers and garbage onto the land.

Roosevelt, however, believed that each generation had a duty to protect and conserve natural resources for future generations.

HISTORY'S VOICES

❝We of an older generation can get along with what we have, . . . but in your full manhood and womanhood you will want what nature once so bountifully supplied and man so thoughtlessly destroyed; and because of that want you will reproach us, not for what we have used, but for what we have wasted.❞

—Theodore Roosevelt

Before Roosevelt's presidency, the federal government had left the nation's natural resources largely unregulated. Business needs had always taken priority over the environment. But Roosevelt recognized that natural resources were limited, and he believed their use needed to be controlled.

In 1903 Roosevelt joined famed naturalist **John Muir** for a camping trip in Yosemite National Park in California. Muir had played a pivotal role in convincing the government to protect and preserve Yosemite. "Unfortunately, God cannot save trees from fools," Muir had observed. "Only the government can do that."

Despite their friendly camping trip, Muir and Roosevelt held different views about conservation. Muir wanted the entire wilderness to be preserved in its natural state. Roosevelt believed that conservation involved the active management of public lands for a variety of uses. Some lands should be preserved as wilderness. Other lands should be put to more directly economical productive uses.

The **Newlands Reclamation Act** of 1902 reflected Roosevelt's beliefs. It allowed the federal government to create irrigation projects to make dry lands productive. The projects would be funded from money raised by selling off public lands. The Roosevelt administration launched more than 20 reclamation projects.

Linking TO Today

National Park System

Theodore Roosevelt will be remembered as the first champion of conservation. Yet before him, some Americans worked to protect natural wonders.

In 1872 Congress passed a law that set aside land in Wyoming, Montana, and Idaho as Yellowstone National Park. Yellowstone became the world's first national park.

Over time, the federal government founded more national parks across the country. In 1919 parts of the Grand Canyon in Arizona became a national park. Shenandoah National Park in Virginia was founded in 1935. Biscayne National Park in Florida was established in 1980, and Cuyahoga Valley National Park in Ohio was created in 2000.

While many parks preserve land and wildlife, other parks throughout the world preserve cultural history. Mesa Verde National Park in Colorado is famous for its Cliff Palace, a settlement built by ancestral Pueblo Indians about 800 years ago. In the Caribbean, Virgin Islands National Park is home to ancient ruins and Danish sugar plantations from the 1700s and 1800s.

In the Yellowstone tradition, national parks have been created in many countries. Meanwhile, debate continues over how to both save and use public lands.

Making Generalizations Why do some national parks preserve cultural elements as well as natural ones?

Visitors enjoy the wonders of Colorado's Mesa Verde National Park.

FEDERAL CONSERVATION LANDS IN THE WEST, 1908

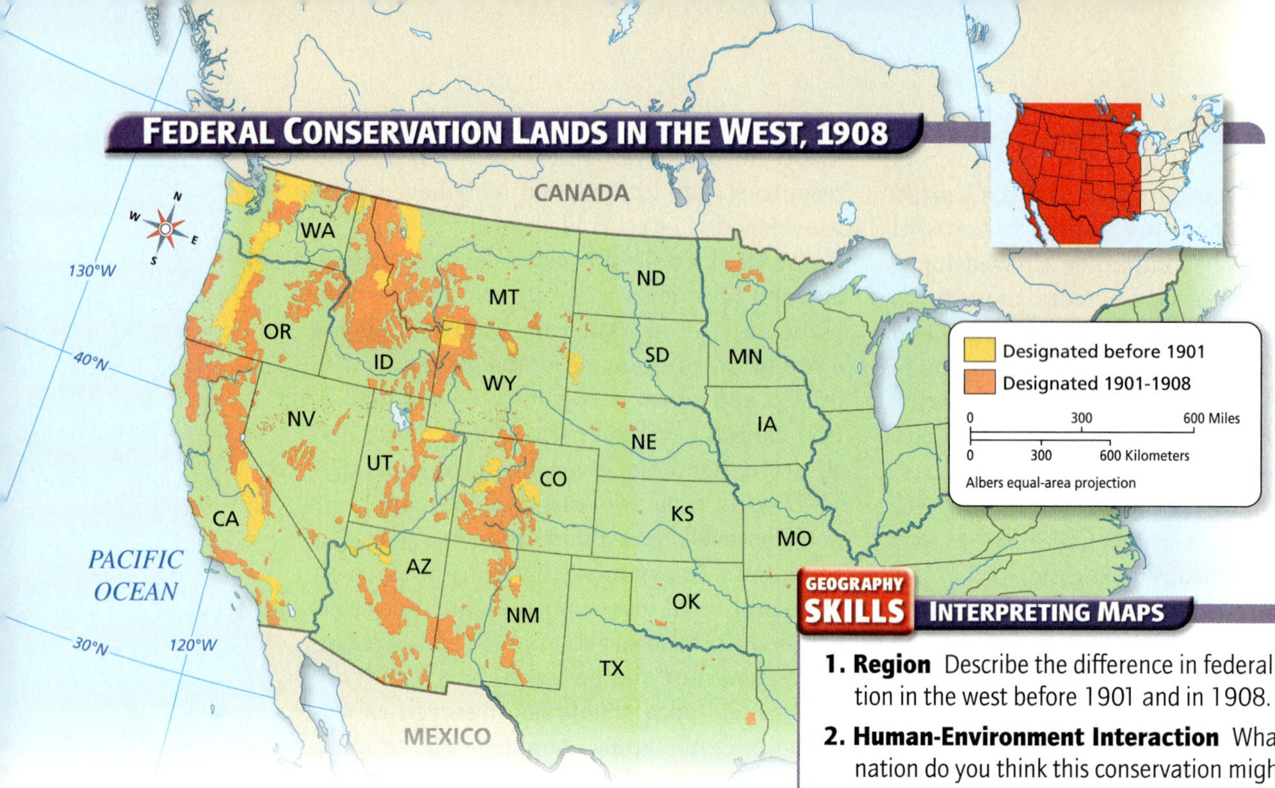

CANADA

WA

MT

ND

OR

ID

SD

MN

WY

NV

IA

UT

NE

CO

CA

KS

MO

AZ

OK

NM

TX

PACIFIC
OCEAN

130°W

40°N

30°N

120°W

MEXICO

Designated before 1901
Designated 1901–1908

0   300   600 Miles
0   300   600 Kilometers
Albers equal-area projection

GEOGRAPHY SKILLS **INTERPRETING MAPS**

1. **Region** Describe the difference in federal land conservation in the west before 1901 and in 1908.
2. **Human-Environment Interaction** What effect on the nation do you think this conservation might have?

See **Skills Handbook**, p. H20

Another conservationist, **Gifford Pinchot** (PIN-shoh), shared Roosevelt's view. Pinchot first came up with the word *conservation* to describe the need to protect the country's natural environment. He wrote: "The conservation of natural resources is the key to the future. It is the key to the safety and prosperity of the American people." Pinchot believed scientific management of natural resources was crucial to sustaining them to serve the nation's needs.

In 1905 the Roosevelt administration established the U.S. Forest Service with Pinchot as its chief. During Roosevelt's presidency, the Forest Service added nearly 150 million acres to the national forests, controlled their use, and regulated their harvest.

The Antiquities Act of 1906 led to the creation of 18 national monuments during Roosevelt's presidency. For many historians, environmental conservation is Roosevelt's greatest legacy.

READING CHECK **Contrasting** How did Roosevelt's and Muir's views of natural resources differ?

SECTION 3 ASSESSMENT

go.hrw.com
Online Quiz
Keyword: SD7 HP16

Reviewing Ideas, Terms, and People

1. **a. Recall** How did Roosevelt use the **bully pulpit** to promote the **Square Deal**?
   b. Evaluate How was Roosevelt's response to the coal strike symbolic of his view of the presidency?

2. **a. Describe** How did Roosevelt engage in trust-busting?
   b. Draw Conclusions Why did the food companies knowingly sell spoiled food?
   c. Predict What impact would Roosevelt's policies have on consumer protection in America?

3. **a. Identify** Who was **Gifford Pinchot**?
   b. Contrast How did Roosevelt's view of natural resources differ from the policies of past presidents?

Critical Thinking

4. **Summarizing** Copy the chart below and record major legislation regulating business during Roosevelt's presidency.

Law	Purpose

FOCUS ON WRITING

5. **Persuasive** As a consumer in 1906, write a letter to Congress supporting the Pure Food and Drug bill.

Taft and Wilson

BEFORE YOU READ

MAIN IDEA

Progressive reforms continued during the Taft and Wilson presidencies, focusing on business, banking, and women's suffrage.

READING FOCUS

1. How did Taft's approach to progressivism split the Republican Party?
2. What was Wilson's New Freedom reform plan?
3. How did women gain the right to vote in national elections?
4. How did progressivism affect African Americans?

KEY TERMS AND PEOPLE

William Howard Taft
Sixteenth Amendment
Hiram W. Johnson
Woodrow Wilson
New Freedom
Federal Reserve Act
Clayton Antitrust Act
Alice Paul
Nineteenth Amendment
Brownsville incident

PI 1.1 Analyze the development of American culture, explaining how ideas, values, beliefs, and traditions have changed over time and how they united all Americans.

THE INSIDE STORY

Can politics and friendship mix? In 1904 Theodore Roosevelt told the country he would not seek re-election as president. He kept his word. Instead, when the 1908 election approached, Roosevelt put forth a successor: his friend and close adviser **William Howard Taft**.

The two men were very different. Roosevelt was an energetic crusader for reform. He held an expansive view of the president's powers and was not afraid to set new precedent. Taft was an easygoing, cautious lawyer with a more restrained view of the presidency. He expressed some discomfort at Roosevelt's activism, saying that Roosevelt "ought more often to have admitted the legal way of reaching the same ends." Still, he served the president loyally for four years as secretary of war and, though his main ambition was to become the chief justice of the Supreme Court, he agreed to run.

Taft didn't enjoy the campaign. He called it "one of the most uncomfortable four months of my life." But he pledged loyalty to the Roosevelt program, and with the president's strong backing he won the 1908 election. In March of 1909 the reluctant candidate found himself living in the White House.

Roosevelt soon regretted his decision. He believed that Taft departed from Progressive ideals on tariffs and the environment. Roosevelt charged that Taft "completely twisted around the policies I advocated." The onetime friends were to become bitter foes. ◢

THE GRANGER COLLECTION, NEW YORK

TAFT Becomes PRESIDENT

▲ Roosevelt crowns his successor, believing Taft will carry on his work.

Progressivism under Taft

In the election of 1908, Taft faced three-time Democratic candidate William Jennings Bryan. The Democrats lost the election by a wide margin in the electoral college and by nearly 1.27 million popular votes.

A cautious man, President Taft worked to secure Roosevelt's progressive reforms rather than to build upon them. Still, he supported several reforms, such as creating a Department of Labor to enforce labor laws and increasing national forest reserves.

The Taft administration also is credited with passage of the **Sixteenth Amendment.** Introduced during the Taft years but ratified in 1913 after Taft left office, the Sixteenth Amendment granted Congress the power to levy taxes based on an individual's income. Progressives had supported a nationwide income tax as a way to pay for government programs more fairly.

Despite these reforms, President Taft lost the support of most Progressive Republicans.

The trouble began early, in April 1909, with the passage of a bill on tariffs, or taxes charged on imports or exports.

The House had passed a version of the bill, which lowered tariffs on imported goods. When the bill went to the Senate, though, Senator Nelson Aldrich of Rhode Island and others added so many amendments that it became a high-tariff bill. Nevertheless, Taft signed the Payne-Aldrich Tariff into law. Progressives were outraged because they saw tariff reduction as a key step in lowering the prices of consumer goods.

Taft also alienated Progressive supporters of conservation. His secretary of the interior, Richard Ballinger, was accused of impeding a government fraud investigation of public coal-land deals in Alaska. When Gifford Pinchot, head of the U.S. Forest Service, charged Ballinger with sabotaging conservation efforts, Taft fired Pinchot.

Progressives believed that the Ballinger-Pinchot affair showed Taft's lack of commitment to conservation. Theodore Roosevelt, who had put forth Taft for the presidency, refused to support Taft after the Ballinger-Pinchot affair.

Split in the Republican Party In the 1910 congressional elections, Roosevelt campaigned for Progressive Republicans who opposed Taft. Roosevelt proposed a program called New Nationalism, a set of laws to protect workers, ensure public health, and regulate business.

Some reformers saw the New Nationalism as a revival of the progressive spirit. Roosevelt's help on the campaign trail was not enough to ensure a Republican victory, though. Republicans lost control of the House of Representatives for the first time in 16 years.

THE ELECTION OF 1912

Candidate	Political Affiliation	Electoral Votes	Popular Votes
Woodrow Wilson	Democratic	435	6,293,454
Theodore Roosevelt	Progressive	88	4,119,538
William Howard Taft	Republican	8	3,484,980

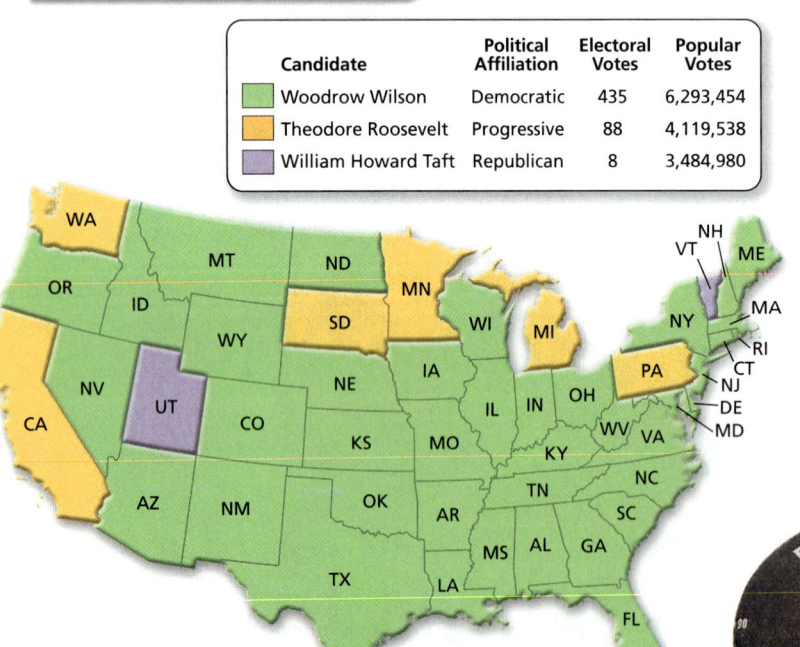

GEOGRAPHY SKILLS INTERPRETING MAPS

Taft made the poorest showing of any president seeking reelection. Wilson won with only about 42 percent of the popular vote.

Region In comparison, how did Wilson fare in the electoral vote?

See **Skills Handbook**, p. H21

By the presidential election of 1912, the Republican Party was badly fractured. Many Republicans continued to support Taft. When the Republican Party nominated Taft as its presidential candidate, the more Progressive Republicans broke away to form the new Progressive ("Bull Moose") Party. Theodore Roosevelt led the ticket, and the popular governor of California, **Hiram W. Johnson**, was their candidate for vice president.

With the Republicans split between Taft and Roosevelt, Democrat **Woodrow Wilson** glided to victory. Wilson received 435 electoral votes, while Roosevelt received 88 and Taft received 8. Socialist candidate Eugene V. Debs won more than 900,000 popular votes but no electoral votes.

READING CHECK Identifying Cause and Effect What effect did the split in the Republican Party have on the election of 1912?

Wilson's New Freedom

Wilson came to office with a reputation as a zealous reformer. As governor of New Jersey, he had fought political machines, approved a law permitting direct primaries, and enacted a program to compensate injured workers. During the campaign, he proposed an ambitious plan of reform that he called the **New Freedom.** The New Freedom platform called for tariff reductions, banking reform, and stronger antitrust legislation—causes dear to the hearts of Progressives.

Tariff reduction Wilson's first priority as president was to lower tariffs. Wilson waged a tireless campaign to persuade Congress. He even appeared at a joint session of Congress, the first president since John Adams to do so. In October 1913 Congress passed the Underwood Tariff Act. This law reduced tariffs to their lowest levels in more than 50 years.

Tariff reduction meant that the government had less income, however. How would the nation make up the shortfall?

The answer was an income tax. The Underwood Tariff Act also introduced a graduated income tax, which would assess people at different rates according to their income levels. Wealthier people would pay more; poorer people would pay less.

Banking reform President Wilson's next target for reform was the banking system. Historically bank failures had been common. Banks collapsed when too many people withdrew their deposits at the same time. What could be done to keep the banks' doors open, while still allowing people to withdraw their money when they wanted to?

The answer was the **Federal Reserve Act.** This law, passed in 1913, created a central fund from which banks could borrow to prevent collapse during a financial panic.

The Federal Reserve Act created a three-tier banking system. At the top was the Federal Reserve Board, a group of officials appointed by the president and charged with running the system. On the second level were 12 Federal Reserve banks, which served other banks rather than individuals. On the third level were the private banks, which could borrow from the Federal Reserve banks as they needed to. The Federal Reserve Act put the nation's banking system under the supervision of the federal government for the first time.

Stronger antitrust laws Congress had passed the Sherman Antitrust Act in 1890 to limit the power of monopolies. But lax enforcement and loopholes in the law allowed a number of unfair business practices to persist.

At President Wilson's urging, Congress passed the **Clayton Antitrust Act,** which clarified and extended the Sherman Antitrust Act. Passed in 1914, the Clayton Antitrust Act prohibited companies from buying the stock of competing companies in order to form a monopoly. The law also supported workers by making strikes, boycotts, and peaceful picketing legal for the first time.

In another effort to make business fairer, Wilson supported the creation of the Federal Trade Commission (FTC) by Congress in 1915. The FTC enforced antitrust laws and got tough on companies that used deceptive advertising. It also had the power to undertake special investigations of businesses. Progressives were displeased, however, when Wilson appointed to the commission a number of people who were sympathetic to business.

READING CHECK Identifying Problems and Solutions What were the three major areas of reform in Wilson's New Freedom?

How to Win the Vote

Suffragist Carrie Chapman Catt believed that women had to work with lawmakers to win the vote.

Alice Paul believed that picketing, imprisonment, and hunger strikes would win suffrage.

" Every day that the Government sends women to prison for holding harmless banners . . . makes the position of the Government more indefensible and therefore strengthens our position."

Alice Paul,
1917

" When thirty-six state associations . . . [agree] to get the Amendment submitted by Congress and ratified by their respective state legislatures; when they live up to their compact by running a red-hot, never ceasing campaign . . . we can get the Amendment through. "

Carrie Chapman Catt,
1916

Skills FOCUS   READING LIKE A HISTORIAN

Identifying Points of View Summarize each woman's approach to the struggle for voting rights.
See **Skills Handbook**, p. H28–H29

Women Gain the Vote

The struggle for women's suffrage took some dramatic turns during Wilson's time in office, highlighted by a split in the ranks of suffrage supporters over the best way to win the vote. The National American Woman Suffrage Association (NAWSA) favored a state-by-state approach. But by 1901 just four western states had given women full voting rights.

Frustrated by this slow progress, in 1913 two activists, **Alice Paul** and Lucy Burns, broke away from NAWSA and formed the Congressional Union for Woman Suffrage. Renamed the National Woman's Party (NWP) in 1916, the group focused on passage of a federal constitutional amendment for women's suffrage. Paul and Burns used new tactics learned from the British suffrage movement. The NWP members picketed the White House in January 1917, chaining themselves to the railings. Many were arrested. Some went on hunger strikes in prison. The dramatic efforts of the NWP protesters brought renewed attention to the suffrage cause.

Meanwhile, the state-by-state approach was gaining momentum. In 1915 Massachusetts, New Jersey, New York, and Pennsylvania held special referendums on women's suffrage. The motions were all defeated, but NAWSA's membership grew to nearly 2 million.

Under the energetic leadership of Carrie Chapman Catt, NAWSA launched a new strategy in 1916 to campaign for suffrage on both the state and federal levels. When the United States entered World War I in 1917, leaders of the movement—along with millions of American women—lent strong support to the war effort. Women's patriotism helped weaken opposition to suffrage.

The work of suffragists convinced members of the House and Senate to support a constitutional amendment. Even President Wilson lent his support, in a speech in 1918. Proposed by Congress in 1919 and ratified in 1920, the **Nineteenth Amendment** finally gave women full voting rights.

READING CHECK   **Contrasting** Explain how the tactics used by NAWSA and the NWP differed.

Progressivism and the Rights of African Americans

The Progressive movement achieved some remarkable successes. But progressive efforts at reform had limits, particularly when it came to securing the rights of African Americans.

Theodore Roosevelt compiled a mixed record concerning the treatment of African Americans. In 1901 he invited Booker T. Washington to the White House, becoming the first U.S. president to entertain an African American as a dinner guest there. Roosevelt also refused to bow to pressure to withdraw his appointment of an African American collector of tariffs in South Carolina.

HISTORY'S VOICES

❝ I cannot consent to take the position that the doorway of hope—the door of opportunity—is to be shut upon any man, no matter how worthy, purely upon the grounds of race or color. Such an attitude would, according to my contentions, be fundamentally wrong. **❞**

—Theodore Roosevelt

However, Roosevelt's reaction to an event in 1906 in Brownsville, Texas, disappointed African Americans. Twelve members of the African American 25th Infantry were accused of going on a shooting spree in town. The members of the 25th were told that if no one accepted responsibility, they would all be dishonorably discharged. None came forward. Roosevelt signed the papers discharging 167 African American soldiers, denying them all back pay and canceling their pensions. Years later, the truth came out that the soldiers involved in the Brownsville incident had been falsely accused. It wasn't until 1972 that their records were corrected to read "honorable discharge."

President Woodrow Wilson had a worse record on civil rights. He opposed a federal anti-lynching law and maintained that the matter should be dealt with at the state level. He also allowed cabinet members to segregate their offices, which had been desegregated since Reconstruction. In addition, during Wilson's administration, Congress passed a law making it a felony for blacks and whites to marry in the District of Columbia.

The outbreak of World War I in Europe in 1914 brought an end to the Progressive Era. As the United States edged closer to war, reformers found that Americans were more interested in the war and less eager to devote their energies to the reform movement. World War I, not progressivism, dominated President Wilson's second term in office.

READING CHECK **Drawing Conclusions** How would you characterize Roosevelt's and Wilson's records in regard to African Americans' rights?

SECTION 4 ASSESSMENT

go.hrw.com
Online Quiz
Keyword: SD7 HP16

Reviewing Ideas, Terms, and People

1. **a. Identify** What was the **Sixteenth Amendment**?
   b. Explain What did Progressives like and not like about Taft?
   c. Evaluate Do you think Roosevelt should have run for a third term, run as the Bull Moose candidate, or not run again?

2. **a. Recall** What was the **New Freedom**?
   b. Compare How did the **Clayton Antitrust Act** expand on the Sherman Antitrust Act?
   c. Predict How might the Federal Reserve Act protect the nation in the future?

3. **a. Identify** What was the **Nineteenth Amendment**?
   b. Elaborate How did the tactics of both NAWSA and the NWP succeed?

4. **a. Recall** What was the **Brownsville incident**?
   b. Make Inferences What do you suppose Wilson's reasons were for not supporting an antilynching law?

Critical Thinking

5. **Analyzing Information** Copy the chart below and record examples of the major elements of Wilson's New Freedom.

Wilson's New Freedom		
Tariff reduction	Banking reform	Antitrust legislation

FOCUS ON SPEAKING

6. **Persuasive** In 1913 Congress debated the bill that would become the Underwood Tariff Act. Suppose you are a member of Congress. Write a short speech in which you support or oppose a graduated income tax. Provide specific examples to support your argument.

Impact of Progressivism

Historical Context The documents below provide different types of information about the muckrakers, turn-of-the-century journalists and activists who publicized corruption and urban problems.

Task Examine the documents and answer the questions that follow. Then you will be asked to write an essay about the goals of muckrakers, using facts from the documents and from the chapter to support the position you take in your thesis statement.

ST 1.2 Analyze the decisions leading to major turning points in United States history. Investigate decisions and actions such as progressive reforms.

ST 3.2 Draw upon literary selections, historical documents, and accounts to analyze the roles played by different individuals and groups during the major eras in New York State and United States history.

DOCUMENT 1

The muckrakers got their nickname from a tool used to scrape up sewage and other unwanted garbage. The cartoon below reflects President Theodore Roosevelt's investigation into unsanitary conditions in meat packing plants. The investigation was sparked by muckraker Upton Sinclair's book *The Jungle*.

A NAUSEATING JOB, BUT IT MUST BE DONE
(President Roosevelt takes hold of the investigating muck-rake himself in the packing-house scandal.)

DOCUMENT 2

One leading muckraker was Lincoln Steffens, who wrote several articles on city corruption between 1902 and 1904. He published the collection as a book titled *The Shame of the Cities*. In this introduction to the book, he reflects on the central problem that faced all of the cities he studied.

"[P]olitics is business. That's what's the matter with it . . . But there is hope, not alone despair, in the commercialism of our politics. If our political leaders are to be always a lot of political merchants, they will supply any demand we may create. All we have to do is to establish a steady demand for good government . . . If we would leave parties to the politicians, and would vote not for the party, not even for men, but for the city, and the State, and the nation, we should rule parties, and cities, and States, and nation. If we would vote in mass on the more promising ticket, or, if the two are equally bad, would throw out the party that is in, and wait till the next election and then throw out the other party that is in—then, I say, the commercial politician would feel a demand for good government and he would supply it. That process would take a generation or more to complete, for the politicians now really do not know what good government is. But it has taken as long to develop bad government, and the politicians know what that is. If it would not 'go,' they would offer something else, and, if the demand were steady, they, being so commercial, would 'deliver the goods.'"

DOCUMENT 3

Florence Kelley was a social worker and lawyer who published numerous studies on urban problems. The following is from a study she conducted with Alzina P. Stevens on child labor in Chicago. It led to the first Illinois laws limiting work hours for women and children.

"The Ewing Street Italian colony furnishes a large contingent to the army of bootblacks and newsboys; lads who leave home at 2:30 A.M. to secure the first edition of the morning paper, selling each edition as it appears, and filling the intervals with blacking boots and tossing pennies, until, in the winter half of the year, they gather in the Polk Street Night-School, to doze in the warmth, or torture the teacher with the gamin [street kid] tricks acquired by day. For them, school is "a lark," or a peaceful retreat from parental beatings and shrieking juniors at home during the bitter nights of the Chicago winter.

There is no body of self-supporting children more in need of effective care than these newsboys and bootblacks. They are ill-fed, ill-housed, ill-clothed, illiterate, and wholly untrained and unfitted for any occupation. The only useful thing they learn at their work in common with the children who learn in school, is the rapid calculation of small sums in making change; and this does not go far enough to be of any practical value."

Skills FOCUS — READING LIKE A HISTORIAN

1. **a. Describe** Look at the political cartoon in Document 1. Describe what is going on.
   b. Interpret Do you think the artist sees the work of muckrakers as positive or negative? Explain.

2. **a. Compare** Refer to Document 2. To what does Steffens compare politics?
   b. Interpret Steffens blames the public for urban problems. Why?
   c. Evaluate Would Steffens's reform work? Explain.

3. **a. Recall** Refer to Document 3. What kinds of work do the boys do?

   b. Analyze Why do you think the boys see no importance in going to school?

4. **Document-Based Essay Question** Consider the question below and form a thesis statement. Using examples from Documents 1, 2, and 3, create an outline and write a short essay supporting your position.
   How did muckrakers change government and society?

   See **Skills Handbook**, p. H28–H29, H31–H33

Visual Summary: The Progressives

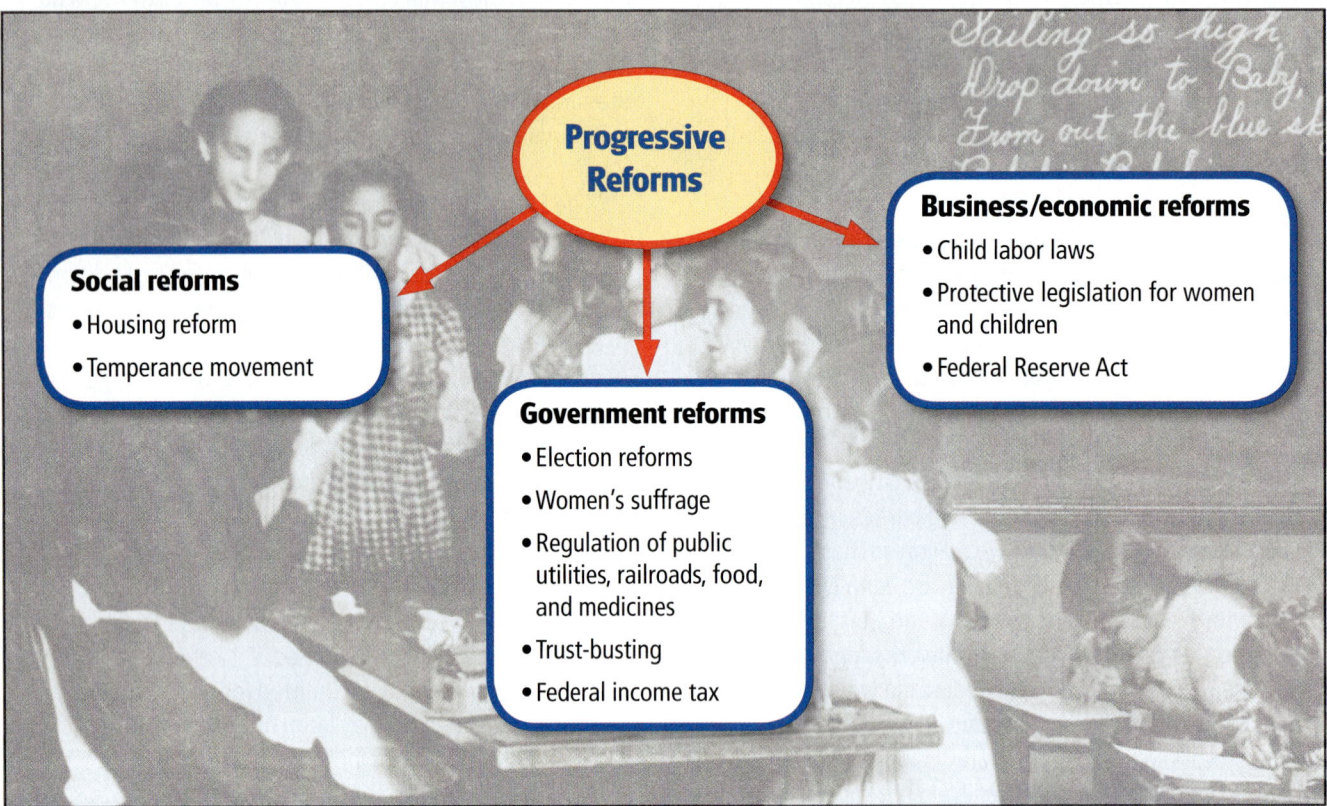

Progressive Reforms

Social reforms
- Housing reform
- Temperance movement

Government reforms
- Election reforms
- Women's suffrage
- Regulation of public utilities, railroads, food, and medicines
- Trust-busting
- Federal income tax

Business/economic reforms
- Child labor laws
- Protective legislation for women and children
- Federal Reserve Act

Reviewing Key Terms and People

Match each lettered definition with the correct numbered item.

a. A law that gave American women the right to vote

b. A reform that gives voters the power to put a proposed law on the ballot for public approval

c. A law that allowed Congress to levy taxes based on an individual's income

d. A law giving voters power to elect senators directly

e. A law that banned the manufacture and sale of alcoholic beverages in the United States

f. A women's organization that fought poverty, segregation, lynchings, and Jim Crow laws

g. Theodore Roosevelt's plan to balance the needs of workers, business, and consumers fairly

h. A law that created a central fund from which banks could borrow to prevent collapse

i. A women's suffrage group that favored a state-by-state approach

1. Eighteenth Amendment

2. Federal Reserve Act

3. initiative

4. National Association of Colored Women

5. National American Woman Suffrage Association

6. Sixteenth Amendment

7. Seventeenth Amendment

8. Nineteenth Amendment

9. Square Deal

History's Impact video program

Review the video to answer the closing question: What impact have labor laws had on American workers and industries?

Comprehension and Critical Thinking

SECTION 1 *(pp. 522–527)*

12. a. Analyze How did the commission plan make city government more effective?

b. Evaluate Why do you think that the city manager plan of government eventually became more popular than the commission plan?

SECTION 2 *(pp. 529–534)*

13. a. Recall What strategy did major women's suffrage organizations use to campaign for the vote?

b. Draw Conclusions How did the Supreme Court influence the decision to use this strategy?

c. Evaluate What were some possible advantages and disadvantages of adopting this strategy?

SECTION 3 *(pp. 535–540)*

14. a. Define What was the Elkins Act?

b. Analyze Why did the U.S. attorney general sue the Northern Securities Company?

c. Elaborate Why do you think that regulating the railroads was such a high priority for Roosevelt?

SECTION 4 *(pp. 541–545)*

15. a. Identify What were the three main reforms called for in the New Freedom?

b. Make Inferences How did all of those reforms relate to business in the United States?

c. Evaluate Why would the president be so concerned about business practices?

Using the Internet

go.hrw.com
Practice Online
Keyword: SD7 CH16

16. Upton Sinclair's novel *The Jungle* had a powerful effect on readers, including President Roosevelt. Using the keyword above, research Roosevelt's reaction to the novel. Then write a paragraph explaining how the novel moved Roosevelt to act.

Analyzing Primary Sources

Reading Like a Historian

This political cartoon shows President Theodore Roosevelt's support for William Howard Taft as his successor.

THE GRANGER COLLECTION, NEW YORK

17. Describe What relationship does the cartoon show?

18. Analyze Do you think the cartoonist supports Roosevelt's action?

Critical Reading

Read the passage in Section 4 that begins with the heading "Women Gain the Vote." Then answer the question that follows.

19. How did Alice Paul and Lucy Burns change the American women's suffrage movement?

A Their decision to adopt a state-by-state approach split the main suffrage organization.

B Their support of NAWSA led to success.

C Their use of tactics from the British movement focused new attention on the suffragists' cause.

D Their attention-getting tactics turned supporters away from the women's suffrage movement.

WRITING FOR THE SAT

Think about the following issue:

Roosevelt believed in achieving a balance between conservation and management of the nation's wilderness areas. He thought that some land should be kept in its natural state and some should be used to meet the nation's needs.

20. Assignment Do you agree with Roosevelt's beliefs about the proper use of the nation's wilderness areas? Write a short essay in which you develop your position on this issue. Support your point of view with reasoning and examples from your reading and studies.

Entering the WORLD STAGE

THE BIG PICTURE U.S. foreign relations took a new turn at the end of the nineteenth century. Global competition for empire led the United States into war against Spain and into military conflicts in Mexico. The United States had forged a new role as a world power.

New York Standards

Key Idea 2 Important ideas, social and cultural values, beliefs, and traditions from New York State and United States history illustrate the connections and interactions of people and events across time and from a variety of perspectives.

Key Idea 3 Study about the major social, political, economic, cultural, and religious developments in New York State and United States history involves learning about the important roles and contributions of individuals and groups.

Skills FOCUS READING LIKE A HISTORIAN

In the Battle of San Juan Hill, future president Theodore Roosevelt leads a band of rough-and-ready volunteers in a famous charge in a war against Spain.

Interpreting Visuals What kind of leader does this painting suggest Roosevelt was? What kind of president do you think he would make?

See **Skills Handbook**, p. H30

U.S.

February 1898
USS Maine explodes in Havana Harbor, triggering the Spanish-American War.

1900

World

1900
Radicals in China stage the Boxer Rebellion to drive away foreigners.

History's Impact video program
Watch the video to understand the impact of the Panama Canal.

1904
The United States begins construction of the Panama Canal.

1911
President Taft promotes "dollar diplomacy."

April 1914
U.S. troops intervene in the Mexican Revolution, occupying Veracruz, Mexico.

August 1914
Panama Canal opens.

1903

1906

1909

1912

1915

1918

1903
Panama declares independence from Colombia.

1905
Japan wins the Russo-Japanese War.

1910
The Mexican Revolution begins.

1917
Russian Revolution begins.

SECTION 1
The Lure of Imperialism

BEFORE YOU READ

MAIN IDEA

The United States entered the imperialist competition late, but it soon extended its power and influence in the Pacific region.

READING FOCUS

1. What inspired the imperialist activity of the late 1800s?

2. How did the United States take control of Hawaii?

3. How did the United States gain influence in China?

4. How did the United States exert influence in Japan?

KEY TERMS AND PEOPLE

imperialism
bayonet constitution
Liliuokalani
Sanford B. Dole
sphere of influence
Open Door Policy
Boxer Rebellion
Russo-Japanese War

 PI 3.4 Understand the interrelationships between world events and developments in New York State and the United States (e.g., causes for immigration, economic opportunities, human rights abuses, and tyranny versus freedom).

THE GRANGER COLLECTION, NEW YORK

▲ Uncle Sam did not have to look far to pluck new territories. This political cartoon suggests that the nation continued to eye neighboring countries.

THE INSIDE STORY

Why did the United States buy Alaska? In the 1890s the United States seemed to be off to a late start in the scramble for colonial possessions. European nations were already busily adding new colonies to their empires. The United States, though, had actually taken its first step toward imperialism back in 1867. While European nations were looking toward Africa and Asia, the United States was expanding in North America and the Pacific.

The huge Alaska landmass lies at the northwestern edge of North America, almost touching northeastern Russia. Russian fur traders were the first foreigners to settle there, in 1784. With a charter from Czar Paul I, the Russian-American Company served as Alaska's government after 1799. Russian, British, and American fur traders all competed amicably. But by 1867, sea otters, which had the most valuable fur, were becoming scarce. In addition, Russia was struggling to recover from the Crimean War. Russia offered to sell the territory to the United States.

At the time, William H. Seward was secretary of state for President Andrew Johnson. He had visions of an American empire and was eager to buy Alaska. He thought it had potential as a resource for fur, timber, and metals. He faced opposition from Congress, though. Unaware of Alaska's rich mineral resources, many people regarded the territory as a frozen wasteland.

Seward finally succeeded in buying Alaska for $7.2 million. Critics joked about Seward's Folly and Seward's Icebox. Later, though, after gold and oil were discovered in Alaska, Americans came to appreciate the bargain they'd gotten.

Alaska was not Seward's only smart acquisition. The very same year—1867—he snapped up the Midway Islands, strategically located west of Hawaii. ◢

Imperialist Activity

From the 1870s to the 1910s, a few industrialized nations actively competed for territory in Africa, Asia, and Latin America. This scramble for territorial control was part of the imperialist mind-set. **Imperialism** involves the extension of a nation's power over other lands.

By the late 1800s, nations such as Great Britain, France, Belgium, Germany, and Japan had all embraced the imperialist spirit. Soon, beginning in Hawaii, the United States would also pursue imperialist policies. What led to this quest for empire?

Economic interests The Industrial Revolution had brought great prosperity to the Western powers. Industrialized nations had flooded their own countries with goods and investment capital. Now they looked to other nations for new customers and new places to invest. Industrialists also began to look to Africa, Asia, and Latin America for new sources of raw materials for their factories.

Military needs Industrialized nations created strong navies to defend their shores and protect their trading interests. But navies needed bases where ships could refuel and make repairs. Industrialized nations sought foreign territory so they could build these coaling stations in strategic places.

Ideology Two popular ideologies also contributed to imperialism. One was a strong sense of nationalism, or love of one's country. Many people felt that territorial conquests enhanced a nation's power and prestige.

The other ideological motive was a feeling of cultural superiority. Because Africa, Asia, and Latin America had less industry and urban development, they seemed "backward" to many Europeans and Americans in the late 1800s.

Social Darwinism fed into this view. Social Darwinists believed that when nations competed against one another, only the fittest would survive. Some people therefore considered it a social responsibility to "civilize" the inhabitants of less developed countries and spread the benefits of Western society. In addition, Protestant Christian missionaries felt they had a moral duty to convert others to their beliefs.

The scramble for territory By the late 1800s, European imperial powers had taken control of vast territories in Africa and Asia, and dominated the economy of Latin America. The British Empire alone ruled about one-quarter of the world's land and population. France, Belgium, Germany, and Japan also controlled huge areas overseas.

Many Americans began to believe it was time for the United States to claim its own territories abroad. The prospect of new markets and military advantages was a powerful attraction. Some Americans, too, wanted to spread the Christian faith and democratic values. Josiah Strong, a Protestant clergyman, expressed this viewpoint eloquently.

HISTORY'S VOICES

" The two great needs of mankind . . . are, first, a pure, spiritual Christianity, and second, civil liberty. Without controversy, these are the forces which, in the past, have contributed most to the elevation of the human race . . . It follows, then, that the Anglo-Saxon [person of British descent], as the great representative of these two ideas . . . is divinely commissioned to be, in a peculiar sense, his brother's keeper. "

—Josiah Strong, *Our Country*, 1885

In the mid-1800s, Americans had believed it was their manifest destiny to expand westward to the Pacific Ocean. Now people sought to move even beyond the shoreline, to claim distant islands farther west.

READING CHECK **Summarizing** What were the three main reasons that industrialized nations became imperialist nations?

ACADEMIC VOCABULARY
ideology set of ideas about human life or culture

CAUSES OF U.S. EXPANSIONISM — QUICK FACTS

CAUSES

- **Economic** Desire for new markets and raw materials
- **Military** Desire for naval bases and coaling stations
- **Ideological** Desire to bring Christianity, western-style culture, and democracy to other peoples

→ United States expansionism

Taking Control of Hawaii

American expansionists became interested in acquiring Hawaii in the late 1800s. Located some 2,000 miles west of California, Hawaii was an ideal spot for coaling stations and naval bases for ships traveling to and from Asia.

Early contact Americans were not the first outsiders to show interest in Hawaii. A British explorer, Captain James Cook, had visited the islands in 1778. Great Britain did not claim Hawaii then, but Captain Cook's voyage brought Hawaii to the attention of the outside world.

Shortly after Cook's arrival, Hawaii's Chief Kamehameha (kah-MAY-hah-MAY-hah) united the eight major islands under his leadership. He established a monarchy and began a profitable trade in sandalwood. In the 1820s U.S. ships began arriving with some frequency, bringing traders and missionaries. Many of the missionaries had come from New England to convert Hawaiians to Christianity. Soon, the missionaries and their families began to settle down and raise crops, particularly sugarcane.

The foreigners also brought diseases, to which Hawaiians had no immunity. The population of Hawaii declined from about 300,000 in the 1770s to about 40,000 by 1893.

Sugar interests gain power As more and more Americans came to the islands, investors in the sugar industry began increasing their control. Americans had a sweet tooth, and sugar planters grew very rich. To keep the sugarcane plantations running, planters needed workers. With so few native Hawaiians left, planters brought in workers from China, Japan, and the Philippines.

Kalakaua became king in 1874. By this time, Americans had gained control over Hawaii's land and economy. But Kalakaua was strongly nationalistic. He resented the Americans' influence over his government and promised to put native Hawaiians back into power.

HISTORY'S VOICES

❝Do not be led by the foreigners; they had no part in our hardships, in gaining the country. Do not be led by their false teachings.❞

—Kalakaua, "Proclamation," 1872

Early in his reign, King Kalakaua allied himself with landowners in his desire to strengthen the Hawaiian economy. He negotiated a treaty in 1875 that allowed Hawaiian sugar to enter the United States tax free. This

Pineapple Industry

James Dole, Sanford Dole's cousin, began growing pineapples in Hawaii in 1901. By the 1930s Dole supplied 90 percent of the world's canned pineapple.

HAWAIIAN
PINEAPPLE

made Hawaiian sugar cheaper than sugar from other places. The treaty gave a real boost to the Hawaiian sugar industry. But the more money that the sugar tycoons made, the more power they wanted over Hawaiian affairs.

Plotting against the king A group of American business leaders, planters, and traders formed a secret society called the Hawaiian League. Its purpose was to overthrow the monarchy and establish a democracy in Hawaii under the control of Americans.

Conflicts between these American business leaders and the king escalated in 1886. The United States wanted the port of Pearl Harbor in exchange for renewing the sugar treaty. But King Kalakaua refused to give up the independence of any part of Hawaii.

Angered, the Hawaiian League forced King Kalakaua to sign a new constitution at gunpoint in July 1887. The king angrily called it the **bayonet constitution**. It severely restricted his power and deprived most Hawaiians of the vote. King Kalakaua was now forced to give Pearl Harbor to the United States. This gave U.S. warships a permanent port in Hawaii.

American sugar planters now had political control over Hawaii. But the economy suffered a heavy blow in 1890. The United States revoked the sugar treaty in order to support sugar producers on the U.S. mainland. American sugar producers in Hawaii believed they had only one option to protect their businesses—become part of the United States. Secretly, they began talks with U.S. officials about annexation.

End of the monarchy When King Kalakaua died in 1891, his sister **Liliuokalani** (LI-lee-uh-woh-kuh-LAHN-ee) became queen. Queen Liliuokalani was a Hawaiian nationalist who wanted to do away with the bayonet constitution. In January 1893, she announced her plan to restore the power of the Hawaiian monarchy. In response, members of the business community plotted to overthrow her. They wanted the islands to be governed as a territory of the United States.

John L. Stevens, the American minister to Hawaii, decided he would help the rebel sugar planters. Without authorization, he ordered four boatloads of U.S. Marines to go ashore. They took up positions around the royal palace, aiming machine guns and cannons at the

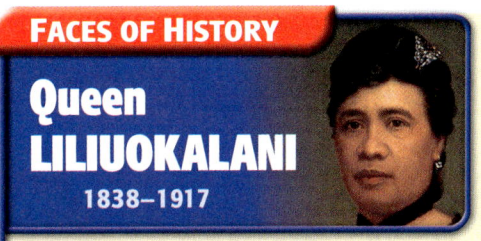

building. The rebels then declared an end to the monarchy. Queen Liliuokalani surrendered under protest on January 17, 1893.

The rebel leaders quickly formed a new regime with **Sanford B. Dole**, a sugar tycoon, as president. John L. Stevens, acting on his own once again, formally recognized the new Republic of Hawaii. He also proclaimed Hawaii to be under U.S. protection, while the Senate considered a treaty to annex the islands.

Annexation Troubled by the events in Hawaii, President Grover Cleveland put the treaty on hold and ordered an investigation. The investigator's report condemned the revolt against Liliuokalani and proposed restoring her to the throne. Cleveland agreed, but Dole refused to step down.

Cleveland was unwilling to use military force to back Liliuokalani. Yet he would not support annexation, either. The matter remained at a standstill until the next president, William McKinley, took office. McKinley favored annexation, and Congress narrowly voted its approval in 1898. Hawaii became an American territory and eventually—in 1959—the fiftieth state. In 1993 Congress apologized for the U.S. role in overthowing Liliuokalani.

READING CHECK **Sequencing** How did American sugar interests gain so much power in Hawaii?

Chinese forces takes European enemy generals prisoner in this Chinese print of the Boxer Rebellion.

Interpreting Visuals How are the foreigners depicted in the image?

Influence in China

Early on, Hawaii had attracted American interest because it was a convenient place to stop for fuel and supplies on the journey to China. American traders had been traveling to China since 1784.

Even so, China stayed nearly isolated from the rest of the world. It strictly controlled foreign trade, allowing foreigners only in the port of Guangzhou. Then in 1842, the British forced China to open five ports to British trade. Two years later, the United States received broader trading privileges as well. For the next 50 years, China's rulers struggled to keep foreign interests from overrunning the country.

The threat was not just from Western nations, however. In 1895 Japan took over the island of Taiwan and tried to seize the Liaotung Peninsula too. European powers—Russia, France, Germany, and Great Britain—quickly carved out their own **spheres of influence** in China. A sphere of influence is a geographic area where an outside nation exerts special economic or political control.

The United States was too late to secure a sphere of influence in China. American leaders feared that the United States would be shut out of the valuable China trade. As a result, Secretary of State John Hay proposed the **Open Door Policy** in 1899. The aim was to give all nations equal trading rights in China. As Senator Henry Cabot Lodge of Massachusetts declared, "We ask no favors; we only ask that we shall be admitted to that great market upon the same terms with the rest of the world."

Hay sent notes recommending the Open Door Policy to Great Britain, Germany, Russia, Japan, France, and Italy. None of them agreed to it, but none rejected it outright. Therefore, Hay felt he could announce in March 1900 that the Open Door Policy had been approved.

With foreign countries now vying for business in China, antiforeigner sentiments grew. A secret group called the Society of Righteous and Harmonious Fists—known to westerners as Boxers—began attacking foreign missionaries and Chinese Christians. In June 1900 the Boxers laid siege to the capital city of Beijing in what became known as the **Boxer Rebellion**.

Western nations rushed 20,000 troops—including 2,000 Americans—to China. They soon quelled the rebellion, and a year later, in September 1901, China signed a humbling settlement agreement.

The Boxer Rebellion increased support for Hay's Open Door Policy. Western nations realized that competition among themselves would hurt their ability to exploit the China trade.

READING CHECK **Identifying Problem and Solution** Why did Hay propose the Open Door Policy?

Influence in Japan

Until Japan seized Taiwan from China in 1895, no one would have thought of the Japanese as imperialists. Since the late 1630s, the country had been inward-looking, shutting itself off from nearly all foreign contact.

By the mid-1800s, though, Japan came under U.S. pressure to open its ports to trade. In 1853 President Millard Fillmore sent Commodore Matthew Perry with a fleet of four ships into Edo (Tokyo) Bay. Japan was not yet industrialized, and Japanese people had never seen steamships before. They were awed by the demonstration of American naval strength.

The Japanese government knew that it could not defend itself against a modern navy. It also realized that it could no longer maintain its isolated position in the world. So in 1854 its leaders agreed to a treaty that opened Japan to trade with the United States.

Japan then embarked on a program of rapid modernization. It transformed itself into an industrial power and built a strong military. After taking over Taiwan, Japan began eyeing Korea and the Chinese province of Manchuria. Russia, meanwhile, also wanted these lands.

In 1904 the **Russo-Japanese War** broke out. The conflict took a toll on both sides, and by the following spring, both sides had had enough.

At Japan's request, President Theodore Roosevelt helped negotiate a peace treaty. He met with representatives of the two countries in Portsmouth, New Hampshire, and hammered out a compromise. Roosevelt received the Nobel Prize for Peace for his efforts in negotiating the Treaty of Portsmouth.

Japan was the clear victor in the war with Russia, and it emerged as a major power. It was now the strongest power in East Asia and a rival to the United States for influence in China and the Pacific region. American leaders knew that Japan remained hungry for territory. It had fewer natural resources than the other imperialist nations. In addition, the Japanese government wanted to expand territorially in order to counterbalance U.S. expansion in the Pacific.

Roosevelt decided to impress upon Japan—and the rest of the world—just how powerful the U.S. military was. In 1907 he sent four squadrons of battleships, known as the Great White Fleet, on a 43,000-mile, around-the-world journey. Led by Rear Admiral Charles Sperry, the fleet stopped at 20 ports on six continents, including a port in Japan, before returning home in 1909.

READING CHECK **Identifying the Main Idea** How did the United States influence Japan's economic policies and its imperialist ambitions?

SECTION 1 ASSESSMENT

Reviewing Ideas, Terms, and People

1. a. Define What is **imperialism**?
b. Summarize What were the main incentives for countries to seek new territories?
c. Evaluate Do you think imperialists who wanted to spread western culture were arrogant or well meaning? Explain.

2. a. Recall Why did its location make Hawaii attractive to Americans?
b. Draw Conclusions What role did sugar play in the desire of many Americans to control Hawaii?
c. Elaborate How did American sugar planters go outside the law to gain control over Hawaii?

3. a. Describe What was the **Open Door Policy**?
b. Explain Why did Americans think they might be at a disadvantage in trading with China?
c. Predict What would have been the likely consequences for the United States if other western powers had divided China into colonies instead of accepting the Open Door Policy?

4. a. Identify Who was Commodore Perry?
b. Analyze Why did the United States want to impress Japan in particular with the Great White Fleet?

Critical Thinking

5. Identifying Cause and Effect Copy the chart below and record the effects of key events in Hawaii's history.

Event	Effect

FOCUS ON WRITING

6. Expository Write an essay about the different perspectives that a Chinese native and a Christian missionary might have had on the Boxer Rebellion. Explain how each might have viewed the Boxers' goals and their means of achieving them.

The Spanish-American War

BEFORE YOU READ

MAIN IDEA

A quick victory in the Spanish-American War gave the United States a new role as a world power.

READING FOCUS

1. How did simmering unrest in Cuba lead to rebellion?
2. Why did Americans get war fever?
3. What happened in the course of the Spanish-American War?
4. Why was annexing the Philippines controversial?

KEY TERMS AND PEOPLE

José Martí
William Randolph Hearst
Joseph Pulitzer
yellow journalism
de Lôme letter
George Dewey
Emilio Aguinaldo
Rough Riders
Battle of San Juan Hill

 P1 2.5 Analyze the United States involvement in foreign affairs and a willingness to engage in international politics, examining the ideas and traditions leading to these foreign policies.

"You Furnish the PICTURES, I'll Furnish the WAR"

THE INSIDE STORY

Did a telegram start a war? In the 1890s rival newspapers owned by William Randolph Hearst and Joseph Pulitzer were competing fiercely. They tried to woo readers with sensational stories and blaring banner headlines.

How far would Hearst go? In January 1897 he sent an artist and reporter team to cover the Cuban rebellion against Spanish rule. Frederic Remington was to send drawings of war scenes. Richard Harding Davis would write the dramatic stories. According to one account, Remington spent some time in Cuba and found that not much was happening in the way of a war. He sent this telegram: "W. R. Hearst, *New York Journal*, N.Y.: Everything is quiet. There is no trouble here. There will be no war. I wish to return. Remington."

Supposedly Hearst answered: "Remington, Havana: Please remain. You furnish the pictures, and I'll furnish the war. W. R. Hearst."

Is the story true? One historian points out that the only source was a journalist named James Creelman, who wrote a book about his life as a foreign correspondent for Hearst. Hearst always denied a role in "manufacturing" the war, but the tale fit with people's belief that he would do anything for a good story. Certainly both the *Journal* and its rival, the *New York World*, played up every incident in Cuba. But Americans were already sympathetic to the Cuban rebels, and perhaps they did not need a push toward war.

▶ War news draws a crowd outside the *New York Journal* offices.

Simmering Unrest in Cuba

By the 1890s Spain had lost all of its colonies in the Western Hemisphere except for Cuba and Puerto Rico. Cubans in particular were not happy to be part of Spain's empire. Since 1868, Cubans had launched a series of revolts against Spanish rule. Spain responded by exiling leaders of the independence movement.

José Martí was one such leader, exiled in 1878. He moved to New York City, where he continued to promote independence and inspire his fellow Cubans. Through newspaper articles and poetry, Martí urged Cubans to fight for their freedom. He also founded the Cuban Revolutionary Party in 1892 and made preparations to return to his homeland.

Cubans rose once more in revolt against Spain in February 1895. Martí joined them in April, but a month later he was killed in battle. By dying for his country, José Martí immediately became one of Cuba's greatest heroes.

As the revolt raged on, Spain sent General Valeriano Weyler to suppress the rebels in 1896. Weyler forced thousands of civilians into camps controlled by the Spanish army to keep them from aiding the rebels. However, nearly one-third of the Cubans in the camps died from starvation or disease. Weyler's mistreatment of these civilians shocked Americans.

READING CHECK **Summarizing** How did José Martí inspire other Cubans to seek independence?

Americans Get War Fever

Many Americans were already sympathetic to the Cuban cause. They believed the Cubans' struggle was similar to their own during the American Revolution. They became even more supportive after learning how Cuban civilians were suffering under General Weyler.

The media's role In this era before radio, television, or the Internet, most people got their news from daily or weekly newspapers. At one point, New York City had as many as 15 daily newspaper editions.

Two of the most widely read papers were the *New York Journal*, published by **William Randolph Hearst,** and the *New York World,* published by **Joseph Pulitzer**. Both papers told scandalous stories and splashed large,

shocking illustrations across their pages. This style of sensationalist reporting became known as yellow journalism, named after the "Yellow Kid," a popular comic strip that ran in the *World*. Determined to compete with the *World* in every way, the *Journal* created its own "yellow kid" comic, and the rivalry between the two papers became a competition between the two "yellow kids."

The *Journal* threw its support behind the Cuban rebels and refused to use any Spanish sources for news stories. Relying only on Cuban sources made the *Journal's* stories biased, but it also made for exciting reading—and sold more papers.

Not to be left behind, the *World* abandoned all attempts at objectivity. It used the same strategy as the *Journal*, and newspaper sales went up. People could not get enough of the dramatic stories printed daily.

The explosion of the *Maine* Hearst felt strongly that the United States should intervene in Cuba. As a result, the *Journal* continued the drumbeat for war. In 1897 Hearst sent artist Frederic Remington to Cuba to create illustrations showing Spanish cruelty. Hearst printed those drawings in his papers to stir up more support for war with Spain.

President William McKinley was reluctant at first to involve the United States in the conflict. Events soon changed McKinley's

FACES OF HISTORY

William R. HEARST
1863–1951

An outgoing and controversial man, William Randolph Hearst built a vast publishing empire. He began his career managing the *San Francisco Examiner.* At the height of his success, he owned 28 major newspapers and 18 magazines, along with various news services, radio stations, and movie companies. Hearst even served in the House of Representatives but was defeated in his efforts to become the mayor of New York City, and later the governor of New York State.

Orson Welles's 1941 film *Citizen Kane* depicted Hearst's extravagant life. It became one of the most popular films of all time.

Drawing Conclusions Many film critics consider *Citizen Kane* to be one of the best movies ever made. Why might Hearst's life make an interesting story?

Editorial

The *New York Journal* published this editorial on February 17, 1898, after the *Maine* exploded.

"To five hundred thousand Cubans starved or otherwise murdered have been added an American battleship and three hundred American sailors lost as the direct result of the dilatory [slow] policy of our government toward Spain. If we had stopped the war in Cuba when duty and policy alike urged us to do[,] the *Maine* would have been afloat today . . .

It was an accident, they say. Perhaps it was, but . . . it was an accident of a remarkably convenient kind for Spain. Two days ago we had five battleships in the Atlantic. Today we have four. A few more such accidents will leave us at the mercy of a Spanish fleet."

Skills FOCUS READING LIKE A HISTORIAN

1. **Analyzing Primary Sources** Whom does the *Journal* blame for the deaths on the *Maine*?

2. **Recognizing Bias** What suggests that the *Journal* is biased against Spain?

See **Skills Handbook**, pp. H28–H29, H33

---

mind. On February 9, 1898, the *Journal* published a letter written by Enrique Dupuy de Lôme, Spain's minister to the United States. The letter had fallen into the hands of a Cuban spy who sold it to Hearst. The **de Lôme letter** ridiculed McKinley for being "weak and catering to the rabble." Americans were outraged at the remarks. The *Journal* called it "the worst insult to the United States in its history."

Furious Americans began clamoring for war with Spain. Then came the final straw: a violent tragedy in Havana Harbor that brought relations with Spain to a breaking point. The battleship USS *Maine* had been sent to Havana to protect American lives and property. On February 15, 1898, the *Maine* mysteriously blew up, killing 260 sailors.

"DESTRUCTION OF THE WAR SHIP MAINE WAS THE WORK OF AN ENEMY!" screamed the *Journal*'s headline, although there was no proof of this. Some historians now believe that a fire in a coal storage room caused the explosion. At the time, however, Americans blamed Spain. "Remember the *Maine*!" became the rallying cry of war supporters.

At the time, an inquiry into the explosion confirmed public perceptions, blaming a Spanish mine for destroying the *Maine*. In late March, President McKinley demanded that Spain grant Cuba its independence. When Spain refused, Congress declared a state of war on April 25, 1898. The Spanish-American War had begun.

READING CHECK **Making Inferences** Why did the *Journal* jump to the conclusion that the Spanish were responsible for the explosion of the *Maine*?

The Course of the War

Although its impact would be felt for years, the Spanish-American War lasted only about four months. It was fought on two fronts: Cuba and the Philippines.

War in the Philippines The Philippines are a group of islands located east of Vietnam between the Philippine Sea and the South China Sea. Spain had claimed the islands since the 1500s.

Before the United States declared war on Spain, Theodore Roosevelt (then the assistant secretary of the navy) sent secret orders to Commodore **George Dewey**, the commander of the U.S. Navy's Asiatic Squadron. If war broke out between the United States and Spain, Dewey's assignment was to attack the Spanish fleet in the Philippines.

Once Dewey received word that war had been declared, his squadron rushed to Manila Bay in the Philippines. Early on the morning of May 1, 1898, the Spanish fleet opened fire, but the American forces were out of range. Dewey had his sailors hold their fire for nearly half an hour, until they came within striking distance of the Spanish ships. Dewey did not want to waste ammunition, because the nearest American point of resupply was in California, some 7,000 miles away.

Finally, Commodore Dewey quietly told Charles Gridley, the captain of the flagship *Olympia*, "You may fire when ready, Gridley." The Americans had the advantage of modern ships with iron and steel hulls, as well as superior weaponry. They were soon inflicting heavy damage on the old-fashioned wooden ships of the enemy.

Then two hours into the battle, Captain Gridley reported that the *Olympia* was low on ammunition. Dewey decided to withdraw from battle so that the ships could redistribute their remaining supplies. To keep morale up, he told his men they were taking a break to eat breakfast. During the break, however, Dewey learned that the report about the ammunition was incorrect. The *Olympia* had plenty of supplies for the rest of the battle.

The Americans continued fighting shortly before noon. Soon the entire Spanish fleet was ablaze and sinking. In a matter of hours, the United States had won a decisive victory. Not a single American life was lost, but nearly 400 Spaniards were injured or killed in the Battle of Manila Bay.

Dewey then began planning an attack on the capital city of Manila. He found a willing partner in **Emilio Aguinaldo**, leader of a rebel army of Filipino patriots. Filipinos had been fighting for independence from Spain for two years. While Dewey's warships remained in the harbor, Aguinaldo's army captured Manila. Cut off by Dewey's fleet and surrounded by Aguinaldo's rebels, Spanish forces in the Philippines surrendered on August 14, 1898.

The war in Cuba Days before declaring war, Congress had recognized Cuba's independence and adopted the Teller Amendment. This stated that once Cuba freed itself from Spanish rule, the United States would "leave the government and control of the Island to its people."

Victory in Cuba proved difficult to achieve, however. The U.S. War Department was not as prepared as it should have been for the conflict.

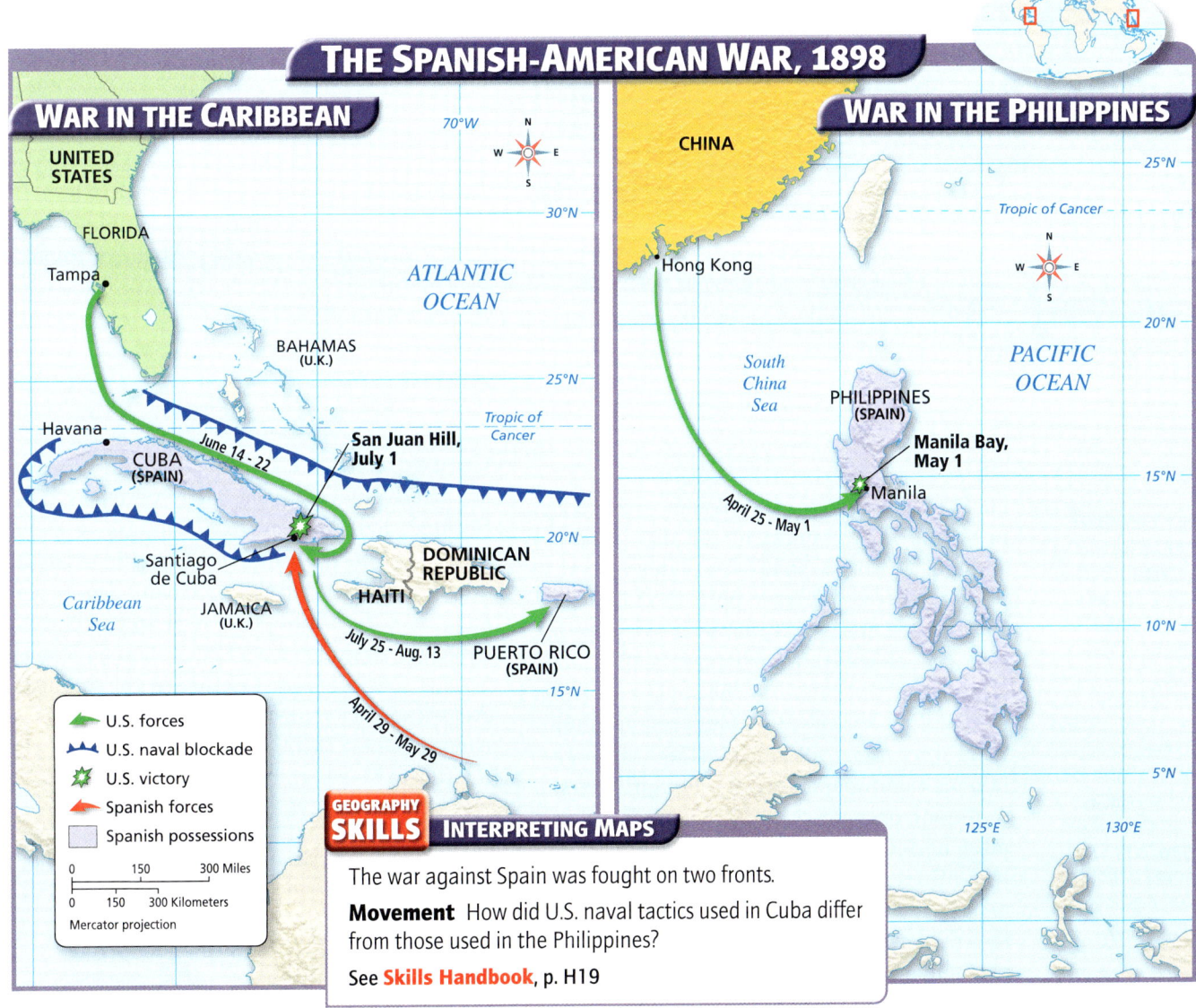

THE SPANISH-AMERICAN WAR, 1898

WAR IN THE CARIBBEAN

UNITED STATES

FLORIDA

Tampa

ATLANTIC OCEAN

BAHAMAS (U.K.)

Tropic of Cancer

Havana

June 14 - 22

San Juan Hill, July 1

CUBA (SPAIN)

Santiago de Cuba

Caribbean Sea

JAMAICA (U.K.)

HAITI

DOMINICAN REPUBLIC

July 25 - Aug. 13

PUERTO RICO (SPAIN)

April 29 - May 29

WAR IN THE PHILIPPINES

CHINA

Hong Kong

Tropic of Cancer

South China Sea

PHILIPPINES (SPAIN)

Manila Bay, May 1

April 25 - May 1

Manila

PACIFIC OCEAN

Legend:
- → U.S. forces
- ⋀ U.S. naval blockade
- ✹ U.S. victory
- → Spanish forces
- ▨ Spanish possessions

0   150   300 Miles
0   150   300 Kilometers
Mercator projection

GEOGRAPHY SKILLS INTERPRETING MAPS

The war against Spain was fought on two fronts.

Movement How did U.S. naval tactics used in Cuba differ from those used in the Philippines?

See **Skills Handbook**, p. H19

READING LIKE A HISTORIAN

Some 10 African American regiments were called to serve in the Spanish-American War. The Ninth and Tenth Cavalries are shown here with the Rough Riders at the Battle of Kettle Hill.

Interpreting Visuals What marks these soldiers as Americans?

FOCUS ON NEW YORK

GOVERNMENT
Before he was secretary of the Navy, Roosevelt was elected to the New York State Assembly. He was later defeated in a bid to become mayor of New York City, but served as president of the New York City Board of Police Commissioners.

For example, it equipped soldiers with woolen uniforms for a summer war in a tropical climate. The mess pans—tin plates issued to soldiers—were left over from the Civil War. The canned meat in Cuba was so sickening that soldiers called it "embalmed beef."

Most of the soldiers who fought in Cuba were enlisted men (also called regulars), but there were many volunteers as well. The most famous volunteers were the **Rough Riders**, a regiment organized by Theodore Roosevelt after he left his navy post. Adventurous college athletes, cowboys, ranchers, and miners all joined the Rough Riders. They expected to fight on horseback, but because the transport ships to Cuba were overbooked, they had to leave their horses behind in America. The Rough Riders ended up functioning as foot soldiers instead of as a cavalry.

The American strategy in Cuba was to capture the port city of Santiago. U.S. troops needed to control the hills around the city. On July 1, one U.S. division seized the hill at El Caney after a four-hour fight.

That same day, some 8,000 U.S. soldiers fought to take control of Kettle and San Juan hills. Experienced African American soldiers of the Ninth and Tenth Cavalries—known as Buffalo Soldiers—led the charge, supported by the Rough Riders and regulars. Theodore Roosevelt described how the Rough Riders stayed the course.

HISTORY'S VOICES

❝We were still under a heavy fire and I got together a mixed lot of men and pushed on . . . , driving the Spaniards through a line of palm-trees, and over the crest of a chain of hills. When we reached these crests we found ourselves overlooking Santiago.❞

—Theodore Roosevelt, *The Rough Riders*, 1902

By nightfall, U.S. troops controlled the ridge above Santiago. For their heroic actions in the **Battle of San Juan Hill**, six of the Buffalo Soldiers and two Rough Riders—including Theodore Roosevelt—received the Medal of Honor.

On July 3, the U.S. Navy sank the entire Spanish fleet off the coast of Cuba in the Battle of Santiago. Two weeks later, Spanish troops in Cuba surrendered. Soon after, U.S. troops defeated Spanish forces in Puerto Rico.

Consequences of the war The terms of the peace treaty proved costly for Spain. The Spanish had to give up all claims to Cuba and cede Puerto Rico and the Pacific island of Guam to the United States. Spain also turned control of the Philippines over to the United States in exchange for a $20 million payment.

For Americans, the victory in the Spanish-American War was sweet. John Hay, the ambassador to Great Britain, summed up his view in a letter to Theodore Roosevelt.

HISTORY'S VOICES

❝It has been a splendid little war; begun with the highest motives, carried on with magnificent intelligence and spirit, favored by that fortune which loves the brave.❞

—John Hay, letter to Theodore Roosevelt

Still, the United States paid a heavy toll for the war. The monetary costs amounted to roughly $250 million. In addition, some 2,000 soldiers died, not from battle wounds but from yellow fever.

Despite the lives lost and the dollars spent, the Spanish-American War had a huge payoff for the United States. Senator Henry Cabot Lodge of Massachusetts noted that although the war was very brief, "its results were many, startling, and of world-wide meaning."

The United States now moved into the ranks of imperialist nations. Its new overseas territories gave it more bases for trade and for resupplying its navy. Within a year, it would capitalize on its new economic and military strength to acquire the Pacific island of Samoa. Expansionists expressed delight over the country's growing power, but the quest for empire troubled many Americans.

READING CHECK **Making Generalizations**
How did the United States benefit from the war?

Annexing the Philippines

After the Spanish-American War, a controversy raged in the United States over whether to annex the Philippines. Some Americans were uneasy with the idea of controlling overseas territories. Others believed that imperialism not only made the United States stronger but also benefited those under colonial rule.

Arguments for annexation Some people who favored annexation believed that the United States had a duty to spread its values overseas. President McKinley, for example, spoke of the need "to educate the Filipinos, and uplift and civilize and Christianize them."

Other Americans wanted the Philippines for their economic and strategic value. Located on the route to China, the Philippines would be useful as a place to refuel and resupply ships. For that reason, many expansionists wanted to annex the Philippines before they fell into the hands of Germany, Japan, or another nation.

COUNTERPOINTS

Annexation of the Philippines

Senator Henry Cabot Lodge argued that the United States should annex the Philippines.

❝ The taking of the Philippines does not violate the principles of the Declaration of Independence, but will spread them among a people who have never known liberty and who in a few years will be . . . unwilling to leave the shelter of the American flag. ❞

Henry Cabot Lodge, 1900

Senator George F. Hoar favored independence for the Philippines.

❝ Now, I claim that under the Declaration of Independence you cannot govern . . . a foreign people . . . against their will, because you think it is for their good, when they do not . . . You have no right at the cannon's mouth to impose on an unwilling people . . . your notions of freedom and notions of what is good. ❞

George F. Hoar, 1899

Skills FOCUS **READING LIKE A HISTORIAN**

Comparing How does each senator invoke the Declaration of Independence in his argument?
See **Skills Handbook**, p. H10

ACADEMIC VOCABULARY

foundation
underlying principle

Opponents' views Americans who opposed annexing the Philippines felt strongly, too. Some reasoned that annexation would violate the ideal of self-government—the underlying foundation of the American system. They formed the Anti-Imperialist League in June 1898.

Many African Americans worried about exporting oppression to the Philippines. A group of activists called the Colored Citizens of Boston argued that with racism and violence still painfully common at home, "the duty of the President and country is to reform these crying domestic wrongs and not attempt the civilization of alien peoples by powder and shot."

Other Americans feared that annexing the Philippines would open the doors to a flood of new immigrants. Samuel Gompers, the leader of the American Federation of Labor, believed that this would hurt American workers.

American rule After a fierce debate, the Senate narrowly approved the treaty calling for annexation of the Philippines. The measure passed on February 6, 1899.

Filipino nationalists were infuriated. They had been fighting for independence from Spain for years. Now they had exchanged one set of rulers for another.

Emilio Aguinaldo had already set up a government and proclaimed himself president of the new Philippine Republic. He warned that he was prepared to take military action if the United States tried to assume control of the Philippines.

To no one's surprise, fighting broke out. For three years, Filipino independence fighters battled U.S. soldiers. Aguinaldo was finally captured by the Americans and forced from power in 1901. By the time the rebellion ended, more than 4,000 U.S. soldiers and some 220,000 Filipinos had died, many from disease.

In taking over the Philippines, the stated goal of the United States was to prepare the islands for independence. Therefore, although Congress put a U.S.-appointed governor in charge, Filipinos were also allowed a voice in governing. At first they could only elect members to the lower house of their legislature. Then in 1916, Filipino voters won the right to elect both houses of their legislature. Three decades later, on July 4, 1946, the United States finally granted full independence to the Philippines.

READING CHECK **Identifying Cause and Effect** What were some of the effects of American annexation of the Philippines?

SECTION 2 ASSESSMENT

go.hrw.com
Online Quiz
Keyword: SD7 HP17

Reviewing Ideas, Terms, and People

1. a. Recall By the 1890s, how did Cubans view Spanish rule?
b. Explain How did **José Martí** promote the Cuban cause from New York City?
c. Evaluate Did General Weyler's actions toward civilians help or hinder the Spanish cause? Explain.

2. a. Define What was **yellow journalism**?
b. Draw Conclusions Why was the sinking of the USS *Maine* significant?
c. Elaborate Was the press irresponsible in covering the buildup to the Spanish-American War? Why or why not?

3. a. Identify What were the key battles during the Spanish-American War?
b. Summarize What were the terms of the peace treaty?
c. Predict If the United States had lost the Spanish-American War, do you think it would have been more or less likely to continue its quest for empire? Explain.

4. a. Recall Why were the Philippines of strategic importance to the United States?

b. Make Inferences Why might **Emilio Aguinaldo** and other Filipino nationalists have felt betrayed by the United States?
c. Evaluate Was the United States justified in not granting immediate independence to the Philippines? Why or why not?

Critical Thinking

5. Contrasting Copy the chart below and record the reasons why some Americans supported annexation of the Philippines and others opposed it.

Supporters	Opponents

FOCUS ON WRITING

6. Narrative Imagine that you were aboard the *Olympia* during the Battle of Manila Bay or that you were with the Rough Riders during the Battle of San Juan Hill. Write a letter to a friend back home telling about your experiences and your feelings.

Roosevelt and Latin America

BEFORE YOU READ

MAIN IDEA

The United States began to exert its influence over Latin America in the wake of the Spanish-American War.

READING FOCUS

1. How did the United States govern Cuba and Puerto Rico?
2. Why and how was the Panama Canal built?
3. What was the Roosevelt Corollary?
4. How did Presidents Taft and Wilson reshape U.S. diplomacy?

KEY TERMS AND PEOPLE

Platt Amendment
protectorate
Foraker Act
Roosevelt Corollary
dollar diplomacy

PI 3.4 Understand the interrelationships between world events and developments in New York State and the United States (e.g., causes for immigration, economic opportunities, human rights abuses, and tyranny versus freedom).

"Speak Softly and Carry a Big Stick"

THE GRANGER COLLECTION, NEW YORK

▲ Roosevelt uses a "big stick" to control the Caribbean region.

THE INSIDE STORY

How did President Roosevelt get the Canal Zone?

Theodore Roosevelt was a man of action with a vigorous foreign policy. He often quoted a West African proverb: "Speak softly and carry a big stick; you will go far."

Roosevelt's "big stick" was naval power. As president, he built up the Great White Fleet. It helped achieve his dream—a canal that would let ships sail between the Atlantic and the Pacific without going around South America. The canal site was in Panama, which was then a province of Colombia.

Under pressure, Colombian diplomats agreed to lease a canal zone across Panama for a one-time payment of $10 million and a yearly fee of $250,000. The Colombian senate, however, rejected the deal and demanded more money.

Then various groups with a stake in the canal stepped in to encourage a revolution in Panama. In November 1903, the USS *Nashville* lingered off the coast. American marines landed to "maintain order," preventing Colombian troops from stopping the rebels. Within three days, the government of newly independent Panama agreed to the original treaty. Work on the canal could begin!

Cuba and Puerto Rico

After the Spanish-American War, the United States began to expand its power in Latin America. To restore order in Cuba and Puerto Rico after the war—and to protect American investments—President William McKinley set up military governments on each island.

Yellow fever in Cuba

President McKinley appointed Leonard Wood as governor of Cuba in 1899. During Wood's term in office, scientists made significant steps toward eliminating yellow fever. The disease had reached epidemic levels among American troops in Cuba. As many as 85 percent of the people infected with yellow fever died.

U.S. Army doctors Walter Reed and William C. Gorgas studied the problem. Cuban doctor Carlos Juan Finlay had theorized that mosquitoes spread yellow fever. Within a year, Reed and Gorgas had proven Finlay's theory. Then Gorgas organized a plan to drain all pools of standing water, where mosquitoes bred. Within six months, yellow fever had been virtually eliminated from the city of Havana.

THE IMPACT TODAY

Government
Since the terrorist attacks of September 11, 2001, the base at Guantánamo has housed prisoners suspected of terrorist activity.

U.S. control over Cuba

Wood also oversaw the drafting of a new Cuban constitution in 1901. The United States had already declared with the Teller Amendment of 1898 that it would not annex Cuba. After the Spanish-American War, however, the United States feared that other imperialist nations might try to take control of Cuba or undercut American business interests there.

As a result, the United States forced Cuba to include the **Platt Amendment** as part of its new constitution. The amendment limited Cuba's ability to sign treaties with other nations. At the same time, it gave the United States the right to intervene in Cuban affairs. The amendment also required Cuba to sell or lease land to the United States for naval and coaling stations. This last clause led to the establishment of a U.S. naval base at Guantánamo Bay.

The Platt Amendment made Cuba a U.S. **protectorate**—a country under the control and protection of another country. After Cuba accepted the Platt Amendment, U.S. troops withdrew. The amendment was eventually repealed, but the United States retained its lease on the naval base at Guantánamo Bay.

PRIMARY SOURCES

Political Cartoon

This cartoon reflects the debate at the end of the Spanish-American War over what should be done with new U.S. territories.

In the caption Uncle Sam says, "These little shavers [kids] seem to like it here. I wonder had I better keep 'em all in the family?"

The children at the table represent lands taken over by the United States in the 1890s.

Lady Liberty was often paired with Uncle Sam in political cartoons, representing America's ideal parents.

THE GRANGER COLLECTION, NEW YORK

Skills FOCUS | **READING LIKE A HISTORIAN**

1. **Interpreting Political Cartoons** Why do you think the artist used a Thanksgiving scene?
2. **Recognizing Bias** How does this cartoon portray the peoples of the acquired lands?

See **Skills Handbook**, pp. H31, H33

Governing Puerto Rico The United States did not make Puerto Rico a protectorate. Instead, it governed Puerto Rico as a territory, as it did the Philippines. The **Foraker Act** of 1900 established that the United States would appoint Puerto Rico's governor and the upper house of its legislature. Puerto Rican voters would elect the lower house.

A 1917 law granted U.S. citizenship to Puerto Ricans. It also allowed Puerto Rican voters to elect all of their legislative representatives. In 1952 Puerto Rico became a self-governing commonwealth of the United States. Today the Puerto Rican government has power over most of its domestic affairs. The U.S. government still controls certain matters though—interstate trade, immigration, and military affairs—just as it does for U.S. states.

READING CHECK **Summarizing** How did Cuba become a U.S. protectorate?

The Panama Canal

For decades, people had dreamed about a faster way to move between the Atlantic and Pacific oceans without having to travel all the way around South America. In the 1880s a French company tried to solve this problem. It began building a canal across the 50-mile-wide Isthmus of Panama, which was then part of the Republic of Colombia. Facing many obstacles, the company eventually went bankrupt and abandoned the canal.

U.S. interest in a canal In 1902 the United States bought the rights to the French canal property and equipment. Secretary of State John Hay began negotiations with Colombia to gain permanent use of the strip of land that the canal would cut through. By 1903 a treaty for a canal zone had been drafted, but Colombia's senate would not ratify it.

Panama's revolution President Theodore Roosevelt had a keen interest in building the canal. Meanwhile, Panamanian revolutionaries were plotting to break free of Colombian

rule. Roosevelt supported the rebellion, and on November 2, it began. The next day, Panama declared its independence, and the United States swiftly recognized the Republic of Panama. Soon afterward, a new treaty with Panama gave the United States complete and unending sovereignty over a 10-mile-wide Canal Zone.

Hardships Faced by Canal Workers
- Yellow fever and malaria
- Accidents
- Lost equipment
- Extreme heat
- Estimated death toll of more than 30,000 workers

Building the Panama Canal American work on the Panama Canal began in May 1904. Harsh working conditions and shortages of labor and materials hampered construction efforts. The situation grew worse when a serious outbreak of yellow fever hit.

To put the project back on track, Roosevelt appointed John F. Stevens as chief engineer and architect. Stevens tackled the technical problems while the army colonel Dr. William C. Gorgas focused on improving sanitation and health. Wiping out yellow fever was one goal, but malaria was an even greater threat. Unlike yellow fever, which gave survivors immunity, malaria could strike people again and again. During the first month of U.S. construction activity, nearly the entire workforce had been stricken with malaria.

Eliminating the mosquitoes that spread malaria was a huge task. Sanitation workers drained swamps, cleared vegetation, spread oil on pools of standing water, and bred spiders, ants, and lizards to feed on the adult mosquitoes. By 1913 malaria was almost eliminated.

Meanwhile, John F. Stevens resigned in 1907, and Lt. Col. George W. Goethals continued the mammoth task of coordinating the construction—not just the canal but all the housing and other facilities needed for workers. His efforts led him to be called the Genius of the Panama Canal.

More than 60 giant steam shovels bit into the land, digging out hundreds of train-car loads of earth each day. Up to 44,000 workers, many recruited from the British West Indies, labored on the project at a time. There were frequent accidents, lost equipment, and deaths—but there was also progress. In August 1914 the SS *Ancon* became the first ship to pass officially through the Panama Canal.

READING CHECK **Drawing Conclusions** Why did the United States get involved in Panama's rebellion against Colombian rule?

The Roosevelt Corollary

The Monroe Doctrine, proclaimed in 1823, declared the Western Hemisphere off-limits to further colonization by European nations. For much of the 1800s, however, the Monroe Doctrine was only an idle threat.

After the Spanish-American War, however, presidents began to back up the Monroe Doctrine with military strength. They wanted to protect American economic interests in Latin America.

In the late 1800s Europeans and Americans invested large sums of money in Latin America, which had a wealth of laborers, consumers, and raw materials. Much of this investment came in the form of high-interest bank loans, which many Latin American countries found difficult to repay. Foreign powers often intervened to collect the loans.

In 1904 the Dominican Republic was unable to repay its European lenders. Fearing that the Europeans would use force to collect

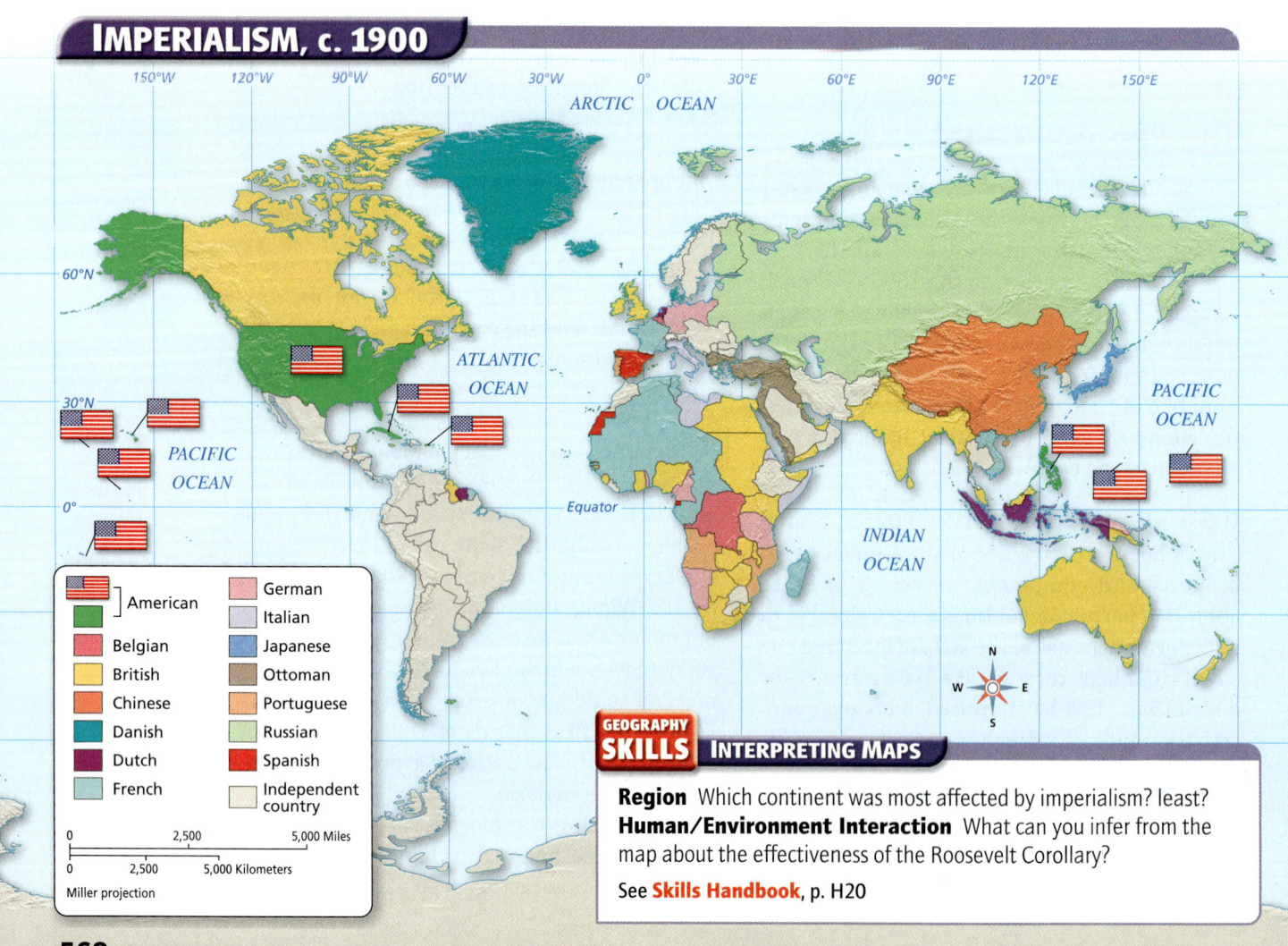

IMPERIALISM, c. 1900

Legend:
- American
- Belgian
- British
- Chinese
- Danish
- Dutch
- French
- German
- Italian
- Japanese
- Ottoman
- Portuguese
- Russian
- Spanish
- Independent country

0   2,500   5,000 Miles
0   2,500   5,000 Kilometers
Miller projection

GEOGRAPHY SKILLS **INTERPRETING MAPS**

Region Which continent was most affected by imperialism? least?
Human/Environment Interaction What can you infer from the map about the effectiveness of the Roosevelt Corollary?

See **Skills Handbook**, p. H20

the debts, President Roosevelt decided to take a tough policy stand. Without seeking approval from any Latin American nation, he issued the **Roosevelt Corollary** to the Monroe Doctrine.

HISTORY'S VOICES

❝Chronic wrongdoing . . . in the Western Hemisphere . . . may force the United States, however reluctantly . . . to the exercise of an international police power.❞

—Theodore Roosevelt, Roosevelt Corollary, 1904

Roosevelt was putting into practice one of his favorite proverbs: "Speak softly and carry a big stick; you will go far." Applying this "big stick" policy to the situation in the Dominican Republic, the United States pledged to use armed forces to prevent any European country from seizing Dominican territory.

Roosevelt hoped to avoid a military confrontation. To ensure that the Europeans were repaid, the United States took control of collecting all Dominican customs duties.

The Roosevelt Corollary succeeded in bringing more stability to the region and keeping other nations out. But America's willingness to use its police power made many Latin Americans uneasy. They worried about continued U.S. involvement in their affairs.

READING CHECK **Identifying Problems and Solutions** Why did Roosevelt decide to announce the Roosevelt Corollary?

Reshaping U.S. Diplomacy

During the presidency of William H. Taft, U.S. influence in Latin America deepened. Taft believed in advancing U.S. interests in other countries through **dollar diplomacy**, a policy of promoting American economic interests in other countries and using that economic power to achieve American policy goals.

To reduce the chances of European interference in Latin America, Taft suggested that Americans buy out European loans. By 1914 Americans had invested more than $1.6 billion in Latin America, mainly in mines, railroads, and banana and sugar plantations.

Dollar diplomacy, however, caused resentment. In Nicaragua, for example, American banks made loans to the government and became heavily involved in the economy. In 1912 President Taft had to send in U.S. troops to quell an uprising against the authorities.

President Woodrow Wilson, who succeeded Taft in 1913, rejected the <u>concept</u> of dollar diplomacy in favor of moral diplomacy, the use of persuasion and American ideals to advance the nation's interests abroad. Nonetheless, he did send in troops when civil unrest shook Haiti in 1915 and the Dominican Republic in 1916. In both cases, U.S. Marines occupied the countries for years.

READING CHECK **Contrasting** How did Taft and Wilson differ in their patterns of diplomacy?

ACADEMIC VOCABULARY

concept abstract notion or idea

go.hrw.com
Online Quiz
Keyword: SD7 HP17

Reviewing Ideas, Terms, and People

1. **a. Recall** How did the United States govern Puerto Rico?
   b. Draw Conclusions Why did the United States make Cuba a **protectorate**?

2. **a. Identify** What was the Panama Canal Zone?
   b. Explain Why was it important to control malaria and yellow fever in Panama?
   c. Predict What effect do you think the Panama Canal had on American military capabilities?

3. **a. Identify** What was the **Roosevelt Corollary**?
   b. Contrast What did the Roosevelt Corollary do that the Monroe Doctrine had not done?

4. **a. Recall** Which president favored **dollar diplomacy**?
   b. Evaluate How effective do you think dollar diplomacy was in Nicaragua?

Critical Thinking

5. **Organizing Information** Copy the table below and fill in the names of Latin American lands discussed in this chapter. Then briefly note how the United States became involved in each.

Country or Territory	U.S. Involvement

FOCUS ON WRITING

6. **Descriptive** Imagine you are a worker helping to build the Panama Canal. Write a diary entry giving details about the task you're doing, the hardships you face, and why you think the project is worthwhile.

Caribbean Sea

Gaillard Cut

At the continental divide, the canal route cuts through the lowest point between two hills, 335.5 feet above sea level. For nearly 9 miles, workers blasted loose the rock. Steam shovels loaded the spoil onto railroad cars to be hauled away.

Lake Gatún

Created by damming the Chagres River, this lake's water feeds the lock system and was once the world's largest human-made lake.

San Francisco

New York

5,200 miles

13,000 miles

Building the Panama Canal

Sailors had dreamed of a canal through Central America since the 1500s, but it wasn't until the early 1900s that engineers had the technology to build it. The canal's planners and builders faced considerable geographic obstacles along the 50-mile path.

New York Standards

ST 4.3 Develop hypotheses about important events, eras, or issues; move from chronicling to explaining historical events and issues.

Madden Lake and Dam

The lake is used to provide more water to the canal system.

How Canal Locks Work

1. A ship enters a lock chamber where the water is level with the body of water the ship is leaving.

2. Gates close behind the ship, and the water level in the chamber rises until level with the next body of water.

3. The gates in front of the boat open to let the vessel pass.

Swamps

When research showed that the malaria-carrying mosquito could not fly far without feeding on vegetation, hundreds of acres were cleared near housing and work sites. To kill the larvae, over 100 square miles of swamps were drained and thousands of gallons of oil were sprayed on the remaining water.

GEOGRAPHY SKILLS **INTERPRETING MAPS**

go.hrw.com
Interactive Map
Keyword: SD7 CH17

1. **Location** What made this part of Panama a good location for a canal?
2. **Human/Environment Interaction** What obstacles made the canal's construction difficult?

See **Skills Handbook**, p. H20

Pacific Ocean

Wilson and the Mexican Revolution

BEFORE YOU READ

MAIN IDEA

American intervention in Mexico's revolution caused strained relations between the two neighbors.

READING FOCUS

1. How did the Díaz dictatorship spark a revolution in Mexico?
2. How and why did the United States intervene in the Mexican Revolution?
3. How did the Mexican Revolution conclude?

KEY TERMS AND PEOPLE

Porfirio Díaz
Francisco Madero
Mexican Revolution
Emiliano Zapata
Francisco "Pancho" Villa
Victoriano Huerta
Tampico incident
Battle of Veracruz
John J. Pershing

PI 2.5 Analyze the United States involvement in foreign affairs and a willingness to engage in international politics, examining the ideas and traditions leading to these foreign policies.

THE INSIDE STORY

Why did Wilson send troops into Mexico? To many people, Francisco "Pancho" Villa was a bandit, a cattle rustler, even a murderer. To many others, he was a folk hero, a kind of Mexican Robin Hood. Legends and ballads told about his deeds. Villa was a brilliant horse rider, leading a cavalry force called Los Dorados ("Golden Ones") in northern Mexico. In 1911 he helped drive Mexico's dictator out of power.

Two years later, Villa was again at the center of a power struggle. This time he was vying with Venustiano Carranza to lead Mexico. When U.S. president Woodrow Wilson recognized Carranza as president, Villa was furious. In 1916 Villa and his men killed a group of American mining engineers in Mexico, and then crossed the border to Columbus, New Mexico. In an attack there, Villa's followers killed more Americans.

Wilson was outraged by the raid on American territory. He sent General John J. Pershing into Mexico with a "punitive expedition." With vehicles and even airplanes, they chased Villa through northern Mexico for almost a year. They never caught him.

By 1917 the United States was preoccupied with war in Europe. American forces left Mexico, and Pancho Villa retired to his ranch. In 1923, however, Villa was ambushed and killed. He died as dramatically as he had lived. ■

PANCHO VILLA WAGES WAR

◀ **Pancho Villa rides to revolution on horseback.**

Dictatorship Sparks a Revolution

When Mexico erupted in revolution in the early 1900s, the United States was drawn into the conflict because of its economic ties with Mexico. But what led to the revolution in the first place?

The Díaz dictatorship For most of the period from 1877 to 1910, the dictator **Porfirio Díaz** ruled Mexico. When Díaz came to power, he brought order to Mexico, which had endured decades of war and unrest. However, order came at a price. Díaz jailed his opponents. He did not permit freedom of the press. He used the army to maintain peace at any cost.

Díaz also got money from foreign investors, including many Americans. Their investments helped modernize Mexico very quickly. Railroads expanded. Production of factory goods doubled. Cotton production also doubled. Still, most Mexicans did not enjoy the benefits of modernization. Wealth became concentrated in the hands of foreign investors and a small Mexican elite. Most Mexicans lived in poverty, and opposition to Díaz grew steadily.

Overthrowing Díaz In 1910 Porfirio Díaz ran for re-election. As in earlier elections, Díaz controlled the outcome. Just before the voting began, he jailed his opponent **Francisco Madero**, a wealthy landowner but a reform-minded idealist. When the ballots were counted, Díaz claimed he had earned a million votes and Madero had earned fewer than 200.

After being released from jail in September 1910, Madero fled over the border to Texas. There he declared himself president of Mexico and called for a revolution. When Madero returned to Mexico in November, he found bands of rebels already active.

The Mexican Revolution unfolded as a series of uprisings in different parts of the country. In the south, **Emiliano Zapata** and his army of mostly Native American peasants—known as Zapatistas—wanted land to be returned to the native peoples. They began to seize land by force. Meanwhile, in northern Mexico, **Francisco "Pancho" Villa** and Pascual Orozco led a large-scale revolt against Díaz. Rebellion spread, and in May 1911, Díaz resigned and went into exile in France.

Shaky leadership In November 1911, Francisco Madero was elected president of Mexico. He tried to establish a democratic government, but he was quickly overwhelmed by the very forces he had unleashed in toppling Díaz. Madero faced challenges from all sides. Even the commander of the government troops, **Victoriano Huerta** (WEHR-tah), proved disloyal. In 1913 Huerta overthrew Madero, imprisoned him, and had him executed soon thereafter. Huerta named himself president of Mexico, but immediately four armies rose up to fight him. The situation in Mexico grew dire.

READING CHECK **Sequencing** What major events occurred between the Mexican election of 1910 and the declaration of Huerta as president?

Turmoil in Mexico

Conflicting visions for Mexico's future led to a series of violent government overthrows.

Porfirio Díaz ruled Mexico as an oppressive dictator from 1877 to 1910. He modernized the country, but kept most of the people impoverished.

Emiliano Zapata led the revolt against Díaz in the south. He and his fellow Zapatistas wanted land returned to Native Americans.

After Díaz fled in the face of revolt, Francisco Madero became president of Mexico. He tried to establish a democratic government.

Victoriano Huerta executed Madero and named himself president. He faced opposition from Mexicans and the United States.

The United States Intervenes

Many European nations recognized Huerta's government, but the United States did not. President Woodrow Wilson viewed Huerta as an assassin with no legitimate claim to power. In February 1914 Wilson authorized arms sales to Huerta's enemies. For a time, Wilson followed a policy of "watchful waiting." Then came an incident that let him move openly against Huerta.

The Tampico incident

On April 9, 1914, nine crew members of the USS *Dolphin* went ashore for supplies in the Mexican port of Tampico. There they were arrested by soldiers loyal to Huerta. The Americans were quickly released unharmed, and Mexican officials apologized. However, U.S. Admiral Henry Mayo demanded more than a formal apology from the Mexican government. He also insisted that the Mexicans give the American flag a 21-gun salute within 24 hours. Huerta refused this humiliating demand.

Because of the Tampico incident, the president asked Congress on April 20 to authorize the use of armed forces against Mexico. Congress approved the request on April 22, but events in Mexico moved faster.

Occupying Veracruz

While waiting for Congress to act, President Wilson learned some alarming news. A German ship loaded with weapons for Huerta was heading for the Mexican port city of Veracruz. Without deliberating further, Wilson ordered the U.S. Navy to seize the city.

Under the cover of a naval bombardment, U.S. Marines then landed at Veracruz. They were met by gunfire from Mexican soldiers, and a violent battle erupted. The Americans had expected to seize control with little bloodshed. Instead, 17 Americans and some 300 Mexicans died during the Battle of Veracruz.

For the next six months, U.S. troops occupied the city. The occupation threatened to plunge the United States and Mexico into war. Crisis was avoided, though, thanks to mediation by Argentina, Brazil, and Chile.

Meanwhile, Huerta struggled to stay in power. In June the mediators called for Huerta's resignation and for the creation of a provisional government. Huerta refused. Pressure mounted against him within Mexico and beyond. In July he resigned and fled to Spain.

READING CHECK **Identifying Cause and Effect** Why did the United States take action against Huerta's government?

The Battle of Veracruz

American sailors aboard a battleship use field artillery to attack Veracruz from their position off the coast. *What prevented the Battle of Veracruz from turning into a full-scale war between the United States and Mexico?*

The Revolution Concludes

With Huerta gone from Mexico, Venustiano Carranza stepped in and declared himself the leader of the Mexican Revolution in August 1914. He faced opposition from Pancho Villa and Emiliano Zapata, however. For some time, it appeared that Villa and Zapata would triumph. This worried American leaders, who feared that U.S. economic interests would be harmed by the land redistribution that Zapata and Villa wanted. President Wilson decided to support the more moderate Carranza.

Pancho Villa retaliated with violence. In March 1916 he led hundreds of troops across the U.S. border to the small, isolated town of Columbus, New Mexico. Striking at dawn, Villa's troops burned the town and killed 17 Americans. This was the first armed invasion of the continental United States since the War of 1812.

Pursuing Pancho Villa President Woodrow Wilson quickly ordered a military expedition to hunt down Villa. Within a week, General **John J. Pershing** led more than 10,000 U.S. troops into Mexico. They searched for 11 months but were never able to capture Pancho Villa. The farther Pershing went into Mexican territory, the more the Mexicans resented the Americans.

By early September 1916, nearly 150,000 U.S. National Guard members were stationed along the Mexican border. Wilson realized that the threat of war increased each day that U.S. troops remained in Mexico. Furthermore, America's attention was shifting to Europe, where World War I was raging. In late January 1917, the president called off the search for Pancho Villa and withdrew U.S. troops from Mexico. Nonetheless, for the rest of Wilson's presidency, relations between Mexico and the United States remained strained.

A new constitution for Mexico In December 1916, Venustiano Carranza called a constitutional convention. A new constitution went into effect on February 5, 1917. The constitution contained the ideas of all the revolutionary groups. It protected the liberties and rights of citizens.

Despite the new constitution, fighting continued in Mexico until 1920. Mexico's economy suffered terribly. Agriculture was disrupted, mines were abandoned, and factories were destroyed. Many Mexican men and women immigrated to the United States in search of work and a more stable life.

READING CHECK **Summarizing** How did Pancho Villa cause trouble for the United States?

FOCUS ON NEW YORK

DAILY LIFE

While many Mexicans originally immigrated to western parts of the United States, they eventually began to immigrate to other parts of the country as well. Today New York City has the eleventh-largest Mexican-American population among major U.S. cities.

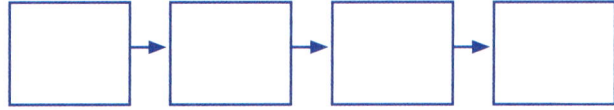

SECTION 4 ASSESSMENT

go.hrw.com
Online Quiz
Keyword: SD7 HP17

Reviewing Ideas, Terms, and People

1. a. Identify Who was **Porfirio Díaz**?
   b. Explain Why did Mexicans rise up against Díaz?
   c. Elaborate Why do you think that **Francisco Madero** and **Victoriana Huerta** both faced challenges after they claimed Mexico's presidency?

2. a. Recall What was the **Tampico incident**?
   b. Analyze How did the Tampico incident draw the United States into armed conflict with Mexico?
   c. Evaluate Was the United States justified in launching the **Battle of Veracruz**? Why or why not?

3. a. Describe What made **Pancho Villa** decide to lead a raid into New Mexico?
   b. Draw Conclusions Why was President Wilson so eager to capture Pancho Villa?
   c. Predict How do you think the expedition to find Pancho Villa affected relations between Mexicans and Americans?

Critical Thinking

4. Sequencing Copy the flowchart below and record the major sequence of events of the Mexican Revolution, from the overthrow of Díaz to the Constitution of 1917. Add as many boxes as you need.

FOCUS ON SPEAKING

5. Persuasive Imagine that you are a Mexican revolutionary in 1911, while Porfirio Díaz is still clinging to power. Prepare a speech to give to people in your community, explaining why you oppose Díaz and whom you support in his place. Encourage your listeners to join you in the fight to overthrow Díaz and bring better leadership to Mexico.

Views on American Expansionism

ST 4.1 Analyze important debates in American history, focusing on the opposing positions and the historical evidence used to support these positions.

ST 4.3 Develop hypotheses about important events, eras, or issues; move from chronicling to explaining historical events and issues; use information collected from diverse sources to produce cogently written reports and document-based essays.

Historical Context The documents below provide information about attitudes regarding American expansion in the late 1800s.

Task Examine the documents and answer the questions that follow. Then write an essay about interaction between imperialists and local peoples. Use facts from the documents and the chapter to support the position you take in your thesis statement.

DOCUMENT 1

Princess Kaiulani, niece of Hawaii's Queen Liliuokalani, visited Washington, D.C., in 1893 to plead for a restoration of the monarchy.

"Seventy years ago, Christian Americans sent over Christian men and women to give religion and civilization to Hawaii. Today, three of the sons of the missionaries are at your capitol, asking you to undo their fathers' work. Who sent them? Who gave them the authority to break the constitution which they swore they would uphold? Today, I, a poor, weak girl, with not one of my people near me and all these statesmen against me, have the strength to stand up for the rights of my people. Even now I can hear their wail in my heart, and I am strong . . . strong in the faith of God, strong in the knowledge that I am right, strong in the strength of seventy million people who in this free land will hear my cry and will refuse to let their flag cover dishonor to mine!"

DOCUMENT 2

John L. Stevens was the U.S. minister to Hawaii in 1893, when Queen Liliuokalani was forced from the throne. That year, he wrote "The Hawaiian Situation. II. A Plea for Annexation."

"The Hawaiian monarchy being thus extinct, and the Hawaiian Islands being not sufficient to constitute an independent nation, all who really understand their situation know that good government is now the first and imperative need . . . [T]hese Islands have become thoroughly Americanized . . . For sixty years the Islands have had the American school system . . . The two principal daily newspapers are edited, owned, and published by Americans. The principal lawyers at the bar and on the bench are Americans . . . and educated in American colleges. More than eighty percent of the trade, amounting to more than twenty million dollars per year, is with the United States. American newspapers, magazines, and books are in as familiar use in the Islands as in the United States . . .

A paramount reason why annexation should not be long postponed is that, if it soon takes place, the crown and government lands will be cut up and sold to American and Christian Caucasian people, thus preventing the Islands from being submerged and overrun by Asiatics, putting an end to Japanese ambitions stimulated by our strong European rival."

Puck was a political magazine that often used humor and satire to address social and political issues. In this magazine cover, the annexation of Hawaii is shown as a marriage between a Hawaiian woman and Uncle Sam. President William McKinley is depicted as a minister, and Alabama senator John T. Morgan stands behind the couple with a shotgun.

ANOTHER SHOTGUN WEDDING, WITH NEITHER PARTY WILLING.

Skills FOCUS — READING LIKE A HISTORIAN

1. **a. Recall** Refer to Document 1. Why does Kaiulani feel that she will be successful?
   b. Contrast In Kaiulani's view, how are the sons of the early missionaries different from their fathers?

2. **a. Identify** Refer to Document 2. What reasons does Stevens give for annexing Hawaii to the United States?
   b. Predict How might Stevens have responded to a statement like that made by Kaiulani?

3. **a. Identify** Refer to Document 3. What expression is shown on the woman's face?

   b. Evaluate How would you describe the cartoonist's opinion of annexation?

4. **Document-Based Essay Question** Consider the question below and form a thesis statement. Using examples from Documents 1, 2, and 3, create an outline and write a short essay supporting your position.
   What factors influenced the decision to annex Hawaii?

See **Skills Handbook**, pp. H28–H29, H31

Visual Summary: Entering the World Stage

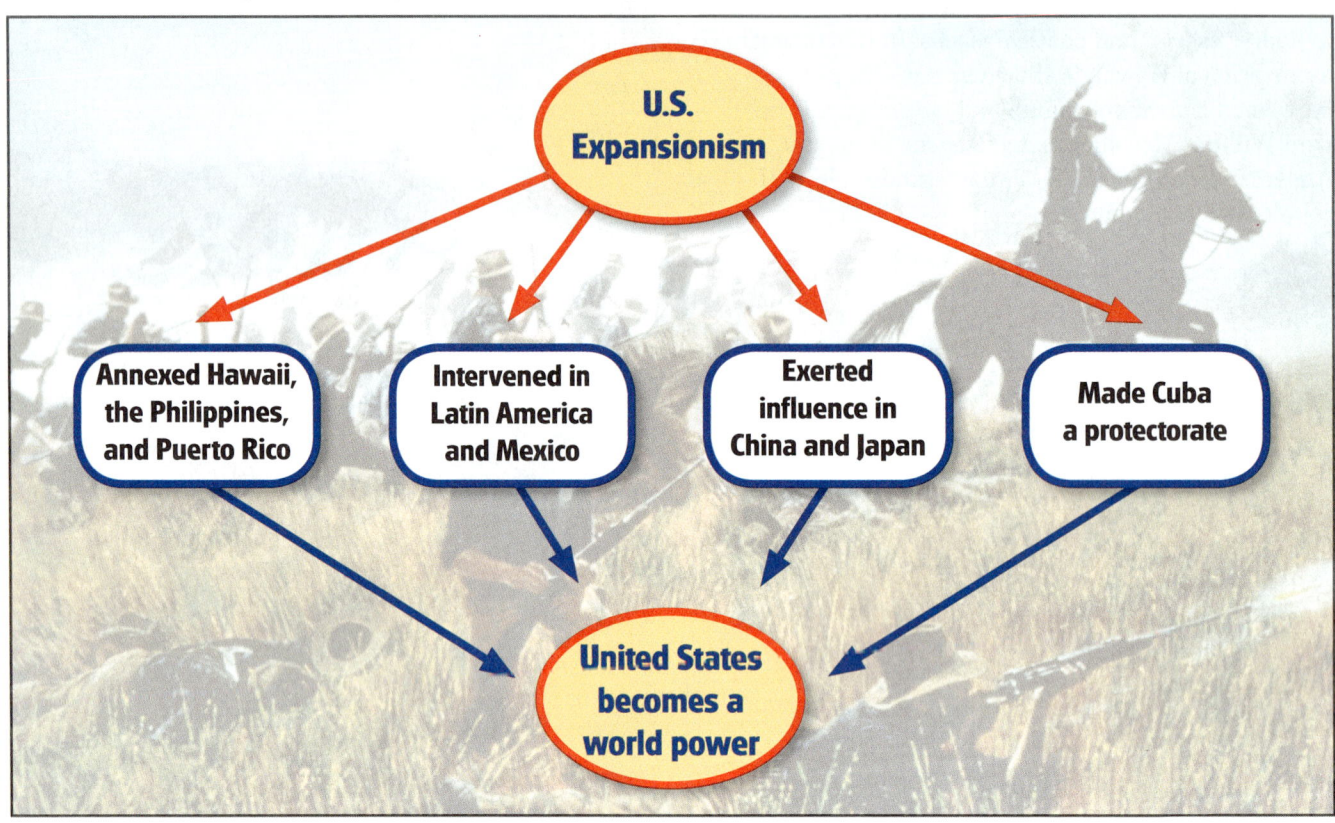

U.S. Expansionism

Annexed Hawaii, the Philippines, and Puerto Rico

Intervened in Latin America and Mexico

Exerted influence in China and Japan

Made Cuba a protectorate

United States becomes a world power

Reviewing Key Terms and People

Complete each sentence by filling the blank with the correct term or name.

1. In 1887 King Kalakaua was forced to sign the _____, which severely restricted his power and denied most Hawaiians the right to vote.

2. Imperialist nations carved out _____ in China—geographic areas where they dominated politics or the economy.

3. The _____ was intended to give all nations equal trading rights in China.

4. The sensationalist style of news coverage called _____ helped sway U.S. public opinion in favor of war with Spain.

5. The _____ gave the United States the right to intervene in Cuban affairs and to buy or lease land for naval and coaling stations.

6. In Latin America and Asia, President Taft practiced _____, a policy of substituting economic power for military force.

7. The Mexican Revolution began as an effort to overthrow the dictator _____.

8. The _____ occurred on April 9, 1914, when nine U.S. sailors were mistakenly arrested by Mexican soldiers.

9. The _____ took place after the United States seized a German ship that was carrying weapons to Mexican president Victoriano Huerta.

Comprehension and Critical Thinking

SECTION 1 *(pp. 552–557)*

10. **a. Identify** Who was Queen Liliuokalani?

b. Explain Why did Liliuokalani's plans for strengthening the monarchy alarm the American business community in Hawaii?

c. Predict How do you think the Japanese reacted to the Great White Fleet? Do you think the fleet had the effect that President Roosevelt wished?

History's Impact video program

Review the video to answer the closing question:
What are two benefits the Panama Canal has
provided for the United States?

SECTION 2 *(pp. 558–564)*

11. a. Recall What was the de Lôme letter?

b. Summarize What were the consequences of the
Spanish-American War?

c. Evaluate How much influence did the media
have in building public support for the Spanish-
American War? Explain.

SECTION 3 *(pp. 565–569)*

12. a. Describe What was the Roosevelt Corollary?

b. Analyze In what various ways did the United
States exert its power in Latin America?

c. Evaluate How did the acquisition of overseas
territory affect the way the United States viewed
its role in the world?

SECTION 4 *(pp. 572–575)*

13. a. Identify Who was Pancho Villa?

b. Contrast As government leaders, how did Porfirio Díaz and Francisco Madero differ?

c. Elaborate Why do you think President Wilson
wished to avoid war with Mexico?

Using the Internet

go.hrw.com
Practice Online
Keyword: SD7 CH17

14. On December 31, 1999, the
United States returned control of the Panama
Canal and the 10-mile-wide Canal Zone to the government of Panama. Using the keyword above, do
research to learn about the events that led to this
historic handover. Then create a report that analyzes the reasons why the United States gave up
the canal and the Canal Zone to Panama.

Analyzing Primary Sources

Reading Like a Historian This painting shows a
pineapple plantation in Hawaii, where pineapples
were typically harvested by hand.

15. Analyzing Visuals
How are the pickers
protecting them-
selves against the
tropical heat?

16. Making Inferences
Why do you suppose
one man is on
horseback?

Critical Reading

*Read the passage in Section 1 that begins with the
heading "Influence in China." Then answer the questions that follow.*

17. Why did the United States propose the Open Door
Policy?

A The United States wanted to prevent China
from refusing to trade with western nations.

B The United States was protesting Japan's seizure of Taiwan.

C The United States hoped the Open Door Policy
would help resolve the Boxer Rebellion.

D Without a sphere of influence of its own, the
United States was afraid of being cut out of the
China trade.

18. Which of the following is a true statement about
the Boxer Rebellion?

A Members of a secret martial arts group in
China demanded more respect for their sport.

B Foreign missionaries and Chinese Christians in
Beijing came under attack.

C An large international military force stopped
the rebellion in 1900 and occupied China for many
years afterward.

D The Boxer Rebellion caused western nations to
reject the Open Door Policy.

FOCUS ON WRITING ✏️

Persuasive Writing *Persuasive writing takes a position for or against an issue, using facts and examples
as supporting evidence. To practice persuasive writing,
complete the assignment below.*

Topic U.S. imperialism in the late 1800s and
early 1900s

19. Assignment Write a paragraph in which you take
a position on the overseas activities of the United
States in the late 1800s and early 1900s. Was the
United States justified in annexing foreign territories and expanding its control over other nations
during this period? Support your point of view
with reasoning and examples from your reading
and studies.

The First WORLD WAR

THE BIG PICTURE

The United States tried to stay neutral when war swept Europe. After the United States joined the Allies in 1917, however, the government quickly mobilized the economy and built public support for the war.

New York Standards

Key Idea 2 Important ideas, social and cultural values, beliefs, and traditions from New York State and United States history illustrate the connections and interactions of people and events across time and from a variety of perspectives.

Key Idea 3 Study about the major social, political, economic, cultural, and religious developments in New York State and United States history involves learning about the important roles and contributions of individuals and groups.

Skills FOCUS **READING LIKE A HISTORIAN**

Artist Frank Schoonover captured a spirit of optimism and determination in the faces of these young Allied soldiers in *Doughboys First.* (A "doughboy" is an infantry member.) The painting was one of a series painted for *The Ladies' Home Journal.*

Interpreting Visuals What do you think the artist wanted to accomplish with this painting?

See **Skills Handbook**, p. H30

U.S.

August 1914
President Wilson declares American neutrality in World War I.

1914

World

June 1914
Archduke Franz Ferdinand is killed in Sarajevo.

August 1914
German troops invade Belgium, and Great Britain declares war on Germany.

History's Impact video program

Watch the video to understand the impact of *Schenck* v. *United States*.

May 1915
German U-boat sinks the *Lusitania*, killing 128 Americans.

April 1917
President Wilson asks Congress to declare war against Germany.

January 1918
President Wilson presents his 14-point plan for world peace.

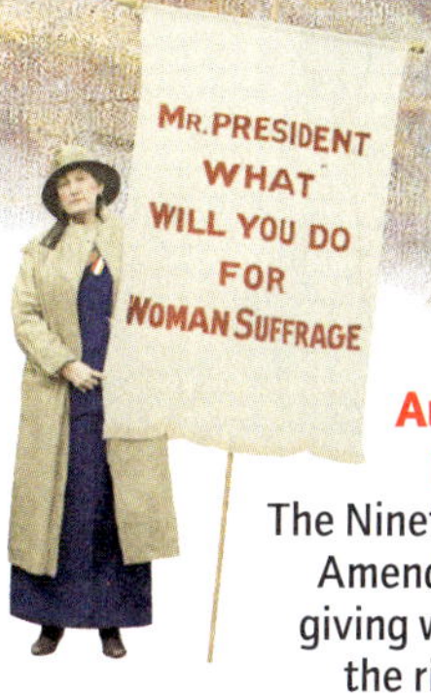

August 1920
The Nineteenth Amendment, giving women the right to vote, is ratified.

| 1915 | 1916 | 1917 | 1918 | 1919 | 1920 |

February 1915
Germany sets up a submarine blockade of England.

November 1917
Lenin's Bolsheviks take control of Russia.

November 11, 1918
The Allies and Germany sign an armistice.

June 1919
The Treaty of Versailles officially ends World War I.

581

BEFORE YOU READ

MAIN IDEA

Rivalries among European nations led to the outbreak of war in 1914.

READING FOCUS

1. What were the causes of World War I?
2. How did the war break out?
3. Why did the war quickly reach a stalemate?

KEY TERMS AND PEOPLE

Archduke Franz Ferdinand
Kaiser Wilhelm II
militarism
Triple Alliance
Triple Entente
balance of power
Central Powers
Allied Powers
trench warfare

PI 3.2 Research and analyze the major themes and developments in New York State and United States history (e.g., colonization and settlement; Revolution and New National Period; immigration; expansion and reform era; Civil War and Reconstruction; the American labor movement; Great Depression; World Wars; contemporary United States).

◄ **Soldiers arrest Archduke Ferdinand's young assassin.**

A WRONG TURN INTO History

THE INSIDE STORY

How does a 19-year-old start a world war? In 1912 Serbian teenager Gavrilo Princip joined the Black Hand terrorist organization. Princip wanted to free his home country, Bosnia and Herzegovina, from Austro-Hungarian rule. He was already a good shot with a pistol—a handy skill for a terrorist.

After years of training and planning, the Black Hand leaders came up with a terrorist plot that they hoped could lead to an independent Bosnia. They heard that **Archduke Franz Ferdinand** of Austria was going to visit the Bosnian

city of Sarajevo. The Black Hand ordered a team of assassins to kill the archduke.

On June 28, 1914, Princip and six other terrorists positioned themselves around Sarajevo as Ferdinand and his wife toured the city in a convertible sedan. Princip was hungry, so he went to buy a sandwich. As he stepped out of the sandwich shop, he could not believe his eyes. There, stopped in front of him, was the car carrying the archduke. Princip dropped his sandwich, reached for his pistol, and fired, killing the archduke and his wife. This single act would propel most of Europe into war within weeks. ■

Causes of World War I

Some 3,000 miles away from Sarajevo, most Americans cared little about the news of Archduke Franz Ferdinand's death. A North Dakota newspaper reported, "One archduke more or less makes little difference." In Europe, however, the death of this archduke made a huge difference. Most of Europe plunged into war within five short weeks. But how could one assassination start a world war?

Long before Princip fired his pistol, a series of political changes in Europe made war almost unavoidable. By 1914 Europe was ripe for war.

Nationalism Nationalism is an extreme pride or devotion that people feel for their country or culture. The spirit of nationalism led to the formation of new nations, such as Germany and Italy during the 1870s. It also led to competition for power.

This struggle for greater power was most visible in the Balkans, a region of southeastern Europe populated by a great number of ethnic groups. The Ottoman Empire, which had ruled the Balkans for hundreds of years, was starting to fall apart during the 1800s. The Austro-Hungarian Empire saw an opportunity to expand and began to push into the region, annexing provinces such as Bosnia and Herzegovina. Many Slavic peoples there, such as the Serbs, rejected the rule of these outsiders.

Some Serbs encouraged other Slavic peoples to revolt against Austria-Hungary, and they received support from Russia, another European power. Russia saw itself as the protector of the Slavs and argued with the Austro-Hungarian rulers about the future of Serbia and control of the Balkans. By the early 1900s tensions in the region were high.

Imperialism Austria-Hungary was not the only nation trying to expand during the late 1800s. Growing nationalism also led nations to compete for overseas colonies. This quest for colonial empires was known as imperialism.

By the late 1800s Great Britain and France already had colonial empires in Africa, the Middle East, and Asia. Colonies provided markets and rich natural resources, so the German emperor, **Kaiser Wilhelm II**, wanted colonies for Germany, too. And to get them, Germany would need a stronger military.

Militarism The world soon also saw the rise of **militarism**—the policy of military preparedness and building up weapons. In 1900 Germany began to build a navy that could take on the world's strongest sea power—Great Britain's Royal Navy.

At the same time, Germany had also enlarged its army. It supplied its troops with the latest weapons, including machine guns and larger artillery.

German army officials also began to draw up war strategies. One such strategy, the Schlieffen Plan, provided precise instructions for waging a two-front war against France and Russia at the same time. The Schlieffen Plan also called for a surprise invasion of France by passing through Belgium, with a subsequent attack on Russia.

Aware of Germany's growing supply of weapons, Great Britain, France, and Russia worried about Germany's intentions. Each country began to build its own military in order to defend itself should war break out.

Many Europeans believed that strong military forces would prevent countries from attacking one another. British admiral Jackie Fisher explained, "I am not for war, I am for peace. That is why I am for a supreme Navy. The supremacy of the British Navy is the best security for the peace of the world."

Alliances For protection, some nations formed alliances, or partnerships. These alliances were created to maintain peace, but they would lead Europe directly into war.

Germany formed a military alliance with Austria-Hungary and Italy. This alliance became known as the **Triple Alliance**. Fearful of Germany's growing power, France and Russia formed a secret alliance with each other. Meanwhile, Great Britain also began to worry about Germany's expanding navy and allied itself with France. Soon Britain, France, and Russia formed the **Triple Entente** (AHN-TAHNT).

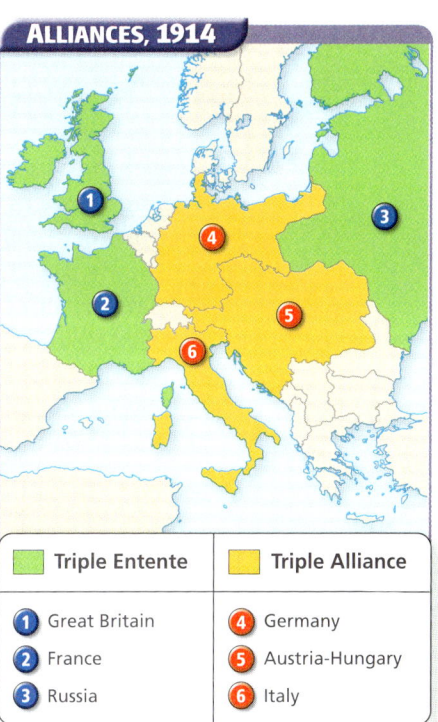

ALLIANCES, 1914

Triple Entente	Triple Alliance
1 Great Britain	**4** Germany
2 France	**5** Austria-Hungary
3 Russia	**6** Italy

ACADEMIC VOCABULARY

subsequent following in time or order

The word *entente* come from French and means "understanding.")

Some European leaders believed that these alliances created a **balance of power**, in which each nation or alliance had equal strength. Many leaders thought that the alliance system would help decrease the chances of war. They hoped that no single nation would attack another out of fear that the attacked nation's allies would join the fight.

The assassination of Archduke Franz Ferdinand exposed the flaws in this thinking. The major European powers' long history of national tensions, imperial rivalries, and military expansion proved too great for alliances to overcome. After this single attack on Austria-Hungary, Europe exploded into war.

READING CHECK **Summarizing** What issues led Europe to the brink of war in 1914?

War Breaks Out

After the assassination, Princip was immediately arrested. While investigating Princip's background, Austro-Hungarian officials learned that the Serbian government had supplied the assassins with bombs and weapons. Furious, Austria-Hungary blamed Serbia for Ferdinand's murder and declared war.

Russia had promised to protect Serbian Slavs. Therefore, the Russian army quickly began to mobilize, or prepare for war. Germany viewed Russia's mobilization as an act of aggression against its ally Austria-Hungary and declared war on Russia. Then Germany declared war on France, Russia's ally. All-out war was about to begin.

The Germans take Belgium Germany made the first move in the war, following the Schlieffen Plan. On August 4, 1914, German troops crossed the border into the neutral country of Belgium. Kaiser Wilhelm II believed Germany needed to make this first move in order to catch Belgium and France by surprise.

Germany's invasion of Belgium drew a new, powerful nation into the conflict. Because the British had pledged to defend Belgium, Great Britain declared war on Germany.

With the entry of Great Britain into the war, most of the major powers of Europe had chosen sides. On one side were Germany,

Austria-Hungary, and the Ottoman Empire, fighting together as the **Central Powers**.

On the other side of the conflict were Great Britain, France, and Russia, who united as the **Allied Powers**, or Allies. Before the conflict's end, another 30 nations, including Italy, would join in what became known as the Great War. Later generations would call it World War I.

At first the Schlieffen Plan worked well for Germany. With only six divisions of troops, Belgian forces were no match for the 38 divisions of the German army, totaling a massive 700,000 soldiers. The tiny Belgian army fought bravely and put up an unexpectedly strong defense, but they were only able to delay the German advance briefly.

The German attack on Belgium was fierce. Germans burned entire villages to the ground. Civilians caught in the fighting, including women and children, were executed. German field marshal Helmuth von Moltke admitted,

MAJOR BATTLES

 Battle of Tannenberg, Aug. 1914
Russia's worst defeat in World War I

 1st Battle of the Marne, Sept. 1914
Allies halted the German advance and saved Paris from occupation

 1st Battle of Ypres, Oct.–Nov. 1914
Last major German offensive until 1918

 3rd Battle of Ypres (Passchendaele), July–Nov. 1917
British forces advanced just five miles at a cost of about 300,000 lives

 Battle of Gallipoli, April–Dec. 1915
Failed attempt of the Allies to knock the Ottoman Empire out of World War I

 Battle of Verdun, Feb.–Dec. 1916
Longest battle of World War I with huge loss of life

 Battle of the Somme, July–Nov. 1916
First major offensive for the British; remembered for its staggering loss of life

 Battle of Caporetto, Oct.–Nov. 1917
Tremendous victory for the Central Powers

"Our advance in Belgium is certainly brutal... all who get in the way must take the consequences."

A new kind of warfare Word of the German invasion of Belgium quickly spread to France and other European countries. French troops mobilized and rushed to meet the approaching German divisions. The French troops who marched to the front looked much as French soldiers had looked more than 40 years earlier, wearing bright red uniforms and heavy brass helmets. The Germans, on the other hand, dressed in gray uniforms that worked as camouflage to help them blend into the battlefield.

French war strategy had also not changed much since the 1800s. In Belgium, French soldiers marched row by row onto the battlefield. With bayonets mounted to their field rifles,

Interactive Map

WORLD WAR I, 1914–1917

Legend:
- Allied Powers
- Central Powers
- Neutral nations
- German U-boat activity
- Allied Powers advance
- Central Powers advance
- Furthest Central Powers advance
- Allied Powers victory
- Central Powers victory
- Undecided outcome

0   150   300 Miles
0   150   300 Kilometers
Lambert azimuthal equal-area projection

BLOCKADE 1914–1917

1st and 3rd Battles of Ypres
Battle of the Somme
1st Battle of the Marne
Battle of Verdun
Battle of Tannenberg
Battle of Caporetto
Battle of Gallipoli

GEOGRAPHY SKILLS **INTERPRETING MAPS**

go.hrw.com
Interactive Map
Keyword: SD7 CH18

Location Where was the Western Front of the war located at this time? What were the outcomes of the major battles fought there?
Movement Describe the movement of the Central Powers. Why did the war have two fronts?

See **Skills Handbook**, p. H20

they were prepared for close combat with the Germans. But when French officers drew their swords and ordered their troops to charge, they were met by a hail of machine gun bullets.

The French military had purchased a small number of machine guns and other new weapons such as the 75-millimeter artillery gun. They were not prepared for Germany's massive firepower.

A well-trained German machine gun team could set up its equipment in just four seconds, and each machine gun's firepower equaled that of 50 to 100 French rifles. Machine guns could fire up to 600 bullets per minute and mow down thousands of troops. In early battles, some 15,000 French soldiers died per day. In short, the Germans were prepared to fight a new kind of war. The French were not.

Many European leaders thought that these modern advances in military technology would result in a short war. German military advisers confidently predicted that France would be defeated in two months.

When the war began in midsummer, Kaiser Wilhelm II promised his German soldiers that they would be home "before the leaves had fallen." The European powers would soon learn that this new kind of war would last much longer than expected, and its devastation would be much more terrible.

The First Battle of the Marne The German army quickly advanced through northern France. After only one month of fighting, the German army was barely 25 miles from Paris. Still, the French troops refused to surrender.

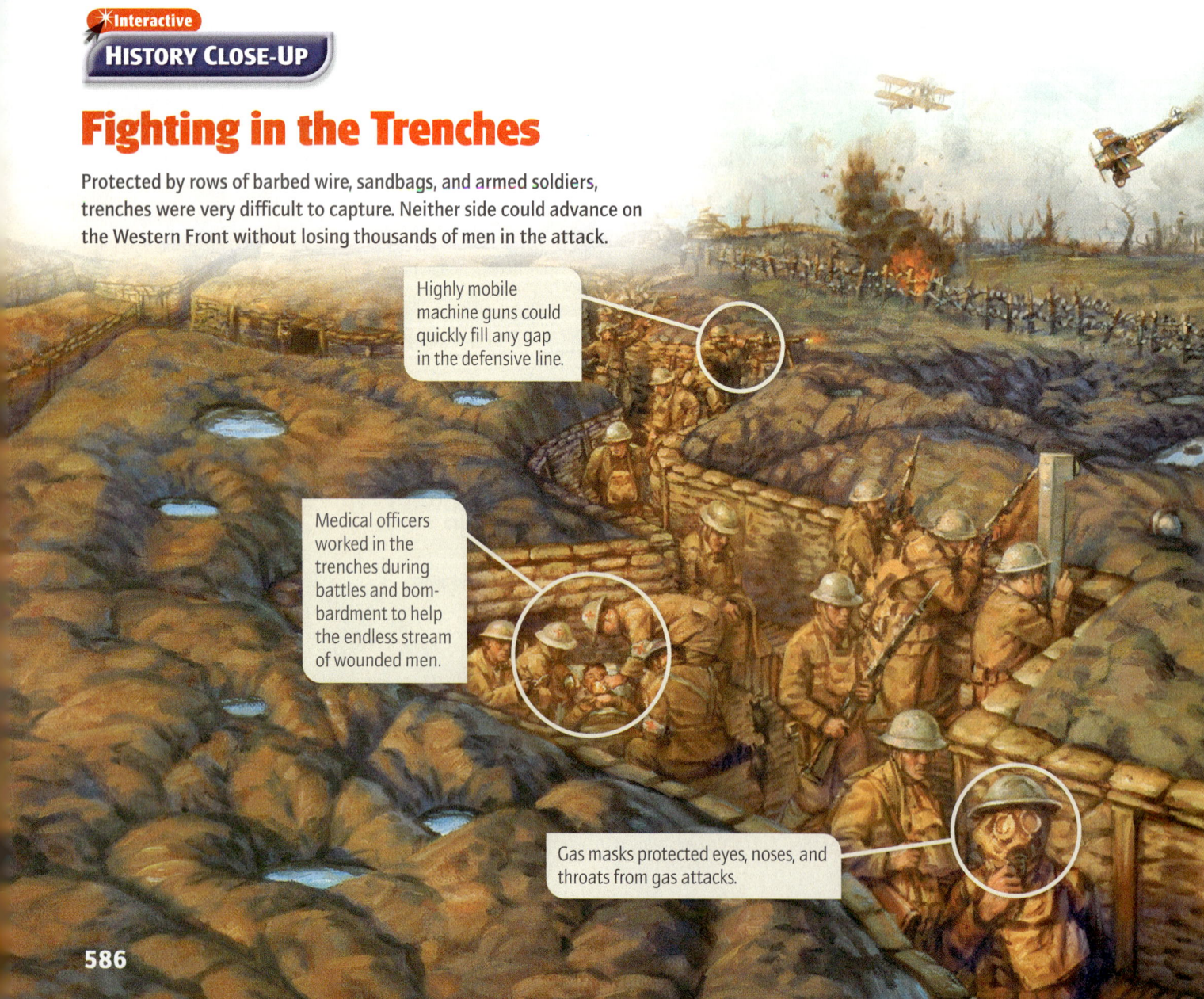

Interactive
HISTORY CLOSE-UP

Fighting in the Trenches

Protected by rows of barbed wire, sandbags, and armed soldiers, trenches were very difficult to capture. Neither side could advance on the Western Front without losing thousands of men in the attack.

Highly mobile machine guns could quickly fill any gap in the defensive line.

Medical officers worked in the trenches during battles and bombardment to help the endless stream of wounded men.

Gas masks protected eyes, noses, and throats from gas attacks.

Desperate for a victory, the French launched a daring counterattack along the Marne River east of Paris on September 7, 1914. In what became known as the First Battle of the Marne, 2 million men fought along a battle-front that stretched 125 miles. After five days and 250,000 lives lost, the French had rallied and pushed the Germans back some 40 miles.

The French had paid a heavy price. A French journalist walking on the battlefield saw what he thought was a field of red poppies. However, these bright patches of red were actually the uniforms of countless fallen French troops.

Despite the cost of the French counterat-tack, it helped the Allies by giving Russia more time to mobilize for war. Once Russia mobilized, Germany had to pull some of its troops out of France. It needed those troops to fight Russia along the Eastern Front, which stretched from the Black Sea to the Baltic Sea.

READING CHECK **Drawing Conclusions** Why was World War I considered a new kind of war?

The War Reaches a Stalemate

The First Battle of the Marne ended in a standoff. Both French and German soldiers dug trenches, or deep ditches, to seek protection from enemy fire and to defend their positions. By the late fall of 1914, two massive systems of trenches stretched for some 400 miles across western Europe. These battle lines of the Western Front extended from Switzerland to the North Sea.

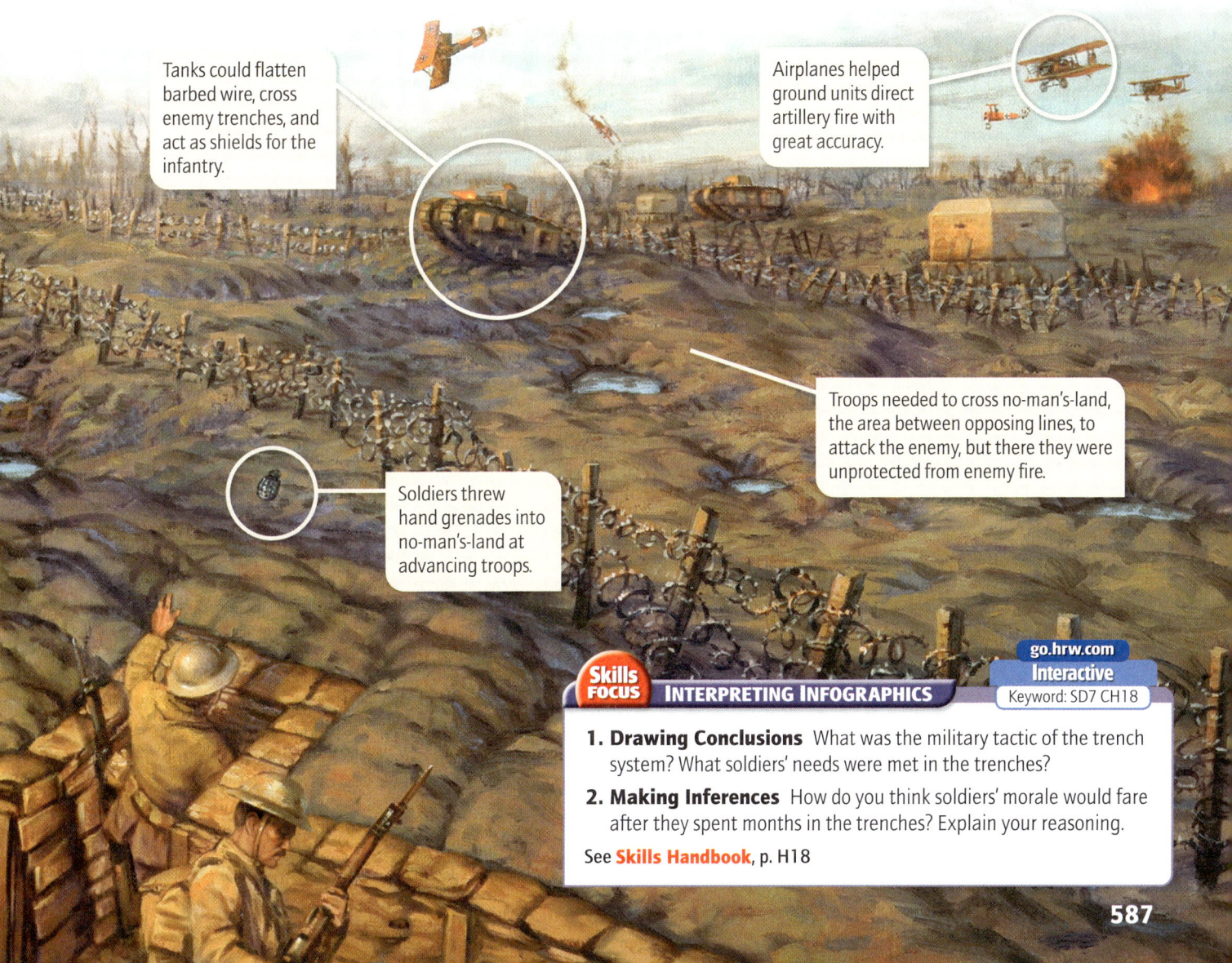

Tanks could flatten barbed wire, cross enemy trenches, and act as shields for the infantry.

Airplanes helped ground units direct artillery fire with great accuracy.

Troops needed to cross no-man's-land, the area between opposing lines, to attack the enemy, but there they were unprotected from enemy fire.

Soldiers threw hand grenades into no-man's-land at advancing troops.

Skills FOCUS **INTERPRETING INFOGRAPHICS**

go.hrw.com
Interactive
Keyword: SD7 CH18

1. **Drawing Conclusions** What was the military tactic of the trench system? What soldiers' needs were met in the trenches?
2. **Making Inferences** How do you think soldiers' morale would fare after they spent months in the trenches? Explain your reasoning.

See **Skills Handbook**, p. H18

The Battle of the Somme

The British made little progress against the Germans' heavy barbed wire and trenches during the Battle of the Somme. After months of fighting, they had advanced only six miles, and hundreds of thousands of soldiers had lost their lives (see table below).

SOMME STATISTICS

Duration of battle: July 1–Nov. 18, 1916

Total Allied casualties: about 630,000

British casualties on day 1: about 57,000

Total German casualties: about 650,000

THE IMPACT TODAY

Science and Technology

Since World War I, improvements in technology have made trench warfare nearly obsolete. Because the military today uses long-distance weapons, radar, and air surveillance, there is less direct combat.

Fighting in the trenches Trench warfare, or fighting from trenches, was not a new strategy. Years earlier American armies had dug trenches during some Civil War battles, including Petersburg. In other wars, armies had dug some trenches in Asia decades before World War I.

However, no soldiers had ever experienced trench warfare on the scale that European forces now did. All across the Western Front, soldiers lived in the trenches, surrounded by machine gun fire, flying grenades, and exploding artillery shells.

Many European military officers thought that a well-motivated army could easily capture the enemy's trenches. They were wrong. Opposing forces had their machine guns aimed at enemy trenches at all times. Any time a helmet or rifle appeared along the trench line, the opposing troops would fire.

Occasionally, soldiers would go over the top to fire at the enemy, but this meant they also lost the protection the trench provided. Soldiers would jump out of their trenches and run across the area between opposing trenches—called no-man's-land—as quickly as they could to attack the other side. But as they ran, thousands of men were chopped down by enemy machine gun fire. No-man's-land became littered with bodies.

As a result, neither the Allies nor the Germans were able to make significant advances. Trench warfare created a stalemate, or deadlock. With the fighting bogged down, both the Allied and Central Powers began looking for new ways to gain an advantage. Many of these new strategies involved the use of new weapons and technology.

New weapons Scientists for both the Allied and Central Powers developed new weapons during World War I in an attempt to win an advantage. German military scientists had been experimenting with poisonous gas as a possible weapon to defeat the Allies.

Although gas seemed to be a breakthrough in military technology, actually using the poisonous gas as a weapon on the battlefield remained a very risky maneuver. Soldiers did not know how much gas to use in an attack. Moreover, a quick change in wind direction could blow the gas back into the troops who had launched it.

The German military eventually found ways to overcome these obstacles, however. In April 1915 German soldiers fired canisters of poisonous gas into Allied trenches. A yellow-green cloud of chlorine gas miles wide enveloped the Allied soldiers. The gas quickly destroyed the soldiers' lungs, and many of them panicked.

Some traditional military officers felt that using poisonous gas was an unfair and barbaric way to fight the war. Even the German commander at the April 1915 attack regretted using the gas, saying, "The plan of poisoning the enemy with gas just as if they were rats . . . disgusted me."

Nevertheless, the Allies could not let the Germans gain an advantage. So British and French forces soon began to develop and use the poisonous gas in their attacks against the Germans as well.

Gas, however, had little effect on the outcome of battles. Soldiers on both sides began to carry gas masks for protection against this new kind of chemical warfare. The gas masks worked well. As long as the soldiers could see the colored gas cloud approaching, they could survive a poisonous gas attack simply by putting on their gas masks.

Once again facing a stalemate, both the Allied and Central Powers began to look for other weapons that could help them win the war. British forces soon developed a motorized armored tank which could maneuver through the dangerous no-man's-land.

These tanks, however, had limited success. In the first battle in which tanks were used, 18 out of 48 tanks became stuck in the mud. Although the tanks frightened the German troops, German military planners were not as impressed. They soon developed strategies to destroy the tanks with artillery fire.

Airplanes proved to be even more useful than tanks. Both sides used airplanes to map enemy positions and trenches and to attack the trenches from above. At first, airplane pilots dropped bricks and heavy objects on enemy troops. Soon, mechanics also figured out how to mount machine guns on planes and launch bombs from the air.

Skilled French and British pilots, or aces, fought German pilots in spectacular air battles called dogfights. Using daring rolls and dives, Allied pilots dueled German aces such as the notorious Baron Manfred von Richthofen, who was known as the Red Baron. The Red Baron shot down 80 Allied planes before he himself was finally shot down in 1918.

Nevertheless, none of the new technologies used in battle gave the Allied or Central Powers the advantage they hoped for. The miserable form of battle known as trench warfare continued. Clearly something would have to change before either side could declare victory in the war.

READING CHECK **Summarizing** Why were the new weapons not very effective in ending trench warfare?

---

go.hrw.com
Online Quiz
Keyword: SD7 HP18

SECTION 1 ASSESSMENT

Reviewing Ideas, Terms, and People

1. **a. Identify** What was **militarism**?
   b. Explain How did the assassination of **Archduke Franz Ferdinand** lead so many nations into war?
   c. Elaborate Why do you think that European nations were willing to go to war so quickly?

2. **a. Recall** What kinds of military technology were new in World War I?
   b. Draw Conclusions At the beginning of the war, how did the new military technology affect the way European leaders thought about the war?
   c. Evaluate Was it reasonable for European leaders to believe the war would be quick? Why or why not?

3. **a. Identify** What was **trench warfare**?
   b. Draw Conclusions How did trench warfare affect the progress of the war?
   c. Elaborate How did soldiers try to overcome the limitations of trench warfare?

Critical Thinking

4. **Identifying Cause and Effect** Copy the chart below and record the four main causes of World War I. Below each cause list two supporting examples.

Cause				
Example				
Example				

FOCUS ON WRITING

5. **Persuasive** Write a letter to the editor of a newspaper that argues either for or against using poison gas and other new military technologies in World War I. Write your letter as if you are a soldier in the war. Use information from the chapter to support your position.

The United States in World War I

BEFORE YOU READ

MAIN IDEA

The United States helped turn the tide for an Allied victory.

READING FOCUS

1. Why did the United States try to stay neutral in the war?
2. Which events showed that America was heading into war?
3. What contributions did Americans make in Europe?
4. How did the war end?

KEY TERMS AND PEOPLE

Lusitania
isolationism
U-boats
Sussex pledge
Zimmermann Note
Selective Service Act
convoy system
Communists

 2.5 Analyze the United States involvement in foreign affairs and a willingness to engage in international politics, examining the ideas and traditions leading to these foreign policies.

THE INSIDE STORY

Would you travel into a war zone? In New York Harbor on Saturday, May 1, 1915, some 1,900 passengers and crew boarded the British luxury ship **Lusitania** and headed for a war zone. The ship's destination was Great Britain. A spokesperson for the ship's company reassured the nervous passengers, "The *Lusitania* … is too fast for any German submarine."

In the early afternoon of May 7, 1915, the *Lusitania* approached the British Isles. Crew member Leslie Morton spotted ominous air bubbles and streaks in the water below. He grabbed a megaphone and shouted, "Torpedoes coming!" But it was too late. A torpedo slammed into the ship's right side. Passengers scrambled for life jackets and lifeboats when the ship began to lean and take on water. As the *Lusitania* slid beneath the waves, parents tried to hold their children above water. Some even tied their children to deck chairs and

wreckage in a futile attempt to save them. As Morton later described the scene, "The turmoil of passengers and life jackets, many people losing hold on the deck and slipping down and over the side … [created] a horrible and bizarre orchestra of death."

The *Lusitania* sank only 18 minutes after it was torpedoed. About 1,200 people died. Among the dead were 128 Americans.

▶ **The sinking of the *Lusitania* killed more than 1,200 people.**

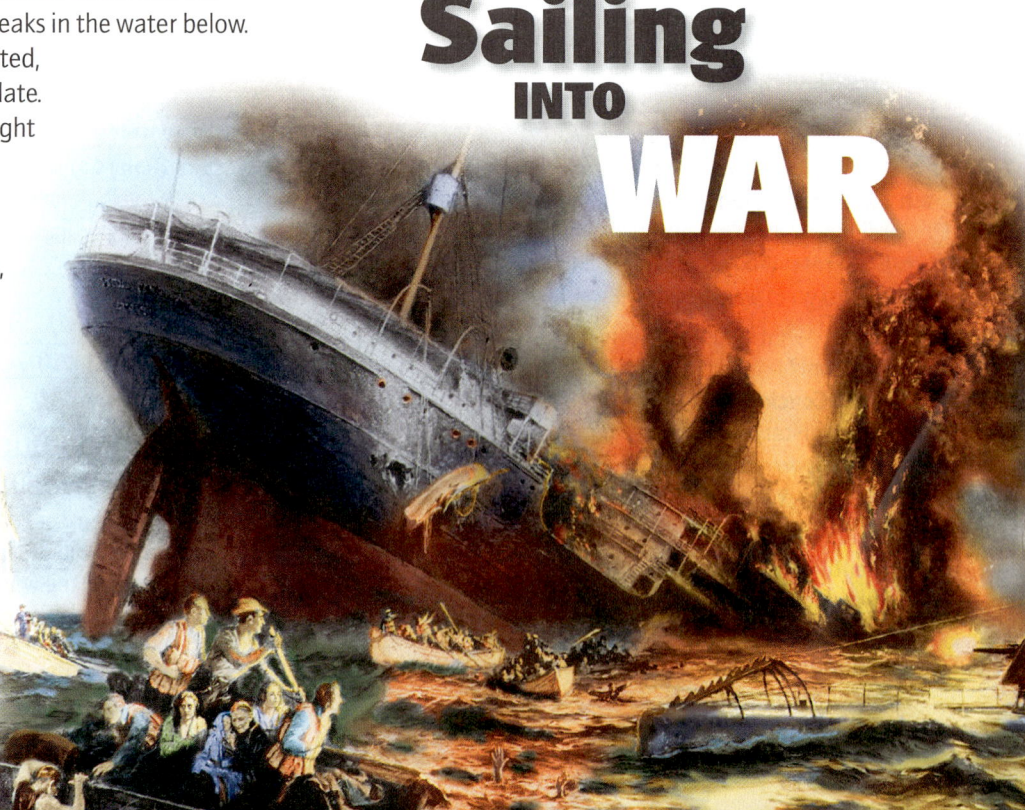

Sailing INTO WAR

United States Stays Neutral

Before the sinking of the *Lusitania*, Americans thought of the war as a European conflict that had little effect on life in the United States. Just after the war began, President Woodrow Wilson declared that the United States would remain <u>neutral</u>. Wilson's response to the war reflected a long-standing American tradition of **isolationism**—a policy of not being involved in the affairs of other nations.

Leaning toward the Allies
Privately, Wilson favored the Allied cause. He was extremely concerned about Germany's war tactics and its invasion of Belgium. Furthermore, the United States historically had greater political, cultural, and commercial ties to Great Britain and France than to Germany.

Financially, the United States was far from neutral. The British fleet had blockaded German ports and transportation routes, and few American businesses could sell goods to German forces. It was far easier, however, to supply the Allies. By 1917 Britain was purchasing nearly $75 million worth of war goods from American businesses each week.

German submarine warfare
Germany suffered greatly under the British blockade, and the German navy began to develop a plan to strike back at Great Britain. Germany planned to wage its naval war with **U-boats**—small submarines named after the German word *Unterseeboot*, which means "undersea boat."

In February 1915 the German government announced that the waters around Great Britain would be a war zone in which Germany would destroy all enemy ships. Germany warned the United States that neutral ships might be attacked as well. This policy of having submarines attack all ships was called unrestricted submarine warfare.

The German plan for unrestricted submarine warfare angered most Americans. Wilson believed that Germany's actions violated the laws of neutrality. He warned Germany that he would hold the nation responsible if American lives were lost. Tensions between the United States and Germany were rising.

READING CHECK **Drawing Conclusions**
Why did American businesses do more business with the Allies than with Germany?

Woodrow Wilson is best known for his peace-making efforts during and after World War I. In fact, Wilson wanted to avoid entering the war at all, but Germany soon challenged American neutrality. In stirring words, Wilson asked Congress for a declaration of war. "The world must be made safe for democracy," he said. "Its peace must be planted upon the tested foundations of political liberty."

After the war Wilson once again addressed Congress, this time with a plan for keeping peace in the postwar world. His Fourteen Points speech called for a League of Nations, an organization for cooperation between countries. Wilson's support of the League of Nations earned him the Nobel Prize for Peace in 1919.

Interpret What did Wilson want to accomplish after World War I?

Heading Toward War

As you read in the "Inside Story," the American public was outraged by the 1915 sinking of the *Lusitania*. President Wilson demanded an end to unrestricted submarine warfare.

Facing international criticism, the German government agreed to attack only supply ships. But less than one year later, Germany attacked the French passenger ship *Sussex* on March 24, 1916, killing about 80 people. After this attack, Wilson threatened to end diplomatic relations with Germany unless it stopped killing innocent civilians. German officials feared that the United States might enter the war, so Germany issued the **Sussex pledge**, which included a promise not to sink merchant vessels "without warning and without saving human lives."

Wilson's re-election
As he campaigned during the election of 1916, Wilson assured Americans that he would not send their sons to die in Europe. Wilson's chief rival, Republican candidate Charles Evans Hughes, took a stronger pro-war stance. The election was very close. In the end, Wilson won by little more than 3 percent of the popular vote.

Once re-elected, Wilson began to work for a peace settlement. In January 1917 he asked the Allied and Central Powers to accept a "peace without victory." This request angered

ACADEMIC VOCABULARY

neutral not aligned with either side in a war or dispute the Allies. They blamed the Central Powers for starting the war and wanted them to pay for wartime damage and destruction.

Any hope for peace ended when Germany resumed unrestricted submarine warfare on February 1, 1917. Two days later, the United States ended diplomatic relations with Germany. Wilson asked Congress for the authority to install guns on U.S. merchant ships.

The Zimmermann Note Meanwhile, German foreign secretary Arthur Zimmermann sent a telegram to a German official in Mexico. The Zimmermann Note proposed an alliance between Germany and Mexico. "We shall make war together, make peace together," the telegram offered. "[In exchange] Mexico is to reconquer the lost territory in New Mexico, Texas, and Arizona." The Germans hoped that an American war with Mexico would keep the United States out of the war in Europe. Since Mexico expressed no interest in fighting, this German strategy backfired.

The British had intercepted the Zimmermann Note, decoded it, and sent it to American officials. On March 1, American newspapers printed excerpts from the telegram. More Americans began to call for war against Germany. Yet Wilson continued to resist, hoping to bring about a lasting peace in Europe.

The United States declares war In mid-March, dramatic events in Russia raised new questions for the United States. An uprising in Russia forced Czar Nicholas II to give up his absolute power over the government. Rebel leaders set up a government based on republican ideals.

These changes made Russia more democratic but also raised questions about how long the new Russian government would continue to fight on the Eastern Front. Many Americans—who believed that the American role in world politics should be to promote democracy—became more supportive of the Allies and the war after the Russian czar lost power.

Then in mid-March 1917, German U-boats sank three American merchant ships. Outraged about the violation of American neutrality, President Wilson called a meeting with his cabinet. Each cabinet member argued for war. On April 2, Wilson asked Congress to declare war on Germany so that the world could "be made safe for democracy."

HISTORY'S VOICES

❝We shall fight for the things which we have always carried nearest our hearts, for democracy ... [and to] bring peace and safety to all nations and make the world itself at last free.❞

—Woodrow Wilson, Speech to Congress, April 2, 1917

From Neutrality to War

Remaining Neutral

Below, a German U-boat prowls the seas. President Wilson opposed the use of unrestricted submarine warfare, but he campaigned for re-election in 1916 (right) with promises to keep America out of the war.

Congress approved President Wilson's request. On April 6, 1917, the United States joined the war on the side of the Allies.

READING CHECK **Drawing Conclusions**
How did the United States respond to war in Europe?

Americans in Europe

Now the United States military began quickly preparing for battle. An army needed to be raised, new recruits needed to be trained for combat, and troops and supplies needed to be shipped to the front.

Raising an army On May 18, 1917, Congress passed the **Selective Service Act**, which required men between the ages of 21 and 30 to register to be drafted into the armed forces. Most young men willingly participated in the draft. A small number of men asked to be classified as conscientious objectors—members of certain religious groups, such as the Quakers, whose moral or religious beliefs prevented them from fighting in a war. But few local draft boards accepted their applications. Once rejected, these men had to take combat positions or face prison.

In the summer of 1917, the new recruits reported for training but found almost nothing ready for them. Many soldiers slept in tents until barracks could be hastily built. Supplies had been ordered but had not yet arrived.

Nevertheless, the training was intense. New recruits spent most of their days learning military rules and practices, marching, and preparing for inspections. Because of a shortage of rifles, they practiced with wooden sticks. Instead of horses, the trainees pretended to ride wooden barrels.

African American soldiers were segregated into separate divisions and trained in separate camps. Many white Army officers and southern politicians objected to the training of African American soldiers to use weapons. They feared that these black soldiers might pose a threat after the war. Because of these beliefs, only a few black regiments were trained for combat.

Latinos also experienced discrimination. Some Hispanic soldiers faced scorn from other American troops and were often assigned menial tasks. Some Latinos who were eager to serve in the war did not speak English fluently. The federal government did not reject them. Instead, the military established special programs in New Mexico and Georgia to help them improve their English skills. After completing such training, the soldiers would fight alongside other American troops.

THE IMPACT TODAY

Government
The Selective Service Act remains in effect today. All men between the ages of 18 and 25 must register to be selected randomly for military service. However, the draft has not been instituted since 1973.

Joining the War

After the United States declared war in 1917, General John J. Pershing led U.S. forces in Europe. Below, Pershing arrives in France with the first soldiers. He spent months establishing the American Expeditionary Forces (right) and setting up communications and supply lines.

Arriving in Europe The American soldiers who went overseas formed the American Expeditionary Forces (AEF), led by General John J. Pershing. The AEF included soldiers from the regular army, the National Guard, and a new larger force of volunteers and draftees.

The first U.S. troops arrived in France in late June 1917. To transport forces safely, Pershing relied on the convoy system, in which troop-transport ships were surrounded by destroyers or cruisers for protection. The convoy system reduced the number of ships sunk and limited the loss of troops and supplies.

When American troops arrived in France, the Allies' situation was grim. German troops occupied all of Belgium and part of northeastern France. Along the Eastern Front, Russia was struggling to defend itself against Germany. The Russians were facing famine and civil war. If Russia fell, many German troops could be sent to fight in France. The Allies desperately needed help and wanted the Americans to start fighting as soon as they arrived.

General Pershing had other plans. He wanted his soldiers to fight as American units and not as individuals in different European regiments. Pershing also wanted to give his troops more training. The American general believed that sending inexperienced soldiers into battle was the same as sending them to die. As a result, Pershing sent his troops to training camps in eastern France.

Allied setbacks Meanwhile, the Allies suffered another blow. In November 1917 a group known as the Bolsheviks took control of Russia's government. The Bolsheviks were Communists—people who seek the equal distribution of wealth and the end of all private property. The new government, led by Vladimir Ilich Lenin, withdrew the Russian army from the Eastern Front and signed a peace agreement with the Central Powers. Now Germany was free to focus on fighting in the west.

In March 1918, German soldiers launched a series of tremendous offensives against the Allies. The Germans were backed by some 6,000 artillery pieces, including "Big Berthas"—massive guns capable of firing a 2,100-pound shell almost 75 miles. By late May the Germans had pushed the Allies back to the Marne River, just 70 miles northeast of Paris.

U.S. troops in action Almost 12 months after arriving in France, American troops finally saw combat. Reaching the front lines, they quickly learned the Allied war strategy. They dug extensive trenches to protect themselves from German gunfire. When Company A

From Neutrality to War, *continued*

Fighting in the War

In June 1918, Belleau Wood, France, became the proving grounds for American soldiers (below). Although a U.S. victory, 8,000 American casualties at the Battle of Belleau Wood made it America's bloodiest battle thus far in the war.

of the 82nd Division reached the front lines, for example, its members had to dig 3,000 yards of trenches and set up 12,000 yards of barbed wire. The soldiers worked in the middle of the night to avoid detection by the enemy. As dawn broke, the exhausted soldiers returned to their temporary shelters. They were covered in mud, and their uniforms were torn to shreds by barbed wire.

Life in the trenches was a painful ordeal. The soldiers stood in deep mud as rats ran across their feet. Enemy planes dropped bombs, artillery shells exploded nearby, and clouds of mustard gas floated into the trenches. "It was an eerie feeling down in that dugout [trench]," one soldier recalled. "No one knew what was going to happen next."

The American troops were a major factor in the war. While defending Paris in June 1918, U.S. troops helped the French stop the Germans at Chateau-Thierry. In northern France, a division of U.S. Marines recaptured the forest of Belleau Wood and two nearby villages. After fierce fighting, the Allies finally halted the German advance. Paris was saved.

American military women The vast majority of Americans who served in the military were men, but some women also signed up to serve overseas. The U.S. Army Signal Corps recruited French-speaking American women to serve as switchboard operators. Known as the Hello Girls, they served a crucial role in keeping communications open between the front line and the headquarters of the American Expeditionary Forces.

During the war, more than 20,000 nurses served in the U.S. Army in the United States and overseas. Women also served in the navy and marines, usually as typists and bookkeepers, although some became radio operators, electricians, or telegraphers.

READING CHECK **Identifying the Main Idea** Why did it take so long for U.S. troops to enter combat?

The War Ends

On July 15, 1918, the Germans launched their last, desperate offensive at the Second Battle of the Marne. During the fighting, the U.S. 3rd Division blew up every bridge the Germans had built across the Marne. The German army retreated on August 3, having suffered some 150,000 casualties.

The Allies began a counterattack in September 1918. For the first time, Americans fought as a separate army. The AEF defeated German troops at Mihiel, near the French-German border.

ACADEMIC VOCABULARY
factor something that contributes to a result

Harlem Hell Fighters

About 42,000 African American soldiers served in combat positions in World War I. The 369th Infantry, also known as the Harlem Hell Fighters, served a record 191 days in the trenches. They fought alongside the French in the 1918 Battle of Meuse-Argonne. After the war, the French awarded the entire unit the Croix de Guerre, a prestigious medal for bravery.

Interactive Map
WORLD WAR I, 1917–1918

GREAT BRITAIN

English Channel

3rd Battle of Ypres, July - Nov. 1917

Brussels

NETHERLANDS

BELGIUM

GERMANY

Battle of Cantigny, May 1918

Seine River

Battle of Belleau-Wood, June 1918

2nd Battle of Marne, July - Aug. 1918

Sedon

LUXEMBOURG

Paris

Battle of Chateau-Thierry, June 1918

Battle of Meuse-Argonne, Sept. - Nov. 1918

Battle of Mihiel, Sept. 1918

FRANCE

go.hrw.com
Interactive Map
Keyword: SD7 CH18

Allied Powers
Central Powers
Neutral nations
German offensive, March - July 1918
Armistice line, Nov. 11, 1918
Allied Powers victory

0   25   50 Miles
0   25   50 Kilometers
Lambert azimuthal equal-area projection

GEOGRAPHY SKILLS **INTERPRETING MAPS**

Movement How did the battles at Cantigny, Belleau Wood, Chateau-Thierry, and the Marne affect the German advance?

See **Skills Handbook**, p. H20

Alvin York's bravery—and capture of 132 Germans—made him the most famous hero of the war.

After the victory, the Allies continued their advance toward the French city of Sedan on the Belgian border. The railway there was the main supply line for German forces. Other Allied forces advanced all along the front.

For more than a month the Allies pushed northward through the rugged Argonne Forest, facing artillery explosions and deadly machine gun fire every step of the way. In the Battle of the Argonne Forest the Americans suffered some 120,000 casualties. By November, however, the Allies reached and occupied the hills around Sedan.

The armistice By late 1918 the war was crippling the German economy; many civilians lacked food and supplies. Food riots and strikes erupted in Germany, and revolution swept across Austria-Hungary. The Central Powers had difficulty encouraging their soldiers to fight. Some soldiers even ran away.

Lacking the will to keep fighting, the Central Powers began to surrender. In early November, Austria-Hungary signed a peace agreement with the Allies. On November 7 a German delegation entered French territory to begin peace negotiations.

The Allies demanded that Germany leave all territories it had occupied. Germany surrendered its aircraft, heavy artillery, tanks, and U-boats. The Allies also forced Germany to allow Allied troops to occupy some German territory. On November 11, 1918, the armistice went into effect, and the guns of war fell silent. An Allied soldier later described the moment when the Great War ended.

HISTORY'S VOICES

❝There came a second of expectant silence, and then a curious rippling sound … It was the sound of men cheering from the Vosges [mountain range] to the sea.❞

—John Buchan, *The King's Grace*, 1935

War tragedies muted some of the celebration. When asked what the armistice meant, one British soldier replied, "Time to bury the dead." People around the world had grown weary of death. Some 8.5 million people had been killed. People everywhere hoped that the Great War would be "the war to end all wars." World leaders soon turned their attention to healing what the American writer W.E.B. Du Bois referred to as the "wounded world."

READING CHECK **Sequencing** What events led to the armistice?

SECTION 2 ASSESSMENT

go.hrw.com
Online Quiz
Keyword: SD7 HP18

Reviewing Ideas, Terms, and People

1. **a. Define** What was isolationism?
   b. Explain Why did the United States pursue a policy of isolationism?
   c. Elaborate How did Germany's actions make the United States begin to consider abandoning isolationism?

2. **a. Recall** What was the Zimmermann Note?
   b. Draw Conclusions How did the Zimmermann Note affect American public opinion about the war?
   c. Evaluate Which event do you think was the most significant in convincing Americans to join the war? Why?

3. **a. Identify** What was the convoy system?
   b. Explain What effect did U.S. troops have on the outcome of the war?

4. **a. Describe** What was the Battle of the Argonne Forest?

   b. Analyze How did the economic effects of the war help bring an end to the fighting?

Critical Thinking

5. **Identifying Cause and Effect** Copy the timeline below. Using information from the section, place on the timeline the major events that led the United States to declare war against Germany.

FOCUS ON WRITING

6. **Expository** What caused the United States to enter World War I? Write a short paragraph in which you explain the events that led the United States to declare war.

American *Literature*

Ernest Hemingway (1899–1961)

About the Reading Ernest Hemingway based his novel *A Farewell to Arms* (1929) on his experiences as an ambulance driver for the American Red Cross in World War I. His novel tells the story of Frederic Henry, an American serving with the Italian ambulance service, who falls in love with Catherine Barkley, a British nurse. In the following passage Frederic describes an atmosphere of confusion and uncertainty as he works to help the wounded.

AS YOU READ **Notice how the narrator remains distant from the "great battle."**

Excerpt from

A Farewell to Arms

by Ernest Hemingway

American snipers on the outskirts of a French town take potshots at German soldiers from the shelter of a shattered building.

The wounded were coming into the post, some were carried on stretchers, some walking and some were brought on the backs of men that came across the field. They were wet to the skin and all were scared. We filled two cars with stretcher cases as they came up from the cellar of the post and as I shut the door of the second car and fastened it I felt the rain on my face turn to snow. The flakes were coming heavy and fast in the rain.

When daylight came the storm was still blowing but the snow had stopped. It had melted as it fell on the wet ground and now it was raining again. There was another attack just after daylight but it was unsuccessful. We expected an attack all day but it did not come until the sun was going down. The bombardment started to the south below the long wooded ridge where the Austrian guns were concentrated. We expected a bombardment but it did not come. It was getting dark. Guns were firing from the field behind the village and the shells, going away, had a comfortable sound.

We heard that the attack to the south had been unsuccessful. They did not attack that night but we heard that they had broken through to the north.

In the night word came that we were to prepare to retreat. The captain at the post told me this. He had it from the Brigade. A little while later he came from the telephone and said it was a lie. The Brigade had received orders that the line of the Bainsizza should be held no matter what happened. I asked about the break through and he said he had heard at the Brigade that the Austrians had broken though the twenty-seventh arms corps up toward Caporetto. There had been a great battle in the north all day.

Skills FOCUS **READING LIKE A HISTORIAN**

1. **Drawing Conclusions** How reliable is the information about the distant battle that the narrator receives?
2. **Literature as Historical Evidence** What larger statement do you think Hemingway is trying to make about the nature of warfare in the twentieth century?

See **Skills Handbook**, pp. H12, H32

The Home Front

BEFORE YOU READ

MAIN IDEA

The United States mobilized a variety of resources to wage World War I.

READING FOCUS

1. How did the government mobilize the economy for the war effort?
2. How did workers mobilize on the home front?
3. How did the government try to influence public opinion about the war?

KEY TERMS AND PEOPLE

Liberty bonds
Bernard Baruch
National War Labor Board
Committee on Public Information
George Creel
propaganda
Schenck v. *United States*

P1 3.1 Compare and contrast the experiences of different ethnic, national, and religious groups, including Native American Indians, in the United States, explaining their contributions to American society and culture.

Pocketbook PATRIOTISM

THE INSIDE STORY

What was a Liberty bond? When the United States entered the war in 1917, President Wilson called on everyone to join the war effort. To help pay for the war, he launched four drives to sell **Liberty bonds**. The bonds, like today's government savings bonds, were a form of loan to the government. In schools, children filled Liberty Books with 25-cent stamps until they were full and could be exchanged for a bond. The slogan was "Lick a Stamp and Lick the Kaiser."

Campaigns to sell bonds were intense. Organizers sent out workers to sell in workplaces, neighborhoods, and theaters. Celebrities from movie stars to baseball players to opera singers appeared at rallies flanked by doughboys in uniform and asked their audiences to buy bonds. Some of the largest rallies were held in Manhattan. In one skit, movie actor Douglas Fairbanks—known for playing swashbuckling heroes—wore boxing gloves labeled Victory and Liberty Bonds as he knocked out the Kaiser.

Artists and advertising experts produced slogans and colorful propaganda posters. They appealed to patriotism, fear, or sympathy for war victims in Europe. One famous poster showed a woman refugee and her children. It read: "Must Children Die and Mothers Plead in Vain—Buy More Liberty Bonds." Another showed a smiling little girl hugging a bond: "My daddy bought me a government bond of the Third Liberty Loan. Did Yours?" In all, the bond drives brought in almost $17 billion. ▪

OVER THE TOP FOR YOU

Buy U.S. Gov't Bonds
THIRD LIBERTY LOAN

Mobilizing the Economy

Going to war was an enormous—and enormously expensive—undertaking. One of the first things that President Wilson and his advisers had to do after joining the war was figure out how to pay for it. First, Congress passed the War Revenue Act of 1917. This law established very high taxes and taxed the wealthiest Americans as much as 77 percent of their annual incomes. It increased federal revenues by 400 percent within two years.

The government also borrowed money to pay for the war. The national debt grew from $1.2 billion in 1916 to $25.5 billion in 1919. More than $20 billion of that debt was owed to Americans who had purchased Liberty bonds. These bonds were essentially a loan from the American people to the federal government.

Regulating industry To make sure that the troops received all the supplies they needed, the Wilson administration prepared the nation's industries for war. Congress created hundreds of administrative boards to regulate both industrial and agricultural production and distribution.

One of the most powerful boards was the War Industries Board (WIB). It had the authority to regulate all materials needed in the war effort. Wall Street business leader **Bernard Baruch**, head of the WIB, explained the board's power: "No steel, copper, cement, rubber, or other basic materials could be used without our approval."

The policies and rules of the WIB managed to increase American industrial production by about 20 percent. The military could select any of the goods that were produced. Once the military's needs were met, any remaining goods could be used by civilians.

Regulating food To make sure that the troops would have plenty of food and supplies, Congress passed the Lever Food and Fuel Control Act. This law gave the government the power to set prices and establish production controls for food and for the fuels needed to run military machines.

Wilson's administration also created agencies to manage and increase food production. Herbert Hoover led the Food Administration, whose slogan was "Food Can Win the War." Hoover's goals were to increase the production of crops and to conserve existing food supplies for the military and for American allies.

Financing the War

Colorful posters that spoke to Americans' sense of patriotism (left), parades (below), and appeals by movie stars such as Charlie Chaplin, Mary Pickford, and Douglas Fairbanks (right), all encouraged the purchase of war bonds. *What other attempts did the government make to finance the war?*

BUY LIBERTY BONDS
BUY NOW
Don't let happen to us what happened in Belgium

In order to encourage wartime production, he promised farmers higher prices for their crops. Farm production soared.

Hoover asked Americans to plant vegetables at home in "victory gardens." He also urged Americans to eat less by participating in "meatless Mondays" and "wheatless Wednesdays." His efforts paid off. By 1918 the United States had so much surplus food that it exported three times as much food as it had prior to the war.

Another proposal to conserve food supplies was a prohibition, or ban, on alcohol. Most alcohol is made with food crops such as grapes and wheat. Days after entering the war, Congress limited the alcohol content of wine and beer so that these crops could be used for food production instead.

Some progressives tried to discourage Americans from drinking beer by linking German Americans to the brewing industry. The progressives hoped that anti-German feelings would lead Americans to stop drinking beer.

As the war continued, the temperance, or anti-alcohol, movement gained strength. In 1919 the Eighteenth Amendment was ratified, banning the "manufacture, sale or transportation" of alcohol in the United States. In 1919 Congress passed the Volstead Act, giving the government the authority to enforce this prohibition on alcohol.

Regulating fuel

After the passage of the Lever Food and Fuel Control Act, the Fuel Administration was established to set production goals and prices for fuels. Its purpose was to make sure that military needs for fuel could always be met.

Harry Garfield, the son of former president James A. Garfield, headed the Fuel Administration. To encourage fuel conservation, Garfield introduced daylight saving time in order to extend daylight hours for those who worked long shifts in the factories. He promoted fuel conservation in other ways, such as through publicity campaigns calling for "gasless Sundays" and "heatless Mondays."

Supplying U.S. and Allied troops

By creating these various boards and agencies, the federal government was quickly able to produce and collect the supplies needed for the

Working for the War Effort

war effort. It was not just American soldiers who benefited from these supplies. The United States also became the major supplier for the Allied Powers. During the war Great Britain alone received more than 1 billion rounds of ammunition, 1.2 million rifles, and more than half a million tons of explosives from the United States. The power of U.S. manufacturing and farming became a much-needed boost for the struggling Allies and a boost for the American economy as well.

READING CHECK **Drawing Conclusions**
How did the Wilson administration change the U.S. economy for the war effort?

Mobilizing Workers

During the war, the profits of many major industrial corporations skyrocketed. This was because the corporations sold their products to the federal government. In turn, the federal government used those products in the war effort. In this way the war created enormous profits for stockholders of industries such as chemicals, oil, and steel.

Women in a gun factory (left) assemble soldiers' pistols in 1918. Below, men at a steel plant make shell casings in 1917. After many male workers went off to fight in the war, women supplied much-needed labor. *How did Wilson aid this transition?*

Wages for factory workers increased as well. The rising cost of food and housing, however, meant that workers were hardly better off than they had been before the war.

Meanwhile, war demands led to laborers working long hours, sometimes in increasingly dangerous conditions. The urgent need to produce materials for the war—and the great financial incentive for companies to do so—led to a faster pace of production.

These harsher working conditions led many workers to join labor unions. Union membership increased by about 60 percent between 1916 and 1919. Union activities boomed as well, with more than 6,000 strikes being held during the war.

National War Labor Board Massive industrial production was essential to the war effort. Leaders feared that industrial protests such as strikes would disrupt the war effort. To keep disruptions to a minimum, the Wilson administration created the National War Labor Board in 1918. This board judged disputes between workers and management. During the short time that the board was in operation (less than a year), it handled some 1,200 cases involving 700,000 workers.

The National War Labor Board also set policies that sought to improve working conditions for all Americans. The board established the eight-hour workday, urged that businesses recognize labor unions, and promoted equal pay for women who did equal work.

Women's war efforts As men left their jobs to fight on the war front, women moved into those jobs to keep the American economy moving. Women took on many jobs traditionally held by men. They worked on railroads, at docks, and in factories. They also built ships and airplanes.

Other women filled more traditional jobs, working as teachers and nurses. Some took on volunteer positions that ranged from helping to sell Liberty bonds to digging victory gardens. In all, about 1 million women entered the workforce during World War I. After the war ended, however, most women left the jobs they had taken. Many women left by choice, but others were forced to leave by employers who wanted to return the jobs to men who had served in the war.

Epidemics

In 1918 and 1919, an influenza epidemic killed millions of people, including some 675,000 Americans. Influenza also spread around the world, killing at least 20 million, and perhaps as many as 40 million people. Travelers carried the disease between countries.

In 2002 a respiratory virus called Severe Acute Respiratory Syndrome (SARS) emerged in China. It also spread to the United States. As with influenza in 1918, travelers are believed to have carried the disease.

Making Inferences How can travel affect the spread of disease?

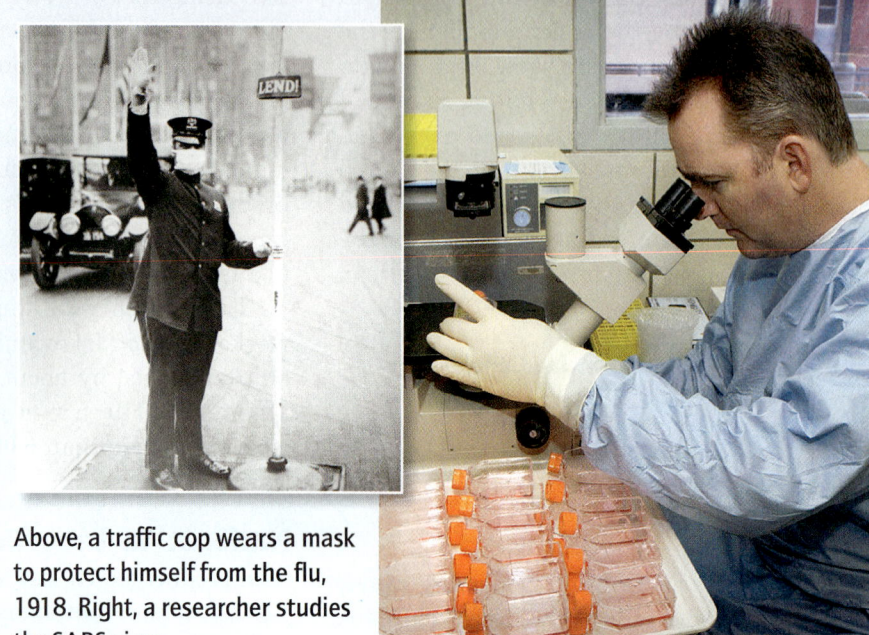

Above, a traffic cop wears a mask to protect himself from the flu, 1918. Right, a researcher studies the SARS virus.

The contributions that women made to the war effort did not go unnoticed. Women's suffrage advocates used these contributions as further justification for granting women the vote. President Wilson also acknowledged women's role in the war effort.

HISTORY'S VOICES

❝This war could not have been fought ... if it had not been for the services of women rendered in every sphere.❞

—President Woodrow Wilson, 1918

Influenza epidemic on the home front

The war's efffort was seriously affected by an extremely severe flu epidemic that broke out between 1918 and 1919. In Europe the disease quickly spread across the Western Front, where crowded and unsanitary trenches were perfect breeding grounds for the disease. In fact, of all the American troops who lost their lives in World War I, about half of them died from influenza.

Soldiers on the front lines, however, were not the only ones to suffer from influenza. On March 11, 1918, an army private in Kansas complained of flulike symptoms. By the end of that week, more than 500 soldiers had come down with influenza. By August, influenza was reported in Philadelphia and Boston.

This was no ordinary flu. Most forms of influenza were simply uncomfortable and unpleasant. But this form of influenza was deadly. It killed healthy people within days. During the month of October 1918 alone, influenza killed nearly 200,000 Americans.

Panicked city leaders canceled public gatherings, but the disease still spread. Rumors spread almost as quickly. Many people, such as Lieutenant Colonel Philip Doane, wrongly blamed Germans for causing the disease. Doane remarked, "It would be quite easy for one of these German agents to turn loose influenza germs in a theater or some other place where large numbers of persons are assembled."

By the time this wave of influenza passed, some 675,000 Americans had lost their lives. It was the deadliest epidemic in U.S. history.

READING CHECK **Identifying the Main Idea** Why did the Wilson administration create the National War Labor Board?

Influencing Public Opinion

President Wilson moved quickly to build public support after Congress declared war. Many Americans had been in favor of the U.S. position of neutrality. Now Wilson had to convince these

THE IMPACT TODAY

Science and Technology

Scientists have reconstructed the 1918 influenza virus and found it to be a bird flu that was transmitted directly to humans. The research team analyzed lung tissue from two people who died in the 1918–1919 epidemic.

Americans that it was their duty to support the war. "It is not an army that we must shape for war … it is a nation," he said.

Winning American support Wilson created the <mark>Committee on Public Information</mark> (CPI) less than two weeks after the United States declared war. He appointed newspaper reporter and political reformer **George Creel** to head the CPI.

Creel began a nationwide campaign of <mark>propaganda</mark>—posters, newspaper stories, speeches, and other materials designed to influence people's opinions. This campaign was meant to encourage Americans to support the war. Creel hired popular movie stars such as Mary Pickford and Douglas Fairbanks to speak on behalf of the war effort.

The CPI also hired artists to create patriotic posters and pamphlets. These posters included James Montgomery Flagg's famous image of Uncle Sam pointing to the viewer and demanding, "I Want You for the U.S. Army."

As many Americans became more patriotic and supportive of the war, some began to distrust all things German as well. Some tried to eliminate all German influence from American culture. Many schools stopped teaching the German language to their students. Many symphonies stopped playing music written by German composers. Even German-sounding items were renamed to sound patriotic. For example, sauerkraut became liberty cabbage, dachshunds became liberty pups, and hamburger became known as liberty steak.

Anti-German feelings continued to grow after reports spread that secret agents from Germany were operating in the United States. In one of the worst acts of sabotage, German agents planted a bomb at a ship-loading terminal in New York City. The bomb destroyed $20 million worth of supplies for the war, killed three dock workers, and shattered windows in buildings across lower Manhattan.

Acts such as these led some Americans to question the loyalty of German Americans in their communities. As a result, some German Americans experienced discrimination and violence. In April 1918, for example, a mob in Illinois lynched socialist coal miner Robert Prager because townspeople suspected him of being a German spy.

PRIMARY SOURCES

Propaganda Poster

To gain support for the war effort, officials in the United States hired skilled artists to create posters that would build public support and increase recruitment. This poster was designed by artist James Montgomery Flagg.

The use of the word *you* as well as Uncle Sam looking and pointing at the viewer makes it clear that the U.S. Army is asking each individual to serve.

Uncle Sam's red, white, and blue clothing tells young men that joining the army is an act of patriotism.

Skills FOCUS **READING LIKE A HISTORIAN**

1. **Drawing Conclusions** What is the main message of this propaganda poster?
2. **Interpreting Visuals** How effective do you think this poster was?

See **Skills Handbook**, p. H30

603

Limiting antiwar speech Prominent Americans, such as reformer Jane Addams and Senator Robert La Follette, spoke out against the war. Addams, a pacifist, also founded the Women's International League for Peace and Freedom. As the Wilson administration built public support, it also tried to limit this public opposition to the war.

In 1917 Congress passed the Espionage Act, which punished people for aiding the enemy or refusing military duty. The next year, Congress passed a related law called the Sedition Act. This law made it illegal for Americans to "utter, print, write, or publish any disloyal … or abusive language" criticizing the government, the flag, or the military.

More than 1,000 opponents of the war were jailed under these laws. Robert Goldstein, who directed a film on the American Revolution called *The Spirit of '76*, was jailed for three years because he refused to remove scenes of British brutality from the movie.

In another case, Socialist Party leader Eugene V. Debs was sentenced to prison for 10 years for criticizing the United States government's prosecution of Americans under the Espionage Act. After the war ended, however, Debs was released from prison by a presidential order.

Some Americans believed that the Espionage Act and the Sedition Act violated the First Amendment. Others, however, thought these laws were essential to protect military secrets, the safety of American soldiers, and the overall U.S. war effort.

The Supreme Court also struggled to interpret the Espionage Act and the Sedition Act. The defining case came when Charles Schenck, an official of the American Socialist Party, was convicted of violating the Espionage Act. Schenck had organized the printing and distribution of some 15,000 leaflets opposing government war policies. He challenged the conviction as a violation of his constitutional right to free speech.

In its first decision interpreting the First Amendment, the Supreme Court upheld Schenck's conviction. Justice Oliver Wendell Holmes Jr. wrote the Court's unanimous opinion in **Schenck v. United States**, explaining the limits to free speech.

In his written opinion, Holmes went on to explain that many things that can safely be said in peacetime can cause problems for the government and danger for soldiers in wartime. For that reason, Holmes argued, some limits needed to be placed on individual free-speech rights during wartime to ensure the country's overall safety. You will read more about *Schenck* v. *United States* on the following page.

READING CHECK **Drawing Conclusions** Why did the Wilson administration place wartime limitations on free speech?

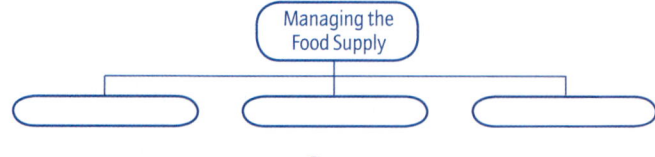

SECTION 3 ASSESSMENT

go.hrw.com
Online Quiz
Keyword: SD7 HP18

Reviewing Ideas, Terms, and People

1. a. Identify What were **Liberty bonds**?
  b. Explain In what two ways did the United States pay for its war effort?

2. a. Describe What happened to the profits of many major corporations during the war?
  b. Compare and Contrast Did workers prosper in the same way that major companies did during the war? Why or why not?
  c. Elaborate Why would the government consider it necessary to get involved in disputes between workers and management?

3. a. Recall What was the **Committee on Public Information**?
  b. Contrast How did the government try to persuade people to support the war and discourage them from opposing it?

c. Evaluate Was the government justified in trying to suppress opposition to the war? Why or why not?

Critical Thinking

4. Identifying Supporting Details Copy the chart below and record the ways in which the United States managed its food supply for the war effort.

Managing the Food Supply

FOCUS ON WRITING

5. Expository Write a short paragraph in which you explain the contributions American women made to the war effort.

ST 1.2 Analyze the decisions leading to major turning points in United States history, comparing alternative courses of action, and hypothesizing, within the context of the historical period, about what might have happened if the decision had been different.

Schenck v. United States (1919)

Why It Matters Schenck was the first major Supreme Court case to consider limits on the First Amendment right of free speech. According to the decision, speech can be limited when it poses a "clear and present danger."

Background of the Case

During World War I, the Espionage Act made it a crime to interfere with the war effort. Charles Schenck, general secretary of the American Socialist Party, distributed thousands of leaflets urging men to oppose the draft. Schenck was convicted of violating the Espionage Act, and he appealed. He argued that the First Amendment protected his right to speak out on this subject.

The Decision

The Supreme Court ruled unanimously against Schenck. Writing for the Court, Justice Oliver Wendell Holmes Jr. looked both at what Schenck said and at the circumstances in which he said it. The Constitution does not protect speech that causes danger to others. For example, the First Amendment

> **"**... would not protect a man in falsely shouting 'Fire' in a theatre and causing a panic.... The question in every case is whether the words used ... create a clear and present danger ...**"**
>
> — Justice Oliver Wendell Holmes Jr.

Certain things that might safely be said during peacetime could be dangerous when the country was at war. Congress can place some limits on the right of free speech in order to protect the country's safety. Schenck's intent was to interfere with the draft, and the First Amendment does not protect this activity.

THE IMPACT TODAY War protesters march in California to mark the first anniversary of the 2003 invasion of Iraq. If this demonstration had taken place in 1919 or 1920, the group could have been arrested under the Espionage Act or the Sedition Act.

CRITICAL THINKING

go.hrw.com
Research Online
Keyword: SS Court

1. **Analyze the Impact** Using the keyword above, research the decision in *Texas* v. *Johnson*. How do the facts in *Johnson* differ from those in *Schenck*? Why did the Court decide in Johnson's favor?

2. **You Be the Judge** While U.S. troops were fighting in Vietnam, Afghanistan, and Iraq, some Americans argued that it is unpatriotic to oppose an ongoing war. Others said that the right to disagree with government policy is essential to democracy. Can Congress constitutionally restrict Americans' right to speak against military actions? Explain your answer.

Peace without Victory

BEFORE YOU READ

MAIN IDEA:

The Allies determined the terms for peace in the postwar world.

READING FOCUS

1. What was President Wilson's Fourteen Points plan for peace?
2. What was resolved at the Paris Peace Conference?
3. Why did Congress fight over the treaty?
4. What was the impact of World War I on the United States and the world?

KEY TERMS AND PEOPLE

Fourteen Points
self-determination
League of Nations
David Lloyd George
Georges Clemenceau
Big Four
reparations
Treaty of Versailles
Henry Cabot Lodge

PI 2.6 Compare and contrast the values exhibited and foreign policies implemented by the United States and other nations over time with those expressed in the United Nations Charter and international law.

THE INSIDE STORY

Will the treaty pass? President Woodrow Wilson had to make many compromises at the peace conference after World War I. The Treaty of Versailles did, however, include his greatest dream—a League of Nations, an international organization that would work to ensure peace. "America shall in truth show the way," Wilson told the Senate, which still had to approve the treaty.

Although he was worn out, Wilson decided to go to the people for support. He set out on an exhausting cross-country speaking tour. In three weeks he traveled 8,000 miles by train from city to city, speaking several times a day. His speeches were eloquent, but they ignored some of the harsh provisions of the treaty. Western audiences were welcoming, which encouraged Wilson to push himself harder.

After speaking in Pueblo, Colorado, on September 25, 1919, Wilson collapsed. A few days later, after returning to Washington, he suffered a stroke that left him partially paralyzed. He carried on some duties but was an invalid, often angry and bitter, for the rest of his presidency. He cut off ties with old friends and political allies. He was openly angry at his opponents. He refused to compromise on changes, and the treaty was defeated. The United States never joined the League of Nations. Perhaps Wilson's only real reward was the 1919 Nobel Peace Prize, which called the League "a design for [bringing] a fundamental law of humanity into present-day international politics."

A Plan for Peace

▶ **President Wilson rides through the streets of San Francisco on his tour to promote the League of Nations.**

The Fourteen Points

As World War I drew to a close, the scale of destruction and massive loss of life was shocking. President Woodrow Wilson wanted a "just and lasting peace" to ensure that a war like the Great War would never happen again.

Wilson outlined his vision of world peace in a speech he made to the U.S. Congress in January 1918, before the war ended. His plan for peace was called the **Fourteen Points**.

HISTORY'S VOICES

> ❝What we demand … is that the world be made fit and safe to live in; and particularly that it be made safe for every peace-loving nation which, like our own, wishes to live its own life, determine its own institutions, be assured of justice and fair dealing by the other peoples of the world as against force and selfish aggression.❞

—President Woodrow Wilson,
Fourteen Points speech, 1918

Wilson's first four points called for open diplomacy, freedom of the seas, the removal of trade barriers, and the reduction of military arms. The fifth point proposed a fair system to resolve disputes over colonies. The next eight points dealt directly with **self-determination**, or the right of people to decide their own political status. For example, Wilson wanted the different ethnic groups within Austria-Hungary to be able to form their own nations.

The fourteenth point, which Wilson believed was the most important, called for the establishment of the **League of Nations**. The League would be an organization of nations that would work together to settle disputes, protect democracy, and prevent future wars.

The components of the Fourteen Points expressed a new philosophy for U.S. foreign policy. The Fourteen Points applied the principles of progressivism to foreign policy. The ideals of free trade, democracy, and self-determination sprang from the same ideals that Progressive reformers supported within the United States. Most importantly, the Fourteen Points declared that the foreign policy of a democratic nation should be based on morality—not just on what was best for that nation.

READING CHECK **Identifying the Main Idea**
What did President Wilson hope to accomplish with his Fourteen Points?

Paris Peace Conference

President Wilson led the group of American negotiators who attended the peace conference that began in Paris in January 1919. By doing so, he became the first U.S. president to visit Europe while in office.

Republicans and others back home criticized Wilson's decision to leave the country. They argued that it was more important for Wilson to stay and help the nation restore its economy after the war than to work toward peace in Europe.

Wilson had a dream of international peace, though, and he wanted to make that dream a reality. He believed that a lasting peace required a fair and unbiased leader, such as himself, to attend the Paris Peace Conference. Otherwise he felt sure that the European powers would continue to squabble over land and colonial rights.

The American delegation arrived in France a few weeks before the conference was scheduled to begin. President Wilson enjoyed a hero's welcome in Paris, when thousands of Parisians lined the streets to cheer his arrival. Before the conference began, Wilson also traveled to London and Rome, and in each city, he received the same heartfelt welcome.

The conference opens The Paris Peace Conference began on January 12, 1919. Leaders from 32 nations—representing about three-quarters of the world's population—attended the conference.

The leaders of the victorious Allies dominated the negotiations. Those leaders—President Woodrow Wilson of the United States, British prime minister **David Lloyd George**, French premier **Georges Clemenceau**, and Italian prime minister Vittorio Orlando—became known as the **Big Four**. Germany and the other Central Powers nations, however, were not invited to participate.

Conflicting needs The delegates arrived at the Paris Peace Conference with competing needs and desires. President Wilson had a vision of a better world where nations dealt with each other openly and traded with each other fairly, while at the same time reducing their arsenals of weapons. Many of the other Allies, however, wanted to punish Germany

ACADEMIC VOCABULARY
component a part of something

for its role in the war. Georges Clemenceau explained the French view in a speech at the conference in June 1919.

HISTORY'S VOICES

❝The conduct of Germany is almost unexampled in human history. The terrible responsibility which lies at her doors can be seen in the fact that not less than seven million dead lie buried in Europe, while more than twenty million others carry upon them the evidence of wounds and sufferings, because Germany saw fit to gratify her [desire] for tyranny by resort to war.❞

—Georges Clemenceau

Other leaders came to the Paris Peace Conference seeking independence. Some wanted to build new nations, such as Yugoslavia and Czechoslovakia. Delegates from Poland, which had been divided between Germany and Russia during the war, wanted to re-establish their nation. A young Vietnamese chef named Ho Chi Minh who worked at the Paris Ritz hotel asked the peacemakers to grant his nation independence from France. Ho Chi Minh would later lead his people in taking Vietnamese independence by force.

The Treaty of Versailles The Allies eventually reached an agreement and presented their peace treaty to Germany in May. The final treaty was much harsher than Wilson had wanted. The treaty forced Germany to disarm its military forces. It required Germany to pay the Allies **reparations**—payments for damages and expenses caused by the war. This amount far exceeded what the German government could actually afford to pay. The Allies also demanded that Germany accept sole responsibility for starting the war.

The treaty did include some of Wilson's Fourteen Points. It would establish a League of Nations. Some ethnic groups in parts of

Wilson's Fourteen Points and the Treaty of Versailles

Some—but not all—of President Wilson's Fourteen Points were reflected in the Treaty of Versailles.

THE FOURTEEN POINTS

1. Public diplomatic negotiations and an end to secret treaties
2. Freedom of navigation on the seas
3. Free trade among nations
4. Reduction of armaments to the level needed for domestic safety
5. Fair resolution of colonial claims that arose because of the war
6. Evacuation of Russia and restoration of its conquered territories
7. Preservation of Belgium's sovereignty
8. Restoration of France's territory, including Alsace-Lorraine
9. Redrawing Italy's borders according to nationalities
10. Divide up Austria-Hungary according to nationalities
11. Redraw the borders of the Balkan states according to nationalities
12. Self-determination for Turks and the other nationalities under Turkish rule
13. Creation of an independent Polish nation
14. Creation of a League of Nations

MAJOR PROVISIONS OF THE TREATY OF VERSAILLES

Military Changes
- Limited the German army to 100,000 men, with no tanks or heavy artillery.
- Limited the German navy to 15,000 men.
- Banned Germany from having an air force.

Territory Changes
- Required Germany to cede land to France, Denmark, Poland, Czechoslovakia, and Belgium.
- Required Germany to surrender all colonies to the control of the League of Nations.
- Germany and Austria were prohibited from uniting.

War-Guilt Provisions
- Held Germany solely responsible for all losses and damages suffered by the Allies during the war.
- Required Germany to pay reparations of 269 billion gold marks, later reduced to 132 billion.

Establishment of the League of Nations
- Did not initially permit Germany to join the League.

The League of Nations

President Wilson exhausted himself traveling the country to win support for the League.

" Why, my fellow citizens, this is one of the great charters of human liberty, and the man who picks flaws in it . . . forgets the magnitude of the thing, forgets the majesty of the thing, forgets that the counsels of more than twenty nations combined . . . in the adoption of this great instrument. "

Woodrow Wilson, 1919

The man who most strongly voiced the opposition to the League was Senator Henry Cabot Lodge.

" We would not have our politics distracted and embittered by the dissensions of other lands. We would not have our country's vigour exhausted or her moral force abated, by everlasting meddling and muddling in every quarrel, great and small, which afflicts the world. "

Henry Cabot Lodge, 1919

Skills FOCUS READING LIKE A HISTORIAN

Identifying Points of View Wilson and Lodge had very different views on the role of the United States in the world. How does each quotation about the League of Nations reflect the speaker's view of relationships between nations?

See **Skills Handbook**, p. H28–H29

Germany, Austria-Hungary, and Russia would receive the right of self-determination. The treaty would create nine new nations, including Czechoslovakia, Poland, and Yugoslavia. The Central Powers also had to surrender control of their colonies to the Allies. The treaty placed some of the colonies under the temporary control of Allied nations until the colonies were deemed ready for independence.

Germany strongly protested the terms of the treaty. Threatened with French military action, however, German officials signed the **Treaty of Versailles** on June 28, 1919. Wilson was disappointed at the treaty's harshness but believed that the League of Nations could resolve any problems the treaty had created.

READING CHECK **Summarizing** How did the Allied leaders at the Paris Peace Conference react to the Fourteen Points?

The Fight over the Treaty

President Wilson returned to the United States on July 8, 1919, and formally presented the treaty to the U.S. Senate two days later. Wilson needed the support of both Republican and Democratic senators to ratify, or approve, the treaty. The Republicans had won control of the Senate in 1918, and getting their support proved difficult for the Democratic president.

The senators quickly divided into three groups. The first consisted of Democrats who supported immediate ratification of the treaty. The second group was the so-called irreconcilables, who urged the outright rejection of U.S. participation in the League of Nations. The last group was the reservationists, who would ratify the treaty only if changes were made.

The reservationists focused their criticism on the part of the League of Nations charter that required its members to use military force to carry out the League's decisions. Some Republicans believed that this conflicted with the constitutional power of the United States Congress to declare war. Senator **Henry Cabot Lodge**, head of the Committee on Foreign Relations, led the reservationists.

Wilson refused to compromise with the reservationists. He took his case directly to the

EUROPE AND THE MIDDLE EAST, 1915

ATLANTIC OCEAN

North Sea

NORWAY
SWEDEN
GREAT BRITAIN
DENMARK
NETHERLANDS
GERMANY
BELGIUM
LUXEMBOURG
FRANCE
SWITZERLAND
ITALY
PORTUGAL
SPAIN
AUSTRIA-HUNGARY
SERBIA
MONTENEGRO
ROMANIA
BULGARIA
ALBANIA
GREECE
RUSSIA
Black Sea
OTTOMAN EMPIRE
AFRICA
Mediterranean Sea
ARABIA

Allied Powers
Central Powers
Neutral nations

0   250   500 Miles
0   250   500 Kilometers
Lambert azimuthal equal-area projection

EUROPE AND THE MIDDLE EAST, 1921

ATLANTIC OCEAN

North Sea

NORWAY
SWEDEN
FINLAND
GREAT BRITAIN
DENMARK
ESTONIA
LATVIA
LITHUANIA
U.S.S.R.
NETHERLANDS
GERMANY
POLAND
EAST PRUSSIA (GERMANY)
BELGIUM
LUXEMBOURG
FRANCE
SWITZERLAND
ITALY
CZECHOSLOVAKIA
AUSTRIA
HUNGARY
ROMANIA
PORTUGAL
SPAIN
YUGOSLAVIA
BULGARIA
ALBANIA
GREECE
Black Sea
TURKEY
AFRICA
Mediterranean Sea
SYRIA
LEBANON
PALESTINE
TRANS-JORDAN
IRAQ
ARABIA

New nations and mandates
Allied-occupied zones

0   250   500 Miles
0   250   500 Kilometers
Lambert azimuthal equal-area projection

GEOGRAPHY SKILLS INTERPRETING MAPS

The map of Europe changed after World War I ended (right). Boundaries changed, and many new nations were created.

Region Where were new nations created? Name them.

See **Skills Handbook**, p. H20

FOCUS ON NEW YORK

GOVERNMENT
After World War II, the United Nations (UN) formed to examine many of the same problems that the League had left unsolved. The United States joined the UN in 1945. The Secretariat Building in New York City became the UN headquarters.

American people. In 22 days Wilson traveled 8,000 miles and gave 32 major speeches, urging the public to pressure Republican senators to ratify the treaty. He warned of serious consequences if the world's nations did not work together in the future.

HISTORY'S VOICES

❝I can predict with absolute certainty that within another generation there will be another world war if the nations of the world do not concert [agree upon] the method by which to prevent it.❞
—President Woodrow Wilson

As you read in the "Inside Story," Wilson's speaking schedule took a heavy toll on his health. After a speech in Pueblo, Colorado, on September 25, 1919, he collapsed. He suffered a stroke in early October and never fully recovered. Wilson spent the rest of his term living privately in the White House, cut off from everyone except his wife and his closest aides.

In November 1919, Senator Lodge presented the treaty to the U.S. Senate for ratification. He included a list of 14 reservations, or con-

cerns about the treaty. Wilson was unwilling to compromise. Following Wilson's instructions, the Senate rejected Lodge's revised treaty on November 19 and again in March 1920.

After Wilson left office in 1921, the United States signed separate peace treaties with Austria, Germany, and Hungary. The United States never joined the League of Nations. Without the United States, the League's ability to keep world peace was uncertain.

READING CHECK **Making Inferences** Why did some Americans oppose the Treaty of Versailles?

The Impact of World War I

World War I was a devastating conflict that shocked the world with its staggering cost. By the end of the war, combat, disease, and starvation had killed more than 14 million people. The war left some 7 million men permanently disabled. The war had cost more than $280 billion—significantly more than any previous war in history.

When the war ended, Americans were eager to return to normal life. But the war had changed the world, and there was no going back to the way things had once been.

Political impact The consequences of World War I were felt far beyond the battlefield. The war led to the overthrow of the monarchies in Russia, Austria-Hungary, Germany, and the Ottoman Empire. It contributed to the rise of the Bolsheviks to power in Russia in 1917. It fanned the flames of revolts against colonialism in the Middle East and in Southeast Asia.

Economic impact World War I devastated European economies. As a result, the United States emerged as the world's leading economic power.

Despite this new financial power, the United States still faced economic challenges at home. The demand for consumer goods increased as Americans raced to buy items that had been in short supply during the war. This increased demand led to inflation, and many Americans struggled to afford ordinary, day-to-day items.

Farmers, who had increased production to meet the needs of European markets during the war, were particularly hard hit when postwar markets no longer need to buy their food. Despite these economic setbacks, most Americans looked forward to the new decade as a time of peace and prosperity.

Social impact The war had drawn more than a million women into the American workforce. Their service to the nation contributed to the passage of the Nineteenth Amendment in 1919, which gave women the right to vote. In 1920 the states ratified the amendment.

The war also encouraged many African Americans to move to northern cities in search of factory work. This changed the population patterns of northern cities and led to new and often uneasy race relations.

Impact in Europe The effects of the war in Europe were devastating. European nations had lost almost an entire generation of young men. France, where most of the combat took place, was in ruins. Great Britain was deeply in debt to the United States and lost its position as the world's financial center. The reparations imposed on Germany by the Treaty of Versailles were crippling.

World War I would not be the "war to end all wars," as many had hoped. Too many issues were left unresolved, and too much anger and hostility would remain. Within a generation, conflict would again break out in Europe, pulling the United States and the rest of the world back into war.

READING CHECK **Summarizing** What economic effects did World War I have on the United States?

Reviewing Ideas, Terms, and People

1. a. Define What was Wilson's **Fourteen Points** plan?
b. Explain Why did Wilson believe the Fourteen Points should be the basis for peace talks?
c. Elaborate How did the Fourteen Points explain a new philosophy of U.S. foreign policy?

2. a. Recall What are **reparations**?
b. Contrast Why did the other Allies reject much of Wilson's plan?
c. Evaluate Whose plan do you believe was most justified—Wilson's or the other Allies'? Explain.

3. a. Identify Who were the reservationists in the U.S. Senate?
b. Drawing Conclusions Why did the reservationists believe that some provisions of the League of Nations were dangerous?
c. Predict What might be the consequence of the United States not joining the League of Nations?

4. a. Describe What are two ways in which World War I made a political impact on the world?
b. Analyzing Information How did World War I propel the United States into a position of greater power in the world?

Critical Thinking

5. Compare Copy the chart below and record examples of the major ways in which World War I had a lasting impact.

	Political Impact	Economic Impact	Social Impact
United States			
The World			

FOCUS ON WRITING

6. Persuasive Should the United States have joined the League of Nations? Write a paragraph supporting your position.

Perspectives on Trench Warfare

Historical Context The three documents below provide different perspectives of trench warfare in World War I.

Task Read the selections and answer the questions that follow. Then write an essay about soldiers' experiences in trench warfare, using facts from the documents provided and from the chapter to support the position you take in your thesis statement.

ST 3.2 Draw upon literary selections, historical documents, and accounts to analyze the roles played by different individuals and groups during the major eras in New York State and United States history.

DOCUMENT 1

In 1929 German author Erich Maria Remarque wrote *All Quiet on the Western Front*, an autobiographical account of the war that became the most celebrated novel of its time. Remarque immigrated to the United States in 1939 after his books were banned by the Nazis and his citizenship was revoked. In the excerpt below, the book's main character, a soldier in whose voice the novel is told, describes a visit home on a leave. Here, he is visiting his mother who is ill in bed.

Suddenly my mother seizes hold of my hand and asks falteringly: "Was it very bad out there, Paul?"

Mother, what should I answer to that! You would not understand, and never realize it. And you never should realize it. Was it bad, you ask.—You, Mother,—I shake my head and say: "No, Mother, not so very. There are always a lot of us together so it isn't so bad."

"Yes, but Heinrich Bredemeyer was here just lately and he said it was terrible out there now, with the gas and all the rest of it."

It is my mother who says that. She says: "With the gas and all the rest of it." She does not know what she is saying, she is merely anxious for me. Should I tell her how we once found three enemy trenches with their garrison all stiff as though stricken with apoplexy? Against the parapet, in the dug-outs, just where they were, the men stood and lay about, with blue faces, dead.

"No, Mother, that's only talk," I answer, "there's not very much in what Bredemeyer says."

DOCUMENT 2

Stull Holt was an American soldier in World War I, fighting in the trenches of France. Below is a letter he wrote home after a frightening experience in which he left his trench and was knocked down by a shell. His gas mask fell off and he was affected by the poison gas.

Sept. 1, 1917
Dear Lois,

At last the long delayed and promised letter. You mustn't complain tho because I wrote to no one . . .

I had a very close call with gas . . . I and this other fellow crawled in a trench alongside the road and waited. We huddled there a long time getting splashed several times by mud thrown by shells exploding, when gas shells started to come in great numbers . . . We started crawling throwing ourselves flat, crawling again (gas masks on of course) . . . I was about buried by a shell and a few seconds later a big gas shell went off within 20 ft of me. Something hit me on the head, making a big dent in my helmet . . . I was dazed, knocked down and my gas mask knocked off. I got several breathes of the strong solution right from the shell before it got diluted with much air. If it hadn't been for the fellow with me I probably wouldn't be writing this letter because I couldn't see, my eyes were running water and burning, so was my nose and I could hardly breathe. I gasped, choked and felt the extreme terror of the man who goes under in the water and will clutch at a straw. The fellow with me grabbed me and led me the hundred yards or so to the post . . . where I felt alright again in a few hours . . . I think the hardest thing I ever did was to go back alone the next night."

This photograph from March 17, 1918, shows U.S. troops of the 168th infantry in the trenches near the town of Badonville, France.

Skills FOCUS   READING LIKE A HISTORIAN

1. **a. Recall** Refer to Document 1. What does the soldier think to himself and not tell his mother?

   b. Interpret *All Quiet on the Western Front* is a novel, but its author, Erich Maria Remarque, drew upon his experiences as a German soldier to write it. In your opinion, which parts of this excerpt might be based on Remarque's own experiences, and which parts of the excerpt might be fiction?

2. **a. Recall** Refer to Document 2. How was Stull Holt's gas mask knocked off?

   b. Make Inferences Why do you think Stull Holt says that walking back alone was the hardest thing he had ever done?

3. **a. Identify** Refer to Document 3. Then review the labeled illustration of trench warfare in Section 1. Identify the following items in Document 3: machine gun, no-man's-land.

   b. Make Inferences What is happening in this photograph? Is there a battle under way? Explain your answer using information in the photograph.

4. **Document-Based Essay Question** Consider the question below and form a thesis statement. Using examples from Documents 1, 2, and 3, create an outline and write a short essay supporting your position.

   What challenges might soldiers face when they returned to peacetime life at home?

   See **Skills Handbook**, p. H28–29, H30, H32

Visual Summary: The First World War

European rivalries lead to the outbreak of war in 1914.
- Nationalism
- Militarism
- Imperialism
- Alliances

The United States enters the war in 1917 and helps turn the tide for an Allied victory.
- Victory in the Battle of Chateau-Thierry
- Stopped German advance at Belleau Wood
- Defeated Germans' last offensive in the Second Battle of the Marne

With the Treaty of Versailles, the Allies determine the terms for peace in the postwar world.
- Forced Germany to pay massive reparations
- Created the League of Nations
- Treaty not ratified by U.S. Senate
- United States did not join the League of Nations

Reviewing Key Terms and People

Match each lettered definition with the correct numbered item below at right.

a. a communication that proposed an alliance between Germany and Mexico to help the Central Powers in case the United States declared war on Germany

b. a military alliance among Germany, Austria-Hungary, and Italy

c. a policy of not being involved in the affairs of other nations

d. payments for damages and expenses caused by the war

e. a military alliance among Great Britain, France, and Russia

f. an extreme pride or devotion that people feel for their country or culture

g. the expansion of arms and the policy of military preparedness

h. posters, newspaper stories, speeches, and other materials designed to influence people's opinions, often during wartime

i. the right of people to decide their own political status

j. the name given to Germany, Austria-Hungary, and the Ottoman Empire during World War I

k. the German promise not to sink merchant vessels without warning

l. the name given to Great Britain, France, and Russia during World War I

1. Allied Powers
2. isolationism
3. Central Powers
4. militarism
5. propaganda
6. Triple Alliance
7. Zimmermann Note
8. *Sussex* pledge
9. self-determination
10. Triple Entente
11. nationalism
12. reparations

History's Impact video program

Review the video to answer the closing question: How does the Supreme Court's decision in *Schenck* v. *United States* explain the limits to free speech?

Comprehension and Critical Thinking

SECTION 1 *(pp. 582–589)*

13. a. Identify What were the main causes of World War I?

b. Analyze How did European leaders discover that a balance of power did not decrease the chances for war among them?

c. Evaluate Which cause of World War I do you believe was the most dangerous? Explain.

SECTION 2 *(pp. 590–596)*

14. a. Recall What did Germany do with its U-boats that violated laws of neutrality?

b. Sequencing Which German actions helped shift U.S. public opinion toward supporting the Allies in the war?

c. Elaborate What effect did U.S. troops have on the Allied fight against the Central Powers?

SECTION 3 *(pp. 598–604)*

15. a. Describe What did the Lever Food and Fuel Control act do?

b. Analyze Why did the U.S. government impose so many regulations on industrial and food production during the war?

c. Elaborate What impact did U.S. industrial and food production have on the war effort for the Allies?

SECTION 4 *(pp. 606–611)*

16. a. Recall What are reparations?

b. Contrasting How did Wilson's goal for the peace treaty differ from that of the other Allies?

c. Elaborate What provisions from Wilson's Fourteen Points were included in the Treaty of Versailles?

Using the Internet

go.hrw.com
Practice Online
Keyword: SD7 CH18

17. The influenza epidemic of 1918 was the deadliest in U.S. history. Using the keyword above, do research to learn about the origins, progression, and final conclusion of this tragic epidemic. Then create a time line of the major events in the progression of the epidemic.

Analyzing Primary Sources

Reading Like a Historian

Propaganda posters like this one encouraged Americans to buy Liberty bonds to support the war effort.

18. Identify What does "Over the Top" mean?

19. Analyze Do you think this was an effective poster? Why or why not?

Critical Reading

Read the passage in Section 1 that begins with the heading "War Breaks Out." Then answer the following question.

20. What was one effect of the German invasion of Belgium?

A It led Russia to join the Central Powers.

B It failed miserably, as Belgium pushed the German forces back across the border.

C It drew Britain into the war against Germany.

D It led the French to surrender to Germany out of fear of being attacked like Belgium.

WRITING FOR THE SAT

Think about the following issue:

The United States had a long-standing foreign-policy tradition of isolationism. As European nations went to war, the United States tried to stay neutral. Eventually, it began leaning toward the Allied side, until in 1917 it joined the war on the side of the Allies.

21. Assignment Given its history of neutrality, was the United States justified in going to war against Germany and the other Central Powers? Write a short essay in which you develop your position on this issue. Support your point of view with reasoning and examples from your reading and studies.

 **The Progressives**
1898–1920

MAIN IDEA During the early 1900s the Progressive movement arose to redress the negative impact of industrialization. Progressives achieved many wide-reaching reforms that affected American political, social, and economic life.

SECTION 1 Progressives focused their attentions on improving the lives of the urban poor, changing dangerous and unfair working conditions, and reforming government.

SECTION 2 Most American women did not have the right to vote in national elections. Nevertheless, many were politically active in reform campaigns for education, children's welfare, temperance, and the vote.

SECTION 3 President Theodore Roosevelt pushed for many Progressive reforms in business and the environment. His program, called the Square Deal, sought to balance the needs of business and industry leaders and those of workers and consumers.

SECTION 4 Progressive reforms continued during the Taft and Wilson presidencies, focusing on business, banking, and certain civil rights reforms. During this time, women won the vote. Despite the many reforms that Progressives campaigned for, they did not fight for the civil rights of African Americans.

CHAPTER 17 **Entering the World Stage**
1898–1917

MAIN IDEA Global competition for empire led the United States into war against Spain and into military conflicts in Mexico. The United States emerged with a new role as a world power.

SECTION 1 The United States joined other industrialized nations in the scramble for empire. For economic, military, and nationalistic reasons, the United States annexed Hawaii and extended its influence in China and Japan.

SECTION 2 The Spanish-American War resulted in a resounding defeat for Spain and the relinquishing of Cuba, Puerto Rico, Guam, and the Philippines to U.S. control. In the aftermath of war, American expansionists and anti-imperialists debated whether to annex the Philippines.

SECTION 3 The United States began to exert its influence over Latin America in the wake of the Spanish-American War. It made Cuba a protectorate and governed Puerto Rico as a territory. Meanwhile, the United States undertook the mammoth task of building the Panama Canal.

SECTION 4 When Mexico exploded into revolution, the United States became drawn into the conflict to protect its economic interests.

 **The First World War**
1914–1920

MAIN IDEA The United States stayed neutral when European nations went to war in 1914. After the United States joined the Allies in 1917, however, the U.S. government quickly mobilized the economy and built public support for the war.

SECTION 1 Rivalries among European nations led to the outbreak of war in 1914. The assassination of an Austrian archduke led to rapid declarations of war, and soon most of Europe was drawn into World War I. Changes in military technology and strategies made World War I a new and deadlier kind of war.

SECTION 2 The United States tried to stay neutral in World War I, but hostile German acts soon convinced President Wilson and Congress that war was inevitable. The United States sent troops to France, where they helped turn the tide for the Allies. The Central Powers agreed to an armistice on November 11, 1918.

SECTION 3 The U.S. government mobilized its resources for the war effort. It sold Liberty bonds to pay for the war and regulated industry to fulfill the needs of the troops overseas. It encouraged women to take on the jobs left vacant by men who joined the military. The government also campaigned to win the support of public opinion and minimize dissent.

SECTION 4 At the Paris Peace Conference, the Allies hammered out a peace treaty. Some, but not all, of Wilson's Fourteen Points were included in the Treaty of Versailles. The treaty also called for Germany to pay heavy reparations for its role in the war. In the United States, the Senate hotly debated the treaty. Many senators objected to the idea of the United States joining the League of Nations, and eventually the Senate rejected the treaty.

A Modern Nation

1919–1940

Themes

Government and Democracy
The nation struggled with postwar labor unrest, radical political ideas, and later, high unemployment brought on by the Great Depression.

Economic Development
Americans experienced a period of great productivity and prosperity, followed by a devastating economic downturn.

Cultural Expressions
The growth of mass media and popular culture, a rebirth in the arts, and the development of a consumer society marked a period of cultural change.

New York City's Times Square is ablaze with electric lights and other signs of progress and prosperity in this 1925 painting.

617

Identifying Problems and Solutions

Find practice for **Identifying Problems and Solutions** in the **Skills Handbook,** p. H11

Historical texts frequently discuss problems that people in the past encountered and the solutions they adopted. Identifying problems and solutions can help you understand what you are reading.

Before You Read
Skim headings to determine a passage's content. What problem do you think will be discussed in this passage?

While You Read
Note the problem cited in the text and the reasons it occurred.

After You Read
Review the problem and the solutions offered.

Bank Failures

As you have read, the collapse of the stock market strained the financial resources of many banks. In the weeks following the crash, a number of banks failed. For ordinary Americans, the collapse of banks was unnerving. Most people did not have money invested in banks, but many had entrusted their savings to banks.

Today, insurance from the federal government protects most people's deposits in the event of bank failure. That is, most Americans do not have to worry that they will lose their savings if their bank goes out of business. In addition, laws today require that a bank keep a greater percentage of its assets in cash, to be paid out to depositors on request.

READING CHECK **Identifying Problems and Solutions** What precautions has the federal government taken to safeguard people's money in banks?

Identify the problem If the problem is large, organize it in smaller parts.

Problem The collapse of banks unnerved many Americans who had entrusted their savings to them.

Solution Federal insurance and laws help protect people's finances today.

Test Prep Tip

Some tests may require you to identify a problem and its solution. In such instances, first try to recognize the problem and its cause and then to identify possible options and solutions for that problem. Then evaluate the effectiveness of the solution.

Reading like a Historian

Interpreting Literature as Historical Evidence

Find practice for **Interpreting Literature as Historical Evidence** in the **Skills Handbook,** p. H32

Literature can be an important source of historical information. It can tell us what life was like in the past and what people believed. But it needs to be read with caution. The author is creating a fictional story not recording facts. Be sure to use your prior knowledge and information from reliable primary and secondary sources when assessing literature as historical evidence.

Strategies historians use:
- Look for descriptive passages that help you understand what life was like in that time and place.
- Examine the author's point of view and any biases by contrasting the types of words used to describe different events.
- Determine whether the literature is meant to describe a certain historical event or to elicit an emotional response.

Steinbeck is describing the migration of people from the Plains to California in the 1930s along Route 66, "the great cross-country highway."

The cars of the migrant people crawled out of the side roads onto the great cross-country highway, and they took the migrant way to the West. In the daylight they scuttled like bugs to the westward; and as the dark caught them, they clustered like bugs near to shelter and to water. And because they were lonely and perplexed, because they had all come from a place of sadness and worry and defeat, and because they were all going to a new mysterious place, they huddled together; they talked together; they shared their lives, their food, and the things they hoped for in the new country. Thus it might be that one family camped for the spring and for company, and a third because two families had pioneered the place and found it good. And when the sun went down, perhaps twenty families and twenty cars were there.

—from *The Grapes of Wrath* by John Steinbeck, 1939

Words like *lonely* and *perplexed* describe how the migrants heading west to California felt. You could check these words against other sources.

The description of families gathering together is fairly neutral. It doesn't seem to betray any bias.

Skills FOCUS — READING LIKE A HISTORIAN

As You Read List historical evidence found in the literature. Then compare the evidence with known facts to arrive at the most complete account of history.

As You Study Use literature to help you understand political and social movements in history. Determine whether the literature recounts history, makes an activist appeal, or has some other purpose.

From WAR to PEACE

THE BIG PICTURE The end of the war brought peace to Americans, but not peace of mind. Dangers seen and unseen troubled the nation—until a new president in the White House and a booming economy seemed to smooth the transition from war to peace.

New York Standards

Key Idea 1 The study of New York State and United States history requires an analysis of the development of American culture, its diversity and multicultural context, and the ways people are unified by many values, practices, and traditions.

Key Idea 2 Important ideas, social and cultural values, beliefs, and traditions from New York State and United States history illustrate the connections and interactions of people and events across time and from a variety of perspectives.

Skills FOCUS READING LIKE A HISTORIAN

This photo, taken in 1924 by the Electric Club of Louisville, Kentucky, shows a few of this appliance store's products. These people are members of the club or employees of the store.
Analyzing Primary Sources What does the fact that Louisville had an Electric Club tell you about how American consumers felt about modern electrical appliances during the 1920s?

See **Skills Handbook**, pp. H28–H29

U.S.

1919
Attorney General Palmer launches anti-radical raids.

1918

WORLD

1918–1919
Influenza epidemic kills millions of people worldwide.

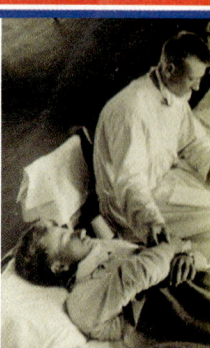

History's Impact video program

Watch the video to understand the impact of women's suffrage.

1920
Promising normalcy, Warren G. Harding wins the presidency.

1924
The U.S. government imposes strict limits on immigration.

1928
Coolidge opts not to seek re-election.

The United States signs the Kellogg-Briand Pact.

1920 • 1922 • 1924 • 1926 • 1928 • 1930

1920
Bolsheviks win a civil war and take control of Russia.

1922
Benito Mussolini establishes a Fascist regime in Italy.

1927
The German stock market collapses.

1928
Scottish doctor Alexander Fleming discovers penicillin.

621

Postwar Havoc

MAIN IDEA

Although the end of World War I brought peace, it did not ease the minds of many Americans, who found much to fear in the postwar years.

READING FOCUS

1. What were the causes and effects of the first Red Scare?
2. How did labor strife grow during the postwar years?
3. How did the United States limit immigration after World War I?

KEY TERMS AND PEOPLE

Bolshevik
communism
Red Scare
A. Mitchell Palmer
Palmer raids
alien
deportation
anarchist

PI 2.3 Compare and contrast the experiences of different groups in the United States.

A DEADLY Epidemic

▼ In March 1918, soldiers in Camp Funston, Kansas, became the first U.S. influenza victims.

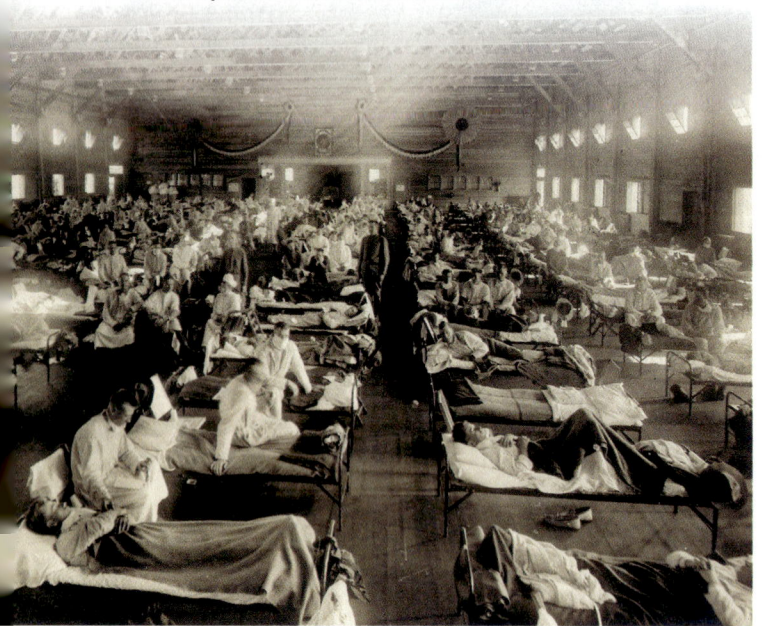

THE INSIDE STORY

How did peace in Europe bring death to the United States? Influenza found breeding grounds in the military camps and the trenches, where soldiers lived in close quarters. It invaded the United States, traveling on troop ships among the healthy and the wounded. In the streets, as hopeful Americans gathered to celebrate the end of World War I, the infection spread quickly. Soon, many were sick and dying—victims of a worldwide influenza epidemic in 1918 and 1919 that would kill some 10 times as many Americans as died in battle in World War I.

Even in the early 1900s, the flu was not generally a serious disease. It caused unpleasant symptoms, and it could be dangerous to the very old and very young. Healthy adults might feel ill for a few days, but they usually recovered quickly. In 1918, however, a powerful new strain of influenza struck with deadly force, eventually infecting more than 1 in 4 Americans. It took an especially heavy toll on men and women in their twenties and thirties. Some victims died within a day or two of getting sick.

The nation's hospitals, already strained with large numbers of wounded soldiers, suddenly had thousands of new patients at their doorsteps. Cities and towns suffered shortages of doctors, nurses, and beds for the sick.

As the winter of 1919 passed, the number of new flu cases began to drop. The crisis had passed, but more than half a million Americans had perished.

As society began to return to normal in the postwar world, many people remained fearful and uneasy. The world was at peace, but Americans were not. As you will read, this feeling would continue for some time. ◼

The First Red Scare

The end of World War I in 1918 brought great rejoicing in America, but it was just the beginning of new problems at home. Besides a terrifying medical crisis, the nation faced economic and political turmoil that cast a dark shadow over the postwar recovery.

Farms and factories that had buzzed with activity during the war now lay silent, as demand for their products suddenly fell. In the slowing economy, returning soldiers had difficulty finding jobs. People began to

Terrorism in the United States

Around noon on September 16, 1920, a horse-drawn cart stopped in front of the offices of financier J.P. Morgan, on Wall Street in New York City. Suddenly, the cart—which had been packed with dynamite—exploded. More than 30 people were instantly killed, and some 300 were injured. Of the cart and horse, only hooves remained.

Detectives took the horseshoes to thousands of stables, but they found no more evidence. Some officials suspected labor organizers and political radicals. Although many people were questioned and even arrested, no one was ever brought to trial.

At about 9 a.m. on April 19, 1995, a homemade bomb exploded inside a truck parked in front of the Alfred P. Murrah Federal Building in Oklahoma City. Nearly 170 people were killed, including children, and more than 500 were injured.

Investigators learned that the Oklahoma City bombing was carried out by two men who opposed earlier government actions against an armed group in Texas. Both were tried and convicted. One received the death penalty, and the other was sentenced to life in prison.

Contrasting How did the outcomes of the two investigations differ?

The 1995 Oklahoma City bombing collapsed the front of the federal building. At the time the bombing was the worst terrorist attack that had occurred on American soil.

---

realize that in many ways, they had traded a painful war for a troubling peace.

HISTORY'S VOICES

❝I felt that when peace came we'd all be so joyful that nothing would weigh upon us again. I find, however, the problems of reconstruction loom so large that we are as much occupied with them as we have been with the problems of war.❞

—Illinois governor Frank Lowden, quoted in *The Harding Era* by Robert K. Murray

The emotional turmoil of the times had disturbing political effects. While World War I had stirred deep feelings of patriotism, it had also ignited hatred toward Germans. These sentiments gave rise to a movement known as 100 Percent Americanism. It celebrated all things American while it attacked ideas—and people—it viewed as foreign or anti-American.

The rise of the Bolsheviks

Americans worried about a new foreign enemy. In 1917 a violent revolution had ripped across Russia. The Red Army of the **Bolsheviks**, which was led by Vladimir I. Lenin, eventually gained control. Five years later Russia would become part of a new nation called the Soviet Union.

Lenin and the Bolsheviks dreamed of establishing a new social system for their people—and for the world. This system, called **communism**, would have no economic classes and no private property. Lenin believed all people should share equally in society's wealth.

American reaction

Many Americans were baffled and frightened by communism. The Soviets called for the overthrow of capitalism. But most Americans embraced the ideals of capitalism, including the freedom to own property. They valued the opportunity to better themselves by hard work or ingenuity.

Lenin predicted that communism would inspire workers throughout the world to rise up and crush capitalism. To some Americans, the threat seemed more ominous than the traditional conflicts of the past.

Throughout World War I, the American public had focused its fear and hatred on "the Hun." Now, public anxiety became fixed on a new target: Communists and others who held radical ideas. They were known as Reds.

Communist parties formed in the United States after the war. Some of their members promoted the violent overthrow of the government. In fact, radicals may have played a role in a 1919 plot in which bombs were mailed to government officials. The plot failed, however. Most historians agree that an internal

Political Cartoon

Hundreds of political cartoons, including this one titled "Put Them Out and Keep Them Out," fueled Red Scare fears. This cartoon originally appeared in the *Philadelphia Inquirer* in October 1919, when the U.S. government was trying to deport many suspected Communist sympathizers.

THE GRANGER COLLECTION, NEW YORK

Political cartoonists often portrayed Communist sympathizers as bearded, sinister-looking characters carrying torches and sometimes weapons.

The torch of anarchy represents the destructive nature of communism. The knife represents the dangers of Bolshevism.

Skills FOCUS   READING LIKE A HISTORIAN

1. **Drawing Conclusions** What do you think the title "Put Them Out and Keep Them Out" means?

2. **Interpreting Political Cartoons** Why do you think the artist showed the character peeking out from under the American flag?

See **Skills Handbook**, p. H12, H31

FOCUS ON NEW YORK

GOVERNMENT
New York's original law against criminal anarchy was passed in 1902 and tested when Benjamin Gitlow was convicted for publishing a socialist pamphlet. The Supreme Court later ruled that states could not abridge rights guaranteed by the First Amendment, setting a precedent for future rulings on free-speech cases.

Communist threat to the nation was probably never great. Yet at the time, the threat seemed very real.

A **Red Scare**, or widespread fear of communism, gripped the nation. One official noted, "I believe it has been 'scared up' considerably by the newspapers, which relate every arrest and incident . . . by printing large scary headlines."

The government took the threat seriously. New York state legislators voted to bar five legally elected socialists from office. New York also passed a law making it a crime to call for the overthrow of the government. In *Gitlow* v. *New York* (1925) the Supreme Court upheld the New York law. But it also held that the Fourteenth Amendment prohibited states from depriving citizens of the right to free speech.

The Palmer raids A. Mitchell Palmer, had been one of the targets of the 1919 bombing plot. Later that year, as attorney general of the United States, Palmer became a key leader of the federal government's anti-Communist campaign. He led an attack on suspected radicals known as the **Palmer raids**.

To justify the raids, Palmer used wartime laws that gave the government broad powers against suspected radicals. For **aliens**—citizens of other countries living in the United States— just belonging to certain groups considered radical could lead to deportation. **Deportation** means removing an alien from one country and sending him or her to another country.

In late 1919 Palmer's forces arrested thousands of members of suspected radical groups. In December 1919, a naval vessel named the *Buford* set sail carrying nearly 250 aliens who were being deported. Many Americans cheered Palmer's actions. Said Leonard Wood, a Republican leader, "I believe we should place them all in ships of stone, with sails of lead."

In time, the Red Scare died down. It became clear that predictions about the radical threat to the country were not coming true. At the same time, Communist movements in Germany and Hungary were failing. These failures dampened fears of worldwide revolution. The nation's anxiety was reduced, but it was not eliminated.

READING CHECK   Sequencing Who replaced "the Hun" as the object of American fear and hatred?

Labor Strife Grows

The year 1919 was one of the most explosive times in the history of the American labor movement. Some 4 million workers took part in more than 3,000 strikes nationwide. In nearly every case, labor lost. Wartime successes and peacetime disappointments set the stage for this catastrophic year for workers.

Postwar difficulties Workers' raised expectations helped create the crisis. During the war, President Wilson had sought good relations with workers who were keeping the troops clothed and equipped. Organized labor won many gains, including shorter hours and higher wages. When the war ended, labor leaders hoped to build on what they had achieved. They were disappointed.

A number of factors combined to frustrate labor's high hopes. Wilson, now focused on promoting his peace plan, paid less attention to events at home and did little to promote workers' causes. Meanwhile, the sinking postwar demand for factory goods hurt many industries. Returning soldiers expected to take their place on the factory floor, but the jobs just weren't there. Unhappy workers, especially strikers, were replaced.

The Red Scare further weakened labor by damaging its reputation. Communism's call to workers to rise up and overthrow their government made many people suspicious of organized labor. Opponents linked labor with the radical ideas that so many people feared.

Labor's losses The showdown between labor and management in 1919 devastated organized labor. Unions lost members and national political power. It would take another decade—and another national crisis—to restore organized labor's reputation, <u>status</u>, and bargaining power in the United States.

Major strikes of the era Among the thousands of union strikes that rocked the country in 1919, a few hold a place in labor history. In Seattle, Washington, labor unrest at the shipyards spread citywide, igniting what became the nation's first major general strike—one in which workers in all industries take part.

The conflict virtually shut down the city. Yet the Seattle general strike of 1919 failed to achieve any gains for workers. In fact, it did great harm. For years afterward, industry, and its jobs, stayed away from Seattle.

On the opposite coast, the city of Boston descended into chaos when its police force went on strike in September 1919 to protest low wages and poor working conditions. Eventually, Massachusetts governor Calvin Coolidge called in the state's militia to end the strike.

Major Strikes, 1919

- **Seattle general strike—** February 6–11
- **Boston police strike—** September 9–13
- **Nationwide steelworkers strike—** September 22, 1919–January 1920

It was another loss for labor, but a great political boost for the Republican governor. In a telegram to the famous labor leader Samuel Gompers, Coolidge wrote, "There can be no right to strike against the public safety by anybody, anywhere, anytime."

The words echoed across a nervous country and made Coolidge a hero. His sudden fame as a champion of law and order elevated his career to the national stage and eventually landed him in the White House.

Other notable strikes hit the steel industry and the coalfields of the eastern United States. The United Mine Workers had kept a "no strikes" pledge during the war. Under the tough new leadership of John L. Lewis, the striking union won a large wage increase.

The workers failed, however, to win other key demands, such as a reduction of their workweek to five days. Lewis recognized the limitations of the union's power at that time.

"We cannot fight the government," the labor leader declared. His miners, like union members throughout the country, would have to wait to press their demands for shorter hours and safer workplaces.

READING CHECK **Summarizing** How successful were the postwar labor strikes?

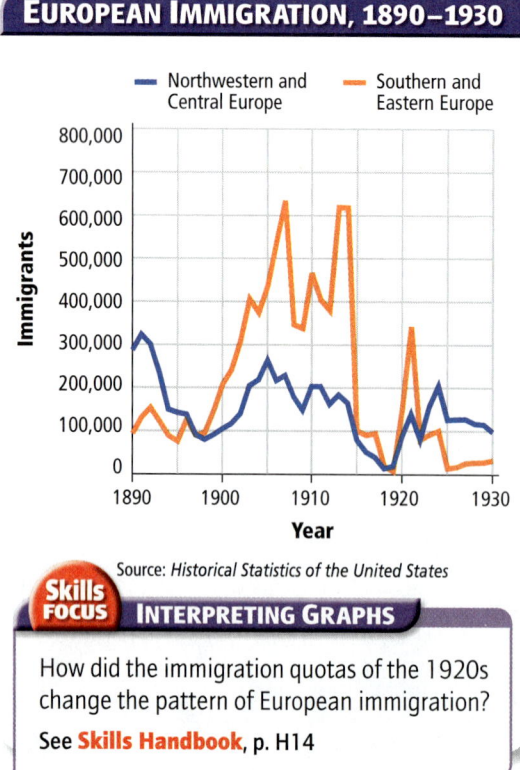

EUROPEAN IMMIGRATION, 1890–1930

— Northwestern and Central Europe   — Southern and Eastern Europe

Source: Historical Statistics of the United States

Skills FOCUS **INTERPRETING GRAPHS**

How did the immigration quotas of the 1920s change the pattern of European immigration?

See **Skills Handbook**, p. H14

Limiting Immigration

Competition for scarce jobs, combined with the Red Scare, triggered an ugly backlash against foreigners in the postwar period. The rise of nativism, or distrust of foreigners, produced a culture clash between the nation's earlier immigrants and its newer ones.

Many nativists were Protestant Christians who had their roots in northern and western Europe, the source of most immigration before 1900. The nativists targeted newer arrivals from southern and eastern Europe, many of whom were Catholics and Jews. Immigrants from these areas of Europe, nativists argued, were less willing to become "Americanized," and should not be welcomed.

Labor leaders, along with the nativists, pushed for immigration restrictions on these groups. New arrivals, often poor and alone, were willing to work for low wages. Unions saw them as a threat.

Immigration control The federal government responded to nativist concern by passing laws to limit immigration. A 1921 law established a quota—an established number—of immigrants to be allowed into the United States from various nations.

The National Origins Act of 1924 went even further. It set quotas for each country at 2 percent of the number of people from that country living in the United States in 1890. The goal was clearly to reduce immigration to the United States from certain countries—mainly southern and eastern European countries. The act also nearly eliminated all immigration from Asian countries.

Nativism also produced a revival in the 1920s of the Ku Klux Klan. The Klan had started as a terror group that targeted African Americans in the South. It reemerged in the postwar years with a broader mission. The hate group now targeted Jews, Catholics, and radicals of all types.

A Klan slogan of the 1920s characterized the group's vision of the nation: "Native white, Protestant supremacy." The new Ku Klux Klan of the 1920s also moved out of the South into other parts of the United States.

Sacco and Vanzetti In the 1920s a court case in Massachusetts dramatically illustrated the nation's struggle with nativist and anti-radical feelings. In May 1920, two men, Nicola Sacco and Bartolomeo Vanzetti, were arrested for armed robbery and murder. The two men were Italian immigrants. More importantly, they proclaimed that they were **anarchists**— radicals who sought the destruction of government.

At the trial, it became clear that the evidence against the two men was weak. It also was apparent that Sacco and Vanzetti were on trial for their political beliefs as well as for bank robbery and murder.

Amid great publicity and protests in Europe and South America as well as in the United States, the two men were convicted and sentenced to die. They were executed in 1927.

Historians still argue over the guilt or innocence of Sacco and Vanzetti. Many agree, however, that the men's political ideas played a prominent role in the trial.

Bartolomeo Vanzetti expressed these same ideas before his trial.

Skills FOCUS **READING LIKE A HISTORIAN**

The artist Ben Shahn based this painting of Sacco and Vanzetti, like many subjects of his paintings, on a newspaper photograph.

Making Inferences Why do you think Shahn chose to use newspaper images?

HISTORY'S VOICES

❝My conviction is that I have suffered for things I am guilty of. I am suffering because I am a radical, and indeed I am a radical; I have suffered because I was an Italian, and indeed I am Italian.❞

—Bartolomeo Vanzetti in court, 1927

The executions of Sacco and Vanzetti were highly controversial at the time. By then, however, the nation had largely recovered from the Red Scare and the turmoil of the postwar years. The 1920s would be very different from the previous decade.

READING CHECK **Identifying Cause and Effect** How did Congress respond to the growing concern about immigration?

SECTION 1 **ASSESSMENT**

go.hrw.com
Online Quiz
Keyword: SD7 HP19

Reviewing Ideas, Terms, and People

1. a. Define What was the Red Scare?
b. Compare How did American attitudes toward "the Hun" relate to attitudes toward Reds?
c. Evaluate Why do you think Americans were able to quickly transfer their feelings about Germans to Communists and radicals?

2. a. Describe Why did labor strife increase after the war?
b. Contrast How did labor fare after the war compared to during the war?

3. a. Define Write a brief definition for each of the following terms: **alien**, **anarchist**
b. Explain What change in immigration in recent decades appeared to concern many Americans in the postwar years?
c. Elaborate How do you think nativism might have related to the Red Scare?

Critical Thinking

4. Comparing and Contrasting Copy the chart below and compare and contrast the public attitudes about radicals, organized labor, and immigrants in the post–World War I era.

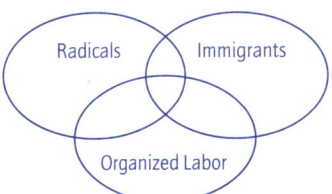

Radicals   Immigrants

Organized Labor

FOCUS ON WRITING

5. Persuasive Write a letter to a member of Congress in which you argue for or against the idea that simply holding a "radical" idea should be against the law.

A New Economic Era

BEFORE YOU READ

MAIN IDEA

New products, new industries, and new ways of doing business expanded the economy in the 1920s, although not everyone shared in the prosperity.

READING FOCUS

1. What role did the Ford Motor Company and Henry Ford play in revolutionizing American industry?

2. How did both the auto industry and the nation change during the 1920s?

3. What were some qualities of the new consumer of the 1920s?

4. What were some weak parts of the economy in the 1920s?

KEY TERMS AND PEOPLE

Henry Ford
assembly line
productivity
welfare capitalism
suburb
installment buying
credit

PI 2.1 Discuss several schemes for periodizing the history of New York State and the United States.

THE INSIDE STORY

How did a department store create an American tradition?

In 1924 Americans were on a shopping spree. The U.S. economy was on the rise, spurred by the American consumer, who was busy spending money on a wide range of exciting new products.

In the middle of this national buying frenzy was Macy's department store in New York City. By 1924 Macy's aisles and displays filled some 1 million square feet of New York real estate. It was said to be the largest store in the world.

In 1924 some Macy's employees came up with the idea to hold a Christmas parade. Many of the employees were recent immigrants from Europe, and they wanted to share their holiday traditions as a gift to the people of their new

country. It wasn't a bad idea for the store, either. The parade would provide an opportunity for Macy's to unveil its enormous Christmas window displays along 34th Street.

The parade kicked off on Thanksgiving Day, 1924, featuring about a thousand employees of the store. Brass bands, clowns, and zoo animals enlivened the scene. Along the route, a quarter million potential shoppers took in the sights and sounds.

The first Macy's parade was a great success. In 1925, on Thanksgiving Day, marchers once again delighted the crowds and welcomed the holiday season. Soon the parade—and the department store itself—was a tradition shared not just by the people of New York but also by visitors from around the world.

Meanwhile, the American consumers who had helped make Macy's a success in New York continued their postwar shopping spree. Indeed, as you will read, for Macy's and other American businesses, the 1920s provided much to be thankful for and to celebrate.

▼ **Macy's first big Christmas parade was held on November 27, 1924.**

Let the PARADE Begin

Ford Revolutionizes Industry

The black automobiles that chugged and sputtered their way down the streets of New York and other cities represented the latest in American technology. During the 1920s, the Ford Model T automobile, like the Macy's parade, would become a fixture of American life.

The first cars appeared in America in the late 1800s, but they remained a toy for the rich through the early 1900s. That changed when a young entrepreneur, **Henry Ford**, began selling his Model T in 1908. It wasn't much to look at. However, it changed American society forever. Ford spelled out his revolutionary vision:

HISTORY'S VOICES

❝ I will build a motor car for the great multitude. It will be large enough for the family but small enough for the individual to run and care for. It will be constructed of the best materials, by the best men to be hired, after the simplest designs that modern engineering can devise. It will be so low in price that no man making a good salary will be unable to own one. ❞

—Henry Ford, announcing plans for his Model T

The assembly line Imagine how expensive cars would be today if every one were custom-made! Ford began by making his cars identical and simple. That brought the cost down, but not enough. So he studied manufacturing processes, from interchangeable parts to the moving belts in meatpacking plants that brought the work to the workers. Then he hired scientific management expert Frederick Winslow Taylor to determine how workers should move, and at what speed, to be most productive.

These ideas combined to produce the first large-scale moving **assembly line**, a production system in which the item being built moves along a conveyor belt to various workstations. On Ford's assembly line, each worker had one of 84 specific jobs, often requiring simple skills.

Ford explained, "The man who puts on a bolt does not put on a nut. The man who puts on the nut does not tighten it." In its first year, the Ford assembly line produced a car every hour and a half.

The car sold for under $500, about half the cost of the first Model Ts. The price was not cheap in its day, but many people could afford it. By the 1920s Ford was rolling out a car every minute, and the price had dropped even lower. By 1929 about 22 million cars bumped along the nation's mostly unpaved roads. People loved the Model T. They wrote songs about it. They formed automobile driving clubs.

Ford realized that his workers also were potential car buyers. He raised his workers' pay to $5 a day, far above average factory wages. This enabled his workers to buy cars.

Workers did pay a price, however. Ford bitterly opposed unions and dealt ruthlessly with anyone who tried to organize workers. Organizers pointed out the boring, repetitive tasks in Ford's clockworklike assembly lines. One labor leader remarked, "Ford workers are not really alive, they are half dead."

The effect on industry During the first quarter of the century, the Ford Motor Company dominated automaking. In the 1920s, more than half the cars in the United States were Fords. Competitors such as General Motors and Chrysler tried to improve on Ford's formula. In an effort to keep costs low, Ford refused to change the Model T's design until 1927, after some 15 million had rolled off the assembly line. New competitors General Motors and Chrysler arose to challenge that formula, bringing out new designs and colors each year. Competition helped the entire industry grow.

Other industries also learned from Ford. Manufacturers of all kinds of consumer goods

THE IMPACT TODAY

Science and Technology

Automakers still use assembly lines to make cars. Industrial robots, instead of people, perform much of the repetitive work. Each machine performs a specific task, much as in Ford's assembly line.

FACES OF HISTORY

Henry FORD
1863–1947

Since he was a young boy, Henry Ford loved to tinker with machines. As a young man, Ford worked as a machinist at the Edison Company plant in Detroit. In 1896 Ford built his first automobile. A few years later, Ford quit his machinist job to start an automobile company. Ford wanted to make cars more affordable. By developing the assembly line and using standardized parts, Ford drastically lowered the cost of manufacturing cars. In turn, he sold his cars at a price the average American could afford. Ford's strategy worked. In 1908 Ford designed the Model T. By 1927, Ford sold more than 15 million Model Ts, transforming American life.

Explain How did Ford build more affordable cars?

Autos Drive the Modern Age

The automobile fostered many changes in American industry, business, and culture.

Service stations gassed up American cars, and the gasoline tax, levied by most states, helped pay for new roads.

The Model T had its competitors—as many as 107 at one time. By the end of the 1920s, however, three competitors dominated the market: General Motors, Chrysler, and Ford.

By 1925 America was producing about five times the number of car and truck tires that it was making a decade earlier.

Like many Americans in the 1920s, these beachgoers in Jacksonville, Florida, took to their cars in pursuit of leisure. America's romance with the open road had its tragic side, too. The rate of traffic fatalities more than doubled during the decade.

Skills FOCUS INTERPRETING INFOGRAPHICS

Mass production of the automobile affected Americans' lives in many ways. *How many can you identify by examining these pictures?*

See **Skills Handbook**, p. H30

began using assembly-line techniques to make goods in large quantities and at lower costs. In the 1920s productivity rose by 60 percent. **Productivity** is a measure of output per unit of input such as labor. American workers were producing more in less time.

The success of business in the 1920s led to a growth of what is called **welfare capitalism**, a system in which companies provide benefits to employees in an effort to promote worker satisfaction and loyalty. For example, many companies offered company-paid pensions—payments made to workers when they retire. Others set up recreation programs for workers. In return, business owners hoped that welfare capitalism would encourage workers to shun unions and accept lower pay. Many did.

READING CHECK **Drawing Conclusions** What innovation by Henry Ford helped transform American industry?

Industry Changes Society

Every time motorists turned the crank handle to start their cars, other industries benefited. Demand for steel, glass, rubber, and other automobile materials soared. Automobile repair shops and filling stations sprang up in cities and towns. Motels and restaurants arose to meet the needs of car travelers.

The simple engines ran on gasoline, a by-product of petroleum. A few of the landowners who found petroleum on their property became rich practically overnight.

Automaking put the city of Detroit, Michigan, on the map. Henry Ford based his manufacturing operations there, and other carmakers followed. In 1910 fewer than 500,000 people lived in Detroit. Within 20 years the population had tripled.

The growth in manufacturing caused a boom in other Midwest cities. Akron, Ohio, the center of the rubber and tire industry, grew from fewer than 70,000 people in 1910 to nearly 210,000 in 1920. For the decade, it was the fastest-growing city in the United States.

As cities grew, so did their **suburbs**, the smaller towns located outside urban areas. Many suburbs had been established since the late 1800s, thanks in part to the construction of trolley lines that carried workers back and forth between home and workplace. Car travel, however, allowed people to live at even greater distances from their jobs. Trolley enterprises, however, suffered during the 1920s, even as suburbs expanded.

Freedom to travel also produced a new tourist industry. Before the auto boom, Florida had a few resorts that attracted mainly wealthy visitors. Automobiles brought tourists by the thousands to discover warm, sunny Florida. Buyers snatched up land, causing prices to rise sharply. Some Florida swamps were drained to put up new housing.

READING CHECK **Identifying Cause and Effect** How did the growth of the auto industry affect related industries?

The New Consumer

During the 1920s Americans witnessed an explosion of new products, new experiences, and new forms of mass communication on a scale never seen before. People were getting into the buying habit and liking it. Companies were happy to supply more new products for them to buy.

New products Using cost-efficient, new manufacturing processes, factories turned out a variety of new electrical appliances, such as refrigerators and vacuum cleaners. The electrification of new areas of the country enabled more people to use the latest home conveniences.

Perhaps the favorite new electronic home technology was the radio. By the end of the 1920s, 4 homes in 10 had a radio. Like the televisions and computers that followed it, the radio opened new worlds to American families. Now, families gathered in the evenings to hear news from around the world as well as dramas and comedy shows.

Radio connected the world as never before. So did a new form of public transportation: the airplane. Aviation had made great advances during World War I. The first passenger airlines appeared over American skies in the 1920s.

The early flights offered little comfort—some passengers wore goggles and helmets. Planes were uninsulated and unpressurized; they couldn't fly over mountains or at night. In fact, for cross-country travel, trains were more comfortable as well as cheaper. For some Americans, though, the thrill of air travel outweighed the early discomforts.

Creating demand Buy! Buy! Buy! On the sidelines of the great American spending spree, advertisers became the cheerleaders. During the 1920s, persuasive advertising gained a major role in the economy. Advertisers paid for space in publications. Companies sponsored popular radio shows, such as the Palmolive Hour and the Maxwell House Concert. Advertising money made these publications and shows available to the public, and advertising gave wide exposure to consumer products.

New ways to pay In the early 1900s, most Americans paid for items in full when they bought them. They might borrow money to buy a house, a piano, or a sewing machine. But as one economist noted, "People who made such purchases didn't talk about them." Borrowing money was not considered respectable.

Setting the stage for today's credit-card society, the generation of the 1920s turned to ==installment buying==—paying for an item over time in small payments. They bought on ==credit==, which is, in effect, borrowing money.

Consumers took quickly to installment buying to purchase the new products on the market. By the end of the decade, 90 percent of durable goods, or long lasting goods such as cars and appliances, were bought on credit. Advertisements encouraged the use of credit, telling consumers they could "get what they want now" and assuring them that with small payments they would "barely miss the money."

READING CHECK **Summarizing** How did life change for consumers in the 1920s?

Consumer Culture

"Everyone owns a car but us"~

You, too, can own an automobile without missing the money, and *now*, is the time to buy it—through the easiest and simplest method ever devised:

Ford Weekly Purchase Plan

Thousands of families, who thought a car was out of the question because of limited incomes, found that they could easily, quickly and surely buy a car of their own under this remarkable plan

You *can* own an automobile, and you *should*. It will mean so much to you. It will add much to the happiness of your family that is worth while. It will bring the most glorious pleasures into your life. It will increase your chances for success. It will give you and your family a social and business prestige that will be invaluable—and which you, and every family, should enjoy. A car is a symbol of success—a mark of achievement, and it brings opportunities to you that you would probably never secure otherwise. You should have a car of your own, and *you can*.

The Ford Plan makes it possible for anyone to own an automobile. It is so easy, simple and practical that many who could easily pay "spot cash" take advantage of it—and buy their car from weekly earnings. The plan is simply wonderful! Before you realize it, you are driving your own automobile. If you have felt that you must make enough to buy a car, you must read The Ford Plan Book. Send for it. See how easy it is to get a car of your own, *now*, and pay for it without missing the money. It seems almost too good to be true, doesn't it? *But it is true.* Get the book—at once. Simply mail the coupon. *Mail it today!*

Give your family the advantages which others have. Get a car of your own. The Ford Plan Book tells you "how" you can buy a car and pay for it without missing the money. Get it! Read it!

COUPON

FORD MOTOR COMPANY
Dept. N-3 Detroit, Michigan
Please send me your book, "The Ford Plan," which fully explains your easy

Hamilton Beach Vacuum Sweeper

'Phone Now and Try It

The advertising industry expanded after World War I. With the help of psychologists, advertising produced glamorous ads that tempted Americans with exciting new products. New payment methods convinced people they could afford to buy them. *What image of Americans is the advertisers portraying?*

Weaknesses in the Economy

The era that brought the boom in cars, consumer goods, radio, and advertising earned the nickname the Roaring Twenties. The name captured a certain excitement of the times. Today, however, historians tend to avoid that nickname because it gives the false impression that all Americans were prosperous and free-wheeling. In fact, many Americans suffered deeply in the postwar period.

American farmers had experienced good times during World War I. Demand for their products was high, and competition from European farmers was low. After the war, however, demand slowed. European farmers returned to their fields. A glut of farm products hit the market. As a result, U.S. farm prices plunged, and American farmers entered a decade of extreme hardship. Farm failures increased. The income of farmers and even the value of farmland declined.

The federal government tried to help. A 1921 tariff made foreign farm products more expensive, which helped raise prices for U.S. products. Yet these measures failed to fully relieve the problems.

In some places, nature added to farmers' woes. An infestation of an insect called the boll weevil destroyed cotton crops throughout the South. As a popular song of the era observed, this plague hit struggling sharecroppers especially hard.

HISTORY'S VOICES

❝Well, the merchant got half the cotton.
The boll weevils got the rest.
Didn't leave the poor farmer's wife
but one old cotton dress.
And it's full of holes, all full of holes.❞

—Carl Sandburg, *the Boll Weevil Song*

Disaster also struck the South in 1927, when the great Mississippi River flooded. Up to a thousand people died, and countless more were left homeless.

In Florida the wild land boom came to a sudden and disastrous end. Demand for land peaked, then collapsed. Then came "The Big Blow"—the strongest hurricane recorded up to that time. The hurricane had winds of 150 miles per hour, and it killed 243 people. Few people heard the warning on South Florida's only radio station. The hurricane was one of the most destructive ever. As a result, Florida sunk into an economic depression even as other parts of the nation enjoyed prosperity.

READING CHECK **Making Generalizations** What was one group that missed out on the booming economy of the 1920s?

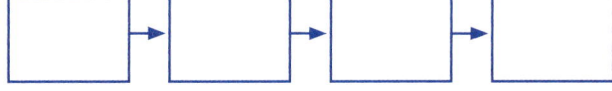

SECTION 2 ASSESSMENT

Reviewing Ideas, Terms, and People

1. **a. Define** What was the **assembly line**?
   b. Explain How did the assembly line affect Ford's ability to make automobiles?
   c. Predict What potential problems might result from industry's rapid increase in **productivity**?

2. **a. Describe** What was the effect of the boom in the auto industry on other industries?
   b. Interpret Why could industrial changes be said to change the map of the United States?
   c. Predict How do you think the rise of the automobile will affect rural areas?

3. **a. Define** Write a brief definition for each of the following terms: **installment buying, credit**
   b. Contrast What change occurred in consumer attitudes in the 1920s compared to earlier times?
   c. Elaborate How did the changes in consumer behavior make possible the growth of the American economy in the 1920s?

4. **a. Identify** What part of the American economy did not enjoy prosperity in the 1920s?
   b. Summarize What factors explain the economic plight of farmers?

Critical Thinking

5. **Sequencing** Copy the chart below and then place events in the chapter in the diagram in the order in which they occurred.

FOCUS ON WRITING

6. **Persuasive** Write a letter to the editor of your local newspaper arguing for or against the use of credit for the purchase of desired goods, such as cars and appliances.

The Harding and Coolidge Presidencies

BEFORE YOU READ

MAIN IDEA

The nation's desire for normalcy and its support for American business was reflected in two successive presidents it chose—Warren G. Harding and Calvin Coolidge.

READING FOCUS

1. What political events and ideas marked the Warren G. Harding presidency?

2. What political events and ideas marked the Calvin Coolidge presidency?

3. What were the lingering effects of World War I on politics in the 1920s?

KEY TERMS AND PEOPLE

Warren G. Harding
Teapot Dome
Calvin Coolidge
reparation
arms race
Charles Evans Hughes
Billy Mitchell
Kellogg-Briand Pact

PI 1.1 Analyze the development of American culture, explaining how ideas, values, beliefs, and traditions have changed over time and how they united all Americans.

A New Time and a New PRESIDENT

THE INSIDE STORY

How did one word help Warren G. Harding become president? The Ohio senator was not known for being an intellectual giant. But behind his appearance of lazy good humor, Warren G. Harding had political smarts. In 1920 he sensed something about the country. He sensed the longing that people have, in times of fear and chaos, for the things that seem familiar and safe. With typical Harding flair, he used a word coined shortly before the Civil War, *normalcy,* rather than the more accepted word *normality.*

Harding was running in the 1920 presidential race when he made a speech in May, in Boston. To recover from World War I, he said, the nation needed healing, restoration, and . . . "normalcy." What did he mean by normalcy? What did it mean to Americans?

People were weary of the great sacrifices they had made during World War I. Soldiers had witnessed unspeakable horrors in the trenches and on the battlefields, and many citizens wondered what the country had gained from

▲ **In a 1920 speech, Harding spoke about America's need for "normalcy."**

it all. After a year of violent labor conflicts and fears of Communist revolution, with factories and family farms in trouble, normalcy—whatever it meant—sounded good to many Americans.

Democrats made fun of what they called Harding's "pompous phrases." But voters wanted a "return to normalcy" nonetheless. They swept Harding into office and inaugurated a decade of Republican rule. ◾

The Harding Presidency

In Marion, Ohio, where newspaper publisher **Warren G. Harding** grew up, people were proud of their small-town values. They did not expect or want the government to solve their problems. They believed in taking care of one another and working hard.

In his political career, however, Harding is not remembered for his work ethic. In fact, his notorious love of leisure produced quite a casual approach to governing. Elected as the U.S. senator from Ohio in 1914, Harding actually skipped more sessions than he attended. He missed historic Senate debates on Prohibition and on women's suffrage. As president, he regarded the job as largely ceremonial and told friends that the job was beyond his skills. On the other hand, his friendly, backslapping manner—and his tendency to avoid taking positions on issues—made him quite popular.

The election of 1920 As Woodrow Wilson's term came to a chaotic end, Republicans knew they had an opportunity to win the White House. At first, Harding was not a leading candidate for his party's nomination. However, he offered a <u>coherent</u> message, one highly appealing to the public. A high point for Harding was inventing the normalcy slogan in his campaign speech in Boston. Harding's candidacy also was aided by the lack of a dominant leader among the Republicans. Theodore Roosevelt, the heart and soul of the party in the early 1900s, had died the year before. Teddy Roosevelt had no clear successor.

Out of this uncertainty, the Republicans named Harding as their candidate. Democrats nominated James Cox, also of Ohio. In the campaign, voters overwhelmingly preferred Harding's vision of normalcy. Harding also helped himself by skillfully avoiding taking a firm stand for or against the League of Nations. The result was a landslide. Harding won more than 60 percent of the vote.

Harding's policies President Harding's answer to the nation's postwar economic troubles was his campaign slogan, "Less government in business and more business in government." To help achieve his pro-business goal, Harding sought to cut the federal budget and to reduce taxes on the wealthiest Americans. Harding and his advisers believed that

ACADEMIC VOCABULARY
coherent clear and logical

PRIMARY SOURCES

Political Cartoon

As the Teapot Dome scandal unfolded, many people began to take a closer look at the illegal activities of the Harding cabinet. This cartoon, titled "Juggernaut," was published in 1924 during the height of the scandal. A "juggernaut" is an indestructible force that crushes everything in its path.

The oil scandal at the heart of Teapot Dome is portrayed as a steamroller.

Skills FOCUS READING LIKE A HISTORIAN

1. **Identifying Points of View** What does the artist's choice of title and imagery say about the power of the scandal?

2. **Making Inferences** What effect does the artist think the scandal might have on the Republican administration?

See **Skills Handbook**, p. H7, H28-H29

The steamroller is headed towards the White House.

THE GRANGER COLLECTION, NEW YORK

it was the wealthy who started and expanded businesses. By taxing them less, the thinking went, business would grow and pull the nation out of the hard times.

To farmers, Harding offered little. He did sign the high Fordney-McCumber Tariff soon after taking office. His <u>motive</u> was to help American farmers by raising the cost of foreign-grown farm products. As the costs for foreign products rose, so did the prices for American products. This helped U.S. farmers in the short term. Yet it also hurt Europeans by making it harder for them to pay back war debts.

The tariff was the only measure Harding would take to help American agriculture. "The farmer," he said, "requires no special favors at the hands of government."

Scandal and sudden death Whatever he lacked in governing skills, Harding attempted to compensate for by appointing highly skilled people to his cabinet. One of his most gifted and respected advisers was Treasury Secretary Andrew Mellon, a multimillionaire business person and philanthropist. Mellon proceeded to reform the nation's tax system during more than a decade in the office. Harding's cabinet included two other highly respected men: Secretary of State Charles Evans Hughes and Commerce Secretary Herbert Hoover.

ACADEMIC VOCABULARY

motive reason to take action

Unfortunately, not all of Harding's choices were so wise. He named a number of old friends from Ohio to lower-level government posts, Some members of this so-called Ohio Gang were later convicted of taking bribes.

The worst Harding-era scandal involved Secretary of the Interior Albert Fall. Fall accepted bribes in return for allowing oil companies to drill federal oil reserves on a piece of federal land known as **Teapot Dome** in Wyoming. Fall was eventually convicted and sent to jail.

Harding was never found to be personally connected to Teapot Dome or the Ohio Gang incidents, and he did not live to see their effects. Distressed by the rumors of scandals, Harding and his wife took a trip to Alaska.

While giving a speech in Seattle at the end of his trip, Harding collapsed. His doctor first diagnosed indigestion. The *New York Times* reassured readers "Harding . . . Rallies From a Slight Indigestion." He had, however, suffered a heart attack. Harding himself expressed concern. "I am worn out," he told his sister at the Palace Hotel in San Francisco, "can't stand the heavy responsibilities and physical work too." In bed that evening, he shuddered and died.

At the time of his death, Harding's popularity was high. Over time, however, the corruption of his administration and Harding's own failings soured his reputation.

READING CHECK **Drawing Conclusions**
What was Harding's goal with regard to business when he became president?

The Coolidge Presidency

"I was awakened by my father coming up the stairs calling my name. I noticed his voice trembled," **Calvin Coolidge** later recalled. To the vice president and the whole country, the news of Harding's death was a shock.

Coolidge received the message after he had gone to bed on the evening of August 2. He walked across town to the nearest telephone to call Secretary of State Charles Evans Hughes, who urged Coolidge to take the oath of office. In the early hours of the morning, by the light of an oil lamp, John Coolidge, a notary public, administered the oath of office to his son, John Calvin Coolidge—now the thirtieth president of the United States.

FACES OF HISTORY

Calvin & Grace COOLIDGE
1872–1933 and 1879–1957

When Calvin Coolidge was only 12 years old, his mother died. Coolidge had to take over many duties on the family farm while going to school. He had another setback when he failed a college entrance exam. He studied hard and finally passed. Coolidge's determination helped him rise in politics from city council member in Northampton, Massachusetts, to president of the United States.

Grace Coolidge's warm, outgoing personality greatly benefited her husband's political career. As first lady, Grace had a striking memory for names and faces. She enjoyed entertaining artists, actors, and writers at the White House. Grace's colorful personality was a welcome contrast to Calvin's quiet demeanor.

Summarize What challenges did Calvin Coolidge overcome?

Native Americans and Citizenship

President Coolidge (left) poses with members of the Blackfoot nation.

Citizenship and voting rights have expanded throughout U.S. history. By 1869 nearly everyone born in the United States, except Native Americans, was a citizen.

The 1887 Dawes Act granted citizenship to some Native Americans, and the Indian Naturalization Act, passed in 1890, allowed Indians to apply for citizenship. In 1901 Congress granted citizenship to Native Americans living on reservations in Oklahoma.

At this time, possibly one-third of Native Americans were not U.S. citizens. In spite of this, thousands of Indians served in the U.S. military during World War I or supported the war effort at home. Still it was not until 1924 when President Coolidge signed the Indian Citizenship Act, that all Indians born in the United States were granted citizenship.

Sequencing What steps did Congress take toward granting citizenship to all Native Americans?

Coolidge's background The Coolidges' rural Vermont home was modest. Calvin Coolige's father ran a store and was active in the local Republican Party. These two interests, business and politics, would stick with Calvin Coolidge throughout his life.

After graduating from college in Amherst, Massachusetts, Coolidge took up law and politics, working his way up the ranks of the Republican Party. Elected governor of Massachusetts in 1918, he achieved national fame for his role in the Boston police strike, as you read in Section 1. The event ignited Coolidge's national career, earning him the vice presidential slot on the 1920 Republican ticket with Harding.

Coolidge in office Coolidge's reputation for honesty helped him deal with the erupting Harding administration scandals. He quickly got rid of officials suspected of corruption. His success overcoming the scandals was proven when he easily defeated Democrat John W. Davis in the 1924 election.

Coolidge's presidency was characterized by his unshakable faith in the power of business and industry. "Those who build a factory build a temple of worship," he said. "Those who work in the factory, worship there."

Business, he believed, would provide the energy and resources to fuel America's growth. Business would promote the arts and sciences. It would fund charities to help society.

The president's faith in the positive power of business was matched by his strong belief that the role of government should be strictly limited. Government, he thought, did not produce things of value and only took away resources that could be used to build businesses. Coolidge believed in lowering taxes and reducing the federal budget. In fact, there were no major budget increases between 1923 and 1929.

One observer noted Coolidge's "active inactivity." Indeed, the president proposed few laws or policies. Among his chief initiatives were efforts to stop congressional plans to help farmers. He also vetoed a bill to provide a bonus to World War I veterans. The costs, he felt, were too great. Coolidge also worked to weaken regulations on industry.

Coolidge the man Serious and straightforward, Coolidge was known as "Silent Cal." He hated small talk, although he did enjoy playing practical jokes on White House staff. His style—and the fairly good times of his era—made him popular at the time.

In his quiet, no-nonsense fashion, Coolidge stunned the nation as the presidential election of 1928 approached. While on vacation he declared, "I do not choose to run for President in 1928."

READING CHECK **Comparing** How did Coolidge's basic beliefs compare to Harding's?

The Past is Behind Us
The Future is Ahead
Let us all strive to
make the future
better and brighter
than the past ever was.

U.S. DEPARTMENT OF LABOR
W.B. WILSON.
Secretary of Labor

This 1918 poster expressed the hope of many Americans that postwar life would soon return to normal.

IMMEDIATE EFFECTS

- Nation desires "normalcy."
- Farmers struggle to recover from postwar slump.
- European countries unable to pay war debts.
- Desire to avoid future wars remains strong.

LONG TERM EFFECTS

- Harding and then Coolidge—who each harken back to an earlier, simpler time—are elected.
- Harding and Congress pass the Fordney-McCumber Tariff. European countries unable to pay war debts.
- United States becomes banker to the nations of Europe.
- United States sponsors Washington Naval Conference and signs the Kellogg-Briand Pact.

The Lingering Effects of World War I

The fighting on the battlefields of World War I ended in 1918, yet the war's effects on national and international politics endured throughout a whole generation and several presidencies. The fight over Wilson's peace plans and the League of Nations consumed the final years of Wilson's presidency. Other questions about the peace played a major role in 1920s politics.

The question of war debt During World War I, the warring nations of Europe had borrowed more than $10 billion from the United States. Americans expected that, when the fighting stopped, the Europeans would repay the money. For the war-torn nations of Europe, this proved very difficult.

The high Fordney-McCumber Tariff made the task that much harder. Europeans had trouble selling their goods in the United States and so could not earn the dollars they needed to pay off their debts. Instead, countries turned to Germany and demanded that it pay extremely high **reparations**, or payments designed to make up for the damage of the war.

Germany was unable to pay what the Allies demanded. This, in turn, left the Allies unable to pay off their war debts. To solve this problem, the United States began to lend money to Germany. In this way, the United States assumed the role of banker to Europe. The loans continued throughout the 1920s, until the German reparations were sharply reduced.

The Washington Naval Conference

Peacetime brought considerable public pressure to reduce the size of U.S. armed forces to save money and reduce the threat of war. On the other hand, people feared that the naval powers of the world, especially Great Britain and Japan, were on the verge of a naval arms race. In an **arms race**, competing nations build more and more weapons in an effort to avoid one nation gaining a clear advantage.

Hoping to head off an arms race, the U.S. government organized the Washington Naval Conference in 1921. The major naval powers of the world were invited. At the conference, the parties agreed to cut back sharply on the size of their navies. Countries actually scrapped existing ships and some that were under construction. The conference also led to agreement on several issues that threatened world peace. These included plans to avoid competition among the world's military powers for the control of China.

Many Americans considered the conference a great success. Secretary of State **Charles Evans Hughes** reported, "We are taking perhaps the greatest forward step in history to establish the reign of peace." As you will read, however, it would not be long before world tensions were rising and nations were again building ships of war.

Billy Mitchell argues for air power

While the United States was scuttling some of its fleet, Brigadier General **Billy Mitchell** was arguing that the United States should invest more in building up its air power. Mitchell had commanded the U.S. air combat operations in World War I. He was a firm believer in the military potential of aircraft.

To demonstrate his point, Mitchell conducted tests in which he used planes to sink two battleships. This, Mitchell thought, proved the superiority of air power over naval power. Other military officials were not convinced. Mitchell's confrontational style hurt him. He was eventually punished for accusing them of "almost treasonable administration of the national defense." He left the military and continued to promote air power until his death in the 1930s.

The Kellogg-Briand Pact

Though the United States had refused to join the League of Nations, a strong interest remained in preventing another catastrophic war. So, when the French proposed a treaty with the United States that would outlaw war between two nations, the United States responded with a bigger idea. Secretary of State Frank Kellogg proposed an agreement that would involve many countries.

The **Kellogg-Briand Pact** was the result. It stated the following:

HISTORY'S VOICES

❝The High Contracting Parties solemnly declare in the names of their respective peoples that they condemn recourse to war for the solution of international controversies, and renounce it, as an instrument of national policy in their relations with one another.❞

—Kellogg-Briand Pact, Article I, 1928

In a world where war had raged across continents throughout human history—a world that had viewed war as a necessity, even a game—the pact represented a high ideal. More than 60 nations signed on. Yet the pact had no system for enforcement. The only thing holding nations to their promise was their word. As you will read, that would not be enough.

READING CHECK **Summarizing** How did America demonstrate its wish to disarm in the 1920s?

THE IMPACT TODAY

Science and Technology

Today the U.S. Air Force is central to the nation's military capability and security. Air power has been a decisive factor in military conflicts such as Afghanistan and Iraq.

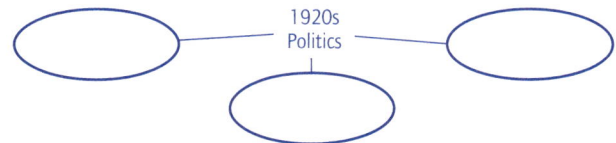

SECTION 3 ASSESSMENT

go.hrw.com
Online Quiz
Keyword: SD7 HP19

Reviewing Ideas, Terms, and People

1. a. Identify What was Teapot Dome?
   b. Analyze What do you think Harding meant when he said that the United States needed "normalcy"?
   c. Evaluate Why do you think so many voters were drawn to Harding's message of normalcy and a return to values of the past?

2. a. Recall Why is Calvin Coolidge known as "Silent Cal"?
   b. Compare How did Coolidge's policies compare to those of Harding?
   c. Rank Who do you think would have had a more positive impression of Coolidge: a farmer or a business owner? Explain.

3. a. Define Write a brief definition for the following term: reparation
   b. Make Inferences Why do you think Billy Mitchell was unable to get a strong commitment to air power in the 1920s?

c. Evaluate Why do you think the United States signed the Kellogg-Briand Pact but did not join the League of Nations?

Critical Thinking

4. Sequencing Copy the chart below, using information from the chapter to complete the diagram.

1920s Politics

FOCUS ON WRITING

5. Persuasive Write a memo to the president in which you argue for or against the agreements made in the Washington Naval Conference.

Tactics of the Red Scare

Historical Context The documents below provide several different perspectives on the U.S. government's actions during the Red Scare.

Task Examine the documents and answer the questions that follow. Then, you will be asked to write an essay about the government's tactics during the Red Scare, using facts from the documents and from the chapter to support the position you take in your thesis statement.

ST 3.2 Draw upon literary selections, historical documents, and accounts to analyze the roles played by different individuals and groups during the major eras in New York State and United States history.

ST 4.1 Analyze important debates in American history, focusing on the opposing positions and the historical evidence used to support these positions.

DOCUMENT 1

Attorney General A. Mitchell Palmer led the government's attack on suspected radicals. He was one of several public officials who had been targeted by bombs suspected of being sent by violent radicals. Among his more controversial policies was the jailing or deportation of people for speech or writings that might lend support for radical actions. In the following magazine article, he explained why people should be arrested for speech, not just actions, against the government.

Like a prairie-fire, the blaze of revolution was sweeping over every American institution of law and order a year ago. It was eating its way into the homes of the American workman, its sharp tongues or revolutionary heat were licking the altars of the churches, leaping into the belfry of the school bell, crawling into the sacred corners of American homes . . . burning up the foundations of society. . . .

Upon these two basic certainties, first that the "Reds" were criminal aliens, and secondly that the American Government must prevent crime, it was decided that there could be no nice distinctions between the theoretical ideals of the radicals and their actual violations of our national laws. . . . Any theory which excuses crime is not wanted in America.

DOCUMENT 2

Not all government officials supported the tactics used to crackdown on suspected Communists. Georgia Senator Thomas W. Hardwick had also been a target of radical bombings. He, his wife, and a maid had all been injured when a mailed bomb exploded in his home. Although Hardwick supported tightening some immigration laws to keep suspected radicals out of the country, he spoke out against Red Scare laws aimed mainly at weakening the power of labor unions, especially the Industrial Workers of the World (IWW). Laws against radical speech were often used against union members who criticized anything about the capitalist system.

I understand that the real, in fact practically the only, object of this [legislation] is to get some men called I.W.W.'s who are operating in a few of the Northwestern states, and you Senators from those states have been exceedingly solicitous [concerned] to have legislation of this kind enacted . . . I dislike to be confronted by a situation in which in the name of patriotism we are asked to justify the fundamental rights and liberties of 100,000,000 American people in order to meet a situation in a few Northwestern states."

This political cartoon refers to the deportation of alien radicals that occurred in December 1919. The ship, the USS *Buford,* pictured in the cartoon, was nicknamed the "Soviet Ark." The bear in the lower left hand corner was a feature that the artist Clifford K. Berryman used in all his cartoons.

A. Mitchell Palmer and J. Edgar Hoover spent four months rounding up alleged alien radicals and others for deportation. In the end, fewer than 300 of the thousands detained were deported. Because they were not citizens, aliens could be deported without a trial or indictment. Most, but not all, of those deported were members of the Union of Russia Workers and supported the Bolshevik revolution in Russia. Emma Goldman, a well known radical and publisher of *Mother Earth* magazine, was among those deported.

1. **a. Describe** Refer to Document 1. To what does Palmer compare the spread of revolution in the United States?
   b. Analyze What is his main justification for the jailing of people for speech?

2. **a. Identify** Refer to Document 2. What region of the country does Hardwick argue will be affected the most from Red Scare laws targeted at labor?
   b. Analyze Why does Hardwick oppose such laws?

3. **a. Identify** Refer to Document 3. How does the cartoonist depict the people on the boat?

   b. Interpret What is the message the cartoonist is trying to send?

4. **Document-Based Essay Question** Consider the question below and form a thesis statement. Using examples from Documents 1, 2, and 3, create an outline and write a short essay supporting your position.
   Were the Red Scare policies of the U.S. government appropriate responses to fears of a Bolshevik revolution?

   See **Skills Handbook**, p. H28–H29, H31

Chapter Review

Visual Summary: From War to Peace

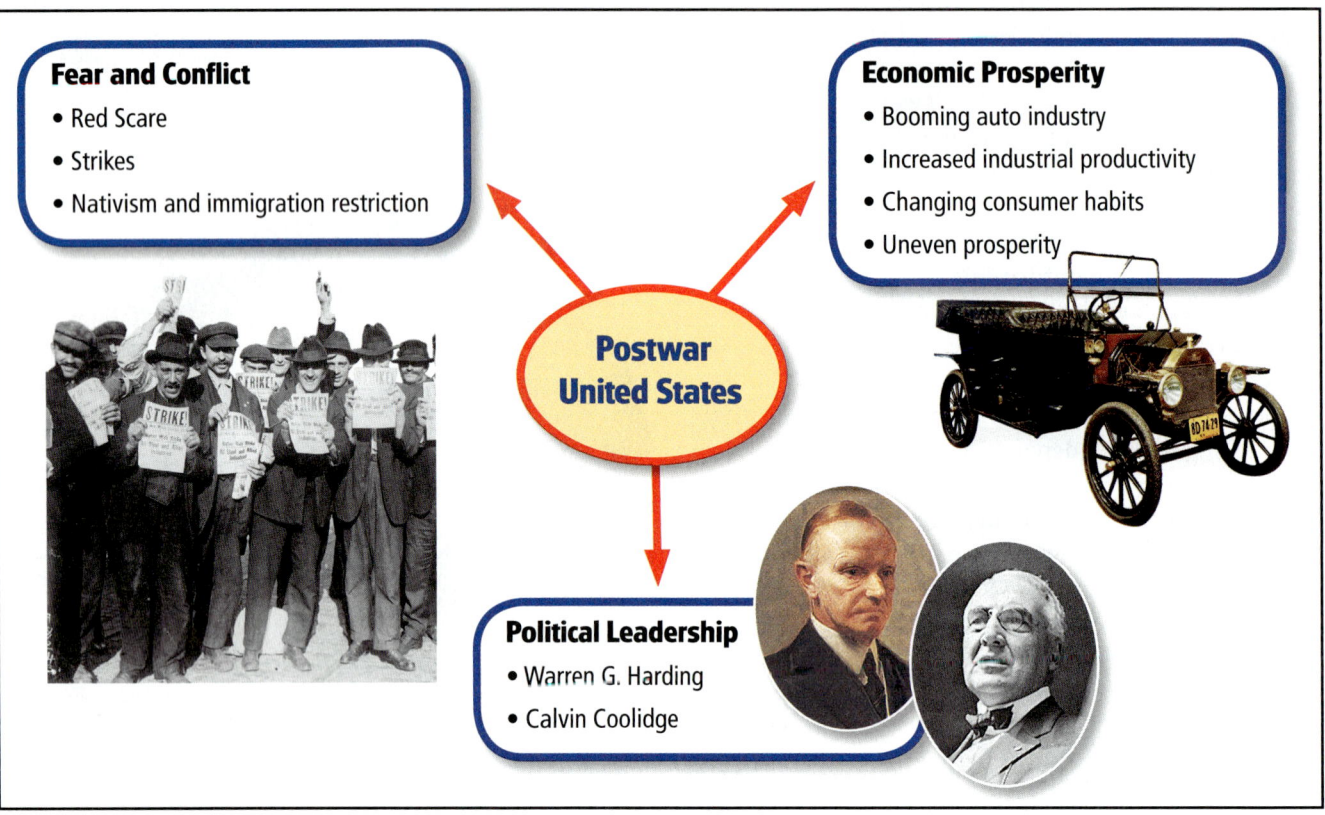

Fear and Conflict
- Red Scare
- Strikes
- Nativism and immigration restriction

Economic Prosperity
- Booming auto industry
- Increased industrial productivity
- Changing consumer habits
- Uneven prosperity

Postwar United States

Political Leadership
- Warren G. Harding
- Calvin Coolidge

Reviewing Key Terms and People

Complete each sentence by filling the blank with the correct term or person.

1. Following World War I, a heightened fear of radicals, or a _____ , gripped the nation.

2. Increasingly, consumers in the 1920s paid for purchases with _____ rather than with cash.

3. _____ became president in 1920 by promising a return to normalcy.

4. The United States government helped Germany pay its high _____ .

5. Vice President _____ skillfully avoided being tainted by the scandals of the Harding administration.

6. The _____ allowed cars to be made in large numbers and at a relatively low cost.

7. The _____ wanted to establish a new social system in their country and in the world.

8. A. Mitchell Palmer's raids led to the _____ of many aliens.

9. _____'s dream was to build a car that the average American could afford.

10. Harding's secretary of the interior was involved in a scandal over a place called _____ .

Calvin Coolidge

Bolsheviks

deportation

Teapot Dome

Henry Ford

credit

Warren G. Harding

reparations

assembly line

Red Scare

History's Impact video program
Review the video to answer the closing question:
How did American women win the right to vote?

Comprehension and Critical Thinking

SECTION 1 *(pp. 622–627)*

11. a. Describe What are some examples of postwar havoc in the United States?

b. Summarize What factors contributed to the postwar havoc?

c. Evaluate Why do you think many Americans reacted to the difficulties of the postwar years by targeting immigrants?

SECTION 2 *(pp. 628–633)*

12. a Describe Describe the significance of the following terms in the 1920s economy: assembly line, welfare capitalism, installment buying.

b. Compare How did the economic performance of agriculture compare to that of industry in the 1920s?

c. Evaluate What was the role of consumer credit in the expansion of the 1920s economy, and why might this pose a problem in the future?

SECTION 3 *(pp. 634–639)*

13. a. Recall Who were the two U.S. presidents who served between 1920 and 1928?

b. Make Generalizations What kind of relationship did the American political leaders of the 1920s promote between business and government?

c. Evaluate Why do you think many people in the United States were so willing to support the pro-business policies of the federal government in the 1920s?

Using the Internet

go.hrw.com
Practice Online
Keyword: SD7 CH19

14. The decade after World War I was a turbulent one. Americans feared the spread of communism. They also were experiencing many political, social, and economic changes at home. Using the keyword above, do research to learn about the changes that were occuring in the United States during the years 1919–1928. Then create a report that describes how political, social, and economic forces combined to create such a sense of uneasiness in the decade after World War I.

Analyzing Primary Sources

Reading Like a Historian

The vacuum cleaner was one of the many new products sold to consumers, often on installment plans, in the 1920s.

15. Identify Who was the primary audience for this advertisement?

16. Analyze Based on the woman's facial expression in the ad, what do you think the ad is claiming the vacuum cleaner will do?

Critical Reading

Read the passage in Section 1 that begins with the heading "American Reaction." Then answer the questions that follow.

17. According to the passage, the fear of Reds in the United States was a continuation of

A wartime prosperity.

B the fight over the League of Nations.

C hatred of "the Hun."

D the rise of labor.

18. In the fourth paragraph of the passage, the text reads, "Some of their members promoted the violent overthrow of the government." In this sentence, the word *promoted* means

A opposed.   **C** achieved.

B stopped.   **D** advocated.

FOCUS ON WRITING

Expository Writing *Expository writing gives information, explains why or how, or defines a process. To practice expository writing, follow the directions below.*

Writing Topic **The impact of the assembly line**

19. Assignment Based on what you have read in this chapter, write a paragraph that explains how Ford's assembly line revolutionized the automobile industry and other industries.

THE ROARING Twenties

THE BIG PICTURE American culture underwent rapid and radical change in the 1920s. Signs of this change were everywhere—in the music and fashions of the day, in the habits and pastimes of Americans, in the art and literature of the country's most creative minds. Large population shifts and new technologies transformed the nation from rural to urban and from traditional to modern.

New York Standards

Key Idea 1 The study of New York State and United States history requires an analysis of the development of American culture, its diversity and multicultural context, and the ways people are unified by many values, practices, and traditions.

Key Idea 2 Important ideas, social and cultural values, beliefs, and traditions from New York State and United States history illustrate the connections and interactions of people and events across time and from a variety of perspectives.

Skills FOCUS READING LIKE A HISTORIAN

This jazz band is supplying not only music but also some food and drink to competitors in a Charleston endurance contest. The Charleston was a new dance that was all the rage in the 1920s. **Interpreting Visuals** What words would you use to describe the mood of the scene captured in this photograph?

See **Skills Handbook**, p. H30

U.S.

1920
First corporate radio station offers music and news.

1920

World

1920
League of Nations holds first meeting in Paris, France.

History's Impact video program

Watch the video to understand the impact of the 1929 stock market crash.

October 29, 1929
Stock market crashes on "Black Tuesday."

1931
Drought that helps produce the Dust Bowl begins on the Great Plains.

June 1932
World War I veterans' "Bonus Army" sets up camp in Washington, D.C.

1930   1931   1932   1933

1931 Japanese army invades Manchuria.

1932
Ibn Saud proclaims himself king of newly created Saudi Arabia.

January 1933
Adolf Hitler becomes chancellor of Germany.

671

The Great Crash

BEFORE YOU READ

MAIN IDEA

The stock market crash of 1929 revealed weaknesses in the American economy and helped trigger a spreading economic crisis.

READING FOCUS

1. What economic factors and conditions made the American economy appear prosperous in the 1920s?
2. What were the basic economic weaknesses in the American economy in the late 1920s?
3. What events led to the stock market crash of October 1929?
4. What were the effects of the crash on the economy of the United States and the world?

KEY TERMS AND PEOPLE

gross national product
Herbert Hoover
buying on margin
Federal Reserve System
Black Tuesday

PI 3.2 Research and analyze the major themes and developments in New York State and United States history (e.g., colonization and settlement; Revolution and New National Period; immigration; expansion and reform era; Civil War and Reconstruction; the American labor movement; Great Depression; World Wars; contemporary United States).

Calm Before the Storm

THE INSIDE STORY

How did Americans behave on the eve of disaster? For many people in the 1920s, investing in the stock market was one big joyride. Week after week, month after month, stock prices steadily rose. After a while, it seemed like making money on Wall Street was a sure thing.

With so many fortunes being made, it was easy to ignore the warning signs that began to appear in the fall of 1929. The economy had began to slump. Consumers weren't buying as much. Products were piling up on factory floors. A handful of experts whispered that trouble lay in store for the stock market.

On Thursday, October 24, 1929, those whispers became reality. By the end of the day, the value of the stocks traded on the New York Stock Exchange had plunged by 9 percent. Years of investment gains—billions of dollars—were wiped out in a few hours.

Major banks and stockbrokers tried to rally the market on Friday. They bought large numbers of stocks, hoping to keep prices from dropping still more. Over the anxious weekend of October 26 and 27, stockbrokers worked quietly to reassure investors. They made phone calls and wrote letters to major investors urging them to buy stocks when the markets reopened on Monday. But nothing could answer the questions on everyone's minds. On Monday morning, which way would prices go—up or down? Were the good times about to come to an end?

▲ Stockholders anxiously gather outside the New York Stock Exchange after news of the crash on October 29, 1929.

An Appearance of Prosperity

The 1920s may not have been good times for everyone. Most farmers, for instance, saw their incomes drop. But for the economy as a whole, the "Roaring Twenties" were a period of impressive and sustained growth. Between 1922 and 1928, the **gross national product** (GNP)—the total value of goods and services produced in a nation during a specific period—rose by 30 percent. At a time when most people's understanding of the economic matters was relatively limited, such rapid growth triggered a feeling of optimism that proved contagious. That optimism, however, led to reckless activities.

The explosive growth of American manufacturing, particularly the new automobile industry, helped drive the expansion of the American economy. By 1929 one in five Americans owned a car. Industries that made products related to automobile production—including steel, oil, and rubber—enjoyed unprecedented business opportunities. Overall, the automobile industry and related industries employed nearly 4 million workers.

As corporate profits swelled, companies hired additional factory workers to keep up with production needs. Unemployment between 1923 and 1929 remained very low, averaging around 3 percent. Low unemployment, in turn, slowed the growth of organized labor. Union membership dropped as employers expanded welfare capitalism programs.

As you read earlier, welfare capitalism is a term for various benefits, such as employer-paid insurance, which companies provide to employees as a way of improving worker loyalty and satisfaction. Such programs helped increase workers' sense of prosperity and well-being in the 1920s.

This feeling of prosperity encouraged many workers to purchase the new products coming off the nation's assembly lines. With their shorter work hours and bigger paychecks, Americans flocked to movie theaters, sporting events, and other leisure activities. Times, it seemed, were good.

Stock market expansion While Americans generally were feeling good about the economy in the 1920s, those who invested in the stock market were overjoyed. The stock market is a place where stocks are bought and sold. *Stock* is ownership in a company, and it is sold in *shares*. In other words, by buying shares of stock, a person is able to buy a piece of a corporation. If the corporation succeeds, its value may rise. This means that the value of its stock also rises. If the corporation does not do well, it may lose value. This would drive the value of the stock down.

ACADEMIC VOCABULARY
specific particular

FOCUS ON NEW YORK

ECONOMICS
The New York Stock Exchange had an unlikely beginning in 1792 when 24 men met under a buttonwood tree on what is now Wall Street. They signed the Buttonwood Agreement, which provided for the trading of securities. In 1817 the exchange was officially formed and became known as the New York Stock and Exchange Board. Its main rival, NASDAQ, is also headquartered in New York City.

The False Sense of Security

Positive economic trends masked the trouble that lay ahead.

- The stock market had been booming for a decade.
- Corporate profits soared.
- Unemployment was low.
- Welfare capitalism and credit increased workers' buying power.

The American stock market performed spectacularly during the 1920s. Although stocks increased at different rates, the general trend in stock prices was sharply upward. Between 1920 and 1929 the overall value of stocks traded at the nation's stock markets quadrupled.

The steep rise in stock prices changed the way many people thought about buying stocks. Since the market never seemed to go down in the 1920s, many people began to act as though it never would.

A growing number of ordinary Americans began to make stock investments. To *invest* means to put money into stocks, land, or some other location in the hope that the value of this money will grow.

The number of shares being traded in the United States rose sharply during the 1920s. The number rose from 318 million in 1920 to more than 1 billion in 1929. Many investors were encouraged by the words of men such as John Raskob, a leader of General Motors.

HISTORY'S VOICES

❝If a man saves $15 a week and invests in good common stocks . . . at the end of 20 years, he will have at least $80,000 and . . . $400 a month. He will be rich. And because income can do that, I am firm in my belief that anyone not only can be rich, but ought to be rich.❞

—John J. Raskob, "Everyone Ought to Be Rich," *Ladies' Home Journal,* August 1929

Faith in business and government For many Americans, the prosperity of the 1920s demonstrated the triumph of American business. Presidents Harding and Coolidge favored policies that gave businesses the maximum freedom to achieve and succeed. As Coolidge once famously remarked, "The chief business of the American people is business."

This approach was popular with the majority of voters. Harding had won a clear victory in the 1920 election, and Coolidge did the same in 1924. Coolidge in particular remained widely popular throughout his term in office. Public confidence in the federal government and in its pro-business policies remained very high.

The election of 1928 Coolidge decided not to run for reelection in 1928, so the Republicans chose **Herbert Hoover** as their candidate. Hoover had never held elective office, but he had an impressive record of public service. He had overseen America's food production during World War I and later directed relief efforts in Europe. He also served as the secretary of commerce under Harding and Coolidge.

By 1928 Hoover had built an outstanding reputation as a businesslike administrator—just the sort of leader who could guide the prosperous nation. Indeed, people thought so highly of Hoover that it troubled him. "They have a conviction that I am sort of superman, that no problem is beyond my capacity," he once said. "If some unprecedented calamity should come upon the nation . . . I would be sacrificed to the unreasoning disappointment of a people who expected too much."

Hoover and the Democratic candidate, Al Smith, presented the nation with a stark contrast. Smith was an outgoing and natural politician. Hoover was quiet and shy by comparison. Smith was a Catholic—the first ever to run for president—and drew much of his support from Catholic urban immigrant

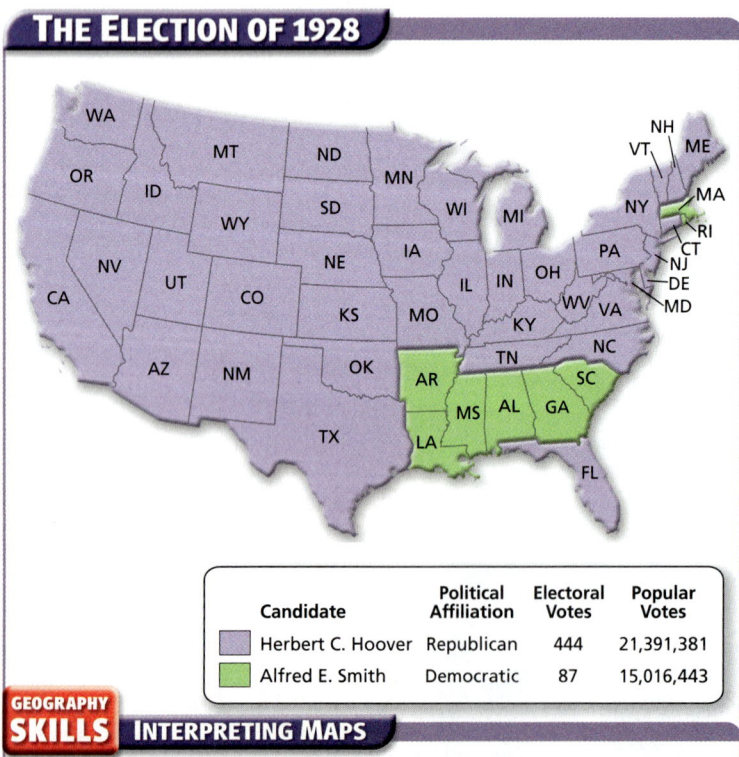

THE ELECTION OF 1928

Candidate	Political Affiliation	Electoral Votes	Popular Votes
Herbert C. Hoover	Republican	444	21,391,381
Alfred E. Smith	Democratic	87	15,016,443

GEOGRAPHY SKILLS INTERPRETING MAPS

The nation was experiencing an era of prosperity under a Republican administration during the 1928 presidential election.

Region Most of the nation voted for the candidate of what party affiliation? In what region was Smith's support concentrated?

See **Skills Handbook**, p. H20

populations. Hoover was a Quaker, and many of his supporters did not trust Catholics. His support was strongest in small towns.

The two men also differed on Prohibition. Smith supported alcohol sales, while Hoover supported Prohibition. In short, the contest represented many of the cultural conflicts that had divided the nation in the 1920s. Hoover won an easy victory.

READING CHECK **Identifying Cause and Effect** How did the rise of the stock market affect American investors?

Economic Weaknesses

The economic prosperity of the 1920s helped define the decade. Yet while many Americans celebrated their financial good fortune, a number of serious problems bubbled just beneath the surface.

Wealth distribution One troubling aspect of the American economy was the vastly uneven distribution of the new wealth that was being created. Despite the boom in business in the 1920s, a surprisingly small number of people had truly prospered. As a group, the wealthiest 1 percent of the population had seen their share of the national income grow 60 percent between 1920 and 1929. Most workers, however, experienced much smaller pay increases—about 8 percent for most job categories.

Workers in certain industries, such as farming and coal mining, were hit particularly hard. By 1929 more than 70 percent of the nation's families had an income below the level they needed for a good standard of living. The personal savings rate declined noticeably during the decade as well.

For much of the decade, the easy availability of credit had allowed many Americans to buy the automobiles, radios, vacuum cleaners, and other products rolling quickly off the nation's assembly lines. By the end of the decade, however, many consumers were reaching the limits of their credit. The pace of purchases slowed. Warehouses became filled with factory goods that no one could afford to buy.

Credit and the stock market Installment credit was not just a tool for buying consumer products. Investors also used credit to purchase

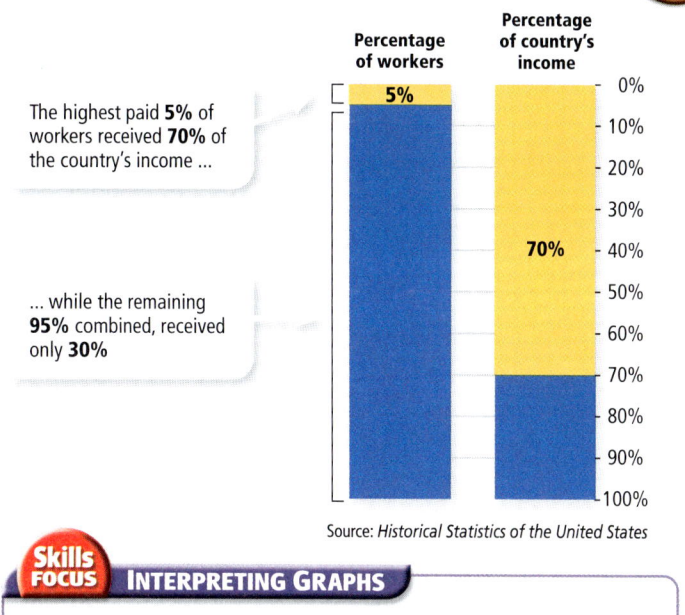

DISTRIBUTION OF WEALTH, 1929

Percentage of workers

Percentage of country's income

The highest paid **5%** of workers received **70%** of the country's income ...

5%

70%

... while the remaining **95%** combined, received only **30%**

0%
10%
20%
30%
40%
50%
60%
70%
80%
90%
100%

Source: *Historical Statistics of the United States*

Skills FOCUS **INTERPRETING GRAPHS**

The 1920s prosperity was more illusion than reality. The uneven distribution of the nation's wealth is shown in this bar graph. *What share of the nation's wealth did the top 5 percent of workers own? What did the remaining 95 percent own?*

See **Skills Handbook**, p. H16

stocks. This risky practice increased during the 1920s as the stock market rose sharply.

Here is how it worked: Imagine an investor wanted to buy 100 shares of stock in Company A at $10 a share. The total purchase price would be $1,000. To make this purchase, the investor would pay just a portion of the $1,000—say, for example, $500. The investor would borrow the other $500 from a stockbroker. The understanding was that the investor would pay off the loan when he or she sold the stock. Buying stocks with loans from stockbrokers is known as **buying on margin.**

As enthusiasm for investing in the stock market grew, brokers began to require lower and lower margins for stock purchases, giving bigger and bigger loans to investors. In 1929 an investor could purchase a stock with as little as a 10 percent margin. In a time when many stocks were gaining value by the day, margin buying seemed like an easy way to make money.

Buying on margin, however, involved enormous risks. Returning to the example of Company A, say its stock price rose to $15 a share. The investor then could sell the stock for $1,500. In this case, the investor would get back the original $500 investment, be able to repay the $500 loan, and still have a $500 profit—doubling the original investment. But if the stock price dropped to $5 a share, the sale then would bring in just $500. All of this would go to pay off the loan. The investor would have no profit and be out the original $500 as well.

The terms of a margin loan made the gamble even riskier for the investor. Under these terms, brokers could force investors to repay their loans if the stock's value fell below a certain point. Such a demand was called a margin call. In theory, margin calls ensured that brokers would get their loans repaid. Margin calls also meant that investors could be in big trouble if their stocks lost value suddenly.

THE IMPACT TODAY

Economics

Today the Federal Reserve Board places strict limits on the practice of buying on margin.

The Federal Reserve The nation's fascination with stocks and with buying on margin drew the concern of the governing board of the **Federal Reserve System**, which serves as the nation's central bank. The Federal Reserve Board takes actions and sets policies to regulate the nation's money supply in order to promote healthy economic activity. In the late 1920s, the Federal Reserve Board decided to make it more difficult and more costly for brokers to offer margin loans to investors.

The Federal Reserve's move was partly successful, at least at first. Borrowing from banks by brokers began to decrease, but it was replaced by money from a new source. Large American corporations began providing brokers with the cash to make margin loans to investors. As a result, the run-up of the stock market continued despite the Federal Reserve's actions.

In September 1929, economist Roger Babson sounded a warning note. "Sooner or later," he said, "a crash is coming, and it may be terrific." The crash he was anticipating was a sudden drop in stock prices, which could devastate those who had borrowed heavily to buy stock.

Many experts, however, dismissed Babson's worries. In October, banker Charles E. Mitchell responded to the warnings of people such as Babson. Mitchell said, famously, "I see no reason for the end-of-the-year slump which some people are predicting." He could not have been more wrong.

READING CHECK **Summarizing** What were some of the weaknesses of the economy in the 1920s?

Crash! October 29, 1929

The Stock Market Crashes

While Babson and Mitchell were making their contrasting predictions about the future of the stock market, American investors looked back on several years of fantastic success. The steady growth of the early and mid-1920s had given way to truly astounding gains as the decade neared its end. One leading measure of the market's value showed a 50 percent gain in 1928 alone. During the following year, 1929, the market gained another 27 percent before reaching its high point on September 3.

Many people in the financial world, however, were beginning to recognize increasing signs of trouble in the economy. Sales of some manufactured goods were sagging badly. Rumors spread that some big investors were getting ready to take their money out of the market. Fears began to grow that current stock prices could soon collapse. The stage was set for an economic disaster.

On Thursday, October 24, 1929, some nervous investors began selling stocks. As others noticed the increased activity, they joined in the selling, afraid to be left behind. A huge sell-off had begun. With few people willing to buy the millions of stocks flooding the market,

Weaknesses in the general economy, combined with unsound financial practices, set the stage for the stock market crash. Worried investors (at left) crowded Wall Street on Black Tuesday to await news.

CAUSES OF THE 1929 STOCK MARKET CRASH

Economic Factors
- Poor distribution of wealth
- Many consumers relied on credit
- Credit dried up
- Consumer spending dropped
- Industry struggled

Financial Factors
- Stock markets rise in mid-1920s
- Speculation in stock increases
- Margin buying encouraged by Federal Reserve policies
- Stock prices rise to unrealistic levels

Stock Market Crash

stock prices plunged, triggering an even greater panic to sell. One newspaper described it as "the most terrifying stampede of selling ever experienced on the New York Stock Exchange."

HISTORY'S VOICES

"Traders on the floor of the Stock Exchange shrieked and howled their offers for desperate minutes before they found takers. Such a roar arose from the Stock Exchange floor that it could be heard for blocks up and down Broad and Wall Streets.**"**

—*Seattle Post-Intelligencer,* October 25, 1929

Toward the end of this terrible day, a number of leading bankers joined together to buy stocks and prevent a further collapse in their prices. This effort succeeded in stopping the panic—for a time. The market returned to normal trading on Friday, and some stocks actually gained value.

When traders returned to work on Monday, however, the good feelings from Friday had completely evaporated. As trading began that day, the market sank like a stone. The next day—Tuesday, October 29—was the worst of all. As panic completely overcame the markets, investors dumped more than 16 million shares of stock. While the sell-offs of earlier days had affected mainly the stocks of weaker businesses, the collapse on **Black Tuesday** affected the stock of even the most solid companies.

The damage was widespread and catastrophic. During October, the stock market dropped in value by about $16 billion. This represented nearly one-half of the market's pre-crash value.

"It was like a thunderclap," one investment banker recalled. "Everybody was stunned."

Devices called ticker-tape machines communicated a steady stream of falling stock prices. One reporter described the scene on October 29 as horrified investors watched the ticker tape.

HISTORY'S VOICES

"[T]he crowds about the ticker tapes, like friends about the bedside of a stricken friend, reflected in their faces the story the tape was telling. There were no smiles. There were no tears either. Just the camaraderie of fellow-sufferers. Everybody wanted to tell his neighbor how much he had lost. Nobody wanted to listen. It was too repetitious a tale.**"**

—*The New York Times,* October 30, 1929

READING CHECK **Sequencing** Briefly describe the events of the stock market crash from October 24 through October 29, 1929.

Banking Crisis
The stock market crash triggered a banking crisis. By 1933 more than 5,000 banks had shut their doors.

$100 WILL BUY THIS CAR MUST HAVE CASH LOST ALL ON THE STOCK MARKET

Gross National Product
In the aftermath of the crash, U.S. GNP fell by nearly one half—from $103.1 billion in 1929 to $55.6 billion in 1933.

World Economy
The effects of stock market crash rippled through the world economy. In Germany, industrial productivity plunged by more than 40 percent.

Fallen on Hard Times
A Wall Street speculator (above) tries to sell his car after losing his wealth in the stock market crash. Margin calls left many such investors desperate for cash. *What other effects did the stock market crash have on individuals?*

The Granger Collection, New York

The Effects of the Crash

In the aftermath of the crash, business and political leaders rushed to calm the panic and reassure the nation. One business executive wrote optimistically in the days following Black Tuesday, "The recent collapse of stock market prices has no significance as regards the real wealth of the American people as a whole." President Hoover also downplayed the effects of the crash. He and many others firmly believed that the economy would soon recover from the shock and return to prosperity.

The impact on individuals
No one denied, however, that the stock market collapse had ruined many individual investors. Some had lost years of gains. Huge fortunes disappeared before their eyes.

Margin buyers were particularly hard hit. When stock prices began to fall, brokers demanded that they pay back the borrowed money. To meet these margin calls, investors were forced to sell their shares for far less than they had paid for them. Some lost their entire savings trying to make up the difference. In the end, investors often owed enormous amounts of money to their brokers for stocks they had been forced to sell below cost.

Effects on banks
The stock market crash triggered a banking crisis. Frightened depositors rushed to withdraw their money, draining banks of funds. Worse, many banks had themselves invested, directly or indirectly, in the stock market. They had purchased stock in companies whose shares were now crumbling in value. In addition, banks had made loans to stockbrokers, who in turn had loaned the money to investors on margin. When individual investors failed to cover their margins, the banks absorbed losses, too.

These loan failures eventually drove many banks out of business. As you will read in the next section, the struggles of the banks would have a deep impact on the American people.

Effects on business The crash delivered a crushing blow to already struggling businesses. With money scarce, banks and investors were suddenly unwilling or unable to provide industry with the money it needed to grow and expand.

At the same time, consumers cut back their spending on everything but essential purchases. With consumers spending less, many companies began to lay off workers. Unemployed workers had even less money to make purchases, and the cycle of layoffs and reduced consumer spending accelerated quickly.

In the year that followed the great crash, Americans saw their wages drop by a total of $4 billion. Nearly 3 million people lost their jobs. Faced with an uncertain future and lower incomes, consumers, who had driven the prosperity of the 1920s, simply stopped spending.

Effects overseas The crisis that began in the United States soon rippled throughout the industrialized world. The fragile economies of Europe, still recovering from World War I, were thrown backward. American banks that had lent heavily to European businesses and governments now called in those loans.

In many cases businesses and governments alike simply did not have the money to pay back the loans. Moreover, with buying power down in the United States, foreign businesses were less able to export their products here. They responded by laying off workers. Just as in the United States, laying off workers in Europe meant that there was less money in the hands of consumers to buy products.

Governments in the United States and in countries around the world moved to protect their own industries by passing high tariffs. A high tariff would make imported goods more expensive than those made at home. Leaders in each country hoped that high tariffs would benefit their local manufacturers.

Unfortunately, the high tariff actually did more harm than good to the American and world economies. As you will read, the decline in world trade that took place in the 1930s created misery around the world. It was one of the several factors that contributed to the nation's slide into what came to be called the Great Depression.

THE IMPACT TODAY

Economics

Today an international organization called the World Trade Organization (WTO) oversees many trade agreements between nations. Its goal is to reduce trade barriers such as tariffs.

READING CHECK **Identifying Cause and Effect** How did the stock market crash affect banks?

Reviewing Ideas, Terms, and People

1. a. Define Write a brief definition for the following term: gross national product
b. Identify Cause and Effect What effect did America's mood have on individuals' financial decisions?
c. Evaluate Defend the widespread American investment in stocks in the 1920s.

2. a. Recall Name two signs of weakness in the American economy in the 1920s.
b. Analyze Why is it significant that much of the nation's wealth was owned by a small number of people?
c. Predict How might the lack of available credit hurt the nation's economy in the 1930s?

3. a. Identify What was Black Tuesday?
b. Sequence Describe how the drop in the stock market brought ruin to so many investors.
c. Elaborate Why would an investor who had not bought stocks on margin have been in a better position to survive the crash than one who had?

4. a. Describe How did the crash affect individual investors, brokers, and banks?

b. Summarize Why did the stock market crash have such a powerful impact on the overall economy?
c. Evaluate Defend Hoover's belief that the economy would soon recover.

Critical Thinking

5. Understanding Cause and Effect Copy the chart below and use information from the section to identify effects of the stock market crash on the American economy.

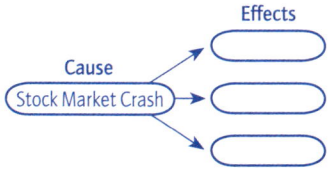

Cause
Stock Market Crash
Effects

FOCUS ON WRITING

6. Persuasive Write a letter to a friend in which you urge him or her to be careful about making stock market investments. Use information from the chapter to support your position.

Americans Face Hard Times

BEFORE YOU READ

MAIN IDEA

The Great Depression and the natural disaster known as the Dust Bowl produced economic suffering on a scale the nation had never seen before.

READING FOCUS

1. How did the Great Depression develop?
2. What was the human impact of the Great Depression?
3. Why was the Dust Bowl so devastating?

KEY TERMS AND PEOPLE

hobo
Great Depression
foreclosure
Hooverville
drought
Dust Bowl
Okie
John Steinbeck
Woody Guthrie

PI 3.2 Research and analyze the major themes and developments in New York State and United States history (e.g., colonization and settlement; Revolution and New National Period; immigration; expansion and reform era; Civil War and Reconstruction; the American labor movement; Great Depression; World Wars; contemporary United States).

Teenage HOBOES

THE INSIDE STORY

Where do you go when you have no place to go? Some of them decided on their own to leave home. Others were told to leave by their parents because there simply was no money to care for them. In either case, tens of thousands of teenagers faced a stark reality during the Great Depression. They had to find their future on the road.

At the height of the Great Depression, as many as a quarter of a million teenagers were wandering the nation, riding the railroads from town to town. With no families to support or protect them, they joined the ranks of the jobless, homeless wanderers known as **hoboes**.

For the young hoboes of the Depression—boys and girls, black and white, some less than 16 years old—the daily task was to survive. The lucky ones found or formed communities with other homeless people, who were primarily adults. The unlucky ones fell prey to abuse and violence.

Young women often disguised themselves as boys in order to reduce the dangers they faced. African Americans often had the threat of racial violence added to the hardships of the road.

Homeless teenagers riding the rails or walking the back roads became a familiar sight in the years of the Great Depression. Along with millions of others, they formed part of the human face of the economic catastrophe that followed the crash. ◼

◀ **Thousands of youths experienced the grim life of a hobo.**

The Development of the Great Depression

With the crash of the stock market, the boom times of the 1920s came to an end. The crash and its aftermath revealed serious flaws in the American economy. These flaws helped transform a stock market crisis into the **Great Depression**, the most severe economic downturn in the history of the United States.

Bank failures As you have read, the collapse of the stock market strained the financial resources of many banks. In the weeks following the crash, a number of those banks failed. For ordinary Americans, the collapse of banks was an especially unnerving new development. Most people did not have money invested in stocks, but many had entrusted their savings to banks.

Today, most Americans do not have to worry that they will lose their savings if their bank goes out of business. Insurance from the federal government protects most people's deposits in the event of bank failure. In addition, laws today require that a bank keep a greater percentage of its <u>assets</u> in cash, to be paid out to depositors on request.

In 1929 there was no such deposit insurance, and with little cash on hand, banks were vulnerable to "runs." A run occurred when nervous depositors, suspecting a bank might be in danger of failing, rushed to withdraw their savings. A run could quickly drain a bank of its cash reserves and force the bank to close.

In the months following October 1929, bank runs struck across the country. Hundreds of banks failed. In late 1930 the rate of failures turned from frightening to disastrous. In December alone almost 350 banks closed. Included was the enormous Bank of the United States, which once had boasted about 400,000 depositors. By 1933 U.S. bank failures had wiped out billions of dollars in savings, on top of losses from the stock market crash.

Farm failures The hard times farmers had faced in the 1920s only worsened with the onset of the Great Depression. Widespread joblessness and poverty reduced Americans' ability to buy food. Many people simply went hungry. With farmers producing more than they could sell, farm prices sank. By 1933 prices were down more than 50 percent from their already low 1929 levels. Lower prices meant lower income for farmers.

ACADEMIC VOCABULARY
asset financial holdings or resources

Economic Impact of the Great Depression

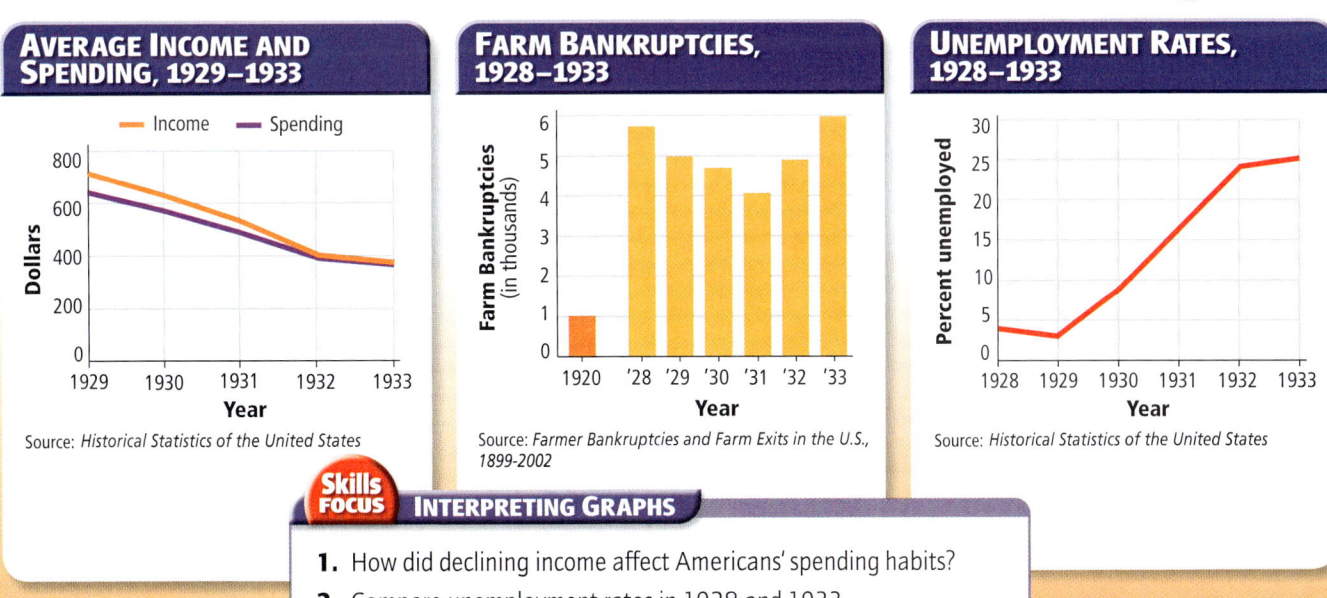

AVERAGE INCOME AND SPENDING, 1929–1933

Source: *Historical Statistics of the United States*

FARM BANKRUPTCIES, 1928–1933

Source: *Farmer Bankruptcies and Farm Exits in the U.S., 1899-2002*

UNEMPLOYMENT RATES, 1928–1933

Source: *Historical Statistics of the United States*

Skills Focus INTERPRETING GRAPHS

1. How did declining income affect Americans' spending habits?
2. Compare unemployment rates in 1928 and 1933.

See **Skills Handbook**, p. H16, H17

It was typical for farmers to borrow money from banks to pay for land and equipment. As their incomes dropped, many farmers were unable to make the payments on their loans. In 1933 alone, some 364,000 farms went bankrupt or suffered foreclosure. **Foreclosure** occurs when a bank or other lender takes over ownership of a property from an owner who has failed to make loan payments.

Unemployment The year following the crash of October 1929 saw a sharp drop in economic activity and a steep rise in unemployment. Such negative trends are not uncommon in a time of economic downturn. What made the Great Depression different was the extent and the stubborn duration of these trends.

By 1933 the gross national product had dropped more than 40 percent from its pre-crash levels. Unemployment reached a staggering 25 percent. In some places and among some groups, the number was even higher. In the African American neighborhood of Harlem in New York City, for example, unemployment reached 50 percent in 1932.

READING CHECK **Making Generalizations**
What happened to the economy in the early 1930s?

The Human Impact of the Great Depression

The Great Depression was an economic catastrophe. Yet statistics tell only part of the story. The true measure of the disaster lies in how it affected the American people.

Hoovervilles and hoboes With millions of people out of work, the competition for jobs became fierce. Thousands of workers would apply for a handful of jobs, and the winners knew they were lucky.

HISTORY'S VOICES

❝I'd get up at five in the morning and head for the waterfront. Outside the Spreckles Sugar Refinery, outside the gates, there would be a thousand men. You know dang well there's only three or four jobs. The guy would come out … 'I need two guys for the bull gang. Two guys to go into the hole.' A thousand men would fight like a pack of Alaskan dogs to get through there.❞

—Ed Paulson, quoted in Studs Terkel's *Hard Times*

For millions of Americans during the Great Depression, the loss of a job meant a quick slide into poverty. To survive, some people begged from door to door. Unable to provide food for

HISTORY CLOSE-UP

Life in a Hooverville

As desperate poverty engulfed people from coast to coast, many formed makeshift communities that they nicknamed Hoovervilles.

The lack of running water and power made tasks such as cooking and cleaning much more difficult and messy.

Most male residents of Hoovervilles had been used to a life of work. For many, idleness led to deep feelings of uselessness and despair.

themselves, some relied on soup kitchens or breadlines—or simply went without.

In the early 1930s, no federal government programs provided food or money to the poor. Local charities and some municipal and state governments provided relief, but these programs were unable to meet the need. In 1932 only 1 in 4 families needing unemployment relief received it.

With no jobs or income, many Americans lost their homes. Property owners evicted tenants who couldn't pay rent, and banks foreclosed on homeowners. In many communities, sprawling neighborhoods of shacks sprang up on the outskirts of town or in public parks to house the newly homeless. These shantytowns came to be known as **Hoovervilles**. This was a bitter reference to President Hoover, whom many people blamed for the Great Depression.

On the streets of America's great cities, some unemployed workers took to selling apples. Charging a nickel an apple, a seller might earn $1.15 on a good day. In the fall of 1930 more than 6,000 unemployed workers sold apples on the streets of New York City alone.

Other Americans took to the road in search of work. Hoboes hopped trains to travel from town to town, often taking their lives in their hands. Not only was boarding a moving train very dangerous, it was also illegal. Many railroads hired "bulls," or guards, to chase hoboes off the trains.

Wherever hoboes went, finding food was a constant challenge. Townspeople often had little food to spare. Approaching homes to beg or steal, hoboes were sometimes met with violence. Across the country, hoboes developed a system of sign language to alert each other to good opportunities—and warn of possible dangers—in a particular town or home.

Most hoboes were men. Many had left behind families that they could no longer care for. During the Great Depression, some families simply broke apart under the strains of poverty and homelessness.

The emotional toll The greatest toll of the Great Depression may have been on the minds and spirits of the American people. Even though millions of people shared the same fate, many of the unemployed saw their situation as a sign of a personal failure. Accepting handouts deeply troubled many proud Americans.

"Shame? You tellin' me?" recalled one person who lived through the Depression. "The only scar it left on me was my pride, my pride." The

MUSEUM OF THE CITY OF NEW YORK

For people living in a Hooverville, reminders of their former homes and the lives they used to lead often were important. Here, pictures provide a touch of beauty to an otherwise grim environment.

Hooverville shacks were generally thrown together with whatever building materials could be found. They were often leaky and drafty.

Skills FOCUS **INTERPRETING INFOGRAPHICS**

Hoovervilles, like this one in New York, were cobbled together with whatever people could salvage.

Drawing Conclusions What hardships might the men in this photograph have endured?

See **Skills Handbook**, p. H18

The Dust Bowl

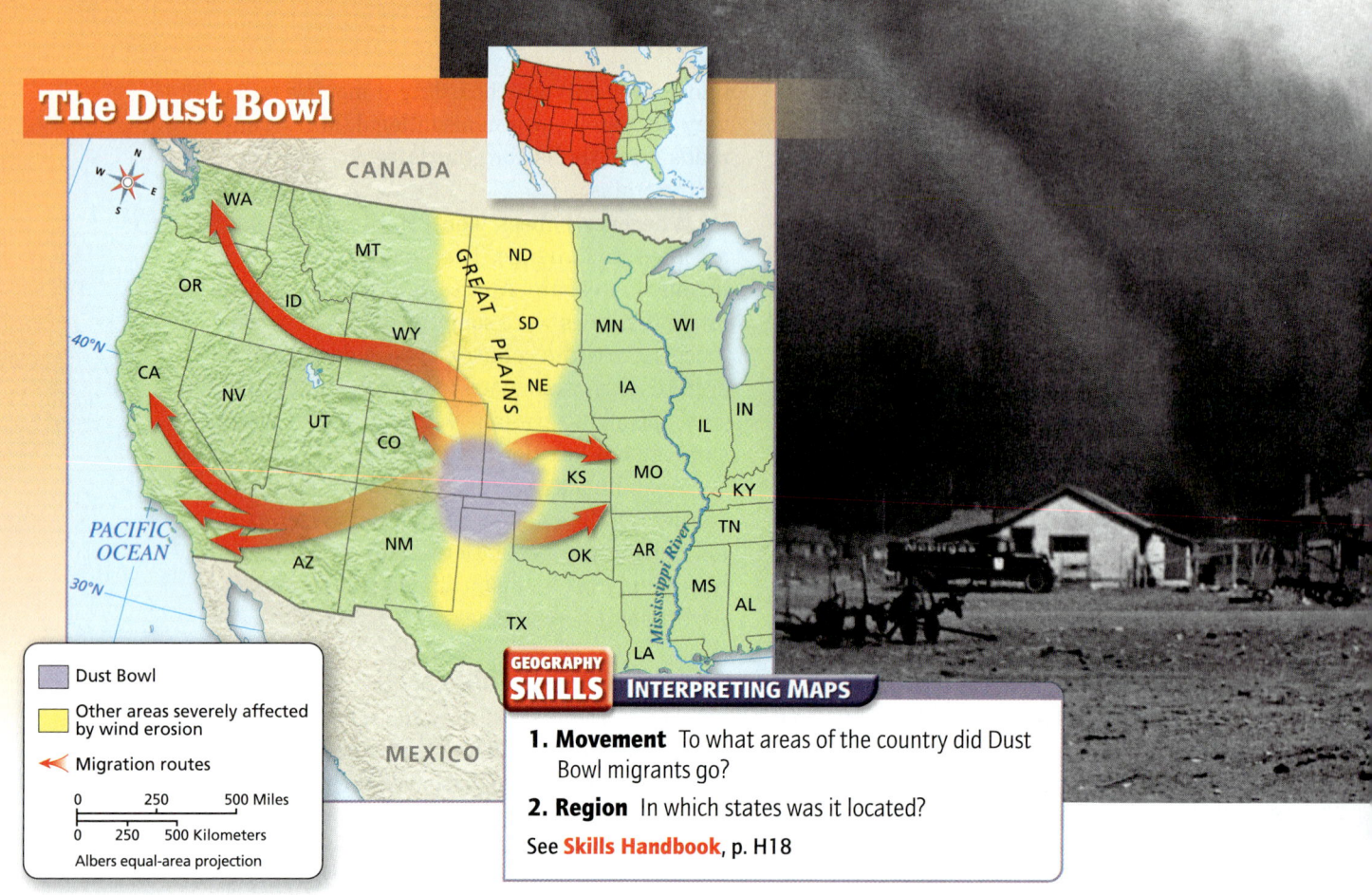

GEOGRAPHY SKILLS INTERPRETING MAPS

1. **Movement** To what areas of the country did Dust Bowl migrants go?
2. **Region** In which states was it located?

See **Skills Handbook**, p. H18

Map legend:
- Dust Bowl
- Other areas severely affected by wind erosion
- Migration routes

0 250 500 Miles
0 250 500 Kilometers
Albers equal-area projection

---

grim despair people felt was reflected in a rise in suicide rates in the early 1930s.

Other people were simply angry. There was a widespread feeling that the nation had failed its hardworking citizens. One popular song of the era summed up the mixture of defiance and shame this way:

HISTORY'S VOICES

"Once I built a railroad, I made it run, made it race against time,

Once I built a railroad; now it's done. Brother, can you spare a dime?"

—"Brother, Can You Spare a Dime,"
Yip and Gorney Harburg, 1931

READING CHECK **Summarizing** In what ways did the Great Depression affect many Americans?

Devastation in the Dust Bowl

In the midst of the economic disaster, nature delivered a cruel blow. Around 1931 much of the Great Plains region entered a long, severe dry spell. This **drought**, or period of below-average rainfall, lasted for several years. By the time it lifted, millions of people had fled the area.

The great dust storms Drought is a part of a weather cycle, naturally occurring on the Great Plains every few decades. By the 1930s, however, careless agricultural practices had left the region vulnerable. Land once covered with grasses now lay bare to the sky with no vegetation to hold the soil in place.

When wind storms came, they stripped away the topsoil and blew it hundreds of miles away. In some of the worst storms, dust reached as far as the Atlantic Coast. Drifting mounds of dust choked crops and buried farm equipment. The fine dust blew into homes through drafty windows and under doors. Year after year, storms came and wreaked destruction. The hardest hit area—including parts of Oklahoma, Kansas, Colorado, New Mexico, and Texas—became known as the **Dust Bowl**.

Fleeing the Plains The terrible drought and dust storms robbed many farmers of their livelihood. Some simply packed up what little they had and moved. By the end of the 1930s, about 2.5 million people had left the Great Plains states. Many headed west along Route 66 to California, where they settled in camps and sought work in farms and orchards.

Pitch-black dust storms, like this one in Springfield, Colorado, drove people out of the Plains on migration routes shown by the arrows on the map. Decades of farming had removed the natural vegetation that had held the soil in place.

The migrants were called **Okies** , after the state of Oklahoma. The term was inaccurate, since the migrants came from a number of different states. It was also meant to be insulting. The Great Plains migrants were often met by resistance and outright discrimination.

The plight of the migrants captured the imagination of some of America's greatest writers and artists, including author **John Steinbeck** and singer-songwriter **Woody Guthrie**. Guthrie's songs about the Dust Bowl describe the disaster's effect on the people it touched.

ACADEMIC VOCABULARY

plight bad situation

HISTORY'S VOICES

❝It's a mighty hard row my poor hands have hoed;
My poor feet have traveled this hot dusty road
Out of your dustbowl and westward we rolled,
Your desert was hot and your mountains were cold.
I've worked in your orchards of peaches and prunes,

Slept on the ground by the light of the moon
On the edge of your city you've seen us and then,
We come with the dust and we're gone with the wind.❞

—Woody Guthrie, "Pastures of Plenty"

Guthrie's lyrics speak to the hardships and struggles not only of the migrants who left the Dust Bowl but also of all Americans hit hard by the Great Depression. For much of the decade the Depression seemingly defied most government efforts to defeat it. The American people were forced to fend for themselves.

READING CHECK **Identifying the Main Idea**
How did the Dust Bowl affect Americans?

SECTION 2 ASSESSMENT

go.hrw.com
Online Quiz
Keyword: SD7 HP21

Reviewing Ideas, Terms, and People

1. a. Identify Briefly describe the **Great Depression** and its main effects.
b. Explain What is the significance of the fact that there were few government relief programs in the early 1930s?
c. Predict How do you think the federal government will respond to the Great Depression?

2. a. Define Write a brief definition for the following term: Hooverville
b. Make Inferences What can you infer from the fact that the shantytowns of homeless Americans came to be known as Hoovervilles?
c. Predict What do you think the political effect of the Great Depression on President Hoover will be? Explain.

3. a. Identify Who were the **Okies**?
b. Compare How were the Okies similar to **hoboes**?

c. Elaborate Do you think those affected by the Dust Bowl were victims of nature or responsible for their own fate?

Critical Thinking

4. Understand Cause and Effect Copy the chart below and use information from the section to identify effects of the Great Depression.

Effects

Cause → (three ovals)

Great Depression

FOCUS ON WRITING

5. Expository Write an essay in which you describe the causes and effects of the Great Depression. Use details from the section to support your account.

American *Literature*

JOHN STEINBECK (1902–1968)

About the Reading Drought, dust storms, and new technology combined to displace tenant farmers during the 1930s. In his Pulitzer Prize-winning 1939 novel *The Grapes of Wrath*, John Steinbeck tells the story of the Joads, a family who lost everything during the Great Depression. Like many other families, the Joads begin migrating from Oklahoma toward California in search of work and a fresh start.

AS YOU READ **Think about the challenges facing farmers and their families as they leave their homes in search of new beginnings.**

Excerpt from

The Grapes of Wrath

by John Steinbeck

Migrant workers, like this family on the road in California's San Joaquin Valley in 1935, were the lowest paid in the nation.

The cars of the migrant people crawled out of the side roads onto the great cross-country highway, and they took the migrant way to the West. In the daylight they scuttled like bugs to the westward; and as the dark caught them, they clustered like bugs near to shelter and to water. And because they were lonely and perplexed, because they had all come from a place of sadness and worry and defeat, and because they were all going to a new mysterious place, they huddled together; they talked together; they shared their lives, their food, and the things they hoped for in the new country. Thus it might be that one family camped for the spring and for company, and a third because two families had pioneered the place and found it good. And when the sun went down, perhaps twenty families and twenty cars were there.

In the evening a strange thing happened: the twenty families became one family, the children were the children of all. The loss of home became one loss, and the golden time in the West was one dream. And it might be that a sick child threw despair into the hearts of twenty families, of a hundred people; that a birth there in a tent kept a hundred people quiet and awe-struck through the night and filled a hundred people with birth-joy in the morning. A family which the night before had been lost and fearful might search its goods to find a present for a new baby. In the evening, sitting about the fires, the twenty were one. They grew to be units of the camps, units of the evenings and the nights. A guitar unwrapped from a blanket and tuned— and the songs, which were all of the people, were sung in the nights.

Skills FOCUS READING LIKE A HISTORIAN

Analyze Do you think Steinbeck was a social activist?

Literature as Historical Evidence In the 1930s many people believed that collective action could be more effective than individual action. How does the excerpt express that point of view?

See **Skills Handbook**, p. H32

Hoover as President

BEFORE YOU READ

MAIN IDEA

Herbert Hoover came to office with a clear philosophy of government, but the events of the Great Depression overwhelmed his responses.

READING FOCUS

1. What was President Hoover's basic philosophy about the proper role of government?
2. What actions did Hoover take in response to the Great Depression?
3. How did the nation respond to Hoover's efforts?

KEY TERMS

associative state
Hoover Dam
cooperative
Reconstruction Finance Corporation
Smoot-Hawley Tariff Act

PI **3.2** Research and analyze the major themes and developments in New York State and United States history (e.g., colonization and settlement; Revolution and New National Period; immigration; expansion and reform era; Civil War and Reconstruction; the American labor movement; Great Depression; World Wars; contemporary United States).

Hoover Seals his DOWNFALL

How did a ragtag army help defeat President Hoover? In 1932 the United States was nearing the low point of the Great Depression. By now Americans had become used to scenes of homeless, jobless people camped out in cardboard shacks in public areas. But the group of some 15,000 World War I veterans who set up camp near the nation's capital in May 1932 was not just another group of men who were down on their luck.

These veterans had come to Washington for a reason. They were trying to put pressure on the federal government to pay them the veteran's bonus, a cash award they had been promised for their service during the war. The bonus, $1.25 for each day served overseas and $1 a day for U.S. service, was not supposed to be paid until 1945. But the men needed the money now, and they believed their request was fair.

The campers settled in, laying out orderly streets and sanitation facilities. As May turned to June, the numbers of so-called Bonus Marchers grew. When Congress failed to agree to their demands, some of the Bonus

Marchers left town, but a core of them remained, along with women and children. In July police and U.S. Army soldiers began clearing the area of the veterans. Violence erupted, and soon the Bonus Marchers' main camp was in flames. Hundreds were injured, and two of the veterans were killed.

Many Americans were deeply disturbed by the sight of U.S. soldiers using weapons against homeless veterans. For President Herbert Hoover, who was already facing complaints that he did not care enough about the plight of the nation's poor, the impact was devastating. As you will read, the Bonus Marchers incident helped complete the public view of Hoover as heartless and helpless in the face of the nation's suffering.

▼ **Bonus Army marchers from Columbus, Georgia, begin their trek to Washington, D.C.**

Herbert Hoover's Philosophy

Herbert Hoover came to the presidency with a set of core beliefs that he had formed over a long career in business and government service. He knew just how he planned to run the country. Yet after less than a year in office, Hoover's plans were upset by the massive stock market collapse. In responding to the growing crisis, Hoover drew on his experience and on the core beliefs that had guided him.

"Rugged individualism" Hoover had served in the administrations of both Warren G. Harding and Calvin Coolidge. He shared many of their ideas about the proper relationship among government, business, and the people. In short, he favored a federal government that played as little role as possible in the affairs of business.

Hoover believed that unnecessary government not only threatened prosperity but also dimmed the very spirit of the American people. A key part of this spirit was what he called "rugged individualism."

THE IMPACT TODAY

Government

In modern times, Republican presidents from Ronald Reagan to George W. Bush have also sought to limit government regulation on businesses.

The Hoover Dam took 21,000 men five years to complete at a cost of $165 million. *How did the project exemplify the associative state?*

HISTORY'S VOICES

❝One of the great problems of government is to determine to what extent the Government itself shall interfere with commerce and industry and how much it shall leave to individual exertion . . . By adherence to the principles of . . . opportunity and freedom to the individual, our American experiment has yielded a degree of well-being unparalleled in all the world.❞

—Herbert Hoover, speech, October 1928

Hoover did not reject the idea of government oversight or regulation of certain business. Nor did he advocate letting people and businesses do exactly as they pleased. Yet he believed deeply that it was vital for the nation's well-being not to destroy people's belief in their own responsibility and power.

The associative state Individualism did not rule out cooperation in Hoover's view. Businesses, he believed, should form voluntary associations that would make the economy fairer and more efficient. Skilled government specialists would then "cooperate with these various associations for the accomplishment of high public purposes." Hoover had a term for his vision of voluntary partnerships between business associations and government. He called it the associative state.

As secretary of commerce in the Harding and Coolidge administrations, Hoover had put these beliefs into practice. He often called together meetings of business leaders and experts to discuss ways to achieve key national goals. He continued to call such conferences after he became president.

Hoover's beliefs were dramatically tested in the construction of what came to be called the Hoover Dam. The dam would harness the Colorado River to provide electricity and a safe, reliable water supply to a vast area that included parts of seven states. The federal government provided funding for the project, which was approved in the 1920s and built in the 1930s. A group of six independent companies joined together to design and construct it. For Hoover, the project's success demonstrated the creative power of partnerships between private business and the federal government.

READING CHECK **Identifying the Main Idea**
Briefly describe the two key features of President Hoover's main beliefs about government.

Hoover's Response to the Great Depression

Hoover's core beliefs shaped many of his early actions as president. Government, Hoover believed, should not provide direct aid. It should find ways to help people help themselves.

Voluntary cooperation Hoover put these beliefs into practice before the stock market crash, when he looked for ways to assist the nation's struggling farmers. He pushed for a program of loans to create and strengthen farm cooperatives. A <mark>cooperative</mark> is an organization that is owned and controlled by its members, who work together for a common goal. The idea behind farmers' cooperatives was that large groups of farmers could buy materials such as fertilizer at lower prices than individual farmers could. Cooperatives also could help farmers market crops in ways that would raise crop prices and increase farmers' income.

After the stock market crash, Hoover continued to rely on his basic belief in voluntary action and cooperation between business and government. He called together many of the nation's top business and government leaders and urged them not to lay off workers or cut wages. If these groups cooperated, Hoover reasoned, workers would have plenty of money to spend on consumer goods, and the worst of the economic crisis would soon pass.

Direct action Unfortunately, the president found it difficult to rally cooperation. In the face of economic disaster, individuals made decisions according to their own economic interests. Businesses cut jobs and wages. State and local governments stopped their building programs, throwing many people out of work. Consumers stopped spending. As a result, the economy plunged into the Great Depression.

The growing crisis eventually persuaded Hoover to break somewhat with his beliefs. At his urging, Congress created in early 1932

PRIMARY SOURCES

Political Cartoon

Most Hoover officials believed the effects of the Great Crash would eventually ease without drastic government action. Treasury Secretary Ogden L. Mills was especially reluctant to fund relief programs. This cartoon appeared three weeks before the 1932 presidential election.

Treasury Secretary Ogden L. Mills attempts to reassure the driver, "U.S. public," that repairs are underway.

President Herbert Hoover, an engineer by training, is unsure how to put the car back together again.

"IT WON'T BE LONG NOW?"

—By Jerry Doyle

READING LIKE A HISTORIAN

Interpreting Political Cartoons What message is the cartoonist trying to convey, and what details in the drawing support that message?

See **Skills Handbook**, p. H31

the **Reconstruction Finance Corporation** (RFC). A key <u>clause</u> in the RFC legislation authorized up to $2 billion in direct government loans to struggling banks, insurance companies, and other institutions. Later that year, Hoover asked Congress to create the Federal Home Loan Bank. The new program encouraged home building and reduced the number of home foreclosures. These measures marked a historic expansion of the role of the federal government in the business of the American people. Still, for many citizens, Hoover's actions were too little, too late.

The Smoot-Hawley Tariff Act One of Hoover's major efforts to address the economic crisis backfired badly. In 1930 he signed the **Smoot-Hawley Tariff Act**. The new tariff raised the cost of imported goods for American consumers, making it more likely that they would purchase the cheaper American goods.

The Smoot-Hawley Tariff Act was a disaster. The tariff rates were set at historically high levels. When European nations responded with tariffs on American goods, trade plunged. By 1934 global trade was down roughly two thirds from 1929 levels.

READING CHECK **Summarizing** What actions did Hoover take to improve the economy during the Great Depression?

FACES OF HISTORY

Herbert HOOVER
1874–1964

Few presidents have entered office seemingly as well prepared and qualified as Herbert Hoover, yet the Great Depression proved too great a challenge for him to master. As an engineer, successful businessman, and humanitarian, Hoover had never met a problem he could not solve through sheer brilliance and dogged hard work. But his failure to make headway against the Depression combined with his reluctance to provide public relief spelled electoral disaster.

Following his defeat, Hoover wrote books and continued to serve with distinction on various government commissions into the 1950s. His work streamling the executive branch for presidents Truman and Eisenhower demonstrated a still potent talent for administration.

Rate How did Hoover's performance as president compare with his earlier public service?

The Nation Responds to Hoover

Hoover had entered office believing that government should seek to avoid direct involvement in the lives of individuals and businesses. Under the pressure of events, he modified his beliefs and began to push for some forms of direct relief. In spite of his efforts, however, Hoover increasingly came under attack for his handling of the Great Depression.

The president loses favor Hoover's frequent optimistic claims about the economy slowly undermined his credibility with voters. Early in the crisis, as millions of people were losing their jobs, he proclaimed the basic economic foundation of the nation to be sound. "I am convinced," he told the nation, "that we have passed the worst." In fact, the worst was yet to come.

Hoover later spoke glowingly about the efforts being made to deal with the Depression. "Industry and business have recognized their social obligation," he said in February 1931. "Never before in a great depression has there been so systematic a protection against distress." Millions of jobless Americans did not share Hoover's assessment of the situation.

Worse, many Americans came to question Hoover's compassion. As economic conditions grew worse, his unwillingness to consider giving direct relief to people became harder and harder for Americans to understand. When Hoover finally broke with his stated beliefs and pushed for programs such as the Reconstruction Finance Corporation, many people wondered why he was willing to give billions of dollars to banks and businesses but nothing to individuals.

Bonus March The Bonus March incident further damaged Hoover's reputation. The photographs of armed soldiers fighting with unarmed, unemployed veterans deeply troubled many observers. As one newspaper of the time observed, "If the Army must be called upon to make war on unarmed citizens, this is no longer America."

Hoover's opposition to paying the Bonus Army marchers stemmed partly from a concern about the federal budget. Hoover believed that the government must have a balanced budget—that is, it must spend no more money than it takes in—in order to achieve financial health. To meet this goal, Hoover pushed for and got a large tax increase in 1932. At a time when people were suffering and asking for government relief, a larger tax burden was highly unpopular.

The voters react The 1930 midterm congressional elections provided an early sign that the public was growing dissatisfied with Hoover's policies. The Republican Party had controlled Congress during the boom years of the 1920s. In 1930, however, Democrats managed to win a majority of the seats in the U.S. House of Representatives. They also came within one seat of matching the Republicans in the Senate.

By the 1932 presidential election, it seemed certain that the voters would reject Hoover at the polls. The Great Depression showed little sign of ending, and Hoover's ability to influence events was nearly gone. The president didn't even bother campaigning until October, little

After Congress refused to approve payment to the Bonus Army marchers, stunned protesters began a "Death March" in front of the Capitol. Finally Hoover moved to disband the camp, and violence broke out. *How did the public respond?*

more than a month before the election. The main question now was who the Democrats would pick to run against him, and what that candidate would do to end the nation's grief.

READING CHECK **Identifying Supporting Details** What were some actions—taken or not taken—that made voters believe Hoover did not care?

Reviewing Ideas, Terms, and People

1. a. Identify What were two key ideas that helped shape Hoover's core beliefs?
b. Compare In what ways were Hoover's basic beliefs similar to those of Presidents Harding and Coolidge?
c. Evaluate What is your opinion about Hoover's belief in the importance of rugged individualism?

2. a. Define Write a brief definition for each of the following terms: **cooperative, Reconstruction Finance Corporation, Smoot-Hawley Tariff Act**
b. Analyze How effective was President Hoover's preferred approach to government in responding to the hardships of the Great Depression?
c. Rate Defend Hoover's commitment to avoiding direct relief to individuals.

3. a. Describe What was the general reaction of the American people to Hoover's performance?
b. Contrast How did Hoover's core beliefs contrast with what many Americans wanted?

c. Design What are some relief programs that Hoover's Democratic opponent might suggest?

Critical Thinking

4. Understanding Cause and Effect Copy the chart below and use information from the section to identify effects of Hoover's personal philosophy on government.

Cause → Effects
Hoover's Philosophies →

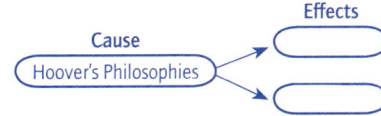
FOCUS ON WRITING

5. Persuasive Write a letter to the editor in which you either defend or criticize Herbert Hoover's approach to the stock market crash and the depression that followed. Use details from the section to support your position.

Life During the Great Depression

Historical Context The documents below provide different types of information on the life during the Great Depression.

Task Examine the documents and answer the questions that follow. Then you will be asked to write an essay about life during the Great Depression, using facts from the documents and from the chapter you just read to support the position you take in your thesis statement.

ST 3.2 Draw upon literary selections, historical documents, and accounts to analyze the roles played by different individuals and groups during the major eras in New York State and United States history.

DOCUMENT 1

During the Depression many families found themselves standing helplessly in lines to get donated food and clothing. A great many of these people never imagined they would be in such a situation. The photograph below shows people standing in a relief line in San Antonio, Texas, to receive aid.

DOCUMENT 2

Charities did what they could to help the needy, but it was often not enough. Social worker Nell Blackshear of Atlanta, Georgia, recalled the relief lines in her city and her experiences providing help to others through a government program.

"That was a sad time when there was a soup line. Men, women, and children would come and go through the soup line once a day—it was bad. They had a black soup line, of course. There was no such thing as just hungry people. Even on relief you had to remember that you were black and they were white. They would have hot soup and sometimes just coffee and bread that was donated from some of the bakeries . . .

[As part of a government program,] I had to buy milk for the families. Even had to buy clothes. We would take the mothers to the stores on Edgewood Avenue . . . We would buy the clothing, then order and pay for the coal, twenty-five-cent bags of coal.

I remember the rear of 210 Butler Street. This was a long tenement house. I would have to go get some groceries in the house, or take coal to give them to make a fire in those little rooms. Sometimes seven or eight people would live in one room. They had a communal toilet outside. It was a deplorable [horrible] sort of thing. And that's where our clients lived, this is the kind of relief and work with families that I started off doing."

DOCUMENT 3

Like African Americans, Asian Americans were targets of discrimination. In California, many Asian American communities were segregated from their white neighbors. They relied heavily on one another. During the 1930s many survived by sharing resources. The photograph at right shows Japanese American migrant workers picking broccoli in Guadalupe, California.

DOCUMENT 4

People showed remarkable generosity during the hard times. Kitty McCulloch, a young seamstress, recalled her experiences.

"There were many beggars, who would come to your back door, and they would say they were hungry. I wouldn't give them money because I didn't have it. But I did take them in and put them in my kitchen and give them something to eat.

One elderly man that had white whiskers and all, he came to my back door. He was pretty much of a philosopher. He was just charming. A man probably in his sixties. And he did look like St. Nicholas, I'll tell you that. I gave him a good, warm meal. He said, 'bring me a pencil and paper and I'll draw you a picture.' So he sketched. And was really good. He was an artist.

A man came to my door. . . He said, 'You don't suppose you could have a couple of shirts you could give me, old shirts of your husband's?' I said, 'Oh, I'm so very sorry, my husband hasn't anything but old shirts, really. That's all he has right now and he wears those.' He said, 'Lady, if I get some extra ones, I'll come back and give them to you.'"

Skills FOCUS READING LIKE A HISTORIAN

1. **a. Describe** Refer to Document 1. Describe the expressions on the people's faces.
   b. Elaborate How do you think these people felt about having to go on relief?

2. **a. Identify** Refer to Document 2. What did Blackshear do as part of her job with the government?
   b. Interpret What did Blackshear mean when she said, "There was no such thing as just hungry people?"

3. **a. Identify** Refer to Document 3. What are the people in the photograph doing?
   b. Analyze How do the field workers reflect the community spirit of Japanese Americans in the 1930s?

4. **a. Identify** Refer to Document 4. What were the beggars who came to McColluch's door seeking?
   b. Elaborate How did the beggars' responses to McColluch reflect the spirit of the times?

5. **Document-Based Essay Question** Consider the question below and form a thesis statement. Using examples from Documents 1, 2, 3, and 4, create an outline and write a short essay supporting your position.
   How did the Great Depression bring people together?

See **Skills Handbook**, p. H28–29, H30

Visual Summary: The Great Depression Begins

Great Depression Begins

- Stock market crashes; banks, businesses fail
- Widespread joblessness and suffering occur
- Drought and dust storms add to suffering

Hoover Responds

- Relies on cooperation, voluntary action
- Later begins using power of government
- Fails to curb spreading economic crisis

Reviewing Key Terms and People

Identify the correct term or person from the chapter that best fits each of the following descriptions.

1. The term for the decisive drop in the stock market at the end of October 1929

2. Hoover's vision of a partnership between private business associations and government

3. The nickname given to a settlement of homeless people during the Great Depression

4. An organization owned and controlled by its members, who work together for a common goal

5. A person who rode the railroads from town to town in search of work

6. The nickname given to refugees from the dust storms of the early 1930s

7. Law originally meant to protect American businesses but that ended up harming the United States and world economies

8. The nickname for the central Plains region struck by a terrible drought and dust storms in the 1930s

9. The widespread practice during the 1920s that increased the danger to investors from a drop in the stock market

10. An organization created by the Hoover administration to aid struggling banks

11. The central bank of the United States

12. A prolonged period of below-normal rainfall

13. What can happen to a home or farm when the owner fails to pay off loans taken to buy the property

14. A singer who described the effects of the Dust Bowl

15. the total value of goods and services produced in a nation during a specific period of time

History's Impact video program
Review the video to answer the closing question:
How do changes made after the 1929 stock market crash help protect the American economy today?

Comprehension and Critical Thinking

SECTION 1 *(pp. 672–679)*

16. a. Recall What was the general experience of investors in stocks in the United States in the mid-1920s?

b. Explain How did the success of the American stock market also increase the dangers of investing in the market?

c. Elaborate How did the collapse of the stock market come to hurt so many people who did not have money invested in stocks?

SECTION 2 *(pp. 680–685)*

17. a. Describe How did the Great Depression affect ordinary Americans?

b. Summarize How did victims of the Great Depression cope with the effects of homelessness and joblessness?

c. Evaluate Why do you think so many people blamed themselves for their misfortune during the Great Depression, in spite of the fact that millions of Americans were in a similar situation?

SECTION 3 *(pp. 687–691)*

18. a. Identify What was President Hoover's basic belief about the proper relationship of citizens to their government?

b. Analyze Why did the Great Depression greatly test Hoover and his fundamental philosophy about how to govern?

c. Evaluate Do you think it was reasonable to expect Hoover to change his philosophy and tactics in response to the crisis the nation faced in the Great Depression? Explain.

Using the Internet

go.hrw.com
Practice Online
Keyword: SD7 CH21

19. The worst day of the Great Crash of 1929 was "Black Tuesday," October 29. During a catastrophic series of workdays preceding Black Tuesday, the American stock market lost nearly one half of its value. Using the keyword above, do research to learn more about what happened to the American economy in October 1929. Then create a report that traces the aftereffects of the stock market crash and explains how it quickly came to affect people throughout the nation, even those who had not invested in stocks.

Analyzing Primary Sources

Reading Like a Historian

This photograph shows an automobile being sold by an investor following the stock market crash of October 1929.

20. Describe What is the significance of the moment shown in this photograph?

21. Draw Conclusions What does this image tell you about how Americans were affected by the crash?

Critical Reading

Read the passage in Section 1 that begins with the heading "An Appearance of Prosperity." Then answer the question that follows.

22. The heading "An Appearance of Prosperity" suggests that

A. there was no prosperity in the United States at all.

B. every American prospered in the 1920s.

C. overall, the economy seemed to be performing very well.

D. in fact, only the auto industry was performing well.

FOCUS ON WRITING

Expository Writing *Expository writing gives information, explains why or how, or defines a process. To practice expository writing, complete the assignment below.*

Writing Topic **Herbert Hoover's Response to the Great Depression**

23. Assignment Based on what you have read in this chapter, write a paragraph that discusses why so many Americans were dissatisfied with Hoover's response to the Great Depression.

The NEW DEAL

THE BIG PICTURE The New Deal was President Franklin D. Roosevelt's plan for overcoming the Great Depression. His plan gave government jobs to the unemployed and increased government regulation of the economy. Although New Deal programs achieved varied levels of success, they did represent a basic change in American society.

New York Standards

Key Idea 1 The study of New York State and United States history requires an analysis of the development of American culture, its diversity and multicultural context, and the ways people are unified by many values, practices, and traditions.

Key Idea 3 Study about the major social, political, economic, cultural, and religious developments in New York State and United States history involves learning about the important roles and contributions of individuals and groups.

Skills FOCUS   READING LIKE A HISTORIAN

Artist Ben Shahn painted this mural for the community center of Jersey Homesteads. The panel shown here celebrates the planning of the New Jersey town, which was built as part of a New Deal program for garment workers. **Interpreting Visuals** Why do you think Shahn included a poster of Roosevelt among the symbols in the mural?

See **Skills Handbook**, p. H30

U.S.

World

March 1933 President Franklin Delano Roosevelt is inaugurated.

1933   1934

March 1933 Germans elect Adolf Hitler as chancellor.

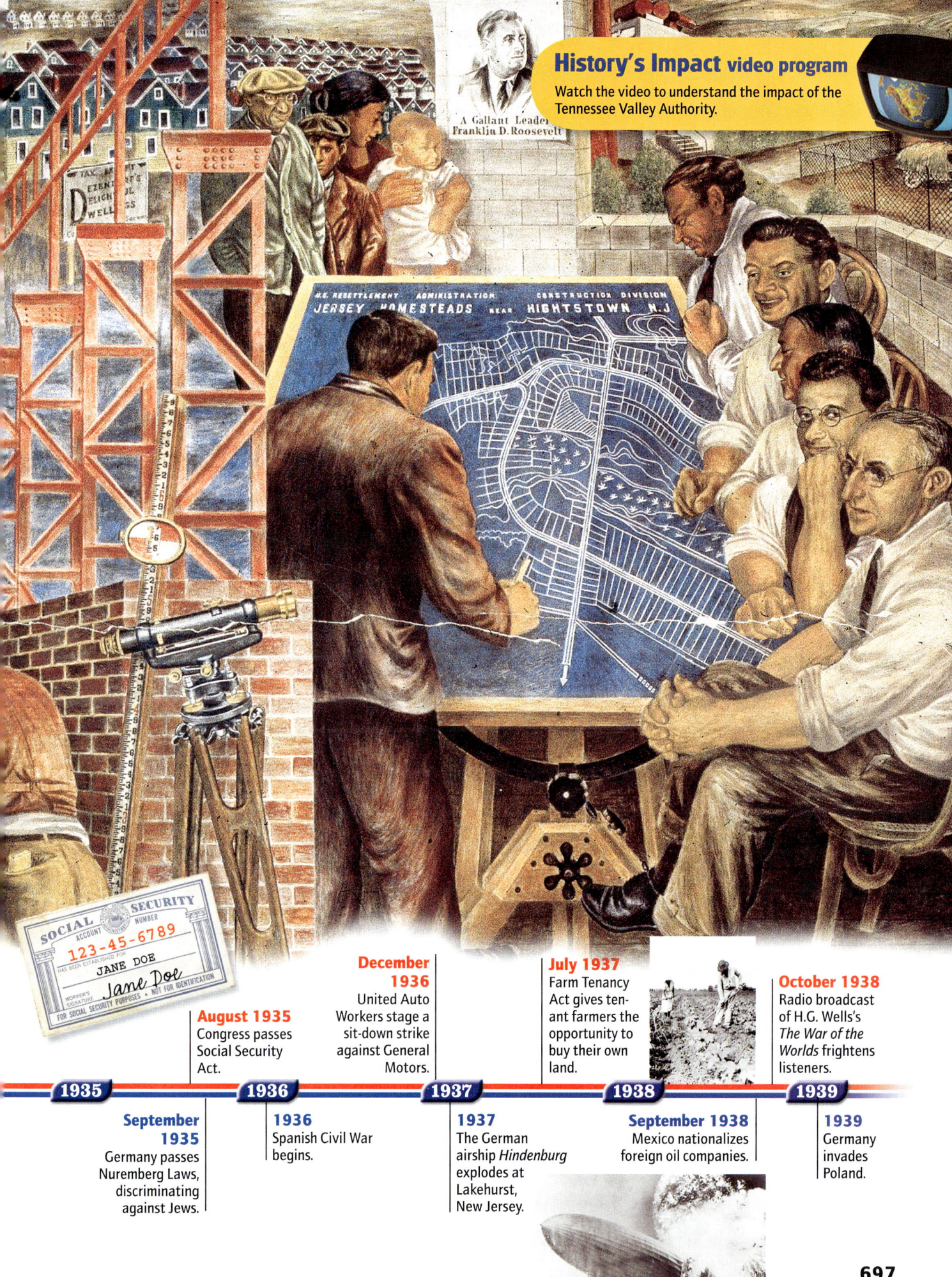

A Gallant Leader
Franklin D. Roosevelt

U.S. RESETTLEMENT ADMINISTRATION CONSTRUCTION DIVISION
JERSEY HOMESTEADS NEAR HIGHTSTOWN N.J.

SOCIAL SECURITY
123-45-6789
JANE DOE
Jane Doe

August 1935
Congress passes Social Security Act.

December 1936
United Auto Workers stage a sit-down strike against General Motors.

July 1937
Farm Tenancy Act gives tenant farmers the opportunity to buy their own land.

October 1938
Radio broadcast of H.G. Wells's *The War of the Worlds* frightens listeners.

| 1935 | 1936 | 1937 | 1938 | 1939 |

September 1935
Germany passes Nuremberg Laws, discriminating against Jews.

1936
Spanish Civil War begins.

1937
The German airship *Hindenburg* explodes at Lakehurst, New Jersey.

September 1938
Mexico nationalizes foreign oil companies.

1939
Germany invades Poland.

697

Launching the New Deal

BEFORE YOU READ

MAIN IDEA

In 1933 Franklin Delano Roosevelt became president of a suffering nation. He quickly sought to address the country's needs, with mixed results.

READING FOCUS

1. What were the key events of the presidential election of 1932?

2. What was the nature of Franklin and Eleanor Roosevelt's political partnership?

3. What initial actions did Roosevelt take to stabilize the economy?

4. How did the New Deal run into trouble in Roosevelt's first term?

KEY TERMS AND PEOPLE

Franklin Delano Roosevelt
public works
fireside chat
Eleanor Roosevelt
Hundred Days
New Deal
subsidy
Huey P. Long
Father Charles Coughlin
Dr. Francis Townsend

PI 1.1 Analyze the development of American culture, explaining how ideas, values, beliefs, and traditions have changed over time and how they united all Americans.

▲ Roosevelt's "forgotten man" speech was as powerful as Maynard Dixon's 1934 painting of the same name.

THE INSIDE STORY

How did it feel to be a forgotten victim of the Great Depression?

Franklin Delano Roosevelt seemed to know. In 1932 Roosevelt was one of several candidates seeking the Democratic presidential nomination. Some critics dismissed him as "an amiable man… without very strong convictions." But in an April 1932 speech, Roosevelt took a strong stand. He criticized the policies of President Hoover as ineffective and wrongly directed at only the "top of the social and economic structure." By contrast, Roosevelt pledged to help the "forgotten man at the bottom of the economic pyramid." Only by helping these people, Roosevelt claimed, would the nation's economic ills be cured.

Roosevelt's speech included few specific proposals. Yet that did not seem to matter to the Depression-weary citizens reading his words or watching the newsreels at the movie houses. Here at last was someone who understood the plight of ordinary citizens. He remembered them, he cared about them, and he seemed to understand that their fate was key to the nation's recovery.

The personal connection Roosevelt established was something few Americans felt they had with Herbert Hoover. It would serve Roosevelt well in the months and years ahead. ◼

The Election of 1932

The 1932 presidential election presented the Democrats with a great opportunity to recapture the White House for the first time in 12 years. With joblessness mounting and banks collapsing in record numbers, many Americans placed the blame squarely on President Hoover. Eager to unseat him, Democrats competed fiercely for their party's nomination. **Franklin Delano Roosevelt** emerged the victor.

Roosevelt's rise Franklin Roosevelt was a distant relative of former president Theodore Roosevelt. He had served as assistant secretary of the navy under Woodrow Wilson. He had also run unsuccessfully for vice president in 1920.

Soon after, the ambitious young politician was stricken with polio. The disease nearly killed him and left him without full use of his legs. Yet Roosevelt rebounded from that experience to become governor of New York in 1929. Many considered Roosevelt's record as governor impressive. He launched a groundbreaking relief program to aid the state's many victims of the Great Depression. By 1932 Roosevelt's program had provided help to 1 of every 10 New York families. His record stood in stark contrast to Hoover's insistence on limited government action.

The 1932 campaign During the campaign, Roosevelt offered some general ideas about what he would do as president. He promised relief for the poor and more **public works** programs—government-funded building projects—that would provide jobs. He also talked about lowering tariffs.

Mainly, though, Roosevelt attacked Hoover and the Republicans for their response to the Great Depression. "For at least two years after the crash," Roosevelt railed in an October 1932 speech, "the only efforts made by the national administration to cope with the distress of unemployment were to deny its existence." At the same time, Roosevelt criticized Hoover for spending too much money, and he promised to cut the federal budget. In general, his speeches laid out the case for change at the White House without tying him down to specific promises or policies.

Though Roosevelt's speeches were vague and sometimes contradictory, they alarmed Hoover. Considering the prospect of Roosevelt's election, he predicted disaster. "The grass will grow in the streets of a hundred cities," cried Hoover. "The weeds will overrun the fields of millions of farms."

A landslide victory Hoover's warnings failed to stir many voters. On election day, the voters handed Roosevelt a clear victory. Roosevelt received more than 57 percent of the popular vote and swept the electoral vote in all but six states. In addition, the Democrats gained 90 seats in the House of Representatives and 13 seats in the Senate to take control of both houses of Congress.

READING CHECK   **Making Generalizations**
What was Franklin Roosevelt's campaign strategy in the election of 1932?

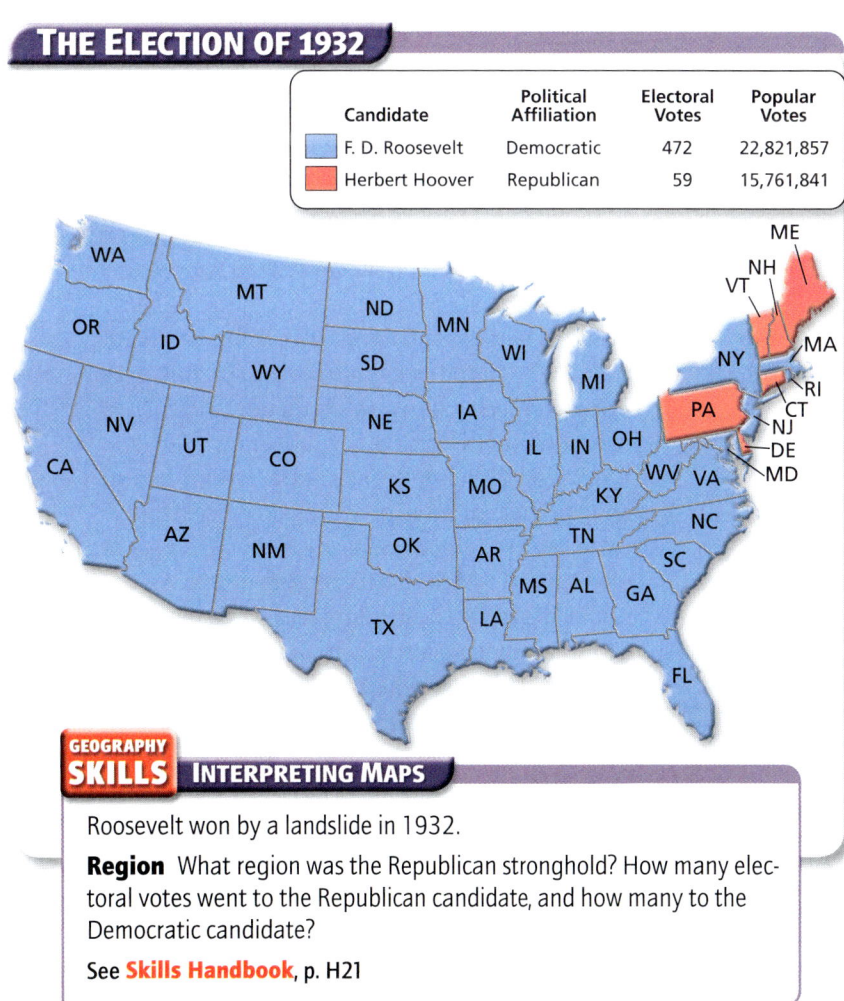

THE ELECTION OF 1932

Candidate	Political Affiliation	Electoral Votes	Popular Votes
F. D. Roosevelt	Democratic	472	22,821,857
Herbert Hoover	Republican	59	15,761,841

GEOGRAPHY SKILLS   **INTERPRETING MAPS**

Roosevelt won by a landslide in 1932.

Region What region was the Republican stronghold? How many electoral votes went to the Republican candidate, and how many to the Democratic candidate?

See **Skills Handbook**, p. H21

Franklin Delano ROOSEVELT
1882–1945

Raised in a wealthy New York family, Franklin Roosevelt had private tutors and traveled to Europe frequently. He won election in 1910 to the New York State Senate, but he resigned in 1913 to serve as President Wilson's assistant secretary of the navy.

Roosevelt's career seemed over when he contracted polio in 1921. With the help of his wife, Eleanor, Roosevelt returned to public service. In 1928 he won the race for governor of New York, serving during the early years of the Depression. His work in easing New Yorkers' suffering helped him win the 1932 Democratic presidential nomination.

Explain How did Roosevelt's experience in New York help him nationally?

A Political Partnership

As a politician, Roosevelt's greatest asset may have been his personality. He had an appealing blend of cheerfulness, optimism, and confidence. These qualities were illustrated by his response to the illness that had left him unable to walk without assistance.

Rather than giving in to his disability, Roosevelt had worked tirelessly to regain strength in his legs and to continue his public career. In this era before television, most Americans were unaware of Roosevelt's handicap. However, his personal struggle gave him a strength that many found very reassuring. In this way, Roosevelt took a personal challenge and turned it into one of his greatest political strengths.

Roosevelt also possessed a warmth and charm that made him an effective communicator. As president, he used the radio to great effect, particularly in his **fireside chats.** As the name suggests, these addresses were meant to sound as though Roosevelt were in the listener's living room, speaking personally with the family. He spoke calmly and clearly and in a way that ordinary people could understand. He conveyed real concern and gave reassurance to millions of troubled Americans.

"I never saw him," recalled one Depression survivor, "but I knew him." This ability to help people feel better during their time of hardship won Roosevelt lasting support with voters.

Roosevelt's philosophy As you have read, Roosevelt sent some unclear signals during his 1932 presidential campaign. Sometimes he attacked Hoover for not doing enough to fight the Depression—and sometimes for doing too much. At heart, however, Roosevelt was a reform-minded Democrat in the tradition of Woodrow Wilson and the Progressives who came before him.

As he had demonstrated as governor of New York, Roosevelt believed that it was the government's job to take direct action to help its people. His basic faith in the ability of government to solve economic and social problems and to help people in need ran deep.

HISTORY'S VOICES

❝I assert that modern society, acting through its Government, owes the definite obligation to prevent the starvation or the dire want of any of its fellow men and women who try to maintain themselves but cannot.❞

—Franklin D. Roosevelt, Campaign Speech, October 13, 1932

Eleanor Roosevelt While still in law school, Franklin Roosevelt had married his distant cousin, **Eleanor Roosevelt**. Their marriage would play a central role in Franklin Roosevelt's political success.

Throughout her husband's career, but especially following his bout with polio in the 1920s, Eleanor served as her husband's "eyes and ears." With his mobility impaired, Franklin Roosevelt relied on his wife to collect and share information gained in her wide travels. He deeply valued his wife's keen insight.

In her own right, Eleanor became a powerful political force. She threw her energies into several major social issues, including the campaign to stop the lynching of African Americans. In the process, she helped change the role of First Lady.

During her husband's presidency, Eleanor began writing her own newspaper column, called "My Day." She received thousands of letters every week. These letters demonstrate the trust and affection many Americans held for the First Lady. They also revealed people's faith in her influence. "Thank you very much for helping me to keep my house," wrote one admirer. "If it wasn't for you, I know I would have lost it."

Not everyone was a fan of Eleanor Roosevelt and her active political role. She was a frequent target of the enemies of her husband's administration. Yet even her critics agreed that no First Lady had ever played such an important role in the government of the nation.

READING CHECK **Summarizing** What did President Roosevelt believe was the proper role of government in the lives of American citizens?

Roosevelt Takes Action

By the time Roosevelt was inaugurated in March 1933, four months had passed since the election. Hoover had struggled during that time to prevent a worsening of the economy. As the loser of the presidential race, however, Hoover had little power to accomplish anything. The crisis deepened.

Rescuing the nation's banking system presented the most immediate challenge facing Roosevelt when he took office. The problems facing the nation's banks had gotten so bad that when leaders gathered in Washington, D.C., for Roosevelt's March 4 inauguration, hotels would not accept checks from out-of-town guests. The hotels feared that the guests' banks might fail before the hotels were able to receive payment.

The banking crisis Roosevelt could see that the nation faced a critical loss of confidence. He wasted no time in addressing the situation. In his inaugural address, the new president sought to calm the public.

HISTORY'S VOICES

❝ So, first of all, let me assert my firm belief that the only thing we have to fear is fear itself— nameless, unreasoning, unjustified terror which paralyzes needed efforts to convert retreat into advance. ❞

—Franklin D. Roosevelt, First Inaugural Address, March 4, 1933

Two days later, Roosevelt took action. The shaky state of the nation's banks had led many people to withdraw all their money from their accounts. They feared losing their savings if the bank collapsed. Such large-scale withdrawals could—and did—ruin even healthy banks. This created more panic, more withdrawals—and more bank failures. To stop this cycle, Roosevelt issued an executive order temporarily closing all of the nation's banks. The president called it a bank holiday.

Next, the president called Congress into emergency session and pushed through the Emergency Banking Act. The law gave government officials power to examine each bank,

"Hoover sent the army; Roosevelt sent his wife."
A World War I veteran

FACES OF HISTORY

Eleanor ROOSEVELT
1884–1962

Orphaned at the age of 10, Eleanor Roosevelt was raised by her mother's relatives. A sad and shy teenager and a serious and scholarly young woman, she married the fun-loving, outgoing Franklin D. Roosevelt.

Eleanor grew into her roles in life, becoming one of the most respected women in America. With dynamic energy, she labored for charities, traveled the world making speeches, and spoke out for women's rights and against racial discrimination. After her husband died in office, Eleanor began a new chapter in life. She served as a delegate to the United Nations, chaired President John F. Kennedy's Commission on the Status of Women, and remained active in American politics.

Make Inferences What choices did Eleanor Roosevelt make in life, and what did those choices reflect about her character?

When a second Bonus Army came to Washington in 1933, Roosevelt sent Eleanor to investigate. Her tour of their camp in Virginia ended in a sing-along.

determine its soundness, take steps to correct problems, and, if necessary, close it. To explain to the worried public what was going on, Roosevelt gave the first of his famed fireside chats.

The plan worked. Within days, banks began to reopen with government assurances that they were on solid footing. Ordinary people, who had been frantically taking money out of their banks, started to return funds. Some banks never did reopen, but the crisis was over. In just over a week, the nation had regained crucial confidence in its financial system.

In the days ahead, Congress enacted additional banking reforms. The Glass-Steagall Act of 1933 created the Federal Deposit Insurance Corporation, or FDIC. This provided government insurance for depositors' savings. Individual depositors no longer needed to fear losing their savings if their bank collapsed.

Reassured by the new law, even more depositors took the money they had stuffed in home safes and under their mattresses and returned it to the banking system. Within a month, about $1 billion in new deposits flowed into the system.

The Hundred Days The resolution of the banking crisis was just the beginning of a critical period of government activity that came to be known as the **Hundred Days**. During this time, Roosevelt pushed Congress to put in place many of the key parts of his program—what he called the **New Deal**.

Roosevelt first used the phrase in a campaign speech in which he promised "a new deal for the American people." The New Deal came to include a wide range of measures aimed at accomplishing three goals:

(1) *relief* for those suffering the effects of the Great Depression;

(2) *recovery* of the depressed economy;

(3) *reforms* that would help prevent serious economic crises in the future.

The Civilian Conservation Corps, or CCC, was typical of the reform programs passed during the Hundred Days. Established in March 1933, it sought to address an immediate problem: unemployment among young men 18 to 25 years old.

Americans enrolled in the CCC were paid to work on a variety of conservation projects, such as planting trees and improving parks. CCC workers lived in army-style camps and were required to send most of their earnings to their families.

Two key recovery programs sought to reinforce the twin pillars of the economy—agriculture and industry. The Agricultural Adjustment Act, or AAA, gave farmers a **subsidy**, or government payment, to grow fewer crops. A smaller

Civilian Conservation Corps workers replant a clear-cut Oregon hillside with seedlings in 1939 (left). The CCC brought immediate relief to families and provided work for 3 million young men. Businesses following fair-practice business codes displayed the NRA's blue eagle emblem (above).

supply of crops on the market would increase demand for those crops. This would drive prices up and help farmers earn more.

The National Industrial Recovery Act (NIRA) mandated that businesses in the same industry cooperate with each other to set prices and levels of production. In the days of Theodore Roosevelt, government had viewed such cooperation as a violation of antitrust laws. Now, with the NIRA, government sought to promote it as a way of helping business.

The NIRA also included $3.3 billion for public-works programs. These were managed through a new agency called the Public Works Administration, or PWA. (The New Deal was famous for creating an "alphabet soup" of government agencies known by their initials.) Labor unions benefited, too, from the NIRA. For the first time, labor got federal protection for the right to organize.

The Federal Securities Act emerged as a major reform effort of the Hundred Days. The measure forced companies to share certain financial information with the public. The purpose was to help investors and to restore confidence in the fairness of the markets.

In 1934 Congress established the Securities and Exchange Commission. The SEC would serve as a government watchdog over the nation's stock markets.

One of the most far-reaching and ambitious programs of the New Deal was the Tennessee Valley Authority, or TVA. Created in May 1933, this massive program was charged with developing the resources of the entire Tennessee River Valley, a vast region in the Southeast United States.

The TVA built dams and other projects along the Tennessee River and its tributaries. These dams controlled floods, aided navigation and shipping along the river, and provided hydroelectric power to be used by industries. (See the History and Geography feature on the TVA at the end of this section.)

Beyond the Hundred Days President Roosevelt had campaigned promising action and "bold, persistent experimentation." He had delivered. Many Americans applauded his efforts. Journalist and former Roosevelt critic Walter Lippmann wrote, "In the hundred days from March to June we became again an organized nation confident of our power."

Amid the successes, there was also much to criticize. Even Roosevelt admitted in a fireside chat, "I do not deny that we make mistakes." Comparing himself to a baseball player, he said, "I have no expectation of making a hit every time we come to bat."

Yet FDR and the Congress kept trying, passing significant legislation in the period after the Hundred Days. In November 1933, for example, the Civil Works Administration (CWA) was created. This agency provided winter employment to 4 million workers. CWA crews built miles of highways and sewer lines, hundreds of airports, and more.

In June 1934 Congress passed the Indian Reorganization Act. It reversed previous policies by recognizing the tribe as the key unit of social organization for Native Americans. It limited the sale of Indian lands and provided assistance to native groups in developing their resources, economy, and culture. It also granted some limited rights of self-rule.

Many Native Americans hailed the new direction. Others viewed it more skeptically, as just another instance of outsiders telling them what to do.

ACADEMIC VOCABULARY mandate require

READING CHECK **Identifying Supporting Details** What were the three main categories of the programs and actions of Roosevelt's New Deal?

Trouble for the New Deal

The New Deal marked a significant shift in the relationship between government and the American people. Never before had government assumed such a central role in the business and personal lives of its citizens. Not surprisingly, this shift triggered strong reactions.

Some reformers and radicals believed the New Deal had not gone far enough in reforming the economy. They wanted a complete overhaul of capitalism. The New Deal, they complained, merely propped up the old banking system and gave new freedoms to business. These, critics charged, were the same people and powers that had led the nation into the Great Depression in the first place.

Conservatives, on the other hand, attacked the New Deal as a radical break with traditional American ideals. Senator Carter Glass of Virginia lamented in 1933 that "Roosevelt is driving this country to destruction faster than it has ever moved before."

Leading critics of the New Deal Over time, several leading critics of the New Deal emerged. Perhaps the most powerful of these was Senator **Huey P. Long** of Louisiana, who believed Roosevelt's policies were too friendly to banks and businesses.

In 1934 Long set up his own political organization, the Share Our Wealth Society. Long's idea, reflected in the slogan "Every Man a King," was to give every family $5,000 to buy a home, plus an income of $2,500 a year. To pay for this, Long proposed heavy taxes on wealthy Americans. Long's organization attracted millions of followers. Roosevelt's advisers feared his possible role in the 1936 election.

Father Charles Coughlin, a Catholic priest, was another one-time Roosevelt supporter who turned against the president. At the peak of Coughlin's popularity, one-third of the nation tuned in to the weekly radio broadcasts of the "radio priest." His program, featuring religious messages and political commentary, was sharply critical of the nation's bankers and financial leaders. When Coughlin concluded that the president was not doing enough to curb their power, he called the president "Franklin Double-Crossing Roosevelt."

Coughlin also began to attack leading Jewish figures in the administration and elsewhere. As his speeches became more extreme,

---

Political Cartoon

The New Deal represented a great change in the role of the federal government in the lives of Americans. Government agencies became involved in people's business and personal lives in many new ways—and not everyone was pleased with the results.

This long line of eager scholars represent government officials carrying out New Deal programs.

UNCLE "GUINEA PIG"

NEW DEAL CLINIC

IT'S MY TURN AFTER YOU!

TRY OUT YOUR EXPERIMENT BEFORE THE PATIENT WAKES UP.

I HOPE THEY DON'T WEAR HIM OUT BEFORE I HAVE A CHANCE TO TRY MY EXPERIMENT.

U.S.A.

ETHER PROPAGANDA

The United States is depicted as a patient under anesthesia.

Skills FOCUS   READING LIKE A HISTORIAN

1. **Interpreting Political Cartoons** What does this cartoon suggest is happening to Uncle Guinea Pig?

2. **Drawing Conclusions** Does this cartoon present a positive view of the New Deal? Explain.

See **Skills Handbook,** p. H31

Coughlin began to lose influence with the American people. Eventually, the Catholic Church forced him to end his radio program.

Dr. Francis Townsend criticized the New Deal for not doing enough for older Americans. He proposed a plan for providing pensions to people over the age of 60. Like Long and Coughlin, Townsend attracted millions of followers. Some of his ideas would later help shape the thinking and policies of President Roosevelt.

The American Liberty League spoke for many conservatives who felt the New Deal had gone too far. The League drew members from both parties, including former Democratic presidential candidate Al Smith. It also included a number of wealthy business leaders, who believed the New Deal's policies were antibusiness. But despite spending thousands of dollars to defeat New Deal candidates in elections, the League met with little success.

Opposition from the courts The American people supported the New Deal's attempts to bring change to the economy. The courts, however, were more skeptical.

The New Deal changed in basic ways the relationship between the American people and their government. It also threatened to alter the balance of power among the president, the Congress, and the courts. Critics feared that the New Deal gave the president too much power over other branches of government. Presidentially appointed administrators, rather than Congress, were now making rules affecting millions of people. Some critics argued that these changes violated the Constitution.

By 1935 New Deal cases were making their way to the Supreme Court. Their decisions delivered a series of sharp blows to Roosevelt's program. For example, in May 1935, the Supreme Court issued a ruling in *Schechter Poultry Corporation* v. *United States* that destroyed key parts of the NIRA. (See the Landmark Supreme Court Cases feature at the end of this section.) In 1936 the court's ruling in *United States* v. *Butler* found a key part of the AAA—the tax used to raise the money for farmer subsidies—unconstitutional.

The courts managed do what the New Deal's critics had failed to accomplish over the course of two years. As Roosevelt faced re-election in 1936, he continued to enjoy wide popularity among voters. Yet parts of his ambitious economic program were in shambles. Meanwhile, the Great Depression remained a grim fact of life for millions of Americans.

READING CHECK **Summarizing** What were the two major types of complaints about the New Deal during Roosevelt's first term in office?

go.hrw.com
Online Quiz
Keyword: SD7 HP22

SECTION 1 ASSESSMENT

Reviewing Ideas, Terms, and People

1. a. Define Write a brief definition for the following term: public works
  b. Explain What factors made Roosevelt a good choice for the Democratic nomination in 1932?
  c. Evaluate Defend Roosevelt's campaign strategy in 1932.

2. a. Describe What were Roosevelt's **fireside chats**?
  b. Analyze How did Franklin Roosevelt's beliefs about government represent a change from those of Hoover?
  c. Compare Compare **Eleanor Roosevelt** to First Ladies who came before her.

3. a. Define Write a brief definition of the following terms: **Hundred Days, New Deal, subsidy**
  b. Draw Conclusions Why do you think Roosevelt's first act as president was to try to restore confidence in the nation's banking system?
  c. Rank Of the three main goals—relief, recovery, and reform—which do you think was most important? Explain.

4. a. Identify Identify at least three major critics of the New Deal in its early years.
  b. Compare What viewpoint did **Huey P. Long, Father Coughlin**, and **Dr. Francis Townsend** share in common?
  c. Predict How do you think the decisions of the Supreme Court will affect Roosevelt in the future?

Critical Thinking

5. Sequence Copy the chart below and use information from the section to record events in sequence.

FDR elected → □ → □ → □

FOCUS ON WRITING

6. Persuasive Write a letter to the editor in which you either defend or criticize Roosevelt's New Deal programs. Use details from the section to support your position.

HISTORY & Geography ★ Interactive

The Tennessee Valley Authority

The Tennessee Valley Authority (TVA) was one of the New Deal's largest projects. It brought affordable electricity to thousands of rural citizens, improved river navigation, controlled flooding, and introduced modern farming techniques to failing farmers. It fit with President Roosevelt's interests in conservation, government-owned utilities, agricultural development, and improving the lives of "Forgotten Americans."

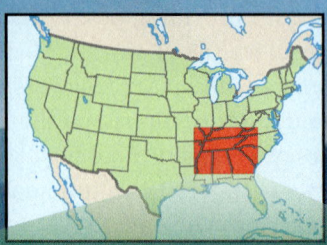

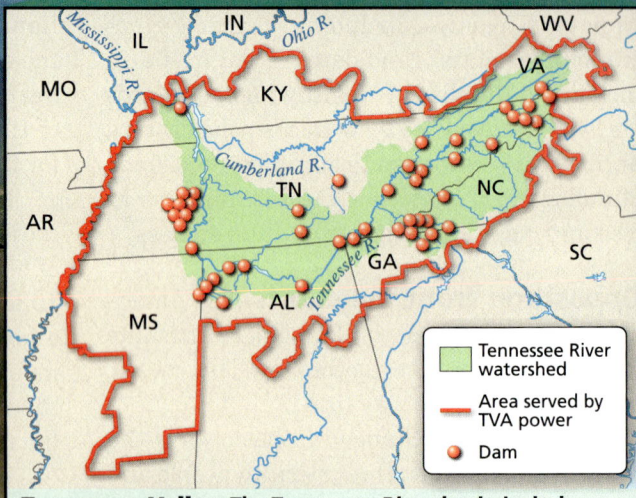

Tennessee Valley The Tennessee River basin includes parts of seven states.

Locks
Locks allow boats to travel past the dams on the river. Today, about 34,000 barges carrying 50 million tons navigate through the locks annually.

Navigational Dams
The dams in the Tennessee River serve to manage navigation and flooding. Droughts, floods, fast currents, and rocky shoals were hazards to earlier shipping. Now nine river dams maintain a water level deep enough for the barges.

New York Standards

ST 1.2 Analyze the decisions leading to major turning points in United States history, comparing alternative courses of action, and hypothesizing, within the context of the historic period, about what might have happened if the decision had been different. Investigate decisions and actions such as: Roosevelt's New Deal.

Electricity for Farms

By the 1930s, only 10 percent of rural dwellers had electricity, while 90 percent of urbanites did. Isolated farmers couldn't keep food cold or turn on a light. The Roosevelt Administration thought the government should provide electricity to citizens not yet served by private companies.

Hydroelectric Dams

The dams built on the rivers that flow into the Tennessee River are high dams backed by huge reservoirs. These dams generated the cheap electricity needed to improve lives and lure industries that would provide jobs to the region.

Farming Practices

Many Tennessee Valley farmers used methods that depleted and eroded the soil. The TVA taught farmers how to use crop rotation and plants like alfalfa and clover to enrich and conserve the soil.

GEOGRAPHY SKILLS INTERPRETING MAPS

go.hrw.com
Interactive Map
Keyword: SD7 CH22

1. Location Why was the Tennessee Valley a good location for this New Deal project?

2. Movement How did the TVA help boats navigate the river?

See **Skills Handbook,** p. H20

ST 1.2 Analyze the decisions leading to major turning points in United States history, comparing alternative courses of action, and hypothesizing, within the context of the historical period, about what might have happened if the decision had been different.

Schechter Poultry Corporation v. United States (1935)

Why It Matters Can Congress broadly delegate its lawmaking authority to the administrative agencies of the executive branch? That was the question the Court faced in *Schechter*. The Court's negative ruling temporarily derailed President Franklin D. Roosevelt's New Deal program. However, it also forced Roosevelt and Congress to tailor future legislation more narrowly.

Background of the Case

In 1933 President Roosevelt created the National Recovery Administration (NRA). The NRA supervised the development of mandatory industry-wide codes for production, prices, and wages. The standards carried the force of law. The Schechter Corporation appealed after it was convicted of violating the minimum wage and maximum hour provisions of the code for the live poultry industry.

The Decision

In its unanimous decision, the Court cited two grounds for finding the mandatory code system unconstitutional. First, it ruled that the delegation of rulemaking authority to an agency of the executive branch violated the constitutional separation of powers. The Constitution places all legislative power in the Congress. Rules or codes having the force of law could only be made by Congress, not by the executive branch.

Second, the Court ruled that the activities of the Schechter Corporation were not subject to congressional regulation. Under the commerce clause, Congress can regulate interstate commerce (conducted in more than one state), not intrastate commerce (conducted entirely within a single state). The Schechter Corporation bought and sold its chickens almost exclusively within New York State. So the commerce clause did not apply to the way that Schecter conducted business.

THE IMPACT TODAY The Supreme Court later took an expanded view of the commerce clause and gave Congress more authority to delegate lawmaking authority to administrative agencies. Today there is widespread governmental regulation of business and economic matters. Much of the regulation is done by administrative agencies within the executive branch. Above, President George W. Bush meets with Senate leaders to discuss energy policy.

go.hrw.com
Research Online
Keyword: SS Court

CRITICAL THINKING

1. **Analyze the Impact** Using the keyword above, read about the Interstate Commerce Commission. What does the Commission do? If *Schechter* had been ruled differently, what aspects of the commission today would have created constitutional problems?

2. **You Be the Judge** The Gun Free School Zones Act of 1990 made it a federal crime for an individual knowingly to possess a firearm in a school zone. Does the act exceed Congress's power to legislate under the Commerce Clause? State the arguments for and against the law's constitutionality.

The Second New Deal

BEFORE YOU READ

MAIN IDEA

A new wave of government initiatives starting in 1935 resulted in some strong successes and stunning defeats for President Roosevelt.

READING FOCUS

1. What were the key programs in the Second Hundred Days?
2. How did New Deal programs help to revive organized labor?
3. What were the key events of the 1936 election?
4. Why was 1937 a troubled year for Roosevelt and the Second New Deal?

KEY TERMS AND PEOPLE

Second New Deal
Social Security
John L. Lewis
CIO
sit-down strike
deficit
John Maynard Keynes

P1 1.2 Describe the evolution of American democratic values and beliefs as expressed in the Declaration of Independence, the New York State Constitution, the United States Constitution, the Bill of Rights, and other important historical documents.

How do you restore hope to the hopeless? The New Deal did not end the Great Depression. Yet the sense of forward movement it created helped give people hope.

Starting in 1935, government increased its commitment to work relief. Earlier programs such as the Civilian Conservation Corps (CCC) had shown how such programs provided not just a source of income but also a sense of purpose and dignity. One worker described how hard work in the CCC transformed his body and mind: "[Y]ou must go through the actual experience before you can really understand the hopeless state of mind most of the prospective members of the CCC were in when we put on our 'G.I.' clothing and

tramped half-heartedly into the forests and fields to plant and cut trees, build dams,… fire breaks and trails, control insect pests, tree diseases, and risk our lives… protecting the forests from the most efficient of destructive forces—Fire. But our don't-care-what-happens attitude didn't last long.… I am making my own way and that is sufficient for the present. What is probably more important is the fact that I am not the undernourished, furtive-eyed, scared kid that went in … over five years ago. Instead, my eyes are clear and my mind is receptive to whatever the future has in store. In short, the CCC has equipped me with the weapons necessary to cope with the innumerable problems that are bound to obstruct my path through life and that must be surmounted before success can be attained."

Working for Dignity

▼ Millions of Americans were uplifted by New Deal work-relief programs.

The Second Hundred Days

With public support for the president and the New Deal running high, the Democratic Party rolled to an unprecedented victory in the congressional elections of 1934. For the first time in U.S. history, the party in control of the White House gained seats in both houses of Congress in a midterm election.

When the new Congress took office in 1935, Democrats held three-quarters of all seats. It was a clear vote of confidence in Roosevelt. As one journalist remarked, "He has been all but crowned by the people."

Roosevelt's victory, however, threatened to be a hollow one. The courts were in the process of finding major parts of the New Deal unconstitutional. The economy was proving stubbornly resistant to recovery. Meanwhile, more-liberal elements in the country were clamoring for the president to do more.

And he did do more. In a flurry of activity in the spring of 1935, during a period called the Second Hundred Days, Roosevelt launched the so-called **Second New Deal**. In short order, Congress passed laws extending government oversight of the banking industry and raising taxes for the wealthy. It funded new relief programs for the still-struggling population.

Emergency relief The major relief legislation of the Second New Deal marked a shift from Roosevelt's earlier programs. The Emergency Relief Appropriations Act largely did away with direct payments to Americans in need. As you have read, the Second New Deal expanded on what had been a small but successful part of the first New Deal: work relief. From now on, said the president, people should work for pay.

HISTORY'S VOICES

❝[C]ontinued dependence upon relief [brings about] a spiritual and moral disintegration . . . destructive to the national fiber. To dole out relief in this way is to administer a narcotic, a subtle destroyer of the human spirit.❞

—Franklin Delano Roosevelt,
State of the Union Address, 1935

The new Works Progress Administration (WPA), created in 1935, was the largest peacetime jobs program in U.S. history. It eventually employed 8.5 million Americans on all kinds of public-works projects at a cost of about $11 billion.

WPA workers built roads, subways, airports, even zoos. They worked in offices, schools, museums, and factories. They ventured into the fields to record the oral histories of former

Murals of the New Deal

Men operating air drills and rope work the dangerously steep slopes of the canyon.

Workers operating a heavy crane hoist a huge conduit above a canyon.

slaves. The WPA even funded the efforts of artists, writers, composers, and actors. A number of soon-to-be-famous figures got their starts in the program, including artist Jackson Pollock and writers Ralph Ellison, Richard Wright, and Eudora Welty.

At its peak, the WPA employed some 3.4 million formerly jobless Americans. This amounted to nearly a fourth of the unemployed people in the country.

As Roosevelt had hoped, getting the opportunity to earn a paycheck rather than get a handout lifted people's spirits. As one worker put it, "You worked, you got a paycheck and you had some dignity."

Social Security A centerpiece of the Second New Deal was the Social Security Act, signed in August 1935. This law created a system called **Social Security**, which provided a pension, or guaranteed, regular payments, for many people 65 and older.

With the creation of Social Security, many retired workers no longer needed to fear hunger and homelessness once they became too old to work. The Social Security Act also included a system of unemployment insurance run jointly by the federal government and the states. This program provided payments to workers who lost their jobs, giving them a financial cushion while they looked for new work. To fund the programs, Congress passed new taxes that affected both workers and employers.

In promoting Social Security, Roosevelt responded to a number of his critics. For example, in helping older Americans, Roosevelt hoped to undermine the attacks of Dr. Francis Townsend, the California doctor whose plan for older Americans had attracted so many supporters. The president hinted to nervous lawmakers that his own plan was preferable to Townsend's more radical design.

Funding Social Security, however, posed problems. To avoid a huge tax hike that could hamper economic recovery, Roosevelt agreed to exclude certain workers from the new program. "Everybody ought to be in on it," Roosevelt had argued. In the end, millions of Americans, including farmworkers, household workers, and government employees, were left out of Social Security.

READING CHECK **Summarizing** What were two major elements of the Second New Deal?

Reviving Organized Labor

After setbacks during the 1920s, the passage of the NIRA during the first New Deal marked a major step forward for organized labor. It guaranteed workers the right to form unions and bargain collectively. Yet many businesses ignored the new rules, vigorously battling the growth of unions. In 1934, unions lost a number of major strikes, as labor-related violence increased.

A cautious FDR was unwilling to push business too hard to accept labor's new powers. In addition, under NIRA's terms, government had little power to force business cooperation.

When NIRA was fatally weakened by the Supreme Court's ruling in *Schechter*, Roosevelt recognized the need to act on behalf of labor. He threw his support behind a new labor law, the Wagner Act (named for its sponsor, Senator Robert Wagner of New York).

The law, also known as the National Labor Relations Act, was stronger than NIRA. The act outlawed a number of antilabor practices, such as the creation of company-sponsored unions. It also established a powerful new National Labor Relations Board. The NLRB was given

Government
The public today has come to depend heavily on Social Security. The cost to workers and employers for funding this program have risen steadily, and payments have risen as more and more Americans live longer and longer lives.

The WPA paid artists to create public art. *Construction of the Dam,* a mural by William Gropper, shows workers on a WPA construction project.

A group of muscular men put together a large section of steel framework.

MAJOR NEW DEAL PROGRAMS

Relief

Civilian Conservation Corps (CCC), 1933 Provided jobs on conservation projects to young men whose families needed relief

Federal Emergency Relief Administration (FERA), 1933 Provided grants to states for direct relief to the needy

Public Works Administration (PWA), 1933 Provided public-works jobs for many of those needing relief

Civil Works Administration (CWA), 1933 Provided public-works jobs for many of those needing relief

Works Progress Administration (WPA), 1935 Provided public-works jobs on a wide range of projects for many of those needing relief

Social Security Act, 1935 Established pensions for retirees, unemployment insurance, and aid for certain groups of low-income or disabled people

Farm Security Administration (FSA), 1937 Provided assistance to tenant farmers to help them purchase land or establish cooperatives

Reform

Emergency Banking Act, 1933 Gave federal government power to reorganize and strengthen banks

Federal Deposit Insurance Corporation (FDIC), 1933 Established an insurance program for deposits in many banks

Securities and Exchange Commission (SEC), 1934 Provided increased government regulation of the trading on stock exchanges

National Labor Relations Act (NLRB), 1935 Established the National Labor Relations Board to enforce labor laws

Fair Labor Standards Act (Wages and Hours Law), 1938 Established minimum wages and maximum hours for many workers

Recovery

Agricultural Adjustment Administration (AAA), 1933 Encouraged farmers to cut production in return for a subsidy

Tennessee Valley Authority (TVA), 1933 Promoted development projects for the Tennessee River Valley—for example, to improve navigation, produce electricity, and control floods

National Industrial Recovery Act (NIRA), 1933 Encouraged cooperation among businesses in establishing production and labor practices

Federal Housing Administration (FHA), 1934 Encouraged loans for renovating or building homes

Rural Electrification Administration (REA), 1935 Encouraged the delivery of electricity to rural areas

Programs in red are still in existence.

the authority to conduct voting in workplaces to determine whether employees wanted union representation. The NLRB could require businesses to accept the voting results. With these new legal tools, organized labor membership surged by millions in the years to come.

The CIO is born The passage of the Wagner Act roughly coincided with a major change in the American labor movement. A new union devoted to the interests of industrial workers arose to challenge the traditional hold of the nation's largest union, the American Federation of Labor (AFL).

The AFL was created as a collection, or federation, of smaller unions representing the interests of skilled workers. These smaller unions were organized within specific crafts rather than across broad industries, such as the auto or steel industries. In general, the AFL looked down on unskilled factory workers, many of whom were immigrants.

The growth of mass production in the 1920s, however, greatly swelled the ranks of unskilled workers. **John L. Lewis**, head of the United Mine Workers, recognized this opportunity. He sought to take advantage of it.

A fiery speaker and organizer, Lewis led a group that broke away from the AFL in 1935 to form the Committee for Industrial Organization, or **CIO.** (The CIO later changed its name to the Congress of Industrial Organizations.) It was not long before Lewis and his new organization would make their mark.

The GM sit-down strike In December 1936 the United Auto Workers, which was part of the CIO, launched a new kind of strike. Workers at the General Motors (GM) plant in Flint, Michigan, simply sat down inside the factory and stopped working.

A **sit-down strike**, as it was called, required the strikers to stay at the factory day and night until the dispute was resolved. They relied on supporters outside the factory to provide food and to look after their families at home.

The sit-down strike created a complicated situation for GM. It could not use traditional methods of strike breaking—bringing in security forces to scatter the picket line and hiring non-union "scab" labor to run the factory. Any effort to take back the factory might turn violent. Valuable property inside the factory could be destroyed, and the risk of negative publicity, such as images of workers being beaten or killed, was too high.

GM asked the state government for help in removing the workers, but Michigan's governor refused. The company tried shutting off heat and water to the factory, but the strikers stayed on. When the police tried shutting off food deliveries to the factory, workers rioted. A brief battle raged between striking workers and the police until the police withdrew.

The sit-down strike was hard on the workers, but it was harder still on GM. The shutdown cost the automaker tens of millions of dollars a week in sales. After a tense six weeks, GM finally gave in and agreed to recognize the union. The workers had won.

It was an enormous victory for labor—and for the CIO. Along with a successful action against the United States Steel Corporation in 1937, the General Motors strike helped establish the CIO as a major force in American organized labor.

HISTORY'S VOICES

❝When [GM executive William] Knudsen put his name to a piece of paper and says that General Motors recognizes UAW-CIO—until that moment we were non-people, we didn't even exist. That was the big one.❞

—Bob Stinson, sit-down striker, recorded in *Hard Times*

The CIO and other labor unions did not win every confrontation with American business in the 1930s. Indeed, unions suffered some serious losses later in the decade. Yet union membership continued to grow. By the early 1940s, nearly one-fourth of the American workforce was unionized.

READING CHECK **Identifying Cause and Effect** How did the Wagner Act work to revive labor?

GM Sit-Down Strike

Strikers make themselves as comfortable as possible on the floor of the GM plant at Flint, Michigan.

GROWTH OF UNION MEMBERSHIP, 1933–1940

Union members (in millions) by Year

Source: *Historical Statistics of the United States*

Skills FOCUS **INTERPRETING GRAPHS**

The NLRB and the CIO strengthened unions. **Compare** What was union membership in 1933? What was it in 1939?

See **Skills Handbook**, p. H17

The Election of 1936

As President Roosevelt entered the election year of 1936, he could look back on a productive 1935. He also knew there was more to be done before he faced the voters in November.

Rural electricity One goal was to provide additional help to rural Americans. Toward this end, Roosevelt in May signed the Rural Electrification Act. It empowered the Rural Electrification Administration (REA) to loan money to farm cooperatives and other groups trying to bring electricity to people living outside of cities and towns. In many areas, for-profit power companies had been unwilling to put in the miles of power lines needed to serve remote, sparsely settled areas. Under the REA, the numbers of rural homes with electricity grew from 10 percent to 90 percent in about a decade. Millions of farmers were finally able to enjoy the benefits of electricity.

Americans re-elect Roosevelt President Roosevelt campaigned on a solid record of legislative achievement. He also pointed to significant improvements in the economy. Unemployment, though still high, had been sliced in half. Personal incomes and corporate earnings were up sharply. New Deal programs had given hope and help to millions, even if they had not brought about full economic recovery.

In the 1936 campaign, Roosevelt virtually ignored the Republican nominee, Governor Alf Landon of Kansas. Landon's mildly reformist positions supporting organized labor and aid to the unemployed and elderly posed no serious threat. Roosevelt also faced no serious competition from the Union Party, a new party formed by Father Charles Coughlin and Dr. Francis Townsend.

Appealing to potential Union Party supporters, Roosevelt gave speeches thundering against big business. Business leaders responded with alarm, again pouring money into the American Liberty League. To some of them, the New Deal amounted to a revolution.

HISTORY'S VOICES

❝The history of these past three years will be written in the future as the history of an American revolution which was engineered and carried on under the unseeing eyes of one hundred and thirty million citizens.❞

—Senator Lester Dickinson,
The American Mercury, February 1936

In a bitterly waged campaign, Republicans attacked Roosevelt's New Deal for being overly bureaucratic and creating a planned economy.

On election day, however, the American voters again handed Roosevelt a tremendous victory. Landon carried only two states. The ineffective Union Party candidate polled less than 2 percent of the popular vote. The Democrats again gained in both houses of Congress. They also won 26 of the 33 races for governor.

The electoral landslide also confirmed a momentous shift in American politics. African Americans in the North switched from the party of Lincoln to the Democratic Party.

READING CHECK **Identifying Supporting Details** What evidence can you find to suggest that the 1936 election showed widespread support for Roosevelt and the New Deal?

THE IMPACT TODAY

Technology

In what is seen as a parallel to rural electrification in the 1930s, Congress has earmarked funds to help bring high-speed Internet service to rural America today.

Historically, African Americans had supported the Republicans, the party of Lincoln. In 1936, however, a majority of African American voters chose Roosevelt and the Democrats—a shift in loyalty that has continued to this day.

Political Cartoon

President Roosevelt was very upset when the Supreme Court struck down some of the key provisions of the New Deal. To protect his new reforms, he attempted to "pack" the Court by adding more justices. Congress stopped this effort, marking one of the few great political defeats for the popular president. Many critics feared that such a change would threaten the balance of powers as spelled out in the U.S. Constitution. The following political cartoon originally included a caption that read, "Oh, So That's the Kind of a Sailor He Is!"

Skills FOCUS   READING LIKE A HISTORIAN

1. **Contrasting** How do the expressions of the captain and the sailor reflect different views of the court-packing plan?
2. **Interpreting Political Cartoons** Why do you think the artist chose this imagery?

See **Skills Handbook**, pp. H10, H31

On a ship, if a compass showed that the vessel was sailing in the wrong direction, the captain would change course, not demand a new compass.

THAT COMPASS DOESN'T POINT THE WAY I WANT TO GO. CHANGE IT. NOW!

The nation is frequently referred to as the "ship of state." The captain of the ship represented Roosevelt. The cartoonist may also have been referring to Roosevelt's early career as assistant secretary of the navy.

The sailor, whose instinct is to obey the ship's captain, represents the Democrat-controlled Congress, which here is shown reacting in alarm.

A Troubled Year

Never before had Roosevelt seemed more in command than when he began his second term. His determination to overcome obstacles to his programs, however, led to a serious misstep.

The court-packing plan Frustrated that the courts had struck down many New Deal programs, Roosevelt surprised Congress with a plan to reorganize the nation's courts. The plan would give the president power to appoint many new judges and expand the Supreme Court by up to six justices. The president argued that changes were needed to make the courts more efficient. Most observers, however, saw it as a clumsy effort to "pack" the Supreme Court with friendly justices—and a dangerous attempt to upset the constitutional balance of power. Even the president's supporters were troubled.

The battle over Roosevelt's proposal occupied Congress for much of 1937. Even members of the president's own party began to desert him. In the end, the president who had begun the year looking invincible ended it with a crushing loss.

HISTORY'S VOICES

❝Roosevelt moved against the court more boldly and directly than any other President had ever done. Public opinion then swung to the defense of the court, and F. D. R. suffered the most humiliating defeat of his career.❞

—Merlo J. Pusey, *American Heritage,* April 1958

Moving forward President Roosevelt lost much of the year in his doomed battle over expanding the Supreme Court. Congress, however, did enact some major legislation in 1937.

The Farm Tenancy Act aided some of the poorest of the nation's poor—tenant farmers and sharecroppers. Many had been forced off the land as a result of New Deal programs that paid landowners to take fields out of production. The new law gave tenants and sharecroppers a chance to buy land of their own.

Roosevelt also won some important victories in an unlikely place—the Supreme Court. Even as he was trying to push through his court-packing plan, the Court handed down rulings that favored key New Deal programs. In March 1937 the Court upheld a rather

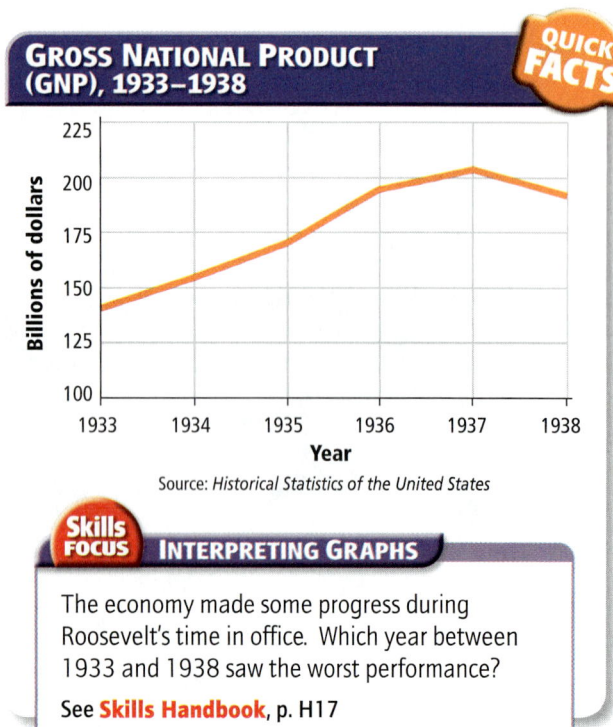

GROSS NATIONAL PRODUCT (GNP), 1933–1938

QUICK FACTS

Source: *Historical Statistics of the United States*

Skills FOCUS INTERPRETING GRAPHS

The economy made some progress during Roosevelt's time in office. Which year between 1933 and 1938 saw the worst performance?

See **Skills Handbook**, p. H17

ACADEMIC VOCABULARY

classical well known, original

controversial Washington State law requiring a minimum wage for workers. The ruling signaled a new willingness to let legislatures regulate the economy—a decision with clear implications for the New Deal.

In April the Court also ruled clearly in favor of a key element of the Wagner Act. In May it declared Roosevelt's Social Security plan to be constitutional.

The favorable rulings pleased Roosevelt. They effectively killed any remaining support for his court-packing plan, however.

Recovery in doubt In the fall of 1937, the nation's economy suffered another setback. It began in a familiar way with a sharp drop in the stock market. By the time the year was over, about 2 million more Americans had lost their jobs.

The return of hard times changed Roosevelt's plans. He had hoped to cut back on government spending, fearing the growing federal budget **deficit**. A deficit occurs when a government spends more money than it takes in through taxes and other income. But as unemployment rose in late 1937 and early 1938, Roosevelt again found himself seeking large sums of money to help the unemployed.

Roosevelt may have been troubled by deficits, but the new spending was supported by the theories of British economist **John Maynard Keynes**. Contrary to <u>classical</u> economic theory, which stressed balanced budgets, Keynes argued that deficit spending could provide jobs and stimulate the economy.

In fact, the economy did begin to rebound in the summer of 1938. By then, however, the positive feelings about Roosevelt and the New Deal had begun to fade.

READING CHECK **Sequencing** What events made 1937 a troubled year for President Roosevelt?

SECTION 2 ASSESSMENT

**go.hrw.com
Online Quiz**
Keyword: SD7 HP22

Reviewing Ideas, Terms, and People

1. a. Identify Identify the significance of the following terms: Second New Deal, Social Security
b. Make Inferences What lessons did Roosevelt draw from the 1934 election?
c. Evaluate What do you think of Roosevelt's decision to cut back on programs that provided relief without work?

2. a. Identify What was the CIO?
b. Explain What factors contributed to labor's growth after 1935?
c. Rank Which do you think was more important in labor's success: the passage of the Wagner Act or the success of the sit-down strikes? Explain.

3. a. Recall What was Roosevelt's 1936 election strategy?
b. Summarize What were the results of the 1936 election?

4. a. Identify Identify the significance of the following: **deficit, John Maynard Keynes**
b. Summarize Why did the court-packing plan cause so much damage to Roosevelt?

Critical Thinking

5. Understand Cause and Effect Copy the chart below and use information from the section to fill it in.

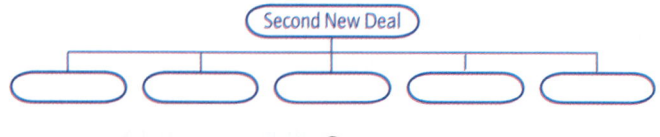

FOCUS ON SPEAKING

6. Persuasive Deliver a speech in which you argue for or against Roosevelt's court-reorganization plan.

Life during the New Deal

BEFORE YOU READ

MAIN IDEA

The Great Depression and the New Deal had a deep impact on American culture during the 1930s.

READING FOCUS

1. How did the public roles of women and African Americans change during the New Deal?

2. How did artists and writers of the era tell the story of the Great Depression?

3. What forms of popular entertainment were popular during the Great Depression?

KEY TERMS AND PEOPLE

Frances Perkins
Black Cabinet
Mary McLeod Bethune
Dorothea Lange
swing

PI 3.1 Compare and contrast the experiences of different ethnic, national, and religious groups, including Native American Indians, in the United States, explaining their contributions to American society and culture.

The Best Woman for the Job

▼ Labor Secretary Frances Perkins on the job

 *How did one woman help to change public views of women in government?*

"[M]en will take advice from a woman, but it is hard for them to take orders from a woman." That was a bit of counsel Franklin Roosevelt received when he was considering naming Frances Perkins to a key post in his administration.

Women's suffrage was not yet a decade old when Roosevelt, as New York's governor, made Perkins the top labor official in the state. When Roosevelt became president, he named Perkins to be his secretary of labor—the first woman ever to serve in the cabinet.

Born in Boston, Massachusetts, Perkins was already a social reformer when she witnessed the Triangle Shirtwaist Factory fire in New York City in 1911. That gruesome tragedy, in which 146 people died, spurred her interest in working to improve conditions in the workplace.

During her time in Washington, her tireless efforts and great skill won her many admirers—and the grudging respect of her enemies. Perkins played a central role in the creation of many New Deal programs, and she led the White House team that created the Social Security system.

Perkins served in Roosevelt's cabinet from 1933 until after his death in 1945. Her example advanced the cause of women in government. ◼

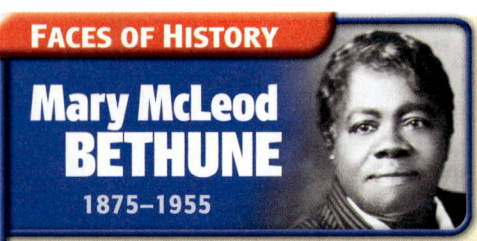
New Roles for Women and African Americans

The New Deal brought great change in American life and society. Under the pressure of an economic emergency, old ways of doing things gave way to new. For women and African Americans, these changes brought hope for an expanded role in public life.

Women in the New Deal As you read in Section 1, Eleanor Roosevelt played a major role in her husband's administration. In addition to her tireless support for her husband's programs, she actively pursued issues of importance to women, helping leaders of women's groups gain access to the president.

THE IMPACT TODAY

Government

Today it is commonplace for women, African Americans, and members of other minorities to fill cabinet and other top government posts. They continue, however, to hold a relatively small share of these positions.

HISTORY'S VOICES

❝When I wanted help on some definite point, Mrs. Roosevelt gave me the opportunity to sit by the president at dinner and the matter was settled before we finished our soup.❞

—Molly Dewson, quoted in *Beyond Suffrage* by Susan Ware, 1981

Other women besides the First Lady served in prominent government posts during the New Deal, none more so than Secretary of Labor **Frances Perkins**. As the first woman to head an executive department, Perkins played a leading role in the formation of major New Deal policies. This included, as you have read, the

Social Security system. Perkins, however, was not the only prominent woman in the government. Ruth Bryan Owen, daughter of three-time presidential candidate William Jennings Bryan, served as minister to Denmark. Roosevelt also appointed women to such posts as director of the U.S. Mint and assistant secretary of the Treasury . Women served as leaders in several New Deal agencies. In short, Roosevelt's record at promoting and recognizing women was simply unmatched for his time.

Still, women faced challenges and discrimination. New Deal programs, for example, generally paid men higher wages than women in work-relief jobs. Men continued to enjoy far more work opportunities. The attitude in the wider world to women in the workforce ranged from grudging acceptance to outright hostility. For example, one journalist put forward his idea for solving unemployment: "Simply fire the women, who shouldn't be working anyway, and hire the men. Presto! No unemployment."

African Americans in the New Deal

Roosevelt's administration also broke new ground in appointing African Americans. William Hastie, for example, became the first black federal judge in U.S. history. African Americans were also hired to fill posts in the government. A group of these officials, known as the **Black Cabinet**, met under the leadership of **Mary McLeod Bethune**, director of Negro Affairs in the National Youth Administration.

The Black Cabinet acted as unofficial advisers to the president. They stood as a powerful symbol of rising African American influence in government. In addition, First Lady Eleanor Roosevelt visibly championed civil rights, frequently staking out bold positions in advance of what her husband felt he could take.

Still, African Americans continued to face tremendous hardships in the 1930s. New Deal programs left largely unchallenged the discrimination that African Americans faced in the larger society. In addition, thousands of African American sharecroppers and tenant farmers suffered terribly. Many never saw real benefit from any New Deal program.

Roosevelt often explained his record with respect to African Americans by saying he was at the mercy of southern Democrats in Congress. Many of these legislators strongly opposed efforts to aid African Americans.

Roosevelt felt that angering southern Democrats would jeopardize the entire New Deal. "They will block every bill I ask Congress to pass to keep America from collapsing," he told the head of the NAACP when he was pressed to support an antilynching law. "I just can't take that risk."

Although President Roosevelt's record was not perfect, African American voters apparently decided that their best hopes lay with the Democratic Party. Staunchly Republican since the Civil War, a majority of African Americans for the first time in history voted Democratic in the 1934 midterm elections. As you have read, this support continued in the 1936 presidential election as well.

READING CHECK **Making Generalizations**
What was the overall effect of Roosevelt's policies on women and African Americans in the 1930s?

Telling the Story of the Depression

Responding to unprecedented economic calamity, artists showed a new interest in social problems and activism. Painters and sculptors fashioned works depicting the struggles of the working class. Authors and playwrights focused on the plight of the rural and urban poor. For example, you read in the last chapter about John Steinbeck's moving tale of Dust Bowl refugees, *The Grapes of Wrath*. Songwriter Woody Guthrie celebrated the grandeur of America and the lives of ordinary people.

The work of Dorothea Lange
Photographer **Dorothea Lange** was another celebrated chronicler of the Great Depression. In her hometown of San Francisco, Lange recorded images of jobless people. Yet her most famous subjects were the rural poor, who were especially hard hit in the 1930s.

Starting in 1935, Lange worked on behalf of the Farm Security Administration. This organization focused on the lives of tenant farmers and sharecroppers. One of her most famous photographs appears at right. These and other pictures helped raise awareness about the poorest of the poor. Indeed, in 1937 the federal government finally began to provide help to tenant farmers and sharecroppers.

IMAGES OF THE GREAT DEPRESSION

Ella Watson, a Washington, D.C. charwoman, with her three children

Gordon Parks

© THE OAKLAND MUSEUM, THE CITY OF OAKLAND

Dorothea Lange

Destitute mother of seven children in California

Skills FOCUS **READING LIKE A HISTORIAN**

Photographers like Gordon Parks and Dorothea Lange were hired to document the plight of the poor and, through their images, gain public support for Roosevelt's New Deal programs.

Interpreting Visuals Do you think these photographs succeed in showing a sympathetic view of their subjects? Explain.

Going to the Movies

At an average of 25 cents a ticket, movies were one of the most affordable forms of entertainment in the 1930s. More than that, movies served the public's emotional needs.

▲ Comedian Charlie Chaplin wrestles with machinery in *Modern Times*, a film that criticized the dehumanizing effects of industry.

Agee, Evans, and *Famous Men* Writer James Agee and photographer Walker Evans also depicted the lives of sharecroppers in the Lower South. Their work, *Let Us Now Praise Famous Men,* focused on a group of families in rural Alabama. This work received little notice when it was first published. Yet Evans's compassionate and unblinking images and Agee's powerful descriptions form a moving record of the reality of rural poverty and the great dignity of those who struggled against it.

READING CHECK **Comparing** How did artists such as Lange, Parks, Agee, and Evans seek to tell the story of the Great Depression?

Popular Entertainment in the 1930s

Despite the hard times of the 1930s, Americans still found the handful of pennies it cost to go to a movie theater. Radio also continued to grow in popularity in the 1930s. A large majority of American households had a radio, and a wide range of programming, including sports, was available.

Movies One study in 1935 showed that nearly 80 million of the nation's 127 million Americans attended a movie each week. Throughout the decade, movie studios produced some 5,000 feature-length films.

A few of these movies focused on the hardships of life during the Great Depression. For example, Steinbeck's *The Grapes of Wrath* was turned into a successful Hollywood film in 1940. Another example of a successful Depression-themed film was *I Am a Fugitive from a Chain Gang*. This told the tale of a jobless man who is lured into a life of crime. *Make Way for Tomorrow* portrayed the financial hardships of an older couple.

For the most part, however, films of the 1930s steered clear of troubling reminders of the hard times gripping the nation. Indeed,

THE GRANGER COLLECTION, NEW YORK

▼ Ginger Rogers and Fred Astaire were the picture of glamour and grace for a downtrodden public.

▲ The Fabulous Fox San Francisco Theatre opened in 1929 with 5,000 seats. Such grand theaters could make moviegoers feel rich, if only for an hour or two at a time.

▲ *King Kong* roared into movie theaters with state-of-the-art special effects in March 1933. In the film's opening week, about 150,000 American moviegoers flocked to the theaters to be frightened by the giant ape.

Skills FOCUS | **INTERPRETING INFOGRAPHICS**

Making Inferences How do you think attending movies like the examples above helped people through the Great Depression? Discuss each example separately, including the theater.

See **Skills Handbook**, p. H7

filmmakers seemed to realize that most Americans went to the movies in an attempt to escape from their own problems—even if only for a couple of hours.

Highly popular in the 1930s were grand musicals featuring glamorous dancers gliding across lavish sets or living it up at posh nightclubs. In the exciting, imaginary lives of characters played by actors such as Fred Astaire and Ginger Rogers, viewers got a glimpse of a life they could only dream about.

Comedy was another popular choice for the public. The Marx Brothers used a zany style to produce a string of hits in the 1930s. Charlie Chaplin continued to be popular. Not only did he make the transition to talkies successfully but he also continued to produce silent movies. The classic *Modern Times* took a hilarious look at a serious subject—the dehumanizing effect of industrial life.

Director Frank Capra captured the spirit of the times in films that combined social themes with a sentimental and comic view of life. Films such as *Mr. Deeds Goes to Town* and *Mr. Smith Goes to Washington* told of the triumph of the "little guy."

The 1930s also saw the introduction of some new moviemaking techniques. For example, Walt Disney's *Snow White and the Seven Dwarfs* was history's first full-length animated feature. It drew huge audiences. *The Wizard of Oz* delighted audiences not only with its charming story and performances but also with the use of color photography and special effects. *Gone with the Wind*, which came out the same year as *The Wizard of Oz*, was also a color blockbuster.

Radio Radio had an important role in American politics. From President Roosevelt's fireside chats to Father Coughlin's rants against the New Deal, radio brought a variety of news and views into millions of American homes.

Of course, radio also provided listeners with religion, music, sports, and other forms of entertainment. Though by today's standards the sound quality was poor, families in living rooms across the country were enthralled by action shows such as *The Lone Ranger* and comedies such as *Fibber McGee and Molly*.

Radio's power to captivate listeners was dramatically demonstrated in October 1938. The actor Orson Welles produced a radio broadcast of the H. G. Wells science fiction tale *The War of the Worlds* that was so realistic, it convinced many panicked listeners that Earth was actually under attack by spaceships from Mars.

Radio helped broaden the appeal of jazz. This vibrant form of music had its roots in African American communities in New Orleans and other big cities. It had spread northward and taken root in cities such as New York. There, performers such as Louis Armstrong dazzled audiences with their ability at improvising.

A new, highly orchestrated type of jazz known as **swing** swept the country in the 1930s. This music tended to feature larger groups of musicians known as big bands. Audiences often danced to the music, performing such steps as the jitterbug or the Lindy Hop (named after Charles Lindbergh).

Swing had its share of African American stars. Duke Ellington and Count Basie were two famous big-band leaders. At the same time, white big-band leaders such as Benny Goodman and the Dorsey Brothers reached audiences that had been untouched by the jazz masters of the 1920s.

Joyous or soulful, the unrestrained moods of jazz were medicine for the times. Said one

critic, "This was the Depression. It was not an easy period. And this was a music that was just pure pleasure. Pure physical pleasure."

Sports in the 1930s The 1920s is widely regarded as the golden age of sports. The Great Depression did limit the ability of many Americans to buy tickets and attend events in person. Nevertheless, interest in sports remained quite strong.

Baseball remained a popular attraction. The legendary Babe Ruth, who had become a huge star in the 1920s, continued his career until the mid-1930s. He was soon replaced on the roster of the New York Yankees by a new star—the great Joe DiMaggio.

Meanwhile, former Ruth teammate Lou Gehrig stirred the emotions of the nation when, stricken with a terrible illness that would soon end his life, he ended his record streak of consecutive games played.

Sports fans also thrilled to the exploits of Babe Didrikson Zaharias. A multisport star, Zaharias won fame for her talents in softball, golf, basketball, and track and field.

Boxing was hugely popular in the 1930s. The big star was heavyweight fighter Joe Louis. His 1938 bout against German Max Schmeling came to represent the growing conflict between Germany and the United States. You will read more about this contest in the next chapter.

READING CHECK **Identifying the Main Idea** How did popular entertainment help Americans cope with the stresses of the Great Depression?

FOCUS ON NEW YORK

DAILY LIFE

One year after acquiring Babe Ruth from the Boston Red Sox, the New York Yankees made another bold move when they announced plans in 1921 for a new ballpark. Yankee Stadium, or "The House That Ruth Built," had a seating capacity of more than 70,000 people and was the sport's first triple-deck ballpark. Its construction signalled the rise of sports entertainment as a big business.

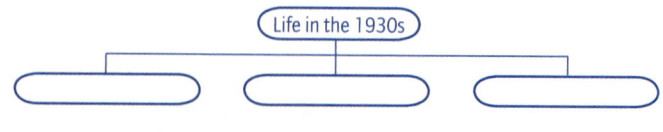

SECTION 3 ASSESSMENT

Reviewing Ideas, Terms, and People

1. a. Identify Who were **Frances Perkins** and **Mary McLeod Bethune**?
b. Make Generalizations How did women and African Americans fare under the policies of the Roosevelt administration?

2. a. Identify Who was **Dorothea Lange**?
b. Make Generalizations Why do you think Lange, Evans, and Agee focused on the plight of sharecroppers and tenant farmers?

3. a. Define Write a brief definition of the following term: **swing**
b. Draw Conclusions What can you conclude about the importance of movies in American life based on the average weekly audience in the 1930s?

Critical Thinking

4. Find Supporting Details Copy the chart below and use information from the section to find supporting details for the main idea given.

Life in the 1930s

FOCUS ON WRITING

5. Descriptive Write a brief description of American popular entertainment in the 1930s, using examples from your reading of the chapter.

Analyzing the New Deal

BEFORE YOU READ

MAIN IDEA

The New Deal had mixed success in rescuing the economy, but it fundamentally changed Americans' relationship with their government.

FOCUS QUESTIONS

1. What was the impact of the New Deal on the nation in the 1930s?
2. In what ways was the impact of the New Deal limited?
3. How did the New Deal come to an end?

KEY TERMS AND PEOPLE

Marian Anderson
minimum wage
incumbent

PI 3.2 Research and analyze the major themes and developments in New York State and United States history (e.g., colonization and settlement; Revolution and New National Period; immigration; expansion and reform era; Civil War and Reconstruction; the American labor movement; Great Depression; World Wars; contemporary United States).

THE INSIDE STORY

How far would white society go to battle racial discrimination in the 1930s? As a musically gifted African American child, **Marian Anderson** got her vocal training the only way she could: singing in the choir at the local church. In time, her talents took her from the choir box to some of the world's most famous concert halls.

Like many African American performers of her day, Anderson went to Europe first to build up her reputation. She returned to America as an international star. But success did not protect her from discrimination at home.

In 1939 Anderson's manager tried to book a concert for her at Constitution Hall in Washington, D.C. The owners of the hall, a prestigious group called the Daughters of the American Revolution (DAR), turned him down, citing a contract clause that said "concert by white artists only."

Many Americans were outraged. Eleanor Roosevelt and other prominent women resigned from the DAR. The First Lady then arranged for Anderson to hold a concert on the steps of the Lincoln Memorial in Washington. Some 75,000 people turned out, hearing Anderson's glorious voice sing the words, "My country, 'tis of thee, sweet land of liberty." Millions heard the national radio broadcast. Anderson later gave a private concert at the White House.

Eleanor Roosevelt's actions on behalf of Marian Anderson were typical of her efforts to aid African Americans. However, the incident also illustrated just how widespread racism was in 1930s America. A principled stand, a public cry of outrage, and groundbreaking symbolism went far in changing attitudes. Indeed, within four years, Constitution Hall changed its whites-only policy and invited Anderson to sing there. Meanwhile, however, there was no move to legally challenge the injustice done to Anderson or the racism it represented. The architects of the New Deal, including President Roosevelt, chose not to fight that battle. ◢

▶ **Marian Anderson performs on the steps of the Lincoln Memorial.**

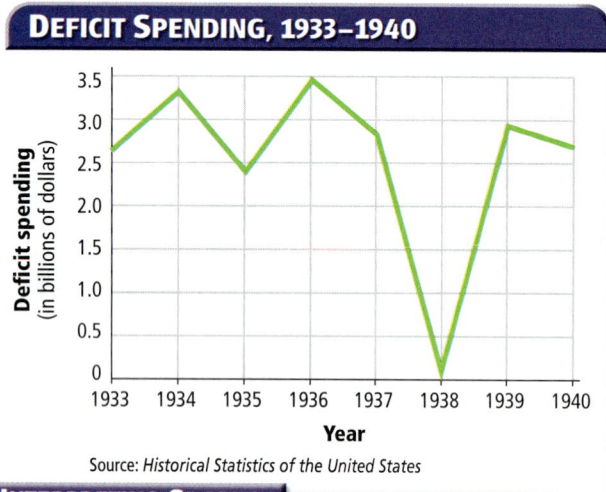

UNEMPLOYMENT, 1933–1940

Percent unemployed

Year

Source: *Historical Statistics of the United States*

DEFICIT SPENDING, 1933–1940

Deficit spending (in billions of dollars)

Year

Source: *Historical Statistics of the United States*

Skills FOCUS INTERPRETING GRAPHS

1. What was the overall trend of unemployment between 1933 and 1940?
2. What was significant about 1938?

See **Skills Handbook**, p. H17

The Impact of the New Deal

From the moment he took office, Franklin Roosevelt knew he faced an economic crisis—and a crisis of spirit. Though he could not hope to please everyone, he knew he had to take action. "Take a method and try it," he said, describing his approach. "If it fails, admit it frankly and try another. But above all, try something."

Relief, recovery, and reform What was the record of the New Deal? Was the promise of relief, recovery, and reform met?

Certainly, the relief programs enacted in 1933 and 1935 put billions of dollars into the pockets of poor Americans. Millions of people enjoyed some form of help, from direct relief to jobs that provided a steady paycheck. Programs such as Social Security and unemployment insurance, moreover, became a fixture of American government.

The New Deal was less successful in delivering economic recovery. Joblessness initially fell from a high of 13 million in 1933 to about 9 million by 1936. Wages, factory output, and other economic indicators rose to levels at or even above those of 1929. Unfortunately, many early gains were wiped out in the downturn of 1937 and 1938. At decade's end, some 10 million workers remained unemployed.

Historians continue to debate the reasons for the New Deal's mixed results. Some argue that Roosevelt's policies, which were never popular with big business, hurt business confidence and slowed the pace of recovery. Others believe that the New Deal was too timid and that real unemployment reduction would have required spending billions more.

New Deal reforms proved more successful—and long-lasting. For example, the Federal Deposit Insurance Corporation helped restore public confidence in the safety of the nation's banks. This was a critical step in stopping the nation's slide into chaos in 1933. The FDIC has continued to serve the nation's economy ever since. Similarly, the Securities and Exchange Commission, established in 1934, helped the public regain faith in the stock markets. Investors today continue to rely on SEC oversight.

The New Deal also left an impressive legacy in the form of thousands of roadways, bridges, dams, and public buildings. The WPA built 2,500 hospitals and nearly 6,000 schools. WPA artists painted over 2,500 murals and erected nearly 18,000 sculptures in public places.

Changing relationships Americans have long argued about whether the New Deal was good or bad for the nation. What is undeniable is that the New Deal changed some basic relationships in American society.

In general, the New Deal changed the link between the American people and their government. The leaders of the 1920s had promoted business as the best way to achieve progress, and they generally viewed government as a barrier to progress. Roosevelt believed that government could help businesses and individuals achieve a greater level of economic security.

The new role for government meant a much bigger government. Dozens of new programs and agencies put people in contact with their government in ways they had not experienced before. Americans now began to look regularly to government for help. Roosevelt and the New Deal were both praised and hated for this. For some, this change brought a welcome shift from the laissez-faire policies of the 1920s. To others, it threatened the basic character that had always held the country together.

HISTORY'S VOICES

❝It cannot be successfully denied that whatever the merits of the New Deal policies, they have, as a whole, caused an appreciable drift away from individual responsibility and self-reliance. They have brought about an excessive, utterly [false] and dangerous reliance upon government.❞

—*Saturday Evening Post*, November 6, 1936

READING CHECK **Making Generalizations** How did the New Deal impact relationships among important segments of American society?

Limits of the New Deal

The New Deal was never as sweeping as its supporters or its opponents claimed. In practice, New Deal programs often compromised—some might say contradicted—Roosevelt's desire to build "a country in which no one is left out."

Relief programs provide a clear example. While they gave aid to millions of people, these programs were never meant to be a permanent solution to joblessness. Nor were they able to provide jobs to all those who needed them.

Roosevelt had hoped the federal government would assist all but about 1.5 million "unemployable" people, who would be left to the states to care for, but some 4.7 million went unserved. Work-relief programs could only provide temporary help. In addition, pay scales were very low. An unskilled worker might make a mere third of what the government deemed a minimum family income. Government leaders did not want wages to be so high that workers would be discouraged from seeking nongovernment jobs.

COUNTERPOINTS

Role of Government in Everyday Life

Although Charles McNary of Oregon was a Republican, he supported most New Deal programs, including the Social Security Act.

❝ I am confident that once the magnitude of this problem is clearly recognized, once we face squarely the fact that it has passed beyond the ability of the individual to master, and is distinctly national in its character, we shall set ourselves to the task of its solution.❞

Senator Charles McNary, 1935

Daniel Reed of New York took a strong stand against Social Security.

❝ I was taught and the people I have the honor to represent believe that the greatest heritage of a free people is the right to transmit that freedom to their children. I loathe this attempt to deceive and betray industry and labor and further fasten upon them this foreign system of regimentation [strict rule].❞

Representative Daniel Reed, 1935

Skills FOCUS **READING LIKE A HISTORIAN**

Analyzing Primary Sources Why does McNary believe that Social Security is needed? Why does Reed oppose it?

See **Skills Handbook**, pp. H28–29

Limits of the New Deal

The New Deal did not lift everyone out of poverty. Many working families, such as these migrant workers in Minnesota (right) or these home-steaders in New Mexico (far right) had little choice but to make the best out of the cramped and impover-ished conditions in which they lived.

The level of government assistance also varied by state. For example, under Aid to Families with Dependent Children, a child in Massachusetts might receive more than $60 a month, while one in Arkansas might get $8.

In addition, New Deal programs sometimes permitted discrimination against African Americans, Hispanic Americans, women, and others. New Deal leaders, Roosevelt included, were unwilling to irritate local populations by requiring programs to go against "local stan-dards"—including discriminatory ones.

READING CHECK **Summarizing** What were some of the limits of the New Deal?

The End of the New Deal

The sense of optimism accompanying Roos-evelt's victory in 1936 withered by 1937. The fight over court-packing cost the president some of his support within his party and with the American public. The economic downturn of 1937–1938 delivered a further blow to his efforts. By the end of 1938, the New Deal era of reform launched in 1933 was, in reality, over.

Weakening support Roosevelt's setbacks emboldened his opponents in Congress. In late 1937, a group of anti–New Deal senators made up of Republicans and southern Democrats issued a direct challenge to Roosevelt's policies. They called on the president to cut taxes, bal-ance the budget, and return more power to the states. This group was strong enough to stop most legislation they disliked.

One target of this group's opposition was the president's plan to reorganize the execu-tive branch of the government. Roosevelt said his goal was to help make the executive branch work more smoothly.

Critics, however, complained that the mea-sure gave too much power to the president. As one member of Congress stated, "This is just a step to concentrate power in the hands of the president and set up a… form of dictatorship." Such a charge carried real weight after the court-packing episode.

Only one major piece of legislation emerged from Congress in 1938: the Fair Labor Stan-dards Act. This law established a **minimum wage**—the lowest wage an employer can legally pay a worker. It also set the maximum number of required hours for a work week at 44. (This was later lowered to 40.) The Fair Labor Standards Act also included a require-ment that workers receive the overtime rate of time-and-a-half—payment at one-and-a-half times their normal rate for any hours over the weekly maximum.

The new law did not cover many large groups, such as farmworkers. Still, it marked a major victory for millions of workers.

Southern Democrats opposed the bill. Southern industry, they argued, depended on paying workers less than in other parts of the country. But Roosevelt worked hard to win passage of the bill. Although he did not know it, the bill would be the last major New Deal law.

The 1938 elections Facing opposition in Congress, President Roosevelt decided his best hope lay in defeating his opponents in the 1938 congressional elections. This included opponents within his own party. He handpicked candidates to fight for the Democratic nominations in several southern states.

President Roosevelt traveled to the South to tell voters he needed new senators to help pass his program. The embattled senators responded by enflaming white fears that African Americans were becoming politically empowered, sponsored by Roosevelt.

Georgia senator Walter George was among those targeted by Roosevelt. He compared the president's attempt to influence the election to the U.S. Army's occupation of the South during post–Civil War Reconstruction. "We answered this question before when federal bayonets stood guard over the ballot box," he observed.

Roosevelt's efforts backfired. In each case, his candidate lost, and the **incumbent** senator—the one presently in office—won the nomination and the November election. In addition, Republicans made gains in the House and Senate, further swelling the ranks of New Deal opponents.

After the New Deal Following the 1938 elections, President Roosevelt lacked the support he needed to pass more New Deal–style laws. Opposition was simply too strong for Roosevelt to overcome.

At the same time, Congress, the president, and the American public turned their attention away from the long struggle against the Great Depression. The possibility of a different kind of struggle lay ahead.

Now Europe appeared to be marching relentlessly toward another war. American factories now began to gear up to arm those who would fight the battles. By the millions, workers returned to the assembly lines and workshops. In a period of months in 1939 and 1940, international conflict produced what years of political struggle had failed to achieve: an end to the Great Depression.

READING CHECK **Sequencing** What events marked the end of the New Deal?

go.hrw.com
Online Quiz
Keyword: SD7 HP22

SECTION 4 ASSESSMENT

Reviewing Ideas, Terms, and People

1. a. Describe On what grounds did people praise and criticize the New Deal?
b. Contrast How did Roosevelt's views about the role of government differ from presidents of the 1920s?
c. Rate Do you think the positive impact of the New Deal outweighed the negative impact? Explain.

2. a. Recall Did the New Deal bring an end to the Depression?
b. Make Inferences Why were New Deal programs able to provide only limited support to the needy?
c. Evaluate Defend the New Deal's approach of honoring local customs in establishing levels of aid.

3. a. Define Write brief definitions of the following terms: minimum wage, incumbent
b. Explain How did Roosevelt's effort to get rid of disloyal Democrats backfire?
c. Elaborate How might Roosevelt have tried to improve relations with Congress and win more support for his efforts?

Critical Thinking

4. Find Supporting Details Copy the chart below and use information from the section to find supporting details for the main idea given.

Evaluating the New Deal

FOCUS ON WRITING

5. Narrative Write a narrative account of the final year of the New Deal. Be sure to include details from the section about the failures and rare successes of Roosevelt as well as the reasons for the end of the New Deal.

Perceptions of Roosevelt

Historical Context The documents below provide different information on perceptions of Franklin Roosevelt.

Task Examine the documents and answer the questions that follow. Then you will be asked to write an essay about perceptions of Franklin Roosevelt, using facts from the documents and from the chapter to support the position you take in your thesis statement.

ST 3.2 Draw upon literary selections, historical documents, and accounts to analyze the roles played by different individuals and groups during the major eras in New York State and United States history.

DOCUMENT 1

To his admirers, Franklin Roosevelt's appeal lay in both his policies and his personality. His energy and enthusiasm helped reassure a country that was going through hard times. Tom Vinciguerra, who grew up during the Great Depression, recalled his family's perceptions of Roosevelt.

"'Depression' was fast becoming a household word to all six of us children. Mother's pretty and usually smiling face now turned grim almost daily. The '29 crash destroyed my father's car-repair business. Survival was dependent on Dad's intermittent part-time jobs, plus welfare. Coal money ran out fast, and we weren't always warm. Hand-me-downs and leftover store bread warded off stark desperation.

In 1931, my nonpolitical mother surprised us with an announcement that the family would attend an election eve rally for Roosevelt in Camden, N.J. At the rally, I watched my mother smile and sing. I was so happy for her. As the troubled '30s rolled on, Roosevelt's alphabet soup—PA, CCC, etc. —worked its magic. Our lives improved.

In 1939, at age 13, I heard the loud wail of sirens while walking to my part-time busboy job in downtown Camden. It was Roosevelt's reelection motorcade. As it reached me, the president doffed his famous hat in my direction. Thrilled, I ran home. When I told my mother, she hugged me. I felt her tremble as she sobbed. Then she looked at me as if through me she could express her deep gratitude to the president. My brothers and sisters treated me like a celebrity. I did not bus dishes that day."

DOCUMENT 2

Some critics argued that Roosevelt's charisma sometimes gave people false hope and hid the details of his political plans. The following editorial appeared in *The Nation* magazine after one of Roosevelt's 1936 speeches, as he was preparing for his re-election.

"Mr. Roosevelt's amazing radio message to Congress has undoubtedly strengthened his campaign fortunes, but leaves his program as unclear as ever. Politically adroit [skilled], and from the standpoint of radio oratory a magnificent achievement, it was intellectually a confused and straddling performance. . . The common man wanted to be let in on a dramatic occasion, and he had his wish. He wanted a fighting speech, and he got it. He was tuning in on history-in-the-making, and the President took pains to make it a good show . . . The President has again used some sort of magic to increase his stature, and by comparison every Presidential possibility on the Republican side seems puny and frustrate[d]. . . .

But a sober rereading of the speech shows how consummately Mr. Roosevelt displayed his talent for leaving almost all the important things unsaid. . . .

In the domestic field Mr. Roosevelt's message was better as a manifesto [a public statement] than as a preface [introduction] to legislative action. It was here that the speech became. . . a political rally, with the business of state being transacted under the klieg lights [bright lights used in making motion pictures]."

Although he grew up wealthy and privileged, President Roosevelt had a strong appeal among many poor Americans, who felt he understood their suffering. The following cartoon reflects this idea.

Some of Franklin Roosevelt's harshest critics were the wealthy, who resented his efforts to redistribute wealth by taxing the rich to help the poor. Some accused him of betraying his class. In this cartoon, a group of wealthy New Yorkers are going to the Trans-Lux, a popular movie theater on Madison Avenue in New York City that showed newsreels about the president.

"Yes, you remembered me."

"Come along. We're going to the Trans-Lux to hiss Roosevelt."

1. **a. Identify** Refer to Document 1. What was the writer's impression of Roosevelt?
b. Analyze How did Roosevelt change this family's life in multiple ways?

2. **a. Describe** Refer to Document 2. According to the writer, what was the main purpose of Roosevelt's speech?
b. Interpret Why was the writer critical of the president for having strong speaking abilities?

3. **a. Identify** Refer to Documents 3 and 4. What are the two different types of people responding to Roosevelt?

b. Contrast What do these two cartoons reflect about the personal appeal of President Roosevelt?

4. Document-Based Essay Question Consider the question below and form a thesis statement. Using examples from Documents 1, 2, 3, and 4, create an outline and write a short essay supporting your position. How did President Franklin Roosevelt's personality shape public perceptions of his presidency?

See **Skills Handbook**, pp. H28–H29, H31

Visual Summary: The New Deal

The New Deal
- Two major plans—in 1933 and 1935
- Established many new government programs
- Popular at first, but limited in its success

Criticism and Resistance
- Political opposition from right and left
- Supreme Court opposition

Lasting Impact
- Forever changes relationship between people and government
- Introduces programs such as Social Security that are still functioning today
- Still controversial

Reviewing Key Terms and People

For each term or name below, write a sentence explaining its significance to the New Deal.

1. public works
2. fireside chat
3. Hundred Days
4. Huey P. Long
5. Social Security
6. CIO
7. deficit
8. John Maynard Keynes
9. Black Cabinet
10. Frances Perkins
11. Mary McLeod Bethune
12. minimum wage

Comprehension and Critical Thinking

SECTION 1 *(pp. 698–705)*

13. a. Recall Who did the Democratic Party choose as its candidate in 1932?

b. Contrast What did the American people seem to like most about Roosevelt's programs? What did they find fault with?

c. Evaluate What can you conclude from the fact that Roosevelt and the New Deal were criticized both for doing too much and for doing too little?

SECTION 2 *(pp. 709–716)*

14. a. Identify What was the Second New Deal?

b. Draw Conclusions What factors undermined support for Roosevelt and his programs?

c. Evaluate Explain this statement: In some ways, President Roosevelt's success contributed to his failure in the late 1930s.

History's Impact video program
Review the video to answer the closing question:
How did the Tennessee Valley Authority change
life in much of the rural South?

SECTION 3 *(pp. 717–722)*

15. a. Recall How did the Roosevelt administration treat women and African Americans?

b. Make Inferences Why do you think Eleanor Roosevelt was able to take a firmer stand for the rights of women and African Americans than her husband did?

c. Rate How do you think Franklin Roosevelt should be evaluated historically in terms of his treatment of women and minorities?

SECTION 4 *(pp. 723–727)*

16. a. Describe What effects did New Deal programs have on the major problems of the Great Depression, such as unemployment?

b. Summarize On what grounds can the New Deal be considered a success? a failure?

c. Rate In your opinion, was the New Deal a success or a failure? Explain.

Using the Internet

go.hrw.com
Practice Online
Keyword: SD7 CH22

17. Photographer Dorothea Lange used a camera to tell stories of life during the Great Depression. Her photographs convey many different moods, show different groups of people and different types of circumstances. Yet the pictures have much in common. Using the keyword above, research Lange's life and study some of her photographs. Then answer these questions: (a) How did Lange's own life affect her work? (b) What do her photographs reveal about the lives of people during the Depression? In your answers, refer to at least two specific photographs by their titles.

Analyzing Primary Sources

Reading Like a Historian This photograph shows Eleanor Roosevelt meeting with several members of the Bonus Army that formed during the early years of the Roosevelt administration.

18. Describe How would you describe the interaction between Eleanor Roosevelt and the Bonus Army marchers?

19. Contrast How did Eleanor Roosevelt's interaction with the Bonus Army differ from Hoover's treatment of the Bonus Army of 1932?

Critical Reading

Read the passage in Section 2 that begins with the heading "The Second Hundred Days." Then answer the question that follows.

20. The issue of Social Security is most closely associated with the criticisms of

A Congress.

B Dr. Francis Townsend.

C voters in 1936.

D African Americans.

WRITING FOR THE SAT

Think about the following issue.

Franklin Roosevelt and the New Deal set off one of the most fundamental debates about government in the nation's history. Not since the debates between the Federalists and Anti-federalists had the country seen such diverging viewpoints as those between Roosevelt and his conservative opponents. The debate is as strong as ever today.

21. Assignment How far should government go to try to improve the lives of citizens? Is it appropriate to use deficit spending when necessary to relieve suffering? What standards would you apply to decide how much help is too little or too much? Support your point of view with reasoning and examples from the chapter.

IN BRIEF

Below is a chapter-by-chapter summary of the main ideas covered in Unit 7.

 **From War to Peace**
1919–1928

MAIN IDEA The years following World War I brought unease over the apparent spread of radical influences. The American people sought leaders who offered a return to peaceful times—and they eagerly contributed to a booming, consumer-driven economy.

SECTION 1 Far from feeling safe and at peace, many Americans in the postwar years saw threats in a variety of forms, including labor unrest, rising immigration, and radical political ideas.

SECTION 2 The increasing availability of consumer goods—from cars to household appliances—helped inspire a growing economic boom in the 1920s.

SECTION 3 Warren G. Harding captured the national mood—and the White House—with his calls for normalcy. His pro-business agenda was expanded upon by his successor, Calvin Coolidge.

 **The Roaring Twenties**
1920–1929

MAIN IDEA The 1920s was a time of widespread cultural change. Music, art, literature, and popular culture reflected dramatic demographic and cultural developments.

SECTION 1 The changing American culture of the 1920s was reflected in new roles for women and an increase in urbanization.

SECTION 2 Centered in New York City's Harlem community, African American culture experienced a renaissance of literature, music, and art.

SECTION 3 The growing popularity of the radio and the movies helped contribute to the rise of a mass popular culture in the 1920s. Americans idolized the stars, both on the screen and off, that emerged from these new forms of entertainment.

The Great Depression Begins
1929–1933

MAIN IDEA Following an era of apparent prosperity, the Great Depression began in 1929. Soon millions of Americans were suffering, and the political landscape of the United States stood on the brink of great change.

SECTION 1 The American stock markets, which had ballooned in value and helped fuel the economic optimism of the 1920s, collapsed in 1929. The crash had effects far beyond the losses by investors.

SECTION 2 In the Great Depression that followed the 1929 stock market crash, millions of people lost their jobs, their savings, and their homes. In some parts of the country, environmental catastrophe added to the suffering.

SECTION 3 President Herbert Hoover believed in limited government action to address the growing national crisis. For many Americans, he came to be the target of much anger and unhappiness.

 **The New Deal**
1933–1940

MAIN IDEA Swept into office in 1932 on his promises of help for the victims of the Great Depression, Franklin Delano Roosevelt pushed forward a series of programs that came to be called the New Deal. These programs met with some success as well as some criticism.

SECTION 1 As president, Roosevelt quickly sought to address the fears of the nation. New Deal laws helped repair the banking system and provide relief for the jobless, though they met with significant criticism.

SECTION 2 The Emergency Relief Appropriation Act and Social Security helped set the pace for the Second New Deal, which helped Roosevelt win re-election as president in 1936.

SECTION 3 The New Deal provided some new opportunities for women and minority groups. It also helped shape the popular and artistic culture of the decade.

SECTION 4 The New Deal had mixed results in solving the economic problems of the Great Depression. However, it unquestionably changed the relationship between the people and their government.

1939–1960

Themes

Global Relations
The United States and the Allies defeated the Axis Powers in World War II, but tensions between the United States and its former ally the Soviet Union led to a long-running Cold War.

Government and Democracy
The United States fought against regimes that opposed democracy during World War II and the Cold War.

Japan formally surrendered aboard the USS *Missouri* on September 2, 1945, bringing World War II to an end.

733

Drawing Conclusions

Find practice for **Drawing Conclusions** in the **Skills Handbook,** p. H12

Good readers can use clues and their own prior knowledge to draw conclusions about various people places, and events mentioned in text. Drawing conclusions helps you remember what you read.

Before You Read
Skim chapter titles, section headings, and visuals to determine what the chapter will be about. Make a mental list of what you already know about the subject matter.

While You Read
Identify facts and ideas in the text. Then look for connections between those facts, ideas and what you already know.

After You Read
Briefly summarize what you have read. Then form a conclusion that makes a decision, judgment, or opinion about what the facts and ideas mean to you.

Mobilizing Industry and Science

The enthusiasm of American fighting forces was important. In order to defeat the Axis armies, however, American troops would need the proper equipment. The nation responded quickly to this need. Many factories that made consumer goods were quickly converted to the production of war supplies.

Rosie the Riveter Producing enough supplies to fight the war required many workers. At the same time, American men were leaving their factory jobs by the millions to join the armed forces.

Women helped provide a solution to this problem. During the war, the number of women working outside the home rose dramatically. Many of these eight million new workers took industrial jobs that had never been open to women before.

READING CHECK **Drawing Conclusions**
How were working women important to the war effort?

The section head tells you that the passage will be about how science and industry were mobilized for war.

Fact To win, American troops needed equipment.

Fact Factories needed workers, but men were leaving to be soldiers.

Test Prep Tip

Short answer and essay questions on tests frequently ask you to draw a conclusion about something you have read. But conclusions are not always stated directly. Try restating a passage from the text as a question that begins, "Why was it important that…?" For example, "Why was it important that many of the eight million new [women] workers took industrial jobs?"

Interpreting Visuals

Find practice for **Interpreting Visuals** in the **Skills Handbook,** p. H30

Many visuals are created for a specific reason. A newspaper photograph may be intended to inform readers, but a war-time **poster** may be a piece of propaganda used to convey a message or a point of view. By interpreting visuals, you can gain insight into different perspectives on historical events.

Strategies historians use:

- Find clues to the artist's point of view. Is the subject treated in a positive or negative light?
- Reflect on who the author's audience might have been.
- Think about the historical context of the image.

The word "Victory" is in large type, and is a different color. this indicates it is more important than the other words on the poster.

The basket is overflowing with fresh food. This creates an impression of abundance, even during a time of shortage.

The woman is dressed as a civilian, but wears a military cap. This calls attention to the war effort at home.

WAR GARDENS FOR VICTORY

GROW VITAMINS AT YOUR KITCHEN DOOR

Enter VICTORY GARDEN CONTEST

REGISTER 404 S. 8th ST. MAY 1-15

CONSUMER INTEREST DIVISION, MINNEAPOLIS DEFENSE COUNCIL—A WAR CHEST AGENCY

Skills FOCUS **READING LIKE A HISTORIAN**

As You Read Examine how the visuals on each page relate to the text that you are reading. How do details in the visuals explain more about those historical events?

As You Study Compare and contrast the visuals in each chapter. Use the visuals to help you understand the progression of historical events.

1939–1941

World War II ERUPTS

THE BIG PICTURE The Treaty of Versailles ending World War I created an uneasy peace. Amid postwar instability, Great Britain and France avoided conflict, and the United States sought to isolate itself from Europe's troubles. Meanwhile, however, Germany, Italy, and Japan fell under the sway of leaders promising order and glory. By the end of the 1930s, their aggression would plunge the world once more into war.

New York Standards

Key Idea 2 Important ideas, social and cultural values, beliefs, and traditions from New York State and United States history illustrate the connections and interactions of people and events across time and from a variety of perspectives.

Key Idea 3 Study about the major social, political, economic, cultural, and religious developments in New York State and United States history involves learning about the important roles and contributions of individuals and groups.

Skills FOCUS **READING LIKE A HISTORIAN**

A crowd salutes German dictator Adolf Hitler as he leads a Reich Party Day celebration in the city of Nuremberg. The annual rallies were held in the city from 1933 to 1938. *Reich* is the German word for *empire*.

Interpreting Visuals What is the focus of this event? What might its purpose be?

See **Skills Handbook**, p. H30

U.S.

September 1939
Congress passes cash-and-carry law to ease the sale of arms to countries at war.

1939

World

September 1939
Germany invades Poland.

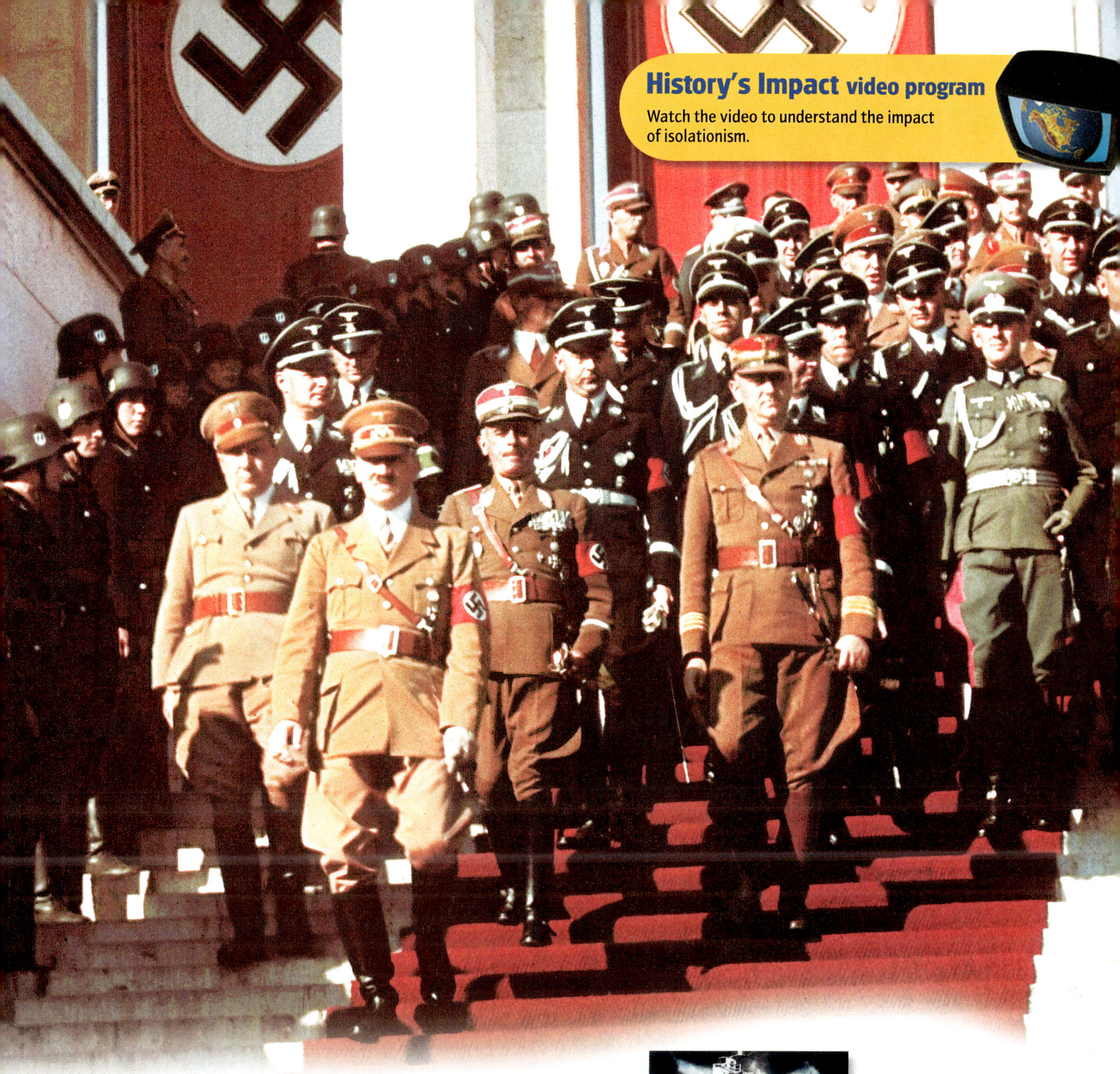

History's Impact video program

Watch the video to understand the impact of isolationism.

1940

May 1940
Winston Churchill becomes UK prime minister.

May–June 1940
Germany conquers the Netherlands, Belgium, and France.

September 1940
Japan joins Axis alliance with Germany and Italy.

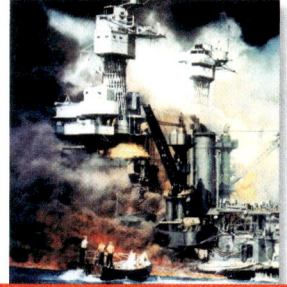

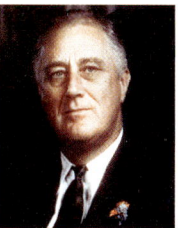

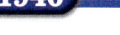

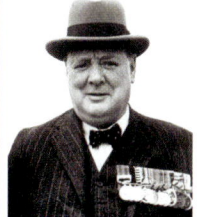

October 1940
Battle of Britain ends with Hitler's forces rebuffed.

December 1940
President Roosevelt declares the United States an "arsenal of democracy."

1941

March 1941
Congress establishes the lend-lease program to deliver arms to Great Britain on credit.

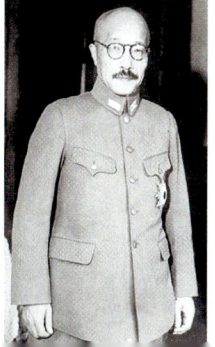

October 1941
General Hideki Tojo becomes Japanese prime minister.

December 7, 1941
Japanese bomb the U.S. Navy's Pacific Fleet at Pearl Harbor, Hawaii.

The Rise of Dictators

BEFORE YOU READ

MAIN IDEA

The shattering effects of World War I helped set the stage for a new, aggressive type of leader in Europe and Asia.

READING FOCUS

1. How did the aftermath of World War I contribute to political problems in Europe?

2. How did the problems facing Europe in the postwar years lead to the rise of totalitarian leaders?

3. What events exemplify the growing use of military force by totalitarian regimes in the 1930s?

4. What alarming actions did Adolf Hitler take in the mid-1930s?

KEY TERMS AND PEOPLE

inflation
Benito Mussolini
fascism
dictatorship
totalitarian
Adolf Hitler
Francisco Franco
Joseph Stalin
Haile Selassie
Neville Chamberlain

 PI 3.3 Prepare essays and oral reports about the important social, political, economic, scientific, technological, and cultural developments, issues, and events from New York State and United States history.

 **THE INSIDE STORY**

How can one man shatter a hateful myth? The 1936 Summer Olympic Games were held in the German capital of Berlin. For German leader Adolf Hitler, the event presented a golden opportunity. Hitler had risen to power telling of the greatness of the German people—and of the racial inferiority of certain other groups, such as Africans. The Olympic Games, many Germans believed, would provide proof of this racist idea for the whole world to see.

The U.S. Olympic team included many African American athletes. Among them was track star Jesse Owens. In an amazing performance, he captured gold medals in the 100- and 200-meter dashes, the long jump, and a relay. As he stood on the podium before the German crowd, he was living proof that Hitler's views on race were wrong.

Unfortunately, Hitler and Germany failed to learn the lessons of Owens's example. Hitler's hold on the German people was strong, and his message of hate, anger, and false pride had taken firm root. As you will read, he was merely one of several powerful and ruthless leaders to emerge during this time of turmoil and uncertainty. ▪

► **Jesse Owens (center) stands above his competitors at the 1936 Olympic Games.**

The "Master Race" Loses the Race

Europe after World War I

In an earlier chapter, you read about some of the difficulties facing the United States after World War I. Economic problems, social change, and the threat of communism helped produce a Red Scare—a fear of aliens and radicals.

Europe faced even more challenges at the end of the war. The war had caused the deaths of millions and the destruction of numerous cities and farms. The European economy was in ruins. It would take years to recover.

Problems with peace The Treaty of Versailles (ver-SY), which had brought the war to an end, left many European nations dissatisfied. France in particular had hoped to use the peace settlement to severely weaken Germany. They felt the treaty was not harsh enough on the Germans. Italy was also unhappy with the treaty. The Italians had been on the winning side in the war. They had hoped to be rewarded with territory as part of the treaty. Instead, they were largely ignored during the peace talks.

German outrage Germany suffered the most as a result of the Treaty of Versailles. Its terms did serious damage to the German economy. It also left the German people—and the German military—feeling humiliated. This helped usher in a period of political upheaval.

The treaty forced Germany to give up control of some of its land, including major industrial regions. As you read earlier, the treaty also required Germany to make heavy reparation payments to other countries. In the early 1920s, these factors helped bring about a period of severe **inflation,** or rising prices. Prices for goods increased at an incredible rate. The chart on this page shows the effects of this economic disaster. By 1923 German currency had simply ceased to have any meaningful value. For millions of Germans, a lifetime's worth of hard work and savings had vanished.

Germany also experienced political turmoil after the war. As you have read before, Communists and Socialists tried to take control of Germany in 1918 and early 1919. This effort failed, and Germany soon established a democratic system of government led by less radical elements. This government was known as the Weimar (VY-mahr) Republic, after the German city where it was established.

German money lost so much value in the early 1920s that children used currency as building blocks.

TALES OF GERMAN HYPERINFLATION

One American dollar could buy about 9 German marks in 1919. At the height of the panic, a dollar could buy more than 4 trillion marks.

By 1923, some 300 paper mills and 2,000 printing presses were working around the clock to print money.

Prices rose extremely fast. One customer at a cafe ordered a cup of coffee at 5,000 marks. By the time he ordered his second, the price had risen to 7,000 marks.

A typical loaf of bread cost about 1 mark in 1920. By November 1, 1923, that bread might cost 3 billion marks. Two weeks later, the price for the bread would have risen to 80 billion marks.

The Weimar Republic, however, was not a very strong government. It faced opposition from the political far left—Communists—and from the far right, which was antidemocratic. Another problem was unhappiness in the German military. It had been greatly reduced in size and power as part of the Treaty of Versailles. These factors helped make the Weimar Republic weak and unstable.

READING CHECK **Identifying Cause and Effect** How did the Treaty of Versailles affect Europe after World War I?

Totalitarian Leaders Arise

European struggles and dissatisfaction during the postwar years had a major effect on European politics. In some countries, a certain type of leader emerged—one who reflected and expressed the people's bitterness and anger. These leaders promised a return to greatness for their nations. This vision was so appealing to their unhappy people that many were willing to give up basic freedoms in return for the hope of future glory.

Mussolini and the birth of fascism

The first of these new leaders to emerge in Europe was the Italian **Benito Mussolini**. He had begun his public life in the early 1900s as a member of a Socialist party in Italy. Unlike many of his fellow Socialists, however, he supported Italy's entry into World War I. By the war's end, Mussolini had moved to the far right of Italian politics. He strongly opposed socialism and communism.

Outraged by the Treaty of Versailles, Mussolini founded a new Italian political party—the National Fascist Party. The term *fascist* comes from a Latin word for "a bundle of rods tied together." The ancient Romans had used this bundle as a symbol of their state. The single rod, Roman thinking went, could be easily broken. When tied together with other rods, however, it was strong.

For Mussolini, **fascism** was a system of government that stressed the glory of the state. He summed up the principle of fascism with the slogan, "Everything in the State, nothing outside the State, nothing against the State." The rights and concerns of individuals were of little importance.

HISTORY'S VOICES

❝Anti-individualistic, the Fascist conception of life stresses the importance of the State and accepts the individual only in so far as his interests coincide with those of the State.❞

—Benito Mussolini and Giovanni Gentile, *The Doctrine of Fascism*, 1932

After World War I, Mussolini used his dynamic public speaking skill to win a seat in Italy's parliament. His vision of a strong, orderly Italy appealed to many people. He also encouraged the use of violence against Communists and Socialists, whom many Italians blamed for the disorder of postwar Italy. By these means, Mussolini gained wide support. In 1922 he became leader of the government.

Europe's New Dictators

740

Once in power, Mussolini established a **dictatorship**—government by a leader or group that holds unchallenged power and authority. He allowed no other political parties and ruthlessly crushed opponents. His government controlled newspapers, schools, and businesses. All power flowed through the man Italians referred to as *Il Duce* (il DOO-chay)—"the leader." Under this **totalitarian** regime, Mussolini had total control over daily life in Italy.

Hitler's rise to power

Another of Europe's aggressive new leaders was Austrian-born **Adolf Hitler**, who had an unremarkable early life. An unsuccessful art student, he was rejected by the Austrian military because they thought him too weak to carry a weapon. With the start of World War I, however, Hitler volunteered for the German army. There he built a solid record as a soldier.

Hitler's anger about the Treaty of Versailles led him into politics. He joined a small political party known as the National Socialists, or Nazis. The party attracted many former soldiers and others who were unhappy with conditions in Germany. It was during this time that

Hitler (left) and Mussolini (above) both used cunning, violence, and repression to achieve and maintain power. Both also possessed a theatrical speaking style that enabled them to achieve great influence over their audiences.

Hitler discovered his talent for public speaking and leadership. Under his guidance, the Nazis gained influence in German politics.

Hitler, however, was impatient for change. In 1923 he organized an effort to seize power in Germany by force. This revolt failed. As a result, Hitler was imprisoned for nine months of a five-year sentence.

While in prison, he produced a book called *Mein Kampf*—German for "My Struggle." The book outlined Hitler's major political ideas. Like Mussolini, Hitler stressed nationalism and devotion to the state. He dreamed of uniting all the Germans of Europe in a great empire. "Germany will either be a world power or there will be no Germany," he wrote.

In *Mein Kampf*, Hitler expressed a belief in the racial superiority of Germanic peoples, whom he called Aryans. In addition, he blamed Jews for many of Germany's problems and believed that they threatened the purity of the Aryan race. (You will read more about Hitler's beliefs in the next chapter.)

HISTORY'S VOICES

> **❝** If we pass all the causes of the German collapse in review, the ultimate and most decisive remains the failure to recognize the racial problem and especially the Jewish menace. **❞**
>
> —Adolf Hitler, *Mein Kampf*, 1924

When he got out of prison, Hitler was determined to gain power through peaceful means. Seizing on public discontent and offering an appealing vision of German greatness, Hitler gradually built support. By 1933 the Nazis were the most powerful party in the nation. Hitler became Germany's chancellor, a top position in the government.

Hitler now moved to establish himself as a totalitarian dictator. Using his political skills—and violence when necessary—he managed to eliminate his political opponents. Meanwhile, Hitler continued to spread the myth of Aryan greatness and the coming German empire. At the center of this myth was Hitler himself. As with Mussolini in Italy, Hitler the man was glorified above all other Germans.

Hitler also began secretly to build up the German armed forces. He knew that these would be useful to him as he sought to fulfill his goal of expanding German territory. The German people, Hitler explained, needed more "living space" in which to grow and prosper.

Totalitarian Dictators

Totalitarian governments are not just a part of the historical past. Today a number of countries are controlled by dictatorial governments.

In Africa, the former British colony of Rhodesia became the independent nation of Zimbabwe in 1980. A guerrilla fighter turned politician named Robert Mugabe gained power.

At first, many people saw him as a reformer. As time passed, however, Mugabe came under sharp criticism. His land-redistribution policies drove out white farm owners and broke up large farms into small plots of land. In recent years, Mugabe has used fear and violence to limit voting rights.

North Korea also has a totalitarian government. Ruled by Kim Jong Il, the government controls all television and radio broadcasts. It does not permit any criticism of the nation's so-called Dear Leader. Rigid economic policies have led to more than 10 years of famine.

In Myanmar, also called Burma, the totalitarian government is run by a group of military officers. The government has suppressed prodemocracy movements since 1988 and ignored the results of a legislative election in 1990.

Drawing Conclusions Would you expect a country with a totalitarian government to have a thriving economy? Explain.

North Korean leader Kim Jong Il

Other regimes Some of the same forces that helped Mussolini and Hitler gain totalitarian power also helped create powerful regimes in other countries. For example, Spain erupted in civil war in the 1930s. Out of this conflict, Fascist general **Francisco Franco** came to power. You will read more about the Spanish Civil War shortly.

In the Soviet Union, communism was already established when **Joseph Stalin** came to power in the mid-1920s. Communism and fascism represent opposite political extremes. Yet there were similarities between the Soviet system under Stalin and the Fascist systems. Like the Fascists, Stalin violently crushed his political opponents.

Also like Hitler and Mussolini, Joseph Stalin created a myth of his own greatness. Throughout the Soviet Union, towns and cities were renamed for him. His portrait was displayed everywhere. "[W]e regard ourselves as the happiest of mortals," gushed one writer in the newspaper *Pravda*, "because we are the contemporary of a man who never had an equal in world history." Stalin's domination of all aspects of Soviet life made him one of the era's most notorious totalitarian dictators.

Japan was another country torn by political and economic conflict. In the early 1930s, military leaders used violence to gain control over the government. They, too, were inspired by nationalistic dreams of Japanese greatness. Such dreams would soon lead to war.

READING CHECK **Comparing** What common factors contributed to the rise of the totalitarian leaders who emerged after World War I?

Totalitarian Governments and Military Force

A common feature of the powerful postwar leaders was a willingness to use violence to gain power. Many were also willing to use military force against other nations.

Japan and Manchuria Among the problems facing Japan in the 1920s was the limited size of its territory. The islands of Japan were growing crowded. Many Japanese wanted to expand their territory and gain greater access to wealth and resources. This desire grew even stronger as a result of the worldwide economic depression of the 1930s.

THE IMPACT TODAY

Government
In 2003 the American-led attack on Iraq was meant in part to remove the totalitarian dictator Saddam Hussein. Like Mussolini, Hitler, and Stalin, Saddam glorified himself with statues and portraits throughout Iraq.

At this time, Japan's government was under civilian control. Many Japanese, however, were unhappy with their leaders. Dissatisfaction was especially high among members of the military who held strong nationalist beliefs.

Some Japanese generals decided it was time to act. In 1931 the army invaded the Chinese province of Manchuria—without the approval of the Japanese government. The goal was to seize Manchuria's land and resources for the use of the Japanese people. Japan's government ordered the army to end the action. The army officers simply refused to obey the order.

The takeover of Manchuria demonstrated the weakness of the Japanese government and the strength of Japan's nationalists. Over the next several years, the military would expand its influence over the government, in part by assassinating its political enemies. In general, the Japanese public supported the increasingly powerful military. As in Germany and Italy, the Japanese people were beginning to believe in the nationalists' dream of expansion.

The League of Nations strongly criticized Japan for the invasion of Manchuria. In response, Japan simply withdrew from the League of Nations, which was unable or unwilling to take any strong action against Japan. The powerlessness of the League was clear for the world to see.

Italy invades Ethiopia
The weakness of the League was soon confirmed by events elsewhere. In 1935 Mussolini's Italy invaded the East African nation of Ethiopia.

Italy's history with Ethiopia was several decades old. Italian efforts to establish a colony there in the late 1800s had ended in a crushing military defeat at the hands of the Ethiopians.

Italy did manage to keep several smaller colonies in East Africa. Some Italians, however, held on to bitter feelings toward Ethiopia for decades.

Those feelings resurfaced when Mussolini came to power with grand plans to rebuild an Italian empire. In 1935 he used a dispute about the border between Ethiopia and an Italian colony as an excuse to launch an invasion.

The Ethiopians were unable to resist the more powerful Italian forces, and Italy soon conquered the country. Ethiopian emperor **Haile Selassie** personally asked the League of Nations for help.

HISTORY'S VOICES

❝It is collective security. It is the very existence of the League of Nations. It is the confidence that each State is to place in international treaties. It is the value of promises made to small States that their integrity and their independence shall be respected and ensured…. In a word, it is international morality that is at stake.❞

—Haile Selassie, Speech to League of Nations, June 1936

Selassie's words failed to sway the League. Again, the international community was unwilling to take a strong stand against aggression.

American leaders, meanwhile, spoke out against Italy's actions, but there was little public support for doing more. President Franklin Roosevelt was unwilling to take formal steps to punish Mussolini.

The Spanish Civil War
Spain in the mid-1930s was troubled by fierce political conflict. On the left were Communists. On the right were Fascists and Nationalists. Most Spaniards held political views somewhere in between these extremes.

In 1936 this conflict led to civil war. The war soon attracted interest and involvement from

THE SPANISH CIVIL WAR

Spanish Civil War
1,000,000 DEAD
$20,000,000,000 LOST
32 MONTHS OF TERROR
RUINED CITIES
WRECKED HOMES
BOMBED FACTORIES
LOST TREASURE
FARMS INJURED

Skills Focus **READING LIKE A HISTORIAN**

The skeleton is dressed in traditional Spanish clothing.

Interpreting Political Cartoons What point is being made by the skeleton's list?

See **Skills Handbook**, p. H31

Appeasement

Prime Minister Chamberlain declared himself "a man of peace to the depths of my soul."

When Chamberlain returned from his meeting with Hitler declaring "peace for our time," Churchill voiced a quite different opinion of events.

66 [W]e should seek by all means in our power to avoid war, by analyzing possible causes, by trying to remove them, by discussion in a spirit of collaboration and good will. I cannot believe that such a programme would be rejected by the people of this country, even if it does mean the establishment of personal contact with dictators. 99

Neville Chamberlain, 1938

66 The Prime Minister desires to see cordial relations between this country and Germany.... You must have diplomatic and correct relations, but there can never be friendship between the British democracy and the Nazi Power. 99

Winston Churchill, 1938

Skills FOCUS   READING LIKE A HISTORIAN

Drawing Conclusions How does Chamberlain's comment hint at why Churchill's warnings went unheeded in 1938?

See **Skills Handbook**, p. H12

---

many other countries in Europe and in North America. For example, Fascist Italy and Nazi Germany sent forces and equipment to fight for the Nationalists, who were led by General Francisco Franco. Opposing the Nationalists were the the so-called Republicans, who controlled the government at the start of the war. They had the support of the Soviet Union, which provided arms and equipment. In addition, volunteers from the United States and many other countries joined the fight on the Republican side.

The fighting in the Spanish Civil War was bloody and brutal. Many hundreds of thousands of people died. This included several hundred American participants in the fighting. By 1939, however, Franco's Nationalists had defeated the Republicans. Spain came under the control of a Fascist dictator.

READING CHECK   Summarizing How did the League of Nations respond to Japan's and Italy's use of military force?

Hitler Takes Action

As soon as Hitler gained power in Germany, he secretly began to rebuild the German military. Before long, however, he was openly stating his plan to re-arm Germany. This was in direct violation of the Treaty of Versailles. Despite this, Hitler managed to convince Great Britain and France to tolerate his actions. In 1935, for example, the British agreed to allow Germany to rebuild its naval forces, including submarines. Hitler claimed that he was building German military strength in order to resist the spread of communism. This was a goal the British supported. In fact, Hitler was already committed to using war to expand his nation.

Militarizing the Rhineland Under the Treaty of Versailles, Germany was required to keep its troops out of an area in the Rhine River valley along the French border. This was meant to protect France against possible German aggression. In 1936, however, Hitler violated the treaty by sending German troops into the Rhineland. As an excuse, Hitler claimed that a recent French military agreement with the Soviet Union threatened Germany.

France was greatly alarmed by the German action. It was unwilling, however, to take military action against Germany. Britain, for its part, had no interest in going to war over the matter. Germany's troops remained in the Rhineland, and Hitler grew bolder.

The *Anschluss*

Two years later, Hitler took action to gain control of neighboring Austria. Hitler was an Austrian by birth. He had long dreamed of uniting all ethnic Germans, including the Austrians. In 1938 he tried to force the Austrian government to agree to *Anschluss* (AHN-shloos)—union with Germany. When the Austrian government refused, Hitler sent troops into the country.

The *Anschluss* was popular among the people of Austria. It was, however, another German violation of the Treaty of Versailles. Germany's neighbors issued strongly worded protests. But they did nothing more to stop Hitler.

The Sudetenland

By now, Hitler was confident that no one would act to stop him. Soon after the *Anschluss*, he began plans to gain control of a German-speaking portion of Czechoslovakia called the Sudetenland. First, he encouraged Germans in the Sudetenland to protest against Czechoslovakian rule. Then he began threatening a military attack.

Hoping to end the crisis, British prime minister **Neville Chamberlain** and French premier Edouard Daladier met with Hitler. As in the past, the British and French seemed most interested in avoiding armed conflict. At a meeting in Munich, Chamberlain and Daladier agreed to allow Hitler to annex the Sudetenland—that is, make it part of Germany. Czechoslovakia, which had no representative at the Munich meeting, protested the agreement. Chamberlain, however, boasted of having achieved "peace for our time." In reality, the world was on the verge of war.

READING CHECK **Summarizing** Explain how France and Great Britain responded to Hitler's actions in the early to mid-1930s.

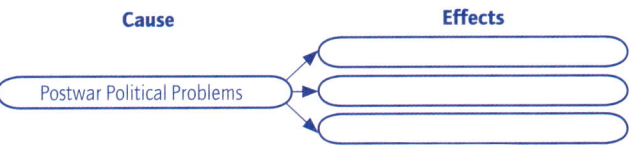

SECTION 1 ASSESSMENT

go.hrw.com
Online Quiz
Keyword: SD7 HP23

Reviewing Ideas, Terms, and People

1. a. Describe How did the conclusion of World War I affect the political climate in Europe?
b. Make Inferences How did the severe **inflation** in Germany affect the population?
c. Evaluate Why do you think it is important for a peace agreement, such as the Treaty of Versailles, to be regarded as fair by all sides?

2. a. Define Write a brief definition for each of the following terms: **fascism, dictatorship, totalitarian**
b. Compare What did **Mussolini, Hitler**, and **Stalin** all share in common?
c. Elaborate Why do you think the three totalitarian dictators worked so hard to build public adoration of themselves?

3. a. Identify What was the significance of Manchuria, Ethiopia, and Spain in the 1930s?
b. Make Generalizations How did other nations react to the aggression of the Japanese and the Italians?
c. Evaluate Why do you think the League of Nations was unwilling to stand up to the aggression of the Japanese and the Italians?

4. a. Describe How did Hitler respond to Germany's obligations under the Treaty of Versailles when he became Germany's leader?

b. Compare How did the reaction of Great Britain and France toward Germany compare to their reaction toward Italy and Japan?
c. Predict How do you think the failure to enforce rules of the League of Nations and the Treaty of Versailles will affect Germany in the future?

Critical Thinking

5. Identifying Cause and Effect Copy the chart below and use information from the section to identify the effects of the rise of dictators.

Cause		Effects
Postwar Political Problems	→	
	→	
	→	

FOCUS ON WRITING

6. Persuasive Assume the position of a delegate to the League of Nations and deliver a speech in which you argue for or against firm action to enforce the League's promises of protection for places such as Manchuria and Ethiopia.

Europe Erupts in War

BEFORE YOU READ

MAIN IDEA

Far from being satisfied by the actions of France and Great Britain, Germany turned to force and triggered the start of World War II.

READING FOCUS

1. How did Germany's actions in 1939 trigger the start of World War II?
2. Where did German forces turn after overrunning Poland in 1939?
3. What developments increased tensions between the United States and Japan in East Asia?

KEY TERMS AND PEOPLE

appeasement
Winston Churchill
blitzkrieg
the Allies
Vichy France
Charles de Gaulle
Luftwaffe
Axis Powers
Hideki Tojo

 PI 3.4 Understand the interrelationships between world events and developments in New York State and the United States (e.g., causes for immigration, economic opportunities, human rights abuses, and tyranny versus freedom).

THE INSIDE STORY

How do you stop an attack that is as fast as lightning? The German war machine began its attack from the air and without warning. Bombers struck at cities, transportation systems, and airfields. Roads became choked with panicked citizens.

Next came the fast-moving columns of German tanks and motorized forces, stabbing deep into the enemy countryside. Defending troops who went out to meet the armored German forces often were attacked by air.

After the tanks came German foot soldiers, fanning out across the land their tanks had just rumbled through. They destroyed or scattered any remaining resistance.

The German method of attack was devastating. The combined effect of speed and armor represented a major innovation over battle techniques used just two decades before in World War I. Starting in 1939, Europe would come to dread the German blitzkrieg, or lightning war. ◼

Blitzkrieg

Fast-moving armored columns struck quickly, driving deeply into enemy territory.

Aircraft bombed airfields, transportation systems, and cities, crippling defenses.

World War II Starts

British prime minister Neville Chamberlain believed that his policy toward Hitler of **appeasement**, or giving in to aggressive demands to maintain peace, had prevented the outbreak of a needless war. "How horrible, fantastic, incredible it is," Chamberlain said after meeting Hitler in Munich, "that we should be digging trenches and trying on gas masks here because of a quarrel in a faraway country." Yet others believed that Hitler was not going to stop after gaining the Sudetenland, as he had promised Chamberlain. One such critic was a rival politician named **Winston Churchill**. He condemned Chamberlain's appeasement as cowardly and likely to lead to war.

Hitler's early moves Churchill was correct. In March 1939 Hitler sent his troops into what remained of Czechoslovakia, capturing it without a fight. Now even Chamberlain realized that Hitler could not be trusted—and that his aggression was far from over.

Hitler's next move was to build alliances that he hoped would help him in the future. First, he established a pact with Italy. Then in August 1939, he announced a nonaggression pact with Stalin's Soviet Union.

With this pact, Hitler had shrewdly won Stalin's agreement to stay out of Germany's way as it continued to expand. In return, Hitler promised not to attack the Soviet Union. He also secretly agreed to give the Soviet Union parts of soon-to-be-conquered territory in Eastern Europe. "I have the world in my pocket!" Hitler triumphantly declared when Stalin agreed to the deal.

This development shocked many in Europe. The British and French had thought that tensions between the Soviets and Germans were rising. They had hoped that Stalin would stand with them against a possible German attack. In fact, the Soviets did fear Hitler's intentions. Stalin, however, believed the deal with the Nazis offered the greatest security.

Hitler attacks Poland Within days of the Nazi-Soviet agreement, Hitler was ready to launch his next strike—the invasion of Poland. To provide an excuse for the attack, Hitler had a German criminal dressed in a Polish military uniform. The man was taken to the German-Polish border and shot. The next morning—September 1, 1939—Germany claimed it had been attacked by Poland, using the dead criminal as proof. German troops immediately launched a massive invasion of Poland.

ACADEMIC VOCABULARY
security the promise of safety

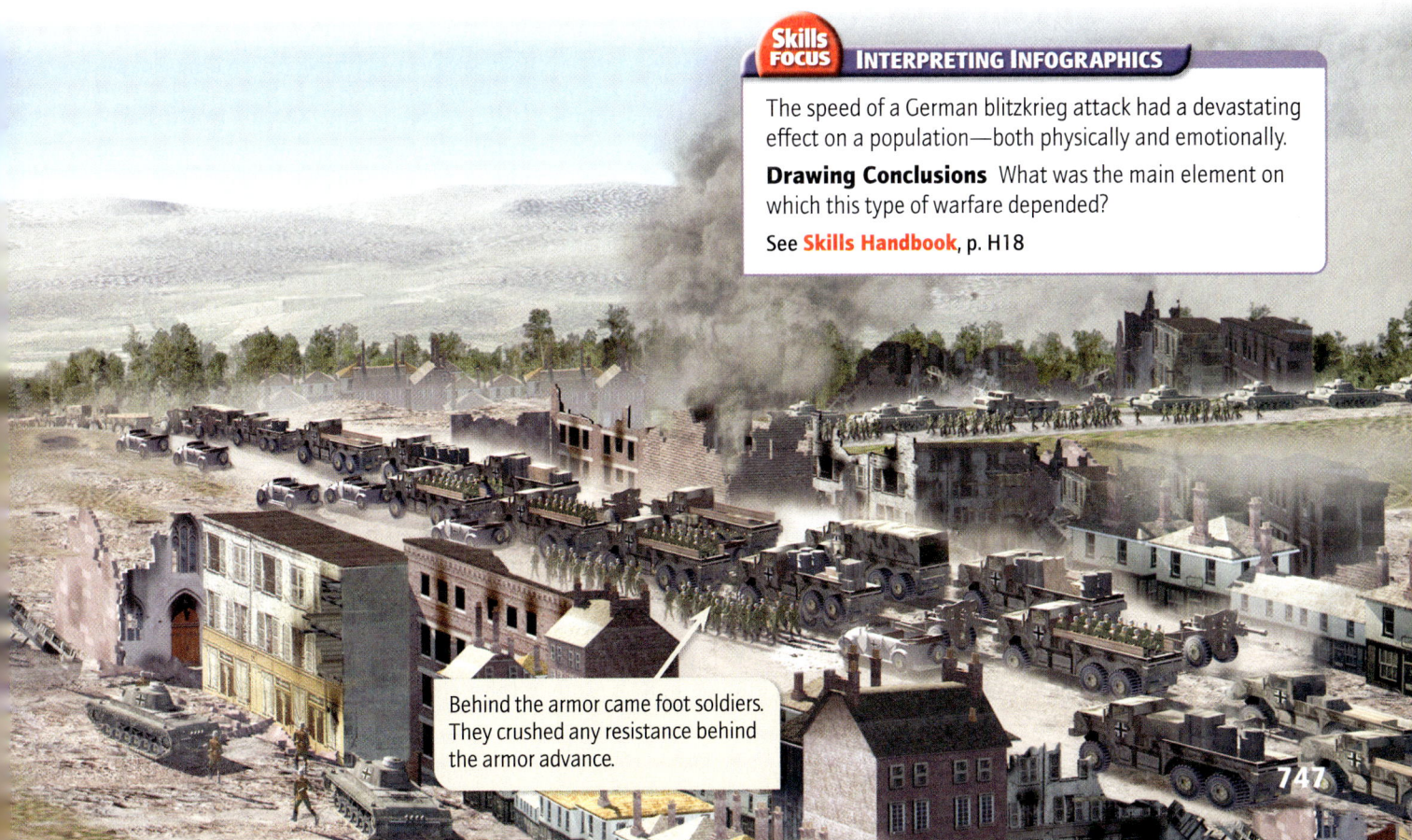

Skills FOCUS INTERPRETING INFOGRAPHICS

The speed of a German blitzkrieg attack had a devastating effect on a population—both physically and emotionally.

Drawing Conclusions What was the main element on which this type of warfare depended?

See **Skills Handbook**, p. H18

Behind the armor came foot soldiers. They crushed any resistance behind the armor advance.

747

Earlier you read about German military tactics. The **blitzkrieg**, German for "lightning war," featured an overwhelming combination of air attack and fast-moving armored strikes to drive deep into enemy territory.

The well-trained Germans used the blitzkrieg to devastating effect in Poland. Although the Poles fought bravely, they could not resist the German onslaught. The Polish landscape offered few natural barriers to slow the speedy invasion, and Polish troops were no match for German armor. In some battles, Polish soldiers on horseback carried swords into battle against German tanks. By the end of the month, Poland was in German hands.

READING CHECK **Sequencing** Outline Hitler's actions in 1939 which led to war.

German Forces Turn to the West

On September 3, 1939, Great Britain and France declared war on Germany. They became known as **the Allies**. There was little they could do, however, to slow Hitler in Poland. And even before the fighting there had ended, Hitler was planning his attack on his new enemies.

The Allies, meanwhile, had been forming their own strategy. They decided not to attack Germany. Instead, they would wait for Hitler's next move. They hoped German forces would weaken by trying to break through what they thought were France's strong defenses.

Allied leaders were surprised that Germany did not attack in the winter of 1939–1940. This period of inaction came to be known as the *sitzkrieg*, or the phony war. In fact, German military leaders were busily making plans for an invasion through the dense Ardennes (ahr-DEN) Forest in northern France and Belgium. Thinking that the forest was too rugged for an army to pass through, the French had concentrated their defenses elsewhere. Some troops were stationed to the north of the Ardennes, along France's border with Belgium. French defenses to the south of the Ardennes featured the famed Maginot (MA-zhuh-noh) Line. This was a string of bunkers and fortresses that lined part of the French-German border.

The lull in the fighting ended in April 1940, when Hitler sent his forces into Denmark and Norway. This move was aimed at improving Germany's access to the Atlantic Ocean. Both countries fell with little resistance. The surprised Allies were unable to do much to help. With Denmark and Norway secured, Hitler was now ready to focus on France.

The Netherlands and Belgium fall The Germans finally made their expected strike toward France in May 1940. Their plan worked to perfection. One group of German troops quickly conquered the Netherlands and stormed into Belgium. There they were met by Belgian, British, and French units.

These forces, however, were unable to stop the German assault. By early June, the Germans had trapped hundreds of thousands of Allied soldiers at the French port of Dunkirk. Included were nearly all British forces in France. In a heroic rescue, Allied ships and hundreds of civilian boats plucked nearly 340,000 troops from the coast and carried them to Great Britain. These rescued forces would prove vital to Great Britain's defense.

France falls France, however, was doomed. While Hitler's troops were capturing the Netherlands and Belgium, more German soldiers were carrying out the planned surprise attack through the Ardennes. When they broke through the forest, they easily overwhelmed the thin French force waiting there. The Maginot Line had simply been bypassed.

Having shattered France's defensive plan, Hitler's troops now raced toward Paris, the capital. By the end of June, France had surrendered to Germany and Italy, which had joined the war earlier that month. German forces now occupied much of France. The rest was placed under the control of French officials who cooperated with Hitler. This unoccupied part of France was known as **Vichy** (VEE-shee) **France**. Many other French leaders, led by General **Charles de Gaulle**, fled to Great Britain. There they organized resistance to German and Vichy control of France.

The Battle of Britain Now Great Britain stood alone against what appeared to be an unstoppable German war machine. The nation was now led by Winston Churchill, who had a great gift for inspiring courage and confidence among the British people.

GERMAN AGGRESSION, 1938–1941

Map of Europe showing German aggression from 1938 to 1941

FINLAND

NORWAY   SWEDEN

North Sea

IRELAND   UNITED KINGDOM

NETHERLANDS

London   1940   DENMARK

BELGIUM   1940   Berlin   EAST PRUSSIA   1939

Paris   1940   GERMANY   Warsaw   POLAND   1941

LUX.   Maginot Line

FRANCE   SWITZ.   AUSTRIA   HUNGARY   CZECHOSLOVAKIA   1941

ATLANTIC OCEAN

ITALY   YUGOSLAVIA   ROMANIA   1941

PORTUGAL   ANDORRA   BULGARIA

SPAIN   ALBANIA   GREECE

Baltic Sea

ESTONIA   1941

LATVIA

LITHUANIA

UNION OF SOVIET SOCIALIST REPUBLICS

Black Sea

TURKEY

Mediterranean Sea

MOROCCO

ALGERIA

SYRIA   IRAQ

LEBANON

PALESTINE   TRANSJORDAN

Legend:
- Axis controlled (1941)
- Allied controlled (1941)
- Neutral (1941)
- Axis troop movements

0   200   400 Miles
0   200   400 Kilometers
Lambert Azimuthal equal-area projection

GEOGRAPHY SKILLS   INTERPRETING MAPS

The Maginot Line was an elaborate fortification built as a permanent line of defense against German invasion into France.
Movement Why did the Maginot Line prove ineffective?
Region How much European territory did the Axis Powers control by 1941?

See **Skills Handbook**, p. H20

HISTORY'S VOICES

❝We shall defend our island whatever the cost may be; we shall fight on beaches, landing grounds, in fields, in streets and on the hills. We shall never surrender…❞

—Winston Churchill, speech before the House of Commons, June 4, 1940

As promised, Churchill refused even to consider trying to negotiate a peace agreement with Germany. Hitler, meanwhile, prepared to invade Great Britain.

The first stage of the German plan was to destroy the British Royal Air Force, or RAF. For the first time in the war, the Germans failed. Using radar, a new technology that used radio waves to detect approaching airplanes, the RAF inflicted heavy damage on German planes. As the battle wore on, the German air force, or

Luftwaffe, began bombing London. The goal was to terrorize the public so that they would lose the will to fight. Though thousands of civilians died in the raids, Churchill helped keep the nation's spirits up. "Little does [Hitler] know the spirit of the British nation," he said, "or the tough fiber of the Londoners."

Americans followed the Battle of Britain through the thrilling radio reports of Edward R. Murrow. He was an American reporter stationed in London. His live broadcasts described the air raids as bombs exploded around him.

By late 1940, the Battle of Britain was over. The British had stopped the Luftwaffe. Hitler was forced to call off the attempted invasion.

READING CHECK   **Summarizing** What was Hitler's experience when he turned his forces to the West in 1940?

THE IMPACT TODAY

Science and Technology

Radar continues to be a major tool in modern armies and navies. Radar allows not only the tracking of enemy aircraft, but also other functions, including detailed weather prediction and guidance for missile systems.

Tensions in East Asia

As you have read, Japanese nationalists expanded their influence in the 1930s. Japan increasingly viewed itself as a great imperial power. In 1934 it began expanding its naval forces. This violated promises made at the Washington Naval Conference in the early 1920s. In 1936 it signed an anticommunism pact with Germany that clearly linked Japan with Europe's Fascist menace.

Then in 1937, Japan began a war against China. The attack was marked by great brutality. For example, Japanese troops massacred an estimated 200,000 to 300,000 Chinese in the capital of Nanjing.

HISTORY'S VOICES

❝ There is probably no crime that has not been committed in this city today…. How many thousands were mowed down by guns or bayoneted we shall probably never know. ❞

—Minnie Vautrin, recorded in her diary, 1937

In 1940 Japan formed a military alliance with Germany and Italy. The three nations became known as the **Axis Powers**.

The next year, Japanese forces, with the agreement of the French Vichy government, moved to take control of French Indochina.

This was a French colony in Southeast Asia that included the modern-day countries of Vietnam, Laos, and Cambodia. Japan's takeover of French Indochina threatened British and American interests in the region. It signaled Japan's intention to seek the oil and other resources of the Dutch East Indies (today known as Indonesia), the Philippines, and other parts of Southeast Asia.

The United States reacted quickly to this move. President Roosevelt took steps to punish Japan economically and to deny it access to vital oil supplies. This was a serious threat to Japan's future plans.

Representatives of the two nations met to try to settle their growing differences. In Japan, a powerful group led by the minister of war, General **Hideki Tojo**, pushed the government not to accept any compromise.

Tojo was a strong nationalist. He was quite willing to go to war in order to build a Japanese empire. In October 1941, strong pressure from Tojo forced Japan's government to resign. Tojo took control of the country. American leaders did not yet realize it, but the time for compromise with Japan was over.

READING CHECK **Identifying Cause and Effect** How did rising tension between the United States and Japan affect politics in Japan?

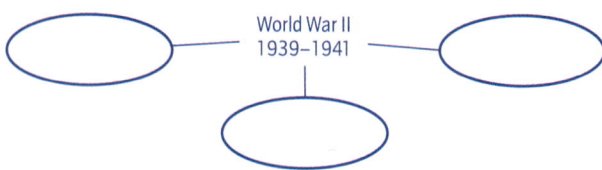

SECTION 2 ASSESSMENT

go.hrw.com
Online Quiz
Keyword: SD7 HP23

Reviewing Ideas, Terms, and People

1. a. Define Write a brief definition for each of the following terms: **appeasement, blitzkrieg**
b. Compare What factor made Germany's blitzkrieg so different from the tactics used in World War I?
c. Develop Based on what you have read about the blitzkrieg, how do you think the Poles might have better defended against it?

2. a. Identify What was the significance of the **Allies, Vichy France,** and **Luftwaffe**?
b. Compare Why do you think the British were able to defend themselves against the Germans but the French were not?
c. Rate Why do you think the leadership abilities of Winston Churchill were so important to the British during the Battle of Britain?

3. a. Describe Briefly describe the relationship between Japan and the United States in the late 1930s and early 1940s.
b. Make Inferences Why do you think the United States was so concerned about Japanese expansion into Southeast Asia?

c. Evaluate Do you think the United States did the right thing by drawing a firm line against Japanese aggression? Explain.

Critical Thinking

4. Identifying the Main Idea Copy the chart below and use information from the section to identify and record key details about the early stages of World War II.

World War II
1939–1941

FOCUS ON WRITING

5. Descriptive Write a description of what you imagine life was like in Great Britain just before and during the Battle of Britain.

The United States Enters the War

BEFORE YOU READ

MAIN IDEA

Isolationist feeling in the United States was strong in the 1930s, but Axis aggression eventually destroyed it and pushed the United States into war.

READING FOCUS

1. Why was a commitment to isolationism so widespread in the 1930s?

2. How did Roosevelt balance American isolationism with the need to intervene in the war?

3. What did the United States do to prepare for war in 1940 and 1941?

4. What were the causes and effects of the Japanese attack at Pearl Harbor?

KEY TERMS AND PEOPLE

pacifist
Neutrality Act
neutral
Quarantine Speech
cash-and-carry
Wendell Willkie
Lend-Lease Act
Atlantic Charter

PI 2.5 Analyze the United States involvement in foreign affairs and a willingness to engage in international politics, examining the ideas and traditions leading to these foreign policies.

THE INSIDE STORY

What threat made even Lucky Lindy nervous?

Ever since his historic 1927 solo flight across the Atlantic, Charles Lindbergh held a place as perhaps the greatest of all American heroes. People admired him not just for his bravery but also for his knowledge about aviation. When he spoke, people listened.

In the early days of World War II, Lindbergh was speaking a lot. Back in the United States after several years living in Europe, the great American flying hero was working hard to keep the country out of the war.

Getting involved in the fighting would be a disaster for the United States, Lindbergh argued. We were safe here in the United States as long as we built our own defenses and minded our own business, he claimed. Danger waited if we got mixed up in the bloody affairs of Europe. There, Lindbergh argued, the mighty German nation, with its superior air force, was poised to win. Lindbergh himself had inspected their aircraft and came away deeply impressed. He concluded that lending support to Hitler's foes was a lost cause that might end up costing us dearly. Americans, Lindbergh insisted, should put "America first." It must avoid giving in to the cries for help from the British and the other doomed people of Europe.

Lindbergh was a powerful voice in American society. His message was well received by millions of people, including many leading politicians. It would take one of the most shocking events in American history to drown it out. ◾

Lindbergh and "AMERICA FIRST"

◀ A soldier snatches a sign from an antiwar demonstrator at the White House in 1941.

American Isolationism

Many Americans had questioned what the Allies' costly victory in World War I had actually achieved. These feelings helped explain why the U.S. Senate was unwilling for America to join the League of Nations. Many feared that the League might drag the United States into future wars. Anti-League feelings remained strong in the 1920s and 1930s.

The desire to avoid involvement in foreign wars was known as isolationism. This view was shared by both liberals and conservatives in the 1930s. Isolationists were not necessarily pacifists, or people who do not believe in the use of military force. Most Americans remained ready to defend their country and its interests. Isolationists simply wanted to preserve America's freedom to choose the time and place for such action.

Franklin D. Roosevelt was not an isolationist. After World War I, for example, he had supported entry into the League of Nations. Though this remained an unpopular position in 1932, Roosevelt easily defeated the staunch isolationist Herbert Hoover in that year's election. This was largely because voting took place in the depths of the Great Depression. Most voters were more concerned with economic issues than with foreign policy.

In his first term, Roosevelt only rarely focused on foreign-policy matters. The United States did establish diplomatic relations with the Soviet Union in 1933. Nearly all of Roosevelt's attention, however, went to his New Deal programs. Meanwhile, when Congress discussed foreign affairs, it was generally to pass isolationist measures, such as the first **Neutrality Act**. Passed in 1935, this law was meant to prevent the nation from being drawn into war as it had been in 1917.

HISTORY'S VOICES

❝Upon the outbreak or during the progress of war between, or among, two or more foreign states…it shall thereafter be unlawful to export arms, ammunition, or [tools] of war to any port of such [warring] states.❞

—Neutrality Act, 1935

Over the next several years, Congress strengthened the Neutrality Act. For example, it outlawed making loans to warring countries.

READING CHECK **Summarizing** Why was isolationism widespread in the years after World War I?

TRACING HISTORY

Isolationism

From the nation's founding, many American leaders have sought to isolate the nation from international politics. Since World War II, however, the United States has increasingly formed alliances with other nations. Study the time line to learn how international events challenged American isolationist impulses.

The USS *Maine* blows up in Havana Harbor.

1898 United States gains control of Puerto Rico, Guam, and the Philippines in the Spanish-American War.

1800

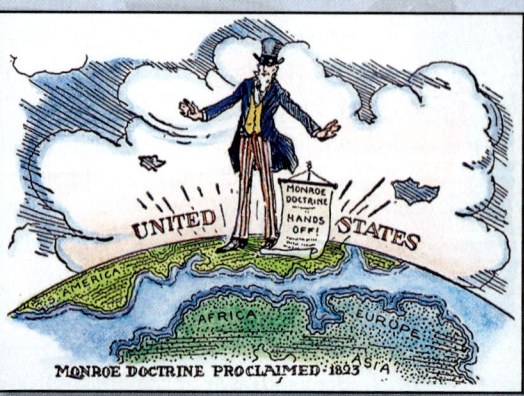

MONROE DOCTRINE PROCLAIMED 1823

THE GRANGER COLLECTION, NEW YORK

1823 Monroe Doctrine pledges neutrality in European disputes but warns European nations not to interfere in the Western Hemisphere.

Political cartoon supporting the Monroe Doctrine

Balancing Isolationism and Intervention

While many Americans focused on their own problems in the 1930s, <u>circumstances</u> overseas were taking an alarming turn. Italy's 1935 invasion of Ethiopia disturbed Roosevelt deeply. He viewed Italy as a dangerous aggressor. Citing the Neutrality Act, he halted arms sales to the two warring countries. This, Roosevelt knew, would hurt only Italy, for Ethiopia was unable to afford weapons. He further urged businesses to voluntarily end oil shipments to Italy. Few listened. Roosevelt, however, could do little more. He feared that taking a stronger stance against Italy would anger isolationists, whose political support he still needed. The isolationists wanted the United States to remain <mark>neutral</mark>—that is, not aid one side or the other.

Other events of the mid-1930s also challenged Roosevelt and his relationship with the isolationists. During the Spanish Civil War, strict neutrality meant not supplying either warring party with arms. Remaining truly neutral, however, was not a simple matter for the United States. Not aiding either side clearly gave an advantage to the Fascists, who were being well supplied by the Italians and Germans. Even the isolationists were unclear how to solve this dilemma.

Another problem was that deep down, President Roosevelt did not want to be neutral. He was deeply disturbed by the increasingly aggressive actions of the world's new group of totalitarian dictators. His willingness to avoid conflict with isolationists in the government was beginning to fade.

After Japan invaded China in 1937, President Roosevelt decided that it was time to speak out. In a speech he delivered in Chicago, he offered his views on recent world events.

HISTORY'S VOICES

> ❝ The peace, the freedom, and the security of 90 percent of the population of the world is being jeopardized by the remaining 10 percent who are threatening a breakdown of all international order and law. ❞
>
> —Franklin D. Roosevelt, October 5, 1937

Roosevelt compared the spread of war to the spread of a contagious disease. Such diseases can be stopped, he said, by a quarantine. This means identifying the sick and separating them from the healthy. Roosevelt urged the United

ST 4.1 Analyze important debates in American history (e.g., United States involvement in foreign affairs and wars), focusing on the opposing positions and the historical evidence used to support these positions.

1918 World War I ends. Isolationists in Congress defeat President Wilson's plan to join the League of Nations.

President Woodrow Wilson

2004 NATO expands to include several countries that had once been part of the Soviet Union.

1900

2000

1945 World War II ends. The United States leads the effort to create the United Nations.

1949 To contain Soviet expansion during the Cold War, the United States joins eleven other nations to form the North Atlantic Treaty Organization (NATO).

President George W. Bush and NATO Secretary General Lord Robertson

Political Cartoon

After the outbreak of World War II, many Americans were sympathetic to the Allies, but few wanted to get involved in another global war. *Chicago Tribune* cartoonist Carey Orr produced this cartoon recommending the American course of action.

THE GRANGER COLLECTION, NEW YORK

The character of Uncle Sam represents the government of the United States.

The character of Democracy pleads with Uncle Sam to stay out of the war.

Across the Atlantic lies Europe.

" STAY OUT! STAY OUT FOR MY SAKE, AS WELL AS YOUR OWN!"

WAR MAD EUROPE

DEMOCRACY

AMERICA, THE LAST REFUGE, OF DEMOCRACY

Skills FOCUS   READING LIKE A HISTORIAN

1. **Interpreting Political Cartoons** What is the artist recommending the United States do?
2. **Drawing Conclusions** Why do you think the artist took this position?

See **Skills Handbook**, pp. H12, H28–H29, H31

States to work with peace-loving countries to quarantine aggressive nations and stop the spread of war. For this reason, the speech was referred to as the **Quarantine Speech**.

READING CHECK   Identifying Problems and Solutions How did Roosevelt strike a balance between isolationism and intervention in the 1930s?

Preparing for War

Roosevelt's Quarantine Speech upset many isolationists. They predicted that his policies would lead to war. North Dakota senator Gerald P. Nye attacked the speech as a "call…upon the United States to police a world that chooses to follow insane leaders." Still, others applauded Roosevelt. Indeed, the president seemed to be gaining strength against the isolationists.

In early 1938, for example, Roosevelt sought from Congress money for building new naval vessels. Isolationists saw warships mainly as a means of fighting wars far from the United States. Some complained about this proposal. Nevertheless, Congress approved the request.

But Adolf Hitler's aggressive actions strengthened Roosevelt's position. Isolationists had cheered Chamberlain's appeasement at Munich. When German forces later invaded Poland, however, Roosevelt got Congress to change the nation's neutrality laws. The change established a new policy known as **cash-and-carry**. Under this policy, countries at war were allowed to purchase American goods as long as they paid cash and picked up their orders in American ports.

Roosevelt had hoped that the cash-and-carry policy would allow the Allies to slow Hitler's advances. German victories in 1940, however, convinced the president that he needed to do more.

As a result, Roosevelt urged a policy of "all aid short of war." The president agreed to trade fifty aging American warships for eight British military bases. Isolationists opposed the deal but were too weak to stop it.

The election of 1940 As Europe was erupting into war, Roosevelt decided to seek a third term as president. Though no one had ever been elected to more than two terms, Roosevelt felt that the world situation required experience in the White House. His opponent was business leader **Wendell Willkie**. In terms of foreign policy, Willkie's views were similar to Roosevelt's. The voters decided to stick with Roosevelt for another term.

Following his re-election, Roosevelt continued his drive to provide aid to the Allies in their fight against Hitler's armies. In a speech at the end of December 1940, Roosevelt declared his goal of making the United States the "arsenal of democracy." An arsenal is a place where weapons are stored. Soon afterward, Congress passed the **Lend-Lease Act**. This allowed the nation to send weapons to Great Britain regardless of its ability to pay.

Ties between the United States and Britain were further strengthened in August 1941. Roosevelt and British leader Winston Churchill met secretly on a ship off the coast of Canada. There the two leaders agreed to the **Atlantic Charter**. This agreement proclaimed the shared goals of the United States and Britain in opposing Hitler and his allies.

Isolationists reacted strongly to these developments. They viewed them as steps leading directly to war. Charles Lindbergh and the America First Committee, which you read about earlier, became leading critics of the president's actions.

In spite of their complaints, however, the United States was looking more and more like a nation at war. Indeed, armed conflict was already taking place on the open seas. As the United States sought to deliver war supplies under the terms of the Lend-Lease Act, German U-boats tried to stop them. In October 1941, torpedoes struck the American destroyer USS *Kearny*. Eleven Americans died. Two weeks later, a German U-boat sank the USS *Reuben James*, killing more than 100 sailors.

Despite the attacks on their ships, many Americans continued to oppose entry into the war. That, however, was about to change.

READING CHECK **Identifying Cause and Effect** Why did the conflict between Roosevelt and the isolationists grow as the United States prepared for the coming war?

Japan Attacks Pearl Harbor

While the situation in Europe troubled many Americans, an even bigger threat to peace was taking shape in the Pacific Ocean. Indeed, by late fall of 1941, American leaders were convinced that war between the United States and Japan was likely. The two nations had earlier come into conflict over French Indochina. Japan had also forged an alliance with Germany and Italy, and Japan's new prime minister, Hideki Tojo, was hostile toward the United States.

The key remaining question was how and where the fighting would start. American officials believed that Japan might attack American bases in the Philippines or British territory in Southeast Asia. In any case, American officials were determined not to fire the first shot. They continued to negotiate with the Japanese. At the same time, they warned American forces throughout the world to be prepared for a possible Japanese attack.

The attack on Pearl Harbor American officials were correct: Japan had decided on war. For months, Japanese military leaders had been developing plans for a surprise attack on the American naval base at Pearl Harbor, Hawaii. This base was home to the United States Navy's Pacific Fleet. The Japanese plan called for aircraft carriers to approach the island of Oahu, where Pearl Harbor was located, from the north. Japanese war planes loaded with bombs and torpedoes would lift off from the carriers and destroy as many American ships and planes as possible.

American military planners had for months believed that an attack on Pearl Harbor was a possibility. In December 1941, however, forces at the base were unready to defend it. This was in part because no single commander was in charge of Pearl Harbor's defenses. In the resulting confusion, routine defensive steps, such as using airplanes to watch for approaching ships, were not in place. The Japanese attack force was able to approach Pearl Harbor undetected.

As the sun rose on Sunday morning, December 7, 1941, the Japanese strike force went into action. The raid was a complete surprise to the Americans. Most American fighter planes in Hawaii never got off the ground. Hundreds were severely damaged or

Attack on Pearl Harbor

In December 1941 military officials throughout the Pacific were on alert for a possible Japanese attack. Yet Pearl Harbor was not considered the most likely target, and the Japanese strike force approached Hawaii undetected. In one stroke, they destroyed the American Pacific battleship fleet. Below, the USS *West Virginia* sinks as sailors rescue a survivor in the water.

go.hrw.com
Interactive Map
Keyword: SD7 CH23

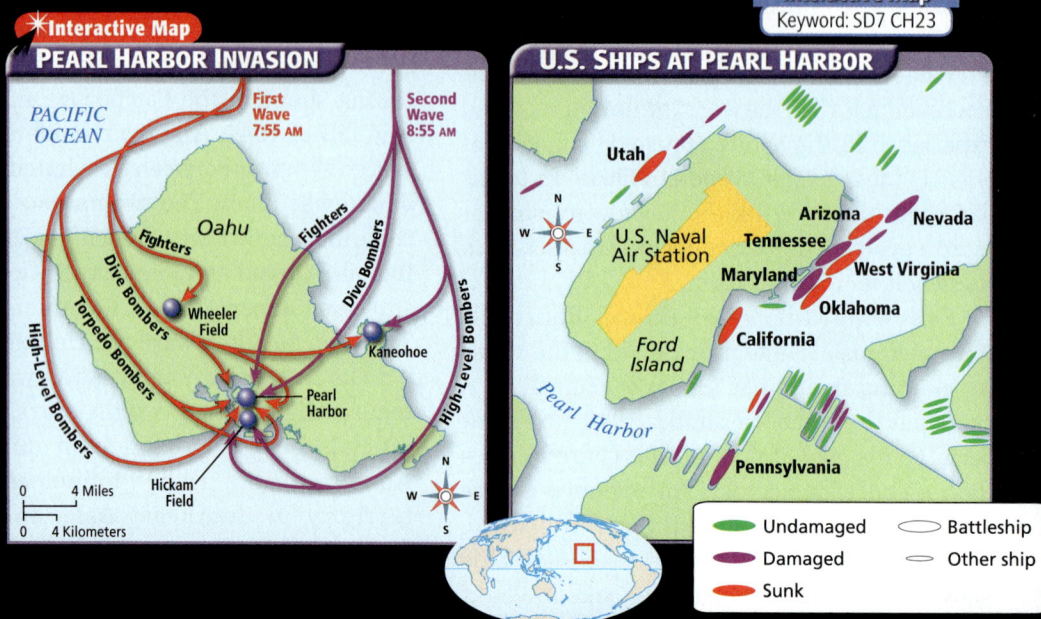

Interactive Map

PEARL HARBOR INVASION

PACIFIC OCEAN

First Wave 7:55 AM
Second Wave 8:55 AM

Oahu

Fighters
Fighters
Dive Bombers
Dive Bombers
Torpedo Bombers
High-Level Bombers
High-Level Bombers

Wheeler Field
Kaneohe
Pearl Harbor
Hickam Field

0   4 Miles
0   4 Kilometers

U.S. SHIPS AT PEARL HARBOR

Utah
U.S. Naval Air Station
Ford Island
Pearl Harbor

Arizona   Nevada
Tennessee
Maryland   West Virginia
Oklahoma
California
Pennsylvania

● Undamaged   ◯ Battleship
● Damaged   ◯ Other ship
● Sunk

Skills FOCUS | **INTERPRETING INFOGRAPHICS**

1. **Making Inferences** What types of ships do you think the Japanese were targeting in their attack?
2. **Interpreting Visuals** How do you think the images of the destruction to the American fleet may have affected the American public?

See **Skills Handbook**, pp. H7, H18, H30

destroyed where they sat. Meanwhile, Japanese bombs and torpedoes took a heavy toll on the American warships anchored in the harbor.

The Japanese attack lasted barely two hours. By the time it was over, however, the Pacific Fleet was a tangled mass of smoking metal. "We felt like crying," said one sailor who survived the raid. "We could see our beautiful fleet upside down and burning up."

The destruction was enormous. All eight battleships in the harbor suffered damage. Four were sunk. Nearly 200 aircraft were completely destroyed, and more were damaged. Some 2,400 Americans were dead. Japan, meanwhile, lost only a handful of submarines and fewer than 30 aircraft. It was a complete defeat for the United States.

American reaction Americans reacted to the devastating attack with anger and fear. Rumors spread that Japanese troops would soon invade the West Coast. Nervous Californians reported seeing submarines off their shores. They strung beaches with barbed wire. As you will read in the next chapter, some people became afraid that Japanese Americans would secretly assist an invasion of the United States mainland.

Roosevelt had expected a Japanese strike, but he also expected a formal declaration of war by Japan. Indeed, Japan's ambassadors had scheduled an appointment to deliver just such a message on the day of the attack. By the time they arrived, however, Pearl Harbor was in flames. Roosevelt was furious that Japan had meant to deceive the United States. On December 8, 1941, he asked Congress for a declaration of war.

HISTORY'S VOICES

❝ Yesterday, December 7, 1941—a date which will live in infamy—the United States of America was suddenly and deliberately attacked by naval and air forces of the Empire of Japan.... Always will we remember the character of the onslaught against us. No matter how long it may take us to overcome this…, the American people in their righteous might will win through to absolute victory. ❞

—Franklin Roosevelt, December 8, 1941

America was now at war with Japan. Three days later, Germany and Italy declared war on the United States. The nation had entered World War II as one of the Allies.

READING CHECK **Drawing Conclusions**
What made Japan's attack on Pearl Harbor so devastating?

FOCUS ON NEW YORK

DAILY LIFE

The terrorist attacks of September 11, 2001 in New York City and Washington D.C., are often compared to the attack on Pearl Harbor. Both took the nation completely by surprise and caused reactions of fear and anger. Both triggered strong surges of patriotism and a commitment to defeat our foes.

---

go.hrw.com
Online Quiz
Keyword: SD7 HP23

SECTION 3 ASSESSMENT

Reviewing Ideas, Terms, and People

1. a. Define Write a brief definition for each of the following terms: pacifist, Neutrality Act
b. Analyze How did World War I contribute to isolationist feeling in the 1920s and 1930s?

2. a. Describe Why were some isolationists skeptical of Roosevelt's foreign policy during his campaign for president?
b. Sequence How did Roosevelt's position toward isolationism change over time?
c. Elaborate Why do you think Roosevelt increasingly came into conflict with isolationists?

3. a. Recall What events explain Roosevelt's continuing shift away from isolationism in the late 1930s?
b. Compare Describe cash-and-carry and the Lend-Lease Act and how they differed from one another.
c. Evaluate Do you think the isolationists were correct in arguing that Roosevelt's policies, including lend-lease, would increase the likelihood of war? Explain.

4. a. Describe What was the attack on Pearl Harbor?
b. Summarize What was the significance of this battle?

Critical Thinking

5. Sequencing Copy the chart below and use information from the section to identify and record the sequence of events that led the United States away from its isolationist position and into World War II.

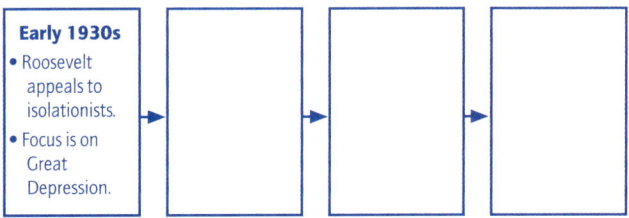

FOCUS ON WRITING

6. Persuasive Write a letter to the editor of a local newspaper from the perspective of a citizen in October 1941, in which you argue either for or against isolationism. Be sure to refer to information from this section and elsewhere in the chapter to support your view.

Mobilizing for War

BEFORE YOU READ

MAIN IDEA

The outbreak of World War II spurred the mobilization of American military and industrial might.

READING FOCUS

1. How did the U.S. armed forces mobilize to fight World War II?

2. What role did American industry and science play in mobilizing to fight World War II?

3. How did mobilization challenge the nation's ideals of freedom?

KEY TERMS AND PEOPLE

George C. Marshall
Oveta Culp Hobby
Rosie the Riveter
Manhattan Project
atomic bomb
J. Robert Oppenheimer
A. Philip Randolph
Bracero Program
zoot suit riots

PI 3.1 Compare and contrast the experiences of different ethnic, national, and religious groups, including Native American Indians, in the United States, explaining their contributions to American society and culture.

THE INSIDE STORY

Can you fight a war by assembly line? Reporters had never seen anything like Willow Run. Inside the giant structure, a person could scarcely see from end to end. "Like infinity," noted an observer, "it stretches everywhere into the distance."

The building these people were describing was the brainchild of business pioneer Henry Ford. Built in the tradition of the great Ford auto factories, Willow Run was a giant, mile-long assembly line for airplanes. As the United States entered World War II, the plant stood as a symbol of the nation's great industrial might. Indeed, the tremendous power of American industry would provide the key to victory against the Axis menace.

It took time for Willow Run to get up to speed. Finding tens of thousands of employees was difficult. Lack of housing was another issue. Over time, however, Ford and the government resolved these problems. Willow Run and its 42,000 workers kicked into high-speed production. By the end of the war, 650 aircraft per month were coming off the Willow Run line.

Willow Run demonstrated the enormous power of American industry—and the mighty effort of American business and government leaders to harness it. As you will read, this was just one part of the nationwide effort to get ready to fight World War II.

Building Victory

▲ B-24 bombers roll off the assembly line in the Willow Run factory.

Mobilizing the Armed Forces

The Japanese bombs and torpedoes that fell on Pearl Harbor had destroyed not only ships and planes, but also most of the remaining isolationist feeling in the United States. Now that the country had entered the war, it had to mobilize, or bring its forces into readiness. This was a huge job.

Fortunately, the United States had made something of a head start. Starting in 1940 the government had sharply increased military spending. This spending, in fact, was largely responsible for ending the Great Depression. Thousands found work in the now-busy factories, making supplies for the military.

The leader of the mobilization effort was Army Chief of Staff, General **George C. Marshall**. Marshall worked closely with President Roosevelt to plan for war. He ensured that American soldiers were well equipped and properly trained. Marshall would also play an important role in developing the nation's military strategy.

Finding soldiers In addition to equipment and supplies, the United States needed soldiers and sailors to fight the Axis Powers. Following Pearl Harbor, the government expanded the draft, which Roosevelt had reinstated in 1940. Many young men, however, did not wait to be called into service. Eager to defend their country, they volunteered by the millions.

HISTORY'S VOICES

❝I wanted to be in it. I was fifteen.... I lied about my age and tried to get in in '43. I was sixteen now. My mother wouldn't sign. ... Then I passed the air corps test at Oak Park High.... Then I figured... you're gonna be two years training, the war'll be over. Go in the Marine Corps.❞

—Roger Tuttrup, quoted in
"The Good War": An Oral History of World War Two, by Studs Terkel

Eventually, some 16 million Americans would enter the armed forces.

Women and the armed forces Although they were not permitted to take part in combat, American women filled a variety of vital roles in the military. Their service helped make more men available for fighting. For example, 10,000 women joined the Women Accepted for Volunteer Emergency Service, or WAVES. This was a navy program in which women did

PRIMARY SOURCES

Propaganda Poster

During World War II the U.S. government produced a wide variety of posters to encourage recruitment and support for the war. This poster for the Army Air Corps was created by artist James Montgomery Flagg, who also created the famous image of Uncle Sam during World War I.

P-38 Lightnings were one of the most popular fighter aircraft used in the war .

The man is clearly enthusiastic to join the fight.

This man's gear identifies him as a pilot.

Coming Right Up!

Skills FOCUS READING LIKE A HISTORIAN

1. **Analyzing Primary Sources** What was the purpose of this image?
2. **Interpreting Visuals** Do you think the image accurately reflects fighter pilots during World War II? Explain.

See **Skills Handbook**, pp. H28–H29, H30

necessary clerical work that would otherwise have to be performed by men. Some 1,000 women joined the Women Airforce Service Pilots, or WASPs. They tested and delivered aircraft. Nearly 40 WASPs gave their lives serving the country.

By far the largest women's unit was the Women's Army Corps, or WAC, in which 150,000 women served. At the start of the war, the unit was known as the Women's Army Auxiliary Corps, or WAAC. Its members worked with, but were not part of, the army. The WAACs repaired equipment, worked as electricians, and performed many other jobs.

By 1943 demand for their services was so great that the army created the Women's Army Corp. WACs were full-fledged members of the army. As such, they were entitled to full army protection and benefits and could serve overseas on nearly every task except combat. They were led by **Oveta Culp Hobby**, who was given the rank of colonel.

New military bases The millions of Americans entering the armed forces all needed training and housing. This required building hundreds of new military bases.

In general, the military looked to build new bases in rural areas where there was plenty of open land. Life on a rural, isolated base often required a big adjustment, especially for those who came from larger cities. It also required some getting used to by local citizens. They had to cope with the presence of thousands of young men in their once quiet neighborhoods.

The military buildup transformed many parts of the country. California became home to more military bases than any other state. Florida, with its warm weather and plentiful land, was also an excellent location for military training. Camp Blanding, with its 55,000 soldiers, became the fourth largest city in Florida almost overnight.

Texans saw 1.2 million troops train at their army bases, including Camp Hood. Some 200,000 air pilots trained at Texas air bases, such as Randolph Air Field. In addition, Texas was a temporary home to over 50,000 German, Italian, and Japanese prisoners of war.

READING CHECK **Identifying Problem and Solution** What were the challenges of mobilizing the armed forces?

Mobilization

Women were essential to the war mobilization effort. They filled many jobs once reserved for men, such as riveting (above).

Mobilizing Industry and Science

The enthusiasm of American fighting forces was important. In order to defeat the Axis armies, however, American troops would need the proper equipment. The nation responded quickly to this need. Many factories that made consumer goods were quickly converted to the production of war supplies.

The federal government spent tens of billions of dollars on weapons and supplies in the months following the outbreak of war. Shortly after Pearl Harbor, Roosevelt set the ambitious goal of building 60,000 new planes in 1942 and a further 125,000 aircraft the following year. He asked for 120,000 new tanks over the same time period. Thanks to the efforts of people such as Henry Ford and the workers of Willow Run, American industry met these goals.

The United States not only had to produce all of these war supplies, it also had to ship them to the armed forces overseas. Cargo

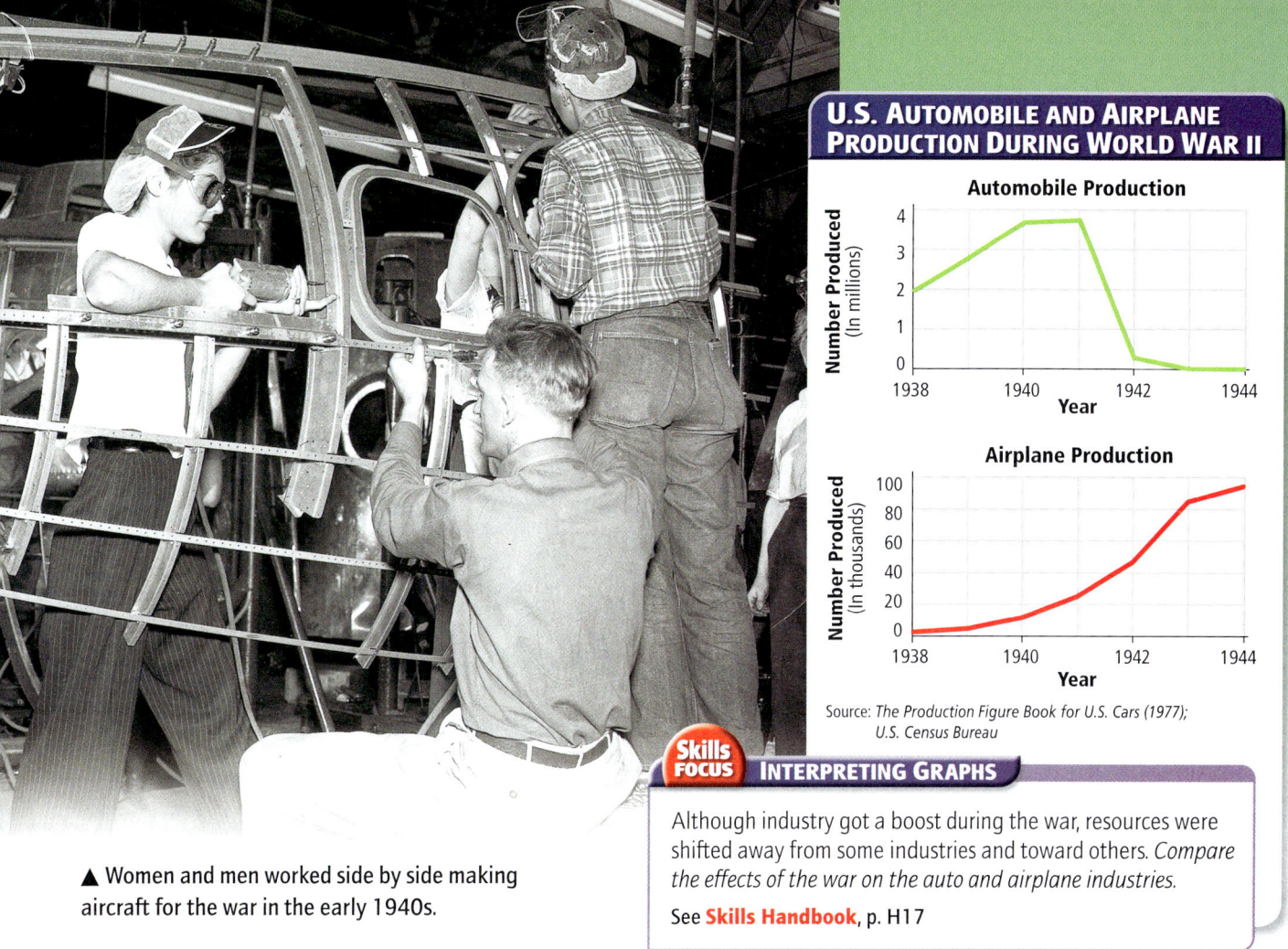

Automobile Production

Airplane Production

Source: *The Production Figure Book for U.S. Cars (1977);*
U.S. Census Bureau

Skills FOCUS **INTERPRETING GRAPHS**

Although industry got a boost during the war, resources were shifted away from some industries and toward others. *Compare the effects of the war on the auto and airplane industries.*

See **Skills Handbook**, p. H17

▲ Women and men worked side by side making aircraft for the war in the early 1940s.

ships, however, were a main target of enemy submarines. Early in the war, submarines took a terrible toll on American shipping. To replace these losses, American shipyards turned out 5,500 vessels over the course of the war.

About half of these ships were the so-called liberty ships built by Henry Kaiser. Before the war, Kaiser was known for such projects as Hoover Dam. He had never built a ship. Yet he created a shipyard in California and used assembly-line techniques to produce massive cargo ships at an astounding rate. His workers once produced a liberty ship in a mere four and a half days.

The federal government created several new agencies to help ensure that American industry would be able to meet the needs of the armed forces. These agencies regulated what products factories produced, what prices they could charge, and how the nation's raw materials would be used. The wartime agencies were staffed in part by American business and labor leaders. Key figures included William Knudsen and Sidney Hillman, who led the

Office of Production Management, and Donald Nelson, who headed the government's War Production Board.

Rosie the Riveter Producing enough supplies to fight the war required many workers. At the same time, American men were leaving their factory jobs by the millions to join the armed forces.

Women helped provide a solution to this problem. During the war, the number of women working outside the home rose dramatically. Many of these 6.5 million new workers took industrial jobs that had never been open to women before.

"I was a woman doing a 'man's job'!" recalled one of these women workers. "I was also very proud of the fact that I was contributing, even in a small way, to the war efforts." Working women of the war came to be represented by the symbolic figure known as **Rosie the Riveter**.

Labor in World War II Government spending during World War II helped end the Great Depression and created millions of new jobs. Many of these workers joined labor unions, but the federal government was concerned that strikes might hamper the war effort.

Just weeks after the nation declared war on Japan, President Roosevelt established the National War Labor Board to help settle labor disputes. In 1943 Congress passed the Smith-Connally Act, giving the president power to take over vital industries in the event of strikes. These measures helped reduce—but not end—labor disputes in the early war years.

Mobilizing science

War planners knew that technology would play an important role in World War II. The Manhattan Project, with laboratories in Los Alamos, New Mexico, was the most significant scientific program of World War II. This was a top-secret American program to build an atomic bomb, a powerful weapon that used energy released by the splitting of atoms.

Research into building an atomic bomb had begun in 1939, motivated by concern that Germany was already working on such a weapon. As you will read later, American scientists led by physicist J. Robert Oppenheimer would win this race. The result would shape world history for decades to come.

READING CHECK **Identifying the Main Idea** What steps did the U.S. government take to mobilize industry and science?

Fighting for Freedom at Home

As in World War I, the United States faced the challenge of fighting for freedom overseas. The nation also faced the challenge of ensuring freedom for Americans at home.

African Americans in the military

Hundreds of thousands of African Americans served with honor during World War II. In the process, they broke down barriers that had long blocked their way. For example, the war saw the enlistment of the first African American marines in U.S. history. The navy commissioned the first African American officers during the war.

At the same time, African Americans continued to suffer discrimination. They were forced to serve in segregated units. Their bravery often went unrecognized. Not a single African American soldier of World War II received the prestigious Medal of Honor. This oversight was corrected nearly 50 years after the fact, when seven African Americans received recognition for their remarkable bravery in battle.

African Americans in the workforce

The war created an enormous demand for factory workers. White women took many of these jobs. African Americans found new opportunities as well. As factories increased

Seeking Equal Opportunity

African American workers wanted an equal opportunity to contribute to the nation's mobization effort and to benefit from the opportunities it created. *How did President Roosevelt respond to African American demands for fair treatment?*

war production, thousands found jobs that had in the past been unavailable to them. Yet even with these new opportunities came harsh reminders of widespread racist attitudes. For example, African Americans were often forced to take the lowest-paying jobs, regardless of their skills or experience.

Union leader **A. Philip Randolph**, head of the Brotherhood of Sleeping Car Porters, noted these developments. In 1941 he called for a march on Washington, D.C., to protest unfair treatment of African Americans. Only after President Roosevelt issued an order outlawing discrimination in government or defense jobs did Randolph call off the march.

Challenges for Hispanic Americans Hispanic Americans experienced opportunities and challenges during World War II. For example, the demand for farm labor led the U.S. and Mexican governments to establish the **Bracero Program** in 1942. This gave some Mexican workers the chance to work temporarily in the United States.

In some communities, unfortunately, the arrival of thousands of Hispanic workers led to increased ethnic tensions. In California, such tensions boiled over into violence. In the **zoot suit riots** of June 1943, white sailors stationed in Los Angeles fought with groups of Mexican American youths during a week of terrible violence. The riot was named after the zoot suit, a flashy style of clothing favored by some Mexican American young men.

In spite of the conflicts, Hispanic Americans remained deeply loyal to the United States and sought opportunities to serve.

HISTORY'S VOICES

66 We know that us Mexican-American boys and girls can do a lot of things to win the war if someone will give us a chance.... [D]iscrimination is the thing that makes the other Americans divide from us. 99

—Letter from Youth Committee for the Defense of Mexican American Youth to Vice President Henry Wallace

Like members of other minority groups, many Hispanic Americans served bravely in the armed forces. They also shared a strong commitment to victory and freedom.

READING CHECK **Identifying Cause and Effect** Explain how mobilization triggered a fight for freedom among minority groups in the United States.

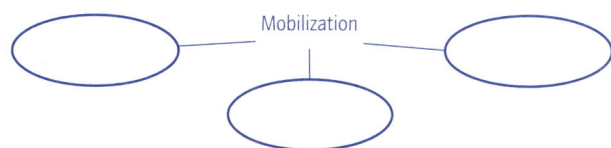

go.hrw.com
Online Quiz
Keyword: SD7 HP23

SECTION 4 ASSESSMENT

Reviewing Ideas, Terms, and People

1. a. Describe Briefly describe the significance of the following to the mobilization effort during World War II: George C. Marshall, Oveta Culp Hobby
b. Explain What effect did the bombing of Pearl Harbor have on the nation's mobilization effort?
c. Evaluate How do you think the changing roles of women in the United States were reflected in their experiences during wartime?

2. a. Define Write a brief definition of each of the following terms: Rosie the Riveter, Manhattan Project, and atomic bomb
b. Summarize Why was mobilization of American industry considered so important to the war effort?
c. Evaluate Do you think the decision of the U.S. government to expand its oversight of American industry would help or hurt industry's ability to meet its goals? Explain

3. a. Recall How did African American military personnel and workers fare during World War II?

b. Draw Conclusions Why do you think World War II created so many opportunities for women and members of minority groups?
c. Predict How do you think the end of the war, when it comes, will affect minority groups? Explain your answer.

Critical Thinking

4. Identifying Supporting Details Copy the chart below and use information from the section to identify and record the details that support the main idea.

Mobilization

FOCUS ON WRITING

5. Descriptive The preparations for World War II brought major changes to life in the United States. Assume the point of view of an American citizen in late 1941 to early 1942. Write a journal entry in which you describe the changes taking place around you.

Reactions to Pearl Harbor

ST 4.1 Analyze important debates in American history, focusing on the opposing positions and the historical evidence used to support these positions.

ST 4.3 Develop hypotheses about important events, eras, or issues; move from chronicling to explaining historical events and issues; use information collected from diverse sources to produce cogently written reports and document-based essays.

Historical Context The documents below provide information on different reactions to the Japanese bombing of Pearl Harbor in Hawaii.

Task Examine the documents and answer the questions that follow. Then you will be asked to write an essay about reactions to the Pearl Harbor attack, using facts from the documents and information from the chapter to support the position you take in your thesis statement.

DOCUMENT 1

The day after the attack on Pearl Harbor, President Franklin Roosevelt asked Congress to declare war on Japan. His simple speech reflected the shock that most Americans felt about the attack.

"Yesterday, December 7, 1941—a date which will live in infamy—the United States of America was suddenly and deliberately attacked by naval and air forces of the Empire of Japan.…

Always will we remember the character of the onslaught against us. No matter how long it may take us to overcome this premeditated invasion, the American people in their righteous might will win through to absolute victory.

I believe I interpret the will of the Congress and of the people when I assert that we will not only defend ourselves to the uttermost but will make very certain that this form of treachery shall never endanger us again.

Hostilities exist. There is no blinking at the fact that our people, our territory and our interests are in grave danger.

With confidence in our armed forces—with the unbounded determination of our people—we will gain the inevitable triumph—so help us God."

DOCUMENT 2

The government used memories of Pearl Harbor to encourage support for the war. The poster below was created to encourage support for war-related work, such as making munitions.

DOCUMENT 3

Most Americans found out about the Pearl Harbor attacks from the radio. Duane T. Brigstock of Battle Creek, Michigan, recalled his reactions upon hearing the news.

"Along with a large contingent [group] of Battle Creek bowlers, I was participating in the Central States tournament in Toledo, Ohio, that fateful Sunday afternoon. As the news broke, the message was relayed to us over the P.A. system: 'The Japanese are bombing Pearl Harbor!' We listened in shocked disbelief and activity halted on the busy alleys. Our first reaction was anger—followed by a great surge of patriotism. Bowling scores were quickly forgotten. As we checked out of our hotel, someone softly started to sing "God Bless America" and soon everyone joined in.

We were a quiet group driving home as we listened to bits of information on our car radios. We dug out our draft registration cards from our billfolds to recheck our numbers and wonder when we would be called up. There was no question in our minds that we would serve—only when."

DOCUMENT 4

While many people reacted to the war by joining the military, those who worked on the home front never forgot the event. Just a few weeks after the attack, these war-production workers took a break from their night shift on New Year's Eve to celebrate the coming year. Instead of shouting "Happy New Year," they shouted "Remember Pearl Harbor!"

Skills FOCUS READING LIKE A HISTORIAN

1. **a. Identify** Refer to Document 1. Why does Roosevelt call December 7, 1941, a "date which will live in infamy?"
   b. Analyze How does Roosevelt try to warn and also to reassure the nation after the attack?

2. **a. Describe** Refer to Document 2. What is going on in this image?
   b. Interpret What kind of effect do you think this image had on wartime workers?

3. **a. Identify** Refer to Document 3. What feelings did the attack immediately stir up for this writer?
   b. Elaborate How do you think that day changed the lives of those who heard about it on the radio?

4. **a. Identify** Refer to Document 4. How did these workers celebrate the new year?
   b. Analyze Why do you think the workers chose that cheer to mark the new year?

5. **Document-Based Essay Question** Consider the question below and form a thesis statement. Using examples from Documents 1, 2, 3, and 4, create an outline and write a short essay supporting your position.
   How did Americans react to the attack on Pearl Harbor?

See **Skills Handbook**, pp. H28–H29, H30

Chapter Review

Visual Summary: World War II Erupts

Rise of Dictators
- Dictators, taking advantage of widespread fear, uncertainty and despair, emerge in the post–World War I era.

Aggression and War
- Aggressive dictators use war to promote their tyrannical goals.

The United States: From Isolationism to War
- Isolationism gives way to the call for war when the United States comes under direct attack.

Mobilizing for War
- The United States musters its tremendous industrial and human might to fight the war.

Reviewing Key Terms and People

Complete each sentence by filling in the blank with the correct term or person.

1. Benito Mussolini introduced a political philosophy known as _____.

2. In the 1930s, many Americans supported _____ rather than an active involvement in affairs overseas.

3. Neville Chamberlain is associated with the _____ of Hitler at Munich.

4. The German attack of Poland demonstrated a tactic known as _____.

5. The symbol for women factory workers during the war was _____ _____ _____.

6. Germany, Italy, and Japan formed the _____ _____.

7. In order to aid the British, Roosevelt promoted the policy of _____.

8. In 1933 _____ _____ became the chancellor of Germany.

9. The _____ _____ was a top-secret program to build an atomic bomb.

10. In the _____ _____, Roosevelt likened the spread of aggression to the spread of disease.

11. The _____ _____ provided an opportunity for workers from Mexico to work in the United States temporarily.

Comprehension and Critical Thinking

SECTION 1 *(pp. 738–745)*

12. **a. Identify** Who were the major totalitarian dictators to emerge following World War I?

  b. Summarize What were the key features of the postwar totalitarian regimes?

  c. Elaborate What do you think was the appeal of fascism, and why did it spread in the post–World War I era?

History's Impact video program

Review the video to answer the closing question: Why did so many Americans favor isolationism before the United States entered World War II?

SECTION 2 *(pp. 746–750)*

13. a. Recall What countries did Germany attack in 1939 and 1940?

b. Make Inferences Based on the events of 1940, what can you infer about the Allies' evaluation of German military strength at the start of World War II?

c. Evaluate Do you think Hitler would have behaved differently had the British and French not appeased him in Munich? Explain.

SECTION 3 *(pp. 751–757)*

14. a. Describe During the 1930s, what was the general attitude among the American public toward events taking place in Europe, Africa, and Asia?

b. Sequence Describe the change in American attitudes toward world events in the period between the late 1930s and the end of 1941.

c. Develop How would you counter the isolationist argument in the late 1930s? Write a brief statement to explain your idea.

SECTION 4 *(pp. 758–763)*

15. a. Describe Describe the key steps in mobilizing the nation for war.

b. Explain What does it mean to say that mobilzation created "opportunities and challenges" for minority groups?

c. Predict How do you think a mobilization effort such as the one that occurred in the early 1940s would affect the United States today? Explain your answer.

Using the Internet

go.hrw.com
Practice Online
Keyword: SD7 CH23

16. Why did people put their faith in totalitarian dictators who propelled their nations into war? Using the keyword above, do some research on the Internet to find some answers to this question. Then create a chart to compare and contrast the reasons why many German, Italian, and Japanese people supported totalitarian dictators in their nations.

Analyzing Primary Sources

Reading Like a Historian

This photograph shows a worker at a defense plant during World War II.

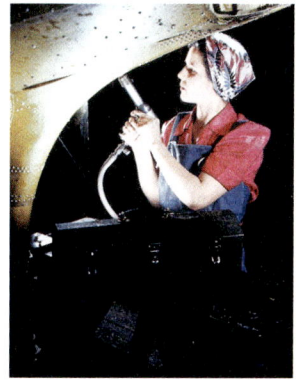

17. Identify What term was used to identify the type of worker shown in this picture?

18. Analyze What is the significance of the fact that this worker is a woman?

Critical Reading

Read the passage in Section 2 that begins with the heading "World War II Starts." Then answer the questions that follow.

19. Winston Churchill believed that

  A. appeasement would lead to war.

  B. it was foolish to get involved in foreign conflicts.

  C. Hitler would stop at the Sudetenland.

  D. Chamberlain correctly handled Hitler.

20. The passage suggests that in return for giving into Chamberlain's demands, Hitler

  A. threatened to invade Great Britain.

  B. promised to support Chamberlain.

  C. promised not to seek further territorial gains.

  D. agreed that Chamberlain was a coward.

FOCUS ON WRITING

Narrative Writing *Narrative writing tells a story. It uses precise detail and often describes events in sequence. To practice narrative writing, complete the assignment below.*

Writing Topic Isolationism in the 1930s

21. Assignment Based on what you have read in this chapter, write a narrative paragraph that retells the story of the rise and fall of isolationist feeling in the United States between World War I and World War II.

The United States in WORLD WAR II

THE BIG PICTURE The United States— including its military forces and its civilian population— succeeded along with the Allies to defeat the Axis powers in Europe and the Pacific. Yet the cost of victory and the discovery of the full horrors of World War II were staggering.

New York Standards

Key Idea 3 Study about the major social, political, economic, cultural, and religious developments in New York State and United States history involves learning about the important roles and contributions of individuals and groups.

Skills FOCUS **READING LIKE A HISTORIAN**

U.S. soldiers in Germany pose on top of an enormous cannon captured from the Germans, pleased to have removed this monster from the enemy's arsenal. These guns were called railway guns because they required one or even two sets of railroad tracks to move their bulk. **Interpreting Visuals** What do the soldiers' poses tell you about their attitudes?

See **Skills Handbook**, p. H30

U.S.

World

January 6
Roosevelt delivers the Four Freedoms speech about the future of the world.

December 7
Japan attacks Pearl Harbor.

1941

June 22
Germany begins its invasion of the Soviet Union.

History's Impact video program

Watch the video to understand the impact of World War II.

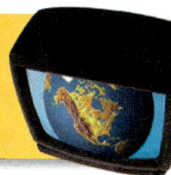

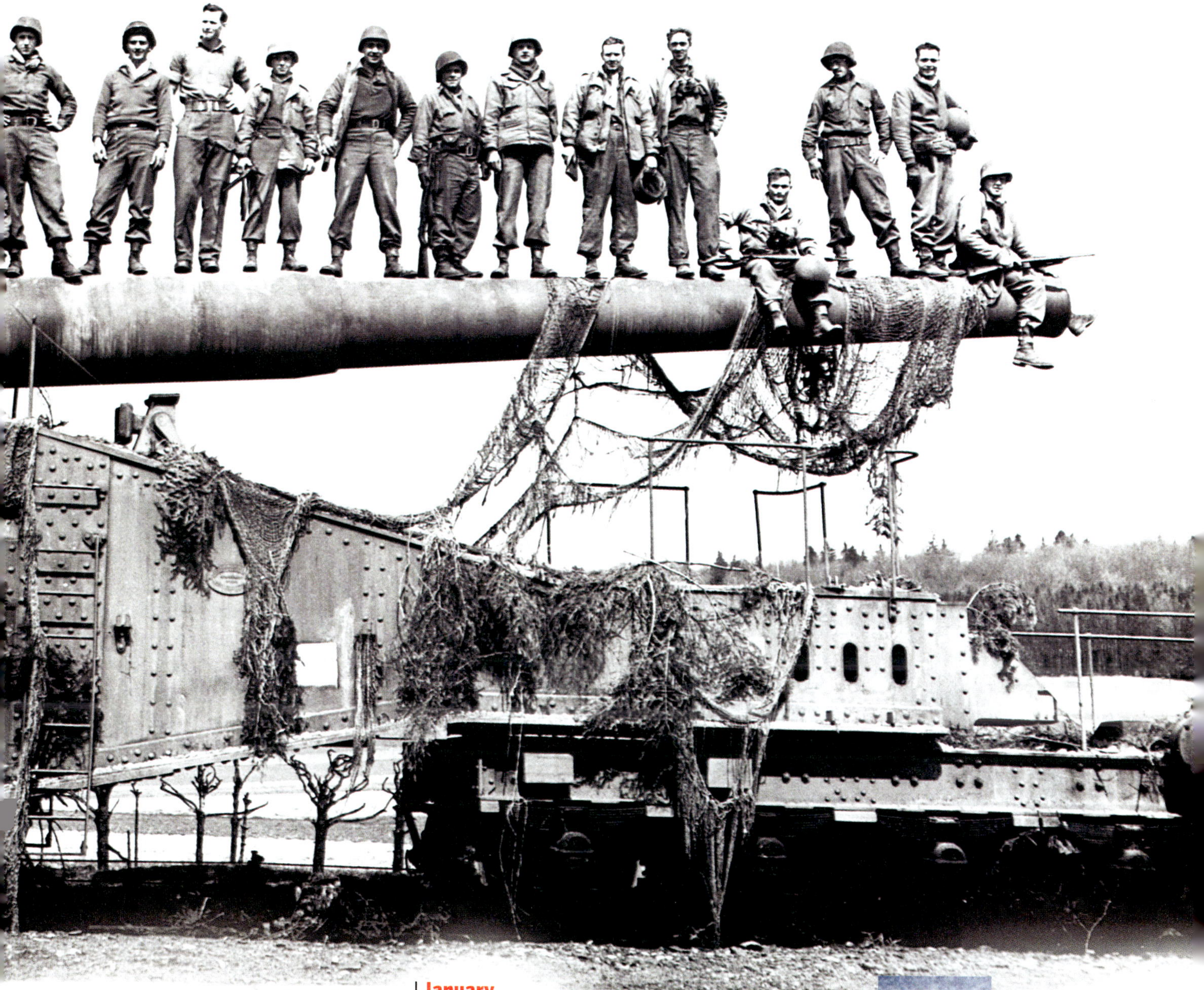

June 4
Americans destroy four Japanese aircraft carriers in the Battle of Midway.

January
Americans win the Battle of Guadalcanal.

July 10
Allies invade Sicily.

June 6
Allies launch invasion of France.

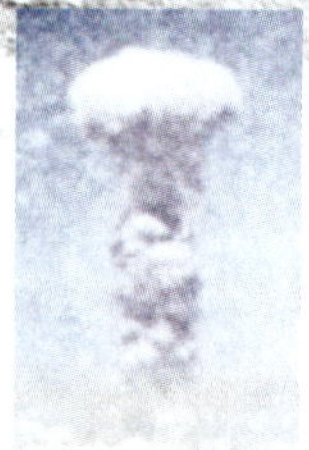

August 15
After the bombings of Hiroshima and Nagasaki, the Japanese surrender.

1942 | 1943 | 1944 | 1945

1942
Hitler and the Nazis formalize plans for exterminating Europe's Jews.

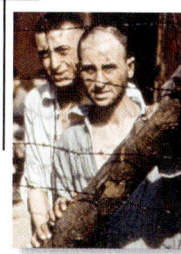

February
The Soviet Union finally defeats the Germans in the Battle of Stalingrad.

June
French Resistance forces aid the Allied invasion of France.

April 30
Adolf Hitler commits suicide in Berlin.

The War in Europe and North Africa

BEFORE YOU READ

MAIN IDEA

After entering World War II, the United States focused first on the war in Europe.

READING FOCUS

1. How and why did the Allies fight the Battle of the Atlantic?
2. What were the key events of the war in the Soviet Union?
3. What did American forces accomplish in North Africa and Italy?
4. What were the events and significance of the Allies' D-Day invasion of France?

KEY TERMS AND PEOPLE

wolf pack
Erwin Rommel
Operation Torch
Dwight D. Eisenhower
Tuskegee Airmen
Operation Overlord
Omar Bradley
D-Day
Battle of the Bulge
George S. Patton

P1 3.1 Compare and contrast the experiences of different ethnic, national, and religious groups, including Native American Indians, in the United States, explaining their contributions to American society and culture.

The Sinking of the Reuben James

▲ The *Reuben James*, the first U.S. vessel destroyed by enemy fire in World War II, lost more than 100 of its crew.

THE INSIDE STORY

What were the hidden dangers of crossing the Atlantic? For ships traveling across the Atlantic Ocean in the early days of World War II, the danger of German submarine attack was always present. Unable to tell whether U-boats, or submarines, were lurking nearby, ships' crews lived in constant fear of attack. When submarines struck without warning, that fear turned to terror.

The crew of the Navy destroyer USS *Reuben James* learned this firsthand in October 1941. At the time, the United States had not yet entered the war. Its ships, however, were serving as escorts to convoys carrying goods from American ports to Great Britain. It was while on such a mission that the *Reuben James* was attacked by a German U-boat. Following a torpedo strike, the ship's ammunition exploded. The *Reuben James* sank quickly. Most of its crew, including all officers, went down with the ship.

A number of crew members, however, were thrown into the sea. They struggled to stay afloat in the freezing water, which was covered with a thick, black layer of oily fuel from the *Reuben James.* Nearby ships rushed to their aid, but the slick oil made it difficult for the sailors to grasp the rescue lines. Reports of another nearby U-boat made the rescue vessels scatter—leaving survivors still bobbing in the sea.

The terrible story of the *Reuben James* would be repeated often in the months ahead. As you will read, the first battles the United States would fight were not on dry land but on the high seas. There it would take time before the United States and its allies would find effective ways to fight their hidden enemy—the German U-boat. ■

The Battle of the Atlantic

For the United States and the Allies, defeating the Axis Powers depended largely on control of the seas. It was only by sea that the United States could deliver soldiers and supplies to the hard-pressed opponents of Hitler. If the Atlantic was not kept safe for shipping, the Axis would soon win the war.

Germany entered World War II with a navy powerful enough to challenge for control of the seas. It featured several new surface ships. Foremost among these was the giant *Bismarck*, the pride of the German fleet. After Great Britain managed to sink the *Bismarck* in 1941, however, Germany began to rely on a familiar weapon—the U-boat.

U-boat attacks In World War I the Allies had learned to protect ships against U-boats by forming convoys. Early in World War II, however, the British (and the Americans) did not have enough vessels to form effective convoys. This made it easy for U-boats to attack supply ships bound for Great Britain. The Germans also developed new tactics to increase U-boat effectiveness. One example was the so-called **wolf pack**, in which U-boats hunted in groups and often attacked at night.

The German U-boat fleet enjoyed what it referred to as the "happy time" in 1940 and 1941. U-boats sent hundreds of ships and tons of supplies to the bottom of the sea. At the same time, the German navy lost only a few dozen U-boats.

After Germany declared war on the United States, U-boat attacks on American shipping increased. German submarines even patrolled the waters off the East Coast of the United States. There they made easy pickings of merchant ships that sailed from American ports without the protection of a full convoy. In a few short months, 360 American ships were sunk compared to just eight German U-boats.

The Allies fight back Despite early losses, America's entry into the war would help turn the tide in the Battle of the Atlantic. Energized American shipyards began producing new ships at an amazing rate. These were used to form larger, better-equipped convoys, which helped cut down on the effectiveness of U-boat

HISTORY CLOSE-UP

The Allied Convoy System

Convoys offered safety in numbers. They could include dozens of ships spread over many miles.

Aircraft flying over the convoy helped spot prowling U-boats in the ocean below. These airplanes used radar to detect U-boats.

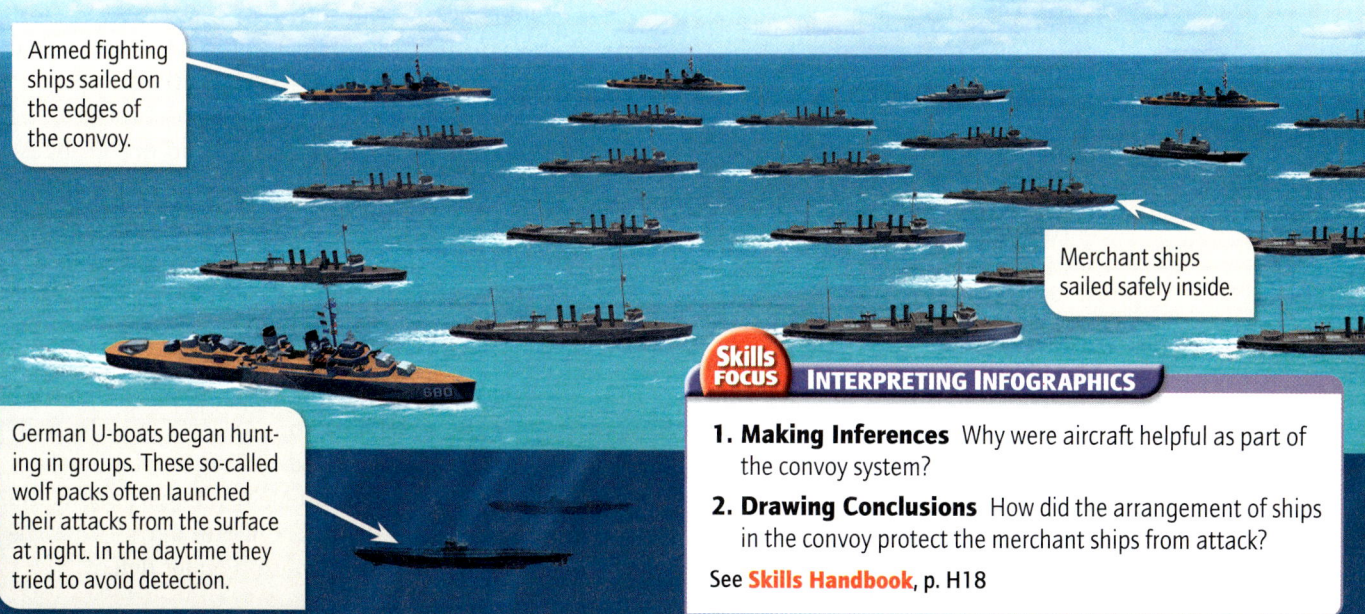

Armed fighting ships sailed on the edges of the convoy.

Merchant ships sailed safely inside.

German U-boats began hunting in groups. These so-called wolf packs often launched their attacks from the surface at night. In the daytime they tried to avoid detection.

Skills FOCUS   **INTERPRETING INFOGRAPHICS**

1. **Making Inferences** Why were aircraft helpful as part of the convoy system?
2. **Drawing Conclusions** How did the arrangement of ships in the convoy protect the merchant ships from attack?

See **Skills Handbook**, p. H18

attacks. At the same time, new Allied aircraft protected convoys from the air. The aircraft and escort ships used radar and other technologies to find and destroy more U-boats.

Another factor in the Allied success was the breaking of Germany's code system, which was called Enigma. After cracking Enigma in 1941, the Allies began to gain vital information about the locations and plans of U-boat formations.

These factors began to give the Allies an advantage over German U-boats. German sailors were soon referring to their ships as "iron coffins." By war's end, some 70 percent of the Germans who had served on a submarine were dead. The Atlantic belonged to the Allies.

READING CHECK **Identifying Problems and Solutions** How did the Allies overcome the German U-boats and win the Battle of the Atlantic?

The War in the Soviet Union

In the summer of 1941, Hitler broke his nonaggression pact with Stalin and sent his forces into the Soviet Union. (The Soviets thus joined the Allies as enemies of the Axis Powers.) For the next several months, German forces stormed across the Soviet countryside. As they had in Poland and France, German tanks, planes, and soldiers steadily pressed the attack. Stalin's forces seemed unable to stop the blitzkrieg.

Though the Soviet Union appeared close to collapse, it did not fall. As autumn came and went, the Soviets were joined by a new ally—the bitterly cold Russian winter. German soldiers and equipment performed poorly in the freezing temperatures, and their invasion slowed.

Still, the Germans held a huge portion of the western Soviet Union. They had also besieged the city of Leningrad. The suffering of the people there was extreme. With little food and fuel, some 200,000 residents died in January and February alone. Hundreds of thousands more would perish in the months ahead.

The Battle of Stalingrad
When spring returned to the Soviet Union, the German armies renewed their assault. One major target was the city of Stalingrad, a major industrial center on the Volga River. The Germans attacked Stalingrad in August 1942. In some of the bloodiest fighting in the history of warfare, the Soviets refused to let Stalingrad fall.

Not only did the Germans fail to take Stalingrad, they also exposed themselves to a Soviet counterattack. In the fighting that followed, 250,000 Axis soldiers were trapped by Soviet forces. The surviving Axis troops were forced to surrender in early 1943. Hitler had suffered a stunning defeat.

Stalingrad marked the beginning of Germany's collapse in the Soviet Union. Thereafter, Soviet forces began to push German forces back toward Germany. The fighting took a terrible toll. Hitler's forces suffered losses of some 2 million, and the Soviets paid an even higher price—12 million soldiers. Millions of civilians also died. In Leningrad alone, as many as 800,000 civilians perished before the siege there was finally lifted in January 1944. Yet the Soviet Union had survived. Now it was fighting toward the final defeat of the Axis.

READING CHECK **Sequencing** Briefly describe the sequence of events of the war in the Soviet Union.

American Forces in North Africa and Italy

Soon after the fall of France in June 1940, the British and Italians began a battle for North Africa. This territory was vital to the Allies. By controlling it, the British could protect shipping on the Mediterranean Sea against Italian attack. This shipping was a lifeline by which the British could efficiently get oil through the Suez Canal from the Middle East. Without oil Great Britain would not be able to defend itself, much less defeat the Axis.

In the early fighting, Italian forces based in Libya tried to drive the British from their stronghold in Egypt. They failed. In fact, the Italians were beaten badly and driven backwards. Hitler was forced to send troops to support the Italians in early 1941. At the head of these forces was the famed German general **Erwin Rommel**. Throughout 1941 and 1942, Rommel's forces and the British fought a back-and-forth battle for control of North Africa. Though Rommel led brilliantly—it was here he earned the nickname Desert Fox—the British ultimately gained control. At the battle of El Alamein (el-a-luh-MAYN), fought about the same time as the Battle of Stalingrad, the British handed the Germans a major defeat.

WORLD WAR II IN EUROPE AND NORTH AFRICA, 1941–1944

NORWAY
SWEDEN
FINLAND
Leningrad 1941
North Sea
ESTONIA
UNITED KINGDOM
IRELAND
Baltic Sea
LATVIA
UNION OF SOVIET SOCIALIST REPUBLICS
DENMARK
LITHUANIA
1940
ATLANTIC OCEAN
NETHERLANDS
EAST PRUSSIA
London
Berlin
1940
Warsaw
1941
Stalingrad 1942-43
BELGIUM
1940
1939
POLAND
1941
Paris
1940
LUX.
GERMANY
CZECHOSLOVAKIA
1941
FRANCE
1940
SWITZ.
AUSTRIA
HUNGARY
ROMANIA
ITALY
1941
PORTUGAL
Black Sea
YUGOSLAVIA
BULGARIA
Rome
Anzio 1944
ALBANIA
SPAIN
1941
From U.S.
1942
1942
1942
1942
1943
1943
GREECE
Casablanca
Algiers
Tunis
Sicily
Crete
MOROCCO
ALGERIA
Kasserine Pass 1943
TUNISIA
Mediterranean Sea

Legend:
- Allied (1942)
- Allied advance
- Axis-controlled (1942)
- Axis advance
- Neutral (1942)
- ★ Major battle

0   200   400 Miles
0   200   400 Kilometers
Lambert Azimuthal equal-area projection

LIBYA
EGYPT
El Alamein 1942-43

go.hrw.com
Interactive Map
Keyword: SD7 CH24

GEOGRAPHY SKILLS INTERPRETING MAPS

1. **Regions** What was the extent of Axis control in 1942?
2. **Movement** Describe the major Allied advances in Africa and the Mediterranean.

See **Skills Handbook**, p. H20

Operation Torch When the United States entered the war in late 1941, President Roosevelt was anxious to make a contribution quickly. Stalin wanted the Allies to invade Europe, to help divide Hitler's attentions. Other Allied leaders, however, resisted calls to rush into Europe unprepared. North Africa, it was decided, was the <u>logical</u> place for American soldiers to enter the fray.

The commander of what came to be called **Operation Torch** was a U.S. lieutenant general named **Dwight D. Eisenhower**. The plan called for American forces to invade the North African countries of Morocco and Algeria in November 1942. France had controlled this territory before 1940. After the fall of France, Vichy leaders were installed there. Still, the Allies hoped that the French in North Africa would side with them in battle. Indeed, the Allies met little resistance upon landing, and French forces soon joined them.

After landing, Allied forces turned east to fight the Germans. In battles at places such as Kasserine Pass, Americans gained valuable combat experience. Some 20,000 Americans were killed or wounded in the six months of North Africa fighting. But by May 1943, they had helped defeat Rommel's forces.

While this fighting was taking place, Allied leaders focused on the war's next phases. Stalin continued to push for a European invasion, and in the planning stages was a massive invasion of France. In early 1943, however, such an operation was still a year away. For now, Allied leaders prepared to cross the Mediterranean and knock the Italians out of the war.

ACADEMIC VOCABULARY

logical based on correct reasoning

On to Italy The first major step in this assault was the July 1943 invasion of the island of Sicily. Soon after the attack began, Roosevelt and Churchill issued a message to the Italian people asking them "whether they want to die for Mussolini and Hitler or live for Italy and civilization." The Italians chose life. By the end of the month, they had turned against dictator Benito Mussolini and forced him from power. The Allies took Sicily a few weeks later. They planned next to occupy the Italian Peninsula.

Hitler, however, was not going to let the Allies simply march through Italy and into Europe. German forces rushed to stop them.

Despite German resistance, the Allies made steady progress at first. Taking part in the fighting were the **Tuskegee Airmen**. This was a segregated unit of African Americans, the first ever to receive training as pilots in the U.S. military.

After its early success, the Allied invasion slowed as it approached Rome. To keep it moving, the Allies planned to land a large force behind enemy lines. The site they chose for this landing was a seafront resort called Anzio.

In late January, the first of some 100,000 Allied soldiers went ashore at Anzio. Fighting raged for the next four months as the Allies were unable to break out of their small coastal beachhead. Finally, Allied forces from the south fought their way to Anzio and freed the trapped soldiers. By then, from 25,000 to 30,000 Allied soldiers had been killed or wounded.

The end of the battle at Anzio, however, did not end the fighting in Italy. It continued for nearly a year. Some 300,000 Allied troops were killed or wounded there.

READING CHECK **Summarizing** What did American forces experience in North Africa and Italy?

Americans in North Africa and Italy

The Tuskegee Airmen's 99th Pursuit Squadron (left) provided air support in both North Africa and Italy. Among their numerous awards, their fighter group was honored for "outstanding performance and extraordinary heroism." In all, the Tuskegee Airmen completed 15,500 missions. Below, elite U.S. Army Rangers charge up an Italian hillside. Rangers, specially trained volunteers who had been serving in Northern Ireland, spearheaded the push through Italy.

D-Day: The Invasion of France

The fighting in Italy was slow and difficult partly because the Allies could not devote all their fighting resources to the battle. Many of these resources were being held for the planned invasion of France. This plan came to be known as **Operation Overlord**.

Planning Operation Overlord

To end the war as quickly as possible, the Allies wanted to launch a large invasion of mainland Europe. Careful planning was vital. The Allies worked for months to select a location for Operation Overlord. They finally settled on the beaches of Normandy, in northern France.

The Allies had to assemble huge numbers of troops, weapons, and other equipment necessary for an invasion. Eisenhower commanded the mission and chose General **Omar Bradley** to lead the American troops. The top British commander was Bernard Montgomery.

While good planning was important, speed was also vital. Of particular concern to the Allies was the expected introduction of two new German weapons, the V1 flying bomb and the V2 rocket. The Allies were able to destroy some rocket-launch sites, but fears of these dangerous weapons forced the Allies onward.

The landing at Normandy

By early June 1944, the Allied force of 3.5 million soldiers was ready for action. Tension ran high. The soldiers knew they had to succeed—and that success was uncertain. They knew that at Normandy they would meet a determined German force.

After a short delay caused by bad weather, **D-Day** finally arrived on June 6, 1944. The attack began with soldiers parachuting behind the German lines to try to secure key sites. Ships offshore rained shells on the coastline to destroy German defenses. Allied aircraft filled the sky to provide cover for the wave of troops to come. A variety of amphibious craft helped deliver equipment and soldiers to the beaches.

In the end, however, the success of Operation Overlord came down to the courage of the individual soldiers who would make the landing. Their job was to wait for their landing-craft gate to open—then to move forward toward shore. By the thousands, they waded through the surf till they hit the sand and then raced

FACES OF HISTORY

Dwight EISENHOWER
1890–1969

Dwight D. Eisenhower was known for his logical mind, a talent for organizing, and an outgoing yet diplomatic attitude. He proved to be the ideal person to lead the Allied military force in World War II.

From his humble childhood in the small farm town of Abilene, Kansas, Eisenhower rose steadily through the ranks of the army. During World War II, General George C. Marshall chose Eisenhower to be Supreme Allied Commander in Europe. In this position Eisenhower planned and commanded Operation Overlord (D-Day), the invasion of France. He also accepted Germany's surrender in 1945.

Explain In what ways do you think Eisenhower's personality helped make him a good leader in World War II?

---

through obstacles, wounded and dead comrades, and a hail of gunfire to find something to hide behind. Then those who managed to get that far gathered their courage, got to their feet, and went forward again. All was chaos and confusion. Little went according to plan. Still, soldiers stuck to their assigned tasks.

HISTORY'S VOICES

> ❝It's amazing what you can do when you're called upon to do it. There was just an overwhelming demand for me to do my duty. Patriotism—that was there. But more, I was filled with a sense of duty. This was my duty, my assigned duty. This is what was expected of me.❞
>
> —Frank Walk, recorded in *War Stories*, by Elizabeth Mullener

Fortunately for the Allies, the Germans were slow to respond to the invasion. Thanks in part to Allied deceptions, Hitler feared that the assault on Normandy was just a trick and that another invasion would take place elsewhere. For precious days, German leaders delayed in sending backup forces to the area. By the time they realized their mistake, the Allies had established a beachhead.

Though the costs were high—an estimated 10,000 Allied casualties, including 6,600 Americans—D-Day had been a success. With each day, more troops and equipment came ashore. By early July, the Allies had landed almost a million soldiers and nearly 180,000 vehicles. The landing area was considered secure enough to send in members of the Women's

D-Day, June 6, 1944

Allied forces landed at five separate sites at Normandy on D-Day of the invasion of France. Omaha Beach was one of two beaches invaded by U.S. forces (see map opposite). As American soldiers moved toward the nearly 100-foot-high cliffs, German guns at the top rained a deadly fire down on them.

Allied aircraft provided cover for the invading forces.

Allied warships fired shells on German positions before and during the landing.

Army Corp. They were to supply support for the forces that would soon fight their way past German defenses at Normandy. This breakthrough occurred in late July. As the German commander reported, "The whole western front has been ripped open."

The Allies were now on the march in France. By the end of August, Paris had been freed from the Germans. Hitler's once mighty war machine was now in full retreat.

The Battle of the Bulge Throughout the fall of 1944, the Allies moved eastward. The Germans fought well in places. For example, the Battle of Hürtgen Forest claimed thousands of Allied lives. Overall, however, the Germans appeared near collapse. As one of Eisenhower's advisers put it in early December, "The battle is over and the German army has had it."

This judgment, it turned out, was premature. On December 16, 1944, the Germans launched a surprise offensive of their own. The attack was known as the **Battle of the Bulge**. This referred to the bulge in the Allied battle lines created by the German advance. For several days, Hitler's forces threatened to win back vital ground from the Allies.

A key moment in the battle came at the Belgian city of Bastogne. This was an important crossroads, and the Germans were determined to take it. Even more determined was the small force of American defenders. Surrounded by Germans, shivering in below-zero temperatures and low on supplies, the Americans clung to survival. But survive they did. On December 26, troops led by Lieutenant General **George S. Patton** arrived to provide relief for the American force. The victory at Bastogne helped blunt the German offensive. It also became a symbol of American strength and determination.

By the end of January 1945, the bulge created by the German offensive had been rolled back. Once again the Allies set their sights on Germany and the defeat of Hitler. Victory was close at hand.

READING CHECK **Drawing Conclusions**
Why did the planning for D-Day take so long?

Guns and firing trenches placed on the bluff enabled the Germans to do terrible damage to the invaders.

German defenses at Omaha Beach included a variety of barriers and explosive mines both on the beach and in the water.

Soldiers who survived the landing climbed the cliffs and tried to take out German firing positions.

Many soldiers were drowned or killed by enemy fire as landing crafts headed into the beach.

ALLIED INVASION

UNITED KINGDOM   London
Portland   South   •
           Hampton   Portsmouth
Dartmouth   •   Shoreham
                            Strait of Dover
English Channel   Calais

                    Sword
                    (U.K.)
          Utah
          (U.S.)

       Omaha   Juno
       (U.S.)   (Canada)
            Gold
            (U.K.)
   0   50 Miles   NORMANDY
   0   50 Kilometers   FRANCE

Skills FOCUS INTERPRETING INFOGRAPHICS

go.hrw.com
Interactive
Keyword: SD7 CH24

1. **Making Generalizations** What advantages did the Germans have at Omaha Beach?

2. **Comparing** What measures did U.S. forces take to counter these advantages?

See **Skills Handbook**, p. H18

SECTION 1 ASSESSMENT

go.hrw.com
Online Quiz
Keyword: SD7 HP24

Reviewing Ideas, Terms, and People

1. **a. Describe** Briefly describe the Battle of the Atlantic.
   b. Explain Why was control of the seas so important for the Allies and the Axis?

2. **a. Identify** Why was the Battle of Stalingrad significant?
   b. Summarize Write one sentence that summarizes the fighting in the Soviet Union between 1941 and 1944.

3. **a. Define** Write brief definitions of the following terms: **Operation Torch, Tuskegee Airmen**
   b. Make Inferences What can you infer from the fact that the Americans' initial battles with the Germans can be described as "learning experiences"?

4. **a. Define** Write brief definitions of the following terms: **Operation Overlord, D-Day, Battle of the Bulge**
   b. Contrast How did Operation Overlord compare to the landing at Anzio?

Critical Thinking

5. **Identifying Cause and Effect** Copy the chart. Use it to identify major battles in the Soviet Union, North Africa, and Europe between 1941 and 1944 and the result of each battle.

Battle	Result
1.	
2.	
3.	
4.	

FOCUS ON WRITING

6. **Expository** Was Operation Overlord a major turning point in the European war? Write a short essay in which you develop your position on this issue.

BEFORE YOU READ

MAIN IDEA

During the Holocaust, Germany's Nazi government systematically murdered some 6 million Jews and 5 million others in Europe.

READING FOCUS

1. What was the history of Nazi anti-Semitism?
2. What was the Nazi government's Final Solution?
3. How did the United States respond to the Holocaust?

KEY TERMS AND PEOPLE

anti-Semitism
Kristallnacht
concentration camp
ghetto
genocide
Final Solution
War Refugee Board
Holocaust
Hermann Göering

PI 3.3 Prepare essays and oral reports about the important social, political, economic, scientific, technological, and cultural developments, issues, and events from New York State and United States history.

A Life-Saving EFFORT

THE INSIDE STORY

How did people in a French village save the lives of thousands of Jews? In 1940 Hitler's German army was rampaging across Europe. By June it had conquered France. The Jewish population there found itself facing what Jews in Germany and Poland had already come to know—government-sponsored persecution, hatred, and brutal mistreatment at the hands of Germany's Nazi Party. Scenes like the one shown above took place throughout France, as Nazis and their followers rounded

◀ **During the Holocaust, the Nazi government targeted European Jews.**

up Jews and sent them to prison camps far from home. These Jews' futures—and their chances of survival—were extremely grim.

During World War II, thousands of non-Jews risked their lives to help save Jews from the Nazis. One such rescue took place in the village of Le Chambon-sur-Lignon (luh shahm-BOHN-soor-leen-yohn) in southern France. In 1942 André Trocmé, the pastor of a local church, called on village residents to give shelter to Jews who asked for help. The residents began to hide Jews in their homes and farms and help them escape to safety in Switzerland. France's Nazi-controlled government demanded that the pastor end the rescue effort. He responded by saying, "These people came here for help and for shelter. I am their shepherd. A shepherd does not desert his flock . . . We do not know what a Jew is; we only know people."

Over the course of the war, the people of Le Chambon helped some 5,000 Jews escape Nazi capture. This was a life-saving effort. As you will read in this section, the persecution of Jews was part of a terrible Nazi plan to murder the entire Jewish population of Europe.

In 1963 the government of Israel began a program to honor those who risked their lives to save Jews. Among those honored were the people of Le Chambon. ◼

Nazi Anti-Semitism

Why did the Nazi government single out Jews especially for mistreatment? The answer has to do with **anti-Semitism**, which is hostility toward or prejudice against Jews.

As you have read, Germany after World War I suffered blows to its economy and pride. Adolf Hitler rose to power in part by promising to return Germany to its former glory. He also told the Germans that they came from a superior race—the Aryans. The idea that Germans had descended from the mythical Aryan people was not new. It was found in German folktales and music. Hitler, however, was effective at using the notion to build support.

In addition to appealing to German pride, Hitler also provided a scapegoat—someone to blame for Germany's woes. The group he singled out was the Jews.

In fact, Jews had lived in Germany for 1,600 years. Christian hostility toward Jews had existed since the Middle Ages. Indeed, many of the anti-Jewish Nazi laws recalled medieval efforts to humiliate Jews. For example, a Nazi law that forced Jews to wear the Jewish Star of David was similar to a 1215 decree that told Jews to dress differently than Christians.

Nazi anti-Semitism combined this medieval Christian hostility with modern—but false—scientific ideas about racial inferiority. Another Nazi law defined anyone with a Jewish grandparent as a Jew, even if the person had no connection with Judaism. Under the Nazis, anti-Semitism changed from prejudice based on religion to hatred based on ancestry.

Hitler in power Hitler began his campaign against Germany's Jews soon after becoming chancellor in 1933. Over the next few years, his Nazi government <u>established</u> a series of anti-Semitic laws. The purpose was to drive the Jews from Germany. For example, in 1935, the Nuremberg Laws stripped Jews of German citizenship and took away most civil and economic rights. The laws also defined who was a Jew and who was an Aryan German.

Attacks on Jews Some Germans were repelled by Hitler's actions. Yet many other people supported his anti-Semitic ideas.

Jewish shopkeepers in Berlin pick up the pieces of their shattered businesses after the destruction of Kristallnacht. *What prompted Germans to attack their Jewish neighbors?*

Discrimination against Jews continued. Violent attacks against Jews also increased.

In 1938, on the nights of November 9 and 10, anti-Jewish riots broke out across Germany. The attack came to be called *Kristallnacht* (KRIS-tahl-nahkt)—the "night of broken glass." The Nazis claimed the attacks were a spontaneous reaction to the assassination of a Nazi official by a Jewish teenager. In fact, the Nazis encouraged the violence. During the rampage, thousands of Jewish businesses and places of worship were damaged. Thugs killed nearly 100 Jews. Over 26,000 more were sent to **concentration camps**—labor camps meant to hold what Hitler called enemies of the state. The Nazis blamed the Jews for Kristallnacht and held them financially responsible. Jews were fined a total of 1 billion marks.

Flight from Germany Kristallnacht sent a strong message to those Jews still in Germany: "Get out!" Over 100,000 managed to leave Germany in the months following the attacks. Many others, however, found it difficult to leave the country. Nazi laws had left many German Jews without money or property, and most countries were unwilling to take in poor immigrants. Other countries, such as the United States, had limited the number of Germans who could enter the country.

READING CHECK **Summarizing** Briefly trace the history of Nazi anti-Semitism.

ACADEMIC VOCABULARY
established created, or brought into being

Toward the Final Solution

When Hitler came to power, Europe was home to 9 million Jews. Few of these people lived under German control. That changed with the outbreak of World War II. As Hitler's armies blazed across Europe, many European Jews came under the control of the Nazi SS. This was the feared police and military force that carried out terror activities for the Nazis. SS treatment of the Jews was overwhelmingly brutal. In the words of one SS leader, the goal was to "incarcerate [jail] or annihilate" the Jews.

Concentration camps and ghettos

The first concentration camps were created in Germany before the start of World War II. These were basically prisons for Jews and others who were considered enemies of Hitler's regime. After the outbreak of World War II, the Nazis established many more camps to hold Jews from the countries that Germany had invaded and occupied. Camps were also set up to house prisoners of war.

As German forces took control of an area, they would arrest the Jews living there. The local population sometimes helped shelter their Jewish neighbors. *The Diary of Anne Frank* is a famous book that tells the story of a young Jewish girl living in the Netherlands whose family hid successfully for two years with the help of neighbors. Like many Jews in German-occupied lands, the Franks were eventually discovered and sent to concentration camps.

Conditions in the Nazi camps were horrific. Inmates received little food and were often forced to perform grueling labor. This combination of overwork and starvation was deliberately designed to kill. Punishment for even the most minor offenses was swift, sure, and deadly. In short, there were many ways to die in a concentration camp. Yet as you will read, the Nazis had only just begun to develop their ghastly killing methods.

Another tactic used by the Nazis to control and punish Jews was to establish ghettos. These are neighborhoods in a city to which a group of people are confined. As in the concentration camps, life in a Jewish ghetto was desperate. Walls or fences kept Jews inside. Those trying to get out were shot. Food was scarce. Diseases spread quickly in the crowded conditions, and many Jews fell ill.

The worst ghetto was in Warsaw, Poland. There, a half-million Jews were crammed into an area less than 1.5 miles square. They lived on a daily ration of thin soup and a slice of bread. In 1941 alone, 43,000 died of hunger. Recalled one survivor, "Every day was men with hand wagons picking up the dead ones from the corners who died of hunger or cold."

In 1943, most of the ghetto residents were sent off to Treblinka, a concentration camp. Those who remained decided to fight back. A group called the Jewish Fighting Organization attacked the Germans with crude weapons. For many Jews it was a proud moment.

HISTORY'S VOICES

❝For the first time since the occupation, we saw Germans clinging to walls, crawling on the ground, running for cover, hesitating before taking a step in the fear of being hit by a Jewish bullet.❞

—Tuvia Borzykowski, recorded in *The Second World War: A Complete History*, by Martin Gilbert

The Warsaw uprising lasted nearly a month. In the end, however, it was crushed. The residents were killed or shipped to concentration camps, where most would die.

The Final Solution

From the first days of World War II, instances of Nazi mass-killings of Jews and other civilians occurred. In many Polish towns, German soldiers rounded up Jews and shot them on the spot. In Bedzin, soldiers forced several hundred Jews into the local synagogue, or Jewish house of worship, and set it on fire. Stories such as these were repeated across Poland.

The German invasion of the Soviet Union in 1941 raised the killing of Jews to a new level. Now Hitler called for the total destruction of all of Europe's Jews. What he proposed—the killing of an entire people—is called genocide. At first, the bloody work was carried out by mobile killing units—*Einsatzgruppen* (EYEN-sahtz-GROOP-uhn). In one incident in the fall of 1941, over 33,000 people were massacred in two days. The bodies were piled into a ravine at Babi Yar, near the Ukrainian city of Kiev.

As bloody as the work of the *Einsatzgruppen* was, Nazi leaders were not satisfied. For them, the killing was not going quickly enough. It was also proving difficult on the men who performed it. Thus, Nazi officials adopted a plan known as the Final Solution. This involved

THE HOLOCAUST, 1939–1945

NETHERLANDS
Amsterdam ✪
BELGIUM
LUX.
Paris ✪
FRANCE
SWITZ.
ITALY

Bergen-Belsen
Berlin ✦
GERMANY
Buchenwald
Dachau

EAST PRUSSIA
POLAND
Treblinka
Chelmno
Warsaw ✪
Sobibor
Auschwitz
Majdanek
Vienna ✪
AUSTRIA
HUNGARY
YUGOSLAVIA

CZECHOSLOVAKIA

ROMANIA

Legend:
● Major concentration camp
• Concentration camp
▢ Extent of German control

0   150   300 Miles
0   150   300 Kilometers
Albers equal-area projection

GEOGRAPHY SKILLS **INTERPRETING MAPS**

The Nazis expanded the number of camps as their conquests brought more Jews under their control.

1. **Place** Which country had the greatest number of camps?

2. **Location** Why do you think the Nazis built so many camps there?

See **Skills Handbook**, p. H20

the establishment of six new camps. These were to be extermination camps for the widespread murder of Jews. Unlike the concentration camps you read about earlier, nearly all inmates at the extermination camps were murdered upon their arrival. The method of killing was by exposure to poison gas in specially built gas chambers. Inmates might also be selected for cruel medical experiments, which often ended in death. Some were also forced to perform labor.

Some 3 million Jews died in Nazi extermination camps. Another 3 million died at Nazi hands by other means. Nazis murdered men, women, and children alike. Wrote Nazi leader Heinrich Himmler, "I did not feel justified in exterminating the men… while allowing the avengers, in the form of their children, to grow up."

In addition to the Jews, the Nazi death machine killed about 5 million others. Among these victims were prisoners of war, disabled people, and the Romany, an ethnic group also known as Gypsies.

READING CHECK **Identifying the Main Idea**
What was the purpose of the Final Solution?

EUROPE'S JEWISH POPULATION

	c. 1933	c. 1950	Percent Decrease
Europe	9,500,000	3,500,000	63
Selected Countries			
Poland	3,000,000	45,000	98.5
Romania	980,000	28,000	97
Germany	565,000	37,000	93.5
Hungary	445,000	155,000	65
Czechoslovakia	357,000	17,000	95
Austria	250,000	18,000	93
Greece	100,000	7,000	93
Yugoslavia	70,000	3,500	95
Bulgaria	50,000	6,500	87

Source: *United States Holocaust Memorial Museum*

Concentration Camp Liberation

As the Allied forces pushed westward across Europe, they came upon the concentration camps that held victims of the Holocaust. Many of the survivors were barely alive. Gerda Weissman was a Jewish prisoner in a Czechoslavakian camp. She recalled the day that American soldiers liberated her camp.

Skills FOCUS   READING LIKE A HISTORIAN

1. **Analyzing Primary Sources** Why was Gerda Weissman so surprised by the soldier's question?

2. **Drawing Conclusions** What did Weissman mean when she said the soldier's gesture "restored me to humanity"?

See **Skills Handbook**, pp. H28–H29

"All of a sudden I saw a strange car coming down the hill, no longer green, not bearing the swastika, but a white star. It was sort of a mud-splattered vehicle but I've never seen a star brighter in my life. And two men sort of jumped out, came running toward us and one came toward where I stood. He was wearing battle gear… I would say it was the greatest hour of my life. And then he asked an incredible question. He said, 'May I see the other ladies?' You know, what… what we have been addressed for six years and then to hear this man. He looked to me like a young god… He held the door open for me and let me precede him and in that gesture restored me to humanity."

The American Response

THE IMPACT TODAY

Government

American leaders continue to face pressure to help populations under attack by their own governments. In the early 2000s, the United States worked to end what was seen as a government-supported effort to destroy the population in Darfur, a region of the African nation of Sudan.

In the 1930s American immigration rules limited the number of Jews who could move to the United States. Although many Americans had read of Kristallnacht and knew about Hitler's policies toward the Jews, they were unwilling to allow large numbers of foreign workers enter the United States during a time when jobs were already scarce. At the time, few truly understood that millions of lives were at stake.

The start of the war eventually brought an end to the economic problems facing American workers, but it did not change American feelings about immigration. That began to change in 1942, when American officials started to learn the horrifying details of what was taking place in Europe. The head of a major Jewish organization in Switzerland told American officials what he had heard about Hitler's Final Solution. The Americans were doubtful at first. One official wrote to another, "The report has earmarks of war rumor inspired by fear." Soon, however, the reality began to sink in.

The fate of Europe's Jews was just one of many issues that preoccupied the United States and its leaders. As you have read, 1943 was a year of difficult fighting in Italy and a time for planning the D-Day invasion. The United States was also fighting hard in the Pacific. These were vital steps in the effort to defeat Hitler and the Axis Powers, which, some argued, might help save millions of lives.

It was not until January 1944 that President Roosevelt announced the creation of the **War Refugee Board**. This organization was told to "take all measures to rescue victims of enemy oppression in imminent [immediate] danger of death." Through the board, the United States was able to help 200,000 Jews who might otherwise have fallen into the hands of the Nazis.

Liberating the Nazi camps As you have read, Allied forces in 1942 started to push back the German advances gained in the beginning of the war. The Soviets made the greatest early progress. In 1944 Soviet troops began to discover some of the Nazi camps that had been set up to house and kill Jews in Poland. In early 1945, they reached the huge extermination camp at Auschwitz. Their reports of the conditions at these camps finally gave the American people proof of Hitler's terrible plan.

American and British forces also encountered death camps. In April 1945 American soldiers came upon several, including the camp at Buchenwald. This was one of the first and largest concentration camps established in Germany. During its existence, some 240,000 prisoners spent time at the camp. Of those, at least 43,000 died. Another 10,000 were shipped elsewhere to be killed.

The Nazis had abandoned Buchenwald shortly before the Americans arrived. Many of the camp's prisoners, however, remained behind. The scenes were appalling. The bodies of victims lay in piles throughout the camp. Many of the survivors were themselves barely alive. One American soldier who was among the first to enter the camp recalled, "They were just one step from their last breath. They weren't able to feel happy. They were so skinny—just skin and bones." Many of these rescued victims were so ill that they could not be saved. At the Bergen-Belsen concentration camp, 13,000 inmates died after they were set free by the British.

Some of the inmates were strong enough to celebrate their freedom. At Dachau, surviving inmates broke out of their prison to meet the approaching American tanks. "Everybody was running—everybody who could run," recalled one survivor. "It looked like somebody from heaven came." Yet within the camp fences was the same horror—the piles of bodies and a great many starving inmates.

The Nuremberg trials Following World War II, many Nazis faced trial for their roles in what is now called the Holocaust—the genocidal campaign against the Jews during World War II. The court, located at Nuremberg, Germany, was called the International Military Tribunal. It was organized by the United States, Great Britain, France, and the Soviet Union.

A total of twenty two Nazis were tried for war crimes. Included were some of the leading Nazis, such as **Hermann Göering** (GEH-ring). Twelve were sentenced to die. Several others served long prison terms.

After Nuremberg, several Nazis have been captured and tried in different courts, including in Israel. These trials demonstrate the commitment of people around the world to remember the Holocaust and the millions of victims of Nazi brutality during World War II.

 **READING CHECK** **Summarizing** How did the United States respond to the reports that the Nazis were attempting to kill all of Europe's Jews?

THE IMPACT TODAY

Government
After World War II, many surviving European Jews were sent to displaced persons' camps. Many made their way to Palestine, where in the late 1940s they took part in the creation of the Jewish nation of Israel.

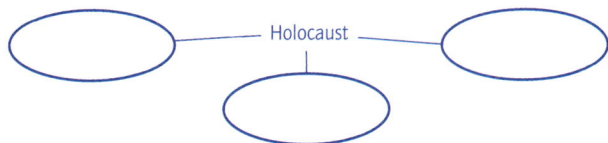

SECTION 2 ASSESSMENT

Reviewing Ideas, Terms, and People

1. **a. Recall** What term describes Hitler's racist attitudes toward the Jews?
   b. Explain Why do you think the German people supported Hitler's anti-Semitic attitudes?
   c. Evaluate Why do you think observers of events in Germany did not do more to help Germany's Jews?

2. **a. Define** Write brief definitions of the following terms: ghetto, Final Solution
   b. Make Generalizations What was the experience of Jews living in territories conquered by the Germans?
   c. Develop How can you explain the participation of so many Germans in the campaign to destroy the Jews?

3. **a. Identify** What was the significance of the War Refugee Board?
   b. Make Inferences Why did it take the United States so long to offer direct help to Europe's Jews?

c. Evaluate Do you think that the best way to help Europe's Jews was to defeat Hitler as quickly as possible? Or should the United States have taken a different approach? Explain.

Critical Thinking

4. **Identifying Supporting Details** Copy the chart below and use information from the section to find supporting details for the main idea given.

Holocaust

 FOCUS ON SPEAKING

5. **Persuasive** Could the United States have done more to prevent the Holocaust? Write a persuasive speech in which you present your position.

American *Literature*

ST 3.2 Draw upon literary selections, historical documents, and accounts to analyze the roles played by different individuals and groups during the major eras in New York State and United States history.

About the Reading Elie Wiesel was born in the small town of Sighet, Romania, in 1928. In 1944 the Nazis began deporting Jewish families from his hometown. In his autobiography, *Night* (1958), he recounts his experiences during his time in Nazi concentration camps. Wiesel became an American citizen in 1963. In this excerpt from *Night*, he describes his journey by train to the camp in Auschwitz, Poland.

 **Think about the reasons why we study the Holocaust today.**

Excerpt from

Night
by Elie Wiesel

Survivors at Buchenwald after their liberation in 1945. Elie Wiesel is on the second bunk from the bottom, seventh from the left.

Pressed up against the others in an effort to keep out the cold, head empty and heavy at the same time, brain a whirlpool of decaying memories. Indifference deadened the spirit. Here or elsewhere—what difference did it make? To die today or tomorrow, or later? The night was long and never ending.

When at last a gray glimmer of light appeared on the horizon, it revealed a tangle of human shapes, heads sunk upon shoulders, crouched, piled one on top of the other, like a field of dust-covered tombstones in the first light of the dawn. I tried to distinguish those who were still alive from those who had gone. But there was no difference. My gaze was held for a long time by one who lay with his eyes open, staring into the void. His livid face was covered with a layer of frost and snow.

My father huddled near me, wrapped in his blanket, his shoulders covered with snow. And was he dead, too? I called him. No answer. I would have cried out if I could have done so. He did not move.

My mind was invaded suddenly by this realization—there was no more reason to live, no more reason to struggle. The train stopped in the middle of a deserted field. The suddenness of the halt woke some of those who were asleep. They straightened themselves up, throwing startled looks around them.

Outside, the SS went by, shouting:

"Throw out all the dead! All corpses outside!"

The living rejoiced. There would be more room. Volunteers set to work. They felt those who were still crouching.

"Here's one! Take him!"

They undressed him, the survivors avidly sharing out his clothes, then two "gravediggers" took him, one by the head and one by the feet, and threw him out of the wagon like a sack of flour.

From all directions came cries:

"Come on! Here's one! This man next to me. He doesn't move."

 READING LIKE A HISTORIAN

Literature as Historical Evidence How does the personal testimony of survivors such as Wiesel help us understand the Holocaust?

See **Skills Handbook**, p. H32

The War in the Pacific

BEFORE YOU READ

MAIN IDEA

After early defeats in the Pacific, the United States gained the upper hand and began to fight its way island by island to Japan.

READING FOCUS

1. Why did the Allies experience a slow start in the Pacific?
2. How did the Allies bring about a shift in their fortunes in the Pacific?
3. What were the major events that marked Allied progress in the late stages of the Pacific war?

KEY TERMS AND PEOPLE

Douglas MacArthur
Bataan Death March
James Doolittle
Chester Nimitz
Battle of Midway
code talker
kamikaze
Battle of Iwo Jima
Battle of Okinawa

PI 3.2 Research and analyze the major themes and developments in New York State and United States history (e.g., colonization and settlement; Revolution and New National Period; immigration; expansion and reform era; Civil War and Reconstruction; the American labor movement; Great Depression; World Wars; contemporary United States).

Why was it so hard to capture a tiny island? Iwo To lies 750 miles south of Japan. The small island, known as Iwo Jima (EE-woh-JEE-muh) until 2007, covers barely eight square miles. Yet during World War II over 100,000 soldiers fought for a month to capture this tiny scrap of land. It was some of the heaviest fighting of the war.

On February 19, 1945, the U.S. Marines stormed the beaches of the island then called Iwo Jima. The marines made easy targets for the Japanese, who had dug miles of tunnels and built dozens of hidden concrete bunkers throughout the island. From these hiding places they could pick off American troops without being exposed.

Also deadly for the Americans were the Japanese guns mounted high on the slopes of Mount Suribachi, an extinct volcano on the southern tip of the island. The Americans knew that they must capture Suribachi or be blown off the island.

On the morning of February 23, a group of Marines finally made it to the top of Mount Suribachi and raised the American flag as thousands of soldiers below watched and cheered. A few hours later a larger flag was raised. This second flag raising is shown in the famous photograph on this page.

Raising the Flag at Iwo Jima

The American flag now flew over Iwo Jima, but fierce fighting lasted for another month before the Americans finally captured the island. An estimated 25,000 American soldiers were killed or wounded. Among the dead were three of the six men who raised the flag atop Mount Suribachi.

◀ **U.S. Marines claim Mount Suribachi with a proud display of the Stars and Stripes.**

A Slow Start for the Allies

The attack on Pearl Harbor had been a tremendous success for the Japanese. They had dealt a blow to the U.S. Pacific Fleet that would take months to overcome. The damage to American sea power—combined with the Allies' decision to focus their energy and resources on defeating the Axis in Europe—would for a time limit the ability of the United States to strike back at the Japanese.

Pearl Harbor also had an enormous emotional impact. For the Japanese, it provided a major boost to national pride and encouraged them to continue their assault. For Americans, it inspired a firm resolve to fight. Some Japanese leaders seemed to sense the dual danger of Japanese confidence and American anger.

HISTORY'S VOICES

❝The fact that we have had a small success at Pearl Harbor is nothing . . . Personally, I do not think it is a good thing to whip up propaganda to encourage the nation. People should think things over and realize how serious the situation is. ❞

—Japanese admiral Isoroku Yamamoto, quoted in *The Second World War: Asia and the Pacific*, Thomas E. Griess, Ed.

Japanese advances In the early days of the war, the Japanese saw little reason to heed Admiral Yamamoto's warning. After all, following Pearl Harbor, Japanese forces won a quick string of impressive victories. In late 1941 they drove American forces from Wake Island and Guam. Elsewhere, they captured the British stronghold at Hong Kong. Then they launched a campaign against the British base at Singapore. The British had believed that this mighty fortress would never fall to invaders. It took the Japanese just two weeks to capture it. In the process, they handed the British what Winston Churchill called "the greatest disaster and capitulation [surrender] in British history."

At the same time, other Japanese forces were easily taking control of the Dutch East Indies (today known as Indonesia) and British Borneo. In the Battle of Java Sea, they caused much damage to the Allied navies. The Japanese also conquered British-controlled Burma as well as a number of key positions in the South Pacific. In this way, they gained control of rich oil reserves, which were vital to their military plans. They also established strategic bases for future operations.

Bataan Death March

Some 70,000 American and Filipino prisoners were force-marched 63 miles in tropical heat with little food or water in the Bataan Death March. Some 7,000 to 10,000 died. The surrender at Bataan was the largest in U.S. history. *Why were the forces defending Bataan so vulnerable?*

The Allies were stunned by the rapid success of the Japanese military in the months after Pearl Harbor. They had not realized that Japanese soldiers were so highly skilled and well trained. The Japanese military also had excellent equipment. For example, Japanese fighter aircraft were as good as—or better than—anything the Allies could produce. Japanese ships and torpedoes were also of high quality. These factors gave the Japanese an important advantage early in the war.

The British were the first to discover the true strength of Japan's military in Hong Kong, Singapore, and Burma. American soldiers were about to learn the same lesson.

The Philippines Japan's attacks on Hong Kong, Singapore, the Dutch East Indies, and Burma were part of a large offensive that had one other major target: the American-controlled islands of the Philippines. General **Douglas MacArthur** led the defense of that island chain. He commanded a small force of Americans, plus a number of poorly trained and equipped Filipino soldiers. In fact, MacArthur's troops were no match for the Japanese invaders, who came ashore in December 1941.

As the Japanese gained ground, MacArthur planned a retreat to the Bataan Peninsula. There he hoped to hold off the Japanese for as long as possible. Simply getting his troops into this defensive position, however, took hard fighting and brilliant leadership. Once there, the soldiers found that food, medicine, and other supplies were terribly short. MacArthur urged Allied officials to send ships to help relieve his starving troops. War planners, however, decided that such a move was too risky. As Secretary of War Henry Stimson grimly noted, "There are times when men have to die."

MacArthur and his forces fought on bravely. Soon, however, illness and hunger began to take their toll. In March 1942 MacArthur was ordered to leave his men. He did so reluctantly, promising, "I shall return." Less than a month later, 10,000 American and 60,000 Filipino troops on Bataan surrendered.

The fighting was over, but the suffering of the soldiers was just beginning. For five days and nights, the Japanese forced the already starving and sick soldiers to march through the steaming forests of Bataan. Those who dropped out of line were beaten or shot. Those

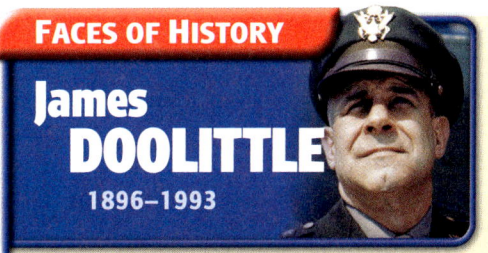

FACES OF HISTORY

James DOOLITTLE
1896–1993

James Doolittle left college to join the army when the United States entered World War I. He became an expert pilot and flight instructor.

After the war he tested and raced aircraft for the Army Air Corps.

Doolittle left the army in 1930 to work as an aviation consultant, but he returned to active duty when World War II began. He led air operations throughout the war, including a courageous bombing attack on Japan in 1942, immortalized in the famous movie *Thirty Seconds Over Tokyo*. The raid was the first attack on the Japanese mainland during the war. Doolittle later commanded bombing raids on Germany, which helped lead to the end of the war in Europe.

Make Inferences Why do you think Doolittle returned to active duty when World War II began?

who fell were left for dead. The Japanese provided little food or water. Thousands of soldiers perished on this so-called **Bataan Death March**. Those who completed this terrible journey did not fare much better. In the Japanese prison camp, lack of food and medicine claimed hundreds more American and Filipino lives.

READING CHECK **Drawing Conclusions**
Why did the Allies experience a slow start in the war in the Pacific?

Fortunes Shift in the Pacific

The loss of the Philippines was a low point for the United States in the Pacific war. Days later, however, Americans finally got some good news. On April 18, 1942, Army Lieutenant Colonel **James Doolittle** led a group of 16 American bombers on a daring air raid of Tokyo and several other Japanese cities. The airplanes had been launched from an aircraft carrier several hundred miles off the coast of Japan.

Doolittle's raid, as the event came to be known, did not do major damage to the Japanese targets. It did, however, have some significant effects. One was to finally give the American people something to celebrate. The other effect was to worry and anger Japan's leaders. Their outrage—and their concern about future attacks—would cloud their judgment and lead to major military mistakes in the months ahead.

The Battle of Coral Sea Americans got something else to cheer about in May 1942, when news reached home about the Battle of Coral Sea. This battle featured the one part of the Pacific fleet that had not been badly damaged at Pearl Harbor—the aircraft carriers.

The Battle of Coral Sea took place as Japanese forces were preparing to invade the British controlled Port Moresby on the island of New Guinea. To prevent this attack, U.S. Admiral **Chester Nimitz** sent two aircraft carriers on the attack. In the battle that followed, the American and Japanese navies both suffered damage. For the Americans, this included the loss of an aircraft carrier and several dozen aircraft. Yet they had stopped the Japanese attack. For the first time, the Japanese advance had been halted.

The Battle of Midway As you have read, Doolittle's raid had troubled Japan's leaders. They were determined to stop any future attacks on the Japanese mainland. To do this, they knew they had to destroy what remained of the United States naval power.

Japanese military planners decided to try to lure the Americans into a large sea battle. The first step would be to attack the American-held Midway Island, which sat in the middle of the Pacific Ocean. They hoped the attack would pull the American fleet into the area. Then the Japanese could destroy it.

The Japanese had a large advantage in the number of ships and carriers they could bring to the battle. The Americans, however, had one great advantage. Naval intelligence officers had broken a Japanese code and learned about the plans for attacking Midway. Americans knew the date for the planned attack—June 3, 1942. They also knew the direction from which the Japanese ships would approach.

The Americans also benefited from the carelessness of Japanese war planners. These planners had recognized possible flaws in their plan. Yet they chose to ignore them. It seemed as though their recent success had led them to believe they could not be defeated.

They were wrong. Using his advance knowledge of Japanese plans, Admiral Nimitz placed his three available aircraft carriers carefully. His goal was to stop a Japanese landing at Midway and to avoid contact with the larger Japanese fleet.

Nimitz's plan worked perfectly. Just as he had expected, the Japanese launched their attack in the early morning hours of June 4, 1942. The first stage was an air attack, meant to prepare Midway Island for a future landing by Japanese forces. The attacking Japanese planes took off from a group of four aircraft carriers that were leading the assault on Midway. American air defenses were waiting and managed to fight off the air raid.

The surviving Japanese planes raced back to their carriers to refuel and rearm. They were followed by American aircraft. The Japanese desperately fought off dozens of American bombers. Finally, several planes from the USS *Enterprise* broke through the Japanese defenses.

The American bombs severely damaged three of the four carriers. The decks of these ships had been cluttered with returning planes, bombs and torpedoes, and fuel, which blew up in the American attack. As Fuchido had predicted, these fires and explosions destroyed all three ships. American aircraft later destroyed the fourth carrier in this group.

During the battle, Japanese planes did manage to destroy one of the American carriers, the USS *Yorktown*. Nimitz, however, had placed the rest of his ships perfectly. The surviving ships of the Japanese battle fleet were too far away to threaten them. As the **Battle of Midway** ended, it was clear the Americans had won a tremendous victory.

The plan to invade Midway had been stopped, and Japan's navy had suffered a terrible blow. Japan's once great advantage on the seas no longer existed.

READING CHECK **Sequencing** What events helped shift the Americans' fortunes in the Pacific?

The Allies Make Progress

The Battle of Midway had changed the entire balance of power in the Pacific. Japanese naval power, which had been a key to its early success, was greatly reduced. Now on a more equal footing with the Japanese, the Americans began to make plans of their own in the Pacific.

Guadalcanal A first step was to win control of territory in the Solomon Islands. The Japanese had moved into these islands in the spring of 1942. This threatened nearby Australia, which was fighting alongside the Allies in the Pacific. An Allied presence in the Solomons would help protect Australia. It would also provide a base for further efforts to push back the Japanese.

A key goal in the Solomons was the capture of an island called Guadalcanal (GWAHD-uhl-KUH-NAL). The Japanese had nearly completed an airfield there, making it a tempting target. The rest of the island, however, offered little. It was covered by swamps and dense jungles. Daytime temperatures regularly reached into the 90s. Millions of disease-carrying insects filled the air. It was a miserable place to fight.

In spite of this, American forces came ashore on Guadalcanal in August 1942. For the next six months, they fought in bloody combat with Japanese forces. The battle took place on land, at sea, and in the air. Each side won small victories until finally, in February 1943, Japanese forces fled the island. It was a key moment in the war. "Before that," recalled one soldier, "we weren't looking for the Japanese, they were looking for us. . . . But from there on out, the Japanese were on the run."

The Allies press on The Allied victory at Guadalcanal set a pattern that was repeated in the coming months. The Allies would use a powerful combination of land, sea, and air forces to capture key islands. These would then

The American Victory at the Battle of Midway

Devastator torpedo bombers lie in wait for the Japanese fleet aboard the USS *Enterprise* (left). Above, a Japanese battle cruiser is destroyed by a hail of American bombs. After Midway, the *Enterprise* received the first Presidential Unit Citation ever awarded to a carrier, the Navy Unit Commendation, and 20 battle stars.

789

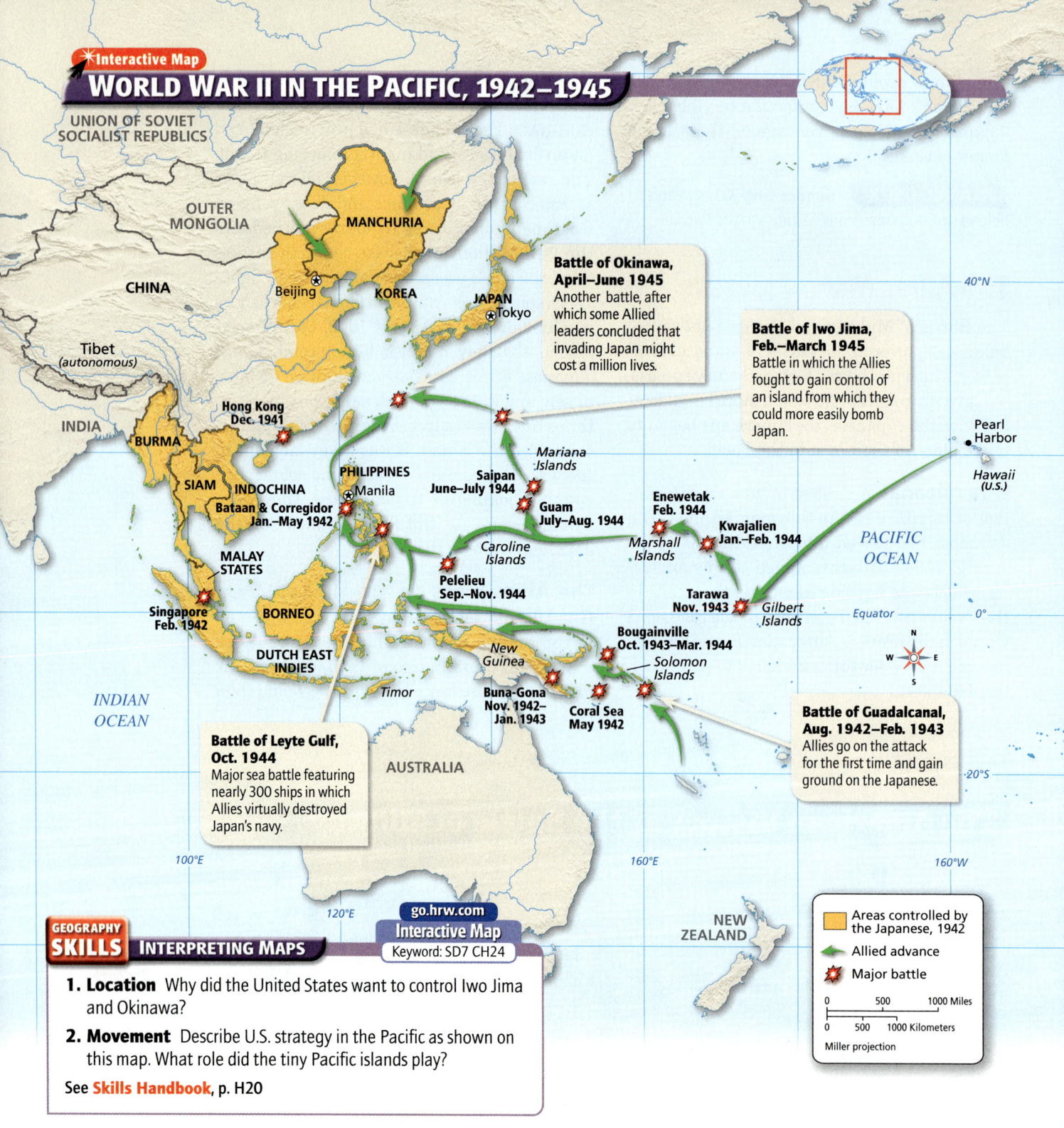

UNION OF SOVIET
SOCIALIST REPUBLICS

OUTER
MONGOLIA

MANCHURIA

CHINA

Beijing

KOREA

JAPAN
Tokyo

40°N

Tibet
(autonomous)

**Battle of Okinawa,
April–June 1945**
Another battle, after
which some Allied
leaders concluded that
invading Japan might
cost a million lives.

**Battle of Iwo Jima,
Feb.–March 1945**
Battle in which the Allies
fought to gain control of
an island from which they
could more easily bomb
Japan.

INDIA

Hong Kong
Dec. 1941

Pearl
Harbor

BURMA

Hawaii
(U.S.)

Mariana
Islands

SIAM

INDOCHINA

PHILIPPINES
Manila

Saipan
June–July 1944

Bataan & Corregidor
Jan.–May 1942

Guam
July–Aug. 1944

Enewetak
Feb. 1944

Kwajalien
Jan.–Feb. 1944

PACIFIC
OCEAN

MALAY
STATES

Caroline
Islands

Marshall
Islands

Pelelieu
Sep.–Nov. 1944

Singapore
Feb. 1942

BORNEO

Tarawa
Nov. 1943

Gilbert
Islands

Equator

0°

DUTCH EAST
INDIES

Bougainville
Oct. 1943–Mar. 1944

Solomon
Islands

INDIAN
OCEAN

New
Guinea

Timor

Buna-Gona
Nov. 1942–
Jan. 1943

Coral Sea
May 1942

**Battle of Guadalcanal,
Aug. 1942–Feb. 1943**
Allies go on the attack
for the first time and gain
ground on the Japanese.

20°S

**Battle of Leyte Gulf,
Oct. 1944**
Major sea battle featuring
nearly 300 ships in which
Allies virtually destroyed
Japan's navy.

AUSTRALIA

N
W   E
S

100°E

160°E

160°W

120°E

NEW
ZEALAND

go.hrw.com
Interactive Map
Keyword: SD7 CH24

Areas controlled by
the Japanese, 1942

Allied advance

Major battle

0   500   1000 Miles
0   500   1000 Kilometers
Miller projection

GEOGRAPHY
SKILLS INTERPRETING MAPS

1. Location Why did the United States want to control Iwo Jima
and Okinawa?

2. Movement Describe U.S. strategy in the Pacific as shown on
this map. What role did the tiny Pacific islands play?

See **Skills Handbook**, p. H20

become the stepping-stones for future military
actions. The Allies focused on Japanese weak
spots and simply skipped over strongholds. In
this way, the Allies made steady progress in the
Southwest Pacific in 1943. In 1944 the Allies
captured locations in the Gilbert, Marshall,
Caroline, and Mariana islands. You can trace
this progress in the map above.

The Allies also began to take advantage of
America's tremendous industrial power. The
fighting in the Pacific was extremely costly, and
both sides lost dozens of ships and thousands
of aircraft. These were losses the Japanese
were unable to replace. Busy American factories, meanwhile, produced planes and ships at
an amazing rate.

American fighters in the Pacific also benefited from Allied gains in Europe. Early in the war, Allied leaders had followed the strategy of focusing their efforts on Europe first. This cut down on the numbers of soldiers, sailors, and supplies available for the Pacific war. Then the Soviets began to push back German advances, and the Allies made gains in North Africa, Italy, and France. This allowed Allied war planners to send more resources to the Pacific.

American ingenuity and diversity also played a role in the Allied success. One example was the hundreds of Native Americans of the Navajo nation who served in the Marines as **code talkers**. Their main job was translating messages into a coded version of the Navajo language. This unwritten language is so complex that the Japanese code-breakers were never able to figure it out. Navajo code talkers could quickly and accurately transmit vital information about troop movements, enemy positions, and more. Their contributions helped the Allies win many major battles.

Back to the Philippines Ever since leaving the Philippines in early 1942, General MacArthur had looked forward to the day when he could fulfill his promise to return. By the middle of 1944, that day was at hand. Allied forces had fought to within striking distance of the Philippines. After much planning, MacArthur was ready to attack.

The first major action took place on the seas—the Battle of Leyte (LAY-tee) Gulf. Here nearly 300 ships took part in the largest naval battle ever fought. By this time, the Allies held a huge advantage in numbers of ships. When the battle was over, the Japanese had lost four carriers, three battleships, and a number of other vessels. What little was left of their fleet would play no major role in the rest of the war.

The Battle of Leyte Gulf also saw the first major use of a new Japanese weapon—the **kamikaze** attack. The term *kamikaze* is a Japanese word meaning "divine wind." It refers to a famous event in Japanese history—a sudden storm that drove off a fleet preparing to invade Japan in the 1200s. In World War II, however, a kamikaze was a pilot who loaded his aircraft with bombs and deliberately crashed it into an enemy ship. It was understood that the attack would lead to the death of the pilot. As a Japanese admiral explained, such tactics were "the only way of assuring our meager strength will be effective to the maximum degree." The kamikaze attacks did not change the outcome of the Battle of Leyte Gulf, but the Allies would come to fear these suicidal attacks.

In late October 1944, MacArthur waded ashore to fulfill his promise to return to the Philippines. It would take his soldiers many more months of tough fighting to gain full control of the islands.

ACADEMIC VOCABULARY
strategy plan of action

Recent Scholarship
The work of the Navajo code talkers was kept secret for years. It was not until recently that they received public recognition. In 2001 the 29 original code talkers received the Congressional Gold Medal for their service.

Linking TO Today

Return to Iwo Jima

Iwo Jima was one of the bloodiest battles of the war in the Pacific. On the 60th anniversary of the battle, it was the site of a reunion of former enemies.

After the month-long battle in early 1945, nearly 7,000 Americans had been killed, along with three times as many Japanese fighters. Around 1,000 Japanese soldiers were captured.

In 2005 American and Japanese veterans returned to Iwo Jima to remember the battle and show how the world has changed. Following World War II, Japan and the United States became close allies. The two nations have a strong trade relationship and work together on international issues.

"Today, 60 years after the battle of Iwo Jima, it gives me deep awe to see Japan and the United States cooperate in fighting terrorism," said Yoshitaka Shinda, whose grandfather was the island's last Japanese commander.

Drawing Conclusions Would Yoshitaka Shinda's grandfather agree with his statement? Explain.

Honoring the war dead on the 60th anniversary of the Battle of Iwo Jima

Iwo Jima and Okinawa Beginning in late 1944 the massive new American B-29 bomber began making regular raids on Japanese cities. Allied bombers dropped many tons of explosives on Tokyo and other centers.

In order to provide a better base from which to launch these raids, American forces set out in February 1945 to capture Iwo Jima. This tiny volcanic island lay some 750 miles south of Tokyo, the capital of Japan. The island's rugged terrain was heavily guarded by Japanese soldiers. American troops greatly outnumbered the defenders. For the first time in the war, however, the Japanese troops were fighting for land that was actually part of Japan. Hidden in caves and tunnels and protected by concrete bunkers, they fought ferociously.

Early in the **Battle of Iwo Jima**, marines managed to capture the island's tallest point, Mount Suribachi. You read about this moment earlier in this section. Some Americans thought that the capture of Mount Suribachi meant that the battle was over, but the Japanese troops refused to surrender. The fighting raged on for several more weeks. By the time it was over, nearly 7,000 Americans were dead and many more were wounded. More than 20,000 Japanese defenders had been on Iwo Jima when the Americans landed. All but a thousand of them fought to the death.

The next American target was Okinawa (OH-kee-NAH-wah). Only 350 miles from Japan, this island was to be the launching pad for the final invasion of Japan itself. First, however, it had to be captured. This would be the bloodiest task the Americans would face in the Pacific.

Allied troops invaded Okinawa on April 1, 1945. The Japanese forces retreated to the southern tip of the island to plan their response. Five days later, they attacked. The island of Okinawa was filled with caves and tunnels. Japanese soldiers used these skillfully to hide and to launch deadly assaults. Over 12,000 Americans died in the **Battle of Okinawa**, and thousands more were injured.

The Japanese lost a staggering 110,000 troops in the fighting. As on Iwo Jima, their willingness to fight on when death was certain filled the Americans with amazement—and dread. "I see no way to get them out," noted one American general, "except to blast them out yard by yard."

In spite of the terrible losses, the Americans finally gained control of the island in June 1945. As you will read, the lessons learned on Okinawa would have a major impact on the final days of the war.

READING CHECK **Summarizing** What factors allowed the Allies to advance in 1944 and 1945?

SECTION 3 ASSESSMENT

go.hrw.com
Online Quiz
Keyword: SD7 HP24

Reviewing Ideas, Terms, and People

1. **a. Recall** What events led up to the **Bataan Death March**?
   b. Analyze What were the key reasons for the early success of the Japanese?
   c. Evaluate How do you think the fighting in Europe may have affected events taking place in the Pacific?

2. **a. Identify** Describe the significance of the following people in World War II: James Doolittle, Chester Nimitz
   b. Explain What was the importance of the American victory at the **Battle of Midway**?
   c. Predict At **Iwo Jima** and **Okinawa**, Japanese troops refused to surrender even when facing certain defeat. How might this reluctance to give in affect the end of the war?

3. **a. Identify** Describe the significance of the following: **code talkers, kamikaze**
   b. Make Generalizations How would you describe the performance of the Japanese in the later battles of the war in the Pacific?

   c. Elaborate What is your opinion about the actions of the kamikaze?

Critical Thinking

4. **Identifying Supporting Details** Copy the chart below and use information from the section to find supporting details for the main idea given.

Slow start	Fortunes shift	Progress

FOCUS ON WRITING

5. **Persuasive** In the early years of the war, should the Allies have committed more resources to the fighting in the Pacific? Write a short essay in which you develop your position on the issue. Include references to events in Europe.

SECTION 4
The Home Front

BEFORE YOU READ

MAIN IDEA

While millions of military men and women were serving in World War II, Americans on the home front were making contributions of their own.

READING FOCUS

1. What sacrifices and struggles did Americans at home experience?
2. How did the U.S. government seek to win American support for the war?
3. What was Japanese internment?
4. How did World War II help expand the role of the government in the lives of the American people?

KEY TERMS AND PEOPLE

rationing
Ernie Pyle
Bill Mauldin
internment

PI 3.1 Compare and contrast the experiences of different ethnic, national, and religious groups, including Native American Indians, in the United States, explaining their contributions to American society and culture.

Gardening for Victory

THE INSIDE STORY

How did vegetable gardens help to win a war? World War II placed huge demands on the United States. Not only did millions of Americans serve in the armed forces, but people at home had to make do with less—including less food and less fuel for harvesting and transporting crops.

To help overcome these shortages and preserve precious resources for the military, Americans by the millions planted "victory gardens." In small towns and large cities, any spare piece of land was likely to be used to grow food. People gardened on the rooftops of apartment buildings and in flower boxes outside their windows. School yards, ball fields, and vacant lots were plowed under. Government agencies and private businesses encouraged the effort with posters, seeds, and instructions for gardening.

Many victory gardens were small and humble but combined they produced big results. In 1943 the nation's 20 million victory gardens yielded an astounding 8 million tons of produce. Grace Bracker's Wisconsin garden was typical. She canned over 400 quarts of fruits and vegetables her first year—more than she and her family could eat.

Victory gardens also helped unite communities. Very young children and older men and women could all help in the preparation, planting, weeding, and harvesting of vegetables. Indeed, the victory gardens became a popular expression of patriotism. They helped Americans at home stay strong during the difficult days of the bloodiest war in human history.

▶ **A few simple tools, some seed, some fertilizer, and a patriotic spirit were nearly all a person needed to grow a victory garden.**

Sacrifice and Struggle at Home

You have read about the amazing courage and sacrifice of the Allied soldiers, sailors, and pilots. By the millions, they risked life and limb so that others could enjoy freedom. Many spilled their blood so that others could live.

World War II, however, made demands of every American. The women, children, and men who remained in the United States played a key role in ensuring success overseas.

HISTORY'S VOICES

❝ Not all of us can have the privilege of fighting our enemies in distant parts of the world ... But there is one front and one battle where everyone in the United States is in action. That front is right here at home. ❞

—Franklin D. Roosevelt, radio address, April 28, 1942

As you read earlier, millions of Americans made contributions to the war effort by taking jobs in factories or offices. In addition, life in the American home changed significantly as citizens of all ages did their part to help the cause of victory in Europe and the Pacific.

Conserving food and other goods Meeting the food needs of the military took top priority in the United States. The planting of victory gardens, which you read about in the "Inside Story," was one way in which Americans filled these needs.

Victory gardens alone did not solve all the nation's food needs. Some foods could not be produced in home gardens, and there was simply not enough of certain products to go around. As a result, the United States began rationing food shortly after the nation entered the war. **Rationing** means limiting the amount of a certain product each individual can get.

During the war, the government rationed products such as coffee, butter, sugar, and meat. Each member of the family received a ration book, which entitled that person to a certain amount of certain foods. Most people willingly accepted the system. Penalties for breaking the rationing rules could be severe.

The war effort also meant shortages of other materials, such as metal, glass, rubber, and gasoline. Gasoline was rationed. Americans helped meet the demand for other materials by holding scrap drives, in which citizens col-

American Support for the War Effort

These children (right) drum up support for the war with a scrap metal drive. Communities enthusiastically responded to such drives by contributing everything from old pots and pans to the statues in their town squares. People also turned out for war bond rallies, such as this one at a navy shipyard in Chicago in 1944 (below). The promotional efforts of movie stars and artists helped sell war bonds to tens of millions of Americans.

lected waste material of all sorts that might be used in the war efforts. Empty tin cans, bits of rubber and glass—anything that could be useful was salvaged. Even women's silk and nylon stockings were recycled to make parachutes.

Scrap drives provided a way for young Americans to help with the war effort. Scouts and other youth organizations helped lead the way in this important national effort.

Investing in victory Americans supported the war effort not just with their trash but also with their treasure. They did this by buying billions of dollars worth of war bonds. The money invested by millions of ordinary citizens helped pay for the the vast quantities of shipping, aircraft, and other weaponry being produced in American factories.

Throughout the war, magazines and newspapers were filled with ads encouraging people to do their <u>civic</u> duty and support the war effort. Inspirational pictures and messages helped promote patriotism and self-sacrifice. "Our fighting forces will do their stuff," promised one ad, "but we at home must do ours."

The result of these appeals was amazing. By war's end, 85 million Americans had purchased war bonds. This represented well over half of the entire population of the country. The total raised was nearly $185 billion. This amount was twice what the entire federal government spent in the year 1945.

Paying the personal price Americans willingly put up with many hardships and made do without many comforts during the war. For many, the hardest part was dealing with the absence of loved ones.

HISTORY'S VOICES

> ❝At first you feel abandoned and you feel angry because they took him when you needed him more at home … [B]ut he went and he was doing his duty, and we figured that was part of our job to give our husband to the war effort and to do the best we could without him.❞
>
> —Jean Lechnir, quoted in *Women Remember the War*, Michael E. Stevens, Ed.

Across the country, families with loved ones in the service showed their sacrifice by displaying a flag with a blue star. If the service member was killed, the blue star was replaced with a gold one.

Families followed the news of the war with great interest. Millions of Americans read the newspaper columns of writer **Ernie Pyle**, who covered the war from the point of view of the men in the field. **Bill Mauldin**, whose cartoons featured two ordinary soldiers named Willie and Joe, also gave folks on the home front a soldier's view of life in the army.

READING CHECK **Identifying Problems and Solutions** What were some of the sacrifices and struggles facing people on the home front?

Winning American Support for the War

American leaders were well aware that public support for the war effort was vital to its success. In the words of one government publication of the time, "Each word an American utters either helps or hurts the war effort." For this reason, the government made a great effort to shape public attitudes and beliefs.

This effort to win American support for the war effort began even before the United States entered the war. In January 1941, President Roosevelt gave a speech in which he observed that the challenge facing the world was a struggle for basic American values. By supporting its allies overseas, Roosevelt argued, the nation would be working to protect what he called the "four freedoms." These were the freedom of speech, freedom of worship, freedom from want, and freedom from fear.

The Office of War Information When the United States officially entered the war, the federal government's need to influence the thoughts, feelings, and actions of the public became even greater. In June 1942, the government created the Office of War Information (OWI). This agency was responsible for spreading propaganda, or information and ideas designed to promote a cause.

The OWI produced dozens of posters and films during the war. Many of these encouraged a positive vision of the United States and stressed positive actions. For example, many posters and films encouraged men to join the fighting forces and women to take jobs in war industries. Others encouraged positive goals, such as saving gasoline and working for racial

ACADEMIC VOCABULARY
civic public or community

harmony. Another famous poster series illustrated the four freedoms that Roosevelt had talked about. These featured paintings by the popular artist Norman Rockwell.

The OWI also issued stark warnings to the public about the dangers they faced. Drawings of Nazi or Japanese soldiers threatening small children were meant to inspire fear in Americans—and the desire to take action against the Axis nations. "We're fighting to prevent this," declared one headline. Below the words was a picture of a giant Nazi boot crushing a little white church.

Another technique was to show the harmful outcomes of improper actions and attitudes, such as talking about sensitive military information. "Someone talked!" accused a drowning American sailor in one poster, moments before he slipped beneath the waves. Films such as *Safeguarding Military Information* dramatized the same ideas.

Hollywood helps out Movies remained enormously popular during the war years. In the early 1940s, some 90 million Americans visited the movie theater each week. As a result, the nation's film industry became a major producer of wartime propaganda.

In general, Hollywood was a willing helper in the war effort. The big movie studios made a series of patriotic films that featured soldiers and workers on the home front. To assist the studios, the OWI produced a guide called "The Government Information Manual for the Motion Picture." This offered tips to ensure that Hollywood films helped promote what the government felt were the right attitudes about the war. The OWI also reviewed movie scripts for the proper messages.

Many leading movie stars devoted time and energy to the war cause. They helped sell war bonds and provided entertainment to the troops at home and overseas.

PRIMARY SOURCES

Propaganda Poster

Office of War Information propaganda posters used bold graphics and simple text to convey their messages. This poster was issued in 1943. It addressed a key priority: the need to safeguard sensitive war-related information when nearly everyone in society was involved in the war effort.

The hand with the swastika suggests that Nazi spies might be hidden in America.

The poster compares bits of information with puzzle pieces that, if combined, could reveal a damaging secret.

Skills FOCUS READING LIKE A HISTORIAN

1. Interpreting Visuals What is the hand doing, and why?

2. Drawing Conclusions What is the main message of this poster?

See **Skills Handbook**, p. H12, H30

The *Barnette* ruling While most Americans willingly supported the war effort, the drive to influence public attitudes sometimes led to conflict. For example, in West Virginia, members of the Jehovah's Witness religious group challenged a law that required students in school to salute the American flag. The Jehovah's Witnesses felt that this requirement went against their religious teachings. In 1943 the Supreme Court of the United States agreed that Americans could not be forced to salute the flag. In *West Virginia Board of Education v. Barnette*, the Court wrote that "no official … can prescribe [require] what shall be orthodox [standard or required belief] in politics, nationalism, religion or other matters of opinion."

READING CHECK **Identifying Supporting Details** What was the mission of the Office of War Information in influencing public opinion?

Japanese Internment

After Pearl Harbor, government officials began to fear that people of German, Italian, and especially Japanese descent would help the enemy. Many Italians and Germans who had immigrated to the United States were forced to carry identification cards. Thousands were placed in prison camps. But the worst treatment was reserved for Japanese Americans.

Executive Order 9066 Right after the bombing of Pearl Harbor, military officials began to investigate the Japanese American community for signs of spying or other illegal activity. They found no evidence of wrongdoing. In spite of this finding, General John L. DeWitt, the Army officer in charge of the western United States, still recommended that all people of Japanese background be removed from the West Coast. "The very fact that no sabotage or espionage has taken place," he warned, "is disturbing and confirming indication that such action will take place."

In response to warnings such as this, President Roosevelt issued Executive Order 9066 on February 19, 1942. This order gave the armed forces the power to establish military zones. It also gave them the power to force people or groups to leave these zones. The clear goal of the order was to remove people of Japanese heritage from the western United States.

The order affected all people of Japanese heritage living in the military zone. Within weeks of the order, soldiers were rounding up Japanese Americans in California, Washington, Oregon, and Arizona. Two-thirds of the 110,000 people affected were American citizens. Many had been born in the United States and had lived here for decades. No hearings or trials were conducted to determine if an individual posed a real threat. The only factor considered was the person's racial background. The Japanese Americans were told they would be taken to one of several camps somewhere in the West. There they would be forced to live for as long as the military decided it was necessary.

This forced relocation and confinement to the camps was called **internment**. It placed many hardships on Japanese Americans. They were allowed to bring only those belongings they could carry. Everything else—homes, businesses, and other property—had to be left behind or sold. Sometimes people were given just days to get rid of their property. As a result, they were forced to accept very low prices for their belongings or were unable to sell them at all. In this way, many Japanese Americans lost their homes and businesses. Confined to camps they were unable to work and pay off loans.

Life in the camps was hard. Many camps were located in barren desert areas with a harsh climate. Barbed wire and armed guards surrounded the facility. Families lived in cramped quarters with few furnishings. Facilities for education and health care were poor.

Japanese American loyalty While interned, Japanese Americans were required to answer questions about their loyalty to the United States. Though German Americans and Italian Americans also faced restrictions during the war, they were not forced to answer such questions.

For many Japanese in America, the desire to prove their loyalty to the country was strong. A number of young people from the camps joined the armed forces to help fight the Axis powers. Many became part of the 442nd Regimental Combat Team, made up entirely of Japanese Americans. This unit fought in Europe and had an outstanding record in battle. For the length of time it served, this unit received more medals and awards than any other of its size in American military history.

Other inmates of the internment camps demonstrated their loyalty in different ways. For some, the greatest statement they could make was in keeping faith in the future and in the promise of the country that had imprisoned them.

HISTORY'S VOICES

❝We are ever hoping that the time will come soon when we can all re-enter the America beyond the relocation camps in order that we make our contributions and be considered as an integral part of the American way of living.❞

—Yoshiko Uchiyama, letter reprinted in the *University of Washington Daily*, January 1943

Not all Japanese Americans accepted their internment peacefully. Incidents of violence and resistance occurred at the camps. In addition, a number of legal challenges were mounted against Japanese internment. One was *Korematsu* v. *United States*, a landmark Supreme Court case that you will read about at the end of this section.

After the war some Japanese Americans continued to speak out against the injustice of their internment. Decades later, the federal government formally acknowledged that it had acted unjustly. Survivors of the internment received letters of apology and a payment from the government.

READING CHECK **Identifying Supporting Details** What was life like in the internment camps?

A New Role for the Federal Government

During the 1930s, the federal government faced the crisis of the Great Depression. With the New Deal, the government grew to have a much larger role in the lives of average Americans than it had in the past. The trend that began in the Great Depression continued during World War II.

You have read about wartime rationing. This program was run by the Office of Price Administration (OPA). The OPA also placed limits on the prices businesses could charge for products and materials.

The War Production Board was another agency involved in the war effort. It was created to make sure that the military got the products and resources it needed to fight the

FOCUS ON NEW YORK

ECONOMICS

New York outpaced all other states in production of wartime goods, manufacturing 12 percent of the nation's military weapons, ammunition, and vehicles, worth $21.5 billion. Only three places in the entire nation produced more war goods than the area around Buffalo.

war. As part of this effort, the board promoted the scrap drives you read about earlier. The War Production Board also placed limits on clothing manufacturers in order to ensure a supply of fabrics, such as cotton, wool, silk, and nylon. Jackets were only allowed to be a certain length. Skirts and dresses were limited in size as well. It was these restrictions on clothing that played a role in the zoot suit riots you read about in the last chapter.

Government spending during the war rose sharply. As you can see from the graph on this page, the high cost of waging war meant a steep increase in the federal budget. Almost all of this increase went to the armed forces.

To help pay for the war effort, the federal government increased income tax rates. Before the war, income taxes had been just for the wealthy, but now millions of Americans paid income taxes for the first time. As one observer noted, "the Kansas wheat farmer, the lumberjack, and the boys around the cracker barrel in the corner grocery are going to have to pay the tax bill this time." As a result American tax revenues jumped from $7.4 billion in 1941 to $43 billion in 1945.

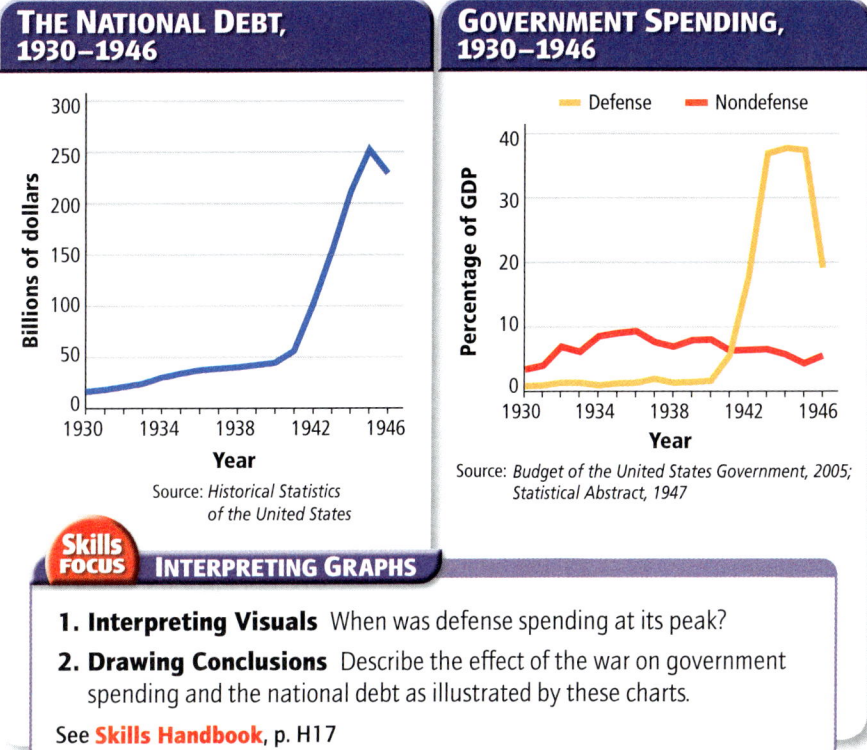

THE NATIONAL DEBT, 1930–1946

Source: *Historical Statistics of the United States*

GOVERNMENT SPENDING, 1930–1946

Source: *Budget of the United States Government, 2005; Statistical Abstract, 1947*

Skills FOCUS **INTERPRETING GRAPHS**

1. **Interpreting Visuals** When was defense spending at its peak?
2. **Drawing Conclusions** Describe the effect of the war on government spending and the national debt as illustrated by these charts.

See **Skills Handbook**, p. H17

READING CHECK **Identifying Supporting Details** Why did income tax rates increase during World War II?

go.hrw.com
Online Quiz
Keyword: SD7 HP24

SECTION 4 ASSESSMENT

Reviewing Ideas, Terms, and People

1. **a. Recall** What were the purposes of **rationing** and scrap drives?
   b. Summarize What kinds of sacrifices were required of people on the home front?
   c. Predict What might have happened had people on the home front been unwilling to support the war?

2. **a. Describe** What did the Office of War Information seek to do?
   b. Draw Conclusions What can you conclude from the fact that the federal government had an organization in charge of propaganda?

3. **a. Recall** What concern led to the **internment** of Japanese Americans?
   b. Explain What factors made the experience of interned Japanese Americans so difficult?

4. **a. Identify** Name two actions the federal government took to support the war effort during World War II.

   b. Compare How did the changes in the federal government during the Great Depression compare to the changes during World War II?

Critical Thinking

5. **Identifying Supporting Details** Copy the chart below and use information from the section to find supporting details for the main idea given.

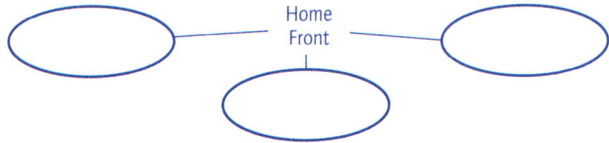

Home Front

FOCUS ON WRITING

6. **Narrative** Based on what you have read in this section, write a one-paragraph account about the internment of Japanese Americans on the West Coast in World War II.

ST 4.1 Analyze important debates in American history, focusing on the opposing positions and the historical evidence used to support these positions.

Korematsu v. United States (1944)

Why It Matters In wartime, citizens are sometimes fearful of those who have common ancestry with the enemy. But the American population includes people from all over the world, and almost all people who live here are loyal to this country. In *Korematsu v. United States,* the U.S. Supreme Court tried to find the right balance between the rights of Japanese Americans and wartime needs.

Background of the Case

In February 1942 President Roosevelt signed an executive order that resulted in the relocation of 110,000 Japanese Americans to internment camps. Fred Korematsu refused the order and was arrested. Korematsu was in his 20s. He was of Japanese ancestry but had been born in Oakland, California, and was an American citizen. In court, Korematsu was found guilty of violating the executive order. He appealed his case to the Supreme Court.

The Decision

The Supreme Court ruled against Korematsu. Writing for the majority, Justice Hugo Black began by noting that "all legal restrictions which curtail [limit] the civil rights of a single racial group are immediately suspect" and must be given "rigid scrutiny." In this wartime situation, however, there was no easy way to separate loyal Americans of Japanese descent from those who might not support the country. The Court ruled that the relocation order was justified as a temporary wartime measure. Black rejected the argument that the relocation was racially motivated.

> **❝** Korematsu was excluded because we are at war with the Japanese Empire ... [W]hen under conditions of modern warfare our shores are threatened by hostile forces, the power to protect must be commensurate [equal] with the threatened danger. **❞**

THE IMPACT TODAY Although Fred Korematsu lost his case, he continued to work for civil rights. He finally succeeded in having his conviction overturned in 1983, and in 1998 he received the Presidential Medal of Freedom from President Bill Clinton. Korematsu died in 2005.

go.hrw.com
Research Online
Keyword: SS Court

CRITICAL THINKING

1. **Analyze the Impact** *Korematsu* v. *the United States* established the idea that classifications based on race are "suspect" and have to be supported by a compelling government interest. Using the keyword above, read about *Loving* v. *Virginia,* a case in which the Supreme Court used "strict scrutiny" to decide whether a state law prohibiting interracial marriage was constitutional. What individual interests did the law violate?

2. **You Be the Judge** The USA Patriot Act, enacted shortly after the terrorist attacks of September 11, 2001, authorizes the Immigration and Naturalization Service to detain immigrants suspected of terrorism for lengthy, or even indefinite, periods. Is this a violation of civil rights or an appropriate use of military authority? Explain your answer in a short paragraph.

World War II Ends

BEFORE YOU READ

MAIN IDEA

While the Allies completed the defeat of the Axis Powers on the battlefield, Allied leaders were making plans for the postwar world.

READING FOCUS

1. How did the Allies defeat Germany and win the war in Europe?
2. How did the Allies defeat Japan and win the war in the Pacific?
3. What challenges faced the United States after victory?

KEY TERMS AND PEOPLE

Yalta Conference
occupy
V-E Day
Harry S Truman
Enola Gay
V-J Day
United Nations
Potsdam Conference

PI 3.2 Research and analyze the major themes and developments in New York State and United States history (e.g., colonization and settlement; Revolution and New National Period; immigration; expansion and reform era; Civil War and Reconstruction; the American labor movement; Great Depression; World Wars; contemporary United States).

THE INSIDE STORY

What happened when the Soviet and American forces met? By April 1945, American forces had crossed Germany's western border and were moving steadily eastward. At the same time, their Soviet allies were driving westward toward the German capital of Berlin. Each side knew that when they met, Hitler's fate would be sealed.

Sometime around noon on April 25, a group of American troops spotted a Soviet force on the other side of the Elbe River. The Americans identified themselves as friendly forces. Once they had made contact, the Americans headed across the Elbe. Some swam and others took boats to the other side. There they met a group of Soviet soldiers for the first time.

The soldiers shook hands, embraced, and offered toasts to the leaders of their countries. They danced and sang. All present promised that they would do everything they could to make sure that their nations would build a lasting peace.

News of the meeting on the Elbe River set off celebrations in the United States and in the Soviet Union. There were still several days of fighting ahead before Germany surrendered, but everyone was convinced that the linking of the two main Allied forces doomed the Germans.

In the days ahead, the scene from that first meeting at the Elbe was repeated many times, as American and Soviet units linked up, posed for pictures and enjoyed their success in the war. Yet these moments of friendship and joy would soon fade away. American forces still had fighting to do in the Pacific. At the same time, tension between the Soviet Union and the United States was growing.

A HISTORIC Meeting

◄ American (left) and Soviet brothers in arms reach out across the Elbe River.

Winning the War in Europe

In the first section of this chapter you read about the Battle of the Bulge. In those few desperate days of combat, over 80,000 Allied troops were killed, wounded, or captured. As bad as those figures were, the result for the German army was even worse. It had risked much in the attack and suffered a crushing defeat. Germany now had few soldiers left to defend the homeland from the 4 million Allied troops poised on its western border. To the east were millions of Soviet soldiers, who had been pushing the Germans westward since the heroic Soviet stand at Stalingrad. They stood waiting to launch a final assault.

The Yalta Conference In January 1945 Franklin D. Roosevelt took the presidential oath of office for the fourth time. He had run in 1944 believing that he needed to see the nation through to victory. A majority of the American voters had agreed.

Shortly after Roosevelt's inauguration, the president left for a conference of the Allied leaders. The meeting was held in the resort town of Yalta, in the Soviet Union. The so-called Big Three—Roosevelt, Winston Churchill, and Joseph Stalin—met to make plans for the end of the war and the peace that was to follow.

A key goal of the **Yalta Conference** was to reach an agreement on what to do with the soon-to-be-conquered Germany. The three leaders agreed to divide the country into four sectors. The Americans, Soviets, British, and French would each occupy one of these sectors. To **occupy** means to take control of a place by placing troops in it. The Soviet Union, which had the largest army, was given the largest zone. It covered most of the eastern half of

Toward Victory in Europe

By the spring of 1945, the Allies were closing in on Hitler. At left, U.S. army infantrymen blast their way through a German city. Below, an American soldier is lifted into the air by Russians celebrating their liberation from a German camp.

Germany. The American, British, and French zones covered the western half. The capital city of Berlin, which lay in the Soviet zone, was similarly divided into four sectors.

Another agreement at Yalta had to do with the fate of Poland and other Eastern European countries now occupied by the Soviets. Stalin agreed to hold elections in these countries following the war. As you will read, this was a promise Stalin would not keep.

Stalin also committed to a third major decision. He said that the Soviet Union would declare war on Japan three months after Germany was defeated.

Though all the participants at Yalta had been allies in the fight to defeat the Axis, the conference had been tense. Friction between the Soviet Union and the other Allies was growing. Nevertheless, Roosevelt cheerfully reported the success of the meeting to the Congress.

HISTORY'S VOICES

> **❝** Of course we know that it was Hitler's hope... that we would not agree, that some slight crack might appear in the solid wall of Allied unity... But Hitler has failed. Never before have the major Allies been more closely united—not only in their war aims but also in their peace aims. **❞**
>
> —Franklin D. Roosevelt, March 1, 1945

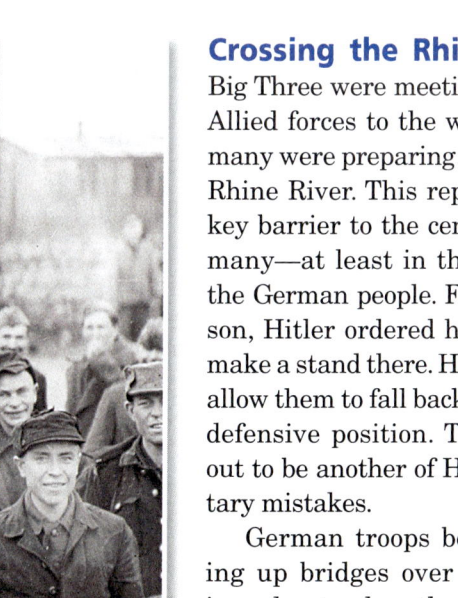

Crossing the Rhine As the Big Three were meeting in Yalta, Allied forces to the west of Germany were preparing to cross the Rhine River. This represented a key barrier to the center of Germany—at least in the minds of the German people. For this reason, Hitler ordered his forces to make a stand there. He refused to allow them to fall back to a better defensive position. This turned out to be another of Hitler's military mistakes.

German troops began blowing up bridges over the Rhine in order to slow the Allies. On March 7, 1945, however, American forces managed to capture a bridge at Remagen. They did this while the Germans were still moving their own forces to the eastern side. The Germans fought desperately to destroy the bridge and keep it out of American hands. They used every weapon in their arsenal against it, including the powerful V-2 rocket. Yet the bridge stood even under this vicious bombardment. Meanwhile, Allied troops and tanks rumbled steadily across.

Once the Allies crossed the Rhine, the foolishness of Hitler's order to defend the river became clear. The Allies were able to surround and capture a quarter million German soldiers. Tens of thousands more were killed.

The question of Berlin With the Rhine crossed, German resistance weakened. Allied planes roamed the skies freely, raining bombs down on German targets. Allied troops began moving speedily across Germany.

Now some Allied leaders, knowing that the Soviets would claim any German land they captured, hoped to claim the prize of Berlin before the Soviets did so. The possibility of beating the Soviets to Berlin had once seemed unlikely. Just days before, the western lines were 200 miles away from the German capital, while the Soviets rested just 30 miles outside the city. Since the Rhine crossing, however, the situation had changed. It was no sure thing the Soviets would get there first.

In spite of these facts, General Eisenhower decided not to make a drive toward Berlin itself. Although German defenses were crumbling, he believed the battle for the city would be a bloody one. He also knew that Allied leaders had already reached an agreement with the Soviets about how to divide Berlin. This meant that some of the territory American soldiers might fight and die for would be turned over to the Soviets anyway. In addition, Eisenhower knew that the war in the Pacific was still raging. He felt it was most important to preserve American forces and supplies and make it as easy as possible to send them to the Pacific when the fighting in Europe was done.

With the decision to leave Berlin to the Soviets made, Eisenhower's forces moved rapidly through Germany. They did receive a blow on April 12, 1945, when President Roosevelt died. Although the president had not been in good health, his death was unexpected. Many American soldiers had known no other president during their adult lives. Roosevelt's death saddened the troops. It did not, however, slow the drive to victory.

Women and Minorities in the Military

At the beginning of World War II, only two African Americans had been line officers in the army. One was Benjamin O. Davis Sr., the first African American general. The other was his son, Benjamin O. Davis Jr., who commanded the famous Tuskegee Airmen, a squadron of African American fighter pilots who flew wartime missions in North Africa and Europe. Like his father, Davis Jr. was eventually promoted to general.

The Davises and other African Americans in World War II served in segregated units. In 1948 President Harry S Truman signed legislation that began racial integration in the military.

Members of women's military units also wanted fair treatment. In most branches of the armed services, women's units did not receive veterans' benefits. Leaders such as Oveta Culp Hobby and Mary Agnes Hallaren fought to change this.

In 1948 Truman signed the Women's Armed Services Integration Act. Still, American women continued to serve in separate units until 1978. Today women make up about 20 percent of the U.S. military.

Drawing Conclusions Why did events in World War II lead Truman to end segregation in the military?

Members of the U.S. Air Force in Iraq during Operation Iraqi Freedom

Hitler's death In the final weeks of April 1945 the steady destruction of the German resistance continued. One by one, units from the Soviet Union met up with other Allied forces. At the same time, Berlin was under heavy bombardment. On April 30 Hitler finally recognized that all hope was lost. He committed suicide in his Berlin bunker.

As news of Hitler's death spread, fighting came to a halt. Berlin surrendered on May 2. The German armies scattered elsewhere gave up the fight. Finally, Karl Dönitz, who had taken over as Germany's leader following Hitler's death, agreed to a surrender on May 7. The surrender was to take effect on May 8. In the United States, this was proclaimed **V-E Day**—Victory in Europe Day.

Celebrations erupted in the United States and throughout Europe. "I was alive! And I was going to stay alive," recalled one soldier of his joyful reaction to the German surrender. This fortunate young American could enjoy the Allied victory. Yet many others still had work to do. This was especially true for those still fighting for their lives in a place called Okinawa.

READING CHECK **Identifying the Main Idea** What was the significance of crossing the Rhine in winning the war in Europe?

Winning the War in the Pacific

As you have read, the Allies did capture Okinawa—but at a terrible cost. The horrors of this combat were reflected in the high rates of battle-related psychological casualties. Thousands of Allied soldiers and sailors suffered from battle fatigue and other disorders. These conditions were serious enough to require medical treatment.

The experience of the Allies in fighting the Japanese made many of them dread the prospect of invading the major islands of Japan. Nevertheless, General MacArthur and Admiral Nimitz went forward with developing plans for a massive invasion. The costs would be enormous. Some officials believed that capturing Japan might produce as many as 1 million Allied casualties.

Japan continues fighting Other Allied military leaders hoped to force Japan to surrender by putting a blockade in place or by bombing Japan heavily. In fact, Allied bombs had already caused severe damage to Japanese cities. In March 1945 Major General Curtis LeMay had experimented with a bombing tactic that was designed to produce a tremendous firestorm in the bombed area. The first of LeMay's raids, on Tokyo, killed nearly 84,000 Japanese and destroyed nearly 270,000 buildings. One American compared the effect of the bombs to "a tornado started by fires." The flames were so intense that river water was heated to the boiling point.

The bombing of Tokyo stunned the people of Japan. The defeat at Okinawa was another blow. Still they vowed to fight on.

Some leaders within the Japanese government saw the need for peace. During June and July of 1945 these officials began to seek contact with the Soviet Union. They hoped that the Soviets could help arrange an agreement for peace with the other Allies. These talks went slowly. Meanwhile, American war plans moved steadily forward.

The atomic bomb You have already read about the U.S. program to build an atomic bomb. The Manhattan Project continued throughout the war. In late 1944 leaders of the project declared that the bomb would be ready by the summer of 1945.

Vice President **Harry S Truman** had become president after Roosevelt's death in April. The new president had known nothing about the bomb prior to assuming the presidency. Now he had to decide whether the United States should use this fearsome new weapon.

Truman formed a group to advise him about using the bomb. This group debated where the bomb should be used and whether the Japanese should be warned. After carefully considering all the options, Truman decided to drop the bomb on a Japanese city. There would be no warning.

Truman and the Allies did, however, give the Japanese one last chance to avoid the bomb. On July 26 they issued a demand for Japan's surrender. Failure to give up, the demand read, would lead to "prompt and utter destruction." The Japanese failed to respond. The plan to drop the atomic bomb went forward.

On August 6, 1945, an American B-29 named the **_Enola Gay_** flew over the city of Hiroshima (hee-roh-SHEE-mah) and dropped its atomic bomb. Seconds later, the bomb exploded.

HISTORY'S VOICES

❝I witnessed a yellowish scarlet plume rising like a candle fire high in the sky surrounded by pitch black swirling smoke… At the same moment… houses levitated [rose] a little and then crushed down to the ground like domino pieces. It was just like a white wavehead coming toward me.❞

—Memoir of Takeharu Terao, Hiroshima survivor

Hiroshima

Nearly everything within a one-mile radius of the blast was destroyed when an atomic bomb hit Hiroshima. Heavy damage extended three miles out. Lighter damage reached as far as 12 miles out from the center of the blast.

Dropping the Atomic Bomb

It fell to Secretary of War Henry Stimson to advise President Truman on whether or not to drop the atomic bomb.

❝ The face of war is the face of death … The decision to use the atomic bomb was a decision that brought death to over a hundred thousand Japanese. No explanation can change that fact and I do not wish to gloss it over. But this deliberate, premeditated destruction was our least abhorrent choice. ❞

Henry Stimson, 1947

Physicist Leo Szilard's work on nuclear reactions was key to the development of the bomb, and he felt a moral responsibility to speak against its use.

❝ Using atomic bombs against Japan is one of the greatest blunders of history. Both from a practical point of view on a ten-year scale and from the point of view of our moral position. I went out of my way and very much so in order to prevent it. ❞

Leo Szilard, 1945

SKILLS FOCUS **READING LIKE A HISTORIAN**

Identifying Points of View Henry Stimson focuses on the immediate need to end the war. What consideration does Leo Szilard emphasize?

See **Skills Handbook**, pp. H28–H29

In a single terrible blast, most of Hiroshima was reduced to rubble. Some 80,000 residents died immediately, and 35,000 were injured. Two-thirds of the city's 90,000 buildings were destroyed. Fires raged everywhere.

In spite of the horror of Hiroshima, Japan's leaders took no action to end the war. For three days, they debated their next step. On August 9 the United States dropped a second bomb on Nagasaki (nah-gah-SAH-kee). The death toll there was 40,000.

Amazingly, even this did not bring an end to the war. Japanese emperor Hirohito (hir-oh-HEE-toh) favored surrender, but military leaders resisted. Some even tried to overthrow the Japanese government and continue the war. They failed. Finally, on August 15—known from then on to the Allies as **V-J Day**—Hirohito announced the end of the war in a radio broadcast. It was the first time the Japanese people had ever heard the emperor's voice.

THE IMPACT TODAY

Government
The United States remains part of the United Nations, an organization it was instrumental in creating, and is a member of the UN Security Council.

READING CHECK **Summarizing** What finally brought victory for the Allies in the war against Japan?

The Challenges of Victory

Winning World War II had been a monumental effort for the United States and its allies. Peace would bring its own challenges.

You have read about the Yalta Conference, where the Allies began to discuss postwar plans for Europe. This planning continued throughout the spring and summer of 1945.

The creation of the United Nations In June 1945 representatives from 50 countries, including the United States, met in San Francisco, California, to establish a new organization—the **United Nations**. Like the League of Nations formed after World War I, the United Nations (UN) was meant to encourage cooperation among nations and to prevent future wars. You will read more about the UN in future chapters.

The Potsdam Conference The next month, leaders of the Allied nations met to carry on the work begun at Yalta. They met at the German city of Potsdam. There was growing American concern that communism and Soviet influence might spread in the postwar world. Truman had hoped that if he met with Stalin, he could get the Soviet leader to live up to his promises from Yalta. In this regard, the **Potsdam Conference** was not a success.

Rebuilding Europe and Japan
The United States also faced the difficult task of helping to rebuild Europe and Japan. In Japan, General Douglas MacArthur directed the effort to create a new, democratic government and rebuild the nation's economy. MacArthur skillfully walked a fine line between showing respect for Japanese traditions and insisting on democratic values. He helped the Japanese create a new constitution that reflected many American ideals, such as equality for women.

As with the Nazis in Europe, Japanese war crimes did not go unpunished. Seven key figures in wartime Japan, including leader Hideki Tojo, were tried and executed for their crimes.

The United States also faced a difficult task in rebuilding war-torn Europe. As you will read in the next chapter, this process resulted in increasing tensions with America's wartime ally, the Soviet Union. In the coming years, this relationship would only grow worse.

READING CHECK **Identifying Problems and Solutions** What was the UN meant to accomplish?

CAUSES AND EFFECTS OF WORLD WAR II
QUICK FACTS

CAUSES

• Isolationism had helped lead the United States not to resist German, Japanese, and Italian aggression in the 1930s.

• Germany invaded Poland, and Japan attacked the United States.

EFFECTS

• The Allies occupied Japan and parts of Europe.

• War led to renewed commitment to the idea of collective security and creation of the United Nations.

• Conflict began between the Soviet Union and the other Allies over the fate of conquered European areas.

• The United States emerged as the world's strongest military power.

SECTION 5 ASSESSMENT

go.hrw.com
Online Quiz
Keyword: SD7 HP24

Reviewing Ideas, Terms, and People

1. a. Identify What is the significance of the following terms: Yalta Conference, V-E Day
b. Explain What were the issues surrounding Eisenhower's decision not to push to Berlin?
c. Evaluate What do you think Eisenhower's greatest responsibility was as the war wound down in Europe? Did he fulfill this responsibility?

2. a. Define Write a brief definition of the following term: V-J Day
b. Make Inferences What can you infer about the atomic bomb from the fact that some people felt that it should not have been dropped without warning?
c. Predict How do you think the decision to drop the bomb will affect the United States in the future?

3. a. Identify What is the significance of the following terms: United Nations, Potsdam Conference

b. Elaborate Why do you think that rebuilding a war-torn country is so difficult?

Critical Thinking

4. Identifying Supporting Details Copy the chart below and use information from the section to find supporting details for the main idea given.

The War Ends

FOCUS ON WRITING

5. Descriptive Write a paragraph in which you describe the circumstances of the end of the war in either Europe or in the Pacific theater.

ISLAND HOPPING
The Route to Japan

In the early weeks of the war, Japan seized key islands in the Pacific to form a defensive barrier. To end the war, the United States planned to bomb and invade the Japanese mainland, but getting there proved enormously difficult and costly. It took nearly four years for the United States to push back the Japanese defenses, one island at a time. Each island captured served as a base to launch air raids or to protect American naval forces, who then moved on to attack the next island. The U.S. strategy was known as "island hopping." This map shows some of the islands that the U.S. forces captured on route to Japan.

HOKKAIDO

Tokyo

Sea of Japan

JAPAN

KYUSHU

CHINA

OKINAWA

TAIWAN

Moving into Range Aircraft carriers were crucial for fighting in the vast Pacific Ocean. U.S. carriers transported fighter planes, torpedo bombers, and dive-bombers, many of which had only a 200-mile range, to battle sites.

Okinawa, April-June, 1945
Okinawa was the southernmost of the Japanese home islands. After costly fighting, U.S. forces seized the island as a base for launching the final invasion of Japan.

New York Standards

ST 4.3 Develop hypotheses about important events, eras, or issues; move from chronicling to explaining historical events and issues.

Bombing Runs The B-29 Superfortress's 5000-mile range was essential in the Pacific Ocean. Air raids on Japan, from the Marianas, began in October 1944.

Iwo Jima, February-March, 1945

In one of the most costly battles in the Pacific, U.S. forces attacked Japanese forces well entrenched in caves and tunnels carved into the island's volcanic rock.

Iwo Jima

Pacific Ocean

Mariana Islands, June-August, 1944

The conquest of the Mariana Islands put American B-29 bombers within reach of Japan. Still, numerous planes were shot down during the 5,000 mile round-trip to Japan. The reason was Iwo Jima—home to a Japanese radar station and fighter planes.

Northern Mariana Islands

Saipan

Island Invasions

Aerial Bombing Bombers from aircraft carriers or nearby land bases "soften up" islands before amphibious assaults.

Storming the Beach Behind further bombardment from offshore battleships, marines storm the beaches.

Establishing Air Bases Once an island was secured, engineers rapidly transform it into a staging area for aerial attacks on nearby islands or on Japan itself.

GEOGRAPHY SKILLS **INTERPRETING MAPS**

go.hrw.com
Practice Online
Keyword: SD7 CH24

1. **Location** What challenges did Iwo Jima's location offer the American invaders?
2. **Movement** What strategy did the U.S. follow in moving toward Japan?

See **Skills Handbook**, p. H20

Perspectives on Life in Uniform

Historical Context The documents below provide different information on the hardships and sacrifices of American military personnel during World War II.

Task Examine the documents and answer the questions that follow. Then write an essay about the hardships U.S. soldiers faced. Use facts from the documents and from this chapter to support the position you take in your thesis statement.

ST 3.2 Draw upon literary selections, historical documents, and accounts to analyze the roles played by different individuals and groups during the major eras in New York State and United States history.

ST 4.3 Develop hypotheses about important events, eras, or issues; move from chronicling to explaining historical events and issues; use information collected from diverse sources to produce cogently written reports and document-based essays.

DOCUMENT 1

Cartoonist Bill Mauldin chronicled the sufferings of the everyday soldier in *Stars and Stripes,* a newspaper published by the U.S. Army. His gritty cartoons featured the characters Willie and Joe, who stood for all ordinary soldiers. Mauldin served during the entire war and was wounded in battle in Sicily.

"Joe, yestiddy ya saved my life an' I swore I'd pay ya back. Here's my last pair of dry socks."

DOCUMENT 2

Army nurses saw much of the worst suffering of the war up close. June Wandrey served as a combat nurse during some of the bloodiest battles in North Africa and western Europe. She helped save many lives and was awarded eight battle stars for her service under fire. She wrote this letter to her family in Wautoma, Wisconsin, in January 1944.

> "We now have a mix of wounded, medical patients, and battle-fatigued soldiers . . . The wounded were happy to be missing only one arm or leg . . . I have a terrible earache but as usual I have to work. The patients need me."

DOCUMENT 3

For many Americans, the war was draining both physically and spiritually. Paul Curtis was from a small town in Tennessee. Fighting in the Italian campaign was unlike anything he had ever experienced. In this letter home from May 1944, he tried to explain his reactions to his brother. Curtis was killed in action shortly after writing this letter.

> "Take a combination of fear, anger, hunger, thirst, exhaustion, disgust, loneliness, homesickness, and wrap that all up in one reaction and you might approach the feelings a fellow has. It makes you feel mighty small, helpless, and alone . . . Without faith, I don't see how anyone could stand this."

DOCUMENT 4

Many African American soldiers faced an extra hardship during the war. In addition to the dangers and shortages experienced by all soldiers, African Americans also encountered racial discrimination. Corporal Rupert Trimmingham wrote the following letter to *Yank,* a weekly magazine published by the U.S. Army. In the letter, Trimmingham refers to "Old Man Jim Crow," a name for the discriminatory laws then in force across much of the United States.

"Myself and eight other Negro soldiers were on our way from Camp Claiborne, La., to the hospital here at Fort Huachuca, Arizona . . . We could not purchase a cup of coffee at any of the lunchrooms around there . . . As you know, Old Man Jim Crow rules. But that's not all; 11:30 A.M. about two dozen German prisoners of war, with two American guards, came to the station. They entered the lunchroom, sat at the tables, had their meals served, talked, smoked, in fact had quite a swell time. I stood on the outside looking on . . . Are we not American soldiers, sworn to fight for and die if need be for this our country?"

DOCUMENT 5

Popular comedian Bob Hope never served in the armed forces, but he traveled throughout the war zones entertaining the troops for the United Service Organizations (USO). In 1944 he wrote *I Never Left Home,* a memoir of his experiences during the war. In the preface he told the public about the soldiers he encountered. President Lyndon Johnson awarded Hope the Presidential Medal of Freedom in 1969. Hope was still entertaining American troops far from home at the age of 90, when he took his act to the Persian Gulf on the eve of the first Persian Gulf War.

"I saw your sons and your husbands, your soldiers and your sweethearts. I saw how they worked, fought, and lived. I saw some of them die. I saw more courage, more good humor in the face of discomfort, more love in an era of hate, and more devotion to duty than could ever exist under tyranny.

I saw American minds, American skill, and American strength breaking the backbone of evil . . . And I came back to find people exulting over the thousand plane raids over Germany… and saying how wonderful they are! Those people never watched the face of a pilot as he read a bulletin board and saw his buddy marked up missing…

Dying is sometimes easier than living through it . . ."

Skills FOCUS — READING LIKE A HISTORIAN

1. **a. Identify** Refer to Document 1. What does the character of Willie offer to Joe in exchange for saving his life?
   b. Interpret What does this cartoon say about the living conditions and supplies for soldiers?

2. **a. Identify** Refer to Document 2. What was Wandrey's job?
   b. Analyze Why were the wounded soldiers happy to be missing only one arm or leg?

3. **a. Identify** Refer to Document 3. What is the overall impression that Curtis gives of his experience?
   b. Elaborate How do you think Curtis's faith helped him during the war?

4. **a. Identify** Refer to Document 4. Why could the African American soldiers not buy coffee at the southern bases?

   b. Analyze How might seeing the German soldiers being treated better than African American soldiers have affected Trimmingham's views of the war?

5. **a. Identify** Refer to Document 5. What was Bob Hope's role in the war?
   b. Explain What did Hope mean when he wrote, "Dying is sometimes easier than living through it"?

6. **Document-Based Essay Question** Consider the question below and form a thesis statement. Using examples from Documents 1, 2, 3, 4, and 5, create an outline and write a short essay supporting your position.
   What kinds of hardships and suffering did American soldiers face during World War II?

See **Skills Handbook**, pp. H28–H29, H31

Visual Summary: The United States in World War II

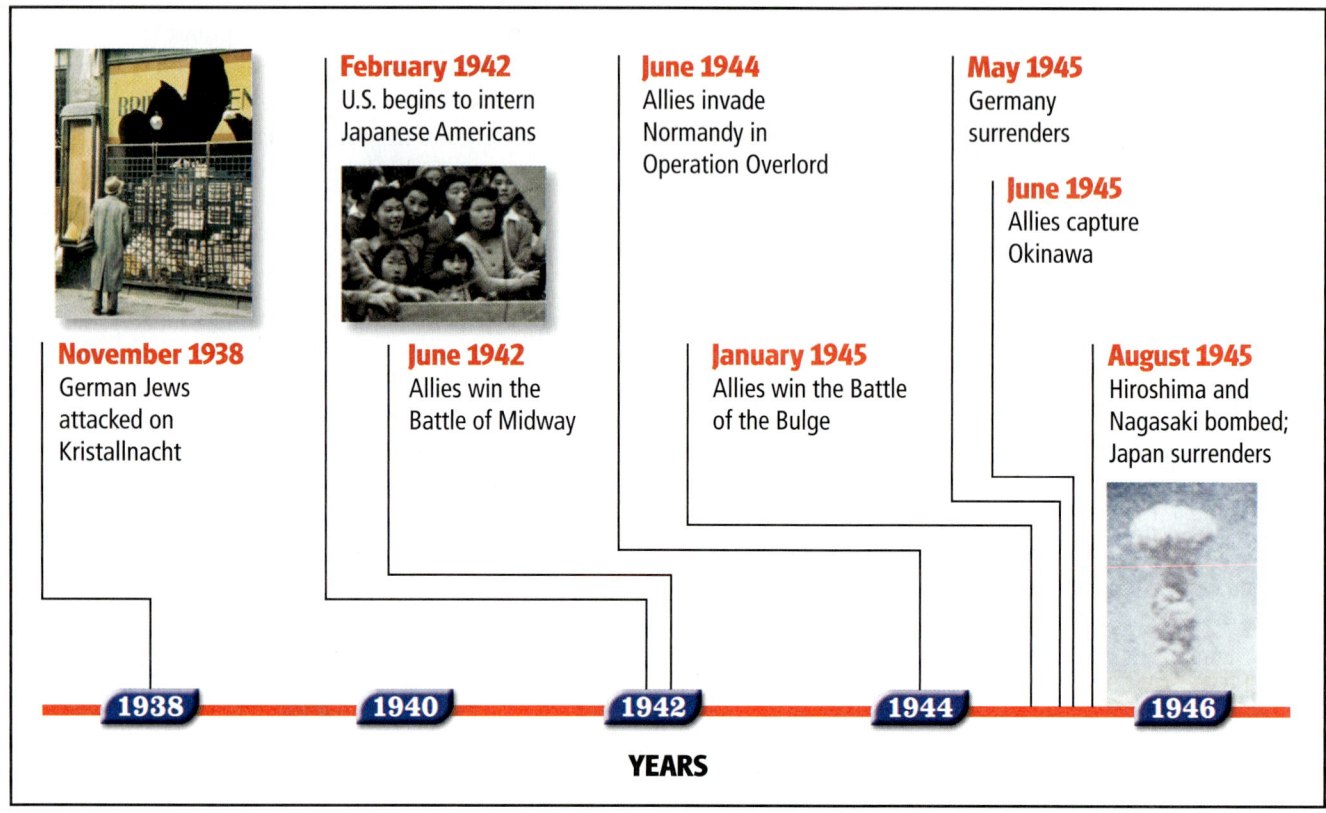

November 1938
German Jews attacked on Kristallnacht

February 1942
U.S. begins to intern Japanese Americans

June 1942
Allies win the Battle of Midway

June 1944
Allies invade Normandy in Operation Overlord

January 1945
Allies win the Battle of the Bulge

May 1945
Germany surrenders

June 1945
Allies capture Okinawa

August 1945
Hiroshima and Nagasaki bombed; Japan surrenders

1938 1940 1942 1944 1946

YEARS

Reviewing Key Terms and People

For each term or name below, write a sentence explaining its significance to World War II.

1. ghetto
2. Operation Overlord
3. Dwight D. Eisenhower
4. internment
5. Final Solution
6. Battle of Okinawa
7. Douglas MacArthur
8. rationing
9. Battle of Midway
10. Tuskegee Airmen
11. Harry S Truman
12. kamikaze

Comprehension and Critical Thinking

SECTION 1 *(pp. 770–777)*

13. **a. Recall** What were Operation Torch and Operation Overlord, and what was their significance?

    b. Sequence Create a brief time line of U.S. involvement in Europe between 1941 and 1944.

    c. Elaborate Explain how American success in the Battle of the Atlantic may have affected the outcome of Operation Overlord.

SECTION 2 *(pp. 778–783)*

14. **a. Describe** What was the Holocaust?

    b. Compare Did Hitler's attitudes toward Jews change over time? Explain.

    c. Evaluate What do you think of Roosevelt's decision to focus all his energy on defeating the Germans and Japanese rather than trying to rescue the Jews in Nazi camps?

History's Impact video program
Review the video to answer the closing question:
Why did the United States emerge as a global
superpower after World War II?

SECTION 3 *(pp. 785–792)*

15. a. Recall Why did the Japanese have early success against the United States in the Pacific?

b. Explain Why was the Battle of Midway such an important victory for the United States?

c. Elaborate Why do you think air and sea power were so important in the Pacific?

SECTION 4 *(pp. 793–799)*

16. a. Recall What sacrifices did Americans on the home front have to make for the war effort?

b. Summarize How did the federal government try to encourage Americans to support the war effort?

c. Elaborate In what ways did World War II increase the power of the American government and its influence in everyday life?

SECTION 5 *(pp. 801–807)*

17. a. Identify Write a brief explanation of the significance of the following terms: V-E Day, V-J Day

b. Contrast How did the behavior of German soldiers compare to the behavior of Japanese soldiers in the final months before each side surrendered?

c. Evaluate How do you think the experience of World War I affected the decisions made at the end of World War II?

Using the Internet

go.hrw.com
Practice Online
Keyword: SD7 CH24

18. The Allied invasion of France, often called D-Day, began on June 6, 1944. Within a few weeks, the Allies had landed nearly a million soldiers on the beaches of Normandy, and Germany's forces were in serious trouble. Using the keyword above, do research to learn more about the events of D-Day. Then create a report that describes the invasion and its importance in ending the war in Europe.

Analyzing Primary Sources

Reading Like a Historian

This photograph was taken after the capture of Mount Suribachi on Iwo Jima. It was soon printed in newspapers all across the United States and became one of the most recognizable images of the war.

19. Describe What is the significance of the moment captured in this photograph?

20. Draw Conclusions Why do you think this image had such a powerful impact on the public?

Critical Reading

Read the passage in Section 4 under the heading "Winning American Support for the War." Then answer the questions that follow.

21. The government demonstrated its need to influence public opinion on the war by

A making Hollywood movies.

B establishing the Office of War Information.

C outlawing religious services.

D forbidding negative talk about the war effort.

22. In the *Barnette* ruling, the Supreme Court held that

A people could be forced to listen to patriotic speeches.

B it was illegal to make movies that did not support the war effort.

C religious groups had to support the war effort.

D people could not be forced to salute the flag.

WRITING FOR THE SAT

Think about the following issue.

Following the Japanese attack on Pearl Harbor, some military and government officials worried about a Japanese attack on the mainland of the United States. Though they had no evidence of any plot, they were especially concerned that such an attack would be aided by some of the many residents of Japanese ancestry then living in the western states.

23. Assignment Was the government right to single out residents of Japanese ancestry as a special threat to the United States? Write a short essay in which you develop your position on this issue. Support your point of view with reasoning and examples from your reading and studies.

25

1945–1953

The COLD WAR Begins

THE BIG PICTURE The Cold War was born in the uneasy World War II alliances between the Soviet Union and democratic nations. After the war, the struggle between democracy and communism led to a long war of ideas with occasional outbreaks of fighting.

New York Standards

Key Idea 2 Important ideas, social and cultural values, beliefs, and traditions from New York State and United States history illustrate the connections and interactions of people and events across time and from a variety of perspectives.

Key Idea 3 Study about the major social, political, economic, cultural, and religious developments in New York State and United States history involves learning about the important roles and contributions of individuals and groups.

Skills FOCUS **READING LIKE A HISTORIAN**

A group of Berliners gaze up at a U.S. military cargo plane bringing them supplies during the Soviet blockade of their city in 1948. The Berlin Airlift, as it was known, lasted until 1949.
Interpreting Visuals What do you think it was like, for Berliners and Americans, during the heightened tensions of this Cold War incident?

See **Skills Handbook**, p. H30

February 1945
President Roosevelt meets with Allied leaders at the Yalta Conference to discuss postwar issues.

U.S.

1945

World

June 1945
Delegates from 50 nations meet in San Francisco to found the United Nations.

History's Impact video program

Watch the video to understand the impact of defense spending.

April 1949
The United States joins the North Atlantic Treaty Organization (NATO).

June 1947
Marshall Plan is established to help Europe rebuild after World War II.

September 1950
UN forces under General MacArthur land at Inchon, South Korea.

April 1951
President Truman fires General MacArthur over Korean War strategy.

1947

1949

1951

1953

March 1947
International Monetary Fund begins operation.

June 1949
Chinese Communists take control of the country.

October 1950
Chinese troops pour into North Korea.

June 1950 North Korean troops invade South Korea.

July 1953
Fighting in Korea ends. United States, North Korea, and China sign an armistice.

The Iron Curtain Falls on Europe

BEFORE YOU READ

PI 2.1 Discuss several schemes for periodizing the history of New York State and the United States.

MAIN IDEA

At the end of World War II, tensions between the Soviet Union and the United States deepened, leading to an era known as the Cold War.

READING FOCUS

1. What were the roots of the Cold War?
2. What was the Iron Curtain?
3. How did the United States respond to Soviet actions in Europe?
4. What was the crisis in Berlin in the late 1940s, and how was it resolved?

KEY TERMS AND PEOPLE

Cold War
Iron Curtain
containment
George F. Kennan
Truman Doctrine
Marshall Plan
Berlin airlift
NATO

THE INSIDE STORY

What does a "man of steel" look like in the flesh? When the Potsdam Conference began in the summer of 1945, President Truman already knew the legend of Soviet leader Joseph Stalin, whose last name meant "man of steel." Stalin's brutal repression of his own people was thought to have led to millions of deaths. His brutality was rivaled perhaps only by Hitler's. Now, on July 17, 1945, this man of steel stood in the doorway across the room from Truman.

As Truman sized up Stalin, he began to realize why Franklin Roosevelt had referred to him as Uncle Joe. The five-foot, five-inch-tall leader was "a little bit of a squirt," Truman would later recall. As Stalin discussed the matters facing the Allied leaders in the days ahead—including the possibility of Soviet entry into the war with Japan and the future of Poland and the rest of Eastern Europe—Truman even found himself admiring the man.

Truman would soon learn that dealing with Stalin was more difficult than he first expected. As you will read, in the months after the Potsdam Conference, Truman would have to deal with Stalin's efforts to expand Soviet power.

President Truman Sizes Up STALIN

▲ President Truman (center) shoulder to shoulder with Stalin

The Roots of the Cold War

Following World War II, the United States and the Soviet Union entered an era of high tension and bitter rivalry known as the **Cold War**. The roots of the Cold War reached back many years. As far back as the 1920s and 1930s, the United States had viewed the Soviet Union as a potential enemy. Americans were hostile to the ideas of communism and had at times feared its spread in the United States.

World War II alliances Despite the American fear of communism, the United States and the Soviet Union joined as allies against Nazi Germany during World War II. The two countries were not truly friends, however. Indeed, after the Germans and Soviets signed their nonaggression pact in 1939, President Roosevelt had worried that the Germans and the Soviets might join forces. He feared the United States might one day be fighting against Stalin and his armies.

Nevertheless, when Hitler's forces invaded the Soviet Union in 1941, the Americans offered to help Stalin by providing military equipment. This was not an expression of support for the Soviet dictator. It was a practical move aimed at helping defeat Hitler, who was seen as a bigger threat. Over time, the Soviets received many tons of American shipments under the Lend-Lease program.

Yet even as the United States sent supplies to the Soviet Union, the two countries argued over military strategy. Early in World War II, Stalin urged the United States and Great Britain to launch an immediate invasion of Europe. This, Stalin believed, would force the Germans to remove some of their troops from the Soviet Union. Several times Roosevelt promised Stalin that the invasion was on its way. With each delay, Stalin fumed. The American and British inaction, he complained, "leaves the Soviet Army . . . to do the job alone." Hard feelings between the Soviets and the Americans and British grew.

The atomic bomb Another issue that created mistrust between the United States and the Soviet Union was the development of the atomic bomb by the United States. As you have read previously, the Manhattan Project was a tightly guarded secret. Nevertheless,

CAUSES OF THE COLD WAR

CAUSES

Philosophical Differences
- Soviet Union: communism, totalitarian dictatorship
- United States: free-enterprise capitalism, republic

World War II Conflicts
- Soviets wanted British and Americans to open a second European front earlier in war.
- United States secretly developed atomic bomb.

Postwar Conflicts
- Soviet Union refused to live up to wartime promises of elections in Eastern Europe.
- United States made efforts to resist Soviet expansion.

The Cold War
- An era of high tension between the United States and the Soviet Union.

Soviet spies had managed to steal the plans and Soviet scientists followed them closely. The Soviets saw the weapon as a threat and soon began to develop an atomic bomb of their own.

READING CHECK **Identifying the Main Idea** What were the roots of the conflict between the United States and the Soviet Union?

The Iron Curtain Descends

After World War II, the United States and Britain were worried about what the Soviet Union might do. In particular, they were concerned that Stalin aimed to gain control of Eastern Europe. This was not a new concern. As you have read, in the Yalta and Potsdam conferences during World War II, American and British leaders pressed Stalin to hold free elections in Soviet-occupied lands, such as Poland.

The Americans and British had good reason to be concerned about Stalin's plans. He had no intention of giving up political and economic control over Eastern Europe. In Stalin's view, he was fully justified in wanting to control Eastern Europe. The Soviet Union had just

ACADEMIC VOCABULARY

justified based on sound reasoning

emerged from a terrible war in which as many as 30 million or more Soviets had died. To Stalin, the German invasion from the West had been part of a long history of attacks originating from Europe. Stalin believed that he could increase the security of his country by creating a line of Soviet-friendly nations between the Soviet Union and its historic enemies in Western Europe.

Communism spreads To achieve his goal in Eastern Europe, Stalin used whatever means necessary. In some cases, he outlawed political parties or newspapers that opposed the Communists. The Soviets also jailed or killed some political opponents and sometimes even rigged elections to ensure the success of Communist candidates. In these ways, the Soviets managed to install Communist governments throughout Eastern Europe during the postwar years.

Soon, every nation in Eastern Europe had a Soviet-friendly Communist government in place. Most of these governments were under the direct control of Stalin and the Soviet Union. The lone exception was the nation of Yugoslavia. There, Josip Broz Tito, who won fame fighting the Nazis during World War II, was firmly in control. Though he was a Communist, Tito refused to take orders from the Soviet Union. His wide popularity in Yugoslavia helped him remain in power.

The United States was also alarmed by the Soviet treatment of Germans living in Poland and the other countries of Eastern Europe. During the war, the Allies had agreed that Germans living in these areas should be removed in an "orderly and humane manner." After the war, however, the Soviets relocated the Germans with great brutality. Several hundred thousand Germans died, as millions were forced to relocate to the western section of Germany, which was occupied by the United States, Britain, and France.

The Iron Curtain American and British leaders were saddened to see Eastern Europeans, who had already suffered greatly during World War II, fall under the control of a dictator. They were also concerned that the Soviet Union would not stop at Eastern Europe.

In response, President Truman urged his secretary of state, James Byrnes, to get tough with the Soviets. "Unless Russia is faced with an iron fist and strong language," Truman wrote, "another war is in the making."

In 1946 former British prime minister Winston Churchill traveled to the United States.

The Iron Curtain in Europe

After World War II, Stalin helped install Communist governments throughout Eastern Europe. Here, a poster of Stalin (center) hangs above a doorway in newly Communist East Germany in 1946. The spread of communism concerned American and British leaders. In a famous speech, British Prime Minister Winston Churchill (far right) described a sharp division between Europe's Communist and non-Communist nations—a division that he famously termed "the Iron Curtain."

THE IRON CURTAIN, 1948

DENMARK
NETHERLANDS
UNITED KINGDOM
POLAND
SOVIET UNION
BELGIUM
EAST GERMANY
CZECHOSLOVAKIA
LUX.
WEST GERMANY
FRANCE
SWITZERLAND
AUSTRIA
HUNGARY
ITALY
ROMANIA
YUGOSLAVIA
BULGARIA
ALBANIA
GREECE

On March 5 he delivered a speech in Fulton, Missouri, in which he sharply attacked the Soviet Union for creating what he called an **Iron Curtain**. The term reflected Churchill's belief that communism had created a sharp division in Europe.

HISTORY'S VOICES

❝A shadow has fallen upon the scenes so lately lighted by the Allied victory. Nobody knows what Soviet Russia and its Communist international organization intends to do in the immediate future, or what are the limits, if any, to their expansive . . . tendencies . . . It is my duty to place before you certain facts about the present position of Europe. From Stettin in the Baltic to Trieste in the Adriatic an iron curtain has descended across the Continent.❞

—Winston Churchill, Speech at Westminster College

In the Soviet Union, Stalin's reaction to Churchill's speech was harsh. He used Churchill's words to help persuade his people that the United States and Great Britain were enemies of the Soviet Union. This became his excuse to rebuild the Soviet Union's military strength—which slowed the pace of rebuilding the shattered Soviet countryside.

READING CHECK **Making Inferences** Why did Churchill use the term *Iron Curtain*?

"An iron curtain has descended upon the Continent."

–Winston Churchill, March 1946

The United States Responds

The end of World War II and the start of the Cold War presented American leaders with a challenge. The United States was now one of the world's two most powerful nations. The other was an increasingly hostile Soviet Union.

American leaders felt they needed a new policy to deal with the situation. That is, the United States had to become the leader of all nations committed to democratic ideals and freedoms, even as the Soviet Union sought to expand its power and influence.

Containment and the Truman Doctrine

The policy that the United States adopted in the late 1940s was known as **containment**. The creator of the containment policy was an American diplomat and expert on the Soviet Union named **George F. Kennan**. Kennan believed the United States should resist Soviet attempts to expand its power and influence wherever those attempts occurred. To Kennan, containment was not limited to military force. It also involved providing economic aid to other countries in order to strengthen them against the Soviet Union.

Kennan's containment policy was put to the test in 1947. That year, President Truman informed Congress of an urgent need to provide emergency economic and military aid to Greece and Turkey. Both countries were facing Soviet pressure. In Greece, Soviet-supported Communists were trying to take advantage of postwar economic problems to gain power. In Turkey, the Soviet government was trying to gain more control.

President Truman argued that providing aid would help both the Greek and Turkish governments resist Soviet expansion. In the process, he issued what came to be called the **Truman Doctrine**:

HISTORY'S VOICES

❝I believe it must be the policy of the United States to support free peoples who are resisting subjugation [forced control] by armed minorities or outside pressures . . .

I believe that our help should be primarily through economic and financial aid which is essential to economic stability and orderly political processes.❞

—Harry S Truman, speech to joint session of Congress, March 12, 1947

THE IMPACT TODAY

Government
Kennan's containment policy guided U.S. foreign affairs for decades, including the decision to send troops to Vietnam in the 1960s.

The Marshall Plan

THE MARSHALL PLAN

Purpose: A U.S. financial aid program to rebuild the economies of European countries in order to create stable conditions for democratic governments.

Total amount of aid: $13.4 billion

Number of countries that received aid: 17

Countries that received the most aid: Great Britain, France, and Italy

Residents lined the streets as the millionth ton of Marshall-Plan goods were paraded through Athens, Greece, in December 1949. The Marshall Plan focused its efforts on struggling countries such as Greece, which was in the midst of a civil war against Communist rebels. The plan, originally called the European Recovery Program, is credited with boosting Western Europe's gross national product by 15 to 25 percent. In 1953 George Marshall received the Nobel Peace Prize for crafting the plan that, noted the prize presenter, "has become inseparably connected with his name."
How would economic recovery discourage communism?

Following Truman's speech, a bipartisan Congress voted in favor of the United States providing hundreds of millions of dollars in aid to Greece and Turkey, to fight Communist influence. In both countries, the Soviets did not succeed in gaining control.

The Marshall Plan The war-related economic problems facing Greece were severe. They were not, however, unusual. Across Europe, World War II had devastated cities and ruined farms. Railroads, factories, and mines lay idle. Though the fighting was over, people were continuing to suffer, and hunger and poverty were widespread.

Many Americans felt moved to help the people of Europe, who had already suffered so much from the war. Americans also realized that, if conditions grew worse, more Europeans might turn to communism. Indeed, as the people of Europe became more desperate, the influence of Soviet communism grew. In several European nations, strong Communist movements were beginning to appear.

In June 1947, George C. Marshall, the former World War II military leader and now secretary of state, gave a speech at Harvard University. In it he called for a massive American program of aid to help Europe rebuild and get back on its economic feet.

HISTORY'S VOICES

"Our policy is directed not against any country or doctrine but against hunger, poverty, desperation, and chaos. Its purpose should be the revival of a working economy in the world so as to permit the emergence of political and social conditions in which free institutions can exist."

—George C. Marshall, commencement address, Harvard University, June 5, 1947

The **Marshall Plan**, as this vision came to be known, was an enormous undertaking. Between 1948 and 1951, the U.S. government spent over 13 billion dollars in 17 different countries. This aid bought food and farm equipment. It also rebuilt factories and homes. Marshall's original plan even offered aid to the Soviet Union and its allies. But Stalin refused the aid.

With the help of the Marshall Plan, Western Europe was soon feeding its hungry and providing jobs for its workers. Western European countries were also able to buy products from American factories, which helped the postwar economy grow in the United States. Finally, the Marshall Plan helped the United States build strong political support in Western Europe. This support would be vital in the Cold War years to come.

READING CHECK **Identifying Cause and Effect** How did the United States respond to the growing tension with the Soviets in the late 1940s?

The Crisis in Berlin

After World War II, the Allies had divided Germany into four zones of occupation—British, French, and American in the western area and Soviet in the east. The capital of Berlin, which lay within the Soviet zone, was also divided into four zones.

With the start of the Cold War, the lines dividing Germany became sharper. It became clear that the Soviets planned to keep their zone under Communist control. The British and Americans, meanwhile, began to take steps to set up a free, democratic government within their zones. The French would later join this effort. The western zone eventually became known as the Federal Republic of Germany, or West Germany. The British and the Americans also took steps to set up a democratic government in West Berlin.

The Soviets block traffic The Soviets were not pleased by the idea of a Western-style government and economy in the middle of the Soviet zone of occupation. In June 1948 they decided to take drastic action. The Soviets announced that they would block any road, rail, or river traffic into West Berlin. Suddenly, West Berlin's 2.1 million residents had been cut off from sources of food, coal, and other basic necessities.

In fact, West Berlin was not completely cut off because there were airstrips in the city. The Western powers could try to supply West Berlin by air. It was a risky plan. Some officials did not believe it was even possible to supply all the needs of a major city by aircraft. Another danger was that the Soviets might try to stop the planes or shoot them down. This could lead to war.

In the end, the Western leaders decided that they had to take the risk. Their only hope for keeping West Berlin free was a massive airlift. The plan went forward.

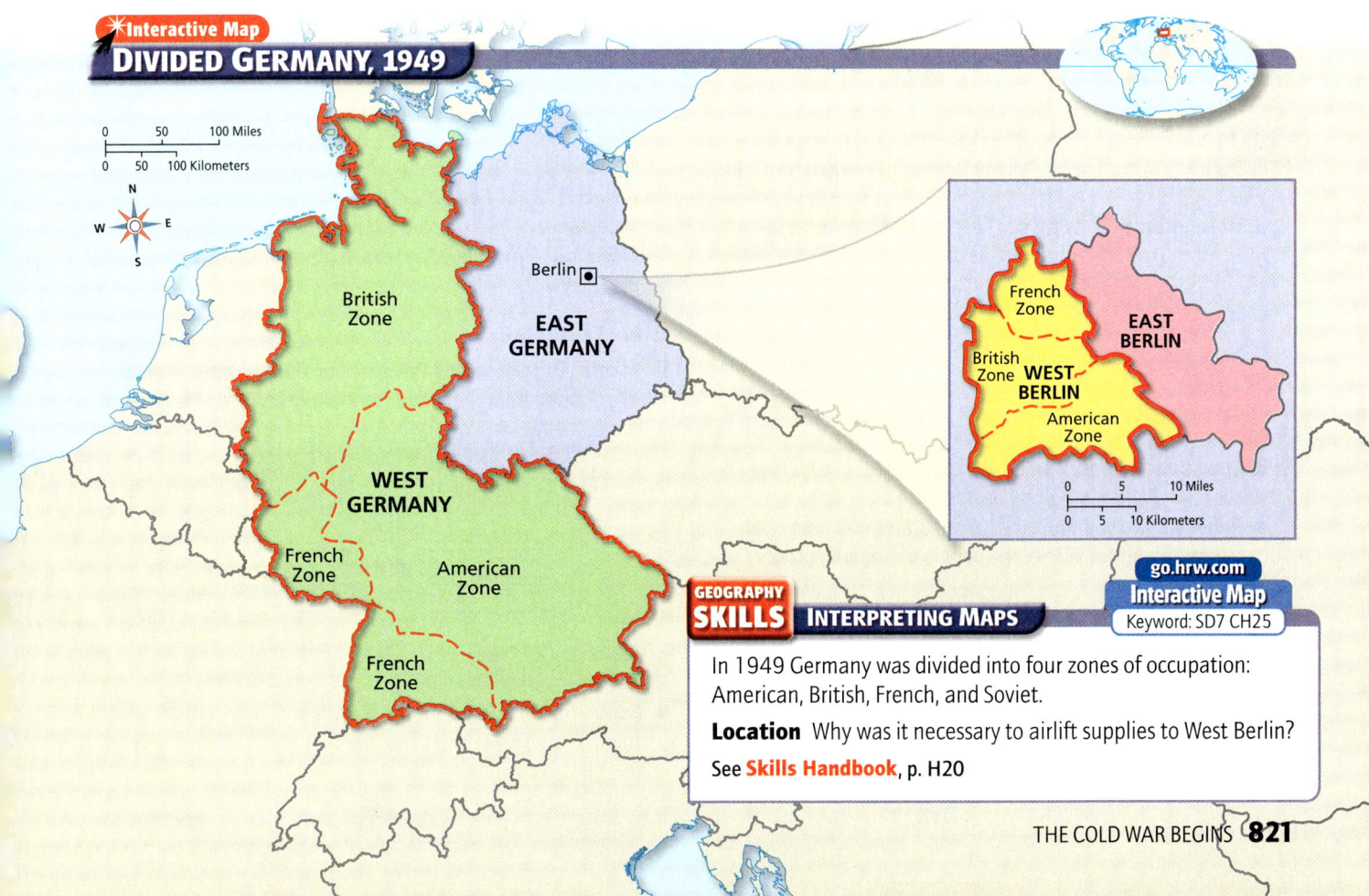

Interactive Map
DIVIDED GERMANY, 1949

British Zone
EAST GERMANY
Berlin
WEST GERMANY
French Zone
American Zone
French Zone

French Zone
EAST BERLIN
British Zone
WEST BERLIN
American Zone

GEOGRAPHY SKILLS **INTERPRETING MAPS**

go.hrw.com
Interactive Map
Keyword: SD7 CH25

In 1949 Germany was divided into four zones of occupation: American, British, French, and Soviet.

Location Why was it necessary to airlift supplies to West Berlin?
See **Skills Handbook**, p. H20

The Berlin airlift begins Within days of the Soviet blockade, British and American airplanes began making deliveries to the people of West Berlin. Every day, the planes flew an average of 7,000 tons of supplies into West Berlin. Hundreds of flights landed, unloaded, and took off again.

To the amazement of the Soviet leaders, the Berlin airlift continued week after week, month after month. The airlift also got bigger. To allow more planes to land, the Allies built another airfield in the French sector of Berlin. In the month of April 1949, nearly 1,400 separate flights took place and nearly 400,000 tons of supplies were delivered.

There were tragedies, however. Some 70 American and British citizens died in airplane crashes. At least five German civilians on the ground were also killed.

In spite of these problems, the airlift continued. Finally, in the face of Allied determination, the Soviet Union lifted its blockade on May 12, 1949. By that time, American, British, and French planes had made nearly 280,000 flights into Berlin. American pilots flew two-thirds of them, leading the way.

NATO forms The widening conflict with the Soviet Union made many Western Europeans very uncomfortable. They realized that if war were to break out, they would be no match for the huge Soviet army. In order to provide a measure of security, Belgium, France, Luxembourg, the Netherlands, and the United Kingdom joined together in a system of common defense in 1948.

The crisis in Berlin helped make other Western nations aware of the wisdom of this action. In April 1949 the United States and six other nations joined the original five to create a new military alliance—the North Atlantic Treaty Organization, or **NATO**. (The other six nations were Canada, Denmark, Iceland, Italy, Norway, and Portugal.) According to the North Atlantic Treaty, an armed attack against one of the member nations would be considered an attack against all.

In the mid-1950s, Greece, Turkey, and the newly created West Germany joined NATO. Today 26 countries, including several former Communist nations, are NATO members.

READING CHECK **Summarizing** What was the crisis in Berlin?

Reviewing Ideas, Terms, and People

1. a. Define Write a brief definition for the following term: **Cold War**

b. Make Inferences What can be inferred from the fact that the United States did not share its plans for building the atomic bomb with the Soviets during the war?

c. Evaluate Do you think the United States should have done more to improve relations with the Soviet Union during World War II? Explain.

2. a. Recall What was the **Iron Curtain**, and why was that term chosen?

b. Draw Conclusions Why do you think western leaders were so concerned about the Iron Curtain?

c. Elaborate Do you think the United States was right to be concerned about the fate of the people of Eastern Europe? Explain.

3. a. Define Write a brief definition for each of the following terms: **containment, Truman Doctrine, Marshall Plan**

b. Analyze What were two different ways that the Marshall Plan benefited the United States?

c. Predict How do you think the Marshall Plan will affect relationships between the United States and the countries of

Western Europe who received the aid? Support your answer with details from the section.

4. a. Recall What was the **Berlin airlift**, and why was it necessary?

b. Explain What were the risks in attempting to supply West Berlin by air?

Critical Thinking

5. Identifying Cause and Effect Copy the chart below and use information from the section to identify causes and effects of the Cold War.

Causes	Effects
Soviet-Western tension	Cold War

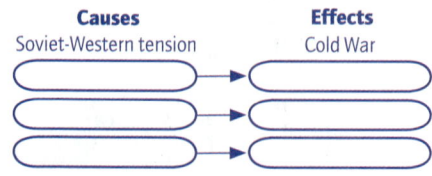

FOCUS ON WRITING

6. Expository Write a paragraph explaining whether or not you think George F. Kennan's containment policy was a good idea for the United States.

Healing the Wounds of War

BEFORE YOU READ

MAIN IDEA

Following the end of World War II, U.S. military forces—and the rest of the country—faced the challenge of returning to life during peacetime.

READING FOCUS

1. What was life like in America after World War II?

2. What happened in politics in post-war America?

3. How did the United States and other countries try to build a better world after the war?

KEY TERMS AND PEOPLE

GI Bill
baby boom
Fair Deal
Universal Declaration of Human Rights
World Bank
International Monetary Fund
General Agreement on Tariffs and Trade

 2.3 Compare and contrast the experiences of different groups in the United States.

Challenges for RETURNING SOLDIERS

▲ **Returning soldiers fight for jobs at a coal-mining operation in 1946.**

THE INSIDE STORY

What did the veterans of World War II have to worry about? In 1946 a popular song told the tale of a soldier returning home from World War II. "Not so long ago when the bullets screamed," went one of the verses, "many was the happy dream I dreamed." Indeed, millions of soldiers had survived the terror of combat by looking forward to their return to a bright future in the United States. Yet as the song continued, it told of a different sort of homecoming for the World War II veteran.

"Now the mighty war over there is won,
Troubles and trials have just begun
As I face that terrible enemy sign, 'No Vacancy.'"

This song tells of just one of the challenges facing veterans of the war, who returned to America by the millions within a few short months of V-J and V-E days. These men and women found shortages of housing—and, as the picture shows above, difficulty finding work. For these veterans who had given so much to their country, the bumpy transition back to life in the United States was a bitter one.

As you will read, however, this troubled transition period was remarkably brief. The federal government did much to help returning soldiers resume their lives and move the country forward beyond the war. American consumers did the rest. ◼

Life in America after World War II

The end of World War II was a joyous occasion for Americans. Yet it was also a time of concern. During the war, the nation's factories had worked overtime to supply the Allied forces. Now the orders for tanks, planes, ships, and weapons dropped sharply. Some experts predicted serious economic trouble.

At the same time, nearly all of the 12 million men and women who had been serving in the armed forces at the end of the war were returning to civilian life. Many of these returning veterans would be looking for jobs. But often jobs simply were not available. In addition, some women workers were pressured to leave their jobs so a male veteran could take their places. In general, however, most veterans did eventually find jobs.

The GI Bill This shift actually began before World War II ended. In June 1944, President Roosevelt signed the Servicemen's Readjustment Act of 1944. The act became known as the **GI Bill**. GI, which stood for "government issue," was a nickname for members of the armed forces.

The GI Bill included several features aimed at helping veterans make a smooth entry into civilian life. For example, it provided money for veterans to attend college or receive advanced job training. It helped arrange for loans for those wishing to buy a home, farm, or business. The GI Bill also provided help in finding work as well as a year's worth of unemployment benefits for those who could not find work. As you have read, the government had promised financial bonuses to World War I veterans but had not delivered. Now, after World War II, veterans were not receiving cash bonuses, but they were receiving immediate benefits.

Increasing demand The GI Bill helped millions of GIs make a successful return to civilian life. At the same time, civilians helped spur the postwar economy. During the war, the federal government took steps to control what products American industry could make. For example, car production stopped so that factories could turn out tanks and equipment.

After the war, demand for consumer goods rose sharply. People who had delayed purchases during the war now decided to buy. Returning veterans built houses, which increased the demand for furniture and appliances.

THE IMPACT TODAY

Government
The GI Bill remains in effect today. Since 1944, about 21 million Americans have received GI Bill tuition benefits, and about 17.5 million Americans have received GI Bill home loans.

The GI Bill in Action

The GI Bill helped millions of World War II veterans earn college degrees. Many attended college while raising their families. Here, veterans celebrate after graduating from the University of Colorado. GI Bill benefits included

- money for college or job training
- loans for homes, farms, or businesses
- unemployment pay of $20 a week for up to a year
- assistance finding jobs

Many more Americans also began having families. The two decades following World War II marked the beginning of the **baby boom**, a dramatic rise in the birthrate. Larger families created demand for larger cars. In this way, the postwar economy made an unexpectedly smooth shift from providing the tools of war to providing the products of peace.

Labor unions after the war

During the war, the government had sought to prevent labor disputes that might affect wartime production. After the war, unions began seeking the increases in wages that had been limited during the war. Starting in 1946, the number of strikes rose sharply. In 1947 Congress passed the Taft-Hartley Act over President Truman's veto. This law greatly reduced the power of labor unions. For example, it empowered the president to stop strikes when the national interest was at stake.

Racial minorities after the war

You have read about efforts early in the war to ensure equal opportunity for African Americans in wartime government and industry jobs. These efforts continued after the war. President Truman was committed to expanding opportunities for African Americans. After meeting strong opposition from members of Congress, he decided to take action on his own. In June 1948, Truman issued Executive Order 9981.

HISTORY'S VOICES

❝It is hereby declared to be the policy of the President that there shall be equality of treatment and opportunity for all persons in the armed services without regard to race, color, religion, or national origin.❞

—Harry S Truman, Executive Order 9981, July 26, 1948

Truman's order ended segregation in the U.S. armed forces. This was a major step forward for African Americans. It would also help pave the way for future gains.

Hispanic Americans were another group seeking opportunities after the war. Several hundred Hispanic veterans joined together in the American GI Forum. This group worked hard to win full access for Hispanic veterans to the benefits they had earned for their military service. In 1948 they won national attention for their efforts on behalf of Felix Longoria, a Mexican American soldier who had been killed

in the last days of World War II. When his body was returned to his Texas hometown, the local funeral home refused to provide services because of Longoria's Mexican background. The GI Forum and its Texas leader, Hector Garcia, accepted Senator Lyndon Johnson's offer that Longoria be buried at Arlington National Cemetery. The case helped highlight the contributions of Hispanic Americans.

READING CHECK **Summarizing** What challenges did the United States face after World War II?

Politics in Postwar America

When President Roosevelt died suddenly in April 1945, Harry S Truman had been vice president for less than three months. In fact, Truman barely knew Roosevelt and had little knowledge of the many issues and decisions the president had been dealing with. After he was sworn in as the new president, Truman told reporters:

HISTORY'S VOICES

❝[I]f you ever pray, pray for me now. I don't know if you fellas ever had a load of hay fall on you, but when they told me what happened yesterday, I felt like the moon, the stars, and all the planets had fallen on me.❞

—Harry S Truman to reporters, April 13, 1945

FOCUS ON NEW YORK

ECONOMICS

One of the largest labor actions occurred in New York City on September 24, 1945, when approximately 15,000 elevator operators, doormen, porters, firemen, and maintenance workers went on strike. More than 1.5 million other workers also did not go to work. After five days, Governor Dewey persuaded the workers and employers to accept arbitration.

Integration and the Military

During World War II, about 1 million African Americans were drafted into the military. All of these soldiers, sailors, and marines served in segregated units.

In 1946 President Harry S Truman appointed the President's Committee on Civil Rights. The committee said that segregation made the armed forces less effective than they would be if they were integrated.

Backed by the committee's report, Truman decided to end racial segregation in the United States military. On July 26, 1948, he signed Executive Order 9981. This executive order required "equality of treatment and opportunity for all persons in the armed services without regard to race, color, religion, or national origin."

Although some military leaders resisted, by 1949 all branches had developed plans for integration. Today all positions in the military are open to people who are qualified, regardless of race or ethnicity.

Making Inferences What might Truman have hoped to gain by ending segregation in the military?

In October 1948, James Leroy Brown (center) became the first African American to receive his wings as a Navy pilot.

Truman faced huge challenges. He had to lead the Allies through the end of the war while guiding the nation through the shift from wartime to peace. He also had to deal with political criticism that came from all sides. Many Democrats compared him unfavorably to their hero, Roosevelt. Republicans saw in Truman someone they thought they could finally defeat.

The 1946 elections in Congress

The attacks on Truman grew stronger as the 1946 elections in Congress approached. One key complaint was inflation, or a rise in prices. During the war, the government had acted to keep prices low. After the war, price controls were relaxed. Prices shot up as a result, and Truman took the blame.

The 1946 elections were a disaster for the Democrats. Republicans gained so many seats that they were now the majority in Congress for the first time since 1930. With this majority, Republicans fought against Truman with increased strength. Truman found it difficult to put in place his own programs. One exception was the Marshall Plan, which you read about in Section 1. His handling of the Berlin Crisis was another of his few accomplishments.

The 1948 presidential election

As the presidential election of 1948 approached, Truman appeared to be in trouble. His popularity with voters was low. Even his fellow Democrats did not fully support him. Liberals broke off to back former vice president Henry Wallace, who ran under the banner of the Progressive Party. Many southern Democrats were angry at Truman's support for civil rights. They supported South Carolina governor Strom Thurmond, who ran as a Dixiecrat.

With his popularity low and his party divided, Truman seemed certain to lose the election. In a poll of 50 political writers published in a leading newsmagazine a few weeks before election day, every single one predicted a Republican victory. Newspapers made fun of him openly. "Mr. Truman is the most complete fumbler and blunderer this nation has seen in high office in a long time," wrote the *Los Angeles Times*. The Republican candidate, Governor Thomas Dewey of New York, was confident of victory.

Refusing to give up, Truman set off on a whirlwind campaign across the country. His tough-talking, plainspoken style had made him the target of many jokes in Washington, D.C. But elsewhere people responded well to Truman's style. He made a special point of criticizing Republicans in the House and Senate. When he complained about the "do-nothing Congress," crowds cheered in support.

In spite of Truman's efforts, most experts did not think he had a chance. Yet on election day, the voters handed Truman a victory. It was one of the most surprising election outcomes in American history.

Having won the election, Truman finally felt strong enough to put forward his own plan for the country. It was called the **Fair Deal**. It included a number of programs in the tradition of the New Deal. This included a federal health insurance program and new funding for education. Congress, however, did not support Truman's program. Few of his Fair Deal ideas ever became law. Meanwhile, new problems in Korea came to dominate the president's attention. You will read about the Korean War in Section 4.

READING CHECK **Drawing Conclusions** Why do you think the Democrats faced problems in the politics of the postwar era?

Trying to Build a Better World

World War II helped give rise to the political tensions of the Cold War. It also gave rise to a strong desire to understand and prevent the causes of war. After two catastrophic conflicts, many people were anxious to find new ways to prevent a third.

One result was the establishment of the United Nations (UN). Its creation started in the final days of the war. Representatives of 50 nations met in June 1945 to create the UN Charter, the written agreement that outlines its aims and principles. The UN Charter was ratified in October 1945. The UN was officially born. Over the years, it would welcome many new members.

The UN Charter committed its members to "save succeeding generations from the scourge of war" and to "reaffirm faith in fundamental human rights." It called for members to respect treaties and agreements and to promote the progress and freedom of all people. Member nations agreed to live in peace and to unite to maintain security. Force would be used only to serve the common interests of the membership. The charter also called for the use of international organizations to promote economic and social advancement.

Human rights Soon after its formation, the United Nations established the Commission on Human Rights. The U.S. representative to this commission was the former first lady Eleanor Roosevelt. She became the chairperson of the commission, helping to soothe tensions between members from different countries. Different countries sometimes had very different ideas about what kinds of human rights all people ought to have and how to achieve them.

PROGRAMS FOR A SAFER WORLD

As World War II came to an end, the countries of the world began seeking ways to prevent the problems and conflicts that helped lead to war. Leaders in the United States and other countries paved the way in establishing the following:

World Bank (1944)	• Organization for providing loans and advice to countries for the purpose of reducing poverty
International Monetary Fund (1944)	• System for promoting orderly financial relationships between countries • Designed to prevent economic crises and to encourage trade and economic growth
United Nations (1945)	• Organization in which member nations agree to settle disputes by peaceful means • Replaced the League of Nations
General Agreement on Tariffs and Trade (1946)	• Agreement among member nations on rules and regulations for international trade • Focused on reducing tariffs and other trade barriers

The democratic United States and Communist Soviet Union, for instance, had different ideas about how to secure basic economic rights.

In December 1948, the commission presented to the UN General Assembly the **Universal Declaration of Human Rights**. This document set high goals for all member nations of the UN. For example, it declared a belief that all human beings are born free and equal. It called for an end to slavery, torture, and inhumane punishment. It demanded a variety of civil rights, including the right to assembly and the right to access to courts. It also stated that elementary education should be free and available to all. The UN General Assembly adopted the declaration and directed member countries to publicize it.

Trade and economic development

World War II had raised a number of concerns about the financial relationships between countries. These problems had helped bring about the Great Depression. Now they threatened to limit trade and create conflict between nations. Many leaders hoped that solving these problems would lead to greater prosperity around the world. This, in turn, would promote peace.

Even before the war was over, representatives of many of the world's great powers met at a conference in Bretton Woods, New Hampshire. Out of this conference came an agreement to create two new organizations—the **World Bank** and the **International Monetary Fund** (IMF).

The World Bank aimed to help poor countries build their economies. It provided grants of money and loans to help with projects that could provide jobs and wealth.

Economic policy was the focus of the International Monetary Fund. Prior to the creation of the IMF, countries often followed economic policies that served their own interests, regardless of whether they hurt other countries. Such practices often had a harmful effect on world trade, which hurt everyone. The IMF was designed to encourage economic policies that promoted international trade. For example, the IMF helped build confidence in the values of different countries' currencies.

The **General Agreement on Tariffs and Trade** (GATT) was another international organization created to promote economic cooperation. The GATT, which took effect in 1948, was designed to reduce barriers to trade.

READING CHECK **Identifying Problems and Solutions** Name some international organizations that aimed to build a better world in the years after World War II.

SECTION 2 ASSESSMENT

go.hrw.com
Online Quiz
Keyword: SD7 HP25

Reviewing Ideas, Terms, and People

1. a. Define Write a brief definition for each of the following terms: **GI Bill, baby boom**
b. Explain Following World War II, how did the United States manage to avoid the severe economic problems that some people had expected?
c. Predict How do you think Truman's decision to desegregate the U.S. armed forces will affect African Americans and their growing demands for civil rights?

2. a. Recall What was the outcome and significance of the elections of 1946?
b. Make Inferences What can you infer about Truman's successful tactic of attacking the "do-nothing Congress"?
c. Elaborate How do you explain the fact that so many political observers were wrong about Truman and the presidential election of 1948?

3. a. Identify What was the UN, and why was it created?
b. Summarize By what means did the United States and other countries seek to make the world better during the postwar era?

c. Elaborate Based on what you have read here and in other chapters, how do you think efforts to improve countries' economies and international trade will help promote peace in the future?

Critical Thinking

4. Identifying the Main Idea Copy the chart below and use information from the section to identify details that support the main idea given.

Postwar United States

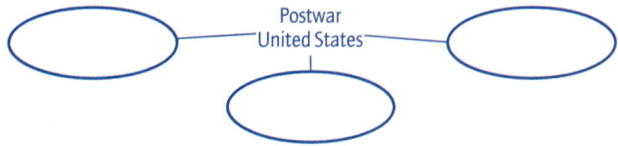

FOCUS ON WRITING

5. Persuasive From the point of view of a member of the Commission of Human Rights, write and present a speech in favor of the Universal Declaration of Human Rights. Use details from the section in your speech.

The Second Red Scare

BEFORE YOU READ

MAIN IDEA

The start of the Cold War and events at home helped trigger a second Red Scare in the late 1940s and early 1950s.

READING FOCUS

1. Why was the fear of communism growing in the late 1940s?
2. What methods and actions did the government use to fight the spread of communism at home?
3. Who was Senator Joseph McCarthy, and what was his role in the second Red Scare?

KEY TERMS AND PEOPLE

Chiang Kai-shek
Mao Zedong
House Un-American Activities Committee
Hollywood Ten
Alger Hiss
Ethel and Julius Rosenberg
Joseph McCarthy
McCarthyism

PI 3.4 Understand the interrelationships between world events and developments in New York State and the United States (e.g., causes for immigration, economic opportunities, human rights abuses, and tyranny versus freedom).

THE INSIDE STORY

How did the White House find out that the Soviets had the atomic bomb? Everyone realized the day would eventually come, though many did not expect it so soon. They even had a code name for describing the situation—Vermont. Still, the realization that the Soviet Union had likely exploded an atomic weapon came as a tremendous shock to most Americans.

For David Lilienthal, head of the Atomic Energy Commission, the news came in the form of a visit from an army general. Lilienthal was on vacation on the island of Martha's Vineyard off the coast of Massachusetts. As he was returning to his home on the evening of September 19, 1949, the general was waiting for him with a grave message: The Soviets had the atomic bomb and had conducted a test explosion.

The next morning, Lilienthal flew to Washington, D.C., to meet with President Truman and several of his advisers. The group debated how to handle the news. Should the public be told? How would they react?

Truman decided that the public must be informed. He presented the information himself several days later. As you will read, the news hit the nation hard. Soon, Americans were in the grips of another Red Scare. ◢

▲ The news that the Soviet Union had tested an atomic bomb sent shock waves of fear through the nation.

THE SPREAD OF COMMUNISM, 1945–1949

Communist countries

EAST GERMANY
POLAND
CZECHOSLOVAKIA
HUNGARY
ROMANIA
YUGOSLAVIA
BULGARIA
ALBANIA

SOVIET UNION

MONGOLIA

NORTH KOREA

CHINA

GEOGRAPHY SKILLS INTERPRETING MAPS

Notice the pattern of Communist nations in Europe.

Place Look at the chart at right. Why do you think the Communist takeover of China worried the United States?

See **Skills Handbook**, p. H20

Growing Fear of Communism

The postwar years were a tense time in the United States. American leaders worried about the spread of communism in Europe. In 1948 the crisis over Berlin drove the tension level even higher.

Then in 1949, two events added greatly to the nation's anxiety. First came the discovery that the Soviet Union possessed an atomic weapon. Then came the news that Communists had gained control of China, the most populous country in the world.

Soviet atomic weapons The first hint of trouble occurred in late August 1949. U.S. aircraft flying over the North Pacific Ocean picked up signs of unusual radioactivity in the atmosphere. American scientists quickly figured out what had happened. In September, President Truman issued a short, terse statement that confirmed the Soviet Union had <u>detonated</u> an atomic bomb.

ACADEMIC VOCABULARY

detonate to cause an explosion

Truman's announcement came as a great shock to the nation. No longer could the country rely on this terribly destructive weapon as the basis of its defense against the Soviets. Soon, Truman would seek to strengthen the nation's military against a possible Soviet threat.

The threat of Communist China Within days of the announcement that the Soviets had atomic weapons, the United States learned that Communists in China had gained nearly full control of the country. The so-called Nationalist government of **Chiang Kai-shek** had fled mainland China for the island of Taiwan. Chiang had been a loyal friend to the United States during World War II. He—and the United States—continued to claim that the Nationalist Party represented the one true government of all China. Now, outside of Taiwan, the Nationalists had no power. China was in the hands of the Communist Party. A new People's Republic of China had been born.

The Communist takeover of China had been many years in the making. At the end of World War II, the defeated Japanese had withdrawn from China. Led by **Mao Zedong**, Chinese Communists used this opportunity to gain control of large areas, especially in northern China.

In a civil war between Nationalists and Communists, the United States supported the Nationalists' effort to defeat communism. Chiang's Nationalist government, however, was riddled with corruption and poor leadership. As a result, Mao's Communists steadily gained power in China.

POPULATION, 1950

QUICK FACTS

NATO Members		Communist Nations	
The United States and Canada	171,550,000	Soviet Union	180,980,000
Western Europe	173,882,000	Eastern Europe	106,055,000
		China	554,760,000
Total	**345,432,000**	**Total**	**841,795,000**

The Communist victory in China delivered another shock to the American people. Americans did not yet know if Chinese communism was equivalent to Soviet communism. Many worried that China would increase the Communist threat to the United States.

READING CHECK **Identifying Cause and Effect** What events helped increase the fear of communism for the American public in the late 1940s?

Fighting the Spread of Communism at Home

The events of 1949 fed an already strong anti-Communist feeling in the United States. Indeed, for several years, concern had been growing about possible Communist influence in American government. Efforts were already underway to root out disloyal people.

Investigating communism Since the 1930s, the House of Representatives had had a **House Un-American Activities Committee**, or HUAC. This committee's original purpose was to investigate the full range of radical groups in the United States, including Fascists and Communists. Over time, however, it came to

focus only on the possible threat of communism in the United States. This focus existed even before the start of the Cold War. It sharpened significantly as the Soviets emerged as the chief enemy of the United States.

The most famous HUAC investigation began in 1947. Its goal was to explore possible Communist influence in the American film industry. The committee collected the names of Hollywood writers and directors who were thought to hold radical political views. Ten of these people, when called before HUAC, refused to answer questions about their beliefs or those of their colleagues. As a result of this refusal, the **Hollywood Ten** were found guilty of contempt of Congress and were sentenced to a year in jail.

The case alarmed others in Hollywood. Many now agreed to provide names of possible Communists to HUAC. Others refused to provide names, and for this they were placed on a blacklist—a list from which all the major Hollywood employers refused to hire. The careers of several hundred writers, actors, directors, and producers were damaged.

In another case that attracted widespread attention, the Atomic Energy Commission accused atomic bomb scientist J. Robert Oppenheimer of Communist sympathies. The commission stripped him of his top-secret security clearance.

ACADEMIC VOCABULARY
equivalent equal in importance

Truman and loyalty The public fear of communism also put pressure on American leaders. No leader wanted to appear weak when dealing with communism. This included the president. Truman felt he had to take action because Republicans in Congress were claiming that Communists were working in the federal government. To help address this charge, Truman created a new plan for ensuring the loyalty of government officials. Under the plan, all federal employees would be investigated. Those found to be disloyal to the United States could be barred from federal employment.

The investigations turned up little evidence of disloyalty. Over the next few years, 3 million people were investigated. A few thousand federal workers resigned, and about 200 were judged disloyal. The investigations troubled some Americans. They made it clear, however, that the Truman administration was serious about fighting communism.

Major Spy Cases

Alger Hiss, 1948

Accused of being a spy for the Soviets, Alger Hiss prepares to testify to HUAC in 1948. Although he denied the charges, evidence later showed Hiss had lied to HUAC. In 1950 he was convicted of perjury, or lying under oath, and sentenced to prison. Soviet documents decoded by American intelligence and declassified in the 1990s confirmed Hiss's guilt in the case.

Klaus Fuchs, 1950

Fuchs, a nuclear physicist, worked on the Manhattan Project. During his work on the development of the atomic bomb, he transmitted information to the Soviet Union, including detailed drawings of "Fat Man," the bomb the United States dropped on Nagasaki, Japan, in World War II. After serving nine years in prison, Fuchs settled in East Germany.

Ethel and Julius Rosenberg, 1951

The Rosenbergs were convicted of passing military secrets to the Soviets, including information from Ethel's brother, who was an employee on the Manhattan Project. They received the death sentence and were executed in 1953. The Rosenbergs were the first U.S. civilians to be executed for espionage.

The Smith Act In 1949 Truman made another show of his commitment to fight communism at home. The government charged several leaders of the Communist Party in the United States under the Smith Act. This 1940 law made it a crime to call for the overthrow of the U.S. government or belong to an organization that did so.

The Communist Party officials were convicted. These convictions, and the Smith Act itself, were upheld in the 1951 Supreme Court ruling in *Dennis* v. *United States*. The Court considered that the domestic danger posed by Communists was "grave and probable" and justified limits on their free speech. (Later, in *Yates* v. *United States,* the Court held that it was a crime only when a person called for specific actions to overthrow the government.)

The McCarran Act In 1950 Congress took further action to fight communism in the United States. The McCarran Internal Security Act required Communist organizations to register with the government and established a special board to investigate Communist involvement. The act also made it illegal to plan for a creation of a totalitarian dictatorship and prevented Communists or other radicals from entering the United States.

Truman vetoed the bill, stating that it "would delight the Communists, for it would make a mockery of the Bill of Rights and of our claims to stand for freedom in the world." But Congress easily overrode Truman's veto.

Spy cases Fear of communism was also fueled by a series of spy cases in the late 1940s. One case involved a former government official named **Alger Hiss**. In 1948 former Communist spy Whittaker Chambers accused Hiss of being part of a 1930s plot to place Communists inside the government. Hiss denied the charges. Then in a dramatic move, Chambers led investigators to his Maryland farm. There, hidden in a hollowed-out pumpkin, they found several rolls of top-secret government microfilm. Chambers said the stolen film had come from Hiss.

Hiss could not be charged with spying—many years had passed since his alleged crime. He was charged, however, with lying under oath. Hiss was eventually convicted and served some years in prison. Future president Richard Nixon played a key role in the investigation.

Another famous case involved the theft of atomic secrets. Klaus Fuchs was a German-born scientist who had worked on the Manhattan Project during World War II. Investigators learned that he gave American atomic secrets to the Soviet Union, including detailed drawings. Fuchs was sentenced to 14 years in prison though he served just 9 years.

The Fuchs case raised fears about atomic spies in the United States. Indeed, investigators soon found several Americans who admitted providing atomic secrets to the Soviets. One of them charged that his sister and brother-in-law—**Ethel and Julius Rosenberg**—were leaders of the spy ring.

At the trial, the Rosenbergs denied the charges. They also refused to answer questions about their political activities, which included past involvement with communism. They were convicted of conspiracy to commit espionage, or spying. The Rosenbergs received the death sentence and were executed in 1953.

READING CHECK **Identifying the Main Idea** Name some examples of efforts to fight communism in the United States in the late 1940s and early 1950s.

Senator Joseph McCarthy

On February 9, 1950, a U.S. senator named **Joseph McCarthy** visited Wheeling, West Virginia to deliver a speech before a Republican women's group. His topic was a familiar one to Americans of that day—the dangers of communism. In his speech, McCarthy claimed that there were 205 known Communists working for the U.S. Department of State. In a later speech, he went a step further. Waving a list before the crowd, he said it contained the names of 57 Communists in the State Department.

The rise of McCarthyism McCarthy's
charges created a sensation. For many Americans, his claim was all too easy to believe. It helped explain recent events, such as the loss of China and the Soviet development of the atomic bomb. But McCarthy never produced the list of names he claimed to be holding in his speech. A Senate committee looked into his charges and found no evidence of Communists in the State Department.

By that time, however, many frightened Americans did not need any evidence. Even if he had been wrong with his first list, they

THE IMPACT TODAY

Recent Scholarship
In 1995 the National Security Agency released information on Soviet spy communications during the Cold War. These files provided further evidence that the Rosenbergs were guilty.

The McCarthy Hearings

COMMUNIST PARTY ORGANIZATION U.S.A-FEB. 9, 1950

Senator Joseph McCarthy presents a map of alleged Communist Party organization to Army counsel Joseph Welch as part of the Army-McCarthy hearing in 1954. *How does McCarthy's use of a map give support to his claims?*

figured, he was clearly on the right track. In this way, just by making accusations, McCarthy had earned for himself a reputation as the nation's top Communist fighter.

With his newfound fame, McCarthy went on the attack. He made many new charges, but none were backed up with any evidence. When people complained about his methods, McCarthy suggested that maybe they had secrets to hide. Truman dismissed him as a "ballyhoo artist who has to cover up his shortcomings by wild charges." One critic, the political cartoonist Herblock, dubbed McCarthy's tactic of spreading fear and making baseless charges **McCarthyism**. The public, however, seemed willing to believe McCarthy.

Then in the 1950 elections, McCarthy made a special effort to bring about the defeat of Maryland senator Millard Tydings. Tydings was one of President Truman's strongest supporters. It was his committee that had investigated McCarthy's first claims and found them to be false. In the Tydings campaign, McCarthy produced faked photographs showing Tydings talking to the head of the American Communist Party. Tydings was defeated.

McCarthyism quickly spread beyond the Senate. In other branches of government, at universities, in labor unions, and in private businesses, the hunt for Communists geared up. The FBI and even private investigators produced names of people with questionable political views. People who refused to help with investigations were also named.

Officials and employers feared that failure to take action would open them to charges of being "soft on communism," in other words, weak in dealing with it. Across the United States, thousands of people were fired for political reasons.

McCarthy's fall Meanwhile, Senator McCarthy continued his campaign from the Senate. He became increasingly wild in his charges. After winning re-election in 1952, he began to go after fellow Republicans. In 1954 he attacked the U.S. Army, claiming that it was protecting Communists. His Senate hearings were televised, which spread his anti-Communist message widely. Still, the public increasingly came to view McCarthy's tactics as unfair. As you will read, the fear of communism in the United States would remain for some time. But the career of Senator Joseph McCarthy—and McCarthyism—would soon fade away.

READING CHECK **Making Generalizations** What did Joseph McCarthy aim to do?

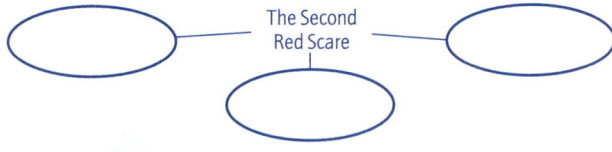

go.hrw.com
Online Quiz
Keyword: SD7 HP25

SECTION 3 ASSESSMENT

Reviewing Ideas, Terms, and People

1. **a. Recall** How did the Communist takeover of China and the Soviet explosion of an atomic bomb affect the United States?
   b. Draw Conclusions Do you think that it was reasonable to conclude from the advance of communism in the late 1940s that communism was "winning"?
   c. Predict How do you think the events of 1949 would affect the U.S. policy toward communism in the future?

2. **a. Identify** Who were the **Hollywood Ten**, and what was their significance in the late 1940s?
   b. Summarize What was the effect of the growing fear of communism at home?
   c. Elaborate Why do you think Julius and Ethel Rosenberg received the death sentence?

3. **a. Define** Write a brief definition of the following term: McCarthyism
   b. Explain Why was Senator McCarthy able to win recognition as a great fighter of communism without actually identifying any Communists?

c. Elaborate Why do you think some people were unwilling to stand up to McCarthy and his hunt for Communists?

Critical Thinking

4. **Identifying the Main Idea** Copy the chart below and use information from the section to identify details that support the main idea given.

The Second Red Scare

FOCUS ON WRITING

5. **Expository** Do you think Truman's investigation of federal employees was justified? Write a short essay in which you explain your position on this issue. Use details from the section to support your explanation.

The Korean War

BEFORE YOU READ

MAIN IDEA

Cold War tensions finally erupted in a shooting war in 1950. The United States confronted a difficult challenge defending freedom halfway around the world.

READING FOCUS

1. What was the situation in Korea before the war began in 1950?
2. What were the circumstances that led to the start of the Korean War?
3. What were the key battles of the Korean War?
4. How did the fighting in the Korean War end?

KEY TERMS AND PEOPLE

38th parallel
Kim Il Sung
Syngman Rhee
police action
Inchon
Panmunjom

PI 3.2 Research and analyze the major themes and developments in New York State and United States history (e.g., colonization and settlement; Revolution and New National Period; immigration; expansion and reform era; Civil War and Reconstruction; the American labor movement; Great Depression; World Wars; contemporary United States).

▲ These soldiers became the first ground troops to enter into combat in Korea.

Crisis in Korea

THE INSIDE STORY

How did the Korean War begin for American troops? The soldiers of Task Force Smith—a group of some 400 soldiers shipped to Korea in 1950—never really had time to be afraid. Just days before, they had been a half-equipped and undertrained unit stationed in Japan. Few of their members had any combat experience—a fact that concerned no one since there was no combat for them to take part in.

That changed with the sudden, surprise invasion of South Korea by North Korean forces in late June 1950. As the North Koreans drove deep into South Korean territory, President Truman authorized the use of American ground forces to stop the advance. That meant Task Force Smith would be transferred from Japan to Korea.

General Douglas MacArthur referred to the soldiers as "that arrogant display of strength." Upon their arrival in South Korea, the troops were greeted with cheers. They drove out to meet the enemy, each soldier carrying two days worth of food and ammunition. They expected that the North Koreans would never dare to do battle with the mighty Americans.

Of course, the North Koreans were not impressed. As you will read, they quickly pushed aside the ill-prepared Task Force Smith. The bloody Korean War was on. ◢

KOREA

CHINA

Yalu River

NORTH
KOREA

Sea of
Japan

40°N

Pyongyang

Present-day
border

Boundary set by
Allies, 1945

38th Parallel

Panmunjom

Seoul

Inchon

Yellow
Sea

SOUTH
KOREA

0   100   200 Miles
0   100   200 Kilometers
Albers equal-area projection

Pusan

35°N

125°E   130°E

GEOGRAPHY SKILLS INTERPRETING MAPS

1. **Location** Why was the 38th parallel chosen as a dividing line?

2. **Place** What nation shares a border with North Korea, besides South Korea? Why is this significant?

See **Skills Handbook**, p. H20

THE IMPACT TODAY

Government

Today Kim Il Sung's son, Kim Jong Il, is the leader of North Korea. North Korea remains a Communist country, while South Korea has a democratic government.

Korea before the War

The 600-mile-long Korean Peninsula lies between China and Japan. The peninsula is also close to Russia, which in 1950 was part of the Soviet Union. China, Japan, and Russia have long held a strong influence over the Korean people. After 1905 Korea came under the control of the Japanese. Japan dominated and occupied the peninsula.

Then in 1945 the Allies defeated the Japanese in World War II. As you have read, the Allies had agreed to divide control of the conquered Germany among several Allied nations. A similar sort of agreement was reached regarding Japanese-occupied Korea. At the Yalta Conference in February 1945, the Allies agreed that Korea should be free following the war. For purposes of accepting the Japanese surrender and providing postwar security in

Korea, however, the Allies also agreed to temporarily divide Korea into northern and southern parts. The dividing line was to be the parallel at 38° north latitude. The Soviet Union would control Korea north of the **38th parallel**. South of it, the Americans would be in charge. In fact, the Soviets played virtually no role in the military defeat of Japan. Stalin did not declare war on Japan until after the dropping of the first atomic bomb at Hiroshima. Nevertheless, after the Japanese surrender, the Soviets took control of North Korea.

The presence of the Soviets and Americans in Korea was meant to be temporary. As in Germany, however, the start of the Cold War led to problems. In North Korea, the Soviet Union tried to establish a Communist system of government. The North called itself the Democratic People's Republic of Korea. Its first leader was **Kim Il Sung**, who sought to reunify North and South Korea under Communist control.

In South Korea, the United States promoted a democratic system. South Korea, known as the Republic of Korea, was led by president **Syngman Rhee**. Although an elected leader, Rhee held dictatorial control over South Korea. Like Kim Il Sung, he hoped the two halves of Korea would be reunified.

Both the North and the South held the goal of bringing together the two Korean halves into one whole, but they had different ideas of how best to reunify the country. Efforts toward unification continued in the late 1940s. In the end, however, these efforts led to war.

READING CHECK **Summarizing** How did the status of Korea prior to June 1950 lead to its division into northern and southern halves?

The Start of the Korean War

In the dark, early hours of June 25, 1950, more than 100,000 North Korean troops crossed the 38th parallel and invaded South Korea. Kim Il Sung had ordered the invasion, hoping to reunify all of Korea under his rule.

The troops carried Soviet-made weapons and drove Soviet-made tanks. In the recent past, some border skirmishes had occurred between North and South Korean troops, but this was different. From the outset it was clear that this was a major attack. The future of South Korea was at stake.

The attack came as a surprise to most leaders in the United States. Tensions on the peninsula had been high, and some observers had noticed a buildup of North Korean forces along the 38th parallel. Still, nobody in the Truman administration had anticipated serious fighting there. In fact, American troops stationed in South Korea since the end of the war had recently completed their withdrawal from the country. This had been part of a large-scale decrease in the size of U.S. armed forces that had been taking place in recent years. Because of this, the United States was not well prepared to fight in Korea. Nevertheless, the decision to fight was made quickly.

The role of the United States

In President Truman's mind, South Korea was where the United States had to take a stand against Communist aggression. South Korea was a small country, unable to defend itself against an enemy supported by the Soviet Union or Communist China. Failure to defend South Korea might send a signal to other nations that the United States would not help defend their freedom. It was even feared that a failure to act could lead to a wider war. In a message to Congress about the situation in Korea, Truman said:

HISTORY'S VOICES

❝For ourselves, we seek no territory or domination over others . . . We are concerned with advancing our prosperity and our well-being as a Nation, but we know that our future is inseparably joined with the future of other free peoples.❞

—Harry S Truman, July 1950

Truman's viewpoint was shared by many others, including World War II hero General Dwight D. Eisenhower. "We'll have a dozen Koreas soon," Eisenhower declared, "if we don't take a firm stand."

Meanwhile, on the battlefield, the situation was getting more serious by the hour. Within days of the invasion, the North Korean force had pushed back the South Korean defenses and captured the capital city of Seoul. Truman realized something had to be done, and it had to be done soon. He ordered American naval and air forces to support South Korean ground troops. Then he asked the United Nations to approve the use of force to stop the North Korean invasion.

The role of the UN

The United Nations Security Council voted unanimously in favor of the use of force. Under the UN rules, five key countries held the power to veto UN Security Council decisions. That is, those five countries could single-handedly vote against a measure and defeat it.

One of the countries holding a veto was the Soviet Union. However, at the time of the UN vote on North Korea, the Soviet representative was absent, in protest over the UN's admission of Nationalist China. Therefore, the soviet representative was not there to veto the use of force against North Korea.

This twist, however, would not be enough to save the South Koreans. It soon became clear that American ground troops were needed. This was a step Truman had been reluctant to take. He feared that sending ground troops might trigger the start of another world war. It soon became clear, however, that there was no other way to stop the North Korean onslaught. On June 30 Truman ordered American ground troops into action.

The military force sent to Korea would be a United Nations force. Technically, the whole effort was referred to as a UN **police action**. The United States never declared war. Its commander was to be none other than General Douglas MacArthur. American soldiers made up the largest part of the force. Some 15 other nations contributed a total of 40,000 troops. This combined force then joined what was left of the South Korean military in a desperate fight to save the country.

READING CHECK **Sequencing** What events occurred at the beginning of the war in Korea?

Key Battles of the Korean War

American soldiers had entered the battle in South Korea. Unfortunately, North Korean troops greatly outnumbered and outgunned South Korea's defenders. Fighting conditions were miserable. Summer heat and heavy rains sapped what little strength the soldiers had after days of desperate combat.

Throughout the month of July, the news from Korea was discouraging. By the end of the month, the North Koreans had pushed UN

FOCUS ON NEW YORK

DAILY LIFE
More than 482,000 New Yorkers served in the armed forces during the Korean War. Today, the New York State Korean War Veterans Memorial in Albany honors their contributions.

forces all the way to the southeastern tip of South Korea. Here the UN forces formed a line around the port city of Pusan. This 130-mile-long line, soldiers were told, needed to be held at all costs.

The Inchon landing In fact, UN forces held the port of Pusan. By early September, the Communist attack had stalled. Meanwhile, thousands of UN troops and tons of equipment were unloading at Pusan daily. Now MacArthur wanted to go on the offensive.

MacArthur's plan was daring and brilliant. It called for UN forces to make an amphibious landing behind North Korean lines at the port city of Inchon, on South Korea's western coast. Inchon was an unlikely place for such an assault. Its natural features made an attack by sea very risky. Chief among these features were the extremely high tides in Inchon's waters.

To MacArthur, the disadvantages of attacking at Inchon only meant that the North Koreans would not expect it. Surprise would be the key to his success. "We shall land at Inchon," he promised, "and I shall crush them."

MacArthur's plan worked beautifully. Within 24 hours of the September 15 invasion at Inchon, a 70,000-troop force had secured a solid landing and regained some ground. See the History Close-Up feature opposite to learn more about the Inchon landing.

North Korea on the run The Inchon landing helped bring about an amazing change in fortunes in South Korea. UN forces quickly moved out from Inchon to recapture Seoul. The North Koreans had stretched themselves too thin chasing the UN forces all the way south to Pusan. They were powerless to stop the force moving out of Inchon.

Meanwhile, the UN launched another offensive from Pusan. This attack broke through the North Korean line and started marching northward. Huge numbers of North Korean troops were destroyed or forced to surrender.

The turnaround was startling. The UN had been facing defeat in August. Only a few months later, by October 1, all of South Korea was back in UN hands.

American leaders now faced the question of whether to stop at the 38th parallel. North Korea's forces were in tatters. MacArthur favored taking all of North Korea. One concern about this plan, however, was the possibility that the Chinese or Soviets might come to the defense of North Korea. A top Chinese official issued just such a warning. But the Americans decided the risk was worth taking. Truman also supported the plan.

Moving into North Korea continued to seem like a good idea through the days of October and November. UN forces made solid progress. There were some reports of Chinese troops filtering into North Korea and joining the battle. By the end of November, however, MacArthur was preparing for a major push. He said his new plan would end the Korean War. Then just as the general's plan was getting under way, it happened: A huge force of 260,000 Chinese troops poured across the Yalu River, which was North Korea's border with China. Again there had been an unexpected turnaround, but this time it favored the North Koreans.

UN forces retreat With the Chinese attack, MacArthur's promise of a quick victory disappeared. In fact, the UN forces suddenly faced defeat. According to MacArthur, the size of the Chinese force was simply too large. Just as in the early days of the war, UN forces were soon in full retreat.

In the case of the 8th Army, this retreat went all the way back south of Seoul. It was the longest such fallback in U.S. military history. To make matters worse, the brutal Korean winter had arrived. Temperatures in some areas dropped well below 0°F. In places such as the Chosin Reservoir, American soldiers suffered terribly under the wintry conditions.

MacArthur is fired As 1951 began, the situation in Korea once again seemed dire for the Americans and the UN. In MacArthur's view, the UN faced a choice between defeat by the Chinese or a major war with them. He called for expanding the war by bombing the Chinese mainland and bringing Nationalist Chinese forces into the fighting. He even called for the use of atomic weapons.

MacArthur, as it turned out, was wrong. In January 1951, a force led by Lieutenant General Matthew Ridgway not only stopped the Chinese onslaught but actually went on the offensive. By April 1951 Ridgway's men had pushed the Chinese back to the 38th parallel.

Interactive
HISTORY CLOSE-UP

Assault on Inchon

The September 1950 invasion at Inchon was a key victory for UN forces in Korea, helping regain territory in South Korea. Territory changed hands frequently during the Korean War (see inset maps at right). UN forces pushed all the way into North Korea but were forced back to the 38th parallel by January 1951.

The tides near Inchon were extreme, and only for short windows of time was water deep enough to allow landing craft to reach the beaches.

The three landing "beaches" were code-named "red," "green," and "blue." They were muddy and rocky and, in some places, had tall sea walls attackers had to climb.

Over 250 ships took part in the assault on Inchon. They had to navigate tricky, swift-moving currents.

	Controlled by North Korea
	Controlled by South Korea
→	North Korean forces
→	United Nations forces

0   200   400 Miles
0   200   400 Kilometers
Albers equal-area projection

THE KOREAN WAR, 1950-1951

June 1950

Pyongyang
Inchon • Seoul
38th parallel
Pusan

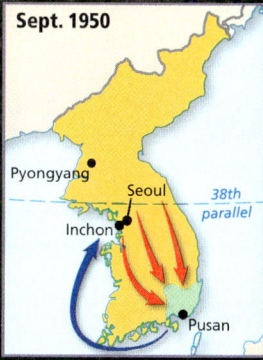

Sept. 1950

Pyongyang
Seoul
38th parallel
Inchon
Pusan

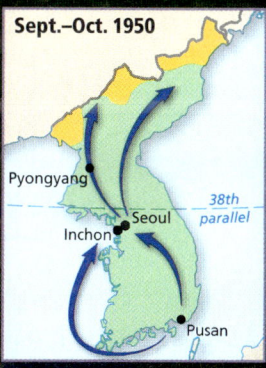

Sept.–Oct. 1950

Pyongyang
Seoul
38th parallel
Inchon
Pusan

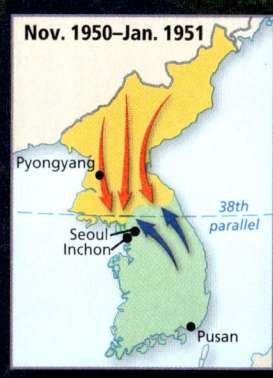

Nov. 1950–Jan. 1951

Pyongyang
38th parallel
Seoul
Inchon
Pusan

go.hrw.com
Interactive
Keyword: SD7 CH25

Skills FOCUS **INTERPRETING INFOGRAPHICS**

Drawing Conclusions How did UN forces overcome geographic obstacles in their invasion of Inchon?

See **Skills Handbook**, p. H18

THE COLD WAR BEGINS **839**

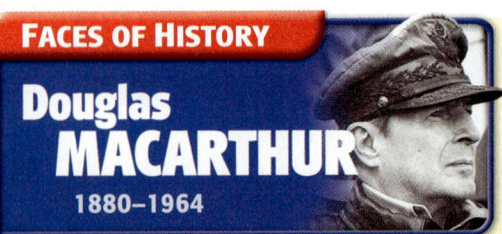

Douglas MACARTHUR
1880–1964

Born to a Civil War veteran who became a high-ranking army officer and raised on a series of military bases across the United States, Douglas MacArthur naturally chose a career in the military. He wrote in his memoirs, "My first memory was the sound of bugles." In 1903 he graduated first in his class at the U.S. military academy at West Point. During World War I he fought in France, where he was promoted to the rank of brigadier general. Known for his bravery and daring on the battlefield, he became the most decorated American soldier of World War I.

As supreme Allied commander in occupied Japan, MacArthur made one of his most important contributions to history—he helped Japan rebuild itself as a democratic nation. After President Truman removed him from command in the Korean War, MacArthur returned home. He died in 1964, still admired for his World War II victories and his leadership in occupied Japan.

Analyze What experiences prepared MacArthur for his leadership roles during World War II and after?

been in a greater danger," warned the *Chicago Tribune*. "It is led by a fool who is surrounded by knaves."

This anger only grew when MacArthur appeared before Congress for a dramatic farewell address. Some 30 million Americans watched his speech on television.

HISTORY'S VOICES

❝In war, there is no substitute for victory. There are some who for varying reasons would appease Red China. They are blind to history's clear lesson, for history teaches with unmistakable emphasis that appeasement but begets new and bloodier war.❞

—General Douglas MacArthur, April 19, 1951

MacArthur closed with the emotional words, "Old soldiers never die; they just fade away." Americans everywhere wept and cheered for their World War II hero.

READING CHECK **Sequencing** What was the sequence of the fighting in Korea from the start of the war through April 1951?

Ridgway's success called into question MacArthur's harsh warnings about the need to expand the war. It especially called into question MacArthur's recommendation to use atomic weapons. Truman began to believe that peace was possible without losing South Korea or triggering a larger war with China or even the Soviets.

MacArthur was dismayed by Truman's attitude. He wanted to see communism defeated in Asia even if meant expanding the scope of the war. Increasingly, he made public statements that challenged the authority of the president. He made threats against the Chinese government even as American officials were exploring ways to stop the fighting in Korea.

Truman faced a serious challenge. To many Americans, MacArthur was a major hero of World War II. They supported his goal of taking the war to the Chinese. Truman, though, wanted to avoid widening the war. Further, he could not allow a general to disobey the president and make his own policy. Truman decided he had to fire MacArthur.

The American public swiftly reacted to the MacArthur firing. While a few leaders supported the president's action, many Americans were outraged. "The American nation has never

ACADEMIC VOCABULARY

scope extent or size

Fighting Ends in Korea

Before long, the uproar over the MacArthur firing died down. Congress investigated the matter. The nation's leading military officers testified that Truman had been right in firing MacArthur.

Meanwhile, in July 1951, the United States entered into peace talks to end the fighting. By this point, 80,000 Americans had been wounded and nearly 14,000 were dead. South Korea and other UN forces had also suffered greatly. So had the Chinese and North Koreans.

Unsuccessful negotiations for peace

One major obstacle during the peace talks was the location of the boundary between North Korea and South Korea. UN forces by that point had actually managed to fight a short distance north of the 38th parallel. The UN wanted the boundary to be there. But the Communists insisted on setting the boundary precisely at the 38th parallel. This dispute helped break off negotiations at the end of the summer.

Meanwhile, the two military forces strengthened their positions. Now and then one side or the other would launch an attack. The goal was not to gain territory but to improve position.

Examples of such actions were the battles of Bloody Ridge and Heartbreak Ridge. These were fought in the late summer and early fall of 1951. Both battles followed a similar pattern: The two forces took turns winning, then losing, key hilltops. Though little was gained, losses were heavy. In these and other battles during this time, the UN suffered 40,000 casualties.

Negotiations resumed in October but again hit a major snag. This time the issue was prisoners of war. Hoping that the UN would continue to fight for unification, Syngman Rhee refused to send North Korean or Chinese prisoners back to Communist countries. This hindered the peace negotiations. Few major moves were happening on the battlefield, but the steady shelling and sniping was a deadly threat.

All of 1952 passed in a similar way. Negotiators meeting in the town of **Panmunjom** (PAHN-MOOHN-JAWM) argued over details of a peace agreement. At the same time, small-scale fighting claimed thousands of casualties.

Events of 1953 Meanwhile, 1952 was a presidential election year in the United States. American voters elected the World War II hero Dwight D. Eisenhower. Eisenhower would be inaugurated in January 1953. You will read more about Eisenhower's presidency in the next chapter.

In his campaign, Eisenhower had promised to end the Korean War. Once in office, he set about achieving this goal. At the same time, the Communists also seemed to want the war to end. Negotiators at Panmunjom worked toward agreement.

Though the end of the conflict was coming, the fighting remained deadly. Indeed, the Communists seemed to step up the fighting in the hope of gaining a last-minute advantage. During the final two months, UN forces suffered 57,000 casualties. The Communists lost 100,000. Finally, however, the guns fell silent on July 27. On that day, negotiators reached an armistice agreement.

The Korean War had left the map of Korea looking much as it had in early 1950, before the war began. The North Koreans had lost only a small amount of territory. The human costs, however, were much more significant. Some 37,000 American soldiers had died. Almost 60,000 UN troops from other countries were killed. Communist forces suffered some 2 million casualties. Perhaps as many as 3 million North and South Korean civilians were killed or injured.

READING CHECK **Sequencing** What events helped bring about the end of the fighting in the Korean War?

Reviewing Ideas, Terms, and People

1. a. Identify Identify the significance of the following term: 38th parallel
b. Explain Why were there two different views about the way in which Korea might be reunified?

2. a. Describe What were the events that started the Korean War?
b. Draw Conclusions Why did Truman believe it was important to defend a small country such as South Korea?
c. Elaborate Why do you think the fighting in Korea was referred to as a **police action**?

3. a. Recall What was the significance of **Inchon** in the war?
b. Make Generalizations How would you describe the major pattern of fighting in the first year of the Korean War?
c. Rate Consider the arguments of both MacArthur and Truman about the possibility of a wider war with China. Which argument do you think was stronger? Explain.

4. a. Identify What is the significance of **Panmunjom**?

b. Make Generalizations What happened to the kind of fighting that took place in the final phase of the war?
c. Evaluate Considering the cost of the war and what was gained, do you think the United States was right to fight in Korea? Explain.

Critical Thinking

5. Sequencing Copy the chart below and use information from the section to sequence the events following the information provided.

| Korea divided Communist North | → | non-Communist South | → | | → | |

FOCUS ON WRITING

6. Expository Write a paragraph in which you explain the events that led to the beginning of the Korean War.

The Cold War at Home

Historical Context The documents below provide different perspectives on the domestic impact of the Cold War.

Task Examine the documents and answer the questions that follow. Then you will be asked to write an essay about the domestic impact of the Cold War, using facts from the documents and from the chapter to support the position you take in your thesis statement.

ST 1.1 Explore the meaning of the United States motto, "E Pluribus Unum," by identifying both those forces that unite Americans and those that potentially divide Americans.

ST 4.3 Develop hypotheses about important events, eras, or issues; move from chronicling to explaining historical events and issues; use information collected from diverse sources to produce cogently written reports and document-based essays.

DOCUMENT 1

In the aftermath of World War II, the House Un-American Activities Committee, or HUAC, investigated possible Communist subversion everywhere, from schools to labor unions to the entertainment industry. The political cartoon below was published in the *Washington Post* in 1947.

"IT'S OKAY—WE'RE HUNTING COMMUNISTS"
from *The Herblock Book* (Beacon Press, 1952)

DOCUMENT 2

In 1947 President Truman signed Executive Order 9835 in order to ban Communists and Fascists from federal employment. The order outlined procedures for investigating the background of federal employees. Although no actual espionage was discovered among government workers, many people were investigated in the years following Executive Order 9835. Below is an excerpt of the order.

"Part I
INVESTIGATION OF APPLICANTS
There shall be a loyalty investigation of every person entering the civilian employment of any department or agency of the executive branch of the Federal Government. …

Part V
STANDARDS [for Employment]
Activities and associations of an applicant or employee which may be considered in connection with the determination of disloyalty may include one or more of the following:
    Membership in, affiliation with or sympathetic association with any foreign or domestic organization, association, movement, group or combination of persons, designated by the Attorney General as totalitarian, fascist, communist, or subversive, or as having adopted a policy of advocating or approving the commission of acts of force or violence to deny other persons their rights under the Constitution of the United States, or as seeking to alter the form of government of the United States by unconstitutional means …"

DOCUMENT 3

This photograph shows a man building a bomb shelter in the backyard of a private home in 1951. These reinforced underground rooms were built for protection in the event of an atomic attack. During the 1950s and 1960s, bomb shelters became increasingly popular as Americans' fears of nuclear war grew.

Skills FOCUS — READING LIKE A HISTORIAN

1. a. Describe Refer to Document 1. What does the car symbolize in this political cartoon?
b. Identify What is happening to the people who are in the car's path?
c. Analyze What point of view does this cartoon present about the House Un-American Activities Committee?

2. a. Identify Refer to Document 2. Name three activities that would exclude a person from working for the federal government in 1947.
b. Interpret Why might President Truman have considered this executive order necessary?

3. a. Identify Refer to Document 3. When finished, how would this structure protect people from a bomb?
b. Analyze What does this photograph suggest about the impact of the Cold War on American society?

4. Document-Based Essay Question Consider the question below and form a thesis statement. Using examples from Documents 1, 2, and 3, create an outline and write a short essay supporting your position.
How did the Cold War affect domestic policy and American society?

See **Skills Handbook**, pp. H28–H29, H30

Visual Summary: The Cold War Begins

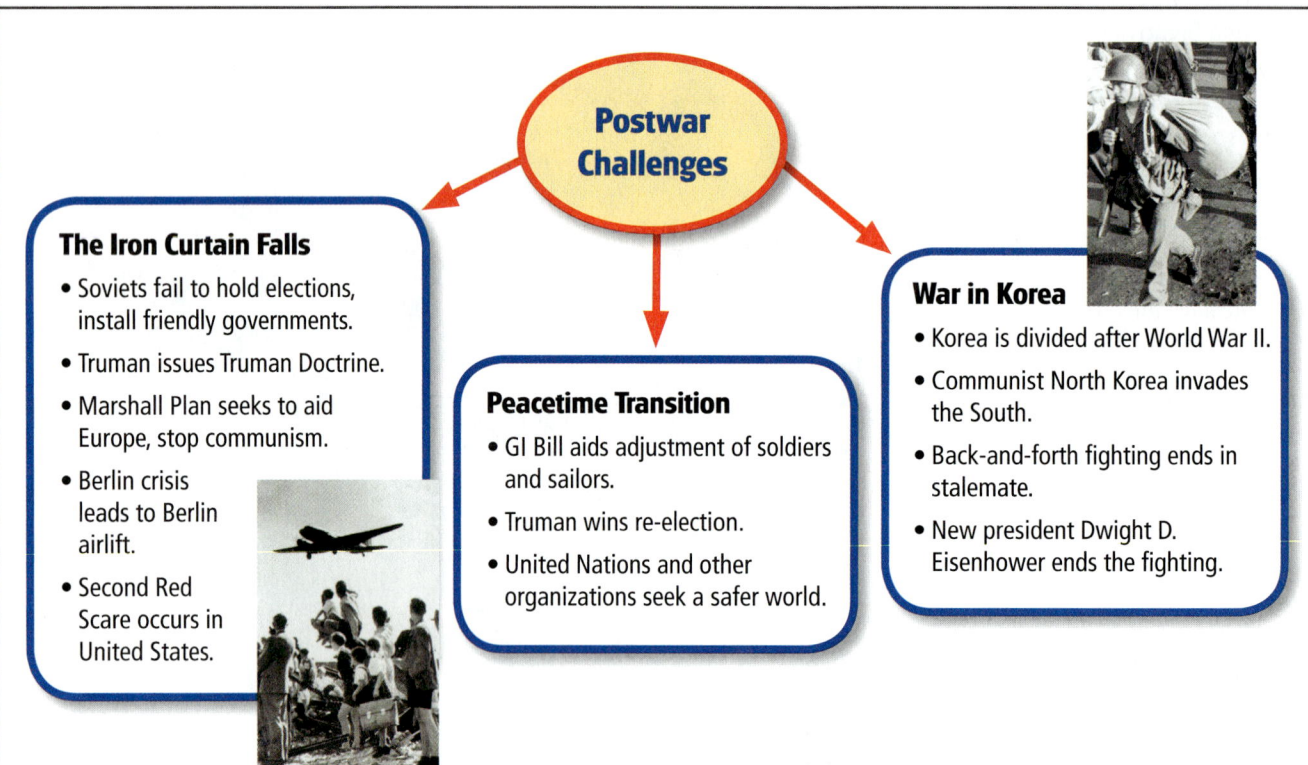

Postwar Challenges

The Iron Curtain Falls

- Soviets fail to hold elections, install friendly governments.
- Truman issues Truman Doctrine.
- Marshall Plan seeks to aid Europe, stop communism.
- Berlin crisis leads to Berlin airlift.
- Second Red Scare occurs in United States.

Peacetime Transition

- GI Bill aids adjustment of soldiers and sailors.
- Truman wins re-election.
- United Nations and other organizations seek a safer world.

War in Korea

- Korea is divided after World War II.
- Communist North Korea invades the South.
- Back-and-forth fighting ends in stalemate.
- New president Dwight D. Eisenhower ends the fighting.

Reviewing Key Terms and People

Identify the correct term or person from the chapter that best fits each of the following descriptions.

1. Truman policy for limiting spread of communism
2. Alliance formed after World War II
3. Postwar rise in U.S. birthrate
4. Effort to help rebuild Europe after World War II
5. Helped many former soldiers get a college education, start a business, or buy a home
6. Term for method of making reckless attacks on people's reputations
7. A major turning point of the Korean War occurred here
8. Communist leader in China
9. Group blacklisted for refusing to help in effort to uncover Communists
10. Accused of spying against the United States
11. The period of high tension between the United States and Soviet Union

a. GI Bill
b. baby boom
c. McCarthyism
d. Inchon
e. containment
f. Mao Zedong
g. Alger Hiss
h. Marshall Plan
i. Cold War
j. Hollywood Ten
k. NATO

Comprehension and Critical Thinking

SECTION 1 *(pp. 816–822)*

12. a. Identify What was the term that described the dividing line between Communist Eastern Europe and non-Communist Western Europe?

b. Sequence What were the events that led up to and marked the beginning phases of the Cold War?

c. Rate What do you think was the most important benefit of the Marshall Plan? Explain your answer.

SECTION 2 *(pp. 823–828)*

13. a. Describe What difficult adjustments faced the people of the United States after the war?

b. Draw Conclusions Why do you think there was so much interest after the war in creating organizations to improve conditions for people in the United States and around the world?

c. Elaborate What was the common idea behind the GI Bill and programs such as the International Monetary Fund and the World Bank established after World War II?

SECTION 3 *(pp. 829–834)*

14. a. Recall What was the second Red Scare?

b. Sequence Identify the sequence of events discussed in the section that contributed to the rising Red Scare.

c. Evaluate How was the second Red Scare similar to and different from the Red Scare of 1919?

SECTION 4 *(pp. 835–841)*

15. a. Describe What events led to the Korean War?

b. Sequence Describe the major events of the war in the order in which they occurred.

c. Rate Do you think the United States and the United Nations in Korea made an effective defense against the spread of communism?

Using the Internet

go.hrw.com
Practice Online
Keyword: SD7 CH25

16. During the twentieth century, the history of the city of Berlin was closely connected with the history of the Cold War. Using the keyword above, do research to learn about Berlin in the twentieth century, beginning after World War II and ending with the fall of the Berlin Wall. Then create a report that explains the significance of Berlin in the Cold War.

Analyzing Primary Sources

Reading Like a Historian

This photograph depicts a parade celebrating the millionth ton of Marshall-Plan goods delivered to Europe.

17. Identify Study the photograph. In what country was it taken?

18. Draw Conclusions Why do you think a parade was held to celebrate this shipment of goods?

Critical Reading

Read the passage in Section 3 that begins with the heading "Truman and loyalty." Then answer the questions that follow.

19. Based on this passage, it seems that

A. Truman was deeply anti-Communist.

B. Truman did not care about communism.

C. Truman took action against communism mainly to satisfy the public.

D. communism was a serious threat.

20. Truman's loyalty investigations produced

A. little evidence of Communist influence in government.

B. thousands of Communists in government.

C. complete support from the public.

D. widespread anger among the public.

FOCUS ON WRITING

Expository Writing *Expository writing gives information, explains why or how, or defines a process. To practice expository writing, complete the assignment below.*

Writing Topic **The Korean War**

21. Assignment Based on what you have read in this chapter, write a paragraph that explains why the United States became involved in the Korean War.

CHAPTER

26

1945–1960

Postwar America

THE BIG PICTURE In the years following World War II, the nation experienced tremendous economic growth and prosperity. Many Americans bought new homes, cars, and televisions as fast as they came on the market, transforming the way middle-class people lived. The Cold War arms race with the Soviet Union, however, cast a dark cloud of anxiety over the Eisenhower years.

New York Standards

Key Idea 2 Important ideas, social and cultural values, beliefs, and traditions from New York State and United States history illustrate the connections and interactions of people and events across time and from a variety of perspectives.

Key Idea 3 Study about the major social, political, economic, cultural, and religious developments in New York State and United States history involves learning about the important roles and contributions of individuals and groups.

Skills FOCUS **READING LIKE A HISTORIAN**

After the war, Americans eagerly bought products that were denied them during the war years. Many people also moved to newly created suburbs. A neat home with a white picket fence came to symbolize middle-class prosperity in the postwar years.
Interpreting Visuals What signs of prosperity can you identify for this family of five?

See **Skills Handbook**, p. H30

U.S.

1947
Bell Laboratories invents the transistor.

1945

World

1945
Nuremberg trials of Nazi leaders begins.

History's Impact video program
Watch the video to understand the impact of television.

June 1951
The first computer comes on the market.

October 1952
The United States tests a hydrogen bomb.

June 1956
Congress approves funds for the Interstate Highway System.

May 1960
Soviets shoot down an American U-2 spy plane.

1948   1951   1954   1957   1960

1948
The nation of Israel is founded.

March 1953
Soviet leader Joseph Stalin dies.

1956
Egypt takes control of the Suez Canal.

1957
Soviets launch *Sputnik*, the first artificial satellite.

847

The Eisenhower Era

BEFORE YOU READ

MAIN IDEA

The presidency of Dwight D. Eisenhower was shaped in large part by the Cold War and related conflicts.

READING FOCUS

1. What were the circumstances of Eisenhower's election in 1952?
2. How did the continuing Cold War affect the Eisenhower administration?
3. What were the Cold War "hot spots" of the 1950s?

KEY TERMS AND PEOPLE

Richard M. Nixon
John Foster Dulles
brinkmanship
massive retaliation
CIA
Nikita Khrushchev
Warsaw Pact
summit
SEATO
Eisenhower Doctrine

PI 2.1 Discuss several schemes for periodizing the history of New York State and the United States.

THE INSIDE STORY

Which party would Eisenhower pick in 1952?
If there was one thing on which Republicans and Democrats could agree in 1952, it was that General Dwight D. Eisenhower would make an excellent president. The World War II hero had an outstanding reputation with voters on both sides of the political divide. Yet as the election year approached, Eisenhower refused to announce whether he would seek the White House. In fact, no one really knew for certain which political party he might belong to.

President Truman seemed to think that Eisenhower might run as a Democrat. After all, the general had worked closely with Truman and with Franklin Roosevelt before that. In 1948 Truman had reportedly even offered to run with Eisenhower—as the vice presidential candidate on a ticket headed by the general. What's more, Truman and Eisenhower shared a strong opposition to the isolationist views of the leading Republican figure of the day, Senator Robert Taft of Ohio. In late 1951 Truman questioned Eisenhower on his willingness to run. He reportedly offered his help in getting Eisenhower the Democratic nomination. Eisenhower replied that he was not interested in politics.

Days later, the nation received startling news. Eisenhower would in fact be seeking the presidency—as a Republican. The entry of the popular war hero into the 1952 presidential race greatly changed the campaign. As you will read, there would be more surprises to follow. ◼

Man without a PARTY

"WE LIKE IKE"

▲ "Likeable Ike" on the campaign trail in 1952

The Election of 1952

Truman's admiration for Eisenhower may have affected his decision not to seek re-election in 1952. The year before, the states had ratified the Twenty-second Amendment. This set a 10-year limit on the number of years a president could serve. Truman was specifically excluded from the amendment's limits. Still, he felt he had served long enough. "In my opinion," he declared, "eight years as president is long enough and sometimes too much for any man to serve in this capacity."

Stevenson vs. Eisenhower With the race wide open, Democrats nominated Illinois governor Adlai Stevenson. Republicans chose Eisenhower, known to the public as "Ike."

On the campaign trail, Eisenhower sharply criticized the Democrats for their handling of the Korean War. Peace talks had been dragging on for months, and soldiers were dying by the thousands. Eisenhower vowed that if elected he would go to Korea to end the war. In response, Democrats noted that if Eisenhower knew how to end the Korean war, he should have done so long ago.

American voters, however, seemed to trust and admire Eisenhower. As election day neared, polls showed him well in the lead.

Nixon and the Checkers speech The Eisenhower campaign did hit one major snag. It involved Ike's vice presidential running mate, **Richard M. Nixon**. Nixon was a senator from California who had made his name as a strong anti-Communist, having led the investigation of Alger Hiss.

During the 1952 campaign, reporters alleged that Nixon had an $18,000 fund made up of gifts from political supporters. At the time, such a fund was not illegal. Nixon's critics, however, implied that he was dishonest.

In a dramatic move, Nixon went on television to defend his conduct. His outstanding performance in the so-called Checkers speech saved his spot on the Republican ticket. With the issue behind them, the Eisenhower campaign moved on to a solid election-day victory.

READING CHECK **Summarizing** What were the key events of the presidential campaign of 1952?

Speech

In what became known as the Checkers speech, Richard M. Nixon admitted having a secret political fund but denied using it improperly. He detailed his personal finances—and admitted to having accepted one special gift in 1952. The speech was well received, and it saved his political career.

"We did get something, a gift, after the election. A man down in Texas heard [my wife] Pat on the radio mention the fact that our two youngsters would like to have a dog, and . . . the day before we left on this campaign trip we got a message from Union Station down in Baltimore, saying they had a package for us. We went down to get it. You know what it was? It was a little cocker spaniel dog, in a crate that he had sent all the way from Texas, black and white, spotted, and our little girl, Tricia, the six-year-old, named it Checkers. And, you know, the kids, like all kids, loved the dog, and I just want to say this, right now, that regardless of what they say about it, we're going to keep it."

Nixon used the image of his daughter and her puppy to build sympathy.

Skills FOCUS **READING LIKE A HISTORIAN**

1. **Analyzing Primary Sources** What was the gift that Nixon admitted to having received?
2. **Drawing Conclusions** Why do you think the speech was effective at ending the scandal?

See **Skills Handbook**, pp. H12, H28–H29

The Cold War Continues

True to his promise, Eisenhower traveled to Korea in December 1952. There he began the task of getting the stalled peace talks going. The effort proved difficult. A cease-fire was not achieved until July 1953. Even with the end of the fighting in Korea, the Cold War continued to rage throughout the 1950s and to dominate Eisenhower's presidency.

Eisenhower's Cold War policies At the center of Eisenhower's foreign policy team was Secretary of State **John Foster Dulles**. Dulles had played a role in the Truman administration.

ACADEMIC VOCABULARY
imply to express indirectly

Before serving in the Truman Administration, John Foster Dulles was a senator from New York. He was appointed by Governor Thomas Dewey following Robert Wagner's resignation in 1949. Dulles failed to win reelection the following year.

Like Eisenhower, he was sharply critical of the Democrats' foreign policy. In particular, Dulles wanted to revise the nation's approach to communism. Rather than merely containing it, as Truman had called for, Dulles spoke of rolling it back.

To stand against the Soviets, Dulles favored building more nuclear weapons. Only the threat of nuclear war, he believed, would stop the Soviets. Dulles's belief was a part of the policy known as **brinkmanship**, the diplomatic art of going to the brink of war without actually getting into war. The practice of brinkmanship involved making threats that were strong enough to bring results without having to follow through on the threats.

Related to this notion was Dulles's concept of **massive retaliation**. This was the pledge that the United States would use overwhelming force against the Soviet Union, including nuclear weapons, to settle a serious conflict.

While Dulles presented the public face of American foreign policy, there was also a secret side. The Central Intelligence Agency, or **CIA**, was formed in 1947 to collect information about—and spy on—foreign governments. The CIA was increasingly active in the 1950s. In addition to collecting information, CIA agents also took part in secret actions against hostile governments. For example, during Eisenhower's first term CIA agents helped overthrow governments in Guatemala and Iran.

Changes in the Soviet Union
In March 1953 longtime Soviet leader Joseph Stalin died. His death brought an end to a terrible period in Soviet history. A ruthless dictator, he had been responsible for the deaths of millions of his own citizens. He had also led the Soviet Union in its domination of Eastern Europe and the start of the Cold War.

Stalin's death raised many questions in the United States. Observers were unsure what policies his successor would pursue. Eventually, **Nikita Khrushchev** emerged as the new leader. Many political prisoners jailed under Stalin were freed. Nevertheless, the Soviet Union remained a Communist dictatorship—and a bitter rival of the United States.

The Warsaw Pact forms
In 1955 the Soviets established a new organization called the **Warsaw Pact**. This was a military alliance with the Soviet-dominated countries of Eastern Europe. It was roughly similar in purpose to NATO. The Warsaw Pact, however, was entirely under the control of the Soviet Union. Warsaw Pact nations stood ready to defend each other and the Soviet Union. At the same time, the pact was a tool that helped the Soviets solidify control in Eastern Europe.

Communist control was firm—and when necessary, ruthless. For example, in June 1956 soldiers violently put down an anti-Communist protest in Poland. Dozens were killed.

Several months later, a larger uprising occurred in Hungary. There, many citizens rose up to demand changes to their harsh, Soviet-style government. Some also sought the return of a former leader, Imre Nagy. Nagy was a Communist, but he favored a more democratic system of government.

Height of the Cold War

In the 1950s Cold War tensions reached new heights as the United States and the Soviet Union maneuvered for power and influence.

This cartoon of Khrushchev and Eisenhower appeared on the cover of *Newsweek* in 1959.

November 1952
Eisenhower is elected president, in part on the strength of his tough anti-Communist stance.

March 1953
Stalin dies; eventually Nikita Khrushchev emerges as the new Soviet leader.

July 1953
Fighting in Korea ends in a stalemate.

In response to public demands, Nagy was named prime minister in late October. Once in office, he promised new reforms for Hungary. He also tried to force the withdrawal of Soviet troops from his country. When these efforts failed, he declared that Hungary would withdraw from the Warsaw Pact.

As demonstrations continued in the Hungarian capital of Budapest, the Soviets used the unrest as an excuse to send in military forces. Soviet tanks rolled through the streets, and planes bombed the city. The Hungarians fought back, but they could not resist the Soviets. The Soviets had sent a powerful message: They were in control in Eastern Europe.

U.S.-Soviet relations

Although the 1950s were a time of Cold War tension, the Americans and Soviets did meet in the first postwar U.S.-Soviet summit in 1955. A **summit** is a meeting of the heads of government. The summit took place in Geneva, Switzerland.

Eisenhower proposed an "open skies" treaty. Under it, both the Soviets and the Americans could fly over each other's territory to learn more about the other's military abilities. Eisenhower believed this would help lower tensions because neither side would have to imagine the worst about the other's military strength. The Soviets, however, rejected the proposal.

This setback did not shake voters' faith in Eisenhower and his handling of international affairs. He easily won re-election in 1956, again defeating Adlai Stevenson.

The Soviet rejection of the open skies proposal did not prevent Eisenhower from seeking information about the Soviet military. The United States sent U-2 aircraft into Soviet airspace to inspect their military facilities. The U-2s carried advanced spying equipment and flew at altitudes thought to be out of reach of Soviet defenses. In 1960, however, the Soviets shot down pilot Francis Gary Powers's U-2 spy plane and captured Powers. Powers was freed in 1962 in exchange for the U.S. release of a captured Soviet spy. The incident greatly damaged U.S.-Soviet relations.

READING CHECK **Identifying Cause and Effect** Identify several events that represent the continuation of the Cold War in the 1950s.

Cold War "Hot Spots"

The Cold War had led to armed conflict in Korea. Cold War tensions also flared in several other spots around the world in the 1950s.

Vietnam and the seeds of war

In 1954 France lost a bloody struggle to keep control of its Southeast Asian colony in Vietnam. After a terrible defeat in the battle of Dien Bien Phu, the French sought peace with the Vietnamese rebels who had been fighting to oust them. Among these rebels were many Communists.

The peace talks between the French and Vietnamese reflected Cold War rivalries. The final agreement divided Vietnam into northern and southern halves. The north came under the control of Communist leader Ho Chi Minh. As in Korea, this division was supposed to be temporary. The peace agreement called for a

Peace talks in Panmunjom stall as the partition between the two Koreas is negotiated.

The military used high-altitude aircraft on spying missions.

© BERNARD CROCHET COLLECTION/PHOTOS12.COM

September 1954
The Southeast Asia Treaty Organization is formed to stop communism in Southeast Asia.

May 1955
The Warsaw Pact is formed between the Soviet Union and the countries it dominated in Eastern Europe.

1956
Poland and Hungary rebel against Communist rule; Egypt seizes the Suez Canal, and Israel, Great Britain, and France attack.

January 1957
The President issues the Eisenhower Doctrine, intended to resist communism in the Middle East; he later sends troops into Lebanon.

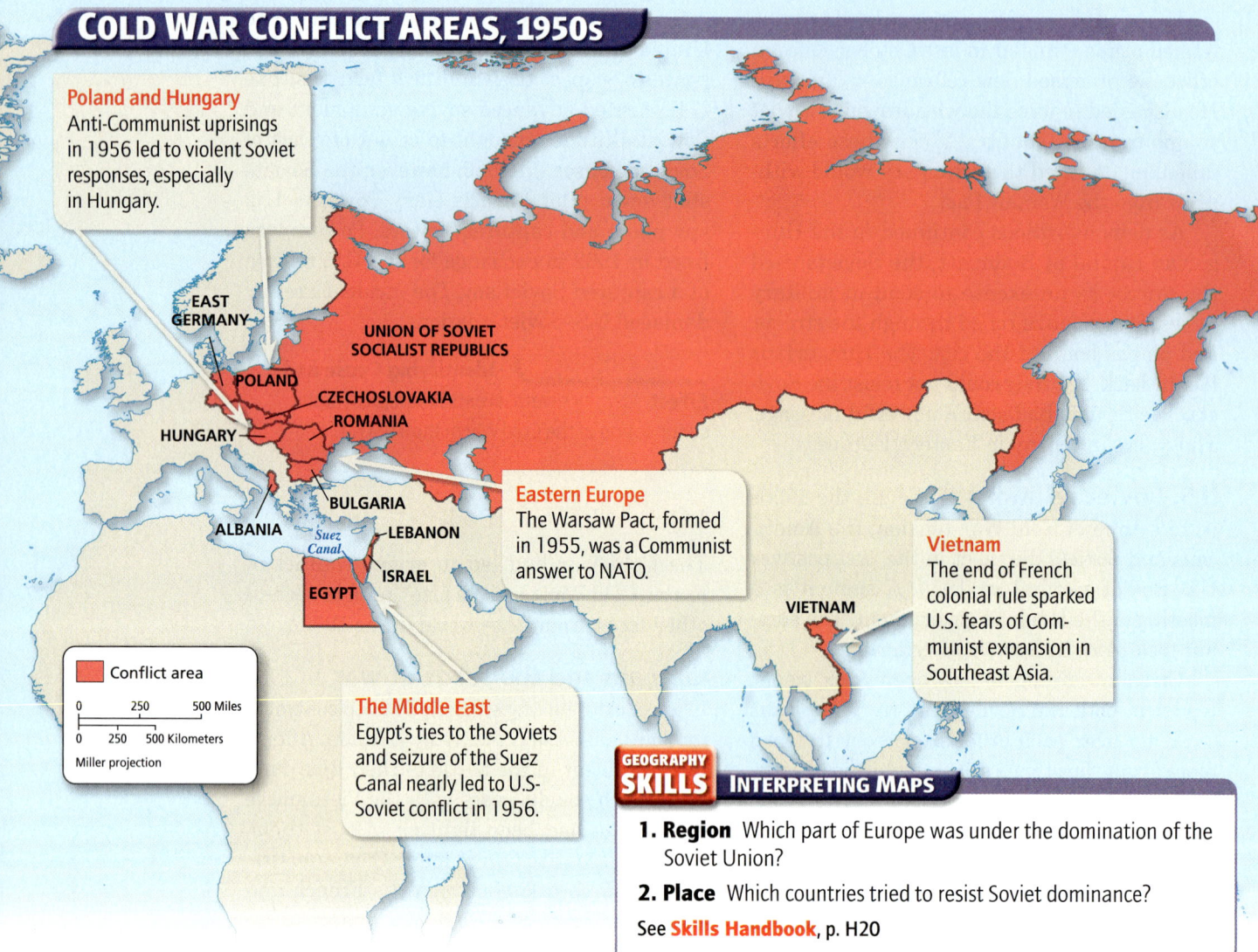

COLD WAR CONFLICT AREAS, 1950s

Poland and Hungary
Anti-Communist uprisings in 1956 led to violent Soviet responses, especially in Hungary.

EAST GERMANY
POLAND
CZECHOSLOVAKIA
ROMANIA
HUNGARY
BULGARIA
ALBANIA
LEBANON
ISRAEL
EGYPT
Suez Canal

UNION OF SOVIET SOCIALIST REPUBLICS

VIETNAM

Eastern Europe
The Warsaw Pact, formed in 1955, was a Communist answer to NATO.

Vietnam
The end of French colonial rule sparked U.S. fears of Communist expansion in Southeast Asia.

Conflict area

0   250   500 Miles
0   250   500 Kilometers
Miller projection

The Middle East
Egypt's ties to the Soviets and seizure of the Suez Canal nearly led to U.S-Soviet conflict in 1956.

GEOGRAPHY SKILLS | INTERPRETING MAPS

1. **Region** Which part of Europe was under the domination of the Soviet Union?
2. **Place** Which countries tried to resist Soviet dominance?

See **Skills Handbook**, p. H20

1956 election. Vietnamese voters would then get to choose for themselves what kind of government they would have.

For Eisenhower, this agreement was unacceptable: An election might lead to a Communist victory. Communism in Vietnam could lead to the spread of communism in the region.

HISTORY'S VOICES

❝You have a row of dominoes set up, you knock over the first one, and what will happen to the last one is the certainty that it will go over very quickly . . .

But when we come to the possible sequence of events, the loss of [Vietnam], of Burma, of Thailand, of the Peninsula, and Indonesia following . . . the possible consequences of the loss are just incalculable to the free world.❞

—Dwight D. Eisenhower, press conference, April 7, 1954

To address this danger, the United States and its anti-Communist allies created a new organization. This was called the Southeast Asia Treaty Organization, or **SEATO**. Members included Australia, Great Britain, France, New Zealand, Pakistan, the Philippines, Thailand, and the United States. SEATO nations agreed to work together to resist Communist aggression.

SEATO and the United States supported the creation of a new anti-Communist nation in 1955: South Vietnam. In the coming years, the United States provided much military and economic support to this government. Unfortunately, its president, Ngo Dinh Diem, angered his own people with his harsh leadership.

Meanwhile, the North Vietnamese were growing impatient. They still wanted to unite all of Vietnam under their control. This set the stage for later armed conflict.

Trouble in the Middle East The Middle East was another region troubled by Cold War tensions. These tensions were heightened by the conflict between Jews and Arabs. This conflict reached a crisis point in 1948, when Israel declared its independence. The creation of Israel followed a UN resolution dividing Palestine into a Jewish and an Arab state.

Israel's Arab neighbors—Egypt, Syria, Jordan, Lebanon, and Iraq—immediately attacked Israel. In the war that followed, Israel won. The land that had been set aside for the Palestinians came under the control of Israel and the nations of Jordan and Egypt.

In 1954 Gamal Abdel Nasser rose to power in Egypt. Nasser sought to unite and strengthen the Arab nations. Toward this goal, he was willing to seek the support of the Soviet Union.

U.S. leaders were unhappy with Nasser's growing relationship with the Soviet Union. In 1956 the United States withdrew its financial support for a major Egyptian building project, the Aswan High Dam.

In response, Nasser seized control of the Suez Canal, the vital waterway between the Mediterranean Sea and the Red Sea. A British-controlled company owned the canal, through which Europe received two-thirds of its petroleum. Britain and France wanted to continue to use the canal and to protect their oil supplies.

Egypt's action in the Suez also blocked Israel's only outlet to the Red Sea. In response, Israel launched a military attack on Egypt. The British and French quickly sent in their forces to take control of the canal. The Soviets then threatened to enter the fight on the side of Egypt. This, Eisenhower knew, might draw the United States into the conflict.

The Suez crisis ended when Eisenhower insisted that the invaders leave Egypt. A wider conflict was averted, although Egypt kept control of the canal. The incident also demonstrated the leadership of the United States over its European allies.

The Suez crisis had not resulted in a larger war over the Suez Canal. Eisenhower was worried, however, about the growing influence of the Soviets in the Middle East. In January 1957 he issued the **Eisenhower Doctrine**. This declared the right of the United States to help, on request, any nation in the Middle East trying to resist armed Communist aggression.

Using the doctrine, Eisenhower sent marines into Lebanon in 1958 to help put down a popular uprising against Lebanon's government. Though no Communists threatened Lebanon, Eisenhower wanted to prevent a wider crisis that might invite Soviet involvement.

READING CHECK **Identifying the Main Idea** What made the Cold War "hot spots" hot?

THE IMPACT TODAY

Economics
Some 25,000 ships pass through the Suez Canal annually, carrying about 14 percent of the world's shipping.

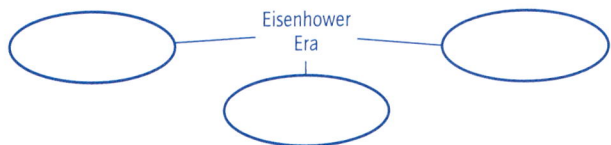

SECTION 1 ASSESSMENT

go.hrw.com
Online Quiz
Keyword: SD7 HP26

Reviewing Ideas, Terms, and People

1. a. Recall What were the key issues and individuals of the 1952 presidential campaign?
b. Elaborate How did Nixon's Checkers speech help the Eisenhower campaign?

2. a. Define Write a brief definition of each of the following terms: **brinkmanship, massive retaliation, Warsaw Pact**
b. Compare How was the Warsaw Pact similar to and different from NATO?
c. Evaluate What do you think were the strengths and weaknesses of Dulles's policy of brinkmanship and massive retaliation?

3. a. Describe How did Cold War tensions contribute to conflicts in Vietnam and in Egypt?
b. Explain What did President Eisenhower mean when he compared Vietnam to a domino?

c. Elaborate Do you think Eisenhower was right to request that Great Britain, France, and Israel end their attack on Egypt during the Suez crisis? Explain.

Critical Thinking

4. Identifying the Main Idea Copy the chart below and use information from the section to record details that support the main idea of the section.

Eisenhower Era

 **FOCUS ON SPEAKING**

5. Persuasive Assume the point of view of President Eisenhower. Make a speech to British, French, and Israeli leaders urging them to end their attack on Egypt.

Atomic Anxiety

BEFORE YOU READ

MAIN IDEA

The growing power of, and military reliance on, nuclear weapons helped create significant anxiety in the American public in the 1950s.

READING FOCUS

1. What was the hydrogen bomb, and when was it developed?
2. What was the arms race, and what were its effects in the United States?
3. How did Americans react to the growing threat of nuclear war?

KEY TERMS AND PEOPLE

hydrogen bomb
ICBMs
Sputnik
satellite
NASA
nuclear fallout

P1 3.4 Understand the interrelationships between world events and developments in New York State and the United States (e.g., causes for immigration, economic opportunities, human rights abuses, and tyranny versus freedom).

Three Rooms, Two Baths, One Bomb Shelter

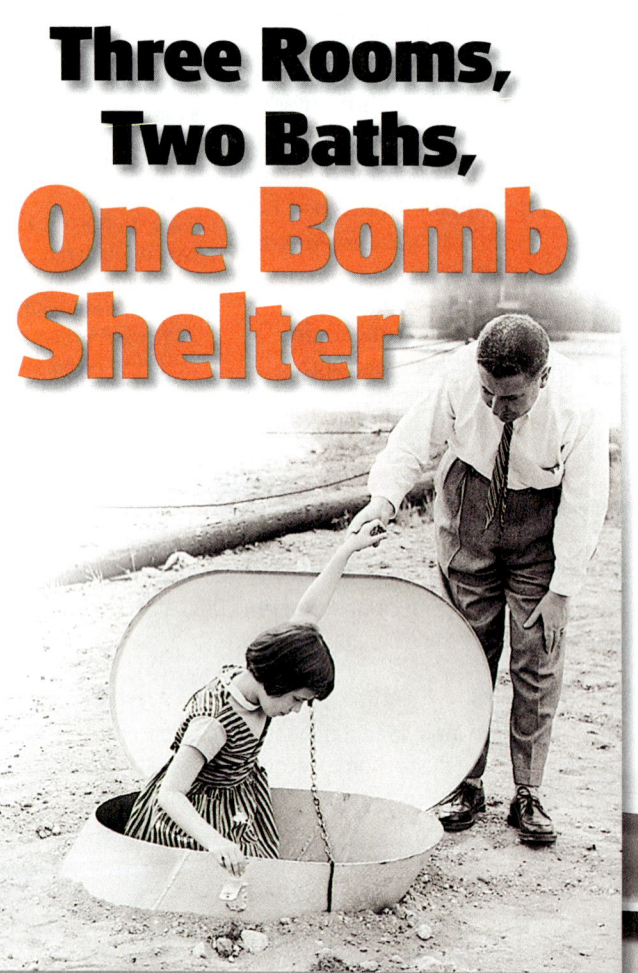

THE INSIDE STORY

Where would you go if the unthinkable happened?
To Americans of the 1950s, war was something that took place in faraway lands. Few people had seriously faced the threat of death and destruction in their own communities. The atomic bomb, however, changed that comfortable feeling. With the bomb came the realization that devastation could come to them with no more warning than the wail of an air-raid siren.

How could Americans living in such a world protect their families? Some sought protection in backyard bomb shelters. Homeowners across the country were urged to install underground bunkers, complete with supplies of food and water that would help them and their loved ones survive a nuclear attack. There were a number of models available on the market. Popular magazines included helpful plans for do-it-yourselfers. For those unable to install an underground shelter, the government provided tips on how to create a bomb-safe area within an existing structure.

Nuclear weapons had brought a kind of peace to the world. They also brought uneasiness. As you will read, this tension colored much of American life in the 1950s. ◼

In theory, a family could survive ▶ up to five days in one of these underground backyard shelters.

Kidde Kokoon

CANNED FOOD

The Hydrogen Bomb

The atomic bombs that the United States used at the end of World War II had changed the world. Their terrible power persuaded Japanese leaders to do what millions of Allied soldiers had been unable to get them to do: surrender. Military strategy would never be the same.

American leaders chose not to use nuclear weapons during the Korean War. Nevertheless, these weapons were clearly a key part of the nation's military future. Even as soldiers were dying in Korea, the United States was building up its atomic stockpile and testing new and improved weapons. Nuclear testing took place in a variety of locations, including New Mexico, Nevada, Colorado, Mississippi, and Alaska.

Among the weapons being studied during this time was a different kind of nuclear device: the **hydrogen bomb**. The atomic bombs that destroyed Hiroshima and Nagasaki used energy that came from splitting apart atoms. The new hydrogen bomb would get its power from the fusing together of hydrogen atoms. Fusion is the same process that creates the energy of the sun and stars. Harnessed into a weapon, fusion had the potential to create a blast hundreds of times more powerful than an atomic bomb. Indeed, the hydrogen bomb—also known as the H-bomb or super bomb—was so potentially devastating that some scientists argued against ever building it.

HISTORY'S VOICES

" In determining not to proceed to develop the super bomb, we see a unique opportunity of providing by example some limitations on the totality of war and thus of limiting the fear and arousing the hopes of mankind. "

—Report of the General Advisory Committee of the Atomic Energy Commission, October 1949

In spite of these concerns, development of the hydrogen bomb went forward in the late 1940s and early 1950s. President Truman had made the final decision. "It is part of my responsibility as commander-in-chief," he declared, "to see to it that our country is able to defend itself against any possible aggressor." Truman did not want to take the chance that the Soviet Union would develop its own hydrogen bomb. That would give the Soviet Union a significant military advantage over the United States.

The first hydrogen bomb, detonated in 1951, was code-named "Mike," for *megaton*.

THE FIRST HYDROGEN BOMB TEST

When detonated: November 1, 1952, Eniwetak Atoll, Marshall Islands

Amount of energy released: 10.4 megatons, equivalent to 10.4 million tons of TNT

Size of fireball: 3 miles in diameter

Height of mushroom cloud: more than 25 miles

By 1952 scientists had solved the difficult technical challenges of building a hydrogen bomb. On November 1 they tested it. The blast was beyond anything they had imagined. The island on which the bomb had been placed simply vanished. "I was stunned," recalled one observer of the explosion. "It looked as though it blotted out the whole horizon."

The explosion of the H-bomb once again put the United States ahead of the Soviet Union in weapons technology. This lead, however, was short-lived. In August 1953 the Soviets successfully tested a hydrogen bomb of their own.

READING CHECK **Drawing Conclusions**
Why did President Truman decide to develop the hydrogen bomb?

The Arms Race

The United States and the Soviets again had roughly the same technology. Each side, however, remained concerned that the other would gain an advantage. To prevent this, both countries began to build stockpiles of weapons. They also sought new and better ways of delivering those weapons to potential targets.

Each improvement or technological advance by one country was met with some response by the other. Thus the United States and Soviet Union began an arms race—an international contest between countries seeking a military advantage over each other.

ACADEMIC VOCABULARY
equipped fitted with; possessing certain equipment

New military strategies The arrival and advance of nuclear weapons forced American leaders to reconsider the way the United States built its military defenses. When Eisenhower took office, he scaled back the nation's reliance on so-called conventional forces, such as soldiers and tanks. In their place, he increased reliance on nuclear weapons. This shift helped lead to the development of John Foster Dulles's policies of brinkmanship and massive retaliation. Instead of resisting its enemies with armies at the point of attack, the United States would seek to prevent its enemies from attacking in the first place by promising a devastating nuclear response.

Eisenhower and Dulles's strategies placed great importance on keeping the lead in the arms race. The American threat of massive retaliation would be more effective if its forces were superior to those of any adversary.

New bombs The first American hydrogen bomb was massive, not just in its destructive power but also in its size. It stood three stories tall and weighed a million pounds. It was so big, there would have been no way to actually use the weapon against an enemy.

Scientists therefore worked hard to reduce the size of the H-bomb. Before long, they had succeeded in making weapons that could be more easily delivered to enemy targets. The first such bomb was tested in 1954.

Early on, the United States focused on aircraft as the means of delivering nuclear weapons. As a result, the U.S. Air Force grew substantially in the 1950s. While Eisenhower was cutting budgets in many other parts of the military, he spent large amounts on new long-range bomber aircraft, such as the B-52. These bombers had the ability to deliver nuclear weapons anywhere in the world.

The U.S. fleet of bombers was spread across dozens of locations in Europe, Africa, and elsewhere. The American nuclear arsenal was constantly on the move. Bombers were always in the air, and those on the ground were ready to take off within 15 minutes. This helped ensure that no enemy would be able to destroy the American ability to launch an attack.

While the United States at first relied on aircraft to carry its nuclear weapons, scientists were hard at work developing missiles that could be equipped with these weapons. The effort involved reducing the size of the weapons themselves. It also involved developing missiles that could reach enemy targets accurately.

The development of missiles represented a major technological challenge. In the early 1950s, American rockets were capable of carrying a small nuclear weapon only a short distance. By the end of the 1950s, Americans had developed intercontinental ballistic missiles, or **ICBMs**. The ICBMs could travel thousands of miles and strike very close to their intended targets. They could also deliver powerful nuclear weapons.

Other new technologies While scientists were exploring the atom's destructive power, they were also learning to use it for other purposes. In 1954 the U.S. Navy launched the first nuclear-powered submarine. On this vessel, the USS *Nautilus*, nuclear fuel heated water to create steam. This steam powered the engine.

Unlike earlier submarines, the *Nautilus* could travel for months without needing to refuel. Thus, vessels such as the *Nautilus* could perform missions over greater distances. Nuclear-powered submarines were also capable of traveling at high speeds underwater.

THE IMPACT TODAY
Science and Technology
In recent times, the United States and other nations have worked to prevent the spread of nuclear weapons to developing countries, including Iran and North Korea.

Several years after launching the *Nautilus*, the United States began fitting its nuclear-powered submarines with nuclear missiles. By sending some of its nuclear weapons underwater and out of reach of enemy attack, the United States had found another way to ensure that any enemy move could be met with a devastating nuclear response.

Nuclear power was put to use for peaceful purposes on land as well. Nuclear power plants in the United States began to produce electricity for homes and businesses in 1957.

Soviet advances in technology The Soviet Union was also improving and expanding its weapons. Throughout the 1950s, the Soviets built new and improved weapons and delivery systems. The Soviets did lag behind the United States in the number of weapons it possessed. Nevertheless, it was well understood that any nuclear attack would lead to terrible destruction for both sides.

Soviet technological skill was demonstrated in shocking fashion in 1957. On October 4 the

The Cold War Arms Race

During the Cold War, the United States and the Soviet Union competed vigorously to achieve superiority in the arms race.

United States

October 1952
Americans explode an H-bomb.

January 1954
United States launches a nuclear-powered sub.

April 1957
United States tests a missile with a 2,000-mile range.

January 1958
United States launches a satellite.

July 1958
NASA is formed to lead U.S. space exploration programs.

May 1960
Francis Gary Powers's U-2 is shot down by the Soviets.

Soviet Union

August 1953
Soviets explode an H-bomb.

August 1957
Soviets test a missile with a 4,000-mile range.

October 1957
Sputnik, the first artificial satellite, is launched.

November 1957
Sputnik II is launched, carrying a dog into space.

SQUEEZE PLAY

possible effects of a nuclear attack on major American urban areas. They took into account the results of the 1954 hydrogen bomb test, in which significant nuclear fallout spread over an area of 7,000 square miles.

The results of the 1955 Operation Alert were deeply disturbing. According to the FCDA's evaluation in the densely populated New York City area, a nuclear attack could leave millions dead and millions more injured and homeless.

In other cities, participation in the tests was inconsistent. In Washington, D.C., for example, the U.S. Congress simply ignored the exercise and continued its work.

In case anyone had had any doubt, Operation Alert made it clear that a true nuclear attack on a major urban area would have terrible, long-lasting results.

HISTORY'S VOICES

❝This demonstration gives new emphasis to President Eisenhower's dictum [statement] that war no longer presented the possibility of victory or defeat, but only the alternative of varying degrees of destruction.❞

—*The New York Times,* June 16, 1955

Nuclear fears The government's efforts did raise preparedness. It also raised fears, leading many Americans to build bomb shelters in their yards. The public also began to express concern over the testing of nuclear weapons and the effects of nuclear fallout. These concerns eventually helped lead to negotiations with the Soviet Union for a treaty limiting nuclear testing. The Limited Test-Ban Treaty was ratified in 1963.

Nuclear fears also affected the culture of the times. A number of 1950s movies had plots that centered on the dangers of radiation. Comic books for young readers featured heroes and villains doing battle in a nuclear world.

The military-industrial complex While the public learned to live with the fear of nuclear attack, President Eisenhower used part of his farewell address in 1961 to inform them of a new danger: the "military-industrial complex." In the past, Eisenhower said, the United States had no permanent arms industry. When war came, factories changed from making cars, for example, to making tanks. By the 1950s, however, that had changed.

"We have been compelled to create a permanent armaments industry of vast proportions," Eisenhower said. While necessary, he noted, it was still a threat to freedom. "The potential for the disastrous rise of misplaced power exists and will persist," Eisenhower warned. Thus, as the 1950s ended and a new decade began, Americans had a new challenge to face.

READING CHECK **Identifying Supporting Details** How were the American people regularly reminded of the threat of nuclear war?

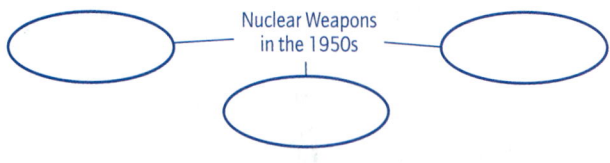

SECTION 2 ASSESSMENT

go.hrw.com
Online Quiz
Keyword: SD7 HP26

Reviewing Ideas, Terms, and People

1. a. Describe How did the **hydrogen bomb** differ from the atomic weapons used on Hiroshima and Nagasaki?
b. Draw Conclusions How do you think a more powerful weapon such as the hydrogen bomb would fit within the policies of brinkmanship and massive retaliation?

2. a. Define Write a brief definition of each of the following terms: **ICBMs**, *Sputnik*, **NASA**
b. Summarize Why was the Soviet development of a **satellite** so significant to the people of the United States?
c. Predict How do you think the race to find an edge in nuclear weapons will affect the nature of nuclear weapons in the decades to come?

3. a. Describe What was the job of the **FCDA**?
b. Contrast How did the nuclear threat differ from the kinds of threats that had faced the American people in the past?

Critical Thinking

4. Identifying the Main Idea Copy the chart below and use information from the section to record details that support the main idea of the section. Refer to the main idea at the beginning of this section.

Nuclear Weapons in the 1950s

FOCUS ON WRITING

5. Narrative Write a brief narrative paragraph that tells the story of the arms race of the 1950s. Include details from this section.

The Television Age

BEFORE YOU READ

MAIN IDEA

Television was a major influence on American culture in the 1950s, mirroring larger changes in technology and culture.

READING FOCUS

1. How did television change American life in the 1950s?
2. What other technological developments occurred during the 1950s?
3. How was American culture changing during the 1950s?

KEY TERMS AND PEOPLE

Lucille Ball
transistor
integrated circuit
Jonas Salk
vaccine
Levittown
Sunbelt
Interstate Highway System

PI 3.3 Prepare essays and oral reports about the important social, political, economic, scientific, technological, and cultural developments, issues, and events from New York State and United States history.

How did a redhead become a star in black-and-white? Television was still quite new in 1951 when the *I Love Lucy* show was first broadcast. The nation quickly fell in love with the zany antics of the show's characters: the redheaded Lucy Ricardo, played by Lucille Ball, and her bandleader husband Ricky, played by Desi Arnaz. At the peak of the show's success, two of three television sets in the country were tuned in for every episode.

The show helped shape the future of television itself. Prior to *I Love Lucy*, TV did not have its own style and distinctive art. Programs were little more than filmed versions of radio programs or vaudeville routines. But under the shrewd guidance of Ball and Arnaz, *I Love Lucy* pioneered new production techniques. For example, the show was filmed rather than broadcast live. This enabled the stars to perfect their comic routines—with hilarious results.

The program also broke ground with its casting. In 1951 Ball was a movie star in decline. Cuban-born Arnaz spoke with a thick Spanish accent. Neither fit the mold of the traditional star of the time. Yet their chemistry—the two were married in real life—was remarkable. Together they produced some of the most memorable moments in TV history. In the process, they helped television revolutionize American life.

FOR THE LOVE OF LUCY

▲ Ball's new ideas changed how TV shows were made.

LOOK

FOOTBALL-1956
THE ALL AMERICA TEAM

A CHRISTMAS EXTRA
ST. PAUL AND CHRISTIANITY

25¢ DECEMBER 25, 1956

An intimate close-up
THE DESI-LUCY
LOVE STORY

Television Changes American Life

Though broadcast television was still young when **Lucille Ball** captured the hearts of the nation, TV technology had existed for a number of years. Scientists had been working on it at least since the 1920s. By the end of World War II, television was ready for home use. Postwar consumers, eager to spend after years of wartime sacrifice, purchased the new devices. Between 1945 and 1950, some 5 million TV sets appeared in American homes.

That was just the beginning. During the 1950s, the number of Americans owning TVs continued to rise. By 1959 more than 40 million American homes had at least one set.

TV and politics One field in which television had an immediate impact was politics. America's leaders quickly learned that TV had great power to change their relationships with the voters. You have read how vice presidential candidate Richard Nixon used television in 1952 to appeal to the voting public. As you will read later, Nixon would also find that TV could do harm to a candidate's image.

Television also altered the career of Senator Joseph McCarthy, the Communist hunter. The televised 1954 Army-McCarthy hearings finally gave the public the chance to see his disgraceful, bullying behavior. The hearings left his once-lofty reputation ruined and his career in tatters.

Television advertising Advertisers were another group that quickly recognized the promise of television. TV's combination of picture and sound gave it more persuasive potential than radio. By 1960 television was the major method of advertising in the country.

Early TV advertising was patterned after radio advertising. A single advertiser sponsored the broadcast of an entire program. On programs such as the *Colgate Comedy Hour,* the line between program and advertisement was blurry. The product being sold was actually a part of the action.

As the cost of producing entire TV programs rose, advertisers shifted to buying just one- or two-minute segments during shows to sell their products. Ads were separated from programming, and the TV commercial was born.

Programming Of course, for most Americans, television was mainly about the programs. Each day and night, audiences tuned in to watch their favorites. The *I Love Lucy* show was only one example of many popular television programs.

Television's first big hit was the *Texaco Star Theater,* starring comedian Milton Berle, which later became the *Milton Berle Show*. Berle's great success earned him the nickname "Mr. Television." His hugely popular program of comedy and music is credited with helping television get established in its earliest days.

The hit show *American Bandstand* got its appeal from another cultural movement of the 1950s: rock and roll music. The show, which began in 1957, featured young people dancing to popular songs. *American Bandstand* remained on television until 1987.

The 1950s also saw the introduction of some of the many categories of programs popular today. Daytime dramas (known as soap operas), crime dramas, and game shows almost all got their start during this decade. To help people keep track of their favorite programs, a magazine called *TV Guide* began publishing.

Concerns about television As television's popularity ballooned, some people began to question its effects. Of special concern was TV's possible impact on children.

On several occasions in the 1950s, Congress looked into the effects of violent content on young viewers. To address this concern, the TV industry adopted its own voluntary standards. For example, the industry promised that law enforcement would always appear in a positive light and that criminals would always be presented as "bad guys." Satisfied, Congress took no formal action to limit television content during the 1950s. Still, Americans would continue to discuss the effect of television on children for years to come.

TV experienced a scandal in the late 1950s when the public learned that a popular game show had been rigged. Congress held hearings into the matter, and one of the contestants involved, Charles Van Doren, wound up leaving his job as a university professor.

READING CHECK **Identifying Cause and Effect** What were some of the effects of television on American life and culture in the 1950s?

ACADEMIC VOCABULARY

categories
groups or classes with members that share common features

THE IMPACT TODAY

Science and Technology

Today most televisions are built to include a device called the V-chip. This device allows concerned adults to block the display of certain programs, such as those that contain violent content.

Milestones in Television History

Television has made history, and it has recorded history. Along the way, many changes have taken place in television. In the 1950s three major networks—ABC, CBS, and NBC—dominated TV broadcasting with shows aimed at the same general audience. Today the major networks share the television market with hundreds of cable networks airing programs tailored to specific age groups and interests.

A 1950 TV set ▲

1950 9 percent of U.S. households have televisions.

1951 Coast-to-coast live television broadcasts begin.

1954 CBS and NBC begin regular color broadcasting,  even though just 1 percent of U.S. households own a color TV set. The NBC "peacock" logo is shown above. ▲

TV Guide magazine is published for the first time.

1960 The first televised presidential debate takes place.

87 percent of U.S. households have televisions. Programming is aimed at a family audience. ▼

1963 ABC, CBS, and NBC broadcast four days of continuous live coverage of the assassination and funeral of President John F. Kennedy. Millions of people around the world watch the state funeral on TV.

1969 *Sesame Street* airs for the first time, breaking new ground in children's educational programming.

An estimated 720 million people watch the first moon landing on live television. ▼

1970 The sitcom *Julia* is the first to feature an African American actor in the title role, played by Diahann Caroll. ▶

1971 Under federal law, cigarette advertising is banned on television and radio.

1972 The first cable network, Home Box Office (HBO), begins broadcasting.

1980 Cable News Network (CNN) offers the first 24-hour news service. ▼

1986 The *Challenger* space shuttle explodes just over a minute after takeoff. Millions of Americans witness the disaster on live TV.

1999 V-chip technology is introduced, allowing parents to block violent or unsuitable television programming from their children.

Today 98 percent of U.S. households have televisions. 76 percent of TV households have more than one set. About 68 percent of TV households have cable TV.

Skills FOCUS **INTERPRETING INFOGRAPHICS**

Making Generalizations In what ways has television changed since the 1950s?

See **Skills Handbook**, p. H18

Other Technological Developments of the 1950s

Television was certainly the most popular technological innovation of the 1950s. A number of other breakthroughs, however, also helped to transform American life.

Transistors and computers Machines have been used to perform calculations for thousands of years. In the 1940s, however, researchers began to build the first of what we might recognize today as computers. These devices used electricity to perform complicated calculations. For example, in Great Britain, scientists used an early type of computer to help break communications codes during World War II.

To build the first computers, scientists used thousands of vacuum tubes. These were glass and metal devices that helped form the complicated electronic workings of the machines. Because computers used so many tubes, they took up hundreds of square feet of floor space. They also drew large amounts of electricity.

In 1947 scientists at Bell Laboratories developed a device called the **transistor**. These devices worked much like tubes but with several advantages. For one, they were smaller. They also did not break as often as tubes did.

The invention of transistors led to the improvement of all kinds of electronics, from radios to televisions. Transistors also made possible smaller and more efficient computers.

In 1951 the first computer available for commercial use hit the market. It was called the UNIVAC, short for universal automatic computer. The UNIVAC earned fame for predicting the outcome of the 1952 presidential election based on early returns.

Use of computers continued to expand in the 1950s. New computer makers, such as International Business Machines (IBM), entered the market. The computers were still large. (A complete UNIVAC system could weigh 30,000 pounds.) Even relatively inexpensive systems cost up to $50,000 or more. Nevertheless, large companies and government agencies purchased computers. By the end of the decade, for example, banks were using computers to help process checks.

Meanwhile, computer technology continued to improve. In 1958 scientists developed the **integrated circuit**, a single piece of material that includes a number of transistors and other electronic components. Also known as computer chips, integrated circuits made possible the dizzying advancement of computer technology in the years ahead.

Linking TO Today

The Computer Revolution

The first general-purpose electronic computer was developed in the 1940s. The Electronic Numerical Integrator and Computer (ENIAC) was about 80 feet long, 8 feet high, and 2 feet deep.

New developments allowed more people to use computers. By the 1980s, Apple Computer had popularized tools such as the mouse, and Compaq had developed a portable computer that weighed 28 pounds.

Today, laptop computers weigh just a few pounds and do not require wires. Powerful computing devices fit in the palm of your hand.

Drawing Conclusions Why was ENIAC not useful to most people?

Today, a computerized gadget that hangs on your keychain has more than a thousand times the data storage of the room-sized ENIAC.

The Salk vaccine Earlier in this book, you read about Franklin D. Roosevelt and his bout with polio. The disease left him without the use of his legs. Another common effect of polio, which often struck children, was an impaired ability to breathe. Many victims died.

Polio was a contagious disease. Outbreaks were all too common in the early 1900s. When polio hit, it spread quickly. For weeks at a time, parents would keep their children out of school or other public places.

The worst year on record for polio in the United States came in 1952. More than 57,000 people came down with the dreaded disease. That year, scientist **Jonas Salk** developed a new polio vaccine. A <mark>vaccine</mark> is a preparation that uses a killed or weakened form of a germ to help the body build defenses against that germ. Vaccines are often given by injection.

The public announcement of the discovery of the polio vaccine came in 1955, and Salk became a hero. Children began receiving the shot, and the number of polio cases plunged.

READING CHECK **Summarizing** What were two major technological developments of the 1950s?

Cultural Change in the 1950s

The 1950s in the United States is often viewed as a time of peace and prosperity. For some, this was true. At the same time, though, the richness and variety of American life formed a more complicated picture.

Boom times The threats of nuclear war and the spread of communism did cause unease for millions of Americans. At the same time, many people took comfort in the nation's stunning economic success. Indeed, in the 1950s the United States had clearly emerged as the world's greatest economic power. The American people made up just 6 percent of the world's population. Yet American workers and farmers produced about one-third of the world's goods and services.

As you have read, the years after World War II saw a sharp increase in birthrates—a baby boom. The baby boom continued throughout the 1950s. To house these growing families, builders such as Bill and Alfred Levitt created whole new communities of individual houses. (See the History Close-Up on the next page.)

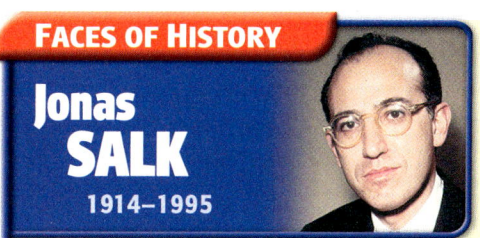

FACES OF HISTORY

Jonas SALK
1914–1995

Jonas Salk dedicated his career to fighting diseases that kill and maim people. After helping develop a vaccine for influenza for the Army during World War II, Salk turned his attention to fighting polio.

Salk worked for eight years to develop a polio vaccine. Confident of success, he tested his vaccine on himself, his wife, and their three sons in 1952. None of them became ill. After further testing, Salk's polio vaccine began to be used for mass vaccinations nationwide.

Salk refused to patent the vaccine. He did not want to profit from it. Rather, he wanted it made available to as many people as possible. Salk later served as a spokesperson for vaccinations. In 1995 he announced a new search—for an HIV vaccine.

Draw Conclusions In what ways was Salk's commitment to ending polio truly heroic?

New homes were filled with new stoves, refrigerators, and washing machines. New TVs ran ads urging people to want and buy even more.

Americans also purchased automobiles by the millions. To help fuel the desire of consumers, carmakers revised the styling of cars regularly. All this buying meant busy factories and high company profits. This, in turn, meant plentiful jobs. Employment was generally high in the 1950s. Wages rose steadily.

Indeed, a leading economist of the time, John Kenneth Galbraith, used the term "affluent society" to describe America in the postwar years. Yet Galbraith's view of the United States was not a positive one. In fact, he criticized an America overly focused on its own wealth.

ACADEMIC VOCABULARY
revise changing or modifying

HISTORY'S VOICES

❝The family which takes its . . . air-conditioned, power-steered, and power-braked automobile out for a tour passes through cities that are badly paved, made hideous by litter, blighted buildings, billboards, and posts for wires that should long since have been put underground.❞
—John Kenneth Galbraith, *The Affluent Society,* 1958

Another critic of the 1950s was Michael Harrington. His book *The Other America,* published in 1962, described the plight of the nation's poor. In his view, people living in poverty had been forgotten amid the economic success of the 1950s.

THE IMPACT TODAY

Daily Life
The postwar baby boom is having a huge effect on society today, as this large population is entering retirement. Health care costs are expected to rise as the "boomers" age and require more services.

Still another critic of the 1950s was William H. Whyte. In his book *The Organization Man,* he observed the push toward "sameness" and the increasing loss of individuality among the growing class of business workers.

New communities Many new homes built in the 1950s were parts of new suburban developments. The most famous of these was the enormous **Levittown**, New York, started in 1947 by Bill and Alfred Levitt.

The key to the success of Levittown and the many similar communities built in the postwar years was affordability: A family could purchase a single-family home at a reasonable price, often financed with the help of the government under the terms of the GI Bill.

Levittown was not a diverse community. Like many builders at the time, the Levitts at first refused to sell to African Americans.

The Levitts later built other communities in New Jersey and Pennsylvania. Overall, however, the U.S. population was beginning a shift in settlement toward the warmer southern and western portions of the United States, the so-called **Sunbelt**. In the 1950s the wide availability of home air conditioning helped make this move practical. This population shift has continued to the present.

California was (and still is) a major Sunbelt destination. At the start of the 1950s, just over 10.5 million people called California home. Over the next 10 years, more than 5 million people moved to the state.

Northern population centers such as New York and Illinois grew much more slowly. The shift from the North to the South and West was dramatized in the late 1950s when two New York baseball teams, the Brooklyn Dodgers and New York Giants, moved to California.

Building Levittown

Levittown, New York was a large community that eventually included more than 17,000 mass-produced homes. Levittown became a symbol for the many similar suburban towns that sprang up during the postwar years.

Developers kept costs down by using mass-production assembly-line techniques.

The houses were fairly inexpensive. Many American families could afford to buy a new, single-family home with little or no down payment.

Although all the houses were similar, builders did use different colors for the siding and roofing.

New highways During the 1950s the United States launched an ambitious building project: the **Interstate Highway System**. This system was designed to be a network of high-speed roads for interstate travel, all built on the same design.

President Eisenhower had long favored such a system. In 1956 Congress finally approved funding for a planned 40,000-mile system. With its construction, the United States reinforced its commitment to cars and trucks as its main means of ground transportation.

The art of rebellion Interestingly, the arts of the 1950s often stressed rebellion against sameness and conformity. Film stars such as Marlon Brando and James Dean built images as rebels who defied social norms. Jack Kerouac and other writers of the Beat generation also took the position of outsiders. They borrowed language from African American jazz music and rejected many social norms.

In popular music, rock and roll represented the rebellion of young people. Early stars such as Elvis Presley shocked many older Americans with his on-stage behavior. (Rock and roll was also influenced by African American musical forms, including jazz and rhythm and blues.)

If America seemed fascinated with the image of the rebel, it was mainly a male image. Women in film and literature tended to fill more traditional roles. It would be several years before women began to make their rebellion from the limits of American cultural norms.

READING CHECK **Summarizing** What were some key features of cultural change in the 1950s?

The Levittown planners created shopping areas, recreation centers, schools, and other attractive features for residents.

Skills FOCUS **INTERPRETING INFOGRAPHICS**

Scenes such as this were common in the 1950s.
Analyzing Information What might make such communities attractive places to live?

See **Skills Handbook**, p. H18

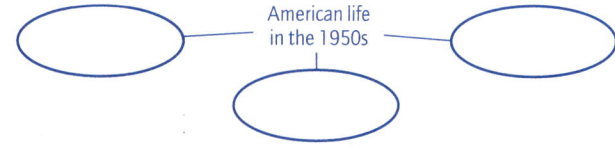

SECTION 3 ASSESSMENT

go.hrw.com
Online Quiz
Keyword: SD7 HP26

Reviewing Ideas, Terms, and People

1. **a. Recall** What was the significance of **Lucille Ball** and Milton Berle in the 1950s?
   b. Draw Conclusions Why do you think Richard Nixon used television as a means of persuading the public that he had done no wrong in 1952?

2. **a. Define** Write a brief definition of each of the following terms: transistor, integrated circuit, vaccine
   b. Make Inferences Why do you think the development of the computer was so important in spite of the fact that only large companies could afford computers in the 1950s?

3. **a. Identify** What was the significance of **Levittown** and the **Sunbelt** in the 1950s?
   b. Contrast How did the concepts of the "affluent society" and the "other America" relate to the general prosperity of the 1950s?

Critical Thinking

4. **Identifying the Main Idea** Copy the chart below and use information from the section to record details that support the main idea of the section.

American life in the 1950s

FOCUS ON WRITING

5. **Descriptive** Assume the point of view of a citizen of the United States in the 1950s. Write a letter to a friend in another country describing the changing life and culture in your country.

Perspectives on Interstate Highways

Historical Context The documents below provide information on the impact of the Interstate Highway System.

Task Examine the documents and answer the questions that follow. Then you will be asked to write an essay about the impact of the Interstate Highway System, using facts from the documents and from the chapter to support the position you take in your thesis statement.

ST 4.3 Develop hypotheses about important events, eras, or issues; move from chronicling to explaining historical events and issues; use information collected from diverse sources to produce cogently written reports and document-based essays.

DOCUMENT 1

The Interstate Highway System was developed in response to public pressure to improve the nation's roads. In this excerpt from a speech given to Congress on February 22, 1955, President Eisenhower discusses the importance of U.S. highways.

"Our unity as a nation is sustained by free communication of thought and by easy transportation of people and goods. The ceaseless flow of information throughout the Republic is matched by individual and commercial movement over a vast system of interconnected highways criss-crossing the Country and joining at our national borders with friendly neighbors to the north and south.

Together, the uniting forces of our communication and transportation systems are dynamic elements in the very name we bear—United States. Without them, we would be a mere alliance of many separate parts.

The Nation's highway system is a gigantic enterprise, one of our largest items of capital investment. Generations have gone into its building. . . . One in every seven Americans gains his livelihood and supports his family out of it. But, in large part, the network is inadequate for the nation's growing needs. . . .

To correct these deficiencies is an obligation of Government at every level. The highway system is a public enterprise. As the owner and operator, the various levels of Government have a responsibility for management that promotes the economy of the nation and properly serves the individual user.**"**

DOCUMENT 2

Within a few short years of the creation of the Interstate Highway System, trucks replaced railroads as the major means of freight transportation. These charts show how the amount of available railroad and highway transportation changed within 50 years.

TRANSPORTATION MILEAGE, 1950–2000

Miles of Railroad in Service

Miles (In thousands) — y-axis: 0, 50, 100, 150, 200, 250
Year — x-axis: 1950, 1960, 1970, 1980, 1990, 2000

Miles of Highway in Service

Miles (In millions) — y-axis: 3.0, 3.2, 3.4, 3.6, 3.8, 4.0
Year — x-axis: 1950, 1960, 1970, 1980, 1990, 2000

Source: *Bureau of Transportation Statistics*

Even with the expansion of air travel, driving by car is still the preferred means of getting around today. People routinely drive to destinations hundreds of miles away. In the year 2000 alone, domestic travelers spent nearly $500 billion visiting other places in the United States. The maps below show how U.S. highways expanded between 1950 and 2000. The red lines indicate interstate highways. Green lines are other highways.

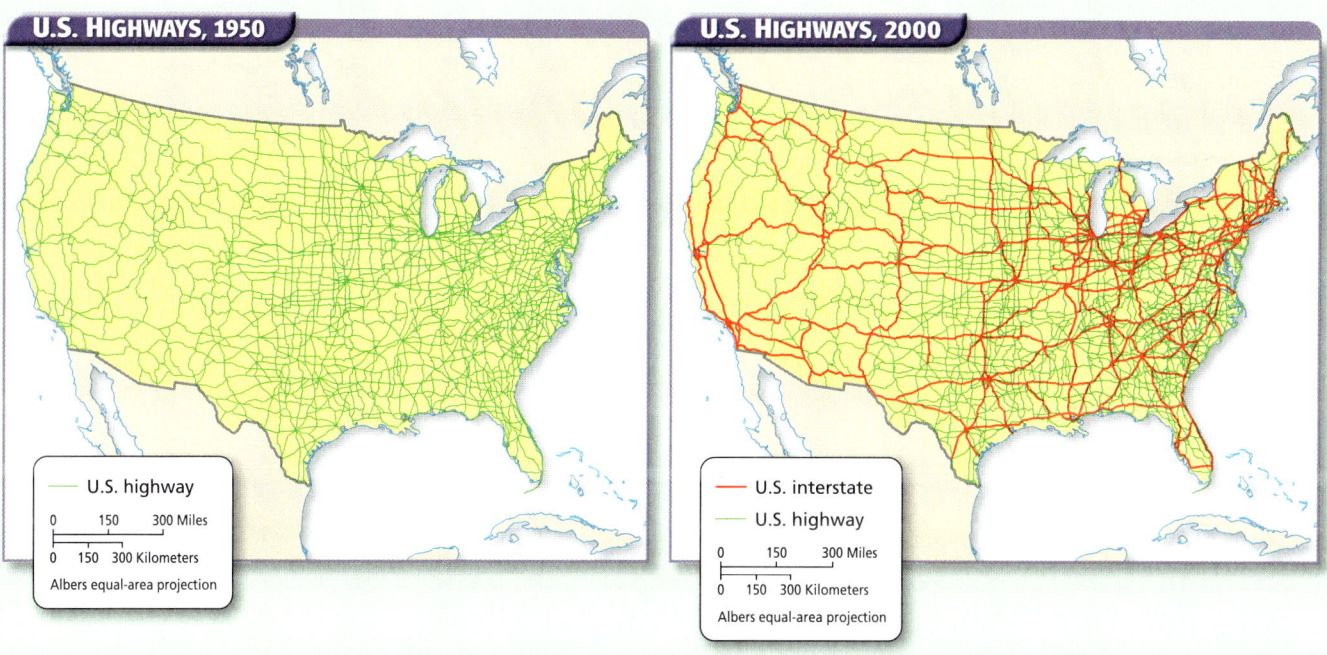

U.S. HIGHWAYS, 1950

U.S. highway

0   150   300 Miles
0   150   300 Kilometers
Albers equal-area projection

U.S. HIGHWAYS, 2000

U.S. interstate
U.S. highway

0   150   300 Miles
0   150   300 Kilometers
Albers equal-area projection

Skills FOCUS READING LIKE A HISTORIAN

1. a. Identify Refer to Document 1. What is Eisenhower's view of the highway system?
b. Elaborate Why do you think Eisenhower thought it was the government's obligation to improve the highway system?

2. a. Describe Refer to Document 2. What happened to railroad and highway mileage during this period?
b. Analyze What do you think were some of the reasons that highways came to replace railroads?

3. a. Describe Refer to Document 3. Where were most highways concentrated in 1950? in 2000?
b. Elaborate What do you think a similar map of highways in 2050 will look like? Explain.

4. Document-Based Essay Question Consider the question below and form a thesis statement. Using examples from Documents 1, 2, and 3, create an outline and write a short essay supporting your position.
How did the expansion of highways affect the United States?

See **Skills Handbook**, pp. H17, H20, H28–H29

Chapter Review

Visual Summary: Postwar America

Arms race anxiety

- Soviets and Americans engage in an arms race.
- Foreign policies are built around the threat of nuclear weapons.
- New technologies emerge, including massive hydrogen bombs.
- Public prepares for worst.

The United States in the 1950s

Eisenhower's presidency

- Ike is elected in 1952 and 1956.
- His presidency is heavily focused on Cold War issues.
- "Hot spots" include Eastern Europe, Southeast Asia, and the Middle East.

Television and cultural change

- Television arrives in full force.
- Scientific advances, such as vaccines, change Americans' lives.
- Population grows and moves.

Reviewing Key Terms and People

For each of the following questions, choose the letter that corresponds to the best available answer.

1. Following the launch of *Sputnik*, the U.S. government established which of the following?

a. SEATO   **c.** ICBMs

b. NASA   **d.** CIA

2. Brinkmanship and massive retaliation are both associated with which person?

a. John Foster Dulles   **c.** Nikita Khrushchev

b. Jonas Salk   **d.** Richard M. Nixon

3. This weapon raised the stakes in the conflict between the United States and the Soviet Union in the Cold War.

a. integrated circuit   **c.** *Sputnik*

b. transistor   **d.** H-bomb

4. Which of the following was under the influence of the Soviet Union?

a. SEATO   **c.** CIA

b. Warsaw Pact   **d.** Interstate Highway System

5. Which term represents the new suburban housing developments that appeared in the postwar years?

a. Sunbelt   **c.** Levittown

b. Interstate Highway System   **d.** integrated circuit

6. Jonas Salk is associated with which of these 1950s inventions?

a. polio vaccine   **c.** transistor

b. satellites   **d.** Sunbelt

History's Impact video program
Review the video to answer the closing question:
How did Americans' knowledge of other places
change after the introduction of the television?

Comprehension and Critical Thinking

SECTION 1 *(pp. 848–853)*

7. a. Identify What is the significance of each of the following to the events described in this section? Hungary, Vietnam, Egypt

b. Contrast How did Eisenhower claim to differ in his ideas about foreign policy compared with Truman?

c. Evaluate Do you think that Eisenhower actually was different from Truman in the way that he claimed? Explain your answer.

SECTION 2 *(pp. 854–860)*

8. a. Describe What was the arms race, and how did it evolve in the 1950s?

b. Summarize How did the arms race in the 1950s change the concept of victory and defeat in war?

c. Evaluate What were some effects of the government's efforts to educate people about how to respond to a nuclear attack? Why do you think people responded this way?

SECTION 3 *(pp. 861–867)*

9. a. Recall What were some of the major technological advancements of the 1950s?

b. Draw Conclusions How did the economic prosperity of the 1950s also present certain challenges to the country?

c. Rank In your opinion, which was the most significant technological change of the 1950s in terms of its long-term impact on the nation? Explain your reasoning.

Using the Internet

go.hrw.com
Practice Online
Keyword: SD7 CH26

10. *I Love Lucy* and other programs captivated the attention of American television audiences during the 1950s. Some of those TV programs are still broadcast on cable and satellite channels today. Using the keyword above, do research to learn more about popular television programs of the 1950s. Then create a report that explains the appeal of those programs in the 1950s and why some of those programs remain popular among some audiences today. Refer to specific examples from your research.

Analyzing Primary Sources

Reading Like a Historian The photograph shows an example of a bomb shelter from the 1950s.

11. Identify Who do you think might be interested and able to buy and install a bomb shelter?

12. Draw Conclusions How long do you think someone could survive in the type of shelter shown here?

Critical Reading

Read the passage from Section 1 under the heading "Cold War 'Hot Spots.'" Then answer the following question.

13. According to this passage, Eisenhower believed that

A it would be foolish to fight over communism in Vietnam.

B it was necessary to fight over communism in Vietnam.

C the French had failed to hold the line against Communist aggression.

D the United States would be better off waiting to see what happened in Vietnam and then reacting.

WRITING FOR THE SAT

Think about the following issue:

In Vietnam, following the departure of the French, it appeared that a truly free election might lead to the election of a Communist regime that was friendly with the Soviet Union.

14. Assignment Was the United States correct to support the creation of an anti-Communist South Vietnam? Write a short essay in which you develop your position on this issue. Support your point of view with reasoning and examples from your reading and studies.

UNIT 8 IN BRIEF

Below is a chapter-by-chapter summary of the main ideas covered in Unit 8.

CHAPTER 23 World War II Erupts
1939–1941

MAIN IDEA After World War I, unsettled conditions in Europe and beyond led to the rise of ruthless dictators. One of these leaders, Germany's Adolf Hitler, led Europe into another great war in 1939. The United States was eventually drawn into World War II after being attacked by Germany's ally, Japan.

SECTION 1 The Treaty of Versailles helped create conditions for the rise of powerful dictators.

SECTION 2 Appeasement failed to stop Hitler's aggression. On September 1, 1939, Germany invaded Poland, starting World War II. Within a year, only Great Britain stood between Hitler and control of Europe.

SECTION 3 As tensions grew in Europe and Asia in the 1930s, President Roosevelt slowly overcame isolationist feeling in the United States. That feeling was shattered completely with Japan's attack on Pearl Harbor on December 7, 1941.

SECTION 4 The United States mobilized its military forces and its industries to fight World War II. The effort changed the nation and gave new opportunities to women and minority groups.

CHAPTER 24 United States in World War II
1941–1945

MAIN IDEA World War II was fought in two theaters. Hard fighting by the Allies brought victory first in Europe and then in the Pacific.

SECTION 1 With the American entry into the war, the Allies focused first on Europe. As the Soviets fought desperately on their home soil, the rest of the Allies invaded North Africa and then, on D-Day, France.

SECTION 2 Adolf Hitler pursued first the persecution of Jews and then their systematic destruction. The resulting Holocaust claimed 6 million innocent lives.

SECTION 3 After early losses, the Allies won a key victory in the Battle of Midway. This was followed by a series of hard-fought victories, including battles at Iwo Jima and Okinawa.

SECTION 4 Americans at home worked hard to support the war. The attack on Pearl Harbor led the government to intern thousands of innocent Japanese Americans.

SECTION 5 By late 1944 the Germans were under pressure from both east and west by the Allies. They finally surrendered in May 1945. Meanwhile, the Japanese only surrendered after the Americans dropped two atomic weapons in early August 1945.

CHAPTER 25 The Cold War Begins
1945–1953

MAIN IDEA After World War II, the United States took its place as a world leader and an adversary of the Soviet Union in the Cold War.

SECTION 1 Tensions between the United States and the Soviet Union that had simmered during the war rose to the surface in the postwar years, resulting in the start of the Cold War.

SECTION 2 The United States helped its own people adjust to the return of peacetime with the GI Bill. It also helped lead the rest of the world toward a more peaceful future through the creation of the United Nations.

SECTION 3 A Communist takeover of China and the Soviet acquisition of an atomic bomb led to a Second Red Scare, led by Senator Joseph McCarthy.

SECTION 4 Cold War tensions led to war in Korea, as the United States and its United Nations allies took a stand against Communist aggression.

CHAPTER 26 Postwar America
1945–1960

MAIN IDEA In the 1950s Cold War conflict and a nuclear arms race worried many Americans, who nevertheless found diversion in television and other new ways of living.

SECTION 1 Dwight D. Eisenhower became president in 1952 and helped bring about a tough approach toward communism.

SECTION 2 The development of the hydrogen bomb and the growing arms race between the United States and the Soviet Union created great anxiety for many people.

SECTION 3 The introduction of the television and other new technologies led to significant changes in the way of life of many Americans.

A Nation Facing Challenges

1954–1975

Themes

Government and Democracy
Government enacted social and economic welfare programs, such as poverty relief, conservation, and urban renewal.

Rights and Responsibilities
Citizens called for racial equality for African Americans and other minorities, equality for women, and social and political reforms.

Global Relations
The threat of communism led to conflicts with the Soviet Union and Cuba and the involvement of the United States in the Vietnam War.

Civil rights leader Martin Luther King Jr. leads a march in Selma, Alabama.

Prepare to Read

Making Generalizations

Find practice for **Making Generalizations** in the **Skills Handbook,** p. H13

A generalization is a broad statement that tells how different examples are similar in some way. Experienced readers make generalizations that enable them to understand and remember what they are reading.

Before You Read
Read the headings to determine what the passage will be about. Then make a mental list of what you already know about the subject matter.

While You Read
List facts from the passage. How do they compare with your prior knowledge of the subject matter?

After You Read
Use your prior knowledge and facts from the reading to make a generalization about what the passage means to you.

Kennedy's Media Strategy

Presidents before and after Kennedy have been masters of the media. Franklin Delano Roosevelt used his radio "fireside chats" to inspire the nation during the Great Depression and World War II. Ronald Reagan, an experienced radio, television, and film actor, became known as the Great Communicator for his skill in conveying his messages directly to the voters. But Kennedy was the first president to consciously use access to the media as part of his strategy for governing the nation.

Image and reality Photographs of the president often showed him engaged in athletic activities like sailing, swimming, or playing touch football. Kennedy understood how such pictures would shape his image and boost his appeal. Like Roosevelt, he understood that images showing him in less-than-top physical shape might lessen the country's confidence in his abilities. In reality, Kennedy struggled with health problems most of his life. He suffered from Addison's disease, a sometimes fatal condition. A bad back kept him in nearly constant pain.

READING CHECK **Making Generalizations**
How is an effective use of the media important to presidents?

> The passage mentions more than one president.

> Kennedy and Roosevelt both tried to convey images of strength.

Test Prep Tip

Some tests may ask you to make generalizations from a given reading passage. Look for clue words such as *all, everyone, many, most, few, generally, never, often, always,* and *usually* that indicate generalizations. Then make sure that the facts in the passage support the entire generalization.

Evaluating Sources

Find practice for **Evaluating Sources** in the **Skills Handbook,** p. H34

Historians evaluate sources in many ways. They consider the author of a source. They think about where, when, and why a source was created. Most historians believe that the closer in time and place an author is to a given event, the more likely it is that the source is a reliable one.

Strategies historians use:

- What was the author's intent in creating the source? Is the source meant to persuade, inform, or entertain?
- What historical events were occurring at the time the source describes? What events does the source depict?
- How soon after the event was the source created? Did the author have firsthand knowledge of the event?

Photojournalism often combines text and a photograph. Its purpose is to inform and express a point of view. The word *savage* has a negative and violent connotation.

Civil rights activists used marches and other forms of nonviolent protest to spur change.

This photograph was taken and published at about the same time that the events were occurring. The photograph is a primary source.

Skills FOCUS   READING LIKE A HISTORIAN

As You Read Try to determine the author of the source, the intended audience, and the author's purpose.
As You Study Use the time-and-place rule to evaluate the reliability of each historical source. Use reliable sources to help you understand historical context.

The New Frontier and the Great Society

THE BIG PICTURE John F. Kennedy proposed a New Frontier to find solutions for "unsolved problems of peace and war, unconquered pockets of ignorance and prejudice, unanswered questions of poverty and surplus." In Lyndon Johnson's Great Society, every citizen had the right to health care, education, housing, and equal opportunities.

New York Standards

Key Idea 2 Important ideas, social and cultural values, beliefs, and traditions from New York State and United States history illustrate the connections and interactions of people and events across time and from a variety of perspectives.

Key Idea 3 Study about the major social, political, economic, cultural, and religious developments in New York State and United States history involves learning about the important roles and contributions of individuals and groups.

Skills FOCUS **READING LIKE A HISTORIAN**

Astronaut John Glenn (right) shows President Kennedy the interior of space capsule *Friendship 7*, the vessel in which Glenn became the first American to orbit the Earth. Winning the race to conquer space was an important Cold War goal for President Kennedy.
Interpreting Visuals What is Kennedy's reaction to the space capsule?

See **Skills Handbook**, p. H30

U.S.

January 1961
President John F. Kennedy is inaugurated.

1961

World

April 1961
Soviets launch the first manned orbiting spacecraft.

August 1961
East Germany closes crossing points between East and West Berlin.

History's Impact video program

Watch the video to understand the impact of space technology.

November 1963
President Kennedy is assassinated. Lyndon B. Johnson becomes president.

July 1964
Congress passes Civil Rights Act of 1964.

July 1965
Congress funds Medicaid and Medicare.

January 1968
U.S. Navy spy ship *Pueblo* is captured by North Korea.

1963   **1965**   **1967**   **1969**

October 1964
Khrushchev is forced to resign as Soviet leader.

January 1966
Indira Gandhi becomes India's first woman prime minister.

August 1968
Soviet army crushes revolt in Czechoslovakia.

877

SECTION 1 Kennedy and the Cold War

BEFORE YOU READ

MAIN IDEA

President Kennedy continued the Cold War policy of resisting the spread of communism by offering help to other nations and threatening to use force if necessary.

READING FOCUS

1. In what ways did Kennedy's election as president suggest change?
2. Why did the Bay of Pigs invasion take place, and with what results?
3. Why did the Berlin crisis develop, and what was its outcome?
4. What caused the Cuban missile crisis, and how was war avoided?
5. How did Kennedy's foreign policy reflect his view of the world?

KEY TERMS AND PEOPLE

John F. Kennedy
Robert Kennedy
Fidel Castro
Bay of Pigs invasion
Lyndon B. Johnson
Cuban missile crisis
Peace Corps
Alliance for Progress
flexible response

PI **2.5** Analyze the United States involvement in foreign affairs and a willingness to engage in international politics, examining the ideas and traditions leading to these foreign policies.

The Great Debates

THE INSIDE STORY

How does television shape public opinion? On September 26, 1960, some 70 million Americans watched Vice President Richard Nixon and Senator John Kennedy in the first televised presidential debate. Nixon was just two weeks out of the hospital. During that time he had covered 15,000 miles, campaigning in 25 states. He had lost so much weight that his shirt collar sagged around his neck. On the day of the debate, he pored over his notes until just before air time.

Kennedy had a leisurely dinner and took a nap before the debate. Still tan from several days of campaigning in sunny California, he refused the traditional TV makeup. Nixon refused makeup too. In his gray suit, Nixon looked pale, ill, and tired. Kennedy's dark suit and deep tan added to his rested and fit appearance.

The hour-long debate was broadcast on both radio and television. Radio listeners thought Nixon narrowly won, while those watching on television gave Kennedy the edge. For days afterward, huge crowds turned out at campaign rallies to see the handsome candidate in the flesh. In contrast, Nixon's staff reassured his supporters that "Mr. Nixon is in excellent health and looks good in person."

Three more debates took place. Although some reporters at the time called them the Great Debates, the Kennedy-Nixon debates probably did not change the outcome of the 1960 election. They did increase the average American's interest in politics, however. The debates also set the standard for modern election campaigns. Voters today expect candidates for office at practically every level to appear in televised debates. ◼

◀ **Kennedy's appearance gave him great appeal to a television audience.**

Kennedy Becomes President

The personal contrasts between **John F. Kennedy** and Richard Nixon were far greater than their political differences in the 1960 presidential campaign. Kennedy was born into a wealthy and politically powerful Massachusetts family, while Nixon was a self-made "common man" from a small town in southern California.

Although the two men were about the same age, Kennedy's movie-star good looks made him appear much younger. During their four television debates, he spoke with ease and authority. To many Americans, the 43-year-old senator represented America's future. Nixon's ties to the 70-year-old Eisenhower made him seem a part of America's past.

The election of 1960 Kennedy emphasized this contrast by adopting the term "new frontier" for his campaign. "There are new frontiers for America to conquer," he declared, "not frontiers on a map, but frontiers of the mind, the will, and the spirit of man."

During the election campaign, Kennedy played on the nation's Cold War fears by claiming the United States had fallen behind the Soviet Union in the development of nuclear missiles. He also claimed that the prosperity of the 1950s was not reaching the poor. "Seventeen million Americans go to bed hungry at night," Kennedy charged. Vice President Nixon defended President Eisenhower's record, which made him appear opposed to new ideas.

Despite Kennedy's personal appeal, some Protestant voters were concerned because he was a Roman Catholic. They feared that Kennedy might put the views of the Catholic Church over those of the American public. The election of 1960 was one of the closest in American history. Fewer than 120,000 votes separated the two candidates out of nearly 69 million ballots cast.

Kennedy's victory by a 303–219 margin in the electoral college was more comfortable. He became the youngest person and the first Catholic elected president. Fifteen southern electors, however, cast their ballots for Virginia's Democratic senator Harry Byrd, who was not even a candidate. This weakness in Kennedy's southern support coupled with his narrow victory in the popular vote would later cause problems for his presidency.

One incident in October might have helped Kennedy's election campaign. Civil rights leader Martin Luther King Jr. was arrested in Georgia during a protest. Kennedy telephoned King's wife, Coretta, to express his concern. **Robert Kennedy**, the candidate's brother, persuaded the judge to release King on bail.

King's father told the press he had planned to vote for Nixon but that Kennedy's call to his daughter-in-law had changed his mind. The Kennedy campaign printed 2 million leaflets that told the story of this incident. The leaflets were passed out in African American churches the Sunday before election day.

Kennedy takes office Kennedy's inaugural address focused on his theme of change. It also took a strong anti-Communist tone.

HISTORY'S VOICES

> ❝Let the word go forth from this time and place, to friend and foe alike, that the torch has been passed to a new generation of Americans—born in this century, tempered by war, disciplined by a hard and bitter peace . . . Let every nation know, whether it wishes us well or ill, that we shall pay any price, bear any burden, meet any hardship, support any friend, oppose any foe, in order to assure the survival and the success of liberty.❞
> —John F. Kennedy, Inaugural Address, January 20, 1961

ACADEMIC VOCABULARY
authority firm self-assurance

Inauguration
Inauguration day was sunny but cold. Despite the 20-degree weather, the Kennedys greeted the American people from an open car in the inaugural parade.

LIFE THE KENNEDY INAUGURATION
JANUARY 27, 1961 20 CENTS

In his inaugural address, Kennedy did not specify his policy goals at home because so much division existed over domestic issues. However, he made accomplishing domestic goals a top priority. "If we are to regain . . . leadership on our domestic problems, it must be presidential leadership," he maintained.

To advance his programs, Kennedy gathered a group of advisers that some people called "the best and the brightest." National Security Adviser McGeorge Bundy had been a dean at Harvard University. Special Assistant Arthur Schlesinger had taught history there. Another adviser was a professor at Massachusetts Institute of Technology (MIT).

Most of Kennedy's advisers were young like he was—some were still in their 30s. Ted Sorensen, who helped develop domestic policies and programs, was just 32 years old. Kennedy called Sorensen his "intellectual blood bank." But no one was closer to the president than his own brother, Robert ("Bobby") Kennedy. He included his 36-year-old brother in his cabinet by making him attorney general.

Except for Bobby, cabinet members had less influence on President Kennedy than did his White House advisers. In foreign affairs, for example, Kennedy relied more on National Security Adviser Bundy than on Secretary of State Dean Rusk or Secretary of Defense Robert McNamara. Kennedy also held cabinet meetings less often than Eisenhower did— only once a month unless Kennedy cancelled the meeting. At an average age of 47, President Kennedy's cabinet was relatively young. Its members averaged 10 years younger than President Eisenhower's.

READING CHECK **Contrasting** How did Kennedy differ from Eisenhower as president?

The Bay of Pigs Invasion

Kennedy would soon need Rusk and McNamara's advice as well as that of Bundy. During the 1960 campaign, Kennedy learned that the Central Intelligence Agency (CIA) was secretly training about 1,500 Cuban exiles in Central America in order to invade Cuba. Many of the trainees were Cuban Americans the CIA had recruited in south Florida. President Eisenhower had authorized the project in the hope of overthrowing Cuba's dictator **Fidel Castro**.

Background to the invasion Fidel Castro came to power in Cuba in 1959 after a two-year guerrilla war against Fulgencio Batista, the U.S.-backed dictator of Cuba. As Castro's followers increased in number, his tactics grew bolder. When his rebel force marched on Havana, Cuba's capital city, Batista fled the country. On January 8, 1959, Castro entered Havana and declared victory.

During his revolt, Castro gained the support of many Cubans by promising to restore people's rights and freedoms. Once in power, however, he

Communist Neighbor
Fidel Castro established the first Communist nation in the Western Hemisphere. He railed against the United States in speeches and forged ties between Cuba and the Soviet Union. *Why did the U.S. government find Castro's actions so alarming?*

followed a more radical course. His government seized private businesses, including American companies on the island. In addition, Castro began making anti-American speeches. U.S.-Cuban relations were further strained when Castro signed a trade agreement with the Soviet Union in February 1960. Eisenhower responded by cutting off American economic and diplomatic ties with Cuba.

The invasion of Cuba The CIA believed an invasion of Cuba would inspire its people to rise up against Castro. Eisenhower doubted this prediction, but he let planning continue to keep all options open. Besides, he knew that the new president would have to make the decision whether to approve an invasion.

Kennedy asked his advisers about the plan to invade Cuba. Opinions were mixed. Schlesinger was openly and strongly opposed. "You would dissipate [lose] all the extraordinary good will . . . toward the new administration throughout the world," he warned.

The president was in a bind. He considered Castro's communism a threat to all of Latin America. In fact, Kennedy had attacked Eisenhower during the campaign for not taking stronger action against Castro. He felt that he could not back down now. When the CIA assured Kennedy that the invasion would succeed, he gave the go-ahead.

The **Bay of Pigs invasion** was a disaster. The *New York Times* reported the plan a week before the invasion began. Kennedy publicly denied the story. Then on April 15, 1961, an air strike by old, unmarked U.S. bombers flown from Nicaragua by Cuban exiles failed to destroy Cuba's air force. Even worse, a bomber damaged in the attack landed at Key West, Florida, instead of returning to Nicaragua. With the U.S. connection now exposed, Kennedy cancelled additional air strikes on Cuba that had been planned for April 16 and 17.

The land invasion on April 17 had little chance of success. Warned by the air attack, Castro was prepared. When the force of Cuban exiles came ashore at the Bay of Pigs, Castro's troops rushed to the scene. Pinned down at their landing site, the invaders fought for nearly three days.

Former vice president Nixon and others urged Kennedy to send U.S. troops to Cuba to rescue the invasion force and overthrow

Skills FOCUS   **READING LIKE A HISTORIAN**

Interpreting Visuals What comment is the cartoonist making on Kennedy's dealings with Cuba? What specific incident do you think the cartoon is referencing?

Castro. Concerned about how such a response might affect U.S.-Soviet relations, the president rejected this advice.

Poor planning and the lack of U.S. air cover had doomed the Bay of Pigs invasion to failure. Also, the CIA had greatly underestimated Castro's support. The expected anti-Castro uprising in Cuba never took place. The nearly 1,200 surviving invaders were captured and put in prison. In December 1962 Kennedy obtained their release in return for $52 million in food and medical aid to Cuba.

Instead of eliminating the threat of communism so close to the United States, the Bay of Pigs incident actually strengthened Castro's ties to the Soviet Union. Increasingly, he looked to the Soviets for protection from the United States. Soviet leader Nikita Khrushchev welcomed the closer relations. "We shall render [the] Cuban government all necessary assistance," he declared.

READING CHECK   **Drawing Conclusions** Why did Kennedy decide to go ahead with the CIA's plan to invade Cuba?

The Berlin Crisis

ACADEMIC VOCABULARY
interpreted understood within the context of the circumstances

One reason Kennedy rejected sending U.S. forces into Cuba was that he feared it would cause Khrushchev to retaliate in Europe. Khrushchev, however, interpreted Kennedy's failure to intervene in Cuba as a sign of weakness. It encouraged Khrushchev to press the United States in Berlin.

The Vienna conference Kennedy invited Khrushchev to meet with him in Vienna, Austria, in June 1961. The president hoped to ease tensions with the Soviet Union. Instead, Khrushchev demanded that the United States and its allies recognize Communist East Germany as an independent nation. He also demanded that the United States withdraw from West Berlin.

Khrushchev said he would sign a treaty with East Germany in December if these demands were not met. He warned that East Germany could then decide for itself what to do about Berlin. Kennedy would not be bullied.

Berlin's significance Berlin had long been a problem for the Soviet Union. The western half of the city was an island of freedom surrounded by East Germany. In the first half of 1961 alone, about 200,000 East Germans escaped communism by slipping past guards to safety in West Berlin.

Some of Kennedy's advisers were concerned that East Germany might use force to gain control of West Berlin. All agreed that Khrushchev was using Berlin to test America's will in Europe and that any action East Germany took would have the approval and backing of the Soviet Union.

Determined to meet the Soviet test, Kennedy acted to show America's strength and resolve. He called reserve troops to active duty, launched a program to build shelters in the United States against nuclear attack, and began a troop buildup in West Germany. Khrushchev responded by threatening to mobilize troops. Realizing how dangerous the situation had become, Kennedy waited for the Soviet leader to make the next move.

The Berlin Wall Khrushchev's response came on August 13, 1961, when Communist forces closed the crossing points between East and West Berlin. Within hours, some 25,000 East German soldiers were in place to guard a hastily erected barbed wire barrier around West Berlin. The temporary fencing was soon replaced with a high concrete wall, to block further escapes to freedom.

Kennedy responded to the construction of the Berlin Wall by sending 1,500 troops from West Germany to West Berlin. Vice President **Lyndon B. Johnson** visited West Berlin to reassure its people that America would not abandon them. Kennedy, however, was relieved. He believed that Khrushchev would now not attempt to seize West Berlin. "A wall is a . . . lot better than a war," he concluded.

The Berlin Wall divided families, neighborhoods, streets, and even cemeteries. As time passed it was extended and fortified. The concrete sections eventually spanned most of the nearly 100 miles around West Berlin. Trenches were dug to keep vehicles from crashing though the wall. The East Germans later built a second wall parallel to the first one. The corridor between the two walls was patrolled by soldiers and attack dogs.

Nearly two years after the crisis was past, Kennedy went to West Berlin to renew his commitment to the city. At an outdoor rally near the Berlin Wall, he gave one of the greatest speeches of his presidency—his *"Ich bin ein Berliner"* ("I am a Berliner") speech. Speaking in English, he noted the wall's importance as a symbol of the failures of communism.

HISTORY'S VOICES

❝There are many people in the world who really don't understand . . . the great issue between the free world and the communist world. Let them come to Berlin. There are some who say that communism is the wave of the future. Let them come to Berlin. And there are some who say in Europe and elsewhere we can work with the communists. Let them come to Berlin.❞

—John F. Kennedy, June 26, 1963

As the huge crowd cheered wildly, Kennedy ended his speech by declaring, "All free men, wherever they may live, are citizens of Berlin, and, therefore, as a free man I take pride in the words *'Ich bin ein Berliner.'*"

READING CHECK **Identifying Cause and Effect** Why was the Berlin Wall constructed?

★ Interactive

HISTORY CLOSE-UP

The Berlin Wall

The Berlin Wall was built in 1961 to block East Germans from escaping to freedom in West Berlin. Part of the wall divided the city itself, separating its democratic and Communist sectors. This scene shows the wall in Berlin as it looked in 1963, the year President Kennedy visited the city.

BERLIN

N W E S

Berlin

GERMAN DEMOCRATIC REPUBLIC (East Germany)

FEDERAL REPUBLIC OF GERMANY (West Germany)

0   100   200 Miles
0   100   200 Kilometers

EAST BERLIN
A fenced "death strip" existed on the East German side of the wall. Persons who entered this zone without permission often were shot.

Only authorized persons could pass into or out of West Berlin. This took place at closely guarded checkpoints.

WEST BERLIN
The Berlin Wall divided families as well as the land itself. Relatives had to settle for distant looks and shouted conversations over the wall. Actual visits were rare.

Watchtowers equipped with searchlights, machine guns, and East German sharpshooters surveyed the death strip. Later, unmanned automatic firing systems were installed that shot any moving thing detected in the death strip.

Tank traps and barbed wire prevented vehicles from crashing through the fence that marked the death strip. They also made escape more difficult for those trying to flee on foot.

Skills FOCUS INTERPRETING INFOGRAPHICS

go.hrw.com
Interactive
Keyword: SD7 CH27

The Berlin Wall was much more than mortar and bricks, but a system of barriers, guards, and deterrents.

Interpreting Visuals What were the methods used to keep people from crossing from East Berlin into West Berlin?

See **Skills Handbook**, p. H18

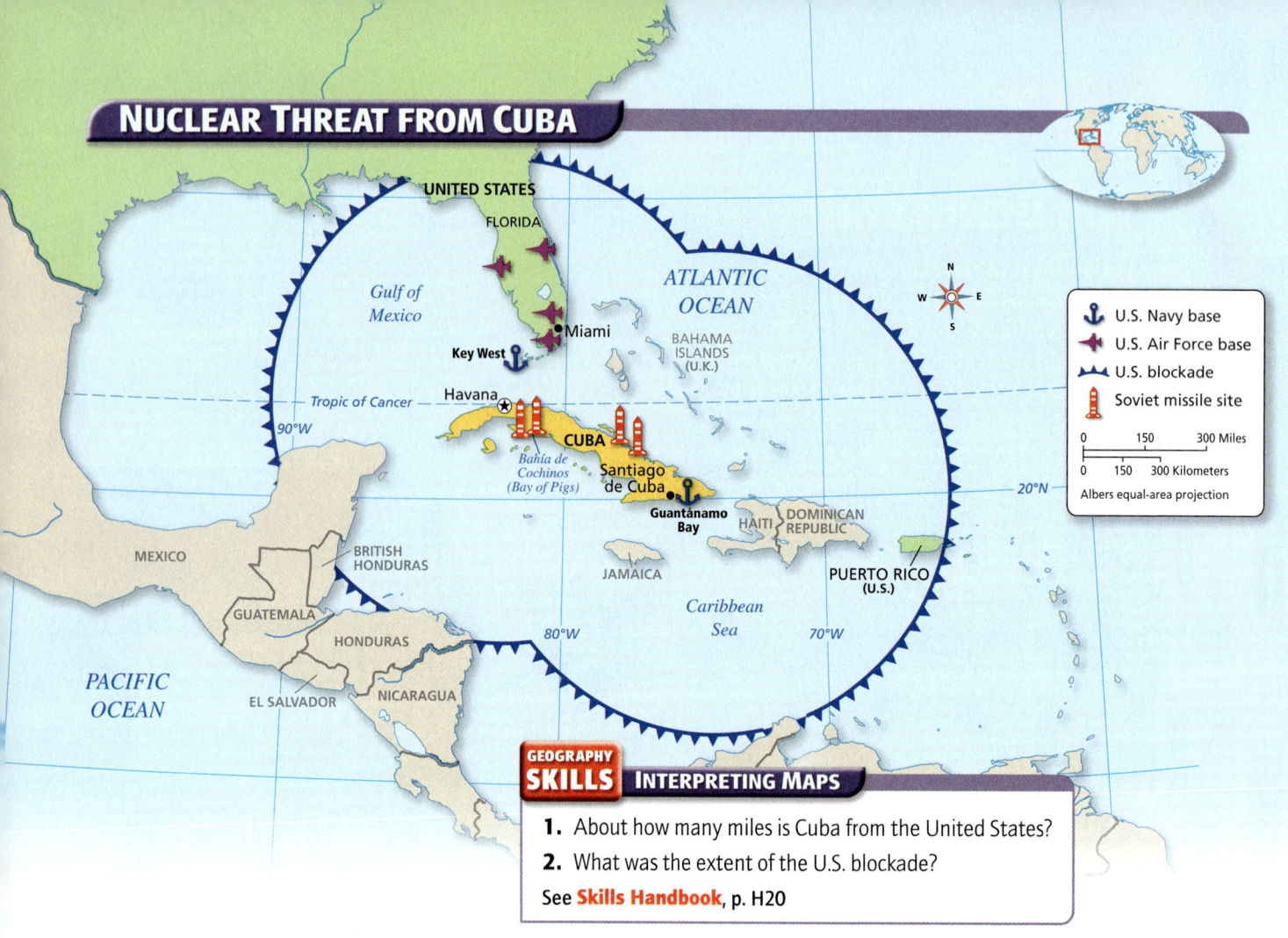

GEOGRAPHY SKILLS INTERPRETING MAPS

1. About how many miles is Cuba from the United States?
2. What was the extent of the U.S. blockade?

See **Skills Handbook**, p. H20

The Cuban Missile Crisis

Khrushchev's continued testing of Kennedy's resolve led to the Cold War's most dangerous crisis. For several days in October 1962, the United States and the Soviet Union teetered on the brink of nuclear war as Kennedy sought a peaceful solution to the Cuban missile crisis.

Buildup to the crisis The origins of the Cuban missile crisis can be found in the policies and politics of both the United States and the Soviet Union. U.S. actions in the Bay of Pigs and Berlin crises encouraged hard-line leaders in the Soviet Union. They pushed Khrushchev to be more aggressive.

Some Americans continued to call for an invasion of Cuba after the Bay of Pigs. This concerned Khrushchev because he had pledged to defend Cuba. The Soviets were also concerned about nuclear missiles the United States had placed in Turkey. Khrushchev thought this threat on the Soviet Union's southwestern border justified putting similar missiles near the southern border of the United States.

Kennedy faced similar pressures. Some American politicians blamed him for the Bay of Pigs disaster and accused him of being "soft on communism." Republicans announced that Cuba would be their main issue in the 1962 congressional election campaign. Khrushchev decided to upgrade Cuba's defenses with antiaircraft weapons called surface-to-air missiles (SAMs). He also convinced Castro to allow the secret installation of offensive nuclear missiles that would be controlled by the Soviet Union.

The crisis begins Republicans' pressure on Kennedy increased as Khrushchev pumped aid into Cuba. Kennedy responded by ordering U-2 spy-plane flights over the island. On August 29, 1962, one of these flights detected the SAMs.

The Soviets pointed out that the SAMs were defensive missiles. They denied charges they were placing offensive missiles in Cuba. Kennedy reported the Soviets' denial to the nation, warning that if it proved untrue, "the gravest issues would arise." Moscow replied that a U.S. attack on Cuba would mean war.

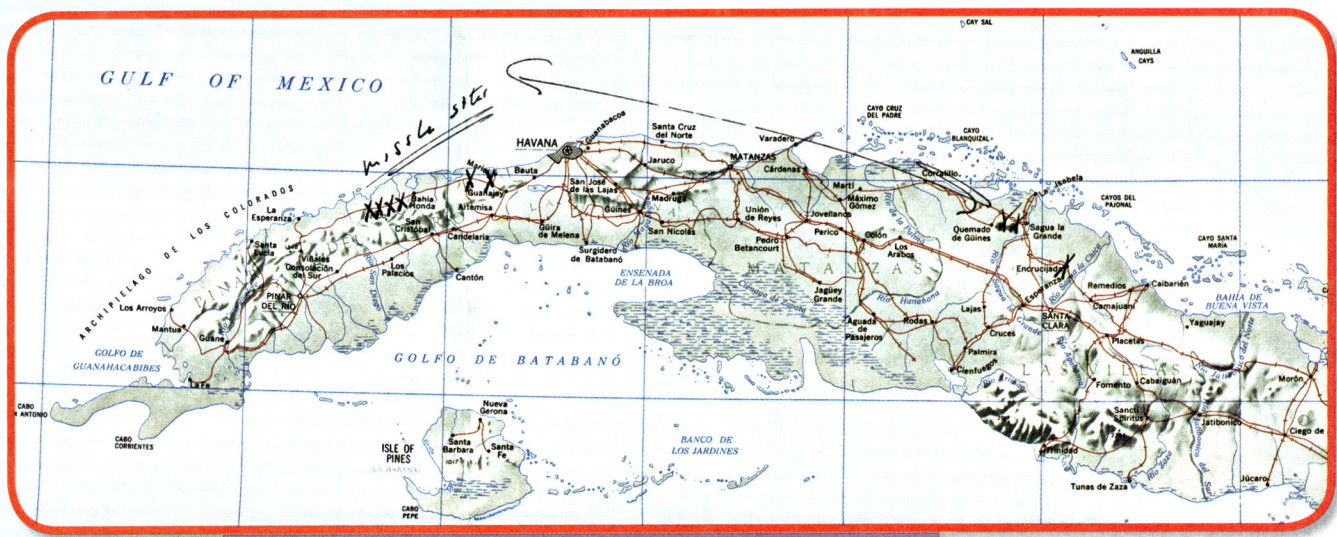

At a Cabinet briefing during the Cuban missile crisis, President Kennedy marked this map of Cuba with a series of X marks, the words *missile sites,* and a black arrow to show locations of Soviet activity as photographed by U-2 spy planes.

As administration officials continued to assure the American people, the spy flights continued. Then on October 14, photos taken from a U-2 plane provided the first solid evidence that the Soviets had lied.

Managing the crisis Kennedy assembled a group of advisers, known as the Ex Comm, to help him decide on a response. He usually did not attend the Ex Comm's daily meetings. He wanted to follow his normal schedule until he was ready to reveal what he knew to the Soviets and to the American people.

Ex Comm's military members favored an air strike against the missile sites, perhaps followed by an invasion of Cuba. Secretary of Defense McNamara and Robert Kennedy argued for a naval blockade instead. Like an air strike, the blockade would be an act of war, but it seemed less likely to provoke a missile launch from Cuba or the Soviet Union. A blockade would also give the Soviets the chance to avoid war by removing the missiles themselves. The president agreed with this reasoning.

On October 22, Kennedy went on television to tell Americans about the Soviet threat. He put U.S. forces on full alert. Some 550 bombers armed with nuclear weapons took to the air and 100,000 troops assembled in Georgia. He wanted to be prepared for war and to show Khrushchev the seriousness of the situation.

As the world nervously watched and waited, several Soviet ships carrying missile parts continued toward Cuba. Khrushchev warned that trying to stop them would mean war. Then on October 24, as they neared the U.S. blockade, they turned back.

Two days later, Kennedy received a letter from Khrushchev offering to remove the missiles if the United States pledged to never invade Cuba. The next day he received a tougher letter from Khrushchev demanding that the United States remove its missiles from Turkey. The Ex Comm advised Kennedy to ignore the second letter and accept the offer in the first letter. The president did so, and Khrushchev announced he would dismantle the missiles.

Effects of the crisis This incident is the closest the world has ever come to nuclear war. Kennedy and Khrushchev both took steps to ease tensions between their countries. In 1963 they set up a hotline to allow U.S. presidents and Soviet leaders to communicate directly in times of crisis. The United States, the Soviet Union, and Great Britain also signed the Limited Nuclear Test Ban Treaty to end the testing of nuclear weapons in the atmosphere and underwater.

Government
Kennedy's pledge that the United States would never invade Cuba caused many Cuban Americans to switch their support to the Republican Party. The Cuban American community remains strongly Republican today.

READING CHECK **Drawing Inferences** Why was the Cuban missile crisis such an important event?

Kennedy's Foreign Policy

In a 1963 speech at American University in Washington, D.C., Kennedy answered those who criticized his foreign policy. He summarized the values he thought should guide America's relations with other nations.

HISTORY'S VOICES

> ❝What kind of peace do we seek? Not a [peace] enforced on the world by American weapons of war . . . not merely peace for Americans but peace for all men and women . . . For, in the final analysis, our most basic common link is that we all inhabit this small planet. We all breathe the same air. We all cherish our children's future. And we are all mortal.❞
>
> —John F. Kennedy, June 10, 1963

Kennedy also tried to express these principles in his foreign policy through programs to help poorer nations. The **Peace Corps** was the most successful. This entity trained and sent volunteers to Africa, Asia, and Latin America to serve for two years as educators, health care workers, and agricultural advisers, or in other jobs that aided the host country's development. The Peace Corps encouraged women and African Americans to volunteer.

ACADEMIC VOCABULARY

entity something that has a separate and distinct existence

Most volunteers were young college graduates. They were instructed not to argue the merits of U.S. foreign policy and to respect the culture of their host country. The program increased goodwill toward the United States throughout the world.

Another of Kennedy's foreign-policy programs was the **Alliance for Progress**. It offered billions of dollars in aid to build schools, hospitals, roads, low-cost housing, and power plants in Latin America. The program was intended to counter communism's influence in the region. It never lived up to its hopes, partly because aid often went to anti-Communist dictators who had little support among their people.

In other areas Kennedy followed the Cold War policies of his predecessors. He continued the nuclear arms buildup begun by Eisenhower as well as Truman's practice of containment. He also developed the strategy of **flexible response**. This involved strengthening conventional American forces so the nation would have other options than nuclear weapons in times of crisis.

READING CHECK **Summarizing** How did the Peace Corps and the Alliance for Progress help other nations?

SECTION 1 ASSESSMENT

go.hrw.com
Online Quiz
Keyword: SD7 HP27

Reviewing Ideas, Terms, and People

1. **a. Define** What did **John F. Kennedy** mean by the term "new frontier"?
   b. Analyze In what ways did Kennedy represent change to the American people?
   c. Elaborate How do you think Kennedy chose his advisers?

2. **a. Describe** Why were U.S.-Cuban relations strained when Kennedy took office?
   b. Make Inferences Why would a strong Soviet alliance with a Latin American nation make the United States uneasy?
   c. Predict Do you think the **Bay of Pigs invasion** could have been more successful? How?

3. **a. Identify** What demands did Khrushchev make at the conference in Vienna?
   b. Draw Conclusions Why was Kennedy relieved when he heard about the Berlin Wall?

4. **a. Recall** What was the immediate set of events that resulted in the **Cuban missile crisis**?
   b. Analyze Why did Kennedy choose a blockade over an air strike in dealing with Soviet missiles in Cuba?

   c. Evaluate Do you think Kennedy handled the Cuban missile crisis well? Is there anything he should have done differently?

Critical Thinking

5. **Identifying Cause and Effect** Review your notes on Cold War crises faced by President Kennedy's administration. Then copy the graphic organizer below and use it to identify the causes and effects of those crises.

Causes	Crisis	Effects

FOCUS ON WRITING

6. **Expository** President Kennedy and many other Americans believed that the Peace Corps was a good way to aid other nations. Would you be interested in becoming a Peace Corps volunteer? Write a paragraph explaining why or why not.

Kennedy's Thousand Days

BEFORE YOU READ

MAIN IDEA

John F. Kennedy brought energy, initiative, and important new ideas to the presidency.

READING FOCUS

1. What was Kennedy's New Frontier?
2. In what ways did the Warren Court change society in the early 1960s?
3. What impact did Kennedy's assassination have on the nation and the world?

KEY TERMS AND PEOPLE

Jacqueline Kennedy
New Frontier
mandate
Earl Warren
Warren Court
Lee Harvey Oswald
Warren Commission

PI 3.3 Prepare essays and oral reports about the important social, political, economic, scientific, technological, and cultural developments, issues, and events from New York State and United States history.

How did the Kennedys bring style and glamour to the White House?

John F. Kennedy brought something to the White House that had not been seen since the early 1900s—young children. The press carried pictures of the president's toddlers playing in the Oval Office and stories of their pony strolling through the White House gardens. The young family was shown sailing on the blue waters off Cape Cod, in Massachusetts. The image of youth and vitality was unmistakable. It was visual reinforcement of what Kennedy had promised at the start of his campaign—a "new generation of leadership."

In addition to youth, the Kennedy White House was a picture of style. The handsome young president was complemented by his glamorous first lady, Jacqueline. The pair dazzled observers with their movie-star appearance. But beyond the glittery exterior was a genuine appreciation of beauty. Jacqueline Kennedy made the White House a showplace for art, music, and theater. State dinners became cultural events. Many Americans responded with enthusiasm to her grace, charm, and sense of style.

Of course, Kennedy could not lead the nation on style alone. As you will read, the outward image of youth and vigor helped set a tone for politics and change that pushed the nation in new directions. ◢

▲ John and Jacqueline Kennedy brought youthful elegance to the White House.

Kennedy's New Frontier

Many Americans were struck by the youth and vitality of the Kennedy White House. Few presidents have been more available to the media. Even fewer have used it as successfully to obtain the public image they desired.

Image and reality Photographs of the president often showed him engaged in physical activities like sailing and swimming. Kennedy understood how such pictures would shape his image and boost his appeal. In reality, he struggled with health problems most of his life. He suffered from Addison's disease, a fatiguing and sometimes painful condition. A bad back kept him in nearly constant pain.

First lady **Jacqueline Kennedy** and the couple's two young children contributed to the sense of glamour and energy that surrounded Kennedy's presidency. Caroline and John Jr. were the first young children to live in the White House since 1908. Although Jacqueline Kennedy tried to protect the children's privacy, the president encouraged the press to photograph and write about them. He knew that this information also would help to create a favorable public opinion of his presidency.

Just 31 years old when Kennedy became president, Jacqueline was, like her husband, very attractive and from a wealthy family. "Jackie" was the more refined of the two and had a great interest in the arts. She made the White House the nation's unofficial cultural center by hosting elaborate events featuring world-famous artists and musicians.

Kennedy and Congress Americans seemed to like the Kennedys more than they liked his **New Frontier**. Because the president had spoken so often of a new frontier during the election campaign, this was the name given to his plans for changing the nation. Most Americans in the early 1960s were not reform minded, however.

The makeup of Congress reflected the American public's mood. Conservative southern Democrats often joined with Republicans to block many of Kennedy's proposals. In addition, Kennedy's narrow victory in the 1960 election denied him the clear **mandate**, or authorization to act, he needed to convince Congress that the people agreed with his plans.

For example, Kennedy asked Congress to reduce taxes to fight rising unemployment. This action would give consumers more money to

---

TRACING HISTORY

Exploration

Early explorers travelled the Earth in search of new places and experiences. Today such curiosity takes people into space and to robotic exploration of the oceans. Study the time line to learn about how key events in American history have transformed the nature of exploration over time.

ST 2.1 Discuss several schemes for periodizing the history of the United States.

ST 4.3 Develop hypotheses about important events, eras, or issues.

1804–1806 Lewis and Clark explore the new territory acquired by the United States in the Louisiana Purchase of 1803. The expedition included Sacagawea, a Shoshone guide.

1927 Charles A. Lindbergh makes the first nonstop transatlantic solo flight from New York to Paris.

1800

1900

1932 Amelia Earhart becomes the first woman to make a solo flight across the Atlantic Ocean. In 1937 she vanishes while attempting to fly around the world.

spend, which would lead businesses to produce more goods and hire more workers. Despite his urgings, Congress failed to act. Congressional leaders also ignored Kennedy's proposals to provide federal aid to education and to create a health care plan for older Americans.

In some cases Kennedy's popularity and presidential powers allowed him to solve problems without depending on Congress. For example, the nation's major steel producers announced big price increases in 1962. Kennedy was concerned this would lead to inflation. When some steel-company executives refused to roll back the price increases, he cancelled government contracts to buy steel from those companies. He also began a vigorous campaign against them in the media. The steel companies soon gave in to the president's pressure and cancelled their price increases.

Although Kennedy was among the nation's wealthiest presidents, he sought ways to help poor Americans. He convinced Congress to pass the Area Redevelopment Act in 1961, which gave financial assistance to economically distressed regions. Congress also created a program to retrain workers in areas with high unemployment and raised the minimum wage from $1.00 to $1.25 per hour.

The space program Kennedy's foreign-policy crises helped to create the program that came to symbolize the New Frontier—the exploration of space. In April 1961 the Soviet Union launched the first human into space in a one-orbit flight. It was nearly a year before U.S astronaut John Glenn matched the Soviet accomplishment.

Khrushchev claimed the Soviet lead in space showed the superiority of communism. Coupled with the Cold War embarrassment of the Bay of Pigs, Americans were dismayed. "Is there any place where we can catch them [the Soviets]?" President Kennedy asked his advisers. In May 1961 Kennedy made a bold proposal to Congress to restore America's world prestige.

HISTORY'S VOICES

❝This nation should commit itself to achieving the goal, before this decade is out, of landing a man on the moon and returning him safely to the earth. No single space project . . . will be more impressive to mankind, or more important for the long-range exploration of space . . . But in a very real sense, it will not be one man going to the moon . . . it will be an entire nation.❞

—John F. Kennedy, May 25, 1961

FOCUS ON NEW YORK

SCIENCE AND TECHNOLOGY

The NASA Goddard Institute for Space Studies (GISS) is located next door to Columbia University. It was established in 1961 to research planetary atmospheres. The GISS studies natural and human-made changes to the environment. A major goal of the GISS is to predict global climate change.

1962 Astronaut John Glenn becomes the first American to orbit the Earth.

1983 Astronaut Sally Ride becomes the first American woman in space on the space shuttle *Challenger*.

2005 Space shuttle engineer John Phillips dazzles the world by repairing the *Discovery* in space.

2000

1985 Robert Ballard discovers the wreck of RMS *Titanic* and revolutionizes undersea exploration by using remotely controlled submersible devices.

1947 USAF Major Chuck Yeager breaks the sound barrier by flying faster than the speed of sound.

1969 Astronaut Neil Armstrong becomes the first person to set foot on the moon.

The president also asked Congress to fund the unmanned exploration of space. These proposals made the space race as much a part of the Cold War as the conflict over Cuba had been. This race, however, was one the United States would win.

READING CHECK **Identifying Cause and Effect** Why did Kennedy propose a mission to the moon and the unmanned exploration of space?

The Warren Court

During Kennedy's presidency, Supreme Court decisions were responsible for major changes in American society. Under the leadership of Chief Justice **Earl Warren**, controversial Court rulings greatly extended individual rights and freedoms. Many historians regard Warren as second only to John Marshall as the most important chief justice. The Supreme Court's influence on the nation increased greatly during Warren's nearly 16 years as chief justice.

Earl Warren did not have a positive record on civil rights when President Eisenhower appointed him chief justice in 1953. As California's attorney general, Warren had called for the internment of Japanese Americans during World War II. Later, as governor of California, he fought against an effort to make the state's Assembly more representative of the people.

Yet as chief justice, Warren led the Court in 1954 to one of the most significant civil rights advances in U.S. history. He persuaded the other justices in *Brown* v. *Board of Education* to ban racial segregation in the nation's schools. You will read more about this landmark case in the next chapter.

Then in the early 1960s, the **Warren Court** issued a series of decisions concerning other reforms. These decisions required some of the legislative reforms Warren had opposed when he had been governor of California.

Voting-rights reform One significant reform made important changes in the way that legislative representation was determined. In the mid-1900s it was standard practice for states not to redraw the boundaries of their legislative districts to reflect changes in the population.

As cities grew, however, their representation in state legislatures did not. In Tennessee, for example, the boundaries of legislative districts had not changed since 1901. By 1960 densely populated urban areas had the same number of state legislators as sparsely populated rural regions.

In *Baker* v. *Carr* (1962), the Court declared that this situation denied urban voters the equal protection of law required by the Fourteenth Amendment. The Court went further in *Westberry* v. *Sanders* (1964) and *Reynolds* v. *Sims* (1964) when it ruled that legislative districts must have equal populations. This reform guaranteed that each citizen's vote has equal weight, a principle known as "one person, one vote."

The rights of the accused The Warren Court also extended the Bill of Rights to the actions of state governments. In *Mapp* v. *Ohio* (1961), the Court established that the search warrants required by the Fourth Amendment apply to state and local police too, not just to searches conducted by federal agents. In *Gideon* v. *Wainwright* (1963), the Supreme Court ruled that states must provide free lawyers to poor persons being tried for crimes. In *Escobedo* v. *Illinois* (1964), the justices decided that a person has a right to a lawyer during police questioning. In 1966 the Court extended these rights again in the case of *Miranda* v. *Arizona*. You will read more about this case in Landmark Supreme Court Cases at the end of this chapter.

Religious freedom In other important cases, the Warren Court defined the religion guarantees of the First Amendment. In *Engel* v. *Vitale* (1962), for example, the justices banned formal prayers in public schools. A year later the Court prohibited daily Bible readings in school. The Supreme Court ruled that both activities violated the First Amendment's guarantee that government would not make any religion the nation's "official" religion.

READING CHECK **Summarizing** How did the Warren Court extend individual rights and freedoms?

The Kennedy Assassination

As 1964 approached, President Kennedy worked to build support for his re-election campaign. To help win the backing of southern Democrats, Kennedy flew to Texas in late 1963. On November 22, President Kennedy rode in an open car of a motorcade through the city of Dallas to the site where he was to deliver a speech. With the first lady by his side, the president waved to the cheering crowds that lined his route.

Then shots rang out from the sixth floor of a schoolbook depository building as the motorcade passed by. Kennedy slumped over, fatally wounded. Within hours, Vice President Johnson, who was with the Kennedys on the trip, was sworn in as president aboard Air Force One.

Kennedy's tragic death shocked the nation and the world. People today still remember what they were doing when they heard the terrible news. Donna Shalala, who later served in President Bill Clinton's cabinet, was working with the Peace Corps in Iran at the time.

Death of a President

Left, President and Mrs. Kennedy shortly before the assassin's bullets struck. Right, Kennedy's widow, Jacqueline, and their children, John and Caroline, wait for the president's funeral to begin. *Why do you think it was important for the nation to have a state funeral?*

" I . . . recall a beggar walking up to me in the street and I said 'No, I don't have any money.' He said, 'I don't want any money. I just want to tell you how sorry I am that your young president died.' "

—Donna Shalala, quoted in *Ordinary Americans*

White House correspondent Helen Thomas later remarked, "The legacy of hope died with him. You never had that same sense again that we were moving forward."

The Warren Commission

Within hours of the shooting, Dallas police arrested **Lee Harvey Oswald**, a troubled loner with connections to the Soviet Union and Cuba. Two days later, as police were transferring Oswald from the Dallas Police Department to the county jail, Oswald was shot to death by Jack Ruby, a Dallas nightclub owner with ties to organized crime. These strange circumstances caused some people to question whether Oswald had acted alone in killing the president.

President Johnson named a commission headed by Chief Justice Earl Warren to investigate the assassination. The **Warren Commission**, after a 10-month investigation, reported that there was no conspiracy and that Oswald and Ruby had each acted alone. Despite lingering suspicions, additional government investigations and many private ones have never found credible evidence of a conspiracy.

An end and a beginning

The Kennedy assassination deeply affected all Americans. The Kennedy family and supporters made a great effort to shape the nation's memory of the fallen president. Jacqueline Kennedy arranged a funeral to rival that of President Lincoln's nearly a century before. Broadcast live on national television, it concluded with the president's burial at Arlington National Cemetery, on a hillside overlooking the capital, with a continuously burning flame at the site.

"In many ways the drama of [Kennedy's] presidency outweighed its achievements," wrote Clark Clifford, an adviser to several presidents. Yet Clifford acknowledged that "[Kennedy] offered a vast promise to a whole new generation of Americans." In world affairs, that promise was realized by improved relations with the Soviet Union following the Cuban missile crisis and the goodwill toward America that the Peace Corps produced.

At home, Kennedy's accomplishments were less impressive. Yet, even during his presidency, Kennedy had acknowledged that the nation's social, economic, and environmental problems would take many years to solve. It remained up to his successor, Lyndon B. Johnson, to carry on his work. As president, Johnson would achieve greater legislative success than Kennedy.

READING CHECK **Drawing Conclusions** What was the purpose and conclusion of the Warren Commission?

SECTION 2 ASSESSMENT

go.hrw.com
Online Quiz
Keyword: SD7 HP27

Reviewing Ideas, Terms, and People

1. a. Describe What public image did Kennedy project?
b. Analyze How did Kennedy deal with the threat of increased steel prices?
c. Evaluate Do you think the space race was an important part of the Cold War? Explain your answer.

2. a. Define What was the "one person, one vote" standard?
b. Predict How do you think the **Warren Court's** decisions would expand people's rights in the future?

3. a. Describe What event made Lyndon Johnson president on November 22, 1963?
b. Make Inferences Why did the fate of President Kennedy affect people so deeply?
c. Evaluate Do you agree that "the drama of [Kennedy's] presidency outweighed its achievements"? Why or why not?

Critical Thinking

4. Analyze Information Review your notes on President Kennedy's proposed programs. Then copy the graphic organizer below and use it to show the results of those ideas.

Kennedy's Ideas	Results

FOCUS ON SPEAKING

5. Expository Explain to a classmate what you see as President Kennedy's legacy to the American people. Support your opinion with facts, arguments, and examples.

BEFORE YOU READ

MAIN IDEA

President Johnson used his political skills to push Kennedy's proposals through Congress and expanded them with his own vision of the Great Society.

READING FOCUS

1. Why was Lyndon Johnson's background good preparation for becoming president?
2. Why was Johnson more successful than Kennedy in getting Congress to enact Kennedy's agenda?
3. In what ways did Johnson's Great Society change the nation?
4. What foreign-policy issues were important in Johnson's presidency?

KEY TERMS AND PEOPLE

War on Poverty
Job Corps
VISTA
Great Society
Barry Goldwater
Medicaid
Medicare
Johnson Doctrine
Pueblo incident

PI 2.4 Examine how the Constitution, United States law, and the rights of citizenship provide a major unifying factor in bringing together Americans from diverse roots and traditions.

THE INSIDE STORY

What made President Johnson an effective leader? Lyndon Johnson had an ability to get what he wanted that few others could match—or were able to resist. The skills that made Johnson a highly effective majority leader in the Senate helped him to quickly become a strong president following President Kennedy's death.

Knowledge was the basic element in Johnson's leadership style. To Lyndon Johnson, information was power. He made it a point to learn everything he could about his subject and about the people with whom he was dealing. He claimed to know the strengths and weaknesses of each senator—how far each could be pushed, in what direction, and by what means.

One of Johnson's most effective methods was what journalists called "The Treatment." One person who received The Treatment described it "as if a St. Bernard had licked your face for an hour [and] had pawed you all over."

First, Johnson closed in on his target, until his face was just a couple of inches away. Then words poured out of him in a torrent as his eyes widened and narrowed. If the target tried to say something, Johnson never allowed the chance. He countered objections before they could even be spoken. "He'd come on just like a tidal wave," one senator reported. "There was nothing delicate about him." Observers of The Treatment called it an almost hypnotic experience that rendered its targets stunned and helpless. ◼

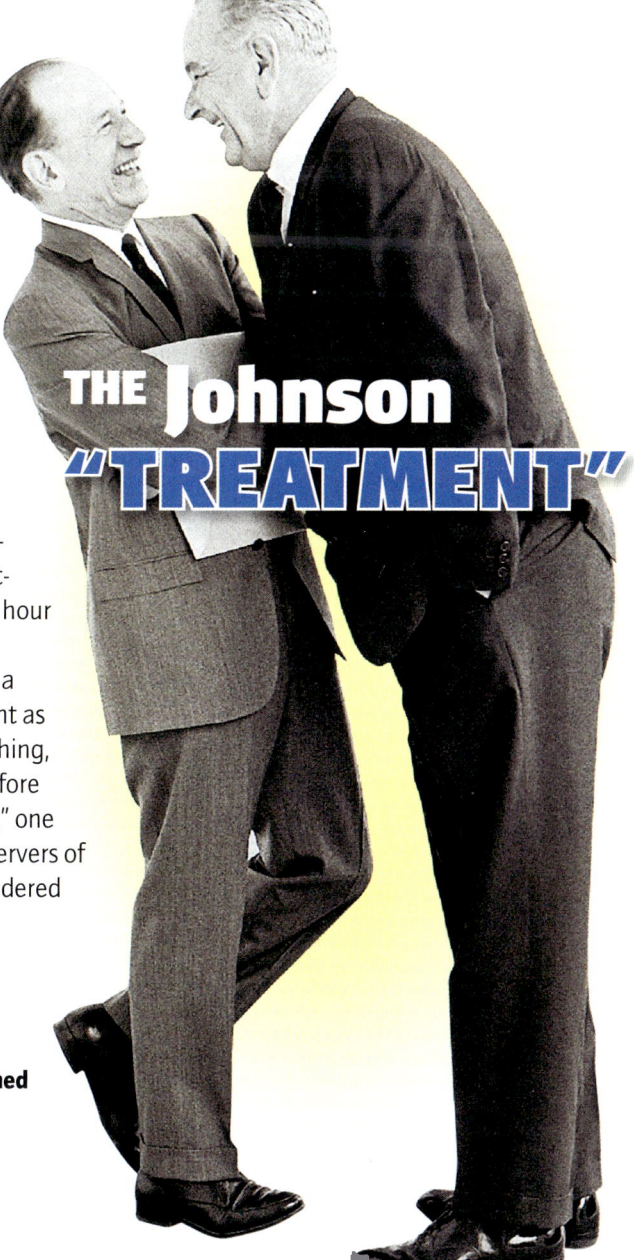

THE Johnson "TREATMENT"

▶ **Johnson (right) overwhelmed friends and opponents alike.**

Johnson Becomes President

As vice president, Lyndon B. Johnson had little opportunity to showcase his political talents. Those talents, however, were one reason John F. Kennedy wanted Johnson as his vice president. Another reason was that Kennedy needed a running mate in 1960 who would help the Democrats win the South. Kennedy might have been better served, however, had Johnson remained in the Senate, where his political skills might have helped to get Kennedy's programs enacted.

Kennedy and Johnson made an unlikely team. A large and intense man, Johnson shared none of Kennedy's good looks, polish, or charm. While Kennedy showed off his beautiful young children to reporters, Johnson was known to display the surgery scars on his abdomen. His often crude language reflected the macho ranching culture from which he came. Born and raised in the rural Hill Country of central Texas, he was hardworking and ambitious. In spite of his sometimes overbearing manner, he had a genuine desire to help others.

Johnson gave up school teaching for government work during the Great Depression. When President Franklin D. Roosevelt created the National Youth Administration (NYA) in 1935, a New Deal agency that found work for young people, Johnson sought the job

of state director for Texas. At age 26 he was the youngest NYA director in the nation. Two years later he ran for Congress, where he served his Hill Country district until 1948. Then Texans statewide elected him to the U.S. Senate.

After just one term as a senator, Johnson's Democratic colleagues made him majority leader in the Senate. He soon developed a close relationship with the Republican president Dwight D. Eisenhower. Johnson used his powerful Senate position and Eisenhower's popularity to force compromises in Congress and pass the first civil rights laws since Reconstruction. By 1960 he had more influence in Washington, D.C., than any other Democrat.

Although Johnson campaigned hard for Kennedy's election in 1960, he was unhappy as vice president. He missed the power he had exercised as Senate majority leader. Even more than Kennedy, Johnson promoted an expanded role for government in making Americans' lives better. He also had a greater concern for the poor and underprivileged. These differences were probably due to the two men's differing backgrounds, including Johnson's experience as part of the New Deal.

Despite his sometimes crude behavior, Johnson was a compassionate man. He was saddened by his inability to comfort Jacqueline Kennedy on the plane ride back from Dallas following her husband's death. When he told the nation in his first speech as president, "All I have I would have given gladly not to be standing here today," he truly meant his words.

READING CHECK **Summarizing** Why was Lyndon Johnson well qualified to be president?

Enacting Kennedy's Agenda

Johnson's mastery of the political process, along with his years of experience in Washington, allowed him to manage the transition of the presidency with great skill and tact. He reassured the nation by promising no great changes from the previous administration. Johnson demonstrated that intent by asking Kennedy's cabinet and advisers to continue serving in the new administration. "I constantly had before me the picture that Kennedy had selected me," he later recalled. "It was my duty to carry on and this meant his people as well as his programs. They were part of his legacy."

FACES OF HISTORY

Lyndon B. JOHNSON 1908–1973

A former Texas high school teacher and long-time member of Congress, Lyndon Johnson ran for the Democratic Party presidential nomination in 1960. Unable to defeat Senator John F. Kennedy of Massachusetts for the nomination, Johnson accepted Kennedy's offer of the vice presidency in order to unite the party.

As president, Johnson carried out an ambitious set of social reforms. After winning the presidential election in 1964, he soon escalated U.S. involvement in Vietnam. Unwilling to let communism advance, he sent American troops into battle. As the Vietnam War dragged on without success, Johnson's popularity with voters decreased. In March 1968 he decided not to run for re-election.

Make Inferences How would Johnson's acceptance of the vice presidency have helped to unite the Democratic Party?

The Job Corps

Among the programs created during the War on Poverty was the Job Corps, a program for young people age 16 to 24 who have not graduated from high school. Today some 60,000 students live on more than 120 Job Corps campuses, where they complete their education and learn a vocation and job-hunting skills.

One of the best-known Job Corps participants is boxer George Foreman. After leaving high school, he joined the Job Corps and learned construction and forestry. A Job Corps counselor also taught Foreman to box, and he went on to win an Olympic gold medal and the heavyweight championship of the world.

Although Foreman's achievements are not typical, Job Corps participants are more successful than other high school dropouts. One study found that Job Corps participants earn about 11 percent more income than dropouts who do not become part of the Job Corps program.

A Job Corps recruiter shares information with high school students in Miami, Florida.

Drawing Conclusions How does the Job Corps represent the ideas of President Johnson's War on Poverty?

The new president also pledged to carry on the New Frontier. Speaking to a joint session of Congress, he called on its members to pass Kennedy's programs, which they had blocked for so long. "Let us here highly resolve that John Fitzgerald Kennedy did not live—or die—in vain," Johnson declared.

HISTORY'S VOICES

❝ John F. Kennedy told his countrymen that our national work would not be finished 'in the . . . life of this administration, nor even perhaps in our lifetime . . . But,' he said, 'let us begin.' Today, in this moment of new resolve, I would say to all my fellow Americans, let us continue. This is our challenge—not to hesitate, not to pause, not to turn about and linger over this evil moment, but to continue on our course so that we may fulfill the destiny that history has set for us. ❞

—Lyndon B. Johnson, speech to Congress, November 27, 1963

The War on Poverty
After Congress passed the Area Redevelopment Act in 1961, Kennedy had told an adviser, "I want to go beyond the things that have already been accomplished." His interest in antipoverty programs was fueled in part by social activist Michael Harrington's influential book published in 1962.

Harrington's *The Other America* was a study of poverty in the United States that shattered the popular belief that all Americans had benefited from the postwar prosperity.

HISTORY'S VOICES

❝ They [the poor] exist within the most powerful and rich society the world has ever known. Their misery has continued while the nation talked of itself as being 'affluent' [wealthy] . . . In this way tens of millions of human beings became invisible. They dropped out of sight and out of mind . . . How long shall we ignore this underdeveloped nation in our midst? ❞

—Michael Harrington, *The Other America*, 1962

Kennedy's staff had begun work on a series of antipoverty programs he wanted to present as part of his 1964 re-election campaign. Johnson was told of Kennedy's planned antipoverty proposals on November 23, 1963, his first full day in office. "Go ahead," the new president ordered. "Give it the highest priority. Push ahead full tilt."

In his first State of the Union Address in January 1964, Johnson declared "unconditional war on poverty" in America. To launch the War on Poverty he asked Congress to pass the Economic Opportunity Act. Congress granted his request in August 1964.

The Economic Opportunity Act funded several new antipoverty programs. The **Job Corps** offered work-training programs for unemployed youth. Volunteers in Service to America, or **VISTA**, was a domestic version of the Peace Corps that provided help to poor communities in the United States. Other programs provided basic education for adults, work opportunities for unemployed fathers and mothers, and help to fight rural poverty and assist migrants. These programs were run directly out of the White House by the newly created Office of Economic Opportunity (OEO). Congress gave the OEO $1 billion to operate them.

Other initiatives passed Johnson also pushed for passage of Kennedy's tax-cut bill and civil rights legislation, both of which had been stalled in Congress. Senate conservatives demanded that the president promise to hold government spending to $100 billion if taxes were cut. Johnson knew the government would not need even that much money. He cleverly told the press, however, how difficult it was to write a budget that met this requirement. Believing it had won a victory, Congress passed the Tax Reduction Act in February 1964.

The law had the effect that Kennedy had hoped for. The nation's economy grew by more than 10 percent, and unemployment declined. As a result, tax <u>revenue</u> actually increased.

The Tax Reduction Act illustrated the difference in the way Kennedy and Johnson approached getting legislation passed.

"Kennedy felt that the way to get the tax cut was to educate the Congress and . . . persuade them to go for it," an aide to both presidents later recalled. "Johnson used his incomparable technique to get the thing through."

"No memorial . . . could more eloquently honor President Kennedy's memory than the earliest possible passage of the civil rights bill for which he fought so long," Johnson told Congress. "We have talked long enough in this country about equal rights . . . It is time now to . . . write it in the books of law." In July, after more than a year of division and debate, Congress passed the landmark Civil Rights Act of 1964. (You will read more about the Civil Rights Act and the circumstances surrounding its passage in the next chapter.)

READING CHECK **Identifying the Main Idea** How did Johnson convince Congress to pass Kennedy's programs?

The Great Society

President Johnson wanted to do more than just follow in Kennedy's footsteps, however. He had ambitious plans of his own. "If you look at my record, you would know that I am a Roosevelt New Dealer," he told an adviser. "As a matter of fact, . . . John F. Kennedy was a little too conservative to suit my taste."

Johnson described his own plans for the nation in a commencement address at the University of Michigan in May 1964.

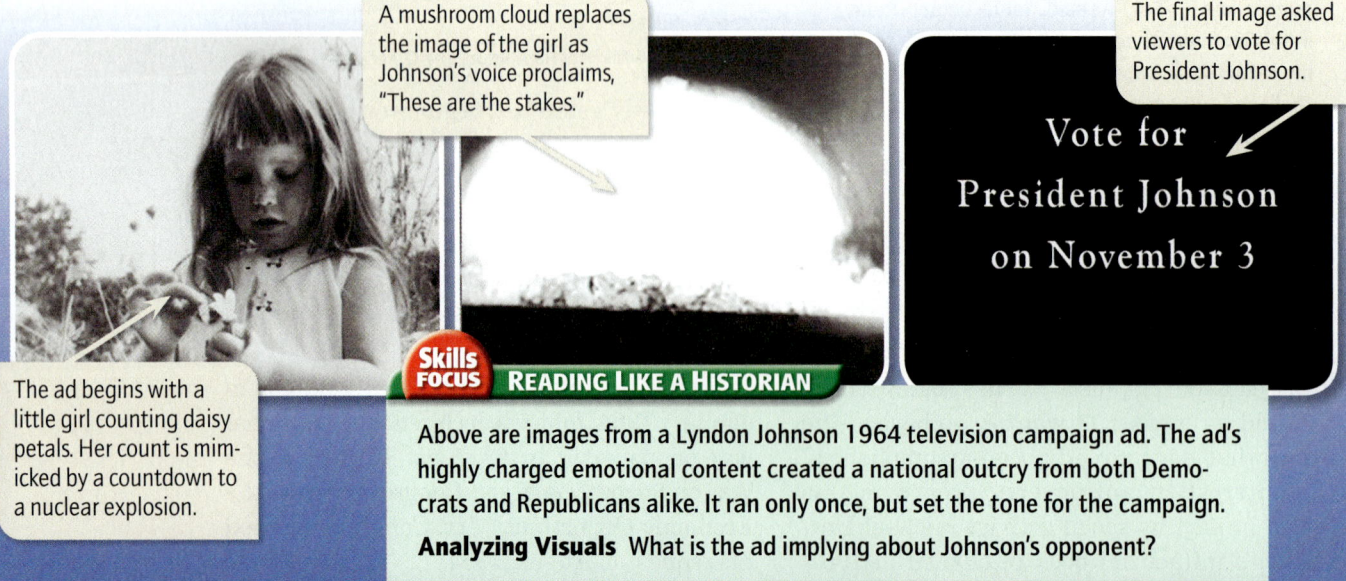

A mushroom cloud replaces the image of the girl as Johnson's voice proclaims, "These are the stakes."

The final image asked viewers to vote for President Johnson.

Vote for President Johnson on November 3

The ad begins with a little girl counting daisy petals. Her count is mimicked by a countdown to a nuclear explosion.

Skills FOCUS **READING LIKE A HISTORIAN**

Above are images from a Lyndon Johnson 1964 television campaign ad. The ad's highly charged emotional content created a national outcry from both Democrats and Republicans alike. It ran only once, but set the tone for the campaign.

Analyzing Visuals What is the ad implying about Johnson's opponent?

Government's Role in Shaping Society

As senator and vice president, Hubert Humphrey acted on his belief that the government should play an active role in society.

❝ [W]e call upon all Americans to join us in making our country a land of opportunity for our young, a home of security and dignity for our elderly, and a place of ... care for our afflicted ... Let us take those giant steps forward ... to build the great society. ❞

Hubert Humphrey, 1964

Senator Barry Goldwater opposed President Johnson's Great Society— which Hubert Humphrey had played a large part in creating.

❝ I've always stood for government that is limited and balanced and against the ever increasing concentrations of authority in Washington ... I believe we must ... not continue drifting endlessly down and down for a time when all of us, our lives, our property, our hopes, and even our prayers will become just cogs in a vast government machine. ❞

Barry Goldwater, 1964

Skills FOCUS — READING LIKE A HISTORIAN

Analyzing Primary Sources In what ways do both speakers try to win support by playing on the emotions of their listeners?

See **Skills Handbook**, pp. H28–H29

HISTORY'S VOICES

❝ We have the opportunity to move not only toward the rich society and the powerful society, but upward to the Great Society. The Great Society rests on abundance and liberty for all. It demands an end to poverty and racial injustice ... I want to talk to you today about three places where we begin to build the Great Society—in our cities, in our countryside, and in our classrooms. ❞

—Lyndon Johnson, May 22, 1964

The 1964 election The phrase Johnson used—Great Society—became the term for the domestic programs of his administration. To achieve his goals for the Great Society, Johnson worked hard to ensure his victory in the 1964 presidential election. He easily won the Democratic Party's nomination for president and chose Hubert Humphrey, a liberal senator from Minnesota, as his running mate. The Republicans selected Senator **Barry Goldwater**, a conservative from Arizona, as their nominee. The vast differences in the two candidates' views gave voters a clear choice.

Goldwater set the tone of the campaign in his acceptance speech at the Republican National Convention by declaring that "extremism in the defense of liberty is no vice." The Democrats portrayed him as a radical who would lead the country into a nuclear war and turn back the clock on the nation's social progress. When Goldwater suggested using nuclear weapons to end the growing war in Vietnam, he convinced many voters that he indeed was a dangerous extremist. (You will read about the Vietnam War in an upcoming chapter.)

Goldwater's attacks on the Great Society also seemed to prove the Democrats' claims about him. "We are all equal in the eyes of God," he proclaimed, "but we are equal *in no other respect*." He charged that government programs to help people were similar to communism and that they posed a threat to the nation's freedom.

In November, the voters provided Johnson with the mandate he sought. The president received 61 percent of the popular vote in the biggest election landslide of the century. His

486–52 victory in the electoral college was even more one-sided. Democrats also strengthened their majorities in both houses of Congress.

Creating the Great Society Now that he had been elected president in his own right, Johnson pushed even harder for his plans. He told aides at an inaugural ball, "Don't stay up late. There's work to be done. We're on our way to the Great Society."

Johnson had a personal interest in providing education for the children of the poor. In 1965 Congress passed the Elementary and Secondary Education Act, the first large-scale program of government aid to public schools. The Higher Education Act created the first federal scholarships for needy college students. In February 1965 the OEO launched Head Start, an education program for the preschool children of low-income parents.

The president also persuaded Congress to pass the Omnibus Housing Act in 1965. To oversee this and other federal housing programs, Congress created the Department of Housing and Urban Development (HUD). Johnson appointed Robert Weaver to head this new department, making him the first African American to be part of a president's cabinet.

In July 1965 Congress authorized funds for states to set up **Medicaid**—a program that provides free health care for poor people. At the same time it created **Medicare**, a health care program for people over age 65. Johnson traveled to Independence, Missouri, to sign the bill into law in front of Harry Truman, the 81-year-old former president who had first proposed such a program. "No longer will older Americans be denied the healing miracle of modern medicine," Johnson declared. "No longer will illness crush and destroy . . . [their] savings."

THE IMPACT TODAY

Economics
Today more than 12 percent of the U.S. population receives health care through Medicaid. Nearly half of those covered are children.

MAJOR GREAT SOCIETY PROGRAMS

Year Enacted	Legislation	Purpose and Provisions
1964	Economic Opportunity Act	Created the Job Corps, VISTA, and eight other programs to fight the "war on poverty"
1964	Tax Reduction Act	Cut income tax rates up to 30%, with the greatest cuts going to lower-income Americans
1964	Civil Rights Act	Outlawed discrimination in housing, employment, and public accommodations; authorized federal government to enforce desegregation
1964	Wilderness Preservation Act	Protected 9.1 million acres of national forest from development
1965	Elementary and Secondary Education Act	Provided aid to school systems based on number of students from low-income homes
1965	Social Security Amendments	Established Medicare and Medicaid
1965	Voting Rights Act	Ended the requirement that voters pass literacy tests and allowed federal supervision of voter registration
1965	Omnibus Housing Act	Provided housing for low-income Americans
1965	Water Quality Act	Required states to clean up rivers and lakes
1965	Clean Air Act Amendments	Established exhaust emission standards for new motor vehicles
1965	Higher Education Act	Provided scholarships and low-interest loans for college students
1966	National Traffic and Motor Vehicle Safety Act	Established safety standards for automobiles and tires
1967	Air Quality Act	Set guidelines on air pollution and increased the federal government's power to enforce clean-air standards

QUICK FACTS

Political Cartoon

President Johnson"s long-standing ties in the Senate and public sympathy after the assassination of President Kennedy helped win support for many issues that had been stalled for months or years. This cartoon, called "Maestro of the 88," reflects on Johnson's relationship with Congress.

Johnson's influence as a senator was so great that he has been called a Master of the Senate. A *maestro* is someone who is a master in the arts, especially music.

These "song lyrics" represent important legislation that Congress passed soon after Johnson became president.

The eighty-eighth Congress met from 1963 to 1965. A piano has 88 keys.

Maestro of the 88   By Karl Hubenthal

Skills FOCUS   READING LIKE A HISTORIAN

Interpreting Political Cartoons What message is the artist trying to convey about Johnson's influence over Congress?

See **Skills Handbook**, p. H31

Many programs of the Great Society were intended to promote a better life for Americans regardless of their economic status. For example, improving the environment was a major emphasis of Johnson's presidency. He signed laws to improve the quality of the air and water as well as other important environmental measures.

Preserving the outdoors and the nation's natural beauty was especially important to Lady Bird Johnson, the first lady. She asked her husband to push the Highway Beautification Act through Congress in October 1965. This law limited advertising along main highways and provided federal funds for landscaping and roadside rest areas. It came to be called Lady Bird's bill.

The decline of the Great Society The peak years for the Great Society were 1965 and 1966. Congress passed 181 of the 200 major bills President Johnson requested during that period. However, some members of Congress expressed substantial concern over the rapid pace of reform called for by Johnson.

The outcome of the midterm elections of 1966 suggested that many Americans shared these concerns. The Democrats retained their majorities in both houses of Congress, but the Republicans gained 47 seats in the House of Representatives and 3 in the Senate. This shift enabled conservatives to slow down Johnson's legislative program.

The new Congress, however, did enact some Great Society proposals into law. One was the Public Broadcasting Act. This law, enacted in 1967, created the Corporation for Public Broadcasting (CPB) to provide public affairs, cultural, and educational programs. The CPB then created the Public Broadcasting System (PBS) for television and National Public Radio (NPR). The programming of PBS and NPR provide alternatives to the offerings of commercial television and radio.

The Truth-in-Lending Act, also passed in 1967, required lenders to inform consumers of actual costs of credit transactions. A 1968 law established the nation's wild and scenic rivers program. These and many other key Great Society reforms continue to provide benefits to Americans today.

READING CHECK   Identifying the Main Idea
What was the overall goal of the Great Society?

Johnson's Foreign Policy

Another factor in the decline of the Great Society was the increasing involvement of the United States in the Vietnam War. You will read more details about the Vietnam War in an upcoming chapter.

At the end of 1966 some 385,000 U.S. combat troops were in Vietnam. The U.S. government was spending about $2.5 billion each month on the war. Budgetary pressures mounted as the nation tried to afford both a major war and expensive social programs at home. As one member of Congress put it, "We cannot have guns and butter."

Johnson chose guns over butter because, like Kennedy, he was fully committed to stopping the spread of communism. Johnson sent 22,000 U.S. troops in 1965 to end a revolt in the Dominican Republic. He justified his actions by declaring that revolutions in Latin America were not just local concerns when "the object is the establishment of a Communist dictatorship." This guideline for intervention became known as the Johnson Doctrine.

As he fought the spread of communism, President Johnson also continued Kennedy's efforts to improve relations with the Soviet Union. In March 1967 the first direct treaty between the two nations since 1917 took effect. The treaty protected each country's diplomats from harassment by authorities in the other country.

A month later, the United States and the Soviet Union joined 58 other nations to ban weapons in outer space. After war broke out between Israel and its Arab neighbors in June, Johnson met Soviet leader Aleksey Kosygin in New Jersey to discuss the situation.

A crisis developed in January 1968 when North Korean forces captured the *Pueblo*, a U.S. Navy spy ship, off the coast of Communist North Korea. U.S. officials claimed the *Pueblo* had been in international waters and demanded its return.

When the North Koreans refused, Johnson ordered the call-up of some 14,000 national guard, air force, and navy reserves. At the same time he sought a negotiated settlement to the *Pueblo* incident. The crisis was resolved in December when the North Koreans released the crew but kept the ship.

READING CHECK **Making Inferences** Why did Johnson involve the United States in the affairs of the Dominican Republic?

SECTION 3 ASSESSMENT

go.hrw.com
Online Quiz
Keyword: SD7 HP27

Reviewing Ideas, Terms, and People

1. a. Identify What were some of Johnson's political accomplishments before he became president?
b. Compare and Contrast In what ways were Johnson and Kennedy alike and different?
c. Predict How do you think Johnson's experiences would help him as president?

2. a. Identify What Kennedy programs did Johnson help pass?
b. Analyze In what ways did the Economic Opportunity Act address poverty?
c. Elaborate Which of the laws and programs Johnson enacted do you think is the most important? Why?

3. a. Describe What were Johnson's main goals for the **Great Society**?
b. Make Inferences Why did some people find **Barry Goldwater's** views threatening?
c. Evaluate How would you rate Johnson's domestic achievements? Explain your answer.

4. a. Identify What were Johnson's most significant foreign-policy concerns?
b. Analyze How did the Vietnam War affect the growth of Johnson's Great Society?
c. Evaluate Do you think Johnson's response to communism in the **Johnson Doctrine** was effective? Why or why not?

Critical Thinking

5. Sequence Review your notes on President Johnson's achievements. Then copy the graphic organizer below and use it to record those achievements in chronological order. You may need to add more boxes.

☐ → ☐ → ☐ → ☐

FOCUS ON WRITING

6. Persuasive Suppose you live in the mid-1960s. Write a letter to your senator expressing support for the Great Society. Your letter should try to convince the senator to support President Johnson's programs.

LANDMARK SUPREME COURT CASES

Constitutional Issue: Due Process

ST 4.1 Analyze important debates in American history, focusing on the opposing positions and the historical evidence used to support these positions.

Miranda v. Arizona (1966)

Why It Matters The Fifth Amendment protects a criminal defendant from being forced to be a witness against himself or herself. The Sixth Amendment gives the right to an attorney in criminal cases. If a suspect is unaware of these rights, the police cannot interrogate him or her without informing the suspect about his or her rights.

Background of the Case

In 1963 Mexican immigrant Ernesto Miranda was arrested in Arizona. Police questioned him for two hours. He confessed to a serious crime, was tried and convicted, and sentenced to jail. The Arizona Supreme Court upheld his conviction.

The U.S. Supreme Court had ruled in *Brown* v. *Mississippi* (1936) that confessions coerced, or forced, by state or local officials violated the due process clause of the Fourteenth Amendment. In *Gideon* v. *Wainwright* (1963), the Court held that a criminal defendant who cannot afford an attorney can have one appointed without charge. Miranda's lawyer argued that police must inform a suspect of these rights before questioning.

The Decision

The Supreme Court ruled that police must protect a suspect's right against self-incrimination before questioning him or her.

> ❝[T]he person must be warned that he has a right to remain silent, that any statement he does make may be used as evidence against him, and that he has a right to the presence of an attorney, either retained or appointed.❞

Police may then question the suspect if he waives these rights. But they must stop if the suspect says he or she wants a lawyer or no longer wants to talk to police. If police do not follow these procedures, any confession or admissions that the suspect makes cannot be used as evidence against him or her at trial in court.

THE IMPACT TODAY *Miranda* was one of the Warren Court's most controversial decisions. Those who disagreed with the ruling warned it could allow guilty people to go free just because of police officers' errors. Today police in the United States carry cards with the Miranda warnings printed on them and routinely "Mirandize" suspects by "reading them their rights" prior to questioning.

CRITICAL THINKING

go.hrw.com
Research Online
Keyword: SS Court

1. **Analyze the Impact** The year after *Miranda* was decided, the Court was faced with the question of whether an accused person is entitled to have counsel present when being shown to prosecution witnesses for identification at a line-up. How is this like the situation in *Miranda?* How is it different? How would you decide this question?

2. **You Be the Judge** Many states have laws requiring a person suspected of committing a crime to identify himself to police. Based on *Miranda,* are such laws constitutional, or does the person have the right to refuse to give police any information? Explain your reasoning in a short paragraph.

The New Frontier and Great Society

Historical Context The documents below provide information on President John F. Kennedy's New Frontier and President Lyndon Johnson's Great Society programs.

Task Examine the documents and answer the questions that follow. Then you will be asked to write an essay about Kennedy's New Frontier and Johnson's Great Society, using facts from the documents and from the chapter to support the position you take in your thesis statement.

ST 3.2 Draw upon literary selections, historical documents, and accounts to analyze the roles played by different individuals and groups during the major eras in New York State and United States history.

ST 3.3 Compare and analyze the major arguments for and against major political developments in New York State and United States history, such as: the Great Society programs of the 1960s.

DOCUMENT 1

President John F. Kennedy came into office with bold ideas and an agenda that came to be known as the New Frontier. He explained some of the goals of this program in his inaugural address.

"[M]an holds in his mortal hands the power to abolish all forms of human poverty and all forms of human life. And yet the same revolutionary beliefs for which our forebears fought are still at issue around the globe . . .

"We dare not forget today that we are the heirs of that first revolution. Let the word go forth from this time and place, to friend and foe alike, that the torch has been passed to a new generation of Americans . . .

"Let every nation know, whether it wishes us well or ill, that we shall pay any price, bear any burden, meet any hardship, support any friend, oppose any foe, to assure the survival and the success of liberty . . .

"To those people in the huts and villages of half the globe struggling to break the bonds of mass misery, we pledge our best efforts to help them help themselves . . . If a free society cannot help the many who are poor, it cannot save the few who are rich . . .

"In your hands, my fellow citizens, more than mine, will rest the final success or failure of our course . . .

"And so, my fellow Americans, ask not what your country can do for you; ask what you can do for your country."

DOCUMENT 2

One component of the New Frontier was the creation of the Peace Corps to help developing countries improve their economies, education, and infrastructure. Thousands of young volunteers heeded Kennedy's call and went to help the poor in foreign countries. Here a Peace Corps volunteer is helping to inoculate children in Bolivia.

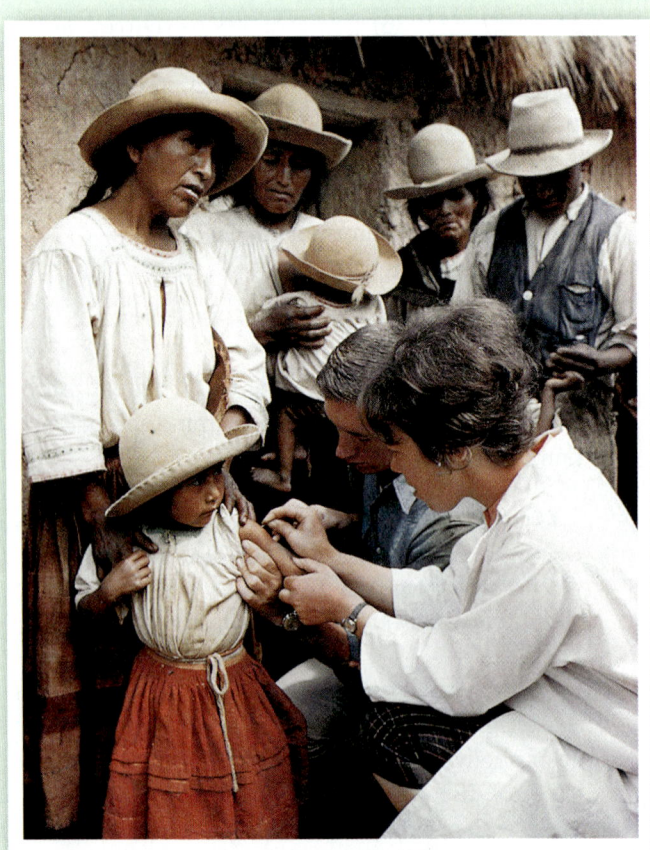

President Lyndon Johnson came into office with his own bold goals, namely the creation of the Great Society, in which problems such as poverty and racism would be wiped out. In the following speech, he explains his War on Poverty, a key element of creating the Great Society.

"We are citizens of the richest and most fortunate nation in the history of the world . . .

"The path has not been an easy one. But we have never lost sight of our goal—an America in which every citizen shares all the opportunities of his society, in which every man has a chance to advance his welfare to the limit of his capacities.

"We have come a long way toward this goal. We still have a long way to go. The distance which remains is the measure of the great unfinished work of our society. To finish that work I have called for a national war on poverty. Our objective: total victory . . .

"The war on poverty is not a struggle simply to support people, to make them dependent on the generosity of others. It is a struggle to give people a chance. It is an effort to allow them to develop and use their capacities, as we have been allowed to develop and use ours, so that they can share, as others share, in the promise of this nation.

"Because it is right, because it is wise, and because, for the first time in our history, it is possible to conquer poverty . . ."

Many conservatives opposed Lyndon Johnson's Great Society programs. His costly programs would increase the size of government, they argued. They feared a larger central government would rob people of their democratic freedoms. Actor Ronald Reagan was new to politics when he delivered the following speech in October 1964. He asked voters to support Republican Barry Goldwater in his campaign for the presidency. Goldwater lost the election to Johnson, but the speech made Reagan a rising star in politics. Reagan would one day become the 40th president of the United States.

In this vote-harvesting time, they use terms like the "Great Society," or as we were told a few days ago by the President, we must accept a greater government activity in the affairs of the people . . .

"This is the issue of this election: Whether we believe in our capacity for self-government or whether we abandon the American revolution and confess that [the government] can plan our lives for us better than we can plan them ourselves . . .

We have so many people who can't see a fat man standing beside a thin one without coming to the conclusion the fat man got that way by taking advantage of the thin one. So they're going to solve all the problems of human misery through government and government planning . . .

No government ever voluntarily reduces itself in size. So governments' programs, once launched, never disappear . . ."

Skills FOCUS — READING LIKE A HISTORIAN

1. **a. Identify** Refer to Document 1. What goals of the New Frontier does Kennedy emphasize in this excerpt?
   b. Elaborate How do you think the Cold War influenced the ideas Kennedy expresses here?

2. **a. Describe** Refer to Document 2. What is happening in this image?
   b. Analyze How does this program help achieve Kennedy's goals?

3. **a. Identify** Refer to Document 3. What does Johnson hope to achieve?
   b. Elaborate Do you think his goal was realistic?

4. **a. Identify** Refer to Document 4. Who do the "fat man" and the "thin one" represent?

b. Explain What did Reagan mean when he said "they're going to solve all the problems of human misery through government and government planning"?

5. **Document-Based Essay Question** Consider the question below and form a thesis statement. Using examples from Documents 1, 2, 3, and 4, create an outline and write a short essay supporting your position.
   How were some of the goal were President Kennedy's New Frontier and President Johnson's Great Society similar to and different from one another?

See **Skills Handbook**, p. H28, H30

Visual Summary: The New Frontier and the Great Society

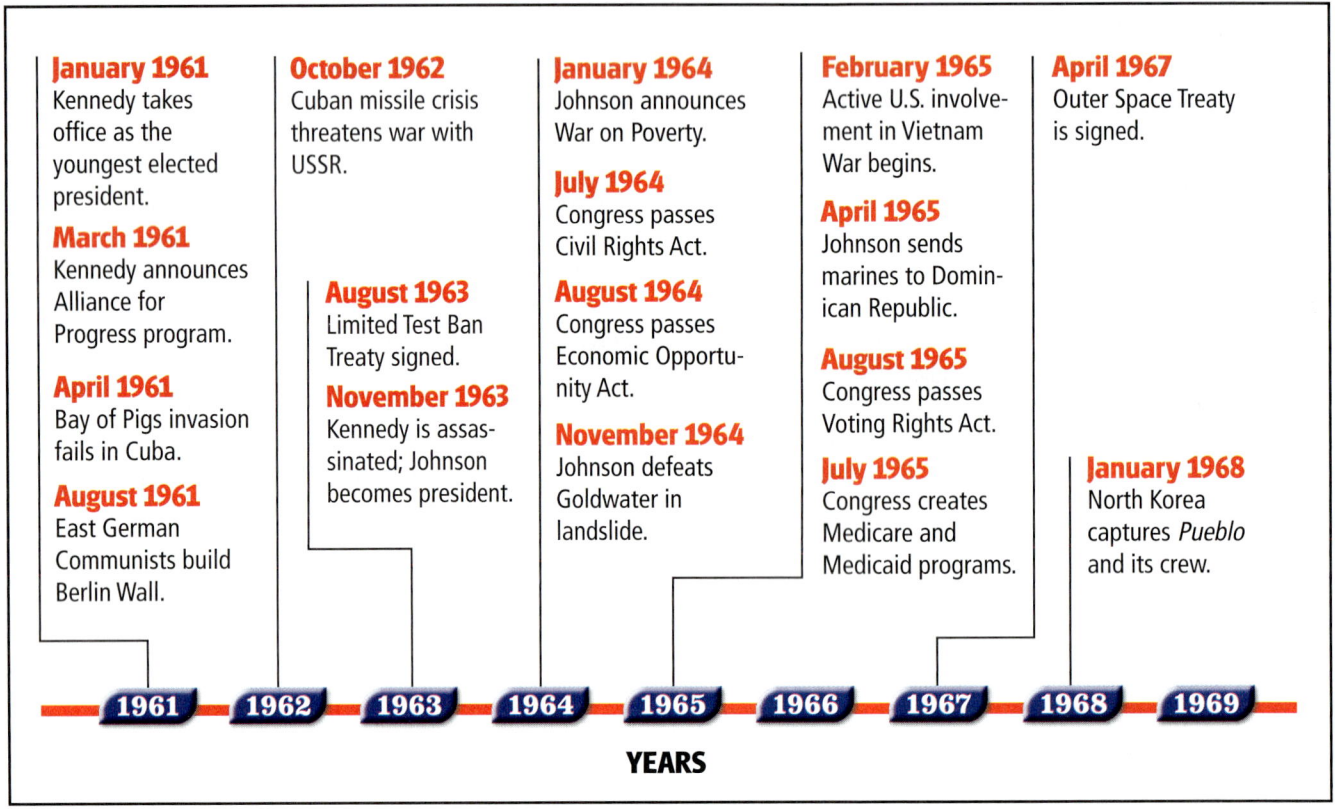

January 1961
Kennedy takes office as the youngest elected president.

March 1961
Kennedy announces Alliance for Progress program.

April 1961
Bay of Pigs invasion fails in Cuba.

August 1961
East German Communists build Berlin Wall.

October 1962
Cuban missile crisis threatens war with USSR.

August 1963
Limited Test Ban Treaty signed.

November 1963
Kennedy is assassinated; Johnson becomes president.

January 1964
Johnson announces War on Poverty.

July 1964
Congress passes Civil Rights Act.

August 1964
Congress passes Economic Opportunity Act.

November 1964
Johnson defeats Goldwater in landslide.

February 1965
Active U.S. involvement in Vietnam War begins.

April 1965
Johnson sends marines to Dominican Republic.

August 1965
Congress passes Voting Rights Act.

July 1965
Congress creates Medicare and Medicaid programs.

April 1967
Outer Space Treaty is signed.

January 1968
North Korea captures *Pueblo* and its crew.

1961 — 1962 — 1963 — 1964 — 1965 — 1966 — 1967 — 1968 — 1969

YEARS

Reviewing Key Terms and People

Complete each sentence by filling in the blank with the correct term or person.

1. The dictator _____ came to power in Cuba in 1959.

2. A disastrous attempt by the CIA to invade Cuba became known as the _____.

3. The _____ brought the United States and the Soviet Union to the brink of nuclear war.

4. Kennedy's strategy of _____ involved strengthening conventional U.S. forces to avoid using nuclear weapons in times of crisis.

5. The _____ offered economic aid to Latin American countries.

6. Because of his narrow victory in 1960, Kennedy never had a strong _____ for his plans.

7. The chief justice of the Supreme Court during Kennedy's presidency was _____.

8. Dallas police arrested _____ for the assassination of President Kennedy.

9. The _____ reported that there was no conspiracy in the assassination of President Kennedy.

10. A domestic version of the Peace Corps called _____ helped poor communities in the United States.

11. Johnson's Republican opponent in the 1964 election was _____.

12. Under the Great Society, a government health care program for people over 65 called _____ was begun.

13. The _____ was resolved when North Korea kept the ship but released its crew.

14. The _____ was the president's justification for U.S. intervention in Latin America when there was the threat of a Communist dictatorship.

History's Impact video program

Review the video to answer the closing question:
How did advances in technology as a result of the space program change American life?

Comprehension and Critical Thinking

SECTION 1 *(pp. 878–886)*

15. a. Describe What happened at the Bay of Pigs invasion?

b. Draw Conclusions In what ways did the Peace Corps increase goodwill for the United States?

c. Evaluate How might the Berlin Wall affect the lives of people in East and West Berlin?

SECTION 2 *(pp. 887–892)*

16. a. Identify What was the Area Redevelopment Act of 1961?

b. Make Inferences Why was Congress willing to fund the space race?

c. Elaborate Why were the reforms of the Warren Court important to the nation?

SECTION 3 *(pp. 893–900)*

17. a. Recall Why did Kennedy choose Johnson as his vice president?

b. Analyze Why did Johnson decide to carry out Kennedy's initiatives?

c. Elaborate Why do you think Americans voted so overwhelmingly for Johnson in the presidential election of 1964?

Using the Internet

go.hrw.com
Practice Online
Keyword: SD7 CH27

18. The Berlin Wall remained in place from 1961 to 1989, when it was finally torn down. Using the keyword above, do research on the significance of the Berlin Wall. Then write a report about the ways the construction and destruction of this barrier changed the world.

Analyzing Primary Sources

Reading Like a Historian In response to criticism of how he handled the Cuban missile crisis, Kennedy made a speech. Read an excerpt from that speech in the History's Voices passage in Section 1 that begins, "What kind of peace do we seek?"

19. Identify What kind of peace does Kennedy reject? What kind of peace does he want?

20. Analyze Why is it important to remember our "common link"?

Critical Reading

Read the passage in Section 3 that begins with the heading "Creating the Great Society." Then answer the questions that follow.

21. According to the passage, one thing limited along major highways by the Highway Beautification Act was

A landscaping.

B rest areas.

C billboards.

D streetlights.

22. The appointment of Robert Weaver as secretary of the Department of Housing and Urban Development was significant because

A he was the first African American to be part of a president's cabinet.

B he was the youngest cabinet member ever.

C Congress had originally rejected his nomination.

D he was a conservative Republican who had previously opposed President Johnson.

FOCUS ON WRITING

Expository Writing *Expository writing gives information, explains why or how, or defines a process. To practice expository writing, complete the assignment below.*

Writing Topic The New Frontier of John F. Kennedy

23. Assignment Based on what you have read in this chapter, write a paragraph that explains what the New Frontier was and how it was presented to the American people.

The Civil Rights MOVEMENT

THE BIG PICTURE In the mid-1900s, many African Americans rose up against the treatment they had endured for decades. They fought discrimination through court cases and through nonviolent resistance, marches, boycotts, and "freedom rides." Their efforts resulted in meaningful government protections of basic civil rights.

New York Standards

Key Idea 2 Important ideas, social and cultural values, beliefs, and traditions from New York State and United States history illustrate the connections and interactions of people and events across time and from a variety of perspectives.

Key Idea 3 Study about the major social, political, economic, cultural, and religious developments in New York State and United States history involves learning about the important roles and contributions of individuals and groups.

Skills FOCUS READING LIKE A HISTORIAN

More than 200,000 civil rights demonstrators gathered peacefully at the Lincoln Memorial in Washington, D.C., in 1963. In his most famous speech, civil rights leader Martin Luther King Jr. told those gathered that "we have come here today to dramatize a shameful condition." **Interpreting Visuals** How do you think this event affected public opinion? Explain.

See **Skills Handbook**, p. H30

U.S.

May 1954
Supreme Court rules that segregation in public schools is unconstitutional.

1954

World

1956
The Soviet army brutally crushes a revolt against Communist rule in Hungary.

History's Impact video program
Watch the video to understand the impact of equal rights and justice for all.

February 1960
Protesters in Greensboro, North Carolina, challenge racial segregation of public facilities.

August 1963
Civil rights protesters stage March on Washington.

July 1964
President Johnson signs the Civil Rights Act of 1964 into law.

April 1968
Civil rights leader Martin Luther King Jr. is killed.

April 1971
The Supreme Court upholds the use of busing to integrate schools.

1958

1962

1966

1970

1974

1960
Nazi war criminal Adolf Eichmann is captured in Argentina.

1967
South African surgeon Christian Barnard performs first successful human heart transplant.

1970
Rhodesian prime minister declares the country an independent and racially segregated republic.

1975
Khmer Rouge leader Pol Pot takes over in Cambodia.

907

Fighting Segregation

BEFORE YOU READ

MAIN IDEA

In the mid-1900s, the civil rights movement began to make major progress in correcting the national problem of racial segregation.

READING FOCUS

1. What was the status of the civil rights movement prior to 1954?
2. What were the key issues in the Supreme Court's ruling in *Brown* v. *Board of Education of Topeka, Kansas*, and what was its impact?
3. How did events in Montgomery, Alabama, help launch the modern civil rights movement?

KEY TERMS AND PEOPLE

CORE
Jackie Robinson
Thurgood Marshall
Little Rock Nine
Rosa Parks
Montgomery bus boycott
Martin Luther King Jr.
SCLC

PI 2.3 Compare and contrast the experiences of different groups in the United States.

Civil Rights PIONEERS

▼ Harry and Eliza Briggs (middle row, at either side of their child Catherine) with plaintiffs and supporters of *Briggs* v. *Elliott*.

THE INSIDE STORY

What does it take to turn ordinary people into activists?

For Harry and Eliza Briggs, it was bad enough that their child had to attend a segregated school in their South Carolina community. But when the school board refused a request for school bus transportation—in spite of the fact that some African American children had to walk as much as 10 miles to school—they had had enough. Harry and Eliza Briggs joined 18 other parents in a legal challenge aimed at ending segregation of the local schools. With the help of the NAACP, they filed *Briggs* v.

Elliott in 1950. Harry and Eliza Briggs paid dearly for their actions. Both of them lost their jobs. Harry had to leave the state to find work to support his family.

Yet their legal challenge went forward. Soon, it was joined together with four other cases, including a case from Topeka, Kansas, for argument before the Supreme Court of the United States. In 2004, Congressional Gold Medals of Honor were awarded posthumously to civil rights pioneers Harry and Eliza Briggs and two other South Carolina citizens, the Reverend Joseph S. DeLaine and Levi Pearson, who were part of their lawsuit. ◼

The Civil Rights Movement Prior to 1954

The Briggses played a key role in launching the modern civil rights movement in the United States. Yet this movement was not really new. You read in earlier chapters about the long struggle for African American rights. This fight had its start with the opposition to slavery in colonial days. It continued in the 1800s with the abolition movement and the Civil War. Slavery ended after the Civil War, and formerly enslaved people enjoyed some rights for a time during Reconstruction.

African American rights suffered setbacks after Reconstruction. In the late 1800s, legalized racism returned to the South. Supported by the Supreme Court's 1896 ruling in *Plessy* v. *Ferguson,* the segregation of African Americans and whites was the law of the land in much of the United States in the early 1900s.

In the late 1800s and early 1900s, a new group of champions joined the battle for civil rights. They included Booker T. Washington and W.E.B. Du Bois. You read about the role of Du Bois in the founding of the National Association for the Advancement of Colored People, or NAACP. This organization formed in 1909. In the decades ahead, it would be a powerful voice in the struggle to improve the legal rights of African Americans. The NAACP also fought to bring an end to racial violence.

The Great Depression of the 1930s presented new challenges to African Americans. Although the entire nation suffered, African Americans fared worse than others. President Roosevelt's New Deal helped win him the support of many African American voters. First Lady Eleanor Roosevelt was a staunch supporter of civil rights. Yet the president was unwilling to push too hard for greater rights for African Americans out of concern that it would anger his southern white supporters.

The 1940s: a decade of progress In earlier chapters, you read about some of the civil rights gains of the 1940s. For example, during World War II, A. Philip Randolph managed to force a federal ban against discrimination

SCHOOL SEGREGATION, 1952

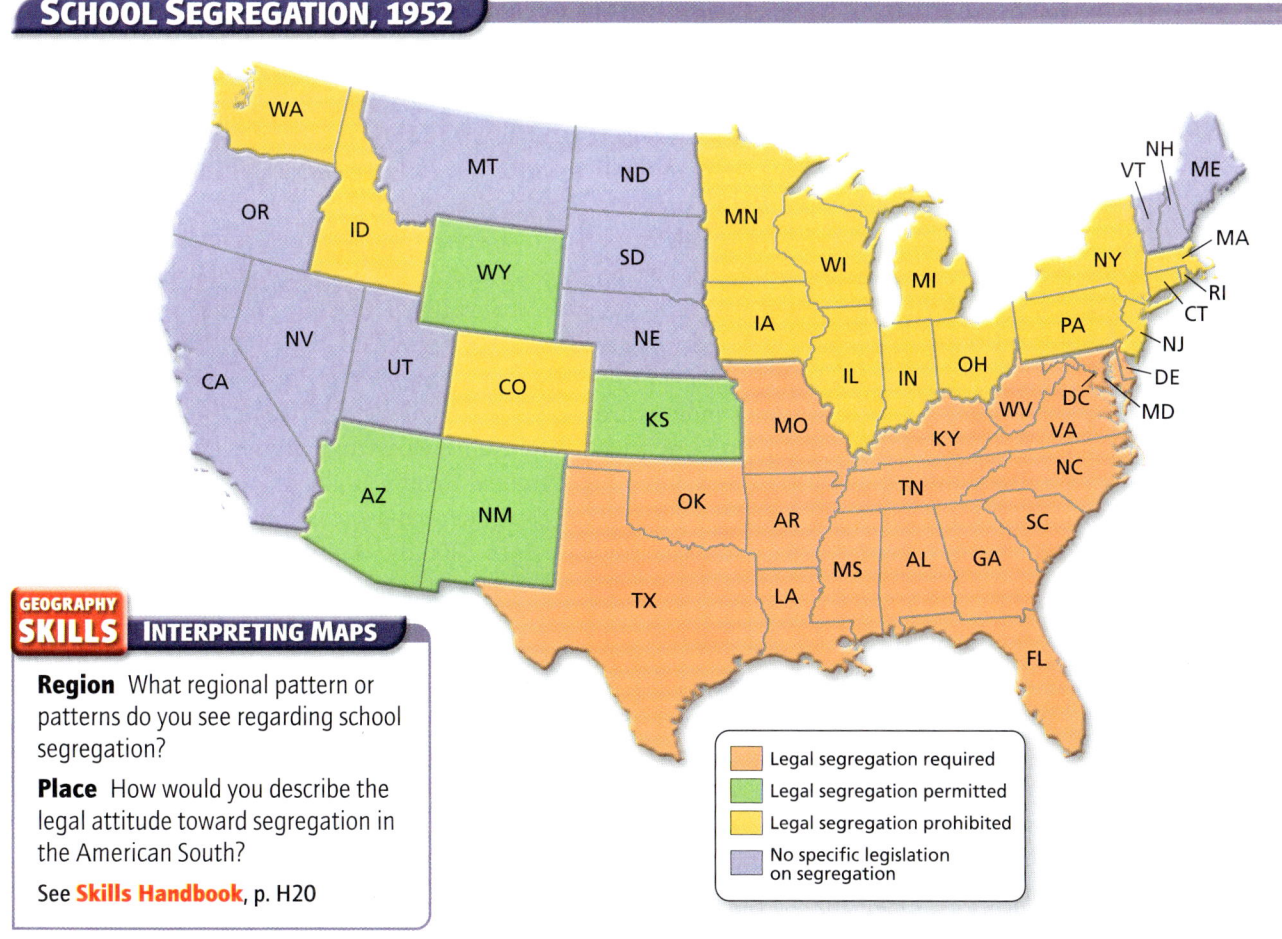

GEOGRAPHY SKILLS **INTERPRETING MAPS**

Region What regional pattern or patterns do you see regarding school segregation?

Place How would you describe the legal attitude toward segregation in the American South?

See **Skills Handbook**, p. H20

Legend:
- Legal segregation required
- Legal segregation permitted
- Legal segregation prohibited
- No specific legislation on segregation

EARLY CIVIL RIGHTS VICTORIES

QUICK FACTS

Early efforts in the civil rights movement included the following gains:	
1940	NAACP Legal Defense Fund founded by Thurgood Marshall
1941	Ban against discrimination in defense industry
1942	Founding of CORE
1947	Integration of Major League Baseball by Jackie Robinson (right)
1948	Desegregation of armed forces

FOCUS ON NEW YORK

GOVERNMENT

New York was a pioneer in civil rights legislation. It was the first state to enact an anti-discrimination law. The 1945 Quinn-Ives Act was an omnibus statute that banned discrimination on the basis of race in employment, housing, credit, places of public accommodation, and non-religious educational institutions.

in defense-related work. Another key development in the 1940s was the founding of the Congress of Racial Equality, or **CORE**. This organization was dedicated to nonviolent protest. Its methods would have a strong effect on civil rights activists in the years ahead.

The end of the 1940s saw several key changes in the march toward greater civil rights. One was President Truman's order to desegregate the armed forces. Another came from popular culture. In 1947 the Brooklyn Dodgers became the first Major League Baseball team to put an African American on its roster. Millions admired **Jackie Robinson** for his great skill as an athlete. Millions more were inspired by his courage. Robinson bore with bravery and dignity the pressure of being an individual so many people wanted to see succeed—and so many others expected to see fail.

Seeking change in the courts While Randolph, Robinson, and others worked to bring change to American society, the NAACP continued its strategy of attacking racism through the courts. This was a method the organization had used from its earliest days to combat such discriminatory practices as the use of grandfather clauses to keep African Americans from voting.

In the 1930s Charles Hamilton Houston began an NAACP campaign to attack the concept of "separate but equal." Houston chose to focus on segregation in education. One of his former students, **Thurgood Marshall**, soon joined him. Marshall knew firsthand the effects of discrimination in education. He was once denied admission to the University of Maryland law school because of his race.

Under Houston and Marshall, NAACP lawyers began to chip away at the 1896 Supreme Court ruling in *Plessy* v. *Ferguson*, which served as the legal basis of segregation. In 1938, for example, in *Missouri ex rel. Gaines* v. *Canada, Registrar of the University of Missouri,* the NAACP successfully argued against Missouri's refusal to offer a law school education to African Americans.

In 1950 the Supreme Court ruled in *Sweatt* v. *Painter* that the separate law school for African Americans at the University of Texas was inferior to the one for whites. The Court also held that just being separate from the white school was likely to harm the preparation of African American students for a career in law.

READING CHECK **Identifying Problems and Solutions** What were some of the methods by which civil rights were expanded in the years before 1954?

Brown v. Board of Education

The NAACP's early success had focused on graduate schools, which affected only a small number of people around the country. In the 1950s Marshall began focusing on the nation's elementary and high schools. At the time, millions of students around the country attended segregated schools. For African Americans, these were almost always inferior schools.

To press its cause, the NAACP needed a case. As you read at the start of this section, it found one in South Carolina, with Harry and Eliza Briggs. NAACP lawyers found another one in the case of Linda Brown, in Topeka, Kansas. You will read about the details of the Kansas case in Landmark Supreme Court Cases later in this section.

The Supreme Court hears *Brown*

In both the *Briggs* and *Brown* cases, the lower courts upheld the practice of segregation. Yet these defeats did not stop Marshall and the NAACP. In fact, they provided an opportunity to bring the issue of school segregation to the Supreme Court. The Court combined the cases and several others from around the country into a single case. It was known as *Brown* v. *Board of Education of Topeka, Kansas*.

The Supreme Court was aware of the case's great significance. It heard arguments over a two-year period. The Court also considered research about segregation's effects on African American children. In one study, black children were shown dolls that were identical except for skin color. The children had more positive feelings about the white-skinned dolls than about the dark-skinned dolls they resembled. This and other tests suggested that segregation had harmed the self-image of young students.

In 1954 Chief Justice Earl Warren issued the Supreme Court's decision. All nine justices agreed that separate schools for African Americans and whites violated the Constitution's guarantee of equal protection of the law.

HISTORY'S VOICES

❝ Education is perhaps the most important function of state and local governments . . . It is doubtful that any child may reasonably be expected to succeed in life if he is denied the opportunity of an education. Such an opportunity . . . is a right that must be made available to all on equal terms . . . Does segregation of children in schools solely on the basis of race . . . deprive the children of the minority group of equal educational opportunities? We believe that it does. ❞

—Chief Justice Earl Warren, *Brown* v. *Board of Education of Topeka, Kansas,* May 17, 1954

American Civil Liberty

Ending Legal Segregation

For many decades following the 1896 Supreme Court ruling in *Plessy* v. *Ferguson,* the concept of "separate but equal" was used to deny African Americans equal protection of the law. Segregation denied African Americans the education—and the dignity—they needed in order to achieve true social equality.

When the NAACP and its lawyers decided to attack the policy of "separate but equal," they knew it would be a long process. They understood that even if they were able to quickly overturn *Plessy*, it would take longer to destroy the attitudes that supported segregation. Instead, they sought to chip away at the *Plessy* ruling and slowly pave the way for true social change.

The strategy worked. By 1954 several cases had weakened the "separate but equal" policy and had in fact begun to break down the walls of segregation in education. The Supreme Court's forceful, unanimous decision in *Brown* v. *Board of Education of Topeka, Kansas,* showed clearly that legally enforced segregation could be challenged.

Identifying Problems and Solutions Why did the NAACP try to chip away at the *Plessy* ruling bit by bit?

Thurgood Marshall (center) and colleagues in front of the Supreme Court building after their victory

The Little Rock crisis At the time of the *Brown* decision, 21 states had schools that were segregated by law. The Supreme Court's ruling declared segregation unconstitutional, but it offered no firm guidance about how or when desegregation should occur.

Some states quickly prepared to integrate their schools. In other states, however, there was strong opposition. Virginia Democratic senator Harry Byrd Jr. organized a movement known as massive resistance, under which officials at all levels pledged to block integration.

In Virginia, for example, the legislature passed laws forcing the closure of any school planning to integrate. Laws also assisted white students wishing to attend private schools. It was more than a year before the federal courts stopped this practice.

Little Rock, Arkansas, was another trouble spot. In 1957 Governor Orval Faubus violated a federal court order to integrate Little Rock's Central High School. Claiming that white extremists were threatening violence, he warned that "blood would run in the streets" if nine African Americans tried to attend the school. Just before the school year was to start, he ordered the Arkansas National Guard to keep them out.

On September 4, 1957, a crowd of angry whites harassed the black students as they arrived for the first day of school. When they reached the door, the soldiers turned them away. The Guard made no effort to protect them from the hostile crowd, who spat at them and tore their clothing.

For nearly three weeks the Guard prevented the African American students, now known as the Little Rock Nine, from entering the school. Meanwhile, President Eisenhower tried to persuade Faubus to back down. Finally, on September 24, Eisenhower went on national television to announce that he was sending federal troops to end the standoff. The next day, protected by U. S. soldiers with fixed bayonets, the Little Rock Nine entered Central High School.

For the rest of the school year, the African American students endured great abuse. Other students constantly shoved them in the halls. Their lives were threatened. The one senior among the Little Rock Nine had to be guarded at graduation. When his name was called at the ceremony, none of his classmates or their families clapped for him.

Meanwhile, Faubus continued to seek ways to stop school integration. In the end he failed. However, the events in Little Rock revealed to many Americans just how strong racism was in some parts of the nation.

READING CHECK **Identifying Problems and Solutions** What kinds of issues faced the Supreme Court in making its *Brown* decision?

ACADEMIC VOCABULARY

integrate to combine two groups in such a way that one becomes fully part of the other

THE IMPACT TODAY

Government

In 1998 Central High School became a national historic site. It continues to educate students and is operated jointly by the Little Rock school district and the National Park Service.

Linking TO Today

Integrating Central High School

The famous photograph at right shows Elizabeth Eckford, one of the Little Rock Nine, walking to Little Rock's Central High School on September 4, 1957. The white girl shouting at Eckford is Hazel Massery. Massery later regretted what she had done. She decided that she did not want to be, as she put it, the "poster child of the hate generation, trapped in the image captured in the photograph." In 1963 Massery apologized to Eckford. The two women later became friends and have spoken publicly together about their experiences.

Identifying the Main Idea Why did Hazel Massery apologize to Elizabeth Eckford?

Eckford and Massery in 1957 (above) and later, after becoming friends (left)

ST 1.1 Explore the meaning of the United States motto, "E Pluribus Unum," by identifying both those forces that unite Americans and those that potentially divide Americans.

ST 3.1 Investigate how Americans have reconciled the inherent tensions and conflicts over minority versus majority rights by researching the civil rights and women's rights movements of the twentieth century.

Brown v. Board of Education of Topeka, Kansas (1954)

Why It Matters By 1950 public schools in many parts of the United States were segregated. Under the Supreme Court's decision in *Plessy* v. *Ferguson*, separate schools for African American and white students were legally acceptable as long as the facilities were equal in quality. In practice, schools for African American children were generally far below the quality of schools for whites.

Background of the Case

Linda Brown, an African American third-grader in Topeka, Kansas, lived just blocks away from the nearest elementary school. However, that was a whites-only school, so she had to walk five blocks and then take a bus for two miles to reach the elementary school for blacks. The NAACP recruited Brown's parents and other Topeka residents to challenge segregation in the public schools. The Supreme Court recognized the harm segregation did to African American students. "The impact is greater when it has the sanction of law," it noted, "for the policy of separating the races is usually interpreted as denoting the inferiority of the Negro group."

The Decision

Chief Justice Earl Warren wrote an opinion for a unanimous Supreme Court that reversed the *Plessy* decision's "separate but equal" doctrine for public schools. Warren wrote that schools segregated by race were unconstitutional:

> **"** We conclude that in the field of public education the doctrine of 'separate but equal' has no place. Separate educational facilities are inherently [by their nature] unequal . . . Such segregation is a denial of the equal protection of the laws. **"**

In 1955 the Supreme Court issued a follow-up decision, now called *Brown II*, ordering that desegregation proceed "with all deliberate speed."

THE IMPACT TODAY A decade after *Brown*, few schools had been integrated. In the early 1970s many communities turned to busing to integrate schools by force. But busing proved highly controversial, and many communities stopped busing by the late 1990s. Nevertheless, by the early 2000s, schools were much more integrated than they had been before *Brown*. Changing demographics were largely responsible for this trend.

go.hrw.com
Research Online
Keyword: SS Court

CRITICAL THINKING

1. **Analyze the Impact** Using the keyword above, read about the Supreme Court's 1971 decision in *Swann* v. *Charlotte-Mecklenburg Board of Education*. How was this case like *Brown*? In what way did the Court's decision in *Swann* move beyond the decision in *Brown*?

2. **You Be the Judge** *Brown* found that separate facilities were inherently unequal in education, but the case did not directly affect other types of legally imposed segregation. After *Brown*, how should a judge rule on a challenge to segregation in public transportation, restaurants, or hotels? Explain your answer in a short paragraph.

A Boycott Begins in Montgomery, Alabama

The Supreme Court's *Brown* decision had an enormous impact on society. Yet it directly affected only schools. Elsewhere in the South, a great variety of other public places and facilities remained segregated.

The Montgomery bus boycott One example of these segregated public facilities was the bus system in Montgomery, Alabama. African American riders, who made up two-thirds of bus passengers, had to pay their fare at the front of the bus, leave the bus, then enter again through the rear doors. They were forbidden from sitting in the front rows, which were reserved for white passengers. If those front rows filled, all African Americans riding in the next row had to give up their seats. Sharing a row with a white passenger was not allowed.

African Americans in Montgomery had endured these conditions for years. Even before the *Brown* ruling, local groups had sought to end segregation on the buses. It was not until 1955 that decisive action was taken, however.

In that year, a local NAACP member named **Rosa Parks** boarded a Montgomery bus after a day of work. She sat in the section reserved for African Americans. The white section soon filled, however. Parks was ordered to give up her seat and make her row available to white riders. She refused and was arrested.

The NAACP recognized the opportunity Parks's arrest presented. With her cooperation, the organization called for a one-day boycott of the city bus system. Some 90 percent of African American riders stayed off the buses that day. This response convinced community leaders to continue the Montgomery bus boycott. To lead this effort, they formed the Montgomery Improvement Association. The group selected as its leader a young minister of a local Baptist church named **Martin Luther King Jr.**

The boycott created hardship for Montgomery's African Americans. Many depended on the buses to get to work and to do errands.

The boycott also hurt the bus system and other white businesses. As a result, many of the city's whites tried to weaken it. Police harassed African Americans who took part in the boycott. When the city's black churches set up car pools to help their members get around, insurers cancelled the auto insurance policies of the cars' owners. King and other African American leaders became targets of violent threats.

Montgomery Bus Boycott

Rosa Parks was arrested for not surrendering her bus seat to a white passenger, setting in motion the Montgomery bus boycott. Below, boycotters wait for rides at a carpool station. The success of the boycott helped make Martin Luther King Jr. a nationally known civil rights leader.

As the boycott continued, court challenges to segregation of city buses also moved forward. The Supreme Court finally ruled on the subject in late 1956. By then, the boycott was a year old. The Court held that segregation on buses was unconstitutional.

Integration of the buses moved forward. There were some tense moments, including threats of violence against buses and local African American leaders. The tension, however, eventually faded. Integrated buses became a fact of life in Montgomery and elsewhere.

Birth of the SCLC The success of the Montgomery bus boycott inspired African Americans elsewhere. In communities across the South, groups organized boycotts of their own.

In January 1957, representatives of the Montgomery Improvement Association and several other groups met in Atlanta, Georgia. The goal was to form a new group that would organize protest activities taking place all across the region. This group became known as the Southern Christian Leadership Conference, or **SCLC**. Martin Luther King Jr., the leader of the successful Montgomery boycott, was elected leader of the SCLC.

As its name suggests, the SCLC was heavily influenced by the Christian faith. Many of its members, such as King, were members of the clergy. However, the SCLC was open to people of all races and faiths. At its heart was a com-

mitment to mass, nonviolent action. You will read more about nonviolent protest in the next section. You will also read about the spread of the campaign to end segregation from the bus stops of Montgomery to other public places throughout the South.

READING CHECK **Making Generalizations**
What was the nature of the movement created by the successful Montgomery bus boycott?

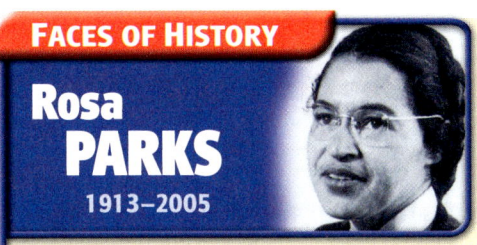

FACES OF HISTORY

Rosa PARKS
1913–2005

When Rosa Parks refused to give up her seat on a bus in 1955, she already had a long history of community activism. In 1943 she became one of the first women to join the local NAACP chapter, where she served as its secretary. She also had experience protesting discrimination on the city's buses. In 1943 her protest of mistreatment on a bus resulted in the driver forcefully removing her from the bus.

In 1957 Parks and her family moved to Detroit. She joined the staff of Representative John Conyers Jr. in 1965, working there for 22 years. For her role in the civil rights movement, Parks received the Presidential Medal of Freedom in 1996 and the Congressional Gold Medal in 1999. After her death in 2005, she became the first woman to lie in honor in the U.S. Capitol rotunda, a tribute only given to the most significant national leaders.

Make Inferences Why was it significant that Rosa Parks had experience as an activist before her 1955 bus protest?

Reviewing Ideas, Terms, and People

1. a. Describe How did Jackie Robinson bring change to American society?
b. Compare How were the NAACP and CORE similar?
c. Predict What do you think will be the final result of Charles Hamilton Houston and Thurgood Marshall's challenges to segregated education?

2. a. Identify What Supreme Court decision had been the legal basis for the segregation of public schools?
b. Make Inferences Why do you think African American students want to attend integrated schools, despite hardships?
c. Evaluate How successful was the *Brown* v. *Board of Education of Topeka, Kansas* decision in desegregating schools?

3. a. Describe What was the goal of the SCLC?
b. Analyze Why was Rosa Parks arrested?

c. Evaluate Did the Montgomery bus boycott achieve its goals? Explain why or why not.

Critical Thinking

4. Categorizing Review your notes on the major events of the early civil rights movement. Then copy the graphic organizer below and use it to list legal and social civil rights victories.

Legal Victories	Social Victories

FOCUS ON WRITING

5. Persuasive Write a flyer encouraging African Americans to join in the Montgomery bus boycott. Make sure your flyer explains why it is important for people to participate.

Freedom Now!

BEFORE YOU READ

MAIN IDEA

The quest for civil rights became a nationwide movement in the 1960s as African Americans won political and legal rights, and segregation was largely abolished.

READING FOCUS

1. What are sit-ins and Freedom Rides, and why were they important in the 1960s?
2. How was the integration of higher education achieved in the South?
3. What role did Albany, Georgia, and Birmingham, Alabama, play in the history of civil rights?
4. What concerns and events led to the passage of the Civil Rights Act of 1964?

KEY TERMS AND PEOPLE

Mohandas Gandhi
James Farmer
SNCC
Freedom Riders
James Meredith
Medgar Evers
Civil Rights Act of 1964

 PI 3.4 Understand the interrelationships between world events and developments in New York State and the United States (e.g., causes for immigration, economic opportunities, human rights abuses, and tyranny versus freedom).

SITTING DOWN FOR CIVIL RIGHTS

▲ Student protesters hold their ground at a lunch counter sit-in.

THE INSIDE STORY

How can you win by being beaten? On May 28, 1963, Anne Moody, Memphis Norman, and Pearlena Lewis, three students from Tougaloo College in Jackson, Mississippi, attempted to place an order at a whites-only lunch counter. The waitress told them to move to the back counter, which was for African Americans. "We would like to be served here," Moody replied. Instead, the waitress closed the counter. The three black students remained seated as a form of protest.

A hostile crowd gathered around the protesters. A man pulled Norman from his stool and beat him. Joan Trumpauer, one of Tougaloo's two white students, took his place. Lois Chaffee, a white faculty member, and John Salter, a Native American professor, soon joined the protesters.

The crowd dumped food on the protesters. Someone hit Salter with brass knuckles, and others poured table salt into his open wound. Still the protesters sat at the counter, refusing to leave or fight back. Finally, fearing greater violence, Tougaloo's president convinced the demonstrators to end their sit-in.

That night the protesters were honored at a huge rally for civil rights. Local NAACP leader Medgar Evers announced that the sit-in was the start of a campaign to end segregation not only in Jackson but throughout Mississippi. ■

Sit-ins and Freedom Rides

The events in Jackson, Mississippi, illustrate tactics that had become common in the civil rights movement in late 1950s and early 1960s. In addition to boycotts, such as the one in Montgomery you read about in Section 1, civil rights workers used other direct, nonviolent methods to confront discrimination and racism. These tactics frequently provoked a violent response from their opponents.

The strategy of nonviolence

Many of the tactics used in the civil rights movement were based on those of **Mohandas Gandhi**. Gandhi, who died in 1948, had been a leader in India's struggle for independence from Great Britain. Gandhi organized actions in which protesters were willing to suffer harm instead of inflicting it. He taught that this nonviolent approach would expose injustice and force those in power to end it. Nonviolent resistance, he believed, was the best way to achieve change in a society in which others held most of the power.

American civil rights leaders such as **James Farmer** of CORE, Martin Luther King Jr. of SCLC, and others shared Gandhi's views. "There is more power in socially organized masses . . . than there is in guns in the hands of a few desperate men," King wrote. "We shall so appeal to your heart and conscience that we will win you in the process."

In the early 1950s, James Lawson, an African American minister, visited India and studied Gandhi's teachings. With King's encouragement, Lawson began conducting workshops on nonviolent methods in Nashville, Tennessee, and on the campuses of African American colleges across the South. He trained hundreds of students, including some whites who supported the civil rights movement. One participant described the weekly workshops.

HISTORY'S VOICES

❝We would practice such things as how to protect your head from a beating and how to protect each other. If one person was taking a severe beating, we would practice other people putting their bodies in between that person and the violence, so that the violence would be more distributed and hopefully no one would get seriously injured. We would practice not striking back if someone struck us.❞

—Diane Nash in *Voices of Freedom* (1990)

The sit-in movement

Lawson was nearly ready to launch a sit-in campaign in Nashville when on February 1, 1960, four college students in Greensboro, North Carolina, began a sit-in of their own after ordering coffee at a lunch counter in a Woolworth's store. Denied service because of their race, the four young men stayed in their seats, expecting to be arrested. When they were not, they remained at the lunch counter until the store closed.

The next day, they returned with more students. By day three, protesters filled 63 of the lunch counter's 66 seats. The daily sit-ins soon attracted hundreds of supporters. The story of these dedicated and well-behaved students, who ended each day's protest with a prayer, quickly became national news. In mid-February, Lawson's Nashville sit-ins began.

The four students who began the sit-in at Greensboro had not attended Lawson's workshops. They had read about his methods, however. The Greensboro protest won important white support. "As long as those who seek a change . . . seek it in a peaceful manner, their power (and their haunting image on the white man's conscience) will not diminish," the *Greensboro Daily News* wrote in an editorial.

FREEDOM RIDES, 1961

MD
Washington, D.C.

VA
Richmond

Greensboro

Nashville
NC

TN

Rock Hill
SC

Anniston

Birmingham
Atlanta

Jackson
GA

Montgomery

LA
MS
AL

New Orleans

ATLANTIC OCEAN

Gulf of Mexico

80°W

90°W

1. May 4: Riders depart Washington, D.C.
2. May 9: Riders assaulted at bus terminal in Rock Hill, SC
3. May 14: Bus attacked in Anniston, AL and set on fire; some riders are beaten
4. May 14: Riders severely beaten in Birmingham, AL
5. May 17: Group of students set out from Nashville, TN to resume rides in Birmingham, AL
6. May 20: Riders meet more violence in Montgomery, AL; federal marshals arrive and Martin Luther King, Jr. leads rally
7. May 25: More than 300 riders are jailed in Jackson, MS
8. New Orleans, LA, the original destination, is never reached

→ Freedom Rides routes

GEOGRAPHY SKILLS INTERPRETING MAPS

1. **Movement** What was the planned route of the Freedom Rides? How far did the riders make it?

2. **Place** Which event seems most significant to you? Explain.

See **Skills Handbook**, p. H19

During the next two months, protesters in about 50 southern cities began to use the sit-in tactic. In many places, white onlookers attacked the participants with food and other objects. Demonstrators, some of whom were white, were sometimes beaten. By April some 2,000 protesters had been arrested. "We do not consider going to jail a sacrifice but a privilege," a jailed demonstrator proclaimed. "Sixty days is not long to spend in jail. We will do it again for a cause as great as this one."

Despite the arrests and violence—or perhaps because of them—sit-ins were generally successful at getting business owners to change their policies. In May several stores in Nashville ended segregation at their lunch counters. The Greensboro sit-ins ended in July with the integration of lunch counters there. In October, Woolworth's and three other national chains integrated lunch counters nationwide.

The sit-ins marked a shift in the civil rights movement. They showed young African Americans' growing impatience with the slow pace of change. Sit-in leaders formed the Student Nonviolent Coordinating Committee, or **SNCC**, to conduct other nonviolent protests.

The Freedom Rides The success of the student sit-ins inspired CORE to plan its own nonviolent action in 1961. In December 1960 the Supreme Court had ordered that facilities in bus stations serving interstate travelers be open to all passengers, regardless of race. The Court's order, however, was not being enforced. Newly elected president John F. Kennedy, though a supporter of civil rights, seemed unwilling to anger southern whites.

Members of CORE decided to draw attention to the situation by sending a group of **Freedom Riders** on a bus trip through the South. At each stop the African American riders would go into the whites-only waiting rooms and try to use facilities such as restrooms and lunch counters. "We felt we could count on the racists of the South to create a crisis so that the federal government would be compelled to enforce the law," James Farmer later explained.

On May 4, 1961, a group of 13 volunteers, including Farmer, left Washington, D.C., by bus, bound for New Orleans, Louisiana. They tried to use the facilities in bus stations in towns they passed through. At first they experienced only mild harassment. Then on May 14, one of the buses was swarmed by a mob outside of Anniston, Alabama. The mob firebombed the bus and beat the Freedom Riders as they escaped. Newspapers nationwide showed the incident on their front pages.

Another Freedom Ride bus reached Birmingham, Alabama, where it was attacked by a group armed with baseball bats and metal pipes. One Freedom Rider suffered permanent brain damage, and another required dozens of stitches to close the wounds to his head. No police arrived to stop the savage beatings. When the bus company refused to sell the Freedom Riders tickets to continue their journey, the CORE-sponsored Freedom Ride disbanded.

Federal intervention SNCC leader Diane Nash refused to give in to the violence, however. She gathered a group of SNCC members to continue the Freedom Rides from Nashville. Fearing death, several of them made out wills or wrote letters of farewell to loved ones before leaving for Birmingham.

Attorney General Robert Kennedy arranged with Alabama's governor to provide police protection for the SNCC volunteers. When their bus reached Montgomery, however, the police disappeared. The SNCC riders were attacked by yet another mob. An aide to President John Kennedy, at the scene as an observer, was among those beaten unconscious. Outraged at the governor's betrayal, the attorney general sent 600 federal marshals to Montgomery to protect the Freedom Riders.

On May 24 the SNCC riders reached Jackson, Mississippi. There they were arrested and jailed for using the bus station's whites-only facilities. The next day more volunteers arrived in Jackson, vowing to continue the rides. They were also arrested.

During the next four months, several hundred Freedom Riders rode buses through the lower South. The protest ended in September 1961, when the federal Interstate Commerce Commission finally issued tough new rules forcing integration of bus and train stations.

READING CHECK **Comparing** In what ways were the sit-ins and the Freedom Rides similar?

Integrating Higher Education

While SNCC and CORE attempted to achieve change using nonviolent protest, the NAACP pushed ahead with its legal campaign against school segregation. By 1960 it had expanded its efforts to include colleges and universities. White lawyers collaborated with the NAACP. In 1961 the organization obtained a court order requiring the University of Georgia to admit two African American students.

Charlayne Hunter and Hamilton Holmes were only in school a few days before they were suspended after white students rioted. A federal judge ordered their reinstatement. Robert Kennedy publicly praised the school for its respect for the law. He called the two students "freedom fighters" for returning to campus

Desegregating Colleges

James Meredith's entrance into the University of Mississippi made him a famous name in civil rights (right). Governor Wallace of Alabama (left) blocks African American students from entering a university. *How did the defiance of state governments affect efforts to desegregate higher education?*

Martin Luther KING Jr.
1929–1968

Martin Luther King Jr. entered Morehouse College in Atlanta, Georgia, at age 15 and graduated in 1948. He became an ordained minister while attending Morehouse. After religious training in Pennsylvania, King attended Boston University, where he completed a doctoral degree in religion in 1955. At all three schools, King studied the teachings on nonviolent protest of Indian leader Mohandas Gandhi.

The powerful speaking abilities for which King was known developed slowly. He received C's in his first public speaking courses in Pennsylvania. By his third year there, however, his professors were praising the impression he made in public speeches and discussions.

In 1953 King married Coretta Scott, an Alabamian he met in Boston. The next year they moved to Montgomery, Alabama, where King became pastor of a Baptist church. The Montgomery bus boycott boosted him to leadership in the civil rights movement. In 1964 King was awarded the Nobel Peace Prize for his work for civil rights.

Draw Conclusions How did King's education prepare him for his role in the civil rights movement?

---

amidst all the threats. Although Hunter especially suffered continuing hostility and taunts, both she and Holmes graduated in 1963.

Greater trouble erupted at the University of Mississippi when **James Meredith** attempted to enroll there in September 1962. A federal court ruled that the university had rejected Meredith's application "solely because he was a Negro," and ordered him to be admitted. On Sunday evening, September 30, Meredith arrived on campus. He was accompanied by 500 federal marshals that Robert Kennedy had ordered to protect him. A mob of 2,500 protesters, many of them nonstudents, met the group with violence.

As the riot worsened, President Kennedy went on national television to announce that he was sending in troops. "The eyes of the nation and the world are upon you," he told Mississippians. "The honor of your university and the state are in the balance." The troops arrived in the predawn hours of Monday morning and finally ended the protest. By then, however, hundreds of people had been injured and two killed. One of the dead was a journalist from France, sent to cover Meredith's enrollment.

In the months that followed, Meredith was frequently harassed by groups of white students. Yet a few students defied their peers and drank coffee with him or sat at his table at mealtimes. A small force of marshals remained at the university to protect Meredith until he graduated in the summer of 1963.

At the University of Alabama, Governor George Wallace in June 1963 physically blocked Vivian Malone and James Hood from enrolling. "This action is in violation of rights reserved to the state by the Constitution of the United States," Wallace proclaimed. However, after his speech and symbolic defiance of a court order to integrate the university, Wallace stepped aside.

READING CHECK **Making Generalizations** How were public universities in Georgia, Mississippi, and Alabama integrated?

Albany and Birmingham

In late 1961 Albany, Georgia, became a battleground in the civil rights movement. SNCC began a sit-in in Albany's bus station in November because local officials were ignoring the Interstate Commerce Commission's new integration rules. When demonstrators were arrested, SNCC notified the U.S. Justice Department. The federal government, however, took no action.

The Albany Movement By mid-December more than 500 protesters had been jailed. Local civil rights leaders brought national attention to the situation by inviting Martin Luther King Jr. to lead more demonstrations. The campaign was called the Albany Movement. "We will wear them down with our capacity to suffer," King promised. He was soon arrested for leading a march on city hall. King refused to pay the fine. He vowed to remain in jail until the city agreed to desegregate. "I hope thousands [of others] will join me," he said.

Albany police chief Laurie Prichett had studied King's tactics, however. "His method was nonviolence . . . to fill the jails, same as Gandhi in India," Prichett said later. "And once they filled the jails, we'd have no capacity to arrest and then we'd have to give in to his demands." Prichett made arrangements with every jail in the surrounding area, so he was able to arrest all the protesters. In addition, when the national press arrived to cover King's sentencing, Prichett had King's fine paid, so King was released instead.

Opponents of integration also took advantage of divisions in the Albany Movement. The local leaders who began it became upset when the SCLC took control. Sensing this, city officials refused to negotiate with anyone but local leaders and would not negotiate at all as long as King was in town. In August 1962, King called off his demonstrations and left Albany. City officials then refused to meet with the local leaders. The protests resumed without King but failed to accomplish their goals.

The nine-month Albany Movement was a major defeat for King. It proved to be an important experience, however. After Albany, King vowed that the SCLC would organize its own campaigns rather than aid campaigns begun by others. His new strategy soon proved successful in Birmingham.

The Birmingham campaign King next focused his efforts on Birmingham, Alabama. Birmingham was known for its strict enforcement of segregation. With help from entertainer Harry Belafonte, King raised several hundred thousand dollars to fund a campaign against Birmingham's segregation laws. Volunteers taught local African Americans the techniques of nonviolence in the city's African American churches.

King's effort began in April 1963 with sit-ins and marches. Authorities quickly arrested the protesters. King had counted on this response to motivate more people to join the protests and focus national attention on the city. At first his strategy worked. On April 12 King and hundreds more were arrested and jailed.

The next day a group of local white clergy took out a full-page ad in the city's newspaper. They attacked King's actions as unwise and untimely. In his jail cell, King rejected these charges with a letter written in the margins of the newspaper. His response gained fame as the "Letter from a Birmingham Jail."

When King was released a few days later, he found fewer adult African Americans willing to risk losing their jobs by going to jail. Another SCLC leader urged King to use children instead. On May 2 demonstrators between the ages six and eighteen sang and chanted as they marched to lines of police set up to stop them. More than 900 were arrested and jailed.

The next day, Birmingham police chief Eugene "Bull" Connor used police and firefighters to break up a group of about 2,500

Witness to Violence

Images of peaceful protesters in Birmingham being attacked by police dogs and swept away by high-pressure fire hoses shocked the nation. *How did President Kennedy react?*

African American students as they gathered for another march. As television cameras and press photographers recorded the scene, the authorities struck. They blasted the protesters with fire hoses. The force of the water knocked the protesters down, tore their clothes, and left some of them bloody on the ground.

Connor repeated these actions for the next several days, as the nation watched on television. Finally, after hundreds of demonstrators had been jailed, federal negotiators succeeded in getting city officials to agree to many of

ACADEMIC VOCABULARY

restore to put something back into its former or original condition

King's demands. King called the agreement "the most magnificent victory for justice we've seen in the Deep South."

Some white people in Birmingham refused to accept the compromise. The motel where King was staying and the home of his brother were bombed. When some African Americans rioted, President Kennedy declared that he would not let extremists on either side destroy the agreement. He sent federal troops to Birmingham to restore order.

READING CHECK **Comparing and Contrasting** How were the Albany and Birmingham campaigns alike, and how did they differ?

MAJOR CIVIL RIGHTS REFORMS — QUICK FACTS

Brown v. Board of Education of Topeka, Kansas (1954)	• declared segregated public schools unconstitutional
Civil Rights Act of 1957	• established a federal Civil Rights Commission to investigate violations of civil rights • created a civil rights division within the Justice Department to enforce civil rights laws • authorized the federal government to prosecute anyone interfering with another person's right to vote
Executive Order 11063 (November 20, 1962)	• banned racial and religious discrimination in housing built or purchased with federal aid
Civil Rights Act of 1964	• banned discrimination in public accommodations • outlawed unequal voting requirements • barred discrimination in employment based on race, gender, religion, or national origin • established the Equal Employment Opportunity Commission • applied federal power to speed integration of schools and other public facilities
Voting Rights Act of 1965	• suspended literacy tests and other devices used to exclude black voters • authorized federal supervision of voter registration • allowed federal workers to register voters
Civil Rights Act of 1968 (Fair Housing Act)	• banned racial discrimination in the sale, rental, or financing of housing • made harming civil rights workers a federal crime

The Civil Rights Act of 1964

You have read about Kennedy's approach on civil rights. He had believed that moving slowly was the best way to make progress. The events in Alabama, however, changed his mind.

HISTORY'S VOICES

> The fires of frustration and discord are burning in every city, North and South . . . We face . . . a moral crisis as a country and as a people . . . We cannot say to 10 percent of the population that . . . the only way . . . to get their rights is to go into the streets and demonstrate. I think we owe them and we owe ourselves a better country than that.
>
> —John Kennedy, June 11, 1963

Kennedy announced that he would ask for sweeping legislation designed to finally end segregation in public accommodations—hotels, restaurants, theaters, and other establishments that serve the public.

The assassination of Medgar Evers A murder just hours after Kennedy's speech helped put the president's concerns into sharp focus. The head of the NAACP in Mississippi, **Medgar Evers**, was shot dead in his front yard. Evers was one of the movement's most effective leaders. His slaying shocked many Americans.

Police quickly arrested a Ku Klux Klan member named Byron De La Beckwith. All-white juries failed to reach a verdict in two trials, and De La Beckwith went free. Some 30 years later, however, authorities tried him yet a third time. In 1994, at the age of 73, De La Beckwith was finally convicted and sentenced to life in prison.

The March on Washington To build support for the civil rights movement, African American leaders planned a huge march on the nation's capital for August 1963. In June, when President Kennedy called for a civil rights law, African American leaders decided to include demands for its passage as one of the march's goals.

The March on Washington for Jobs and Freedom took place on August 28, 1963. It was the largest civil rights demonstration ever held in the United States. More than 200,000 people of all races covered the National Mall. Major civil rights figures addressed the crowd from the steps of the Lincoln Memorial. Gospel singer Mahalia Jackson, folk singer Joan Baez, and other popular entertainers of the day performed for the crowd.

Martin Luther King Jr. delivered the last speech at the day-long rally. He started by reviewing African Americans' long struggle throughout history for freedom. Then, urged on by Mahalia Jackson and other listeners nearby, King put aside his prepared remarks and began to speak from his heart. His speech became known as the "I Have a Dream" speech.

HISTORY'S VOICES

❝I have a dream that one day this nation will rise up and live out the true meaning of its creed: 'We hold these truths to be self-evident; that all men are created equal.' . . . I have a dream that my four little children will one day live in a nation where they will not be judged by the color of their skin, but the content of their character. I have a dream today!❞

—Martin Luther King Jr., August 28, 1963

Passing the Civil Rights Act The good feeling produced by the March on Washington was short-lived. The next month a bomb exploded in a Birmingham church, killing four young African American girls. Then in November, President Kennedy was assassinated. His vice president, Lyndon Johnson, took office.

President Johnson supported passage of a strong civil rights bill. Although some southerners in Congress fought hard to kill it, Johnson signed it into law on July 2, 1964. The **Civil Rights Act of 1964** banned discrimination in employment and in public accommodations.

Government

The conviction in Evers's killing has encouraged the FBI to reopen other old cases from the civil rights movement. In 2002 a jury convicted a man long suspected in the Birmingham church bombing.

READING CHECK **Summarizing** Why did a strong civil rights bill finally become law in 1964?

Reviewing Ideas, Terms, and People

1. a. Identify What civil rights tactic was based on the ideas and actions of **Mohandas Gandhi**?
b. Summarize What was the basic belief behind the tactic of nonviolence?
c. Elaborate Why do you think the sit-ins were successful?

2. a. Describe How did the NAACP work for the integration of colleges and universities?
b. Make Inferences Why did so many federal marshals accompany **James Meredith** to the University of Mississippi?
c. Predict Do you think the rioting at the University of Mississippi affected people's opinions about segregation? Why or why not?

3. a. Identify What began the Albany Movement?
b. Make Inferences Why did Martin Luther King Jr. decide to focus on Birmingham?
c. Elaborate Why did federal negotiators want Birmingham officials to agree to many of King's demands?

4. a. Define What was the goal of the March on Washington?
b. Analyze What inspired President Kennedy to begin focusing on civil rights?

c. Evaluate Do you think the **Civil Rights Act of 1964** went far enough? Explain why or why not. What substitute or additional provisions might the law have contained?

Critical Thinking

5. Identify Cause and Effect Review your notes on the Civil Rights Act of 1964. Then copy the graphic organizer below and use it to list the causes and effects of the law. You may need to add more circles.

FOCUS ON WRITING

6. Persuasive Write a letter to your representative in Congress, explaining why he or she should vote for the Civil Rights Act of 1964. Be sure to include in your letter persuasive arguments that support your position.

American *Literature*

ST 1.3 Read Dr. Martin Luther King's "Letter from Birmingham Jail" and discuss how this letter expresses the basic ideas, values, and beliefs found in the United States Constitution and Bill of Rights.

MARTIN LUTHER KING JR. (1929–1968)

About the Reading While protesting segregation in Birmingham, Alabama, Martin Luther King Jr. was arrested and held in a Birmingham jail. The following is an excerpt from a letter that King wrote in response to a full-page ad in a local newspaper. The ad, taken out by eight members of the clergy, denounced the protests. King's letter clearly presents his philosophy on nonviolence.

AS YOU READ Consider the dangers that Martin Luther King Jr. as well as other social activists faced by standing up for the causes they believed in.

Excerpt from

Letter from a Birmingham Jail

by Martin Luther King Jr.

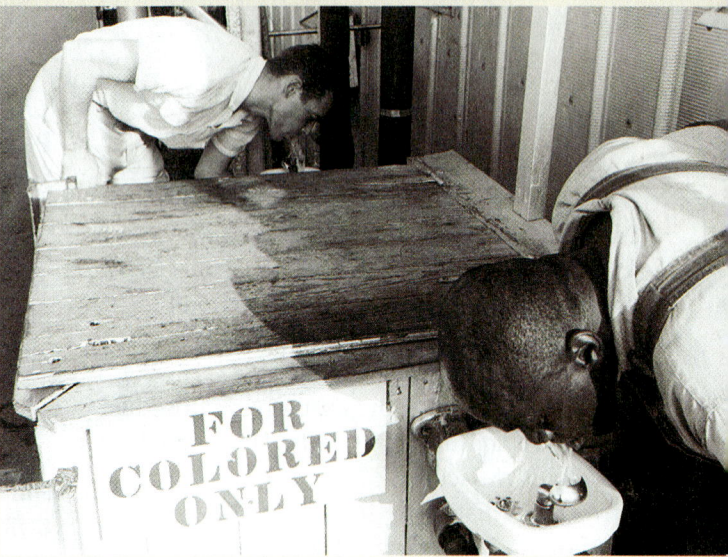

Men drinking from segregated water fountains in the South

You express a great deal of anxiety over our willingness to break laws. This is certainly a legitimate concern. Since we so diligently urge people to obey the Supreme Court's decision of 1954 outlawing segregation in the public schools, at first glance it may seem rather paradoxical for us consciously to break laws. One may well ask: "How can you advocate breaking some laws and obeying others?" The answer lies in the fact that there are two types of laws: just and unjust. I would be the first to advocate obeying just laws. One has not only a legal but a moral responsibility to obey just laws. Conversely, one has a moral responsibility to disobey unjust laws. I would agree with St. Augustine that "an unjust law is no law at all."

Now, what is the difference between the two? How does one determine whether a law is just or unjust? A just law is a man-made code that squares with the moral law or the law of God. An unjust law is a code that is out of harmony with the moral law. To put it in the terms of St. Thomas Aquinas: An unjust law is a human law that is not rooted in eternal law and natural law. Any law that uplifts human personality is just. Any law that degrades human personality is unjust.

All segregation statutes are unjust because segregation distorts the soul and damages the personality. It gives the segregator a false sense of superiority and the segregated a false sense of inferiority. Segregation, to use the terminology of the Jewish philosopher Martin Buber, substitutes an "I-it" relationship for an "I-thou" relationship and ends up relegating persons to the status of things. Hence segregation is not only politically, economically and sociologically unsound, it is morally wrong and sinful. Paul Tillich said that sin is separation. Is not segregation an existential expression of man's tragic separation, his awful estrangement, his terrible sinfulness? Thus it is that I can urge men to obey the 1954 decision of the Supreme Court, for it is morally right; and I can urge them to disobey segregation ordinances, for they are morally wrong.

Skills FOCUS **READING LIKE A HISTORIAN**

Literature as Historical Evidence How does King's letter show the importance of religious thought in the civil rights movement?

See **Skills Handbook**, p. H32

Voting Rights

BEFORE YOU READ

MAIN IDEA

In the 1960s, African Americans gained voting rights and political power in the South, but only after a bitter and hard-fought struggle.

READING FOCUS

1. What methods did civil rights workers use to gain voting rights for African Americans in the South?
2. How did African American political organizing become a national issue?
3. What events led to passage of the Voting Rights Act?

KEY TERMS AND PEOPLE

Voter Education Project
Twenty-fourth Amendment
Freedom Summer
Mississippi Freedom Democratic Party
Fannie Lou Hamer
Voting Rights Act of 1965

PI 2.3 Compare and contrast the experiences of different groups in the United States.

THE INSIDE STORY

What did the 2000 election in Selma symbolize? On March 7, 1965, about 600 people marching for voting rights were attacked and beaten by police as they crossed the Edmund Pettus Bridge in Selma, Alabama. The savage attack gained national attention and became one of the most notorious events of the civil rights movement.

Thirty-five years later, in 2000, Selma made national news again when James Perkins became the city's first African American mayor. Perkins was twelve years old when the march took place. He wanted to join, but his parents, fearing that violence might erupt, refused to let him go. However, like many other Selma residents, Perkins never forgot that fateful and bloody day.

The candidate Perkins defeated in 2000, Joe Smitherman, had been Selma's mayor in 1965. He did not take part in the beatings at the bridge. But back then, Smitherman opposed voting rights for African Americans. He later apologized for his views. This helped him stay in office for ten terms, as the number of African American voters in his city increased from 150 in 1964 to 9,000—some 65 percent of Selma's voters—in 2000.

Perkins focused his campaign in 2000 on economic issues instead of race, but some Selma residents organized their own effort to defeat Smitherman. For months, demonstrators stood at the Edmund Pettus Bridge holding signs reading "Remember the Blood" and shouting to passing cars, "Joe gotta go!"

Within minutes of the announcement of James Perkins's victory, thousands of his supporters poured back and forth across the bridge in cars and on foot, honking and cheering. "This is the final step of the march over the bridge," said one supporter about the election's significance. "This is the dream that Dr. King wanted."

SELMA, Now and Then

◄ **Selma mayor James Perkins, with the Edmund Pettus Bridge in the background**

Gaining Voting Rights

James Perkins and the many other African Americans who hold elective offices across the nation today owe much to the civil rights struggles of the 1960s. Voting rights for African Americans, like other victories of the civil rights movement, were achieved at great human cost and sacrifice.

Registering voters The nonviolent methods of the civil rights movement troubled the Kennedy administration because of the violent reactions they provoked. After the brutal attacks on the Freedom Riders in 1961, Attorney General Robert Kennedy met with SNCC leaders. He urged them to focus on voter registration rather than on protests. The vote was the key to changing things in the South, Kennedy claimed. He said that civil rights workers could count on federal government protection if they took this approach.

In 1962 SNCC, CORE, and other groups founded the **Voter Education Project** (VEP) to register southern African Americans to vote. However, the groups soon discovered that opposition to African American suffrage was as great as opposition to ending segregation. Marches to register voters were attacked by mobs or broken up by the police. Project workers routinely were beaten or jailed.

Mississippi presented the greatest challenge. VEP workers there lived in daily fear for their safety. A local farmer helping one voter registration drive was killed. The state legislator who shot him was aquitted. The lone African American witness to the crime was later found shot to death.

In spite of such terror tactics, the Voter Education Project was a success. In 1962 fewer than 1.4 million of the South's 5 million African American adults were registered to vote. By 1964 the VEP had registered more than a half million more African American voters. Only in Mississippi were results discouraging. "We are powerless to register people in significant numbers anywhere in the state," SNCC organizer Robert Moses told the VEP in a report.

The Twenty-fourth Amendment Congress passed the **Twenty-fourth Amendment** to the Constitution in August 1962 and submitted it to the states for ratification. The amendment banned states from taxing citizens to vote. Many southern states required these poll taxes as a way to keep African Americans from voting. Because the tax was not based on gender or race, it was constitutional. But since more African Americans than whites were poor, it affected them most.

Although the Twenty-fourth Amendment's ban on poll taxes applied only to elections

TRACING HISTORY

Civil Rights

The Declaration of Independence says that all people are born with "unalienable rights," but it took nearly 200 years to see that promise extended to all Americans. Study the time line to learn about key events in the struggle for civil rights.

ST 3.1 Investigate how Americans have reconciled the inherent tensions and conflicts over minority versus majority rights by researching the abolitionist and reform movements of the nineteenth century, the civil rights and women's rights movements of the twentieth century, or the social protest movements of the 1960s and 1970s.

1865–1870 The Thirteenth, Fourteenth, and Fifteenth Amendments abolish slavery, grant citizenship to African Americans, and give the vote to African American men.

1700

1800

1791 The First Amendment in the Bill of Rights guarantees freedom of religious worship.

An Islamic prayer service

for president or Congress, it increased hopes that change was on the way. As the proposed amendment worked its way through the ratification process, voting rights leaders planned more projects, concentrating on Mississippi.

Freedom Summer The Twenty-fourth Amendment became part of the Constitution in January 1964. A call went out for college students willing to spend their summer in Mississippi, registering African Americans to vote.

When school let out, hundreds of volunteers gathered at an Ohio college to train for a project called **Freedom Summer**. Most of the trainers—mainly SNCC workers—were from poor southern African American families. The student volunteers were mainly white, northern, and upper middle class. One volunteer later recalled why he took part.

HISTORY'S VOICES

❝ I grew up in New York City. I had been raised in a family where being Jewish was important in terms of identifying with the underdog, with people who were suffering repression and discrimination . . . It was tremendously impressive and exciting. For me, it was a tremendous privilege to be allowed to participate in this movement for racial justice. At eighteen years old, to be able to be involved in this kind of a struggle was very important to me. **❞**

—Peter Orris in *Voices of Freedom* (1990)

Volunteers were trained to register voters or to teach at summer school. Mississippi spent about $82 per year to educate each white student but less than $22 per black student. In addition, many black schools in Mississippi closed during the cotton harvest to provide cheap child labor. The project's Freedom Schools offered African American students much-needed help in reading and math as well as instruction in black history and the civil rights movement.

Besides educating children and registering voters, project workers hoped to start a freedom movement in Mississippi that would continue after the volunteers left. Project leader Robert Moses had another goal: Just getting everyone through the summer alive would be an accomplishment, he said.

Crisis in Mississippi The first 200 volunteers arrived in Mississippi on June 20, 1964. The very next day one of them went missing. Andrew Goodman, a college student from New York, had gone with two CORE workers, James Chaney and Michael Schwerner, to inspect an African American church that had recently been bombed. They were arrested for speeding in Philadelphia, Mississippi, and held in jail until evening. After paying a fine, the three men drove off into the night. They were never heard from again.

Intercollegiate women's basketball game

1964 The Civil Rights Act of 1964 guarantees voting rights and prohibits gender-based discrimination.

1972 Title IX of the Higher Education Act prohibits gender discrimination in all areas of higher education, including athletics.

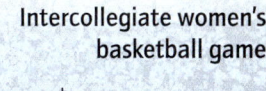

1920 The Nineteenth Amendment guarantees women the right to vote.

Georgia Supreme Court Chief Justice Leah Ward Sears

2005 Leah Ward Sears becomes the chief justice of the Georgia Supreme Court, the first African American woman chief justice in the country.

American Civil Liberty

Twenty-fourth Amendment

In 1870 the Fifteenth Amendment granted African American men the right to vote in federal elections. Still, many states set requirements that made voting difficult for African Americans. One example was the poll tax. Many people could not afford this tax. Often, however, anyone whose father or grandfather had been eligible to vote did not have to pay it. In this way, many whites avoided the tax. Many African Americans could not.

One result of the civil rights movement of the 1950s and 1960s was a new amendment to the Constitution. The Twenty-fourth Amendment outlawed poll taxes in federal elections. This amendment was reinforced by a 1966 Supreme Court decision that poll taxes were illegal in state and local elections.

Identifying Cause and Effect In what ways would the Twenty-fourth Amendment increase the political power of African Americans?

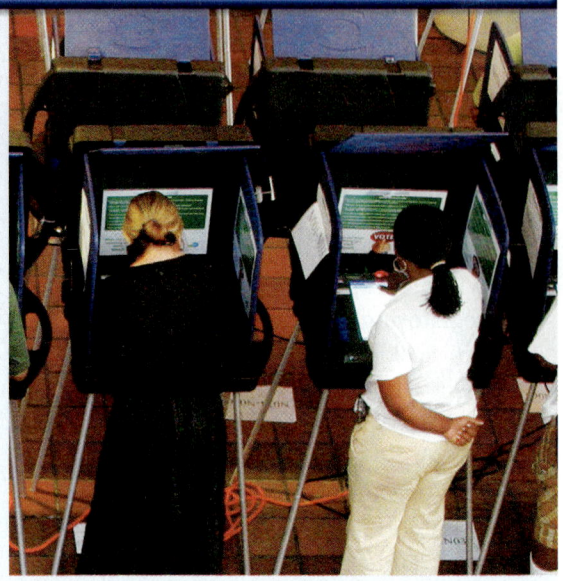

All Americans today cast their ballots free of the poll tax.

President Lyndon Johnson ordered a massive hunt for the three young men. In August their bodies were found in an earthen dam near Philadelphia, Mississippi. The incident cast gloom over Freedom Summer. Two-thirds of the volunteers went home. Many of those who remained suffered through shootings, beatings, bombings, and arrests.

In December the FBI arrested 21 suspects in the murders of Goodman, Chaney, and Schwerner. Most were members of the Ku Klux Klan. When the state dropped all charges, they were brought to trial in federal court for violating civil rights laws. Seven were convicted and received prison sentences ranging from 4 to 10 years. They were the first convictions ever in Mississippi for killing a civil rights worker.

In spite of the violence, organizers considered Mississippi's Freedom Summer project a success. The Freedom Schools taught 3,000 students, and more than 17,000 African Americans in Mississippi applied to vote. When state elections officials accepted only about 1,600 of these applications helped to show that a federal law was needed to secure voting rights for African Americans.

Government

In 2005 another of the killers was convicted and sentenced to prison for the murders of Goodman, Chaney, and Schwerner.

READING CHECK **Summarizing** What steps were taken to help African Americans register to vote?

Political Organizing

Freedom Summer was often overshadowed by the 1964 presidential election campaign. Most African American leaders wanted Johnson to defeat the Republican candidate Barry Goldwater, who had voted against the Civil Rights Act of 1964. You read about the election in the previous chapter. To help Johnson, Martin Luther King Jr. and other civil rights leaders agreed to suspend their protests until after election day.

SNCC, however, refused to agree. SNCC leaders wanted to protest segregation within the Democratic Party itself. "It is time for the Democratic Party to clean itself of racism," John Lewis, the head of SNCC, told the press.

As part of Freedom Summer, SNCC helped the **Mississippi Freedom Democratic Party** (MFDP) to organize. The MFDP elected sixty-eight delegates to the Democratic National Convention in August 1964. They arrived at the convention and asked to be seated instead of the all-white delegation sent by the state's Democratic Party.

The convention's credentials committee held a hearing to decide which delegates should represent Mississippi. **Fannie Lou Hamer**, an MFDP leader, presented her group's case. Her testimony was carried live on national television. Hamer, a poor sharecropper, told how on the day she registered to vote she was fired from the plantation where she had lived for 18 years. She described how she was beaten in jail after being arrested for attending a voter registration meeting. Hamer wept as she concluded her powerful statement.

❝All this on account of us wanting to register, to become first-class citizens, and if the Freedom Democratic Party is not seated now, I question America. Is this America, the land of the free and the home of the brave where we have to sleep with our telephones off the hooks because our lives be threatened daily because we want to live as decent human beings in America?❞

—Fannie Lou Hamer, August 22, 1964

While Hamer's powerful testimony was on the air, President Johnson was trying to control any political damage to the Democratic Party. In a quickly arranged news conference, he offered to compromise with the MFDP.

The compromise that party leaders proposed was to seat two members of the MFDP delegation and classify the rest as nonvoting "guests" of the convention. Although the NAACP and SCLC supported the compromise, SNCC and the MFDP opposed it. "We didn't come all this way for just two votes," Hamer declared. "We must stop playing the game of token recognition for real change," the MFDP said in a statement rejecting the compromise.

The MFDP's challenge failed in the end. It also helped widen a split that was developing in the civil rights movement. But it helped pave the way for future increases in the power of minorities and women in American politics.

READING CHECK **Identifying Problems and Solutions** How did the MFDP represent the drive for political organization among African Americans?

The Voting Rights Act

Following passage of the Civil Rights Act of 1964, the SCLC shifted its main focus to voting rights for African Americans. "The right to vote was the issue, replacing public accommodation as the mass concern of a people hungry for a place in the sun," Martin Luther King Jr. later wrote of the movement's new focus.

The Selma campaign In January 1965 King began a campaign to gain voting rights for African Americans by organizing marches in Selma, Alabama. "We will dramatize the situation to arouse the federal government by marching by the thousands to the places of registration," he declared.

By the end of January more than 2,000 marchers had been arrested. Police acted with restraint. They did not want to give King the confrontation he was seeking. King then repeated a tactic he had used earlier in Birmingham. He forced police to jail him along with several hundred other marchers, including many children.

King's arrest had the desired effect. The national media swarmed into Selma. The mass arrests and images of children being sent off to jail began appearing on the networks' evening news programs.

March from Selma

Above, police lay in wait for civil rights marchers as they cross the Edmund Pettus Bridge, March 7, 1965. Right, John Lewis, the SNCC leader who organized the first Selma march, is beaten by state troopers after crossing the bridge on what came to be known as Bloody Sunday.

THE CIVIL RIGHTS MOVEMENT **929**

Tensions rose in mid-February, when police attacked a march in nearby Marion, Alabama. Two state troopers shot and killed a marcher. A few days later King announced a four-day march from Selma to Montgomery, the state capital, to protest police brutality. Governor George Wallace issued an order prohibiting the march. "[It] will not be tolerated," he warned.

The Selma march On Sunday, March 7, 1965, about 600 African Americans began the 54-mile march. Just across the Edmund Pettus Bridge, on the way out of Selma, city and state police blocked their way. After firing tear gas at the marchers, police attacked with clubs, chains, and electric cattle prods. TV networks showed film of the savage violence.

King was not present on the March 7 march. He announced that it would resume on March 9. In a controversial decision, he led the group only to the base of the bridge—not across it. The pause was only temporary, however. After receiving promises of federal protection, the marchers finally reached Montgomery on March 25.

The Voting Rights Act of 1965 A week later, President Johnson gave a nationally televised address to a joint session of Congress. "At times history and fate meet . . . to shape a turning point in man's unending search for freedom," he observed. "So it was last week in Selma, Alabama." The president asked for quick passage of a tough voting rights law. "It is wrong—deadly wrong—to deny any of your fellow Americans the right to vote," Johnson declared. "Outside this chamber is the outraged conscience of a nation."

The **Voting Rights Act of 1965** passed in Congress by large majorities. King, James Farmer, Rosa Parks, and other civil rights leaders attended the president's signing ceremony on August 6.

The law proved to be one of the most important pieces of civil rights legislation ever passed. It gave the federal government powerful tools with which to break down longstanding barriers to African American voting rights. The impact was felt quickly. Within three weeks more than 27,000 African Americans in Mississippi, Alabama, and Louisiana registered to vote. African American candidates were soon elected to state and local offices, helping to break the long-held political power of those who supported segregation.

READING CHECK **Identifying Cause and Effect** How did the Selma march help to secure passage of the Voting Rights Act of 1965?

SECTION 3 ASSESSMENT

go.hrw.com
Online Quiz
Keyword: SD7 HP28

Reviewing Ideas, Terms, and People

1. **a. Identify** What was the goal of the **Voter Education Project**?
   b. Compare How were the obstacles faced by the Voter Education Project and **Freedom Summer** workers similar?
   c. Elaborate Why do you think African American voter registration efforts faced such fierce resistance?

2. **a. Describe** Who was **Fannie Lou Hamer** and what was her goal?
   b. Analyze Why did some civil rights groups suspend their protests before the election of 1964?
   c. Evaluate Do you think the **Mississippi Freedom Democratic Party** was right to reject President Johnson's compromise? Explain your viewpoint.

3. **a. Define** What was the Selma campaign?
   b. Make Inferences How did the media help the marchers' cause in Selma?
   c. Elaborate Why do you think so many members of Congress supported the **Voting Rights Act of 1965**?

Critical Thinking

4. **Analyze Information** Review your notes on African Americans' struggle for political equality. Then copy the graphic organizer below and use it to list the events in the struggle, what injustice each event targeted, and the effects of those actions.

Event	Injustice	Effects

FOCUS ON SPEAKING

5. **Expository** Make a short speech supporting either the Twenty-fourth Amendment or the Voting Rights Act of 1965. In your speech, explain the likely benefits of the new law.

ST 1.2 Analyze the decisions leading to major turning points in United States history, comparing alternative courses of action, and hypothesizing, within the context of the historic period, about what might have happened if the decision had been different.

Reynolds v. Sims (1964)

Why It Matters *Reynolds* v. *Sims* provided the Court's philosophy behind the "one person, one vote" standard. Because of this ruling, all states had to change their methods for electing state legislators.

Background of the Case

By 1960 about three-fourths of Alabama voters lived in cities, but rural voters still controlled both houses of the legislature. A group of Birmingham citizens sued, claiming that their votes had substantially less impact than the votes of people from rural counties.

In earlier cases the Supreme Court ruled that federal courts could not tell state legislatures how to handle representation issues. But in 1960 the Court struck down an Alabama law designed to keep African American votes from deciding elections. This case opened the door to judicial review of apportionment decisions. However, the Birmingham plaintiffs still had to convince the Court that Alabama's legislative districts were so unfair as to be unconstitutional.

The Decision

Chief Justice Earl Warren wrote the opinion of the Court. He emphasized that the individual citizen is the key component of a democratic society:

> **❝Legislators represent people, not trees or acres. Legislators are elected by voters, not farms or cities or economic interests . . . A citizen, a qualified voter, is no more nor no less so because he lives in the city or on the farm. This is the clear and strong command of our Constitution's Equal Protection Clause.❞**

The Court held that seats in both branches of state legislatures had to be apportioned based on population. Each elected official in a particular state had to represent approximately the same number of voters. This "one person, one vote" standard has become a hallmark of democracy.

THE IMPACT TODAY Members of New York's state assembly wrap up a legislative session. Based on *Reynolds* v. *Sims*, seats in state legislatures must be apportioned based on population. The U.S. Census Bureau provides guidelines to assist states in gathering population data to redraw their district boundaries.

go.hrw.com
Research Online
Keyword: SS Court

CRITICAL THINKING

1. **Analyze the Impact** Using the keyword above, read about the decision in *Baker* v. *Carr*, decided two years before *Reynolds*. What was the issue in *Baker*? How did that decision pave the way for the plaintiffs in *Reynolds* to bring their case?

2. **You Be the Judge** The New York Education Law said that only the parents or guardians of public school children—or the owners or renters of property—could vote in school district elections. A man living in the Union School District No. 15 brought suit after he was not allowed to vote in a school district election. He was not a parent of a student and he neither rented nor owned property in the district. Does New York's law deny him equal protection? How should the court rule on his claim? Explain your reasoning in a paragraph.

Changes and Challenges

BEFORE YOU READ

MAIN IDEA

Continued social and economic inequalities caused many young African Americans to lose faith in the civil rights movement and integration and seek alternative solutions.

READING FOCUS

1. Why did the civil rights movement expand to the North?

2. What fractures developed in the civil rights movement, and what was the result?

3. What events led to the death of Martin Luther King Jr., and how did the nation react?

KEY TERMS AND PEOPLE

de jure segregation
de facto segregation
Kerner Commission
Stokely Carmichael
Black Power
Black Panther Party
Malcolm X

PI 3.2 Research and analyze the major themes and developments in New York State and United States history (e.g., colonization and settlement; Revolution and New National Period; immigration; expansion and reform era; Civil War and Reconstruction; the American labor movement; Great Depression; World Wars; contemporary United States).

The March Against Fear

▼ King (left) and Carmichael (right) on the March Against Fear in Mississippi

THE INSIDE STORY

How did the March Against Fear widen a split in the civil rights movement? In June 1966 James Meredith, the University of Mississippi's first African American graduate, began a 27-day march from Memphis, Tennessee, to Jackson, Mississippi, to encourage African Americans to register to vote. On the second day of what he called his March Against Fear, Meredith was shot and wounded. About 150 SCLC and SNCC members gathered to finish his march. Among them were Martin Luther King Jr. of SCLC and SNCC's young new leader, Stokely Carmichael.

The march was a harrowing experience. Vehicles swerved at the marchers, forcing them off the highway. People threw bottles, rocks, and firecrackers. "What are we waiting for, till they kill some of us?" some marchers began to ask. "I'm not much for that nonviolence stuff any more," an angry marcher announced on the highway one day.

As they marched, demonstrators shouted the SCLC's familiar call-and-response chant: "What do we want?" "Freedom now!" Soon, however, SNCC marchers began offering a new response: "Black power!" Whenever the chant began, each side tried to drown out the other. Finally, King and Carmichael agreed to abandon the chant for the rest of the march. Journalists accompanying the march had already noticed the conflict, however. They reported this visible break in the unity of the civil rights movement.

De Facto Segregation

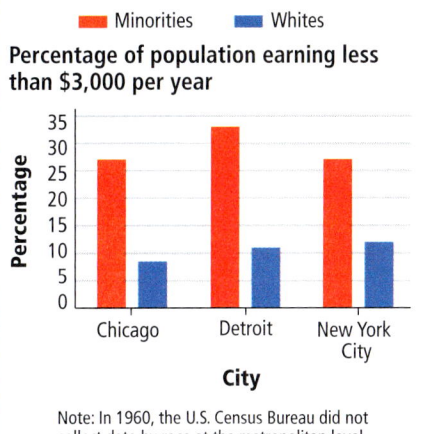
About 350 demonstrators, guarded by police, march through an all-white Chicago neighborhood to protest housing discrimination in the Chicago real estate industry in 1966. Housing discrimination was a form of de facto segregation.

Expanding the Movement

The March Against Fear marked a turning point in the drive for civil rights. The movement had done much to bring an end to **de jure segregation**, or segregation by law, in the South. However, Meredith's shooting provided grim evidence that changes in laws had not altered attitudes. Especially outside the South, African Americans were challenging the movement's tactics. Many began to question whether non-violent protest was the best means to genuine and permanent change.

Conditions outside the South

African Americans in the South and outside the South faced similar but slightly different conditions. Most states did not deny African Americans voting rights. Nor did they require segregated public accommodations. Yet segregation was widespread in America. In most places it was **de facto segregation**—segregation that exists through custom and practice rather than by law. De jure segregation ends when the laws that create it are repealed. De facto segregation can be more difficult to overcome.

Most African Americans outside the South lived in cities. However, they often faced conditions like those faced by black southerners. For example, few real estate agents would take African Americans to homes for sale in white neighborhoods. White homeowners willing to show their house to African American buyers incurred the anger of their neighbors. As a result, African Americans often had no choice but to live in all-black parts of town.

In addition, discrimination by banks made it hard to borrow money to buy or improve property in African American neighborhoods. This caused homeownership there to be low and many buildings to decay. Job discrimination against African Americans led to high unemployment and poverty in these neighborhoods, making the situation worse.

Urban unrest

Frustration over these conditions exploded into violence. From 1964 to 1967, racial unrest erupted in most of the nation's large cities. Some of the worst violence took place in the poor, African American neighborhood of Watts in Los Angeles. In 1965, about 35,000 African Americans took part in a six-day riot that destroyed entire city blocks. Some 3,000 people were arrested and 34 were killed before police and troops restored order.

A week of violence in Detroit in July 1967 resulted in 43 deaths and thousands of injuries and arrests. After the riot, President Johnson

Divisions within the Movement

Black Power

At the 1968 Summer Olympics, African American members of the U.S. track team Tommie Smith (left) and John Carlos (right) gave the Black Power salute as they received their medals. Many saw the Black Power movement as threatening because it abandoned the concept of non-violence.

Black Panther Party

The Black Panther Party formed in Oakland, California, in 1966 as a militant group that called for an armed revolution to achieve African American liberation.

Nation of Islam

Elijah Muhammad led the Nation of Islam from 1934 to 1975. Here he is speaking to a group of followers. The Nation of Islam promoted economic independence for African Americans as well as racial separation.

appointed the **Kerner Commission** to study the causes of urban rioting. Its report placed the blame on poverty and discrimination. "Our nation," the report warned, "is moving toward two societies, one black and one white—separate and unequal."

The movement moves north The riots convinced King that the movement's gains in the South had bypassed millions of African Americans. This awareness spurred him to focus his attention on Chicago in 1966.

The SCLC's Chicago campaign lasted eight months. It was one of King's biggest failures. Chicago's African Americans did not share his civil rights focus. They had the right to vote, and they did not consider themselves segregated. Their concerns were mainly economic.

Chicago authorities also failed to provide the confrontations that worked so well for King in the South. Chicago police had strict orders against using force. Without such brutality, King found it hard to attract the media attention on which he relied to sway public opinion.

In July, King took his marches into Chicago's white neighborhoods. This tactic worked. Residents showered marchers with rocks and bottles. Unlike in the South, however, police protected the marchers. In addition, King's new strategy weakened his northern white support. He found that some whites who had criticized racism in the South had no interest in seeing it exposed in the North. In August, King hollowly declared victory and left Chicago.

READING CHECK **Summarizing** What did King hope to accomplish by expanding the civil rights movement into Chicago?

Fractures in the Movement

Most white Americans viewed the civil rights movement as a unified effort. In fact, it was made up of diverse groups united by the goal of ending racial discrimination. By the mid-1960s, however, conflicts among these groups had developed.

The first signs of trouble arose from Freedom Summer in 1964. As harassment of SNCC and CORE workers in Mississippi increased, some of them rejected the philosophy of nonviolence. As you have read, unity was further weakened when the NAACP, CORE, and the

Tactics of Change

Malcolm X was blunt and uncompromising. He inspired hatred from some and respect from others.

Martin Luther King's commitment to nonviolence never wavered.

❝ [V]iolence . . . seeks to annihilate rather than convert . . . Nonviolence is a powerful and just weapon . . . which cuts without wounding and ennobles the man who wields it. ❞

Martin Luther King Jr., 1964

❝ [N]ow you're facing a situation where the young Negro's coming up. They don't want to hear that 'turn-the-other-cheek' stuff, no. . . . There's new thinking coming in. There's new strategy coming in . . . It'll be ballots, or it'll be bullets. It'll be liberty, or it will be death. ❞

Malcolm X, 1964

Skills FOCUS **READING LIKE A HISTORIAN**

Identifying Points of View What does King mean when he says that nonviolence "cuts without wounding"? To what is Malcolm X referring when he speaks of "ballots" or "bullets"?

See **Skills Handbook**, pp. H28–H29

SCLC favored the compromise offered the Mississippi Freedom Democratic Party at the Democratic National Convention. SNCC members accused the other groups of betrayal.

Black Power Cracks in the movement widened in May 1966, when **Stokely Carmichael** replaced the moderate John Lewis as head of SNCC. Under Carmichael's leadership, SNCC abandoned the philosophy of nonviolence.

Carmichael's support of aggressive action became clear during the March Against Fear in June 1966. The SNCC leader was among those arrested when the marchers stopped in Greenwood, Mississippi. After being released, Carmichael addressed a rally of about 3,000 protesters. With his arm raised in a clenched-fist salute, he shouted his defiance.

HISTORY'S VOICES

❝ This is the twenty-seventh time I have been arrested—and I ain't going to jail no more. The only way we're going to stop them white men from whippin' us is to take over. We been saying freedom for six years—and we ain't got nothin'. What we gonna start now is 'Black Power!' ❞

—Stokely Carmichael, June 17, 1966

As onlookers cheered, Carmichael yelled, "What do you want?" "Black power!" the crowd roared back. The next day the slogan became newspaper headlines across the nation.

Many critics believed the Black Power movement to be a call to violent action. Carmichael rejected this interpretation. He explained **Black Power** as African Americans' dependence on themselves to solve problems. "Integration is irrelevant," he declared. "Political and economic power is what black people have to have." He called on African Americans to form their own separate political organizations.

Like SNCC, CORE also abandoned nonviolence and endorsed Black Power in 1966. In 1967 CORE gave up its commitment to being a multiracial organization.

The Black Panthers Black Power appealed to many young African Americans. It inspired two young community activists, Huey Newton and Bobby Seale, to found a group called the **Black Panther Party** in Oakland, California, in October 1966. The Panthers rejected nonviolence and called for violent revolution as a means of African American liberation.

To achieve some of their goals, the Panthers carried guns and monitored African American neighborhoods to guard against police brutality. Confrontations between Black Panthers and the police in the late 1960s led to several shootouts resulting in deaths on both sides.

Black Muslims One of the largest and most influential groups expressing the ideas of Black Power was the Nation of Islam. Based on the Islamic religion, it was founded in 1930. Its members were called Black Muslims.

The group's leader, the Honorable Elijah Muhammad, preached a message of black nationalism, self-discipline, and self-reliance. Rules forbade smoking, gambling, and alcohol and stressed cleanliness and thrift. Men and women dressed conservatively. During the Great Depression, Black Muslims would not accept any government assistance.

By the 1960s the Nation of Islam had as many as 65,000 followers. Young African Americans, especially from the North's urban slums, were drawn to the Black Muslims' image and to a fiery minister known as **Malcolm X**. (Some Black Muslims took the surname "X" to represent the loss of their original, African identities.) Malcolm X offered a message of hope, defiance, and black pride. "Revolutions are never based upon . . . begging a corrupt society or a corrupt system to accept us into it," Malcolm X said. "Revolutions overturn systems."

At first, Malcolm X was also critical of King and nonviolence. "Any Negro who teaches other Negroes to turn the other cheek is disarming the Negro . . . [of] his natural right to defend himself," he charged. Many white Americans found his message frightening. King and other civil rights leaders thought him an extremist.

In 1964, however, Malcolm X broke with Elijah Muhammad and the Black Muslims. He visited Islam's holy sites in Saudi Arabia and returned a changed man. Although Malcolm X continued to preach Black Power, he began cooperating with other civil rights leaders and called for racial harmony. "If the white people realize what the alternative is," he noted, "perhaps they will be more willing to hear Dr. King." In February 1965, a few weeks after making this observation, Malcolm X was assassinated by Black Muslims who considered him a traitor to their cause.

READING CHECK **Identifying Supporting Details** How did Black Muslims reflect fractures in the civil rights movement?

The Death of Martin Luther King Jr.

Moments after Martin Luther King Jr. was shot, his aides frantically pointed to the source of the gunshots (left).

The Assassination of King

King's disappointing Chicago campaign increased his awareness that economic issues must be part of the civil rights movement. With this in mind, he went to Memphis, Tennessee, in March 1968 to aid African American sanitation workers who were on strike against discrimination in the city's work and pay policies. King led a march to city hall on March 28 and then remained in Memphis to speak at a rally on April 3.

The next day James Earl Ray, a white sniper with a high-powered rifle, shot and killed King as he stood on the balcony of his motel. Within hours, rioting erupted in more than 120 cities as enraged African Americans across the nation responded to the assassination. Within three weeks, 46 people were dead, some 2,600 were injured, and more than 21,000 were arrested. Nearly 55,000 troops were required to restore order. One civil rights leader noted that King would have been outraged by the violent reaction to his death.

Robert Kennedy, who was running for president at the time, was about to give a campaign speech in an African American neighborhood of Indianapolis, Indiana, when he learned of the shooting. After informing the audience of the tragedy, he recalled King's message while making an impassioned appeal for calm.

HISTORY'S VOICES

❝ You can be filled with bitterness and with hatred and a desire for revenge. We can move in that direction as a country, in great polarization, black people amongst blacks and white people amongst whites, filled with hatred toward one another. Or we can make an effort, like Martin Luther King did, to understand and to comprehend, and replace that violence, that stain of bloodshed that has spread across the land, with . . . compassion and love. ❞

—Robert Kennedy, April 4, 1968

READING CHECK **Summarizing** What were the circumstances of King's death?

King's widow, Coretta Scott King, mourns at his funeral (left). Below, mules pull King's casket, symbolizing his work on behalf of the poor. Some 50,000 mourners joined the procession.

SECTION 4 ASSESSMENT

go.hrw.com
Online Quiz
Keyword: SD7 HP28

Reviewing Ideas, Terms, and People

1. **a. Describe** What did the **Kerner Commission** conclude?
   b. Contrast What is the difference between **de jure segregation** and **de facto segregation**?
   c. Predict How do you think urban unrest could have been prevented or stopped?

2. **a. Identify** What was the **Black Panther Party**?
   b. Contrast How were the goals of supporters of the **Black Power** movement different from those of other civil rights groups?
   c. Elaborate Why do you think many African Americans were drawn to leaders such as **Stokely Carmichael** and **Malcolm X**?

3. **a. Describe** Why did Martin Luther King Jr. go to Memphis, Tennessee, in March 1968?
   b. Make Inferences Why would King have been upset about the public reaction to his death?
   c. Predict What long-term effect do you think King's death will have on the civil rights movement?

Critical Thinking

4. **Categorizing** Review your notes on the Black Power movement. Then copy the graphic organizer below and use it to list traditional and Black Power civil rights groups and leaders.

Traditional	Black Power

FOCUS ON WRITING

5. **Expository** Write a paragraph either for or against Black Power. Explain why you would or would not have supported its goals and methods.

The Movement Continues

BEFORE YOU READ

MAIN IDEA

The civil rights movement was in decline by the 1970s, but its accomplishments continued to benefit American society.

READING FOCUS

1. How did the SCLC's goals change and with what results?

2. For what reasons did the Black Power movement decline?

3. What civil rights changes took place in the 1970s, and what were their results?

KEY TERMS AND PEOPLE

Poor People's Campaign
Ralph Abernathy
Civil Rights Act of 1968
affirmative action
John Lewis
Andrew Young
Jesse Jackson

PI 3.1 Compare and contrast the experiences of different ethnic, national, and religious groups, including Native American Indians, in the United States, explaining their contributions to American society and culture.

Would you endure miserable conditions to seek changes that you believed to be right? A covered wagon pulled by mules would have attracted attention on the streets of Washington, D.C., even if not accompanied by tens of thousands of demonstrators protesting their poverty. Another strange sight was the community of tents and shacks that 2,500 of these protesters—African Americans, Native Americans, Hispanic Americans, and whites among them—occupied on the National Mall. They called their settlement Resurrection City.

Longtime SCLC leader Ralph Abernathy explained why the protesters were there. "The poor are no longer divided. We're not going to let the white man put us down any more," he declared. "It's not white power, and I'll give you some news, it's not black power, either. It's poor power and we're going to use it."

Unusually heavy spring rains quickly put Resurrection City ankle-deep in mud, making sanitation and trash collection difficult. Each day, however, determined groups of demonstrators organized marches from their miserable surroundings to federal agencies throughout the city. The marches were designed to demand that the government do more to combat poverty. "We have business on the road to freedom," Abernathy encouraged one group of protesters as they marched toward Capitol Hill: "We must prove to white America that you can kill the leader but you cannot kill the dream." ◾

▶ The Poor People's Campaign set off to combat economic inequality as the next phase of the civil rights movement.

The Poor People's Campaign

A Change in Goals

The **Poor People's Campaign** marked an important expansion of the civil rights movement. By 1967 changes in the law had achieved basic rights for African Americans. Martin Luther King Jr. believed, however, that most African Americans were still prevented from achieving equality because they were poor. He decided to alert the nation to the economic plight not only of African Americans, but of all poor people.

King's death prevented him from leading this effort. That task fell to his successor as the head of the SCLC, **Ralph Abernathy**. In May 1968, thousands of protesters came to the nation's capital to be part of the Poor People's Campaign. A Mississippi woman explained why she joined the protest.

HISTORY'S VOICES

❝I'm here because when I was a child, I got taken out of school and put to work on the farm helping my family . . . Then I got married and had kids, and my husband worked in the cotton fields . . . But he got sick and don't work much no more and there ain't hardly no cotton to get picked by hand anyway . . . So I came here with the Campaign to tell people that we got to be treated like human beings—that we have a right to live because we've earned that right but we've yet to be paid.❞

—Henrietta Franklin, quoted in the *Washington Post*, May 24, 1968

The Poor People's Campaign turned out to be a disaster. Besides bad weather, the SCLC experienced terrible media relations. Some Resurrection City residents harassed reporters. About 200 protesters turned out to be members of inner-city gangs. The campaign's organizers eventually sent them home. After six weeks of problems, police used tear gas to empty Resurrection City and then tore it down.

Without King's eloquence and leadership, the Poor People's Campaign also failed to express clearly the protesters' needs and demands. Some conservative members of Congress believed they saw elements of communism in the campaign's beliefs and goals. All these factors combined to cause the SCLC and its role in the civil rights movement to decline.

READING CHECK **Identifying the Main Idea** How did the Poor People's Campaign represent a change of goals for the civil rights movement?

The Decline of Black Power

The civil rights movement took place at the height of the Cold War, when the nation's fear of communism was at its height. FBI director J. Edgar Hoover was convinced that the major civil rights groups were led by Communists.

In 1956 Hoover created a secret program within the FBI to keep an eye on many types of groups that were involved in the unrest that was plaguing society. Spies and informers working for the FBI posed as supporters of these groups and reported the groups' plans and activities back to the government.

At first, King was Hoover's main target in the civil rights movement. As the Black Power movement grew, however, he instructed his agents to disrupt and otherwise interfere with the activities of other civil rights groups he considered a threat to American society.

For example, to disrupt SNCC—and at the same time weaken the Black Panthers—FBI spies in SNCC spread false rumors that the Panthers intended to kill SNCC leaders. The FBI also forged harmful posters, leaflets, and correspondence that appeared to come from the groups it had targeted.

Hoover was especially concerned about the Black Panthers. The FBI encouraged local authorities to combat the Panthers by any means possible. Police raided the Panthers'

The Congressional Black Caucus

Retired North Carolina Supreme Court Chief Justice Henry Frye swears in members of the Congressional Black Caucus of the 109th Congress. Founded in 1970 as an organization of African American members of the House of Representatives, the group's mission is to address legislative concerns of black and minority citizens.

AFRICAN AMERICAN GAINS IN THE CIVIL RIGHTS MOVEMENT

African American Elected Officials:
1,469 in 1970; 9,040 in 2000

African Americans Not Living in Poverty:
45% in 1960; 78% in 2000

African American College Graduates:
3.3% in 1960; 16.5% in 2000

headquarters in cities across the country. Since Black Panthers usually were armed, violent conflict sometimes resulted. Law enforcement authorities also sometimes shot Black Panther members whether they resisted or not. By the early 1970s, armed violence had led to the killing or arrest of many Black Panther leaders. Others had fled the United States in order to avoid arrest.

SNCC also collapsed with FBI help. In 1967, H. Rap Brown replaced Stokely Carmichael as head of SNCC. Urged on by his staff—many of whom were on the FBI's payroll—Brown took increasingly radical and shocking positions. As a result, SNCC's membership declined rapidly. The group disbanded in the early 1970s.

READING CHECK **Identifying Main Ideas** How did federal action help lead to a decline of the Black Power movement?

New Changes and Gains

In spite of the challenges, the civil rights movement did make gains in the late 1960s. For example, just a week after Martin Luther King Jr.'s death, President Johnson signed the **Civil Rights Act of 1968**. Also called the Fair Housing Act, the law banned discrimination in the sale or rental of housing.

Busing and political change Despite the 1954 *Brown* decision, urban schools were still largely segregated in the late 1960s. This was a result of de facto segregation. Years of housing discrimination had contributed to segregated neighborhoods in many cities.

The Fair Housing Act was a step toward ending this situation. However, it would take years to overcome decades of discrimination and to achieve integrated neighborhoods. Meanwhile, many city schools would remain segregated.

To speed integration of city schools, courts began ordering that some students be bused from their neighborhoods to schools in other parts of the city. Busing met fierce opposition, especially in the North. Court-ordered busing in Boston in 1974, for example, led to two years of sometimes violent protests. Denver opponents of busing burned school buses.

Forced busing speeded the migration of whites from cities to suburbs. This development increased the political power of African Americans. By 1974 Cleveland, Detroit, Los Angeles, Washington, Atlanta, and several smaller cities had elected black mayors.

Affirmative action As you read in Section 2, the Civil Rights Act of 1964 banned discrimination in employment. By the late 1960s, the U.S. Justice Department was taking legal action against employers for violating this law. At the same time, the government helped businesses and colleges set up **affirmative action** programs that gave preference to minorities and women in hiring and admissions. These programs were designed to help make up for past discrimination against these groups.

Affirmative action and busing were divisive issues in the 1970s. It is difficult to assess clearly their contribution to the Republican Party's success in the late 1900s and early 2000s. However, backlash against these programs helped Republicans lure two important groups of voters away from the Democratic Party—white southerners and urban, working-class whites.

The new Black Power

As African Americans in the South exercised their newly won voting rights—and were more politically active nationwide—it became clear that Black Power did not die in the 1970s. It merely took on a new form and meaning.

By 1970 the populations of more than 100 counties in the South were at least 50 percent African American. The African Americans who took over elected offices in these and other places governed as well as the white officials they replaced. In addition, many African Americans who played important roles in the civil rights movement later provided other services to the nation. For example, Thurgood Marshall, the NAACP lawyer who argued the *Brown* case before the Supreme Court, later became the Court's first African American justice.

John Lewis took part in some of the first sit-ins in 1960. He was also a Freedom Rider in 1961 and participated in the Selma march in 1965. The head of SNCC in the early 1960s, Lewis was elected in 1986 to the first of many terms representing the people of Atlanta, Georgia, in Congress.

As a staff member of the SCLC and a close adviser to King, **Andrew Young** played a key role in the 1963 Birmingham campaign and in the Selma march. In 1972 he became Georgia's first African American member of Congress since Reconstruction. Young later served as U.S. ambassador to the United Nations and as mayor of Atlanta. You will read more about Young's career later in this book.

Jesse Jackson was another young activist who went on to leave his own mark on the nation. Jackson founded his own civil rights organization, Operation PUSH, and became an international figure for his work on behalf of poor and oppressed peoples around the world. His campaigns for the Democratic presidential nomination in the 1980s raised the real possibility that the nation might one day have an African American president.

READING CHECK **Summarizing** What political changes did busing, affirmative action, and Black Power bring to America in the 1970s?

ACADEMIC VOCABULARY
assess determine the importance of

SECTION 5 ASSESSMENT

go.hrw.com
Online Quiz
Keyword: SD7 HP28

Reviewing Idea, Terms, and People

1. a. Identify Who succeeded Martin Luther King Jr. as head of the SCLC?
   b. Analyze Why did the **Poor People's Campaign** fail?
   c. Elaborate Why did Martin Luther King Jr. treat poverty as a civil rights issue?

2. a. Describe How did J. Edgar Hoover and the FBI weaken the Black Panthers?
   b. Make Inferences How did the Cold War influence Hoover and the FBI's attitude about the Black Power movement?

3. a. Define What was busing, and what was its purpose?
   b. Contrast How was the role of Black Power different during and after the 1970s than before the 1970s?
   c. Elaborate Why do you think many people have opposed affirmative action?

Critical Thinking

4. Identifying Supporting Details Review your notes on the decline of the civil rights movement. Then copy the graphic organizer below and use it to list gains and losses for African Americans that accompanied the movement's decline.

Gains	Losses

FOCUS ON WRITING

5. Expository Write a statement suggesting ways to prevent the civil rights movement from declining. Include an assessment of whether the civil rights movement is needed today.

The Government and Equal Rights

Historical Context The documents below provide information on views of government intervention for equal rights.

Task Examine the documents and answer the questions that follow. Then you will be asked to write an essay about the federal government's role in establishing equal rights for Americans, using facts from the documents and from the chapter to support the position you take in your thesis statement.

ST 4.1 Analyze important debates in American history, focusing on the opposing positions and the historical evidence used to support these positions.

ST 4.3 Develop hypotheses about important events, eras, or issues; move from chronicling to explaining historical events and issues; use information collected from diverse sources to produce cogently written reports and document-based essays.

DOCUMENT 1

Many white southerners viewed integration as a social question that should not be answered by the federal government. Some argued that segregation would eventually end on its own. Federal intervention, they argued, would only create hostility and resentment. Robert Patterson was a white Mississippi native who opposed government-enforced integration. In the following interview, he explained his views on the integration of restaurants and motels.

> "That's not social integration, that's forced integration under the might of the federal government. . . . To be subjected to integration is one thing, but to submit to it is something else entirely. We are being subjected to integration; we're not submitting to it. And you will find that white people do not frequent places where there are a whole lot of Negroes through choice. And I think gradually . . . things will resegregate themselves."

DOCUMENT 2

Some people who supported civil rights cautioned that the federal government risked a backlash if it moved too fast to change society. Clifford H. Baldowski was a white editorial cartoonist for the *Atlanta Journal-Constitution* who supported civil rights. The following cartoon, published in 1963, depicts Attorney General Robert F. Kennedy trying to ensure the success of needed federal civil rights legislation.

". . . Wait a minute . . . Somebody has gotta keep this thing on the track!"

Many African Americans did not believe that white officials in the South would protect equal rights unless the federal government forced them to do so. Fannie Lou Hamer called on the federal government to intervene in Mississippi, a state in which a majority black population was largely prevented from participating in local and state government. In the following interview, she recalled how Byron De La Beckwith, the assassin of civil rights leader Medgar Evers, was set free by two all-white juries.

"America that is divided against itself cannot stand, and we cannot say that we have all this unity they say we have when black people are being discriminated against in every city in America I have visited.

"I was in jail [for protesting] when Medgar Evers was murdered and nothing, I mean nothing has been done about that . . . We can no longer ignore the fact that America is NOT the 'land of the free and the home of the brave.'"

Some African American leaders warned the federal government that it needed to enforce equal rights not just because it was the right thing to do but in order to prevent violence. In the following speech from 1964, Malcolm X urged government leaders to enforce equal rights before people took matters into their own hands.

"America is the only country in history in a position to bring about a revolution without violence and bloodshed. But America is not morally equipped to do so.

Why is America in a position to bring about a bloodless revolution? Because the Negro in this country holds the balance of power and if the Negro in this country were given what the Constitution says he is supposed to have, the added power of the Negro in this country would sweep all of the racists and segregationists out of office. It would change the entire political structure of the country. It would wipe out the southern segregationism that now controls America's foreign policy, as well as America's domestic policy.

And the only way without bloodshed that this can be brought about is that the black man has to be given full use of the ballot in every one of the 50 states. But if the black man doesn't get the ballot, then you are going to be faced with another man who forgets the ballot and starts using the bullet."

Skills FOCUS · READING LIKE A HISTORIAN

1. **a. Identify** Refer to Document 1. To Patterson, what is the difference between "subjected" and "submitting"?
   b. Elaborate Do you think Patterson sees voluntary integration ever taking place without force? Explain.

2. **a. Describe** Refer to Document 2. Who is driving?
   b. Interpret What does this cartoon reflect about the role that Robert F. Kennedy played in civil rights legislation?

3. **a. Identify** Refer to Document 3. What is the main hypocrisy that Hamer sees?
   b. Analyze How does the example of Byron De La Beckwith support Hamer's call for federal intervention?

4. **a. Describe** Refer to Document 4. To Malcolm X, what was the most important right that the government needed to protect for African Americans?
   b. Elaborate Do you think Malcolm X's reasons for needing government intervention are valid? Explain.

5. **Document-Based Essay Question** Consider the question below and form a thesis statement. Using examples from Documents 1, 2, 3, and 4, create an outline and write a short essay supporting your position. What role should the government have in enforcing equal rights for Americans?

See **Skills Handbook**, pp. H28–H29, H30

Visual Summary: The Civil Rights Movement

Fighting Segregation
- Early civil rights groups included the NAACP and CORE.
- In 1954 the Supreme Court ordered an end to racial segregation in public schools.
- A bus boycott in Montgomery, Alabama, launched the SCLC and the modern civil rights movement.

Freedom Now!
- Sit-ins and Freedom Rides provoked violent reactions from some white southerners.
- Violent response to marches in Birmingham, Alabama, shocked the nation.
- The March on Washington helped lead to the Civil Rights Act of 1964.

Voting Rights
- Some white southerners tried to block efforts of African Americans to vote.
- African Americans in Mississippi organized to increase their political power.
- A brutal attack on a protest in Selma, Alabama, helped win support for the Voting Rights Act of 1965.

Changes and Challenges
- Civil rights leaders began attacking de facto segregation in the North in the mid-1960s.
- Differences within the civil rights movement weakened it and led to the rise of Black Power.
- The assassination of Martin Luther King Jr. caused urban unrest.

The Movement Continues
- King's death and the Poor People's Campaign helped lead to the decline of SCLC.
- Internal divisions and an FBI campaign weakened some civil rights groups.
- The civil rights movement resulted in important gains for African Americans.

Reviewing Key Terms and People

Identify the correct term or person from the chapter that best fits each of the following descriptions.

1. Law banning discrimination in employment and in public facilities
2. Leader of SNCC in the 1960s who many years later was elected to Congress from the state of Georgia
3. A type of discrimination that exists through custom and practice instead of by law
4. Groups of people who traveled through the South challenging segregation at bus stations
5. Project for college students to spend their summer vacation registering African Americans to vote in Mississippi
6. African American politician and civil rights leader who campaigned for the Democratic presidential nomination in the 1980s
7. Minister and civil rights leader who supported nonviolent resistance
8. NAACP leader who was murdered at his home by a member of the Ku Klux Klan
9. Part of the Constitution banning states from taxing citizens to vote in elections

Comprehension and Critical Thinking

SECTION 1 *(pp. 908–915)*

10. **a. Recall** What civil rights gains were made in the 1940s?

    b. Analyze How did the African American community support the Montgomery bus boycott?

    c. Elaborate How did Thurgood Marshall and the NAACP's earlier work contribute to the *Brown* v. *Board of Education of Topeka, Kansas,* decision?

History's Impact video program

Review the video to answer the closing question: How did civil rights activists push for equality during the 1950s and 1960s?

SECTION 2 *(pp. 916–923)*

11. a. Identify What were the goals of SNCC?

b. Draw Conclusions What effect did racial violence have on President Kennedy's approach to civil rights?

c. Evaluate What do you think made the strategy of nonviolence effective?

SECTION 3 *(pp. 925–930)*

12. a. Describe What did Freedom Summer accomplish?

b. Draw Conclusions Why did Martin Luther King Jr. resume the march from Selma to Montgomery, Alabama after it met with violence?

c. Predict How do you think the actions of the Mississippi Freedom Democratic Party affected the Democratic Party?

SECTION 4 *(pp. 932–937)*

13. a. Identify What slogan did Stokely Carmichael introduce at a SNCC rally?

b. Compare How were conditions similar for African Americans in the South and in the North?

c. Elaborate Why is the legacy of Martin Luther King Jr. so important?

SECTION 5 *(pp. 938–941)*

14. a. Describe How did civil rights leaders such as John Lewis and Andrew Young continue serving the nation after the 1960s?

b. Analyze Why did SNCC collapse?

c. Predict What could have made the Poor People's Campaign more successful?

Using the Internet

go.hrw.com
Practice Online
Keyword: SD7 CH28

15. The policy of affirmative action resulted from the civil rights movement, but it remains controversial today. Using the keyword above, do research to learn about court cases and controversies related to affirmative action. Then create a report that analyzes how these questions and decisions have shaped affirmative action policies today.

Analyzing Primary Sources

Reading Like a Historian Read the History's Voices passage in Section 2 from Diane Nash that begins: "We would practice such things …" Nash was training to take part in civil rights demonstrations.

16. Identify What were the civil rights workers practicing?

17. Draw Conclusions Why do you think civil rights workers needed this kind of training?

Critical Reading

Read the passage in Section 4 that begins with the heading "Fractures in the Movement." Then answer the question that follows.

18. The first major signs of trouble in the civil rights movement occurred when some workers

  A rejected the philosophy of nonviolence.

  B split off and formed their own groups.

  C made speeches in favor of Black Power.

  D disagreed at the 1964 Democratic National Convention.

WRITING FOR THE SAT

Think about the following issue.

Martin Luther King Jr. was an inspiring leader who was highly effective at communicating and motivating African Americans and whites. He was clearly the most important and influential leader of the civil rights movement in the mid-1950s through the late 1960s.

19. Assignment Did King's death bring an end to the civil rights movement? Write a short essay in which you develop your position on this issue. Support your point of view with reasoning and examples from your reading and studies.

The Vietnam War

THE BIG PICTURE It was the first war to invade American homes via television. For years TV brought the U.S. fight against the horrors of jungle warfare into American living rooms. Seemingly unwinnable, the U.S. war effort brought down a president and bitterly divided the nation.

New York Standards

Key Idea 2 Important ideas, social and cultural values, beliefs, and traditions from New York State and United States history illustrate the connections and interactions of people and events across time and from a variety of perspectives.

Key Idea 3 Study about the major social, political, economic, cultural, and religious developments in New York State and United States history involves learning about the important roles and contributions of individuals and groups.

Skills FOCUS **READING LIKE A HISTORIAN**

Members of the 1st Squadron, 9th Cavalry, burst out of their helicopter and into action in Chu Lai, South Vietnam, in 1967. While Americans at home may have been divided about the war, U.S. involvement was reaching its peak at this time.

Interpreting Visuals What does this photo suggest about soldiers' commitment to the war?

See **Skills Handbook**, p. H30

U.S.

1953
United States aids France in Indochina War.

1954

World

May 1954
French forces at Dien Bien Phu surrender to the Vietminh.

History's Impact video program

Watch the video to understand the impact of public opinion on foreign policy.

1960
The United States starts supplying military assistance to South Vietnam.

August 1964
Congress passes the Tonkin Gulf Resolution, expanding U.S. involvement in Vietnam.

April 1965
Antiwar demonstration in Washington, D.C., draws more than 200,000 protesters.

January 1973
The United States agrees to withdraw all troops from South Vietnam.

END THE DRAFT

1958

1962

1966

1970

1974

January 1959
Communist guerillas, led by Fidel Castro, take control of Cuba.

January 1968
Communist forces launch the Tet Offensive.

April 30, 1975
South Vietnam surrenders to North Vietnam.

The War Develops

BEFORE YOU READ

MAIN IDEA

Concern about the spread of communism led the United States to become increasingly involved in Vietnam.

READING FOCUS

1. How did Southeast Asia's colonial history produce increased tensions in Vietnam?

2. What policies did Presidents Truman and Eisenhower pursue in Vietnam after World War II?

3. What events and conditions caused growing conflicts between North Vietnam and South Vietnam?

4. Why did Presidents Kennedy and Johnson increase U.S. involvement in Vietnam?

KEY TERMS AND PEOPLE

Ho Chi Minh
Vietminh
domino theory
Dien Bien Phu
Geneva Conference
Ngo Dinh Diem
Vietcong
Tonkin Gulf Resolution

PI 3.2 Research and analyze the major themes and developments in New York State and United States history (e.g., colonization and settlement; Revolution and New National Period; immigration; expansion and reform era; Civil War and Reconstruction; the American labor movement; Great Depression; World Wars; contemporary United States).

THE INSIDE STORY

How did President Woodrow Wilson disappoint Ho Chi Minh? Paris in 1919 was an exciting place to be for 28-year-old Nguyen That Thanh (NY-uhn TAHT TAHN). He was one of some 50,000 Southeast Asians from the colony of French Indochina who were living in France at the end of World War I. Most of these Vietnamese worked in factories, aiding the French war effort.

Nguyen That Thanh, however, had come for a different reason: to convince the other Vietnamese in France to support Vietnam's independence. He was inspired by the Fourteen Points that U.S. president Woodrow Wilson had issued during World War I. Wilson's Fourteen Points called for self-determination for all people—that is, letting people decide how they want to be governed.

Wilson was among the leaders who met in Paris in 1919 to negotiate the peace treaty and plan the postwar world. Nguyen wrote to the president asking that his Fourteen Points be applied to the people of Southeast Asia. He hand-delivered his letter to American officials at the peace conference, but he was turned away.

There was little chance that Wilson could have convinced France to give up its control of Vietnam. Yet Nguyen was very disappointed that the president ignored his letter. He bitterly complained of being deceived by Wilson's "song of freedom." Nguyen left France in 1923. In 1941 he returned to Vietnam to lead its fight for independence. By then he was known by a new name: Ho Chi Minh. ◼

A Disappointed FAN

▲ As a young man in France, Nguyen That Thanh began working toward Vietnamese independence.

Colonial Vietnam

The Southeast Asian nation of Vietnam is bordered by China to the north and by Laos and Cambodia to the west. Rich agricultural resources have long made the country ripe for foreign invasion. China invaded northern Vietnam's Red River Delta around 200 BC. The Vietnamese people struggled for independence for centuries, finally driving out Chinese rulers in the early 1400s.

Vietnam's independence again was threatened in the mid-1800s, as European powers competed to build colonial empires. Despite fierce resistance from the Vietnamese, France gained control of Vietnam by 1883. The French later combined Vietnam with Laos and Cambodia to form French Indochina.

A nationalist leader Many Vietnamese were driven into poverty under French rule. The French raised taxes and gave the Vietnamese no civil rights under French authority.

These conditions helped to fuel a growing nationalist movement in Vietnam. Nguyen That Thanh emerged as one of its leaders. He came to be known by a new name, **Ho Chi Minh**, meaning "He Who Enlightens."

Ho Chi Minh was born in a village in central Vietnam in 1890. He participated in several tax revolts against the French before leaving home and traveling around the world in the early 1900s. After President Wilson declined to meet him at the Paris Peace Conference, Ho Chi Minh joined the French Communist Party. "It was patriotism, not communism, that inspired me," he claimed.

While living in China and the Soviet Union in the 1920s and 1930s, Ho Chi Minh continued to work for Vietnam's independence and to study communism. He came to believe that a Communist revolution was a way Vietnam could gain freedom from foreign rulers.

Changing rulers Control of Vietnam again changed hands during World War II, when the Japanese army occupied Indochina. Ho Chi Minh returned to Vietnam in 1941 and organized a group to resist the Japanese occupation. The group was called the League for the Independence of Vietnam, or the **Vietminh** (vee-eht-MIN). The Vietminh was led by Communists, but the group was open to non-Communists who were committed to independence. During World War II, the Vietminh attacked Japanese forces and were able to liberate parts of northern Vietnam.

In 1945 Japan surrendered to the Allies and withdrew from Indochina. The Vietminh took the opportunity to declare Vietnam an independent country. Thousands of people gathered in Hanoi, Vietnam's capital, to hear Ho Chi Minh speak on September 2. Hoping to gain American support for Vietnam's independence, he quoted from the Declaration of Independence.

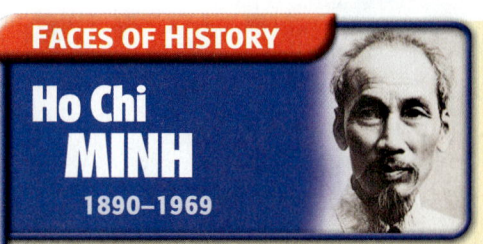

Ho Chi MINH
1890–1969

Ho Chi Minh was a rebel from a young age. The school he attended taught that France was trying to improve Vietnam. Ho Chi Minh told other students that France was actually an invader, a view he formed by reading banned books. He was soon kicked out of school.

When he was 21 he went to London, where he met Asian workers who he believed were overworked and underpaid. In France he became a Communist, but he criticized the French Communist Party for not opposing colonialism more strongly. He called for revolution in Southeast Asia and moved to south China to train Vietnamese exiles. He amassed an army of supporters who would eventually wage the twentieth century's longest and costliest battle against colonialism.

Draw Conclusions Why did Ho adopt Communist beliefs?

HISTORY'S VOICES

❝All men are created equal. They are endowed by their Creator with certain unalienable Rights; among these are Life, Liberty, and the pursuit of Happiness . . . The whole Vietnamese people, animated [driven to action] by a common purpose, are determined to fight to the bitter end against any attempt by the French colonialists to reconquer their country. We are convinced that the Allied nations, which . . . have acknowledged the principles of self-determination and equality of nations, will not refuse to acknowledge the independence of Vietnam.❞

—Ho Chi Minh, September 2, 1945

Ho Chi Minh believed that Vietnam's fight for independence from France was similar to the American colonies' struggle for independence from Great Britain. He expected that the United States would support the Vietnamese nationalist movement.

READING CHECK **Drawing Conclusions** Why did Ho Chi Minh work for Vietnam's independence from France?

Vietnam after World War II

As Ho Chi Minh feared, the French reclaimed Vietnam as a colony after World War II. In December 1946 the Vietnamese people again began battling French rule.

The first Indochina war President Harry Truman disappointed Ho Chi Minh after World War II, as Wilson had after World War I. Truman saw the situation in Indochina in terms of the struggle against communism. He decided to support France, a key ally in the effort to block Communist expansion in Europe. He was also unwilling to back the Vietminh because many of its members were Communists.

Events in Asia soon revealed the extent of Communist expansion. The Communist army of Mao Zedong seized China in 1949. The next year, Communist North Korea invaded South Korea. At the same time, several Communist-led nationalist revolts were raging in Indonesia, Malaya, and the Philippines. These events strengthened the U.S. commitment to contain communism in Southeast Asia.

The domino theory After Dwight D. Eisenhower became president of the United States in 1953, he warned that if Vietnam fell to communism, other Southeast Asian countries would quickly follow. The belief that communism would spread to neighboring countries was called the domino theory. "You have a row of dominoes set up," Eisenhower explained. "You knock over the first one, and what will happen to the last one is a certainty that it will go over very quickly."

The United States sent arms, ammunition, supplies, and money to the French forces in Vietnam. By 1954 the United States was paying more than 75 percent of the cost of France's war. Despite the massive U.S. aid, the French were losing, suffering defeat after defeat.

The Vietminh used guerrilla tactics effectively. They attacked French forces without warning and then disappeared into the jungle. Ho Chi Minh compared this type of warfare to a fight between a tiger and an elephant.

HISTORY'S VOICES

❝If the tiger ever stands still, the elephant will crush him with his mighty tusks. But the tiger does not stand still . . . He will leap upon the back of the elephant, tearing huge chunks from his hide, and then the tiger will leap back into the dark jungle. And slowly the elephant will bleed to death. That will be the war of Indochina.❞

—Ho Chi Minh, quoted in *America Inside Out* by David Schoenbrun. Copyright © 1994 by McGraw-Hill Companies, Inc. All rights reserved. Reprinted by permission of the publisher.

France is defeated The French soldiers made a last stand in a valley in northwestern Vietnam called **Dien Bien Phu** (DYEN BYEN FOO). About 40,000 Vietminh troops surrounded 15,000 French troops. The French commander clung to the hope of a U.S. rescue, telling his soldiers, "The 'free world' will not let us down."

Eisenhower, however, had no intention of sending U.S. soldiers into another war in Asia so soon after the Korean War. The French forces at Dien Bien Phu surrendered to the Vietminh on May 7, 1954.

In eight years of fighting, the two sides had lost nearly 300,000 soldiers. Surviving Vietnamese forces had gained valuable experience fighting a guerrilla war against an enemy with superior weapons and technology. This would prove to be an important factor in the years ahead.

The Geneva Conference After the French surrender, representatives from France, Vietnam, Cambodia, Great Britain, Laos, China, the Soviet Union, and the United States gathered in Geneva, Switzerland. The goal of the **Geneva Conference** was to work out a peace agreement and arrange for Indochina's future.

The Geneva Accords were signed in July 1954. A cease-fire was worked out, and Vietnam was temporarily divided at the 17th parallel. Vietminh forces would control the northern part of Vietnam, and the French would withdraw from the country. A demilitarized zone (DMZ) along the 17th parallel would act as a buffer zone to prevent fighting between the north and south.

According to the Geneva Accords, general elections were to be held in July 1956. These elections would reunify the country under one government. The United States, however, believed that Ho Chi Minh and the Communists would win a nationwide election. The United States therefore never fully supported the peace agreements.

China's Communist government had been aiding the Vietminh in the war and hoped to limit U.S. influence in the region. The United States, meanwhile, did not want to see all of Vietnam fall under Communist control.

READING CHECK **Identifying Cause and Effect** Why did the United States support France instead of Vietnam after World War II?

INDOCHINA, 1950

GEOGRAPHY SKILLS **INTERPRETING MAPS**

The political and cultural influence of both India and China on the region gave Indochina its name.

1. **Region** What countries formed Indochina?
2. **Place** What were the capitals of North and South Vietnam?

See **Skills Handbook**, p. H20

Growing Conflict in Vietnam

With North Vietnam in the control of Ho Chi Minh and his Communist forces, President Eisenhower hoped to at least prevent communism from spreading to South Vietnam. He pinned his hopes on the South Vietnamese leader, **Ngo Dinh Diem** (NGOH DIN dee-EM).

Vietnam's leaders Diem, a Roman Catholic, had served as a high-ranking official in the colonial government under French rule. He was taken hostage by the Vietminh in 1945 and brought to see Ho Chi Minh. Ho asked

Diem to become part of his Communist government, believing Diem would bring support from Catholics. Diem, whose brother had been murdered by the Vietminh, refused the offer. Despite Diem's refusal to cooperate, he was released.

Vietminh forces later tried unsuccessfully to assassinate Diem. He then fled Vietnam and traveled for several years. He spent two years in the United States, where he met American leaders. Diem impressed them with his strong anti-Communist views. He returned to Vietnam after France's defeat in 1954 and became the president of South Vietnam.

Very soon, however, U.S. officials became disappointed with Diem's corrupt and brutal leadership. In a presidential election in 1955, Diem claimed to have won more than 98 percent of the vote. In Saigon, the capital of South Vietnam, election results showed he received 200,000 more votes than there were registered voters in the city.

Diem's government was unpopular from the start. He showed favoritism toward Catholics, which upset South Vietnam's large Buddhist majority. He handed out top government jobs to members of his family. In addition, Diem's land policies favored wealthy landowners at the expense of the peasants. His security forces tortured and imprisoned his political opponents. American leaders were disturbed by these and other actions by Diem. Nevertheless, they preferred Diem's government to a Communist takeover.

In North Vietnam, Ho Chi Minh's leadership became increasingly totalitarian and repressive. Forsaking his earlier commitment to human rights, he struck with brutal force, breaking up the estates of large colonial landowners. He gave the land to the peasants, which made him immensely popular.

Fearing that Ho Chi Minh would win the 1956 election set by the Geneva Accords, Diem barred the election in South Vietnam. Like Germany and Korea, Vietnam continued to be divided into separate Communist and non-Communist countries. This was unacceptable to Ho Chi Minh, who wanted to unite Vietnam as a nation under one Communist government.

A civil war By the late 1950s, Diem's opponents in South Vietnam were in open revolt. In 1959 Communist leaders in North Vietnam began supplying weapons to Vietminh rebels

Growing Divisions in Vietnam

who had remained in the south after the defeat of the French.

The following year, the Vietminh in South Vietnam formed the National Liberation Front (NLF). The NLF's military forces were called **Vietcong**, meaning Vietnamese Communists. Not all members of the NLF were Communists, but they were united in the goal of overthrowing Diem's regime.

Some peasants joined the Vietcong because they opposed Diem's government, but others did so because they feared retaliation from the Vietcong if they did not. The Vietcong assassinated thousands of South Vietnamese government officials. Soon, much of the countryside was under Vietcong control.

In 1960 Ho Chi Minh expanded the effort to reunify North and South Vietnam. More supply routes leading to South Vietnam were established. North Vietnamese Army (NVA) forces also began coming into the country to fight alongside the Vietcong.

President Eisenhower decided to <u>intervene</u> in the conflict in 1955. The United States began supplying South Vietnam with money and weapons. Eisenhower began sending military advisers to train South Vietnam's army—the

In mid-1963 Buddhists began protesting Diem's oppression of their religion. At left, Buddhist demonstrators clash with police. In a terrible protest that focused world attention on Diem, Buddhist monk Quang Duc set himself on fire at a busy Saigon intersection.

Army of the Republic of Vietnam (ARVN)—to use American weaponry.

By the end of Eisenhower's presidency, there were about 900 U.S. military advisers in South Vietnam. Many of these advisers had become frustrated with the corruption and inefficiency present in the ARVN.

READING CHECK **Summarizing** Why was Ngo Dinh Diem's government unpopular?

Increasing U.S. Involvement

Elected in 1960, President John F. Kennedy was a firm believer in the domino theory. Kennedy was eager to display U.S. strength in Vietnam.

You read in an earlier chapter about the two Cold War disasters that began Kennedy's presidency, the Bay of Pigs invasion and the building of the Berlin Wall. In the aftermath of these incidents, Kennedy hoped that aiding South Vietnam would be a sign of continued U.S. resolve and strength. "Now we have a problem in making our power credible," he warned, "and Vietnam is the place [to do so]."

President Kennedy hesitated to send official combat forces into South Vietnam, however. Instead, he decided to increase the number of military advisers and army special forces, or Green Berets, in that country. In December 1961 there were about 3,000 U.S. advisers in South Vietnam. By 1963 that number had increased to about 16,000.

The advisers were not supposed to take part in combat, but many did. For example, helicopter pilots fired rockets and machine guns at Vietcong targets. Green Berets often accompanied the ARVN on dangerous ambush operations. As Vietcong attacks mounted, Kennedy authorized U.S. personnel to engage in direct combat. The number of Americans killed or wounded climbed steadily. In 1961 some 14 Americans were killed. In 1963 the number rose to nearly 500.

Diem's overthrow Meanwhile, Diem's government grew more and more unpopular. When Buddhist leaders opposed his rule, Diem struck back by arresting and killing Buddhist protesters. To bring attention to the situation, several Buddhist monks killed themselves by publicly setting themselves on fire. Gruesome photographs were printed in newspapers around

ACADEMIC VOCABULARY
intervene get involved in, get in the middle of

QUICK FACTS

CAUSES OF THE VIETNAM WAR

- **Vietnam's desire for freedom from colonial rule** France reclaimed Vietnam as a colony after World War II. The Communist-led Vietminh fought against French rule.

- **U.S. fears of the spread of communism (the domino theory)** Fearing that communism would spread throughout Southeast Asia if Communists took over Vietnam, the United States supported France. Despite U.S. aid, French rule of Vietnam ended in 1954.

- **South Vietnam's failure to comply with the Geneva Accords** After the French surrender, Vietnam was temporarily divided. North Vietnam was controlled by the Vietminh. Under the Geneva Accords, elections to unify the country under one government were set for 1956, but South Vietnam's leader refused to hold them.

- **Efforts by North Vietnam to reunite the nation under Communist rule** By 1959 North Vietnam began sending weapons to Vietminh in South Vietnam with the goal of unifying the country under a Communist government.

- **U.S. support for the anti-Communist government of South Vietnam** The United States supported South Vietnam with military advisers and later with troops.

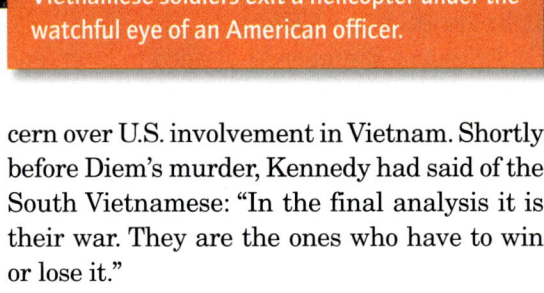

Early in the war, U.S. personnel served primarily as military advisers and trainers. Here, South Vietnamese soldiers exit a helicopter under the watchful eye of an American officer.

the world. The images shocked Americans, and public opinion turned sharply against Diem.

American officials threatened to withdraw support unless Diem changed his policies. Yet he refused to alter his stand against Buddhists.

In response, U.S. leaders secretly began to support a plot within the South Vietnamese army to overthrow Diem. The U.S. ambassador to South Vietnam, Henry Cabot Lodge Jr., sent a cable to Washington describing the situation.

HISTORY'S VOICES

> **❝** We are launched on a course from which there is no respectable turning back: the overthrow of the Diem government. There is no turning back because there is no possibility, in my view, that the war can be won under a Diem administration. **❞**
>
> —Henry Cabot Lodge Jr., August 29, 1963

In November 1963 the South Vietnamese plotters murdered Diem. Although Kennedy and his top advisers supported Diem's overthrow, they did not seek his assassination. The removal of Diem from power, however, did nothing to ease President Kennedy's growing con-

cern over U.S. involvement in Vietnam. Shortly before Diem's murder, Kennedy had said of the South Vietnamese: "In the final analysis it is their war. They are the ones who have to win or lose it."

It cannot be known for sure whether Kennedy would have changed U.S. policy toward Vietnam. Just three weeks after Diem's death, President Kennedy himself was assassinated in Dallas, Texas.

The Tonkin Gulf Resolution When Vice President Lyndon B. Johnson took over as president, he inherited a rapidly deteriorating situation in South Vietnam. Although the ARVN had about 300,000 soldiers, the South Vietnamese government was on the brink of collapse. North Vietnamese forces were slipping into South Vietnam at an ever-increasing rate. By March 1964 the Vietcong controlled about 40 percent of South Vietnam.

President Johnson became convinced that only an expanded U.S. military involvement in South Vietnam could prevent a Communist victory. To increase the American military effort there, however, Johnson needed to obtain authority from the U.S. Congress. In 1964 an incident off the coast of North Vietnam gave him the opportunity to ask for this authority.

Near midnight on August 4, 1964, President Johnson appeared on national television. He made the dramatic announcement that on August 2 the USS *Maddox*, a navy destroyer, had been attacked by North Vietnamese torpedo boats in the Gulf of Tonkin, off the North Vietnamese coast.

Johnson said that the attack on the *Maddox* "was repeated today by a number of hostile vessels attacking two U.S. destroyers [the *Maddox* and the *C. Turner Joy*] with torpedoes." He called for a swift military response.

HISTORY'S VOICES

❝Repeated acts of violence against the Armed Forces of the United States must be met not only with alert defense, but with positive reply. That reply is being given as I speak to you tonight. Air action is now in execution against gunboats and certain supporting facilities in North Vietnam which have been used in these hostile operations.❞

—Lyndon B. Johnson, speech on August 4, 1964

Later it was learned that President Johnson did not present a completely accurate picture of the incident in the Gulf of Tonkin. Johnson was in the middle of his 1964 presidential election campaign against Senator Barry Goldwater, a strong anti-Communist. Johnson wanted to avoid charges from Senator Goldwater and the Republicans that he was soft on communism.

The president claimed that the attack on the USS *Maddox* was unprovoked. In fact, the *Maddox* had been on a spying mission and had fired first.

As for the second attack, U.S. sailors may have mistaken interference on their radar and sonar for enemy boats and torpedoes. At the time, however, most members of Congress did not know the factual details surrounding the two incidents.

The **Tonkin Gulf Resolution** was approved by Congress on August 7. The resolution <u>enabled</u> the president to take "all necessary measures to repel any armed attack against forces of the United States." Johnson and his advisers now had authority to expand the war.

Senator Wayne Morse of Oregon was one of only two senators to oppose the Tonkin Gulf Resolution. "I believe that history will record we have made a great mistake," he predicted. "We are in effect giving the President war-making powers in the absence of a declaration of war."

ACADEMIC VOCABULARY

enable to give enough power, opportunity, or ability

READING CHECK **Identifying Cause and Effect** What circumstances led Congress to pass the Tonkin Gulf Resolution?

---

go.hrw.com
Online Quiz
Keyword: SD7 HP29

SECTION 1 ASSESSMENT

Reviewing Ideas, Terms, and People

1. a. Define What was French Indochina?
b. Analyze How did French rule influence **Ho Chi Minh**'s decision to embrace communism?
c. Elaborate Do you think Ho Chi Minh's comparison of Vietnam after World War II and colonial America was valid? Explain.

2. a. Describe According to the **domino theory**, what did American leaders think might happen if Vietnam became a Communist country?
b. Make Inferences Do you think the Geneva Accords eased American concerns about a domino effect in Southeast Asia? Why or why not?

3. a. Identify Who were the **Vietcong**?
b. Analyze Cause and Effect What was Eisenhower's response to the growing strength of the Vietcong?
c. Evaluate Do you think the United States was justified in supporting **Ngo Dinh Diem**? Why or why not?

4. a. Describe What happened to the USS *Maddox* in the Gulf of Tonkin?

b. Predict How might the **Tonkin Gulf Resolution** affect the power of the presidency?

Critical Thinking

5. Draw Conclusions Review your notes on the leaders of North Vietnam and South Vietnam. Then copy the graphic organizer below and use it to list the causes for the decline in popularity of Ngo Dinh Diem's government.

Cause	Effect
	The popularity of Ngo Dinh Diem's government declined.

FOCUS ON WRITING

6. Expository Suppose that you are the communications director in the Kennedy or Johnson White House. Write a press release that explains the president's decision to increase U.S. military involvement in Vietnam.

U.S. Support of the War at Home and Abroad

BEFORE YOU READ

MAIN IDEA

As the United States sent increasing numbers of troops to defend South Vietnam, some Americans began to question the war.

READING FOCUS

1. Why did U.S. superiority in the air war fail to win quickly in Vietnam?

2. What made the ground war in Vietnam so difficult to fight?

3. How were U.S. forces mobilized for the war?

4. How and why did public opinion about the war gradually change?

KEY TERMS AND PEOPLE

Operation Rolling Thunder
Ho Chi Minh Trail
William Westmoreland
pacification
doves
hawks
J. William Fulbright

PI **2.5** Analyze the United States involvement in foreign affairs and a willingness to engage in international politics, examining the ideas and traditions leading to these foreign policies.

THE INSIDE STORY

Why do some people risk their lives to serve their country?
The young men who volunteered to fight in Vietnam came mostly from rural America or from industrial neighborhoods in the nation's cities. Many recruits were the sons of American soldiers who had fought in World War II or the Korean War. For young men fresh out of high school, serving in Vietnam seemed to be an adventure as well as a patriotic duty.

Eighteen-year-old Rod Kane was just such a person. After graduating from high school in 1964, he went to see the recruiter. "I want to be in the infantry, like my Uncle Paul . . . Maybe I should do something like save people, like medics," Kane said.

"If you volunteer for three years, I can guarantee you medics school," the recruiter promised. "Remember what President Kennedy said," he urged. "'Ask not what your country can do for you. Ask what you can do for your country.'"

It sounded good to Kane. In 1965, army infantry member and medic Rod Kane arrived in Vietnam.

Signing Up

New recruits pledge to "support and defend" the United States.

The Air War

The first major direct U.S. military activity in Vietnam took place in the air. President Johnson ordered **Operation Rolling Thunder**, a bombing campaign over North Vietnam, in March 1965. He wanted to weaken the enemy's ability and will to fight. He also wanted to assure South Vietnam of his commitment to its independence.

U.S. pilots bombed military targets in North Vietnam, such as army bases and airfields. They also bombed anything North Vietnam would find useful in the war effort, including bridges, roads, railways, and power plants.

Rolling Thunder

U.S. Air Force pilots flying Vietnamese Skyraiders drop napalm on Vietcong targets. Operation Rolling Thunder aimed to weaken the enemy, disrupt the Ho Chi Minh Trail, and defoliate the countryside. *Why did U.S. involvement in Vietnam begin with air power instead of ground troops?*

One of the main targets of Operation Rolling Thunder was the **Ho Chi Minh Trail**. The trail was a network of paths that began in North Vietnam, snaked through Laos and Cambodia, and ended in South Vietnam. The North Vietnamese used the trail to send weapons, soldiers, food, and other supplies to the Vietcong and NVA forces in South Vietnam.

Much of the Ho Chi Minh Trail ran through thick jungle areas, making movement along it all but invisible from the air. American planes began spraying jungle areas with defoliants, or chemicals that destroy vegetation. The goal of this spraying was to expose enemy supply routes and hiding places. A chemical called Agent Orange was the most widely used type of defoliant.

American forces used several other types of weapons in the air war. Napalm, a jellied form of gasoline, was used to create firebombs that destroyed farms and forests. "Cluster bombs" sprayed sharp metal fragments when they exploded. Pilots also carried out attacks called carpet bombing, a strategy in which strings of bombs dropped from high altitudes destroy large areas of land with no specific target.

The bombing did not succeed in its goal of weakening the enemy's war effort, however.

Instead of cutting off aid to the Vietcong, the flow of troops and supplies from North Vietnam to the south actually increased. When roads or bridges on the Ho Chi Minh Trail were damaged, the Vietcong quickly repaired them or did without them. They also had underground bunkers that protected soldiers and supplies.

Another reason the Communist forces were able to withstand the bombing was that they received massive support from the Soviet Union and China. Both Communist powers provided North Vietnam with soldiers, economic aid, and high-tech weapons, including radar and antiaircraft guns.

Frustrated by the lack of progress, Johnson broadened the air war. By late 1968 more than 1 million tons of bombs had been dropped on North Vietnam. Targets in Laos, Cambodia, and parts of South Vietnam were also bombed.

One unintended effect of the American bombing campaign was that it led many South Vietnamese to join the Vietcong. Soon the forces opposing American troops included an increasing number of South Vietnamese.

READING CHECK **Identifying the Main Idea**
What did U.S. forces hope to accomplish by bombing the Ho Chi Minh Trail?

The Ground War

THE IMPACT TODAY

Government

In part because of Vietnam, the question of U.S. involvement in a foreign war comes under intense scrutiny today. Recent presidents have been pressured to make the case for a compelling national interest before sending U.S. forces to hostile overseas situations.

As the war continued, Johnson called for an escalation, or buildup, of U.S. ground forces in Vietnam. The number of American troops in South Vietnam grew from 185,000 at the end of 1965 to 486,000 two years later.

U.S. strategy In response to the guerrilla tactics used by Communist forces, General **William Westmoreland**, the commander of U.S. ground troops in South Vietnam, ordered thousands of search-and-destroy missions to drive enemy forces out of their hideouts. Ground troops located Vietcong and NVA positions and then called in air strikes to bomb them. Once an area was "cleared" the ground patrols moved on to search for other enemy positions.

American troops on search-and-destroy missions often cut through the thick jungle, fighting foes they rarely saw. Other times, they waded through rice paddies or searched rural villages. One U.S. commander, Captain Myron Harrington, described what it was like to lead a company of 100 marines.

HISTORY'S VOICES

❝After a while, survival was the name of the game as you sat there in the semidarkness, with the firing going on constantly, like at a rifle range. And the horrible smell. You tasted it as you ate your rations, as if you were eating death . . . You went through the full range of emotions, seeing your buddies being hit, but you couldn't feel sorry for them because you had the others to think about.❞

—Captain Myron Harrington,
quoted in *Vietnam* by Stanley Karnow

After search-and-destroy patrols left an area, villages seldom remained clear for long. Returning Vietcong and NVA troops sometimes terrorized civilians they believed had aided the Americans.

To improve rural security, U.S. forces instituted a program of <mark>pacification</mark>. Its goal was to "win the hearts and minds" of the South Vietnamese people—to pacify, or calm, opposition—especially in the countryside.

Nonmilitary pacification involved construction projects to improve the country's infrastructure and economy. Militarily, pacification involved moving people out of their villages when Vietcong were concentrated

ACADEMIC VOCABULARY

instituted established or started

nearby. Villagers were relocated to safe camps and given food and housing. American troops then burned the village to prevent the Vietcong from using it.

U.S. planners hoped that driving out the Vietcong would help win the support of South Vietnamese civilians. Many civilians, however, resented being moved off their land and having their villages destroyed.

As armies fought from village to village, it was difficult for U.S. military leaders to show progress on a map. Instead, they measured success with body counts, or the number of enemy killed. It often was difficult for troops to make accurate counts in the midst of hectic jungle firefights. Also, high military officials sometimes inflated the body counts reported by units in the field.

Declining troop morale The first U.S. ground troops in Vietnam were convinced that they would succeed. Marine lieutenant Philip Caputo remembered his early confidence.

HISTORY'S VOICES

❝Our expectations were, we were going to stay there a month to 90 days, help the South Vietnamese recover, and then we would get out . . . We got this idea that the United States was invincible . . . that, being U.S. Marines, our mere presence in Vietnam was going to terrify the enemy into quitting.❞

—Lieutenant Philip Caputo, CNN interview, June 1996

In reality, American troops confronted many of the same challenges the French had faced. Aided by NVA troops, the Vietcong struck at U.S. patrols and government-held villages and then melted back into the jungle. Some Vietnamese peasants seemed peaceful by day but aided or even became the Vietcong at night. The Vietcong also had the major advantage of knowing the local geography.

U.S. combat soldiers faced constant danger. Each path could lead into an enemy ambush. Each step could trip a deadly mine or a booby trap such as Punji stakes, which were sharpened bamboo sticks concealed in a hole or mud. On patrol, American troops found it nearly impossible to tell the difference between a Vietcong fighter and a civilian.

Caputo later described the sense of uncertainty he and his fellow marines felt when interacting with Vietnamese civilians.

Vietcong Tunnels

The Vietcong had a vast system of underground tunnels some of which had been built in the 1940s. The tunnels served as hiding places during combat. They also served as living quarters, places to store food and weapons, and locations to tend wounded soldiers. This illustration depicts a typical complex in one of the larger tunnel systems. By 1965 the tunnels stretched underground from Saigon to the Cambodian border, a distance of about 120 miles.

Firing Post

The Vietcong used tunnel meeting rooms to plan attacks on U.S. soldiers.

Air Vents

Bomb Shelter

Kitchen

Dormitory

Special doors were installed to protect against bomb blasts and poison-gas attacks.

Bicycle-powered generators provided electricity for tunnel rooms.

Some tunnels held traps that would injure invaders.

Hospital

Weapons Storage

Wells were dug to provide fresh water inside the tunnel system.

Skills FOCUS INTERPRETING INFOGRAPHICS

The Vietcong could not compete in firepower, but they used tunnels and other types of guerrilla warfare.

Drawing Conclusions How did the tunnel structure meet the military and personal needs of the Vietcong?

See **Skills Handbook**, p. 18

"You didn't and couldn't really trust them," he said. "You did develop this intense suspicion. You were constantly watching them, and that got to be kind of wearing after a while."

Despite these obstacles, U.S. troops inflicted enormous casualties on the Communist forces. This did not lead to victory, however. With the continued aid of China and the Soviet Union, North Vietnam was able to send a steady stream of supplies and soldiers to the South.

The Vietcong also refilled their ranks by recruiting civilians. Some South Vietnamese began to help the Communists or join the Vietcong. Destruction from American air strikes and the pacification policy turned many peasants into Vietcong fighters.

READING CHECK **Summarizing** What fighting strategies did the NVA and the Vietcong use?

U.S. Forces Mobilize

More than 2.5 million Americans served in the Vietnam War. On average, the soldiers who served in Vietnam were slightly younger than the U.S. troops who fought in Korea and World War II. Most Vietnam soldiers were not well educated. Some 80 percent of the American troops had a high school education or less.

The draft At the start of the war, most American troops were professional soldiers—volunteers who enlisted in the armed forces. As the American force in Vietnam steadily increased, however, the U.S. government depended more and more heavily on drafted soldiers.

About 25 percent of the young men who registered for the draft were excused from service for health reasons. Another 30 percent received deferments, or postponements of service. Men enrolled in college were able to get deferments. Enrollment at American colleges and universities skyrocketed as a result. Draft boards monitored student progress, however, and could cancel a deferment if a student's grades were too low.

Because college students could get draft deferments, young men from higher-income families were less likely to serve in Vietnam. Poor Americans served in numbers greater than their proportion of the general population. "I'm bitter," said one firefighter whose son died in the war. "The college types, the professors, they go to Washington and tell the government what to do . . . But their sons, they don't end up in the swamps over there, in Vietnam."

Large numbers of African Americans traditionally enlisted in the military. For this reason, a high percentage of soldiers in combat positions were African American during the war's early years, when much of the fighting was done by volunteers. Therefore, the casualty rates of black soldiers at first were very high. For example, African Americans accounted for at least one fifth of all U.S. battle deaths in 1965 even though they made up 11 percent of the American population.

As the war continued, however, the draft largely ended this inequity. In 1969 the government made an attempt to reform the makeup of the military by instituting a lottery system for the draft. This lottery system drafted men based on birth dates chosen at random.

By putting an end to many deferments, it made the draft fairer, because now income levels were less important in determining who had to serve. Finally, in 1973 the government ended the unpopular draft and returned to filling its ranks with volunteers.

About 3 percent of eligible young men escaped the draft altogether during the Vietnam War, either by refusing to register or by leaving the United States. Thousands of American men went to Canada to avoid being sent to Vietnam.

One young man who fled to Canada commented on his experience. "I ran into quite a few Americans on the run from the draft," he reported. "They were scared . . . Most had been cut off from their parents who branded them cowards and traitors."

Noncombat positions Most Americans who went to Vietnam served in non-combat positions, such as those in administration, communications, engineering, medical care, and transportation. Even in these noncombat roles, however, soldiers faced dangers from the fighting. Enemy rockets and mortars often struck seemingly safe positions.

About 10,000 American military women served in noncombat positions, mostly as nurses. Some 20,000 to 45,000 more women worked in civilian capacities, many as volunteers for the Red Cross or other humanitarian relief organizations.

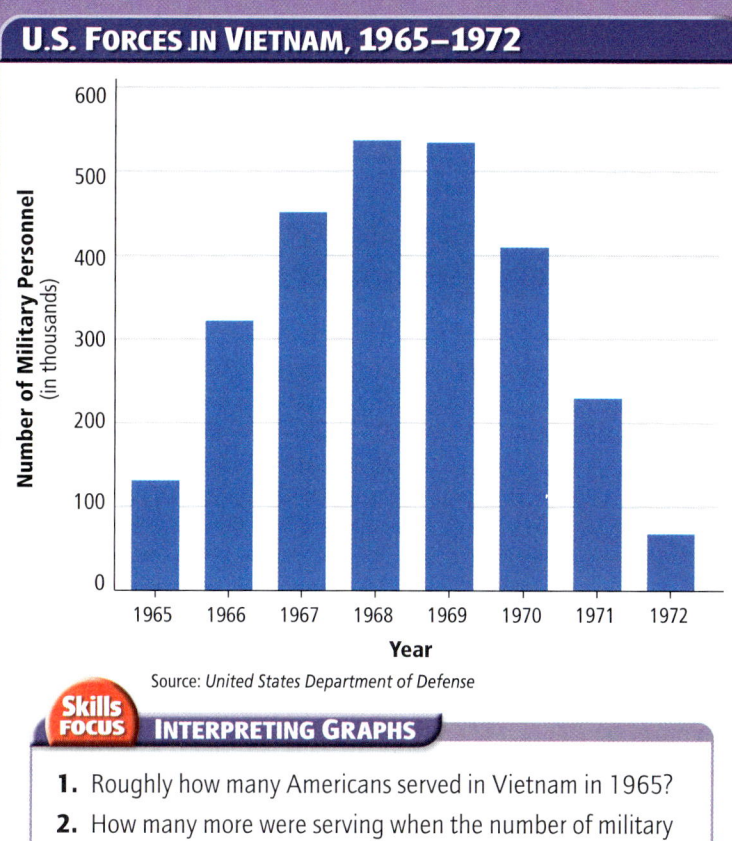

U.S. FORCES IN VIETNAM, 1965–1972

Number of Military Personnel (in thousands)

Year

Source: United States Department of Defense

Skills FOCUS **INTERPRETING GRAPHS**

1. Roughly how many Americans served in Vietnam in 1965?
2. How many more were serving when the number of military personnel reached its peak?

See **Skills Handbook**, p. H16

U.S. military involvement in Vietnam peaked in 1968. Above, military nurses prepare wounded U.S. soldiers at a Saigon military base for their journey home in 1967.

Sylvia Lutz Holland was one of many nurses assigned to evacuation hospitals, where wounded troops were brought by helicopter. She had the heavy responsibility of deciding who to treat first.

"You'd look at the wounds, check the vital signs, and just make a decision—he's a go or he can wait," the nurse recalled. "We had to move fast."

Although nurses did not carry guns into battle, they were exposed to the horrors of combat on a daily basis.

HISTORY'S VOICES

❝ If the Army took a hill, we saw what was left over. I remember one boy who was brought in missing two legs and an arm, and his eyes were bandaged. A general came in later and pinned a Purple Heart on the boy's hospital gown, and the horror of it all was so amazing that it just took my breath away. ❞

—nurse Edie Meeks, *Newsweek* interview, March 8, 1999

READING CHECK **Making Inferences** How did the draft change the U.S. force in Vietnam?

Public Opinion Shifts

Most Americans supported U.S. involvement in the Vietnam War at first. By the end of 1968, however, more than 16,000 Americans had been killed in combat. A growing number of Americans began to question the wisdom of U.S. policy regarding involvement in Vietnam.

The media's impact News media coverage of the Vietnam War had a strong impact on American public opinion. During previous wars the military had imposed tight restrictions on the press. In Vietnam, however, reporters and television crews accompanied soldiers on patrol and interviewed people throughout South Vietnam.

Television coverage brought scenes of firefights and burning villages into Americans' living rooms. For this reason, the Vietnam War has been called the first "living room war."

The U.S. government allowed TV crews to cover the war, hoping television reports would show Americans that U.S. forces were making

Views on the Vietnam War

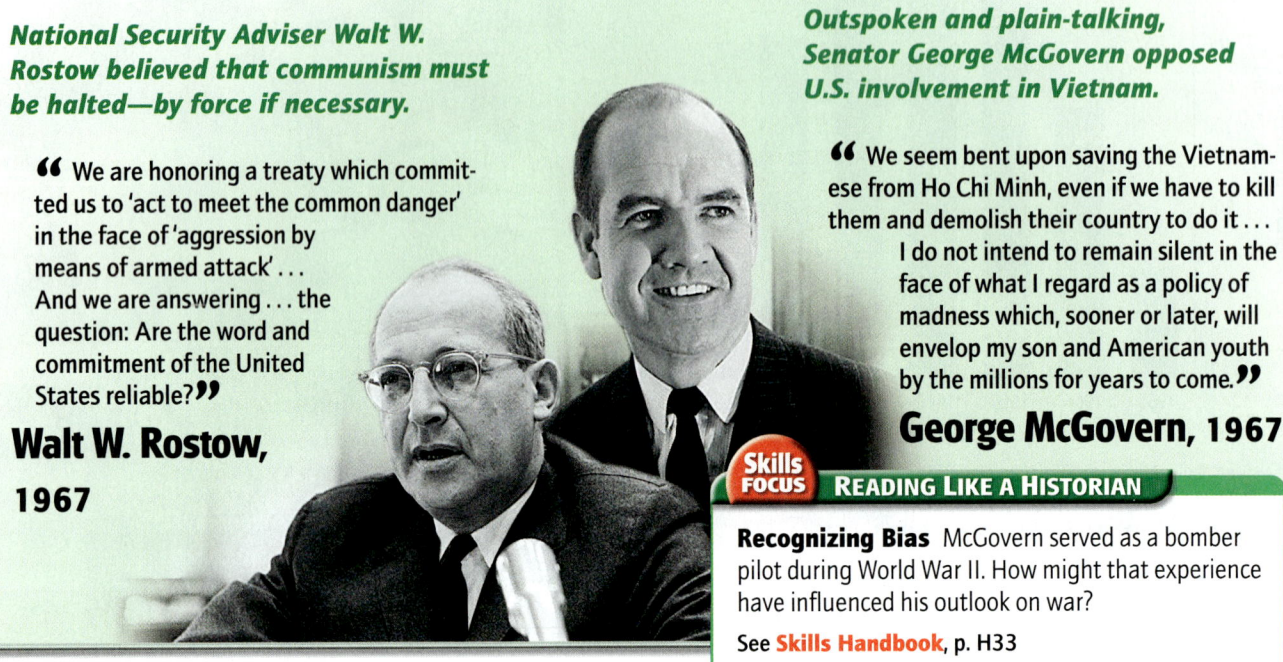

National Security Adviser Walt W. Rostow believed that communism must be halted—by force if necessary.

❝ We are honoring a treaty which committed us to 'act to meet the common danger' in the face of 'aggression by means of armed attack' . . . And we are answering . . . the question: Are the word and commitment of the United States reliable?❞

Walt W. Rostow, 1967

Outspoken and plain-talking, Senator George McGovern opposed U.S. involvement in Vietnam.

❝ We seem bent upon saving the Vietnamese from Ho Chi Minh, even if we have to kill them and demolish their country to do it . . . I do not intend to remain silent in the face of what I regard as a policy of madness which, sooner or later, will envelop my son and American youth by the millions for years to come.❞

George McGovern, 1967

Skills FOCUS **READING LIKE A HISTORIAN**

Recognizing Bias McGovern served as a bomber pilot during World War II. How might that experience have influenced his outlook on war?

See **Skills Handbook**, p. H33

---

progress in Vietnam. But to many Americans, the images they saw on television contradicted the optimistic government reports on the progress of the war. Some reporters questioned or criticized the government's reports as well. They reported on the ineffectiveness of South Vietnamese troops. In addition, they accused the U.S. government of inflating body counts to create the appearance of success.

Hawks and doves As the gap between official reports and media accounts widened, debate at home increased. Johnson was criticized by both **doves**—people who opposed the war—and **hawks**—people who supported the war's goals. Some hawks disapproved of the government's handling of the war. They believed more troops and heavier bombing were necessary to victory. Air force general Curtis LeMay expressed this view. "Here we are at the height of our power. The most powerful nation in the world. And yet we're afraid to use that power."

Doves had a variety of reasons for opposing the war. Diplomat George Kennan, for example, argued that Vietnam was not crucial to

American national security. Pediatrician and author Dr. Benjamin Spock and others claimed that the United States was fighting against the wishes of a majority of Vietnamese. Martin Luther King Jr. expressed concern that the war was draining needed resources from Great Society programs.

HISTORY'S VOICES

❝ I watched the [antipoverty] program broken and eviscerated [gutted] as if it were some idle political plaything of a society gone mad on war, and I knew that America would never invest the necessary funds or energies in rehabilitation of its poor so long as Vietnam continued to draw men and skills and money like some demonic, destructive suction tube.❞

—Martin Luther King Jr., sermon opposing the Vietnam War, 1967

Many other civil rights activists argued that it was unfair to expect African Americans to fight for democracy in a foreign land when discrimination continued at home. Polls showed that African Americans were much more likely than whites to believe that U.S. involvement in the war was a mistake.

Doves in Congress also became more vocal as the war continued. **J. William Fulbright** of Arkansas, head of the Senate Foreign Relations Committee, criticized Johnson's policies as too extreme. He held televised committee hearings in 1966 to give the war's critics a public voice.

The antiwar movement

As opposition to the war grew, a large antiwar movement developed. The movement attracted a broad range of people, including students, civil rights workers, doctors, homemakers, retirees, and teachers.

Much of the antiwar activity took place on college campuses, where students held antiwar rallies and debates. Faculty members held teach-ins, where they sought to educate students about the war. Student opponents of the war also protested the draft and the presence of the Reserve Officers' Training Corps (ROTC) on campus.

One of the most vocal antiwar groups was Students for a Democratic Society (SDS). By the end of 1965, the SDS had members on 124 college campuses across the country. In April 1965, SDS members led the first national antiwar demonstration. More than 20,000 people marched to the Capitol in Washington, D.C., where they delivered a petition to Congress demanding that lawmakers "act immediately to end the war." The SDS and other antiwar groups also protested against universities that conducted research for the military. Some young men protested the draft by burning their draft cards, which the government sent to each man at the time he registered for the draft.

President Lyndon Johnson responded to the protests by insisting that the United States was protecting an ally against an aggressor. Secretary of State Dean Rusk put it this way: If the United States failed to support South Vietnam, what ally would ever trust the United States again?

While antiwar protesters were highly visible, they made up a small percentage of the U.S. population. Many Americans opposed the antiwar movement, especially the actions of the extreme groups. They were particularly angered by the burning of draft cards or American flags. Many veterans of previous wars spoke out against men who avoided the draft. Some opponents of the antiwar movement held rallies in support of the war, carrying signs with messages such as "America, Love It or Leave It" and "My Country, Right or Wrong."

READING CHECK **Identifying Cause and Effect** How and why did television affect public opinion about the Vietnam War?

SECTION 2 ASSESSMENT

go.hrw.com
Online Quiz
Keyword: SD7 HP29

Reviewing Ideas, Terms, and People

1. a. Identify What was Operation Rolling Thunder?
b. Draw Conclusions Why do you think Operation Rolling Thunder failed to lead to a quick victory?

2. a. Describe What dangers did American soldiers face in Vietnam?
b. Analyze Why did the U.S. program of pacification fail?
c. Elaborate How do you think the pacification program might have been improved?

3. a. Recall Who was most likely to be drafted to serve in the Vietnam War?
b. Draw Conclusions How do you think American soldiers fighting in Vietnam felt about the young men who tried to avoid being drafted?
c. Elaborate What factors would a young man have weighed in deciding whether to flee the United States to avoid the draft?

4. a. Describe What were the views of the doves and the hawks during the Vietnam War?

b. Evaluate Do you think groups such as the SDS had much influence on public opinion about the Vietnam War? Why or why not?

Critical Thinking

5. Contrast Review your notes on the tactics of U.S. soldiers in the Vietnam War. Then copy the graphic organizer below and use it to contrast U.S. military strategies with those of the North Vietnamese Army and Vietcong.

U.S. Military	North Vietnamese Army, Vietcong

FOCUS ON WRITING

6. Persuasive Either as an antiwar or pro-government demonstrator, write a speech that you would give at a rally about the Vietnam War.

THE VIETNAM WAR **963**

1968: A Turning Point

BEFORE YOU READ

MAIN IDEA

As the Vietnam War dragged on and increasingly appeared to be unwinnable, deep divisions developed in American society.

READING FOCUS

1. What was the Tet Offensive?
2. What were the effects of the Tet Offensive?
3. How did President Johnson try to find a solution to the war?
4. How did the election of 1968 illustrate divisions in American society?

KEY TERMS AND PEOPLE

Tet Offensive
Robert S. McNamara
Eugene McCarthy
Hubert Humphrey
George Wallace

PI 3.3 Prepare essays and oral reports about the important social, political, economic, scientific, technological, and cultural developments, issues, and events from New York State and United States history.

THE INSIDE STORY

Why did an attack on the U.S. Embassy become so important in the war? At 2:45 a.m. on January 31, 1968, two vehicles approached the compound that housed the U.S. embassy in Saigon, South Vietnam's capital city. At the compound's entrance, 19 Vietcong fighters jumped out and opened fire with automatic weapons. The two American military police (MP) officers guarding the entrance returned fire as they backed through the heavy steel gate and locked it. Then they radioed Signal 300, the code for an enemy attack.

Suddenly, a huge explosion shook the neighborhood as the attackers blew a hole in the high concrete wall surrounding the compound. "They're coming in—help me!" one MP shouted into his radio. Then the radio went silent.

Both MPs were killed as the Vietcong poured through the hole in the wall. The MPs, however, had managed to delay the attackers long enough to allow the marines inside the compound to seal the main embassy building. Other U.S. troops rushed to the scene. A fierce firefight spread across the grounds of the compound.

By 9:15 a.m. the fighting was over. All but two of the Vietcong were dead, along with five American soldiers.

General William Westmoreland arrived a few minutes later. "It's a relatively small incident," he declared. His assessment proved to be wrong. The assault on the embassy was part of a much larger attack that ultimately changed the course of the Vietnam War.

▼ Saigon erupted into a battle zone in the months following the attack on the U.S. Embassy.

Under Attack

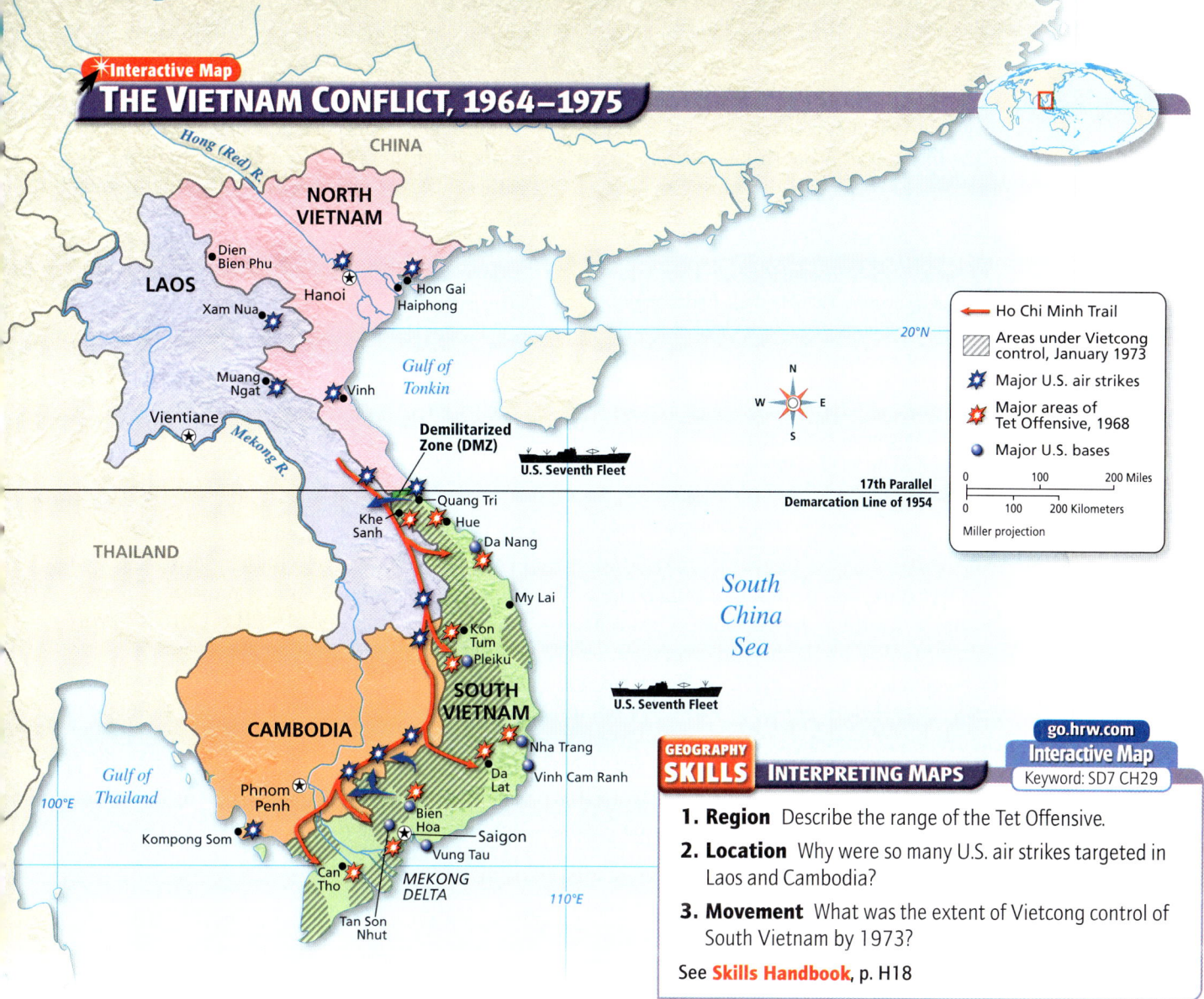

CHINA

Hong (Red) R.

NORTH VIETNAM

LAOS

Dien Bien Phu
Hanoi
Xam Nua
Hon Gai
Haiphong

Muang Ngat
Vinh

Vientiane

Mekong R.

Gulf of Tonkin

THAILAND

Demilitarized Zone (DMZ)

U.S. Seventh Fleet

Quang Tri
Khe Sanh
Hue
Da Nang

My Lai

Kon Tum
Pleiku

SOUTH VIETNAM

South China Sea

CAMBODIA

U.S. Seventh Fleet

Nha Trang

Da Lat
Vinh Cam Ranh

Gulf of Thailand

Phnom Penh

Kompong Som

Bien Hoa
Saigon
Vung Tau

Can Tho

MEKONG DELTA

Tan Son Nhut

20°N

17th Parallel
Demarcation Line of 1954

100°E

110°E

N W E S

→ Ho Chi Minh Trail
Areas under Vietcong control, January 1973
✦ Major U.S. air strikes
✦ Major areas of Tet Offensive, 1968
● Major U.S. bases

0   100   200 Miles
0   100   200 Kilometers
Miller projection

GEOGRAPHY SKILLS   **INTERPRETING MAPS**

go.hrw.com
Interactive Map
Keyword: SD7 CH29

1. **Region** Describe the range of the Tet Offensive.
2. **Location** Why were so many U.S. air strikes targeted in Laos and Cambodia?
3. **Movement** What was the extent of Vietcong control of South Vietnam by 1973?

See **Skills Handbook**, p. H18

The Tet Offensive

The Vietcong assault on the U.S. Embassy marked the start of the **Tet Offensive**, a series of massive coordinated attacks throughout South Vietnam. The Tet Offensive caused 1968 to become a critical year in the Vietnam War.

Khe Sanh In late 1967 U.S. military leaders began noticing increased traffic on the Ho Chi Minh Trail. They suspected a major assault was coming. In January 1968 thousands of NVA and Vietcong troops struck an isolated U.S. military base in Khe Sanh (KAY sahn), in northwestern South Vietnam. Communist troops surrounded the base and pounded it with artillery fire. News reporters compared the siege to the French battle at Dien Bien Phu in 1954. After the 77-day siege ended, however, the Americans still held Khe Sanh.

General Westmoreland concluded that preparations for the Khe Sanh assault explained the increased Ho Chi Minh Trail traffic. In fact, Khe Sanh and other rural attacks were diversions. Their purpose was to draw U.S. and ARVN forces away from urban areas, where the major strikes were planned.

The main attacks The main Communist offensive began on January 30, 1968. This was the start of Tet, the Vietnamese New Year. In previous years, the opposing sides had observed a cease-fire during the holiday, with many South Vietnamese soldiers actually going home to celebrate.

In 1968 the Vietcong and North Vietnamese troops took advantage of this moment to launch an offensive. During the crippling campaign, some 84,000 Communist soldiers attacked 12 U.S. military bases and more than

100 cities across South Vietnam. The U.S. Embassy was one of several Saigon sites attacked on the first night. A South Vietnamese government official recalled the assault.

HISTORY'S VOICES

> **"**Embassy staff, covered in blood, were being treated by doctors. Humble clerks had changed their pens for guns. There were dead bodies everywhere—some American, but mostly Viet Cong. They lay in heaps on the lawn, staining the green grass red with blood . . . Chunks of stone and concrete were strewn about, and the once beautiful white walls of the embassy were now full of bullet holes.**"**
>
> —Tran Van Huong, quoted in *Nam: The Vietnam Experience, 1965–75*

North Vietnamese leaders hoped the Tet Offensive would inspire South Vietnamese civilians to rise up against their government. However, the expected public support did not materialize. Many civilians were left homeless from the damage caused by the attacks. The Communists also slaughtered South Vietnamese people they believed were helping the Americans. This also turned many civilians against the Vietcong.

General Westmoreland described the Tet Offensive as a decisive defeat for the Communists. After more than a month of fighting, the cities captured by the Vietcong and NVA were retaken, and about 45,000 enemy soldiers were killed. About 1,100 American and 2,300 ARVN troops also died. Despite suffering such heavy losses, however, the Communists showed that they were determined to keep fighting.

READING CHECK **Identifying the Main Idea** Why did the Communists launch the Tet Offensive?

Effects of the Tet Offensive

The Tet Offensive showed that no part of South Vietnam was safe from attack. This shattered many people's belief that Communist forces were weakening and that the United States would soon win the war.

Walter Cronkite, the respected anchor of *CBS Evening News,* said privately, "I thought we were winning the war! What . . . is going on?" In February 1968 Cronkite broadcast a television report in which he offered the American public his personal assessment of the situation in Vietnam.

Linking TO Today

Battlefield Reporting

Photographs of Civil War battlefields and newsreels from World War II helped to inform civilians about those wars. Yet frequently this information was well out of date by the time it reached the American public.

As technology improved, the way people learned about wars changed. During the Vietnam War, relatively lightweight cameras and improved shipping service meant that stories could be filmed and flown back to the United States within 24 hours. The evening news brought dramatic and disturbing images of the war into American homes.

During the Iraq War in 2003, reporters relied on laptop computers and satellite videophones. News traveled around the world almost instantly, reaching the United States via the Internet as well as by television.

Working conditions also changed for reporters. In Vietnam, journalists often traveled with troops, but they were not officially connected to the military. During the Iraq War, reporters could choose to be "embedded" with a military unit. They received training and an honorary rank. Journalists gained greater access to troops. However, critics charged that the arrangement compromised the objectivity and scope of their reporting.

Drawing Conclusions What were the biggest changes in war coverage during the last 150 years?

A U.S. news photographer during the Iraq War uses a computer, generator, and satellite phone to send his images back to the office.

" We have been too often disappointed by the optimism of the American leaders . . . For it seems now more certain than ever that the bloody experience of Vietnam is to end in a stalemate. **"**

—Walter Cronkite on CBS television, February 27, 1968

Growing doubts The president despaired when he heard Cronkite's words. "If I've lost Cronkite I've lost middle America," Johnson said. Major national magazines such as *Time* and *Newsweek* also expressed doubts about the war and began to call for its end.

Public criticism of the government's policies grew louder and more intense. Johnson felt trapped as picketers surrounded the White House chanting, "Hey, hey, LBJ, how many kids did you kill today?"

Many leaders within the Johnson administration also became critical of his policies. As secretary of defense for both Presidents Kennedy and Johnson, **Robert S. McNamara** had played a key role in shaping U.S. strategy in Vietnam. By 1968, however, he had become discouraged by America's lack of success in the war. He began openly seeking ways to launch peace negotiations to end it.

Democratic challengers As Johnson sought re-election in 1968, roughly 3 out of 4 Americans opposed his policies in Vietnam. The president found himself facing challengers for his party's nomination. Minnesota senator **Eugene McCarthy**, a vocal critic of the war, finished a strong second to Johnson in the New Hampshire primary in March. Soon afterward, New York senator Robert Kennedy, the former U.S. attorney general, entered the race.

Shaken by the divisions in his party, an exhausted Johnson made a shocking announcement during a speech on national television.

" With America's sons in the fields far away, with America's future under challenge right here at home . . . I do not believe that I should devote an hour or a day of my time to any personal partisan causes . . . Accordingly, I shall not seek, and I will not accept, the nomination of my party for another term as president. **"**

—Lyndon Johnson, March 31, 1968

READING CHECK **Identifying Cause and Effect** How did the media react to the Tet Offensive?

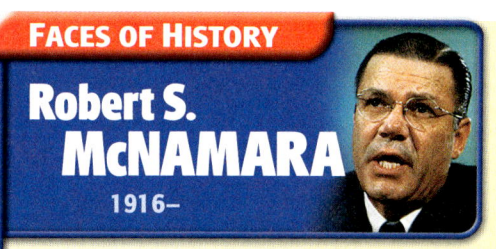

FACES OF HISTORY

Robert S. McNAMARA

1916–

After college, Robert McNamara attended Harvard University, earning a master's degree in business administration. He then taught for a few years until he joined the military during World War II. Following the war, McNamara took a job at Ford, helping to make the automobile company more profitable.

In 1961 McNamara joined President Kennedy's cabinet as head of the Defense Department. He introduced modern business practices to the military and strengthened its conventional fighting capability. As the conflict in Vietnam grew, McNamara became the leading spokesperson and chief prosecutor of what some called McNamara's war. By 1968, however, he had doubts about the war. He resigned as defense secretary and took a position as head of the World Bank.

Summarize What changes did McNamara make to the military?

Johnson Seeks a Solution

General Westmoreland argued that the Tet Offensive had been devastating to the enemy. He believed that if more ground troops were sent to Vietnam, he could deliver a crushing blow to the weakened Communists. In March 1968 he sent President Johnson a request for 206,000 more soldiers.

When the *New York Times* reported Westmoreland's request, many Americans were outraged. They wondered why more U.S. troops were needed if the war was being won, as the government had been insisting. In part because of the strong public outcry, the president denied Westmoreland's request.

Johnson knew he needed to reassess his entire war strategy, but his own advisers could not agree on the best course. Many U.S. military leaders believed that the administration was not doing all that could be done to win the war. In particular, some officers felt that Johnson's decision not to invade North Vietnam with ground troops unfairly limited them in fighting the war.

Even before the Tet Offensive, McNamara and some other government leaders had come to believe that Johnson's war policies were too extreme. McNamara suggested limiting the air strikes and reversing the escalation of the war.

❝The picture of the world's greatest superpower killing or seriously injuring 1,000 non-combatants a week, while trying to pound a tiny backward nation into submission on an issue whose merits are hotly disputed is not a pretty one.❞

—Robert S. McNamara, letter to President Johnson, May 19, 1967

Johnson agreed it was time to try to negotiate with North Vietnam. In the same televised speech in which he stated he would not run for re-election, he announced that he would seek a peace agreement to end the war.

In May 1968 delegates from North Vietnam and the United States met in Paris. Immediately the talks stalled over two issues. The United States wanted all NVA troops out of South Vietnam, and North Vietnam would not accept a temporary South Vietnam government that included the U.S.-backed president, Nguyen Van Thieu. The two sides would not reach an agreement for several more years.

READING CHECK **Summarizing** How did President Johnson try to end the Vietnam War before the conclusion of his presidency?

The Election of 1968

After Johnson withdrew from the 1968 presidential campaign, his vice president, **Hubert Humphrey**, entered the race. The Vietnam War was a key issue among voters. Humphrey defended the administration's war policies. His Democratic rivals, Senators Eugene McCarthy and Robert Kennedy, called for a rapid end to the war. When Kennedy announced his candidacy, he explained his position on Vietnam.

HISTORY'S VOICES

❝The reality of recent events in Vietnam has been glossed over with illusions . . . I have tried in vain to alter our course in Vietnam before it further saps our spirit and our manpower, further raises the risks of wider war, and further destroys the country and the people it was meant to save. I cannot stand aside from the contest that will decide our nation's future and our children's future.❞

—Robert F. Kennedy, March 16, 1968

The Democratic primary fight Kennedy quickly gained ground in the race by winning primaries in Indiana and Nebraska. In June

A Year of Turmoil: 1968

❶ Johnson does not seek reelection

Wearied by events during the Vietnam War, Johnson declines to seek another term. His vice president, Hubert Humphrey, joins the race.

❷ Robert Kennedy enters the race for president

Kennedy, the Democratic frontrunner, celebrates his victory in the California primary with a speech at the Ambassador Hotel.

❸ Kennedy is assassinated

Moments later Kennedy is gunned down in the hotel kitchen. Restaurant worker Juan Romero comforts the fatally wounded senator.

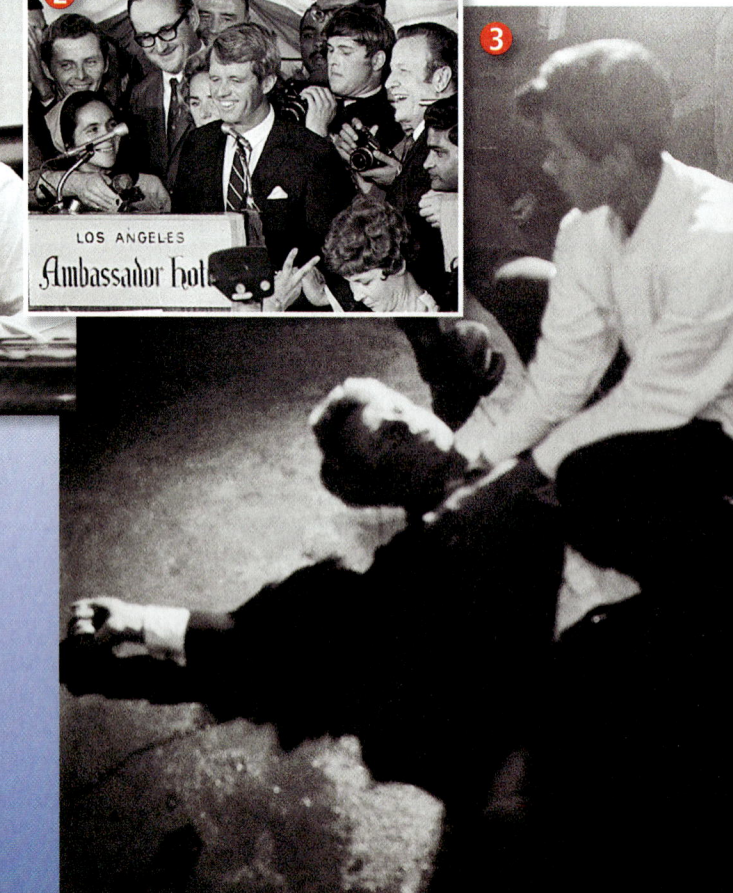

he won the crucial California primary. This made him the favorite to win the Democratic presidential nomination.

As he finished his victory speech in a Los Angeles hotel, Kennedy flashed a victory sign to the audience and declared, "On to Chicago, and let's win there." Chicago was the location for the upcoming Democratic National Conention, where delegates would choose the party's presidential candidate.

After Senator Robert Kennedy walked off the stage, a gunman shot him three times. He died less than 24 hours later. The assassin, Sirhan Sirhan, was a Jordanian immigrant who was angry about Kennedy's support for the nation of Israel.

The Democratic Convention In August, the remaining candidates fought for the nomination at the Democratic National Convention. Inside the convention hall, the delegates debated between McCarthy and Humphrey. Some people thought McCarthy's position on the war showed personal weakness. Others disliked Humphrey because he was too close to Johnson's failed war policies.

Outside the hall, chaos erupted in the streets of Chicago. About 10,000 protesters from across the country had gathered to demand an immediate end to the war and to pressure the delegates to reject Johnson's Vietnam policies. They held rallies and chanted antiwar slogans calling for "Peace now!"

Chicago mayor Richard Daley dispatched thousands of police and national guard troops to maintain order. The situation soon exploded into violence, when a huge group of demonstrators attempted to march on the convention hall. Some protesters threw rocks and bottles at the police. Daley described them as "a lawless violent group of terrorists menacing the lives of millions of our people."

The police clubbed demonstrators with rifle butts and clubs and used tear gas to disperse the crowd. Scuffles even broke out inside the convention hall. Many people, including innocent bystanders, were injured as well.

Television reporters and camera crews recorded the violence. They showed that in some instances police officers reacted with excessive force. Viewers watching the live coverage on television were shocked at the brutality. The

❹ Protests at the Democratic Convention

Antiwar delegates inside the Chicago convention hall pressured candidates to support a quick end to the war.

❺ Chaos erupts outside the convention

In the streets of Chicago, emotional protests met with a brutal police response. Radical activists, the so-called Chicago Seven, were found guilty of conspiring to incite riots, but their convictions were later overturned.

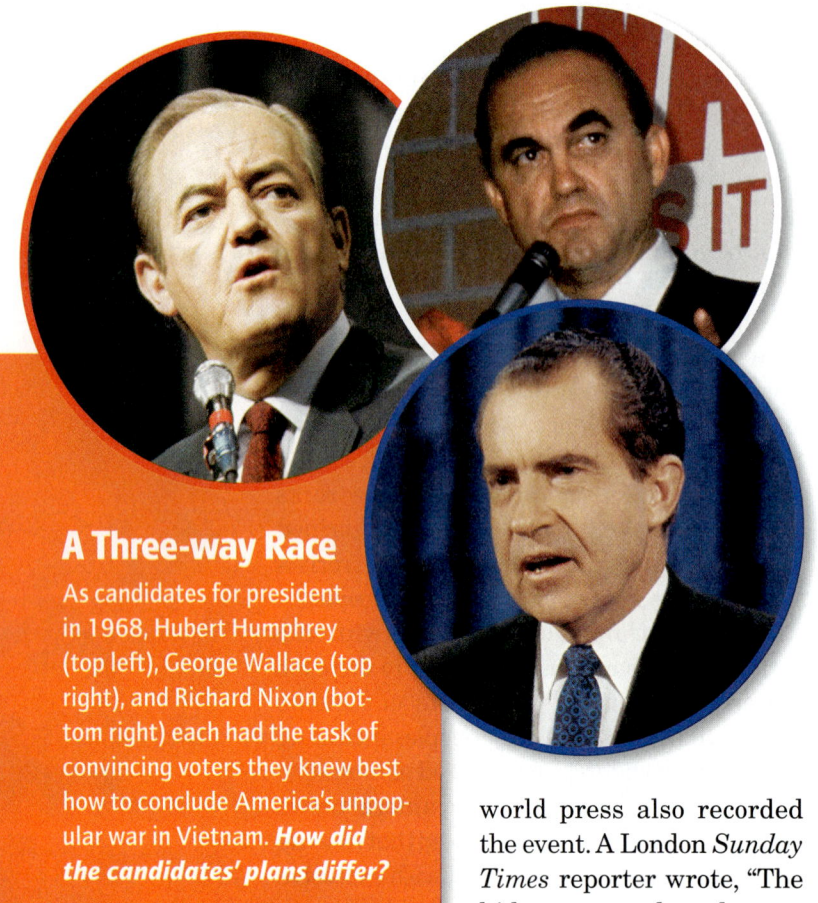

Miami Beach, Florida. Nixon chose Maryland Governor Spiro Agnew of Maryland as his running mate. He made this choice, in part, to attract conservative southern voters.

Nixon appealed to the patriotism of many mainstream Americans. Even people who were sympathetic to the antiwar movement had been put off by the behavior of protesters at the Democratic National Convention in Chicago. In a time of chaos, many Americans appreciated Nixon's promise of "law and order."

Nixon told voters that the "war must be ended. It must be ended honorably." He claimed to have a secret plan to end the war. He refused to explain his plan, saying that doing so might interfere with Johnson's efforts to achieve a peace settlement. Many voters were skeptical of a plan they could learn nothing about.

George Wallace, independent

Another serious candidate in the race was former Alabama governor **George Wallace**. Earlier in the 1960s Wallace had gained national attention for his staunch opposition to the civil rights movement and school desegregation. Wallace was nominated for president by the American Independent Party. In his speeches, he raged against war protesters.

Wallace's strongest supporters were Democrats who opposed liberal policies. Many of these voters were conservative Democratic white southerners and working-class whites from across the nation. Although Wallace was a Democrat, Republicans feared that Wallace might take votes from Nixon.

The election campaign

Nixon led in the polls for most of the campaign. As election day neared, though, his lead narrowed. Humphrey made some gains in the polls in September, after a speech in which he finally separated himself from Johnson's Vietnam policies. Humphrey said that he believed the bombing of North Vietnam should be stopped. He also argued that more responsibility for the war should go to South Vietnamese forces.

In addition, progress was made in the peace talks in Paris. The North Vietnamese agreed to include South Vietnamese representatives in the discussions if the air strikes on North Vietnam were stopped. Just days before the vote, President Johnson announced an end to the bombing of North Vietnam.

world press also recorded the event. A London *Sunday Times* reporter wrote, "The kids screamed and were beaten to the ground . . . I saw one girl surrounded by cops, screaming, 'Please God, help me. Help me.'"

More than 600 Chicago protesters were arrested. Despite the disturbances, convention delegates reached a decision and nominated Hubert Humphrey. He chose Senator Edmund Muskie of Maine as his running mate.

The chaos at the Democratic National Convention was one symptom of a growing "generation gap" over government, politics, and the Vietnam War. Many teenagers and young adults of the 1960s found themselves at odds with their parents, who had experienced the Great Depression and World War II. Young people accused the previous generation of valuing material comfort over justice and equality. Younger Americans also increasingly distrusted their political leaders, while older Americans urged them to have confidence in their government.

Richard Nixon, Republican

A divided Democratic Party improved the Republicans' chances of winning the presidency. Former vice president Richard Nixon swept the Republican primaries and easily won the nomination at the Republican National Convention in

The election results The results of the popular election in November were very close. Just 510,000 votes separated Nixon and Humphrey, out of 73 million cast. Nixon received 43.4 percent of the vote, while Humphrey received 42.7 percent. As expected, Wallace was an important factor in the race, as nearly 10 million people, or 13.5 percent of electorate, voted for him.

In the electoral college, Nixon's margin of victory was wider. He carried the heavily populated states of California, Illinois, Ohio, and Florida and won many more electoral votes than the other two candidates combined. Nixon received 301 electoral votes to Humphrey's 191. Wallace, who won five states, received 46 electoral votes. This and his percentage of the popular vote made him one of the most successful third-party candidates in U.S. history.

Nixon's comfortable victory in the electoral college provided him with a mandate that the popular vote denied him. This sense of approval gave Nixon the confidence to pursue new policies to achieve victory in Vietnam—policies that would raise divisions over the war to a level not yet seen.

READING CHECK **Drawing Conclusions** How did events at the 1968 Democratic National Convention illustrate the divisions that existed within the Democratic Party?

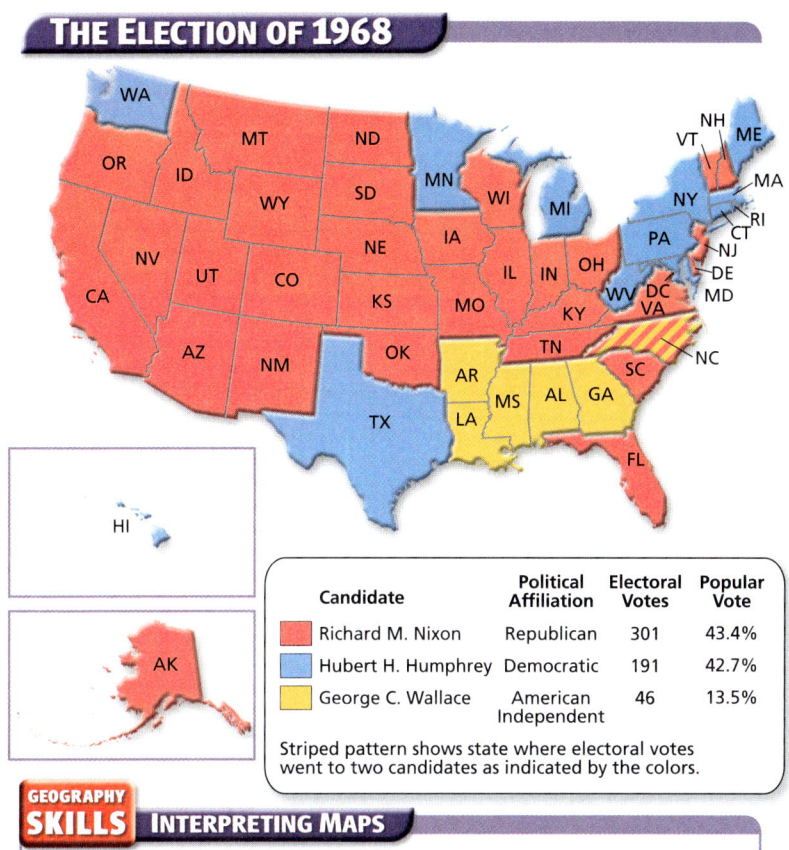

THE ELECTION OF 1968

Candidate	Political Affiliation	Electoral Votes	Popular Vote
Richard M. Nixon	Republican	301	43.4%
Hubert H. Humphrey	Democratic	191	42.7%
George C. Wallace	American Independent	46	13.5%

Striped pattern shows state where electoral votes went to two candidates as indicated by the colors.

GEOGRAPHY SKILLS **INTERPRETING MAPS**

1. **Region** What effect did the presence of a third-party candidate have on the outcome of the race between the two major party candidates? Explain.

2. **Place** How did the electoral vote differ in North Carolina?

See **Skills Handbook**, p. H21

---

go.hrw.com
Online Quiz
Keyword: SD7 HP29

SECTION 3 ASSESSMENT

Reviewing Ideas, Terms, and People

1. **a. Recall** Why did NVA and Vietcong forces attack the U.S. military base at Khe Sanh?
   b. Contrast How did the **Tet Offensive** differ from previous fighting in Vietnam?
   c. Evaluate Do you think the Tet Offensive should be considered a turning point in the Vietnam War? Why or why not?

2. **a. Identify** What were **Walter Cronkite**'s views on the war after the Tet Offensive?
   b. Analyze Why did President Johnson decide not to run for re-election in 1968?
   c. Elaborate Why do you think **Robert S. McNamara** changed his mind about the Vietnam War?

3. **a. Recall** How did Americans view General William Westmoreland's March 1968 request for more troops?
   b. Design What advice would you have given President Johnson about how to proceed with the war in 1968? Why?

4. **a. Identify** Who won the presidential election of 1968?

b. Analyze What was the goal of the protesters at the 1968 Democratic National Convention?
c. Predict How might the election of 1968 affect the course of the Vietnam War?

Critical Thinking

5. **Sequence** Review your notes on the main events of the Vietnam War in 1968. Then copy the graphic organizer below and use it to put the events in the correct sequence.

FOCUS ON SPEAKING

6. **Descriptive** As a television news journalist, deliver a report giving Americans an update on the events of either the Tet Offensive or the Democratic National Convention.

SECTION 4 The War Ends

BEFORE YOU READ

MAIN IDEA
President Nixon eventually ended U.S. involvement in Vietnam, but the war had lasting effects on the United States and in Southeast Asia.

READING FOCUS
1. How did President Nixon's policies widen U.S. involvement in the war?
2. How and why did protests against the war increase?
3. How did Nixon achieve an end to U.S. involvement in Vietnam?
4. What was the war's legacy in the United States and in Vietnam?

KEY TERMS AND PEOPLE
Henry Kissinger
Vietnamization
silent majority
My Lai massacre
Pentagon Papers
George McGovern
Twenty-sixth Amendment
Khmer Rouge
War Powers Act

 PI 2.3 Compare and contrast the experiences of different groups in the United States.

Appealing to the Silent Majority

▼ **Nixon greets a crowd of enthusiastic supporters in 1969.**

THE INSIDE STORY

Who was the silent majority, and what role did it play in the Vietnam War?

In October 1969 thousands of protesters converged on Washington to voice their opposition to the Vietnam War. In Congress, demands increased that President Nixon withdraw American forces from Vietnam. Even some of the president's supporters joined the calls to end American involvement in the war.

Despite these events, Nixon remained convinced that most Americans still supported the war. He was confident that these hardworking, law-abiding citizens were simply too busy supporting their families and too intimidated by the radical antiwar protests to make their voices heard.

Nixon asked the television networks for airtime to deliver a major address. Contrary to the usual practice, no advance copies of his speech were released to the media. Speculation was immense. Was the president about to announce a U.S. troop withdrawal from Vietnam? Instead, on November 3, 1969, he went on television to denounce the antiwar protesters and appeal to the American people.

"To you, the great silent majority of my fellow Americans, I ask for your support," Nixon said. "Because, let us understand: North Vietnam cannot defeat or humiliate the United States. Only Americans can do that."

Nixon's speech renewed support for the war effort and dealt a setback to the antiwar movement. Although these effects proved only temporary, the "silent majority" speech bought Nixon time to find a way out of Vietnam.

Widening the War

During his presidential campaign, Nixon had pledged that if elected he would end the war in Vietnam. Once in office, he and National Security Adviser **Henry Kissinger** devised plans to fulfill this promise. In 1969 Kissinger began secret peace negotiations in Paris with North Vietnamese revolutionary Le Duc Tho (LAY duhk TOH). "I don't look back on our meetings with any great joy," Kissinger later said of these tense talks. "Yet he was a person of substance and discipline who defended the position he represented with dedication."

Vietnamization Kissinger's secret negotiations were part of a larger U.S. strategy aimed at achieving what Nixon called "peace with honor." A part of this plan was a strategy called <mark>Vietnamization</mark>. This involved turning over more of the fighting in Vietnam to the South Vietnamese while gradually bringing U.S. ground troops home.

Nixon's hope was that Vietnamization would give South Vietnamese leaders enough time to create a stable anti-Communist government. If this could not be achieved, Nixon wanted to delay the collapse of the South Vietnamese government until after the U.S. troops were gone. This would at least help to avoid the appearance of an embarrassing U.S. defeat.

Nixon began slowly withdrawing American forces from South Vietnam. When he took office in 1969, there were some 540,000 U.S. troops in that country. By the end of 1972, the number had been reduced to just over 24,000.

Antiwar activists opposed Nixon's plan for Vietnamization because it did not immediately end the war. Yet Nixon was convinced that he had the firm backing of the <mark>silent majority</mark> of Americans who he believed disapproved of antiwar protesters and generally supported the government's goals in Vietnam.

Laos and Cambodia Although he withdrew U.S. troops from Vietnam, Nixon at the same time also secretly expanded the war. In early 1969 he ordered the bombing of Cambodia, with the goal of disrupting supply lines along the Ho Chi Minh Trail. Nixon also wanted to demonstrate to North Vietnam that he was willing to widen the war in order to gain more favorable terms at the negotiating table.

He concealed the air strikes from the American people—including members of Congress and even some key military leaders.

The war expanded further in 1970, when Nixon sent U.S. and ARVN troops into Cambodia, and into Laos the following year, to destroy North Vietnamese army bases. Nixon also renewed the bombing of North Vietnam, hoping to pressure the country's leaders into seeking peace. "I call it the Madman Theory," he told his chief of staff, H. R. Haldeman. "I want the North Vietnamese to believe that I've reached the point where I might do anything to stop the war."

As Johnson had done before him, Nixon underestimated the opposition's resolve, which survived even the death of Ho Chi Minh in 1969. North Vietnam staged a major invasion in March 1972, driving deep into South Vietnam.

READING CHECK **Identifying the Main Idea**
Why did Nixon order the bombing of Cambodia?

Tough Negotiators
President Nixon's national security adviser, Henry Kissinger (left), and North Vietnamese leader Le Duc Tho (right) negotiated an end to the war in secret meetings in Paris. *What other strategies did Nixon plan to bring an end to the war?*

Increasing Protests

On April 30, 1970, Nixon announced that he had ordered U.S. troops into Cambodia. Antiwar protests intensified around the country, especially on college campuses. "As much as we hated the war on April 29, we hated it more on April 30," said Tom Grace, a student at Kent State University in Ohio.

Campus violence On May 2, 1970, antiwar demonstrators at Kent State University set fire to the campus Reserve Officers' Training Corps (ROTC) building. The governor of Ohio sent National Guard troops to control further demonstrations. On May 4, students gathered in a grassy area on campus for an antiwar rally. The troops ordered the students to disperse. When some students threw rocks and shouted insults at the soldiers, several soldiers began firing into the crowd. Four students were killed, and nine others were injured. Some of those who were shot were not protesting but simply passing by on the way to class.

Nine days later, a similar incident occurred at Jackson State College in Mississippi. State police fired at protesters inside a dormitory, killing two students and wounding nine.

Americans were horrified by the images of young people shot dead on college campuses. Students and faculty members on campuses nationwide went on strike. These protests forced hundreds of colleges and universities to shut down temporarily.

The antiwar movement grows Nixon was convinced that the antiwar protesters represented only a minority of Americans. "I recognize that some of my fellow citizens disagree with the plan for peace that I have chosen," he said. "I would be untrue to my oath of office to be dictated by the minority." Nevertheless, by late 1969 polls showed that more than half of Americans opposed the war.

As public opinion turned increasingly against the war, the peace movement began to seem more mainstream and respectable to many middle-class Americans. It gradually became clear that the opponents of the war included more than just college students and other young Americans.

In 1969, for example, a coalition of antiwar groups consisting of clergy, trade unionists, and veterans established October 15 as a nationwide day of protest. Millions of people

FOCUS ON NEW YORK

DAILY LIFE

In 1965 about 25,000 people gathered in New York City to protest ongoing United States involvement in the Vietnam War. Two years later, about 400,000 protesters marched from Central Park to the United Nations building. In 1970, and in response to U.S. troops in Cambodia, a New York City Art Strike prompted more than 50 galleries and museums to close.

Americans React to the War

Below, demonstrators show their support for the war. Right, an antiwar rally turns tragic at Kent State University in Ohio, leaving four students dead. At far right, war protesters take their cause to the nation's capital.

took part in peaceful demonstrations on what was called Moratorium Day, calling for a moratorium, or halt, to the war.

A month later more than 250,000 protesters gathered in Washington, D.C., for the largest antiwar demonstration in U.S. history. Police lined up buses in front of the White House to form a barrier between Nixon, who was inside, and the thousands of marchers in the streets.

In an especially emotional demonstration in April 1971, members of Vietnam Veterans Against the War gathered in front of the Capitol. Some 800 veterans threw down their war medals to protest the war. Never before had returning U.S. soldiers so strongly opposed a war that was still being fought.

Radical protests A small minority of protesters believed that demonstrations and marches did not go far enough to end the war. Some radical antiwar groups turned to violent measures. A group called the Weathermen set off more than 5,000 bombs in places such as the New York City police department, the Pentagon, and the Capitol.

In October 1969 the Weathermen carried out the Days of Rage, a failed attempt to shut down the city of Chicago. Group members

armed with clubs, lead pipes, chains, and gas masks clashed with police. Six Weathermen were shot, and many more were arrested. The negative reaction to the Days of Rage showed that most antiwar protesters did not support extremist groups or terrorist measures.

Troubling revelations In late 1969 Americans learned about a dark episode in the war's history. In March 1968 U.S. troops under the command of Lieutenant William Calley had entered the village of My Lai (mee l y) on a search-and-destroy mission to find Vietcong fighters. Although none were found, the soldiers killed at least 450 women, children, and elderly men.

The **My Lai massacre** was initially kept quiet by high-ranking military officials, but eventually former soldiers began talking about what they had witnessed. Calley was charged with murder in September 1969.

The My Lai atrocities further intensified the divisions between war supporters and opponents. Calley insisted that he had merely been doing his duty in the war on communism. "We weren't in My Lai to kill human beings, really," he said. "We were there to kill ideology that is carried by—I don't know—pawns." Calley was convicted of murder and sentenced to life in prison. He was paroled in 1974.

In 1971 another news story boosted the momentum of the antiwar movement. The *New York Times* published a collection of secret government documents that traced the history of U.S. military involvement in Vietnam since the Truman years. Known as the **Pentagon Papers**, they revealed that government officials had been misleading the American people about the war for years. The leak angered and embarrassed President Nixon. Government lawyers failed to persuade the U.S. Supreme Court to suppress their publication.

Daniel Ellsberg, a former official at the Department of Defense, leaked the papers to the press. Ellsberg had originally been a supporter of the war. While spending time in Vietnam, however, he analyzed the effects of American policy and concluded that few South Vietnamese civilians supported the U.S.-backed government.

READING CHECK **Contrasting** How did radical groups differ from other antiwar protesters?

End of U.S. Involvement

In 1972 Nixon campaigned for re-election while continuing his efforts to achieve peace with honor in Vietnam. His Democratic challenger, Senator **George McGovern** of South Dakota, was well known for his outspoken criticism of the war.

The 1972 election McGovern insisted that the Vietnam War be brought to an immediate end. "We have heard many times that Vietnam will no longer be an issue by the time the fall election approaches," he said in July 1972. "For the sake of the thousands of Vietnamese peasants still dying from American bombing raids, the GIs still dying . . . the American POWs [prisoners of war] rotting in the jails of Hanoi, I sincerely hope it will not be an issue."

McGovern hoped the ratification of the **Twenty-sixth Amendment** would boost his election chances. Passed in 1971, the amendment lowered the voting age from 21 to 18. Many of McGovern's supporters were young people.

As he had done in 1968, Nixon stressed law and order at home and assured voters that he would bring a quick end to the war. Just weeks before the election, Henry Kissinger announced a breakthrough in the long negotiations in Paris. "Peace is at hand," he declared. This announcement helped Nixon win by a landslide, with 60.7 percent of the popular vote to McGovern's 37.5 percent. In the electoral college, McGovern carried only Massachusetts and the District of Columbia.

A peace agreement Despite Kissinger's prediction, the peace talks stalled. To force North Vietnam to make concessions, Nixon ordered around-the-clock bombings of the North Vietnamese cities of Hanoi and Haiphong in late December 1972. The intense two-week air campaign, the so-called Christmas bombing, failed to sway the North Vietnamese. Nixon called off the bombing, and the talks resumed.

Officials from North Vietnam, South Vietnam, and the United States finally reached a settlement in January 1973. The United States agreed to withdraw all of its troops from South Vietnam and to help rebuild Vietnam. Both sides agreed to release all prisoners of war. But the agreement did not settle the key issue behind the war from the start: the political future of South Vietnam.

READING CHECK Identifying the Main Idea
What were the terms of the 1973 peace agreement?

The Legacy of Vietnam

Two years after U.S. troops were withdrawn, North Vietnamese troops invaded South Vietnam. In April 1975 they reached Saigon. The

A former prisoner of war in Vietnam has a joyful reunion with his family. American casualties from the war included:
- 600 American POWs
- 300,000 wounded
- 58,000 dead
- 2,500 missing

U.S. military rushed to evacuate Americans still working in the city. As North Vietnamese troops overran the American embassy, helicopters airlifted thousands of people to safety on U.S. warships offshore.

Many of the Vietnamese who had helped the Americans were also desperate to leave South Vietnam. They feared they would be jailed or killed by North Vietnamese officials as punishment for their actions. Some 130,000 Vietnamese were evacuated and flown to the United States. Many more were left behind.

On April 30, 1975, South Vietnam surrendered. The North Vietnamese then set up a Communist government in the south. After more than two decades of "temporary" division, Vietnam became a reunited country.

Violence consumes Cambodia The fall of Saigon did not end the fighting in Southeast Asia. In 1975 Communist forces called the **Khmer Rouge** (kuh-MER ROOZH) gained control of Cambodia. In a brutal campaign of slaughter, the Khmer Rouge killed 1.5 million people in an attempt to subdue the country. Following a border dispute, Vietnamese forces invaded Cambodia in 1979. They overthrew the Khmer Rouge and installed a puppet government. The Vietnamese occupation lasted until 1989, when UN peacekeeping forces were deployed to monitor the fragile peace.

Effects on Southeast Asia The Vietnam War was devastating to the people of Southeast Asia. About 185,000 South Vietnamese soldiers and 450,000 South Vietnamese civilians were killed in the war. The number of Vietcong and NVA war dead is estimated at about 1 million.

The war also caused severe environmental damage in Vietnam. U.S. planes dropped some 8 million tons of bombs in the region as well as defoliants that contaminated food and water.

More than 1.5 million South Vietnamese fled the country after the fall of Saigon. Many of these refugees braved the open sea in tiny, crowded boats. Other Southeast Asian refugees, such as the Hmong (MUHNG) from Laos, also escaped postwar conditions in Southeast Asia. About 700,000 Southeast Asian refugees eventually settled in the United States.

Le Ly Hayslip was one of the many Vietnamese refugees who started a new life in America. Born in a village near Da Nang in 1949,

Autobiography

In 1967 navy pilot and future Arizona senator John McCain was shot down over North Vietnam. He spent more than five years as a prisoner of war, much of it in solitary confinement. In his memoirs he recalled how he and the other prisoners developed a tapping system so that they could secretly send each other messages.

"The punishment for communicating could be severe, and a few POWs, having been caught and beaten for their efforts, had their spirits broken as their bodies were battered. Terrified of a return trip to the punishment room, they would lie still in their cells when their comrades tried to tap them up on the wall. Very few would remain uncommunicative for long. To suffer all this alone was less tolerable than torture . . . Almost all would recover their strength in a few days and answer the summons to rejoin the living."

—from *Faith of My Fathers: A Family Memoir,* by John McCain and Mark Salter

Skills FOCUS **READING LIKE A HISTORIAN**

Analyzing Primary Sources How did McCain's captors try to stop soldiers from communicating?

See **Skills Handbook**, pp. H28–H29

she grew up amid constant warfare. In her book *When Heaven and Earth Changed Places*, Hayslip offered a message.

HISTORY'S VOICES

❝Do not feel sorry for me—I made it; I am okay. Right now, though, there are millions of other poor people around the world—girls, boys, men, and women—who live their lives the way I did in order to survive. Like me, they did not ask for the wars which swallowed them. They ask only for peace—the freedom to love and live a full life— and nothing more.❞

—Le Ly Hayslip, *When Heaven and Earth Changed Places*

Effects on veterans About 58,000 Americans were killed in the Vietnam War. Around 600 others were held as POWs. Some POWs spent several years in North Vietnamese jails, where they often endured long periods of torture and solitary confinement.

Vietnam Veterans Memorial

The Vietnam Veterans Memorial includes the Wall (left) and the Three Servicemen Statue (below). The smooth, black-granite wall, nearly 500 feet long, lists the 58,249 names of the military men and women who died or were listed as missing in action.

The Wall was designed by a Yale architecture student, Maya Ying Lin (right).

About 2,500 American soldiers were reported missing in action in the war. Some 300,000 U.S. soldiers were wounded. Because of improving emergency medical services, many who would have died from serious wounds in previous wars were saved. As a result, a great number of paralyzed and otherwise severely disabled veterans returned home.

Some U.S. soldiers exposed to dangerous defoliants later developed cancer and other diseases. Their children born after the war have had high rates of birth defects. In 1984 the makers of Agent Orange were forced to create a fund to help veterans and their families.

Unlike the veterans of previous American wars, soldiers returning from Vietnam were not greeted with celebrations and ticker-tape parades. On the contrary, Vietnam War veterans often became targets for the anger or shame many of their fellow citizens felt about the war. Veterans told of being verbally abused and of people spitting on them. After having served their country in horrendous circumstances,

veterans were stunned by the negative reception. One Vietnam War veteran later described how painful it was to be made a scapegoat for an unpopular war.

HISTORY'S VOICES

"I wondered if my country would ever welcome us back. Welcome all of us in body and spirit. Or would we always remain a flaw in America's vision of itself."

—Frederick Downs Jr.,
Aftermath: A Soldier's Return from Vietnam

Some veterans had trouble readjusting to civilian life. Many suffered from a condition called post-traumatic stress disorder. Memories of their horrible experiences caused nightmares, violent behavior, or flashbacks. The war's aftermath tore families apart.

"When I got back everything was changed," said one veteran. "I have flashbacks and people can't understand me sometimes. I sit by myself and I just think. You try to talk to somebody about it, they think you're out of your mind."

The war's political impact In the end, the United States failed to prevent the Communists from taking over South Vietnam. The U.S. government spent more than $150 billion on the Vietnam War. The spending added greatly to the national debt and fueled inflation. It also diverted funds that might have gone to domestic programs, such as education.

The war changed how many Americans viewed government. Some were angry about officials misleading them. Some thought both Johnson and Nixon had exceeded their constitutional powers by waging an undeclared war.

Seeking to prevent another Vietnam, Congress passed the War Powers Act in 1973. This law reaffirms Congress's constitutional right to declare war. It sets a 60-day limit on the presidential commitment of U.S. troops to foreign conflicts without a specific authorization by Congress or a declaration of war.

Another legacy of the Vietnam War is the impact it has had on the way Americans think about foreign conflicts. Before committing troops to a foreign conflict, leaders and the public often debate whether or not the nation is getting into another Vietnam.

Healing from the war Coming to terms with the Vietnam conflict has been an ongoing process for Americans. An important step was taken with the dedication of the Vietnam Veterans Memorial in Washington, D.C., in 1982. The memorial was designed by Maya Ying Lin, a Chinese American who was a 21-year-old architecture student at Yale University when her design was chosen.

The memorial is a long wall of polished black granite, inscribed with the names of the more than 58,000 Americans who died or went missing in Vietnam. Bruce Weigl explained why he and many other veterans were drawn to the memorial's dedication ceremony. "We came to find the names of those we lost in the war, as if by tracing the letters cut into the granite we could find what was left of ourselves."

Vietnam veterans in government were among the leaders of a subsequent effort to rebuild relations between the United States and Vietnam. The two countries resumed normal relations in 1995. In 1997 Douglas "Pete" Peterson, a former air force pilot who spent six years as a POW in North Vietnam, became the new U.S. ambassador to Vietnam. "It's a tragic history that we've shared as two peoples," he observed. "No one can change that, but there is a great deal we can all do about the future."

READING CHECK **Identifying Cause and Effect** What effects has the Vietnam War had on American veterans?

Reviewing Ideas, Terms, and People

1. a. Describe What was President Nixon's Madman Theory?
b. Analyze What role did Henry Kissinger have in the Vietnam War?
c. Rate How well do you think Nixon's Vietnamization strategy worked? Explain.

2. a. Identify What was the silent majority?
b. Make Generalizations How did Americans react to the My Lai massacre?
c. Elaborate Why do you think Daniel Ellsberg leaked the Pentagon Papers?

3. a. Recall What issues helped President Nixon win re-election in 1972?
b. Draw Conclusions Why do you think Nixon defeated George McGovern by so wide a margin in the 1972 election?
c. Evaluate Did Nixon's bombing of North Vietnam achieve its goal? Explain.

4. a. Identify What was the War Powers Act?
b. Make Inferences Why did so many people leave Vietnam after the fall of Saigon?

Critical Thinking

5. Categorize Review your notes on the effects of the Vietnam War. Then copy the graphic organizer below and use it to list the effects of the war on different groups of people.

Group	Effect
North Vietnamese	
South Vietnamese	
Americans	

FOCUS ON WRITING

6. Narrative Write a poem that honors the fallen American soldiers who served in the Vietnam War.

The Tet Offensive

Historical Context The documents below provide a look at the Tet Offensive in 1968, one of the key turning points in the Vietnam War.

Task Examine the documents and answer the questions that follow. Then write an essay about the effects of the Tet Offensive on the Vietnam War. Use facts from the documents and from the chapter to support the position you take in your thesis statement.

ST 4.3 Develop hypotheses about important events, eras, or issues; move from chronicling to explaining historical events and issues; use information collected from diverse sources to produce cogently written reports and document-based essays.

DOCUMENT 1

The Tet Offensive was a surprise attack during the Vietnamese New Year. The North Vietnamese Army (NVA) and the Vietcong (VC) achieved tactical surprise but sustained high casualties. This table shows the casualties for each side.

TET OFFENSIVE CASUALTIES

Force	Killed in Action	Wounded in Action	Missing in Action	Captured in Action
U.S. Forces	1,536	7,764	11	unknown
ARVN	2,788	8,299	587	unknown
NVA/VC	45,000	unknown	unknown	6,691

Source: Combat Area Casualty File of 11/93, National Archives

DOCUMENT 2

General William Westmoreland commanded U.S. forces in Vietnam from 1964 to 1968. In 1976 he published his memoirs of the war in a book titled *A Soldier Reports.* In this excerpt he discusses a press conference he held at the U.S. Embassy following the defeat of the Tet Offensive.

". . . I took the opportunity to try to put the Embassy raid and the countryside attacks into perspective. Contrary to rumor, I said, none of the Viet Cong had gotten inside the Chancery. Damage to the building was superficial. As for the big offensive throughout the country, the enemy, by coming out into the open, was exposing himself to tremendous casualties. Fully conscious of American and South Vietnamese strength and ability, I had no hesitation in saying that the enemy was inviting defeat.

"My efforts at perspective went for nought. The attack on the Embassy, Don Oberdorfer wrote later, 'seemed to give the lie to the rosy projections and victory claims that Westmoreland and others had been dishing out'. Oberdorfer said that the reporters could hardly believe their ears. 'Westmoreland was standing in the ruins and saying everything was great'.

"That attitude on the part of the American reporters undoubtedly contributed to the psychological victory the enemy achieved in the United States. What would they have had me say, that the walls were tumbling down when I knew they were not? That the enemy was winning when I knew he was on the verge of a disastrous military defeat?"

DOCUMENT 3

On February 24, 1968, the Department of Defense began the process of drafting 48,000 more soldiers for the Vietnam War. This cartoon by Hugh Haynie appeared in the Louisville, Kentucky *Courier-Journal* a few days later.

Suspended here in Asia . . .
We think back
with chagrin . . .

VIETNAM

How difficult
the getting out . . .
How easy getting in . . .

© 1968 L. A. TIMES SYNDICATE
The Courier-Journal

February 27, 1968

DOCUMENT 4

Walter Cronkite was the anchor for CBS News from 1962 to 1981. In February 1968 Cronkite traveled to Vietnam to see firsthand the conditions following the Tet Offensive. In his broadcast on February 27, 1968, he offered a personal assessment of the situation.

"Who won and who lost in the great Tet offensive against the cities? I'm not sure. The Vietcong did not win by a knockout, but neither did we. The referees of history may make it a draw . . .

"We have been too often disappointed by the optimism of the American leaders, both in Vietnam and Washington, to have faith any longer in the silver linings they find in the darkest clouds . . .

"To say that we are closer to victory today is to believe, in the face of the evidence, the optimists who have been wrong in the past. To suggest we are on the edge of defeat is to yield to unreasonable pessimism. To say that we are mired in stalemate seems the only realistic, yet unsatisfactory, conclusion. On the off chance that military and political analysts are right, in the next few months we must test the enemy's intentions in case this is indeed his last big gasp before negotiations. But it is increasingly clear to this reporter that the only rational way out then will be to negotiate, not as victors, but as an honorable people who lived up to their pledge to defend democracy, and did the best they could."

Skills FOCUS READING LIKE A HISTORIAN

1. **a. Identify** Refer to Document 1. Which group experienced the largest number of battle-related deaths?

   b. Analyze Based solely on the casualty statistics, which side was victorious?

2. **a. Identify** Refer to Document 2. What did General Westmoreland hope to achieve in the press conference?

   b. Interpret What opinion does Westmoreland have of the press?

3. **a. Identify** Refer to Document 3. What is the Vietnam War compared with in this political cartoon?

   b. Analyze Why might this cartoon be seen as a response to the increase in the draft?

4. **a. Identify** Refer to Document 4. What outcome does Cronkite predict for the war?

   b. Elaborate What course of events does Cronkite suggest in order to achieve that outcome?

5. **Document-Based Essay Question** Consider the question below and form a thesis statement. Using examples from Documents 1, 2, 3, and 4, create an outline and write a short essay supporting your position.
   How did the Tet Offensive affect Americans' perceptions of the situation in Vietnam?

See **Skills Handbook**, pp. H28–H29, H31

Chapter Review

Visual Summary: The Vietnam War

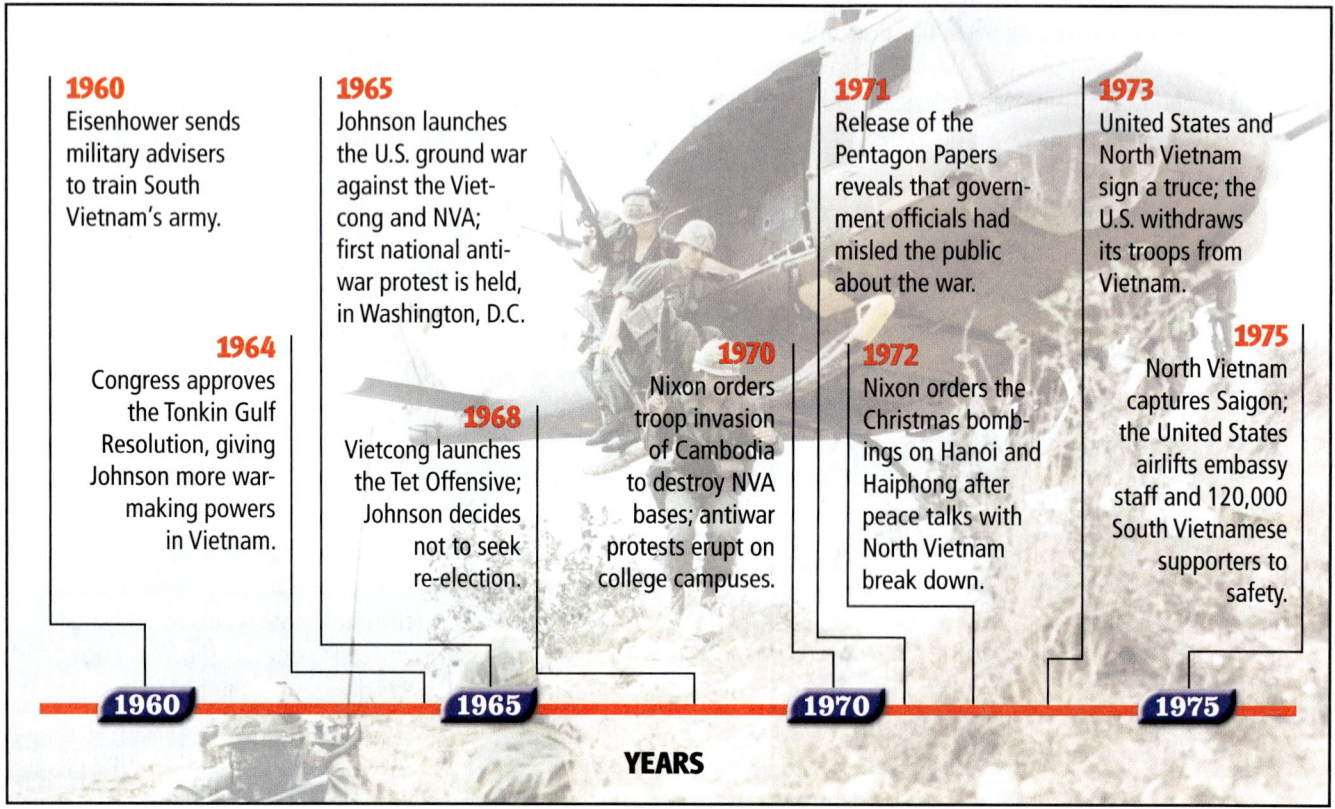

1960
Eisenhower sends military advisers to train South Vietnam's army.

1964
Congress approves the Tonkin Gulf Resolution, giving Johnson more war-making powers in Vietnam.

1965
Johnson launches the U.S. ground war against the Viet-cong and NVA; first national anti-war protest is held, in Washington, D.C.

1968
Vietcong launches the Tet Offensive; Johnson decides not to seek re-election.

1970
Nixon orders troop invasion of Cambodia to destroy NVA bases; antiwar protests erupt on college campuses.

1971
Release of the Pentagon Papers reveals that government officials had misled the public about the war.

1972
Nixon orders the Christmas bomb-ings on Hanoi and Haiphong after peace talks with North Vietnam break down.

1973
United States and North Vietnam sign a truce; the U.S. withdraws its troops from Vietnam.

1975
North Vietnam captures Saigon; the United States airlifts embassy staff and 120,000 South Vietnamese supporters to safety.

1960   1965   1970   1975

YEARS

Reviewing Key Terms and People

Complete each sentence by filling the blank with the correct term or person.

1. Communist forces called the _____ took over the Cambodian government and slaughtered about 1.5 million people.

2. _____ _____ was the Democratic presidential candidate in 1968.

3. Nixon called people who disapproved of antiwar protesters and generally supported the government's Vietnam goals the _____.

4. Ho Chi Minh originally founded the _____ to resist the Japanese occupation of Vietnam.

5. Secretary of Defense _____ _____ at first supported and carried out the war in Vietnam but later tried to find a way to end it.

6. The _____ lowered the voting age in the United States from 21 to 18.

7. The French army was defeated by the Vietminh at _____.

8. In a campaign called _____, U.S. pilots bombed and destroyed much of North Vietnam.

9. Chicago mayor _____ _____ ordered police and National Guard troops to keep order during the 1968 Democratic Convention.

10. General _____ _____ commanded U.S. ground troops in South Vietnam.

11. The _____ was the reason the United States wanted to defeat communism in Vietnam.

12. After the French were defeated in 1954, representatives from several nations met at the _____ to work out a peace agreement for Indochina.

13. The strategy of _____ was designed to keep Vietnamese civilians safe and win their support.

History's Impact video program

Review the video to answer the closing question: What role did American public opinion play during the Vietnam War?

Comprehension and Critical Thinking

SECTION 1 *(pp. 948–955)*

14. a. Identify What kinds of tactics did the Vietminh use to fight the French?

b. Analyze What were the terms of the 1954 Geneva Accords? What was the purpose of the proposed 1956 election?

c. Elaborate Why do you think President Kennedy wanted to show U.S. resolve in Vietnam?

SECTION 2 *(pp. 956–963)*

15. a. Describe How did American troops try to disrupt the Ho Chi Minh Trail?

b. Analyze Why did many civil rights advocates oppose the Vietnam War?

c. Predict Do you think Americans' opinions about the Vietnam War would have been different had there been no television reporting? Explain your answer.

SECTION 3 *(pp. 964–971)*

16. a. Describe What happened to protesters during the Democratic National Convention in 1968?

b. Analyze Why did Johnson's negotiations with North Vietnam fail to result in a peace agreement?

c. Elaborate Why do you think the Tet Offensive had such a strong effect on public opinion in the United States?

SECTION 4 *(pp. 972–979)*

17. a. Identify What was Vietnamization?

b. Compare How were the incidents at Kent State University and Jackson State College similar?

c. Evaluate Was the Vietnam War a success for the United States? Why or why not?

Using the Internet

go.hrw.com
Practice Online
Keyword: SD7 CH29

18. During the Vietnam War, U.S. air strikes used dangerous chemicals such as napalm and Agent Orange. Using the keyword above, do research to find out what was known about them at the time and about the short- and long-term effects of these chemicals. Then create a report that analyzes the ways in which veterans, Vietnamese civilians, the U.S. military, and other groups have responded to these effects.

Analyzing Primary Sources

Reading Like a Historian In Section 2, read the History's Voices passage from Myron Harrington that begins "After a while, survival was the name of the game." He described his experience in Vietnam.

19. Describe What was Harrington's experience in Vietnam like?

20. Draw Conclusions Based on details in the source, what was Harrington's role in the war?

Critical Reading

Read the passage near the end of Section 4 that begins with the heading "The war's political impact." Then answer the questions that follow.

21. According to the passage, the Vietnam War has made Americans today

A open to accepting large numbers of refugees.

B likely to suffer post-traumatic stress disorder.

C debate whether they are getting into another Vietnam before committing troops to a conflict.

D eager to fight communism in Southeast Asia.

22. Which of the following resulted from government spending on the Vietnam War?

A inflation and a higher national debt

B the fall of Saigon

C the passage of the War Powers Act

D the rise to power of the Khmer Rouge

FOCUS ON WRITING

Persuasive Writing *Persuasive writing takes a position for or against an issue, using facts and examples as supporting evidence. To practice persuasive writing, complete the assignment below.*

Writing Topic **The response to the protests at the 1968 Democratic National Convention**

23. Assignment Based on what you have read in this chapter, write a brief editorial to convince people that Chicago mayor Richard Daley's response to the protests was either necessary or too extreme.

A Time of Social Change

THE BIG PICTURE Inspired by the African American civil rights movement, women, Native Americans, and Latinos all stood up against social, political, and economic inequality in the 1960s. At the same time a youthful counterculture turned its back on mainstream society in search of a new way of life.

New York Standards

Key Idea 2 Important ideas, social and cultural values, beliefs, and traditions from New York State and United States history illustrate the connections and interactions of people and events across time and from a variety of perspectives.

Key Idea 3 Study about the major social, political, economic, cultural, and religious developments in New York State and United States history involves learning about the important roles and contributions of individuals and groups.

Skills FOCUS **READING LIKE A HISTORIAN**

These farmworkers call out from a picket line. Beginning in the 1960s, farmworkers began organizing, using strikes and initiating boycotts to fight for better working conditions and better wages.

Interpreting Visuals What does this photograph tell you about the workers' commitment and determination?

See **Skills Handbook**, p. H30

U.S.

1964
Title VII of the Civil Rights Act of 1964 outlaws gender discrimination in employment.

1963

World

1964
South African rebel leader Nelson Mandela is sentenced to life in prison.

History's Impact video program
Watch the video to understand the impact of the right of assembly.

1965
Farmworkers begin a strike in Delano, California.

WOODSTOCK
3 DAYS OF PEACE
AND MUSIC...AND LOVE

1969
400,000 attend the Woodstock Music and Art Fair in upstate New York.

1972
Congress approves the Equal Rights Amendment.

1973
Federal marshals and Indian activists face off at Wounded Knee, South Dakota.

1965	1967	1969	1971	1973	1975

1967
Israel defeats Egypt, Jordan, and Syria in the Six-Day War.

1971
The UN recognizes Communist China and expels Nationalist China (Taiwan).

1973
Egypt and Syria attack Israel, beginning the Yom Kippur War.

1975
Saigon, capital of South Vietnam, falls to North Vietnam, ending the Vietnam War.

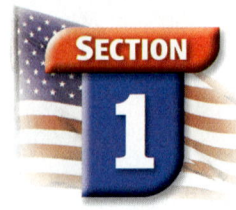

Women and Native Americans Fight for Change

BEFORE YOU READ

MAIN IDEA

In the 1960s women and Native Americans struggled to achieve social justice.

READING FOCUS

1. What led to the revival of the women's movement?

2. Which issues were important to the women's liberation movement?

3. What were the lives of Native Americans like by the early 1960s?

4. How did Native Americans fight for fairness?

KEY TERMS AND PEOPLE

Betty Friedan
feminism
National Organization for Women
Equal Rights Amendment
Phyllis Schlafly
Roe v. *Wade*
American Indian Movement
Russell Means

PI 2.4 Examine how the Constitution, United States law, and the rights of citizenship provide a major unifying factor in bringing together Americans from diverse roots and traditions.

A Failed Amendment

THE INSIDE STORY

What did labor unions have to do with women's rights?

"Equality of rights under the law shall not be denied or abridged by the United States or by any state on account of sex." This was the wording of a constitutional amendment that Congress proposed in 1972.

Many Americans regarded this Equal Rights Amendment (ERA) as long overdue. After all, Congress had been considering it for 49 years.

When the Nineteenth Amendment extended suffrage to women in 1920, an amendment guaranteeing equality with men in other areas had seemed a logical next step. The ERA was first introduced in Congress in 1923 and then introduced again in every subsequent session. The result was always the same—defeat. Powerful labor unions opposed the ERA because they feared it would undo protections they had won for women workers.

In the 1960s the civil rights movement changed everything. Hoping to weaken support for the proposed Civil Rights Act, which aimed to ban racial discrimination in employment, opponents added a ban on gender discrimination. To their dismay, the bill passed anyway.

Passage of the Civil Rights Act of 1964 pumped new life into the ERA. With special protections for women workers now outlawed by the Civil Rights Act, the unions no longer had a reason to oppose the ERA. In fact, they gradually reversed their position and backed it.

Representative Martha Griffiths of Michigan, a state where unions were strong, lobbied hard for the ERA. Congress finally passed it in 1972 and submitted it to the states for ratification. In the states, though, supporters of the ERA would fight a losing battle.

▼ Demonstrators show their support of the Equal Rights Amendment at a rally in Washington, D.C., in 1981.

Revival of the Women's Movement

After the Nineteenth Amendment gave women the right to vote in 1920, the organized movement for women's rights declined. In the 1960s, some women began to question once more why they were still considered unequal—and what should be done about it.

Experiences at work To understand the revival of the women's movement, it is important to know what many women's lives were like in the 1950s and early 1960s. Throughout the 1950s more women began to join the workforce. By 1963, nearly one-third of American workers were women.

Yet on average, women in 1963 earned only 60 percent of what men earned. One reason for this difference was that most women worked in service jobs, such as retail sales, clerical work, and domestic service. These jobs typically paid poorly. Many of the better-paying jobs, such as those in manufacturing and construction, were considered men's domain. Even when women had the same jobs as men, however, they often received lower wages than men did.

In 1961 President John F. Kennedy ordered a formal <u>inquiry</u> into the position of women in American society. The Presidential Commission on the Status of Women reported that women did experience discrimination at work. Employers paid women less than men and promoted them less often. This report opened many people's eyes to the need for change.

Experiences at home Even though increasing numbers of women entered the workforce, many other women remained full-time homemakers. A popular idea in the 1950s was that women would be happiest as wives, mothers, and homemakers. Women tended to marry young; their average age at marriage was 20 years old. Many women who delayed marriage and built careers often left their jobs once they got married.

ACADEMIC VOCABULARY
inquiry investigation, examination

American Women: A Statistical Profile

During the latter half of the twentieth century, women began playing a greater role in public life, working at paid employment in greater numbers than ever before and attaining higher levels of education. *How do you think these experiences would lead women to seek social equality?*

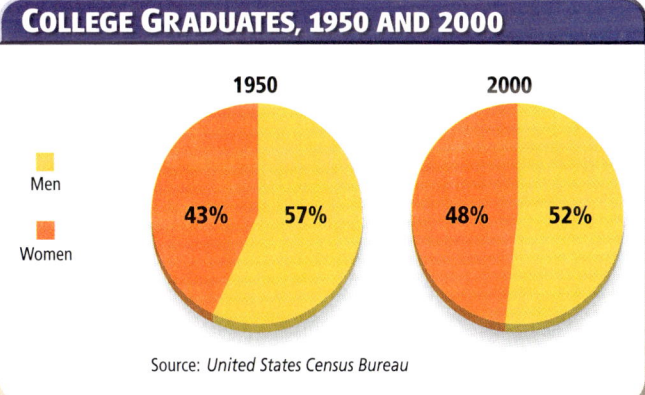

COLLEGE GRADUATES, 1950 AND 2000

1950: Women 43%, Men 57%
2000: Women 48%, Men 52%

Men
Women

Source: *United States Census Bureau*

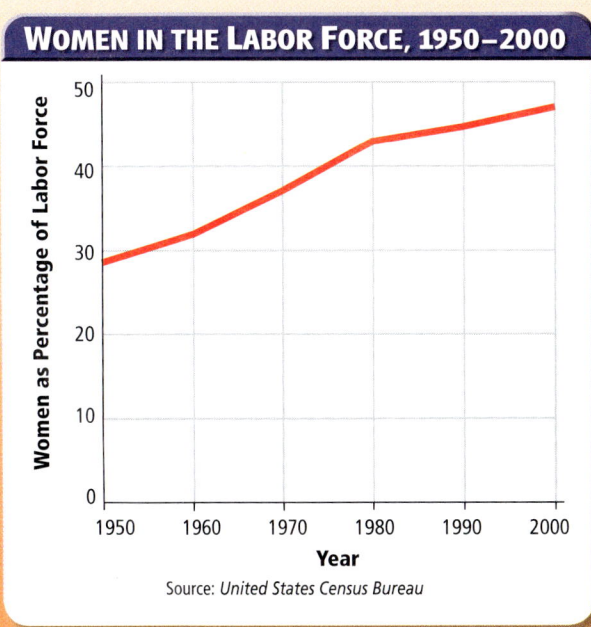

WOMEN IN THE LABOR FORCE, 1950–2000

Women as Percentage of Labor Force / Year

Source: *United States Census Bureau*

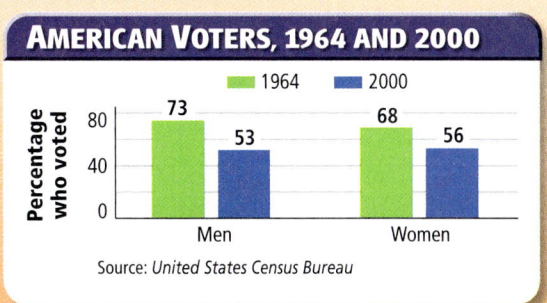

AMERICAN VOTERS, 1964 AND 2000

1964 / 2000

Percentage who voted

Men: 73, 53
Women: 68, 56

Source: *United States Census Bureau*

SKILLS FOCUS INTERPRETING GRAPHS

Did a higher percentage of men or women vote in the year 2000?

See **Skills Handbook**, pp. H16, H17

Betty FRIEDAN
1921–2006

After graduating from Smith College, Betty Friedan settled in New York and became a journalist. This was during World War II, when women were filling the jobs of men who had left to fight. Friedan discovered that women reporters were being paid less than men doing the same work. When Friedan requested maternity leave, her employer fired her.

Friedan became a pioneer of the women's movement with her best-selling book, *The Feminine Mystique.* She has remained a vocal feminist leader, calling for reforms to aid women and families, such as increased childcare, flexible work schedules, and equal pay.

Analyze A popular saying of the women's movement was "The personal is political." How did this fit Friedan's own life?

Life as a homemaker did not make all women happy, however. **Betty Friedan** (free-DAN) conducted a survey of college-educated women and found that many were dissatisfied with their lives. Nearly all of the survey respondents were full-time homemakers. In her 1963 book, *The Feminine Mystique*, Friedan concluded that many women felt trapped by domestc life, rather than fulfilled by it.

Consciousness raising By the late 1960s, *The Feminine Mystique* had sparked a national debate about the roles and rights of women. Some women organized small group discussions. In these consciousness-raising sessions, women discovered that the discrimination they experienced individually was part of a larger pattern of discrimination based on gender. More and more women came to feel like second-class citizens.

Ironically, even the civil rights movement—a movement aimed at eliminating discrimination—harbored discriminatory attitudes toward women. In 1964 two female volunteers for the Student Nonviolent Coordinating Committee (SNCC) noted that SNCC's "assumption of male superiority" was "as widespread and . . . as crippling to . . . women as the assumptions of white supremacy are to the Negro."

READING CHECK **Summarizing** What factors contributed to the revival of the women's movement?

The Women's Liberation Movement

In the late 1960s and 1970s, the movement for women's rights was known by several different names—the women's liberation movement, the feminist movement, and the equal rights movement. The core belief of the women's liberation movement was **feminism**, the conviction that women and men should be socially, politically, and economically equal.

Feminists cheered the passage of the Civil Rights Act of 1964. The act banned gender discrimination in employment and created the Equal Employment Opportunity Commission to enforce the law. Yet it soon became clear that many government officials gave low priority to fighting gender-based discrimination.

NOW In 1966 a group of feminists formed the **National Organization for Women** (NOW). This women's rights organization fought gender discrimination in the workplace, schools, and justice system. It also worked to end violence against women and to achieve abortion rights.

Members of NOW used many tactics to achieve their goals. They lobbied government officials to change the laws. They filed lawsuits to seek equality through the justice system. They also staged rallies, marches, and other nonviolent protests.

The first president of NOW was Betty Friedan. She and Pauli Murray—the first African American woman Episcopal priest and a co-founder of NOW—wrote NOW's original Statement of Purpose.

HISTORY'S VOICES

❝We believe that women will do most to create a new image of women by acting now, and by speaking out in behalf of their own equality, freedom, and human dignity . . . in an active, self-respecting partnership with men. By so doing, women will develop confidence in their own ability to determine actively, in partnership with men, the conditions of their life, their choices, their future and their society.❞

—NOW's Statement of Purpose, 1966

The Equal Rights Amendment NOW actively campaigned for passage of the **Equal Rights Amendment** (ERA). This proposed amendment to the Constitution promised equal treatment for men and women in all spheres, not just employment. Before it could take effect, though, the ERA had to be ratified by at least 38 states.

At first ratification seemed certain. NOW organized a 1978 march in support of the ERA that drew more than 100,000 people to Washington, D.C. Some people, however, viewed the ERA as a threat to traditional family life. Critics warned that the ERA would cancel laws that distinguished between men and women. They argued that women would be drafted into the military and that men and women would have to share public restrooms.

Conservative groups launched a campaign to defeat the ERA. One of the most outspoken critics of the ERA was **Phyllis Schlafly**. She argued that it would take away legal protections that women already had without conferring any new benefits. By the 1982 deadline set by Congress, the ERA was three states short of ratification. It failed to become law.

Roe v. Wade Another significant issue for the women's movement was the campaign for abortion rights. The Supreme Court struck down state laws that banned abortion in the 1973 landmark case **Roe v. Wade**. The Court ruled that such laws violated a constitutional right to privacy.

The decision sparked a debate that continues to this day. Supporters argued that women could not achieve equality until they could control when or whether to have children. Supporters also believed that legal abortion was necessary to protect women's health. They argued that many women would otherwise resort to inept, "back-alley" practitioners who often botched the procedure.

Many people opposed the decision because of religious or moral beliefs that fetal life was sacred and should be protected. Other opponents of the ruling argued that the Court's assumption of a right to privacy strayed too far from the original intent of the Constitution.

THE IMPACT TODAY

Government

For more than 20 years after its failure to become law, the ERA continued to be reintroduced into every session of Congress, but failed to pass again.

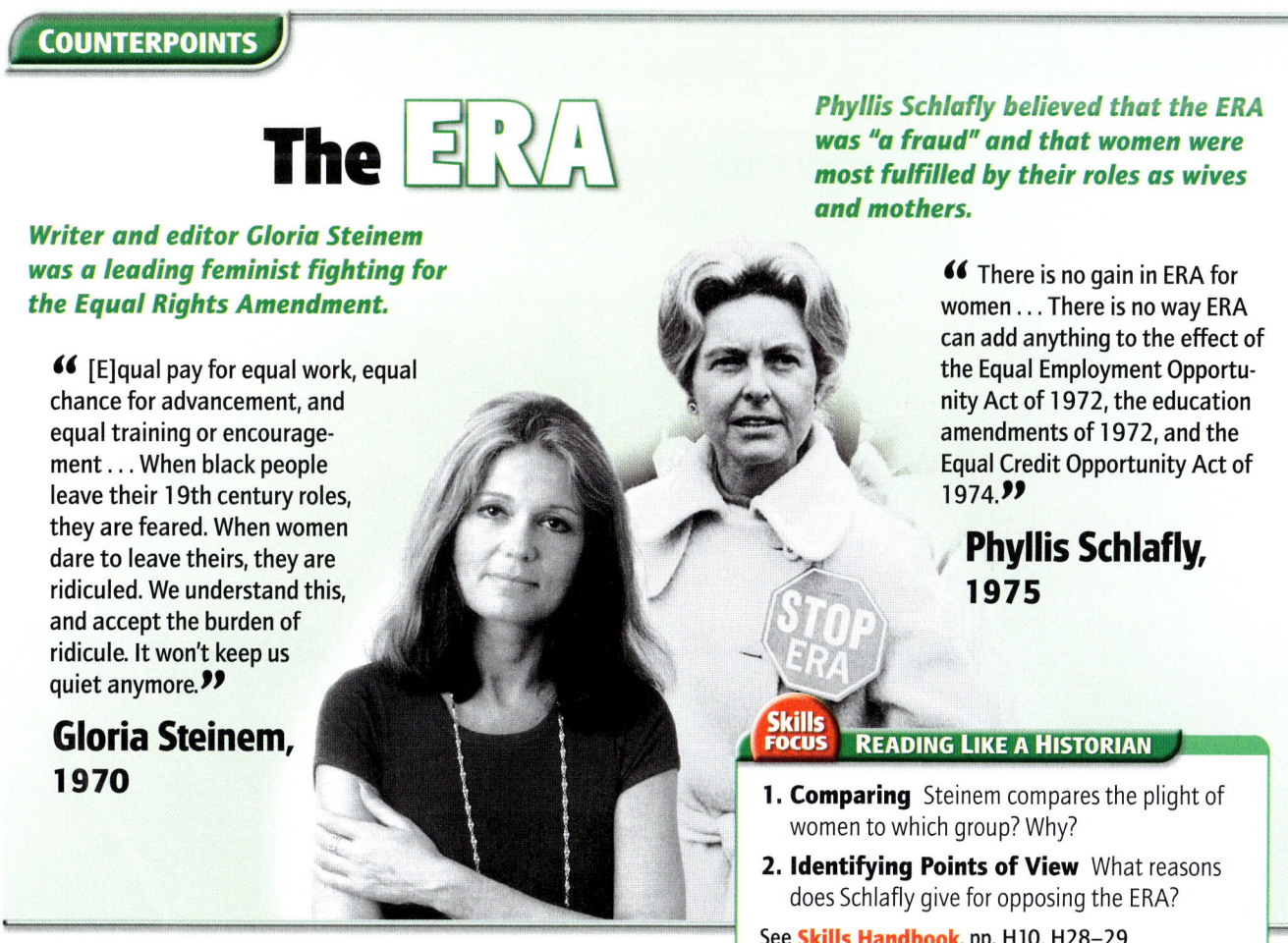

COUNTERPOINTS

The ERA

Writer and editor Gloria Steinem was a leading feminist fighting for the Equal Rights Amendment.

❝ [E]qual pay for equal work, equal chance for advancement, and equal training or encouragement . . . When black people leave their 19th century roles, they are feared. When women dare to leave theirs, they are ridiculed. We understand this, and accept the burden of ridicule. It won't keep us quiet anymore. ❞

Gloria Steinem, 1970

Phyllis Schlafly believed that the ERA was "a fraud" and that women were most fulfilled by their roles as wives and mothers.

❝ There is no gain in ERA for women . . . There is no way ERA can add anything to the effect of the Equal Employment Opportunity Act of 1972, the education amendments of 1972, and the Equal Credit Opportunity Act of 1974. ❞

Phyllis Schlafly, 1975

Skills FOCUS — **READING LIKE A HISTORIAN**

1. **Comparing** Steinem compares the plight of women to which group? Why?
2. **Identifying Points of View** What reasons does Schlafly give for opposing the ERA?

See **Skills Handbook**, pp. H10, H28–29

Effects of the women's movement

The women's movement had many notable successes in the 1970s. By the end of the decade, the number of women holding professional jobs had increased, although most women still held low-paying jobs. For example, in 1970 just 5 percent of the nation's lawyers were women. A decade later, 12 percent of American lawyers were women.

More women also began to move into senior positions in government. More female politicians were elected to Congress, although they still made up less than 5 percent of its members. Representatives Bella Abzug and Shirley Chisholm of New York received national attention. Abzug became an outspoken supporter of women's issues in Congress. In 1972 Shirley Chisholm—the first African American woman elected to Congress—became the first African American woman to run for president.

The pace of the feminist movement slowed in the late 1970s, however. There was a perception that its leaders and its beneficiaries were mainly wealthy white women. Many working-class and nonwhite women felt that the movement offered little to address the problems they faced.

READING CHECK **Summarizing** What were the arguments for and against the ERA?

FOCUS ON NEW YORK

GOVERNMENT

Displaying a manner she characterized as "unbought and unbossed," Shirley Chisholm became known as a leader. Born in Brooklyn in 1924, Chisholm became a powerful speaker who worked for civil rights, served on education and labor committees, and spoke out about the political and economic rights of women. In 1993 Chisholm was inducted into the National Women's Hall of Fame.

The Lives of Native Americans

Just as many women felt they were held back in mid-twentieth-century America, so did many Native Americans. Indian groups had suffered injustices since colonial times. During the 1950s, negative stereotypes of Indians still persisted, and hardships abounded.

Living conditions

Native Americans did not share the prosperity many Americans experienced in the 1950s. As a group, they suffered some of the highest unemployment rates in the nation. The average income of Native American men was less than half that of white American men. Mary Crow Dog recalled growing up poor on a Sioux reservation in South Dakota: "We had no shoes and went barefoot most of the time. I never had a new dress."

The Native American population suffered disproportionately from poor health. Rates of alcoholism and tuberculosis were alarmingly high. Native Americans had lower life expectancy than other Americans, and their children were more likely to die in infancy.

Termination policy

During the presidency of Dwight D. Eisenhower, the federal government began a policy called termination. The

---

TRACING HISTORY

Native American Policy and Activism

Native American peoples have struggled to retain their ways of life ever since European colonists first arrived in America. Study the time line to learn more about Native Americans and government policies.

1838 Some 18,000 Cherokee embarked upon the Trail of Tears as they were forced to move from the Southeast to Oklahoma.

1800

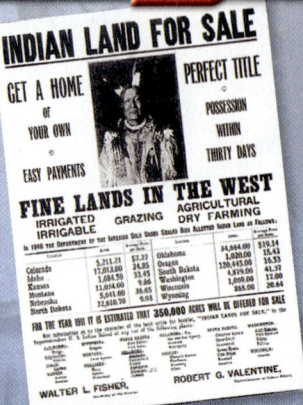

INDIAN LAND FOR SALE

1887 The Dawes Act split Native American land into individual plots and allowed surplus land to be sold to settlers.

goal was to "end the status of Indians as wards of the government and grant them all the rights and prerogatives pertaining to American citizenship." The architects of the policy hoped to draw Native Americans out of their isolated reservations and into mainstream society. The method for doing this, however, was to stop federal services to reservations and relocate Native Americans to the cities.

Between 1952 and 1967, some 200,000 Native Americans were resettled in this way. However, the government failed to <u>allocate</u> resources to help them adjust to urban life. The results were disastrous. Most of the Native Americans affected by termination remained desperately poor.

A movement emerges Many Native Americans believed the time had come for an organized movement for Native American rights. In 1961 a group of about 700 Native Americans from 64 nations held a conference in Chicago to oppose the termination policy and create a political agenda for change.

At the conference a Chippewa-Cree activist named D'Arcy McNickle drafted the Declaration of Indian Purpose. This document condemned termination. It also boldly stated Native Americans' intention to take control over their own lives.

HISTORY'S VOICES

❝Since our Indian culture is threatened by presumption of being absorbed by the American society, we believe we have the responsibility of preserving our precious heritage . . . What we ask of America is not charity . . . We ask only that the nature of our situation be recognized and made the basis of policy and action.❞

—Declaration of Indian Purpose, June 1961

The declaration marked the beginning of what became known as the Red Power movement. A new sense of unity arose among Native Americans as different groups joined forces to confront common challenges.

READING CHECK **Identifying the Main Idea** What factors led Native Americans to begin an organized fight for their rights?

ACADEMIC VOCABULARY

allocate set aside for a specific purpose

Native Americans Fight for Fairness

In 1968 President Lyndon B. Johnson declared his support for Indian self-determination. He established the National Council on Indian Opportunity to get Native Americans more involved in setting policy regarding Indian affairs. Real change, though, came through the efforts of Native American political activists.

1953 Congress adopted the termination policy, moving many Native Americans to cities and cutting aid to reservations.

1969 Occupation of Alcatraz began, awakening the public to Native Americans' struggle for self-determination.

ST 2.3 Examine the effects of immigration on various Native American groups.

ST 3.1 Investigate how Americans have reconciled the inherent tensions and conflicts over minority versus majority rights by researching the social protest movements of the 1960s and 1970s.

1900

2000

1934 The Indian Reorganization Act set up Tribal Business Councils and stopped the sale of tribal lands.

1972 The Indian Education Act established culturally appropriate educational programs for Native American students.

2005 Nearly 40 percent of federally recognized Indian nations earn money and create jobs by running gambling casinos.

The occupation of Alcatraz In 1969 a group of Native Americans tried to reclaim Alcatraz Island, the site of an abandoned federal prison in San Francisco Bay. They claimed that the 1868 Treaty of Fort Laramie gave them the right to use any surplus federal territory.

The highly publicized occupation lasted nearly 18 months, until federal marshals removed the Indians by force. Although they did not succeed in gaining ownership of Alcatraz, the occupiers did draw attention to the plight of Native Americans. Partly as a result, New Mexico returned 48,000 acres of the Sacred Blue Lake lands to the Taos Pueblo in 1970. Indian nations in Washington State, Maine, and Connecticut also settled land claims.

John Trudell, a Santee Sioux, found the Alcatraz occupation to be a transforming experience. "Alcatraz put me back into my community and helped me remember who I am. It was a rekindling of the spirit. Alcatraz made it easier for us to remember who we are."

AIM The Alcatraz Island takeover helped invigorate the **American Indian Movement** (AIM), founded in Minnesota in 1968 by Dennis Banks, Clyde Bellecourt, and others. Originally focused on urban Native Americans, AIM became the major force behind the larger Red Power movement. AIM called for renewal of traditional cultures, economic independence, and better education for Indian children.

Russell Means, one of AIM's best-known leaders, summarized the organization's importance to Native Americans in an interview in a 2002 PBS television documentary.

HISTORY'S VOICES

❝Before AIM, Indians were dispirited, defeated and culturally dissolving. People were ashamed to be Indian . . . We put Indians and Indian rights smack dab in the middle of the public consciousness for the first time since the so-called Indian Wars . . . [AIM] laid the groundwork for the next stage in regaining our sovereignty and self-determination as a nation.❞

—Russell Means, "Alcatraz Is Not an Island"

In an era when many civil rights groups used nonviolent strategies, AIM sometimes used more forceful tactics. In November 1972, for example, AIM and several other Native American rights groups staged a protest called the Trail of Broken Treaties. Protesters marched to the Bureau of Indian Affairs (BIA) in Washington, D.C., to demand changes in the relationship between Native Americans and the government. Angered by the government's lack of support, the protesters took over BIA headquarters. Officials were embarrassed by the media coverage and agreed to appoint a committee to study the demands. In return, the protesters ended the occupation.

In February 1973, AIM took its most dramatic action on the Pine Ridge Reservation in Wounded Knee, South Dakota. This was where U.S. soldiers had killed more than 300 Sioux in 1890. Now, some 80 years later, conflict unfolded again. The Oglala Sioux president, Richard Wilson, had banned all AIM activities on the reservation, calling AIM a "lawless" band of "social misfits." AIM believed that Wilson's tribal government was corrupt. About 200 AIM members occupied Wounded Knee in order to force the federal government to investigate the tribal government. They also wanted an investigation of alleged misconduct at the Bureau of Indian Affairs.

After AIM members seized Wounded Knee, federal agents arrived to drive them out. For 71 days AIM and U.S. marshals faced off. Finally, after two AIM activists had been killed and a federal marshal wounded, the government agreed to consider AIM's grievances. The siege ended, but the government did not follow through on its promise to AIM.

FACES OF HISTORY

Clyde BELLECOURT
1939–

It is little wonder that Clyde Bellecourt became a Native American activist. He developed a passion for social justice early on, listening to his mother tell stories about attending boarding school and being punished for speaking her native language.

Bellecourt has been influential in many Native American organizations, including AIM, the Indian School System, and the International Indian Treaty Council, which seeks to protect traditional cultures and sacred lands. More recently, he helped organize the National Coalition on Racism in Sports and the Media, which demonstrates against sports teams whose names perpetuate racial and cultural stereotypes. Bellecourt believes that things are destined to change for Native Americans, that there is "a spiritual rebirth going on."

Explain How has Bellecourt helped Native Americans?

Other organizations AIM was not the only organization fighting for Native American rights at this time. Many other organizations focused on particular needs.

The National Indian Education Association, formed in 1969, fought to improve access to education for Native Americans. The Native American Rights Fund, founded in 1971, provided legal services to Native Americans. The Council on Energy Resource Tribes helped its member nations gain control over their natural resources and choose whether to protect or develop them.

These groups, and others like them, worked to protect Native Americans' rights, improve standards of living, and do it all in a manner consistent with Native Americans' cultures and traditions. Today reservations are home to many Indian-owned businesses, including oil and natural gas companies. Tourism is booming on Indian lands, and Native American arts and crafts have increased in value.

Assessing progress During the era of Red Power activism, Native Americans made important legislative gains. Congress passed a number of laws in the 1970s to enhance education, health care, voting rights, and religious freedom for Native Americans.

The Red Power movement also instilled greater pride in Native Americans and generated wider appreciation of Native American

MAJOR NATIVE AMERICAN LEGISLATION

Alaska Native Claims Settlement Act, 1971
This act turned over 44 million acres of land to Alaska Natives and provided $962.5 million to settle other land claims by Alaska Natives.

Indian Self-Determination and Education Assistance Act, 1975
This act allowed tribes to implement their own education, health, and housing programs with government funding.

Indian Child Welfare Act, 1978
This act set standards for adoptions of Native American children, giving preference to relatives, members of the tribe, and Native American foster parents over white families.

culture. N. Scott Momaday, a Kiowa author, won the prestigious Pulitzer Prize for Fiction in 1969. Fritz Scholder led the New American Indian Art movement, which depicted Native American life in a fresh way, free of clichés.

Despite their accomplishments, Native Americans continued to face many problems. Unemployment rates remained high in the 1970s, averaging 40 percent and reaching as high as 90 percent on some reservations. The high school dropout rate among Native Americans was the highest in the nation.

READING CHECK **Identifying Cause and Effect** What were the results of the Indian occupation of Alcatraz Island?

SECTION 1 ASSESSMENT

go.hrw.com
Online Quiz
Keyword: SD7 HP30

Reviewing Ideas, Terms, and People

1. a. Identify What was *The Feminine Mystique*?
b. Explain How did *The Feminine Mystique* inspire the women's movement?
c. Elaborate What expectations were placed on women at home and in the workplace during the 1950s?

2. a. Define What is feminism?
b. Draw Conclusions Why was *Roe* v. *Wade* controversial?
c. Evaluate Given the failure of the Equal Rights Amendment to be ratified, was the women's movement of the 1960s and 1970s a success or a failure? Explain.

3. a. Recall What was the Declaration of Indian Purpose?
b. Make Inferences How do you think Native Americans felt about the federal government's termination policy?

4 a. Describe What was the American Indian Movement?
b. Analyze How did the occupation of Alcatraz affect AIM?

c. Evaluate How successful was the Native American fight for fairness? Explain.

Critical Thinking

5. Organizing Information Copy the chart below and record key characteristics of the women's movement and the Red Power movement in the 1960s and 1970s.

Movement	Goals	Leaders	Key Issues

FOCUS ON WRITING

6. Persuasive Suppose it is 1960. Write a letter to the editor opposing the U.S. government's policy of termination and suggesting reforms.

Latinos Fight for Rights

BEFORE YOU READ

MAIN IDEA

In the 1960s Latinos struggled to achieve social justice.

READING FOCUS

1. What were the lives of Latinos like in the early 1960s?
2. What event launched Latinos' struggle for social justice?
3. What were the main goals of the movements for Latino rights?

KEY TERMS AND PEOPLE

social justice
César Chávez
Chicano
Rodolfo "Corky" Gonzales
José Angel Gutiérrez
La Raza Unida Party
boricua

PI 3.2 Research and analyze the major themes and developments in New York State and United States history (e.g., colonization and settlement; Revolution and New National Period; immigration; expansion and reform era; Civil War and Reconstruction; the American labor movement; Great Depression; World Wars; contemporary United States).

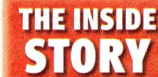
THE INSIDE STORY

How did farmworkers improve their lives? In 1965, Filipino workers began a strike against grape growers around Delano, California, in the state's agricultural San Joaquin Valley. Demanding a 15-cent increase in their hourly wages, they asked Mexican American farmworkers to join them. Dolores Huerta and César Chávez, co-founders of the National Farm Workers Association, a union of Mexican American farmworkers, agreed to help. Some 5,000 grape workers walked off their jobs.

The now-famous Delano Grape Strike lasted five years. It was bitter and hard-fought. Strikers picketed the fields to convince the nonstriking workers to join them. Growers sprayed the picketers with farm chemicals and drove tractors through the fields to choke them with dust.

To build support for the strike, Chávez led a 250-mile march to the state capital at Sacramento. As the march passed through towns along the way, many farmworkers joined it. By the time it reached Sacramento, the number of marchers had grown from just a few hundred to more than 5,000.

The Great GRAPE BOYCOTT

▲ **César Chávez (right) leads striking farmworkers.**

When picketing and marches did not win the strike, Huerta sent union activists around the nation to set up local boycott committees. Committee members stood outside supermarkets to tell customers about conditions for workers in the fields. They urged shoppers to support the strike by not buying California grapes.

The Great Grape Boycott proved successful. By 1969 it had even spread to Great Britain. As people in other European nations considered joining the boycott, the growers gave in and finally settled with the union. The Delano Grape Strike was the first major victory in a long, difficult struggle to improve the lives and working conditions of migrant farmworkers. ◾

The Lives of Latinos

In 1960 more than 900,000 Latinos lived in the United States. A Latino is any person of Latin American descent. Latinos may also be called Hispanics, but *Hispanic* has a slightly different meaning. It encompasses all people of Spanish-speaking ancestry, including those whose families came from Spain.

The U.S. Latino population increased sharply during the 1960s. This was partly because the Immigration Act of 1965 gave preference to immigrants with relatives already in the country. Eligible Latinos, especially Mexicans, streamed in.

Latinos, however, often struggled in the United States. In 1960 one-third of Mexican American families lived below the poverty line. Twice as many Mexican Americans as white Americans were unemployed. About 80 percent of Mexican Americans worked in low-paying, unskilled jobs, such as farm labor, household service, construction, or factory work.

Latinos faced discrimination in education too. Their children often attended schools with less qualified teachers, fewer resources, and shabbier facilities than other American schools. Few of their teachers were Hispanic or able to speak Spanish. In this discouraging environment, about 75 percent of Latino students dropped out before finishing high school.

In politics Latinos had far less power than the size of their population would warrant. State legislatures drew the boundaries of election districts in ways that kept Latino voices scattered. The number of Latinos in political office was very small. In addition, Latinos were often excluded from serving on juries.

READING CHECK **Comparing and Contrasting** How did Latinos' living standards compare to those of other Americans in the early 1960s?

Launching the Struggle for Social Justice

As other groups began campaigning for their rights, Latinos also sought **social justice**, or the fair distribution of advantages and disadvantages in society. One of the earliest efforts was made in the farm fields of California. Migrant

THE IMPACT TODAY

Government

In 2003 the U.S. Census Bureau announced that Latinos had become the nation's largest minority group. The political power that comes with such numbers is apparent as major political parties now make serious efforts to attract Latino voters.

Hispanic Americans: A Statistical Profile

According to the U.S. census taken in 2000, more than half of all immigrants to the United States that year came from Latin America. Specifically, one fourth of all immigrants that year came from Mexico.

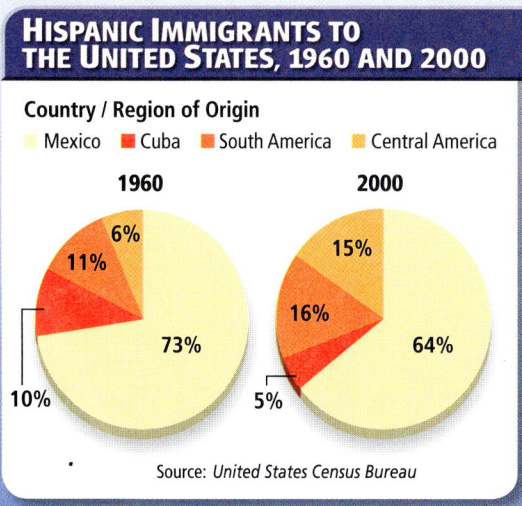

HISPANIC IMMIGRANTS TO THE UNITED STATES, 1960 AND 2000

Country / Region of Origin
- Mexico
- Cuba
- South America
- Central America

1960
- 6%
- 11%
- 73%
- 10%

2000
- 15%
- 16%
- 64%
- 5%

Source: *United States Census Bureau*

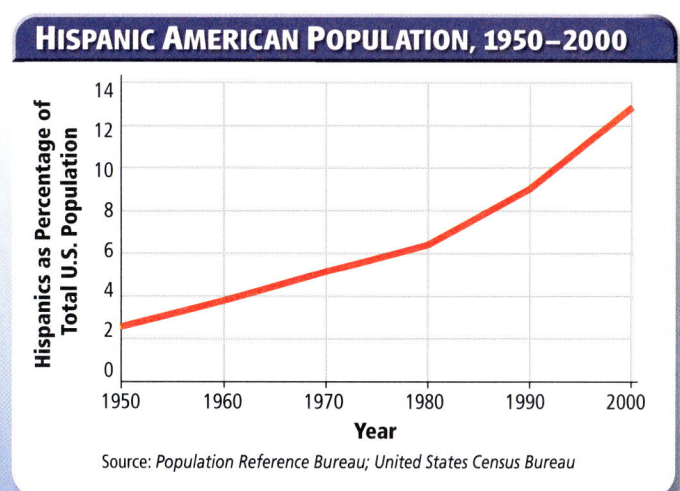

HISPANIC AMERICAN POPULATION, 1950–2000

Hispanics as Percentage of Total U.S. Population

Year

Source: *Population Reference Bureau; United States Census Bureau*

Skills FOCUS **INTERPRETING GRAPHS**

1. How has the place of origin of Hispanic immigrants changed since 1960?

2. How has the rate of Hispanic immigration changed over time?

See **Skills Handbook**, pp. H16, H17

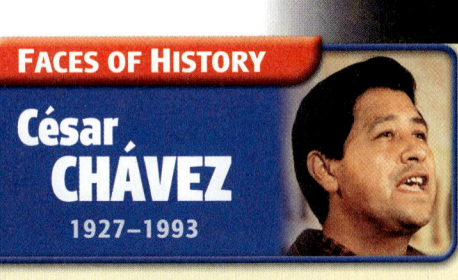

César CHÁVEZ
1927–1993

César Chávez spent his early years on his family's small farm in Arizona. When the farm failed during the Great Depression, his family moved to California and lived in migrant labor camps. Chávez left school in the eighth grade to work in the fields. After serving in the navy, he returned to California and to the life of a migrant worker.

In 1952 Chávez began a career as an activist, joining the Community Service Organization and registering Mexican Americans to vote. In 1962 he co-founded the National Farm Workers Association to help migrant farmworkers unionize. In the photo at right, Chávez (center) is talking with grape pickers. After his success in the grape strike, Chávez turned to organizing workers in California's lettuce fields and migrant fruit pickers in Florida's citrus groves.

Make Inferences Why was Chávez so successful in his efforts to organize migrant farmworkers?

agricultural workers, many of whom were Latinos, received low wages for backbreaking labor. In 1965 farmworkers went on strike in Delano, California. The National Farm Workers Association soon joined the strike, under the leadership of **César Chávez** and Dolores Huerta.

Chávez and Huerta knew that the strike needed publicity. Simply stopping work in the fields would not draw enough attention to their cause. So, as you read at the beginning of this section, union activists and sympathetic volunteers stood in front of grocery stores nationwide, urging Americans not to buy grapes.

HISTORY'S VOICES

❝Grapes must remain an unenjoyed luxury for all as long as the barest human needs and basic human rights are still luxuries for farm workers. The grapes grow sweet and heavy on the vines, but they will have to wait while we reach out first for our freedom. The time is ripe for our liberation.❞

—Dolores Huerta, "Proclamation of the Delano Grape Workers for International Boycott Day," 1969

The success of the strike made César Chávez a national figure, respected for his tireless support of migrant workers and his commitment to nonviolent protest. Chávez's leadership inspired many Mexican Americans to fight discrimination in their lives. The union's symbol, a black Aztec eagle, came to represent the Mexican American civil rights movement that developed during the late 1960s.

READING CHECK **Identifying Main Idea and Details** How did farmworkers enlist the help of consumers to achieve better working conditions?

Movements for Latino Rights

César Chávez proved the effectiveness of mass action. While he fought for farmworkers, other Latino activists pursued different agendas.

Defining the Chicano movement In the late 1960s some Mexican Americans began to embrace a form of cultural nationalism similar to the Black Power movement supported by black nationalists. They called themselves **Chicanos**, a shortened form of *mexicanos*. The name conveyed their ethnic pride and commitment to political activism.

In earlier generations the term *Chicano* had carried a negative connotation. Now Chicanos adopted the name proudly. They used the term

Mexican American to describe someone who had assimilated—someone who held American views rather than Mexican ones.

Alianza One early Chicano leader was Reies López Tijerina. He formed the Alianza Federal de Mercedes (Federal Alliance of Land Grants) to focus on the enduring issue of land rights.

After winning the Mexican-American War in 1848, the United States had signed the Treaty of Guadalupe Hidalgo, promising to respect Mexicans' land claims in territories it annexed. Despite this promise, Mexican Americans had lost tens of thousands of acres over the years—often through fraud or deception. In Rio Arriba County, New Mexico, for example, some 60 percent of the land once belonging to Mexican Americans had been taken away— much of it by the federal government.

In 1967 Tijerina and his followers charged into the Rio Arriba County courthouse to demand justice. A gun battle broke out, and two police officers were wounded. The incident focused national attention on the unfair seizure of Mexican American lands. However, Tijerina was later arrested because of his activities, and Alianza eventually broke up.

The Crusade for Justice Another leading figure in the Chicano movement was **Rodolfo "Corky" Gonzales**. A former boxer, Gonzales became active in Democratic Party politics and antipoverty programs in Denver, Colorado, during the late 1950s and early 1960s. Over time, though, he grew to believe that mainstream politics did little to help Mexican Americans.

In 1966 Gonzales founded the Crusade for Justice, a group that promoted Mexican American nationalism. Operating out of an old church, the group provided legal aid, a theater for enhancing cultural awareness, a Spanish-language newspaper, and other community services. It also ran a school that offered children free bilingual classes and lessons in Chicano culture.

Gonzales credited the Crusade for Justice with igniting the "nationalism that now exists here in the Southwest. It has been a dream of the past, but we're now creating a reality out of it." He popularized the use of the nationalist term *Chicano*. Gonzales also composed a poem, "I Am Joaquín," which served as an anthem for the Chicano movement.

In March 1969 Gonzales and the Crusade for Justice sponsored the National Chicano Liberation Youth Conference. Conference delegates produced *El Plan Espiritual de Aztlán*, or the Spiritual Plan of Aztlán. The plan called upon Chicanos to reclaim the lands of the Southwest. The ultimate goal was to build a unified Chicano community that was empowered to determine its own future.

MAYO Mexican Americans in Texas also turned to protest during the 1960s. In 1967 a group of college students in San Antonio formed the Mexican American Youth Organization (MAYO). The founders of MAYO, including **José Angel Gutiérrez**, wanted to achieve economic independence for Mexican Americans, to gain local control over the education of Hispanic children, and to achieve power for Latinos through the creation of a third political party.

Under Gutiérrez's leadership, MAYO organized school walkouts and mass demonstrations to protest discrimination against Mexican Americans. MAYO's aggressive tactics were a departure from the moderate approach of more established contemporary Latino organizations, such as the League of United Latin American Citizens.

"Most of our traditional organizations will sit there and pass resolutions and mouth off at conventions, but they'll never take on the gringo [white American]," Gutiérrez charged.

Culture
Spanish-language newspapers have become big business in the United States. In 2002 there were 35 dailies with a combined circulation of more than 1.7 million.

ACADEMIC VOCABULARY

contemporary existing during the same period of time

"They'll never stand up to him and say, 'Hey man, things have got to change . . . We've had it long enough!'"

Not all Latinos approved of MAYO's tactics. Henry B. Gonzalez, a member of Congress from San Antonio, was a vocal critic. "MAYO styles itself . . . [as all] good and the Anglo-American as . . . [all] evil. That is not merely ridiculous, it is drawing fire from the deepest wellsprings of hate," Gonzalez declared. "One cannot fan the flames of bigotry one moment and expect them to disappear the next."

MAYO did force changes, though, especially in education. In 1969 Gutiérrez helped organize a student protest in Crystal City, Texas, where about 80 percent of the population was Mexican American. Many local high school students fumed about discrimination. They wanted more Mexican American teachers and a bilingual education program. They also wanted their cheerleaders and homecoming queen to be elected by the students, not appointed by teachers.

The protest began when teachers appointed two Anglo students as cheerleaders. Chicano students' complaints to school officials had no effect. Gutiérrez helped the students organize a boycott of the school. The U.S. Justice Department intervened to resolve the crisis. The settlement required the school board to meet most of the students' demands, including bilingual and bicultural education.

The success at Crystal City inspired students in other Texas schools. MAYO supported numerous student walkouts to protest the crumbling conditions of schools, the lack of Latino teachers, and rules against speaking Spanish. After many of these boycotts, students gained the reforms they were seeking.

La Raza Unida After his success in Crystal City, Gutiérrez formed **La Raza Unida Party** (RUP). (The name means "the united people.") The party campaigned for bilingual education, improved public services, education for children of migrant workers, and an end to job discrimination. In 1970, RUP candidates were elected to offices in several Texas cities with large Chicano populations.

HISTORY CLOSE-UP

The Chicano Movement

During the 1960s and 1970s Mexican Americans forged political power by embracing their cultural identity.

Dolores Huerta

Dolores Huerta took an interest in social activism from a young age. In her early 20s she was active in a Mexican American self-help group called the Community Service Organization. It was there that she first met César Chávez. Together they founded the National Farm Workers Association. In the late 1960s she met feminist leader Gloria Steinem, whose influence led Huerta to incorporate feminist ideals into the Chicano movement.

La Raza Unida

José Angel Gutiérrez (above) founded La Raza Unida to spur political change in Crystal City, Texas. The party moved to the state level in 1972, backing Ramsey Muñiz for governor and supporting many Chicana candidates for other offices. Although Muñiz did not win his race, La Raza Unida successfully changed the landscape of Texas politics.

Rodolfo Gonzales also organized a Colorado branch of the RUP. The Colorado party did not have many election victories, but it drew attention to Chicano causes. The RUP expanded into other parts of the Southwest as well. In Arizona, New Mexico, and California, it registered some 10,000 new voters and ran candidates for several state offices.

In the late 1970s, disagreements among RUP leaders caused the party to fall apart. However, for the better part of a decade it symbolized growing Chicano power.

The Brown Berets In the late 1960s the Brown Berets emerged as one of the most militant organizations in the Chicano movement. Founded by working-class Chicano students in Los Angeles in 1967, the Brown Berets began their activism by protesting against police brutality in East Los Angeles.

Soon the group also began fighting for bilingual education, better school conditions, Chicano studies, and more Chicano teachers. In school walkouts in California, the Brown Berets protected striking students by standing between them and the police. "When the cops moved in," one observer noted, "it was the Berets that were dragged behind bars."

The Brown Berets also supported the efforts of Chicanos in New Mexico to recover their historic lands. They lent their support to the United Farm Workers' campaigns, and they protested the high death rate of Chicano soldiers in the Vietnam War. They worked with African American civil rights groups as well, such as the Black Panther Party and the Southern Christian Leadership Conference.

The Brown Berets received much media attention because of their strong rhetoric and action-oriented protests. They also gained the notice of law enforcement officials, who tracked their activities and infiltrated the group. The publicity strengthened the Chicano movement in California and helped it spread farther. By 1970 there were 60 Brown Beret groups across the Southwest.

In the Brown Berets, as in many Chicano organizations, men held positions of leadership and women often struggled to have their voices heard. Women participated in marches and

Corky Gonzales

Rodolfo "Corky" Gonzales, boxer turned activist, knew firsthand the plight of many poor Mexican Americans. Born to migrant farmworkers, Gonzales urged Mexican Americans to embrace their cultural heritage. He saw Chicano nationalism as a way for his people to gain economic independence and political power.

Student Activism

In 1969 some 700 Mexican American high school students in Crystal City, Texas, boycotted class. The strike began as a protest of the mainly Anglo cheerleading squad, but it grew to include broader educational issues. The students' action forced the school to abandon its discriminatory policies.

Skills FOCUS **INTERPRETING INFOGRAPHICS**

Chicanos were among the many groups of Americans fighting for their rights in the 1960s and 1970s.

Drawing Conclusions Why do you think Chicanos wanted their own political party?

See **Skills Handbook**, p. H18

Mural

Some Chicano artists expressed their cultural pride by creating murals. This art form has a long history in Mexico, dating to Aztec times. Today hundreds of public buildings throughout the West contain murals celebrating Chicanos' heritage . This scene from a California mural shows the economic transformation of Mexican Americans.

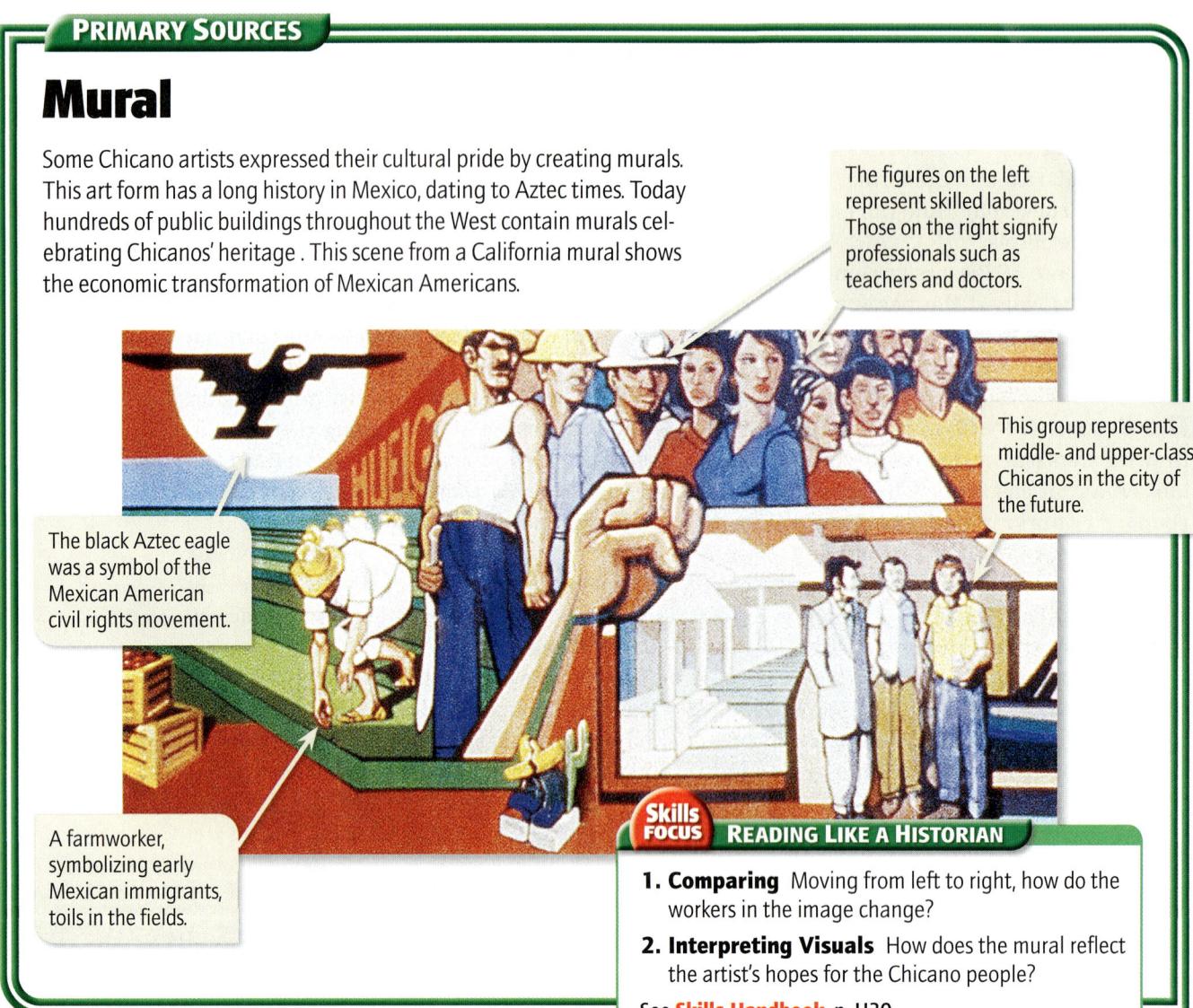

The figures on the left represent skilled laborers. Those on the right signify professionals such as teachers and doctors.

This group represents middle- and upper-class Chicanos in the city of the future.

The black Aztec eagle was a symbol of the Mexican American civil rights movement.

A farmworker, symbolizing early Mexican immigrants, toils in the fields.

Skills FOCUS   READING LIKE A HISTORIAN

1. **Comparing** Moving from left to right, how do the workers in the image change?
2. **Interpreting Visuals** How does the mural reflect the artist's hopes for the Chicano people?

See **Skills Handbook**, p. H30

---

demonstrations, but those actions were always led by men. As one female member noted, "They [the men] wanted to make all the decisions and we always got the [unpleasant] jobs."

The Brown Berets disbanded in 1972 after a series of demonstrations turned violent. Public opinion within the Mexican American community began to turn against their activities. Although the Brown Berets were not successful in ending police brutality in East Los Angeles, the group succeeded in raising awareness of the struggles Chicanos often faced.

The boricua movement Boricua is the name by which many Puerto Ricans refer to themselves. Like the term *Chicano,* it expresses ethnic pride and support for political activism.

The island of Puerto Rico has been governed as a U.S. territory since the United States acquired the island from Spain after the Spanish-American War in 1898. Slow economic growth and lack of opportunity in Puerto Rico in the early 1900s prompted some Puerto Ricans to migrate to the mainland United States.

The pace of migration increased after World War II, as many Puerto Ricans hoped to share in the economic boom the United States experienced after the war. Some U.S. companies even recruited workers from Puerto Rico, viewing the island as a source of cheap labor. New York, Chicago, and several other U.S. cities developed large Puerto Rican communities. In New York, for example, Puerto Ricans made up more than 9 percent of the city's population by 1964.

Like other minority groups, Puerto Ricans in the United States experienced social and economic discrimination. Holding low-paying jobs, many had to live in run-down neighborhoods and send their children to overcrowded, substandard schools. In the 1950s and 1960s, they organized to seek change.

The boricua movement sprang from the calls of some Puerto Ricans, both in Puerto Rico and on the mainland, for the island's independence. When this demand failed to gain much support, even within the Puerto Rican community, the movement's goals gradually shifted to self-government for Puerto Rico and better conditions for all Puerto Ricans.

Among those pushing for social justice for Puerto Ricans were the Young Lords, a militant boricua organization inspired by the Black Panthers. In 1969 the New York City chapter of the Young Lords barricaded streets until the city promised more frequent trash pickups in Puerto Rican neighborhoods. The Young Lords also called for local control of Puerto Rican communities, as well as better health care, employment, and educational opportunities.

Other boricua groups shared some of the Young Lords' goals but not their methods. One group called Taller Boricua (meaning "Puerto Rican Workshop") was founded in 1970 as a community arts organization in New York. It provided art education programs as a means of encouraging cultural, social, and economic development in the Puerto Rican community. Similar groups now exist in many other American cities.

Cuban Americans After Fidel Castro seized power in Cuba in 1959, many well-to-do Cubans fled Castro's Communist government for the United States. After 78,000 Cubans left in 1962, Castro banned further emigration. The exodus continued nonetheless. About 50,000 people left on flights allowed by the Cuban government between 1965 and 1973. However, most refugees made dangerous, illegal voyages to the United States in small boats.

The majority of Cubans who arrived during this period were professionals and business people. Unlike most other Latinos, they had left their homeland for political reasons, not economic ones. Therefore, they did not generally suffer the economic disadvantages that prompted other Latino groups to demand social justice. Instead, most Cuban Americans who organized for change were seeking changes for Cuba—the overthrow of Castro and communism—and not for themselves.

READING CHECK **Making Generalizations** What issues were most important to the movements for Latino rights?

SECTION 2 ASSESSMENT

go.hrw.com
Online Quiz
Keyword: SD7 HP30

Reviewing Ideas, Terms, and People

1. a. Recall What is the difference between the terms *Hispanic* and *Latino*?
   b. Summarize What economic, educational, and political challenges did many Latinos face in the early 1960s?
   c. Elaborate Do you think that speaking Spanish was an asset or a drawback for Latinos in the 1960s? Explain.

2. a. Identify Who were **César Chávez** and Dolores Huerta?
   b. Explain How did farmworkers pressure grape growers to address their demands?
   c. Predict Do you think the grape boycott would have turned out differently if strikers had used violent tactics? Explain.

3. a. Describe What do the terms *Chicano* and *boricua* have in common?
   b. Sequence What experiences led **José Angel Gutiérrez** to form a new political party?
   c. Rank With which issue do you think the Latino rights movements had the most success? Explain.

Critical Thinking

4. Comparing and Contrasting Copy the chart below and record the similarities and differences between MAYO and **La Raza Unida Party**.

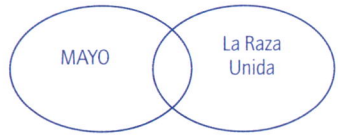

MAYO   La Raza Unida

FOCUS ON WRITING

5. Expository Reread the excerpt from **Rodolfo Gonzales**'s poem, "I Am Joaquín." In your own words, analyze the excerpt. What past hardships does Gonzales describe? How have the conditions of his people changed, and why? What emotions are conveyed in his poem? Why would this poem be considered an anthem of the Chicano movement?

Culture and Counterculture

PI 2.3 Compare and contrast the experiences of different groups in the United States.

BEFORE YOU READ

MAIN IDEA

The counterculture that emerged in the 1960s and 1970s left a lasting impact on American life.

READING FOCUS

1. What led to the rise of the counter-culture?
2. What was life like in the counter-culture?
3. How did mainstream American society react to the counterculture?
4. What legacy did the counterculture leave behind?

KEY TERMS AND PEOPLE

counterculture
Establishment
Free Speech Movement
flower children
Summer of Love
pop art

THE INSIDE STORY

How would hosting a huge public event affect a small town?

The word was out. Some rich music promoters needed a place to hold a rock concert. In tiny Bethel, New York, resort owner Ed Tiber had a permit from town officials for a small music and arts festival to attract business to his resort hotel. He put the concert's organizers in touch with Max Yasgur, a nearby dairy farmer. They paid Yasgur $75,000 to hold their concert in one of his fields.

As workers prepared the site, Bethel's 3,900 residents became concerned that the expected 100,000 concert-goers might overwhelm their town. Signs went up: "Buy No Milk. Stop Max's Hippie Music Festival." There was no turning back, though. Too many tickets to the concert had already been sold—nearly 190,000!

Despite opposition, the Woodstock Music and Art Fair began on schedule, on August 15, 1969. By then it had snowballed into a four-day event attended by more than 400,000 people. Woodstock astounded Bethel and became a defining experience for a whole generation.

Rock Concert in a Small Town

▼ The band Jefferson Airplane rocks for a crowd that stretches as far as the eye can see.

Student protest leader Mario Savio makes a peace sign with his hand at a rally at the University of California, Berkeley. Students at Berkeley fought the school administration for free-speech rights and inspired campus protests nationwide.

Rise of the Counterculture

The **counterculture** of the 1960s was a rebellion of teens and young adults against mainstream American society. These young Americans, called hippies, believed that society's values were hollow and its priorities were misplaced. Turning their backs on the mainstream— which they called the **Establishment**—hippies wanted to create an alternative culture based on peace and love.

The youth culture

Where did the counterculture come from? First of all, the number of teens and young adults in the United States rose dramatically in the 1960s. Between 1960 and 1970 the number of Americans aged 15 through 24 increased almost 50 percent.

Second, these young people were living in turbulent times. They blamed their parents' generation for the problems the nation faced— the threat of nuclear war, racial discrimination and segregation, the Vietnam War, and environmental pollution. They vowed to do things differently.

Rebellion against the dominant culture was not something new. The Beat generation of the 1950s also broke with mainstream America. Beatniks questioned traditional values, challenged authority, and experimented with nonconformist lifestyles. Although beatniks were few in number, the Beat generation would influence the hippie culture that arose later.

Rising student activism

On college campuses in the 1960s, students enjoyed newfound independence. They began rebelling against school policies they considered restrictive, unjust, or not relevant. At the University of California at Berkeley, students had often used one of the entrances to the campus as a place for speech making and political organizing. In September 1964, university officials banned that activity at the campus entrance. Students protested loudly. They picketed and held sit-ins, nonviolent demonstrations in which they sat down and refused to move.

On October 1, 1964, a former student named Jack Weinberg set up a table in the banned area to collect donations for CORE, a civil rights group. Police arrived to arrest him for trespassing. Hundreds of students surrounded the police car so that it could not move. Student Mario Savio climbed on top of the car and urged more students to join the protest.

For 32 hours the students surrounded the car and prevented the police from taking Weinberg away. Other students protested at the main administration building. However, university officials refused to drop the charges against Weinberg. California governor Edmund Brown issued a statement: "This will not be tolerated. We must have—and will continue to have—law and order on our campuses." Some 500 police officers were called out as the crowd swelled to more than 7,000 demonstrators.

Counterculture Life

Hippie clothing and hairstyles tended to be loose and flowing, but the main characteristics were individuality and low cost. Flowers worn in the hair were also a mainstay of hippie expression.

Members of the Family of the Mystic Arts (above) lived in this Oregon commune for over a year. Communes had high ideals but were often short-lived.

FOCUS ON NEW YORK

DAILY LIFE

Students at universities all over New York State took part in the Free Speech Movement during the 1960s. One of the most famous demonstrations took place in April 1968, when over 1,000 protesting students occupied five buildings of Columbia University. The students' actions forced the school to shut down until protesters were removed by police.

The protest came to a nonviolent end when university officials agreed to consider students' grievances. A few weeks later, though, the university decided to discipline Savio and another organizer of the protest, Arthur Goldberg. In response, about a thousand students took over the campus administration building in a massive sit-in. On December 3, more than 600 police arrested nearly 800 students.

For the next few days, a student strike shut down the campus. As pressure mounted—from the faculty as well as the student body—administrators finally agreed to ease restrictions on students' political activities.

The events in Berkeley marked the beginning of the **Free Speech Movement**, which swept campuses across the nation. Arthur Goldberg summed up the goal this way: "We ask only the right to say what we feel when we feel like it. We'll continue to fight for this freedom, and we won't quit until we've won." Students used the tactics of civil disobedience to protest a variety of injustices. In the process, they shocked mainstream Americans, who expected young people not to question authority.

READING CHECK Summarizing What major influences led to the rise of the counterculture?

Life in the Counterculture

Throughout the 1960s, thousands of teens and young adults abandoned school, jobs, and traditional home life in search of a more freewheeling existence. Like the beatniks of the 1950s, hippies rejected the materialism and work ethic of older generations. Instead, they wanted to live simply and "do your own thing."

Some hippies formed communities in run-down urban neighborhoods, such as San Francisco's Haight-Ashbury district. Haight-Ashbury became the most famous center of the counterculture. Young people flocked there because of the cheap rents and flourishing hippie culture. Urban hippie communities in general attracted many newcomers because of the promise of a new lifestyle. Writer Carol Brightman spoke about the freedom of moving to Berkeley in 1970.

HISTORY'S VOICES

❝Coming to California and settling in the Bay Area, [I] was . . . looking for a cultural experience outside the mainstream . . . Berkeley was like a liberated zone, you know . . . You were on the edge there.❞

—Carol Brightman, interview with David Gans, 1999

This detail from a poster by the artist Peter Max (left) is an example of pyschedelic art, or art that mimics a drug-induced state. Below is the psychedelic album cover to the Broadway musical *Hair*, which celebrated the counterculture and shocked the Establishment.

Other hippies "dropped out" of society by joining rural communes—collectively run communities—where they attempted to live in harmony with nature. Residents of communes often avoided modern conveniences. They grew their own food and shared all property. Their intention was to build communities based on peace and love.

Hippie culture Hippies sought new experiences in a variety of ways. Some looked for enlightenment through Eastern religions, such as Buddhism. Others searched for answers through astrology or the occult. Many others experimented with illegal drugs, such as marijuana and LSD, or "acid." Timothy Leary, a former Harvard University psychology instructor, promoted the use of LSD as a way to open and expand the mind. Leary urged others to "tune in, turn on, and drop out."

Hippies expressed their sense of freedom through a casual and colorful style of clothing. Bright, tie-dyed T-shirts were popular. Many African Americans adopted the dashiki, a pullover-style African shirt usually decorated with vivid colors. Some men wore beads as a rejection of the traditional necktie. Men also began wearing longer hair and beards. Some African Americans sported Afros, a hairstyle that came to symbolize racial pride. Other hippies wore flowers in their hair and called themselves **flower children**.

The counterculture's decline The height of the hippie movement was the summer of 1967. In San Francisco, this was known as the **Summer of Love**. A generation proclaimed the dawning of a blissful new age. Although the country was at war in Vietnam and wracked by racism and sexism, hippies professed peace, love, and harmony.

These ideals were difficult to achieve, however. The freedom that hippies sought often led to serious problems. Many young people struggled with drug addiction—or worse. Singer Janis Joplin and guitarist Jimi Hendrix died from overdoses of drugs, as did other less-famous members of the counterculture.

Hippies expected to find mellow living by moving to communes and places such as Haight-Ashbury. However, many hippies had no means of supporting themselves. The lack of rules often led to conflict. The counterculture also attracted sinister characters such as Charles Manson, who moved to Haight-Ashbury in 1967. Two years later Manson and a handful of his followers committed a mass murder in California that horrified the nation.

READING CHECK **Contrasting** How did the counterculture lifestyle differ from that of traditional, middle-class Americans?

Mainstream Society Reacts

Some observers of the counterculture were put off by the unkempt appearance of hippies. George Harrison, a member of the legendary British music group the Beatles, recalled his surprise when he visited Haight-Ashbury in 1967. "I expected them to all be nice and clean and friendly and happy." Instead, he saw them as "hideous, spotty little teenagers" who "were all terribly dirty and scruffy."

On a deeper level, many mainstream Americans objected to the unconventional values of the counterculture. They viewed hippies' attitudes and actions as disrespectful, uncivilized, and threatening. Some believed that American society as a whole was losing its sense of right and wrong.

THE IMPACT TODAY

Daily Life

Blue jeans were considered work clothing until hippies began wearing them. Today people of all ages and economic backgrounds wear jeans regularly.

To many in the Establishment, it appeared that society was unraveling. Unrest on college campuses particularly troubled FBI director J. Edgar Hoover.

A daring television comedy called *All in the Family* dramatized both the older generation's distrust of the counterculture and the younger generation's desire to change society. Premiering in 1971, the program featured a bigoted, working-class character named Archie Bunker. Archie bluntly criticized hippies, Vietnam War protesters, and anyone else who didn't fit his view of what Americans should be. Archie's son-in-law, Mike Stivic, was a college student fighting against the Establishment. The lack of understanding between Archie Bunker and Mike Stivic was symbolic of the divisions in American society at the time.

READING CHECK Identifying the Main Idea
Why did many Americans find the counterculture to be so alarming?

The Counterculture's Legacy

The counterculture did not last long. However, it did make a lasting impact on American culture, particularly in attitudes, art, and music.

Attitudes The permissiveness of the counterculture affected the wider American society. Many Americans became more casual in the way they dressed and more open-minded about lifestyles and social behavior. Attitudes toward sexual behavior loosened. In movies, on television, and in books and magazines, people wanted to explore topics that had once been taboo, including sexual activity and violence.

PRIMARY SOURCES

Political Cartoon

The attitudes and lifestyles of the counterculture shocked many Americans. As this cartoon depicts, some Americans believed hippies were defiant youths with no respect for authority.

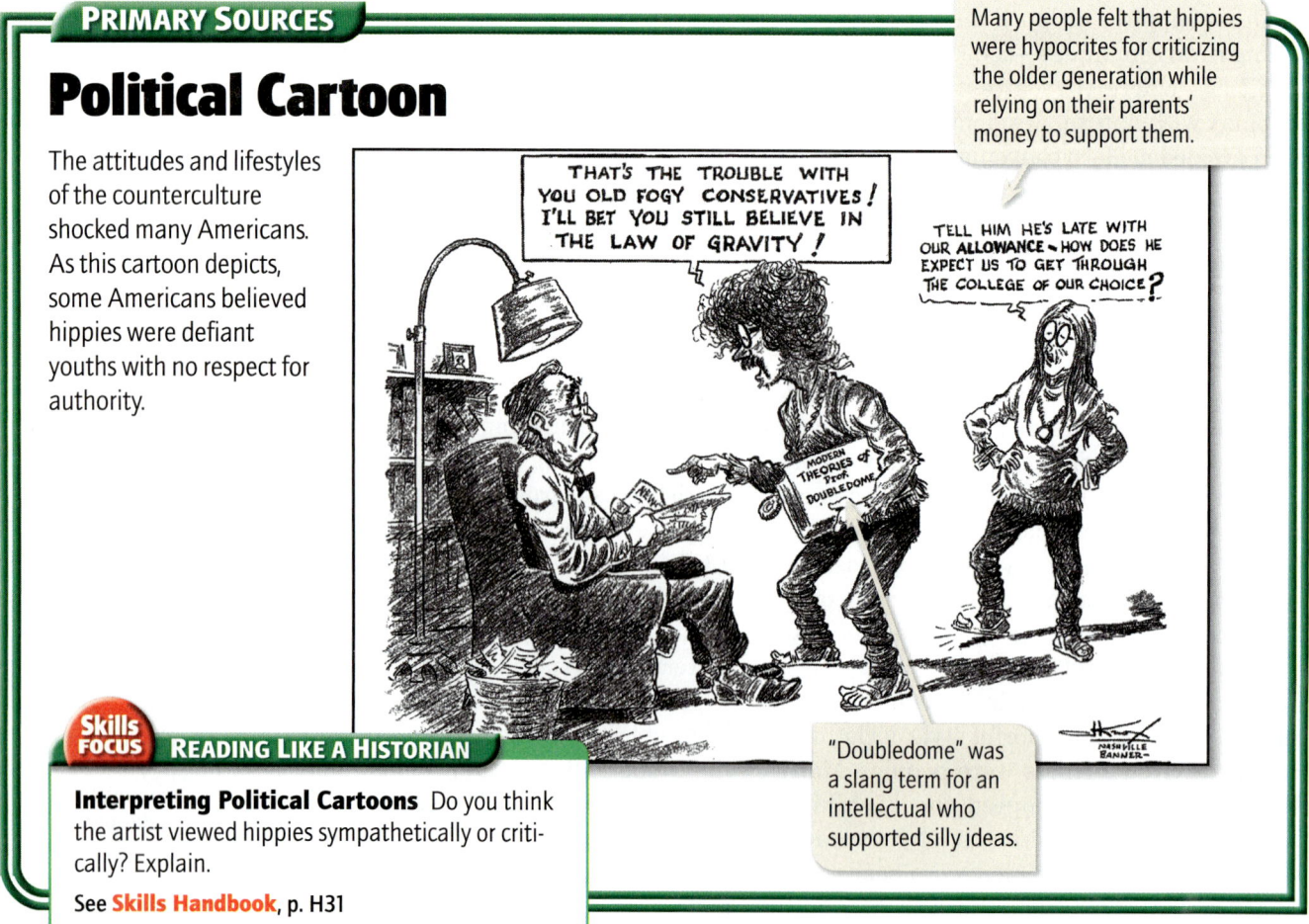

Many people felt that hippies were hypocrites for criticizing the older generation while relying on their parents' money to support them.

"Doubledome" was a slang term for an intellectual who supported silly ideas.

Skills FOCUS **READING LIKE A HISTORIAN**

Interpreting Political Cartoons Do you think the artist viewed hippies sympathetically or critically? Explain.

See **Skills Handbook**, p. H31

Art and film The counterculture's questioning of tradition and authority extended into the art world. Many artists of the 1960s argued that art had become a slave to elite tastes. They claimed that established artists created works only to please a few cultural critics.

In this period, a new style developed called **pop art.** Aiming to appeal to popular tastes, artists took inspiration from elements of the popular culture, including advertising, comic books, and movies. Andy Warhol led the pop art movement. He painted common, mass-produced objects such as Campbell Soup cans and Coke bottles. He also produced works featuring brightly colored likenesses of celebrities such as Marilyn Monroe and John F. Kennedy.

Film also underwent a broadening of subject matter as censorship rules relaxed. The film industry adopted a rating system ranging from G to X to inform audiences about the content of movies. The rating system was designed to gain favor with the viewing public, who wanted more information about what they would see on screen. Some people argued, however, that moral standards began to decline, because movies rated for mature audiences drew larger crowds than family-oriented films.

Music The counterculture had a tremendous influence on popular music. Rock and roll became an outlet for young people to express their discontent and their desire for change.

The Beatles, for example, moved from love songs like "I Want to Hold Your Hand" to more topical songs such as "Revolution." The group also brought new ideas and techniques to rock and roll music. Their performances electrified audiences and influenced countless other musicians.

Bob Dylan was another key figure on the music scene. Hailed as the spokesperson of his generation, Dylan found audiences wildly responsive to political songs like "The Times They Are A Changin'" and "Masters of War."

One of the most significant events of the period was the Woodstock Music and Art Fair, commonly known as Woodstock. In August 1969, some 400,000 people attended the music festival in rural upstate New York. Massive traffic jams led officials to close the roads leading to the area. Those who made it to Woodstock had to deal with driving rain, knee-deep mud, and shortages of food and water.

Despite the enormous crowds, the festival was peaceful. Over four days, many of the most popular musicians and bands performed, including Jimi Hendrix, Janis Joplin, Joan Baez, and the Grateful Dead. Woodstock was more than just a rock concert. It was the celebration of an era, and it marked the high point of the counterculture movement.

READING CHECK **Drawing Conclusions** How did the values of the counterculture influence art and music?

SECTION 3 ASSESSMENT

go.hrw.com
Online Quiz
Keyword: SD7 HP30

Reviewing Ideas, Terms, and People

1. a. Identify What factors contributed to the rise of the **counterculture** in the 1960s?
b. Make Inferences Why did university officials at Berkeley want to shut down the **Free Speech Movement**?
c. Evaluate Did university officials handle the conflict with students appropriately? Explain.

2. a. Recall Who were the **flower children**?
b. Analyze What were members of the counterculture trying to achieve?
c. Evaluate Was the decline of the counterculture avoidable? Why or why not?

3. a. Identify Who was Archie Bunker?
b. Interpret Why would J. Edgar Hoover describe student activism as "revolutionary terrorism"?

4. a. Describe What was Woodstock?
b. Summarize What effects did the counterculture have on the broader society?

Critical Thinking

5. Identifying Cause and Effect Copy the chart below and record the causes and effects of the counterculture.

The Counterculture

FOCUS ON SPEAKING

6. Persuasive What would you have said if you were addressing the crowd at the Berkeley student protests in 1964?

The Women's Movement

Historical Context The documents below provide different information on the women's movement during the late 1960s and early 1970s.

Task Examine the documents and answer the questions that follow. Then write an essay about the women's movement. Use facts from the documents and from the chapter to support the position you take in your thesis statement.

ST 4.3 Develop hypotheses about important events, eras, or issues; move from chronicling to explaining historical events and issues; use information collected from diverse sources to produce cogently written reports and document-based essays.

DOCUMENT 1

In 1969 students protested at the University of Chicago after it refused to extend the appointment of Marlene Dixon, a professor known for her radical political views. The Chicago Women's Liberation Union issued this statement in support of the protests.

"What does women's freedom mean? It means freedom of self-determination, self-enrichment, the freedom to live one's own life, set one's own goals, the freedom to rejoice in one's own accomplishments. It means the freedom to be one's own person in an integrated life of world, love, play, motherhood: the freedoms, rights, and privileges of first class citizenship, of equality in relationships of love and work: the right to choose to make decisions or not to: the right to full self-realization and to full participation in the life of the world. That is the freedom we seek in women's liberation.

To achieve these rights we must struggle as all other oppressed groups must struggle: one only has the rights one fights for. We must come together, understand the common problems, despair, anger, the roots and processes of our oppression: and then together, win our rights to a creative and human life.

At the U of C we see the *first large action, the first important struggle of women's liberation*. This university—all universities—discriminate against women, impede their full intellectual development, deny them places on the faculty, exploit talented women and mistreat women students."

DOCUMENT 2

Bill Mauldin created drawings that commented on current events for the *St. Louis Post-Dispatch* and the *Chicago Sun-Times*. In this cartoon, he comments on the challenges facing the women's movement.

"WELL, GIRLS, AT LEAST THE ONLY WAY WE CAN GO IS UP."

Over the past several decades, women's lives have changed in many ways. This table presents statistics that indicate women's progress in education, employment, athletics, and government service.

EDUCATION AND EARNINGS	1970	2002
Number of female college students (approximate)	3,000,000	9,300,000
Percentage of college students who were women	40.5 percent	56.4 percent
Percentage of undergraduate and graduate degrees received by women	40.8 percent	57.8 percent
Percentage of doctoral degrees received by women	13.3 percent	45.5 percent
Women's earnings compared to every dollar earned by men	59.4 cents	76.6 cents
ATHLETICS	1970	2002
Number of female participants in high school athletics	294,000	2,856,350
Percentage of participants in high school athletics who were women	7.4 percent	41.7 percent
CORPORATE LEADERSHIP AND GOVERNMENT SERVICE	1970	2002
Number of female chief executive officers of Fortune 500 companies	0	6
Percentage of female federal civilian employees	30.3 percent	45 percent
Number of women elected to U.S. House of Representatives	10	59
Number of women elected to U.S. Senate	1	13

Sources: Statistical Abstract of the United States, 1976, 2004–2005; National Federation of State High School Associations Participation Figure History; National Committee on Pay Equity; femmx, Volume 10, issue 1, May 2002

Skills FOCUS   READING LIKE A HISTORIAN

1. a. Recall Refer to Document 1. Why are the protests important, according to the Chicago Women's Liberation Union?
b. Interpret How does this statement encourage cooperation with other groups?

2. a. Describe Refer to Document 2. How does Mauldin portray equal rights for women?
b. Analyze Based on this cartoon, what is Mauldin's attitude toward the women's movement?

3. a. Identify Refer to Document 3. Which category shows the least change over time?

b. Make Inferences How might changes in educational achievement and changes in government employment be related?

4. Document-Based Essay Question Consider the question below and form a thesis statement. Using examples from Documents 1, 2, and 3, create an outline and write a short essay supporting your position.
How did the women's movement contribute to change in the United States?

See **Skills Handbook**, pp. H15, H28–H29, H31

Visual Summary: A Time of Social Change

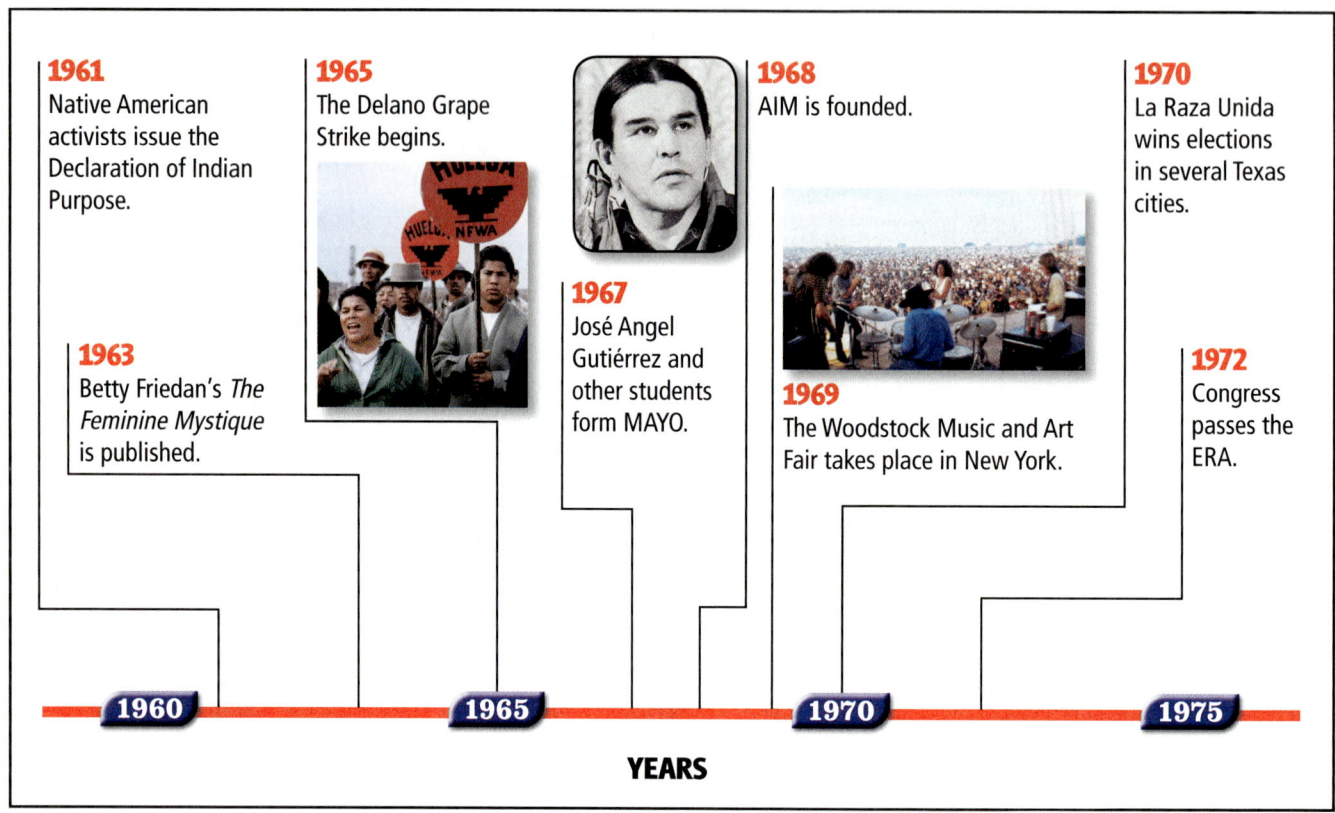

1961
Native American activists issue the Declaration of Indian Purpose.

1963
Betty Friedan's *The Feminine Mystique* is published.

1965
The Delano Grape Strike begins.

1967
José Angel Gutiérrez and other students form MAYO.

1968
AIM is founded.

1969
The Woodstock Music and Art Fair takes place in New York.

1970
La Raza Unida wins elections in several Texas cities.

1972
Congress passes the ERA.

1960   1965   1970   1975

YEARS

Reviewing Key Terms and People

Match each lettered definition with the correct numbered item at right.

a. Rebellion of teens and young adults against mainstream American society

b. Another popular name for hippies

c. Name by which many Puerto Ricans refer to themselves

d. A leader of the American Indian Movement

e. Conservative leader who opposed the ERA

f. Founder of MAYO who campaigned against anti-Latino discrimination in Texas schools

g. Chicano founder of the Crusade for Justice and author of the poem "I Am Joaquín"

h. Organization founded by José Angel Gutiérrez to strengthen Latinos' political power

i. Chicano labor leader who championed the rights of migrant farmworkers

1. boricua
2. counterculture
3. José Angel Gutiérrez
4. Phyllis Schlafly
5. flower children
6. Rodolfo "Corky" Gonzales
7. Russell Means
8. César Chávez
9. La Raza Unida Party

History's Impact video program

Review the video to answer the closing question:
How has the right of assembly allowed Americans
to have a voice in social and political change?

Comprehension and Critical Thinking

SECTION 1 *(pp. 986–993)*

10. a. Recall What was the ERA?

b. Summarize What gains did Native Americans make in the 1970s?

c. Elaborate Not all women supported NOW, nor did all Native Americans support AIM. Why was this the case?

SECTION 2 *(pp. 994–1001)*

11. a. Identify Who were the Brown Berets?

b. Compare and Contrast What did Chicano and Puerto Rican activists have in common, and how did they differ from Cuban Americans?

c. Develop Why do you think that the issue of fairness in education was so important to the Latino movements for equal rights?

SECTION 3 *(pp. 1002–1007)*

12. a. Describe What were the goals of the counterculture?

b. Analyze Why did some people find the counterculture threatening?

c. Evaluate Did the counterculture have more positive or negative effects on American culture and society? Explain.

Using the Internet

go.hrw.com
Practice Online
Keyword: SD7 CH30

13. President Bill Clinton awarded César Chávez the Presidential Medal of Honor in 1994. Using the keyword above, do research to learn about Chávez's activism after the Delano Grape Strike. Then write a short biography of Chávez, highlighting the important achievements of his leadership after the strike.

Analyzing Primary Sources

Reading Like a Historian The epic poem "I Am Joaquín" called on Chicano youths to find strength and pride in their culture and history. Reread the excerpt in Section 2.

14. Describe How does the poet describe the lives of Mexican Americans in the past?

15. Draw Conclusions What made this poem inspirational to a generation of Chicanos?

Critical Reading

Read the passages in Section 1 that discuss the occupation of Alcatraz and AIM. Then answer the questions that follow.

16. Why was the Indian occupation of Alcatraz Island significant?

A Congress gave Native Americans the right to use any surplus government property.

B It led to the founding of the American Indian Movement.

C It drew attention to injustices against Native Americans and encouraged AIM activists.

D The Bureau of Indian Affairs agreed to consider Native Americans' grievances.

17. Which of the following statements is true?

A The goals of AIM were to protect Native Americans' traditional ways of life, foster economic independence, and improve educational opportunities.

B The American Indian Movement was founded with the intention of helping Native Americans who lived on reservations.

C AIM activists seized Wounded Knee in retaliation for the killing of 300 Sioux in 1890.

D AIM's tactics were limited to nonviolent marches and demonstrations.

WRITING FOR THE SAT

Think about the following issue:

Throughout the 1960s, thousands of teens and young adults rebelled against mainstream American society. They abandoned school, jobs, and traditional home life in search of a more freewheeling existence. They wanted to live simply and "do your own thing."

18. Assignment Was the counterculture a bold experiment in nontraditional living or a self-indulgent escape from reality? Write a short essay in which you develop your position on this issue. Support your point of view with reasoning and examples from your reading and studies.

 **The New Frontier and the Great Society**
1961–1969

MAIN IDEA Both Presidents Kennedy and Johnson pushed for major changes in American society while confronting the threat of communism overseas.

SECTION 1 President Kennedy fought communism by supporting West Berlin when the Communists erected the Berlin Wall. He turned back a Communist threat to the United States when he faced down the Soviet Union in the Cuban missile crisis.

SECTION 2 Kennedy was a youthful, popular president whose thousand days in office showed promise. His assassination in 1963 deeply shocked the nation and the world.

SECTION 3 President Johnson convinced Congress to pass several of Kennedy's programs after his death. Johnson built on these reforms with programs of his own in an effort to create a Great Society in America.

 **The Civil Rights Movement**
1954–1975

MAIN IDEA The civil rights movement won key victories in gaining racial equality for African Americans.

SECTION 1 The civil rights movement's early successes included efforts to end segregation in education, including the landmark *Brown* decision, and the Montgomery bus boycott.

SECTION 2 Nonviolent protests often met with violent responses. The March on Washington in August 1963 called for a federal law to end segregation. The Civil Rights Act of 1964 banned discrimination in employment and public accommodations.

SECTION 3 The Twenty-fourth Amendment inspired increased efforts to gain voting rights for southern African Americans. Violent responses to a voter registration drive in Mississippi and a peaceful march in Selma, Alabama, gained national attention, helping to secure passage of the Voting Rights Act of 1965.

SECTION 4 Divisions developed in the civil rights movement in the late 1960s over such issues as tactics and de facto segregation. The assassination of Martin Luther King Jr. further weakened the movement.

SECTION 5 Busing and affirmative action programs in the 1970s continued to combat segregation and discrimination.

 **The Vietnam War**
1954–1975

MAIN IDEA The Vietnam War began as an effort to resist the spread of communism. As it continued, divisions arose over U.S. involvement in the war.

SECTION 1 American involvement in Vietnam began as support for France against a Communist-led war for independence. When the French were defeated and Vietnam was divided, U.S. support shifted to the anti-Communist government of South Vietnam.

SECTION 2 In 1965 President Johnson sent the first U.S. fighting forces to South Vietnam. The war escalated as U.S. troop strength increased. Ground troops faced great challenges in fighting North Vietnamese and Viet Cong forces that used unconventional tactics.

SECTION 3 The Tet Offensive in 1968 led increasing numbers of Americans to question U.S. involvement in Vietnam. The issue provoked growing protest and shaped the presidential election of 1968.

SECTION 4 President Nixon negotiated an end to U.S. involvement in the war in 1973. Fighting continued, however, and South Vietnam surrendered to North Vietnam in 1975.

 **A Time of Social Change**
1963–1975

MAIN IDEA The 1960s and 1970s were a time of great social and political change for many groups in American society.

SECTION 1 Women and Native Americans formed new organizations to promote political, social, and economic equality in American society.

SECTION 2 Latinos sought equality through the peaceful, nonviolent tactics of César Chávez, as well as the more militant methods of groups like MAYO and the Brown Berets.

SECTION 3 The counterculture of the 1960s grew out of a youth movement rooted in the beliefs of peace and love.

Looking Toward the Future

1968–Present

Themes

Government and Democracy
Public trust in government was tested by political scandals, and Americans re-examined the role of government in the United States.

Global Relations
The end of the Cold War presented new challenges in foreign affairs, and the United States and other countries confronted international terrorism.

Science and Technology
Innovations such as the Internet affected nearly all areas of everyday life.

Fireworks light the sky above the Capitol at a Fourth of July celebration in Washington, D.C.

Prepare to Read

Summarizing

Find practice for **Summarizing** in the **Skills Handbook,** p. H6

Summarizing helps you understand and remember what you read. In a summary you use your own words to restate your reading. Summaries should use fewer words and highlight only the key points.

Before You Read
Skim headings and visuals to preview the text and form a general idea of its content.

While You Read
Pick out main ideas and key details that support the main ideas.

After You Read
Write a summary of the reading, restating in your own words the key ideas contained in the text and images.

Crises Overwhelm Carter

In his first years in office, Carter enjoyed some successes and suffered through some failures. In 1979, however, a series of events occurred that seemed to overwhelm his entire presidency.

The Soviets invade Afghanistan In 1978 the government of Afghanistan was toppled in a coup. Afghanistan's new Communist leaders were friendly to the Soviet Union. Yet this new pro-Soviet Afghan government was not stable. When it showed signs of crumbling, the Soviets acted. In December 1979, they invaded Afghanistan.

READING CHECK **Summarizing** How would you describe President Carter's final two years in office?

This heading tells you the topic—problems that President Carter encountered.

Main Idea A series of events plagued Carter's presidency.

Detail A coup and instability in the Afghan government led the Soviets to invade Afghanistan in 1979.

Test Prep Tip

Tests often ask you to choose the best summary of a particular reading passage. Before reading the answer options, try summarizing the passage in your own words. Then read the choices and determine which one best fits your summary.

Reading like a Historian

Making Oral and Written Presentations

Find practice for **Making Oral and Written Presentations** in the
Skills Handbook, pp. H40–41

Presentations are written or verbal reports on a topic that you have researched. There are specific steps to follow for any kind of presentation, as well as some skills that apply to oral presentations and some that apply only to written presentations.

1. Identify a topic that you wish to learn more about for your presentation.
2. Formulate a hypothesis. This will be the main idea of your presentation.
3. Organize facts, data, and details to support your hypothesis.
4. Express your ideas and arguments clearly and persuasively.

Strategies historians use:

- Choose a central idea or theme on which to focus your presentation. This theme should be specific to help structure your research.
- Keep a bibliography of all of the sources you consult in your research. You should always know where you found your facts.
- Proofread your presentation, whether it is written or oral, to ensure that it is well organized and grammatically correct.

This is the topic of the presentation. All the facts should relate to the topic, "Reaganomics."

Oral Presentation Notes, American History

Reaganomics:

(1) President Ronald Reagan, 1980-1988

(2) tax cuts and smaller federal government

(3) increased military spending,

(4) supply-side economics, "voodoo economics"

(George H. W. Bush)

(5) 1981-1982 – worst economic recession since the Great

~~Depressive~~ Depression

Whenever you use a quote, be sure to label the its source.

Proofreading is important, even in oral presentation notes like these. Reading the wrong word can confuse both you and your audience.

 READING LIKE A HISTORIAN

As You Read Make an index card for each fact or piece of data you find. Be sure to include the source information.
As You Study Write an outline that shows how your presentation will be organized. Make sure that all of your facts support your main idea in a meaningful way.

A Search for ORDER

THE BIG PICTURE Both Presidents Nixon and Carter achieved great diplomatic successes—but also made decisions that ended their presidencies. Nixon, accused of lying and covering up a crime, was forced to resign. Carter was denied a second term for failing to provide strong leadership in relations with Iran and the Soviet Union.

New York Standards

Key Idea 2 Important ideas, social and cultural values, beliefs, and traditions from New York State and United States history illustrate the connections and interactions of people and events across time and from a variety of perspectives.

Key Idea 3 Study about the major social, political, economic, cultural, and religious developments in New York State and United States history involves learning about the important roles and contributions of individuals and groups.

Skills FOCUS **READING LIKE A HISTORIAN**

New York City celebrates the return of astronauts Neil A. Armstrong, Michael Collins, and Edwin E. "Buzz" Aldrin (right to left) with a grand ticker-tape parade in the summer of 1969. The trio recently completed a historic trip to the moon—a first for humans.
Making Inferences How might great achievements affect a society searching for order?

See **Skills Handbook**, p. H7

July 20, 1969
Neil Armstrong becomes the first man to walk on the moon.

U.S. **1968** Richard Nixon is elected president.

1968

World

1969 The ruling council of the Palestine Liberation Organization elects Yasser Arafat to head the PLO.

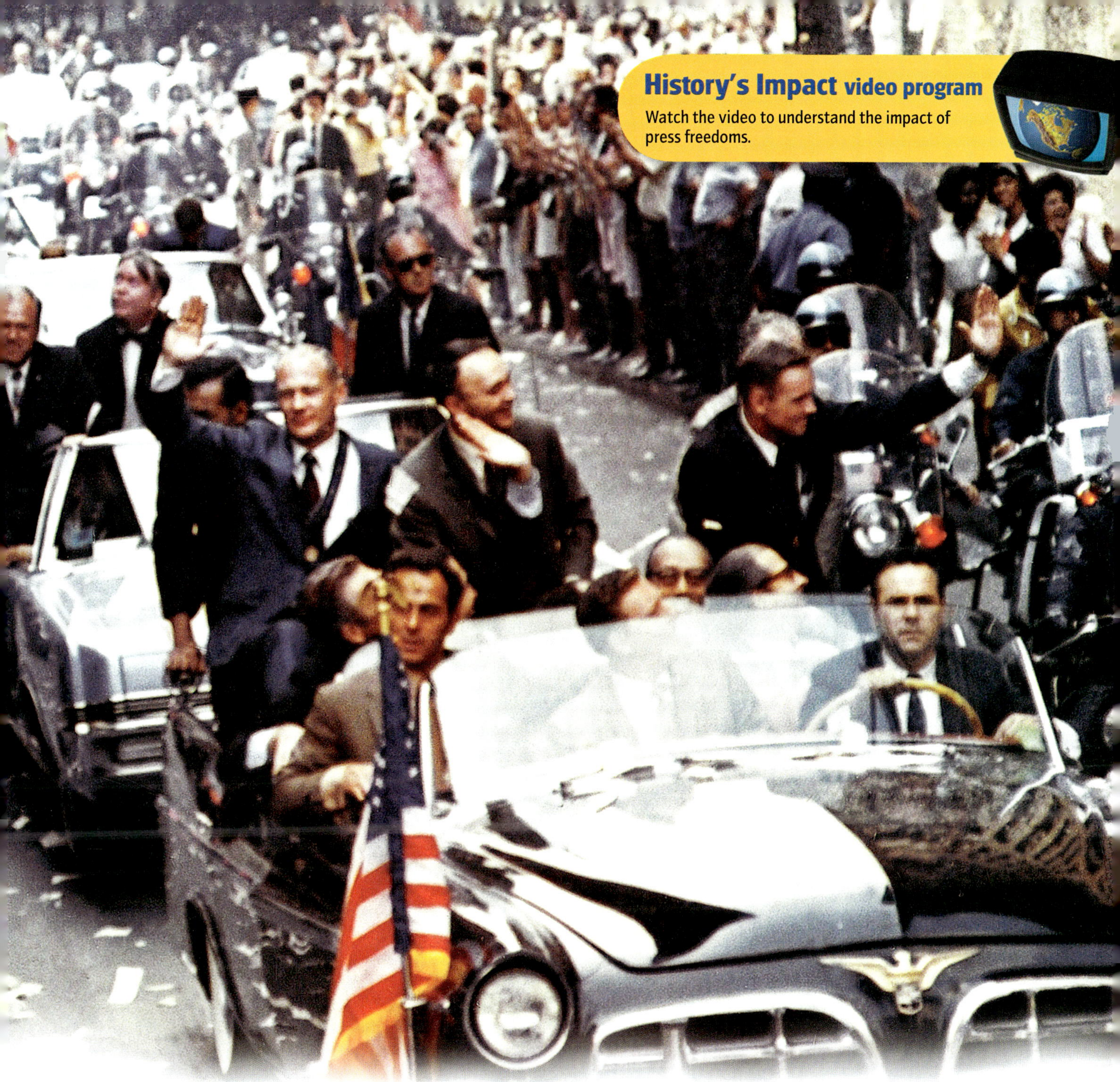

History's Impact video program
Watch the video to understand the impact of press freedoms.

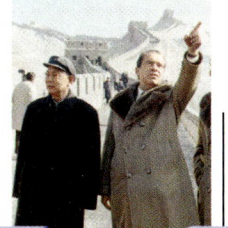

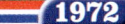

February 1972
Nixon makes a historic trip to the People's Republic of China.

August 1974
Nixon resigns the presidency.

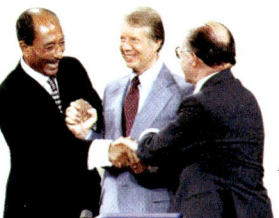

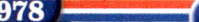

September 1978
President Carter helps negotiate the Camp David Accords between Israel and Egypt.

March 1980
Carter announces a U.S. boycott of the Olympic Games in Moscow.

1970 — 1972 — 1974 — 1976 — 1978 — 1980

1971
The People's Republic of China invites the U.S. table tennis team to Beijing.

1975
Refugees called "boat people" begin fleeing Vietnam.

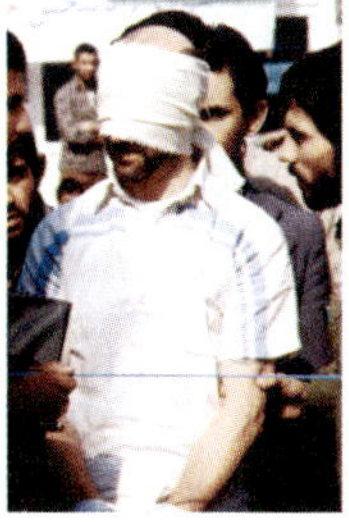

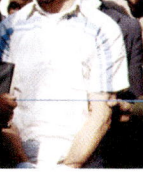

November 1979
An Iranian mob seizes American embassy in Tehran.

December 1979
The Soviet Union invades Afghanistan to prop up its Communist government.

The Nixon Years

BEFORE YOU READ

MAIN IDEA

Beyond the ongoing turmoil of the Vietnam War, the Nixon administration did enjoy some notable success.

READING FOCUS

1. What were the key features of Nixon's politics and domestic policies?
2. How did Nixon carry out his foreign policies with regard to China and the Soviet Union?
3. How did trouble in the Middle East affect the Nixon administration?
4. What were some of the major social and cultural events at home in the Nixon years?

KEY TERMS AND PEOPLE

realpolitik
détente
SALT I
OPEC
shuttle diplomacy
Apollo 11
Neil Armstrong

PI 2.5 Analyze the United States involvement in foreign affairs and a willingness to engage in international politics, examining the ideas and traditions leading to these foreign policies.

THE INSIDE STORY

How did Nixon bounce back from crushing defeat? By 1962 Richard Nixon seemed to be an utterly defeated man. Still recovering from having lost the presidential election of 1960 to John F. Kennedy, Nixon had sought the governor's office in his home state of California. Again, however, he suffered a humiliating defeat. In a surprising move, he announced his retirement from politics the day after the election. "You won't have Dick Nixon to kick around anymore," he angrily told reporters, whom he had blamed for his defeat. The man who had once been the second most powerful man in the world and who had come within a few thousand votes of being president was now a bitter man.

But Nixon was far from finished in politics. Out of office and out of the spotlight, he remained active in Republican politics in the 1960s. After wins in the 1968 presidential primaries, it became clear that he was an electable candidate. He won his party's nomination. Then, as the Democrats squabbled and divided over the Vietnam War and civil rights, he emerged as the winner in a close election.

Nixon had made a remarkable political comeback. Far from being through with politics, the most memorable years of his political career lay ahead of him. These included achievements in the 1970s for which he is favorably remembered. ◾

Nixon's Comeback to Success

▶ Richard Nixon gives the victory salute that would become his trademark gesture.

Nixon's Politics and Domestic Policies

Richard Nixon's 1968 political comeback high-lighted what had already been a long and successful career. Before his losses in 1960 and 1962, he had built a reputation as a strong opponent of communism and as a solid conservative. Recall that in American politics, conservatives tend to favor smaller, less active government. They also favor what are seen as more traditional values.

Nixon the conservative Indeed, Nixon entered the presidency promoting a number of conservative ideas. For example, he had campaigned on the belief that the federal government had grown too large.

HISTORY'S VOICES

❝[W]e have been deluged by government programs for the unemployed, programs for the cities, programs for the poor, and we have reaped from these programs an ugly harvest of frustrations, violence and failure across the land . . . I say it's time to quit pouring billions of dollars into programs that have failed in the United States of America.❞

—Richard Nixon, Acceptance Speech, August 8, 1968

"It's time," Nixon continued, "to have power go back from Washington to the states and to the cities of this country all over America." The solution he proposed came to be called the New Federalism. A key feature of this proposal was the concept of revenue sharing. This meant that money collected by the federal government would be shifted to states and cities. Local governments, Nixon believed, would do a better job of spending the taxpayers' money than the federal government would.

The southern strategy Early in his career, Nixon had supported civil rights for African Americans. As president, however, he crafted a "southern strategy" designed to appeal to former segregationists in the South. Nixon's goal was to ensure electoral success by expanding his support in the traditionally Democratic region. Based on this strategy, Nixon tried unsuccessfully to weaken the 1965 Voting Rights Act. He urged a slowdown in forced integration in the South. He also opposed the busing of students from their home neighborhoods to schools in another part of the city. This had been a court-

FACES OF HISTORY

Richard NIXON
1913–1994

Richard Nixon accomplished much in a political career that spanned nearly three decades. In addition to his accomplishments, he also won a reputation for tough political tactics.

Born and raised in California, Nixon excelled in college and law school. After serving in the navy in World War II, he pursued a political career. In 1946 he won election to Congress in part on the strength of a strong anti-Communist message. As a House member, he won national attention for his role in the trial of accused spy Alger Hiss. This political success was followed by a 1950 campaign for a Senate seat. He won this election after accusing his opponent of being soft on communism.

Now a national figure, Nixon served as vice president for two terms under Dwight D. Eisenhower. He only narrowly missed winning election to the presidency in 1960. Yet this and his 1962 loss in the race for governor of California left their mark on Nixon. His fear of another loss would lead him to campaign excesses in the future.

Explain How did Nixon's experiences in 1960 and 1962 affect the way he approached political campaigns?

ordered way of integrating schools in places where neighborhoods were all-black or all-white. Nixon favored letting local governments take action rather than having the federal government force them to act.

As a result of action at the state level, many communities made real progress toward desegregation. Still, de facto segregation—that is, segregation in fact though not by law—continued in many places, including in many northern cities, for some time. Nixon, meanwhile, gained the favor of many white voters in the South.

Drugs and crime Nixon also took a firm stand against crime and drug use. "Time is running out for the merchants of crime and corruption in American society," he promised. He shared conservatives' concern about federal court rulings that put limits on the powers of the police. (Recall what you have read about rulings such as *Miranda* v. *Arizona*.) He therefore sought to name conservative judges for openings on the federal courts. Though the Senate rejected two of his Supreme Court nominees, Nixon was able to fill four openings on the court.

The other side of Richard Nixon While Nixon had a solid conservative record, he was sometimes willing to take more liberal stances. For example, he expanded the role of the federal government by increasing funding for programs such as food stamps, which helped people with low incomes buy groceries. He also increased payments for Social Security.

Nixon's environmentalism Nixon also took a special interest in the environment. Concern about pollution had been growing in the United States for several years. In 1962 author Rachel Carson had published *Silent Spring*, which warned of the harmful effects of chemicals on the natural world.

By 1970 widespread concern led to massive Earth Day demonstrations all across the country. Millions of Americans took part in these events, at which information and ideas about the environment were shared.

Nixon responded to this growing national issue. In 1970 he signed the Clean Air Act, which sought to regulate levels of air pollution created by factories and other sources. That same year, Nixon worked to establish the Environmental Protection Agency to help carry out the nation's environmental laws and policies.

Other Nixon policies Late in 1970 Nixon signed the Occupational Safety and Health Act. This created a large new organization within the federal government. At its heart was the Occupational Health and Safety Administration, or OSHA, which worked to prevent work-related injury and illness. OSHA set and enforced safety standards in the workplace and provided safety training and education.

While Nixon pursued his southern strategy, he also took steps to advance affirmative action. As you have read, this refers to active measures taken by the government to overcome the effects of past discrimination against minority groups.

Early in his administration, Nixon encouraged the setting of specific hiring goals and timetables for overcoming discrimination in companies doing business with the government. He also extended affirmative action programs to the hiring of women.

THE IMPACT TODAY

Government

In its first three decades, OSHA helped reduce workplace fatalities by 60 percent—at the same time that the size of the American workforce more than doubled.

ACADEMIC VOCABULARY

innovations new ideas or advances

READING CHECK **Summarizing** How did Nixon's basic political beliefs affect his domestic policies?

Nixon's Foreign Policies

When Nixon was running for office in 1968, the war in Vietnam was the major issue facing the voters. You have read about Nixon's troubled efforts to bring that crisis to a close. Yet Vietnam was only one of the foreign-policy issues facing Nixon during his presidency. In general, Nixon met these challenges with great success.

Henry Kissinger and realpolitik Henry Kissinger, who helped negotiate an end to the Vietnam War, was deeply involved in shaping much of Nixon's foreign policy. Nixon named Kissinger as his national security adviser in 1969. Kissinger later became secretary of state. In both roles, he was guided by the notion of realpolitik. **Realpolitik** means basing foreign policies on realistic views of national interest rather than on broad rules or principles.

Kissinger believed the United States should consider each foreign-policy conflict or question from the standpoint of what is best for America. The government should not, Kissinger believed, be bound by promises to fight communism or promote freedom wherever it is threatened. Henry Kissinger's realpolitik marked a significant change from earlier policies such as containment.

Détente Nixon had built his reputation as a tough opponent of communism. Voters knew they were electing a strong and forceful leader. However, as Nixon once remarked, "Sometimes those on the right can do things which those on the left can only talk about." Indeed, as president Nixon took steps to ease tensions with Cold War enemies. These efforts were referred to as **détente** (day-TAHNT).

The policy of détente was strongly influenced by Henry Kissinger's realpolitik. The goal was to build a more stable world in which the United States and its adversaries accepted one another's place.

In 1969 Nixon entered into discussions with the Soviets to slow the ongoing arms race. These were known as the Strategic Arms Limitation Talks (SALT). In addition to increasing numbers of weapons, the United States and the Soviet Union each had recently made innovations in weapons technology. For example, each had recently built antiballistic missile, or ABM, defense systems. Many people considered ABM systems to be a threat to peace. It was feared they would undermine the power balance that helped prevent nuclear war during the Cold War. If one side thought it could survive a nuclear attack, the thinking went, it might be more likely to launch one itself.

The SALT meetings dragged on for several years. Finally, in 1972 Nixon visited Moscow for a summit. At that meeting, Nixon and Soviet leader Leonid Brezhnev agreed to an ABM treaty that bound each country to strict limits in the building of missile systems.

Nixon and Brezhnev also agreed to a five-year slowdown in building new offensive weapons. Following the end of these talks—now called **SALT I**—negotiators began a second round of discussions on arms limitation. These became known as SALT II. You will read more about them later.

Nixon in China Shortly after taking office, President Nixon told his closest advisers about one of his key goals for his presidency: improving relations with the Communist People's Republic of China. At that time, the People's Republic had little contact with the United States and most of the rest of the world.

Yet Nixon saw great opportunity in improving relations with the Communist giant. Such a step would put pressure on the Soviet Union. Both China and the Soviets practiced communism, but they had become bitter rivals in recent years. Nixon knew that by becoming friendlier with China, he could make the Soviets uncomfortable and pressure them into a more cooperative relationship with the United States.

Nixon had to move carefully. The United States did not formally recognize the People's Republic of China. It considered the Republic of China on Taiwan to be the true Chinese government. Thus, the effort to reach out to the People's Republic took place in secrecy.

Nevertheless, Nixon's plan went forward. In 1971 the People's Republic made a surprise invitation to an American table tennis team to play in a tournament. The team members became the first Americans to visit mainland China since 1949.

Later, Kissinger made a secret trip to the People's Republic to explore a possible

Nixon Visits China

- **January 1969** Nixon informs key staff of his desire to improve relations with the People's Republic of China.

- **May 1969** Using Pakistan as a go-between, U.S. officials begin talking with Communist Chinese representatives.

- **April 1971** A U.S. table tennis team visits the People's Republic of China.

- **July 1971** Kissinger makes a secret trip to the People's Republic of China to pave the way for Nixon's visit.

- **February 1972** Nixon travels to the People's Republic and meets with Communist leader Mao Zedong.

◀ Nixon tours the Great Wall of China in February 1972.

presidential visit. The meeting went well. In July 1971, Nixon announced that he would go to the People's Republic in early 1972.

The news shocked some Americans and pleased others. Some were upset that Nixon seemed to be abandoning Nationalist China and embracing the Communists. Nixon assured these critics that that was not the case. Many Americans, however, supported the move.

In February Nixon's team took off for China. There he met with top Chinese leaders, including the aging Mao Zedong. The visit was a huge success for Nixon. He and Mao recognized the benefits of a closer relationship. Toward that end, they agreed to disagree about Taiwan.

The trip also seemed to have the hoped-for effect on the Soviets. Shortly after the China visit, Nixon and Brezhnev reached agreement in the SALT I meetings.

ACADEMIC VOCABULARY
region an area of the world

READING CHECK **Identifying the Main Idea** What was the primary goal of Richard Nixon's foreign policy with regard to the Soviet Union and China?

Trouble in the Middle East

The Middle East had been a point of conflict for many years. In 1967 Israel went to war against several of its Arab neighbors. As a result of the Six-Day War, Israel occupied territory that had belonged to or been controlled by the Arab nations of Egypt, Syria, and Jordan.

Following the war's end, the United Nations passed a resolution that called for Israel to withdraw from these occupied lands and for Arab states to recognize Israel's right to exist. However, there was disagreement on exactly what the resolution required. Israel—with U.S. support—continued to dispute with its Arab neighbors for the next several years.

In 1973 this ongoing conflict finally erupted in war. On the Jewish holy day of Yom Kippur, Egypt and Syria attacked Israel.

The fighting affected the United States in a number of ways. One effect was the threat of Soviet involvement. In response to events on the battlefield, the Soviet Union offered supplies to the Egyptians and the Syrians.

The United States in turn sent supplies to the Israelis. The Soviets also threatened to send troops to aid the embattled Egyptians. Conflict in the region threatened to turn into a superpower confrontation.

Oil embargo Another effect of the war was the decision of several Arab nations to impose an oil embargo. An embargo is the refusal by a country to ship a product or products from its ports.

Shortly after the start of the Yom Kippur War, the Arab oil-producing countries of the Middle East jointly agreed not to ship any oil to the United States and certain other countries. This was a response to American support for Israel. The Arab countries were part of a group called the Organization of Petroleum Exporting Countries, or **OPEC**.

At the time of the embargo, the United States was dependent on OPEC oil for a significant amount of its large petroleum needs. That dependence was growing. In 1970 the United States had gotten just over a fifth of its oil from foreign sources. By 1973 that figure had risen to about a third.

The Arab oil embargo contributed to an energy crisis in the United States. As gasoline became scarce, drivers sometimes had to wait in long lines at gas stations to fill their tanks. When they got to the pump, they often found that prices for gasoline had risen sharply.

The oil embargo affected more than just people who drove cars. For example, it drove up the cost of operating machines in factories. It cost farmers more to harvest their crops. The embargo also increased the cost of

CAUSES AND EFFECTS OF THE YOM KIPPUR WAR

QUICK FACTS

CAUSES
- Israel occupied Arab-controlled land in the Six-Day War.
- The United Nations passed a resolution urging Israel to leave occupied lands and Arab nations to recognize Israel.
- Arabs and Israelis were unable to reach agreement on either point of the UN resolution.

EFFECTS
- Tension between United States and the Soviet Union grew.
- Arab oil-producing nations decided on an oil embargo.

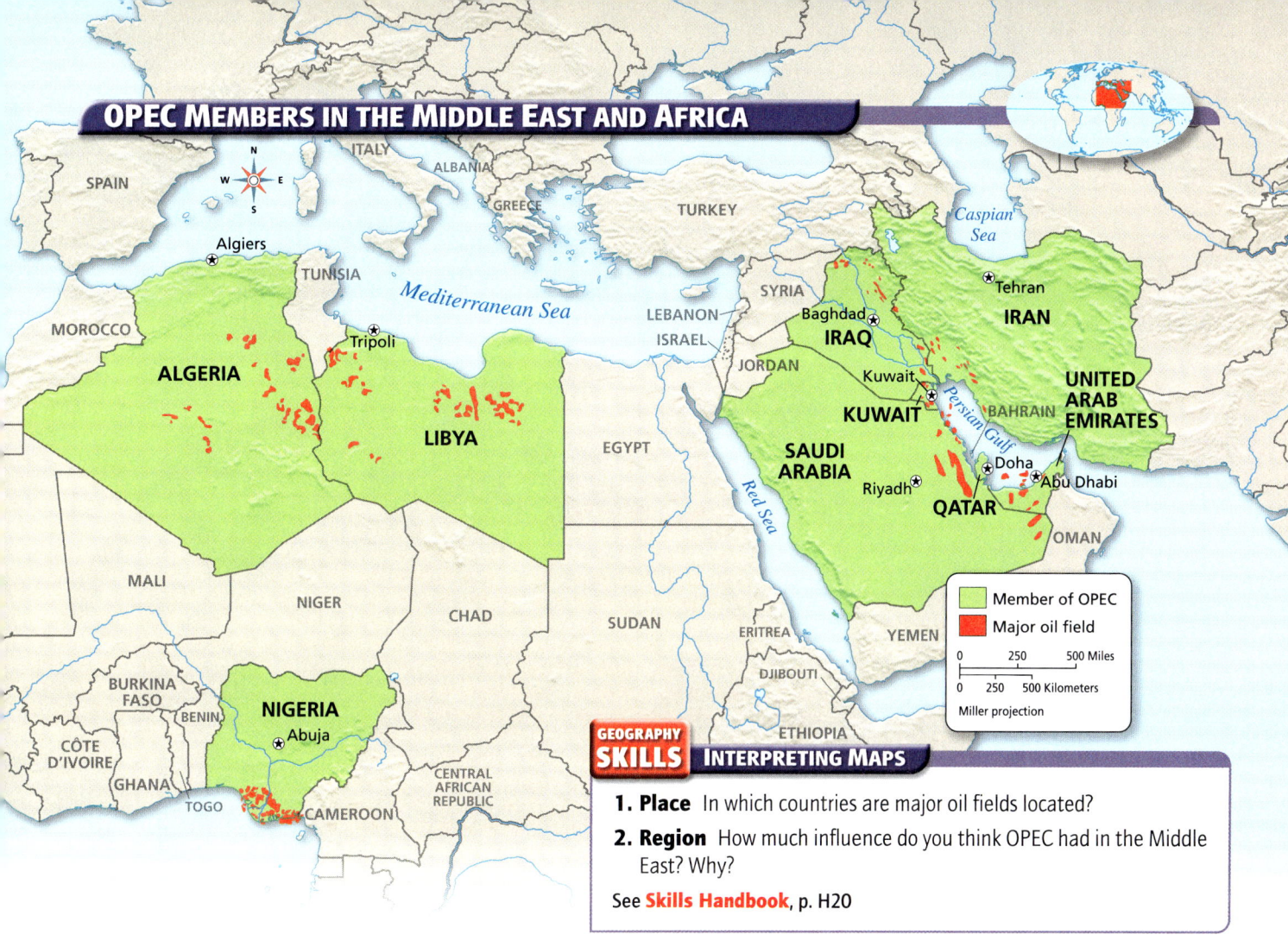

Member of OPEC

Major oil field

0   250   500 Miles

0   250   500 Kilometers

Miller projection

GEOGRAPHY SKILLS INTERPRETING MAPS

1. **Place** In which countries are major oil fields located?

2. **Region** How much influence do you think OPEC had in the Middle East? Why?

See **Skills Handbook**, p. H20

transporting products from farms and factories to stores. Prices for all kinds of products thus began to rise. As you will read, this rapid rise in prices would cause serious problems throughout the U.S. economy.

Kissinger and shuttle diplomacy

To help resolve the crisis in the Middle East, Henry Kissinger went to work. Unable to get all the parties involved to meet together to discuss possible solutions, he started what came to be called **shuttle diplomacy**. That is, he traveled—shuttled—from group to group, trying to work out separate agreements to end the fighting. For example, he negotiated peace between Israel and Egypt. Then he helped bring about a separate deal between Israel and Syria. In this way, the military conflict came to an end. Eventually, the oil embargo was also lifted.

READING CHECK **Identifying Cause and Effect** How did the trouble in the Middle East affect the United States in the early 1970s?

Major Events at Home

In an earlier chapter, you read about the American program to put astronauts on the moon. During the Nixon years, the United States finally achieved this history-making goal.

Throughout the mid-1960s, the American public followed the progress of the NASA astronauts with great interest. Every few months brought another launch and another step toward the goal of a lunar landing. These triumphs were also marred by tragedy. In 1967 three astronauts died in a terrible launchpad fire. In spite of this setback, the Apollo space program continued.

The climax came in July 1969. On the 16th of that month, a flight known as *Apollo 11* made a successful liftoff from Cape Kennedy, also known as the Kennedy Space Center, in Florida. On board were three modern-day pioneers—astronauts **Neil Armstrong**, Edwin "Buzz" Aldrin, and Michael Collins.

The First Moon Landing

The successful landing of human beings on the surface of the moon was a triumph of technology— and of the American will and spirit of exploration.

The lunar module was designed to withstand the low gravitational forces of the moon, which were one-sixth those of Earth.

The large amounts of equipment made the interior of the lunar module cramped and noisy.

The large footpads were designed to ensure the module did not sink into the soft lunar soil.

UNITED STATES

Skills FOCUS **INTERPRETING INFOGRAPHICS**

go.hrw.com
Interactive
Keyword: SD7 CH31

1. **Making Inferences** Why do you think conditions were so cramped in the lunar landing module?

2. **Drawing Conclusions** What factors made landing on the moon difficult?

See **Skills Handbook**, pp. H12, H18

After a journey of several days, the crew of *Apollo 11* swung into orbit around the moon. As their spacecraft sailed miles above the moon's surface, a separate craft split off from the main part. One part was the control module *Columbia*, in which Collins remained. The other part was a lunar module called the *Eagle*, which carried Aldrin and Armstrong.

On July 20 the *Eagle* landed on the moon's surface. Back on Earth, millions of viewers watched the flawless landing on television. Several anxious hours later, Neil Armstrong made his way out of the module. Wearing a heavy space suit, he slowly backed down a ladder. "That's one small step for a man," crackled his voice over the radio as he stepped onto the moon, "one giant leap for mankind." The mission started years before by President John F. Kennedy had been achieved at last.

Soon Armstrong was joined by Aldrin. The pair set up a camera and carried out a variety of tasks. This included planting an American flag in the lunar soil.

HISTORY'S VOICES

“ So many people have done so much to give us this opportunity to place this American flag on the surface. To me it was one of the prouder moments of my life, to be able to stand there and quickly salute the flag. ”

—Edwin "Buzz" Aldrin, news conference, August 12, 1969

Inflation and price controls

The success of the lunar landing gave the nation and Nixon a lift. However, Nixon knew that it was not enough to ensure his future in office. As the memory of *Apollo 11* faded and the election of 1972 approached, Nixon grew concerned.

A particular worry was the high rate of inflation, or the overall rise in prices. In the months leading up to the 1972 election, this stood at an unacceptable 5 percent, and it was rising. Unemployment was also at an uncomfortably high level.

Nixon had traditionally favored limited government involvement in the economy. Now, however, he believed action was needed. In August 1971 he announced a 90-day freeze of wages and prices. That is, businesses could not increase the prices they charged for their products or the wages they paid their workers. This, Nixon hoped, would act as a brake on inflation.

The immediate impact of Nixon's measures was positive. Inflation did appear to slow, at least for a while. Nixon seemed to have successfully addressed a major economic concern of the voters.

Unfortunately, Nixon had not solved the problem of inflation permanently. The oil crisis of 1973–1974 would soon send prices sharply higher again. The wage and price controls that had worked before failed to bring relief. Meanwhile, the second term Nixon had worked so hard to secure dissolved into scandal. You will read about this in the next section.

READING CHECK **Summarizing** What were two major events affecting the United States during Nixon's first term in office?

Science and Technology

NASA's moon explorations ended in the early 1970s. In early 2004 President George W. Bush announced a new goal for U.S. space exploration: a return to the moon and, eventually, human missions to the planet Mars.

SECTION 1 ASSESSMENT

go.hrw.com
Online Quiz
Keyword: SD7 HP31

Reviewing Ideas, Terms, and People

1. **a. Identify** What kind of political reputation did Nixon have when he was elected president in 1969?
   b. Draw Conclusions Why do you think Nixon sometimes favored conservative policies and sometimes took more liberal positions?

2. **a. Define** Write a brief definition of each of the following terms: realpolitik, détente
   b. Interpret What do you think Nixon meant when he said, "Sometimes those on the right can do things which those on the left can only talk about"?

3. **a. Describe** What were the key events in the Middle East that occurred in 1973?
   b. Sequence What was the sequence of events surrounding the Arab oil embargo?

4. **a. Identify** What is the significance of *Apollo 11*?
   b. Compare How did Nixon's handling of the inflation problem match his overall political philosophies?

Critical Thinking

5. **Identifying the Main Idea** Copy the chart below and use information from the section to record details that support the section's main idea.

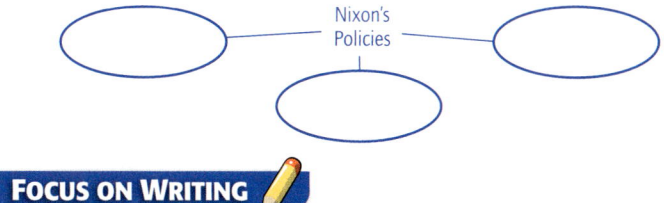

Nixon's Policies

FOCUS ON WRITING

6. **Descriptive** Based on the events described in this section, write a brief descriptive paragraph about Nixon's performance, including details of his major policies and accomplishments.

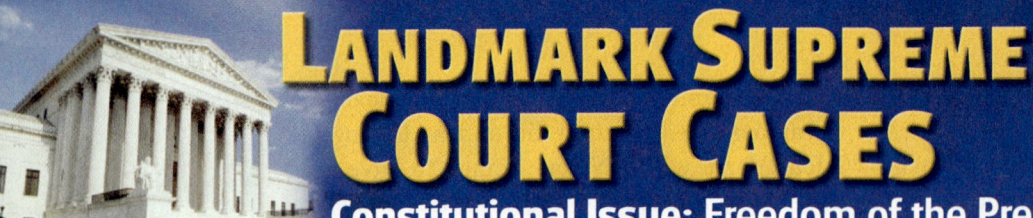

ST 1.2 Analyze the decisions leading to major turning points in United States history, comparing alternative courses of action, and hypothesizing, within the context of the historic period, about what might have happened if the decision had been different.

New York Times Co. v. United States (1971)

Why It Matters This case considered whether newspapers could be prevented from publishing information that the government did not want disclosed to the public on the grounds that it might harm national security.

Background of the Case

In 1971 the *New York Times* began publishing portions of a secret Defense Department study of the Vietnam War. The Pentagon Papers had been leaked by former Defense Department economist Daniel Ellsberg. The Nixon administration went to court to prevent publication of the information.

The Decision

In its ruling the Court noted the strong presumption that "prior restraint"—that is, prevention of speech or the publication of information—is unconstitutional. The government therefore had a "heavy burden" to show that blocking publication is justified. The government failed to do so, the Court held.

There were several separate concurring or dissenting opinions. Some justices argued that under the First Amendment the government can never restrict publication of news. Others argued that government sometimes has the right to keep certain matters secret in the interest of national security but that this was not such a case. One justice suggested that the publishers might be prosecuted but only after publication.

In the end, however, the ruling upheld the key role of the press in educating and informing the public:

> ❝ [T]he only effective restraint upon executive policy and power in the areas of national defense and international affairs may lie in an enlightened citizenry—in an informed and critical public opinion which alone can here protect the values of democratic government. ❞
>
> — Justice Potter Stewart

THE IMPACT TODAY The issue of prior restraint of news and the possible threat to national security in the release of certain information in newspapers and other news outlets remains a difficult one. Since the terrorist attacks of September 11, 2001, for example, the government and the press have differed over ways to manage the release of information about the nation's ongoing fight against terrorism.

CRITICAL THINKING

go.hrw.com
Research Online
Keyword: SS Court

1. **Analyze the Impact** Using the keyword above, read about *New York Times Co.* v. *Sullivan,* another important First Amendment case involving the same newspaper. What is the ruling of the case? Why did the Court allow the media greater flexibility in writing about public figures than in stories about private individuals?

2. **You Be the Judge** The events of September 11, 2001, and the ongoing war on terrorism have raised new concerns about the proper balance between governmental secrecy and open disclosure and discussion in the press. How might these contemporary concerns affect the decision in a case like *New York Times Co.* v. *United States* today? Explain your answer in a short paragraph.

From Watergate to Ford

BEFORE YOU READ

MAIN IDEA

The Nixon presidency became bogged down in scandal, leading to the first presidential resignation in American history and the administration of Gerald Ford.

READING FOCUS

1. What were the main events of the presidential election of 1972?
2. How did the Watergate scandal unfold?
3. Who was Gerald Ford, and what were the highlights of his presidency?

KEY TERMS AND PEOPLE

Watergate scandal
executive privilege
Saturday night massacre
transcript
Spiro T. Agnew
Gerald R. Ford
Nelson Rockefeller

 3.2 Research and analyze the major themes and developments in New York State and United States history (e.g., colonization and settlement; Revolution and New National Period; immigration; expansion and reform era; Civil War and Reconstruction; the American labor movement; Great Depression; World Wars; contemporary United States).

A Piece of Tape Brings Down a Presidency

 **THE INSIDE STORY**

How did a little piece of tape trigger one of history's great scandals? When security guard Frank Wills first noticed the piece of tape covering a door latch in the garage of the Watergate hotel-office complex on June 17, 1972, he was not alarmed. He figured that someone during the day had probably been making deliveries and had wanted to keep the door from locking. Wills removed the tape and continued to patrol the building.

Later, however, Wills returned to the door and checked it again. Someone had replaced the tape he had removed earlier. This time, Wills called the police.

When the police arrived, they began their search for the intruders they suspected were in the building. Eventually, they surprised a group of five men who had broken into the offices of the Democratic National Committee, which were housed in the Watergate. The group was in the process of installing or repairing advanced eavesdropping equipment. They also had cameras and appeared to be planning to photograph the contents of filing cabinets.

It was not clear at first exactly why the burglars had broken into the office. Nor was it known right away whether they had been working on behalf of some other people or group. In fact, many dismissed the incident as nothing more than the bumbling handiwork of petty crooks. As you will read, however, the story caught the attention of reporters at the *Washington Post*. As a result of their efforts, Watergate would soon be a household word. ◢

▶ **Frank Wills made the discovery that led to the arrest of the Watergate burglars.**

The Election of 1972

Richard Nixon's first term had been eventful. Though he had experienced his share of troubles, Nixon had also enjoyed many triumphs.

This was fortunate for Nixon, for he was deeply concerned about his political future. Indeed, many of his first-term actions had been aimed at shoring up support with the voters. Having both lost and won the presidency by tiny margins, he was leaving nothing to chance in 1972. In fact, he was prepared to support illegal actions to help ensure re-election.

Nixon had a well-earned reputation as a political scrapper from his days in Congress. At times Nixon's supporters used underhanded tactics during the first term of his presidency.

To do his political dirty work, Nixon advisers John Ehrlichman and H. R. Haldeman had created a group that came to be known as the "Plumbers." Their job was to respond to "leaks" of secret information—and to investigate Nixon's political enemies.

In 1971, for example, the Plumbers broke into the offices of Daniel Ellsberg's psychiatrist. Ellsberg was a former government official who had leaked key documents about the Vietnam War to the *New York Times*. These were the so-called Pentagon Papers. The Plumbers had hoped to find information they could use to embarrass Ellsberg and damage his reputation and credibility.

In 1972 Nixon and his team turned their attention to the upcoming presidential election. Nixon's chances for re-election seemed very good. Many of his recent moves, such as his trip to China, had been highly popular with the voters.

Still, Nixon's team did not rest easy. In early 1972, they hatched a plan to send a team of burglars to break into the offices of the Democratic National Committee at the Watergate hotel-office complex. The purpose of the burglary appeared to be to collect information about Democratic strategy that might be useful in the president's re-election campaign.

As you have read, the Watergate plot ended with the arrest of five men. The break-in and arrest barely made the news at the time. Even after facts began to emerge linking the burglars to the president, national news organizations continued to give the story little coverage.

The story did not die, however. Two young reporters on the staff of the *Washington Post*, Bob Woodward and Carl Bernstein, continued to investigate the break-in. They began to uncover troubling facts about the burglars' links to the White House. In August they reported that one of the Watergate burglars had received a $25,000 check that had been originally sent to the president's re-election campaign. By October the *Post* was reporting that the Watergate break-in was actually part of a widespread spying effort by members of the Nixon campaign.

TIME LINE

Watergate

June 17, 1972 Burglars were caught during a break-in at the Watergate (left).

June 18, 1972 Carl Bernstein and Bob Woodward helped report the first in a series of stories on the break-in (below).

November 7, 1972 Nixon won re-election in a landslide (above).

May 18, 1973 The Senate Watergate Committee began televised hearings into the scandal.

July 13, 1973 Alexander Butterfield revealed the existence of the White House taping system.

If the public noticed the *Post* stories at this time, it did not <u>affect</u> their voting. In November Nixon was handed one of the most overwhelming victories in U.S. history. His opponent, South Dakota senator and Vietnam War critic George McGovern, managed to carry only Massachusetts and the District of Columbia.

READING CHECK **Making Inferences** What can you infer about Nixon's level of confidence about the election of 1972 based on his actions?

The Scandal Unfolds

With his re-election, Nixon may have believed any trouble related to the Watergate break-in was behind him. He was wrong. Indeed, the scandal was just about to break.

By February 1973 seven men involved with the break-in had been convicted or had pleaded guilty to a variety of crimes. Among them were several officials who had worked in the White House and for Nixon's re-election campaign. During the burglars' trials questions emerged about what other White House officials may have been involved in illegal activities. People began to wonder whether Nixon had known about the wrongdoing taking place around him and helped to cover it up.

Meanwhile, the *Washington Post* continued to investigate the story. Now the public—and members of Congress—were paying attention to the stories.

In response to the growing controversy, Nixon ordered his staff to conduct a full investigation. In April 1973 Haldeman and Erlichman resigned from their White House jobs, as did Nixon's attorney general. In addition, Nixon fired John Dean, the lawyer he had appointed to investigate what was now called the <mark>Watergate scandal</mark>. The moves were meant to signal the president's tough action against wrongdoing. "There can be no whitewash at the White House," he declared.

These actions calmed many Republicans in Congress. For example, Representative Gerald Ford praised Nixon for "cleaning house." He declared, "I am absolutely positive he had nothing to do with this mess."

Democrats were not so sure. They demanded that the president appoint someone who was not part of his own administration to look into the scandal. This sort of independent investigator is now known as a special prosecutor. In May Nixon agreed to take this step. Nixon's attorney general Elliot Richardson appointed a Harvard Law School professor named Archibald Cox to the job.

Butterfield's bombshell Also in May, a Senate committee began its own investigation. The committee held televised hearings. Millions of viewers tuned in to get answers to the famous question of Tennessee Republican senator Howard Baker: "What did the president know, and when did he know it?"

ACADEMIC VOCABULARY
affect to change or influence something

THE IMPACT TODAY

Government
In May 2005 Americans learned the name of a key but secret figure in the Watergate story as reported by the *Washington Post.* Mark Felt, a former top FBI official, was revealed as the secret source for many *Washington Post* stories about the scandal.

October 20, 1973
In the Saturday night massacre, Nixon fired the special prosecutor.

April 30, 1974
The White House released edited transcripts of the tapes (left).

July 24, 1974
The Supreme Court ruled that the White House must turn over the tapes.

August 8, 1974
Richard Nixon announced his resignation from the presidency (right).

Washington Star-News
ON TV AT 9 TONIGHT
Nixon Resigning

Skills FOCUS **INTERPRETING TIME LINES**
Which event suggests that the public was not immediately concerned by the events of June 1972?
See **Skills Handbook**, p. H14

Political Cartoon

At the height of the Watergate scandal in 1973, President Richard Nixon held a press conference to declare his innocence in the case. This political cartoon appeared shortly after that press conference.

President Nixon was famous for raising his arms and making the "V for Victory" sign with his fingers.

A sanctuary refers to a safe place for someone fleeing the law.

Speaking of sanctuaries . . .

COPYRIGHT 1973, LOS ANGELES TIMES SYNDICATE. REPRINTED WITH PERMISSION.

Skills FOCUS — READING LIKE A HISTORIAN

1. **Interpreting Political Cartoons** What is the "sanctuary" that Nixon is hiding behind?
2. **Identifying Points of View** What is the message that the artist is trying to send?

See **Skills Handbook**, pp. H28–H29, H31

The hearings produced plenty of drama. For example, early in June, John Dean told the committee that he had talked many times with Nixon about Watergate and its cover-up. These statements appeared to go against the president's own words. Then on July 16, 1973, a former presidential aide named Alexander Butterfield revealed that since 1971 Nixon had tape-recorded all conversations in his offices.

The Saturday night massacre News of the existence of White House tapes caused great excitement. Investigators realized that the recordings might answer many outstanding questions about the president's actions.

Nixon, however, did not want to give up the tapes. He argued that the constitutional separation of powers and the principle of executive privilege gave him the right to withhold them. **Executive privilege** holds that a president must be able to keep official conversations and meetings private. Such guarantees of privacy, the thinking goes, help ensure that the president gets open and honest advice.

Investigators rejected Nixon's claim of executive privilege. They argued that the tapes they were interested in hearing did not involve official presidential business. Rather, the investigators wanted to listen to Nixon's discussions of political matters—his re-election campaign—and possible illegal actions. Such conversations were not protected by executive privilege, investigators claimed.

Special Prosecutor Cox and the Senate Watergate committee continued to seek the tapes. They both issued subpoenas demanding Nixon hand them over. A subpoena is a legal order requiring the recipient to bring a certain item to court.

Nixon's response was harsh. In the so-called **Saturday night massacre**, he ordered attorney general Elliot Richardson to fire Special Prosecutor Cox. Richardson refused to do so and instead quit his job. Then Nixon ordered Richardson's assistant to fire Cox. He also refused and resigned. Nixon finally persuaded the third-ranking official in the Justice Department to fire Cox.

Many people were stunned by Nixon's actions. Not only did his innocence seem in doubt, it appeared that the president was challenging the constitutional system itself.

" Whether ours shall continue to be a government of laws and not of men is now for Congress and ultimately the American people to decide. "

—Archibald Cox, October 20, 1973

The crisis continues Public confidence in the president was very low. Yet a determined Nixon continued to deny his involvement in either the break-in or the cover-up. "People have got to know whether or not their president is a crook," he said. "Well, I'm not a crook." Meanwhile, he continued to delay release of the tapes. The White House also revealed that a critical, 18-minute portion of the tapes had been unexplainably erased.

Nixon's presidency was now in serious trouble. There were calls for impeachment and for Nixon to resign as president. As the pressure mounted in the spring of 1974, Nixon released some transcripts of the tapes. A **transcript** is a written record of a spoken event. Though Nixon denied it, the pages seemed to contain many suggestions that he had known about and covered up illegal activity. At the same time, the release of the transcripts did not satisfy investigators. They continued legal action aimed at gaining access to the tapes themselves.

Nixon resigns The Supreme Court of the United States finally settled the question of the White House tapes. In late July the Court ruled that Nixon had to obey the subpoenas and produce the tapes. Without waiting for the president to comply, the House Judiciary Committee voted to recommend impeachment of the president. The reasons included Nixon's alleged obstruction of justice and his failure to obey subpoenas.

Nixon could see that his support in Congress was thin. He must also have known that the tapes would reveal clear evidence of his own wrongdoing. On August 8, 1974, he spoke to the American people. For the first time in American history, a president resigned the office. "By taking this action," he said, "I hope that I will have hastened the start of the process of healing . . ."

READING CHECK **Sequencing** What was the key sequence of events as the Watergate scandal unfolded?

Gerald Ford's Presidency

Watergate was only one of the problems facing Richard Nixon. In early 1973, just as the Watergate scandal was about to explode, investigators began exploring the activities of Vice President **Spiro T. Agnew**, former governor of Maryland. Agnew was eventually accused of taking payments in return for political favors and cheating on his taxes. After pleading no contest to the tax charge, he resigned in disgrace. Agnew became only the second U.S. vice president to resign.

To replace Agnew, Nixon chose the Republican leader in the House of Representatives, **Gerald R. Ford**. With Nixon's resignation, Ford became president. He was the first person ever to become president without having been elected either president or vice president.

At his swearing in on August 9, 1974, Ford noted, "I am acutely aware you have not elected me as your President." Still, he urged the nation and the government to move forward.

" My fellow Americans, our long national nightmare is over.

Our Constitution works; our great Republic is a government of laws and not of men. Here the people rule. "

—Gerald R. Ford, August 9, 1974

Ford appointed **Nelson Rockefeller**, former Republican governor of New York, as vice president.

Ford pardons Nixon Less than a month after taking office, President Ford granted a full pardon to Richard Nixon for any crime he may have committed. A pardon is a formal, legal forgiveness for a crime. Ford's action ensured that Nixon could not be tried in court or punished for any of his actions involving the Watergate affair. Many Americans reacted to the pardon with outrage. Some even wondered

Ford said he pardoned Nixon to shift attention "from the pursuit of a fallen President to the pursuit of the urgent needs of a rising nation." *Why did many people question this decision?*

FOCUS ON NEW YORK

GOVERNMENT
Nelson Rockefeller led the liberal wing of the national Republican Party. During his four terms as New York governor, he helped expand the state university system and establish a modern highway network. Both Ford and Rockefeller became vice president through the Twenty-fifth Amendment, which holds that when the office is vacant, the president may appoint a nominee to fill the position.

openly whether Ford had promised to pardon Nixon prior to his resignation.

There was no evidence of such a deal, and Ford denied it flatly. He also took the unusual step of testifying about the pardon before a congressional committee.

Ford as president Ford, a Republican, found that his job as president was made more difficult by the fact that the Democrats controlled Congress. For example, he believed that inflation was a serious problem for the economy. To help fight it, he proposed cutting the amount of money that the U.S. government spent—spending that he felt drove prices even higher.

Congress, however, passed many spending bills against his wishes. Ford used his power to veto these spending bills on dozens of occasions. In spite of these efforts, inflation continued at a high rate.

In foreign affairs, President Ford had to overcome problems of the past. The experience of the Vietnam War had caused Congress to place limits on the powers of the president. In 1975 South Vietnam was about to fall to North Vietnam. Ford tried to send aid to the South Vietnamese, but Congress blocked this effort. The president did, however, help nearly 250,000 people flee South Vietnam before the arrival of the Communists.

Congress also refused to allow Ford to aid forces fighting Cuban-backed Communists in the African country of Angola. Ford complained about the loss of presidential power, but he seemed powerless in the matter.

Ford was able to take action when a Cambodian naval ship seized the American cargo ship *Mayaguez* and its 39-man crew. A military raid did recover the ship and crew, though 41 Americans died in the operation.

One of Ford's first acts as president had been to announce that Henry Kissinger would remain as his secretary of state. Ford also worked to maintain the Nixon policy of détente. He and Soviet leader Leonid Brezhnev agreed to new and larger limits on nuclear weapons.

Also during Ford's presidency, the United States and the Soviet Union worked jointly on a space project. The highlight was a meeting in space between U.S. and Soviet astronauts.

An election challenge In spite of his successes, Ford faced serious political problems. In the 1976 election, he faced opposition even from within his own party. In the primary elections to determine the Republican nominee, former California governor Ronald Reagan did well.

Ford won the nomination, but only after a close struggle. Clearly, the contest for the White House, in which he would face Governor Jimmy Carter of Georgia, would be difficult.

READING CHECK **Evaluating** How did the Watergate scandal affect Gerald Ford's presidency?

SECTION 2 ASSESSMENT

go.hrw.com
Online Quiz
Keyword: SD7 HP31

Reviewing Ideas, Terms, and People

1. **a. Describe** What were the circumstances of the break-in at the Watergate?
   b. Draw Conclusions Why might members of one political campaign want to spy on or steal information from another campaign?

2. **a. Define** Write a brief definition of each of the following terms: special prosecutor, **executive privilege**, subpoena
   b. Make Generalizations Why do you think the **Saturday night massacre** troubled many Americans?
   c. Elaborate Why do you think many people accused Nixon of acting as if he were above the law?

3. **a. Recall** How did the decision to **pardon** Nixon affect Ford?
   b. Make Inferences What can you infer from the fact that Ford issued so many vetoes?

Critical Thinking

4. **Identifying Cause and Effect** Copy the chart below and use information from the section to give effects of the causes given.

Cause	Effect
Watergate burglars arrested	
Butterfield reveals existence of tapes	
Nixon ordered to hand over tapes	
Ford pardons Nixon	

FOCUS ON SPEAKING

5. **Persuasive** Deliver a speech in which you argue either for or against President Ford's decision to pardon former President Nixon. Be sure to use information from the section in making your argument.

Carter's Presidency

BEFORE YOU READ

MAIN IDEA

Jimmy Carter used his reputation for honesty to win the presidency in 1976, but he soon met challenges that required other qualities as well.

READING FOCUS

1. What were some of the difficult domestic challenges facing Carter and the nation in the late 1970s?
2. What were Carter's greatest foreign-policy triumphs and challenges?
3. How did international crises affect Carter's presidency?

KEY TERMS AND PEOPLE

James Earl "Jimmy" Carter
SALT II
Camp David Accords
Ayatollah Ruhollah Khomeini

PI 2.4 Understand the interrelationships between world events and developments in New York State and the United States (e.g., causes for immigration, economic opportunities, human rights abuses, and tyranny versus freedom).

THE INSIDE STORY

How can the world's most powerful man show a common touch? In American politics, an inaugural parade is typically a moment of great pomp and circumstance. But for **James Earl "Jimmy" Carter**, it was another opportunity to remind the American people that he would be a different kind of leader from the ones they had been used to in their recent, difficult past. It was a message Carter had stressed throughout his successful 1976 presidential campaign against President Gerald Ford.

Following his swearing in—at which the new president had asked to use the nickname Jimmy rather than his more formal, full name—Carter set off on the ceremonial trip down Pennsylvania Avenue from the Capitol to the White House. Jimmy Carter, however, would not make this trip in the traditional way. Rather than riding in a limousine, separated from the people by a layer of steel and bulletproof glass, he would walk. Surprising all observers, Carter, new first lady Rosalynn Carter, and their young daughter, Amy, left their limousine behind and strode among the crowd. All the while, the new leader of the most powerful nation on earth waved to the people and flashed his warm smile.

Carter's inaugural walk was without precedent in modern American political history. It was clear that he aimed to be a different type of president—one who did not consider himself above the people. Later, Carter would reinforce this message by refusing to allow the traditional playing of the song "Hail to the Chief" to announce his arrival at important events.

Jimmy Carter succeeded at creating the image of a down-to-earth, honest man. But he would soon learn that a reputation for trustworthiness was not enough to lead the nation through difficult times.

WALKING to the White House

▼ The Carters charmed the nation by walking to the White House on inauguration day.

Oil Consumption

In 1973 an oil embargo by Arab nations and higher prices led to long lines at American gas stations. Then in 1979 another energy crisis began.

A revolution in Iran stopped oil exports from that country. Exports later resumed but at a lower level than before. Other countries raised the price of their oil exports too, and prices skyrocketed in the United States. In response, President Carter urged Americans to consume less oil.

Although many people have worked during the last few decades to limit their use of oil, consumption has continued to increase. Today the United States has less than 5 percent of the world's population but uses a quarter of its oil. Many people fear that the nation depends too heavily on foreign oil.

Most nations use oil primarily for heat and power. In the United States, however, transportation accounts for about two-thirds of oil use. During the Iraq War and following Hurricanes Katrina and Rita in 2005, rising gasoline costs troubled many consumers.

Making Inferences How might an oil embargo affect the United States today?

Cars streaming through their daily rush-hour commute in New York City

Challenges Facing the Nation

As he strode along the parade route on inauguration day, Jimmy Carter seemed in many ways to be the right man at the right time for the United States. The former peanut farmer and Georgia governor came across as an honest man of deep religious faith. He had never worked in Washington, D.C. His simple promise—"I'll never lie to you"—was just what the weary American public wanted to hear.

Carter wasted no time trying to help the nation heal some of the wounds from the past. A day after being sworn in as president, he issued a pardon to thousands of American men who had avoided the draft during the Vietnam War. The pardon enabled many men who had fled the country to return home without fear of being charged with a crime. Not everyone supported this action. Yet with it, Carter fulfilled one of his campaign promises.

The economy and energy Carter also tried to tackle problems in two other areas that had troubled earlier administrations. One was the economy. Inflation and unemployment stood at unacceptably high levels. Carter tried to address both concerns. During his time in office, the economy added many new jobs. Yet, as you will read, Carter was unable to bring down inflation. Indeed, the problem only seemed to get worse.

Carter had more success in addressing the nation's energy problems. Recalling the oil crisis of 1973–1974 and fearing another one, he made the development of a national energy policy a top priority.

HISTORY'S VOICES

❝I know some of you may doubt that we face real energy shortages. The 1973 gasoline lines are gone, and our homes are warm again. But our energy problem is worse tonight than it was in 1973 or a few weeks ago in the dead of winter. It is worse because more waste has occurred, and more time has passed by without our planning for the future.❞

—Jimmy Carter, April 18, 1977

Carter's goals included easing dependence on foreign oil through energy conservation, developing new energy supplies, and loosening government regulation of the American oil industry. To help develop and carry out his new policies, he pushed for the establishment of a new cabinet-level Department of Energy.

Carter also sought to change the habits and attitudes of the American people. He urged Americans to conserve fuel. Citizens were asked to turn down their heat and air conditioning and drive fewer miles. Car buyers were urged to buy models that offered greater fuel efficiency. U.S. automakers were offered incentives to build cars that met new, tougher fuel-efficiency standards.

Carter promoted the development of alternative energy sources, such as solar and wind power. He promoted laws by which Americans were able to lower their taxes by installing energy-saving equipment in their homes.

These and other Carter energy policies were successful at helping reduce American dependence on foreign oil. American production of energy also increased under Carter.

Environmental concerns Carter was concerned not only about energy but also about the environment. He believed that conserving fuel was a key way to avoid "mounting pressure to plunder the environment." In order to prevent this from happening, the president led a years-long battle to win passage of the Alaska National Interest Lands Conservation Act. This law helped protect more than 100 million acres of land and doubled the size of the nation's park and wildlife refuge system.

But the Carter years were also marred by environmental questions and crises. In 1979 a mishap at a nuclear power plant located at Three Mile Island in Pennsylvania terrified the nation. For a time, officials seemed unsure how to correct problems that threatened a massive release of radiation into the environment. Some people in the immediate area of the plant were evacuated. In the end, very little radiation was released, and no one suffered any ill effects. However, public concern about the safety of nuclear power continued to grow.

Another environmental disaster was uncovered at Love Canal in New York. There, long-buried chemicals left behind by a chemical company began seeping up through the ground. Exposure to the chemicals was linked to the high rates of birth defects in the community. To solve the problem, the state of New York bought the homes of some 200 residents. The government then began the costly task of cleaning up the mess. Experts warned that there were likely many more toxic waste sites like Love Canal around the country.

READING CHECK Identifying Supporting **Details** Find two examples of how energy created major challenges for Carter and the nation.

Carter's Foreign Policy

Jimmy Carter came to office with no real foreign-policy experience and no background in federal government. He brought his own ideas to the field of foreign affairs with mixed results.

Carter also brought some new faces. Among them was Andrew Young. An African American with a background in the civil rights movement, Young served as American ambassador to the United Nations. His appointment helped highlight Carter's strong civil rights background. Indeed, Carter made dozens of top-level appointments of African Americans, women, and Hispanic Americans.

A focus on human rights During the presidential campaign, Carter had promised that the concept of human rights would be at the forefront of his foreign policy. This promise was repeated in his inaugural address when he declared, "Our commitment to human rights must be absolute." By human rights Carter meant the basic ideas of human freedom as outlined in the United Nations Declaration of Human Rights. For Carter, friends and enemies alike would be expected to uphold the highest standards in the treatment of their citizens.

ACADEMIC VOCABULARY

efficiency the ability to produce a desired result with little waste

THE IMPACT TODAY

Science and Technology
The Three Mile Island incident helped dampen interest in nuclear energy. Throughout the 1980s, 1990s, and early 2000s, the United States planned or built hardly any new nuclear power facilities.

Andrew Young at the UN

Andrew Young first rose to prominence during the civil rights movement in the 1950s and 1960s. *Why do you think Young's background helped prepare him to represent Carter's foreign policy?*

THE CAMP DAVID ACCORDS

The Camp David Accords were a major breakthrough in relations between Egypt and Israel, two countries that had fought several costly, bloody wars. Anwar el-Sadat, Jimmy Carter, and Menachem Begin (left to right) shake hands at the successful conclusion of their meeting at Camp David. Key parts of the accords declared that:

- Egypt and Israel, along with Jordan and Palestinian representatives, would agree to work to resolve questions about the Palestinians' future.

- Israel and Egypt would agree to work to negotiate a peace treaty.

- Egypt and Israel would agree to grant each other full recognition.

Soviet relations The Soviet Union was one target of President Carter's criticism about human rights violations. In a letter written to Soviet leader Leonid Brezhnev just days after taking office, Carter mentioned his concerns. Brezhnev's response politely but firmly declared that each side should stay out of the other's internal affairs.

In spite of disagreements over human rights, American and Soviet negotiators did conclude a treaty in 1979 known as **SALT II**. Talks on this treaty had begun at the end of SALT I, which you read about in Section 1. SALT II called for limits on certain kinds of nuclear weapons.

The Panama Canal treaties Another early Carter foreign-policy effort involved the Panama Canal. American control of the canal had been the source of conflict between the United States and Panama for some time. In 1977 Carter and Panama's leader reached an agreement by which Panama would take control of the canal by the end of 1999. The Senate narrowly approved the treaties Carter had negotiated. For many Americans, however, the loss of control of the canal represented a decline in American power.

Recognizing China In 1979 Carter took the final step in a process that had begun during the Nixon administration. He formally recognized the government of the Communist People's Republic of China. This move required the United States to formally end its official recognition of the Republic of China on Taiwan, which claimed to be the true Chinese government. Under Carter's action, however, the United States would officially recognize only one China—the Communist People's Republic.

The Camp David Accords Carter's greatest foreign-policy achievement centered on the long-standing conflict between Israel and Egypt. The two nations had fought frequently in recent decades. Fighting had occurred in 1967 and in the Yom Kippur War. In the aftermath of the 1973 war, Israel still occupied Egyptian territory on the Sinai Peninsula. Egypt still did not recognize Israel's right to exist. These were just some of the issues dividing the nations.

In 1978 Carter invited Egyptian president Anwar el-Sadat (AHN-wahr el-suh-DAHT) and Israeli prime minister Menachem Begin (men-AH-kem BAY-gin) to explore solutions to their bitter divisions. The meeting took place at Camp David, a presidential retreat located in Maryland. At the meeting, Carter painstakingly guided Sadat and Begin to a historic agreement. This came to be known as the **Camp David Accords**. For their efforts, Begin and Sadat were awarded the Nobel Peace Prize in 1979.

READING CHECK **Summarizing** What were the main highlights of Carter's foreign policy?

International Crises

In his first years in office, Carter enjoyed some success and suffered through some difficulties. In 1979, however, a series of events occurred that seemed to overwhelm his presidency.

Soviets invade Afghanistan

In 1978 the government of Afghanistan was toppled in a coup. The Communist leaders who took power were friendly to the Soviet Union. Yet this new pro-Soviet Afghan government was not stable. When it showed signs of crumbling in late 1979, the Soviets invaded. Their goal was to ensure continued Communist rule in Afghanistan.

The Soviet invasion of Afghanistan caused great anxiety within the United States. The attack not only threatened the U.S.–Soviet relationship. It also called into question Carter's ability to respond effectively to Soviet aggression. Carter's national security adviser summarized the problem in a memo to the president days after the invasion: "Soviet 'deci-siveness'," he wrote, "will be contrasted with our restraint, which will no longer be labeled as prudent but increasingly as timid."

Several days after the invasion, Carter detailed the American response. It included the decision to block shipment of grain to the Soviet Union. In addition, Carter announced that the United States would not take part in the Olympics, set to take place in the Soviet Union in the summer of 1980.

Both the Olympic boycott and the grain embargo were unpopular with the public. To some they appeared to hurt the United States at least as much as they hurt the Soviet Union. As a result, Carter and the United States appeared weak.

Iranian hostage crisis

While the Afghanistan crisis upset many Americans, it was not the major news story of the day. That story came from the country of Iran.

Early in 1979, a revolution in Iran had led to the overthrow of that country's long-time

---

COUNTERPOINTS

Resolving the Hostage Crisis

National security adviser Zbigniew Brzezinski (ZBIG-nyoo bruzh-IN-skee) focused on U.S. interests.

❝ [I]t is important that we get our people back. But [our] greater responsibility is to protect the honor and dignity of our country and its foreign policy interests. At some point that greater responsibility could become more important than the safety of our diplomats. I hope we never have to choose between the hostages and our nation's honor in the world, but… [we] must be prepared for that occurrence. ❞

Zbigniew Brzezinski, 1979

Negotiation and compromise were well-known trademarks of Secretary of State Cyrus Vance.

❝ The President and this nation will ultimately be judged by our restraint in the face of provocation, and on the safe return of our hostages. We have to keep looking for ways to reach Khomeini and peacefully resolve this. ❞

Cyrus Vance, 1979

Skills FOCUS | **READING LIKE A HISTORIAN**

Identifying Points of View When the Carter administration launched a military mission to rescue the hostages, Vance resigned his post. How do the quotes help you to understand this fact?

See **Skills Handbook**, pp. H28–H29

ruler, known as the shah. The shah had long enjoyed American support, but among his people he had built a reputation for brutal repression. After his overthrow, Iran came under the control of an Islamic religious leader known as the **Ayatollah Ruhollah Khomeini** (eye-uh-TOHL-uh roo-HAHL-uh koh-MAYN-ee). Khomeini preached a strongly anti-American message.

In October 1979 the American government allowed the shah to enter the United States to receive treatment for cancer. This action enraged many Iranians. On November 4 a mob attacked the American embassy in Tehran, Iran's capital. They captured several dozen American employees. It soon became clear that Iran's leaders supported this attack.

In the United States, the hostage-taking was greeted with outrage. Newscasts fueled American anger by showing nightly scenes of Iranian protesters burning American flags.

President Carter appeared powerless to end the Iranian hostage crisis. His efforts to negotiate the safe return of the hostages went nowhere. He then approved a military mission to rescue the hostages. This failed tragically when mechanical problems led to a helicopter crash that killed eight soldiers. The scenes of smoldering American wreckage in the Iranian desert hurt Carter's chances for re-election.

A crisis of confidence The hostage crisis dragged on throughout the presidential election year of 1980. To make matters worse for Carter, the events in Iran had disrupted the production of oil there. As a result, gasoline prices shot up in 1979. This helped drive up prices for many goods in the United States. Inflation soared. The economy struggled badly.

Carter was in serious trouble politically. Even he seemed to recognize the threat as he described the downcast mood of the country in a major speech.

HISTORY'S VOICES

❝It is a crisis of confidence.

It is a crisis that strikes at the very heart and soul and spirit of our national will. We can see this crisis in the growing doubt about the meaning of our own lives and in the loss of a unity and purpose for our nation.❞

—Jimmy Carter, July 15, 1979

Carter's view of the mind-set of the nation was not incorrect. What he did not realize was that many voters held him responsible for this crisis of confidence.

READING CHECK **Making Inferences** Why did the events of 1979 and 1980 seem to overwhelm Carter's presidency?

SECTION 3 ASSESSMENT

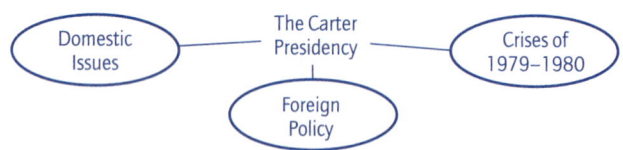

go.hrw.com
Online Quiz
Keyword: SD7 HP31

Reviewing Ideas, Terms, and People

1. a. Identify What were the key domestic issues facing the Carter administration?
b. Explain Explain how energy was at the center of so many of the challenges facing the United States in the late 1970s.
c. Predict How successful do you think President Carter would be in his call for the American people to change their energy habits?

2. a. Recall What was the guiding principle behind Jimmy Carter's foreign policy?
b. Draw Conclusions Why do you think the **Camp David Accords** are considered Carter's greatest foreign-policy success?
c. Elaborate How did Carter's focus on human rights in foreign policy differ from the policy of realpolitik stressed by Nixon and Ford?

3. a. Identify Who was **Ayatollah Ruhollah Khomeini**?
b. Make Generalizations How did the American people interpret Carter's responses to the crises of 1979–1980?

Critical Thinking

4. Identifying the Main Idea Copy the chart below and use information from the section to record details that support the main idea of the section.

Domestic Issues — The Carter Presidency — Crises of 1979–1980 — Foreign Policy

 **FOCUS ON WRITING**

5. Descriptive Using information from the section, write a brief description of what you think Jimmy Carter was like as a president. Include information about how you think his style and personality helped and hurt him.

Regents of the University of California v. *Bakke* (1978)

Why It Matters Affirmative action programs have helped create opportunities for many minorities. However, favoring a minority applicant for a job or for a spot in graduate school may also mean that a qualified majority applicant will be turned down. *Bakke* was the first Supreme Court case to consider the constitutionality of what is called "reverse discrimination."

Background of the Case

A white male named Alan Bakke applied to the medical school of the University of California at Davis and was not accepted. The school had a special program that set aside a certain number of spots for minority applicants. Under this program, some minority students with lower qualifications than Bakke were admitted to the school. Bakke sued, and the Supreme Court of California agreed that it was unconstitutional to discriminate in favor of the minority applicants. The university appealed to the Supreme Court.

The Decision

In a 5–4 ruling, the Court found that the University's "set-aside" program was unconstitutional because it totally excluded white applicants from consideration for certain spots. The Court ordered Bakke admitted to the university. The Court also held that the school could consider race as one factor in future admissions decisions.

Bakke did not resolve the question of just what role affirmative action could play in university admissions. This means that the *Bakke* decision did not offer clear guidance on how affirmative action could properly be used. However, the opinion did help focus national attention on this difficult question.

THE IMPACT TODAY Affirmative action programs such as those that led to the *Bakke* case have played a part in increasing diversity in many graduate school programs, including the law school at the University of Michigan. (The photo above is from a class at that university.) The question of just where the line lies between reasonable affirmative action and improper reverse discrimination continues to stir controversy in the United States.

go.hrw.com
Research Online
Keyword: SS Court

CRITICAL THINKING

1. **Analyze the Impact** Using the keyword above, read about the Supreme Court's decision in *Sweatt v. Painter* (1950). How did the issues in *Sweatt* differ from the issues in *Bakke*? What changes had taken place in the country between the decisions?

2. **You Be the Judge** After *Bakke*, the University of Michigan Law School began giving extra consideration in the admissions process to African Americans, Hispanic Americans, and Native Americans. These applicants therefore had a greater chance of admission than students with similar qualifications from other groups. Is this policy constitutional? Write a short paragraph explaining your answer.

The Watergate Crisis

Historical Context The documents below provide information about taped conversations in the White House, which became an important part of the Watergate investigation.

Task Examine the documents and answer the questions that follow. Then write an essay on the proposed topic. Use facts from the documents and from the chapter to support the position you take in your thesis statement.

ST 4.3 Develop hypotheses about important events, eras, or issues; move from chronicling to explaining historical events and issues; use information collected from diverse sources to produce cogently written reports and document-based essays.

DOCUMENT 1

The Gallup Organization is a polling group. One of the statistics they regularly track is a president's job-approval rating—the percentage of people who agree with the president's actions and decisions. This graph shows changes in job-approval ratings for President Nixon during the Watergate crisis.

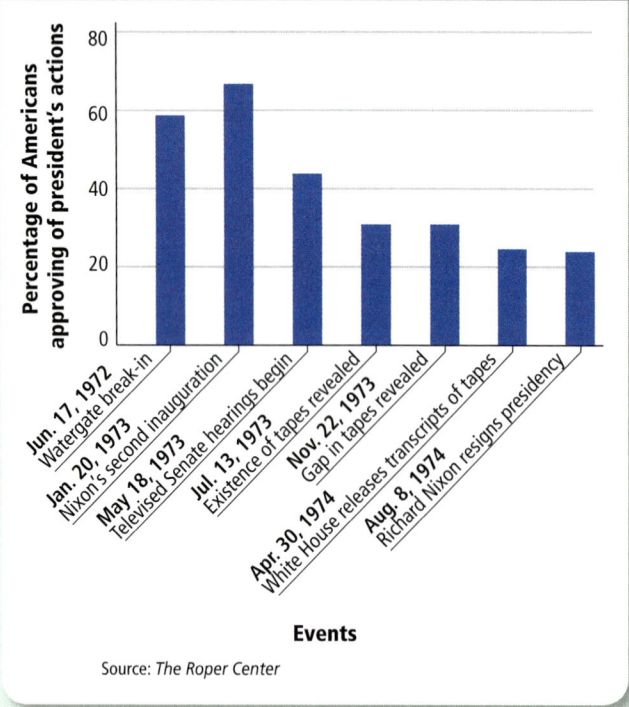

PRESIDENTIAL APPROVAL RATINGS AND THE WATERGATE CRISIS

Percentage of Americans approving of president's actions

Events

Source: *The Roper Center*

DOCUMENT 2

On April 29, 1974, President Nixon addressed the nation. He talked about the subpoena demanding additional transcripts for tape recordings made in the White House and his decision to obey the subpoena.

"Ever since the existence of the White House taping system was first made known last summer, I have tried vigorously to guard the privacy of the tapes. I have been well aware that my effort to protect the confidentiality of Presidential conversations has heightened the sense of mystery about Watergate and, in fact, has caused increased suspicions of the President. Many people assume that the tapes must incriminate the President, or that otherwise, he would not insist on their privacy.

"But the problem I confronted was this: Unless a President can protect the privacy of the advice he gets, he cannot get the advice he needs . . .

I want there to be no question remaining about the fact that the President has nothing to hide in this matter . . . "

I realize that these transcripts will provide grist for many sensational stories in the press. Parts will seem to be contradictory with one another, and parts will be in conflict with some of the testimony given in the Senate Watergate committee hearings . . .

In giving you these records—blemishes and all—I am placing my trust in the basic fairness of the American people."

DOCUMENT 3

Cartoonist Herbert Block, known as Herblock, created many cartoons commenting on Nixon's presidency and the Watergate crisis. This cartoon ran in newspapers on May 24, 1974.

From *Herblock: A Cartoonist's Life* (TIMES BOOKS, 1998)

DOCUMENT 4

In this transcript of one of the White House tapes, President Richard Nixon talks with White House Chief of Staff H. R. Haldeman. The two men discuss the FBI investigation, specifically mentioning acting FBI director L. Patrick Gray and assistant director Mark Felt. This exchange, which took place on June 23, 1972, is known as the Smoking Gun conversation.

Haldeman: Okay—that's fine. Now, on the investigation, you know, the Democratic break-in thing, we're back to the—in the, the problem area because the FBI is not under control . . . and . . . their investigation is now leading into some productive areas . . . And, and it goes in some directions we don't want it to go. . . [T]he way to handle this now is for us to have [Deputy Director of the CIA Vernon A.] Walters call Pat Gray and just say, "Stay . . . out of this . . . this is ah, business here we don't want you to go any further on it." That's not an unusual development . . .

President: Um huh.

Haldeman: . . . and, uh, that would take care of it.

President: What about Pat Gray . . . ?

Haldeman: He'll call Mark Felt in . . . and say, "We've got a signal from across the river to, to put the hold on this." And that will fit rather well because the FBI agents who are working the case, at this point, feel that's what it is. This is CIA.

Skills Focus · READING LIKE A HISTORIAN

1. **a. Identify** Refer to Document 1. What event corresponds to Nixon's lowest job-approval rating?
   b. Interpret How did developments in Watergate affect public opinion regarding President Nixon?

2. **a. Identify** Refer to Document 2. Why does the president say he is releasing the transcripts?
   b. Evaluate Why do you think the president may have decided to make this speech to the American people?

3. **a. Identify** Refer to Document 3. What is shown in the cartoon?
   b. Elaborate What is the cartoonist's opinion of Nixon?

4. **a. Identify** Refer to Document 4. Why does Haldeman refer to the break-in as a "problem area"?
   b. Explain How does the president respond to Haldeman's suggestion to end the FBI investigation?
   c. Analyze Why was this called the Smoking Gun conversation?

5. **Document-Based Essay** Consider the question below and form a thesis statement. Using examples from Documents 1, 2, 3, and 4, create an outline and write a short essay supporting your position.
   What role did the White House tapes play in the Watergate crisis?

See **Skills Handbook**, pp. H17, H28–H29, H31

Visual Summary: A Search for Order

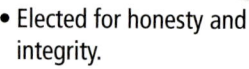

The Search for Order 1968–1980

Nixon's Presidency

- Conservative policies included New Federalism.
- Liberal policies included support for environment and wage and price controls.
- Sought détente with the Soviets, dialogue with Chinese.
- Shuttle diplomacy helped end Yom Kippur War and oil embargo.
- Moon landing a highlight.

Watergate and Ford

- Scandal with roots in the 1972 presidential campaign haunted Nixon.
- Nixon eventually forced to resign for lying and covering up White House crime.
- Ford became president, but lost support for pardoning Nixon.

Carter's Presidency

- Elected for honesty and integrity.
- Focused on saving energy.
- Built foreign policy around human rights.
- Helped secure Camp David Accords.
- Response to Soviet actions in Afghanistan and Iran hostage crisis seen as weak.

Reviewing Key Terms and People

Complete each sentence by filling the blank with the correct term or person.

1. Nixon at first refused to hand over the Watergate tapes, but he did offer to provide a _____.

2. Henry Kissinger practiced something called _____ rather than following broad rules for the conduct of foreign policy.

3. Carter helped bring about the _____ between Israel and Egypt.

4. The nation watched in wonder as _____ fulfilled its mission to the moon.

5. During the _____ Nixon ordered the firing of the special prosecutor.

6. The organization called _____ organized an oil embargo against the United States.

7. _____ holds that a president must be able to keep official conversations and meetings private.

8. Following the overthrow of the shah, _____ became the leader of Iran.

9. During Nixon's administration, the United States and the Soviets reached an agreement limiting nuclear weapons known as _____.

10. The improvement in relations between the United States and the Soviet Union in the early 1970s was known as _____.

Comprehension and Critical Thinking

SECTION 1 *(pp. 1018–1025)*

11. **a. Describe** What was the significance of President Nixon's trip to the People's Republic of China in 1972?

   b. Contrast In what ways did Nixon's policies while president differ from some of his previously stated positions?

History's Impact video program

Review the video to answer the closing question: Why is freedom of the press a crucial part of a democratic society?

c. Elaborate What do you think were the reasons for Nixon's willingness to pursue goals and programs that varied greatly from his past conservative beliefs?

SECTION 2 *(pp. 1027–1032)*

12. a. Recall What was the purpose of the break-in at the Watergate Hotel?

b. Summarize How would you summarize the conflict between Nixon and those investigating the Watergate scandal?

c. Predict Do you think Nixon could have survived had he admitted early in the scandal that his office had been involved in the Watergate break-in? Explain.

SECTION 3 *(pp. 1033–1038)*

13. a. Describe What qualities did Jimmy Carter use to win public support in the election of 1976?

b. Make Generalizations How did Carter come to be regarded by the public by the end of his term?

c. Predict How do you think Carter's opponents will attack his record in the election of 1980?

Using the Internet

go.hrw.com
Practice Online
Keyword: SD7 CH31

14. The Iran hostage crisis that began in 1979 caused public outrage—and deep concern about the waning prestige of the United States. Using the keyword above, do research to learn more about the hostage crisis. Then create a time line and brief report on its effects on the presidential election of 1980.

Analyzing Primary Sources

Reading Like a Historian This picture shows Jimmy Carter, his wife Rosalynn, and daughter Amy walking to the White House on the day of his inauguration.

15. Describe How did Carter's actions differ from those of presidents who came before him?

16. Make Inferences What kind of message do you think Carter tried to send through his decision to walk?

Critical Reading

Read the passage in Section 2 that begins with the heading "The Saturday night massacre." Then answer the questions that follow.

17. Nixon sought to have the special prosecutor fired because

A. he revealed information about the Watergate tapes.

B. he sought to obtain the tapes in spite of Nixon's refusal to hand them over.

C. he was not doing enough to get to the bottom of the Watergate scandal.

D. he was thought to be part of the cover-up.

18. Which of the following most closely represents Nixon's argument against handing over the tapes?

A. The tapes included no relevant information.

B. He was afraid the tapes would prove his guilt.

C. He believed it was his legal right as president to keep official conversations private.

D. He did not believe that the Constitution permitted the creation of a special prosecutor.

FOCUS ON WRITING

Expository Writing *Expository writing gives information, explains why or how, or defines a process. To practice expository writing, complete the assignment below.*

Writing Topic Ford's Pardon of Nixon

19. Assignment Based on what you have read in this chapter, write a paragraph that describes the public's reaction to President Ford's pardon of Richard Nixon.

A Conservative ERA

THE BIG PICTURE Ronald Reagan won the presidency in 1980 by appealing to a discontented electorate with the promise to return to a simpler time and conservative values. Reagan and his successor, George H. W. Bush, presided over the end of the Cold War and huge changes in economic and social policy.

New York Standards

Key Idea 2 Important ideas, social and cultural values, beliefs, and traditions from New York State and United States history illustrate the connections and interactions of people and events across time and from a variety of perspectives.

Key Idea 3 Study about the major social, political, economic, cultural, and religious developments in New York State and United States history involves learning about the important roles and contributions of individuals and groups.

Skills FOCUS READING LIKE A HISTORIAN

Reagan loved a crowd, and the crowds loved him. His vitality, gentle humor, and dynamic speaking style charmed even his opponents. In his journey from actor to president, Reagan used all his skills to reach out to voters and persuade America to move in a new direction. **Interpreting Visuals** What can you infer about Reagan's personality from this photograph?

See **Skills Handbook**, p. H30

U.S.

September 1981
Sandra Day O'Connor becomes first female U.S. Supreme Court Justice.

1980

World

1980
Lech Walesa's Solidarity trade union leads protests in Poland.

History's Impact video program
Watch the video to understand the impact of the collapse of the Berlin Wall.

1982
Deepest U.S. recession since the Great Depression begins.

November 1985
Reagan and Gorbachev meet in the first of their arms reduction summits.

January 1989
George H. W. Bush becomes president.

February 1991
In First Gulf War, U.S.-led coalition ousts Iraq from Kuwait.

1982   1984   1986   1988   1990   1992

October 1983
Suicide bombers attack U.S. peacekeepers in Lebanon, killing 241.

March 1985
Mikhail Gorbachev becomes leader of the Soviet Union.

June 1989
China crushes pro-democracy protests in Tiananmen Square.

November 1989
Berlin Wall falls as protests bring down Communist regimes in Eastern Europe.

1045

1 Reagan's First Term

BEFORE YOU READ

MAIN IDEA

In 1980 Americans voted for a new approach to governing by electing Ronald Reagan, who powerfully promoted a conservative agenda.

READING FOCUS

1. As the 1980 presidential election approached, why was America a nation ready for change?
2. What was the Reagan revolution, and who supported it?
3. What were the key ideas of Reagan's economic plan, and what were its effects?

KEY TERMS AND PEOPLE

Ronald Reagan
New Right
Jerry Falwell
Nancy Reagan
David A. Stockman
supply-side economics
budget deficit

PI **2.4** Examine how the Constitution, United States law, and the rights of citizenship provide a major unifying factor in bringing together Americans from diverse roots and traditions.

"A City UPON A HILL"

▼ Reagan's ease in front of an audience and gifted speaking style gave him wide appeal.

 *What event marked the rise of the Reagan revolution?*
As California governor **Ronald Reagan** faced an audience in Washington, D.C., on January 25, 1974, he was witnessing something new. It was the first-ever Conservative Political Action Conference. Reagan was among friends.

Modern conservative politics had been born in defeat. Senator Barry Goldwater of Arizona, whom Reagan had supported, lost the 1964 presidential race in spectacular fashion. Richard Nixon had brought some conservative credentials into office when he was elected president in 1968, but his administration had been wracked with scandals. By 1974 conservatives were looking for someone to lead them.

Ronald Wilson Reagan was the man they were looking for. As he spoke to the crowd, Reagan laid out themes that would become familiar to the nation in the years ahead. He spoke of the need for greater military strength. He criticized the size and inefficiency of government. He praised the accomplishments of American business and the wonder of the free enterprise system.

Drawing on his gift at using stories to illustrate his points, Reagan reached back into American history to a sermon given in 1630 by John Winthrop, the first governor of Massachusetts Bay Colony. He reminded his listeners that Winthrop had compared the colony to "a city upon a hill" with "the eyes of all people upon us." Driven by hope and a love of freedom, America was Reagan's vision of that "city upon a hill."

Reagan's day in the national spotlight was still years away. Yet on that January day in 1974, it was possible to see it coming.

A Nation Ready for Change

When Ronald Reagan declared in a 1974 speech that "We are not a sick society," he sounded a theme that would carry him throughout his political career. When he proclaimed that "we are today, the last best hope of man on earth," he set a positive tone that would define his two-term presidency.

America in low spirits The scene was set for change as the 1980 presidential election approached. Opinion polls showed a lack of confidence in government. Political observers said America had fallen into a state of malaise, a depressed or uneasy mood. Indeed, there were plenty of reasons to be uneasy.

The turbulence of the 1960s had been followed by the Watergate scandal. Under President Carter, the United States seemed powerless as the Soviets invaded Afghanistan and Iranian militants took American embassy workers hostage. At home, Americans waited in long gasoline lines and wondered why foreign forces had so much power over their lives.

President Carter responded to the growing public discontent in a television speech on July 15, 1979. He said the nation faced a "crisis of confidence." While accepting a large dose of blame, he urged citizens to control their appetite for consumer goods to ease inflation and reduce reliance on foreign oil. Critics accused Carter of blaming Americans instead of fixing the problems. The president's appeal became known as the malaise speech.

Beneath the malaise, however, a political movement was gathering force during the 1970s. Its roots lay deeper than any temporary anger over crises such as gas lines and the hostage situation. The growing conservative movement opposed liberal social and racial policies, including abortion rights, forced busing to achieve school desegregation, welfare, and affirmative action. This opposition, combined with general discontent with Carter, spelled electoral trouble for the president.

The 1980 election Projecting energy and youth at age 69, Republican presidential nominee Ronald Reagan tried to turn voters' attention away from the nation's problems. He said the country needed to return to a simpler time of low taxes, smaller government, a stronger military, and conservative moral values. His message focused on five words: "family, work, neighborhood, peace, and freedom."

ACADEMIC VOCABULARY

welfare public assistance to the needy

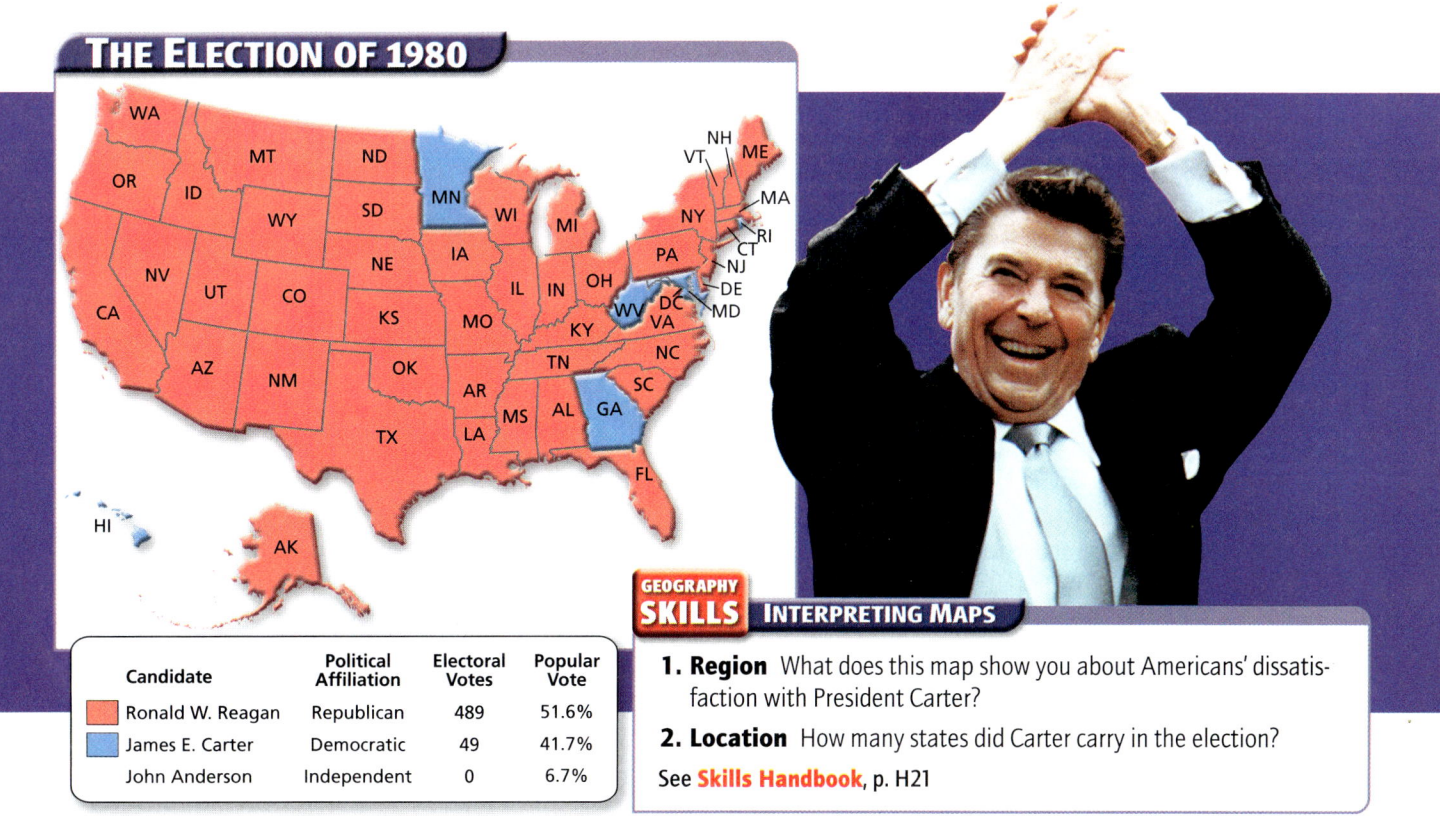

THE ELECTION OF 1980

Candidate	Political Affiliation	Electoral Votes	Popular Vote
Ronald W. Reagan	Republican	489	51.6%
James E. Carter	Democratic	49	41.7%
John Anderson	Independent	0	6.7%

GEOGRAPHY SKILLS | **INTERPRETING MAPS**

1. **Region** What does this map show you about Americans' dissatisfaction with President Carter?

2. **Location** How many states did Carter carry in the election?

See **Skills Handbook**, p. H21

In a debate with Carter, Reagan asked, "Are you better off today than you were four years ago?" For many, struggling with 13 percent inflation, high taxes, and a seemingly powerless government, the answer was "No."

Despite the entrance of Republican representative John Anderson as a third-party candidate, Reagan and his running mate, George H. W. Bush, won in a landslide of electoral votes. Republicans also won control of the Senate for the first time since 1955. In what seemed to be a final insult to Carter, the American hostages in Iran were released just hours after Reagan was sworn in as president.

READING CHECK **Identifying Cause and Effect** What factors led to Carter's downfall in the election of 1980?

The Reagan Revolution

One word will forever be linked to the name of Ronald Wilson Reagan: optimism. By all accounts—even those of his political opponents—Reagan had an infectiously cheerful outlook on life and the world. Yet beneath his relaxed manner, Reagan possessed a deep determination to reshape not only the United States, but also the world.

From actor to governor During his career as a modestly successful movie actor, Reagan was a union leader and an active member of the Democratic Party. During the 1950s as spokesperson for the General Electric Company, he sharpened his public-speaking skills and became a champion of free enterprise. He grew to be increasingly at odds with Democratic policies, and in 1962 he found his home in the Republican Party.

Reagan adopted the conservative cause with zest. In a 1964 speech urging support for Senator Goldwater, Reagan delivered a powerful critique of liberal government, from the New Deal to the Great Society. On taxes, he warned: "Today, 37 cents out of every dollar earned in this country is the tax collector's share." Government, he declared, "does nothing as well or as economically as the private sector of the economy." He warned against appeasing the Soviets, calling communism "the most dangerous enemy that has ever faced mankind."

American Civil Liberty

Smaller Government

In his inaugural address in 1981 Ronald Reagan said, "All of us need to be reminded that the federal government did not create the states; the states created the federal government." With these words, Reagan introduced his goal of reducing the power of the federal government.

Reagan believed that federal spending was too high and that complex laws intruded on free enterprise and personal freedoms. "Our citizens feel they have lost control of even the most basic decisions made about the essential services of government, such as schools, welfare, roads, and even garbage collection," he said. He slashed price controls and regulations.

Reagan hoped to expand the economic choices available to Americans by cutting taxes and reducing government spending. During his presidency, taxes were cut, but the bureaucracy increased in size and spending skyrocketed. By the time Reagan left office, the federal government was not only bigger but it was also unable to pay for itself without massive borrowing.

Drawing Conclusions How did Ronald Reagan hope to increase liberty for Americans?

"LEAVE THE FACADES—IT'LL BE JUST LIKE HOLLYWOOD." © 1981 HERBLOCK IN *THE WASHINGTON POST*. COURTESY THE HERBLOCK FOUNDATION

On the strength of the speech, California Republicans recruited him to run for governor in 1966. Reagan easily defeated the incumbent Democrat, Edmund "Pat" Brown.

As governor, Reagan had trouble meeting his goals for cutting the size of government. He expressed frustration with the job of controlling a large bureaucracy. After serving two terms, Reagan set his sights on a bigger job. "I feel I'm better qualified to be president than governor," he told a supporter.

Reagan would have to wait. He lost the Republican presidential nomination twice, to Richard Nixon in 1968 and to Gerald Ford in 1976. By 1980, however, Reagan had a strong and growing base of support.

Reagan's conservative support Ronald Reagan's journey from New Deal Democrat to conservative Republican made him a hero of a growing movement called the **New Right**. This was a coalition of conservative media commentators, think tanks, and grassroots Christian groups. Many of the groups had been formed to oppose specific liberal causes, such as the abortion rights gained under *Roe* v. *Wade*.

The New Right <u>advocated</u> major reversals in liberal government, economic, and social policies. The movement endorsed school prayer, deregulation, lower taxes, a smaller government, a stronger military, and the teaching of a Bible-based account of human creation. It opposed gun control, abortion, homosexual rights, school busing to achieve desegregation, the Equal Rights Amendment, affirmative action, and nuclear disarmament.

The New Right grew in influence with the rise of televangelism, or TV ministries led by evangelical Christians. One televangelist leader of the New Right, the Rev. **Jerry Falwell**, founded a political activist organization called Moral Majority in 1979. The name came from the group's belief that a majority of Americans agreed with conservative moral values.

Reagan gave the New Right an eloquent and persuasive voice. He drew many Americans to his side, including a large number of Democrats. These so-called Reagan Democrats shifted their allegiance from the Democratic Party in the elections of 1980 and 1984. They voted for Reagan to express their frustration with the Democratic Party's stands on social and racial issues and on national security.

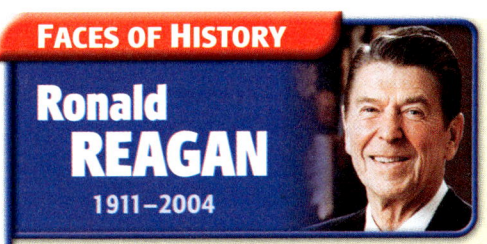

FACES OF HISTORY

Ronald REAGAN
1911–2004

Ronald Reagan earned the nickname the Great Communicator because of his speaking ability and sharp wit. During the 1980 election, after a debate with Jimmy Carter, a reporter asked Reagan if he had been nervous being on stage with the president.

"No, not at all," Reagan replied. Referring to his career as an actor, he added, "I've been on the stage with [acting legend] John Wayne."

Reagan entered politics after a long career in Hollywood. As governor of California and president, Reagan powerfully articulated conservatives' desires to reshape the government, reverse Great Society reforms, and battle communism. As the USSR began to reform, Reagan worked with Soviet leaders, helping to end the Cold War.

Explain Why was Reagan known as the Great Communicator?

A powerful personality The stage presence Reagan developed as an actor served him well in politics. On the campaign trail he became known as the Great Communicator. As president he gained the nickname the Great Persuader. To gain support for his programs, he threw his energies and charm into winning over conservative southern and western Democrats in Congress. If that didn't work, he spoke directly to voters through skillful television addresses. The newsmagazine *Time* referred to him as "the velvet steamroller."

Perhaps Reagan's greatest ally was his wife, **Nancy Reagan,** a former actor. She played a major role in running of the White House. She advised her husband on policy issues and fiercely protected his interests. As First Lady, she headed a "Just Say No" antidrug campaign.

Reagan's presidential agenda Reagan's chief goals were largely those of the New Right. He pledged to reduce the federal bureaucracy, deregulate certain industries, cut taxes, increase the defense budget, take a hard line with the Soviet Union, and appoint conservative judges to the federal judiciary.

In his first few months, the president got much of what he wanted. Congress passed a tax cut, eliminated some social programs, reduced the budgets of many federal agencies, and passed the largest-ever peacetime increase in

ACADEMIC VOCABULARY
advocate support, endorse

the defense budget. As head of the executive branch, Reagan could carry out some of his reforms without going to Congress. For example, he instructed federal agencies to roll back regulations on many industries. With each step toward achieving his agenda, Reagan seemed to be answering those who had felt the nation could no longer be governed effectively.

Reagan's image only grew stronger when he survived an assassination attempt in 1981. With a bullet in his left lung, the 70-year-old president kept his sense of humor. "Honey," he told the First Lady, "I forgot to duck." Reagan's positive outlook in the face of adversity created goodwill that helped him achieve his agenda.

Reagan's easygoing manner did not prevent him from taking decisive action. In August 1981 Reagan faced a strike by the nation's air traffic controllers. As federal employees, the 13,000 members of the Professional Air Traffic Controllers' Organization (PATCO) were forbidden to strike. Reagan warned them—and then he fired them all. Despite the resulting confusion at airports, the public generally approved of the president's uncompromising actions.

READING CHECK **Summarizing** How did Reagan want to change the federal government?

Reaganomics

- Reaganomics: Reagan's plan for tax and spending cuts
- supply-side economics: theory that breaks for businesses will increase supply of goods and services, aiding the economy

Below, Reagan meets with budget director David A. Stockman.

Reagan's Economic Plan

Reagan's blueprint for remaking government required a new economic plan. It was nicknamed Reaganomics. The plan had two goals: 1) reduce taxes to stimulate economic growth, and 2) cut the federal budget. Reagan appointed a controversial young budget director, **David A. Stockman**, to sell his plan to a skeptical Congress. Stockman's job was to get Congress to put the Reagan plan into effect in 40 days.

Supply-side economics Reaganomics was based on an economic theory known as supply-side economics. According to that theory, tax cuts and business incentives stimulate investment. Investment encourages economic growth. A growing economy, in turn, results in an increased supply of goods and services. Supply-side theory appealed to conservatives, who supported free enterprise and minimal government regulation.

Stockman pressed Congress for tax cuts for upper-income Americans and for businesses. Supply-side supporters believed that the tax relief would produce a series of benefits. Individuals would invest their tax savings. Businesses would use investment funds to expand and hire more workers. Expanding businesses would generate more tax revenue, allowing the government to eliminate any budget deficit. A budget deficit is the amount by which government spending for a year exceeds government income.

Stockman succeeded in getting Congress to pass numerous major components of Reaganomics. During Reagan's first six years as president, tax rates on the wealthiest Americans dropped from 70 percent of their income to 28 percent. Critics claimed that the tax breaks simply made the rich richer. They predicted that little of the new wealth would "trickle down" to the working class, as Reaganomics predicted. Critics also warned that tax cuts, combined with increases in military spending, would drive the federal deficit higher, increasing the national debt.

Reagan's own vice president, George H. W. Bush, had questioned the plan to cut taxes and boost military spending at the same time. Back in 1980, when Bush was competing with Reagan for the Republican nomination, he had labeled Reagan's plan "voodoo economics."

Recession and recovery Events did not go quite according to Reagan's plan. In 1981 and 1982, the nation suffered the worst recession since the Great Depression. Unemployment rose, and government revenues plunged. Meanwhile, federal spending soared, largely because of huge defense increases. With less tax money to pay for the increased government spending, the federal budget deficit skyrocketed. Stockman told a magazine that "None of us really understands what's going on with all these numbers." He left the administration and later wrote a critique of Reaganomics.

The actions of the Federal Reserve Board contributed to the recession. The Federal Reserve had steadily raised interest rates from 1979 to 1982 in an effort to reduce inflation. Higher interest rates made it more expensive for businesses to borrow money to expand.

By 1983, with inflation at a low 4 percent, the Federal Reserve had reduced interest rates. The collapse of OPEC's ability to set high oil prices also helped lower inflation. The economy began to grow at a brisk pace. Economic growth was uneven, however, and largely favored the wealthy. Unemployment eased. Nevertheless, federal revenues lagged far behind spending. Faced with a severe budget crisis, Congress put the brakes on federal spending. In 1985 it passed the Balanced Budget and Emergency

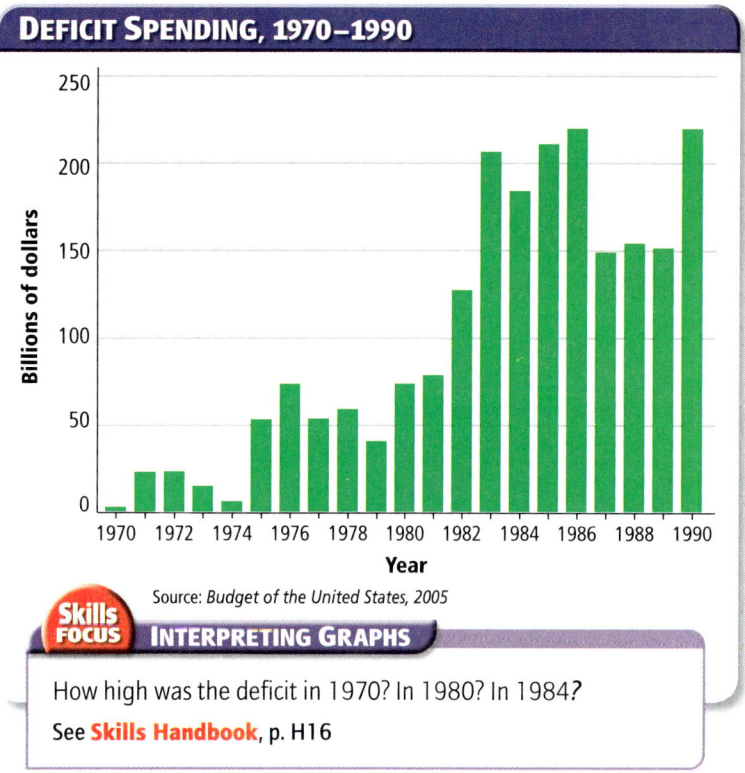

DEFICIT SPENDING, 1970–1990

Billions of dollars / Year

Source: *Budget of the United States, 2005*

Skills FOCUS **INTERPRETING GRAPHS**

How high was the deficit in 1970? In 1980? In 1984?

See **Skills Handbook**, p. H16

Deficit Control Act, or the Gramm-Rudman-Hollings Act. The measure required mandatory budget cuts to curb the deficit.

READING CHECK **Summarizing** What were the key elements of Reaganomics?

Reviewing Ideas, Terms, and People

1. a. Recall Why was America said to be in a state of malaise in the late 1970s?
   b. Make Inferences What do you think Carter was trying to accomplish in his malaise speech, and why did it backfire?
   c. Rate What made Reagan's message so effective among voters?

2. a. Recall What types of groups and individuals supported Reagan's rise to the presidency?
   b. Analyze What skills earned Reagan his nicknames the Great Communicator, the Great Persuader, and the Velvet Steamroller?
   c. Evaluate How did conservative ideas represent a change from the recent past?

3. a. Define Write a brief definition for each of the following terms: **Reaganomics, supply-side economics**
   b. Contrast How did the assumptions of Reaganomics differ from the outcomes?

c. Predict What effect would the Gramm-Rudman-Hollings bill have on funding of federal programs?

Critical Thinking

4. Identifying the Main Idea Copy the web diagram below and use information from the section to show what types of changes conservatives wanted to make.

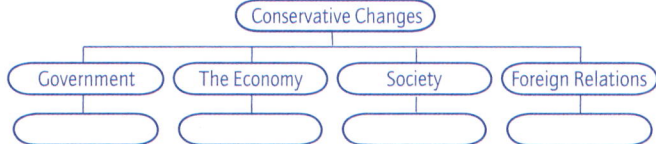

Conservative Changes

Government | The Economy | Society | Foreign Relations

FOCUS ON SPEAKING

5. Expository President Reagan communicated strong ideas to the American public. Choose one of his ideas and write a brief speech explaining it, using facts to support your account.

ST 1.2 Analyze the decisions leading to major turning points in United States history, comparing alternative courses of action, and hypothesizing, within the context of the historic period, about what might have happened if the decision had been different.

New Jersey v. *T.L.O.* (1985)

Why It Matters Under the Fourth Amendment, police must have probable cause before they can conduct a search. In this case, the Supreme Court ruled that school officials may search a student without violating the Fourth Amendment if there is reasonable suspicion that the student has broken the law or a specific school rule.

Background of the Case

In 1980 a New Jersey high school student whose initials were T.L.O. was accused of smoking in the school bathroom. When T.L.O. claimed that she did not smoke, the assistant principal looked in her purse and found cigarettes. Then he noticed a package of rolling papers. Searching further he found marijuana and letters indicating that T.L.O. was selling drugs. T.L.O. later admitted to selling marijuana, and the State of New Jersey brought delinquency charges against her. She was sentenced to one year of probation. T.L.O. appealed her conviction, arguing that there was no probable cause to search her purse. She asked for a new trial at which the evidence from her purse could not be used against her.

The Decision

The Supreme Court ruled that the Fourth Amendment's prohibition on unreasonable searches and seizures does apply to searches conducted by public school officials. In addition, schoolchildren do have legitimate expectations of privacy, and their belongings may not be searched unreasonably. However, school officials are not required to follow the same standards as police. School officials need only reasonable grounds for *suspecting* that the search will turn up evidence that the student has violated school rules. The search must be conducted in ways that are reasonably related to the goal of the search. Judged by this standard, the search of T.L.O.'s purse was reasonable and did not violate the Constitution.

THE IMPACT TODAY Based on the Fourth Amendment arguments used in the *T.L.O.* case, the Supreme Court has issued rulings permitting school officials to conduct random screenings for weapons using metal detectors (above) and to conduct random drug testings of students wishing to participate in extracurricular sports and clubs. Many school boards are developing guidelines for how to interpret and carry out the Court's rulings on these controversial topics.

go.hrw.com
Research Online
Keyword: SS Court

CRITICAL THINKING

1. **Analyze the Impact** Using the keyword above, read about the 1961 decision in *Mapp* v. *Ohio*. In what ways was the reasoning in *Mapp* important to the decision in *New Jersey* v. *T.L.O.*?

2. **You Be the Judge** Based on *New Jersey* v. *T.L.O.*, should a school be allowed to require student athletes to submit to random drug testing, or does that policy violate the reasonable search provision of the Fourth Amendment? Explain your answer in a short paragraph.

Reagan's Foreign Policy

BEFORE YOU READ

MAIN IDEA

President Reagan took a hard line against communism around the world.

READING FOCUS

1. How did President Reagan help to bring about the end of the Cold War?
2. What foreign trouble spots persisted during Reagan's presidency?
3. How did the Iran-Contra Affair undermine the president?

KEY TERMS AND PEOPLE

Strategic Defense Initiative
Lech Walesa
Solidarity
Mikhail Gorbachev
INF Treaty
apartheid
Iran-Contra affair
Oliver North

PI 3.4 Understand the interrelationships between world events and developments in New York State and the United States (e.g., causes for immigration, economic opportunities, human rights abuses, and tyranny versus freedom).

THE INSIDE STORY

Can simple words knock down a cement wall? For the United States and its allies in the West, the Berlin Wall had long been a symbol of the harsh reality of life in the Soviet empire. The massive wall dividing Communist East Berlin from the free West told a stark tale of two systems. On one side, citizens freely approached the wall and turned its entire length into an exuberant canvas of colorfully painted designs and slogans. On the other, armed guards and barriers kept citizens away for fear that they might escape to freedom in the West.

In 1987, some 25 years after the Berlin Wall was constructed, Ronald Reagan gave a speech at a famous Berlin Wall landmark known as the Brandenburg Gate. Reagan's speech went out not only to the people of West Berlin, whom he addressed directly, but also to the people in East Berlin. Loudspeakers carried his words into the air and over the wall.

President Reagan's message was clear and simple. He called out the name of the Soviet leader.

"Mr. Gorbachev, open this gate. Mr. Gorbachev—Mr. Gorbachev, tear down this wall!"

The message of defiance and confrontation would characterize Reagan's hard-line Cold War stance throughout his first term. Gorbachev, for his part, did not respond immediately to Reagan's demand in Berlin. But in time, the Soviet leader indeed would have to answer. ◢

"Mr. Gorbachev, Tear Down This Wall!"

▶ In West Berlin, citizens exercised freedom of expression on their side of the Berlin Wall.

Reagan and the Cold War

Staunch opposition to communism was a bedrock principle that shaped Ronald Reagan's political life. Yet as president, Reagan joined in a complex relationship with a new Soviet leader to help end the 40-year Cold War.

The "Evil Empire"
President Reagan rejected the policies of containment and détente pursued by previous presidents. He did not want to accommodate communism. He wanted to destroy it. He used thundering language to condemn the Soviet Union as "the focus of evil in the modern world."

HISTORY'S VOICES

"I urge you to beware the temptation ... to ignore the facts of history and the aggressive impulses of an evil empire, to simply call the arms race a giant misunderstanding and thereby remove yourself from the struggle between right and wrong and good and evil."

—President Ronald Reagan,
"Evil Empire" speech, March 8, 1983

Reagan's strong position worsened relations with the Soviets during his first term. But it also won considerable praise. He forged bonds with like-minded foreign leaders, including conservative British prime minister Margaret Thatcher and Polish-born Pope John Paul II. Still, critics viewed Reagan's approach as reckless. At a time when the two superpowers had their fingers on the nuclear trigger, some people feared he would set off World War III.

Military spending soars
Urging "peace with strength," Reagan obtained massive increases in defense spending. Between 1981 and 1985 the Pentagon budget grew from about $150 billion to some $250 billion.

Much of the new spending went to nuclear weapons. In 1981 the president unveiled a plan to add thousands of new nuclear warheads. Two years later, the U.S. military installed new nuclear missiles in Europe. The presence of new weapons aimed at Soviet cities angered the USSR. It ended arms control talks and boycotted the 1984 Olympic Games in Los Angeles.

In 1983 Reagan initiated the creation of a new defensive weapon: a shield in space to protect the United States against incoming Soviet missiles. Reagan put all his persuasive skills to work to promote the concept, named the **Strategic Defense Initiative** (SDI).

Opponents, including many scientists, scoffed at SDI, saying it would be too expensive and would not work. They nicknamed it Star Wars, after the popular science-fiction

Reagan's Defense Buildup

This cartoon, like many critics, charged that Reagan's massive military spending came at the expense of other valuable programs.

DEFENSE SPENDING, 1980–1988

Source: *Budget of the United States Government, 2005*

Skills FOCUS **INTERPRETING GRAPHS**

Compare defense spending in 1980, shortly before Reagan took office, with that near the end of his presidency in 1988.

See **Skills Handbook**, pp. H16

movie. The Soviets viewed SDI as an offensive weapon rather than a defensive one, saying it would allow the United States to launch a first strike without fear of retaliation.

Reagan hoped SDI would ease the growing pressures for disarmament. Across the United States and Europe, hundreds of thousands of supporters of a nuclear freeze—a halt in production of all atomic weapons—marched in massive demonstrations.

"I would agree to freeze if only we could freeze the Soviets' global desires," Reagan said. Yet increasingly, the Soviet Communists were less concerned with global conquest than with their own political survival.

A weakened Soviet Union The long rule of Leonid Brezhnev, from 1964 to 1982, saw the USSR rise to the height of its power and then begin to decline. By the late 1970s, the Soviet economy was shrinking. Industrial and farm production, population growth, education, medical care, and other indicators of prosperity fell sharply. A country rich in farmland became an importer of food. Government corruption was rampant.

Soviet weakness became strikingly clear in 1980 when the USSR failed to contain a dramatic series of events in Poland. Under the leadership of an electrician named **Lech Walesa**, some 17,000 workers in the city of Gdansk locked themselves in a factory to protest steep rises in food prices. The daring move riveted the world. The strikes spread, finally forcing the Soviet-backed government to legalize independent trade unions. Walesa was elected to lead a new, independent union called **Solidarity**. More than a union, Solidarity was a freedom movement.

U.S.-Soviet relations warm The death of Leonid Brezhnev and two other Soviet leaders in quick succession brought a visionary new leader to power in 1985. **Mikhail Gorbachev** believed that the only way to salvage the Soviet economy was to strike a deal with America.

The emergence of Gorbachev gave Reagan an opportunity. In the 1984 election, the Reagan-Bush ticket had beaten former Vice President Walter Mondale and his running mate, Representative Geraldine Ferraro of New York. As he began his second term, Reagan was ready to negotiate with the Soviets.

Speech

On June 6, 1984, Ronald Reagan spoke in France to observe the fortieth anniversary of the Normandy invasion on D-Day. This passage from his "Boys of Pointe du Hoc" speech reflects Reagan's speaking style and foreign-policy views.

"The men of Normandy had faith that what they were doing was right, faith that they fought for all humanity, faith that a just God would grant them mercy on this beachhead or on the next … [T]here is a profound moral difference between the use of force for liberation and the use of force for conquest. You [U.S. veterans of D-Day] were here to liberate, not to conquer, and so you and those others did not doubt your cause. And you were right not to doubt.

You all knew that some things are worth dying for. One's country is worth dying for, and democracy is worth dying for, because it's the most deeply honorable form of government ever devised by man. All of you loved liberty. All of you were willing to fight tyranny, and you knew the people of your countries were behind you."

Skills FOCUS   **READING LIKE A HISTORIAN**

1. **Identifying Points of View** According to Reagan, what proved that the Normandy invasion was the right action?
2. **Analyzing Primary Sources** What does this speech reflect about Reagan's political views?

See **Skills Handbook**, p. H28–29

In four meetings from 1985 through 1988, Reagan and Gorbachev changed the superpower relationship. Their talks produced the Intermediate-Range Nuclear Forces (INF) Treaty, the first agreement to actually reduce nuclear arms instead of simply halting production. The **INF Treaty**, ratified in 1988, ordered the destruction of a whole class of weapons—more than 2,500 missiles, many of which faced each other in Europe.

In 1988 Reagan stood in Moscow's Red Square and embraced the leader of the once "evil empire." The Cold War was almost over.

READING CHECK   **Summarizing** What actions did Reagan take to help end the Cold War?

Nicaragua

Lebanon

Trouble Spots Abroad

Regional conflicts often force presidents to choose where to become involved militarily. Reagan's choices reflected his view of American interests in the world in the 1980s.

Upheaval in Latin America Nowhere was the fight against communism more urgent to Reagan than Latin America. The United States supported several anti-Communist governments and rebel groups in the region during the Reagan years. Some of these regimes were repressive, but Reagan believed U.S. support was necessary to prevent the spread of communism in those countries. U.S. actions focused on two Central American nations, El Salvador and Nicaragua.

In tiny El Salvador, peasants were caught in a violent civil war between Marxist guerrillas and government troops supported by armed extremist groups. The Reagan administration gave its support to a relatively moderate leader who won election in 1984, José Napoleón Duarte. The civil war dragged on until peace was reached in 1992.

Meanwhile, a civil war in neighboring Nicaragua drew the president's staff into what would become the most serious crisis to affect the Reagan White House. The United States had at one time supported Nicaraguan dictator Anastasio Somoza Debayle. In 1979 a Marxist-leaning group known as the Sandinistas, with aid from Cuba's Communist government, ousted Somoza. At first the Sandinista governed as part of a coalition of political groups, but soon Sandinista dominance became clear.

When Reagan took office, he cut off aid to Nicaragua, saying that the Sandinistas were supported by the USSR. In 1981 Reagan approved $20 million for the Central Intelligence Agency (CIA) to equip and train a Sandinista opposition group, the Contras. The effort stalled when the CIA conducted sabotage operations in Nicaragua, including laying mines in two Nicaraguan ports, without informing Congress. As the secret activities came to light, Congress cut off funds to the Contras and banned all direct or indirect U.S. military support for them.

Reagan remained determined to help the Contras. He told his national security adviser, Robert McFarlane, "I want you to do whatever you have to do to help these people [the Contras] keep body and soul together." His staff took this as a signal to find a way around Congress's restrictions. Americans would soon learn that the White House continued to fund the Contras despite the congressional ban.

ACADEMIC VOCABULARY

regime
government, administration

At far left, a Contra rebel wears a baseball cap that shows U.S. support of his struggle against the Sandinista government in Nicaragua. At near left, the U.S. embassy in Beirut, Lebanon, is damaged following a suicide attack on April 18, 1983, in which 63 people were killed. *What other conflicts was the United States involved in during the Reagan administration?*

Tragedy in Lebanon

President Reagan believed that American interests required stability in the Middle East. For years the Mediterranean coastal country of Lebanon had been ripped apart by civil war. Muslim and Christian factions battled for control of the country. Various groups, including the Palestine Liberation Organization (PLO), used Lebanon as a base for attacks against Israel to the south. In 1982 Israel invaded and occupied southern Lebanon to expel the PLO and try to form a new, reliably friendly government. The invasion threatened to turn Lebanon's civil war into a general Middle East war.

In 1983 an international peacekeeping force, including some 800 U.S. Marines, arrived in Lebanon's capital, Beirut. On October 23, a suicide bomber drove a truck full of explosives into the marine barracks in Beirut. The blast leveled the building, killing 241 sleeping soldiers inside. This tragedy and the bombing of the U.S. embassy a few months earlier were the first suicide terrorist attacks against the United States.

The incidents ignited an intense debate in America about the role of the military in violent, unstable regions. Reagan decided to withdraw the troops from Lebanon. Anti-American groups claimed victory.

Victory in Grenada

A few days before the bombing in Lebanon, a violent Communist coup took place in the tiny Caribbean country of Grenada (gruh-NAY-duh). Cuban troops were helping build an airstrip on the island, raising fears that it could become a Communist outpost. Reagan also worried about the fate of some 800 U.S. students in medical school there.

Two days after the Lebanon bombing, with the nation still in shock, Reagan sent 5,000 marines to invade Grenada. They took the island in two days, with a loss of 19 soldiers. The victory aided Reagan in the 1984 election.

Apartheid in South Africa

Reagan took a less activist position in confronting the South African government. For decades, the official policy of **apartheid** ("apartness") had enforced legalized racial segregation throughout South African society. Under apartheid the minority white population enjoyed great privileges. Meanwhile, the government forcibly relocated millions of people categorized as nonwhite to desolate frontier lands. Nonwhites were banned from decent jobs, schools, and housing and were prohibited from owning land, voting, or traveling freely.

American companies and investments in the resource-rich land helped keep the white regime in power. Starting in the 1970s, anti-apartheid groups urged nations to divest, or withdraw investments, from South Africa.

Reagan preferred a policy of "constructive engagement"—that is, maintaining business ties while offering incentives for reform and engaging in diplomacy with the government. Critics charged that the policy enriched a corrupt, white minority regime. In 1986 Congress overrode a Reagan veto to pass the Comprehensive Anti-Apartheid Act, which imposed trade limits and other sanctions.

READING CHECK **Summarizing** How did the Reagan administration respond to crises in Lebanon, Grenada, and South Africa?

The Iran-Contra Affair

Despite the congressional ban on U.S. funds for the Contras' war against the Nicaraguan government, Reagan's national security staff sought to continue the funding. The United States was then facing terrorism in the Middle

THE IMPACT TODAY

Government

Terrorists have used suicide bombings to strike in Israel and in Iraq. The terrorist attacks against the United States on September 11, 2001, also were suicide attacks.

REAGAN'S FOREIGN POLICY

Latin America	• U.S. backs moderate Duarte in El Salvador civil war. • Reagan backs anti-Communist Contras in Nicaragua. • White House defies Congress ban on Contra funding.
Lebanon	• Following civil war, U.S. sends 800 peacekeepers. • October 1983: Suicide bomber hits marine barracks. • 241 Americans killed; U.S. withdraws from Lebanon.
Grenada	• 1983 Communist coup strands 800 U.S. students. • Cuba's role and students' safety concern Reagan. • U.S. launches two-day invasion, restores democracy.
South Africa	• Reagan prefers "constructive engagement" with white minority government to combat apartheid. • 1986: Congress imposes sanctions over Reagan veto.

East, where American civilians in Lebanon were being kidnapped by pro-Iranian groups.

In 1985 the situations in Nicaragua and the Middle East became linked. National Security Adviser Robert McFarlane persuaded Reagan to approve sales of weapons to Iran, hoping that Iran would help obtain the release of U.S. hostages in Lebanon. This violated a U.S. arms embargo as well as Reagan's own principle of refusing to negotiate with terrorists.

The **Iran-Contra affair** unfolded when members of the National Security Council staff secretly diverted money from the illegal Iran arms sales to the Contras in Nicaragua. Vice Admiral John Poindexter and Lieutenant Colonel **Oliver North** carried out the plan.

When the scheme was revealed in 1986, Congress wanted to know if anyone higher up was involved. It launched an investigation modeled after the Watergate probe of Nixon.

Reagan admitted authorizing the Iran arms sales but denied knowledge of the diversion of funds to the Contras. Vice President Bush, Defense Secretary Caspar Weinberger, and other staff made similar statements.

The full details of the affair are not known because members of the administration engaged in a cover-up of their actions. North admitted destroying key documents. High-level Reagan staff were found to have lied in testimony to Congress and withheld evidence. North was convicted of destroying government documents and perjury. The conviction later was overturned on technicalities.

READING CHECK **Sequencing** Trace the significant events that led to prosecutions in the Iran-Contra affair.

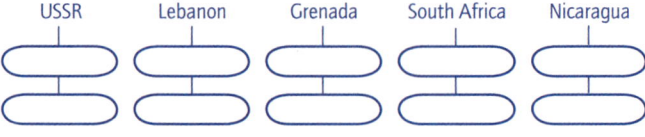

SECTION 2 ASSESSMENT

go.hrw.com
Online Quiz
Keyword: SD7 HP32

Reviewing Ideas, Terms, and People

1. a. Identify Explain how each of these terms and people relates to the ending of the Cold War: **Strategic Defense Initiative, Lech Walesa, Solidarity, Mikhail Gorbachev**
b. Make Inferences What influence do you think SDI and U.S. defense spending had on Soviet leaders' thinking about the Cold War?
c. Evaluate To what extent do you think Reagan and Gorbachev shaped the events of the Cold War, and to what extent did they encounter changes already in progress?

2. a. Define Write a brief definition for this term: **apartheid**
b. Contrast Contrast the reasons for U.S. involvement in Lebanon, Grenada, and South Africa.
c. Evaluate What do you think were the advantages and disadvantages of Reagan's "constructive engagement" policy in South Africa?

3. a. Recall What was Oliver North's role in the **Iran-Contra affair?**
b. Make Inferences What can you infer about Reagan's relationship with Congress from the Iran-Contra Affair?

c. Rate Do you think North's actions were justifiable given (a) circumstances in Nicaragua or (b) pressure from the president to help the Contras?

Critical Thinking

4. Making Decisions Copy the chart below and use information from the section to identify the choices Reagan had to make in various conflicts.

Reagan Foreign-Policy Choices

USSR	Lebanon	Grenada	South Africa	Nicaragua

FOCUS ON WRITING

5. Descriptive As a reporter covering the appearance of Reagan and Gorbachev in Red Square in 1988, describe the historic meeting of former enemies.

A New World Order

BEFORE YOU READ

MAIN IDEA

In 1988 Reagan's vice president, George H. W. Bush, won election to a term that saw dramatic changes in the world.

READING FOCUS

1. What factors influenced the election of 1988?

2. How did Soviet society become more open?

3. What chain of events led to the collapse of the Soviet empire?

4. What other global conflicts emerged near the end of the Cold War?

KEY TERMS AND PEOPLE

George H. W. Bush
glasnost
perestroika
velvet revolution
Boris Yeltsin
Tiananmen Square massacre
Saddam Hussein
Operation Desert Storm
Nelson Mandela

PI 2.1 Discuss several schemes for periodizing the history of New York State and the United States.

THE INSIDE STORY

How do you make the transition from vice president to commander in chief?

On December 7, 1988, Vice President **George H. W. Bush** was basking in the glory of his victory in the 1988 presidential election. Yet he was still second in command to a very powerful and popular Ronald Reagan.

Thus the summit taking place that day on Governor's Island in New York Harbor had clear symbolic meaning. The Americans were there to meet with Soviet leader Mikhail Gorbachev. Ronald Reagan was still president, and he would conduct the discussions with his Soviet counterpart. Bush, however, was a living symbol of a change soon to take place: the orderly, democratic transfer of power in the U.S. government.

Before the formal talks began, the three men informally answered questions from reporters. Reagan gave his positive reaction to the recently announced decision by Gorbachev to reduce the number of troops in Europe. Bush was then asked for his reaction. His first response was similar to one he had given for the previous eight years: He supported whatever the president said. But then, with a reference to his upcoming January 20 inauguration, Bush extended an invitation to the assembled reporters: "Give me a ring on the 21st."

Indeed, the Reagan era would soon be over. The presidency of George H. W. Bush was about to begin. ◢

Passing the Torch

▼ **Gorbachev, Reagan, and Bush meet under the watchful eye of Lady Liberty.**

The Election of 1988

George Herbert Walker Bush came from a wealthy and powerful family. In World War II he had served with distinction as a navy pilot. Following careers in banking and oil, Bush entered politics in 1967 as a member of Congress from Texas. He served under presidents Nixon, Ford, and Reagan—as U.S. ambassador to the United Nations, as head of the Central Intelligence Agency, and as vice president.

In 1988 the Republican Party nominated George H.W. Bush as its presidential candidate and Indiana senator Dan Quayle as his running mate. They joined a presidential race that was notable for its lack of public attention. Excitement peaked early in the election year when an African American candidate, the Reverend Jesse Jackson, ran for the Democratic Party's nomination.

Jackson, a major civil rights leader and a liberal candidate, had run in 1984 with little success. This time, however, he achieved an upset, winning the most votes on Super Tuesday, the day when most states hold primary elections. Jackson's candidacy earned significant support from both white and black voters. In the end, however, Governor Michael Dukakis of Massachusetts won the most delegates and became the Democratic Party's nominee.

Many people attribute the low 50.1 percent voter turnout in the general election to the negativity of the campaign. The Democratic ticket of Michael Dukakis and his running mate, Texas senator Lloyd Bentsen, challenged Bush on the weak economy. The Bush campaign shot back with a series of advertisements that portrayed Dukakis as soft on crime. The tough ads contrasted with Bush's stump speech calling for a "kinder, gentler" America.

Despite a shaky economy, Bush earned support with his promise to continue the Reagan economic plan: "Read my lips: No new taxes." The Bush-Quayle ticket beat Dukakis and Bentsen by 426 electoral votes to 111.

When George Bush suceeded Ronald Reagan as president, the world stood on the verge of a democratic awakening. In four short years President Bush would take part in intense dramas around the globe.

THE IMPACT TODAY

Science and Technology
A 2005 Chernobyl Forum report on the 20-year impact of the disaster revealed that only about 50 deaths could be directly linked to the accident, rather than thousands as previously estimated. Still, the report predicted that as many as 4,000 people could eventually die from radiation exposure, and some 5 million live in contaminated areas.

READING CHECK **Summarizing** What events triggered the most interest in the 1988 election?

The Opening of the USSR

For nearly 70 years, citizens in the closed Soviet society risked great danger in speaking out or acting against the government. Dissidents—those who protested Soviet rule—were imprisoned and exiled. Basic freedoms of speech, religion, and association were nearly nonexistent. Mikhail Gorbachev sought to change Soviet society, opening it not only to the West but also to internal dissent.

Glasnost and perestroika As part of his plan to reform the failing Soviet system, Gorbachev announced a new era of *glasnost*, or "opening." He lifted media censorship, allowing public criticism of the government. Gorbachev held press interviews, a stunning contrast to the secrecy in which the Kremlin had operated.

Soviet citizens, cautious at first, began to speak openly. They complained about the price of food, of empty store shelves, and of their sons dying in the Soviet occupation of Afghanistan.

Gorbachev also undertook the huge process of *perestroika*, the "restructuring" of the corrupt government bureaucracy. The program was launched with much excitement and hope.

To restructure the shattered economy, Gorbachev dismantled the Soviet central planning system, giving local officials more authority over farm and factory production. He fired about 40 percent of regional officials and pushed through a flurry of reforms:

- 1986: Soviet scientist and dissident Andrey Sakharov was released from exile.
- 1989: Free elections took place for the first time since 1917.
- 1989: The Soviet Union withdrew from Afghanistan.
- 1989: Gorbachev visited China, easing tensions along the Soviet-Chinese border.

One glaring exception to *glasnost* occurred in 1986, when the Soviets attempted to cover up the world's worst nuclear accident. The meltdown of the Chernobyl nuclear plant near Kiev, the capital of Ukraine, was detected when deadly radiation drifted across Europe. The lead caused deaths and widespread illness. About 350,000 people had to be relocated from the region. The site remains uninhabitable.

READING CHECK **Identifying Cause and Effect** What effects did *glasnost* and *perestroika* have on the Soviet economy, government, and society?

Soviet Shortages

The Soviet Union experienced healthy economic growth after World War II, but it did not last. Soviet leaders focused on expanding heavy industry instead of creating adequate supplies of consumer goods. Store shelves were often empty, creating a thriving black market in food and other goods.

The Soviet Empire Collapses

The call for *glasnost* and *perestroika* awakened hopes for freedom throughout the Soviet empire. A spirit of nationalism, long repressed and feared by Soviet authorities, rose in the subject nations of Eastern Europe.

Eastern Europe crumbles
Gorbachev knew the USSR could no longer afford to support the ailing Eastern European economies. He ordered a large troop pullback from the region and warned local leaders to adopt reforms.

Dissidents and ordinary citizens didn't wait for reforms. They created their own paths to freedom. All across Eastern Europe, dreams of a better life inspired revolutions in the late 1980s. The Polish trade union Solidarity forced the government to hold elections, and in December 1990 Lech Walesa became to president. Hungarian officials opened their country's border with Austria in August 1989, and people streamed to the West. In Czechoslovakia, a nonviolent **velvet revolution**—so called because it was peaceful—swept the Communists from power in November 1989. Dissident playwright Vaclav Havel became president.

In Romania, revolution turned violent. Demonstrations brought down the government of one of the Soviet bloc's cruelest dictators, Nicolae Ceausescu, in December 1989. Ceausescu and his wife, Elena, were executed.

The fall of the Berlin Wall
Gorbachev's call for openness made him very popular in Europe, especially in East and West Germany. Protesters at a fortieth anniversary celebration of the East German state in October 1989 chanted "Gorby, help us!"

But still the Berlin Wall remained, the repressive symbol of Soviet communism. With so many barriers falling, could the Berlin Wall continue to divide the German people?

Hoping to calm rising protests, the East German government flung open the gates of the Berlin Wall on November 9, 1989. Thousands of East Berliners poured through to freedom. As border guards looked on helplessly, jubilant Berliners scaled the wall from both sides. They pulled down the razor wire, climbed atop the wall, and danced on it. With axes and sledgehammers and their bare hands, they spontaneously began ripping down the wall.

Writing on the tenth anniversary of the fall of the Berlin Wall, one reporter looked back on the spectacular sights and sounds of history being made.

HISTORY'S VOICES

❝ And then I hear the noise. Pick, pick, pick. Chuck, chuck, chuck. Growing louder and louder as hundreds of hammers and chisels attack the wall, taking it down chip by chip. I laugh and laugh—and cry at the same time. ❞

—BBC reporter Tim Weber, November 9, 1989

An Empire Falls

Pressured by U.S. threats and the dead weight of his ailing Soviet empire, Gorbachev cracked open a door to democracy—and millions of oppressed people rushed through.

1 Poland

Electrician Lech Walesa leads a strike and starts a revolution.

- In 1989, Solidarity forces the government to hold elections.
- Walesa is elected president in 1989; the Communists fall.

2 Romania

One of the cruelest Communist regimes falls the hardest.

- In December 1989 violent protests sweep the country.
- Dictator Ceausescu and his wife are executed.

People around the world watched in awe as TV cameras recorded the triumph of democracy. Less than a year later, on October 3, 1990, East Germany and West Germany were reunified as one nation.

The end of the Soviet Union With the Soviet empire crumbling, Communist Party officials in the USSR stood to lose power, prestige, and wealth. The world waited anxiously to see how far they would allow Gorbachev to go. With Gorbachev preparing to sign a treaty granting partial freedoms to the Soviet republics in 1991, hard-line Communist Party leaders had had enough. They seized Gorbachev in a coup d'état.

Help for the captive president came from **Boris Yeltsin**, leader of the Russian Republic. Yeltsin had quit the Communist Party and was actually a liberal opponent of Gorbachev. Now, however, he led a popular revolt against the Communist coup. As soldiers and tanks rolled into Red Square to arrest Yeltsin, a mass of unarmed Russians flooded the plaza, surrounding them. What would happen? At a tense moment, Yeltsin climbed atop a tank and addressed the cheering crowd. Soldiers looked the other way. Some even joined the protest.

The balance of power tipped, and the army backed down. Gorbachev was released and restored to power in the Kremlin. But, he would not stay long. The forces that Gorbachev had unleashed quickly overwhelmed him. Beginning in 1990, Soviet republics had begun declaring their independence. In late 1991 most of the former Soviet republics, including Russia, formed a loose federation called the Commonwealth of Independent States (CIS).

Gorbachev resigned as president, and no one was named to replace him. The Soviet Union dissolved. Yeltsin now led a severely weakened superpower. A journalist later assessed Gorbachev's place in history:

HISTORY'S VOICES

❝One can argue about what degree of direct credit Mr. Gorbachev deserves for ending the nuclear arms race or for bringing down the Berlin wall. It can credibly be suggested that Russia itself, pinned mercilessly beneath the staggering burdens of Bolshevism, could not have moved in any other direction and that Mr. Gorbachev just happened to be there when the society began to collapse. But he was there, and it is hard to imagine that history won't reward him handsomely for his role.❞

—"A Visionary Who Put an Era Out of Its Misery," *The New York Times,* January 7, 1997

It was fitting that George Bush, former head of America's Cold War spy agency, the CIA, was the president who would preside over the ending of the Cold War. Less than one month after the fall of the Berlin Wall, Bush and Gorbachev met to discuss arms reduction. In 1991 they agreed on a Strategic Arms Reduction Treaty (START) to cut stockpiles of long-range nuclear weapons.

Two months after the collapse of the USSR, Bush and Yeltsin met at Camp David. They issued a joint statement declaring that the United States and Russia no longer regarded each other as "potential adversaries." The leaders signed a START II agreement in 1993. Bush said START II offered "a future free from fear." Yeltsin called it "a treaty of hope."

READING CHECK **Making Generalizations** How did Gorbachev's call for *glasnost* and *perestroika* help bring down the Soviet Union?

Other Bush-Era Conflicts

President Bush guided the nation through other foreign-policy challenges. By 1991 he spoke hopefully of creating a "new world order," free of the Cold War rivalries.

China: democracy crushed Inspired in part by events in the Soviet Union, a generation of Chinese students called on their Communist leaders to embrace reforms. In April 1989 they led huge pro-democracy demonstrations that filled Tiananmen Square in the Chinese capital of Beijing. For two hope-filled months, Chinese officials tolerated the protests. Change seemed possible. Then hard-line officials ran out of patience.

On June 4 a line of tanks rolled toward Tiananmen Square. As cameras recorded the scene, a man ran into the street and stood in front of the tanks. For half an hour, he halted their progress. The image of the lone rebel defying Chinese authority sent a powerful message around the world. Then the man melted back into the crowd. The tanks surrounded the protesters and opened fire. Hundreds of unarmed people, including children, were gunned down in the Tiananmen Square massacre.

President Bush announced an arms embargo but said America had to stay "engaged" with China. Democratic reform would take much longer in China than in the rest of the Communist world. But the protests showed a desire for freedom that was heard by China's leaders.

THE IMPACT TODAY

Government

In 2002 President George W. Bush and Russian President Vladimir Putin replaced START II with the SORT, Strategic Offensive Reduction Treaty, which calls for cuts to overall arsenals rather than to specific weapon types.

Panama: a dictator falls During the 1980s, Colonel Manuel Noriega basically ran the country of Panama. As head of the armed forces, he brutally suppressed opposition. Evidence that he was involved in smuggling drugs to the United States led a U.S. court to indict him in 1988. In 1989 Noriega seized direct control of Panama and declared a state of war with the United States. At stake was the security of the Panama Canal, which was scheduled to be turned over to Panamanian control in 1999.

When Noriega's soldiers shot and killed a U.S. marine in December 1989, President Bush ordered an invasion of Panama. U.S. troops arrested Noriega and moved him to Florida. He was later convicted of drug trafficking and other charges.

The Persian Gulf War In August 1990 the ruthless dictator of Iraq, **Saddam Hussein**, invaded the neighboring country of Kuwait.

The attack on the tiny, oil-rich kingdom shocked the United States and other Western countries—which depended on petroleum supplies from Kuwait—as well as the Arab nations in the region. Concerns rose further when reports surfaced of atrocities by Iraqi troops against Kuwaiti civilians. President Bush vowed that Saddam's "aggression would not stand."

The UN imposed sanctions on Iraq and set a deadline of January 15, 1991, for the withdrawal of Iraqi troops. Meanwhile, President Bush used his diplomatic skills to assemble a strong multinational military coalition.

Saddam remained defiant. The deadline passed. On January 16, 1991, the U.S.-led force attacked, starting with heavy bombing raids on targets in Kuwait and Iraq. On the Iraq–Saudi Arabia border and on warships in the Persian Gulf, a force of some 690,000 troops from the United States, Britain, France, and a number of Arab nations prepared to strike.

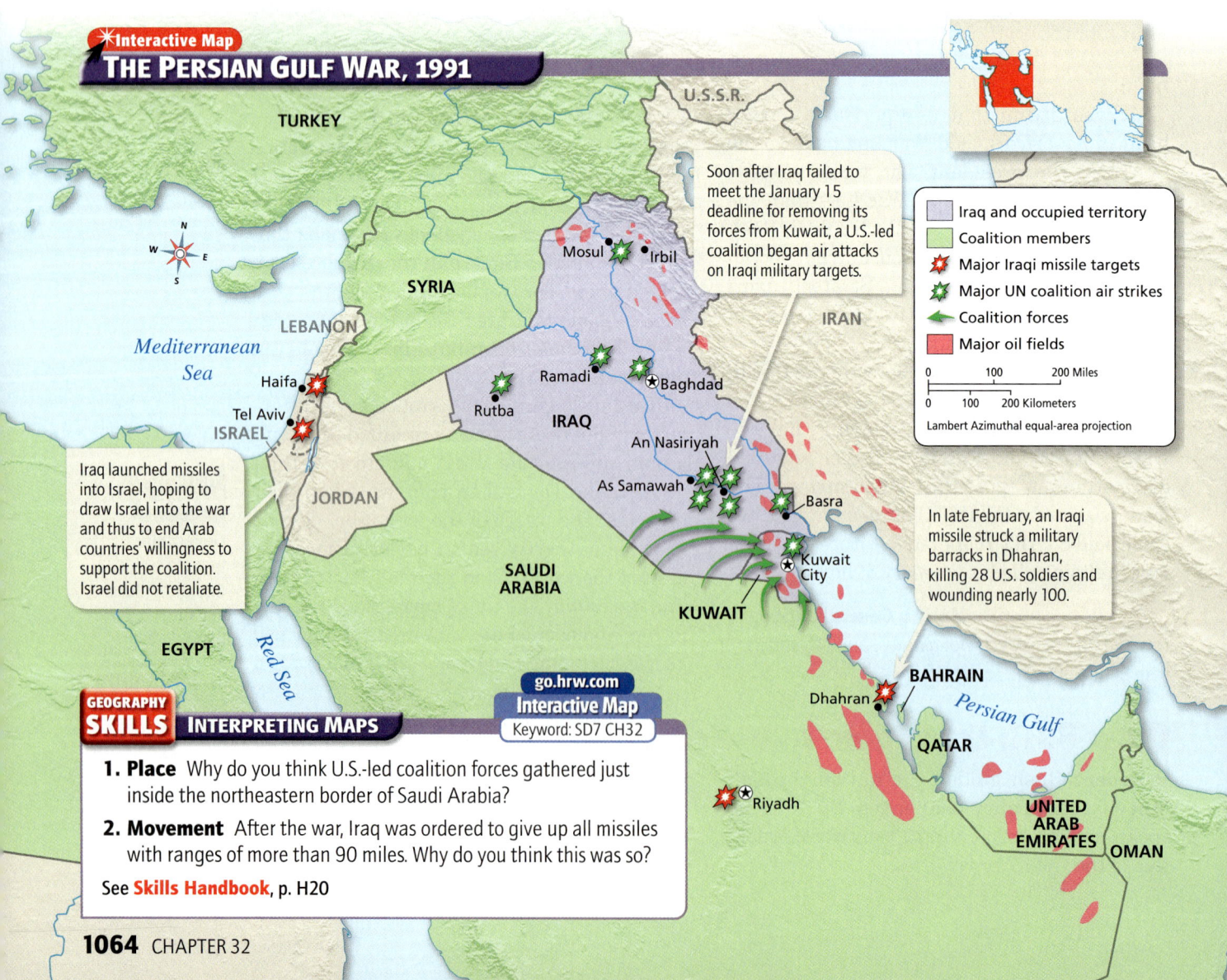

Interactive Map
THE PERSIAN GULF WAR, 1991

Soon after Iraq failed to meet the January 15 deadline for removing its forces from Kuwait, a U.S.-led coalition began air attacks on Iraqi military targets.

Iraq launched missiles into Israel, hoping to draw Israel into the war and thus to end Arab countries' willingness to support the coalition. Israel did not retaliate.

In late February, an Iraqi missile struck a military barracks in Dhahran, killing 28 U.S. soldiers and wounding nearly 100.

Legend:
- Iraq and occupied territory
- Coalition members
- Major Iraqi missile targets
- Major UN coalition air strikes
- Coalition forces
- Major oil fields

0   100   200 Miles
0   100   200 Kilometers
Lambert Azimuthal equal-area projection

GEOGRAPHY SKILLS INTERPRETING MAPS

go.hrw.com
Interactive Map
Keyword: SD7 CH32

1. **Place** Why do you think U.S.-led coalition forces gathered just inside the northeastern border of Saudi Arabia?
2. **Movement** After the war, Iraq was ordered to give up all missiles with ranges of more than 90 miles. Why do you think this was so?

See **Skills Handbook**, p. H20

The ground war, launched on February 23, was short and swift. Iraqi troops retreated and scattered. Coalition forces returned Kuwait's royal family to power within a few days.

The campaign, **Operation Desert Storm**, was a conventional (non-nuclear) war. But it was unlike any war before it. The harsh desert terrain and long distances between targets made high technology airpower the most effective military tool. Nearly radar-proof Stealth bombers launched laser-guided bombs from afar. And long-range cruise missiles soared hundreds of miles from ships in the Gulf to hit targets in downtown Baghdad, the Iraqi capital.

Because so much of the campaign took place from the air, little of the violence appeared on the world's television sets, despite widespread coverage. The coalition tallied fewer than 500 casualties, including 148 Americans. An estimated 20,000 Iraqi soldiers and some 2,400 Iraqi civilians died.

The Persian Gulf War would not be the last conflict to involve the United States and Iraq. As you will read in the next chapter, U.S. involvement in Iraq would continue.

South Africa: new freedom

While Eastern Europe was throwing off its chains, a similar miracle was occurring in South Africa. In 1989 the white government elected F. W. de Klerk as president. Like Gorbachev, de Klerk triggered a chain of events that resulted in a new system of government.

De Klerk sought a gradual, orderly lifting of apartheid. He released political prisoners including **Nelson Mandela**, a former guerrilla fighter imprisoned in 1964. Despite threats of civil war by white opposition, de Klerk and Mandela worked to end apartheid. A new constitution followed, and in 1994 the nation's first all-race elections were held. Mandela and his African National Congress party won.

Sharing the Nobel Peace Prize with de Klerk in 1993, Mandela praised the work of Dr. Martin Luther King Jr., whose call to nonviolent protest had inspired the antiapartheid movement. In language echoing the American Declaration of Independence, he saw a better day:

HISTORY'S VOICES

" Thus shall we live, because we will have created a society which recognizes that all people are born equal, with each entitled in equal measure to life, liberty, prosperity, human rights and good governance. "

—Nelson Mandela, Nobel lecture, December 10, 1993

READING CHECK **Identifying Main Ideas** What victories and setbacks for democracy occurred near the end of the Cold War?

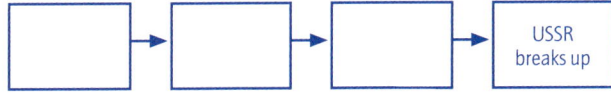

SECTION 3 ASSESSMENT

Reviewing Ideas, Terms, and People

1. a. Identify Who were the main candidates in the 1988 presidential election?
b. Make Inferences What can be inferred from the low voter turnout in the 1988 election?
c. Develop Why did Jesse Jackson's big victory in the primaries generate so much excitement?

2. a. Define Write a brief definition for each of the following terms: *glasnost*, *perestroika*
b. Analyze Why did Mikhail Gorbachev believe that *glasnost* and *perestroika* were necessary?
c. Predict Why was it dangerous for Gorbachev to launch such big social and economic changes in the USSR?

3. a. Identify How did **Boris Yeltsin** come to power?
b. Compare and Contrast How did Czechoslovakia's **velvet revolution** compare with the other Soviet-bloc uprisings?
c. Rate What year do you think was the biggest turning point in ending the Cold War?

4. a. Describe What roles did Manuel Noriega, **Nelson Mandela**, and **Saddam Hussein** have in Bush-era conflicts?
b. Rank Which Bush-era conflicts turned out to be the best and worst for the spread of democracy? Explain your choices.

Critical Thinking

5. Identifying Cause and Effect Copy the chart below and use information from the section to identify the causes of the fall of the Soviet empire.

```
[   ] → [   ] → [   ] → [ USSR
                          breaks up ]
```

FOCUS ON WRITING

6. Descriptive Suppose you were one of the young people who climbed atop the Berlin Wall in triumph. Write a letter to an American friend describing the experience.

Life in the 1980s

BEFORE YOU READ

MAIN IDEA

The 1980s and early 1990s saw major technological, economic, and social changes that produced both progress and intense conflicts.

READING FOCUS

1. How did new technologies such as the space shuttle affect society?
2. How did changes in the economy of the 1980s affect various groups of Americans?
3. What other changes and challenges did U.S. society face in the 1980s?

KEY TERMS AND PEOPLE

Steve Jobs
Bill Gates
space shuttle
Alan Greenspan
savings and loan crisis
Sandra Day O'Connor
Geraldine Ferraro
Clarence Thomas

PI 3.2 Research and analyze the major themes and developments in New York State and United States history (e.g., colonization and settlement; Revolution and New National Period; immigration; expansion and reform era; Civil War and Reconstruction; the American labor movement; Great Depression; World Wars; contemporary United States).

Dawn of the Digital Age

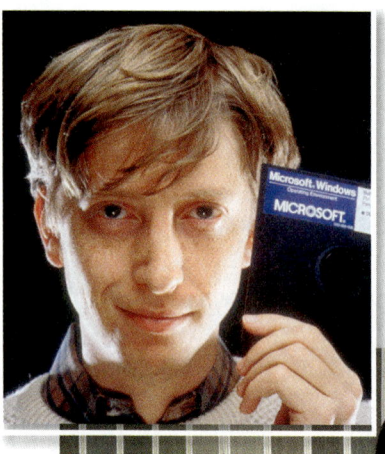

The innovations of Bill Gates (left) and Steve Jobs (below) changed the way Americans live, work, and play.

THE INSIDE STORY

How did two guys in a garage change the world? Try to envision the technology—or lack of it—in the year 1980. There were no home computers, CDs, DVDs, or plasma-screen TVs; no cell phones or e-mail. Microwaves and VCRs were still quite new. In 1980 people rushed to buy a new game played right on the television: Pac Man.

All that would change in the 1980s. New inventions brought immense changes in the way people lived—changes as significant, perhaps, as the invention of the printing press and the automobile.

While some revolutions start on a battlefield or in a laboratory, the personal computer revolution started in a garage in Cupertino, California. That's where **Steve Jobs**, a restless college dropout, and a friend, Steve Wozniak, started a small business called Apple Computer. The Apple II home computer was introduced in 1977. More a toy than a tool at first, Apple computers soon transformed the way Americans lived and worked.

Computers existed already, but Apple made them smaller—small enough to be usable at home on a desktop. Jobs's genius was in recognizing that computers could have appeal far beyond the community of scientists, military engineers, and other academics already using them.

Like Steve Jobs, **Bill Gates** was born in 1955 and dropped out of college to form a company. His Seattle-based company, Microsoft, invented a new type of computer-operating software. The time was ripe for his innovation. When Gates leased the software to the largest computer manufacturer, IBM (International Business Machines), a business giant was born. Microsoft soon became the world leader in computer software. ■

The Space Shuttle Blasts Off

Besides the computer, one of the more stunning technological developments of the 1980s was a new type of spacecraft. Unlike previous spacecraft, the new **space shuttle** could be reused after each flight. It lifted off like a rocket but returned to Earth like an airplane. Engineers at the National Aeronautics and Space Administration (NASA) had been developing a reusable spacecraft since the 1970s. They saw the space shuttle as a workhorse, carrying satellites and scientific experiments into space on a routine basis.

On April 12, 1981, millions of television viewers around the world watched the triumphant liftoff of the first shuttle, *Columbia*, from Cape Kennedy, Florida. At Air Force Plant 42 in Palmdale, California, where *Columbia* was built, "There was not a dry eye in the whole place," former plant commander Joe Davies recalled.

On January 28, 1986, tragedy struck the shuttle program when *Challenger* exploded after liftoff. All seven astronauts on board died, including the first private passenger, schoolteacher Christa McAuliffe. President Reagan led the nation in mourning.

Under President Reagan, NASA explored military and commercial uses for the space shuttle. This shift in priorities, along with proposals for the Star Wars (SDI) missile defense program, raised concerns about the militarization of space. The first military satellite was launched by the space shuttle in 1985.

Beyond space exploration, the shuttle program also benefited society more directly. Technologies developed or discovered by scientists on the program led to the development of such products as infrared cameras for detecting fires and a treatment for brain tumors.

READING CHECK **Summarizing** What hopes and disappointments did the space shuttle create?

The *Challenger* Space Shuttle Tragedy

The large picture shows the *Challenger* space shuttle launch on January 28, 1986. Just 73 seconds after liftoff, the *Challenger* exploded, killing the crew. Spectators reacted with horror as they watched the explosion. The *Challenger* crew included the space program's first civilian passenger, New Hampshire schoolteacher Christa McAuliffe (back row, second from left).

The Economy of the 1980s

Like most periods in American history, the 1980s witnessed both good and bad economic trends. Some were not apparent until the late 1980s and the early 1990s.

Uneven economic growth The 1980s marked the longest period of U.S. peacetime economic growth up to that time. The gross domestic product (GDP), the total value of goods and services produced by the nation, grew at an average annual rate of 3.5 percent from 1982 to 1989. The stock market, too, rose to then historic highs, slowed only temporarily by a crash in 1987.

The strong growth was achieved without the high inflation that had troubled the country throughout the 1970s. The deep recession of 1982 helped to slash inflation, though at the cost of high unemployment. Moves by the Federal Reserve Board also helped. Under chairperson Paul Volcker and his successor, **Alan Greenspan**, "the Fed," as it is known, actively raised and lowered interest rates to help avoid either recession or inflation.

Following the recovery, inflation stayed under 5 percent during the rest of the 1980s and early 1990s. Unemployment slowly dropped as well. Some people credit Reaganomics for many of the positive economic trends of the 1980s. Others point to the Federal Reserve Board.

But the strong economic growth of the 1980s was unevenly distributed. Many farmers, for example, did poorly during the decade. In 1986 and 1988 droughts struck the Midwest, turning cropland into wasteland. The droughts were followed by destructive floods. Meanwhile, crop and farmland prices declined. Farmers became mired in debt.

The recession of 1982–83 had struck older U.S. industries, such as steel and automobile production, particularly hard. Many factories closed, throwing tens of thousands out of work. Bankruptcies rose 50 percent in one year. Homelessness increased sharply in many cities. Yet the relief provided by the Reagan tax cuts mainly benefited wealthier Americans.

Rising deficits Reagan's tax cuts, coupled with increased military spending, threatened to undermine the success in combating inflation. With expenditures far outstripping tax revenue, the government's annual budget deficit nearly tripled, from $74 billion in 1980 to $221 billion in 1986. The national debt grew from about $1.2 trillion to $5.7 trillion. The interest alone on the debt increased 61 percent between 1980 and 1986. The huge government borrowing needed to fund the deficit raised fears of renewed inflation.

Another troubling economic sign was the rising U.S. trade deficit, the difference between the value of American exports and imports. The trade deficit grew throughout the 1980s as Asian economies roared to life, producing high quality goods such as automobiles by using cheaper labor and new, efficient processes.

Financial deregulation The deregulation of financial services under Reagan led to innovative business practices that changed the face of American business. Led by business tycoons such as Ivan Boesky, corporate raiders bought declining companies at a low price. They restructured them by merging them, selling off pieces of them, or dissolving them. They then sold the new entities at high prices. This corporate downsizing resulted in huge employee layoffs. Not all firms wanted to be purchased, so corporate raiders engaged in hostile takeovers. Supporters maintained that corporate raiders weeded out weak companies and improved productivity.

Savings and loan crisis The deregulation of the savings and loan (S&L) industry showed some of the risks of deregulation. S&Ls traditionally had used the money deposited to make home mortgage loans. Deregulation allowed S&Ls to offer other services, such as credit cards and investment management.

During a 1980s housing boom, deregulated S&Ls loaned out too much of their wealth. When the boom went bust, borrowers defaulted on their loans. S&Ls went bankrupt on a massive scale. The savings and loan crisis forced the federal government to step in and guarantee the deposits. The bailout cost taxpayers an estimated $152 billion.

Bush and the economy The S&L crisis and a recession that began in late 1990 forced President Bush to break his campaign pledge of "no new taxes." The tax hike did not prevent the deficit from climbing to $271 billion in 1992.

THE IMPACT TODAY

Government
In 2005 Ben S. Bernanke became chair of the Federal Reserve Board. Bernanke succeeded Alan Greenspan, who retired after heading the Federal Reserve Board for 18 years.

The Savings and Loan Crisis

Some members of Congress had grave concerns about the specific costs and methods of the S&L bailout.

Many lawmakers believed the government had to bail out savings and loans and restore depositors' money, despite the cost.

“ The current bailout law raises funds according to a costly 'borrow and spend' philosophy that adds billions to the bailout cost in interest. It drives up interest rates and the budget deficit. It also places the bulk of the bailout burden on those who can least afford to bear it: America's working and poor families. ”

Rep. Joseph P. Kennedy II

(D., MA), 1990

“ The deposit insurance grew out of the hard-learned lesson of the banking crisis that helped trigger the Great Depression. A failure to stand behind federally insured deposits would condemn us to repeat the mistakes of the past. People would lose their money and their faith in their Government, and there would be a bank panic rivaling the runs on deposits 60 years ago. ”

Rep. James McDermott

(D., WA), 1989

Skills FOCUS | **READING LIKE A HISTORIAN**

Identifying Points of View How did the two legislators differ? Were they necessarily in complete opposition to one another? Explain.

See **Skills Handbook**, pp. H28–H29

Unemployment and poverty rose significantly during his term. Despite his foreign-policy successes, economic troubles at home proved to be Bush's political downfall.

READING CHECK **Identifying Supporting Details** List major economic trends of the 1980s.

Changes and Challenges in American Society

Social issues proved increasingly divisive in the 12 years of the Reagan and Bush administrations. Political controversies opened new cultural battle lines in America.

Milestones During the elections of the 1980s, pollsters identified a gender gap in voting patterns. Women were voting in greater proportions than men, and they voted more Democratic. Politicians began to pay more attention to women voters and their interests.

Several women in politics achieved notable milestones. In 1981 President Reagan chose an Arizona judge, **Sandra Day O'Connor**, to be the first woman on the U.S. Supreme Court. Reagan also appointed a woman, Jeane Kirkpatrick, to serve as ambassador to the United Nations. In 1984 Democratic presidential candidate Walter Mondale named the first woman, New York Congresswoman Geraldine Ferraro, to run on a major party ticket.

Another milestone of the era was the passage of the Americans with Disabilities Act. The law, signed by President Bush in 1990, represented the culmination of years of work by activists for disabled Americans. It outlawed discrimination on the basis of physical impairment and required employers to make "reasonable accomodations" for people with disabilities.

Changes in immigration law New waves of refugees from Southeast Asia and from poverty and upheaval in Cuba, Haiti, and other parts of Latin America triggered revisions

FOCUS ON NEW YORK

GOVERNMENT
Geraldine Ferraro earned her law degree by attending Fordham University Law School at night while teaching elementary school during the day. In 1975, she helped create New York City's Special Victims Bureau to prosecute domestic violence cases and crimes against the elderly.

in U.S. immigration policy during the 1980s. Laws passed in 1980 and 1986 increased legal immigration limits and granted legal status to nearly 3 million undocumented immigrants living in the United States. It also toughened penalties on employers who knowingly hired undocumented workers. Despite these measures, illegal immigration continued to grow.

Court battles over social issues During the Reagan and Bush administrations, the Supreme Court ruled on several sensitive landmark cases. The rulings in these cases are still being felt today.

In the 1985 case *New Jersey* v. *T.L.O.*, the Court ruled that schools have the right to search students' belongings without being in violation of the Fourth Amendment's prohibition of unreasonable searches. You can read more about this case in the Landmark Supreme Court Cases in Section 1 of this chapter.

In *Westside Community School District* v. *Mergens*, the Supreme Court in 1990 ruled that a high school in Omaha, Nebraska, had to allow students to form an after-school Christian group that could meet on school grounds. Upholding the Equal Access Act, the ruling required schools that receive federal funding to provide equal access to student groups seeking to express "religious, political, philosophical, or other content."

Following the 1973 *Roe* v. *Wade* decision legalizing abortion, the Court issued rulings that further defined the scope of *Roe*. In the 1992 case *Planned Parenthood of Southeastern PA* v. *Casey*, the Court ruled that a state could require a woman seeking an abortion to give informed consent, to wait 24 hours, and in the case of a minor, to obtain parental consent.

In another sensitive case, the Court set a precedent in cases involving the removal of life-support equipment from a critically ill patient. Nancy Cruzan sustained severe brain damage in a car accident and was said to be in a "persistent vegetative state," kept alive by a feeding tube and other medical means. The 1990 ruling in *Cruzan* v. *Director, Missouri Dept. of Health* recognized an adult's right to refuse medical treatment. But it ruled that the state could require "clear and convincing evidence" that the patient would have wanted to have life support removed under the circumstances.

Battles over Supreme Court nominees
President Reagan had the rare opportunity to fill three seats on the Supreme Court. He also

American Religious Liberty

Churches and Politics

In recent decades, Christian conservatives have been a powerful political force. Christian fundamentalism and evangelism became popular in the 1920s and gained new power when Reagan came to office. Fundamentalists and evangelicals believe in a strict interpretation of the Bible as a source of clear direction and values in society.

One leading Baptist fundamentalist minister, Jerry Falwell, called for conservative Christians to become more active in politics. He believed that the country was facing problems because its political leaders had turned away from the Christian values upon which,

he said, the United States was founded. Falwell and other conservative Christians, including the Reverend Pat Robertson and Eagle Forum founder Phyllis Schlafly, maintained that they were promoting their right to practice religion. Some opponents felt that the increased influence of religion in politics threatened the separation of church and state. The nation continues to seek ways to balance the rights of religious groups with the rights of those who have other opinions and beliefs.

Identifying the Main Idea What is the basic disagreement between some fundamentalists and their critics?

Falwell began his career at the Thomas Road Baptist Church.

appointed about half the judges in the federal court system. Both Reagan and Bush sought to appoint conservative judges, at times setting off furious confirmation clashes in the Senate.

In 1987 Reagan nominated Robert Bork, a law professor and appeals court judge. Bork advocated a strict interpretation of the Constitution. Many senators and liberal groups feared he would roll back *Roe* v. *Wade* and civil rights laws. After angry hearings, the Senate rejected Bork. It later confirmed Reagan's next nominee, Anthony Kennedy.

Another battle took place over a Bush nominee to the Supreme Court in 1991. This nominee was **Clarence Thomas**, a conservative African American judge and former head of the federal Equal Opportunity Employment Commission (EEOC). In televised hearings, the Judiciary Committee investigated charges by law professor Anita Hill that Thomas had sexually harassed her when she worked for him at the EEOC. Hill underwent aggressive questioning by Republican senators defending Thomas, which offended many women. Thomas narrowly won confirmation.

A deadly disease In 1981 scientists identified what has since become one of the worst outbreaks of infectious disease in human history: acquired immunodeficiency syndrome, or AIDS. The deadly disease is caused by the human

Clarence Thomas's confirmation hearings were dominated by the accusation of sexual harassment. Critics were also concerned over his level of experience and his reluctance to reveal his stance on controversial issues.

immunodeficiency virus (HIV). AIDS first appeared among homosexual men and intravenous drug users, and the means of contracting it was not known. As a result, people with AIDS suffered discrimination. Scientists eventually determined that the disease is spread through transmission of bodily fluids, including sexual contact. AIDS has since spread to millions of men and women around the world.

READING CHECK **Summarizing** What major social changes occurred in the 1980s and early 1990s?

SECTION 4 ASSESSMENT

go.hrw.com
Online Quiz
Keyword: SD7 HP32

Reviewing Ideas, Terms, and People

1. a. Identify What pioneering roles did **Steve Jobs** and **Bill Gates** have in American society?
b. Make Inferences How do you think people reacted to the rapid technological changes brought about by the invention of personal computers?
c. Evaluate Do you think Reagan's emphasis on using the **space shuttle** for military and commercial purposes was wise, or should it have been reserved for scientific use only?

2. a. Recall What role did **Alan Greenspan** have in the changing U.S. economy?
b. Analyze Explain the connection between deregulation and trends such as hostile takeovers and the **savings and loan crisis**.
c. Evaluate How would you characterize the overall impact of Reaganomics?

3. a. Identify What firsts did Geraldine Ferraro and **Sandra Day O'Connor** achieve?
b. Predict What would be the long-term effects of Reagan's decision to nominate conservative justices to the Supreme Court?

Critical Thinking

4. Identifying Cause and Effect Copy the chart below, and complete it with the causes and effects.

```
[        ] → | Rising       | → [        ]
             | National Debt |
```

FOCUS ON WRITING

5. Persuasive Make the case for or against "trickle down" economic policies, using facts from the section.

Wealth in the 1980s

Historical Context The documents below provide different information about wealth in the 1980s: getting it, losing it, and being fascinated by it.

Task Examine the documents and answer the questions that follow. Then you will be asked to write an essay about how Americans viewed wealth in the 1980s, using facts from the documents and from the chapter to support the position you take in your thesis statement.

ST 4.3 Develop hypotheses about important events, eras, or issues; move from chronicling to explaining historical events and issues; use information collected from diverse sources to produce cogently written reports and document-based essays.

DOCUMENT 1

The rising stock market created enormous wealth for American stockholders. Some corporate managers became more concerned with companies' stock prices and profits than with their products. In the 1987 movie *Wall Street*, corporate raider Gordon Gekko, based on real-life characters such as Ivan Boesky, tells stockholders that his takeover of their company will benefit them because he will hire managers who will maximize profits for investors.

"Well, ladies and gentlemen, we're not here to indulge in fantasy, but in political and economic reality. America—America has become a second-rate power. Its trade deficit and its fiscal deficit are at nightmare proportions. Now, in the days of the free market, when our country was a top industrial power, there was accountability to the stockholder. The Carnegies, the Mellons, the men that built this great industrial empire, made sure of it because it was their money at stake. Today, management has no stake in the company! . . .

"The new law of evolution in corporate America seems to be survival of the unfittest. Well, in my book you either do it right or you get eliminated. . . .

"I am not a destroyer of companies. I am a liberator of them! The point is, ladies and gentleman, is that greed—for lack of a better word—is good. Greed is right. Greed works. Greed clarifies, cuts through, and captures the essence of the evolutionary spirit. Greed, in all of its forms—greed for life, for money, for love, knowledge—has marked the upward surge of mankind. And greed—you mark my words—will not only save Teldar Paper, but that other malfunctioning corporation called the USA."

DOCUMENT 2

Corporate raiders bought vulnerable companies in order to reorganize and sell them or to break them up and sell off their valuable parts. Other tactics that produced great wealth on Wall Street included investments in junk bonds as well as greenmail—a tactic of tricking other investors into buying stock at a high price. The 1985 cartoon below comments on these tactics. It is titled "Invasion of the Corporate Body Snatchers," a spoof on a popular movie about aliens who take over the world.

"INVASION OF THE CORPORATE BODY SNATCHERS" FROM *HERBLOCK AT LARGE* (PANTHEON BOOKS, 1987)

DOCUMENT 3

The economic boom of the 1980s saw an increase in incomes for many families without the high inflation that had wiped out most income increases in the 1970s. Some of the biggest beneficiaries of the 1980s boom were richer families, who saw their incomes increase, largely from successful investments. The chart below shows the changes in wealth for families in the lowest, middle, and highest income brackets.

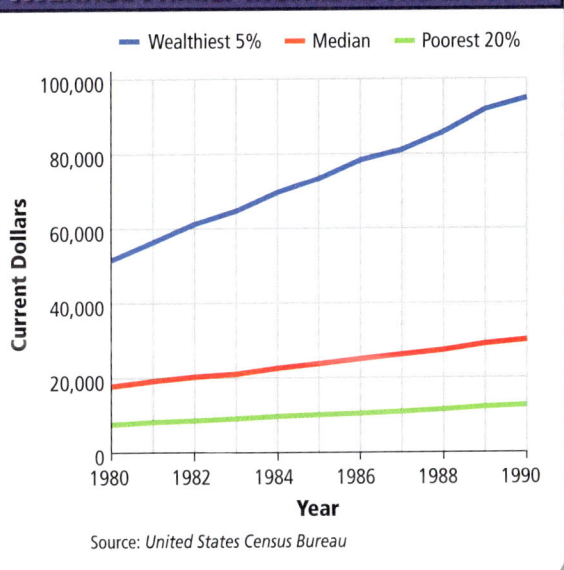

AVERAGE FAMILY INCOME IN THE 1980s

— Wealthiest 5%   — Median   — Poorest 20%

Current Dollars / Year

Source: *United States Census Bureau*

DOCUMENT 4

Americans were fascinated by the wealthy in the 1980s. Young people throughout the country copied the preppy look, imitating fashions associated with wealthy families of the East Coast. The most popular television shows were nighttime soap operas like *Dallas* and *Dynasty* that portrayed glamorous, if troubled, lives of rich families. In *Dynasty*, the large, oil-rich Carrington family lived an opulent lifestyle, yet they personified the saying that wealth doesn't bring happiness. Millions of viewers tuned in each week to watch the Carrington spouses, parents, and children viciously fight and plot against one another.

Skills Focus — READING LIKE A HISTORIAN

1. a. Summarize Refer to Document 1. What does Gekko say about greed?
b. Interpret What point is Gekko trying to make about the American economy?

2. a. Describe Refer to Document 2. How does the cartoonist portray corporate tactics?
b. Analyze What message is the cartoonist trying to send about the effects of such tactics on businesses?

3. a. Make Generalizations Refer to Document 3. What trends in income took place during this time period?
b. Elaborate How did the income gap between the richest and poorest families change from 1980 to 1990?

4. a. Contrast Refer to Document 4. How does the picture convey the image of wealth?
b. Elaborate How do you think the public's fascination with wealthy families on television reflected their views of wealth in the real world?

5. Document-Based Essay Question Consider the question below and form a thesis statement. Using examples from Documents 1, 2, 3, and 4, create an outline and write a short essay supporting your position.
How did American culture reflect fascination with and concerns about wealth during the 1980s?

See **Skills Handbook**, pp. H28–29, H31, H16

Visual Summary: A Conservative Era

Reagan's First Term
- Under President Reagan, people have renewed confidence in America.
- Conservative policies begin, such as smaller government and increased defense spending
- Supply-side economics, lower taxes, and big deficits occur.

Reagan's Foreign Policy
- The Soviet Union becomes a partner in arms control.
- Staunch anti-communism leads to the invasion of Grenada and the Iran-Contra scandal.

The Reagan and Bush Administrations

The New World Order
- George H. W. Bush becomes president.
- Soviet empire collapses, although China remains Communist.
- "New world order" proves dangerous, as United States goes to war with Iraq.

Life in the 1980s
- Good economic times, although not for all.
- Social issues divide society and lead to Supreme Court battles.

Reviewing Key Terms and People

For each term or name below, write a sentence explaining its significance.

1. Sandra Day O'Connor
2. velvet revolution
3. Bill Gates
4. space shuttle
5. Tiananmen Square massacre
6. New Right
7. Lech Walesa
8. Clarence Thomas
9. Strategic Defense Initiative
10. Iran-Contra affair
11. David A. Stockman
12. Ronald Reagan

Comprehension and Critical Thinking

SECTION 1 *(pp. 1046–1051)*

13. a. Identify Write a brief explanation of the following terms: supply-side economics, Reaganomics.

b. Analyze How did Ronald Reagan represent the conservative response to the liberalism of the 1960s?

c. Rank How important were social changes to conservatives? How important were economic and governmental changes?

SECTION 2 *(pp. 1053–1058)*

14. a. Recall What was Solidarity? How did it rise to power?

b. Draw Conclusions How was the success of Solidarity an early indicator of troubles for the Soviet Union?

c. Evaluate Was Ronald Reagan successful in increasing pressure on the Soviet Union for change? Explain.

History's Impact video program

Review the video to answer the closing question: What did the collapse of the Berlin Wall signify for both the United States and the rest of the world?

SECTION 3 *(pp. 1059–1065)*

15. a. Describe How did *glasnost* and *perestroika* come about in the Soviet Union? What were they meant to accomplish?

b. Sequence What major foreign-policy challenges occurred during the administration of President George H. W. Bush?

c. Elaborate Why did the START talks represent such a major change in U.S.–Soviet relations?

SECTION 4 *(pp. 1066–1071)*

16. a. Identify Explain the significance of the following: Alan Greenspan, savings and loan crisis.

b. Generalize What major trends occurred in the American economy during the 1980s?

c. Evaluate In 1980 Ronald Reagan asked the country, "Are you better off than you were four years ago?" How do you think most Americans would have answered that question at the end of his presidency?

Using the Internet

go.hrw.com
Practice Online
Keyword: SD7 CH32

17. First Lady Nancy Reagan was a complicated figure in American politics and history. She was criticized for the way she ran the White House and influenced her husband. She also was greatly admired by many Americans. Using the keyword above, research and write a short biography of Nancy Reagan that emphasizes her impact on the country and on her husband's administration.

Analyzing Primary Sources

Reading Like a Historian Reread the quotation from President Reagan's "evil empire" speech in Section 2. Then answer the following questions.

18. How did Reagan distinguish his view of the Soviet Union from others' views?

19. What words does Reagan use to emphasize his opinion of the Soviet Union and its goals?

Critical Reading

Read the American Civil Liberty feature in Section 1 titled "Smaller Government." Then answer the questions that follow.

20. Ronald Reagan opposed big government because he believed that

A taxes on poor people were too high.

B government did not control industries such as petroleum and airlines.

C government did not provide enough services.

D government spent too much and regulated too much.

21. Reagan wanted to change government by

A increasing the budget deficit.

B deregulating industries and cutting taxes.

C placing restrictions on key industries.

D increasing spending on social programs.

WRITING FOR THE SAT

Think about the following issue.

To battle apartheid in South Africa, the Reagan administration preferred a policy of "constructive engagement." Critics wanted to cut off relations with the white government and withdraw U.S. investments in the South African economy. Reagan disagreed, saying that if the United States withdrew, it would have no bargaining power with which to influence government policy. Congress opposed Reagan and placed a boycott on some South African products.

22. Assignment When a government such as South Africa pursues repressive policies against its people, should the United States punish it harshly by boycotting its products and severing government relations? Or, should it allow U.S. businesses to continue to operate in the country, using the threat of withdrawal to force the government to change its ways? Support your answer with reasoning and facts.

Into the Twenty-First Century

THE BIG PICTURE Americans faced the twenty-first century with hope, determination, and a readiness to embrace challenges at home and abroad. While always remembering and learning from the past, they looked forward to a future of change and opportunity.

New York Standards

Key Idea 2 Important ideas, social and cultural values, beliefs, and traditions from New York State and United States history illustrate the connections and interactions of people and events across time and from a variety of perspectives.

Key Idea 3 Study about the major social, political, economic, cultural, and religious developments in New York State and United States history involves learning about the important roles and contributions of individuals and groups.

Skills FOCUS READING LIKE A HISTORIAN

Tens of thousands of runners race across the Verrazano-Narrows Bridge during the annual New York City Marathon. Some 2 million spectators cheer them on, and 260 million television viewers tune in across the globe.
Interpreting Visuals How do you think the terrorist attacks of September 11, 2001, affected interest in this event?

See **Skills Handbook**, p. H30

U.S.

January 1993
Bill Clinton becomes president.

1992

World

1993
Israel and the PLO sign the Oslo Accords.

1994
UN forces land in Haiti to restore democracy.

History's Impact video program
Watch the video to understand the impact of September 11, 2001.

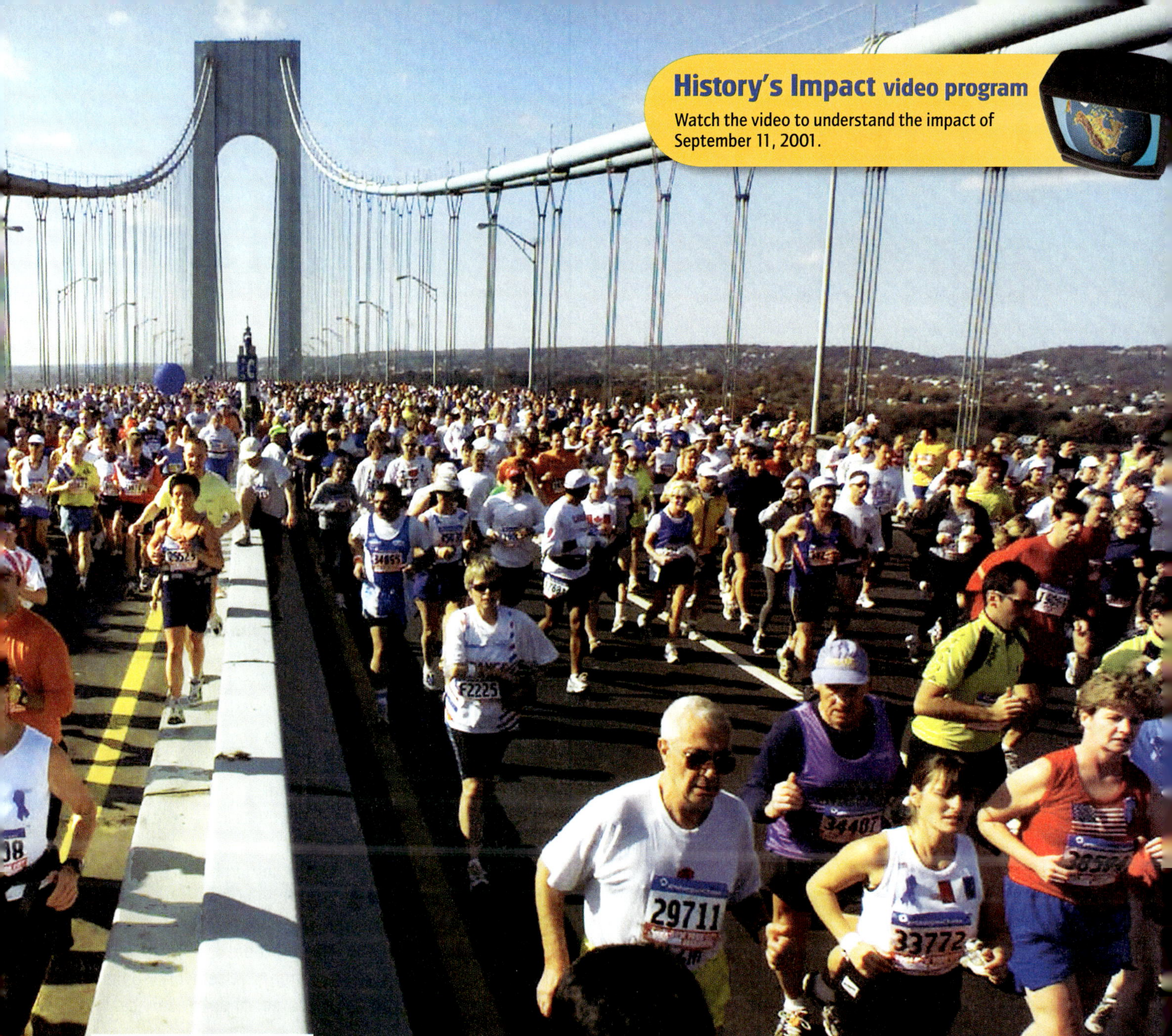

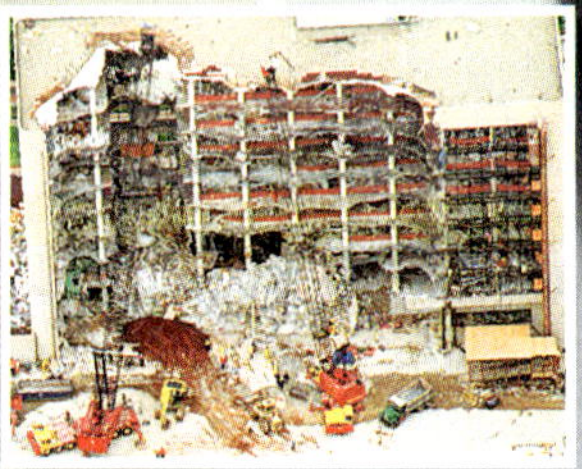

April 1995
A terrorist bomb destroys the Federal Building in Oklahoma City, killing 168 people.

1998
Serbian leader Slobodan Milosevic sends troops into Kosovo to drive ethnic Albanians from the region.

December 1998
The U.S. House of Representatives votes to impeach President Clinton.

January 1999
The United States and NATO stop "ethnic cleansing" of Kosovo.

September 11, 2001
Foreign terrorists attack the World Trade Center and the Pentagon.

March 2003
President George W. Bush orders invasion of Iraq to remove Saddam Hussein from power.

November 2004
President George W. Bush wins re-election.

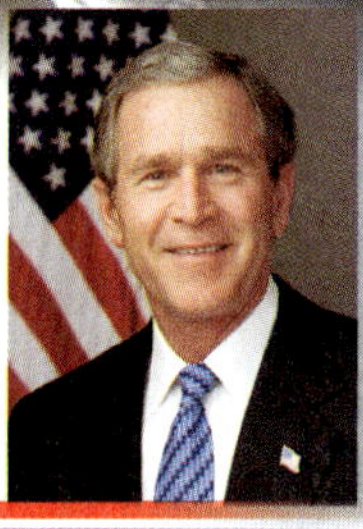

1995 — 1998 — 2001 — 2004

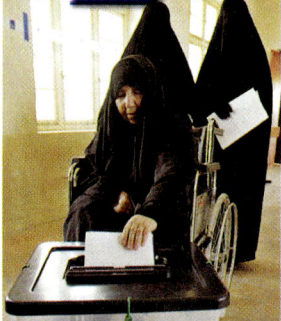

October 2005
Iraqis approve a new constitution.

The Clinton Years

MAIN IDEA

Bill Clinton was a new type of Democrat, and his administration faced challenges for a new millennium— and scandals as old as politics.

READING FOCUS

1. What were the key events in the political rise of Bill Clinton?

2. What were some major domestic-policy questions facing Clinton?

3. What were some major foreign-policy challenges facing Clinton?

4. What events led to scandal and impeachment proceedings during the Clinton presidency?

KEY TERMS AND PEOPLE

Bill Clinton
Hillary Rodham Clinton
Al Gore
H. Ross Perot
Contract with America
terrorism
NAFTA

PI 2.5 Analyze the United States involvement in foreign affairs and a willingness to engage in international politics, examining the ideas and traditions leading to these foreign policies.

Shaking History by the Hand

▼ **Sixteen-year-old Bill Clinton, a future president, shakes hands with President Kennedy.**

THE INSIDE STORY

Can one handshake change someone's life? Yes, it can, according to **Bill Clinton**. Clinton was a high school senior in Arkansas when he had the opportunity to travel to Washington, D.C., for a youth leadership conference. A highlight of the trip was a visit to the White House, where participants lined up to meet President John F. Kennedy. Among the first to shake the president's hand was Bill Clinton. Nobody at the time knew it, but the handshake, captured by photographers, linked two men who would one day be viewed as key figures in the second half of the twentieth century.

The young Clinton realized it was a central moment in his life. That handshake, he later recalled, changed him. He had long been interested in leadership and politics. But meeting John F. Kennedy in person instilled in him a new commitment: to serve the nation by leading it as president.

Clinton wasted little time in reaching for his dream. After working his way through college and law school, he began a career of public service. ◼

Bill Clinton's Political Rise

Bill Clinton did become a successful politician, rising to the highest positions in state government as a very young man. When he was just 30 years old, he became attorney general of Arkansas. Two years later, at the age of 32, he became the nation's youngest governor. Politically, Clinton represented a new kind of Democrat. He was not as conservative as many Republicans but not as liberal as many other Democrats. In other words, he was a centrist.

Clinton's reputation grew steadily. In the late 1980s, he chaired the National Governors Association. There he focused on issues such as improving public education and reforming the welfare system. He also chaired the Democratic Leadership Council, an organization of centrists. Clearly, Clinton was a Democrat on the rise.

Clinton the candidate It was no surprise, then, when Clinton sought the Democratic nomination for the presidency in 1992. During his campaign, he stressed the need for a national health-care system and middle-class tax cuts. He also skillfully deflected questions about his past. These included charges that he had evaded the draft during the Vietnam War.

Clinton's campaign also featured a major role for his wife, **Hillary Rodham Clinton**. She was regarded as one of the country's top lawyers. Clinton made it clear that his <u>administration</u> would rely on her skill and guidance.

The 1992 election Clinton won the Democratic nomination and ran against President George H.W. Bush. Clinton named a fellow southerner, Senator **Al Gore** of Tennessee, as his running mate. The race also featured independent candidate **H. Ross Perot**.

In the campaign, Clinton presented himself as the protector of the middle class. His message helped produce a solid victory. He won 370 electoral votes to Bush's 168, although Clinton received less than 50 percent of the popular vote. Although Perot received 19 percent of the popular vote, he carried no state.

READING CHECK **Identifying Cause and Effect** What were some of the key factors in Clinton's rise to the presidency?

Domestic Policy Issues

During his campaign, Bill Clinton made a number of promises about domestic matters. His record in fulfilling those promises was mixed.

Deficit reduction As you have read, Clinton proposed cutting taxes for middle class Americans during the 1992 campaign. Soon after taking office, however, he changed his plan. Citing budget deficits, which continued to rise sharply, he pushed through a major increase in taxes.

Clinton's move was criticized by some Republicans. They predicted the tax increase would hurt the economy. "The deficit four years from now will be higher than it is today, not lower," claimed Senator Phil Gramm of Texas.

This prediction turned out to be false. In fact, the United States in 1993 was entering a time of prosperity. As the decade continued, the nation experienced a long period of low unemployment and interest rates. Other features of the booming 1990s economy are shown in the graphs on the next page.

Health-care reform Reform of the nation's health-care system was another major 1992 campaign issue for Clinton. In 1992 health-care costs were rising sharply. Meanwhile, Clinton observed, tens of millions of Americans

The Clinton Style

Bill Clinton's warmth and charm made him an effective candidate. He won both the 1992 and 1996 presidential elections. In his State of the Union address at the start of his second term (inset), Clinton stated that the country had recovered not only its economic strength but also its optimism.

had little or no health insurance. The public, it seemed, was anxious for change.

To explore solutions to these problems, Clinton named a special task force headed by First Lady Hillary Clinton. After months of study, the group proposed a government-sponsored program of health care. Response to the proposal was mixed. The plan offered coverage to all Americans, but many people were unwilling to risk major changes to the health-care system. The plan was defeated after months of debate.

The 1994 elections The defeat of Clinton's health-care plan reflected a discontent with Clinton's leadership. The new president had failed to deliver on several campaign promises. The tax hike of 1993 was also unpopular.

The discontent helped contribute to a major Republican victory in the 1994 midterm elections. Many Republicans, led by Representative Newt Gingrich of Georgia, campaigned with a document they called the Contract with America. The Contract included plans to balance the budget, fight crime, and provide tax cuts for many Americans. The Contract with America appealed to many voters. Republicans gained 54 seats in the House and 8 seats in the Senate. They took control of both houses of Congress for the first time in 40 years.

Welfare reform In spite of this defeat, Clinton bounced back. He did this by addressing several issues the Republicans had raised, including reform of the welfare system. Since the Great Depression, welfare programs had paid cash to poor families. Many people, however, had come to believe that this system was often misused. The Contract with America included plans for welfare reform. Democrats, including Clinton, opposed the plan proposed by the Contract with America.

In 1996, however, Clinton proposed his own welfare-reform plan. It limited the time people could receive benefits and required most recipients to find work within two years of getting benefits. Congress approved this plan.

Other challenges During the 1990s, the Internet emerged as a major means of communication and commerce. It also presented challenges, however. For example, many adults were concerned that children would be exposed

The Economy in the 1990s

Left, shoppers enjoy the benefits of a strong economy at a mall. Disposable income— that is, income available for spending or saving—grew during the 1990s. Americans' rate of savings fell drastically in the 1990s.

FEDERAL DEFICITS AND SURPLUSES, 1980–2000

Source: *Budget of the United States Government, 2005*

STOCK MARKET, 1980–2000

— NASDAQ — Dow Jones

Source: Global Financial Data; New Trading Ideas

Skills Focus INTERPRETING GRAPHS

1. How high were the federal deficits before Clinton took office? How did the federal deficit change in the late 1990s?

2. Compare the rate of growth in the stock market in the 1980s and the 1990s.

See **Skills Handbook**, pp. H16, H17

to inappropriate material on the Internet. The White House helped push a 1996 law to limit the use of the Internet for transmitting certain sexually explicit material. In *Reno* v. *ACLU*, however, the Supreme Court struck down this law as a violation of the freedom of speech.

Clinton also faced the task of helping the nation cope with tragedy. In 1995 terrorists exploded a bomb in the Murrah Federal Building in Oklahoma City, Oklahoma. **Terrorism** is the use of violence by individuals or groups to advance political goals.

The Oklahoma City blast killed 168 people, including many children. More than 500 people were injured. Two Americans, Timothy McVeigh and Terry Nichols, were convicted for their roles in the crime. (McVeigh was executed in 2001. Nichols was sentenced to life in prison.)

Another challenge facing Clinton was re-election. In 1996 he defeated Republican senator Bob Dole of Kansas. H. Ross Perot again ran, this time on the Reform Party ticket.

READING CHECK **Summarizing** In what sense was Clinton's success in domestic policy "mixed"?

Foreign Policy Challenges

When Bill Clinton came into office, the United States was still struggling to understand the post–Cold War world. With the threat of communism gone, Clinton had to determine where American interests lay and how to protect them. The new environment would present its share of challenges to the new president.

Early success in the Middle East In September 1993, Clinton hosted a ceremony for the signing of a major peace agreement between Israel and the Palestinians. The agreement was known as the Oslo Accords. Israeli prime minister Yitzhak Rabin and Palestinian chairman Yasser Arafat agreed to self-rule for the Palestinians in certain areas. The Palestinians agreed to recognize Israel's right to exist. The agreement also set the stage for ongoing negotiations in the Middle East.

Much of the promise of the Oslo Accords was never realized. Yitzhak Rabin died at the hands of an assassin in 1995. Still, the signing was a historic high point in President Clinton's first term.

Somalia Early in his term, Clinton faced a difficult challenge in the African country of Somalia. Before Clinton took office, President Bush had sent American forces there to help a UN program distribute food to starving Somali victims of a civil war within their country.

By 1993 the UN's mission had grown. Now UN forces were working to end the fighting itself. A number of American forces died in the violence. The worst incident occurred in October 1993. In a bloody battle in the Somali capital of Mogadishu, 18 Americans were killed and 84 were wounded. Many Somalis also died. Clinton chose to withdraw American forces. The bitter experience helped discourage Clinton from sending forces to the African country of Rwanda in 1994 to stop a terrible genocide that claimed hundreds of thousands of lives.

Haiti In 1994 the UN acted to settle a violent dispute in the Caribbean nation of Haiti. The goal was to remove a military dictator who had taken over Haiti's government by force. Clinton pledged the use of American troops to lead the UN effort. In September, the force landed in Haiti. Their presence helped bring about a generally peaceful change in government.

The former Yugoslavia Yugoslavia was a country that had formed after World War I. Within its borders lived several ethnic groups that were historical enemies and that had dreams of their own independence. During the

Government
One topic left for future negotiation under the Oslo Accords was the presence of Israeli settlements in the occupied territories. In 2005, Israel removed the settlements in the Gaza Strip, which had long caused conflict with the Palestinians.

Views on Free Trade

In the early days of his administration, President Clinton worked hard to persuade Congress and the American people to support the North American Free Trade Agreement (NAFTA).

Business leader H. Ross Perot opposed NAFTA and free trade during his independent campaign for the presidency in 1992.

66 [U]nder NAFTA more jobs will stay home here in America and more American exports will head to Mexico . . . If you want to create more American jobs, if you want to lower the differences in cost of production in America and Mexico, if you want to take down barriers in Mexico to exports, then you should want NAFTA. 99

President Clinton, 1993

66 You implement that NAFTA, the Mexican trade agreement, where they pay people a dollar an hour, have no health care, no retirement, no pollution controls . . . and you're going to hear a giant sucking sound of jobs being pulled out of this country. 99

H. Ross Perot, 1992

Skills FOCUS **READING LIKE A HISTORIAN**

Analyzing Primary Sources Why does Clinton think NAFTA will create American jobs? Why does Perot expect the opposite?

See **Skills Handbook**, p. H28–H29

THE IMPACT TODAY

Economics

In August 2005, President George W. Bush signed the Central American-Dominican Republic Free Trade Agreement, or CAFTA-DR. The agreement is designed to break down trade barriers between the United States and several Latin American neighbors.

Cold War, the country was held together by its leader, Josip Broz Tito. Soon after Tito's death in 1980, however, the country began to unravel. By the 1990s Yugoslavia no longer existed. In its place were several smaller countries. Within and between these countries, violence raged.

Clinton was deeply involved in efforts to end the bloodshed. In 1995 he helped bring about the Dayton Accords, an agreement aimed at ending fighting in the new country of Bosnia and Herzegovina. In 1999 he urged NATO to act against Serbia, another country formed from the former Yugoslavia. His goal was to stop the Serb army's attempt to force ethnic Albanians from the Serbian region of Kosovo. NATO forces conducted a bombing campaign that forced Serb troops to leave Kosovo.

Promoting international trade Another issue awaiting Bill Clinton when he took office was the North American Free Trade Agreement, or **NAFTA**. Under this agreement, the

United States, Mexico, and Canada became one large free-trade zone. This meant that most products could be sold across the borders of these countries without tariffs or trade barriers. President Bush had completed negotiations on the agreement before he left office. It became Clinton's job to win congressional approval. Facing stiff opposition, Clinton fought for and won passage of NAFTA in the fall of 1993.

Some critics believed NAFTA would cost American jobs. They argued that because Mexican factories paid lower wages, they could make and sell goods at a lower cost than American-made goods. Without tariffs to make Mexican goods more expensive, many feared American factories would go out of business.

Clinton and supporters of NAFTA believed the agreement would increase trade, which would help the economy. Indeed, increasing trade was a major Clinton goal. During his presidency, the United States took part in the creation of the World Trade Organization (WTO).

The WTO replaced the General Agreement on Tariffs and Trade (GATT). It was meant as a means of settling trade disputes and forming rules for global trade. Clinton pushed for other trade agreements as well. For example, he fought for permanent normal trade status for China, the world's most populous country.

 READING CHECK **Identifying Supporting Details** How did the end of the Cold War affect Clinton's foreign policy?

Scandal and Impeachment

Clinton had won the presidency in spite of questions about his past. His election, however, did not end the controversy. Soon came even more scandal.

Throughout his first term, Clinton faced investigation about an investment he and his wife had made in a failed real estate project in the 1970s. The project was known as Whitewater. Among several legal questions related to Whitewater, observers wondered whether the Clintons and their business partners had acted improperly in getting and using loans.

Special prosecutor Kenneth Starr led the Whitewater investigation. Though he never filed any Whitewater-related charges against Clinton, three former Clinton business associates were found guilty of various crimes.

Clinton also faced charges that while he was governor of Arkansas, he had sexually harassed a female state employee. That woman, named Paula Jones, brought a lawsuit against the president. In the course of this case, information emerged suggesting that the president had conducted an improper relationship with a 21-year-old White House intern named Monica Lewinsky. Starr then extended the scope of his investigation to include Clinton's relationship with Lewinsky.

Eventually, Clinton was accused of lying under oath about his relationship with Lewinsky. He was also accused of trying to influence Lewinsky's testimony. Clinton later admitted he had conducted an improper relationship, but he said he did not lie under oath.

The House of Representatives responded by approving two articles of impeachment against Clinton in November 1998. Clinton was the first president to face a Senate impeachment trial since Andrew Johnson in 1868.

In order to remove a president from office, a two-thirds majority in the Senate must vote to convict. In early 1999 the Senate voted 55–45 against conviction on the first article of impeachment and voted 50–50 on the second article. Clinton remained in office to complete his term.

READING CHECK **Sequencing** What role did scandal play in Bill Clinton's presidency?

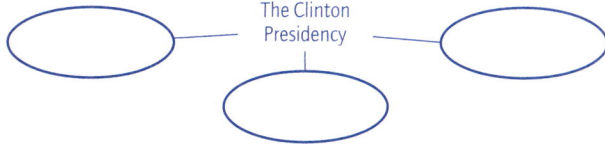

SECTION 1 ASSESSMENT

go.hrw.com
Online Quiz
Keyword: SD7 HP33

Reviewing Ideas, Terms, and People

1. a. Recall Who were the key figures in the election of 1992?
b. Make Inferences What can you infer from the performance of H. Ross Perot in the 1992 election?

2. a. Define Write a brief definition of the following term: Contract with America
b. Summarize What do you think were Clinton's greatest successes and his greatest failures during his time in office?

3. a. Identify What were the major foreign-policy issues facing the Clinton administration?
b. Make Generalizations Toward what goals did the United States use military force during Clinton's time in office?

4. a. Identify Identify and briefly describe the significance of the Whitewater scandal.
b. Explain On what grounds did the House of Representatives approve articles of impeachment against Clinton?

Critical Thinking

5. Identifying the Main Idea Copy the chart below and use information from the section to record details that support the main idea of the section.

The Clinton Presidency

FOCUS ON WRITING

6. Narrative President Clinton was known for overcoming setbacks to achieve political success. Write a brief paragraph telling of some of the setbacks and recoveries of the Clinton administration.

LANDMARK SUPREME COURT CASES

Constitutional Issue: Search and Seizure

ST 1.2 Analyze the decisions leading to major turning points in United States history, comparing alternative courses of action, and hypothesizing, within the context of the historical period, about what might have happened if the decision had been different.

Vernonia School District v. *Acton* (1995)

Why It Matters The Fourth Amendment prevents the government from making unreasonable searches. In this case, the Supreme Court found it reasonable to "search" student athletes by making them submit to drug testing.

Background of the Case

Officials in the Vernonia School District in Oregon were concerned about the extent of drug use by students. The school district adopted a rule requiring student athletes to submit to random drug testing. When James Acton signed up to play seventh-grade football, he and his parents refused to sign the consent form for drug testing. The school did not let him play, so Acton sued, arguing that the drug testing violated the search and seizure clause of the Fourth Amendment. The trial court ruled that he had no valid constitutional claim and dismissed his case, but the court of appeals reinstated the case. The school district then appealed to the Supreme Court.

THE IMPACT TODAY Public high schools can now require student athletes to submit to drug testing as a condition of playing sports. The Supreme Court's decision gives schools more power to detect and discourage drug abuse by student athletes.

The Decision

The Supreme Court ruled that random drug testing of student athletes is not a violation of the Fourth Amendment's search and seizure clause. First, the Court held that drug testing is a "search" under the Fourth Amendment. The question was whether the search was reasonable. The Court decided that the school district had a legitimate concern about student drug use and that the testing program was designed to have a minimal impact on students' privacy. Finally, the Court held that students were not required to go out for sports, and those who did should expect some intrusions on their privacy. The manner and extent of the search were reasonable, the Court held, so the drug testing was lawful under the Constitution.

go.hrw.com
Research Online
Keyword: SS Court

CRITICAL THINKING

1. **Analyze the Impact** Using the keyword above, find and read the text of the Fourth Amendment. Could the Supreme Court have found that the school drug testing was not a search within the meaning of the Constitution?

2. **You Be the Judge** Based on the *Vernonia School District* decision, should a school be allowed to require drug testing for students who participate in nonsports activities, such as the yearbook or chess club? Explain your answer in a short paragraph.

George W. Bush's Presidency

BEFORE YOU READ

MAIN IDEA

Following a troubled election, Republican George W. Bush won the White House and strongly promoted his agenda.

READING FOCUS

1. What were the unusual circumstances of the election of 2000?

2. What were key components of George W. Bush's domestic policy?

3. What were the key components and figures in Bush's foreign policy?

KEY TERMS AND PEOPLE

George W. Bush
budget surplus
Bush v. *Gore*
dot-com
dividend
Colin Powell
Condoleezza Rice

 P1 3.3 Prepare essays and oral reports about the important social, political, economic, scientific, technological, and cultural developments, issues, and events from New York State and United States history.

 ### What happened on the night of the 2000 presidential election?

For **George W. Bush**, it had been a night of great tension. At the end of a hard-fought campaign for president, the Republican candidate sat down with his family to watch the election returns on TV.

First came news that Democratic candidate Al Gore had apparently won the popular vote in Florida—a state that was key to the outcome of the election. Two hours later, the news organizations that had made this report took an extraordinary step—they retracted their announcement and declared the winner in Florida uncertain. Then at around 2 a.m., these same news organizations announced that Bush had won Florida—and with it the presidency. Gore, following the election-night custom, called Bush to acknowledge Bush's victory and congratulate the new president-elect.

But the drama was not yet over. An hour after Gore's telephone call, the news organizations switched their call again! Florida was once more considered too close to call. Gore called his opponent once again—this time taking back his admission of defeat. The election in Florida was over, but who had won the presidency? It would take more than a month to determine the answer. ◾

An Election Night to Remember

▼ **George W. Bush (center) awaits results with his father, former president George H. W. Bush, and brother Jeb.**

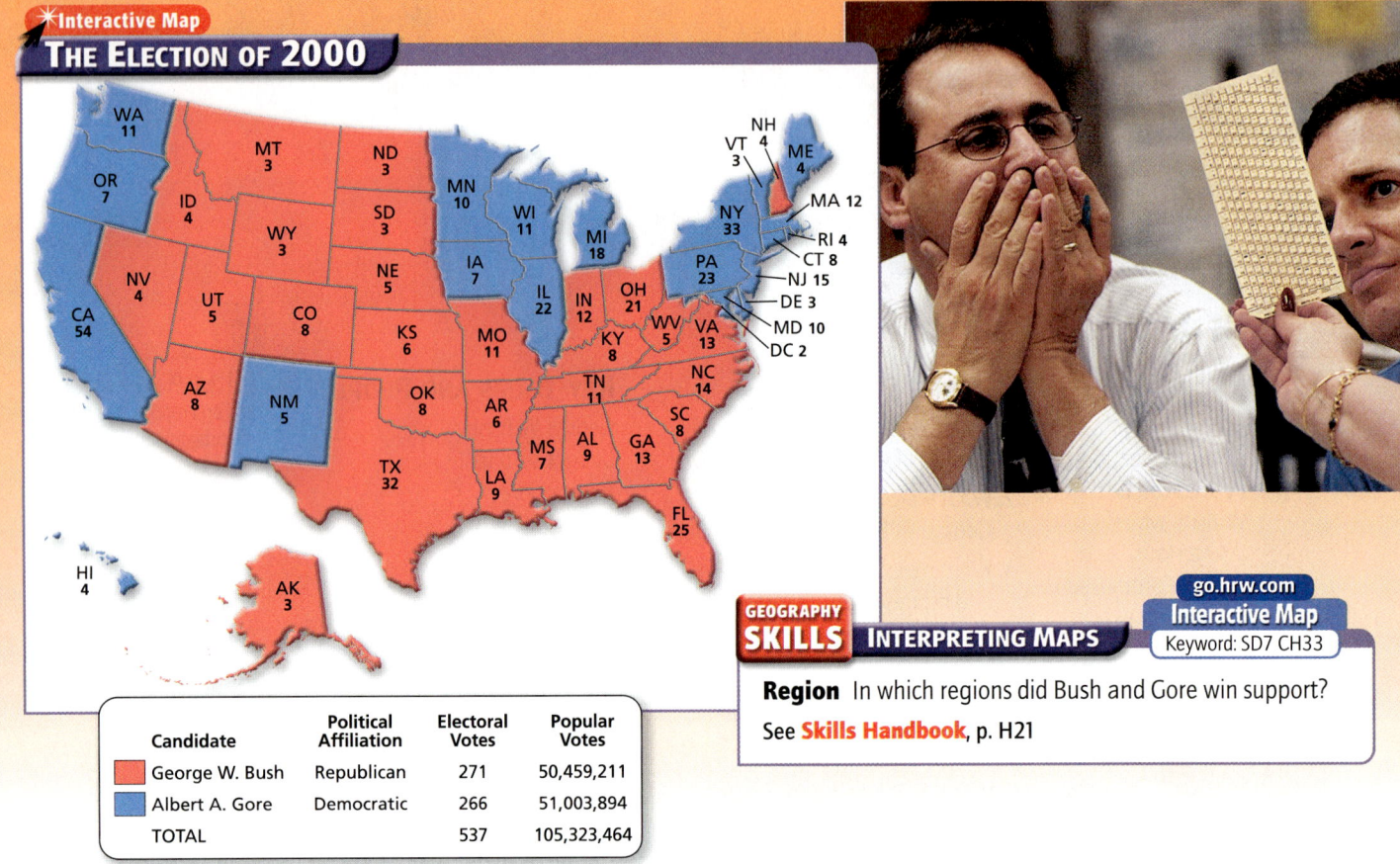

Interactive Map

THE ELECTION OF 2000

Candidate	Political Affiliation	Electoral Votes	Popular Votes
George W. Bush	Republican	271	50,459,211
Albert A. Gore	Democratic	266	51,003,894
TOTAL		537	105,323,464

GEOGRAPHY SKILLS | **INTERPRETING MAPS**

go.hrw.com
Interactive Map
Keyword: SD7 CH33

Region In which regions did Bush and Gore win support?
See **Skills Handbook**, p. H21

The Election of 2000

With President Clinton finishing his second term, both parties knew the 2000 race was wide open. It turned out to be one of the closest, most controversial elections in U.S. history.

The nominees During Clinton's presidency, the American economy prospered. The federal government had a **budget surplus**, which meant that its income exceeded its spending. Although the country's future looked bright, some Democrats were uncomfortable with Clinton's image.

Nobody understood the situation better than Clinton's vice president, Al Gore. As the Democratic nominee in the 2000 presidential race, Gore wanted to claim credit for the success of the past. He also needed to set himself apart from Clinton. "We're entering a new time," he declared as he accepted his party's nomination. "We're electing a new president. And I stand here tonight as my own man." For his running mate, Gore made a historic choice: Connecticut senator Joe Lieberman, who became the first Jewish American to seek that high office.

The Republicans chose George W. Bush as their candidate. The son of former president George H.W. Bush, he had served six years as governor of Texas. Bush's running mate was Dick Cheney of Wyoming. Cheney had a long record that included service in Congress and in several previous administrations.

The 2000 election also featured the third-party candidacy of Ralph Nader. A longtime advocate for American consumers, Nader ran as the leader of the Green Party, a liberal party that supported environmental causes.

A troubled election As election day 2000 approached, polls indicated a tight race. The polls were correct. Election-night returns showed a close popular and electoral vote. It soon became clear that the race hinged on the outcome in a single state—Florida. Whoever won there would win the election.

As you have read, election returns in Florida were amazingly close. The result was confusion, with news organizations changing their reports several times about who had won the state. The matter remained unresolved through the night and into the next morning.

A pair of reporters examine an incorrectly punched ballot during a manual election recount in Fort Lauderdale, Florida, in early December 2000. Controversy over incorrectly punched ballots and so-called butterfly ballots stalled election results. *How was the outcome finally decided?*

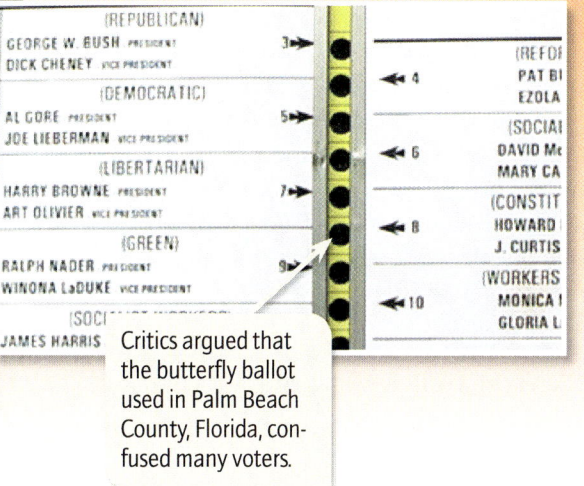

Critics argued that the butterfly ballot used in Palm Beach County, Florida, confused many voters.

Recounts and legal wrangling Florida election officials quickly performed a recount of the ballots. As with the original vote count, this was performed by machine. The recount gave Bush a lead of just over 300 votes out of a total of nearly 6 million Florida ballots cast.

Meanwhile, Democrats were raising questions about the Florida balloting. One concern was that thousands of ballots had gone uncounted by vote-counting machines. Many ballots had been rejected because voters had made mistakes in marking them. For example, some ballots required voters to make their choices by punching a hole in the ballot. In some cases, the hole was not clean or complete enough for the counting machine to read. Democrats argued that in many cases, the choice of the voters was obvious even though the ballot-counting equipment did not count the ballot. Because the race was so close, they said, it made sense to recount all ballots by hand. They hoped that among the uncounted ballots they would gain enough votes to win the state.

Another type of punch-card ballot used in Florida was the butterfly ballot shown above.

Some observers argued that the butterfly ballot's design led some voters to mistakenly select someone other than their intended choice.

Republicans were generally opposed to hand recounts of ballots. One reason was that hand counting introduced the role of human error and individual judgment. They also objected to Democratic plans to recount only in areas that were thought to be heavily Democratic.

Over the next few days, Democrats and Republicans took turns filing lawsuits aimed at forcing or preventing recounts. In some counties, recounts were completed. Absentee ballots were also tallied, some of which were challenged by Democrats.

Bush v. Gore On December 8, Gore won what seemed like a key legal victory. The Florida Supreme Court ordered that hand recounts had to take place in certain Florida counties.

The Bush campaign appealed the ruling to the U.S. Supreme Court. The Court issued its decision in *Bush* v. *Gore* on December 12, 2000. The ruling held that the Florida Supreme Court's recount order was unconstitutional because it failed to provide clear standards by which the ballots were to be counted. Further, the Court held, there was no time to create standards for use statewide.

The day after the decision, Gore publicly accepted his defeat in the race. That evening, George W. Bush addressed the nation on television as the president-elect. He urged Americans to unite for the future.

HISTORY'S VOICES

❝ I was not elected to serve one party, but to serve one nation.

The president of the United States is the president of every single American, of every race and every background.

Whether you voted for me or not, I will do my best to serve your interests and I will work to earn your respect. ❞

—George W. Bush, December 13, 2000

On January 20, 2001, Bush was sworn in as president. He became only the fourth person in American history to have won the presidency in spite of having received fewer popular votes than his opponent.

 **READING CHECK** **Sequencing** What was the sequence of key events in the election of 2000?

THE IMPACT TODAY

Government

In 2002 President Bush signed into law the Help America Vote Act, which provided funds to help states replace punch-card voting machines with electronic voting systems. The law required states to have the new voting systems in place by 2006. However, criticism has arisen over the electronic voting machines' accuracy, reliability, and security. For this reason, several states have begun keeping paper trails of electronic voting or providing optional paper ballots.

Bush's Domestic Policy

The 1990s had been a prosperous time. By the time Bush took office, however, the picture was beginning to change. For example, even before the election, the once booming stock market had begun to fall. This was due in large part to the collapse in the price of many Internet-related stocks.

In the 1990s the Internet represented a whole new way of doing business. Many investors had hoped to make big money buying shares of Internet pioneers. These companies were known as dot-coms, after the .com that appears in many Internet addresses. Investors gambled billions on dot-coms. They paid high prices for the stock of companies that had never earned a profit. They expected the companies to make money one day. When the profits failed to appear, however, investors began to sell their stocks. As a result, prices dropped.

Stock prices were also hurt by a series of scandals that hit several large corporations in the early 2000s. The scandals involved dishonest accounting methods designed to make the companies more attractive to investors.

In addition to the drop in the stock market, the overall economy began to slow. Shortly after Bush took office, the United States was officially entering a recession. Though Bush was not responsible for this development, it did affect his domestic policies.

Tax cuts During the campaign, Bush had promised to cut taxes. At that time, the country enjoyed a budget surplus. When he took office, he quickly urged Congress to take action.

HISTORY'S VOICES

" You see, the growing surplus exists because taxes are too high and government is charging more than it needs. The people of America have been overcharged and on their behalf, I'm here asking for a refund. "

—George W. Bush, February 27, 2001

Bush also argued that cutting taxes would help spur the now slumping economy. By lowering taxes and letting Americans keep more of their income to spend, Bush reasoned, business would improve. He believed this would provide more jobs and higher incomes.

By June, the Republican-controlled Congress had delivered on Bush's request. In addition to cutting tax rates, the new law addressed some long-standing complaints about the tax code. For example, it helped reduce the so-called marriage penalty. This is a part of the tax code that causes many married people to pay higher taxes than they would if they were single. The new law also lowered the estate tax, a tax on property inherited after a person's death.

Despite Bush's tax cuts, however, the economy did not improve. Instead, it went into recession. This recession was made worse by the terrorist attacks of September 11, 2001, which you will read about in the next section.

By 2003 Bush was again looking to cut taxes in hopes of promoting economic growth. Congress again passed a tax cut, which included the elimination of taxes on dividends. A dividend is a portion of a company's profits paid to its shareholders.

Education, health care, and more

Shortly after taking office, Bush announced a major plan for improving education. The plan became the basis for a 2001 law, the No Child Left Behind (NCLB) Act. A key part of NCLB was a requirement that states develop academic standards and test students annually to ensure that those standards are met.

Another early Bush program was the White House Office of Faith-Based Initiatives. This office helps religious community-service organizations of all faiths develop greater access to federal funding. Bush viewed religious groups as effective tools for delivering services to needy groups such as the homeless, troubled youth, and former prison inmates. Critics, however, worried that the program might cross the constitutional line separating church and state.

In 2003 Bush signed into law a major update to the Medicare program. Included in this update was a new benefit to help Medicare recipients pay for prescription medicines.

Bush's second term In 2004 Bush ran for a second term in office. The Democrats nominated Senator John Kerry of Massachusetts. In addition to attacking Bush's foreign policy, Kerry criticized Bush's handling of the economy. He noted that the government was again running large deficits—that is, spending more than it takes in. In spite of these attacks, Bush won re-election in another close contest.

No Child Left Behind

In 2001 Congress passed an amendment to the Elementary and Secondary Education Act of 1965. Known as No Child Left Behind (NCLB), the law is intended to improve education across the United States.

No Child Left Behind says that all students should reach at least minimal proficiency on state academic achievement standards and state academic tests. Under the law, students will take standardized tests every year to show what they have learned. The results will be used to decide whether students are getting the education they need.

Many states already had testing programs in place before NCLB was put into effect. Remaining states had until the 2005–2006 school year to make sure that their tests addressed their state's academic standards.

Not everyone agrees that NCLB is the solution to improving education. In 2003 the National Education Association, a teachers' union, filed a lawsuit arguing that the federal government was not providing enough money to support the required changes. A lawsuit filed by the state of Connecticut in 2005 also opposed the idea that states should pay for federal education goals.

Making Inferences Why might leaders feel that standardized testing is a useful tool for measuring what students have learned?

High school students take a standardized test.

Bush soon announced a top priority for his second term: reform of Social Security. Recall that this system uses money collected from taxpayers to help fund payments to retired Americans. Bush noted that in the future, taxpayers would be unable to pay all the benefits due to retirees. He proposed reforms that would allow taxpayers to create private accounts to fund their retirement. The plan, however, faced considerable public opposition. By late 2005 Congress had not acted on it.

Bush also faced decisions over Supreme Court vacancies. In 2005, Justice Sandra Day O'Connor announced her retirement and Chief Justice William Rehnquist died. To replace Rehnquist as Chief Justice, Bush nominated John Roberts, who won Senate confirmation in September 2005. To replace O'Connor, Bush nominated conservative judge Samuel Alito. On January 31, 2006, Alito won Senate confirmation in a 58-42 vote, one of the tightest margins in recent history.

READING CHECK **Identifying Problems and Solutions** What were some of the problems Bush hoped to address with his domestic policies?

Bush's Foreign Policy

Even before taking office in 2001, Bush assembled his foreign-policy staff. He chose **Colin Powell** as secretary of state. Powell had been a general in the army and chair of the Joint Chiefs of Staff during the Persian Gulf War of 1991. Bush named **Condoleezza Rice** as his national security adviser. Rice had been on the faculty of Stanford University and had served in the administration of George H. W. Bush.

Soon after the 2004 election, Powell resigned and Rice became secretary of state. For secretary of defense, Bush selected Donald Rumsfeld, who had earlier held this post and other key government posts. In 2006 Rumsfeld resigned as well, and Robert Gates became the new secretary of defense.

During the 2000 election campaign, Bush had promised to limit the use of American troops for what he termed "nation building." For example, he criticized Clinton's use of troops in Somalia and Haiti.

With this in mind, Bush called for a review of the nation's armed forces. He wanted to ensure that the military was prepared to fight the kinds of conflicts the United States might face.

Colin POWELL
1937–

Born to Jamaican immigrants in New York City, General Colin Powell became the youngest man to serve as the Chairman of the Joint Chiefs of Staff in 1989. His experience as a key advisor to President George H. W. Bush during the Gulf War would prove invaluable to Powell in the future. In 2001 Powell became the first African American to hold the office of secretary of state when he was unanimously confirmed by the U.S. Senate. He served in that capacity until 2004. Powell spent much of his tenure as secretary of state dealing with issues in the Middle East. One of Powell's first duties was to try and negotiate peace between Israel and the Palestinians. After the September 11 terrorist attacks in 2001, Powell helped win support for U.S. action against Afghanistan, the Taliban forces, and the March 2003 invasion of Iraq.

Infer How might Powell's experience in the military have helped him as secretary of state?

Bush also decided to cancel the 1972 Anti-Ballistic Missile (ABM) Treaty. This agreement had been forged with the Soviet Union during the Cold War. Bush argued that the nation no longer faced a nuclear threat from Russia. Instead, he believed the danger was from some terrorist state. Therefore, Bush planned to move forward with development of a missile defense system. At the same time, Bush planned steep cuts in the nation's nuclear arsenal. This, he said, signaled his own commitment to reducing the threat to other nations.

The decision on the ABM treaty caused some friction with Russia and China. In general, however, Bush worked to build better relations with both countries. For example, he relied heavily on China's cooperation in putting pressure on North Korea to end its program for building nuclear weapons.

Bush also helped promote the so-called Middle East road map to peace. This historic document established a two-state vision—that is, an independent Palestinian state as well as the Jewish state of Israel.

The peace plan, brokered by the United States, the European Union, Russia and the United Nations, required the Palestinian Authority to appoint a prime minister free from the control of long-time leader Yasir Arafat and end terrorism in exchange for statehood. For their part the Israelis would have to recognize the new Palestinian government and end the so-called "settlement movement" in the occupied territories of the West Bank and the Gaza Strip. However, violence between both sides continued and Israel renewed work on a security barrier around the occupied territories, over protest by Palestinians.

Arafat's death paved the way for the election of Mahmoud Abbas as the new Palestinian president in 2005 and a negotiated cease-fire. Secretary of State Condoleezza Rice later brokered a deal opening the border between the Gaza Strip and Egypt. By far, however, the most important foreign-policy event of the Bush administration occurred on September 11, 2001. This event set in motion a series of events that continue to affect the United States today. You will be reading about September 11 in the next section.

READING CHECK **Contrasting** How did Bush's foreign policy differ from Clinton's?

SECTION 2 ASSESSMENT

go.hrw.com
Online Quiz
Keyword: SD7 HP33

Reviewing Ideas, Terms, and People

1. **a. Describe** What factors made the 2000 election unusual?
   b. Contrast How did the positions of the Democrats and Republicans differ in the 2000 election with regard to hand recounting of ballots?

2. **a. Define** Write a brief definition of each of the following terms: **budget surplus, dot-com, dividend**
   b. Analyze How did the change in the economic situation in the United States affect George W. Bush's presidency?

3. **a. Identify** Besides the terrorist attacks of September 11, 2001, what were the major foreign-policy issues facing the Bush administration?
   b. Make Generalizations How did Bush's foreign policy reflect the realities of a post-Cold War world?

Critical Thinking

4. **Identifying the Main Idea** Copy the chart below and use information from the section to record details that support the main idea of the section.

The Bush Presidency

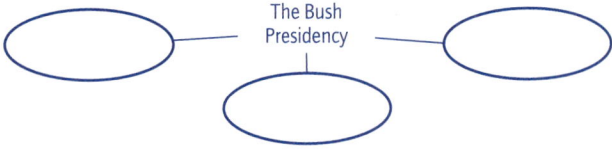

5. **Narrative** Write and deliver a news story about the key events of the 2000 presidential election. The account should tell what made the election so unusual in American politics.

How September 11, 2001, Changed America

BEFORE YOU READ

MAIN IDEA

A horrific attack on September 11, 2001, awakened the nation to the threat of terrorism and changed America's view of the world.

READING FOCUS

1. What happened on September 11, 2001?
2. What was the background to the September 11 attacks?
3. How did the United States respond to the attacks?
4. How did the 9/11 attacks eventually lead to war with Iraq?

KEY TERMS AND PEOPLE

9/11
Rudolph Giuliani
Osama bin Laden
al Qaeda
Taliban
Department of Homeland Security
USA PATRIOT Act

PI 3.4 Understand the interrelationships between world events and developments in New York State and the United States (e.g., causes for immigration, economic opportunities, human rights abuses, and tyranny versus freedom).

Attack on the World Trade Center

THE INSIDE STORY

What would you do if terrorists struck your neighborhood? On September 11, 2001, students at Stuyvesant High School in New York City were not at all prepared for terror to strike their community. Yet that morning, just as school was getting started, an aircraft slammed into one of the Twin Towers of the World Trade Center, about five blocks away. A short while later, a second airplane struck the second tower.

The students fled the school in search of safety. Among them was Ethan Moses, the photographer for the Stuyvesant High School newspaper, *The Spectator*. When he left the school, he took his camera along. As a student journalist, he felt driven to record what was taking place in his neighborhood—even though he was terrified by the tragedy unfolding before him. Before turning to run for his own safety, he snapped the image you see here of one of the Twin Towers collapsing.

Moses knew that he must preserve the images of what took place that day. Like Americans throughout the country, he overcame his horror and faced the September 11 attacks with courage and resolve. ◼

◀ **The horror of September 11, 2001, changed the way Americans looked at themselves and the world.**

September 11, 2001

Shortly after 8:45 A.M. on September 11, 2001, people around the country began to hear startling reports of a terrible crash in New York City. An airliner had slammed into one of the 110-story-tall Twin Towers of the World Trade Center. This complex housed thousands of offices and businesses.

A deliberate attack Just 17 minutes after the first jet crashed, a second aircraft flew into the second of the Twin Towers. It became clear that the crashes were part of a deliberate attack. President Bush appeared before reporters to issue a brief statement. "Today we've had a national tragedy," he declared. He then assured the public that he had ordered the "full resources of the federal government" to respond to the disaster.

In fact, the attack—and its devastating effects—had just begun. In New York, fire-fighters and police officers rushed to the World Trade Center to help get people out of the burning towers. Military officials launched fighter aircraft to guard against any further attack. The Federal Aviation Administration (FAA) frantically gathered information about other possible hijackings. Hijacking is a terrorist act in which a plane is forced to go somewhere other than its intended destination. To prevent terrorists from getting control of more planes, the FAA also halted all commercial flights.

Unfortunately, there was nothing the FAA could do to stop the deadly flight of planes already in the air. Less than an hour after the first plane hit in New York, another slammed into the Pentagon, the mammoth headquarters of the Department of Defense located just outside Washington, D.C.

The Twin Towers collapse By now, millions of people were watching events unfold on television or listening to the news on the

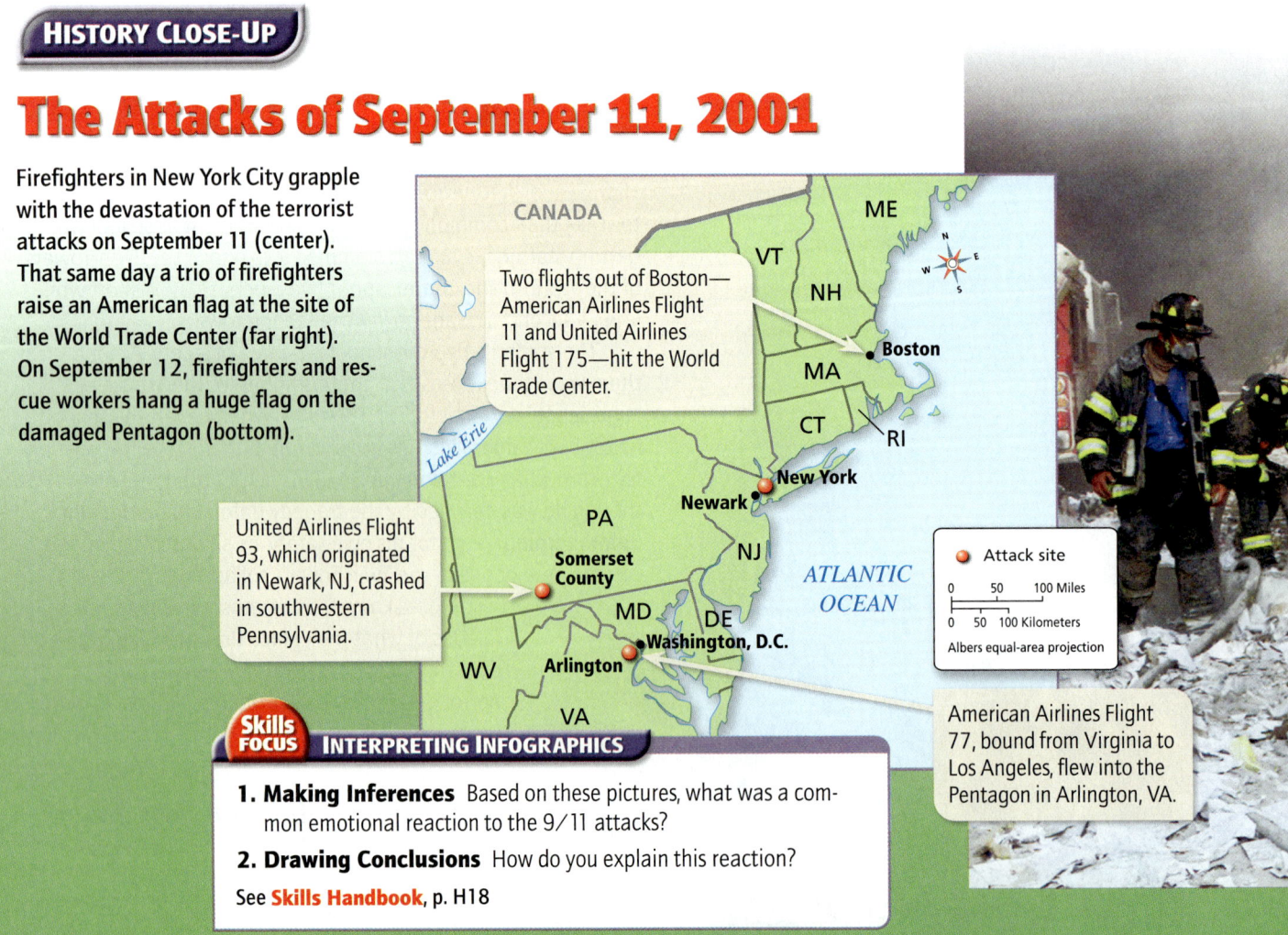

HISTORY CLOSE-UP

The Attacks of September 11, 2001

Firefighters in New York City grapple with the devastation of the terrorist attacks on September 11 (center). That same day a trio of firefighters raise an American flag at the site of the World Trade Center (far right). On September 12, firefighters and rescue workers hang a huge flag on the damaged Pentagon (bottom).

CANADA

Two flights out of Boston—American Airlines Flight 11 and United Airlines Flight 175—hit the World Trade Center.

United Airlines Flight 93, which originated in Newark, NJ, crashed in southwestern Pennsylvania.

American Airlines Flight 77, bound from Virginia to Los Angeles, flew into the Pentagon in Arlington, VA.

ME
VT
NH
MA
Boston
CT
RI
New York
Newark
PA
NJ
ATLANTIC OCEAN
Somerset County
Lake Erie
MD
DE
WV
Arlington
Washington, D.C.
VA

Attack site

0   50   100 Miles
0 50 100 Kilometers
Albers equal-area projection

Skills FOCUS INTERPRETING INFOGRAPHICS

1. **Making Inferences** Based on these pictures, what was a common emotional reaction to the 9/11 attacks?

2. **Drawing Conclusions** How do you explain this reaction?

See **Skills Handbook**, p. H18

radio. But the worst was yet to come. Ten minutes after the Pentagon crash came the shocking collapse of the World Trade Center's South Tower. Fires caused by the plane's nearly full fuel tanks had caused a fatal weakening of the building's structure. The horrifying event was captured by TV cameras for viewers everywhere to see. Shortly after that came news of a fourth plane crash, this one in a field in the Pennsylvania countryside. Then at about 10:30 A.M., the North Tower collapsed in a massive cloud of dust and debris.

The stunned nation did not know it yet, but the worst was over. Later in the day, another building that had been damaged when the Twin Towers came down collapsed. But there were no more hijackings or plane crashes.

The death toll The nation next turned to face the horrible reality of what had taken place. To begin with, the four planes had carried 265 people, including passengers and crew. All were dead. In addition, at the Pentagon, 125 people were killed by the plane's impact and the fires that followed. The number of victims at the World Trade Center was not known, but the estimates were in the thousands. (After several years of investigation, the New York death toll stood at 2,749.) It was clear that the attacks of **9/11** would surpass Pearl Harbor and other great disasters of American history in terms of lives lost.

The nation reacts The nation was overcome by a wave of grief and anger. At the same time, recognition of the bravery of those who responded to the disaster gave people comfort and strength. Americans were awestruck by the heroism of New York's rescue workers. Several hundred firefighters and police officers had run willingly into the burning towers, only to perish when they collapsed. Many also admired the steady leadership of the mayor of New York, **Rudolph Giuliani**. Giuliani inspired millions by stating, "Tomorrow New York is going to be here. . . . I want the people of New York to be an example to the rest of the country, and the rest of the world, that terrorism can't stop us."

DAILY LIFE

In 2004 New Yorker Michael Arad's design "Reflecting Absence" was chosen as the memorial to those who lost their lives during the September 11 World Trade Center terrorist attacks. The design features two large voids with recessed pools where the two towers once stood.

ACADEMIC VOCABULARY

rational based on reason

There were also reports that the plane that crashed in Pennsylvania may have been forced down by the heroic actions of its passengers. Telephone calls from passengers aboard the plane indicated they knew about the other attacks and had decided to stop the terrorists on board from hitting their next target.

Inspired by these stories, Americans reached out to the victims of 9/11. Blood collection centers received two-and-a-half times the normal donations in the days after 9/11. Millions of dollars poured into charities. Rescue workers from around the country traveled to New York to help with the recovery efforts at Ground Zero, the site where the Twin Towers had stood. Six months after the attacks one of the first memorials to the victims of 9/11 was unveiled in New York City. Called the "Tribute in Light", twin beams of searchlights were set up about a block from Ground Zero. The shafts of light were pointed up into the sky, representing the lost towers.

While honoring the victims, Americans also strengthened their resolve to face the challenge ahead. Patriotic feelings soared, and millions of people displayed American flags. It was clear that the United States was now engaged in a new kind of war: a war on terrorism.

READING CHECK **Sequencing** What were the key events of September 11, 2001?

In the days following the attacks, New Yorkers placed several memorials such as this one in Manhattan's Union Square Park to remember the victims of 9/11.

Background to the Attacks

Investigators, meanwhile, were trying to determine who was responsible for the attacks. One rational theory focused on **Osama bin Laden**. A member of a wealthy Saudi Arabian family, bin Laden had gone to Afghanistan in the 1980s to help fight Soviet invaders. During this time, he adopted the goal of promoting a worldwide Islamic revolution. Islam is one of the world's major religions, and it is based on the teachings of the prophet Muhammad, who lived about AD 570–632. Achieving an Islamic revolution, bin Laden claimed, required the destruction of the United States. Bin Laden had also been angered by the presence of American military forces in Saudi Arabia during the Persian Gulf War. This he saw as an insult to Islam.

To carry out his campaign against his enemies, bin Laden developed a terrorist network. This was known as **al Qaeda**, or "the base." By 2001 bin Laden and al Qaeda were well known to American officials. During the 1990s, these terrorists had made a number of threats against the United States and announced the goal of killing Americans. Bin Laden had links to a 1993 bombing at the World Trade Center that killed six people. He was also accused of helping to train some of the attackers who killed 18 American soldiers in Mogadishu, Somalia, in 1993. In August 1998 bombings at the U.S. embassies in the African countries of Kenya and Tanzania killed 224. After establishing a link between the bombings and bin

FACES OF HISTORY

Rudolph W. GIULIANI
1944–

Rudolph (Rudy) Giuliani had been the popular and sometimes controversial mayor of New York City for eight years when the terrorist attacks occurred on September 11, 2001. Giuliani already had proven himself to be a tough and decisive leader, cutting New York's crime rate by two-thirds. His battle with prostate cancer in 2000 also showed his will and determination.

Giuliani's leadership, however, was tested on and after the attacks of September 11. He once again proved himself to New Yorkers and also to people across the country by making quick, sound decisions and providing frequent announcements and updates to worried New Yorkers. Giuliani visited frightened families in hospitals and inspired hope by promising to build a stronger New York and even in the middle of what he believed to be a terrorist attack, he called on New Yorkers to show tolerance. Through his heroic actions on that terrible day, Giuliani became known as "America's Mayor."

Make Inferences How do you think Mayor Giuliani's previous experiences prepared him for September 11?

Laden's network, President Clinton launched a missile attack into a suspected al Qaeda training camp in Afghanistan. Bin Laden and his organization survived. In 2000 they carried out a bomb attack on an American naval vessel, the USS *Cole*, which was visiting a port in the Middle Eastern country of Yemen. Seventeen Americans died in the blast.

Meanwhile, investigators later learned, al Qaeda was busy planning the 9/11 attacks. As part of this plan, terrorists began entering the United States in early 2000. They enrolled in American flight schools, where they learned the basics of flying airliners.

By September 11 they were ready to act. In the morning hours, they boarded flights at several East Coast airports. They chose long, cross-country routes so that the planes would be fully loaded with fuel. Once in the air, the hijackers—19 in total—seized control of the aircrafts. To do so, they used ordinary box cutters as weapons. It was a complicated plan that used simple methods. Tragically, it worked just as they had planned.

READING CHECK **Identifying the Main Idea**
What is Osama bin Laden's background and his reasons for using terrorism?

The United States Responds

Fires were still burning in New York and at the Pentagon when President Bush issued a clear warning to the world. "We will make no distinction between the terrorists who committed these acts and those who harbor them," he declared. With suspicion quickly focusing on Osama bin Laden and his al Qaeda network, Bush's warning seemed especially directed toward the nation of Afghanistan.

War in Afghanistan Afghanistan had endured terrible suffering in the late 1900s. The 1979 invasion by the Soviet Union had been followed by years of bloody fighting and civil war. Out of this chaos, a group known as the **Taliban** had gained control over most of the country. The Taliban governed according to a strict application of Islamic law. For example, women were required to wear clothing that covered nearly every inch of their bodies. They were forbidden from attending school or leaving home without a male relative. Punishment for offenses was swift and harsh.

The Taliban also enjoyed a close relationship with Osama bin Laden. Recall that bin Laden operated al Qaeda training camps in

Responding to the Attacks

President Bush meets with his National Security Council on September 12, 2001, to plan America's response to the terrorist attacks on the nation. Attention focused on Afghanistan (see map below), a landlocked country in south-central Asia with a mountainous terrain and extreme climate.

AFGHANISTAN

TURKMENISTAN
UZBEKISTAN TAJIKISTAN
Herat
Jalalabad
Kabul
Tora Bora
AFGHANISTAN
PAKISTAN
IRAN
Kandahar

0   100   200 Miles
0 100 200 Kilometers

U.S. soldiers in the Khakeran Valley of Afghanistan search a house for weapons in June 2005 in a continuing effort to root out Taliban presence in the region.

THE IMPACT TODAY

Government

The creation of the Department of Homeland Security marked one of the most far-reaching government reorganizations in American history. It was followed by a planned overhaul of the nation's entire intelligence structure.

Afghanistan. This was done with the cooperation of the Taliban. For his part, bin Laden provided support to the Taliban in its struggle to control Afghanistan.

When it became clear that bin Laden and al Qaeda were likely responsible for the 9/11 attacks, Bush put pressure on the Taliban. He insisted that Taliban leaders seize bin Laden and hand him over to the United States.

In spite of this pressure, the Taliban remained defiant. By the end of September, it was clear they would not give in to American demands. So, on October 7, 2001, the United States, along with ally Great Britain, launched a military attack on Taliban strongholds throughout Afghanistan.

HISTORY'S VOICES

❝We're a peaceful nation. Yet, as we have learned, so suddenly and so tragically, there can be no peace in a world of sudden terror. In the face of today's new threat, the only way to pursue peace is to pursue those who threaten it.❞

—George W. Bush, October 7, 2001

In fighting the Taliban, the United States relied heavily on fighters of Afghanistan's Northern Alliance. This armed group opposed the Taliban and controlled a small part of Afghanistan. Within weeks, anti-Taliban forces captured the capital of Kabul. By early December, the Taliban was defeated.

Less successful was the hunt for Osama bin Laden. American and Northern Alliance forces at one point thought they had him trapped in the mountainous Tora Bora region of Afghanistan. The site was bombed heavily. Bin Laden, however, managed to avoid capture.

In spite of this setback, the American operation in Afghanistan was considered a success. At the end of December, representatives of several major groups in Afghanistan met to select a new interim leader for the country. They made plans to create a new constitution and government. Presidential elections took place in 2004, and parliamentary elections went forward in 2005. Afghanistan would continue to face serious problems. These included continued fighting by surviving members of the Taliban. However, the country's role as a terrorist base was greatly reduced.

Fighting terrorism at home While American troops were fighting in Afghanistan, President Bush and Congress were working to fight terrorism at home. To coordinate these efforts, Bush and Congress began work on what would become the **Department of Homeland Security**. This cabinet-level organization combined 22 government agencies and 180,000 employees. Its functions included maintaining a color-coded warning system for terrorist threats.

Also in the days after 9/11, the nation experienced a frightening introduction to another kind of terrorist threat: biological agents. In several locations in the eastern United States, 18 people came down with a rare but deadly infection caused by the anthrax bacteria. Five people died. The anthrax had apparently been sent through the mail in a deliberate attempt to infect people. For several anxious weeks, Americans wondered how widespread the anthrax attacks had been. It soon became clear that the crisis was limited to a handful of specific locations. For a nation still recovering from 9/11, however, the incident was alarming.

In Congress, lawmakers took up the question of how to prevent future terrorist attacks. One solution proposed by the White House was to strengthen the powers of law-enforcement to investigate possible terrorists. These proposals became the basis of the **USA PATRIOT Act**. This law made it easier for law enforcement to secretly collect information about suspected terrorists. Indeed, some critics complained that the USA PATRIOT Act gave law enforcement too much power and posed a threat to basic freedoms. To address these concerns, Congress agreed to let some provisions of the law expire after a certain period of time.

READING CHECK **Identifying Problems and Solutions** How did the U.S. government respond to the threat of terrorism after 9/11?

War in Iraq

Following the success in Afghanistan, President Bush delivered his State of the Union address in January 2002. "What we have found in Afghanistan," he said, "confirms that, far from ending there, our war against terror is only beginning." Further, he identified Iraq as a possible future foe.

Following the Persian Gulf War in 1991, Iraq had agreed to destroy its weapons of mass destruction. To ensure that Iraq's leader, Saddam Hussein, was living up to this agreement, the UN placed weapons inspectors inside the country. With each passing year, however, the Iraqi leader grew more and more uncooperative with these inspection efforts. In response, the UN removed its inspectors entirely in 1998.

Since that time, observers believed the Iraqis had been busy building banned weapons. Given the events of 9/11, this greatly concerned President Bush. "The United States will not permit the world's most dangerous regimes to threaten us with the world's most destructive weapons," he declared.

Throughout the fall of 2002 and the winter of 2003, Bush sought to build support for forceful action against Saddam Hussein. Under this pressure, Iraq allowed a new round of UN weapons inspections. This turned up no weapons of mass destruction. Bush, however, insisted that Iraq had failed to account for weapons it was known to have possessed after

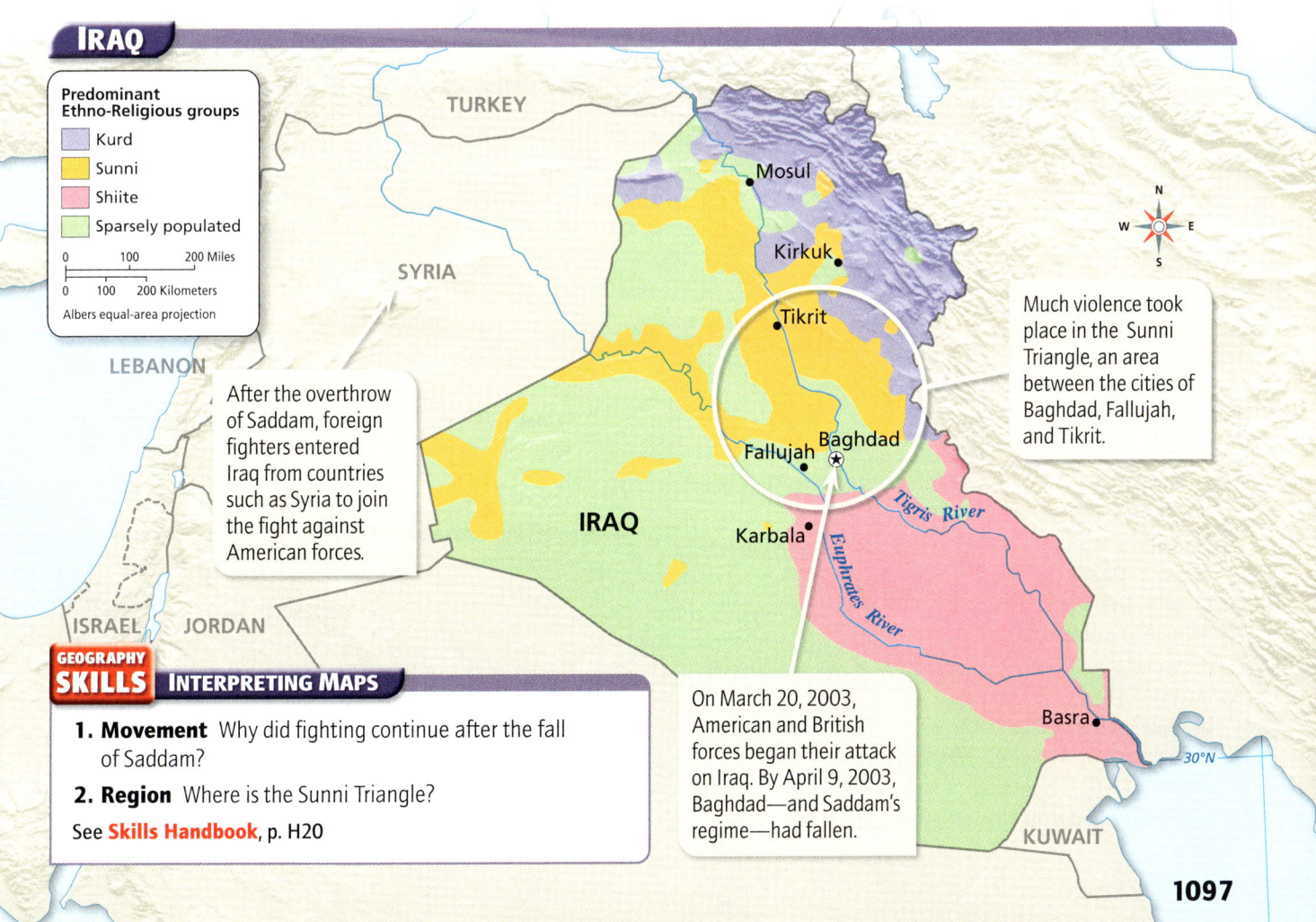

IRAQ

Predominant Ethno-Religious groups
- Kurd
- Sunni
- Shiite
- Sparsely populated

0   100   200 Miles
0   100   200 Kilometers
Albers equal-area projection

TURKEY

Mosul

Kirkuk

Tikrit

Baghdad

Fallujah

Karbala

Basra

SYRIA

LEBANON

ISRAEL   JORDAN

IRAQ

KUWAIT

Tigris River

Euphrates River

30°N

After the overthrow of Saddam, foreign fighters entered Iraq from countries such as Syria to join the fight against American forces.

Much violence took place in the Sunni Triangle, an area between the cities of Baghdad, Fallujah, and Tikrit.

On March 20, 2003, American and British forces began their attack on Iraq. By April 9, 2003, Baghdad—and Saddam's regime—had fallen.

GEOGRAPHY SKILLS **INTERPRETING MAPS**

1. **Movement** Why did fighting continue after the fall of Saddam?
2. **Region** Where is the Sunni Triangle?

See **Skills Handbook**, p. H20

George W. Bush did not initially seek a life in politics. Though his father, George H. W. Bush, had served as a member of Congress and in other government posts, Bush decided to pursue a business career. A failed bid for Congress in 1978 did nothing to change his mind. Then following his father's term as president, Bush won the race for governor of Texas and was re-elected in 1998. His campaign for the presidency followed two years later. Bush was re-elected to a second term in 2004. After 9/11, Bush's primary focus as president became protecting the nation against the threat of terrorism. His administration will forever be defined by his leadership in the wake of the 9/11 attacks.

Explain How did the 9/11 attacks change Bush's presidency?

the Persian Gulf War. Members of his administration also claimed to have information about new Iraqi weapons systems. Many of America's longtime allies argued against going to war. Still, Bush insisted the Iraqi threat must be countered. With the support of Great Britain and several other countries, American forces stormed into Iraq in March 2003.

The United States and its allies made quick work of Iraq's military. By early April, Saddam Hussein's regime had fallen. Saddam was captured in late 2003.

The United States then moved to establish a new Iraqi government. In June 2004 American officials handed control over to an interim Iraqi government. American forces remained to help keep order and train a new Iraqi security force.

Elections in early 2005 began the process by which Iraqis would create a new constitution. Conflict between rival religious and ethnic groups complicated the process. In October 2005, voters approved a new constitution.

Iraq, however, continued to experience serious problems. Terrorists, who included former Saddam loyalists and religious extremists, continued to take a terrible toll on American soldiers and on Iraqi civilians and those who joined the new police and security forces.

The ongoing violence created political problems for Bush. He also faced criticism when it became clear that Saddam Hussein had apparently not possessed weapons of mass destruction at the start of the war.

The president overcame these questions to win re-election in 2004. He reminded voters that Saddam had been a brutal dictator and that his removal from power made the world a safer place. He assured Americans that progress was being made toward a more peaceful, democratic Iraq. He also made clear that U.S. forces would remain in Iraq for as long as necessary to ensure peace and order there.

READING CHECK **Sequencing** Describe the events leading up to and following the war in Iraq.

SECTION 3 ASSESSMENT

go.hrw.com
Online Quiz
Keyword: SD7 HP33

Reviewing Ideas, Terms, and People

1. **a. Describe** What is the significance of **9/11**?
   b. Summarize How would you summarize the reaction of the American people to the attacks of 9/11?

2. **a. Identify** Who or what are the following: **Osama bin Laden, al Qaeda**
   b. Make Inferences Why do you think Osama bin Laden decided to try to destroy the United States?

3. **a. Describe** Why did the United States attack Afghanistan in 2001?
   b. Make Inferences What can you infer from the fact that the United States received wide support for its attack on Afghanistan?

4. **a. Recall** Why did the United States attack Iraq in 2003?

b. Explain Why did Bush think that removing Saddam Hussein was important?

Critical Thinking

5. **Identifying Cause and Effect** Copy the chart below and use information from the section to record the effects of the cause given.

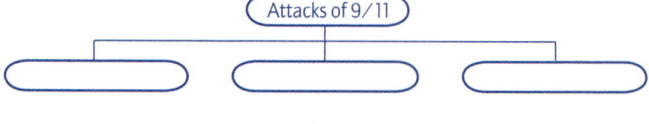

Attacks of 9/11

FOCUS ON WRITING

6. **Narrative** Write a brief narrative that recounts the major events of September 11, 2001, and its aftermath.

BEFORE YOU READ

MAIN IDEA

The dawn of a new century found the United States facing a new era of opportunity and challenge.

READING FOCUS

1. What recent issues have Americans faced at home and abroad?
2. What trends and advances are reshaping life in the United States?
3. What challenges will confront the United States in the future?

KEY TERMS AND PEOPLE

Hurricane Katrina
Antonio Villaraigosa
IT
genetic engineering

PI 3.2 Research and analyze the major themes and developments in New York State and United States history (e.g., colonization and settlement; Revolution and New National Period; immigration; expansion and reform era; Civil War and Reconstruction; the American labor movement; Great Depression; World Wars; contemporary United States).

THE INSIDE STORY

What can a hurricane reveal about the spirit and strength of Americans? In the small town of Port Sulphur, Louisiana, people eagerly gathered in October 2006 to watch a high school homecoming parade. The event was a major celebration. It marked not only homecoming but the survival and renewal of three towns: Boothville-Venice, Buras, and Port Sulphur. Only 14 months before, Hurricane Katrina—the most destructive hurricane in U.S. history—had slammed into the three Gulf Coast towns, all but erasing them. Yet residents refused to give up. Slowly, they began to rebuild, and businesses reopened. With their high schools destroyed, the three communities came together and formed a combined high school, South Plaquemines.

The new school was housed in temporary buildings on the campus of a destroyed school. In a show of determination, the 266 students chose *Hurricanes* as the name of their sports teams. When the high school opened in August 2006, the cafeteria and gym were not yet ready, and the football team did not have a field. Most of the students and their families were still living in temporary trailers. By homecoming, though, a new field had been completed. That night, the football team played its first home game since the hurricane. The strength, spirit, and unity that these Americans and countless others displayed after Hurricane Katrina are the characteristics that will keep the United States strong in the future. ◢

RISING to the CHALLENGE

▶ **Members of the Hurricanes watch their teammates during the season opener game.**

At Home and Abroad

The story of the United States is the story of a people who have overcome many challenges. Although the challenges have changed with time, the spirit of Americans remains strong both at home and abroad.

Hurricane Katrina One major challenge of the new century was <mark>Hurricane Katrina</mark>, which struck the Gulf Coast on August 29, 2005. This massive hurricane was the most devastating natural disaster in U.S. history. Katrina left a path of death and destruction across Louisiana, Mississippi, Alabama, and Florida. In some areas, whole communities were wiped out.

The worst devastation related to the hurricane occurred in New Orleans, Louisiana, which lies below sea level. A mandatory evacuation order for the city had been issued before the storm. However, thousands of residents stayed—many because they had no way to leave. Heavy rains then broke some of the city's levees, the walls holding back surrounding waters. As floodwaters poured through the failed levees, much of New Orleans was submerged. Thousands of residents were left stranded. Many people went for days with little or no food and water before being rescued.

The human suffering that resulted from Hurricane Katrina was immense. More than 1,500 people died—most of them in New Orleans—and hundreds of thousands of people lost their homes and sources of livelihood. Damage estimates were as high as $80 billion.

The hurricane's economic impact extended far beyond the Gulf Coast. Interruption of oil production sent fuel prices soaring. In addition, the major flow of products through the port of New Orleans was disrupted. To make matters worse, a second hurricane—Rita—struck Louisiana and Texas just weeks later, adding to the overall devastation.

Americans rallied to help with rescue and relief efforts. Volunteer organizations and individuals donated time, money, and supplies. The government response, led by the Federal Emergency Management Agency (FEMA), involved agencies at all levels. Some parts of this response received high praise, such as the Coast Guard's heroic rescue work. But the disaster's extent overwhelmed many other agencies, including FEMA. In addition, some critics claimed that government agencies responded slowly because many of the worst-hit areas were populated largely by poor African Americans. In response to such criticism,

A Determined Nation

Hurricane Relief and Recovery

Water covers much of New Orleans, Louisiana, following Hurricane Katrina in August 2005 (below). This makeshift shop in Waveland, Mississippi (left), helps storm survivors begin to piece their lives back together.

FEMA's director stepped down. The federal government then began an overhaul of the nation's emergency response system.

Recovery from Katrina and Rita has been slow and will take years. The devastation led many residents to leave the Gulf Coast. Others returned to rebuild, though, and most Americans feel confident the region will recover.

Continuing war in Iraq As Americans dealt with the aftermath of Katrina and Rita, they continued to face challenges in Iraq. U.S. and Iraqi officials had been working to establish a democratic government and to rebuild the country. However, deep divisions among religious and ethnic groups in Iraq led to internal fighting and rising violence. These problems threatened the new government's stability. At the same time, rebels and terrorists in Iraq increased their attacks, particularly against civilians. Casualties rose, with civilians suffering the heaviest losses. In response, hundreds of thousands of Iraqis fled the country.

Meanwhile, in 2006 an Iraqi court tried Saddam Hussein, the country's former dictator. Saddam was sentenced to death for his role in a brutal massacre of Iraqis in the 1980s. On December 30, 2006, he was executed.

The growing violence and lack of progress in Iraq led to fierce debate at home. As American casualties in Iraq mounted, support for the war began to decrease. Critics accused the administration of President George W. Bush of having exaggerated the danger Iraq posed and of mishandling the war. A growing number of Americans also began pressing for the withdrawal of U.S. troops from Iraq. At the same time, many Americans continued to support the war.

The 2006 elections The worsening situation in Iraq caused Bush's approval rating to drop drastically. In the 2006 midterm elections, many voters showed their displeasure with the Republican administration by voting for Democrats. As a result, the Democratic Party gained a majority in both houses of Congress.

The outcome of the elections led Donald Rumsfeld, the secretary of defense, to resign. Bush replaced him with Robert Gates. In addition, Bush increased the number of U.S. troops in Iraq in an effort to reduce the violence. The new Congress responded by calling for a plan to withdraw U.S. troops from Iraq.

READING CHECK **Summarize** What issues have Americans faced recently at home and abroad?

The Iraq War
U.S. soldiers and Iraqi security troops patrol a busy open-air market in Baghdad, the capital of Iraq (below).

Democratic Control of Congress
In January 2007 the U.S. House of Representatives elected Nancy Pelosi (above), a Democrat from California, as Speaker of the House. She is the first woman to hold the post.

Trends and Advances

As Americans address the issues of today, they continue to look toward the future. But what does the future hold? Current trends and advances provide some insight.

ACADEMIC VOCABULARY

diverse including great variety

Tomorrow's Population The U.S. census, which measures the population every 10 years, reveals several trends changing the face of America. For example, a comparison of 1980 and 2000 census data (see below) shows that the U.S. population has grown more <u>diverse</u>, a trend expected to continue.

Ethnic minorities—such as African, Asian, and Hispanic Americans—currently make up about 30 percent of the U.S. population. By 2050 these groups are expected to form about half of the population. The number of Asian Americans is expected to more than triple. Hispanic Americans are expected to become nearly one-fourth of the U.S. population.

The nation's growing minority groups will very likely play a leading role in the future. In Los Angeles, the second-largest U.S. city, the growing number of Latino residents helped elect **Antonio Villaraigosa** (vee-uh-ry-GOH-suh) as mayor in 2005. Villaraigosa was the city's first Hispanic mayor since 1872.

The U.S. population's growing diversity has led to other changes as well. You have read about the growing resistance, mainly among white Americans, to affirmative action programs. Such programs are designed to help minority groups overcome discrimination. In California, voters passed Proposition 209 in 1996. This amendment to the state's constitution outlawed the use of racial, ethnic, or gender preferences in decisions such as university admissions.

Another trend reshaping American society is a change in where people live. Census officials predict that between 2000 and 2030, the population of the warmer regions of the South and West will grow at a faster rate than the colder Northeast and Midwest. Lower energy and labor costs in the South and West are two reasons. Between 2000 and 2030 the populations of Nevada and Arizona are expected to double. Texas, Florida, and California could each gain 9 million residents. Meanwhile, the Northeast is expected to grow by a mere 7.6 percent, and the Midwest by only 10 percent.

The American population is also aging. Today people 64 and older are the country's fastest-growing age group. Between 2000 and 2050 the 65-to-84 age group is expected to double. This rate of growth is four times that expected for the 20-to-40 age group.

The nation's diverse population is reflected in the faces of these recent Presidential Scholars, honored for their academic achievement in high school.

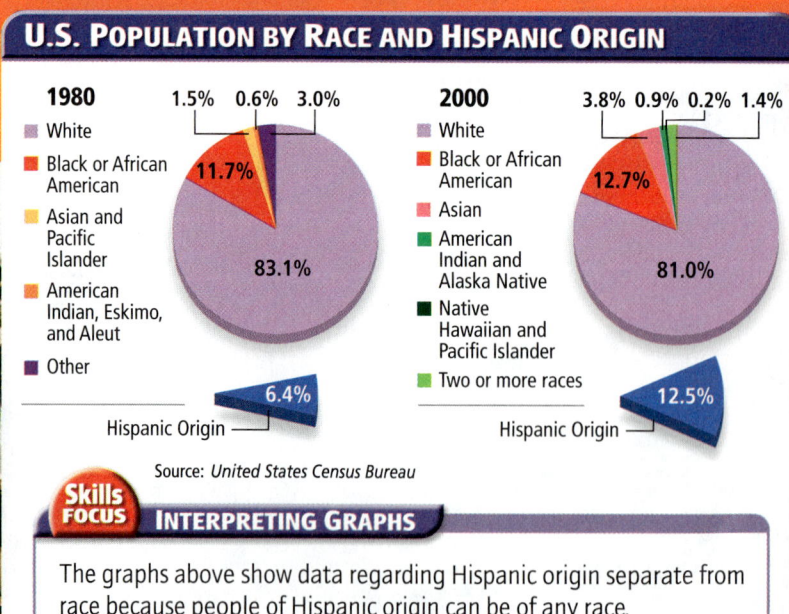

U.S. POPULATION BY RACE AND HISPANIC ORIGIN

1980
- White
- Black or African American
- Asian and Pacific Islander
- American Indian, Eskimo, and Aleut
- Other

1.5% 0.6% 3.0%
11.7%
83.1%
Hispanic Origin — 6.4%

2000
- White
- Black or African American
- Asian
- American Indian and Alaska Native
- Native Hawaiian and Pacific Islander
- Two or more races

3.8% 0.9% 0.2% 1.4%
12.7%
81.0%
Hispanic Origin — 12.5%

Source: *United States Census Bureau*

Skills FOCUS   INTERPRETING GRAPHS

The graphs above show data regarding Hispanic origin separate from race because people of Hispanic origin can be of any race. What has been the most dramatic change in the U.S. population?

See **Skills Handbook**, p. H16

Immigration and Religion

Immigrants coming to the United States have always brought their cultures, languages, and traditions with them. They also bring their religious beliefs. Most settlers in the original English colonies were Protestant Christians. Later immigration increased the numbers of Catholics, Jews, and other groups. Recently, new immigrants have brought even greater religious diversity. As more immigrants come from Asia and Africa, various cultures and religions have been introduced to the United States.

Today about 80 percent of people in the United States identify themselves as Christians. Among organized religions, the next largest group is Judaism, with about 2 percent of the population. Religions such as Islam, Buddhism, and Hinduism are growing, although members of each faith still make up less than 1 percent of the total U.S. population.

The First Amendment of the U.S. Constitution guarantees the "free exercise" of religion, which means that anyone may practice his or her beliefs. By guaranteeing freedom of religion, the Constitution has enabled the United States to become increasingly diverse in terms of religion.

Drawing Conclusions How is the Constitution connected to growing religious diversity?

The U.S. Constitution guarantees this convention attendee the right to openly practice his Sikh religion.

The promise of technology Throughout history, technological advances have helped keep the nation strong, prosperous, and secure. Computer technology is one area increasingly affecting life in the United States. In 1980, less than 1 percent of Americans owned a computer. Today more than 60 percent do. In addition, most of these computers are connected to the Internet, and most libraries and schools provide Internet access as well. The infrastructure that supports these connections now covers nearly the entire United States.

Many everyday devices such as cars and household appliances now contain tiny computers. One example of the melding of computers with everyday devices is the telephone. Use of computerized wireless phones is growing rapidly in the United States. In fact, by 2005 the number of wireless phone lines had surpassed the number of landline phones.

Computerized information technology, or **IT**, is also bringing change to American business. IT enables businesses to organize and examine information in more-productive ways. For example, an IT system makes it possible for a company's sales, manufacturing, and shipping departments to share the exact same information on their computer screens. Customers can then use their own computers to check on the status of orders or to shop online. These capabilities can help a business be more efficient, which helps increase profits.

Genetic research Advances in genetic research continue to change science, medicine, and agriculture. By studying human genetic information, such as DNA sequence, medical researchers, for instance, hope to learn how to cure or better treat diseases such as cancer.

Another leading area of genetic research is **genetic engineering**, or the artificial modification of genes. By altering the genes of a species of plant, for example, scientists can produce new varieties of the plant that have desirable features such as resistance to pests. Scientists have also learned how to modify bacteria to create vaccines and other medicines.

Like many other technological changes, genetic engineering has created controversy. Some people worry about possible health effects of genetically modified crops. Another concern is that altered genes might introduce dangerous traits into other organisms.

READING CHECK **Identifying Supporting Details** How do you think advances in technology will affect the United States in the future?

ACADEMIC VOCABULARY
infrastructure the basic facilities of a community for transportation, communication, and more

Challenges for the Future

Americans are blessed with the drive, talent, and abundant resources needed to create a better future. This future, like the past, will hold many challenges—and opportunities.

Health care One major challenge for the future is health care. Advances in medical science are helping Americans to live longer. The nation's average life expectancy today is 78 years. By 2025 it is expected to be about 80. You have also read that the U.S. population is aging. People typically require more health care as they age. Thus, as older Americans make up a larger part of the population, health-care issues will affect more people.

At the same time, the costs of health care and health insurance are rising. Some Americans, particularly among the elderly, cannot afford adequate health care. A large number of Americans lack sufficient health insurance as well. How to ensure the availability of health care and what role the government should play are likely to be major concerns in the United States for years to come.

Medical conditions such as HIV infection and AIDS are another health-care challenge. Experts estimate that tens of millions of people worldwide will die from HIV/AIDS in the coming decades. In Africa in particular, HIV threatens to devastate entire countries.

Social Security Another challenge Americans face is how to maintain the nation's Social Security system. Benefits paid to retirees come from the taxes on workers' wages. As the population ages, more people will retire, leaving fewer workers to pay taxes. In time, experts predict that Social Security payouts will exceed the amount of taxes collected. Americans will have to decide how to address this issue.

Energy and the environment Other challenges for the future involve energy and the environment. The United States is by far the world's largest consumer of energy. In fact, the gap between how much energy the United States uses and how much it produces is widening. To fill this gap, the United States imports about a third of its energy. The result has been a growing dependance on foreign oil.

Americans also continue to debate how best to balance the need for energy with the need to protect the environment. The use of fossil fuels such as coal and oil creates pollution and harms the environment. Many experts also think that the carbon dioxide gas released when people use fossil fuels is building up and causing global warming. Americans will continue to search for solutions to these challenges.

READING CHECK **Comparing** How are the challenges facing the United States today similar to and different from challenges of the past?

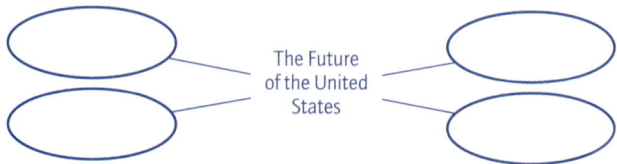

SECTION 4 ASSESSMENT

go.hrw.com
Online Quiz
Keyword: SD7 HP33

Reviewing Ideas, Terms, and People

1. **a. Describe** What were the major effects of **Hurricane Katrina** on the Gulf Coast and the nation?
   b. Explain How did the course of the Iraq War affect the Bush administration and the Republican Party?

2. **a. Identify** What are two major trends in the makeup of the American population?
   b. Make Generalizations What are some areas in which technology is likely to change American life in the future?

3. **a. Recall** What is the general trend in the overall health of the nation as measured by life expectancy?
   b. Summarize What major health-care issues will Americans likely face in the coming decades?
   c. Evaluate On what basis is it safe to predict that the United States will meet the challenges it faces in the future?

Critical Thinking

4. **Identifying the Main Idea** Copy the chart below and use information from the section to record details that support the main idea of the section. You may need to add ovals.

The Future of the United States

FOCUS ON WRITING

5. **Persuasive** Write a letter to an elected official in which you try to persuade him or her to support or oppose an action related to one of the issues discussed in this section.

ST 3.2 Draw upon literary selections, historical documents, and accounts to analyze the roles played by different individuals and groups during the major eras in New York State and United States history.

About the Reading Amy Tan drew on the experiences of family members in her 1989 novel, *The Joy Luck Club*, which tells the stories of four Chinese women and their Chinese American daughters. In the following excerpt Lindo Jong, one of the main characters, recalls her first days after arriving in the United States in the 1940s.

AS YOU READ Consider the difficulties involved with moving to a new place.

Excerpt from

The Joy Luck Club

by Amy Tan

Chinatown in San Francisco during a Chinese New Year festival

When I arrived, nobody asked me questions. The authorities looked at my papers and stamped me in. I decided to go first to a San Francisco address given to me by this girl in Peking. The bus put me down on a wide street with cable cars. This was California Street. I walked up this hill and then I saw a tall building. This was Old St. Mary's. Under the church sign, in handwritten Chinese characters, someone had added: "A Chinese Ceremony to Save Ghosts from Spiritual Unrest 7 a.m. and 8:30 a.m." I memorized this information in case the authorities asked me where I worshipped my religion. And then I saw another sign across the street. It was painted on the outside of a short building: "Save Today for Tomorrow, at Bank of America." And I thought to myself, This is where American people worship. See, even then I was not so dumb! Today that church is the same size, but where that bank used to be, now there is a tall building, fifty stories high, where you and your husband-to-be work and look down on everybody.

My daughter laughed when I said this. Her mother can make a good joke.

So I kept walking up this hill. I saw two pagodas, one on each side of the street, as though they were the entrance to a great Buddha temple. But when I looked carefully, I saw the pagoda was really just a building topped with stacks of tile roofs, no walls, nothing else under its head. I was surprised how they tried to make everything look like an old imperial city or an emperor's tomb. But if you looked on either side of these pretend-pagodas, you could see the streets became narrow and crowded, dark, and dirty. I thought to myself, Why did they choose only the worst Chinese parts for the inside? Why didn't they build gardens and ponds instead? Oh, here and there was the look of a famous ancient cave or a Chinese opera. But inside it was always the same cheap stuff.

So by the time I found the address the girl in Peking gave me, I knew not to expect too much.

Skills FOCUS READING LIKE A HISTORIAN

1. **Summarizing** How would you characterize Lindo Jong's first reactions to Chinatown in San Francisco?
2. **Literature as Historical Evidence** How does this excerpt describe the struggle of immigrants to adapt to a new culture?

See **Skills Handbook**, p. H32

CASE STUDY
HISTORY & Geography

New York Standards

ST 2.2 Explain the contributions of specific groups of people to American society and culture.

Hispanic Growth and Influence

Hispanics, with a population of 40.4 million at the end of 2004, make up 14 percent of the total U.S. population. They are the country's largest and fastest growing minority group. By 2020 Hispanics will total an estimated 60.4 million and account for half of the growth of the U.S. labor force. With their rising numbers have come newfound political and economic powers. Many people point to the Hispanic vote as a key factor in recent presidential elections.

HISPANIC POPULATION GROWTH, 1960 - 2000

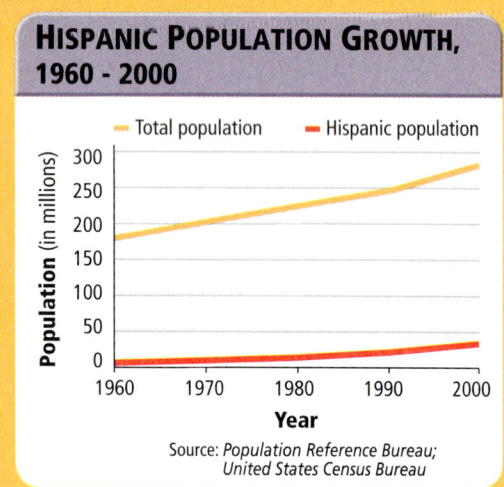

— Total population   — Hispanic population

Population (in millions)

300
250
200
150
100
50
0

1960   1970   1980   1990   2000

Year

Source: *Population Reference Bureau; United States Census Bureau*

PERCENTAGE HISPANIC POPULATION, 2000

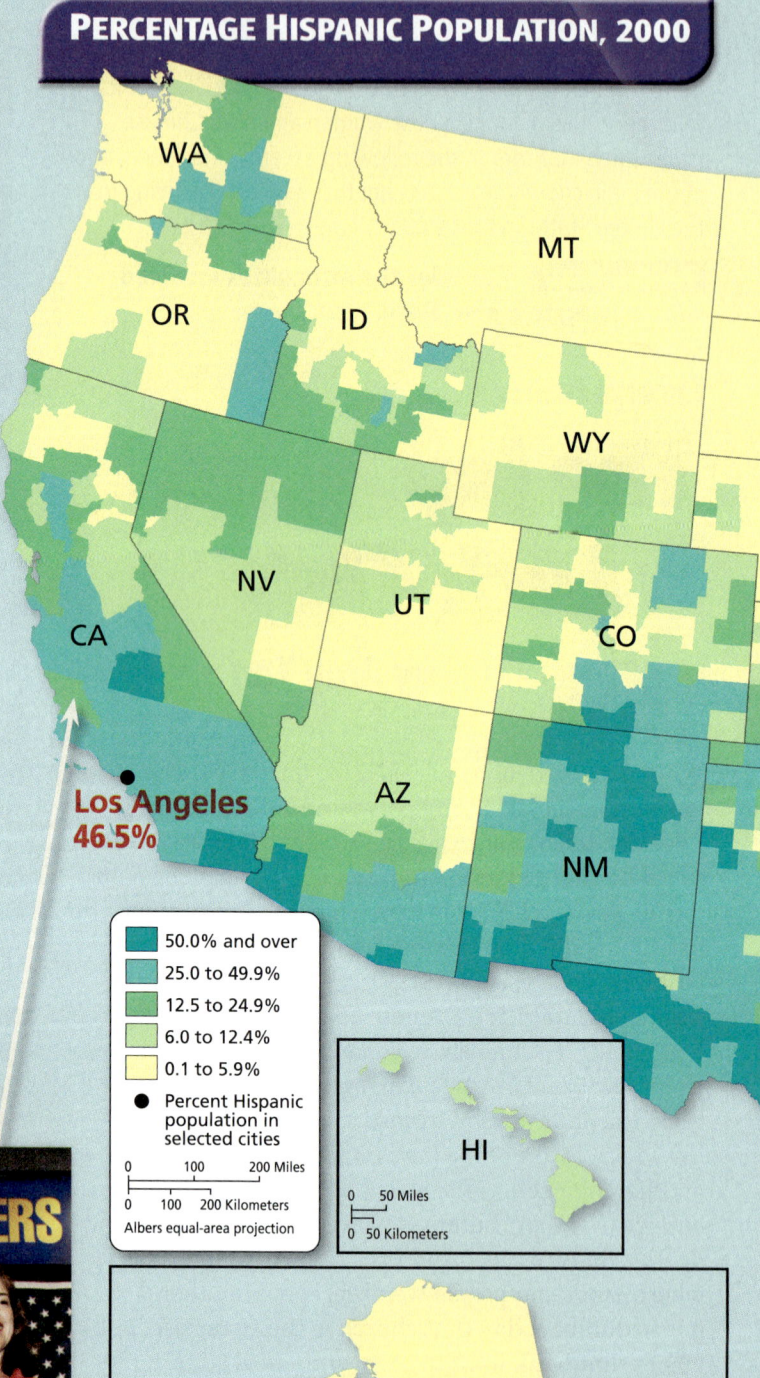

WA
MT
OR
ID
WY
NV
UT
CA
CO
Los Angeles 46.5%
AZ
NM
HI
AK

Legend:
- 50.0% and over
- 25.0 to 49.9%
- 12.5 to 24.9%
- 6.0 to 12.4%
- 0.1 to 5.9%
- ● Percent Hispanic population in selected cities

0   100   200 Miles
0   100   200 Kilometers
Albers equal-area projection

0   50 Miles
0   50 Kilometers

0   200 Miles
0   200 Kilometers

Winning Elections

Californians Loretta and Linda Sanchez are the first sisters to serve together in the U.S. Congress. They joined 22 other Hispanic Americans serving in the House of Representatives and over 6,000 Hispanic Americans holding elected office.

Spending Power

Illinois's Hispanic population grew by 650,000 from 1990 to 2000, with most settling in Chicago. Overall Hispanic spending power has grown, too. To attract a larger piece of the Hispanic market, Chicago's Tribune Company turned its Spanish-language weekly, *¡Exito!*, into the daily *Hoy.*

College Bound

As the number of U.S.-educated Hispanics has risen, so has the proportion of those who attend college. To better serve the area's Dominican population, which is larger than the population of the Dominican Republic, the City University of New York offers a degree in Dominican Studies.

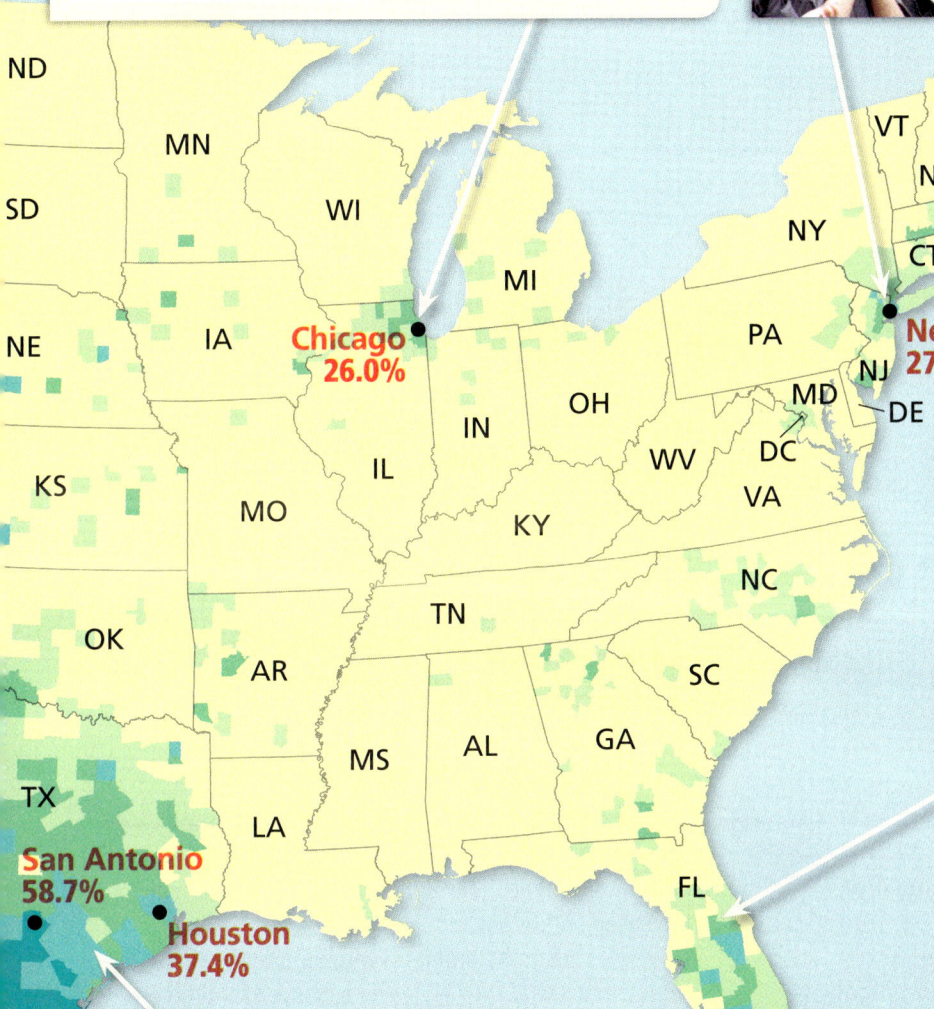

ND

MN

SD

WI

NE

IA

**Chicago
26.0%**

KS

MO

IL

IN

MI

OH

WV

KY

OK

AR

TN

MS

AL

TX

LA

GA

SC

NC

VA

DC

MD

DE

NJ

PA

NY

CT

RI

NH

MA

VT

ME

**New York
27.0%**

FL

**San Antonio
58.7%**

**Houston
37.4%**

Immigration

After California, Texas has the largest Hispanic population, mostly of Mexican origin. Unlike with earlier European immigrants, Mexican immigration has not come in a single wave, but rather in a continuous flow for over a century.

Swing Voters

Mel Martinez immigrated to Florida from Cuba at age 15. In 2004 he became the first Cuban American elected to the U. S. Senate. In 2000 President Bush took Florida by 537 votes, but he won 80 percent of the Cuban vote.

GEOGRAPHY SKILLS   INTERPRETING MAPS

1. **Location** Look at some of the major areas of Hispanic American concentration. Why might these areas have been attractive? Why might other areas be unattractive?

2. **Movement** Why might Mexican immigration be occurring in a continuous flow instead of a single wave?

See **Skills Handbook,** p. H20

The Global Economy and Society

Historical Context The documents below provide different information on the effects of globalization on economics and society.

Task Examine the documents and answer the questions that follow. Then write an essay about globalization. Use facts from the documents and from the chapter to support the position you take in your thesis statement.

ST 4.3 Develop hypotheses about important events, eras, or issues; move from chronicling to explaining historical events and issues; use information collected from diverse sources to produce cogently written reports and document-based essays.

DOCUMENT 1

This cartoon comments on the increase in outsourcing—sending local jobs overseas in order to take advantage of lower labor costs in other countries.

"The last step says to dismantle the whole thing and ship all the jobs overseas."

DOCUMENT 2

In 2003 the editor in chief of *Reason* magazine interviewed author Tyler Cowen about his book *Creative Destruction: How Globalization Is Changing the World's Cultures*. Cowen's book suggests that globalization benefits most people around the world.

"Reason: Give an example that characterizes the sort of cultural exchange . . . you discuss . . .

"Tyler Cowen: The first point to make is that all examples characterize it. The only question is, how much of it do we already see? Look at a book and ask yourself, where does paper come from, where does printing come from, where do the ideas in the book come from? What's the religious background of the author? You're already talking about the Middle East, China, Europe, the United States. Just about anything you can find

reflects a synthetic [not natural; made by humans] culture based on trade . . .

"*Reason*: One of the problems with arguments about cultural loss is that they are often advanced for protectionist reasons. So, for instance, we have the French decrying [complaining about] U.S. cultural imperialism and insisting on domestic-content rules and the like. What are the effects of trying to hold back cultural creative destruction?

"Tyler Cowen: The good news is that it cannot easily be held back . . . Look at the French. For all the noise they make, Paris is remarkably open to African and Middle Eastern cultures—and to Hollywood movies, for that matter. . . As a whole, the world has been moving toward freer trade for quite a while."

Economic changes have affected people all over the world. This *Newsweek* article, published in 2001, examines the effects of globalization on women in different countries.

"For European women, globalization's fallen trade barriers, blurred national boundaries and new technology have brought the best of times—and the worst. The European Union's freedom of movement created more career opportunities, but increased competition, and with it, stress . . . Creeping Americanization has shaken up antique boardroom attitudes—but also ushered in a 24/7 work schedule. Leaner company structures make it easier to negotiate part-time work, but harder to get paid maternity leave or a pension. A boom economy means women have little trouble finding jobs, but with cuts in education and health, they may have trouble getting trained for good ones—or finding child care while they're at them."

Mark Rice-Oxley is a reporter for *The Christian Science Monitor*. In this article, published in 2004, he discusses how the spread of American culture affects societies around the world.

"Stick a pin in a map and there you'll find an example of U.S. influence. Hollywood rules the global movie market, with up to 90 percent of audiences in some European countries. Even in Africa, 2 of 3 films shown are American. Few countries have yet to be touched by McDonald's and Coca-Cola . . .

"America's preeminence is hardly surprising. Superpowers throughout the ages sought to perpetuate their way of life: from the philosophy and mythology of the ancient Greeks to the law and language of the Romans; from the art and architecture of the Tang dynasty and Renaissance Italy to the sports and systems of government of the British . . .

"So how much good does American culture bring to the world? And how long will it last? Ian Ralston cautions against sweeping dismissals of U.S. pop culture. British television may be saturated with American sitcoms and movies, but while some are poor, others are quite good, he says . . . Others note that it is not all one-way traffic. America may feast largely on a diet of homegrown culture, but it imports modestly as well: soccer, international cuisine, Italian fashion, and, increasingly, British television."

Skills FOCUS — READING LIKE A HISTORIAN

1. **a. Identify** Refer to Document 1. What are the boys in the cartoon building?
   b. Interpret How does this cartoon illustrate changes in employment patterns?
2. **a. Identify** Refer to Document 2. What example does Cowen use to support his point that globalization creates synthetic cultures?
   b. Interpret Based on this excerpt, what is Cowen's opinion about the effects of free trade on culture?
3. **a. Identify** Refer to Document 3. How has the spread of technology affected work habits in foreign countries?
   b. Analyze Do you think the article would conclude that globalization has benefited or harmed European women?

4. **a. Identify** Refer to Document 4. How, according to the article, is the spread of American culture similar to that of past empires?
   b. Elaborate How does this article suggest that the spread of culture affects people in the United States and other countries?
5. **Document-Based Essay Question** Consider the question below and form a thesis statement. Using examples from Documents 1, 2, 3, and 4, create an outline and write a short essay supporting your position. How does the global economy affect cultures and societies around the world?

See **Skills Handbook**, pp. H28–H29, H30

Visual Summary: Into the Twenty-first Century

The Clinton Administration

- Welfare reform was achieved, but health-care reform was not.
- The nation became drawn into conflicts in Somalia, Haiti, and the former Yugoslavia.
- Despite impeachment, President Clinton completed his two terms.

The Bush Administration

- President Bush won a controversial election in 2000 and re-election in 2004.
- His domestic policy focused on tax cuts, education, and Medicare reform.
- His foreign policy was dominated by response to the terrorist attacks of September 11, 2001, and the Iraq War.

The 1990s and Beyond

Terrorism and War

- The attacks of September 11, 2001, shifted national focus to terrorism.
- In the war on terror, the United States attacked Afghanistan and Iraq.
- The United States created the Department of Homeland Security and passed new laws to fight terrorism.

Looking Ahead

The twenty-first century should bring:

- demographic changes—greater diversity and an aging population.
- technological changes in communication, medicine, and agriculture.
- challenges in health care, energy, and the environment.

Reviewing Key Terms and People

Identify the correct term or person from the chapter that best fits each of the following descriptions.

1. Law passed in the aftermath of 9/11 aimed at enhancing investigative powers
2. Trade agreement involving Mexico and Canada
3. Elected mayor of Los Angeles in 2005
4. Terrorist believed responsible for 9/11
5. Nickname for the type of Internet company that appeared in the 1990s
6. Republican package of proposals and legislation from 1994
7. New cabinet-level organization created in the aftermath of 9/11
8. Payments made by corporations to stockholders
9. A technology designed to improve agriculture by altering the genetic material of plants
10. Use of computer technology to efficiently use information
11. Supreme Court case that finally settled the presidential election of 2000

Comprehension and Critical Thinking

SECTION 1 *(pp. 1078–1083)*

12. **a. Describe** How would you describe the basic political beliefs of Bill Clinton?

   b. Make Inferences What can you infer from the fact that Clinton was able to survive so many political scandals?

   c. Evaluate Do you think Clinton's willingness to adopt policies of his political opponents was a strength or a weakness?

History's Impact video program

Review the video to answer the closing question: How have the events of September 11, 2001, changed life in the United States?

SECTION 2 *(pp. 1085–1090)*

13. a. Recall What were President George W. Bush's major goals for domestic policy?

b. Summarize What reasons did President Bush give for wanting to cut taxes?

c. Elaborate How do you think the circumstances of Bush's election in 2000 affected his ability to govern? Explain your answer.

SECTION 3 *(pp. 1091–1098)*

14. a. Recall What is the significance of the date September 11, 2001?

b. Make Generalizations Describe the emotional reactions of the American people to the catastrophe of September 11th.

c. Evaluate How effective do you think the terrorist attacks were in damaging the United States? Explain your answer.

SECTION 4 *(pp. 1099–1104)*

15. a. Recall What major challenges has the United States faced at home and abroad in recent times?

b. Summarize What are some of the causes and effects of the increase in the population of older Americans?

c. Rank Do you think the challenges facing the United States today are more or less significant than the challenges this country has faced in previous eras? Explain your answer.

Using the Internet

go.hrw.com
Practice Online
Keyword: SD7 CH33

16. Choose of one of the following topics: communication, medicine, agriculture, transportation, or industry. Using the keyword above, do research to learn how technology has affected the topic of your choice. Then write a brief report that summarizes your findings. In your report, include at least three ways that technology has an impact on the topic you chose.

Analyzing Primary Sources

Reading Like a Historian After the 2000 presidential election, officials in many Florida communities struggled to read ballots that had been rejected by the automatic vote-counting machines.

17. Describe What do you think these election officials are trying to figure out by looking at this ballot?

18. Explain Why do you think the hand counting of ballots as shown here was a controversial process?

Critical Reading

Read the passage in Section 3 that begins with the heading "The United States Responds." Then answer the question that follows.

19. Why did the United States invade Afghanistan?

A. to take revenge on the people of Afghanistan

B. to remove the Taliban regime that had harbored Osama bin Laden

C. to use Afghanistan as a military base for the war on terrorism

D. to help distract the American public from their problems at home

FOCUS ON WRITING

Descriptive Writing *Descriptive writing uses concrete details to help a reader visualize a person, place, or thing. To practice descriptive writing, complete the assignment below.*

Writing Topic **The Future of the United States**

20. Assignment Based on what you have read in this chapter, write a paragraph that describes the United States 20 years from now.

10 IN BRIEF

Below is a chapter-by-chapter summary of the main ideas covered in Unit 10.

CHAPTER 31 · A Search for Order
1968–1980

MAIN IDEA Richard Nixon achieved notable successes during his time in office, such as improving relations with the People's Republic of China. His involvement in the Watergate scandal, however, led to his resignation. His successors, Presidents Gerald Ford and Jimmy Carter, sought to help the nation recover from Watergate and face ongoing economic and foreign-policy challenges, which included high inflation and the continuing Cold War.

SECTION 1 Early in his presidency, Richard Nixon was able to promote improved relations with Communist China and the Soviet Union. He also had some success in pursuing domestic policies, including his stance on civil rights, the environment, and the economy.

SECTION 2 In his second term, Nixon's presidency unraveled in the Watergate scandal, as the nation slowly learned of his role in a criminal conspiracy to spy on his political opponents—and to cover it up. His successor, Gerald Ford, struggled to escape the scandal's undertow.

SECTION 3 Jimmy Carter came to office hoping to help the nation move beyond its troubled past. However, his presidency foundered on familiar problems, including economic trouble and foreign-policy crises with Iran and the Soviet Union.

CHAPTER 32 · A Conservative Era
1980–1992

MAIN IDEA Ronald Reagan and his successor George H. W. Bush dominated the 1980s with their conservative message of smaller government and a tougher stance against communism. During this time, the Cold War came to an end and the United States faced a new set of economic and foreign-policy challenges.

SECTION 1 Ronald Reagan came to office on the strength of his personality and a strong conservative message. He led a national reconsideration of many of the basic questions about the relationship between government and its people.

SECTION 2 A staunch anti-Communist, Reagan increased defense spending and spoke strongly against the Soviet Union. Foreign difficulties in Grenada, South Africa, Lebanon, and Iran characterized his time in office as well.

SECTION 3 George H. W. Bush presided over the end of the Cold War. He was also the first president to face the challenges of the post–Cold War world, when he led the nation—and numerous allies—into war against Iraq in the Persian Gulf War of 1990.

SECTION 4 The 1980s were a time of economic ups and downs, technological advances, and controversial cases in the Supreme Court.

CHAPTER 33 · Into the Twenty-first Century
1992–Present

MAIN IDEA Americans faced the twenty-first century with hope, determination, and a readiness to confront challenges at home and abroad.

SECTION 1 Bill Clinton used his political skills and voter dissatisfaction with George H. W. Bush's handling of the economy to reach the White House. Clinton's presidency was a time of economic growth, complex foreign-policy challenges—and political scandal.

SECTION 2 George W. Bush won a controversial election in 2000. He faced an economic downturn, which he countered with tax cuts and his own domestic-policy agenda. Following his re-election in 2004, Bush launched an initiative to reform the Social Security system.

SECTION 3 On September 11, 2001, the United States became the target of international terrorists. The attacks refocused the nation on a new enemy and led to war overseas and significant governmental changes at home.

SECTION 4 American society is changing as a result of a more diverse population and new advances in technology. The nation continues to face its challenges with a spirit of determination.

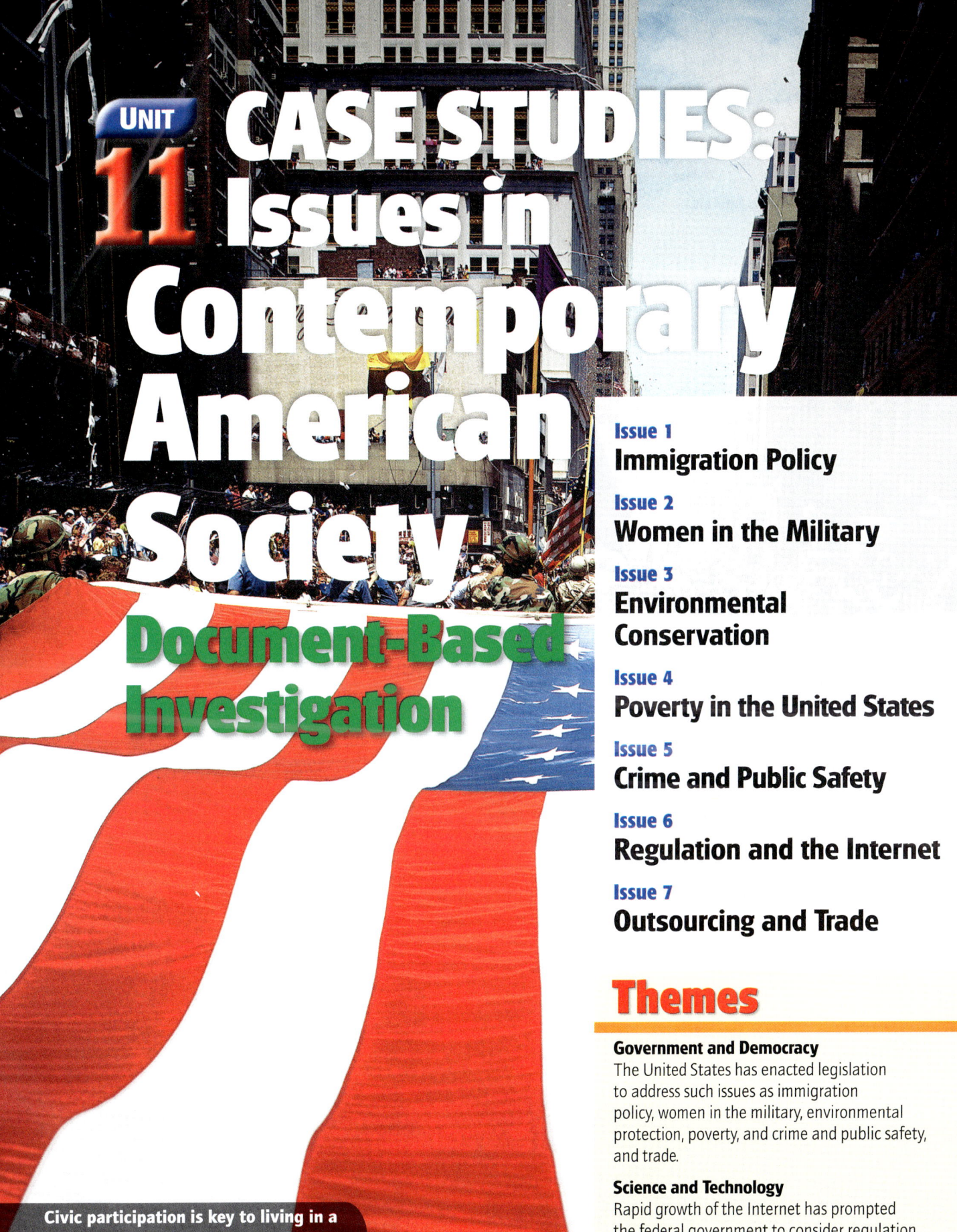

UNIT 11

CASE STUDIES: Issues in Contemporary American Society

Document-Based Investigation

Issue 1
Immigration Policy

Issue 2
Women in the Military

Issue 3
Environmental Conservation

Issue 4
Poverty in the United States

Issue 5
Crime and Public Safety

Issue 6
Regulation and the Internet

Issue 7
Outsourcing and Trade

Themes

Government and Democracy
The United States has enacted legislation to address such issues as immigration policy, women in the military, environmental protection, poverty, and crime and public safety, and trade.

Science and Technology
Rapid growth of the Internet has prompted the federal government to consider regulation to protect users and consumers.

Civic participation is key to living in a democracy. Here, the American flag is part of a parade in New York City.

1113

Prepare to Read

Making Inferences

Find practice for **Making Inferences** in the **Skills Handbook,** p. H7

To make sense of what you read, you often need to go beyond what is stated directly and make an inference, or informed judgement, about what a passage means. When making an inference, use your prior knowledge, clues in the text, and your common sense .

Before You Read
Skim the text to determine its subject. Then think about what you already know about the subject.

While You Read
Note ideas directly stated in the reading, as well as those that may be implied. Look for clues to guide your interpretation.

After You Read
Review ideas in the text and make connections to your prior knowledge.

Medical Service

During the Civil War, a number of women, including Clara Barton and Dorothea Dix, helped train nurses and care for wounded and ill soldiers. These female nurses were not a part of the military. They served with, not in, the Union Army.

In the Spanish-American War, thousands of U.S. soldiers contracted diseases such as typhoid, malaria, and yellow fever. The urgent need for qualified medical personnel led army hospitals to hire 1,500 civilian, or nonmilitary, female nurses. Impressed by their performance, the military created the Army Nurse Corps in 1901, followed by the Navy Nurse Corps seven years later. A corps is a military group. This was the first time in more than 100 years of service that women were officially allowed into the military. However, these female nurses received neither military rank nor benefits.

READING CHECK **Making Inferences** What can you infer about women's roles in the military in the 1800s?

Implied idea Women were needed as nurses, not as replacements for thousands of ill soldiers.

Directly stated idea An urgent need for qualified nurses arose after thousands of U.S. soldiers contracted diseases in the Spanish-American War.

Inference Women were not allowed to serve in the military in the 1800s.

Test Prep Tip

Tests often contain passages from which you may be asked to infer meaning. Because making inferences means choosing the most likely explanation from the facts available, try to balance information in the text with prior knowledge so that you arrive at the most informed inference.

Evaluating Sources

Find practice for **Evaluating Sources** in the **Skills Handbook,** p. H34

Historians understand that every source reflects a point of view. Therefore, historians must evaluate all sources. Understanding how an author's bias and purpose influence a source allows historians to know how to evaluate its usefulness.

Strategies historians use:

- Who created the source? Was the author impartial in his or her writing, or influenced by his or her interests?
- What was the purpose of the source? Was it supposed to convey public or private information? Did the author want to inform or persuade others?
- Compare the source with other sources of information, including both primary and secondary sources. Are they consistent?

Note that the purpose of the sources is to persuade. What techniques does each source use to persuade you?

Identify how bias affects each source. What kinds of bias do the selections, presentations, and discussions of evidence show?

Drilling for oil in Alaska

"Drilling in the Arctic represents a real and significant threat to a wide range of species including caribou, snow geese, musk oxen, and other wildlife. It would be a terrible mistake to drill in ANWR, truly one of America's national treasures, for. . . [an] insignificant supply of oil. . ."

—Senator Maria Cantwell, D-Alaska, in a speech to the U.S. senate, 2002

"ANWR opponents say that you can't have responsible development on the coastal plain. We know that's not true. We can have a healthy balance between production and conservation—between development and a concern for the world we are developing. We work hard to strike this balance in Alaska. . ."

—Senator Lisa Murkowski, R-Alaska, in a speech to the Alaska legislature, 2005

Does the source present logical arguments? Are the cause-and-effect relationships sound? Are conclusions rational or emotional?

Skills FOCUS   READING LIKE A HISTORIAN

As You Read Evaluate each source and decide whether you would use it to draw conclusions or make generalizations about the historical period or subject.

As You Study After you have evaluated the source, determine the extent to which it relates to your study. Then decide how, or if, the source should contribute to your historical understanding, and use it accordingly.

CASE STUDIES: Issues in Contemporary American Society

By now you have read about many issues in United States history. What issues continue to face Americans today? In the following seven sections you will read about some key twenty-first century challenges, both at home and abroad. Some of these topics are new developments of long-running debates; others are surfacing for the first time.

Issue 1 Immigration Policy
How should the United States respond to legal and illegal immigration into the country?

Issue 2 Women in the Military
What should be the role of women in the military?

Issue 3 Environmental Conservation
How should the federal government balance environmental protection with the use of needed resources?

Issue 4 Poverty in the United States
What are some ways to reduce poverty?

Issue 5 Crime and Public Safety
What are some ways to reduce crime?

Issue 6 Regulation and the Internet
How should the Internet be regulated?

Issue 7 Outsourcing and Trade
What are the advantages and disadvantages of outsourcing?

Immigrant advocates rally at Liberty State Park in Jersey City, New Jersey, in 2003.

Immigration Policy

New York Standards

ST 4.1 Analyze important debates in American history (e.g., restrictions on immigration), focusing on the opposing positions and the historical evidence used to support these positions.

ST 4.3 Develop hypotheses about important events, eras, or issues; move from chronicling to explaining historical events and issues; use information collected from diverse sources to produce cogently written reports and document-based essays.

FOCUSING ON THE ISSUE

How should the United States respond to legal and illegal immigration into the country?

KEY TERMS
immigrant, refugee, assimilation, ethnicity, quota, migrant, green card, amnesty, political asylum

Assistant Attorney General Viet Dinh, the country's first Vietnamese American to hold the post, swears in new U.S. citizens on Ellis Island.

THE INSIDE STORY

Viet Dinh was 10 years old when his family fled war-torn Vietnam in a small fishing boat. After 12 days at sea without food, the group swam ashore in Malaysia, but not before Dinh's mother used an ax to chop a hole in the side of the boat. By sinking the boat, she kept her family of six children from being forced back to sea and took a decisive step on a journey that eventually led them to the United States.

Like many **immigrants,** or people who settle in a new country, Dinh left his home country in the hope of finding new opportunities. He graduated from Harvard Law School, and in 2001 the Bush administration named him assistant attorney general.

From the Pilgrims on the *Mayflower* to Cubans arriving on the beaches of Miami, immigration has long been an important part of American culture. Many immigrants come to the United States as **refugees,** or people seeking protection from religious and political persecution. Others come for economic opportunity. Over time, U.S. immigration law has changed, often in response to such events as labor shortages, economic difficulties, or terrorist attacks.

1907
"Gentleman's Agreement" reached in which the United States will not prohibit Japanese immigration and Japan will not issue passports to laborers.

1900

In colonial times, immigrants from Western Europe were the equivalent of Vietnamese refugees like Dinh and his family. British, Scots-Irish, and German immigrants sought refuge in the British colonies in such numbers that by 1790, Congress passed a Naturalization Act requiring a two-year residence before immigrants could become citizens. In 1795 this residency requirement was raised to five years. In time, the Alien Act called for the expulsion of foreigners who posed a threat to U.S. interests. Even Benjamin Franklin, a statesman and a diplomat, was concerned about how to control "the stream of these people" who entered the new nation.

Chinese workers, like the ones photographed here in 1882, provided cheap labor for the often dangerous task of building railroads.

Two waves of immigration Franklin's so-called stream, however, did not diminish, and immigrants arrived in waves throughout the 1800s and early 1900s. Between 1840 and 1920, the country experienced its largest period of immigration, an influx of 37 million people. Because of the potato famine and European upheavals, Irish and German arrivals dominated in the mid- and later nineteenth century.

New arrivals, however, often received a chilly reception from earlier immigrants. The Know-Nothing political party of the 1850s, for example, was a group who played on anti-immigrant and anti-Catholic prejudices.

In the early 1900s, the largest number of immigrants were from southern and central Europe. The new federal immigration station at Ellis Island processed the arrival of many of these immigrants. The Immigration Service could deny entrance to those who lacked money or family connections in America. For many of the newcomers, the key to success in America was **assimilation**, or blending in with the established culture. Immigrants worked to learn the language and customs of their newly adopted land.

Closing the door Just as Europeans at Ellis Island had sought a better life, so too did Chinese immigrants who came to the United States to escape grinding poverty. News of the California gold rush had reached China, and many Chinese came to California seeking work in the mid-1800s. Chinese workers labored in mines, and they helped build the Central Pacific Railroad.

1943
Bracero Program provides temporary agricultural work to Mexican citizens. Chinese Exclusion Act is repealed.

1986
Immigration Reform and Control Act includes employer sanctions for knowingly hiring illegal immigrants.

2001
USA PATRIOT Act authorizes detention of noncitizens suspected of terrorism.

1925

1950

1975

2000

1924
Immigration Act establishes quota system favoring admission of northern and western Europeans.

1965
Immigration and Nationality Act amendments discontinue quotas based on national origins.

1990
Immigration Act of 1990 increases total immigration to 700,000, which will be gradually reduced to 675,000 people per year.

Migrant agricultural workers pick sugar beets near Stockton, California. Mexican migrants in the Bracero Program carried identification cards like the one shown here.

However, Chinese immigrants also faced discrimination in the form of mine and poll taxes. They were barred from testifying in court and had to attend separate schools. Anti-Chinese sentiment increased during the economic depression of the 1870s. Labor unions argued that the Chinese competed with American workers for jobs. This sentiment led to the Chinese Exclusion Act, the first American law to ban immigration by ethnicity—national, religious, language, or cultural origin. Passed in 1882, the act barred all Chinese immigration for 10 years. Those already in the country were denied citizenship, becoming "permanent aliens." The act was not repealed until 1943.

A "Gentleman's Agreement"

When Californians complained about Japanese immigration, President Theodore Roosevelt negotiated a "Gentlemen's Agreement" in 1907. By this arrangement, the Japanese government agreed not to issue passports to laborers. Immigration from Japan was completely eliminated after World War I, when the United States passed laws establishing quotas. These laws set limits on the number of people who could enter the United States from each country and favored admissions from northern and western Europe.

World War II also affected immigration policy. Wartime labor shortages led to an increase in the number of Mexican agricultural workers. The Bracero Program, begun in 1942, encouraged migrant laborers to take temporary work in the United States and then return to Mexico. This policy created a circular migration pattern that was supported until the program ended in 1964.

Present-day policies

U.S. immigration patterns changed fundamentally in 1965 with the passage of the Immigration and Nationality Act, which abolished national-origin quotas. Since that time, European immigration has slowed; immigrants today are primarily from Latin America, the Caribbean, and Asia. The goal for these immigrants is often a Permanent Resident Card, called a green card—evidence of an immigrant's legal right to live and work in the United States.

In the 1980s concern over illegal immigration led to stricter U.S. policy that was supposed to penalize employers who hired illegal aliens. This provision also provided amnesty, or forgiveness, to illegal aliens who had lived in the United States for many years, allowing them to gain legal status. Other policies made provisions for the admission of immigrants seeking political asylum, a kind of protection for humanitarian reasons.

In response to the terrorist attacks of September 11, 2001, Congress passed the USA PATRIOT Act. Among its many provisions, the act authorized indefinite detention of immigrants suspected of terrorist activities. Critics assert that the provisions of the PATRIOT Act violate Americans' civil rights as well as those of foreign citizens. However, the PATRIOT Act's chief author, former Vietnamese refugee Viet Dinh, claims that it is needed to "fight the common fight against terrorism."

The issue of how much immigration should be permitted in the United States and to whom citizenship should be granted are topics of ongoing debate. The documents that follow explore these issues by presenting different points of view and arguments. Examine the documents, keeping in mind what you have read about the history of U.S. immigration, and answer the questions that follow.

DOCUMENT 1

In 1992 the *Los Angeles Daily News* asked California's candidates for the U.S. Senate to describe their positions on several issues, including immigration. Candidates' responses were printed in the newspaper.

GRAY DAVIS
California must receive its fair share of federal funds to deal with the tremendous influx of immigrants into California. We must demonstrate that there is a serious price to pay for sanctioning illegal immigration and employment.

DIANNE FEINSTEIN
The vitality and diversity of immigrant communities is one of our greatest national strengths. I realize that immigrants face particular problems upon arrival in this country, including finding adequate housing, health care, education and jobs. But I feel that illegal immigration should be stopped for the simple reason that California is hard-pressed and cannot afford to take care of everyone else's problems at this time.

DAVID KEARNS
We need stricter enforcement of existing laws, and help with the related social programs by which we try to deal humanely with this problem. The federal government owes California a lot of help (send money). Citizenship for children of foreign-national parents should be restricted to those whose parents become American citizens within seven years . . . The long-range, real solution for this historical trend is to economically develop northern Mexico.

—*Los Angeles Daily News,* May 25, 1992

Analyzing the Document
What do Davis, Feinstein and Kearns believe the role of the federal government should be in immigration? On what do they base their positions?

DOCUMENT 2

At a meeting of the American Immigration Lawyers Association, former chairperson Carl Shusterman spoke about proposed cutbacks in immigration.

Americans have traditionally been hostile to new waves of immigrants, yet immigration has been vital to the development of our national character. . . .
In California, in particular, the economy flourished as immigrants—legal or otherwise—worked the fields of the world's largest agricultural economy. Wealthy immigrants sent their children to U.S. universities where they stayed to help give America a technological edge over the Russians. U.S. scientists, both American and foreign-born, worked side-by-side developing transistors, microchips, genetically engineered pharmaceuticals and ever more powerful computers. Immigrants were prominent in each new cutting-edge industry. Its large immigrant population established Los Angeles as the Capital of the Pacific Rim.

. . . Globalism, with its free movement of ideas and peoples, is as inevitable in the 21st Century as industrialization was in the 1800s. . . . A country where the population density is one of the lowest in the world, where legal immigrants include the world's best and brightest talent, and where present quotas allow for only a fraction of one percent of the population to immigrate annually, has not reached "carrying capacity."

—Carl Shusterman, December 9, 1996

Analyzing the Document
Why does Shusterman argue that immigrants are important to the growth of the U.S. economy?

In 2004 President George W. Bush presented proposals that would provide legal status to many undocumented workers as well as increase the number of green cards available to immigrants.

Analyzing the Document
What are the values and ideals that President Bush expects from new immigrants?

> In the process of immigration reform, we must also set high expectations for what new citizens should know. An understanding of what it means to be an American is not a formality in the naturalization process; it is essential to full participation in our democracy. My administration will examine the standard of knowledge in the current citizenship test. We must ensure that new citizens know not only the facts of our history, but the ideals that have shaped our history. Every citizen of America has an obligation to learn the values that make us one nation: liberty and civic responsibility, equality under God, and tolerance for others.
>
> —President George W. Bush, January 7, 2004

The U.S. census shows that foreign-born people are concentrated in "gateway" areas of the United States, including southwestern border states, the New York City and Miami areas, the Pacific Northwest, and metropolitan Washington, D.C. Miami-Dade County, Florida, was the only county in the United States in which the foreign-born population constituted a majority.

FOREIGN-BORN POPULATION BY STATE, 2000

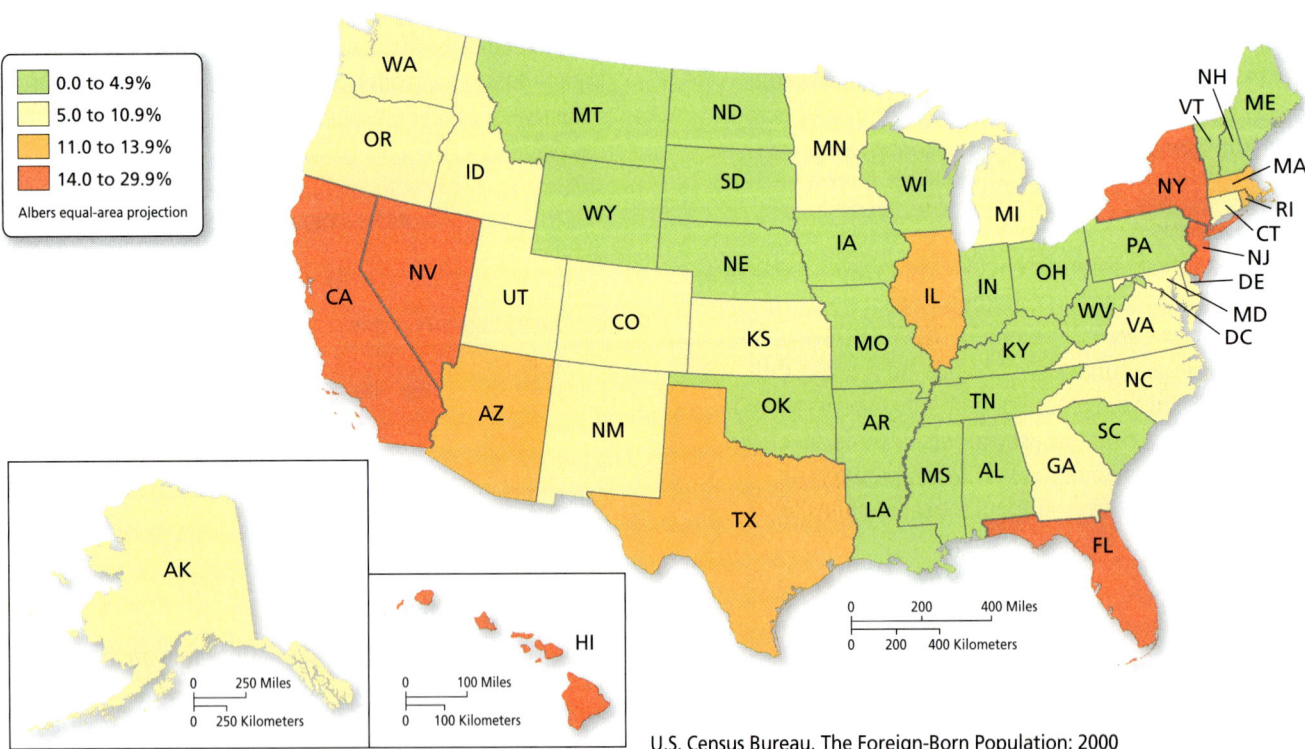

Legend:
- 0.0 to 4.9%
- 5.0 to 10.9%
- 11.0 to 13.9%
- 14.0 to 29.9%

Albers equal-area projection

U.S. Census Bureau, The Foreign-Born Population: 2000

Analyzing the Document
How do you think the patterns of immigration seen on the map might affect American culture?

Newsweek columnist Robert J. Samuelson looked at some of the issues associated with high levels of immigration.

Americans rightly glorify our heritage of absorbing immigrants. Over time, they move into the economic, political and social mainstream; over time, they become American rather than whatever they were—even though immigrants themselves constantly refashion the American identity. But no society has a boundless capacity to accept newcomers, especially when many are poor and unskilled. There are now an estimated 34 million immigrants in the United States, about a third of them illegal. About 35 percent lack health insurance and 26 percent receive some sort of federal benefit, reports Steven Camarota of the Center for Immigration Studies. To make immigration succeed, we need (paradoxically) to control immigration.

... [Low skilled] workers are inevitably crammed into low-wage jobs: food workers, janitors, gardeners, laborers, farm workers

... For today's [low skilled] immigrants (legal or illegal), the closest competitors are tomorrow's [low skilled] immigrants (legal or illegal). The more who arrive, the harder it will be for existing low-skilled workers to advance.

—Robert J. Samuelson, "The Hard Truth of Immigration," *Newsweek*, June 13, 2005

Analyzing the Document
How might unskilled immigrants affect poor, low-skilled workers already in the United States?

Although the Bracero Program ended in 1964, many migrant workers still come to the United States with the intention of working and sending money back to their families in their home countries.

Analyzing the Document
What does this political cartoon say about circular migration and how some people view immigrant laborers in the United States?

ANALYZING THE ISSUES

go.hrw.com
Research Online
SD7 Case Study

1. Review the documents presented in this issue. What do they show about the current U.S. reception of immigrants?

2. What do the documents lead you to believe about the economic impact of immigration to the United States? Analyze the documents discussed and note those that encourage this economic activity and those that seem concerned that American businesses will suffer from new waves of immigration.

3. Do library research to find out how immigration has affected your state in recent years. Has immigration increased or decreased in your state over the past five years?

4. Do library or online research to find two recent news articles about immigration trends in your state. Write a paragraph about your findings.

Women in the Military

New York Standards

ST 4.1 Analyze important debates in American history, focusing on the opposing positions and the historical evidence used to support these positions.

ST 4.3 Develop hypotheses about important events, eras, or issues; move from chronicling to explaining historical events and issues; use information collected from diverse sources to produce cogently written reports and document-based essays.

FOCUSING ON THE ISSUE

What should be the role of women in the military?

KEY TERMS

combat, corps, yeomen, prisoners of war

THE INSIDE STORY

In Colorado, Major Carrie Acree is a teacher, wife, and mother of three. In northwest Baghdad, Iraq, where she was deployed, or sent, with the U.S. Army's 443rd Civil Affairs Unit, Acree delivered school supplies to Iraqi children. Acree's unit also works in many other ways to improve Iraqis' daily lives.

Major Acree took the same oath that all men and women take when they join the armed forces. They make the same commitment to defend their country. But for many, the similarities end there.

Airborne Specialist Shelby Bixler, for example, would be idle if her paratrooper unit entered into **combat**, or fighting. Army rules restricting women from combat frustrate trained soldiers like Bixler, who would prefer to share combat risk.

These rules, however, do not mean that women are free from danger. More than 30 U.S. servicewomen had been killed in Iraq by March 2005, despite the combat ban.

Some people think that women should not face the same military risks as their male counterparts, especially when it comes to combat situations. Others think that when women join the military, they should be given the same opportunities and responsibilities as men. The role of women in the military is a debate that directly affects women in the service today. ◼

1901
U.S. Army establishes the first female Nurse Corps.

1900

A female soldier helps with the helicopter evacuation of another soldier wounded in the 1991 Persian Gulf War.

When Robert Shurtliff enlisted in, or joined, the Continental army to fight the British in 1782, no one knew that he was really 21-year-old Deborah Sampson in disguise. When Sampson was wounded in battle, she treated her own injuries rather than reveal her secret. It was only when she was hospitalized for a fever that the doctor caring for her learned her true identity. Sampson received an honorable discharge. Eventually, through the lobbying of Patriots such as Paul Revere, Sampson was awarded a government pension.

Deborah Sampson's experience was unusual. Although women have a long history of military service in the United States, much of it has come in supporting, rather than in fighting, roles.

Medical service During the Civil War, a number of women, including Clara Barton and Dorothea Dix, helped train nurses and care for wounded and ill soldiers. These nurses were not a part of the military. They served with, not in, the Union army.

In the Spanish-American War, thousands of U.S. soldiers contracted diseases such as typhoid, malaria, and yellow fever. The urgent need for qualified medical personnel led army hospitals to hire 1,500 civilian, or nonmilitary, female nurses. Impressed by their performance, the military created the Army Nurse Corps in 1901, followed by the Navy Nurse Corps seven years later. A **corps** is a military group. This was the first time in more than 100 years of

Nurses Are Needed Now!

FOR SERVICE IN THE
ARMY NURSE CORPS

IF YOU ARE A REGISTERED NURSE AND NOT YET 45 YEARS OF AGE
APPLY TO THE SURGEON GENERAL, UNITED STATES ARMY,
WASHINGTON 25, D. C., OR TO ANY RED CROSS PROCUREMENT OFFICE

Recruiting posters like this World War II army one helped fill the critical need for military nurses in both World Wars.

service that women were officially allowed into the military. However, these nurses received neither military rank nor benefits.

World wars bring changes On the eve of the U.S. entry into World War I, Secretary of the Navy Josephus Daniels asked a question that would stir debate for decades to come. Faced with a shortage of navy clerks, who were called **yeomen**, he asked his legal advisers, "Is there any law that says a yeoman must be a man?" The answer was no, and for the first time, the U.S. Navy and the Marine Corps enlisted women. Although they earned full military status and benefits, these women were not allowed to advance beyond the rank of sergeant.

1941
More than 350,000 women serve in World War II, not only as nurses but also as administrative and clerical personnel.

1976
Women are admitted to military academies.

1925 — **1950** — **1975** — **2000**

1917–18
Women serve as army and navy nurses, and almost 12,000 women enlist as navy yeomen to serve stateside.

1948
The Women's Armed Services Integration Act makes permanent women's right to join the military.

1990
Approximately 40,000 servicewomen are deployed during the Persian Gulf War in noncombat roles.

Women who worked with the U.S. Army, however, were civilian employees working as typists and performing other clerical duties without rank or benefits. Although most women served in the United States, a few went overseas. General John J. Pershing, the commander of the Allied forces, requested bilingual women to work communication centers in France. Known as Hello Girls, they transferred messages from headquarters to the front lines and back again. Women's service in these jobs meant that men typically responsible for them could be free to fight. But when the war ended, all women on active military duty were discharged, except for some nurses.

It was not until World War II that all branches of the armed forces enlisted women in special divisions for the first time. These women served in new capacities as truck drivers, supply plane pilots, air traffic controllers, electricians, and in other noncombat roles. Many of these women earned full military status. All told, about 350,000 women served in the military during World War II.

Unlike the end of World War I, the close of World War II did not bring a halt to women's military careers. Many women served again as nurses in the Korean War. Women remained a permanent part of the military, but laws limited their number, rank, and roles. These restrictions on women remained until the 1970s.

New roles for servicewomen During the Vietnam War, women made inroads into new service areas, including communications, intelligence, and finance. After the war, opportunities for women in the military continued to expand. Servicewomen became military police, helicopter pilots, chaplains, and construction equipment operators.

In 1970 Anna Mae Hays, chief of the Army Nurse Corps, and Elizabeth P. Hoisington, Women's Army Corps director, were the first women to attain the rank of brigadier general. Six years later, the first women were admitted to the military academy at West Point. However, military women still were not permitted to take any assignment with a high likelihood of direct combat.

Then in the 1990s more than 40,000 servicewomen were deployed during the Persian Gulf War. Women ran facilities for prisoners of war, or captured enemy troops; directed artillery; and served in port security units. But with increased opportunities came increased risk. Although the Persian Gulf War lasted a little more than a month, nearly twice as many servicewomen died during it as in the Korean and Vietnam Wars combined.

Servicewomen deployed to the Middle East after the terrorist attacks on September 11, 2001, have been allowed to fly in combat missions. However, they still cannot serve on submarines or on the ground in direct combat. In Iraq there are no frontlines, and women may unexpectedly find themselves in combat positions. Leigh Ann Hester of Kentucky did, and as a result of her heroic response she was awarded the Silver Star for valor in combat.

Today women play an accepted and valuable role in the U.S. military. But the debate over women's involvement in combat continues. For proponents of placing women in combat, it is an issue of fairness, of equal rights translating to equal responsibility and risk. Opponents, however, regard the idea that a woman, especially a mother, would be willing to kill or possibly be killed as a moral conflict that cannot be resolved.

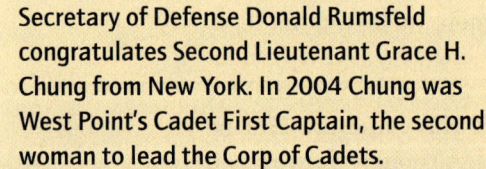

Secretary of Defense Donald Rumsfeld congratulates Second Lieutenant Grace H. Chung from New York. In 2004 Chung was West Point's Cadet First Captain, the second woman to lead the Corp of Cadets.

The role of women in the military raises many questions. The documents that follow explore this issue by presenting different points of view and arguments. Examine the documents, keeping in mind what you have read about the history of women in the military, and answer the questions that follow.

DOCUMENT 1

Lorry M. Fenner is a colonel in the air force. She has taught at the National War College as well as served as Vice Wing Commander of the 70th Intelligence Wing. The following is an excerpt from her portion of *Women in Combat: Civic Duty or Military Liability?*, a book Fenner cowrote with Marie E. deYoung. In the book the two women express their opposing points of view on women in the military.

Most of the arguments (regarding women in the military) presume that not only American women but American society will be harmed by exposing women to danger in combat ... Yet the integration of women into the armed forces to date has not only been of benefit to women but has been essential to military effectiveness and our nation's defense. Continuing their integration by eliminating the barriers to service that remain will keep faith with our security needs, our democratic heritage, and our political philosophy.

We put our young men at risk, even in times of ostensible [apparent] peace, and we have regarded their participation in the draft registry as an obligation of citizenship. We put our young women at risk as well in support positions that are "noncombat" on paper but are well within the range of even the crudest military or quasi-military weapons. We thereby limit our options, while sustaining the myth that military women are not in "harm's way" and denying them the opportunity to contribute to their fullest capability. Opening remaining military positions to all qualified individuals (determined by relevant tests, not sex) and requiring young women to register for the draft if we require young men to do so are simply the next logical ... steps in our military's and our nation's evolution toward our ideal of civic responsibility and equality.

—Lorry M. Fenner, *Women in Combat: Civic Duty or Military Liability?*, 2001

Analyzing the Document

What does Fenner think women's role in the military should be? On what basis does she make her argument?

DOCUMENT 2

Marie E. deYoung, the coauthor of *Women in Combat: Civic Duty or Military Liability?*, is a captain in the U.S. Army Reserves. The following excerpts from the book express her point of view regarding women's role in the military.

The most persistent myth to propel the argument for allowing women in ground combat is the mistaken belief that our high-tech military equipment will spare American combatants from the ravages of war because such gadgetry makes physical inferiority irrelevant to combat success.

Our nation and women would be better served if we begin to rethink the notion that combat service should confer special privileges, rights, and entitlements. Women, elderly persons, physically disabled persons, and children should not be relegated to second-class citizenship because they are not fit for ground combat assignments.

A time may come when the average woman can perform hard physical duties and handle physical and emotional trauma with the same resiliency as men. That moment has not arrived. In this moment in history, female soldiers suffer tremendously with every step taken to lift the combat exclusion. Therefore, I respectfully conclude that the ground combat exclusion for women should not be lifted.

—Marie E. deYoung, *Women in Combat: Civic Duty or Military Liability?*, 2001

Analyzing the Document

What is deYoung's opinion of women serving in ground combat? How does she support her argument?

DOCUMENT 3

Over time, women have played an important, although restricted, role in the military. The table below shows how women's roles in the military have changed since the mid-1900s.

Year	Ruling	Effect
1948	**Women's Armed Services Integration Act**	Women received permanent military status, but they could only make up 2 percent of the total force, and they had restrictions in duties and benefits.
1951	**Executive Order 10240**	Military branches discharged women who were pregnant or who had minor children at home.
1967	**Public Law 90-130**	It modified the Armed Services Integration Act by removing the 2 percent cap and lifting some pay and career restrictions.
1976	**Public Law 94-106**	Service academies opened to women for the first time.
1976	***Crawford v. Cushman***	U.S. Court of Appeals case ruled the discharge of pregnant marines violated the Fifth Amendment.
1980	**Defense Officer Manpower Personnel Act**	The DOMPA eliminated separate job standards for men and women. Promotions were done by selection instead of appointment.
1991	**Kennedy-Roth Amendment**	It repealed a ban in the Defense Authorizations Act so that women were allowed to serve on combat aircraft.
1993	**Order by Secretary of Defense Les Aspin**	It ordered the navy to open more ships to women after Congress repealed the law barring women from combat ships.

Source: Women in Military Service for America Memorial Foundation

Analyzing the Document
How has legislation changed women's roles in the military?

DOCUMENT 4

A Gallup poll asked Americans the following question: Do you think women in the armed services should get combat assignments on the same terms as men, should they be able to get combat assignments only if they want to, or should they never get combat assignments? The responses to that question are shown in the circle graph on the right.

Analyzing the Document
From this poll, what conclusion can you draw about American support of women in combat?

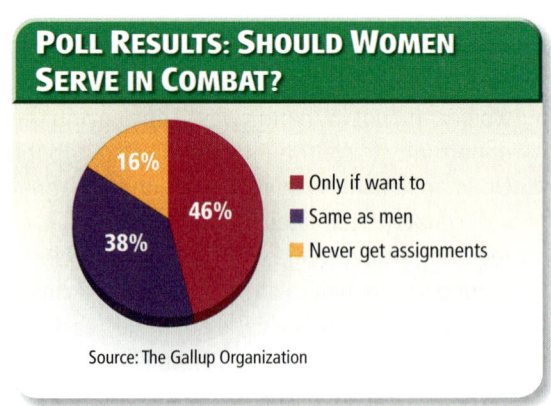

POLL RESULTS: SHOULD WOMEN SERVE IN COMBAT?

- 16%
- 46%
- 38%

■ Only if want to
■ Same as men
■ Never get assignments

Source: The Gallup Organization

The following excerpts are from the congressional debate surrounding the opening of combat positions to women. The first is from Representative Patricia Schroeder, D-Colorado, the first woman to serve on the House Armed Services Committee. The second is from Elaine Donnelly, the president of the Center for Military Readiness.

I believe I have heard all the objections to women holding combat positions. They vary from emotional to practical, but the competence of military women's performances as individuals has already been acknowledged . . . It is pure opinion, at this point, that women can't be effective in combat jobs. The fact is, however, that the combat exclusion policy tends to limit a woman's career opportunities. More importantly, the exclusionary policies deny the military the services of qualified personnel. It is time for military service to be based on qualifications, not gender.

—Rep. Patricia Schroeder, January 1990

As I see it, the issue at stake here is not support or admiration for the professionalism and patriotism of the women in the military. I share that support and admiration. The question, rather, is whether women should be directly involved in long-term ground combat in a future conventional war. The Army employs thousands of people, but it is not just another equal opportunity employer whose functions would be essentially the same in wartime as in peacetime . . . Military units should not be slowed down or deployed short-handed because some soldiers cannot march as fast, carry the same load, or are absent because of pregnancy or lack of childcare. No military power in the world—including Israel—has fought and won a war with women in combat roles.

—Elaine Donnelly, September 1990

Analyzing the Document

On what point do both Schroeder and Donnelly agree? Which items in these statements are facts? Which items are opinions?

The following is an excerpt from a 1994 recommendation by Secretary of Defense Les Aspin to broaden assignments to women in the armed forces. Aspin's recommendation partially overturned the so-called risk rule, which prohibited women from serving in combat roles.

We've made historic progress in opening up opportunities for women in all of the Services. Expanding roles for women in the military is right, and it's smart. It allows us to assign the most qualified individual to each military job. In all these actions, our overall aim remains the same, a high-quality, ready-to-fight force.

Women will still be barred from jobs that involve direct ground combat. The new policy defines direct ground combat for the Services uniformly for the first time. The definition has three parts, all of which must be present to prevent service by women. Women may not serve in units that (1) engage an enemy on the ground with weapons, (2) are exposed to hostile fire and (3) have a high probability of direct physical contact with the personnel of a hostile force.

—Secretary of Defense Les Aspin, January 13, 1994

Analyzing the Document

What do you think of Aspin's policy recommendation for women in the military?

Over time, women have made significant gains in the roles they perform in the military. The table on the right shows the rank order in the air force and the percentage of women who make up each rank. The total number of women is 13,479.

Analyzing the Document
What trends do you notice within the table? Explain your answer.

Air Force Rank Structure	Percentage That Are Women
Lieutenant General	0
Major General or Brigadier General	0.5
Colonel	3
Lieutenant Colonel	10
Major	18
Captain	35
1st Lieutenant	15.5
2nd Lieutenant	18

Source: U.S. Department of Defense, Active duty Personnel Report, 2003

The Vietnam Women's Memorial in Washington, D.C., honors an estimated 11,000 women who served in the Vietnam War. The sculpture depicts three uniformed nurses. In the first picture, one nurse gives medical aid and comfort to a wounded male soldier while another looks to the sky for help from incoming helicopters. The second picture shows the other side of the sculpture, where a third nurse is believed to be kneeling in prayer or thought.

Analyzing the Document
If an observer knew nothing about the history of women in the U.S. military, what might he or she conclude from this memorial about the role of women during the Vietnam War?

This line graph shows the total number of women enlisted in the U.S. Armed Forces from 1953 to 2003.

Analyzing the Document
What has been the trend regarding women's enlistment in the armed forces?

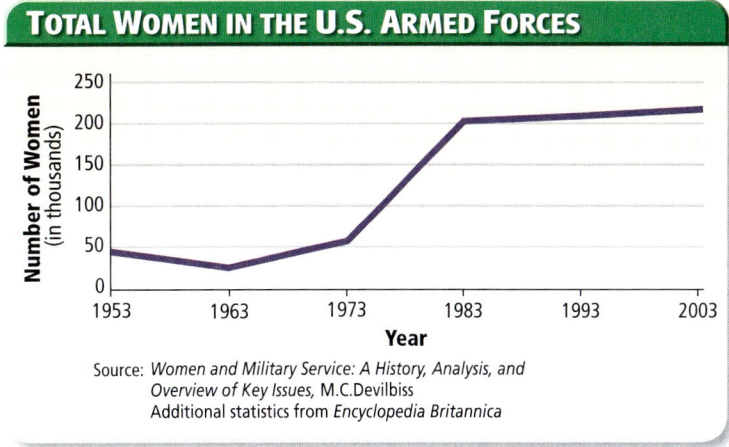

TOTAL WOMEN IN THE U.S. ARMED FORCES

Source: *Women and Military Service: A History, Analysis, and Overview of Key Issues*, M.C.Devilbiss
Additional statistics from *Encyclopedia Britannica*

Army Specialist Shoshana Johnson was held as a prisoner of war after her unit was ambushed in Iraq in 2003. At the time of her capture, Johnson was in a noncombat role as a cook. The following is an excerpt from an interview with Johnson.

Analyzing the Document
From Johnson's experience, what can you infer about the difference in the risk involved with military support roles and military combat roles?

At first they didn't realize I was a female, so their treatment was pretty rough. But once they realized I was a female, I was separated and I received medical care. I was shown kindness and some respect. There were some guards who were not as kind, but then there were some that interceded on my behalf. I think I was pretty lucky. The guys did not get as good treatment as myself . . . And I'll never really understand why. Was it because I was female? Was it because I was black, because I was a black female? I don't know. But I'm just thankful for it.

—Shoshana Johnson, National Public Radio, "Talk of the Nation," March 1, 2005

ANALYZING THE ISSUES

go.hrw.com
Research Online
SD7 Case Study

1. In what ways have women's roles in the military followed a pattern of development? What does that pattern imply for the future?

2. Knowing that combat has changed and that today being in a military support position in a war theater can put women in dangerous positions, how would you suggest that the issue of women in combat be resolved?

3. Do library or online research to find out how women in your state have recently served in the military. Write a short summary of your findings. Include the military branch, the location of the service, and the nature of the assignment.

4. Write a letter to the editor in which you explain the pros and cons of allowing women to serve in combat missions. Include different ideas regarding the role of women in the military.

Environmental Conservation

ST 4.1 Analyze important debates in American history, focusing on the opposing positions and the historical evidence used to support these positions.

ST 4.3 Develop hypotheses about important events, eras, or issues; move from chronicling to explaining historical events and issues; use information collected from diverse sources to produce cogently written reports and document-based essays.

FOCUSING ON THE ISSUE

How should the federal government balance environmental protection with the use of needed resources?

KEY TERMS

national park, conservation, extinction, public lands, taking

John Anderson grows alfalfa on a 600-acre farm in Oregon's Klamath Basin. The basin is dry and cannot support crops without irrigation.

A century ago the federal government dug canals to bring water from the Klamath River to new farms in the basin. When Anderson inherited the family farm, he expected to stay on the land. But a drought in 2000 and 2001 challenged his expectations.

Water levels in the Klamath River dropped, threatening the salmon that the Yurok Indians used for food. The U.S. government, with a duty to preserve salmon as a threatened species and food source, diverted water from farms to increase the water level for fish. Deprived of irrigation water, the farm fields dried up.

A generation ago, farmers' needs would have been the only consideration. But in 2001 the federal government had to consider wildlife and treaty obligations to the Yurok as well as crops.

Eventually, water flowed to the farms. But the crisis shows why it is hard to agree on how to use resources and who has the right to them. ■

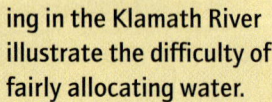

The dead salmon floating in the Klamath River illustrate the difficulty of fairly allocating water.

1903
The nation's first wildlife refuge is established at Florida's Pelican Island.

1900

1905
The National Forest system is established to conserve forest resources.

Hundreds of years before workers arrived to dig the Klamath canals, millions of bison roamed the Great Plains. An 1832 traveler wrote, "As far as my eye could reach the country seemed . . . blackened by . . . [the] herds."

After the Civil War, however, railroad tracks and settlers moved west. Soon, the bison population dropped. By 1892 only a few dozen bison were left on the Great Plains. The U.S. government sheltered the remaining animals in Yellowstone National Park. A **national park** is a natural area set aside by the federal government. This action may have saved the bison, but it was an unusual act at a time when conservation was not important to the federal government or to most Americans.

An endless frontier

During most of the 1800s, the idea of preserving land or wildlife seemed unnecessary to most people. The United States was a huge country, with wilderness extending as far as the eye could see. Animals were everywhere in endless numbers.

The land overflowed with natural resources, things found in nature that are useful to people. Forests and wildlife as well as rich deposits of gold, silver, and copper could be found. Settlers wasted no time in putting these resources to use. They logged and plowed, hunted and mined. As one of the few people of the time who favored **conservation**, or the careful use of resources, George Perkins Marsh wrote, "Man is everywhere a disturbing agent."

Marsh, however, was one of the few voices of concern in the mid-1800s. After all, many believed that if the land were spoiled or if animals were killed off in one valley, there were sure to be more in the next valley.

At that time, the U.S. government's main goal was settling land, not saving it. The federal government gave away land to anyone who would live, farm, or build on it. Homesteaders, railroads, and mining and logging companies received generous grants or bought huge acreages for bargain prices. By 1900 the federal government had given away half the land it had owned only 50 years before.

Early conservation efforts

During the late 1800s the frontier of the United States was filling up rapidly. Industry was growing, fueled by the

Yosemite Falls is a well-loved feature of Yosemite National Park, which was established in 1890.

1925	1950	1975	2000

1946
The Bureau of Land Management (BLM) is formed.

1976
The Federal Land Policy and Management Act strengthens the BLM's power to regulate federal lands.

1970s
The Sagebrush Rebellion spreads in the West to defend property rights against federal regulation.

1934
Yearbook of Agriculture states that 100 million acres of the Great Plains had lost its topsoil, and another 125 million acres was rapidly losing topsoil.

1988
The Wise Use movement is organized to roll back environmental regulations.

2000
President Clinton creates several new national monuments, covering millions of acres of western land.

This farmer's field shows the devastation caused by erosion. To prevent further erosion, a windbreak stretching from Texas to Canada and made up of 217 million trees was planted.

extraction of coal, iron, and other resources. The government saw land and resources as tools to boost development, and it considered regulation an unnecessary obstacle.

There were signs of trouble, however. Bison and beaver had disappeared from areas of the West. Logging and mining had left land bare and scarred. More and more people began to express concern.

As a result, the federal government took the first steps toward preserving land, wildlife, and resources. It set aside certain wilderness areas as national parks. The spectacular landscape in the northwest corner of Wyoming became Yellowstone National Park in 1872.

Congress also passed laws to protect some forests. Some restrictions also were put on mining, but these laws were not strongly enforced.

New challenges
The conservation movement received a boost from Theodore Roosevelt, the former Progressive governor of New York State, who became president in 1901. An adventurer who loved the outdoors, Roosevelt was the first president to make wildlife and resource conservation a priority. Roosevelt formed the nation's first national wildlife refuge in 1903 at Pelican Island in Florida. He also set aside millions of acres of western forest that later formed the core of a new system of national forests.

Many ranchers, miners, and loggers were unhappy with the national forests and with the new system of national parks that followed in 1916. They did not think conservation measures were necessary. Instead, they interpreted such measures as a seizure of land by the federal government. They claimed that the new national forests and parks would restrict or eliminate access to millions of acres of resources.

In the 1930s environmental disaster on the Great Plains led to increased regulation. To settlers of the mid-1800s, the western Plains were an unappealing land—flat, brown, and dry. They passed over it in favor of greener lands farther west. But unusually wet weather in the early 1900s led cattle ranchers and farmers to take another look at the western Plains. Ranchers moved in with cattle that overgrazed native grasses. What the cattle did not eat, farmers plowed under to plant wheat.

When drier weather returned in the 1930s, the crops dried up. Without natural grasses to hold the topsoil in place, wind whipped up the soil into large dust clouds that blackened the skies. The Dust Bowl was most severe in Kansas, Oklahoma, Texas, New Mexico, and Colorado. It drove farmers and ranchers from the land. It also led the federal government to develop new regulations to decrease soil erosion.

In 1934 the Taylor Grazing Act placed 140 million acres of the most damaged grazing land under stricter control. Although the law was not well enforced, it did decrease the number of cattle grazing on federal lands. It also upset ranchers who had grazed cattle there for decades.

An effort began to remove grazing lands from federal control and give them to the states, but that effort failed. However, the effort was an indication of the larger clashes to come between the dueling issues of conservation and property rights.

The environmental movement By the 1960s the quality of America's air, water, and land was suffering from decades of abuse. Smog hung over cities. Several animals, such as the grizzly bear and bald eagle, were in danger of **extinction**, or complete disappearance as a species.

Then in 1969 Americans saw pictures of an Ohio river so polluted with chemicals that it burst into flames. Conservationists said that something had to be done. In 1970 the first Earth Day celebration helped raise the public's awareness of environmental issues.

Backed by public support, the federal government passed several important environmental laws in the 1960s and 1970s. One of the earliest was the Wilderness Act, which preserved millions of acres of forest, desert, and wetlands. Later, Congress passed the Endangered Species Act to protect those plants and animals in danger of extinction. The Clean Air and Clean Water Acts were created to fight air and water pollution.

Sagebrush rebels The rise of environmental laws and regulation of public lands triggered a backlash in the West in the late 1970s known as the Sagebrush Rebellion. The goal of the new regulations was to protect forests and wildlife, conserve grazing land, and protect water supplies. For most people who used the land, however, the new regulations were the first real restrictions on the use of public lands that they had known. **Public lands** are federal lands that were never sold or made into protected areas such as national parks or wilderness areas.

Sometimes, regulations to protect endangered species also restricted activities on private land. "It really is like being in a colony," one Nevada resident complained.

The ranchers considered these government laws and regulations a "taking," based on the "takings clause" of the Fifth Amendment to the U.S. Constitution. A **taking** occurs when regulations restrict use of land so much that owners believe that the government has essentially taken the land.

Ranchers whose cattle grazed on federal grasslands believed that the use of resources on public lands was a right the government could not restrict or take away—that land access should remain much as it had been when the West was first settled. They disapproved of the permits, fees, and rules designed to decrease environmental damage. The issue is complicated by the fact that on some public lands the government owns the land but individuals may own water, mineral, or other rights.

The Sagebrush Rebellion gained an advocate in 1980 with the election of President Ronald Reagan. Declaring, "I am a sagebrush rebel," Reagan decreased the regulation of federal lands in the West. In the 1990s the rebellion against federal regulations continued.

An ongoing struggle For more than a decade, the federal government has shifted positions on the issue of how best to balance environmental protection with the commercial use of natural resources.

Conservation has been effective. Air and water are cleaner today than they have been in previous years. Several endangered species have been saved from extinction. Millions of acres of wilderness remain undeveloped. President Bill Clinton believed that environmental regulation was good for the country, and his administration strengthened environmental laws. Clinton's successor, George W. Bush, believed in encouraging resource development to boost the American economy. He has increased logging, mining, and grazing on public lands.

Rachael Carson's 1962 book *Silent Spring* focused attention on the dangers posed by pesticides—particularly DDT. She pointed out that pesticides are not selective poisons but can affect everything they touch.

Is it possible to use resources without harming the environment? Can land, water, and mineral resources be protected while also preserving people's rights to use them? The documents that follow explore these questions by presenting different points of view. Examine the documents, keeping in mind what you have just read about resource use and conservation. Then answer the questions that follow.

DOCUMENT 1

This map shows the location of federal lands in the United States.

FEDERAL LANDS IN THE UNITED STATES

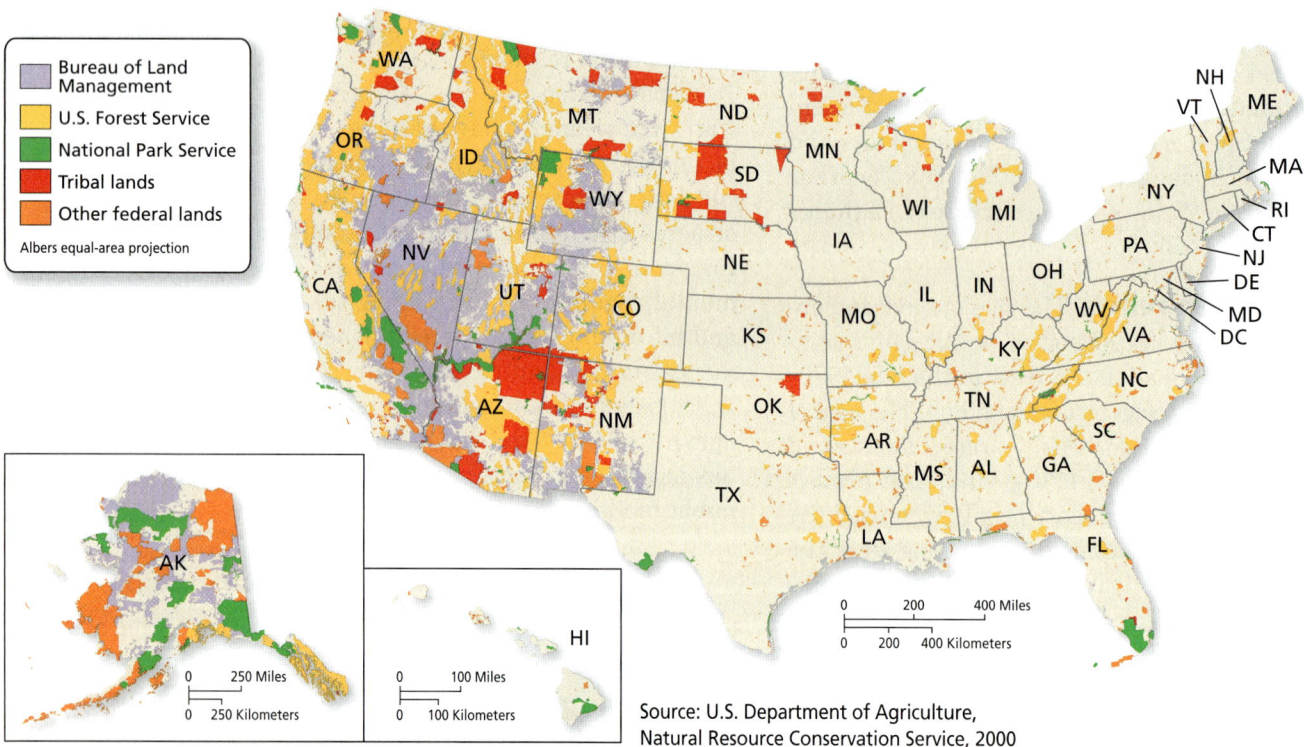

Legend:
- Bureau of Land Management
- U.S. Forest Service
- National Park Service
- Tribal lands
- Other federal lands

Albers equal-area projection

Source: U.S. Department of Agriculture, Natural Resource Conservation Service, 2000

Analyzing the Document

From the map, what can you conclude about the locations of the Sagebrush Rebellion?

Senator Lisa Murkowski (R., Alaska) offers her opinion on oil drilling in Alaska's Arctic National Wildlife Refuge. This excerpt is taken from a speech she made to the Alaska state legislature.

> The question we have to answer is how to create a state for our children that is better than the one we know today. The future that we want will be funded in part by our resources, and I hope that a portion of that will be from ANWR...
>
> It's... important that we let people in the Lower 48 know that a majority of Alaskans want ANWR open and that when it comes to balancing development with care for our environment, we do it right...
>
> ANWR opponents say that you can't have responsible development on the coastal plain. We know that's not true. We can have a healthy balance between production and conservation—between development and concern for the world we are developing. We work hard to strike this balance in Alaska...
>
> Our resources serve two objectives. First, they fulfill our role as one of fifty states that share in the responsibility of advancing the country. We advance as a country because of the unique contributions of each one of the states—Alaska's contribution to energy security is through domestic production.
>
> Secondly, our resources serve the objective of lessening our reliance on federal funds and providing financial security for the state. Our resources are an opportunity to create long term, local and sustainable [sources of income].
>
> —Senator Lisa Murkowski,
> speech to Alaska legislature, March 30, 2005

Analyzing the Document

What state and national benefits does Senator Murkowski see to drilling in ANWR?

This letter to the editor of the *Atlantic Monthly* expresses the writer's point of view regarding a rancher's right to use public land without restrictions.

> Dear Editors:
> Cattle grazing has a ... negative impact on any landscape, especially across the arid US west. [Cattle] cross the landscape in search of food and water, eating most everything available, in many cases down to the bare ground ... Grazing causes not only the destruction of plants and native grasses, but unleases erosion that hinders the health of rivers, degrading habitat essential to fish and other aquatic species.
>
> ... In addition to the subsidized rent on public land ... ranchers also get subsidized fencing, and subsidized eradication of so called "nuisance" species such as coyote, and even wolves—all on land that belongs to you and me. Further, in ... Montana, where a vast expanse of public land is used for grazing, a recent economic study at the University of Montana states that, "federal grazing is responsible for about one quarter of one percent of all income in Montana." To characterize grazing on public land in the west as a sole source of income for family ranchers is off base, and on the whole, grazing on public lands in the west subjects a fragile landscape to a tremendous beating for a very small return. It is also key to note that the vast majority of acres grazed on public lands are still held by very large corporate operations that cover millions of acres.
>
> While there are standouts that should be encouraged for their efforts, ... they represent only a small strand in the web of public lands grazing ... It is not about the so-called loss of cowboy culture, but instead it is about the opportunity for people to enjoy a landscape that has not been ravaged ... Grazing on our land, public land, is not a right, but instead a privilege.
>
> —TW, Letter to the Editor,
> *Atlantic Monthly,* November 1999

Analyzing the Document

Does this writer think that rules and regulations on grazing public land are needed?

The cartoon expresses the artist's point of view about the government's record in balancing resource use and conservation in the national forests.

Analyzing the Document

Does the artist think that there is a balance between resource use and environmental conservation in the national forests? Explain your answer.

COPYRIGHT 1999. REPRINTED BY PERMISSION OF STEVE GREENBERG.

The Bureau of Land Management oversees the public land in the United States. This land can be used for grazing, natural resource collection, habitat preservation, and recreation, sometimes all at once. This chart shows the amount of money generated in 2004 by the Bureau of Land Management.

COMMERCIAL ACTIVITIES SUMMARY

Public/Federal Land Commercial Activity	Value FY 2004 (millions $)	Federal Revenue Generated FY 2004 (millions $)
Oil and Gas, Geothermal, and Helium	14,217	1,620
Coal	3,645	545
Other Leasable 3 and Salable Materials	943	46
Grazing	62	9
Timber	33	22
Total	18,900	2,242

Source: Bureau of Land Management, 2004 Annual Report

Analyzing the Document

What are the benefits to using land for multiple purposes? In your opinion, does oil and gas drilling fit well with the purpose of recreation and habitat preservation? Explain your answer.

This table shows the major types of federal lands and their uses.

MAJOR TYPES OF FEDERAL LANDS AND THEIR USES

Federal Lands	National Forests	National Wildlife Refuges	National Parks	Public Lands	National Wilderness Areas
Size (in acres)	190 million	95 million	80 million	260+ million	160 million
Number of Sites	155 forests; 20 grasslands	542	58		600
Purpose	Conservation of forests, in part as a source of timber	Protection of fish and wildlife and their habitats	Preservation of natural, historic, and cultural sites for public enjoyment	Broad resource use as well as recreation and wildlife protection	Preservation of land largely untouched by human activity
Activities Allowed	Recreation, logging, grazing	Recreation, including hunting and fishing	Recreation, including fishing and camping	Livestock grazing, mining, logging, recreation	Recreation, scientific study, conservation
Activities Prohibited			Hunting, mining, logging, and other resource development		Commercial activities: mining, logging, use of motor vehicles, and building of permanent roads and structures

Source: Federal Land and Resource Management: A Primer, Congressional Research Service Report, 1998

Analyzing the Document
Which types of federal lands offer the greatest protection to land and wildlife? Which types offer the greatest opportunity to use timber and mineral resources? How would the formation of a new wilderness area affect people who graze cattle or cut trees on the land? How might that affect their point of view on the formation of new wilderness areas?

ANALYZING THE ISSUES

go.hrw.com
Research Online
SD7 Case Study

1. From the information in this issue, what can you conclude is the main reason for regulation of federal lands?

2. In your opinion, should the federal government own large tracts of land, or should it sell the land to private interests? Would a private company have an advantage in balancing environmental and resource issues? Refer to the documents to explain your answer.

3. Select and research federal lands in or near your state. Discover how the managers of these lands protect the environment. Find out whether activities such as mining or grazing are permitted.

4. Research important dates in the movement to conserve public lands. Then construct a time line of events. Then use the time line to write a summary of developments in the public-lands conservation movement.

Poverty in the United States

New York Standards

ST 3.2 Draw upon literary selections, historical documents, and accounts to analyze the roles played by different individuals and groups during the major eras in New York State and United States history.

ST 4.3 Develop hypotheses about important events, eras, or issues; move from chronicling to explaining historical events and issues; use information collected from diverse sources to produce cogently written reports and document-based essays.

FOCUSING ON THE ISSUE

What are some ways to reduce poverty?

KEY TERMS
poverty threshold, welfare, working poor, food insecurity, disparity, cost of living, minimum wage

William Henderson of the Green Bay Packers hands out gifts to a woman at a food bank in Green Bay, Wisconsin. Many of the working poor depend on aid, especially at the end of the month.

THE INSIDE STORY

Pamela Reed-Loy lives with her family of five in a cramped hotel room in Washington, D.C. Although her husband, Archie Loy, works full time as a mechanic, the family struggles to make ends meet. Pamela must stay home to care for her three daughters, one of whom suffers from frequent asthma attacks.

"It's stressful, living all in one room—you can't get away from anybody," she said. Each month, the Loy family gets two free bags of groceries from a local church's food bank. "I know people who won't go to the food bank—who don't want to be seen. But why not? I'd never let my kids go hungry."

The Loy family and millions like them live in poverty, or the condition of having insufficient income or resources to acquire basic needs. Much more than a simple lack of money, poverty is a complex social, political, and personal issue. Poverty profoundly affects not only the poor but the society that supports and surrounds them.

1904
Robert Hunter's book *Poverty* is one of the first American efforts to measure poverty.

1900

These men line up for a free meal. Soup kitchens fed many of the unemployed during the Great Depression.

Poverty as we know it today was not recognized as a national issue until the early 1900s, when the U.S. government had to confront problems created by the rapid growth of industry and cities. At the end of the nineteenth century, Americans' lives were changing dramatically. The growth of industries led people to move from rural areas to the cities. Immigrants flocked to New York City and other places in search of jobs and financial security. What many found, however, was overcrowding, low wages, long hours, and dangerous working conditions.

The Great Depression Many families had prospered during the 1920s but lost their jobs and savings in the Great Depression. Children and the elderly were among the most vulnerable, much as they still are today. At the peak of the Great Depression, one in four Americans was unemployed. Nearly 250,000 young people were homeless.

President Franklin D. Roosevelt proposed the New Deal, a far-reaching set of initiatives designed to stimulate the economy and provide relief to the millions in poverty by putting people back to work. Social Security was created to protect the elderly, people with disabilities, and families with children.

The Other America The U.S. economy recovered and then grew during World War II. Men, women, and minorities all worked in the war effort. The United States became the richest nation in the world as Americans earned more and spent more, factories produced more, and more jobs were created. By the 1950s a sprawling middle class had emerged.

But some political activists, such as Michael Harrington, saw a different America. Millions of people continued to struggle economically, especially the elderly. In 1962 Harrington exposed a "culture of poverty"—some 40 to 50 million Americans suffering in inner cities, in rural Appalachia, and elsewhere—in a book called *The Other America*. Harrington's book influenced the social policies of Presidents John F. Kennedy and Lyndon Johnson.

President Johnson's Great Society In his 1964 election campaign, President Johnson introduced the Great Society program, an extension of Roosevelt's New Deal. President

1933
President Roosevelt announces the New Deal.

1935
Social Security is signed into law.

1962
The Other America is published.

1965
Medicare and the first Head Start program begin.

1980–82
Spending on domestic social programs falls by $101 billion.

1925

1929
The stock market crashes, plunging the nation into the Great Depression.

1950

1964
President Johnson announces the Great Society.

1975

2000

1996
Welfare reform is initiated.

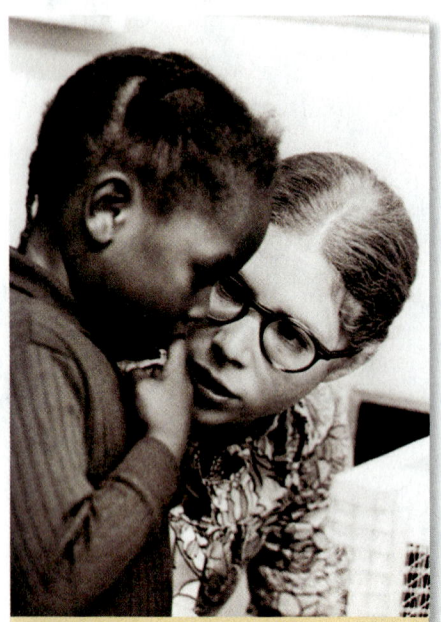

A teacher talks with a student in a New York Head Start Program. The program's goal is to increase the school readiness of children from low-income families.

Johnson said his Great Society was "a place where men are more concerned with the quality of their lives than the quantity of their goods." The goals of the Great Society were abundance and liberty for all, an end to poverty, and an end to racial injustice.

War on Poverty In his first State of the Union address, Johnson declared an official War on Poverty. He proposed the Economic Opportunity Act of 1964, under which programs to aid the poor were born. A new housing act provided rent supplements and created the Department of Housing and Urban Development. Medicare, a health insurance program for the elderly, and Medicaid, health-insurance assistance for the poor, were created. Head Start provided free preschool for poor children. Food stamps were introduced. Millions of Americans continue to benefit from these programs today.

The War on Poverty made measuring poverty a priority in order to determine who qualified for aid and how much they should receive. A social scientist, Mollie Orshansky, formed a strategy. She developed a **poverty threshold**, also called a poverty line, to statistically measure the number of people living in poverty. The poverty threshold became the government's official definition of poverty. In 2004 the poverty threshold for a family of four was an annual income of $19,157. Families subsisting on less than that were considered poor.

Welfare reform Throughout the 1970s and 1980s, little change was made in the official definition of poverty. President Ronald Reagan's administration focused on reducing the number of families receiving **welfare**, or financial assistance from the government, and helping the unemployed find work. Many families, however, continued to struggle.

The poverty rate fell substantially in the 1990s as the country's economy boomed. Policy-makers discussed measuring poverty and whether benefits received by the poor should count as income, and if so, whether the poverty line should be raised. The 1996 welfare-reform law brought massive change, as the emphasis shifted from providing income to helping parents find jobs. Welfare became welfare-to-work. Temporary Assistance for Needy Families (TANF) replaced Aid to Families with Dependent Children (AFDC) and placed limits on the amount of time a family could receive public assistance.

Poverty now and in the future Many people believe that the United States was built on the American Dream, the idea that those who work hard can earn enough to achieve prosperity. Yet more than two-thirds of the nation's poor children have at least one parent who works. The Reed-Loy family in Washington, D.C., is part of this new and growing type of poverty in the United States. They are known as the **working poor**—those who are employed but cannot earn enough to lift themselves out of poverty.

The United States has the highest rate of poverty in the developed world. The progress made in fighting poverty in the 1990s ended in 2001. Although the economy improved after that date, the poverty rate rose. In 2004 it reached 12.7 percent. A 2003 survey found 36 million suffering from **food insecurity**, or the inability to buy enough healthy food.

Over the last 20 years, the incomes of the richest 1 percent of Americans have more than doubled. The incomes of the poorest one-fifth, however, grew by only 9 percent. Some people think that such a gap, or **disparity**, between the rich and poor is responsible for lack of progress in reducing the poverty rate. They also think that the **cost of living**, or the amount of income required to buy basic necessities, is too high.

Many Americans have conflicting views on how to reduce poverty. Some think that the federal government needs to provide more assistance to low-income people and to mandate a higher **minimum wage**, or the minimum amount a company must pay its employees. Others think that such measures would make the problem worse by creating dependence on the government.

The issue of how to reduce poverty continues to be debated. The documents that follow explore this issue by presenting different points of view and arguments. The documents reflect the social, economic, and governmental efforts to define and lessen poverty and its effects on people. Examine the documents, keeping in mind what you have read about the history of poverty in the United States, and answer the questions that follow.

DOCUMENT 1

On May 22, 1964, President Johnson gave a speech at the University of Michigan introducing the Great Society. Following is an excerpt of his speech.

The purpose of protecting the life of our Nation and preserving the liberty of our citizens is to pursue the happiness of our people. Our success in that pursuit is the test of our success as a Nation.

For a century we labored to settle and to subdue a continent. For half a century we called upon unbounded invention and untiring industry to create an order of plenty for all of our people.

The challenge of the next half century is whether we have the wisdom to use that wealth to enrich and elevate our national life, and to advance the quality of our American civilization.

Your imagination, your initiative, and your indignation will determine whether we build a society where progress is the servant of our needs, or a society where old values and new visions are buried under unbridled growth. For in your time we have the opportunity to move not only toward the rich society and the powerful society, but upward to the Great Society.

The Great Society rests on abundance and liberty for all. It demands an end to poverty and racial injustice, to which we are totally committed in our time.

—President Lyndon Johnson, commencement speech at the University of Michigan, May 22, 1964

Analyzing the Document
What was President Johnson's goal in creating the Great Society?

DOCUMENT 2

In this editorial cartoon, Larry Wright of the *Detroit News* offers his opinion on the condition of Social Security, the safety net designed to help protect senior citizens from poverty.

Analyzing the Document
How does this cartoon portray Social Security's future?

Nationally, more than 12 percent of U.S. residents are considered to be poor, meaning they fall below the poverty threshold assigned by the U.S. Census Bureau. The map shows, however, that poverty rates vary from region to region.

POVERTY IN THE UNITED STATES

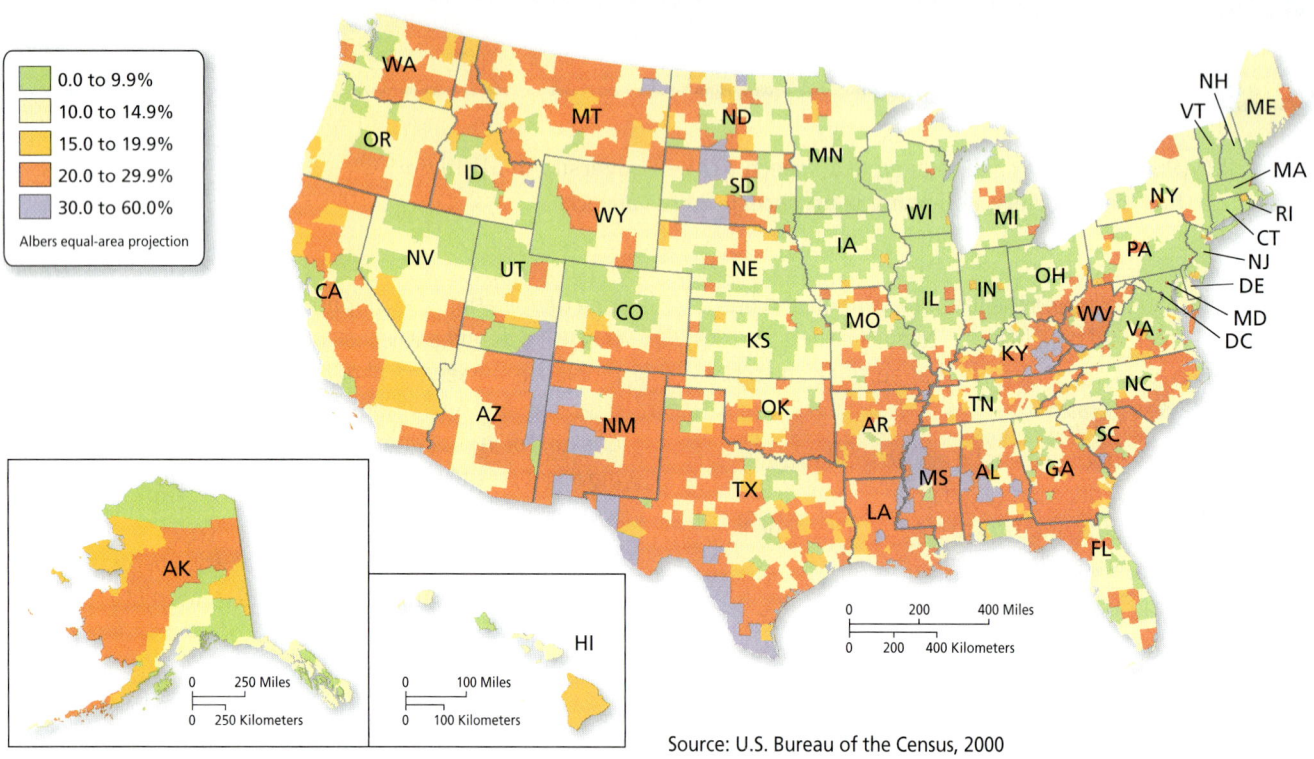

0.0 to 9.9%	
10.0 to 14.9%	
15.0 to 19.9%	
20.0 to 29.9%	
30.0 to 60.0%	

Albers equal-area projection

Source: U.S. Bureau of the Census, 2000

Analyzing the Document
What areas of the country are most affected by poverty?

The Center on Budget and Policy Priorities analyzed government studies of the living conditions of poor and near-poor families. This graph represents the percentage of U.S. households with children that experienced what the authors termed hardships: hunger or food insecurity, crowded living space, loss of utilities such as phone or water, and the total experiencing any combination of these factors.

Analyzing the Document
What percentage of poor families reported going hungry? What percentage of near-poor families reported overcrowding? From the information in the graph, what might you conclude about living conditions just above the federal poverty line?

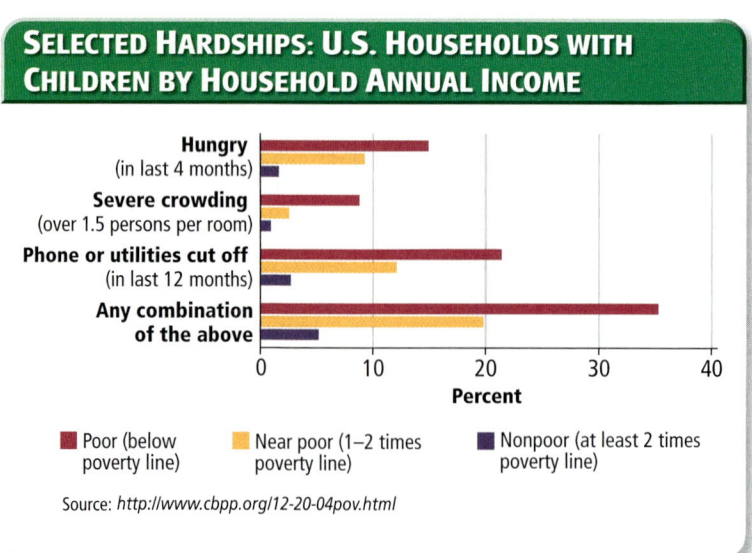

SELECTED HARDSHIPS: U.S. HOUSEHOLDS WITH CHILDREN BY HOUSEHOLD ANNUAL INCOME

Hungry (in last 4 months)
Severe crowding (over 1.5 persons per room)
Phone or utilities cut off (in last 12 months)
Any combination of the above

Percent

■ Poor (below poverty line)   ■ Near poor (1–2 times poverty line)   ■ Nonpoor (at least 2 times poverty line)

Source: http://www.cbpp.org/12-20-04pov.html

This document is an excerpt from a White House position paper promoting the Welfare Reform Law of 1996.

Over the past 15 years or so, Congress has expanded a series of programs that provide support to low-income working families. These programs include Medicaid, childcare, the child tax credit, the EITC (Earned Income Tax Credit), and food stamps. Taken together, these programs convert even a minimum wage job into the equivalent of a job paying $8 per hour with benefits. More specifically, if a mother with two children works almost full time at the minimum wage, she earns about $10,000 per year. But thanks to $4,000 in cash from the EITC and around $2,000 in food stamps, the mother and children have a total income of $16,000. In addition, the mother has Medicaid coverage for up to a year after she leaves welfare and the children have Medicaid coverage for as long as the mother has a low income. Moreover, the mother may benefit from the $17 billion in annual federal funding for childcare. The fundamental goal of welfare reform since 1996 has been to help each family achieve its highest degree of self-sufficiency.

—Working toward Independence, White House Position Paper, Februrary 2002

The U.S. Department of Agriculture provides people with low incomes food stamps, which are used to purchase grocery items, excluding alcohol and tobacco. The food-stamp program helps lessen food insecurity by giving people with lower incomes access to healthy food. The government considers food stamps "the first line of defense against hunger." The average monthly benefit for a family with children is $242. But not all eligible families decide to participate in the food-stamp program.

TOP TEN STATES RECEIVING FOOD STAMPS IN 2003

State	Number of People Receiving Food Stamps	Number of People Living in Poverty
Texas	1,872,000	3,705,000
California	1,709,000	4,634,000
New York	1,436,000	2,707,000
Florida	1,041,000	2,148,000
Illinois	954,000	1,592,000
Ohio	855,000	1,226,000
Michigan	838,000	1,125,000
Pennsylvania	823,000	1,279,000
Georgia	750,000	1,014,000
Tennessee	728,000	829,000

Source: *U.S. Department of Agriculture, Food and Nutrition Service, 2005* (rounded to the nearest thousand)

Analyze the Document

How does the federal government believe that welfare-to-work helps families? Do you agree or disagree? Explain your answer.

Analyzing the Document

Which state in the table above has the most people in poverty? Which has the most people receiving food stamps? What might be some reasons that not all poor people receive food stamps?

ANALYZING THE ISSUES

go.hrw.com
Research Online
SD7 Case Study

1. After you have examined all of the documents, think about the following questions: How might redrawing poverty lines affect poorer Americans?

2. How should we balance the needs of people with lower incomes against other, possibly conflicting, priorities? Who should decide?

3. Research the programs available to people living in poverty in your community. What programs established as part of President Johnson's Great Society are still in effect? Which ones are newer?

4. Look at the map of poverty in the United States and find the percentage for your area. How does your community try to reduce poverty's effects? Write a proposal for an event that you could organize to assist local families living in poverty.

Crime and Public Safety

New York Standards

ST 4.1 Analyze important debates in American history, focusing on the opposing positions and the historical evidence used to support these positions.

ST 4.3 Develop hypotheses about important events, eras, or issues; move from chronicling to explaining historical events and issues; use information collected from diverse sources to produce cogently written reports and document-based essays.

FOCUSING ON THE ISSUE

What are some ways to reduce crime?

KEY TERMS
criminal code, Second Amendment, militia, rehabilitation, discretion

THE INSIDE STORY Derek Ali was many things to many people: father, teacher, newspaper reporter, and community volunteer, to name a few. One night in September 2004, he was wearing yet another hat: DJ for a private party. As he packed his gear in the parking lot after the show, Ali heard gunshots. He pushed the woman beside him to the ground, but he was struck in the chest by a bullet and died. Police said that Ali was a victim of random gunfire. That night a 15-year-old girl lost a father, reporters lost a beloved coworker, and a community lost a leader.

But the toll of the events of that September night goes beyond personal tragedy. People and governments at all levels bear the direct and indirect costs of crime, harmful or dangerous acts as defined by law. In 2001 all levels of government spent more than $167 billion, or about $600 per person, for police, jails and prisons, and judicial and legal activities.

The price of being a crime victim is also high. In 1996 the U.S. Department of Justice estimated the annual cost to victims in medical expenses, lost earnings, and other factors at $450 billion. Given the enormous costs, the decisions we make about how best to fight crime are crucial to our social and financial welfare. ◼

Fremont Police Crime Scene Specialist Donna Gott investigates evidence left behind at a crime scene.

1907
Federal Bureau of Investigation established.

1900

EXPLORING THE PAST

Over time, the kinds of crimes people commit and ideas about how to treat offenders, or convicted criminals, have changed along with social and economic conditions. Understanding the history of crime and the various attempts to reduce it may help us make more effective decisions about crime control today.

The police began wearing copper badges like this early one from Philadelphia beginning in the late 1840s.

Crime in the colonies
The American colonies based their system of law and law enforcement on that of England. Local community leaders wrote laws, and juries decided guilt or innocence at trials presided over by judges.

Penalties for crimes were generally severe by modern standards. Besides the death penalty, they included branding, flogging, and forced labor. In 1682 William Penn, the Quaker leader and founder of Pennsylvania, introduced the Great Law, which treated prisoners more humanely. It limited the use of the death penalty and made hard labor the most common form of punishment.

Cities and states fight crime
The first police officers, or cops, walked a beat in New York City. They got their nickname from the copper badges that they wore to identify themselves. As more and more people moved to cities, the crime rates in urban areas increased. In the early 1800s cities throughout the Northeast formed professional police departments.

On the state level, legislators began to standardize laws across communities. New York's 1881 **criminal code**, or standard set of laws, became a model for other states.

By the mid-1800s small, easily hidden handguns were being mass produced. Cities and states tried to control urban crime by targeting these concealed weapons, the first attempts at gun control. Associations of gun owners also arose, including the National Rifle Association, which formed in 1871. In 1911 New York passed the Sullivan Act, which made carrying a concealed weapon illegal and tightened gun-permit procedures.

Crime and gun control
National events would shape the efforts to control crime throughout the 1900s. To meet the challenge on the national level, the federal government established the Federal Bureau of Investigation in 1907 and the Federal Bureau of Prisons in 1929. These agencies brought greater resources as well as professionalism to the fight against crime.

Following the assassination of Robert F. Kennedy in 1968, the Gallup poll found that for the first time respondents ranked crime as the nation's most pressing issue, and Congress passed the Gun Control Act of 1968. This law

---

1924
Congress establishes the FBI's Identification Division to consolidate fingerprint files.

1938
Gun Control Act passed in response to assassinations.

1984
Crime Control Act expands the death penalty and funds crime prevention measures.

1994
Violent Crime Control and Law Enforcement Act bans assault weapons.

1925   **1950**   **1975**   **2000**

1934
National Firearms Act, the first federal gun-control law, is passed.

1972
National Sheriffs' Association establishes neighborhood watch.

2004
Congress allows ban on assault weapons to expire.

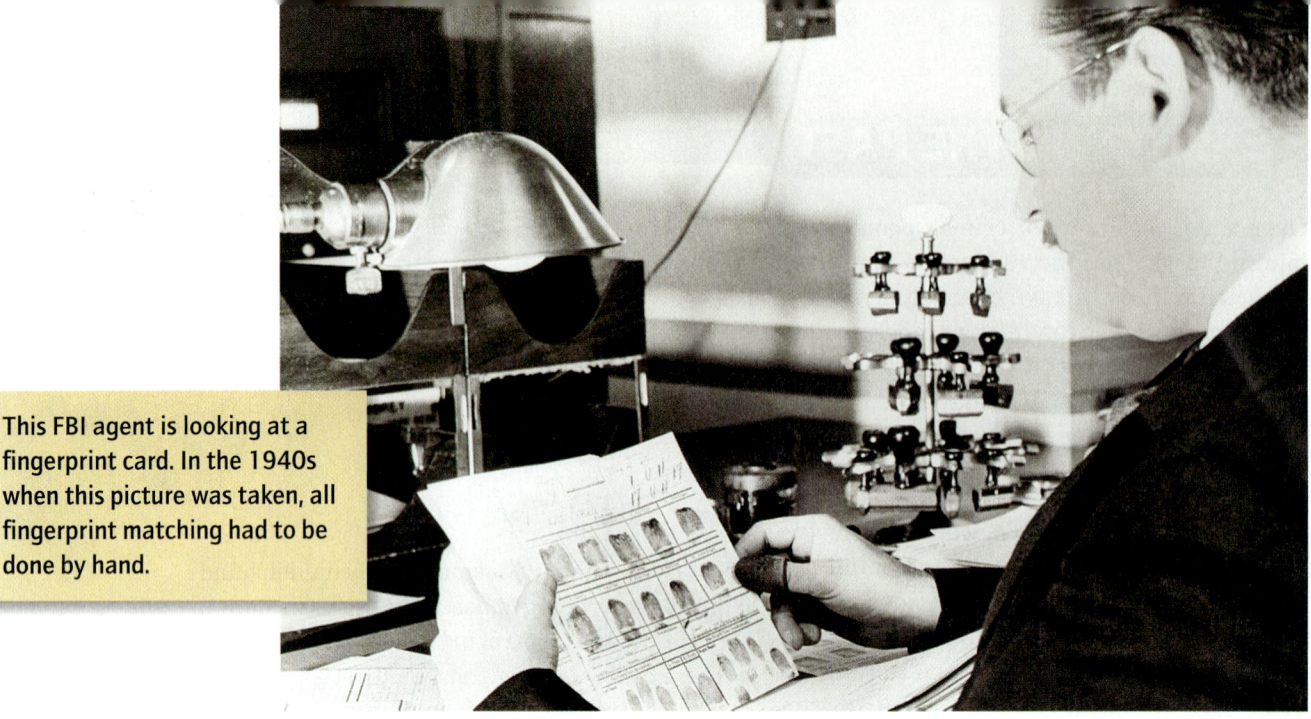

This FBI agent is looking at a fingerprint card. In the 1940s when this picture was taken, all fingerprint matching had to be done by hand.

prohibited felons and others—such as illegal aliens, unlawful users of controlled substances, and inmates of mental institutions—from buying guns and required licensing of gun dealers and outlawed some types of guns, such as fully automatic civilian machine guns.

What does "the right to keep and bear arms" mean?
The Second Amendment of the Constitution states that "the right to keep and bear arms shall not be infringed." But what exactly does this mean? Are a person's rights infringed, or interfered with, if a state requires gun owners to carry a permit or restricts the sales of certain types of guns?

Gun-control advocates point to the phrase "a well-regulated militia" as evidence that Congress meant only to guarantee the right of states to organize their own armed militias. Other Americans believe that the Second Amendment protects the private ownership of guns.

New solutions to combat crime
The number of violent crimes, such as homicide, or the deliberate killing of another person, more than doubled from 1965 to 1975. During that period, violent crime topped 1 million incidents for the first time and continued increasing into the early 1990s, when the number of violent crimes peaked at 1.9 million in 1992.

Violence associated with the drug trade played a large role in this increase. Shootings in post offices, businesses, and schools increased concerns about violence. Since 1992, however, violent crime has fallen, reaching the lowest level ever recorded in 2004.

As violence rose, efforts to use criminal sentencing as a means of rehabilitation, or reforming offenders into contributing members of society, came under increasing criticism. More and more, legislators responded to citizens' worries with "get tough" approaches.

Governments try various approaches
Choices about possible punishments for crimes begin with the legislators who write the laws. Sometimes the law gives a judge discretion, or the freedom to decide on an appropriate sentence for each individual within certain guidelines. In other cases, the judge must give a mandatory, or required, sentence to each offender convicted of a particular crime.

Theories about punishment influence sentencing. A retribution and incapacitation approach favors strict mandatory sentencing laws, the expansion of prisons, and the use of the death penalty as deterents and ways of preventing offenders from commiting another crime. This approach has led to over 2 million Americans being incarcerated in 2004. A rehabilitation approach favors programs such as boot camps and drug treatment programs as ways of changing the offender's behavior. Governments also try to prevent crime. Community policing and citizen watch groups are examples of programs designed to stop crime before it happens.

The issue of how best to reduce crime in the United States is a serious topic of debate. The documents that follow explore these issues by presenting different points of view and arguments. Examine the documents, keeping in mind what you have read about the history of crime and the government's response to it, and answer the questions that follow.

DOCUMENT 1

The causes of crime are complex, and many factors contribute to rising or falling crime rates, argues Marc Mauer, assistant director of The Sentencing Project in the late 1990s. In his book *Race to Incarcerate,* Mauer points out that creating tougher sentencing laws is only one of many policy options available for reducing the amount of crime.

> Over half of all state and federal prison inmates are currently serving time for a non-violent drug or property offense. While many of these offenders have had prior criminal convictions, the policy decision regarding their sentencing involves a consideration of whether spending $20,000 a year to incarcerate them [keep them in prison] is the wisest course of action. The alternative is not to do nothing but, rather to explore whether some combination of community supervision [probation], victim restitution [repayment], required treatment, and other conditions would more effectively respond to the needs of both victim and offender.
>
> —Marc Mauer, *Race to Incarcerate,* 1999

Analyzing the Document
What might government or other institutions do to determine which measures actually influence the crime rate?

DOCUMENT 2

Theories about the reasons for crime often affect approaches to punishment. Morgan O. Reynolds, a senior fellow and director of the National Center for Policy Analysis, argues that tough sentences for convicted criminals in the 1990s helped reduce the crime rate during that decade.

> What explains the sudden decline in crime after a long rise? Better economic conditions? Cultural changes? A more convincing explanation is at hand: Courts have been handing out tougher punishment for crime, and potential criminals know and fear it . . . some Americans fail to see the connection between new get-tough policies and recent improvements in the crime rate. "Crime keeps on falling, but prisons keep on filling," a *New York Times* headline declared . . . Crime is falling because prisons are filling.
>
> —Morgan O. Reynolds, "Does Punishment Deter?," National Center for Policy Analysis, 1998

Analyzing the Document
Use this excerpt to contrast the basis for attempting to rehabilitate prisoners with the basis for continuing get-tough policies.

Two high school students, Dylan Klebold and Eric Harris, killed 13 people and injured another 24 in a 1998 attack at Columbine High School in Littleton, Colorado. Many people were disturbed to learn of the killers' obsession with violent video games, music, and movies.

Analyzing the Document

What do you think the cartoonist thinks about the causes of youth violence, such as school shootings? Do you agree or disagree? Explain your answer.

Editor Carol Wekesser collected conflicting viewpoints about violence in television and films for her collection of essays, *Violence in the Media*. The following excerpt from her introduction helps explain the issues that violent media raises for parents and society at large.

Analyzing the Document

How might children be affected by viewing so many violent acts in the media?

Those who believe that media violence is largely responsible for societal violence can cite many startling statistics and cases that support their view. For example, the American Psychological Association states that by seventh grade the average child has seen seven thousand murders and one hundred thousand acts of violence on television. Several murders and attacks have been connected to movies and television.

Yet, while such statistics and cases are alarming, the vast majority of American children who grow up viewing violent television programs and movies also grow up to be normal, healthy adults.

—Carol Wekesser, ed., *Violence in the Media*, 1995

This line graph from the Department of Justice's Bureau of Crime Statistics shows the total number of robberies and aggravated assaults reported to police in the United States from 1960 to 2000.

Analyzing the Document
About how many incidents of robbery does the graph show happened in 1990? During what decade are the numbers for both crimes the highest? During what decade are the numbers of both crimes the most similar?

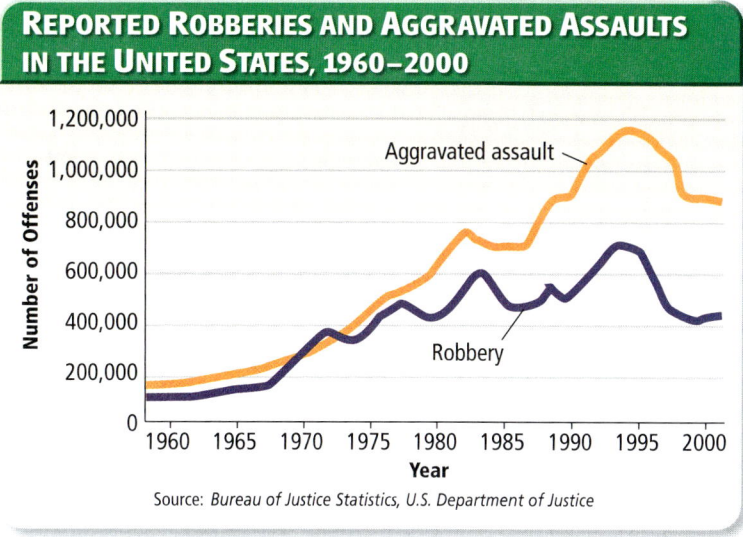

REPORTED ROBBERIES AND AGGRAVATED ASSAULTS IN THE UNITED STATES, 1960–2000

Source: *Bureau of Justice Statistics, U.S. Department of Justice*

A recent response to crime is the introduction of community-oriented policing. According to the Department of Justice, the goal of community-oriented policing is to "address the causes and reduce the fear of crime and social disorder through problem-solving tactics and community-police partnerships." This photograph illustrates ways that community-oriented police officers interact with those they serve and protect.

Analyzing the Document
What changes might occur in a neighborhood as a result of community policing? How might those changes lead to lower crime rates?

ANALYZING THE ISSUES

go.hrw.com
Research Online
SD7 Case Study

1. What do you think is the best way to reduce crime? Explain your answer.

2. Where should efforts to reduce crime originate— with governments, individuals, or society? Explain.

3. Research recent crime-control laws in your state. Describe what kinds of crime they target and whether crime rates have fallen since these laws were passed.

4. Survey people in your community to find out where crime ranks among their concerns and which crime reduction method they favor. Research similar national data and compare it with your results.

6 DOCUMENT-BASED INVESTIGATION

Regulation and the Internet

New York Standards

ST 4.1 Analyze important debates in American history, focusing on the opposing positions and the historical evidence used to support these positions.

ST 4.3 Develop hypotheses about important events, eras, or issues; move from chronicling to explaining historical events and issues; use information collected from diverse sources to produce cogently written reports and document-based essays.

FOCUSING ON THE ISSUE

How should the Internet be regulated?

KEY TERMS
packet switching, protocol, encryption

THE INSIDE STORY Before 17-year-old Jeremy gets up for school, his mom checks the news headlines and weather on her computer's Internet home page. At school, Jeremy's physics class uses the Internet to visit university Web sites, looking for information about the forces created by roller coasters. After school, Jeremy and his friends use their computers to send each other electronic mail, more commonly referred to as e-mail. After Jeremy goes to bed, his mother uses the computer to do some shopping and to send messages to her real estate clients. Like most people his age, Jeremy has never known a world without the Internet.

The Internet is a network of computers that connects many smaller networks around the world. People can use Internet technologies to communicate, conduct research, buy and sell goods and services, bank, pay bills, and access news and entertainment. Since its beginnings, the Internet has transformed the way millions of people live, work, and do business.

The Internet has affected human culture and commerce in many positive ways. However, some people have taken advantage of the new technologies to exploit Internet users. For example, unwanted messages clog e-mail in-boxes. Identity theft, copyright infringement, and illegal accessing of government or corporate information, known as hacking, also are serious problems. Such problems present many challenges to government, law enforcement, and computer scientists. ▪

Tens of millions of Americans use the Internet at home, work, and school as well as at public places such as Internet cafes and libraries. One of the most common uses of the Internet is sending electronic mail.

The technological developments that led to the Internet originated in the Cold War conflict between the United States and the former Soviet Union. To help maintain a lead in science and technology, the U.S. Department of Defense started the Advanced Research Projects Agency (ARPA) in 1958. Many people credit ARPA for establishing the foundations of the Internet.

In 1969 ARPA organized one of the first general-purpose computer networks, called ARPANET, to connect computers at research sites supported by the government. ARPANET took advantage of a new technology called **packet switching**. Instead of sending a large chunk of information in a single message, a computer could send the message in smaller packets. The packets then travel separately along the fastest routes to the receiving computer, which reassembles the message.

Scientists at ARPANET also developed innovative new **protocols**, or formats for sending data from one computer to another. These included the "simple message transfer protocol" (SMTP), used to send e-mail. By the early 1980s researchers had established standard protocols for connecting, or internetting, the different networks.

The Internet expands Several important innovations helped take the Internet from a purely academic research tool to the familiar component of daily life that it is today. The first

This map shows the geographical distribution of computer networks in 1993, when the Mosaic browser was released.

was the development of the personal computer in the mid-1980s.

The second was the creation of the World Wide Web, a computer program that allows users to create, store, and connect information in documents called Web pages. The third innovation was the Web browser, which enables users to find, display, and interact with documents on the Web. The first widely available browser, called Mosaic, was released in 1993.

The Internet expanded quickly during the 1990s. The U.S. government was active in the early years of the Internet. But it gradually withdrew, allowing commercial interests to take over. By 1995 the Internet was largely controlled by private companies.

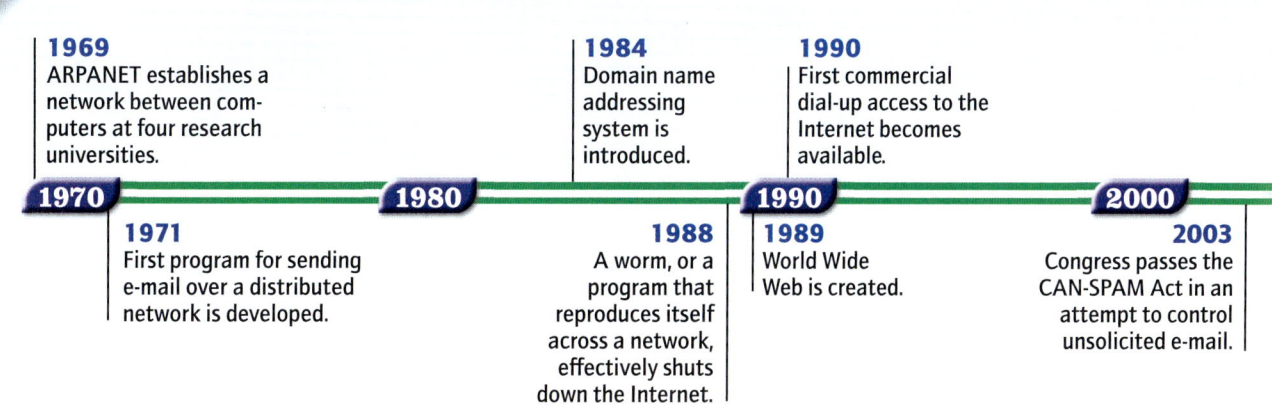

1969
ARPANET establishes a network between computers at four research universities.

1971
First program for sending e-mail over a distributed network is developed.

1984
Domain name addressing system is introduced.

1988
A worm, or a program that reproduces itself across a network, effectively shuts down the Internet.

1990
First commercial dial-up access to the Internet becomes available.

1989
World Wide Web is created.

2003
Congress passes the CAN-SPAM Act in an attempt to control unsolicited e-mail.

1970 — 1980 — 1990 — 2000

Uses of the Internet The Internet has been so successful because it appeals to a large cross section of society. The government has used the Internet to distribute information and to automate procedures, such as tax filing. Schools have used the Internet for research and online courses. Many businesses have advertised, bought, sold, and provided customer service online. The Internet also has made it easier for businesses to support telecommuting. Some employees can telecommute by working away from their office on a computer connected to the Internet.

Problems in cyberspace The growth of cyberspace—a term often used for the online world of the Internet—occurred with great speed. This has left government and law-enforcement agencies little time to consider whether or how the Internet should be regulated. This relative lack of regulation has left the Internet and millions of users vulnerable.

Internet users are bombarded with unwanted e-mail advertisements, called spam. Spam wastes the time and money of users, who are forced to separate spam from legitimate e-mails. Criminals also have used spam to spread computer viruses, programs designed to damage recipients' computers. Another feature of the Internet that invites abuse is the online availability of image, audio, and video files. Sharing of such files can violate copyright laws.

Identity theft and privacy issues Today technologies exist that allow outside observers to monitor Internet users' Web browsing, e-mail, and even every keystroke they enter on their keyboards. A serious abuse of monitoring technologies is identity theft, or the theft of someone's personal information, such as credit card or social security numbers, for illegal use.

Computer scientists have worked to find technical solutions to these problems. Encryption technology, which transforms data to make it indecipherable to an outside observer, is one such solution.

Problems also arise in trying to define the legitimate uses of both monitoring and encryption tools. Government and law enforcement want to use the tools to protect citizens from illegal activity. Employers want to use them to monitor employees' behavior. Businesses are also interested in using such tools to identify the economic habits of consumers in order to better market their goods and services. Privacy and civil liberties advocates, however, cite the potential for abuse.

State, national, and international governments and organizations are trying to create a reasonable legal environment for Internet activities. Bills have been introduced in the U.S. Congress to regulate the Internet. Legislatures in Canada, Australia, and the European Union are also at work trying to solve Internet problems.

One bill introduced in Congress to protect Americans from the growing crime of identity theft is the Social Security Number Misuse Prevention Act. The bill was sponsored by Senator Judd Gregg (R-New Hampshire), Senator Dianne Feinstein (D-California), and Senator Patrick Leahy (D-Vermont).

Issues surrounding Internet regulation are still being debated. The following documents reflect the social, economic, and governmental perspectives on Internet regulation. Examine the documents, keeping in mind what you have read about the history of the Internet. Then answer the questions that follow.

DOCUMENT 1

The Internet Crime Complaint Center is a government agency set up in 2000 to provide a way for people and law-enforcement agencies to report and collect information about Internet crimes. At right is a chart showing reported Internet fraud cases over a five-year period.

Analyzing the Document
What can you conclude about reported cases of Internet fraud from 2000 through 2004?

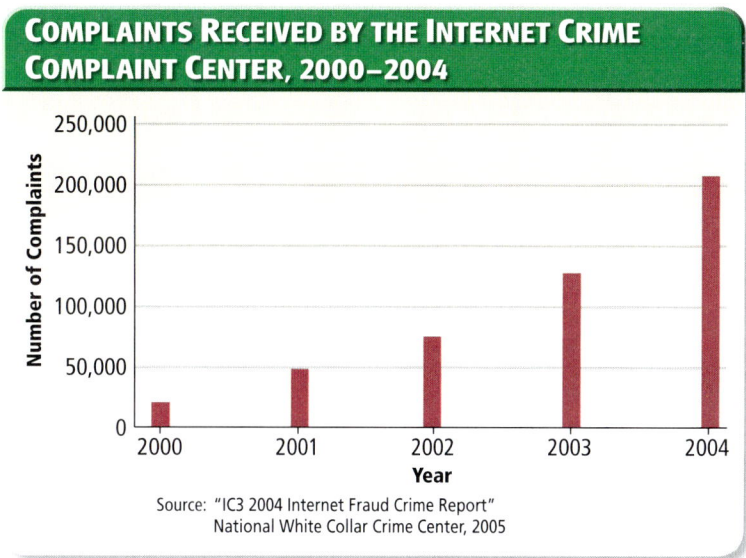

COMPLAINTS RECEIVED BY THE INTERNET CRIME COMPLAINT CENTER, 2000–2004

Source: "IC3 2004 Internet Fraud Crime Report" National White Collar Crime Center, 2005

DOCUMENT 2

This newspaper article from the *Chicago Tribune* points out the difficulty of controlling spam, even with the CAN-SPAM law that was passed in 2004.

Seeking to shut down a University of Texas student listed as the fourth-worst e-mail spammer in the world, the Texas attorney general . . . filed a civil lawsuit against the man potentially seeking nearly $500 million in damages . . .

[The target of the suit] . . . owns a $450,000 home in an exclusive Austin neighborhood and several luxury automobiles. [The attorney general said the student] earns up to $28 each time a recipient clicks on one of his e-mails and fills out a form seeking personal information—a bounty paid by mortgage and insurance brokers for each legitimate lead . . .

[The student's attorney said he and his partner] "are Internet marketers and are no different from the bulk mailers" who flood postal mailboxes with unsolicited offers . . .

The CAN-SPAM Act, passed by Congress to slow the torrent of unwanted e-mails that by some estimates account for 85 percent of all Internet traffic, does not ban unsolicited commercial solicitations . . .

"Spam is the front end of a lot of things," said Dan Larkin, the unit chief of the FBI's Internet Crime Complaint Center. "It can lead to identity theft or getting spyware downloaded to your computer. These guys are not just nuisances. They are making a lot of money, they are disrupting e-commerce and they are involved in malicious code that leads to high-impact attacks on the Internet infrastructure. We are going after them."

—*Chicago Tribune,* January 13, 2005

Analyzing the Document
Why would controlling unsolicited e-mail be important for the success of Internet commerce?

This political cartoon addresses the issue of copyrighted material, such as music, being shared on the Internet free of charge, without payment going to the copyright holder.

Analyzing the Document
What effect might downloading music files have on people who make their living from music, including artists and record companies? Might it affect some groups differently than others?

MIKE KEEFE, *NETWORK WORLD.* REPRINTED BY PERMISSION

In 2005 three researchers from the University of Pennsylvania's Annenberg Public Policy Center conducted a phone survey of 1,500 American adults who had used the Internet in the previous month. They asked 17 true-false questions about Internet commerce and privacy. An excerpt from the report follows.

Most Americans who use the Internet have little idea how vulnerable they are to abuse by online and offline marketers and how the information they provide can be used to exploit them . . . Americans' lack of knowledge about marketplace rules puts them at risk. We found that:

- 68% of American adults who have used the Internet in the past month believe incorrectly that "a site . . . that compares prices on different airlines must include the lowest airline prices."

- 49% could not detect illegal "phishing"—the activity where crooks posing as banks send emails to consumers that ask them to click on a link wanting them to verify their account.

- 66% could not correctly name even one of the three U.S. credit reporting agencies (Equifax, Experian, and TransUnion) that could keep them aware of their credit worthiness and whether someone is stealing their identity . . .

- 75% do not know the correct response—false—to the statement, "When a website has a privacy policy, it means the site will not share my information with other websites and companies."

—"Open to Exploitation: American Shoppers Online and Offline," by Joseph Turow, Lauren Feldman, and Kimberly Meltzer, Annenberg Public Policy Center, University of Pennsylvania

Analyzing the Document
According to this survey, what conclusion can you draw about Americans' understanding of online commerce? What facts led you to this conclusion?

This cartoon uses a depiction of students passing notes to one another to comment on unwanted e-mail.

Analyzing the Document

What are some possible effects of spam on people's lives?

Mike Keefe, *The Denver Post.* Reprinted by Permission

Research conducted by Don McCabe, the founder of the Center for Academic Integrity, has shown that Internet plagiarism is widespread in colleges. In 2005 the Center released results from its nationwide survey on academic integrity in which nearly 50,000 undergraduates on more than 50 campuses took part.

Internet plagiarism is a growing concern on all campuses as students struggle to understand what constitutes acceptable use of the Internet. In the absence of clear direction from faculty, most students have concluded that "cut and paste" plagiarism—using a sentence or two (or more) from different sources on the Internet and weaving this information together into a paper without appropriate citation—is not a serious issue. While 10% of students admitted to engaging in such behavior in 1999, almost 40% admit to doing so in the Assessment Project surveys. A majority of students (77%) believe such cheating is not a very serious issue.

—Center for Academic Integrity, Duke University

Analyzing the Document

According to the document, how serious an issue is Internet plagiarism in American schools? In what way does the Internet play a role in student cheating and plagiarism?

ANALYZING THE ISSUES

go.hrw.com
Research Online
SD7 Case Study

1. After you examine the above documents, think about the following question: How much privacy should people expect when they use the Internet? Explain your answer.

2. How much protection should a consumer expect when buying goods and services on the Internet?

3. What are some possible consequences of restricting access to private information? Do research on state-level attempts to regulate the Internet. How would the same restrictions affect you in your state?

4. How would you go about trying to stop Internet plagiarism?

Outsourcing and Trade

New York Standards

ST 4.1 Analyze important debates in American history (e.g., regulation of big business), focusing on the opposing positions and the historical evidence used to support these positions.

ST 4.3 Develop hypotheses about important events, eras, or issues; move from chronicling to explaining historical events and issues; use information collected from diverse sources to produce cogently written reports and document-based essays.

FOCUSING ON THE ISSUE

What are the advantages and disadvantages of outsourcing?

KEY TERMS
outsourcing, comparative advantage, protectionism, NAFTA

THE INSIDE STORY

Natasha Humphries worked for three years as a software engineer at one of the world's leading producers of handheld computing devices. When overseas workers were hired to perform testing, Humphries was assigned to manage a team in India. In 2003, however, she lost her job when all of the work that Humphries did was transferred to the very group in India that she had helped train.

Humphries' story is a familiar one. In recent years, thousands of American jobs have been outsourced overseas to countries such as India where labor costs are lower than in the United States. **Outsourcing** is the practice of using workers from outside a company. Proponents contend that lower overall labor costs mean savings for consumers in the form of lower prices for goods and services. The practice of outsourcing jobs to overseas workers has attracted increased criticism, however, from people who believe American businesses should employ American workers. ■

1930
Smoot-Hawley Tariff Act places high tariffs on foreign goods.

1920

This customer service call center in Bangalore, India, provides 24-hour telephone support for customers in the United States and England.

EXPLORING THE PAST

Outsourcing has roots in international trade. From colonial times through American independence, trade was largely discouraged. Governments granted monopolies and subsidies to protect merchants, farmers, and manufacturers from competition.

In 1776 Scottish economist and philosopher Adam Smith challenged such practices in his book *Inquiry into the Nature and Causes of the Wealth of Nations*. Smith described how free trade, competition, and choice would lead to economic development and improve people's lives. The system he proposed laid the groundwork for free trade throughout the 1800s.

Comparative advantage In 1817 English economist David Ricardo explained the theory of comparative advantage. A nation has a **comparative advantage** when it can produce a certain good or service more cheaply than another country. According to this theory, nations gain when they trade those items that they are most efficient at producing. For example, in Country A it might be difficult to make computer parts but easy to make clothing. In Country B both are easily produced. If Country B decides to focus on producing computer parts, it can trade its excess to Country A for clothing. Both countries benefit.

If imports cost less and exports earn more, trade seems to benefit everyone. People can buy goods more cheaply and get jobs in booming industries. But what happens to those people who became expert clothing makers in Country A? What happens if Country B does

not earn as much selling computer parts as it spends for clothing? Historically, governments have managed such risks by regulating trade.

Restrictions on trade When economies are strong and relationships between nations are good, trade has remained open. During financial or political hard times, governments adopt **protectionism**, or the restriction of trade, to protect their producers.

In 1890 Congress protected U.S. businesses by passing the McKinley Tariff. As with other tariffs, it raised the cost of foreign products so that consumers were more likely to buy comparable American goods. Thus, U.S. industries profited from tariffs at home. However, they suffered losses when other countries began imposing tariffs on U.S. goods.

Trade with other countries helped establish the United States as a world power. This view of New Orleans in 1841 was made to show the importance of the city as a thriving port. New Orleans remains an important port city today.

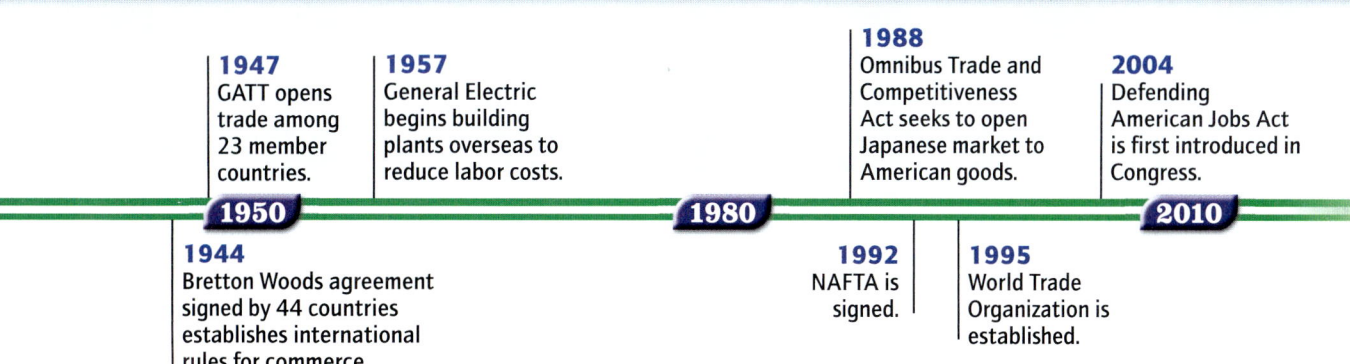

1944
Bretton Woods agreement signed by 44 countries establishes international rules for commerce.

1947
GATT opens trade among 23 member countries.

1950

1957
General Electric begins building plants overseas to reduce labor costs.

1980

1988
Omnibus Trade and Competitiveness Act seeks to open Japanese market to American goods.

1992
NAFTA is signed.

1995
World Trade Organization is established.

2004
Defending American Jobs Act is first introduced in Congress.

2010

Chief trade representatives for Mexico, the United States, and Canada hold NAFTA treaties that have just been signed by Mexican president Carlos Salinas de Gortari (left), President George H.W. Bush (center), and Canadian prime minister Brian Mulroney (right).

At the World Economic Conference in 1927, several countries decided to stop imposing tariffs on one another. After the stock market crash in 1929, however, the United States broke with this policy by passing the Smoot-Hawley Tariff, the highest protective tariff in American history. Other countries responded by imposing high tariffs on American goods, worsening the effects of the Great Depression.

Creating a global marketplace

After World War II interest renewed in trading cooperatively with other nations. An organization called the General Agreement on Tariffs and Trade (GATT) was formed in 1947. (In 1995 GATT was replaced by the World Trade Organization.) Member nations opened their markets and reduced tariffs. U.S. manufacturing boomed as demand increased from European nations whose industries had been largely destroyed in the war. The United States dominated world markets through the 1960s.

Worldwide tariff reductions continued to expand trade in the latter half of the 1900s. Nations such as Japan and Mexico became increasingly competitive in world markets. The United States responded by looking for new markets. For example, President Richard Nixon opened trade relations with China. In the late 1980s President George H.W. Bush broadened U.S. access to markets in Japan.

In 1992 the United States, Canada, and Mexico formed **NAFTA**, or the North American Free Trade Agreement. Its purpose was to remove tariffs among the three countries.

Proponents of NAFTA say that it has led to lower prices in the United States and higher sales of American goods, resulting in higher-paying and higher-skilled U.S. jobs. Opponents contend that it has resulted in the exporting of jobs from the United States to Mexico, where labor costs are less expensive.

Increase in outsourcing

As globalization has increased, so too has competition. Demand for domestic goods decreased in the 1980s as less expensive goods were imported from regions such as Asia. To save money, companies reduced their manufacturing workforces.

As American factory workers protested, they were reassured that they would find better jobs. Employees who already held such jobs rested easy—until the 1990s, when new technologies like e-mail and the Internet made it possible to outsource those jobs.

At first, companies outsourced narrowly defined higher-level tasks, such as customer service, to supplement domestic staff during peak times. As outsourcing's benefits became clearer, companies began moving entire divisions overseas. More than half of all Fortune 500 corporations have moved jobs outside the United States. The reason? Analysts estimate outsourcing saves companies between 30 and 70 percent annually in costs.

Analyzing the effects

Supporters of outsourcing contend that it benefits the U.S. economy. By employing people in previously impoverished regions, outsourcers are creating new consumers who want and can afford American products. Proponents further contend that, as jobs move overseas, Americans will develop new areas in which U.S. workers can specialize. Long-term losses will be minimal, they argue, because 70 percent of American jobs, such as those in hospitals, must be performed locally.

Outsourcing opponents say that although companies are profiting, people are not. They claim that displaced workers are not being rehired for equal or better jobs. To guard against future outsourcing, more than 50 U.S. representatives have sponsored the Defending American Jobs Act of 2004. The act proposes to cut federal funding from companies that lay off workers at higher rates in the United States than abroad.

The issue of outsourcing raises many questions. The documents that follow explore this issue by presenting different points of view and arguments. Examine the documents, keeping in mind what you have read about the history of outsourcing, its costs, and its benefits. Then answer the questions that follow each document.

DOCUMENT 1

David Ricardo's theory of comparative advantage is frequently cited by proponents to explain the logic of outsourcing's benefits. In this article, the author examines how well—or if—Ricardo's theory applies today.

> Economists are blind to the loss of American industries and occupations because they believe these results reflect the beneficial workings of free trade. Whatever is being lost, they think, is being replaced by something as good or better. This thinking is rooted in the doctrine of comparative advantage put forth by economist David Ricardo in 1817 . . .
>
> Today's economists can't identify what the new industries and occupations might be that will replace those that are lost, but they're certain that those jobs and sectors are out there somewhere. What does not occur to them is that the same incentive that causes the loss of one tradable good or service—cheap, skilled foreign labor—applies to all tradable goods and services. There is no reason that the "replacement" industry or job, if it exists, won't follow its predecessor offshore.
>
> For comparative advantage to work, a country's labor, capital, and technology must not move offshore. This international immobility is necessary to prevent a business from seeking an absolute advantage by going abroad.
>
> —Paul Craig Roberts, "The Harsh Truth about Outsourcing," *Business Week,* March 22, 2004

Analyzing the Document
Why does the author feel that Ricardo's theory is outdated?

DOCUMENT 2

In this political cartoon called "The New American Patriotism," men in business suits launch small boats out to sea. The boats are labeled "US Jobs." On the shore is a building labeled "IBM etc." Study the cartoon and then answer the question that follows.

The New American Patriotism

Analyzing the Document
Does this cartoon support unlimited or restricted outsourcing? Explain your answer.

Because companies are not required to keep records, no one knows how many jobs have been sent overseas. It is estimated, however, that by 2015 more than 3 million American jobs will have been outsourced. While companies are seeing the benefits of outsourcing in the short term, unemployed workers are feeling its costs.

Analyzing the Document
What are some disadvantages of outsourcing?

This is an excerpt from an article published by the National Conference of State Legislatures. State lawmakers have been raising concerns over government contracts being awarded to companies that use taxpayer money to hire workers overseas. The author explains some of the benefits of supporting companies that outsource.

The outsourcing dispute is rooted in the debate over free trade and jobs. Proponents argue that through outsourcing, American goods get into more foreign markets, only lower-level jobs are lost, and American workers move into more advanced jobs. They also argue that outsourcing is a scapegoat, that the loss of most jobs can be attributed to a poor economy and increased productivity and cyclical changes in employment.

Using overseas workers is beneficial to the United States in four ways, says a recent report in the McKinsey Quarterly . . .

First is cost savings. The report states that "for every dollar of spending on business services that move offshore, U.S. companies save 58 cents."

Second is new revenues. The rise of office services in the developing world creates demand for goods that are often purchased here, including computers, telecommunications equipment, and legal, financial, and marketing services . . . These profits can be used to expand business in the United States or be returned to investors. Third is repatriated earnings. Profits that American companies generate operating in the low-cost overseas markets are sent back to the United States through taxes on these additional earnings.

Fourth is the redeployment of labor. Sending lower-level, lower-skilled jobs overseas permits the American workforce to move into higher paying occupations.

—National Conference of State Legislatures,
State Legislatures, May 2004

Analyzing the Document
According to the report, how does helping businesses help the economy?

Outsourcing is not just one way. According to the Organization of International Investment, over the past 15 years more corporations have moved jobs to the United States than have moved jobs outside the United States.

Analyzing the Document

According to the graphs, how does the rate of increase of insourced jobs compare to that of outsourced jobs? Why is the percentage of manufacturing job growth higher than the percentage growth in the total number of jobs?

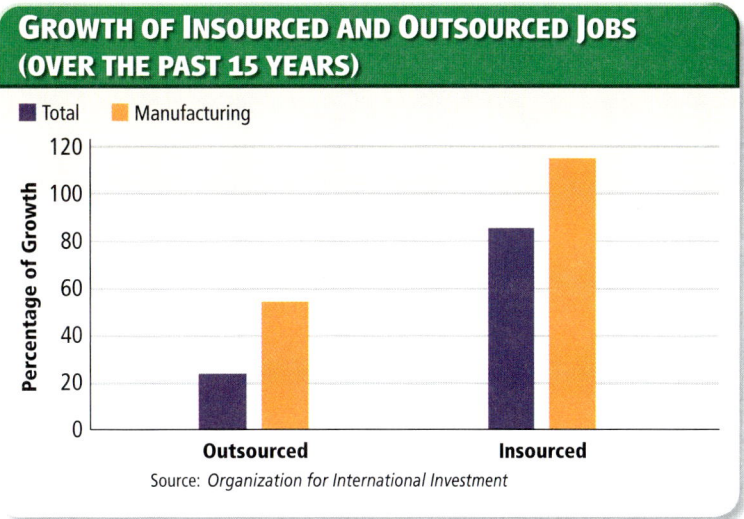

GROWTH OF INSOURCED AND OUTSOURCED JOBS (OVER THE PAST 15 YEARS)

Source: *Organization for International Investment*

As companies have seen the benefits of outsourcing outweigh its costs, their ideas surrounding its potential have expanded. This table features data from Forrester Research, Inc., showing plans for future outsourcing of jobs by industry.

Analyzing the Document

According to the table, which industries will be most affected by outsourcing in the future? How might such changes affect workers?

How Much Pain?

As more U.S. employers embrace white-collar globalization . . .

Share of 1,000 largest U.S. companies that say they plan to:	2003	2008
Do virtually no white-collar offshoring	63%	46%
Offshore to some degree	33%	44%
Offshore any white-collar work possible	4%	10%

. . . more nonfactory jobs will move abroad.

Job Type	2002 employment	Share moving offshore by		
		2004	2008	2015**
Computer	3 million	5%	9%	20%
Legal	1 million	1%	3%	9%
Business	5 million	1%	3%	8%
Architecture	2 million	1%	2%	8%
Office	23 million	1%	3%	7%
Life sciences	1 million	0	1%	4%
Management	7 million	0	1%	4%
Art, Design	2 million	0	1	2%
Sales	13 million	0	0	2%
Total	57 million jobs	1%, or 546,000 jobs	2%, or 1.2 million jobs	6%, or 3.4 million jobs

Source: Forrester Research Inc.   **Estimates

DOCUMENT 7

In this excerpt from a 2004 campaign speech, President Bush discusses the need for U.S. workers to rise to the challenge against foreign competition.

There is a temptation in Washington to say the solution to jobs uncertainty is to isolate America from the world. It's called economic isolationism, a sense that says, well, we're too pessimistic, we don't want to compete—as opposed to opening up markets, let's close markets, starting with our own. That is very dangerous . . .

And so the fundamental question is, do we keep our market open, or do we close it? My attitude is, we keep it open, but make sure others open theirs, too . . . One way to make sure jobs don't go overseas, and one sure way to make sure we're vibrant here at home is to insist that other people lower their barriers so we can compete. That's all we ask. Just give us a chance. Americans can rise to the challenge, trust me.

—President George W. Bush, March 2004

Analyzing the Document
Explain President Bush's point of view regarding government's role in job protection.

DOCUMENT 8

Senator John Kerry (D–Mass.) ran against President Bush in the 2004 election. In a campaign speech Senator Kerry advocated for a system in which the federal government would enforce its trade agreements and help end the outsourcing of certain jobs.

I won't let America wage the fight for our economic future with one hand tied behind our back. No one should misunderstand me: I am not protectionist—but I am a competitor. American workers are the most competitive in the world—and they deserve a government that's as competitive as they are. We will demand our trading partners play by the rules they've agreed to and show them that America means business when it comes to enforcing our trade agreements . . .

It is time to insist on and enforce real worker and environmental provisions in the core of every trade agreement so that we don't exploit workers in other countries or sell them out here at home. And it's time to break the deadlock in Congress and pass real tax breaks for our manufacturing industries.

—Senator John Kerry, campaign speech, March 26, 2004

Analyzing the Document
How does Senator Kerry's approach to job protection differ from President Bush's?

ANALYZING THE ISSUES

go.hrw.com
Research Online
SD7 Case Study

1. What are the primary arguments put forth in support of and against outsourcing?

2. Are the benefits of outsourcing worth the costs? Explain your position.

3. Write an editorial in which you explain the pros and cons of outsourcing. Include different perspectives regarding the short-term as well as the long-term effects of outsourcing.

4. Do research and write a report describing the outsourcing trends that have taken place in your state in the past decade. Include an examination of the efforts made by state and local governments in support of and restricting further outsourcing.

REFERENCE SECTION

go.hrw.com
Research Online
Keyword: SS World Almanac

Regents Review of American History

The World Almanac Regents Review of American History is a brief summary of important turning points in the history of the nation. It provides a capsule description of an event or movement along with brief accounts of its significance. Use this section to review the content in *American Anthem, New York Edition*.

12,000 B.C.E. Migrations to America

The first people arrived in North America at least 14,000 years ago, during the last Ice Age. With much of Earth's water frozen in ice sheets, sea levels dropped and a land bridge connected Asia and North America. Hunters from Siberia migrated over the land bridge to North America.

Significance The migration brought the first people to the Western Hemisphere. Archaeologists think that by about 11,000 years ago Native Americans were living in both North and South America.

1492–1502 Columbus's Voyages

In 1492 Italian-born explorer Christopher Columbus sailed west from Europe with the goal of finding a sea route to Asia. His ships landed on the Caribbean island of Hispaniola. Believing he had reached the Indies, Columbus called the people he met "Indians." Columbus made three more journeys to the Americas, exploring Caribbean islands and making stops in Central and South America.

Significance Columbus' voyages opened the Western Hemisphere to exploration and conquest by Spain and other European powers. They also led to the Columbian Exchange—an exchange of plants, animals, and diseases between the Western Hemisphere and Europe and Africa.

1607 Settlement of Jamestown

Founded in Virginia in 1607, Jamestown was the first permanent English colony in North America. Plagued by an unhealthy location, the colony barely managed to survive. Captain John Smith provided critical leadership. John Rolfe planted tobacco in Jamestown, giving the colony a cash crop that was in high demand in England. A small group of enslaved Africans arrived in Jamestown in 1619.

Significance After Jamestown, the English established other colonies along the east coast of North America. Successful tobacco farming in Jamestown led to the growth of plantation agriculture and slave labor. The Virginia House of Burgesses, established in 1619, was America's first elected legislature.

1620 Pilgrims arrive at Plymouth

The Pilgrims were religious dissenters from the Church of England who sought the freedom to worship according to their beliefs. In 1620 they traveled to North America on the *Mayflower*. The Pilgrims founded a colony at Plymouth, Massachusetts, which survived with the aid of friendly Wampanoag Indians. The colony marked its first harvest with a feast which forms the basis for the Thanksgiving holiday.

Significance The Pilgrims were the first colonists motivated to found a colony by a desire to freely practice their own religion. This became an important motivation for several other groups of colonists, and eventually the free practice of religion became a fundamental principle of the U.S. Constitution.

1651–1673 Navigation Acts

The Navigation Acts were a series of trade laws passed by the English government between 1651 and 1673. The laws sought to control trade with England's colonies to the benefit of the mother country. Among other things, the laws required that colonial goods be shipped only on English ships.

Significance England got what it wanted from the Navigation Acts—raw materials and tax revenues from the colonies. Colonists, on the other hand, were angered by the laws and often avoided paying taxes by smuggling goods into and out of the colonies.

1730s–1740s The Great Awakening

The Great Awakening was a religious revival in the English colonies that began in the 1730s. One of its leading voices was the colonial Puritan clergyman Jonathan Edwards, who appealed to his listeners' fears and emotions. Another was the English Methodist minister George Whitefield, who moved large audiences to cry and confess their sins.

Significance The Great Awakening countered the spread of Enlightenment ideas in the colonies, which were causing some people to question long-accepted religious beliefs. It led to the growth of new Protestant denominations in America, including the Methodist, Baptist, and Presbyterian churches.

1754–1763 French and Indian War

The Seven Years' War was the fourth and decisive war fought between Britain and France for control of land in North America. It's European phase is known as the Seven Years' War, but colonists called this conflict the French and Indian War because France and its Indian allies battled Britain and the colonists. After several early setbacks, the British won the crucial Battle of Quebec in 1759. France surrendered the following year.

Significance The French and Indian War marked the end of French power in North America. Britain gained all of France's lands east of the Mississippi River, helping to establish the basis for a mighty British empire. British leaders tried to recover some of cost of the war by taxing colonists, a policy which led to growing tensions between Britain and its colonies in America.

1765 Stamp Act

Passed by Parliament in 1765, the Stamp Act was a tax designed to raise money from colonists to help pay the cost of protecting the colonies. Resentful colonists called this "taxation without representation" because they had no voice in Parliament. In October 1765, delegates from nine colonies met at the Stamp Act Congress to protest the tax. Parliament repealed the Stamp Act in 1766.

Significance The Stamp Act was the first time Parliament had directly taxed the colonists. Colonial leaders from different regions, who were not used to working together, united to protest the tax. The united action of leaders from different colonies would become a model for future action.

1770 Boston Massacre

Tensions between British soldiers and the people of Boston were growing in early 1770. This anger exploded on March 5, 1770, when a group of British soldiers opened fire on a colonial mob that was taunting and threatening them. Local colonial leaders called the event the Boston Massacre, describing it as a deliberate attack on innocent civilians.

Significance The Boston Massacre served the cause of radicals like Samuel Adams who were eager to paint the British as cruel oppressors. The Massacre became a rallying cry for proponents of independence from Britain.

1775–1783 American Revolution

The American colonies' fight for independence from Britain began in April 1775 with the Battles of Lexington and Concord. Over the next six years, George Washington led the often undermanned and poorly equipped Continental Army. The American victory at the Battle of Saratoga in 1777 was a pivotal turning point; it convinced the French to join the war on the American side. The last significant battle was Washington's defeat of Lord Cornwallis' army at Yorktown, Virginia, in 1781.

Significance The Treaty of Paris, which ended the war in 1783, acknowledged the independence of the United States. The American Revolution was the first successful democratic revolution against a colonial ruler. A direct result was the establishment of the United States of America as a independent democratic republic.

1776 Declaration of Independence

Written largely by Thomas Jefferson in June 1776, the Declaration of Independence explained the reasons colonial leaders decided to break free from Britain and declared the United States to be an independent country. It was presented to Congress on July 2, 1776, and members voted to declare independence on that day. Two days later, on July 4, Congress approved the Declaration of Independence.

Significance The Declaration marked a point of no return for Americans—people were now forced to take sides in the struggle between Patriots and Loyalists. In addition, the Declaration boldly stated the principles of government that form the basis for American democracy, and it has been an inspiration to other freedom movements ever since.

1786 Shays's Rebellion

High taxes forced many Massachusetts farmers into heavy debt in the 1780s. When a court ordered their farms and homes be sold to pay the debts, Daniel Shays, a Revolutionary War veteran, led a rebellion. After some success delaying court proceedings, the rebellion was quickly put down by state militia.

Significance Shays's Rebellion frightened many Americans and helped convince them that the central government under the Articles of Confederation was not strong enough to deal with the country's problems. This fueled the movement to form a stronger federal government, which led to the Constitutional Convention.

1787 Northwest Ordinance

Congress passed the Northwest Ordinance to encourage orderly settlement and the formation of new states on the land north and west of the Ohio River. The law promised settlers religious freedom and barred slavery. It also set up a system for the eventual admission of new states.

Significance The Northwest Ordinance created a pattern for settlement in western territory, leading to a rapid expansion of the population of these lands. It also barred slavery from the Northwest Territory, which later became the states of Ohio, Indiana, Illinois, Michigan, Wisconsin, and part of Minnesota.

1787 Constitutional Convention

Delegates came to the convention in Philadelphia to discuss ways to strengthen the Articles of Confederation. Instead they drafted an entirely new plan of government, the United States Constitution.

Significance Ratified in 1788, the Constitution defined a plan of government—with checks and balances between three branches of government—that has endured for well over 200 years. The Bill of Rights, ten amendments protecting the freedoms of individual Americans, was ratified in 1791.

1803 *Marbury v. Madison*

The case of *Marbury* v. *Madison* was brought by William Marbury, who was appointed to a judgeship in 1801 by outgoing President John Adams. When incoming President Thomas Jefferson refused to give Marbury his commission, Marbury sued to get it. The Supreme Court ruled that it did not have the power to force Jefferson to deliver the commission. The Justices also declared that the law that had given the Court that power—the Judiciary Act of 1789—was unconstitutional.

Significance *Marbury* v. *Madison* established the Supreme Court's right to declare that a law violates the Constitution. This power, known as judicial review, greatly expanded the influence of the Supreme Court.

1803 Louisiana Purchase

President Jefferson sent James Monroe to France to try to attempt to buy New Orleans, a port of critical importance to western farmers. Much to Monroe's surprise, the French offered to sell all of Louisiana, stretching from the Mississippi River to the Rocky Mountains. The final price of the Louisiana Purchase was about $15 million.

Significance The Louisiana Purchase almost doubled the size of the United States, opening up huge new tracts of land to future American settlement. It also removed an important foreign power as an obstacle for American expansion in North America.

1812 The War of 1812

The War of 1812 between Great Britain and the United States actually lasted three years, from 1812-1815. It arose from a dispute over American

rights to trade with France, Britain's enemy in the Napoleonic Wars. Native American efforts, aided by the British, to resist United States expansion also played a role in triggering conflict. The war ended with no clear winner.

Significance The war's conclusion reaffirmed American independence and spurred a period of intense patriotic feeling. Two of its military heroes, William Henry Harrison and Andrew Jackson, later went on to become presidents. Francis Scott Key wrote "Star-Spangled Banner," the national anthem, to celebrate American resistance to British bombardment of Fort McHenry in Baltimore harbor.

1820s–1830s Second Great Awakening

The Second Great Awakening was a national religious movement that was especially strong in the North. Americans attended revivals, embraced religious teachings, and joined churches in record numbers. New religious denominations, including the Mormon Church, were formed at this time.

Significance By 1850 the majority of Americans considered themselves to be Protestant. The Second Great Awakening helped launch the Reform Era, which lasted from about 1830 to 1860. Inspired by religious ideals, Americans attempted to reshape society by promoting temperance, improved education, and other reforms.

1820 Missouri Compromise

Missouri's desire to join the Union as a slave state sparked a crisis, because the Union was then balanced between slave states and free states. In 1820 Congress reached a compromise: Missouri was admitted to the union as a slave state, while Maine entered the Union as a free state. In addition, the Missouri Compromise banned slavery in the Louisiana Territory north of a line stretching west from the southern border of Missouri.

Significance The Missouri Compromise temporarily defused the tension between free and slave states, but it did not end the debate over slavery in western lands. The crisis illustrated the intense feelings of sectionalism that would eventually split the nation in two.

1823 Monroe Doctrine

After the former Spanish colonies in Latin America won their independence, U.S. leaders were concerned that Britain and other European nations might try to expand their influence in the Western Hemisphere. In 1823 President James Monroe issued the Monroe Doctrine, declaring that the Western Hemisphere was no longer open to colonization by European countries. Any attempt to do so, Monroe declared, would be viewed as a hostile act directed against the United States.

Significance The Monroe Doctrine was a bold statement for the young United States to make. European powers did not welcome the policy, but for the most part they did not challenge it. In the decades after the Monroe Doctrine, the United States continued to expand its influence in Latin America.

1825 Completion of the Erie Canal

The 363-mile long Erie Canal ran across New York State, connecting the Great Lakes with the Hudson River. The canal provided a quick and economical way to ship manufactured goods to the west and farm products to the east.

Significance Trade generated by the Erie Canal helped make New York City into a great trading and financial center. The success of the canal set off a "canal craze" in the United States. Within 15 years a network of canals crisscrossed the northeast. These transportation improvements contributed to rapid economic growth.

1830 Indian Removal Act

In 1830 President Andrew Jackson signed the Indian Removal Act, which called for the relocation of five Indian tribes from the Southeast to an area west of the Mississippi River. Though the Supreme Court declared the forced relocation unconstitutional, Jackson refused to follow the Court's decision.

Significance The Indian Removal Act demonstrated that Native Americans had little protection under the law in the United States. U.S. Army troops supervised the removal of the tribes to Indian Territory. The forced removal of the Cherokee became known as the Trail of Tears, as thousands died on the miserable journey west.

1835–1836 Texas Revolution

In the 1820s a small group of Americans moved to Texas at the invitation of the Mexican government. The new residents clashed with Mexican authorities, who banned slavery and wanted all residents to follow Roman Catholicism. When the Texans moved to armed resistance, Antonio López de Santa Anna, the dictator of Mexico, marched an army into Texas to crush the revolt. The Texans defeated Santa Anna, and declared their independence.

Significance Texas became an independent country known as the Republic of Texas. The United States annexed Texas in 1845, angering Mexican leaders. This set in motion a chain of events that led to the Mexican-American War.

1846–1848 Mexican-American War

A dispute over the southern boundary of Texas led to the outbreak of the Mexican-American War in 1846. American forces drove through Mexican defenses and captured Mexico City. Under the terms of the Treaty of Guadalupe Hidalgo, which ended the war in 1848, Mexico was forced to cede more than half a million square miles of land to the United States. This land included areas that became the states of Arizona, New Mexico, and California.

Significance The Mexican Cession vastly increased the size of the United States and helped fulfill the claims of manifest destiny. California became part of the United States just as gold was discovered there. The war also contributed to poor relations with Mexico for many years to come.

1848 Seneca Falls Convention

Held in July 1848 in Seneca Falls, New York, the Seneca Falls Convention was the country's first women's rights convention. It was organized by Lucretia Mott and Elizabeth Cady Stanton. Stanton wrote the Seneca Falls Declaration, which stated that "all men and women are created equal."

Significance The Seneca Falls Convention marked the beginning of an ongoing national campaign for women's rights. One of the main goals was women's suffrage, which was achieved in 1920 with the passage of the Nineteenth Amendment.

1849 California Gold Rush

In 1848 a carpenter discovered gold in the American River in northern California. People as far away as Asia, South America, and Europe heard the news and headed to California, dreaming of striking it rich. The mass migration to California of miners—and business people who made money off the miners—is known as the Gold Rush. By 1854 300,000 people had migrated to California.

Significance The Gold Rush resulted in the rapid growth of California, which became a state in 1850. It also contributed to the wealth of a nation and helped fuel the dream of instant riches that has become part of American culture.

1854 The Birth of the Republican Party

The Republican Party began when former members of the Whig, Free Soil, and Democratic parties came together in opposition to the Kansas Nebraska Act. The main issue uniting Republicans was opposition to the expansion of slavery in the West.

Significance By 1860 and the election of Abraham Lincoln as president, the Republican Party had become what it remains today, one of the two major political parties in the United States.

1857 The *Dred Scott* Decision

Dred Scott was an enslaved person owned by Dr. John Emerson, an army surgeon from Missouri. In the 1830s, Emerson brought Scott to Illinois and other free areas of the North. After returning to Missouri, Scott sued for his freedom, arguing that by living where slavery was illegal, he had become free. The Supreme Court ruled against Scott in 1858. Chief Justice Roger Taney noted that the Fifth Amendment to the Constitution protected the property rights of slaveholders. In addition, the Court ruled that since the Constitution forbade Congress from making laws depriving people of their property, the Missouri Compromise was unconstitutional.

Significance The Dred Scott decision added to the explosive tension between the North and South over slavery. Most white Southerners saw the ruling as a great victory. Many Northerners were outraged, fearing the government now lacked the authority to bar slavery in any territory.

1860–1861 Secession of the South

On December 20, 1860, soon after Abraham Lincoln's election as president, South Carolina became the first state to secede. Mississippi, Florida, Alabama, Georgia, Louisiana, Texas followed quickly. In response to the fall of Fort Sumter in April 1861, Lincoln called on the remaining states to supply soldiers to put down the southern rebellion. Rather than comply, Virginia, North Carolina, Tennessee, and Arkansas seceded and joined the Confederacy.

Significance The secession of the southern states, along with Lincoln's determination to hold the Union together, resulted in the Civil War.

1861–1865 The Civil War

The Civil War began in April 1861 with the Confederate attack on Fort Sumter. The South won key early battles, largely thanks to the superior military skill of its generals. Northern victories at Vicksburg and Gettysburg in 1863 helped turn the tide of the war. The fighting ended in April 1865, when Confederate commander General Robert E. Lee surrendered to Union commander General Ulysses S. Grant at Appomattox Court House, Virginia.

Significance More than 600,000 Americans died in the Civil War, making it the costliest war in U.S. history. Fighting left the South's farms, factories, and transportation system in ruins. The Northern victory ensured the preservation of the Union and led to the end of slavery everywhere in the United States.

1862 Homestead Act

The Homestead Act allowed any head of a household over the age of 21 to claim 160 acres of public land. Each homesteader had to build a home on the land, make improvements, and farm the land for five years before gaining full ownership of the land. In the 124 years the Act was in force, nearly two million people tried to claim land under its provisions.

Significance The Homestead Act led to rapid settlement of the Great Plains, which had previously been considered a "Great American Desert." Settlers turned this into one of the most productive farming regions in the world. Many of the settlers were immigrants from northern Europe, whose descendants still populate the Great Plains today.

1862 Emancipation Proclamation

Announced in September 1862, Lincoln's Emancipation Proclamation declared that as of January 1, 1863, all slaves in areas of the South in rebellion against the Union would be free. Its immediate impact was limited, since unconquered areas of the South were not effected. It also did not free slaves in the Border States, which were still in the Union.

Significance The Emancipation Proclamation widened the goals of the war to include the end of slavery. It also helped assure the neutrality of Great Britain, which had been expected to enter the war on the side of the Confederacy. Strong anti-slavery sentiment in Great Britain made any plans to aid the Confederacy unfeasible.

1865 Assassination of Lincoln

Lincoln was assassinated on April 14, 1865, five days after Lee's surrender. He was attending a play at Ford's Theater when John Wilkes Booth, a well known actor and a bitter Confederate sympathizer, entered Lincoln's box and shot him in the head. Booth escaped from the scene, but was hunted down and died in a shoot out with Union troops.

Significance Lincoln's death produced a national outpouring of grief. As a successful wartime leader, Lincoln might have been able to push his relatively lenient Reconstruction plan through Congress. Vice President Andrew Johnson, a southerner, had far less influence with Republican congressional leaders. A fierce battle between Johnson and Congress over the direction of Reconstruction soon began.

1865–1877 Reconstruction

Reconstruction was the process of readmitting the Southern states into the Union after the Civil War. After Southern leaders passed Black Codes to limit the rights of African Americans, the Republican controlled Congress passed the Reconstruction Acts. These acts divided the South into five military districts under the control of the U.S. Army and required southern states to ratify the Fourteenth Amendment and write new state constitutions guaranteeing freedmen the right to vote. A major political struggle over Reconstruction policy between President Andrew Johnson and Congress led to Johnson's impeachment and near conviction.

Significance Reconstruction included three Constitutional amendments that initially helped African Americans. But enforcement of these reforms was dependent on the presence of the Union Army in the South. When the army withdrew in 1877, reconstruction collapsed and African Americans were denied their civil rights. Reconstruction also contributed to the lasting bitterness between North and South.

1865-1870 Reconstruction Amendments

The Thirteenth Amendment abolished slavery in the United States. The Fourteenth Amendment conferred citizenship on all persons born in the United States, thus extending citizenship to all freed African Americans. It also said that people could not be deprived of life, liberty or property without due process of law. The Fifteenth Amendment made it unconstitutional to deprive a citizen of the the right to vote because of "race, color, or previous condition of servitude."

Significance The three amendments helped make full citizens of freed African Americans during Reconstruction. With the collapse of Reconstruction, however, African Americans lost most of their rights until the Civil Rights Movement of the mid-1900s.

1869 Completion of the Transcontinental Railroad

In 1862 Congress provided land for the building of a transcontinental railroad to connect the East and West coasts of the United States. Workers for the Union Pacific Railroad laid tracks west from Nebraska while Central Pacific Railroad built tracks east from California. The workforce was made up largely of immigrants from China, Ireland, and Germany, as well as African Americans and Native Americans. On May 10, 1869, the two rail lines met at Promontory Summit in Utah Territory.

Significance The rail line helped speed up the settlement of the West by making it easier to move people, goods, and resources across the country. It helped unite the country, both physically and economically. Other transcontinental railroads were soon built, and regional railroads expanded.

1876 Invention of the Telephone

In 1876 Scottish-born Alexander Graham Bell patented his design for a "talking telegraph," or, as it came to be known, telephone. Companies quickly found it to be an essential business tool, and people wanted them in their homes.

Significance Along with inventions such as the telegraph and typewriter, the telephone was part of a communication revolution in the 1800s. By 1900 more than a million telephones had been installed in offices and homes across the nation.

1880s–1910s New Wave of Immigrants

Prior to 1880 most immigrants had come to the United States from northern and western Europe. Beginning in the 1880s, waves of immigrants came from southern and eastern Europe. Millions came every decade until 1920. Thousands of immigrants came from Asia as well.

Significance Between 1880 and 1910, nearly 18 million newcomers came to the United States. The new immigrants helped power America's growing industries. The wave of immigration also changed the makeup of the American population. By 1910 nearly one out of every seven Americans was foreign-born.

1883 Pendleton Civil Service Act

The Pendleton Civil Service Act was designed to end the spoils system, a long-standing practice of filling government jobs with supporters of the winning political party. The law required that federal appointments be based on merit, not on political connections. It also guaranteed the rights of people to compete for jobs regardless of race, religion or national origin.

Significance The new law initially applied to only 10 percent of federal jobs, but was still an important first step in reducing corruption in the federal government. By 1980 the law applied to more than 90 percent of all federal positions.

1886 Formation of the AFL

Samuel Gompers formed the American Federation of Labor (AFL) in 1886. The AFL was a coalition of skilled workers in trade and craft unions. Unlike more radical unions, the AFL was more concerned with better wages and working conditions than with pushing larger political reforms.

Significance The AFL became the most powerful union of its time. Gompers used collective bargaining and strikes to gain higher wages and shortened work hours for union workers.

1887 Dawes Act

The Dawes Act divided up Native American reservation lands, allotting small individual plots to families. The goal of the law was to encourage Native Americans to value private property and live more like typical American farmers. The land many Native Americans received included desert or near-desert lands unsuitable for farming. Many who did want to farm could not afford the tools, animals, seed, and other supplies necessary to get started.

Significance Under the Dawes Act, land not allotted to Native Americans was sold, thus decreasing the amount of land under Indian control. Native American traditional life was weakened, and poverty on reservations became more widespread.

1890 Formation of the National American Woman Suffrage Association

The National American Woman Suffrage Association was the largest suffrage group in the United States. NAWSA activists worked to persuade state legislatures to grant women the vote.

Significance NAWSA's membership grew to nearly 2 million under the leadership of Carrie Chapman Catt. Working at both the state and federal levels, the organization played a key role in pressuring Congress to pass the Nineteenth Amendment, granting women full voting rights. A successor organization, the League of Women's Voters, exists today.

1890 Sherman Anti-Trust Act

Though the United States had a tradition of laissez-faire capitalism, in the late 1800s the federal government became concerned about the power of expanding corporations. The Sherman Antitrust Act made it illegal for corporations to form trusts that interfered with free trade.

Significance The Sherman Anti-Trust Act was the first federal action taken against trusts. The act was vaguely written, however, and corporations were easily able to avoid prosecution. The government soon stopped trying to enforce the Sherman Act. Consolidation of corporations continued. Congress later toughened the regulation of trusts by passing the Clayton Antitrust Act in 1914.

1896 *Plessy v. Ferguson*

Plessy v. *Ferguson* provided the legal justification for segregation in the South. The Supreme Court ruled that "separate but equal" facilities for blacks and whites did not violate the equal protection clause of the Fourteenth Amendment.

Significance *Plessy* v. *Ferguson* gave the force of federal law to the segregation practices that had been initiated in the South after the end of Reconstruction. The ruling was overturned in 1954 by the Supreme Court's decision in the *Brown* v. *Board of Education of Topeka, Kansas* case.

1898 Spanish-American War

The Spanish-American War was a four-month conflict in which American forces defeated Spain in Cuba and the Philippines. In the treaty ending the war, the United States gained control of Cuba, Puerto Rico, Guam, and the Philippines. Cuba was quickly granted independence, but remained under American influence.

Significance The Spanish-American War marked the establishment of the United States as a major international power. The capture of colonies set off a broad debate in the United States between expansionists and anti-imperialists. In the Philippines, Filipino nationalists rebelled against American rule. United States forces eventually crushed the rebellion in a war that lasted 15 years and claimed the lives of hundreds of thousands of Filipinos and over 4,000 U.S. soldiers.

1899 Open Door Policy

In the late 1890s Japan and European powers carved out spheres of influence in China. Fearing the United States would be shut out of trade with China, U.S. Secretary of State John Hay proposed the Open Door Policy. This policy would give all nations equal trading rights in China.

Significance The Open Door Policy was neither accepted nor rejected right away by other imperialist powers. The Boxer Rebellion, however, convinced Western nations that competing among themselves threatened their ability to exploit China. This led to increased support for the Open Door Policy.

1903 Invention of the Airplane

Orville and Wilbur Wright, two bicycle mechanics from Dayton, Ohio, built the first successful airplane. On December 17, 1903, at Kitty Hawk, North Carolina, Orville Wright became the first man ever to fly an airplane.

Significance Orville Wright's first flight lasted just 12 seconds, but it was the first true airplane flight in history. The Wright brothers and others began manufacturing airplanes. Air travel quickly changed transportation, increased demand for oil, and affected warfare.

1908 Henry Ford Begins selling Model T Automobiles

Henry Ford's goal was to build a car that most working Americans could afford. He achieved this in 1908 with the introduction of his Model T. Ford used the assembly line to produce cars quickly and cheaply, lowering the Model T's price to less than $500.

Significance By 1929 there were almost 30 million cars in the country. The auto industry created huge spin-off industries, such as road construction, oil refining, and gasoline retailing. The invention of the assembly line changed the way goods were produced. The wide availability of cars made it easier for more people to live some distance from their jobs, which led to the rise of suburbs.

1909 Founding of NAACP

A multiracial group of activists, including Ida Wells-Barnett, W.E.B. Du Bois, and Jane Addams, formed the National Association for the Advancement of Colored People (NAACP), to fight for the rights of African Americans. Early actions included defending African Americans falsely accused of crimes and protesting segregation in the federal government.

Significance The NAACP was the first national civil rights organization. In 1954 NAACP lawyers won the case of *Brown* v. *Board of Education of Topeka, Kansas*, in which the Supreme Court declared segregation in public schools to be unconstitutional.

1913 Passage of Sixteenth Amendment

The Sixteenth Amendment gave Congress the power to levy taxes based on personal income. The Treasury Department set up the Internal Revenue Service to collect income taxes.

Significance Under the first income tax laws, less than one percent of the population paid income taxes. This percentage, along with income tax rates, rose as government grew and the nation faced challenges such as World Wars I and II.

1914 Opening of the Panama Canal

Work on the Panama Canal began in May 1904 and lasted until 1914. The 50-mile canal across the Isthmus of Panama connected the Atlantic and Pacific Oceans, greatly shortening maritime travel times.

Significance The Panama Canal helped make the United States a great naval power by allowing the U.S. fleet to move more quickly from the Atlantic to the Pacific. It also greatly facilitated world trade. Protecting the canal and other economic interests became a central element of U.S. foreign policy in Latin America.

1914–1918 World War I

Increasingly intense rivalries in Europe, along with growing feelings of nationalism and a system of military alliances, led to the start of World War I. The primary opponents were the Central Powers (Germany, Austria-Hungary and Italy) and the Allied Powers (Great Britain, France and Russia). New technology such as machine guns and poison gas made this the deadliest war the world had seen to that point. The United States entered the war in 1917, helping the Allies gain eventual victory.

Significance World War I caused levels of casualties far higher than any previous war—combat, disease, and starvation killed more than 14 million people. Another 7 million men were left permanently disabled. The war led to the overthrow of monarchies in Russia, Austria-Hungary, Germany, and Turkey, and contributed to the rise of the Communists to power in Russia. The Treaty of Versailles, which ended the war, imposed harsh penalties on Germany, causing bitterness that later contributed to the outbreak of World War II.

1910s–1920s The Great Migration

In the early 1900s most African Americans lived in the South, where strict segregation laws kept them in a separate but unequal world. The Great Migration was a massive movement of African Americans from the South to the North, where they hoped to find economic opportunity and greater personal freedom. This movement accelerated with the outbreak of World War I, as northern factories needed workers to meet the demand for war supplies.

Significance The Great Migration was the largest internal migration in American history. Hundreds of thousands of African Americans streamed into northern cities such as New York, Chicago, and Detroit. This led to a mixing of cultures, and transformed race from a regional to a national issue.

1919 Treaty of Versailles

The Treaty of Versailles ended World War I. Against the advice of President Woodrow Wilson, Germany was forced to make large reparations payments to the Allies. The treaty also created nine new nations and established the League of Nations, an international organization designed to settle disputes, protect democracy, and prevent future wars.

Significance It is widely believed that the harsh terms of the Treaty of Versailles contributed to the rise of the Nazis in Germany and, therefore, the start of World War II. In the United States, Wilson's unwillingness to compromise with the Senate led to rejection of the treaty by the United States.

1920–1933 Prohibition

Prohibition was a period lasting from 1920 to 1933 during which the manufacture, transportation, and sale of alcohol was outlawed by the 18th Amendment. Prohibition proved unenforceable and was repealed by the 21st Amendment in 1933.

Significance Prohibition led to the creation of organized criminal groups who defied the law. It also led to strengthening of the Bureau of Investigation, forerunner to today's FBI, to combat crime. Its failure widely discredited efforts to legislate what many considered an area of private morality.

1919 The Palmer Raids

During the Red Scare that followed World War I, fear of Communists and radicals grew to an intense level in the United States. The Palmer Raids, led by U.S. Attorney General Mitchell Palmer, were a series of government raids on suspected radicals. Thousands of suspects were arrested, in some cases without proper legal authority.

Significance Far from criticizing the Palmer raids, many Americans cheered, or demanded even tougher action. This demonstrated the level of fear that existed in American society. The Red Scare gradually died out as it became clear that radicals had little power or support in the United States.

1920s Harlem Renaissance

The Harlem Renaissance was a creative movement of African American writers, musicians and artists that took place in the New York City neighborhood of Harlem in the 1920s. Important writers of the movement included James Weldon Johnson, Zora Neale Hurston, and Langston Hughes. Jacob Lawrence and William Johnson were two artists who won fame, as did such musicians as Paul Robeson, Louis Armstrong, and Duke Ellington.

Significance The Harlem Renaissance enriched American culture. Writers and artists made important contributions to American culture. Jazz swept the nation, contributing to a major cultural movement in the 1920s.

1930s The Dust Bowl

In the 1930s, drought and poor farming practices led to massive dust storms that turned portions of the Great Plains into what became known as the Dust Bowl. It was one of the worst ecological disasters in American history.

Significance The Dust Bowl contributed to a mass migration west among displaced farmers. The refugees from Dust Bowl states such as Oklahoma, sometimes called "Okies," came to represent the difficulties of the 1930s. The Dust Bowl led to improved efforts at soil conservation.

1929 Stock Market Crash

Despite underlying weakness in the economy, the stock market continued to rise in 1929. In September, prices began to weaken. The great crash came on "Black Tuesday," October 29, 1929, when stock prices collapsed.

Significance Both individual investors and businesses were devastated by the stock market crash. The crash marked the beginning of large decline in the economy that became known as the Great Depression. The crash also led to reforms of the stock market, including the creation of the Securities and Exchange Commission.

1930 Smoot-Hawley Tariff

The Smoot-Hawley Tariff was intended to ease the plight of American farmers by raising tariffs on imported farm products. This tariff also raised tariff rates on many kinds of manufactured goods. The tariff rates under Smoot-Hawley were higher than at any point in American history.

Significance European nations responded to the American tariff with high tariffs of their own. International trade dropped 66 percent from its 1929 levels, causing economies everywhere to suffer. In this way, the tariff can be said to have deepened the Great Depression worldwide.

1932 Franklin D. Roosevelt elected President

As the 1932 presidential election approached, many Americans blamed President Herbert Hoover for causing the Great Depression, or at least for failing to provide relief from the crisis. Democratic nominee Franklin D. Roosevelt promised swift government action to improve the economy. Roosevelt won the election in a landslide.

Significance In addition to winning the White House, the Democratic Party gained firm control of both houses of Congress. This gave President Roosevelt the ability to push though his New Deal legislation, which changed the role of government in American life.

1933–1945 The Holocaust

Soon after gaining power in Germany in 1933, Adolf Hitler began using the power of the government to persecute German Jews. German conquests early in World War II brought nearly all of Europe's 9 million

Jews under Nazi control. The Nazis attempted to exterminate the entire Jewish population of Europe. This became known as the Holocaust.

Significance The Nazis murdered 6 million Jews in the Holocaust, decimating the Jewish population of Europe. Nazis also killed about 5 million others, including prisoners of war, disabled people, and Gypsies. After the war, many of the Nazi leaders were convicted of war crimes by an international court. These trials were meant to demonstrate the commitment of people around the world to prevent a repetition of the Holocaust.

1935 Passage of the Social Security Act

Signed into law by President Roosevelt on August 14, 1935, the Social Security Act created a program that provided pensions for many Americans age 65 and older. These pensions were paid for by a new tax on workers and employers.

Significance The Social Security Act marked a significant expansion of the role of government in the lives of Americans. Its passage showed that government intended to take a greater share of responsibility for the well-being of citizens.

1935 Passage of the Wagner Act

Named for its sponsor, Senator Robert F. Wagner, the Wagner Act outlawed many of the anti-labor strategies in wide use among business leaders in the 1930s. The act created the National Labor Relations Board (NLRB), which had the power to investigate unfair labor practices and assure employees the right to collective bargaining.

Significance The Wagner Act was a major victory for organized labor. In the four years after the act's passage, union membership jumped from under 3.8 million members to over 6.5 million members.

1939-1945 Manhattan Project

The Manhattan Project was a top-secret government program to develop an atomic bomb during World War II. It was motivated by the danger that Germany might be the first to develop atomic weapons. Manhattan Project scientists worked in Los Alamos, New Mexico. They successfully tested the first atomic bomb near Alamogordo, New Mexico, on July 16, 1945.

Significance The Manhattan Project initiated the age of nuclear weapons. In August 1945, U.S. planes dropped atomic bombs on the Japanese cities of Hiroshima and Nagasaki, forcing Japan's surrender in World War II. During the Cold War that followed World War II, the United States and Soviet Union competed in a nuclear arms race.

1941 Lend-Lease Act

Passed by Congress during World War II, the Lend-Lease Act gave the U.S. government authority to make weapons available to Great Britain without regard for its ability to pay. Lend-lease aid was extended to the Soviet Union after the Nazis invaded Soviet territory in March 1941.

Significance At the time the Lend-Lease Act was passed, Britain was standing alone against Germany in World War II and desperately needed the assistance. Lend-Lease aid helped both Britain and the Soviet Union resist German attacks. It also moved the United States one step closer to full participation in World War II.

1941 Attack on Pearl Harbor

On Sunday morning, December 7, 1941, Japanese forces launched a surprise attack on the American naval base at Pearl Harbor, Hawaii. Catching American forces completely unprepared, Japanese planes inflicted devastating damage on U.S. aircraft and ships at Pearl Harbor. Some 2,400 Americans were killed in the attack.

Significance The Pearl Harbor attack shocked and outraged Americans, erasing isolationist feeling in the United States. The United States immediately declared war on Japan. Japan's ally, Germany, declared war on the United States. United States forces played a major role in winning World War II, the largest and deadliest war in world history.

1942 Japanese American Internment

Fearing that Japanese Americans living along the West Coast might aid an attack by Japan, in March 1942 the federal government forcibly removed some 110,000 people of Japanese ancestry—most of them American citizens—to desolate inland internment camps. Most evacuees remained confined until the internment order was lifted in December 1944.

Significance Many of the internees lost their homes and belongings—some $400 million in property—as well as their jobs. In 1988 President Ronald Reagan signed a bill authorizing the payment of $20,000 to each surviving Japanese American evacuees and apologized for the violation of their civil liberties.

1942 Battle of Midway

Fought in the Pacific Ocean between June 3 and 6, 1942, the Battle of Midway was a major World War II naval battle between U.S. and Japanese forces. Using intelligence gained from intercepted and decoded Japanese messages, U.S. aircraft carrier-based planes surprised and sank four Japanese aircraft carriers with a loss of only one carrier.

Significance The Battle of Midway was a major turning point in the war in the Pacific. Japanese naval power, which had been a key to its early success, was greatly reduced. American forces were able to begin gaining back territory from Japan.

1944 D-Day

June 6, 1944, was D-Day—the day the Allies invaded Nazi-held Western Europe. In the largest combined air and sea invasion in history, more than 150,000 soldiers stormed the beaches at Normandy, France. Facing fierce German resistance, the Allies gained a beachhead from which to begin their massive invasion of Europe.

Significance D-Day was a major turning point of the war in Europe. The United States and Britain drove toward Germany from the west, while the Soviet Army attacked from the east. Germany was forced to surrender in May 1945.

1948-1949 Berlin Airlift

In June 1948, the Soviets suddenly blocked road, rail, and river traffic into West Berlin, cutting off the city's people from sources of food and fuel. In the Berlin Airlift, American and British pilots flew around the clock, bringing necessities into West Berlin by air. They sustained the effort until May 1949, when the Soviets lifted their blockade.

Significance The Berlin Airlift demonstrated how deeply committed the United States was to opposing the expansion of communism and Soviet power. This commitment became the central theme of U.S. foreign policy throughout the Cold War.

1947-1951 Marshall Plan

Named for its architect, U.S. Secretary of State George C. Marshall, the Marshall Plan was a U.S. program to help the nations of Western Europe recover World War II. The United States government spent over 13 billion to buy food and farm equipment and to rebuild factories and homes.

Significance The Marshall Plan was very successful in helping Western European economies recover from the devastation of World War II. The program also strengthened political and economic ties between the United States and Western Europe.

1950-1953 Korean War

The Korean War began in 1950 when communist North Korea invaded South Korea. A United Nations force, made up mostly of American troops, entered the war to block the North Korean invasion. Chinese troops fought alongside the North Koreans. After several major back and forth battles, the war ended in 1953 with North and South Korea divided along almost the same border as before the war.

Significance The Korean War was the first "shooting war" in the Cold War between Communists and U.S. forces. The United States defended South Korea to show it would protect nations from Communist attack. U.S. troops are still stationed in South Korea, more than fifty years after the fighting ended.

1954 *Brown v. Board of Education of Topeka, Kansas* Decision

The "Brown" in this landmark Supreme Court case was an African American third-grader named Linda Brown, who was forced to travel a long distance to a segregated school in Topeka, Kansas. NAACP lawyers sued, demanding that Brown be allowed to enroll in an all-white school that was much closer to her home. In 1954 The Supreme Court ruled unanimously that separate schools for African American and white students were by their nature unequal, and thus unconstitutional.

Significance By declaring that segregation in public schools was a violation of the Constitution's guarantee of equal protection of the law, the Court reversed *Plessy* v. *Ferguson* (1896), which had established the constitutionality of segregated facilities. This victory was just the beginning of the civil rights movement that changed the nation in the 1950s and 1960s.

1955–1956 Montgomery Bus Boycott

In December 1955 Rosa Parks, an African American woman, was arrested in Montgomery, Alabama, for refusing to move to the back of a segregated city bus. African Americans, led by Martin Luther King Jr., organized the Montgomery Bus Boycott to protest Parks' arrest and segregation on city buses. After more than a year, the boycott achieved its goal when the Supreme Court ruled the segregation policy unconstitutional.

Significance Beyond achieving local goals in Montgomery, the bus boycott made a national impact by inspiring similar boycotts in other southern cities. Martin Luther King Jr. gained nationwide attention and became a powerful leader of the growing civil rights movement.

1958 Formation of NASA

In 1957 the Soviet Union shocked the United States by launching Sputnik, the first-ever artificial satellite, into space. The United States responded in 1958 with the creation of the National Aeronautics and Space Administration (NASA), a government agency dedicated to the exploration of space.

Significance NASA led the United States past the Soviet Union in the space race, moving quickly from single satellites to manned flights orbiting the Earth to the Apollo program that successfully landed men on the moon. NASA exhibited the success of American technology and boosted American pride and confidence during the Cold War.

1950s Television changes American life

Television ownership exploded in the 1950s, and by the end of the decade over 40 million American homes had at least one television set. Watching television became a favorite national pastime, as families across the country tuned in to the same comedies, game shows, and music programs.

Significance Television, like radio and movies, provided Americans with common cultural experiences. By 1960 TV had become the major means of advertising in the country. Politicians quickly learned that TV had an enormous power to impact their relationship with voters.

1954–1973 Vietnam War

In the Vietnam War the United States fought to try to prevent Communist forces from taking over all of Vietnam. U.S. troops supported non-Communist South Vietnam against Communist North Vietnam and guerilla forces known as the Vietcong. Though U.S. troop levels in Vietnam topped 500,000 in 1968, victory seemed nowhere in sight. With the American public turning against the war, the government began gradually withdrawing troops from Vietnam. The last soldiers left in 1973. In 1975 North Vietnam succeeded in taking over all of Vietnam.

Significance More than 58,000 Americans died in Vietnam, and more than 2 million Vietnamese soldiers and civilians were killed. The war caused bitter divisions in American society, as some protested the fighting, while others backed the government. Misleading statements by military and government leaders about the progress of the war caused many Americans to lose some faith in their government.

1962 Cuban Missile Crisis

In April 1961 Cuban exiles, backed by the United States, tried to invade Cuba and overthrow its dictator, Fidel Castro. The invasion of the Bay of Pigs failed. In October 1962 U.S. spy planes discovered that the Soviet Union was installing nuclear missiles in Cuba. The missiles would be able to strike almost any location in the United States. President John F. Kennedy demanded that the missiles be removed and announced that U.S. warships would enforce a naval blockade of Cuba. For several days the world watched and waited for the Soviet response. The crisis finally lifted when Khrushchev agreed to dismantle the Soviet missiles in Cuba in return for a U.S. promise not to invade the island.

Significance The Cuban missile crisis marked the closest the world has ever come to the outbreak of nuclear war. Sobered by the experience, Kennedy and Khrushchev took steps to ease Cold War tensions. They set up a hot line that would allow American and Soviet leaders to communicate directly during times of crisis, and signed the Limited Nuclear Test Ban Treaty, banning the testing of nuclear weapons in the atmosphere and underwater.

1963 March on Washington

In the aftermath of police violence against civil rights protests, on August 28 about 250,000 people from across the country, about a quarter of them white, took part in the March on Washington for Jobs and Freedom. The march brought together several major civil rights organizations to demand school desegregation, jobs programs, a minimum wage, and various civil rights laws.

Significance Part protest and part celebration, the demonstration was the largest ever in Washington and the first to be covered on television. It is remembered for the peacefulness of the event and for the stirring "I Have a Dream" speech by Martin Luther King Jr., one of the most famous in U.S. history.

Civil Rights Act of 1964

Following the assassination of President Kennedy, the new president, Lyndon Johnson, secured passage of a landmark civil rights bill first proposed by President Kennedy. The Civil Rights Act of 1964 banned segregation in public places and discrimination in employment. It set up the Equal opportunity Commission to end job discrimination—another provision allowed the government to withhold federal funds from school districts that violated integration orders.

Significance The Civil Rights Act of 1964 has been called the most significant civil right law since the Reconstruction amendments. The Civil Rights Act, along with the Voting Right Act of 1965, were major victories for the civil rights movement. These new laws gave the federal government the power to prevent racial discrimination.

1965 Passage of Medicare & Medicaid

Established in 1965, Medicaid and Medicare were parts of President Lyndon B. Johnson's ambitious program of domestic reform known as the Great Society. Medicaid is a government program that provides free or low-cost health care for poor people. Medicare is a government funded health care program for people over age 65.

Significance Medicare and Medicaid have helped provide health services for millions of Americans. Like New Deal programs of the 1930s, Johnson's Great Society programs expanded the role of the federal government in American society.

1965–1970 United Farm Workers Grape Boycott

In 1965 farm workers in California went on strike when their employer cut their pay during the grape harvest. César Chávez and Dolores Huerta, cofounders of the National Farm Workers Association (NFWA), helped lead a nationwide grape boycott to support striking farm workers. Millions of Americans refused to buy grapes.

Significance The pressure on the grape growers eventually forced them to negotiate a settlement. The success of the grape boycott brought César Chávez to national prominence as a leader in the fight for civil rights for Hispanic Americans.

1965 Immigration Act of 1965

This act repealed the national-origin immigration quotas in effect since 1924 and set hemisphere-based quotas instead. Priority was given to those applicants with relatives already in the United States and possessing desired job skills. The effect was to open up immigration to people from countries that had previously been denied entry to the United States.

Significance The act triggered a new wave of immigration to the United States from Asian and Latin American nations which has altered the cultural mix in the United States.

1966 Formation of National Organization for Women (NOW)

The National Organization for Women (NOW) is a women's rights organization founded by women's rights leaders in 1966. NOW actively campaigned for passage of the Equal Rights Amendment (ERA). Though the ERA eventually failed, NOW helped women make important gains in the 1970s.

Significance The organization continues to be an influential voice in American politics. NOW's goals include fighting discrimination in the workplace, schools, and the justice system. It also works to end violence against women and to protect women's reproductive rights.

1969 Apollo 11 Moon Landing

The goal of NASA's Apollo program was to land American astronauts on the moon. The program achieved this goal with the Apollo 11 mission. On July 20, 1969, Neil Armstrong and Buzz Aldrin became the first humans to walk on the moon. Millions of amazed viewers around the world watched the moon landing on television.

Significance The Apollo 11 mission fulfilled a bold promise made by President Kennedy at the start of the 1960s to place a man on the moon in that decade. It was a triumph for American technology and was a source of wonder and pride to all Americans.

1970 Creation of the Environmental Protection Agency

In 1970 Congress established the Environmental Protection Agency (EPA) to research, monitor, and set and enforce standards on air and water quality and noise and radiation pollution. The EPA administers the "Superfund" toxic waste cleanup act, established in 1980.

Significance The creation of the EPA was one of Richard M. Nixon's presidential legacies. The agency has overseen the restoration of polluted waterways, the creation of antipollution standards for industries, and the cleanup of toxic waste sites throughout the country.

1972 Nixon Goes to China

As part of his "realpolitik" approach to foreign policy, President Richard Nixon made a historic visit to communist China in 1972. Nixon hoped that improved U.S.-China relations would spur the Soviets also to seek better relations with the United States.

Significance The visit was a huge success for Nixon. Not only did U.S.-China relations improve, but the trip also had the hoped-for effect on the Soviets: shortly after the China visit, Nixon and Soviet leaders reached a nuclear arms control agreement. This opened a period of détente, a time of easing Cold War tensions.

1972–1974 Watergate Scandal

The Watergate Scandal began when five burglars broke into the Democratic Party headquarters in the Watergate Hotel in Washington, D.C. Officials in the Nixon White House worked to cover up their role in the Watergate break-in. As the House of Representatives began the impeachment process against the president, Nixon resigned from office August 9, 1974.

Significance Nixon became the first president in

American history to resign from office. Watergate caused a sharp drop in the percentage of Americans who said they trusted the government.

1979 Iran Hostage Crisis

On November 4, 1979, a student-led Islamic revolutionary group seized the U.S. Embassy in Iranian capital, Tehran. The rebels held 52 Americans hostage for 444 days. President Jimmy Carter imposed economic penalties, conducted diplomatic negotiations, and ordered a rescue attempt, which failed. The hostages were released on the day of Ronald Reagan's inauguration, January 20, 1981.

Significance The crisis, and the poorly executed military rescue attempt, traumatized the country and strongly contributed to Carter's election defeat.

1982 Strategic Arms Reduction Talks

After more than a decade of work to limit increases in the superpowers' nuclear forces, President Ronald Reagan and Soviet leader Mikhail Gorbachev began negotiations aimed at reducing the huge stockpiles of atomic weapons. The talks resulted in the Strategic Arms Reduction Treaty (START), signed by Gorbachev and President George H. W. Bush in 1991.

Significance START took place during the collapse of the Soviet empire and the end of the Cold War. START II, signed by Bush and Russian President Boris Yeltsin in 1993, was never ratified by the United States, but the two countries have far exceeded the nuclear reduction goals of START I and II.

1991 Collapse of the Soviet Union

In the 1980s economic and political reforms by Soviet leader Mikhail Gorbachev led to calls for greater freedom in the Soviet Union and Eastern Europe. Under this pressure, communist governments in Eastern Europe began collapsing in 1989. In 1991 the Soviet government itself collapsed as former Soviet republics declared their independence.

Significance The fall of the Soviet Union marked the end of the Cold War. Millions of people in Eastern Europe and the former Soviet Union gained freedom from communist dictatorships. The United States was left as the world's only superpower.

1991 Operation Desert Storm

In August 1990 Iraqi dictator Saddam Hussein invaded and conquered the neighboring oil-rich nation of Kuwait. President George H.W. Bush built an international coalition of allies to oppose the Iraqi action. In Operation Desert Storm, a U.S.-led coalition drove Hussein's troops out of Kuwait.

Significance The U.S.-led forces succeeded in freeing Kuwait from Iraqi control, demonstrating the effectiveness of international cooperation. Saddam Hussein, however, remained in power in Iraq. Just over 12 years later, the United States would be at war with Hussein again.

1993 Passage of NAFTA

Passed in 1993, the North American Free Trade Agreement (NAFTA) eliminated trade barriers between the United States, Mexico, and Canada. This allowed most products to be sold across borders without tariffs. The agreement caused controversy, with critics arguing it would cost American jobs, and supporters insisting it would increase trade.

Significance The debate over NAFTA was part of a larger debate about international trade and globalization. This will continue to be a major issue for Americans as the world's economies become more interconnected.

2001 Terrorist Attacks of 9/11

On September 11, 2001, terrorists hijacked four planes, crashing two of them into the towers of the World Trade Center in New York City and a third into the Pentagon near Washington, D.C. A fourth plane crashed in Pennsylvania after passengers attempted to take back the plane from the terrorists. A total of about 3,000 people were killed in these attacks.

Significance President George W. Bush declared a war on terror. U.S. officials identified the hijackers as members of al Qaeda, an extremist Islamic terrorist group led by Osama bin Laden and based in Afghanistan. In October 2001, U.S. forces invaded Afghanistan, driving out the Taliban government, which had supported bin Laden.

2003 Iraq War

Fearing that Iraqi leader Saddam Hussein was building weapons of mass destruction that could be used against the United States or given to a terrorist, President Bush called for Iraq to disarm. Saddam, however, refused to fully cooperate with UN weapons inspections. Though many of America's allies argued against going to war, Bush insisted the Iraqi threat must be countered. With the support of Great Britain and several other allies, American forces invaded and quickly conquered Iraq in 2003. Saddam was captured in late 2003.

Significance In June 2004, American officials handed control over to an Iraqi government. Iraqis began electing their own leaders in 2005. The violence continued, however, as insurgents carried out deadly attacks against American troops and Iraqis. To date, American and international teams have found no weapons of mass destruction.

Presidents

1 GEORGE WASHINGTON
Born: 1732   Died: 1799
Years in Office: 1789–97
Political Party: None
Home State: Virginia
Vice President:

2 JOHN ADAMS
Born: 1735   Died: 1826
Years in Office: 1797–1801
Political Party: Federalist
Home State: Massachusetts
Vice President: Thomas Jefferson

3 THOMAS JEFFERSON
Born: 1743   Died: 1826
Years in Office: 1801–09
Political Party: Republican*
Home State: Virginia
Vice Presidents: Aaron Burr,
George Clinton

4 JAMES MADISON
Born: 1751   Died: 1836
Years in Office: 1809–17
Political Party: Republican
Home State: Virginia
Vice Presidents: George Clinton,
Elbridge Gerry

5 JAMES MONROE
Born: 1758   Died: 1831
Years in Office: 1817–25
Political Party: Republican
Home State: Virginia
Vice President: Daniel D. Tompkins

6 JOHN QUINCY ADAMS
Born: 1767   Died: 1848
Years in Office: 1825–29
Political Party: Republican
Home State: Massachusetts
Vice President: John C. Calhoun

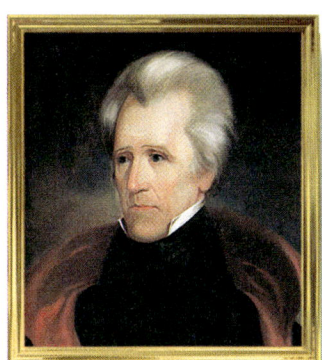

7 ANDREW JACKSON
Born: 1767   Died: 1845
Years in Office: 1829–37
Political Party: Democratic
Home State: Tennessee
Vice Presidents: John C. Calhoun,
Martin Van Buren

8 MARTIN VAN BUREN
Born: 1782   Died: 1862
Years in Office: 1837–41
Political Party: Democratic
Home State: New York
Vice President: Richard M. Johnson

* The Republican Party of the third through sixth presidents is not the party of Abraham Lincoln, which was founded in 1854.

9 WILLIAM HENRY HARRISON
Born: 1773 **Died:** 1841
Years in Office: 1841
Political Party: Whig
Home State: Ohio
Vice President: John Tyler

10 JOHN TYLER
Born: 1790 **Died:** 1862
Years in Office: 1841–45
Political Party: Whig
Home State: Virginia
Vice President: None

11 JAMES K. POLK
Born: 1795 **Died:** 1849
Years in Office: 1845–49
Political Party: Democratic
Home State: Tennessee
Vice President: George M. Dallas

12 ZACHARY TAYLOR
Born: 1784 **Died:** 1850
Years in Office: 1849–50
Political Party: Whig
Home State: Louisiana
Vice President: Millard Fillmore

13 MILLARD FILLMORE
Born: 1800 **Died:** 1874
Years in Office: 1850–53
Political Party: Whig
Home State: New York
Vice President: None

14 FRANKLIN PIERCE
Born: 1804 **Died:** 1869
Years in Office: 1853–57
Political Party: Democratic
Home State: New Hampshire
Vice President: William R. King

15 JAMES BUCHANAN
Born: 1791 **Died:** 1868
Years in Office: 1857–61
Political Party: Democratic
Home State: Pennsylvania
Vice President: John C. Breckinridge

16 ABRAHAM LINCOLN
Born: 1809 **Died:** 1865
Years in Office: 1861–65
Political Party: Republican
Home State: Illinois
Vice Presidents: Hannibal Hamlin, Andrew Johnson

17 ANDREW JOHNSON
Born: 1808 **Died:** 1875
Years in Office: 1865–69
Political Party: Republican
Home State: Tennessee
Vice President: None

18 ULYSSES S. GRANT
Born: 1822   Died: 1885
Years in Office: 1869–77
Political Party: Republican
Home State: Illinois
Vice Presidents: Schuyler Colfax,
Henry Wilson

19 RUTHERFORD B. HAYES
Born: 1822   Died: 1893
Years in Office: 1877–81
Political Party: Republican
Home State: Ohio
Vice President: William A. Wheeler

20 JAMES A. GARFIELD
Born: 1831   Died: 1881
Years in Office: 1881
Political Party: Republican
Home State: Ohio
Vice President: Chester A. Arthur

21 CHESTER A. ARTHUR
Born: 1829   Died: 1886
Years in Office: 1881–85
Political Party: Republican
Home State: New York
Vice President: None

22 GROVER CLEVELAND
Born: 1837   Died: 1908
Years in Office: 1885–89
Political Party: Democratic
Home State: New York
Vice President: Thomas A. Hendricks

23 BENJAMIN HARRISON
Born: 1833   Died: 1901
Years in Office: 1889–93
Political Party: Republican
Home State: Indiana
Vice President: Levi P. Morton

24 GROVER CLEVELAND
Born: 1837   Died: 1908
Years in Office: 1893–97
Political Party: Democratic
Home State: New York
Vice President: Adlai E. Stevenson

25 WILLIAM McKINLEY
Born: 1843   Died: 1901
Years in Office: 1897–1901
Political Party: Republican
Home State: Ohio
Vice Presidents: Garret A. Hobart,
Theodore Roosevelt

26 THEODORE ROOSEVELT
Born: 1858   Died: 1919
Years in Office: 1901–09
Political Party: Republican
Home State: New York
Vice President: Charles W. Fairbanks

27 WILLIAM HOWARD TAFT
Born: 1857 **Died:** 1930
Years in Office: 1909–13
Political Party: Republican
Home State: Ohio
Vice President: James S. Sherman

28 WOODROW WILSON
Born: 1856 **Died:** 1924
Years in Office: 1913–21
Political Party: Democratic
Home State: New Jersey
Vice President: Thomas R. Marshall

29 WARREN G. HARDING
Born: 1865 **Died:** 1923
Years in Office: 1921–23
Political Party: Republican
Home State: Ohio
Vice President: Calvin Coolidge

30 CALVIN COOLIDGE
Born: 1872 **Died:** 1933
Years in Office: 1923–29
Political Party: Republican
Home State: Massachusetts
Vice President: Charles G. Dawes

31 HERBERT HOOVER
Born: 1874 **Died:** 1964
Years in Office: 1929–33
Political Party: Republican
Home State: California
Vice President: Charles Curtis

32 FRANKLIN D. ROOSEVELT
Born: 1882 **Died:** 1945
Years in Office: 1933–45
Political Party: Democratic
Home State: New York
Vice Presidents: John Nance Garner, Henry Wallace, Harry S Truman

33 HARRY S TRUMAN
Born: 1884 **Died:** 1972
Years in Office: 1945–53
Political Party: Democratic
Home State: Missouri
Vice President: Alben W. Barkley

34 DWIGHT D. EISENHOWER
Born: 1890 **Died:** 1969
Years in Office: 1953–61
Political Party: Republican
Home State: Kansas
Vice President: Richard M. Nixon

35 JOHN F. KENNEDY
Born: 1917 **Died:** 1963
Years in Office: 1961–63
Political Party: Democratic
Home State: Massachusetts
Vice President: Lyndon B. Johnson

36 LYNDON B. JOHNSON
Born: 1908   Died: 1973
Years in Office: 1963–69
Political Party: Democratic
Home State: Texas
Vice President: Hubert H. Humphrey

37 RICHARD M. NIXON
Born: 1913   Died: 1994
Years in Office: 1969–74
Political Party: Republican
Home State: California
Vice Presidents: Spiro T. Agnew, Gerald R. Ford

38 GERALD R. FORD
Born: 1913   Died: 2006
Years in Office: 1974–77
Political Party: Republican
Home State: Michigan
Vice President: Nelson A. Rockefeller

39 JIMMY CARTER
Born: 1924
Years in Office: 1977–81
Political Party: Democratic
Home State: Georgia
Vice President: Walter F. Mondale

40 RONALD REAGAN
Born: 1911   Died: 2004
Years in Office: 1981–89
Political Party: Republican
Home State: California
Vice President: George Bush

41 GEORGE BUSH
Born: 1924
Years in Office: 1989–93
Political Party: Republican
Home State: Texas
Vice President: J. Danforth Quayle

42 BILL CLINTON
Born: 1946
Years in Office: 1993–2001
Political Party: Democratic
Home State: Arkansas
Vice President: Albert Gore Jr.

43 GEORGE W. BUSH
Born: 1946
Years in Office: 2001–
Political Party: Republican
Home State: Texas
Vice President: Richard B. Cheney

Supreme Court Decisions

Gibbons v. Ogden (1824)

Significance: The first case to deal with the commerce clause of the Constitution, *Gibbons v. Ogden* reaffirmed Congress's exclusive power to regulate interstate and foreign commerce.

Background: Aaron Ogden held a monopoly license issued by New York state to operate a steamboat ferry service between New Jersey and New York. Thomas Gibbons had a federal license to travel along the coast and began operating a competing ferry between New York and New Jersey. Ogden sued to protect his monopoly and won. Gibbons appealed the decision to the Supreme Court.

Decision: By a vote of 6–0, the Court ruled in favor of Gibbons. Chief Justice John Marshall wrote the opinion. The Court determined that the states could regulate transportation within their own borders but not between states. The power to regulate commerce between states belonged only to Congress, so Gibbons's federal license was valid. The ruling broadly defined commerce to include more than simply the exchange of goods, but also the transportation of people and the use of new inventions such as the steamboat.

Worcester v. Georgia (1832)

Significance: This case showed the limits of the Court's power to enforce one of its decisions if it chose not to use further legal action to compel cooperation. As a result, Georgia and other states continued to force American Indian tribes off lands protected by treaties with the federal government.

Background: The state of Georgia wanted to remove Cherokee Indians from lands the Indians held by federal treaty. Samuel Worcester, a mis-sionary who worked with the Cherokee Nation, was arrested and convicted for refusing to leave the lands. Worcester appealed, charging that Georgia had no legal authority on Cherokee lands.

Decision: This case was decided in favor of Worcester by a 5–1 vote. Chief Justice John Marshall spoke for the majority, which ruled that the Cherokee Nation was "a distinct community occupying its own territory." Under the Constitution and the treaties between the United States and the Cherokees, only the federal government, and not the state of Georgia, had the power to control dealings with the Cherokee people. Georgia defied the decision, and President Andrew Jackson refused to act to uphold the Supreme Court's decision.

Civil Rights Cases (1883)

Significance: This decision limited Congress's ability to outlaw "whites only" facilities. As a result, blacks in many areas continued to be subject to inferior treatment. This situation continued until the Civil Rights Movement of the 1950s and 1960s led to new civil rights laws based on the commerce clause rather than on the Fourteenth Amendment.

Background: After the Civil War, many facilities of public accommodation like hotels, theaters, restaurants, and buses were restricted to whites only, or had separate (and often inferior) sections for blacks. In the Civil Rights Act of 1875, Congress attempted to outlaw this race-based discrimination. The U.S. government and blacks who had been denied admission to these facilities brought a series of cases seeking to enforce the Act. The cases were appealed to the U.S. Supreme Court and were combined for decision.

Justice Scalia

Justice Ginsberg

Justice Souter

Justice Roberts

Justice Alito

Decision: In an opinion by Justice Joseph P. Bradley, the Court ruled that although the Fourteenth Amendment prohibited racial discrimination by the state and federal governments, it did not give Congress the power to outlaw discrimination by private individuals or businesses. Because the law went beyond Congress's authority, it was ruled unconstitutional.

Justice John Harlan wrote a strong dissent, arguing that many states were refusing to protect the basic rights of black people and that Congress should have the power under the Fourteenth Amendment to make all citizens equal.

Wabash, St. Louis & Pacific R.R. v. Illinois (1886)

Significance: The ruling marked the end of railroad regulation by the individual states and led to the passage of the federal Interstate Commerce Act the following year. In preventing individual states from interfering with national commerce, the case helped develop a more unified national economy.

Background: In *Munn v. Illinois* (1877) the Supreme Court had allowed states to regulate areas of interstate commerce where Congress had not acted. Following the logic of that ruling, Illinois passed a law allowing it to control railroad rates by regulating the shipping contracts of railroads passing through Illinois. The state sued the Wabash, St. Louis & Pacific Railroad for not following the law. The railroad responded that the law did not apply to shipments going from Illinois to another state.

Decision: In a 6–3 decision written by Justice Samuel F. Miller, the Court drew back from *Munn v. Illinois* and overruled Illinois's railroad law. The commerce clause, the Court ruled, prevents states from imposing direct burdens on interstate commerce. This meant that states could not enact laws that interfered with the free flow of goods across the country.

United States v. E.C. Knight Co. (1895)

Significance: The ruling was a major setback for federal antitrust regulation. Freed by this case from the fear of federal prosecution, manufacturers began a period of significant merger and consolidation. Manufacturing monopolies continued largely unrestricted until President Theodore Roosevelt tackled "trust busting" in the early 1900s.

Background: In the early 1890s, the American Sugar Refining Company bought out its major competitors. The purchases gave American Sugar Refining, owned by E.C. Knight Co., almost total control over the manufacturing of refined sugar in the United States. The U.S. government sued, claiming the company had violated the Sherman Antitrust Act. This act, passed in 1890, outlawed monopolies and prohibited "restraint of trade" in interstate commerce.

Decision: The Supreme Court ruled 8–1 in favor of Knight. Chief Justice Melville Fuller wrote the majority opinion, taking a very narrow view of commerce that distinguished the manufacture of goods from their sale. Under this analysis, Congress could regulate sales under the commerce clause, but it did not have the power to regulate manufacturing.

In Re Debs (1895)

Significance: This case confirmed the federal government's power to get an injunction (court order) to end unlawful strikes and force striking workers to return to work. The government used injunctions to stop major strikes for the next 30 years.

Background: In 1894 workers making railroad cars at the Pullman Company rebelled against poor working conditions. After the company hired armed guards to subdue the protesters, the American Railroad Union refused to handle trains with Pullman cars. The strike disrupted rail service nationwide,

Justice Stevens

Justice Breyer

Justice Thomas

Justice Kennedy

and railroad managers sought federal intervention. The government claimed the strike was impeding interstate trade and interfering with delivery of the U.S. mail—a federal offense. When the union ignored a court order to stop the strike, the union's leader, Eugene V. Debs was jailed for contempt of court. He petitioned for release on the grounds that the order was unconstitutional.

Decision: The Supreme Court ruled unanimously against Debs. Justice David Brewer wrote that the federal government has control over interstate commerce and the delivery of the mails and therefore had the right to ask a judge to stop the strike. The strike created a public nuisance by interfering with the mail, so the judge acted correctly in ordering it stopped and in jailing Debs for contempt when he refused to obey the order.

Northern Securities Co. v. United States (1904)

Significance: This ruling revived the federal government's power to prohibit monopolies, a power that had been undercut by *United States* v. *E.C. Knight Co.* (1895). The government's victory in this case resulted in the dissolution of the Northern Securities Company and paved the way for stricter regulation of large corporations.

Background: In 1901 three competing railroads that ran from the Pacific Northwest to the Great Lakes agreed to merge by turning over their stock to a new holding company, the Northern Securities Company. The U.S. government sued under the Sherman Antitrust Act. It claimed that the holding company was created to reduce competition in the railroad business and therefore violated the Sherman Act's prohibition on restraint of commerce. The Northern Securities Company argued that it merely owned the railways' stock and did not itself engage in commerce. It was a state-chartered corporation, and federal interference would violate state powers protected by the Tenth Amendment.

Decision: In a 5–4 decision, the Supreme Court sided with the government. The states can charter corporations, but corporations are still subject to federal law, and the Sherman Antitrust Act did apply in this case. The Court interpreted the act broadly, ruling that a business combination was illegal if it restrained commerce in any way, even if it didn't directly engage in commerce.

Lochner v. New York (1905)

Significance: This decision limited the states' ability to regulate labor and industry. For more than 30 years, *Lochner* was used as a precedent to strike down state laws such as minimum-wage laws, child labor laws, and regulations on the banking and transportation industries.

Background: In 1895 the state of New York passed a labor law limiting bakers to working no more than 10 hours per day or 60 hours per week. The purpose of the law was to protect the health of bakers, who worked in hot, damp conditions and breathed in large quantities of flour dust. In 1902 Joseph Lochner, the owner of a small bakery in New York, claimed that the state law violated his Fourteenth Amendment due process rights by depriving him of the freedom to make contracts with employees.

Decision: The case was decided in Lochner's favor by a 5–4 vote. The Supreme Court ruled that the right to sell and buy labor was implicit in the Fourteenth Amendment's concept of personal liberty. Thus any state law restricting that right was unconstitutional. The Court rejected the argument that limited work hours were necessary to prevent worker exploitation.

Muller v. Oregon (1908)

Significance: This was the first case in which the Supreme Court recognized social conditions (in this case, women's health) as a factor in judging the constitutionality of state laws. The decision marked the beginning of the Court's gradual retreat from the strict doctrine of *Lochner* v. *New York* (1905), which had appeared to prohibit state regulation of the workplace.

Background: In 1903 Oregon passed a law limiting workdays to 10 hours for women workers in laundries and factories. In 1905 Curt Muller's Grand Laundry was found guilty of breaking this law. Muller appealed, arguing (as Lochner successfully had) that the state law violated his freedom of contract. When the matter came to the Supreme Court, lawyer Louis D. Brandeis presented Oregon's case in a novel and compelling way. He supplied not only legal arguments, but also medical, social, and economic data on the impact of long working hours on women's health.

Decision: In 1908 a unanimous Supreme Court upheld the Oregon law. The Court agreed that the government had a legitimate interest in women's well-being and concluded that the 10-hour law was a valid way of protecting that interest. Although the Court did not overrule *Lochner*, it did show a willingness to accept some workplace regulation as justifiable.

Watkins v. United States (1957)

Significance: This decision recognized limits on congressional investigations. Congress may not expose the private affairs of citizens unless they pertain to a legitimate legislative inquiry.

Background: In 1954 the House Un-American Activities Committee was investigating communists. The committee subpoenaed John Watkins, a labor organizer, to testify. Watkins was willing to answer questions about his affiliation with the Communist Party and also to identify current party members. He refused, however, to name people who had left the party. Watkins was convicted for contempt of Congress, a federal offense.

Decision: Chief Justice Earl Warren wrote the Court's 6–1 decision holding that Watkins's conviction violated the due process clause of the Fifth Amendment. Watkins did not have to answer questions unrelated to the official inquiry of the committee. The Court ruled that the committee failed to clearly define the scope of its inquiry and to establish the relevance of questions about former members of the Communist Party.

Mapp v. Ohio (1961)

Significance: This decision created the legal rule that states cannot use evidence obtained from an illegal search in state criminal proceedings.

Background: In 1957 the police forced their way into Dollree Mapp's house without a search warrant. They were looking for a suspected bomber, but instead they found obscene pictures. Mapp was arrested and convicted for possession of pornography—a crime in Ohio. Mapp appealed to the Supreme Court, which had ruled in 1914 that evidence illegally obtained by the police could not be used in a federal criminal prosecution. The purpose of this "exclusionary rule" was to encourage the police to respect individuals' Fourth Amendment rights. However, until the *Mapp* case, states could decide for themselves whether to follow the exclusionary rule.

Decision: The Supreme Court ruled in Mapp's favor, 6–3. The majority held that the due process clause of the Fourteenth Amendment makes the protections of the Fourth Amendment apply to the states. Thus the exclusionary rule applies in state criminal cases as well as in federal court.

Baker v. Carr (1962)

Significance: This decision held that federal courts could review apportionment, or the distribution of seats, in state legislatures. The case led to the widespread redrawing of legislative districts to equalize representation and ensure "one person, one vote." As a result, political power shifted from rural to urban areas in most states.

Background: Many states had kept the same legislative district lines for decades, despite dramatic population shifts as people moved from the country to the cities. In Tennessee rural voters made up a minority of the population, but they had far more representatives in government than urban voters. Charles Baker and others brought suit against Joseph Carr, the Tennessee secretary of state, claiming that as urban dwellers, their votes were so diluted that they were denied equal protection under the law. The case reached the Supreme Court after being dismissed by the federal district court, which considered apportionment a political question to be decided by the legislature.

Decision: The Supreme Court did not rule on the legality of Tennessee's voting districts. However, it affirmed that the courts can indeed consider such cases. Justice William Brennan wrote that a state's failure to apportion its legislative districts equally would violate the equal protection clause of the Fourteenth Amendment. Thus Baker's constitutional rights were at stake, and the case went back to the federal district court for trial.

Engel v. Vitale (1962)

Significance: This was a landmark case on the subject of religious freedom. In a ruling that remains highly controversial, the Supreme Court held that state-sponsored prayer in public schools is unconstitutional. Attempts have since been made to amend the Constitution to permit prayer, but none have succeeded.

Background: The New York Board of Regents wrote a short, nondenominational prayer for students to say at the beginning of the school day. A group of parents sued, arguing that the prayer violated the establishment clause of the First Amendment—the clause banning the establishment of religion. Although students could remain silent during the prayer, the parents claimed they would always feel pressure to join in the recitation.

Decision: By a 7–1 margin, the Court agreed with the parents and invalidated the school prayer. Justice Hugo Black wrote for the majority. He pointed out that prayer is clearly a religious activity and that under the First Amendment, promoting prayer "is no part of the business of government." The lone dissenter, Justice Potter Stewart, argued that the establishment clause forbids only the creation of an official state religion; it should not be interpreted to deny schoolchildren the opportunity to pray voluntarily.

Gideon v. Wainwright (1963)

Significance: This case established the right of all criminal defendants to be given a lawyer if they cannot afford one. The ruling reflected a growing concern to ensure equal justice for the poor.

Background: Clarence Earl Gideon was accused of robbery in Florida. Gideon could not afford a lawyer for his trial, and the judge refused to supply him with one for free. Gideon tried to defend himself and was found guilty. He eventually appealed to the U.S. Supreme Court, claiming that the lower court's denial of a court-appointed lawyer violated his Sixth and Fourteenth Amendment rights.

Decision: The Supreme Court ruled unanimously in Gideon's favor in 1963. The Court agreed that the Sixth Amendment's right to counsel requires the government to provide a lawyer if the defendant cannot afford one. The Court also agreed that the due process clause of the Fourteenth Amendment makes the Sixth Amendment's right to counsel binding on the states as well as on the federal government.

Heart of Atlanta Motel v. United States (1964)

Significance: This decision upheld the Civil Rights Act of 1964, which banned racial discrimination in places of public accommodation.

Background: The owner of the Heart of Atlanta Motel, a whites-only facility that served many interstate travelers, sued to overturn the Civil Rights Act of 1964. His primary argument was that the law went beyond Congress's authority to regulate interstate commerce under the commerce clause. A trial court ruled against the motel, and the owner appealed to the Supreme Court.

Decision: The Supreme Court found that Congress had carefully limited Title II of the Civil Rights Act to facilities that had a direct and substantial relation to the interstate flow of goods and people. Testimony before Congress had shown that Americans were increasingly mobile and that black travelers in particular often faced difficulty finding accommodations. Writing for a unanimous court, Justice Tom C. Clark concluded that Title II was therefore a valid exercise of congressional power under the commerce clause.

Tinker v. Des Moines Independent Community School District (1969)

Significance: This case established the right of public school students to express political opinions at school.

Background: Some high school and junior high school students in Des Moines, Iowa, planned to wear black armbands to school to show their opposition to the Vietnam War. Two days before they were going to start this protest, the school board created a new policy forbidding armbands at school. Three students, including Mary Beth Tinker and John Tinker, wore the armbands and were suspended. They sued the school district, claiming that the armband rule violated their First Amendment right of free speech.

The Decision: By a 7–2 margin, the Court agreed with the students. Justice Abe Fortas wrote that students do not "shed their constitutional rights to freedom of speech . . . at the schoolhouse gate." Protected speech includes not only spoken words but also "symbolic speech," or acts that express an opinion. Although school officials have the right to set rules, these rules must respect the First Amendment. Here the students had not been disruptive and their armbands did not interfere with anyone else's rights. Also, students were allowed to wear other political symbols, such as campaign buttons. School officials could not constitutionally pick which opinions students could express and which would be prohibited.

Reed v. Reed (1971)

Significance: This was the first case to hold that gender discrimination violates the Fourteenth Amendment equal protection clause. *Reed* v. *Reed* case was later used to strike down other statutes that discriminated against women.

Background: Cecil and Sally Reed were separated when their son Richard died. Each parent asked to be appointed administrator of Richard's modest estate. According to Idaho law at that time, when picking between two equally qualified administrators, "males must be preferred to females." When the judge appointed Cecil as the law required, Sally sued, challenging the gender preference in the law.

Decision: Chief Justice Warren Burger wrote the unanimous Supreme Court decision. Although some distinctions based on gender are permissible, the distinction must be reasonable rather than arbitrary. Because there is no reason to assume that men will be better administrators than women, the law did not have any rational basis. The Court therefore ruled that the law was unconstitutional. This did not mean that Sally would automatically get appointed, but it did require the probate judge to assess her qualifications and make a considered choice between her and Cecil.

Roe v. Wade (1973)

Significance: This case established a woman's right to an abortion as part of the constitutional right of privacy. The decision led to an ongoing battle in American politics between "pro-life" and "pro-choice" voters.

Background: In 1970 an unmarried, pregnant Texas woman filed suit to overturn the state's anti-abortion law. Texas, like many other states, had made it a crime for anyone to perform an abortion except to save the life of the mother. The case was argued before the Supreme Court in 1971 and then reargued at the Court's request in 1972. The plaintiff was called by a fictitious name, Jane Roe, to protect her privacy.

Decision: The Court voted 7–2 to invalidate the Texas law. Writing for the majority, Justice Harry Blackmun concluded that a woman's rights to privacy and control over her own body needed to be balanced against the state's interest in protecting maternal health and preserving the potentiality of human life. During the first trimester (three-month period) of pregnancy, abortion would be at the discretion of the woman and her physician. During the second trimester the state could impose restrictions related to the woman's health. In the final trimester the state could prohibit abortions entirely except where medically necessary to protect the life or health of the mother. Blackmun also concluded that the fetus did not have rights under the Fourteenth Amendment because the original intent of the Constitution and of that amendment was not to consider an unborn child as a "person." Justice Byron White wrote a strong dissent saying that nothing in the Constitution guaranteed the right to abortion.

United States v. Nixon (1974)

Significance: This decision led to the resignation of President Richard Nixon. The case confirmed that the president is not above the law and that the Supreme Court makes the final decision on constitutional questions.

Background: In 1972 senior Nixon administration officials helped plan, and then cover up, a break-in at the Democratic Party's campaign headquarters in the Watergate building in Washington. After the break-in came to light, a special prosecutor began a criminal investigation. He subpoenaed President Nixon to turn over secret tape recordings of conversations with his aides, but Nixon refused. He claimed "executive privilege," a right that past presidents had asserted to withhold information from other branches of government in order to protect confidentiality or the public good.

Decision: In a unanimous opinion written by Chief Justice Warren Burger, the Supreme Court ordered President Nixon to deliver his secret Oval Office tapes to the special prosecutor. The Court insisted that the president is not immune from the judicial process. Executive privilege may be invoked under certain circumstances, but in this case, President Nixon did not claim that military, diplomatic, or sensitive national security matters were at stake. Moreover, under the constitutional separation of powers, the legitimate needs of the courts in criminal proceedings may outweigh the President's need for confidentiality.

Texas v. Johnson (1989)

Significance: This case decided whether the First Amendment allows the burning of the U.S. flag as a form of symbolic speech. The decision has been controversial because it involves the flag, one of our national symbols. Since this case was decided, several amendments banning flag burning have been proposed in Congress but have not been adopted.

Background: Gregory Lee Johnson burned an American flag as part of a political demonstration during the 1984 Republican National Convention in Dallas, Texas. Johnson was convicted of violating a Texas law that made it a crime to desecrate, or treat disrespectfully, the national flag. He was sentenced to one year in prison and fined $2,000. The Texas Court of Criminal Appeals reversed Johnson's conviction, reasoning that burning the flag was a form of symbolic speech protected by the First Amendment. Texas then appealed to the U.S. Supreme Court.

Decision: The Court ruled for Johnson, 5–4, in an opinion written by Justice William Brennan. Brennan accepted the argument that flag burning is constitutionally protected as a form of symbolic speech—like the students wearing armbands in *Tinker* v. *Des Moines Independent Community School District* (1969). Brennan recognized that many people might be deeply upset by Johnson's actions, but he wrote that "government may not prohibit the expression of an idea [because it is] offensive." Chief Justice William Rehnquist dissented, writing that "for more than 200 years, the

American flag has occupied a unique position as the symbol of our Nation, a uniqueness that justifies a governmental prohibition against flag burning in the way respondent Johnson did here."

Cruzan v. Director, Missouri Department of Health (1990)

Significance: This was the first "end of life" medical treatment case to reach the Supreme Court. In its ruling, the Court recognized that even unconscious patients have the right to refuse medical care (through their parents or guardians). At the same time, the Court allowed the states flexibility in setting standards for deciding whether to approve the termination of treatment.

Background: Nancy Cruzan was seriously injured in an auto accident. Because she was unable to swallow, her doctors put in a feeding tube to give her food and liquids. She remained unconscious in a persistent vegetative state for years afterwards. Eventually, when it became clear that she had virtually no chance of improvement, her parents asked the Missouri Supreme Court to instruct the doctors to stop administering food and liquids artificially. This action would have ended Cruzan's life. The state court denied the parents' request because they had not presented "clear and convincing" evidence of what their daughter would have wanted, as required by Missouri law. The parents then asked the U.S. Supreme Court to hear the case.

Decision: Chief Justice William Rehnquist wrote for the majority in a 5–4 decision. He stated that Missouri could constitutionally decline to grant the parents' request where they had not presented "clear and convincing" evidence that Cruzan herself would have wanted feeding and hydration discontinued. Although the Court upheld the state's right to set standards for deciding when medical treatment can be terminated, it also was willing to assume that people have a constitutional right to refuse life-sustaining medical treatment such as feeding by a tube. The decision left open the possibility that the parents could return to the trial court with more conclusive evidence of their daughter's wishes, which they eventually did. The trial court ultimately authorized removal of the feeding tube, and Cruzan died soon afterwards.

Planned Parenthood of Southeastern Pennsylvania v. Casey (1992)

Significance: This case upheld the basic premise of *Roe* v. *Wade,* even though the Supreme Court had become more conservative with the appointment of several new justices. The decision introduced a more flexible legal approach that gave state legislatures more leeway in imposing restrictions on abortions.

Background: Pennsylvania's 1982 Abortion Control Act outlined three conditions that had to be met before an abortion could be performed. First, under an "informed consent" rule, doctors were required to tell women the health risks and possible complications of having an abortion. This information had to be provided at least 24 hours in advance of the procedure. Second, a "spousal notification" rule required married women to notify their husbands. Third, a "parental notification" rule required minors to notify their parents. Five abortion clinics and one physician brought suit to challenge the constitutionality of these requirements.

Decision: The Supreme Court issued a plurality decision, meaning that no single opinion had the support of a majority of the justices. Justices Sandra Day O'Connor, Anthony Kennedy, and David Souter wrote the plurality opinion and other justices joined in various parts. The decision created a new "undue burden" standard for abortion cases, saying that abortion laws must not have "the purpose or effect of placing a substantial obstacle in the path of a woman seeking an abortion of a nonviable fetus." Using this standard, the Court invalidated the spousal notification requirement because it gave husbands too much control over their wives' medical decisions and would be dangerous in cases of spousal abuse. However, the Court accepted the 24-hour waiting period and the informed consent and parental notification requirements, finding that none of these imposed an undue burden on abortion seekers.

Vernonia School District v. Acton (1995)

Significance: This decision allowed schools to administer drug tests to all students who wanted to play sports. The case paved the way for *Board of Education* v. *Earls* (2002), which allowed drug testing for students in all extracurricular activities.

Background: In an effort to reduce drug use, particularly among student athletes, the Vernonia (Oregon) School District started a program for random urinalysis drug testing of students participating in sports. Jason Acton signed up for seventh grade football, but he and his parents refused to sign the consent form for drug testing. When he was not allowed to play, he sued the school district. In his view, the drug testing constituted an unreasonable search of his body, in violation of the Fourth Amendment. The trial court dismissed the case but an appellate court reinstated it. Eventually the case went to the Supreme Court.

Decision: In a 6–3 decision, the Supreme Court upheld the school district's drug testing policy. Justice Antonin Scalia wrote that the district's collection and testing of urine amounted to a reasonable search. Vernonia students could choose whether or not to go out for sports, and those who did could expect some restrictions and intrusions on their privacy. The urine samples were collected in ways that minimized the violation of students' privacy. Moreover, given the government's interest in reducing student drug use, the extent of the search was reasonable and permissible. In dissent, Justice Sandra Day O'Connor argued that the blanket testing of student athletes was more intrusive and less reasonable than a suspicion-based testing of students who actually appeared to be using drugs.

Bush v. Gore (2000)

Significance: As a practical matter, this case decided the 2000 presidential election, confirming George W. Bush as the winner. The question before the Court was whether ballots that could not be read by voting machines should be recounted by hand. The broader issue was whether the Supreme Court would overrule the Florida Supreme Court on its interpretation of Florida state law.

Background: The 2000 presidential election between Democrat Al Gore and Republican George W. Bush was extremely close. As the votes were counted, it became clear that the winner of Florida's electoral votes would win the election. According to the first count, Bush won the state of Florida by a few hundred votes, and Florida's Election Commission declared Bush the victor. However, about 60,000 ballots were not counted because of problems reading them mechanically. Gore challenged the outcome, and the Florida Supreme Court ordered counties to recount all those votes by hand. Bush appealed to the U.S. Supreme Court, which ordered a halt to the recounts while it considered the case.

The Decision: On December 12, 2000, the Supreme Court voted 5–4 to end the hand recount of votes. The majority said that the Florida Supreme Court had ordered the recount without clarifying what was a valid vote. The contested ballots were not always clearly marked, and different vote counters might use different standards to tally them. The Court said that this inconsistency meant that votes were treated arbitrarily, based on a counter's choice rather than on fixed standards. This arbitrariness violated the due process and equal protection clauses of the Constitution. Furthermore, because the deadline for counting the votes under Florida law had expired, there was no time for the state to create new rules for the recount.

Hamdi v. Rumsfeld and Rasul v. Bush (2004)

Significance: These cases considered whether the Constitution's promise of due process applies to Americans or foreigners accused of fighting against the United States in its war on terror. The prisoners in both cases sought access to lawyers and the right to have their incarceration reviewed by an American court.

Background **Detaining American Citizens:** Yaser Hamdi, an American citizen, was captured in Afghanistan in 2001 and accused of fighting for the Taliban against the United States. The U.S. military declared Hamdi an "enemy combatant" and claimed the right to hold him indefinitely without trial and without access to an attorney.

Detaining Foreigners at Guantanamo Bay: Shafiq Rasul and two other foreign nationals were captured abroad and confined for over two years at Guantanamo Bay Naval Base in Cuba. They tried to challenge the legality of their detention in the U.S. courts. Cuba leases the base to the United States. In a World War II era case, the Court had ruled that "if an alien is outside the country's sovereign territory, then . . . the alien is not permitted access to the courts of the United States to enforce the Constitution."

Decisions: Although there was no majority decision in *Hamdi,* the Court ruled 6–3 that Hamdi had a right to a limited hearing at which he could contest the government's determination that he was an enemy combatant. Justice Sandra Day O'Connor wrote that "a state of war is not a blank check for the president when it comes to the rights of the nation's citizens." Hamdi was ultimately released to Saudi Arabia in October, 2004, after agreeing to give up his U.S. citizenship.

In *Rasul,* a six-justice majority concluded that the prisoners had the right to go to the federal courts for review of their claims that they were unlawfully held in indefinite detention. The government eventually released two of the prisoners in *Rasul* and announced its intention to try the third before a military tribunal. Other cases have been filed challenging the constitutionality of the military tribunals.

Facts About the States

State	Year of Statehood	2005 Population	Area (Sq. Mi.)	Population Density (Sq Mi.)	Capital
Alabama	1819	4,527,166	50,744	89.2	Montgomery
Alaska	1959	661,110	571,951	1.2	Juneau
Arizona	1912	5,868,004	113,635	51.6	Phoenix
Arkansas	1836	2,777,007	52,068	53.3	Little Rock
California	1850	36,038,859	155,959	231.1	Sacramento
Colorado	1876	4,617,962	103,718	44.5	Denver
Connecticut	1788	3,503,185	4,845	723.1	Hartford
Delaware	1787	836,687	1,954	428.2	Dover
District of Columbia*	—	551,136	61	9,035.0	—
Florida	1845	17,509,827	53,927	324.7	Tallahassee
Georgia	1788	8,925,796	57,906	154.1	Atlanta
Hawaii	1959	1,276,552	6,423	198.7	Honolulu
Idaho	1890	1,407,060	82,747	17.0	Boise
Illinois	1818	12,699,336	55,584	228.5	Springfield
Indiana	1816	6,249,617	35,867	174.2	Indianapolis
Iowa	1846	2,973,700	55,869	53.2	Des Moines
Kansas	1861	2,751,509	81,815	33.6	Topeka
Kentucky	1792	4,163,360	39,728	104.8	Frankfort
Louisiana	1812	4,534,310	43,562	104.1	Baton Rouge
Maine	1820	1,318,557	30,862	42.7	Augusta
Maryland	1788	5,600,563	9,774	573.0	Annapolis
Massachusetts	1788	6,518,868	7,840	831.5	Boston
Michigan	1837	10,207,421	56,804	179.7	Lansing
Minnesota	1858	5,174,743	79,610	65.0	St. Paul

*Note: The District of Columbia is a Federal District; it is not a state.

State	Year of Statehood	2005 Population	Area (Sq. Mi.)	Population Density (Sq Mi.)	Capital
Mississippi	1817	2,915,696	46,907	62.2	Jackson
Missouri	1821	5,765,166	68,886	83.7	Jefferson City
Montana	1889	933,005	145,552	6.4	Helena
Nebraska	1867	1,744,370	76,872	22.7	Lincoln
Nevada	1864	2,352,086	109,826	21.4	Carson City
New Hampshire	1788	1,314,821	8,968	146.6	Concord
New Jersey	1787	8,745,279	7,417	1,179.1	Trenton
New Mexico	1912	1,902,057	121,356	15.7	Santa Fe
New York	1788	19,258,082	47,214	407.9	Albany
North Carolina	1789	8,702,410	48,711	178.7	Raleigh
North Dakota	1889	635,468	68,976	9.2	Bismarck
Ohio	1803	11,477,557	40,948	280.3	Columbus
Oklahoma	1907	3,521,379	68,667	51.3	Oklahoma City
Oregon	1859	3,596,083	95,997	37.5	Salem
Pennsylvania	1787	12,426,603	44,817	277.3	Harrisburg
Rhode Island	1790	1,086,575	1,045	1,039.8	Providence
South Carolina	1788	4,239,310	30,109	140.8	Columbia
South Dakota	1889	771,803	75,885	10.2	Pierre
Tennessee	1796	5,965,317	41,217	144.7	Nashville
Texas	1845	22,775,044	261,797	87.0	Austin
Utah	1896	2,417,998	82,144	29.4	Salt Lake City
Vermont	1791	630,979	9,250	68.2	Montpelier
Virginia	1788	7,552,581	39,594	190.8	Richmond
Washington	1889	6,204,632	66,544	93.2	Olympia
West Virginia	1863	1,818,887	24,078	75.5	Charleston
Wisconsin	1848	5,554,343	54,310	102.3	Madison
Wyoming	1890	507,268	97,100	5.2	Cheyenne

American Flag Etiquette

The American flag is a symbol of the nation. It is recognized instantly, whether as a big banner waving in the wind or a tiny emblem worn on a lapel. The flag is so important that it is a major theme of the national anthem, "The Star-Spangled Banner." One of the most popular names for the flag is the Stars and Stripes. It is also known as Old Glory.

THE MEANING OF THE FLAG

The American flag has 13 stripes—7 red and 6 white. In the upper-left corner of the flag is the union—50 white five-pointed stars against a blue background.

The 13 stripes stand for the original 13 American states, and the 50 stars represent the states of the nation today. According to the U.S. Department of State, the colors of the flag also are symbolic:

Red stands for courage.

White symbolizes purity.

Blue is the color of vigilance, perseverance, and justice.

DISPLAYING THE FLAG

It is customary not to display the American flag in bad weather. It is also customary for the flag to be displayed outdoors only from sunrise to sunset, except on certain occasions. In a few special places, however, the flag is always flown day and night. When flown at night, the flag should be illuminated.

Near a speaker's platform, the flag should occupy the place of honor at the speaker's right. When carried in a parade with other flags, the American flag should be on the marching right or in front at the center. When flying with the flags of the 50 states, the national flag must be at the center and the highest point. In a group of national flags, all should be of equal size and all should be flown from staffs, or flagpoles, of equal height.

The flag should never touch the ground or the floor. It should not be marked with any insignia, pictures, or words. Nor should it be used in any disrespectful way—as an advertising decoration, for instance. The flag should never be dipped to honor any person or thing.

SALUTING THE FLAG

The United States, like other countries, has a flag code, or rules for displaying and honoring the flag. For example, all those present should stand at attention facing the flag and salute it when it is being raised or lowered or when it is carried past them in a parade or procession. A man wearing a hat should take it off and hold it with his right hand over his heart. All women and hatless men should stand with their right hands over their hearts to show their respect for the flag. The flag should also receive these honors during the playing of the national anthem and the reciting of the Pledge of Allegiance.

THE PLEDGE OF ALLEGIANCE

The Pledge of Allegiance was written in 1892 by Massachusetts magazine (*Youth's Companion*) editor Francis Bellamy. (Congress added the words "under God" in 1954.)

I pledge allegiance to the flag of the United States of America and to the republic for which it stands, one nation under God, indivisible, with liberty and justice for all.

Civilians should say the Pledge of Allegiance with their right hands placed over their hearts. People in the armed forces give the military salute. By saying the Pledge of Allegiance, we promise loyalty ("pledge allegiance") to the United States and its ideals.

Biographical Dictionary

Abernathy, Ralph (1926–1990) Martin Luther King Jr.'s successor as head of the Southern Christian Leadership Conference; he led the Poor People's Campaign after King's death. (p. 939)

Adams, Abigail (1744–1818) Wife of President John Adams, mother of President John Quincy Adams, writer, and American feminist, she was also the first First Lady to live in what was later known as the White House. (p. 120)

Adams, John (1735–1826) American statesman; he was a delegate to the Continental Congress, a member of the committee that drafted the Declaration of Independence, vice president to George Washington and second president of the United States. (p. 115)

Adams, John Quincy (1767–1848) Son of President John Adams and secretary of state to James Monroe; he largely formulated the Monroe Doctrine. He was the sixth president of the United States and later became a representative in Congress. (p. 241)

Adams, Samuel (1722–1803) American revolutionary who led the agitation that led to the Boston Tea Party; he signed the Declaration of Independence. (p. 107)

Addams, Jane (1860–1935) American social worker and activist; she was the co-founder of Hull House, an organization that focused on the needs of immigrants. She won the Nobel Peace Prize in 1931. (p. 498)

Aguinaldo, Emilio (1869–1964) Self-proclaimed President of the new Philippine Republic in 1899; he fought for Filipino independence from the United States. (p. 561)

Anderson, Marian (1897–1993) Singer who fought discrimination in the 1930s; Eleanor Roosevelt arranged for her to perform on the steps of the Lincoln Memorial in 1939. (p.723)

Anderson, Robert (1805–1871) Union commander in charge of Fort Sumter when it was attacked by the Confederacy. (p. 357)

Anthony, Susan B. (1820–1906) American social reformer; she was active in the temperance, abolitionist, and women's suffrage movements and was co-organizer and president of the National Woman Suffrage Association. (p. 532)

Armstrong, Louis (1901–1971) Leading African American jazz musician during the Harlem Renaissance; he was a talented trumpeter whose style influenced many later musicians. (p. 659)

Armstrong, Neil (1930–) American astronaut; he was the first man to set foot on the moon. (p. 1023)

Arthur, Chester A. (1829–1886) Vice president of the United States in 1880; he became the twenty-first president of the United States upon the death of James Garfield (p. 502)

Austin, Moses (1767–1828) American banker who requested land in Texas from the Mexican government on which to build a colony; he died before he received the land and his son, Stephen Austin, later founded a colony there. (p. 303)

Austin, Stephen F. (1793–1836) American colonizer in Texas; after helping Texas win independence from Mexico, he became secretary of state for the Texas Republic. (p. 303)

Ball, Lucille (1911–1989) Actress and star of the television comedy series *I Love Lucy*, one of the most popular programs of the 1950s. (p. 862)

Baltimore, Lord (1580?–1632) (also known as George Calvert) English and the first Lord Baltimore; he requested land to establish a colony for Catholics in America, but died before it was granted. His son, the second Lord Baltimore later established a settlement in Maryland in 1632. (p. 65)

Barton, Clara (1821–1912) Founder of the American Red Cross; she administered care to the Union soldiers during the American Civil War. (p. 378)

Baruch, Bernard (1870–1965) American business leader and head of the War Industries Board during World War I; he later advised many American political leaders. (p. 599)

Beecher, Catharine (1800–1878) American educator and the daughter of Lyman Beecher; she promoted education for women in such writings as *An Essay on the Education of Female Teachers*. She founded the first all-female academy. (p. 282)

Bell, Alexander Graham (1847–1922) American inventor and educator; his interest in electrical and mechanical devices to aid the hearing-impaired led to the development and patent of the telephone. (p. 479)

Bell, John (1797–1869) American politician; he was nominated for president in 1860 by the Constitutional Union Party because of his moderate pro-slavery and pro-Union views. (p. 342)

Bethune, Mary McLeod (1875–1955) African American leader and advocate; she served as Director of Negro Affairs in the National Youth Administration and led the Black Cabinet of unofficial African American advisors to Franklin D. Roosevelt. (p. 718)

bin Laden, Osama (1957–) Founder of al Qaeda, the terrorist network responsible for the attacks of September 11, 2001 and other attacks. (p. 1094)

Booth, John Wilkes (1838–1865) Actor and Confederate supporter who assassinated Abraham Lincoln. (p. 407)

Bradford, William (1590–1657) Leader of the Pilgrims who came to New England aboard the Mayflower and established a colony at Plymouth; he served as the governor of Plymouth from 1621 to 1656. (p. 52)

Bradley, Omar (1893–1981) American general who led the Allied troops in Operation Overlord during World War II. (p. 775)

Breckinridge, John C. (1821–1875) American politician; he served as vice president under President James Buchanan and ran for president as a Southern Democrat in 1860. (p. 342)

Brown, John (1800–1859) American abolitionist; he started the Pottawatomie Massacre in Kansas to revenge killings of abolitionists. He later seized the federal arsenal at Harpers Ferry, Virginia, to encourage a slave revolt. He was tried and executed. (p. 331)

Brutus Name used by Robert Yates (1738–1801), an American lawyer and leader of the Antifederalists, when writing letters to the Constitutional Convention in opposition of the Constitution. (p. 159)

Bryan, William Jennings (1860–1925) American lawyer and Populist politician, he favored the free coinage of silver, an economic policy expected to help farmers. He was a Democratic candidate for president in 1896 and was defeated by William McKinley. He later led the prosecution in the Scopes Trial. (p. 505)

Buchanan, James (1791–1868) American politician and fifteenth president of the United States; he was chosen as the Democratic nominee for president in 1854 for being politically experienced and not offensive to slave states. (p. 332)

Burr, Aaron (1756–1836) American soldier, lawyer, senator, and vice president of the U.S. (1801–1805); he shot and killed Alexander Hamilton in a duel in 1804, was arrested for treason against the U.S. in 1807 and later acquitted. His trial ended his political career. (p. 215)

Bush, George H. W. (1924–) American politician and the forty-first president of the United States; he was president at the end of the Cold War and during Operation Desert Storm. (p. 1059)

Bush, George W. (1946–) American politician and the forty-third president of the United States; the son of former president George H.W. Bush. (p. 1085)

Calhoun, John C. (1782–1850) American politician and supporter of slavery and states' rights; he served as vice president to Andrew Jackson and was instrumental in the South Carolina nullification crisis. (p. 249)

Carmichael, Stokely (1941–1998) Civil rights activist in the United States; he was an important leader of the black nationalism movement in the 1960s. (p. 935)

Carnegie, Andrew (1835–1919) American industrialist and humanitarian; he focused his attention on steelmaking and made a fortune through his vertical integration method. (p. 469)

Carter, James Earl "Jimmy" (1924–) Thirty-ninth president of the United States; he negotiated a peace agreement between Israel and Egypt. He was awarded the Nobel Prize for Peace in 2002 for his work in international diplomacy. (p. 1033)

Castro, Fidel (1926–) Communist political leader of Cuba; he helped overthrow the Cuban government in 1959 and seized control of the country, exercising total control of the government and economy. (p. 880)

Chamberlain, Neville (1869–1940) British prime minister; he supported the policy of appeasement, allowing Hitler to gain land and power in the 1930s. (p. 745)

Chaplin, Charlie (1889–1977) British comedian and movie star; he became famous for playing the character of the "Little Tramp" in silent movies in the 1920s. (p. 662)

Chávez, César (1927–1993) American activist; he co-founded the National Farm Workers Association as part of his commitment to improving the working conditions of migrant workers on American farms. (p. 996)

Chiang Kai-shek (1887–1975) Leader of the Chinese Nationalist government and a strong U.S. ally; his government was defeated by the Communists in 1949. (p. 830)

Chief Joseph (c.1840–1904) Chief of the Nez Percé tribe; he led resistance against white settlement in the Northwest. He eventually surrendered, but his eloquent surrender speech earned him a place in American history. (p. 442)

Churchill, Winston (1874–1965) British prime minister; he opposed the policy of appeasement and led Great Britain through World War II. (p. 747)

Clark, George Rogers (1752–1818) American Revolutionary soldier and frontier leader; he captured the British trading village of Kaskaskia during the Revolution and encouraged Indian leaders to remain neutral. (p. 133)

Clark, William (1770–1838) American soldier and friend of Meriwether Lewis; he was invited to explore the Louisiana Purchase and joined what became known as the Lewis and Clark expedition. (p. 219)

Clemenceau, Georges (1841–1929) French Premier during World War I; he was a member of the Big Four at the Paris Peace Conference after World War I. (p. 607)

Cleveland, Grover (1837–1908) Twenty-second and twenty-fourth president of the United States; he promoted civil service reform and a merit system of advancement for government jobs. (p. 476)

Clinton, Hillary Rodham (1947–) American politician and lawyer; she was a particularly influential First Lady during her husband Bill Clinton's presidency. She was elected to the U.S. Senate in 2000. (p. 1079)

Clinton, William Jefferson "Bill" (1946–) Forty-second president of the United States; he became the second U.S. president to be impeached. (p. 1078)

Columbus, Christopher (1451–1506) Italian explorer who reached the Americas in 1492 while searching for a western sea route from Europe to Asia. (p. 30)

Coolidge, Calvin (1872–1933) Thirtieth president of the United States; he became president upon the death of President Warren G. Harding. He was known for his honesty and his pro-business policies. (p. 636)

Cornwallis, Charles (1738–1805) (Also known as Lord Cornwallis) British general and commander of the British army at the battle of Yorktown in 1781. After the defeat of the British army he was forced to surrender to the Americans, ending the American Revolution. (p. 134)

Coronado, Francisco Vázquez de (1510?–1554) Spanish explorer who explored parts of the southwestern United States in search of the legendary Seven Cities of Gold. (p. 42)

Cortés, Hernán (1485–1547) Spanish conquistador; he conquered Mexico and brought about the fall of the Aztec Empire. (p. 41)

Coughlin, Father Charles (1891–1979) Catholic priest and popular radio broadcaster; his broadcasts praised Hitler and criticized Franklin D. Roosevelt's New Deal policies. (p. 704)

Creel, George (1876–1953) Newspaper reporter and political reformer; he was appointed by President Woodrow Wilson to head the Committee on Public Information. (p. 603)

Custer, George Armstrong (1839–1876) American army officer in the Civil War; he became a Native American fighter in the West and was killed with his troops in the Battle of the Little Bighorn. (p. 441)

Darrow, Clarence (1857–1938) Famous American criminal lawyer; he defended John Scopes's right to teach evolution in the Scopes Trial. (p. 651)

Davis, Jefferson (1808–1889) First and only president of the Confederate States of America after the election of President Abraham Lincoln in 1860 led to the secession of many southern states. (p. 347)

Debs, Eugene V. (1855–1926) Leader of the American Railway Union and supporter of the Pullman strike; he was the Socialist Party candidate for president five times. (p. 476)

Dewey, George (1937–1917) Commander of the U.S. Navy's Asiatic Squadron; he led the attack in the Pacific during the Spanish-American War. (p. 560)

Díaz, Porfirio (1830-1915) Mexican general and politician; he was president and dictator of Mexico for a total of 30 years. He ruled the people of Mexico harshly but encouraged foreign investment. (p. 573)

Dix, Dorothea (1802–1887) American philanthropist and social reformer; she helped change the prison system nationwide by advocating the development of state hospitals to treat the mentally ill instead of imprisonment. (p. 269)

Dole, Sanford B. (1844–1926) American sugar tycoon; he helped overthrow Queen Liliuokalani and later served as president and governor of Hawaii. (p. 555)

Doolittle, James (1896–1993) U.S. Army officer; he won a promotion for leading a bombing raid on Tokyo and other Japanese cities during World War II. (p. 787)

Douglas, Stephen A. (1813–1861) American politician and pro-slavery nominee for president; he debated Abraham Lincoln about slavery during the Illinois senatorial race. He proposed the unpopular Kansas-Nebraska Act, and he established the Freeport Doctrine, upholding the idea of popular sovereignty. (p. 325)

Douglass, Frederick (1817–1895) American abolitionist and writer, he escaped slavery and became a leading African American spokesman and writer. He published an autobiography, *The Narrative of the Life of Frederick Douglass*, and founded the abolitionist newspaper, the *North Star*. (p. 289)

Drake, Edwin L. (1819–1880) He drilled the first commercial oil well in the United States, drawing oil prospectors to the West. (p. 461)

Drake, Sir Francis (c.1540–1596) English naval captain; he circumnavigated the globe in 1577, plundering Spanish ships and towns as he sailed. (p. 45)

Du Bois, W. E. B. (1868–1963) African American educator, editor, and writer; he led the Niagara Movement, calling for economic and educational equality for African Americans. He helped found the National Association for the Advancement of Colored People (NAACP). (p. 509)

Dulles, John Foster (1888–1959) Secretary of State under President Dwight D. Eisenhower; he favored building up the American nuclear arsenal as part of an effort to decrease Soviet influence around the world. (p. 849)

BIOGRAPHICAL DICTIONARY

Earhart, Amelia (1897–1937?) American pilot; she was the first woman to fly across the Atlantic Ocean and set many speed and distance records. She disappeared over the Pacific Ocean in 1937. (p. 663)

Edison, Thomas Alva (1847–1931) American inventor of over 1,000 patents; he invented the light bulb and established a power plant that supplied electricity to parts of New York City. (p. 480)

Edwards, Jonathan (1703–1758) Important and influential revivalist leader in the Great Awakening religious movement; he delivered dramatic sermons on the choice between salvation and damnation. (p. 86)

Eisenhower, Dwight D. (1890–1969) Thirty-fourth president of the United States; he led the Allied invasion of North Africa and the D-Day invasion of France and commanded the Allied forces in Europe during World War II. He faced many Cold War challenges as president. (p. 773)

Emerson, Ralph Waldo (1803–1882) American essayist and poet; he was a supporter of the transcendentalist philosophy of self-reliance. (p. 269)

Equiano, Olaudah (c.1750–1797) African American abolitionist; he was an enslaved African who was eventually freed, became a leader of the abolitionist movement, and wrote *The Interesting Narrative of the Life of Olaudah Equiano*. (p. 82)

Eriksson, Leif (c.980–?) Viking seaman who was the first European to land on the continent of North America (p. 30)

Evers, Medgar (1925–1963) Head of the NAACP in Mississippi, he was shot and killed in front of his home in 1963 by a member of the Ku Klux Klan. (p. 922)

Falwell, Jerry (1933–2007) American evangelist; he founded an organization called the Moral Majority that is known for its conservative views. (p. 1049)

Farmer, James (1920–1999) American civil rights leader and founder of the Congress of Racial Equality (CORE); he believed in the practice of nonviolence as a means of achieving his organization's goals. (p. 917)

Fillmore, Millard (1800–1874) Thirteenth president of the United States; he oversaw the passage of the Compromise of 1850. (p. 325)

Ferraro, Geraldine (1935–) Democratic representative of New York; in 1984 she became the first female vice presidential candidate on a major party ticket. (p. 1069)

Finney, Charles Grandison (1792–1875) American clergyman and educator; he became influential in the Second Great Awakening after a dramatic religious experience and conversion. (p. 267)

Fitzgerald, F. Scott (1896–1940) American writer famous for his novels and stories, such as *The Great Gatsby*, capturing the mood of the 1920s. He gave the decade the nickname the "Jazz Age." (p. 664)

Ford, Gerald R. (1913–2006) Thirty-eighth president of the United States; he became President after the resignation of Richard Nixon. (p. 1031)

Ford, Henry (1863–1947) American business leader; he revolutionized factory production through use of the assembly line and popularized the affordable automobile. (p. 629)

Franco, Francisco (1892–1975) Fascist dictator of Spain; he led the nationalists to victory in the Spanish Civil War in the 1930s and controlled the Spanish government for nearly 40 years. (p. 742)

Franklin, Benjamin (1706–1790) American statesman; he was a philosopher, scientist, inventor, writer, publisher, first U.S. postmaster, and member of the committee to draft the Constitution. (p. 84)

Franz Ferdinand, Archduke (1863–1914) Heir to the throne of Austria-Hungary whose assassination by a Serb nationalist started World War I. (p. 582)

Frémont, John (1813–1890) American explorer, army officer, and politician; he was chosen as the first Republican candidate for president. Against the spread of slavery, he was rejected by all but the free states as a "single issue" candidate in the election of 1856. (p. 332)

Friedan, Betty (1921–2006) American feminist and writer; her book, *The Feminine Mystique*, explored the frustrations of women with their domestic lives in the 1950s and 1960s. (p. 988)

Fulbright, J. William (1905–1995) American politician, he was a U.S. senator from Arkansas who was chairman of the Senate Foreign Relations Committee from 1959 to 1974 and strongly advocated peace talks in the Vietnam War. (p. 963)

Fulton, Robert (1765–1815) American engineer and inventor; he built the first commercially successful full-sized steamboat, the *Clermont*, which led to the development of commercial steamboat ferry services for goods and people. (p. 255)

Gálvez, Bernardo de (1746–1786) Governor of Spanish Louisiana; he captured key cities from the British, greatly aiding the American Patriot movement and enabling the Spanish acquisition of Florida. (p. 134)

Gandhi, Mohandas (1869–1948) Leader of India's struggle for independence from Great Britain; he taught nonviolent resistance, which was later practiced by many civil rights leaders in the 1950s and 1960s. (p. 917)

Garfield, James A. (1831–1881) Twentieth president of the United States; he was elected in 1880 but was assassinated only months after inauguration. (p. 502)

Garrison, William Lloyd (1805–1879) American journalist and reformer; he published the famous antislavery newspaper, the *Liberator*, and helped found the American Anti-Slavery Society, promoting immediate emancipation and racial equality. (p. 288)

Garvey, Marcus (1887–1940) African American leader who promoted self-reliance for African Americans; he started the Universal Negro Improvement Society (UNIA), which urged African Americans to take pride in their heritage. (p. 656)

Gates, Bill (1955–) American computer programmer and entrepreneur; he co-founded Microsoft Corporation, the world's largest computer software company. (p. 1066)

Gaulle, Charles de (1890–1970) French military and political leader; he led the Free French government and army in World War II. He remained an important figure in France's postwar government. (748)

George, David Lloyd (1863–1945) British prime minister during World War I; he was a member of the Big Four at the Paris Peace Conference in 1919. (p. 607)

Geronimo (1829–1909) Chiricahua Apache leader; he evaded capture for years and led an opposition struggle against white settlements in the American Southwest until his eventual surrender. (p. 442)

Gershwin, George (1898–1937) Composer whose famous piece "Rhapsody in Blue" showed the impact of jazz music on the 1920s. (p. 665)

Giuliani, Rudolph (1944 –) American lawyer and politician; he was the mayor of New York City from 1993 to 2002 and was praised for his leadership after the terrorist attacks of September 11, 2001. (p. 1093)

Glidden, Joseph (1813–1906) Farmer who received a patent for barbed wire in 1874. (p. 448)

Göering, Hermann (1893–1946) German Nazi leader and one of Hitler's top assistants; he played a key role in persecuting Jews and in making Germany a totalitarian Nazi state before and during World War II. (p. 783)

Goldwater, Barry (1909–1998) American politician; he was a U.S. senator from Arizona and the Republican Party's presidential candidate in 1964. He was known for his extreme conservatism. (p. 897)

Gompers, Samuel (1850–1924) American labor leader; he helped found the American Federation of Labor to campaign for workers' rights. (p. 475)

Gonzales, Rodolfo "Corky" (1928–2005) Politician and activist; he founded an urban civil rights group called the Crusade for Justice and was a leader in the Chicano movement in the 1960s. (p. 997)

Gorbachev, Mikhail (1931–) Russian politician; he was the last president of the Soviet Union before the country's collapse in 1991. (p. 1055)

Gore, Al (1948–) American politician; he was vice president under President Clinton and the Democratic presidential candidate in the 2000 election. (p. 1079)

Grant, Ulysses S. (1822–1885) Eighteenth president of the United States; he received a field promotion to lieutenant general in charge of all Union forces. He accepted General Robert E. Lee's surrender at Appomattox Courthouse, ending the Civil War. (p. 366)

Greene, Nathaniel (1742–1786) American general during the Revolution and commander of the Army of the South; he is credited with having saved the Southern colonies from the British army. (p. 134)

Greenspan, Alan (1926–) American economist; he became Federal Reserve Board Chairman in 1987. (p. 1068)

Grenville, George (1712–1770) English politician whose policy of taxing the American colonists contributed to the start of the American Revolution. (p. 94)

Griffith, D.W. (1875–1948) Filmmaker who produced *Birth of a Nation* during World War I, which introduced many advanced filmmaking techniques. (p. 662)

Guthrie, Woody (1912–1967) American singer and songwriter; he wrote and performed songs about the experiences of common people during the Great Depression. He wrote the song "This Land Is Your Land." (p. 685)

Guitierrez, Jose Angel (1944–) American activist; he was among a group of students to found the Mexican American Youth Organization (MAYO) to work for Mexican American rights. (p. 997)

Hamer, Fannie Lou (1917–1977) American civil rights activist; she was a prominent leader of the Mississippi Freedom Democratic Party. (p. 928)

Hamilton, Alexander (1755–1804) American statesman and member of the Continental Congress and the Constitutional Convention; he was an author of the *Federalist Papers*, which supported ratification of the Constitution. He was the first secretary of treasury under George Washington and developed the Bank of the United States. (p. 204)

Harding, Warren G. (1865–1923) Twenty-ninth president of the United States; his policies favored business, but his administration was known for scandals. (p. 635)

Harrison, William Henry (1773–1841) American politician; he served as the governor of Indian Territory and fought Tecumseh in the Battle of Tippecanoe. He was the ninth president of the United States. (p. 225)

Hayes, Rutherford B. (1822–1893) Nineteenth president of the United States; he was a Civil War general and hero and, in the disputed presidential election of 1876, he was chosen president by a special electoral committee. (p. 426)

Hearst, William Randolph (1863–1951) American journalist; he was famous for sensational news stories, known as yellow journalism, that stirred feelings of nationalism and formed public opinion for the Spanish-American War. (p. 559)

Hiss, Alger (1904–1996) Former U.S. government official who was accused in 1948 of participating in a Communist spy ring. He denied the charges, but was convicted of lying under oath in 1950. (p. 832)

Hitler, Adolf (1889–1945) Totalitarian dictator of Germany; his invasion of European countries led to World War II. He believed in the supremacy of the German Aryan race and was responsible for the mass murder of millions of Jews and others in the Holocaust. (p. 741)

Ho Chi Minh (1890–1969) Vietnamese revolutionary leader and president of the Democratic Republic of Vietnam from 1945 to 1969; he wanted to bring communism to South Vietnam. (p. 949)

Hobby, Oveta Culp (1874–1964) Director of the Women's Army Corps during World War II; she held the rank of colonel. She later became the second woman cabinet member by serving as secretary of health, education, and welfare. (p. 760)

Hoover, Herbert (1874–1964) Thirty-first president of the United States; he helped save Europe from starvation after World War I but as president failed to deal effectively with the Great Depression. (p. 674)

Houston, Sam (1793–1863) American lawyer, politician, and soldier; he led U.S. settlers in a fight to secure Texas against Mexico and was instrumental in Texas' admission to the United States in 1845. (p. 306)

Huerta, Victoriano (1854–1916) Mexican general and politician; he overthrew Madero as Mexican president and faced revolts with many revolutionary leaders. His government was not recognized by the United States. (p. 573)

Hughes, Charles Evans (1862–1948) American politician who served as secretary of state and participated in the Washington Naval Conference. He served on the Supreme Court and helped the court deal with controversial New Deal laws. (p. 639)

Hughes, Langston (1902–1967) African American poet who described the rich culture of African American life using rhythms influenced by jazz music. He wrote of African American hope and defiance, as well as the culture of Harlem and had a major impact on the Harlem Renaissance (p. 657)

Humphrey, Hubert (1911–1978) American politician, he was vice president under President Johnson, and presidential candidate of the Democratic Party in 1968 after Johnson decided not to seek re-election. (p. 968)

Hurston, Zora Neale (1891–1960) African American writer and folklore scholar who played a key role in the Harlem Renaissance. (p. 654)

Hussein, Saddam (1937–2006) President of Iraq from 1979–2003; he began wars with Iran and Kuwait, and established a brutal dictatorship in Iraq. He was captured and removed from power in 2003 by American-led forces; in 2006 he was convicted by an Iraqi tribunal of crimes against humanity and was executed. (p. 1064)

Hutchinson, Anne (1591–1643) Puritan leader who angered other Puritans by claiming that people's relationship to God did not need guidance from ministers; she was tried and convicted of undermining church authorities and was banished from Massachusetts colony; she later established the colony of Portsmouth in present-day Rhode Island. (p. 54)

Isabella, Queen (1451–1504) Queen of Spain who, together with her husband, King Ferdinand II, believed in uniting Spain under Catholicism; she funded Columbus' expedition in search of the New World. (p. 26)

Jackson, Andrew (1767–1845) Nicknamed Old Hickory, he was an American hero in the Battle of New Orleans. He defeated the Creek Indians, securing 23 million acres of land and his election as the seventh president of the United States marked an era of democracy called Jacksonian Democracy. (p. 227)

Jackson, Jesse (1941–) American civil rights leader, minister, and politician; he was an adviser to Martin Luther King Jr. He became famous for his work on behalf of underprivileged peoples around the world, and mounted campaigns for the Democratic presidential nomination in the 1980s. (p. 941)

Jackson, Thomas "Stonewall" (1824–1863) American Confederate general; he led the Shenandoah Valley campaign and fought with Lee in the Seven Days' Battles and the First and Second Battles of Bull Run. (p. 364)

Jay, John (1745–1829) American statesman and member of the Continental Congress; he authored some of the Federalist Papers and negotiated Jay's Treaty with Great Britain to settle outstanding disputes. (p. 160)

Jefferson, Thomas (1743–1826) American statesman; he was member of two Continental Congresses, chairman of the committee to draft the Declaration of Independence, the Declaration's main author and one of its signers, and the third president of the United States. (p. 115)

Jobs, Steve (1955–) American entrepreneur; he founded Apple Computer in 1977, a company that helped popularize personal computers. (p. 1066)

Johnson, Andrew (1808–1875) American politician who became the seventeenth president of the United States upon the assassination of Lincoln. He was impeached for his unpopular ideas about Reconstruction and held onto the office by a one-vote margin. (p. 407)

Johnson, Hiram W. (1866–1945) Governor of California and U.S. senator; he helped form the Progressive Party, or Bull Moose Party, and ran as its vice presidential candidate with Theodore Roosevelt in 1912. (p. 543)

Johnson, James Weldon (1871–1938) NAACP leader and writer; he wrote poetry and, with his brother, the song "Lift Every Voice and Sing." He was a key figure in the Harlem Renaissance. (p. 657)

Johnson, Lyndon B. (1908–1973) Thirty-sixth president of the United States; he took office after the assassination of John F. Kennedy. (p. 882)

Kearney, Denis (1847-1907) Irish immigrant leader of the Workingmen's Party; he opposed Chinese immigration in California in the late 1870s. (p. 494)

Kearny, Stephen (1794–1848) American general who fought in the Mexican-American War, leading forces that captured New Mexico and helping in the capture of California from Mexico. (p. 310)

Kennan, George F. (1904–) American diplomat and expert on the Soviet Union; he developed the U.S. policy of containment to counter Soviet expansion after World War II. (p. 819)

Kennedy, Jacqueline (1929–1994) American First Lady; she was the wife of President Kennedy and was known for her style and social grace. (p. 888)

Kennedy, John F. (1917–1963) Thirty-fifth president of the United States; he was the youngest person and the first Roman Catholic elected president. He was assassinated in Dallas, Texas in 1963. (p. 879)

Kennedy, Robert (1925–1968) American politician; he was Attorney General during his brother President Kennedy's presidency, and was assassinated during his bid for the 1968 Democratic presidential nomination. (p. 879)

Keynes, John Maynard (1883–1946) British economist; his revolutionary economic theory provided the basis for some of Franklin D. Roosevelt's successful policies. (p. 716)

Khomeini, Ayatollah Ruhollah (1900?–1989) Islamic leader who led a revolution to overthrow Iran's government in 1979; he ruled the country for the next ten years on a strongly anti-American platform. (p. 1038)

Khrushchev, Nikita (1894–1971) Leader of the Soviet Union during the building of the Berlin Wall and the Cuban Missile Crisis. He and President Kennedy signed the Limited Nuclear Test Ban Treaty in 1963, temporarily easing Cold War tensions. (p. 850)

Kim Il Sung (1912–1994) Communist leader of North Korea; his attack on South Korea in 1950 started the Korean War. He remained in power until 1994. (p. 836)

King, Martin Luther Jr. (1929–1968) American civil rights leader; he was a celebrated and charismatic advocate of civil rights for African Americans in the 1950s and 1960s. He was assassinated in 1968. (p. 914)

Kissinger, Henry (1923–) German-born political scientist; he was an important foreign policy advisor during the 1960s and 1970s. He won the Nobel Prize for Peace for negotiating the cease-fire agreement that ended the Vietnam War. (p. 973)

La Follette, Robert M. (1855–1925) Progressive American politician; he was active in local Wisconsin issues and challenged party bosses. As governor, he began the reform program called the Wisconsin Idea to make state government more professional. (p. 527)

Lafayette, Marquis de (1757–1834) French statesman and officer who viewed the American Revolution as important to the world; he helped finance the Revolution and served as major general. (p. 130)

Lange, Dorothea (1895–1965) American photographer who recorded the Great Depression by taking pictures of the unemployed and rural poor. (p. 719)

Lee, Robert E. (1807–1870) American general; he refused Lincoln's offer to head the Union Army and agreed to lead Confederate forces. He successfully led several major battles until his defeat at Gettysburg, and he surrendered to the Union's Commander General Grant at Appomattox Courthouse. (p. 335)

Lewis, John L. (1880–1969) American labor leader, president of the United Mine Workers, and founder of the Congress of Industrial Organizations (CIO); he helped win labor victories through strategies such as the sit-down strike. (p. 712)

Lewis, John (1940–) American politician and civil rights activist; he took part in major protest and sit-ins in the 1960s and became the head of the Student Nonviolent Coordination Committee (SNCC). He was elected to Congress in 1986. (p. 941)

Lewis, Meriwether (1774–1809) Former army captain selected by President Jefferson to explore the Louisiana Purchase; he lead the expedition that became known as the Lewis and Clark expedition. (p. 219)

Liliuokalani (1838–1917) Queen of the Hawaiian Islands; she opposed annexation by the United States but lost power in a U.S.-supported revolt, which led to the installation of a new government in Hawaii. (p. 555)

Lincoln, Abraham (1809–1865) Sixteenth president of the United States; he promoted equal rights for African Americans in the famous Lincoln-Douglas debates. He issued the Emancipation Proclamation and set in motion the Civil War, determined to preserve the Union. He was assassinated in 1865. (p. 338)

Lindbergh, Charles A. (1902–1974) American pilot; he became the first person to fly alone across the Atlantic Ocean nonstop in 1927. He was a hero to millions of Americans. (p. 662)

Little Turtle (1752–1812) Chief of the tribe of Miami and Shawnee Native Americans; he won the greatest victory Native Americans had ever achieved over white armies in 1791. (p. 211)

Lodge, Henry Cabot (1850–1924) U.S. senator and head of the Committee of Foreign Relations; he led the reservationists in opposition to the League of Nations. (p. 609)

Long, Huey P. (1893–1935) Louisiana politician and senator; he criticized the New Deal and set up the Share Our Wealth Society. He wanted to tax wealthy Americans and give more money to poor Americans. (p. 704)

Longstreet, James (1809–1865) Confederate general who commanded Pickett's Charge at the Battle of Gettysburg. (p. 384)

Lowell, Francis (1775–1817) American industrialist who developed the Lowell system. He hired young women to live and work in his mill. (p. 253)

Lucas, Eliza (1722–1793) Plantation manager in the Carolinas; she was the first person to successfully grow Indigo in the colonies. (p. 81)

Luther, Martin (1483–1546) German monk who protested against the Catholic Church in 1517; which led to calls for reform and the movement known as the Reformation. (p. 25)

MacArthur, Douglas (1880–1964) American general, he commanded U.S. troops in the Southwest Pacific during World War II and administered Japan after the war ended. He later commanded UN forces at the beginning of the Korean War until he was removed by President Truman. (p. 787)

Madero, Francisco (1873–1913) President of Mexico after Porfirio Díaz fled the country; he tried to establish a democratic government in Mexico. (p. 573)

Madison, James (1751–1836) American statesman; he was a delegate to the Constitutional Convention, the fourth president of the United States, and the author of some of the *Federalist Papers*. He is called the "father of the Constitution" for his proposals at the Constitutional Convention. (p. 151)

Malcolm X (1925–1965) Well-known supporter of the Nation of Islam and black leader; he spoke in support of black separatism, black pride, and the use of violence for self-protection. (p. 936)

Mandela, Nelson (1918–) Former guerrilla fighter who helped end apartheid; he became the first black president of South Africa. (p. 1064)

Mann, Horace (1796–1859) American educator; he is considered the father of American public education. (p. 268)

Mansa Musa (died 1332) Leader of Mali who held power from 1307 to 1332. (p. 19)

Mao Zedong (1893–1976) Leader of the Chinese Communists, he led a successful revolution and established a Communist government in China in 1949. (p. 830)

Marshall, George C. (1880–1959) American general and politician; he led U.S. mobilization for World War II and helped plan the nation's war strategy. He also developed the postwar European Recovery Program called the Marshall Plan. (p. 759)

Marshall, Thurgood (1908–1993) American jurist; he was the first African American to serve on the Supreme Court. (p. 910)

Martí, José (1853–1895) Cuban writer and independence fighter; he was killed in battle but became a symbol of Cuba's fight for freedom. (p. 559)

Mauldin, Bill (1921–2003) American cartoonist whose World War II cartoons gave people at home a soldier's point of view on life in the army. (p. 795)

McCarthy, Eugene (1916–) American politician, he was a U.S. senator who vied for the 1968 Democratic presidential nomination against President Johnson. (p. 967)

McCarthy, Joseph (1908–1957) U.S. senator from Wisconsin who gained national fame in the late 1940s and early 1950s by aggressively charging that communists were working in the U.S. government. He lost support in 1954, after making baseless attacks on U.S. Army officials. (p. 833)

McClellan, George (1826–1885) American army general put in charge of Union troops and later removed by Lincoln for failure to press Lee's Confederate troops in Richmond. (p. 364)

McGovern, George (1922–) American politician; he was the Democratic candidate for the presidency in 1972 losing to Richard Nixon. (p. 976)

McKinley, William (1843–1901) Twenty-fifth president of the United States; he enacted protective tariffs in the McKinley Tariff Act of 1890 and acquired Cuba, Puerto Rico, Guam, and the Philippines during his administration. He was later assassinated. (p. 505)

McNamara, Robert S. (1916–) American businessman and public official; he was the U.S. secretary of defense from 1961–1968. (p. 967)

McNickle, D'Arcy (1904–1977) Native American activist; he drafted the Declaration of Indian Purpose, a document that asserted the rights of Native Americans in the United States. (p. 991)

McPherson, Aimee Semple (1890–1944) American fundamentalist preacher who was well-known for her glamorous presentation. (p. 650)

Meade, George (1815–1872) American army officer; he served as a Union general at major Civil War battles. He forced back General Lee's Confederate army at Gettysburg but failed to obtain a decisive victory. (p. 384)

Means, Russell (1939–) One leader of the American Indian Movement. (p. 992)

Meredith, James (1933–) Civil rights activist who entered the University of Mississippi after being denied admission because of his race. His entrance led to violent riots on the school's campus. (p. 920)

Minuit, Peter (1580–1638) Director General of the Dutch colony of New Netherland; he bought Manhattan from the Native Americans. (p. 45)

Mitchell, Billy (1879–1936) American general who supported the development of air power in the military. (p. 639)

Monroe, James (1758–1831) Leading Revolutionary figure, negotiator of the Louisiana Purchase, and the fifth president of the United States. He put forth the Monroe Doctrine that became the foundation of U.S. foreign policy. (p. 241)

Morse, Samuel F.B. (1791–1872) American artist and inventor; he applied scientists' discoveries of electricity and magnetism to develop the telegraph. (p. 255)

Mott, Lucretia (1793–1880) American reformer; she planned the Seneca Falls Convention with Elizabeth Cady Stanton, the first organized meeting for women's rights in the United States. (p. 283)

Muhammad, Askia (?–1538) Ruler of the West African kingdom of Songhai from 1493–1528; he was known for encouraging a revival of Muslim learning during his rule. (p. 20)

Muir, John (1838–1914) Naturalist who believed the wilderness should be preserved in its natural state. He was largely responsible for the creation of Yosemite National Park in California. (p. 539)

Mussolini, Benito (1883–1945) Italian Fascist leader; he ruled as Italy's dictator for more than 20 years beginning in 1922. His alliance with Adolf Hitler brought Italy into World War II. (p. 740)

Nation, Carry (1846–1911) Temperance advocate; she took extreme measures to further her cause by entering saloons in her native state of Kansas and smashing bottles of alcohol with a hatchet. (p. 531)

Nast, Thomas (1840–1902) American political cartoonist; he helped turn public attention to the corruption of Tammany Hall and Boss Tweed. (p. 501)

Ngo Dinh Diem (1901–1963) Vietnamese political leader; he became president of South Vietnam in 1955. He was assassinated in 1963. (p. 951)

Nimitz, Chester (1885–1966) American admiral; he won major victories in the Battle of the Coral Sea and the Battle of Midway, stopping the Japanese advance during World War II. (p. 788)

Nixon, Richard M. (1913–1994) Thirty-seventh president of the United States and vice-president under President Eisenhower; he resigned from his second term because of the Watergate scandal. (p. 849)

North, Oliver (1943–) Officer in the U.S Marines, he is known for his role in the Iran-Contra affair. (p. 1058)

O'Connor, Sandra Day (1930–) First woman on the Supreme Court; she was appointed by President Reagan in 1981 and announced her resignation in 2005. (p. 1069)

Oglethorpe, James (1696–1785) English soldier and humanitarian; he founded the colony of Georgia as a haven where debtors from England could come and begin new lives. (p. 63)

Oliver, James (1823–1908) American plow maker who developed a new plow with a sharper edge that helped farmers plow their fields with much less effort. (p. 453)

Olmsted, Frederick Law (1822–1903) American landscape architect; he designed New York City's Central Park, Boston's "Emerald Necklace" network of parks, and other urban parks. (p. 496)

Oppenheimer, J. Robert (1904–1967) American physicist; he led the Manhattan Project laboratory in Los Alamos, which developed the first nuclear bomb. (p. 762)

Oswald, Lee Harvey (1939–1963) The accused assassin of President Kennedy. (p. 892)

Otis, Elisha (1811–1861) American mechanic and inventor, he invented the mechanized safety elevator. (p. 496)

Paine, Thomas (1737–1809) American political philosopher and author; he urged an immediate declaration of independence from England in his anonymously and simply written pamphlet, *Common Sense*. (p. 117)

Palmer, A. Mitchell (1872–1936) U.S. attorney general and opponent of communism; he ordered the Palmer raids against radicals and aliens during the Red Scare of 1919 and 1920. (p. 624)

Parks, Rosa (1913–2005) American civil rights activist; she was arrested in 1955 after refusing to give her seat on a public bus to a white man. Her arrest led to a widespread bus boycott that was an important chapter in the civil rights movement. (p. 914)

Patton, George S. (1885–1945) American general; he was involved in North Africa, Italy, and the Battle of the Bulge during World War II. (p. 776)

Paul, Alice (1885–1977) American social reformer, suffragist, and activist; she was the founder of the National Woman's Party (NWP) that worked to obtain women's suffrage. (p. 544)

Penn, William (1644–1718) Quaker leader who founded a colony in Pennsylvania; the colony provided an important example of representative self-government and became a model of freedom and tolerance. (p. 60)

Perkins, Frances (1882–1965) First American woman to head an executive or cabinet department; she served as secretary of labor in Franklin D. Roosevelt's administration. She played an important role in shaping New Deal jobs programs and labor policy. (p. 718)

Pershing, John J. (1860–1948) American army commander; he commanded the expeditionary force sent into Mexico to find Pancho Villa. He was the major general and commander in chief of the American Expeditionary Forces in World War I. (p. 575)

Pierce, Franklin (1804–1869) Fourteenth president of the United States; he condemned Kansas's free-soil government as rebels, which led to the Sack of Lawrence in 1856. (p. 331)

Pike, Zebulon M. (1779–1813) Army officer sent on a mission to explore the West, he was ordered to find the headwaters of the Red River. He attempted to climb what is now known as Pikes Peak in Colorado. (p. 219)

Pinchot, Gifford (1865–1946) Conservationist who was chief of the Forest Service. Under his leadership millions of acres of land were added to the national forests under his leadership. (p. 540)

Pocahontas (c.1595–1617) Algonquian princess; she saved the life of John Smith when he was captured and sentenced to death by the Powhatan. She was later taken prisoner by the English, converted to Christianity, and married colonist John Rolfe. (p. 47)

Polk, James (1795–1849) Eleventh president of the United States; he negotiated the establishment of the Oregon Territory for the U.S. and acquired much land as a result of the Mexican-American War. (p. 299)

Pitt, William (1708–1778) English leader in Parliament who opposed taxing American colonists, but also opposed their requests for independence. (p. 93)

Ponce de León, Juan (1460–1521) Spanish explorer who explored Puerto Rico and became its governor in 1509. In 1513 he discovered landed off the east coast of Florida while looking for a fabled "fountain of youth" and claimed the region for Spain. (p. 41)

Pontiac (c.1720–1769) Ottawa chief who united the Great Lakes' Indians to try to halt the advance of European settlements. He attacked British forts in a battle known as Pontiac's Rebellion and eventually surrendered in 1766. (p. 94)

Popé Indian shaman who led a revolt of Pueblo Indiana in 1680 against the Spanish in present-day New Mexico, driving out the Spanish and restoring the Pueblo way of life. The Spanish retook the area upon his death in 1692, but the Pueblo culture remained a part of this region. (p. 44)

Powderly, Terence V. (1849–1924) American labor leader for the Knights of Labor; he removed the secrecy originally surrounding the organization, so it became the first truly national American labor union. (p. 474)

Powell, Colin L. (1937–) Chairman of the Joint Chiefs of Staff and later Secretary of State; he was instrumental in forming U.S. foreign policy in the Middle East. (p. 1089)

Powhatan (1550?–1618) Algonquin Indian chief who was the head of the Powhatan Confederacy of Algonquin Peoples; he was also the father of Pocahontas. (p. 47)

Publius (1811–1861) The author name used by James Madison, Alexander Hamilton, and John Jay when writing the *Federalist Papers*. (p. 160)

Pulitzer, Joseph (1847–1911) American journalist and newspaper publisher; he established the Pulitzer Prize for public service and advancement of education. (p. 559)

Pyle, Ernie (1900–1945) American journalist and war correspondent; he reported on World War II from the point of view of an ordinary soldier. (p. 795)

Randolph, A. Philip (1889–1979) African American union and civil rights leader; his protests during World War II led President Roosevelt to ban discrimination in government and defense jobs. (p. 763)

Reagan, Nancy (1921–) Wife of President Ronald Reagan; she headed a campaign against drugs. (p. 1049)

Reagan, Ronald (1911–2004) American politician and the fortieth president of the United States; his presidency focused on arms control, economics, and the end of the Cold War. (p. 1046)

Revels, Hiram (1822–1901) American clergyman, educator, and politician; he became the first African American in the U.S. Senate. (p. 418)

Rice, Condoleezza (1954–) American educator and politician; she was national security adviser (2001–2005) and secretary of state (2005–) under President George W. Bush. (p. 1089)

Riis, Jacob (1849–1914) Newspaper reporter, reformer, and photographer; his book, *How the Other Half Lives*, shocked Americans with its descriptions of slum conditions and led to tenement housing legislation in New York. (p. 522)

Robeson, Paul (1898–1976) African American actor and singer who promoted African American rights and left-wing causes. (p. 659)

Robinson, Jackie (1919–1972) American baseball player; he was the first black player in the major leagues. (p. 910)

Rochambeau, Count de (1725–1807) French general who led troops against the British Army during the Revolutionary War. (p. 134)

Rockefeller, John D. (1839–1937) American industrialist and philanthropist; he made a fortune in the oil business and used vertical and horizontal integration to establish a monopoly on the steel business. (p. 468)

Rockefeller, Nelson (1908–1979) Republican governor of New York and vice president under Ford. (p. 1031)

Rolfe, John (1585–1622) English colonist who was the first tobacco grower in Virginia, he helped make tobacco a profitable export to England; he married the Algonquian princess Pocahontas. (p. 48)

Rommel, Erwin (1891–1944) German general during World War II; he commanded the Afrika Korps and was nicknamed the Desert Fox for his leadership. (p. 772)

Roosevelt, Eleanor (1884–1962) Wife of President Franklin D. Roosevelt, social reformer, writer, and diplomat; she supported equal rights for women and African Americans. She served as the first U.S. ambassador to the United Nations. (p. 700)

Roosevelt, Franklin Delano (1882–1945) Thirty-second president of the United States; he was elected president four times. He led the United States during the major crises of the Great Depression and World War II. (p. 699)

Roosevelt, Theodore (1858–1919) Twenty-sixth president of the United States; he focused his efforts on trust busting, environmental conservation, and strong foreign policy. (p. 535)

 S

Sacagawea (1786?–1812) Shoshone woman who, along with French fur trapper husband, accompanied and aided Lewis and Clark on their expedition. (p. 219)

Salk, Jonas (1914–1995) Scientist who developed the polio vaccine in 1952. (p. 865)

Santa Anna, Antonio López de (1794–1876) Mexican general, president and dicatator; he fought in the Texas Revolution and seized the Alamo but was defeated and captured by Sam Houston at San Jacinto. (p. 305)

Schlafly, Phyllis (1924–) American conservative columnist; she is known for speaking out for conservative causes, such as her opposition to the Equal Rights Amendment (ERA). (p. 989)

Scott, Winfield (1786–1866) American army general who fought in the War of 1812, the Mexican-American War, and the Civil War; he also ran for president in 1852 but lost the election. (p. 311)

Seymour, Horatio (1810–1886) Democratic governor of New York; he was a presidential candidate in 1868. (p. 415)

Selassie, Haile (1892–1975) Emperor of Ethiopia; he resisted the Italian invasion of Ethiopia during World War II and later helped modernize Ethiopia. (p. 743)

Sherman, William Tecumseh (1820–1891) Union army officer; his famous March to the Sea captured Atlanta, Georgia, an important turning point in the war. (p. 391)

Sinclair, Upton (1878–1968) Novelist whose 1906 book, *The Jungle*, depicted the unsanitary conditions at a meatpacking plant. Public outcry from the book led to consumer-protection laws. (p. 538)

Singleton, Benjamin "Pap" (1809–1892) African American leader, community builder, and former slave; he encouraged African Americans to build their own communities in the West. He later supported Black Nationalism and encouraged African Americans to move to Africa. (p. 452)

Sitting Bull (c.1831–1890) Native American leader who became head chief of the entire Sioux nation. He encouraged other Sioux leaders to resist government demands to buy lands. (p. 441)

Slater, Samuel (1768–1835) English industrialist who brought a design for a textile mill to America; known as the founder of the American cotton industry. (p. 251)

Smith, Bessie (1898?–1937) African American blues singer during the Harlem Renaissance. (p. 659)

Smith, John (c.1580–1631) English colonist to the Americas who helped found Jamestown Colony. (p. 47)

Stalin, Joseph (1879–1953) Totalitarian dictator of the Soviet Union; he led the Soviet Union through World War II and created a powerful Soviet sphere of influence in Eastern Europe after the war. (p. 742)

Stanton, Elizabeth Cady (1815–1902) American suffrage leader; she organized the Seneca Falls Convention, the first organized meeting for women's rights in the United States. (p. 532)

Steffens, Lincoln (1866–1936) Muckraker and managing editor of *McClure's* magazine; he exposed government corruption in his 1904 book, *The Shame of the Cities*. (p. 523)

Stevens, Thaddeus (1792–1868) American lawyer and politician; he was the leader of the Radical Republicans in the Reconstruction effort and was an opponent and critic of Andrew Johnson's policies. (p. 406)

Stockman, David A. (1946–) American politician; he was appointed by President Reagan to help put his economics plan into action. (p. 1050)

Stowe, Harriet Beecher (1811–1896) American author and daughter of Lyman Beecher; she was an abolitionist and author of the famous antislavery novel, *Uncle Tom's Cabin*. (p. 325)

Stuyvesant, Peter (1612–1672) Director General of the Dutch colony of New Netherland; he surrendered New Netherland to England in 1664. (p. 61)

Sunday, Billy (c.1862–1935) American fundamentalist minister; used colorful language and powerful sermons to drive home the message of salvation through Jesus and to oppose radical and progressive groups. (p. 650)

Syngman Rhee (1875–1965) Korean leader who became president of South Korea after World War II and led South Korea during the Korean War. (p. 836)

T

Taft, William Howard (1857–1930) Twenty-seventh president of the United States; he angered progressives by moving cautiously toward reforms and by supporting the Payne-Aldrich Tariff. He lost Roosevelt's support and was defeated for a second term. (p. 541)

Tarbell, Ida (1857–1944) Investigative journalist; she wrote a report condemning the corrupt business practices of John D. Rockefeller in *McClure's* magazine. These articles became the basis for her book, *The History of the Standard Oil Company*. (p. 523)

Taylor, Zachary (1874–1850) American general and twelfth president of the United States, he led American troops during the Mexican-American War. He was the first president elected after the Mexican-American War, but died only 16 months after taking office. (p. 310)

Tecumseh (1768–1813) Shawnee chief who attempted to form an Indian confederation to resist white settlement in the Northwest Territory. (p. 225)

Thomas, Clarence (1948–) Associate justice on the Supreme Court; in 1991 he became the second African American to serve on the court. (p. 1071)

Thoreau, Henry David (1817–1862) American writer and philosopher; he wrote "Civil Disobedience," as well as his famous book, *Walden Pond*. (p. 270)

Tocqueville, Alexis de (1805–1859) French philosopher, politician and author; his work, *Democracy in America*, encouraged Americans to form their own culture rather than mimicking that of Europeans. (p. 239)

Tojo, Hideki (1884–1948) Japanese nationalist and general; he took control of Japan during World War II. He was later tried and executed for war crimes. (p. 750)

Townsend, Dr. Francis (1867–1960) New Deal critic who focused on the needs of older Americans; his ideas for a pension plan for retirees contributed to the formation of Social Security. (p. 705)

Travis, William (1809–1836) American lawyer and commander of Texas forces at the Alamo. (p. 306)

Truman, Harry (1884–1972) Thirty-third president of the United States; he became president upon the death of President Franklin D. Roosevelt. He led the United States through the end of World War II and the beginning of the Cold War. (p. 805)

Truth, Sojourner (1797–1883) African American abolitionist; she traveled the nation giving speeches about slavery and women's rights. (p. 288)

Tubman, Harriet (c.1820–1913) American abolitionist who escaped slavery and assisted other enslaved Africans to escape. She is the most famous Underground Railroad conductor. (p. 286)

Turner, Frederick Jackson (1861–1932) American historian; he developed the idea that the existence of the frontier made the United States distinctive. (p. 451)

Turner, Nat (1800–1831) American slave leader; he claimed that divine inspiration had led him to end the slavery system. He led the most violent slave revolt in U.S. history; he was tried, convicted, and executed. (p. 286)

Tweed, William Marcy (1823–1878) American politician, he gained control of New York City's Tammany Hall became known as Boss Tweed. He was convicted of stealing from the New York City treasury. (p. 501)

Tyler, John (1790–1862) Tenth president of the United States; he favored annexation of Texas and signed the joint resolution of Congress into law three days before his term ended in 1845. (p. 309)

V

Van Buren, Martin (1782–1862) Eighth president of the United States; he extended the 10-hour work day plan, initiated by Jackson, to include other groups in 1840. (p. 277)

Vanderbilt, Cornelius (1794–1877) American business leader who controlled the New York Central Railroad and up to 4,500 miles of railroad track; he later donated $1 million to a Tennessee university. (p. 470)

Villa, Francisco "Pancho" (1878–1923) Mexican bandit and revolutionary leader; he led revolts against Carranza and Huerta. He was pursued by the United States but evaded General Pershing. (p. 573)

Villaraigosa, Antonio (1953–) Latino mayor of Los Angeles, elected to office in 2005. (p. 1102)

Walesa, Lech (1943–) Polish labor leader and electrician, he was president of Poland from 1990–1995. (p. 1055)

Wald, Lillian (1867–1940) Founder of the Henry Street Settlement house in New York City. (p. 498)

Wallace, George (1919–1998) American politician; he was a four-time governor of Alabama who fought against segregation in the South in the 1960s. (p. 970)

Walker, David (1785–1830) African American abolitionist; he wrote the anti-slavery treatise *An Appeal to the Colored Citizens of the World*. (p. 288)

Warren, Earl (1891–1974) American jurist and politician, he was Chief Justice of the Supreme Court from 1953 to 1969. Under his leadership the court made many decisions that extended individual rights. (p. 890)

Washington, Booker T. (1856–1915) African American educator and civil rights leader; he was born into slavery and later became head of the Tuskegee Institute for career training for African Americans. (p. 509)

Washington, George (1732–1799) First president of the United States; he served as a representative to the Continental Congresses and commanded the Continental Army during the Revolutionary War. (p. 90)

Watie, Stand (1806–1871) Cherokee leader and Confederate general; he was the only Native American on either side to hold such rank in the war. (p. 382)

Webster, Noah (1758–1843) American author who published works on American grammar and language, his most famous work was *An American Dictionary of the English Language*, published in 1828, which included thousands of words that had not been previously defined in other dictionaries. (p. 240)

Westmoreland, William (1914–) American general in the U.S. Army; he was the commander of U.S. ground troops in South Vietnam during the Vietnam War. (p. 958)

Whitefield, George (1714–1770) British minister who held religious open-air meetings throughout the American colonies during the Great Awakening. (p. 86)

Whitney, Eli (1765–1825) American inventor whose cotton gin changed cotton harvesting procedures and enabled large increases in cotton production; he introduced the technology of mass production through the development of interchangeable parts in gun-making. (p. 256)

Wilhelm II, Kaiser (1859–1941) German emperor and king of Prussia; his militarism helped cause and prolong World War I. (p. 583)

Wilkie, Wendell (1892–1944) Franklins Roosevelt's opponent in the 1940 Presidential election. (p. 755)

Willard, Frances (1839–1898) Temperance and women's suffrage advocate, she was a leader in the Women's Christian Temperance Union (WCTU) and the Prohibition Party. (p. 531)

William and Mary King William III (1650–1702) and Queen Mary II (1662–1694); Rulers of Great Britain who replaced King James II as a result of the Glorious Revolution. (p. 74)

Williams, Roger (1603–1683) Puritan Separatist who was banished from the Massachusetts Bay Colony in 1635 for preaching that government and religion should be separate, and that settlers should compensate Native Americans for their land, rather than taking it. He later established a colony in Providence, Rhode Island in 1636 where all religions were welcome. (p. 54)

Wilson, Woodrow (1856–1924) Twenty-eighth president of the United States; he proposed the League of Nations after World War I. His reform legislation included direct election of senators, prohibition, and women's suffrage. He also created the Federal Reserve System and the Federal Trade Commission, and he enacted child labor laws. (p. 543)

Winthrop, John (1588–1649) Leader of the Massachusetts Bay Colony who led Puritan colonists to Massachusetts to establish an ideal Christian community; he later became the colony's first governor. (p. 53)

Wright, Orville (1871–1948) and **Wilbur** (1867–1912) American pioneers of aviation; they went from experiments with kites and gliders to piloting the first successful gas-powered airplane flight.

Young, Andrew (1932–) American politician with a background in the civil rights movement; he served as American ambassador to the United Nations under President Carter. (p. 941)

Yeltsin, Boris (1931–) Russian politician and president of Russia in the 1990s; he was the first popularly elected leader of the country. (p. 1062)

Zapata, Emiliano (1879–1919) Mexican revolutionary, he led the revolt against Porfirio Díaz in the south of Mexico during the Mexican Revolution. (p. 573)

The United States of America: Political

CANADA

WASHINGTON
- Puget Sound
- Seattle
- Tacoma
- Olympia ★
- Spokane
- Portland
- Franklin D. Roosevelt Lake
- Pend Oreille
- Columbia River

OREGON
- Salem ★
- Eugene

IDAHO
- Boise ★
- Sun Valley
- Pocatello
- Snake River

MONTANA
- Great Falls
- Helena ★
- Billings
- Flathead Lake
- Fort Peck Lake
- Missouri River
- Yellowstone River

NORTH DAKOTA
- Lake Sakakawea
- Bismarck ★

SOUTH DAKOTA
- Lake Oahe
- Pierre ★
- Rapid City

WYOMING
- Yellowstone Lake
- Cheyenne ★

NEBRASKA
- Platte River

NEVADA
- Pyramid Lake
- Reno
- Carson City ★
- Lake Tahoe
- Great Salt Lake
- Ogden
- Salt Lake City ★
- Provo
- Utah Lake

CALIFORNIA
- Cape Mendocino
- Goose Lake
- Shasta Lake
- Sacramento River
- Berkeley
- Oakland
- San Francisco
- San Francisco Bay
- Monterey Bay
- San Jose
- Sacramento ★
- San Joaquin River
- Fresno
- Las Vegas
- Santa Barbara
- Ventura
- Los Angeles
- Riverside
- Long Beach
- Palm Springs
- Anaheim
- Santa Ana
- San Diego
- Channel Islands
- Salton Sea

UTAH
- Green River

COLORADO
- Boulder
- Vail
- Denver ★
- Aspen
- Colorado Springs
- Pueblo
- Arkansas River

KANSAS

ARIZONA
- Flagstaff
- Phoenix ★
- Casa Grande
- Tucson
- Lake Powell
- Lake Mead
- Colorado River
- Gila River

NEW MEXICO
- Taos
- Santa Fe ★
- Albuquerque
- Las Cruces
- El Paso
- Canadian River

OKLAHOMA
- Oklahoma ★
- Amarillo
- Lawton

TEXAS
- Lubbock
- Abilene
- Fort Worth
- Midland
- Odessa
- Brazos River
- Pecos River
- Colorado River
- Amistad Reservoir
- Rio Grande
- San Antonio
- Austin
- Corpus Christi
- Laredo

PACIFIC OCEAN

MEXICO

To understand the relative locations of Alaska and Hawaii, as well as the vast distances separating them from the rest of the United States, see the world map.

HAWAII
- Kauai
- Niihau
- Oahu
- Honolulu
- Molokai
- Lanai
- Maui
- Kahoolawe
- Hilo
- Hawaii
- PACIFIC OCEAN

Scale:
0   75   150 Miles
0   75   150 Kilometers
Projection: Mercator

ALASKA
- ARCTIC OCEAN
- Arctic Circle
- Bering Strait
- RUSSIA
- Nome
- Yukon River
- St. Lawrence Island
- St. Matthew Island
- Nunivak Island
- Fairbanks
- Anchorage
- Valdez
- CANADA
- Skagway
- Juneau
- Kodiak Island
- Gulf of Alaska
- Alexander Archipelago

- Attu Island
- Bering Sea
- PACIFIC OCEAN

Scale:
0   250   500 Miles
0   250   500 Kilometers
Projection: Albers Equal Area

CANADA

MINNESOTA

Grand Forks
Fargo
Duluth
Superior
Marquette
Sault Ste. Marie

Red River
Minnesota River
Mississippi River

Lake Superior

MICHIGAN

Lake Huron

MAINE
Augusta
Portland

Burlington
Montpelier
VT
NH
Concord
Manchester
Boston
Worcester
Providence
Cape Cod

Lake Champlain
Hudson R.
Connecticut R.

WISCONSIN
Minneapolis
St. Paul
Green Bay
Madison
Milwaukee
Grand Rapids
Lansing
Saginaw
Detroit
Ann Arbor

Lake Ontario
Rochester
Syracuse
Albany
Springfield
MA
Hartford
CT RI
New Haven
Bridgeport
Jersey City
Newark
Yonkers
New York City
Long Island Sound
Long Island

NEW YORK
Buffalo
Lake Erie

Sioux Falls
Sioux City
IOWA
Cedar Rapids
Davenport
Des Moines

Rockford
Chicago
Gary
South Bend
Fort Wayne
Peoria

Toledo
Cleveland
Youngstown
Akron

OHIO
Columbus
Dayton
Cincinnati

PENNSYLVANIA
Allentown
Harrisburg
Pittsburgh
Philadelphia
Camden
Trenton
NJ
Atlantic City

Susquehanna River

Lake Michigan
Lake Erie

maha
ncoln
Topeka
Wichita
Kansas City
Kansas City

MISSOURI
Springfield
St. Louis
East St. Louis

ILLINOIS
Springfield
Indianapolis

INDIANA

Illinois River
Missouri River

Jefferson City
Lake of the Ozarks

Louisville
Evansville
Frankfort
Lexington

KENTUCKY

WEST VIRGINIA
Charleston
Washington, D.C.
Baltimore
MD
Annapolis
DE
Dover
Delaware Bay

Chesapeake Bay

VIRGINIA
Richmond
Newport News
Norfolk
Virginia Beach

ATLANTIC OCEAN

Ohio River
Lake Barkley
Kentucky Lake
Kentucky River

Keystone Lake
Tulsa
Fayetteville

Springfield

Nashville
Knoxville

TENNESSEE
Chattanooga
Memphis
Huntsville

Asheville
Winston-Salem
Greensboro
Durham
Raleigh
NORTH CAROLINA
Charlotte
Greenville

Cape Hatteras

35°N

Eufaula Lake
Lake Texoma

ARKANSAS
Little Rock
Pine Bluff

SOUTH CAROLINA
Columbia
Charleston

Savannah River
Sea Islands

National capital
State capitals
Other cities

0   100   200 Miles
0 100 200 Kilometers
Projection: Albers Equal Area

Dallas
Naco

MISSISSIPPI
Vicksburg
Jackson

ALABAMA
Meridian
Montgomery
Birmingham

GEORGIA
Atlanta
Columbus
Macon
Savannah

Shreveport

Red River

30°N

Toledo Bend Reservoir
Beaumont
Houston
Galveston

LOUISIANA
Baton Rouge
New Orleans
Biloxi
Chandeleur Islands

Mobile
Pensacola
Tallahassee
Jacksonville

Chattahoochee R.

Gainesville

FLORIDA

Cape Canaveral

THE BAHAMAS

Gulf of Mexico

N
W   E
S

Orlando
Tampa
St. Petersburg
Lake Okeechobee

Fort Lauderdale
Fort Myers
Miami

Cape Sable
Florida Keys
Straits of Florida

25°N

95°W
90°W
85°W
80°W
75°W
70°W

The United States of America: Physical

CANADA

Mount Rainier 14,410 ft. (4,392 m)

Puget Sound

Pend Oreille Lake

Flathead River

Flathead Lake

Lewis Range

Milk River

Missouri River

Lake Sakakawea

Franklin D. Roosevelt Lake

Clark Fork

Columbia River

COAST RANGES

CASCADE RANGE

Bitterroot Range

Salmon River

CONTINENTAL

ROCKY

Fort Peck Lake

Yellowstone River

Lake Oahe

GREAT

Salmon River Mts.

Snake River

Columbia Plateau

Sawtooth Mts.

Grand Tetons

Yellowstone Lake

Bighorn Mts.

Powder River

Cheyenne River

Black Hills

White River

Cape Mendocino

Klamath River

Goose Lake

Shasta Lake

Pyramid Lake

Great Salt Lake

Gannett Peak 13,804 ft. (4,207 m)

Wind River

Wind River Range

MOUNTAINS

North Platte River

Niobrara – River

INTER

Sacramento River

SIERRA NEVADA

Lake Tahoe

GREAT BASIN

Utah Lake

Wasatch Range

Uinta Mts.

Green River

DIVIDE

Front Range

South Platte River

Platte River

Republican River

San Francisco Bay

Central Valley

San Joaquin River

COLORADO

Lake Powell

Colorado River

Mount Elbert 14,433 ft. (4,400 m)

Pikes Peak 14,110 ft. (4,301 m)

Smoky Hill River

PLAINS

Monterey Bay

Mount Whitney 14,494 ft. (4,419 m)

Death Valley

Mojave Desert

PLATEAU

San Juan River

San Luis Valley

Sangre De Cristo Mts.

Coast Ranges

Lake Mead

Grand Canyon

Painted Desert

DIVIDE

Canadian River

PACIFIC OCEAN

Channel Islands

Salton Sea

Imperial Valley

Colorado River

Gila River

River

Sonoran Desert

CONTINENTAL

Rio Grande

Pecos River

Colorado River

Gulf of California

Amistad Reservoir

Rio Grande

Nueces River

MEXICO

To understand the relative locations of Alaska and Hawaii, as well as the vast distances separating them from the rest of the United States, see the world map.

Kauai

Niihau

Oahu

HAWAII

Molokai

Maui

Lanai

Kahoolawe

PACIFIC OCEAN

Mauna Kea 13,796 ft. (4,206 m)

Hawaii

| 0 | 75 | 150 Miles |
| 0 | 75 | 150 Kilometers |

Projection: Mercator

ARCTIC OCEAN

RUSSIA

Arctic Circle

BROOKS RANGE

Bering Strait

St. Lawrence Island

St. Matthew Island

Yukon River

Tanana River

ALASKA RANGE

Mount McKinley 20,320 ft. (6,194 m)

CANADA

Nunivak Island

Kuskokwim River

Bering Sea

Attu Island

Gulf of Alaska

Kodiak Island

Alexander Archipelago

| 0 | 250 | 500 Miles |
| 0 | 250 | 500 Kilometers |

Projection: Albers Equal Area

PACIFIC OCEAN

CANADA

Red River

Minnesota River

Mississippi River

Mesabi Range

Isle Royale

Lake Superior

Lake Michigan

Lake Huron

Wisconsin River

Missouri River

Des Moines River

Illinois River

P L A I N S

Kansas R.

Lake of the Ozarks

OZARK PLATEAU

Keystone Lake

Eufaula Lake

Arkansas River

White River

Wabash River

Scioto River

Ohio River

Lake Barkley

Kentucky Lake

Cumberland River

Tennessee River

Ouachita Mts.

Lake Texoma

Trinity River

Sabine River

Red River

Toledo Bend Reservoir

Mississippi River

Pearl River

Tombigbee River

Alabama R.

Coosa River

Chattahoochee River

G U L F   C O A S T A L   P L A I N

Chandeleur Islands

Mississippi Delta

Gulf of Mexico

Lake Ontario

Lake Erie

Allegheny R.

PLATEAU

Susquehanna River

Adirondack Mts.

Catskill Mts.

St. Lawrence River

St. Lawrence River

St. Lawrence Seaway

Lake Champlain

Green Mts.

White Mts.

Longfellow Mts.

St. John River

Penobscot River

Connecticut River

Hudson River

Delaware River

Cape Cod

Long Island Sound

Long Island

A P P A L A C H I A N   M O U N T A I N S

ALLEGHENY

Monongahela R.

Kanawha River

Potomac River

James River

Roanoke River

Great Smoky Mts.

BLUE RIDGE MOUNTAINS

Cumberland Plateau

P I E D M O N T

Oc0nee River

Savannah River

Altamaha River

Delaware Bay

Chesapeake Bay

ATLANTIC OCEAN

Pamlico Sound

Cape Hatteras

Sea Islands

Okefenokee Swamp

FLORIDA PENINSULA

Cape Canaveral

Lake Okeechobee

The Everglades

Cape Sable

Florida Keys

Straits of Florida

THE BAHAMAS

N
W   E
S

40°N

70°W

35°N

80°W

85°W

90°W

95°W

25°N

75°W

25°N

ELEVATION

Feet	Meters
13,120	4,000
6,560	2,000
1,640	500
656	200
(Sea level) 0	0 (Sea level)
Below sea level	Below sea level

0   100   200 Miles
0   100   200 Kilometers

Projection: Albers Equal Area

ATLAS

Boundaries

⊛ National capitals

• Other cities

0   500   1,000 Miles

0   500 1,000 Kilometers

Projection: Mollweide

COUNTRY	CAPITAL
1 Antigua and Barbuda	St. Johns
2 St. Kitts and Nevis	Basseterre
3 Dominica	Roseau
4 St. Lucia	Castries
5 St. Vincent and the Grenadines	Kingstown
6 Barbados	Bridgetown
7 Grenada	St. George's

0   200   400 Miles

0   200   400 Kilometers

Projection: Mercator

ARCTIC OCEAN

EUROPE

RUSSIA

Moscow

Astana

KAZAKHSTAN

ASIA

MONGOLIA   Ulaanbaatar

Harbin

NORTH KOREA   P'yŏngyang   Seoul   JAPAN   Tokyo   Nagoya

SOUTH KOREA

40°N

60°N

GEORGIA   Almaty   KYRGYZSTAN

Istanbul   ARMENIA   Baku   UZBEKISTAN   Tashkent   TAJIKISTAN

Ankara   TURKEY   AZERBAIJAN   TURKMENISTAN   Ashgabat

Tunis   Nicosia   SYRIA   Tehran   Kabul   Islamabad

CYPRUS   Damascus   IRAQ   IRAN   AFGHANISTAN

TUNISIA   Tripoli   LEBANON   Beirut   Baghdad   KUWAIT   PAKISTAN   NEPAL   Kathmandu   BHUTAN

Cairo   Jerusalem   ISRAEL   JORDAN   Amman   BAHRAIN   Delhi   New   BANGLADESH   Naypyidaw

LIBYA   EGYPT   SAUDI ARABIA   QATAR   OMAN   Karachi   Delhi   Dhaka   Calcutta

Riyadh   UNITED ARAB EMIRATES   Mumbai (Bombay)   INDIA   MYANMAR (BURMA)   LAOS   Hanoi

CHINA   Beijing   Tianjin   Wuhan   Chongqing   Shanghai   Guangzhou   Hong Kong   TAIWAN   Taipei

Tropic of Cancer   20°N

Northern Mariana (U.S.)

PACIFIC OCEAN

MARSHALL ISLANDS

Guam (U.S.)

AFRICA   NIGER   CHAD   Khartoum   ERITREA   Asmara   YEMEN   Sanaa

N'Djamena   SUDAN   DJIBOUTI   Addis Ababa

NIGERIA   Abuja   CENTRAL AFRICAN REPUBLIC   ETHIOPIA   SOMALIA

Lagos   CAMEROON   DEMOCRATIC REPUBLIC OF THE CONGO   UGANDA   KENYA   Nairobi

GABON   REP. OF THE CONGO   RWANDA   BURUNDI   TANZANIA   Dodoma   Dar es Salaam

Kinshasa   Luanda   ANGOLA   MALAWI   COMOROS   SEYCHELLES

ZAMBIA   Lusaka   MOZAMBIQUE   MADAGASCAR   Antananarivo

NAMIBIA   ZIMBABWE   Harare

Windhoek   BOTSWANA   Gaborone   Pretoria   SWAZILAND   Maputo   MAURITIUS   Réunion (FRANCE)

Johannesburg   Bloemfontein   LESOTHO

SOUTH AFRICA   Cape Town

Chennai (Madras)   SRI LANKA   Colombo   MALDIVES

Yangon (Rangoon)   THAILAND   Bangkok   CAMBODIA   VIETNAM   Phnom Penh   Ho Chi Minh City   Manila   PHILIPPINES

Kuala Lumpur   MALAYSIA   BRUNEI   PALAU

Singapore   SINGAPORE   INDONESIA

Jakarta   Surabaya

EAST TIMOR   PAPUA NEW GUINEA   Port Moresby   SOLOMON ISLANDS

FEDERATED STATES OF MICRONESIA

Equator   0°   NAURU   KIRIBATI   TUVALU

INDIAN OCEAN

VANUATU   FIJI

New Caledonia (FRANCE)   20°S

AUSTRALIA   Tropic of Capricorn

Sydney   Canberra   NEW ZEALAND   Melbourne   Wellington

Tasmania

60°S

ANTARCTICA

20°E   40°E   60°E   80°E   100°E   120°E   140°E   160°E

ATLAS

COUNTRY	CAPITAL
1 Czech Republic	Prague
2 Slovakia	Bratislava
3 Slovenia	Ljubljana
4 Croatia	Zagreb
5 Bosnia and Herzegovina	Sarajevo
6 Macedonia	Skopje
7 Serbia	Belgrade
8 Montenegro	Podgorica
9 Lithuania	Vilnius
10 Latvia	Riga
11 Estonia	Tallinn

0   250   500 Miles
0   250   500 Kilometers
Projection: Mollweide

Arctic Circle

ICELAND   Reykjavik

NORWAY   SWEDEN   FINLAND   Helsinki

60°N   Oslo   Stockholm   11   St. Petersburg   RUSSIA

North Sea   DENMARK   Copenhagen   10   Minsk   Moscow

UNITED KINGDOM   NETHERLANDS   Amsterdam   Berlin   9   BELARUS

Dublin   The Hague   GERMANY   Warsaw   POLAND   Kiev

IRELAND   London   Brussels   BELGIUM   1   UKRAINE

50°N   Paris   LUXEMBOURG   2   MOLDOVA   Chişinău

ATLANTIC OCEAN   Bern   AUSTRIA   Vienna   Budapest   HUNGARY   ROMANIA

FRANCE   SWITZERLAND   LIECHTENSTEIN   3   4   5   7   Bucharest

MONACO   ITALY   SAN MARINO   6   BULGARIA   Sofia   Black Sea

Corsica (FRANCE)   Rome   8   Tiranë   ALBANIA

PORTUGAL   ANDORRA   VATICAN CITY   Sardinia (ITALY)   GREECE

Madrid   Balearic Is. (SPAIN)   Mediterranean   Sea   Athens

Lisbon   SPAIN   40°N   Sicily   Crete

Gibraltar (U.K.)   MALTA

10°W   0°   10°E   20°E   30°E   40°E   50°E   60°E   70°E   80°E

ATLAS

North America: Political

ARCTIC OCEAN

ASIA

EUROPE

North Pole

+

ICELAND

Point
Barrow

ALASKA
(U.S.)

Queen
Elizabeth
Islands

Greenland
(DENMARK)

St.
Lawrence
Island

Bering
Strait

Nunivak
Island

Beaufort
Sea

Banks
Island

Ellesmere Island

Baffin
Bay

Denmark Strait

Anchorage

Yukon
River

Victoria
Island

Baffin Island

Cape
Farewell

Kodiak
Island

Gulf of
Alaska

Great Bear
Lake

Mackenzie
River

Davis Strait

Alexander
Archipelago

Juneau

Great Slave
Lake

Southampton
Island

Hudson Strait

Labrador
Sea

Queen
Charlotte
Islands

Peace
River

Coats
Island

Mansel
Island

PACIFIC
OCEAN

Edmonton

CANADA

Hudson
Bay

Anticosti
Island

Newfoundland

Vancouver
Island

Calgary

Lake
Winnipeg

St. Lawrence R.

Gulf of
St. Lawrence

St. Pierre and
Miquelon (FRANCE)

Vancouver

Winnipeg

Lake
Superior

Prince
Edward
Island

Cape
Breton
Island

Seattle

Portland

Columbia
River

Lake
Huron

Quebec

Montreal

Snake
River

Minneapolis

Lake
Michigan

Ottawa
Toronto

Lake
Ontario

Boston
Cape Cod

ATLANTIC
OCEAN

Cape Mendocino

Great
Salt
Lake

Salt Lake
City

Milwaukee

Chicago

Detroit

Lake Erie

Cleveland

Columbus

New York City
Philadelphia

San Francisco

San
Jose

Denver

Platte
River

Kansas City

Indianapolis

St. Louis

Baltimore
Washington, D.C.

Los Angeles
San Diego
Tijuana

Colorado River

UNITED STATES

Ohio R.

Norfolk

Cape
Hatteras

Bermuda
(U.K.)

Phoenix

Memphis

Red River

Atlanta
Birmingham

Rio Grande

Dallas

Mississippi River

Austin
San
Antonio

Houston

New Orleans

Jacksonville

Cape Canaveral

Tropic of Cancer

Gulf of
California

Gulf of
Mexico

Florida
Keys

Miami

THE
BAHAMAS

Nassau

Turks and Caicos
Islands (U.K.)

DOMINICAN
REPUBLIC

Puerto Rico (U.S.)

ST. KITTS & NEVIS

Monterrey

Straits of
Florida

San
Juan

ANTIGUA &
BARBUDA

MEXICO

Havana

CUBA

Guadeloupe
(FRANCE)

Guadalajara

Mexico
City

Mérida

Cayman Is.
(U.K.)

Kingston

HAITI

Port-au-
Prince

Santo Domingo

Virgin Is.
(U.S.; U.K.)

DOMINICA

Puebla

JAMAICA

Martinique (FRANCE)

BARBADOS

Balsas R.

ST. LUCIA

Belmopan

BELIZE

ST. VINCENT AND
THE GRENADINES

Netherlands
Antilles
(NETHERLANDS)

GRENADA

GUATEMALA

HONDURAS

Guatemala City

Tegucigalpa

San Salvador

NICARAGUA

EL SALVADOR

Managua

Caribbean Sea

Aruba (NETHERLANDS)

Panama
Canal

TRINIDAD AND TOBAGO

San José

Panama City

COSTA
RICA

PANAMA

SOUTH
AMERICA

Legend

	Boundaries
⊛	National capitals
•	Other cities

0   300   600 Miles

0   300   600 Kilometers

Projection: Azimuthal Equal Area

N
W   E
S

0° Equator

South America: Political

CENTRAL AMERICA

Caribbean Sea

Barranquilla
Cartagena

Caracas

Lake Maracaibo

VENEZUELA

Orinoco River

Georgetown
Paramaribo
Cayenne

GUYANA

SURINAME

FRENCH GUIANA (FRANCE)

ATLANTIC OCEAN

Medellín

Bogotá

COLOMBIA

Cali

Malpelo Island (COLOMBIA)

Quito

ECUADOR

Guayaquil

Galápagos Islands (ECUADOR)

Equator 0°

Río Negro

Amazon River

Amazon River

Belém

Equator 0°

Trujillo

PERU

Marañón River

Ucayali River

Callao
Lima

Arequipa

Lake Titicaca

La Paz

Lake Poopó

BOLIVIA

Sucre

BRAZIL

Brasília

São Francisco River

Recife

Salvador

Belo Horizonte

PACIFIC OCEAN

Paraguay River

PARAGUAY

Asunción

Campinas
São Paulo

Curitiba

Rio de Janeiro

Tropic of Capricorn

Tropic of Capricorn

San Ambrosio Island (CHILE)

San Félix Island (CHILE)

CHILE

Paraná River

Uruguay River

Pôrto Alegre

Córdoba

Juan Fernández Islands (CHILE)

Valparaíso
Santiago

Rosario

URUGUAY

Montevideo

ATLANTIC OCEAN

Buenos Aires

Río de la Plata

ARGENTINA

Legend

- Boundaries
- ⊛ National capitals
- • Other cities

0   250   500 Miles
0   250   500 Kilometers
Projection: Azimuthal Equal Area

Strait of Magellan

Falkland Islands (U.K.)

Tierra del Fuego

South Georgia Island (U.K.)

ATLAS

Europe: Political

Legend:
- Boundaries
- ✪ National capitals
- • Other cities

0   150   300 Miles
0   150   300 Kilometers
Projection: Azimuthal Equal Area

SOUTHWEST ASIA

ASIA

URAL MOUNTAINS

RUSSIA

Ural River
Volga River
Don River
Nizhny Novgorod
Moscow
St. Petersburg

Caspian Sea
Black Sea

FINLAND
Helsinki

ESTONIA
Tallinn
Gulf of Finland

LATVIA
Riga

LITHUANIA
Vilnius

RUSSIA

BELARUS
Minsk

UKRAINE
Kiev

MOLDOVA
Chişinău

ROMANIA
Bucharest

BULGARIA
Sofia

Dnipro River
Danube River

MACEDONIA
Skopje

SERBIA
Belgrade

GREECE
Athens

ALBANIA
Tirane

Aegean Sea
Rhodes
Crete

SWEDEN
Stockholm
Göteborg

NORWAY
Oslo
Bergen

DENMARK
Copenhagen

POLAND
Warsaw
Krakow

SLOVAKIA
Bratislava

HUNGARY
Budapest

CROATIA
Zagreb

BOSNIA AND HERZEGOVINA
Sarajevo

MONTENEGRO
Podgorica

Adriatic Sea

North Cape

ARCTIC OCEAN

White Sea
Barents Sea
Gulf of Bothnia
Baltic Sea

GERMANY
Berlin
Dresden
Hamburg
Cologne
Bonn
Munich

CZECH REPUBLIC
Prague

AUSTRIA
Vienna

SLOVENIA
Ljubljana

Elbe River
Rhine River
Danube River

LIECHTENSTEIN
Vaduz

SWITZERLAND
Bern

THE NETHERLANDS
Amsterdam
The Hague

BELGIUM
Brussels

LUXEMBOURG
Luxembourg

ALPS

ITALY
Rome
Milan
Naples

SAN MARINO
San Marino

VATICAN CITY

MONACO
Monaco

MALTA
Valletta

Sicily

Corsica (FRANCE)
Sardinia (ITALY)

North Sea

UNITED KINGDOM
London
Liverpool
Edinburgh

SCOTLAND
ENGLAND
WALES
NORTHERN IRELAND
Belfast

IRELAND
Dublin

Shetland Islands
Faeroe Islands (DENMARK)

British Isles
Channel Islands (U.K.)
English Channel
Thames R.

FRANCE
Paris
Lyon
Marseille

Seine River
Loire River
Rhône River

PYRENEES
ANDORRA
Andorra la Vella

Bay of Biscay

ICELAND
Reykjavik

SPAIN
Madrid
Barcelona
Valencia
Seville

PORTUGAL
Lisbon

Balearic Islands (SPAIN)

Gibraltar (U.K.)
Strait of Gibraltar

Tagus River

ATLANTIC OCEAN

Mediterranean Sea

AFRICA

N E S W

ATLAS

Asia: Political

Boundaries
※ **National capitals**
• **Other cities**

Miles
0 250 500 750
0 250 500 750 Kilometers
Projection: Two-Point Equidistant

PACIFIC OCEAN

RUSSIA

EUROPE

Moscow

URAL MOUNTAINS

Yekaterinburg
Chelyabinsk
Omsk

Novosibirsk

Yakutsk

Irkutsk

Lake Baikal

Vladivostok

Sakhalin Island

Kuril Islands (RUSSIA)

Aleutian Islands

Bering Sea

Sea of Okhotsk

Sapporo

JAPAN
Tokyo
Yokohama
Nagoya
Osaka
Kobe
Hiroshima
Nagasaki

NORTH KOREA
Pyongyang

SOUTH KOREA
Seoul
Pusan

MONGOLIA
Ulaanbaatar

Harbin
Changchun
Fushun
Dalian
Shenyang

CHINA
Beijing
Great Wall of China
Qingdao
Nanjing
Shanghai
Wuhan
Xi'an
Chengdu
Chongqing
Guangzhou
Hong Kong
Macao
Hainan

Yellow Sea
East China Sea
South China Sea

TAIWAN
Taipei

Ryukyu Islands (JAPAN)

Tropic of Cancer

PHILIPPINES
Manila

New Guinea

Arafura Sea

AUSTRALIA

EAST TIMOR

INDONESIA
Medan
Ujung Pandang
Jakarta
Semarang
Surabaya
Bandung

Java Sea
Celebes Sea
Banda Sea

BRUNEI
Bandar Seri Begawan

MALAYSIA
Kuala Lumpur

SINGAPORE
Singapore

Gulf of Thailand

VIETNAM
Hanoi
Ho Chi Minh City

LAOS
Vientiane

CAMBODIA
Phnom Penh

THAILAND
Bangkok

MYANMAR (BURMA)
Naypyidaw
Yangon (Rangoon)
Mandalay

Andaman Sea

Andaman Islands (INDIA)

Nicobar Islands (INDIA)

Bay of Bengal

BANGLADESH
Dhaka
Chittagong

BHUTAN
Thimphu

NEPAL
Kathmandu

INDIA
Delhi
New Delhi
Jaipur
Ahmadabad
Bhopal
Nagpur
Kolkata (Calcutta)
Hyderabad
Bangalore
Chennai (Madras)
Mumbai (Bombay)

Lakshadweep (INDIA)

SRI LANKA
Colombo

MALDIVES
Male

INDIAN OCEAN

Arabian Sea

PAKISTAN
Islamabad
Lahore
Faisalabad
Karachi

AFGHANISTAN
Kabul

KAZAKHSTAN
Astana
Almaty

UZBEKISTAN
Tashkent

KYRGYZSTAN
Bishkek

TAJIKISTAN
Dushanbe

TURKMENISTAN
Ashgabat

Lake Balkhash

Aral Sea

Caspian Sea

IRAN
Tehran
Mashhad
Isfahan
Shiraz

AZERBAIJAN
Baku

ARMENIA
Yerevan

GEORGIA
T'bilisi

TURKEY
Ankara
Istanbul
Izmir

Black Sea

IRAQ
Baghdad
Basra
Mosul

SYRIA
Damascus
Aleppo

LEBANON
Beirut

ISRAEL
Tel Aviv
Jerusalem

CYPRUS
Nicosia

JORDAN
Amman

Mediterranean Sea

SAUDI ARABIA
Riyadh
Mecca
Jidda

KUWAIT
Kuwait City

BAHRAIN
Manama

QATAR
Doha

UNITED ARAB EMIRATES
Abu Dhabi

OMAN
Masqat (Muscat)

YEMEN
Sanaa

Red Sea

Gulf of Aden

Socotra (YEMEN)

Persian Gulf

AFRICA

0° Equator

Arctic Circle

North Pole

Kara Sea

Barents Sea

Ob River
Irtysh River
Lena River
Yenisey River
Amur River
Huang He (Yellow R.)
Chang Jiang (Yangtze R.)
Mekong River
Brahmaputra River
Ganges River
Indus River
Tigris River
Euphrates River
Nu River

Africa: Political

EUROPE

SOUTHWEST ASIA

Mediterranean Sea

Azores (PORTUGAL)

Strait of Gibraltar

Madeira (PORTUGAL)

Canary Islands (SPAIN)

Casablanca • ⊛ Rabat
Algiers Tunis
TUNISIA
Tripoli

MOROCCO

El Aaiún

WESTERN SAHARA (Claimed by Morocco)

ALGERIA

LIBYA

Alexandria
Giza • ⊛ Cairo
Suez Canal
EGYPT

Lake Nasser

Nile River

Red Sea

Gulf of Aden

Tropic of Cancer

CAPE VERDE

Praia

MAURITANIA
Nouakchott

Niger River

MALI

NIGER

CHAD

Khartoum
⊛

SUDAN

ERITREA
⊛ Asmara

DJIBOUTI
Djibouti

SENEGAL
Dakar • ⊛
Banjul
GAMBIA
Bamako
GUINEA BISSAU
Bissau
Conakry
Freetown
SIERRA LEONE
Monrovia
LIBERIA

GUINEA

BURKINA FASO
Ouagadougou
Niamey

Lake Chad

N'Djamena

CÔTE D'IVOIRE
Yamoussoukro
GHANA
Abidjan
Accra

BENIN
TOGO
Lomé
Porto-Novo
Lagos

NIGERIA
Abuja ⊛

Gulf of Guinea

Malabo

CENTRAL AFRICAN REPUBLIC
Bangui

ETHIOPIA
Addis Ababa •

SOMALIA
Mogadishu

CAMEROON
Yaoundé ⊛

EQUATORIAL GUINEA

SÃO TOMÉ AND PRÍNCIPE
São Tomé

Libreville ⊛
REPUBLIC OF THE CONGO
GABON

Congo River

Kisangani

DEMOCRATIC REPUBLIC OF THE CONGO

UGANDA
Kampala ⊛
KENYA
Nairobi ⊛

RWANDA
⊛ Kigali
BURUNDI
Bujumbura

Lake Victoria

Equator

INDIAN OCEAN

Victoria
SEYCHELLES

Brazzaville ⊛
CABINDA (ANGOLA)
Kinshasa ⊛

Luanda

ATLANTIC OCEAN

St. Helena (U.K.)

ANGOLA

TANZANIA
Dodoma ⊛
Dar es Salaam
Mombasa
Pemba
Zanzibar

Lake Tanganyika

Lake Malawi (Nyasa)

Lubumbashi •

ZAMBIA
Lusaka ⊛

MALAWI
Lilongwe ⊛

COMOROS
⊛ Moroni

Zambezi River

ZIMBABWE
Harare ⊛
Bulawayo

MOZAMBIQUE

Antananarivo ⊛
MAURITIUS
Port Louis ⊛
MADAGASCAR
Réunion (FRANCE)

NAMIBIA
Windhoek ⊛

BOTSWANA
Gaborone ⊛

Pretoria ⊛
Maputo
Mbabane
SWAZILAND

Johannesburg •
Bloemfontein
Maseru
LESOTHO

Orange River

Tropic of Capricorn

SOUTH AFRICA

Cape Town

Legend

	Boundaries
⊛	National capitals
•	Other cities

0   250   500 Miles
0   250   500 Kilometers
Projection: Azimuthal Equal Area

Australia and New Zealand: Political

NORTH AMERICA

NORTH PACIFIC OCEAN

ASIA

Philippine Sea

South China Sea

Bonin Islands (JAPAN)

Volcano Islands (JAPAN)

Northern Marianas (U.S.)

Guam (U.S.) · Agana

Koror · PALAU

Christmas Island (AUSTRALIA)

Truk Is.

FEDERATED STATES OF MICRONESIA

Palikir

MICRONESIA

Eniwetok I.

MARSHALL ISLANDS

Kwajalein Island

Majuro

Wake Island (U.S.)

Gilbert Islands

Tarawa

Yaren

NAURU

Midway Island (U.S.)

Johnston Island (U.S.)

Hawaiian Islands

Hawaii (U.S.)

Kingman Reef (U.S.)

Palmyra Island (U.S.)

Washington Island

Fanning Island

Jarvis I. (U.S.)

Howland I. (U.S.)

Baker I. (U.S.)

Phoenix Islands

McKean I.

Gardner

KIRIBATI

Starbuck Island

Manihiki Island

Cook Islands (NEW ZEALAND)

Rarotonga Island

POLYNESIA

Marquesas Islands (FRANCE)

Tuamotu Archipelago (FRANCE)

French Polynesia

Society Islands (FRANCE)

Tahiti (FRANCE)

Papeete

Tubuai Islands (FRANCE)

Rapa Island (FRANCE)

Pitcairn (U.K.)

Pitcairn Island

Ducie Island

Easter Island (CHILE)

Tropic of Capricorn

Equator

Tropic of Cancer

International Date Line

Tokelau (N.Z.)

SAMOA · Apia

American Samoa

Pago Pago

Wallis & Futuna (FR.)

TUVALU

Funafuti

Niue (N.Z.)

TONGA

Nuku'alofa

FIJI

Suva

Port-Vila

VANUATU

Malekula I.

Espiritu Santo I.

Loyalty Islands (FRANCE)

New Caledonia (FRANCE)

Noumea

SOLOMON ISLANDS

Honiara

Guadalcanal I.

MELANESIA

Bismarck Archipelago

PAPUA NEW GUINEA

Port Moresby

New Guinea

Coral Sea

Arafura Sea

Timor Sea

Darwin

Kermadec Islands (N.Z.)

Norfolk Island (AUSTRALIA)

NEW ZEALAND

North Island

Auckland

Wellington

Christchurch

South Island

Chatham Islands (N.Z.)

Bounty Islands (N.Z.)

Auckland Islands (NEW ZEALAND)

SOUTH PACIFIC OCEAN

Tasman Sea

AUSTRALIA

Flinders R.

Darling R.

Lachlan R.

Murray R.

Brisbane

Sydney

Canberra

Melbourne

Hobart

Adelaide

Perth

INDIAN OCEAN

N E W

S

Legend

Boundaries
⊛ National capitals
· Other cities

1,000 Miles
1,000 Kilometers
500
500
0

Projection: Mercator

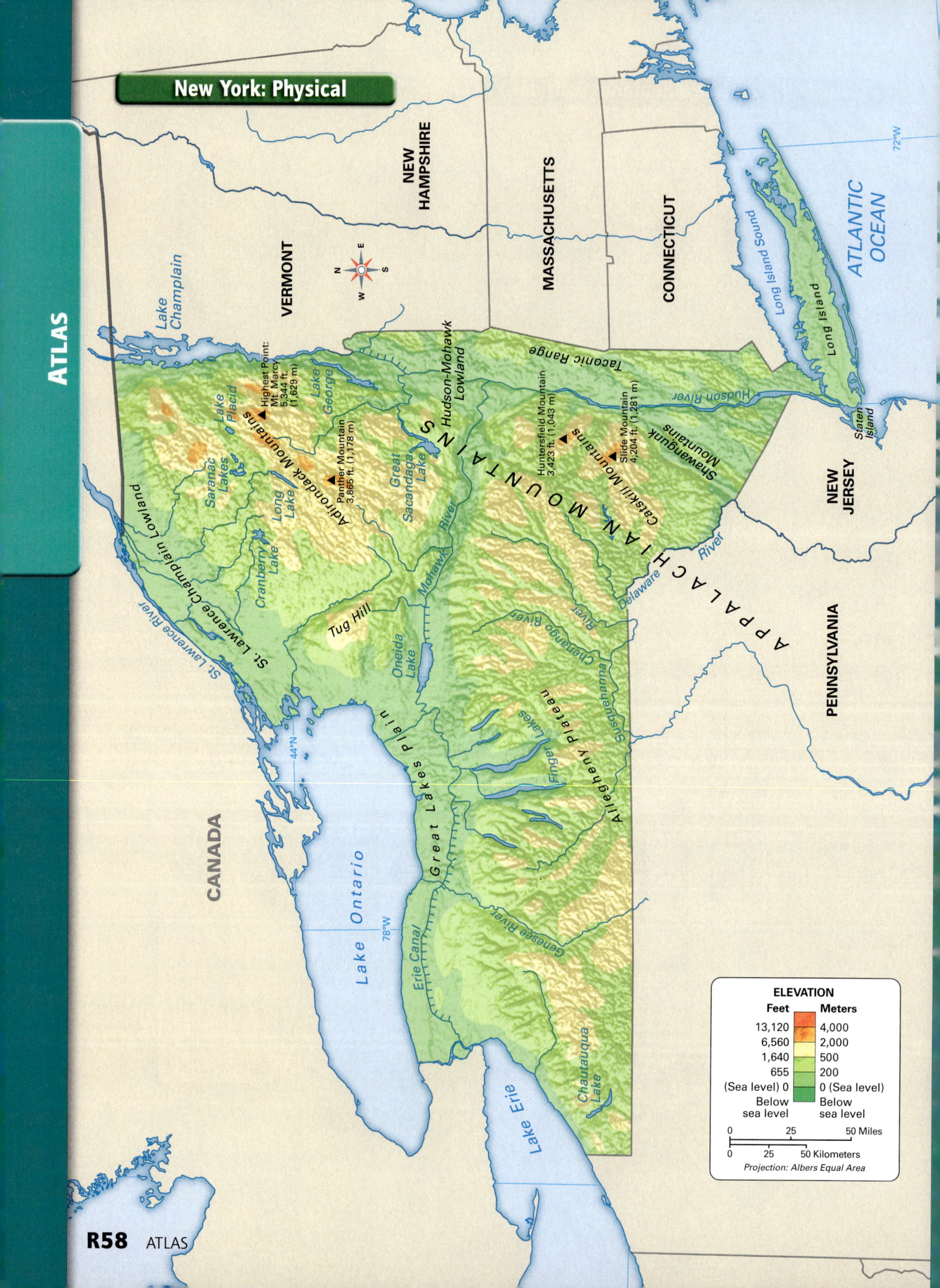

New York: Physical

NEW HAMPSHIRE

MASSACHUSETTS

CONNECTICUT

ATLANTIC OCEAN

72°W

VERMONT

Lake Champlain

Long Island Sound

Long Island

N
W E
S

Highest Point: Mt. Marcy 5,344 ft. (1,629 m)

Lake Placid

Lake George

Hudson-Mohawk Lowland

Taconic Range

Hudson River

Staten Island

Saranac Lakes

Adirondack Mountains

Panther Mountain 3,865 ft. (1,178 m)

Great Sacandaga Lake

A P P A L A C H I A N   M O U N T A I N S

Hunters field Mountain 3,423 ft. (1,043 m)

Slide Mountain 4,204 ft. (1,281 m)

Catskill Mountains

Shawangunk Mountains

NEW JERSEY

Long Lake

Cranberry Lake

St. Lawrence Champlain Lowland

Mohawk River

Delaware River

Tug Hill

Oneida Lake

Chenango River

Susquehanna River

Allegheny Plateau

PENNSYLVANIA

St. Lawrence River

44°N

Erie Canal

Great Lakes Plain

Finger Lakes

CANADA

Lake Ontario

78°W

Genesee River

Chautauqua Lake

Lake Erie

ELEVATION

Feet		Meters
13,120		4,000
6,560		2,000
1,640		500
655		200
(Sea level) 0		0 (Sea level)
Below sea level		Below sea level

0   25   50 Miles
0   25   50 Kilometers
Projection: Albers Equal Area

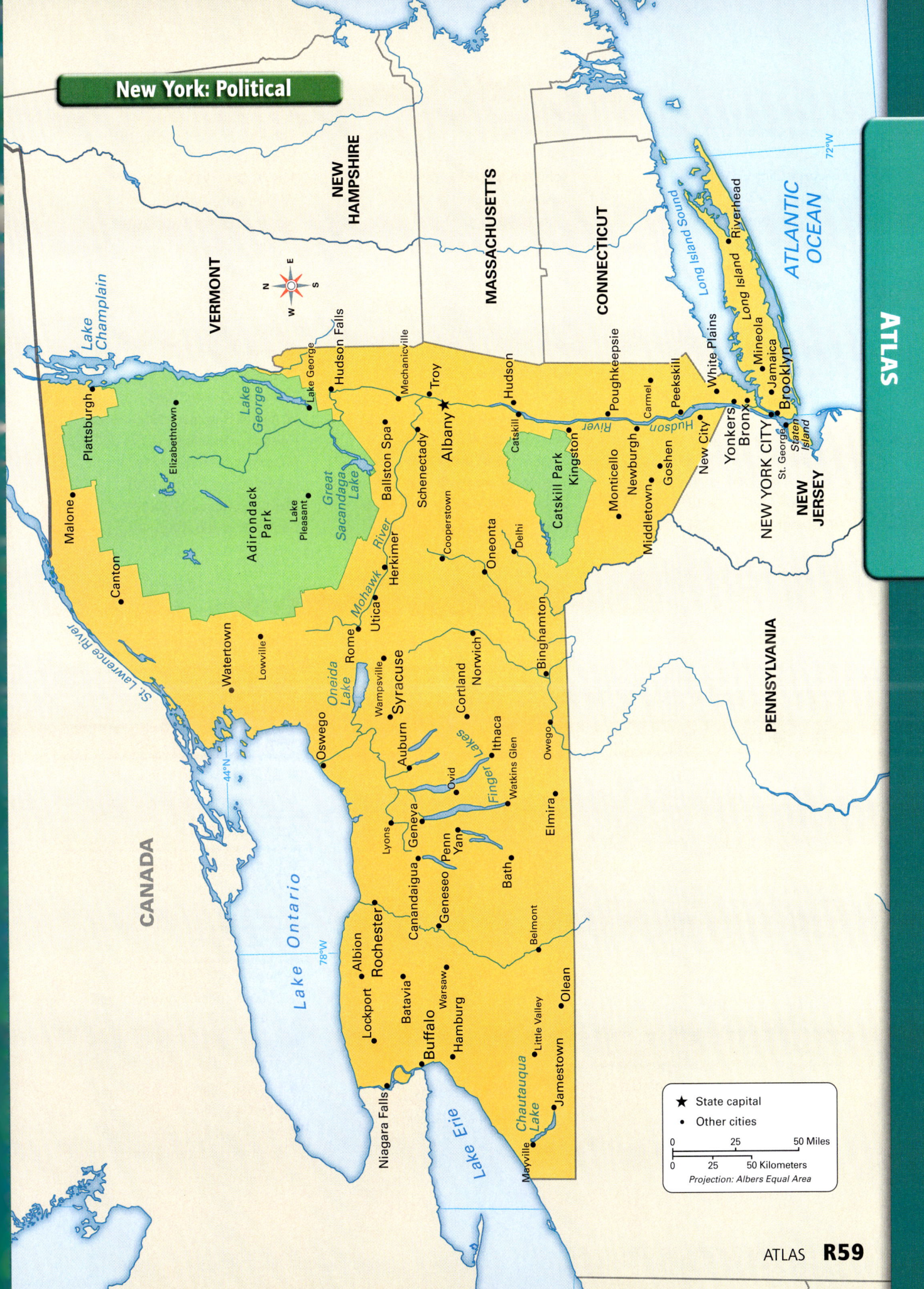

New York: Political

VERMONT

NEW HAMPSHIRE

MASSACHUSETTS

CONNECTICUT

CANADA

PENNSYLVANIA

NEW JERSEY

ATLANTIC OCEAN

Lake Champlain

Lake George

Great Sacandaga Lake

St. Lawrence River

Lake Ontario

Oneida Lake

Mohawk River

Finger Lakes

Lake Erie

Chautauqua Lake

Long Island Sound

Hudson River

Adirondack Park

Catskill Park

Malone

Plattsburgh

Elizabethtown

Canton

Watertown

Lowville

Lake Pleasant

Lake George

Hudson Falls

Mechanicville

Troy

Albany ★

Ballston Spa

Schenectady

Herkimer

Utica

Rome

Cooperstown

Oneonta

Delhi

Catskill

Kingston

Monticello

Newburgh

Middletown

Goshen

Carmel

Poughkeepsie

Peekskill

White Plains

New City

Yonkers

Bronx

NEW YORK CITY

St. George

Staten Island

Brooklyn

Jamaica

Mineola

Long Island

Riverhead

Oswego

Wampsville

Syracuse

Auburn

Cortland

Norwich

Binghamton

Owego

Ovid

Ithaca

Watkins Glen

Elmira

Lyons

Geneva

Penn Yan

Bath

Canandaigua

Geneseo

Belmont

Rochester

Albion

Lockport

Batavia

Warsaw

Buffalo

Hamburg

Little Valley

Olean

Niagara Falls

Mayville

Jamestown

Hudson

44°N

78°W

72°W

ATLAS

Legend

★ State capital

• Other cities

| 0 | 25 | 50 Miles |
| 0 | 25 | 50 Kilometers |

Projection: Albers Equal Area

New York Governors

George Clinton (1777–1795)
John Jay (1795–1801)
George Clinton (1801–1804)
Morgan Lewis (1804–1807)
Daniel D. Tompkins (1807–1817)
John Tayler (1817)
De Witt Clinton (1817–1822)
Joseph C. Yates (1823–1824)
De Witt Clinton (1825–1828)
Nathaniel Pitcher (1828)
Martin Van Buren (1829)
Enos T. Throop (1829–1832)
William L. Marcy (1833–1838)
William H. Seward (1839–1842)
William C. Bouck (1843–1844)
Silas Wright (1845–1846)
John Young (1847–1848)
Hamilton Fish (1849–1850)
Washington Hunt (1851–1852)

Horatio Seymour (1853–1854)
Myron H. Clark (1855–1856)
John A. King (1857–1858)
Edwin D. Morgan (1859–1862)
Horatio Seymour (1863–1864)
Reuben E. Fenton (1865–1868)
John T. Hoffman (1869–1872)
John A. Dix (1873–1874)
Samuel J. Tilden (1875–1876)
Lucius Robinson (1877–1879)
Alonzo B. Cornell (1880–1882)
Grover Cleveland (1883–1884)
David B. Hill (1885–1891)
Roswell P. Flower (1892–1894)
Levi P. Morton (1895–1896)
Frank S. Black (1897–1898)
Theodore Roosevelt (1899–1900)
Benjamin B. Odell, Jr. (1901–1904)
Frank W. Higgins (1905–1906)

Charles E. Hughes (1907–1910)
Horace White (1910)
John A. Dix (1911–1912)
William Sulzer (1913)
Martin H. Glynn (1913–1914)
Charles S. Whitman (1915–1918)
Alfred E. Smith (1919–1920)
Nathan L. Miller (1921–1922)
Alfred E. Smith (1923–1928)
Franklin D. Roosevelt (1929–1932)
Herbert H. Lehman (1933–1942)
Charles Poletti (1942)
Thomas E. Dewey (1943–1954)
W. Averell Harriman (1955–1958)
Nelson A. Rockefeller (1959–1973)
Malcolm Wilson (1973–1974)
Hugh L. Carey (1975–1982)
Mario M. Cuomo (1983–1994)
George E. Pataki (1995–)

New York Government

Executive Branch

Carries out the laws and policies of state government

The Governor

- Elected by voters to a four-year term
- No term limits
- Appoints officials and some judges
- Can veto whole laws or items of laws regarding budgets

Lieutenant Governor

- Elected along with governor
- Various jobs include replacing governor should he or she leave office

The Cabinet

- Consists of officials appointed by governor
- Offers advice to governor on specific areas of knowledge

Legislative Branch

Makes state laws

Bicameral System

- Has two houses — State Senate and Assembly
- Both houses take part in law-making
- Legislature can override the governor's veto with a two-thirds vote in both houses

The State Senate

- 62 Senators
- Serve two-year terms
- No limit on number of terms

The Assembly

- 150 Assembly members
- Serve two-year terms
- No limit on number of terms

Judicial Branch

Decides conflicts and questions about the law

Trial Courts

- Hear civil and criminal cases
- Five divisions of superior courts

Appellate Courts

- Hear and determine appeals from the lower courts
- Four divisions of appellate courts

Circuit Courts

- Determines statewide principles of law in deciding specific lawsuits
- Focuses on broad issues of law, not individual factual disputes
- Has one Chief Judge and six Associate Judges
- Appointed by governor with approval of the Senate
- Serve 14-year terms

New York Facts

State tree	Sugar maple
State bird	Bluebird
State marine animal	Trout
State animal	Beaver
State insect	Ladybug
State fossil	Sea scorpion
State shell	Bay scallop
State flower	Rose
State fruit	Apple
Capital	Albany
Year of Statehood	1788 (11th State)
Nickname	The Empire State
Motto	Excelsior (Ever Upward)
Song	"I Love New York"
Highest Elevation	Mt. Marcy, 5,344 feet above sea level
Lowest Elevation	Sea level
Total Area	54,475 sq. miles
National Rank in Land Area	27
Total Coastline	1,850 miles (includes every bay & inlet on Long Island) 127 miles (Atlantic coastline only)
Largest City	New York City
Largest Lake	Lake Oneida
Number of Counties	62
Longest River	Hudson River
Population	19,190,115 (as of 2003)
National Rank in Population	3
Length (North to South)	310 miles
Width (East to West)	440 miles [including Long Island]

rose

Mapping the Earth
Using Latitude and Longitude

A **globe** is a scale model of the earth. It is useful for showing the entire earth or studying large areas of the earth's surface.

A pattern of lines circles the globe in east-west and north-south directions. It is called a **grid**. The intersection of these imaginary lines helps us find places on the earth.

The east-west lines in the grid are lines of **latitude**. Lines of latitude are called **parallels** because they are always parallel to each other. These imaginary lines measure distance north and south of the **equator**. The equator is an imaginary line that circles the globe halfway between the North and South Poles. Parallels measure distance from the equator in **degrees**. The symbol for degrees is °. Degrees are further divided into **minutes**. The symbol for minutes is ´. There are 60 minutes in a degree. Parallels north of the equator are labeled with an N. Those south of the equator are labeled with an S.

The north-south lines are lines of **longitude**. Lines of longitude are called **meridians**. These imaginary lines pass through the Poles. They measure distance east and west of the **prime meridian**. The prime meridian is an imaginary line that runs through Greenwich, England. It represents 0° longitude.

Lines of latitude range from 0°, for locations on the equator, to 90°N or 90°S, for locations at the Poles. Lines of longitude range from 0° on the prime meridian to 180° on a meridian in the mid-Pacific Ocean. Meridians west of the prime meridian to 180° are labeled with a W. Those east of the prime meridian to 180° are labeled with an E.

Lines of Latitude

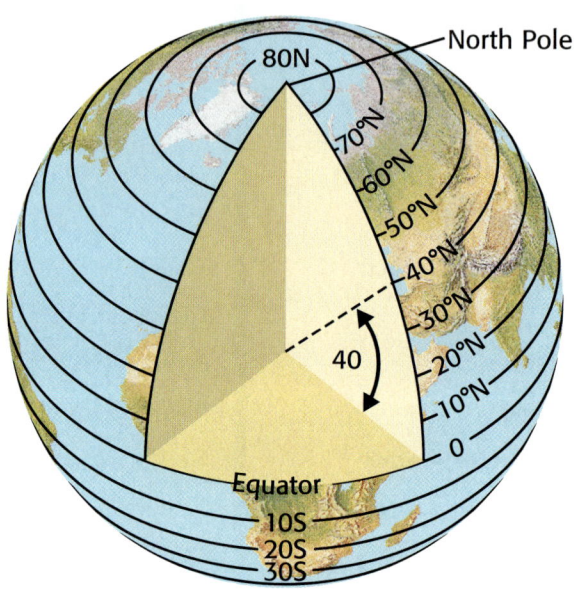

Lines of Longitude

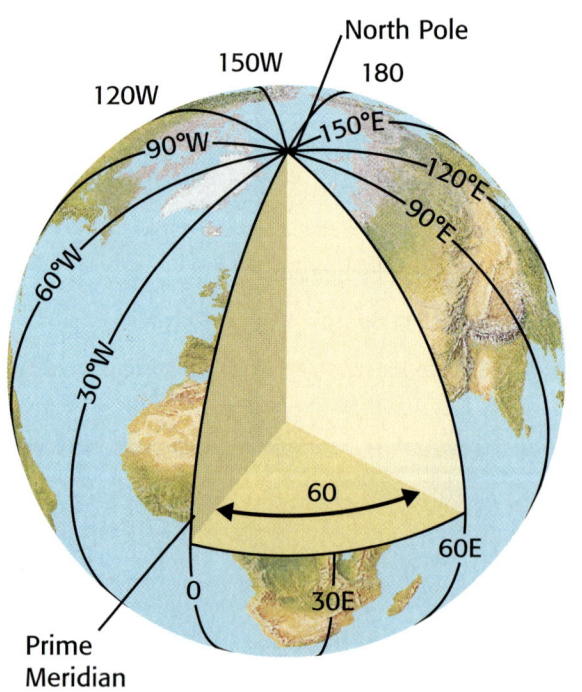

The equator divides the globe into two halves, called **hemispheres**. The half north of the equator is the Northern Hemisphere. The southern half is the Southern Hemisphere. The prime meridian and the 180° meridian divide the world into the Eastern Hemisphere and the Western Hemisphere. However, the prime meridian runs right through Europe and Africa. To avoid dividing these continents between two hemispheres, some mapmakers divide the Eastern and Western hemispheres at 20°W. This places all of Europe and Africa in the Eastern Hemisphere.

Our planet's land surface is divided into seven large landmasses, called **continents**. They are identified in the maps on this page. Landmasses smaller than continents and completely surrounded by water are called **islands**.

Geographers also organize Earth's water surface into parts. The largest is the world ocean. Geographers divide the world ocean into the Pacific Ocean, the Atlantic Ocean, the Indian Ocean, and the Arctic Ocean. Lakes and seas are smaller bodies of water.

Northern Hemisphere

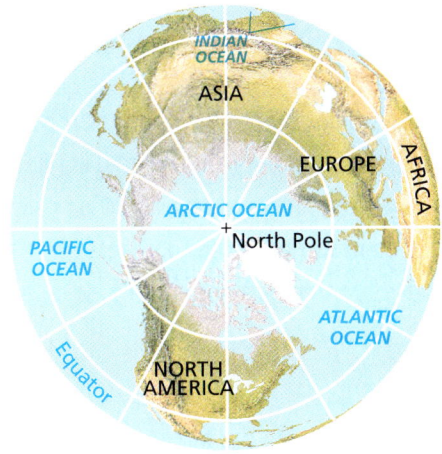

Southern Hemisphere

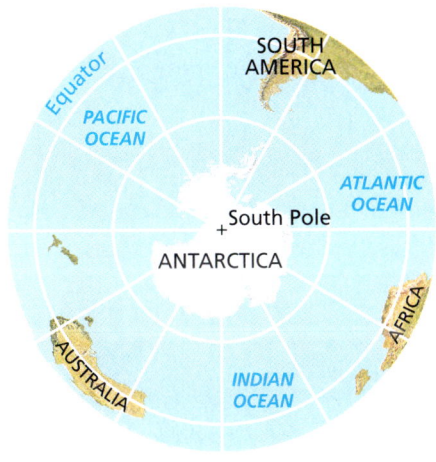

Western Hemisphere

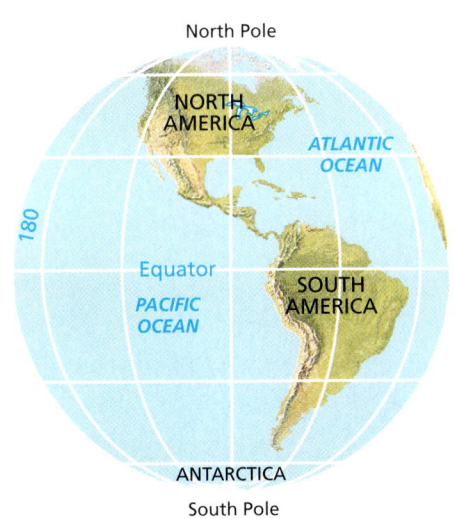

Eastern Hemisphere

Mapmaking
Understanding Map Projections

A **map** is a flat diagram of all or part of the earth's surface. Mapmakers have created different ways of showing our round planet on flat maps. These different ways are called **map projections**. Because the earth is round, there is no way to show it accurately in a flat map. All flat maps are distorted in some way. Mapmakers must choose the type of map projection that is best for their purposes. Many map projections are one of three kinds: cylindrical, conic, or flat-plane.

Paper cylinder

Cylindrical Projections

Cylindrical projections are based on a cylinder wrapped around the globe. The cylinder touches the globe only at the equator. The meridians are pulled apart and run parallel to each other instead of meeting at the Poles. This causes landmasses near the Poles to appear larger than they really are. The map below is a Mercator projection, one type of cylindrical projection. Navigators use the Mercator projection because it shows true direction and shape. However, it distorts the size of land areas near the Poles.

Mercator projection

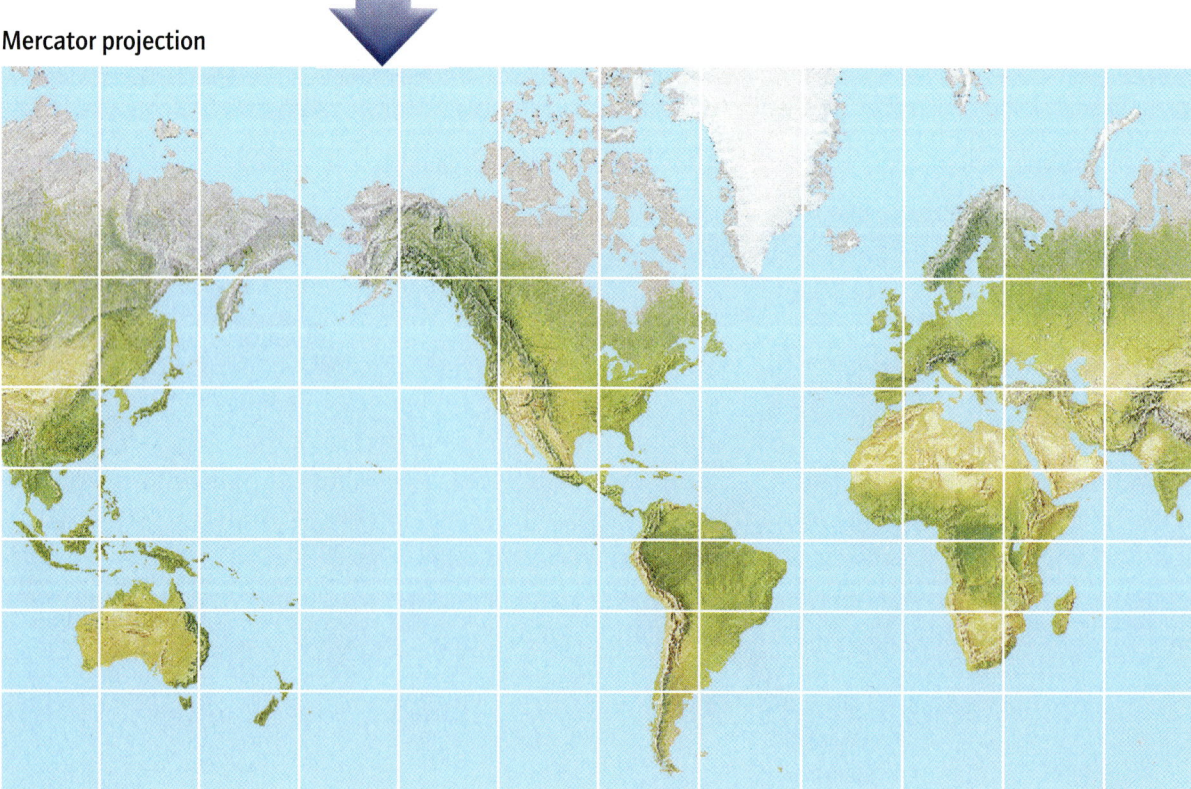

Conic Projections

Conic projections are based on a cone placed over the globe. A conic projection is most accurate along the lines of latitude where it touches the globe. It retains almost true shape and size. Conic projections are most useful for showing areas that have long east-west dimensions, such as the United States.

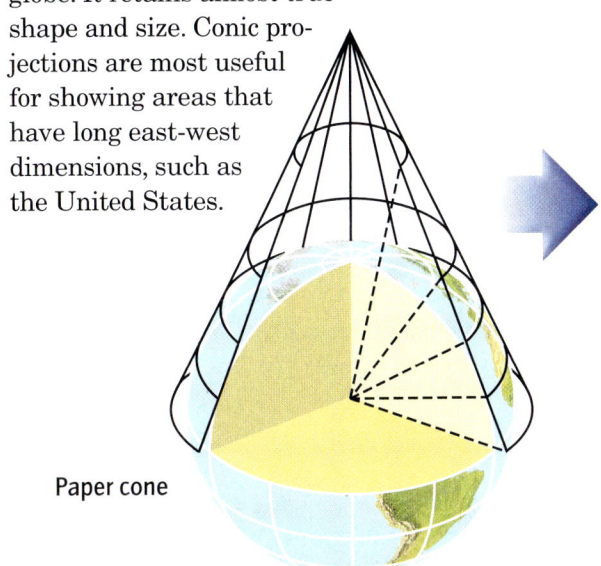

Paper cone

Conic projection

Flat-plane Projections

Flat-plane projections are based on a plane touching the globe at one point, such as at the North Pole or South Pole. A flat-plane projection is useful for showing true direction for airplane pilots and ship navigators. It also shows true area. However, it distorts the true shapes of landmasses.

Flat plane

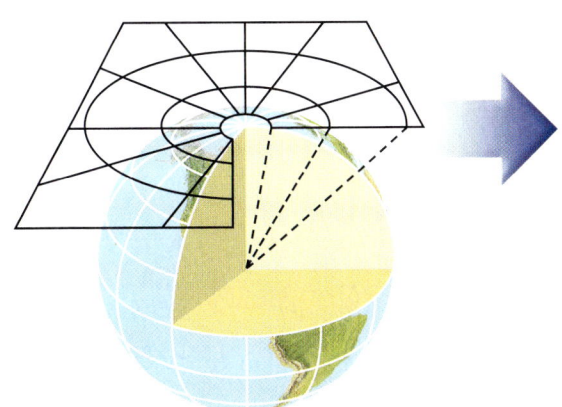

Flat-plane projection

Map Essentials
How to Read a Map

Maps are like messages sent out in code. Mapmakers provide certain elements that help us translate these codes. These elements help us understand the message they are presenting about a particular part of the world. Of these elements, almost all maps have titles, directional indicators, scales, and legends. The map below has all four of these elements, plus two more—a locator map and an interactive keyword.

1 Title

A map's **title** shows what the subject of the map is. The map title is usually the first thing you should look at when studying a map, because it tells you what the map is trying to show.

Interactive Map

BATTLES OF THE AMERICAN REVOLUTION, 1775 TO 1778

Battle of Quebec

Montreal

Battle of Ticonderoga, 1775

Burgoyne

Capture of Ticonderoga, 1777

NH

Battle of Concord

Battle of Lexington

Battle of Saratoga

Battle of Bunker Hill

Lake Ontario

Capture of Fort Stanwix

Albany

MA

Boston

NY

RI

CT

3
- → Colonial troop movement
- ✶ Colonial victory
- → British troop movement
- ✶ British victory

4
0   40   80 Miles
0   40   80 Kilometers
Albers equal-area projection

Washington

Battle of Harlem Heights

40°N

PA

New York

Philadelphia

Valley Forge

Battles of Trenton and Princeton

NJ

70°W

MD

Howe

DE

6

go.hrw.com
Interactive Map
Keyword: SE7 CH4

VA

N
W   E
S

2

GEOGRAPHY SKILLS   INTERPRETING MAPS

1. Location How does the the pattern of battles and troop movements reflect Britain's war strategy?

2. Movement Why was the Battle of Saratoga a turning point?

See **Skills Handbook**, p. H19

❷ Compass Rose

A directional indicator shows which way north, south, east, and west lie on the map. Some mapmakers use a "north arrow," which points toward the North Pole. Remember, "north" is not always at the top of a map. The way a map is drawn and the location of directions on that map depend on the perspective of the mapmaker. Most maps in this textbook indicate direction by using a compass rose. A **compass rose** has arrows that point to all four principal directions, as shown.

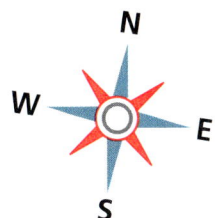

❸ Legend

The **legend**, or key, explains what the symbols on the map represent. Point symbols are used to specify the location of things, such as cities, that do not take up much space on the map. Some legends show colors that represent elevations. Other maps might have legends with symbols or colors that represent things such as roads, the movement of military forces and battles. Legends can also show political divisions, economic resources, land use, population density, and climate.

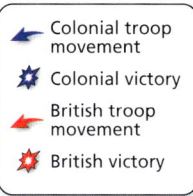

❹ Scale

Mapmakers use scales to represent the distances between points on a map. Scales may appear on maps in several different forms. The maps in this textbook provide a bar **scale**. Scales give distances in miles and kilometers. The scale is often found in the legend. In this textbook, the type of projection used to make the map is shown below the scale bar.

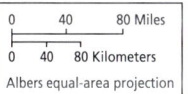

To find the distance between two points on the map, place a piece of paper so that the edge connects the two points. Mark the location of each point on the paper with a line or dot. Then compare the distance between the two dots with the map's bar scale. Because distances on a scale are given in large intervals, you may have to approximate the actual distance.

❺ Locator Map

A **locator** map shows where in the world the area on the map is located. The area shown on the main map is shown in red on the locator map. The locator map also shows surrounding areas so the map reader can see how the information on the map relates to neighboring lands.

❻ Interactive Keyword

Some maps in this textbook are interactive. If you go online to the Holt website and type in the map's keyword, you can learn more about the places and events shown on the map.

Working with Maps
Using Different Kinds of Maps

The Atlas in this textbook includes both physical and political maps. **Physical maps** show the major physical features in a region. These features include things like mountain ranges, rivers, oceans, islands, deserts, and plains. **Political maps** show the major political features of a region, such as countries and their borders, capitals, and other important cities.

Historical Map

In this textbook most of the maps you will study are historical maps. Historical maps, such as the one below, show information about the past. This information might be which lands a country controlled, where a certain group of people lived, what large cities were located in a region, or how a place changed over time. Often colors are used to indicate the different things on the map. Be sure to look at the map title and map legend first to see what the map is showing. What does this map show?

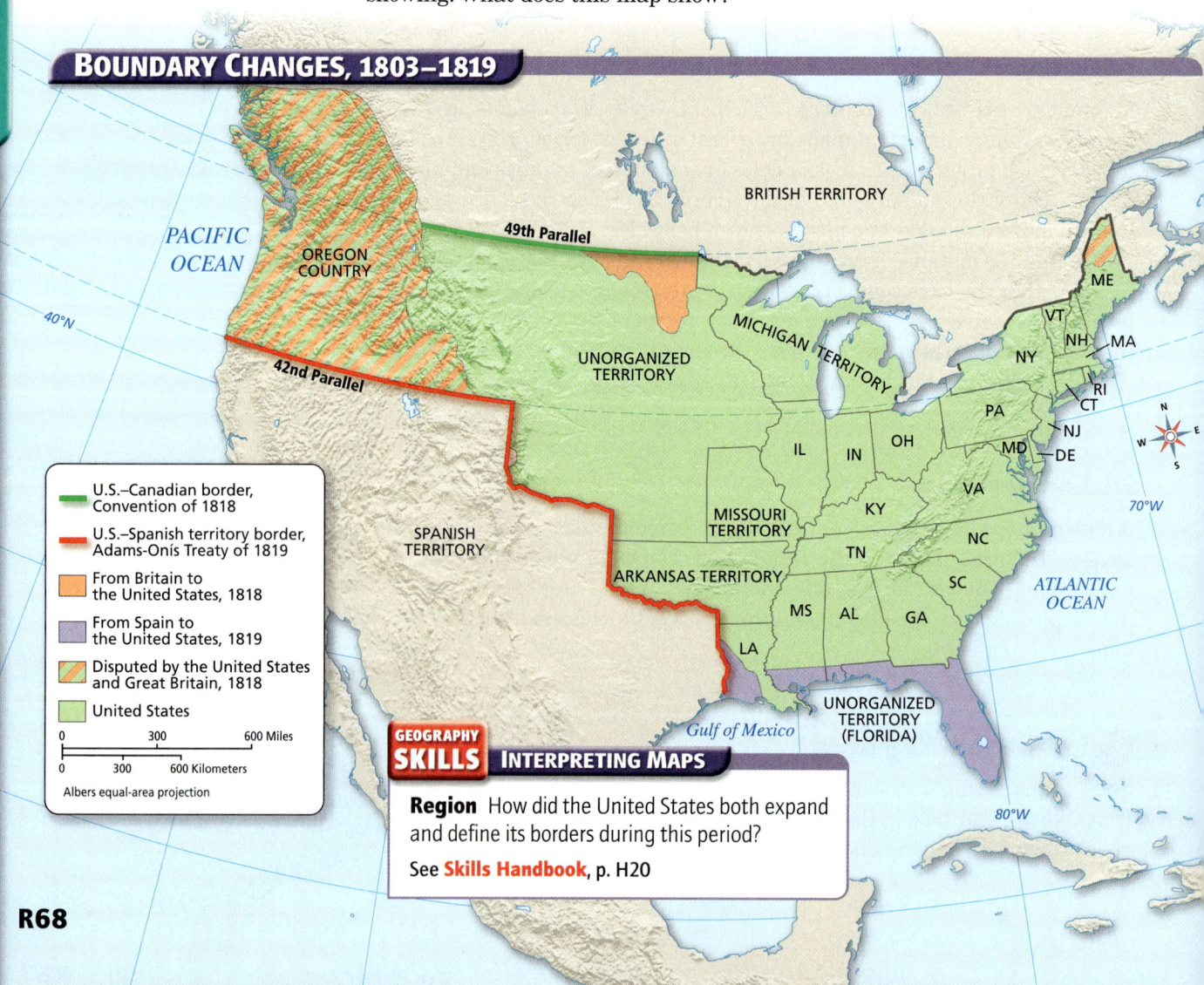

BOUNDARY CHANGES, 1803–1819

Legend:
- U.S.–Canadian border, Convention of 1818
- U.S.–Spanish territory border, Adams-Onís Treaty of 1819
- From Britain to the United States, 1818
- From Spain to the United States, 1819
- Disputed by the United States and Great Britain, 1818
- United States

0   300   600 Miles
0   300   600 Kilometers
Albers equal-area projection

GEOGRAPHY SKILLS | INTERPRETING MAPS

Region How did the United States both expand and define its borders during this period?

See **Skills Handbook**, p. H20

Interactive Map

THE LOUISIANA PURCHASE AND WESTERN EXPEDITIONS

Legend:
- U.S. states and territories in 1804
- Louisiana Purchase (acquired 1803)
- Lewis and Clark's expedition, 1804–1806

0   200   400 Miles
0   200   400 Kilometers
Albers equal-area projection

GEOGRAPHY SKILLS   INTERPRETING MAPS

go.hrw.com
Practice Online
Keyword: SE7 CH6

1. **Movement** About how long was Lewis and Clark's route?
2. **Region** What new problems do you think the Louisiana Purchase might present for the United States and for Native Americans?

See **Skills Handbook**, p. H19

Route Map

One special type of historical map is called a route map. A route map, like the one above, shows the route, or path, that someone or something followed. Route maps can show things like trade routes, invasion routes, or the journeys and travels of people. The routes on the map are usually shown with an arrow. If more than one route is shown, several arrows of different colors may be used. What does this route map show?

The maps in this textbook will help you study and understand history. By working with these maps, you will see where important events happened, where empires rose and fell, and where people moved. In studying these maps, you will learn how geography has influenced history.

Geographic Dictionary

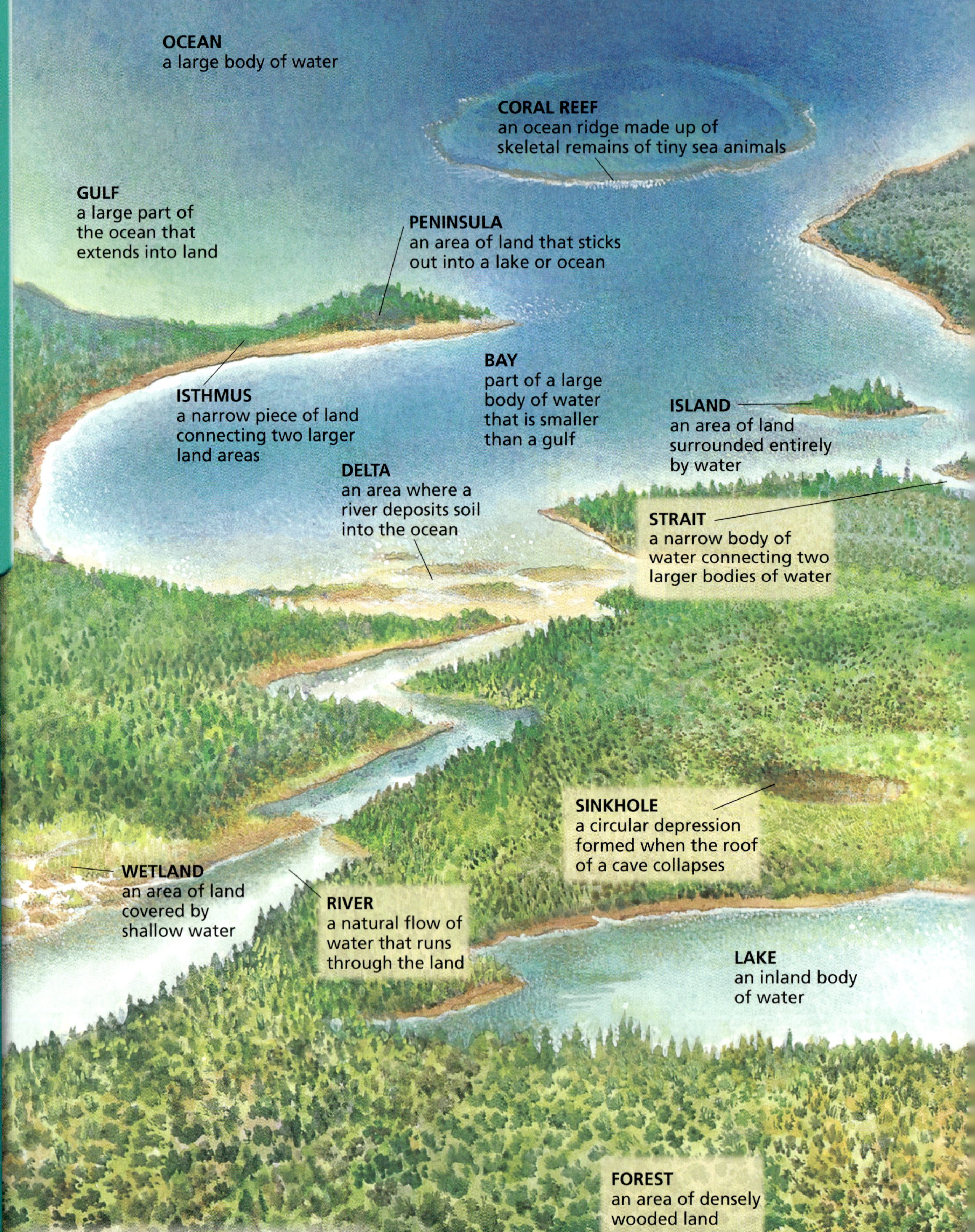

OCEAN
a large body of water

CORAL REEF
an ocean ridge made up of
skeletal remains of tiny sea animals

GULF
a large part of
the ocean that
extends into land

PENINSULA
an area of land that sticks
out into a lake or ocean

BAY
part of a large
body of water
that is smaller
than a gulf

ISLAND
an area of land
surrounded entirely
by water

ISTHMUS
a narrow piece of land
connecting two larger
land areas

DELTA
an area where a
river deposits soil
into the ocean

STRAIT
a narrow body of
water connecting two
larger bodies of water

SINKHOLE
a circular depression
formed when the roof
of a cave collapses

WETLAND
an area of land
covered by
shallow water

RIVER
a natural flow of
water that runs
through the land

LAKE
an inland body
of water

FOREST
an area of densely
wooded land

COAST
an area of land near the ocean

MOUNTAIN
an area of rugged land that generally rises higher than 2,000 feet

VALLEY
an area of low land between hills or mountains

GLACIER
a large area of slow-moving ice

VOLCANO
an opening in Earth's crust where lava, ash, and gases erupt

CANYON
a deep, narrow valley with steep walls

HILL
a rounded, elevated area of land smaller than a mountain

PLAIN
a nearly flat area

DUNE
a hill of sand shaped by wind

OASIS
an area in the desert with a water source

DESERT
an extremely dry area with little water and few plants

PLATEAU
a large, flat, elevated area of land

Themes and Essential Elements of Geography

by Dr. Christopher L. Salter

To study the world, geographers have identified 5 key themes, 6 essential elements, and 18 geography standards.

"How should we teach and learn about geography?" Professional geographers have worked hard over the years to answer this important question.

In 1984 a group of geographers identified the 5 Themes of Geography. These themes did a wonderful job of laying the groundwork for good classroom geography instruction. Teachers used the 5 Themes in classrooms, and geographers taught workshops on how to apply the 5 Themes in everyday life.

By the early 1990s, however, some geographers felt the 5 Themes were too broad. They created the 18 Geography Standards and the 6 Essential Elements. The 18 Geography Standards include more detailed information about what geography is, and the 6 Essential Elements are like a bridge between the 5 Themes and 18 Standards.

Look at the chart to the right. It shows how each of the 5 Themes connects to the 6 Essential Elements and 18 Geography Standards. For example, the theme of Location is related to The World in Spatial Terms and, through it, to the first three Standards. Study the chart carefully to see how the other Themes, Elements, and Standards are related.

The last Essential Element and the last two Standards cover The Uses of Geography. These key parts of geography were not covered by the 5 Themes. They emphasize how geographical knowledge can be applied to the study of history and current events and also be used to plan for the future.

5 Themes of Geography

Location The theme of location describes where something is.

Place Place describes the features that make a site unique.

Regions Regions are areas that share common characteristics.

Movement This theme looks at how and why people and things move.

Human-Environment Interaction People interact with their environment in many ways.

6 Essential Elements

18 Geography Standards

I. The World in Spatial Terms

1. How to use maps and other tools
2. How to use mental maps to organize information
3. How to analyze the spatial organization of people, places, and environments

II. Places and Regions

4. The physical and human characteristics of places
5. How people create regions to interpret Earth
6. How culture and experience influence people's perceptions of places and regions

III. Physical Systems

7. The physical processes that shape Earth's surface
8. The distribution of ecosystems on Earth

IV. Human Systems

9. The characteristics, distribution, and migration of human populations
10. The complexity of Earth's cultural mosaics
11. The patterns and networks of economic interdependence on Earth
12. The patterns of human settlement
13. The forces of cooperation and conflict

V. Environment and Society

14. How human actions modify the physical environment
15. How physical systems affect human systems
16. The distribution and meaning of resources

VI. The Uses of Geography

17. How to apply geography to interpret the past
18. How to apply geography to interpret the present and plan for the future

MAGNA CARTA, 1215

In the early 1200s King John of England angered the nobility when he imposed high taxes. The nobles joined forces with the Archbishop of Canterbury and in 1215 forced the king to sign the Magna Carta (Latin for "Great Charter"). The main point established by the Magna Carta was that the king, like all other people in England, was subject to the rule of law. The document also established the due process of law and the right to a fair and speedy trial as basic rights enjoyed by all people in England. These principles endured as part of English law and became part of American law in the Bill of Rights.

1. In the first place have granted to God, and by this our present charter confirmed for us and our heirs for ever that the English church shall be free, and shall have its rights undiminished and its liberties unimpaired . . . We have also granted to all free men of our kingdom, for ourselves and our heirs for ever, all the liberties written below, to be had and held by them and their heirs of us and our heirs.

2. If any of our earls or barons or others holding of us in chief by knight service dies, and at his death his heir be of full age and owe relief he shall have his inheritance on payment of the old relief, namely the heir or heirs of an earl 100 for a whole earl's barony, the heir or heirs of a baron 100 for a whole barony, the heir or heirs of a knight 100s, at most, for a whole knight's fee; and he who owes less shall give less according to the ancient usage of fiefs.

3. If, however, the heir of any such be under age and a ward, he shall have his inheritance when he comes of age without paying relief and without making fine.

40. To no one will we sell, to no one will we refuse or delay right or justice.

41. All merchants shall be able to go out of and come into England safely and securely and stay and travel throughout England, as well by land as by water, for buying and selling by the ancient and right customs free from all evil tolls, except in time of war and if they are of the land that is at war with us . . .

42. It shall be lawful in future for anyone, without prejudicing the allegiance due to us, to leave our kingdom and return safely and securely by land and water, save, in the public interest, for a short period in time of war—except for those imprisoned or outlawed in accordance with the law of the kingdom and natives of a land that is at war with us and merchants (who shall be treated as aforesaid).

62. And we have fully remitted and pardoned to everyone all the ill-will, indignation and rancour that have arisen between us and our men, clergy and laity, from the time of the quarrel. Furthermore, we have fully remitted to all, clergy and laity, and as far as pertains to us have completely forgiven, all trespasses occasioned by the same quarrel between Easter in the sixteenth year of our reign and the restoration of peace. And, besides, we have caused to be made for them letters testimonial patent of the lord Stephen archbishop of Canterbury, of the lord Henry archbishop of Dublin and of the aforementioned bishops and of master Pandulf about this security and the aforementioned concessions.

63. An oath, moreover, has been taken, as well on our part as on the part of the barons, that all these things aforesaid shall be observed in good faith and without evil disposition. Witness the above-mentioned and many others. Given by our hand in the meadow which is called Runnymede between Windsor and Staines on the fifteenth day of June, in the seventeenth year of our reign.

Source: "English Bill of Rights." Britannica Online. Vers. 99.1. Encyclopedia Britannica. 1994–1999. Encyclopedia Britannica, Inc.

The Mayflower Compact, 1620

In 1620 the Pilgrims left England bound for Virginia. A storm blew the Mayflower off course, and the Pilgrims made landfall in present-day Massachusetts. In Virginia the Pilgrims would have come under the laws governing that colony. In Massachusetts there were no laws, so the Pilgrims drew up a framework for self-government.

We whose names are underwritten, the loyal subjects of our dread Sovereign Lord King James, by the Grace of God of Great Britain, France and Ireland, King, Defender of the Faith, etc.

Having undertaken, for the Glory of God and advancement of the Christian Faith and Honour of our King and Country, a Voyage to plant the First Colony in the Northern Parts of Virginia, do by these presents solemnly and mutually in the presence of God and one of another, Covenant and Combine ourselves together into a Civil Body Politic, for our better ordering and preservation and furtherance of the ends aforesaid; and by virtue hereof to enact, constitute and frame such just and equal Laws, Ordinances, Acts, Constitutions and Offices, from time to time, as shall be thought most meet and convenient for the general good of the Colony, unto which we promise all due submission and obedience. In witness whereof we have hereunder subscribed our names at Cape Cod, the 11th of November, in the year of the reign of our Sovereign Lord King James, of England, France and Ireland the eighteenth, and of Scotland the fifty-fourth. Anno Domini 1620.

Source: *Of Plymouth Plantation.* William Bradford, 1630–1654. Samuel Eliot Morison, Ed., 1952. Pp. 75-76

> **VOCABULARY**
> **covenant** enter into a binding agreement

Fundamental Orders of Connecticut, 1639

In January 1639 settlers in Connecticut, led by Thomas Hooker, drew up the Fundamental Orders of Connecticut. An agreement among the settlers about how they would rule themselves, it included a body of laws. It is considered to by America's first written constitution.

Forasmuch as it hath pleased the All-mighty God by the wise disposition of his divyne pruvidence so to Order and dispose of things that we the Inhabitants and Residents of Windsor, Harteford and Wethersfield are now cohabiting and dwelling in and upon the River of Conectecotte and the Lands thereunto adioyneing [adjoining]; As also in our Civell Affaires to be guided and governed according to such Lawes, Rules, Orders and decrees as shall be made, ordered & decreed, as followeth:--

1. It is Ordered . . . that there shall be yerely two generall Assemblies or Courts, the one the second thursday in Aprill, the other the second thursday in September, following; the first shall be called the Courte of Election, wherein shall be yerely Chosen . . . soe many Magestrats and other publike [public] Officers as shall be found requisitte: which choise shall be made by all that are admitted freemen and have taken the Oath of Fidelity, and doe cohabitte within this Jurisdiction, (having beene admitted Inhabitants by the major part of the Towne wherein they live,) or the major parte of such as shall be then present . . .

Source: Federal and State Constitutions. F. N. Thorpe, Ed., Vol.1. 1909. p. 519.

> **VOCABULARY**
> **cohabiting** living
> **magestrats (magistrates)** local judges
> **requisitte (requisite)** essential or necessary
> **jurisdiction** an area over which a court or other government body has authority

ENGLISH BILL OF RIGHTS, 1689

In 1689, after the change of government known as the Glorious Revolution, Parliament passed the English Bill of Rights. This act ensured that Parliament would have power over the monarchy. The bill also protected the rights of English citizens. This part of the document contains a list of royal wrongdoings that would no longer be permitted.

By assuming and exercising a power of dispensing with and suspending of laws and the execution of laws without consent of Parliament; . . .

By levying money for and to the use of the Crown by pretence of prerogative for other time and in other manner than the same was granted by Parliament;

By raising and keeping a standing army within this kingdom in time of peace without consent of Parliament, and quartering soldiers contrary to law; . . .

And excessive bail hath been required of persons committed in criminal cases to elude the benefit of the laws made for the liberty of the subjects;

And excessive fines have been imposed;

And illegal and cruel punishments inflicted;

And several grants and promises made of fines and forfeitures before any conviction or judgment against the persons upon whom the same were to be levied;

All which are utterly and directly contrary to the known laws and statutes and freedom of this realm . . .

Source: "English Bill of Rights." Britannica Online. Vers. 99.1. Encyclopedia Britannica. 1994–1999. Encyclopedia Britannica, Inc.

VIRGINIA STATUTE FOR RELIGIOUS FREEDOM, 1786

The Virginia Statute for Religious Freedom, written by Thomas Jefferson and passed by Virginia's legislature in 1786, was an early statement of the rights of citizens to worship freely without experiencing coercion from government. The act was an inspiration to writers of the Bill of Rights.

. . . to compel a man to furnish contributions of money for the propagation of opinions which he disbelieves, is sinful and tyrannical; that even the forcing him to support this or that teacher of his own religious persuasion, is depriving him of the comfortable liberty of giving his contributions to the particular pastor . . . that our civil rights have no dependence on our religious opinions, any more than our opinions in physics or geometry; that therefore the proscribing any citizen as unworthy the public confidence by laying upon him an incapacity of being called to Offices of trust and emolument, unless he profess or renounce this or that religious opinion, is depriving him injuriously of those privileges and advantages to which in common with his fellow-citizens he has a natural right . . .

Be it enacted by the General Assembly, That no man shall be compelled to frequent or support any religious worship, place, or ministry whatsoever, nor shall be enforced, restrained, molested, or burthened in his body or goods, nor shall otherwise suffer on account of his religious opinions or belief; but that all men shall be free to profess, and by argument to maintain, their opinion in matters of religion, and that the same shall in no wise diminish enlarge, or affect their civil capacities.

. . . yet we are free to declare, and do declare, that the rights hereby asserted are of the natural rights of mankind, and that if any act shall be hereafter passed to repeal the present, or to narrow its operation, such act shall be an infringement of natural right.

Source: *Statutes at Large of Virginia*. W.W. Hening, Ed., Vol. 12. 1823. Pp. 84–86.

FEDERALIST PAPER No. 10, 1787

The Federalist Papers were a series of essays written in favor of ratifying the United States Constitution. The Papers were written by James Madison, Alexander Hamilton and John Jay. In Federalist Paper No. 10, *James Madison addressed critics who said that the United States was too large to be governed by a strong central government. Critics claimed there were too many interest groups, or "factions," to be ruled by a democratically elected government. Madison acknowledged the presence and problem of factions. He argued however, that the republican form of government under the Constitution was best able to deal with the problem by helping different factions negotiate solutions.*

By a faction, I understand a number of citizens, whether amounting to a majority or a minority of the whole, who are united and actuated by some common impulse of passion, or of interest, adversed to the rights of other citizens . . .

The latent causes of faction are thus sown in the nature of man; and we see them everywhere brought into different degrees of activity, according to the different circumstances of civil society. A zeal for different opinions concerning religion, concerning government, and many other points, as well of speculation as of practice; an attachment to different leaders ambitiously contending for pre-eminence and power; or to persons of other descriptions whose fortunes have been interesting to the human passions, have, in turn, divided mankind into parties, inflamed them with mutual animosity, and rendered them much more disposed to vex and oppress each other than to co-operate for their common good . . .

The inference to which we are brought is, that the CAUSES of faction cannot be removed, and that relief is only to be sought in the means of controlling its EFFECTS . . . A republic, by which I mean a government in which the scheme of representation takes place, opens a different prospect, and promises the cure for which we are seeking.

The two great points of difference between a democracy and a republic are: first, the delegation of the government, in the latter, to a small number of citizens elected by the rest; secondly, the greater number of citizens, and greater sphere of country, over which the latter may be extended . . .

The effect of the first difference is, on the one hand, to refine and enlarge the public views, by passing them through the medium of a chosen body of citizens, whose wisdom may best discern the true interest of their country, and whose patriotism and love of justice will be least likely to sacrifice it to temporary or partial considerations . . . [I]t may well happen that the public voice, pronounced by the representatives of the people, will be more consonant to the public good than if pronounced by the people themselves, convened for the purpose.

. . . [I]t clearly appears, that the same advantage which a republic has over a democracy, in controlling the effects of faction, is enjoyed by a large over a small republic, is enjoyed by the Union over the States composing it.

Source: *The Federalist* or *The New Constitution.* Papers by Alexander Hamilton, James Madison, and John Jay. New York Heritage Press. Introduction by Carl Van Doren. 1945.

VOCABULARY

latent hidden

animosity dislike

vex anger

discern understand or recognize

convened brought together

PRIMARY SOURCE LIBRARY

OBJECTIONS TO THIS CONSTITUTION OF GOVERNMENT, 1787

George Mason played a behind-the-scenes role in the Revolutionary War and wrote Virginia's Declaration of Rights. He attended the Constitutional Convention in 1787. Mason criticized the proposed Constitution for allowing slavery, creating a strong central government, and lacking a bill of rights. As a result, he refused to sign the Constitution. In the following excerpt, Mason explains why he would not sign the Constitution.

There is no Declaration of Rights, and the laws of the general government being para- mount to the laws and constitution of the several States, the Declarations of Rights in the separate States are no security. Nor are the people secured even in the enjoyment of the benefit of the common law.

In the House of Representatives there is not the substance but the shadow only of representation . . .

The Senate have the power of altering all money bills, and of originating appropriations of money, and the salaries of the Officers of their own appointment, in conjunction with the president of the United States, although they are not the representatives of the people or amenable to them . . .

The Judiciary of the United States is so constructed and extended, as to absorb and destroy the judiciaries of the several States; thereby rendering law as tedious, intricate and expensive, and justice as unattainable, by a great part of the community, as in England, and enabling the rich to oppress and ruin the poor.

The President of the United States has no Constitutional Council, a thing unknown in any safe and regular government. He will therefore be unsupported by proper informa- tion and advice, and will generally be directed by minions and favorites; or he will become a tool to the Senate . . .

The President of the United States has the unrestrained power of granting pardons for treason, which may be sometimes exer- cised to screen from punishment those whom he had secretly instigated to commit the crime, and thereby prevent a discovery of his own guilt . . .

Source: Gunston Hall Plantation

WASHINGTON'S FAREWELL ADDRESS, 1796

In 1796, at the end of his second term as president, George Washington wrote his farewell address with the help of Alexan- der Hamilton and James Madison. In it he spoke of the dangers facing the young nation. He warned against the dangers of political parties and sectionalism, and he advised the nation against permanent alliances with other nations.

In contemplating the causes, which may disturb our Union, it occurs as matter of serious concern, that any ground should have been furnished for characterizing parties by geographical discriminations—Northern and Southern—Atlantic and Western . . .

To the efficacy and permanency of your Union, a government for the whole is indispensible. No alliances, however strict, between the parts can be an adequate sub- stitute; they must inevitably experience the infractions and interruptions which all alli- ances in all times have experienced . . .

The great rule of conduct for us, in regard to foreign nations, is, in extending our com- mercial relations, to have with them as little political connexion [connection] as possible. So far as we have already formed engage- ments, let them be fulfilled with perfect good faith. Here let us stop . . .

Source: *Annals of Congress*, 4th Congress, pp. 2869–2880. American Memory Library of Congress. 1999.

JEFFERSON'S FIRST INAUGURAL ADDRESS, 1801

In 1800 Thomas Jefferson, representing the Democratic-Republican Party, defeated the Federalist candidate, President John Adams. Jefferson used his inaugural address of March 1801 to try to bridge the gap between the new political parties and to reach out to the Federalists.

Friends and Fellow-Citizens:

Called upon to undertake the duties of the first executive Office of our country, I avail myself of the presence of that portion of my fellow-citizens which is here assembled to express my grateful thanks for the favor with which they have been pleased to look toward me, to declare a sincere consciousness that the task is above my talents, and that I approach it with those anxious and awful pre-sentiments which the greatness of the charge and the weakness of my powers so justly inspire. A rising nation, spread over a wide and fruitful land, traversing all the seas with the rich productions of their industry, engaged in commerce with nations who feel power and forget right, advancing rapidly to destinies beyond the reach of mortal eye when I contemplate these transcendent objects, and see the honor, the happiness, and the hopes of this beloved country committed to the issue, and the auspices of this day, I shrink from the contemplation, and humble myself before the magnitude of the undertaking . . .

I repair, then, fellow-citizens, to the post you have assigned me. With experience enough in subordinate Offices to have seen the difficulties of this the greatest of all, I have learnt to expect that it will rarely fall to the lot of imperfect man to retire from this station with the reputation and the favor which bring him into it. Without pretensions to that high confidence you reposed in our first and greatest revolutionary character, whose preeminent services had entitled him to the first place in his country's love and destined for him the fairest page in the volume of faithful history, I ask so much confidence only as may give firmness and effect to the legal administration of your affairs.

Source: Inaugural Addresses of the Presidents of the United States. 1989. Bartleby Library.

VOCABULARY

presentiments feeling about something that will happen in the future

transcendent uplifting

auspices protection, support

reposed placed trust in

preeminent finest, the best

JOHN QUINCY ADAMS'S FOURTH OF JULY ADDRESS, 1821

John Quincy Adams, then Secretary of State to President James Monroe, made this Fourth of July speech to the House of Representatives in 1821. His topic was the role of the United States in world affairs. He begins by speaking of the "elder world," or the old world of Britain and Europe.

And now, friends and countrymen, if the wise and learned philosophers of the elder world, the first observers of nutation and aberration, the discoverers of maddening ether and invisible planets, the inventors of Congreve rockets and Shrapnel shells, should find their hearts disposed to enquire what has America done for the benefit of mankind?
Let our answer be this: America, with the same voice which spoke herself into existence as a nation, proclaimed to mankind the inextinguishable rights of human nature, and the only lawful foundations of government. She has abstained from interference in the concerns of others, even when conflict has been for principles to which she clings, as to the last vital drop that visits the heart . . .

[America's] glory is not dominion, but liberty. Her march is the march of the mind. She has a spear and a shield: but the motto upon her shield is, Freedom, Independence, Peace. This has been her Declaration: this has been, as far as her necessary intercourse with the rest of mankind would permit, her practice.

Source: Future of Freedom Foundation

VOCABULARY

nutation nodding one's head

aberration abnormality, irregularity, oddness

congreve rockets an early rocket used by the British in the War of 1812

shrapnel shells an anti-personnel weapon invented by Sir Henry Shrapnel and first used by the British army in 1803.

dominion supreme power

DENMARK VESEY DOCUMENT, 1822

Some enslaved African Americans tried to strike back against the slave system in the South. Denmark Vesey, a free African American living in Charleston, South Carolina, was accused of planning a massive and violent revolt in 1822. Vesey and others were caught and executed. Today some scholars have questioned if the conspiracy was real, arguing that Vesey was framed. Included below is an excerpt from an observer of the time.

At the head of this conspiracy stood Denmark Vesey, a free negro; with him the idea undoubtedly originated. For several years before he disclosed his intentions to any one, he appears to have been constantly and assiduously engaged in endeavoring to embitter the minds of the colored population against the white. He rendered himself perfectly familiar with all those parts of the Scriptures, which he thought he could pervert to his purpose; and would readily quote them, to prove that slavery was contrary to the laws of God; that slaves were bound to attempt their emancipation, however shocking and bloody might be the consequences, and that such efforts would not only be pleasing to the Almighty, but were absolutely enjoined, and their success predicted in the Scriptures . . .

In the selection of his leaders, Vesey showed great penetration and sound judgment. Rolla was plausible, and possessed uncommon self-possession; bold and ardent, he was not to be deterred from his purpose by danger. Ned's appearance indicated that he was a man of firm nerves, and desperate courage. Peter was intrepid and resolute, true to his engagements, and cautious in observing secrecy where it was necessary; he was not to be daunted nor impeded by difficulties, and though confident of success, was careful in providing against any obstacles or casualties which might arise, and intent upon discovering every means which might be in their power if thought of before hand. Gullah Jack was regarded as a Sorcerer, and as such feared by the natives of Africa, who believe in witchcraft.

He was not only considered invulnerable, but that he could make others so by his charms; and that he could and certainly would provide all his followers with arms. He was artful, cruel, bloody; his disposition in short was diabolical. His influence amongst the Africans was inconceivable. Monday was firm, resolute, discreet and intelligent . . .

As Vesey, from whom all orders emanated, and perhaps to whom only all important information was conveyed, died without confessing any thing, any opinion formed as to the numbers actually engaged in the plot, must be altogether conjectural; but enough has been disclosed to satisfy every reasonable mind, that considerable numbers were concerned. Indeed the plan of attack, which embraced so many points to be assailed at the same instant, affords sufficient evidence of the fact.

Source: *A NARRATIVE OF THE Conspiracy and Intended Insurrection, AMONGST A PORTION OF THE Negroes in the State of South-Carolina, In the Year 1822*

MONROE DOCTRINE, 1823

In 1823 President James Monroe proclaimed the Monroe Doctrine. Designed to end European influence in the Western Hemisphere, it became a cornerstone of United States. foreign policy.

With the existing colonies or dependencies of any European power we have not interfered and shall not interfere. But with the governments who have declared their independence and maintained it, and whose independence we have, on great consideration and on just principles, acknowledged, we could not view any <u>interposition</u> for the purpose of oppressing them, or controlling in any other manner their destiny, by any European power in any other light than as the <u>manifestation</u> of an unfriendly <u>disposition</u> toward the United States . . .

Our policy in regard to Europe, which was adopted at an early stage of the wars which have so long agitated that quarter of the globe, nevertheless remains the same, which is not to interfere in the internal concerns of any of its powers; to consider the government <u>de facto</u> as the legitimate government for us; to cultivate friendly relations with it, and to preserve those relations by a frank, firm, and manly policy, meeting in all instances the just claims of every power, submitting to injuries from none.

Source: "The Monroe Doctrine" by James Monroe reprinted in *The Annals of America: Volume 5, 1821–1832.* Encyclopedia Britannica. 1976.

VOCABULARY
interposition placing in the middle
manifestation a sign or appearance
disposition attitude
de facto actual

SENECA FALLS DECLARATION OF SENTIMENTS, 1848

One of the first documents to express the desire for equal rights for women was the Declaration of Sentiments, issued in 1848 at the Seneca Falls Convention in Seneca Falls, New York. Led by Elizabeth Cady Stanton and Lucretia Mott, the delegates adopted a set of resolutions modeled on the Declaration of Independence.

When, in the course of human events, it becomes necessary for one portion of the family of man to assume among the people of the earth a position different from that which they have <u>hitherto</u> occupied, but one to which the laws of nature and of nature's God entitle them, a decent respect to the opinions of mankind requires that they should declare the causes that impel them to such a course.

We hold these truths to be self-evident: that all men and women are created equal; that they are endowed by their Creator with certain inalienable rights; that among these are life, liberty, and the pursuit of happiness; that to secure these rights governments are instituted, <u>deriving</u> their just powers from the consent of the governed. Whenever any form of government becomes destructive of these ends, it is the right of those who suffer from it to refuse allegiance to it, and to insist upon the institution of a new government, laying its foundation on such principles, and organizing its powers in such form, as to them shall seem most likely to effect their safety and happiness.

Source: "Seneca Falls Declaration on Women's Rights" reprinted in *The Annals of America: Volume 7, 1841–1849.* Encyclopedia Britannica. 1976.

VOCABULARY
hitherto previously
deriving receiving from a source

VOCABULARY
equilibirium balance
subjugation con-
quest

In March 1850 the Senate debated the admission of California into the Union as a free state. The debate eventually led to the Compromise of 1850, brokered by Senator Henry Clay of Kentucky, known as the "Great Compromiser." Senator John C. Calhoun of South Carolina, opposed the Compromise. Too ill to speak or even walk, he was carried into the Senate, where another senator read his speech. It was Calhoun's last appearance in the Senate. A few weeks later, he died. On March 7, Senator Daniel Webster of Massachusetts replied to Calhoun. Excerpts from both speeches are given below.

From the speech of John C. Calhoun:

The question then recurs: What is the cause of this discontent? It will be found in the belief of the people of the Southern States, as prevalent as the discontent itself, that they can not remain, as things now are, consistently with honor and safety, in the Union. The next question to be considered is: What has caused this belief?

One of the causes is, undoubtedly, to be traced to the long-continued agitation of the slave question on the part of the North, and the many aggressions which they have made on the rights of the South during the time. I will not enumerate them at present, as it will be done hereafter in its proper place.

There is another lying back of it—with which this is intimately connected—that may be regarded as the great and primary cause. This is to be found in the fact that the equilibrium between the two sections in the government as it stood when the Constitution was ratified and the government put in action has been destroyed. At that time there was nearly a perfect equilibrium between the two, which afforded ample means to each to protect itself against the aggression of the other; but, as it now stands, one section has the exclusive power of controlling the government, which leaves the other without any adequate means of protecting itself against its encroachment and oppression.

The result of the whole is to give the Northern section a predominance in every department of the government, and thereby concentrate in it the two elements which constitute the federal government: a majority of States, and a majority of their population, estimated in federal numbers. Whatever section concentrates the two in itself possesses the control of the entire government . . .

It is a great mistake to suppose that disunion can be effected by a single blow. The cords which bind these States together in one common Union are far too numerous and powerful for that. Disunion must be the work of time. It is only through a long process, and successively, that the cords can be snapped until the whole fabric falls asunder. Already the agitation of the slavery question has snapped some of the most important, and has greatly weakened all the others.

If the agitation goes on, the same force, acting with increased intensity, as has been shown, will finally snap every cord, when nothing will be left to hold the States together except force. But surely that can with no propriety of language be called a Union when the only means by which the weaker is held connected with the stronger portion is force. It may, indeed, keep them connected; but the connection will partake much more of the character of subjugation on the part of the weaker to the stronger than the union of free, independent, and sovereign States in one confederation, as they stood in the early stages of the government, and which only is worthy of the sacred name of Union.

Source: National Center for Public Policy Research

From the speech of Daniel Webster:

Mr. President [of the Senate], I wish to speak to-day, not as a Massachusetts man, nor as a Northern man, but as an American, and a member of the Senate of the United States . . . I speak to-day for the preservation of the Union . . .

Mr. President, I should much prefer to have heard from every member on this floor declarations of opinion that this Union could never be dissolved, than the declaration of opinion by any body, that, in any case, under the pressure of any circumstances, such a dissolution was possible. I hear with distress and anguish the word "secession," especially when it falls from the lips of those who are patriotic, and known to the country, and known all over the world, for their political services. Secession! Peaceable secession! Sir, your eyes and mine are never destined to see that miracle. The dismemberment of this vast country without convulsion! The breaking up of the fountains of the great deep without ruffing the surface! Who is so foolish, I beg every body's pardon, as to expect to see any such thing? . . .

There can be no such thing as peaceable secession. Peaceable secession is an utter impossibility. Is the great Constitution under which we live, covering this whole country, is it to be thawed and melted away by secession, as the snows on the mountain melt under the influence of a vernal sun, disappear almost unobserved, and run off? No, Sir! No, Sir! I will not state what might produce the disruption of the Union; but, Sir, I see as plainly as I see the sun in heaven what that disruption itself must produce; I see that it must produce war, and such a war as I will not describe, in its twofold character.

Peaceable secession! Peaceable secession! The concurrent agreement of all the members of this great republic to separate! A voluntary separation, with alimony on one side and on the other. Why, what would be the result?

Where is the line to be drawn? What States are to seceded? What is to remain American? What am I to be? An American no longer? Am I to become a sectional man, a local man, a separatist, with no country in common with the gentlemen who sit around me here, or who fill the other house of Congress? Heaven forbid! Where is the flag of the republic to remain? Where is the eagle still to tower? or is he to cower, and shrink, and fall to the ground? Why, Sir, our ancestors, our fathers and our grandfathers, those of them that are yet living amongst us with prolonged lives, would rebuke and reproach us; and our children and our grandchildren would cry out shame upon us, if we of this generation should dishonor these ensigns of the power of the government and the harmony of that Union which is every day felt among us with so much joy and gratitude . . .

And now, Mr. President, instead of speaking of the possibility or utility of secession, instead of dwelling in those caverns of darkness, instead of groping with those ideas so full of all that is horrid and horrible, let us come out into the light of day; let us enjoy the fresh air of Liberty and Union; let us cherish those hopes which belong to us; let us devote ourselves to those great objects that are fit for our consideration and action; let us raise our conceptions to the magnitude and the importance of the duties that devolve upon us; let our comprehension be as broad as the country for which we act, our aspirations as high as its certain destiny; let us not be pigmies in a case that calls for men. Never did there devolve on any generation of men higher trusts than now devolve upon us, for the preservation of this Constitution and the harmony and peace of all who are destined to live under it.

Source: Dartmouth College

FREDERICK DOUGLASS'S "THE SIGNIFICANCE OF EMANCIPATION IN THE WEST INDIES," 1857

On August 3, 1857, Frederick Douglass gave a speech in Canadaigua, New York in which he discussed freedom for slaves in the West Indies. In this speech Douglass described what he called his "philosophy of reform," which was that successful struggles for liberty always require tremendous effort and sacrifice.

Let me give you a word of the philosophy of reform. The whole history of the progress of human liberty shows that all concessions yet made to her august claims, have been born of earnest struggle. The conflict has been exciting, agitating, all-absorbing, and for the time being, putting all other tumults to silence. It must do this or it does nothing. If there is no struggle there is no progress. Those who profess to favor freedom and yet depreciate agitation, are men who want crops without plowing up the ground, they want rain without thunder and lightening. They want the ocean without the awful roar of its many waters.

This struggle may be a moral one, or it may be a physical one, and it may be both moral and physical, but it must be a struggle.

Power concedes nothing without a demand. It never did and it never will. Find out just what any people will quietly submit to and you have found out the exact measure of injustice and wrong which will be imposed upon them, and these will continue till they are resisted with either words or blows, or with both. The limits of tyrants are prescribed by the endurance of those whom they oppress. In the light of these ideas, Negroes will be hunted at the North, and held and flogged at the South so long as they submit to those devilish outrages, and make no resistance, either moral or physical. Men may not get all they pay for in this world; but they must certainly pay for all they get. If we ever get free from the oppressions and wrongs heaped upon us, we must pay for their removal. We must do this by labor, by suffering, by sacrifice, and if needs be, by our lives and the lives of others."

Source: *The Frederick Douglass Papers. Series One: Speeches, Debates, and Interviews. Volume 3: 1855–63.* Edited by John W. Blassingame. New Haven: Yale University Press, p. 204.

LINCOLN'S FIRST INAUGURAL ADDRESS, 1861

Abraham Lincoln knew that his victory in the 1860 presidential election threatened to tear the country apart. In his inaugural address on March 4, 1861, Lincoln pledged that there would be no war unless the South chose to begin one. In the excerpt below, he explains his reasons for believing secession to be unconstitutional and urges the South not to destroy the Union.

Fellow-Citizens of the United States:

In compliance with a custom as old as the Government itself, I appear before you to address you briefly and to take in your presence the oath prescribed by the Constitution of the United States to be taken by the President "before he enters on the execution of this Office." . . .

I have no purpose, directly or indirectly, to interfere with the institution of slavery in the States where it exists. I believe I have no lawful right to do so, and I have no inclination to do so. Those who nominated and elected me did so with full knowledge that I had made this and many similar declarations and had never recanted them; and more than this, they placed in the platform for my acceptance, and as a law to themselves and to me, the clear and emphatic resolution which I now read:

. . . In any law upon this subject ought not all the safeguards of liberty known in civilized and humane jurisprudence to be introduced, so that a free man be not in any case surrendered as a slave? And might it not be well at the same time to provide by law for the enforcement of that clause in the Constitution which guarantees that "the citizens of each State shall be entitled to all privileges and immunities of citizens in the several States?" . . .

It follows from these views that no State upon its own mere motion can lawfully get out of the Union; that resolves and ordinances to that effect are legally void, and that acts of violence within any State or States against the authority of the United States are insurrectionary or revolutionary, according to circumstances.

I therefore consider that in view of the Constitution and the laws the Union is unbroken, and to the extent of my ability, I shall take care, as the Constitution itself expressly enjoins upon me, that the laws of the Union be faithfully executed in all the States . . .

One section of our country believes slavery is right and ought to be extended, while the other believes it is wrong and ought not to be extended. This is the only substantial dispute.

Physically speaking, we can not separate. We can not remove our respective sections from each other nor build an impassable wall between them. A husband and wife may be divorced and go out of the presence and beyond the reach of each other, but the different parts of our country can not do this.

This country, with its institutions, belongs to the people who inhabit it. Whenever they shall grow weary of the existing Government, they can exercise their constitutional right of amending it or their revolutionary right to dismember or overthrow it . . .

In your hands, my dissatisfied fellow-countrymen, and not in mine, is the momentous issue of civil war. The Government will not assail you. You can have no conflict without being yourselves the aggressors. You have no oath registered in heaven to destroy the Government, while I shall have the most solemn one to "preserve, protect, and defend it."

I am loath to close. We are not enemies, but friends. We must not be enemies. Though passion may have strained it must not break our bonds of affection. The mystic chords of memory, stretching from every battlefield and patriot grave to every living heart and hearthstone all over this broad land, will yet swell the chorus of the Union, when again touched, as surely they will be, by the better angels of our nature.

Source: Inaugural Addresses of the Presidents of the United States. 1989. Bartleby Library.

PRIMARY SOURCE LIBRARY

THE EMANCIPATION PROCLAMATION

After the Union army victory at the Battle of Antietam, President Abraham Lincoln decided to issue the Emancipation Proclamation, which freed all enslaved people in states under Confederate control. The proclamation, which went into effect on January 1, 1863, was a step toward the Thirteenth Amendment (1865), which ended slavery in all of the United States.

That on the 1st day of January, in the year of our Lord 1863, all persons held as slaves within any state or designated part of a state, the people whereof shall then be in rebellion against the United States, shall be then, thenceforward, and forever free; and the executive government of the United States, including the military and naval authority thereof, will recognize and maintain the freedom of such persons and will do no act or acts to repress such persons, or any of them, in any efforts they may make for their actual freedom . . .

And I further declare and make known that such persons of suitable condition will be received into the armed service of the United States to garrison forts, positions, stations, and other places, and to man vessels of all sorts in said service. And upon this act, sincerely believed to be an act of justice, warranted by the Constitution upon military necessity, I invoke the considerate judgment of mankind and the gracious favor of Almighty God.

Source: "Emancipation Proclamation" by Abraham Lincoln. Reprinted in *The Annals of America: Volume 9, 1858–1865*. Encyclopedia Britannica, Inc. 1976.

LINCOLN'S GETTYSBURG ADDRESS, 1863

VOCABULARY
score twenty years
consecrated made holy

On November 19, 1863, Abraham Lincoln addressed a crowd gathered to dedicate a cemetery at the Gettysburg battlefield. His short speech, which is excerpted below, reminded Americans of the ideals on which the Republic was founded.

Four score and seven years ago our fathers brought forth on this continent a new nation, conceived in liberty and dedicated to the proposition that all men are created equal.

Now we are engaged in a great civil war, testing whether that nation or any nation so conceived and so dedicated can long endure. We are met on a great battlefield of that war. We have come to dedicate a portion of that field as a final resting-place for those who here gave their lives that that nation might live. It is altogether fitting and proper that we should do this.

But in a larger sense, we cannot dedicate—we cannot consecrate—we cannot hallow—this ground. The brave men, living and dead, who struggled here have consecrated it far above our poor power to add or detract. The world will little note nor long remember what we say here, but it can never forget what they did here. It is for us, the living, rather, to be dedicated here to the unfinished work which they who fought here have thus far so nobly advanced.

It is rather for us to be here dedicated to the great task remaining before us—that from these honored dead we take increased devotion to that cause for which they gave the last full measure of devotion; that we here highly resolve that these dead shall not have died in vain; that this nation, under God, shall have a new birth of freedom; and that government of the people, by the people, for the people shall not perish from the earth.

Source: "The Gettysburg Address" by Abraham Lincoln. *Reprinted in The Annals of America: Volume 9, 1858–1865.* Encyclopedia Britannica, Inc. 1976.

LINCOLN'S SECOND INAUGURAL ADDRESS, 1865

VOCABULARY
deprecated made little of
malice desire to cause injury; hatred

On March 4, 1865, President Lincoln laid out his approach to Reconstruction in his second inaugural address. As the excerpt below shows, Lincoln hoped to peacefully reunite the nation and its people.

At this second appearing to take the oath of the Presidential Office there is less occasion for an extended address than there was at the first. Then a statement somewhat in detail of a course to be pursued seemed fitting and proper. Now, at the expiration of four years, during which public declarations have been constantly called forth on every point and phase of the great contest which still absorbs the attention and engrosses the energies of the nation, little that is new could be presented. The progress of our arms, upon which all else chiefly depends, is as well known to the public as to myself, and it is, I trust, reasonably satisfactory and encouraging to all. With high hope for the future, no prediction in regard to it is ventured.

On the occasion corresponding to this four years ago all thoughts were anxiously directed to an impending civil war. All dreaded it, all sought to avert it. While the inaugural address was being delivered from this place, devoted altogether to saving the Union without war, urgent agents were in the city seeking to destroy it without war—seeking to dissolve the Union and divide effects by negotiation. Both parties deprecated war, but one of them would make war rather than let the nation survive, and the other would accept war rather than let it perish, and the war came . . .

With malice toward none, with charity for all, with firmness in the right as God gives us to see the right, let us strive on to finish the work we are in, to bind up the nation's wounds, to care for him who shall have borne the battle and for his widow and his orphan, to do all which may achieve and cherish a just and lasting peace among ourselves and with all nations.

Source: Inaugural Addresses of the Presidents of the United States. 1989. Bartleby Library.

DECLARATION OF RIGHTS FOR WOMEN

Included below are excerpts from a speech made by Susan B. Anthony on July 4, 1876. Anthony used the occasion—the 100th anniversary of the approval of the Declaration of Independence—to speak out in support of rights for women.

Susan B. Anthony, July 4, 1876

While the nation is buoyant with patriotism, and all hearts are attuned to praise, it is with sorrow we come to strike the one discordant note, on this one-hundredth anniversary of our country's birth. When subjects of kings, emperors, and czars from the old world join in our national jubilee, shall the women of the republic refuse to lay their hands with benedictions on the nation's head? . . . Yet we cannot forget, even in this glad hour, that while all men of every race, and clime, and condition, have been invested with the full rights of citizenship under our hospitable flag, all women still suffer the degradation of disfranchisement.

The history of our country the past one hundred years has been a series of assumptions and usurpations of power over woman, in direct opposition to the principles of just government, acknowledged by the United States as its foundations, which are:

First–the natural rights of each individual
Second–the equality of these rights
Third–that rights not delegated are retained by the individual
Fourth–that no person can exercise the rights of others without delegated authority
Fifth–that the non-use of rights does not destroy them

And for the violation of these fundamental principles of our government, we arraign our rulers on this Fourth day of July, 1876 . . .

These articles of impeachment against our rulers we now submit to the impartial judgment of the people. To all these wrongs and oppressions woman has not submitted in silence and resignation. From the beginning of the century, when Abigail Adams, the wife of one president and the mother of another, said, "We will not hold ourselves bound to obey laws in which we have no voice or representation," until now, woman's discontent has been steadily increasing, culminating nearly thirty years ago in a simultaneous movement among the women of the nation, demanding the right of suffrage . . .

And now, at the close of a hundred years, as the hour hand of the great clock that marks the centuries points to 1876, we declare our faith in the principles of self-government; our full equality with man in natural rights . . . We ask of our rulers, at this hour, no special favors, no special privileges, no special legislation. We ask justice, we ask equality, we ask that all the civil and political rights that belong to citizens of the United States, be guaranteed to us and our daughters forever.

Source: *History of Women's Suffrage,* Elizabeth C. Stanton et al., eds., Vol.III, 1887.

VOCABULARY

buoyant cheerful, capable of floating
jubilee a special anniversary
benedictions blessings
usurpations takings by force and without right

THE FOURTEEN POINTS, 1918

On January 8, 1918, nearly a year before the end of World War I, Woodrow Wilson presented his plan for a postwar peace to the U.S. Congress. Wilson came to the Paris Peace Conference in 1919 with these same 14 points.

1. Open covenants of peace, openly arrived at, after which there shall be no private international understandings of any kind but diplomacy shall proceed always frankly and in the public view.
2. Absolute freedom of navigation upon the seas, outside territorial waters, alike in peace and in war . . .
3. The removal, so far as possible, of all economic barriers and the establishment of an equality of trade conditions . . .
4. Adequate guarantees given and taken that national armaments will be reduced to the lowest point consistent with domestic safety.
5. A free, open-minded, and absolutely impartial adjustment of all colonial claims, based upon a strict observance of the principle that in determining all such questions of sovereignty the interests of the populations concerned must have equal weight with the equitable claims of the government whose title is to be determined.
6. The evacuation of all Russian territory . . .
7. Belgium . . . must be evacuated and restored, without any attempt to limit . . . sovereignty . . .
8. All French territory should be freed and the invaded portions restored, and the wrong done to France by Prussia in 1871 in the matter of Alsace-Lorraine, which has unsettled the peace of the world for nearly fifty years, should be righted, in order that peace may once more be made secure in the interest of all.
9. A readjustment of the frontiers of Italy should be effected along clearly recognizable lines of nationality.
10. The peoples of Austria-Hungary . . . should be accorded the freest opportunity of autonomous development.
11. Rumania, Serbia, and Montenegro should be evacuated . . .
12. The Turkish portions of the present Ottoman Empire should be assured a secure sovereignty, but the other nationalities which are now under Turkish rule should be assured an undoubted security of life and an absolutely unmolested opportunity of an autonomous development,
13. An independent Polish state should be erected which should include the territories inhabited by indisputably Polish populations
14. A general association of nations must be formed under specific covenants for the purpose of affording mutual guarantees of political independence and territorial integrity to great and small states alike.

Source: Avalon Project of Yale University Law School

FOUR FREEDOMS SPEECH, 1941

In January 1941, while World War II raged in Europe and Asia, many Americans hoped the United States would stay out of the war. President Franklin D. Roosevelt understood this public feeling, but believed it was important that the United States help Great Britain resist Nazi Germany. Roosevelt gave this speech on January 6, 1941 to win greater support for his policy of providing aid to the enemies of Germany and Japan.

I have called for personal sacrifice. I am assured of the willingness of almost all Americans to respond to that call.

A part of the sacrifice means the payment of more money in taxes. In my Budget Message I shall recommend that a greater portion of this great defense program be paid for from taxation than we are paying today. No person should try, or be allowed, to get rich out of this program; and the principle of tax payments in accordance with ability to pay should be constantly before our eyes to guide our legislation.

If the Congress maintains these principles, the voters, putting patriotism ahead of pocketbooks, will give you their applause.

In the future days, which we seek to make secure, we look forward to a world founded upon four essential human freedoms.

The first is freedom of speech and expression—everywhere in the world.

The second is freedom of every person to worship God in his own way—everywhere in the world.

The third is freedom from want—which, translated into world terms, means economic understandings which will secure to every nation a healthy peacetime life for its inhabitants—everywhere in the world.

The fourth is freedom from fear—which, translated into world terms, means a worldwide reduction of armaments to such a point and in such a thorough fashion that no nation will be in a position to commit an act of physical aggression against any neighbor—anywhere in the world.

That is no vision of a distant millennium. It is a definite basis for a kind of world attainable in our own time and generation. That kind of world is the very <u>antithesis</u> of the so-called new order of tyranny which the dictators seek to create with the crash of a bomb.

Source: Franklin D. Roosevelt Presidential Library and Museum

JOHN F. KENNEDY INAUGURAL ADDRESS, 1961

President John F. Kennedy took office on January 20, 1961, at the height of the Cold War. In his inaugural address, Kennedy spoke of the immense responsibility entrusted to his generation of Americans.

The world is very different now. For man holds in his mortal hands the power to abolish all forms of human poverty and all forms of human life. And yet the same revolutionary beliefs for which our <u>forebears</u> fought are still at issue around the globe—the belief that the rights of man come not from the generosity of the state, but from the hand of God.

We dare not forget today that we are the heirs of that first revolution. Let the word go forth from this time and place, to friend and foe alike, that the torch has been passed to a new generation of Americans—born in this century, tempered by war, disciplined by a hard and bitter peace, proud of our ancient heritage—and unwilling to witness or permit the slow undoing of those human rights to which this Nation has always been committed, and to which we are committed today at home and around the world.

Let every nation know, whether it wishes us well or ill, that we shall pay any price, bear any burden, meet any hardship, support any friend, oppose any foe, in order to assure the survival and the success of liberty . . .

In the long history of the world, only a few generations have been granted the role of defending freedom in its hour of maximum danger. I do not shrink from this responsibility—I welcome it. I do not believe that any of us would exchange places with any other people or any other generation. The energy, the faith, the devotion which we bring to this endeavor will light our country and all who serve it—and the glow from that fire can truly light the world.

And so, my fellow Americans: ask not what your country can do for you—ask what you can do for your country.

My fellow citizens of the world: ask not what America will do for you, but what together we can do for the freedom of man.

Source: Avalon Project of Yale University Law School

VOCABULARY
proprietor owner
coerce force

First proposed by President Kennedy, the Civil Rights Act faced fierce opposition from Southern senators who opposed federal legislation to end segregation. After Kennedy's assassination in 1963, Vice President Lyndon Johnson became president. Johnson, who had served as the Senate majority leader, used his extensive legislative experience to help push the Civil Right Act through Congress. He signed it into law on July 2, 1964. The new law banned segregation in public places.

Title II
Sec. 201. (a) All persons shall be entitled to the full and equal enjoyment of the goods, services, facilities, privileges, advantages, and accommodations of any place of public accommodation, as defined in this section, without discrimination or segregation on the ground of race, color, religion, or national origin. (b) Each of the following establishments which serves the public is a place of public accommodation within the meaning of this title if its operations affect commerce, or if discrimination or segregation by it is supported by State action:

(1) any inn, hotel, motel, or other establishment which provides lodging to transient guests, other than an establishment located within a building which contains not more than five rooms for rent or hire and which is actually occupied by the proprietor of such establishment as his residence;

(2) any restaurant, cafeteria, lunchroom, lunch counter, soda fountain, or other facility principally engaged in selling food for consumption on the premises, including, but not limited to, any such facility located on the premises of any retail establishment; or any gasoline station;

(3) any motion picture house, theater, concert hall, sports arena, stadium or other place of exhibition or entertainment;

Sec 202. All persons shall be entitled to be free, at any establishment or place, from discrimination or segregation of any kind on the ground of race, color, religion, or national origin, if such discrimination or segregation is or purports to be required by any law, statute, ordinance, regulation, rule, or order of a State or any agency or political subdivision thereof.

Sec. 203. No person shall (a) withhold, deny, or attempt to withhold or deny, or deprive or attempt to deprive, any person of any right or privilege secured by section 201 or 202, or (b) intimidate, threaten, or coerce, or attempt to intimidate, threaten, or coerce any person with purpose of interfering with any right or privilege secured by section 201 or 202, or (c) punish or attempt to punish any person for exercising or attempting to exercise any right or privilege secured by section 201 or 202.

Source: U.S. Statutes at Large 78 (1964): 241.

In 1968 Martin Luther King, Jr. went to Memphis to march in support of striking sanitation workers. The strikers were mostly African American. On April 3, 1968, King gave the following speech. He makes reference to an earlier incident in which he was stabbed by a deranged woman. The wound was so close to King's heart, doctors announced, that that if he had sneezed, he would have died. The day after delivering this speech, King was assassinated.

April 3, 1968, Memphis, Tennessee

And I want to say tonight, I want to say that I am happy that I didn't sneeze. Because if I had sneezed, I wouldn't have been around here in 1960, when students all over the South started sitting-in at lunch counters. And I knew that as they were sitting in, they were really standing up for the best in the American dream. And taking the whole nation back to those great wells of democracy which were dug deep by the Founding Fathers in the Declaration of Independence and the Constitution. If I had sneezed, I wouldn't have been around in 1962, when Negroes in Albany, Georgia, decided to straighten their backs up. And whenever men and women straighten their backs up, they are going somewhere, because a man can't ride your back unless it is bent. If I had sneezed, I wouldn't have been here in 1963, when the black people of Birmingham, Alabama, aroused the conscience of this nation, and brought into being the Civil Rights Bill. If I had sneezed, I wouldn't have had a chance later that year, in August, to try to tell America about a dream that I had had. If I had sneezed, I wouldn't have been down in Selma, Alabama, been in Memphis to see the community rally around those brothers and sisters who are suffering. I'm so happy that I didn't sneeze . . .

Well, I don't know what will happen now. We've got some difficult days ahead. But it doesn't matter with me now. Because I've been to the mountaintop. And I don't mind. Like anybody, I would like to live a long life. Longevity has its place. But I'm not concerned about that now. I just want to do God's will. And He's allowed me to go up to the mountain. And I've looked over. And I've seen the promised land. I may not get there with you. But I want you to know tonight, that we, as a people, will get to the promised land. And I'm happy, tonight. I'm not worried about anything. I'm not fearing any man. Mine eyes have seen the glory of the coming of the Lord.

Source: American Federation of State, County and Municipal Employees

César Chávez Speech, 1984

In 1962 César Chávez formed the United Farm Workers, a labor union for migrant farm workers. In the 1984 speech excerpted below, Chávez described the goals that motivated his life's work and spoke of the contribution the farm workers movement had made to improving lives for Hispanic Americans everywhere.

VOCABULARY
implements tools
chattel personal property a slave

All my life, I have been driven by one dream, one goal, one vision: To overthrow a farm labor system in this nation which treats farm workers as if they were not important human beings. Farm workers are not agricultural implements. They are not beasts of burden to be used and discarded . . .

I'm not very different from anyone else who has ever tried to accomplish something with his life. My motivation comes from my personal life—from watching what my mother and father went through when I was growing up; from what we experienced as migrant farm workers in California.

That dream, that vision, grew from my own experience with racism, with hope, with the desire to be treated fairly and to see my people treated as human beings and not as chattel. It grew from anger and rage—emotions I felt 40 years ago when people of my color were denied the right to see a movie or eat at a restaurant in many parts of California. It grew from the frustration and humiliation I felt as a boy who couldn't understand how the growers could abuse and exploit farm workers when there were so many of us and so few of them . . .

I began to realize what other minority people had discovered: That the only answer—the only hope—was in organizing. More of us had to become citizens. We had to register to vote. And people like me had to develop the skills it would take to organize, to educate, to help empower the Chicano people . . .

All Hispanics—urban and rural, young and old—are connected to the farm workers' experience. We had all lived through the fields—or our parents had. We shared that common humiliation. How could we progress as a people, even if we lived in the cities, while the farm workers—men and women of our color—were condemned to a life without pride? How could we progress as a people while the farm workers—who symbolized our history in this land—ere denied self-respect? . . .

The UFW was the beginning! We attacked that historical source of shame and infamy that our people in this country lived with. We attacked that injustice, not by complaining; not by seeking handouts; not by becoming soldiers in the War on Poverty.

Farm workers acknowledged we had allowed ourselves to become victims in a democratic society—a society where majority rule and collective bargaining are supposed to be more than academic theories or political rhetoric. And by addressing this historical problem, we created confidence and pride and hope in an entire people's ability to create the future . . .

The union's survival—its very existence—sent out a signal to all Hispanics that we were fighting for our dignity, that we were challenging and overcoming injustice, that we were empowering the least educated among us—the poorest among us . . . I didn't really appreciate it at the time, but the coming of our union signaled the start of great changes among Hispanics that are only now beginning to be seen.

I've traveled to every part of this nation. I have met and spoken with thousands of Hispanics from every walk of life—from every social and economic class. One thing I hear most often from Hispanics, regardless of age or position—and from many non-Hispanics as well—is that the farm workers gave them hope that they could succeed and the inspiration to work for change . . . And Hispanics across California and the nation who don't work in agriculture are better off today because of what the farm workers taught people about organization, about pride and strength, about seizing control over their own lives.

Source: The Cesar E. Chavez Foundation is the intellectual property owner of Cesar's name, voice, image, and likeness, speeches and writings. Permission to reproduce said intellectual property for publication purposes may be obtained by contacting the: Cesar E. Chavez Foundation, 634 S. Spring St., Su. 727, Los Angeles, CA, 90014, (213) 362-0267, fax: (213) 362-0265, info@cecfmail.org

ADDRESS TO THE NATION, SEPTEMBER 11, 2001

Terrorists attacked the United States on the morning of September 11, 2001, crashing planes into the World Trade Center in New York City and the Pentagon building near Washington, D.C. At 8:30 on the evening of September 11, President George W. Bush addressed the nation from the White House.

Good evening. Today, our fellow citizens, our way of life, our very freedom came under attack in a series of deliberate and deadly terrorist acts. The victims were in airplanes, or in their offices; secretaries, businessmen and women, military and federal workers; moms and dads, friends and neighbors. Thousands of lives were suddenly ended by evil, despicable acts of terror.

The pictures of airplanes flying into buildings, fires burning, huge structures collapsing, have filled us with disbelief, terrible sadness, and a quiet, unyielding anger. These acts of mass murder were intended to frighten our nation into chaos and retreat. But they have failed; our country is strong.

A great people has been moved to defend a great nation. Terrorist attacks can shake the foundations of our biggest buildings, but they cannot touch the foundation of America. These acts shattered steel, but they cannot dent the steel of American resolve. America was targeted for attack because we're the brightest beacon for freedom and opportunity in the world. And no one will keep that light from shining.

Today, our nation saw evil, the very worst of human nature. And we responded with the best of America—with the daring of our rescue workers, with the caring for strangers and neighbors who came to give blood and help in any way they could.

Immediately following the first attack, I implemented our government's emergency response plans. Our military is powerful, and it's prepared. Our emergency teams are working in New York City and Washington, D.C. to help with local rescue efforts.

Our first priority is to get help to those who have been injured, and to take every precaution to protect our citizens at home and around the world from further attacks.

The functions of our government continue without interruption. Federal agencies in Washington which had to be evacuated today are reopening for essential personnel tonight, and will be open for business tomorrow. Our financial institutions remain strong, and the American economy will be open for business, as well.

The search is underway for those who are behind these evil acts. I've directed the full resources of our intelligence and law enforcement communities to find those responsible and to bring them to justice. We will make no distinction between the terrorists who committed these acts and those who harbor them.

I appreciate so very much the members of Congress who have joined me in strongly condemning these attacks. And on behalf of the American people, I thank the many world leaders who have called to offer their condolences and assistance.

America and our friends and allies join with all those who want peace and security in the world, and we stand together to win the war against terrorism. Tonight, I ask for your prayers for all those who grieve, for the children whose worlds have been shattered, for all whose sense of safety and security has been threatened. And I pray they will be comforted by a power greater than any of us, spoken through the ages in Psalm 23: "Even though I walk through the valley of the shadow of death, I fear no evil, for You are with me."

This is a day when all Americans from every walk of life unite in our resolve for justice and peace. America has stood down enemies before, and we will do so this time. None of us will ever forget this day. Yet, we go forward to defend freedom and all that is good and just in our world.

Thank you. Good night, and God bless America.

Source: The White House

> **VOCABULARY**
> **despicable** wicked, shameful

American Anthem Correlation to Holt's Social Studies Library

Holt's Social Studies Library provides a rich array of reading experiences for students of American history. Use the table below to find which title in the Holt Library corresponds to a particular unit in *American Anthem, New York Edition*. Read one or all of the books listed to supplement your understanding of American history.

UNIT	Title / Author	Time, and Place, and Summary of Plot
UNIT 1 BEGINNINGS OF AMERICA	**The United States: Change and Challenge** *edited by Holt, Rinehart and Winston*	A content-area reader that covers the colonial period to the present. ***Anthology***
UNIT 2 FORMING A NEW NATION, 1763–1815	**The Scarlet Letter** *by Nathaniel Hawthorne*	(New England, 17th century) A young woman named Hester must wear a scarlet A for committing adultery in a puritan New England town. ***Fiction***
UNIT 3 DEVELOPING A NATIONAL IDENTITY, 1815–1860	**Narrative of the Life of Frederick Douglass, an American Slave** *by Frederick Douglass*	(America, 1818–1841) In this autobiography, Douglass tells of his life as an enslaved person in the American South and his escape to freedom in the North. ***Nonfiction***
	A Paradise Called Texas *by Janice Jordan Shefelman*	(Texas, 1845) This is the story of young Mina, who immigrated with her parents from Germany in 1845—the year that the Republic of Texas became a state. ***Fiction***
UNIT 4 THE UNION IN CRISIS, 1850–1877	**The Adventures of Huckleberry Finn** *by Mark Twain*	(Southern United States, late 1800s) This story is about a young boy who travels down the Missouri river with a black man in pursuit of adventure. ***Fiction***
	The Glory Field *by Walter Dean*	(America) This story is about a black family and a history that spans generations—from the day the first members of the family disembarked from a slave ship to the year 1994. ***Fiction***
	The Red Badge of Courage *by Stephen Crane*	(America, during the Civil War) This novel tells the story of a young man and his psychological and unconscious response to the battlefront. ***Fiction***
	A Stillness at Appomattox *by Bruce Catton*	(America, during the Civil War) This book presents a history of the Union Army of the Potomac as it drives toward victory in the Civil War. ***Nonfiction***
UNIT 5 AN INDUSTRIAL NATION, 1860–1920	**The Adventures of Tom Sawyer** *by Mark Twain*	(Missouri, late 1800s) In this novel, Tom Sawyer and his friend Huckleberry Finn get involved with a murder, meet unsavory characters, and spend three days hiding in a cave. ***Fiction***
	Call of the Wild *by Jack London*	(Canada's Yukon Territory, late 1800s) This book is about a dog that is stolen from his comfortable home in California and made to be a part of a dog sled for an abusive man who seeks gold in the Klondike. ***Fiction***
	Cold Sassy Tree *by Olive Ann Burns*	(America, 1906) The marriage of a widower and a young woman challenge the sense of propriety in a parochial Georgia town. ***Fiction***
Unit 6 BECOMING A WORLD POWER, 1898–1920	**Things Fall Apart** *by Chinua Achebe*	(Nigeria, 1890s) This novel uses the story of one man's life to show how "things fell apart" when his culture was colonized by the British. ***Fiction***
	Animal Farm *by George Orwell*	(England) A fable-like satire of the Russian Revolution centers on a rebellion of farm animals. ***Fiction***
	Ethan Frome *by Edith Wharton*	(New England, early 1900s) The narrator of this novel, set in a small New England town, investigates the life of a mysterious local named Ethan Frome, who had a tragic accident some twenty years earlier. ***Fiction***

UNIT	Title / Author	Time, and Place, and Summary of Plot
UNIT 7 **A MODERN NATION, 1919–1940**	**Bud, Not Buddy** *by Christopher Paul Curtis*	(Michigan, 1936) This story is about an orphaned African-American living in Flint, Michigan, during the Great Depression. **Fiction**
	To Kill a Mockingbird *by Harper Lee*	(Alabama, 1930s) This novel tells the story of its young narrator, "Scout" Finch, and her family when a young black man is arrested and tried for the rape of a white woman. **Fiction**
UNIT 8 **A CHAMPION OF DEMOCRACY, 1939–1960**	**Wish You Well** *by David Baldacci*	(New York City, 1940) This is a story about a precocious twelve-year-old girl living in the hectic New York City of 1940 with her underpaid writer father, her mother, and younger brother Oz. **Fiction**
	A Separate Peace *by John Knowles*	(New England, during World War II) A young man's visit to his preparatory school triggers a flashback to his experiences during the summer session when he was sixteen years old. **Fiction**
	Night *by Elie Wiesel*	(Romania, various Nazi death camps, 1940s) Wiesel recounts his experiences as a young man in the death camps of Auschwitz, Buna, Buchenwald and Gleiwitz during the Holocaust. **Nonfiction**
	The Chosen *by Chaim Potok*	(Brooklyn, 1940s) The novel tells the story of a friendship between two young men—a Hasidic Jew and a more liberal Jewish teenager—in Brooklyn at the end of World War II. **Fiction**
	El Bronx Remembered *by Nicholasa Mohr*	(The Bronx, 1940s and 1950s) This is a collection of twelve short stories that depict the harsh reality of many Puerto Ricans who lived in El Barrio. **Fiction**
	A Raisin in the Sun *by Lorraine Hansberry*	(Chicago, late 1950s) In this play an African American family struggles to hold on to its dreams for a better life. **Drama**
UNIT 9 **A NATION FACING CHALLENGES, 1954–1975**	**Barrio Boy** *by Ernesto Galarza*	(Mexico and California, mid 1900s) In this memoir, Galarza recalls how his life changed when his family moved from Mexico to the United States. **Nonfiction**
	The Fire Next Time *by James Baldwin*	(America, 1960s) In this book Baldwin gives a brutal analysis of race relations and calls for all Americans to accept the fact that America is a multiracial society. **Nonfiction**
	Fallen Angels *by Walter Dean Myers*	(South Vietnam, 1960–70s) The sole support of his family, a seventeen-year-old puts aside his dreams of college and a writing career in order to join the army and go into active combat in Vietnam. **Fiction**
	Barefoot Heart *by Elva Treviño Hart*	(America, mid-1900s) This memoir focuses on the author's childhood as the daughter of Mexican immigrants who worked as migrant workers to feed their six children. **Nonfiction**
Unit 10 **LOOKING TOWARD THE FUTURE, 1968–Present**	**Long Walk to Freedom** *by Nelson Mandela* *(abridged)*	(South Africa, contemporary) Nelson Mandela's own story of the anti-apartheid movement and his long struggle to bring racial justice to his country, South Africa. **Nonfiction**
	Necessary Roughness *by Marie G. Lee*	(America, contemporary) This is a coming-of-age story that revolves around Chan Kim and his twin sister, Young, as they cross the continent to get to their new home. **Fiction**
	1984 *by George Orwell*	(London, 1984) Written in 1949, this novel is about a future society in which Big Brother controls all aspects of every person's life. **Fiction**
	Great American Stories *edited by Holt, Rinehart, and Winston*	This is a collection of stories by American authors. **Fiction**

English and Spanish Glossary

TIME LINE:
Hispanic Immigration to New York

1900
Total immigration to New York state from all of Latin America is under 10,000 people.

1960
Migrants from Puerto Rico and immigrants from the West Indies and Cuba make up the three largest Spanish-speaking groups in the state.

1980s
Immigrants from the Dominican Republic outnumber those from Cuba nationwide and become the largest Caribbean immigrant group.

2000
About 650,000 Dominicans live in New York state, accounting for about half of the Hispanic population.

2000
Almost 3 million Hispanics live in New York State, about 15 percent of the population.

1900 — **1950** — **2000**

1917
U.S. Congress passes the Jones Act granting U.S. citizenship to all Puerto Ricans.

1930
Hispanic immigration to the state reaches 35,000.

1970
More than 250,000 foreign-born Spanish speakers live in the state, nearly 20 percent of the Spanish-speaking population.

1970
More than 52,000 immigrants arrive in New York state from the Dominican Republic.

1990
Eighteen percent of immigrants to the state are of Hispanic origin.

A

abolition movement movement to end slavery in the United States (p. 288)
movimiento abolicionista movimiento para poner fin a la esclavitud en Estados Unidos

Adams-Onís Treaty (1819) an agreement in which Spain gave East Florida to the United States (p. 241)
tratado de Adams y Onís (1819) acuerdo en el que España cedió el territorio del este de la Florida a Estados Unidos

affirmative action programs that gave preference to minorities and women in hiring and admissions (p. 941)
acción afirmativa programas que les daban preferencia a los grupos minoritarios y a las mujeres en cuestión de empleos y de ingreso en la universidad (pág. 941)

agricultural revolution a change in way of life that occurred about 7,000 years ago, when hunter-gatherer societies began to stay in one place and grow their own food (p. 7)
revolución agrícola un cambio en el estilo de vida que ocurrió hace unos 7,000 años atrás, cuando las sociedades de cazadores y recolectores comenzaron a establecerse en un solo sitio y a cultivar sus alimentos

Al Qaeda Osama bin Laden's terrorist network (p. 1094)
Al Qaeda red terrorista de Osama bin Laden

Alamo Spanish mission in San Antonio, Texas; the site of a famous battle of the Texas Revolution in 1836 (p. 306)
El Álamo misión española en San Antonio, Texas; escenario de una famosa batalla durante la Revolución Texana de 1836

Albany Plan of Union (1754) first plan for uniting the colonies; proposed by Ben Franklin (p. 92)
Plan de Unión de Albany (1754) primer plan para unir a las colonias propuesto por Ben Franklin.

alien citizen of another country living in the United States (p. 624)
extranjero ciudadano de otro país que reside en Estados Unidos

Alien and Sedition Acts (1798) laws passed by Congress that allowed the government to deport foreigners and jail critics (p. 213)
Leyes de Extranjeros y Sedición (1798) leyes aprobadas por un Congreso que permitían al gobierno deportar a los extranjeros y encarcelar a las personas que lo criticaban

Alliance for Progress President Kennedy's program to provide economic aid to Latin America (p. 886)
Alianza para el Progreso programa iniciado por el presidente Kennedy mediante el cual se le brindó ayuda económica a América Latina

Allied Powers alliance between Britain, France, and Russia; later joined by the United States in World War I (p. 584)
potencias aliadas alianza formada durante la Primera Guerra Mundial entre Inglaterra, Francia y Rusia, a la que luego se unió Estados Unidos

the Allies the alliance of Britain, France, and Russia in World War II (p. 748)
Aliados alianza entre Inglaterra, Francia y Rusia durante la Segunda Guerra Mundial

American Federation of Labor (AFL) labor organization that united skilled workers into national unions for specific industries (p. 475)
Federación Estadounidense del Trabajo (AFL, por sus siglas en inglés) organización que unió a los obreros especializados en sindicatos nacionales para industrias específicas

American Indian Movement (AIM) organization founded in 1968 by Native American leaders calling for a renewal of Native American culture and recognition of Native Americans' rights (p. 992)
Movimiento Indígena Norteamericano (AIM, por sus siglas en inglés) organización fundada en 1968 por líderes de los indígenas norteamericanos que fomentó la renovación de la cultura indígena norteamericana y el reconocimiento de los derechos de los indígenas

Americanization process in which Native Americans were forced to abandon their traditional cultures and adopt the culture of white America (p. 442)
americanización proceso mediante el cual se obligó a los indígenas norteamericanos a abandonar su cultura tradicional y a adoptar la cultura de los estadounidenses blancos

amnesty forgiveness to illegal aliens who had lived in the United States for many years, allowing them to gain legal status (p. CS4)
amnistía perdón concedido a extranjeros ilegales que habían vivido en Estados Unidos durante muchos años, permitiéndoles legalizar su situación

Anaconda Plan name given to the Civil War plan devised by Union General Winfield Scott to seal the South off from the rest of the world (p. 360)
Anaconda Plan nombre que se le dio al plan de guerra concebido por el general norteño Winfield Scott para aislar al Sur del resto del mundo

anarchist radicals who believe in the destruction of government (p. 627)
anarquista radical que cree en la destrucción del go-bierno

Angel Island an island in the San Francisco bay that was an entry point for many Asian immigrants to the United States beginning in 1910 (p. 492)
isla Angel isla en la bahía de San Francisco que fue el punto de ingreso para muchos inmigrantes asiáticos a partir de 1910

Antifederalists people who opposed ratification of the Constitution (p. 158)
antifederalistas personas que se oponían a la ratificación de la Constitución

anti-Semitism anti-Jewish beliefs (p. 779)
antisemitismo creencias en contra de los judíos

apartheid the South African government's official policy of legalized racial segregation throughout society (p. 1057)
apartheid política oficial del gobierno sudafricano de segregación racial legalizada en toda la sociedad

Apollo 11 U.S. space mission, which, in 1969, landed the first person, Neil Armstrong, on the moon (p. 1023)
Apollo 11 misión espacial estadounidense que en el año 1969 llevó a la primera persona, Neil Armstrong, a la Luna

appeasement giving in to the demands of uncompromising powers to avoid war (p. 747)
apaciguamiento aceptar a las exigencias de las potencias que no quieren ceder, con el fin de evitar la guerra

arms race competition between nations to gain an advantage in weapons (p. 638)
carrera armamentista competencia entre varios países para obtener una ventaja en las armas

Articles of Confederation (1777) the document that created the first central government for the United States; it was replaced by the Constitution in 1789 (p. 146)
Artículos de la Confederación (1777) documento que creó el primer gobierno central en Estados Unidos; fue reemplazado por la Constitución en 1789

artillery large, mounted guns (p. 357)
artillería grandes armas colocadas en una base

assembly line a mass-production process in which a product moved forward through many work stations (p. 629)
cadena de montaje proceso de producción masiva en el que el producto avanza de puesto en puesto

assimilation blending in with the established culture (p. CS3)
asimilación mezcla con la cultura estabecida

associative state the term for President Hoover's vision of voluntary partnership between business associations and the government (p. 688)
estado asociativo término que usó el presidente Hoover para referirse al vínculo voluntario entre las asociaciones empresariales y el gobierno

Atlantic Charter (1941) a statement of American and British goals for the defeat of the Nazis and their vision for the postwar world (p. 755)
Carta del Atlántico (1941) declaración de las metas estadounidenses y británicas para derrotar a los nazis, y de su visión para el mundo después de la guerra

atomic bomb a bomb which uses energy released by splitting atoms to create an enormous explosion (p. 762)
bomba atómica artefacto explosivo que usa energía liberada por la división de los átomos, creando así una explosión enorme

Axis Powers the alliance of Germany, Italy and Japan in World War II (p. 750)
potencias del Eje la alianza formada entre Alemania, Italia y Japón durante la Segunda Guerra Mundial

Aztec a Mesoamerican society that lived in the central valley of present-day Mexico from about the 14th through 16th centuries (p. 9)
azteca sociedad mesoamericana que vivió en el valle central de lo que hoy es México entre los siglos XIV y XVI, aproximadamente

baby boom a dramatic rise in the birthrate following World War II (p. 825)
baby boom aumento marcado en la tasa de natalidad después de la Segunda Guerra Mundial

Bacon's Rebellion (1676) an atttack led by Nathaniel Bacon against American Indians and the colonial government in Virginia (p. 50)
Rebelión de Bacon (1676) ataque encabezado por Nathaniel Bacon contra los indígenas norteamericanos y el gobierno colonial en Virginia

balance of power a system in which each nation or alliance has equal strength (p. 584)
equilibrio del poder sistema en el que cada país o alianza tiene igual poderío

balance of trade the relationship between a country's imports and exports (p. 73)
balanza comercial relación entre lo que el país importa y exporta

Bank of the United States a national bank chartered by Congress in 1791 to provide security for the U.S. economy (p. 207)
Banco de Estados Unidos banco nacional formado por el Congreso en 1791 para dar estabilidad a la economía de Estados Unidos

barter an exchange of goods without using money (p. 16)
trueque intercambio de bienes sin dinero

Bataan Death March (1942) forced march of American and Filipino prisoners of war captured by the Japanese in the Philippines during World War II (p. 787)
Marcha de la Muerte de Bataan (1942) marcha forzada de prisioneros de guerra estadounidenses y filipinos capturados por los japoneses en las Islas Filipinas durante la Segunda Guerra Mundial

Battle of Antietam (1862) a Union victory in the Civil War that marked the bloodiest single-day battle in U.S. military history (p. 370)
batalla de Antietam (1862) victoria del ejército de la Unión durante la Guerra Civil que fue la batalla de un solo día más sangrienta de la historia militar de Estados Unidos

Battle of Atlanta (1864) Civil War battle which led to the Union army's siege and capture of Atlanta and the final phase of the war (p. 391)
batalla de Atlanta (1864) batalla de la Guerra Civil tras la que el ejército de la Unión sitió y capturó la ciudad de Atlanta al final de la guerra

Battle of the Bulge (1944) World War II battle between Germany and the Allied forces; the German advance created a "bulge" in the Allied battle lines, though the Allies eventually prevailed (p. 776)
batalla del Bulge (de Árdenas) (1944) batalla de la Segunda Guerra Mundial entre Alemania y las fuerzas aliadas; la ofensiva alemana creó una especie de "acu-malción" o "bulge"en las líneas aliadas, aunque los aliados salieron victoriosos al final

Battle of Bunker Hill (1775) a Revolutionary War battle in Boston that showed the colonists could fight well against the British army (p. 116)
batalla de Bunker Hill (1775) batalla de la Guerra de Independencia estadounidense en Boston que demostró que los colonos podían luchar bien contra el ejército británico

Battle of Chancellorsville (1863) Civil War battle that was one of the Confederate army's major victories (p. 384)
batalla de Chancellorsville (1863) batalla de la Guerra Civil que fue una las mayores victorias del Ejército Confederado

Battle of Chickamauga (1863) Confederate victory during the Civil War; one of the bloodiest battles as a result of a Union campaign to capture Chattanooga (p. 387)
batalla de Chickamauga (1863) victoria de la Confederación durante la Guerra Civil que también fue una de las batallas más sangientas, resultado de una campaña de la Unon para apoderarse de Chattanooga

Battle of Cold Harbor (1864) Civil War battle which caused nearly 7,000 Union army casualties (p. 391)
batalla de Cold Harbor (1864) batalla de la Guerra Civil en la cual murieron casi 7,000 soldados del ejército de la Unión

Battle of Fallen Timbers (1794) battle between U.S. troops and an American Indian confederation that ended Indian efforts to halt white settlement in the Northwest Territory (p. 212)
batalla de Fallen Timbers (1794) batalla entre las tropas estadounidenses y una confederación de indígenas norteamericanos que puso fin a los intentos de los indígenas por detener el establecimiento de los blancos en el Territorio del Noroeste

Battle of Gettysburg (1863) a Union Civil War victory that turned the tide against the Confederates at Gettysburg, Pennsylvania (p. 384)
batalla de Gettysburg (1863) victoria del ejército de la Unión durante la Guerra Civil que cambió el curso de la guerra en contra de los confederados en Gettysburg, Pensilvania

Battle of Glorieta Pass (1862) Civil War battle in which Union troops and volunteers stopped a Confederate invasion in northern New Mexico (p. 382)
batalla de Glorieta Pass (1862) batalla de la Guerra Civil, en la Unión y voluntarios detuvieron la invasión de la Confederación en la parte norte de Nuevo México

Battle of Iwo Jima (1945) a World War II battle between Japanese forces and invading U.S. troops (p. 792)
batalla de Iwo Jima (1945) batalla de la Segunda Guerra Mundial entre las fuerzas japonesas y las fuerzas estadounidenses invasoras

Battle of the Little Bighorn (1876) Battle in which Sioux forces led by Chief Sitting Bull defeated a U.S. Army troop led by Lieutenant Colonel George Armstrong Custer (p. 441)
batalla de Little Bighorn (1876) batalla en la que guerreros de la tribu sioux comandados por el jefe Sitting Bull derrotaron a las tropas del ejército estadounidense comandadas por el teniente coronel George Armstrong Custer

Battle of Midway (1942) a key naval and air battle between Japan and the United States in World War II (p. 788)
batalla de Midway (1942) batalla naval y aérea clave entre Japón y Estados Unidos durante la Segunda Guerra Mundial

Battle of New Orleans (1815) the greatest U.S. victory in the War of 1812; actually took place two weeks after a peace treaty had been signed ending the war (p. 227)
batalla de Nueva Orleáns (1815) la mayor victoria estadounidense en la Guerra de 1812; tuvo lugar dos semanas después de que se firmara el tratado de paz en el que se declaraba el final de la guerra

Battle of Okinawa (1945) World War II battle between Japanese forces and invading U.S. troops (p. 792)
batalla de Okinawa (1945) batalla de la Segunda Guerra Mundial entre las fuerzas japonesas y las tropas estadounidenses invasoras

Battle of Pea Ridge (1862) the Civil War's biggest battle west of the Mississippi River, in Arkansas (p. 382)
batalla de Pea Ridge (1862) la batalla más importante de la Guerra Civil al oeste del río Mississippi, en Arkansas

Battle of San Juan Hill (1898) battle in the Spanish-American War in which 8,000 U.S. soldiers fought to seize control over San Juan Hill (p. 562)
batalla de San Juan Hill (1898) batalla de la Guerra Hispanoamericana en la cual 8,000 soldados estadounidenses lucharon para apoderarse de la loma de San Juan

Battle of Saratoga (1777) a Revolutionary War battle in New York that resulted in a major defeat of British troops (p. 128)
batalla de Saratoga (1777) batalla de la Guerra de Independencia estadounidense que tuvo lugar en Nueva York y en la que las fuerzas británicas sufrieron una de sus peores derrotas

Battle of Shiloh (1862) a Civil War battle in Tennessee in which the Union army gained greater control over the Mississippi River valley (p. 366)
batalla de Shiloh (1862) batalla de la Guerra Civil en Tennessee en la que el ejército de la Unión adquirió mayor control sobre el valle del río Mississippi

Battle of Spotsylvania (1864) an 11-day series of clashes in the Civil War (p. 391)
batalla de Spotsylvania (1864) serie de combates durante 11 días en la Guerra Civil

Battle of Veracruz (1914) major conflict in the Mexican Revolution (p. 574)
batalla de Veracruz (1914) importante conflicto en la Revolución Mexicana

Battle of the Wilderness (1864) Civil War battle that was so fierce, the woods where it was fought caught fire and burned, killing many wounded soldiers (p. 391)
batalla de Wilderness (1864) batalla de la Guerra Civil que fue tan feroz que el bosque en la cual se peleó se incendió hasta no quedar nada, causando la muerte de muchos soldados heridos

Battle of Yorktown (1781) a three-week-long siege by the Americans and French that trapped most of the British Army at Yorktown, Virginia (p. 135)
batalla de Yorktown (1781) asedio de tres semanas en el que los estadounidenses y los franceses atraparon a la mayor parte del ejército británico en Yorktown, Virginia

Bay of Pigs invasion (1961) the failed attempt of Cuban exiles backed by the U.S. to overthrow the Cuban socialist government of Fidel Castro (p. 881)
invasión de la Bahía de Cochinos (1961) intento fallido de exiliados cubanos respaldados por Estados Unidos de derrocar al gobierno socialista cubano de Fidel Castro

bayonet constitution (1887) a constitution the king of Hawaii was forced to sign which severely restricted his power and deprived most Hawaiians of the vote (p. 555)
constitución de las bayonetas (1887) constitución que el rey de Hawai se vio obligado a firmar restringiendo gravemente su poder y privando a la mayoría de los hawaianos del voto

Bear Flag Revolt (1846) a revolt against Mexico by American settlers in California who declared the territory an independent republic (p. 311)
Rebelión de Bear Flag (1846) rebelión en contra de México iniciada por colonos estadounidenses que declararon al territorio de California una república independiente

benevolent society an aid organization set up by residents of a community to help its immigrants (p. 493)
sociedad benéfica organización de ayuda organizada por residentes de una comunidad para ayudar a sus inmigrantes

Berlin Airlift a program in which the United States and Britain shipped supplies by air to West Berlin during a Soviet blockade of all routes to the city; lasted from 1948-1949 (p. 822)
Puente Aéreo de Berlín programa mediante el cual Estados Unidos e Inglaterra enviaban suministros a Berlín Occidental durante un bloqueo soviético de todas las rutas hacia la ciudad; duró de 1948 a 1949

Bessemer process a process developed in the 1850s that led to faster, cheaper steel production (p. 461)
proceso Bessemer proceso de producción de acero más económico y rápido, desarrollado en la década de 1850

Big Four name given to the leaders of the Allied Powers who dominated the Paris Peace Conference following the Allied victory in World War I (p. 607)
Cuatro Grandes nombre que se les dio a los líderes de las potencias aliadas que dominaron la Conferencia de Paz en París tras la victoria de los Aliados en la Primera Guerra Mundial

Bill of Rights the first 10 amendments to the United States Constitution; ratified in 1791 (p. 159)
Declaración de Derechos primeras 10 enmiendas hechas a la Constitución de Estados Unidos.; aprobada en 1791

Black Cabinet group of African Americans Franklin D. Roosevelt appointed to key government positions; they served as unofficial advisors to the president (p. 718)
Gabinete Negro un grupo de afroamericanos que Franklin D. Roosevelt designó para que ocuparan cargos importantes en el gobierno; fueron asesores extraoficiales del presidente

Black Codes laws passed in the southern states during Reconstruction that greatly limited the freedom and rights of African Americans (p. 411)
Códigos Negros leyes aprobadas en los estados sureños en la época de la Reconstrucción que limitaron en gran medida la libertad y los derechos de los afroamericanos

Black Panther Party a group formed in 1966, inspired by the idea of Black Power, that provided aid to black neighborhoods; often thought of as radical or violent (p. 935)
Partido Black Panther grupo formado en 1966, inspirado en la noción del poder negro, que prestó ayuda en barrios predominantemente negros; a menudo fue considerado un grupo radical o violento

Black Power an African American social movement in the late 1960s that advocated unity and self-reliance to address injustice (p. 935)
poder negro movimiento social afroamericano que surgió a fines de la década de 1960; partidario de la unidad e interdependencia para enfrentar la injusticia

Black Tuesday Tuesday, October 29, 1929, the day that the stock market crashed (p. 677)
martes negro martes 29 de octubre de 1929, día en que se desplomó el mercado de valores

blacklist a list or register of people who are being denied a particular freedom or privilege (p. 475)
lista negra lista de personas a quienes se les niega una libertad o privilegio particular

Bleeding Kansas (1856) nickname given to Kansas after violence erupted between anti-slavery and pro-slavery groups (p. 330)
La sangriá de Kansas (1856) sobrenombre dado al estado de Kansas luego de que estalló la violencia entre grupos a favor y en contra de la esclavitud

blitzkrieg a German word meaning "lightning war" (p. 748)
blitzkrieg palabra en alemán que significa "guerra relámpago"

Bolsheviks a group of Russian radicals, led by Vladimir I. Lenin, who played a major role in the 1917 revolution in Russia (p. 623)
bolsheviques grupo de radicales rusos, dirigidos por Vladimir I. Lenin, que tuvo un rol muy importante en la Revolución Rusa de 1917

bonanza farm large-scale farm with expensive machinery, professional managers, and hired laborers working at specialized tasks (p. 453)
granja de bonanza granja de gran escala con maquinaria costosa, administradores profesionales y obreros contratados para hacer tareas especializadas

bootlegger people who smuggled liquor during the Prohibition (p. 652)
contrabandista persona que comerciaba clandestinamente con licores durante la época de la Prohibición

border states Delaware, Kentucky, Maryland, and Missouri; slave states in between the North and the South that did not join the Confederacy during the Civil War (p. 358)
estados fronterizos Delaware, Kentucky, Maryland y Missouri; estados esclavistas entre el Norte y el Sur y que no se unieron a la Confederación durante la Guerra Civil

boricua the name by which many Puerto Ricans refer to themselves; it expresses pride, empowerment, and certain political beliefs (p. 1000)
boricua nombre con el que se refieren muchos puertorriqueños a ellos mismos; expresa orgullo, poderío y ciertas creencias políticas

Boston Massacre (1770) an incident where British soldiers fired into a crowd of colonists, killing five people (p. 109)
Masacre de Boston (1770) incidente en el que los soldados británicos dispararon contra una multitud de colonos, matando a cinco personas

Boxer Rebellion (1900) a siege of a foreign settlement in Beijing by Chinese nationalists who were angry at foreign involvement in China (p. 556)
Rebellión de los Boxers (1900) asentamiento extranjero en Beijing por parte de un grupo de nacionalistas chinos que estaban en desacuerdo con la participación extranjera en China

Bracero program (1942) program allowed poor Mexican workers to work temporarily in the U.S. (p. 763)
programa de braceros (1942) programa que les dio a los trabajadores mexicanos pobres la oportunidad de trabajar temporalmente en Estados Unidos

brinkmanship a strategy that involves countries getting to the verge of war without actually going to war (p. 850)
política arriesgada estrategia que implica que los países llegan al borde de la guerra sin entrar en batalla

Brownsville incident (1906) the accusation of twelve members of the African American 25th Infantry of a shooting spree in Brownsville, Texas (p. 545)
incidente de Brownsville (1906) acusación de doce soldados del batallón 25 de Infantería, compuesto de afroamericanos de una matanza en Brownsville, Texas

budget deficit the amount by which government spending for a year exceeds government income (p. 1050)
déficit presupuestario cantidad en la cual los gastos del gobierno superan sus ingresos en un año determinado

budget surplus when a government's income exceeds its spending (p. 1086)
excedente presupuestario cuando los ingresos de un gobierno son mayores que sus gastos

bully pulpit a platform used to publicize and seek support for important issues (p. 536)
tribuna plataforma usada para promocionar y solicitar apoyo para temas de importancia

Bureau of Indian Affairs (BIA) the federal agency that managed the Native American reservations (p. 442)
Oficina de Asuntos Indígenas (BIA, por sus siglas en inglés) agencia federal que administraba las reservas de indígenas norteamericanos

Bush v. Gore Supreme Court case that ruled the Florida Supreme Court's recount in the 2000 presidential election was unconstitutional (p. 1087)
Bush contra Gore caso en el que la Corte Suprema decidió que el recuento efectuado por la Corte Suprema de Florida en la elección presidencial de 2000 fue in-constitucional

Butterfield Trail a 2,800 mile long trail that carried mail and passengers between St. Louis and San Francisco (p. 301)
camino de Butterfield camino de 2,800 millas por el que se transportaban correo y pasajeros entre St. Louis y San Francisco (pág. 301)

buying on margin buying stocks with loans from brokers (p. 675)
comprar a crédito comprar acciones con dinero prestado por los corredores

cabinet group of advisors that heads the executive branch of government (p. 203)
gabinete grupo de asesores que encabeza la rama ejecutiva del gobierno

California Trail an overland trail that led migrants to California during the Gold Rush (p. 299)
camino de California camino por tierra que llevó a los emigrantes a California durante la fiebre del oro

Camp David Accords (1978) peace agreement mediated by President Carter between Egyptian President Anwar Sadat and Israeli Prime Minister Menachem Begin (p. 1036)
Acuerdos de Camp David (1978) acuerdos de paz entre el presidente egipcio Anwar Sadat y el primer ministro israelí Menachem Begin en los que el presidente Carter actuó como mediador

capitalism economic system in which most businesses are privately owned (p. 467)
capitalismo sistema económico en el que la mayoría de las empresas son de propiedad privada

caravel a sailing vessel that uses square and triangular sails to help it sail against the wind (p. 27)
carabela barco con velas cuadras y triangulares que sirven para navegar contra el viento

carpetbagger derogatory nickname given by Southern critics to northern Republicans who came south during Reconstruction (p. 417)
carpetbagger apodo despectivo que les dieron los críticos sureños a los republicanos norteños que vinieron al Sur durante Reconstrucción

cash-and-carry (1939) law aimed at aiding the Allies during World War II, allowed countries at war to purchase American goods as long as they paid cash and picked up their orders in American ports (p. 754)
pague y lleve (1939) ley cuyo objetivo era ayudar a los Aliados durante la Segunda Guerra Mundial; permitía que los países en guerra compraran productos estadounidenses siempre y cuando pagaran en efectivo y recogieran sus pedidos en puertos estadounidenses

cash crops agricultural products grown to be sold (p. 80)
cultivos comerciales productos agrícolas que se cultivan para venderlos

casualties military term for those killed, wounded, or missing in action (p. 364)
bajas término militar que se refiere a los muertos, heridos o desaparecidos en acción

cavalry soldiers who fight on horseback (p. 365)
caballería soldados que luchan montados a caballo

Central Powers alliance between Germany, Austria-Hungary and the Ottoman Empire (p. 584)
poderes centrales alianza entre Alemania, Austria-Hungría y el Imperio otomano

checks and balances the Constitutional system that prevents any branch of government from becoming too powerful (p. 155)
equilibrio de poderes sistema establecido por la Constitución para evitar que ninguna rama del gobierno adquiera demasiada autoridad en relación con las demás

Chicano name adopted by Mexican Americans in the late 1960s to refer to a person of Mexican descent living in the U.S. (p. 996)
Chicano nombre adoptado por los mexicano-americanos a fines de la década de 1960 para referirse a una persona de ascendencia mexicana que reside en Estados Unidos

Chinese Exclusion Act law that banned Chinese immigration for 10 years declaring that no Chinese people already in the United States could become citizens (p. 494)
Ley de Exclusión de los Chinos ley que prohibió la inmigración china durante 10 años y declaró que ningún chino que ya residiera en Estados Unidos podía obtener la ciudadanía estadounidense

Chisholm Trail a trail that ran from San Antonio, Texas, to Abilene, Kansas, established by Jesse Chisholm in the late 1860s for cattle drives (p. 448)
camino de Chisholm camino desde San Antonio, Texas hasta Abilene, Kansas, creado por Jesse Chisholm a finales de la década de 1860 para arrear ganado

CIA Central Intelligence Agency; collects intelligence information and takes part in secret actions against foreign targets (p. 850)
CIA Agencia Central de Inteligencia; recoge información y participa en acciones secretas contra objetivos en el exterior del país

CIO a group that broke away from the AFL to form the Committee for Industrial Organization (p. 712)
CIO grupo que se separó de la AFL para formar la Comisión para la Organización Industrial

Civil Rights Act (1866) law that gave African Americans legal rights equal to those of white Americans (p. 413)
Ley de Derechos Civiles (1866) ley que les dio a los afroamericanos derechos legales igualés a los de los estadounidenses blancos

Civil Rights Act of 1964 act signed it into law on July 2, 1964 that banned discrimination in employment and in public accommodations (p. 923)
Ley de Derechos Civiles de 1964 ley firmada el 2 de julio de 1964 que prohibió la discriminación en el empleo y en los establecimientos públicos

Civil Rights Act of 1968 law that banned discrimination in the sale or rental of housing (p. 940)
Ley de Derechos Civiles de 1968 ley que prohibió la discriminación en la venta y alquiler de viviendas

clan a group of people related by blood (p. 10)
clan grupo de personas emparentadas entre sí por la misma sangre

Clayton Antitrust Act (1914) law that made illegal certain monopolistic business practices; it also legalized strikes, boycotts, and peaceful picketing (p. 543)
Ley Clayton Antimonopolios (1914) ley que prohibió ciertas práticas comerciales monopolísticas y legalizó las huelgas, los boicots y los piquetes pacíficos

code talkers Navajos who served as radio operators in the Marines during World War II translating important military messages into the Navajo language (p. 791)
codificadores navajos que durante la Segunda Guerra Mundial prestaron servicios en la marina estadou-nidense como operadores de radio, traduciendo importantes mensajes militares al idioma navajo

Cold War an era of high tension and bitter rivalry known between the United States and the Soviet Union following the end of World War II (p. 817)
Guerra Fría era de grandes tensiones y gran rivalidad entre Estados Unidos y la Unión Soviética después de concluida la Segunda Guerra Mundial

colonization the establishing of colonies, regions governed by a foreign power (p. 31)
colonización establecimiento de colonias, regiones gobernadas por potencias extranjeras

Columbian Exchange the transfer of plants, animals, and diseases between the Americas and Europe, Asia, and Africa (p. 33)
intercambio colombino intercambio de plantas, animales y enfermedades entre las Américas y Europa, Asia y África

combat fighting (p. CS8)
combate batalla

Committee on Public Information created by President Wilson, this committee's objective was to maximize national loyalty and support for World War I (p. 603)
Comité de Información Pública creado por el presidente Wilson; su objetivo era aprovechar al máximo la lealtad y el apoyo de la nación durante la Primera Guerra Mundial

committees of correspondence committees created by the Massachusetts House of Representatives in the 1760s to help towns and colonies share information about resisting British laws (p. 109)
comités de correspondencia comités creados por la Cámara de Representantes de Massachusetts en la década de 1760 para que los pueblos y las colonias compartieran información que los ayudara a resistirse a las leyes británicas

Common Sense (1776) a pamphlet written by Thomas Paine that criticized monarchies and convinced many American colonists of the need to break away from Britain (p. 117)
Sentido común (1776) folleto escrito por Thomas Paine en el que criticaba a las monarquías con el fin de convencer a los colonos estadounidenses de la necesidad de independizarse de Gran Bretaña

communism economic and political system in which governments own the means of production and control economic planning (p. 623)
comunismo sistema económico y político en el que los gobiernos poseen los medios de producción y controlan la planificación económica

Communists people who seek the equal distribution of wealth and the end of all private property (p. 594)
comunistas personas que buscan una distribución igualitaria de la riqueza y el fin de todo tipo de propiedad privada

comparative advantage the ability of a nation, region or company to produce a certain good or service more cheaply than any other country (p. CS43)
beneficio comparativo competencia de una nación, region, o compañía a producer algún bien o servicio más barato que cualquiera país

Compromise of 1850 Henry Clay's proposed agreement that allowed California to enter the Union as a free state and divided the rest of the Mexican Cession into two territories where slavery would be decided by popular sovereignty
Compromiso de 1850 acuerdo redactado por Henry Clay en que se permitía a California entrar en la Unión como estado libre y se proponía la división de la Cesión Mexicana en dos partes donde la esclavitud sería reglamentada por soberanía popular

Compromise of 1877 an agreement to settle the disputed presidential election of 1876; Democrats agreed to accept Republican Rutherford B. Hayes as president in return for the removal of federal troops from the South (p. 427)
Compromiso de 1877 acuerdo en el que se resolvió la disputa de las elecciones presidenciales de 1876; los demócratas aceptaron al republicano Rutherford B. Hayes como presidente a cambio del retiro de las tropas federales del Sur

Comstock Lode Nevada gold and silver mine discovered by Henry Comstock in 1859 (p. 445)
veta de Comstock mina de oro y plata descubierta en Nevada por Henry Comstock en 1859

concentration camp a detention site created for military or political purposes to confine, terrorize, and, in some cases, kill civilians (p. 779)
campo de concentración lugar de detención creado con fines militares o políticos para recluir, atemorizar y, en algunos casos, asesinar a civiles

Confederate States of America the nation formed by the southern states when they seceded from the Union (p. 347)
Estados Confederados de América nación formada por los estados del Sur cuando se separaron de la Unión

confederation a group in which each member keeps control of internal affairs but all member cooperate cooperate on certain issues, such as defense (p. 75)
confederación grupo en el que cada miembro retiene el control de sus asuntos internos pero todos juntos colaboran en ciertos asuntos, como la defensa

conquistadors Spanish soldiers and explorers who led military expeditions in the Americas and captured land for Spain (p. 41)
conquistadores soldados y exploradores español que encabezó expediciones militares en América y capturó territorios en nombre de España

conservation the careful use of resources (p. CS16)
conservación uso prudente de los recursos

conscription required service in the military (p. 376)
conscripción servicio militar obligatorio

Constitutional Convention (1787) a meeting held in Philadelphia at which delegates from the states wrote the Constitution (p. 151)
Convención Constitucional (1787) encuentro en Filadelfia en el que los delegados de los estados redactaron la Constitución

containment U.S. policy adopted in the late 1940s to stop the spread of Communism by providing economic and military aid to countries opposing the Soviets (p. 819)
contención política adoptada por Estados Unidos a fines de la década de 1940 para detener la diseminación del comunismo proporcionando ayuda económica y militar a los países que se oponían a los soviéticos

Continental Army the army created by the Second Continental Congress in 1775 to defend the American colonies from Britain (p. 115)
Ejército Continental ejército creado por el Segundo Congreso Continental en 1775 para defender las colonias estadounidenses de Gran Bretaña

convoy system a military technique of transport in which ships were surrounded by destroyers or cruisers for protection (p. 594)
sistema de convoy grupo de varios barcos o vehículos, incluso naves de combate armadas, que por ser numeroso ofrece seguridad

cooperative an organization that is owned and controlled by its members (p. 689)
cooperativa organización que pertenece y es controlada por sus miembros

Copperheads a group of northern Democrats who opposed abolition and sympathized with the South during the Civil War (p. 377)
copperheads grupo de demócratas del Norte que se oponían a la abolición de la esclavitud y simpatizaban con los sureños durante la Guerra Civil

CORE Committee of Racial Equality; an organization dedicated to the practice of nonviolent protest (p. 910)
CORE Comité por la Igualdad Racial; organización dedicada a la práctica de protestas no violentas

corps a military group (p. CS9)
cuerpo grupo militar

cost of living the amount of income required to buy basic necessities (p. CS26)
costo de vida ingresos necesarios para comprar las necesidades básicas

Cotton Belt a region stretching from South Carolina to east Texas where most U.S. cotton was produced during the mid-1800s (p. 257)
cinturón algodonero zona que se extiende desde Carolina del Sur hasta el este de Texas, en la que se producía la mayor parte del algodón cosechado en Estados Unidos a mediados del siglo XIX

cotton diplomacy the South's use of cotton as a tool of foreign policy during the Civil War (p. 362)
diplomacia del algodón el uso del algodón por parte del Sur como recurso de política exterior durante la Guerra Civil

cotton gin a machine invented by Eli Whitney in 1793 to remove seeds from short-staple cotton (p. 257)
desmotadora de algodón máquina inventada por Eli Whitney en 1793 para separar las semillas del algodón de fibra corta

counterculture a rebellion of teens and young adults against mainstream American society in the 1960s (p. 1003)
contracultura rebelión de adolescentes y jóvenes adultos contra la corriente dominante de la sociedad estadounidense durante la década de 1960

credit system of borrowing money from banks to make purchases, then paying it back later with interest (p. 632)
crédito sistema de tomar prestado dinero de un banco para hacer compras y luego pagarlo con intereses

criminal code code standard set of laws (p. CS32)
código penal conjunto estandarizado de leyes

Crittenden Compromise (1860) plan created by Senator John Crittenden which proposed amending the Constitution to ban slavery north of the old Missouri Compromise line and to guarantee that it would not be interfered with south of that line (p. 348)
Compromiso de Crittenden (1860) plan creado por el senador John Crittenden en el que se proponía enmendar la Constitución prohibiendo la esclavitud al norte de la antigua línea del Compromiso de Missouri garantizando que no se interferiría al sur de esa línea

Crusades (1091–1295) a series of holy wars led by Christian kings to regain parts of the Middle East from the Muslim Turks (p. 24)
cruzadas (1091–1295) serie de guerras santas dirigidas por los reyes cristianos con el fin de recuperar de los musulmanes turcos partes del Oriente conocidas como Tierra Santa

Cuban missile crisis (1962) confrontation between the United States and the Soviet Union over Soviet missiles in Cuba (p. 884)

crisis de los misiles de Cuba (1962) enfrentemiento entre Estados Unidos y la Unión Soviética provocado por la instalación de misiles soviéticos en Cuba

cult of domesticity a movement that arose during the Industrial Revolution urging women to remain in the home environment (p. 281)

culto de la domesticidad movimiento que surgió durante la Revolución Industrial que fomentaba que las mujeres permanecieran en el hogar

Dawes Act (1887) legislation passed by Congress that split up Indian reservation lands among individual Indians and promised them citizenship (p. 443)

Ley de Dawes (1887) ley aprobada por el Congreso que dividía el terreno de las reservas indígenas entre sus habitantes y les prometía la ciudadanía

D-day (1944) June 6, 1944, the first day of the Allied invasion of Normandy in World War II (p. 775)

Día D (1944) 6 de junio de 1944, primer día de la invasión de Normandía por parte de los Aliados en la Segunda Guerra Mundial

de facto segregation segregation that exists through custom and practice rather than by law (p. 933)

segregación de facto segregación que existe por costumbre y práctica y no por ley

de jure segregation segregation by law (p. 933)

segregación de jure segregación establecida por ley

de Lôme letter (1898) letter written by Spain's minister to the United States ridiculing President McKinley that was published in a major newspaper (p. 560)

carta de Lôme (1898) carta escrita por el ministro español en los Estados Unidos ridiculizando al presidente McKinley, publicada en los periódicos más importantes

debt peonage system where workers are tied to their jobs until they can pay off debts they owe their employer (p. 510)

peonaje por deudas sistema mediante el cual los trabajadores no pueden abandonar su empleo sino hasta que terminen de pagar las deudas que le deben a su empleador

deficit when a government spends more money than it takes in (p. 716)

déficit cuando el gobierno gasta más dinero del que recauda

delegated powers powers given to each branch of the national government by the Constitution (p. 163)

poderes delegados poderes que la Constitución le otorga a cada rama del gobierno nacional

Democratic Party a political party formed by supporters of Andrew Jackson after the presidential election of 1824 (p.246)

Partido Demócrata partido político formado por partidarios de Andrew Jackson después de las elecciones presidenciales de 1824

Democratic-Republicans a political party founded in the 1790s by Thomas Jefferson, James Madison, and other leaders who wanted to preserve the power of the state governments and promote agriculture (p. 208)

demócratas-republicanos un partido político fundado en la década de 1790 por Thomas Jefferson, James Madison y otros líderes que deseaban conservar el poder de los gobiernos estatales y promover la agricultura

Department of Homeland Security U.S. government department created by the Bush administration after the attacks of September 11, 2001, to protect the United States (p.1096)

Departmento de Seguridad Nacional departamento del gobierno estadounidense creado por el gobierno de Bush luego de los ataques del 11 de septiembre de 2001 para proteger al país

deportation being sent back to one's country of origin (p. 624)

deportación ser devuelto al país de origen

détente efforts President Nixon took in the late 1960s and early 1970s to lower Cold War tensions (p. 1020)

distensión campaña del presidente Nixon para reducir las tensiones de la Guerra Fría a finales de los años 60 y principios de los años 70

dictatorship government by a leader or group that holds unchallenged power and authority (p. 741)

dictadura forma de gobierno en la que el poder y la autoridad ilimitados se se concentran en una persona o grupo

Dien Bien Phu site of a battle between the French and the Vietminh in 1954; the French lost the battle and control of Vietnam (p. 951)

Dien Bien Phu aldea en Vietnam donde los franceses y el Vietminh lucharon una batalla en 1954; los franceses perdieron la batalla y el control de Vietnam

discretion the freedom to decide on an appropriate sentence for each individual within certain guidelines (p. CS32)

discreción libertad de decidir la sentencia adecuada para cada persona dentro de ciertas relgas generales

discrimination treatment based on race, class, or category rather than individual merit (p. CS4)

discriminación trato que se basa en la raza, la clase o la categoría y no en el mérito individual

disparity gap (p. CS26)

disparidad distancia o brecha

dividend a payment made by a company to its shareholders (p. 1088)

dividendo cantidad que una compañía paga a sus accionistas

division of labor when certain people do certain kinds of work (p. 16)

división del trabajo cuando ciertas personas hacen ciertos tipos de trabajos

dollar diplomacy President Taft's policy of influencing Latin America through economic intervention (p. 569)

diplomacia del dólar política creada por el presidente Taft para influir en América Latina mediante la intervención económica

domino theory a belief that if Vietnam fell to Communists, other countries of Southeast Asia would follow (p. 950)

teoría del dominó creencia de que si Vietnam caía en manos comunistas, también caerían otros países del sureste asiático

dot-coms companies whose products or services are marketed on the Internet (1088)

punto coms empresas cuyos productos o servicios se comercializan en Internet

doves people opposed to a war (p. 962)

palomas personas que se oponen a la guerra

ENGLISH AND SPANISH GLOSSARY

Dred Scott decision (1857) a U.S. Supreme Court ruling that African Americans were not U.S. citizens, that the Missouri Compromise's restriction on slavery was unconstitutional, and that Congress did not have the right to ban slavery in any federal territory (p. 333)
decisión *Dred Scott* (1857) decisión de la Corte Suprema dictaminando que los afroamericanos no eran ciudadanos estadounidenses, que las restricciones sobre la esclavitud del Compromiso de Missouri eran inconstitucionales y que el Congreso no tenía el derecho de prohibir la esclavitud en ningún territorio federal

drought a period of very dry weather (p. 684)
sequía período de tiempo muy seco

dugout shelter dug out of the sides of hills (p. 453)
refugio lugar excavado de la ladera de una colina

Dust Bowl a nickname for the Great Plains regions hit by drought and dust storms in the early 1930s (p. 684)
Tazón de Polvo apodo dado a las regiones de las Grandes Planicies azotadas por la sequía y las tormentas de polvo a principios de la década de 1930

Eighteenth Amendment (1919) a constitutional amendment that outlawed the production and sale of alcoholic beverages in the United States; repealed in 1933 (p. 532)
Decimoctava enmienda (1919) enmienda constitucional que prohibió la producción y venta de bebidas alcohólicas en Estados Unidos; revocada en 1933

Eisenhower Doctrine (1957) declared the right of the United States to help, on request, any nation in the Middle East trying to resist armed Communist aggression (p. 853)
Doctrina Eisenhower (1957) declaró el derecho de Estados Unidos de ayudar, cuando se lo solicitaran, a cualquier país del Medio Oriente en su resistencia contra la agresión armada de los comunistas

Elkins Act (1903) law passed by Congress which prohibited railroads from accepting rebates from their best customers (p. 538)
Ley de Elkins (1903) ley aprobada por el Congreso para prohibirles a los ferrocarriles recibir a devoluciones de dinero de sus mejores clientes

Ellis Island an island in New York harbor that was an entry point for immigrants coming to the United States between 1892 and 1954 (p. 491)
isla Ellis isla en el puerto de Nueva York que fue el punto de ingreso de inmigrantes a Estados Unidos entre 1892 y 1954

emancipation freeing of the slaves (p. 372)
emancipación liberación de los esclavos

Emancipation Proclamation (1862) an order issued by President Abraham Lincoln freeing the slaves in areas rebelling against the Union (p. 372)
Proclamación de Emancipación (1862) decreto emitido por el presidente Abraham Lincoln para liberar a los esclavos en las regiones rebeladas contra la Unión

embargo the banning of trade with a country (p. 362)
embargo prohibición del comercio con un país

Embargo Act (1807) a law that prohibited American merchants from trading with other countries (p. 225)
Ley de Embargo (1807) ley que prohibía a los comerciantes estadounidenses comerciar con otros países

empresarios contractors who recruited settlers and established colonies for the Mexican government (p. 304)
empresarios contratistas que reclutaban colonos y establecían colonias para el gobierno mexicano

encryption technology that transforms data to make it indecipherable to an outside observer (p. CS38)
codificación tecnología que transforma los datos de modo que sean imposibles de descifrar por un observador externo

Enforcement Acts group of laws passed by Congress in 1870 and 1871 that banned the activities of groups like the Ku Klux Klan; empowered the army and courts to capture and punish KKK members (p. 425)
Leyes de Acatamiento grupo de leyes aprobadas por el Congreso en 1870 y 1871 que prohibieron las actividades de grupos como el Ku Klux Klan; autorizó al ejército y las cortes federales a capturar y castigar a los miembros del Ku Klux Klan

English Bill of Rights document drafted by Parliament to set limits on the monarch's powers (p. 74)
Declaración de Derechos inglesa documento redactado por el Parlamento para establecer límites a los poderes de los monarcas

Enlightenment movement that began in Europe in the late 1600s as people began examining the natural world, society, and government; also called the Age of Reason (p. 85)
Ilustración movimiento que comenzó en Europa a fines del siglo XVII cuando la gente empezó a estudiar el mundo natural, la sociedad y el gobierno; también se conoce como la Edad de la Razón

Enola Gay the nickname of the American plane that dropped the atomic bomb on the Japanese city of Hiroshima in World War II (p. 805)
Enola Gay nombre del avión desde el cual se lanzó la bomba atómica sobre la ciudad japonesa de Hiroshima durante la Segunda Guerra Mundial

entrepreneur risk taker who starts new ventures within the economic system of capitalism (p. 297, 467)
empresario persona que toma riesgos y emprende nuevas operaciones dentro del sistema económico del capitalismo

Equal Rights Amendment (ERA) a proposed constitutional amendment barring discrimination on the basis of sex (p. 988)
Enmienda de Igualdad de Derechos (ERA, por sus siglas en inglés) enmienda constitucional propuesta que prohibía la discriminación basada en el sexo

Erie Canal canal running from Albany to Buffalo, New York; completed in 1825 (p. 254)
canal de Erie canal que va desde Albany a Búfalo, en el estado de Nueva York; se terminó de construir en 1825

Establishment the social, economic, and political leaders of a nation who hold power and influence (p. 1003)
clase dirigente líderes sociales, económicos y políticos de un país que tienen poder e influencia

ethnicity identification with a culturally distinct group. Ethnic groups may be defined in terms of shared culture, language, heritage or country of origin. (p. CS4)
éthnicidad identificación con un grupo cultural diferenciado. Los grupos étnicos se pueden definir por la cultura, lenguaje, pasado o país de origen compartidos

evolution theory which holds that inherited characteristics of a population change over generations and that as a result of these changes, new species sometimes arise (p. 650)
evolución teoría que explica que la características heredadas de una población cambian de una generación a otra y que, como consecuencia de esos cambios, a veces surgen nuevas especies

executive branch the division of the federal government that includes the president and the administrative departments (p. 145)
poder ejecutivo división del gobierno federal que incluye al presidente y a los departamentos administrativos

executive privilege policy that a president must be free to keep his or her official conversations and meetings private (p. 1030)
privilegio ejecutivo política que afirma que un presidente debe contar con la libertad de mantener la confidencialidad de sus conversaciones y reuniones oficiales

Exodusters African Americans who settled western lands in the late 1800s (p. 452)
Exodusters afroamericanos que se establecieron en el oeste a finales del siglo XIX

extinction complete disappearance of a species (p. CS19)
extinción desaparición total de una especie

Fair Deal plan proposed by President Truman that included a number of programs in the tradition of the New Deal (p. 827)
Trato Justo plan propuesto por el presidente Truman que incluyó una serie de programas en la tradición del New Deal

fascism a system of government that focuses on the good of the state rather than on the individual citizens (p. 740)
fascismo sistema de gobierno que se concentra en el bienestar del estado en lugar del bienestar de los ciudadanos

The Federalist collection of essays on the principles of government written in defense of the Constitution in 1787 (p. 160)
El federalista colección de ensayos sobre los principios de gobierno escritos en defensa de la Constitución en 1787

Federalists people who supported ratification of the Constitution (p. 158)
federalistas personas que apoyaban la ratificación de la Constitución

Federal Reserve System the nation's central bank (p. 676)
Sistema Reserva Federal banco central de la nación

Federal Reserve Act (1913) law that created a central fund from which banks could borrow to prevent collapse during a financial panic (p. 543)
Ley de la Reserva Federal (1913) ley que creó un fondo central del cual los bancos tomarían prestados fondos para evitar el colapso durante un pánico económico

feminism the principle that women and men should have equal social, political, and economic rights (p. 988)
feminismo principio según el cual las mujeres y los hombres deben gozar de igualdad de derechos sociales, políticos y económicos

Fifteenth Amendment (1870) gave African American men the right to vote (p. 415)
Decimoquinta enmienda (1870) otorgó a los hombres afroamericanos el derecho al voto

Final Solution the Nazi Party's plan to murder the entire Jewish population of Europe and the Soviet Union (p. 780)
Solución Final plan del partido nazi de asesinar a toda la población judía de Europa y la Unión Soviética

fireside chat conversational radio addresses given by President Franklin D. Roosevelt (p. 700)
charlas informales discursos radiales a modo de conversación que daba Franklin D. Roosevelt

First Battle of Bull Run (1861) the first major battle of the Civil War, resulting in a Confederate victory (p. 364)
primera batalla de Bull Run (1861) un gran batalla de la Guerra Civil, que resultó en una victoria de la Confederación

First Continental Congress (1774) a meeting of colonial delegates in Philadelphia to decide how to respond to the abuses of authority by the British government (p. 110)
Primer Congreso Continental (1774) reunión de delegados de las colonias en Filadelfia para decidir cómo responderían a los abusos de la autoridad del gobierno británico

flapper a young woman in the 1920s who wore her hair bobbed, wore makeup, dressed in flashy, skimpy clothes, and lived a life of independence and freedom (p. 648)
flapper jovencita que en la década de 1920 lucía el pelo a la moda, usaba maquillaje, se ponía ropa elegante y escasa, y vivía una vida de independencia y libertad

flexible response a response strategy to nuclear tensions that involved strengthening conventional U.S. forces so the nation would have options other than nuclear weapons in times of crisis (p. 886)
respuesta flexible estrategia de repuesta a las tensiones nucleares que implicó fortalecer las fuerzas convencionales de Estados Unidos para que el país contara con otras opciones además de las armas nucleares en cualquier época de crisis

flower children a slang term for hippies (p. 1005)
niños de las flores expresión popular para los hippies

food insecurity the inability to buy enough healthy food (p. CS26)
inseguridad alimenticia incapacidad de comprar una cantidad suficiente de alimentos saludables

Foraker Act (1900) established that the United States would appoint the upper house of Puerto Rico's legislature, as well as its governor (p. 567)
Ley de Foraker (1900) estableció que Estados Unidos designaría a los miembros de la cámara alta de la legislatura de Puerto Rico así como su gobernador

foreclosure when a lender takes over ownership of a property from an owner who has failed to make loan payments (p. 682)
ejecución hipotecaria cuando el prestamista se apodera de una propiedad porque el propietario no ha pagado las cuotas del préstamo

Fourteen Points President Woodrow Wilson's plan for organizing post-World War I Europe and for avoiding future wars (p. 607)
Catorce Puntos plan del presidente Woodrow Wilson para organizar Europa después de la Primera Guerra Mundial y para evitar futuras guerras

Fourteenth Amendment (1866) gave full rights of citizenship to all people born or naturalized in the United States, except for American Indians (p. 414)
Decimocuarta enmienda (1866) otorga derechos totales de ciudadanía a todas las personas nacidas en Estados Unidos o naturalizadas estadounidenses, con excepción de los indígenas norteamericanos

free blacks African Americans who were not slaves (p. 286)
　negros libres afroamericanos que no eran esclavos

Free Speech Movement counterculture movement during the 1960s (p. 1004)
　Movimiento por la Libertad de Expresión movimiento en contra de la cultura dominante que tuvo lugar en la década de 1960

freedmen a term for emancipated slaves (p. 373)
　libertos término para referirse a los esclavos emancipados

Freedmen's Bureau an agency established by Congress in 1865 to help poor people throughout the South (p. 404)
　Oficina de Libertos agencia creada por el Congreso en 1865 para ayudar a los pobres en el Sur

Freedom Riders activists who challenged segregation in bus terminals in the South in 1961 (p. 918)
　Pasajeros de la Libertas activistas que en 1961 desafia-ron la segregación en las terminales de autobuses del sur

Freedom Summer a volunteer project in which college students spent their summer vacation in Mississippi, registering African Americans to vote (p. 927)
　Verano de la libertad proyecto voluntario en el que un grupo de estudiantes universitarios pasaron sus vacaciones de verano en el estado de Mississippi, inscribiendo a afroamericanos para votar

Freeport Doctrine (1858) a statement made by Stephen Douglas during the Lincoln-Douglas debates stating how people could use popular sovereignty to determine if their state or territory should permit slavery (p. 341)
　Doctrina de Freeport (1858) declaración hecha por Stephen Douglas durante los debates Lincoln-Douglas que señalaba que el pueblo podía usar la soberanía popular para decidir si su estado o territorio debía permitir la esclavitud

free-soilers members of a political party called the Free-Soil Party; it was formed in 1848 by antislavery northerners (p. 327)
　free-soilers integrantes de un partido político llamado Free-Soil Party (partido de las tierra libre); formado en 1848 por norteños opuestos a la esclavitud

Fugitive Slave Act (1850) a law that made it a crime to help runaway slaves (p. 325)
　Ley de los Esclavos Fugitivos (1850) ley que hacía que ayudar a un esclavo a escapar de su amo fuera un delito

fundamentalism a belief in the literal interpretation of a particular religion's doctrine or holy books (p. 650)
　fundamentalismo creencia en la interpretación literal de la doctrina o de los libros sagrados de una religión

General Agreement on Tariffs and Trade (GATT) international organization that works to reduce tariffs and other barriers to trade (p. 828)
　Acuerdo General sobre Aranceles y Comercio (GATT, por sus siglas en inglés) organización internacional que trabaja para reducir los aranceles y otras barreras para el comercio

genetic engineering artificial modification of genes or genetic material (p. 1103)
　ingeniería genética modificación artificial de los genes o del material genético

Geneva Conference (1954) international meeting in Geneva, Switzerland to restore peace in Indochina (p. 951)
　Convención de Ginebra (1954) cumbre internacional celebrada en Ginebra, Suiza, para restablecer la paz en Indochina

genocide the killing of an entire people (p. 780)
　genocidio exterminio de un pueblo entero

Gentlemen's Agreement pact made between the United States and Japan in which Japan agreed to limit immigration to the U.S., and in exchange President Roosevelt agreed to put pressure on the city of San Francisco to rescind an order that forced children of Japanese parents to attend segregated schools (p. 494)
　Acuerdo entre Caballeros pacto alcanzado entre Estados Unidos y Japón por el que Japón se comprometió a limitar la inmigración a Estados Unidos y a cambio el presidente Roosevelt se comprometió a presionar a la ciudad de San Francisco para que revocara una orden que obligaba a los hijos de padres japoneses a acudir a escuelas segregadas

ghetto an area where people from a specific ethnic background live as a group (p. 780)
　gueto lugar en el que vive una comunidad de personas de un origen étnico particular

GI Bill (1944) act that helped veterans make a smooth entry into civilian life by providing money for attending college or for advanced job training (p. 824)
　Ley de Veteranos (1944) ley que facilitó la reintegración de los veteranos a la vida civil con ayudas económicas que les permitieron ir a la universidad u obtener formación profesional avanzada

glasnost Russian word for "opening"; refers to a new era of media freedom on the Soviet Union under Mikhail Gorbachev (p. 1060)
　glasnost palabra rusa que significa "apertura"; se refiere a una nueva era de libertad en los medios que se vivió en la Unión Soviética bajo Mikhail Gorbachev

Glorious Revolution (1688) a nonviolent revolution in which leaders of Britain's Parliament invited Mary, daughter of King James II, and her husband, the Dutch ruler William of Orange, to replace King James II (p. 74)
　Revolución Gloriosa (1688) revolución pacífica por la que los líderes del Parlamento británico invitaron a María, hija del rey James II y a su esposo, el gobernante holandés Guillermo de Orange, a reemplazar al rey James II

gold rush (1849) the mass migration of people to California after gold was discovered there (p. 299)
　fiebre del oro (1849) la migración masiva de personas a California tras el descubrimiento de oro allí

grandfather clause a law added to the Constitution of many Southern states, stating that a man could vote if he, his father, or his grandfather had been eligible to vote before January 1, 1867 (p. 508)
　cláusula de los abuelos ley agregada a la Constitución de muchos estados del Sur que establecía que un hombre podía votar si él, su padre o su abuelo habían tenido derecho al voto antes del 1º de enero de 1867

Great Awakening a religious movement in the American colonies in the 1730s and 1740s (p. 86)
　Gran Despertar movimiento religioso que tuvo gran popularidad en las colonias estadounidenses en las décadas de 1730 y 1740

Great Compromise (1787) an agreement worked out at the Constitutional Convention establishing that a state's population would determine representation in the lower house of the legislature, while each state would have equal representation in the upper house (p. 154)
　Gran Compromiso (1787) acuerdo redactado durante la Convención Constitucional en el que se establece que la población de un estado debe determinar su represen-tación en la cámara baja de la asamblea legislativa y que cada estado debe tener igual representación en la cámara alta

Great Depression (1929- 1930s) the most severe economic downturn in the history of the United States (p. 681)
Gran Depresión (de 1929 a la década de 1930) la crisis económica más grave de la historia de Estados Unidos

Great Irish Famine period in Ireland during the mid-1880s, when a blight on the potato crop caused about 1 million people to die of starvation (p. 273)
Gran Hamburna Irlandesa período de la historia de Irlanda a mediados de la década de 1880 durante el cual una plaga en la cosecha de papas (patatas) hizo morir de hambre a aproximadamente 1 millón de personas

Great Migration the movement of nearly 16,000 Europeans from Europe to New England from 1620 to 1643 (p. 53); the major relocation of African Americans from 1910 into the 1920s to northern cities (p. 655)
Gran Migración translado de casi 16,000 europeos de Europa a Nueva Inglaterra entre 1620 y 1643; gran translado de afroamericanos a las ciudades del Norte desde 1910 hasta la década de 1920

Great Society the term for the domestic programs of the Johnson administration (p. 897)
Gran Sociedad término que se refiere a los programas de política doméstica del gobierno del presidente Johnson

green card Permanent Resident Card (p. CS4)
tarjeta verde tarjeta de residencia permanente

gross national product (GNP) the total value of all goods and services produced in the nation (p. 673)
producto interior bruto (PIB, por sus siglas en español) el valor total de todos los bienes y servicios producidos en el país

guerrilla war fighting marked by sabotage, ambushes, and other surprise attacks (p. 332)
guerra de guerrillas enfrentamientos marcados por el sabotaje, las emboscadas y otros ataques por sorpresa

habeas corpus the constitutional protection against unlawful imprisonment (p. 377)
hábeas corpus protección constitucional contra el encarcelamiento ilegal

hard-rock mining mining that requires cutting deep shafts in solid rock to extract the ore (p. 446)
minería de roca dura explotación minera en la que es necesario hacer huecos profundos en la roca sólida para extraer el mineral

Harlem Renaissance a blossoming of African American art and literature that began in the 1920s (p. 656)
Renacimiento de Harlem florecimiento del arte y la literatura afroamericanas que comenzó en la década de 1920

hawks people who are supportive of a war's goals (p. 962)
halcones personas que apoyan los objetivos de una guerra

headrights 50-acre grants of land offered by the Virginia Company beginning in 1618 in order to attract settlers to the New World (p. 49)
concesiones áreas de tierra de 50 acres ofrecidas por Virginia Company a partir de 1618 para atraer pobladores al Nuevo Mundo

Hepburn Act (1906) law that authorized the Interstate Commerce Commission to set maximum railroad rates and gave it the power to regulate other companies engaged in interstate commerce (p. 538)
Ley Hepburn (1906) ley que autorizó que la Comisión Interestatal de Comercio fijara precios máximos para el ferrocarril y le dio el poder para regular otras empresas que participaban en el comercio interestatal

hobo a homeless person, typically one who is traveling in search of work (p. 680)
vagabundo persona sin hogar que por lo general viaja de un sitio a otro en busca de trabajo

Ho Chi Minh Trail a network of paths from North Vietnam to South Vietnam (p. 957)
Ruta de Ho Chi Minh red de senderos que comunica Vietnam del Norte con Vietnam del Sur

Hollywood Ten Hollywood writers and directors who were thought to be radicals and called before HUAC; they refused to cooperate and were sentenced to short prison terms (p. 931)
los diez de Hollywood escritores y directores de Hollywood considerados radicales y convocados por el HUAC; se negaron a cooperar y fueron condenados a corto tiempo en prisión

Holocaust the killing of millions of Jews and others by Nazis during World War II (p. 783)
Holocausto asesinato de millones de judíos y de otras personas por parte de los nazis durante la Segunda Guerra Mundial

Homestead Act (1862) a law passed by Congress to encourage settlement in the West by giving government-owned land to small farmers (p. 450)
Ley de Heredad (1862) ley aprobada por el Congreso para fomentar la colonización del oeste del país mediante la cesión de tierras del gobierno a pequeños agricultores

Hoover Dam a dam built in the 1930s with funding from the federal government to control the Colorado River (p. 688)
Presa Hoover presa construida en la década de 1930 con financiamiento del gobierno federal para controlar el río Colorado

Hooverville makeshift shantytowns that sprung up during the Great Depression (p. 683)
Hooverville barriadas improvisadas que surgieron durante la Gran Depresión

horizontal integration owning all the businesses in a certain field (p. 468)
integración horizontal ser dueño de todas las empresas de un campo específico

House of Burgesses America's first law-making body, formed in July 1619 by representatives from the different communities in Virginia (p. 49)
Cámara de Burgueses la primera cámara legislativa de Estados Unidos; formada en julio de 1619 por representantes de las distintas comunidades de Virginia

House Un-American Activities Committee (HUAC) committee formed in the House of Representatives in the 1930s to investigate radical groups in the United States; it later came to focus on the threat of communism in the United States during World War II and the Cold War (p. 834)
Comité de Actividades Antiestadounidenses (HUAC, por sus siglas en inglés) comité formado en la Cámara de Representantes en la década de 1930 para investigar a los grupos radicales en Estados Unidos; más tarde se enfocó en la amenaza comunista en Estados Unidos durante la Segunda Guerra Mundial y la Guerra Fría

ENGLISH AND SPANISH GLOSSARY

Hundred Days (1933) the first hundred days of Franklin Roosevelt's term as president (p. 702)
Cien Días (1933) primeros cien días del gobierno de Franklin Roosevelt como presidente

hunter-gatherers people who hunt animals and gather wild plants to provide for their needs (p. 7)
cazadores y recolectores personas que satisfacen sus necesidades cazando animales y recolectando plantas silvestres

Hurricane Katrina massive hurricane that struck the Gulf Coast on August 29, 2005 and resulted in immense destruction and more than 1,500 deaths (p. 1100)
Huracán Katrina huracán masivo que arremetió contra la costa del golfo el 29 de agosto de 2005 y que causó inmensos daños y más de 1,500 muertes

hydraulic mining method of mining that uses water under high pressure to blast away gravel and dirt to expose the minerals underneath (p. 446)
minería hidráulica método de explotación minera que utiliza agua con alta presión para hacer volar la grava y la tierra, y así exponer el mineral que se oculta debajo.

hydrogen bomb a nuclear weapon that gets its power from the fusing together of hydrogen atoms (p. 855)
bomba de hidrógeno arma nuclear que obtiene su energía de la fusión de átomos de hidrógeno

ICBM intercontinental ballistic missiles; guided missiles that could travel thousands of miles and strike targets accurately (p. 856)
MBIC misiles balísticos intercontinentales; misiles guiados que podían recorrer miles de millas y alcanzar objetivos con precisión

immigrant a person who settles in a new country (p. CS2)
inmigrante persona que se establece en un nuevo país

impeachment the process used by a legislative body to bring charges of wrongdoing against a public official (p. 415)
acusación proceso utilizado por un grupo legislativo para presentar cargos en contra de un funcionario público

imperialism the practice of extending a nation's power by gaining territories for a colonial empire (p. 553)
imperialismo práctica de ampliar el poder de una nación mediante la anexión de otros territorios para formar un imperio colonial

impressment the practice of forcing people to serve in the army or navy (p. 225)
leva práctica que obligaba a las personas a servir en el ejército o la marina

Inca American Indian society that lived in the Andes Mountains of South America from about the 12th century, until Spanish conquest in the mid-16th century (p. 9)
incas sociedad indígena americana que vivió en la cordi-llera de los Andes, en América del Sur, aproximadamente desde el siglo XII hasta la conquista española a mediados del siglo XVI

Inchon a port city in western South Korea on the Yellow Sea; site of major battle in the Korean War (p. 839)
Inchon ciudad portuaria en el oeste de Corea del Sur a orillas del mar Amarillo; fue el lugar de una importante batalla de la Guerra de Corea

incumbent the person who currently holds a public office (p. 727)

titular la persona que ocupa un puesto oficial actualmente

indentured servants people whose employers pay for passage to the country they wish to emigrate to, food, and shelter; in return the indentured servants agree to work for the employer for a certain number of years (p. 49)
sirvientes por contrato personas a los que sus empleadores les pagaban el pasaje al país al que deseaban emigrar, la comida y el alojamiento; a cambio, los sirvientes por contrato se comprometían a trabajar para el empleador durante un determinado número de años

Indian Removal Act (1830) a congressional act that authorized the removal of Native Americans who lived east of the Mississippi River (p. 247)
Ley de Expulsión de Indígenas (1830) ley redactada por el Congreso que autorizaba la expulsión de los indígenas norteamericanos que vivían al este del río Mississippi

Industrial Revolution a period of rapid growth in the use of machines in manufacturing and production that began in the mid-1700s (p. 252)
Revolución Industrial período de rápido desarrollo debido al uso de maquinaria en la fabricación y producción que comenzó a mediados del siglo XVIII

infantry foot soldiers (p. 364)
infantería soldados de a pie

inflation increased prices for goods and services combined with the reduced value of money (pp. 129, 739)
inflación alza en los precios de los bienes y servicos al mismo tiempo que se produce una reducción en el valor del dinero

initiative a method of allowing voters to propose a new law on the ballot for public approval (p. 527)
iniciativa método que permite a los votantes proponer una ley en la boleta electoral para la aprobación del público

installment buying paying for an item over a period of time with a series of small payments (p. 632)
compra a plazos pagar por un artículo a lo largo de un período de tiempo mediante una serie de pequeños pagos

integrated circuit a computer chip that includes a number of transistors and other electronic components (p. 864)
circuito integrado chip de computadora que contiene un número de transistores y de otros componentes electrónicos

Intermediate-range Nuclear Forces (INF) Treaty a treaty between the United States and the Soviet Union that ordered the destruction of thousands of missiles (p. 1055)
Tratado de Fuerzas Nucleares de Alcance Intermedio (FNAI) tratado entre Estados Unidos y la Unión Soviética que ordenó la destrucción de miles de misiles

International Monetary Fund organization designed to encourage economic policies that promote international trade (p. 828)
Fondo Monetario Internacional organización diseñada para fomentar políticas económicas que promueven el comercio internacional

internment the forced relocation and confinement of Japanese-Americans to concentration camps (p. 797)
internamiento el traslado forzoso y el confinamiento de los japoneses-americanos en campos de concentración

Interstate Highway System a network of high-speed roads built to make interstate travel faster and easier (p. 867)
sistema de autopistas interestatales red de carreteras de alta velocidad construidas para facilitar y agilizar los viajes interestatales

Intolerable Acts (1774) laws passed by Parliament to punish the colonists for the Boston Tea Party and to tighten government control of the colonies (p. 110)
Leyes Intolerables (1774) leyes apropadas por el Parlamento inglés para castigar a los colonos que participaron en el Motín del Té de Boston y para aumentar su control sobre las colonias

Iran-Contra affair secret U.S. sales of weapons to Iran in an attempt to secure the release of U.S. hostages held in Lebanon in 1986 (p. 1058)
asunto Irán-Contra venta secreta de armas de Estados Unidos a Irán para lograr la liberación de los rehenes estadounidenses detenidos en el Líbano en 1986

Iron Curtain term coined by Winston Churchill in 1946 to describe an imaginary line dividing Communist countries in the Soviet bloc from countries in Western Europe during the Cold War (p. 819)
cortina de hierro término creado por Winston Churchill en 1946 para describir la línea imaginaria que dividía a los países comunistas del bloque soviético de los países de Europa occidental durante la Guerra Fría

ironclads armored gunboats covered with iron plates up to three inches thick (p. 366)
acorazados barcos armados y cubiertos con placas de hierro de hasta tres pulgadas de espesor

Iroquois Native American group of the Northeast (p. 14)
iroqueses grupo indígena norteamericano del Norest

Iroquois League an alliance of Native Americans (p. 92)
Liga de los Iroqueses alianza de indígenas norteamericanos

Islam the Muslim religion (p. 19)
Islam religión de los musulmanes

isolationism a policy in which a nation avoids entanglement in foreign wars (p. 591)
aislacionismo política por la que una nación evita participar en guerras ajenas

IT computerized information technology (p. 1103)
TI tecnología de información computarizada

Jacksonian Democracy an expansion of voting rights during the Andrew Jackson administration (p. 246)
democracia jacksoniana ampliación del derecho al voto durante el gobierno del presidente Andrew Jackson

Jay's Treaty (1794) an agreement negotiated by John Jay to work out problems between Britain and the United States over northwestern lands, British seizure of U.S. ships, and U.S. debts owed to the British (p. 211)
Tratado de Jay (1794) acuerdo negociado por John Jay para resolver los problemas entre Gran Bretaña y Estados Unidos por los territorios del noroeste, por la incautación británica de barcos estadounidenses y por las deudas estadounidenses con los ingleses

jazz type of American music that blends several different musical forms from the Deep South (p. 659)
jazz typo de musical estadounidense que mezcla varias formas musicales del Sur y sureste del país

Jim Crow laws laws that enforced segregation in the southern states (p. 508)
leyes de Jim Crow leyes que impusieron la segregación racial en los estados sureños

Job Corps program under President Johnson that offered work-training programs for unemployed youth (p. 896)
Job Corps programa del presidente Johnson que ofrecía programas de formación laboral a los jóvenes desempleados

Johnson Doctrine President Johnson's philosophy that revolutions in Latin America were not just local concerns when "the object is the establishment of a Communist dictatorship" (p. 900)
Doctrina Johnson filosofía del presidente Johnson según la cual las revoluciones en América Latina dejaban de ser un asunto de interés local cuando "el objetivo es el establecimiento de una dictadura comunista."

joint-stock companies businesses formed by groups of people who jointly make an investment and share in the profits and losses (p. 47)
sociedades por acciones empresas formadas por grupos de personas que invierten conjuntamente y comparten las ganancias y las pérdidas

judicial branch the division of the federal government that is made up of the national courts (p. 145)
poder judicial división del gobierno federal formada por las cortes nacionales

judicial review the Supreme Court's power to declare acts of Congress unconstitutional (p. 220)
revisión judicial poder de la Corte Suprema para declarar inconstitucionales las acciones del Congreso

Judiciary Act of 1789 legislation passed by Congress that created the federal court system (p. 204)
Ley de Judicatura de 1789 ley aprobada por el Congreso para crear el sistema federal de tribunales

Judiciary Act of 1801 act passed by Congress that created new positions in the judicial branch (p. 220)
Ley de Judicatura de 1801 ley aprobada por el Congreso para crear nuevos puestos en el poder judicial

kamikaze in World War II, a pilot who agreed to load his aircraft with bombs and crash it on an enemy ship (p. 791)
kamikaze en la Segunda Guerra Mundial, piloto que accedía a cargar su avión con bombas para estrellarlo contra un barco enemigo

Kansas-Nebraska Act (1854) a law that allowed voters in Kansas and Nebraska to choose whether or not to allow slavery (p. 326)
Ley de Kansas y Nebraska (1854) ley que permitió a los votantes de Kansas y Nebraska decidir si permitirían o abolición de la esclavitud

Kellogg-Briand Pact treaty signed in 1928 that rejected war as a way of solving problems between countries (p. 639)
Pacto de Kellogg-Briand tratado firmado en 1928 que rechazó la guerra como un medio para solucionar los problemas entre países

Kerner Commission committee appointed to study the causes of urban rioting after violence in Detroit in July 1967 (p. 934)
Comisión Kerner comité nombrado para estudiar las causas de los disturbios urbanos ocurridos después de actos de violencia en Detroit en julio de 1967

Khmer Rouge Communists who took over Cambodia in 1975 (p. 977)
Khmer Rouge comunistas que arrebataron el poder en Camboya en 1975

King Cotton name given by Southerners to indicate the economic and political importance of cotton production in the southern states (p. 258)
Rey Algodón nombre utilizado por los habitantes del Sur para indicar la importancia económica y política de la producción de algodón en los estados sureños

King Philip's War (1675) war fought between the Wampanoag and English settlers in southern New England, led by a Wampanoag leader named Metacomet, known to the English as "King Philip" (p. 56)
Guerra del Rey Felipe (1675) guerra entre los indios wampanoag y los pobladores ingleses del sur de Nueve Inglaterra liderados por el jefe wampanoag llamado Metacomet, conocido por los ingleses como "Rey Felipe"

kinship family relationship (p. 15)
parentesco relación de familia

Knights of Labor secret society that became the first truly national labor union in the United States (p. 474)
Knights of Labor sociedad secreta que se convirtió en el primer sindicato verdaderamente nacional en Estados Unidos

Know-Nothings a mid-1800s secret anti-immigration fraternal organization; this group later became a political party called the American Party (p. 275)
Know-Nothings hermandad secreta antiinmigrantes de mediados del siglo XIX; más tarde, el grupo se convirtió en un partido político llamado Partido Americano

Kristallnacht (1938) a German word for broken glass; an event that occurred on the nights of November 9 and 10 in which Hitler's Nazis encouraged Germans to riot against Jews, and nearly 100 Jews died (p. 779)
Kristallnacht (1938) palabra en alemán que significa vidrios de los cristales rotos; acontecimiento que tuvo lugar las noches del 9 y 10 de noviembre en que los nazis de Hitler animaron a los alemanes a participar en disturbios callejeros contra los judíos y murieron cerca de cien judíos

Ku Klux Klan a secret society that used terror and violence to keep African Americans from obtaining their civil rights (p. 412)
Ku Klux Klan sociedad secreta que usaba el terror y la violencia para impedir que los afroamericanos obtuvieran sus derechos civiles

Kwakiutl Native American group of the Pacific Northwest (p. 12)
kwakiutl grupo de indígenas norteamericanos de la costa noroeste del Pacífico

La Raza Unida Party organization formed in the 1960s aimed at helping Mexican Americans (p. 998)
Partido La Raza Unida organización formada en la década de 1960 con el motivo de ayudar a los mexicano americanos

labor movement reform movement working to secure higher wages, shorter hours, and safer working conditions (p. 276)
movimiento obrero movimiento reformista que buscaba obtener salarios más altos, jornadas más cortas y condiciones laborales más seguras

laissez-faire in French, meaning "allow to do"; a business system where companies are allowed to conduct business without interference by the government (p. 467)
laissez-faire "dejar hacer" en francés en el mundo de los negocios un sistema en el que las compañías llevan a cabo sus actividades comerciales sin interferencia del gobierno

Land Ordinance of 1785 legislation passed by Congress authorizing surveys and the division of public lands in the western region of the country (p. 149)
Ordenanza de Territorios de 1785 ley aprobada por el Congreso en el que se autorizaron las mediciones de terreno y la división de territorios públicos en el oeste del país

League of Nations international body of nations formed in 1919 to prevent wars (p. 607)
Liga de las Naciones organización internacional de naciones formada en 1919 con el fin de prevenir las guerras

Lecompton Constitution a pro-slavery state constitution written by delegates to the constitutional convention in the Kansas territory in 1857 (p. 334)
Constitución de Lecompton constitución estatal a favor de la exclavitud redactada por delegados de la convención constitucional en el territorio de Kansas en 1857

legislative branch the division of the federal government that proposes bills and passes them into laws (p. 145)
poder legislativo división del gobierno federal que propone proyectos de ley y los aprueba para convertirlos en leyes

Lend-Lease Act (1940) program that gave the government power to make weapons available to Great Britain without regard for its ability to pay (p. 755)
Ley de Préstamo y Arriendo (1940) programa que le dio al gobierno la autoridad para poner armas a disposición de Gran Bretaña sin importar si podía pagarlas

Levittown a New York town of mass-produced homes, which became a symbol for many similar suburban towns built during the post-World War II years (p. 866)
Levittown pueblo de Nueva York formado por viviendas fabricadas en serie que se convirtió en el símbolo de muchos pueblos suburbanos similares que se construyeron tras la Segunda Guerra Mundial

Lewis and Clark Expedition an expedition led by Meriwether Lewis and William Clark that began in 1804 to explore the Louisiana Purchase (p. 219)
expedición de Lewis y Clark expedición encabezada por Meriwether Lewis y William Clark que partió en 1804 para explorar el territorio adquirido en la Compra de Luisiana

Liberal Republicans group of Republicans that broke with the Republican party over the Enforcement Acts scandals of the Grant administration (p. 425)
republicanos liberales grupo de republicanos que se separaron del partido republicano a raíz de los escándalos de las Leyes de Acatamiento del gobierno del presidente Grant

Liberty bonds bonds that American citizens bought to help pay for the costs of World War I (p. 598)
bonos Liberty bonos que compraron los ciudadanos de Estados Unidos para ayudar a pagar los costos de la Primera Guerra Mundial (pag. 598)

Lincoln-Douglas debates a series of debates between Republican Abraham Lincoln and Democrat Stephen Douglas during the 1858 U.S. Senate campaign in Illinois (p. 341)
debates Lincoln-Douglas serie de debates entre el republicano Abraham Lincoln y el demócrata Stephen Douglas durante la campaña de 1858 para el Senado estadounidense en Illinois

lineage ancestry (p. 20)
linaje ascendencia

literacy test a test that determines a person's ability to read (p. 494)
prueba de alfabetización prueba que determina la capacidad de leer de una persona (p. 494)

Little Rock Nine nine African American students who first integrated Central High School in Little Rock, Arkansas, in 1957 (p. 912)
los nueve de Little Rock primeros nueve estudiantes de raza negra en integrar Central High School en Little Rock, Arkansas, en el año 1957

longhouse a large wooden building built by the Iroquois (p. 14)
longhouse edificio grande de madera construido por los iroquois

loose construction a way of interpreting the Constitution that agrees with the federal government taking actions that the Constitution does not specifically forbid (p. 206)
interpretación flexible interpretación de la Constitución que permite al gobierno federal tomar acciones que la Constitución no prohíbe de manera específica

Louisiana Purchase (1803) the purchase of land between the Mississippi River and the Rocky Mountains that doubled the size of the United States (p. 218)
Compra de Luisiana (1803) compra del territorio localizado entre el río Mississippi y las montañas Rocosas que duplicó el tamaño de Estados Unidos

Lowell girls name given to women who worked in Lowell textile mills (p. 253)
Lowell girls nombre dado a las mujeres que trabajaban en las fábricas textiles de Lowell

Loyalist a colonist who sided with Britain in the American Revolution (p. 116)
leal colono que se puso de parte de Gran Bretaña durante la Guerra de Independencia estadounidense

Luftwaffe the German air force (p. 749)
Luftwaffe fuerza aérea alemana

Lusitania British ship sunk by a German U-Boat in 1915 (p. 590)
Lusitania banco británico hundido por un submarino alemán U-Boat en 1915

lynching the murder of an individual by a group or mob (p. 509)
linchamiento el asesinato de una persona por un grupo o una muchedembre

Magna Carta (1215) a charter of liberties agreed to by King John of England, it made the king obey the same laws as citizens (p. 24)
Carta Magna (1215) carta de libertades firmada por el rey Juan de Inglaterra que estableció que el rey debía obedecer las mismas leyes que los ciudadanos

mandate authorization to act (p. 888)
mandato autorización para actuar

Manhattan Project the top-secret program to build an atomic bomb during World War II (p. 762)
Proyecto Manhattan programa secreto para construir una bomba atómica durante la Segunda Guerra Mundial

manifest destiny a belief shared by many Americans in the mid-1800s that the United States should expand across the continent to the Pacific Ocean (p. 297)
destino manifiesto creencia de muchos estadounidenses a mediados del siglo XIX de que Estados Unidos debía expandirse por todo el continente hasta llegar al océano Pacífico

Marshall Plan (1947) plan for the reconstruction of Europe after World War II; announced by the U.S. Secretary of State George C. Marshall (p. 820)
Plan Marshall (1947) plan para la reconstrucción de Europa después de la Segunda Guerra Mundial; anunciado por el secretario de estado estadounidense George C. Marshall

martial law type of rule in which military commanders are in control and citizens' rights and freedoms are suspended (p. 358)
ley marcial tipo de gobierno en el que las fuerzas militares toman el control y se suspenden los derechos y libertades de los ciudadanos

mass transit public transportation systems that carry large numbers of people (p. 478)
transporte público sistemas de transporte colectivo que llevan a grandes cantidades de personas

massive retaliation the United States' willingness to use nuclear force to settle disputes (p. 850)
represalia masiva disposición de Estados Unidos a usar armas nucleares para resolver disputas

matrilineal tracing ancestry through the mother (p. 15)
matrilineal establecimiento de los antepasados a través de la madre

Maya Mesoamerican society that lived in present-day Mexico from about the 3rd century through the 14th century (p. 8)
mayas sociedad mesoamericana que vivió en lo que hoy es México desde el siglo III hasta el siglo XIV aproximadamente

Mayflower Compact (1620) a document written by the Pilgrims establishing themselves as a political society and setting guidelines for self-government (p. 51)
Pacto del Mayflower (1620) documento redactado por los peregrinos en el que formaban una sociedad política y establecían los principios para gobernarse a sí mismos

McCarthyism the name critics gave to Joseph McCarthy's tactic of spreading fear and making baseless charges (p. 834)
macarthismo nombre que los críticos dieron a la táctica empleada por Joseph McCarthy para infundir miedo y hacer acusaciones sin fundamento

McCulloch v. Maryland (1819) Supreme Court case that declared the Second Bank of the United States was constitutional (p. 240)
McCulloch contra Maryland (1819) caso de la Corte Suprema que declaró que el banco Segundo Banco de Estados Unidos era constitucional

Meat Inspection Act (1906) law that required government inspection of meat shipped across state lines (p. 538)
Ley de Inspección de la Carne (1906) ley que exigió que el gobierno inspeccionara la carne que se enviaba de un estado a otro (pág. 538)

Medicaid a government program that provides free health care for poor people (p. 898)
Medicaid programa del gobierno que brinda atención médica gratuita a los pobres

Medicare a health care program for people over age 65 (p. 898)
Medicare programa de atención médica para personas mayores de 65 años

mercantilism economic system used from about the 1500s to the 1700s; held that a nation's power was directly related to its wealth (p. 73)
mercantilismo sistema económico usado entre los siglos XVI y XVIII aproximadamente; sostenía que el poder de una nación estaba directamente relacionado con su riqueza

Mexican Cession more than 500,000 square miles of land turned over to the United States by Mexico after the Mexican-American War (p. 311)
Cesión Mexicana más de 500,000 millas cuadradas de territorio cedido a Estados Unidos por México después de la Guerra contra México

Mexican Revolution a revolution led by Francisco Madero in 1910 that eventually forced the Mexican dictator Porfirio Díaz to resign (p. 573)
Revolución Mexicana revolución encabezada por Francisco Madero en 1910 que al final obligó a renunciar al dictador mexicano Porfirio Díaz

Mexican-American War (1846-1848) war fought between the United States and Mexico in which the U.S. gained more than 500,000 square miles of land in the United States (p. 310)
Guerra contra México (1846-1848) guerra librada entre Estados Unidos y México en la que los primeros conquistaron más de 500,000 millas cuadradas de territorio para Estados Unidos

Middle Ages period of European history, from the fall of the Roman Empire to the Renaissance (p. 24)
Edad Media período de la historia europea desde la caída del Imperio romano hasta el Renacimiento

Middle Passage a voyage that brought enslaved Africans across the Atlantic Ocean to North America and the West Indies (p. 79)
Paso Central viaje a través del océano Atlántico que trajo a los africanos esclavizados a América del Norte y a las Antillas

migrant person who moves from one place to another (p. CS4)
emigrante persona que se muda de un lugar a otro

militarism the expansion of arms and the policy of military preparedness (p. 583)
militarismo aumento de la cantidad de armas y política de preparación militar para la guerra

militia a military organization made up of civilians (p. CS32)
milicia organización militar compuesta de civiles

minimum wage the lowest wage an employer can legally pay a worker (p. 726)
salario mínimo salario más bajo que un patrón puede pagar legalmente a un trabajador

minutemen American colonial militia members ready to fight at a minute's notice (p. 110)
milicianos del minuto miembros de la milicia norteamericana en la época colonial preparados para combatir con aviso de un minuto

missionary people sent by their church to teach and convert others to their religion (p. 42)
misionero personas enviadas por su iglesia a enseñar y convertir a otras a su religión

mission system a way of living used by the Spanish in the Americas, in which settlements were designed to convert local Indians to Catholicism and make them into loyal Spanish subjects (p. 303)
sistema de las misiones forma de vida usada por los españoles en las Américas, bajo la cual los asentamientos se diseñaban con el propósito de convertir a los indígenas locales al catolicismo y obligarlos a ser fieles servidores de España

Mississippi Freedom Democratic Party a political party created in 1964 with the purpose of winning seats at the 1964 Democratic National Convention (p. 928)
Partido Demócrata por la Libertad de Mississippi partido político creado en 1964 con el fin de obtener puestos en la Convención Nacional Demócrata de 1964

Missouri Compromise (1820) an agreement that allowed Missouri to enter the Union as a slave state and Maine to enter as a free state and outlawed slavery in any territories or states north of 36°30′ N. latitude (p. 243)
Compromiso de Missouri (1820) acuerdo redactado en el que se aceptaba a Missouri en la Unión como estado esclavista y a Maine como estado libre y prohibía la esclavitud en los territorios o estados ubicados al norte del paralelo 36°30′ N

monopoly having complete control in the marketplace, without any outside competition (p. 468)
monopolio control absoluto del mercado, sin competencia externa

Monroe Doctrine (1823) President James Monroe's statement forbidding further colonization in the Americas and declaring that any attempt by a foreign country to colonize would be considered an act of hostility (p. 242)
Doctrina Monroe (1823) declaración hecha por el presidente James Monroe en la que se prohibía la colonización adicional del continente americano a partir de entonces y en que se declaró que cualquier intento de colonización por parte de otro país se consideraría un acto hostil

Montgomery bus boycott (1955) a boycott of the Montgomery, Alabama bus system in response to the racial segregation of city buses (p. 914)
boicot de los autobuses en Montgomery (1955) boicot del sistema de autobuses de Montgomery, Alabama, como reacción a la segregación racial en los autobuses de la ciudad

Mormon Trail 1,300-mile-long route used by Mormons to travel west to Utah (p. 299)
Ruta de los Mormones ruta de 1,300 millas que usaron los mormones para viajar hacia el oeste a Utah

Morrill Act (1862) a federal law passed by Congress that gave land to western states to encourage them to build colleges (p. 450)
Ley Morrill (1862) ley federal aprobada por el Congreso para otorgar tierras a los estados del oeste con el fin de fomentar la construcción de universidades

muckrakers a term coined for journalists who "raked up" and exposed corruption and problems of society (p. 523)
muckrakers término creado para llamar a los periodistas que se dedicaban a investigar y exponer la corrupción y los problemas de la sociedad

Muslims followers of Islam (p. 19)
musulmanes seguidores del Islam

My Lai Massacre (1968) a massacre of hundreds of unarmed Vietnamese civilians by American soldiers during the Vietnam War (p. 975)
Masacre de My Lai (1968) matanza de cientos de civiles vietnamitas desarmados a manos de soldados estadounidenses durante la Guerra de Vietnam

NASA National Aeronautics and Space Administration; agency in charge of the United States' programs for exploring outer space (p. 858)
NASA (por sus siglas en inglés) Administración Nacional de Aeronáutica y el Espacio; agencia encargada de los programas estadounidenses de exploración del espacio exterior

National American Woman Suffrage Association (NAWSA) an organization founded by Elizabeth Cady Stanton and Susan B. Anthony in 1890 to obtain women's suffrage (p. 534)
Asociación Nacional Estadounidense para el Sufragio Femenino (NAWSA, por sus siglas en inglés) organización fundada en 1890 por Elizabeth Cady Stanton y Susan B. Anthony para obtener el derecho al voto de las mujeres

National Association for the Advancement of Colored People (NAACP) an organization founded in 1909 by W. E. B. Du Bois and other reformers to bring attention to racial inequality (p. 509)
Asociación Nacional para el Progreso de la Gente de Color (NAACP, por sus siglas en inglés) organización fundada en 1909 por W. E. B. Du Bois y otros reformadores para dirigir la atención hacia la desigualdad racial

National Association of Colored Women an organization founded in 1896 that worked to fight poverty, segregation, lynchings, and the persistence of Jim Crow laws (p. 532)
Asociación Nacional de Mujeres de Color organización fundada en 1896 para combatir la pobreza, la se-gregación, los linchamientos y las leyes de Jim Crow

National Grange a social and educational organization for farmers (p. 503)
Granja Nacional organización social y educativa para los agricultores

nationalism sense of pride and devotion to a nation (p. 240)
nacionalismo sentimiento de orgullo y lealtad a una nación

National Organization for Women (NOW) a women's rights group formed in 1966 (p. 988)
Organización Nacional de la Mujeres (NOW, por sus siglas en inglés) grupo defensor de los derechos de la mujer creado en 1966

national park a natural area set aside by the federal government (p. CS17)
parque nacional área natural protegida por el gobeirno federal

National Road also called the Cumberland Road, when it was completed in 1841 it stretched from Cumberland, Maryland 800 miles west to Vandalia, Illinois (p. 253)
Camino Nacional también llamado Camino de Cumberland cuando se terminó en 1841, cubría 800 millas al oeste, desde Cumberland, Maryland, hasta Vandalia, Illinois

National War Labor Board (1918) this board mediated disputes between workers and management (p. 601)
Junta Nacional del Trabajo en Tiempos de Guerra (1918) esta junta mediaba en los conflictos entre trabajadores y patronos

nativism an opposition to immigration by the citizens living in a country (p. 274); distrust of foreigners (p. 626)
nativismo oposición a la inmigración por parte de los ciudadanos que viven en un país; desconfianza hacia los extranjeros

NATO North Atlantic Treaty Organization; an international defense alliance formed in 1949 (p. 822)
OTAN Organización del Tratado del Atlántico Norte; alianza internacional de defensa formada en 1949

Navigation Acts series of laws passed between 1651 and 1663 by Parliament stating that all goods coming from Europe or Africa to the colonies had to travel on British ships manned with a British crew (p. 73)
Leyes de Navegación serie de leyes aprobadas entre 1651 y 1663 por el Parlamento; las leyes afirmaban que todos los bienes provenientes de Europa o África con destino a las colonias tenían que viajar en barcos británicos comandados por una tripulación británica

neutral in a war, not aiding either side (p. 753)
neutral en una guerra, que no ayuda a ningún bando

Neutrality Act (1935) a United States act aimed at helping prevent the nation from being drawn into a war (p. 752)
Ley de Neutralidad (1935) ley estadounidense creada para ayudar a impedir que la nación se viera involucrada en una guerra

Neutrality Proclamation (1793) a statement made by President George Washington that the United States would not side with any of the nations at war in Europe following the French Revolution (p. 210)
Proclamación de Neutralidad (1793) declaración en la que el presidente George Washington anunció que Estados Unidos no sería aliado de ninguna de las naciones europeas en guerra después de la Revolución Francesa

New Deal a plan by President Franklin Roosevelt intended to bring economic relief, recovery, and reforms to the country after the Great Depression (p. 702)
Nuevo Trato plan del presidente Franklin Roosevelt para traer ayuda, recuperación y reformas económicas al país después de la Gran Depresión

New Freedom Woodrow Wilson's plan of reform which called for tariff reductions, banking reform, and stronger antitrust legislation (p. 543)
Nueva Libertad plan de reformas de Woodrow Wilson que abogaba por reducciones arancelarias de los aranceles, reformas bancarias y leyes antimonopolio más estrictas

New Frontier the nickname given to President Kennedy's plans for changing the nation (p. 888)
Nueva Frontera apodo dado a los planes del presidente Kennedy para transformar a la nación

New Jersey Plan a proposal to create a unicameral legislature with equal representation of states rather than representation by population (p. 153)
Plan de Nueva Jersey propuesta para la creación de un gobierno de una sola cámara que contara con la misma representación por parte de cada estado, sin basarse en el número de habitantes

New Right a coalition of conservative media commentators, think tanks, and grassroots Christian groups (p. 1049)
Nueva Derecha coalición de analistas conservadores de los medios de asesoría estretégica, grupos de estudiosos y organizaciones cristianas de base popular

New South name used by some Southerners to describe the South after Reconstruction (p. 427)
Nuevo Sur nombre usado por algunos sureños para describir el Sur después de la Reconstrucción (pág. 427)

Newlands Reclamation Act (1902) law that allowed the federal government to build irrigation projects to make marginal lands productive (p. 539)
Ley de Reclamación de Nuevas Tierras (1902) ley que permitía al gobierno federal llevar a cabo proyectos de irrigación para hacer productivas las tierras de poco rendimiento

9/11 terrorist attacks on the World Trade Center in New York City and the Pentagon in Washington, D.C., that took place on September 11, 2001 (p. 1093)
9/11 ataques terroristas contra el World Trade Center en la ciudad de Nueva York y el Pentágono en Washington, D.C., que tuvieron lugar el 11 de septiembre de 2001

Nineteenth Amendment (1920) gave women the right to vote (p. 544)
Decimonovena enmienda (1920) otorgó a la mujer el derecho al voto

nomads people who move from place to place (p. 7)
nómadas personas que se trasladan de un lugar a otro

North American Free Trade Agreement (NAFTA) (1993) an agreement in which the United States, Mexico, and Canada became one large free-trade zone (p. 1082, CS44)
Tratado de Libre Comercio de América del Norte (TLCAN) (1993) acuerdo según el cual Estados Unidos, México y Canadá se convirtieron en una gran zona de libre comercio

Northwest Ordinance (1787) legislation passed by Congress to establish a political structure for the Northwest Territory and create a system for the admission of new states (p. 149)
Ordenanza del Noroeste (1787) ley aprobada por el Congreso para establecer una estructura política en el Territorio del Noroeste y crear un proceso para la incorporación de nuevos estados

nuclear fallout harmful particles of radioactive material produced by nuclear explosions (p. 858)
lluvia radiactiva partículas dañinas de material radiactivo producido por explosiones nucleares

nullification the act of declaring something void (p. 214)
anulación acto de declarar que algo es inválido

nullification crisis a dispute led by John C. Calhoun that said that states could ignore federal laws if they believed those laws violated the Constitution (p. 250)
crisis de anulación controversia liderada por John C. Calhoun que argumentaba que los estados no tenían que obedecer las leyes federales si consideraban que esas leyes desobedecían la Constitución

occupy to take control of a place by placing troops in it (p. 802)
ocupar tomar el control de un lugar colocando tropas allí

Okie nickname for a farmer who left the Dust Bowl in search of work (p. 685)
Okie apodo dado a los granjeros que se fueron de Tazón de Polvo en busca de trabajo

Olmec one of the first major American Indian societies in Mesoamerica (p. 8)
olemcas una de las primeras sociedades indígenas norteamericanas de importancia en Mesoamérica

OPEC Organization of Petroleum Exporting Countries; organization that coordinates petroleum policies of major producing countries (p. 1022)
OPEP Organización de Países Exportadores de Petróleo; organización que coordina las políticas petroleras de los principales países productores

Open Door policy a policy established by the United States in 1899 to promote equal access for all nations to trade in China (p. 556)
política de puertas abiertas política establecida por Estados Unidos en 1899 para promover el acceso igualitario por igual a todas las naciones al comercio con China

Operation Desert Storm U.S.-led war to end Iraq's occupation of Kuwait in 1990-1991 (p. 1065)
Operación Tormenta del Desierto guerra dirigida por Estados Unidos para ponerle fin a la ocupación de Kuwait por parte de Irak entre 1990 y 1991

Operation Overlord (1944) the code name for the Allied invasion of mainland Europe in World War II, starting with the D-Day landings (p. 775)
Operación Overlord (1944) nombre en clave de la invasión de Europa continental por parte de los Aliados en la Segunda Guerra Mundial; empezó con los desembarcos del Día D

Operation Rolling Thunder a U.S. bombing campaign in North Vietnam in March 1965 (p. 956)
Operación Trueno Galopante ofensiva de bombardeos estadounidenses en Vietnam del Norte en marzo de 1965

Operation Torch (1942) the code name for the Allied invasion of North Africa during World War II (p. 773)
Operación Antorcha (1942) nombre en clave de la invasión del norte de África por parte de los Aliados durante la Segunda Guerra Mundial

oral tradition unwritten history passed down through stories and legends (p. 19)
tradición oral historia no escrita transmitida a través de relatos y leyendas

Oregon Trail a 2,000-mile trail through the Great Plains from western Missouri to the Oregon Territory (p. 298)
Sendero de Oregón ruta de 2,000 millas que cruzaba las Grandes Planicies desde el oeste de Missouri hasta el Territorio de Oregón

outsourcing the practice of using workers from outside a company (p. CS42)
subcontratación práctica de usar trabajadores que no forqman parte de la compañía

Pacific Railway Act (1862) congressional measure which gave land to railroad companies to help facilitate the construction of a railroad and telegraph line from the Missouri River to the Pacific Ocean (p. 450)
Ley del Ferrocarril del Pacífico (1862) medida del Congreso por la que se entregaban terrenos a las compañías de ferrocarriles para facilitar la construcción de un ferrocarril y de una línea de telégrafo desde el río Missouri hasta el océano Pacífico

pacification a program in the Vietnam War in which U.S. troops would move South Vietnamese from their villages and burn the villages down (p. 958)
pacificación programa durante la Guerra de Vietnam en el que las tropas de Estados Unidos sacaban a los vietnamitas del Sur de sus aldeas y las incendiaban

pacifist a person who does not believe in the use of military force (p. 752)
pacifista persona que no cree en el uso de la fuerza militar

packet switching the ability of a computer to send messages in smaller packages, allowing the packets to travel separately along the fastest routes to the receiving computer, which reassembles the message (p. CS37)
conmutación de paquetes capacidad de una computadora de enviar mensajes en paquetes más pequeños, permitiendo así que los paquetes viajen por separado por las rutas más rápidas hasta la computadora de destino, donde se vuelve a armar el mensaje

Palmer raids (1918) a series of government attacks on suspected radicals in the United States led by the U.S. Attorney General, A. Mitchell Palmer (p. 624)
redadas de Palmer (1918) serie de ataques del gobierno sobre supuestos radicales de Estados Unidos dirigidos por el secretario de justicia, A. Mitchell Palmer

Panmunjom town in the demilitarized zone between North and South Korea where peace talks took place following the Korean War (p. 841)
Panmunjom pueblo ubicado en la zona desmilitarizada entre Corea del Norte y Corea del Sur, donde se llevaron a cabo las negociaciones para firmar un tratado de paz después de la Guerra de Corea

Peace Convention (1861) a meeting called by Virginia leaders after the defeat of the Crittendon Compromise to deal with the issue of slavery in the United States
Convención de Paz (1861) reunión convocada por los líderes de Virginia para tratar el asunto de la esclavitud en Estados Unidos después del rechazo del Compromiso de Crittenden

Peace Corps a program that trains and sends volunteers to poor nations to serve as educators, health care workers, agricultural advisers, and in other jobs (p. 886)
Cuerpo de Paz programa que entrena y envía voluntarios a países pobres de todo el mundo para trabajar como educadores, trabajadores de salud, consejeros agrícolas y en otros trabajos

Pentagon Papers papers that revealed that government officials had been misleading the American people about the progress of the Vietnam War for many years (p. 975)
Papeles del Pentágono documentos que revelaron que los funcionarios del gobierno engañaron al pueblo durante muchos años con respecto al progreso de la guerra de Vietnam

Pequot War (1637) war between the Pequot Indians and the Dutch settlers and their Naragansett and Mohegan Indian allies (p. 56)
Guerra Pequot (1637) guerra entre los indígenas pequot y los pobladores holandeses y sus aliados, los indígenas naragansett y mohegan

perestroika Russian word for "restructuring;" refers to the restructuring of the corrupt government bureaucracy in the Soviet Union under Mikhail Gorbachev (p. 1060)
perestroika palabra rusa que significa "reestructuración", se refiere a la reestructuración bajo Mikhail Gorbachev de la burocracia gubernamental corrupta de la Unión Soviética

Pickett's Charge (1863) a failed Confederate attack during the Civil War led by General George Pickett at the Battle of Gettysburg (p. 386)
ataque de Pickett (1863) ataque fallido del ejército confederado, al mando del general George Pickett, en la batalla de Gettysburg de la Guerra Civil

Pinckney's Treaty (1795) an agreement between the United States and Spain that changed Florida's border and made it easier for American ships to use the port of New Orleans (p. 211)
Tratado de Pinckney (1795) acuerdo entre Estados Unidos y España que modificó los límites de la Florida y facilitó a los barcos estadounidenses el uso del puerto de Nueva Orleáns

placer mining searching for gold by using pans or other devices to wash gold nuggets out of loose rock (p. 446)
minería con bandeja manera de buscar el oro con bandejas u otros utensilios que con la ayuda del agua separan las pepitas de oro de las piedras sueltas

plantation a large farm that usually specialized in growing one kind of crop for profit (p. 21)
plantación granja de gran tamaño que por lo general se especializa en un cultivo específico con el fin de obtener ganancias

platform a declaration of the principles for which a group stands (p. 342)
plataforma declaración de los principios en los que cree un grupo

Platt Amendment a part of the Cuban constitution that limited Cuba's right to make treaties, gave the United States the right to intervene in Cuban affairs, and required Cuba to sell or lease land to the U.S. (p. 566)
Enmienda Platt parte de la constitución cubana redactada bajo la supervisión de Estados Unidos que limitaba el derecho de Cuba a firmar tratados, otorgaba a Estados Unidos el derecho a intervenir en los asuntos cubanos y exigía a Cuba vender o arrendar tierras a Estados Unidos

Plessy v. Ferguson (1896) U.S. Supreme Court case that established the separate-but-equal doctrine for public facilities (p. 508)
Plessy contra Ferguson (1896) caso en el que la Corte Suprema estableció la doctrina de "separados pero iguales" en los lugares públicos

pocket veto a presidential power to prevent a bill passed in the last 10 days of a legislative session from becoming law by simply ignoring it (p. 406)
veto de bolsillo poder del presidente que le permite impedir la aprobación de un proyecto de ley aprobado en los 10 días anteriores de una sesión legislativa al no hacerle caso

police action phrase to describe the U.S. intervention in Korea in 1950 (p. 837)
acción policial frase usada para describir la intervención de Estados Unidos en Corea en 1950

political asylum protection for immigrants for humanitarian reasons (p. CS4)
asilo político protección dada a immigrantes por motivos humanitarios

poll tax a special tax that a person had to pay in order to vote (p. 508)
impuesto electoral impuesto especial que debía pagar una persona para poder votar

Pony Express a system of messengers that carried mail between relay stations on a route 2,000 miles long in 1860 and 1861 (p. 301)
Pony Express sistema de mensajeros que transportaban el correo entre estaciones de relevo a lo largo de una ruta de 2,000 millas entre 1860 y 1861

Poor People's Campaign an expansion of the civil rights movement that tried to raise awareness about poverty among people of all races (p. 939)
Campaña por los Pobres ampliación del movimiento de los derechos civiles que intentaba crear una mayor conciencia sobre la pobreza entre las personas de todas las razas

pop art a style of art in the 1950s and 1960s intended to appeal to popular tastes (p. 1007)
arte pop estilo artístico de las décadas de 1950 y 1960 que pretendía atraer a los gustos populares

popular sovereignty the idea that political authority belongs to the people (p. 326)
soberanía popular idea de que la autoridad política pertenece al pueblo

Populist Party a political party formed in 1892 that supported free coinage of silver, work reforms, immigration restrictions, and government ownership of railroads and telegraph and telephone systems (p. 505)
Partido Populista partido político formado en 1892 que apoyaba la libre producción de monedas de plata, reformas laborales y restricciones de la inmigración, además de apoyar que el gobierno fuera dueño de los sistemas ferroviario, telegráfico y telefónico

Potsdam Conference (1945) meeting among leaders of the Allies near the end of World War II (p. 807)
Conferencia de Potsdam (1945) encuentro de los líderes aliados celebrado poco antes del final de la Segunda Guerra Mundial

Pottawatomie Massacre (1856) an incident in which abolitionist John Brown and seven other men murdered pro-slavery Kansans (p. 332)
Mascare de Pottawatomie (1856) incidente en el que el abolicionista John Brown y siete hombres más asesinaron a varios habitantes pro esclavistas de Kansas

poverty threshold a line that statistically measures the number of people living in poverty (p. CS26)
umbral de pobreza línea que mide estadísticamente la cantidad de personas que viven en la pobreza

prisoner of war captured enemy troops (p. CS10)
prisionero de guerra soldado capturado por tropas enemigas

Proclamation of 1763 law created by British officials that prohibited colonists from settling in areas west of the Appalachian Mountains (p. 95)
Proclamación de 1763 ley creada por los funcionarios británicos que prohibía a los colonos asentarse al oeste de los montes Apalaches

productivity the amount of product made by a worker or a machine (p. 631)
productividad cantidad de un producto fabricada por un trabajador o una máquina

progressivism group of reform movements of the late 1800s that focused on urban problems, the plight of workers, and corrupt political machines (p. 523)
progresivismo grupo de movimientos reformistas de finales del siglo XIX que se concentraba en los problemas urbanos, como las dificultades de los trabajadores y las maquinarias políticas corruptas

prohibition a ban on alcohol that became law in 1920; the ban was lifted in 1933 (p. 531)
prohibición suspensión de la venta de bebidas alcohólicas que se convirtió en ley en 1920; se elimnó en 1933

propaganda information designed to influence public opinion (p. 603)
propaganda información diseñada para influir en la opinión pública

proprietary colonies grants of land given by the King to his loyal friends (p. 61)
colonias en propiedad concesiones de tierra otorgadas por el rey a sus amigos leales

protectorate a country that is controlled by an outside government (p. 566)
protectorado país controlado por un gobierno externo

Protestants reformers who protested certain practices of the Catholic Church (p. 26)
protestantes reformistas que protestaban por ciertas prácticas de la Iglesia católica

protocol formats for sending data from one computer to another (p. CS37)
protocolo formatos utilizados para enviar datos de una computadora a otra

provisional temporary (p. 347)
provisional temporal

public lands federal lands that were never sold or made into protected areas such as national parks (p. CS19)
tierras públicas tierras federales que nunca se vendieron ni se convirtieron en áreas protegidas como los parques nacionales

public works government-funded building projects (p. 699)
obras públicas proyectos de construcción financiados por el gobierno

pueblo a word meaning "town" in Spanish (p. 9)
pueblo palabra en español que significa "ciudad"

Pueblo Native American group of the Southwest (p. 12)
pueblo grupo indígena norteamericano del Suroeste

Pueblo incident North Korean capture of the Pueblo, a Navy spy ship, off the coast of Communist North Korea (p. 900)
incidente del Pueblo captura por parte de Corea del Norte del Pueblo, un barco espía de la armada, cerca de la costa de Corea del Norte, un país comunista

Pure Food and Drug Act (1906) law that forbade the manufacture, sale, or transportation of food and patent medicine containing harmful ingredients, and required that containers of food and medicines carry ingredient labels (p. 538)
Ley de Alimentos y los Medicamentos Puros (1906) ley que prohibió la fabricación, venta o transporte de alimentos y de medicamentos patentados con ingredientes dañinos y que requirió que los envases de los alimentos y los medicamentos llevaran etiquetas con los ingredientes

Puritans a group of English Protestants who wanted to "purify" the Church of England through reforms (p. 52)
puritanos grupo de protestantes ingleses que querían "purificar" la Iglesia de Inglaterra con reformas

push-pull model of immigration example of immigration where factors that cause people to leave their homeland are "pushes," and factors that encourage people to travel to another country are called "pulls" (p. 273)
modelo de inmigración de expulsión y atracción ejemplo de inmigración en el que los factores que explican la salida de la gente de sus países de origen se llaman factores "de expulsión" y los que animan a la gente a trasladarse a otro país se llaman factores "de atracción"

Quaker member of a Protestant sect founded in the 1640s in England (p. 60)
cuáquero miembro de una secta protestante fundada en la década de 1640 en Inglaterra

Quarantine Speech (1937) Franklin D. Roosevelt's speech following the Japanese attack on China in which he called on America to take clear sides in the current world conflicts (p. 754)
Discurso de la Cuarentena (1937) discurso pronunciado por Franklin D. Roosevelt después del ataque japonés a China en el instó a los estadounidenses a tomar una posición clara en los conflictos mundiales del momento

quota limit on the number of people who can enter the United States from each foreign country (p. CS4)
cuota límite a la cantidad de personas que pueden entrar a Estados Unidos de cada país extranjero

racial etiquette strict rules of behavior that governed the social and business interactions of white and black Americans (p. 509)
etiqueta racial reglas estrictas de conducta que regían la interacción social y comercial entre estadounidenses blancos y negros

radical a person with extreme views (p. 325)
radical persona con puntos de vista extremos

Radical Republicans members of Congress who felt that southern states needed to make great social changes before they could be readmitted to the Union (p. 412)
republicanos radicales miembros del Congreso convencidos de que los estados del Sur necesitaban realizar grandes cambios sociales antes de poder a ser readmitidos en la Unión

rationing limiting the amount of a certain product each individual can get (p. 794)
racionamiento limitación de la cantidad de cierto producto que puede obtener cada persona

realpolitik basing foreign policies on realistic views of national interest rather than on broad rules or principles (p. 1020)
realpolitik basar la política exterior en perspectivas realistas de los intereses nacionales en lugar de basarla en reglas o principios generales amplios

recall a vote to remove an official from office (p. 527)
destitución votación para retirar a un funcionario de su cargo

Reconstruction Acts (1867-68) the laws that put the southern states under U.S. military control and required them to draft new constitutions (p. 414)
Leyes de Reconstrucción (1867-68) leyes que pusieron a los estados del Sur bajo el control militar estadounidense y los obligaron a reformar sus constituciones

Reconstruction Finance Corporation a program that provided aid to struggling banks and other institutions during the Great Depression (p. 690)
Corporación Financiera de la Reconstrucción programa que proporcionó ayuda a los bancos y demás instituciones que se encontraban en dificultades durante la Gran Depresión

Redcoats British soldiers who fought against the colonists in the Revolutionary War (p. 126)
casacas rojas soldados británicos que lucharon contra los colonos en la Guerra de Independencia estadounidense

Redeemers name taken in the late 1870s by democrats who now controlled southern states p. 425)
redentores nombre adoptado a finales de la década de 1870 por los demócratas que entonces controlaban los estados del Sur

Red Scare widespread fear of communism (p. 624)
terror rojo temor generalizado al comunismo

referendum a procedure that allows voters to approve or reject a law already proposed or passed by government (p. 527)
referéndum medida que permite a los ciudadanos votar para aprobar o rechazar una ley previamente propuesta o aprobada por el gobierno

Reform Era (1830-1860) period during which thousands of Americans sought to reshape American life (p. 267)
Era de la Reforma (1830-1860) período durante el cual miles de estadounidenses quisieron cambiar la forma de vida en Estados Unidos

reform societies groups that were organized to promote social reforms (p. 281)
sociedades reformistas grupos que se formaban para promover reformas sociales

Reformation a religious movement within the Catholic Church in the 1500s; led to the establishment of the Protestant Church (p. 26)
Reforma movimiento religiosa dentro de la Iglesia católica en el siglo XVI; condujo al establecimiento de la Iglesia protestante

rehabilitation reforming offenders into contributing members of society (p. CS32)
rehabilitación reforma de los delicuentes para que pasen a ser miembros útiles de la sociedad

Renaissance an era of learning and creativity that began in Italy in the 1300s and spread throughout Europe (p. 25)
Renacimiento era de aprendizaje y creatividad que empezó en Italia en el siglo XIV y se extendió por el resto de Europa

reparations payments designed to make up for the damage of something (p. 608, 638)
indemnizaciones pagos designados para compensar el daño causado por algo

republic a political system in which the citizens of a region elect representatives to run the government (p. 145)
república sistema político en el que los ciudadanos de una región eligen representantes para dirigir el gobierno

Republic of California name taken by California after American settlers declared it independent from Mexico in 1846 (p. 310)
República de California nombre adoptado por California después de que los pobladores estadounidenses declararon el territorio independiente de México en 1846

Republic of Texas name taken by Texas after it won its independence from Mexico in 1836 (p. 307)
República de Texas nombre adoptado por Texas después de lograr independizarse de México en 1836

Republican Party a political party formed in the 1850s to stop the spread of slavery in the West (p. 328)
Partido Republicano partido político formado en la década de 1850 para detener la expansión de la esclavitud hacia el Oeste

ENGLISH AND SPANISH GLOSSARY

reserved powers powers in the Constitution not specifically given to the federal government but instead left to the states (p. 163)
　poderes reservados poderes establecidos en la Constitución y no otorgados específicamente al gobierno federal, sino a los estados

Restoration (1660–1685) name given to the period of reign of the English King Charles II; the monarchy was restored in England with his ascension to the throne (p. 61)
　Restauración (1660–1685) nombre dado al período del reinado de Carlos II de Inglaterra porque al subir él al trono, se restauró la monarquía en Inglaterra

Roe v. Wade (1973) Supreme Court decision that made abortion legal in the United States (p. 989)
　Roe contra Wade (1973) decisión de la Corte Suprema que legalizó aborto en Estados Unidos

Roosevelt Corollary a change to the Monroe Doctrine, saying that the United States could intervene in the internal affairs of Latin American nations (p. 569)
　Corolario de Roosevelt cambio en la Doctrina Monroe en la que se declaraba que Estados Unidos podía intervenir en los asuntos internos de los países latinoamericanos

Rosie the Riveter a popular symbol for working women of World War II (p. 761)
　Rosie la remachadora símbolo popular de las mujeres trabajadoras durante la Segunda Guerra Mundial

Rough Riders a cavalry regiment organized by Theodore Roosevelt (p. 562)
　Jinetes Rudos regimiento de caballería organizado por Theodore Roosevelt

royal colony a colony under direct control of the king (p. 55)
　colonia real colonia bajo el control directo del rey

Russo-Japanese War (1904–1905) war between Russia and Japan over Manchuria (p. 557)
　Guerra Ruso-Japonesa (1904–1905) guerra por Manchuria entre Rusia y Japón

SALT I discussions between the United States and the Soviets to slow the ongoing arms race in the late 1960s and early 1970s (p. 1021)
　SALT I conversaciones entre Estados Unidos y la Unión Soviética para frenar la carrera armamentista a finales de la década de 1960 y comienzos de la década de 1970

SALT II continuing discussions in 1979 between the United States; SALT II set limits on certain kinds of nuclear weapons (p. 1036)
　SALT II conversaciones entre Estados Unidos y la Unión Soviética en 1979; SALT II fijó límites sobre ciertos tipos de armas nucleares

salutary neglect idea that the colonies benefited by being left alone, without too much British interference (p. 76)
　abandono saludable ideea que sostenía que las colonias se beneficiaban si se les daba más libertad, sin demasiada interferencia británica

Sand Creek Massacre (1864) U.S. Army's killing of about 150 Cheyenne elderly, women, and children at Sand Creek Reservation in Colorado Territory (p. 440)
　Masacre de Sand Creek (1864) matanza por parte del ejército de Estados Unidos de unos 150 ancianos, mujeres y niños cheyenes en la reserva de Sand Creek en el territorio de Colorado

Santa Fe Trail an important trail west from Independence, Missouri to Santa Fe, New Mexico (p. 297)
　Sendero de Santa Fe importante ruta que va hacia el oeste desde Independence, Missouri, hasta Santa Fe, Nuevo México

satellite an object that orbits around a planet (p. 858)
　satélite objeto que gira alrededor de un planeta

Saturday night massacre part of the Watergate Scandal in which Nixon ordered his attorney general to fire special prosecutor Archibald Cox (p. 1030)
　masacre del sábado en la noche parte del escándalo Watergate en la que Nixon ordenó a su secretario de justicia que despidiera al fiscal especial Archibald Cox

savings and loan crisis a financial disaster in which the federal government had to step in and pay back loans for many S & L institutions (p. 1068)
　crisis de ahorro y préstamo catástrofe financiera en la que el gobierno federal se vio obligado a intervenir y pagar los préstamos de muchas instituciones de ahorro y préstamo

scalawag name given by former Confederates to southerners who supported the shift in power to Congress and the army in the South during Reconstruction (p. 416)
　scalawag nombre dado por los antiguos confederados a aquellos habitantes del Sur que apoyaron el cambio del poder al Congreso y al ejército en el Sur durante la Reconstrucción

Schenck v. United States (1917) court case that explained the limits of the First Amendment (p. 604)
　Schenck contra Estados Unidos (1917) juicio en el que se explicaron los límites de la Primera enmienda

SCLC Southern Christian Leadership Conference; a group formed in Georgia in 1957 to organize civil rights protest activities (p. 915)
　SCLC Conferencia del Liderazgo Cristiano del Sur; grupo formado en Georgia en 1957 para organizar las actividades de protesta en favor de los derechos civiles

SEATO Southeast Asia Treaty Organization; group of nations that agreed to work together to resist Communist aggression (p. 852)
　SEATO Organización del Tratado del Sureste Asiático; grupo de naciones que se comprometieron a trabajar juntas para resistir la agresión comunista

secede break away from (p. 250)
　secesión separación

Second Amendment Constitutional amendment granting Americans the right to bear arms (p. CS32)
　Segunda enmienda enmienda constitucional que garantiza a los estadounidenses el derecho a portar armas

Second Bank of the United States a national bank created by Congress in 1816 and overseen by the federal government, its purpose was to regulate state banks (p. 248)
　Segundo Banco de Estados Unidos banco nacional creado por el Congreso en 1816 y supervisado por el gobierno federal con la función de reglamentar los bancos estatales

Second Continental Congress (1775) a meeting of colonial delegates in Philadelphia to decide how to react to fighting at Lexington and Concord (p. 115)
　Segundo Congreso Continental (1775) reunión de delegados coloniales en Filadelfia para tomar decisiones acerca de los enfrentamientos en Lexington y Concord

Second Great Awakening a period of religious evangelism that began in the 1790s and became widespread in the United States by the 1830s (p. 267)
Segundo Gran Despertar período de evangelización religiosa iniciado en la década de 1790 que se extendió por Estados Unidos para la década de 1830

Second New Deal (1935) a new set of programs in the spring of 1935 including additional banking reforms, new tax laws, new relief programs (p. 710)
Segundo Nuevo Trato (1935) nuevo conjunto de programas de la primavera de 1935 que incluyó reformas bancarias, nuevas leyes sobre impuestos y nuevos programas de ayuda social

sectionalism devotion to the interests of one geographic region over the interests of the entire country (p. 213, 240)
regionalismo dedicación a los intereses de una región geográfica y no a los del país

Selective Service Act (1921) act which required men between the ages of 21 and 30 to register to be drafted into the armed forces (p. 593)
Ley del Servicio Militar Selectivo (1921) ley que exigía que los hombres entre los 21 y los 30 años se inscribieran para ser reclutados por las fuerzas armadas

self-determination the right of people to decide their own political status (p. 607)
autodeterminación derecho de las peronas a decidir su propia situación política

Seneca Falls Convention (1848) the first national women's rights convention at which the Declaration of Sentiments was written (p. 282)
Convención de Seneca Falls (1848) primera convención nacional a favor de los derechos de la mujer, en la cual se redactó la Declaración de Sentimientos

settlement house neighborhood center staffed by professionals and volunteers for education, recreation, and social activities in poor areas (p. 498)
organización de servico a la comunidad centro social en el que trabajan profesionales y voluntarios que promueven la educación, la recreación y las actividades sociales en las zonas pobres

Seventeenth Amendment (1913) allowed American voters to directly elect U.S. senators (p. 527)
Decimoséptima enmienda (1913) permite a los votantes estadounidenses elegir directamente a los senadores de Estados Unidos

sharecropping a system used on southern farms after the Civil War in which farmers worked land owned by someone else in return for a small portion of the crops (p. 421)
Cultivo de aparcería sistema usado en las granjas del sur después de la Guerra Civil en el cual los agricultores labraban las tierras de otra persona a cambio de una pequeña porción de la cosecha

Sherman Antitrust Act (1890) a law that made it illegal to create monopolies or trusts that restrained free trade (p. 473)
Ley Antitrust Sherman (1890) ley que prohibió la creación de monopolios o consorcios que restringieran el libre comercio

shuttle diplomacy negotiation style in which a mediator shuttles between groups, trying to work out agreements to end a disagreement (p. 1023)
diplomacia de ir y venir estilo de negociación en la que el mediador va y viene entre distintos grupos para intentar alcanzar acuerdos que pongan fin a un desacuerdo

silent majority phrase used by President Nixon to describe people who supported the government's Vietnam policies but did not express their opinions publicly (p. 973)
mayoría silenciosa frase utilizada por el presidente Nixon para describir a las personas que apoyaban la política del gobierno en Vietnam pero no expresaban su opinión en público

sit-down strike a strike in which workers refuse to work or leave the workplace until a settlement is reached (p. 713)
huelga de brazos caídos huelga en la que los trabajadores se niegan a trabajar o a abandonar el lugar de trabajo hasta que se alcance un convenio laboral

Sixteenth Amendment (1913) law that allowed Congress to levy taxes based on an individual's income (p. 542)
Decimosexta enmienda (1913) ley que permitió al Congreso recaudar impuestos en base a los ingresos de una persona

Smoot-Hawley Tariff Act (1930) extremely high tariff on farm products and manufactured goods (p. 690)
Ley Arancel Smoot-Hawley (1930) arancel muy alto sobre los productos agrícolas y los bienes fabricados

SNCC Student Nonviolent Coordinating Committee; student civil rights organization in the 1960s (p. 918)
SNCC Comité Coordinador No Violento de Estudiantes; organización estudiantil de derechos civiles de la década de 1960

social contract an agreement between a people and their government or ruler, stating that if a government (or ruler) did not protect citizens and their rights, they were justified in overthrowing it (p. 85)
contrato social acuerdo entre un pueblo y su gobierno o gobernante que establece que si el gobierno (o el gobernante) no protege a sus ciudadanos y sus derechos, el pueblo tiene justificación para derrocarlo

social Darwinism a view of society based on Charles Darwin's scientific theory of natural selection (p. 467)
darwinismo social visión de la sociedad basada en la teoría científica de la selección natural de Charles Darwin

Social Gospel the idea that religious faith should be expressed through good works (p. 498)
evangelio social idea según la cual la fe religiosa se debe expresar por medio de buenas obras

social justice the fair distribution of advantages and disadvantages in a society (p. 995)
justicia social distribución justa de las ventajas y desventajas en una sociedad

Social Security a system for providing pensions for many Americans age 65 and older (p. 711)
Seguro Social sistema para proporcionar pensiones a la mayoría de estadounidenses mayores de 65 años

sod house home built from squares of turf and soil of the prairie, stacked up like bricks (p. 449)
casa de tepe casa construida con cuadrados de césped y tierra de las praderas, apilados como ladrillos

Solidarity an independent labor union founded in Soviet-controlled Poland in 1980 (p. 1055)
Solidaridad sindicato obrero independiente fundado en Polonia en 1980, cuando el país todavía estaba controlado por la Unión Soviética

Solid South name given to the South after Reconstruction, because it was so heavily Democratic (p. 427)
Sólido Sur nombre dado al Sur después de la Reconstrucción debido a que los demócratas representaban una mayoría aplastante

ENGLISH AND SPANISH GLOSSARY

Southern Homestead Act (1866) law that set aside 45 million acres of government-owned land in southern states to provide free farms for African Americans (p. 420)
Ley de Heredad del Sur (1866) ley que reservó 45 millones de acres de terrenos controlados por el gobierno en los estados del sur para entregar granjas gratuitas a los afroamericanos

space shuttle a reusable spacecraft able to land on the ground like an airplane, and that could be used to transport people and supplies into space (p. 1067)
transbordador espacial nave espacial reutilizable capaz de aterrizar en la tierra igual que un avión y que se puede utilizar para transportar personas y suministros al espacio

speakeasy illegal bars where alcohol was served during Prohibition (p. 653)
bar clandestino bar ilegal donde se servían bebidas alcohólicas durante la época de la Prohibición

sphere of influence an area where foreign countries control the trade or natural resources of another nation or area (p. 556)
esfera de influencia zona de un país cuyos recursos naturales y comercio son controlados por otro país o zona

spoils system a politicians' practice of giving government jobs to his or her supporters (p. 246)
Tráfico de influencias o amiguismo práctica de los políticos de dar empleos en el gobierno a las personas que los apoyan

Sputnik (1957) the first artificial satellite; launched by the Soviets (p. 858)
Sputnik (1957) primer satélite artificial; lanzado por la Unión Soviética

Square Deal Theodore Roosevelt's 1904 campaign slogan; expressed his belief that the needs of workers, business, and consumers should be balanced (p. 536)
Square Deal lema de la campaña de Theodore Roosevelt de 1904; expresaba su creencia en el equilibrio entre las necesidades de los trabajadores, los empresarios y los consumidores

Stamp Act (1765) a law passed by Parliament that raised tax money by requiring colonists to pay for an official stamp whenever they bought paper items (p. 107)
Ley del Sello ley aprobada por el Parlamento para recaudar impuestos en la que se obligaba a los colonos a pagar un sello oficial cada vez que compraran artículos de papel

states' rights belief that the power of the states should be greater than the power of the federal government (p. 249)
derechos estatales creencia de que el poder de los estados debe ser mayor que el del gobierno federal

Stono Rebellion (1739) rebellion by about 100 enslaved African Americans in South Carolina against Southern planters (p. 83)
Rebelión de Stono (1739) rebelión de unos 100 esclavos negros en Carolina del Sur contra hacendados sureños

Strategic Defense Initiative President Reagan's proposed defensive space shield that would knock out incoming Soviet missiles (p. 1054)
Iniciativa de Defensa Estratégica escudo protector espacial propuesto por el presidente Reagan con la idea que pudiera bloquear los misiles soviéticos que se acercaran

strict construction a way of interpreting the Constitution that allows the federal government to take only those actions the Constitution specifically says it can (p. 206)
interpretación estricta interpretación de la Constitución que sólo permite al gobierno federal realizar las acciones permitidas de manera específica en ella

subsidy a government payment that is aimed at achieving some public benefit (p. 702)
subsidio pago del gobierno destinado a lograr un beneficio parar el público

suburb smaller towns that are located outside a larger urban area (p. 631)
suburbio pueblos más pequeños ubicados en las afueras de una ciudad

Summer of Love the height of the hippie movement during the Summer of 1967 in San Francisco (p. 1005)
Verano del Amor punto máximo del movimiento hippie que tuvo lugar durante el verano de 1967 en San Francisco

summit a meeting of the heads of government (p. 851)
cumbre encuentro de jefes de estado

Sunbelt the southern and western portions of the United States (p. 866)
Sunbelt (cinturón del sol) estados del sur y el oeste de Estados Unidos

supply-side economics the economic theory that tax cuts and business incentives will stimulate the economy (p. 1050)
economía de la oferta teoría económica según la cual los recortes de impuestos y los incentivos para las compañías estimularán la economía

***Sussex* pledge** a pledge Germany issued which included a promise not to sink merchant vessels "without warning and without saving human lives" (p. 591)
promesa de *Sussex* compromiso de Alemania que incluía la promesa de que no hundirían los barcos mercantes "sin avisar ni sin salvar las vidas humanas"

sweatshop small workshop set up in a tenement rather than in centralized factories (p. 473)
fábrica explotadora pequeño taller montado en una casa de vecindad en lugar de en fábricas centralizadas

swing a type of jazz music popular in the 1930s (p. 722)
swing tipo de música de jazz popular en la década de 1930

Taino Arawakan Indian group living on the islands of the present-day Greater Antilles when Christopher Columbus arrived there in 1492 (p. 31)
taíno grupo indígena arahuaco que vivía en las islas que hoy son las Antillas Mayores cuando Cristóbal Colón llegó en 1492

taking an action that occurs when regulations restrict use of land so much that the government has essentially taken the land (p. CS19)
apoderarse acción que occure cuando las leyes limitan hasta tal punto el uso de la tierra que es como si el gobierno se hubiera apropiado de ella

Taliban group that took control over most of Afghanistan following the Soviet occupation in 1979 (p. 1095)
Talibán grupo que tomó el control de la mayor parte de Afganistán tras la ocupación soviética de 1979

Tampico incident (1914) confrontation between the U.S. and Mexico at Tampico Bay, Mexico, involving the arrest of American sailors by the Mexican government (p. 574)
incidente de Tampico (1914) enfrentamiento entre Estados Unidos y México en la bahía de Tampico, México, durante lel cual el gobierno mexicano arrestó a unos marineros estadounidenses

Teapot Dome a federally owned piece of land in Wyoming that was the site of a government scandal in 1921 when President Harding's Secretary of the Interior accepted bribes in return for allowing oil companies to drill for oil there (p. 636)
Teapot Dome nombre de un terreno federal en Wyoming que fue el centro de un escándalo gubernamental en 1921; el secretario del interior del presidente Harding aceptó sobornos para permitir que las empresas petroleras excavaran pozos allí

Tejanos Texans of Mexican heritage (p. 304)
tejanos texanos de ascendencia mexicana

telegraph a machine perfected by Samuel F. B. Morse in 1832 that uses pulses of electric current to send messages across long distances through wires (p. 255)
telégrafo máquina perfeccionada por Samuel F. B. Morse en 1832 que emplea impulsos eléctricos transmitidos por cables para enviar mensajes a grandes distancias

temperance movement a social reform effort begun in the mid-1800s to encourage people to drink less alcohol (p. 267)
movimiento de templaza movimiento de reforma social iniciado a mediados del siglo XIX para fomentar la disminución en el consumo de bebidas alcohólicas

tenant farming system of farming where farmers rented their land from the landowner and were allowed to grow whatever crop they chose (421)
agricultura de arriendo sistema de agricultura en el que los agricultores arriendan la tierra del propietario y pueden cultivar lo que quieran

tenement poorly built, overcrowded housing where many immigrants lived (p. 276)
casa de vecinos casas mal construidas donde vivían amontonados una gran cantidad de inmigrantes

Ten-Percent Plan President Abraham Lincoln's plan for Reconstruction (p. 405)
Plan del Diez por Ciento plan de Reconstrucción del presidente Abraham Lincoln

terrorism the use of violence by individuals and groups to advance political goals (p. 1081)
terrorismo uso de la violencia por parte de individuos y grupos con el fin de alcanzar metas políticas

Tet Offensive a series of major attacks launched by Communist forces in South Vietnam in 1968 (p. 955)
ofensiva del Tet serie de ataques importantes realizado por fuerzas comunistas en Vietnam del Sur en 1868

Texas Revolution (1835-1836) war of independence fought by Texans to gain independence from Mexico (p. 306)
Revolución Texana (1835-1836) guerra de independencia luchada por los texanos para independizarse de México

Thirteenth Amendment (1865) outlawed slavery (p. 391)
Decimotercera enmienda (1865) abolió la esclavitud

38th parallel line of latitude that divides North and South Korea (p. 836)
paralelo 38 línea de latitud que divide a Corea del Norte de Corea del Sur

Three-Fifths Compromise (1787) an agreement stating that enslaved people would be counted as three-fifths of a person when determining a state's population for representation in the lower house of Congress (p. 154)
Compromiso de los Tres Quintos (1787) acuerdo en el que se estableció que las personas exclavizadas contarían como tres quintas partes de una persona para determinar la representación de ese estado en la cámara baja del Congreso

Tiananmen Square massacre (1989) a large pro-democracy protest in China that resulted in the government using military force, killing hundreds (p. 1063)
Masacre de la Plaza de Tiananmen (1989) gran manifestación de protesta a favor de la democracia en China, en la que el gobierno usó fuerzas militares y dio muerte a cientos de personas

Toleration Act (1649) a Maryland law that made restricting the religious rights of Christians a crime (p. 65)
Ley de Tolerancia (1649) ley de Maryland que hizo ilegal la restricción de los derechos religiosos de los cristianos

Toltec people who dominated central Mexico around AD 900; known for their skills as warriors, artisans, and builders (p. 8)
toltecas grupo que dominó la zona central de México alrededor del año 900 d. de C.; eran reconocidos por sus destrezas como guerreros, artesanos y constructores

Tonkin Gulf Resolution (1964) congressional resolution that authorized military action in Southeast Asia (p. 955)
Resolución del Golfo de Tonkin (1964) resolución del Congreso que autorizó las acciones militares en el sureste de Asia

totalitarian form of government in which the person or party in charge has absolute control over all aspects of life (p. 741)
totalitario forma de gobierno en la que la persona o el partido que está a cargo tiene control absoluto sobre todos los aspectos de la vida

Trail of Tears (1838-39) an 800-mile forced march made by the Cherokee from their homeland in Georgia to Indian Territory (p. 248)
Sendero de las Lágrimas (1838-39) marcha forzada de 800 millas que realizó la tribu cherokee desde su territorio natal en Georgia hasta el Territorio Indígena

transatlantic crossing the Atlantic Ocean (p. 662)
transatlántico que atraviesa el océano Atlántico

transcendentalist movement movement whose members believed that knowledge is not found only by observation of the world, but also through reason, intuition, and personal spiritual experiences (p. 269)
movimiento trascendentalista movimiento cuyos miembros creían en la convicción de que el conocimiento no se obtiene sólo observando el mundo, sino mediante la razón, la intuición y las experiencias espirituales personales

transcontinental railroad a railroad system that crossed the continental United States (p. 463)
ferrocarril transcontinental sistema de trenes que cruzaba la parte continental de Estados Unidos de un extremo a otro

transcript a written record of a spoken event (p. 1031)
transcripción registro escrito de un suceso oral

transistor small electrical devices that can be found in computers and other machines (p. 864)
transistores pequeños dispositivos eléctricos de las computadoras y otras máquinas

Treaty of Ghent (1814) a treaty signed by the United States and Britain ending the War of 1812 (p. 227)
Tratado de Gante (1814) tratado firmado por Estados Unidos y Gran Bretaña para dar fin a la Guerra de 1812

Treaty of Greenville (1795) an agreement between Native American confederation leaders and the U.S. government that gave the United States Indian lands in the Northwest Territory (p. 212)
Tratado de Greenville (1795) acuerdo entre los líderes de la confederación de indígenas norteamericanos y el gobierno estadounidense que otorgó a Estados Unidos parte del Territorio del Noroeste

Treaty of Guadalupe Hidalgo (1848) a treaty that ended the Mexican-American War and gave the United States much of Mexico's northern territory (p. 311)
Tratado de Guadalupe Hidalgo (1848) tratado que daba por terminada la Guerra mexicano-estadounidense y daba posesión a Estados Unidos de gran parte del norte del territorio mexicano

Treaty of Paris (1763) agreement that ended the Seven Years' War in Europe and divided up the land in North America between Britain, France, and Spain (p. 93)
Tratado de París (1763) convenio que puso fin a la Guerra de los Siete Años en Europa y que repartió las tierras de América del Norte entre Gran Bretaña, Francia y España

Treaty of Paris (1783) agreement that officially ended the Revolutionary War and established British recognition of the independence of the United States (p. 136)
Tratado de París (1783) acuerdo de paz que oficialmente daba por terminada la Guerra de Independencia estadounidense y en el que Gran Bretaña reconocía la independencia de Estados Unidos

Treaty of Tordesillas (1494) agreement between Spain and Portugal that created an imaginary north-south line which divided the territory of the Americas (p. 40)
Tratado de Tordesillas (1494) acuerdo entre España y Portugal mediante el cual se creó una línea imaginaria que atravesaba de norte a sur y dividía el territorio de las Américas

Treaty of Versailles (1919) treaty ending World War I that required Germany to pay huge war reparations and established the League of Nations (p. 609)
Tratado de Versailles tratado que puso fin a la Primera Guerra Mundial, que le impuso a Alemania el pago de indemnizaciones económicas y que estableció la Liga de las Naciones

trench warfare a form of combat in which soldiers dug trenches, or deep ditches, to seek protection from enemy fire and to defend their positions (p. 588)
guerra de trincheras forma de combate en la que la que los soldados excavan trincheras o zanjas profundas para protegerse del fuego enemigo y defender sus posiciones

Trent affair (1861) incident in which two Confederate leaders secretly boarded a British ship named the Trent en route to Britain, and were then captured by Union forces and brought back to the United States (p. 381)
asunto del Trent (1861) incidente en el que dos líderes confederados abordaron clandestinamente el Trent, un barco británico que llevaba el correo hacia Gran Bretaña; las fuerzas de la Unión los capturaron y los devolvieron a los Estados Unidos

triangular trade trading networks in which goods and slaves moved among England, the American colonies, and Africa (p. 79)
comercio triangular redes de intercambio de esclavos y bienes entre Inglaterra, las colonias americanas y África

Triple Alliance a military alliance between Germany, Austria-Hungary and Italy (p. 583)
Triple Alianza alianza militar entre Alemania, Austria-Hungría e Italia

Triple Entente a military alliance between Great Britain, France, and Russia (p. 584)
Triple Entente alianza militar entre Gran Bretaña, Francia y Rusia

Truman Doctrine (1947) President Truman's pledge to provide economic and military aid to countries threatened by communism (p. 819)
Doctrina Truman (1947) promesa del presidente Truman de dar ayuda económica y militar a los países amenazados por el comunismo

Tuskegee Airmen unit of African American pilots that fought in World War II (p. 774)
Aviadores de Tuskegee unidad de pilotos afroamericanos que combatió en la Segunda Guerra Mundial

Twelfth Amendment stated that electors must cast separate ballots for president and vice president (p. 216)
Decimosegunda enmienda dice que los electores deben votar de forma separada para los cargos de presidente y vicepresidente

Twenty-fourth Amendment (1964) banned states from taxing citizens to vote in elections (p. 926)
Vigésimocuarta enmienda (1964) prohibió a los estados cobrarles impuestos a los ciudadanos por votar en las elecciones

Twenty-sixth Amendment (1971) lowered the legal voting age from 21 to 18 (p. 976)
Vigésimosexta enmienda (1971) redujo la edad legal para votar de 21 a 18 años

two-party system a system of government in which there are two groups with differing political opinions (p. 208)
sistema bipartidista sistema de gobierno en el que hay dos grupos con diferentes opiniones políticas

U-boats small submarines named after the German word unterserboot, which means "undersea boat" (p. 591)
U-boat pequeño submarino cuyo nombre proviene de la palabra alemana unterserboot, que significa "bote submarino"

Uncle Tom's Cabin (1852) an antislavery novel written by Harriet Beecher Stowe (p. 325)
La cabaña del tío Tom (1852) novela abolicionista escrita por Harriet Beecher Stowe

Underground Railroad a network of people who helped enslave people escape to the North (p. 286)
Tren Clandestino red de personas que ayudó a los esclavos a escapar hacia el Norte

United Nations an international organization that encourages cooperation among nations (p. 806)
Naciones Unidas (ONU) organización internacional que fomenta la cooperación entre países

Universal Declaration of Human Rights (1948) document that stated all human beings are created free and equal; tried to set standards for human rights (p. 828)
Declaración Universal de los Derechos Humanos (1948) documento que afirma que todos los seres humanos nacen libres e iguales e intentó establecer normas para los derechos humanos

urban working class social class made up of poor and uneducated workers (p. 276)
clase trabajadora urbana clase social compuesta por trabajadores pobres y con pocos estudios

USA PATRIOT Act (2001) law passed by Congress making it easier for the FBI and other law enforcement agencies to collect information about suspected terrorists (p. 1097)
Ley Patriota Estadounidense (2001) ley aprobada por el Congreso que facilita al FBI y a otros agentes de la ley recoger en secreto información acerca de presuntos terroristas

utopian movement movement during the late 1700s and into the mid-1899s whose members worked to establish a perfect society through utopian communities (p. 270)
movimiento utópico movimiento cuyos miembros se esforzaron por establecer una sociedad perfecta mediante comunidades utópicas que tuvieron popularidad Estados Unidos a fines del siglo XVIII y a comienzos y mediados del siglo XIX

vaccine a preparation that uses a killed or weakened form of a germ to help the body build its own defenses against that germ (p. 865)
vacuna preparación que utiliza una forma muerta o debilitada de un germen para ayudar al cuerpo a desa-rrollar sus propias defensas contra dicho germen

Valley Forge location in Pennsylvania where the Continental Army spent the winter of 1777-1778 under extremely harsh conditions (p. 129)
Valley Forge lugar en Pensilvania donde el Ejército Continental pasó el invierno de 1777 a 1778 bajo condiciones extremadamente rigurosas

values the key ideas and beliefs a person holds (p. 649)
valores ideas y creencias claves de una persona

V-E day (1945) May 8, 1945; the date when the Allies celebrated victory in Europe World War II (p. 804)
Día del Armisticio (1945) 8 de mayo de 1945, fecha en que los Aliados celebraron la victoria en Europa de la Segunda Guerra Mundial

velvet revolution a quick, peaceful revolution that swept the Communists from power in Czechoslovakia in 1989 (p. 1061)
revolución de terciopelo revolución breve y pacífica que en 1989 sacó del poder a los comunistas en Checoslovaquia

vertical integration the business practice of owning all of the businesses involved in each step of a manufacturing process (p. 468)
integración vertical práctica empresarial de poseer todas las empresas implicadas en cada paso de un proceso de fabricación

Vichy France French government set up with the Germans that ruled the southern half of France during World War II (p. 748)
Francia Vichy gobierno establecido en Francia en cooperación con Alemania, que gobernó la mitad sur de Francia durante la Segunda Guerra Mundial

Vietcong the military forces of the National Liberation Front, a group that wanted to overthrow the government in Vietnam (p. 953)
Vietcong fuerzas militares del Frente de Liberación Nacional, un grupo Grupo que quería derrocar el gobierno de Vietnam

Vietminh a group that resisted the Japanese occupation in Vietnam (p. 949)
Vietminh grupo que se resistió a la ocupación japonesa de Vietnam

Vietnamization a plan to end the Vietnam war that involved turning over the fighting to the South Vietnamese while U.S. troops gradually pulled out (p. 973)
vietnamización plan para dar fin a la guerra de Vietnam que conllevaba el traspaso de la lucha a los vietnamitas del sur mientras las tropas de Estados Unidos se retiraban gradualmente

Vikings sea raiders from Scandinavia (p. 30)
vikingos piratas escandinavos

Virgina and Kentucky Resolutions resolutions drafted by Jefferson and Madison arguing that the Alien and Sedition Acts were unconstitutional (p. 214)
Resoluciones de Virginia y Kentucky resoluciones redacradas por Jefferson y Madison que sostenían que las Leyes de Extranjeros y Sedición eran inconstitucionales

Virginia Declaration of Rights (1776) a declaration of citizens' rights issued by the Virginia Convention (p. 118)
Declaración de Derechos de Virginia (1776) declaración de derechos civiles proclamada por la Convención de Virginia

Virginia Plan (1787) the plan for government in which the national government would have supreme power and a legislative branch would have two houses with representation determined by state population (p. 152)
Plan de Virginia (1787) plan de gobierno según el cual el gobierno nacional tendría poder supremo y habría un poder legislativo con dos cámaras en las que la representación de cada estado sería determinada por el número de habitantes

VISTA a domestic version of the Peace Corps that provided help to poor communities in the U.S. in the 1960s (p. 896)
VISTA versión nacional e interna del Cuerpo de Paz que ayudó a las comunidades pobres de Estados Unidos durante la década de 1960

V-J Day (1945) August 15, 1945; the date when the Allies declared victory over Japan in World War II (p. 806)
Día V-J (1945) 15 de agosto de 1945; fecha en que los Aliados declararon la victoria sobre Japón durante la Segunda Guerra Mundial

ENGLISH AND SPANISH GLOSSARY

Voter Education Project group founded in 1962 to register southern African Americans to vote (p. 926)
Proyecto para la Educación de Votantes grupo fundado en 1962 para inscribir como votantes a los afroamericanos del sur

Voting Rights Act of 1965 civil rights law that banned literacy tests and other practices that discouraged blacks from voting (p. 930)
Ley del Derecho al Voto de 1965 ley de derechos civiles que prohibió las pruebas de lectura y escritura y otras prácticas que trataban de impedir que los afroamericanos votaran

Wade-Davis Bill (1864) a reconstruction plan that required a majority of a southern state's white male citizens to pledge loyalty to the United States before elections could be held (p. 406)
proyecto de ley Wade-Davis (1864) plan de reconstrucción que requería que una mayoría de los ciudadanos varones blancos de un estado sureño prometieran lealtad a Estados Unidos antes de que se pudieran celebrar elecciones

wage earner person who is paid a set amount by a business owner instead of making income from his or her own enterprise (p. 276)
asalariado persona que recibe una cantidad de dinero fija del propietario de una empresa en vez de obtener sus ingresos a través de una empresa propia

War Hawks American politicians who called for war in response to the incident with the Chesapeake and the Leopard (p. 226)
Halcones de Guerra políticos estadounidenses que ejercieron presión para que se declarara la guerra como respuesta al incidente con el Chesapeake y el Leopard

War on Poverty set of programs introduced by President Johnson to fight poverty (p. 895)
Guerra contra la Pobreza conjunto de programas introducidos por el presidente Johnson para combatir la pobreza

War Powers Act (1973) law that set a 60-day limit on the presidential commitment of U.S. troops to foreign conflicts (p. 979)
Ley de Poderes de Guerra (1973) ley que limita a 60 días el plazo de envío de tropas estadounidenses a conflictos internacionales por parte del presidente

War Refugee Board a group established by President Franklin D. Roosevelt that helped 20,000 Jews who might otherwise have fallen into the hands of the Nazis (p. 782)
Junta de Refugiados de Guerra grupo establecido por el Presidente Franklin D. Roosevelt que ayudó a 20,000 judíos que de otra manera podrían haber caído en manos de los nazis

Warren Commission a commission headed by Chief Justice Earl Warren to investigate the assassination of President Kennedy (p. 892)
Comisión Warren comisión presidida por el presidente de la Corte Suprema Earl Warren para investigar el asesinato del presidente Kennedy

Warren Court a term that refers to the years when Earl Warren served as Chief Justice of the Supreme Court (p. 890)
Coret de Warren término que hace referencia a los años en que Earl Warren ocupó el cargo de juez presidente de la Corte Suprema

Warsaw Pact a military alliance established in 1955 of the Soviet-dominated countries of Eastern Europe (p. 850)
Pacto de Varsovia alianza militar establecida en 1955 por los países de Europa oriental controlados por la Unión Soviética

Watergate scandal a political scandal that resulted in President Nixon's resignation in 1974 (p. 1029)
escándalo Watergate escándalo político que produjo la renuncia del presidente Nixon en 1974

welfare financial assistance from the government (p. CS26)
asistencia social ayuda financiera proporcionada por el gobierno

welfare capitalism system in which companies provided fringe benefits to employees in an effort to promote worker satisfaction and loyalty (p. 631)
capitalismo del bienestar sistema por el que las empresas proporcionan prestaciones a sus empleados para promover la satisfacción y lealtad de los trabajadores

Whiskey Rebellion (1794) a protest of small farmers in Pennsylvania against new taxes on whiskey (p. 208)
Rebelión del Whisky (1794) protesta de pequeños agricultores de Pensilvania contra los nuevos impuestos sobre el whisky

wildcatters name given to oil prospectors who came to Pennsylvania in the mid and late 1800s (p. 461)
cazadores de pozos nombre dado a los prospectores de petróleo que llegaron a Pensilvania a mediados y a finales del siglo XIX

wolf pack a submarine tactic in which submarines hunt as a group and attack at night (p. 771)
manada de lobos táctica de los submarinos por la que éstos buscan al enemigo en grupo y atacan de noche

Women's Christian Temperance Movement reform organization that led the fight against alcohol in the late 1800s (p. 531)
Movimiento Cristiano Femenino por la Abstinencia oranización reformista que lideró la lucha en contra del consumo de alcohol a fines del siglo XIX

Worcester v. Georgia (1832) the Supreme Court ruling that stated that the Cherokee nation was a distinct territory over which only the federal government had authority (p. 248)
Worcester contra Georgia (1832) decisión de la Corte Suprema que estableció que la nación cherokee era un territorio distinto sobre el que sólo el gobierno federal tenía autoridad

working poor those who are employed but cannot earn enough to lift themselves out of poverty (p. CS26)
trabajadores pobres personas que trabajan pero que no ganan lo suficiente como para salir de la pobreza

World Bank helps poor countries build their economies by providing grants and loans to help with projects that could provide jobs and wealth (p. 828)
Banco Mundial ayuda a los países pobres a desrrollar sus economías mediante subsidios y préstamos para invertir en proyectos que pueden generar empleos y riqueza

Wounded Knee Massacre (1890) the U.S. Army's killing of approximately 300 Sioux at Wounded Knee Creek in South Dakota (p. 441)
Masacre de Wounded Knee (1890) matanza de aproximadamente 300 indios sioux en Wounded Knee Creek, Dakota del Sur.

writs of assistance (1767) law that gave British customs officers the right to search colonists' homes for smuggled goods without a search warrant (p. 108)
orden judicial de asistencia (1767) ley que dio a los funcionarios de aduanas británicos el derecho a registrar las casas de los colonos en busca de bienes de contrabando sin una orden de registro

xenophobia fear of foreigners (p. 475)
xenofobia miedo a los extranjeros

XYZ Affair (1797) an incident in which French agents attempted to get a bribe and loans from U.S. diplomats in exchange for an agreement that French privateers would no longer attack American ships (p. 213)
asunto XYZ (1797) incidente en el que funcionarios franceses intentaron obtener sobornos y préstamos de diplomáticos estadounidenses a cambio de un acuerdo por el cual los barcos corsarios franceses no atacarían más a los barcos estadounidenses

Yalta Conference (1945) meeting between Franklin Roosevelt, Winston Churchill, and Joseph Stalin to reach agreement on what to do with Germany after World War II (p. 802)
Conferencia de Yalta (1945) cumbre celebrada entre Franklin Roosevelt, Winston Churchill y Joseph Stalin para llegar a un acuerdo acerca de lo que harían con Alemania después de la Segunda Guerra Mundial

yellow journalism the reporting of exaggerated stories in newspapers to increase sales (p. 559)
prensa amarillista reporraje de artículos exagerados en la prensa para aumentar las ventas

yeoman in the colonies, farmers living on small farms rather than on large plantations (p. 81, CS9)
campesino en las colonias, los granjeros que vivían en pequeñas granjas en lugar de en grandes plantaciones

Zimmermann note a telegram sent to a German official in Mexico before World War I; it proposed an alliance between Germany and Mexico (p. 592)
nota de Zimmermann telegrama enviado a un funcionario alemán en México antes del inicio de la Primera Guerra Mundial; proponía una alianza entre Alemania y México

zoot suit riot a series of riots in Los Angeles, California during World War II, between soldiers stationed in the city and Mexican American youths because of the zoot suits they wore (p. 763)
disturbios de *zoot suit* serie de ataques contra mexicano-americanos por parte de marineros estadounidenses en Los Angeles

Index

INDEX

INDEX

INDEX

G

INDEX

L

INDEX

Q

R

INDEX

Credits and Acknowledgments

reasononline: From "Really Creative Destruction: Economist Tyler Cowen argues for the cultural benefits of globalization" from *reasononline,* August–September 2003, available at http://www.reason.com/0308/cr.ng.really.shtm, October 28, 2005. Copyright © 2003 by reasononline.

Estate of Paulette Goddard Remarque: From *All Quiet on the Western Front* by Erich Maria Remarque. Copyright 1929, 1930 by Little, Brown and Company; copyright renewed © 1957, 1958 by Erich Maria Remarque. All rights reserved. "Im Westen Nichts Neues" copyright 1928 by Ullstein A. G.; copyright renewed © 1956 by Erich Maria Remarque.

The Richmond Organization (TRO): From "Pastures of Plenty" words and music by Woody Guthrie. Copyright © 1960, 1963 by TRO-Ludlow Music, Inc.

Scribner, an imprint of Simon & Schuster Adult Publishing Group: From *The Great Gatsby* by F. Scott Fitzgerald. Copyright 1925 by Charles Scribner's Sons. Copyright renewed 1953 by Frances Scott Fitzgerald Lanahan. From *A Farewell to Arms* by Ernest Hemingway. Copyright 1929 by Charles Scribner's Sons; copyright renewed © 1957 by Ernest Hemingway.

Law Office of Carl Shusterman: From "Immigration: America Stands Unique in the World" from *Law Offices of Carl Shusterman,* available online at http://www.shusterman.com/history.html, May 17, 2005. Copyright © 1996 by Carl Shusterman.

Texas A & M University Press: From "The Death of Davy Crockett" from *With Santa Anna in Texas: A Personal Narrative of the Revolution / José Enrique de la Peña* by Carmen Perry. Copyright © 1997 by Carmen Perry.

20th Century Fox: From the movie *Wall Street* by Stanley Weiser and Oliver Stone. Copyright © 1987 by 20th Century Fox.

United States Holocaust Memorial Museum: From "Gerda Weissmann Klein: Born 1924: Bielsko, Poland" from "Personal Histories: Liberation," as available at http://www.ushmm.org/museum/exhibit/online/phistories, on July 14, 2005. Copyright © United States Holocaust Memorial Museum, Washington, D.C.

The University of Georgia Press: Quote by Nell Blackshear from *Living Atlanta: An Oral History of the City 1914–1948* by Clifford Kuhn, Harlon Joye, and E. Bernard West. Copyright © 1990 by the University of Georgia Press, Athens, GA 30602.

University of Washington Press: From "Poem # 32" by Anonymous from *Island: Poetry and History of Chinese Immigrants on Angel Island, 1910–1940* by Him Mark Lai, Genny Lim, and Judy Yung. Copyright © 1991 by University of Washington Press.

Viking Penguin, a division of Penguin Group (USA), Inc.: From *The Grapes of Wrath* by John Steinbeck. Copyright 1939 and renewed © 1967 by John Steinbeck

Washington Post Company: From "A Tip of That Hat" by Tom Vinciguerra from "Remembering Franklin Delano Roosevelt" from *The Washington Post Online,* available http://www.washingtonpost.com/wp-srv/local/longterm/tours/fdr/, 7/14/05. Copyright © 1997 by The Washington Post Company.

Estate of William C. Westmoreland: From *A Soldier Reports* by General William C. Westmoreland. Copyright © 1976 by William C. Westmoreland.

WGBH Educational Foundation: From letter by June Wandrey from "War Letters" available at http://www.pbs.org/wgbh/amex/warletters/letters/warletter_09.html, on July 14, 2005. Copyright © 1999–2001 by PBS Online/WGBH.

Sources Cited:

From "Roger Tuttrup" from *The Good War: An Oral History of World War Two* by Studs Terkel. Published by Ballantine Books, New York, 1985.

From *Anxious Decades: America in Prosperity and Depression 1920–1941* by Michael E. Parrish. Published by W. W. Norton & Company, New York, 1992.

Quotes by Myron Harrington and Tran Do from *Vietnam: A History* by Stanley Karnow. Published by Penguin Books, New York, 1983.

From "Puttin' On Ole Massa" from *Narrative of William Wells Brown: A Fugitive Slave written by himself.* Published by Prentice-Hall, Inc., Englewood Cliffs, NJ, 1963.

Quotes by Zbigniew Brzezinski and Cyrus Vance from *Crisis: The Last Year of the Carter Presidency* by Hamilton Jordan. Published by G. P. Putnam's Sons, New York, NY, 1982.

From "A Black GI" (retitled "An African American GI in Vietnam (1969-1970)" from *Everything We Had: An Oral History of the Vietnam War* by Al Santoli. Published by Random House, Inc., New York, 1981.

From *Patriots: The Vietnam War Remembered from All Sides* by Christian G. Appy. Published by Viking Penguin, New York, NY 2003.

From "Honor and Humiliation" by Ben Isaacs from *Hard Times: An Oral History of the Great Depression* by Studs Terkel. Published by Washington Square Press, New York, NY, 1970.

From "Pete Peterson - Assignment Hanoi" from web site accessed at http://www.pbs.org/hanoi/home.htm., on June 30, 2005. Published by WGBH Educational Foundation, Boston, MA, 1999.

From the June 1993 Gateway Greens' Compost-Dispatch Speech at the May Day rally against NAFTA, read by Rainbow Coalition member Gene Bruskin for Reverend Jesse Jackson.

From "Artist's Statement" by Joel Meyerowitz from *After September 11 Images from Ground Zero* at http://www.911exhibit.state.gov/artist_statement.cfm, July 19, 2005.

"A Personal Record of Hiroshima A-bomb Survival (No. 1) re-post: Takeharu Terao 91/03/03 13:32" from http://www.coara.or.jp/~ryoji/abomb/a-bomb1.html, July 8, 2005.

Photo Credits

Cover: Joseph Sohm/PictureQuest.
Front Matter: Page ii, (Schulzinger) Bill Salaz/HRW Photo; ii, (Ayers) Ian Bradshaw/HRW Photo; ii, (de la Teja) Sam Dudgeon/HRW; ii, (Gray-White) Michael Denora/ HRW Photo; ii, (Wineburg) HRW Photo/Gary Benson Photography; v, The Granger Collection, New York;vi, ©Superstock/SuperStock; vii (t), Private Collection/PRC Archive; vii (t), Thomas Cole, *A View of the Mountain Pass Called the Notch of the White Mountains*, Andrew w. Mellon Fund, Photograph © 2005 Board of Trustees, National Gallery of Art, Washington, DC; (b) Gallery of the Republic; viii, The Art Archive/ Culver Pictures;ix (t), Smithsonian American Art Museum, Washington, DC/Art Resource, NY; ix (b), Library of Congress, Detroit Publishing Company Collection, LC-USZC4-1584; x (tl), Janice L. and David J. Frent Collection of Political Americana;x (tr), Janice L. and David J. Frent Collection of Political Americana;x (c), Janice L. and David J. Frent Collection of Political Americana; x (b), Courtesy The Delaware Military Heritage and Education Foundation, Inc.; xi (Robeson) ©Photo by Sasha/Getty Images; (Smith) ©Bettmann/CORBIS; (Armstrong) ©Reuters/STR/Getty Images; xi (b), Culver Pictures, Inc.; xii (t), ©US Air Force/Collection of David Ethell; xii (b), © Photo by Walter Sanders/Time Life Pictures/Getty Images; xiii, © Matt Herron/Take Stock; xiv (t), © Arthur Schatz/Time Life Pictures/Getty Images; xiv (b), © Pete Saloutos/CORBIS; xv, © CORBIS; xvi, Library of Congress; xix, © CORBIS; xxi, Retrofile.com/Getty Images; xxii, Gladys City Museum, Beaumont, Texas; xxvi (t), HRW Photo/Gary Benson Photography; xxvi, (b) National Portrait Gallery, Smithsonian Institution, Washington, DC/Art Resource, NY; xxxii, (c) Brand X Pictures, (all others) Image Club Graphics; H1, Smithsonian American Art Museum, Washington, DC/Art Resource, NY; H16 (bc), Harvey Schwartz/Index Stock Imagery; H16 (b), © Tom Nebbia/CORBIS; H16 (c), © London Aerial Photo Library/CORBIS; H16 (t), Earth Satellite Corporation/Science Photo Library/Photo Researchers, Inc.; H16 (tc), © Frans Lemmens/The Image Bank/Getty Images; H24 (l), © Robert W. Kelley/Time Life Pictures/Getty Images; H24 (c), © Bettmann/CORBIS; H24 (r), Photo by Hugo Jaeger/Timepix/Time Life Pictures/Getty Images; H25 (tr), The Museum of American Political Life, University of Hartford, West Hartford,CT; H25 (br), © Mike Segar/REUTERS/CORBIS; H25 (tl), Picture Research Consultants & Archives; H26 (tl), ©Michael Ventura/Folio, Inc.; H26 (b), © Bettmann/CORBIS; H26 (tr), Ric Francis/AP/Wide World Photos; H27 (tl), © Lonny Shavelson/Zuma Press Photos; H27 (bl), © Bettmann/CORBIS; H27 (tr), © CORBIS; H27 (br), © Justin Sullivan/Getty Images; H29, Collection of the American Numismatic Society, New York; H30, © Woburn Abbey Collection, Bedford Estate; H31, The Granger Collection, New York; T6, The Granger Collection, New York; T7, The Granger Collection, New York; T23, Library of Congress; T24 (l), © Bettmann/CORBIS; T24 (r), Picture Research Consultants & Archives. **Unit One**: Page 1, The Granger Collection, New York. **Chapter 1**: Pages 4 - 5 (t), ©Steve Vidler/SuperStock; 5 (cl), © Richard A. Cooke /CORBIS; 5 (cr), Cahokia Mounds Historic Site; 5 (b), © Royalty-Free/CORBIS; 06 (l), Dr. George Frison, Hell Gap Prehistoric Site, University of Wyoming; 6 (r), Arizona State Museum, University of Arizona; 8 (t), © Kevin Schafer/CORBIS; 8 (c), © David Muench/CORBIS; 8 (b), © Richard A. Cooke /CORBIS; 09 (tl), Cahokia Mounds Historic Site; 9 (tr), BMI/Michael Zabe; 9 (b), © Stuart Westmoreland/CORBIS; 11, © John Griffin/Florida Museum of Natural History; 14 (t), © Royalty-Free/CORBIS; 14 (b), © Marilyn "Angel" Wynn/Nativestock Pictures; 15, National Museum of the American Indian, Smithsonian Institution, Washington, DC. Photo #092104PRWL047; 17 (l), © John Bigelow Taylor. Franck H. McClung Museum, the University of Tennessee. ; 17 (r), The Field Museum of Natural History, [neg. A29TC], Chicago; 18, National Geographic Image Collection; 20, Giraudon/Art Resource, NY; 21, © MARCEL MOCHET/AFP/Getty Images; 23, North Wind Picture Archives; 24, National Archives; 25, HIP /Art Resource, NY; 29, Wolverhampton Art Gallery, West Midlands, UK/ Bridgeman Art Library; 30, SuperStock; 32, Architect of the Capitol. **Chapter 2**: Pages 34-35, © Burstein Collection/CORBIS; 34 (t), © Dan Heller Photography; 34 (b), Jacka Photography; 36, Library of Congress/ PRC Archive; 38 (c), The Granger Collection, New York; 38 (b), Michel Zabe; 39 (b), Private Collection; 40, The Art Archive / Marine Museum Lisbon / Dagli Orti; 41, The Granger Collection, New York; 44, © Woburn Abbey Collection, Bedford Estate; 46, The Granger Collection, New York; 48, Private Collection; 49, Library of Congress; 51, Private Collection; 54 (l), © Bettmann/CORBIS; 54 (r), American Antiquarian Society; 55, Art Ref: PRC Archive; 57 (t), Yale Collection of American Literature, Beinecke Rare Book and Manuscript Library. Photo by Carl Van Vechten, published by permission of the Carl Van Vechten Trust; 57 (b), © Peabody Essex Museum, Salem, MA/ Bridgeman Art Library; 58, © Kevin Fleming/CORBIS; 59, © Raymond Gehman/CORBIS; 60 (l), Historical Society of Pennsylvania; 60 (r), Historical Society of Pennsylvania; 61 (l), Museum of London, Great Britain, HIP/Art Resource, NY; 61 (r), Victoria & Albert Museum, London/Art Resource, NY; 61 (b), Cheltenham Art Gallery & Museums, Gloucestershire, UK/Bridgeman Art Library; 64, © Stapleton Collection/CORBIS; 65, State Capitol, Commonwealth of Virginia, Courtesy Library of Virginia, image altered.; 66 (l), National Portrait Gallery, Smithsonian Institution, Washington, DC/Art Resource, NY; 66 (r), New York State Office of General Services, Executive Mansion, Albany, New York; 67, ©Buena Vista Pictures/Courtesy Everett Collection ; 68 (r), The Granger Collection, New York; 68 (l), Private Collection. **Chapter 3**: Pages 70 - 71, "View of Boston Common" (detail) about 1750. Object Place: Boston, Massachusetts, United States. Hannah Otis, 1732–1801. Wool, silk, metallic threads, and beads on linen ground; predominately tent stitch; original frame and glass. 61.59 x 133.98 cm (24 1/4 x 52 3/4 in.). Museum of Fine Arts, Boston. Gift of a Friend of the Department of American Decorative Arts and Sculpture, a Supporter of the Department of American Decorative Arts and Sculpture, Barbara L. and Theodore B. Alfond, and Samuel A. Otis; and William Francis Warden Fund, Harriet Otis Cruft Fund, Otis Norcross Fund, Susan Cornelia Warren Fund, Arthur Tracy Cabot Fund, Seth K. Sweetser Fund, Edwin E. Jack Fund, Helen B. Sweeney Fund, William E. Nickerson Fund, Arthur Mason Knapp Fund, Samuel Putnam Avery Fund, Benjamin Pierce Cheney Fund, and

Mary L. Smith Fund. 1996.26; 70 (b), Peter Newark's American Pictures; 71 (c), National Portrait Library, London/Bridgeman Art Library; 71 (b), Private Collection/ The Bridgeman Art Library; 72, PHOTOGRAPH COURTESY PEABODY ESSEX MUSEUM [detail neg. #17530]; 73, PHOTOGRAPH COURTESY PEABODY ESSEX MUSEUM] [neg. #M11588]; 74, Massachusetts State Archives ; 75, HIP/Art Resource, NY; 77, The Granger Collection, New York; 82, Royal Albert Memorial Museum, Exeter, Devon, UK/The Bridgeman Art Library; 84, Picture Research Consultants & Archives; 86, The Granger Collection, New York; 88, A Bicentennial Gift to America from a Grateful Armenian-American People, 1978. #1978.15.12, Photograph © The Metropolitan Museum of Art; 90-91, The Union League of Philadelphia; 92, American Antiquarian Society; 95, The Granger Collection, New York; 96 (l), © British Museum, London; 96 (r), Smithsonian Institution, Washington, DC, photo #93-2845; 97, Abby Aldrich Rockefeller Folk Art Collection, Colonial Williamsburg Foundation; 98, Picture Research Consultants & Archives. **Unit Two**: Page 101, ©Superstock/SuperStock. **Chapter 4**: Pages 104-105 (t), Sinclair Hamilton Collection, Department of Rare Books and Special Collections/ Princeton University Libraries; 104 (b), The Granger Collection, New York; 105 (cl), © Bettmann/ CORBIS; 105 (cr), © Superstock/ SuperStock; 105 (b), Private Collection/Bridgeman Art Library; 106, Picture Research Consultants & Archives; 107, Library of Congress/PRC Archive; 109, © Bettmann/ CORBIS; 111, Library of Congress/PRC Archive; 114, Colonial Williamsburg Foundation; 116, *Attack on Bunker's Hill, with The Burning of Charlestown*. Gift of Edgar William and Bernice Chrysler Garbisch, Photograph by Richard Carafelli, Image © 2005 Board of Trustees, National Gallery of Art, Washington, DC; 119 (l), Private Collection; 119 (r), © New-York Historical Society, New York, USA/ Bridgeman Art Library; 120, Courtesy of the Massachusetts Historical Society; 121-124 (border), © Richard Cummins/CORBIS; 125, Rhode Island Historical Society; 126 (l), ©Kathy McLaughlin/The Image Works; 126 (r), © Kelley-Mooney Photography/CORBIS; 127, Reunion de Musees Nationaux/Art Resource, NY; 130, Chicago Historical Society, #138885; 131 (t), © Bettmann/ CORBIS; 131 (b), North Wind Picture Archives; 132, (detail) Art Gallery, Williams Center, Lafayette College, Easton, PA. Gift of Mrs. John Hubbard; 137 (both), National Archives/PRC Archive; 138 (l), Courtesy of the John Carter Brown Library at Brown University; 138 (r), Trustees of the Boston Public Library; 139, Library of Congress/PRC Archive; 140, ,Sinclair Hamilton Collection, Department of Rare Books and Special Collections/Princeton University Libraries. **Chapter 5**: Pages 142-143, ©Superstock/SuperStock; 142 (c), National Archives/PRC Archive; 142 (b), Culver Pictures, Inc.; 143 (c), © Dennis Degnan/CORBIS; 143 (b), Reunion de Musees Nationaux/Art Resource, NY; 144 (t), Eric P. Newman/Numismatic Education Society; 144 (bl), Picture Research Consultants & Archives; 144 (r), Collection of the American Numismatic Society, New York; 145, Private Collection/PRC Archive; 147 (l), © MPI/Getty Images; 147 (r), Painting by Gregory Stapko, Collection of the Supreme Court of the United States; 150, The Granger Collection, New York; 151, Library of Congress/PRC Archive; 152-153, Hall of Representatives, Washington, DC/ Bridgeman Art Library; 155 (l), © Royalty Free/ CORBIS; 155 (c), Image Copyright ©2007 PhotoDisc, Inc.; 155 (r), © Royalty Free/CORBIS; 157 (b), Independence National Historical Park . Detail, "Rising Sun" chair; 157 (inset), Hall of Representatives, Washington, DC/ Bridgeman Art Library; 159, American Antiquarian Society; 160 (l), Charles Willson Peale, *James Madison*, 1792, oil on canvas, 0126.1006, From the Collection of Gilcrease Museum, Tulsa; 160 (r), Colonial Williamsburg Foundation; 162, Jill Brady/Maine Sunday Telegram; 166 (l), National Archives/ PRC Archive; 166 (r), Hall of Representatives, Washington, DC/ Bridgeman Art Library. **Constitution**: Pages 168-169, ©2009 Jay Mallin; 170-197 (border), © Richard Cummins/ CORBIS; 174 (l), Dennis Cook/AP/Wide World Photos; 174-75 (bc), © Mark Wilson/Getty Images; 175 (r), © Brooks Kraft/CORBIS; 176, © Royalty-Free/ CORBIS; 186 (l), © Yang Liu/CORBIS; 186 (r), Norm Detlaff, Las Cruces Sun-News/AP/Wide World Photos; 187 (l), ©Bettmann/CORBIS; 187 (c), © David Young-Wolff/PhotoEdit; 187 (r), © Bettmann/CORBIS; 191, Library of Congress/PRC Archive; 193, Library of Congress; 195 (l), © Bettmann/CORBIS; 195 (r), © Oscar White/ CORBIS; 196 (tl), Dr. Hector P. Garcia Papers, Special Collections & Archives, Texas A&M University-Corpus Christi, Bell Library; 196 (bl), Texas State Library & Archives Commission; 196 (r), ©1978 Matt Herron/TakeStock; 199, Texas State Library & Archives Commission. **Chapter 6**: Pages 200-201 (t), Virginia Historical Society; 200 (b), Giraudon/Art Resource, NY; 201 (bl), © New-York Historical Society/Reuters/Corbis; 201 (br), The Granger Collection, New York; 202, National Portrait Gallery, Smithsonian Institution, Washington, DC/Art Resource, NY; 203, 205, 206 (both), The Granger Collection, New York; 207, (t), John Trumbull, "Alexander Hamilton", oil on canvas, 1806, The Granger Collection, New York; 207 (b), Lauros/Giraudon/ Bridgeman Art Library; 209, Reunion de Musees Nationaux/Art Resource, NY; 210, HRW Photo Research Library; 211, Courtesy Ohio Historical Society; 213, The Granger Collection, New York; 215 (l), © Bettmann/CORBIS; 215 (r), The Art Archive/ Chateau de Blernacourt/Dagli Orti; 218 (t), The Granger Collection, New York; 218 (b), (detail) *Mission San Carlos Del Rio Carmelo* by Oriana Day, oil on canvas 20 x 30 (50,8 x 76.2 cm), Gift of Mrs. Eleanor Martin. Fine Arts Museum of San Francisco; 219 (tl), ©SUPERSTOCK/SuperStock; 219 (tr), Lake County (IL) Museum / Curt Teich Postcard Archive; 219 (b), Oregon Historical Society, #OrHi 1645; 218-219 (bkgd),, Used by permission, Utah State Historical Society, all rights reserved; 220, [#1867.306] Collection of The New-York Historical Society; 221 (t), Getty Images; 221 (b), William J. Hennessy Jr.; 222 (tl), © Connie Ricca/CORBIS; 222 (b), © Bob Rowan/ Progressive Image/CORBIS; 223 (t), © Tom Bean/ CORBIS; 223 (b), North Wind Picture Archives; 224 (l), The Granger Collection, New York; 224 (r), © Bettmann/ CORBIS; 225, The Field Museum of Natural History, [neg. #A993851], Chicago; 229, The Granger Collection, New York; 230 (both), The Granger Collection, New York. **Unit Three**: Page 233, ©SuperStock, Inc./SuperStock. **Chapter 7**: Pages 236-237, Historical Society of Pennsylvania, Fourth of July Celebration in Center Square by John Lewis Krimmel (Bc 882 K897); 236 (b), Bildarchive Preussischer Kulturbesitz/Art Resource, NY; 237 (bl), United Nations; 237 (br), © Stapleton Collection/CORBIS; 238, Private Collection/PRC Archive; 239, Thomas Cole, *A View of the Mountain Pass Called the Notch of the White Mountains*, Andrew w. Mellon Fund, Photograph © 2005 Board of Trustees, National Gallery of Art, Washington, DC; 240 (tl), New York State Office of Parks, Recreation and Historic Preservation, Clermont State Historic Site, Taconic Region; 240 (tr), National Portrait Gallery, Smithsonian Institution, Washington, DC/Art Resource, NY; 240 (cl), Private Collection; 240 (cr), ©Superstock/ Superstock; 240 (b), Chicago Historical Society, #P&S 1995.008; 244 (t), Getty Images; 244 (b), © Lief Skoogfors/CORBIS; 245, Library of Congress/ PRC Archive; 246, Memphis Brooks Museum of Art; 248, Sinclair Hamilton Collection, Department of Rare Books and Special Collections, Princeton University Library; 249, [neg. 46519] Collection of The New-York Historical Society; 251, Picture Research Consultants & Archives; 252 (t), National Museum of American History, Smithsonian Institution, Washington, DC, neg. no 73-11287; 252 (l), Division of History and Technology/ National Museum of American History, Smithsonian Institution, Washington, DC. Photo # 86-9625 by Eric Long; 252 (r), National Museum of American History, Smithsonian Institution, Washington, DC. Photo # 2005-10045; 253 (tl), The Granger Collection, New York; 253 (r), Charles Phillips; 253 (b), Jack Naylor Collection/Picture Research Consultants & Archives; 254, [#34684] Collection of The New-York Historical Society; 256, © Bettmann/ CORBIS; 258, (detail) *Hauling the Whole Week's Pickings* by William Henry Brown. The Historic New Orleans Collection; 260, North Wind Picture Archives; 261, The Granger Collection, New York; 263, Private Collection/PRC Archive. **Chapter 8**: Pages 264-265 (t), [neg. #44227] Collection of The New-York Historical Society; 265 (cr), Private Collection; 265 (b), *Coffin Ships-Below Decks* by Rodney Charman. Albert F. Egan Jr. & Dorothy Egan Foundation, Inc. Nantucket, Mass.; 266 (cl), Trenton Psychiatric Hospita/Photo by Josh Nefsky; 266 (c), Onondaga Historical Association, #19981.21.171B; 266 (revival), Library of Congress/PRC Archive; 267 (all), Oberlin College Archives, Oberlin, Ohio; 268, Picture Research Consultants & Archives; 269, Trenton Psychiatric Hospital/Photo by Josh Nefsky; 271 (t), Courtesy of Concord Free Public Library; 271 (b), © Royalty-Free/CORBIS; 272, Lester S. Levy Collection, Milton S. Eisenhower Library, Johns Hopkins University; 273, *Coffin Ships-Below Decks* by Rodney Charman. Albert F. Egan Jr. & Dorothy Egan Foundation, Inc. Nantucket, Mass.; 274 (l), Jane White Johnson, her husband, Thomas Johnson and baby, Jenna c. 1850, #93.49.1, Museum of the City of New York; 274 (r), [#41082] Collection of The New-York Historical Society; 276, Zuma Press Photos; 277, © Bettmann/ CORBIS; 278, Library of Congress; 279 (t), Courtesy of the Bostonian Society/Old State House279 (bl), *Irish immigrants on board the Odessa, ship's cook* by Rodney Charman. Albert F. Egan Jr. & Dorothy Egan Foundation, Inc. Nantucket, Mass.; 280, Coline Jenkins/Elizabeth Cady Stanton Trust; 283, The Granger Collection, New York; 287, Library of Congress/PRC Archive; 288, Photographie portrait of Sojourner Truth, holding daguerreotype in lap, Courtesy of the Massachusetts Historical Society; 289, Onondaga Historical Association, #19981.21.171B; 291 (l), Library of Congress; 291 (r), Library of Congress ; 293, [neg. #44227] Collection of The New-York Historical Society. **Chapter 9**: Pages 294-295 (t), Albert Bierstadt, "The Oregon Trail", oil on canvas. Butler Institute of American Art; 295 (cl), Gallery of the Republic; 295 (cr), © George F. Mobley/Getty Images; 295 (b), Library of Congress/PRC Archive; 296, Colorado Historical Society (10025774/F20280) All Rights Reserved; 299, Seaver Center for Western History Research, Natural History Museum of Los Angeles County; 300, Smithsonian American Art Museum, Washington, DC/Art Resource, NY; 302, #di_ 01943, The Center for American History, The University of Texas at Austin; 303, Texas State Library and Archives Commission; 304, The Granger Collection, New York; 308, © Bettmann/ CORBIS; 310, Society of California Pioneers; 313 (l), Courtesy Everett Collection ; 313 (r), © Touchstone Pictures/Everett Collection ; 314 (t), Colorado Historical Society; 314 (b), Society of California Pioneers. **Unit Four**: Page 317, The Art Archive/ Culver Pictures; Chicago Historical Society, #P&S 1955.0398. **Chapter 10**: Pages 320-321 (t), © Bettmann/CORBIS; 320 (b), © CORBIS; 321 (c), Chicago Historical Society, #i22204; 321 (b), India Office Library & Records, The British Library; 322 (t), © Hulton-Deutsch Collection/ CORBIS; 322 (b), Library of Congress; 325 (t), Chicago Historical Society, #i22204; 325 (b), Picture Research Consultants & Archives; 328, © Benjamin Lowy/CORBIS; 329, Kansas State Historical Society; 333, The Granger Collection, New York; 334, Missouri Historical Society; 335, Boston Athenaeum; 336 (t), Getty Images; 336 (b), Dennis Cook/AP/Wide World Photos; 337, The Granger Collection, New York; 338 (l), Abraham Lincoln Birthplace National Historic Site; 338 (c), Library of Congress; 338 (r), Courtesy The Lilly Library, Indiana University, Bloomington, Indiana; 340 (l), Library of Congress; 340 (r), Library of Congress/PRC Archive; 342, Sally Andersen-Bruce, Museum of American Political Life; 344 (t), © Bettmann/CORBIS; 344 (b), Kansas Museum of History; 346, Library of Congress/PRC Archive; 347, Chicago Historical Society, #1920.175; 351, Library of Congress, LC-USZ62-1959. ; 352, © Bettmann/CORBIS. **Chapter 11**: Pages 354-355 (t), State Museum of Pennsylvania, Pennsylvania Historical and Museum Collection; 354 (c), © CORBIS; 354 (b), The Granger Collection, New York; 355 (cl), © SuperStock; 355 (cr), National Geographic Image Collection; 355 (b), Courtesy of the International Red Cross; 356, The Museum of the Confederacy Richmond, Virginia. Photography by Katherine Wetzel; 357, Anne S.K. Brown Military Collection, Brown University Library; 358, Courtesy of The Lincoln Museum, Fort Wayne, IN (#0-42); 361, Library of Congress/PRC Archive; 363, Library of Congress; 364 (l), Picture Research Consultants & Archives; 364 (c), © Bettmann/CORBIS; 364 (r), Naval Historical Center; 365 (l), The Museum of the Confederacy Richmond, Virginia. Photography by Katherine Wetzel; 365 (r), Ron Rubles Enterprises; 367, Chicago Historical Society, #1932.27; 368,

National Park Service; 371, U.S. Capitol Historical Society; 372 (b), Library of Congress, Brady Civil War Collection; 372 (br), Courtesy of the Massachusetts Historical Society; 373, © Larry Kolvoord/The Image Works; 374, Rochester Museum & Science Center, Rochester, NY; 375, Anne S.K. Brown Military Collection, Brown University Library; 376, National Archives (NARA); 377, Gettysburg National Military Park; 378, © Bettmann/CORBIS; 379 (t), Used by permission of Orchard House/Louisa May Alcott Memorial Association; 379 (b), National Archives/ PRC Archive; 380, © SuperStock; 381, Library of Congress; 389 (r), Naval Historical Center; 390, National Archives (NARA); 391 (l), National Archives (NARA); 391 (r), Library of Congress; 392, Yale University Art Gallery, New Haven, CT/ Bridgeman Art Library; 395, National Geographic Image Collection; 396 (l), Library of Congress, #LC-B8184-10037; 396 (r), Collection of Kean E. Wilcox; 398 (l), Anne S.K. Brown Military Collection, Brown University Library; 398 (c), National Park Service; 398 (r), National Geographic Image Collection. **Chapter 12**: Pages 400-401, Courtesy of the Charleston Renaissance Gallery, Robert M. Hicklin Jr., Inc. Charleston, SC ; 400 (b), The Granger Collection, New York; 401 (c), Herbert F. Johnson Museum of Art, Cornell University; 401 (bl), © Michael Maslan Historic Photographs/CORBIS; 401 (br), © Hulton-Deutsch Collection/CORBIS; 402, Chicago Historical Society, #P&S 1955.0398; 403, Library of Congress; 405, The Western Reserve Historical Society, Cleveland, Ohio; 406, Library of Congress; 407, Anne S.K. Brown Military Collection, Brown University Library; 409 (t), Getty Images; 409 (b), © Sketch by Art Lein/Pool/Reuters/CORBIS; 410, Library of Congress/PRC Archive; 412, Cook Collection, The Valentine Museum; 413, The Granger Collection, New York; 415, The Granger Collection, New York; 416, Chickamauga and Chattanooga National Military Park; 417, Library of Congress/PRC Archive; 418, Herbert F. Johnson Museum of Art, Cornell University; 419 (tr), The Valentine Museum; 419 (cr), © Bettmann/ CORBIS; 419 (cl), Cook Collection, The Valentine Museum; 419 (b), © CORBIS; 421, Brown Brothers; 422, Brown Brothers; 423, The Granger Collection, New York; 424, Library of Congress/ PRC Archive; 426 (t), © CORBIS; 426 (b), © Bettmann/CORBIS; 429 (l), [neg. 50473] Collection of The New-York Historical Society; 429 (r), Collection of Thomas H. Gandy and Joan W. Gandy; 430, Courtesy of the Charleston Renaissance Gallery, Robert M. Hicklin Jr., Inc. Charleston, SC. **Unit Five**: Page 433, The Granger Collection, New York.; **Chapter 13**: Pages 436-437 (t), National Archives (NARA); 437 (cl), © Bettmann/CORBIS; (cr), © Bettmann/CORBIS; 437 (b), © Hulton-Deutsch Collection/CORBIS; 438, National Anthropological Archives, Smithsonian Institution, Washington, D.C., neg. #81-9626; 439, Smithsonian American Art Museum, Washington, DC/Art Resource, NY; 442, National Anthropological Archives, Smithsonian Institution, Washington DC, neg. 43201-B; 443 (both), National Anthropological Archives, Smithsonian Institution, Washington DC; 444, University of Washington Libraries, UW 4770; 446, Colorado Historical Society (F2276) All Rights Reserved; 447, Courtesy of Texas Department of Transportation; 449, ©Topham/The Image Works; 450 (l), Archives & Manuscript Division of the Oklahoma Historical Society; 450-451, Archives & Manuscript Division of the Oklahoma Historical Society; ; 451 (r), Archives & Manuscripts Division of the Oklahoma Historical Society; 452, Kansas State Historical Society; 453, History of Technology Division, National Museum of American History, Smithsonian Institution, Washington, DC. Photo # 76-9598. 454, Chicago Historical Society, neg #i21030; 455, Library of Congress, # Portfolio 134, folder 13, ephemera; 456 (both), Archives & Manuscript Division of the Oklahoma Historical Society; 457, (detail) University of Washington Libraries, UW 4770. **Chapter 14**: Pages 458-459 (t), © Bettmann/ CORBIS; 458 (b), © Hulton Archive/ Getty Images; 459 (c), © Bettmann/CORBIS; (b), © Archivo Iconografico, S.A./CORBIS; 460, National Archives; 461, Gladys City Museum, Beaumont, Texas; 465 (t), © Bettmann/CORBIS; 466, Photo © Richard Cheek for Preservation Society of Newport County; 467 (l), The Granger Collection, New York; (r), Library of Congress; 469, Collection of The New-York Historical Society; 470, © Bettmann/CORBIS; 471, (t) Sears Modern Home mail order catalogue, 1918; (b) © Steve Warble; 472-473, Library of Congress; 474 (t), Courtesy Gore Place; (b), George Meany Memorial Archives; 475 (l), © Roger Ressmeyer/CORBIS; (r), Brian Kersey/UPI Photo/NewsCom; 474-475 (bkgd) Library of Congress, Bain Collection; 477, National Air & Space Museum, Smithsonian Institution, Washington, D.C., #A26767B-2; 478 (t), Los Angeles Public Library; (b), Reed Saxon/ AP/Wide World Photos; 480, Ford Archives, Henry Ford Museum; 481, 483 Picture Research Consultants & Archives; 485, Library of Congress, #LC-DIG-NCLC-01581. **Chapter 15**: Pages 486-87 (t), Library of Congress, Detroit Publishing Company Collection ; 486 (b), National Museum of American History, Cultural History Division, Smithsonian Institution, Washington, DC. Cat# 31979.0131.01; 486 © National Archives; 487 (b), © Bettmann/CORBIS; 488, Keystone-Mast Collection/University of California at Riverside/ California Museum of Photography, #X97322; 490 (l), © Charles E. Rotkin/CORBIS; (r), Trustees of the Watts Gallery, Compton, Surrey, UKThe Bridgeman Art Library; 491 (t), National Archives (NARA); (b), © Spencer Grant/PhotoEdit; 490-491 (bkgd), © Bill Ross/CORBIS; 493, Copyright The New York Public Library / Art Resource, NY; 495, ©Kindra Clineff Photography; 498, University of Illinois at Chicago, The University Library, Jane Addams Memorial Collection, JAMC neg. 109; 499, Library of Congress/PRC Archive; 500, Picture Research Consultants & Archives; 502, Chicago Historical Society, #DN0000739; 503, Library of Congress; 504, Nebraska Historical Society; 505, Kansas State Historical Society, Topeka; 506, Picture Research Consultants & Archives; 507, Brown Brothers; 508, Tusekegee University Library; 509 (l), Brown Brothers; (r), The Schomburg Center for Research in Black Culture, New York Public Library, Astor, Lenox and Tilden Foundations; 510, Texas State Library & Archives Commission; 511 (t), Getty Images; (b), © Jeff Greenberg/PhotoEdit; 513, San Francisco History Center, San Francisco Public Library; 514 (tl), Trustees of the Watts Gallery, Compton, Surrey, UK/ Bridgeman Art Library; (tr), Picture Research Consultants & Archives; (bl), Copyright The New York Public Library / Art Resource, NY; (br), Chicago Historical Society, #DN0000739; 515, Keystone-Mast Collection/ University of California at Riverside/California Museum of Photography, #X97322. **Unit Six**: Page 517, Museum of the City of New York, USA / Bridgeman Art Library; 519, North Wind Picture Archives. **Chapter 16**: Pages 520-521 (t), Library of Congress; 520 (c), Keystone-Mast Collection/California Museum of Photography /University of California at Riverside/; (b), © Bettmann/ CORBIS; 521 (c), Brown Brothers; (b), © Bettmann/n CORBIS; 522, *How the Other Half Lives: an old rear tenement in Roosevelt Street, 1890*, Jacob Riis, Museum of the City of New York; 525 (inset), © Underwood & Underwood/CORBIS; 526, Brown Brothers; 528 (t), © Hulton-Deutsch Collection/ CORBIS; 528 (b), Library of Congress; 529, Sophia Smith Collection, Smith College; 530 (l), New York State Historical Association, Cooperstown; (r), Picture Research Consultants & Archives; 531 (t), Brown Brothers; (bl), Picture Research Consultants & Archives; (r), © Jeff Greenberg/PhotoEdit; 530-531, (bkgd), © Bettmann/CORBIS; 532, Coline Jenkins/Elizabeth Cady Stanton Trust; 533, Library of Congress; 535, Theodore Roosevelt Collection/ Harvard Library; 537 (l), Keystone-Mast Collection/ California Museum of Photography /University of California at Riverside/; (r), The Granger Collection, New York; 538, Library of Congress; 539, © Joseph Sohm/Chromosohm, Inc./CORBIS; 541, The Granger Collection, New York; 542 (all), Janice L. and David J. Frent Collection of Political Americana; 544 (l), Library of Congress; (r), Library of Congress/ PRC Archive; 546, North Wind Picture Archives; 548, Library of Congress; 549, The Granger Collection, New York. **Chapter 17**: Pages 550-551 (t), National Guard Bureau.; Pages 550 (b), Picture Research Consultants & Archives; 551 (cl), © Underwood & Underwood/ CORBIS; (cr), © Hulton-Deutsch Collection/ CORBIS; (b), Brown Brothers; 552, Library of Congress; 554, Lake County (IL) Museum /Curt Teich Postcard Archives; 555, © Douglas Peebles/ CORBIS; 556, Snark/Art Resource, NY; 558, © Bettmann/CORBIS; 559, © CORBIS; 562, Chicago Historical Society; 563 (both), Library of Congress; 565, 566, The Granger Collection, New York; 567, © Underwood & Underwood/CORBIS; 572, Brown Brothers; 573 (tl, tr), © Bettmann/CORBIS; (bl), © CORBIS; (br), © Underwood & Underwood/ CORBIS; 574, © Hulton-Deutsch Collection/ CORBIS; 577, C. J. Taylor, artist. Courtesy The Bishop Museum; 578 (bkgd), National Guard Bureau; 579, Lake County (IL) Museum /Curt Teich Postcard Archives. **Chapter 18**: Pages 580-581 (t), Courtesy The Delaware Military Heritage and Education Foundation, Inc.; 580 (b), Picture Research Consultants & Archives; 581 (cl), ©SuperStock; (cr), Library of Congress; (b), The Art Archive/Imperial War Museum; 582, © CORBIS; 588, Retrofile.com/Getty Images; 590, ©SuperStock; 591, © CORBIS; 592 (l), © Trustees of the Imperial War Museum, London, #Q53033; (r), © CORBIS; 593 (l), © Bettmann/CORBIS; (r), © Trustees of the Imperial War Museum, London; 594 (both), National Archives; 596, Brown Brothers; 597 (t), Charles Scribner's Sons/AP/Wide World Photos; (b), National Archives, War & Conflict #615; 598 (t), Library of Congress; 598-599, Brown Brothers; 599 (r), © Bettmann/ CORBIS; 600, Brown Brothers; 601, Picture Research Consultants & Archives; 602 (l), Culver Pictures, Inc.; (r), © CDC/PHIL/CORBIS; 603, National Archives/PRC Archive; 605 (t), Getty Images; (b), AP/Wide World Photos; 606, © Bettmann/ CORBIS; 609 (l), Picture Research Consultants & Archives; (r), Photo by Keystone/ Getty Images; 613, AP/Wide World Photos; 614 (l), Retrofile.com/Getty Images; (c), National Archives/ PRC Archive; (r), © Bettmann/CORBIS; 615, Library of Congress. **Unit Seven**: Page 617, © New-York Historical Society/ Bridgeman Art Library. **Chapter 19**: Pages 620-621 (t), Caulfield & Shook Collection #CS71790, Photographic Archives, University of Louisville; 620 (b), National Museum of Health & Medicine, Armed Forces Institute of Pathology; 621 (bl), ©Culver Pictures/SuperStock; (c), © Bettmann/CORBIS; (br), © Photo by Wolf Suschitsky/ Pix Inc./ Time Life Pictures/Getty Images; 622, National Museum of Health & Medicine, Armed Forces Institute of Pathology; 623, David Longstreath/ AP/Wide World Photos; 624, The Granger Collection, New York; 625, © Bettmann/CORBIS; 627, Digital Image © the Museum of Modern Art/ Licensed by SCALA/Art Resource, NY. © Estate of Ben Shahn/Licensed by VAGA, New York, NY ; 628, Macy's Federated Department Stores; 629, © CORBIS; 630 (tl), General Motors Corp. Used with permission, GM Media Archives; (bl), Akron University Archives/Goodyear Photo Collection; (c), National Museum of American History, Smithsonian Institution, Washington, DC, Behring Center. Neg. # 71-181; (tr), © Bettmann/CORBIS; 630-631, Curt Teich Postcard Archives, Lake County Museum, Illinois; 632 (l), Library of Congress/ PRC Archive; (r), Picture Research Consultants & Archives; 634, © Bettmann/ CORBIS; 635, The Granger Collection, New York; 636 (l), White House Historical Association (White House Collection); (r), White House Historical Association (White House Collection)/ Photo by National Geographic Society; 637, © CORBIS; 638, Library of Congress; 642 (l), © Bettmann/CORBIS; (r), National Museum of American History, Smithsonian Institution, Washington, DC, Behring Center. Neg. # 71-181; 642 (b), White House Historical Association (White House Collection); 643, Picture Research Consultants & Archives. **Chapter 20**: Pages 644-645, Brown Brothers.; 644 (b), Picture Research Consultants & Archives.; 645 (cl), Library of Congress; (cr), Picture Research Consultants & Archives; (b), ©SuperStock; 646, © Bettmann/CORBIS; 647 (l), Lewis Wickes Hine/ George Eastman House; (r), HRW Photo Research Library; 648, Lake County (IL) Museum /Curt Teich Postcard Archives; 650 (l), The Granger Collection, New York; (r), AP/Wide World Photos; 651, University of Tennessee Library Special Collections, Robinson and Hicks Collections; 652 (l), Kansas State Historical Society, Topeka; (r), © Bettmann/CORBIS; 653, © Bettmann/CORBIS; 654, Photo by Carl Van Vechten, courtesy Carl Van Vechten Trust. With the permission of the Zora Neale Hurston Trust. The Beinecke Rare Book and Manuscript Library, Yale University Library; 656 (t), Crisis Publishing Co., Inc.; (b), The publisher wishes to thank The Crisis Publishing Co., Inc., the publisher of the magazine of the National Association for the Advancement of Colored People for the use of this work that was first published in the April 1923 issue of "The Crisis Magazine." General Research and